The International Directory of Little Magazines and Small Presses

Len Fulton, Editor

27TH EDITION, 1991–1992

DUSTBOOKS

CONTENTS

Dustbooks would like to thank the many people who by advice and criticism have helped make this Directory a more useful and readable publication.

PAPER: $25.95/copy ISBN 0-916685-23-3
$88.00/4-year subscription
CLOTH: $41.95/copy ISBN 0-916685-24-1
$126.00/4-year subscription

Published annually by Dustbooks, P.O. Box 100, Paradise, CA 95967, also publishers of the *Directory of Editors, Small Press Record of Books in Print, Directory of Poetry Publishers* and the *Small Press Review* (monthly). Systems design, typesetting format and computer programming by Neil McIntyre, 15 Letty Court, Sacramento, CA 95833.

Pressure sensitive or cheshire labels are available from the International Directory data base. These can be sorted alphabetically or by Zip Code.

ON THE OTHER HAND . . .

If you are interested in only one or two of our information titles, but would like to beat inflation and get onto an automatic subscription basis (folks who did this four years ago received this 27th edition for about $13.00!) here are our '91-'92 four-year subscription prices -- again as with the Info Library, good if you use the order blank below.

■International Directory . . $88.00/4 years (paper)
■Directory of Editors . . $63.00/4 years (pa only)
■Small Press Record . . . $126.00/4 years (cl only)
■Directory of Poetry Publishers $48/4 yrs (pa only)
■Small Press Review (monthly) . . . $52.00/4 years

Dustbooks, PO Box 100, Paradise, CA 95967

Enclosed find $_____ for four-year sub-
scription(s) to:_____
_____
_____
_____
_____

Subscription to start with _____ edition.

NAME_____

ADDRESS_____

_____

_____

Listings are of three basic kinds: those for **magazines** (periodicals, printed in all caps), those for **presses** (book publishers), and **cross-references**.

The **cross-references** are simply publisher imprints (usually presses but sometimes magazines) which have no listing data of their own but which are designed to lead you to a listing for that publisher which does have such data.

A complete **magazine** listing would include, in the following order: Name of magazine, name of press, name(s) of editor(s), address, phone number, founding year, type of material used, additional comments by editors including recent contributors, circulation, frequency of publication, number of issues published in 1990, expected in 1991 and 1992, one-year subscription price, single copy price, sample copy price, back issues price, discount schedules, average number of pages, page size, production method (mi-mimeo, lo or of- offset; lp-letterpress), length of reporting time on manuscripts, payment rates, rights purchased and/or copyright arrangements, number of reviews published in 1990, areas of interest for review materials, ad rates (page/half page) and membership in small mag/press organizations.

A complete **press** listing would include, in the following order: Name of press, name of magazine (if any), names(s) of editor(s), address, founding year, type of material used, additional comments by editors including recent contributions, average press run, number of titles published in 1990, expected in 1991 and 1992, average copy price, in cloth, paperback and "other," discount schedules, average number of pages, average page size, printing method (mi-mimeo, lo or of-offset; lp-letterpress), length of reporting time on manuscripts, payment or royalty arrangements, rights purchased and/or copyright arrangements, number of titles listed in the current edition of the **Small Press Record of Books in Print**, and membership in publishing organizations.

Certain special abbreviations apply to listings from the United Kingdom: px-postage is extra; pf-postage is free; pp-pages; p-pence.

In some cases in this edition we received no report by press time but had a reasonable sense that the magazine or press was still going. In such cases a ‡ is used before the name. Query before sending money or material, however.

The following additional indicators are used in this edition to simplify yes or no in the listings: † means the magazine or press does its own printing; § before a listing of areas of interest for review materials indicates the magazine wishes to receive materials for review.

For those who wish to list a magazine or press in future editions of this *Directory* or our new *Directory of Poetry Publishers*, Dustbooks provides a special form. Please write to us for it. Write to us also for a form to list books, pamphlets, broadsides, posters, and poem-cards (i.e. *non*-periodicals) in our annual *Small Press Record of Books in Print*. However, once a report form has been filled out for the *Directory*, further forms and requests for information will be sent automatically. A "proof-sheet" is sent in February of each year for updating *Directory* listings, and for updating *Record* listings. Deadline is April 1st of each year.

A

A, Alphabox Press, Jeremy Adler, Flat 1, 41 Mapesbury Road, London NW2 4HJ, England. 1969. *"A* (1970); *AB* (1973); *ABC* (1975); *ABCD* (1977). Envelope magazine of visual poetry. Pages usually supplied by respective contributors. Contributors include: Bob Cobbing, Peter Finch, Bill Griffiths, D.S.H., Jackson MacLow, Peter Mayer, B.P. Nichol, Nannuci, P.C. Fencott, Paul Dutton, Paula Claire etc." circ. 300. Irregular. Pub'd 1 issue 1990. sub. price: 75p plus p&p; per copy: 75p plus p&p; sample: 75p plus p&p. 40pp; size A4; mi, of, silkscreen. Reporting time: 2 months. Payment: 3 copies. Copyrighted. No ads accepted. ALP, CULP.

A as A Publishing, Alicia E. Guzman Russell, 212 1/2 E. Portland Street, Phoenix, AZ 85004-1837. 1988. Fiction, non-fiction. "A as A Publishing was founded for the purpose of producing exclusively proreason fiction and nonfiction quality editions. We hold that a work's literary style must follow its philosophic function and that theme, plot, and characterization in fiction should be implicitly rationally delineated throughout; i.e., *nothing* is accidental in the conceptual art. Criteria for our children's imprint, Child of Reason, are no less exacting. Our first title, *Honor Student* by Michael Russell, represents precisely what we desire in fiction—please do not submit writing for publication unless you are familiar with it." avg. press run 5M. Expects 1 title 1991, 1 title 1992. 1 title listed in the *Small Press Record of Books in Print* (20th Edition, 1991-92). avg. price, cloth: $18. Discounts: 2-9 copies 30%, 10-99 40%, 100-199 42%, 200-299 44%, 300-399 46%, 400-499 48%, 500+ 50%, payment with order, FOB 03302. 224pp; 5½×8¼; of. Reporting time: 6 weeks. Payment: 10%-15% royalty on retail. Copyrights for author.

A.J. Books, Alan J. Goldberg, Tony DiMarco, 3415 Lebon Drive, #237, San Diego, CA 92122. 1986. "We publish one or two books a year and self distribute. Our books are generally action fiction; however, we are planning one nutrition book and one computer book for 1988." 1 title listed in the *Small Press Record of Books in Print* (20th Edition, 1991-92).

A.R.A. JOURNAL, Ion Manea, Dr. Miron Butariu, 4310 Finley Avenue, Los Angeles, CA 90027, 213-666-8379. "Yearly publication that contains Romanian studies of interest to American intellectuals" circ. 500. 1/yr. Pub'd 1 issue 1990; expects 1 issue 1991, 1 issue 1992. price per copy: $12. Back issues: $10. Discounts: 10%. 250pp; 5½×8½. Copyrighted, does not revert to author. §East-Central Europe.

Aa To Zz Publishing Co., Frank W. Pandozzi, Debra J. Pandozzi, 506 Valley Drive East, Chittenango, NY 13037, 315-687-9631. 1990. Articles, non-fiction. "We will be expanding into sales motivational material with newsletters and books. No sex, interested in articles and manuscripts on salesmanship. Any material on abuses in the insurance industry, preferably within the health insurance industry will be looked at." avg. press run 1M. Pub'd 1 title 1990; expects 2 titles 1991, 4 titles 1992. 1 title listed in the *Small Press Record of Books in Print* (20th Edition, 1991-92). avg. price, paper: $9.95. Discounts: standard industry rates. mi, of, lp. Reporting time: 30-60 days. Payment: contact editors for specifics. Copyrights for author. COSMEP, PO Box 703, San Francisco, CA 94101.

Aames-Allen Publishing Co., Peggy Glenn, 1106 Main Street, Huntington Beach, CA 92648, 714-536-4926. 1980. Non-fiction. avg. press run 5M. Pub'd 1 title 1990; expects 1 title 1991. 5 titles listed in the *Small Press Record of Books in Print* (20th Edition, 1991-92). avg. price, cloth: varies; paper: varies. Discounts: trade 42% (47% prepaid) over 5 copies; bulk 50% over 50 copies with no resale in a store setting, jobbers 20% - 50% depending on number of copies purchased. Pages vary; size varies; of. AAP, ABA, Publishers Marketing Association (PMA).

Aangstrom Publishing Company, Kelly L. Frey, 600 New Hampshire Avenue NW, Ste. 450, Washington, DC 20037, 202-298-8929. 1991. Fiction. "Consider only first novels by serious authors. Submissions are reviewed by academics for literary merit. Selection is based solely on literary merit, not commercial value of work." avg. press run 3M-5M. Expects 4-6 titles 1991, 4-6 titles 1992. avg. price, other: $59.85 to $89.85 Gold stamped, leather bound deluxe editions. Discounts: none. Pages vary; size varies. Reporting time: 3-4 months. Payment: outright purchase; $15,000 to $35,000 payable upon date of shipment of first printing. Copyrights for author.

Aardvark Enterprises (see also BREAKTHROUGH!), J. Alvin Speers, 204 Millbank Drive S.W., Calgary, Alta T2Y 2H9, Canada, 403-256-4639. 1977. Poetry, fiction, articles, photos, cartoons, interviews, reviews, letters, news items, non-fiction. "Open to proposals. We publish for hire at reasonable rates, which is advantageous for special short run projects, or other. Over twenty books with successful results" avg. press run varies. Pub'd 6 titles 1990; expects 6 titles 1991, 6 titles 1992. 22 titles listed in the *Small Press Record of*

Books in Print (20th Edition, 1991-92). avg. price, paper: $8.95; other: $4.95 booklets. Discounts: inquiries invited - quantity discounts only. 100pp; 5½×8½; †quality photocopying. Reporting time: fast, return mail usually. Payment: by arrangement on individual project. Copyrights for author. American Booksellers Exchange.

AAS HISTORY SERIES, Univelt, Inc., R. Cargill Hall, Series Editor, PO Box 28130, San Diego, CA 92128, 619-746-4005. 1977. Non-fiction. "History of Science (esp. Space Science and Technology). Science Fiction and Space Futures. An irregular serial. Standing orders accepted. Vols 1-7 published." circ. 600-2M. Irregular. Pub'd 3 issues 1990; expects 2 issues 1991, 2 issues 1992. sub. price: varies. Back issues: no. Discounts: 20% and more by arrangement; reduced prices for classroom use. 200-500pp; 7×9½; of. Reporting time: 90 days. Payment: 10% (if the volume author). Copyrighted, authors may republish material with appropriate credits given. No advertising.

AASLH Press (see also HISTORY NEWS), Mary Bray Wheeler, Managing Editor for Publication Services; Joanne Jaworski, Assistant Director for Publication Services, 172 Second Avenue N., Suite 202, Nashville, TN 37201, 615-255-2971. 1940. Non-fiction. "AASLH Press welcomes manuscripts of interest to readers who work at historical sites, history museums, or educational agencies that advance knowledge, understanding, and appreciation of the North American experience. We also publish books that aid historians (academic or non-academic) in exploring the history around them. Recent titles include *Directory of Historical Organizations in the United States and Canada, Fourteenth Edition,* edited by Mary Bray Wheeler and *Local Businesses: Exploring Their History* by K. Austin Kerr, et al. We do not consider manuscripts that are primarily about historical events or persons." avg. press run 2.5M. Pub'd 3 titles 1990; expects 7 titles 1991, 7 titles 1992. 50 titles listed in the *Small Press Record of Books in Print* (20th Edition, 1991-92). avg. price, cloth: $21; paper: $12. Discounts: member discount 10%; trade: 1-5 copies 20%, 6 or more 40%. 200pp; 6×9; of. Reporting time: 2 months. Payment: paid every 6 months—10% of discounted price (usually). Copyrights for author.

Aatec Publications, Christina Bych, PO Box 7119, Ann Arbor, MI 48107, 313-995-1470. 1980. Non-fiction. "We specialize in the alternative energies, current emphasis on photovoltaics. Aatec books offer background and working knowledge to the serious alternative energy user." avg. press run 5M. Pub'd 3 titles 1990; expects 4 titles 1991, 5 titles 1992. 3 titles listed in the *Small Press Record of Books in Print* (20th Edition, 1991-92). avg. price, paper: $16.95. Discounts: write for schedules. 200+pp; 6×9; of. Reporting time: 2-3 weeks. Payment: 15% of monies received, annual. Copyrights for author. COSMEP.

AAUG Press (see also ARAB STUDIES QUARTERLY; MIDEAST MONITOR), Abbas Alnasrawi, 556 Trapelo Road, Belmont, MA 02178, (617) 484-5483. 1967. Articles, interviews, non-fiction. "Information papers, monographs, anthologies, bibliographies on Arab affairs, U.S. Middle East policy, Arab-American affairs, the Arab-Israeli conflict; vary in length from under 10 pages to over 500 pages" avg. press run 3M. Pub'd 4 titles 1990; expects 3 titles 1991, 4 titles 1992. 10 titles listed in the *Small Press Record of Books in Print* (20th Edition, 1991-92). avg. price, paper: $8.00. Discounts: bookstores & wholesalers: 40% on over 9 copies; others, 20% on large orders. 150pp; 6×9; of. Reporting time: 4-5 weeks. Payment: varies from author to author. Sometimes copyrights for author.

ABACUS, Potes & Poets Press Inc, Peter Ganick, 181 Edgemont Avenue, Elmwood, CT 06110. 1984. Poetry. "Features one writer per issue, favors language poets. We have published Ron Silliman, Charles Bernstein, Bruce Andrews, Jackson MacLow among others." circ. 150. 8/yr. Pub'd 8 issues 1990; expects 8 issues 1991, 8 issues 1992. sub. price: $17; per copy: $3; sample: $3. 16pp; 8½×11.

Abattoir Editions, Bonnie O'Connell, Library Room 100, University of Nebraska, Omaha, NE 68182, 402-554-2787. 1972. Poetry, fiction, art, long-poems, collages, non-fiction. "Recent authors under editorship of Harry Duncan: Richard Duggin, Art Homer, Ben Howard, Judith Root, William Logan, James Merrill. Forthcoming titles (under new editorship) from the following contributors: Sam Pereira, Brenda Hillman, Ardyth Bradley, Lynn Emanuel, Bernard Cooper, Ann Deagon" avg. press run 200-300. Pub'd 2 titles 1990; expects 2-3 titles 1991, 2-3 titles 1992. 11 titles listed in the *Small Press Record of Books in Print* (20th Edition, 1991-92). avg. price, cloth: $25-$60; paper: $12-$30. 15-120pp; †lp. Reporting time: 2 weeks - 2 months. Payment: 10% of edition. Copyrights for author.

ABBEY, White Urp Press, David Greisman, 5360 Fallriver Row Court, Columbia, MD 21044. 1971. Poetry, articles, art, interviews, criticism, reviews, letters. "*Abbey* is the Molson's Ale of Small Press rags. Recent contributors: Ann Menebroker, Gretchen Johnsen, Peter Wild, John Elsberg, Ron Androla, Richard Peabody, Harry Calhoun, Cheryl Townsend, Vera Bergstrom, Wayne Hogan, Joan Payne Kincaid, and Sister Mary Ann Henn" circ. 200. 3-4/yr. Pub'd 4 issues 1990; expects 4 issues 1991, 4 issues 1992. sub. price: $2; per copy: 50¢; sample: 50¢. Back issues: 50¢. 18pp; 8½×11; of. Reporting time: 2 minutes-2 years. Payment: nothing. Copyrighted, reverts to author. Pub's reviews: 12-20 in 1990. §Poetry, running. Ads: $10/$5.

ABBEY NEWSLETTER: Bookbinding & Conservation, Abbey Publications, Ellen McCrady, 320 E. Center Street, Provo, UT 84606, 801-373-1598. 1975. Articles, reviews, letters, news items, non-fiction. "The

AN is a professionally-oriented medium of communication for book conservators, amateur bookbinders and preservation-minded librarians" circ. 1.2M. 8/yr. Pub'd 8 issues 1990; expects 8 issues 1991, 8 issues 1992. sub. price: $37 indiv., $45 instit.; per copy: $3.50; sample: free. Back issues: $3.50. Discounts: dealer 12%. 20pp; 8½x11; of. Reporting time: receipt acknowledged within 2 weeks, acceptance reporting time varies. Most contributions are invited. Copyrighted. Pub's reviews: 2 in 1990. §Bookbinding and preservation of library materials. Ads: No ads except for jobs: $50 heading and first 10 lines and $2 each additional line. none.

Abbey Publications (see also ABBEY NEWSLETTER: Bookbinding & Conservation; ALKALINE PAPER ADVOCATE), Ellen R. McCrady, 320 East Center, Provo, UT 84606, 801-373-1598.

THE ABER BULLETIN, Hugh T. Law, 1216 Lillie Circle, Salt Lake City, UT 84121, (801) 262-4586. 1971. Articles, photos, letters. "Several ancestral lines of the Abers were extended and published. Many families of descendants were published with birthplaces and dates. 28 issues were published by Autumn 1982 when publication ceased. However, I have copies of many issues and can make photocopies of those out of stock" circ. 100. 2/yr. price per copy: $1.85. Back issues: $1.85 per issue (24 or more pages, with excellent photos). Discounts: 20%. 24pp; 8½x11; of. Payment: none. Not copyrighted. §U.S., Canada, England. COSMEP.

THE ABIKO QUARTERLY RAG, Anna Livia Plurabelle, Managing Editor; DC Palter, Fiction Editor; Vincent Broderick, Poetry Editor, 8-1-8 Namiki, Abiko-shi, Chiba-ken 270-11, Japan, 0471-84-7904. 1989. Poetry, fiction, articles, art, photos, cartoons, interviews, satire, criticism, reviews, music, letters, pai ts-of-novels, long-poems, collages, plays, concrete art, news items, non-fiction. "All types of fiction considered. Fiction contest in Fall. First prize Y30,000. Especially want essays on anything Joycean, w/emphasis on Finnegans Wake" circ. 300. 4/yr. Pub'd 4 issues 1990; expects 4 issues 1991, 4 issues 1992. sub. price: Y5,000; per copy: Y1,500; sample: Y1,500. 100pp; size A4; of. Reporting time: 1 month. Payment: 5 contributors copies, fiction contest in the fall. Not copyrighted. Pub's reviews. §Books relating to the life of James Joyce or analysis of Finnegan's Wake. Ads: Y10,000/Y5,000.

Ability Workshop Press, Audrey Cheney, Richard Vaughan, 24861 Alicia Parkway #292, Laguna Hills, CA 92653, 714-661-5779. 1987. Fiction, non-fiction. "We publish primarily self help, psychology oriented books which align with the topics of the many workshops taught by our Parent Company—Ability Workshops. For example, burnout, learning disabilities, self-esteem; we also publish spiritually oriented fiction." avg. press run 5M. Pub'd 2 titles 1990; expects 6 titles 1991, 8 titles 1992. 5 titles listed in the *Small Press Record of Books in Print* (20th Edition, 1991-92). avg. price, paper: $16.95. Discounts: standard trade, 0-55% based on volume. 150pp; 8½x11; of. Reporting time: 2 months. Payment: standard royalties, 7½ to 15%. Copyrights for author. COSMEP.

Able Publishing, Mindy Bingham, Robert Shafer, 3463 State Street, Suite 219, Santa Barbara, CA 93105. 1990. Non-fiction. "Trade and Textbooks for Secondary and College age." avg. press run 10M. Pub'd 3 titles 1990; expects 3 titles 1991, 3 titles 1992. 5 titles listed in the *Small Press Record of Books in Print* (20th Edition, 1991-92). avg. price, paper: $19.95. Discounts: 6-35 books 40%; 36-90 books 50%; 91-500 books 52%; over 500 books 55%. 288pp; 8½x11. Reporting time: 3-4 months. Payment: varies. Copyrights for author. PMA.

ABRAXAS, Abraxas Press, Inc., Ingrid Swanberg, Editor; Warren Woessner, Senior Editor; David Hilton, Contributing Editor, 2518 Gregory Street, Madison, WI 53711, 608-238-0175. 1968. Poetry, articles, art, photos, satire, criticism, reviews, letters, collages, concrete art. "*Abraxas* has re-converted to a format featuring poetry. We are no longer considering unsolicited reviews and are no longer accepting unsolicited poems. *Abraxas* will announce submission policies as projects arise. *Abraxas Press* has published an anthology of Jazz Poetry, *Bright Moments* ($4.00). Inquiries on guidelines and poetry manuscripts should be sent to Ingrid Swanberg (2518 Gregory St., Madison, WI 53711); inquiries on reviews to Warren Woessner, (34 W. Minnehaha Parkway, Minneapolis, MN 55419), or to Ingrid Swanberg. We have recently published Cesas Vallejo, Charles Bukowski, Denise Levertov, Roberta Hill Whiteman, Gerald Locklin, William Stafford, Ivan Arguelles, Andrei Codrescu" circ. 500+. Irregular: 4 single issues or 2 double issues. Pub'd 2 issues 1990; expects 2 issues 1991, 2 issues 1992. sub. price: $12/4 issues; per copy: $3; sample: $4 double issues; $2 single issue. Back issues: Catalog on request. SASE please. Discounts: 20% 1-5 copies; 40% on orders of more than 5 copies. 80pp, 120pp double issues; 6x9; of. Reporting time: 2-5 months, sometimes longer. Payment: copies. Copyrighted, reverts to author. Pub's reviews. §Criticism reviews of small press poetry books. Ads: $60/$35. CLMP.

Abraxas Press, Inc. (see also ABRAXAS), Ingrid Swanberg, Editor, 2518 Gregory Street, Madison, WI 53711, 608-238-0175. 6 titles listed in the *Small Press Record of Books in Print* (20th Edition, 1991-92).

Abrazo Press (see also ECOS: A Journal of Latino People's Culture), Carlos Cumpian, c/o Movimiento Artistico Chicano, Inc., PO Box 2890, Chicago, IL 60690-2890, 312-935-6188. 1981. Poetry, photos, interviews, criticism, reviews, plays. "We publish chapbooks of poetry and full books perfectbound" avg. press run 1M. Pub'd 1 title 1990; expects 2 titles 1991, 1 title 1992. 6 titles listed in the *Small Press Record of*

3

Books in Print (20th Edition, 1991-92). avg. price, paper: $5 chapbooks; other: $7. Discounts: 20-50 10%. 52pp; 8½×5; of, or laser printer. Reporting time: 6-9 weeks for submissions. Payment: 3-5 copies. Does not copyright for author.

Abundance Press, Susan Middleton, 70 Granby Heights, Granby, MA 01033, 413-467-2231. 1 title listed in the *Small Press Record of Books in Print* (20th Edition, 1991-92).

AC Projects, Inc., Old Harding Road, Box 5106, Franklin, TN 37064, 615-646-3757. 1977. "Not accepting ms until further notice" avg. press run 3M-25M. Pub'd 1 title 1990; expects 1 title 1992. 4 titles listed in the *Small Press Record of Books in Print* (20th Edition, 1991-92). avg. price, cloth: $9.95-$35; paper: $9.95. Discounts: inquire please. 44-691pp.

Academy Chicago Publishers, Anita Miller, President Editor; Jordan Miller, Vice President, 213 West Institute Place, Chicago, IL 60610, 312-751-7302. 1975. Fiction, art, non-fiction. "Strong anti-sexist bias. Mysteries, History" avg. press run 5M. 80 titles listed in the *Small Press Record of Books in Print* (20th Edition, 1991-92). avg. price, cloth: $14.95; paper: $6.95. Discounts: Returns: 1-4 copies, 20%; 5-24 copies, 40%; 25-49 copies, 42%; 50-99 copies, 43%; 100-999 copies, 45%; 1000+copies, 46%;No returns: 10-49 copies, 45%; 50-249 copies, 48%; 250-999 copies, 50%; 1000+ copies, 51%. Libraries: 1-9 copies, 10%; 10+ copies, 15%. 150-300pp; 5½×8½, 4¼×7; varies. Reporting time: 12 weeks. Payment: standard paperback/hardcover royalties c. 7-10%. Copyrights for author. COSMEP.

Acadia Publishing Company, Frank Matter, PO Box 170, Bar Harbor, ME 04609, 207-288-9025. 1985. Fiction, non-fiction. "Our first few years were spent publishing and marketing books for the area we know best-Acadia National Park, Bar Harbor, Maine. Between 1985 and 1987 we published four titles and purchased the remaining stock of another. Following this pattern we published 8 titles in 1988. In 1989 we began to publish books with a Main/New England theme selected for an Atlantic Coast/national audience. In 1991 we are returning to our roots with 3 titles on Acadia/Maine. Our titles include previously unpublished works such as the award winning book *Discovering Acadia, A Guide for Young Naturalists* by Margaret Scheid; as well as previously published works such as *A Romance of Mount Desert* a novel by A.A. Hayes. Literary titles planned for 1989-90 include: *The Eloquent Edge, an Anthology of 15 Maine Women Writers*, *The Lost Tales of Horatio*, *Aqurhega*, a historical novel, *Dabbler and the Purple Cup*, a childrens picture book, and two juvenile chapter books *Fair Play* and *Growing Up Summer*. Our emphasis is on high quality both in the written word and the photographs and illustrations. Royalties are paid quarterly and we work closely with our authors to ensure a long term relationship. Writers quidelines and booklists are available upon request." avg. press run 1.5M-4M. Pub'd 10 titles 1990; expects 3 titles 1991, 16 titles 1992. 25 titles listed in the *Small Press Record of Books in Print* (20th Edition, 1991-92). avg. price, cloth: $21.95; paper: $8.95. Discounts: standard. 220pp; 6×9; as appropriate. Reporting time: 9-10 weeks. Payment: negotiable with author. Copyrights for author. COSMEP, PMA, Maine Writers Alliance.

ACCCA Press, Milli Janz, 19 Foothills Drive, Pompton Plains, NJ 07444, 201-835-2661. 1978. Articles. "*Culture Without Pain or Money* is now in a new 2nd edition, and is being distributed in Haiti, Japan, The Philippines and Egypt. It is being used currently in many parts of the U.S. as a blueprint for initiating, developing and continuing cultural centers in communities. (Especially where art services are exchanged in lieu of money). Because the book is in a smaller edition, the price for the book and mailing will remain at $4 each." 1 title listed in the *Small Press Record of Books in Print* (20th Edition, 1991-92). avg. price, paper: $3.00 plus postage ($4.00). Discounts: 10%. 8½×11. Payment: when other writers will join me, I will offer a per page fee.

Accent on Music, Mark Hanson, Greta Pedersen, PO Box 417, Palo Alto, CA 94302, 415-856-0987. 1985. Music. avg. press run 5M. Pub'd 1 title 1990; expects 1 title 1991, 1 title 1992. 2 titles listed in the *Small Press Record of Books in Print* (20th Edition, 1991-92). avg. price, other: $16.95 with instruction cassette. 72pp; 9×12; of. Reporting time: 4-6 weeks. Payment: royalties paid annually; contract negotiable. Copyrights for author.

‡**Acheron Press,** Robert E. Pletta, Bear Creek at the Kettle, Friendsville, MD 21531, 301-746-5885. 1981. Poetry, fiction, articles, art, cartoons, interviews, satire, criticism, reviews, letters, parts-of-novels, long-poems, collages, plays, non-fiction. "Authors encouraged to have familiarity with Acheron's publications to judge appropriateness before submitting" avg. press run 1M. Expects 5 titles 1991, 6 titles 1992. 7 titles listed in the *Small Press Record of Books in Print* (20th Edition, 1991-92). avg. price, paper: $7.00. Discounts: please inquire. 25-150pp; 5½×8½; †of, lp. Reporting time: depends on time of year. Acheron does not reply during June, July and August. Payment: individual arrangements. Copyrights for author.

Achievement Press, Anna Louise Matthews, Box 608, Sheridan, WY 82801, 307-672-8475. 1984. Non-fiction. avg. press run 5M-10M. Expects 1 title 1991, 1 title 1992. avg. price, paper: $12.95. Discounts: 1-2 books 20%, net 14 days; 3-23 40%, net 60 days with returns; 24+ 55%, net 60 days with returns. 160pp; 5½×8½. Reporting time: 8 weeks. Payment: 10% of net receipts. Does not copyright for author. PMA.

4

Acid Rain Foundation, Inc., 1410 Varsity Drive, Raleigh, NC 27606, 919-828-9443.

ACM (ANOTHER CHICAGO MAGAZINE), Left Field Press, Barry Silesky, 3709 N. Kenmore, Chicago, IL 60613, 312-248-7665. 1976. Poetry, fiction, articles, art, photos, cartoons, interviews, satire, criticism, reviews, long-poems. "Recent contributors have included Tom McGrath, Marge Piercy, Peter Michelson, John Knoepfle, Phyllis Janik, Sterling Plumpp, Ralph J. Mills Jr. and Marilyn Krysl" circ. 1.2M. 2/yr. Pub'd 3 issues 1990; expects 2 issues 1991, 2 issues 1992. sub. price: $15; per copy: $8; sample: $8. Back issues: $5. Discounts: 50% on 10 or more. 196pp; 8½x5½; of. Reporting time: 8 weeks. Payment: minimum of $5 + copy. Copyrighted, reverts to author. Pub's reviews: 20 in 1990. §Small press poetry, fiction, literary reviews or criticism, works on politics and art. Ads: $150/$75. COSMEP, CCLM.

Acorn Publishing, Mary O. Robb, Box 7067-D, Syracuse, NY 13261, 315-689-7072. 1985. Non-fiction. "Distributed by The Countryman Press, Woodstock, Vermont, 800-457-1049" avg. press run 2M. Pub'd 1 title 1990; expects 1 title 1991, 2 titles 1992. 4 titles listed in the *Small Press Record of Books in Print* (20th Edition, 1991-92). avg. price, paper: $10.95. Discounts: 1 (prepaid) 20%, 2-4 books 30%, 5-24 40%, 25-99 45%, 100+ 50%. 160pp; 5½x8½; of. Reporting time: 6 weeks. Payment: on case by case basis. Does not copyright for author.

Acre Press (see also FELL SWOOP), Joel Dailey, 1521 N. Lopez Street, New Orleans, LA 70119. 1980. Poetry. "Have seen the light of day: *New Sky* by Gordon Anderson; *Red Hats* by Mark Chadwick; *Arthur Zen Comes To America* by Robb Jackson; *Between The Eyes* by Randall Schroth; *Angry Red Blues* translations from the Martian poet, S. Zivvit 57; *Minigolf* by Anselm Hollo. You are welcome to submit after you purchase a title; three bucks American" avg. press run 200. Pub'd 1 title 1990; expects 2 titles 1991, 3 titles 1992. 5 titles listed in the *Small Press Record of Books in Print* (20th Edition, 1991-92). avg. price, paper: $3 all titles. Discounts: 50%. 20pp; 5½x8½; of. Reporting time: fast. Payment: copies, % of run. Does not copyright for author.

Acrobat Books, Tony Cohan, PO Box 870, Venice, CA 90294, 213-578-1055. 1975. Fiction, art, photos, non-fiction. "Non fiction brooks in the creative arts. *Stolen Moments,* by Tom Schnabel *Directing the Film,* by Eric Sherman, *Nine Ships, A Book of Tales* by Tony Cohan; *Street Writers: A Guided Tour of Chicano Graffiti* by Gusmano Cesaretti; *Outlaw Visions* ed. by Tony Cohan/Gordon Beam; *The Record Producer's Handbook* by Done Gere; *A Twist Of The Wrist* and *The Soft Science* by Keith Code; *Frame By Frame* by Eric Sherman" avg. press run 4M. Pub'd 3 titles 1990; expects 4 titles 1991, 5 titles 1992. 5 titles listed in the *Small Press Record of Books in Print* (20th Edition, 1991-92). avg. price, cloth: $19.95; paper: $14.95. Discounts: 1-5 copies 20%, 6-49 40%. 196pp; 5¼x8¼; of. Reporting time: 60 days. Payment: negotiable. Copyrights for author.

ACROSTICS NETWORK, Will Mock, 1030-A Delaware Street, Berkeley, CA 94710, 415-549-0659. 1989. "We publish original acrostic puzzles" circ. 200. 6/yr. Pub'd 4 issues 1990; expects 6 issues 1991, 6 issues 1992. sub. price: $12.50; per copy: $2.50; sample: free. Back issues: mostly not available. Discounts: none. 12pp; 8½x11; †photo copy. Reporting time: 2 months. Payment: none. Copyrighted, reverts to author. Ads: by arrangement.

ACS Publications (see also ASTROFLASH), Maritha Pottenger, Editorial Director, PO Box 16430, San Diego, CA 92116, 619-297-9203. 1982. Articles, interviews, reviews. "Please submit OUTLINE only" avg. press run 3M. Pub'd 6 titles 1990; expects 6 titles 1991, 6 titles 1992. 7 titles listed in the *Small Press Record of Books in Print* (20th Edition, 1991-92). avg. price, cloth: $29.95; paper: $12.95. Discounts: trade. 200pp; 5⅜x8⅜; of/lo. Reporting time: 1 month - 6 weeks. Payment: usual. Copyrights for author.

ACTA VICTORIANA, Emma Thom, 150 Charles Street West, Toronto, Ontario M5S 1K9, Canada, 416-585-4973. Poetry, fiction, articles, art, photos, interviews, satire, criticism, long-poems, collages, plays. circ. 1.5M. 2/yr. Pub'd 2 issues 1990; expects 2 issues 1991, 2 issues 1992. sub. price: $9; per copy: $3; sample: $3. 40pp; 9x12. Reporting time: about 3 months. Payment: 1 free issue. Copyrighted, reverts to author.

Acting World Books (see also THE HOLLYWOOD ACTING COACHES AND TEACHERS DIRECTORY; THE AGENCIES-WHAT THE ACTOR NEEDS TO KNOW), Lawrence Parke, PO Box 3044, Hollywood, CA 90078, 213-466-4297. 1981. "Publications and career guidance for the acting community. Publishes books and periodicals of career and acting methodology natures. Typical is the six-volume 'seminars to go' series on six different 'how to' topics involved in the actor's career building processes. Book: *Since Stanislaviski and Vakhtangov: The Method as a System for Today's Actor* (April, 1986) $12.95, 300 pages, paperback. In-house publishing and waiting" avg. press run 2M. Expects 1 title 1991, 2 titles 1992. 1 title listed in the *Small Press Record of Books in Print* (20th Edition, 1991-92). avg. price, paper: $10-$12.50; other: Seminar series $10. Discounts: trade, 40% booksellers. 40pp; 8½x11; †photocopy. Does not copyright for author. COSMEP.

ACTINIDIA ENTHUSIASTS NEWSLETTER, Michael Pilarski, Friends of the Trees Society, PO Box 1064, Tonasket, WA 98855. 1984. Articles. circ. 2M. 1/yr. Pub'd 1 issue 1990; expects 1 issue 1991, 1 issue

1992. price per copy: $5- latest publication $10. Back issues: $3. 60-115pp; 8½x11; of. Payment: none. Pub's reviews: 50 in 1990. AEN.

ACTION DIGEST, J. Flores Publications, Eli Flores, PO Box 163001, Miami, FL 33116, 305-559-4652. 1990. Articles, interviews, non-fiction. "800-4,000 words on guns, self-defense, crime stories, law enforcement, military history, elite units, and adventure." circ. 10M. 4/yr. Expects 4 issues 1991, 4 issues 1992. sub. price: $12; per copy: $2.95; sample: $3.95. Discounts: 40%. 48pp; 8½x11; of. Reporting time: 30 days. Payment: $50-$200 on publication. Copyrighted, reverts to author. Pub's reviews. §Guns, outdoors, military, law enforcement, adventure (non-fiction only). Ads: $850/$479/$1 per word.

ACTIVIST, Collective, DSA Youth Section, 15 Dutch Street, Suite 500, New York, NY 10038-3708. 1979. Articles, art, photos, cartoons, satire, criticism, reviews, letters, news items. "Articles should be submitted on DOS or Mac disk, no longer than 1500 words. Contributions are generally only accepted from members of the DSA Youth Section, though socialist contributors writing about current affairs, and student politics in particular, will be considered." circ. 3M. 4/yr. Pub'd 4 issues 1990; expects 4 issues 1991, 4 issues 1992. sub. price: $8; per copy: $1; sample: $1. Back issues: $1. 40pp; 8½x11. Reporting time: within several months. Payment: none. Not copyrighted. Pub's reviews: several in 1990. §Student and youth politics, foreign and domestic policy, urban poverty, national health insurance, racism, feminism, gay and lesbian issues, socialism. Ads: $20 2x2/$30 2x3/$45 3x3.

ACTS, David Levi Strauss, Editor; Benjamin Hollander, Associate Editor, 514 Guerrero, San Francisco, CA 94110-1017, 415-431-8297. 1982. Poetry, fiction, articles, art, photos, interviews, criticism, reviews, music, letters, parts-of-novels, long-poems, collages, plays, concrete art, news items, non-fiction. "*Acts* is a journal of contemporary radical poetry & poetics, "analytic lyric"word/image work and reviews. Also book issues on selected poets (Jack Spicer, Paul Celan, Robert Duncan) and Subjects. Recent contributors include Michael Palmer, Susan Howe, Robert Creeley, Leslie Scalapino, Norma Cole, Aaron Shurin. We do not publish unsolicited work." circ. 650-3M. 1 or 2. Pub'd 1 issue 1990; expects 2 issues 1991, 2 issues 1992. 1 title listed in the *Small Press Record of Books in Print* (20th Edition, 1991-92). sub. price: $12 (2 issues) individual/$16 (2 issues) institutional & foreign; per copy: $10; sample: $10. Back issues: Acts 1-OP; Acts 2 & 3-$5; Acts 4 + 5, $6; Acts 7, $8; Acts 8/9, $15.95. Discounts: 60/40. 140pp; 7x10; of/lo. Reporting time: ASAP (we do not publish unsolicited pieces). Payment: in copies. Copyrighted, reverts to author. Pub's reviews. §Poetry & poetics. Ads: $100. CCLM (Coordinating Council of Literary Magazines).

THE ACTS THE SHELFLIFE, Xexoxial Endarchy, Miekal And, Elizabeth Was, 1341 Williamson, Madison, WI 53703, 608-258-1305. 1986. Poetry, fiction, articles, art, photos, interviews, criticism, music, letters, parts-of-novels, long-poems, collages, plays, concrete art, news items. "*The Acts The Shelflife* is an assembling project devoted to accessing information and commentary about new and experimental literature. Sort of a hybrid of Kostelanetz' work with the assembling idea and Andrews & Bernstein's *L=A=N=G=U=A=G=E.* An ongoing project, each issue will have a general theme for exploration. The magazine will be issued twice a year, and each issue will remain in print after the initial edition is exhausted. #1—Networking Visual/Verbal Lit. #2—Polyartistry. #3—Graphism. #4—Improvisation (deadline: Jan 1988). Interested contributors should query in advance" circ. 200. 2/yr. Pub'd 2 issues 1990; expects 2 issues 1991, 2 issues 1992. sub. price: $16/2 years; per copy: $4 + $1 p/h; sample: $4.50. Back issues: $4.50. Discounts: 20% discount and postage and handling free with multiple orders of 5 or more. 80pp; 7x8½; †xerox. Payment: 5 copies. Not copyrighted. Ads: $50/$30.

Adams-Hall Publishing, Sue Ann Bacon, Marketing Director, PO Box 491002, Los Angeles, CA 90049, 213-399-7137; 800-888-4452. Pub'd 2 titles 1990; expects 2 titles 1991, 2 titles 1992. 1 title listed in the *Small Press Record of Books in Print* (20th Edition, 1991-92).

ADAPTED PHYSICAL ACTIVITY QUARTERLY (APAQ), Human Kinetics Pub. Inc., Geoffrey D. Broadhead, Box 5076, Champaign, IL 61825-5076, 217-351-5076. 1984. Articles, reviews. "Study of physical activity for special populations of all ages" circ. 750. 4/yr. Pub'd 4 issues 1990; expects 4 issues 1991, 4 issues 1992. sub. price: $28 individual, $56 institution; per copy: $7 indiv., $15 instit.; sample: free. Back issues: $7 indiv., $15 instit. Discounts: 5% agency. 94pp; 6x9; of. Reporting time: 2 months. Payment: none. Copyrighted. Pub's reviews: 5 in 1990. §Sport, sport science, and physical education related to disabilities and rehabilitation. Ads: $170/$102 (4X rate).

Adaptive Living, Angela Van Etten, PO Box 60857, Rochester, NY 14606. 1988. avg. press run 4M. Expects 1 title 1992. 1 title listed in the *Small Press Record of Books in Print* (20th Edition, 1991-92). avg. price, paper: $15.95. Discounts: 2-20%; 5-30%; 10-40%; 25-42%; 50-44%; 100-48%. 200pp; 8 inches; desk-top, laser print, camera-ready. Payment: negotiable. Copyrights for author. COSMEP.

Adastra Press, Gary Metras, 101 Strong Street, Easthampton, MA 01027, 413-527-3324. 1978. Poetry. "All books are hand-set letterpress printed and hand-sewn with square binding of paper wrapper. Each book is individually designed with the poetry in mind. I pay attention to the craft and art of printing and expect poets to

6

pay attention to their art. Interested authors should query first. The poetry should have some bite to it and be grounded in experience. Poem cycles, thematic groups and long poems are always nice to produce in chapbook format. Reading period for manuscripts is during the month of February only. Send queries with samples in the fall; if I like the sample, I'll ask you to send the manuscript in February. Manuscripts should have 12 to 18 pages; nothing longer; no full-length manuscripts will be considered. Accepted authors can expect to help with publicity. Payment is copies. *Adastra Press* is a one man operation, paying for itself as it goes without grants of any kind, and I am always overworked and booked in advance. Chances of acceptance are slim, but there's no harm in trying. Some titles to date are: *The Adastra Reader: Collected Chapbooks*; *Something More Than Force*, Zoe Anglesey; *Sea Fire*, Judith Neeld; *Twelve Poems with Preludes and Postludes*, Joseph Langland; *The Ballad of Harmonic George & Other Poems*, David Raffeld." avg. press run 200-500. Pub'd 2 titles 1990; expects 3 titles 1991, 3 titles 1992. 18 titles listed in the *Small Press Record of Books in Print* (20th Edition, 1991-92). avg. price, cloth: $15; paper: $5-$10; other: $10-$25, signed and numbered. Discounts: bookstores 30%, distributors 40%, more than 1 copy, 20% on cl/signed editions. 18pp; 5×8; †lp. Reporting time: 1-2 weeks on queries. Payment: usually percent of print run, but each arrangement made individually. Does not copyright for author.

ADDICTION & RECOVERY, Brenda L. Lewison, Editor, 4959 Commerce Parkway, Cleveland, OH 44128, 216-464-1210. 1980. Articles, cartoons, interviews, reviews, news items. circ. 30M. 6/yr. Pub'd 6 issues 1990; expects 6 issues 1991, 6 issues 1992. sub. price: $28; per copy: $7.50; sample: same. Back issues: $7 each. 48pp; 8⅛×10⅞; of. Payment: 1 yr. subscription and 6 copies of issue. Copyrighted, reverts to author. Pub's reviews: 40 in 1990. §Alcoholism, other drug addiction and recovery subjects. Ads: $4,250/$2,850/$150 per inch.

ADIRONDAC, Adirondack Mountain Club, Inc., Neal S. Burdick, Editor, Rd. #3, Box 3055, Lake George, NY 12845-9523, 518-668-4447. 1936. Poetry, articles, art, photos, interviews, reviews, letters, news items, non-fiction. "Avg. length: 1000-3000 words, with conservation, education, and recreation focus, representing different stances on issues of concern to the Adirondack and Catskill constitutionally-protected Forest Preserves. Contributors include ADK members, state authorities, Forest Preserve historians, outdoor recreationists, etc." circ. 11.5M. 6/yr. Pub'd 8 issues 1990; expects 6 issues 1991, 6 issues 1992. sub. price: $20; per copy: $2.25; sample: $2.50. Back issues: $4.25. Discounts: retailers 40% (min. 10 copies); libraries $12/yr. 44pp; 8½×11; of. Reporting time: 3 months. Payment: none. Copyrighted, does not revert to author. Pub's reviews: approx. 36 in 1990. §Natural history, conservation, "muscle-powered" recreation, Adirondack or Catskill history and lore. Ads: 1x: $489, 3x: $437/1x: $259, 3x: $230/request rate sheet for other sizes. COSMEP.

Adirondack Mountain Club, Inc. (see also ADIRONDAC), Neal S. Burdick, Adirondac Editor; Metzger Crosby, Publications Director, RR 3, Box 3055, Lake George, NY 12845, 518-668-4447. 1935. Fiction, non-fiction. "—DO NOT WISH TO BE LISTED—We publish guidebooks (canoe guides, natural history guides, trail guides) as well as fiction about the Forest Preserve of New York State (which includes the Adirondacks and Catskills). We also publish history of the Forest Preserve and are planning to expand our publications division to include other types of guidebooks. Between 1985 and 1987 we will be releasing 7 guidebooks, which will cover all of the hiking trails in the Adirondack Park" avg. press run 2.5M. Pub'd 6 titles 1990; expects 4 titles 1991, 4 titles 1992. 18 titles listed in the *Small Press Record of Books in Print* (20th Edition, 1991-92). avg. price, cloth: $17; paper: trade $8. Discounts: retail: 1-4 net; 5-9, 20%; 10-99, 40%; 100+, 42%. Schools & Libraries: 1-4, net; 5 or more, 20%. (Retail STOP: 30%) Wholesalers: 1-4, net; 5-24, 40%; 25-99, 42%; and 100+, 46%. 200pp; 4⅜×5⅛ (guidebooks only); of. Reporting time: 2 weeks to 3 months (decided by Committee). Payment: typical is 7½% royalty. Copyrights for author. COSMEP.

Ad-Lib Publications, John Kremer, 51 North Fifth Street, Fairfield, IA 52556, 515-472-6617. 1982. Non-fiction. "Length of material: 96-360 pages. We are primarily into illusions, fairytales, fables, and anything to do with words and writing and publishing" avg. press run 3M. Pub'd 5 titles 1990; expects 4 titles 1991, 4-6 titles 1992. 11 titles listed in the *Small Press Record of Books in Print* (20th Edition, 1991-92). avg. price, cloth: $19.95; paper: $14.95. Discounts: 2-4 books 20%, 5-24 40%, 25-49 43%, 50-99 45%, over 100 50%. 200pp; 8½×11; of. Reporting time: 2 weeks. Payment: 8%, no advance. Copyrights for author. COSMEP, PMA, American Booksellers Association, Mid-America Publisher Group, Upper Midwest Booksellers Association, Minnesota Independent Publishers Association.

ADOLESCENCE, Libra Publishers, Inc., 3089C Clairemont Dr., Suite 383, San Diego, CA 92117, 619-581-9449. 1960. Articles. circ. 3M. 4/yr. Pub'd 4 issues 1990; expects 4 issues 1991, 4 issues 1992. sub. price: $50/$40; per copy: $12; sample: $14. Back issues: $12. Discounts: 10% to subscriber agents. 256pp; 6×9; of. Reporting time: 3 weeks. Payment: none. Copyrighted, does not revert to author. Pub's reviews: 60 in 1990. §Behavioral sciences. Ads: $300/$175.

ADRIFT, Thomas McGonigle, 239 East 5th Street #4D, New York, NY 10003. 1982. Poetry, fiction, interviews, satire, criticism, reviews, letters, parts-of-novels, long-poems. "Interested in Irish, Irish-American, and other. Remembrance and reflection and despair. The final irreducible experience of the individual. James Liddy, Francis Stuart, Hannah Green" circ. 1M+. 2/yr. Pub'd 2 issues 1990; expects 2 issues 1991, 2 issues 1992. 1 title listed in the *Small Press Record of Books in Print* (20th Edition, 1991-92). sub. price: $8; per copy: $4; sample: $5. Back issues: #1 & #2 $6 each. Discounts: usual 60/40. 32pp; 8½×11; of. Reporting time: as soon as possible. Payment: yes. Copyrighted, rights revert with permission. Pub's reviews: 12 in 1990. §Irish and other fiction poetry. Ads: rates upon request.

THE ADROIT EXPRESSION, Xavier F. Aguilar, PO Box 73, Courtney, PA 15029. 1986. Poetry, fiction, art, reviews, letters. circ. 25-75. 2/yr. Pub'd 1 issue 1990; expects 3 issues 1991, 2 issues 1992. sub. price: $5; per copy: $3; sample: $3. 6-8pp; 8½×11; mi. Reporting time: 1 month. Payment: free copy, byline. Not copyrighted. Pub's reviews. Ads: by request.

ADVANCES IN THE ASTRONAUTICAL SCIENCES, Univelt, Inc., H. Jacobs, Series Editor, PO Box 28130, San Diego, CA 92128, 619-746-4005. 1957. "Space and related fields. An irregular serial. Publishers for the American Atronautical Society. Vols. 1-62 published. Standing orders accepted." circ. 500-600. Irregular. Pub'd 2 issues 1990; expects 4 issues 1991, 5 issues 1992. sub. price: varies. Back issues: no. Discounts: normally 20% but more by arrangement. Discounts for classroom use. 400-700pp; 7×9½; of. Reporting time: 60 days. Payment: none. Copyrighted, authors may republish material with appropriate credits given. No advertising.

Adventure Printing Inc., 3441 Halifax Street, PO Box 29543, Dallas, TX 75229. 1 title listed in the *Small Press Record of Books in Print* (20th Edition, 1991-92).

THE ADVOCATE, Liberation Publications, Inc., Richard Rouilard, Editor-in-Chief; Gerry Kroll, Editor, PO Box 4371, Los Angeles, CA 90078-4371, 213-871-1225. 1967. Articles, art, photos, cartoons, interviews, letters, news items, non-fiction. "Consumer magazine. Query first, most materials assigned. For advertising rates, call advertising offices in Los Angeles for current rates" circ. 75M. 26/yr. Pub'd 26 issues 1990; expects 26 issues 1991, 26 issues 1992. sub. price: $39.97; per copy: $2.95; sample: $3.95. Back issues: last 10 issues only $3.95 each. Discounts: none. 172pp; 8×10¾; web of. Reporting time: 6 weeks. Payment: inquire. Copyrighted. Pub's reviews: 50 in 1990. §All areas. Ads: $1830/$1030/$1.25. GPA (Gay Press Association), Magazine Publishers Assn. (MPA), Western Publishers Assn. (WPA).

THE ADVOCATE, Les Breeding, Ellen Barfield, HCR 2, Box 25, Panhandle, TX 79068, 806-335-1715. 1986. Poetry, articles, photos, cartoons, reviews, letters. circ. 1M. 6/yr. Pub'd 5 issues 1990; expects 6 issues 1991, 6 issues 1992. sub. price: $5; per copy: $1; sample: $1. Back issues: pay postage. 16pp; 8½×11; of. Payment: none. Not copyrighted. Pub's reviews: 22 in 1990. §Peace and justice, social change, disarmament. Ads: $75/$50/$10 business card.

AEGEAN REVIEW, Barbara Fields, Dino Siotis, Wire Press, 220 West 19th Street, Suite 2A, New York, NY 10011. 1986. Poetry, fiction, articles, art, photos, interviews, reviews, letters, parts-of-novels, non-fiction. "*Aegean Review* provides a showcase for Greeks, non- and would-be Greeks who have been touched by the Greek muse—Alice Bloom, Jorge Luis Borges, C.P. Cavafy, Truman Capote, Andrei Codrescu, Lawrence Durrell, Stratis Haviaras, Irving Layton, David Solway" circ. 2.5M. 2/yr. Pub'd 1 issue 1990; expects 2 issues 1991, 2 issues 1992. sub. price: $10; per copy: $5; sample: $5. Back issues: $8. Discounts: 40%. 72pp; 7×10; of. Reporting time: 6 weeks. Payment: $25. Not copyrighted. Pub's reviews: 4 in 1990. §Any books okay, magazines on Greece—ancient or modern. Ads: $265 (6 X 8½)/$145 (3 X 8½)/$85 1/4 page (3 X 4¼). CCLM, Modern Greek Studies Assoc.

Aegina Press, Inc., Ira Herman, Managing Editor, 59 Oak Lane, Spring Valley, Huntington, WV 25704, 304-429-7204. 1984. Poetry, fiction, non-fiction. "Publishes fiction, strongly encourages new authors. Also publishes poetry and nonfiction originals and reprints, in perfect-bound paperbacks. Manuscripts should be book-length (45-400 page typescript). Will consider all types of fiction, nonfiction and poetry, as long as quality is high. No racist, sexist, or hate materials. Primarily interested in novels, short story collections, and volumes of poetry. Enclose SASE for return of material. Reports in about one month. Simultaneous and photocopied submissions are acceptable. A 1-2 page synopsis is helpful. Presently reading in all categories for upcoming list. Often publishes material by new writers. Recent authors include Ken Winslett, Kirk Judd, and James Kelsh. During the next year, at least, we will be doing some subsidized publication. On subsidized books, author receives all sales proceeds until breakeven point. Then, a 40% royalty begins. Attempts to help and establish new authors" avg. press run 500-1M. Pub'd 15 titles 1990; expects 25 titles 1991, 25 titles 1992. 5 titles listed in the *Small Press Record of Books in Print* (20th Edition, 1991-92). avg. price, paper: $6.00. Discounts: 40% to libraries, bookstores and jobbers on orders of 5 or more copies. Free examination copies to potential adopters and distributors. 64-300pp; 5½×8½; of. Reporting time: 1 month. Payment: depends on author and subject matter; up to 15% royalty on nonsubsidized books. Copyrights for author.

The Aegis Group, T. Joe Willey, 155 W. Hospitality Lane #230, San Bernardino, CA 92408, 714-381-4800. 1987. "We are looking for books or manuscripts on labor management subject. Especially on temporary help or employee contracting concepts and work styles" Expects 3 titles 1991. avg. price, paper: $37.50; other: $87.50. Discounts: up to 43% in greater than 50 orders. 200pp; 8½×11; †of. Reporting time: 3 months. Payment: negotiable. Copyrights for author. National Staff Leasing Association.

Aeolus Press, Inc. (see also KITE LINES), Valerie Govig, Publisher & Editor, PO Box 466, Randallstown, MD 21133-0466, 301-922-1212; fax 301-922-4262. 1977. Articles, art, photos, interviews, reviews, letters, news items. avg. press run 13M. Expects 4 titles 1991. avg. price, paper: $3.95. Discounts: $2.55 each to kite and bookstores (20 minimum). 64pp; 8¾×10⅞; of. Reporting time: 2 weeks to 3 months. Payment: $0-$100 + copies. Does not copyright for author. BPA, Small Magazine Publishers Group.

AERIAL, Rod Smith, P.O. Box 25642, Washington, DC 20007, (202) 333-1544. 1984. Poetry, fiction, articles, art, photos, cartoons, interviews, satire, criticism, reviews, music, letters, parts-of-novels, long-poems, collages, plays, concrete art, news items, non-fiction. "Aerial #6 includes new work by, and an interview with, John Cage. Aerial #5 features Carla Harryman/Lyn Hejininan collaboration and an interview with Tina Darragh. Aerial #4 is the Douglas Messerli issue. *The best form of government is no government at all.*" circ. 1M. 1/yr. Pub'd 1 issue 1990. sub. price: $17/3 issues; per copy: varies; sample: $7. Discounts: 40% to retailers. 150pp; 6×9; of. Reporting time: 1 week-2 months. Payment: contributors copies. Copyrighted, reverts to author. Pub's reviews: 12 in 1990. §Lit. mags, poetry, fiction, criticism, art. Ads: $100/$60/will consider exchanges. CLMP.

AERO SUN-TIMES, Linda Hays, 44 N. Last Chance Gulch #9, Helena, MT 59601, 406-443-7272. 1974. Poetry, articles, art, photos, cartoons, interviews, criticism, reviews, letters, news items, non-fiction. "Length: 15 to 20 typed pages (single spaced, 20 pages); Biases: we promote sensible, appropriate, low-cost and decentralized applications of renewable energies, sustainable agriculture and local sustainable economic development; Recent contributors: Wilbur Wood, Steve Coffel, Miguel A. Altieri" circ. 1M. 4/yr. Expects 4 issues 1992. 5 titles listed in the *Small Press Record of Books in Print* (20th Edition, 1991-92). sub. price: $15/yr, magazine is part of $25 yearly membership in our non-profit tax-exempt educational organization; per copy: $2.50; sample: $2.50. Back issues: $1.25-$2.50. Discounts: none. 16pp; 8½×11; of. Reporting time: variable. Payment: solicited material done on either consulting or contracted basis; unsolicited material can seldom be paid for. Pub's reviews. §Sustainable alternatives to conventional agriculture, *sustainable* local economic development, pesticide/food issues. Ads: $85-$100/$50-$60/$35/$8 col in, minimum $8.

AFFAIRE DE COEUR, Brandywyne Books, Barbara Keenan, 5660 Roosevelt Place, Fremont, CA 94538, 415-357-5665. 1981. Articles, reviews, non-fiction. "*Affaire de Coeur* is a publication for romance readers and writers. It contains book reviews, articles, author profiles and other pertinent publishing news" circ. 15M. 12/yr. Pub'd 12 issues 1990; expects 12 issues 1991, 12 issues 1992. sub. price: $25 3rd class, $28 1st class, $32 out of state; per copy: $2; sample: same. Back issues: limited # issues available $3 each. Discounts: 40% return, 50% non-return. 16-24pp; 8×10; of. Reporting time: 2-3 months. Payment: $10-$25. Copyrighted. Pub's reviews: 600 in 1990. §Romance books and women's general fiction. Ads: $430/$270/$55. ABA.

Affiliated Writers of America, Inc., Jay Fraser, PO Box 343, Encampment, WY 82325, 307-327-5328. 1988. Fiction, non-fiction. avg. press run 4M. Pub'd 2 titles 1990; expects 6 titles 1991, 10 titles 1992. 5 titles listed in the *Small Press Record of Books in Print* (20th Edition, 1991-92). avg. price, cloth: $19.95; paper: $11.95. Discounts: trade. 300pp; 6×9; of. Copyrights for author.

Affinity Press, Judithann H. David-Carrea, 73 Brookwood Road #18, Orinda, CA 94563-3310, 415-253-1889. 1987. Non-fiction. "All current books are on the 'Michael Teaching,' a philosophical/spiritual view of the universe. We are a group of 6 authors and have printed 7 books to date" avg. press run 5M. Pub'd 2 titles 1990; expects 3 titles 1991, 2 titles 1992. avg. price, paper: $8.95, $11.95. Discounts: 40% to retail stores, 50% to catalogs, and 55% to distributors. 200pp; 6×9. Reporting time: 2 months. Payment: 37%, they pay all cost of advertising and printing. Copyrights for author. NAPRA.

Affinity Publishers Services, A. Doyle, Founder, PO Box 570213, Houston, TX 77257. 1981. avg. press run 55. avg. price, cloth: $3.95; paper: $1.95. Discounts: standard. 12pp; 8½×11. Reporting time: 7 weeks.

Affordable Adventures, Inc., Christine Boyce, Barbara McCang, PO Box 129, Brookfield, WI 53008-0129. 1982. Non-fiction. "Travel books, soon to be specializing in exotic travel. Regional and state books with emphasis on outdoor activity" avg. press run 5M. Pub'd 5 titles 1990; expects 12 titles 1991, 20 titles 1992. avg. price, paper: $5.95. Discounts: 40% 5-49 books, 50% 50+ books. 150-200pp; 4½×6, 8×11; †of. Reporting time: 4-6 weeks. Payment: advance $250-$1,000, 10% royalties, payment quarterly. Copyrights for author. American Association of Travel Writers.

AFRICA NEWS, Reed Kramer, Managing Editor, P.O. Box 3851, Durham, NC 27702, 919-286-0747. 1973. Articles, photos, interviews, reviews, news items. "All of the above items relate to current African developments" circ. 3M. 24/yr. Pub'd 8 issues 1990; expects 24 issues 1991, 24 issues 1992. sub. price: $30 individuals, $48 non-profit; per copy: $1.50; sample: 1 copy free; $5 two month trial. Back issues: rates upon request. Discounts: 3 rates, basically: individuals get special rate for (new) subscribers — 9 months for $24.

12pp; 8½×11; †of. Reporting time: 2 weeks. Payment: 8¢/word published. Copyrighted, does not revert to author. Pub's reviews: 0 in 1990. §Africa, Third World generally. No ads.

AFRICA TODAY, Edward A. Hawley, Exec. Editor; George W. Shepherd, Jr., Tilden J. LeMelle, c/o G.S.I.S, Univ of Denver, Denver, CO 80208. 1954. Articles, reviews, letters. "Scholarly articles on Africa *only* 2000-6000 words, book reviews (Africa titles only)–450-1800 words. We no longer publish poetry" circ. 1.5M. 4/yr. Pub'd 4 issues 1990; expects 4 issues 1991, 4 issues 1992. sub. price: $15 indiv., $40 instit.; per copy: $3.50 plus $.50 postage and handling charge; sample: no charge. Back issues: write for list. Discounts: 15% to established sub. agencies only; bulk rates available. 96pp; 5½×8¾; of. Reporting time: 3-4 months. Payment: copies in which article appears. Copyrighted, does not revert to author. Pub's reviews: 44 in 1990. §Contemporary Africa-various aspects: political, economic, geographic, literary. Ads: $140/$75/$40 1/4 page.

Africa World Press, Inc., Kassahun Checole, PO Box 1892, Trenton, NJ 08607, 609-771-1666, FAX 609-771-1616. 1983. Poetry, photos, interviews, criticism, reviews, non-fiction. "*A.W.P.* publishes books on current issues related to the African world. Our focus is on human rights, development problems and allied subjects. Among our authors are reknowned writers such as Ngugi wa Thiong'o and Sonia Sanchez, Nzongola-Ntalaja, Ann Seidman, Kofi Hadjor, Carole Davies, Immanuel Wallerstein, Horace Campbell, Basil Davidson, Molefi Asante, John Saul, Jean Suret-Carole, Lina Magaia, William Minter, Peter Katjavivi, Jan Carew, Bernard Magubane, Cecil Abrahams, Mokubung Nkomo, Robert Edgar" avg. press run 5M. Pub'd 50 titles 1990; expects 92 titles 1991, 100 titles 1992. 31 titles listed in the *Small Press Record of Books in Print* (20th Edition, 1991-92). avg. price, cloth: $45; paper: $14.95. Discounts: 40% trade, jobbers 20%, individual orders must be prepaid. 250pp; 5½×6½; of. Reporting time: upon receipt of a manuscript, once it is accepted for publication, within 1 year we go to press. Payment: negotiable — average 7½% royalty on both editions. Copyrights for author. ABA, ASA, ALA.

African American Images, Jawanza Kunjufu, 9204 Commercial, Suite 308, Chicago, IL 60617. 1980. Non-fiction. avg. press run 5M. Pub'd 2 titles 1990; expects 2 titles 1991, 2-4 titles 1992. 19 titles listed in the *Small Press Record of Books in Print* (20th Edition, 1991-92). avg. price, paper: $7. Discounts: 5-75 40%, 76-99 46%, 100+ 50%. 125pp; 5½×8½; of. Reporting time: 2 months to respond. Payment: 10% net. Copyrights for author. COSMEP.

THE AFRICAN BOOK PUBLISHING RECORD, Hans Zell Publishers, Hans M. Zell, Editor; Mary Jay, Deputy Editor, PO Box 56, Oxford 0X13EL, England, 0865-511428. 1975. Articles, interviews, criticism, reviews, news items. "Largely a bibliographic tool, providing information on new and forthcoming African published materials; plus 'Notes & News', 'Magazines', 'Reports', 'Reference Sources' sections and interviews; normally one major article on aspects of publishing and book development in Africa per issue. Major book review section. (Ca. 50 reviews per issue)." circ. 800. 4/yr. Pub'd 4 issues 1990; expects 4 issues 1991, 4 issues 1992. sub. price: £75 ($130); per copy: £12 - $21.50; sample: gratis. Back issues: £48-$86 per volume; £12-$21.50 per issue. Discounts: 15% to adv. agents/10% to subs. agents. 84pp; size A4; of/li. Reporting time: 6-8 weeks. Payment: £50-£80 ($90-$140) for major articles. Copyrighted. Pub's reviews: 312 in 1990. §Books published in Africa only, with an emphasis on scholarly books, creative writing, reference tools, and children's books. Ads: £110 ($220)/ £70 ($140)/ £120 ($240) cover 3 & 4.

AFRICAN STUDIES, Witwatersrand University Press, W.D. Hammond-Tooke, WITS, 2050 Johannesburg, Republic of South Africa. 1921. Articles, criticism, reviews. "(Former title: *Bantu Studies*). African anthropology and linguistics." circ. 800. 2/yr. Pub'd 2 issues 1990; expects 2 issues 1991, 2 issues 1992. sub. price: individual R15, institutions R35; per copy: individual R8.00; insititutions R18.00; sample: on application. Back issues: on application. Discounts: 10% to booksellers and agents. 100pp; 21×15cm (A5); of. Reporting time: 3 months. Payment: none. Copyrighted, does not revert to author. Pub's reviews: 19 in 1990. §African anthropology and linguistics. Ads: R100/R50.

AFRO-HISPANIC REVIEW, Marvin A. Lewis, Edward J. Mullen, Romance Languages, Univ. of Missouri, 143 Arts & Science Building, Columbia, MO 65211, 314-882-2030. 1982. Poetry, fiction, articles, interviews, criticism, reviews, letters, news items. "We also publish translations" circ. 500. 3/yr. Pub'd 3 issues 1990; expects 3 issues 1991, 3 issues 1992. sub. price: $9 indiv., $15 instit.; per copy: $5; sample: $5. Back issues: $5. Discounts: 40%. 32pp; 8½×11; of. Reporting time: 60 days. Payment: 5 copies of issue containing contribution. Copyrighted, does not revert to author. Pub's reviews: 6 in 1990. §Afro-Hispanic history, literature and sociology. Ads: $100/$50/50¢.

Afta Press (see also CROW MAGAZINE; CROW—The Alternative Magazine), Bill Dale Marcinko, 47 Crater Avenue, Wharton, NJ 07885, 201-828-5467. 1977. Articles, art, photos, interviews, satire, criticism, reviews, music. avg. press run 1M. Expects 3 titles 1991, 3 titles 1992. avg. price, paper: $5.95. Discounts: 50% off w/returns; 60% without returns; minimum order per title-5. 8½×11; of. Reporting time: 1 week. Payment: in contributor's copies, first rights only. Does not copyright for author.

AFTERIMAGE, Visual Studies Workshop, Nathan Lyons, Editor; David Trend, Managing Editor, 31 Prince

Street, Rochester, NY 14607, 716-442-8676. 1972. Articles, photos, interviews, criticism, reviews, letters, news items. "Features, reviews, news, notices of exhibitions. Recent contributors: Paul Byers, Howard Becker, Michael Lesy, A.D. Coleman, Les Krims, Nam June Paik, Richard Rudisill" circ. 4.2M. 9/yr. Pub'd 9 issues 1990; expects 9 issues 1991, 9 issues 1992. sub. price: $25; per copy: $2.25 single, $4.00 double; sample: gratis. Back issues: $2.25. Discounts: Classrooms (10 or more subscriptions) 20% — Trade 40%. 24pp; 11×17; †of. Reporting time: 2-3 weeks. Copyrighted, reverts to author. Pub's reviews: 54 long, 248 short in 1990. §Photography, film, video, and visual books. No advertising. ◡CLM,.

AGADA, Reuven Goldfarb, Editor; Yehudit Goldfarb, Associate Editor; Danielle Lanier-Shelley, Managing Editor, 2020 Essex Street, Berkeley, CA 94703, 415-848-0965. 1981. Poetry, fiction, articles, art, interviews, criticism, parts-of-novels. "We have a limit of 6M words on our fiction and articles but also print much shorter pieces. We publish as much poetry as prose and like a spiritual point of view. We generally select for publication work whose subject matter is in some way related to the Jewish experience, its values and aspirations. We draw from Classical sources—Scriptural, Rabbinic, Kabbalistic, and Chassidic—for translations and for inspiration but cultivate a contemporary sensibility in regard to how we shape this material. Recent contributors: The magazine is well illustrated with Thomas Friedmann, Daniel Spicehandler, Marcia Tager, Florence Wallach Freed, Julie Heifetz, Yael Mesinai, Robert Stern and Roger White graphic art" circ. 1M. 2/yr. Pub'd 1 issue 1990; expects 1 issue 1991, 1 issue 1992. sub. price: $12/12 issues; per copy: $6.50; sample: $6.50. Back issues: $6/$5/$4—inquire for more details. Discounts: Bookstores: 40% discount ($3.90 each); Agents: $3.25 each on orders of 25 or more. 64pp; 7×10; of. Reporting time: 3-4 months, more or less. Payment: only to illustrators, at present. Copyrighted, reverts to author. Ads: $100/$50/$25 1-4 page—no classifieds accepted. CCLM/COSMEP.

Again + Again Press (see also REMARK), Charles Fabrizio, Editor, PO Box 20041, Cherokee Station, New York, NY 10028.

AGAPE, Truth Center, Roselyn Witt, Filip Field, 6940 Oporto Drive, Los Angeles, CA 90068, 213-876-6295. 1970. Articles. "Religious articles by W. Norman Cooper and his students" circ. 3M-4M. 6/yr. Pub'd 6 issues 1990; expects 6 issues 1991, 6 issues 1992. sub. price: any donation to world-wide work of Truth Center; per copy: donation; sample: no charge upon request. Back issues: 75¢. 8-12pp; 5½×8½; lp. Not copyrighted. Do not accept ads.

Agathon Press, Burton Lasky, Publisher & Production Editor, 225 West 34th Street, New York, NY 10122-0072. 1959. Non-fiction. "Publisher of scholarly books. Releases include 10 titles in political science, 2 titles in early education, and the first 6 volumes of an annual series on higher education" avg. press run 2M. Pub'd 3 titles 1990; expects 2 titles 1991, 2 titles 1992. 21 titles listed in the *Small Press Record of Books in Print* (20th Edition, 1991-92). avg. price, cloth: $35; paper: $15. Discounts: 1-4 copies 20%, 5+ copies 25%, occasional trade discounts on special titles. of. Reporting time: 2 weeks to 4 months. Payment: 10% net. Copyrights for author. COSMEP.

THE AGE OF AQUARIUS, Gerina Dunwich, 7131 Owensmouth Avenue #066, Canoga Park, CA 91303-2008. 1990. Poetry, articles, art, photos, cartoons, satire, reviews, letters, news items, non-fiction. "*The Age of Aquarius* is a Neo-Hippie journal of poetry, psychedelic art, love, New Age spirituality, and flower-power. We seek (but are not limited to) poetry, far-out artwork, and articles that deal with ecology, mind-expanding drugs, war, free love, the occult, the re-surgence of the Hippie culture in the 1990's, and other related topics. *Taboos*: anything that is sexist, racist, ageist, punk, or yuppie. 50 lines maximum for poetry. To order samples, etc., please send cash or make checks and money orders payable to Gerina Dunwich. Recent contributors include Karma Kosmic, Don Lewis (artwork), and the flower-child Gypsy Electra." circ. 300. 4/yr. Expects 4 issues 1991, 4 issues 1992. sub. price: $8; per copy: $2; sample: $2. 20pp; 5½×8½; †Canon PC method (desktop publishing). Reporting time: 1-3 weeks. Payment: 1 free contributor's copy. Copyrighted, reverts to author. Pub's reviews. §Poetry, 60's nostalgia, New Age/occult, counter-culture and anything off-beat. Ads: $20/$10/classified 25¢ per word; we also accept ads on an exchange basis with other magazines.

THE AGENCIES-WHAT THE ACTOR NEEDS TO KNOW, Acting World Books, Lawrence Parke, PO Box 3044, Hollywood, CA 90078, 213-466-4297. 1981. "Occasional articles by and or about subject material people, orgns, currently recommended procedures, etc" circ. 1.2M. 6/yr. Pub'd 6 issues 1990; expects 6 issues 1991, 6 issues 1992. sub. price: $40; per copy: $10. Back issues: not available. Discounts: 40% bookstore. 35pp; 8½×11; †of. Reporting time: 2 weeks. Payment: as and if negotiated. Copyrighted, reverts to author. Ads: $500 1/2 page/special 6 months in both pub's, rate $800.

AGENDA, Agenda Editions, William Cookson, Peter Dale, 5 Cranbourne Court, Albert Bridge Road, London, England SW11 4PE, England, 071-228-0700. 1959. Poetry, articles, art, photos, interviews, satire, reviews, long-poems. "Poetry must be in recognizable contemporary English. 'More than usual emotion, more than usual order'. At least half magazine devoted to reviews. Special issues on individual poets or themes. Art & photos: we usually have a reproduction on our covers, except for special issues where we use photographs"

11

circ. approx. 1.5M. 4/yr. Pub'd 4 issues 1990; expects 4 issues 1991. sub. price: £16 indiv., £22 instit., overseas £18 ($38) indiv., £24 ($50) instit.; per copy: £4 ($9); sample: £3.50 ($7.50). Most back issues £4 ($9); these vary according to rarity, (double issues £7.50 $18). Discounts: 33⅓% for editions; 15% for magazine issues. 80pp; 7×5; lp. Reporting time: 3 months. Payment: £12 per page of poetry. Copyrighted, reverts to author. Pub's reviews: 12 in 1990. §Contemporary poetry, neglected poetry from past. Ads: £250/£125.

Agenda Editions (see also §AGENDA), William Cookson, Peter Dale, 5 Cranbourne Court, Albert Bridge Rd, London, England SW114PE, England, 01-228-0700. 1971. Poetry. "New poetry; translations" avg. press run 500-1M. Expects 2 titles 1991. 24 titles listed in the *Small Press Record of Books in Print* (20th Edition, 1991-92). avg. price, cloth: £12-£15; paper: £6.60; other: £25-£50 depending on author & length. Discounts: 33⅓%. 60-80pp; 7×5; lp. Reporting time: 3 months. Payment: 10% after costs.

AGNI, Askold Melnyczuk, Editor; Sharon Dunn, Advisory Editor, Boston Univ-Creative Writing Program, 236 Bay State Road, Boston, MA 02215, 617-353-5389. 1972. Poetry, fiction, parts-of-novels, long-poems. "Derek Walcott, James Fenton, Seamus Heaney, Marilynne Robinson, Ai, Carolyn Chute, Diane Wakoski, Sven Birkerts,Olga Broumas, Joyce Carol Oates, George Scialabba, Tom Sleigh, Eavan Boland, Alfred Alcorn, Robert Pinsky, Dzvinia Orlowsky are among past contributors" circ. 2M. 2/yr. Pub'd 2 issues 1990; expects 2 issues 1991. sub. price: $12; per copy: $7; sample: $7. Back issues: varies. 350pp; 5½×8½; of. Reporting time: 1-4 months. Payment: $10 per page. Copyrighted, reverts to author. Pub's reviews: 5-6 in 1990. §Politics & literature. Ads: upon request. CLMP, AWP.

AGOG, Scott Gray, 340 22nd Street, Brooklyn, NY 11215, 718-965-3871. 1990. Poetry, fiction, art, photos, cartoons, interviews, criticism, reviews, plays. "Biases: I have my share of 'em. Recent contributors: Erin Van Rheenen, Dondi DeMarco" circ. 100. 4/yr. Expects 4 issues 1991, 4 issues 1992. price per copy: $2. 45pp; 5½×8½; †mi. Reporting time: 1 week. Payment: color copies. Copyrighted, reverts to author. Pub's reviews: 1 in 1990. §Fun stuff, whatever.

AGRICULTURAL HISTORY, University of California Press, Morton Rothstein, University of California Press, 2120 Berkeley Way, Berkeley, CA 94720, 415-642-4191. 1926. Articles, reviews, non-fiction. "Editorial address: Agricultural History Center, University of California, Davis, CA 95616. Copyrighted by Agricultural History Society." circ. 1.25M. 4/yr. Pub'd 4 issues 1990; expects 4 issues 1991, 4 issues 1992. sub. price: $25 indiv., $43 instit., $15 students; per copy: $6.25 indiv.; $10.75 instit., $4 students. Back issues: $6.25 indiv.; $10.75 instit., $4 students. Discounts: foreign subs. agent 10%, one-time orders 10+ 30%, standing orders (bookstores): 1-99 40%, 100+ 50%. 106pp; 6×9; of. Reporting time: 2-3 weeks. Payment: varies. Copyrighted, does not revert to author. Pub's reviews: 100 in 1990. §Agricultural history and economics. Ads: $200/$120.

AHA Books (see also MIRRORS - IN THE SPIRIT OF HAIKU), Jane Reichhold, PO Box 767, Gualala, CA 95445, 707-882-2226. 1987. "Haiku and renga books of more than 80 pages. Not into mini-chapbooks." avg. press run 200-1M. Pub'd 2 titles 1990; expects 9 titles 1991, 14 titles 1992. 15 titles listed in the *Small Press Record of Books in Print* (20th Edition, 1991-92). avg. price, paper: $10. Discounts: 40%. 125-400pp; 5×8; of. Reporting time: 2 weeks. Payment: individually arranged. Copyrights for author.

THE AHFAD JOURNAL: Women And Change, Amna El Sadik, The Ahfad University for Women, 4141 N. Henderson Rd., Suite 1216, Arlington, VA 22203, (703) 525-9045. 1984. Articles, reviews. "6 to 8 pages for main articles, mostly reports of original research; 1-2 pages for research notes; 1-2 pages for book reviews: focus on women in developing countries, particularly Sudan, Africa and the Middle East; roles of women in national development. Editorial address: PO Box 167, Ahfad University for Women, Omdurman, Sudan, Africa. 6 months required because all editorial decisions are made in Sudan, where the Journal is published and from which it is distributed by airmail to subscribers" circ. 400. 2/yr. Pub'd 2 issues 1990; expects 2 issues 1991, 2 issues 1992. sub. price: 40; per copy: $20; sample: free. Discounts: 10%. 84-88pp; 6⅝×9½; lp. Reporting time: 6 months. Payment: none. Copyrighted, reverts to author. Pub's reviews: 12 in 1990. §Books only; women in developing countries, women's roles in development, Sudan, Africa, Middle East. No ads.

Ahsahta, T. Trusky, O. Burmaster, D. Boyer, Boise State University, Department of English, Boise, ID 83725, 208-385-1246 or 1999. 1975. Poetry. "We publish only work by Western poets—this does not mean paeans to the pommel or songs of the sage, but quality verse which clearly indicates its origin in the West. Samplers (15 poems) sent SASE read Jan-Mar." avg. press run 500. Pub'd 3 titles 1990; expects 3 titles 1991, 3 titles 1992. 39 titles listed in the *Small Press Record of Books in Print* (20th Edition, 1991-92). avg. price, paper: $6.45 postpaid; other: $7.45 Ahsahta Cassette Sampler, postpaid. Discounts: 40% to trade, bulk, jobber, classroom; no returns. 60pp; 6×8½; †of. Reporting time: 2 months. Payment: copies of book; royalties begin on third printing; titles in-print eternally. Copyrights for author. COSMEP.

AIGA Publications, Kenneth Lindsay, Executive Editor, PO Box 148, Laie, HI 96762, 808-293-5277. 1980. Non-fiction. "Specializing in bilingual public health information, cultural anthropology, contract bridge, and small computers, including computer software" avg. press run 500-2M. Expects 3 titles 1991, 2 titles 1992. avg. price, paper: $8.50; other: 20 pp pamplets-free. Discounts: Progressive discounts with increasing quantities, up to maximum of 50%. Schedule varies with title. 170pp; 5½×8½. Reporting time: 1-6 weeks. Payment: subsidy only, unless a manuscript is *very exceptional*. Usually copyrights for author.

AIKI NEWS, Aiki News, Stanley Pranin, Editor-in-Chief; Diane Bauerle, English Editor, Lions Mansion #204, Tamagawa Gakuen 5-11-25, Machida-shi, Tokyo-to 194, Japan, 81(427)24-9119. 1974. Articles, photos, interviews, reviews, non-fiction. "English editorial office: Yasuda Co-op #201, 4-14-10 Shimo-Shakujii, Nerima-ku, Tokyo 177, Japan. Most of our material is generated in-house. Unsolicited manuscripts will not be accepted." circ. 6M. 4/yr. Pub'd 4 issues 1990; expects 4 issues 1991, 4 issues 1992. sub. price: $30; per copy: $5. Back issues: $7. Discounts: 40% on prepaid orders of more than 10 copies. 70pp; 8½×11; of. Copyrighted, does not revert to author. Pub's reviews: 3 in 1990. §Aikido, Daito-ryu Aikijujutsu, Japanese Martial Arts. Ads: full page $1,098 color/$698 b/w/1/2 page $783 color/$398 b/w/$215 1/4 page b/w. PMA, COSMEP.

Aiki News (see also AIKI NEWS), Stanley Pranin, Editor-in-Chief; Diane Bauerle, English Editor, Lions Mansion #204, Tamagawa Gakuen 5-11-25, Machida-shi, Tokyo-to 194, Japan, 81(427)9119. 1988. Articles, photos, interviews, reviews, non-fiction. "English editorial office: Yasuda Co-op #201, 4-14-10 Shimo-Shakujii, Nerima-ku, Tokyo 177, Japan. Most of our material is generated in-house. Unsolicited manuscripts will not be accepted." avg. press run 4166. Pub'd 1 title 1990; expects 3 titles 1991, 3 titles 1992. 2 titles listed in the *Small Press Record of Books in Print* (20th Edition, 1991-92). avg. price, paper: $18.42. Discounts: 6-9 copies 15%, 10-24 25%, 25-49 35%, 50-99 45%, 99+ 50%. 194pp; 8½×11; of. Copyrights for author. PMA, COSMEP.

AILERON, A LITERARY JOURNAL, Edwin Buffaloe, Cynthia Farar, PO Box 891, Austin, TX 78767-0891. 1980. Poetry, fiction, articles, art, satire, criticism, long-poems. "No limitations as to form or content. All submissions must have name & address on each page. SASE required. Copies of work accepted are not returned. ART: Black & White only, 5 X 7 to 8 X 10, originals only. Originals of art will be returned. We are no longer able to publish photographs" circ. 300. 1/yr. Pub'd 1 issue 1990; expects 1 issue 1991, 1 issue 1992. sub. price: $7; per copy: $3.50; sample: $4. Back issues: issues prior to 1984 $10 each; first issue unavailable. Discounts: 50%. 60pp; 5½×8½; †xerox. Reporting time: 10 weeks. Payment: 1 copy. Copyrighted, reverts to author. Ads: negotiable.

AIM MAGAZINE, Ruth Apilado, Editor; Myron Apilado, Managing Editor, PO Box 20554, Chicago, IL 60620. 1973. "Our readers are those wanting to eliminate bigotry and desiring a world without inequalities in education, housing, etc. Because of the threat of nuclear war, people are seeking out ways for survival. They are feeling more alienated from society and are more conscious of the importance of getting together.— Recently we sponsored an essay contest on "Where is God?" The apartheid practices in South Africa prompted it. Dr. William Lawlor from the University of Wisconsin won the prize. The title of his article was "God And The Disinherited." We sponsor short story contests. We're looking for compelling, well-written pieces with lasting social significance. The story should not moralize. Length: 4,000 words" circ. 10M. 4/yr. Pub'd 4 issues 1990; expects 4 issues 1991, 4 issues 1992. sub. price: $8; per copy: $2; sample: $3.50. Back issues: $4. Discounts: 30%. 48pp; 8½×11. Reporting time: 1 month. Payment: $25 articles and stories. Not copyrighted. Pub's reviews: 2 in 1990. §Black and Hispanic life. Ads: $250/$150/$90 1/4 page.

Aircraft Owner Organization, David Sakrison, PO Box 337, Iola, WI 54945, 800-331-0038. 1 title listed in the *Small Press Record of Books in Print* (20th Edition, 1991-92).

AIRLINERS, World Transport Press, John Wegg, PO Box 52-1238, Miami, FL 33152, 305-477-7163. 1988. Articles, satire, reviews, news items, non-fiction. "Articles concerning commercial aviation only" circ. 15M. 4/yr. Pub'd 4 issues 1990; expects 4 issues 1991, 4 issues 1992. sub. price: $15.95; per copy: $3.95; sample: $3.95. Back issues: $3.95 if available. Discounts: contact publisher. 72pp; 8½×11; of. Reporting time: 3 months. Payment: yes, contact publisher. Not copyrighted. Pub's reviews: 28 in 1990. §Commercial aviation. Ads: $550/$325/$35 column inch. COSMEP.

AIRLINERS MONTHLY NEWS, World Transport Press, John Wegg, PO Box 52-1238, Miami, FL 33152, 305-477-7163. 1989. News items. "Commercial aviation news and news photos" circ. 2M. 12/yr. Pub'd 12 issues 1990; expects 12 issues 1991, 12 issues 1992. sub. price: $39.95; per copy: $3.95; sample: $3.95. Back issues: $3.95. Discounts: contact publisher. 20pp; 8½×11; of. Reporting time: 1 month. Payment: none. Not copyrighted. Ads: $40 column inch.

AIRPORT P0CKET GUIDE UNITED STATES EDITION, 67 S. Bedford Street, Ste 400W, Burlington, MA 01803-5166. "ISSN 0894-1513. A publication for frequent flyers contains top 100 major U.S. airportterminal diagrams-Intl symbols show location of airport services. Plus travel information including 80 listings" 4/yr. sub. price: US $39.95, CAN $43.95, O/S $59.95; per copy: $12.95 $1.55 S & H. 180pp; 4¼×8½.

Aka Press, M.J. Harden, Jill Engledow, PO Box 1372, Wailuku, HI 96793, 808-242-4173. 1987. Non-fiction. "Recently published a 368-page guidebook to Maui. Might do other Hawaii books or other travel guides" avg. press run 5M. Pub'd 1 title 1990; expects 1 title 1991, 1 title 1992. 1 title listed in the *Small Press Record of*

Books in Print (20th Edition, 1991-92). avg. price, paper: $9.95. Discounts: 5-55% depending on amount ordered. 300pp; 6×9; of. Reporting time: 1 month. Payment: variable. COSMEP.

Akiba Press, Sheila Baker, PO Box 13086, Oakland, CA 94661, 415-339-1283. 1978. Fiction, photos. "Will publish historical fiction and non-fiction, as well as juveniles on same themes. Up to 400 pp." avg. press run 2.5M. Expects 2 titles 1991. avg. price, cloth: $10; paper: $5.95. Discounts: 20% libraries, 40% bookstores. 250pp; 6×8; ip. Reporting time: 3 months. Payment: 10% royalty, no advance. Copyrights for author.

‡**AKWEKON: A National Native American Literary & Arts Journal, Akwesasne Notes,** Alex Jacobs, Peter Blue Cloud, Dan Thompson, Salli Benedict, PO Box 223, Hogansburg, NY 13655, 518-358-9531/9535. 1985. Poetry, fiction, articles, art, photos, cartoons, interviews, satire, criticism, reviews, music, letters, parts-of-novels, long-poems, collages, plays, concrete art, news items, non-fiction. "Accepting: poetry, short stories, prose, works in progress, experimental, reviews of all media concerning Native people & issues, critical pieces, satire, humour, artwork, photos, artist profiles/interviews, listings paid advertising, classifieds, until income established, payment in copies. $7 single issue by mail order, $20 individual sub, $25 institution sub, $7 cover price, need distributors/sellers." circ. 1M. 4/yr. Expects 4 issues 1991, 4 issues 1992. sub. price: $20 individual, $25 institution US & Foreign & Canada. Canadian orders in Canadian currency: $25 individual, $30 institution; per copy: $7 regular issue; $10 double issue #2/3; sample: $5 for review or request for group to purchase bulk. Back issues: $11 AKWEKON #1; $10 #2/3; $7 #4. Discounts: 40% 4 and more. 72pp; 8½×11, 7½×10; of. Reporting time: 4-8 weeks. Payment: copies (2-3). Copyrighted, reverts to author. Pub's reviews: 32 in 1990. §Native American Literature, arts. Ads: $150/$85/1/4-$55, 1/8-$30, column inch-$5.

‡**AKWEKON LITERARY JOURNAL, Akwesasne Notes,** Alex Jacobs, Peter Blue Cloud, Dan Thompson, Salli Benedict, PO Box 223, Hagansburg, NY 13655, 518-358-9531. 1984. Poetry, fiction, articles, art, photos, cartoons, interviews, satire, criticism, reviews, music, parts-of-novels, long-poems, collages, plays, concrete art, news items, non-fiction. "Priority: Native North American Native writers/artists; international indigenous writers/artists; 6 poems; 1-8 page short story/fiction; b/w art/photos; color cover art selected from slide or print; art exhibits/shows/reviews; music/artists; video/performing arts reviews, essays, articles, listings; resource & contacts listings in Indian Country, publishers, media, fine and commercial art, products. John Trudell, Linda Hogan, Lance Henson, Joe Bruchac, Wendy Rose, Barney Bush, Bill Oandasan, Ray Young Bear. PO Box 191, St. Regis, Quebec H0M 1A0 or Mohawk Nation, Rooseveltown, NY 13683-0196" circ. 1M. 4/yr. Pub'd 3 issues 1990; expects 4 issues 1991. sub. price: $20; per copy: $7; sample: $7. Back issues: AKWEKON #1 $7; AKWEKON #2/3 $10; AKWEKON #4 $7. Discounts: bookstore 40% regular; 25% double issue/classes 25%. 72pp; 8½×11; of. Reporting time: 4-6 weeks. Payment: copies, subscriptions. Copyrighted, reverts to author. Pub's reviews: 32 in 1990. §Native North American art, literature, media, culture, non-native publishers, businesses, groups aiming for native audience. Ads: $150/$85/$55 1/4 page/$30 1/8 page/$5 per column inch.

‡**Akwesasne Notes (see also AKWEKON: A National Native American Literary & Arts Journal; AKWEKON LITERARY JOURNAL),** Peter Blue Cloud, Alex Jacobs, PO Box 196, Rooseveltown, NY 13683, 518-358-9531. 1968. Poetry, articles, art, photos, interviews, criticism, reviews, music, letters, long-poems, news items, non-fiction. "An international journal for native & natural peoples; USA, Canada, Central-South America, other indigenous and folk cultures. Native land rights, religion, philosophy, politics, economy, culture, poetry, artwork. Bio-regional, Green Party, permaculture, Peace Movement, appropriate technology, North American legislation, human rights, international arms market, international indigenous conferences, Native women, children, elders, Iroquois Confederacy & Great Law of Peace. Ward Churchill, Hank Adams, Winona LaDuke, Jack Forbes, John Mohawk, Vine Deloria, Elders Circle, Coyote, Bill Wahpepah. Poetry, photos, artwork, reviews, articles, essays for, by, about native people, rights cultures. 2 double space pages = 1 column in *NOTES*, 9-12 columns maximum. *INDIAN TIME*: local newspaper, 1200 every two weeks" avg. press run 10M. Expects 2-3 titles 1992. 6 titles listed in the *Small Press Record of Books in Print* (20th Edition, 1991-92). avg. price, cloth: $8; paper: $5; other: $3, $5, $5.50, $6.95. Discounts: 40% bulk 12 or more; 25% small orders for classes, groups. 95pp; 6×9; of. Reporting time: 4-8 weeks. Payment: individual contracts. Copyrights for author. APS.

ALA Social Responsibilities Round Table (see also ALA/SRRT NEWSLETTER), c/o Eubanks, Brooklyn College Library, Brooklyn, NY 11210.

ALA/SRRT NEWSLETTER, ALA Social Responsibilities Round Table, c/o Eubanks, Brooklyn College Library, Brooklyn, NY 11210. 1969. "News-little outside material solicited. Bias-small press & movement press for libraries." circ. 1.2M. 4-5/yr. Expects 4 issues 1991. sub. price: individual $3/yr, institution $20; sample: 1 free. Back issues: $1 ea. 8pp; 8½×11, fold; of. Payment: none. Pub's reviews: 4 in 1990. §Movement-general, literary-only gay, women. No ads. COSMEP.

ALABAMA DOGSHOE MOUSTACHE, dbqp, Ge(of Huth), po.ed.t, 317 Princetown Road, Schenectady, NY 12306-2022. 1987. Poetry, cartoons, collages, concrete art. "*Alabama Dogshoe Moustache (ADM)* is a quarterly poetry magazine publishing mostly visual and language poetry. Subscriptions can be of any amount—cost (which varies) per issue will be subtracted when mailed" circ. 100. 4/yr. Pub'd 4 issues 1990; expects 4 issues 1991, 4 issues 1992. sub. price: varies by complexity of issue—about $5 per year; per copy: 75¢-$2.75; sample: 75¢-$2.75. Discounts: none. 5pp; size varies; †photocopy, rubberstamp printing. Reporting time: 2 weeks. Payment: at least 2 copies; 1/4 of press run is divided among contributors. Copyrighted, reverts to author.

ALABAMA LITERARY REVIEW, Theron E. Montgomery III, Editor; James G. Davis, Associate Editor, Smith 253, Troy State University, Troy, AL 36082, 205-566-8112 Ext. 3307. 1987. Poetry, fiction, articles, art, photos, cartoons, interviews, criticism, reviews, parts-of-novels, long-poems, plays. "No bias against style or length of poetry, fiction or drama. First issue included Eve Shelnutt and Elise Sanguinetti" circ. 600+. 2/yr. Expects 1 issue 1991, 1-2 issues 1992. sub. price: $9; per copy: $4.50; sample: $4.50. 100pp; 6×9; of, hand spine. Reporting time: 4-6 weeks. Payment: copies. Copyrighted, reverts to author. Pub's reviews: 6 in 1990. §All kinds, particularly poetry and fiction by new authors and/or smaller presses.

ALABAMA REVIEW, Sarah Woolfolk Wiggins, Editor, PO Box 1209, University of Alabama, Tuscaloosa, AL 35486-1209. 1947. "Published in cooperation with the Alabama Historical Assn. The journal includes articles on Alabama history and culture and book reviews on Alabama and Southern history and culture." 4/yr. Pub'd 4 issues 1990; expects 4 issues 1991, 4 issues 1992. sub. price: $15; per copy: $5.50. 80pp. Payment: none. Copyrighted, does not revert to author. Pub's reviews: 75 in 1990. §Alabama history.

Alamo Square Press, Bert Herrman, PO Box 14543, San Francisco, CA 94114, 415-252-0643. 1988. Non-fiction. "Book length, gay, non-pornographic, social or spiritual importance only" avg. press run 5M. Expects 2 titles 1991, 2 titles 1992. 3 titles listed in the *Small Press Record of Books in Print* (20th Edition, 1991-92). avg. price, paper: $9. Discounts: 40% retail, 55% distributor. 144pp; 5½×8½; of. Reporting time: 2 weeks. Payment: negotiable. Copyrights for author. COSMEP.

Alan Wofsy Fine Arts, Milton J. Goldbaum, Zeke Greenberg, Adios Butler, PO Box 2210, San Francisco, CA 94126, 415-986-3030. 1969. Art, cartoons. avg. press run 500. Pub'd 4 titles 1990; expects 4 titles 1991, 5+ titles 1992. 14 titles listed in the *Small Press Record of Books in Print* (20th Edition, 1991-92). avg. price, cloth: $95; paper: $20. Discounts: 20-40. 300pp; 9×12; of. Payment: varies. Copyrights for author.

ALASKA ASSOCIATION OF SMALL PRESSES, Fathom Publishing Co., Constance Taylor, PO Box 821, Cordova, AK 99574. 1984. Articles, interviews, criticism, reviews, letters, non-fiction. "Recent contributors, Norm Bolotin, Sharon Haney, Tee Loftin, John Mitchell. Accept articles of interest to small presses, writers, and photographers" circ. 200. 4-6/yr. Pub'd 1 issue 1990; expects 1 issue 1991, 4 issues 1992. sub. price: $10; per copy: free; sample: free. Back issues: free with sub, otherwise $1. 8pp; 8½×11; †of. Reporting time: 1 month. Copyrighted, reverts to author. Pub's reviews. §All areas of publishing with emphasis on small presses. Ads: $5 col. in camera ready, $7 col. in not camera ready. 40+.

Alaska Native Language Center, Tom Alton, Box 900111, University of Alaska, Fairbanks, AK 99775-0120, 907-474-7874. 1972. Non-fiction. "We publish materials in or about Alaska Native languages only" avg. press run 1M-2M. Pub'd 6 titles 1990; expects 6 titles 1991, 6 titles 1992. 13 titles listed in the *Small Press Record of Books in Print* (20th Edition, 1991-92). avg. price, paper: $12. Discounts: wholesalers 40% on 5 or more items. 150pp; 8½×11, 6×9, 8½×7, 5½×8½; of. Reporting time: varies. Payment: varies. Sometimes copyrights for author. Alaska Association of Small Presses (AASP), Box 821, Cordova, AK 99574.

ALASKA QUARTERLY REVIEW, Ronald Spatz, Fiction Editor, Executive Editor; James Jakob Liszka, Philosophy Editor, Executive Editor; Thomas Sexton, Poetry Editor, English Department, Univ. of Alaska, 3221 Providence, Anchorage, AK 99508, 907-786-1731. 1981. Poetry, fiction, criticism, reviews, parts-of-novels. "We are looking for high quality traditional and unconventional fiction and poetry, as well as perceptive essays, critical articles and reviews of contemporary literature and philosophy. Unsolicited manuscripts welcome between August 15 and May 15" circ. 1M. 2/yr. Expects 2 issues 1992. 1 title listed in the *Small Press Record of Books in Print* (20th Edition, 1991-92). sub. price: $8; per copy: $4; sample: $3. Back issues: $5. 136pp; 6×9; of. Reporting time: 6-12 weeks. Payment: 1 contributor's copy. Copyrighted. Pub's reviews. §Fiction, poetry, criticism and philosophy. Ads: $100/$50. CCLM.

ALASKA WOMEN, Lory B. Leary, Editor-in-Chief; G.R. Gardner, Assistant Editor, HCR 64 Box 453, Seward, AK 99664, 907-288-3168. 1990. Poetry, articles, art, photos, cartoons, interviews, criticism, reviews, non-fiction. "We accept features on Alaskan Women only, written by or about. Feature articles limited to 1,500 words. Photos must be B/W; exception, cover photo in full color." 4/yr. Expects 2 issues 1991, 4 issues 1992. sub. price: $30; per copy: $10; sample: free. Back issues: $10, when available. Discounts: 50% plus postage/shipping on 100 or more; lesser amounts 30% plus postage/shipping. 36-40pp; 8½×11; Webb Press. Reporting time: 2 weeks. Payment: by-line and 1 year's subscription. Copyrighted, reverts to author. Pub's reviews: several in 1990. §books written by or about Alaska Women; submissions must include copy of book and b/w photo. Ads: none. COSMEP (International Association of Independent Publishers).

THE ALBANY REVIEW, Theodore Bouloukos II, Lyn Lifshin, Poetry Editor; Thomson H. Littlefield, Fiction Editor, Albany Review Associates, Inc., 80 Willett Street #1, Albany, NY 12210-1010. 1987. Poetry, fiction, art, photos, cartoons, interviews, satire, criticism. "Subscription price covers first-class mail only" circ. 15M. 10/yr. Pub'd 5 issues 1990; expects 5 issues 1991, 10 issues 1992. sub. price: $15; per copy: $1; sample: $1.50. Discounts: as negotiated. 60pp; 11×14. Reporting time: 6 weeks. Payment: 2 copies. Copyrighted, reverts to author. Pub's reviews: 24 in 1990. §Current fiction, nonfiction. Ads: $1045/$530.

ALBATROSS, Anabiosis Press, Richard Smyth, Richard Brobst, 125 Horton Avenue, Englewood, FL 33981. 1986. Poetry, art, interviews, long-poems. "Continuous deadline. Send 3-5 poems, 200 line max. Published in spring and fall, 2 issues/year. $3/issue; $5/2 issues. Recent contributors: Duane Locke, Walter Griffin, Stephen Meats, Janet McCann. Tend to be biased towards ecological concerns" circ. 500. 2/yr. Pub'd 2 issues 1990; expects 2 issues 1991, 2 issues 1992. sub. price: $5; per copy: $3; sample: $3. Back issues: $2. Discounts: $2/copy if 10 or more ordered. 36pp; 5½×8½; of. Reporting time: 3-4 months. Payment: 2 copies. Copyrighted, reverts to author (credit given to ALB.). CCLM.

ALBERTA HISTORY, Historical Society of Alberta, Hugh A. Dempsey, 95 Holmwood Ave NW, Calgary Alberta T2K 2G7, Canada, 403-289-8149. 1953. Articles, reviews, non-fiction. "3.5M to 7M word articles on Western Canadian History" circ. 2.2M. 4/yr. Pub'd 4 issues 1990; expects 4 issues 1991. sub. price: $15; per copy: $4; sample: free. Back issues: $4. Discounts: 1/3 off. 32pp; 7×10; of. Reporting time: 1 month. Payment: nil. Not copyrighted. Pub's reviews: 16 in 1990. §In our field-Western Canadian History. No ads. AASLH, CHA.

ALCATRAZ, Alcatraz Editions, Stephen Kessler, Hollis deLancey, 133 Towne Terrace, Santa Cruz, CA 95060. 1978. Articles, art, photos, interviews, criticism, reviews, letters, long-poems. "No unsolicited mss. until further notice" circ. 1M. Irregular. price per copy: varies; sample: free to writers. Discounts: 40% to booksellers on orders of 3 or more. 300pp; 6×9; of. Payment: copies. Copyrighted, reverts to author. Pub's reviews: 5 in 1990. §Poetry, translations, cultural commentary, criticism, biography. No ads.

Alcatraz Editions (see also ALCATRAZ), Stephen Kessler, Hollis deLancey, 133 Towne Terrace, Santa Cruz, CA 95060. 1978. Long-poems. "See *Alcatraz 3* for current biases. No new books until further notice" avg. press run 500. Pub'd 1 title 1990. 5 titles listed in the *Small Press Record of Books in Print* (20th Edition, 1991-92). avg. price, paper: $6.00. Discounts: 40% to trade on orders of 3 or more. 80-120pp; of.

THE ALCHEMIST, Marco Fraticelli, PO Box 123, LaSalle, Quebec H8R 3T7, Canada. 1974. Poetry, fiction, art, photos, collages, concrete art, non-fiction. "No biases in terms of length of material or number of works submitted. Although we publish good 'traditional' works we are more interested in those which explore the possibilities" circ. 500. 2/yr. Pub'd 2 issues 1990; expects 2 issues 1991. 1 title listed in the *Small Press Record of Books in Print* (20th Edition, 1991-92). sub. price: $12; per copy: $4; sample: $2. 48pp; 5½×8½; of. Reporting time: 1 month. Payment: copies only. Copyrighted, reverts to author.

Alchemist/Light Publishing, Bil Paul, PO Box 5183, San Jose, CA 95150-5183, 408-723-6108. 1972. Fiction, photos, non-fiction. "Books" avg. press run 2M. Expects 1 title 1992. 2 titles listed in the *Small Press Record of Books in Print* (20th Edition, 1991-92). avg. price, paper: $4.00. Discounts: 40% bookstores. 100pp; size varies; of, lp. Reporting time: 1 week. Copyrights for author.

Alchemy Books, Kenneth P. Cameron, President; Graham Philips, Submissions Editor, PO Box 479, Marlborough, CT 06447. 1977. Poetry, fiction, art, photos, cartoons, satire, long-poems, news items, non-fiction. "We are planning now to develop a line of science fiction novels and anthologies. We publish mainly non-fiction books with strong political or philosophical overtones, but remain open to anything. Recent works include: *Timeless Faces* by Valentino Luciani, *The Law & The Travel Industry* by Alexander Anolik, esq, *Calculated Chaos* by Butler Shaffer, and *Armageddon Sunrise* by Larry Buettner" avg. press run 5M. Pub'd 34 titles 1990; expects 50 titles 1991. 33 titles listed in the *Small Press Record of Books in Print* (20th Edition, 1991-92). avg. price, cloth: $12.95; paper: $5.95. Discounts: Retailers: 1-5 copies 20%; 6 or more copies 40%, Wholesalers: 1 or more 50%. 200pp; 5½×8½ usually, can vary; †of. Reporting time: 8 months. Payment: rates vary - no advances. Copyrights for author.

Alchemy Press (see also FRAGMENTS), Fred Calero, 1789 Macdonald Avenue, Brooklyn, NY 11230, 212-303-8301; 718-339-4168. 1986. Poetry, fiction, articles, art, photos, cartoons, interviews, satire, criticism, reviews, music, letters, collages, news items, non-fiction. "Experimental poetry, art, surrealism. Recent contributors: Jonathan Leake, Jim Feast, Fred Calero, Eve Teitelbaum, Simon Perchik, Richard Kostelanetz" avg. press run 1M. Pub'd 3 titles 1990; expects 4 titles 1991, 6 titles 1992. 1 title listed in the *Small Press Record of Books in Print* (20th Edition, 1991-92). avg. price, paper: $2. Discounts: $1. 40pp; 11×8½, 5½×8½; †xerox. Reporting time: 60 days at least. Payment: 5 copies. Copyrights for author.

Alegra House Publishers, Robert C. Peters, Managing Editor; Linda Marado, Co-Editor; Edward Amicucci, Co-Editor, PO Box 1443-D, Warren, OH 44482, 216-372-2951. 1985. Non-fiction. "Major goals/objectives: 1)

16

Provide self-help adult and childrens' books(divorce, war, learning, relaxation), 2) self-help cassette tape (divorce, learning, relaxation)" avg. press run 5M. Pub'd 4 titles 1990; expects 6 titles 1991, 2 titles 1992. 11 titles listed in the *Small Press Record of Books in Print* (20th Edition, 1991-92). avg. price, cloth: $14.95; paper: $9.95. Discounts: bookstores 40%, distributors 50%. 224pp; 8½x5½, 6x9. Reporting time: 6 weeks. Payment: 7% of cover price on paperback; 10%. Copyrights for author. COSMEP, PMA.

Algamut Press, Marie Lande, PO Box 2293, Edison, NJ 08818, 201-549-1543. 1987. Fiction. 1 title listed in the *Small Press Record of Books in Print* (20th Edition, 1991-92). avg. price, cloth: $14.95; paper: $5.95. Discounts: usual industry discount. 169pp; 5½x8½.

Algol Press (see also SCIENCE FICTION CHRONICLE), Andrew Porter, Editor & Publisher, PO Box 2730, Brooklyn, NY 11202-0056, 718-643-9011. 1963. Articles, art, photos, reviews, letters, news items, non-fiction. "Not soliciting material" avg. press run 2M. 2 titles listed in the *Small Press Record of Books in Print* (20th Edition, 1991-92). avg. price, cloth: $15; paper: $5.95; other: S.F. Chronicle $2.75. Discounts: 40% trade, write publisher. 196pp; 5½x8½; of. Reporting time: 1-3 weeks. Payment: royalties percentage of gross cover price. Copyrights for author.

Alice James Books, Marjorie Fletcher, President; Cooperative, 33 Richdale Avenue, Cambridge, MA 02140, 617-354-1408. 1973. Poetry. "A writers' cooperative in which the authors whose work is published by the press share the responsibilities of running the business, *Alice James Books* has been issuing books by contemporary poets for over 15 years. Because of this work commitment,the Beatrice Hawley Award is offered to poets who cannot meet the work commitment due to geographical or financial restraints. During regular submissions, only poets who live in the New England area may have their manuscripts considered. Although the cooperative has published books by men, we emphasize the publication of poetry by women. We strongly encourage submissions by women of color. We issue about four titles each year." avg. press run 1.2M. Pub'd 4 titles 1990; expects 4 titles 1991, 4 titles 1992. 68 titles listed in the *Small Press Record of Books in Print* (20th Edition, 1991-92). avg. price, cloth: $15.95; paper: $8.95. Discounts: 20% jobbers, 50% distributors, no discounts for libraries, bookstores 1-4 books 20%, 5+ 40%. 72pp; 5½x8½; of. Reporting time: 2 months. Payment: no royalties; author receives 100 books as part of cooperative's contract with author. Copyrights for author. COSMEP.

Alioth Press, Mark Dominik, PO Box 1554, Beaverton, OR 97075, 503-644-0983. 1987. "Alioth Press specializes in works on English literature—criticism and reprints of early editions. We regret we cannot accept unsolicited submissions" avg. press run 500. Expects 2 titles 1991, 1 title 1992. 3 titles listed in the *Small Press Record of Books in Print* (20th Edition, 1991-92). avg. price, cloth: $22.50. Discounts: 20% to library wholesalers. 2-300pp; 5½x8½.

ALKALINE PAPER ADVOCATE, Abbey Publications, Ellen R. McCrady, Abbey Publications, 320 East Center, Provo, UT 84606, 801-373-1598. 1988. Articles, letters, news items, non-fiction. "This is not a publishing outlet for poets and writers of fiction, but a source of information on long-lasting paper for libraries, papermakers, and small (and large) publishers" circ. 520. 6/yr. Pub'd 6 issues 1990; expects 6 issues 1991, 6 issues 1992. sub. price: $30; per copy: $5; sample: free. Discounts: 12% to agents. 10pp; 8½x11; of. Reporting time: 1-150 days. Payment: none. Copyrighted. §Paper permanence and related topics. No ads.

All American Press, Elizabeth Byrum, PO Box 20773, Birmingham, AL 35216, (205) 822-8263. 1986. Non-fiction. "Small paperback books around 50 pages. Subjects are contemporary and thrust is usually a How-to-do-it approach. Not requesting submissions at this time" avg. press run 2M. Pub'd 1 title 1990; expects 2-4 titles 1991, 2-4 titles 1992. 3 titles listed in the *Small Press Record of Books in Print* (20th Edition, 1991-92). avg. price, paper: $6.00. 50pp; 8½x5½; variable based on project.

ALL AVAILABLE LIGHT, McOne Press, Jason Freeman, PO Box 50174, Austin, TX 78763. 1989. Poetry, fiction, articles, art, criticism, reviews, letters, parts-of-novels, long-poems, non-fiction. "Looking for luminescent literature with spiritual content. Unspoken connection with some higher power, shown through actions within the work. Not religious, spiritual. Do you dedicate your life to spirit?" circ. 200-300. 2/yr. Pub'd 1 issue 1990; expects 2 issues 1991, 2 issues 1992. sub. price: $6; per copy: $3; sample: $3. Discounts: 40% distributor. 50pp; 5½x8½; of. Reporting time: 2-3 weeks. Payment: 2 copies and half price on purchases of extras. Copyrighted, reverts to author. Pub's reviews: 1 in 1990. §Spiritual literary magazines. Ads: $100/$60.

ALL OF THE ABOVE, C. Lee Graham, PO Box 36023, Grosse Pointe, MI 48236-0023. 1990. Fiction, articles, art, cartoons, reviews, letters. "Average submission length is between 6 and 8 pages, biased towards fantasy and science fiction role playing games, preferably G.U.R.P.S. from Steve Jackson games" circ. 30. 6/yr. Pub'd 2 issues 1990; expects 6 issues 1991, 6 issues 1992. Back issues: cost for non-members is $1 above cost to reproduce & mail. This will usually be around $5 (for the immediate future). Discounts: will trade one for one for zines of similar material, other than that I've never thought about it. 40pp; 8½x11; †xerox. Reporting time: within a month. Payment: none, but issue is sold to them at member rate. Copyrighted, reverts to author. Pub's reviews. §Conspiracy theory, fringe (or fortean) fantasy, science fiction, or horror fiction, anything to do with role playing games. Ads: $5/$3.50.

Allardyce, Barnett (Agneau 2), Fiona Allardyce, Publisher; Anthony Barnett, Editor, 14 Mount Street, Lewes, East Sussex, BN7 1HL, England, 0273 479393. 1981. Poetry, fiction, art, criticism, music. "USA distribution: Small Press Distribution, Inc.,1814 San Pablo Avenue, Berkeley, CA. 415-549-3336. Substantially important books in letters, art, music. 1st book: J.H. Prynne *Poems*, 320 pages, cloth ISBN: 0-907954-00-6, UK £12.00, USA $24.00, paperback ISBN: 0-907954-01-4, UK £8.95 (revised price), USA $15.00. Published May 1982. We cannot encourage unsolicited work because of finanical constrictions" avg. press run 500-1.5M. Pub'd 1 title 1990; expects 2 titles 1991. 8 titles listed in the *Small Press Record of Books in Print* (20th Edition, 1991-92). Discounts: usual, on application. 8¼x5¾; of. Reporting time: immediate. Payment: information is available only to authors. Copyrights for author. ALP.

Allegheny Press, Bonnie Henderson, John Tomikel, Box 220, Elgin, PA 16413, 814-664-8504. 1967. Non-fiction. "We will be considering only outdoor books in the future." avg. press run 2M. Pub'd 6 titles 1990; expects 5 titles 1991, 5 titles 1992. 12 titles listed in the *Small Press Record of Books in Print* (20th Edition, 1991-92). avg. price, cloth: $10; paper: $6. Discounts: 10%-40% depending on size of order. 154pp; 6x9; lp. Reporting time: 3 weeks. Payment: 10%-15%. Copyrights for author.

ALLEGHENY REVIEW, Vern A. Maczuzak, Co-Editor; Richardson K. Prouty, Co-Editor, Box 32, Allegheny College, Meadville, PA 16335, 814-332-6553. 1983. Poetry, fiction, photos, long-poems, plays. "Editorial staff changes yearly. Publish work by undergraduate college students only, from across the country. *Allegheny Review* has been used as a classroom text. National edition founded 1983; a local version under similar names has been published since 1893" circ. 1M. 1/yr. Pub'd 1 issue 1990; expects 1 issue 1991, 1 issue 1992. sub. price: $3.50; per copy: $3.50; sample: $3.50. Back issues: $2. Discounts: 25 copies, $2.00 each for use in classroom. 100pp; 6x9; of. Reporting time: 2 months after deadline. Payment: in copies (2), $50 to contest winners (best submission each genre; poetry, fiction, artwork). Copyrighted, rights revert if requested by author.

Alleluia Press, Jose M. de Vinck, Owner, Box 103, 672 Franklin Turnpike, Allendale, NJ 07401, 201-327-3513. 1969. Poetry, criticism. "Very few outside MSS. are accepted since we have our own authors. We produce books and offer our imprint and distribution *only* in the case of scholars whose works are up to our high standards and who can finance first costs of production. No limit to length: we have 1,250 pp. and 850 pp. books. Some recent contributors: Rev. Casimir Kucharek, Rama, Sask., Can.; Liturgical Commission, Ruthenian Dioceses of Pittsburgh, Parma & Passaic; Archbishop Joseph Raya, Combermere, Ont., Can., etc. We specialize in very high quality religious books, generally printed in Belgium, but accept other works, for instance a photographic album. Our distribution, however, is geared mainly to religious customers of the Byzantine Rite, Orthodox and Catholic, and to the general Christian readership. Do not send manuscripts." avg. press run 1M-10M. Pub'd 4 titles 1990; expects 1 title 1991, 3 titles 1992. 19 titles listed in the *Small Press Record of Books in Print* (20th Edition, 1991-92). avg. price, cloth: $6-$24.75; paper: $2.00-$16.75; other: $35.00-Deluxe Morocco, $107.50 Byzantine lectionaries. Discounts: below $20 25%, $20 or over 40%, discount on all codes BW.Net $8.75; special discounts on very large orders; 20% on codes BBP. From 32 to 1,250pp depending on type of book; 6x9, 7x10 and others; of, lp. Reporting time: 1 week. Payment: individual contracts. Does not copyright for author.

Allergy Publications, Gale Alpin, PO Box 640, Menlo Park, CA 94026, 415-322-1663. 1976. Articles. avg. press run 3M. Pub'd 1 title 1990; expects 1 title 1991. 1 title listed in the *Small Press Record of Books in Print* (20th Edition, 1991-92). avg. price, paper: $15. Discounts: trade 40%, bulk 50%, agent 12%. 150pp; 5½x8½, 8½x11; of. Reporting time: 6 weeks. Payment: 10% of money received. Copyrights for author. COSMEP.

Ally Press, Paul Feroe, 524 Orleans St., St. Paul, MN 55107, 612-227-1567. 1973. Poetry. "The Ally Press is a publisher and distributor of books and tapes, by Robert Bly. It will seek to maintain a blacklist of all Bly material in print through its mail-order service. In addition it will publish an occasional newsletter detailing Bly's current reading schedule. Those desiring these free mailings can write care of the press. Ally Press is not accepting any manuscripts at this time. Our most recent title is *An Almost Human Gesture* by Louis Jenkins. $6.95. Co-published with Eighties Press" avg. press run 1.5M. Expects 2 titles 1992. 9 titles listed in the *Small Press Record of Books in Print* (20th Edition, 1991-92). avg. price, paper: $6.50. Discounts: 1-4, 20%; 4-49, 40%. 60pp; 5¼x8; of, lp. Payment: in copies. Copyrights for author.

Almar Press, Alfred N. Weiner, 4105 Marietta Drive, Vestal, NY 13850, 607-722-0265 (6251). 1977. Non-fiction. "Prefer to see an outline and one main chapter instead of an entire manuscript. *MUST include a stamped self-addressed envelope for a reply and return of items sent otherwise items are destroyed.* We publish consumer, regional, business, technical information. No specific length" avg. press run 2M. Pub'd 9 titles 1990; expects 9 titles 1991, 10 titles 1992. 13 titles listed in the *Small Press Record of Books in Print* (20th Edition, 1991-92). avg. price, paper: $11.95. Discounts: average 30-55. 200pp; 5½x8½, 8½x11; of. Reporting time: average 30 days. Payment: 10% of net selling price paid twice each year. Copyrights for author.

Alms House Press, Alana Sherman, Lorraine S. DeGennaro, PO Box 668, Stony Point, NY 10980. 1985. Poetry. "16-24 pages of poetry that works as a collection. We seek variety and excellence in many styles. Each year we publish one or two chapbooks from an open competition. Costs: $7 handling/reading fee. Chapbook sent to each contributor. Recent winners include Sandra Marshburn and Martin Anderson." avg. press run 200. Pub'd 4 titles 1990; expects 3-4 titles 1991, 3-4 titles 1992. 4 titles listed in the *Small Press Record of Books in Print* (20th Edition, 1991-92). avg. price, paper: $3.95. Discounts: 50% bookstores; $15 set of five. 20pp; 5½×8½. Reporting time: 3 months. Payment: 15 copies to the author. Copyrights for author.

Alpenglow Press, PO Box 1841, Santa Maria, CA 93456, 805-928-4904. 1985. Non-fiction. "Self-help, aging, relationships & travel (humor)" avg. press run 10M. Expects 4 titles 1992. 2 titles listed in the *Small Press Record of Books in Print* (20th Edition, 1991-92). avg. price, paper: $9.95. Discounts: standard. 176pp; 5½×8½; of. Reporting time: query first. Payment: open. Copyrights for author. COSMEP, PMA.

Alpha Beat Press (see also ALPHA BEAT SOUP), Dave Christy, 68 Winter, Scarborough, Ont. M1K 4M3, Canada. 1987. Poetry, fiction, articles, art, photos, interviews, long-poems. avg. press run 500. Pub'd 4 titles 1990; expects 7 titles 1991, 4 titles 1992. 11 titles listed in the *Small Press Record of Books in Print* (20th Edition, 1991-92). avg. price, paper: $5. 50pp; size varies; †IBM-PS2. Reporting time: immediately. Copyrights for author. Index of American Periodical Verse.

ALPHA BEAT SOUP, Alpha Beat Press, Dave Christy, Alpha Beat Press, 68 Winter, Scarborough, Ont. M1K 4M3, Canada, 416-261-7390. 1987. Poetry, fiction, articles, art. "Diane di Prima, George Dowden, Charles Bukowski, Richard Nason, Diane Wakoski, Ken Babbs, Herschel Silverman, are recent contributors. ABS features beat generation, post-beat independent and other international writings" circ. 600. 2+. Expects 2 issues 1991, 2 issues 1992. sub. price: $10; per copy: $5; sample: $5. Back issues: $5. Discounts: 1/2 of cover price to dealers. 75pp; 7×8½; †IBM-PS2. Reporting time: immediately. Payment: copies. Copyrighted, rights remain with author. Pub's reviews: 2 in 1990. §Beat literature. Index of American Periodical Verse.

Alphabox Press (see also A), Jeremy Adler, Flat 1, 41 Mapesbury Road, London NW2 4HJ, England. 1974. Poetry, long-poems, collages, concrete art. "Other publications in association with Pirate Press and Writers Forum. To publish otherwise unpublishable visual poetry; poetry combining traditional techniques with experimentation; translations; at cost (non profit-making) prices. Contributions not solicited, but considered if accompanied by SAE." avg. press run 100-300. Pub'd 2 titles 1990; expects 3 titles 1991. 5 titles listed in the *Small Press Record of Books in Print* (20th Edition, 1991-92). avg. price, paper: $2-$3. Discounts: 33%, 40% booksellers. 20pp; size A4, A3; †of, lp. Reporting time: 2 months. Payment: copies. ALP, CULP.

Alpine Guild, PO Box 183, Oak Park, IL 60303. 1977. Non-fiction. "Publish books only, aimed at specific identifiable, reachable audiences. The book must provide information of value to the audience" Pub'd 2 titles 1990; expects 2 titles 1991, 2 titles 1992. 8 titles listed in the *Small Press Record of Books in Print* (20th Edition, 1991-92). avg. price, cloth: $18.95; paper: $9.95. Discounts: standard. of. Reporting time: within 30 days. Payment: depends on book, audience, etc. Copyrights for author. ABC, MAPA, DMA, COSMEP.

Alpine Press, S.F. Achenbach, PO Box 1930, Mills, WY 82644, 602-986-9457. 1985. Non-fiction. *"How To Be Your Own Veterinarian (Sometimes),* by Ruth B. James, D.V.M. We do not read unsolicited manuscripts." avg. press run 15M. Pub'd 2 titles 1990; expects 1 title 1991, 2 titles 1992. 2 titles listed in the *Small Press Record of Books in Print* (20th Edition, 1991-92). avg. price, paper: $19.95. Discounts: 1-2 copies $15.97, 3-9 $14.97, 10+ $13.97, freight paid with prepaid orders. 300pp; 8½×11; of. Reporting time: long. Payment: negotiated individually on merits of book. Copyrights for author.

Alpine Publications, Betty McKinney, Managing Editor, 214 19th Street, SE, Loveland, CO 80537, 303-667-2017. Non-fiction. "We publish nonfiction hardback & trade paperback how-to books for the dog, horse, and pet markets. About half of our sales are by mail order. Our books are high quality, in-depth, thorough coverage of a specific subject or breed. Authors must know their field and be able to provide useful, how-to information with illustrations." avg. press run 2M. Pub'd 7 titles 1990; expects 10 titles 1991. 36 titles listed in the *Small Press Record of Books in Print* (20th Edition, 1991-92). avg. price, cloth: $22; paper: $8. Discounts: 2-9 20%; 10-74 40%; 75 or more 45%. 200pp; 6×9, 8½×11; of. Reporting time: 8-12 weeks. Payment: royalty. Copyrights for author. COSMEP, Rocky Mountain Publishing Association.

Alta Napa Press, Carl T. Endemann, 1969 Mora Avenue, Calistoga, CA 94515, 707-942-4444. 1977. Poetry, fiction, articles, photos, parts-of-novels, long-poems. "Reply only if SASE. *Gondwana Books* is now a division of *Alta Napa Press.* As to restrictions, for details you can use Writers Digest 'Poetry Market'" avg. press run 1M-2M. Pub'd 4 titles 1990; expects 2 titles 1991, 4 titles 1992. 13 titles listed in the *Small Press Record of Books in Print* (20th Edition, 1991-92). avg. price, cloth: $15; paper: $4.95-$9.95. Discounts: trade 40%, bulk 50%. 48-144pp; 5×8½, 6×9; of, lp. Reporting time: 1 month. Payment: yes. Copyrights for author. COSMEP.

Alta Research, Reed White, PO Box 1001-D, Sebastopol, CA 95473, 707-829-1001. 1983. Photos, non-fiction. "Desire write-ups and information on recreation within easy access of airports in the western states" avg. press

19

run 10M. Pub'd 4 titles 1990; expects 3 titles 1991, 3 titles 1992. 1 title listed in the *Small Press Record of Books in Print* (20th Edition, 1991-92). avg. price, other: $24.95. Discounts: 2 books 20%, 3-25%, 6-30%, 12-35%, 24-40%, 48-50%. 384pp; 4×6; of. Reporting time: 30 days. Payment: negotiable. Does not copyright for author.

Altamont Press, Inc. (see also FIBERARTS), 50 College Street, Ashville, NC 28801, 704-253-0468. 1973. Art, photos. "Looking for a broad spectrum of high quality crafts/arts books." avg. press run 7.5M. Pub'd 8 titles 1990; expects 10 titles 1991, 16 titles 1992. 13 titles listed in the *Small Press Record of Books in Print* (20th Edition, 1991-92). avg. price, cloth: $25; paper: $15. Discounts: all depend on volume. 150+pp; 8½×10; of. Reporting time: 1-2 months. Payment: 5%+. Copyrights for author.

THE ALTERED MIND, Ariel Rowen, Co-Editor; Aillinn Lune, Co-Editor, PO Box 1083, Claremont, CA 91711, 714-949-9531. 1989. Poetry, fiction, articles, art, photos, cartoons, interviews, criticism, reviews, music, letters. "Our primary focus is underground/independent and local music. Submissions from *anywhere* are welcome." circ. 500-1M. 6/yr. Pub'd 6 issues 1990; expects 6 issues 1991, 6 issues 1992. sub. price: $8; per copy: $1.50; sample: $1.50. Back issues: generally unavailable; for those in print $1.50. Discounts: none. 20pp; 8½×11; of. Reporting time: 1 week to 2 months (but no longer than 2 months). Payment: barter system. Not copyrighted. Pub's reviews: 5-10 in 1990. §Celtic studies, underground music, unconventional fiction. Ads: $40/$25/$50 back cover/$15 1/4 page/$10 business card.

Alternating Crimes Publishing (see also SCREAM MAGAZINE), Russell Judd Boone, PO Box 10363, Raleigh, NC 27605, 919-834-7542. 1985. Poetry, fiction, art, cartoons, long-poems, non-fiction. "Graphic novels, comicbooks, poetry chapbooks, short story collections, novels" avg. press run 500. Expects 2 titles 1992. avg. price, paper: $7. Discounts: 40%, full returns, 50% quan. 100. 64pp; 6×9; of. Reporting time: 16 weeks. Payment: 50% of net profit. Copyrights for author. COSMEP, N.C. Writer's Network, Carolina Crime Writer's Assoc.

ALTERNATIVE PRESS INDEX, Collective, Alternative Press Center, Inc., PO Box 33109, Baltimore, MD 21218, 301-243-2471. 1969. "The *Alternative Press Index* is a quarterly subject index to alternative and radical publications" circ. 500. 4/yr. Pub'd 4 issues 1990; expects 4 issues 1991, 4 issues 1992. sub. price: $125 libraries, $30 individuals; sample: free. Back issues: 50% discount if 3 or more back volumes are purchased. Discounts: $30 individuals, high schools, movement groups; $75 new subs., 1st yr. institutions. 130pp; 8½×11; of. Copyrighted. No ads accepted.

Alternative Press Syndicate, R.J. Smith, Editor, PO Box 1347, Ansonia Station, New York, NY 10023. 1975. Articles, cartoons, interviews, criticism, reviews, news items. "Subscription rate $7.50" avg. press run 7M. Pub'd 2 titles 1990; expects 4 titles 1991, 4 titles 1992. 1 title listed in the *Small Press Record of Books in Print* (20th Edition, 1991-92). avg. price, paper: $2.00. Discounts: $1.00 to distributor. 44pp; 8½×11. Reporting time: 3 weeks. Payment: $50-$100 feature articles, $25-$50 news & reviews. Copyrights for author. APS.

ALURA, Ruth Lamb, Editor, PO Box 44, Novinger, MO 63559, 816-488-5216. 1975. Poetry. "Poems and reviews must be understandable. Length: prefer poems of no more than 48 lines & spaces. Will use longer if exceptionally good. Biases: no porn, didactic, racial, or overly religious. We publish all styles...traditional, modern, haiku. Do not send poems in large manila envelopes. SEND poems and mail in regular business envelopes (#10). Enclose four (4) loose stamps. *Alura* is now international, we receive poems and subscriptions from all over the world" circ. 325-350. 4/yr. Pub'd 4 issues 1990; expects 4 issues 1991, 4 issues 1992. sub. price: $10; per copy: $3; sample: $3. Back issues: please inquire. Discounts: Have not had bulk orders. 10% off. 51pp; 5½×8½; of. Reporting time: 2 months. Payment: 2 copies. Copyrighted, reverts to author. §Poetry. Michigan State Poetry Society.

ALWAYS JUKIN', Always Jukin', Mike Baute, Sally Baute, 221 Yesler Way, Seattle, WA 98104. 1985. Articles, photos, interviews, reviews, music, letters, news items, non-fiction. "*Always Jukin*' is a hobby magazine. It is read by a few thousand people in 20 countries who own, collect, repair, buy, sell & trade all vintages of jukeboxes and jukebox parts & related items (records). Each issue averages 10-15 pages of letters, photos, stories, technical tips, and general jukebox related information. Each issue also contains 20-30 pages of ads for all of the above. 90% of the articles are written by the subscribers. The current issue has 12 contributors. All articles must relate to the general area of 'jukeboxes & music'" circ. 3M. 12/yr. Pub'd 12 issues 1990; expects 12 issues 1991, 12 issues 1992. sub. price: $27; per copy: $3; sample: $4. Back issues: $4. Discounts: $1 per issue, net cost. 40pp; 10×16; web. Reporting time: same day received. Payment: as negotiated. Copyrighted, reverting rights revert. Pub's reviews: 12 in 1990. §Books and mags relating to jukeboxes and records. Ads: $150/$85/8.5¢ per word.

Always Jukin' (see also ALWAYS JUKIN'), Mike Baute, Sally Baute, 221 Yesler Way, Seattle, WA 98104. 1986. Photos, non-fiction. "We publish books & booklets relating to jukeboxes. In 1988 we published the first *Guide to Collectible Jukeboxes* with over 300 pictures and prices for same. We are now putting together 'How To Repair' manuals for specific jukeboxes. We will do as many manuals as are submitted each year and will do a yearly update of the *Guide to Collectible Jukeboxes*. We also plan to do a 250 page 'Coffee Table' book on the history of jukeboxes: 4 colors and hundreds of photos" avg. press run 5M. Pub'd 1 title 1990; expects 1 title 1991, 2 titles 1992. 1 title listed in the *Small Press Record of Books in Print* (20th Edition, 1991-92). avg. price, paper: $14.95. Discounts: 40/45/50. 60pp; 8½×11; web. Reporting time: 2 weeks. Payment: 50% of net profit. Does not copyright for author.

Alyson Publications, Inc., Sasha Alyson, 40 Plympton Street, Boston, MA 02118, 617-542-5679. 1977. "We publish trade paperbacks for gay and lesbian readers. We occasionally do co-publishing with other publishing houses. Also publishes children's books aimed at kids with lesbian and gay parents" avg. press run 6M. Pub'd 15 titles 1990; expects 15 titles 1991, 15 titles 1992. 99 titles listed in the *Small Press Record of Books in Print* (20th Edition, 1991-92). avg. price, paper: $8.95. Discounts: standard 40% trade. 120-250pp; 5½×8½; of. Reporting time: 4-6 weeks average. Payment: 6-10%. Copyrights for author.

Amador Publishers, Adela Amador, Harry Willson, PO Box 12335, Albuquerque, NM 87195, 505-877-4395. 1986. Fiction. "What began in 1986 as self-publishing, for Adela Amador and harry Willson, now includes a type of "risk" publishing, in which the author shares some of the risk. Besides three titles by Willson, six other titles have been issued and all authors have become active sales reps. We still are looking at full-length fiction with some kind of southwest tie-in. Query first" avg. press run 3M. Pub'd 3 titles 1990; expects 3 titles 1991, 3 titles 1992. 11 titles listed in the *Small Press Record of Books in Print* (20th Edition, 1991-92). avg. price, cloth: $17; paper: $9. Discounts: bookstores 40%, wholesalers 50%. 176-250pp; 5½×8½; lp. Reporting time: varies. Payment: varies. Copyrights for author. COSMEP, Poets & Writers, RGWA, Rocky Mtn. Book Publishers Ass'n.

Amana Books, Samir Abed-Rabbo, Publisher, 58 Elliot Street, Brattleboro, VT 05301, 802-257-0872. 1984. Poetry, fiction, non-fiction. "Amana Books publishes scholarly works on world issues and intercultural understanding. Areas of current focus include The Middle East, Islam, and Africa" avg. press run 5M. Pub'd 10 titles 1990; expects 12 titles 1991, 12 titles 1992. 43 titles listed in the *Small Press Record of Books in Print* (20th Edition, 1991-92). avg. price, cloth: $19.95; paper: $12.50. Discounts: inquire. 200pp; 5⅜×8¼; of. Reporting time: 1-2 months from receipt. Payment: 10% net for first 5,000 sold, 12½% net for next 5,000 sold, 15% net from then on. Copyrights for author.

AMANECER IN ENGLISH, New York CIRCUS, Inc., New York CIRCUS Collective, PO Box 37, Times Square Station, New York, NY 10108, 212-928-7600; FAX 212-927-2757. 1975. "Testimonies of Christian in Latin America" circ. 3M. Pub'd 6 issues 1990; expects 6 issues 1991, 6 issues 1992. price per copy: $2 Lucha, $5 Amanecer. Discounts: bulk rate 40%. 40pp; 8½×11. Payment: none.

AMANITA BRANDY, W. Paul Ganley: Publisher, W. Paul Ganley, PO Box 149, Amherst Branch, Buffalo, NY 14226-0149, 716-839-2415. 1980. Poetry. "Features weird fantasy poetry originally accepted for *Weirdbook*." circ. 150. sub. price: $6 4 issues; per copy: $2; sample: $2. 32pp; 5½×8½; mi.

THE AMARANTH REVIEW, Windov· Publications, Dana L. Yost, PO Box 56235, Phoenix, AZ 85079, 846-5567. 1989. Poetry, fiction, art, photos, reviews, long-poems, non-fiction. "No minimum or maximum length on poetry. 3500 word maximum on fiction. No reprints." circ. 1M. 2/yr. Expects 2 issues 1991, 2 issues 1992. sub. price: $10 USA; per copy: $5.50; sample: $5.50. Discounts: 40%. 80pp; 8½×11; of. Reporting time: 4 weeks. Payment: 2 copies; 40% discount on extras. Copyrighted, reverts to author. Pub's reviews: 2 in 1990. §Poetry, short fiction, nonfiction of interest to writers. Ads: $250/$100/$1, occasional special rates, write for details.

AMATEUR COMPUTERIST, Ronda Hauben, Bill Rohler, Norman Thompson, Michael Hauben, PO Box 4344, Dearborn, MI 48126, 313-278-0246. 1987. Poetry, fiction, articles, art, cartoons, satire, criticism, reviews, letters, news items, non-fiction. "Programs (computer programs in BASIC, C, etc.), how-to articles, fiction, essays related to computers, etc. Issues concerning technology or computers, history of computers, bbs discussions, pro labor, pro amateur orientation. Recent titles include *Commodore County USA, The Spirit of Babbage, CoCo Corner, Why Learn to Program, Jobs: Hours and Sense, BBS Discussion on the War, May Day Poem*" circ. varies. 4/yr. Pub'd 4 issues 1990; expects 4 issues 1991, 4 issues 1992. sub. price: $5; per copy: $1.50; sample: $1. Back issues: $1.50 each. Discounts: inquire. 12pp; 8½×11; †xerox. Reporting time: 3-4 months. Payment: free issue. Not copyrighted. Pub's reviews: 1 in 1990. §Computers (any area), technology. Ads: inquire.

AMAZING HEROES, Fantagraphics Books, Thomas Harrington, 7563 Lake City Way, Seattle, WA 98115. 1981. Articles, photos, cartoons, interviews, criticism. "The class act of comics fanzines, *Amazing Heroes* is devoted to comic new and reviews, interviews, and upcoming previews" circ. 12M. 13/yr. Pub'd 26 issues 1990; expects 13 issues 1991, 13 issues 1992. sub. price: $32; per copy: $2.50; sample: $2.50. 76pp; 7×10; of. Reporting time: 1-2 months. Payment: 1.5¢-2.5¢ per word. Copyrighted, reverts to author. Pub's reviews: 200 in 1990. §Comics and comics-related publications, film, etc. Ads: $150. COSMEP.

AMBASSADOR REPORT, John Trechak, PO Box 60068, Pasadena, CA 91116, 818-798-6112. 1976. Articles, photos, interviews, reviews, letters, news items. "ISSN: 0882-2123. We are primarily a publisher of exposes dealing with the following subjects: Armstrongism, The Worldwide Church of God, Ambassador College, and the problem of religious cults" circ. 2.5M. 4/yr. Pub'd 2 issues 1990; expects 4 issues 1991, 4 issues 1992. sub. price: $20 (contribution); per copy: $5.00; sample: $5.00. Back issues: $5.00. Discounts: negotiable. 12pp; 8½×14; of. Reporting time: 1 month maximum. Payment: usually in copies, but will negotiate for quality research. Copyrighted, rights revert if requested. Pub's reviews: 2 in 1990. §Anything on mind control and cults. Ads: negotiable (We do not usually run ads).

AMBERGRIS, Mark Kissling, PO Box 29919, Cincinnati, OH 45229. 1987. Poetry, fiction, art, photos. "We prefer works of fiction 5,000 words or less. We favor works about everyday experience showing psychological penetration of character. We give special consideration to works with a Midwestern flavor. Recent contributors: Rick Stansberger, Frankie Paino, Richard Hague, John Gerlach" circ. 1M. 1/yr. Pub'd 2 issues 1990; expects 2 issues 1991, 1 issue 1992. sub. price: $6; per copy: $4; sample: $4. Back issues: $3. Discounts: trade with other magazines. 120pp; 5½×8½. Reporting time: 3 months. Payment: 2 copies of the issue in which they appear. Copyrighted, reverts to author. Ads: $50/$25. Coordinating Council of Literary Magazines and Press (CLMP).

AMBIT, Martin Bax, 17 Priory Gardens, London, N6 5QY, England, 01-340-3566. 1959. Poetry, fiction, art, photos, reviews, long-poems. "Always looking for material which excites and interests. Suggest contributors read the magazine before they submit" circ. 1.5M. 4/yr. Pub'd 4 issues 1990; expects 4 issues 1991, 4 issues 1992. sub. price: £20 libraries and institutes, all other sub's $20; per copy: £5; sample: £5. Back issues: recent back nos. £5. Discounts: 25% 1-11, 12+ 33%. 96pp; 9½×7½; of. Reporting time: 3 months. Payment: by arrangement. Copyrighted, reverts to author. Pub's reviews: 30+ in 1990. §Poetry, novel. Ads: £12/£60/£35 1/4 page. ALP.

AMC Publishing, Chin-ning Chu, G. Vrla, 10 Milland Drive #B-4, Mill Valley, CA 94941-2546. 1988. News items, non-fiction. "Recent contributors: *Artificial Intelligent for Perfect Sex* by Laurie Enzer Sone, MA, *The Chinese Mind Game - Best Kept Trade Secret in the East* and *Travel in China: The Real Story* by Chin-ning Chu, and *Knowledge Translator I* by Curt Paulson. Seeking computer artificial intelligent expert system writers." Pub'd 2 titles 1990; expects 5 titles 1991, 5-8 titles 1992. 4 titles listed in the *Small Press Record of Books in Print* (20th Edition, 1991-92). Discounts: wholesale-with marketing programs 55%, wholesale-without marketing programs 50%, retail-from 40-45%. 250pp; 6×9; of. Payment: contact publisher. Northwest Publishing Association.

AMELIA, Amelia Press, Frederick A. Raborg, Editor, 329 'E' Street, Bakersfield, CA 93304, 805-323-4064. 1983. Poetry, fiction, articles, art, photos, cartoons, interviews, satire, criticism, reviews, parts-of-novels, long-poems, plays, non-fiction. "Fiction to 4M words; poetry to 100 lines, any form; strong satire; belles lettres to 1M words; criticism to 2M words; translations of both fiction and poetry, same lengths; reviews of small press interest; pen and ink sketches and line drawings; b/w photos with artistic merit. We welcome newcomers and have published the first works in both fiction and poetry of several new writers. *Amelia* sponsors the following annual contests: The Amelia Awards (poetry of all types to 100 lines); The Reed Smith Fiction Prize; The Willie Lee Martin Short Story Award; The Bernard Ashton Raborg Prize for Criticism; The Ralph Kreiser Non-Fiction Award; The Charles Katzman Journalism Award; The Frank McClure One-Act Play Award; The Hildegarde Janzen Prize for Oriental Forms of Poetry; The Lucille Sandberg Haiku Award; The Eugene Smith Prize for Sonnets; The Charles William Duke Longpoem Award; The Georgie Starbuck Galbraith Prize for Light/Humorous Verse; The Amelia Chapbook Awards (names of past winners of each award and the dates of issues in which they appear will be furnished for an SASE marked accordingly). When submitting to *Amelia* be professional in your approach; it is a high quality magazine which uses the very best material available to it. Neatness is always appreciated. More important, have something to say, say it well and economically. Contributors include Pattiann Rogers, Florri McMillan, David Ray, Gary Fincke, Ben Brooks, Lawrence P. Spingarn, Larry Rubin, Maxine Kumin, Judson Jerome, Merrill Joan Gerber, Knute Skinner, James Steel Smith, Fredrick Zydek, Bruce Michael Gans, Charles Bukowski, Stuart Friebert, and many others" circ. 1.25M. 4/yr. Pub'd 4 issues 1990; expects 4 issues 1991, 4 issues 1992. sub. price: $25; per copy: $7.95 ppd.; sample: $7.95 ppd. First two years are sold out. Discounts: contributors' discount: 20% on 5 or more copies; classroom: 25%. 136pp; 5½×8½; of. Reporting time: 2 weeks-3 months (the latter if under serious consideration). Payment: $35 for fiction; $2-$25 for poetry on acceptance (also contests). Copyrighted, reverts to author. Pub's reviews: 4 in 1990. §Poetry and fiction, drama, photography, essays. Will consider university press and small press (quality) ads on exchange basis or $300/$175. Will consider other outside quality ads and reading notices (80¢ per word, payable with copy). CCLM.

Amelia Press (see also AMELIA; CICADA; SPSM&H), 329 'E' Street, Bakersfield, CA 93304, 805-323-4064. 1983. Poetry, fiction, articles, art, photos, cartoons, interviews, satire, criticism, reviews, parts-of-novels, long-poems, plays, concrete art. avg. press run 500-1250. Pub'd 2 titles 1990; expects 3 titles 1991, 4 titles 1992. 17 titles listed in the *Small Press Record of Books in Print* (20th Edition, 1991-92). avg.

price, paper: $4.50-$7.95. Discounts: bookstore 40%. 20-152pp; 5½x8; of. Reporting time: 2 weeks to 3 months. Payment: varies. Copyrights for author. CCLM.

Amen Publishing Co., G.M. Weinstein, President, Box 3612, Arcadia, CA 91006, 818-355-9336. 1981. Cartoons, non-fiction. avg. press run 10M. Pub'd 1 title 1990; expects 1 title 1991, 3 titles 1992. 2 titles listed in the *Small Press Record of Books in Print* (20th Edition, 1991-92). avg. price, cloth: $12.95; paper: $6.95; other: varies. Discounts: 50% wholesalers, 40% retailers. 340pp; lp. Reporting time: 30 days. Payment: varies. Copyrights for author.

Amen-Ra Publishing Company, Box 3481, Columbus, OH 43210, 614-444-4460. 1990. Non-fiction. "Not accepting material at this time." avg. press run 1M. Expects 1 title 1991, 2 titles 1992. 1 title listed in the *Small Press Record of Books in Print* (20th Edition, 1991-92). avg. price, paper: $13.95. Discounts: 2-199 40%, 200-499 50%, 500+ less 55% less 25%. 200pp; 5½x8½; of.

AMERICA, George W. Hunt, Editor-in-Chief; Francis W. Turnbull, Managing Editor; Patrick H. Samway, Poetry Editor, 106 West 56th Street, New York, NY 10019, 212-581-4640. 1909. *"America* is a journal of opinion that frequently publishes original poetry." circ. 37M. 44/yr. Pub'd 44 issues 1990; expects 44 issues 1991, 44 issues 1992. sub. price: $33; per copy: $1.25; sample: $1.25. Back issues: $1.25. Discounts: up to 50% for over 200 ordered. 24pp; 8¼x10½; of. Reporting time: indeterminate. Payment: yes. Copyrighted, reverts to author. Pub's reviews: 200+ in 1990. §General interest. Ads: $800/$455/50¢. CPA (Catholic Press Association).

America West Publishers, Desiree Stevens, Marketing Director, PO Box 986, Tehachapi, CA 93581. 1986. Non-fiction. "New Age, new science & technology, new spirituality, metaphysics." avg. press run 5M. Expects 23 titles 1991, 25 titles 1992. 30 titles listed in the *Small Press Record of Books in Print* (20th Edition, 1991-92). avg. price, paper: $11.95. Discounts: bookstores 40%, distributors 50-60%, bulk (over 500) 50%, libraries 20%. 250pp; 5½x8½; †of. Reporting time: 60 days. Payment: twice yearly—10% of wholesale net, 5% of retail price. Copyrights for author. ABA, PMA, NAPRA.

AMERICAN AMATEUR JOURNALIST, Camel Press, James Hedges, HC 80, Box 160, Big Cove Tannery, PA 17212, 717-573-4526. 1937. Articles, interviews, reviews, news items, non-fiction. "The editor and address change yearly, in October. 'Official Editor' is an elective office in the publishing organization (American Amateur Press Association)" circ. 330. 6/yr. Pub'd 6 issues 1990; expects 6 issues 1991, 6 issues 1992. sub. price: $10; per copy: $2. 16pp; 5½x8½; †of. Reporting time: 1 week. Payment: none. Not copyrighted. Pub's reviews: a few in 1990. §Amateur (hobby) journalism, printing history. No ads. AAPA, APA.

American & World Geographic Publishing, Mark Thompson, Director of Publications; Carolyn Cunningham, Editor, PO Box 5630, Helena, MT 59601, 406-443-2842. 1970. "We have a line of geographic books by state. These are 1/3 to 1/2 text and the remainder photography. The concept behind these titles is to bridge travel guides and photo books with well illustrated information about places. We also have a line of market-oriented photo books and general interest regional publications" Pub'd 15 titles 1990; expects 12 titles 1991, 18 titles 1992. avg. price, cloth: $15.95. 104pp; 11x8½; of. Reporting time: 4 weeks. Payment: varies, we have photo-editorial mix. Copyrights for author. PNBA, RMBPA.

AMERICAN ATHEIST, American Atheist Press, R. Murray-O'Hair, Editor, PO Box 140195, Austin, TX 78714-0195, 512-458-1244. 1958. Poetry, fiction, articles, art, photos, cartoons, interviews, satire, criticism, reviews, letters, news items, non-fiction. "Street address: 7215 Cameron Road #C, Austin, TX 78752-2973. The *American Atheist* focuses on subjects of particular concern or interest to Atheists: state/church separation and relations, religious history and criticism, the history of Atheism, and the Atheist lifestyle. It also reports on current Atheist activism" circ. 30M. 12/yr. Pub'd 12 issues 1990; expects 12 issues 1991, 12 issues 1992. sub. price: $25 domestic, $35 foreign; per copy: $2.95; sample: free. Back issues: $1.50. Discounts: 50% for dealers and libraries. 52pp; 8½x11; †of. Reporting time: 6-12 weeks. Payment: 15 contributors' copies or 1 year subscription for first timers, $15 per thousand words thereafter. Copyrighted, reverts to author. Pub's reviews: 6 in 1990. §Atheism, freethought, state/church relations, religious history/criticism. Ads: $250/$150/$100 1/4 page/$20 per inch/25¢ per word. COSMEP.

American Atheist Press (see also AMERICAN ATHEIST), R. Murray-O'Hair, Jon G. Murray, PO Box 140195, Austin, TX 78714-0195, 512-458-1244. 1958. Poetry, fiction, articles, cartoons, satire, criticism, non-fiction. "Street address: 7215 Cameron Road #C, Austin, TX 78752-2973. The American Atheist Press publishes paperback books, booklets, pamphlets, and the monthly *American Atheist*. It releases reprints of Atheist classics as well as new works of particular interest to the Atheist community, on subjects such as Atheist history, state/church separation, and criticism of religion. Recent books include *The X-Rated Bible* by Ben Edward Akerley and *Christianity Before Christ* by John G. Jackson. Paperbacks are usually between 150 and 350 pages in length." Pub'd 6 titles 1990; expects 8 titles 1991, 12 titles 1992. 59 titles listed in the *Small Press Record of Books in Print* (20th Edition, 1991-92). avg. price, paper: $8; other: $3-$4 for booklets. Discounts: trade 1 copy 30%, 2-4 33.3%, 5-99 40%; wholesale and jobber 46%, library 20%, textbook 25%, drop shipment 20%. 200pp; 5½x8½; †of. Reporting time: 6-12 weeks. Payment: 5-8% on retail sales.

Copyrights for author. COSMEP.

American Audio Prose Library (non-print), Kay Bonetti, Director, PO Box 842, Columbia, MO 65205, 314-443-0361/447-2275. 1980. Fiction, interviews, parts-of-novels, non-fiction. "The *American Audio Prose Library* records an annual series of distinguished American prose artists who read from their own work and discuss their life, work, and related matters in a thoroughly researched, in-depth interview conducted by Director Kay Bonetti. Tapes are then distributed nationally for mail order sale to appropriate individuals and institutions. Some tapes are also edited for public radio broadcast (The American Prose Series). A cross section of published writers are invited by *AAPL* to record each year, chosen for balance as to venerability, prominence, genre, region, racial or ethnic background, and gender. *AAPL* 's ultimate goal: comprehensiveness. *AAPL* does accept for consideration submissions of extant recordings of good technical quality, both for archival and distribution puposes. All *AAPL* materials are reposited with the Western Manuscript Collection of the State Historical Society of Missouri, which serves as *AAPL* 's official listening facility." Pub'd 6 titles 1990; expects 10 titles 1991, 16 titles 1992. avg. price, other: $12.95 for the reading cassette, $12.95 for the interview cassette, $23 for the two cassette set. Discounts: for retail outlets only: 40% for AAPL tapes only. audio recordings of the writer. Payment: royalty 8% of net receipts. Copyrights for author.

AMERICAN BOOK COLLECTOR, The Moretus Press, Inc., Bernard McTigue, Editor, PO Box 1080, Ossining, NY 10562, 914-941-0409. 1933. Fiction, articles, photos, cartoons, interviews, reviews, news items, non-fiction. circ. 3.8M. 11/yr. Pub'd 6 issues 1990; expects 12 issues 1991, 11 issues 1992. sub. price: $33; per copy: newsstand $3.75; sample: $4. Back issues: $5. Discounts: 30% to trade or bulk; extra 20% to jobber. 56pp; 7×10; of. Reporting time: 2-6 weeks. Payment: $50 per 1M words, on publication. Copyrighted, does not revert to author. Pub's reviews: 200-250 in 1990. §Book collecting, bibliography, small presses, publishing history, bookbinding. Ads: $300/$175/$1.

THE AMERICAN BOOK REVIEW, Ronald Sukenick, Publisher; Don Laing, Managing Editor; Rochelle Ratner, John Tytell, Russell Hoover, Publications Center Box 494, English Dept., Colorado University, Boulder, CO 80309, 303-492-8947. 1977. Articles, art, photos, cartoons, criticism, reviews. "Length: ideally, 750-1.5M words. Reviewers should be primarily writers. We would like to see more reviews, or review articles, departing from the traditional review form—more innovative material. Contributors: Jamie Gordon, Fanny Howe, Seymour Krim, Andrei Codrescu, etc." circ. 15M. 6/yr. Pub'd 6 issues 1990; expects 6 issues 1991, 6 issues 1992. sub. price: $18, $28 (2 years), $23 libraries & institutions, $26 foreign; per copy: $3.00; sample: 3.00. Back issues: $3.00. 32pp; 11½×16; of. Reporting time: 2 months. Payment: $50 honorarium per review. Copyrighted. Pub's reviews: 167 in 1990. §Literary or closely allied fields. Ads: $190/$115.

AMERICAN BUDDHIST, Dr. Kevin O'Neil, 301 West Forty-Fifth Street, New York, NY 10036, 212-489-1075. 1980. Poetry, articles, interviews, reviews, news items, non-fiction. circ. 10M. 12/yr. Pub'd 12 issues 1990; expects 12 issues 1991, 12 issues 1992. sub. price: $15, institutions $20; per copy: $5; sample: $5. Back issues: Volume 1 & 2 $35. 16pp; 8×11. Reporting time: 2 months. Payment: none. Copyrighted, does not revert to author. Pub's reviews: 70 in 1990. §Buddhism, Asian studies, meditation, new age self-help, Buddhist art, spiritual, psychology. Ads: $1,908/$954. ABM.

American Business Consultants, Inc., Wilfred F. Tetreault, Robert W. Clements, 1540 Nuthatch Lane, Sunnyvale, CA 94087-4999, 408-732-8931/738-3011. 1979. Non-fiction. "These books written by the above authors covers thoroughly business opportunities, business training, and general education in the art of appraising, buying, operating, and selling any business. The material in these books has been thoroughly researched and approved by California, Washington, DC, Maryland, Connecticut, South Dakota, Ohio, Kansas, Wisconsin, Oregon, Florida, Utah, and Nevada Department of Real Estate, California board of accountancy, and California Board of Equalization. Endorsed by Society of Certified Business Opportunity Appraisers. Conducts seminars every week in major cities in U.S." avg. press run 5M. Pub'd 1 title 1990; expects 14 titles 1991, 16 titles 1992. 19 titles listed in the *Small Press Record of Books in Print* (20th Edition, 1991-92). avg. price, cloth: $35; paper: $1-$14.95. Discounts: standard. 6-300pp; 8½×11; †of. Reporting time: 2-6 weeks. Payment: standard. Copyrights for author.

AMERICAN COLLEGIATE POETS, International Publications, Val M. Churillo, Editor, PO Box 44044-L, Los Angeles, CA 90044, (213) 755-1814. 1975. "Published twice a year, Spring and Fall. A compilation of *student poetry* entered in 'National College Poetry Contest'. Five cash prizes with literary comments by editor; about 50 honorable mentions, the rest special awards. Please write for copy of rules. Published in English. Foreign language poems accepted. Maximum length of submissions: 14-16 lines" circ. 500. 2/yr. Pub'd 2 issues 1990; expects 2 issues 1991, 2 issues 1992. sub. price: $12.50. 5½×8½; of. Reporting time: 2-3 weeks following contest deadline. Payment: five cash prizes paid each title (see copy of rules for breakdown).

American Cooking Guild, Karen N. Perrino, President; Dan Perrino, Vice President, 6-F East Cedar Avenue, Gaithersburg, MD 20877, 301-949-6787. 1982. "We specialize in the publication of small cookbooks and will

24

accept manuscripts in that area" avg. press run 8M. Pub'd 4 titles 1990; expects 2 titles 1991, 2 titles 1992. 23 titles listed in the *Small Press Record of Books in Print* (20th Edition, 1991-92). avg. price, paper: $2.95-$5.95. Discounts: 50% or better to trade. 64-96pp; 5½×8½, 8¼×9; of. Reporting time: 2-3 months. Payment: upon request. Copyrights for author.

American Council for the Arts/ACA Books (see also UPDATE; VANTAGE POINT), Robert Porter, Director of Publishing, 1285 Avenue of the Americas, Third Floor, New York, NY 10019, 212-245-4510. 1968. Articles, art, news items. "Interested in material on arts administration, legislation affecting all the arts, news on all art forms. Arts research & policy studies" avg. press run 3M. Pub'd 8 titles 1990; expects 10 titles 1991, 10 titles 1992. 15 titles listed in the *Small Press Record of Books in Print* (20th Edition, 1991-92). avg. price, cloth: $22.95; paper: $14.95. Discounts: ACA Members: 10%. Volume discounts also available. Bookstores: 1-4 20%, 5+49 40% 50+42%, Wholesales: 1-4 25%, 5-49 45% 50+50%. 200pp; 6×9, 8½×11. Payment: none for magazines; varies for books. Copyrights for author.

AMERICAN DANCE GUILD NEWSLETTER, Rima Sokoloff, Lawrence Epstein, Karen Deaver, 33 West 21st Street, New York, NY 10010, 212-627-3790. 1956. Articles, interviews, criticism, reviews, letters, news items. circ. 1M. 6/yr. Pub'd 6 issues 1990; expects 5 issues 1991, 6 issues 1992. 3 titles listed in the *Small Press Record of Books in Print* (20th Edition, 1991-92). Regular membership $40, student & retired $25; price per copy: $1; sample: $1. Back issues: $10. Discounts: none. 14pp; 8½×11; of. Reporting time: 2 months. Payment: none. Not copyrighted. Pub's reviews: 15-18 in 1990. §Performing arts, arts management, arts education, dance. Ads: $80/$45/$25 fourth/$20 eighth. CCLM.

AMERICAN DANE, Jennifer C. Denning, Editor-in-Chief; Jerome L Christensen, Administrative Editor, Danish Brotherhood in America, 3717 Harney Street, Omaha, NE 68131-3844, 402-341-5049. 1916. Poetry, fiction, articles, photos, reviews, non-fiction. *"Must be of Danish context"* circ. 10M. 12/yr. Pub'd 12 issues 1990; expects 12 issues 1991, 12 issues 1992. sub. price: $12, $15 foreign; per copy: $1; sample: $1. Back issues: inquire about availability. Discounts: given upon inquiries. 24pp; 8¼×11; lp. Reporting time: 2 weeks. Payment: immediately following publication. Copyrighted, reverts to author. Pub's reviews: 2 in 1990. §Must concern Danish history, traditions, etc. Ads: $330/$192.50/$110 1/4 page/$66 1/8/$44 1/16.

American Family Foundation (see also CULT OBSERVER; CULTIC STUDIES JOURNAL), PO Box 336, Weston, MA 02193, 617-893-0930. 1979. 2 titles listed in the *Small Press Record of Books in Print* (20th Edition, 1991-92). Discounts: 50% to distributors. 120pp; 6×9.

AMERICAN FORESTS, Bill Rooney, Editor; Norah Deakin Davis, Managing Editor, PO Box 2000, Washington, DC 20013, (202) 667-3300. 1894. Articles, art, photos, news items, non-fiction. "We are looking for factual articles that are well written, well illustrated, and will inform, entertain, and perhaps inspire. *We rarely accept fiction or poetry.* We welcome informative news stories on controversial topics as long as they are well documented and present the issue fairly. Feature stories have a better chance when quotes and anecdotes liven the text. Articles should be neither too elementary nor too technical. A written query is suggested. Manuscripts should be typewritten, double-spaced, and should not exceed 2,000 words. Include SASE with submissions" circ. 26M. 6/yr. Pub'd 6 issues 1990; expects 6 issues 1991, 6 issues 1992. sub. price: $24; per copy: $2.50; sample: $1 postage w/ SASE. 80pp; 8¼×10⅞; web. Reporting time: 6 weeks. Payment: full length feature articles, *with photo or other illustrative support* ranges from $300 to $700; cover photos $300. Copyrighted, reverts to author. Pub's reviews: 28 in 1990. §Trees, forests, forest policy, nature guides, forestry. Ads: available on request.

American Handwriting Analysis Foundation, Sheila Lowe, Editor, PO Box 6201, San Jose, CA 95150. 1967. News items, non-fiction. "Patricia Wellingham-Jones is in charge of publications." avg. press run 100-200. Pub'd 3 titles 1990; expects 1 title 1991, 1 title 1992. 7 titles listed in the *Small Press Record of Books in Print* (20th Edition, 1991-92). avg. price, paper: $6.95-$32.95. Discounts: 40% for 5 of 1 title. 22-212pp; 8½×11, 7×8½, 6½×8½; of. Does not copyright for author.

AMERICAN HIKER, The American Hiking Society, Wayne Curtis, 1015 31st Street NW, Washington, DC 20007, 703-385-3252. circ. 51M. 4/yr. Pub'd 4 issues 1990; expects 4 issues 1991, 4 issues 1992. sub. price: $10. 32pp.

The American Hiking Society (see also AMERICAN HIKER), Wayne Curtis, 1015 31st Street, N.W., Washington, DC 20007, 703-385-3252. 1977. Photos, cartoons, interviews. avg. press run 10M. Pub'd 2 titles 1990; expects 2 titles 1991, 2 titles 1992. 4 titles listed in the *Small Press Record of Books in Print* (20th Edition, 1991-92). Discounts: please inquire. 96pp; 8½×10¾; of, web. Reporting time: 6 weeks. Payment: none. Does not copyright for author.

American Impressions, Dixie Ingram, Marilyn Childers, PO Box 3706, Hickory, NC 28603, 704-324-1416. 1990. "American Impressions was established March, 1990. It is the publishing division of A-1 Quick Print which was founded in 1987. As a newcomer, we are seeking every opportunity to gain acceptance in the publishing field. Currently, we have 2 books in process" Expects 5 titles 1991. 11×17; †of, high speed duplicator. Copyrights for author.

AMERICAN INDIAN BASKETRY, Institute for the Study of Traditional American Indian Arts Press, John M Gogal, Editorial advisory board of nationwide experts, PO Box 66124, Portland, OR 97266, 503-233-8131. 1979. Articles, photos, interviews, criticism, reviews, non-fiction. "Seeking photo essays on Native American basket weavers showing the step-by-step method of weaving baskets, or of gathering the native materials used in weaving. Should be accompanied by information on the basket weaver, her weaving tradition, tribal background, and appropriate accurate commentary and analysis of this type of basketry. Also, short pieces with accompanying photo of Native American basket weavers, living or dead." circ. 5M. 4/yr. Pub'd 4 issues 1990; expects 4 issues 1991, 4 issues 1992. sub. price: $30; per copy: $7.95; sample: $6.95. Back issues: inquire. Discounts: 50% on 10 or more copies of latest issue, others 40%. 36pp; 8½×11; of. Reporting time: 1 month. Payment: inquire. Copyrighted, does not revert to author. Pub's reviews: 20 in 1990. §American Indian, South and Central American Indian arts as well as North American history, arts, and crafts. Ads: $800/$450/$250.

THE AMERICAN JOURNAL OF PSYCHOANALYSIS, Plenum Publishing Corporation, Mario Rendon, 233 Spring Street, New York, NY 10013, (212) 741-3087. 1941. Articles, reviews, non-fiction. "*The American Journal of Psychoanalysis* was founded by Dr. Karen Horney, and is sponsored by the Association for the Advancement of Psychoanalysis of the Karen Horney Psychoanalytic Institute and Center. Its purpose is to communicate modern concepts of psychoanalytic theory and practice, and related investigations in allied fields. All correspondence concerning subscriptions should be addressed to: American Journal of Psychoanalysis, Fulfillment Dept., Agathon Press, Inc., 49 Sheridan Avenue, Albany, NY 12210. Address manuscripts, editorial correspondence, and books for review to: Mario Rendon, M.D., Editor, The American Journal of Psychoanalysis, 329 East 62nd Street, New York, NY 10021" circ. 1M. 4/yr. Pub'd 4 issues 1990; expects 4 issues 1991, 4 issues 1992. sub. price: indiv. $24, instit. $50; per copy: $12. Back issues: 1974-87 (Vols. 34-47, 4 issues ea.), $42 per vol. Discounts: 10% discount to subscription agents. 96pp; 6½×9½; of. Reporting time: 3 months. Payment: none. Copyrighted, does not revert to author. Pub's reviews: 3 in 1990. §Books on psychology, psychoanalysis, and psychoanalysts. Ads: $225/$140. COSMEP.

AMERICAN LITERARY REVIEW: A National Journal of Poems and Stories, Scott Cairns, University of N. Texas Press, PO Box 13615, Denton, TX 76203, 817-565-2124. 1990. Poetry, fiction. "Recent contributors: Pattiann Rogers, Gordon Weaver, Gerald Haslam, Patricia Goedicke, Betty Adcock, Miller Williams" 2/yr. Expects 2 issues 1991, 2 issues 1992. sub. price: $10; per copy: $5. Back issues: $5, if available. Discounts: standard. 128pp; 7×10; of. Reporting time: 4-6 weeks. Payment: 2 copies. Copyrighted, reverts to author. Ads: $150/$75/$50 must be camera ready. AWP.

AMERICAN LITERATURE, Cathy N. Davidson, Editor; Michael Moon, Associate Editor, 304 E. Allen Building, Duke University, Durham, NC 27706, 919-684-3948. 1929. Articles, criticism, reviews. "*American Literature only*" circ. 5M. 4/yr. Pub'd 4 issues 1990; expects 4 issues 1991, 4 issues 1992. sub. price: $20 individuals, $35 institutions, foreign add $8 postage; per copy: $9. Back issues: single, $9; Volume $35. 185pp; 6×9; lp. Reporting time: 3 months. Payment: 50 reprints. Copyrighted, rights optional with author. Pub's reviews: 140 in 1990. §American literary criticism, scholarship, bibliography. Ads: $300/$200.

AMERICAN LIVING, Angela Mark, Michael Shores, PO Box 901, Allston, MA 02134, 617-522-7782. 1982. Art, collages. "*American Living* is a visual magazine consisting of original collages and drawings done by Angela Mark and Michael Shores. We do a collaborative issue once a year taking submissions from anyone interested" circ. 150. 4/yr. Pub'd 4 issues 1990; expects 4 issues 1991, 4 issues 1992. 7 titles listed in the *Small Press Record of Books in Print* (20th Edition, 1991-92). sub. price: $7; per copy: $2; sample: $1. Back issues: $1-$2. Will trade for other magazines. 32pp; 5½×8½; †xerox. Reporting time: about 2 months. Payment: free issue. Copyrighted, reverts to author.

American Malacologists, Inc., Dr. R. Tucker Abbott, PO Box 2255, Melbourne, FL 32902-2255, 407-725-2260. 1974. Articles, non-fiction. "Publish books shells and conchology. Latest *Compendium of Landshells*" avg. press run 5M. Pub'd 2 titles 1990; expects 2 titles 1991, 2 titles 1992. 7 titles listed in the *Small Press Record of Books in Print* (20th Edition, 1991-92). avg. price, cloth: $38; paper: $4.95; other: $9.95 waterproof paper. Discounts: 40-65%. 250pp; size varies; of. Copyrights for author.

American Montessori Consulting, PO Box 5062, 11961 Wallingsford Road, Rossmoor, CA 90721, 213-598-2321. 2 titles listed in the *Small Press Record of Books in Print* (20th Edition, 1991-92).

AMERICAN POETRY ANTHOLOGY, American Poetry Association, PO Box 51007, Seattle, WA 98115-1007. 1981. Poetry. "We are interested in seeing work from poets of all levels of skill and experience, especially those who are new, not-yet published or little known. Up to 1 poem per poet. English language only. 20 lines or less. Any form. Any subject except sexually explicit. Photocopy, simultaneous submissions OK. Poems can not be returned. *American Poetry Anthology* is published by American Poetry Association, formed

26

to encourage the writing and appreciation of poetry. Accepted poets may be requested to purchase a copy of the anthology in which poem appears. Copy of booklet, *Poet's Guide to Getting Published*, available free upon request with S.A.S.E." circ. 3M-4M. 4/yr. Pub'd 4 issues 1990; expects 5 issues 1991, 6 issues 1992. price per copy: $40; sample: $40. Back issues: $25.00. Discounts: 40%. 325pp; 8½×11; of. Reporting time: 3-4 weeks. Payment: none, but all poems considered in APA Contest—Grand Prize $1,000, 140 other prizes. Copyrighted, reverts to author. COSMEP.

American Poetry Association (see also AMERICAN POETRY ANTHOLOGY), PO Box 51007, Seattle, WA 98115-1007, 408-429-1122. 1981. Poetry. "Any style of poem, on any subject, one original poem, 20 line limit" avg. press run 3M. Pub'd 4 titles 1990; expects 5 titles 1991, 6 titles 1992. 17 titles listed in the *Small Press Record of Books in Print* (20th Edition, 1991-92). avg. price, cloth: $40. 350-400pp; 8¼×10⅞. Reporting time: 3-4 weeks. Payment: no royalties; payment for prize winners only. Copyrights for author. COSMEP.

AMERICAN POETRY REVIEW, Arthur Vogelsang, David Bonanno, Stephen Berg, 1721 Walnut St., Philadelphia, PA 19103, 215-496-0439. 1972. Poetry, fiction, articles, art, photos, cartoons, interviews, satire, criticism, reviews, music, letters, parts-of-novels, long-poems, collages, plays, concrete art, news items, non-fiction. circ. 20M. 6/yr. Pub'd 6 issues 1990; expects 6 issues 1991. sub. price: $12; per copy: $2.50; sample: $2.50. Back issues: $5 and $2. Discounts: Through Eastern News for stores and newsstands. 48pp; 9¾×13¾; of. Reporting time: 12 weeks. Payment: $1 line for poetry; $75 tabloid page for prose. Copyrighted, reverts to author. Pub's reviews: 30 in 1990. §Literary. Ads: $600/$360. CCLM.

American Poets In Profile Series, Steven Ford Brown, PO Box 2764, Boston, MA 02208. 1983. "A series of profiles of American poets and their work. Contributors to the various books have included: Marvin Bell, Fred Chappell, Hayden Carruth, Paul Christensen, Karla Hammond, Terry Hummer, Judith Johnson, Rod Jellema, Laura Jensen, Merrill Leffler, Larry McMurtry, John Montague, Robert Morgan, Carol Muske, Sister Bernetta Quinn, Dennis Schmitz, Dabney Stuart, David Wojahn. Books in the series to date include: *The Giver of Morning: On the Poetry of Dave Smith*, ed. Bruce Weigl; *Dissolve To Island: On the Poetry of John Logan*, ed. Michael Waters; *Earth That Sings: On the Poetry of Andrew Glaze*, ed. William Doreski; *Poet As Zimmer, Zimmer As Poet: On the Poetry of Paul Zimmer*, ed. Jan Susina; *Heart's Invention: On the Poetry of Vassar Miller*, ed. Steven Ford Brown; *An Answering Music: On the Poetry of Carolyn Kizer*, ed. David Rigsbee. Forthcoming volumes are planned on Fred Chappell, Jack Kerouac, and Lorene Neidecker." avg. press run 1.5M-3M. Pub'd 1 title 1990; expects 2 titles 1991, 3 titles 1992. avg. price, paper: $15.95. Discounts: standard 40% for 5+ copies, 20% 1-4. 256-300pp; 5½×8¼; of. Reporting time: 1 month. Payment: copies, percentages. Copyrights for author. COSMEP; Small Press Center-NY.

AMERICAN POP, Steve White, Editor & Publisher, 154 Woodland Drive, Hanover, MA 02339, 617-982-9567. 1990. Articles, photos, interviews, reviews, news items, non-fiction. circ. 2M. 12/yr. Pub'd 9 issues 1990; expects 12 issues 1991, 12 issues 1992. sub. price: $12; per copy: $1.25; sample: $2. Back issues: $2-$6. Discounts: 60/40 split with stores. 16pp; 8×10; †of. Reporting time: 2 weeks. Payment: $25. Not copyrighted. Pub's reviews: 3 in 1990. §1960's culture (music, film, TV, politics, counterculture, fashion, etc.). Ads: $125/$70/$40 1/4 page/$15 1/8.

American Press, Jim Wyzard, PO Box 127, Odessa, MO 64076. 1987. Poetry, fiction, articles, non-fiction. "We seek book length material for publication on a subsidy and self-publishing basis. We also publish anthologies of poetry averaging 2-4 per year." avg. press run 300-500. Pub'd 5 titles 1990; expects 75 titles 1991, 175 titles 1992. avg. price, paper: $5.95. 65pp; 5½×8½; of. Reporting time: 2 weeks. Payment: none. Copyrights for author.

American Samizdat Editions, Herman Berlandt, PO Box 886, Bolinas, CA 94924, 415-868-9224. 1990. Poetry. "We invite poems from colleagues beyond our borders in good English translations." avg. press run 2M. Pub'd 1 title 1990; expects 2 titles 1991, 2 titles 1992. 1 title listed in the *Small Press Record of Books in Print* (20th Edition, 1991-92). avg. price, other: $5 per copy tabloid. Discounts: 50%. 24-28pp; 11×15; of. Reporting time: no special deadlines. Payment: 2 free copies + 40% royalty to translators. Does not copyright for author. PEN - Oakland.

THE AMERICAN SCHOLAR, The William Byrd Press, Joseph Epstein, 1811 Q Street NW, Washington, DC 20009, 202-265-3808. 1932. Poetry, articles, criticism, reviews, letters. "3,000 to 4,000 words best" circ. 28M. 4/yr. Pub'd 4 issues 1990; expects 4 issues 1991, 4 issues 1992. sub. price: $21; per copy: $5.75; sample: $5.75. Back issues: $5 and up. Discounts: vary. 160pp; 5½×8; of. Reporting time: 4-8 weeks. Payment: $500 per article. Copyrighted. Pub's reviews: 32 in 1990. §Literary, cultural, contemporary. Ads: $675/$425.

American Source Books, PO Box 280353, Lakewood, CO 80228, 303-980-0580. 1988. Non-fiction. avg. press run 3M. Expects 2 titles 1991, 3 titles 1992. 2 titles listed in the *Small Press Record of Books in Print* (20th Edition, 1991-92). avg. price, paper: $17; other: $35. Discounts: 2-4 20%, 5-24 40%, 25-49 42%, 50-99 45%, 100+ 50%. 250pp; 6×9, 8½×11; of. Reporting time: 1 month. Payment: 6-15% royalty on net. Does not copyright for author. COSMEP, PMA, Rocky Mtn Book Publishers Assn.

AMERICAN SQUAREDANCE, Stan Burdick, Cathie Burdick, Burdick Enterprises, PO Box 488, Huron, OH 44839, 419-433-2188. 1945. Poetry, fiction, articles, art, photos, cartoons, interviews, satire, reviews, letters, news items, non-fiction. *"Must* deal with some phase of the square dance activity" circ. 20M. 12/yr. Pub'd 12 issues 1990; expects 12 issues 1991, 12 issues 1992. sub. price: $15; per copy: $1.50; sample: free. Back issues: 75¢. 100-110pp; 5½x8½; of. Reporting time: 2 weeks. Payment: on publication. Copyrighted, does not revert to author. Pub's reviews: 12 in 1990. §Square dance activity. Ads: $330/$175.

AMERICAN THEATRE MAGAZINE, Theatre Communications Group, Jim O'Quinn, 355 Lexington Avenue, New York, NY 10017, 212-697-5230. 1984. Articles, interviews, letters, plays, news items. circ. 14M. 11/yr. Pub'd 11 issues 1990; expects 11 issues 1991, 11 issues 1992. sub. price: $27; per copy: $3.50; sample: $3.50. 56pp; 8½x11. Reporting time: 2 months lead time. Payment: negotiated per article. Copyrighted. Pub's reviews: 30 in 1990. §Theatre-related titles also performing arts. Ads: $660/$415/50¢ per word ($20 min.).

THE AMERICAN VOICE, Frederick Smock, Sallie Bingham, 332 West Broadway, #1215, Louisville, KY 40202, 502-562-0045. 1985. Poetry, fiction, articles, photos, interviews, criticism. "We publish daring new writers, and the more radical work of established writers from Canada, the U.S., *and* South America. At least half of our contributors are women; we also have an interest in beginning writers. Recent contributors include Marge Piercy, Sergio Ramirez, Isabel Allende, Joan Givner, Jamake Highwater, Wendell Berry, Bienvenido Santos, Ernesto Cardenal, Chaim Potok, Key Boyle, Sharon Doubiago, Linda Hogan, Olga Broumas. We are open to all forms." circ. 2M. 4/yr. Pub'd 4 issues 1990; expects 4 issues 1991, 4 issues 1992. sub. price: $12; per copy: $4; sample: $5. Back issues: $5. 100pp; 6x9; of. Reporting time: 6 weeks. Payment: poems $150/prose $400/translators $75-$150. Copyrighted, reverts to author. Pub's reviews. Swap full-page ads only. CLMP.

AMERICAN WRITING: A MAGAZINE, Nierika Editions, Alexandra Grilikhes, 4343 Manayunk Avenue, Philadelphia, PA 19128, 215-483-7051. 1990. Poetry, fiction, articles, interviews, criticism, letters, parts-of-novels, long-poems, collages, plays, concrete art, non-fiction. "We are open to all forms. We encourage experimentation in writing and welcome the innovative idea. We are more interested in the new work itself than in the fame or publication credits of the writers. The subtext of much of what we publish has to do with the powers of intuition. It's a good idea to look at an issue before submitting- but certainly not required. 3000 word max for prose." circ. 1M. 2/yr. Pub'd 2 issues 1990; expects 2 issues 1991, 2 issues 1992. $8/yr; $15/yr institutions; price per copy: $5; sample: $5. Back issues: $5. Discounts: negotiable. 80pp; 5⅜x8½; of. Reporting time: 2 months average, sometimes 3-4. Payment: copies; discount to contributors on additional copies. Copyrighted, reverts to author. Ads: on request.

Americana & Collectibles Press, Ted Hake, PO Box 1444, York, PA 17405, 717-848-1333. 1977. Non-fiction. "Books dealing with American Popular Culture Collectibles" avg. press run 3M. Pub'd 2 titles 1990; expects 2 titles 1992. avg. price, cloth: $30; paper: $20. Discounts: 6 copies 40%, 100+ 60%. 200pp; 8½x11; †of. Reporting time: 2 weeks. Payment: 10% on selling price (wholesale or retail).

American-Canadian Publishers, Inc., Arthur Goodson, Editorial Director; Arlene Zekowski, Stanley Berne, Herman Zaage, Art Director, PO Box 4595, Santa Fe, NM 87502-4595, 505-983-8484. 1972. Poetry, fiction, articles, art, photos, interviews, satire, criticism, reviews, music, letters, parts-of-novels, long-poems, collages, plays, concrete art, news items, non-fiction. "We are categorically against realism in the novel simply because it is by now a bankrupt form. We reject orthodox "story" because it generally tortures the truth to fit the formula. We support the novel that investigates "inner consciousness," that is multi-dimensional and open-structured in language and thought: the novel for the year 2000. Interested? Send SASE for free Catalog full of new examples. *No unsolicited manuscripts"* avg. press run 1.5M-3M. Pub'd 2 titles 1990; expects 2 titles 1991, 6 titles 1992. 11 titles listed in the *Small Press Record of Books in Print* (20th Edition, 1991-92). avg. price, cloth: $22.95; paper: $15; other: $10-$100. Discounts: 40% to dealers; 50% bulk-class adoptions: rates negotiable. 200pp; 6x9; of. Payment: negotiable. Copyrights for author. Santa Fe Writers Coop, COSMEP.

THE AMERICA'S REVIEW, Arte Publico Press, Julian Olivares, University of Houston, Houston, TX 77204-2090, 713-749-4768. 1972. Poetry, fiction, articles, art, photos, interviews, satire, criticism, reviews, long-poems, plays. *"The Americas Review* is a journal of Hispanic literature and art of the USA that also publishes articles of literary criticism, folklore, and popular culture. We publish the most renowned Hispanic writers as well as beginning writers." circ. 3.5M. 2+. Pub'd 4 issues 1990; expects 4 issues 1991, 4 issues 1992. sub. price: $15 individuals, $20 institutions; per copy: $5/$10 double; sample: $5. Back issues: $10. Discounts: 40% bookstores & distributors. 128-198pp; 5½x8½; of. Reporting time: immediate acknowledgement; delayed acceptance or rejection (3-6 months). Payment: only on basis of grants; no fixed rate. Copyrighted, reverts to author. Pub's reviews: 16 in 1990. §Hispanic literature, art, culture, etc. Ads: $200/$125. CCLM.

AMERICAS REVIEW, Gerald Gray, Kenneth Kitch, Moira Hughes, Box 7681, Berkeley, CA 94707, 415-845-2089. 1985. Poetry, fiction, art, cartoons, satire, long-poems, plays. "Poems range from one page to twelve pages. Stories vary in length. Content generally has a political sense, dealing with events in the U.S. since the Civil Rights Movement and the countries in Europe and Latin America since about the same time." circ. 1M. 1/yr. Pub'd 1 issue 1990; expects 1 issue 1991, 1 issue 1992. sub. price: $4 individual, $6 institution; per copy: same; sample: $4 indiv., $6 institution. Back issues: 3 indiv., $5 inst. 75pp; 6×9; photo offset. Reporting time: 3 months. Payment: $10. Copyrighted, reverts to author. Ads: $75/$35.

Americas Society (see also REVIEW. LATIN AMERICAN LITERATURE & ARTS), Alfred Mac Adam, Editor; Daniel Shapiro, Managing & Poetry Editor, 680 Park Avenue, New York, NY 10021. 1968. Poetry, fiction, articles, art, interviews, criticism, reviews. "Latin American literature in translation." avg. press run 4.5M. Pub'd 1 title 1990; expects 2 titles 1991, 2 titles 1992. avg. price, paper: $7. Discounts: agency 15%. 88pp; 8½×11; lp. Reporting time: 4-6 weeks. Payment: $50 per review, $100-$200 per article. Copyrights for author.

Amethyst Press, Stan Leventhal, 70A Greenwich Avenue, New York, NY 10011-8307, 212-629-8140. 1989. Poetry, fiction, art. "Dennis Cooper, David Trinidad, Bo Houston, Kevin Killian, Stan Leventhal, Mark Ameen, Patrick Moore, John Gilgun" avg. press run 3M. Pub'd 5 titles 1990; expects 6 titles 1991. avg. price, paper: $9.95. 150pp; 5½×8½; of. Copyrights for author.

Amherst Media, Craig Alesse, 418 Homecrest Drive, Amherst, NY 14226, 716-874-4450. 1979. "We publish how-to photography books. Also books on video and astronomy. We distribute for 20 other presses into photo retailers" avg. press run 5M. Pub'd 4 titles 1990; expects 4 titles 1991, 4 titles 1992. avg. price, paper: $17.95. Discounts: 40% stores, 20% schools. 192pp; 9×8, 8½×11; of. Reporting time: 6 weeks. Payment: negotiable. Copyrights for author. COSMEP.

Amherst Writers & Artists Press, Inc. (see also PEREGRINE), PO Box 1076, Amherst, MA 01004, 413-253-3307. 1983. Poetry, fiction. "We do not want manuscripts at this time." avg. press run 500-1M. Pub'd 2 titles 1990; expects 3 titles 1991, 3 titles 1992. 7 titles listed in the *Small Press Record of Books in Print* (20th Edition, 1991-92). avg. price, paper: $8. Discounts: 40%. 5½×8; of. Reporting time: 3-6 months. Payment: in copies only. Copyrights for author. Amherst Writers and Artists.

THE AMICUS JOURNAL, Peter Borrelli, Editor; Beth Hanson, Managing Editor; Brian Swann, Poetry Editor, 40 West 20th Street, New York, NY 10011, 212-727-2700. 1979. Poetry, articles. "We are the journal of the *Natural Resources Defense Council*. Publish poems rooted in nature, no more than five per issue. Poems should be no more than one manuscript page in length. Please enclose SASE when you send to Brian Swann, Poetry Editor, c/o the address above. Some recent contributors: William Stafford, Duane Niatum, Gary Snyder, Ben Howard, Peter Cooley, Peter Wild, Peter Blue Cloud, David Wagoner. We will not be reading any poetry until 1992" circ. 130M. 4/yr. Pub'd 4 issues 1990; expects 4 issues 1991, 4 issues 1992. sub. price: $10; per copy: $4.00; sample: complimentary with 9 X 12 SASE (90¢ postage). Back issues: $4. Discounts: none. 48pp; 7½×10½; of. Reporting time: 2 months. Payment: $25 on publication. Copyrighted. Pub's reviews: 10 in 1990. §Environment, energy, pollution: water, air; land conservation.

Amnos Publications, Ann Lampros, 2501 South Wolf Road, Westchester, IL 60154, 312-562-2744. 1984. Non-fiction. "We publish historical studies of the early Christian Church, based upon the teachings of the Eastern Orthodox Church." avg. press run 7M. Pub'd 2 titles 1990; expects 2 titles 1991, 2 titles 1992. 1 title listed in the *Small Press Record of Books in Print* (20th Edition, 1991-92). avg. price, paper: $7.95. Discounts: trade. 175pp; 6×9. Does not copyright for author.

Ampersand Press (see also CALLIOPE), Martha Christina, Director, Creative Writing Program, Roger Williams College, Bristol, RI 02809, 401-253-1040, ext. 2217. 1980. Poetry, fiction. "Chapbooks and single volume collections of poetry and fiction. We are not accepting unsolicited manuscripts at this time" avg. press run 250-1M. Pub'd 3 titles 1990; expects 3 titles 1991, 3 titles 1992. 20 titles listed in the *Small Press Record of Books in Print* (20th Edition, 1991-92). avg. price, paper: $10 full-length collections; other: $2.50 chapbooks (though longer chapbooks, say over 24pp cost more). Discounts: 40% bookstores, distributors; libraries and individuals pay full list price. 52-136pp full-length, 20-40pp chapbook; 5½×8½, 6×9; of. Payment: usually 10% of 1st press run for chapbooks, standard 15% for full-length; royalties on subsequent printings. Copyrights for author. CLMP.

AMRA, Owlswick Press, Box 8243, Philadelphia, PA 19101. 1956. Poetry, fiction, satire, criticism, reviews, non-fiction. "This is a very specialized magazine, dealing with the writings of Robert E. Howard and similar heroica. We strongly advise writers to familiarize themselves with the magazine before submitting anything. If you have to ask who Robert E. Howard is or what sort of thing he wrote, this is not the market for you. The identity of the editor is normally cloaked in mystery." circ. 1.2M. Irregular. Expects 1 issue 1991, 1-2 issues 1992. sub. price: $9/5 issues; per copy: $2; sample: $2. Back issues: #1-3, #46-69 $1.50 each; #70 onward, $2 each. Add $1 shipping per order. Discounts: inquire. 40pp; 7×10; of. Reporting time: 1 week. Payment: 2¢ per word for fiction and non-fiction. Copyrighted, reverts to author. Pub's reviews. §Robert E. Howard and related heroic fantasy.

29

Amrita Foundation, Inc., Priscilla Alden, PO Box 8080, Dallas, TX 75205, 214-522-5224 (TX); 415-527-6813, 1-800-526-7746 (CA). 1978. "Additional address: PO Box 9869, Berkeley, CA 94709" 11 titles listed in the *Small Press Record of Books in Print* (20th Edition, 1991-92).

AN SEANRUD, Sunburst Press, Rudi Holzapfel, c/o Sunburst Press, 25 Newtown Avenue, Blackrock, Co. Dublin 882575, Ireland. 1987. Poetry, articles, satire, criticism, reviews. circ. 300. Occasional. Expects 1 issue 1992. price per copy: free. Discounts: variable. 30-80pp; size normal octavo; †of. Reporting time: 3 months. Payment: if anything, by special arrangement. Not copyrighted. Pub's reviews. §Poetry, private press, art, bibliography, Irish interest, lit. crit. No ads.

Anabiosis Press (see also ALBATROSS), Richard Smyth, Richard Brobst, 125 Horton Avenue, Englewood, FL 33981. "Send chapbook ms with name, address, and phone# on title page. 16-20 pages of poetry. $5 reading fee, for which entrants receive one copy of winner's chapbook and one copy of *Albatross*. Send between Sept. 1-Dec. 31 of each year. Winners gets $50 and 25 copies. Send ms to Chapbook Contest, R. Brobst, Ed. 125 Horton Avenue, Englewood, FL 34223" avg. press run 1. Expects 1 title 1991, 1 title 1992. avg. price, paper: $3. 16-20pp; 5½×8½; OF. Payment: $50 to winner and 25 copies. Copyrights for author. CCLM.

Anaphase II, Lily Splane, Box 6157, Chula Vista, CA 91909, 619-661-2528. 1987. Art, satire, non-fiction. "Main publishing interests are handbooks and manuals by previously unpublished authors who are considered experts in their fields. We have 2 books in print: *Nutritional Self Defense* by Lily Splane, M.N., and *Physiology Lab Handbook* by Michael B. Clark. We are planning to publish, more titles this year. Other interests include books for young adults (13-18 years) written *by* young adults" avg. press run 500. Pub'd 1 title 1990; expects 2 titles 1991, 5 titles 1992. 3 titles listed in the *Small Press Record of Books in Print* (20th Edition, 1991-92). avg. price, paper: $12. Discounts: 4-10 copies 10%, 11-25 15%, 26-50 17%, 51-100 20%, 101-150 22%, 150+ 25%. 150pp; 8½×11; of, xerox. Reporting time: 6-8 weeks. Payment: negotiable. Copyrights for author.

ANARCHY: A JOURNAL OF DESIRE ARMED, Lev Chernyi, A. Hacker, S. Hickory, Toni Otter, Noa, Mikell Zhan, Avid Darkly, PO Box 1446, Columbia, MO 65205-1446, 314-442-4352. 1980. Poetry, fiction, articles, art, photos, cartoons, satire, criticism, reviews, letters, collages, news items, non-fiction. "Features: 1,000 to 4,500 words. Reviews: 200-750 words (unless previously queried-up to 1,500 words). Short fiction: 1,000 to 3,000 words" circ. about 3M. 4/yr. Pub'd 4 issues 1990; expects 4 issues 1991, 4 issues 1992. sub. price: $6-$10; per copy: $2.50; sample: $2.50. Back issues: $2.50 for 1st, $2 each for additional back issues. Discounts: 6-19 copies 40%, 20-59 45%, 60-99 50%, 100+ 60%; 20% to other continents for 6-19, & 40% for 20 or more. 40pp; 10½×14½; web. Reporting time: 1 week to 4 months. Payment: free subscriptions for now and/or multiple copies. Not copyrighted. Pub's reviews: 24 books, 357 magazines in 1990. §Anarchist, libertarian/anti-authoritarian books, sexual liberation, feminism, ecology, radical history. No ads. COSMEP.

ANCESTRY NEWSLETTER, Ancestry Publishing, Robb Barr, Editor, PO Box 476, Salt Lake City, UT 84110, 801-531-1790. 1984. Articles, non-fiction. "Non-fiction topics of special interest to genealogical hobbyist and professional; strong 'how-to' focus. The newsletter is interested in articles that instruct (how-to, research techniques, etc.) and inform (new research sources, new collections, etc.). Basically, any article that can help genealogists with the advancement of their pursuit has a place in the newsletter. However, the newsletter does not solicit family histories, genealogies, or pedigree charts. The newsletter solicits original works only, but revised or updated articles, or pieces drawn from lectures, are welcome" circ. 8.2M. 6/yr. Pub'd 6 issues 1990; expects 6 issues 1991, 6 issues 1992. sub. price: $12; per copy: $2.50; sample: 3 25¢ stamps. 16pp; 8½×11; lp. Reporting time: 1 month. Payment: $50 on publication. Copyrighted, does not revert to author. No ads.

Ancestry Publishing (see also ANCESTRY NEWSLETTER; GENEALOGICAL COMPUTING), Robb Barr, Editor; Robert Welsh, Managing Editor; Robert Passaro, Editor, PO Box 476, Salt Lake City, UT 84110, 801-531-1790. 1983. "Our interest at present is in books and articles on how to conduct successful genealogical research. Source references, methodology, immigration/emigration studies, and library guidebooks are also wanted" avg. press run 5M. Pub'd 4 titles 1990; expects 6 titles 1991, 6 titles 1992. 1 title listed in the *Small Press Record of Books in Print* (20th Edition, 1991-92). avg. price, cloth: $30; paper: $12. Discounts: 1-4 25%, 5-24 40%, 25-49 41%, 50-99 42%, 100+ 43%. 400pp; 6×9; of. Reporting time: 4-6 weeks. Payment: variable, based on gross sales. Copyrights for author.

Ancient City Press, Mary A. Powell, President; Robert F. Kadlec, Vice-President; Marta Weigle, Secretary-Treasurer, Editor, PO Box 5401, Santa Fe, NM 87502, 505-982-8195. 1961. Non-fiction. "Booklets through book-length." avg. press run 2M-5M. Pub'd 5 titles 1990; expects 6 titles 1991, 5 titles 1992. 38 titles listed in the *Small Press Record of Books in Print* (20th Edition, 1991-92). avg. price, cloth: $24; paper: $10; other: $10. Discounts: 40% trade; standard for individuals; 50% distributors. 48pp booklet, 200pp book; 5½×8½. Reporting time: 1-4 months. Payment: contracts negotiated individually, royalties paid once a year. Copyrights for author. Rocky Mountain Book Publishers Association.

ANCIENT CONTROVERSY, Spencer's Int'l Enterprises Corp., PO Box 43822, Los Angeles, CA 90043.

1988. "A newsletter for society's leaders. Leadership in society ancient and present is a living dynamic change under the control of the Most High God" 8-10pp.

AND, Writers Forum, Bob Cobbing, John Rowan, 89A Petherton Road, London N5 2QT, England, 01-226-2657. 1952. Poetry, fiction, articles, art, photos, music, concrete art. "No submissions wanted." circ. 500. Very irregular. Expects 1 issue 1991, 1 issue 1992. price per copy: varies. Back issues: £1.50. 32pp; size varies; †photo-copy. Payment: copies. Not copyrighted. ALP, COLP.

and books, Janos Szebedinszky, Editor, 702 South Michigan, Suite 836, South Bend, IN 46601. 1978. Art, photos, non-fiction. "Encourage non-fiction mss on computers, new age, alternative materials. Please query first with outline" avg. press run 2M. Pub'd 10 titles 1990; expects 10 titles 1991, 15 titles 1992. 28 titles listed in the *Small Press Record of Books in Print* (20th Edition, 1991-92). avg. price, paper: $8.95. Discounts: 1-4 copies 10%, 5-14 30%, 15+ $40%. 200pp; 6×9; of. Reporting time: 1 month. Payment: 6%-10%. Copyrights for author.

Ander Publications, View Pointe Lane, Suite 202, LaGrange, GA 30240. 1977. Expects 1 title 1991. 2 titles listed in the *Small Press Record of Books in Print* (20th Edition, 1991-92). avg. price, cloth: $29.95; paper: $14.95. Discounts: standard. 190pp; 8½×11. Does not copyright for author.

Anderson Press, Barbara S. Anderson, President; Martin B. Tittle, Admin. Ass't., 706 West Davis, Ann Arbor, MI 48103, 313-995-0125; 994-6182. 1987. Photos, criticism, reviews, music, non-fiction. "Specialized music books welcome" avg. press run 1M. Pub'd 2 titles 1990; expects 2 titles 1991, 2 titles 1992. 2 titles listed in the *Small Press Record of Books in Print* (20th Edition, 1991-92). avg. price, cloth: $14.95; paper: $7.95. Discounts: Regular: 1-2 net; 3-99, 40%; 100, 45%; returnable; for non-returnable, 5% add'l Short: 1-2 net; 3, 20%; returnable; no add'l disc for non-returnable; both schedules + shipping. 32-400pp; 5×7, 9×12; of/lo. Reporting time: 3 month. Royalties accrue on sales but are not paid until our out-of-pocket costs are recovered. Copyrights for author.

And/Or Press, Inc., PO Box 2246, Berkeley, CA 94702, 415-548-2124. 1974. Non-fiction. "No unsolicited mss" avg. press run 10M. Pub'd 5 titles 1990; expects 6 titles 1991. 10 titles listed in the *Small Press Record of Books in Print* (20th Edition, 1991-92). avg. price, paper: $11.95. Discounts: 1-5 - 10%; 6-50 - 40%; 51-200 - 45%; over 500 - 55%. Pages vary; size varies; electronic. Reporting time: 3 months. Payment: standard arrangement. Copyrights for author.

ANDROGYNE, Androgyne Books, Ken Weichel, 930 Shields, San Francisco, CA 94132, 586-2697. 1971. Poetry, fiction, art, collages. circ. 500. 1/yr. sub. price: $5; per copy: $4; sample: $4. Back issues: No. 1, $5; No. 2, $2; No. 3, $2. Discounts: 40/60. 60pp; 5×8; †of. Reporting time: 3 weeks. Payment: 2 copies. Copyrighted, reverts to author. Pub's reviews: 2 in 1990. §Poetry, collages, criticism. COSMEP, IE.

Androgyne Books (see also ANDROGYNE), Ken Weichel, 930 Shields, San Francisco, CA 94132, 586-2697. 1971. Poetry, fiction, articles, art, photos, criticism, collages, plays. avg. press run 500. Pub'd 2 titles 1990; expects 4 titles 1991. 24 titles listed in the *Small Press Record of Books in Print* (20th Edition, 1991-92). avg. price, cloth: $4; paper: $4; other: $4. Discounts: 40% bookstores; 50% wholesalers. 65pp; 5×7½; †of. Reporting time: 3 weeks. Payment: 10% of press run. Copyrights for author. COSMEP.

ANEMONE, Nanette Morin, Editor, PO Box 369, Chester, VT 05143. 1979. Poetry, fiction, articles, art, photos, interviews, satire, criticism, reviews, long-poems, collages. circ. 12M. 4+. Pub'd 4 issues 1990; expects 4 issues 1991, 4 issues 1992. sub. price: $10; per copy: $2.50; sample: $2.50. Back issues: $3. 32pp; 10×15; of. Reporting time: erratic 1 day-1 year. Payment: in issues and 1 yrs. subscription. Copyrighted, reverts to author. Pub's reviews: 25 in 1990. §Poetry, women, authors, politics, art. Ads: $150/$75. Mass. Council on the Arts and Humanities, New England Foundation for the Arts, Vermont Council on the Arts, CLMP, COSMEP.

ANERCA/COMPOST, Adeena Karasick, Kedrick James, Wreford Miller, 3989 Arbutus Street, Vancouver, B.C. V6J 4T2, Canada, (604) 732-1648. 1986. Poetry, interviews, criticism, reviews, letters, long-poems. "Interested in language centered poetry and essays on post structural theory" circ. 500. 4/yr. Pub'd 1 issue 1990; expects 4 issues 1991, 6 issues 1992. sub. price: $12/4 issues; per copy: $3; sample: $3 Cdn. 30pp; 8×11½; †of. Reporting time: 2 months. Payment: copies. Copyrighted, reverts to author. Pub's reviews: 5 in 1990. §Contemporary verse, tending to experimental, language centered. Ads: $30/$15/negotiable.

ANGELSTONE, Angelstone Press, Beth Bradley, Sandra S. Thompson, Toney Teague, Carol Dennison Segal, 316 Woodland Drive, Birmingham, AL 35209, 205-870-7281. 1977. Poetry. "Prose poetry. We are looking for imagistic poems with interesting use of the language. First issue featured Alabama residents and natives, future issues not limited to Alabama. Contributors must include SASE or poems will not be returned. Recent contributors: Sonia Sanchez, Pier Giorgio DiCicco, Terry Stokes, Susan Fromberg Schaeffer, Lyn Lifshin, David Spicer, Joe Rosenblatt, Carolyn Smart, Phillip Foss, etc." circ. 200. 1/yr. Expects 1 issue 1991, 1 issue 1992. No subscriptions; price per copy: $4; sample: $4. Back issues: $2.50 - *Angelstone 1* and *Angelstone 2* out of print. Discounts: Negotiable. 30-40pp; 7×10; of. Reporting time: 1 week - 3 months.

31

Payment: 1 copy. Not copyrighted.

Angelstone Press (see also ANGELSTONE), Beth Bradley, Sandra S. Thompson, Toney Teague, Carol Dennison Segal, 316 Woodland Drive, Birmingham, AL 35209, 205-870-7281. 1977. Poetry. "Chapbooks by Carol Dennison Smith, Sandra S. Thompson, Robert Lynn Penny and Pier Giorgio DiCicco" avg. press run 200. Expects 1 title 1991, 1 title 1992. avg. price, paper: $3.50. Discounts: negotiable. 30-40pp; size varies; of. Reporting time: 1-3 months. Payment: negotiable, according to the individual. Does not copyright for author.

ANGRY, Tyger Press, Steven Marks, 325 Captain's Walk, Room 301, New London, CT 06320, 442-1835. 1990. Fiction, articles, art, photos, cartoons, interviews, satire, criticism, reviews, letters, non-fiction. "This is the place for you to get angry about politics, government, education, the 'poisonous pedagogy', obscurantism, hypocrisy and any other 'ism' in which somebody is trying to pull the wool over your eyes." circ. 500. 4-5/yr. Pub'd 2 issues 1990; expects 4-5 issues 1991, 4-5 issues 1992. price per copy: $4; sample: $4. 20pp; 8½×11; †xerox. Reporting time: 3 months. Payment: 25% of yearly sales distributed equally among contributors. Not copyrighted. Pub's reviews. §Alternative non-fiction, literature. Ads: $15 1/4 page/$8 1/8 page/$5 business card. COSMEP.

Angst World Library, Thomas Carlisle, Kathleen Carlisle, PO Box 593, Selma, OR 97538-0593. 1974. Fiction, parts-of-novels, non-fiction. "Please query prior to submitting ms. and *always* enclose SASE. *Tragedy of the Moisty Morning* by Jessica Salmonson; *The Twenty-fifth Hour* by Lawrence Russel" avg. press run 100-500. Expects 2 titles 1991, 3 titles 1992. 6 titles listed in the *Small Press Record of Books in Print* (20th Edition, 1991-92). avg. price, paper: $4-$6. Discounts: 40% on purchases over 5 copies; 40% to retailers. Pages vary; 5×8; of. Reporting time: 1-2 months. Payment: 25% of net profit + 5 copies, and/or outright purchase. Copyrights for author.

Anhinga Press, Van K. Brock, PO Box 10595, Tallahassee, FL 32302-5144, 904-575-5592. 1973. Poetry. "The Anhinga Prize is open to all poets writing in English who have not yet published a second full-length book of poetry, carries an award of $500 plus publication, requires an entry fee of $17, and is judged anonymously. Send SASE for complete details. Aside from the contests, we publish very few manuscripts" avg. press run 500-1M. Pub'd 1 title 1990; expects 2 titles 1991, 2 titles 1992. 13 titles listed in the *Small Press Record of Books in Print* (20th Edition, 1991-92). avg. price, cloth: $14.95; paper: $8. Discounts: 40%. 32-64pp; 5½×8½; of. Reporting time: varies greatly; contest submissions—6-9 months. Payment: varies. Copyrights for author.

ANIMA: The Journal of Human Experience, Anima Publications, Harry Buck, Barbara D. Rotz, 1053 Wilson Avenue, Chambersburg, PA 17201, 717-267-0087. 1974. Poetry, articles, art, photos, interviews, criticism, reviews, music, long-poems. "*Anima,* The Journal of Human Experience celebrates the sources of our separate identity in the common soul of us all. Articles on feminism, Eastern religion, Jungian psychology, and human wholeness present a cross-cultural perspective. The magazine is itself a physical example of its themes, with experimental design and art work by many new photographers, poets, and artists. Authors creating new traditions from immediate experience are welcome" circ. 1M and growing. 2/yr. Expects 2 issues 1991. sub. price: $9.95; per copy: $5.95; sample: $3.95. Back issues: $3.95. Discounts: 5 copies-40%, no returns. 72pp; 8½×8½; of. Reporting time: 12 weeks. Payment: copies and offprints only. Copyrighted. Pub's reviews: 4 in 1990. §Psychology, religion, women. Ads: $150/$95.

Anima Publications (see also ANIMA: The Journal of Human Experience), Harry M Buck, Executive Editor, c/o Concocheague Associates, Inc., 1053 Wilson Avenue, Chambersburg, PA 17201, 717-267-0087. 1974. Non-fiction. avg. press run 2M. Pub'd 4 titles 1990; expects 4 titles 1991, 4 titles 1992. 42 titles listed in the *Small Press Record of Books in Print* (20th Edition, 1991-92). avg. price, cloth: $14; paper: $10. Discounts: 5+ copies 20%. 200pp; 5½×8½; of. Reporting time: 3 months. Payment: yes. Copyrights for author.

ANIMAL LIFE, ANIMAL WORLD, Michaela Miller, RSPCA, Causeway, Horsham, West Sussex RH12 1HG, England, 0403-64181. Fiction, articles, photos, interviews, reviews, letters, news items, non-fiction. "All material originated and written in house." circ. 29M-35M. 4/yr. Pub'd 4 issues 1990; expects 4 issues 1991, 4 issues 1992. sub. price: £3, £4 overseas; per copy: 50p; sample: free. Discounts: bulk orders. 32pp; size A4; web (heat set). Not copyrighted. Pub's reviews: 6 in 1990. §Animals, animal welfare. Ads: £610/£370/£200 1/4/£130 1/8 page.

ANIMAL TALES, Berta I. Cellers, PO Box 2220, Payson, AZ 85547-2220. 1989. "Manuscripts from 2,000 to 6,000 words (fiction) about animals and the people who love them. Must be suitable for all age groups. Light verse poetry. Currently seeking stories and poems that are accompanied by artwork. Do not accept stories about deceased pets or material that gives an animal human abilities. *Animal Tales* is for people who like to read short fiction and true stories about animals. We want original, previously unpublished fiction stories and poems with animals (dogs, cats, horses, birds and wildlife) as the primary focus of interest. We are looking for unique material that communicates to an adult readership the animal/human relationship in the format of adventure, fantasy, historical, humorous, mystery and true stories." circ. 1M+. 6/yr. Pub'd 6 issues 1990; expects 6 issues

1991, 6 issues 1992. sub. price: $19.95; sample: $4.95. Back issues: $5.95. 32pp; 7¼x9¾. Reporting time: 6-8 weeks. Payment: on publication. Copyrighted, reverts to author. Pub's reviews. §Related to animals and pets. Ads: $85/$50/$30 1/4 page/$20 1/8.

ANIMAL WORLD, ANIMAL LIFE, Michaela Miller, RSPCA, Causeway, Horsham, West Sussex RH12 1HG, England, 0403-64181. "Material originated and written in house. Animal welfare-orientated" circ. 70M. 6/yr. Pub'd 6 issues 1990; expects 6 issues 1991, 6 issues 1992. sub. price: £3, £4 overseas; per copy: 50p; sample: free. Discounts: bulk orders. 32pp; size A4; web (heat set). Not copyrighted. Pub's reviews: 24 in 1990. §Animals, animal welfare.

THE ANIMALS' AGENDA, Kim Bartlett, Editor; Mary Jean Bernabucci, 456 Monroe Turnpike, Monroe, CT 06468, 203-452-0446. 1979. Poetry, articles, photos, cartoons, interviews, satire, criticism, reviews, letters, collages, concrete art, news items, non-fiction. "News + discussion concerning animal rights and environmental issues—hunting, fur-trapping, food animals, lab animals. *Clearing House* magazine for animal rights movement supporters also presents ideas, strategies, & tactics for political change" circ. 30M. 10/yr. Pub'd 10 issues 1990; expects 10 issues 1991, 10 issues 1992. sub. price: $22 US,$28 Canada & Mexico, $35 other foreign; per copy: $2.75; sample: $2.75. Back issues: $2.75. Discounts: write for bulk rates. 64pp; 8⅛x10⅞; of. Reporting time: 8 weeks. Payment: 10¢ a word or donation. Copyrighted. Pub's reviews: 25 in 1990. §Animals, environmental, general progressive. Ads: $891/$520/$1.

ANIME SHOWER SPECIAL, Ianus Publications, Inc., Claude J. Pelletier, 33, Prince Street #243, Montreal, Quebec H3C 2M7, Canada, 514-397-0342. 1990. Articles, art, photos, cartoons. "Special issue about shower and erotic scene in Japanese animations and comics. For mature readers. Color insert" circ. 10M. 1/yr. Pub'd 1 issue 1990; expects 1 issue 1991, 1 issue 1992. price per copy: $3; sample: $3.50. Back issues: $3.50. 40pp; 6¾x10; of. Reporting time: 2 months. Payment: none. Copyrighted, reverts to author. Ads: $175/$150/$75 1/4 page/$300 back cover/$200 inside cover.

Anjou, Richard Lush, Roger Greenwald, Two Sussex Avenue, Toronto M5S 1J5, Canada, 416-537-1569. 1980. Poetry. "Mainly broadsides. Submissions by solicitation only." Pub'd 1 title 1990; expects 1 title 1991, 1 title 1992. 2 titles listed in the *Small Press Record of Books in Print* (20th Edition, 1991-92). avg. price, other: $15. Discounts: 20% to bookstores. size varies; of. Payment: copies. Copyrights for author.

THE ANNALS OF IOWA, Marvin Bergman, 402 Iowa Avenue, Iowa City, IA 52240, 319-335-3916. 1863. Articles, reviews. circ. 1M. 4/yr. Pub'd 4 issues 1990; expects 4 issues 1991, 4 issues 1992. sub. price: $20; per copy: $6; sample: none. Discounts: 40% for resale. 120pp; 6x9. Reporting time: 90 days. Payment: none. Copyrighted, does not revert to author. Pub's reviews: c. 80 in 1990. §History of Iowa and the Midwest; other relevant state and local history. CELJ, Conference of Historical Journals.

ANNA'S HOUSE: THE JOURNAL OF EVERYDAY LIFE, Roland Wulbert, PO Box 438070, Chicago, IL 60643-8070, 312-881-4907. 1989. Articles, art, photos, letters, non-fiction. "Essays on, or set in, everyday life. Travel writing welcome. No political analyses or literary criticism. First person nonfiction narratives welcome. No poetry or fiction, please. 500-5,000 words. Black and white representational drawings of everyday objects and events." circ. 2M. 2/yr. Pub'd 1 issue 1990; expects 2 issues 1991, 2 issues 1992. sub. price: $6; per copy: $3.95; sample: $2. Back issues: $2. Discounts: 35%. 64pp; 8½x11; of. Reporting time: 2 weeks. Payment: 3 contributor's copies. Not copyrighted. Pub's reviews: 10 in 1990. §Essays, travel. Ads: $150/$80. ILPA.

Annick Press Ltd., Anne W. Millyard, Rick Wilks, 15 Patricia Avenue, Willowdale, Ontario M2M 1H9, Canada, 416-221-4802. 1975. Fiction. "We cannot accept unsolicited manuscripts any longer." avg. press run 10M. Pub'd 20 titles 1990; expects 33 titles 1991, 24 titles 1992. 79 titles listed in the *Small Press Record of Books in Print* (20th Edition, 1991-92). avg. price, cloth: $12.95; paper: $4.95; other: 99¢ (Annikins - 3 X 3). Discounts: order from Firefly Books Ltd. 250 Sparks Avenue, Willowdale, Ontario M2H 2S4, or your favorite supplier. 24-32pp; 8x8, 8¼x10½; of. Payment: twice a year. Copyrights for author. ACP, CBIC, Children's Book Centre.

Another Chicago Press, Lee Webster, PO Box 11223, Chicago, IL 60611, 312-848-6333. 1985. Poetry, fiction. avg. press run 1.5M. Pub'd 4 titles 1990; expects 6 titles 1991, 8 titles 1992. 21 titles listed in the *Small Press Record of Books in Print* (20th Edition, 1991-92). avg. price, cloth: $19.95; paper: $10.95. 200pp; 8½x5½; of. Reporting time: 8-12 weeks. Copyrights for author.

ANQ: A Quarterly Journal of Short Articles, Notes, and Reviews, Dr. Arthur Wrobel, University of Kentucky, English Department, Office Tower 1321, Lexington, KY 40506, 606-257-6975. Articles, criticism, reviews. "*ANQ*, formerly titled *American Notes and Queries* is a medium of exchange for bibliographers, biographers, editors, lexicographers, and textual scholars. From sources and analogues to the identification of allusions, from variant manuscript readings to previously neglected archives, from Old English word studies to *OED* supplements, from textual emendations to corrections of bibliographies and other scholarly reference works, *ANQ* provides a needed outlet for short factual research concerning the language and literature of the

English-speaking world. We publish signed reviews of critical studies, new editions, and recently published bibliographies. Manuscripts offering only explicit de textes are not appropriate. Manuscript length should not exceed 1,600 words in length; must be accompanied by loose stamps and a self-addressed envelope for the return mailings; and must follow the MLA documentation style that includes parenthetical citations in the text and an alphabetized list of Works Cited as described in *The MLA Style Manual* by Walter S. Achtert and Joseph Gibaldi (specifically chapters 4, 5, and 6). *ANQ* also publishes queries related to scholarly research; replies to queries should be sent to the editor for publication in future issues. Authors are responsible for reading and correcting proofs." circ. 650. 4/yr. Pub'd 4 issues 1990; expects 4 issues 1991, 4 issues 1992. sub. price: $14; per copy: $4; sample: same. Back issues: $4. 56pp; 6×9; of. Reporting time: 1 month. Payment: 2 copies of the issue in which the author's contribution appears. Copyrighted, rights revert only upon request. Pub's reviews: 25 in 1990. §Bibliographies, new scholarly editions of the major poets, novelists, essayists, and men-of-letters of the English-speaking world. Ads: $125.

Ansuda Publications (see also HOR-TASY; THE PUB), Daniel R. Betz, Editor, Box 158, Harris, IA 51345. 1978. Poetry, fiction, satire, long-poems, non-fiction. "No limits on length, style, or material. We just stress originality and quality. We do chapbooks by one author/poet, and work continuously on our 'psycho-horror' and 'pure fantasy' anthologies entitled *Hor-Tasy*, in which we request work from a number of writers. If the writer has something really different that other publishers are uninterested in or afraid of trying, we welcome a query from him/her with an open mind, but query first. We are also very interested in fantasy novels" avg. press run 400. Expects 2 titles 1991, 2 titles 1992. 8 titles listed in the *Small Press Record of Books in Print* (20th Edition, 1991-92). avg. price, paper: $1.35 on poetry chapbooks. Discounts: query. 24pp; 5½×8½; †mi, of. Reporting time: immediate, 2 weeks, sometimes 2-3 months. Payment: we must see material first. Copyrights for author.

ANT FARM, Kate Bremer, PO Box 15513, Santa Fe, NM 87506, 505-473-0290. 1990. Fiction. "Poems of 4 lines or less. Looking for immediacy, impact, image, energy" circ. 250. 2/yr. Expects 2 issues 1991, 2 issues 1992. sub. price: $8; per copy: $3; sample: $3. 40pp; 4×5; xerox pages, print cover, typeset. Reporting time: 6 weeks before publication. Payment: 1 copy per poem. Copyrighted, reverts to author.

ANT SPOIM/SMASH APATHY, Rising Sun, PO Box 1216, Fairlawn, NJ 07410. 1981. Poetry, fiction, articles, art, cartoons, collages, news items, non-fiction. circ. 300. 2/yr. Pub'd 2 issues 1990; expects 2-4 issues 1991, 2-4 issues 1992. sub. price: free; per copy: free. Discounts: free or trade. 12-14pp; 5½×8½. Payment: none. Not copyrighted. Pub's reviews. §Anything. Ads: free.

ANTAEUS, The Ecco Press, Daniel Halpern, Editor-in-Chief; Cathy Jewell, Managing Editor, 26 West 17th Street, New York, NY 10011, 212-645-2214. 1970. Poetry, fiction, interviews, letters, parts-of-novels, long-poems, non-fiction. "Contributors: Czeslaw Milosz, Paul Bowles, Robert Hass, Louise Gluck, Robert Pinsky, Seamus Heaney, Paul Muldoon, Joyce Carol Oates, W.S. Merwin, James Merrill, Carolyn Forche, Zbigniew Herbert, Mark Strand, Charles Simic" circ. 7M. 2/yr. Pub'd 2 issues 1990; expects 1 issue 1991, 2 issues 1992. sub. price: $30/4 issues (2 years); per copy: $10 varies; sample: available for cover price. Discounts: 33⅓% trade. 250pp; 6×9; of, perfect binding, four color cover. Reporting time: 6-8 weeks. Payment: $10 per page. Copyrighted, will assign copyright upon author's request. Ads: $500/$300. CCLM, NYSSPA, NESPA.

ANTI-APARTHEID NEWS, Alan Brooks, Editor; Karen Livingston, Assistant Editor, 13 Mandela Street, London NW1 0DW, England, 071 387 7966. 1965. Articles, photos, cartoons, interviews, reviews, letters, news items, non-fiction. "News and analysis from Southern Africa, support for liberation movements of Southern Africa, and news of British and international anti-apatheid action" circ. 20M. 10/yr. Pub'd 10 issues 1990; expects 10 issues 1991, 10 issues 1992. sub. price: UK indiv. £10, orgs. £13.50; Europe indiv. £15, org. £25; outside Europe surface: indiv. £12, org. £17, airmail £24, £26; per copy: 40p; sample: free. Back issues: £1. Discounts: 33⅓%. 12pp; 17×12; of, web. Reporting time: copy date second Wednesday in month before cover date. Payment: nil. Not copyrighted. Pub's reviews: 25 in 1990. §Southern Africa. Ads: £500/£300/£5 per 25 words. Anti-Apartheid Movement.

Antietam Press, Ellen M. Dorosh, 51 East Antietam Street, Hagerstown, MD 21740, 301-797-5155. 1978. Poetry. "Especially interested in working with self-publishing authors in all phases from writing through promotion and distribution" avg. press run 500-1M. Expects 5 titles 1991, 5 titles 1992. avg. price, paper: $4. Discounts: In keeping with present industry practices. 100-250pp; 5½×8½; of. Reporting time: 2-3 weeks. Payment: negotiated with individual author. Copyrights for author.

ANTIETAM REVIEW, Ann B. Knox, Fiction Editor; Crystal Brown, Poetry Editor; Susanne Kass, Managing Editor, 82 W. Washington Street, 3rd Floor, Hagerstown, MD 21740, 301-791-3132. 1982. Poetry, fiction, photos, interviews, parts-of-novels. "Our stories average about 3,000 words—min. 1,500, max. 5,000. We look for well-crafted literary work. In fiction we like relevant detail and significant emotional movement within the story—something happening to the characters. We expect dialogue, gesture, and image to carry emotional content without resorting to abstract language. Poems to 40 lines. We take work of writers from MD, VA, WV, PA, DE and the District of Columbia" circ. 1M. 1/yr. Pub'd 1 issue 1990; expects 1 issue 1991, 2 issues 1992. sub. price: $5; per copy: $5; sample: $2.50. Back issues: $2.50. 42pp; 8½×11; of. Reporting time: 4-12 weeks. Payment: $100/story; $20/poem. Copyrighted, reverts to author. CLMP.

THE ANTIGONISH REVIEW, George S. Sanderson, St Francis Xavier University, Antigonish, Nova Scotia B2G1CO, Canada. 1970. Poetry, fiction, articles, art, interviews, criticism, reviews. "All submissions from U.S. must be accompanied by Postal Reply Coupons; submissions accompanied by U.S. postage will not be returned" circ. 800. 4/yr. Expects 4 issues 1991. sub. price: $18; per copy: $5; sample: $3 accompanied by postage. Back issues: $3. Discounts: 20%. 150pp; 9×6; of. Reporting time: 3 months. Payment: 2 copies only. Copyrighted. Pub's reviews: 40 in 1990. §Literary, biographies and autobiographies of poets, writers, artists. No ads. The Canadian Periodical Publishers Association.

ANTI-ISOLATION/NEW ARTS IN WISCONSIN, Xexoxial Endarchy, Miekal And, Elizabeth Was, 1341 Williamson, Madison, WI 53703. 1984. Poetry, fiction, articles, art, photos, interviews, reviews, music, plays, concrete art, news items, non-fiction. "Experimental Artzine with emphasis on new arts in Wisconsin, each issue features several otherwise isolated artists; articles, interviews, actual art reprinted; resources, contacts, networking" circ. 1M. Irregular. Pub'd 1 issue 1990; expects 1 issue 1991, 2 issues 1992. sub. price: $5/4 numbers; per copy: $1; sample: $2.50 double, $1.50 single + $1 p/h. Back issues: $1. Discounts: None. 32pp; size varies; †xerox. Reporting time: 1 week. Payment: 5 copies. Not copyrighted. Pub's reviews: 30 in 1990. §Esperimental arts & multimedia. Ads: $150/$75.

THE ANTIOCH REVIEW, Robert Fogarty, Editor; David St. John, Poetry Editor; Tom Holyoke, Book Review Editor; Nolan Miller, Associate Editor, PO Box 148, Yellow Springs, OH 45387, 513-767-6389. 1941. Poetry, fiction, articles, satire, criticism, reviews, long-poems, non-fiction. "Recent contributors: James Purdy, Stephen Dixon, Annie Dillard, Tess Gallagher, Heather McHugh, Alvin Greenberg, Cynthia Fuchs Epstein, Edward J. Shoben Jr., Lynda Lloyd, Stuart Dybek, Andrew M. Greeley, Emile Capouya, Gordon Lish, Margaret Dickson." circ. 5M. 4/yr. Pub'd 4 issues 1990; expects 4 issues 1991. sub. price: $20 ($25 foreign), $30 institutional ($35 foreign); per copy: $5; sample: $5. Back issues: $5. Discounts: 20% to agents. 160pp; 9×6; of. Reporting time: fiction 1-6 weeks, poetry 2-3 months. Payment: $15 per page (approx. 425 words). Copyrighted, reverts when requested. Pub's reviews: 200 in 1990. §General interest social science, fiction, contemporary affairs. Ads: $250/$150. CCLM, OAC.

Anvil Press (see also SUB-TERRAIN), PO Box 1575, Station A, Vancouver, B.C. V6C 2P7, Canada. "We publish broadsheets and pamphlets."

Anvil Press Poetry, Peter Jay, Editor; Julia Sterland, Editorial Assistant, 69 King George St., London SE10 8PX, England, 01-858-2946. 1968. Poetry. "All titles for which Anvil holds us rights are stoks by: Small Press Distribution Inc 1814 San Pablo Avenue Berkeley CA 94702" avg. press run 800. Pub'd 2 titles 1990; expects 10 titles 1991, 10 titles 1992. 117 titles listed in the *Small Press Record of Books in Print* (20th Edition, 1991-92). avg. price, cloth: £12; paper: £5.95. Discounts: inquire. Pages vary; 216×138mm; of/lo. Reporting time: 1 month. Payment: royalty. Copyrights for authors in U.K. ALP.

APAEROS, Kathe Burt, Clerk; John Burt, Clerk, 960 SW Jefferson Avenue, Corvallis, OR 97333. 1985. Poetry, fiction, articles, art, photos, cartoons, interviews, satire, criticism, reviews, letters, news items, non-fiction. "*Apaeros* is an unedited reader-written forum about sex and erotics: what turns us on and off and why; relating to partners (het, lesbian, or gay); nudism; SM; birth control; VD and rape prevention; pornography-erotica; etc. *Apaeros* is for sharing our knowledge, insights, questions, problems, stories, fantasies, and feelings. Each subscriber may but needn't contribute two photo-ready pages per issue which will be published unedited at no extra charge. Send SASE for sample and guidelines *before* submitting" circ. 125. 6-8/yr. Pub'd 8 issues 1990; expects 8 issues 1991. sub. price: minium 5 issues $10; per copy: $2 cash; sample: $3 and state over 18. 32pp; 8½×5½ (reduced to half size); photocopy. Reporting time: up to a couple of months. Payment: none. Copyrighted, reverts to author. Pub's reviews: 7 in 1990. §Sex, relationships, erotic fiction, erotic poetry. Ads: exchange only.

Apalachee Press (see also APALACHEE QUARTERLY), Barbara Hamby, Pamela Ball, Claudia Johnson, Bruce Boehrer, Paul McCall, PO Box 20106, Tallahassee, FL 32316. 1 title listed in the *Small Press Record of Books in Print* (20th Edition, 1991-92).

APALACHEE QUARTERLY, Apalachee Press, Barbara Hamby, Pamela Ball, Claudia Johnson, Bruce Boehrer, Paul McCall, PO Box 20106, Tallahassee, FL 32316. 1972. Poetry, fiction, articles, art, photos, parts-of-novels, long-poems, plays. "We always need manuscripts of poetry and fiction. Send 3-8 poems and prose up to 30 pages. We often write short criticisms on our rejection notices, but unless we specifically ask you to try us again it would be better if you tried your luck elsewhere after the first attempt. We're extremely selective about what goes in to the *A.Q.* Be selective in submitting. We don't read during the summer" circ. 500. 3/yr. Pub'd 4 issues 1990; expects 4 issues 1991, 4 issues 1992. sub. price: $15 indiv., $20 instit.; per copy:

$5 includes p/h; sample: $5 includes p/h. Back issues: query by issue number. Discounts: 40% discount to bookstores. 100-200pp; 6¼×9¼. Reporting time: 3 months. Payment: 2 copies. Copyrighted, reverts to author. Pub's reviews: 20 in 1990. §Fiction, poetry, novels, literary biography, essay, interviews. Ads: $100. CCLM.

APKL Publications (see also LIGHTNING SWORD), Stephen Mark Rafalsky, PO Box 371, Woodstock, NY 12498. 1977. "APKL is an acronym of the Greek *apokalypsis*, which means uncovering or revelation. We find buried in the collective unconscious of the human race the central archetype of existence; we declare this to be Jesus Christ the resurrected and living creator, and we publish those works that illuminate the human condition in this light. We are not religious, but creators of consciousness. See also, *Lightning Sword*, a magazine we publish. No unsolicited manuscripts, please. Inquiries with SASE accepted." avg. press run 10-200. Expects 1 title 1991. avg. price, paper: $2. 3-100pp; 5½×8½; †of. Payment: negotiable. Copyrights for author.

APPALACHIA, Appalachian Mountain Club Books, Sandy Stott, 5 Joy Street, Boston, MA 02108, 617-523-0636. 1876. Poetry, fiction, articles, art, photos, cartoons, interviews, reviews, letters, long-poems, news items, non-fiction. circ. 8.5M. 2/yr. Pub'd 2 issues 1990; expects 2 issues 1991, 2 issues 1992. sub. price: $10; per copy: $5; sample: $5. Back issues: $5. Discounts: 10+copies 20%. 160pp; 6×9; of. Reporting time: 1-3 months. Payment: none. Not copyrighted. Pub's reviews: 17 in 1990. §Outdoor recreation, mountaineering, water sports, hiking, mountain history. Ads: $265/$165/$110 1/4 page.

Appalachian Consortium Press, A 14-member publications committee acts as editorial board, University Hall, Appalachian State University, Boone, NC 28608, 704-262-2064, 704-262-2076. 1973. Poetry, fiction, articles, art, photos, interviews, criticism, music, non-fiction. "We publish occasional works of poetry but, most often, *non-fiction* relating to the Appalachian region. Payment: Varies, sometimes we do not pay royalties. Generally a % of gross receipts after a certain number of copies are sold." avg. press run 2M. Pub'd 3 titles 1990; expects 5 titles 1991, 4 titles 1992. 30 titles listed in the *Small Press Record of Books in Print* (20th Edition, 1991-92). avg. price, cloth: $13.95; paper: $6.95. Discounts: on purchases for resale, 1-3 books 25%, 4+ 40%. 150pp; 6×9¼; of. Reporting time: at least 6 months. Payment: a negotiable 5-10% percentage of sales. Copyrights for author.

APPALACHIAN HERITAGE, Sidney Saylor Farr, Hutchins Library, Berea College, Berea, KY 40404, 606-986-9341 ext. 5260. 1973. Poetry, fiction, articles, art, photos, interviews, non-fiction. "1,500-2,000 words. Material must have Appalachian topics and the art work and/or photos should be scenic or have people and backgrounds similar to that found in Southern Appalachia" circ. 1,050. 4/yr. Pub'd 4 issues 1990; expects 4 issues 1991, 4 issues 1992. sub. price: $16; per copy: $5; sample: $5. Back issues: $4. 80pp; 6⅞×9½; of. Reporting time: 4-6 weeks. Payment: 3 copies. Copyrighted, reverts to author. Pub's reviews: 8-10 in 1990. §Appalachian subjects. Ads: $150/$85/$50 1/4 page.

Appalachian Mountain Club Books (see also APPALACHIA), Susan Cummings, Publisher, 5 Joy Street, Boston, MA 02108, 617-523-0636. 1897. Photos, non-fiction. "We publish nonfiction books and maps." avg. press run 5M. Pub'd 6 titles 1990; expects 4 titles 1991, 8 titles 1992. avg. price, cloth: $29.95; paper: $12.95; other: $3.50 map. Discounts: 2-4 copies 20%, 5-19 40%, 20-34 41%, 35-49 42%, 50-99 43%, 100-149 44%, 150-299 45%, 46%, 300+; wholesale 55% for 100+ copies, nonreturnable. 256pp; 6×9; of. Reporting time: 1-4 months. Payment: royalty 10% of list price, paid twice a year. Copyrights for author. Bookbuilders of Boston.

THE APPLE BLOSSOM CONNECTION, Peak Output Unlimited, Mary M. Blake, J.D. Scheneman, PO Box 325, Stacyville, IA 50476, 515-737-2269. 1987. Poetry, fiction, articles, art, photos, cartoons, interviews, reviews, plays, news items, non-fiction. "Poetry to 36 lines, fiction to 2,000 words, non-fiction to 1,200 words. Nothing off-color or tasteless. Like good, clean, finished manuscripts" circ. 3M. 12/yr. Pub'd 12 issues 1990; expects 12 issues 1991, 12 issues 1992. sub. price: $15 (+ $5/yr outside USA); per copy: $5, applicable toward subscription ordered within one month; sample: $5. Back issues: to contributors while supplies last; query. Discounts: available on request plus SASE. 36pp; 5½×8½; †of. Reporting time: 4-6 weeks. Payment: varies. Copyrighted, reverts to author. Pub's reviews: 2 in 1990. §All aspects of professional writing and publishing, poetry & short fiction collections. Ads: query. Mid-America Publishers Association.

Applezaba Press, D.H. Lloyd, Shelley Hellen, Rachel Viray, PO Box 4134, Long Beach, CA 90804, 213-591-0015. 1977. Poetry, fiction, satire. avg. press run 1M. Pub'd 3 titles 1990; expects 3 titles 1991, 3 titles 1992. 30 titles listed in the *Small Press Record of Books in Print* (20th Edition, 1991-92). avg. price, cloth: $15; paper: $6.95; other: $20 numbered and signed, cloth. Discounts: 20%-55% depending on quantity purchased. 78pp; 6×9; of. Reporting time: 2 months. Payment: 8-15% + copies. Copyrights for author.

Applied Probability Trust (see also MATHEMATICAL SPECTRUM), D. W. Sharpe, Department of Probability and Statistics, The University, Sheffield S3 7RH, England, England. 1968. Articles, reviews, letters.

Applied Publishing, Paul M. Palmer, Constance Palmer, PO Box 672, Chanhassen, MN 55317, 612-470-1837. 1983. "Additional address: PO Box 269, Excelsior, MN 55331. We are particularly interested in material that would be able to fit into our T.I.P.S. (Techniques and Ideas on Purchasing and Selling) trademark. To date real estate and investing are two areas we have concentrated on." avg. press run 10M. Pub'd 1 title 1990; expects 1 title 1991, 3 titles 1992. avg. price, cloth: $16.95; paper: $9.95; other: Manual- $14.95. Discounts: wholesalers and distributors receive 50% for any order over 48 books, 20-47 45%, 10-19 42% & 1-9 40%. 275pp; 5½x7½. Reporting time: 60 days. Payment: negotiable. Copyrights for author. ABE, PMA, MIPA (Minnesota Independant Publishers Assoc.), MACI.

AQUARIUS, Eddie S. Linden, Flat 10, Room A, 116 Sutherland Avenue, London W9, England. 1968. Poetry, fiction, articles, reviews. "Special all Irish issue forthcoming with Seamus Heaney" circ. 1.5M. 2/yr. sub. price: $40; per copy: $6; sample: £2.50 - $9. Back issues: $5. Discounts: 33% trade. 120pp; lp. Payment: special issues only. Pub's reviews: 40 in 1990. §Poetry, biography. Ads: £40/£20.

AQUATERRA, WATER CONCEPTS FOR THE ECOLOGICAL SOCIETY, Jacqueline Froelich, Route 3, Box 720, Eureka Springs, AR 72632. 1986. Poetry, articles, art, cartoons, letters, news items. "Water related information particularly compost toilet information and innovative conservation" circ. 3M. 2/yr. Pub'd 2 issues 1990; expects 2 issues 1991, 2 issues 1992. sub. price: $10; per copy: $5.95; sample: $5.95. Back issues: $5.95. Discounts: inquire. 64pp; 8x5; †varies. Payment: none. Copyrighted, reverts to author. Pub's reviews: 1 in 1990. §Submissions related to technical and/or spiritual experiences with water articles, research, interviews, ceremonies, prose, poetry, artwork, summaries of water organizations. Ads: inquire.

ARAB STUDIES QUARTERLY, AAUG Press, Samih K. Farsoun, 556 Trapelo Road, Belmont, MA 02178, (617) 484-5483. 1979. Articles, interviews, criticism, reviews, non-fiction. "Scholarly articles and book reviews on Arab affairs, the Middle East, and U.S. foreign policy" circ. 2.5M. 4/yr. Pub'd 4 issues 1990; expects 4 issues 1991, 4 issues 1992. sub. price: $20 individual, $40 institution; per copy: $6.00; sample: same. Back issues: $6.00. Discounts: 15% for subscription agencies. 100pp; 6x9; of. Reporting time: 3 months. Payment: none. Copyrighted, does not revert to author. Pub's reviews: 25 in 1990. §Arab politics, economy, society, culture; Mideast conflict; U.S. Mideast policy. Ads: $250/$140.

ARABIAN HORSE TIMES, Marian Studer, Route 3, End of Eighth Street N.E., Waseca, MN 56093, (507) 835-3204. 1970. Poetry, articles, interviews, criticism, reviews, news items, non-fiction. circ. 20M. 12/yr. Pub'd 12 issues 1990; expects 12 issues 1991, 12 issues 1992. sub. price: $25; per copy: $4; sample: $2. 325pp; 7½x10½. Reporting time: 3 weeks to 3 months. Payment: from $25 to $350. Copyrighted, does not revert to author. Pub's reviews: 6 in 1990. §Arabian horses, equine management and care. Ads: 4-color: full $945/half $595; b/w: $395/$250. American Horse Publications.

ARARAT, Ararat Press, Leo Hamalian, Armenian General Benevolent Union, 585 Saddle River Road, Saddle Brook, NJ 07662. 1960. Poetry, fiction, articles, art, criticism, reviews, parts-of-novels. "We prefer material in some way pertinent to Armenian life and culture." circ. 2.2M. 4/yr. Pub'd 4 issues 1990; expects 4 issues 1991, 4 issues 1992. sub. price: $24; per copy: $7; sample: $4. Back issues: $4. Discounts: 15%. 74pp; 9x12; of. Reporting time: 4 months. Payment: $10 a printed page (roughly). Copyrighted, reverts to author. Pub's reviews: 10 in 1990. §Ethnic Armenian. Ads: $250/$125. CCLM.

Ararat Press (see also ARARAT), Leo Hamalian, Editor, Armenian General Benevolent Union, 585 Saddle River Road, Saddle Brook, NJ 07662. 1960. Poetry, fiction, articles, reviews. "Material by Armenians or about Armenians: articles, fiction, poetry and book reviews" avg. press run 2M. 14 titles listed in the Small Press Record of Books in Print (20th Edition, 1991-92). avg. price, cloth: $14, $27/2 years. Discounts: 10%. 76pp; 8½x11; of. Reporting time: 3 months. Payment: on publication. Copyrights for author.

ARBA SICULA, Arba Sicula, Inc., Gaetano Cipolla, c/o Modern Foreign Languages, St. John's University, Jamaica, NY 11439-0002. 1979. Poetry, fiction, articles, art, photos, reviews, music, letters, long-poems, collages, plays, news items, non-fiction. "Bilingual ethnic oriented material in the Sicilian language with a lyrical English translation" circ. 1.5M. 2/yr. Pub'd 2 issues 1990; expects 2 issues 1991, 2 issues 1992. sub. price: $20; per copy: $10; sample: $10. Back issues: we'll give you a quote. Discounts: ask for quote. 90pp; 5½x8½; laser, of. Reporting time: flexible. Payment: none. Copyrighted, does not revert to author. Pub's reviews: several in 1990. §Sicilian ethnic worldwide. Ads: $150/$75.

Arba Sicula, Inc. (see also ARBA SICULA; SICILIA PARRA), Gaetano Cipolla, c/o Modern Foreign Languages, St. John's University, Jamaica, NY 11439. 1979. Poetry, fiction, articles, art, photos, interviews, satire, criticism, reviews, music, letters, long-poems, collages, plays, concrete art, non-fiction. "We come out with various supplements. Sicilian—English Press Bilingual" avg. press run 1.5M. Pub'd 4 titles 1990. avg. price, paper: $10. Discounts: ask for quote. Pages vary; 5½x8½; laser. Payment: none.

Arbiter Press, Christine Blackwell, Editor & Publisher, PO Box 592540, Orlando, FL 32859, 407-380-8617; 345-3803. 1988. Fiction. "Prefer original fiction that will equal 128 pages in published form. Like to publish new writers. Recent contributors include: J. Whitebird, author of Heat and Other Stories, 1990; Joy Williams, Bob Schacochis, Padgett Powell, Harry Crews, and others in New Visions: Fiction by Florida Writers, 1989" avg. press run 1M. Pub'd 2 titles 1990; expects 1 title 1991, 1 title 1992. avg. price, paper: $7.95. Discounts: 40% to bookstores only. 128-288pp; 5½×8; of. Reporting time: 8 weeks. Payment: free copies and 50% of subsidiary rights sold. Copyrights for author. Florida Publishers Group.

The Archives Press, Jim Harris, Managing; Triona Watson, Graphics & Production; Canyon Draper, Public Relations-Sales; Hank Challas, Editor-in-Chief, 334 State Street #536, Los Altos, CA 94022. 1967. Fiction, non-fiction. "Mystic and New Age- Tarot, Holy Grail, but not corny. Jungian bias, Zen, motorcycles, pit bulls, horses, etc.; ecology, mystery, Irish history" avg. press run 1M-5M. Pub'd 3 titles 1990; expects 3 titles 1991, 3 titles 1992. avg. price, cloth: $18.95; paper: $16.95. Discounts: jobber 30-40%, some 55%, library 40%, min. order $50. 240pp; 8½×11; 7×9; full text press. Reporting time: 2 months. Payment: 50% of net profit only. Copyrights for author. COSMEP, APA, PEN, LMP.

ARCTIC—Journal of the Arctic Institute of America, University of Calgary Press, Karen M. McCullough, The Arctic Institute of N. America, University of Calgary, Calgary, Alberta T2N 1N4, Canada, 403-220-4050. 1948. Articles, photos, reviews, news items. "Original scholarly papers in the life, physical and social sciences, humanities, engineering and technology are included, as are book reviews, commentaries on public policy and biographical sketches of significant northern historical and contemporary figures." circ. 2.4M. 4/yr. Pub'd 4 issues 1990; expects 4 issues 1991, 4 issues 1992. sub. price: $37 indiv., $79 instit., $21 retired/student, add G.S.T., outside Canada price in U.S. dollars; per copy: $10 + G.S.T. Back issues: $25 + G.S.T./$25 US—supplement to Vol. 40. Discounts: 10% agents (subscriptions). 100pp; 8½×11; of. Reporting time: 5 weeks. Payment: none. Copyrighted, does not revert to author. Pub's reviews: 32 in 1990. §All areas of Arctic study. Ads: write for info. C.A.L.J.

Arden Press, Inc., Frederick Ramey, Editor; Susan Holte, Editor, PO Box 418, Denver, CO 80201, 303-239-6155. 1980. Criticism, non-fiction. "We are most actively pursuing film criticism/history/theory and women's topics of either scholarly/historical import or contemporary significance, but we would gladly consider any non-fiction title, including reference works and guides." avg. press run 3M. Pub'd 2 titles 1990; expects 3 titles 1991, 4 titles 1992. 8 titles listed in the *Small Press Record of Books in Print* (20th Edition, 1991-92). avg. price, cloth: $24; paper: $14. Discounts: 40% to trade. 250pp; size varies. Reporting time: 1 month. Payment: standard royalty. Copyrights for author.

AREOPAGUS, Robert Paul Roth, Ph.D., Editor, Tao Fong Shan Road, PO Box 33, Shatin, New Territories, Hong Kong, 06- 10 54. 1987. Poetry, articles, art, photos, cartoons, interviews, criticism, reviews, letters, news items. "*Areopagus* is a full-color magazine on spirituality and mission in which Christians engage in dialogue with persons of all faiths and ideologies. Writers analyze traditional and contemporary religious movements, as well as New Age, gurus and news events from all parts of the world. Features include interviews, dialogue, testimonies, icon prints, prayers and liturgies." circ. 2M+ in 50 countries. 4/yr. Pub'd 4 issues 1990; expects 4 issues 1991, 4 issues 1992. sub. price: $24 US; $120 HK; 145 NOK; per copy: $5 US; sample: free. Discounts: Free or discount to certain Third World Countries. 56pp; 8¼×11¼; laser/computer. Reporting time: 2-4 weeks. Payment: writers-none; photos-US $12.50. Copyrighted, reverts to author. Pub's reviews: 4 in 1990.

Argo Press (see also ARGONAUT), Michael E. Ambrose, PO Box 4201, Austin, TX 78765-4201. 1972. Fiction. "All submissions are by solicitation only" avg. press run 200. Pub'd 1 title 1990. 1 title listed in the *Small Press Record of Books in Print* (20th Edition, 1991-92). avg. price, paper: $2. Discounts: 5 or more, %40. 16-20pp; size varies; of. Payment: individual terms. Copyrights for author. SPWAO.

ARGONAUT, Argo Press, Michael E. Ambrose, Editor and Publisher, PO Box 4201, Austin, TX 78765-4201. 1972. Poetry, fiction, art, photos. "Looking for original, literate science fiction and weird fantasy. Some poetry used. Prospective contributors should send SASE for guidelines" circ. 500. 1/yr. Expects 1 issue 1991, 1 issue 1992. sub. price: $5; per copy: $5; sample: $3. Back issues: 3/$8/4/$10. Discounts: 5 copies or more, 40%. 56pp; 5¼×8½; of. Reporting time: 6-8 weeks. Payment: for all material used, 2 copies. Copyrighted, reverts to author. §SF & fantasy, small press publications and books. Ads: $50/$30/inquire. SPWAO.

Argonauts/Misty Isles Press, Jo Anton, Bob Ness, Joseph Thomas, Publisher, 1616 NW 67th Street, Seattle, WA 98117, 206-783-5447. 1980. "Book length: 200-300pp. Biases: Political issues, Asian-American pre-Columbian contacts. *Nu Sun* by Gunnar Thompson" avg. press run 1.5M. Pub'd 2 titles 1990; expects 1 title 1991, 2 titles 1992. 2 titles listed in the *Small Press Record of Books in Print* (20th Edition, 1991-92). avg. price, cloth: $25; paper: $13. Discounts: trade 40%, jobber 30% and up, bulk 40-50%. 2-300pp; size varies; contract of. Reporting time: 6 weeks. Payment: variable. Copyrights for author. COSMEP.

Ariadne Press, Carol F. Hoover, Editor, 4817 Tallahassee Avenue, Rockville, MD 20853, 301-949-2514. 1974. Fiction. "Ellen Moore *Lead Me to the Exit* publication date 12-01-77. Michael Marsh, *The Rudelstein Affair*, publication date 6/1/81. Henry Alley, *The Lattice*, publication date 3/15/86. Writers Mentor Group, ed. Carol Hoover, *How to Write an Uncommonly Good Novel*, publication date 6/1/90" avg. press run 1M. Expects 1 title 1991. 4 titles listed in the *Small Press Record of Books in Print* (20th Edition, 1991-92). avg. price, cloth: $19.95; paper: $12.95. Discounts: 20-40% to booksellers or libraries ordering in quantity. 208pp; 5½×8½, 6×9;

of. Reporting time: 2 months. Payment: 10% of list price. Copyrights for author. Writer's Center, Bethesda, Md.

ARIEL—A Review of International English Literature, University of Calgary Press, V.J. Ramraj, The University of Calgary Press, Calgary, Alberta T2N 1N4, Canada, 403-220-4657. 1970. Poetry, articles, reviews. "Critical and scholarly perspectives on literatures in English from around the world" circ. 925. 4/yr. Pub'd 4 issues 1990; expects 4 issues 1991, 4 issues 1992. sub. price: $14 indiv., $22 instit., payable in Canadian funds; per copy: $6 + G.S.T. Canada, add G.S.T. in Canada; sample: $5 + G.S.T. Canada. Back issues: $25 indiv., $30 instit., payable in Cdn. funds, add G.S.T. in Canada. Discounts: $1 for agents, claim period is 6 months. 110pp; 6×9; of. Reporting time: 2 months. Payment: none. Copyrighted, contact editor. Pub's reviews: 10-12 in 1990. §English literature. Ads: write for information. C.A.L.J.

Ariel Vamp Press, Jolene Babyak, PO Box 3496, Berkeley, CA 94703, 415-654-4849. 1987. Interviews, music, non-fiction. "Prefer display-size, well-researched, historical non-fiction" avg. press run 4M. Expects 1 title 1991, 1 title 1992. 1 title listed in the *Small Press Record of Books in Print* (20th Edition, 1991-92). avg. price, paper: $10.95. Discounts: 1-3 books 20%, 4-250 40%, 251-600 45%, stop orders 20-40%. 135pp; 8½×11; of. Reporting time: 2-3 months. Payment: negotiable. Copyrights for author.

ARISTOS, Louis Torres, Editor and Publisher; Michelle Marder Kamhi, Associate Editor, PO Box 1105, Radio City Station, New York, NY 10101, 212-678-8550. 1982. Articles, photos, interviews, criticism, reviews, letters. "Publisher: The Aristos Foundation. *Aristos* is dedicated to the preservation and advancement of traditional values (as opposed to modernism and post-modernism) in the arts, and to objective standards in scholarship and criticism. Advocates positive humanistic values in literature; realism in the visual arts; melody and tonality in music; intelligibility in all the arts. Feature articles range from 1,500 to 3,500 words; other items vary in length. Indexed in *The American Humanities Index, Bibliography of the History of Art* and *Artbibliographies Modern*. (An annotated table of contents is available.) In the words of *Library Journal* 'The value is there, particularly as the point of view is unique.' *Magazines for Libraries* (6th ed.) calls *Aristos* 'a scholarly but gutsy little periodical.'" 6/yr. Pub'd 1 issue 1990; expects 4 issues 1991, 6 issues 1992. sub. price: $25 individuals, $30 institutions; per copy: $4; sample: $3 individuals; free to institutions. Back issues: available to individual subscribers upon request. 6pp; 8½×11; of. Reporting time: 4-6 weeks. Payment: $25-$100 honorarium, paid upon publication. Copyrighted, does not revert to author. Pub's reviews: 1 in 1990. §All the fine, literary, and performing arts; especially if the treatment is compatible with our editorial philosophy. No ads.

ARIZONA COAST, Gerald Hale, Hale Communications, Inc., 912 Joshua Avenue, Parker, AZ 85344, 602-669-6464. 1988. Articles, art, photos, reviews, news items. "Short stories" circ. 20M. 6/yr. Pub'd 6 issues 1990; expects 6 issues 1991, 6 issues 1992. price per copy: free; sample: same. Back issues: $1 for shipping & handling. 40pp; 5½×8½; of. Reporting time: 60 days. Payment: varies. Copyrighted. Pub's reviews: 1 in 1990. §Travel, old west, business/finance. Ads: $303/$215/$160 1/4 page.

ARIZONA GREAT OUTDOORS, SINGLE SCENE, Janet L. Jacobsen, Box 6243, Scottsdale, AZ 85257, 602-945-6746. 1989. "Articles related to hiking and camping in Arizona; news-oriented. Article length 600-1200 words." circ. 23M. 4/yr. Pub'd 4 issues 1990; expects 4 issues 1991, 4 issues 1992. sub. price: $6; per copy: free; sample: $2. Back issues: $2. Discounts: contact editor. 12pp; 10¼×14; web. Reporting time: up to 2 months. Payment: not currently paying for material. Copyrighted, reverts to author. Pub's reviews: 1 in 1990. §Camping, outdoor cooking. Ads: $800/$480/40¢ word classified.

ARIZONA QUARTERLY, Albert F. Gegenheimer, Shirley Crowell, Editorial Assistant, Univ. Of Arizona, Tucson, AZ 85721, Main Library B541 602-621-6396. 1945. Articles, criticism, reviews. "No fiction, no poetry" 4/yr. Pub'd 4 issues 1990; expects 4 issues 1991. sub. price: $12; per copy: $5; sample: $5. Back issues: regular price available. 96pp; 6×9; of. Reporting time: 3-4 months. Payment: copies. Copyrighted. Pub's reviews: 2 in 1990. §Modern literature, literary criticism. Ads: $200 full page. Conference of Editors of Learned Journals.

Arjuna Library Press (see also JOURNAL OF REGIONAL CRITICISM), Joseph A. Uphoff, Jr., Director, 1025 Garner Street, D, Space 18, Colorado Springs, CO 80905-1774. 1983. Fiction, art, photos, long-poems, non-fiction. "We want to explore the subtle ways in which mass media fiction has an effect on our perceptual environment, a direct displacement of the individual; myths and rumors arise from this strange, dynamic quality in an experimental social structure that can result in catastrophe, revolution, or prototypes for success. How has the real supernatural affected technological inception? These speculations will be centering on the story of Pegasus. In performance art the structure of the kata (formal practice) is being extended from karate (empty hand practice) into jujitsu (precision arts) and judo (grappling and throwing). We are asserting, as the conceptual plexism, a form to be adapted in the extemporaneous struggle. All principles remain limited as previously stated, general audience (adult suitable for children), volunteers, no deliberate injury or distress complaint (about submission rules), news about reality." Pub'd 10 titles 1990; expects 2 titles 1991, 6 titles

1992. 16 titles listed in the *Small Press Record of Books in Print* (20th Edition, 1991-92). avg. price, paper: $2-$5; other: $1 if available. 30pp; 5×7; †xerography. Reporting time: indefinite. Payment: dependent on market, profit sharing. Does not copyright for author.

THE ARK, The Ark, Geoffrey Gardner, 35 Highland Avenue, Cambridge, MA 02139-1015, 617-547-0852. 1970. Poetry, long-poems. "We are primarily publishers of poetry. *The Ark 14* is a special 400 page issue in honor of Kenneth Rexroth, illustrated by Morris Graves and including work by some 100 contributors. *The Ark 15* is *From Down To The Village* by David Budbill, a full-length book of poems with ink and wash drawings by Lois Eby. We publish only full-length books. We only read solicited manuscripts. Query first" circ. 1.5M+. 1/yr. Pub'd 1 issue 1990; expects 1 issue 1991, 2 issues 1992. sub. price: $5; per copy: No. 14: $10; No. 15: $5; sample: none available. Discounts: 40% to bookstores, otherwise none. 116pp; 5½×8½; of. Reporting time: at once to 3 months. Payment: varies with the nature of each issue. Copyrighted, reverts to author.

The Ark (see also THE ARK), Geoffrey Gardner, 35 Highland Avenue, Cambridge, MA 02139, 617-547-0852. 1970. Poetry, long-poems. "This is a highly selective press" avg. press run 1.5M+. Pub'd 1 title 1990; expects 1 title 1991, 2 titles 1992. 2 titles listed in the *Small Press Record of Books in Print* (20th Edition, 1991-92). avg. price, cloth: $10; paper: $5. Discounts: 40% to bookstores only. 116pp; 5½×8½; of. Reporting time: at once to 3 months. Payment: unique to each project and by arrangement with each author. Copyrights for author.

Arlotta Press, 6340 Millbank Dr., Dayton, OH 45459. 1977. Non-fiction. avg. press run 1M. 1 title listed in the *Small Press Record of Books in Print* (20th Edition, 1991-92). avg. price, paper: $3. Discounts: 40% bookstores, standard libraries. 80pp; 5½×8½; of.

THE ARMCHAIR DETECTIVE, The Armchair Detective Library, Katherine Daniel, Editor-in-Chief, 129 West 56th Street, New York, NY 10019, 212-765-0902. 1968. Articles, photos, interviews, criticism, reviews, letters. "Journal of mystery fiction: interviews, criticism, short fiction" circ. 4M. 4/yr. Pub'd 4 issues 1990; expects 4 issues 1991, 4 issues 1992. sub. price: $26; per copy: $7.50; sample: $7.50. Back issues: $7.50. Discounts: 5 copies +, 40% to dealers. 128pp; 8½×11; of. Reporting time: 6-8 weeks. Payment: 2 copies of issue in which article appears plus $10 printed page/nonfiction; fiction-negotiable. Copyrighted, reverts to author. Pub's reviews: 500 in 1990. §Mystery fiction & critical works. Ads: $425/$275/40¢ word $20 min.

The Armchair Detective Library (see also THE ARMCHAIR DETECTIVE), Ed Strosser, 129 West 56th Street, New York, NY 10019, 212-765-0923. 2 titles listed in the *Small Press Record of Books in Print* (20th Edition, 1991-92). 250pp; 5½×8½; of. Reporting time: 6-8 weeks. Payment: standard. Copyrights for author.

ARMED FORCES & SOCIETY, Claude Welch, PO Box 27, Cabin John, MD 20818, (301) 320-2130. 1974. Non-fiction. circ. 2M+. 4/yr. Pub'd 4 issues 1990; expects 4 issues 1991, 4 issues 1992. sub. price: $40; per copy: $10.50. Back issues: depends on year of publication. Discounts: 10% to subscription agencies. 160pp; 6×9; of. Copyrighted, does not revert to author. Pub's reviews: 16 in 1990. Ads: $200/$125/no classified.

ARNOLD ANCESTRY, Kinseeker Publications, Victoria Wilson, PO Box 184, Grawn, MI 49637, 616-276-6745. 1986. Articles, reviews, news items, non-fiction. circ. 50. 4/yr. Pub'd 4 issues 1990; expects 4 issues 1991, 4 issues 1992. sub. price: $7.50; per copy: $2; sample: same. Back issues: $2. Discounts: none. 8pp; 8½×11; †xerox (photocopy). Reporting time: 2 weeks. Payment: varies. Not copyrighted. Pub's reviews: 2 in 1990. §Genealogy.

Aroc Publishing, Anna Mazos, Publisher, PO Box 550, Elm Grove, WI 53122-0550, 414-541-3407. 1989. avg. press run 3M. Pub'd 1 title 1990; expects 1 title 1991, 1 title 1992. 1 title listed in the *Small Press Record of Books in Print* (20th Edition, 1991-92). avg. price, paper: $14.95. Discounts: 2-4 copies 20%, 5-9 30%, 10-49 40%, 50-99 42%, 100-299 44%. 184pp; 5½×8½.

Arrow Publishing, Cynthia Schubert, Editorial Director, 405 W. Washington St., Suite 26, San Diego, CA 92103, 619-296-3201. 1985. "A recent title published was called *Winning The Confidence Game* about how to increase your self-confidence. Self-help, psychology and motivational titles. Query first" avg. press run 2M. Pub'd 1 title 1990; expects 1 title 1991, 2 titles 1992. 1 title listed in the *Small Press Record of Books in Print* (20th Edition, 1991-92). avg. price, paper: $9.95. Discounts: 3-9 books: 30%, 10-49 books: 40%, 50-99 books: 45%, 100+ books: 50%. 100pp; 8½×11; of. Reporting time: negotiable upon acceptance. Copyrights for author. A.B.E.-American Bookdealers Exchange.

Arrowood Books, Lex Runciman, Deborah J. Runciman, PO Box 2100, Corvallis, OR 97339, 503-753-9539. 1985. Poetry, fiction, plays, non-fiction. "Our newest poetry title, *The Light Station on Tillamook Rock*, by Madeline DeFrees, is a trade version on the original fine print edition published by the Press of Appletree Alley. It features illustrations by Rosalyn Richards" avg. press run 1M. Pub'd 2 titles 1990; expects 2 titles 1991, 2 titles 1992. 7 titles listed in the *Small Press Record of Books in Print* (20th Edition, 1991-92). avg. price, cloth: $15; paper: $8. Standard discounts to bookstores, distributors and jobbers; classroom adoption rates available. Pages vary; size varies; of. Reporting time: 2 months. Payment: negotiated. Copyrights for author.

Arrowstar Publishing, R. Punley, 10134 University Park Station, Denver, CO 80210-0134, 303-692-6579. 1984. Non-fiction. avg. press run 10M. Expects 2 titles 1991, 50 titles 1992. 5 titles listed in the *Small Press Record of Books in Print* (20th Edition, 1991-92). avg. price, cloth: $25; paper: $20; other: $10. Discounts: Variable. 350pp; 5½x8½; †of. Reporting time: 3 weeks. Payment: negotiable. Copyrights for author.

Arsenal Pulp Press, Ltd., Linda Field, #100-1062 Homer St., Vancouver, B.C. V6B 2W9, Canada, 604-687-4233. 1982. Poetry, fiction, non-fiction. "Admittedly, our bias is toward Canadian authors and material, but we will look at international submissions" avg. press run 1M-1.5M. Pub'd 8 titles 1990; expects 11 titles 1991, 12 titles 1992. 54 titles listed in the *Small Press Record of Books in Print* (20th Edition, 1991-92). avg. price, paper: $10.95. Discounts: trade 20% under 5, 40% 5+; jobber/wholesaler subject to negotiation. 120pp; 5½x8½; of. Reporting time: 1-3 months. Payment: 15% of net. Copyrights for author. Association of Canadian Publishers (ACP), Literary Press Group (LPG), Association of Book Publishers of B.C. (ABPBC).

ART CALENDAR, Carolyn Blakeslee, PO Box 1040, Great Falls, VA 22066, 703-430-6610. 1985. Articles, art, photos, interviews, news items. "Marketing and career management journal for visual artists. Articles on marketing, art law, psychology of creativity; interviews with dealers, curators. Professional listings: grants, residencies, juried shows, museums, etc. reviewing portfolios" circ. 50M. 11/yr. Pub'd 11 issues 1990; expects 12 issues 1991, 12 issues 1992. sub. price: $29; per copy: $4; sample: $4. Back issues: $3.50. 32-52pp; 8½x11; of. Reporting time: varies. Copyrighted, rights revert if requested. Pub's reviews: +/-10 in 1990. §For visual artists, career management books. Ads: inquire. COSMEP.

ART HAZARDS NEWS, Michael McCann, 5 Beekman Street, New York, NY 10038, 212-227-6220. 1978. Articles, non-fiction. "Interested only in articles related to health & safety issues in visual art, performing arts & museums" circ. 4M. 10/yr. Pub'd 10 issues 1990; expects 10 issues 1991, 10 issues 1992. sub. price: $15; per copy: $1; sample: free with SASE. Back issues: free. Discounts: 40%. 4pp; 8½x11; of. Payment: none. Copyrighted, reverts to author. Pub's reviews: 2 in 1990. §Occupational health, industrial hygiene.

ART INFORMATION REPORT, Alan Laming, 496 La Guardia Place, New York, NY 10012, 212-505-2004. 1987. "Short items of trade news for professionals in the art world" circ. 1.1M. 10/yr. Pub'd 10 issues 1990; expects 10 issues 1991, 10 issues 1992. sub. price: $95; per copy: $9.50; sample: free. Back issues: $9.50. Discounts: 10%. 8pp; 8½x11; of. Payment: varies. Copyrighted, does not revert to author. Pub's reviews: 16 in 1990. §art, design, photography, architecture, antiques. No advertising.

Art Metropole, 217 Richmond Street West, Toronto, Ontario M5V 1W2, Canada, (416) 362-1685. 1972. Art, interviews. "We do not usually publish unsolicited material." avg. press run 3M. Pub'd 3 titles 1990; expects 2 titles 1991, 2 titles 1992. 14 titles listed in the *Small Press Record of Books in Print* (20th Edition, 1991-92). avg. price, paper: $5. Discounts: 35 percent bulk orders, 5 or more. 64pp; 10¾x14; of. Reporting time: varies. Payment: varies. Copyright reverts to authors.

ART PAPERS, Glenn Harper, Editor; Carolyn Griffin, Managing Editor, PO Box 77348, Atlanta, GA 30357, 404-588-1837. 1977. Articles, art, photos, interviews, criticism, reviews, news items, non-fiction. "Features: 2,500-3,500 words. Reviews: 500-1,500 words. Recent art. Jean Baudrillard, Dick Higgins, Kathy Acker, and Benny Andrews. Additional Address: PO Box 77348, Atlanta GA 30357" circ. 5M-7M. 6/yr. Pub'd 6 issues 1990; expects 6 issues 1991, 6 issues 1992. sub. price: $18; per copy: $4.50; sample: free. Back issues: $4.50 per copy. Discounts: Group subscriptions to groups of 10 or more. 80pp; 10x13½; of. Reporting time: 6 weeks. Payment: copies, fees range from $10 to $200. Copyrighted, reverts to author. Pub's reviews: 5 in 1990. §Contemporary visual arts, dance, new music, theater, performance, video, film. Ads: $572/$322/$15 per column inch/free.

ART TIMES, Raymond J. Steiner, PO Box 730, Mount Marion, NY 12456-0730, 914-246-6944. 1984. "Other address: 7484 Fite Road, Saugerties, NY 12477. *Art Times* is a monthly journal of and for the arts. Although the bulk is written by Staff members, we solicit poetry and short stories from free-lancers around the world (we are listed in *Writer's Market, Literary Market, Poet's Market*, etc). Fiction: short stories up to 1,500 words. No excessive sex, violence or racist themes. High literary quality sought. Poetry: up to 20 lines. All topics; all forms. High literary quality sought. Readers of *Art Times* are generally over 40, affluent and art conscious. Articles in *Art Times* are general pieces on the arts written by staff *and are not solicited.* General tone of paper governed by literary essays on arts—no journalistic writing, press releases. *Always include SASE.* Guidelines: business size envelope, 1 first class stamp" circ. 15M. 11/yr. Pub'd 11 issues 1990; expects 11 issues 1991, 11 issues 1992. sub. price: $15, $20 foreign; per copy: $1.75 on newsstands; sample: SASE + 3 first class stamps. Back issues: same. Discounts: bulk is sent free to arts organizations, museums and similar distribution points. 20pp; 10x14; of. Reporting time: 6 months (24-36 months for publication). Payment: poetry 6 free issues + 1 yr. sub.; short stories $15 + 1 yr. sub. Copyrighted, reverts to author. Pub's reviews: 25-30 in 1990. §We only review art books. Ads: $725/$375/$195 1/4 page/$150 3/16/$100 1/8/$55 1/16/contract rates available.

Arte Publico Press (see also THE AMERICA'S REVIEW), Nicolas Kanellos, Publisher, University of

Houston, Houston, TX 77204-2090, 713-749-4768. 1980. Poetry, fiction, art, photos. avg. press run 3M. Pub'd 22 titles 1990; expects 20 titles 1991, 20 titles 1992. 99 titles listed in the *Small Press Record of Books in Print* (20th Edition, 1991-92). avg. price, paper: $5-$12. Discounts: 40% trade. 120pp; 5½x8½; of. Reporting time: 4 months. Payment: varies per type of book. Copyrights for author. CCLM, COSMEP.

Artek Press, Inc., Dick Gahler, 3474 Ebba Street, White Bear Lake, MN 55110, 612-777-4829. 1980. "Book is called *Getting A Job In The Post Office*. Bright cover, highly illustrated text. A study guide for passing the U.S. Postal Service Examinations. 128 pages of memory codes, study guides, techniques, etc. Also a directory of U.S. Postal Job Information offices." avg. press run 3M. Pub'd 1 title 1990; expects 2 titles 1991. 2 titles listed in the *Small Press Record of Books in Print* (20th Edition, 1991-92). avg. price, paper: $13. Discounts: 55%. 128pp; 8½x11; of. Copyrights for author.

ARTEMIS, Judy Light Ayyildiz, Maurice Ferguson, Carol Murphey, Bob Walter, Robert Fishburn, Dan Gribbon, Stuart Dabney, Special Poetry Editor; George Garrett, Special Fiction Editor; Anna Fariello, Art Juror; Linda Adkinson, Design Editor, PO Box 8147, Roanoke, VA 24014, 703-774-8440 or 977-3155. 1977. Poetry, fiction, art, photos. "*Artemis* features writers and artists from the Blue Ridge Mountains and Virginia. Without conscious persuasion toward any style or school, *Artemis* seeks the works of both published and unpublished writers. Past contributors include Mary North, Jeanne Larsen, Rosanne Coggeshall, Catherine Hankla, Joseph Garrison, Lisa Ress, Ann Stanford, Walter James Miller, Kurt Rheinheimer, Nikki Giovanni, Caroline Forche" circ. 1M. 1/yr. Pub'd 1 issue 1990; expects 1 issue 1991, 1 issue 1992. sub. price: $6; per copy: $6. Discounts: $2.50 to bookstores or for 10+ copies. 92pp; 8x7½; lp. Reporting time: 2 months. Payment: 1 copy. Copyrighted.

Artemis Press, Inc., Jyoti Masters, PO Box 4295, Boulder, CO 80306, 303-443-9289. 1989. "Artemis Press is a new publishing enterprise founded for the purpose of promoting healing of the individual, the community, and the planet. We specialize in publishing books and software programs based on sound, ecological, and holistic healing methods using nature's cornucopia of medical plants and foods." avg. press run 3-4M. Expects 2 titles 1991, 3 titles 1992. 2 titles listed in the *Small Press Record of Books in Print* (20th Edition, 1991-92). avg. price, paper: $12.95-$39.95. Pages vary; size varies; of. Reporting time: 2 weeks to 1 month. Payment: negotiable. Copyrights for author. COSMEP, PMA.

ARTFUL DODGE, Daniel Bourne, Editor; Karen Kovacik, Editor, Department of English, College of Wooster, Wooster, OH 44691. 1979. Poetry, fiction, articles, art, photos, cartoons, interviews, satire, criticism, reviews, parts-of-novels, long-poems, collages, plays. "According to *Library Journal*, our interviews (Borges, Sarraute, Milosz, Merwin, Lee Smith, William Matthews, Stanislaw Baranczak) are "much more perceptive and informative than most." Translations are heartily encouraged; we like to print special sections of contemporary writing (especially East European and Third World) beyond America's extensive, though not infinite, linguistic/cultural borders, and in general like to see work which accomplishes broader vision and breadth than is standard practice today, but which is grounded in an awareness of the accomplishment of contemporary poetics in the illumination of the particular. We are initiating a 'poet as translator' series, featuring the original poetry and translations of such prominent and emerging practitioners as William Stafford, Stuart Friebert, Nicholas Kolumban and Len Roberts" circ. 750-1M. 1-2/yr. Pub'd 1 double-issue issues 1990. sub. price: indiv. $10, instit. $16; per copy: $5; sample: recent issues are double ones available for $5. Older sample copies are $2.75 for one issue or $5 for 5 issues. Discounts: 20%. 150pp; 5½x8½; of. Reporting time: 5 months maximum. Payment: 2 copies, plus at least $5 honorarium, thanks to Ohio Arts Council. Copyrighted, reverts to author. Pub's reviews: 3 in 1990. §Poetry, fiction, plays, criticism, arts, social commentary, translation. Ads: $50/$30/$20 1/4 page. CCLM.

ARTICHOKE HEART, Bonita House, 1419 Bonita Avenue, Berkeley, CA 94709, 415-526-4765. 1991. Poetry, fiction, art, cartoons. "Art and literature from the mental health community" circ. 500. 1/yr. Expects 1 issue 1991, 1 issue 1992. sub. price: $5; per copy: $5; sample: $5. 12pp; 8½x11; †of. Reporting time: no submissions. Payment: none. Copyrighted, does not revert to author.

Artifact Press, Ltd., 900 Tanglewood Drive, Concord, MA 01742, 508-369-8933. 1991. Poetry, fiction. "First title was an anthology of L.A. poetry" avg. press run 1M. Expects 1 title 1991, 1-2 titles 1992. avg. price, paper: $12.95. Discounts: standard. 215pp; 6x9; of. Reporting time: 4 weeks. Payment: not yet determined. COSMEP, PMA.

ARTISTAMP NEWS, Banana Productions, Anna Banana, PO Box 3655, Vancouver, B.C. V6B 3Y8, Canada, 604-876-6764. 1991. Articles, art, criticism, reviews, letters. "This newsletter's objective is to present current and past history of the artist use of the stamp format, profiles of artists, and articles about techniques used in producing stamp art. Includes section of mail-art show & project listings & Classified section" circ. 500. 2/yr. Pub'd 1 issue 1990; expects 2 issues 1991, 2 issues 1992. sub. price: $12; per copy: $5; sample: $5. Discounts: 50% wholesale. 7pp; 11x17 folded to 8½x11; of. Reporting time: 6 months. Payment: 10 copies only. Copyrighted, reverts to author. Ads: 45¢/word.

ART/LIFE, Art/Life Limited Editions, Joe Cardella, Editor; Gayle Beede, Poetry Editor, PO Box 23020, Ventura, CA 93002, 805-648-4331. 1981. Poetry, art, photos, collages, concrete art. "Poetry and prose should be sent to Gayle Beede, Poetry Editor, 7773 Bradford Drive, Goleta, CA 93117" circ. 500-1M. 11/yr. Pub'd 11 issues 1990; expects 11 issues 1991, 11 issues 1992. sub. price: $450; per copy: $50; sample: $50. Back issues: $50. Discounts: 30% wholesale-minimum 2. 50pp; 8½x11. Reporting time: 1-6 weeks. Payment: each contributor receives a copy of the issue in which his work appears. Copyrighted, reverts to author. No ads.

Art/Life Limited Editions (see also ART/LIFE), Joe Cardella, Editor; Gayle Beede, Poetry Editor, PO Box 23020, Ventura, CA 93002, 805-648-4331. 1981. Poetry, art, photos, collages, concrete art. "Poetry and prose should be sent to Gayle Beede, 7773 Bradford Drive, Goleta, CA 93117" avg. press run 200. Pub'd 11 titles 1990; expects 11 titles 1991, 11 titles 1992. avg. price, other: $50 per copy. Discounts: 30% wholesale-minimum 2. 50pp; 8½x11. Reporting time: 1-6 weeks. Payment: each contributor receives a copy of the issue in which their work appears. Copyrights for author.

ARTPAPER, Jan Zita Grover, Editor; Vince Leo, Associate Editor, 2402 University Avenue W., Ste. 206, Saint Paul, MN 55114-1701. 1980. Art, criticism, letters, concrete art, news items. "Recent contributors include: Kate Ellis, Jan Zita Grover, Harvey Wasserman, Howard Hampton, Donna Kossey, and Jon Held. In addition to articles, reviews, and news, each issue contains extensive listings of regional, national, and international grants, competitions, commissions, and other opportunities for visual artists." circ. 10M. 10/yr. Pub'd 10 issues 1990; expects 10 issues 1991, 10 issues 1992. sub. price: $20; per copy: $2.75; sample: $2.75. Back issues: $2.75. Discounts: jobbers 40-50%, bulk $2/issue. 32pp; 11½x17½; of. Reporting time: 30 days. Payment: feature articles $200-$300, essays $100-$150, artist projects $100, reviews $75, news $50. Copyrighted, reverts to author. Pub's reviews: 10 in 1990. §Visual arts, cultural activism, social issues. Ads: $500/$250/$150 1/4/$90 1/8.

ARTPOLICE, F. Gaard, A. Baird, Jon West, NY Editor; Robert C. Corbit, Associate Editor; Ann Morgan, Editor; Rolanda Nash, Music Editor, 5228 43rd Avenue S, Minneapolis, MN 55417-2210, 612-331-1721. 1974. "We are now in our 16th year of continuous publication" circ. 1M. 3/yr. Pub'd 3 issues 1990; expects 3 issues 1991, 3 issues 1992. sub. price: $10/4 issues; per copy: $1; sample: $1 + 2 25¢ stamps. Back issues: by donation. Discounts: none. 20pp; size varies; of. Reporting time: 2 or 3 months. Payment: 30 books to each contributor. Copyrighted. No advertising.

Arts End Books (see also NOSTOC), Marshall Brooks, Editor, Box 162, Newton, MA 02168. 1979. Poetry, fiction, parts-of-novels, long-poems, non-fiction. "Send a SASE for our catalog describing our subscription package program. Most recent title: *Blackness of a White Night, Fiction & Poetry,* by Sherry Mangan." avg. press run 500. Pub'd 2 titles 1990; expects 2 titles 1991, 2 titles 1992. 10 titles listed in the *Small Press Record of Books in Print* (20th Edition, 1991-92). avg. price, cloth: $8; paper: $3. Discounts: on request. Pages vary; size varies; of, lp. Reporting time: within a few weeks, usually. Payment: worked out on an individual basis with each author, for each project. Copyrights for author.

ART'S GARBAGE GAZZETTE, Art Paul Schlosser Books, Tapes, & Garbage Gazzette, Art Paul Schlosser, 214 Dunning, Madison, WI 53704, 608-249-0715. 1990. Poetry, fiction, articles, art, cartoons, satire, letters, news items, non-fiction. 6/yr. Pub'd 9 issues 1990; expects 6 issues 1991, 6 issues 1992. sub. price: $3.90; per copy: 85¢; sample: 50¢. Back issues: $3.90 for every issue (March 90-March 91). 8pp; 3½x4¾. Payment: a free subscription and their name in the issue. Copyrighted, reverts to author. Ads: none.

ARTSFOCUS PERFORMING ARTS MAGAZINE, Cydney Gillis, 1514 Western, Seattle, WA 98101, 206-624-6113. 1985. Poetry, interviews, criticism, reviews. "*ArtsFocus* is a performing arts magazine devoted to Seattle's theater, dance and music. We print short reviews (300-600 words) and features (1,500-2,000) on events and performers" circ. 5M. 6/yr. Pub'd 4 issues 1990; expects 6 issues 1991, 12 issues 1992. sub. price: $10; sample: free. Back issues: $1. 16pp; 10x13; of. Payment: none, volunteered writing and help. Copyrighted, reverts to author. Pub's reviews. §Non-fiction on theater, dance, music or personalities (bias) of people in these fields. Ads: $350/$140/$75 1/4 page/$40 1/8 page.

As Is/So & So Press (see also SO & SO), John Marron, 123 North 8th Avenue, Highland Park, NJ 08904, (201) 985-5565. 1973. Poetry, fiction, art, photos, interviews, long-poems, collages, concrete art, non-fiction. "Additional address: 1625 Curtis, Berkeley, CA 94702" avg. press run 500-1M. Pub'd 4 titles 1990; expects 4 titles 1991, 4 titles 1992. avg. price, cloth: $16; paper: $8; other: $8 calendar (stapled). Discounts: direct mail (add $1.50); trade 40/60; Small Press Distribution 50/50. 80-150pp; 5x8; of. Reporting time: 2 months. Payment: 10% of print run in contributor copies; 5% of production costs; combination thereof. Copyrights for author. Small Press Distribution, COSMEP, CCLM, Before Columbus, Poets & Writers, PEN, CPITS, CAC, St. Mark's Newsletter, Poetry Flash, Dustbooks.

ASC NEWSLETTER, Michael Schauff, 730 11th Street NW, 2nd Floor, Washington, DC 20001, 202-347-2850. 1972. Articles, photos, interviews, reviews, letters, news items. "*ASC Newsletter* carries articles, newsnotes, book reviews and job ads relevent to biologists in the broad field of systematic biology, or to those whose interests are peripheral to systematics. Articles are reviewed. Submissions detailing techniques applicable to systematics in general, museum computer projects, collection resources, etc. are encouraged" circ. 1.2M. 6/yr. Pub'd 6 issues 1990; expects 6 issues 1991, 6 issues 1992. 10 titles listed in the *Small Press Record of Books in Print* (20th Edition, 1991-92). sub. price: $17 indiv., $32 instit.; 2 yr. sub—$28 indiv., $55 instit.; per copy: $3; sample: $3. Back issues: $2 each issue; $10/yr. thru 1983. 16pp; 9×12; †of. Reporting time: 3 week. Payment: none. Copyrighted, does not revert to author. Pub's reviews: 9 in 1990. §Botany, zoology, natural history. Ads: write for rate/format sheet.

Ascension Publishing, Shirley Kuhn, Betsy Thompson, Box 3001-323, Burbank, CA 91508, 818-848-8145. 1990. "Approx. 160 pages. Work is generally concerned with proposing new possibilities for coping with modern living through ideas that offer greater serenity" avg. press run 5M. Expects 1 title 1991, 2 titles 1992. 1 title listed in the *Small Press Record of Books in Print* (20th Edition, 1991-92). avg. price, paper: $8.95. Discounts: bookstore 40%; other 3-199 40%, 200-499 50%, 500+ 65%. 160pp; 5½×8½. Copyrights for author. PMA, COSMEP.

ASH, David R. Wyder, 121 Gregory Avenue, #B-7, Passaic, NJ 07055, 201-471-8378. 1989. Poetry, fiction, art, satire, reviews, collages, non-fiction. "Short poems and short stories with an erotic and sexual tone are favored. However, *Ash* is not limited to that respect. Recent contributors include Cheryl Townsend, Judson Crews, Paul Weinman, Dan Nielsen, Dan Adams and T. Kilgore Splake." circ. 125. 4/yr. Pub'd 4 issues 1990; expects 4 issues 1991, 4 issues 1992. sub. price: $4; per copy: $1.50; sample: $1. Back issues: $1. Discounts: sold only through the mail, discounts for contributors on five or more copies. 32pp; 8½×11; photocopy. Reporting time: 2 weeks. Payment: 1-2 copies. Not copyrighted. Pub's reviews: 40 in 1990. §Sex and erotica. Ads: none.

Ash Lad Press, Bill Romey, 14 West Main Street, Canton, NY 13617, 315-386-8820. 1975. Non-fiction. avg. press run 1.5M. Pub'd 1 title 1990; expects 2 titles 1991. 4 titles listed in the *Small Press Record of Books in Print* (20th Edition, 1991-92). avg. price, paper: $4.95. Discounts: trade 40% for orders of over 5, 20% for 1-4, texts 20%, libraries 25%. 150pp; 6×9; of. Payment: cooperative sharing of costs and income. Copyrights for author. COSMEP.

Ash Tree Publishing, Susun Weed, PO Box 64, Woodstock, NY 12498, 914-246-8081. 1986. Non-fiction. "We publish eco-feminist, alternative health (wise woman tradition), and woman-spirit, goddess-centered material" avg. press run 5M. Pub'd 1 title 1990; expects 1 title 1991, 1 title 1992. 3 titles listed in the *Small Press Record of Books in Print* (20th Edition, 1991-92). avg. price, paper: $9.95. Discounts: 10% 1-4 copies, 30% 5-9, 40% 10-51, 45% 1 case, 50% 2 cases, 55% 5 cases. 240pp; 5½×8½; Belt press. Reporting time: 2-6 weeks. Payment: standard. Copyrights for author. COSMEP, PMA.

ASHES, Howling Dog Press, Michael Annis, PO Box 5987, Westport Station, Kansas City, MO 64111. "*Ashes* is a chapbook series featuring one writer per issue." 56pp.

The Ashland Poetry Press, Robert McGovern, Editor, Ashland University, Ashland, OH 44805, 419-289-5110. 1970. Poetry. "Thematic anthologies and occasional individual books of poems by a single poet; series of lectures by AU annual writer-in-residence. Manuscripts by invitation only" avg. press run 1M. Pub'd 2 titles 1990; expects 1 title 1991, 1 title 1992. 15 titles listed in the *Small Press Record of Books in Print* (20th Edition, 1991-92). avg. price, paper: $6. Discounts: 40% to book companies. 70pp; 8½×5; of. Payment: 10%. Does not copyright for author.

Ashley Books, Inc., Gwen Costa, Associate Editor, 4600 West Commercial Boulevard, Fort Lauderdale, FL 33319, 305-739-2221. 1971. Fiction, non-fiction. "Always looking for controversial material. Our list consists of approximately 350 titles ranging from general fiction, gay literture, Black literature, and biography, to life after death and medicine. Urgently seeking manuscripts dealing with medical subjects and controversy" avg. press run 2.5M-10M. Pub'd 30 titles 1990; expects 30 titles 1991, 30 titles 1992. 3 titles listed in the *Small Press Record of Books in Print* (20th Edition, 1991-92). avg. price, cloth: $19.95-$22.95; paper: $12.95-$13.95. Discounts: please inquire. 250-350pp; 5½×8½. Reporting time: 8-15 weeks. Payment: 10%, 12.5%, 15% depending on number of copies sold. Copyrights for author. Association of American Publishers.

Ashod Press, Jack Antreassian, PO Box 1147, Madison Square Station, New York, NY 10159, 212-475-0711. 1980. Poetry, fiction, satire, plays. "Range of interest includes translations from the Armenian, and other material related to Armenian culture, history, and literature. We usually commission work" avg. press run 1M. Pub'd 3 titles 1990; expects 3-4 titles 1991, 3-4 titles 1992. 25 titles listed in the *Small Press Record of Books in Print* (20th Edition, 1991-92). avg. price, cloth: $12; paper: $7.50; other: $15. Discounts: 35%. 150pp; 6×9; of. Reporting time: 1-2 months. Payment: 9%. Copyrights for author.

Asian CineVision, Inc., 32 East Broadway, New York, NY 10002. 1 title listed in the *Small Press Record of Books in Print* (20th Edition, 1991-92).

ASIAN LITERARY MARKET REVIEW, Jaffe Publishing Management Service, Kunnuparambil P.

44

Punnoose, Kunnuparambil Buildings, Kurichy, Kottayam 686549, India, 91-4826-470. 1975. Interviews, criticism, reviews. *"Asian Literary Market Review* is a book promotion journal specialising in promoting the sale of American small press books and magazines in India and other Asian countries" circ. 3M. 4/yr. Pub'd 4 issues 1990; expects 4 issues 1991, 4 issues 1992. sub. price: $10; per copy: $2.50; sample: same. Back issues: not available. Discounts: 15% on the annual subscription price. 48pp; 8½×11; †lp. Reporting time: 3 months. Payment: in copies. Copyrighted, reverts to author. Pub's reviews: 200 in 1990. §All subjects of human interest. Ads: $200/$125.

Asian Studies Center, Michigan State University (see also JOURNAL OF SOUTH ASIAN LITERATURE), Michigan State University, Oakland University, East Lansing, MI 48224.

ASIAN SURVEY, University of California Press, Robert A. Scalapino, Leo E. Rose, University of California Press, 2120 Berkeley Way, Berkeley, CA 94720, 415-642-4191. 1960. Non-fiction. circ. 3M. 12/yr. Pub'd 12 issues 1990; expects 12 issues 1991, 12 issues 1992. sub. price: $38 indiv., $79 instit., $22 students ($9 foreign postage); per copy: $6.75; sample: free. Back issues: $6.75. Discounts: 10% foreign agents, 30% 10+ one time orders, standing orders (bookstores): 1-99 40%, 100+ 50%. 96pp; 6×9; of. Reporting time: 1-2 months. Payment: varies. Copyrighted, does not revert to author. Ads: $200/$120.

ASIA-PACIFIC ENVIRONMENT NEWSLETTER, Sahabat Alam Malaysia (Friends of the Earth Malaysia), 43 Salween Road, 10050 Penang, Malaysia, (04) 375705, 376930. 1983. "The various articles are contributed by various organizations, individuals in the various Asia-Pacific countries so as to make this newletter a very accurate reporting of issues in the various counties in this region" circ. 3M. 4/yr. Pub'd 4 issues 1990; expects 4 issues 1991, 4 issues 1992. sub. price: 8 issues (2 years) US$24 by airmail US$20 by seamail; per copy: US$3; sample: US$3. Back issues: US$2. 16pp; 10¼×15½; of. Reporting time: 3 months. Payment: none, as we are a non-profit group. Not copyrighted. Pub's reviews: 20 in 1990. §Development, environment, labour, toxic chemicals, science, natural resources, wildlife, health, working environment, urban environment, energy. Ads: free.

Ask Publishing, Linda Faye Joyner, PO Box 502, Newport News, VA 23607. 1991. Poetry, articles, long-poems, non-fiction. "I would like to receive manuscript submissions. For typing, proofreading and correctional editing for short stories, articles, books, etc.; also repetitive letters, labels, envelopes, poetry, addressing, letters, invoices, inserting. $1.50/page." avg. press run 2-3M. Expects 6 titles 1991, 12 titles 1992. 1 title listed in the *Small Press Record of Books in Print* (20th Edition, 1991-92). avg. price, cloth: $12.95; paper: $6.95. Discounts: 15-25%. 65pp; 6⅛×9¼. Reporting time: 4-6 weeks. Payment: not at this time, possible in the future. Copyrights for author.

Aslan Publishing, Dawson Church, PO Box 887, Boulder Creek, CA 95006-0887, 408-338-7504. 1987. Non-fiction. "Non-fiction material combining spiritual/New Age approaches with mainstream approaches in the fields of health, religion, business, education, communication, etc. Upward looking approaches, illustrating integrity in all endeavors" avg. press run 4M. Pub'd 8 titles 1990; expects 5 titles 1991, 7 titles 1992. 11 titles listed in the *Small Press Record of Books in Print* (20th Edition, 1991-92). avg. price, paper: $11; other: audiotapes $9.95. Discounts: trade 40-46%, distributors 55-60%. 200pp; 6×9, 5⅜×8⅜; web. Reporting time: 2-6 months. Payment: 5%+/- of cover price. Copyrights for author. Publisher's Marketing Association (PMA), 2401 E. Pacific Coast Hwy #206, Hermosa Beach, CA 90254, Santa Cruz County Publishers Assn., COSMEP.

ASPECTS, Steve Polsz, Lucy Polsz, 5507 Regent Street, Philadelphia, PA 19143, 215-726-9746. 1989. Poetry, articles, criticism, reviews, music, non-fiction. "Articles vary from 1-4 pages. Recent contributors: Calvin Murry, Richard Miller, David Castleman. *Aspects* is intended as a neo-renaissance manual for personal development and advancement of consciousness level" circ. 1M. 12/yr. Pub'd 12 issues 1990; expects 12 issues 1991, 12 issues 1992. sub. price: free except for mailing cost. 30pp; 8½×11; xerox. Reporting time: 1 week. Payment: none. Copyrighted, reverts to author. Pub's reviews: 30 in 1990. §Metaphysics. Ads: none.

Aspiring Millionaire, Hunter William Bailey, PO Box 661540, Sacramento, CA 95825, 916-973-8181. 1 title listed in the *Small Press Record of Books in Print* (20th Edition, 1991-92). avg. price, paper: $14.95. 150pp; 5½×8½. Payment: none.

ASSEMBLING, Assembling Press, Charles Doria, Publisher, Editor; Jude Schwendenwein, Associate Editor; Andrea von Milbacher, Associate Editor; Andrea Schwartz, Intern; Richard Kostelanetz, Editor, PO Box 1967, Brooklyn, NY 11202. 1970. Poetry. "*Assembling* is a collaborative magazine. Contributors print 1M copies of up to three 8½ x 11 pages of anything they wish at their own initiative and expense. Contribution is by invitation. Those wishing invitations are invited to send sample manuscripts. Acceptance comes in the form of an invitation. Editors of *Assembling* are really compilers. Fourteen *Assembling* annuals have collected an unprecedented variety of avant-garde printed art. Individual books extend the press. Send SASE for catalogue. Since 1985, Assembling Press has been affiliated with Mason Gross School of the Arts, Rutgers University, New Brunswick, NJ 08903" circ. 200. 1/yr. Pub'd 1 issue 1990; expects 1 issue 1991, 1 issue 1992. sub. price: $30; per copy: $10 for all editions. 2 sample *Assembling*; sample: $10 for a sample. Back issues: complete set of Assembling $150. Discounts: 40% discount to retailers paying in advance, and incl. postage. We do not send consignments as past issues are scarce. No returns accepted. All sales final. 300pp; size varies; mi, of, lp. Reporting time: 1 month. Payment: copies only. Copyrighted. CCLM.

Assembling Press (see also ASSEMBLING), Charles Doria, PO Box 1967, Brooklyn, NY 11202. 1970. "Assembling Press, now in its twentieth year, publishes and distributes poetry, fiction (experimental and otherwise), criticism, artists' books and anthologies. We sponsor readings and other events, and arrange for the publication of *ASSEMBLING ANNUAL*, a collective anthology of artists and writers. We also distribute records and tapes or any other interesting art object that we can conveniently handle. We work closely with our authors to insure that each book is as close to the original concept as possible, without needless editorial intervention. Our publications have been reviewed, exhibited and distributed around the world" avg. press run 700. Expects 3 titles 1992. 8 titles listed in the *Small Press Record of Books in Print* (20th Edition, 1991-92). Request catalogue for prices; avg. price, paper: $8; other: $10 hardbound. Discounts: 40% to dealers paying in advance. No returns accepted. All sales final. Pages vary; size varies; variable. Reporting time: one month. Payment: 10% of edition. Copyrights for author. CCLM, COSMEP.

Associated Writing Programs (see also AWP CHRONICLE), D.W. Fenza, AWP c/o Old Dominion University, Norfolk, VA 23529-0079. 1967. Articles, interviews, criticism, news items. "Articles pertaining to contemporary literature, writing, and the teaching of writing welcome. Book reviews, news items, grants & awards, magazine submission notices. Occasional interviews" avg. press run 13M. Pub'd 6 titles 1990; expects 4 titles 1991, 6 titles 1992. avg. price, cloth: $3.50; paper: $3.50; other: $3.50. Discounts: none. 24pp; 10×15; web of. Reporting time: 2 months. Payment: copies and honorarium, $5/100 words for accepted articles; no kill-fees. Copyrights for author.

Astarte Shell Press, Eleanor H. Haney, PO Box 10453, Portland, ME 04104, 207-871-1817. 1989. Poetry, non-fiction. "Purpose: publication of books and other materials on feminist spiritual, politics and related themes" avg. press run 4M. Expects 1 title 1991, 1 title 1992. avg. price, paper: $11. Discounts: 55% for distributors. 200pp; 6×9; of. Reporting time: 1 month. Payment: 7% of retail price. Copyrights for author. Feminist Bookstore News, 456 14th St. #6, PO Box 882554, San Francisco, CA 94188.

Astonisher Press, James E. Bunstock, Editor, Publisher, PO Box 80635, Lincoln, NE 68501, 402-477-2800. 1985. Fiction, art, photos, cartoons, satire, non-fiction. avg. press run 5M. Pub'd 1 title 1990; expects 5 titles 1991, 10 titles 1992. 1 title listed in the *Small Press Record of Books in Print* (20th Edition, 1991-92). avg. price, paper: $5.95. 120pp; 4×6; of. Reporting time: 60 days. Copyrights for author. COSMEP (PO Box 703, San Francisco, CA 94101).

Astro Artz (see also HIGH PERFORMANCE), Steven Durland, Editor, 1641 18th Street, Santa Monica, CA 90404-3807, 213-315-9383. 1977. Articles, art, photos, interviews, criticism, reviews. avg. press run 6M. Pub'd 4 titles 1990; expects 4 titles 1991, 4 titles 1992. 6 titles listed in the *Small Press Record of Books in Print* (20th Edition, 1991-92). avg. price, paper: $6. Discounts: 25-50%. 88pp; 8½×11; of. Reporting time: 3 months. Payment: variable. Copyrights for author.

Astro Black Books, Charles Luden, P O Box 46, Sioux Falls, SD 57101, 605-338-0277. 1976. Poetry. "Our first book published is *Virgin Death* by Charles Luden (Feb. 1977). Will not be reading any new manuscripts" avg. press run 1M. Pub'd 1 title 1990; expects 1 title 1991, 1 title 1992. 4 titles listed in the *Small Press Record of Books in Print* (20th Edition, 1991-92). avg. price, cloth: $15; paper: $5; other: $25 signed, numbered edition. Discounts: 35% to trade (stores), 45% to jobbers. 75-130pp; 5½×8½; of. Reporting time: 1 month. Payment: negotiable. Copyrights for author.

ASTROFLASH, ACS Publications, Maritha Pottenger, PO Box 16430, San Diego, CA 92116. Articles, interviews, reviews. circ. 20M.

ASYLUM, Asylum Arts, Greg Boyd, PO Box 6203, Santa Maria, CA 93456. 1985. Poetry, fiction, articles, art, satire, criticism, reviews, letters, parts-of-novels, collages. circ. 600. 2/yr. Pub'd 4 issues 1990; expects 4 issues 1991, 2 issues 1992. sub. price: $10; per copy: $5; sample: $3. Discounts: 40%. 100pp; 5½×8½; of. Reporting time: 2 weeks to 3 months. Payment: copies; some small cash awards to critics and reviewers. Copyrighted, reverts to author. Pub's reviews: 25 in 1990. §Any small press publication, especially poetry, translations, fiction, art. Ads: $50/$25. CLMP.

Asylum Arts (see also ASYLUM), Greg Boyd, PO Box 6203, Santa Maria, CA 93456, 805-928-8774. 1990. Fiction, art, photos, criticism, parts-of-novels, collages, plays. "Asylum Arts publishes high-quality literary titles—fiction, plays, translations, essays, and an occasional book of poems—in attractive trade paperback format. All our books are printed on acid-free paper and are smyth-sewn for durability. Our most recent titles are *Friends: More Will and Magna Stories* by Stephen Dixon, and *How We Danced While We Burned*, two plays by Kenneth Bernard" avg. press run 1.5M. Expects 2 titles 1991, 5 titles 1992. 7 titles listed in the *Small Press Record of Books in Print* (20th Edition, 1991-92). avg. price, cloth: $15.95; paper: $7.95. 128pp; 5½×8½;

46

of. Reporting time: 2-6 months. Payment: varies from book to book. Copyrights for author. CLMP.

ATALANTA, PO Box 5502, Atlanta, GA 30307. 1973. Articles, art, cartoons, interviews, criticism, reviews, letters, news items, non-fiction. *"Atalanta* is the newsletter of the Atlanta Lesbian Feminist Alliance. We publish information by and about lesbians." circ. 250. 12/yr. Pub'd 12 issues 1990; expects 12 issues 1991, 12 issues 1992. sub. price: $15 or ALFA membership sliding scale $20-$100; sample: 49¢ SASE. Back issues: 49¢ SASE. 14pp; 8½×11; photocopy. Reporting time: 2 months (provide SASE for response). Payment: none. Copyrighted. Pub's reviews: 50 in 1990. §Lesbian fiction, lesbian theory, feminist books in general. Ads: $20/$10/$5 -1/4 page. Atlanta Lesbian Feminist Alliance.

Atelier De L'Agneau (see also MENSUEL 25), Robert Varlez, Francoise Favretto, 39 Rue Louis Demeuse, 4400 Herstal, Belgium, (41) 363722. 1972. Poetry, fiction, articles, art, photos, cartoons, interviews, criticism, reviews, collages. Pub'd 5 titles 1990; expects 5 titles 1991, 5 titles 1992. 80pp; †of. Payment: 25 books for the author. Does not copyright for author.

ATHA NEWSLETTER, Pam Smith, Editor, 1676 SW 11th Street, Miami, FL 33135, (305) 541-0218. 1980. Poetry, articles, art, cartoons, reviews, news items, non-fiction. "Magazine for Association of Traditional Rug Hooking Artists" circ. 1.5M. 6/yr. Pub'd 6 issues 1990; expects 6 issues 1991, 6 issues 1992. sub. price: $12 includes *ATHA* membership (payable on Sept. 1); per copy: $1; sample: 60¢. Back issues: $2. 18-20pp; 8½×11; of. Reporting time: 1 week for notice of receipt. Copyrighted, reverts to author. Pub's reviews: 2 in 1990. §Traditional hooking, textile news, preservation of textiles, hooking history and techniques. Ads: $30/$16/1-4 page $9; $3.00 add'l fee for non-members, ads must relate to our rug-hooking craft.

Athelstan Publications, Suzanne Kemmer, PO Box 8025, La Jolla, CA 92038-8025. 1986. Non-fiction. "Focus on technology and language learning" avg. press run 1.5M. Pub'd 1 title 1990; expects 2 titles 1991, 3 titles 1992. 4 titles listed in the *Small Press Record of Books in Print* (20th Edition, 1991-92). avg. price, cloth: $23.95; paper: $15. 200pp; of. Copyrights for author. PMA.

ATHENA, Ronald K. Jones, PO Box 5028, Thousand Oaks, CA 91360, 805-379-3185. 1988. Poetry, fiction, articles, art, cartoons, interviews, plays, news items. "Subtitled: 'World's Only International Newspaper for Victory over Domestic Violence.' (Feminist oriented)" circ. 10M+. 2/yr. Pub'd 2 issues 1990; expects 2 issues 1991, 2 issues 1992. sub. price: USA $3, $5 instit., foreign $7, Canada & Mexico $6 (all copies sent 1st class); per copy: $1.50; sample: $2 USA, $3 foreign. Discounts: 40%. 32pp; 11×13½; of. Reporting time: 4-6 weeks. Payment: contributors' copies. Copyrighted, reverts to author. Pub's reviews: 2 in 1990. §Child Abuse, incest, wife battering. Ads: $500/$250/$65 business card size.

ATINDEX, John Noyce, Publisher, John Noyce, G.P.O. Box 2222T, Melbourne, Vic. 3001, Australia. 1980. 4/yr. Pub'd 4 issues 1990; expects 4 issues 1991, 4 issues 1992. sub. price: £49 Sterling. 64pp; size A5; †xerox.

The Atlantean Press, Patricia LeChevalier, 354 Tramway Drive, Milpitas, CA 95035, 408-262-8478. 1990. Poetry, fiction, plays. "We are very particular. Writers should study *The Romantic Manifesto* by Ayn Rand before submitting" avg. press run 5M. Expects 1 title 1991, 3 titles 1992. 1 title listed in the *Small Press Record of Books in Print* (20th Edition, 1991-92). avg. price, cloth: $30; paper: $18; other: $85 handbound. Discounts: 2-4 copies 20%, 5-24 40%, 25-49 43%, 50-99 46%, 100+ 50%. 450pp; 6×9; of. Reporting time: 1 month. Payment: individual arrangements. Does not copyright for author. COSMEP, PMA.

Atlantic Publishing Company, Robert Coomery Montgomery, Managing Editor, 7458 N.W. 33rd Street, Lauderhill, FL 33319, 1-800-541-1336. 1980. Non-fiction. avg. press run 5M. Pub'd 10 titles 1990; expects 12 titles 1991. 1 title listed in the *Small Press Record of Books in Print* (20th Edition, 1991-92). avg. price, cloth: $49.95. Discounts: normal, standard industry. 300pp; 8½×11; †of. Reporting time: 2 months. Payment: open. Copyrights for author. ALA, COSMEP, P.M.A., MSPA.

ATLANTIS: A Women's Studies Journal/Journal d'etudes sur la femme, Deborah C. Poff, Editor, Mount Saint Vincent University, Halifax, Nova Scotia, B3M 2J6, Canada. 1975. Poetry, fiction, articles, art, photos, criticism, reviews, non-fiction. circ. 1M. 2/yr. Pub'd 2 issues 1990; expects 2 issues 1991, 2 issues 1992. sub. price: individual $20 Can, $30 US, $35 overseas; institution $30 Can, $40 US, $45 overseas; per copy: $7.50 + postage/handling. Back issues: $6 or $7.50 (depending on issue). 200pp; 8×10; †photo-typeset. Reporting time: 6-8 months. Payment: 1 complimentary issue. Copyrighted, reverts to author. Pub's reviews: 35 in 1990. §Women's studies. Ads: $150/$75/$50. CMPA.

Atrium Society Publications, Tom Funk, PO Box 816, Middlebury, VT 05753, 802-388-0922. 1984. Art. "We focus exclusively on understanding conflict in its many forms (internal, interpersonal, international) and helping readers—particularly young readers—learn to resolve their differences nonviolently. We publish no unsolicited written material but are often interested in seeing samples of illustrative work for our non-fiction children's books." avg. press run 3M. Pub'd 4 titles 1990; expects 2 titles 1991, 2 titles 1992. 10 titles listed in the *Small Press Record of Books in Print* (20th Edition, 1991-92). avg. price, cloth: $15.95; paper: $9.95. Discounts: 40-46% trade, 20% to libraries and schools, 50% to wholesalers. 150pp; of. Reporting time: 1

month. Payment: not applicable. Copyrights for author. Publishers Marketing Assoc. (PMA), 2401 Pacific Coast Hwy., Suite 109, Hermosa Beach, CA 90254; COSMEP, PO Box 703, San Francisco, CA 94101.

ATROCITY, Hank Roll, 2419 Greensburg Pike, Pittsburgh, PA 15221. 1979. Fiction, articles, art, cartoons, satire, reviews, letters, concrete art, news items. "Length of material: very short. Biases: funny. Recent contributor: Joe Lintner" circ. 250. 12/yr. Pub'd 12 issues 1990; expects 12 issues 1991, 12 issues 1992. sub. price: $10; per copy: $1; sample: $1. Back issues: $1. 7pp; 11×8½; †Mita copier. Reporting time: month. Payment: copies. Copyrighted, reverts to author. Pub's reviews: 3 in 1990. §Humor, cartoons. Ads: $50/$25/$5 2 lines, 50¢/word.

AT-SOURCE-TA, Hannie Korthof, PO Box 41, 6700 AA Wageningen, Holland, 08370-12217/25033. 1972. Articles, interviews, reviews. "One issue consists of 40 pages, published in an english and french version, 4 times a year" circ. 2M. 4/yr. Pub'd 4 issues 1990; expects 4 issues 1991, 4 issues 1992. sub. price: Dfl 35; per copy: Dfl 9; sample: free. Back issues: Dfl 7. 40pp; 21×27cm; of. Payment: none. Not copyrighted. Pub's reviews: 8 in 1990. §Appropriate technology, environment, health. Ads: Dfl 550 1/2 page/Dfl 275 1/4.

Attic Press, Ailbhe Smyth, 44 East Essex Street, Dublin 2, Ireland. 1984. Fiction, non-fiction. avg. press run 3M. Pub'd 25 titles 1990; expects 35 titles 1991, 50 titles 1992. avg. price, cloth: $20; paper: $10. Discounts: wholesale 50%; retail trade 35%. 160pp. Reporting time: 3 months. Copyrights for author. CLE (Irish Book Publishers Assoc.).

Atticus Press (see also ATTICUS REVIEW), Harry Polkinhorn, 720 Heber Avenue, Calexico, CA 92231-2408, 619-357-5512. 1981. Poetry, fiction, articles, art, photos, criticism, collages, concrete art. "Books, Chapbooks, Broadsides. Most titles signed. Some titles handbound. Recent publications by Karl Kempton, Richard Kostelanetz, Pete Carver" avg. press run 150. Pub'd 1 title 1990; expects 1 title 1991, 1 title 1992. 3 titles listed in the *Small Press Record of Books in Print* (20th Edition, 1991-92). avg. price, cloth: $15; paper: $7; other: $3 broadsides. Discounts: 1 copy 10%, 2-4 20%, 5+ 40%; cash orders, any quantity 40%; jobbers 40%. 40+pp; 6×9; lp, of. Reporting time: 30 days. Payment: copies of work. Copyrights for author.

ATTICUS REVIEW, Atticus Press, Harry Polkinhorn, 720 Heber Avenue, Calexico, CA 92231-2408, 619-357-5512. 1983. "Recent contributors: Guy Beining, Michael Helsem, Karl Kempton and Winter Damon. Biases: Lean toward experimental works, cut-up writing" circ. 100. 2/yr. Pub'd 2 issues 1990; expects 4 issues 1991, 2 issues 1992. sub. price: $8; per copy: $4; sample: $4. Discounts: 1 copy 10%, 2-4 20%, 5+ 40%; cash orders, any quantity 40%. 60pp; 8½×11; of. Reporting time: 30 days. Payment: copies of magazine. Copyrighted, reverts to author. Pub's reviews: 2 in 1990. §Poetry, fiction, experimental writing, art. Ads: $30/$15.

Audacious Press, LaVita Williams, Editor, PO Box 1001, Bridgeport, CT 06601, 203-579-4322. 1987. Poetry. "Not accepting submissions until 1989" avg. press run 5M. Pub'd 1 title 1990; expects 1 title 1991, 1 title 1992. 2 titles listed in the *Small Press Record of Books in Print* (20th Edition, 1991-92). avg. price, paper: $10. 40-60pp; 5½×8½; of. Copyrights for author. COSMEP.

AUFBAU, Henry Marx, Editor, 2121 Broadway, New York, NY 10023, 212-873-7400. 1934. Poetry, art, interviews, criticism, reviews, music, plays, news items, non-fiction. *"AUFBAU is mainly read by and published for the German-speaking Jewish refugees who came to this country during WWII. AUFBAU used to be the leading publication for German exile literature and was connected with names like Albert Einstein, Thomas Mann, Hannah Arendt et al. The weekly tabloid covering cultural and political events in Europe and the U.S. is read mainly in the United States, Germany, and Israel."* circ. 20M. 26/yr. Pub'd 26 issues 1990; expects 26 issues 1991, 26 issues 1992. sub. price: USA $48.50; per copy: $2; sample: free. Back issues: varies from $2.00 to $20.00 depending upon year and volume. Discounts: special discounts for teachers upon request. 24pp; 11½×13¼; †of. Reporting time: 2-4 weeks. Payment: monthly for freelancers, weekly for staff. Copyrighted, does not revert to author. Pub's reviews: 200 in 1990. §American literature (fiction, poetry), Judaica, German Literature. Ads: $1040/$520/$1.30 per 14 pica line.

AUM U.S.A. Co. Ltd., Joyu Fumihiro, 8 East 48th Street #2E, New York, NY 10017-1005, 212-226-5030. 1988. Non-fiction. Expects 2 titles 1991, 4 titles 1992. 1 title listed in the *Small Press Record of Books in Print* (20th Edition, 1991-92). avg. price, paper: $5.95. 232pp; 5½×8½; mi. Copyrights for author.

Aunt Lute Books (see also Spinster's Book Company), Joan Pinkvoss, PO Box 410687, San Francisco, CA 94141, 415-558-8116. 1978. Fiction, criticism, plays, non-fiction. "We publish only multicultural, feminist material. Recent authors: Audre Lorde, Gloria Anzalua, Melanie Kaye-Kantrowitz, Cherry Muhanji. Aunt Lute Books is part of the Aunt Lute Foundation, which is the non-profit entity that grew out of the work of Spinsters/Aunt Lute Book Co." avg. press run 3M-5M. Pub'd 6 titles 1990; expects 7 titles 1991, 5 titles 1992. 12 titles listed in the *Small Press Record of Books in Print* (20th Edition, 1991-92). avg. price, cloth: $18.95; paper: $9.95. Discounts: bookstores 40% on 5+ books, 50+ mixed titles 45%; distributors 50-55%, classroom 20%, no rate for single orders from library, jobbers, etc. 40% on STOP orders, 2-5 copies 20%. 185pp; 5½×8;

48

of. Reporting time: 3 months. Payment: 7% on first 5M, increased thereafter. Copyrights for author. Bookbuilders West.

AURA Literary/Arts Review, David Good, Steven Smith, Box 76, University Center, Birmingham, AL 35294, 205-934-3216. 1974. Poetry, fiction, articles, art, photos, interviews, reviews, plays. "No limits as to poem length, 7,000 word limit on prose. Recent contributors include Andrew Glaze, Jon Silkin, Fred Bonnie, Steven Ford Brown" circ. 500. 2/yr. Pub'd 2 issues 1990; expects 2 issues 1991, 2 issues 1992. sub. price: $6; per copy: $3; sample: $2.50. Back issues: $3. 100pp; 6×9; lp. Reporting time: 5-12 weeks. Payment: 2 copies. Copyrighted, reverts to author. Pub's reviews: 3 in 1990. §fiction, poetry.

Auromere Books and Imports (see also PURNA YOGA), Atmaniketan Ashram, 1291 Weber Street, Pomona, CA 91768, 714-629-8255. 1974. "Sri Aurobindo Books, classical Indian Spiritual Texts, Children's Books, and Health books, including Ayurveda Other addresses: Auromere, Inc., c/o Atmaniketan Ashram, Merschstrasse 49, 4715. Ascheberg-Herbern, W. Germany, Phone (02599) 1364. Also carry a number of side lines including imported bookmarks and incense. We are the exclusive U.S. representative of a number of publishers from India and their titles are significantly more in number. Including: Ganesh & Co.; National Book Trust of India; Samata Books: Hemkunt Books; All India Press; Children's Book Trust of India. In addition we also represent Sri Aurobindo Books Distribution Agency and here in the U.S., plus Vedanta Press of Hollywood list has over 1M titles. We do not accept submissions, as we publish existent classical texts. A free catalog of our books is available on request" avg. press run 5M-10M. Pub'd 1 title 1990; expects 3 titles 1991. 14 titles listed in the *Small Press Record of Books in Print* (20th Edition, 1991-92). avg. price, cloth: $18; paper: $7.95. Discounts: Trade 40%, $50 minimum order after discount; Jobbers, Distributors by arrangement $25 minimum order even % discount. 200pp; 5⅜×8⅜. Payment: variable. Copyrights for author. AAIP.

AURORA, SF3**, PO Box 1624, Madison, WI 53701-1624, 233-0326. 1975. Poetry, fiction, articles, art, photos, cartoons, interviews, satire, criticism, reviews, letters, collages, non-fiction. "Science Fiction from a feminist perspective" circ. 500. Irregular. Pub'd 2 issues 1990; expects 2 issues 1991, 2 issues 1992. sub. price: $10 for 3 issues; per copy: $4; sample: $5 postpaid. Back issues: prices on request. Discounts: available on request. 40pp; 8½×11; of. Reporting time: 1 month. Payment: contributor's copy. Copyrighted, reverts to author. Pub's reviews: 20 in 1990. §Feminism, science fiction, fantasy. Ads: $86.00/$44.00.

Aurora Press, PO Box 573, Santa Fe, NM 87504, 505-989-9804. 1982. Non-fiction. "We do not accept submissions without a letter first" avg. press run 3M-20M. Pub'd 3-4 titles 1990; expects 3 titles 1991, 3 titles 1992. avg. price, paper: $9.95. Discounts: all sales through our distributors: Weiser—PO Box 612, York Beach, ME 03910; New Leaf; Bookpeople. 200pp; 5½×8½; printers. Reporting time: 3 months approx. Payment: varies. Copyrights for author. ABA.

AUSTIN SENIOR CITIZEN, Rental Business Press, Elizabeth T. Winn, Senior Service Press, 5600 Cedro Trail, Austin, TX 78731, 512-338-1712. 1987. Articles, art, photos, cartoons, interviews, criticism, reviews, music, letters, news items, non-fiction. "Tabloid designed to provide Austin senior citizens and their families with resource information on social and medical related topics. Regular departments address safety, travel, Social Security, medicine, taxes, legislation, living alone, grandparenting, housing, insurance, events calendar, local discounts, book reviews—local advertisers featured." circ. 5M. 12/yr. Expects 1 issue 1991, 12 issues 1992. sub. price: $7; per copy: $1; sample: free (when available). Discounts: none. 10pp; 11×17; of. Reporting time: 3 weeks. Payment: none; by-line provided. Copyrighted, does not revert to author. Pub's reviews. §Any social or medical issues that affect or are of interest to senior citizens. Publishers Marketing Assoc. (PMA), 2401 Pacific Coast Hwy, Suite 206, Hermosa Beach, CA 90254, International Assoc. of Independent Publishers (COSMEP), PO Box 703, San Francisco, CA 94101.

Australian American Publishing, B.L. Redgrave, 228 Fragrant Harbor Court, San Jose, CA 95123, 408-226-4056. 1986. Art, photos, non-fiction. "Australia; photography; art education. Not seeking submissions in 1991 or 92" avg. press run 500-5M. Expects 2 titles 1991, 2 titles 1992. 2 titles listed in the *Small Press Record of Books in Print* (20th Edition, 1991-92). avg. price, cloth: $8.95; paper: $5.95. Discounts: trade—1 up 55% net 30 days; library; ind. retail cash with order; shipping and handling-$1.35 + 25¢ per book. 200pp; 8½×5½; of. Payment: negotiable. Copyrights for author. COSMEP.

THE AUTHOR, Society Of Authors, Derek Parker, 84 Drayton Gardens, London, England SW10 9SB, England. 1890. "The main journal of professional writers in Britain. N.B./NO unsolicited material, contributions only by invitation." circ. 5M. 4/yr. Pub'd 4 issues 1990. sub. price: £10; per copy: £4.50; sample: £4.50. Discounts: 10%. 36pp; size A4; of, lp. Reporting time: 6 weeks. Payment: £50 per 1M words. Copyrighted, reverts to author. Pub's reviews: 12-15 in 1990. §Authorship. Ads: inquire.

Author's Unlimited, J. Hill Renais, 3324 Barham Boulevard, Los Angeles, CA 90068, 213-874-0902. 1983. "General book publishing, all subjects" avg. press run 2M. Pub'd 15 titles 1990; expects 25 titles 1991, 25 titles 1992. 29 titles listed in the *Small Press Record of Books in Print* (20th Edition, 1991-92). avg. price, cloth: $19.95; paper: $11.95; other: $17.95. Discounts: 2-5 copies 20%, 6-10 30%, 11-25 40%, 26-74 45%, 75+ 50%.

200pp; 5½×8½; of. Reporting time: 1 month. Payment: varies. Copyrights for author. PMA, ABA.

THE AUTOGRAPH COLLECTOR'S MAGAZINE, Joe Kraus, Editor & Publisher, PO Box 55328, Stockton, CA 95205, (209) 473-0570. 1986. Articles, photos, cartoons, interviews, news items, non-fiction. "The magazine serves collectors of autographs, signed photos, letters and historical documents. It has an international readership and includes libraries, universities and historical societies throughout the world. Recent contributors includes California Supreme Court Justice Stanley Mosk, comic book artist Bob Burden and Todd Axelrod, the world's largest manuscript dealer. The subject is autographs but topics include world history, entertainment, science and invention, the arts and the military. Included in each issue is news from all the autograph collecting clubs. Also featured are 200 VIP addresses in each issue" circ. 4M. 8/yr. Pub'd 6 issues 1990; expects 8 issues 1991, 10 issues 1992. sub. price: $20 in U.S., $25 Canada/Mexico; $30 all other countries; per copy: $3; sample: same. Back issues: $3. Discounts: 40% in orders of 10 or more. 64pp; 8½×11; of. Reporting time: 2-3 weeks. Payment: 5¢ per word on publication, $10 photos, $3 photocopies. Copyrighted, reverts to author. Pub's reviews: 5 in 1990. §Autographs & historical documents, history & entertainment books that relate to subject areas. Ads: $140/$80/$57 1/3 page/$30 1/6 page/$20 1/12 page. COSMEP.

Autonomedia, Inc. (see also SEMIOTEXT(E)), Jim Fleming, Lewanne Jones, PO Box 568, Brooklyn, NY 11211, 718-387-6471. 1983. Fiction, criticism, non-fiction. "essays. Post-Marxist theory, post-structuralist theory, philosophy, politics and culture" avg. press run 5M. Pub'd 7 titles 1990; expects 7 titles 1991, 10 titles 1992. 4 titles listed in the *Small Press Record of Books in Print* (20th Edition, 1991-92). avg. price, cloth: $21.95; paper: $9.95. Discounts: Trade 40%, Distributors 50%. 300pp; 6×9; of. Reporting time: 6 weeks. Payment: arranged per title for royalties. Copyrights for author. CCLM/PMA.

Avalanche Press, James Vallance, James Rubow, Lewis Anderson, PO Box 30815, Gahanna, OH 43230. 1989. Poetry, fiction, non-fiction. avg. press run 5M. Pub'd 1 title 1990; expects 5 titles 1991. 1 title listed in the *Small Press Record of Books in Print* (20th Edition, 1991-92). avg. price, paper: $10. Discounts: 2-4 copies 20%, 5-9 30%, 10-6 35%, 61+ 40%. 250pp; †of. Reporting time: 4 weeks. Payment: negotiable, usually split 50/50. Copyrights for author. TARC, BISG, COSMEP.

AVALOKA: A Journal of Traditional Religion and Culture, Arthur Versluis, 249 Maynard NW, Grand Rapids, MI 49504. 1986. Reviews, non-fiction. "Contributors include Ananda Coomaraswamy, Rene Guenon, Frithjof Schuon, Masao Abe, Titus Burckhardt, Robert Aitken Roshi, James Cowan and Arthur Versluis. Essay subjects range from Buddhist symbolism to the sacred function of poetry to the symbolism of the Sun-cross in Christianity to Hakuin Zenji's *Four Wisdoms*. We also accept select translations—and have published a new English translation of Tozan's *Five Ranks*. It is advisable to read the journal before submitting an essay" circ. 500. 1/yr. Pub'd 2 issues 1990; expects 1 issue 1991, 1 issue 1992. sub. price: $12; per copy: $12; sample: $12. Back issues: $9. Discounts: 33% for stores. 100pp; 5½×8½; of. Reporting time: 1 month. Payment: free copies. Copyrighted, reverts to author. Pub's reviews: 7 in 1990. §Eastern religion—particularly Buddhist, Taoist and Vedantic texts, Hermetica, traditional studies.

AVEC, Cydney Chadwick, PO Box 1059, Penngrove, CA 94951, 707-762-2370. 1988. Poetry, fiction, art, photos, parts-of-novels, plays. "*Avec* is interested in experimental writing that makes unusual use of language. We are also interested in translation, particularly in translations of French writing. Recent contributors: David Bromige, Lydia Davis, Jackson Mac Low, Claude Royet-Journoud, Leslie Scalapino" circ. 1M. 2/yr. Pub'd 1 issue 1990; expects 2 issues 1991, 2 issues 1992. sub. price: $12; per copy: $7.50; sample: $4.50. Back issues: $4.50. Discounts: 40% to bookstores; 50% to distributors. 160pp; 8½×11; perfectbound with color cover. Reporting time: 1-3 months. Payment: copies. Copyrighted, reverts to author. Ads: $130/$65. CLMP.

Avery Color Studios, Anita McCollum, Hoyt Avery, Star Route, Box 275, AuTrain, MI 49806, 906-892-8251. 1956. Fiction, photos, non-fiction. "History, folklore, shipwrecks, pictorials. Contributors: Frederick Stonehouse; Thomas Avery, Anita McCollum, Larry B. Massie, Cully Gage" avg. press run 3M. Pub'd 2 titles 1990; expects 4 titles 1991, 2 titles 1992. 41 titles listed in the *Small Press Record of Books in Print* (20th Edition, 1991-92). avg. price, paper: $7.95 & $8.95. Discounts: 40% trade. 185pp; 5½×8½, 7×10; †of. Reporting time: 30 days. Payment: negotiable. Copyrights for author.

Avery Publishing Group, Inc., Rudy Shur, Managing Editor, 120 Old Broadway, Garden City Park, NY 11040, 516-741-2155. 1976. Non-fiction. avg. press run 5M-10M. Pub'd 35 titles 1990; expects 35 titles 1991, 35 titles 1992. avg. price, cloth: $25; paper: $8.95. Discounts: college 20%, trade 20% to 45%. 200pp; 6×9; of. Reporting time: 1 month. Payment: 10% of net, paid semi-annually. Copyrights for author.

Aviation Book Company, W.P. Winner, 25133 Anza Drive, Suite E, Santa Clarita, CA 91355-2999. 1964. Non-fiction. "Aviation only." avg. press run 3M. Expects 3 titles 1991. 11 titles listed in the *Small Press Record of Books in Print* (20th Edition, 1991-92). avg. price, cloth: $15; paper: $10. Discounts: distributor, dealer, school, public library. 192pp; 8×10; of. Reporting time: 90 days. Payment: usually 10% of list price. Copyrights for author.

50

AVSTAR Publishing Corp., Robert Alan, Managing Editor, PO Box 537, Lebanon, NJ 08833, 201-236-6210. 1989. avg. press run 5M. Pub'd 3 titles 1990; expects 2 titles 1991, 3 titles 1992. 4 titles listed in the *Small Press Record of Books in Print* (20th Edition, 1991-92). avg. price, cloth: $12.95; paper: $4.95. Discounts: 20+ 50%. 64-128pp. Reporting time: 3 months. Payment: standard royalty schedule. Copyrights for author. COSMEP, PMA.

Awareness Publications, Joe Vitale, PO Box 300792, Houston, TX 77230, 713-434-2845. 1985. Non-fiction. "How-to books, inspirational; short, direct, practical information designed to get results" avg. press run 1M. Pub'd 1 title 1990; expects 1 title 1991, 1 title 1992. 2 titles listed in the *Small Press Record of Books in Print* (20th Edition, 1991-92). avg. price, paper: $9.95. Discounts: 40%. 112pp; 5½x8¼; †1p. Reporting time: 2 weeks. Payment: negotiable. Copyrights for author. Association For Authors.

AWP CHRONICLE, Associated Writing Programs, D.W. Fenza, c/o Old Dominion University, Norfolk, VA 23529-0079. Articles, interviews, criticism, news items. circ. 13M. 6/yr. Pub'd 6 issues 1990; expects 6 issues 1991, 6 issues 1992. sub. price: $18; per copy: $3.50; sample: $2.50. Back issues: $4. Discounts: For classroom use-20+ is $1.50 per copy. 24pp; 10x15. Reporting time: 2 months. Payment: honorarium and copies, $5/100 words. Copyrighted, reverts to author. Pub's reviews: 10 in 1990. §Nonfiction books on contemporary authors, 20th Century authors, anthologies, pedagogy of creative writing, and lit. crit. Ads: $685 (full); $325 (6½ X 8); $140 (3⅛ X 4).

AXEFACTORY, Axefactory Press (A.K.A. The Axefactory), Joseph Farley, 2653 Sperry Street, Philadelphia, PA 19152. 1986. Poetry, art, interviews, satire, criticism, reviews, collages, non-fiction. "Publication comes out in even numbered years and alternates between anthology/magazine and chapbook formats. 1986 issue was *The Axefactory Review*, 1988 issue was a chapbook *The Year I Learned to Drive* (poetry) by Greg Geletu; 1990 issue was *Axefactory III* (anthology), 1992 issue will be a chapbook by Jeff Vetock (poetry/art). Contents are primarily by invitation. Future issues will be theme oriented. Past contributors: Ann Mennbroker, Tina Barr, Henry Braun, Suzy Flory, Al Masarik, Gerald Locklin, Lynne Savitt, Charles Bukowski, Etheridge Knight, William Stafford, Len Roberts, Stephen Dunn, and more. Not looking at unsolicited material prior to June 1992." circ. 200. Published on even numbered years. Pub'd 1 issue 1990; expects 1 issue 1992. price per copy: $5; sample: $5. Back issues: 1986 sold out, 1990 issue available for $5 each. Discounts: none. 60pp; size varies; of. Reporting time: 2 weeks. Payment: 2 copies. Copyrighted, reverts to author. Pub's reviews: 2 in 1990. §Poetry (original and translations), Chinese & Japanese philosophy and history, ecology, aesthetics, literary theory and criticism, race relations. Ads: we'll publish acknowledgement of mags we recommend along with addresses.

Axefactory Press (A.K.A. The Axefactory) (see also AXEFACTORY), Joseph] Farley, 2653 Sperry Street, Philadelphia, PA 19152. 1985. Poetry, art, interviews, criticism, collages, non-fiction. "Most work is solicited. Not reading again until late 1992. Expect poetry/chapbook by Jeff Vetock out in '92." avg. press run 150-200. Pub'd 1 title 1990; expects 1 title 1992. avg. price, paper: $5. Pages vary; size varies; of. Reporting time: 2 weeks. Payment: 25-33% of run, minimum of 50 copies, possible discounts for purchase of additional copies. Copyrights for author.

Axelrod Publishing of Tampa Bay, Sally Axelrod, 1304 De Soto Avenue, PO Box 14248, Tampa, FL 33690, 813-251-5269. 1985. Fiction, photos, music, non-fiction. avg. press run 1.5M-5M. Pub'd 4 titles 1990; expects 4 titles 1991, 5 titles 1992. avg. price, cloth: $20; paper: $10. Discounts: 40-55% net 30-60 to be determined at point of purchase. 200pp; 6x9; sheetfed offset. Reporting time: 2-4 weeks, prefer cover letter, outline & SASE. Payment: author subsidizes cost of production. Publisher is paid percentage of sales for marketing, sales and fulfillment. Copyrights for author. COSMEP.

Axiom Information Resources, Terry Robinson, PO Box 8015, Ann Arbor, MI 48107, 313-761-4842. 1987. Non-fiction. avg. press run 10M. Pub'd 1 title 1990; expects 1 title 1991, 5 titles 1992. 2 titles listed in the *Small Press Record of Books in Print* (20th Edition, 1991-92). avg. price, paper: $12.95. Discounts: 10 or more copies 40%. 182pp; 5½x8½. Copyrights for author. COSMEP, P.M.A.

Axiom Press, Publishers, Erik Jorgensen, PO Box L, San Rafael, CA 94913, 415-956-4859. 1977. Non-fiction. "*Successful Real Estate Sales Agreements* is the ultimate authoritative guide for Real Estate agents, brokers, and investors for structuring and understanding transactions, contracts, and negotiation. It is both a day-to-day realtor's handbook and an essential reference book for school and business libraries. It is an excellent second text for real estate and business courses. Additionally, this 4th Edition has been substantially revised and expanded to include discussion of and instruction about creative financing, new disclosures and comparison of printed forms in common use, etc. This Edition matches the diversity of the free-flowing and difficult investment market, and successfully decodes its complexities. Realtors across the country have found this book a "must" for each day's challenges, and many schools structure courses around the information it offers" avg. press run 5M. Pub'd 2 titles 1990; expects 2 titles 1991. 1 title listed in the *Small Press Record of Books in Print* (20th Edition, 1991-92). avg. price, paper: $17.95. Discounts: 2-4, 20%; 5-9, 30%;10-99, 40%; 100+,

50%. 370pp; 6×9; of. Reporting time: 2 weeks. Payment: royalty. Copyrights for author. COSMEP, PMA.

AXIOS, Axios Newletter, Inc., Daniel John Gorham, 800 South Euclid Avenue, Fullerton, CA 92634, 714-526-4952; 526-1913. 1981. Articles, art, photos, interviews, criticism, reviews, letters, parts-of-novels, non-fiction. *"Axios* is published for the purpose of explaining the world-wide Orthodox Catholic faith and religious practices to those who would wish to have a better understanding of it. *Axios* carries articles that help to give a religious solution to world and personal problems. We criticize the half stupid ideas put forth by the 'reasonable men of this world'! Now read in 32 countries" circ. 8,462. 10/yr. Pub'd 12 issues 1990; expects 10 issues 1991, 6 issues 1992. sub. price: $10; per copy: $2; sample: $2. Back issues: $2. Discounts: 40%. 24pp; 8½×11; †of. Reporting time: 2 to 4 weeks. Payment: varies. Copyrighted. Pub's reviews: 15 in 1990. §Religion, all types! (Our book reviews are well read in religious book stores.). Ads: $85/$55. COSMEP, OCPA, ACP.

Axios Newletter, Inc. (see also AXIOS; GORHAM; THE VORTEX (A Historical and Wargamers Jornal)), Daniel John Gorham, Joseph T. Magnin, 800 South Euclid Avenue, Fullerton), CA 92634, 714-526-1913. 1981. Poetry, articles, art, photos, cartoons, interviews, satire, criticism, reviews, letters, parts-of-novels, news items, non-fiction. "We publish Orthodox Christian books, art and pamplets, also philosophy and historical books. Republish old out of print books, in some cases—would like to see some religious history of Russia, Greece, Albania, Bulgaria, Finland, Rumania, and also America, if it pertains to the Orthodox Christian." avg. press run varies. Pub'd 3 titles 1990; expects 5 titles 1991. 1 title listed in the *Small Press Record of Books in Print* (20th Edition, 1991-92). avg. price, cloth: $10.95; paper: $3.75-$6.95. Discounts: 40% trade. 355pp; size varies; †of. Reporting time: 2-4 weeks. Payment: negotiated. Copyrights for author. COSMEP, OCPA, ACP.

THE AZOREAN EXPRESS, Seven Buffaloes Press, Art Cuelho, PO Box 249, Big Timber, MT 59011. 1985. Poetry, fiction, art, photos, cartoons, collages. "Although I have a strong focus on rural America and working people, I also consider non-rural material and everything of literary value. Prefer fiction to be 5 or 6 double-space pages. Will accept stories up to 10 double-space pages." circ. 500. 2/yr. Pub'd 1 issue 1990; expects 2 issues 1991, 2 issues 1992. sub. price: $5 p.p.; per copy: $2.50 p.p.; sample: $2.50 p.p. Back issues: $2.50 p.p. 24-30pp; 5½×8½; †of. Reporting time: 1 day to 2 weeks. Payment: copies. Copyrighted, reverts to author. CLMP.

AZTLAN: A Journal of Chicano Studies, Chicano Studies Research Center Publications, Raymund A. Paredes, Carroll B. Johnson, Edit E. Villarreal, Guillermo E. Hernandez, University of California-Los Angeles, 405 Hilgard Avenue, Los Angeles, CA 90025, 213-825-2642. 1970. Articles, criticism, reviews, news items. *"Aztlan* is the oldest continuously published journal in the field focusing on the Mexican experience in the U.S. and Mexico." circ. 1M. 2/yr. Pub'd 2 issues 1990; expects 2 issues 1991, 2 issues 1992. sub. price: $15 individuals, $25 libraries & institutions; per copy: $7.50-$12.50. Back issues: complete set of available issues $100 (26 issues). 200pp; 6×9; of. Reporting time: 6 months. Payment: books in quantity. Copyrighted, reverts to author. Pub's reviews: 4 in 1990. §Books on Mexican-Americans, Mexican immigrants, artistic production of Mexican-Americans. No ads. So Calif Bookbuilders.

B

THE BABY CONNECTION NEWS JOURNAL, Parent Education for Infant Development, Gina G. Morris, Drawer 13320, San Antonio, TX 78213, 512-493-6278. 1986. Poetry, fiction, articles, photos, cartoons, interviews, reviews, letters, news items, non-fiction. "Our publication is for new and expectant parents and their babies, 0-5 years of age. Prefer writing that is extremely friendly and conversational. No judgmental or harsh, 'preachy-how to' articles. However, how-to articles are welcome from professionals in the field of infant development. I want articles that will make a parent feel supported and inspired. Father perspectives greatly encouraged. Can always use drawings, art, cartoons, photos of babies and families. Photos of babies looking at reader only. Photos for cover receive cover credit. Please, nothing over 2,000 words. Prefer short, sweet, simple. 2-3 double spaced typed pages. Write for us, please! Include your bio telling readers who you are. Make it personable." circ. 36M. 6/yr. Pub'd 12 issues 1990; expects 6 issues 1991, 12 issues 1992. sub. price: $10; per copy: $2; sample: $3-Request writer's kit, includes forms, guidelines, pre-routed return envelopes. Back issues: up to 3 copies $3 ea., 4-10 $2 ea.; samplings all different issues. Discounts: bulk subs. For $25 per year—10 copies per issue for 6 issues. 16pp; 10×15¾; of, web. Reporting time: immediately. Payment: pays in copies or $5 to $25 articles, photos in b/w 8 X 10 cover $10-$30. Copyrighted, reverts to author. Pub's reviews: 25-45 in 1990. §Families, infant/toddler development, nursing & physician oriented articles/books, inspirational, real-life day-to-day family experiences. Ads: $12 column inch 1⅝" wide up to 6 columns wide/50¢ word classified or set size of 3-5/16" wide X 3-13/16" deep = $48 per issue. Newspaper Marketing

Association, National Infant Development Education Association, Internatinal Childbirth Education Association, Parent Action, Family Resource Coalition, La Lecheth League International, International Montessori Society, National Association Education Young Children, National Association of Neonatal Nurses, National Center for Clinical Infant Programs.

BABY SUE, Don W. Seven, PO Box 1111, Decatur, GA 30031, 404-875-8951. 1985. Poetry, cartoons, interviews, satire, reviews, music. "We mainly feature bizarre adult cartoons, although we feature poetry, interviews, and reviews as well. Recent cartoonists who have contributed work are Mary Fleener, Roy Tompkins, and Ace Backwords." circ. 5M. 2/yr. Pub'd 2 issues 1990; expects 2 issues 1991, 2 issues 1992. sub. price: $8; per copy: $1.50; sample: free (send 29¢ stamp). Back issues: $2. 18-20pp; 5½x8½; †of. Reporting time: 1 month. Payment: 1 free copy of magazine in which work appears. Copyrighted, reverts to author. Pub's reviews: 10 in 1990. §Cartoons, music magazines, cassettes, CDs and vinyl. Ads: $50/$30.

Bacchus Press Ltd., James M. Gabler, 1421 Jordan Street, Baltimore, MD 21217, 301-576-0762. 1983. Non-fiction. "We publish books on the subject of wine and wine relate subjects" avg. press run 5M. Pub'd 1 title 1990; expects 1 title 1991, 2 titles 1992. 2 titles listed in the *Small Press Record of Books in Print* (20th Edition, 1991-92). avg. price, cloth: $19. Discounts: 40% libraries; 50% booksellers. 400pp; 7x10; lp. Payment: 20%. Copyrights for author. COSMEP, PASCAL, ABA.

BACKBOARD, backspace ink., Joanne Shwed, 1131 Galvez Drive, Pacifica, CA 94044, 415-355-4640. 1986. Poetry, articles, art, interviews, reviews, music, news items. "Brief, newsworthy, creative" circ. 200. 1/yr. Expects 1 issue 1992. sub. price: free; per copy: free; sample: free. Back issues: free. 4-8pp; 8½x11; of. Reporting time: 1 month. Payment: client basis. Copyrighted, reverts to author. §All areas. No ads at present.

backspace ink. (see also BACKBOARD), Joanne Shwed, 1131 Galvez Drive, Pacifica, CA 94044, 415-355-4640. 1985. Poetry, art, music. "Recent contributors: Thomas A. Ekkens, San Francisco poet, artist and musician; Mark S. Johnson, Bay Area writer; Chappell Rose Holt, Bay Area artist" avg. press run 200. Expects 1 title 1992. 1 title listed in the *Small Press Record of Books in Print* (20th Edition, 1991-92). avg. price, cloth: $12. Discounts: trade. 96pp; 5½x8½; of. Reporting time: client basis. Payment: client basis. Copyrights for author.

Backwoods Books (see also NATURALLY YOURS), Marci Cunningham, McClellan Lane, PO Box 9, Gibbon Glade, PA 15440, 412-329-4581. 1982. avg. press run 2M. Pub'd 4 titles 1990; expects 1 title 1991. 4 titles listed in the *Small Press Record of Books in Print* (20th Edition, 1991-92). avg. price, paper: $10. Discounts: 40% for 10 or more. Reporting time: 2 weeks. ABE, COSMEP, PMA.

BAD HAIRCUT, Kimberlea Goforth, Ray Goforth, 3115 SW Roxbury, Seattle, WA 98126. 1987. Poetry, fiction, articles, art, photos, cartoons, interviews, satire, criticism, reviews, letters, news items, non-fiction. "Fiction and nonfiction—2,000 words max. Focus exclusively on politics, human rights and environmental issues" circ. 1M. 1-3/yr. Pub'd 4 issues 1990; expects 4 issues 1991, 1 issue 1992. sub. price: $14; per copy: $4; sample: $4. Back issues: contact us. Discounts: contact us. 30-200pp; 5x7 to 8x10; of. Reporting time: 1 day to 1 month. Payment: tearsheets, copies, small cash sometimes, advertising. Copyrighted, reverts to author. Pub's reviews: 1 in 1990. §Politics, Dada, rock, music. Ads: $20/$10/negotiable.

THE BAD HENRY REVIEW, 44 Press, Inc., Michael Malinowitz, Evelyn Horowitz, Mary du Passage, Box 150045, Van Brunt Station, Brooklyn, NY 11215-0001. 1981. Poetry, long-poems. "Recent contributors: John Ashbery, Stephen Sandy, Colette Inez, Jill Hoffman, Muhammad Ali. No biases" circ. 1M. 1/yr. Pub'd 1 issue 1990; expects 1 issue 1991, 1 issue 1992. sub. price: $12/2 issues; per copy: $6; sample: $5. Discounts: query; 1/2 price for contributors. 64pp; 5½x8½; of. Reporting time: 6 months. Payment: 1 copy. Copyrighted, reverts to author. Ads: $100/$50. COSMEP, CODA.

BAD NEWZ, Bob Z, PO Box 14318, San Francisco, CA 94114. 1986. Fiction, articles, art, photos, cartoons, interviews, satire, criticism, reviews, music, letters, collages, concrete art, news items, non-fiction. "Short (under 1,000 words is best), never use anything over 3,000 words." circ. 1M. Published whenever. Pub'd 3 issues 1990; expects 2 issues 1991. sub. price: $8; per copy: $3; sample: $3. Back issues: $3. Discounts: wholesale 40%, 10 or more 50%. 58pp; 8½x11; †of. Reporting time: 6 months. Payment: copies. Copyrighted, reverts to author. Pub's reviews: lots of in 1990. §Music, underground, radical culture. Ads: $19/$11/$7 1/4 page.

THE BADGER STONE CHRONICLES, Seven Buffaloes Press, Art Cuelho, PO Box 249, Big Timber, MT 59011. 1987. Poetry. "This literary newsletter is dedicated to the life and artistic times of the late Michael Lynn Cuelho—pen name: Badger Stone. Each issue special theme. #2 issue, Family Farm." 2/yr. sub. price: $2.50. 8pp; 8½x11.

BAHLASTI PAPER, Chen, PO Box 15038, New Orleans, LA 70115, 504-899-7439. 1985. Fiction, articles, art, photos, cartoons, interviews, satire, criticism, reviews, letters, parts-of-novels, collages, plays, non-fiction. "*The Bahlasti Papers* is the newsletter of the Kali Lodge of the Ordo Templi Orientis. We print articles on the occult; on sociology, psychology, etc. We look for the creative and extraordinary point-of-view, with an eye for inspiration, honesty, and healing. Many of the articles are bitingly humorous. All of them seem to be written with the lunatic fringe in mind. Recent contributors: Steve Cannon, Darius James, Lionell Snell. Anything longer than 4 columns will be serialized." circ. 100. 12/yr. Pub'd 12 issues 1990; expects 12 issues 1991, 12 issues 1992. sub. price: $27; per copy: $2.25; sample: $2.25. Back issues: $3.50. Discounts: none. 8pp; 8½×11. Reporting time: 2-4 weeks. Payment: none, copy of issue in which article appears. Not copyrighted. Pub's reviews: 4 in 1990. §Occult, mythology, sociology, psychology, anthropology, ethnomusicology, ethnobiology. Ads: none. OTO.

Bain-Dror International Travel, Inc. (BDIT), Eli Dror, Joseph H. Bain, PO Box 1405, Port Washington, NY 11050, 513-944-5508; fax 516-944-7540. 1984. Non-fiction. avg. press run 10M. Pub'd 1 title 1990; expects 2 titles 1991, 3 titles 1992. 2 titles listed in the *Small Press Record of Books in Print* (20th Edition, 1991-92). avg. price, paper: $16.95. Discounts: trade 40%, jobber 50%, distributors 55%. 400pp; 5½×8½.

Baker Publishing, Douglas Kirkpatrick, 16245 Armstead Street, Granada Hills, CA 91344. 1983. Non-fiction. avg. press run 3M. Expects 1 title 1991, 1 title 1992. 2 titles listed in the *Small Press Record of Books in Print* (20th Edition, 1991-92). Discounts: 2-4 books 20%, 5-99 40%, 100-199 45%, 200+ 50%. of.

BAKER STREET GAZETTE, Baker Street Publications, Sharida Rizzuto, Sidney J. Dragon, Thomas Schellenberger, PO Box 994, Metailie, LA 70004, 504-734-8414. 1983. Poetry, fiction, articles, art, photos, cartoons, interviews, satire, criticism, reviews, letters, long-poems, collages, plays, news items, non-fiction. circ. under 10M. 3/yr. Pub'd 3 issues 1990; expects 3 issues 1991, 3 issues 1992. sub. price: $25; per copy: $6.90; sample: $6.90. Back issues: $6.90. Discounts: trade with other like publications. 80pp; digest size; of, photo copy, excellent quality offset covers. Reporting time: 2-6 weeks. Payment: free copies, fees paid to all contributors negotiable. Copyrighted, reverts to author. Pub's reviews: 16 in 1990. §Sherlock Holmes and Victorian Times. Ads: free. NWC, SPWAO, HWA, Literary Markets, MWA, Western Writers of America (WWA), Arizona Author Association (AAA).

Baker Street Publications (see also THE VAMPIRE JOURNAL; THE HAUNTED JOURNAL; SLEUTH JOURNAL; HORIZONS BEYOND; POISON PEN WRITERS NEWS; NOCTURNAL NEWS; BAKER STREET GAZETTE; HORIZONS WEST), Sharida Rizzuto, Sidney J. Dragon, Thomas Schellenberger, Robert Jr. Dyer, PO Box 994, Metairie, LA 70004, 504-734-8414. 1983. Poetry, fiction, articles, art, photos, cartoons, interviews, satire, criticism, reviews, letters, long-poems, collages, plays, news items, non-fiction. "We plan to publish a few story anthologies this year. Next year we are expanding to non-fiction books and novels. We are interested in published writers and talented newcomers" avg. press run 500-1M. Expects 5 titles 1991, 5-7 titles 1992. 6 titles listed in the *Small Press Record of Books in Print* (20th Edition, 1991-92). avg. price, paper: under $10; other: card stock covers, under $10. Discounts: trades, organizations, bookstores. 100-200pp; 8½×11, digest size; of. Reporting time: 2-6 weeks. Payment: 50% after printing costs. Copyrights for author. National Writers Club (NWC), Western Writers of America (WWA), Arizona Authors Associaiton (AAS), Small Press Writers And Artists Organization (SPWAO), Horror Writers of America (HWA), Literary Markets, Mystery Writers of America.

Walter H. Baker Company (Baker's Plays), John B. Welch, 100 Chauncy St., Boston, MA 02111, 617-482-1280. 1845. Plays. "Seeking one-act, full length, musicals, chancel and children's plays" avg. press run 1M. Expects 18 titles 1991, 25 titles 1992. 2 titles listed in the *Small Press Record of Books in Print* (20th Edition, 1991-92). avg. price, paper: $2.25-$4.50. Discounts: 20-40%. 50pp. Reporting time: 3-4 months. Payment: varies, 50/50 split amateur rights; 80/20 split professional rights; 10% book royalty. Copyrights for author.

Bakhtin's Wife Publications, Brian C. Clark, 47 Noe #6, San Francisco, CA 94114, 415-978-9737. 1984. "I publish mags, chapbooks, broadsides, and mail art around the world. I'm interested in publishing radical reinterpretations of knowledge, communication, ideology: be it in the form of essays, novels, poetry, or what have you. Send complete ms, SASE, and a cover letter filled with interesting information. Try reading Mary Daly first. Sample publications are free for postage: 9x12 inch SAE and 90¢ postage. Always wanting to look at more collections of black and white art (though I'll consider color), music and writing about music, plays. Will consider collective editing and publishing. Looking for mss concerned with the thought of Mikhail Bakhtin, and other early Soviets" avg. press run 320. Pub'd 4 titles 1990; expects 4 titles 1991, 4 titles 1992. avg. price, paper: free for postage; other: various formats. Discounts: contact editor. 32pp; 8½×11; †photocopy, off-set; silk-screen. Reporting time: 2 weeks to 2 months. Payment: varies; in the past, copies, or copies with honorarium. Does not copyright for author.

BAKUNIN, Jordan Jones, 2025 Plato Court, Simi Valley, CA 93065, 805-526-8900. 1990. Poetry, fiction, articles, art, interviews, criticism, parts-of-novels, long-poems, plays, non-fiction. "Recent contributors:

Benjamin Saltman, J.T. Ledbetter, Norman Mallory, Greg Boyd. Submission quantity: 1-5 poems. A magazine for the dead Russian anarchist in all of us. Read a sample copy before submitting." circ. 200-400. 4/yr. Expects 4 issues 1991, 4 issues 1992. sub. price: $12, $16 institutional and foreign; per copy: $4; sample: $4. Discounts: 40% bookstores, 50% wholesalers and jobbers. 48pp; 5½x8½; of. Reporting time: 2-6 weeks. Payment: 2 contributor's copies. Copyrighted, reverts to author. Ads: $60/$30.

BALDER, Coxland Press, Stephen B. Cox, Nautonier; Stig Wolfton, Editor, c/o 60 Elmhurst Road, Reading, Berkshire RG1 5HY, England, 0734-323105 incl. Fax/answerphone. 1990. Poetry, articles, letters, news items, non-fiction. "Additional address: Jens Johansson, Knight Commander Scandinavia, Planvagen 12, 88100, Solleftea, Sweden. The magazine is the monthly journal of an international Pan-European Brotherhood (incl. Canada, USA, Australia, New Zealand) of education and esoteric studies. Not for sale to the public. Subscribers must be 18 years or over. Applications for membership to the editor. Membership includes research facilities, workshops, study programmes, grades, visits to our school in England, discounts on books access to The European Library, and special access/discount to The Albion Pilgrimage—a magickal study holiday in England, etc. All contributors are members of *Balder* or else leading members of organizations with which we have a working dialogue. Articles vary between 2 and 5 pages and ongoing series/instructional programmes. *Balder* has now launched 'The European Library,' a repository and study centre for all aspects of pan-European culture and esoterica. The Library now receives regular donations from publishers world-wide. Publishers are invited to donate one copy of each title (in English and any other languages the title is released in). Publishers sponsoring the Library are listed in a Roll of Honour. Additionally, *Balder* will distribute to its mall-list information on suitable forthcoming titles by publishers who sponsor this educational initiative. Updates/donations published monthly in *Balder*. Complete inventory published three times a year, inserted in *Balder*." 12/yr. Pub'd 4 issues 1990; expects 12 issues 1991, 12 issues 1992. sub. price: $70, £33; sample: $6. Back issues: $10. Discounts: none. 28+pp; 5⅞x8¼; †xerography. Payment: none. Copyrighted, reverts to author. Pub's reviews: 7 in 1990. §History, masonry, folklore, occult, mythology, religion, European archaeology and ethnography, classicism, mystic art, culture, legends, rural/farming tradition, esoterica, the E.E.C., ethnic cultural revivals, Euro-languages/philology, pan-Europeans and their landscape; folk arts/crafts/music, etc. Ads: only by special agreement.

Ballena Press, Sylvia Brakke Vane, Lowell John Bean, Thomas C. Blackburn, 823 Valparaiso Avenue, Menlo Park, CA 94025, 415-323-9261. 1973. Non-fiction. "We publish works on the anthropology of the western United States, especially California and the Southwest. We are interested only in books demonstrating the highest level of scholarship. Unsolicited manuscripts will not be returned to the author" avg. press run 1M. Pub'd 2 titles 1990; expects 2-4 titles 1991, 4 titles 1992. 2 titles listed in the *Small Press Record of Books in Print* (20th Edition, 1991-92). avg. price, cloth: $39.95; paper: $19.95. Discounts: resale only 20% for 1 book, 40% for more than 1 book. 100-400pp; 6x9, 8¼x10½; of. Reporting time: 1 month to 1 year. Payment: varies. Copyrights for author.

BALLOT ACCESS NEWS, Richard Winger, 3201 Baker Street, San Francisco, CA 94123, 415-922-9779. 1985. News items. "Bias in favor of voter's right to vote for the party of his or her choice. Bias against laws which interfere with this right." circ. 520. 13/yr. Pub'd 13 issues 1990; expects 13 issues 1991, 13 issues 1992. sub. price: $6; per copy: free; sample: free. Back issues: 50¢ per issue. 6.25pp; 8½x11. Payment: none. Copyrighted, does not revert to author. Pub's reviews: 2-3 in 1990. §Political parties. Ads: none.

Balmy Press (see also THE FOOTLOOSE LIBRARIAN), Wiliam J. Cutts, Box 972, Minneapolis, MN 55440, 612-874-8108.

Bamberger Books, W.C. Bamberger, PO Box 1126, Flint, MI 48501-1126, 313-232-5396. 1984. Fiction. "I'm not able to look at unsolicited manuscripts at this time. Distributed by Small Press Distribution, Inc" avg. press run 800. Pub'd 4 titles 1990; expects 2 titles 1991, 2 titles 1992. 9 titles listed in the *Small Press Record of Books in Print* (20th Edition, 1991-92). avg. price, cloth: $14; paper: $7.50; other: signed $25. 90pp; 5½x8½, 5x7¼; of. Payment: varies. Copyrights for author.

BAMBOO RIDGE, THE HAWAII WRITERS' QUARTERLY, Bamboo Ridge Press, Eric Chock, Darrell Lum, PO Box 61781, Honolulu, HI 96839-1781. 1978. Poetry, fiction, articles, parts-of-novels, plays, non-fiction. "Particular interest in literature reflecting the multi-ethnic culture of the Hawaiian islands" circ. 600-1M. 3/yr. Pub'd 3 issues 1990; expects 3 issues 1991, 3 issues 1992. sub. price: $16 institutions, $12 individual; per copy: $4; sample: $4. Back issues: varies. Discounts: 40%. 125pp; 6x9; of. Reporting time: 3-6 months. Payment: usually $10/poem; $20/prose piece. Copyrighted, reverts to author. Ads: $100/$60. CCLM.

Bamboo Ridge Press (see also BAMBOO RIDGE, THE HAWAII WRITERS' QUARTERLY), Eric Chock, Darrell Lum, PO Box 61781, Honolulu, HI 96839-1781. 1978. Poetry, fiction, plays. "Particular interest in island writers and writing which reflects the multi-ethnic culture of Hawaii" avg. press run 1M. Pub'd 1 title 1990; expects 1 title 1991, 1 title 1992. 12 titles listed in the *Small Press Record of Books in Print* (20th Edition, 1991-92). avg. price, paper: $8. Discounts: 40%. 125-200pp; 6x9; of. Reporting time: 6 months.

Payment: 10% of press run. Copyrights for author. CCLM.

Banana Productions (see also ARTISTAMP NEWS; ENCYCLOPEDIA BANANICA; INTERNATION-AL ART POST), Anna Banana, PO Box 3655, Vancouver, BC V6B 3Y8, Canada, 604-876-6764. 1974. Poetry, fiction, articles, art, photos, cartoons, satire, reviews, letters, collages, concrete art, news items. avg. press run 1M. Pub'd 2 titles 1990; expects 1 title 1991. 2 titles listed in the *Small Press Record of Books in Print* (20th Edition, 1991-92). Discounts: 40% on consignment, 50% wholesale. 32-40pp; 8½x11; of. Reporting time: 1-3 months depending on busy-level here. Payment: copies only. Does not copyright for author.

Bandanna Books, Sasha Newborn, 319 Anacapa Street, Santa Barbara, CA 93101, 805-962-9915. 1975. Articles, art, non-fiction. "Looking for translations of humanist classics in any tradition; also Greek works" avg. press run 1M. Pub'd 3 titles 1990; expects 6 titles 1991, 9 titles 1992. 25 titles listed in the *Small Press Record of Books in Print* (20th Edition, 1991-92). avg. price, paper: $4. Discounts: Credits 1-4 copies - no discount; 5+ 40%; short discount for colleges (25%). 120pp; 2½x3½; †of. Reporting time: 2 months. Payment: by agreement. Copyrights for author.

Bank Street Press, Mary Bertschmann, Maurice Hart, 24 Bank Street, New York, NY 10014, 212-255-0692. 1984. Poetry, fiction, articles, art, long-poems, plays. avg. press run 1M. Pub'd 1 title 1990; expects 4 titles 1991, 8 titles 1992. 7 titles listed in the *Small Press Record of Books in Print* (20th Edition, 1991-92). avg. price, paper: $6. Pages vary; 5½x8½; of. Reporting time: 6 weeks. Copyrights for author. ISBN, PAPL (Port Authority Poetry League); The Small Press Center, New York, COSMEP.

THE BANNER, CRC Publications, Galen Meyer, 2850 Kalamazoo SE, Grand Rapids, MI 49560, (616) 241-1691. 1865. Poetry, fiction, articles, photos, cartoons, interviews, reviews, letters, news items, non-fiction. "Religion-in the Reformed-Presbyterian tradition" circ. 46M. 46/yr. Pub'd 46 issues 1990; expects 46 issues 1991, 46 issues 1992. sub. price: $25; per copy: $1.50. 32pp; 8½x11; †of. Reporting time: 2 weeks. Copyrighted, reverts to author. Pub's reviews: 20 in 1990. §Religion. Ads: $1290/$735/$56 per column inch. ACP, EPA.

Banner Press International, Inc., Barry W. Greenberg, PO Box 21195, Midtown Station, New York, NY 10129, 212-459-4525. 1978. Fiction, non-fiction. "Prefer manuscripts of 150-250pp" avg. press run 4M. Pub'd 2 titles 1990; expects 4 titles 1991, 4 titles 1992. avg. price, cloth: $19.95; paper: $9.95. Discounts: 40% trade, 20% classroom, 50-55% distributors & jobbers. 200pp; 5½x8½; of. Reporting time: usually 1 month. Payment: flexible contractual agreement. Does not copyright for author. COSMEP.

Banyan Tree Books, 1963 El Dorado Avenue, Berkeley, CA 94707, 415-524-2690. 1975. "We are not accepting any mss. at present" avg. press run 4.5M. 3 titles listed in the *Small Press Record of Books in Print* (20th Edition, 1991-92). avg. price, cloth: $14; paper: $6.95. Discounts: Bookpeople's. of.

The Barbizon Foundation (see also BARBIZON MAGAZINE), Don Elzer, Barbizon House, Rural Route One, Lumby, B.C. V0E 2G0, Canada, (604) 547-6621.

BARBIZON MAGAZINE, The Barbizon Foundation, Small Press International, Don Elzer, Steven Dafoe, Nobu Ono, Jerry Billstrom, Barbizon House, Rural Route One, Lumby, B.C. V0E 2G0, Canada, (604) 547-6621. 1983. Poetry, fiction, articles, art, photos, cartoons, interviews, criticism, reviews, music, letters, parts-of-novels, concrete art, news items, non-fiction. "*Barbizon* is a *whole earth* publication for the pacific region, material should take such a slant. Articles furthering the creative and artistic expression of all aspects of the human experience remain the priority, interpependence and "Green" alternatives as well. Length can be from 600 words to 3,500, typed double space. Contributors receive our inter-collective newsletter *The Lobby*. Recent articles in *Barbizon* include: Interview with Masanabu Fukoaka, Green Dollar Exchange System, New Science and the New Age, Seed Saving, Permaculture Village, Direct Action in the Pacific Region, numerous organic farming articles, natural living, and preventative health care. Regular contributors include: D.H. Elzer, Jerry Billstrom, Jeane Manning, Murray Kennedy, Cheryl Prurdey, Jill Bend, Dale Lakevold, and Cindy Hanson" circ. 2.5M. 8/yr. Pub'd 4 issues 1990; expects 8 issues 1991, 8 issues 1992. sub. price: $15; per copy: $2, $3.75, $1; sample: $2.50. Back issues: 2 back issues with subscription, special offer. Discounts: 25% off. Bulk distributors get 50% off cover price. 32+pp; 8½x11. Reporting time: various. Payment: open to negotiation on features but usually no payment. Copyrighted, reverts to author. Pub's reviews: 40 in 1990. §Whole-earth ecology, arts, politics, self-reliance, education, history, aboriginal, human rights, economics. Ads: $240/$135/120 word directory ad with graphic-$43.

Barca De Vela Publishing, PO Box 37168, Phoenix, AZ 85069-7168, 602-864-9493. 1986. Non-fiction. avg. press run 2M. Pub'd 1 title 1990; expects 1 title 1991, 1 title 1992. 1 title listed in the *Small Press Record of Books in Print* (20th Edition, 1991-92). avg. price, paper: $14.95. Discounts: 3+ 40%, 200+ 50%, 500+ 55%. 350pp; 5½x8½; of. Does not copyright for author. COSMEP.

Barclay House, Lawrence Ferrara, 35-19 215th Place, Bayside, NY 11361, 718-225-5178. 1986. Non-fiction. "We publish books on death & dying education, aging, and grieving, music, education." avg. press run

56

2M-10M. Pub'd 3 titles 1990; expects 3 titles 1991, 4 titles 1992. 1 title listed in the *Small Press Record of Books in Print* (20th Edition, 1991-92). avg. price, cloth: $28; paper: $11.95. Discounts: 40% bookstores, net to libraries, 52% jobber. 190-400pp; 5½×8½; of. Reporting time: 2-3 months. Payment: 10% on net sales paid annually. Copyrights for author.

Bard Press (see also WATERWAYS: Poetry in the Mainstream), Richard Spiegel, Editor, 393 St. Paul's Avenue, Staten Island, NY 10304-2127, 718-442-7429. 1974. Poetry, art, long-poems. "Chapbooks containing the work of one poet, most recently Ida Fasel and Joanne Seltzer. Most poets come to us through our magazine *Waterways*." avg. press run 300. Pub'd 2 titles 1990; expects 2 titles 1991, 2 titles 1992. 5 titles listed in the *Small Press Record of Books in Print* (20th Edition, 1991-92). avg. price, paper: $3.50. Discounts: 40% to booksellers. 32pp; 4×5½; †xerox. Reporting time: 1-2 months if manuscript is sent with SASE. Payment: in copies. Copyrights for author. NYSWP.

BARDIC RUNES, Michael McKenny, 424 Cambridge Street South, Ottawa, Ontario K1S 4H5, Canada, 613-231-4311. 1990. Poetry, fiction, art. "*Traditional and high fantasy only*. Prefer short stories but use some poems. Setting must be pre-industrial, either historical or of author's invention. Length: 3,500 words or less. Art: only illustrations of stories, usually contracted from Ottawa fantasy artists" circ. 300. 2/yr. Pub'd 2 issues 1990; expects 2 issues 1991, 2 issues 1992. sub. price: $7; per copy: $3.50; sample: $3.50. Back issues: $3.50. 43pp; size digest. Reporting time: normally within 2 weeks. Payment: on acceptance, 1/2¢ per word. Copyrighted, reverts to author. Ads: none. Small Press Writers & Artists Organization (SPWAO).

Barefoot Press, Kirsty Beauchamp, Managing Editor, 1856 Cherry Road, Annapolis, MD 21401. 1987. Fiction, art, photos. "We are concerned with publishing high quality, *lasting* graphics and children's literature (posters, cards and picture books). As such, we print on acid free paper wherever possible (as in our *California Girls* poster). We are a private publisher and do not solicit manuscripts." avg. press run 5M. Expects 1 title 1992. avg. price, other: $20 (California Girls poster). of.

Barn Owl Books, Gina Covina, P.O. Box 226, Vallecitos, NM 87581, 505-582-4226. 1983. Fiction, non-fiction. "Book length only. Barn Owl Books aims to encourage the fusion of spiritual mystery with practical action, through publication of books that defy categorization as either 'how-to' or 'how-come', and through active involvement of authors in the publishing process. Send queries only, with SASE" avg. press run 6M-10M. Pub'd 1 title 1990; expects 1 title 1991, 1 title 1992. 2 titles listed in the *Small Press Record of Books in Print* (20th Edition, 1991-92). avg. price, paper: $12. Available to book trade through distributors (Bookpeople, Inland Book Co., etc.), to libraries through Baker & Taylor, please inquire about classroom and other bulk sales. Also available through Pacific Publishers' Cooperative. 240pp; 5½×8½; of. Reporting time: 2 months. Payment: individually arranged according to extent of author's participation in publishing process. Copyrights for author.

‡**BARNWOOD, The Barnwood Press**, Sheila Coghill, Tom Koontz, Thom Tammaro, 600 E. Washington Street, Muncie, IN 47305. 1980. Poetry, criticism, reviews, letters, news items. "Poetry, reviews, brief essays. Each issue features five or six poems that we believe our readers will be very pleased to have received. Recent authors include Robert Bly, Grace Butcher, Jared Carter, Siv Cedering, Phyllis Janowitz, Lyn Lifshin, Marge Piercy, Paul Ramsey, William Stafford, Lewis Turco." circ. 500. 4/yr. Pub'd 4 issues 1990; expects 4 issues 1991, 4 issues 1992. sub. price: $2.50/4 issues; per copy: $1; sample: $1. 12pp; 8½×7½; of. Reporting time: 1 month. Payment: $10/poem. Copyrighted, reverts to author. Pub's reviews: 8 in 1990. §Poetry. CCLM.

‡**The Barnwood Press (see also BARNWOOD)**, Tom Koontz, Thom Tammaro, Sheila Coghill, 600 E. Washington Street, Muncie, IN 47305. 1975. Poetry, fiction, articles, art, interviews, criticism, reviews, letters, long-poems, concrete art, news items. "Our organization is a nonprofit cooperative in support of contemporary poetry. Criterion is artistic excellence. Recent authors include: Baker, Bly, Carter, Friman, Guedicke, Jerome, Mathis-Eddy, Robinson, Ronnow, Stafford." avg. press run 1M. Pub'd 4 titles 1990; expects 8 titles 1991, 5 titles 1992. 37 titles listed in the *Small Press Record of Books in Print* (20th Edition, 1991-92). avg. price, paper: $5.00; other: $1. Discounts: 40% to stores, 50% to members. 64pp; 6×9; of. Reporting time: varies from 2 weeks to 6 months. Payment: 10% of income or copies. Copyrights for author.

Barr-Randol Publishing Co., G.F. Coats, 136A N. Grand Avenue, West Covina, CA 91791, 818-339-0270. 1985. Non-fiction. "Essential reading for those interested in trust deeds (mortgages) in California, but applies to other states as well. For real estate lenders, investors, real estate brokers, escrow. Easy to read style. Tricks of trade, as well as fundamentals of business" avg. press run 4M. Expects 1 title 1991, 1 title 1992. 1 title listed in the *Small Press Record of Books in Print* (20th Edition, 1991-92). avg. price, paper: $23.50. Discounts: 4-9 35%, 10+ 50%. 302pp; 7×10; of. Reporting time: 2 months. Payment: negotiated. Copyrights for author. PMA.

BASEBALL: OUR WAY, Our Way Publications, Dale Jellings, 5014 Starker Avenue, Madison, WI 53716, 608-241-0549. 1984. Poetry, fiction, articles, art, cartoons, interviews, satire, news items, non-fiction. "We're interested in seeing any type, form or variety of baseball talk. Picture, if you will, a nation-wide network of sports buffs spouting off, discussing, arguing, concurrung, and generally dispensing information unique to each contributer. Background articles, statistical articles, updates, articles of favorite teams and players, histories, ratings, systems, and other trivia. We also encourage the submission of poetry and short fiction which deals with Baseball.'' circ. 20-100. 10/yr. Pub'd 10 issues 1990; expects 10 issues 1991, 10 issues 1992. sub. price: $9; per copy: $1; sample: $1. Back issues: $1. 8pp; 8½x11; †photocopy. Reporting time: 1 month. Payment: copies. Copyrighted. Pub's reviews: 1 in 1990. §Sports, sports biography, sports reference, etc. Ads: $30/$15/$10.

Basement Graphics, 37 Wendell Street, Cambridge, MA 02138, 617-868-0685. 1 title listed in the *Small Press Record of Books in Print* (20th Edition, 1991-92).

The Battery Press, Inc., PO Box 3107, Uptown Station, Nashville, TN 37219, 615-298-1401. 1976. ''We reprint scarce military unit histories. Inquire for a list of reprints'' avg. press run 1M. Pub'd 15 titles 1990; expects 10 titles 1991, 15 titles 1992. 37 titles listed in the *Small Press Record of Books in Print* (20th Edition, 1991-92). avg. price, cloth: $29.95; other: $10-$15. Discounts: 1-4 copies 20%, 5+ 40%. 200-300pp; size varies; various methods of production. Payment: varies. Copyrights for author.

William L. Bauhan, Publisher, William L. Bauhan, PO Box 443, Dublin, NH 03444-0443, 603-563-8020. 1960. Poetry, art. ''Specialize in New England regional books; authors, non-fiction. Recent titles: *North of Monadnock* by Newton F. Tolman, *The Constant God* poems by Henry Chapin, *The Invisible Giant* poems by Dorothy Richardson, *Seat in a Wild Place* by Erik Brown, *Early American Homes* by Congdon, *First Year Alone* by Gordon, *As Does New Hampshire* by Sarton - Nora Unwin'' avg. press run 1.5M-2.5M. Pub'd 8 titles 1990; expects 7 titles 1991, 8 titles 1992. 74 titles listed in the *Small Press Record of Books in Print* (20th Edition, 1991-92). avg. price, cloth: $10; paper: $7.95. Discounts: 40% off on 5 or more copies, flat 20% off on textbooks, ltd. editions. 150pp; 5½x8½; of, lp. Reporting time: month or so. Payment: 10% of list price; less on poetry & small editions. Copyrights for author. NESPA.

Bay Area Poets Coalition, Inc. (see also POETALK), Maggi H. Meyer, Editor, POETALK, 1527 Virginia Street, Berkeley, CA 94703, 415-845-8409. 1974. Poetry. ''Send 4 with SASE (20 lines, 3 X 4 max); 1 will generally be used (at least); payment in copy'' Pub'd 1 title 1990; expects 1 title 1991, 1 title 1992. 1 title listed in the *Small Press Record of Books in Print* (20th Edition, 1991-92). Membership: $12/year (includes letter, *Poetalk* & *BAPC Anthology*, etc.). of. Reporting time: 2 months. Payment: none. Copyrights for author.

Bay Press, Thatcher Bailey, 115 West Denny Way, Seattle, WA 98119, 206-284-5913. 1981. Criticism. ''Contemporary cultural criticism'' avg. press run 5M. Pub'd 3 titles 1990; expects 3 titles 1991, 3 titles 1992. 14 titles listed in the *Small Press Record of Books in Print* (20th Edition, 1991-92). avg. price, cloth: $17.95; paper: $14.95. Discounts: trade 20-50%. 192pp; 5¼x8; of. Reporting time: 2 weeks. Payment: 5-8% on cover price, payable quarterly. Copyrights for author.

BAY WINDOWS, Rudy Kikel, Co-Editor; Patricia A. Roth, Co-Editor, 1523 Washington Street, Boston, MA 02118, 617-266-6670, X211. 1983. Poetry. ''We're looking for short poems (1-36 lines) by gay men or lesbians on themes of interest to gay men or lesbians'' circ. 13M. 51/yr. Pub'd 51 issues 1990; expects 51 issues 1991, 51 issues 1992. sub. price: $35; per copy: $1; sample: $1. Back issues: $1. 44pp; 10⅛x15½. Reporting time: 4 weeks. Payment: copies. Copyrighted, reverts to author. Pub's reviews: 51 in 1990. §Gay or lesbian—fiction, non-fiction, poetry. Ads: $716.10/$346.50/$173.25 1/4 page/$92.40 1/8 page.

BB Books (see also GLOBAL TAPESTRY JOURNAL), Dave Cunliffe, 1 Spring Bank, Longsight Road, Copster Green, Blackburn, Lancs BB1 9EU, England, 0254 249128. 1963. Poetry, fiction, articles, art, long-poems. ''Mainly publish poetry collections, short novels, anarchic counter-culture theoretics & mystic tracts (zen,tantra, etc.).'' avg. press run 800. Pub'd 4 titles 1990; expects 4 titles 1991, 4 titles 1992. 10 titles listed in the *Small Press Record of Books in Print* (20th Edition, 1991-92). avg. price, paper: $4. Discounts: 1/3 to trade. 44pp; 8x6; †of. Reporting time: soon. Payment: 10%. Copyrights for author. NWASP.

B-CITY, Connie Deanovich, B-City Press, 619 West Surf Street, Chicago, IL 60657, 312-871-6175. 1983. Poetry, fiction, interviews. ''Query before submitting. Recent contributors include: Paul Hoover, Jack Skelley, Maxine Chernoff, Elaine Equi. Spring 1989 issue includes new work B4 *Clark Coolidge*. 'Little magazines keep the heart of writing located, and this one is a first stop for anybody who wants to know what's happening' says Robert Creeley. It covers a lot of ground just like the rest of us, but thankfully it keeps on talking'' circ. 250. 1/yr. Pub'd 1 issue 1990; expects 1 issue 1991, 1 issue 1992. sub. price: $5; per copy: $4; sample: $4. Back issues: $4, #6 1988 issue. Discounts: 5% bulk discount. 100pp; 7x9; †of. Reporting time: 1-3 weeks during Sept/Oct only. Payment: contributors copies. Copyrighted, reverts to author. §Poetry. Ads: $100 or exchange/. CCLM.

Beacon Press, 25 Beacon Street, Boston, MA 02108, 617-742-2110. 1854. ''No original fiction or poetry accepted. We publish books on scholarly topics that have an interest for the general reader, and trade books with potential scholarly uses. Subjects: women's studies, psychology, environmental studies, religious studies, gay and lesbian studies, Afro-american studies, anthropology, politics and current affairs, history, philosophy, education. Submit 2 sample chapters (typed double-spaced) with table of contents, synopsis, and curriculum vitae.'' avg. press run varies widely. Pub'd 60 titles 1990; expects 50 titles 1991, 60 titles 1992. avg. price, cloth: $22.95; paper: $12.95. Discounts: trade discount, nonreturnable and returnable special bulk, text...all different. Reporting time: 8 weeks. Payment: negotiated separately. Copyrights for author.

Beaconlamp Books, PO Box 182, Bronxville, NY 10708, 914-699-7155. 1 title listed in the *Small Press Record of Books in Print* (20th Edition, 1991-92).

Bean Avenue Publishing (see also TUCSON MOTOR NEWS), Bruce A. Kaplan, PO Box 1055, Tucson, AZ 85702, 602-882-8323. 1990. ''Erick Andersen, syndicated cartoonist, creator of *No Exit*, is our first author. Looking for off-beat humor, theory or investigation.'' avg. press run 5M. Expects 1 title 1991. avg. price, paper: $6.95. Discounts: 1-4 books 40%, 5-10 48%, 11-25 50%, 26-50 52%, 51-100 54%, 100+ 55%. 96pp; 9×6; of. Payment: depends on the project. Copyrights for author. PMA, Tucson Book Publishers Assn.

BEAN ZINE, Derek Cerovski, 1359 Oxford Avenue, Kingsville, Ontario N9Y 2S8, Canada, 519-733-4875. 1988. Fiction, articles, art, photos, cartoons, interviews, reviews, music, collages, concrete art, news items, non-fiction. ''Currently working on 20th edition. Very small circulation. Usually short material but long material if sufficient accepted. Contributors of stories, articles, photos, essays art.'' circ. 125. 6/yr. Pub'd 12 issues 1990; expects 7-8 issues 1991, 7-8 issues 1992. sub. price: free or trade; per copy: free or trade; sample: free or trade. Back issues: $1.50. 20pp; 5½×8½; †photocopying. Payment: none. Not copyrighted. Pub's reviews: 6 in 1990. §Preferably magazines (small press usually). Ads: $10/$5.

Bear & Company, Inc., Barbara Clow, Box 2860, Santa Fe, NM 87504, 505-983-5968. 1981. Art, photos, interviews, criticism, non-fiction. avg. press run 7.5M. Pub'd 6 titles 1990; expects 6 titles 1991, 12 titles 1992. 7 titles listed in the *Small Press Record of Books in Print* (20th Edition, 1991-92). avg. price, paper: $9.95. Discounts: 5-24 40%; 25-99 42%; 100-249 44%. 240pp; 5½×8½; web, cameron belt. Reporting time: 8 weeks SASE only. Payment: 8%-10% of net. Copyrights for author. Rocky Mountain Book Publishers Assoc., ABA.

Bear Creek Publications, Kathleen Shea, Editor, 2507 Minor Avenue East, Seattle, WA 98102, 206-322-7604. 1985. Non-fiction. avg. press run 4M. Pub'd 1 title 1990; expects 1 title 1991, 1 title 1992. 2 titles listed in the *Small Press Record of Books in Print* (20th Edition, 1991-92). avg. price, paper: $5.50. Discounts: 2-4 20%, 5-24 40%, 25-49 43%, 50-99 46%, 100+ 50%. 72pp; 5½×8½; of. Reporting time: 3 months. Payment: negotiable. PMA, PNBA, PNBPA, NWPC.

Bear Flag Books, Lachlan P. MacDonald, Editor, PO Box 840, Arroyo Grande, CA 93421-0840, 805-473-1947. 1974. ''California history, travel and nature studies'' avg. press run 2M. Pub'd 3 titles 1990; expects 3 titles 1991, 4 titles 1992. 3 titles listed in the *Small Press Record of Books in Print* (20th Edition, 1991-92). avg. price, cloth: $18.95; paper: $9.95. Discounts: 12+ 40%. 160pp; 6×9; of. Reporting time: 2 weeks on queries, 2 months on mss. Payment: paper 6-8%, hardcover 10%; semiannual payments. Copyrights for author. PMA.

Bear House Publishing (see also LUCIDITY), Ted O. Badger, Route 2, Box 94, Eureka Springs, AR 72632-9505, 501-253-9351. 1985. Poetry, fiction, criticism. ''Contract Publication/write for prices and parameters'' avg. press run 50-200. Pub'd 10 titles 1990; expects 10 titles 1991, 10 titles 1992. 17 titles listed in the *Small Press Record of Books in Print* (20th Edition, 1991-92). avg. price, paper: $4. Discounts: negotiable. 60pp; 5½×8½; of. Reporting time: 90 days or less. Payment: primarily a press for self-publishing, but we do some promotion. Copyrights for author.

Bear Tribe Publishing (see also WILDFIRE: A NETWORKING MAGAZINE), Sun Bear, Publisher; Matt Ryan, Editor, PO Box 9167, Spokane, WA 99209, 509-326-6561. 1985. Poetry, articles, art, photos, interviews, reviews. ''Books on native philosophy, religion, self reliance, environment'' avg. press run 5M. Pub'd 3 titles 1990; expects 4 titles 1991, 4 titles 1992. 6 titles listed in the *Small Press Record of Books in Print* (20th Edition, 1991-92). avg. price, paper: $3.50 or $3.75. Discounts: write to Bear Tribe. 70pp; 8½×11; of. Reporting time: 2-5 months. Payment: standard. Copyrights for author. ABA, COSMEP.

The Bear Wallow Publishing Company, Jerry Gildemeister, PO Box 370, Union, OR 97883, 503-562-5687. 1976. Art, photos, non-fiction. ''Primarily, Bear Wallow is for in-house publishing projects; however, we work with authors wishing to self-publish; and consider special projects that fit our style. Specialize in one-of-a-kind, limited edition printing'' avg. press run 5M-10M. Pub'd 1 title 1990; expects 1 title 1991, 1 title 1992. 5 titles listed in the *Small Press Record of Books in Print* (20th Edition, 1991-92). avg. price, cloth: $20-$40. Discounts: school, library 20%; trade 40%. 96-208pp; 9×8, 12×9, 11×11, varies by project; of. Reporting time: promptly. Payment: 5-10%, quarterly. Copyrights for author.

THE BEAST, Howling Dog Press, Michael Annis, PO Box 5987, Westport Station, Kansas City, MO 64111. ''*The Beast* is a magazine featuring up to 100 writers per issue. It is social/political protest work.'' 216pp.

BEAT SCENE, Beat Scene Press, Kevin Ring, 27 Court Leet, Binley Woods, Coventry, Warwickshire CV3

2JO, England, 0203-543604. 1988. Poetry, fiction, articles, art, interviews, criticism, reviews, music, letters, parts-of-novels, news items, non-fiction. "Short reviews, articles, interviews, mod USA writing, heavy accent on Jack Kerouac, Burroughs, Bukowski, Fante, Ginsberg, Snyder. Recent contributors include Miles, Neal Cassady, Carolyn Cassady, Thea Snyder. Only couple of poems at most in each issue" circ. 200. 7/yr. Expects 7 issues 1991, 10 issues 1992. sub. price: $24/4 issues; per copy: $6; sample: $6. Discounts: 25% on 5+ copies. 36pp; 6×8½. Payment: copies. Copyrighted, reverts to author. Pub's reviews. §Beat generation material, mod USA lit, film, art, poetry. Ads: £10 ($17)/£5 ($8).

Beat Scene Press (see also BEAT SCENE), Kevin Ring, 27 Court Leet, Binley Woods, Coventry, Warwickshire CV3 2JO, England, 0203-543604. 1988. Fiction, articles, interviews, criticism, reviews, letters, parts-of-novels, news items. "First title from Beat Scene Press was Gerald Nicosia's *The Two Lowells of Jack Kerouac*. Nicosia is the author of the Kerouac bio *Memory Babe* 115 copies printed limited edition July 1988" avg. press run 150. Pub'd 1 title 1990; expects 3 titles 1991, 3 titles 1992. avg. price, other: chapbook $6 incs airmail post. Discounts: 25% for 5+ copies. 36pp; 6×8½. Payment: 50% after costs. Copyrights for author.

Beautiful America Publishing Company, Michael Brugman, 9725 South West Commerce Circle, PO Box 646, Wilsonville, OR 97070, 503-682-0173. 1986. Poetry, photos, non-fiction. "Length of material: 72 page softcover to 144 page hardcover. Recent contributors: Bill and Jan Moeller, Kenneth Naversen, Howard Rainer, Frank Murdoch" avg. press run 5M-10M. Pub'd 7 titles 1990; expects 7 titles 1991, 10 titles 1992. avg. price, cloth: $29.95, $34.95, $39.95; paper: $10.95. Discounts: 40%-50%-55%. 144pp; 8½×11½; of. Reporting time: 3 months. Payment: varies. Copyrights for author.

Beekman Publishers, Inc., Joanne Michaels, Stuart Ober, Po Box 888, Woodstock, NY 12498, 914-679-2300. 1972. Fiction. "Beekman is largely a distributor of titles published in England and other European countries. We do not accept unsolicited manuscripts. Beekman published an original novel (A Spartan Education by Albert Werder), but this was its first. We are known for our business & finance, medical and other technical lines. No unsolicated mss." avg. press run 2M. Pub'd 5 titles 1990; expects 10 titles 1991, 20 titles 1992. 40 titles listed in the *Small Press Record of Books in Print* (20th Edition, 1991-92). avg. price, cloth: $25; paper: $15. Discounts: 20%. 300pp; of. Reporting time: 6 months. Payment: 8-10%. Copyrights for author.

BEGINNING: THE MAGAZINE FOR THE WRITER IN THE COMMUNITY, Writers House Press, Richard L. Collett, Jr., Editor & Publisher, 1530 Bladensburg Road, Ottumwa, IA 52501-9066, 515-682-4305. 1982. Poetry, fiction, articles, art, photos, cartoons, interviews, satire, criticism, reviews, music, letters, parts-of-novels, long-poems, collages, plays, concrete art, news items, non-fiction. "ALL OPERATIONS ARE SUSPENDED. NO NEW MEMBERSHIPS, SUBSCRIPTIONS, MANUSCRIPT SUBMISSIONS WILL BE ACCEPTED UNTIL FURTHER NOTICE. *Beginning* is a publication of the Community Writers Association. Annual dues are $30/year, $20/year for students, "subscription only" is available at $12/year. Benefits: 1) subscription to *Beginning*; 2) personal critiques & comment of manuscripts submitted to the mag; non-members receive limited critique 3) discount prices on poetry, fiction, non-fiction, 'how-to-write' books, market books such as the one you're reading and Writers Market from the Association's bookstore; 4) the opportunity to participate in Writing Workshops thru the mail; 5) Critique and feedback service: offering feedback on a continuing basis beyond yearly quota of 'free' critiques, described above, at a very modest price—in most cases, 80% lower cost than other criticism services. Our critiques are based on artistic rather than market considerations. We believe a work must first be good art; we do not compromise art for the market; and 6) out-of-print and rare book search service. All writers are welcome to join the Association and/or submit material regardless of writing ability. *You don't have to be a member to submit ms.* We comment on all ms submitted. We don't believe in form rejection letters. Many writers have been published after revision. We are geared toward the general public (the writer in the community) and beginning writers. We are a service organization designed to help you develop your writing and help you publish. You don't have to be a W.S. Merwin or an Andre Gide to get published in our mag. We have a special interest in poetry & prose on feminist & social issues, material exploring the depth of human experience, & New Age topics. We are, however, open to any topic, style of writing, or school of thought. Please send SASE with all correspondence and manucripts. Include a one paragraph bio and a telephone number with all submissions. More info available on request about our benefits listed above & our book publishing services. Recent contributors: Morty Sklar, Jim Mulac, Chuck Miller, John Sjoberg, and Phoebus Delphis. *Beginning* magazine is recommended by Judson Jerome of Writer Digest Books and is listed in his Poet's Market; Where to Publish Your Poetry. To give writers a better opportunity to publish full-length manuscripts in book form, subscription will include 1 double-issue magazine (for individual submissions) and two books per year. The double-issue magazine will publish about the same number of writers and poets as the previous quarterly issues." circ. 1M. 1/yr. Pub'd 2 issues 1990; expects 1 issue 1991, 1 issue 1992. sub. price: $20 libraries, add $3 foreign surface + $10 foreign air delivery, (*subscription only* is available to non-members at $15/yr); per copy: $6-9; sample: $6-$9. Back issues: $3-$6, rare issues $25. Discounts: sell in bulk (5 or more) to schools, libraries, organizations at 30% discount. 30% to bookstores; examination copy is free desk copy to instructors ordering 10 or more for classroom. Subscription services 20%. 125pp; 5½×8½; of. Reporting time: 3 minutes to 3 months. Payment: copies plus money when

60

available. Copyrighted, reverts to author. Pub's reviews: 0 in 1990. §Poetry, non-fiction, on social issues, psychology, New Age topics. Ads: $75.00/$50.00/$2.00.

Belhue Press, Perry Brass, John Hammond, Box 1081, Ridgefield, CT 06877, 203-438-2528. 1990. "Belhue Press's first book is *Sex-charge*, gay writing by Perry Brass. Sex-charge deals with issues important to gay men now: relationships, love, our own community, censorship, AIDS, and sex. It integrates humor, pathos, and eros. Belhue Press was started to publish books for a gay audience, or an audience interested in quality gay material. We are a small press, but now there is an audience for gay books, expecially ones outside of what is becoming an increasingly bland publishing situation." avg. press run 3M. Expects 2 titles 1991, 2 titles 1992. 2 titles listed in the *Small Press Record of Books in Print* (20th Edition, 1991-92). avg. price, paper: $8.95. Discounts: standard discounts to distributors, trade, and for bulk. 120pp; 5½×8½. Reporting time: reasonable, punctual with SASE. Payment: standard. Copyrights for author.

Bell Publishing, Burton E. Lipman, 15 Surrey Lane, East Brunswick, NJ 08816, 201-257-7793. 1982. Non-fiction. "We specialize in technical + semi-technical books for business people, as well as 'self-improvement' books for business people" avg. press run varies. Pub'd 2 titles 1990; expects 2 titles 1991, 2 titles 1992. 5 titles listed in the *Small Press Record of Books in Print* (20th Edition, 1991-92). avg. price, cloth: $38.50; paper: $24.95. Discounts: inquire. 200pp; 8½×11; of. Reporting time: 1 month. Payment: open. Copyrights for author.

Bell Springs Publishing, Bernard Bear Kamoroff, Box 640 Bell Springs Road, Laytonville, CA 95454, 707-984-6746. 1976. "Printing, sizes, page, prices vary. No submissions wanted" 4 titles listed in the *Small Press Record of Books in Print* (20th Edition, 1991-92). Discounts: bookstores 40%; wholesalers 50%. of. COSMEP, AM Booksellers ASSN.

Belleridge Press, Caryl W. Krueger, 28455 Meadow Mesa Lane, Escondido, CA 92026, 619-749-2122. 1980. avg. press run 10M. avg. price, paper: $12. Discounts: 20%-50%. 324pp; 6×9; of, lp. Reporting time: 14 days. Payment: different each time. Copyrights for author. COSMEP.

BELLES LETTRES, Janet Mullaney, Editor, Publisher, 11151 Captain's Walk Ct., North Potomac, MD 20878, 301-294-0278. 1985. Poetry, fiction, articles, art, photos, cartoons, interviews, satire, criticism, reviews, letters, news items. "We do reviews, interviews, retrospectives, and rediscoveries; short stories & fiction will published also. Contributors must query first. Recent contributors include Susan Koppelman, Merrill Joan Gerber, Dale Spender, and Faye Moskowitz. Reviews may be written by men, but only women-authored books are reviewed. Reviews due 90 days before print month. Work by multicultural women and women from the 'Southern Hemisphere' is especially solicited." circ. 5M. 4/yr. Pub'd 4 issues 1990; expects 4 issues 1991, 4 issues 1992. sub. price: $20/indiv. domestic, foreign add $9 to subscription, $40/institution, $15/student ID; per copy: $5; sample: $5. Back issues: write for price schedule. Discounts: classroom—10 + copies @ $4 each. 2 or more subscriptions—$12.50 each. 64pp; 8½×11; of. Reporting time: 4-6 weeks. Payment: copies & complimentary subscription. Copyrighted, rights revert, except for rights to anthologies. Pub's reviews: 40-50 per issue in 1990. §Women-authored books—all genres (fiction and poetry predominate). Ads: $800/$450/$325(1/3), 1/4/$250, 1/8/$100, 1/16. MLA.

Bellevue Press, Gil Williams, Deborah H. Williams, 60 Schubert Street, Binghamton, NY 13905. 1973. Poetry, art, photos. "All publication by our invitation only. Authors should write ahead. Recently published artists and authors include: Matt Phillips, Marcia Falk, Ursula K. LeGuin, Stephen Sandy, Philip Dow, Kirby Congdon, Mac Hammond, Patricia Wilcox, Barbara Unger, Tom Disch, David Posner, Harriet Zinnes, Albert Glover, John Gardner." avg. press run 65-125 on broadsides, 200-2.5M on post-cards, 150-750 on books. Expects 2 titles 1991. 211 titles listed in the *Small Press Record of Books in Print* (20th Edition, 1991-92). avg. price, paper: $3 to $20 for books (many autographed editions); other: $5 to $7.50 for broadsides, 25¢ for postcards. Discounts: 40 percent off to all bookdealers on regular editions, 20% off on signed. No discount to libraries, handling and postage added. 25-80pp; of. Reporting time: usually within 8 weeks concerning manuscripts, longer for letters and misc. correspondence. Payment: 10% of published edition to authors, plus $5 for each accepted poetry post-card poem, $10 for broadside poems. Payments to illustrators or for introductions varies. Copyright remains with authors; we only print one edition of our books or cards, no reprints.

THE BELLINGHAM REVIEW, Signpost Press Inc., Susan Hilton, Editor; Edna Faye Kiel, Assistant Editor; Irene Bernstein, Assistant Editor; Knute Skinner, Advisory Editor, 1007 Queen Street, Bellingham, WA 98226, 206-734-9781. 1975. Poetry, fiction, art, photos, reviews, parts-of-novels, long-poems, plays. "No fiction over 5M words." circ. 800. 2/yr. Pub'd 2 issues 1990; expects 2 issues 1991, 2 issues 1992. sub. price: $5/2 issues, $9.50/4 issues, $12.50/6 issues; per copy: $2.50; sample: $2.50. Discounts: 25% on 5 + copies. 60pp; 5½×8½; of. Reporting time: 1-3 months. Payment: one copy plus one-year subscription. Copyrighted, reverts to author. Pub's reviews: 0 in 1990. §Poetry volumes & books of fiction.

BELLOWING ARK, Bellowing Ark Press, Robert R. Ward, Editor, PO Box 45637, Seattle, WA 98145, 206-545-8302. 1984. Poetry, fiction, art, photos, letters, parts-of-novels, long-poems, plays, non-fiction.

"*Bellowing Ark* publishes high-quality literary works that affirm the fact that life has meaning. We are interested in poetry, fiction, essays and work in other forms that extends the philosophical ground established by the American Romantics and the transcendentalists. Our belief is that the techniques developed in the last 60 years (and particularly the last 20) are just that, technique; for us polish is a secondary consideration and work in the "modern" vein need not apply (i.e. stories should have a plot; poetry should contain a grain of universal truth). Our desire is to expand the philosophical and literary marketplace of ideas, not to be its arbiters—but we have very definite ideas about what our mission entails. Please write for a sample copy or subscription if you have any doubts. While form is generally not a consideration for selection we have one regular feature, "Literal Lives", which presents well-developed autobiographical stories. Other work particularly featured in the past have been serializations and sequences; long and narrative poems; stories of childhood; and love, nature and erotic poetry. Our contributors over the past year have included Nelson Bentley, Harold Witt, Natalie Reciputi, John Elrod, Mark Allan Johnson, Bethany Reid, Jon Jech" circ. 1M+. 6/yr. Pub'd 6 issues 1990; expects 6 issues 1991, 6 issues 1992. sub. price: $12; per copy: $2; sample: SASE (9 X 12 please) with 85¢ postage, or $2. Back issues: $2. Discounts: negotiable. 24pp; 11½×16; of. Reporting time: 6 weeks to 2 months. Payment: in copy at present. Copyrighted, reverts to author on request only.

Bellowing Ark Press (see also BELLOWING ARK), Robert R. Ward, Editor-in-Chief; Dianne Schoenberg, Publisher, PO Box 45637, Seattle, WA 98145, 206-545-8302. 1987. "As we are just beginning book publishing, we are not currently able to consider unsolicited manuscripts; however, we are interested in any work with a philosophical bent as described under the listing for the magazine we publish, *Bellowing Ark*. At this time the best approach would be to submit work to *Bellowing Ark* with a cover letter describing the complete project; also, *BA* has in the past published chapbook-length poetry manuscripts and has serialized complete book-length works" avg. press run 1M. Pub'd 2 titles 1990; expects 5 titles 1991, 4 titles 1992. 5 titles listed in the *Small Press Record of Books in Print* (20th Edition, 1991-92). avg. price, paper: $4-$10. Discounts: will negotiate. 48-192pp; 6×9; of. Reporting time: usually within 2-3 months. Payment: negotiable (currently 10% of net). Copyrights for author.

Bellwether Productions, Inc., Donna LaBrecque, 1888 Century Park, E, #1924, Los Angeles, CA 90067-1723, 213-392-1964. 1987. Non-fiction. avg. press run 5M+. Pub'd 1 title 1990; expects 3 titles 1991, 5 titles 1992. avg. price, paper: $14.95. Discounts: 40%. 250pp; 8½×11; web. Reporting time: open. Payment: differing with authors, to be discussed. Copyrights for author. Publish, Publishers Weekly.

BELLYWASH, Craig Michaels, PO Box 151481, Altamonte Springs, FL 32715, 407-339-6965. 1991. Poetry, art, photos, cartoons, interviews, reviews, music, letters, collages. "Looking for computer-generated artwork of a surreal, absurd or silly nature. Music preference is experimental, electronic and/or difficult" circ. 300. 4/yr. Expects 4 issues 1991, 4-6 issues 1992. sub. price: $12; per copy: $3; sample: $3. Back issues: issue #1 $1.50. Discounts: not yet considered. 32pp; 8½×11; †mi, computer (Macintosh). Payment: free copies. Not copyrighted. Pub's reviews: 6 in 1990. §Music, computer art, art, "general absurdity or silliness"

BELOIT FICTION JOURNAL, Clint McCown, Box 11, Beloit College, Beloit, WI 53511, 608-363-2308. 1984. Fiction. "We publish new contemporary short fiction. Theme and subject matter open, except we will not print pornography, political propaganda, or religious dogma. Length of stories range from about three to thirty pages. Recent contributors include Tony Ardizzone, Maura Stanton, Gary Fincke, Erin McGraw, David R. Young, William F. Van Wert, Alvin Greenberg, David Michael Kaplan, Scott Russell Sanders, T.M. McNally" circ. 700. 2/yr. Pub'd 2 issues 1990; expects 2 issues 1991, 2 issues 1992. sub. price: $9; per copy: $5; sample: $5. Back issues: $5 each, all issues available. 144pp; 6×9. Reporting time: varies, 2 weeks to 2 months. Payment: in copies. Copyrighted, reverts to author.

BELOIT POETRY JOURNAL, The Latona Press, Marion K. Stocking, Box 154, RFD 2, Ellsworth, ME 04605, 207-667-5598. 1950. Poetry. "We publish the best of the poems submitted. No biases as to length, form, subject, or school. Occasional chapbooks on special themes, such as the recent chapbook of New Chinese. Some recent contributors: Albert Goldbarth, A.G. Sobin, T. Alan Broughton, Thomas Frosch, Brooks Haxton, Lola Haskins, Susan Tichy." circ. 1.2M. 4/yr. Pub'd 4 issues 1990; expects 4 issues 1991, 4 issues 1992. sub. price: $8; per copy: $2; sample: $2. Back issues: $5 for chapbooks, most others $2. List available. Discounts: by arrangement. 40pp; 5½×8½; of. Reporting time: immediately to 4 months. Payment: 3 copies. Copyrighted, reverts to author. Pub's reviews: 23 in 1990. §Books by and about poets, mags with poetry, all reviews written by editor. CCLM.

The Bench Press, Warren Slesinger, 1355 Raintree Drive, Columbia, SC 29210, 803-781-7232. 1985. Poetry, fiction, parts-of-novels. "New poetry + fiction; essays + memoirs; letters. Need to reprint in paperback important work by established writers to build backlist. Wm Stafford, John Haines, Josephine Jacobsen" avg. press run 1M-2M. Expects 1 title 1991, 1 title 1992. avg. price, cloth: $18; paper: $8. Discounts: 40% store; 50% distributor; individuals must prepay. 75-100pp; of. Reporting time: 3 weeks. Payment: copies, no royalties. Copyrights for author.

R.J. Bender Publishing (see also THE MILITARY ADVISOR), R.J. Bender, J.R. Angolia, D. Littlejohn, H.P. Taylor, PO Box 23456, San Jose, CA 95153, 408-225-5777. 1967. Non-fiction. avg. press run 5M. Expects 4 titles 1991, 4 titles 1992. 13 titles listed in the *Small Press Record of Books in Print* (20th Edition, 1991-92). avg. price, cloth: $32.95. Discounts: 33%-55%. 400pp; 6×9; of. Reporting time: 1-2 years. Payment: variable. Copyrights for author.

Benjamin Press, John D. Riley, PO Box 112, Northampton, MA 01061. 1985. "We are reprinting history books and welcome suggestions on out of print books in all fields. Our first book is *A History Of Chess* by H.J.R. Murray" avg. press run 2M. Expects 1 title 1991, 3 titles 1992. 1 title listed in the *Small Press Record of Books in Print* (20th Edition, 1991-92). Discounts: 20% 1 copy; 40% trade 2 or more; 10% libraries. of.

Bennett & Kitchel, William Whallon, PO Box 4422, East Lansing, MI 48826. 1990. Poetry. "We do poetry of form; we leave free verse, blank verse, and hiaku to other houses" avg. press run 600. Expects 3 titles 1991, 3 titles 1992. 5 titles listed in the *Small Press Record of Books in Print* (20th Edition, 1991-92). avg. price, cloth: $9. Discounts: 33⅓%. 68pp; 5½×8½; photolithography. Reporting time: 1 week on queries, 1 month on submissions. Payment: negotiable. Copyrights for author.

Bennett Books, James Tomarelli, PO Box 1553, Santa Fe, NM 87504, 505-986-1428. 1988. Non-fiction. "High quality paperbacks. Occasional hardbacks. Spiritually oriented material, sacred traditions" avg. press run 3M. Expects 3 titles 1991, 5 titles 1992. 4 titles listed in the *Small Press Record of Books in Print* (20th Edition, 1991-92). avg. price, cloth: $24; paper: $11. 128pp; 6×9; of. Reporting time: 2 months. Payment: between 5-10% list price, quarterly. Does not copyright for author. Rocky Mountain Book Publishers Association, COSMEP.

Bergin & Garvey Publishers, Sophy Craze, 1420 South East Street, Amherst, MA 01002, 413-253-9980. 1977. Criticism, non-fiction. "An imprint of the Greenwood Publishing Group" avg. press run 4.5M. Pub'd 20 titles 1990; expects 20 titles 1991, 20 titles 1992. 20 titles listed in the *Small Press Record of Books in Print* (20th Edition, 1991-92). avg. price, cloth: $35.95; paper: $14.95. Discounts: please write for trade bookstore discount schedule. 256pp; 6×9. Reporting time: 1-2 weeks. Payment: 7.5%-15% of net income. Copyrights for author. AAP.

THE BERKELEY MONTHLY, Karen Klaber, Publisher; Teresa Cirolia, Editor, 1301 59th Street, Emeryville, CA 94608, 415-848-7900. 1970. Poetry, fiction, articles, art, photos, cartoons, interviews, satire, criticism, reviews, music, letters, parts-of-novels, long-poems, non-fiction. "Since 1970, *The Monthly* has established a reputation for outstanding graphics and design, and for the high level of its editorial content. We publish first rate interviews, and nonfiction articles, (please send written query). We are no longer able to take unsolicited fiction manuscripts. Recent contributors include: Kevin Berger, Susan Lydon, Stephanie von Buchan, Mal and Sandra Sharpe." circ. 80M. 12/yr. Pub'd 12 issues 1990; expects 12 issues 1991, 12 issues 1992. sub. price: $10; per copy: $1; sample: $1 if available, with SASE (needs 50¢ postage for 2nd class). Back issues: query. Discounts: query. 40-52pp; 11½×15; desktop. Reporting time: as soon as possible. Payment: nonfiction $100-$400, photos and art work negotiated on sliding scale. Copyrighted, *The Monthly* buys only first publication rights, and option to anthologize. Pub's reviews: 8 in 1990. §We consider all subjects and prefer a Bay Area connection. Ads: query.

BERKELEY POETRY REVIEW, Natalia Apostolos, Editor; Jonathan Brennan, Editor, 700 Eshleman Hall, University of California, Berkeley, CA 94720. 1973. Poetry, art, photos, interviews, criticism, reviews, long-poems. "While the *BPR* is biased towards new poets and writers who reside in the San Francisco Bay Area, we are happy to consider all submissions. Please include a SASE, up to five poems and a short biography. Recent contributors: Thom Gunn, Robert Hass, Philip Levine, Ron Loewinsohn, Czeslaw Milosz, Leonard Nathan, Robert Pinsky, William Stafford, Gary Soto. Double issue coming out March 20, 1990" circ. 750. 1/yr. Pub'd 2 issues 1990; expects 1 issue 1991, 1 issue 1992. sub. price: $10; per copy: for upcoming double issue-$8, regular issues $4-$6. Back issues: $3.50. Discounts: 40% trade. 120-150pp; 5½×8½; of. Reporting time: 3-4 months. Payment: contributor's copy. Copyrighted, reverts to author. Pub's reviews: 15 in 1990. §Poetry, criticism, film, literature. Ads: $55/$30. CCLM.

Berkeley Poets Workshop and Press, Charles Entrekin, Managing Editor, PO Box 459, Berkeley, CA 94701, 415-843-8793. 1969. Poetry, fiction, art, photos, parts-of-novels, long-poems, plays. "Book manuscripts are considered only when funds permit" avg. press run 500. Pub'd 2 titles 1990; expects 2 titles 1991, 2 titles 1992. 27 titles listed in the *Small Press Record of Books in Print* (20th Edition, 1991-92). avg. price, paper: $6.95. Discounts: 40% trade. 64pp; 5½×8½; of. Reporting time: 1 month. Payment: 50 copies plus 50% of profit. Copyrights for author. CCLM, AAP.

THE BERKELEY REVIEW OF BOOKS, H.D. Moe, Deborah Zike, Managing Editor, 1731 10th Street, Apt. A, Berkeley, CA 94710, 415-528-8713. 1988. Poetry, fiction, articles, art, photos, interviews, satire, criticism, reviews, music, letters, parts-of-novels, long-poems, collages, plays, concrete art, non-fiction. "We want reviews (200-300 words) of what isn't reviewed; art, poems, fiction that couldn't have been possibly written or drawn. Open to any kind of books, very interested in experimental writing, art (*not* the language prose/poetry sponsored by the university presses—'Our American professors like their literature clear, cold and very dead'—Sinclair Lewis). Recent contributors: Jenifer Stone, Ivan Arguelles, Lisa Chang, D. McNaughton, Larry Eigner, Mary Rudge, Hadassal Haskale, David Meltzer, Denise du Roi, Norman Moser" circ. 500-1M. 3-4/yr. Pub'd 1 issue 1990; expects 3 issues 1991, 4 issues 1992. sub. price: $20/4 issues; per copy: $7; sample: $7. Back issues: $7. Discounts: 30%-70%. 100-150pp; 7×8½; xerox, litho. Reporting time: 1 week to 2 months. Payment: none as of now. Copyrighted, reverts to author. Pub's reviews: 50 in 1990. §All subjects. Ads: $100/$60/$40 1/4 page/$25 1/8.

Berkeley West Publishing, Claire Burch, Mark Weiman, 2847 Shattuck Avenue, Berkeley, CA 94705. 1987. Non-fiction. avg. press run 2.5M. Pub'd 1 title 1990; expects 1 title 1991, 1 title 1992. 1 title listed in the *Small Press Record of Books in Print* (20th Edition, 1991-92). avg. price, cloth: $18.95; paper: $12.95; other: $9.95. Discounts: 55% (Bookpeople, Inland, New Leaf, The Distributors, Metamorphous). 225pp; 5½×8½. COSMEP.

BERKELEY WOMEN'S LAW JOURNAL, University of California Press, Boalt Hall Students of the Univ. of Calif., 2 Boalt Hall, Univ. of Ca., School of Law, Berkeley, CA 94720, 415-642-6263. 1985. *"The Journal* is an interdisciplinary law journal focusing on the legal concerns of women, which are underrepresented in traditional literature." circ. 550. 1/yr. Pub'd 1 issue 1990; expects 1 issue 1991, 1 issue 1992. sub. price: $16 individuals, $35 institutions, $8 students (+ $3 foreign postage); per copy: $16, $35, $8; sample: free. Back issues: same. Discounts: call Univ of Calif Press Periodicals for info at 415-642-4191. 400pp; 6¾×10; lp. Payment: none. Copyrighted, does not revert to author. Pub's reviews: 3 in 1990. §Feminism, women's studies, gay/lesbian studies, disability issues. Ads: $200 (5½ X 8)/$120 (5½ X 4).

The Bess Press, Dr. Ann Louise Rayson, PO Box 22388, Honolulu, HI 96823, 808-734-7159. 1979. Cartoons, non-fiction. *"The Bess Press* is a regional, educational publisher which is seeking manuscript materials for the el-hi, college markets. We have several books and workbooks on Hawaiian history published these last five years. We are actively seeking regional materials, especially introductory Asian/Pacific language books and/or cassettes" avg. press run 5M. Pub'd 6-7 titles 1990; expects 14 titles 1991, 10 titles 1992. 69 titles listed in the *Small Press Record of Books in Print* (20th Edition, 1991-92). avg. price, cloth: $16; paper: $7. Discounts: standard. 200pp; 6×9, varies. Reporting time: usually less than 4-6 weeks. Payment: standard 10%. Copyrights for author. COSMEP.

Bet Alpha Editions, PO Box 20042, Rochester, NY 14602, 716-442-0570. avg. press run 5M. Expects 1 title 1991. 2 titles listed in the *Small Press Record of Books in Print* (20th Edition, 1991-92). avg. price, cloth: $175; paper: trade $175. Discounts: 2-4 copies 20%, 5-99 40%, 100+ 50%. 177pp; 9¼×14; of. Copyrights for author. COSMEP.

Betelgeuse Books, David Pelly, Glenna Munro, 193-55 McCaul Street, Toronto Ont. M5T 2W7, Canada. 1980. Fiction, non-fiction. "We are a small press specializing in 'northern wilderness literature.' No unsolicited manuscripts" avg. press run 3M. Expects 1 title 1991, 1 title 1992. avg. price, paper: $19.95. Discounts: 40% trade. 192pp; 6×9. Payment: varies.

BETWEEN C & D, Joel Rose, Catherine Texier, 255 East 7th Street, New York, NY 10009. 1984. Fiction. "Note well: *Between C & D* will not be reading manuscripts this year. Writers on the edge. Recent contributors: Patrick McGrath, Kathy Acker, Dennis Cooper, David Foster Wallace Lynne Tillman, Reinaldo Povod. Sex, drugs, violence, danger, computers" circ. 600. 3/yr. Pub'd 3 issues 1990; expects 3 issues 1991, 3 issues 1992. sub. price: $15; per copy: $4 ($5 by mail or outside NY); sample: $5. Back issues: $9, complete set Vol. I or II $30, Vol. III or IV $25. Discounts: 40%. 50pp; 10×12; †dot-matrix computer printer. Reporting time: 6 weeks. Payment: magazine copies. Copyrighted, reverts to author. CCLM.

Between The Lines, Sheila Nopper, 394 Euclid Avenue, Toronto, Ontario M6G 2S9, Canada, 416-925-8260. 1977. Photos, interviews, criticism, non-fiction. "Popular non-fiction, national and international history, economics, politics, theory and practice, women, enviroment, Third World" avg. press run 2M. Pub'd 8 titles 1990; expects 10 titles 1991, 8 titles 1992. 52 titles listed in the *Small Press Record of Books in Print* (20th Edition, 1991-92). avg. price, cloth: $29.95; paper: $14.95. Discounts: for university bookstore corse orders 20%, trade stores 5 copies and over 40%, no library discount, except to library services. 240pp; 6×9, 5½×8½; of. Reporting time: 2-3 months. Payment: variable. Copyrights for author. ACP (Assoc. of Canadian Publishers).

Beynch Press Publishing Company, Alyce P. Cornyn-Selby, 1928 S.E. Ladd Avenue, Portland, OR 97214, 503-232-0433. 1986. Non-fiction. avg. press run 1M. Pub'd 2 titles 1990; expects 4 titles 1991, 4-6 titles 1992. 9 titles listed in the *Small Press Record of Books in Print* (20th Edition, 1991-92). avg. price, paper: $7.50-$9.95. 100pp; 4¼×5½. Reporting time: 1 month. Payment: each is different, $ and # of copies. Copyrights for author. Pacific Northwest Book Publishers Assn., Willamette Writers, Oregon Writers Colony, PMA.

Beyond Athletics, K.A. Lynch, In House Editor, 414 Aspen Court, Medford, NJ 08055, (609) 654-4050. 1986. Non-fiction. avg. press run 500. Pub'd 1 title 1990; expects 2 titles 1991. 1 title listed in the *Small Press Record of Books in Print* (20th Edition, 1991-92). avg. price, other: $29.95 + shipping. Discounts: 1/3. 175pp; 5½×8½; of. Payment: variable. Copyrights for author.

Beyond Baroque Foundation Publications (see also FOREHEAD: Writing & Art Journal), Benjamin Weissman, Editor, PO Box 2727, Venice, CA 90291, 213-822-3006. 1968. Poetry, fiction, art, criticism, reviews, non-fiction. "Books published occasionally: *Chinese Folk Poetry* translated by Cecilia Liang, 1982. *Harbinger,* fiction and poetry by Los Angeles writers, 1990. *Beyond Baroque Literary Small Press Library* consists of over 3M small press literary publications. Calendar of Events, Library borrowing privileges and *Membership* in Beyond Baroque Foundation available for $30 a year. The Library serves as an important link between the independent publisher and the public. It strongly urges publishers to contribute books and magazines to this lending library. In exchange Beyond Baroque will send its literary publications. The Los Angeles Public Library System has put *Beyond Baroque Library* on the SCAN system, one of California's regional resource centers. Beyond Baroque Small Press Bookstore is a distribution and marketing center for literary books and magazines. Interested publishers please send catalogue. Terms are consignment 60/40, payments quarterly. *Forehead* and Beyond Baroque Foundation Publications do publish unsolicited manuscripts" avg. press run 1M. Pub'd 1 title 1990; expects 1 title 1991, 1 title 1992. 2 titles listed in the *Small Press Record of Books in Print* (20th Edition, 1991-92). avg. price, paper: $6.50. No discounts. 150pp; 6×8; of. Payment: copies only. Copyrights for author. CCLM.

Beyond Words Publishing, Inc., Cynthia Black, Editor, 13950 NW Pumpkin Ridge Road, Hillsboro, OR 97123, 503-647-5109; 647-5114 FAX. 1983. Photos, non-fiction. "Photo books contain 100-200 photos and text of 20,000 words. Softcover titles 200 pages of text" avg. press run 10M. Pub'd 6 titles 1990; expects 8 titles 1991, 10 titles 1992. 21 titles listed in the *Small Press Record of Books in Print* (20th Edition, 1991-92). avg. price, cloth: $60, $39.95; paper: $12.95; other: $9.95 childrens. Discounts: bookstore standad 40%-high volume up to 45%. 200pp; 10×12, 9×7; of. Reporting time: 60 days. Payment: 10% royalty. Copyrights for author if requested. ABA, PMA.

Biblia Candida, 4466 Winterville Road, Spring Hill, FL 34606, 904-686-3527. 1986. Fiction. avg. press run 1M. Expects 2 titles 1991. 2 titles listed in the *Small Press Record of Books in Print* (20th Edition, 1991-92). avg. price, paper: $6.95. Discounts: standard. 100pp; 5×8: of.

Biblio Press, Doris B. Gold, Editor and Publisher, 1140 Broadway, R. 1507, New York, NY 10001, 212-684-1257. 1979. Non-fiction. "Jewish women's studies, (non-fiction) and significant reprint fiction; bibliographies, and reference materials on Jewish women. No poetry. Authors should not submit mss. Query first." avg. press run 1M-3M. Pub'd 3 titles 1990; expects 2 titles 1991, 1 title 1992. 5 titles listed in the *Small Press Record of Books in Print* (20th Edition, 1991-92). avg. price, cloth: $16; paper: $3.50-$11.95. Discounts: Women's bookstores get 40% plus other special discounts off;jobbers 25% or more, Judaica & religion bookstores 20% and up; our distributors generously discount. Up to 350pp; 6×9, 7×10; of. Reporting time: 3 weeks for queries. Payment: flat fee for mss and limited royalty arrangement. Copyrights for author. Assn. of Jewish Book Publishers, Distributors: Inland Book Co., East Haven, CT; Bookpeople, Berkeley, CA, Stermatzky, Israel, Bookslingers, Minneapolis; New Leaf Distrib; Atlanta.

Bibliographies Unlimited, PO Box 873, Conifer, CO 80433, 303-838-6964. 1989. Fiction, non-fiction. avg. press run 5M. Pub'd 2 titles 1990; expects 5 titles 1991. 2 titles listed in the *Small Press Record of Books in Print* (20th Edition, 1991-92). avg. price, other: $29.95. Discounts: please write. 200pp; 8½×11; laser-print/loose leaf bound. Reporting time: 30 days. Payment: please write. Does not copyright for author. COSMEP, PMA.

THE BIBLIOTHECK, H. Wright, c/o L.H. Davies, Glasgow Univ. Library, Hillhead Street, Glasgow G12 8QE, Scotland, 041-667-1011 X6732. 1956. Articles, reviews. circ. 300. 3/yr. Pub'd 3 issues 1990; expects 3 issues 1991, 3 issues 1992. sub. price: £10.25, $22 individual; £13, $27.50 institutional; per copy: £3.50, $8; sample: free. Discounts: reductions for bulk orders. 30pp; 6×8; of. Reporting time: 1 month. Payment: 6 offprints. Copyrighted, copyright to publishers and contributors. Pub's reviews: 8 in 1990. §Scottish bibliography. Ads: £40/£28.

BIBLIOTHEQUE D'HUMANISME ET RENAISSANCE, Librairie Droz S.A., A. Dufour, Librairie Droz S.A., 11r.Massot, 1211 Geneve 12, Switzerland. 1934. Articles, criticism, reviews. "History of 16th century" circ. 1M. 3/yr. Pub'd 3 issues 1990; expects 3 issues 1991. sub. price: 90 SW.FR ($73)-yr; per copy: 30 SW.FR. ($24). 300pp; 16×24cm; typography. Pub's reviews: 100 in 1990. §15th and 16th Centuries.

Bicentennial Era Enterprises, PO Box 1148, Scappoose, OR 97056, 503-684-3937. 1978. Criticism, news items. "The press is part of a larger operation designed to educate people to their monetary rights and to document the errors and false policies of government which have led to a loss of those rights." avg. press run 5M. Pub'd 1 title 1990. 2 titles listed in the *Small Press Record of Books in Print* (20th Edition, 1991-92). avg.

price, paper: $5; $8. Discounts: trade 40%; bulk and class 10%; agent, jobber by agreement. 166pp; 6×9; of. Reporting time: 2-4 weeks. Payment: by agreement. Does not copyright for author. none.

Bicycle Books (Publishing) Inc., Rob Van der Plas, PO Box 2038, Mill Valley, CA 94941, 415-381-2515. 1985. Photos, news items, non-fiction. "Length of material: 200 pages. Biases: only bicycle related books. Recent contributor: Samuel Abt, Jim Langley" avg. press run 8M. Pub'd 4 titles 1990; expects 4 titles 1991, 4 titles 1992. 17 titles listed in the *Small Press Record of Books in Print* (20th Edition, 1991-92). avg. price, cloth: $19.95; paper: $9.95. Discounts: 1-2 25%, 3-99 40%, 100-249 45%, 250 + 50%. 160pp; 6×9; Ventura publisher, linotype. Reporting time: 6 months. Payment: on an individual basis 7.5% retail or 15% net. Copyrights for author. PMA, MSPA, ABA.

The Bieler Press, Gerald Lange, USC-Research Annex 122, 3716 South Hope Street, Los Angeles, CA 90007-4377, 213-743-3939. 1975. 15 titles listed in the *Small Press Record of Books in Print* (20th Edition, 1991-92).

BIG CIGARS, Jose Padua, Stephen Ciacciarelli, Michael Randall, The P.O.N. Press, 1625 Hobart Street NW, Washington, DC 20009. 1986. Poetry, fiction, art, photos, cartoons, collages. "Length: Poems of any length. Fiction pieces are usually brief, but we will use longer works on occasion. Biases: No academic self-indulgence. Our favorite writers are Bukowski, Beckett, and Bowles. These people, of course, refuse to have anything to do with us. On the other hand, William Burroughs said of us, 'They publish the best biker fiction east of the Mississippi, but I hear they're moving on to bigger and better things now.' Recent contributors: Patrick McKinnon, Jennifer Blowdryer, Todd Moore, Ron Kolm, Bina Sharif" circ. 300. 2/yr. Pub'd 1 issue 1990; expects 2 issues 1991, 2 issues 1992. price per copy: $4; sample: $5 pp. Back issues: none. Discounts: none. 40pp; 8½×11; xerox, with printed plastic covers. Reporting time: 4-5 months. Payment: copy of magazine. Copyrighted, reverts to author.

BIG HAMMER, David Roskos, Editor, PO Box 1698, New Brunswick, NJ 08901, 908-249-2645. 1988. Poetry, art, photos, cartoons. "I believe that a good writer knocks the wind out of her/his readers, puts them through an emotional experience, cuts through all the crap and goes straight to the heart of the situation, breaks reality down to its lowest common denominator with the precision of a surgeon's scalpel. Slice of life cut with a chainsaw. Autobiographical writings that come out of experience; fragments of memory from survivors of child abuse, domestic violence, rape, war, racism, poverty, institutionalized medicine/the A.M.A., etc. listening for what Blake called 'the voice of the devil,' poems with a sense of urgency. A blend of objectivism and lyricism, 'compassionate realism.' I also like straightup lyrical poems, love poems, sonnets, industrial and work poems, ecopoetry, and poems by children. *Big Hammer* is very eclectic. Your best bet is to read a copy before mailing on mss." circ. 750-1M. Published every 2 years. Expects 1 issue 1991. sub. price: $6 + 29¢ stamp; per copy: same; sample: $6 + 29¢ stamp. Back issues: same. Discounts: 60/40. 100-140pp; 8½×11; of. Reporting time: 1 day to 6 months. Payment: 1 or 2 copies. Copyrighted, reverts to author. Ads: $150/$70/$40 1/4 page/$25 business card.

Big River Publishing, John Derevlany, 1321 Washington Street, Hoboken, NJ 07030, 201-798-7800. 1987. News items, non-fiction. "Interested in real estate and urban-related issues. We like material that is timely and human, rather than academic" avg. press run 10M. Expects 1 title 1991, 1 title 1992. 1 title listed in the *Small Press Record of Books in Print* (20th Edition, 1991-92). avg. price, paper: $7.95. Discounts: 40% to stores, 50% to distributors, 50% for orders of 100+ books. 208pp; 6×9; of. Reporting time: 4 months. Payment: negotiable. Copyrights for author.

BIG SCREAM, Nada Press, David Cope, 2782 Dixie S.W., Grandville, MI 49418, 616-531-1442. 1974. Poetry, fiction, art. "We include 2-5 pages of each writer publ.- some longpoems tend to have imagist bias; prefer *personal* poems. Contributors: David Cope, Andy Clausen, James Ruggia,Janet Cannon, Jim Cohn, Antler, Jeff Poniewaz, Bob Rixon, Allen Ginsberg, George Drury. Poets and writers *must* include SASE with their submissions." circ. 100-150. 1/yr. Pub'd 2 issues 1990; expects 1 issue 1991, 1 issue 1992. sub. price: $3; per copy: $3; sample: $3. Back issues: $3 per copy. 35pp; 8½×11; photo offset. Reporting time: 1 week - 1 month. Payment: 1 copy, more if requested.

Big Sky Press, 653 N. Laurel Avenue, Los Angeles, CA 90048, 213-653-0444. 1 title listed in the *Small Press Record of Books in Print* (20th Edition, 1991-92).

BikePress U.S.A./BikePress Canada, Phillip Norton, Editor & Publisher, 492 Covey Hill Road, Franklin Centre, P.Q. J0S 1E0, Canada, 412-625-1180. 1982. Photos, non-fiction. "Backpacking, canoeing, nature, environmental issues, outdoor sports, especially bicycling. Planning a series entitled *Bikepacking Into Countrysides & Lifestyles* - each edition to cover a different part of the world. The first edition covers Eastern North America. Newly published book of reprinted articles on forest decline and acid rain, the only reference on the topic for the non-scientific community. 1988" avg. press run 1.5M. Expects 1 title 1991, 1 title 1992. 1 title listed in the *Small Press Record of Books in Print* (20th Edition, 1991-92). avg. price, paper: $5.50 U.S.; $6.50 Canada. Discounts: Wholesale 50%, stores 40%, libraries 20%. 112pp; 6×9; of. Reporting time:

immediate with SASE. Copyrights for author.

BIKEREPORT, Daniel D'Ambrosio, PO Box 8308, Missoula, MT 59807, (406) 721-1776. 1974. Fiction, articles, cartoons, interviews, news items, non-fiction. circ. 18M. 9/yr. Pub'd 9 issues 1990; expects 9 issues 1991, 9 issues 1992. 24pp; 8¾×10⅞; of. Reporting time: 1 month. Payment: 3¢/word. Copyrighted, reverts to author. Ads: $900/$495.

Bilingual Review/Press (see also BILINGUAL REVIEW/Revista Bilingue), Gary D. Keller, General Editor; Karen S. Van Hooft, Managing Editor, Hispanic Research Center, Arizona State University, Tempe, AZ 85287-2702, 602-965-3867. 1976. Poetry, fiction, articles, criticism, plays. "We publish U.S. Hispanic creative literature (fiction, poetry, drama) and scholarly monographs and collections of articles in the following areas: U.S. Hispanic language and literature, Chicano and Puerto Rican studies, contemporary methods of literary analysis" avg. press run 1M cloth, 2M paper. Pub'd 10 titles 1990; expects 12 titles 1991, 12 titles 1992. 87 titles listed in the *Small Press Record of Books in Print* (20th Edition, 1991-92). avg. price, cloth: $18; paper: $10. Discounts: 20% for textbooks; trade—1-4 copies 20%, 5-24 40%, 25-99 42%, 100+ 43%. 256pp; 5½×8½; of. Reporting time: 8-10 weeks. Payment: varies from author subsidy with repayment to author from royalties on copies sold, to standard 10% royalty with no subsidy, depending on commercial prospects of book. We copyright in our name. COSMEP, CCLM.

BILINGUAL REVIEW/Revista Bilingue, Bilingual Review/Press, Gary D. Keller, Editor; Karen S. Van Hooft, Managing Editor, Hispanic Research Center, Arizona State University, Tempe, AZ 85287-2702, 602-965-3867. 1974. Poetry, fiction, articles, interviews, criticism, reviews. "Research and scholarly articles dealing with bilingualism, primarily but not exclusively Spanish-English; U.S.-Hispanic literature; English-Spanish contrastive linguistics; fiction, poetry, etc., concerning Hispanic life in the U.S." circ. 1M. 3/yr. Pub'd 3 issues 1990; expects 3 issues 1991, 3 issues 1992. sub. price: $16 individuals, $26 institutions; per copy: $9 institutions, $6 individuals; sample: $9 institutions; $6 individuals. Back issues: depends on issue. Discounts: none. 96pp; 7×10; of. Reporting time: 6-8 weeks. Payment: 2 complimentary copies of issue. Copyrighted, does not revert to author. Pub's reviews: 9 in 1990. §Books dealing with our primary areas of interest: bilingualism, U.S. Hispanic literature. Ads: $150/$90/2-pg spread $250, back cover $200, inside back cover $175. CCLM, COSMEP.

Bilingue Publications, Robert C. Medina, PO Drawer H, Las Cruces, NM 88004, 505-526-1557. 1975. Fiction, plays. avg. press run 1M. Pub'd 1 title 1990; expects 1 title 1991, 1 title 1992. 4 titles listed in the *Small Press Record of Books in Print* (20th Edition, 1991-92). avg. price, paper: $3.50. Discounts: 40%. 140pp; 6×8. Reporting time: 3 months. We help authors with copyright.

BIOLOGY DIGEST, Plexus Publishing, Inc., Mary Suzanne Hogan, 143 Old Marlton Pike, Medford, NJ 08055, 609-654-6500. 1977. Non-fiction. "*Biology Digest* is an abstracting journal with subject and author indexes. Each issue also contains a full-length original feature article on some life science subject of particular timely interest. We also publish an annual cumulative index" circ. 2M. 9/yr. Pub'd 9 issues 1990; expects 9 issues 1991, 9 issues 1992. sub. price: $125; per copy: $15; sample: $15. Back issues: same. Discounts: $5 subscription agency. 170pp; 8½×11; of. Reporting time: 60 days. Payment: $250 per article. Copyrighted, does not revert to author. Pub's reviews: 32 books in 1990. §Biology, life sciences, medicine, health, ecology. Ads: $200.

Bio-Probe, Inc., Sam Ziff, PO Box 580160, Orlando, FL 32858-0160, 407-299-4149. 1984. Non-fiction. "Last book 448 pages. Heavy metals, toxicity, biochemistry, dental materials and their effect on health. Most subjects dealing with health" avg. press run 5M. Pub'd 2 titles 1990; expects 1 title 1991, 2 titles 1992. avg. price, cloth: $18.95; paper: $14.95. Discounts: universal. 225-448pp; 6×9. Payment: negotiated % on wholesale—every 6 months. Copyrights for author. National Association of Independent Publishers (NAIP), PO Box 850, Moore Haven, FL 33471; Florida Publishers Group (FPG), PO Box 262261, Tampa, FL 33685.

Birch Brook Press, Tom Tolnay, RD 1 Box 620, Delhi, NY 13753, 212-353-3326. 1982. Poetry, fiction. "Birch Brook Press does not solicit or read unsolicited manuscripts. We have our own complete letterpress print shop and we use monies from commercial work to do some original books on a project-by-project basis, soliciting material for each. Our latest, for example, are *Baseball & The Game of Life* and *Editors in the Stream*. Both projects are now completed. We also do some printing/typesetting (in metal)/designing for other publishers, and sometimes do books of unusual quality on a co-op basis. Though popular culture is our main interest, we do two books of literary poetry each year. Recent titles include *Abreactions* by Marcus Rome and *Immigrant* by Stanley Nelson. Some of our books are made entirely by hand, and these are sold as limited editions." avg. press run 250-1M. Pub'd 4 titles 1990; expects 4 titles 1991, 4 titles 1992. 5 titles listed in the *Small Press Record of Books in Print* (20th Edition, 1991-92). avg. price, cloth: $25; paper: $10; other: $40-$100 limited editions. Discounts: 1 copy 32%, 2-4 36%, 5-9 38%, 10-15 40%; these discounts do not apply to limited editions. 64-232pp; 5½×8½; †lp. Payment: 5-10%. Copyrights for author. Small Press Center, NYC.

BIRD WATCHER'S DIGEST, Mary Beacom Bowers, PO Box 110, Marietta, OH 45750, 614-373-5285.

1978. Poetry, articles, art, photos, cartoons, interviews, reviews, letters, news items, non-fiction. "600-3,000 words; we publish only material that deals with birds or bird watching, although of course conservation and environmental issues figure importantly. Recent contributors: John K. Terres, Donald Stokes, Peter Dunne, Alan Pistorius; Roger Tory Peterson writes a regular feature for each issue" circ. 85M. 6/yr. Pub'd 6 issues 1990; expects 6 issues 1991, 6 issues 1992. sub. price: $15.95; per copy: $2.75; sample: $3.50. Back issues: $17 for volume of 6. 136pp; 5x8; of. Reporting time: 8 weeks. Payment: from $50 per article (original); $25 for reprints upon publication. Copyrighted, reverts to author. Pub's reviews: 50 in 1990. §Cnly on birds, bird watching, or related natural history field (staff-written). Ads: B&W $921.25, 4-color $1834/$1.50 per word (20 word min.). ASME, SRDS.

Birdalone Books, Viola Roth, 508 N. College Avenue, Suite #333, Bloomington, IN 47404-3831, 812-333-0167. 1988. Poetry, fiction, criticism, music, long-poems, non-fiction. "Primary interest is in the facsimile reprinting, via offset lithography, of obscure out-of-print literature (e.g. William Morris) and music. Specialty is in high-*quality* production, especially of the binding, which is all done by hand. Any volume is also available in half- or full-leather (goat or calf), completely hand-sewn and hand-bound, with authentic, *sewn* silk headbands. All acid-free papers and boards; skins are pared by hand (no bonded leather!). Bindery will also do repairs and restoration of customers' other books, at competitive prices. No unsolicited mss., please." avg. press run 500. Pub'd 1 title 1990; expects 1 title 1991, 1 title 1992. 1 title listed in the *Small Press Record of Books in Print* (20th Edition, 1991-92). avg. price, cloth: $35; other: $35-pa binders' boards; $90-half goat; $115-half calf;$125-full goal;$150, full calf. Discounts: 1 copy 10%, 5+ copies 20%. 306pp; 4⅛x6¼; of.

BIRMINGHAM POETRY REVIEW, Robert Collins, Editor; Randy Blythe, Associate Editor, English Department, University of Alabama-Birmingham, Birmingham, AL 35294, 205-934-8573. 1988. Poetry. "Poetry of any length or style. We are interested in publishing work on the cutting edge of contemporary poetry." circ. 500. 2/yr. Expects 2 issues 1991, 2 issues 1992. sub. price: $3; per copy: $1; sample: $2. 50pp; 6x9; of. Reporting time: 1-3 months. Payment: 2 copies, plus a one year subscription. Copyrighted, reverts to author.

Birth Day Publishing Company, PO Box 7722, San Diego, CA 92107, 619-296-3194. 1975. Poetry, articles, art, photos, interviews, reviews, letters, non-fiction. "We publish material dealing with spirituality in general and, in particular, the life and teachings of an Indian holy man named Sri Sathya Sai Baba. Published material has been book length, non-fiction. Recent contributors include Samuel H. Sandweiss, M.D., Dr. John S. Hislop, Ph.D, and Howard Murphet. Ms by invitation only" avg. press run 5M. Pub'd 2 titles 1990; expects 3 titles 1991, 3 titles 1992. 9 titles listed in the *Small Press Record of Books in Print* (20th Edition, 1991-92). avg. price, paper: $6.40/$9. Discounts: book trade 40%, bulk 50%, classroom/library 40%, jobber 50%. 225pp; 5½x8½; of. Payment: usually none. Copyrights for author. COSMEP, SSA.

The Biting Idge/Miracle Press (Chrysalis Publications), N.L. ('Sam') Stricker, Publisher and Editor, 581 South 6th Street, German Village, Columbus, OH 43206-1274. 1982. Fiction, satire, non-fiction. "Fiction titles illustrated" avg. press run varies. Expects 2 titles 1991, 2 titles 1992. 3 titles listed in the *Small Press Record of Books in Print* (20th Edition, 1991-92). avg. price, paper: $4.95; other: $6.95 for hard/handbound. 100pp; 5½x8½; †of.

BITTERROOT, Menke Katz, Editor-in-Chief, PO Box 489, Spring Glen, NY 12483. 1962. Poetry, reviews. "We shall always discourage stereotyped forms in poetry which imitate fixed patterns and leave no individual mark. We shall inspire all poets who seek their own identity through original poetry, realistic or fantastic. Many of our poets see *Bitterroot* as a palm in a desert" circ. 1M. 3/yr. Pub'd 3 issues 1990; expects 3 issues 1991, 3 issues 1992. sub. price: $15/1 yr, $25/2 yrs, $36/3 yrs. Foreign & Canada please add $3 per year for postage & handling; per copy: $6; sample: $6. Back issues: complete set of 90 issues/$950. Discounts: 10%. 72pp; 5½x8½; of, computer printing. Reporting time: about 1 month-6 weeks, must send SASE. Payment: 1 copy. Copyrighted, reverts to author. Pub's reviews: 36 in 1990. §Poetry. Ads: $100/$50. CLMP, COSMEP.

BkMk Press, Dan Jaffe, Director, University of Missouri-Kansas City, 109 Scofield Hall, Kansas City, MO 64110, 276-2558. 1971. Poetry, long-poems, plays, concrete art. "*BkMk Press* ordinarily publishes non-commercial materials of high quality & cultural significance, poetry, translations, etc" avg. press run 750. Pub'd 5 titles 1990; expects 6 titles 1991. 36 titles listed in the *Small Press Record of Books in Print* (20th Edition, 1991-92). avg. price, cloth: $9; paper: $6. Discounts: Trade, 40%. 75pp; 5½x8½; of. Reporting time: 5 months. Payment: permission fee & free copies. Copyrights for author.

BLACK AMERICAN LITERATURE FORUM, Joseph Weixlmann, Indiana State University, Dept. of English, Terre Haute, IN 47809, 812-237-2968. 1967. Poetry, articles, art, photos, interviews, criticism, reviews. circ. 1250. 4/yr. Pub'd 4 issues 1990; expects 4 issues 1991, 4 issues 1992. sub. price: $20 individuals, $32 institutions (foreign add $5); per copy: $8.50; sample: $8.50. Back issues: $8.50. Discounts: 40%. 200pp; 6x9; †of. Reporting time: 3 months. Payment: 1 copy, plus offprints. Indiana State Univ. holds copyright on entire issue, author on individual article/poem. Pub's reviews: 19 in 1990. §Black American literature. Ads:

68

$150/$90. CCLM, COSMEP, Society for Scholarly Publishing.

Black & White & Read All Over Publishing Co., Irene Schultz, PO Box 452, Lake Bluff, IL 60044, 312-295-1077. 1984. Fiction. "Children's full-length novels for 8 through 14 year olds reading at a 2nd grade recreational level. Set sells at $26.70. Not accepting manuscripts at this time" avg. press run 2M. Pub'd 6 titles 1990; expects 6 titles 1991, 6 titles 1992. avg. price, paper: $4.95; other: $26.70 set. Discounts: none. 128pp; 5½×7¾; of. CRRT, IRC, ACLD.

Black Bear Publications (see also BLACK BEAR REVIEW), Ave Jeanne, Ron Zettlemoyer, 1916 Lincoln Street, Croydon, PA 19021-8026, 215-788-3543. 1984. Poetry, articles, art, reviews. "Chapbook publications depends upon funding at present times. Usually no more than 3 per year. Manuscripts should reflect Black Bear image. Contributors should have a good knowledge of Black Bear and have worked with us before. Query with cover letter, bio and samples. "Be prepared to get honest comments". We have recently published *Our National Tapestry* by Steven Levi and *The Governor's Office* by James Doyle. Samples available for $3 ppd. in the US and Canada. Illustrators receive cash payment on acceptance for illustrating our chapbooks. Query for current titles. Our main objective is to get more poets into print and off the streets. If we can't print you, we will help you find a market who will. "Talk to us, we actually listen"" avg. press run 500. Pub'd 3 titles 1990; expects 3 titles 1991, 3 titles 1992. 8 titles listed in the *Small Press Record of Books in Print* (20th Edition, 1991-92). avg. price, paper: $4. 30pp; 5½×8½; of. Reporting time: 1 month. Payment: in copies. Copyrights for author.

BLACK BEAR REVIEW, Black Bear Publications, Ave Jeanne, Poetry & Art Editor; Ron Zettlemoyer, Black Bear Publications, 1916 Lincoln Street, Croydon, PA 19021, 215-788-3543. 1984. Poetry, art, reviews, collages. "We like to see poetry that is potent. Forms used are avant-garde, free verse and haiku. Length limit of 100 lines. We would like to see artwork in black & white, (no originals, prefer photocopies) signed by author. Poets published: John Elsberg, Ivan Arguelles, Andrew Gettler, John Grey, Jon Daunt, A. D. Winans. Artists published: Nancy Glazer, deMerle, James Michael Dorsey, Robert Bixby" circ. 500. 2/yr. Expects 2 issues 1991, 2 issues 1992. sub. price: $9; per copy: $5; sample: $5. Back issues: $3. Discounts: 40%. 64pp; 5½×8½; of. Reporting time: 2 weeks. Payment: contributor copy. Copyrighted, reverts to author. Pub's reviews: 25 in 1990. §Social, political, ecological. Ads: $45/$25.

Black Buzzard Press (see also VISIONS, International, The World Journal of Illustrated Poetry; BLACK BUZZARD REVIEW), Bradley R. Strahan, 1110 Seaton Lane, Falls Church, VA 22046. 1979. Poetry, art. "No unsolicited manuscripts! *The Black Buzzard Illustrated Chapbook Series* currently has 10 volumes inprint: *Dada Dog* by Larry Couch, *In Wicked Times* by Aaron Kramer, *New Love Songs For An Age of Anxiety* by B.R. Strahan, *The Copper Lantern* by K. Freivalds, *Native Steel* by Tom Wells, and *White Lies* by Lane Jennings. *Picnics* by David Breeden, *Silvija, A Riga Nocturine* by Karlis Freivalds" avg. press run 200-700. Expects 1 title 1991, 1 title 1992. 9 titles listed in the *Small Press Record of Books in Print* (20th Edition, 1991-92). avg. price, paper: $4. Discounts: 20 or more 40%. 32pp; 5½×8½; of. Reporting time: 2 weeks to 2 months. Payment: by arrangement. Copyrights for author. CLMP.

BLACK BUZZARD REVIEW, Black Buzzard Press, Bradley R. Strahan, 1110 Seaton Lane, Falls Church, VA 22046. 1988. Poetry. "We decided to publish this informal journal as a supplement to our successful, long running international magazine *Visions*, which has become more and more occupied with translations and special projects. *BBR* prints only original work in English (poetry) no translations, no reprints, *rarely* will do non U.S.A. work. We are *wide open* to a wide variety of poems. All poems should be less than 40 lines, not previously published or submitted elsewhere and *must include a SASE* with adequate postage. Strongly suggest reading a sample before submitting work. A sample is worth a thousand words of description" circ. 300. 1/yr. Pub'd 1 issue 1990; expects 1 issue 1991, 1 issue 1992. sub. price: $2.50 w/sub. to *Visions* (total would be $16/yr); per copy: $4.50; sample: $3.50. Discounts: none. 32pp; 8½×11; of. Reporting time: 2 days to 2 months. Payment: copy. Not copyrighted. VIAS, CLMP.

THE BLACK FLY REVIEW, Wendy Kindred, Roland Burns, University of Maine at Fort Kent, Fort Kent, ME 04743, 207-834-3162. 1980. Poetry, fiction. "So far we have only published poetry and short fiction but we remain open to other possibilities. Preference for concise writing and strong imagery. Recent contributors include Terry Plunkett, Susan Atherton, Norma Voorhees Sheard, Robert M. Chute, Walter McDonald" circ. 1M. 1/yr. Pub'd 1 issue 1990; expects 1 issue 1991, 1 issue 1992. sub. price: $3; per copy: $3; sample: $3. Back issues: $3. Discounts: by arrangement. 60pp; 5½×8½. Reporting time: 1-4 months, manuscripts received Sept-Dec. only. Payment: in copies (5). Copyrighted, reverts to author. MPW.

Black Hat Press (see also RAG MAG), Beverly Voldseth, Editor & Publisher, Box 12, Goodhue, MN 55027, 612-923-4590. 1989. Poetry, fiction, articles, art, photos, cartoons, interviews, satire, criticism, reviews, letters, long-poems, plays, non-fiction. "Just send your best stuff" avg. press run 200. Pub'd 2 titles 1990; expects 1 title 1992. 5 titles listed in the *Small Press Record of Books in Print* (20th Edition, 1991-92). avg. price, paper: $6. Discounts: 40%. 80pp; 5½×8½; of. Reporting time: 2-3 months. Payment: varies. Does not copyright for author. CCLM, COSMEP.

BLACK HERITAGE UNVEILED NEWSLETTER, Spencer's Int'l Enterprises Corp., PO Box 43822, Los Angeles, CA 90043. 1989. "Research in black heritage and notes and subjects that encourage creating a worldwide goal for people of black heritage to rise above their present condition" 2-4pp.

Black Heron Press, Jerry Gold, PO Box 95676, Seattle, WA 98145. 1984. Fiction. "May do something other than fiction, if it appeals to us" avg. press run 1M. Pub'd 2 titles 1990; expects 2 titles 1991, 2 titles 1992. 8 titles listed in the *Small Press Record of Books in Print* (20th Edition, 1991-92). avg. price, cloth: $17.50; paper: $8.50. Discounts: 2-4 copies 20%, 5-9 30%, 10-24 40%, 25-49 42%, 50-74 44%, 75-99 46%, 100-199 48%, 200+ 50%. 170pp; 5½x8½; of. Reporting time: 2-3 months. Payment: 10% of retail price of book, payment semiannually. Copyrights for author. COSMEP.

BLACK ICE, Ronald Sukenick, Editor; Dallas Wiebe, Associate Editor, English Department Publications Center, Box 494, University of Colorado, Boulder, CO 80309-0001, 617-484-2048. 1984. Fiction. "Fiction only. The best work of fiction published in the issue will receive the $500 Margaret Jones Fiction Award. Guidelines: very innovative work only. We suggest familiarity with th magazine, as in appropriate work will be returned without comment. All submissions must be under 35 pages (total), with SASE. Computer print-outs OK. Contributors include: Steve Katz, Tom Glynn, Alain Arias-Misson, Mark Amerika, Erik Belgum, DC Berry, Welch Everman, Lissa McLaughlin *Black Ice* is distributed by Bookslinger" circ. 500. 3/yr. Pub'd 1 issue 1990; expects 3 issues 1991, 3 issues 1992. 4 titles listed in the *Small Press Record of Books in Print* (20th Edition, 1991-92). sub. price: 3 issues $15 (3 years); per copy: $7; sample: $7. Back issues: $4, $5, $6. Discounts: standard to distributors. 90pp; 5½x8½; of. Reporting time: 3 months. Payment: 2 copies. Copyrighted, reverts to author.

BLACK JACK & VALLEY GRAPEVINE, Seven Buffaloes Press, Art Cuelho, Box 249, Big Timber, MT 59011. 1973. Poetry, fiction, art, photos, interviews, reviews, parts-of-novels, long-poems, collages. "*Black Jack*: rural poems & stories from anywhere in America, especially the West, the Appalachias, Oklahoma, and the Ozarks. Work that tells a story, a craft that shows experience, not only of the head (technique), but of the heart (passion and compassion). I'm more than prejudiced against poems that are made up or forced, even when they are concocted out of the supposed wisdom of some established school. A 'school' is nothing more than a group of individuals sitting in one communal literary lap. Give me a loner on his foggy mountaintop; at least the fog is from the mountain, not from his song or his tale to tell. *Valley Grapevine* takes material native to Central California...the San Joaquin and Sacramento Valleys. Especially want work from small town farming communities, but will look at non-rural city work too.Focus on Okies, hoboes, ranch life, migrant labor, the Dustbowl era, and heritage and pride. Want writers and poets who write predominately of the valley of their birth. Contributors: Gerry Haslam, Wilma McDaniel, Richard Dokey, Dorothy Rose, Morine Stanley, Frank Cross, William Rintoul." circ. 750. 1/yr. Pub'd 1 issue 1990; expects 1 issue 1991, 1 issue 1992. price per copy: $5 to $6.75 postpaid; sample: $4.75. Back issues: none. Discounts: 1-4, 0%; 5 copies or over, 40%. 80pp; 5½x8½; †of. Reporting time: within a week, often a day or two. Payment: copies, often other free copies. Copyrighted, reverts to author. No ads. CLMP.

Black Light Fellowship, PO Box 5369, Chicago, IL 60680, 312-722-1441. 1976. Non-fiction. "Street address: Black Light Fellowship, 2859 W. Wilcox, Chicago, IL, 60612" avg. press run 6M. Pub'd 2 titles 1990; expects 2+ titles 1991. 6 titles listed in the *Small Press Record of Books in Print* (20th Edition, 1991-92). avg. price, paper: $12. Discounts: 20% short, 40% trade, 50% distributors. 200pp; 5½x8½.

BLACK MOUNTAIN REVIEW, Lorien House, David A. Wilson, PO Box 1112, Black Mountain, NC 28711-1112. 1987. Poetry, fiction, articles, non-fiction. "The themes are American writers. An SASE gives current themes, requirements, and payment rate. *Please* do not submit until you read the guidelines. Coming up are Hemingway, Williams, Sandburg." circ. 200. 1/yr. Pub'd 2 issues 1990; expects 1 issue 1992. sub. price: $4 per issue; per copy: $4; sample: $4 + $1 shipping. Back issues: $3.50. Discounts: 40% 5 copies/write for info. 48pp; 8½x5½; †of. Reporting time: 1 week queries. Payment: yes, listed on guidelines. Copyrighted, revert 1 year after publication. Pub's reviews: 1 in 1990. §books that fit the themes. Ads: $80/$45/$25 (1/4 page.

BLACK MULLET REVIEW, Jubilee Press, Gina Bergamino-Frey, PO Box 22814, Tampa, FL 33622. 1986. Poetry, fiction, art, reviews, concrete art. "Prefers poems less than 1 page; short, clever, fiction; welcomes black and white art. Recent contributors: Patrick McKinnon, Lyn Lifshin, Michael Hathaway" circ. 250. 2/yr. Pub'd 1 issue 1990; expects 2 issues 1991, 2 issues 1992. price per copy: $3.00; sample: $3.00. Back issues: $3.00. Discounts: bulk orders of 10+ receive 40% discount. 32-48pp; 5¼x8½; †of. Reporting time: 2 weeks on most. Payment: 2 copies. Copyrighted, reverts to author. Pub's reviews. §Poetry, fiction, art.

Black Oak Press, Tom Jennings, May Richards, PO Box 4663, University Place Station, Lincoln, NE 68504. 1978. Poetry. "Experimental, satirical material, children's stories. dada/surrealism. Query before submission" avg. press run 1M. Pub'd 2 titles 1990; expects 3 titles 1991, 3-5 titles 1992. 9 titles listed in the *Small Press Record of Books in Print* (20th Edition, 1991-92). avg. price, cloth: $6; paper: $3. Discounts: 20%. 64pp;

5½×8½; of, lp. Reporting time: 3-6 weeks. Payment: negotiable. Copyrights for author.

BLACK RIVER REVIEW, Kaye Coller, Editor; Deborah S. Glaefke, Associate Editor, 855 Mildred, Lorain, OH 44052, 216-244-9654. 1985. Poetry, fiction, articles, art, cartoons, satire, criticism, reviews, non-fiction. "Our main focus is contemporary poetry, fiction, and essay. Too much of what we get seems to have the same style, expression, tone, and/or subject matter. I feel sometimes as if I were reading the same mss over and over. Therefore, besides technical excellence, we look for writing that has a unique voice, energy, freshness, and depth. Please send prose and poetry separately if possible. Recent contributors: James Margorian, Adrian Louis, Stephen Dunning, Catherine Hammond, Sylvia Foley, Leslie Leyland Fields, Richard Kostelanetz. We also need black & white, camera-ready artwork" circ. 400. 1/yr. Pub'd 1 issue 1990; expects 1 issue 1991, 1 issue 1992. price per copy: $3.50 (any 2 issues $6). Back issues: $3. 60pp; 8½×11; of. Reporting time: submission period is January 1 to May 1, we report in June. Payment: copies. Copyrighted, reverts to author. Pub's reviews: 5 in 1990. §Poetry, fiction, non-fiction (relating to the arts). Ads: $100/$50/$30¼/$20⅛/$10 business card.

Black Rose Books Ltd. (see also OUR GENERATION), D. Roussopoulos, 3981 St. Laurent Blvd., #444, Montreal, Que H2W 1Y2, Canada, 514-844-4076. 1970. Non-fiction. "USA address: 340 Nagel Drive, Cheektowaga, NY 14225, (716) 683-4547. Published over 100 books" avg. press run 3M. Pub'd 10 titles 1990; expects 12 titles 1991, 10 titles 1992. 50 titles listed in the *Small Press Record of Books in Print* (20th Edition, 1991-92). avg. price, cloth: $29.95; paper: $14.95. Discounts: regular trade discount. 200pp; 6×9; of. Reporting time: 6 months. Payment: 10% of list price. Copyrights for author. Association of Canadian Publishers.

THE BLACK SCHOLAR: Journal of Black Studies and Research, Robert Chrisman, Editor; JoNina M. Abron, Managing Editor; Tony M. Tingle, PO Box 2869, Oakland, CA 94609, 415-547-6633. 1969. Poetry, articles, art, photos, interviews, criticism, reviews, music. "Manuscripts for full-length articles may range in length from 2M to 5M words, include brief biographical statement, typewritten, double spaced. Articles may be historical and documented, they may be analytic and theoretical; they may be speculative. However, an article should not simply be a 'rap'; it should present a solid point of view convincingly and thoroughly argued. Recent Contributors: Jesse Jackson, Manning Marable, Jayne Cortez, Sonia Sanchez, Jack O'Dell, Audre Lorde" circ. 15M. 4/yr. Pub'd 4 issues 1990; expects 4 issues 1991. sub. price: $30 individual, $50 institution; per copy: $5. Back issues: $6. Discounts: Publishers discount of 10% off above rates. 80pp; 7×10; of. Reporting time: 1-2 months. Payment: in contributors copies of magazine and 1 year subscription. Rights become property of the *Black Scholar*. Pub's reviews: 22 in 1990. §The black experience or black related books. Ads: $1,100/$660/quarter page $500/classified $200 for 50 words or less, over 50 words add $22 per line per 7 words. CLMP.

Black Sparrow Press, 24 Tenth Street, Santa Rosa, CA 95401. 1966. Poetry, fiction, criticism, letters. "See our publications." avg. press run 2.5M. Pub'd 11 titles 1990; expects 12 titles 1991, 12 titles 1992. 192 titles listed in the *Small Press Record of Books in Print* (20th Edition, 1991-92). avg. price, cloth: $20; paper: $12. Discounts: trade 20%-46%. 150-300pp; 6×9; of, lp. Reporting time: 60 days. Payment: royalty on sales. Copyrights for author.

Black Swan Books Ltd., John J. Walsh, Publisher, PO Box 327, Redding Ridge, CT 06876, 203-938-9548. 1978. Poetry, fiction, art, music, letters. avg. press run 1M. Pub'd 6 titles 1990; expects 10 titles 1991, 10 titles 1992. 45 titles listed in the *Small Press Record of Books in Print* (20th Edition, 1991-92). avg. price, cloth: $17.50; paper: $6/$7.50. Discounts: bookstores 1-4 20%, 5-9 30%, 10-50 40%, 51-99 43%, 100+ 45%. 120pp; 5½×8½; of, lp. Copyrights for author.

Black Tie Press, Peter Gravis, Publisher, Editor; John Dunivent, Art Consultant; Harry Burrus, Associate Editor & Designer, PO Box 440004, Houston, TX 77244-0004, 713-789-5119. 1986. Poetry, art, photos, collages. "We are not a magazine, we publish books. Send ms. with 30-60 poems. We like the unusual, the wild, and rough, sensual and erotic. Narrative poems must provoke, startle. No rhymed material. We want writing that sits in the flame, that ignites the reader's imagination" avg. press run 250+. Pub'd 7 titles 1990; expects 7-12 titles 1991, 5-7 titles 1992. 17 titles listed in the *Small Press Record of Books in Print* (20th Edition, 1991-92). avg. price, cloth: $19.95, limited editions are more; paper: $10.50; other: $28 signed and lettered. Discounts: available upon request, 40% bookstores, special discounts for libraries and foreign bookstores. Much smaller discounts on limited editions. 40-112pp; 6×9, 5½×8½; offset, limited editions may be letter press. Reporting time: 2-12 weeks depending on material, time of year. Sometimes, due to the volume we receive, it may be several months before a writer hears from us regarding his ms. We acknowledge receipt straight away. Payment: may depend on material and author, usually 10% of press run. Copyrights for author. COSMEP, Small Press Center (NY).

THE BLACK WARRIOR REVIEW, Glenn Mott, Editor; James H.N. Martin, Poetry Editor; Nicola Williams, Fiction Editor, P.O. Box 2936, University of Alabama, Tuscaloosa, AL 35487, 205-348-4518. 1974. Poetry, fiction, art, photos, interviews, reviews, parts-of-novels, long-poems. "Publish high quality contemporary fiction and poetry. Recent contributors include Tony Ardizzone, Jorie Graham, Sherod Santos,

Linda Gregg, Dennis Johnson" circ. 1.5M. 2/yr. Pub'd 2 issues 1990; expects 2 issues 1991. sub. price: $9; per copy: $5; sample: $5. Back issues: $3.50. Discounts: none at present. 144pp; 6×9; of. Reporting time: 4 weeks to 3 months. Payment: 2 copies of magazine; 2 annual $500 prizes; varies. Copyrighted, transferred on request. Pub's reviews: 8 in 1990. §Serious poetry and fiction. Ads: $150/$85. CCLM, COSMEP, AWP.

Blackberry, Gary Lawless, Chimney Farm, R.R. 1, Box 228, Nobleboro, ME 04555, 207-729-5083. 1974. Poetry, fiction, articles, art, interviews, reviews, parts-of-novels. "Especially interested in native American work, and bioregionalism work arising from the natural world. Recent and forthcoming contributors: Peter Blue Cloud, Mary Tall Mountain, Elizabeth Coatsworth, James Koller, Theodore Enslin, Miriam Dyak, Gary Lawless. Also reprinting the Maine novels of Ruth Moore and several other Maine titles" avg. press run 200-500. Pub'd 1 title 1990; expects 20 titles 1991, 20+ titles 1992. 9 titles listed in the *Small Press Record of Books in Print* (20th Edition, 1991-92). avg. price, paper: $9.95; other: $2. Discounts: Bookstore 40%, jobber 50%. 250pp; 5½×8½; of. Reporting time: 1-3 weeks. Payment: usually 10% in cash or copies. Copyrights for author. Maine Writers & Publishers Alliance.

BLACKJACK FORUM, R.G.E. Publishing, Arnold Snyder, Alison Finlay, 414 Santa Clara Avenue, Oakland, CA 94610, 415-465-6452. 1981. Articles, news items. "All articles, items, etc., relate to casino blackjack and/or systems for beating the game. From short news items to 1.5M word max" circ. 1.8M. 4/yr. Pub'd 4 issues 1990; expects 4 issues 1991, 4 issues 1992. sub. price: $30, $35 by 1st class mail; per copy: $7.50; sample: $5. Back issues: Vol. I #1-4, $3 each, Vol. II, III, $4.95 each, Vol. IV, V, VI, VII $6 each. Discounts: 40% in quantities of 4 or more (same issue). 52pp; 5½×8½; of. Reporting time: 2-6 weeks. Payment: $25 to $100 for articles of 500 words to 1.5M words. Copyrighted, reverts to author. Pub's reviews: 15 in 1990. §Gambling in general, blackjack in particular. Ads: $600/$350/$1 classified word. COSMEP.

THE BLACKLIST, Dave Paul, David Woodworth, Ian Probasco, PO Box 1417, Salt Lake City, UT 84110, 972-6739. 1989. Poetry, fiction, articles, art, long-poems, non-fiction. "*The Blacklist* is a bi-monthly open forum for all types of creative expression reproducible in black and white." circ. 500. 6/yr. Pub'd 6 issues 1990; expects 6 issues 1991, 6 issues 1992. sub. price: $3; per copy: 50¢; sample: 50¢ (or stamp). Back issues: not available. Discounts: can be worked out with editors. 8pp; 8½×11; of. Reporting time: a few weeks to 2 months. Payment: free subscription. Copyrighted, reverts to author. §§35/$25/$5 business card. 73/37.

BLADES, JoAnn Balingit, Francis Poole, Poporo Press, 182 Orchard Road, Newark, DE 19711-5208. 1977. Poetry, fiction, art, satire, letters, collages, news items. "*Blades* is a tiny magazine, so send short poems (15 lines=one page). Occasionally we publish longer ones, 3 or 4 pages. We publish surrealism (drawings too), satire, humor, linguistically interesting work. Very short stories, dreams, and cultural documents also sought; prose should be short. We are interested in non-English poems, also." circ. 175. 2/yr. Pub'd 1 issue 1990; expects 2 issues 1991, 2 issues 1992. sub. price: $1 or exchange of publications and SASE. Donations accepted; per copy: free with SASE; sample: free, or for exchange, enclose SASE. Back issues: $1. 36pp; 4¼×3¾; †offset or photocopy. Reporting time: 2 months. Payment: copies. Copyrighted, reverts to author. Exchange ads free.

BLAKE: AN ILLUSTRATED QUARTERLY, Morris Eaves, Morton D. Paley, Dept. of English, Univ. of Rochester, Rochester, NY 14627, 716-275-3820. 1967. Poetry, articles, art, photos, criticism, reviews, letters, news items. "Our orientation is scholarly, though we have published some non-scholarly material. Blake was both poet and artist, and we welcome material on either or both aspects of his work: news items on exhibitions, publications, etc.; essays, and notes that run from one to many pages, discussion articles for the exchange of opinion; minute particulars, which are mini-notes; reviews of books about Blake; biographical material. Many of the articles are illustrated" circ. 600. 4/yr. Pub'd 4 issues 1990; expects 4 issues 1991, 4 issues 1992. sub. price: $20 individuals, $40 institutions, $6 surcharge for foreign surface mailing, additional $15 foreign air mail; per copy: $6; sample: $6. Back issues: whole nos. 1-16, 19-21, 31, 37, 41-42, 50 $5; whole nos. 22-30, 32-36, 38-current, $6; whole nos. 17-18/$10. Discounts: agency 15%. 60pp; 8½×11; of. Reporting time: 4-6 weeks. Payment: copies only. Copyrighted, does not revert to author. Pub's reviews: 25 in 1990. §Scholarship. Ads: $120/$80. CELJ.

Blake Publishing, Vicki Leon, Publications Director, 2222 Beebee Street, San Luis Obispo, CA 93401, 805-543-6843. 1984. Photos, non-fiction. "We publish full-color nature books, heavily pictorial. Most books are written and produced in-house; however, we do entertain outside submissions. We do welcome photos for review; no unsolicited photos please. Call first: within California 800-727-8558" avg. press run 10M. Pub'd 4 titles 1990; expects 2 titles 1991, 2 titles 1992. avg. price, paper: $5.95 and up. Discounts: standard. 40-64pp; 8½×11; †of. Reporting time: varies. Payment: flat fee usually. Copyrights for author.

BLANK GUN SILENCER, Dan Nielsen, 1240 William Street, Racine, WI 53402, 414-639-2406. 1991. Poetry, art, cartoons, collages, concrete art. "I'm looking for poetry and art that makes me laugh that special kind of laugh, the nervous kind, the guilty kind. Recent contributors: Gerald Locklin, John Yamrus, Ron Androla, Mark Weber, Charles Bukowski." circ. 200. 3/yr. Expects 3 issues 1991, 3 issues 1992. sub. price: $6; per copy: $2; sample: $2. Discounts: will trade in most cases. 28pp; 5½×8½. Reporting time: 2 weeks.

Payment: contributor copy. Copyrighted, reverts to author. Pub's reviews. §Art, lit, poetry.

BLIND ALLEYS, Seventh Son Press, Glenford H. Cummings, Charles Lynch, Aissatou Mijiza, Michael S. Weaver, Rutgers Univ, Box 29, Camden, NJ 08102, 609-757-6117. 1982. Poetry, fiction, art, photos, interviews, reviews. "We are especially sensitive to, though not exclusively devoted to, the needs of minority writers and artists. Recent contributors have been Juan Felipe Herrera, Joseph Bruchac, Rikki Lights, E. Ethelbert Miller, and Frank Marshall Davis. Fiction should be limited to 1500 words. Poetry should be submitted in batches of five" circ. 500. 2/yr. Expects 1 issue 1991, 2 issues 1992. sub. price: $11; per copy: $6; sample: $6. Back issues: none. Discounts: 40% to bookstores, libraries, and jobbers. 7Cpp; 6×9. Reporting time: 3-6 months. Payment: 2 copies. Copyrighted, reverts to author. Pub's reviews. §Poetry, fiction, drama. Ads: $125/$75. CCLM.

Blind Beggar Press, Gary Johnston, C. D. Grant, Box 437 Williamsbridge Station, Bronx, NY 10467, 914-683-6792. 1976. Poetry, fiction, art, photos, parts-of-novels, long-poems, plays. "No length on material. Recent contributors: Judy Simmons, Fatisha, Sandra Marie Esteres, Louis Reyes Rivera, Askia Toure" avg. press run 1M. Pub'd 2 titles 1990. Expects 4 titles 1991, 5 titles 1992. 17 titles listed in the *Small Press Record of Books in Print* (20th Edition, 1991-92). avg. price, paper: $2.95-$9.95. Discounts: 50% on bulk orders of 5 or more copies for retailers and distributors. 60-150pp; 5½×8½, 6×9; computer. Reporting time: 1-2 months. Payment: in copies. Copyrights for author. BCA.

Bliss Publishing Company, Inc., Stephen H. Clouter, PO Box 920, Marlboro, MA 01752, 508-779-2827. 1989. Non-fiction. "Booklength manuscripts" avg. press run 2M. Expects 4 titles 1991, 4 titles 1992. avg. price, paper: $10.95. Discounts: 40% trade. 220pp; 6×9. Reporting time: 8 weeks. Payment: negotiated. Copyrights for author.

BLITZ, Mike McDowell, Editor & Publisher, PO Box 48124, Los Angeles, CA 90048-0124, 818-360-3262. 1975. Articles, photos, interviews, criticism, reviews, music, letters, news items. "Magazine is billed as 'The Rock and Roll Magazine For Thinking People'. Emphasis is on artists who are not being afforded enough exposure via other forms of the media. Magazine covers all forms of aesthetically meritous rock and roll music, with slant towards the academic. Deadline for submissions is 15th day before publication" circ. 3M. 6/yr. Pub'd 6 issues 1990; expects 2 issues 1991, 4 issues 1992. sub. price: $10.50 for 6 issues; per copy: $1.95; sample: $1.95. Back issues: varies with each title, information supplied upon request. Discounts: $1.25 per copy on orders of ten or more; overseas $1.25 per copy, US Currency in advance only (cover lists price of 95p for U.K.). 28pp; 8½×11; of. Reporting time: 6 weeks. Payment: all submissions are non-solicited, no financial remuneration. Copyrighted, reverts to author. Pub's reviews: 25 in 1990. §Music, music related films and publications. Ads: $200/$120/$10 for insert any size. COSMEP.

THE BLOATED TICK, Paul N. Dion, 24 Main Street, S. Grafton, MA 01560, 508-839-3221. 1988. Poetry, fiction, articles, art, photos, cartoons, satire, reviews, music, letters, long-poems, collages. "No porn published at all" circ. 50+/-. 12/yr. Pub'd 12 issues 1990; expects 12 issues 1991, 12 issues 1992. sub. price: SASE plus 1st class stamp; per copy: same; sample: same. Back issues: same. Discounts: free in trade. 10-15pp; 8½×11; †photocopy. Payment: none. Copyrighted. Pub's reviews: 5 in 1990. §Anything. Ads: $10/$5.50/on request.

Drew Blood Press Ltd., Drew Blood, 3410 First Street, Riverside, CA 92501, 714-788-4319. 1980. Poetry, fiction, articles, art, photos, cartoons, interviews, long-poems, collages, non-fiction. "Over the past 11 years, DBPL has published all subjects. Also have 2 spoken word and music cassettes. Currently working on a chap with Paul Weinman/White Boy & Drew Blood. Recent chaps include 2 various poets collections. Too many closets (mostly gay writers) and comp book. Also I've done 4 so far with A. Razor and 4 with Paul Weinman/White Boy. About 10 chaps are in the planning stages at the moment. Recent poets are John H. Pofall, Max Hoffman, A. Razor, paul Weinman and Holly Day." avg. press run 100-200. Pub'd 14 titles 1990; expects 16 titles 1991, 20 titles 1992. Discounts: yes I trade or reg. bulk $1 per or 50¢ per depending on which work. 28pp; 5½×8½; †mi, xerox. Reporting time: 3 weeks. Payment: free copies if used in a various, 1/2 of press run if a whole chap is done with one poet. All copyright belongs to author.

BLOODROOT, Bloodroot, Inc., Joan Eades, Editor; Linda Ohlsen, Editor; Dan Eades, Editor, PO Box 891, Grand Forks, ND 58206-0891, 701-775-6079. 1976. Poetry, fiction, articles, art, parts-of-novels, long-poems. "Beginning and established writers are read with equal care - particularly when the writing is well-crafted. In poetry our bias is toward length - both of line and poem. In fiction we look for honest stories - traditional or experimental - which read like stories rather than undistilled autobiography. In both, we tend to prefer the honest and energetic to the careful and lifeless. We are open to the poetry and fiction of all schools, but reviewers have noticed an affinity to work with a strong voice. We occasionally use interviews that we have assigned, and writers should query before submitting them. Though *BLOODROOT* is growing, we still try to respond individually. We need two line drawings (preferably pen and ink) for each issue: one for the cover and one for the frontpiece. We'll look at photocopies, but the original must be available if accepted. Drawings should be of a shape to suit 6 X 9 size" circ. 800. Irregular. Pub'd 1 issue 1990; expects 2 issues 1991. sub.

price: $9 for 3 issues; per copy: $3 plus 50¢ for postage and handling; sample: $3 plus 50¢ for p/h. Back issues: $5. Discounts: standard. 72pp; 6×9; of. Reporting time: one week to six months. Payment: 6 copies or, grants permitting, $5 per page. Copyrighted, reverts with credit given. CCLM, COSMEP.

Bloodroot, Inc. (see also BLOODROOT), Dan Eades, Editor; Joan Eades, Editor; Linda Ohlsen, Editor, PO Box 891, Grand Forks, ND 58206-0891, 701-746-5858. 1977. Poetry, fiction. "Our chapbook series is open to writers published in *BLOODROOT*" avg. press run 500. Expects 1 title 1991, 2 titles 1992. 3 titles listed in the *Small Press Record of Books in Print* (20th Edition, 1991-92). avg. price, paper: $1.50, poetry; $2.50, fiction. Discounts: standard. 24pp poetry, 60pp fiction; 5½×8½; of. Reporting time: 3 week to 6 months. Payment: according to NEA guidelines whenever possible. Copyrights for author. CCLM, COSMEP.

Bloody Twin Press, Brian Richards, Publisher, 4525 Blue Creek Road, Stout, OH 45684, 513-549-4162. 1982. Poetry. "Recent books include: *Dirty Dogs* by Joe Sheffler, *Zero Bonding* by Earl Butler, *Apocalyptic Talkshow* by Tom Clark, *The Drivers* by Carl Thayler, *Provocateur* by Joel Lipman. *Tell Me About It* by Anne Waldman, by Howard McCord, *Pranks* by Steve Kowit. Bridge Thrashing Through History" avg. press run 300. Pub'd 3 titles 1990; expects 3 titles 1991. avg. price, paper: $8. Discounts: standard. 30pp; 6×8; †lp. Reporting time: return mail. Payment: 10% of edition plus 20 review copies. Copyrights for author.

THE BLOOMSBURY REVIEW, Tom Auer, Publisher, Editor-in-Chief; Marilyn Auer, Associate Publisher, 1028 Bannock Street, Denver, CO 80204, 303-892-0620. 1980. Poetry, fiction, articles, art, photos, interviews, reviews, letters, long-poems, non-fiction. "We do not publish original fiction at this time" circ. 50M. 8/yr. Pub'd 6 issues 1990; expects 8 issues 1991, 8 issues 1992. sub. price: $18; per copy: $3; sample: $3.50. Back issues: $3.50. Inquiries about distribution are welcome. 32pp; 10½×15¼; of. Reporting time: 3 months. Payment: $10 per review, $5 poetry, $20 features. Copyrighted, reverts to author. Pub's reviews: 900 in 1990. §Literature, history, biography, poetry, autobiography, politics-All subject areas. Ads: $2,790/$1,490/$40 first 15 words—$1 each additional word.

Blue Arrow Books, Terri Katahn, PO Box 1669, Pacific Palisades, CA 90272, 213-447-5951. 1989. Non-fiction. "Our first book is a how-to related to the film and television industry, titled Reading For A Living, How to be a Professional Story Analyst for Film and Television. We plan to start publishing fiction next year. We hope someday to begin accepting submissions." avg. press run 3.5M. Expects 1 title 1991, 1 title 1992. 1 title listed in the *Small Press Record of Books in Print* (20th Edition, 1991-92). avg. price, paper: $12.95. Discounts: currently Samuel French Trade is our exclusive distributor to bookstores and wholesalers like Ingram. 192pp; 5½×8½. PMA, COSMEP.

Blue Bird Publishing, Cheryl Gorder, 1713 East Broadway, #306, Tempe, AZ 85282, 602-968-4088. 1985. Fiction, non-fiction. "Encouraging submission of manuscripts of non-fiction topics, both adult and juvenile levels. We specialize in home education topics, and are looking for good educational manuscripts for parents teaching their children. Also interested in manuscripts on current social issues." Pub'd 6 titles 1990; expects 6 titles 1991, 6 titles 1992. 12 titles listed in the *Small Press Record of Books in Print* (20th Edition, 1991-92). avg. price, paper: $11.95. Discounts: usually 40%. 208pp; 6×9; of. Reporting time: 6-12 weeks. Payment: standard. Copyrights for author. PMA.

BLUE BUILDINGS, Tom Urban, Ruth Doty, Guillaume Williams, Department of English, Drake University, Des Moines, IA 50311-3005, 515-274-9103. 1978. Poetry, long-poems. "Poetry, translations. Recent contributors include Michael Benedikt, George Hitchcock, Mekeel McBride, Robert Peters, Marge Piercy, Richard Shelton, Jane Shore, David Wagoner, Peter Wild, Roger Weingarten, and many others. Five chapbooks published to date: *Rainbow*, by Peter Wild, *Notes on Continuing Light*, by Michael Simms, *Rounds* by Thomas Swiss. *Goldbarth's Book of Occult Phenomena* by Alberth Goldbarth, *Tables of the Meridian* By Roger Weingarten, *The Coat in The Heart* by Gary Fincke Please query before submitting chapbook manuscripts" circ. 700. 2/yr. Pub'd 2 issues 1990; expects 2 issues 1991, 2 issues 1992. 6 titles listed in the *Small Press Record of Books in Print* (20th Edition, 1991-92). sub. price: $10 (2 issues); per copy: $8; sample: $4. Discounts: 40% trade. 40-60pp; 8½×11; of. Reporting time: 3 months—sometimes longer. Payment: copies. Copyrighted, reverts to author. CCLM/COSMEP/CLMP.

Blue Crane Books, Mrs. Alvart Badalian, Publisher, PO Box 291, Cambridge, MA 02238, 617-926-8585. 1991. "Street address: 36 Hazel Street, Watertown, MA 02172." avg. press run 5M. Expects 2 titles 1991, 5 titles 1992. 1 title listed in the *Small Press Record of Books in Print* (20th Edition, 1991-92). avg. price, cloth: $25; paper: $15. Discounts: available. 200pp; 6×9. Reporting time: 3 months. Payment: 5-10%, quarterly or semiannually. We sometimes copyright for author.

Blue Dolphin Press, Inc., Paul M. Clemens, PO Box 1908, Nevada City, CA 95959, 916-265-6923. 1976. Non-fiction. "We are also Blue Dolphin Publishing, Inc. We publish books on spiritual traditions, personal growth, self-help, and health" avg. press run 3M-5M. Pub'd 10+ titles 1990; expects 10+ titles 1991. avg. price, cloth: $19.95; paper: $12.95. Discounts: 40-55%. 200+pp; 5½×8½; †of. Reporting time: 3-6 months, bids 1 week. Payment: 10%. Copyrights for author.

THE BLUE GUITAR, Richard Kearns, 3022 North 5th Street, Harrisburg, PA 17110. 1989. Poetry, fiction, photos. "Publish mostly poetry and some short fiction. Have published works by Gary Fincke, Nancy Tiley, Eugene Howard, Jack Veasey, Jennifer Bitner and others. Prefer strong writing—no greeting card or light verse" circ. 250-300. 4/yr. Pub'd 2 issues 1990; expects 4 issues 1991, 4 issues 1992. sub. price: $12; per copy: $3; sample: $3. 45pp; 5×8; of. Reporting time: 3-4 months. Payment: 2 copies. Copyrighted, reverts to author. Ads: $50/$25.

Blue Heron Press (see also COMPUTER EDUCATION NEWS), Carol J. Anderson, PO Box 5182, Bellingham, WA 98227, 206-671-1155; 206-676-3954. 1985. Fiction, non-fiction. "Blue Heron Press is dedicated to provide educational materials for able students. (i.e., gifted, advanced, excellerated). Interested in science materials and non-fiction. Blue Heron Press is also interested in Marine related non-fiction" avg. press run 5M-10M. Pub'd 1 title 1990; expects 5 titles 1991, 5-10 titles 1992. 2 titles listed in the *Small Press Record of Books in Print* (20th Edition, 1991-92). avg. price, cloth: $19.95; paper: $10.95. 200-250pp; 8½×11. Reporting time: 2 months. Payment: 10%. Copyrights for author if requested. COSMEP, PMA.

Blue Heron Publishing, Inc. (see also WRITER'S N.W.), Linny Stovall, Dennis Stovall, Media Weavers, Route 3, Box 376, Hillsboro, OR 97124, 503-621-3911. 1985. "Reprints and new books from Walt Morey (author of *Gentle Ben*)." avg. press run 5M-6M. Pub'd 1 title 1990; expects 8 titles 1991, 3 titles 1992. 10 titles listed in the *Small Press Record of Books in Print* (20th Edition, 1991-92). avg. price, cloth: $6.95-14.95; paper: $6.95-$14.95. 135-200pp; 6×9. Payment: royalty, no advance. Northwest Association of Book Publishers.

BLUE HORSE, Blue Horse Publications, Jacqueline T. Bradley, Editor & Publisher; G. Warren Weissmann, Editor At Large; Eugenia P. Mallory, Graphics Editor, P.O. Box 6061, Augusta, GA 30906, 404-798-5628. 1964. Poetry, fiction, satire. "*Blue Horse* is a magazine of satire, misanthropy and scurrilous language without regard to sex, religion, age, race, creed, or I.Q. *Blue Horse* is the periodical of Blue Horse Movement which recognizes the folly of human life and the inutility of politics. *Blue Horse* sees writers as the victims of their own art. Currently publishing only solicited chapbooks." circ. 500. Irregular. Expects 1 issue 1992. price per copy: $3.50; sample: $2. Back issues: $4 except Vol. l, $8. Discounts: prisoners pay postage only. 36pp; 5½×8½; of. Reporting time: 30-60 days. Payment: copies. Copyrighted. Exchange ads.

Blue Horse Publications (see also BLUE HORSE), Jacqueline Bradley, Editor & Publisher, PO Box 6061, Augusta, GA 30906, 404-798-5628. 1964. Poetry, fiction, satire. avg. press run 500. Expects 1 title 1992. 7 titles listed in the *Small Press Record of Books in Print* (20th Edition, 1991-92). avg. price, paper: $4. Discounts: 25%. 36pp; 5½×8½; of, lp. Reporting time: 30-60 days. Payment: mutual agreement.

BLUE LIGHT RED LIGHT, Alma Rodriguez, Joy Parker, Stephen Rutherford, Design Director, 496A Hudson Street, Suite F42, New York, NY 10014, 201-432-3245. 1988. Poetry, fiction, articles, art, photos, interviews, criticism, reviews, letters, parts-of-novels, non-fiction. "*Blue Light Red Light* is dedicated to the publication of magic realism, speculative fiction, surrealism, and experimental fiction. Unlike other journals, we seek not to isolate these literary genres but to discover the points of contact between them and to explore their connections to mainstream writing itself. We believe the resurgence of interest in the imaginative literatures is part of a compensating process taking place in the human psyche today. As contemporary life becomes more fragmented, the search for meaning, for personal myths, becomes all the more intense. We want to participate in this search for meaning. We are accepting short stories, poetry, film and book reviews, and literary essays with SASE only" circ. 2M. 3/yr. Pub'd 2 issues 1990; expects 3 issues 1991, 3-4 issues 1992. sub. price: $15; per copy: $5.50; sample: $5.50. Back issues: $4.50. Discounts: 40% to libraries and bookstores ordering 10 or more copies; 25% to individuals ordering 10 or more, special distributor discounts available. 177pp; 6×9; desktop publishing. Reporting time: 1-3 months. Payment: copies. Copyrighted, reverts to author. Pub's reviews: 2 in 1990. §experimental lit., Third World literature, New Wave science fiction, fantasy, surrealism, speculative fiction, feminist lit. Ads: $250/$150. COSMEP/CCLM.

BLUE LIGHT REVIEW, Paul Dilsaver, PO Box 1621, Pueblo, CO 81002. 1983. Poetry, fiction, long-poems. circ. 200. 2/yr. Pub'd 1 issue 1990; expects 2 issues 1991. sub. price: $6; per copy: $4; sample: $4. Discounts: 30% for 5 or more copies. 48pp; 8½×5½; of. Reporting time: 6 months. Payment: copy. Copyrighted. Pub's reviews: 15 in 1990. §Poetry, fiction.

BLUE LIGHTS, Blue Lights Publications, Victoria Onstine, Vicki Hessel Werkley, Christ Menefee, Founding Editor, 4945 U Street, c/o Lil Sibley, Sacramento, CA 95817, 916-452-2024. 1987. Poetry, fiction, articles, art, photos, cartoons, interviews, criticism, reviews, letters, news items. "Additional addresses: 2405 Togo Street, Eureka, CA 95501; 16563 Ellen Springs Drive, PO Box 1953, Lower Lake, CA 95457. Length of material: varies according to topic, maximum of 2-3 pages per item. Submissions to be concerning the movie and/or TV series Starman, television industry, movies, science-fiction related topics." circ. 150-200. 4/yr. Pub'd 4 issues 1990; expects 4 issues 1991, 4 issues 1992. sub. price: $24; per copy: $6; sample: $6. Back issues: $6. Discounts: trade. 50pp; 8½×11; photocopy. Reporting time: 3-4 weeks. Payment: occasional complimentary copies at discretion of editors. Copyrighted, reverts to author. Pub's reviews: 15-20 in 1990.

§Non-fiction and fiction related to the movie and/or TV series Starman. Ads: $10/$5/$2.50 1/4 page/$5 1/3 page.

Blue Lights Publications (see also BLUE LIGHTS), Christine Menefee, Chief Editor; Victoria Onstine, Co-Editor; Vicki Hessel Werkley, Co-Editor, c/o Vicki Werkley, 16563 Ellen Springs Drive, Lower Lake, CA 95457. 1987. Poetry, fiction, articles, art, photos, cartoons, interviews, satire, criticism, reviews, music, letters, parts-of-novels, plays, news items, non-fiction. "Publications include: quarterly newsletterzine with quarterly supplements; special editions of collected essays, short stories, etc. by multi-authors; single author pieces. Open forum for all ideas on improving human relations." avg. press run 150. Pub'd 10 titles 1990; expects 10 titles 1991, 10 titles 1992. avg. price, other: $6. Discounts: trade. 50pp; 8½×11; photocopy. Reporting time: 3-4 weeks. Payment: copies; some expenses. Copyrights for author.

Blue Mouse Studio, Rex Schneider, Chris Buchman, 26829 37th Street, Gobles, MI 49055, 616-628-5160. 1980. Cartoons. "No unsolicited manuscripts" avg. press run 2M. Pub'd 1 title 1990; expects 1 title 1991, 1 title 1992. 1 title listed in the *Small Press Record of Books in Print* (20th Edition, 1991-92). avg. price, paper: $3.95. Discounts: wholesalers-50%; retailers-40%. 80pp; 5¼×7¼; of.

The Blue Oak Press, Maria Campbell, PO Box 27, Sattley, CA 96124, 916-994-3397. 1967. Poetry, fiction, criticism, long-poems. "Recent contributors: Cornel Lengyel, Edith Snow, William Everson, Robinson Jeffers, Randy White, John Berutti, Bill Hotchkiss, K'os Naahaabii, Stan Hager. Our bias would be toward the poetry of contemporary Western America; and we have drawn a significant focus on the work of Robinson Jeffers as the seminal figure of this developing tradition. Price is extremely variable, from one special edition at $30 to paperbacks at $3.95. We do not invite submissions" avg. press run 500. Pub'd 4 titles 1990; expects 3-4 titles 1991. 8 titles listed in the *Small Press Record of Books in Print* (20th Edition, 1991-92). avg. price, cloth: $15; paper: $10; other: special editions, cloth, $15-$30. Discounts: 40% to bookstores and dealers; 20% to libraries; 30% on consignment; short discounts on special editions. 80-100+pp; 6×9; †of, lp. Payment: no specific policy. Copyrights for author.

Blue Poppy Press, Bob Flaws, Honora Lee Wolfe, 1775 Linden Avenue, Boulder, CO 80304, 303-442-0796. 1981. Non-fiction. "Material is mostly translations from chinese medical source texts. Most contributors are Chinese, Korean, Japanese, etc." avg. press run 1M-5M. Pub'd 4 titles 1990; expects 3-4 titles 1991, 4-6 titles 1992. 5 titles listed in the *Small Press Record of Books in Print* (20th Edition, 1991-92). avg. price, paper: $8.95-$16.95. Discounts: 55% consignment to distributors; 40% to stores, other. 100-300pp; 6×9; of. Reporting time: 3 weeks. Payment: 10% of all sales, paid quarterly. Copyrights for author. ABI.

Blue Raven Publishing, Frances Colbert, PO Box 973, Woodinville, WA 98072, 206-485-0000. 1983. Photos. avg. press run 5M. Expects 1 title 1991. avg. price, other: $60. Discounts: All books are 40% of the retail price. 176pp; 11¼×9½; of. Payment: author fee. Does not copyright for author.

Blue Sky Marketing, Inc., Vic Spadaccini, Editor, PO Box 21583, Saint Paul, MN 55121-0583, 612-456-5602. 1982. Non-fiction. avg. press run 4M. Pub'd 1 title 1990; expects 2 titles 1991, 2 titles 1992. 3 titles listed in the *Small Press Record of Books in Print* (20th Edition, 1991-92). avg. price, paper: $9.95. Discounts: distributed by Adventure Publications, Ingram. 96pp; size varies; of. Reporting time: 30 days. Payment: negotiable. Copyrights for author on request. MIPA, PMA.

Blue Swan Communications, Randall Cornish, Kimberly Swan, PO Box 9925, San Diego, CA 92169-0925, 619-272-5718. 1990. 1 title listed in the *Small Press Record of Books in Print* (20th Edition, 1991-92). avg. price, paper: $7.95. 32pp; 8½×11.

BLUE UNICORN, Ruth G. Iodice, Daniel J. Langton, Harold Witt, 22 Avon Road, Kensington, CA 94707, 415-526-8439. 1977. Poetry, art. "*Blue Unicorn* is a journal looking for excellence of the individual voice whether that voice comes through in a fixed form or an original variation or in freer lines. We publish poets who are established and those who are less known but deserve to be known better, and we are also proud to welcome new talent to our pages. We like poems which communicate in a memorable way whatever is deeply felt by the poet, and we believe in an audience which is delighted, like us, by a lasting image, a unique twist of thought, and a haunting music. We also use a limited number of expert translations. Among recent contributors to our tri-quarterly are: John Ciardi, Rosalie Moore, Charles Edward Eaton, James Schevill, John Ditsky, Janemarie Luecke, Don Welch, Barbara A. Holland, Lawrence Spingarn, A.D. Winans, Eve Triem, William Dickey, Adrianne Marcus, Stuart Silverman, Josephine Miles. Please send only unpublished poems." circ. 500. 3/yr. Expects 3 issues 1991. 1 title listed in the *Small Press Record of Books in Print* (20th Edition, 1991-92). sub. price: $12, $18 foreign; per copy: $4; add $2 mailing for foreign copies; sample: $4; $6 foreign. Back issues: $3.50. 48-60pp; 4¼×5½; of. Reporting time: 1-3 months. Payment: 1 copy. Copyrighted, reverts to author. §Poetry. CCLM.

Blue Water Publishing, Inc., Gretchen D. Lingle, Brian L. Crissey, Pam Meyer, PO Box 230893, Tigard, OR 97224, 503-684-9749. 1988. Fiction, non-fiction. avg. press run 5M. Pub'd 1 title 1990; expects 3 titles 1991, 6 titles 1992. 10 titles listed in the *Small Press Record of Books in Print* (20th Edition, 1991-92). avg. price, cloth: $19.95; paper: $12.95. Discounts: bookstores 40%, wholesalers 55%. 256pp; 5½×8½; of. Reporting time: 4 weeks. Payment: 7.5% of gross revenues. Copyrights for author. Northwest Ass'n of Book Publishers.

BLUEFISH, Anselm Parlatore, 4621 Westcott Drive, Friday Harbor, WA 98250-9733. 1983. Poetry, fiction, articles, interviews, criticism, reviews, letters, parts-of-novels, long-poems. circ. 1M. 2/yr. Pub'd 1 issue 1990; expects 2 issues 1992. sub. price: $20; per copy: $5.00; sample: $5. Back issues: please inquire. Discounts: please inquire. 100pp; 9×6; of. Reporting time: immediate. Payment: yes. Copyrighted, reverts to author. Pub's reviews: 3 in 1990. §Poetry. Ads: please inquire.

BLUELINE, Anthony Tyler, Editor, State University College, English Dept., Potsdam, NY 13676, 315-267-2006. 1979. Poetry, fiction, articles, art, reviews, parts-of-novels, plays, non-fiction. "We are interested in material that has some relationship, either literal or in spirit, to the Adirondack mountain region in upstate New York. We are willing to interpret that relationship broadly. Short fiction and essays should be no more than 2.5M words, poems 44 lines or less. Recent contributors include Joseph Bruchac, Paul Corrigan, Joanne Seltzer, Ursulu Hegi, Roger Mitchell, Kurt Rheinheimer, Ina Jones, David Swickard, Philip Booth, L.M. Rosenberg, Maurice Kenny. We occasionally publish reviews." circ. 700. 1/yr. Expects 2 issues 1991, 1 issue 1992. sub. price: $6; per copy: $6.50; sample: $6.50. Back issues: $5.50. Discounts: $4 per copy to distributors. 96-120pp; 6×9; photo, of. Reporting time: 4-10 weeks. Payment: copies. Copyrighted, revert with permission of publisher. Pub's reviews: 1 in 1990. §Short fiction, novels, poetry, essays about the Adirondacks. No ads. COSMEP, CLMP.

Bluestocking Press, Jane A. Williams, PO Box 1014, Dept. LF, Placerville, CA 95667-1014, 916-621-1123. 1987. Fiction, non-fiction. "UPS address: 3333 Gold Country Drive, Placerville, CA 95667. Query with SASE for reply" avg. press run 4M. Pub'd 1 title 1990; expects 2 titles 1991, 3 titles 1992. 5 titles listed in the *Small Press Record of Books in Print* (20th Edition, 1991-92). avg. price, paper: $7.95 perfect. Quantity discounts available to booksellers, wholesalers, catalogers. 5½×8½; desk top publishing. Reporting time: 3 months. Payment: by agreement. Does not copyright for author.

BOA Editions, Ltd., A Poulin, Jr., 92 Park Avenue, Brockport, NY 14420, 716-637-3844. 1976. Poetry. "Generally not accepting unsolicited manuscripts. Major poets invited to select and introduce new poets. Contributors include: W. D. Snodgrass, Anthony Piccione, Archibald MacLeish, William B. Patrick, John Logan, Isabella Gardner, Michael Waters, Richard Wilbur, Joseph Stroud, Peter Makuck, Emanuel di Pasquale, Carolyn Kizer, Lucille Clifton, Li-Young Lee, Bill Tremblay, Anne Hebert, Yannis Ritsos." avg. press run 500 cloth, 2.5M paper. Expects 6 titles 1991. avg. price, cloth: $18; paper: $9; other: $50-$100 signed. Discounts: bookstores 40%, 20% for signed editions. 60-80pp; 6×9; of. Reporting time: 4-6 weeks. Payment: advance and royalty. Copyrights for author.

BOGG, Bogg Publications, John Elsberg, USA Editor; George Cairncross, British Editor; Sheila Martindale, Canadian Editor, 422 N Cleveland Street, Arlington, VA 22201. 1968. Poetry, articles, art, interviews, satire, reviews, letters. "U.K. Address: 31 Belle Vue ST., Filey , N. Yorks, UK YO14 9HU. Canadian address: 532 Pall Mall Street, London, Ontario N5Y 2Z6. Essays on British and American small press history and experience; mainly short reviews. The magazine puts out a series of free (for postage) pamphlets of poetry, prose, comics. The magazine contains roughly equal amounts of British/Canadian/Australian and American work. ISSN 0882-648X" circ. 750. 2-3/yr. Pub'd 2 issues 1990; expects 3 issues 1991, 3 issues 1992. sub. price: £5 ($12)/3 issues; per copy: £2 ($4.50); sample: $3. Back issues: negotiable. Discounts: 40% 10 copies or more. 64pp; 6×9; of. Reporting time: 1 week. Payment: 2 copies of issue. Copyrighted, reverts to author. Pub's reviews: 30 in 1990. §Small press publications, U.K. and U.S. CCLM.

Bogg Publications (see also BOGG), John Elsberg, George Cairncross, Sheila Martindale, 422 North Cleveland Street, Arlington, VA 22201. 1968. Poetry, cartoons, satire. "Only solicited mss considered" avg. press run 300. Pub'd 2 titles 1990; expects 2 titles 1991, 2 titles 1992. 8 titles listed in the *Small Press Record of Books in Print* (20th Edition, 1991-92). avg. price, paper: free-for-postage (first printings); other: $3 (2nd and subsequent printings). 20pp; size varies; of. Payment: 25% of print run (in copies). Copyrights for author. CCLM.

Boise State University Western Writers Series, James Maguire, Wayne Chatterton, Department of English, Boise State University, Boise, ID 83725, 208-385-1246. 1972. Criticism. "Each of the pamphlets in the Western Writers Series provides a brief introduction to the life and work of a writer who has made a significant contribution to the literature of the American West." avg. press run 1M. Pub'd 5 titles 1990; expects 5 titles 1991, 5 titles 1992. avg. price, paper: $3.95. Discounts: 40%. 50pp; 5×7½; †of. Reporting time: 1 month, but contact readers before submission. Payment: none. The WWS holds the copyright.

Bolchazy-Carducci Publishers, Inc., Ladislaus J. Bolchazy, Ph.D., S. Casey Fredericks, Ph.D., 1000 Brown Street, Wauconda, IL 60084, 708-526-4344. 1981. Non-fiction. "We are also interested in translations of classics from any language in addition to translations of Eastern European works of merit. Book-length proposals only: 25,000 word minimum. Prefer word-processed manuscripts available on diskettes. Any serious, intelligent work of non-fiction will be given a thorough, professional review.'' avg. press run 2M. Pub'd 10 titles 1990; expects 10 titles 1991, 10 titles 1992. avg. price, cloth: $20; paper: $10. Discounts: 20% bookstores, 40% to qualified distributors and representatives. 200pp. Reporting time: 4 weeks. Payment: negotiable. Copyrights for author. Our connections are solely with universities and libraries.

BOLD PRINT, Kyle Hogg, 2211 Stuart Avenue, 1st Floor, Richmond, VA 23220. 1982. Poetry, fiction, art, photos, cartoons, interviews, satire, criticism, reviews, music, collages, non-fiction. "Be yourself when writing. Impress yourself and let it flow. Don't write over your own head. That's not impressive, it's confusing'' circ. 800. 1/yr. Pub'd 1 issue 1990; expects 1 issue 1991, 1 issue 1992. price per copy: $3; sample: $3. 10-15pp; 8½×11; †mi. Payment: issue. Not copyrighted. §Anything I can get for free, I'll take. No ads unless I really like the ad subject—then free ad space.

Bold Productions, Mary Bold, PO Box 152281, Arlington, TX 76015, 817-468-9924. 1983. Non-fiction. "Our Children's Resources Series has been expanded to include newsletters as well as books. All of these materials are non-fiction, geared to the elementary school market and parents buying for children. We also produce the Publishing Decisions Report Series as well as books and workbooks for self-publishers and writers. Watercolor artist Carol Brown Small is the author of *Concepts for Children*, the fifth title in our Children's Resources Series.'' avg. press run 2M. Pub'd 1 title 1990; expects 2 titles 1991, 1 title 1992. 6 titles listed in the *Small Press Record of Books in Print* (20th Edition, 1991-92). avg. price, paper: $8.95. Discounts: discounts to wholesalers begin at 40%; free shipping on orders of 10+ books. 100pp; 5½×8½; of. Reporting time: 1 month. Payment: negotiable. Copyrights for author. NAIP, Florida Publishers Group, Book Publishers of Texas.

The Bold Strummer Ltd., Nicholas Clarke, Mary Clarke, PO Box 2037, Westport, CT 06880-0037, 203-226-8230. 1974. Cartoons, interviews, music. "The Bold Strummer actively seeks and promotes music books for publication, with an emphasis on guitars and related instruments and equipment. Also importer and distributor of books of same.'' avg. press run 2M. Pub'd 2 titles 1990; expects 6 titles 1991, 6 titles 1992. 15 titles listed in the *Small Press Record of Books in Print* (20th Edition, 1991-92). avg. price, cloth: $24.95; paper: $8.95. Discounts: 40%. 130pp; 8½×11; of. Payment: royalty 10% of retail. Copyrights for author. NAMM.

Bolton Press, Amanda Bolton, 3606 El Camino Court, Largo, FL 34641, 813-535-4668. 1987. Fiction, non-fiction. "Hardbound and softbound books'' avg. press run 5M. Pub'd 2 titles 1990; expects 1 title 1991, 2 titles 1992. 1 title listed in the *Small Press Record of Books in Print* (20th Edition, 1991-92). avg. price, cloth: $15; paper: $9. Discounts: 40% trade, 50% jobber. 250pp; 6×9; of. Reporting time: 6 weeks. Payment: negotiated. Copyrights for author. COSMEP.

BOMB MAGAZINE, Betsy Sussler, Editor-in-Chief; Ameena Meer, Managing Editor, 594 Broadway, Suite 1002A, New York, NY 10012, 212-431-3943. 1981. Poetry, fiction, art, photos, interviews, parts-of-novels. circ. 60M. 4/yr. Pub'd 4 issues 1990; expects 4 issues 1991, 4 issues 1992. sub. price: $16; per copy: $5; sample: $5. Back issues: #1, NY Film $10/#4 Painters & Writers $10/#6, Sculpture & Fiction $8/#8, Drawing $5. Discounts: trade 40%, classroom 30%. 90pp; 11×15; of. Reporting time: 3 months unsolicited. Payment: yes. Copyrighted, reverts to author. Ads: $1,200/$720/1/4 page $550. CCLM.

Bomb Shelter Propaganda (see also **MALLIFE**), Mike Miskowski, Editor, PO Box 17686, Phoenix, AZ 85011, 602-279-3531. 1981. Poetry, fiction, art, interviews, long-poems, collages, plays, concrete art. avg. press run 50-500. Pub'd 10 titles 1990; expects 3 titles 1991, 3 titles 1992. 22 titles listed in the *Small Press Record of Books in Print* (20th Edition, 1991-92). avg. price, cloth: $20; paper: $2-$5. Discounts: standard with dealers and distributors. 40pp; size varies; †of, photocopy. Reporting time: 3-8 weeks. Payment: inquire. Copyrights for author.

Bombshelter Press (see also **ONTHEBUS**), Michael Andrews, Jack Grapes, 6421-1/2 Orange Street, Los Angeles, CA 90048, 213-651-5488. 1975. Poetry. "Other address: 1092 Loma Drive, Hermosa Beach, CA 90254, 213-374-7672. We publish California poets, most specifically poets from the Los Angeles area. Poets should not send manuscripts without sending a query letter first. Recent books by Macdonald Carey, Doraine Poretz, Michael Andrews, John Oliver Simon, Lee Rossi, Ko Wan, Jack Grapes, Bill Mohr, and James Krusoe. We will be publishing an anthology of 60 new Los Angeles poets in the summer of 1989. *Onthebus* is a biannual literary magazine—open to submissions from anyone.'' avg. press run 800. Pub'd 3 titles 1990; expects 3 titles 1991, 3 titles 1992. 5 titles listed in the *Small Press Record of Books in Print* (20th Edition, 1991-92). avg. price, paper: $8. Discounts: 40% consignment to bookstores, etc., 50% to distributors. 60pp; 5½×8½; of, mostly jobbed out, lp. Reporting time: 3-4 months. Payment: free copies (usually 50) plus 10% of profits from sales. Copyrights for author.

BONE & FLESH, Frederick Moe, Editor; Lester Hirsh, Editor; Bob Shannahan, Production Assistant, c/o Lester Hirsh, PO Box 349, Concord, NH 03302-0349. 1988. Poetry, fiction, articles, art, reviews, letters, long-poems. "We publish work that is thought provoking and aesthetic. All styles, prose poems, haiku,

78

concrete, avant-garde, experimental are welcome. Themes should focus on the substance of our lives, or the link with other lives and times. We are oriented towards inner (spiritual) journeys and interpersonal relationships. Poetry: length open. Fiction: to 2,000 words. Reviews/essays: to 1,200 words." circ. 250-300. 2/yr. Pub'd 2 issues 1990; expects 2 issues 1991, 2 issues 1992. sub. price: $8; sample: $5. Back issues: $5. Discounts: 10% off orders of two or more publications. 75-100pp annual issue, 32pp aside issue; 8½×11 annual, 5×7 aside issue; mi, xerography. Reporting time: 1-3 months. Payment: 1 contributors copy minimum. Copyrighted, reverts to author. Pub's reviews: 5 in 1990. §Literary magazines, chapbooks. No ads.

Bonus Books, Inc., Sharon Turner Mulvihill, Assistant Editor; Lawrence Razbadouski, Assistant Editor, 160 East Illinois Street, Chicago, IL 60611, 312-467-0580. 1985. Non-fiction. avg. press run 5M-10M. Pub'd 16 titles 1990; expects 21 titles 1991, 25 titles 1992. 59 titles listed in the *Small Press Record of Books in Print* (20th Edition, 1991-92). avg. price, cloth: $16.95; paper: $7.95. Discounts: please inquire. 240pp; 6×9; of. Reporting time: 1 month (send SASE). Payment: standard scale. Copyrights for author.

Bookcraft, Margaret E. Haller, PO Box 605, Fiskdale, MA 01518-0605, 413-245-7459. 1990. Non-fiction. "Bookcraft, formed to answer a specific need with a book on small-town library buildings, will in the future be interested in publishing other material. Title of first book: *Libraries in New England*, published January, 1991." avg. press run 2M. Pub'd 1 title 1990; expects 2 titles 1991, 3 titles 1992. 1 title listed in the *Small Press Record of Books in Print* (20th Edition, 1991-92). avg. price, paper: $17.95. Discounts: available to libraries everywhere, please inquire. 188pp; 9¾×8¼; of. Copyrights for author.

BOOK DEALERS WORLD, North American Bookdealers Exchange, Al Galasso, Editorial Director; Judy Wiggins, Senior Editor; Russ von Hoelscher, Associate Editor, PO Box 606, Cottage Grove, OR 97424-0026. 1979. Articles, news items, non-fiction. "Articles of interest to self-publishers, writers, and mail order book dealers and information sellers. 1000-2000 words length." circ. 20M. 4/yr. Pub'd 4 issues 1990; expects 4 issues 1991, 4 issues 1992. sub. price: $16; per copy: $4; sample: $2. Back issues: 2 for $3. Discounts: 35% off 1 yr. sub or $10.40 for agents, trade, bulk, etc. 32pp; 8½×11; of. Reporting time: 2 weeks. Payment: ad space in exchange for contributions or $20 to $50 for articles depending on length. Copyrighted, reverts to author. Pub's reviews: 100+ in 1990. §Money-making and money-saving books of all types, how-to, male-female relationships, health & diet. Ads: $300/$150/$7.50-15 words.

BOOK FORUM, Driskill Clarence, Editor, Crescent Publishing Co., Inc., PO Box 585, Niantic, CT 06357. 1974. Articles, interviews, criticism, reviews. circ. 5.2M. 4/yr. Pub'd 4 issues 1990; expects 4 issues 1991, 4 issues 1992. sub. price: $18; per copy: $6; sample: $3. Back issues: $6. Discounts: 40% to bookstores. 48pp; 8½×11; of. Reporting time: 3-4 weeks. Payment: $25-$100. Copyrighted. Pub's reviews: 75 in 1990. §Non fiction, literary bio, criticism, world affairs. No poetry, fiction. Ads: $200 full-page. NBCC.

BOOK MARKETING UPDATE, Open Horizons Publishing Company, John Kremer, PO Box 1102, Fairfield, IA 52556, 515-472-6130. 1986. Articles, art, photos, cartoons, interviews, reviews, letters, news items, non-fiction. "News, stories, and resources to help other publishers market their books more effectively." circ. 3M. 6/yr. Pub'd 6 issues 1990; expects 6 issues 1991, 6 issues 1992. sub. price: $48; per copy: $8; sample: $8. 32pp; 8½×11; of. Reporting time: 1 week. Payment: none. Copyrighted, reverts to author. Pub's reviews: 3-4 in 1990. §Book publishing, marketing, direct mail, graphics, printing, publicity, directories. Ads: $350/$175/$125 1/4 page. PMA, COSMEP, MAP, MSPA, UMBA, ABA, MIPA.

BOOK NEWS & BOOK BUSINESS MART, Premier Publishers, Inc., Neal Michaels, Owen Bates, PO Box 330309, Fort Worth, TX 76163, 817-293-7030. 1971. Articles, reviews, news items. "Recent contributors: Lee Howard, author and president of *Selective Books*; Galen Stilson, consultant and publisher of *The Direct Response Specialist*. Character of circulation: distributed to mail order dealers, suppliers to mail order firms, new entrants to mail order and new opportunity seekers. Doubles as advertising forum for mail order distributors, news magazine and wholesale catalog" circ. 50M. 4/yr. Pub'd 4 issues 1990; expects 4 issues 1991, 4 issues 1992. sub. price: $4; per copy: $2; sample: $2. 80pp; 8½×11; of, web. Payment: negotiable. Copyrighted, reverts to author. Pub's reviews: 2 in 1990. §Self-improvement, do-it-yourself, how-to, success oriented how-to, or instruction manual how-to. Ads: $400/75¢.

The Book Peddlers, Vicki Lansky, Editor & President, 18326 Minnetonka Boulevard, Deephaven, MN 55391, 612-475-3527. 1983. Non-fiction. "Parenting area" avg. press run 5M. Expects 4 titles 1991, 2 titles 1992. 9 titles listed in the *Small Press Record of Books in Print* (20th Edition, 1991-92). avg. price, paper: $7.95. 132pp; size varies. Reporting time: varies. Payment: percent of net receipts. Sometimes copyrights for author. ABA.

THE BOOK REPORT: Journal for Junior & Senior High School Librarians, Linworth Publishing, Inc., Carolyn Hamilton, Publisher & Editor; Annette Thorson, Book Review Editor; Marlene Woo-Lun, President; Jenifer Wilson, Marketing Manager, 5701 N. High Street, Suite One, Worthington, OH 43085, 614-436-7107; FAX 614-436-9490. 1982. Articles, reviews. circ. 11M. 5/yr. Pub'd 5 issues 1990; expects 5 issues 1991, 5 issues 1992. sub. price: $39 US, $47 Canada, $59 foreign; per copy: $9; sample: no charge. Back issues: $9.

Discounts: 5%. 68pp; 8½×11. Reporting time: 2 weeks. Payment: none. Copyrighted, does not revert to author. Pub's reviews: 450 in 1990. §Books suitable for school libraries, grades 6-12. Ads: $812/$528/$325 1/3 page (b/w), 4-color full page 2nd, 3rd & 4th cover $1712 (1x). EDPress.

BOOK RIGHTS REPORT, Owen J. Hurd, 1947 W. Leland #2, Chicago, IL 60640, 312-769-3769. 1990. Reviews, news items. "News of interest to acquisitions editors of book publishing houses. Lists available book and subsidiary rights. Reviews books for the publishing and writing industries." circ. 5M. 6/yr. Pub'd 1 issue 1990; expects 6 issues 1991, 6 issues 1992. sub. price: free. 6pp; 8½×11; of. Payment: none. Not copyrighted. Pub's reviews: 1 in 1990. §Book publishing industry or writer's reference. Ads: $594/$297/$200 1/4 page. American Booksellers Assn. (ABA), Publishers Marketing Assn. (PMA), COSMEP, Mid-American Publishers Assn. (MAPA).

BOOK TALK, Carol A. Myers, 8632 Horacio Pl NE, Albuquerque, NM 87111, 505-299-8940. 1972. Articles, reviews. "300-1M words. All contributors actively engaged in a book-related field (editors, librarians, booksellers, publishers, authors (of books), etc.). ISSN: 0145 627X" circ. 500. 5/yr. Pub'd 5 issues 1990; expects 5 issues 1991, 5 issues 1992. sub. price: $7.50; per copy: $1.00; sample: free. Back issues: $1.00 for existing issues, $2.00 for issues needing reproduction. 12pp; 8½×11; of. Reporting time: 1 month. Payment: none - all donated by subscribers or interested bookpeople. Not copyrighted. Pub's reviews: 120 in 1990. §Southwestern non-fiction (area defined as TX, NM, AZ, CA, UT, CO and OK). Ads: $100/$50. New Mexico Book League.

BookNotes :(TM) Resources for Small & Self-Publishers, HearSay Press TM, Cliff Martin, Editor, PO Box 3877, Eugene, OR 97403-0877. 1984. "*BookNotes (TM)* is a monthly newsletter created especially as a resource for marketing and promoting small and self-publisher's books. Coverage includes conventional sales (like libraries, bookstores, direct mail), and unusual markets (like premium sales, specialty markets, selling rights, etc.). Irregular "bonus" special issues" circ. 1.5M. 6/yr. Pub'd 6 issues 1990; expects 6 issues 1991, 6 issues 1992. sub. price: $45; per copy: $4; sample: same. Back issues: same. Discounts: write for details. 4pp; 8½×11; of. Payment: none. Copyrighted, does not revert to author. Pub's reviews: 12 in 1990. §Books and periodicals on publishing, bookselling, business, mail order, writing, graphics, and printing. COSMEP, NW Book Publishing Association, AM Book Council, Int. Association Book Trade Consultants.

BOOKS AND RELIGION: A Quarterly Review, Christopher Walters-Bugbee, Trinity Church, 74 Trinity Place, New York, NY 10006. 1971. Reviews. "Subscriptions ordered from *Books & Religion*, PO Box 3000, Dept. LL, Denville, NJ 07834" circ. 3.5M. 4/yr. Pub'd 6 issues 1990; expects 4 issues 1991, 4 issues 1992. sub. price: $20; per copy: $5; sample: free on request. Back issues: $3.00. 40pp; 9¾×13¾; of. Reporting time: 3-4 weeks. Payment: negotiable. Copyrighted, reverts to author. Pub's reviews: 200 in 1990. §Religion, philosophy, history, psychology, general humanities. Ads: $450/$250.

Books for All Times, Inc. (see also EDUCATION IN FOCUS), Joe David, PO Box 2, Alexandria, VA 22313, 703-548-0457. 1981. Fiction, non-fiction. "At this time overstocked. Will only consider at a future date (always query) books of lasting quality (non-fiction and fiction). Modern classics of mentally healthy and efficacious characters achieving. Example: *The Fire Within* by Joe David." avg. press run 3M. Pub'd 1 title 1990; expects 1 title 1991, 1 title 1992. 2 titles listed in the *Small Press Record of Books in Print* (20th Edition, 1991-92). avg. price, paper: $5.95. Discounts: 40% bookstores; 50% wholesalers and distributors; write publisher for details. 250pp; 5¼×8½; of. Reporting time: query always, 4 weeks at the most. Payment: to be negotiated. Copyrights for author.

BOOKS OF THE SOUTHWEST, W. David Laird, Editor, Box 40850, Tucson, AZ 85717, 602-326-3533. 1957. Reviews. circ. 500. 12/yr. Pub'd 12 issues 1990; expects 12 issues 1991, 12 issues 1992. sub. price: $20 indiv., $30 instit., $45 foreign; per copy: $3; sample: free. Back issues: ask for quote. Discounts: none. 18pp; 5×8; of. Payment: none. Copyrighted. Pub's reviews: 600 in 1990. §Anything Southwest. No ads.

THE BOOKWATCH, Diane C. Donovan, Editor, 166 Miramar Avenue, San Francisco, CA 94112, 415-587-7009. 1980. Reviews. "*The Bookwatch* publishes short (approx. 100 words) reviews, bias towards titles which would appeal to a general readership. Reviews outline the scope of each title with notations on how it compares to similar publications. Only titles which are recommended are reviewed. The bulk of *The Bookwatch* lies in nonfiction, but other major sections include science fiction and fantasy and young adult fiction. A section is also devoted to audiocassettes." circ. 5M. 12/yr. Pub'd 12 issues 1990; expects 12 issues 1991, 12 issues 1992. sub. price: $12; per copy: $1.50; sample: $1.50. Back issues: $1.50 each. Discounts: 40% bookstores. 12pp; 8½×11; of. Reporting time: 4-6 weeks. Payment: 1 copy of issue in which review appears. Copyrighted, reverts to author. Pub's reviews: 800+ in 1990. §General-interest nonfiction (science, history/culture, health, travel), SF and Fantasy, Young adult fiction. Ads: $504/$327.60/write for smaller size rates.

Bookworm Publishing Company, Barbara Redin, Editor-In-Chief, PO Box 3037, Ontario, CA 91761. 1975. Non-fiction. "We publish books of interest in the fields of natural and social ecology, broadly defined. Current titles include *Earthworms For Ecology And Profit, Don't Call It Dirt!*, by Gordon Baker Lloyd. *House Plants and Crafts For Fun & Profit* by Derek Fell, *Living Off the Country For Fun & Profit* by John L. Parker. Other titles cover the fields of vermology, gardening, and botany. We are looking for well-written how-to-do-it type books on any topic related to gardening & agriculture, including business, and family self-sufficiency'' Pub'd 4 titles 1990; expects 10 titles 1991. 9 titles listed in the *Small Press Record of Books in Print* (20th Edition, 1991-92). avg. price, cloth: $9.95; paper: $5.95; other: $5.95. Discounts: 1-5, 20%; 6-10, 33%; 11-25, 40%; 26-50, 44%; 51-100, 48%. 200pp; 5½x8½. Reporting time: 6 weeks. Payment: royalty, 5-10% of revenue. Copyrights for author. BPASC, BPSC.

BOOMBAH HERALD, Loren D. Geiger, 15 Park Boulevard, Lancaster, NY 14086. 1973. Articles, photos, reviews, music, non-fiction. "The *Boombah Herald* is devoted entirely to preservation of *band music history*, with emphasis on composer biographies, band literature, and stories on contemporary military and concertbands. Publish reviews of records, 2 last year, possible review (military band music)." circ. 100. 2/yr. Pub'd 2 issues 1990; expects 2 issues 1991, 2 issues 1992. sub. price: $10; per copy: price varies; sample: postage. Back issues: varies with date from 50¢ - $5. 4-18pp; 8x11; of. Payment: none. Copyrighted, does not revert to author. Pub's reviews: 1 in 1990. §Band music, band history, records of band music. Ads: $10.

Borderland Sciences Research Foundation (see also JOURNAL OF BORDERLAND RESEARCH), Thomas Joseph Brown, Alison Davidson, P.O. Box 429, Gaberville, CA 95440, 724-2043. 1945. Articles, photos, reviews, news items. "We publish the researches of our associates on alternate energy, alternate medicine, UFOs, fortean phenomenon, ether physics." avg. press run 2.5M. Pub'd 3 titles 1990; expects 5 titles 1991, 10 titles 1992. 7 titles listed in the *Small Press Record of Books in Print* (20th Edition, 1991-92). avg. price, paper: $9.95. Discounts: 40% to qualified retail outlets. 120pp; 5½x8½; web. Reporting time: 30-60 days. Payment: varies—average 10% of net. Copyrights for author.

BORDER/LINES, 183 Bathurst Street, #301, Toronto, Ontario M5T 2R7, Canada, 416-360-5249. 1984. Articles, art, photos, cartoons, interviews, criticism, reviews, parts-of-novels, collages, non-fiction. "Critical commentary on culture and politics, art, music" circ. 2M. 4/yr. Pub'd 3 issues 1990; expects 4 issues 1991, 4 issues 1992. sub. price: $16 indiv., $14 low income, $35 instit.; per copy: $5; sample: $5. Back issues: $5. Discounts: 30% to distribution, retailers. 52pp; 15⅜x9; lp. Reporting time: 6 weeks. Payment: at present to Ontario writers only. Copyrighted, reverts to author. Pub's reviews: 24 in 1990. §Culture, arts, music, communications, film, TV, radio, political movements. Ads: $500/$300/1/4 $175. CPPA/Marginal.

Borealis Press Limited (see also JOURNAL OF CANADIAN POETRY), Frank Tierney, Glenn Clever, 9 Ashburn Drive, Nepean Ontario, Canada, 613-224-6837. 1970. Poetry, fiction, criticism, plays, non-fiction. "With few exceptions publish only material Canadian in authorship or orientation. Query first." avg. press run 1M. Pub'd 4 titles 1990; expects 4 titles 1991, 4 titles 1992. 3 titles listed in the *Small Press Record of Books in Print* (20th Edition, 1991-92). avg. price, cloth: $25; paper: $13. Discounts: 40% to retail; 20% to jobbers. 150pp; 5½x8½; of. Reporting time: 6 months. Payment: 10% once yearly. Does not copyright for author.

The Borgo Press, Robert Reginald, Publisher; Mary Burgess, Editorial Director; Daryl F. Mallett, Assistant Editor, Box 2845, San Bernardino, CA 92406, (714) 884-5813. 1975. Criticism, non-fiction. "We publish and distribute scholarly books in the Humanities and Social Sciences for the library and academic markets. All of our books are published in open-ended, monographic series, including: The Milford Series: Popular Writers of Today; Stokvis Studies in Historical Chronology and Thought; I.O. Evans Studies in the Philosophy and Criticism of Literature; Clipper Studies in the American Theater; Borgo BioViews; Bibliographies of Modern Authors; etc." avg. press run 300. Pub'd 100 titles 1990; expects 100 titles 1991, 100 titles 1992. avg. price, cloth: $19.95-$49.95; paper: $9.95-$39.95. Discounts: 20% for trade sales, 50-99 copies 22%, 100-199 24%, 200+ 25%. Payment in advance required for all sales to bookstores and individuals. Pages vary; 5¼x8¼; of. Reporting time: 2 months minimum. Payment: royalty 10%, no advances; we pay once annually. Copyrights for author.

Don Bosco Multimedia, Rev. James Hurley, Publisher; Michael Mendl, Salesian Studies Editor; John Serio, Editorial Director, 475 North Avenue, Box T, New Rochelle, NY 10802, 914-576-0122. 1952. Non-fiction. "Books and pamphlets for religious education and popular reading. Emphasis on youth." avg. press run 2.5M. Pub'd 3 titles 1990; expects 6 titles 1991, 18 titles 1992. 38 titles listed in the *Small Press Record of Books in Print* (20th Edition, 1991-92). avg. price, cloth: $24.95; paper: $13.95; other: $1.50 picture books. Discounts: 1 10%, 2-4 25%, 5-9 35%, 10-99 40%, 100-249 42%, 250-499 44%. 225pp; 5¼x7¾, 6x9; of/lo. Reporting time: 6 weeks. Payment: negotiable. Copyrights for author. Catholic Book Publishers Association.

BOSTON LITERARY REVIEW, Gloria Mindock, Editor, PO Box 357, West Somerville, MA 02144. 1984. Poetry, fiction. "*Boston Literary Review (BLuR)* emphasizes poetry, with one short story per issue. Preference is for work with a strong voice, and that has unique form or content. Experimental work is welcome, as are series of poems. Writers may submit 5-10 poems, and fiction under 2500 words. *BLuR* has published Stuart Friebert, Richard Kostelanetz, Eric Pankey, David Ray and Ron Silliman." circ. 500. 2/yr. Pub'd 2 issues 1990;

expects 2 issues 1991, 2 issues 1992. sub. price: $6; per copy: $4; sample: $4. Back issues: none. 24pp; 5½×13; of. Reporting time: 2-4 weeks. Payment: 2 copies. Copyrighted, reverts to author. No ads.

The Boston Mills Press, John Denison, President, 132 Main Street, Erin, Ontario N0B 1T0, Canada, 519-833-2407. 1974. Non-fiction. "Historical subjects, e.g: transportation, pioneer life, community histories and lifestyles—Canadian and American." avg. press run 2M. Pub'd 7 titles 1990; expects 20 titles 1991, 20 titles 1992. 50 titles listed in the *Small Press Record of Books in Print* (20th Edition, 1991-92). avg. price, cloth: $24.95; paper: $14.95. Discounts: 40% wholesale. 160pp; 8×11; of. Reporting time: 2 weeks. Payment: negotiable. Copyrights for author. CBIC, ABA, CBA, OHS.

BOSTON REVIEW, Margaret Ann Roth, Editor; Sophie Glazer, Managing Editor; Garen Daly, Advertising Editor, 33 Harrison Avenue, Boston, MA 02111-2008, 617-350-5353. 1975. Poetry, fiction, articles, art, photos, interviews, criticism, reviews, parts-of-novels, long-poems. "Bi-monthly publication of art and culture" circ. 10M. 6/yr. Pub'd 6 issues 1990; expects 6 issues 1991, 6 issues 1992. sub. price: $15 individuals, $18 institutions; per copy: $2.50; sample: $4. Back issues: $4. Discounts: bookstores 50%. 32-40pp; 11⅜×14½; of. Reporting time: 2 months. Payment: $50-$200 according to subject, author, length. Copyrighted, reverts to author. Pub's reviews: 70 in 1990. §Poetry, fiction, criticism, all the arts, politics, culture. Ads: $800/$450/Class: $1 per word, $10 minimum. CCLM.

BOTH SIDES NOW, Free People Press, Elihu Edelson, Editor, Rt 6, Box 28, Tyler, TX 75704, 903-592-4263. 1969. Poetry, fiction, articles, art, photos, cartoons, interviews, satire, criticism, reviews, music, letters, news items, non-fiction. ""An Alternative Journal of New Age/Aquarian Transformations." Articles on current events and thinkpieces with emphasis on alternatives which have implicit spiritual content. Unique spiritual/political synthesis related to such concepts as 'New Age politics' and 'the Aquarian conspiracy.' Editorial concerns include nonviolence, pacifism, decentralism, green politics, human rights, social justice, alternative lifestyles & institutions, healing, economics, appropriate technology, organic agriculture, philosophy, prophecy, psychic pheanomena, the occult, metaphysics, and religion. Reprints of important material which deserves wider circulation" Irregular. sub. price: $9/10 issues, $5/5 issues; per copy: $1; sample: $1. Back issues: price list on request with SASE. 8pp; 8½×11; photocopied. Reporting time: erratic. Payment: copies. Copyrighted, reverts to author. Pub's reviews: 0 in 1990. §'New Age', pacifism, anarchism, religion, the occult, radical and "Green" politics, general alternatives. Ads: $50 (7½ X 10)/smaller sizes pro-rated/classifieds 20¢/word. APS.

Bottom Dog Press, Larry Smith, c/o Firelands College of BGSU, Huron, OH 44839, 419-433-5560. 1984. Poetry, fiction, parts-of-novels, long-poems. "We do a combined chapbook series (three chapbooks bound as one) and collections of stories, personal essays and photography. A chapbook of poetry should be 20-40 poems with a unified theme and form. We are particularly interested in the work of Ohio writers—our Ohio Writers Series—and in the writing of the Midwest—Our Midwest Writers Series. We expect the writer to work with us on the production and distribution of the book. Publication payment is either through royalties, copies, or co-op arrangement. Our slant is towards writing that is direct and human with clean, clear images and voice. We prefer the personal, but not the self-indulgent, simple but not simplistic, writing of value to us all. Our bias is towards sense of place writing—being who you are, where you are, and here. Authors we've published: Robert Flanagan, Philip F. O'Connor, Jack Matthews, Robert Fox, Wendell Berry, Scott Sanders, David Shevin, Joe Napora, Roy Rentley, Diane Kendig, Annie Dillard." avg. press run 600 poetry, 1M fiction. Pub'd 2 titles 1990; expects 3 titles 1991, 3 titles 1992. 16 titles listed in the *Small Press Record of Books in Print* (20th Edition, 1991-92). avg. price, paper: $3-$9. Discounts: 1-4 30%, 5-9 copies 35%, 40% 10+ copies. 160pp; 5½×8½; of, lp. Reporting time: 1-2 months. Payment: negotiated. Copyrights for author.

THE BOTTOM LINE PUBLICATIONS, Weems Concepts, Kay Weems, Editor, Star Route, Box 21AA, Artemas, PA 17211, 814-458-3102. 1988. "This is a huge market listing for poets and writers. Offers over 100 listings per month, complete with guidelines and entry forms. Complete guidelines given for writers and poets on contests, etc." circ. 100. 12/yr. Pub'd 12 issues 1990; expects 12 issues 1991, 12 issues 1992. sub. price: $25; per copy: $3; sample: $2.50. Back issues: $2.50. 30-50pp; 8½×11; †Sharp copier. Reporting time: 3-5 weeks. Ads: info furnished upon request. PA Poetry Society, Walt Whitman Guild, UAPAA, National Arts Society, National Federation of State Poetry Societies, New Horizons Poetry Club, Southern Poetry Assoc.

BOTTOMFISH MAGAZINE, Robert Scott, 21250 Stevens Creek Blvd., Cupertino, CA 95014, 408-996-4538, 996-4547. 1976. Poetry, fiction, parts-of-novels, long-poems, plays. "Adrianne Marcus, Thom Gunn, Stephen Vincent, Paul Shuttleworth, Frank Cady, Wm. Dickey, Joseph Stroud, Frances Mayes." circ. 500. 1/yr. Pub'd 1 issue 1990; expects 1 issue 1991, 1 issue 1992. sub. price: free to libraries, small press racks, schools, but is $4 per copy to individual requests which covers only the cost of printing; per copy: $4; sample: $4. Back issues: $2.00. Discounts: none, free on request to libraries, mags. 50-70pp; 7×8½; †of. Reporting time: 6-8 weeks, (not operating during the summer). Payment: 2 copies of magazine. Not copyrighted. Ads: none. COSMEP.

BOULEVARD, Richard Burgin, Editor, Opojaz, Inc., 2400 Chestnut Street, #2208, Philadelphia, PA 19103, 215-561-1723. 1985. Poetry, fiction, articles, art, photos, cartoons, interviews, criticism, music, parts-of-novels, long-poems, plays, non-fiction. "Contributors: I.B. Singer, John Updike, Tess Gallagher, Kenneth Koch, Tom Disch, Allen Ginsberg, Joyce Carol Oates, Alice Adams, David Mamet, Donald Hall, John Ashbery, Phillip Lopate. *Boulevard* is committed to publishing the best of contemporary fiction, poetry, and non-fiction." circ. 2.5M. 3/yr. Pub'd 3 issues 1990; expects 3 issues 1991, 3 issues 1992. sub. price: $12; per copy: $5 + $1 p/h; sample: $5 + $1 p/h. Back issues: $5. Discounts: 50% agency. 200pp; 5⅜×8½; of. Reporting time: 8-12 weeks. Payment: $25-$100 (poetry), $50-$150 (fiction), plus contributor's copies. Copyrighted, reverts to author. §Fiction, poetry, lit. criticism, art/music criticism. Ads: $100/$500 for back cover. CCLM.

THE BOUND SPIRAL, Mr. M. Petrucci, M. Schneider, 72 First Avenue, Bush Hill Park, Enfield, Middlesex, EN1 1BW, England. 1988. Poetry, articles, art, criticism, reviews, letters. "Generally poems any length, some short fiction. All art received will be considered, but must be photo-copy tolerant." circ. 100-200. 2/yr. Pub'd 1 issue 1990; expects 2 issues 1991, 2 issues 1992. sub. price: £4; per copy: £2; sample: £2. Back issues: £1.50. Discounts: 10% for 5+. 40pp; 5¾×8¼; Xerox, high quality. Reporting time: 1-4 months (dependent on sub-editors). Payment: 1 complimentary copy. Copyrighted, reverts to author. Pub's reviews: 2 in 1990. §Poetry, but available review space is limited. Ads: £10/£5.

BOUNDARY, Ray Darlington, 23 Kingsley Road, Runcorn, Cheshire, WA7 5PL, England, Runcorn 63624. 1984. Poetry, fiction, articles, art, photos, interviews, satire, reviews, letters, long-poems, collages. "Non-Fiction about Literature. Short-stories max 1200 words. No bias (intentional that is) no racist or sexist material will be accepted. We accept contributions of poetry, short-stories, prose and artwork—all must be accompanied by an S.A.E. for return of unused Mss. Our current issue is issue seven. We do publish articals about literature also letters which care to comment on *Boundary*. Artwork must be no larger than A4 line drawings black on white. We do music and theatre reviews along with magazines. Although we can not print plays we will offer critisism on plays sent to us. A number of individual collections of poetry, prose, and song lyrics are available too" circ. 250. 3/yr. Pub'd 3 issues 1990; expects 3 issues 1991, 3 issues 1992. sub. price: £1.50; per copy: 50p; sample: large S.A.E. 11pp; 104.5×148.5mm (A5); duplication. Reporting time: aproximately 14 days. Payment: complimentary copy of magazine. Copyrighted, reverts to author. Pub's reviews: approx. 6 per issue in 1990. §Poetry, short-stories, prose, fanzines. FAIM, FWWCP, MAWW.

BOWBENDER, Kathleen E. Windsor, 65 McDonald Close, PO Box 912, Carstairs, Alberta T0M 0N0, Canada, 403-337-3023. 1983. Articles, art, photos, cartoons, interviews, criticism, reviews, letters, news items, non-fiction. "Up to 3,000 words. Must be Canadian game in hunting articles. Recent contributors: Russell Thornberry, Dr. Valerius Geist, George R. Bradford. Editorial guidelines available for SASE on request. Content is Canadian, archery, hunting, equipment, animals" circ. 47M. 5/yr. Pub'd 4 issues 1990; expects 5 issues 1991, 5-6 issues 1992. sub. price: $11; per copy: $2.50; sample: $2.95 (Cdn). Back issues: $2.95 each. 48+pp; 8¼×10⅞; sheet fed. Reporting time: every other Friday. Payment: 10¢/word (includes photo complement). Copyrighted, first NA Serial Rights only. Pub's reviews: 1-2 in 1990. §Archery, hunting, wildlife, how-tos in these areas. Ads: Canadian 1X b/w: $1316/$784/available on request. OWC.

BOX 749 MAGAZINE, The Printable Arts Society, Inc., David Ferguson, Editor In Chief; P. Raymond Marunas, Art Editor; Thomas Garber, Music Editor; Brian Padol, Amy H. Gateff, Betty B. Kcein, Ann Tucker, 411 West 22nd Street, New York, NY 10011, 212-98-0519. 1972. Poetry, fiction, art, photos, cartoons, satire, music, parts-of-novels, long-poems, collages, plays. "*Box 749* is a magazine of the printable arts—open to all kinds of writing, graphic art and music. We have no particular stylistic or ideological bias. We will consider—and have serialized—long fiction; we have published one-act plays and will consider plays that are full length. (We have also printed the first two poems, with art work, of a six-part broadside series.)" circ. 3.5M. 1/yr. Expects 1 issue 1991, 1 issue 1992. sub. price: $7/4 issues; per copy: Vol 2, double issue, numbers 2&3, $2.50 ($3.25 mail); sample: $2.50 ($3.25 for mail orders). Back issues: $6 each ($6.75 for mail orders). Discounts: 4-issue subscription is $6 to libraries. No discounts for single copies. 100pp; 8½×11; of. Reporting time: 1-3 months. Payment: copies. Copyrighted, reverts to author. No ads. CCLM, COSMEP, NESPA.

Box Turtle Press (see also MUDFISH), Jill Hoffman, Poetry Editor; Vladimir Urban, Art Editor, 184 Franklin Street, New York, NY 10013. 1983. avg. press run 1.5M. Pub'd 1 title 1990; expects 2 titles 1991. avg. price, cloth: $8. Discounts: 1983. 168pp; 6⅞×8¼. Reporting time: immediately to 6 months.

The Boxwood Press, Ralph Buchsbaum, Editor, 183 Ocean View Blvd, Pacific Grove, CA 93950, 408-375-9110. 1952. Non-fiction. "FAX: 408-375-0430. *Books*: science & natural history, misc." avg. press run 1M. Pub'd 8 titles 1990; expects 8 titles 1991. 24 titles listed in the *Small Press Record of Books in Print* (20th Edition, 1991-92). avg. price, cloth: $25; paper: $9.95. Discounts: 20% on texts, 40% trade. 200pp; 5½×8½, 6×9; of, photo type setting-digital. Reporting time: 30 days. Payment: 10% royalty. Copyrights for author.

Betty Boyink Publishing, Betty Boyink, Brent A. Boyink, 818 Sheldon Road, Grand Haven, MI 49417,

616-842-3304. 1982. "Primarily self-publisher but also publishes selective materials for other authors which fall into the category of "Ideas, patterns and techniques for making quilts." Do not market through traditional book channels of sale, but rather through quilt, fabric and needlework shops as well as direct response and direct mailing advertising" avg. press run 5M. Pub'd 1 title 1990; expects 2 titles 1991, 1 title 1992. 12 titles listed in the *Small Press Record of Books in Print* (20th Edition, 1991-92). avg. price, paper: $12.50, both saddle stitch and perfect bound. Discounts: 40% to retail trades, 50-60% distribution. 60-80pp; 8½×11; of. Reporting time: 2-4 weeks on queries. Payment: 5% payable quarterly. Copyrights for author.

BOYS & GIRLS GROW UP, Amy Crehore, Tom Campagnoli, 904 Forestview Drive, Richmond, VA 23225. 1981. Art, photos, cartoons. circ. 1.2M. 0/yr. 1 title listed in the *Small Press Record of Books in Print* (20th Edition, 1991-92). price per copy: $2.50. Back issues: #1 $5; #2-#5 $2.50. Discounts: 30% retail stores, standard wholesale discounts. 35pp; 8½×11. Payment: free copies of book, others at cost. Copyrighted, reverts to author.

Boz Publishing, Richard Simonds, Ron Really, 163 Third Ave., Suite 127, New York, NY 10003, 212-795-1800. 1988. Poetry, fiction, long-poems. "We are looking for works of exceptional originality by writers in the New York area." avg. press run 500. Pub'd 1 title 1990; expects 1 title 1991, 2 titles 1992. Discounts: 40% on all orders at wholesale; full list price on all mail-order sales. Reporting time: 3 months. Payment: negotiable. Copyrights for author. COSMEP.

BP REPORT, Kenneth S. Giniger, PO Box 7430, Wilton, CT 06897. 1983. "All staff written. Business and circulation address: Knowledge Industry Publications, 701 Westchester Ave, White Plains, NY 10604. Length of material: 4 pages, telegraphic style. Events, news items, contact names and addresses, bi-annual Calendar of Events. Categories: publishing events, import/export, marketing, economic news, rights, copyright, piracy, merger, acquisition, expansion, book manufacturing, new technologies, editorial, travel advisory, personnel" 12/yr. Pub'd 12 issues 1990; expects 12 issues 1991, 12 issues 1992. sub. price: $125 US, $140 foreign; sample: free. Back issues: $15. Discounts: 10% agency commissions. 5pp; 8½×11; of. Payment: none. Copyrighted, does not revert to author. Pub's reviews: 85 in 1990. §Book publishing, marketing, editorial reference. No ads. IPN.

THE BRADFORD POETRY QUARTERLY, Clare Chapman, 9, Woodvale Way, Bradford, West Yorkshire BD7 2SJ, England. 1984. Poetry. "Any style of poetry considered. Would prefer fairly short poems—this is owing to lack of space, not dislike of epics." circ. 100. 4/yr. Pub'd 2 issues 1990; expects 3 issues 1991, 3-4 issues 1992. sub. price: £2; per copy: 70p; sample: 50p. Back issues: anything I can negotiate. 30pp; size A5; mi. Reporting time: about a month. Payment: complimentary copies of magazines; can't afford fees. Copyrighted, reverts to author. §Would be interested to see other small poetry magazines, if they are offered free. No ads. WYFSP, West Yorkshire Federation of Small Presses, Flat 7, 4, Chestnut Avenue, Leeds LS6 1BA England.

Brain Books, 2075 Buffalo Creek Road, Lake Lure, NC 28746, 704-625-9153. 1987. Non-fiction. "Our first title, *The Creative Brain,* is a book that is geared toward individuals who want to gain full access to his or her mental capabilities, and learn how this can be a very creative process. The author has been a trainer of trainers in a corporate setting for over 20 years. Basing his work on brain dominance theory. The author has developed a model of thinking styles which can be used in training or for an individual's quest to know more about him or her self." avg. press run 5M. Pub'd 1 title 1990; expects 1 title 1992. 1 title listed in the *Small Press Record of Books in Print* (20th Edition, 1991-92). avg. price, cloth: $34.95; paper: $24.95. Discounts: trade 2-7 20%, 8-32 40%, 40-48 43%, 56-104 46%, 105-160 50%, 161+ 55%. 480pp; 11×8½; of. Copyrights for author. ABA.

BRAIN/MIND BULLETIN, Interface Press, Marilyn Ferguson, Publisher & Executive Editor, P O Box 42211, Los Angeles, CA 90042, 213-223-2500; 800-553-MIND. 1975. Articles, interviews, reviews, news items. "Except for 'Letters,' BMB is staff-written" circ. 10M. 12/yr. Pub'd 12 issues 1990; expects 12 issues 1991, 12 issues 1992. sub. price: $35, $40 outside N.America; per copy: $2 (minimum of 2); sample: free. Back issues: $35 for 12 in sequence — otherwise $3 each. Also BMB 'Collections' and BMB 'ThemePacks' Discounts: inquire. 8pp; 8½×11; of. Payment: none. Copyrighted. Pub's reviews: 50+ in 1990. §Psychology, psychiatry, consciousness, brain research, learning, human potential, creativity, health, etc. Ads: none.

Branch Redd Books (see also BRANCH REDD REVIEW), William David Sherman, 4805 B Street, Philadelphia, PA 19120. 1976. Poetry. "No unsolicited contributions please." avg. press run 400. Pub'd 1 title 1990; expects 1 title 1991, 3 titles 1992. 6 titles listed in the *Small Press Record of Books in Print* (20th Edition, 1991-92). avg. price, paper: $10. Discounts: none. Pages vary; size varies. Copyrights for author.

BRANCH REDD REVIEW, Branch Redd Books, William David Sherman, 4805 "B" Street, Philadelphia, PA 19120. 1976. Poetry. "No unsolicited contributions, please." circ. 400. Irregular. Expects 1 issue 1991. sub. price: No subscriptions available; per copy: $10; sample: none. Back issues: *Branch Redd* poetry chapbooks #1 & #3, still in-print: *The Leer* by Allen Fisher $2, *Four Poems* by John Lobb $2. Both for $3. Discounts: none. Pages vary; size varies. Payment: copies. Copyrighted, reverts to author after publication.

Branden Publishing Company, Adolph Caso, 17 Station Street, Box 843, Brookline Village, MA 02147, 617-734-2045; FAX 617-734-2046. 1965. Fiction, art, music, letters, long-poems, plays, non-fiction. "See our latest catalogue. No manuscripts accepted, only queries with SASE" avg. press run 5M. Pub'd 15 titles 1990; expects 10 titles 1991, 15 titles 1992. 49 titles listed in the *Small Press Record of Books in Print* (20th Edition, 1991-92). avg. price, cloth: $15; paper: $8; other: $3. Discounts: from 1 copy 10% to 101+ copies 48%. 215pp; 6×9. Reporting time: 1 week. Payment: 10% on monies from sales; 50% on monies from sales of rights. Copyrights for author. NEBA.

Brandywyne Books (see also AFFAIRE DE COEUR), Barbara Keenan, 1555 Washington Avenue, San Leandro, CA 94577. 1984. "Brandywyne Books are limited special collectors editions. As of this date, they have all been previously published titles" avg. press run 500-1M. Pub'd 4 titles 1990. avg. price, cloth: $15-$25; paper: $2.25. Discounts: 40%. 250pp; of. Reporting time: 12 months. Copyrights for author. ABA.

Branyan Press, PO Box 764, Elburn, IL 60119, 312-442-7907. 1 title listed in the *Small Press Record of Books in Print* (20th Edition, 1991-92).

Brason-Sargar Publications, Sondra Anice Barnes, Publisher, PO Box 872, Reseda, CA 91337, 818-701-0809. 1978. Poetry, art. "We are primarily interested in gift books which express psychological truths. Must use as few words as possible. We publish thoughts, observations or statements expressing human truths written in a style which visually looks like poetry but is not poetry per se. If the poet reads our books *Life Is The Way It Is* or *We Are The Way We Are* and can write in this style, then we are interested and will negotiate payment." avg. press run 2M 1st printing, up to 20M subsequent printings. Pub'd 1 title 1990; expects 4 titles 1991, 19 titles 1992. 2 titles listed in the *Small Press Record of Books in Print* (20th Edition, 1991-92). avg. price, paper: $5. Discounts: 40% bookstores, 50% distributers. 96pp; 5½×8½; of. Reporting time: 30 days. Payment: to be negotiated. Copyrights for author. WNBA.

BRAVO, THE POET'S MAGAZINE, John Edwin Cowen, Ltd., Jose Garcia Villa, John Cowen, Publisher, 1081 Trafalgar Street, Teaneck, NJ 07666. 1980. Poetry. "Jose Garcia Villa, Editor, 780 Greenwich Street, New York, NY 10014. BRAVO believes that 1. poetry must have formal excellence; 2. poetry must be lyrical; 3. poetry is not prose. Recent contributors: Robert Levine, John Cowen, Gloria Potter, Nick Joaquin, and Filipino poets: Virginia Moreno, Alex Hufana, Jolico Cuadra, and Hilario Francia. ISSN 0275-6080" circ. 500, *Bravo #2* 1M. 2/yr. Expects 2 issues 1991. price per copy: $3.50; sample: $3.50 + 50¢ handling in USA. Back issues: $3.50. Discounts: 15%. 48pp; 6×9; of. Reporting time: 2 weeks to 1 month. Payment: 2 copies of magazine. Copyrighted, reverts to author. Ads: $150/$75. NYSSPA.

THE BREAD AND BUTTER CHRONICLES, Seven Buffaloes Press, Art Cuelho, PO Box 249, Big Timber, MT 59011. 1986. Art, photos, news items. "Special three-page feature in every issue entitled 'Rural American Hall of Fame'; inductees taken from poets, writers, and artists in rural and working people. There's a farm column by Frank Cross where he covers rural American literature at large. I list contests, mags looking for special materials, special anthologies being sought. New publications just born. Events, etc. *New focus* is on *rural essays.*" circ. 500. 2/yr. Expects 2 issues 1991, 2 issues 1992. sub. price: $2.50 pp; per copy: $1.25; sample: $1. Back issues: $1.25. 8pp; 8½×11; †of. Reporting time: 1 day to 2 weeks. Payment: copies. Copyrighted, reverts to author. CLMP.

BREAKFAST WITHOUT MEAT, Gregg Turkington, Lizzy Kate Gray, PO Box 15927, Santa Fe, NM 87506. 1983. Poetry, fiction, art, photos, cartoons, interviews, satire, criticism, reviews, music, letters. "*Breakfast Without Meat* started out as a San Francisco punk/underground fanzine, but has evolved into a childishly self-indulgent 'mak de Heck-bub'. We have featured interviews (with Meat Puppets, 101 Strings, Pete Townshend, Flipper, Jimmy Webb, Tiny Tim, Canned Heat), oddball fiction, record, concert, and movie reviews, art, and way offbeat poems. People considering submitting material should first become familiar with the tone of the magazine to avoid wasting time that could better be spent raking up Kraft cheese from the trecheele in their backyard" circ. 1M. Pub'd 1 issue 1990; expects 2 issues 1991, 2 issues 1992. sub. price: $8/3 issues; per copy: $3; sample: $3. Back issues: $1.75. Discounts: inquire. 24pp; 8½×11; of. Reporting time: 6 weeks (with SASE). Payment: copies, unusual gifts. Copyrighted. Pub's reviews. §Everything, but especially records and books on music and art. Ads: $75/$40/$50 back cover.

BREAKTHROUGH!, Aardvark Enterprises, J. Alvin Speers, 204 Millbank Drive S.W., Calgary, Alberta T2Y 2H9, Canada, 403-256-4639. 1982. Poetry, fiction, articles, photos, cartoons, interviews, reviews, letters, news items, non-fiction. "Approximately 2,500 words max. Up-beat tone, motivational positive outlook, serious or funny, lessons of life, making best of what we have, etc" circ. 250 and growing. 4/yr. Pub'd 4 issues 1990; expects 4 issues 1991, 4 issues 1992. sub. price: $15; per copy: $4; sample: $4. Back issues: $4. Discounts: none. 52pp; 5½×8½; †quality photocopying. Reporting time: return mail. Payment: small cash honorarium to best 3 items per issue by readers vote; no other payment at present. Copyrighted, reverts to author. Pub's reviews: 10 in 1990. §General interest items with up-beat theme in line with our own. Ads: $28/$14/$8 1/8 page. American Booksellers Exchange.

Breitenbush Books, Inc., Patrick Ames, Editor-in-Chief, P.O. Box 82157, Portland, OR 97282. 1977. Poetry, fiction, non-fiction. "Reading manuscripts 4/87" avg. press run 2.5M-5M. Pub'd 8 titles 1990; expects 8 titles 1991, 10 titles 1992. 15 titles listed in the *Small Press Record of Books in Print* (20th Edition, 1991-92). avg. price, cloth: $14.95; paper: $6.95. Discounts: Standard to bookstores. 64-350pp; 6×9; of. Reporting time: 3 months, SASE only! Payment: varies, depending upon author. Copyrights for author. PNWBPA, ABA.

Brennen Publishing Company, William K. Beaver, Ashland University, Clayton Hall, Ashland, OH 44805. 1987. News items, non-fiction. "Brennen Publishing Company is especially interested in receiving manuscripts dealing with the martial arts" Expects 3 titles 1991, 3 titles 1992. of. Reporting time: 2-3 weeks. Payment: varies, negotiable. Copyrights for author. COSMEP.

Brenner Information Group, Robert C. Brenner, Editor-in-Chief; Lee Rathbone, Editor, 9282 Samantha Court, San Diego, CA 92129, 619-538-0093. 1988. Non-fiction. "50-300 page published. How-to subjects (all categories including computers, engineering, and science). Recently published *The Silent Speech of Politicians - Body Language in Government*, how to read a politician like a book. In process: *Home Office Handbook*." avg. press run 5M. Pub'd 2 titles 1990; expects 4 titles 1991, 4 titles 1992. 7 titles listed in the *Small Press Record of Books in Print* (20th Edition, 1991-92). avg. price, paper: $7.95-$39.95. Discounts: 0-60%. 128-245pp; 7×9, 8½×11, 5½×8½; of. Reporting time: 4-6 weeks. Payment: 10%-17%. Copyrights for author. COSMEP, San Diego Pagemaker Users Group, Book Publicists of Southern California.

BRICK, Barry Carpenter, PO Box 1153, Russellville, AL 35653. 1988. Articles, cartoons, news items. "A newsletter which trys to encourage direct action to reinforce one's opinion. Carries a monthly calendar of anarchist history in each issue, or upcoming events of interest to anarchist activists." circ. 100. 4/yr. Pub'd 4 issues 1990; expects 4 issues 1991, 4 issues 1992. sub. price: $2; per copy: 50¢; sample: donation or 50¢. Back issues: none. Discounts: trades/stamps accepted, free to prisoners and those with no money; distributors 25¢/copy for 5 copies minimum. 8pp; 4¼×5½; photocopy. Reporting time: none. Payment: copy(s). Not copyrighted. Pub's reviews: 3 in 1990. §'Leftist' politics, anarchist (history, theory, fiction, etc.). Ads: trade for ad space only.

BRICK: A Journal Of Reviews, Linda Spalding, Box 537, Station Q, Toronto, Ontario M4T 2M5, Canada, 519-666-0283. 1976. Articles, criticism, reviews. "The review finds its own length. Experiment with form, according to what the book requires" circ. 1.2M. 3/yr. Pub'd 3 issues 1990; expects 3 issues 1991, 3 issues 1992. sub. price: $10 Canadian (+ $5 for foreign postage); per copy: $4; sample: $4. Back issues: $4. Discounts: bookstores 40%. 64pp; 8½×11; web. Reporting time: varies. Payment: varies. Copyrighted, reverts to author. Pub's reviews: 49 in 1990. §All areas. No ads. CMPA.

Brick Books, Stan Dragland, Don McKay, Box 38, Station B, London, Ontario N6K 4V3, Canada. 1975. Poetry. "Brick Books isn't looking for unsolicited manuscripts." avg. press run 500. Pub'd 4 titles 1990; expects 7 titles 1991, 4 titles 1992. 44 titles listed in the *Small Press Record of Books in Print* (20th Edition, 1991-92). avg. price, paper: $9.95. Discounts: 40% trade, 40% distributors, 20% 3+ books to libraries, 40% 3+ books to individuals. 56pp; size varies; of, lp. Reporting time: 3 months. Payment: 10% of print run in books. Copyrights for author. ACP, LPG.

Brick House Publishing Co., Inc., Robert Runck, PO Box 2134, Acton, MA 01720, 508-635-9800. 1976. Non-fiction. avg. press run 2.5M. Pub'd 12 titles 1990; expects 10 titles 1991, 12 titles 1992. avg. price, cloth: $24.95; paper: $12.95. Discounts: 1-4 20%, 5-24 40%, 25-49 45%, 50+ 50%. 200pp; 6×9; of. Reporting time: 3 months. Payment: Royalty paid 6 months from pub date. Net royalty. Copyrights for author.

Brick Row Publishing Co. Ltd., Oswald Kraus, L., PO Box 100-057, Auckland 10, New Zealand, 410-6993. 1978. avg. press run 3M-5M. Pub'd 3 titles 1990; expects 4 titles 1991, 4 titles 1992. 7 titles listed in the *Small Press Record of Books in Print* (20th Edition, 1991-92). avg. price, cloth: $24.95; paper: $12.95. Discounts: trade: 35%. of. Reporting time: 4 weeks. Payment: standard. Copyrights for author.

Bright Ring Publishing, Mary Ann F. Kohl, PO Box 5768-SP, Bellingham, WA 98227, 206-734-1601. 1985. Fiction, non-fiction. "We are looking for material for teachers using learning centers, individualized classrooms, and creative thinking. Preferably early childhood and primary. Should transfer easily to use at home. Creative, independent, open-minded. We are also looking for bright, creative children's materials that inspire independent thought in a wholesome way. No violence, monsters, anything too trendy or commercial. First contribution, *Scribble Cookies And Other Independent Creative Art Experiences for Children*, 144 pages, black line drawings (120), 11 X 8½, suitable for teachers, parents, children, and others who work with children ages 2-forever." avg. press run 5-10M. Pub'd 1 title 1990; expects 1 title 1991, 1 title 1992. 3 titles listed in the *Small Press Record of Books in Print* (20th Edition, 1991-92). avg. price, paper: $13.95. Discounts: bulk. 150pp; 8×11; of. Reporting time: 4 weeks. Payment: 5-10% of retail and wholesale annually. Does not copyright for author. PMA, COSMEP, Pacific Northwest Assoc. of Publishers.

Brighton & Lloyd, PO Box 2903, Costa Mesa, CA 92626, 714-540-6466. 2. avg. press run 10M. Pub'd 1 title

1990; expects 3 titles 1991, 5 titles 1992. 2 titles listed in the *Small Press Record of Books in Print* (20th Edition, 1991-92). avg. price, paper: $3.25. 132pp; 5×8. Copyrights for author. PMA.

BRILLIANT IDEAS FOR PUBLISHERS, Naomi K. Shapiro, Editor & Publisher, PO Box 44237, Madison, WI 53744, 608-233-2669. 1982. *"Short,* ideas; tips. Specifically designed for, and aimed at newspaper top management. Any articles have to be very familiar with this industry and current problems, topics, and interest areas. We don't encourage submissions" circ. 17M. 6/yr. Pub'd 6 issues 1990; expects 6 issues 1991, 6 issues 1992. sub. price: $10 US, $20 Canada, $30 foreign; per copy: $2 US, $3 Canada, $4 foreign; sample: send catalog envelope with 4 1st class stamps. Back issues: $69.95 for *all* back issues. 24pp; 8½×11; web of. Payment: negotiable. Copyrighted, rights revert to author depending on arrangement made. Pub's reviews: 5 in 1990. §Sales, marketing, promotions, creative thinking, advertising, newspaper industry. Ads: $1495/$934.60/ $49.98 per col. inch.

BRILLIANT STAR, Candace Moore Hill, General Editor, Baha'i National Center, Wilmette, IL 60091. 1969. Poetry, fiction, articles, art, photos, cartoons, interviews, reviews, music, plays, non-fiction. "Material should not generally exceed 1000 words. We do publish unpublished writers. Prefer articles & fiction which reflect racial and cultural diversity. Request NO queries. Stories with moral or religious theme should not be 'preachy' or heavy-handed in conveying a lesson" circ. 2.5M. 6/yr. Pub'd 6 issues 1990; expects 6 issues 1991, 6 issues 1992. sub. price: $12 (US); per copy: $2.50; sample: free with 9 X 12 SASE with postage for 5 oz. Back issues: $2.50. Discounts: negotiable on request for special needs. 33pp; 8½×11; †of. Reporting time: 6-8 weeks. Payment: none. Copyrighted, reverts to author if they specify that they are retaining copyright. Pub's reviews: 6 in 1990. §Children's or young adult. No ads.

Bristlecone Publications, Mary Cram, 2405 Whirlaway, Las Vegas, NV 89108, 702-648-4710. 1989. Fiction. "Not accepting submissions at this time" Expects 2 titles 1991. 2 titles listed in the *Small Press Record of Books in Print* (20th Edition, 1991-92). avg. price, paper: $7.50. Discounts: 2-5 20%, 6-24 25%, 24-49 30%, 50-99 35%, 100-199 40%, 200+ 46%. 23-141pp; 5½×8½, 7½×9½. Payment: royalty 10%. Copyrights for author. COSMEP, Small Press Center, North American Bookdealers Exchange.

BRITISH BOOK NEWS, Jennifer Creswick, 65 Davies Street, London W1Y 2AA, England, 01-930-8466. 1940. Articles, reviews, news items. "W.e.f. April '87 reviews of periodicals, plus bibliographical survey articles and classified listings of 1000 new titles monthly. (No solus new book notices)" circ. 7M. 12/yr. Pub'd 12 issues 1990; expects 12 issues 1991, 12 issues 1992. sub. price: individuals UK £33.50, overseas £44.50, US & Canada US$81, Europe £40; institutions UK £46, overseas £61, US & Canada US$111, Europe £55; per copy: individuals UK £3, £4 overseas, $6.75 US & Canada; institutions UK £4.50, overseas £5.40, $9 US & Canada; sample: free. Back issues: same as current single copy price. Discounts: 5% on 6-12 ads with 12 months. 80pp; 268×181mm type area; of. Reporting time: 1 month. Payment: by negotiation. Copyrighted. Pub's reviews: 3M in 1990. §Most areas, level should be educational/academic. Ads: £425/£248.

BRITISH JOURNAL OF AESTHETICS, Oxford University Press, T.J. Diffey, Journal Subscription Department, Pinkhill House, Southfield Road, Eynsham, Oxford, OX8 1JJ, United Kingdom. 1960. Articles, reviews, letters. "For ad rates write Oxford University Press, Oxford Journals, Production Department, Pinkhill House, Southfield Road, Eynsham, Oxford OX8 1JJ, United Kingdom." circ. 1.3M. 4/yr. Pub'd 4 issues 1990; expects 4 issues 1991, 4 issues 1992. sub. price: $90; per copy: $27; sample: free. 96pp; 234×155mm; of. Reporting time: normally 3 months. Payment: 20 free offprints. Copyrighted, copyright held by Oxford U Press. Pub's reviews. §Aesthetics, philosophy of art, theory of art, theory of art and literary criticism; reviews are commissioned, unsolicited reviews not accepted. Ads: £205($370)/£120($215)/£85($155) 1/4 page.

British Society For Social Responsibility In Science (see also SCIENCE FOR PEOPLE), 25 Horsell Road, London N5 1XL, United Kingdom, 01-607-9615. 1969. avg. press run 2M.

BROADSHEET, Broadsheet Collective, P.O. Box 56-147, Dominion Rd., Auckland, New Zealand, 09-608-535. 1972. Poetry, fiction, articles, art, photos, cartoons, interviews, satire, criticism, reviews, music, letters, news items. "New Zealand's only feminist magazine covering the women's movement. Comment on current events mainly in New Zealand, theoretical articles on feminism, fiction and poetry. Trying to get a mass of women as well as feminists so present attractively with good graphics and photos" circ. 4M. 10/yr. Pub'd 10 issues 1990; expects 10 issues 1991. sub. price: $62 overseas, $50 NZ inland; per copy: $4.50 N.Z.; sample: $4.50 N.Z. Back issues: complete set $100 N.Z. plus postage. Discounts: 10%. 48pp; 21×29.5cm; lose type. Reporting time: 2 months. Payment: none. Copyrighted, reverts to author. Pub's reviews: 33 in 1990. §women, feminism, abortion, women's art-culture, novels by women, poetry, children's books, women's health, racism, indigenous people frowning on women. Ads: $710/$380/50¢ per word.

Broadway Press, David Rodger, 12 W. Thomas Street, Shelter Island, NY 11964-1037, 516-749-3266. 1983. Non-fiction. "Specializes in publishing information books for Theatre and Film professionals; personnel directories, buyers guides, etc. Recent editors: The Association of Theatrical Artists and Craftspeople. ISBN Publisher identifier 0-911747" avg. press run 1M-5M. Pub'd 2 titles 1990; expects 3 titles 1991, 3-4 titles 1992.

8 titles listed in the *Small Press Record of Books in Print* (20th Edition, 1991-92). avg. price, paper: $10-$20. Discounts: 40% to the trade, quantity discounts available. 300pp; 6×9, 8½×11; of. Reporting time: 6 weeks. Payment: negotiated. Copyrights for author. COSMEP, PMA.

Broken Jaw Press, Joe Blades, M.A.P. Productions, 467 Waterloo Row, Suite 201, Fredericton, N.B. E3B 1Z6, Canada, 506-454-5127. 1985. Poetry, art, photos, collages, concrete art. "Publishes artist books, poetry chapbooks, and anthologies. Not open to unsolicited mss except for New Muse of Contempt magazine." avg. press run 500. Pub'd 3 titles 1990; expects 7 titles 1991, 4 titles 1992. 9 titles listed in the *Small Press Record of Books in Print* (20th Edition, 1991-92). avg. price, paper: $6. Discounts: trade 40% on 5 or more, library 20% on 4 or more. 40pp; 7×8½ 5½×8½ 11×8½ 4¼×5-0/2 varies; of, lp, xerographic. Payment: 10% of press run. Authors retain copyright on their work. Small Press Action Network-Eastern Region.

Broken Mirrors Press, Bryan Cholfin, Box 473, Cambridge, MA 02238. 1989. Fiction. "I am interested in publishing challenging, demanding, top-notch science fiction and fantasy of a commercially questionable sort. I have one open anthology currently in progress. Otherwise not accepting unsolicited material." avg. press run 1M. Pub'd 2 titles 1990; expects 1 title 1991, 4 titles 1992. avg. price, cloth: $25-$45; paper: $10. 160-200pp; 5½×8½; of. Reporting time: less than 1 week. Payment: 10% with small advance. Copyrights for author.

Broken Moon Press, John Ellison, Lesley Link, PO Box 24585, Seattle, WA 98124-0585, 206-548-1340. 1982. Poetry, fiction, art, photos, interviews, letters, parts-of-novels, long-poems, collages, concrete art. avg. press run 1M-4M. Pub'd 6 titles 1990; expects 6 titles 1991, 6 titles 1992. 15 titles listed in the *Small Press Record of Books in Print* (20th Edition, 1991-92). avg. price, cloth: $15-$30; paper: $8-$19.95. Discounts: 20%-40% to bookstores. 200pp; of, lp. Reporting time: 6 months. Payment: 10%, paid yearly. Copyrights for author.

Broken Rifle Press, Gerald R. Gioglio, Publisher, PO Box 749, Trenton, NJ 08607, 201-846-3750. 1987. Non-fiction. avg. press run 3.5M. Expects 1 title 1991. 2 titles listed in the *Small Press Record of Books in Print* (20th Edition, 1991-92). Discounts: 1-4 20%, 5-24 43%, 25-49 46%, 50-99 48%, 100-more 50%. 5-12/ X 8½; lo. Publishers Marketing Assn; COSMEP (International Assn of Independent Publishers).

The Broken Stone (see also **The Forces of Magic; Pebbles**), D. Steven Conkle, Senior Editor; Annabel Conkle, PO Box 246, Reynoldsburg, OH 43068. 1984. Poetry. "*The Broken Stone* and its two imprints, Pebbles and The Forces of Magic, publish poetry chapbooks, broadsides, folios, and postcards. Recent contributors include Taelen Thomas, Arthur Winfield Knight, d steven conkle and Gary Snyder. Our standards are extremely high, and we are heavily backlogged. With all of this in mind, if you want to give us a try - good luck. SASE, of course. A good way to approach us is to enter our poemcard contest. Send SASE for guidelines. Those wishing samples of our publications should send $5-$10 for a selection of stuff" avg. press run varies. Pub'd 4 titles 1990; expects 5 titles 1991, 5 titles 1992. avg. price, paper: $5; other: $3 broadsides, $1 poemcards. Discounts: Negotiable. Pages vary; size varies; of, lp. Reporting time: fast, but getting slower. Payment: by arrangement. Copyrights for author. COSMEP.

BROKEN STREETS, Ron Grossman, 57 Morningside Drive East, Bristol, CT 06010. 1979. Poetry. "Christian/contemporary reflections of the city, life, peop;le, feelings, etc. No four letter words. Recent contributors: Bettye K. Wray, Ruth W Schuler. 5-16 lines, but will read longer works. Open editor, 'born-again' christian. Also uses prose, prayers and journal entries." circ. 100. 4/yr. Pub'd 4 issues 1990; expects 3 issues 1991, 4 issues 1992. sub. price: $12; per copy: $3.50; sample: $3.50. Back issues: $2. 45pp; 6×9; lp. Reporting time: 1 week. Payment: none. Copyrighted, reverts to author. Ads: $10/$5.

BRONG'S BUSINESS SUCCESS NEWS, John Mix, Gerald Brong, PO Box 9, Ellensburg, WA 98926-0009, 509-962-8238. Articles, satire, criticism, reviews, news items, non-fiction. "Reader focus is business success for the owner/manager of small businesses." circ. 30-50M. 12/yr. Expects 600,000 issues 1991, 600,000 issues 1992. sub. price: $29.95; per copy: $5; sample: free. 16pp; lp. Reporting time: 7 days+. Copyrighted. Pub's reviews. Ads: $1400; 1/2 $750.

Bronx Books, Alan Mandel, PO Box 100, Bronx, NY 10463, (212) 548-4050. 1986. Non-fiction. "In July 1987, *Bronx Books* published *The S.E.X. Blackjack System*. This is the first book to provide detailed information on the psychological and physical aspects of playing the casino game—Blackjack! *Bronx Books* will continue to publish books that explore subjects in a way that *has not* been done before!!!" avg. press run 5M. Pub'd 1 title 1990; expects 2 titles 1991, 3 titles 1992. 1 title listed in the *Small Press Record of Books in Print* (20th Edition, 1991-92). avg. price, paper: $12.95. Discounts: runs from 25 to 50% off retail price depending on quantity ordered; schedule will be provided on request. 224pp; 5½×8½; of, cameron belt press. Reporting time: 3 months. Payment: 5%. Does not copyright for author. Network of Independent Publishers, New York, NY.

Brooding Heron Press, Samuel Green, Co-Publisher; Sally Green, Co-Publisher, Bookmonger Road, Waldron Island, WA 98297. 1984. Poetry. "Limited interest in unsolicited manuscripts. New work by Dave Lee, John Haines, and Barry Sternlieb. Forthcoming by Denise Levertov." avg. press run 300. Pub'd 2 titles 1990;

expects 2 titles 1991, 3 titles 1992. 7 titles listed in the *Small Press Record of Books in Print* (20th Edition, 1991-92). avg. price, cloth: $25; paper: $10; other: $30-$35 signed editions. Discounts: 30% to bookstores for tradepaper copies only. 36-54pp; size varies; †lp. Reporting time: 6 weeks. Payment: copies, 10% of run. Copyrights for author. None.

Brook Farm Books, Donn Reed, PO Box 246, Bridgewater, ME 04735. 1981. Fiction, cartoons, satire, non-fiction. "Especially interested in home-school material" avg. press run 1M. Pub'd 2 titles 1990; expects 2 titles 1991, 2 titles 1992. 1 title listed in the *Small Press Record of Books in Print* (20th Edition, 1991-92). avg. price, paper: $15. Discounts: 1-4 30%, 5+ 40%, 10+ 50%. 80-200pp; 7×8, 5×7, 8½×11; of. Reporting time: 2 months. Payment: 10%; no advance. Copyrights for author.

Brook House Press, Inc., Peter Haber, Senior Editor, Mills Pond House, PO Box 52, St. James, NY 11780, 516-584-6948. 1987. Poetry, fiction, criticism, long-poems, plays, non-fiction. "We no longer accept unsolicited mss. We do accept queries—one page, letter format. No samples. Must enclose an SASE. Quality fiction, nonfiction, poetry" avg. press run 1M-3M. Pub'd 3 titles 1990; expects 3-5 titles 1991, 3-5 titles 1992. 3 titles listed in the *Small Press Record of Books in Print* (20th Edition, 1991-92). avg. price, cloth: $15-$25; paper: $10-$15. Pages vary; size varies; of. Reporting time: 4-6 months. Payment: standard. Copyrights for author. COSMEP, PMA.

Brooke-Richards Press, Audrey Bricker, Editor, 9420 Reseda Blvd., Suite 511, Northridge, CA 91324, 818-893-8126. 1989. "Books for reluctant readers." avg. press run varies. Pub'd 2-3 titles 1990. 2 titles listed in the *Small Press Record of Books in Print* (20th Edition, 1991-92). Discounts: 20%. 160pp.

BROOMSTICK: A PERIODICAL BY, FOR, AND ABOUT WOMEN OVER FORTY, Mickey Spencer, Polly Taylor, 3543 18th Street, #3, San Francisco, CA 94110, 415-552-7460. 1978. Poetry, fiction, articles, art, cartoons, interviews, reviews, non-fiction. "*Broomstick* is a feminist political journal. We only publish material which is by, for, and about women over forty. Our first priorities are that material convey clear images of midlife and long-living women that are positive, that it take a stand against the denigration of women which our culture surveys, and that it offers us alternatives which will make our lives better. Our intention is to form a network among women over forty which will help us all develop understanding of our life situations and to acquire the skills to improve both our individual lives and the social conditions which affect all of us." circ. 3M. 4/yr. Pub'd 6 issues 1990; expects 4 issues 1991, 4 issues 1992. sub. price: $15 (sliding scale for women over forty only); per copy: $5; sample: $5. Back issues: through 1981, $2.00/back issues; 1982 on all back issues $3.00. Discounts: 40% to bookstores, no minimum order. 40pp; 8½×11; of. Reporting time: 12 weeks. Payment: 2 copies of issue in which work appears. Copyrighted. Pub's reviews: 20 in 1990. §Feminism, women over forty (women authors only). Ads: $10 column inch (2¼ column) or $2 per 27 character line.

Harrison Brown, Publishers, Inc., Jay Moore, PO Box 151574, Tampa, FL 33684, 813-963-2959. 1989. Fiction. "Harrison Brown, Publishers Inc., is part of SMI financial research reports. We will be publishing mostly work of fiction for up and coming young authors across the country and hope to place in the market place, at least four or more books per year, all hard cover with at least 250 page counts." avg. press run 5-10M. Pub'd 1 title 1990; expects 1 title 1991, 4 titles 1992. 1 title listed in the *Small Press Record of Books in Print* (20th Edition, 1991-92). avg. price, cloth: $16.95. Discounts: 2-4 20%, 5-99 40%, 100+ 50%. 275pp; 5×8; †of. Reporting time: 6 weeks. Payment: 7-10%. Copyrights for author.

Brunswick Publishing Corporation, Rt. 1, Box 1A1, Lawrenceville, VA 23868, 804-848-3865. 1973. Poetry, fiction, articles, parts-of-novels, long-poems, plays, non-fiction. "Most categories apply. We accept or reject upon examination on individual basis" avg. press run 500-1M. Pub'd 32 titles 1990; expects 35 titles 1991, 35 titles 1992. 40 titles listed in the *Small Press Record of Books in Print* (20th Edition, 1991-92). avg. price, cloth: $22; paper: $11. Discounts: 40% jobber. 200pp; 5¼×8¼; †of. Reporting time: 2 weeks. Payment: send for statement of philosophy and purpose. Does not copyright for author.

Carol Bryan Imagines (see also THE LIBRARY IMAGINATION PAPER!), 1000 Byus Drive, Charleston, WV 25311.

B-SIDE MAGAZINE, Sandra Garcia, Carol Schutzbank, PO Box 1860, Burlington, NJ 08016-7460. 1986. Articles, interviews, reviews, music, letters, news items. "Secondary address: PO Box 15921, Philadelphia, PA 19103" circ. 10M. 6/yr. Pub'd 6 issues 1990; expects 6 issues 1991, 6 issues 1992. sub. price: $13; per copy: $3; sample: same. Back issues: $2.25 per issue. 52pp; 9×12; of. Reporting time: 1 month. Payment: in copies. Copyrighted, does not revert to author. Pub's reviews. §Entertainment, culture. Ads: $400/$220.

BUCKNELL REVIEW, Pauline Fletcher, Editor, Bucknell Hall, Bucknell University, Lewisburg, PA 17837, 717-524-1184. 1941. Articles, criticism. "An interdisciplinary book-journal, each issue is devoted to a major theme or movement in humanities or sciences." circ. 500. 2/yr. Pub'd 2 issues 1990; expects 2 issues 1991, 2 issues 1992. sub. price: $42; per copy: $21; sample: $21. Discounts: for agencies only 10%. 192pp; 6×9. Reporting time: 4-8 weeks. Payment: 1 complimentary copy of issue, contributor may xerox the essay.

Copyrighted, does not revert to author. No ads.

Buddha Rose Publications (see also THE SCREAM OF THE BUDDHA), Dr. Scott Shaw, PO Box 902, Hermosa Beach, CA 90254, 213-543-3809. 1989. Poetry, fiction, art, non-fiction. avg. press run 5M. Pub'd 12 titles 1990; expects 20 titles 1991, 20 titles 1992. avg. price, cloth: $20; paper: $10.95. Discounts: 2-4 copies 20%, 4-10 30%, 10-20 40%, 20+ 50%. 200pp; 8½×5½; of. Reporting time: 1 month. Payment: depends on the type of book, quality, and author's reputation. Copyrights for author.

BUDDHISM AT THE CROSSROADS, 86 Vaughan Road, Toronto, Ont. M6C 2M1, Canada, 416-658-0137. 1981. Articles, art, photos, interviews, news items. "Other mailing address: Zen Buddhist Temple - Ann Arbor, 1214 Packard Road, Ann Arbor, MI 48104. U.S.A. *Buddhism at the Crossroads* is a quarterly journal devoted to examining the rich traditions of Buddhism and their contemporary expressions in thorough articles by well-known teachers and scholars." circ. 1.5M. 3/yr. Pub'd 1 issue 1990; expects 3 issues 1991. sub. price: $20/year, $50/3 yrs; per copy: $5.50; sample: $5.50. Discounts: none. 48pp; 8×11; of. Payment: none. Copyrighted, reverts to author. Pub's reviews: 1 in 1990. §Buddhism related topics - historical and contemporary. Ads: $500/$250.

Buddhist Study Center Press, Ruth M. Tabrah, 876 Curtis Street #3905, Honolulu, HI 96813, 808-536-7633. 1979. "We publish translations of Pure Land Buddhist texts and commentaries, also such biographical material as our 1991 title—*Memories of a Woman Buddhist Missionary in Hawaii* by Shigeo Kikuchi. We are not taking submissions at this time, but welcome query letters" avg. press run 3.5M. Pub'd 1 title 1990; expects 1 title 1991, 1-2 titles 1992. 13 titles listed in the *Small Press Record of Books in Print* (20th Edition, 1991-92). avg. price, cloth: $12.95; paper: $6.95. 75-125pp; 6×9.

Buddhist Text Translation Society (see also VAJRA BODHI SEA; PROPER DHARMA SEAL; SOURCE OF WISDOM), Dharma Realm Buddhist Assn., City of 10,000 Buddhas, Talmage, CA 95481-0217, 707-462-0939. 1959. Poetry, fiction, articles, art, photos, non-fiction. "Buddhist Text Translation Society began publishing in 1972 with the goal of making the principles of Buddhist wisdom available to the American reader in a form that can be put directly into practice. BTTS translators are not only scholars but are practicing Buddhists who encounter every day the living meaning of the works they translate. Each translation is accompanied by a contemporary commentary. On the publishing list are standard Buddhist classics such as the *Shurangama Sutra,* the *Lotus Sutra,* and the *Vajra Sutra;* esoteric works such as the *Earth Store Bodhisattva Sutra* and the *Shurangama Mantra;* books of informal instruction in meditation; and books, including fiction, that have grown out of the American Buddhist experience. Beginning in 1979 the Society started publishing translations of Buddhist Scriptures bilingually (Chinese and English). Some of the works available bilingually include chapters from the *Avatamsaka Sutra, The Heart Sutra* and the *Brahma Net Sutra.* Extensive commentaries accompany each of these works, in both languages. The Society also plans to publish more works in other languages in the future. In 1980 the Society published two translation works into Spanish and will be publishing works in French, German and Italian in the near future." avg. press run 4M. Pub'd 10 titles 1990; expects 10 titles 1991, 10 titles 1992. 91 titles listed in the *Small Press Record of Books in Print* (20th Edition, 1991-92). avg. price, paper: $8. Discounts: 10% up to $49, 20% $50-$149, 30% $150-$249, 40% $250+. 200pp; 5½×8½; of. Payment: none-non profit org. Copyrights for author.

The Builders Publishing Company (see also THE BUILDERS QUARTERLY), Patricia Paulsen, Editor-in-Chief; Tricia Dunham, Promotions Editor; Dawn King, General Editor, PO Box 2122, Oasis, NV 89835. 1975. Photos, non-fiction. avg. price, cloth: $16.95; paper: $10.95. Discounts: 30% consignment, 40% bookstores, 50% distributors. 496pp; 5½×8. Reporting time: 1 month. Payment: none. Does not copyright for author.

THE BUILDERS QUARTERLY, The Builders Publishing Company, Dawn King, General Editor, PO Box 2122, Oasis, NV 89835. circ. 200. 4/yr. Pub'd 4 issues 1990; expects 4 issues 1991, 4 issues 1992. price per copy: $2.50. 20pp; †desktop. Reporting time: 1 month. Payment: none. Not copyrighted.

Bull Publishing Co., David C. Bull, P O Box 208, Palo Alto, CA 94302, 415-322-2855. 1974. "Texts in health sciences; books in nutrition and health, child care and cancer patient education." avg. press run 7M. Pub'd 7 titles 1990; expects 4 titles 1991, 4 titles 1992. 35 titles listed in the *Small Press Record of Books in Print* (20th Edition, 1991-92). avg. price, cloth: $19.95; paper: $14.95. Discounts: trade distributor: Publishers Group West, 4065 Hollis St., Emeryville, Ca. 94608. 300pp; 5½×8½, 8½×11; web or sheet feed press-usually in the Midwest. Reporting time: 1 week. Copyrights for author. PMA, NCBPA, NCBA.

BULLETIN OF ANARCHIST RESEARCH, John Moore, Editor; T.V. Cahill, Networking Editor; John Mason, Production Editor, PO Box 556, London SE5 0RL, England. 1985. Articles, interviews, criticism, reviews, letters, news items. "Length of material: maximum 2,500 words. Biases: non-sectarian anarchist research; aims to be a forum of ideas for, and to help facilitate networking of, anarchist intellectuals and researchers of anarchism. Some recent contributors: John Moore, Tom Cahill, David Goodway, Bob Black, Ed Lawrence, Leigh Burton, Sharif Gemie, Gareth Bellaby, George Crowder. Unsolicited material welcome, although the majority of pieces are written by subscribers." circ. 200. 4/yr. Pub'd 4 issues 1990; expects 4 issues 1991, 4 issues 1992. sub. price: £5, £6 foreign-6 issues; per copy: £1.50; sample: £1. Back issues: 75p. Discounts: negotiable. 30pp; 11¾×8¼; mi. Reporting time: 1 month maximum. Payment: none. Copyrighted, reverts to author. Pub's reviews: 32 in 1990. §Anarchism & related areas (eg., spirituality, feminism, arts, social movements, radical ideas, ecology, animal liberation, small press activity). Ads: £40/£20.

BULLETIN OF HISPANIC STUDIES, Liverpool University Press, Dorothy Sherman Severin, Ann L. Mackenzie, Dept. Of Hispanic Studies, The University, PO Box 147, Liverpool L69 3BX, England, 051 794 2774/5. 1923. Articles, reviews. "Specialist articles on the languages and literatures of Spain, Portugal and Latin America, in English, Spanish, Portuguese and Catalan" circ. 1M. 4/yr. Expects 4 issues 1991. sub. price: inland (European community) indiv. £18.50, instit. £47, overseas indiv. US $40, instit. US $95; per copy: £10. Back issues: £20.00 per volume. 112pp; metric crown quarto; of. Reporting time: 3 months max. Payment: none. Not copyrighted. Pub's reviews: 200 in 1990. §Languages and literatures of Spain, Portugal and Latin America. Ads: £200/£100/£50 1/4 page. CELJ.

BULLETIN OF THE BOARD OF CELTIC STUDIES, University Of Wales Press, D. Ellis Evans, J. Beverley Smith, R. G. Livens, Univ. of Wales Press, 6 Gwennyth Street, Cathays, Cardiff CF2 4YD, Wales, 231919. 1922. Articles. "Articles on language and literature, history and law, archealogy and art." circ. 450. 1/yr. Pub'd 2 issues 1990; expects 1 issue 1991, 1 issue 1992. sub. price: £12 one volume; per copy: £12; sample: £12. Back issues: £8 per part. Discounts: 10%. 187pp; size Cr8vo; of. Payment: none. UWP.

THE BULLISH CONSENSUS, R. Earl Hadady, Publisher, Editor, 1111 S. Arroyo Parkway, Suite 410, PO Box 90490, Pasadena, CA 91109-0490, (818) 441-3457. 1964. Articles, news items, non-fiction. "A weekly poll—neither fundamental nor technical analysis, but the direct approach to analyzing the commodity markets" circ. 600. 51/yr. Expects 51 issues 1991, 51 issues 1992. sub. price: $345; per copy: $5. 1 page; 8½×11; †photocopy. Copyrighted.

The Bunny & The Crocodile Press, Robert Sargent, Grace Cavalieri, David Bristol, PO Box 416, Hedgesville, WV 25427-0416, 304-754-8847. 1976. Poetry. "Other address: Suite #6061W, 4201 Mass. Avenue NW, Washington DC 20016." avg. press run 500-1M. Pub'd 2 titles 1990; expects 1 title 1991. 1 title listed in the *Small Press Record of Books in Print* (20th Edition, 1991-92). avg. price, paper: $7. Discounts: would, but haven't had occasion. 77pp; 5½×8½; of. Payment: to date authors obtain grants to publish, get 100% of sales. Author owns copyright. Small Press Center, Writers Center.

Burning Books, Melody Sumner, Kathleen Burch, Michael Sumner, 690 Market Street, Suite 1501, San Francisco, CA 94104, 415-788-7480. 1979. Poetry, fiction, art, interviews, music. "Our idea is to publish books that extend possibilities in literature, music, art, and ideas. We use volunteer labor, donated professional services, and income from previous publications, and advance sales to create our books.*The Guests Go In To Supper* is about seven American composers who use words as an integral part of their compositions. It includes texts, and scores of new works as well as interviews with: John Cage, Robert Ashley, Yoko Ono, Laurie Anderson, Charles Amirkhanian, Michael Peppe, and K. Atchley. Music seems to be one of the most dynamic arenas of art right now, particularly music in combination with language and ideas. Each of the composers included in the book was chosen for his or her powerful vision, and the catalytic effect of that vision in combination with music and/or sound. Other titles include: *The Time Is Now*, eleven stories with tab dividers and illustrations—by Melody Sumner; *One of One*, stories, diagrams, and photographs—a book in magazine format by Sheila Davies and Patrick James; *Home Cooking* by Barbara Golden-recipes, songs, and poems" avg. press run 1M-3M. Pub'd 1 title 1990; expects 1 title 1991, 1 title 1992. 6 titles listed in the *Small Press Record of Books in Print* (20th Edition, 1991-92). avg. price, paper: $10-$25. Discounts: 40/60. 84-450pp; 8×10; of, lp. Reporting time: 2 years. Payment: varies. Copyrights for author. PCBA (Pacific Center for the Book Arts, PO 6209, San Francisco, CA 94101).

Burning Deck Press, Keith Waldrop, Rosmarie Waldrop, 71 Elmgrove Avenue, Providence, RI 02906. 1962. Poetry. "Order from Small Press Distribution." avg. press run 350-1M. Pub'd 5 titles 1990; expects 2 titles 1991, 2 titles 1992. 83 titles listed in the *Small Press Record of Books in Print* (20th Edition, 1991-92). avg. price, cloth: $15; paper: $8; other: $4. Discounts: see schedule of Small Press Distribution. 20-80pp; 6×9; †lp. Reporting time: 2 months. Payment: 10% of edition (copies). Does not copyright for author.

BURNT SIENNA, Charles Heimler, PO Box 7495, Berkeley, CA 94707. 1979. Poetry, art, photos, interviews, reviews, collages, concrete art. "*Burnt Sienna* takes its name after the color first produced in Italy. Issues focus on migration; Wm. Everson-Kenneth Rexroth-Gary Snyder-Phil Whalen sense of poetics; alternative lifestyles; bioregional aesthetics. Welcome submissions" circ. 1M. 1/yr. Pub'd 1 issue 1990; expects 1 issue 1991, 1 issue 1992. sub. price: $2.50; per copy: $2.50; sample: $2.50. 50-100pp; 7×8½; of. Reporting time: 2-3 months. Payment: 2 copies. Copyrighted, reverts to author. Pub's reviews: 4 in 1990. §Contemporary poetry and visual arts. negotiable. COSMEP.

BURWOOD JOURNAL, Survival News Service, Christopher Nyerges, Vernon Devans, Box 41834, Los

Angeles, CA 90041, 213-255-9502. 1981. Articles, art, photos, cartoons, reviews, letters, news items, non-fiction. "Focus of *Burwood Journal* is to educate city dwellers in realistic, practical ways to 'survive' (re, earthquake preparation, arrest crime, economic survival, city gardens and compost pits, alternative energy, wild foods, etc.). No payment to contributors per se, but we can exchange advertising, give copies. We allow authors full rights, etc., and we ask that we can use at will also." circ. 2.5M. 4/yr. Pub'd 1 issue 1990; expects 4 issues 1991, 4 issues 1992. sub. price: $8.50; sample: free. Discounts: available to schools in bulk amounts for $1.00 each. 12pp; 8½×11; of. Reporting time: 1 month. Payment: none. Copyrighted. Pub's reviews. §Survival, gardening, alternate energy, co-ops, credit unions, recycling. Ads: $100/$60/$1 for 3 lines; $1 per line thereafter.

BUT A TWIST OF THE LIP, Lainie Duro, 1003 Avenue X, Apt. A, Lubbock, TX 79401, 806-744-7412. 1986. Articles, cartoons, interviews, satire, criticism, reviews, music, letters, news items, non-fiction. "Mostly of a humorous bond. Serious topics, but humorous writing" circ. 500. 1-2/yr. Pub'd 2 issues 1990; expects 2 issues 1991, 2 issues 1992. price per copy: $2; sample: $2. 32pp; 11×8½; †xerox. Reporting time: 3-4 months. Payment: none. Not copyrighted. Pub's reviews: 100+ in 1990. §Music, poetry, political humor, comics. Ads: trade for ad space.

BYLINE, Marcia Preston, Editor & Publisher; Kathryn Fanning, Managing Editor, PO Box 130596, Edmond, OK 73013, 405-348-5591. 1981. Poetry, fiction, articles, cartoons, interviews, non-fiction. circ. 2.5M. 11/yr. Pub'd 11 issues 1990; expects 11 issues 1991, 11 issues 1992. sub. price: $20; per copy: $3 p.p.; sample: $3 (incl. p/h). Back issues: $3. 28pp; 8½×11; of. Reporting time: 4-8 weeks. Payment: up to 10¢ per word, on acceptance. Copyrighted, reverts to author. Ads: $300/$150/$1 word.

The William Byrd Press (see also THE AMERICAN SCHOLAR), Joseph Epstein, 1811 Q Street NW, Washington, DC 20009, 202-265-3808.

C

C & T Publishing, Diane Pedersen, 5021 Blum Road #1, Martinez, CA 94553, 415-370-9600. 1983. Non-fiction. "We publish how-to quilting books, most of which are softcover with an average of 96 pages. Most books have a color section of 16 pages." avg. press run 15M. Pub'd 7 titles 1990; expects 5 titles 1991, 8 titles 1992. 11 titles listed in the *Small Press Record of Books in Print* (20th Edition, 1991-92). avg. price, cloth: $34.95; paper: $14.95. Discounts: 1-3 books 20%, 4-12 40%, 13-50 43%, 50+ 50%, COD or prepaid add'l 2%. 96pp; 8½×11. Reporting time: 4 weeks. Payment: 8% retail price, monthly. Does not copyright for author. Northern Calif. Booksellers Assn. (NCBA), Berkeley, CA.

C.C. Publishing Co., Clyde Crum, 5410 Davis, Dallas, TX 75211, 214-330-4845. 1991. Fiction, articles, non-fiction. avg. press run 500-1M. Expects 4 titles 1991, 8 titles 1992. avg. price, paper: $16.50. Discounts: 2-25 40%, 26-50 42%, 51-100 44%, 100+ 46%. 300pp; 6×9; of. Reporting time: 2-4 weeks. Payment: coop. publishing. Does not copyright for author. Book Publishers of Texas.

C.J.L. Press (see also CHASTITY AND HOLINESS), Cecil Justin Lam, Editor, Box 22006, 45 Overlea, Thorncliff Post Office, Toronto, Ont. M4H 1N9, Canada. 1988. Poetry. "Welcome all Christianic poetry and poems. The editor encourages submissions of poetry with no assumption of material gains from this press; all rewards are in spiritual form." avg. press run 50. Pub'd 50 titles 1990. 1 title listed in the *Small Press Record of Books in Print* (20th Edition, 1991-92). Discounts: 80% per 100 or negotiable. 90pp; 11×8½; †photoset/copy. Reporting time: 3 months on the average. Payment: minimal, but lots of prayers in reward.

C.S.P. WORLD NEWS, Edition Stencil, Guy F. Claude Hamel, Editor & Publisher, c/o Guy F. Claude Hamel, 1307 Bethamy Lane, Gloucester, Ont. K1J 8P3, Canada, 613-741-8675. 1962. Poetry, satire, reviews. "Recent Contributors: Hundreds of poets. Best Book of the Year (1977) Contest: Wm. B. Eerdmans, publishers; Poet of the Year (1977) Teresa Peirinska, televised series *Poetry Ottawa* by Hamel Theatre Productions. C.S.P. World News Poet of the Year: 1975, Alexandre L. Amprimoz, Winnipeg, Man.; 1976, Lynda Rostad, Toronto, Ont.; 1977, Teresinka Pereira, Boulder, CO.; 1978, Sheila Sommer, Toronto, Ont.; 1979, Marilyn Carmen, Mechanicsburg, PA.; Book of the Year Contest Winners: 1977, Wm. B. Eerdmans, Grand Rapids, MI.; 1978, Rasheed Mohammed, New York, NY. *Poet of the Year* 1980: Bluebell S. Phillips, Dorval, P. Que. Carl T. Endemann, *1981* Calistoga California. Eda Howink, *1982* St. Louis, Missouri. Ken Stone, *1983* Portland, NY, George Orwell (1984)-posthumously. Pope John Paul II (1985). Robert L.J. Zenik, Sudbury, Ontario (1986), Ida Fawers, Haifa, Israel (1987), Elsie M. Brien, Montreal (1988), H.H. Claudius I, universal patriarch of the Old Catholic churches, Ottawa (1989)" circ. 2M. 12/yr. Pub'd 12 issues 1990; expects 12 issues 1991, 12 issues 1992. 1 title listed in the *Small Press Record of Books in Print* (20th Edition,

1991-92). sub. price: $15. 20pp; 8×14; †of. Reporting time: 2 weeks. Copyrighted. Pub's reviews: 312 in 1990. §All types books, LP's and tapes. Ads: not available. International News Registry.

C. Salway Press, PO Box 4115 A, Menlo Park, CA 94026, 415-368-7882; FAX 415-368-2287. 1988. avg. press run 1.5M. Pub'd 1 title 1990; expects 1-3 titles 1992. 1 title listed in the *Small Press Record of Books in Print* (20th Edition, 1991-92). avg. price, cloth: $16.95. 48pp; 8½×10½. COSMEP, PMA, ABA, MSPA, WNBA, NCBA, NCBPA.

Cable Publishing, PO Box 75575, Honolulu, HI 96836, 808-536-6697. 1989. avg. press run 2M. 1 title listed in the *Small Press Record of Books in Print* (20th Edition, 1991-92). avg. price, paper: $11.95. Discounts: 50%. 54pp; 6½×10. Reporting time: 3 weeks. Copyrights for author.

Cacanadadada Press Ltd., J. Michael Yates, Senior Editor; R. Hatch, President, 3350 West 21st Avenue, Vancouver, B.C. V6S 1G7, Canada, 604-738-1195. 1988. Poetry, fiction, art, photos, satire, parts-of-novels, long-poems, collages, plays, concrete art, non-fiction. avg. press run 1.2M-2M. Pub'd 3 titles 1990; expects 5 titles 1991, 6 titles 1992. 7 titles listed in the *Small Press Record of Books in Print* (20th Edition, 1991-92). avg. price, cloth: $29.95 CDN; paper: $11 CDN. Discounts: trade 40%, libraries 20%, wholesale (bulk) 50%. 108pp; 5¼×8. Reporting time: 1 month. Payment: 10% of retail, royalties negotiated at contract signing. Copyrights for author. APBC, ACP, LPG.

CACANADADADA REVIEW, Jack Estes, PO Box 1283, Port Angeles, WA 98362, 206-325-5541. 1989. Poetry, fiction, articles, art, photos, cartoons, interviews, satire, criticism, reviews, letters, parts-of-novels, long-poems, collages, non-fiction. "5-6 pages maximum recommended. *Tone* is important: irreverent, parodic, humorous, unusual and innovative material sought. Recent contributors: William Slaughter, Dick Bakken, John Grey, Susan Musgrave, J. Michael Yates, David Ray." circ. 300+. 2/yr. Expects 2 issues 1991, 2 issues 1992. sub. price: $6; per copy: $3.50; sample: $4. Back issues: $4. Discounts: 25%-50%. 50pp; 8½×11; of. Reporting time: 6 weeks. Payment: 1 copy plus small financial honorarium. Copyrighted, reverts to author. Pub's reviews: 2 in 1990. §Unusual fiction, non-fiction, poetry. Ads: $100/$60/$10 minimum.

Caddo Gap Press (see also EDUCATIONAL FOUNDATIONS; TEACHER EDUCATION QUARTERLY), Alan H. Jones, Publisher; Susan Holtzer Jones, Editor, 915 L Street, Suite C-414, Sacramento, CA 95814. 1989. "Caddo Gap Press is primarily a publisher of educational books and journals, with particular interest in the fields of teacher education and the social foundations of education; we also publish books related to environmental education, ecology, communications and journalism." avg. press run 2M. Pub'd 5 titles 1990; expects 6 titles 1991, 6 titles 1992. 5 titles listed in the *Small Press Record of Books in Print* (20th Edition, 1991-92). avg. price, paper: $15. Discounts: 20% to institutions and college bookstores, trade discounts based on quantity. 150pp; size varies; of. Reporting time: 1 month. Payment: to be arranged, usually 10%. Copyrights for author. COSMEP, EDPRESS.

CADENCE: THE REVIEW OF JAZZ & BLUES: CREATIVE IMPROVISED MUSIC, Robert D. Rusch, Cadence Building, Redwood, NY 13679, 315-287-2852 (FAX 315-287-2860). 1975. Articles, photos, interviews, criticism, reviews, music, news items. "We run about 36 interviews or oral histories a year. Have covered more than 19,000 record releases (reviews) since 1976. January 1, 1991 is Volume 17, #1. We also publish a yearly index." circ. 5M+. 12/yr. Pub'd 12 issues 1990; expects 12 issues 1991, 12 issues 1992. sub. price: $25; per copy: $2.50; sample: $2.50. Back issues: $3 each. Discounts: Distributors only 5-10 $1.69; 11-15 $1.62; 16-20 $1.56; 20-49 $1.44; 50 $1.31; 100 or more $1.25. 96pp; 5½×8½; of. Reporting time: 2 weeks. Payment: varies. Copyrighted, does not revert to author. Pub's reviews: 1.4M in 1990. §Jazz, blues and related areas. Ads: $130/$75/50¢.

Cadmus Editions, Jeffrey Miller, PO Box 687, Tiburon, CA 94920. 1979. Poetry, fiction, music, parts-of-novels. "Distribution in U.S. by: Inland Book Company Inc., PO Box 261, East Haven, CT 06512, telephone 203-467-4257. Distribution in U.K. by: Airlift Books, 26/28 Eden Grove, London N78EL. Telephone: 01-607-5792." avg. press run 2M. Pub'd 3 titles 1990; expects 3 titles 1991, 3 titles 1992. 16 titles listed in the *Small Press Record of Books in Print* (20th Edition, 1991-92). avg. price, paper: $7.00; other: $25 signed/ltd. Discounts: 2-4 10%, 5-9 20%, 10+ 40%. Additional 2% on prepaid orders. Always add est. shipping. Net 30 days. 150pp; 6×9; lp, of. Reporting time: 30 days. Payment: negotiable; paid annually. Copyrights for author.

CAESURA, R.T. Smith, Caesura Press, English Dept. Auburn University, Auburn, AL 36849, 205-826-4620. 1984. Poetry, fiction, criticism, reviews. "We're not interested in sentimental or conventional religious verse, but in all forms of serious poetry. Recent contributors: Fred Chappell, Jordan Smith, Jared Carter, David Citino, Julie Suk, James Applewhite, Jim Wayne Miller, Allen Hoey." circ. 500. 2/yr. Pub'd 2 issues 1990; expects 2 issues 1991, 2 issues 1992. sub. price: $8; per copy: $5; sample: $5. Discounts: none. 70pp; 5½×8½; of. Reporting time: 8 weeks. Payment: small honorarium. Copyrighted, reverts to author. Pub's reviews: 1 in 1990. §Poetry. Ads: $35/$20. COSMEP South.

THE CAFE REVIEW, Steve Luttrell, Mark Souders, c/o Yes Books, 20 Danforth Street, Portland, ME 04101. 1989. Poetry, art, photos, interviews, criticism. circ. 250. 12/yr. Pub'd 12 issues 1990; expects 12 issues 1991, 12 issues 1992. sub. price: $24; per copy: $2; sample: $2. 40pp; 5½x8½; †of. Reporting time: 2-4 months. Payment: copies. Copyrighted, reverts to author. Pub's reviews: 0 in 1990. §Poetry, essays on poetry. Ads: $90/$45/1/3 page $30. MWPA.

Cajun Publishing, Don Thornton, Suzi Thornton, Route 4, Box 88, New Iberia, LA 70560, 318-365-6653; 364-2752. 1985. Poetry, fiction, art. "Additional address: Don Thornton, 1504 Howard Street, New Iberia, LA 70560" avg. press run 1M. Pub'd 3 titles 1990; expects 2 titles 1991. avg. price, cloth: $3; paper: $3. Discounts: on arrangement. 50pp; 5½x8½; †of. Copyrights for author.

CAL NEWSLETTER, Conservatory of American Letters, Harley Fetzer, PO Box 123, South Thomaston, ME 04858. 1986. Poetry, fiction, articles, art, interviews, satire, criticism, reviews, letters, news items. circ. approx. 1M-1.5M. 4/yr. Pub'd 4 issues 1990; expects 4 issues 1991, 4 issues 1992. sub. price: $4; per copy: $2; sample: $2. Back issues: $3. Discounts: none. 8pp; 8½x11; of. Reporting time: 1 week to 2 months. Payment: we pay cash for all acceptances, except letters, range from $2-$20 depending on length, quality, relevancy, etc. Copyrighted, does not revert to author. Ads: $98/$54.

Calapooia Publications, Margaret Standish Carey, Co-Owner, Co-Editor; Patricia Hoy Hainline, Co-Owner, Co-Editor, PO Box 160, Brownsville, OR 97327, 503-369-2439. 1976. Non-fiction. "Not accepting book manuscripts at this time. Will consider historical newsletter submissions, SASE, pay in copies. Began publishing *Northwest Passages*, historical newsletter Sept. 1985, bi-monthly, subscriptions $12/year" avg. press run 1M. Expects 1-2 titles 1991. 7 titles listed in the *Small Press Record of Books in Print* (20th Edition, 1991-92). avg. price, paper: $7.95. Discounts: 40% to dealers on orders of 5 books or more, mixed titles OK. 150pp; 5½x8½; of. Reporting time: variable. Payment: negotiable. Copyrights for author.

CALAPOOYA COLLAGE, Thomas L. Ferte, PO Box 309, Monmouth, OR 97361, 503-838-6292. 1981. Poetry, fiction, articles, photos, interviews, reviews, non-fiction. "Sponsor of annual $700 Carolyn Kizer Poetry Awards. Recent contributors: Robert Bly, Joseph Bruchac, Octavio Paz, Marge Piercy, William Stafford, Ursula K. LeGuin, Patricia Goedicke, Colleen J. McElroy, David Wagoner, Warren French, David Ray." circ. 1.5M. 1/yr. Pub'd 1 issue 1990; expects 1 issue 1991, 1 issue 1992. sub. price: $4; per copy: $4; sample: $4. Back issues: $4. 48pp; 11¼x17½; laser/offset. Reporting time: 4-8 weeks. Payment: copies. Copyrighted, reverts to author. Pub's reviews: 9 in 1990. §Poetry. Ads: $300/$150/$80 1/4 page.

Calgre Press, Division of Calgre Inc., Edward Francis Woodmansee, PO Box 711, Antioch, CA 94509, 415-754-4916. 1988. Non-fiction. "Send SASE for ms guidelines; unused ms are returned; good copies or computer print out ms accepted. Contact: Diane Power, 415-754-4916, Calgre, Inc., 40 Sara Lane, Walnut Creek, CA 94598" avg. press run 10M. Pub'd 1 title 1990; expects 4 titles 1991, 4 titles 1992. 1 title listed in the *Small Press Record of Books in Print* (20th Edition, 1991-92). avg. price, cloth: $24; paper: $12. Discounts: 20-50%. 160pp; 5½x8½; of. Reporting time: 9 months; queries 2 weeks. Payment: 5-20% of list price. Copyrights for author. PMA, COSMEP.

Caliban Press, Mark McMurray, Patricia McMurray, 114 Westview Road, Montclair, NJ 07043, 201-744-4453. 1985. Fiction, letters, plays. avg. press run 100-250. Pub'd 3 titles 1990; expects 2 titles 1991, 2 titles 1992. 8 titles listed in the *Small Press Record of Books in Print* (20th Edition, 1991-92). avg. price, other: $25-100 limited edition. Discounts: 30% trade. 10-70pp; size varies; †lp. Reporting time: 6-9 months. Payment: 5-10% part cash, part copies. Copyrights for author.

Calibre Press, Inc., Charles Remsberg, President; Dennis Anderson, Vice President, 666 Dundee Road, Suite 1607, Northbrook, IL 60062-2727, 312-498-5680. 1979. Non-fiction. avg. press run 5M. Expects 1 title 1991, 1 title 1992. 2 titles listed in the *Small Press Record of Books in Print* (20th Edition, 1991-92). avg. price, cloth: varies, over $25. Discounts: varies with book. 400pp; size varies. Reporting time: 1 month. Payment: varies with project, author. Nat'l Assn. of Independent Publishers; Nat'l Direct Mail Order Assn.; Assn. Midwest Publishers; Publishers Marketing Assn.

California Bound Books, PO Box 613, Port Washington, NY 11050, 1-800-475-7046. 1 title listed in the *Small Press Record of Books in Print* (20th Edition, 1991-92).

CALIFORNIA LAW REVIEW, University of California Press, Students of Boalt Hall School of Law, University of California Press, 2120 Berkeley Way, Berkeley, CA 94720, 415-642-4191. 1912. Articles, reviews, non-fiction. "Editorial address: 14 Boalt Hall School of Law, University of CA, Berkeley, CA 94720. Copyrighted by California Law Review, Inc." circ. 1.9M. 6/yr. Pub'd 6 issues 1990; expects 6 issues 1991, 6 issues 1992. sub. price: $35 (+ $8 foreign postage); per copy: $9; sample: free. Back issues: $9. Discounts: foreign subs. agent 10%, one-time order 10+ 30%, standing orders (bookstores): 1-99 40%, 100+ 50%. 300pp; 7x10; of. Reporting time: 1-2 months. Payment: varies. Copyrighted, does not revert to author. Pub's reviews: 6 in 1990. Ads: $200/$120.

THE CALIFORNIA QUARTERLY, Jack Hicks, Acting Editor; Jordan Jones, Poetry Editor; Mark Wisniewski, Fiction Editor; Michael Ishii, Managing Editor, 100 Sproul Hall, Univ of Calif, Davis, CA 95616. 1971. Poetry, fiction, art, photos, interviews, parts-of-novels, long-poems. "Stories should not exceed 5M words, though we make exceptions. We publish whatever we think is good and recommend that authors glance at past issues. Recent contributors include Charles Simic, Robert Kelly, Karl Shapiro, James Bertolino, Marjorie Grene, Jerry Bumpus, Sandra Gilbert, Rosellen Brown, Ann Stanford, Joyce Carol Oates, Ruth Stone, Flossie Lewis. Recently published fiction has been reprinted in *O'Henry Prize Fiction* 1983 and *Best American Short Stories* 1983." circ. 600. 2-4/yr. Pub'd 1 single issues 1990; expects 1 tri, 1 dbl, 1 sin issues 1991, 3 singles issues 1992. sub. price: $14 4 issues; Single issue $4, double issue $8; sample: $4. Back issues: #1 $5.00; #2-10 $4.00; #11-26 $3.00. 80pp; 8½x5½; of. Reporting time: 6 weeks to 3 months. Payment: $4/page poetry & graphics; $3/page prose. Copyrighted, reverts to author. Ads: $40 page/$25 1/2. CCLM, COSMEP.

CALIFORNIA STATE POETRY QUARTERLY (CQ), John Brander, 1200 East Ocean Blvd #64, Long Beach, CA 90802, 213-495-0925. 1973. Poetry. circ. 700. 3-4/yr. Pub'd 1 issue 1990; expects 2 issues 1991, 2 issues 1992. sub. price: $12 (3 issues); per copy: $5; sample: $5. Back issues: $5. 84pp; 4x5½. Reporting time: 2-3 months. Payment: one copy of magazine. Copyrighted, reverts to author.

CALLALOO, Callaloo Poetry Series, Charles H. Rowell, Editor, English Dept, Wilson Hall, University of Virginia, Charlottesville, VA 22903, (804) 924-6637; 924-6616. 1976. Poetry, fiction, articles, art, photos, interviews, criticism, reviews, parts-of-novels, long-poems, plays, news items, non-fiction. "Short one act plays. Journal is sponsored by The University of Virginia, but published by The John Hopkins University Press" circ. 1M. 4/yr. Expects 4 issues 1991, 4 issues 1992. 4 titles listed in the *Small Press Record of Books in Print* (20th Edition, 1991-92). sub. price: $16; per copy: $7; sample: $7. Back issues: $7, $10 for photo copies of issues out-of-stock. 200pp; 7x10; of. Reporting time: 3 months. Payment: 2 copies. Copyrighted, reverts to author. Pub's reviews: 5 in 1990. §Creative literature by Black writers and critical works about Black literature. Ads: $300/$150. CCLM.

Callaloo Poetry Series (see also CALLALOO), Department of English, University of Virginia, Charlottesville, VA 22903. 1976. 4 titles listed in the *Small Press Record of Books in Print* (20th Edition, 1991-92).

CALLBOARD, Jean Schiffman, 657 Mission Street #402, San Francisco, CA 94105, 415-621-0427. 1976. Articles, photos, interviews. "Open to short articles (750-2,000 words) related to theatre. No reviews. Essays, features, interviews with theatre personalities." circ. 10M. 12/yr. Pub'd 12 issues 1990; expects 12 issues 1991, 12 issues 1992. sub. price: $32; per copy: $3.75; sample: $3.75. Back issues: $3.75. 40pp; 5x8; of. Reporting time: 2 months. Payment: $75/article; $75/cover art. Copyrighted, does not revert to author. Pub's reviews: 40-50 in 1990. §Theatre: production, administration, playwrighting, plays, acting, etc. Ads: $446/$236/$31 line classified.

CALLIGRAPHY REVIEW, Karyn L. Gilman, Nancy R. Block, 1624 24th Avenue SW, Norman, OK 73072, 405-364-8794. 1982. Articles, art, reviews. circ. 5M. 4/yr. Pub'd 4 issues 1990; expects 4 issues 1991, 4 issues 1992. 2 titles listed in the *Small Press Record of Books in Print* (20th Edition, 1991-92). sub. price: $36; per copy: $11; sample: $11. Back issues: $10 each, $8 4 or more. Discounts: 60/40 for outlets, others negotiable. 64pp; 8½x11; of. Reporting time: 8 weeks or less. Payment: on publication. Copyrighted, reverts to author. Pub's reviews: 10+ in 1990. §Calligraphy, graphic arts, typography, book arts. Ads: $550/$400/$25 classified/all one time/4x rate available.

CALLIOPE, Ampersand Press, Martha Christina, Editor, Creative Writing Program, Roger Williams College, Bristol, RI 02809, 401-253-1040, ext. 2217. 1977. Poetry, fiction, interviews, long-poems. "Interested in good new writers as well as established ones. We look for work that is strong, imagistically. We prefer concrete to abstract and like poems without inflated diction. Equally attracted to the lyric and the narrative. Some recent contributors: Gary Finke, Lynda Sexson, Mark Doty, Mark Cox, Wm. Virgil Davis, Brendan Galvin, Maggie Valentine, Kate Dougherty, Lynne deCourcy, Geraldine North" circ. 300. 2/yr. Pub'd 2 issues 1990; expects 2 issues 1991, 2 issues 1992. per copy: $3; sample: $1. Back issues: Vol 1/1&2, Vol 2/1&2, Vol 3/1, Vol 4/1, Vol 5/1&2, Vol 6/1&2, Vol 7/2, Vol 8/1, Vol 10/1 unavailable; others $1 while they last. Specify thematic issue desired: *Place, Colors, Food*. Other issues are eclectic. Discounts: 40% bookstores. 48-80pp; 5½x8½; of. Reporting time: immediately to 3 months. Payment: 2 copies and yr's subscription. Copyrighted, reverts to author. No ads. CLMP.

CALLIOPE: World History for Young People, Cobblestone Publishing, Inc., Carolyn P. Yoder, Editor-in-Chief; Sarah E. Hale, Assistant Editor, 30 Grove Street, Peterborough, NH 03458, 603-924-7209. 1990. "The magazine will accept freelance articles related to themes covered" circ. 8M. 5/yr. Expects 5 issues 1991, 5 issues 1992. sub. price: $17.95/yr + $5 foreign; per copy: $3.95. 48pp; 7x9.

CALLI'S TALES, The Quarterly for Animal Lovers of All Ages, Annice E. Hunt, Editor, Box 1224, Palmetto, FL 34220, 813-722-2202. 1981. Poetry, fiction, articles, cartoons, interviews, reviews, news items, non-fiction. "Additional address: 2103-5th Street W., Palmetto, FL 33561. A quarterly for animal lovers of all ages. Brief stories, articles and poems. We have a big backlog of poetry, fiction and non-fiction" 4/yr. Pub'd 7 issues 1990; expects 4 issues 1991, 4 issues 1992. 1 title listed in the *Small Press Record of Books in Print* (20th Edition, 1991-92). sub. price: $8; per copy: $2; sample: $2. 18pp; 8½×11; †of. Reporting time: 2 months. Payment: 1 copy. Copyrighted, reverts to author. Pub's reviews: 2 in 1990. §Nature subjects for all ages, conservation, animal protection, wildlife, pets. Ads: $15/10¢ display/word, 5¢ classifed/word.

CALYPSO: Journal of Narrative Poetry and Poetic Fiction, Susan Richardson, 1829 Arnold Way #503, Alpine, CA 91901-3708. 1988. Poetry, fiction, articles, interviews, criticism, reviews. "Emphasis on narrative poetry and poetic fiction, though we will consider all types. Biased toward originality, rhythm, energy and purity in metaphor. Would also like interviews with those who write both poetry and fiction well and essays on narrative poetry and poetic fiction." 1/yr. Pub'd 1 issue 1990; expects 1 issue 1991, 1 issue 1992. sub. price: $6; per copy: $6; sample: $6. Back issues: $6. Discounts: $5 each for orders of 20 or more. 60-100pp; 6×9; of. Reporting time: 2 months. Payment: copies. Copyrighted, reverts to author. Pub's reviews: 1 in 1990. §Poetry, fiction, essays, criticism, creative writing in general. CLMP.

CALYX: A Journal of Art and Literature by Women, Calyx Books, Margarita Donnelly, Managing Editor; Beverly McFarland, Editor; Catherine Holdorf, Editor, PO Box B, Corvallis, OR 97339, 503-753-9384. 1976. Poetry, fiction, art, photos, criticism, reviews, parts-of-novels. "*Calyx* is the Major West Coast publication of its kind. Recently reviewed as 'undoubtedly...one of the best literary mags in the U.S.'—New Pages Press. (128 pages). Manuscript queries and submissions must be accompanied by a SASE. The journal is no longer open to submissions all year round. Open reading dates for journal submissions are April 1 to May 30, and Oct. 1 to Nov. 30 annually. Be sure to include brief bio statement with all submissions" circ. 3M. 2/yr. Pub'd 2 issues 1990; expects 2 issues 1991, 2 issues 1992. sub. price: $18 indiv., institutional & library $22.50 (subs are 3 issues but take 18 months to complete); per copy: $8 + $1.50 p/h; sample: $8 + $1.50 p/h. Back issues: Spring 86 & 87 double issues, $12 + $1.25 postage (supply limited). Discounts: trade 40%. 112-125pp; 8×7; of. Reporting time: 1-6 months. Payment: in copies. Copyrighted, rights revert on request. Pub's reviews: 32 in 1990. §Feminist criticism, reviews of books, films & poetry by women. Ads: $550/$285/75¢. CCLM, WCA, COWO.

Calyx Books (see also CALYX: A Journal of Art and Literature by Women), Margarita Donnelly, Managing Editor, PO Box B, Corvallis, OR 97339. 1985. Poetry, fiction, art, non-fiction. avg. press run 5M. Pub'd 3 titles 1990; expects 4 titles 1991, 3 titles 1992. 12 titles listed in the *Small Press Record of Books in Print* (20th Edition, 1991-92). avg. price, cloth: $20; paper: $12. Discounts: 20% 1-4 books, 40% 5-49, 43% 50-99, 45% 100+. 5½×8½; of. Reporting time: 1 year. Payment: individually contracted. Copyrights for author. CLMP, COWO.

CAMBRENSIS: THE SHORT STORY QUARTERLY MAGAZINE OF WALES, Arthur Smith, 41 Heol Fach, Cornelly, Bridgend, Mid-Glamorgan, CF334LN South Wales, United Kingdom, 0656-741-994. 1987. Fiction, art, cartoons. "Uses only short stories, under 2,500 words, by writers born or resident in Wales; no poetry used; cartoons/black & white artwork sharp-contrast used." circ. 500. 4/yr. Pub'd 4 issues 1990; expects 4 issues 1991, 4 issues 1992. sub. price: £6; per copy: £1.50; sample: IRC. Back issues: £1.25. Discounts: 20%. 64pp; size A5; of. Reporting time: by return. Payment: none at present time—copies given. Copyrighted, reverts to author. Ads: £25/£15/£10 1/4 page. ALP, BAPA, Welsh Academy.

Cambric Press, Joel Rudinger, Publisher, 901 Rye Beach Road, Huron, OH 44839, 419-433-5660; 419-929-8767. 1975. Poetry, fiction, non-fiction. "Self-publishing, book manufacturer." avg. press run 500-1M. Pub'd 2 titles 1990; expects 2 titles 1991, 2 titles 1992. 7 titles listed in the *Small Press Record of Books in Print* (20th Edition, 1991-92). avg. price, paper: $8.95. Discounts: 40% on bulk orders over 10; 30% under 10. 64-80pp; 5½×8½; of. Reporting time: 4 weeks. Payment: 100% to author. Copyrights for author.

Camel Press (see also DUST (From the Ego Trip); AMERICAN AMATEUR JOURNALIST), James Hedges, Editor, HC 80, Box 160, Big Cove Tannery, PA 17212, 717-573-4526. 1984. Articles, non-fiction. "Autobiography, 1-2.5M words." avg. press run 500. Expects 3 titles 1991, 2 titles 1992. 7 titles listed in the *Small Press Record of Books in Print* (20th Edition, 1991-92). avg. price, paper: $2. Discounts: on request. 20pp; 4¼×5¾; †lp. Reporting time: 1 week. Payment: 50 free copies, page charges may be requested from author. Copyrights for author. AAPA, APA.

CAMELLIA, Tomer Inbar, Dan Alter, PO Box 4092, Ithaca, NY 14852. 1989. Poetry, fiction, cartoons. "We try to keep fiction to 1 or 2 pages. Poetry to 1 or 2 pages." circ. 1M. 4/yr. Pub'd 4 issues 1990; expects 4 issues 1991, 4 issues 1992. sub. price: $5; per copy: free (52¢ SASE if requested by mail); sample: 52¢ SASE. 20pp; 8½×11; †xerox. Reporting time: asap. Payment: copy. Copyrighted, reverts to author.

CAMERA OBSCURA: A Journal of Feminism and Film Theory, Janet Bergstrom, Elisabeth Lyon, Constance Penley, Lynn Spigel, Sharon Willis, University of Rochester, R Rhees Library, Rochester, NY 14627. 1976. Articles, photos, interviews, criticism, reviews, letters. "Johns Hopkins University Press." circ.

3M. 3/yr. Pub'd 2 issues 1990; expects 3 issues 1991, 3 issues 1992. sub. price: individual $18.50, institution $37 (foreign postage: Canada & Mexico + $6, outside North America + $6); per copy: $7.50, $13 institutions; sample: $7.50. Back issues: No. 3/4 $9.50 individual, $15 institutions; No. 8/9/10 $11.50 individual, $17 institutions; No. 13/14 $9.50, $15 institutions. Discounts: 40% bookstores. 150-180pp; 5½×8½; of. Reporting time: 1 month. Payment: none. Copyrighted, does not revert to author. Pub's reviews: 12 in 1990. §Film, feminist theory, political theory, popular culture, psychoanalysis, photography, video. CK w/JHUP (301)338-6982.

Campaign For Press & Broadcasting Freedom (see also FREE PRESS), 9 Poland Street, London W1V 3DG, England, 01 437 0189; 01 437 2795. 1979. Articles, photos, cartoons, interviews, criticism, reviews, letters, news items, non-fiction. "CPBF publishes its own booklets on specific media issues, and co-publishes larger works with other publishers. Recent CPBF publications: *Media Hits The Pits*—analysis of media coverage of the 84/5 coal dispute, £1.50. *Women In Focus*—guidelines on eliminating media sexism, £1.50. *Right Of Reply Pack*—folder of posters, info sheets and booklets on how to counter media bias and distortion, £2.95. Joint publications: *Bending Reality: The State of the Media*—various authors (all CPBF members) with Pluto Press, £5.95. We also produce videos" avg. press run 2M-3M. Expects 3 titles 1991. Discounts: normal trade. Pages vary; size A4; of, lp. Reporting time: Jan. 8 for Feb 1 issue, March 8 for April 1 issue. Payment: by agreement.

CAMPUS REVIEW, Jeff Renander, 336 S. Clinton #16, Iowa City, IA 52240, 319-338-1532. 1983. Articles, cartoons, interviews, satire, criticism, reviews, music, letters, news items. "Primary focus is on college scene. Has conservative/libertarian bias. Lots of humor and original cartoons. Interviewed nearly all U.S. presidential candidates in 1988." circ. 9M. 12/yr. Pub'd 10 issues 1990; expects 10 issues 1991, 14 issues 1992. sub. price: $10; per copy: $1; sample: $1. 20pp; 11×15; web press. Payment: $15-$30 per article published. Copyrighted, reverts to author. Pub's reviews: 40 in 1990. §Politics, fiction, humor. Ads: $300/$150/$75 1/4 page. Collegiate Network.

CANADIAN AUTHOR & BOOKMAN, Gordon E. Symons, Editor; Sheila Martindale, Poetry Editor; Geoff Hancock, Fiction Editor, 121 Avenue Road, Suite 104, Toronto, Ontario M5R 2G3, Canada, 416-926-8084. 1919. Poetry, articles, reviews. "Want Canadian literary doings-writing craft articles from any writer. Only Canadian fiction & poetry" circ. 5M. 4/yr. Pub'd 4 issues 1990; expects 4 issues 1991. sub. price: $12.50 individual, $20 institution, (U.S. subscribers add $5 for postage); per copy: $3.50; sample: $4.50. Back issues: $4.50. Discounts: 15%. 32pp; 8⅛×10⅞; of. Reporting time: up to 90 days. Payment: $30/printed page, $15/poem. Copyrighted. Pub's reviews: 24 in 1990. §Whatever we review must be approached from point of view of writer's craft. Ads: $400/$250/$25 per col inch. CPPA.

CANADIAN CHILDREN'S LITERATURE, Mary Rubio, Elizabeth Waterston, Francois Pare, Department of English, University of Guelph, Guelph, Ontario N1G 2W1, Canada. 1975. Articles, interviews, criticism, reviews. "*CCL* publishes critical articles and in-depth reviews of books written for Canadian children and adolescents." circ. 1.5M. 4/yr. Expects 4 issues 1991. 3 titles listed in the *Small Press Record of Books in Print* (20th Edition, 1991-92). sub. price: $22 (plus $8 postage outside Canada); per copy: $6; sample: $6 (plus $2 postage outside Canada). Back issues: prices available upon request. Discounts: none. 100pp; 6×9; of. Reporting time: 2 months. Payment: none. Copyrighted. Pub's reviews: 40 in 1990. §Books written for Canadian children and adolescents. CMA.

CANADIAN DIMENSION, Editorial Board, 707-228 Notre dame Avenue, Winnipeg, Manitoba R3B 1N7, Canada, 957-1519. 1965. Articles, art, photos, cartoons, criticism, reviews, music. circ. 5M. 8/yr. Pub'd 9 issues 1990; expects 8 issues 1991, 8 issues 1992. sub. price: Canadian rate: regular $24.50; student, pensioner, unemployed $18.50; libraries, institutions, organizations $35. U.S. rate: regular $30.50; libraries, institutions, organizations $35; per copy: $3.25; sample: $1.50. Back issues: $2 per issue. Discounts: 33% to bookstores, 40% to distributors. 48pp; 8½×11; of. Reporting time: 2 Months. Payment: fees paid by agreement on publication if writer makes exclusive living on writing. Copyrighted, does not revert to author. Pub's reviews: 27 in 1990. §Politics, economics, contemp. topics. Ads: $350/$228. CPPA, CMPA.

CANADIAN FICTION MAGAZINE, Geoffrey Hancock, PO Box 946, Station F, Toronto, Ontario M4Y 2N9, Canada. 1971. Fiction, interviews, criticism, reviews, parts-of-novels. "We publish work of writers and artists resident in Canada and Canadians living abroad. No restriction on length, subject matter or style though we tend to prefer fiction that astonishes both through technique & meaning. We offer an annual $500.00 contributors prize. Recent contributors include Derk Wynand, Michel Tremblay, Jacques Ferron, Felix Leclerc, George Woodcock, Matt Cohen, Rikki, Joyce Marshall, Leon Rooke, Hugh Hood, Robert Harlow, Jane Rule, John Metcalf, Yves Theriault, Robert Kroetsch, Robertson Davies, Mavis Gallant, Susan Musgrave, Josef Skvorecky." circ. 1.8M. 4/yr. Pub'd 4 issues 1990; expects 4 issues 1991. sub. price: $40 Canada, $46 US & institution; per copy: $9.95; sample: $7.95 in Canadian funds (inc. postage for current issue). Back issues: price on request; average price $5 (inc. postage). Discounts: 5% agent, 40% consignment to stores. 160pp; 6×9; of. Reporting time: 4-6 weeks. Payment: $10 per printed page on publication. Buys first North American serial rights. Pub's reviews: 35 in 1990. §Surrealism & magic realism in short fiction, also Canadian short stories & novellas, French-Canadian writers in translation, interviews, forums of future of fiction. Ads: $100/$65. CMPA.

CANADIAN JOURNAL OF DRAMA AND THEATRE, University of Calgary Press, Roberta Bramivell, Department of Drama, The University of Calgary, Calgary, Alberta T2N 1N4, Canada, 403-220-3849. 1991. Articles, photos, interviews, criticism, music. "Qualitative, quantitative, analytical and historical studies of drama and theatre" circ. 50. 2/yr. Expects 2 issues 1991, 2 issues 1992. sub. price: $16 + G.S.T. Canada, outside Canada price in U.S. dollars; per copy: $8. 60pp; 6×9; of. Reporting time: 4 months. Payment: none. Copyrighted, does not revert to author. Ads: write for info.

CANADIAN JOURNAL OF LAW AND SOCIETY/Revue canadienne de droit et societe, C. Thomassett, Department des sciences juridiques, c.p. 8888, succ. A., Quebec Univ., Montreal, P.Q. H3C 3PA, Canada, 514-987-8397. 1985. Articles, reviews. "A bilingual refereed journal dedicated to the promotion and publication of writing on law and the legal system" circ. 300. 1/yr. Pub'd 1 issue 1990; expects 2 issues 1991, 1 issue 1992. sub. price: $18 indiv., $30 instit., add G.S.T. Canada; outside Canada price in U.S. dollars; per copy: $18. 175pp; 6×9; of. Reporting time: 2 months. Payment: none. Copyrighted, does not revert to author. Pub's reviews: 10 in 1990. §Law and the legal system. Ads: write for info.

CANADIAN JOURNAL OF PHILOSOPHY, University of Calgary Press, W. Cooper, Managing Editor, Department of Philosophy, University of Alberta, Edmonton, Alberta T6G 2E5, Canada, 403-492-3307. 1970. Articles. "Publishes philosophical work of high quality in any field of philosophy" circ. 2.3M. 4/yr. Pub'd 4 issues 1990; expects 4 issues 1991, 4 issues 1992. sub. price: $20 indiv., $35 instit., $13 student, add G.S.T. Canada; other: $20US indiv., $36US instit., $13US student; per copy: $9 + G.S.T. Canada, $9US. Back issues: back volume of 4 issues $30 + G.S.T. Canada, $30 US. Discounts: agent $2 off institution price. 160pp; 6×9; of. Reporting time: 2 months. Payment: none. Copyrighted, does not revert to author. Ads: write for info.

CANADIAN JOURNAL OF PROGRAM EVALUATION/Le Revue canadienne d'evaluation de programme, University of Calgary Press, R.M. Grinnell, Jr., Faculty of Social Welfare, The University of Calgary, Calgary, Alberta T2N 1N4, Canada, 403-220-6154. 1986. Articles, criticism. "Publishes all aspects of the theory and practice of evaluation including research and practice notes." circ. 1.3M. 2/yr. Pub'd 2 issues 1990; expects 2 issues 1991, 2 issues 1992. sub. price: $55 + G.S.T. Canada; outside Canada price in U.S. dollars; per copy: $11 + G.S.T. Canada. 110pp; 6×9; of. Reporting time: 3 months. Payment: none. Copyrighted, does not revert to author. Ads: write for info. Canadian Evaluation Society.

CANADIAN LITERATURE, W.H. New, University of British Columbia, 2029 West Mall, Vancouver, B.C. V6T 1Z2, Canada, 604-822-2780. 1959. Poetry, criticism, reviews. "Criticism and reviews focus primarily on Canadian writers" circ. 2M. 4/yr. Pub'd 4 issues 1990; expects 4 issues 1991, 4 issues 1992. sub. price: indiv. $30, institution $45 plus postage (outside Canada) $5; per copy: $10; sample: $5-$10. Back issues: may be obtained from Journal. Discounts: $1 for agencies. 192pp; 6¾×9¾; lp. Reporting time: 1 month. Payment: $5 a page. Copyrighted. Pub's reviews: 107 in 1990. §Canadian writers and writing. Ads: $300/$200/$135/$75. CMPA.

CANADIAN MONEYSAVER, Dale L. Ennis, Box 370, Bath, Ontario K0H 1G0, Canada. 1981. Articles, interviews, non-fiction. circ. 27M. 11/yr. Pub'd 10 issues 1990; expects 11 issues 1991, 11 issues 1992. sub. price: Canada $19.95, U.S. $33, others US $40; per copy: $3; sample: $3. Back issues: none. Discounts: up to 40% off for large orders (100+). 36pp; 8×10½; †web. Reporting time: 3 weeks. Payment: none. Copyrighted, reverts to author. Pub's reviews: 25-30 in 1990. §Finance, money management, investment, consumer savings. Ads: $2,000/$1,200. CMPA.

CANADIAN PUBLIC POLICY- Analyse de Politiques, Nancy Olewiler, Editor, Room 039, MacKinnon Bldg., University of Guelph, Guelph, Ontario N1G 2W1, Canada, 519-824-4120 ext. 3330. 1975. Articles, reviews. "A journal for the discussion of social and economic policy in Canada." circ. 2M. 4/yr. Pub'd 5 issues 1990; expects 4 issues 1991, 5 issues 1992. sub. price: $35 indiv., $33 members, $19 students, $55 institutions, + GST in Canada, + $9 for mailing outside Canada; per copy: $10; sample: free. Discounts: can be arranged. 128pp; 7×10; of. Reporting time: 35 days. Copyrighted, does not revert to author. Pub's reviews: 74 in 1990. §Public policy. Ads: $295/$195/on request.

CANADIAN SLAVONIC PAPERS, E.W. Dowler, Centre for Russian and East European Studies, University of Toronto, Toronto, Ontario M5S 1A1, Canada. 1956. Articles, reviews. "We publish scholarly articles in all disciplines of Russian, Soviet & East European studies. Manuscripts-no longer than 30 typewritten double spaced pages. Directory." circ. 1M. 4/yr. Pub'd 4 issues 1990; expects 4 issues 1991. 1 title listed in the *Small Press Record of Books in Print* (20th Edition, 1991-92). sub. price: $40 for Canada, $45 for USA & overseas; per copy: $12; sample: $12. Back issues: varies. Discounts: none. 150pp; 6×9; of. Reporting time: 3 months. Payment: none. Copyrighted, does not revert to author. Pub's reviews: 145 in 1990. §Russian & East European studies. Ads: $300/$150 for camera-ready copy.

98

CANADIAN WOMAN STUDIES/les cahiers de la femme, Carol Greene, 212 Founders College, York Univ., 400 Keele Street, Downsview, Ontario M3J 1P3, Canada, (416) 736-5356. 1978. Poetry, fiction, articles, art, photos, cartoons, interviews, reviews, non-fiction. "We do not publish sexist, racist, homophobic, or any other discriminatory material. Length of articles: 10 typed, double-spaced pages." circ. 3M. 4/yr. Pub'd 4 issues 1990; expects 4 issues 1991, 4 issues 1992. sub. price: $30 indiv. (Cdn), $40 instit. (Cdn), $36 indiv. outside Canada, $46 instit. outside Canada; per copy: $8; sample: $3. Back issues: usually $3 per issue unless out of print. 112pp; 8½×11; of. Reporting time: 3 months. Payment: complimentary copy of issue in which work appears. Copyrighted, reverts to author. Pub's reviews: 50 in 1990. §Women's studies, women's issues, feminism, literary works and criticism. Ads: $200/$100/$75 1/3 page/$50 1/6 page. CMPA.

CANDELABRUM POETRY MAGAZINE, Red Candle Press, M.L. McCarthy, 9 Milner Road, Wisbech PE13 2LR, England, tel: 0945 581067. 1970. Poetry. "Provides an outlet for poets using traditional verse-forms though also open to good-quality free-verse. We believe that the purpose of poetry is to delight and exalt through the pattern of language & the beauty of imagery. As the English language is heavily accented, English poetry has developed as metrical verse; the disciplines imposed by the structure & accentuation of the language must be observed for sustained artistry to be possible in poetry. Authors keep the copyright. We send the usual British copyright copies." circ. 1M. 1 double number every year. Pub'd 1 issue 1990; expects 1 issue 1991, 1 issue 1992. sub. price: £2, US $12 by cheque, $4 in bills; per copy: same; sample: £2, US $12 by cheque, $4 in bills. Back issues: Back numbers before 1986, as available: £1 (US $8 by cheque, $2 in bills). Please note: the higher US price is to cover the bank-charge on dollar cheques. 40pp; 8½×5½; of. Reporting time: 1-2 months. Payment: 1 free copy, no cash payment. Copyrighted, reverts to author. Pub's reviews. §Poetry. Ads: £20/£10 (US $46/$26 by cheque, $40/$20 in bills).

Candle Publishing Company, Lynn Sims, PO Box 5009-136, Sugar Land, TX 77478, 713-242-6162. 1986. Pub'd 2 titles 1990; expects 3 titles 1991. 3 titles listed in the *Small Press Record of Books in Print* (20th Edition, 1991-92). avg. price, cloth: $17.95; paper: $12.95. 175-250pp; 5⅜×8⅛. Copyrights for author. Book Publishers of Texas, Publishers Marketing Assn., NAPRA.

Cane Hill Press, Steven Schrader, 225 Varick Street, New York, NY 10014. 1987. Fiction. avg. press run 1.5M. Pub'd 2 titles 1990; expects 3 titles 1991, 3 titles 1992. 9 titles listed in the *Small Press Record of Books in Print* (20th Edition, 1991-92). avg. price, paper: $8.95. Discounts: 1-4 copies 20%, 5-49 copies 40%, 50+ 43%. Freight: $1 for one, 35¢ for additional; UPS: $1.50 for one, $1.75 for additional. 150pp; 5½×8½; of. Reporting time: usually within 1 month. Payment: flat fee paid on acceptance, no royalty, additional flat fee for each reprinting. Copyrights for author.

CANTU'S COMEDY NEWSLETTER, John Cantu, PO Box 590634, San Francisco, CA 94159-0634, 415-668-2402. Articles, cartoons, interviews, satire, criticism, letters, news items. "Strictly oriented to stand-up comedy, comedians and comedy writing (for stand-up comics or for other areas)" circ. 2M. 2/yr. Pub'd 2 issues 1990; expects 2 issues 1991, 3 issues 1992. sub. price: free; per copy: free; sample: free for SASE. Back issues: $1. 6-8pp; 8½×11; †of. Reporting time: send 1-page query letter w/SASE first. Payment: the respect and admiration of peers. Not copyrighted. Pub's reviews. §Only dealing with stand-up comedy or comedy writing in any area (writing humor for ads, greeting cards, etc.). Ads: neg.

CANVAS, Mark V. Cushman, William Perry, 6189 Helen C. White Hall, Madison, WI 53703. 1987. Poetry, fiction, art, photos. circ. 500. 1/yr. Pub'd 1 issue 1990; expects 1 issue 1991, 1 issue 1992. sub. price: $1; per copy: $1; sample: $1. Discounts: negotiable. 100pp; 5½×8¼; of. Reporting time: 4 months. Payment: only as awards. Not copyrighted.

CANVAS CHAUTAUQUA MAGAZINE, Ted Willi, PO Box 361, Bloomington, IN 47402, 812-333-4542. 1990. Poetry, articles, art, cartoons, reviews, letters, non-fiction. "*Canvas Chautauqua* is interested in canvas shelters (or other nomadic shelters), hair (or other expressions of body/personality), belief systems (or what people think is reality), canoes/bicycles (or other ecologically-sound vehicles). Poems should be less than a page; articles should be 1-3 pages; black and white artwork preferred over greys. Recently published work by John Skoyles, Elizabeth Holtam, and Swami Tapasya." circ. 250. 4/yr. Pub'd 2 issues 1990; expects 4 issues 1991, 4 issues 1992. sub. price: $4; per copy: $1; sample: $1. Back issues: $1. Discounts: 1/2 price in quantities of 20 or more. 16-24pp; 5½×8½; mi. Reporting time: 2 weeks. Payment: free year's subscription. Copyrighted, reverts to author. Pub's reviews: 48 in 1990. §Native American traditions, world religions, anarchic philosophies, the occult, nomadics. Ads: $20/$10/$5 1/4 page. National Association for the Cottage Industry, PO Box 14850, Chicago, IL 60614.

Cape Cod Writers Inc (see also SANDSCRIPT), Barbara Renkens Dunning, Editor, Box 333, Cummaquid, MA 02637. 1977.

THE CAPE ROCK, Harvey Hecht, English Dept, Southeast Missouri State, Cape Girardeau, MO 63701, 314-651-2500. 1964. Poetry, photos. "Our criterion for selection is the quality of the work, not the bibliography of the author. We consider poems of almost any style on almost any subject and favor poems under 75 lines.

Each submission should have the author's name and complete address, preferably in the upper right hand corner. A self-addressed, stamped envelope (SASE) is required to guarantee return. We do not read submissions in June, July, and August. We feature the work of a single photographer in each issue; submit 20-25 thematically organized 5 x 7 B & W glossies. Submissions, subscriptions, and queries should be addressed to *The Cape Rock*, Harvey Hecht, Editor, Southeast Missouri State University, Cape Girardeau, MO 63701." circ. 600. 2/yr. Pub'd 2 issues 1990; expects 2 issues 1991. sub. price: $5; per copy: $3; sample: $3. Discounts: 25% off on orders of 20 or more (our cost plus postage). 64pp; 5½x8¾; †of. Reporting time: 1-4 months. Payment: $100 for photography, $200 for best poem, in each issue. Other payment in copies. Copyrighted, rights to contents released to authors and artists upon request, subject only to their giving credit to *The Cape Rock* whenever and wherever else the work is placed. *The Cape Rock* retains reprint rights. No ads. CCLM, COSMEP, NESPA.

THE CAPILANO REVIEW, Pierre Coupey, 2055 Purcell Way, North Vancouver, B.C. V7J3H5, Canada, 604-986-1911; FAX 604-984-4985. 1972. Poetry, fiction, art, photos, interviews, parts-of-novels, long-poems, plays, concrete art. *"The Capilano Review* is a tri-annual literary and visual art magazine, publishing only what its editors consider to be the very best work being produced. The magazine is published at considerable cost, and the editors collectively put in a great deal of energy in order to give writers and other artists the best possible presentation and circulation of their work. Sample issues are available at the regular $8.00 per single copy cost. The most intelligent way of seeing if your material is likely to interest us is to read the magazine. (It is also available in over 100 major libraries in Canada, the U.S., and other countries.) We are most interested in publishing artists whose work has not yet received the attention it deserves. We are not interested in imitative, derivative, or unfinished work. We have no format exclusions" circ. 1M-1.5M. 3/yr. Pub'd 4 issues 1990; expects 2 issues 1991, 3 issues 1992. sub. price: $16 individual, $25 libraries, add $5 postage for U.S. & overseas; per copy: $8; sample: $8. Back issues: $7 per copy. Discounts: 40% to bookstores. 100pp; 9x6 (approx); of. Reporting time: up to 4 months. Copyrighted, reverts to author. Ads: $150/$75/$50 1/3 page/exchange in other little magazines.

Capra Press, Noel Young, PO Box 2068, Santa Barbara, CA 93120, 805-966-4590; FAX 805-965-8020. 1969. Fiction, interviews, satire, criticism, letters, non-fiction. "A general trade press with a focus on the West. *No poetry.*" avg. press run 5M. Pub'd 12 titles 1990; expects 12 titles 1991. 71 titles listed in the *Small Press Record of Books in Print* (20th Edition, 1991-92). avg. price, cloth: $19; paper: $10.95. Discounts: distributors 1-4 20%, 5-24 42%, 25-99 44%. 96-300pp; 5½x8½, 6x9, 7⅜x9¼; of. Reporting time: 6 weeks average. Payment: royalties negotiated. Copyright in author's name. COSMEP, AAP, ABA.

Caravan Press, Jonah Cain, 15445 Ventura Boulevard #10279, Sherman Oaks, CA 91403-3005. 1980. Poetry, fiction, photos, non-fiction. "We look for high quality manuscripts with a socially redeeming benefit. Very 'current' styles are preferred. We have strong liaisons in the entertainment industry and thusly we are media oriented. Only strong writers with some sort of track record should submit. Professionalism, style and quality are the keys to submission here." avg. press run 3M-10M poetry, 50M calendars. Pub'd 4 titles 1990; expects 5 titles 1991, 5 titles 1992. 5 titles listed in the *Small Press Record of Books in Print* (20th Edition, 1991-92). avg. price, cloth: $19.95; paper: $9.95. Discounts: trade 2-4 20%, 5-9 30%, 10-24 40%, 25-49 45%, 50-99 50%; schools and libraries less added 5%. 112pp; 5½x8½; of, lp. Reporting time: 2-6 weeks. Payment: 5-10% on sales + guarantee and expenses: see Standard Writers Union Contract. Copyrights for author.

Cardinal Press, Inc., Mary McAnally, 76 N Yorktown, Tulsa, OK 74110, 918-583-3651. 1978. Poetry, art, photos, long-poems. "Bias for Midwest/Southwest poets, for women, prisoners, minorities. Will not publish any racist or sexist material. Socialist/humanist orientation, no unsolicited manuscripts." avg. press run 300. Expects 1 title 1991, 2-4 titles 1992. 3 titles listed in the *Small Press Record of Books in Print* (20th Edition, 1991-92). avg. price, paper: $5. Discounts: 3-5 15%; 6-10 25%; 11+ 35%. 48pp; 6x9; of. Reporting time: 1-3 months. Payment: copies. Does not copyright for author.

Career Publishing, Inc., PO Box 5486, Orange, CA 92613-5486, 714-771-5155; 800-854-4014. 1972. Non-fiction. "Truck driving course, guidance material, medical office management, real estate dictionary, career guidance, Wordstar step by step, Wordperfect step-by-step, HyperCard, CDL manuals, desktop publishing" avg. press run 5M-10M. Pub'd 8 titles 1990; expects 6 titles 1991, 10 titles 1992. 12 titles listed in the *Small Press Record of Books in Print* (20th Edition, 1991-92). avg. price, paper: $25; other: guidance booklets $2.50 each, pack of 20 for $37.50, no discount. Discounts: classroom 20% textbooks, guides no discount. 350-500pp; 8½x11; of. Reporting time: 1 month or longer. Payment: 10%. Does not copyright for author. ABA, PMA.

CARIBBEAN NEWSLETTER, Box 20392, Park West Station, New York, NY 10025. 1981. Articles, cartoons, news items. "Length of material: 8-14 pages" circ. 500. 6/yr. Pub'd 6 issues 1990; expects 6 issues 1991, 6 issues 1992. sub. price: $10; per copy: $2; sample: $1. 10pp; 8½x11; of. Not copyrighted. Pub's reviews: 3 in 1990. §Caribbean issues or biographies.

CARIBBEAN REVIEW, Barry B. Levine, 9700 SW 67th Avenue, Miami, FL 33156, 305-284-8466. 1969. Poetry, fiction, articles, art, photos, cartoons, interviews, satire, criticism, reviews, long-poems, non-fiction. "(1) and (2) used less frequently than other categories" circ. 5M. 4/yr. Pub'd 2 issues 1990; expects 4 issues 1991, 4 issues 1992. sub. price: $20; per copy: $6. Back issues: $8.50. Discounts: 15% Agency discount. 48pp; 8½×11; of. Reporting time: 6 weeks. Payment: contributor's copies. Copyrighted, reverts to author on request. Pub's reviews: 45 in 1990. §Caribbean Latin America and their emigrant groups. Ads: $975/$595 (full color); $750/$450 (b/w). Florida Magazine Association.

THE CARIBBEAN WRITER, Erika J. Smilowitz, Caribbean Research Institute, RR 2, Box 10,000, Univ of Virgin Islands, Kingshill, St. Croix, VI 00851, 809-778-0246 X20. 1987. Poetry, fiction, art, photos, reviews, parts-of-novels. "*The Caribbean Writer* is an international magazine with a regional focus. The Caribbean should be central to the work or the work should reflect a Caribbean heritage, experience or perspective" circ. 1M. 1/yr. Pub'd 1 issue 1990; expects 1 issue 1991, 1 issue 1992. sub. price: $7 + $1.50 postage; per copy: $7 + $1.50 postage; sample: same. Back issues: none. Discounts: 12-24 copies 30%, 25+ 40%. 120pp; 6×9; of. Reporting time: authors of accepted mss are notified in February. Payment: 1 copy. Copyrighted, reverts to author. Pub's reviews: 10 in 1990. §Caribbean fiction, poetry, or related reference materials. Ads: $225/$150/$100 1/4 page/no classifieds.

Carlton Books, Graham Carlton, PO Box 333, Evanston, IL 60204, (312) 328-0400. 1986. Fiction. Expects 10 titles 1992. avg. price, other: tape $9.95. Discounts: negotiable. 60-90 minute tape; cassette. Reporting time: depends. Payment: negotiable. COSMEP.

‡**CARN (a link between the Celtic nations), Celtic League,** P.A. Bridson, J.B. Moffatt-General Secretary, Celtic League-24, St. Germain's Place, Peel, Isle of Mann, 0306 2484 3135. 1973. Poetry, articles, interviews, criticism, reviews, letters, news items. "500-1M words per article, 2000 for one or two in each issue. -1/3 to -1/4 of the material in Celtic languages, rest in English, CARN is the organ of the Celtic League which fosters co-operation & solidarity between the Celtic nations. Additional address: P.A. Bridson, 33 Bothar Bancroft, Tamklacht, Dublin, Eire" circ. 1.3M-1.5M. 4/yr. Pub'd 4 issues 1990; expects 4 issues 1991, 4 issues 1992. sub. price: £6 (Ireland), £5 UK & Europe, $14 USA; per copy: 80p; sample: 80p + postage. Back issues: 40p per copy. Discounts: 25 percent bookshops. 24pp; 8½×12; of. Reporting time: up to 3 months. Payment: none. Copyright remains with *Carn*. Pub's reviews: 8 in 1990. §History of the Celtic nations, history of the Celtic languages, movements for national freedom and language restoration, bilingual education. Ads: £4.00 column inch.

The Carnation Press, H.K. Henisch, B.A. Henisch, PO Box 101, State College, PA 16804, 814-238-3577. 1966. Plays, non-fiction. "1 facsimile reprint; 3 non-fiction; 1 play, 1 poetry. Among the contributors: Prof. Robert Lima, Dept. of Spanish, PSU; Prof. Robert Snetsinger, Dept. of Entymology, PSU." avg. press run 500-2.4M. Expects 1 title 1992. 5 titles listed in the *Small Press Record of Books in Print* (20th Edition, 1991-92). avg. price, cloth: $13; paper: $5. Discounts: 40% (10 copies or more); 30% (single copies). 150pp; 6×9; of. Reporting time: 1 month. Payment: no royalties to break even point; 25% of net receipts after that. Copyright negotiable.

Carnival Enterprises, Rosemary Wallyer, Editor, c/o H. Jaffee, 15th Floor, 350 Park Avenue, New York, NY 10022. 1981. Fiction, art. "*Carnival Enterprises* is a Minnesota and Connecticut-based packager of juvenile materials for commercial publishers. Our stories are edited in a way that makes the picturebook format a medium of entertainment for all ages" Pub'd 3 titles 1990; expects 20 titles 1991, 30 titles 1992. 8 titles listed in the *Small Press Record of Books in Print* (20th Edition, 1991-92). We do not market our titles. 32pp; size varies. Payment: various—negotiated advance and royalty or occasional work-for-hire.

Carnival Press, Julie Zuckman, 351 Pleasant Street, Suite 277, Northampton, MA 01060. 1988. Satire, criticism, non-fiction. "Interested in non-fiction only, especially informed essays, non-academic cultural criticism, and commentary on science, American culture and folkways. New England emphasis for cultural/regional titles." avg. press run 500-1M. Expects 1 title 1991, 1 title 1992. 1 title listed in the *Small Press Record of Books in Print* (20th Edition, 1991-92). avg. price, paper: $8.95. Discounts: standard trade terms. 96-192pp; 5½×7½; of. Reporting time: 2-3 months, SASE required—mss not returned w/o. Prefer query letter first. Payment: negotiated by the project. Copyrights for author.

A CAROLINA LITERARY COMPANION, Nellvena Duncan Eutsler, Executive Editor; Michael M. Parker, Fiction Editor; Dr. Hal J. Daniel III, Poetry Editor, Community Council for the Arts, PO Box 3554, Kinston, NC 28501, (919) 527-2517. 1985. Poetry, fiction. "Fiction published is short story length (maximum 20 8½ X 11 ms. pp., longest poems published are 3 8½ X 11 ms. pp.); priority given to writers from Southeast region. Contributors divided between established and emerging writers." circ. 500. 2/yr. Pub'd 2 issues 1990; expects 1 issue 1991, 2 issues 1992. sub. price: $8.50; per copy: $5; sample: $4.25. Back issues: $4 Issues 2,3,4,5 and 6 available. Discounts: trade 3-4 copies 33%, 5+ copies 40%. 70pp; 5×8¼; of Local presses. Reporting time: depending on submission date; Fall deadline 10/1, Spring 2/15. Payment: 2 contributor's copies. Copyrighted, reverts to author. No ads. Coordinating Council of Literary Magazines (CCLM), 666 Broadway, New York, NY 10012-2301, North Carolina Writers' Network (NCWN), PO Box 17079, Durham, NC 27705.

CAROLINA QUARTERLY, David Kellogg, CB# 3520 Greenlaw Hall, Univ of N. Carolina, Chapel Hill, NC 27599-3520, 9l9-962-0244. 1948. Poetry, fiction, art, photos, reviews, long-poems. "'Looking for the well-crafted poem or story.' Recent contributors: William Harmon, Rick Bass, Ian MacMillan, Larry Brown, Michael Waters, R.T. Smith'' circ. 1M. 3/yr. Pub'd 3 issues 1990; expects 3 issues 1991. sub. price: $10 indiv., $12 instit.; per copy: $5; sample: $5 (postage paid). Back issues: $4. Discounts: 20% local stores, agent 10%. 100pp; 6×9; of. Reporting time: 4-6 months. Payment: $15 per author. Copyrighted, reverts to author. Pub's reviews: 1 in 1990. §Short stories, poems. Ads: $95/$60. CCLM.

The Carolina Wren Press, Elaine Goolsby, Editor-in-Chief & Non-Fiction Editor; Shelley Day, Fiction Editor; Marilyn Bulman, Poetry Editor; Kurt Heins, Innovative Editor, PO Box 277, Carrboro, NC 27510, 919-560-2738. 1976. Poetry, fiction, letters, long-poems, plays, non-fiction. "Our goal is to publish high-quality, non-stereotyping literature that is both intellectually and artistically challenging. Our publishing priorities are: works which are written by women and/or minorities, works which deal with issues of concern to those same groups, works which are innovative and/or experimental. *Dead on Arrival* (Jaki Green). *Rituals of Our Time* Herron; *Poems in One Part Harmony* Reddy; *Brinktown* Ramirez. *Rose, A Color of Darkness* (Liner); *Light of the Red Horse* P. B. Newman, *Rainbow Roun Mah Shoulder* Bragg, *Bombs* Randee Russell, *Wind Over Ashes* Randolph." avg. press run 1M. Pub'd 2 titles 1990; expects 2 titles 1991, 3 titles 1992. 23 titles listed in the *Small Press Record of Books in Print* (20th Edition, 1991-92). avg. price, paper: $6. Discounts: 40% to bookstores after 5 copies, (1-4 full price). 150pp; 6×9; of. Reporting time: 3-6 months. Payment: 10% of printrun. Copyright belongs to Carolina Wren; condition of IRS status. North Carolina Writers Network.

CAROUSEL, The Writer's Center, Allan Lefcowitz, Editor, 7815 Old Georgetown Road, Bethesda, MD 20814-2415, 301-654-8664. 1976. Articles, interviews, letters, news items. "We are staff produced. We will publish manuscript needs, and news of interest in the small press world, i.e. contests, new magazines, things of use to the literary community. Write for a brochure on typesetting services and advertising." circ. 6M. 6/yr. Pub'd 6 issues 1990; expects 6 issues 1991, 6 issues 1992. sub. price: $25. Back issues: out of print almost immediately. 16pp; 10¼×13¼; of. Reporting time: 30 days. Payment: copies. Copyrighted. Pub's reviews: 6 in 1990. §Books about writing. Ads: write for rate sheet.

Carousel Press, Carole Terwilliger Meyers, Editor & Publisher; Gene Howard Meyers, Publisher & Sales Manager, PO Box 6061, Albany, CA 94706, 415-527-5849. 1976. Articles, photos, non-fiction. "We are interested in family-oriented travel guides and related books. 150-250 pages. We are also interested in reprinting family-oriented travel articles. And we distribute family-oriented travel guides and travel game books from other publishers through our mail-order catalog subsidary: *The Family Travel Guides Catalogue*." avg. press run 5M. Pub'd 1 title 1990; expects 1 title 1991, 1 title 1992. 3 titles listed in the *Small Press Record of Books in Print* (20th Edition, 1991-92). avg. price, cloth: $8.95; paper: $11.95; other: $3-4/article. Discounts: trade, bulk, jobber 40% 5-12 books; 41% 13-24; 42% 25-49; 43% 50-99; library 10% prepaid. 250pp; 5½×8½; of, web. Reporting time: 6 weeks, include return postage. Payment: royalties and flat payments. Copyrights for author. Northern California Book Publicists' Association, Publishers Marketing Assn.

Carpenter Press, Bob Fox, Publisher & Editor, PO Box 14387, Columbus, OH 43214. 1973. Poetry, fiction, art, photos. "Full-length fiction and poetry, chapbooks, S-F. Interested in vision primarily. Publish traditional as well as experimental fiction and poetry. Full-length fiction by Hugh Fox, Jerry Bumpus, and Curt Johnson; poetry by Steve Kowit and David Shevin. Tenth anniversary first novel competition winner, Jane Piirto's *The Three-Week Trance Diet*, published in 1985. Query first. I will not read photocopied inquiries or dot matrix submissions and will not return material without SASE." avg. press run 500-1.5M. Pub'd 1 title 1990; expects 1 title 1991, 1 title 1992. 14 titles listed in the *Small Press Record of Books in Print* (20th Edition, 1991-92). avg. price, paper: $7.95; other: $3 chapbooks. Discounts: trade. Chapbooks 32pp, full-length poetry 96pp, full-length fictions 144pp; 6×9; of, lp. Reporting time: several months. Payment: by contract. Copyrights for author. AWP.

The Carrefour Press, Douglas Reid Skinner, Editor, PO Box 2629, Cape Town, 8000, Republic of South Africa. 1988. "A carrefour is a place where roads meet, a crossroads, a meeting place. The Carrefour Press is an independent publishing house dedicated to the publishing of new volumes, selections and anthologies of English poetry by South Africans" avg. press run 1M. Pub'd 5 titles 1990; expects 8 titles 1991, 3 titles 1992. 12 titles listed in the *Small Press Record of Books in Print* (20th Edition, 1991-92). avg. price, paper: R17.95. Discounts: 35%. 96pp; 138×212mm; of. Reporting time: by invite only. Does not copyright for author. Independent Publishers Association of South Africa.

Carriage House Press, Florence Kulick, Publisher, 1 Carriage Lane, East Hampton, NY 11937, 516-267-8773. 1987. avg. press run 1.5M. Expects 3 titles 1992. 4 titles listed in the *Small Press Record of Books in Print* (20th Edition, 1991-92). avg. price, paper: $20; other: text $83. Text 450pp, poetry 60-100pp; 8½×5½;

typsetting-gallery-prints. Reporting time: 1 week. Copyrights for author.

Carroll & Graf Publishers, Inc., Kent Carroll, Executive Editor, 260 Fifth Avenue, New York, NY 10001, (212) 889-8772. 1983. Fiction, criticism, non-fiction. Pub'd 76 titles 1990; expects 87 titles 1991, 100 titles 1992. 275pp; of. Reporting time: 2 weeks. Copyrights for author.

CARROLL CABLES, Kinseeker Publications, Victoria Wilson, PO Box 184, Grawn, MI 49637, 616-276-6745. 1987. Articles, reviews, news items, non-fiction. circ. 40. 4/yr. Pub'd 4 issues 1990; expects 4 issues 1991, 4 issues 1992. sub. price: $10; per copy: $2.50; sample: same. Back issues: $2.50. 10pp; 8½×11; †photocopy. Reporting time: 2 weeks. Payment: varies. Not copyrighted. Pub's reviews: 3 in 1990. §Genealogy.

CARTA ABIERTA, Relampago Books Press, Juan Rodriguez, Center for Mexican American Studies, Texas Lutheran College, Seguin, TX 78155, 512-379-4161 X331. 1975. Articles, interviews, criticism, reviews, letters, news items. "News about the Chicano literary world" circ. 1M. 4/yr. Pub'd 4 issues 1990; expects 4 issues 1991, 4 issues 1992. sub. price: $10; per copy: $5; sample: $2. Back issues: $5. 6pp; 8×11½; †of. Reporting time: immediate. Copyrighted, reverts to author. Pub's reviews: 250 in 1990. §Chicano literature in particular, but will review third world literature also. Ads: $50/$25/10¢.

CASE ANALYSIS, Progresiv Publishr, Kenneth H. Ives, 401 E 32nd, #1002, Chicago, IL 60616, 312-225-9181. 1977. Articles, reviews. "Retain non-exclusive reprint rights, sharing resulting royalties." circ. 100. 1/yr. Pub'd 1 issue 1990; expects 1 issue 1991, 1 issue 1992. sub. price: $20 indiv, $30 instit; per copy: $3.50 indiv., $5 instit. for Vol. 1, $5 indiv., $7 instit. for Vol. 2; $8 indiv., $12 instit. for Vol. 3; sample: Vol 1: $3.50 indiv., $5 instit. Back issues: Volume I & II: Individuals $25, Institutions $40. 80-100pp; 7×8½; xerox. Reporting time: 1-3 months. Payment: 1 copy of issue plus 10 reprints. Copyrighted. Pub's reviews: 1 in 1990.

Cassandra Press, Gurudas, PO Box 868, San Rafael, CA 94915, 415-382-8507. 1985. Non-fiction. "FAX: 415-382-7758. We publish only New Age and metaphysical and holistic health books. I like to see the full manuscript before making a final decision, although this isn't necessarily true with an established author. We are now actively looking for new titles to expand next year. We are not accepting novels or children's books." avg. press run 8M-12M. Pub'd 6 titles 1990; expects 6 titles 1991. 19 titles listed in the *Small Press Record of Books in Print* (20th Edition, 1991-92). avg. price, paper: $9.95. Discounts: 40% to stores, 1-3 copies 20%. 150-230pp; size varies. Reporting time: 1-2 months. Payment: varies. Copyrights for author if asked. PMA, COSMEP.

Cassell Communications Inc. (see also FREELANCE WRITER'S REPORT), Dana K. Cassell, PO Box 9844, Ft. Lauderdale, FL 33310, 305-485-0795; 800-351-9278. 1977. Articles, interviews, news items, non-fiction. "Prefers titles/material on freelance writing/photography business management and development, professional development" avg. press run 2.2M. Pub'd 3 titles 1990; expects 4 titles 1991, 6 titles 1992. 3 titles listed in the *Small Press Record of Books in Print* (20th Edition, 1991-92). avg. price, paper: $15. Discounts: 40% to bookstores. 96pp; 8½×11; of. Reporting time: 1 month. Payment: arranged individually. Copyrights for author. Florida Publishers Group, Florida Magazine Assn., NAIP.

'THE CASSETTE GAZETTE', An Audio Magazine, Handshake Editions, Jim Haynes, Jack Henry Moore, Atelier A2, 83 rue de la Tombe-Issoire, Paris 75014, France, 4327-1767. 1971. Poetry, interviews, music, long-poems, collages, plays. "*The Cassette Gazette* is an audio 'magazine' - two hours in length - and contains contributions from Germaine Greer, Lawrence Ferlinghetti, Charles Bukowski, Grandma Haynes, Heathcote Williams, Charles de Gaulle, Shawn Phillips, Tuli Kupferberg, Hyde Manhattan, etc etc. Cheques to be paid to: Jim Haynes." circ. 1M. 4/yr. Pub'd 4 issues 1990; expects 4 issues 1991, 4 issues 1992. sub. price: $40 for 4 issues; per copy: $10; sample: $10. 90 minutes. Payment: copies. Copyrighted, reverts to author.

CASSIE'S EXPRESS, Laura Winter, 112 Conway Street, So. Deerfield, MA 01373.

Castalia Publishing Company, Scot G. Patterson, Editor-in-Chief, PO Box 1587, Eugene, OR 97440, 503-343-4433. 1975. Non-fiction. "We are publishers of psychology books and related materials that are used by parents, therapists, and researchers. We specialize in research-based materials that emphasize social learning or cognitive-behaviored approaches." avg. press run 2M. Pub'd 2 titles 1990; expects 3 titles 1991, 5 titles 1992. 8 titles listed in the *Small Press Record of Books in Print* (20th Edition, 1991-92). avg. price, cloth: $30; paper: $15. Discounts: 25% to bookstores and book jobbers, we pay shipping on prepaid U.S. orders. 250pp; 8½×11, 6×9; of/lo. Reporting time: allow up to 3 months. Payment: we pay approx. 12% royalty on actual cash received (net after discounts allowed). Copyrights for author. PNWBPA, COSMEP, PMA.

Castle Peak Editions, Judith Shears, William Hotchkiss, Editor-in-Chief, 1670 E. 27th Avenue, Eugene, OR 97403, 503-342-2975. 1971. Poetry, fiction, non-fiction. "We are a *book-length* publisher of poetry, fiction, criticism of a literary nature; secondary, we do textbooks for community college adoptions, often in close conjunction with teacher/authors. Example: *Great Upheaval* (poetry), *The Short Hall* (paperback reprint), *Sancho's Guide* and *Tilting at Windmills* (both grammar/rhetoric texts)." avg. press run 500-1M. Pub'd 6 titles

1990; expects 8 titles 1991, 8 titles 1992. avg. price, cloth: $18; paper: $15; other: $15-$17 texts. Discounts: libraries 20%; 30 days; inquire for other schedules. 5×7, 7×9; of, lp. Reporting time: 30 days. Payment: 10%, publisher's net. Copyrights for author.

THE CATALOG CONNECTION, Holly Pasiuk, PO Box 1427, Guilford, CT 06437. 1988. Reviews, non-fiction. circ. 1.5M. 1/yr. Pub'd 1 issue 1990; expects 1 issue 1991, 1 issue 1992. sub. price: $7.50; per copy: $7.50. 54pp; 8½×11. Copyrighted.

CATALYST, Laocoon Books, M. Kettner, Editor; David Lloyd Whited, Editor; Kathleen K., Consulting Editor, PO Box 20518, Seattle, WA 98102, 206-323-7268. 1980. Poetry, fiction, art, photos, cartoons, satire, parts-of-novels, long-poems, collages, plays, concrete art, non-fiction. "We continuously review submissions, both general and erotic. Inquiries welcome." circ. 1M-4M. 1-3/yr. Pub'd 1 issue 1990; expects 1 issue 1991, 1 issue 1992. sub. price: $9/3 consecutive issues; per copy: write for individual price lists; sample: 2nd Erotic Collection: $3, 3rd Erotic Collection: $4; *Mary Jane* $3. Back issues: full price. Discounts: 55% to distributor; 40% to retail outlets (2 to 20) 50% on 20+. 12-60pp; size varies; of. Reporting time: 2-10 weeks. Payment: copies. Copyrighted, reverts to author.

CATALYST, A Magazine of Heart and Mind, Pearl Cleage, 34 Peachtree Street, Ste. 2330, Atlanta, GA 30303, 404-730-5785. 1986. Poetry, fiction, photos, interviews, satire, criticism, reviews, letters, long-poems, non-fiction. "Limit for contributions is 3,000 words (15 typed pages). Focus is primarily on Southern writers, but accepts work from all writers. Recent contributors include: Nikky Finney, Nikky Giovanni, Robert Earl Price, Vern E. Smith." circ. 5M. 2/yr. Pub'd 2 issues 1990; expects 2 issues 1991, 2 issues 1992. sub. price: $5; per copy: $2.50; sample: $2.50. Back issues: $2.50. 110pp; 7¾×10¾; †lo. Reporting time: 2 months prior to publication. Payment: $10-$200. Copyrighted, reverts to author. Pub's reviews: 1 in 1990. §Literature, film, poetry. CLMP.

Catbird Press, Robert Wechsler, 44 North Sixth Avenue, Highland Park, NJ 08904, 908-572-0816. 1987. Fiction, non-fiction. "Our specialties are Czech literature in translation and humor, particularly about travel and the law, and solely written humor." avg. press run 3.5M. Pub'd 5 titles 1990; expects 3 titles 1991. avg. price, cloth: $19.95; paper: $12.95. Discounts: Independent Publishers Group schedule (our distributor). 300pp; of. Reporting time: 1 month. Payment: up to 10% gross. Copyrights for author.

THE CATHARTIC, Patrick M. Ellingham, PO Box 1391, Ft Lauderdale, FL 33302, 305-474-7120. 1974. Poetry, art, photos, reviews. "*The Cathartic* is a small poetry magazine devoted to the unknown poet with the understanding that most poets are unknown in America. There is no set type of poem that I use. I do not use poems that are racist or sexist in nature. Poems should speak with and to true human emotion in a way, and with an intensity, that readers can recognize and feel. I would really like to see some poems that are willing to take chances with both form and language and also forget self for once and see what's happening in the world around us and make something of it that causes people to feel and react to it. Poems from the darker side of human experience, intense, focused and powerful, are what I'm moving towards. Rhyme for the sake of rhyme does not interest me. Recent contributors include: Joy Walsh, Paul Weinman, Lyn Lifshin, Sue Walker, Stefan Anders and Eileen Eliot." circ. 200-300. 2/yr. Pub'd 2 issues 1990; expects 2 issues 1991, 2 issues 1992. sub. price: $5; per copy: $3; sample: $3. Back issues: $3 per back issue starting with #9. Discounts: none. 28pp; 5½×8½; of. Reporting time: 1 month. Payment: one contributor's copy. Not copyrighted. Pub's reviews: 0 in 1990. §Books of poetry from small presses are always welcome for review or at least listing. No ads. CCLM.

Cat's Pajamas Press, John Jacob, 527 Lyman, Oak Park, IL 60304. 1968. Poetry, fiction, criticism, parts-of-novels, long-poems. "Our most recent titles include *Hojo Supreme* by Bernie Bever and *Scar Mirror* by Derek Pell, the first a short book of violent poems, the second a Robbe-Grilletain fantasy narrative. Our books by Ken Smith, John Oliver Simon, Tom Montag, Eric Felderman, and Thomas Michael Fisher are still in-print. We have maintained our broadside series with the most recent publication of poems by Sara Plath. The broadside series soon will be available as a set. We plan to publish a title or two per year and lean toward extremely short, unified manuscripts, whether poetry or prose. We will also publish very limited print runs, usually between 100 and 250. We don't like a lot of what we read and we want to retain validity as a true alternative to mainstream material. The press is a guerrilla press that will use whatever means available to suit our aesthetic ends, whether cheap xerography or cloth bindings and expensive papers." avg. press run 100-1M. Pub'd 1 title 1990. 7 titles listed in the *Small Press Record of Books in Print* (20th Edition, 1991-92). avg. price, cloth: $2.50; paper: $1; other: $5. Discounts: 40% on multiples. 8-32pp; 5×8, 8×11; mi, of, lp. Reporting time: 4-6 weeks. Payment: min. 20% print run. Copyrights for author.

Cave Books, Richard A. Watson, Editor, 756 Harvard Avenue, Saint Louis, MO 63130, 314-862-7646. 1957. Fiction, non-fiction. "Any prose (fiction, non-fiction) to do with caves, karst, and speleology. We actively solicit manuscripts and receive very few. Almost nobody in America writes books on caves. Are we the only press in America begging for submissions?" avg. press run 1.5M. Pub'd 4 titles 1990; expects 4 titles 1991, 4 titles 1992. 2 titles listed in the *Small Press Record of Books in Print* (20th Edition, 1991-92). avg. price, cloth:

$15; paper: $10. Discounts: 40% trade. 150pp; size varies; of, lp. Reporting time: 3 months. Payment: 10%. Copyrights for author.

Wm Caxton Ltd, Kubet Luchterhand, Box 709, Sister Bay, WI 54234, 414-854-2955. 1986. Poetry, criticism, letters, non-fiction. "We have 14 titles in print, 2 more in press now, and a total of 6 more in various stages of editing/typesetting/proofing. We publish book-length manuscripts, and reprint some books (6 of our titles so far); most titles so far are non-fiction, though we have published 1 book of poetry (*Green Whistle* by David Koenig) and are looking for more good poetry. We're especially interested in northern mid-West material of all kinds; we have two philosophy titles; one book about theatre technique (*Chamber Theatre* by Robert Breen); a reprint of a classic Wisconsin economic history book (*Empire In Pine* by Robert Fries). In a phrase, we will consider publishing any book that is actually *about* something." avg. press run 700-2M. Pub'd 3 titles 1990; expects 5 titles 1991, 5-9 titles 1992. 14 titles listed in the *Small Press Record of Books in Print* (20th Edition, 1991-92). avg. price, cloth: $25; paper: $12.95. Discounts: booksellers 40% nonreturnable, 20% returnable for orders of five copies or more, returns must be in saleable condition, unmarked in any way, returned within 6 months of invoice date. 230pp; 5½x8½, 6x9, 8½x11; of. Reporting time: 1-3 months, depending upon season. Payment: varies widely; prefer subvention coupled with much higher than average royalty structure on first printing, guarantee to keep in print for 5 years, high but not as high as original on later printings. Copyrights for author.

Cayuse Press, Margaret Switzer, 1523 Valley Road, Kensington, CA 94707, 415-525-8515. 1985. Fiction. "We publish short story collections and novels of high quality with respect to craft and literary content. Author is expected to take a full role in publishing on a cooperative basis." avg. press run 2M-3M. Pub'd 1 title 1990; expects 4 titles 1991, 4 titles 1992. 4 titles listed in the *Small Press Record of Books in Print* (20th Edition, 1991-92). avg. price, cloth: $12.95-$15.95; paper: $7-10. Discounts: jobbers 20%, bookstores 1 20%, 2-4 30%, 5-49 40%, 50-99 44%, 100+ 48%. 200-300pp; 6x9; of. Reporting time: 1 month. Payment: based on individual book. Copyrights for author. NCBPA, California Writer's Club.

CCR Publications, Richard Soos, 2745 Monterey Road #76, San Jose, CA 95111. 1974. "Currently publishing 48 page paperbacks by single authors. Persons with new projects in mind should contact me. $2.95 + 65¢ postage. Current authors include Ella Blanche, Kay Clossom, Kimon Friar, and Don MacQueen. Will publish non-fiction books also, starting 1988" avg. press run 1M. Expects 1 title 1991, 3 titles 1992. avg. price, paper: $2.95. †of. Reporting time: 1 month. Payment: 10% cover price. Copyrights for author.

Cedar Ridge Publications, 73 Cedar Ridge Road, Broken Arrow, OK 74011. Pub'd 1 title 1990. 2 titles listed in the *Small Press Record of Books in Print* (20th Edition, 1991-92).

CEILIDH: AN INFORMAL GATHERING FOR STORY & SONG, Ceilidh, Inc., Patrick S. Sullivan, Publisher, Editor; Perry Oei, Editor; Denise E. Sullivan, Director of Marketing, PO Box 6367, San Mateo, CA 94403, 415-591-9902. 1981. Poetry, fiction, art, photos, parts-of-novels, long-poems, plays, non-fiction. "Short stories and non-fiction preferably 2-3 M words, but will consider longer pieces. We are looking for poetry, stories and art that have a sense of 'voice', and can stand on their own even after many readings or viewings. For more information and deadlines send SASE. You might want to order a copy of *Ceilidh* to see the kind of work we publish." circ. 300. 2/yr. Pub'd 1 issue 1990; expects 2 issues 1991, 2 issues 1992. sub. price: $15; per copy: $5; sample: $5. Back issues: $5. Discounts: 20-40%. 32-64pp; 5½x8½; of. Reporting time: 8 weeks. Payment: 2 copies. Copyrighted, reverts to author. Pub's reviews. §Modern literature. Ads: $50/$30/or exchange. CCLM.

Ceilidh, Inc. (see also CEILIDH: AN INFORMAL GATHERING FOR STORY & SONG), Patrick S. Sullivan, Publisher & Editor; Perry Oei, Editor; Denise E. Sullivan, Director of Marketing, P.O. Box 6367, San Mateo, CA 94403, 415-591-9902. 1981. "(Non-profit corporation)" avg. press run 300. Pub'd 2 titles 1990. avg. price, cloth: $12; paper: $7. Discounts: 40%. 30pp; 8½x11; of. Reporting time: 8 weeks. Copyrights for author.

CELEBRATION, William J. Sullivan, 2707 Lawina Road, Baltimore, MD 21216, 301-542-8785. 1975. Poetry. "All styles, we hope to be as unbiased as contributors will permit. Recent contributors: Terry Kennedy, Michael L. Johnson, Lisa Yount, Tim Houghton, Sheila E. Murphy, Ivan Arguelles." circ. 300. Occasional. Expects 1 issue 1991, 1 issue 1992. sub. price: $8/4 issues; per copy: $2; sample: $2. Back issues: $2. 30pp; 5½x8½; of. Reporting time: 12 weeks. Payment: copies. COSMEP.

Celestial Gifts Publishing, Ron Dalrymple, PO Box 414, RD 1, Box 80F, Chester, MD 21619, 301-643-4466. 1976. Fiction, satire. avg. press run 5M. Pub'd 1 title 1990; expects 2 titles 1991. 2 titles listed in the *Small Press Record of Books in Print* (20th Edition, 1991-92). avg. price, paper: $10. Discounts: standard industry. 112pp; 5x8; of. Reporting time: not presently accepting unsolicited manuscripts. Copyrights for author. COSMEP, ABA, Publishers Marketing, NAPRA.

Celestial Otter Press (see also MAGIC CHANGES), John Sennett, Editor, PO Box 658, Warrenville, IL 60555, 708-416-3111. 1978. Poetry, fiction, art, photos, cartoons, interviews, satire, criticism, reviews, music, long-poems, plays. avg. press run 200. Pub'd 1 title 1990; expects 1 title 1992. avg. price, paper: $5. Discounts: inquire. 64pp; 5½×8½; †lp. Reporting time: 2 months. Payment: negotiable. Copyrights for author.

CELFAN Editions Monographs (see also REVUE CELFAN REVIEW), Dept. of French & Italian, Tulane University, New Orleans, LA 70118. 6 titles listed in the *Small Press Record of Books in Print* (20th Edition, 1991-92).

Celo Valley Books, Diana M. Donovan, 346 Seven Mile Ridge Road, Burnsville, NC 28714, 704-675-5918. 1989. Poetry, fiction, non-fiction. avg. press run 50-6M. Pub'd 2 titles 1990; expects 8 titles 1991, 8 titles 1992. 9 titles listed in the *Small Press Record of Books in Print* (20th Edition, 1991-92). avg. price, cloth: $18; paper: $10. 176pp; size varies; of. Reporting time: 1 month. Payment: so far all our titles are paid for by the author; within 5 years, though, we hope to do some titles in a more traditional way. Copyrights for author. Coop America, NC Writer's Network.

Celtic Heritage Press, Inc., PO Box 637, Woodside, NY 11377, 718-478-8162. 1983. Non-fiction. "Desired works are approximately 150 pages." Expects 1 title 1991, 1 title 1992. 2 titles listed in the *Small Press Record of Books in Print* (20th Edition, 1991-92). avg. price, paper: $7.95. Discounts: 30%. 90pp; 5½×4¼; of. Reporting time: 3 weeks. Payment: varies with each contributing author. Copyrights for author. COSMEP.

‡**Celtic League (see also CARN (a link between the Celtic nations)),** P.A. Bridson, J.B. Moffatt-General Secretary, Celtic League-24, St. Germain's Place, Peel, Isle of Mann, Dublin 373957. 1973. Poetry, articles, interviews, criticism, reviews, letters, news items. "additional address: P.A. Bridson, 33 Bothar Bancroft, Tamklacht, Dublin, Eire" avg. press run 2M. Pub'd 4 titles 1990; expects 4 titles 1991, 4 titles 1992. 1 title listed in the *Small Press Record of Books in Print* (20th Edition, 1991-92). avg. price, paper: 80p. Discounts: 25% to shops. 24pp; 8½×12; of. Reporting time: up to 3 months. Payment: none. Copyrights for author.

THE CENTENNIAL REVIEW, R.K. Meiners, Editor; Cheryllee Finney, Managing Editor, 312 Linton Hall, Mich. State Univ., E. Lansing, MI 48824-1044, 517-355-1905. 1955. Poetry, articles. "Topics cover English literature, soc. sci, sciences, humanities, 3M words, double-spaced. Contributors:Joseph Needham, Susan Fromberg Schaeffer." circ. 1M. 3/yr. Pub'd 4 issues 1990; expects 3 issues 1991. sub. price: $10; per copy: $5; sample: $5. Back issues: $5. 160pp; 6×9; of, linotype (metal). Reporting time: 3-6 months. Payment: year's free subscription. Copyrighted, reverts to author. Ads: $75/$50. CELJ.

CENTER, Center Press, Carol Berge, Editor & Publisher, 307 Johnson Street, Santa Fe, NM 87501. 1970. Fiction, articles, satire, criticism, reviews, letters, parts-of-novels, non-fiction. "*Innovative prose only*. No poetry. From short sections to longer prose books. New writers *must* query before submitting, *and must have read any issue* of *Center* magazine. Enclose SASE (8½ x 11, $1.05)." circ. 2M. 2/yr. Pub'd 1 issue 1990; expects 2 issues 1991. No subscriptions issued; price per copy: $10 & SASE to individuals, $15 to libraries; sample: $6 & SASE. Back issues: first 3 issues not available. Other back issues: $10 each, (when available), plus SASE with book rate postage ($1.05). Discounts: none. 76pp; 8½×11; of. Reporting time: 2 weeks. Payment: $3-$4.50 pg. when possible. Copyrighted, revert to authors 6 mos. after pubn. Pub's reviews: 0 in 1990. §Innovative prose & fiction, social science fiction, philosophy, physics, geophysics, contemporary satire. No ads. CLMP, SFRA, Popular Culture Assn, NEA, NYSCA (New York State Council on Arts).

Center Book Publishers, Inc., 301 N. Harrison Street, Suite 298, Princeton, NJ 08540, 609-924-6328. 1986. Non-fiction. "These are engineering reference books authored by the instructors of The Center for Professional Advancement (E. Brunswick, NJ) and other engineering instructors" avg. press run 1M. Expects 1 title 1991, 3 titles 1992. 1 title listed in the *Small Press Record of Books in Print* (20th Edition, 1991-92). avg. price, cloth: $80. 300pp; 5½×8½; standard book mfgr. Payment: 15%. Copyrights for author. PMA.

Center for Arab and Islamic Studies (see also THE SEARCH - JOURNAL FOR ARAB AND ISLAMIC STUDIES), Samir Abed-Rabbo, Box 543, Bratttleboro, VT 05301, 802-257-0872.

Center for Public Representation, Kathy Parks, Publications Manager, 121 S. Pinckney Street, Madison, WI 53703-1999, 608-251-4008. 1974. Articles, non-fiction. "The Center for Public Representation (CPR) is a nonprofit, public interest law firm founded in 1974 to provide advocacy, research, and training on behalf of a broad range of citizen groups. Special areas of interest: rights of consumers, citizens, and the elderly; health care cost containment; and maternal and child health. Most of our publications are generated through our own organization, but we will also consider manuscripts on appropriate subjects. A copy of our free publications catalog is available on request. Please include stamped, self-addressed envelope when sending manuscript." avg. press run 1M. Pub'd 4 titles 1990; expects 2 titles 1991, 2 titles 1992. 1 title listed in the *Small Press Record of Books in Print* (20th Edition, 1991-92). avg. price, paper: $15. Discounts: 40% to stores, 50% and up to distributors, 20-40% institutional on bulk orders of same title. 100-200pp; 8½×11, 5½×8½; of. Reporting time: 3 months. Payment: arrangements vary. Does not copyright for author.

Center For Self-Sufficiency, A.C. Doyle, Founder, c/o Prosperity and Profits Unlimited, Box 570213, Houston, TX 77257. 1982. "Distributed by Prosperity and Profits Unlimited" avg. press run 2M. 10 titles listed in the *Small Press Record of Books in Print* (20th Edition, 1991-92). avg. price, cloth: $6.95; paper: $4.95. Discounts: 25% to libraries & bookstores. 36pp; 5½x8½; †of. Reporting time: 8 weeks.

The Center For Study of Multiple Birth, Donald M. Keith, Louis G. Keith, 333 East Superior Street, #464, Chicago, IL 60611, 312-266-9093. 1977. Articles, news items, non-fiction. *"The Center for Study of Multiple Birth publishes & distributes non-fiction for parents of twins and triplets and for twins and triplets."* avg. press run 5M-50M. Pub'd 1 title 1990; expects 2 titles 1991, 3 titles 1992. 3 titles listed in the *Small Press Record of Books in Print* (20th Edition, 1991-92). avg. price, paper: $10. Discounts: please write for schedule. 160pp; 4x7; lp. Reporting time: 4 weeks. Payment: sliding depending on total sales, negotiable. Does not copyright for author.

Center for the Art of Living, Gary Michael Durst, Box 788, Evanston, IL 60204, 312-864-8664. 1979. Non-fiction. "Book length mss, philosophical, psychological topics" avg. press run 5M. Expects 2 titles 1991. 2 titles listed in the *Small Press Record of Books in Print* (20th Edition, 1991-92). avg. price, cloth: $15; paper: $9, $15. Discounts: 40% to trade, 40% to wholesalers. 230pp; 5¼x8½, 8½x11. Payment: no arrangement yet made. Copyrights for author.

Center Press (see also EXIT), Frank Judge, Editor & Publisher; Mary Whitney, Art Director, 232 Post Avenue, Rochester, NY 14619-1313. 1977. Poetry, fiction, art, photos, interviews, reviews, concrete art. "See entry under *Exit*" avg. press run 1M. avg. price, paper: $4. 5½x8½; of. Reporting time: 1-2 months. Payment: in copies. Copyrights for author. COSMEP.

Center Press (see also CENTER), Carol Berge, Editor & Publisher, 307 Johnson Street, Santa Fe, NM 87501. 1970. Fiction, articles, satire, criticism, reviews, letters, parts-of-novels, non-fiction. "Also Center Press Novels. (Innovative prose only). From short sections to longer prose chapbooks. New writers (must) query before submitting (and must have read current chapbook). Enclose $1 SASE and $10 for Chapbook." avg. press run 300-600. Pub'd 2 titles 1990; expects 2 titles 1991, 2 titles 1992. 7 titles listed in the *Small Press Record of Books in Print* (20th Edition, 1991-92). avg. price, paper: $10 + SSAE; other: depending on availability. Discounts: none. 76pp; 8½x11; of. Reporting time: 2 weeks. Payment: $3-$5 per page as specified in Grant, plus copies. Copyright reverts to authors 6 months after publication. NEA, CLMP, NYSCA, Natl Press Women, NMAD.

Centerplace Publishing Co., Paul J. Lyons, Publisher, PO Box 901, Lake Oswego, OR 97034, 800-96-CHILD. 1987. "Focus is on books, information kits, games for parents of children age 2-12." avg. press run 2M. Pub'd 1 title 1990; expects 1 title 1991, 3 titles 1992. 1 title listed in the *Small Press Record of Books in Print* (20th Edition, 1991-92). avg. price, cloth: $15; paper: $12. Discounts: 40% to retailers, 55% to wholesalers, 20% to non-profits in quantities up to 10 then 40%. 60pp; 6x9. Reporting time: 30 days. Payment: 10% to authors paid quarterly. Copyrights for author. Northwest Association of Book Publishers (NWABP).

CENTRAL AMERICA REPORT, Inforpress Centroamericana, 9a. Calle "A" 3-56, Zona 1, Ciudad de Guatemala, Guatemala, 29432,81997. 1974. News items. circ. 500. 49/yr. Pub'd 49 issues 1990; expects 49 issues 1991, 49 issues 1992. sub. price: US $205; per copy: $4.25; sample: free. Back issues: $4.25. Discounts: 20% agents. 8pp; 8½x11; †of. Payment: none. Copyrighted.

CENTRAL PARK, Stephen-Paul Martin, Fiction Editor; Richard Royal, Fiction Editor; Eve Ensler, Poetry Editor, P.O. Box 1446, New York, NY 10023. 1979. Poetry, fiction, articles, art, photos, interviews, satire, criticism, reviews, parts-of-novels, long-poems, collages, plays, non-fiction. "Our primary interest at this point is experimental writing. We are also looking for essays that move beyond conventional disciplinary borders and avoid genteel academic posturing. We are not in any way interested in workshop poetry and fiction. Writers are advised to query before submiting" circ. 1M. 2/yr. Pub'd 1 issue 1990; expects 2 issues 1991, 3 issues 1992. sub. price: $9; per copy: $5; sample: $5. 150pp; 8x10; of. Reporting time: 6 weeks. Payment: 1 copy. Copyrighted, reverts to author. Pub's reviews: 2 in 1990. §Poetry, fiction, socio-political commentary, criticism, music, visual arts. Ads: rates vary.

Ceres Press (see also TRUE FOOD), David Goldbeck, Nikki Goldbeck, PO Box 87, Woodstock, NY 12498. 1977. "Unsolicited mss. cannot be returned unless S.A.S.E." avg. press run 5M. Pub'd 1 title 1990; expects 1 title 1991. 4 titles listed in the *Small Press Record of Books in Print* (20th Edition, 1991-92). avg. price, paper: $4.95. Discounts: normal trade. of. Reporting time: 2 months. Payment: as agreed.

CERTAIN GESTURES, David Tiffen, Andrea James, 55 Perowne Street, Aldershot, Hants. GU11 3JR, England, 316170. 1982. Fiction, articles, art, photos, collages, non-fiction. circ. 300. Erratic. Pub'd 1 issue 1990; expects 1 issue 1991. price per copy: 40p; sample: 60p or willing to exchange. 20pp; size varies; of. Payment: nil. Not copyrighted. Small Press Group of Britain, BM Bozo, London WC1 3XX, England.

Cerulean Press (Subsidiary of Kent Publications) (see also SAN FERNANDO POETRY JOURNAL), Richard Cloke, Editor; Lori C. Smith, Associate Editor; Shirley J. Rodecker, Associate Editor; Blair H. Allen, Associate Editor, 18301 Halsted St., Northridge, CA 91325. 1980. Poetry, fiction, long-poems. "This press is

107

generally along the same lines as Kent Publications & its other subsidiary, *San Fernando Poetry Journal*, although under a different financial structure." avg. press run 500. Pub'd 2 titles 1990; expects 1 title 1991, 2 titles 1992. avg. price, paper: $6.75. Discounts: 40% trade; 30% stores; 20% libraries. 600pp; 5½x8½; of. Reporting time: immediate. Payment: copies. Copyrights for author. CLMP.

CHAKRA, Liz Camps, PO Box 8551, Dept. 106, FDR Station, New York, NY 10022. 1988. Poetry, fiction, articles, art, photos, cartoons, interviews, satire, criticism, reviews, letters, parts-of-novels, long-poems, collages, plays, concrete art, non-fiction. "Poetry: any length. Short stories: 1000-4000 words, excerpts. Editor is drawn to the erotic surreal, occult, experimental,and mystical." circ. 200-1M. 2-4/yr. Pub'd 1-2 issues 1990; expects 2-4 issues 1991. sub. price: $3.80 2 issues, $5.50 3 issues; per copy: $2; sample: $2. Back issues: $2. Discounts: will sometimes trade, please inquire. 28pp; 8½x11; †mi. Reporting time: 3 months or less. Payment: $1 per page + collector's copy. Copyrighted. Pub's reviews. §Eroticism, mysticism, esoteric politics, surrealism, occult, cybershamanism. Ads: $60/$30/ $15 1/4 page/$8 1/8 page.

CHALK CIRCLE, J. Monaco, B. Carpenter, D. Augsberger, R. Kinerk, PO Eox 5038, Hoboken, NJ 07030, 201-420-9235. 1988. "We have an interest in progressive politics and welcome works of literary merit that deal with sexism, racism and oppression of children, among other issues" circ. 500. 4/yr. Pub'd 1 issue 1990; expects 4 issues 1991, 4 issues 1992. sub. price: $15; per copy: $4; sample: $4. Back issues: $3. Discounts: negotiable. 72pp; 7x8½. Reporting time: 6 weeks. Payment: 2 copies. Not copyrighted. Pub's reviews. §Political. Ads: $50/$27/$15 1/4 page.

CHALLENGE: A Journal of Faith and Action in Central America, Epica, Minor Sinclair, Catherine Collins, 1470 Irving Street NW, Washington, DC 20010, 202-332-0292. 1989. Articles, interviews, non-fiction. "*Challenge* publishes original material from Central American theologians and activists reflecting on their faith and vision for justice. Article length is from 1,000-7,500 words. Submissions in English or Spanish. Recent contributors include Lutheran Bishop Medardo Gomez, human rights activist Mirna Anayn, theologian Raquel Rodriguez." circ. 2M. 3/yr. Pub'd 1 issue 1990; expects 3 issues 1991, 4 issues 1992. sub. price: $10; per copy: $3.50; sample: free. Back issues: $3.50 each. Discounts: 10 copies or more $1. 16pp; 8½x11; of. Reporting time: 3 weeks. Payment: none. Copyrighted, reverts to author. Pub's reviews: 2 in 1990. §Central American politics and faith, U.S. solidarity to Central America. Ads: $100/$65/$40 1/4 page.

Challenger Press, PO Box 919, Solvang, CA 93464, 805-688-4439. 1989. Non-fiction. "Additional phone: 800-726-0061. FAX: 805-686-1340. Less than 25,000 words, self-help subjects with a strong positive, encouraging theme. Self-help for lifes crisis not just addictive behaviors. Written for the average reader, suggest a ninth-grade reading level, no overly technical language. Simple to read, easy to understand." avg. press run 5M. Expects 2 titles 1991, 2-3 titles 1992. 3 titles listed in the *Small Press Record of Books in Print* (20th Edition, 1991-92). avg. price, paper: $11. Discounts: 35-55%. 150pp; 6x9; litho; lp. Reporting time: 2-4 weeks. Payment: negotiated. Copyrights for author. PMA/ NABE.

CHAMINADE LITERARY REVIEW, Loretta D. Petrie, James Jr. Robinson, James Kraus, 3140 Waialae Avenue, Honolulu, HI 96816-1578, 808-735-4723. 1987. Poetry, fiction, articles, art, photos, criticism, parts-of-novels, concrete art. "Special consideration to Hawaii writers and/or subject matter. Recent contributors: William Heyen, Rob Wilson, Cathy Song, Nell Altizer, William Stafford, Marjorie Sinclair." circ. 350. Pub'd 2 issues 1990; expects 2 issues 1991, 2 issues 1992. sub. price: $10; per copy: $5. 175pp. Reporting time: varies. Payment: 1 year's subscription. Copyrighted, reverts to author. Ads: $50; 1/2 $25. CCLM.

Chance Additions, Marc Lecard, 3064 Richmond Boulevard, Oakland, CA 94611. 1983. Poetry, fiction, art, photos, long-poems, collages. "Prefer query first" avg. press run 350. Pub'd 1 title 1990; expects 1 title 1991, 1 title 1992. 4 titles listed in the *Small Press Record of Books in Print* (20th Edition, 1991-92). avg. price, paper: $4.00. Discounts: 60/40%. 50pp; 5x7; of. Reporting time: 3 months. Payment: copies. Copyrights for author.

Chandler & Sharp Publishers, Inc., Jonathan Sharp, 11A Commercial Blvd., Novato, CA 94949, 415-883-2353. 1972. "We are strictly book publishers. Adult non fiction trade books and college textbooks in the social sciences and humanities" avg. press run 3M. Pub'd 6 titles 1990; expects 6 titles 1991, 6 titles 1992. 35 titles listed in the *Small Press Record of Books in Print* (20th Edition, 1991-92). avg. price, cloth: $25; paper: $10.95. Discounts: trade books 40%, textbooks 20%, wholesalers 50%. 192pp; 6x9; of. Reporting time: 2-6 weeks. Payment: royalties. Copyrights for author on request. AAA.

CHANGE: The Journal of the Synergetic Society, Synergetics Press, Art Coulter, 1825 North Lake Shore Dr, Chapel Hill, NC 27514, 919-942-2994. 1954. Articles, criticism, reviews, letters. "Synergetics is the art and science of evoking synergy in the human mind, in small groups, and in other complex systems." circ. 200. 5/yr. Pub'd 5 issues 1990; expects 5 issues 1991. sub. price: $10; per copy: $2; sample: free. 25pp; 8½x11; †of. Reporting time: 30 days. Payment: copies only. Not copyrighted. Pub's reviews: 5 in 1990.

CHANGING MEN, Feminist Mens' Publications, Rick Cote, Managing Editor; Michael Biernbaum, Managing Editor; Peter Bresnick, Business Manager, 306 N. Brooks #305, Madison, WI 53715, 608-256-2565.

108

1979. Poetry, articles, art, photos, reviews, letters, news items, non-fiction. "Send fiction to Jeff Kirsch, Dept. of Spanish/Portugese, Tulane University, New Orleans, LA 70118. Send non-fiction to Rick Cote, PO Box 639, Durham, NH 03824-0639. ISSN 0889-7174. *Changing Men* is dedicated to discussing issues important to changing men, affirming a healthy, life-loving non-oppressive masculinity, and supporting the network of men and women working to end sexism. Articles in *Changing Men* are intended to speak to the collective and individual experiences and interests of its readers, and it is from those experiences and interests that we urge contributors to the journal to draw their words and images. We encourage the use of straightforward English, first-person narration, and the honest expression of feelings. Writers and artists are encouraged to contribute personal accounts, reports on men and their activities, poetry, letters, analytical essays, book reviews, humor, and graphics (cartoons, line drawings, photographs). We are committed to printing materials from both well-known men's movement writers and our readers. All written contributions should be typewritten and double spaced. Feature articles should not exceed 3000 words. Writers and artists should not send more than three works at a time. All materials must be signed, and include an address and phone number where you can be contacted. When sending in previously published items, include the original publisher's name, and provide us with copyright permission (or instructions for obtaining permission). Materials are not returned unless accompanied by SASE. Final disposition of an article may take three to twelve months. The editors work with authors in any necessary editing or revising; final substantive changes are subject to the author's approval. We take pride in the quality of our art & graphic selections. All graphic material is printed b/w, though single color cover images have been used successfully. Graphic material need not literally reflect copy content, though this is the principle placement criterion. Foremost, we are interested in the quality and dramatic content of the composition itself. Drawings or photos with particularly strong content or feeling are frequently placed independent of text. Any work that is visually intriguing or intellectually/politically stimulating is appreciated in its own right. Given the weightiness of some of the subjects covered in the text, humorous, whimsical or comedy pieces are particularly welcomed. We will work with you to assure a satisfactory representation of your work. Our current budget permits us to pay $15 (or a 4-issue subscription) for each inside graphic used, $30-$50 for cover art, plus 2 copies of the issue in which your work is presented, mailed First Class." circ. 4M. 2/yr. Pub'd 2 issues 1990; expects 2 issues 1991, 3 issues 1992. sub. price: $12, normal 4-issue sub. is $24; per copy: back issue $4.50; sample: $6. Back issues: complete set is presently $60. Discounts: 40% to bookstores, 50% to distributors, possibly higher in near future. 52pp; 8½×10½; of. Reporting time: 6 months. Payment: some for artwork, free issue. Copyrighted, rights revert by arrangement. Pub's reviews: 6 in 1990. §Men's issues, feminism, gay rights, psychology of masculinity today. Ads: $350/$190/$20, progressive rates, classifieds, exchanges.

Chantry Press, Dee Patrick, PO Box 144, Midland Park, NJ 07432. 1981. Poetry, fiction, long-poems. "No biases. Quality important. Published: Maria Gillan's *Flowers From the Tree of Night* (1981), Laura Boss' *Stripping*, Ruth Lisa Schecter's *Speedway*, and Anne Bailie's *In the Soul's Riptide*, Joanne Riley's *Racing the Moon*, Maria Gillen's *Winter Light*, Ruth Lisa Schechter's *Chords*." avg. press run 500-1M. Expects 1 title 1991, 5 titles 1992. 7 titles listed in the *Small Press Record of Books in Print* (20th Edition, 1991-92). avg. price, paper: $5.95. Discounts: 1-5 books 20%, 5+ 40%. 72pp; 5½×8; of. Reporting time: 6 months. Payment: standard. Copyrights for author. COSMEP.

THE CHAOS NETWORK, Mark Michaels, PO Box 4100, Urbana, IL 61801, 217-328-0032. 1989. "We are interested in articles and reviews of articles and books concerning the application of the science of chaos to social systems. Articles should be 500-1,000 words long. We also review articles on chaos-based subjects in the newsletter. Submission on disk in ASCII or WordPerfect format preferred." circ. 200+. 4/yr. Pub'd 4 issues 1990; expects 4 issues 1991, 6 issues 1992. sub. price: $49; sample: free. Discounts: distributors $39 for 10+; bulk $39 for 10+, $35 for 15+ (per subscription). 12pp; 8½×11. Reporting time: 1 month. Payment: none, free subscription possible. Copyrighted, does not revert to author. Pub's reviews: 15+ in 1990. §Science of chaos, business and management, artificial intelligence, community and economic development. Ads: none.

CHAPMAN, Joy M. Hendry, 4 Broughton Place, Edinburgh EH1 3RX, Scotland, 031-557-2207. 1970. Poetry, fiction, articles, art, interviews, criticism, reviews, long-poems. "Literary material, philosophical orientation, Scottish bias, but *not* exclusive. High standards." circ. 2.5M. 4/yr. Expects 4 issues 1991. 24 titles listed in the *Small Press Record of Books in Print* (20th Edition, 1991-92). sub. price: £9.50 (£12.50 overseas, US$21); per copy: £3 ($6); sample: £3 ($6). Back issues: list available. Discounts: variable. 104pp; 6×8½; of. Reporting time: ASAP. Payment: £9 per page. Copyrighted. Pub's reviews: 70 in 1990. §Literature (general), politics. Ads: £75/£40. Scottish Publishers Association, Association of Little Presses.

THE CHARIOTEER, Pella Publishing Co, Carmen Capri-Karka, 337 West 36 Street, New York, NY 10018, 212-279-9586. 1960. Poetry, fiction, articles, art, criticism, reviews, letters, plays. "Purpose: to bring to English-speaking readers information on, appreciation of, and translations from modern Greek literature, with criticism and reproductions of modern Greek art and sculpture." circ. 1M. 1/yr. Pub'd 1 issue 1990; expects 1 issue 1991, 1 issue 1992. sub. price: $15; per copy: $15; sample: $15. Back issues: $9-single; $15-double. Discounts: Jobbers-20%, bookstores-20%. 160pp; 5½×8½; †1p. Reporting time: 1 year. Payment: 20 offprints.

Copyrighted, reverts to author if requested. Pub's reviews: 0 in 1990. §Modern Greek Literature & Poetry. Ads: $125/$75/Outside Back Cover-$250/Inside Covers-$200.

CHARITON REVIEW, Chariton Review Press, Jim Barnes, Northeast Missouri State University, Kirksville, MO 63501, 816-785-4499. 1975. Poetry, fiction, art, photos, reviews. "We try to keep open minds, but admit a bias to work that relies more on strong imagery than talkiness. We are very interested in translation, particularly translations of modern poets and especially those from languages other than French or Spanish though we have used numerous translations from those two languages. Recent contributors include Gordon Weaver, Steve Heller, Elizabeth Moore, Lynn Thorsen, Lucien Stryk, Brian Bedard, Greg Johnson, Lewis Horne, David Ray, Quinton Duval, James Welch, Paul Zimmer, translations of Belli, Koteski, Huchel, Paulovski, Sabines, Aleixandre, Elytis, Nick. No xerox or carbons or dot matrix." circ. 650+. 2/yr. Pub'd 2 issues 1990; expects 2 issues 1991. sub. price: $5/yr, $9 2/yr; per copy: $2.50; sample: $2.50. Back issues: Vol. 1 No. 1 $50; Vol. 1 No. 2 $20; Vol. 2 No. 1 $20; Vol. 2 No. 2 $50; others $2. Discounts: on request. 104pp; 6×9; electronic type. Reporting time: 1 month or less. Payment: $5 page up to $50 and 1 copy. Copyrighted, returned to author on request. Pub's reviews: 6 in 1990. §Modern poetry, fiction, translation. Ads: $100/$50. CCLM.

Chariton Review Press (see also CHARITON REVIEW), Jim Barnes, Northeast Missouri State University, Kirksville, MO 63501, 816-785-4499. 1978. Poetry. "Submitters should query before sending manuscripts. We like our books to run between 100 and 125 pages. We have absolutely no desire to print chapbooks. Our first full length collection of poetry—*The Tramp's Cup*, by David Ray — won the 1979 William Carlos Williams Award from The Poetry Society of America, which allowed us to go into a second edition with a print run of 1,200 copies. Our second book, *Summons and Sign: Poems by Dagmar Nick* won a Translation Award from the Translation Center of Columbia University in 1980. Funds permitting, we plan to do one book per year. We are interested only in solid contemporary poetry and fiction of first rank. We pay 10% royalty, or a flat rate (usually between 300 and 500 dollars)." avg. press run 700. Pub'd 1 title 1990; expects 1 title 1992. 6 titles listed in the *Small Press Record of Books in Print* (20th Edition, 1991-92). avg. price, paper: $5. Discounts: on requests. 125pp; 6×9; of, lp. Reporting time: 1 week to 1 month (submitter must query first). Payment: 10% or flat rate. Copyrights for author. CCLM.

Charlemagne Press, J. Fred Farrell, PO Box 771, Arcadia, CA 91006, 818-357-7236. 1987. Poetry, criticism. avg. press run 3.5M. Pub'd 1 title 1990; expects 1 title 1991, 1 title 1992. 1 title listed in the *Small Press Record of Books in Print* (20th Edition, 1991-92). avg. price, paper: $7.95. Discounts: 2-3 20%, 4-5 30%, 6-50 40%, 51+ 50%. 144pp; of.

Deborah Charles Publications (see also INTERNATIONAL JOURNAL FOR THE SEMIOTICS OF LAW; LAW AND CRITIQUE; LIVERPOOL LAW REVIEW), B.S. Jackson, 173 Mather Avenue, Liverpool L18 6JZ, United Kingdom, 051-724 2500. 1986. Non-fiction. "Mainly legal theory" avg. press run 300. 2 titles listed in the *Small Press Record of Books in Print* (20th Edition, 1991-92). Discounts: 10% subscription agents, 25% bookshops. 112pp; size royal octavo; desktop publishing Macintosh. IPG, COSMEP.

Charnel House, Crad Kilodney, c/o Crad Kilodney, PO Box 281, Station S, Toronto, Ontario M5M 4L7, Canada, 416-924-5670. 1979. Poetry, art. "To the best of my knowledge, I am the only author in the world who not only publishes his own books but also sells them on the street as his sole occupation. For a sample book, send $5. Only material wanted at this time is bad poetry for series of anthologies of bad poetry...and I mean really bad. Lately I have been producing cassette tapes of my street encounters recorded secretly with a concealed mike. These are 90-minute cassettes for $10." avg. press run 1M. Pub'd 1 title 1990; expects 2 titles 1991, 2 titles 1992. 3 titles listed in the *Small Press Record of Books in Print* (20th Edition, 1991-92). avg. price, paper: $4. Discounts: query. 52pp; 6×9; of. Reporting time: soon. Payment: no set policy.

Charter Oak Press, Thomas W. Horn, PO Box 7783, Lancaster, PA 17604, 717-898-7711. 1984. Non-fiction. "Business, legal, real estate and career subjects. Interested in unique reference books, and 'how-to' books—well-organized, practical, step-by-step presentations which teach a skill or produce a specific end result. Send query with detailed outline, sample chapters, market study for book, and SASE. No unsolicited mss." avg. press run 15M. 1 title listed in the *Small Press Record of Books in Print* (20th Edition, 1991-92). avg. price, cloth: business titles - $20-$125; other: $5.95-$14.95. Discounts: write for current information. Pages vary; of. Reporting time: 1-2 weeks on queries. Payment: flat fee or variable percentage on actual wholesale or retail receipts. COSMEP, ABA.

CHASQUI, Ted Lyon, Dept of Spanish, Brigham Young University, Provo, UT 84602. 1971. Poetry, fiction, articles, interviews, criticism, reviews, parts-of-novels. "*Chasqui* accepts creative writing written in Spanish or Portuguese. All other material may be in either English, Spanish or Portuguese. Subscription information should be directed to Howard Fraser, Dept. of Modern Language, College of William and Mary, Williamsburg, Virginia 23185." circ. 500. 2/yr. Pub'd 2 issues 1990; expects 2 issues 1991, 2 issues 1992. sub. price: $9; per copy: $4; sample: $4. Back issues: $5. Discounts: none. 130pp; 6×9; laser. Reporting time: 3 months. Payment: none. Copyrighted, reverts to author. Pub's reviews: 65 in 1990. §Brazilian and Spanish American literature,

110

literary criticism, theory. Ads: $50/$35. CCLM.

CHASTITY AND HOLINESS, C.J.L. Press, Cecil Justin Lam, Box 22006, 45 Overlea, Thorncliff Post Office, Toronto, Ont. M4H 1N9, Canada, 423-6781. 1988. Poetry, art, long-poems. "Specializes in revival and original Christianity. With emphasis in poetic testimonial theology. Religious comparison in the spiritual context. Therefore, all religious submissions poetical welcome" circ. 100. 2/yr. Pub'd 2 issues 1990; expects 2 issues 1991, 2 issues 1992. sub. price: $12; per copy: $5; sample: $5. Back issues: $5. Discounts: 80% per 100, or negotiable. 30pp; 7×8½; †photoset/copy. Reporting time: 2 months on the average. Payment: reward in prayers and minimal payment. Copyrighted. Ads: $100/$50/$25 1/4 page.

Chatham Publishing Company, Karl R. Koenig, PO Box 283, Burlingame, CA 94010, 415-348-0331. 1961. Articles, photos, reviews, letters, news items. "ISBN prefix 0-89685" avg. press run 10M. 5 titles listed in the *Small Press Record of Books in Print* (20th Edition, 1991-92). Discounts: trade 40%. 8½×11; of. Reporting time: 1 month. Payment: negotiated. Copyrights for author.

Chatsworth Press, Scott Brastow, Publisher, 9135 Alabama Avenue #B, Chatsworth, CA 91311-6913, 818-341-3156. 1980. Non-fiction. *"Chatsworth Press* is a publisher of human sexuality information, as well as erotica." avg. press run 15M. Pub'd 2 titles 1990; expects 4 titles 1991, 4 titles 1992. 4 titles listed in the *Small Press Record of Books in Print* (20th Edition, 1991-92). avg. price, other: $14.95-trade paper. Discounts: 42%-retail; 50% wholesale. 30pp; 7¼×10¾; †of. Reporting time: 90 days. Payment: negotiable, mostly work-for-hire contracts. if necessary, not usually. Publishers Marketing Association (PMA) 2401 Pacific Coast Highway, Hermosa Beach, CA 90254. COSMEP, PO Box 703, San Francisco, CA 94101.

THE CHATTAHOOCHEE REVIEW, Lamar York, DeKalb College, 2101 Womack Road, Dunwoody, GA 30338-4497, 404-551-3019. 1980. Poetry, fiction, art, interviews, reviews, non-fiction. "Fred Chappell, Ann Deagon, Madison Jones, Peter Taylor, Andrew Lytle, Anne Rivers Siddons, John Stone, David Madden, David Bottoms, Terry Kay, Leon Rooke, Doug Marlette, and Vinnie Williams, as well as a handful of students, faculty, and writers in this area and elsewhere have appeared in the *Review.*" circ. 1M. 4/yr. Pub'd 4 issues 1990; expects 4 issues 1991, 4 issues 1992. sub. price: $15/yr or $25/2 yrs; per copy: $4; sample: $4. Back issues: $2. Discounts: 30% to retailers. 90pp; 6×9; of. Reporting time: 6 months. Payment: copies. Copyrighted, reverts to author. Pub's reviews: 6 in 1990. §Poetry, fiction and literary magazines. Ads: $125/$75. COSMEP, CCLM.

Chax Press, Charles Alexander, 101 West 6th Street #4, Tucson, AZ 85701, 602-622-7109. 1984. Poetry, fiction, long-poems, concrete art, non-fiction. "1. Fine Press, handmade books emphasizing experimentation and innovation in both writing and book arts. 2. Literary Trade (offset-printed) books; innovations in contemporary writing; books by American and Canadian writing; at least one book per year by a southwestern writer, and at least one book per year by a Canadian writer. In fiction, only experimental fiction. Recent books by bp Nichol, Charles Alexander, Lyn Hejinian, Kit Robinson, Charles Bernstein. Forthcoming books by Karen Mac Cormack, Sheila Murphy, Karl Young, Ron Silliman, Nathaniel Mackey, Mei-Mei Berssenbrugge, Eli Goldblatt, Beverly Dahlen, Tom Mandel, Leslie Scalapino, Norman Fischer. Mostly books 140-180 pages; some titles 64-80 pages." avg. press run 75-125 handmade, 800-1.2M offset-printed. Pub'd 4 titles 1990; expects 6 titles 1991, 6 titles 1992. avg. price, paper: $12; other: $100 handmade. Discounts: (on trade literary books) bookstores 30%, distributors 50%. 168pp offset, 24-60pp handmade; 5×8; †lp. Reporting time: 2 months; usually sooner. Payment: royalties or copies; to be negotiated. Copyrights for author.

CHELSEA, Sonia Raiziss, Editor; Alfredo de Palchi, Associate Editor; Richard Foerster, Associate Editor; Caila Rossi, Associate Editor, Box 5880, Grand Central Station, New York, NY 10163. 1958. Poetry, fiction, articles, art, photos, interviews, criticism, parts-of-novels, long-poems, concrete art, non-fiction. "Stress on quality, originality, style, variety...superior translations. No special biases, no requirements but prefer fiction under 25 pages. Flexible attitudes, eclectic material. Recent contributors: Lucille Clifton, Rita Dove, Colette Inez, Laura (Riding) Jackson, William Van Wert, Rosemarie Waldrop, Len Roberts, Roberta Allen, Jascha Kessler." circ. 1.3M. 2/yr. Pub'd 1 issue 1990; expects 2 issues 1991, 2 issues 1992. sub. price: $11/2 consecutive issues as published or one double issue, $14 foreign; per copy: $6 (500-page *Retrospective* double issue—$9); sample: $5. Back issues: prices range from $3 to $15 if rare. Discounts: agency discount: 30%; bookstores: 25% or adjusted terms. 150pp; 6×9; of. Reporting time: 3 weeks to 3 months. Payment: copies plus $5 per printed page. Copyrighted, reverts to author. Ads: $125/$75/exchange ads with other literary mags. CLMP.

Chelsea Green Publishing Company, Ian Jr. Baldwin, Michael Moore, Associate Editor, PO Box 130, Post Mills, VT 05058, 802-333-9073. 1984. Fiction, non-fiction. "Emphasis on non-fiction: nature, biography, travel, outdoors. Serious fiction (literary)" avg. press run 5M. Pub'd 7 titles 1990; expects 10 titles 1991, 12 titles 1992. 25 titles listed in the *Small Press Record of Books in Print* (20th Edition, 1991-92). avg. price, cloth: $19; paper: $12. Discounts: under 5 35% prepaid, 5-9 40%, 10-24 42%, 25-49 43%, 10-99 45%, 100+ 46%. 200pp; size varies; of. Reporting time: 2-3 months. Payment: varies. Copyrights for author. NEBA, ABA.

Cheops Books, Kay Bognar, Gary Bennet, Alice Bognar, Larry Bognar, 977 Seminole Trail, Suite 179, Charlottesville, VA 22901, 804-973-7670. 1990. Fiction. "Believe it or not, we publish only historical fiction. No genre westerns, family sagas, romances, or series books. We don't consider anything concerning the post-1914 world historical enough for our purposes. We even prefer unusual time periods and settings, the more exotic the better (but no pure fantasy or self-created worlds please). Our first offering is *To Follow the Goddess* by Linda Cargill, a tale of the Trojan War from the point-of-view of Helen. Tip: Find a voice. Pretend the main character is telling the story to you as did the bards and story-tellers of old. You can hear it. We are very fond of the novels of Mary Renault and Robert Graves. What will their fans do now that both are dead? We think that in this country in particular historical fiction is in the doldrums, particularly fictional biography and autobiography. The French have it all over us in this regard. Computer submissions only on laser printer. No literary agents please." avg. press run 2-3M. Expects 1 title 1991, 1 title 1992. 1 title listed in the *Small Press Record of Books in Print* (20th Edition, 1991-92). avg. price, cloth: $19.95; paper: $9.95. Discounts: 2-4 books 20%; 5-9 30%; 10-24 40%; 25-49 42%; 50-74 44%; 75-99 46%; 100-199 48%; 200 or more 50% (to the book trade & libraries), wholesale 55%. 200-400pp; 5½x8½; of. Reporting time: 3-4 months. Payment: 7% net of all copies sold. Copyrights for author. PMA.

Cherokee Publishing Company, Alexa Selph, PO Box 1730, Marietta, GA 30061, 404-424-6210. 1968. "Additional address: 1800 Sandy Plains Parkway #226, Marietta, GA 30066, 1-800-548-8778" avg. press run 3M. Pub'd 10 titles 1990; expects 15 titles 1991, 15 titles 1992. avg. price, cloth: $16.95; paper: $9. of. Reporting time: 3 months. Payment: usually 12.5% of net. Copyrights for author. PMA, COSMEP, ABA, ALA, PAS, GA Pub Assoc-President.

CHESAPEAKE BAY MAGAZINE, Betty Rigoli, Editor; Jean Waller, Executive Editor, 1819 Bay Ridge Avenue, Annapolis, MD 21403, 301-263-2662. 1971. Fiction, articles, art, photos, cartoons, interviews, reviews, letters, news items. circ. 35M. 12/yr. 1 title listed in the *Small Press Record of Books in Print* (20th Edition, 1991-92). sub. price: $19.95; per copy: $2.50; sample: $2. 88pp; 8½x11; of. Reporting time: 6-8 weeks. Payment: yes. Copyrighted, reverts to author. Pub's reviews: 8 in 1990. §Marine related, boating. Ads: $1857/$1174/$30-20 words. MPA, BPA.

Cheshire Books, Michael Riordan, 1855 Mintwood Place NW #2, Washington, DC 20009-1941. 1976. Non-fiction. "We are now publishing material from the writing public at large, and authors are invited to submit manuscripts in fields of art, architecture, energy & the environment, and science. Accepting non-fiction only. Most recent book's are *The Wind Power Book*, *The Ecology of Freedom*, and *The Day After Midnight*" avg. press run 10M. Expects 1 title 1991, 2 titles 1992. 5 titles listed in the *Small Press Record of Books in Print* (20th Edition, 1991-92). avg. price, cloth: $19.95; paper: $9.95. Discounts: Trade distribution through selected Small Press Distributors including Book People in Berkeley, CA, and Inland Book Co., East Haven, CT. 300pp; size varies; of. Reporting time: two months. Payment: 6-10% of list price, small advance payable on delivery. Copyrights for author.

Chess Enterprises, Inc. (see also EN PASSANT), B.G. Dudley, 107 Crosstree Road, Coraopolis, PA 15108. Non-fiction. "Only chess; no beginner text." avg. press run 1.2M. Pub'd 12 titles 1990; expects 12 titles 1991, 12 titles 1992. 16 titles listed in the *Small Press Record of Books in Print* (20th Edition, 1991-92). avg. price, paper: $6.50. Discounts: trade 35%, 25+ copies 45%. 100pp; 5x8; †of. Reporting time: 30 days. Payment: flat fee up front. Copyrights for author.

CHESS IN INDIANA, Roger E. Blaine, Editor-President, 214 S. 4th Street, Elkhart, IN 46516, 219-293-2241. 1988. Articles, art, photos, cartoons, interviews, reviews, letters, news items. circ. 250. 5/yr. Pub'd 5 issues 1990; expects 5 issues 1991, 5 issues 1992. sub. price: $8 (with ISCA membership $10); sample: $1. 24pp; 5½x8½; of. Reporting time: 3 weeks. Payment: none. Not copyrighted. Pub's reviews. §Chess. Ads: $25/$15/no classified.

CHESS LIFE, U.S. Chess Federation, Glenn Petersen, United States Chess Federation, 186 Route 9W, New Windsor, NY 12553, (914) 562-8350. 1958. Articles, photos, cartoons, interviews, reviews, news items, non-fiction. "Incorporates *Chess Review*; until 1960 name was *Chess Life & Review*. Chess must be central to all material submitted. Very little fiction used." circ. 57M. 12/yr. Pub'd 12 issues 1990; expects 12 issues 1991, 12 issues 1992. sub. price: $30; per copy: $2.95; sample: (free with req. for writer guidelines). 68pp; 8¼x10¾; of. Reporting time: 1 month. Payment: on publication. Copyrighted, does not revert to author. Pub's reviews: 8-10 in 1990. Ads: $2145/$1180/$1 per word, min. $15.

Chicago Democratic Socialists Of America (see also THE DIGGER; SOCIALISM AND SEXUALITY; ECOSOCIALIST REVIEW), 1608 N. Milwaukee #403, Chicago, IL 60647.

CHICAGO REVIEW, Andy Winston, Editor; Angela Sorby, Managing Editor, 5801 South Kenwood, Chicago, IL 60637, 312-702-0887. 1946. Poetry, fiction, articles, art, photos, interviews, criticism, reviews, parts-of-novels, plays, non-fiction. "*CR* has an international readership; submissions from unknown writers are welcome. *CR* looks for poetry and fiction which participates in and tests the bounds of these respective traditions. It seeks essays, reviews and interviews which address contemporary literary and cultural questions and problems. SASE expected (including subs. from agents). Recent numbers include the poetry of Turner Cassity, Jim Powell, Eavan Boland, and Andrew Hudgins; interviews with Paul Muldoon and Diane Johnson; and fiction by Bo Ball" circ. 2M. 4/yr. Pub'd 2 issues 1990; expects 4 issues 1991, 4 issues 1992. sub. price: $16 individuals, $20 institutions + $2.50/yr postage to Canada, $2.50 to Mexico, $4.50/yr postage to other foreign countries; per copy: $5; sample: $5. Back issues: yes, on inquiry. Discounts: agency 5% subscription. 95-125pp; 6×9; of. Reporting time: 3 months or more with fiction. Payment: primarily in contributors copies. Copyrighted, reverts to author only on request. Pub's reviews. §Literature & the arts. Ads: $150/$75. CCLM, COSMEP.

Chicano Studies Library Publications Unit, Lillian Castillo-Speed, Series Editor; Carolyn Soto, Managing Editor, 3404 Dwinelle Hall, University of California, Berkeley, CA 94720, 415-642-3859. 1976. "Major bibliographies. Our major publication is the *Chicano Periodical Index* published yearly. Presently producing 1990 index. This is equivalent to *Readers Guide...* but indexes Chicano articles. Also includes Chicano references in mainstream journals. Other publications are bibliographies on Chicano topics: Chicano literature, US-Mexico Immigration, etc." avg. press run 500. Pub'd 2 titles 1990; expects 2 titles 1991, 3 titles 1992. 3 titles listed in the *Small Press Record of Books in Print* (20th Edition, 1991-92). avg. price, cloth: $100; paper: $16; other: $90 Chicano Periodical Index. Discounts: 10% libraries, 20% trade. 600pp; 8½×11; of. Reporting time: 60 days. Payment: no royalties, copies of book by agreement. Copyrights for author.

Chicano Studies Research Center Publications (see also AZTLAN: A Journal of Chicano Studies), Raymund A. Paredes, University of California-Los Angeles, 405 Hilgard Avenue, Los Angeles, CA 90024, 213-825-2642. 1970. Articles, criticism, reviews, news items. "Original research and analysis related to Mexicans and Mexican Americans." avg. press run 1M. Pub'd 2 titles 1990; expects 3 titles 1991, 3 titles 1992. 14 titles listed in the *Small Press Record of Books in Print* (20th Edition, 1991-92). Discounts: retailers 40%. 200pp; 6×9; of. Reporting time: 6 mo. Payment: books in quantity. Copyrights for author. SCB.

Chicory Blue Press, 795 East Street North, Goshen, CT 06756, 203-491-2271. 1987. Poetry, fiction, art, interviews, letters, parts-of-novels, non-fiction. "Chicory Blue Press specializes in writing by women" avg. press run 3.5M, 2M for poetry. Expects 2 titles 1991, 1 title 1992. 3 titles listed in the *Small Press Record of Books in Print* (20th Edition, 1991-92). avg. price, paper: $14.95. Discounts: 3-199 40%, 200-499 50%, 500+ 55%. printer. Payment: negotiable. Copyrights for author. COSMEP, PMA.

The Chicot Press, Randall P. Whatley, Box 53198, Atlanta, GA 30355, 404-640-9918. 1978. Non-fiction. avg. press run 2M. Expects 3 titles 1991, 5 titles 1992. 2 titles listed in the *Small Press Record of Books in Print* (20th Edition, 1991-92). avg. price, paper: $10. Discounts: 1-4 copies 20%, 5-9 30%, 10-99 40%, 100-499 45%, 500+ 50%. 100pp; 6×9; of. Reporting time: 60 days. Payment: percentage of profits. Copyrights for author. ABA, PMA.

Children Of Mary (see also FIDELIS ET VERUS), Ella McBride, Fidelis Et Verus, RR 10, Box 13517, Tallahassee, FL 32310-9803, 904-576-0817; 800-749-1925. 1981. Non-fiction. "Orthodox Roman Catholic views reflected in commentary apparitions of Jesus and Mary in Bayside, NY (1970-85) are completely recorded in two volumes *Roses* and also published in *Fidelis et Verus*, a Catholic quarterly newspaper, $10/yr." avg. press run 10.5M. Pub'd 2 titles 1990; expects 1 title 1991, 2 titles 1992. 1 title listed in the *Small Press Record of Books in Print* (20th Edition, 1991-92). avg. price, cloth: $19.50; paper: $13.50. Discounts: 40% trade, bulk, classroom, agent, jobber, etc. 592pp; 8½×11; of. Reporting time: 3 months. Payment: voluntary. Does not copyright for author.

CHILDREN'S ALBUM, EGW Publishing Company, Margo Lemas, PO Box 6086, Concord, CA 94524, 415-671-9852. 1984. Fiction, articles, art, photos, cartoons, criticism, reviews, letters, plays, non-fiction. "*The Children's Album* is a collection of stories and plays written by children ages 8-14. It is designed to promote literacy and encourage creative writing. Educational, entertaining fillers are included, along with adult input regarding tips and examples of improving writing. Covers are often designed by children in this age group, and illustrations accompany the stories and plays. Some pieces can run up to four pages. *Children's Crafts* is a prominent part of this publication" circ. 25M. 6/yr. Pub'd 6 issues 1990; expects 6 issues 1991, 6 issues 1992. sub. price: $15; per copy: $2.95; sample: same. 32pp; 8⅛×10⅞. Reporting time: 2-8 weeks. Payment: children - 1-year subscription, $50 U.S. for best writer and best artist; adults - $35 per published page, $5-$20 for fillers (adults, children). Copyrighted, reverts to author. No ads.

Children's Book Press, Harriet Rohmer, 6400 Hollis Street #4, Emeryville, CA 94608-1028. 1975. "We publish myths, legends, folklore and contemporary stories of the different peoples who live in America today. Most of our books are bilingual in Spanish, Chinese, Tagalog (Pilipino), Korean or Vietnamese. We do not solicit manuscripts" avg. press run 7.5M. Pub'd 5 titles 1990; expects 6 titles 1991, 6 titles 1992. 22 titles listed in the *Small Press Record of Books in Print* (20th Edition, 1991-92). avg. price, cloth: $12.95; paper: $5.95. Discounts: 40% trade, other rates on request. 32pp; 9×9½; of. Payment: yes. Copyrights for author.

113

CHILDREN'S LITERATURE IN EDUCATION, Plenum Publishing Corporation, Anita Moss, US & Canada; Geoff Fox, United Kingdom, 233 Spring Street, New York, NY 10013, (212) 741-3087. 1970. Articles, interviews, criticism, reviews. *"Children's Literature in Education* features interviews with noted children's authors, literary criticism of both classic and contemporary writing for children, and articles about successful classroom reading projects. All correspondence concerning subscriptions should be addressed to: Children's Literature in Education, Fulfillment Dept., Agathon Press, Inc., 49 Sheridan Avenue, Albany, NY 12210. All editorial correspondence, manuscript submissions, and review copies should be addressed as follows: In North America, to Anita Moss, English Dept., Univ. of N. Carolina at Charlotte, UNCC Station, Charlotte, NC 28223; In the UK and elsewhere outside North America, to Geoff Fox, Exeter Univ. School of Education, St. Luke's, Exeter EX1 2LU, Devon, England'' circ. 2.5M. 4/yr. Pub'd 4 issues 1990; expects 4 issues 1991, 4 issues 1992. sub. price: ind. & schools K-12 $18, inst. $32; per copy: $12; sample: $2 (send to NYC). Back issues: 1977-86 (Vols. 8-17), 4 issues ea., $32/vol.; 1970-76, issues numbered serially, 1-23. Discounts: 10% discount to subscription agents. 64pp; 7×10; of. Reporting time: 3 months. Payment: none. Copyrighted, does not revert to author. Pub's reviews: 1 in 1990. §Recent titles of professional interest to educators on reading-related topics. Ads: $250/$150. COSMEP.

CHINESE LITERATURE, Chinese Literature Press, He Jingzhi, 24 Baiwanzhuang Road, Beijing 100037, People's Republic of China, 892554. 1951. circ. 50M. 4/yr. Pub'd 4 issues 1990; expects 4 issues 1991, 4 issues 1992. sub. price: $10.50. 200pp; 21.5×14cm; †photo of. Copyrighted. Pub's reviews: 4 in 1990. §Chinese literature and art areas.

Chinese Literature Press (see also CHINESE LITERATURE), He Jingzhi, 24 Baiwanzhuang Road, Beijing 100037, People's Republic of China. 1951. avg. press run 50M. Pub'd 4 titles 1990; expects 4 titles 1991, 4 titles 1992. 65 titles listed in the *Small Press Record of Books in Print* (20th Edition, 1991-92). 200pp; 21.5×14cm; †li. Payment: in Chinese and foreign currency. Copyrights for author.

CHIPS OFF THE WRITER'S BLOCK, FICTION FORUM, Wanda Windham, PO Box 83371, Los Angeles, CA 90083. 1984. Poetry, fiction, articles, cartoons, interviews, news items, non-fiction. "How-to articles on all aspects of writing and selling, personal experience, short fiction (less than 1,000 words), some poetry" circ. 500+. 7/yr. Pub'd 6 issues 1990; expects 7 issues 1991, 7 issues 1992. sub. price: $12; per copy: $2; sample: $2. Back issues: none. Discounts: to be arranged. 14pp; 8½×11; †photocopy. Reporting time: 2-3 weeks. Payment: copy only. Copyrighted, reverts to author. Pub's reviews: 4 in 1990. §Books on all aspects of writing. Ad rates can be arranged. Subscribers ads are free.

Chiron Press (see also CHIRON REVIEW), Michael Hathaway, 1514 Stone, Great Bend, KS 67530-4027, 316-792-5025. 1987. Poetry, fiction, non-fiction. "We are always on the lookout for excellent manuscripts" avg. press run 100-200. Pub'd 1 title 1990; expects 2 titles 1991. 4 titles listed in the *Small Press Record of Books in Print* (20th Edition, 1991-92). avg. price, paper: $6. Discounts: 40% bookstores & distributors. Pages vary; 8½×5½; of. Reporting time: quick—between 1 week and 1 month. Payment: 25% of press run, no royalties. Copyrights for author.

CHIRON REVIEW, Chiron Press, Michael Hathaway, Editor; Jane Hathaway, Assistant Editor; Jay Dougherty, Non-Fiction Editor; Gerald Locklin, Contributing Editor (Poetry); Ray Zapeda, Contributing Editor (Fiction), 1514 Stone, Great Bend, KS 67530-4027, 316-792-5025. 1982. Poetry, fiction, articles, art, photos, interviews, satire, criticism, reviews, letters, long-poems, collages, concrete art, news items, non-fiction. "Presents the widest possible range of contemporary creative writing—fiction and non-fiction, traditional and off-beat—in an attractive, professional tabloid format, including artwork and photographs of featured writers. All submissions are invited; no taboos. Recent contributors include Charles Bukowski, Marael Johnson, Edward Field, William Stafford, Lyn Lifshin, and a host of others, both well-known and new. Also, about a quarter of each issue is devoted to news, views, and reviews of interest to writers and the literary community. We are always on the lookout for intelligent non-fiction, as well as talented reviewers who wish to write in-depth, analytical reviews of literary books and magazines (500-1000 words). Artwork suitable for cover and/or illustrations also needed. We hold yearly poetry contests; query or send for sample copy of magazine. *Be sure to include self-addressed, stamped envelope with all correspondence and submissions.* Make all checks payable to Michael Hathaway." circ. 2.5M. 4/yr. Pub'd 4 issues 1990; expects 4 issues 1991, 4 issues 1992. sub. price: $8 ($16 overseas), $20 instit.; per copy: $2 ($4 overseas), $4 instit.; sample: $2 ($4 overseas), $4 instit. Back issues: $2. Discounts: 50%. 24-32pp; 10×13; †photocomposition, of. Reporting time: 1-4 weeks. Payment: 1 copy. Copyrighted, reverts to author. Pub's reviews: 79 in 1990. §Literary magazines, poetry, fiction, essays—all areas. Ads: SASE for rates.

Chockstone Press, George Meyers, Merrill Wilson, PO Box 3505, Evergreen, CO 80439, 303-377-1970. 1982. Non-fiction. avg. press run 4M. Pub'd 5 titles 1990; expects 6 titles 1991, 6 titles 1992. 12 titles listed in the *Small Press Record of Books in Print* (20th Edition, 1991-92). avg. price, cloth: $25; paper: $10; other: $18. Discounts: 40% wholesale, 55% distributor. 325pp; 6×9; of. Reporting time: 1 month. Payment: 12% semi-annually. Copyrights for author. COSMEP.

Christian Classics, Inc., John J. McHale, 77 W. Main, Box 30, Westminster, MD 21157, 301-848-3065. 1966. "Interested in average trade books on religious subjects, chiefly Roman Catholic." avg. press run 2M. Pub'd 14 titles 1990; expects 10 titles 1991. 14 titles listed in the *Small Press Record of Books in Print* (20th Edition, 1991-92). avg. price, cloth: $20; paper: $10. Discounts: 40% to trade for 5 or more books. 250pp; 5×8; of. Reporting time: 3 weeks. Payment: 10% on 10M; 12% thereafter. Copyrights for author. Catholic Publishers Assoc.

CHRISTIAN FAMILY, Elm House Christian Communications Ltd, Clive Price, Editor, 37 Elm Road, New Malden, Surrey KT3 3HB, England, 01-942-9761. 1982. circ. 12M. 12/yr. Pub'd 12 issues 1990; expects 12 issues 1991, 12 issues 1992. sub. price: £15.90; per copy: £1.20; sample: same. Back issues: £1.20. size A4.

THE CHRISTIAN LIBRARIAN, Ron Jordahl, Assoc. of Christian Librarians, Three Hills, Alberta T0M 2A0, Canada. 1957. Articles, interviews, reviews, letters, non-fiction. "1,500-3,500 words. Looking for articles of Christian interpretation of librarianship; philosophy, theory, and practice of library science; bibliographic essays" circ. 450. 4/yr. Pub'd 4 issues 1990; expects 4 issues 1991, 4 issues 1992. sub. price: $20; per copy: $5; sample: same. 36pp; 8½×11; of. Reporting time: 2 weeks. Not copyrighted. Pub's reviews: 120 in 1990. §Library science, reference, religion. Ads: $50/$30/$22 col./$12 half col. EPA, (Evangelical Press Association), PO Box 4550, Overland Park, KS 66204.

CHRISTIAN*NEW AGE QUARTERLY, Catherine Groves, PO Box 276, Clifton, NJ 07011. 1989. Articles, reviews, letters, news items, non-fiction. *"Christian*New Age Quarterly* is a lively forum exploring the similarities and distinctions between Christianity and the New Age movement. Essentially a vehicle for communication—to draw the two ideological groups into genuine dialogue—articles must quickly cut through superficial divisions to explore the substance of our unity. Pertinent controversy is fine. Garbage thinking (ie., 'I'm right - you're wrong') makes the editor frown. Submissions should sparkle with both insight and creativity. Article lengths vary from 400 to 1500 words (longer pieces accepted if excellent). Guidelines available." 4/yr. Pub'd 4 issues 1990; expects 4 issues 1991, 4 issues 1992. sub. price: $12.50; per copy: $3.50; sample: $2.50 for writers *only*. Back issues: $3.50. Discounts: available by subscription only. 20pp; 7×8½; photocopy. Reporting time: 4 weeks (and we always respond, if SASE enclosed). Payment: in subscription or copies (depending on nature of article). Copyrighted, reverts to author. Pub's reviews: 9 in 1990. §Books which address both Christian and New Age issues. Before sending review copies, write for reviewer's address. Ads: $35/$25/$15 1/4 page/$10 business card/cheap classifieds!

Christmans, Lana Newlin, Senior Editor, PO Box 510, Pittsburg, KS 66762, 417-842-3322. 1988. Non-fiction. "Prefer to work with wholesome subject matter directed towards family life, self-sufficient living, crafts and hobbies, caring for the earth, education K-12, and innovative children's fiction and non-fiction. No gay, new age, or astrology. Query adult books. Send manuscript on children's lit. SASE for return of manuscripts and queries." avg. press run 2M-5M. Pub'd 1 title 1990; expects 1 title 1991, 4 titles 1992. 1 title listed in the *Small Press Record of Books in Print* (20th Edition, 1991-92). Discounts: industry standards. Pages vary; size varies; of. Reporting time: 2 weeks on queries, 8 weeks on manuscripts. Payment: offers advance, some books bought outright, pays 8-12% on retail price. Copyrights for author.

THE...CHRONICLE, Nathaniel M. Naske, William O. Fuller, PO Box 80721, Fairbanks, AK 99708, 907-479-2966. 1988. Articles, cartoons, interviews, satire, criticism, reviews, music, letters, collages, news items, non-fiction. "We will look at anything!" circ. 500+. 2/yr. Pub'd 2 issues 1990; expects 2 issues 1991, 2 issues 1992. price per copy: $3; sample: $3. Back issues: #1,2 $2 each, #3-7 $3 each. Discounts: if over 100 ordered, $2 per issue. 44pp; 8½×11; Qwik-copy xerox. Reporting time: 2 months. Payment: none, volunteer basis. Not copyrighted. Pub's reviews: 50+ in 1990. §Splatterpunk, Fortean, alternative news, mayhem, true crime, fringe religion, UFO's, junk culture. Ads: $100/$60/$40 1/4 page/$20 business card.

Chronicle Books, Jack Jensen, General Manager; William LeBlond, Editor, 275 Fifth Street, San Francisco, CA 94103, 415-777-7240. 1966. Non-fiction. *"Chronicle Books* continues to publish regional outdoor and western guidebooks. West Coast history, art and architecture, natural history" avg. press run 7.5M. Expects 17 titles 1991, 45 titles 1992. 90 titles listed in the *Small Press Record of Books in Print* (20th Edition, 1991-92). avg. price, cloth: $25; paper: $7.95(Chron). Discounts: 10, 40%; 50, 42%; 100, 43%; 250, 45%; 600, 46%. 160pp; 8×9, 10×13; of. Reporting time: 2 months. Payment: 8% paid twice yearly. Copyrights for author.

CHRYSANTHEMUM, Goldfish Press, Koon Woon, Allan Hikida, Sandra Schroeder, 416-1/2 7th Avenue South, Seattle, WA 98104. 1989. Poetry, fiction, articles, interviews, satire, criticism, reviews, letters, parts-of-novels, long-poems, plays, non-fiction. "We want to hear from minorities, women, working class and others who believe that literature arises from and elevates human experiences. We are interested in both phenomena and essence. We want poetry, short fiction, essays, reviews, and nonfiction. We consider material of any length. What you have to say is more important than style. We have a bias for self-awareness and for literature combined with philosophy." circ. 1M. 1/yr. Pub'd 1 issue 1990; expects 1 issue 1991, 2 issues 1992. sub. price: $2.50; per copy: $2.50; sample: $2.50. Back issues: $5 Inaugural issue. Discounts: negotiable.

20-30pp; 11½×16; of. Reporting time: 2 weeks to 2 months, longer if seriously under consideration. Payment: 2 copies. Copyrighted, reverts to author by request. Pub's reviews. §Minority literature. Ads: $100/$50/ negotiable.

THE CHURCH, FARM AND TOWN, Archdeacon John Peacock, Box 368, RR 4, Amherst, NS B4H 3Y2, Canada, 902-667-4006. 1943. Poetry, articles, cartoons, reviews, letters, news items, non-fiction. "Biases: Small is beautiful, small community, ecology (anti-nuclear), pro-Peace, farming (non-technical), home schooling vis-a-vis State Education, music in general, criticism of politics, the "end" of Economy." circ. 420. 10/yr. Pub'd 10 issues 1990; expects 10 issues 1991, 10 issues 1992. sub. price: $2. Back issues: postage. 19pp; 8½×11; †mi. Reporting time: 1-2 months. Payment: none. Not copyrighted. Pub's reviews: 0 in 1990. §The economy, rural living, environment, philosophy, theology, art, church music.

CICADA, Amelia Press, Frederick A. Raborg, Jr., Editor, 329 'E' Street, Bakersfield, CA 93304, (805) 323-4064. 1985. Poetry, fiction, articles, art, cartoons, reviews. "Haiku, senryu and other Japanese forms, traditional or experimental; fiction to 3,000 words which in some way uses the haiku form or pertains to Japanese culture; essays to 2,000 words on the history and techniques of the forms; pen & ink sketches and line drawings as well as well-perceived cartoons with oriental themes. We welcome newcomers. Sponsors the annual Lucille Sandberg Haiku Awards and The Hildegarde Janzen Prizes for Oriental Forms of Poetry. Reviews collections of haiku and books about the forms. Contributors include: Roger Ishii, H.F. Noyes, Katharine Machan Aal, David Ray, Ruth Shigezawa, Ryokufu Ishizaki, and many others" circ. 600. 4/yr. Pub'd 4 issues 1990; expects 4 issues 1991, 4 issues 1992. sub. price: $14; per copy: $4.50 ppd; sample: $4.50 ppd. Back issues: $4 when available. Discounts: contributor's discount, 20% on five or more copies. 20pp; 5½×8½; of. Reporting time: 2 weeks. Payment: none, except three *best of issue* poets each receive $10 on publication, plus copy. Copyrighted. Pub's reviews: 12 in 1990. §Collections of haiku and books on the form. Will consider ads based on $60/$40/$25.

Cider Mill Press, Napoleon St. Cyr, P O Box 211, Stratford, CT 06497. 1966. "CMP does not consider unsolicited mss. It selects its authors, and publishes only once in a while." 7 titles listed in the *Small Press Record of Books in Print* (20th Edition, 1991-92).

CIMARRON REVIEW, Deborah Bransford, Managing Editor; Gordon Weaver, Editor-in-Chief; David Major, Associate Editor; Kathy Bedwell, Fiction Editor; Steffie Corcoran, Fiction Editor; Dennis Bormann, Fiction Editor; E.P. Walkiewicz, Essay Editor; Thomas Reiter, Poetry Editor; Randy Phillis, Poetry Editor; Sally Shigley, Poetry Editor; Thomas E. Kennedy, European Editor, 205 Morrill Hall, Oklahoma State University, Stillwater, OK 74078-0135, 405-744-9476. 1967. Poetry, fiction, articles, interviews, satire, criticism, reviews, long-poems, non-fiction. "$30 for 3 years ($40 in Canada) plus $2.50 for all international postage" circ. 700. 4/yr. Pub'd 4 issues 1990; expects 4 issues 1991, 4 issues 1992. sub. price: $12 ($15 in Canada); per copy: $3; sample: $3. Back issues: half-price. Discounts: none. 96-128pp; 6×9; †of. Reporting time: 4-6 weeks. Payment: in copies and 1-year subscriptions; occasionally small cash stipends if we have a grant. Copyrighted, does not revert to author. Pub's reviews: 11 in 1990. §Poetry, fiction, articles, art, satire, nonfiction. No ads. CCLM, MLA, CELJ.

Cin Publications, Clifford Cannon Cin, PO Box 11277, San Francisco, CA 94101. 1978. Articles, art, long-poems, news items. "*Cin Publications* are 'tight', i.e. concentrated, succinctly informative, because they are mainly for people who hate tomes, who live fast, who read only to make life decisions, who appreaciate expert. Capsulated info. Present titles include: *Welcome, Hot Plate!* (ways to live thriftily); *The Vitamin Guide; Natural Living Book; Alpha Shorthand: 3-Hour Self-Instructor; How to I-N-C-R-E-A-S-E Gas Mileage; Rejuvevate Thyself; Unusual Original Salads; Naturopathic Formulary* (natural cures & therapies); The 21st Century Do-It-Yourself Health Control Manual. Writers should inquire before submitting mss, as our material is prepared in-house as a rule. A book may be 2 pages to 64 pages-we like it tight. Cin Pubs. Get around by work of mouth. We sell books, print broadsides to give free. We have yet to publish for profit, editor has outside job" avg. press run varies. Pub'd 2 titles 1990; expects 2 titles 1991, 2 titles 1992. 4 titles listed in the *Small Press Record of Books in Print* (20th Edition, 1991-92). avg. price, paper: $5. 2-64pp; †of, lp. Reporting time: in ten days, if ms was requested. Payment: in books only at this time; other arrangements possible.

CINCINNATI POETRY REVIEW, Dallas Wiebe, Dept of English (069), University of Cincinnati, Cincinnati, OH 45221, 513-556-3922. 1975. Poetry. "*CPR* is eclectic. Takes all kinds of poetry. Each issue features one writer or a group of writers. Send $2 for sample copy." circ. 1M. 2/yr. Pub'd 2 issues 1990; expects 2 issues 1991, 2 issues 1992. 1 title listed in the *Small Press Record of Books in Print* (20th Edition, 1991-92). price per copy: $3; sample: $2. Back issues: Complete set (20 issues) $40. Discounts: 40% on consignment. 64-72pp; 6×9; of. Reporting time: 2-4 months. Payment: 2 copies of issue. Copyrighted, reverts to author.

Cinco Puntos Press, Bobby Byrd, Co-Publisher; Lee Merrill Byrd, Co-Publisher, 2709 Louisville, EL Paso, TX 79930, 915-566-9072. 1985. "Cinco Puntos Press will center its energies on the literature (poetry, fiction) of the Southwest. We will also publish non-fiction books of regional/national interest which we believe have commercial possibilities" avg. press run 2M-3M. Pub'd 3 titles 1990; expects 5 titles 1991, 6 titles 1992. 14 titles listed in the *Small Press Record of Books in Print* (20th Edition, 1991-92). avg. price, paper: $9.95. Discounts: 40%+ depending on quantity. 128pp; 6×9. Reporting time: 3 months. Payment: 10% of gross-quarterly. Copyrights for author.

CIN-DAV, Inc., David L. Dodge, Route 1, Box 778, Starke, FL 32091, 904-964-5370; 904-392-1631. 1990. Photos, interviews, criticism, reviews, music, non-fiction. avg. press run 3M. Pub'd 1 title 1990; expects 1 title 1991, 2 titles 1992. 1 title listed in the *Small Press Record of Books in Print* (20th Edition, 1991-92). avg. price, paper: $14.95. Discounts: bulk. 384pp; 6×9. Copyrights for author.

CINEASTE MAGAZINE, Gary Crowdus, Dan Georgakas, Karen Jaehne, Robert Sklar, Leonard Quart, Tina Margolis, Advertising Rep., 200 Park Avenue South, New York, NY 10003, 212-982-1241. 1967. Articles, photos, interviews, satire, criticism, reviews, letters. "Offers a social & political perspective on the cinema—everything from the latest hollywood flicks & the American independent scene to political thrillers from Europe and revolutionary cinema from the Third World. Query before submitting." circ. 7M. 4/yr. Pub'd 4 issues 1990; expects 4 issues 1991, 4 issues 1992. sub. price: $15 (institutions $30); per copy: $5; sample: $5. Back issues: $4 to subscribers/$5 to others. Discounts: 25%. 64pp; 8½×11; of. Reporting time: 2-3 weeks. Payment: reviews $12, articles $20 and up. Not copyrighted. Pub's reviews: 53 in 1990. §Social, political perspective on all aspects of movies. Ads: $400/$300.

CIP Communications (see also CONSTRUCTION COMPUTER APPLICATIONS NEWSLETTER (CCAN)), Royal H. Maul, 6585 Commerce Blvd, Suite E-292, Rohnert Park, CA 94928, 707-792-2223. 1 title listed in the *Small Press Record of Books in Print* (20th Edition, 1991-92).

Circa Press, Robert Brooks, PO Box 482, Lake Oswego, OR 97034, 503-636-7241. 1985. Fiction, non-fiction. "We are looking for nonfiction titles that are written on serious subjects for adults. We are especially interested in new ideas, new information and works that make difficult, but important, topics more easily understood." avg. press run 2M. Pub'd 2 titles 1990; expects 3 titles 1991, 4 titles 1992. 6 titles listed in the *Small Press Record of Books in Print* (20th Edition, 1991-92). avg. price, cloth: $14.95; paper: $9.95. Discounts: trade: prepaid 1-10 copies 40%; 2-5 25%, 6-10 30%, 11-25 40%, 26-75 45%, 76-99 50%, 100+ 55%. 200pp; 5½×8½; of. Reporting time: 2 months. Payment: no advance; royalty about 10% of list price, terms negotiable. Copyrights for author. NWABP.

Circumpolar Press, Jane Niebergall, Box 221955, Anchorage, AK 99522, 907-248-7323. 1990. Fiction, articles, non-fiction. "We focus upon Alaskan educational materials. We will produce a broader scope of titles (Early Action (pre-school) and Old Believer Cookbook). We are looking for Alaskan material for teachers and student level K-12." avg. press run 1M-5M. Expects 4 titles 1991, 10 titles 1992. 2 titles listed in the *Small Press Record of Books in Print* (20th Edition, 1991-92). avg. price, paper: $7-$12. Discounts: 10%-20%-30%-40%. 100-300pp; 5×7, 8½×11; †of. Reporting time: within 1 quarter. Payment: per individual contract. Copyrights for author.

Citeaux Commentarii Cistercienses (see also CITEAUX: COMMENTARII CISTERCIENSES), Fr. Jean-Francois Holthof, c/o Br. Anthony Weber, Abbey of the Genesee, Piffard, NY 14533. 1950. Articles, art, photos, reviews, non-fiction. "Publishes scholarly books pertaining to the history, art, law, etc. of the Cistercian monastic order. French address: Abbaye de Citeaux, 21700 Nuits-St. Georges, France." avg. press run 800. Expects 1 title 1991, 1 title 1992. avg. price, cloth: $55. 375pp; of. Reporting time: 6 months or less. Payment: 5%, or in free copies of book if author wishes. Does not copyright for author.

CITEAUX: COMMENTARII CISTERCIENSES, Citeaux Commentarii Cistercienses, Fr. Jean-Francois Holthof, Editor-in-Chief, c/o Br. Anthony Weber, Abbey of the Genesee, Piffard, NY 14533. 1950. Articles, art, photos, reviews, non-fiction. "Scholarly journal, publishing articles, notes, book reviews on all aspects of Cistercian monastic life. French address: Abbaye de Citeaux, 21700 Nuits-St. Georges, France." circ. 500+. 2/yr. Pub'd 2 issues 1990; expects 2 issues 1991, 2 issues 1992. sub. price: $38. Back issues: 15. 200pp; 16cm X 24.5cm; of. Reporting time: depends on when submitted; editorial board meets July & January. Payment: none. Copyrighted, reverts to author. Pub's reviews. §All aspects of Cistercian life, history, literature, law, arts, etc.

City Lights Books (see also CITY LIGHTS JOURNAL), Lawrence Ferlinghetti, Nancy J. Peters, Robert Sharrard, Attn: Bob Sharrard, Editor, 261 Columbus Avenue, San Francisco, CA 94133, 415-362-8193. 1955. Poetry, fiction, articles, non-fiction. avg. press run 3M. Pub'd 5 titles 1990; expects 5 titles 1991. 73 titles listed in the *Small Press Record of Books in Print* (20th Edition, 1991-92). avg. price, cloth: $10.95; paper: $4.00. 100pp; size varies; of. Reporting time: 4 weeks. Payment: varies. Copyrights for author. COSMEP.

CITY LIGHTS JOURNAL, City Lights Books, Lawrence Ferlinghetti, Nancy J. Peters, Robert Sharrard, 261 Columbus Avenue, San Francisco, CA 94133, 415-362-8193. "1 issue every 2 years, infrequent." No subscriptions available.

City Miner Books, Michael Helm, P.O. Box 176, Berkeley, CA 94701, 415-841-1511. 1976. Fiction. "Bias toward Northern California writers" avg. press run 2.5M. Expects 2 titles 1991, 2 titles 1992. 11 titles listed in the *Small Press Record of Books in Print* (20th Edition, 1991-92). avg. price, cloth: $14; paper: $7.95. Discounts: 1-4 books 20%, 5-9 40%, 10-24 42%, 25-49 43%, 50+ 45%. 175pp; 8½x5½, 6x9; of. Reporting time: 6 weeks. Payment: graduated royalty, 10-25% of income received. Copyrights for author.

City Publications Ltd. (see also ECONOMIC AFFAIRS), Robert Miller, Editor, 15 Mantilla Road, London SW17 8DY, United Kingdom, 01-767-1005. 1980. Music. "Studies of neglected composers or of neglected aspects of the work of better-known composers. Also collections of the writings of composers and other musicians" avg. press run 2.5M-3M. Pub'd 5 titles 1990; expects 2 titles 1991, 10 titles 1992. avg. price, cloth: $25; paper: $10. Discounts: 30/35%; more for bulk purchases. US distributors for some titles. 250pp; 5½x8¼; of. Reporting time: 2-3 months. Payment: no advance; 10% author's royalties on all standard sales. Copyrights for author if desired.

CITY RANT, McOne Press, John McElhenney, PO Box 50174, Austin, TX 78763, 512-477-2269. 1989. Poetry, fiction, letters, long-poems, non-fiction. "Caffeine stimulated prose and poetry dealing intensely with city-life-stress-work-blues. Emotion/image packed stuff only. SASE for guidelines" circ. 200-400. 6/yr. Pub'd 6 issues 1990; expects 6 issues 1991, 6 issues 1992. sub. price: $6; per copy: $1; sample: $1. Discounts: 40% seller. 40pp; 5½x8½; mi. Reporting time: 2-3 weeks. Payment: 2 copies and 50% on extra copies. Copyrighted, reverts to author. Ads: $100/$60.

City Spirit Publications (see also CONNECTICUT NATURALLY; NEW JERSEY NATURALLY; NEW YORK NATURALLY), Jerome Rubin, Editor-in-Chief & Publisher; Kenny Schiff, Managing Editor, 590 Pacific Street, Brooklyn, NY 11217, 718-857-1545. 1984. Poetry, articles, photos, interviews, non-fiction. "Wide range of material relating to a natural life-style, focus on New York, New Jersey, and Connecticut. We publish 3 annual books in January (formerly 1)." avg. press run 100M. Pub'd 1 title 1990; expects 3 titles 1991, 3 titles 1992. avg. price, paper: $3.50. 5x8; web press. Reporting time: 2 weeks. Payment: varies. Does not copyright for author.

Cityhill Publishing, Bob Briggs, 4600 Christian Fellowship Road, Columbia, MO 65203, (314) 445-8567. 1986. Non-fiction. avg. press run 5M. Expects 2 titles 1991, 4-6 titles 1992. 19 titles listed in the *Small Press Record of Books in Print* (20th Edition, 1991-92). avg. price, paper: $6.95-$8.95; other: $12.95-$14.95. Discounts: Distributor: 55%, Retail: 40%. 150pp; 5⅜x8⅜; of. Reporting time: 8 weeks. Payment: annual, negotiated rate. Does not copyright for author. CBA.

THE CIVIL ABOLITIONIST, Oak Tree, Bina Robinson, Box 26, Swain, NY 14884, 607-545-6213. 1983. Poetry, articles, art, photos, cartoons, interviews, criticism, reviews, letters, news items, non-fiction. "A 1-year subscription to *The CIVIS Report* for $15 also includes occasional *Civis Bullet-ins* which usually run over 60 pages includes *The Civil Abolitionist* which is $5 by itself" circ. 2M. 4/yr. Pub'd 4 issues 1990; expects 4 issues 1991, 4 issues 1992. sub. price: $15 with Civis Report; per copy: $1; sample: $1. Back issues: $1. 8pp; 8½x11; †of. Payment: none. Not copyrighted. Pub's reviews: 9 in 1990. §Human health in relation to animal experimentation.

THE CIVIL WAR NEWS, C. Peter Jorgensen, PO Box C, Arlington, MA 02174-0001, 617-646-2010. 1974. Articles, photos, interviews, reviews, letters, news items. "Articles and photos on authors, collectors, book reviews, research and preservation projects, coming events listing related to American Civil War" 9/yr. Pub'd 9 issues 1990; expects 9 issues 1991, 9 issues 1992. sub. price: $15, $21 overseas; per copy: 50¢; sample: $2. Back issues: $2. Discounts: agent 10%. 40pp; 10x16; of. Reporting time: 1 month. Payment: minimal. Not copyrighted. Pub's reviews: 90+ in 1990. §American Civil War Era. Ads: $5 col. inch, SAU column widths volume and frequency discounts.

CJE NEWSLETTER (Newsletter of the Coalition for Jobs & the Environment), Rob Conrad, Coordinator, 114 Court Street, PO Box 645, Abingdon, VA 24210-0645, 703-628-8996. 1990. Interviews, letters, news items, non-fiction. "We are a small, heavily-edited bi-monthly. We have regular columns entitled 'Action Needed,' 'Calendar,' 'Reports from Member Groups,' 'Resources,' which take up most of the space. We are always interested in hearing of successful methods for pollution reduction or elimination." circ. 300. 6/yr. Pub'd 3 issues 1990; expects 6 issues 1991, 6 issues 1992. sub. price: $6 individuals, $12 groups, free w/membership; per copy: $1; sample: one 29¢ stamp. Back issues: $1 per issue. Discounts: on request, depends who asks. 10pp; 8½x11; high-speed xerox. Reporting time: 4 weeks. Payment: none, low budget, volunteer organization. Not copyrighted. Pub's reviews: 19 in 1990. §Alternative economics, democratic reform & education, pollution reduction and elimination. Ads: none.

Clamshell Press, D.L. Emblen, 160 California Avenue, Santa Rosa, CA 95405. 1973. "We do not read unsolicited mss." avg. press run 250-500. Pub'd 1 title 1990; expects 2 titles 1991, 2 titles 1992. 6 titles listed in the *Small Press Record of Books in Print* (20th Edition, 1991-92). avg. price, paper: $15. 48pp; 5½x8½; †lp. Copyrights for author.

Claridge Press (see also SALISBURY REVIEW), Roger Scruton, Jessica Douglas-Home, 6 Linden Gardens, London W2 4ES, United Kingdom. 1987. Criticism, non-fiction. avg. press run 1M. Pub'd 9 titles 1990; expects 6 titles 1991. 11 titles listed in the *Small Press Record of Books in Print* (20th Edition, 1991-92). avg. price, cloth: £12.95; paper: £8.95. Discounts: bookstores 20%, 33% 2+ books. 200pp; size A5; of. Payment: 10% of income. Copyrights for author.

CLARITY, J.M. Sprague, 26 Valleyside, Hemel Hempstead, Herts. HP1 2LN, England. 1968. Poetry, articles, criticism, reviews, letters. "Length of material approx. 750-2500 words. Aimed at intelligent non-specialist who is interested in Christianity; interdenominational, covering a broad spectrum of views & attitudes. *Clarity* is the house magazine of the MENSA Christian Group, for MENSA members who are interested in Christianity. Contributors are mainly group members, but outside contributors & subscribers are welcome" circ. 200+. 6/yr. Pub'd 6 issues 1990; expects 6 issues 1991. sub. price: £3.50 UK, £4 US surface mail; $12 US air mail; sample: $7.50. 24pp; 1/2 flscp; †photocopy. Copyrighted. Pub's reviews: 9 in 1990. §Religious, social science, psychology. MCG.

Clarity Press, 3277 Roswell Road NE, Suite 469, Atlanta, GA 30305. 1984. Fiction, non-fiction. "Prefer nonfiction on political, social, minority, and human rights issues." avg. press run 3M. Pub'd 3 titles 1990; expects 2 titles 1991, 4 titles 1992. 8 titles listed in the *Small Press Record of Books in Print* (20th Edition, 1991-92). Discounts: 40% bookstores, 20% jobbers and college bookstores. 150pp; 5½x8½; of. Reporting time: 2 months. Payment: negotiable. Copyrights for author. COSMEP, PMA.

Arthur H. Clark Co., Robert A. Clark, PO Box 14707, Spokane, WA 99214, 509-928-9540. 1902. Non-fiction. "Documentary source material and non-fiction dealing with the history of the Western U.S." avg. press run 750-1.5M. Pub'd 7 titles 1990; expects 10 titles 1991, 9 titles 1992. 10 titles listed in the *Small Press Record of Books in Print* (20th Edition, 1991-92). avg. price, cloth: $30. Discounts: 1-2 copies 15%; 3-4 25%; 5+ 40%. 250pp; 6¼x9½; of, lp. Reporting time: 2 months. Payment: 10% generally. Copyrights for author.

CLASSIC IMAGES, Sue Laimans, PO Box 809, Muscatine, IA 52761. 1962. Articles, art, photos, cartoons, interviews, criticism, reviews, letters, news items. "No standard." circ. 3M. 12/yr. Pub'd 12 issues 1990; expects 12 issues 1991, 12 issues 1992. sub. price: $27.50; per copy: $3.50; sample: $3. Back issues: $3.50 each. 80pp; 9⅛x12⅞; †of. Payment: none. Copyrighted. Pub's reviews: approx. 120 in 1990. §Film, video tape, books. Ads: $132/$72/classified $3.50 1st 20 words, 15¢ per word after 20.

Classic Theatre For Children, Publishers, Forrest M. Stone, 225 West 83rd Street #11A, New York, NY 10024-4903. 1986. Plays. "Faithful adaptations of classic plays, written for teachers and students with little experience of directing or acting. Uses drama/theatre to teach language arts and social studies. Special features include: easy-to-follow diagrams suggesting actors' movements; zero-budget staging ideas; open-ended questions that improve problem-solving skills. Teacher's edition contains: ideas for language arts and social studies projects; alternatives to full staging. These textbooks are a lively introduction to the original classics and their history. Recommended for grades 5-12 and Gifted Programs" Pub'd 10 titles 1990. 6 titles listed in the *Small Press Record of Books in Print* (20th Edition, 1991-92). avg. price, paper: $9.95 Director's edition, $5.95 Actor's edition. 8½x11.

CLASSICAL ANTIQUITY, University of California Press, Tom Habinek, Univ of California Press, 2120 Berkeley Way, Berkeley, CA 94720, 415-642-4191. 1981. Non-fiction. "Editorial address: Department of Classics, Univ. of CA, Berkeley, CA 94720." circ. 650. 2/yr. Pub'd 2 issues 1990; expects 2 issues 1991, 2 issues 1992. sub. price: $24 indiv.; $48 instit. (+ $3 foreign postage); per copy: $12 indiv.; $24 instit.; sample: free. Back issues: $12 indiv.; $24 instit. Discounts: 10% foreign subs., 30% one-time orders 10+, standing orders (bookstores): 1-99 40%, 100+ 50%. 200pp; 7x10; of. Reporting time: 3 months. Payment: none. Copyrighted, does not revert to author. Ads: $200/$120.

THE CLASSICAL OUTLOOK, Richard A. LaFleur, Department of Classics, The University of Georgia, Athens, GA 30602, 404-542-9257. 1923. Poetry, articles, criticism, reviews. circ. 4M. 4/yr. Pub'd 4 issues 1990; expects 4 issues 1991, 4 issues 1992. sub. price: $25; per copy: $7.50; sample: $7.50. Back issues: same. 34pp; 8½x11; †lp. Reporting time: 6 months. Payment: complimentary copies and/or offprints. Copyrighted, does not revert to author. Pub's reviews: 30 in 1990. §Latin, classical Greek, classical studies. Ads: $210/$135. American Classical League.

Clay Press, Inc. (see also LLAMAS MAGAZINE), PO Box 100, Herald, CA 95638, 916-448-1668.

Claycomb Press, Inc., Mary H. Claycomb, President & Publisher, PO Box 70822, Chevy Chase, MD 20813-0822, 301-656-1057. 1985. Fiction, non-fiction. avg. press run 3M. Expects 8 titles 1991, 8-10 titles 1992. 10 titles listed in the *Small Press Record of Books in Print* (20th Edition, 1991-92). avg. price, cloth: $15.95; paper: $8.95. Discounts: 1 copy - 20%; 2-4 - 30%; 5-24 - 40%; 25 or more - 44%. 288pp; 5½x8½; of.

119

Reporting time: varies - 6 weeks. Payment: royalties standard - 10% on first 5,000 copies; to 12.5% to 15%; v. small advance. Copyrights for author. Women's National Book Assn. (WNBA) Washington Chapter, c/o Diane Ullins, Pres. 3508 Leland Street., Chevy Chase, MD 20815; Small Press Center, New York City.

CLEANING BUSINESS MAGAZINE, Cleaning Consultants Serv's, Inc., Martha Ireland, Editor; William R. Griffin, PO Box 1273, Seattle, WA 98111-1273, (206) 622-4241. 1980. Poetry, articles, art, photos, cartoons, interviews, news items. "A small business quarterly written specifically for self-employed cleaning and maintenance contractors. We buy articles on related technical and management subjects. Sample issue and submissions guidelines, send $3." circ. 5M. 4/yr. Pub'd 4 issues 1990; expects 4 issues 1991, 4 issues 1992. sub. price: $20; per copy: $5; sample: $3. Back issues: $5 each if available. Discounts: none on singles; multiples-25%. 72pp; 7×8½; †of. Reporting time: 4-6 weeks. Payment: to $90. Copyrighted, rights revert in some cases. Pub's reviews: 30 in 1990. §Cleaning, maintenance, self-employers, supervision, marketing. Ads: $215/$107. NWBPA, ASCR, BOMA.

Cleaning Consultants Serv's, Inc. (see also CLEANING BUSINESS MAGAZINE), William R. Griffin, PO Box 1273, Seattle, WA 98111-1273. 1976. Articles, non-fiction. "Formerly *Service Business*. Publish books on cleaning, maintenance and self-employment. Both management and technical subjects. Especially interested in technical side of fire, damage, and building contents restoration (at this time). Also computer rooms, clean rooms, high tech manufacturing. Also purchase articles for quarterly publication, cleaning business magazine." avg. press run 2M-5M. Pub'd 4 titles 1990; expects 6 titles 1991, 2 titles 1992. †of. Reporting time: 4-6 weeks. Payment: 5-15%. NWBPA.

Cleis Press, Frederique Delacoste, Felice Newman, PO Box 8933, Pittsburgh, PA 15221. 1980. Fiction, non-fiction. "—Aquisitions Editior (Po Box 14684, San Francisco CA 94114)—*Cleis Press* operates from two offices - East and West. All mss & queries regarding mss should be sent to Cleis West. Cleis East address is above. Cleis West address: PO Box 14684, San Francisco, CA 94114. Full-length book manuscripts only. Please include SASE w/complete ms. or sample chapter(s). Welcome manuscripts or query letters from feminist writers. Cleis Press is committed to publishing progressive nonfiction and fiction by women. Cleis East now handles all orders, marketing, and publicity. Cleis West handles acquisitions" avg. press run 5M. Pub'd 5 titles 1990; expects 7 titles 1991, 7 titles 1992. 26 titles listed in the *Small Press Record of Books in Print* (20th Edition, 1991-92). avg. price, cloth: $24.95; paper: $9.95. Discounts: standard bookstore & distributor, please write for terms. 150-300pp; 5½×8½; of. Reporting time: 2-3 months. Payment: please write us for information on royalty. Copyrights for author.

Cleveland State Univ. Poetry Center, Nuala Archer, Poetry Center Director; Leonard Trawick, Editor; David Evett, Dept English, Cleveland State Univ, Cleveland, OH 44115, 216-687-3986. 1962. Poetry, concrete art. "1 local (Ohio) poetry series—46 published since 1971—24 pp-100. 2 national series, 32 published since 1971; have already published Stuart Friebert, Thomas Lux, Stratis Haviaris, David Young, Jan Haagensen, Mark Jarman, Marilyn Krysl, Jeanne Walker, Valery Nash, Lynn Luria-Sukenick, Ralph Burns, J.B. Goodenough, Martha Collins, Roger Mitchell, Robert Hill Long, Trish Reeves, Stephen Tapscott, Sarah Provost, Thylias Moss. Query before submitting. Submit only Dec.-Feb. each year. $10 reading fee for national series. $1000 prize for best manuscript each year. About 50-100 pp. Free catalog on request" avg. press run 500 local series, 1M national series. Pub'd 4 titles 1990; expects 4 titles 1991, 4 titles 1992. 67 titles listed in the *Small Press Record of Books in Print* (20th Edition, 1991-92). avg. price, cloth: $12; paper: $8; other: $4 chapbooks. Discounts: 40% for bulk orders. National series distributed by National Association of College Stores, Oberlin, Ohio 44074; Bookslinger, 213 East Fourth Street, St. Paul, MN 55101; Spring Church Book Co., PO Box 127, Spring Church, PA 15686. 32-100pp; size varies; †of. Reporting time: 4-6 months. Payment: national series 100 copies, local series 50 copies + $300. Copyrights for author.

CLIENT MAGAZINE, JB & Me Publishing, Jack Bernstein, Publisher; Marilyn Elkind, Managing Editor, PO Box 3879, Manhattan Beach, CA 90266. 1986. Articles, interviews, news items. "This publication is for advertising agencies, print and broadcast media, and corporate marketing personnel" circ. 10M. 6/yr. Pub'd 6 issues 1990; expects 6 issues 1991, 6 issues 1992. sub. price: $25; per copy: $5; sample: $5. Back issues: $5 per issue. Discounts: none. 24pp; 8½×10½; of. Reporting time: varies. Payment: none. Copyrighted, rights revert on request. Pub's reviews. §Sales/business travel/marketing. Ads: $900/$500/$350 1/3 p./$250 1/4 p./$125 1/8 p.

Cliffhanger Press, Nancy Chirich, P.O. Box 29527, Oakland, CA 94604-9527, 415-763-3510. 1985. Fiction. "Manuscripts will not be returned without adequate postage affixed to adequate wrapping. Mystery and suspense; book-length mystery novels." avg. press run 3M. Pub'd 2 titles 1990; expects 2 titles 1991, 2 titles 1992. 9 titles listed in the *Small Press Record of Books in Print* (20th Edition, 1991-92). avg. price, paper: $9.95. Discounts: 40% + freight retail stores; 45% + freight to jobbers and wholesalers, prepaid; 15% free shipping to libraries. 208pp; 5½×8½; of. Reporting time: immediately on query or sample chaps with SASE, could be a year with unsolicited full manuscripts, solicited mss 2 months. Payment: 8% of list price with paperbacks, no advances. Copyrights for author. NCBPA (Northern California Book Publicists Association), WNBA, COSMEP, Mystery Writers of America.

THE CLIMBING ART, The FreeSolo Press, David Mazel, Editor; Pat Ament, Contributing Editor; John Gill, Contributing Editor; Barry Greer, Contributing Editor, PO Box 816, Alamosa, CO 81101, 719-589-5579. 1986. Poetry, fiction, articles, art, photos, cartoons, interviews, satire, criticism, reviews, letters, parts-of-novels, long-poems, collages, news items, non-fiction. "We will consider material of any length, and will even serialize book-length mss. We publish only material that is well written and of interest to those who live in, travel in, or climb mountains. Recent contributors include Reg Saner, David Craig and Grant McConnell" circ. 1M. 4/yr. Pub'd 4 issues 1990; expects 4 issues 1991, 4 issues 1992. sub. price: $10; per copy: $2.75; sample: $2.75. Back issues: inquire. Discounts: 1-4 copies 20%, 5-24 40%, 25-49 43%, 50-99 46%, 100+ 50%; jobbers up to 55%. 32pp; 8½x11; of. Reporting time: 2 months. Payment: up to $200. Copyrighted, reverts to author. Pub's reviews: 5 in 1990. §The mountains, mountaineering and rock-climbing, mountain-area histories, biographies of figures associated with the mountains. Ads: $100/$60/$3.50 per column inch.

CLINTON ST., David Milholland, Editor, Box 3588, Portland, OR 97208, 503-222-6039. 1979. Fiction, articles, cartoons, interviews, satire, non-fiction. "The *Clinton St.* features an eclectic blend of writing on politics, art, and the times we live in. We are especially interested in writing which explores intense personal experience and offers ways for others to understand and relect on it. Most of our writers come from or live in the Western U.S. though we're looking for the best work we can obtain from any source" circ. 50M. 6/yr. Pub'd 4 issues 1990; expects 6 issues 1991, 6 issues 1992. sub. price: $12/6 issues; per copy: $3; sample: $3. Back issues: inquire for costs. 48pp; 11x17. Reporting time: 2 weeks-2 months. Payment: range is from $40-$150. Copyrighted, reverts to author. Pub's reviews: 8-10 in 1990. §Contemporary political issues, sex and sexism, writing about the Western U.S., small/med. press novels, humor, U.S. involvements abroad. Ads: $1000/$600/write for ad rates and contract discounts.

CLIPS FROM BEAR'S HOME MOVIES, Dancing Bear Productions, Craig Ellis, c/o Dancing Bear Productions, PO Box 733, Concord, MA 01742, 617-369-5592. 1985. "See primary listing at Dancing Bear Productions for further information" circ. 500. Irregular. sample price: $4.

CLOCKWATCH REVIEW, Clockwatch Review Press, James Plath, Editor & Publisher, James Plath, English Department, Illinois Wesleyan University, Bloomington, IL 61702, 309-556-3352. 1983. Poetry, fiction, art, interviews, music. "*Clockwatch* wants poetry to 32 lines, fiction to 4M words. In any case, we look for strong voice and characterization which is believable and colorful without being cliched. We seek material which can straddle two worlds: the literary and the popular. Recent contributors include Greg Kuzma, Rita Dove, Ellen Munnicutt, Stuart Dybek, Rosellen Brown, and Peter Wild. Our emphasis is on excellence, but we prefer upbeat and the offbeat, or things which do what all art attempts: to leave a lingering shadow of learning within a work which entertains." circ. 1.4M. 2/yr. Pub'd 1 issue 1990; expects 2 issues 1991, 2 issues 1992. sub. price: $8-$10; per copy: $4-$5; sample: $4-$5. Back issues: $5 each. Discounts: Wholesalers, 50% plus shipping; Retailers, 40%. 80pp; 5½x8½; of. Reporting time: 2 weeks; to 2 months if under serious consideration. Payment: 3 copies, small cash awards—presently $50 fiction, $10 poetry. Copyrighted, reverts to author. Ads: $300/$150. CCLM, ILPA.

Clockwatch Review Press (see also CLOCKWATCH REVIEW), James Plath, Department of English, Illinois Wesleyan University, Bloomington, IL 61702, 309-556-3352. 1983. Poetry, fiction. "Our first book title, *Under a Cat's-Eye Moon*, poems by Martha M. Vertreace, will appear in Fall, 1991. Thereafter, we will continue to seek out and publish quality fiction and poetry manuscripts. At the present time, we will only consider material from writers who have published extensively in literary magazines. Query first, with SASE." avg. press run 1.5M. Expects 1 title 1991, 1-2 titles 1992. 1 title listed in the *Small Press Record of Books in Print* (20th Edition, 1991-92). avg. price, paper: $5.95. Discounts: 50% wholesale, 40% classroom. 80pp; 6x9; of. Reporting time: 1-2 months on queries. Payment: 100 copies plus 10% after expenses have been met. Copyrights for author. CLMP, ILPA.

Clothespin Fever Press, Jenny Wrenn, Carolyn Weathers, 5529 N. Figueroa, Los Angeles, CA 90042, 213-254-1373. 1985. Poetry, fiction, art, photos, satire, long-poems. "We are interested in work by lesbians who are usually turned down by mainstream publishers who say 'We like it but it's not mainstream,' and feminist publishers who say, 'We like it but it's not issue oriented.' Profit is obviously not the prevailing raison d'etre of Clothespin Fever Press. Instead, the motive of our press is to gain exposure for quality work by lesbians. Each work is carefully designed for a limited edition printing faithful to the author's intention. *Leaving Texas, A Memoir* by Carolyn Weathers, *Self-Portraits: Viewing Myself as an Adult Child of an Alcoholic* by Jenny Wrenn 1986, *Shitkickers and other Texas Stories* by Carolyn Weathers 1987. Planned for 1988: lesbian anthology, *A Dyke's Bike Repair Handbook* by Jill Taylor, *Crazy* by Carolyn Weathers. Please no poems or books on AIDS." avg. press run 1M. Pub'd 4 titles 1990; expects 2 titles 1991, 3 titles 1992. 11 titles listed in the *Small Press Record of Books in Print* (20th Edition, 1991-92). avg. price, paper: $8.95. Discounts: 40% to bookstores. Pages vary; 5½x7¼; of. Reporting time: 4-6 weeks. Payment: in copies or 10% royalty. Copyrights for author. COSMEP.

CLOUDLINE, Wind Vein Press, Scott Preston, PO Box 462, Ketchum, ID 83340, 208-788-3704. 1985.

Poetry, fiction, art, collages. *"Cloudline* is interested in material that deals primarily with the contradiction of man's presence in the natural world, especially as it affects life in the Western U.S. Our next issue will deal with the problem of maintaining the integrity of the land while making a living off it. I like and use a number of styles, but prefer work that is informed with an immediacy of voice-I do not care for academically contrived verse forms as found in *The New Yorker*. Recent contributors include: Gary Snyder, Keith Wilson, Drummond Hadley, Barbara Einzig. I like work from the N. Rockies/Intermountain Region" circ. 300. Published every other year. Expects 1 issue 1991. price per copy: $6; sample: $6. Discounts: due to the high quality of the book's production, we can only offer 20% on orders of 3 or more copies. 56pp; 7×9; of. Reporting time: 2-3 months. Payment: 2 or 3 copies, depending on amount of work accepted. Copyrighted, reverts to author. §The West, especially alternative western literatures: Native American, Immigrant.

Clover Press (see also GREEN'S MAGAZINE), David Green, Box 3236, Regina, Saskatchewan S4P 3H1, Canada. 1975. "Capable of limited-run production; type by compositor; no reduction capability; noncoated stock. Will not undertake distribution except in conjunction with *Green's Magazine*. Mail, art extra." avg. press run 1M. Pub'd 2 titles 1990; expects 1 title 1991, 2 titles 1992. 12 titles listed in the *Small Press Record of Books in Print* (20th Edition, 1991-92). avg. price, paper: $3. 60pp; size up to 11×14 (full sheet); †of. Reporting time: 8 weeks. Payment: negotiable. Copyrights for author.

CLUBHOUSE, Elaine Trumbo, Your Story Hour, PO Box 15, Berrien Springs, MI 49103, (616) 471-9009. 1951. Poetry, fiction, cartoons, non-fiction. "1,200 word limit, psychologically "up", can-do, kids-are-neat philosophy. No Halloween, Santa-elves, Easter-bunny-eggs, etc. material. Prefer action-oriented stories in which kids are clever, wise, kind, etc. Religious backdrop, but not overtly stated. Age group 9-14 years old." circ. 10M. 6/yr. Pub'd 5 issues 1990; expects 6 issues 1991, 6 issues 1992. sub. price: $5; sample: free with SASE for 3 oz. Discounts: none. 32pp; 6×9; web. Reporting time: 4-8 weeks. Payment: $30-$35 stories, $10-$12 cartoons, puzzles, $10 poems. Copyrighted, reverts to author. No ads.

The Clyde Press, Catherine Harris Ainsworth, 373 Lincoln Parkway, Buffalo, NY 14216, 716-875-4713/834-1254. 1976. Fiction, non-fiction. "The Clyde Press has published collections of superstitions, jump rope verses, riddles, folktales and legends, calendar customs, games & lore, *American Folk Foods*, *Family Life of Young Americans*." avg. press run 1-2M. Pub'd 2 titles 1990; expects 1 title 1991, 2 titles 1992. 14 titles listed in the *Small Press Record of Books in Print* (20th Edition, 1991-92). avg. price, paper: $4 and $10. Discounts: 40%; postage paid in U.S.; for 2 or more books, 40%. 200-224pp; 5½×8½, 8½×11; of, lp. Reporting time: no delay. Payment: special arrangements. Copyrights for author.

CNL/WORLD REPORT, Griffon House Publications/Bagehot Council, PO Box 81, Whitestone, NY 11357. 1974. "Part of CNL membership" circ. 1M. 1/yr. Pub'd 1 issue 1990; expects 1 issue 1991, 1 issue 1992. sub. price: $35 USA, $45 others, with membership to Council on National Literatures; per copy: $15 + $2 p&h; sample: same. Back issues: same. Discounts: 10% agencies only, only on membership dues. 16-24pp; 5½×8½; of. Reporting time: 2-4 months. Payment: 6 copies. Not copyrighted. Pub's reviews. §Multination critical perspectives. Multinational Literary Studies, Non-Western Studies, International Programs in Educations.

Coach House Press, Stan Bevington, David Young, Alberto Manquez, Gail Scott, Michael Ondaatje, Robert Wallace, Jason Sherman, Dennis Reid, David McFadden, Christopher Dewdney, 401 Huron Street (rear), Toronto, Ontario M5S 2G5, Canada, 416-979-7374. 1964. Poetry, fiction, art, photos, satire, parts-of-novels, long-poems, collages, plays. avg. press run 750. Pub'd 18 titles 1990; expects 10 titles 1991, 15 titles 1992. 73 titles listed in the *Small Press Record of Books in Print* (20th Edition, 1991-92). avg. price, cloth: $30; paper: $12.50. Discounts: Bookstores & the trade 1-4, 20%; 5 up, 40%; 5+ non-returnable, 50%; Libraries and institutions: 20%. 175pp; 6×9; †of. Reporting time: 10-12 weeks. Payment: 10% normally. Copyrights for author.

COACHING SLO'PITCH SOFTBALL, GDE Publications, PO Box 304, Lima, OH 45802.

COACHING VOLLEYBALL, Human Kinetics Pub. Inc., Scott Wikgren, Box 5076, Champaign, IL 61825-5076, 217-351-5076. 1987. Articles, interviews, reviews, letters, news items, non-fiction. circ. 3.2M. 6/yr. Pub'd 2 issues 1990; expects 6 issues 1991, 6 issues 1992. sub. price: $18 indiv., $30 instit.; per copy: $4 indiv., $6 instit.; sample: free. Back issues: $4 indiv., $6 instit. Discounts: 5%. 32pp; 8½×11; of. Reporting time: 2 months. Payment: none. Copyrighted. American Volleyball Coaches Association.

COACHING WOMEN'S BASKETBALL, Human Kinetics Pub. Inc., Scott Wikgren, Box 5076, Champaign, IL 61825-5076, 217-351-5076. 1987. Articles, interviews, reviews, letters, news items, non-fiction. circ. 3.2M. 6/yr. Pub'd 2 issues 1990; expects 6 issues 1991, 6 issues 1992. sub. price: indiv. $18, instit. $30; per copy: $4 indiv., $6 instit.; sample: free. Back issues: $4 indiv., $6 instit. Discounts: 5%. 32pp; 8½×11; of. Reporting time: 2 months. Payment: none. Copyrighted. Women's Basketball Coaches Association.

COALITION FOR PRISONERS' RIGHTS NEWSLETTER, Tracy Kimball, Mara Taub, PO Box 1911,

Santa Fe, NM 87504, 505-982-9520. 1976. Articles, cartoons, interviews, letters, news items, non-fiction. "Length of material: 250+/- words. Politically progressive. Half of each issue is excerpts of letters from prisoners" circ. 1.5M-2M. 12/yr. Pub'd 11 issues 1990; expects 12 issues 1991, 12 issues 1992. sub. price: $6, free to prisoners and their families; per copy: free; sample: free. Back issues: $1 an issue to non-prisoners. 8pp; 7×8½; lp. Reporting time: 6 weeks. Payment: none. Not copyrighted. Ads: none.

Coast to Coast Books Inc., Mark Beach, 2934 NE 16th Avenue, Portland, OR 97212-3345, 503-232-9772. 1979. Non-fiction. avg. press run 10M-20M. Pub'd 2 titles 1990. 4 titles listed in the *Small Press Record of Books in Print* (20th Edition, 1991-92). avg. price, paper: $25. 160pp; 8½×11; of. Reporting time: 4 weeks. Payment: higher than industry standards. Copyrights for author.

Coastline Publishing Company, Beatrice Hamilton, Henry Calero, PO Box 223062, Carmel, CA 93922, 625-9388. 1984. Fiction, non-fiction. "Book length novels or self-help. We are particularly interested in spiritual books, both fiction and non-fiction. By spiritual we do not mean religious, nor do we wish to receive any religious type material. Our recent release *The Sedona Trilogy* is a splendid example of the type of work we publish" avg. press run 5M. Expects 3 titles 1991, 6 titles 1992. 3 titles listed in the *Small Press Record of Books in Print* (20th Edition, 1991-92). avg. price, paper: $7.95. Discounts: 40% 1-4 copies. 150-200pp; 5½×8½. Reporting time: 2 months. Payment: to be discussed. Copyrights for author. Book Builders West.

COBBLESTONE: The History Magazine for Young People, Cobblestone Publishing, Inc., Beth Weston, Editor, 30 Grove Street, Peterborough, NH 03458, 603-924-7209. 1979. Poetry, fiction, articles, art, photos, interviews, reviews, music, plays, non-fiction. "Material must be written for children ages 8-14. Most articles do not exceed 1M words, write Editor for guidelines as we focus each issue on a particular theme" circ. 47M. 12/yr. Pub'd 12 issues 1990; expects 12 issues 1991, 12 issues 1992. sub. price: $22.95 + $6/yr for foreign and Canada; per copy: $3.95; sample: $3.95. Back issues: $3.95, annual set $44.95, includes slipcase and cumulative index. Discounts: 20% to agency; schools only: 5 subs @ $14 each/year. 48pp; 7×9; of. Reporting time: within 4-6 weeks. Payment: on publication. Copyrighted, *Cobblestone* buys all rights. Pub's reviews: 60-80 in 1990. §History books for children, ages 8-14, American history related only. No ads. Classroom Assoc./Ed Press.

Cobblestone Publishing, Inc. (see also COBBLESTONE: The History Magazine for Young People; FACES: The Magazine About People; CALLIOPE: World History for Young People), Carolyn P. Yoder, Editor-in-Chief, 30 Grove Street, Peterborough, NH 03458, 603-924-7209. avg. press run 8M-12M. 2 titles listed in the *Small Press Record of Books in Print* (20th Edition, 1991-92). 40-48pp; 7×9. Reporting time: 4-6 weeks (*Faces*). We own copyright.

The Cobham and Hatherton Press, Roderick Boyd Porter, 1770 The Huntington Building, Cleveland, OH 44115, 216-589-4960. 1979. Poetry, fiction, photos, satire, music, letters, long-poems. "We are interested in very high-quality material primarily in fiction and poetry, capable of high-quality fine press printing in classical formats, letterpress, and small runs (not usually more than 1500). Recent books: *The Persian Letters,* by George Lord Lyttelton; *Honor Bright,* by Sue Morgan; *What's Wrong,* by Laurie Blossom" avg. press run 500-1.5M. Pub'd 4 titles 1990; expects 6 titles 1991, 6 titles 1992. avg. price, cloth: $20-$75; paper: $15. Discounts: 20%. 120pp; 6×9; †lp. Reporting time: 6 months. Payment: negotiable. Copyrights for author.

CODA: The Jazz Magazine, Bill Smith, Box 87 Stn. J., Toronto, Ont. M4J4X8, Canada, 416-593-7230. 1958. Articles, photos, interviews, criticism, reviews, news items. "Our emphasis is on the art rather than the commerce of the music (i.e. we concentrate on non-commercialism) and we cover jazz of all styles and areas." circ. 4M. 6/yr. Expects 6 issues 1991. sub. price: $24 Canada & US, elsewhere $21CAN; per copy: $4; sample: $4. Back issues: $10 for 10. Discounts: agency discount (subscriptions only) 20%. 40pp; 8¼×10⅜; of. Reporting time: 1 month to 2 years. Payment: none. Not copyrighted. Pub's reviews: 22 in 1990. §Jazz, blues. Ads: $300/$160/75¢ (min. $15).

COFFEE & DONUTS, Douglas Firs, PO Box 6920, Alexandria, VA 22306. 1990. Articles, art, cartoons, criticism, reviews, letters, news items. "Most of our contributors use alias like 'Agent Cooper,' 'Diane,' 'Douglas Firs'" circ. 500-5M. 6/yr. Pub'd 3 issues 1990; expects 9-10 issues 1991. price per copy: 50¢; sample: 50¢, overseas $1. Back issues: 50¢. Discounts: fan club rate—5 of same issue for $2, overseas wholesale 10 for $3. 4pp; 8½×11; laser printed and photocopied. Reporting time: 2 weeks to 1 month, except art. Payment: free issues. Copyrighted, reverts to author. Pub's reviews: 1 in 1990. §Twin Peaks, Lynch, Frost, etc. *only*. Ads: none.

Coffee House Press, Allan Kornblum, 27 N. 4th Street, #400, Minneapolis, MN 55401, 612-338-0125. 1984. Poetry, fiction, art, long-poems. "Books may be ordered directly from publisher." avg. press run 1M. Pub'd 6 titles 1990; expects 10 titles 1991, 10 titles 1992. 82 titles listed in the *Small Press Record of Books in Print* (20th Edition, 1991-92). avg. price, cloth: $19.95; paper: $9.95; other: $10 handsewn chapbooks. Discounts: paperback: 2-5 copies, 25%; 6-9 copies, 35%, 10-49, 40%; 42% for 50 or more books (bookstores); libraries, standing orders 10%. 150pp; poetry 6×9, fiction 5½×8½; †lp, of. Reporting time: 8-12 weeks. Payment: 8% of list for trade books 10% of run for chapbooks. Copyrights for author. CBA MCBA.

COFFEEHOUSE POETS' QUARTERLY, Ray Foreman, Editor; Barbara Shukle, Associate Editor, PO Box 15123, San Luis Obispo, CA 93406, 805-541-4553. 1990. Poetry. "Prefer poems less than 45 lines, but will consider longer poems. We look for fresh imaginative free verse that shakes conventional thought, stirs the imagination and rattles the spirit. We like poems of everyday experience and psychological penetration that develop images, thoughts, and events without the use of cliches and contrived archaism. We don't like poems that say, 'guess what I mean,' or 'look what I know.'" circ. 300. 4/yr. Pub'd 1 issue 1990; expects 4 issues 1991, 4 issues 1992. sub. price: $8; per copy: $2; sample: $2. Back issues: $2 pp. Discounts: retail less 40% to trade. 40pp; 5½×8½; Xerography. Reporting time: 2 weeks. Payment: discount on quantities of 5. Not copyrighted.

COKEFISH, Ana Pine, PO Box 683, Long Valley, NJ 07853, 908-876-3824. 1990. Poetry, art, cartoons. "Limit poems to one page. Reading fee $1 per 3 poems. Do not want to see violence, religion, or rhyme. Recent contributors are Lyn Lifshin, Bukowski, Joy Walsh, Paul Weinman." circ. 150. 12/yr. Expects 12 issues 1991, 12 issues 1992. sub. price: $17; per copy: $4; sample: $4. 60pp; 8½×11. Reporting time: immediate to 1 week. Payment: copy. Not copyrighted. Ads: $15/$10/$5 by line.

Coker Publishing House, Editorial Board, 625 N. Riverside Drive, Grapevine, TX 76051, 817-488-6764. 1970. Fiction, non-fiction. avg. press run 5M. Pub'd 4 titles 1990; expects 6-10 titles 1991, 10-12 titles 1992. 6 titles listed in the *Small Press Record of Books in Print* (20th Edition, 1991-92). avg. price, cloth: $12.95; paper: $6.95. Discounts: 20% to retailers, 50% to jobbers. 150pp; 5½×8½. Reporting time: 4-6 weeks. Payment: negotiable. Copyrights for author.

COLD-DRILL, Cold-Drill Books, Tom Trusky, 1910 University Drive, Boise, ID 83725, 208-385-1999. 1970. Poetry, fiction, articles, art, photos, cartoons, parts-of-novels, plays, concrete art, non-fiction. "Material by Idaho residents and by non-residents. Submission deadline: December 1st for March 1 issue. Send xerox (we notify by Jan. 15 only if accepted)." circ. 500. 1/yr. Pub'd 1 issue 1990; expects 1 issue 1991, 1 issue 1992. sub. price: $8.50 (inc. p/h); per copy: $8.50 (inc. p/h); sample: $8.50 (inc. p/h). Back issues: same. Discounts: none. 150pp; 6×9; †of. Reporting time: by January 1, each year. Payment: copy of magazine. Copyrighted, reverts to author. CCLM, CSPA, RMCPA.

Cold-Drill Books (see also COLD-DRILL), Tom Trusky, Dept. of English, Boise State University, Boise, ID 83725. 1980. "Prior publication in *Cold-Drill Magazine* required. Interested in multiple artist's books editions." avg. press run 50-1M. Pub'd 1 title 1990; expects 1 title 1991. 3 titles listed in the *Small Press Record of Books in Print* (20th Edition, 1991-92). avg. price, cloth: varies; paper: varies. Discounts: 40%, no returns. Pages vary; size varies; †varies. Reporting time: 4 months. Payment: 25% on third printing. Copyrights for author.

Earl M Coleman Enterprises, Inc, Ellen Coleman, PO Box T, Crugers, NY 10521, 914-271-5124. 1977. Articles, reviews. "Publisher of original books in the social sciences, political science, human rights, and reprints in the fields of horticulture, maritime affairs, indian legal materials, and schorarly journals" avg. press run varies. Pub'd 10 titles 1990; expects 30 titles 1991. 33 titles listed in the *Small Press Record of Books in Print* (20th Edition, 1991-92). avg. price, cloth: varies. Discounts: contact publisher. Pages vary; size varies; of. Reporting time: 2-6 weeks. Payment: varies depending upon type of book.

COLLABORATION, Jeanne Korstange, Gordon Korstange, Sri Aurobindo Assn., PO Box 297, Saxtons River, VT 05154, 802-869-2789. 1974. Poetry, articles, art, photos, reviews, letters, news items. "*Collaboration* is devoted to the philosophy of Sri Aurobindo, with extracts from his works and relevant material by others. Also includes news of the city of Auroville and Sri Aurobindo centers around the world" circ. 1M. 3/yr. Pub'd 2 issues 1990; expects 2 issues 1991, 2 issues 1992. sub. price: by contribution ($12); per copy: $3; sample: free. Back issues: some available. 24pp; 8×10½; of. Reporting time: 2 weeks. Payment: copies. Copyrighted, reverts to author. Pub's reviews: 3 in 1990. §Relevant to Sri Aurobindo and his philosophy, and Auroville, futurology. No ads. COSMEP.

COLLAGES & BRICOLAGES, Marie-Jose Fortis, 212 Founders Hall, Clarion University of PA, Clarion, PA 16214, 814-226-2340. 1986. Poetry, fiction, articles, art, photos, interviews, satire, criticism, reviews, parts-of-novels, collages, plays, non-fiction. "Alternate address (best used during summer): PO Box 86, Clarion, PA 16214. Short plays only. Art must be in black and white. We try to be a forum for writers who produce high-quality, literary material; for authors (artists & writers) who are honest and uncompromising with their mode of expression. Recent contributors include Marilou Awiakta, Aisha Esche, and Karen Douglas" circ. 400. 1/yr. Pub'd 1 issue 1990; expects 1 issue 1991, 1 issue 1992. sub. price: $5; per copy: $5; sample: $5. Back issues: $2.50/copy. 130pp; 11×18; of. Reporting time: 2 weeks to 3 months. Payment: 2 copies/author. Copyrighted, reverts to author. Pub's reviews: 1 in 1990. §Fiction, poetry, criticism, literary magazines. Ads: on an exchange basis. CLMP.

124

COLLECTORS CLUB PHILATELIST, E.E. Fricks, Editor, 22 East 35th Street, New York, NY 10016, 212-683-0559. 1922. Articles, photos, interviews, reviews, news items, non-fiction. "Average single article 15 pages. Some extended articles continued to suceeding issues" circ. 3M. 6/yr. Pub'd 6 issues 1990; expects 6 issues 1991, 6 issues 1992. sub. price: $30; per copy: $5; sample: $5. Back issues: $5. Discounts: 40% to the trade for 5 or more. 80pp; 6½x9; of. Reporting time: 2-6 weeks. Payment: varies with length, content; average $200. Copyrighted, reverts to author by special arrangement only. Pub's reviews: 40 in 1990. §Stamp collecting (philately), history. Ads: $225/$125/ask for rate card. AAP.

COLLECTRIX, Alida Roochvarg, 389 New York Avenue, Huntington, NY 11743, 516-424-6479. 1982. "The complete reference guide to new books about antiques and collectibles. Fifty pages of annotated previews, by subject, of all new books, magazines, newsletters in every area of collecting. Feature articles, reviews, and a special section on out-of-print books. *Collectrix*: a recognized selection and reference resource for libraries: an essential tool for the advanced and beginning collector." circ. 1M. 3/yr. Pub'd 3 issues 1990; expects 3 issues 1991, 3 issues 1992. sub. price: $10; per copy: $4.50; sample: same. 30pp; 8x10; of. Pub's reviews: 546 in 1990. §Books about antiques and collectibles. Ads: $150/$100 15¢ a word.

COLLEGE ENGLISH, National Council of Teachers of English, James C. Raymond, Drawer AL, University of Alabama, Tuscaloosa, AL 35487, 205-348-6488. 1939. Poetry, articles, criticism, reviews, letters. circ. 16M. 8/yr. Pub'd 8 issues 1990; expects 8 issues 1991, 8 issues 1992. sub. price: $35, includes membership in NCTE, student rate $10.50; per copy: $4.50; sample: $4.50. Back issues: $4.50. 100pp; 7½x9½; of. Reporting time: 16 weeks. Payment: none. Copyrighted, reverts to author. Pub's reviews: 16 in 1990. §Literary theory, linguistic theory, theory of learning and pedagogy, history of English studies, studies of works of literature. Ads: $435/$280 one time.

Colonial Press, Carl Murray, Ken Hensley, Bradley Twitty, Poetry Editor, 3325 Burningtree Drive, Birmingham, AL 35226-2643. 1957. Poetry, fiction, non-fiction. "We solicit black authors, young poets, and do a number of scholarly works." avg. press run 500. Pub'd 7 titles 1990; expects 10 titles 1991, 15 titles 1992. 6 titles listed in the *Small Press Record of Books in Print* (20th Edition, 1991-92). avg. price, cloth: $14.95; paper: $7.50. Discounts: 40% trade, 50% jobber. 200pp; 5½x9; of. Reporting time: 6 months. Payment: negotiable. Copyrights for author.

COLOR WHEEL, 700 Elves Press, William Szostak, Frederick Moe, 4 Washington Court, Concord, NH 03301. 1990. Poetry, fiction, art, long-poems, collages, non-fiction. "We are interested in esoteric poetry, prose, artwork expressing spiritual or ecological themes. Some thematic webs might include: Native American spirituality, Goddess inspired writings, spiritual journeys, gnosticism, healing, meditation, creativity, mythology, ritual, Mother Earth, ecology, women's issues, men's issues, peace, anti-nuclear, anti-war themes. Length of material is open." circ. 300. 2/yr. Expects 2 issues 1991, 2 issues 1992. sub. price: $8; per copy: $5; sample: $5. 40pp; 8½x11; of. Reporting time: 4-6 weeks. Payment: copies. Copyrighted, reverts to author. Ads: $100/$75.

COLORADO NORTH REVIEW, Student Media Corporation, Mitchell Clute, Editor, University Center, University of Northern Colorado, Greeley, CO 80639, 303-351-1333. 1964. Poetry, fiction, art, photos, plays. "Preference toward original intaglio. On written request of author copyright is reassigned. Poetry, art, and fiction up to 20 typed pages. Brief biographical sketch requested." circ. 2.5M. 2/yr. Pub'd 2 issues 1990; expects 2 issues 1991, 2 issues 1992. sub. price: $8; per copy: $4; sample: $4. Discounts: none. 120-180pp; 6x9; of. Reporting time: 2-10 weeks. Payment: 2 copies. Copyrighted, reverts to author on written request. Ads: $100/$60. COSMEP, CLMP.

COLORADO REVIEW: A Journal of Contemporary Literature, Bill Tremblay, Poetry & General Editor; David Milofsky, Fiction Editor; Mary Crow, Translations Editor, 322 Eddy, English Department, Colorado State University, Fort Collins, CO 80523, 303-491-6428. 1955. Poetry, fiction, articles, interviews, criticism, reviews, parts-of-novels, long-poems. "We are attempting a new format: we will publish two issues per year including fiction, poetry, translations, interviews, reviews, and articles on contemporary literary culture. Our readers will consider mss. from Sept. 1 to April 1 each year. Allow until end of reading period for reply. *Colorado Review* is listed in both the *American Humanities Index* and the *Index of American Periodical Verse*. It is distributed nationally by Ingram Periodicals, Inc. and by DeBoers in the New York City area. Libraries may use Faxon or Ebsco" circ. 1M. 2/yr. Pub'd 2 issues 1990; expects 2 issues 1991, 2 issues 1992. 2 titles listed in the *Small Press Record of Books in Print* (20th Edition, 1991-92). sub. price: $9; per copy: $5; sample: $5. Back issues: $5. Discounts: 50% to distributors, 40% to bookstores, classes, other orders of 10 or more copies. 160pp; 6x9; of. Reporting time: 3 months. Payment: 2 copies plus one free subscription; $10 per printed page. Copyrighted, reverts to author. Pub's reviews: 6 in 1990. §Contemporary fiction & poetry. Ads: $100/$50. CCLM.

Colormore, Inc., Susan Koch, PO Box 111249, Carrollton, TX 75011-1249, 316-636-9326. 1987. Art, non-fiction. avg. press run 2.5M. Pub'd 1 title 1990; expects 4 titles 1991, 6 titles 1992. 6 titles listed in the

Small Press Record of Books in Print (20th Edition, 1991-92). avg. price, paper: $4.95. Discounts: 1-4 copies 20%, 5-14 40%, 15-49 42%, 50-99 43%, 100-499 45%, 500-749 46%, 750+ 48%. 32pp; 8½×11; of. Reporting time: 1 month. Payment: 8% of retail sales price. Copyrights for author. COSMEP, Publishers Marketing Association.

Columbia Publishing Company, Inc. (see also TRIBE: An American Gay Journal), Bernard Rabb, 234 East 25th Street, Baltimore, MD 21218, 301-366-7070. 1973. "Lengths vary. Trim sizes vary. We publish casebound and paperbound editions. Recent authors include William Herrick, Vincent Abraitys, Rainer Esslen, John Sinclair, Bernard Jacobson, Jerome Eckstein" avg. press run 3M. Expects 2 titles 1991, 4 titles 1992. avg. price, cloth: $18; paper: $10. 240pp; 6×9. Reporting time: 3 months. Payment: yes. Copyrights for author.

COLUMBUS FREE PRESS, Duane Jager, Publisher & Editor, 1066 North High Street, Columbus, OH 43201-2440, 614-228-5796. 1970. Articles, art, photos, cartoons, interviews, satire, criticism, reviews, music, letters, collages, news items. "Nothing which might offend on the basis of race or sex. Loosely left perspective. Must have local application" circ. 15M. 12/yr. Pub'd 12 issues 1990; expects 12 issues 1991, 12 issues 1992. sub. price: $10; per copy: $1; sample: free. Back issues: $1. 12pp; 10½×14; of. Reporting time: 1 month-forever if no SASE. Copyrighted, reverts to author. Pub's reviews: unknown in 1990. §All non-fiction esp. politics, energy and other current event stuff. Ads: $650/$400/free non-commercial classifieds. APS.

COLUMBUS SINGLE SCENE, Jeanne Marlowe, Publisher and Managing Editor, Box 30856, Gahanna, OH 43230, 614-476-8802. 1985. Poetry, fiction, articles, art, photos, cartoons, interviews, satire, criticism, reviews, music, letters, parts-of-novels, collages, plays, concrete art, news items, non-fiction. "I would love to receive anything—articles, poems, stories, book reviews—dealing with singles and/or relationships. No longer have space for long (over 40 lines) poems." circ. 7M. 12/yr. Pub'd 12 issues 1990; expects 12 issues 1991, 12 issues 1992. sub. price: $10; per copy: $2; sample: $2. Back issues: $2. Discounts: 10 for $10. 24pp; 8½×11; web of. Reporting time: within 1 month. Payment: in copies and advertising. Copyrighted, reverts to author. Pub's reviews: 12 in 1990. §Singles, relationships, love, self help. Ads: $250/$135/50¢ per word. Singles Press Assoc.

Combat Ready Publishing, Belva O. Brown, Senior Editor, 6049 West 95th Street, Oak Lawn, IL 60453. Non-fiction. "Non-fiction books on Vietnam War" Expects 2 titles 1991. avg. price, paper: $16.95. 500pp; 6×9. Does not copyright for author. COSMEP.

Combs Vanity Press, Coburn Corelli, 925 Lakeville Street, Suite 295, Petaluma, CA 95492, 707-795-4797. 1989. Reviews, news items. "Interested in similar manuscripts for publishing in Taiwan." avg. press run 1M-2M. Pub'd 1 title 1990; expects 2 titles 1991, 3 titles 1992. 1 title listed in the *Small Press Record of Books in Print* (20th Edition, 1991-92). avg. price, paper: $14.95. Discounts: 40% cash 30 days, 50% paid at time of order. 250pp; of. Reporting time: 30 days. Payment: to be discussed. Copyrights for author. USTP, CSPT.

COME-ALL-YE, Legacy Books (formerly Folklore Associates), Richard Burns, Editor; Lillian Krelove, Assistant Editor, P.O. Box 494, Hatboro, PA 19040, 215-675-6762. 1977. Art, music, parts-of-novels, news items. "' . . . contains reviews and book selection news of publications in the fields of folklore/folklife, social history, studies investigating the culture, fabric and spirit of people in communities. The journal seeks to provide a reference selection and advisory guide to inform professionals, faculty, scholars, students and the general interested public of significant current publications.'—from the masthead. No submissions, staff produced." circ. 2M-3M. 4/yr. Pub'd 4 issues 1990; expects 4 issues 1991, 4 issues 1992. sub. price: $6; per copy: $1.25; sample: $1. Back issues: $1. Discounts: none. 16pp; 8¼×11; of. Reporting time: no outside reviews. Payment: none. Copyrighted, reverts to author. Pub's reviews: 300 in 1990. §Folklore, social history, local history, regional surveys, music (all but classical), American culture, Black studies, anthropology, ethnic culture, music and ethnic studies. Ads: $150/$85/1/4 page $50, camera-ready. COSMEP/ABA.

Comforter Publishing, Raymond Ashton, Karen Chin, 515 Crocker Avenue, Daly City, CA 94014, 415-584-3329. 1991. Fiction, satire, criticism, plays, non-fiction. "Comforter Publishing was established to compete against the commonplace commercial tide of publishing that panders to the crude, biological drives of the average reader, and to publish and promote works that aspire to cultivating interest in the higher, sophisticated sensibilities that distinguish us from the beasts, and on which the comfort, survival, and advancement of our race depends." avg. press run 1M-2M. Expects 2 titles 1991, 4+ titles 1992. 1 title listed in the *Small Press Record of Books in Print* (20th Edition, 1991-92). avg. price, paper: $8-$12 quality editions. Discounts: customary schedule. 5½×8½; of. Reporting time: 1 month or more. Payment: escalating royalty rate policy, i.e., as sales increase so does royalty rate. Does not copyright for author.

THE COMICS JOURNAL, Fantagraphics Books, Gary Groth, 7563 Lake City Way, Seattle, WA 98115. 1976. Articles, cartoons, interviews, criticism, reviews. "*The Comics Journal* is a monthly magazine devoted to news and reviews of the comic book trade, both mainstream and independent publishing" circ. 10M. 12/yr. Pub'd 6 issues 1990; expects 8 issues 1991, 8 issues 1992. sub. price: $35 USA; per copy: $3.50; sample: $3.50. 132pp; 8½×11; of. Reporting time: 1-2 months. Payment: 1½¢ per word. Copyrighted, reverts to author. Pub's reviews: 75 in 1990. §Comics, comics-related publications and productions. Ads: $120. COSMEP.

126

COMICS REVUE, Rick Norwood, PO Box 336 -Manuscript Press, Mountain Home, TN 37684-0336, 615-926-7495. 1984. Cartoons. "We publish syndicated comic strips: Batman, Flash Gordon, Calvin & Hobbes, Bloom County, Modesty Blaise, The Phantom, Teenage Mutant Ninja Turtles, Gasoline Alley, and Latigo. We are not interested in looking at submissions unless they are better than what is available from the syndicates. No submissions can be returned. Submissions are discouraged, but if you must submit a comic strip, send xerox copies only and include a SASE for a reply. Additional address: Fictioneer Books, Ltd., #1 Screamer Mountain, Clayton, GA 30525." circ. 4M. 12/yr. Pub'd 12 issues 1990; expects 14 issues 1991, 12 issues 1992. sub. price: $45; per copy: $5; sample: same. Back issues: $5 for single copies, $45 for 12 copies, current or old. Discounts: 10-99 copies 40% off, 100-499 copies 50% off, 500+ copies 60% off. 64pp; 8½×11; of. Reporting time: indefinite. Payment: $5 per page. Copyrighted, reverts to author. Pub's reviews: 10-12 in 1990. §Comic strip reprints. Ads: $125/$70.

COMMON BOUNDARY, Anne Simpkinson, 7005 Florida Street, Chevy Chase, MD 20815, 301-652-9495. 1980. Articles, art, photos, interviews, criticism, reviews, letters, news items, non-fiction. "1,500-3,000 average article. Prefer journalistic style when writing about spiritual/psychotherapeutic experiences." circ. 20M. 6/yr. Pub'd 6 issues 1990; expects 6 issues 1991, 6 issues 1992. sub. price: $22; per copy: $5; sample: same. Back issues: individual articles $1.50, whole issue $5. Discounts: 15% for teachers who sign up 10 students (all receive discount). 48pp; 8½×11; of, Web press. Reporting time: 6 months. Payment: $50-$500. Copyrighted, reverts to author. Pub's reviews: 20 in 1990. §Psychology, spirituality, new age, religion, Jung, pastoral counseling and meditation practice. Ads: $800/$450/$325 1/3 page/$260 1/4/$195 1/6/$135 1/12. ASME.

COMMON LIVES / LESBIAN LIVES, PO Box 1553, Iowa City, IA 52244. 1981. Poetry, fiction, articles, art, photos, cartoons, interviews, satire, criticism, reviews, music, letters, parts-of-novels, plays, non-fiction. "Journal entries, diaries, correspondence etc. The everyday writings of ordinary women, oral history." circ. 3M. 4/yr. Pub'd 4 issues 1990; expects 4 issues 1991, 4 issues 1992. 1 title listed in the *Small Press Record of Books in Print* (20th Edition, 1991-92). sub. price: $15; per copy: $5; sample: $5. Back issues: $3.50 + $1 p/h. Discounts: 40% to bookstores. 128pp; 5½×8½; of. Reporting time: maximum 90 days. Payment: 2 copies of issue in which her piece appears. Copyrighted, reverts to author. Pub's reviews: 10-15 in 1990. §Lesbian-authored work, esp. small press. Ads: $100/$50/20¢.

COMMON SENSE, C. Pinsonngault, Managing Editor; T. Paine, Editor, PO Box 520191, Miami, FL 33152-0191, 305-221-0154. 1971. Articles, news items. "Recent contributors: Robert Brakeman, Roy Childs, David Bergland" circ. 600. 5/yr. Pub'd 6 issues 1990; expects 5 issues 1991. sub. price: $10/1 year, $18/2 years via bulkrate; $22 3 years; per copy: $1.50; sample: $1. Discounts: not available at this time. 12pp; 8½×14; of, desktop publishing. Reporting time: 2 months prior to printing (usually first of the month). Payment: 2 year subscription. Not copyrighted. Ads: $24/$12/10¢. COSMEP.

Commonwealth Press Virginia (see also THE LYRIC), Bonnie Clark, Jean Willcox, 415 First Street, Box 3547, Radford, VA 24141. 1954. "General fiction & nonfiction. Recent books: *Appalachian Heritage cookbook, Hold 'Em Poker Bible, There Will Never Be Another You, Murder On The Appalachian Trail.* Reprints on special arrangement." avg. press run 2M. Pub'd 16 titles 1990; expects 14 titles 1991. avg. price, cloth: $12.95; paper: $6.95. Discounts: 5 copies 40%, 100-249 45%, Bulk shipments to wholesalers (1,000 copies and up) 50%. 176pp; 5½×8½; †of. Payment: some of our books are done on contract with historical societies, others on royalty, still more on coop with other publishers.

Communication Creativity, Rebecca Atkinson, 425 Cedar, PO Box 909, Buena Vista, CO 81211, 719-395-8659. 1977. Non-fiction. "Communication Creativity Books are designed to be both entertaining and informational. They deal primarily with subjects in the fields of business. Not soliciting submissions" avg. press run 5M. Pub'd 3 titles 1990; expects 3 titles 1991, 4 titles 1992. 7 titles listed in the *Small Press Record of Books in Print* (20th Edition, 1991-92). avg. price, cloth: $19.95; paper: $9.95. Discounts: from 20% to 55%. 224pp; 5½×8½, 6×9; cameron belt, of. Payment: negotiable. Copyrights for author. PMA, COSMEP, Rocky Mountain Book Publishers Assn.

The Communication Press, Randall Harrison, PO Box 22541, San Francisco, CA 94122, 415-386-0178. 1977. Cartoons. "Our focus is on humorous how-to, such as our *How To Cut Your Water Use—and Still Stay Sane and Sanitary.* We also are interested in art, psychology and communication. We're probably a poor market for free lancers as we already have as many projects as we can handle for the next few years; and we hope to stay small and quality oriented." avg. press run 5M. Pub'd 1-2 titles 1990. 11 titles listed in the *Small Press Record of Books in Print* (20th Edition, 1991-92). avg. price, cloth: $7.50; paper: $3.50. Discounts: 40% trade. 96-128pp; 5×8; of. Reporting time: 6-8 weeks. Payment: variable. Copyrights for author. COSMEP.

Communication Trends Inc., E. Sigel, 2 East Avenue, Larchmont, NY 10538. 1983. Non-fiction. Pub'd 3 titles 1990; expects 6 titles 1991, 10 titles 1992. avg. price, other: $1,300. 100pp; 8½×11; of. Reporting time: query first. Payment: negotiable. Does not copyright for author.

Communicom Publishing Company, Donna Matrazzo, 19300 NW Sauvie Island Road, Portland, OR 97231,

503-621-3049. 1984. Non-fiction. "We publish and distribute books (and other items) related to business communications, specializing in writing and audio visual work. Title published: *The Corporate Scriptwriting Book*, Donna Matrazzo; Titles distributed: *Organizational TV News*, Tom Thompson; *Editing Your Newsletter*, Mark Beach, *Getting It Printed*, Mark Beach, *Thinking on Your Feet*, Marian Woodall, *Speaking to a Group*, Marian Woodall." avg. press run 5M. Expects 2 titles 1992. 1 title listed in the *Small Press Record of Books in Print* (20th Edition, 1991-92). avg. price, paper: $20. Discounts: 20% to schools, bookstore discount varies by volume. 250pp; 5½×8½. Reporting time: no specification. Payment: arrangements made on book-by-book basis. Copyrights for author. Northwest Association of Book Publishers (Portland, OR).

Communitas Press, Gregory Calvert, Ken Carpenter, PO Box 3784, Eugene, OR 97403, 503-485-0776. 1991. Non-fiction. "Communitas Press promotes the publishing of works relating to political and social change grounded in spiritual and ecological values. It recently published *Democracy From The Heart: Spiritual Values, Decentralism, and Democratic Idealism in the Movement of the 1960s*, by Gregory Nevala Calvert. We are especially interested in books on radical history, ecology and decentralist political philosophy. Other areas we will consider include gay and lesbian studies, Latin American history and politics, Third-world studies, and the theory and practice of non-violence." avg. press run 3M-5M. Expects 2 titles 1991, 2 titles 1992. avg. price, cloth: $29.95; paper: $14.95. Discounts: trade 20-40%. 300pp; 5⅜×8⅜; of. Reporting time: 6-12 weeks. Payment: varies. Copyrights for author.

COMMUNITIES, Laird Schaub, Managing Editor, Route 1, Box 155, Rutledge, MO 63563, 816-883-5543. 1972. Articles, art, photos, interviews, reviews, letters. "Bias: limited to contributions relating to aspects of cooperative living" circ. 1M. Periodic. Pub'd 2 issues 1990; expects 1 issue 1991, 2 issues 1992. sub. price: $18/4 issues; per copy: $5; sample: $5. Back issues: full available set (approx. 35) $35. Discounts: 3-4 copies 25%, 5-9 30%, 10-24 35%, 25-49 40%, 50+ 50%. 56pp; 8½×11; of. Reporting time: 60 days. Payment: none. Copyrighted, reverts to author. Pub's reviews. §Intentional communities, alternative culture. Ads: $250/$150/proportionals. COSMEP.

Community Collaborators, Virginia A. Decker, Managing Editor, PO Box 5429, Charlottesville, VA 22905, 804-977-1126. 1977. Articles. "*The Funding Process: Grantsmanship & Proposal Development*, *Creating Interagency Projects: School & Community Agencies*, *Community Involvement For Classroom Teachers*, *Managing Federalism: Evolution and Development of the Grant-In-Aid System*, *A Directory of Publishing Opportunities For Teachers of Writing*, *Foundations of Community Education*." avg. press run 5M. Expects 1 title 1991, 1 title 1992. 5 titles listed in the *Small Press Record of Books in Print* (20th Edition, 1991-92). avg. price, cloth: $11.50; paper: $3. Discounts: bulk 10+, 20%; 25+ copies, 30%. 100pp; 6×9, 8½×11½; of. Reporting time: 2 weeks. Payment: range 10-15%. Copyrights for author. COSMEP.

COMMUNITY DEVELOPMENT JOURNAL, Oxford University Press, Gary Craig, Foldyard House, Pinkhill House, Southfield Road, Naburn, York YO1 4RU, England, 0632-367142. 1966. Articles, photos, cartoons, reviews, news items, non-fiction. "Articles (should be sent) to Editorial address above. For subs, advertising, back nos., write Journal Manager, Oxford Univ. Press, Pinkhill House, Southfield Road, Eynsham, Oxford OX8 1JJ, United Kingdom. Copyright held by Oxford University Press." circ. 1M. 4/yr. Pub'd 4 issues 1990; expects 4 issues 1991, 4 issues 1992. sub. price: $70; per copy: $21; sample: free of charge. Back issues: negotiable. Discounts: on request for more than 20 copies. 80pp; 23×15cm; cold metal/photosetting. Reporting time: 8 weeks approx. Payment: none, except one copy of journal and eight off-prints free. Copyrighted. Pub's reviews: 45 in 1990. §Community problems, politics, policy making, planning, programming, participation, action. Ads: £205($370)/£120($215)/£85($155) 1/4 page.

COMMUNITY ECONOMICS, Institute For Community Economics, Kirby White, Lisa Berger, 151 Montague City Road, Greenfield, MA 01301, 413-774-7956. 1983. Non-fiction. "We run feature stories on community land trusts and loan funds in various parts of the country, on related conferences, workshops, seminars, and community development projects. There are some more general and philosophical essays or talk excerpts/condensations on these subjects that are written or edited in-house" circ. 7.5M. 4/yr. Pub'd 2 issues 1990; expects 4 issues 1991, 4 issues 1992. sub. price: suggested donation: $10/year for individuals, $20/year for institutions; free upon request; per copy: $1; sample: free. Back issues: $1.50 for *Land and Housing* and *Community Investment* reprints. 16pp; 8½×11; lp. Payment: none. Not copyrighted. Pub's reviews: 10 in 1990. §Community development, land distribution, socially responsible investing.

Community Resource Institute Press, 1442-A Walnut #51, Berkeley, CA 94709, 415-526-7190. 1 title listed in the *Small Press Record of Books in Print* (20th Edition, 1991-92).

Community Service, Inc. (see also COMMUNITY SERVICE NEWSLETTER), Jane Morgan, Director, Box 243, Yellow Springs, OH 45387, 513-797-2161, 767-1461. 1940. Articles, reviews, letters, non-fiction. avg. press run 500 for newsletter, 1M for pamphlets. Pub'd 2 titles 1990; expects 1 title 1991. 33 titles listed in the *Small Press Record of Books in Print* (20th Edition, 1991-92). avg. price, paper: $5. Discounts: write for them 40% off for 10. 35pp; of/lo. Reporting time: 2 weeks. Does not copyright for author.

COMMUNITY SERVICE NEWSLETTER, Community Service, Inc., Jane Morgan, Director, Box 243, Yellow Springs, OH 45387, 513-767-2161. 1940. Articles, reviews, letters, non-fiction. circ. 400. 6/yr. Pub'd 6 issues 1990; expects 2 issues 1991, 6 issues 1992. sub. price: $20; per copy: $1; sample: free. Back issues: $1. Discounts: write for 40% on 10 or more. 12pp; 7×8½; of. Reporting time: 2 weeks. Payment: copies. Copyrighted, reverts to author. Pub's reviews: 8 or 9 in 1990. §Community, alternatives in community, society, economy, education, land trusts and land reform. exchange ads.

Community Workshop on Economic Development, 100 South Morgan, Chicago, IL 60607. 1 title listed in the *Small Press Record of Books in Print* (20th Edition, 1991-92).

A COMPANION IN ZEOR, Karen Litman, Route 5, Box 82, Ashland Avenue, Pleasantville, NJ 08232, 609-645-6938. 1978. Poetry, fiction, art, cartoons, interviews, letters, news items. "Contributions based on the universes of Jacqueline Lichtenberg. Any and all universes she has created or worked in. Preferred, nothing obscene—no homosexuality unless relevant to story line. Science-fiction oriented." circ. 300. Irregular. Expects 1 issue 1991, 2 issues 1992. price per copy: issues are different prices, SASE for flyer, can negotiate for free issues on occasion. Discounts: willing to discuss and arrange. 60pp; 8½×11; †mi, of, photocopy. Reporting time: 1 month. Payment: contributor copy, possibly more than one if arranged. Copyrighted, reverts to author after 5 years to the contributor. Pub's reviews: 1 in 1990. §Almost anything but romance type, science fiction preferred for my own reading. free.

The Compass Press, W.D. Howells, Box 9546, Washington, DC 20016, 202-333-2182. 1988. Articles, interviews, non-fiction. "Contemporary history with special interest in institutional biography and generational change. Current public and political affairs with special interest in decision process" avg. press run 2.5M. Expects 1-2 titles 1991, 2 titles 1992. 3 titles listed in the *Small Press Record of Books in Print* (20th Edition, 1991-92). avg. price, cloth: $26; paper: $14. Discounts: 3-10 20%, 10-20 40%, 20+ 50%, no freight, no return. 250pp; 6×9; of. Reporting time: immediate acknowledgement, decision 2-4 weeks. Payment: various, modest advance for completed mss. Copyrights for author. SSP, PMA, Washington Book Publishers.

CompCare Publishers, Margaret Marsh, Managing Editor, 2415 Annapolis Lane, Minneapolis, MN 55441, 612-559-4800; 800-328-3330. 1976. Non-fiction. avg. press run 10M. Pub'd 25 titles 1990; expects 25 titles 1991, 20 titles 1992. avg. price, paper: $9.95. Discounts: various. 150pp; 5¼×8¼, 6×9; of. Reporting time: 2-3 months. Payment: negotiated. Copyrights for author.

COMPOST NEWSLETTER (CNL), Valerie Walker, 729 Fifth Avenue, San Francisco, CA 94118. 1978. Fiction, articles, cartoons, interviews, satire, criticism, reviews, letters, non-fiction. "Subjects: Wiccan & pagan politics, rituals, mythology, controversies, humor; fitness and health; food; herbs; magick; aging; fashion & bad taste; science fiction, fantasy, horror and tales of the bizarre; social commentary. Length of articles: 1,000 words or less, longer articles will be serialized. Recent contributors: Jess River, Will Downing, Leah Samul, Brent Gilman, Ron Miller, Aldyth Beltane, Ron Frakes, Andraste, Gabriel of BloodRose" circ. 100. 8/yr. Pub'd 8 issues 1990; expects 8 issues 1991, 8 issues 1992. sub. price: $10; per copy: $2; sample: $2. Discounts: none. 20pp; 7×8½; †xeroxed laserprint. Reporting time: 1 month. Payment: 1 free copy. Not copyrighted. Pub's reviews: 4-5 in 1990. §Witches, herbs, magick, ritual, pagans, humor, science-fiction, fantasy. Ads: $10/$5.

Comprehensive Health Education Foundation (CHEF), Robynn Rockstad, Steven Goldenberg, 22323 Pacific Highway South, Seattle, WA 98198, 206-824-2907. 1974. Fiction, non-fiction. "We are publishers of health education materials and curriculum, which include books and videos. Most of our titles are children's and young adult books. We usually have our books written to specifically augment our teaching materials. We aren't actively soliciting manuscripts." avg. press run 10M-15M. Pub'd 6 titles 1990; expects 2 titles 1991, 3 titles 1992. 11 titles listed in the *Small Press Record of Books in Print* (20th Edition, 1991-92). avg. price, paper: $5.95-$10.95. Discounts: 2-4 copies 20%, 5-24 40%, 25-49 42%, 50-99 43%, 100-249 44%, 250+ 45%. 40-100pp; 6¾×9; of. Reporting time: within 2 months. Payment: depends on project. Copyrights for author. Book Publishers Northwest (BPN), PO Box 31236, Seattle, WA 98103, Publishers Marketing Association, 2401 Pacific Coast Hwy, Suite 109, Hermosa Beach, CA 90254.

COMPUTER BOOK REVIEW, Maeventec, Carlene Char, Editor & Publisher, 735 Ekekela Place, Honolulu, HI 96817, 808-595-7089. 1983. "Critically reviews the latest microcomputer books, all subjects, most publishers. 70 reviews per issue, plus annual index. Electronic edition available on News Net. Reviews written in-house, no queries or reviews accepted at this time" 12/yr. Pub'd 12 issues 1990; expects 12 issues 1991, 12 issues 1992. sub. price: $25; per copy: $2; sample: $2. 6pp; 8½×11; of. Copyrighted, does not revert to author. Pub's reviews: 600 in 1990. §Computer-related books. No ads.

COMPUTER EDUCATION NEWS, Blue Heron Press, Carol Anderson, PO Box 5182, Bellingham, WA 98227, 206-676-3954. 1985. Art, photos, reviews, non-fiction. "This is a newsletter for anyone in computer education. From elementary school teachers to corporate trainers. Includes new product reviews, training tips, hardware information, and industry advancements" circ. 5M-10M. 12/yr. Expects 12 issues 1991, 12 issues 1992. sub. price: $69; per copy: $3; sample: same. 8pp; 8½×11; of. Reporting time: 2 months. Payment: varies per submission. Copyrighted. Pub's reviews. §Computer books and programs. No ads. PMA, COSMEP.

COMPUTER GAMING WORLD, Russell Sipe, Editor-in-Chief; Johnny Wilson, Editor, PO Box 4566, Anaheim, CA 92803, (714) 535-4435. 1981. Articles, interviews, reviews, letters, news items. *"CGW* provides reviews and information on commercially available computer games" circ. 30M. 12/yr. Pub'd 12 issues 1990; expects 12 issues 1991, 12 issues 1992. sub. price: $24; per copy: $3.50; sample: same. Back issues: same. Discounts: bulk 40%, agent 33%. 64pp; 8½×11; of. Payment: 5¢ per word. Copyrighted, reverts to author. §Computers and/or entertainment. Ads: $1090/$630. Small Magazine Publisher's Group.

Computer Musician Coalition, Ronald A. Wallace, 1024 West Willcox Avenue, Peoria, IL 61604, 309-685-4843. 1987. Articles, art, photos, cartoons, interviews, criticism, reviews, music, letters, news items. "Any reference to computers and music acceptable. Professional, beginner, educational" avg. press run 1M. Pub'd 6 titles 1990; expects 6 titles 1991, 6 titles 1992. 1 title listed in the *Small Press Record of Books in Print* (20th Edition, 1991-92). avg. price, cloth: $75. Discounts: none. 300pp; 8×11; of. Reporting time: 60 days. Payment: 3¢ per published, edited word. Does not copyright for author.

COMPUTING SYSTEMS, University of California Press, Michael O'Dell, University of California Press, 2120 Berkeley Way, Berkeley, CA 94720, 415-642-4191. 1988. Articles, non-fiction. "Membership in the USENIX Assn. includes a subscription to *Computing Systems."* circ. 4.5M. 4/yr. Expects 4 issues 1991, 4 issues 1992. sub. price: $43; per copy: $11 ($5 foreign postage); sample: free. Back issues: $11. Discounts: 10% foreign agents, 30% 10+ one time orders, standing orders (bookstores): 1-99 40%, 100+ 50%. 124pp; 7×10; of. Copyrighted, does not revert to author. Ads: $300/$150.

Comstock Bonanza Press, 18919 William Quirk Memorial Drive, Grass Valley, CA 95945, 916-273-6220. 1979. Non-fiction. "We're not soliciting any new material for publication by Comstock Bonanza Press—but we will assist authors who wish to self-publish their own books." avg. press run 2M. Pub'd 1 title 1990; expects 1 title 1992. 8 titles listed in the *Small Press Record of Books in Print* (20th Edition, 1991-92). avg. price, cloth: $12.50-$21.50; paper: $8.75-$10.75; other: $12.50-$17.50. Discounts: 40% trade and wholesale; 15% schools and libraries. 160-400pp; standard sizes; of.

Conari Press, Mary Jane Ryan, 1339 61st Street, Emeryville, CA 94608, 415-596-4040. 1987. Non-fiction. "Distribution: Publishers Group West, Ingram, Raincoast Books (Canada)" avg. press run 10M-30M. Pub'd 3 titles 1990; expects 4 titles 1991, 10 titles 1992. 11 titles listed in the *Small Press Record of Books in Print* (20th Edition, 1991-92). avg. price, cloth: $19.95; paper: $8.95. Discounts: standard. Pages vary; size varies; litho. Reporting time: 1 month. Payment: varies. Copyrights for author. COSMEP, PMA.

CONCHO RIVER REVIEW, Terence A. Dalrymple, Fort Concho Museum Press, English Dept., Angelo State Univ., San Angelo, TX 76909, 915-942-2253. 1986. Poetry, fiction, articles, criticism, reviews, non-fiction. "Fiction and non-fiction: 1500-5000 words; reviews: 500-1500 words; poetry open. We read all submissions carefully but generally publish only material by writers of Texas and the Southwest or about Texas and the Southwest. Circulation office: Fort Concho Museum Press, 213 East Ave. D, San Angelo, TX 76903." circ. 300. 2/yr. Pub'd 2 issues 1990; expects 2 issues 1991, 2 issues 1992. sub. price: $12; per copy: $7; sample: $5. Back issues: $5. Discounts: query. 115pp; 6×9; of. Reporting time: 2-6 weeks. Payment: copies. Copyrighted, reverts to author. Pub's reviews: 10 in 1990. §Fiction, poetry, nonfiction by writers of Texas and the Southwest or about Texas and the Southwest. Ads: query.

Concourse Press, Robert Reed, Editor-in-Chief, PO Box 28600, Overbrook Station, Philadelphia, PA 19151, 215-649-2207. 1979. Poetry, fiction, satire, criticism, long-poems. "Minimum pages for manuscript 50-60 pages, preferably 64-80. The bias of the press is toward an integrative view of life that includes artistic/literary/philosophical/psychological/social elements. We would publish any good literature, but encourage publication of material with literary/artistic value regardless of business/financial considerations. We like to help unestablished writers who have a hard time making it through the commercial big market. We are committed to progressive cultural-social goals and encourage the alternative culture and counter-culture goals dedicated to the deeper human values and humanistic non-commercial outlooks on life. Recent contributors have included John High, William Dickey, Bahman Sholevar, Robert Hazel (jacket blurbs), Denise Levertov (jacket blurb)" avg. press run 1M-5M. Pub'd 3 titles 1990; expects 2 titles 1991, 5 titles 1992. avg. price, cloth: $13; paper: $5.95. Discounts: large orders/wholesalers 40%; small orders/individual orders 20% to stores. 100pp; 6×9; of. Reporting time: 1 month on invited manuscripts. Payment: negotiable up to 10% of the cover price. Copyrights for author.

CONDITIONED RESPONSE, Conditioned Response Press, John McKinley, Editor, PO Box 3816, Ventura, CA 93006. 1983. Poetry. "Not accepting unsolicited submissions at this time. Unsolicited material will be returned unread. Recent contributors are Belinda Subraman, Arthur Winfield Knight, Judsen Crews, and Michael Wilds" circ. 200+. 2/yr. Pub'd 1 issue 1990; expects 2 issues 1991, 2 issues 1992. sub. price: $6/3 issues; per copy: $2; sample: $2. Back issues: $2 each, $5 for 3 different issues. Discounts: 50% on orders to bookstores. University libraries receive normal subscription rate. 24pp; 5½×8½; of. Reporting time: 2 weeks-2 months. Payment: 1 contributor copy. Copyrighted, reverts to author. Pub's reviews. §lit mags, chapbooks, poetry, fiction art. No ads.

Conditioned Response Press (see also CONDITIONED RESPONSE), John McKinley, Editor, PO Box 3816, Ventura, CA 93006. 1983. Poetry. "No unsolicited manuscripts accepted." avg. press run 200+. Pub'd 1 title 1990; expects 1 title 1991, 1 title 1992. 6 titles listed in the *Small Press Record of Books in Print* (20th Edition, 1991-92). avg. price, paper: $2. Discounts: 50% for 5 copies or more to bookstores. 24pp; 5½x8½; of. Reporting time: 1-2 months. Payment: 5 free copies (split press run). Copyrights for author.

Confluence Press, Inc., James Hepworth, Director, Lewis-Clark State College, 8th Avenue & 6th Street, Lewiston, ID 83501-2698, 208-799-2336. 1975. Poetry, fiction, articles, art, photos, interviews, criticism, music, non-fiction. "Poetry, fiction, literary criticism" avg. press run 1M-3M. Pub'd 5 titles 1990; expects 8 titles 1991, 8 titles 1992. 36 titles listed in the *Small Press Record of Books in Print* (20th Edition, 1991-92). avg. price, cloth: $14.95; paper: $8.95; other: chapbooks (limited editions) pa $20, cl $50. Discounts: 20% libraries, 40% bookstores, 50% jobbers and wholesalers. 96-200pp; 5½x8½, 6x9; of. Reporting time: 1-3 months. Payment: 10% or 10% of press run. Copyrights for author.

CONFRONTATION, Martin Tucker, English Department, C.W. Post of Long Island Univ., Greenvale, NY 11548, 516-299-2391. 1968. Poetry, fiction, articles, interviews, parts-of-novels, long-poems, plays. circ. 2M. 2/yr. Expects 2 issues 1991. 7 titles listed in the *Small Press Record of Books in Print* (20th Edition, 1991-92). sub. price: $10; per copy: $6; sample: $3. Back issues: $6 to $8. 190pp; 6x9; lp. Reporting time: 6-8 weeks. Payment: $15-$100 stories, $5-$50 poetry. Copyrighted, reverts to author. Pub's reviews: 30 in 1990. §Fiction, poetry. COSMEP, CCLM.

CONJUNCTIONS, Bradford Morrow, Editor, 33 W. 9th Street, New York, NY 10011. 1981. "Contributing editors include: Walter Abish, Mei-mei Berssenbrugge, Guy Davenport, William H. Gass, Kenneth Irby, Ann Lauterbach, Nathaniel Tarn. Among most recently published authors are: John Ashbery, William Burroughs, Mary Caponegro, Maxine Hong Kingston, David Foster Wallace, John Hawkes, Rachel Blau DuPlessis, Robert Kelly, Harry Mathews, Joseph McElroy, Paul West" circ. 6.5M. 2/yr. Pub'd 2 issues 1990; expects 2 issues 1991, 2 issues 1992. sub. price: $18 paper, $24 institution rate; $45 cloth, individual and institution; per copy: $9.95; sample: $9.95, $22.95 cloth. Discounts: 1-2 copies 20%; 3-4 copies 30%; 5 or more copies 40%. Special rates to distributors. 300pp; 6x9; of, lp covers—2 colors + four color. Reporting time: solicited mss immediate, unsolicited 4-6 weeks. Payment: 3 paper copies of issue + $100. Copyrighted, reverts to author. Pub's reviews: 35 in 1990. §Poetry, fiction, literary criticism, drama, music, translated literature, the arts. Ads: $350. MacMillan Co.

CONNECTICUT NATURALLY, City Spirit Publications, Jerome Rubin, Publisher & Editor-in-Chief; Kenny Schiff, Managing Editor, 590 Pacific Street, Brooklyn, NY 11217, 718-857-1545. 1984. Poetry, articles, photos, interviews, non-fiction. "Wide range of material relating to a natural life-style, focus on New York, New Jersey, and Connecticut. We publish 3 annual books in January (formerly 1)." circ. 25M. 1/yr. Pub'd 1 issue 1990. price per copy: $3.50; sample: $2.50. 80pp; 5x8; web press. Reporting time: 2 weeks. Payment: varies. Copyrighted, reverts to author. §Natural lifestyle, health, environmentalism, natural foods/cooking, new age.

THE CONNECTICUT POETRY REVIEW, J. Claire White, Co-Editor; James Chichetto, Co-Editor, PO Box 3783, Amity Station, New Haven, CT 06525. 1981. Poetry, interviews, satire, criticism, reviews. "Reviews: 700 words. Poems: 10-40 lines. But we do make exceptions. We look for poetry of quality which is both genuine and original in content. That is all we seek. We will consider any new and interesting book of poems mailed to us for a review. Some past and recent contributors: Cornelia Veenendaal, Nikki Giovanni, Walter Mac Donald, Laurel Speer, John Updike, Dona Stein, James Sallis, Celia Gilbert, Diane Wakoski, Stuart Friebert, Felice Picano, Joseph Bruchac, W.D. Ehrhart, Joel Chace, Anna Maxwell, James Chichetto, Marge Piercy, Steve Abbott, Rochelle Ratner, Dan Duffy, A.R. Ammons, Mark Johnson, Jefferson Peters, Greg Kuzma, Diane Kruchkow, Daniel Langton, M. Marcuss Oslander, Robert Peters, Philip Fried, Emily Glen, Andrew Holleran, Edwin Honig, Rudy Kikel, F.D. Reeve, Dennis Cooper, Richard Kostelanetz, Charles Edward Eaton, Clifton Snider, Wm. Virgil Davis, John Tagliabue, Edward Butscher, Allen Ginsberg, Margaret Randall, Barry Spacks, J. Kates, Eugenio de Andrade, Susan Fromberg Schaeffer, Claudia Buckholts, Simon Perchik, Odysseus Elytis." circ. 400. 1/yr. Pub'd 1 issue 1990; expects 1 issue 1991, 1 issue 1992. 1 title listed in the *Small Press Record of Books in Print* (20th Edition, 1991-92). sub. price: $3; per copy: $3; sample: $3. Back issues: $25 first issue. Discounts: none. 40-45pp; 4¼x8½; lp. Reporting time: 3 months. Payment: $5 per poem, $10 per review. Copyrighted, reverts to author. Pub's reviews: 0 in 1990. §Poetry, poetry, poetry. CCLM, Indexed in the Index of American Periodical Verse (Metuchen, NJ: Scarecrow P.), American Humanities Index (Troy, NY: Whitson PC).

CONNECTICUT RIVER REVIEW: A National Poetry Journal, Robert Isaacs, Editor; Kristin Aronson, Associate Editor; Patricia Forgnoli, Associate Editor; Madeleine Hennessy, Associate Editor; Arlene Kindilien,

Managing Editor, Robert Isaacs, Editor, PO Box 2171, Bridgeport, CT 06608. 1978. Poetry. "We publish only the highest quality poetry, with authentic poetic music the criterion; poetry in which logic and emotion, fact and imagination are one and *truly felt*. We use 40-60 poems an issue; receive about 2,000 submissions. No simultaneous submissions, but will look at previously published work if author retains copyright. Send 3-5 poems, 40 lines or under. Recent contributors: Joseph Bruchac, Donald Jenkins, Simon Peachik, Vivian Shipley, Ann Yarmel, Paul Zimmer." circ. 500. 2/yr. Pub'd 2 issues 1990; expects 2 issues 1991, 2 issues 1992. sub. price: $10; per copy: $5; sample: $5. Back issues: $4 + $1 postage. 35-50pp; 6×9; of. Reporting time: 2 weeks to 3 months. Payment: 1 copy. Copyrighted, reverts to author. No ads. CCLM, 666 Broadway, New York, NY 10012-2301.

CONNEXIONS, Collective, 4228 Telegraph, Oakland, CA 94609, 415-654-6725. 1981. Poetry, fiction, articles, art, photos, cartoons, interviews, letters, news items, non-fiction. "Articles on women around the world, compiled from the international feminist and alternative press" circ. 5M. 4/yr. Pub'd 4 issues 1990; expects 4 issues 1991, 4 issues 1992. sub. price: $15 individual, $24 institutions; per copy: $4. Back issues: 4 for $10. Discounts: bookstores 40%. 32pp; 9×12; of. Payment: none. Not copyrighted. §Feminism, int'l issues. Ads: $540/$270.

CONNEXIONS DIGEST, Connexions Information Services, Inc., Ulli Diemer, 427 Bloor Street West, Toronto, Ontario M5S 1X7, Canada, 960-3903. 1976. Articles, art, photos, cartoons, interviews, criticism, reviews, letters, news items. "We are an abstract service linking groups working for social justice-we are interested in materials that include reflection, analysis, report on action—always with a *Canadian* focus." circ. 1.2M. 4/yr. Pub'd 4 issues 1990; expects 4 issues 1991, 4 issues 1992. sub. price: $25 individual; per copy: $17.95 for directory issue; sample: $1. Back issues: $1. Discounts: 40% for re-sale; other negotiable. 48pp; 8½×11; of. Reporting time: 3 months maximum. Payment: none. Not copyrighted. Pub's reviews: 46 in 1990. §Social justice struggles/analysis. Ads: $175/$100/$35. Canadian Periodical Publishers Association;.

Connexions Information Services, Inc. (see also CONNEXIONS DIGEST), Ulli Diemer, Managing Editor, 427 Bloor Street West, Toronto, Ontario M5S 1X7, Canada, 416-960-3903. 1975. 3 titles listed in the *Small Press Record of Books in Print* (20th Edition, 1991-92).

Conscious Living (see also STRESS MASTER), Dr. Tim Lowenstein, PO Box 9, Drain, OR 97435. 1976. Articles, music, non-fiction. avg. press run 3M. Pub'd 2 titles 1990; expects 3 titles 1991, 5 titles 1992. avg. price, paper: $9.95. 96pp; 8½×11; of. Copyrights for author.

Conservatory of American Letters (see also CAL NEWSLETTER; Dan River Press; Northwoods Press), Robert Olmsted, Executive Director; Richard S. Danbury III, Senior Editor; Harley Fetzer, Newsletter Editor; Deborah S. Benner, Business Manager, PO Box 123, So. Thomaston, ME 04858, 207-354-6550. 1982. "CAL is the owner of Dan River Press and Northwoods Press, who offer publication of poetry, fiction, local history. We don't charge a reading fee, but require a donation, whatever you can afford. If you can afford nothing, convince us and we'll read free. We use anything *not* seditious, pornographic, evangelical religious, stupid" avg. press run 1M. Expects 12 titles 1991, 12 titles 1992. avg. price, cloth: $19.95; paper: $6.95; other: collector's $75. Discounts: 2% X No. of paperback books ordered to maximum of 50% for 25 or more. No discount on hardcovers. 150pp; 5½×8½; of. Reporting time: 1 week to 1 month. Payment: minimum advance on books - $250 payable on contracting, minimum 10% royalties from first sale; for anthologies, minimum is $5 per page (pro-rated). Copyrights for author.

THE CONSTANTIAN, Randall J. Dicks, The Constantian Society, 123 Orr Road, Pittsburgh, PA 15241, 412-831-8750. 1970. Articles, photos, interviews, letters, news items, non-fiction. "The Constantian Society is a monarchist organization with educational goals and activities. Our journal, *The Constantian*, published four times a year or more, offers news, historical articles, genealogical information, interviews, profiles, book reviews, and commentaries on *monarchy* and *royalty*. Format is tabloid, 8 1/2 X 11, 12-16 pages per issue. Black and white illustrations used, also maps, drawings, heraldry, ornaments. Recent articles include the Imperial Family of Japan, and interviews with Archduke Otto and Archduke Karl of Austria-Hungary. ISSN 0270-532X. Our journal is produced on a Macintosh computer." circ. 400+. 4+. Pub'd 4 issues 1990; expects 4 issues 1991, 4 issues 1992. sub. price: $8 (membership $15); per copy: $2.50; sample: $1. Back issues: $2 each generally (list available). 12pp; 8 1/2×11; of. Reporting time: generally 2 weeks. Payment: limited funds available for honoraria. Copyrighted, reverts to author. Pub's reviews: 12 in 1990. §Monarchs, royalty, historical subjects related to monarchy/royalty, biography, political theory of monarchy. Ads: $50/$30/no classifieds.

THE CONSTRUCTION CLAIMS CITATOR, Construction Industry Press, Bruce Jervis, Editor, PO Box 9838, San Rafael, CA 94912, 415-927-2155. "*The Citator* is a monthly compilation of cases dealing with construction contract claims and bid disputes. It is the most comprehensive source available for this specialized information. Every effort is made to abstract all pertinent cases from all jurisdictions including 12 Federal Boards like Corp of Engineers. It is designed as an index for legal research" 12/yr. Pub'd 6 issues 1990. sub.

price: $315. Back issues: Sets available at discount. 16pp; 8½×11; of.

CONSTRUCTION COMPUTER APPLICATIONS NEWSLETTER (CCAN), CIP Communications, Royal H. Maul, 6585 Commerce Blvd., Suite E-292, Rohnert Park, CA 94928, 707-792-2223. 1981. *"CCAN* covers construction uses of computers for everyone in the industry. It provides the only source of the latest news on the fast changing technology and new applications for the computer. It's an education for new users and those expanding the benefits they get from automation. But experienced users and software companies subscribe because they know that one new idea or product tip can be worth thousands of dollars to them. *CCAN* also reviews software and analyzes the newest programs available" 12/yr. Pub'd 12 issues 1990; expects 12 issues 1991, 12 issues 1992. sub. price: $89/1 yr, $158/2 yrs, $227/3 yrs; add $20 each for foreign subscriptions; sample: free. Back issues: sets available at discount. 6pp; 8½×11; of. Reporting time: 2 weeks. Copyrighted, does not revert to author. Pub's reviews. §Computers, software.

Construction Industry Press (see also CONTRACTOR PROFIT NEWS (CPN); THE CONSTRUCTION CLAIMS CITATOR), Roderick P. Crandall, Bruce Jervis, 6585 Commerce Blvd #E-292, Rohnert Park, CA 94928, 415-927-2155. 1981. 8-16pp; 8½×11.

CONSTRUCTIVE ACTION NEWSLETTER, Shirley Burghard, Act/Action, B 1104 Ross Towers 710 Lodi St., Syracuse, NY 13203, 315-471-4644. 1960. "We prefer material that shows people how they can help themselves to new and better lives via the use of selfhelp poetry therapy, selfhelp art therapy, selfhelp creative writing therapy, selfhelp pet therapy, selfhelp horticulture therapy, selfhealth natural food recipe therapy, selfhealth supplemental vitamin and mineral therapy etc. We are primarily constructive in nature, but we are against the therapeutic state, the new gods known as psychiatrists, the great mental illness-mental health rip off of the psychoquackiatrists, the psychofrauds and the mental health racketeers. We are against state mental institutions because of the abuse, assaults, atrocities committed in them by the staff against the patient. We believe not only in the right to treatment but the right to refuse treatment when it consists of brain cell destroying electric convulsive shock treatment and over tranquilization to a zombie state and brain surgery" circ. 250. 12/yr. Pub'd 12 issues 1990; expects 12 issues 1991, 12 issues 1992. sub. price: $10; per copy: $1.50; sample: $1.50. No back issues available. Discounts: none. 18-20pp; 8½×14; †mi. Reporting time: about 3 weeks. Payment: copy. Not copyrighted. Pub's reviews: 3 in 1990. §Self-help, self-health or the fucking over of little people by the big psychiatric profession. Ads: 5¢/word, $5 extra for line drawing illustrations.

Consumer Education Research Center, Robert L. Berko, PO Box 336, 350 Scotland Road, Orange, NJ 07050. 1969. Non-fiction. "Books that will aid consumers in coping with the marketplace and modern society" avg. press run 10M-20M. Pub'd 6 titles 1990; expects 6 titles 1991, 6 titles 1992. avg. price, paper: $12. Discounts: 25-60% depending on amount and payment arrangements. 200pp; 8½×10, 4½×7½; web. Payment: subject to negotiation. Copyrights for author. CERC.

The Consumer's Press, Inc., Alvin Lewitas, 1050 N. State Street #200, Chicago, IL 60610, 312-943-0770. 1991. Non-fiction. avg. press run 5M-10M. Expects 3 titles 1991, 6 titles 1992. 1 title listed in the *Small Press Record of Books in Print* (20th Edition, 1991-92). avg. price, paper: $19.95. Discounts: 40%-55%. 250-300pp; 8½×11; lp. Reporting time: 2-4 weeks. Payment: 15% of wholesale—negotiable. Copyrights for author.

CONTACT/11: A Poetry Review, Contact II: Publications, Maurice Kenny, J.G. Gosciak, PO Box 451, Bowling Green Station, New York, NY 10004. 1976. Poetry, articles, art, photos, cartoons, interviews, satire, criticism, reviews, letters, news items, non-fiction. *"CONTACT/11: A Bimonthly Poetry Review* gives voice in magazine format to poetry and poets regardless of region, school, or subject matter. We try to be as open-minded and fair as humanly possible with all submissions. We try to limit material (other than poems) to a 2-page spread. Poems are poems and we do not edit. We are always interested in reviews, criticism, articles on poetry. Recent contributors include: Barbara A. Holland, Rochelle Ratner, Patricia Wilcox, Lyn Lifshin, Siv Cedering, Richard Longchamps, John Brandi, Kirby Congdon, James Purdy, Duane Niatum, Wendy Rose, Theodore Enslin, Keith Wilson, Joseph Bruchac, Joe Johnson, William Packard, Robert Peters, Tom Montag, George Hitchcock, Mei-Mei Berssenbrugge, Olga Cabral, Jerome Rothenberg, Ted Joans, June Jordan, Tom Disch" circ. 250. 4/yr. Pub'd 4 issues 1990; expects 4 issues 1991, 4 issues 1992. sub. price: $8/$14 institutions; per copy: $6.00. Back issues: $5.00 each where available, unless otherwise specified. Discounts: 40%. 76pp; 8½×11; of, web. Reporting time: 3 months. Payment: in copies. Copyrighted, reverts to author. Pub's reviews: 75 in 1990. §Poets, poetry, works by or about poets. Ads: $500/$310/$10. CCLM, NYSCA, NEA.

Contact II: Publications (see also CONTACT/11: A Poetry Review), Maurice Kenny, J.G. Gosciak, PO Box 451, Bowling Green Station, New York, NY 10004. 1976. Poetry. *"Nuke Chromicles,* a brief anthology of poems by Allen Ginsberg, Joseph Bruchac, Tuli Kupferberg, Carter Revard, Ron MacFarland, Ed Sanders. *Toll Bridge,* a new collection of poems by Wilma Elizabeth McDaniel, William Packard *The Haiku's of Teaching,* Elizabeth Marraffine *Blue Moon For Ruby Tuesday,* Steve Kewit *Cutting Our Loses,* and James Purdy *Brooklyn Branding Parlors"* avg. press run 1.5M journal, 750 poetry books. Pub'd 4 titles 1990; expects 4 titles 1991, 4 titles 1992. 16 titles listed in the *Small Press Record of Books in Print* (20th Edition, 1991-92). avg. price, paper: $4. Discounts: standard. 32pp; 5½×8½; of. Reporting time: 3 months. Payment: copies. Copyrights for author. CCLM, NYSCA, NEA.

Contemporary Curriculums, PO Box 152, Lockport, IL 60441. 1973. "Creativity lessons for elementary grades (Ideabooks)" avg. press run 1M. Pub'd 1 title 1990; expects 1 title 1991, 1 title 1992. 5 titles listed in the *Small Press Record of Books in Print* (20th Edition, 1991-92). avg. price, paper: $6. Discounts: 30%. 75pp; 8½×11; of. Reporting time: 6 weeks. Payment: varies. Copyrights for author.

CONTEMPORARY LITERATURE, L.S. Dembo, 7141 Helen C. White Hall, University of Wisconsin, Madison, WI 53706. 1960. Criticism, reviews. "Scholarly literary criticism" circ. 2M+. 4/yr. Expects 4 issues 1992. sub. price: individuals $20/yr, institutions $47; per copy: varies. Back issues: write for details. Discounts: 5% subscription agency. 136pp; 6×9; of. Reporting time: varies. Payment: none. Copyrighted, does not revert to author. Pub's reviews. §All reviews commissioned. Ads: $150/$80.

CONTEMPORARY WALES, University Of Wales Press, G. Day, G. Rees, 6 Gwennyth Street, Cathays, Cardiff CF2 4YD, Wales, 231919. 1987. Articles. "Available in North America from Humanities Press, Inc." circ. 500. 1/yr. Pub'd 1 issue 1990; expects 1 issue 1991, 1 issue 1992. sub. price: £6.50; per copy: £7.50; sample: £7.50. Discounts: booksellers 10%. 100pp; size A5; of. Payment: none. Copyrighted. Ads: £75/£37.50. UWP.

Context Publications, Ron Kennedy, PO Box 2909, Rohnert Park, CA 94927, 707-576-0100. 1979. Non-fiction. avg. press run 10M. Pub'd 6 titles 1990; expects 7 titles 1991, 8 titles 1992. 8 titles listed in the *Small Press Record of Books in Print* (20th Edition, 1991-92). avg. price, cloth: $19.90; paper: $9.95. Discounts: 40% over 20 copies, 20% 1-9 copies, 30% 10-19 copies. 250pp; 6×9. Reporting time: 3 weeks. Payment: royalties only (10%). Copyrights for author. COSMEP.

CONTEXT SOUTH, David Breeden, Poetry Editor; Craig Taylor, Fiction; J.F. Smith, Non-Fiction; Paul Hadella, Assistant Poetry Editor, Box 2244, State University, AR 72467, 501-972-6095. 1989. Poetry, fiction, art, photos, interviews, criticism, reviews, concrete art, non-fiction. "We believe art must build a culture not kick its corpse. Recent contributors: Wayne Dodd, William Greenway, Andrea Budy, Fred Dings" circ. 300. 2-3/yr. Expects 2 issues 1991, 3 issues 1992. sub. price: $10; per copy: $5; sample: $5. 65pp; 4¼×5½; of. Reporting time: 4-6 weeks. Payment: 1 copy. Copyrighted, reverts to author. Pub's reviews. §Small press, contemporary poets, aesthetics. Ads: $50/$25. CLMP.

Continuing Education Press, Portland State University, PO Box 1491, 1633 SW Park, Portland, OR 97207. 1968. Non-fiction. avg. press run 5M. Pub'd 2 titles 1990; expects 2 titles 1991, 2 titles 1992. 5 titles listed in the *Small Press Record of Books in Print* (20th Edition, 1991-92). avg. price, paper: $15. Discounts: 2-5 20%, 6-49 40%, 50+ 50%. 100pp; 8½×11; of. Reporting time: 2 months. Payment: contract terms by arrangement. Can copyright for author. Northwest Association of Book Publishers (NWABP).

Continuing Education Publications, Tony Midson, PO Box 1491, Portland State University, Portland, OR 97207. Non-fiction. "Authors must be authority in their field" Pub'd 2 titles 1990; expects 1 title 1991, 2 titles 1992. 4 titles listed in the *Small Press Record of Books in Print* (20th Edition, 1991-92). avg. price, paper: $12. Discounts: usual trade. of. NWABP.

CONTRACTOR PROFIT NEWS (CPN), Construction Industry Press, Roderick P. Crandall, PO Box 9838, San Rafael, CA 94912, 415-927-2155. *"CPN* is designed to make you money. It now includes more on marketing—getting and keeping customers. There are profit tips and more interviews from experts and top-notch consultants in every issue. Plus, we talk to owners and architects to show you how customers buy construction." 12/yr. Pub'd 12 issues 1990; expects 12 issues 1991, 12 issues 1992. sub. price: $116/1 yr, $219/2 yrs; add $20 each for foreign subs; sample: free. Back issues: sets available at discount. 8pp; 8½×11; of. Reporting time: 2 weeks. Copyrighted, does not revert to author. Pub's reviews. §Productivity, management and marketing.

CONVERGING PATHS, Kyril Oakwind, PO Box 63, Mt. Horeb, WI 53572. 1986. Fiction, articles, art, photos, cartoons, interviews, satire, reviews, letters, non-fiction. "Length: 2-6 single spaced pages but will serialize longer pieces. Must be Neo-Pagan or Wiccan oriented, may use positive occult or magic (ceremonial) material. Material returned only with SASE. Contributors should send for submission guidelines and see an issue before submitting." circ. 600. 4/yr. Pub'd 4 issues 1990; expects 4 issues 1991, 4 issues 1992. sub. price: $14, $22 foreign; per copy: $4, $6 foreign; sample: same. Back issues: $4 special pricing for back issue sets. 32pp; 8½×11; of. Reporting time: 6-8 weeks. Payment: contributor copy only. Copyrighted, reverts to author. Pub's reviews: 10 in 1990. §Pagan, Wiccan, magick. Ads: $25 1/2 page/$14 1/4 page/$8 1/8 page. Wiccan/Pagan Press Alliance (WPPA), PO Box 1392, Mechanicsburg, PA 17055.

COOKBOOK SERIES, Fell Publishers, Inc., Sherri Adelman, Elizabeth Wyatt, 2131 Hollywood Boulevard, Hollywood, FL 33020, 305-925-5242. 1943. Non-fiction. "We are the leading publisher of one-shot magazines

134

in the United States. We have four categories in which we publish. These are diet & health, health, cookbook series and financial planning series. We are looking for full manuscripts that would lend itself to these areas" circ. 50M. 8/yr. Pub'd 8 issues 1990; expects 8 issues 1991, 8 issues 1992. price per copy: $2.95. Back issues: cover price. Discounts: I.D. Distribution, Kable News Company-national distributor. 128pp; 5-3/16×7⅞; of. Reporting time: 3 months. Payment: negotiated. Copyrighted, reverts to author. Ads: $2,000. PBAA, ACIDA.

THE COOL TRAVELER, Bob Moore, PO Box 11975, Philadelphia, PA 19145, 215-440-0592. 1988. Poetry, fiction, articles, art, photos, cartoons, interviews, letters, news items, non-fiction. "Recent contributors include Addie Lee, Arthur Winfield Knight, Marion Homer Painter, and Gary Waller. We like material about 'place' including diaries written when travelling, and letters, info, articles about where one lives. Material can be any length." circ. 500. 4-6/yr. Pub'd 5 issues 1990; expects 5 issues 1991, 6+ issues 1992. sub. price: $10; per copy: $3; sample: $3. Back issues: $3. Discounts: negotiable. 25pp; 4¼×11; of. Reporting time: 2 weeks. Payment: sometimes—well written articles or unique info about places. Copyrighted, reverts to author. Pub's reviews: 4 in 1990. §Travel, art shows happening internationally (cultural events). Ads: $40/$25/classified $5 40 or so words.

COOP. ANTIGRUPPO SICILIANO, Sicilian Antigruppo/Cross-Cultural Communications, Nat Scammacca, Crescenzio Cane, Ignazio Navarra, Villa Schammachanat, Via Argentaria Km 4, Trapani, Sicily, Italy, 0923-38681. 1968. Poetry, articles, satire, criticism, reviews, letters, long-poems, collages, concrete art. "3-5 pages in English and Italian. A poetry review of the Sicilian Antigruppo, a populist movement of pluralistic commitment, leftist. Contributors: Crescenzio Cane, Nat Scammacca, Lollini, Jack Hirschman, Guiseppe Zagarrio, Mariella Bettarini, Pietro Terminelli, Ignazio Apolloni, Carmelo Pirrera, Santo Cali, Enzo Bonventre, Ignazio Navarra." circ. 1M. 3/yr. Expects 3 issues 1991. sub. price: $15; per copy: $5; sample: free. Back issues: $6. 44pp; 6×8; of, lp. Reporting time: 1 month. Payment: none. Copyrighted, reverts to author. Pub's reviews: 5 in 1990. §Poetry, poetics, criticism.

Cooper House Publishing Inc. (see also POET MAGAZINE), Peggy Cooper, Michael Hall, Joy Hall, PO Box 54947, Oklahoma City, OK 73154, 405-949-2020. 1990. Poetry, art, photos. "We sponsor the Annual Chapbook Competition and the grand prize winner receives publication of his/her manuscript in book form. Other book projects include poetry books and in the future, self-help and how-to books." avg. press run varies. Pub'd 1 title 1990; expects 2 titles 1991, 4 titles 1992. Discounts: available upon request. Pages vary; size varies; of. Reporting time: 3-6 months. Payment: winner of chapbook competition receives 50 free books; other arrangements would vary. Copyrights for author. COSMEP.

Cooperative Children's Book Center, Kathleen T. Horning, Ginny Moore Kruse, PO Box 5288, Madison, WI 53705, 608-262-3930. 1982. "The *Alternative Press Publishers of Children's Books: A Directory*, 4th edition(1991) lists with annotations, 205 alternative presses publishing one or more books for children in the U.S. and Canada. The *Directory* includes the following indexes: Distributors and the presses they serve, geographical index, index of presses publishing bilingual books and a subject index. Note: The Cooperative Children's Book Center is a children's literature examination and research library for adults." Expects 1 title 1991. avg. price, paper: $15, $18 outside U.S.

Copper Beech Press, M.K. Blasing, Director; Randy Blasing, Editor, Box 1852 Brown Univ., English Department, Providence, RI 02912, 401-863-2393. 1973. Poetry, fiction, long-poems. avg. press run 350-1M. Pub'd 3 titles 1990; expects 3 titles 1991, 3 titles 1992. 45 titles listed in the *Small Press Record of Books in Print* (20th Edition, 1991-92). avg. price, paper: $7.95. Discounts: bookstores, jobbers, etc. 1-5 20%; 6-9 33%; 10+ 40%. Poetry 48-75pp, fiction 80-150pp; size varies; of. Reporting time: ASAP, usually within 1 month. Payment: copies, 10%. Does not copyright for author.

Copper Canyon Press, Sam Hamill, Editor; Tree Swenson, Publisher; Mary Jane Knecht, Managing Editor, P.O. Box 271, Port Townsend, WA 98368. 1973. Poetry, long-poems. "We no longer read unsolicited mss. Queries should include SASE. Books distributed to the trade by Consortium, 287 E. 6th Street, Suite 365, St. Paul, MN 55101, 800-283-3572" avg. press run 2.5M. Pub'd 6 titles 1990; expects 6 titles 1991, 7 titles 1992. 65 titles listed in the *Small Press Record of Books in Print* (20th Edition, 1991-92). avg. price, cloth: $15; paper: $9. Discounts: standard 40%, returnable. 80pp; 6×9; of, lp. Reporting time: 1 month. Payment: 10% of edition. Copyrights for author.

Copyright Information Services (see also Umbrella Books), Jerome K. Miller, President, PO Box 1460-A, Friday Harbor, WA 98250, 217-356-7590. 1983. Non-fiction. "A division of Harbor View Publications Group. Limited to books and audiovisual material on the application of the copyright law to schools, colleges, libraries and churches. Unsolicited manuscripts MUST be accompanied by return postage or the manuscript will be returned COD with a $10.00 service charge, plus postage!" avg. press run 1M. Pub'd 4 titles 1990; expects 4 titles 1991, 4 titles 1992. 8 titles listed in the *Small Press Record of Books in Print* (20th Edition, 1991-92). avg. price, cloth: $30; other: audio seminars - $28. Discounts: 1-4 copies at list price; 5-10 items 30%, 11-25 items 40%, 26-75 items 45%, 76- items 50%. 200pp; 5½×8½; of. Reporting time: 1 month. Payment: negotiable.

135

Does not copyright for author.

Cordelia Press, Kim Van Alkemade, PO Box 11066, Milwaukee, WI 53211, 414-264-4018. 1990. Poetry. "No unsolicited manuscripts" avg. press run 500. Pub'd 1 title 1990; expects 1 title 1991, 1 title 1992. avg. price, paper: $10. Discounts: 20%. 70pp; 5½×8½; of.

Corfa Books, Sam Carr Polk, PO Box 3658, Santa Monica, CA 90408-3658, 213-829-7039. 1988. Fiction, non-fiction. "If the owner/author's first book is successful, other works will then be considered in the same field: national revitalization through basic, peaceful change—constitutional revision, electoral reform, political party reform, etc." Expects 1 title 1991. 1 title listed in the *Small Press Record of Books in Print* (20th Edition, 1991-92). Discounts: 2-9 20%, 10-29 30%, 30-59 40%, 60+ 50%.

CorkScrew Press, Bill Cates, Publisher; Richard Lippman, President, 2915 Fenimore Road, Silver Spring, MD 20902, 301-949-6787. 1988. Non-fiction. "We specialize in humor books" avg. press run 10M. Expects 2 titles 1991, 4 titles 1992. 2 titles listed in the *Small Press Record of Books in Print* (20th Edition, 1991-92). avg. price, paper: $8.95. Discounts: 42% trade, 50%+ jobber subject to change. 144pp; 8×8; of. Reporting time: 2 months. Payment: upon request. Copyrights for author. ABA, PMA.

Cornell Maritime Press, Inc., PO Box 456, Centreville, MD 21617, 301-758-1075. 1938. 1 title listed in the *Small Press Record of Books in Print* (20th Edition, 1991-92). Discounts: on request.

CORNERSTONE, Dawn Herrin, Editor, 939 W. Wilson, Chicago, IL 60640, 312-989-2080. 1972. Poetry, fiction, articles, art, photos, cartoons, interviews, satire, criticism, reviews, music, letters, parts-of-novels, long-poems, news items, non-fiction. "Call publication." circ. 50M. 6/yr. Pub'd 5 issues 1990; expects 6 issues 1991, 6 issues 1992. sub. price: $6.95; per copy: $2; sample: $2. Back issues: not available. Discounts: bulk - $12.50 for 50 copies. 40pp; 11×15; web, of. Reporting time: 6-8 weeks. Payment: varies. Copyrighted, reverts to author. Pub's reviews: 50-60 in 1990. §Religious, social, political. Ads: $1,400/$700.50/50¢ classified. EPA.

Cornerstone Press (see also IMAGE MAGAZINE), Anthony J. Summers, James J. Finnegan, PO Box 388, Arnold, MO 63010-0388. 1974. Poetry, fiction, articles, art, cartoons, interviews, reviews, collages, plays, concrete art, news items. "We have published 10 books to date. We are looking for works of art no matter how they are produced. Submit only things that will stand on their own" avg. press run 500-600. Pub'd 4 titles 1990; expects 3 titles 1991, 4 titles 1992. 9 titles listed in the *Small Press Record of Books in Print* (20th Edition, 1991-92). avg. price, cloth: $4-5; paper: $1-$3. Discounts: one free to any prisoner requesting. 48-72pp; 5½×8½; of. Reporting time: 2 weeks to 6 months, *query first*. Payment: money and copies to be arranged. Copyrights for author. CCLM.

CORNFIELD REVIEW, Stuart Lishan, English Dept, Ohio State Univ., 1465 Mount Vernon Avenue, Marion, OH 43302-5695, 614-389-6786. 1974. Poetry, fiction, articles, art, photos, criticism. "*The Cornfield Review* showcases 'midwestern writers.' Recent contributors: David Citino, Donald M. Hassler, Patricia Klas, E.L. Sauselen. We consider this magazine as an outlet for new and established writers with vision" circ. 750. 1/yr. Pub'd 1 issue 1990; expects 1 issue 1991, 1 issue 1992. sub. price: $4.50; per copy: $4.50. Discounts: 40% to stores. 64pp; 6×9; of. Reporting time: 5 months maximum. Payment: 2 copies. Copyrighted, reverts to author on written request. No ads.

CORONA, Lynda Sexson, Co-Editor; Michael Sexson, Co-Editor; Sarah Merrill, Managing Editor, Dept. of Hist. & Phil., Montana State University, Bozeman, MT 59717, 406-994-5200. 1980. Poetry, fiction, articles, art, photos, cartoons, satire, music, collages, plays, non-fiction. "Journal of arts and ideas; imaginative treatment of cultural issues. Looking particularly for work that transcends categories. We are interested in everything from the speculative essay to recipes for the construction or revision of things; we publish art and ideas that surprise with their quality and content. Recent contributors: Frederick Turner, William Irwin Thompson, James Hillman, Rhoda Lerman, Philip Dacey, Ivan Doig, Donald Hall, A.B. Guthrie, Jr., Richard Hugo, William Matthews, Stephen Dixon, James Dickey, Rayna Green, Fritjof Capra, Wendy Battin, Charles Edward Eaton, Nick Johnson." circ. 2M. 0-1/yr. Expects 1 issue 1992. sub. price: $7; per copy: $7; sample: $7. Back issues: $7. Discounts: trade, classroom, 30% (orders of 10 or more). 130pp; 10×7; of. Reporting time: 1 week to 6 months. Payment: nominal honorarium, 2 copies. Copyrighted. Pub's reviews: 10 in 1990. §All aspects of current thought, technology & the imagination, metaphor, art, religion. Ads: $150/$95/$65/back cover (inside) $200.

Corona Publishing Co., David Bowen, 1037 S. Alamo, San Antonio, TX 78210. 1977. Poetry, fiction, non-fiction. "We are a regional, independent, trade publishing house...operated for profit" avg. press run 2.5M-3.5M. Pub'd 6 titles 1990; expects 5 titles 1991, 6 titles 1992. 5 titles listed in the *Small Press Record of Books in Print* (20th Edition, 1991-92). avg. price, cloth: $15.95; paper: $8.95. Discounts: 30-45% to retail; 50% wholesale. 200pp; size varies; of. Reporting time: 6 weeks. Payment: 10% of net and up. Copyrights for author. Book Publishers of Texas, 3404 S. Ravinia Dr., Dallas, TX 75233.

Corporeal Studio Ltd. (see also ENSEMBLE, THE NEW VARIETY ARTS REVIEW), J.R. Moore, One Hudson Street, New York, NY 10013.

CORVALLIS STREETS POETRY MAGAZINE, Arnie Wolman Co., Arnie Wolman, PO Box 2291, Corvallis, OR 97339, 758-8244. 1989. Poetry, fiction, articles, art, interviews, reviews, parts-of-novels, long-poems, plays, news items, non-fiction. "We are putting out our second issue in tabloid form and it will contain poetry and short stories, satire and childrens stories by Arnie Wolman, James Magorian, Rochelle Holt and others yet to be decided upon." circ. 3M. Pub'd 100 issues 1990; expects 1 issue 1991, 2-10 issues 1992. sub. price: $24; per copy: $2.50; sample: $2. 8-16pp; 16×32; of. Reporting time: 2 weeks to 1 month. Payment: none—some by 1992. Copyrighted, reverts to author. Pub's reviews: 2 in 1990. §Herbs, metaphysics, poetry, travel, children, science. Ads: $350/$190/$98 1/4 page/50¢ per word classified. STREET, Poets Society of America.

CORVETTE FEVER MAGAZINE, Paul Zazarine, Editorial Director, Dobbs Publishing Group, PO Box 6320, Lakeland, FL 33807, 813-646-5743. 1978. Fiction, articles, photos, cartoons, interviews. "Must relate to the Chevrolet Corvette" circ. 50M. 12/yr. Pub'd 6 issues 1990; expects 10 issues 1991, 12 issues 1992. sub. price: $23.97; per copy: $3.95. Back issues: $5. Discounts: direct dealer rates available; inquire. 100pp; 8¼×10⅞; of. Reporting time: 3 months. Payment: upon pub - within 30 days. Copyrighted, we buy 1st rights & non-exclusive reprint rights. Pub's reviews: 6 in 1990. §Books about corvettes.

COSMEP NEWSLETTER, Richard Morris, PO Box 420703, San Francisco, CA 94142-0703, 415-922-9490. 1968. "Information for Publishers. Published for COSMEP members. Membership is $60 per year. Membership 1.5M." circ. 2.5M. 12/yr. Pub'd 12 issues 1990; expects 12 issues 1991, 12 issues 1992. sub. price: $60; per copy: $5; sample: free to publishers. Back issues: $5 each. Discounts: 20% subscription agencies. 8pp; 8½×11; of. Reporting time: 1 week. Payment: $60 for articles, query first. Copyrighted, reverts to author. Pub's reviews: 40 in 1990. §Books of interest to publishers. No ads.

Cosmic Circus Productions (see also SPIRIT MAGAZINE), Rey King, Editor, 414 So 41st Street, Richmond, CA 94804, 415-451-5818. 1974. Fiction, articles, photos, cartoons, interviews, satire, music, collages, plays. "We have interest in articles on cults, movements, conspiracies and the future" avg. press run 2M. Pub'd 1 title 1990; expects 2 titles 1991, 1 title 1992. 1 title listed in the *Small Press Record of Books in Print* (20th Edition, 1991-92). avg. price, paper: $5. Discounts: 40% off wholesale. 80pp; 7¾×10; of, web. Reporting time: 6 months. Payment: on publication. Copyrights for author. Artist Network.

Cosmic Footnotes Publications, Gayle Bachicha, 2575 S. Syracuse Way, #J-203, Denver, CO 80231. 1987. Poetry, fiction, non-fiction. "Additional address: PO Box 22594, Denver, CO 80222. We are a new press just recently established. We hope to have one or more books published by the fall of 1988. We will publish paperback books that deal with new age subjects such as metaphysics, esotenic astrology and related subjects" avg. press run 2M-3M. Expects 2-3 titles 1991, 5 titles 1992. avg. price, paper: $8.95. 200-450pp; 5½×8½.

COSMIC KALUDO, Rikki Leeson, Rikki Leeson, PO Box 581, Seattle, WA 98111. 1988. Fiction, art, cartoons, letters. "*Cosmic Kaludo* contains self-authored, self-drawn science fiction comic strips." circ. 44. Irregular. Pub'd 1 issue 1990. price per copy: $2; sample: $2. Back issues: inquire. Discounts: inquire. 36pp; 6½×10; photocopy. Copyrighted, reverts to author. Ads: inquire.

Cosmoenergetics Publications, Rick Blanchard, Betty Laing, PO Box 86353, San Diego, CA 92138, 619-295-1664. 1981. Non-fiction. "Biases: *Interrelationships*, metaphysics and science, symbolism and language, psychology and health, mind and healing" avg. press run 5M. Expects 3 titles 1991, 2 titles 1992. 6 titles listed in the *Small Press Record of Books in Print* (20th Edition, 1991-92). avg. price, paper: $9.95. Discounts: bookstores-40%; wholesalers-55%; 2-4 books-20%; 5-9 30%; 10-24 40%. 250pp; 5½×8½; arcata. Reporting time: 2-3 weeks. Payment: 10% quarterly. Copyrights for author. PMA (was PASCAL) 2401 Pacific Coast Hwy, Ste. 206, Hermosa Beach, CA 90254; BPSD, Box 220, Carlsbad, CA 92008; NAPRA, Po Box 9, Eastsound, WA 98245.

COSMOPOLITAN CONTACT, Romulus Rexner, Editor-in-Chief; Irene Anders, Managing Editor, PO Box 89300, Honolulu, HI 96830-9300. 1962. Articles, cartoons, interviews, criticism, reviews, letters. "*Cosmopolitan Contact*-a polyglot magazine, promotes intercultural understanding & intellectual growth as means toward the reduction of intergroup and international tension and conflict. Worldwide, friendly exchange of letters, hobbies, gifts, ideas, hospitality, information and other mutual travel or trade assistance among members. As a result of listings in this directory, in Writers' Markets, etc. more and better literary material is being contributed and more space will be allocated to literary material relevant to the philosophy and objectives of Planetary Legion for Peace (P.L.P.) and Planetary Universalism. It is the publication's object to have as universal appeal as possible — students, graduates and others interested in international affairs, cooperation, contacts, travel, friendships, trade, exchanges, self-improvement and widening of mental horizons through multicultural interaction. This publication has world wide distribution and participation, including the Communist countries. We need material designed to promote across all frontiers bonds of spiritual unity, intellectual understanding and sincere friendship among people by means of correspondence, meetings, publishing activities, tapes, records, exchange of hospitality, books, periodicals in various languages, hobbies and other contacts. Most of the material is not written by experts to enlighten or to amuse the readers, but it is written by the readers who also are freelance writers. The material is didactic, provocative, pragmatic — not art-for-art's sake — and tries to answer the reader's question: 'What can I do about it?' (Not what our leaders should do about the problem or need.) If a writer wants us to be interested in him, he/she should also be interested in our aims. Many writers are mainly preoccupied with their own self-aggrandisement and not interested in participating continuously in our work. The addresses of all contributors are published in order to facilitate global contacts among our contributors, editors and readers/members. Instead of writing e.g. about Lincoln or history, it is better to be an emancipator and to make history by promoting high ideals of mankind. Consequently, the material submitted to us should not be only descriptive, but it should be analytical, creative, action and future-oriented. Expose, preferably concentrating on government, education, etc., informational, inspiration, personal experience, travel, opinion. 'Silence is not always golden; sometimes it is yellow'. However, an average individual who wants to express publicly his own views or experiences finds out that the means of communication are controlled either by indoctrinated government officials, or by profit-seeking businessmen. The pages of 'Cosmopolitan Contact' are open to its readers who are invited to write regarding matters of general interest. These letters and articles will be published as far as space permits. Maximum 500 words. We are not interested in any contribution containing vulgar language, extreme, intolerant, pro-Soviet or anti-American opinions." circ. 1.5M. 2-3/yr. Pub'd 2-3 issues 1990; expects 2-3 issues 1991. sub. price: $4; per copy: $2; sample: $2. 8 back issues $3. Discounts: 40%. 32pp; 6×9; of. Reporting time: 6 weeks. Payment: copies only. Pub's reviews: 1 in 1990. §International affairs. Ads: $3 per inch/10¢. Pantheon Press—General Enterprises.

Coteau Books (see also Thunder Creek Publishing Co-operative), Shelley Sopher, Managing Editor, 401-2206 Dewdney Avenue, Regina, Sask. S4R 1H3, Canada, 306-777-0170. 1975. Poetry, fiction, interviews, criticism, long-poems, plays, non-fiction. "Coteau Books was established to publish prairie and Canadian writing: poetry, fiction, songs, plays, children's books and literary criticism. We do *not* consider manuscripts from non-Canadian writers. Coteau Books is committed to publishing the work of new as well as established writers and two series of books are devoted to new writers' work" avg. press run 3M. Pub'd 8 titles 1990; expects 9 titles 1991, 10 titles 1992. 25 titles listed in the *Small Press Record of Books in Print* (20th Edition, 1991-92). avg. price, cloth: $21.95; paper: $10.95; other: $6.95 mass market format. Discounts: 40% retail, 20% to schools and universities on 10 or more of same title. 80-400pp; 6×9, 4¼×7, 8×8, 8½×11; of. Reporting time: 3-6 months. Payment: normally 10% royalties. Copyrights for author. Sask. Publishers Group (SPG), Association of Canadian Publishers (ACP), Literary Press Group (LPG), Can. Book Information Centre (CBIC), Can. Telebook Agency (CTA), Can. Booksellers Association (CBA).

Cottage Books (see also THE ISLAND), Eddie Stack, C.B. Ni Sharachain, 731 Treat Avenue, San Francisco, CA 94110, 415-826-7113. 1987. Fiction, non-fiction. "Most recent publication - *Failure Free Activities for the Alzheimer Patient*, Author: Carmel Sheridan, M.A., A How-to book, 112 pages. Next book - Collection of Irish Folktales, edited by E.S." avg. press run 2.5M. Expects 2 titles 1991, 4 titles 1992. 2 titles listed in the *Small Press Record of Books in Print* (20th Edition, 1991-92). avg. price, paper: $10. Discounts: 60/40. 150pp; 5½×8½; of. Reporting time: 3 months. Payment: negotiable. Copyrights for author. COSMEP, PMA.

Cottage Press, PO Box 1207, Stockbridge, MA 01262. 1984. avg. press run 5M. Pub'd 1 title 1990; expects 2 titles 1991. 2 titles listed in the *Small Press Record of Books in Print* (20th Edition, 1991-92). avg. price, paper: $20. Discounts: 40% to bookstores on orders of more than 5 copies; up to 50% for wholesalers depending on size of order. 200pp; 8½×11. Reporting time: 60 days. Payment: to be arranged. Copyrights for author.

Cottage Publications, Inc., Don Wright, 24396 Pleasant View Drive, Elkhart, IN 46517, 219-875-8618. 1986. Articles, photos, non-fiction. avg. press run 20M. Pub'd 2 titles 1990; expects 3 titles 1991, 4 titles 1992. 2 titles listed in the *Small Press Record of Books in Print* (20th Edition, 1991-92). avg. price, paper: $14.95. Discounts: standard trade. 600pp; 5×7; of. Reporting time: 3 months. Payment: negotiable. Copyrights for author.

Cottontail Publications (see also THE PRESIDENTS' JOURNAL), Ellyn R. Kern, R 1, Box 198, Bennington, IN 47011, 812-427-3914. 1979. News items, non-fiction. avg. press run 1M. Expects 1 title 1991, 1 title 1992. 1 title listed in the *Small Press Record of Books in Print* (20th Edition, 1991-92). avg. price, paper: $7. Discounts: 2-50 40%. 90pp; 8½×11, 5½×7; of. Reporting time: 6 weeks or less. Payment: to be negotiated. Copyrights for author. COSMEP, NWC.

COTTONWOOD, George F. Wedge, Editor; Jane Garrett, Fiction Editor; Philip Wedge, Poetry Editor, Box J, Kansas Union, Univ. of Kansas, Lawrence, KS 66045, 913-864-3777. 1965. Poetry, fiction, art, photos, interviews, reviews. "Formerly *Cottonwood Review*. We publish a wide variety of styles of poetry and fiction but tend not to accept academic writing, workshop produce, or rhymed poetry. We generally prefer work that comes from experience. We are particularly interested in work from or about the 'Kansas midwest.' Poetry submissions should be limited to the five best, fiction to one story, as a rule. Past issues have included interviews with William Burroughs, Gwendolyn Brooks and Seamus Heaney. We have published recent work by Allen Ginsberg, Rita Dove, Patricia Traxler, William Stafford, Jared Carter, Victor Contoski, Robert Day,

W.S. Merwin, and Edwin Moses. We welcome submissions of photos, graphics, short fiction, poetry, and reviews of books from authors or presses in the midwest." circ. 500-600. 3/yr. Pub'd 2 issues 1990; expects 3 issues 1991, 3 issues 1992. 19 titles listed in the *Small Press Record of Books in Print* (20th Edition, 1991-92). sub. price: $12, $15 overseas; per copy: $5; sample: $3. Back issues: $2. Discounts: 30% trade, bulk negotiable. 112pp; 9×6; computer, of. Reporting time: 2-5 months, poetry; 3-6 months, fiction. Payment: 1 copy; eligibility for yearly Alice Carter Awards in poetry and fiction. Copyrighted. Pub's reviews: 8 in 1990. §Kansas Midwest, national, poetry or fiction chapbooks. No ads. CCLM.

COTTONWOOD MONTHLY, Cottonwood Press, Inc., Cheryl Thurston, 305 West Magnolia, #398, Fort Collins, CO 80521, 303-493-1286. 1987. Articles, non-fiction. *"The Cottonwood Monthly* contains articles, games, composition ideas, lessons, and teacher tips for junior high/middle school language arts teachers. Material can be as short as one paragraph (for teacher tips) or as long as 1,000 words (for lessons or articles). We want practical material that is useful for busy teachers, material that will make their lives easier. Some recent titles: 'Slang Is Here To Stay', 'Vocabulary Study Doesn't Need To Be Boring', 'Rap Can Motivate Reluctant Poets.'" circ. 300. 9/yr. Pub'd 3 issues 1990; expects 9 issues 1991, 9 issues 1992. sub. price: $21.95; per copy: $3; sample: free with SASE, 6 X 9. Back issues: $3 per issue. 6pp; 8½×11; of. Reporting time: 1-4 weeks. Payment: $10 for short tips to $20-$25 for lessons or short articles. Copyrighted, does not revert to author.

Cottonwood Press, W.E. Black, PO Box 1947, Boulder, CO 80306, (303) 433-4166. 1976. Non-fiction. "Additional address: PO Drawer 112, Crawford, NE 69339. Focus is on scholarly/historical and literary/western Americana and posthumous works of Mari Sandoz. How-to guides include foodbook and travel in Turkey. No submissions ever accepted without prior query letter and response affirming interest" avg. press run 1M. Pub'd 1 title 1990; expects 5 titles 1991, 2 titles 1992. avg. price, cloth: $24.95; paper: $9.95. Discounts: standard. Pages vary; 5¼×8¼; of. Payment: standard contract. COSMEP, PMA.

Cottonwood Press, Inc. (see also COTTONWOOD MONTHLY), Cheryl Thurston, 305 West Magnolia, Suite 398, Fort Collins, CO 80521, 303-493-1286. 1986. Poetry, plays, non-fiction. "We are interested primarily in practical books for language arts teachers. For example, the *Cottonwood Composition Book* is a book of ready-to-photocopy composition assignments for middle school and junior high classrooms. We are open to other material as well. We recently published a book of poems about teaching, for example. We like to see anything involving humor, anything that can make a teacher's life easier." avg. press run 500. Pub'd 3 titles 1990; expects 3 titles 1991, 3-5 titles 1992. 8 titles listed in the *Small Press Record of Books in Print* (20th Edition, 1991-92). avg. price, paper: $15.95. 50pp; 8½×11; of. Reporting time: 2-4 weeks. Payment: outright purchase, $200-$500. Copyrights for author.

Cougar Books, Ruth Pritchard, Editorial Director, PO Box 22879, Sacramento, CA 95822, 916-442-1434. 1973. Non-fiction. "Publish books in primarily health & parenting" avg. press run 5M. Pub'd 2 titles 1990; expects 2 titles 1991, 2 titles 1992. 4 titles listed in the *Small Press Record of Books in Print* (20th Edition, 1991-92). avg. price, paper: $7.95. Discounts: 1-4, 20; 5-49, 40%; 50-99, 42%. 160pp; 5½×8½; of. Reporting time: 2 months. Payment: 5% to 10%. Copyrights for author. AAP, NCBPA, WBPA.

Michael E. Coughlin, Publisher (see also THE DANDELION), Michael E. Coughlin, 1985 Selby Avenue, St Paul, MN 55104, 612-646-8917. 1978. avg. press run 1M. Pub'd 1 title 1990; expects 1 title 1991, 1 title 1992. 6 titles listed in the *Small Press Record of Books in Print* (20th Edition, 1991-92). avg. price, cloth: $25; paper: $5.95. Discounts: 40% to bookstores ordering 3 or more copies. 300pp; 6×9; †lp. Reporting time: 2 months. Payment: negotiated. Copyrights for author.

Council For Indian Education, Hap Gilliland, 517 Rimrock Road, Billings, MT 59102, 406-252-7451. 1963. Fiction, non-fiction. "Small books on themes related to American Indian life and culture, both fiction and non-fiction, also Indian crafts, and small books on teaching. Book ordering address: PO Box 31215, Billings, MT 59107" avg. press run 2M. Pub'd 6 titles 1990; expects 6 titles 1991, 6 titles 1992. 45 titles listed in the *Small Press Record of Books in Print* (20th Edition, 1991-92). avg. price, cloth: $9.95; paper: $3.95. Discounts: 1-10 20%, 11+ 40% to bookstores only. 44pp; 6×9; of. Reporting time: 1-5 months. Payment: 10% of wholesale price or 1½¢ per word. We furnish author with copyright forms.

Council Oak Books, Sally Dennison, Publisher, 1428 S. St. Louis, Tulsa, OK 74120, 918-587-6454. 1984. "We no longer accept unsolicited queries & manuscripts" avg. press run 4M. Pub'd 4 titles 1990; expects 4 titles 1991, 7 titles 1992. 31 titles listed in the *Small Press Record of Books in Print* (20th Edition, 1991-92). avg. price, cloth: $19.95; paper: $9.95. Discounts: trade 1-3 20%, 4-49 43%, 50-99 44%, 100-249 45%, 250-299 46%, 500+ 47%; wholesale 50%. 220pp; size varies. Reporting time: varies. Payment: standard percentages of retail sales. Copyrights for author. ABA, Oklahoma Booksellers Association, South Central Booksellers Assn.

Council on Interracial Books For Children (see also INTERRACIAL BOOKS FOR CHILDREN BULLETIN), Melba Kgositsile, Executive Director, 1841 Broadway, New York, NY 10023, 212-757-5339.

1966. "Interested in materials that give insights to children on institutional racism and sexism" avg. press run 5M. Pub'd 3 titles 1990; expects 4 titles 1991. 13 titles listed in the *Small Press Record of Books in Print* (20th Edition, 1991-92). avg. price, paper: $2.95. 128pp; 8½×11; of. Reporting time: 3 months. Payment: yes. Copyrights for author. COSMEP.

The Counter-Propaganda Press, Box 365, Park Forest, IL 60466, 312-534-8679. 1982. Non-fiction. avg. press run 5M. Expects 1 title 1991, 1 title 1992. 1 title listed in the *Small Press Record of Books in Print* (20th Edition, 1991-92). avg. price, paper: $14.95. Discounts: 1-2 20%, 5+ 40%. 208-224pp; 6×9; of.

THE COUNTRYMAN, Christopher Hall, Sheep Street, Burford, Oxford OX8 4LH, England, Burford 2258. 1927. Poetry, articles, art, photos, cartoons, reviews. "1.5M words max. Concern with country life of all kinds, but no sentimentalising" circ. 70M. 6/yr. Pub'd 6 issues 1990. sub. price: £10.50, $25, £11.50 overseas rate; per copy: £1.80; sample: £1.80 plus mailing costs. Back issues: £1 + mailing costs. 200pp; 120mm x 175mm; photocomposition. Reporting time: 1-2 weeks. Payment: £40 for 1M words and upwards. Copyrighted, does not revert to author. Pub's reviews: 250 in 1990. §Country life, wildlife, rural history and economics, hiking, gardening, architecture. Ads: £660/£355/80p (minimum 15 words). PPA.

Countryman Press, Louis Kannenstine, Editorial Director, PO Box 175, Woodstock, VT 05091, 802-457-1049. 1973. Poetry, fiction, non-fiction. avg. press run 5M. Pub'd 21 titles 1990; expects 28 titles 1991. 183 titles listed in the *Small Press Record of Books in Print* (20th Edition, 1991-92). avg. price, cloth: $17.95; paper: $9.95. Discounts: 40% 5-24 copies, 42% 25-49, 43% 50-99, 44% 100-199, 45% 200+, 47% 200+ to one location. 6×9; of. Reporting time: 8 weeks. Payment: usual contract terms. Copyrights for author. AAP.

CountrySide Business Publications, Marcia Hodson, PO Box 115, Galveston, IN 46932, 219-626-2131. 1990. Non-fiction. "Recently started small press publishing company and self-published first book *Word Processing Plus: Profiles of Home-Based Success.* Am interested in publishing works that will be of help and interest to women (and men) in the area of home-based business, businesses which use word processing/desktop publishing skills. Also interested in women's health issues." avg. press run 2.5M. Expects 3 titles 1991, 5 titles 1992. 1 title listed in the *Small Press Record of Books in Print* (20th Edition, 1991-92). avg. price, paper: $15.95. Discounts: wholesale/jobbers 55%, libraries 20%. 240pp; 5½×8½; of. Reporting time: 4-6 weeks. Payment: 4-10% of royalties. Copyrights for author. PMA.

Cove View Press, Mereda Kaminski, 375 Tudor Street, Ashland, OR 97520. 1977. avg. press run 500. Pub'd 1 title 1990; expects 2 titles 1991. 6 titles listed in the *Small Press Record of Books in Print* (20th Edition, 1991-92). Discounts: less than 3 - 20%; 3 or more - 30%; any 10 or more (paid) - 50%. of. Reporting time: 1-4 weeks. Payment: 10% of net. Copyrights for author.

John Edwin Cowen, Ltd. (see also BRAVO, THE POET'S MAGAZINE), Jose Garcia Villa, 1081 Trafalgar Street, Teaneck, NJ 07666. 1977. "Biases: (1) Poetry must have formal excellence, (2) Poetry must be lyrical, (3) Poetry is not prose. Books Published: *Introducing Mr. Vanderborg* poems by Arthur Vanderborg; *Appassionata: Poems in Praise of Love,* Jose Garcia Villa; (forthcoming) *The Collected Poems of Jose Garcia Villa* by Jose Garcia Villa, and *Parlement of Giraffes,* by Jose Garcia Villa, selected by John Cowen. Mss by invitation only" avg. press run 1.5M. Pub'd 1 title 1990; expects 1 title 1991, 1 title 1992. 2 titles listed in the *Small Press Record of Books in Print* (20th Edition, 1991-92). avg. price, cloth: $10; paper: $4.95. Discounts: 40%. 96pp; 6¼×9½; lp. Payment: by arrangement with author. Copyrights for author. NYSSPA.

Coxland Press (see also BALDER), Stephen B. Cox, 60 Elmhurst Road, Reading, Berkshire RG1 5HY, England. 1990. Poetry, fiction, articles, non-fiction. "Our press deals mainly with the fields of history, mythology, folklore, occult, religion, culture, etc., and especially manuscripts which are rare and normally unavailable; for example, which provide a sensitive service to groups releasing their material to the public for the first time in history. Upcoming books include material from a society in Turkey, also in USA, and Sweden" avg. press run 1M. Pub'd 2 titles 1990; expects 4 titles 1991, 5 titles 1992. 6 titles listed in the *Small Press Record of Books in Print* (20th Edition, 1991-92). avg. price, paper: £9; other: £24 computer style manual. Discounts: 35% on orders over 10. 50-252pp; 5⅞×8¼; †of. Payment: 10% of sale price after publication. Copyrights for author.

COYDOG REVIEW, Candida Lawrence, Editor, PO Box 2608, Aptos, CA 95001, 408-761-1824. 1984. Poetry, fiction, articles, art, interviews, satire, criticism, reviews, parts-of-novels, long-poems, collages. "Length open. Works published by *Coydog* may have appeared elsewhere. The editor has a preference for material she can understand but is willing to look at anything" circ. 300. 1/yr. Pub'd 1 issue 1990; expects 1 issue 1992. price per copy: $7; sample: $5. Back issues: $5. 100pp; 7½×10; of. Reporting time: 2 months or less. Payment: 2 copies. Copyrighted, reverts to author. Pub's reviews: 0 in 1990. §Very good work by relatively unpublished authors. IWWG/NWU.

CRAB CREEK REVIEW, Linda J. Clifton, Carol Orlock, Fiction Editor, 4462 Whitman Avenue North,

Seattle, WA 98103, 206-633-1090. 1983. Poetry, fiction, art, satire, non-fiction. "Prefer poems under 40 lines, fiction and articles under 3M words. Like work that reads well aloud, has an authentic voice, presents clear and compelling images, makes us look at the world again with a new perception, displays a sense of wit and work-play. Accept free verse and verse written in form. Recent contributors include, William Stafford, Sam Hamill, Laurel Speer, Maxine Kumin, T.S. Wallace, Robert Bringhurst, Shuntaro Tanakawa. Maximum story length is 3,200 words. Need non-fiction - essays in the tradition of Thoreau, Dillard, Didion, Selzer. Not seeking mss. until 1993." circ. 300. 3/yr. Pub'd 3 issues 1990; expects 3 issues 1991, 3 issues 1992. sub. price: $8; per copy: $3; sample: $3. 32pp; 6⅜x10; of. Reporting time: 8-12 weeks. Payment: 2 copies; hope to expand to be able to pay in cash. Copyrighted, reverts to author but request mention of *Crab Creek Review* with subsequent printings. Ads: $120/$65. CLMP.

CRAFTS NSW, Helen Zilko, 88 George Street, Sydney, N.S.W. 2000, Australia, 612-247-9126. 1964. Articles, art, photos, interviews, criticism, reviews, letters, news items. "Aims to provide info. relevant to prof. crafts practice in NSW/Australia" circ. 1M. 4/yr. Pub'd 6 issues 1990; expects 4 issues 1991, 4 issues 1992. sub. price: AUS$30 to libraries only, AUS$68 companies; per copy: AUS$3.50 plus postage; sample: $AUS4. Back issues: $4. Discounts: 40%. 16pp; size A4; computer typeset. Reporting time: 1 month. Payment: none. Copyrighted, reverts to author. Pub's reviews: 20 in 1990. §Art, craft, allied areas such as marketing, etc. Ads: $AUS220/$AUS130.

Craftsman Book Company, Gary Moselle, Publisher; Laurence Jacobs, Editor, 6058 Corte Del Cedro, Carlsbad, CA 92009, 619-438-7828. 1952. Non-fiction. "Craftsman Book Company publishes *practical references for professional builders*. Craftsman books are loaded with step-by-step instructions, illustrations, charts, reference data, checklists, forms, samples, cost estimates, rules of thumb, and examples that solve actual problems in the builder's office or in the field. Every book covers a limited construction subject fully, becomes the builder's primary reference on that subject, has a high utility-to-cost ratio, and will help the builder make a better living in his profession. Length is variable but should be at least 500 manuscript pages including illustrations and charts. We see queries and outlines and will consider material in nearly all construction areas and trades, including electrical, heating and air conditioning, lath and plaster, painting, prefab housing construction, heavy construction, estimating, and costing" avg. press run 5M. Pub'd 8 titles 1990; expects 12 titles 1991, 12 titles 1992. 20 titles listed in the *Small Press Record of Books in Print* (20th Edition, 1991-92). avg. price, paper: $19. Discounts: trade 1-4 copies 33%, 5-49 copies 40%, 50+ copies 45%. 297pp; 8½x11. Reporting time: 3 weeks. Payment: 12½% of all books sold, no advance. Copyrights for author. Publishers Marketing Assn.

CRAMPED AND WET, Kidd Smiley, 1012 29th, Sioux City, IA 51104. 1988. Poetry, fiction, art. "Stuff that shows tractor-driven passion—stuff that practices self-parody like some practice self-discipline—stuff that hits." circ. 150. 4/yr. Pub'd 3 issues 1990; expects 4 issues 1991, 4 issues 1992. price per copy: $1.50; sample: $1.50. Back issues: $1.50. 28pp; 5½x8; †of. Reporting time: varies. Payment: copy. Not copyrighted.

The F. Marion Crawford Memorial Society (see also THE ROMANTIST), John C. Moran, Editor; Steve Eng, Co-Editor; Jesse F. Knight, Co-Editor; Don Herron, Contributing Editor; Richard Dalby, Contributing Editor, Saracinesca House, 3610 Meadowbrook Avenue, Nashville, TN 37205. 1975. Poetry, articles, art, photos, interviews, criticism, reviews, music, letters, long-poems, collages. "H. Warner Munn, Donald Sidney-Fryer, Clark Ashton Smith, Robert E. Howard, George Sterling, and kindred authors. Purview is Modern Romanticism, especially Imaginative Literature (emphasis upon Fantasy) ; contains a regular section on F. Marion Crawford (1854-1909). Publishes mostly traditional (rimed) poetry. No fiction" avg. press run 300 (limited and numbered). Pub'd 1 title 1990; expects 1 title 1991, 1 title 1992. 5 titles listed in the *Small Press Record of Books in Print* (20th Edition, 1991-92). avg. price, paper: $12.50 incl postage. Discounts: 20% to 40% depending upon quantity. 100-120pp; 8½x11; of, lp. Reporting time: within 1 month (query on all articles). Payment: 1 copy (at present). Does not copyright for author.

CRAWLSPACE, Robert Spencer, Steve Urbaniak, Box 10911, Portland, ME 04104. 1991. "We are restricted by our size and also our own aesthetic inclinations to shorter works. That includes short prose poems, dialogues, and modern fables of a 'Kafka-esque' nature." 4/yr. Expects 2 issues 1991, 4 issues 1992. sub. price: $11; per copy: $3; sample: $1. 36pp; 5½x8½; †photocopy. Reporting time: 2-10 weeks. Payment: copies. Copyrighted, reverts to author. Maine Writers and Publishers Alliance (MWPA), 19 Mason Street, Brunswick, ME 04011.

CRAZYHORSE, Zabelle Stodola, Managing Editor; Judy Troy, Fiction Editor; Ralph Burns, Poetry Editor; Dennis Vannatta, Review and Criticism Editor, 2801 S. University, Dept. of English, Univ. of Arkansas-Little Rock, Little Rock, AR 72204, 501-569-3160. 1960. Poetry, fiction, interviews, criticism, reviews, parts-of-novels, long-poems. "Past Contributors include James Wright, Louis Simpson, Richard Hugo, Philip Levine, Maura Stanton, Jorie Graham, William Matthews, Frederick Busch, Raymond Carver, Andre Dubus, Bobbie Ann Mason, John Updike, etc." circ. 1M. 2/yr. Pub'd 2 issues 1990; expects 2 issues 1991, 2 issues 1992. sub. price: $10; per copy: $5; sample: $4. Back issues: $2-$4. Discounts: agencies, 30%; bookstores, 40%. 150pp; 6x9; of. Reporting time: 2-8 weeks. Payment: $10 per printed page, also $500 awards for best poem and story we publish each year. Copyrighted. Pub's reviews: 2 in 1990. §Contemporary poetry, fiction and criticism of the same. Ads: $85/$50. CCLM.

CRAZYQUILT LITERARY QUARTERLY, Marsh Cassady, Editor-in-Chief & Fiction; Jim Kitchen, Managing Editor; Nancy Churnin Demac, Drama Editor; Jackie Ball (Cicchetti), Poetry Editor; Leif Fearn, Nonfiction Editor; Edee Suslick, Art Editor; Steve Smith, Fiction Co-Editor, CrazyQuilt Press, PO Box 632729, San Diego, CA 92163-2729, 619-688-1023. 1986. Poetry, fiction, articles, art, photos, interviews, satire, criticism, parts-of-novels, long-poems, non-fiction. "Prefer fiction under 4,000, shorter poems, will accept longer. Nonfiction: about writing, writers or literary criticism preferred. Black and white photos. Simultaneous submissions okay. Contributors: Louis Phillips, William Marael Johnson, Sue Saniel Elkind, Huchman." circ. 200. 4/yr. Pub'd 4 issues 1990; expects 4 issues 1991, 4 issues 1992. sub. price: $14.95; per copy: $4.50; sample: $4.50 current issue. Back issues: $2.50. Discounts: 40%. 90pp; 5×8; of. Reporting time: 10-12 weeks. Payment: 2 copies. Copyrighted, reverts to author. Pub's reviews: 2 in 1990. §Writers, writing, art, drama, fiction, poetry. Ads: $40/$25/$15 1/4 page. CLMP, 666 Broadway, New York, NY 10012-2301.

CRC Publications (see also THE BANNER), Harvey Smit, Galen Meyer, 2850 Kalamazoo SE, Grand Rapids, MI 49560. 1979. Poetry, fiction, articles, art, photos, cartoons, interviews, criticism, reviews, music, non-fiction. "Religion-in the Reformed-Presbyterian tradition" avg. press run varies. Pub'd 40 titles 1990; expects 50 titles 1991, 60 titles 1992. Discounts: 15-30% to qualified bookstores/distributors. Pages vary; †of. Reporting time: varies. Does not always copyright for author. PCPA, CBA.

CRCS Publications, Julie Pickerill, PO Box 1460, Sebastopol, CA 95473-1460. 1975. Non-fiction. "We are specializing in the production of high-quality, aesthetically-pleasing astrological books, with a psychological and spiritual slant, & books on health, herbology, Taich, yoga" avg. press run 5M. Pub'd 5 titles 1990; expects 4 titles 1991, 3 titles 1992. 39 titles listed in the *Small Press Record of Books in Print* (20th Edition, 1991-92). avg. price, cloth: $9.95-14.95; paper: $4.95-$9.95. Discounts: 40% off orders of 5 or more books to dealers; 40% off all pre-paid orders from dealers, in any quantity; 10% to libraries if requested. Free shipping on pre-paid orders for 25 or more books. 200+pp; size varies; of. Reporting time: 8 weeks - must inquire before sending ms. Payment: royalties plus large discounts on books. Copyrights for author. COSMEP.

THE CREAM CITY REVIEW, Valerie Ross, Editor, PO Box 413, English Dept, Curtin Hall, Univ. of Wisconsin, Milwaukee, WI 53201. 1975. Poetry, fiction, photos, interviews, criticism, reviews, parts-of-novels, long-poems, plays. "We publish a variety of writers and writings, offering a range of perspectives, styles, and contents from new and well-known writers. Each issue also features a forum for debate on a literary topic. We prefer prose of 25 pages or less, though we'll consider longer pieces. Please submit no more than one work of prose, or up to five poems. Personal essays, non-academic literary essays, and short small press book reviews are especially welcome, as are b/w camera-ready art and photos. Recent contributors: Marge Piercy, Maxine Kumin, Ted Kooser, William Matthews, Eugenio de Andrade, George Garrett, Jerome Mazzaro, Stuart Dybek, Charles Altieri, Ihab Hassan, Amy Clampitt, Houston Baker, Herbert Blau, and F.D. Reeve." circ. 1M-1.5M. 2/yr. Pub'd 2 issues 1990; expects 2 issues 1991, 2 issues 1992. sub. price: $10; per copy: $6; sample: $4.50. Back issues: $5. 200pp; 5½×8½; of. Reporting time: 4-8 weeks, sometimes longer. Payment: varies, 2 copies. Copyrighted, reverts to author. Pub's reviews: 20 in 1990. §Poetry, prose, criticism. Ads: $50/$25/no classified word rate. CCLM, COSMEP.

CREATING EXCELLENCE, David Robinson, New World Publishing, Inc., PO Box 2048, South Burlington, VT 05407. 1987. Articles, art, photos, cartoons, interviews, non-fiction. "Prefer nonfiction inspirational articles on people or ideas related to *personal development* in Vermont. Average length 1,500 words. Prefer positive approach toward ways to improve relationships, business and personal success" circ. 20M. 6/yr. Pub'd 6 issues 1990; expects 6 issues 1991, 6 issues 1992. sub. price: $12; per copy: $2.75; sample: same. Back issues: $3.75 individually $2.50 in volume. 48pp; 8⅜×10⅞; of, web. Reporting time: 3-4 weeks. Payment: upon publication. Copyrighted, reverts to author. Ads: $1400/$775.

CREATION/EVOLUTION JOURNAL, Frederick Edwords, PO Box 146, 7 Harwood Drive, Buffalo, NY 14226, 716-839-5080. 1980. Articles, criticism, reviews, letters, news items. circ. 2M. 4/yr. Pub'd 3 issues 1990; expects 4 issues 1991, 4 issues 1992. sub. price: $12 (outside USA $15); per copy: $3; sample: same. Back issues: $3 for each back issue; 10 copies or more of only 1 back issue $2 per copy. 44pp; 5¼×8½; †of. Reporting time: 1 month. Payment: none; free issues are provided. Copyrighted, reverts to author. Pub's reviews: 5 in 1990. §The creation/evolution controversy.

Creative Concern Publications, Richard Hughes, Editor, 12066 Suellen Circle, West Palm Beach, FL 33414, 305-793-5854. 1984. Fiction, non-fiction. "General office: 3208 East Mayaguana Lane, Lantana, FL 33462" avg. press run 5M. Pub'd 2 titles 1990; expects 2 titles 1991, 2 titles 1992. 3 titles listed in the *Small Press Record of Books in Print* (20th Edition, 1991-92). avg. price, paper: $3.95. Discounts: 40% wholesalers, 30% bookstores. 250pp; 5½×8¾; of. Reporting time: 6 months. Payment: subsidize press. Copyrights for author. NWC, FFWA.

142

CREATIVE KIDS, GCT Inc., Fay L. Gold, PO Box 6448, Mobile, AL 36660, 205-478-4700. 1980. Poetry, fiction, articles, art, photos, cartoons, interviews, reviews, music, plays. "All work must be original and by children ages 5-18. None other will be considered" circ. 12M. 8/yr. Pub'd 8 issues 1990; expects 8 issues 1991, 8 issues 1992. sub. price: $23.97 (foreign postage, add $6); per copy: $3; sample: $3. Discounts: price on request. 32pp; 8½x11; of. Reporting time: ASAP. Payment: none. Copyrighted, reverts to author. Pub's reviews: 20 in 1990. §Books, materials for children 5-18, especially items dealing with creativity. Ads: $500/$275. Edpress.

CREATIVE LOAFING, Deborah Eason, 750 Willoughby Street, Atlanta, GA 30312-1124, 404-873-5623. 1972. Poetry, articles, interviews, reviews, news items. circ. 100M. 52/yr. Pub'd 52 issues 1990; expects 52 issues 1991, 52 issues 1992. sub. price: $32; per copy: free; sample: free. Back issues: free. 100pp; tabloid; web of. Reporting time: 1 week. Payment: $2.50/inch approx. $4 for cover. Copyrighted, reverts to author. Pub's reviews: 26 in 1990. §Non-fiction. Ads: $2475/$350/$12 1st 15 words, 60¢ each additional word.

Creative Roots, Inc., Lloyd deMause, PO Box 401, Planetarium Station, New York, NY 10024, 212-799-2294. 1975. Non-fiction. "Book publishing" avg. press run 2M. Pub'd 1 title 1990; expects 2 titles 1991, 5 titles 1992. 2 titles listed in the *Small Press Record of Books in Print* (20th Edition, 1991-92). avg. price, cloth: $25; paper: $10. Discounts: 2 or more-20%. 350pp; 6x9; of. Reporting time: 1 month. Payment: variable. Copyrights for author. COSMEP.

Creative With Words Publications (CWW), Brigitta Geltrich, Editor & Publisher, PO Box 223226, Carmel, CA 93922-3226, 408-649-1682. 1975. Poetry, fiction, cartoons, satire. "Length: brevity is the key word. Submittals by all ages. Query with SASE is a MUST. Annual Poetry Contest" avg. press run varies. Pub'd 2 titles 1990; expects 2 titles 1991, 2 titles 1992. 16 titles listed in the *Small Press Record of Books in Print* (20th Edition, 1991-92). avg. price, cloth: $5-$8; paper: price varies $8 and below; other: varies. Discounts: schools, libraries, and senior citizens receive rates, inquire; authors receive 20% off; on orders 10 or more 10% off. Pages vary (approx. 50); 5½x8½, 5½x11; mi, xerox, laser printer. Reporting time: 1-2 months - SASE is always a must; if a seasonal anthology reporting time is 6 months. Payment: 20% reduction of regular cost to participants, no payment in copies; small fee for guest artists. Copyrights for author. SCBW.

THE CREATIVE WOMAN, Helen E. Hughes, Governors State University, University Park, IL 60466, 312-534-5000, Ext. 2524. 1977. Poetry, fiction, articles, art, photos, interviews, criticism, reviews, letters, news items. circ. 1M. 3/yr. Pub'd 3 issues 1990; expects 3 issues 1991, 3 issues 1992. sub. price: $12; per copy: $4; sample: $4. Back issues: $5. Discounts: 40%. 48pp; 8½x11; †of. Reporting time: 6 months or less. Payment: 4 copies. Copyrighted, reverts to author. Pub's reviews: 8 in 1990. §Women's involvement in creative endeavors, any aspect of creativity in any field applied to women. No ads.

CREATIVITY CONNECTION, Marshall J. Cook, Room 224 Lowell Hall, Wisconsin Univ., 610 Langdon Street, Madison, WI 53703, 608-262-4911. 1990. Articles, photos, cartoons, interviews, reviews, news items, non-fiction. "We publish articles and art about and illustrating the creative process in writers, photographers, and print designers." circ. 1M. 3/yr. Pub'd 3 issues 1990; expects 3 issues 1991, 3 issues 1992. sub. price: $6.95; per copy: $2; sample: $2. Back issues: $1. Discounts: we can negotiate with classrooms. 8-12pp; 8½x11; †of. Reporting time: 2 weeks. Payment: 10 copies. Copyrighted, reverts to author. Pub's reviews: 6 in 1990. §Creativity, writing (how-to), writers (auto & bio). Ads: none.

Creatures At Large Press, John Stanley, PO Box 687, 1082 Grand Teton Drive, Pacifica, CA 94044, (415) 355-READ. 1981. Fiction, reviews. "We now have 3 books: *Lost in Time and Space with Lefty Feep* by Robert Bloch, *Revenge of the Creature Features Movie Guide* by John Stanley, *Them Ornery Mitchum Boys* by John Mitchum" avg. press run 5M-10M. Pub'd 3 titles 1990. 4 titles listed in the *Small Press Record of Books in Print* (20th Edition, 1991-92). avg. price, cloth: $40; paper: $12. Discounts: available on request. 400-500pp; size varies; of. Payment: varies from project to project but usually 8-10-12%. Copyrights for author. COSMEP, PMA, Writers Connection, 10601 S. DeAnza Blvd, Suite 301, Cupertino, CA 95014.

CREDIT REPORT, CreditPower Publishing Co., Daniel K. Berman, 44 Montgomery Street, 5th floor, San Francisco, CA 94104, 415-955-2650.

CreditPower Publishing Co. (see also CREDIT REPORT), Daniel K. Berman, 44 Montgomery Street, 5th Floor, San Francisco, CA 94104, 415-955-2650. 1987. "CreditPower is the nation's only publishing company focusing on issues relating to consumer credit, a growing and important niche. Any subject within the realm of personal finance may be considered" avg. press run 5M. Pub'd 1 title 1990; expects 3 titles 1991, 7 titles 1992. 1 title listed in the *Small Press Record of Books in Print* (20th Edition, 1991-92). avg. price, other: $25-$50 comb-bound. Discounts: 40%. 200pp; 8½x11. Reporting time: 2 weeks for manuscripts. Payment: negotiable. PMA.

CREEPING BENT, Joseph Lucia, 1023 Main Street, Apt. 5, Bethlehem, PA 18018, 215-866-5613. 1984. Poetry, fiction, reviews. "We will be publishing very little (possibly no) unsolicited work during 1991-92.

Though we will publish poetry on any subject, we take a special interest in poems that articulate a vision of the continuities and discontinuities in the human relationship to the natural world. We are open to the work of unpublished and beginning writers, but we look for the marks of developed talent in everything we select to print. This means that we like technically-accomplished poems that make use of the varied resources of the medium, and that we look especially for verse that demonstrates a poet's deep engagement with language, with the world outside the self, and with other poetry. Above all, we are eclectic in our tastes." circ. small but growing. 1-2/yr. Pub'd 1 issue 1990; expects 1 issue 1991, 2 issues 1992. sub. price: $6 individual, $8 libraries; per copy: $3; sample: $3. Discounts: 40% plus postage to bookstores; 20% to jobbers. 56pp; 5½x8½; of. Reporting time: generally 1 month, but may be longer. Payment: copies. Copyrighted, reverts to author. Pub's reviews: 2 in 1990. §Small press and university press poetry. CCLM.

Creighton-Morgan Publishing Group, Fay Faron, Po Box 470862, San Francisco, CA 94147-0862. 1989. avg. press run 5M. Pub'd 1 title 1990; expects 3 titles 1991. 3 titles listed in the *Small Press Record of Books in Print* (20th Edition, 1991-92). avg. price, cloth: $48; paper: $15.95. Discounts: 40%. 300pp; 8½x11; OF. Reporting time: do not submit. Does not copyright for author. COSMEP.

THE CRESCENT REVIEW, Guy Nancekeville, Editor, PO Box 15065, Winston-Salem, NC 27113, 919-924-1851. 1983. Fiction, art. *"The Crescent Review* is a short-story magazine. All styles, all subjects. We solicit southern (esp. NC), minority (esp. black and native Am.), and previously unpublished writers, but all are welcome to submit." circ. 300. 2/yr. Pub'd 2 issues 1990; expects 2 issues 1991, 2 issues 1992. sub. price: $10; per copy: $5 next issue; sample: $6 back issue. 128pp; 6x9; of. Reporting time: 6 weeks. Payment: 2 contributor copies. Copyrighted, reverts to author. Pub's reviews. §Short-story collections and anthologies only. Ads: $120/$65/bookstores carrying *Crescent Revew* get free mention. CCLM.

CRICKET, THE MAGAZINE FOR CHILDREN, Marianne Carus, Publisher & Editor-in-Chief, PO Box 300, Peru, IL 61354, 815-224-6643. 1973. Poetry, fiction, articles, art, music, plays, non-fiction. "Word limit for fiction: 1500 words; for non-fiction: 1200 words." circ. 130M. 12/yr. Pub'd 12 issues 1990; expects 12 issues 1991, 12 issues 1992. sub. price: $29.97; per copy: $3; sample: $2. Back issues: $3. 80pp; 7x9; of. Reporting time: approximately 3 months. Payment: stories and articles up to 25¢ per word (1500 max), poems up to $3 per line. Copyrighted, reverts to author. Pub's reviews: 40 one-paragraph reviews in 1990. §Any good children's books: fiction or non-fiction. Magazine Publishers Assn., 575 Lexington Avenue, New York, NY 10022.

Crime and Social Justice Associates, Inc. (see also SOCIAL JUSTICE: A JOURNAL OF CRIME, CONFLICT, & WORLD ORDER), Gregory Shank, PO Box 40601, San Francisco, CA 94140, 415-550-1703. 1974. Articles, interviews, reviews. "Send editorial material to: Social Justice, PO Box 40601, San Francisco, CA 94610. Ordering information: Social Justice, PO Box 40601, San Francisco, CA 94140." avg. press run 3M. Pub'd 4 titles 1990; expects 4 titles 1991, 4 titles 1992. 2 titles listed in the *Small Press Record of Books in Print* (20th Edition, 1991-92). avg. price, paper: $10. Distribution handled through: DeBoer, Ingram, Far East Periodicals. 168pp; 6x9; of. Reporting time: 1-3 months. Payment: varies. Copyrights for author.

Crisp Publications, Inc., Carol Harris, 95 First Avenue, Los Altos, CA 94022, 415-949-4888. 1984. Non-fiction. "Prefer self-help books suitable for industrial training markets. Length between 64-256 pages. Practical, self-help guides" avg. press run 5M+. Pub'd 8 titles 1990; expects 20 titles 1991, 20 titles 1992. 7 titles listed in the *Small Press Record of Books in Print* (20th Edition, 1991-92). avg. price, paper: $9.95/$6.95. Discounts: write for details. 64-320pp; 8x10; of. Reporting time: very fast. Payment: varies, normally 10% of net selling price. Copyrights for author.

CRITICAL REVIEW: An Interdisciplinary Journal, Jeffrey M. Friedman, 942 Howard Street, San Francisco, CA 94103, 415-465-4985. 1987. "Uniquely, *Critical Review* offers its contributors the opportunity to explore, develop and criticize neo-liberal political and social theory at length. It welcomes extended scholarly essays and review essays that conform to its style sheet (available on request). Of particular interest are developments and criticisms of ideas informed by classical liberalism, including public choice theory, Austrian-school economics, and spontaneous order analysis. *CR* is the only journal in the world that confronts such ideas in every field with the most sophisticated scholarship drawn from other intellectual traditions." circ. 2M. 4/yr. Pub'd 4 issues 1990; expects 4 issues 1991, 4 issues 1992. sub. price: $29, libraries $49; per copy: $8; sample: $8. Back issues: $10. 180pp; 5½x8½; of. Reporting time: 2 months. Payment: none. Copyrighted, rights revert if arranged. Pub's reviews: 28 in 1990. §Economics, anthropology, jurisprudence, political science, history, philosophy, sociology. Ads: $50/$35.

THE CRITICAL REVIEW, S. L. Goldberg, Editor; T. B. Tomlinson, Managing Editor, Philosophy Dept, Research School of Social Science, Australian Nat'l Univ., GPO Box 4, Canberra, A.C.T. 2601, Australia. 1958. Criticism. "c. 7M-8M words or less. No footnotes or notes at end. Critical articles on English literature and related topics; also review articles, commentaries, etc" circ. 1.6M. 1/yr. Expects 1 issue 1991. sub. price:

$8 U.S.; per copy: $8. Discounts: 10%. 120pp; size B5; lp. Reporting time: 2 months. Payment: 6 off prints of article. Copyrighted, reverts to author. No ads.

Croissant & Company, Duane Schneider, P.O. Box 282, Athens, OH 45701-0282. 1968. Poetry, fiction, criticism. "Currently publishing no new work." avg. press run 500. 6 titles listed in the *Small Press Record of Books in Print* (20th Edition, 1991-92). avg. price, cloth: $10-$12 trade; $30-$50 signed ltd. Discounts: 40% on trade books; 20% on scholarly books; 30% on signed, limited editions. 40+pp; 5½×8; of, lp. Reporting time: variable. Payment: negotiable. Copyrights for author.

Crones' Own Press, Elizabeth Freeman, Publisher, PO Box 488, Durham, NC 27702, 919-688-3521. 1982. Poetry, fiction, art, photos. "—ADDITIONAL ADDRESS; 209 Watts Street #1, Durham, NC 27701—Publish works of mid-life and older women. Published *Pacific Soul* by Bonnie Davidson, San Francisco poet Margaret Budicki's poetry in *Splinters,* F. Zarod Rominski's *Seven Windows, Stories of Women, Button, Button: Who Has the Button,* by Ruth Harriet Jacobs, *WIDDERSHINS* by Judith W. Monroe." avg. press run 1.5M. Expects 1 title 1992. 4 titles listed in the *Small Press Record of Books in Print* (20th Edition, 1991-92). avg. price, paper: $10. Discounts: booksellers 1c 20%, 2-5 30%, 6+ 40%; distributors 1c 30%, 2-5 40%, 6+ 50%. 150pp; 5½×8½, 6×9; of. Reporting time: 1-6 months. Payment: 10% of net royalty. Does not copyright for author. COSMEP.

CROOKED ROADS, Wheel of Fire Press, Carl Bettis, Chief Editor; Sharon Eiker, Poetry & Art Editor, PO Box 32631, Kansas City, MO 64111. 1989. Poetry, fiction, articles, art, photos, cartoons, interviews, satire, letters, long-poems, news items, non-fiction. "Prose, prefer 500-5000 words. Poetry, no limit (dislike haiku and fragments). Recent works by Carl Bettis, Dorian Helmar, Neal Wilgus, Garry De Young" circ. 180. 3/yr. Pub'd 1 issue 1990; expects 3 issues 1991, 3 issues 1992. sub. price: $5; per copy: $2; sample: $1.50. Back issues: $1.50 when available. Discounts: None, but willing to work some out. 20-30pp; 8½×11; †laserprinting and photocopy. Reporting time: 2-4 weeks. Payment: issue copies, occasional small ($5-$20) honoraria. Copyrighted, reverts to author. Ads: $12/$6/10¢ per square inch under half page.

CROP DUST, Crop Dust Press, Edward C. Lynskey, Route 5, Box 75, Warrenton, VA 22186-8614, 703-642-6055. 1978. Poetry, fiction, reviews. "*Crop Dust* hopes to begin publishing issues again in 1991. Past contributors include William Heyen, Greg Kuzma, Ted Kooser, Judson Jerome, William Packard, Michael Waters, Kathleen Norris, Wm. Virgil Davis and Peter Wild." circ. 500. 2/yr. sub. price: $5/yr; per copy: $3 + postage; sample: none are available. Back issues: no back issues are available. Discounts: negotiate. 40-50pp; 8½×11; †of. Reporting time: 2-3 days. Payment: copy of issue work appears in. Copyrighted, reverts to author. Pub's reviews. §We are interested in small press publications, chapbooks, etc. Willing to exchange ads with other mags. CCLM.

Crop Dust Press (see also CROP DUST), Edward C. Lynskey, Route 5, Box 75, Warrenton, VA 22186-8614, 703-642-6055. 1978. Poetry. "By invitation only. Interested in putting together concept chapbook-length publications." avg. press run 500+. 1 title listed in the *Small Press Record of Books in Print* (20th Edition, 1991-92). avg. price, paper: $3.50. Discounts: will negotiate. 50pp; 5×8; †of. Reporting time: 6 months when start chapbook series. Copyrights for author. CCLM.

Cross Cultural Press, Kenneth Feuter, 1166 South 42nd St., Springfield, OR 97478, 503-746-7401. 1984. Non-fiction. "Must deal with cross cultural experience. Primarily American-Japanese may deal with prejudice in any form. Most recent fook was about american society's prejudice against persons living with AIDS." avg. press run 2M. Pub'd 2 titles 1990; expects 2 titles 1991, 2 titles 1992. 6 titles listed in the *Small Press Record of Books in Print* (20th Edition, 1991-92). avg. price, paper: $11. Discounts: 40-60%. 200+pp; 6×9; of. Reporting time: 2-3 weeks. Payment: 5-10%. Copyrights for author.

CROSS CURRENTS: Religion & Intellectual Life, William Birmingham, Joseph Cunneen, College of New Rochelle, New Rochelle, NY 10805, 914-654-5425. 1950. Articles, reviews, non-fiction. "Relation of religion and ethics to contemporary intellectual, political, cultural, philosophical questions. Published by Convergence, Inc." circ. 5.2M. 4/yr. Pub'd 4 issues 1990; expects 4 issues 1991. 2 titles listed in the *Small Press Record of Books in Print* (20th Edition, 1991-92). sub. price: $17.50, libraries $25; per copy: $5; sample: same. Back issues: $5. 144pp; 6×9; computer. Reporting time: 1 month. Payment: no. Copyrighted, reverts to author. Pub's reviews: 65 in 1990. §Theology, philosophy, world politics, literature, and arts. Ads: $350/$200/$100 1/4 pg.

CROSS TIMBERS REVIEW, Monte Lewis, Editor; Cleatus Rattan, Poetry Editor; Ken Hammes, Fiction Editor; Lawrence Clayton, Criticism, (Lit); Kenneth Neighbours, History Editor, Cisco Junior College, Cisco, TX 76437, 817-442-2567. 1983. Poetry, fiction, articles, criticism, parts-of-novels, non-fiction. "10-25 pages, typed and double-spaced. Fiction, poetry, history, biography, literary criticism. Serious works for a general, serious audience. Recent contributors: Elmer Kelton, Paul Ruffin, Walt McDonald, Don Graham, William Pilkington, Warren C. Miller" circ. 250. 2/yr. Expects 4 issues 1991, 2 issues 1992. sub. price: $6; per copy: $3; sample: $3. Back issues: $5. Discounts: 100 @ $250. 70pp; 9½×6; †of. Reporting time: 2 months. Payment: 3 copies. Copyrighted, reverts to author. §Southwestern literature, history, and biography. Ads: $50/$30.

145

CROSS-CANADA WRITERS' MAGAZINE, Ted Plantos, Editor, Cross-Canada Writers, Inc., Box 277, Station F, Toronto, Ontario M4Y 2L7, Canada. 1978. Poetry, fiction, articles, art, photos, cartoons, interviews, satire, reviews, letters, parts-of-novels, long-poems. "Poetry, short fiction, interviews with writers, usual maximum about 3M words for articles, stories. Recent contributors:Glen Sorestad, Susan Musgrave, Al Purdy, W.P. Kinsella, Bronwen Wallace, Ralph Gustafson, Lorna Crozier, Susan Ioannou, Gwendolyn MacEwen, Anne Marriott, Irving Layton, Raymond Souster, John Metcalf, P.K. Page, Joy Kogawa" circ. 2M. 3/yr. Pub'd 4 issues 1990; expects 3 issues 1991, 3 issues 1992. sub. price: $12 individual, $16 outside Canada; $18 institutions, $21 outside Canada; per copy: $4.50; sample: $4. Back issues: $3. Discounts: arrangements must be made on an individual basis with the editor. 32pp; 8½x11; of. Reporting time: 6-8 weeks. Payment: honorarium. Copyrighted, reverts to author. Pub's reviews: 49 in 1990. §We prefer Canadian poetry, fiction, and literary reference books for full-length reviews. Ads: $200/$110/1/12 $45. CPPA.

Cross-Cultural Communications, 239 Wynsum Avenue, Merrick, NY 11566. 2 titles listed in the *Small Press Record of Books in Print* (20th Edition, 1991-92).

CROSSCURRENTS, Bob Fink, 516 Ave K South, Saskatoon, Saskatchewan, Canada. 1975. Art, satire, criticism, music, news items. *"Crosscurrents* is a newsletter that makes news. It has a local, national and international circulation list published for 15 years. The nature of *Crosscurrents* is to deal with local issues in a way that expresses an underlying universal theme, usually political & about freedom. Universal or broader issues are given a local relevance as well. As a result, many issues of *Crosscurrents* can, and have been, reprinted without need for change, even years later, and can be enjoyed and be relevant far from the place where they were written" circ. 500-5M depending upon the subject and reprints. 12/yr. Pub'd 12 issues 1990; expects 12 issues 1991, 12 issues 1992. sub. price: $10 for 12 issues; per copy: $.25 plus postage (50¢); sample: $.25 plus postage (50¢). Back issues: $5 for 9 from 1975 to present. Discounts: none. 4pp; 7x8½; †mi, of. Reporting time: forever. Payment: copies. Copyrighted, reverts to author. Pub's reviews: 1 in 1990. §Arts and politics.

CROSSCURRENTS, A QUARTERLY, Linda Brown Michelson, Editor-in-Chief, 2200 Glastonbury Road, Westlake Village, CA 91361, 818-991-1694. 1980. Fiction, art, photos. "Fiction to 6M words: no heavy erotica, science fiction or western. Xerox O.K., but no simultaneous submission. We review unsolicited manuscripts from June 1 through Nov. 30, each year. Recent contributors: Alice Adams, Joyce Carol Oates, John Updike, Josephine Jacobsen, Margaret Atwood, Saul Bellow. Please note: Re poetry, *Crosscurrents* no longer regularly uses poetry. We will, however, feature special issues devoted to in-depth looks at poetry, from time to time. I do want to stem the voluminous flow of poetry submissions, as I hate to waste submittor's postage when there is little to no chance of acceptance" circ. 3M. 4/yr. Pub'd 4 issues 1990; expects 4 issues 1991, 4 issues 1992. 1 title listed in the *Small Press Record of Books in Print* (20th Edition, 1991-92). sub. price: $18; per copy: $6; sample: $6. Back issues: $6. Discounts: wholesale and retail. 176pp; 6x9; of. Reporting time: 6 weeks. Payment: 1 contributors copy, fiction $35, graphics $10-$25. Copyrighted, reverts to author. Ads: $70/$35. CCLM, PMA, AWP, PSA.

The Crossing Press, Jane Somers, Promotions Director; John Gill, Elaine Gill, Dennis Hayes, Marketing Director, PO Box 1048, Freedom, CA 95019-1048, 408-722-0711. 1966. Poetry, fiction. "Recently moved into newer, larger warehouse and offices" avg. press run 5M-10M. Pub'd 36 titles 1990; expects 24-30 titles 1991, 30-36 titles 1992. 27 titles listed in the *Small Press Record of Books in Print* (20th Edition, 1991-92). avg. price, cloth: $18.95; paper: $8.95. Discounts: 1-4 books, 25%, 5-24 40%, 25-49 42% and free freight, wholesale-jobbers negotiable. 64-300pp; 8½x5½, 6x9, 8¼x9; of. Reporting time: 4-6 weeks. Payment: royalties. Copyrights for author.

Crossroads Communications, Del Wilson, Senior Editor, PO Box 7, Carpentersville, IL 60110. 1980. Non-fiction. "Interested in American history 50M-100M words in length. Must be well researched. Some biographies. Recent contributors: Ira Morton, (Red Grange biography), A. Richard Crabb (Everett Mitchell memoirs)" avg. press run 2M. Pub'd 3 titles 1990; expects 3 titles 1991, 3 titles 1992. 15 titles listed in the *Small Press Record of Books in Print* (20th Edition, 1991-92). avg. price, cloth: $12.50; paper: $9.95. Discounts: 40% bulk, to the trade. 260pp; 5½x8½; of. Reporting time: 4 weeks. Payment: each separate, negotiable. Does not copyright for author.

Crossroads Publications, Inc., Mae F. Mead, Col. Rodney L. Cron, William I. Yeagy, Sr., PO Box 842, Greenwood, IN 46142, 317-639-5474. 1989. Poetry, fiction, non-fiction. "Additional addresses: 322 S. Oakwood Drive, Greenwood, IN 46142 (Res.); 320 N. Meridian Street, Indianapolis, IN 46204 (Office)." avg. press run 3.5M. Pub'd 3 titles 1990; expects 3 titles 1991, 3+ titles 1992. 240pp; 6x9. Copyrights for author.

Crossway Books, Jan Dennis, Editor-in-Chief; Ted Griffin, Managing Editor, 9825 W. Roosevelt Road, Westchester, IL 60154, 312-345-7474. 1979. Fiction, non-fiction. "Publish books with an orthodox Christian perspective, including novels, contemporary issues, theology, and the family" Pub'd 30 titles 1990; expects 30 titles 1991, 30 titles 1992. avg. price, paper: $8.95. Discounts: trade, jobber. 192pp; 5½x8½; of. Reporting time:

4 months. Copyrights for author. CBA, ECPA.

CROTON REVIEW, Ruth Lisa Schechter, Executive Editor; Gloria Scalzo, Business Manager; David M. Stanton, Associate Editor; Linda Ashear, Associate Editor; Elsa Colligan, Associate Editor; Gerry Rosenzweig, Editorial Associate, P.O. Box 277, Croton on Hudson, NY 10520. 1978. Poetry, fiction, interviews, letters. "Prefer evidence of language, craft, originality welcome. Short-short stories, general poetry, literary essays, interviews. We seek quality, diversity, substance,...unpublished work of known and unknown writers in our area and elsewhere in the U.S. Contributors: Marge Piercy, Clarence Major, T. Alan Broughton, Yvonne, Carol Emshwiller, Harold Witt, Stephen Dixon, Susan Fromberg Shaeffer, Robert Phillips, David Evanier, William Jay Smith, Lyn Lifshin, Carolyn Forche. CR is tax-exempt and tax deductible. Our issues include interviews of distinguished writers (not solicited). Tenth Anniversary Issue off press Spring '87. Announcing; *#11/Special Awards/Anthology Issue: 1988 "A Tribute To Anne Sexton"*, includes award winners, HM poems, fiction, Sexton scholars, Maxine Kumin, Kathleen Spivack memoir. Queries are welcome with SASE. *Please Note: Croton Review staff will be on an editorial hiatus temporarily after Issue #11, 1988 and will not be reading mss until further notice. Please watch literary newsletters for our future publishing schedule and editorial needs"* circ. 2M. 1/yr. Pub'd 1 issue 1990; expects 1 issue 1991, 1 issue 1992. sub. price: $10 sponsor, $25 patron, $50 benefactor, $12 libraries/2 issues; per copy: issues #4-10 $3-$4 + 75¢ postage, issue #11 $5 ppd; sample: none. Back issues: same. Discounts: standard. 64-80pp; 7×10; of, typeset, perfectbound, laminated cover print. Reporting time: from 4-16 weeks or sooner. Payment: 1 copy at publication time. Copyrighted, reverts to author. Ads: 10¢ word-listings, 3 lines under Patrons, $35.00, Benefactors: $50 (until further notice). COSMEP, CCLM.

CROW—The Alternative Magazine, Afta Press, Bill-Dale Marcinko, Afta Press, Inc., 47 Crater Avenue, Wharton, NJ 07885-2023, 201-828-5467. 1978. Fiction, articles, art, photos, cartoons, interviews, satire, criticism, reviews, news items. *"Crow* is basically a review magazine of popular culture: books, films, records, television and comic books with short news items, reviews and interviews of a recent nature. We also cover the anti-nuke, pro-gay, and feminist movements. We will trade subscriptions with other small press editors." circ. 25M. 6/yr. Pub'd 2 issues 1990; expects 6 issues 1991, 6 issues 1992. sub. price: $18.95; per copy: $4.50; sample: $2. Back issues: none available. Discounts: 10 copies: $20 postpaid. 144pp; 8½×11; of. Reporting time: 1 week. Payment: free copy of issue. Copyrighted, reverts to author. Pub's reviews: 70 in 1990. §Humor, critical essays, review magazines, film reviews, videocassette reviews, record reviews. Ads: $500/$250/25¢.

CROW MAGAZINE, Afta Press, Bill-Dale Marcinko, 47 Crater Avenue, Wharton, NJ 07885, 201-828-5467. 1977. Articles, art, photos, interviews, satire, criticism, reviews. circ. 5M. 6/yr. Pub'd 1 issue 1990; expects 6 issues 1991, 6 issues 1992. sub. price: $19.95; per copy: $4.50; sample: $4.50. Back issues: none available. Discounts: over 10 copies purchased—50% off cover w/returns, 60% off without returns. 132pp; 8½×11. Reporting time: 1 week. Payment: contributor's copies. Copyrighted, reverts to author. Pub's reviews: 50 in 1990. §Film, video, comics, television, gay issues. Ads: $495.

CRS Consultants Press, PO Box 490175, Key Biscayne, FL 33149. 1982. Non-fiction. "New press—publish only specific works of interest to engineering and scientific consultants. Submissions not usually considered—commissioned works only at present" avg. press run 500. Expects 1 title 1991, 2 titles 1992. 1 title listed in the *Small Press Record of Books in Print* (20th Edition, 1991-92). avg. price, paper: $10. Discounts: available on request. 50pp.

CRUCIBLE, Terrence L. Grimes, English Department, Barton College, Wilson, NC 27893, 237-3161 X217. 1964. Poetry, fiction, non-fiction. "Short stories should not exceed 8,000 words" circ. 300. 1/yr. Pub'd 1 issue 1990; expects 1 issue 1991, 1 issue 1992. sub. price: $5; per copy: $5; sample: $5. Back issues: $4. Discounts: none. 70pp; 6×9; of. Reporting time: 2 months. Payment: none. Copyrighted, reverts to author.

CRYPTOSYSTEMS JOURNAL, Tony Patti, Editor & Publisher, 9755 Oatley Lane, Burke, VA 22015, 703-451-6664. 1988. Articles, reviews, letters, news items. "A unique international journal devoted to the implementation of cryptographic systems (i.e. secret codes, encryption, decryption) on IBM Personal Computers (and compatible clones) for the purpose of education and research in the subject matter areas of computer science, mathematics, engineering, and communications. Each issue includes one or more computer diskettes containing computer programs with complete source code listings" Irregular. sub. price: $45/yr U.S. & Canada, $80/yr International Surface Mail, $90/yr International Air Mail. 60pp; 8½×11; †photocopy machine. Reporting time: 2 weeks. Payment: 2 free copies of the issue in which contribution appears. Copyrighted, does not revert to author. Pub's reviews: 6 in 1990. §Cryptology, computer security, secret codes, encryption.

Crystal Press, Ltd., William A. Mandel, Editor & Publisher, PO Box 215, Crystal Bay, NV 89402, 702-831-3846. 1981. Fiction, non-fiction. "Must be well-written and of general interest. No religious or poetry" avg. press run 5M+. Pub'd 1 title 1990; expects 1 title 1991, 1 title 1992. 1 title listed in the *Small Press Record of Books in Print* (20th Edition, 1991-92). avg. price, paper: $3.95. Discounts: trade: 40%, others

50%. of. Reporting time: 1 month. Payment: standard 10%-12½%-15%. Copyrights for author. COSMEP.

Crystal Publishers, Inc., Frank Leanza, 4947 Orinda Court, Las Vegas, NV 89120, 702-434-3037. 1985. Music. avg. press run 5M. Pub'd 2 titles 1990; expects 2 titles 1991, 5 titles 1992. 5 titles listed in the *Small Press Record of Books in Print* (20th Edition, 1991-92). avg. price, paper: $13.95. Discounts: 46-55% wholesaler. 224pp; 6×9; of. Reporting time: 6-8 weeks. Payment: semi-annual. Copyrights for author. COSMEP, PO Box 703, San Francisco, CA 94101.

CRYSTAL RAINBOW, Louise M. Turmenne, The Mirrored Image, 340 Granada Drive, Winter Park, FL 32789. 1987. Poetry, fiction, articles, non-fiction. "Anything pertaining to relationships (friendship, etc.). Length of material: poetry-24 lines max., articles-300 words max. Regular columns available and needing contributions. General readership: teen-elderly. Publication is at least (perhaps more than) 1 year from date of acceptance. Writing contests each quarter: small cash prizes. Seasonal themes. Sample and guidelines available for $3.50 and SASE (75¢ postage)" circ. 160. 4/yr. Pub'd 4 issues 1990; expects 4 issues 1991, 4 issues 1992. sub. price: $11.75; per copy: $3.50; sample: $3.50 & SASE (75¢ postage). SASE *must* accompany request with check for sample copy. Back issues: $2.50. 28pp; 7×8½; †photocopy. Reporting time: 1-6 months. Payment: 2 copies of issue. Copyrighted. Ads: $100/$50/$25 1/4 page/$18 1/6/$12 1/8.

Crystal Spring Publishing, Lynn Davis, Bruce Muncy, Michael Muncy, PO Box 8814, Roanoke, VA 24014, 703-982-2029. 1988. Photos, non-fiction. "Specialty in bed and breakfast travel writing. Books heavily photographic." avg. press run 10M. Pub'd 1 title 1990; expects 1 title 1991, 1 title 1992. 2 titles listed in the *Small Press Record of Books in Print* (20th Edition, 1991-92). avg. price, paper: $15.95. Discounts: 40% 4 or more copies. 120pp; 8½×11; †photo offset. Reporting time: 3 months. Payment: negotiable. Copyrights for author. Public Relations Society of America, 845 Third Avenue, New York, NY 10022.

CSS Publications, Rebecca S. Bell, C. Sherman Severin, PO Box 23, Iowa Falls, IA 50126, 515-282-4379; 648-2716. 1977. Fiction. "CSS Publications publishes volumes of poetry annually. The poems are selected from among those submitted to its spring poetry contests which are nationwide in emphasis. CSS Publications bears all the cost of publishing these perfectly bound paper volumes. The next volume contains works of 160 poets, has 240 pages and will be released in October. Price is $9.95. CSS Publications also publishes the works of individual authors. The 1982 release is *The Rhyme & Reason of Curt Sytsma* in hardcover, $14.95. Also publishes 'How To' books" avg. press run 2M. Pub'd 2 titles 1990; expects 3 titles 1991, 5 titles 1992. 8 titles listed in the *Small Press Record of Books in Print* (20th Edition, 1991-92). avg. price, cloth: $14.95; paper: $9.95; other: $3.95 "How To" books. Discounts: 40%. 200pp; 5½×8½; of. Reporting time: 4 months maximum; average 2½ months. Payment: for collections of poetry—prizes and books; individual author-negotiable. Copyrights for author. COSMEP, CODEL.

Cube Publications Inc, George L. Manthe, Katherine B. Glean, 1 Buena Vista Road, Port Jefferson, NY 11777, 516-331-4990. 1982. Fiction, satire, non-fiction. avg. press run 1M. Expects 4 titles 1991, 4+ titles 1992. 1 title listed in the *Small Press Record of Books in Print* (20th Edition, 1991-92). avg. price, cloth: $16; paper: $9.95. Discounts: inquire. 200pp; 6×9; of. Reporting time: 90 days. Payment: variable. Copyrights for author. COSMEP.

Culinary Arts Ltd., Cheryl Long, PO Box 2157, Lake Oswego, OR 97035, 503-639-4549. 1979. "Published magazine prior to 1983. Changed to books in that year. Culinary areas of interest are our forte. Unusual subjects, hard-to-find, or new concepts, specialty in microwave area, food hobbies" avg. press run 2.5M. Pub'd 2 titles 1990; expects 3 titles 1991, 3-4 titles 1992. 11 titles listed in the *Small Press Record of Books in Print* (20th Edition, 1991-92). avg. price, paper: $7. Discounts: 40% trade with 6 book minimum, titles can be mixed, etc. 96pp; 5½×8½; of. Reporting time: apx. 1 month, query first! Payment: quarterly. Does not copyright for author. Northwest Assoc. of Book Publishers (NWABP), Publishers Marketing Assn. (PMA).

Culpepper Press, David Tripp, Don Leeper, 2901 Fourth Street SE, Minneapolis, MN 55414, 617-378-2116. 1982. Non-fiction. avg. press run 5M. Pub'd 5 titles 1990; expects 2 titles 1991, 2 titles 1992. avg. price, cloth: $8.95; paper: $10. Discounts: wholesalers 50%, bookstores: 1-2 books 20%, 3-9 40%, 10-99 43%, 100-299 44%. 200pp; 6×9; varies. Reporting time: 1 month. Payment: varies. Copyrights for author. UMBA.

CULT OBSERVER, American Family Foundation, Robert E. Schecter, PO Box 336, Weston, MA 02193, 617-893-0930. 1979. circ. 850. Discounts: 50% to distributors. 120pp; 6×9.

CULTIC STUDIES JOURNAL, American Family Foundation, Michael D. Langome, PO Box 336, Weston, MA 02193, 617-893-0930. 1979. circ. 1.1M. Discounts: 50% to distributors. 120pp; 6×9.

THE CULTURAL FORUM, Lucien Graves, PO Box 709, Holbrook, NY 11741, 516-472-2191. 1987. Criticism, reviews, non-fiction. "We publish articles which critique all aspects of modern day culture, i.e. the art, literature, music, etc. of the day." circ. 8M. 4/yr. Expects 4 issues 1991, 4 issues 1992. sub. price: $10; per copy: $2.75; sample: free. 12pp; 11×17; of. Reporting time: 2 months. Copyrighted, reverts to author. Pub's reviews: 2-4 per issue in 1990. §High quality fiction, non-fiction, poetry. Ads: $100/$50/$25 1/4 page or

148

business card. COSMEP, STAC.

Cultural Survival, Inc. (see also CULTURAL SURVIVAL QUARTERLY), Leslie Baker, Managing Editor, 53-A Church Street, Cambridge, MA 02138, 617-495-2562. 1972. *"Since its formation in 1972, Cultural Survival* has supported projects on five continents to help indigenous peoples survive, both physically and culturally, the changes brought by contact with expanding industrial society. Project evaluations, research and dissemination of research results serve to educate the public, influence development theory and policy, and stimulate debate among academics, planners and indigenous people" avg. press run 2M. Pub'd 2 titles 1990; expects 2 titles 1992. avg. price, paper: $9.95; other: $4 for magazine. Discounts: write for info. 200pp; 6×9. Reporting time: 3 weeks or longer. Payment: no royalties. Copyrights for author.

CULTURAL SURVIVAL QUARTERLY, Cultural Survival, Inc., Leslie Baker, Managing Editor, 53-A Church Street, Cambridge, MA 02138, 617-495-2562. 1976. "Since 1976, *Cultural Survival Quarterly* has addressed issues of both immediate and long-term concern to indigenous peoples throughout the world. *The Quarterly* serves to inform the general public and policy makers in the United States and abroad to stimulate action on behalf of tribal people and ethnic minorities. Length: 8-10 double spaced pages" circ. 25M. 4/yr. Pub'd 4 issues 1990; expects 4 issues 1991, 4 issues 1992. sub. price: $25; per copy: $4 current; sample: $4. Back issues: $5. Discounts: 50% to distributors, 40% to retail outlets. 80pp; 8½×11; web. Payment: none. Copyrighted, reverts to author. No paid ads accepted.

CULTURE CONCRETE, C.E. Petroni, Editor & Publisher, 2141-C Mission Street #305, San Francisco, CA 94110-9839, 415-285-4286. 1991. Poetry, fiction, articles, art, photos, cartoons, interviews, satire, criticism, reviews, music, news items, non-fiction. "Poetry, no more than a typed, double-space page, 8½ x 11 per poem; short stories, up to 3,500 words each; essays, up to 3,500 words each; investigative journalism, length negotiable. Reading fees: short stories, essays and articles $5, poetry $3 per submission. Every poem and short story published is automatically given entry in our Annual Awards with cash prizes for every category up to $500." circ. 14M. 4/yr. Expects 4 issues 1991, 6 issues 1992. sub. price: $16; per copy: $5; sample: $5. Back issues: $5 plus $2 handling and first class mailing. Discounts: distributors 50%, bookstores 40%. 60pp; 12×18; of. Reporting time: 4-6 weeks. Payment: $10-$100 plus copies and complimentary subscription. Copyrighted, reverts to author. Pub's reviews: 8-10 pages per issue in 1990. §Fiction (both novels and short stories), poetry, politics, social sciences, media, etc., and biographies. Ads: $1,200/$750/$450 1/4 page/$300 1/8 page.

CULTWATCH RESPONSE, Vicki Copeland, PO Box 1842, Colorado Springs, CO 80901. 1989. Articles, interviews, criticism, reviews, letters, news items, non-fiction. "Pagan publication aimed at non-pagans. Deals with the subjects of 'occult related crime,' police training material, media misinformation, etc. from a Wiccan perspective. Recent contributors include Vicki Copeland, Hal Mansfield, and San Francisco Police office Sandi Daly Gallant" circ. 120. 6/yr. Pub'd 6 issues 1990; expects 6 issues 1991, 6 issues 1992. sub. price: $12; per copy: $2; sample: $2. Back issues: $2. 12pp; 7×8½; xerox. Reporting time: 2 months. Payment: none. Not copyrighted. Pub's reviews: 12 in 1990. §Books on occult crime, police training material, etc. Ads: none. Wiccan/Pagan Press Alliance (WPPA), Mechanicsburg, PA.

Cumberland (see also CUMBERLAND), 7652 Sawmill Road, Suite 194, Dublin, OH 43017. 1976. Poetry, fiction. *"No unsolicited manuscripts"* avg. press run 500. 5 titles listed in the *Small Press Record of Books in Print* (20th Edition, 1991-92). avg. price, paper: $5; other: $5. 104pp; 5×8; of. Reporting time: 2 weeks. Copyrights for author.

CUMBERLAND, Cumberland, George Myers, Jr., 7652 Sawmill Road, Suite 194, Dublin, OH 43017. 1976. Interviews, criticism, reviews, music, letters, parts-of-novels. "Contributors: Russell Edson, James Wright, David Ignatow, Margaret Atwood, Richard Kostelanetz, Joseph Napora, Gretchen Johnsen, Serge Gavronsky, Warren C. Miller, Richard Grayson. Thematic issues announced. No unsolicted manuscripts" circ. 300. 1/yr. sub. price: $5; per copy: $5; sample: $5. Back issues: $5. Discounts: none. 104pp; 6×9; of. Reporting time: 1-2 weeks usually. Payment: copy. Copyrighted, reverts to author. Pub's reviews: 300 in 1990. §Criticism, essays, prose poems.

CUMBERLAND POETRY REVIEW, Editorial board, Poetics, Inc., PO Box 120128 Acklen Station, Nashville, TN 37212, 615-373-8948. 1981. Poetry, reviews. "Translations, poetry criticism. Recent contributors include Laurence Lerner, Donald Davie, Seamus Heaney, X.J. Kennedy and Emily Grosholz. *CPR* presents poets of diverse origins to a widespread audience. Our aim is to support the poet's effort to keep up the language" circ. 500. 2/yr. Pub'd 2 issues 1990; expects 2 issues 1991, 2 issues 1992. sub. price: $12 (individuals), $15 (institutions), $21 (overseas); per copy: $6; sample: $6. Back issues: Vol. I, #1, unavailable; all others $5. Discounts: 30% to bookstores. 100pp; 6×9; lp. Reporting time: 3 months. Payment: 2 copies. Copyrighted, reverts to author on request. §Review on a poet's entire work. No ads. CCLM.

Curbstone Press, Alexander Taylor, Judy Doyle, 321 Jackson Street, Willimantic, CT 06226, 423-9190. 1975. "Curbstone Press is an incorporated, non-profit publishing house founded in 1975. Our primary goal is to publish important works by writers and translators which might not find a voice in the commercial publishing

149

channels. Curbstone has published poetry, short stories and novels. We aim for conceptual integrity — so that, ideally, in each book the feel, look and words reflect and extend one another. We have a particular bias toward poetry of the left and literature in translation. We do not ask for unsolicited ms." avg. press run 1M-3M. Pub'd 4 titles 1990; expects 9 titles 1991, 6 titles 1992. 62 titles listed in the *Small Press Record of Books in Print* (20th Edition, 1991-92). avg. price, cloth: $15; paper: $9.95; other: $25-$50 signed, limited. Discounts: all trade orders are handled by ImBook. Poetry 96pp, prose 200pp; 6×9, 5½×8½; of. Reporting time: 2-3 months on unsolicited mss. Payment: we pay a royalty (10%) in copies or in annual cash payments. Copyrights for author, the author retains all rights. COSMEP, CLMP.

The Curlew Press (see also POETRY QUARTERLY), P.J. Precious, Hare Cottage, Kettlesing, Harrogate, Yorkshire, England, Tel: Harrogate 770686. 1975. Poetry, fiction, articles, art, photos, cartoons, interviews, satire, criticism, reviews, letters, parts-of-novels, long-poems, collages, plays, concrete art, news items, non-fiction. "One author booklets and poem sheets published occasionally. Do *not* send American stamps with mss" avg. press run variable. Pub'd 2 titles 1990; expects 2 titles 1991. avg. price, paper: £1.75/$3.50. Pages variable; size varies; printing and xerox. Reporting time: by return of post when possible. Payment: none. Copyrights for author in U.K. YFSP (Yorkshire Federation of Small Presses).

CURLEY, Sheila K. Smith, PO Box 23521, Providence, RI 02903. 1990. Poetry, fiction, interviews, reviews, long-poems. 4/yr. Expects 4 issues 1991, 4 issues 1992. sub. price: $8; per copy: $2; sample: $2. 40pp; 5×8. Reporting time: 4 weeks. Payment: issue in which work appears - 2 copies. Copyrighted, reverts to author. Pub's reviews. Ads: $10.

CURRENTS, Eric Leaper, National Organization for River Sports, Box 6847, Colorado Springs, CO 80934, 719-473-2466. 1979. Articles, photos, cartoons, reviews, letters, news items, non-fiction. "Street address: 314 N. 20th Street, Colorado Springs, CO 80904. Subscription includes membership in NORS. We have a writer's guideline sheet, which includes info for photogrpahers too" circ. 10M. 4/yr. Pub'd 3 issues 1990; expects 4 issues 1991, 4 issues 1992. sub. price: $15; per copy: $1; sample: $1. Back issues: $1 plus 9X12 SASE (75¢ p/h). Discounts: 50¢ each to dealers; 5 order minimum. 24pp; 8×10½; of. Reporting time: 10-30 days. Payment: $10-$90. Copyrighted, reverts to author. Pub's reviews: 7 in 1990. §Whitewater river running, kayaking, canoeing, rafting. Ads: $329/$257/$15 - 3 lines.

CURTAINS, Pressed Curtains, Paul Buck, 4 Bower Street, Maidstone, Kent ME16 8SD, England, 0622-63681. 1971. Poetry, fiction, articles, art, photos, interviews, criticism, reviews, music, parts-of-novels, long-poems, plays. "Presents mainly French writings in translation. Blanchot, Bataille, Noel, Faye. Though English & American poetry also strongly featured" circ. 450. 1/yr. Pub'd 1 issue 1990; expects 1 issue 1991. price per copy: $7. 200pp; size A4; of, colored inks. Reporting time: days. Payment: copies. Copyrighted. Pub's reviews: 4 in 1990. No ads. ALMS, Set International.

CUTBANK, Peter Fong, Co-Editor; Dennis Held, Co-Editor; Claire Davis, Fiction Editor; Marnie Bullock, Poetry Editor, English Dept., University of Montana, Missoula, MT 59812. 1973. Poetry, fiction, articles, art, photos, interviews, criticism, reviews, long-poems. "Recent contributors include Rick DeMarinis, Lowell Jaeger, William Kittredge, Sheryl Noethe, William Stafford, Melanie Roe Thon" circ. 400. 2/yr. Pub'd 2 issues 1990; expects 2 issues 1991, 2 issues 1992. sub. price: $12; per copy: $5.95; sample: $4. Back issues: write for current information. Discounts: trade rates for bulk orders. 120+pp; 5½×8½; of, perfect bound. Reporting time: 8-12 weeks. Payment: 1 issue. Copyrighted, rights revert with provision *CutBank* is credited. Pub's reviews: 10 in 1990. §Poetry, fiction, criticism. Ads: $75/$45. CCLM.

CUTTING EDGE QUARTERLY, Richard T. Julius, Editor-in-Chief, PO Box 3430, Ann Arbor, MI 48106, 313-995-8637. 1985. Poetry, fiction, articles, art, photos, cartoons, interviews, satire, criticism, reviews, letters, long-poems, collages, plays. "We are accepting poetry, fiction, graphics, humor. We cannot accept responsibility for any unsolicited manuscripts not accompanied by a self-addressed, stamped envelope" circ. 150-200. 4/yr. Pub'd 4 issues 1990; expects 4 issues 1991, 4 issues 1992. sub. price: $12; per copy: $4; sample: $4. Back issues: $5. 40-60pp; 8½×5½; of. Reporting time: 4 weeks. Payment: in copies. Copyrighted, reverts to author. No ads.

CWM, Ge(of Huth), geologian; David C. Kopaska-Merkel, geologian, 112 South Market Street, Johnstown, NY 12095, 518-374-7143. 1989. Poetry, fiction, articles, art, photos, cartoons, interviews, satire, criticism, reviews, letters, parts-of-novels, long-poems, collages, plays, concrete art, non-fiction. "Additional address: David C. Kopaska-Merkel, 4801 Cypress Creek Drive, Apt. 1004, Tuscaloosa, AL 35405. *CWM*, a journal of the reproducible arts, aims to publish portfolios of divergent works held together loosely by themes. Not tied down by ideas of proper style, form or substance, *CWM* will judge writing and art on quality rather than genre. Response time will be as short as possible, but any work accepted for *CWM* must be accepted by both geologians, who live in different sections of the country. The theme for the issue out in early 1992 will be 'What lies beneath the surface.'" circ. 100. 1/yr. Expects 1 issue 1991, 1 issue 1992. sub. price: $3; per copy: $3; sample: $3. Discounts: flexible. 8½×7; photocopy. Reporting time: 2-8 weeks. Payment: at least 1 contributor's copy. Copyrighted, reverts to author. Pub's reviews. §Poetry, fiction, the arts.

Cypres Publishing House, Beate Zilversmidt, Heemraadschapslaan 33, Amstelveen, Holland 1181 T2, The Netherlands, 31-20-6410388. 1986. Fiction, criticism, non-fiction. avg. press run 2M. Pub'd 1 title 1990; expects 1 title 1991, 1 title 1992. avg. price, cloth: $10. Discounts: 33%. 150pp. Reporting time: 1 month. Copyrights for author.

D

D.B.A. Books, Mark Hetherington, D.M. Bellavance, 323 Beacon Street, Boston, MA 02116, 617-262-0411. 1980. Non-fiction. avg. press run 5M. Pub'd 3 titles 1990; expects 4 titles 1991, 4 titles 1992. 3 titles listed in the *Small Press Record of Books in Print* (20th Edition, 1991-92). avg. price, paper: $14.95. Discounts: 2-5 10%, 6-9 15%, 10+ 20%. 100pp; 6×8½; of. Reporting time: 2 weeks. Payment: by contract. Does not copyright for author.

THE D.H. LAWRENCE REVIEW, Dennis Jackson, Department of English, University of Delaware, Newark, DE 19716, 302-454-1480/302-451-2361. 1968. Articles, art, photos, interviews, criticism, reviews. *"The D.H. Lawrence Review* publishes scholarly and critical articles, review essays, bibliography, and news relating to D.H. Lawrence and his circle. The average length of an accepted article is about 15 pages in manuscript, double-spaced, but we are flexible enough on special occasions to accept larger and smaller articles (we do publish short critical 'notes'). Material submitted should follow *The MLA Style Manual* (1985) and be accompanied by return self-addressed envelope and postage. We are eclectic in approach from various critical perspectives and in subjects treated within our area of interest. Please send two copies of the manuscript" circ. 750. 3/yr. Pub'd 3 issues 1990; expects 3 issues 1991. sub. price: individuals $14, foreign $15, institutions $20; per copy: $5; sample: $5. Back issues: $5 single, $15 volume. Discounts: $1 off to agencies. 120pp; 6×9; of. Reporting time: 3 months. Payment: 2 copies of issue plus about 10 offprints of article. Copyrighted, does not revert to author. Pub's reviews: 50 in 1990. §D.H. Lawrence and his circle, modern literature. Ads: $120/$60.

D.I.N. Publications, Jim Parker, Editor; Christina Dye, Managing Editor, PO Box 27568, Tempe, AZ 85285-1126. 1967. Articles, art, photos, cartoons, interviews, reviews, letters, news items, non-fiction. "Write to editor for guidelines before sending material" avg. press run 20M-50M. Pub'd 130 titles 1990; expects 145 titles 1991, 160 titles 1992. 13 titles listed in the *Small Press Record of Books in Print* (20th Edition, 1991-92). avg. price, paper: 25¢ per pamphlet; $1-$1.50 per booklet, $9.95-$14.95 books. Discounts: quantity. 6-40pp; size varies; †of. Reporting time: varies, 2 weeks to 2 months. Payment: available, but not often; must be special material. Copyrights for author.

DADA/SURREALISM, Mary Ann Caws, Rudolf Kuenzli, 425 EPB, University of Iowa, Iowa City, IA 52242. 1971. Articles. "Essays on special topics, which are announced three years in advance" circ. 700. 1/yr. sub. price: $12. Back issues: $10. Discounts: 40%. 200pp; 6×9; of. Reporting time: 2 months. Payment: none. Copyrighted, does not revert to author. Ads: $100.

DAEDALUS, Journal of the American Academy of Arts and Sciences, Stephen R. Graubard, Editor, American Academy of Arts and Sciences, 136 Irving Street, Cambridge, MA 02138, 617-491-2600. 1958. Articles. "No unsolicited mss." circ. 20M. 4/yr. Pub'd 4 issues 1990; expects 4 issues 1991, 4 issues 1992. sub. price: individual—$25, $45/2 yrs, $65/3 yrs; institution—$40, $70/2 yrs, $100/3 yrs; per copy: $6.95; sample: same. Back issues: $6.95. 270pp; 6×9; of. Reporting time: 1 month. Copyrighted, does not revert to author. No ads.

Daedalus Press (see also WHOLE NOTES), Nancy Peters Hastings, PO Box 1374, Las Cruces, NM 88004, 505-382-7446. 1988. Poetry. "Each year Daedalus Press features the work of a single poet in a chapbook. Submissions to the Daedalus Chapbook Series are welcomed. Send a sampler of 5-10 poems along with a stamped, self-addressed envelope. Recent chapbooks by Glenna Luschei and Keith Wilson." avg. press run 400. Pub'd 1 title 1990; expects 1 title 1991, 1 title 1992. 2 titles listed in the *Small Press Record of Books in Print* (20th Edition, 1991-92). avg. price, other: $3 chapbook. Discounts: available upon request. 20pp; 5½×8½; lp. Reporting time: immediately. Payment: author will receive 25 copies of the chapbook. Copyrights for author. CLMP.

THE DALHOUSIE REVIEW, Alan Andrews, Editor; J.A. Wainwright, Fiction & Poetry Editor, Alan Andrews, Editor, Sir James Dunn Bldg. Suite 314, Halifax, Nova Scotia B3H 3J5, Canada. 1921. Poetry, fiction, articles, criticism, reviews. "Authors change with each issue" circ. 1M. 4/yr. Pub'd 4 issues 1990; expects 4 issues 1991, 4 issues 1992. sub. price: $17 within Canada, outside $25 includes GST; per copy: $6 +

handling (double issue $12); sample: $6 + handling ($12 double issue). Back issues: vary from $6 to $25 plus handling. Discounts: none. 155pp; 9×6½; lp. Reporting time: varies. Payment: fiction $1 per page (honorarium only), $3 for 1st poem used and $2 for each subsequent poem per issue. Copyrighted, rights are held by both publisher and author. Pub's reviews: 30-40 in 1990. §All areas would be examined. Ads: $175/$100.

Dalkey Archive Press (see also THE REVIEW OF CONTEMPORARY FICTION), John O'Brien, Steven Moore, 5700 College Road, Lisle, IL 60532. 1984. Fiction. "No unsolicited manuscripts." avg. press run 2M. Pub'd 15 titles 1990; expects 15 titles 1991, 15 titles 1992. 58 titles listed in the *Small Press Record of Books in Print* (20th Edition, 1991-92). avg. price, cloth: $20; paper: $9. Discounts: 10% bookstores, 50% on 10 or more copies; payment in advance. 180pp; 6×9; of. Reporting time: 1 month. Payment: 10%. Copyrights for author.

D-Amp Publications, Dennis V. Damp, PO Box 1243, Coraopolis, PA 15108, 412-262-4531. 1985. Articles, non-fiction. avg. press run 5M. Pub'd 2 titles 1990; expects 4 titles 1991, 4 titles 1992. 4 titles listed in the *Small Press Record of Books in Print* (20th Edition, 1991-92). avg. price, paper: $11.95. Discounts: 1-3 books 20%, 2-199 40%, 200+ 50%. 90pp; 8½×11, 5⅜×8½. Reporting time: 6 weeks. Payment: negotiable. Copyrights for author. Publishers Marketing Assoc. (PMA).

Dan River Press (see also Conservatory of American Letters), Richard S. Danbury III, Editor, PO Box 88, Thomaston, ME 04861. 1978. "Request 15 point program SASE-2 stamps. Anything except porn & evangelical. We don't charge a reading fee, but require a donation, whatever you can afford. If you can't afford any donation, convince us and we'll read free" avg. press run 1M. Pub'd 3 titles 1990; expects 5 titles 1991, 5 titles 1992. 17 titles listed in the *Small Press Record of Books in Print* (20th Edition, 1991-92). avg. price, cloth: $19.95; paper: $10; other: $75 collector's. Discounts: no. of paperback books ordered X2%. Maximum 50% for 25 or more copies. No discount on hardcovers. 145-180pp; 5½×8½; of. Reporting time: 1-3 weeks, usually one. Payment: minimum advance $250, payable on contracting; minimum royalty 10% from first sale. Copyrights for author.

Dancing Bear Productions (see also CLIPS FROM BEAR'S HOME MOVIES), Craig Ellis, Nancy Lundy, PO Box 733, Concord, MA 01742, 617-369-5592. 1983. Poetry, fiction, art, photos, cartoons, satire, music, collages, plays, concrete art. "Dancing Bear Productions grows out of 16 years of small press activity. In present incarnation, we are an independent publisher, and bookseller. So far, we've put out work by Larry Eigner, James Schevill, Robert Creeley, Ted Enslin, Jonathan Williams, etc. A catalog of publications by other presses, available from us, is due Fall 1989. More & more, these daze, we are interested in the political, the social, the psychological... On the other hand, art counts most. And we have an abiding affection for what used to be called Modernism. I.e., we think *RAW* is a great mag. Postcards, chapbooks, whatever it takes. Work forthcoming from Jonathan Strong and Fielding Dawson" avg. press run 1-1M (500). Pub'd 2 titles 1990; expects 3 titles 1991, 6 titles 1992. 5 titles listed in the *Small Press Record of Books in Print* (20th Edition, 1991-92). Discounts: available on request — generally standard trade. of, lp, silkscreen. Reporting time: 12+ weeks, query is strongly suggested, SASE necessary. Payment: negotiable, usually copies, as % of edition. Copyrights for author. COSMEP.

THE DANDELION, Michael E. Coughlin, Publisher, Michael E. Coughlin, 1985 Selby Ave, St Paul, MN 55104, 612-646-8917. 1977. Articles, cartoons, satire, criticism, reviews, letters. *"The Dandelion* is an occasional journal of philosophical anarchism which welcomes a wide variety of articles, cartoons, reviews, satire, criticism and news items. Prefers shorter articles, but will consider major pieces if appropriate. A sample copy is available at no cost to prospective authors" circ. about 400. 2/yr. Pub'd 1 issue 1990; expects 2 issues 1991, 2 issues 1992. sub. price: $4.50; per copy: $1.50; sample: 50¢. Back issues: $1.50. Discounts: 25% off listed price for bulk orders. 28pp; 5½×8½; †lp. Reporting time: 1 month. Payment: copies of the magazine. Not copyrighted. Pub's reviews: 2 in 1990. §Anarchist/libertarian history, biographies, philosophy. Ads: none.

John Daniel and Company, Publishers, John Daniel, Publisher; Susan Daniel, Sales Manager, PO Box 21922, Santa Barbara, CA 93121, (805) 962-1780. 1985. Poetry, fiction, non-fiction. "We will look at anything, but we specialize in belles lettres. Our current best-selling authors are Hildegarde Flanner, Janet Lewis, Mary Jane Moffat, and Joan Baez, Sr. Our books are sold and distributed to the trade nationwide by National Book Network" avg. press run 2M. Pub'd 10 titles 1990; expects 10 titles 1991, 10 titles 1992. 33 titles listed in the *Small Press Record of Books in Print* (20th Edition, 1991-92). avg. price, cloth: $17.95; paper: $9.95. Discounts: trade 1-4 20%, 5+ 40%; library 10%; jobber 1-9 20%, 10+ 50%. 144pp; 5½×8½; of. Reporting time: 6-8 weeks. Payment: no advance; 10% of net receipts. Copyrights for author.

DARK TOME, Scareware, Michelle Marr, PO Box 705, Salem, OR 97308, 503-371-8647. 1990. Fiction, art. "Horror to 6,000 words. Supernatural slant preferred. Make checks payable to Michelle Marr only" circ. 100+. 6/yr. Pub'd 6 issues 1990; expects 6 issues 1991, 6 issues 1992. sub. price: $10; per copy: $2; sample: $2. Discounts: will trade with other publications. 40pp; 5½×8½; †xerox. Reporting time: 1 month. Payment: $2-$10 or sub + copy. Copyrighted, reverts to author. Ads: $25/$15/will trade.

DAUGHTER OF SARAH, Reta Finger, 3801 North Keeler, Chicago, IL 60641, 312-736-3399. 1974. Poetry,

152

fiction, articles, art, photos, cartoons, interviews, satire, criticism, reviews, music, letters, news items, non-fiction. "Must be Christian feminist. No more than 2,000 words; mostly nonfiction articles" circ. 6.5M. 6/yr. Pub'd 6 issues 1990; expects 6 issues 1991, 6 issues 1992. sub. price: $18; per copy: $3.50; sample: $3.50. Back issues: $2-$3.50 plus p/h. 32pp; 5½x8½; of, sheet fed. Reporting time: 1-2 months. Payment: approx. $15 per printed page. Copyrighted, reverts to author. Pub's reviews: 25-35 in 1990. §On Christian feminism. Ads: $250/$125/50¢. ACP (Assoc. Church Press), SMPG (Small Mag Publishing Group).

Steve Davis Publishing, Steve Davis, PO Box 190831, Dallas, TX 75219, 214-558-4702. 1982. Non-fiction. avg. press run 2.5M-10M. Pub'd 2 titles 1990; expects 4 titles 1991, 4 titles 1992. 2 titles listed in the *Small Press Record of Books in Print* (20th Edition, 1991-92). avg. price, cloth: $19.95; paper: $7.95-$19.95. 300pp; 8½x11, 7x9, 6x9, 5½x8½. Reporting time: 2-4 weeks if we're interested. Payment: normally 10% of sales, paid semi-annually. Copyrights for author. ABA.

The Dawn Horse Press (see also THE LAUGHING MAN: The Alternative to Scientific Materialism and Religious Provincialism), Carolyn Lee, Editor, PO Box 3680, Clearlake, CA 95422. 1972. avg. press run 5M. Pub'd 3 titles 1990; expects 6 titles 1991, 6 titles 1992. avg. price, cloth: $24.95; paper: $12.95. Discounts: 5-25 copies 40%/26-50 copies 41%/50-100 copies 42%/100 up copies 43%. 250pp; 5¼x8½, 9x6, 4x7; of. Reporting time: 2-3 weeks. Payment: royalties 10%. Copyrights for author.

Dawn Rose Press, 12470 Fiori Lane, Sebastopol, CA 95472, 707-874-2001. 1990. 1 title listed in the *Small Press Record of Books in Print* (20th Edition, 1991-92).

Dawn Sign Press, Joe Dannis, 2124 Kittredge Street #107, Berkeley, CA 94704-1436, 415-430-9419. 1983. Fiction, parts-of-novels, non-fiction. "We publish educational materials for pre-school, elementary, and parents—sign language related and for college students" avg. press run 5M-20M. Pub'd 2 titles 1990; expects 1 title 1991, 2 titles 1992. 10 titles listed in the *Small Press Record of Books in Print* (20th Edition, 1991-92). avg. price, paper: $20; other: games $15.95. Discounts: write for details. 100pp; 10½x8; of. Reporting time: 120 days. Payment: varies. Copyrights for author.

Dawnwood Press, John Welch, 387 Park Avenue South, 5th Floor, New York, NY 10016-8810, 212-532-7160; fax 212-213-2495; 800-367-9692. 1983. Fiction. "Recent contributor: Paul Kuttner. More to come. No unsolicited mss." avg. press run 2.5M. Pub'd 1 title 1990; expects 1 title 1991, 1 title 1992. 4 titles listed in the *Small Press Record of Books in Print* (20th Edition, 1991-92). avg. price, cloth: $14.95. Discounts: 42% - books returnable after six months by trade; 20% - to schools and libraries; 50% - to jobbers - returnable after one year. 250-500pp; 6x9 (average); of. Reporting time: agents' submissions - 6 weeks. Payment: yes - outright, depends on sales appeal of novel. Copyrights for author.

W.S. Dawson Co., C.W. Tazewell, PO Box 62823, Virginia Beach, VA 23462, 804-499-6271. 1983. Non-fiction. "Publisher uses 21st century, zero-level inventory, shoe-string concepts, on paper, floppy disk and on-line services. 'A shoe-string publisher' (each item special order)." avg. press run varies. Pub'd 13 titles 1990; expects 17 titles 1991, 10 titles 1992. 33 titles listed in the *Small Press Record of Books in Print* (20th Edition, 1991-92). avg. price, cloth: $13; paper: $11. Discounts: trade 20%; libraries, institutions and government 10% (if paid in 30 days). 90pp; 8½x11; xerox. Reporting time: 1 month. Payment: negotiable. Copyrights for author.

DAYSPRING, The Dayspring Press, Inc., John C. Brainerd, 18600 West 58 Avenue, Golden, CO 80403-1070, 303-279-2462. 1983. Poetry, fiction, articles, art, photos, cartoons, interviews, satire, criticism, reviews, music, letters, parts-of-novels, long-poems, collages, plays, concrete art, non-fiction. circ. 980. 12/yr. Pub'd 12 issues 1990; expects 12 issues 1991, 12 issues 1992. sub. price: $12; per copy: $2; sample: $2. Back issues: $2. Discounts: 1/3 over 15 copies. 60pp; 5½x8½; †photo offset. Reporting time: 1-4 weeks. Copyrighted, rights reverting is negotiable. Pub's reviews: 10 in 1990. §Theology, philosophy, history, education. Ads: $35//$5 per inch.

The Dayspring Press, Inc. (see also DAYSPRING; NEW ANGLICAN REVIEW; NEW CATHOLIC REVIEW; FICTION FORUM; POET'S FORUM), John C. Brainerd, 18600 West 58 Avenue, Golden, CO 80403-1070, 303-279-2462. 1983. "Dayspring is a little-literary and religious forum. We publish almost everything received (or find its natural market), especially short lyrics, up to five-page narrative poems, literary criticism, short, and extended fiction that trades in the deeper human sensibilities. No prurient, scandalous, or malicious material will be published" avg. press run 500. Pub'd 2 titles 1990; expects 3 titles 1991, 1 title 1992. 8 titles listed in the *Small Press Record of Books in Print* (20th Edition, 1991-92). avg. price, paper: $5.95. Discounts: 1/3 over 15 copies. 227pp; 5½x8½; †of. Reporting time: 1-4 weeks. Payment: 50% after expenses (accountable) or by mutual agreement. Copyrights for author.

dbqp (see also ALABAMA DOGSHOE MOUSTACHE; SOCKS, DREGS AND ROCKING CHAIRS; THE SUBTLE JOURNAL OF RAW COINAGE; A VOICE WITHOUT SIDES), Ge(of Huth), po.ed.t, 317 Princetown Road, Schenectady, NY 12306-2022. 1987. Poetry, satire, collages, concrete art. "Recent contributors: John M. Bennett, Greg Evason, Daniel f. Bradley, David C. Kopaska-Merkel. dbqp: the overarching press, which includes magazines, pamphlet series, and other series. &: occasional series of small leaflets & cards which publishes mostly short language poetry; about 50 published per year. dbqprescard: irregular series of postcards, mostly visually, printed by rubberstamp, photography, photocopy; about 2 titles per year. goodbooqpres: press responsible for publishing booklets mostly of short poetry. QCXK: publishes original eraser carvings—actual prints of the carvings—about 3 titles per year. Chron: series of handwriting printed publications, 3 per year. Objecta: series of writing published as and on objects—wood, erasers, etc. dboudbledb: series publishing two poems (one by each of two poets) brought together by the whim of the editor. Cautionary Pamplet of the Chemung County Geodesic Society for the Preservation and Proliferation of Mark Twain: series of satiric and parodying pamphlets, not necessarily (or even ever) about Twain. dbqp is interested in publishing linguistically daring work only (what people might call visual, language or surrealistic poetry). dbqp publishes short poetry (a page long at most & usually less). Any chapbooks submitted to goodbooqpres should be no more than 30 pages & of very short poetry. dbqp does not have the ability to publish large manuscripts. Subscriptions can be of any dollar amount—cost (which varies) per issue will be subtracted when mailed. Catalog of all dbqp publications is available for SASE." avg. press run 100. Pub'd 30 titles 1990; expects 30 titles 1991, 30 titles 1992. 1 title listed in the *Small Press Record of Books in Print* (20th Edition, 1991-92). avg. price, other: $2. 30pp; size varies; †mi, of, photocopy, rubberstamp type, photography (actual prints), handwriting, hand typing, spirit duplicating, hectography, Gocco printing, dot-matrix, laser printing. Reporting time: 2 weeks. Payment: author receives 1/4 of press run. Copyrights for author.

dbS Productions, Bob Adams, PO Box 1894, University Station, Charlottesville, VA 22903, 804-977-1581. 1990. Non-fiction. "Outdoor skill related, first-aid, survival; biology skills; video production." avg. press run 10M. Pub'd 3 titles 1990; expects 4 titles 1991, 5 titles 1992. 2 titles listed in the *Small Press Record of Books in Print* (20th Edition, 1991-92). avg. price, paper: $19. Discounts: 20% bulk, 40% retail. 60pp; 4×7. Reporting time: 1 month. Payment: 10% biannual. Copyrights for author.

DE NAR, Erik Van Der Veken, Kris Wauters, PO Box 104, 1210 Brussels 21, Belgium. 1986. Poetry, articles, art, criticism, reviews, music, letters, news items, non-fiction. "Any alternative news is published. Many publications and addresses. Information..." circ. 500. 12/yr. Pub'd 12 issues 1990; expects 12 issues 1991, 12 issues 1992. sub. price: 200BEF; per copy: 15BEF; sample: free. 16-32pp; 15×21cm. Payment: none, free contribution. Not copyrighted. Pub's reviews: 278 in 1990. §Alternative small publishes, art, action, politics. Ads: free contribution.

Dead Angel Press, Chuck Oliveros, 1206 Lyndale Drive SE, Atlanta, GA 30316, 404-624-1524. 1982. Poetry, fiction, parts-of-novels, plays. avg. press run 500. Pub'd 1 title 1990; expects 1 title 1991, 1 title 1992. 1 title listed in the *Small Press Record of Books in Print* (20th Edition, 1991-92). avg. price, paper: $5. No discounts. 54pp; 5½×8½; of. Reporting time: 3 months. Payment: negotiated. Copyrights for author.

" "...A DEAD BEAT POET PRODUCTION, James Phipps, 500 North River Oaks, Indialantic, FL 32903, 407-952-0563. 1990. Poetry, fiction, articles, art, photos, cartoons, interviews, satire, criticism, reviews, long-poems, collages, plays, concrete art, non-fiction. "This magazine Iguanna is just one of many one to two to three issue mags from the dead beat poets. They reflect our continued desire to explore reality, and maybe change it. I am interested in getting more members involved in various creative urges. Right now there are artists, musicians, and political radicals in our group, but mainly on a local level. I would like to at least go state in about 4 months. You may have noticed that there are many different areas we cover, that's just the way we are. Praise dead beat poets!" circ. 100-150. 6+. Pub'd 2 issues 1990; expects 10 issues 1991, 10-15 issues 1992. sub. price: donation; per copy: $2 ppd; sample: on request. Back issues: if someone wants a back issue and it's available, $2 plus postage. Discounts: will trade, free for anyone who contributes, anyone who wishes to join the dead beat poets. 12+pp; 4½×5½; mi. Reporting time: continuously accepting submissions. Payment: no. Not copyrighted. Pub's reviews: 5-7 in 1990. §Many in the same field as mine, plus gay and lesbian erotica, art. Ads: all ad prices negotiable; free for political groups, and individual artists, sample product advertised for larger groups.

DEAD OF NIGHT MAGAZINE, L. Lin Stein, 916 Shaker Road #143, Longmeadow, MA 01106-2416. 1989. Poetry, fiction, articles, art, cartoons, interviews, reviews, letters. "Recent contributors: J.N. Williamson, John Maclay, Jim Kisner, Barbara Parker, Yvonne Navarro, Edward Lodi. Preferred length: Articles & fiction 500-1500 words. Poetry up to 32 lines. We publish only Vampire-related fiction, features, reviews, etc." circ. 300+. 4/yr. Expects 4 issues 1991, 4 issues 1992. sub. price: $15; per copy: $3.95; sample: $3.95. Back issues: $3. Discounts: none. Pages vary; 8½×11. Reporting time: 4-6 weeks. Payment: fiction $12, articles $8, poetry $4, 'fillers' 1/2-3¢ word, varies, plus contributor copy. Copyrighted, reverts to author. Pub's reviews: 5 in 1990. §Horror (general), fantasy, Vampire-related novels, non-fiction Vampire lore, non-fiction how-to (write horror, etc.). Ads: send for rates. SPWAO, HWA, COSMEP.

S. Deal & Assoc., Shirley Herd Deal, 1629 Guizot Street, San Diego, CA 92107. 1977. Pub'd 1 title 1990; expects 1 title 1991, 3 titles 1992. 1 title listed in the *Small Press Record of Books in Print* (20th Edition,

154

1991-92). avg. price, paper: $9; other: poly vinyl notebook $16. Discounts: 5 books-40%; classroom-20%; wholesaler-55% for 100 or more. 255pp.

DEANOTATIONS, Dean Blehert, 11919 Moss Point Lane, Reston, VA 22094. 1984. Poetry. *"Deanotations* is a poetry letter. It contains poems by me, drawings by my wife, Pamela Coulter Blehert. It goes out every 2 months to about 400 addresses. The first issue went out in Aug. 1984. There have been 40 issues so far, plus 2 'bonus issues' sent to contributors. The first issue went to about 90 people. They sent me names of friends they thoought would enjoy it, and thus my mailing list grew. It was free for over 6 years. With issue 40, it is sent to subscribers only." circ. 2.8M. 6/yr. Pub'd 6 issues 1990; expects 6 issues 1991, 6 issues 1992. sub. price: $10; sample: free. Back issues: $1. Discounts: 2 yrs, $17.50, will exchange for other publications. 4pp; 8½×11; of. Copyrighted.

DECEMBER MAGAZINE, Curt Johnson, Box 302, Highland Park, IL 60035. 1958. Fiction, articles, art, photos, interviews, satire, criticism, reviews, non-fiction. circ. 1M. Irregular. Pub'd 2 issues 1990; expects 2 issues 1991, 2 issues 1992. sub. price: $25 4 issues; per copy: $7.50; sample: $5. Back issues: twice cover price. Discounts: 20% 10 or more, agency 20%. 228pp; 6×9; of. Reporting time: 15-20 weeks. Payment: free copies. Copyrighted, reverts to author. Pub's reviews: 0 in 1990. §Fiction. Ads: $100/$60. COSMEP, PMA.

DECENTRALIZE!, Carol Moore, PO Box 1608, Washington, DC 20013-1608. 1986. News items, non-fiction. "Short letters and news items (under 300 words) on non-violent decentralist networking and strategy" circ. 500. 4/yr. Pub'd 4 issues 1990; expects 4 issues 1991, 4 issues 1992. sub. price: $4; per copy: $1; sample: same. Back issues: $1 each. Discounts: 5 plus, 75¢ each. 6pp; 8½×11; †of. Reporting time: no report back, may receive copy of publication. Payment: none. Not copyrighted. Pub's reviews: 15 in 1990. §Decentralism, greens, bioregionalists, anarchists, libertarians, gandhi, feminism. No ads.

The Dedalus Press (see also TRACKS), John F. Deane, 24 The Heath, Cypress Downs, Dublin 6, Ireland. 1985. Poetry. "Poetry in translation by Irish poets, original poetry. Recent contributors: Robert Greacen, Rory Brennan, Macdara Woods, Tomas Transtromer, Marin Sorescu, Miguel Hernandez, Richard Kell, Tom Mac Intyre, Dennis O'Driscoll" avg. press run 750. Pub'd 6 titles 1990; expects 6 titles 1991, 6 titles 1992. 2 titles listed in the *Small Press Record of Books in Print* (20th Edition, 1991-92). avg. price, cloth: £5.70; paper: £3.60. Discounts: 33⅓% on 3+. 64pp; size A5; of. Reporting time: 1 month. Payment: 10% royalties, (or) cash payments. Copyrights for author.

DeerTrail Books, Jack Campbell, 637 Williams Court, PO Box 171, Gurnee, IL 60031, 312-367-0014. 1988. Non-fiction. "Interested in non-fiction m.s.—books only—of approx. 40-100,000 words. Subjects are open, but no poetry, religious tracts, personal life philosophies, autobiographies; and other subjects of only interest to the writer. We *don't* want to see a m.s. first. Write a one-page letter (if you can) describing your subject, your reader, and your thrust and treatment. We'll tell you if *we* want to invest our funds and energy into publishing it for or with you. We are *not* a vanity publisher. Please include SASE to facilitate reply" avg. press run 2M-5M. Pub'd 1 title 1990; expects 3-4 titles 1991, 4-5 titles 1992. 1 title listed in the *Small Press Record of Books in Print* (20th Edition, 1991-92). avg. price, cloth: $17; paper: $12. Discounts: standard trade. 144-250pp; size varies; of. Reporting time: 90 days. Payment: negotiable. Copyrights for author. Heartland Press Association, MidAmerica Publishers Group.

De-Feet Press, Inc., Burton S. Schuler, 2401 W. 15th Street, Panama City, FL 32401. 1981. Non-fiction. "We are mostly interested in biography and travel books. Also any non-fiction work where the writer can show us a ready market via mail order" avg. press run 500. Pub'd 1 title 1990; expects 2 titles 1991, 3 titles 1992. avg. price, cloth: $15.95; paper: $12.95. 150pp; 6×9. Payment: no advance. COSMEP.

Delancey Press, Inc., Wesley Morrison, Editorial Director, PO Box 40285, Philadelphia, PA 19106. "Delancey Press, a new trade publisher, is now accepting queries and proposals from authors. Our needs include both specialized and general non-fiction, humor, and how-to. Regional focus is encouraged but not required. Delancey Press will publish both pamphlets and books, and we will consider projects of up to 40,000 words. Delancey Press is presently looking at queries and proposals only; do not send full manuscripts. Writers should direct all correspondence to Wesley Morrison, Editorial Director, at the address above." Payment: negotiable, based on both the size of the manuscript and the scale of the project.

DELIRIUM, Judith Shannon Paine, Route one, Box 7x, Harrison, ID 83833, 714-689-3726. 1989. Poetry, fiction, art, photos, cartoons, reviews. "Recent contributors: John Sjoblom, Cliff Burns, Elliot Richmen, and Judy Widener. Length: 250 to 2500 words. Distinct editorial preference for shorter, free verse poetry. Material should be lively, well-crafted, neat. Send me your best, please. No religious, political rant, violence, or juvenile. Subscription and sample copy requests should be addressed to Muggwart Press, Frank L. Nicholson, Publisher, PO Box 7814, Riverside, CA 92503." circ. 150. 4/yr. Pub'd 4 issues 1990; expects 4 issues 1991, 4 issues 1992. sub. price: $16; per copy: $4; sample: $4. Back issues: at the discretion of the press or $4. 60pp; †laser. Reporting time: 90 days at the very latest. Payment: copies and nominal (very) cash on publication. Copyrighted, reverts to author. Pub's reviews. §No religious, political rant, juvenile or violence, anything else is

155

o.k; poetry especially o.k.

Delta Publishing Company, Geoff Daigle, John van Geldern, 316 California Avenue #134, Reno, NV 89509, 702-329-9995. 1990. "We prefer full-length novels which have unusual story lines and characters and in which there is a strong philosophical message. We also entertain non-fiction book-length writings and political satire." avg. press run 15M. Expects 3 titles 1991, 5-8 titles 1992. 1 title listed in the *Small Press Record of Books in Print* (20th Edition, 1991-92). avg. price, cloth: $22; paper: $10. Discounts: conventional quantity trade discounts, STOP orders and wholesale distributor discounts. 200pp; 6½×9; of. Reporting time: 60 days. Payment: industry standard but we encourage author participation in pub. work for greater royalties. Copyrights for author. ABA.

Deltiologists of America (see also POSTCARD CLASSICS), Dr. James Lewis Lowe, PO Box 8, Norwood, PA 19074, 215-485-8572. 1960. "We publish books about picture postcards only" avg. press run 1.5M. Expects 3 titles 1991, 3 titles 1992. 6 titles listed in the *Small Press Record of Books in Print* (20th Edition, 1991-92). avg. price, cloth: $15; paper: $10. Quantity discounts to booksellers. Reporting time: 60 days. Payment: by arrangement. Does not copyright for author.

Dembner Books, S. Arthur Dembner, 61 4th Avenue, 3rd Floor, New York, NY 10003-5202. 1978. Fiction, non-fiction. "We are a small trade publisher (hardcover and trade paperback). We publish books that are worth reading and even worth keeping. Our non-fiction includes popular reference works, *The Complete Book of U.S. Presidents*, and medical self-help, such as *A Doctor's Prescription for Getting the Best Medical Care* and *Your Skin: From Acne to Zitts*. Our fiction includes the mystery series by John Riggs *The Garth Ryland Mystery Series* and *One Cried Murder*" avg. press run 3.5M-10M. Pub'd 12 titles 1990; expects 12 titles 1991, 12-15 titles 1992. 1 title listed in the *Small Press Record of Books in Print* (20th Edition, 1991-92). avg. price, cloth: varies; paper: varies. Discounts: we are distributed by W.W. Norton. Their discount schedule is 1-9 copies 20%, 10-24 40%, 25-99 42%, 100-499 44%, 500-1499 46%. Pages vary; 5½×8¼, 6×9; of. Reporting time: 8 weeks. Payment: standard royalties—10% first 5,000 sold, 12½% next 5,000, 15% thereafter. Copyrights for author. Assoc. of American Publishers.

DEMOCRATIC LEFT, Michael Harrington, Founding Editor; Michael Lighty, Managing Editor, 15 Dutch Street, Suite 500, New York, NY 10038, 212-962-0390. 1972. Articles, photos, cartoons, interviews, criticism, letters, news items. "Almost all of the articles are written from a democratic socialist perspective" circ. 10M. 6/yr. Pub'd 6 issues 1990; expects 6 issues 1991, 6 issues 1992. sub. price: $8; per copy: $1.50; sample: 25¢. Back issues: $1.50. Discounts: 40% to bookstores for order of 20 or more, prepaid. 20pp; 8½×11; desktop. Reporting time: 1 month lead time. Payment: none. Not copyrighted. Pub's reviews: 6 in 1990. §Political science, socialist stragies, history. Ads: $50 col inch/$2 line.

The Denali Press, Alan Edward Schorr, Editorial Director and Publisher, 1704 Willow Drive, Juneau, AK 99801, 907-586-6014. 1986. Non-fiction. "Firm publishes only reference and scholarly publications oriented toward library (academic and public) market, with modest sales directly to stores and indivduals. Principally interested in: directories, guides, handbooks, indexes/abstracts as well as scholarly academic works, principally in the area of cultural diversity, ethnic and minority groups as well as occasional titles on Alaskana. Emphasis on books about ethnic groups and refugees. Exclusive distributor in US for Hull University Press, Libris, and Meridian Books. Recent titles include national resource directories for Hispanics and refugees/immigrants, as well as books on Jewish refugee children and US policy in Micronesia." avg. press run 1.5M. Pub'd 3 titles 1990; expects 4 titles 1991, 4 titles 1992. 11 titles listed in the *Small Press Record of Books in Print* (20th Edition, 1991-92). avg. price, cloth: $37.50; paper: $25. Discounts: 20%. 320pp; 8½×11, 5¼×8½, 6×9; of. Reporting time: 5 weeks. Payment: 10%. Does not copyright for author. PMA, COSMEP, American Library Assn., Soc. for Scholarly Publ., Alaska Assn. of Small Presses, Small Press Center of NY.

DENVER QUARTERLY, Donald Revell, Editor, University of Denver, Denver, CO 80208, 303-871-2892. 1966. Poetry, fiction, articles, interviews, satire, criticism, reviews, parts-of-novels, long-poems, non-fiction. "Essays: Carl Dennis, David Wojahn, Lee Upton, James Longenbach. Fiction: Charles Baxter, Joanne Greenberg. Poems: James Tate, Philip Booth, Jane Miller, Stanley Plumly" circ. 1M. 4/yr. Pub'd 4 issues 1990; expects 4 issues 1991, 4 issues 1992. sub. price: $18/institutions, $15/individuals; per copy: $5; sample: $5. Back issues: cost is based on cover price of the individual issue; usually $4 or $5. 160pp; 6×9; of. Reporting time: 2-3 months. Payment: $5 per page. Copyrighted, reverts to author. Pub's reviews: 32 in 1990. §Literature of last 100 years and contemporary fiction and poetry. Ads: $150/$75. CCLM, Council of Editors of Learned Journals.

Depot Press, Steve Eng, Literary Editor; Ted P. Yeatman, Nonfiction Editor, PO Box 60072, Nashville, TN 37206, 226-1890. 1981. Poetry, articles, photos, non-fiction. "Must relate to the Old West, or Civil War, or within limits, Southern Regional history or literature, all interested parties should query first. Recent: *Jesse James and Bill Ryan at Nashville* (1981); *The Hunter of Time* verse by Lucile Coleman 1984; *Toreros* verse by John Gawsworth (1990)" avg. press run 500. Pub'd 1 title 1990; expects 1 title 1991, 1 title 1992. 3 titles listed

156

in the *Small Press Record of Books in Print* (20th Edition, 1991-92). avg. price, cloth: $8; paper: $3. Discounts: standard dealer. 30-70pp; 5×8; of. Reporting time: 3 weeks, and only if queried first. Payment: standard, but by arrangement. Generally copyrights for author. TWHFS, NOLA, BMI.

DESCANT, Betsy Feagan Colquitt, Editor; Stanley Trachtenberg, Editor; Harry Oppenheimer, Editor, English Department, TCU, Box 32872, Fort Worth, TX 76129. 1955. Poetry, fiction. *"Descant* does not publish poetry volumes" circ. 500. 2/yr. sub. price: $8; per copy: $4.50; sample: $4. Back issues: $4. 80-100pp; 6×9; of. Reporting time: 6 weeks. Payment: in copies. We retain copyright. No ads.

DESCANT, Karen Mulhallen, PO Box 314, Station P, Toronto, Ontario M5S 2S8, Canada. 1970. Poetry, fiction, articles, art, photos, interviews, long-poems, plays. circ. 1M. 4/yr. Pub'd 4 issues 1990; expects 4 issues 1991, 4 issues 1992. sub. price: $21-$29 plus $6 per year outside Canada ($22.47 = $21 + $1.47 GST; $31.03 = $29 + $2.03 GST) GST *in Canada only*; per copy: $7.50; sample: $7.50 + $2 outside Canada. Back issues: inquire. 200pp; 6×8; of. Reporting time: 6-12 weeks. Payment: varies. Not copyrighted. §Poetry, quality fiction, arts and letters. Ads: inquire. COSMEP, CPPA.

DESDE ESTE LADO/FROM THIS SIDE, Frances Negron, Luz Borrero, Juan David Acosta, Luis Hernandez, PO Box 18458, Philadelphia, PA 19120. 1987. Poetry, fiction, art, photos, interviews, criticism, reviews, music, collages, plays, non-fiction. "Latino writers or Latino-related topics. Pieces should not exceed 10 double-spaced pages." circ. 700. 1/yr. Expects 1 issue 1991, 1 issue 1992. sub. price: $10; per copy: $5; sample: free when applicable. 60pp; of. Reporting time: depends. Payment: copies. Copyrighted, reverts to author. Pub's reviews. §Literature in general (Latinos in particular), film, art. Ads: none.

DESIGN AND TECHNOLOGY TEACHING, Trentham Books, John Eggleston, Unit 13/14, Trent Trading Pack, Botteslow St., Hanley, Stoke-on-Trent, Staffordshire ST1 3LY, England, 0203-523848. 1966. Articles, photos, cartoons, interviews, criticism, reviews, letters, concrete art, news items. "Prints articles on new developments and practice of design education in schools and colleges." circ. 2.5M. 3/yr. Pub'd 2 issues 1990; expects 2 issues 1991, 3 issues 1992. sub. price: £20; per copy: £7; sample: £7. Back issues: £7. Discounts: 10% series disc/w ads. 64pp; 30×21cm; of. Reporting time: max 1 month usually 2 weeks. Payment: none. Copyrighted, rights held by magazine. Pub's reviews: 66 in 1990. §Craft, art, design, education. Ads: £300/£150/£1.

DESIGN BOOK REVIEW, Elizabeth Snowden, Co-Editor; Richard Ingersoll, Co-Editor; John Parman, Founding Publisher; Michael Zavala Tobriner, Managing Editor, 1418 Spring Way, Berkeley, CA 94708, 415-486-1956; fax 415-540-1057. 1983. Articles, art, photos, criticism, reviews, letters. *"Design Book Review* is a leading magazine of ideas in the design field. Each quarter we provide our readers with essays, interviews, design criticism, and reviews of the latest and most significant books and exhibitions on architecture, design, urbanism, and landscape architecture. Subscriptions, advertising inquiries, address changes and mailing list correspondence should be addressed to: *Design Book Review,* MIT Press Journals, 55 Hayward Street, Cambridge, MA 02142. Books for review and editorial correspondence should be sent to the Berkeley address." circ. 7M. 4/yr. Pub'd 3 issues 1990; expects 4 issues 1991, 4 issues 1992. sub. price: $30 indiv., $55 instit., outside US add $14 per year. Discounts: schedules on request. 96pp; 8½×11; sheetfed offset. Reporting time: 6 weeks. Payment: in copies. Pub's reviews: 240 in 1990. §Architecture design, landscape architecture, urban design, decorative arts. Ads: write for rates. COSMEP.

Design Enterprises of San Francisco, Donald McCunn, Editor, PO Box 14695, San Francisco, CA 94114. 1977. "How-to books related to clothing design and programing personal computers. Also books on Chinese Americans. Send letters of inquiry only." avg. press run 5M. Expects 2 titles 1991. 6 titles listed in the *Small Press Record of Books in Print* (20th Edition, 1991-92). avg. price, cloth: $10.95; paper: $6.95. Discounts: 1 copy 20%, 2-4 30%, 5-19 40%, 20+ 45%. 200pp; 8½×11; of.

DESIGNING NEW CIVILIZATIONS, Leon Vickman, 16255 Ventura Blvd., #605, Encino, CA 91436, 818-788-1136. 1983. Articles, letters, non-fiction. circ. 80. 12/yr. Pub'd 12 issues 1990; expects 12 issues 1991, 12 issues 1992. sub. price: $20; per copy: $2; sample: $1. 50pp; 8½×11; †xerox. Reporting time: 1 month. Payment: none. Not copyrighted. Ads: none.

THE DESIGNMENT REVIEW, Todd Lord, 4928 109th Street SW, Tacoma, WA 98499, 206-584-6309. 1986. "Floor plans and illustrations" circ. 10M. 1/yr. Pub'd 1 issue 1990; expects 1 issue 1991, 1 issue 1992. sub. price: $8; per copy: $8; sample: no charge. Discounts: 5-10 books 20%, 11-50 50%, larger quantities write. 70pp; 8½×11; of. Payment: fees negotiable. Copyrighted, reverts to author. Pub's reviews. §Home construction manuals. Ads: $10,000 (full-page sponsorships only).

DEVIANCE, Lin Collette, PO Box 1706, Pawtucket, RI 02862. 1987. Poetry, fiction, articles, cartoons, interviews, satire, criticism, reviews, letters, long-poems, non-fiction. "Checks *must* be made out to Lin Collette. Published Katharyn Machan Aal, Kerry L. Fare, Delta Zahner, Joe Cardillo, Zach Rombakis among others. *Deviance* is a magazine dedicated to publishing work by persons espousing views that may not be

157

popular with 'middle America.' This includes feminist, lesbian/gay, non-religious/religious (atheistic, pagan, or unorthodox views of mainstream religions such as Judaism or Christianity), political (anarchist, socialist, or similar), and material by people of color. We really, really need non-fiction! For return of manuscripts, *make sure* you enclose an SASE—otherwise, tough luck'' circ. 500. 3/yr. Pub'd 2 issues 1990; expects 3 issues 1991, 3 issues 1992. 1 title listed in the *Small Press Record of Books in Print* (20th Edition, 1991-92). sub. price: $13; per copy: $5; sample: $5. Discounts: can be negotiated. 40pp; 8½×11; xerox machine. Reporting time: 2-6 weeks. Payment: 1-2 copies. Copyrighted, reverts to author. Pub's reviews: 1 in 1990. §Religion, politics, feminism, racism, gay/lesbian, fiction, history, psychology. Ads: classifieds 30¢ per word.

Devida Publication, 6 Darby Road, East Brunswick, NJ 08816-3407, 201-257-7257. 1981. Non-fiction. "Most recent of books was *Ignore Your Teeth and They'll Go Away, by Dr. Sheldon B. Sydney, The Consumers Complete Guide To Gum Disease.*" avg. press run 4M. Expects 1 title 1991, 2 titles 1992. avg. price, paper: $15.95. Discounts: available upon request and specific per type, i.e. wholesaler vs. trade. 130pp; 6×9; of. Reporting time: 60 days. Payment: upon request. Copyrights for author. COSMEP.

Devil Mountain Books, Clark Sturges, PO Box 4115, Walnut Creek, CA 94596, 415-939-3415. 1984. 4 titles listed in the *Small Press Record of Books in Print* (20th Edition, 1991-92).

THE DEVIL'S MILLHOPPER, The Devil's Millhopper Press, Stephen Gardner, Editor; Carol Jennings, Assistant Editor, 171 University Parkway, College of Humanities/USC at Aiken, Aiken, SC 29801-6399, 803-648-6851. 1976. Poetry, art, photos. "Submission periods: Sept. 1 to Oct. 15 of each year" circ. 500. 1/yr. Pub'd 1 issue 1990; expects 1 issue 1991, 1 issue 1992. sub. price: $5, $9 for 2 years; per copy: $3; sample: $3. Back issues: $3. 36pp; 5½×8½; of. Reporting time: 2-3 months. Payment: 3 cash prizes—$150, $100, $50. Copyrighted, reverts to author.

The Devil's Millhopper Press (see also THE DEVIL'S MILLHOPPER), Stephen Gardner, Editor; Carol Jennings, Assistant Editor, 171 University Parkway, College of Humanities/USC at Aiken, Aiken, SC 29801-6399, 803-648-6851. 1984. Poetry. "The chapbook and most of the poems in our magazine issue are received and published as the results of our yearly contests. Send SASE for guidelines. Submission periods: Chapbooks-the month of January of each year; Magazine-Sept. 1 to Oct. 15 of each year" avg. press run 500. Pub'd 2 titles 1990; expects 2 titles 1991, 2 titles 1992. 6 titles listed in the *Small Press Record of Books in Print* (20th Edition, 1991-92). avg. price, paper: $3.50 (chapbook). Discounts: for 5 copies or more, $1 off per copy price. 28-40pp; 5½×8½; of. Reporting time: 2-3 months. Payment: chapbook—$50 + 50 copies. Copyrights for author.

Devin-Adair, Publishers, Inc., Jane Andrassi, 6 North Water Street, Greenwich, CT 06830. 1911. Photos, cartoons, criticism, non-fiction. "Publishing in these areas exclusively: 1) Political and national affairs, 2) Health and ecology, 3) Irish topics, 4) Americana, 5) Cooking and gardening, 6) photography" avg. press run 4M. Pub'd 14 titles 1990; expects 16 titles 1991, 22 titles 1992. 3 titles listed in the *Small Press Record of Books in Print* (20th Edition, 1991-92). avg. price, cloth: $16.95; paper: $12.95. Discounts: 3-5 books 20%, 6-9 40%, 10-24 41%, 25-99 42%, 100+ individual discounts arranged 50%+. 220pp; size varies; web printing, internal typesetting, w/freelance designers. Reporting time: 1-2 months. Payment: 10% royalty. Copyrights for author. APA, ABA, SWGA, SACIA, Small Press Center.

The Devon Publishing Co., Inc., Pauline Innis, 2700 Vol Avenue NW, Washington, DC 20037. 1980. Poetry, non-fiction. avg. press run 2M. Pub'd 2 titles 1990; expects 2 titles 1991, 2 titles 1992. avg. price, cloth: $15; paper: $10. Discounts: 40%. Payment: varies. Copyrights for author. Washington Independent Publishers.

The Devonshire Publishing Co., Jonathon Fried, PO Box 85, Elgin, IL 60121-0085, 708-242-3846; fax 708-879-0308. 1984. Fiction, art, photos, non-fiction. "Prefer letters of inquiry as opposed to mss—must include SASE" avg. press run 1M-5M. Expects 4 titles 1991, 1 title 1992. 5 titles listed in the *Small Press Record of Books in Print* (20th Edition, 1991-92). avg. price, cloth: $10.95; paper: $6.95. Discounts: wholesale & retail 1-5 20%, 6-49 40%, 50-100 55-60%, +3% for all prepaid orders. 200pp; 5½×8½; of. Reporting time: 1 month for letters/2 months for mss. Payment: usually no advance, 10% of net paid quarterly; different % for books sold at more than 50% discount. Copyrights for author. COSMEP, PMA.

Devyn Press, 3600 Chamberlain Lane #230, Louisville, KY 40241, 502-895-1354. 1979. Non-fiction. "All of our books are currently on the game of bridge and sports; we are largest publisher of bridge books in U.S." avg. press run 4M. Pub'd 8 titles 1990; expects 5 titles 1991, 6 titles 1992. 2 titles listed in the *Small Press Record of Books in Print* (20th Edition, 1991-92). avg. price, paper: $8.95. Discounts: generally 50%. 300pp; 5×8. Payment: 7-10% of retail. Copyrights for author.

DEWITT DIGEST & REVIEW, G. DeWitt, Box 355, Seal Beach, CA 90740. 1986. Articles, criticism, reviews, letters. "Biases: intrinsic critical theory—from new criticism to deconstructionism. Orientation toward functional diction—metaphor, pun, etc. Emphasis in essays on economic democracy, ending arms race, developing a national health care system, remedies to the effects of deregulation, and philosophy (especially philosophies of history)'' circ. 1,049. 3/yr. Pub'd 1 issue 1990; expects 3 issues 1991, 3 issues 1992. sub. price: free to libraries and educational institutions; no yearly sub. price; per copy: free to libraries and educational institutions; $3 for others; sample: free. Back issues: $3. 36pp; 5½×8½; †of, camera-ready copy prepared on letter-quality computer laser printer. Reporting time: 1 month. Payment: $5 per piece, without regard to type or length. Copyrighted. Pub's reviews: 15 in 1990. §Theoretical physics, critical/aesthetic theory, international affairs, philosophy, linguistics. No ads.

DHARMA COMBAT, Jim Keith, PO Box 20593, Sun Valley, NV 89433. 1988. Fiction, articles, art, cartoons, interviews, satire, criticism, reviews, letters, collages, concrete art, news items, non-fiction. *"Dharma Combat* is a non-denominational magazine about spirituality, philosophy, metaphysics (and conspiracies)'' circ. 1M. 4/yr. Pub'd 2 issues 1990; expects 4 issues 1991, 4 issues 1992. sub. price: $10; per copy: $3; sample: $3. 32pp; 11×17; †of. Reporting time: 1+ week. Payment: none. Copyrighted, reverts to author. Pub's reviews. §Spirituality, religion, metaphysics, reality, anarchism, conspiracies. Ads: please write for info.

Dharma Publishing (see also GESAR-Buddhism in the West), Tarthang Tulku, President; Elizabeth Cook, Publisher's contact, 2425 Hillside Avenue, Berkeley, CA 94704. 1972. Articles, art, photos, interviews, reviews, news items. "91 titles currently in print; over 100 reproductions of Tibetan in full color. Sepcializes in books on Buddhism. We have our own photo-typesetting and offset printing facilities. 8 titles for 1991'' avg. press run 5M. Pub'd 3 titles 1990; expects 8 titles 1991, 10 titles 1992. 63 titles listed in the *Small Press Record of Books in Print* (20th Edition, 1991-92). avg. price, cloth: $12.95-$20.95; paper: $5.95-$10.95; other: $2.95 Gesar, $10 Tibetan art prints. Discounts: bookstores 1 book 0%, 2-4 20%, 5-25 40%, 26-49 42%, 50-99 43%, 100-250 45%; 40% maximum on returnable books; distributors by contract; libraries 20%; class adoptions 20%. 32-250pp; 5½×8½, 8½×11, 7×10; †of. Reporting time: 2 months. Payment: subject to individual arrangement. ABA, COSMEP, PMA.

DIAL-A-POEM POETS LP'S, Giorno Poetry Systems Records, John Giorno, 222 Bowery, New York, NY 10012, 212-925-6372; fax 212-966-7574. 1967. Poetry, photos, cartoons, music. "LP records of over 300 poets reading their work." circ. 7M-10M. 4/yr. Pub'd 4 issues 1990; expects 4 issues 1991, 4 issues 1992. price per copy: $8.98 single album or cassette, $12.98 double album, $13.98 for double cassette or compact disc, videopak $39.95. Discounts: 40% for book and record stores. record, compact disc, cassette, videopak. Payment: $400 to each poet. CCLM.

DIAMOND HITCHHIKER COBWEBS, Nuclear Trenchcoated Subway Prophets Publications, Lake Rain Vajra, Ellis Dee, 118 E. Goodheart Avenue, Lake Mary, FL 32746. 1986. Poetry, fiction, articles, art, photos, cartoons, interviews, reviews, music, letters, long-poems, collages, plays, concrete art, non-fiction. "Psychedelic nightmares, erotic suicide notes, surreal manifestatements, psychotic hallucinations, bizarre drug/sex experiences, morbid trancewritings, punk requiems, long nocturnal ramblings, obscure meditations/ chants/magick, tantra, phallic sufism, s/m, theatre ov cruelty, psychedelics, virtual reality, TOPY, angels-vampyrs-graveyards-goths-punks" circ. 500. 6/yr. Pub'd 6 issues 1990; expects 6 issues 1991, 6 issues 1992. sub. price: none; per copy: $3; sample: $3. Back issues: $3. 100+pp; size varies; †varies. Reporting time: w/SASE 1-2 weeks, w/o SASE your whole life. Payment: contributor copy, my undying l-ov-e. Not copyrighted. Pub's reviews: 60 in 1990. §Occult, eastern studies, poetry, fiction, non-fiction, avant-garde, anarchist, dada/surrealism, beats, erotica, horror, sf, fantasy, mythology, drugs, counter culture, music, art. Ads: $10/$5/trade/free classifieds. SM, LSD, OTO, MDMA, TOPY.

DIAMOND INSIGHT, Guido Giovannini-Torelli, 790 Madison Avenue, Suite 602, New York, NY 10021, 212-570-4180; FAX 212-772-1286. 1988. Articles, photos, interviews, reviews, news items, non-fiction. "Publisher: Tryon Mercantile, Inc." 11/yr. Pub'd 11 issues 1990; expects 11 issues 1991, 11 issues 1992. sub. price: $295; sample: free. 8pp; 8½×11½; mi. Reporting time: 4 weeks. Payment: copies. Copyrighted, reverts to author. Pub's reviews: 5 in 1990. §Diamonds, precious stones, jewelry.

Diane Publishing Company, Herman Baron, 600 Upland Avenue, Upland, PA 19015, 215-499-7415. 1987. Fiction, articles, interviews, non-fiction. "Interested in non-fiction, articles, and interviews regarding foreign investment in U.S., Americans view of Asians and other foreigners. Will republish o.p. books and copyright-free material. Fiction accepted if related to Vietnam, Korea or military subjects. Also religion and health. Especially interested in terrorism, security, law enforcement, AIDS and entrepreneurship" avg. press run 10M. Pub'd 5 titles 1990; expects 7 titles 1991, 9 titles 1992. avg. price, cloth: $19.95; paper: $11.95. Discounts: 25% trade, 60% bulk. 75-115pp; 5½×8½; web. Reporting time: 3 weeks. Payment: 10% 1st 5,000, 15% over 5,000. Does not copyright for author. SSP, ABA.

DIARIST'S JOURNAL, Ed Gildea, 102 West Water Street, Lansford, PA 18232, 717-645-4692. 1988. "We print excerpts from diaries people are keeping today. Articles about diaries and diarists, reviews of books relating to diaries. 'True things happening to ordinary people.'" circ. 800. 4/yr. Pub'd 12 issues 1990; expects 4 issues 1991, 4 issues 1992. sub. price: $12; per copy: $3; sample: $3. Back issues: $1 each for 10 or more. 32pp; 11×13; of. Reporting time: 1 month. Payment: copies. Not copyrighted. Pub's reviews: 10 in 1990.

§Diaries, diarists, journals. Ads: $180/$90/$5 per column inch.

THE DICK E. BIRD NEWS, Dick E. Mallery, PO Box 377, Acme, MI 49610, 800-255-5128. 1987. Poetry, fiction, articles, art, photos, cartoons, interviews, criticism, reviews, letters, news items. "Short—300 words" circ. 5M. 12/yr. Pub'd 12 issues 1990; expects 12 issues 1991, 12 issues 1992. sub. price: $12; per copy: $1; sample: $1. Back issues: $1 copy. Discounts: 75% for wholesalers. 16pp; 11½×17; of. Reporting time: 30 days. Payment: $50-$125. Copyrighted, reverts to author. Pub's reviews: 7 in 1990. §Birds, ecology. Ads: none.

DIE FAT PIGGY DIE, Billy Rotten, John Utjsen, PO Box 134, Waynesville, MO 65583, 319-774-2822. 1990. Art, cartoons, satire, criticism, music, letters, collages, news items, non-fiction. "Strict leaning toward classical philosophy and Zen through psychology" 52/yr. Pub'd 52 issues 1990; expects 52 issues 1991, 52 issues 1992. sub. price: $8; per copy: 50¢; sample: 2 stamps. Back issues: same (list alternatives). Discounts: write for details. 12pp; 9×5¾; mi. Reporting time: unlimited. Payment: none. Copyrighted, reverts to author. Pub's reviews: 75 in 1990. §New Zealand, medieval, Zen, sex, gore, intelligences. Ads: $5/$2.

DIET & HEALTH SERIES, Fell Publishers, Inc., Sherri Adelman, Elizabeth Wyatt, 2131 Hollywood Boulevard, Hollywood, FL 33020, 305-925-5242. 1943. Non-fiction. "We are the leading publisher of one-shot magazines in the United States. We have four categories in which we publish. These are diet & health, health, cookbook series and financial planning series. We are looking for full manuscripts that would lend itself to these areas" circ. 50M. 8/yr. Pub'd 8 issues 1990; expects 8 issues 1991, 8 issues 1992. price per copy: $2.95. Back issues: cover price. 128pp; 5-3/16×7⅞; of. Reporting time: 3 months. Payment: negotiated. Copyrighted, reverts to author. Ads: $2,000. PBAA, ACIDA.

A DIFFERENT DRUMMER, Nicholas Stix, 84 Bay 28th Street, Brooklyn, NY 11214, 718-372-4806. 1989. Poetry, fiction, articles, art, photos, cartoons, interviews, satire, reviews, letters, parts-of-novels, long-poems, non-fiction. "Current submission limit: 3,000 words. I am particularly interested in short fiction with an urban slant, and humorous and satirical essays, especially those mocking the pretensions of art cliques and political movements. I will not read dot-matrix submissions, nor any sent without an SASE. I have recently published work by Bob Balo, Alysia Harpootian, Clara Pierre, Geoffrey Weil, et al." circ. 6M. 3/yr. Pub'd 1 issue 1990; expects 3 issues 1991, 3 issues 1992. sub. price: $9; per copy: $4; sample: $4. Back issues: same. Discounts: 30% on consignment, 50% with advance payment. 83pp; 8×11. Reporting time: 3 months. Payment: copies. Copyrighted, does not revert to author. Pub's reviews: 13 in 1990. §Litmags and political/cultural magazines, film, fiction, philosophy, race relations, Judaism, Germany, urban affairs. Ads: $400/$225/$125 1/4 page/$90 business card.

THE DIGGER, Chicago Democratic Socialists Of America, Robert Hinde, Chicago DSA, 1608 N. Milwaukee #403, Chicago, IL 60647. 1990. Articles, art, photos, cartoons, interviews, criticism, reviews, letters, news items, non-fiction. "We are a democratic socialist student magazine based at the University of Chicago." circ. 3M. 5/yr. Pub'd 1 issue 1990; expects 5 issues 1991, 5 issues 1992. sub. price: $15; per copy: $2; sample: $2. Back issues: $2. Discounts: none. 8pp; 11×17; of. Reporting time: 1 month. Payment: 1 copy. Not copyrighted. Pub's reviews: 1 in 1990. §Liberal, radical, socialist politics. Ads: $200/$125/$75 1/4 page/$50 1/8 page.

DIGIT, Permeable Press, Brian Clark, 47 Noe Street #6, San Francisco, CA 94114-1017, 415-978-9759. 1984. Poetry, fiction, articles, art, photos, cartoons, interviews, satire, criticism, reviews, music, letters, parts-of-novels, long-poems, collages, plays, concrete art, news items, non-fiction. "Political, apocalyptic, cut-throat and beautiful. Contributors include Hugh Fox, Daren Peabody, Bob Black. Length is open. Subscriptions should be sent to: 350 Townsend Street, Suite 409-A, San Francisco, CA 94107." circ. 1M. 3/yr. Pub'd 1 issue 1990; expects 3 issues 1991, 3 issues 1992. sub. price: $20; per copy: $8; sample: $8. Discounts: 40%. 24pp; 11×17; †silkscreen, color copier. Reporting time: 2 weeks. Payment: copies, honorarium. Copyrighted, usually. Pub's reviews: 30 in 1990. §Small press, alternative living/energy, gay and lesbian, political. Ads: call for rates.

THE DILETTANTE FORUM, Harris Stonehouse Press, Joan E. Stone, 142 Woodlawn Drive, Marietta, GA 30067-4016. 1987. Poetry, fiction, articles, art, photos, cartoons, interviews, criticism, reviews, music, letters, parts-of-novels, long-poems, non-fiction. "*The Dilettante Forum* is for and about creative people. We accept fiction, articles, music, poetry which we publish along with a ballot at the end of each piece. The ballots, numbered from 1-10, are designed for the reader to grade the piece according tot his taste by circling a number. The piece getting the highest score in each category goes back into the following magazine. Any piece, ie. music, poem, story, whatever, winning three times running is published in an anthology of the best works for that year. Monthly prizes are paid each month to the winners of each category" 12/yr. Expects 12 issues 1991, 12 issues 1992. sub. price: $25; per copy: $4; sample: $4. 50pp; 11×14; †laser. Reporting time: 90 days. Payment: prizes to winners. Copyrighted, does not revert to author. Ads: $600/$350/call for rates.

DIMENSION, A. Leslie Willson, Editor, Box 26673, Austin, TX 78755, 512-345-0622. 1968. Poetry, fiction, art, parts-of-novels, long-poems, plays. "Contributions in German with English translations" circ. 1.2M. 3/yr.

160

Pub'd 3 issues 1990; expects 3 issues 1991, 3 issues 1992. 1 title listed in the *Small Press Record of Books in Print* (20th Edition, 1991-92). sub. price: $20 indiv, $24 instit; per copy: $10; sample: $10. Back issues: query. Discounts: 20% to agencies and bookdealers. 150-200pp; 6x9; of. Reporting time: 3-6 months. Payment: yes (not to translators). Copyrighted, does not revert to author. CCLM.

Dimi Press, Dick Lutz, 3820 Oak Hollow Lane, SE, Salem, OR 97302, 503-364-7698; fax 503-364-9727. 1981. Non-fiction. "We publish both books and tapes. Although many of our books/tapes deal with the use of relaxation, this is not an exclusive interest for us. We are interested in self-help books/tapes that are of immediate, practical use to the reader. Also, other interesting non-fiction" avg. press run 1.5M. Pub'd 1 title 1990; expects 2 titles 1991, 3 titles 1992. 8 titles listed in the *Small Press Record of Books in Print* (20th Edition, 1991-92). avg. price, paper: $10; other: $9.95 cassette. Discounts: 1-4 20%, 5+ 40%; libraries 20%. 130pp; 5½x8½; of. Reporting time: 1 month. Payment: will negotiate (5-10% royalties). Copyrights for author. COSMEP, PMA, NWABP.

DIRECT RESPONSE, Craig A. Huey, Publisher; Kent Komae, Editor, PO Box 2100, Rolling Hills Estates, CA 90274, 213-212-5727. 1977. Reviews, news items, non-fiction. circ. 1M. 12/yr. Pub'd 12 issues 1990; expects 12 issues 1991, 12 issues 1992. sub. price: $79; per copy: $10; sample: same. Back issues: $5. 12pp; of. Not copyrighted. Pub's reviews: 10 in 1990. §Marketing, advertising, business.

Directed Media, Inc., J.D. Lodato, Dale Lambert, 246 N. Wenatchee Avenue, Box 3005, Wenatchee, WA 98801, 509-662-7693. 1979. Non-fiction. "Primarily Northwest social studies but expanding into new fields each year" avg. press run 3M. Pub'd 4 titles 1990; expects 4 titles 1991, 5 titles 1992. 9 titles listed in the *Small Press Record of Books in Print* (20th Edition, 1991-92). avg. price, cloth: $16; paper: $6.95; other: comb: $5.95. Discounts: trade 40%+; wholesale 50-55%. 200pp; 6x9, 4x7; †of. Reporting time: 2 weeks. Payment: negotiated contract. Copyrights for author. PNWBPA-Seattle.

DIRECTORY MARKETPLACE, Todd Publications, Barry Klein, Nancy Rout, PO Box 301, West Nyack, NY 10994, 914-358-6213. 1987. Reviews, news items. circ. 100M. 3/yr. Pub'd 3 issues 1990; expects 3 issues 1991, 3 issues 1992. sub. price: $25; per copy: $10; sample: free. Back issues: $10. 16pp; 8½x11; of. Reporting time: 2 weeks. Payment: none. Copyrighted, does not revert to author. Pub's reviews: 25-50 in 1990. §Directories and reference books, business guides and manuals. Ads: $950/$600/$350 1/4 page/$200 1/8 page.

Dirigo Books, Inc., Edward L. Francis, PO Box 343, Bryant Pond, ME 04219, 207-665-2133. 1988. Non-fiction. "Non-fiction books with upcountry New England themes and content. Specialties in herb gardening and white mountain books" avg. press run 3M. Pub'd 1 title 1990; expects 3 titles 1991, 3 titles 1992. avg. price, cloth: $21; paper: $14. Discounts: trade 20%-50% depending on quantity. 250pp; 6x9; of. Reporting time: 2 weeks. Payment: 10% of net, payment twice per year. Copyrights for author. COSMEP, NEBA.

DIRTY LINEN, Paul Hartman, PO Box 66600, Baltimore, MD 21239-6600, 301-583-7973; fax 301-665-5144. 1983. Articles, photos, cartoons, interviews, reviews, music, news items, non-fiction. "Folk, electric folk, traditional and world music. Record and concert reviews: preferably 200-300 words, max. 400 words. Feature articles and interviews: 1,000-2,000+ words depending on topic" circ. 5M. 6/yr. Pub'd 5 issues 1990; expects 6 issues 1991, 6 issues 1992. sub. price: $20; per copy: $3.50; sample: $3.50. Back issues: $3.50. Discounts: distributors 50%, retail stores 40%. 68pp; 8¼x10⅞; of. Payment: none, we expect to start paying as finances allow. Copyrighted, reverts upon request. Pub's reviews: 12 in 1990. §Music. Ads: $300/$160/$85 1/4 page/$60 1/6/$450 back cover. COSMEP, NAIRD.

Dirty Rotten Press, Kurt Brecht, 4401 San Leandro Street #36, Oakland, CA 94601, 415-533-2051. 1989. Poetry, non-fiction. "Under 100 pages. Perfect and saddle bound stitched. Trying to stick to books by vocalists and musicians. Recent contributors: Mark Sperry, Dave McCord, Kurt Brecht" avg. press run 1M. Expects 7 titles 1991, 7 titles 1992. 7 titles listed in the *Small Press Record of Books in Print* (20th Edition, 1991-92). avg. price, paper: $3.50. Discounts: retailers and wholesalers $1.85-$2.50 price. 80pp; 5½x8½; of. Reporting time: 2 weeks. Payment: author gets 75% till break point-then 50%. Does not copyright for author.

DISC GOLF WORLD NEWS, Rick Rothstein, Editor-Publisher; Lynne Rothstein, Editor-in-Chief, Disc Golf World, PO Box 30011, Columbia, MO 65205, (314) 874-2981. 1984. Articles, photos, cartoons, interviews, reviews, letters, news items, non-fiction. circ. 800. 4/yr. Pub'd 4 issues 1990; expects 4 issues 1991, 4 issues 1992. sub. price: $12 US ($16.50 1st class), $16 Can., $18 Europe, $20 Australia & Japan; per copy: $4.25 N. America, $5.25 rest; sample: same. 48pp; 5½x8½; of. Reporting time: 1-2 weeks. Payment: rarely. Copyrighted, reverts to author. Pub's reviews. §New sports and games, psychology of individual sports (especially golf), flying disc subjects. Ads: $110/$70/$40 1/4 page.

DISCOMBOBULATION, Maynard Xenolith, Zep O'Klep, PO Box 240474, Montgomery, AL 36124. 1989. Poetry, articles, cartoons, reviews, letters, collages. "Ad space is limited. Articles should be no more than 4 7x8½ pages. Recent contributors include Paul Weinman, Matt Sivils, Edward Mycue, Jack Little, and Adam

Smith." circ. 300. 6/yr. Pub'd 3 issues 1990; expects 6 issues 1991, 6 issues 1992. sub. price: $4/4 issues; per copy: $1.50; sample: $1.50. Back issues: varies, check with us about the issue desired. Discounts: negotiable. 32pp; 7×8½; photocopying. Reporting time: 3-6 weeks. Payment: copy of issue work appears in. Not copyrighted. Pub's reviews: 14 in 1990. Ads: $20/$12/$7 1/4 page/$4 1/8 page. 217/168/907/215/33/819/50/66/73/75/79/816/814.

Discovery Enterprises, Ltd., Kenneth M. Deitch, JoAnne B. Weisman, 134 Middle Street, Suite 210, Lowell, MA 01852, 508-459-1720; fax 508-937-5779. 1990. Non-fiction. "Children's nonfiction for ages 6-12. Series of biographies. Length: 32-48 pages; full color. Also, Discovery Enterprises, Ltd. supplies book design and production to other small publishers as well as full service marketing and advertising." avg. press run 30M-100M. Pub'd 3 titles 1990; expects 5 titles 1991, 6 titles 1992. 6 titles listed in the *Small Press Record of Books in Print* (20th Edition, 1991-92). avg. price, cloth: $17.95; paper: $7.95; other: $3.50 Perspectives on History, 48 page paperbacks. Discounts: 3-5 20%, 6-100 40%, 101-500 50%, 501+ 55%, returns by 120 days. 48pp; 9×12; †of. Reporting time: 6 weeks. Payment: negotiable; co-publishing for new authors. Copyrighting for author optional. COSMEP, ABA, PMA, ALA, ABC.

Distinctive Publishing Corp., K. Ancona, PO Box 17868, Plantation, FL 33318-7868, 305-975-2413. 1986. Fiction, art, interviews, satire, criticism, music, news items, non-fiction. avg. press run 2M-5M. Expects 20 titles 1991, 50 titles 1992. 6 titles listed in the *Small Press Record of Books in Print* (20th Edition, 1991-92). 225pp; 5½×8½. Reporting time: 4-6 weeks. Payment: 8-15%. Copyrights for author. National Association of Independent Publishers, Fl Publishers Group, Am Booksellers Association.

DR. DOBB'S JOURNAL, M & T Publishing, Jonathan Erickson, Editor, 501 Galveston Drive, Redwood City, CA 94063-4728, 415-366-3600. 1976. Articles, interviews, criticism, reviews, letters, news items. "A journal of software tools for advanced microcomputer programmers" circ. 78M. 14/yr. Pub'd 14 issues 1990; expects 14 issues 1991, 14 issues 1992. sub. price: $29.97; per copy: $2.95; sample: $2.95. Back issues: $5. Discounts to resellers and subscription agencies. 130pp; 8½×11; web. Reporting time: 3 months. Payment: fee for articles varies. Copyrighted, does not revert to author. Pub's reviews: §technical books & products for programmers. Ads: $4,400/$3,300 (1 time b&w).

Doctor Jazz Press, A.J. Wright, 617 Valley View Drive, Pelham, AL 35124-1525, 205-663-3403. 1979. Poetry, art. "DJ Press continues to issue poetry broadsides. No submissions, please; I am still overstocked. Until next time, this is Doctor Jazz signing off" avg. press run 100. Pub'd 2 titles 1990; expects 8 titles 1991. 10 titles listed in the *Small Press Record of Books in Print* (20th Edition, 1991-92). avg. price, paper: $1; other: $2.50, 3 broadsides. 1 page; 8½×11; of. Reporting time: less than a month. Payment: 25 copies. Copyrights for author.

DOCTOR-PATIENT STUDIES, J. Hughes, 5627 S. Drexel, Chicago, IL 60637, 312-752-3562. 1990. Articles, reviews, news items. "We generally accept only contributions of articles and books related to research on the doctor-patient relationship for review" circ. 200. 6/yr. Pub'd 5 issues 1990; expects 6 issues 1991, 6 issues 1992. sub. price: $12; per copy: $2; sample: $2. Back issues: $5 for set. 20pp; 8½×11; †photocopied. Reporting time: within several weeks. Payment: none. Not copyrighted. Pub's reviews: hundreds in 1990. §Health care and medicine, medical ethics, medical sociology. Ads: none.

Dog Hair Press (see also LUNA TACK), David Duer, Editor, PO Box 372, West Branch, IA 52358, 319-643-7324. 1981.

DOG RIVER REVIEW, Trout Creek Press, Laurence F. Hawkins, Jr., Editor, 5976 Billings Road, Parkdale, OR 97041, 503-352-6494. 1981. Poetry, fiction, art, interviews, satire, criticism, reviews. "Poetry: any length considered, but prefer 2-30 lines. Fiction: to 2.5M words. Art: B/W only" circ. 300. 2/yr. Pub'd 2 issues 1990; expects 2 issues 1991, 2 issues 1992. sub. price: $6; per copy: $3 postpaid; sample: $2. Back issues: $2. Discounts: bookstores 40%. 60pp; 5½×8; †of. Reporting time: 2-3 months. Payment: copies. Copyrighted, reverts to author. Pub's reviews: 8 in 1990. §Poetry, fiction, art. CCLM.

Dog-Eared Publications, Nancy Field, Publisher, PO Box 863, Middleton, WI 53562, 608-831-1410. 1978. Art, non-fiction. "Dog-Eared Publications creates and produces materials about nature and the environment for children. To date we have not accepted others' work." avg. press run 4M-10M. Pub'd 1 title 1990; expects 2 titles 1991, 3 titles 1992. 8 titles listed in the *Small Press Record of Books in Print* (20th Edition, 1991-92). avg. price, paper: $3.95. Discounts: 2-5 20%, 6-10 25%, 11-199 40%, 200+ 45%. 32pp; 8½×11; of. Reporting time: 2 weeks. Copyrights for author.

Doggerel Press, Laureal Williams, Janet Lockhart, PO Box 985, Salem, OR 97308, 503-588-2926. 1990. Cartoons, satire. "We publish offbeat/mainstream, mass-market humor, visual (illus. cartoon books). Recent contributors: Irene Turk, Mark McCoin" avg. press run 5M-10M. Pub'd 1 title 1990; expects 1 title 1991, 3 titles 1992. 1 title listed in the *Small Press Record of Books in Print* (20th Edition, 1991-92). avg. price, paper: $6.95. 100pp; 8¼×5½; full web. Reporting time: 2-3 months (SASE). Payment: per agreement. Copyrights for

162

author.

Do-It-Yourself Legal Publishers, Benji Anosike, Executive Editor, 298 Fifth Avenue #403, New York, NY 10001. 1978. Non-fiction. "We specialize in self-help 'how-to' legal books and manuals for the non-lawyer" avg. press run 1.2M. Pub'd 5 titles 1990; expects 5 titles 1991, 5 titles 1992. 11 titles listed in the *Small Press Record of Books in Print* (20th Edition, 1991-92). avg. price, paper: $9. Discounts: bookstores, 40%; libraries, 25%. 100pp; 7⅜×9¼; of. Reporting time: 6 weeks. Payment: 10%. Copyrights for author.

Dollarpoems, Ken Hanly, Box 5, Brandon University, Brandon, Manitoba R7A 6A9, Canada. 1983. Poetry. "We request 24-30 pages of poetry from which 12 pages are selected. Most are published by invitation only. Unfortunately the Manitoba Arts Council which provides a grant limits the series to Canadian authors. We usually like to see about half of the work unpublished; however, this has varied in actual production from 0% to 100% previously published" avg. press run 140-180. Pub'd 6 titles 1990; expects 10+ titles 1991. 40 titles listed in the *Small Press Record of Books in Print* (20th Edition, 1991-92). avg. price, paper: $1. Authors may purchase copies at 40% discount. Booksellers: no discount 1-9 copies; 10-19 titles - may be mixed - 30%; 20 and over 40% discount. 12pp; 5½×8½; xerography. Reporting time: variable. Payment: 15% of printing is given to author in lieu of royalties; this applies to subsequent printings as well; authors may purchase additional copies at 40%. Copyright remains with author.

Dolphin-Moon Press, James Taylor, President, PO Box 22262, Baltimore, MD 21203. 1973. Poetry, fiction, art, photos, cartoons. "Books and chapbooks with unusual design formats by poets, fiction writers and dramatists. In addition, anthologies, record albums, cassette tapes, note cards, and other art objects have also been published by the press. The press also publishes a comic book series" avg. press run 750. Pub'd 1 title 1990; expects 7 titles 1991, 7 titles 1992. 39 titles listed in the *Small Press Record of Books in Print* (20th Edition, 1991-92). avg. price, cloth: $16; paper: $8; other: $1.50 (pamphlets, etc.). Discounts: negotiable. 60-100pp; size varies; of. Reporting time: 1 month. Payment: percentage of print run. Copyrights for author.

Dominion Press (see also MASTER THOUGHTS; THEOLOGIA 21), A. Stuart Otto, PO Box 37, San Marcos, CA 92079-0037, 619-746-9430. 1966. "*Theologia 21* is religious (Alternative Christianity). No outside contributors. Published quarterly. Our books are also in the same field. No mss accepted." avg. press run 1M-1.5M. Pub'd 1 title 1990; expects 1 title 1991, 1 title 1992. 20 titles listed in the *Small Press Record of Books in Print* (20th Edition, 1991-92). avg. price, paper: $10; other: $25, vinyl. Discounts: 40% to dealers in quantities. 50-200pp; 8½×11, 5½×8½; of. Payment: none, non-profit organization, staff on salary.

The Donning Company / Publishers, Robert S. Friedman, Publisher, 184 Business Park Drive #106, Virginia Beach, VA 23462-6533. 1974. Fiction, art, non-fiction. "Pictorial histories, cookbooks, science fiction and fantasy, metaphysical, general interest" avg. press run 5M. Pub'd 18 titles 1990; expects 20 titles 1991, 25 titles 1992. 64 titles listed in the *Small Press Record of Books in Print* (20th Edition, 1991-92). avg. price, cloth: $14.95; paper: $5.95. Discounts: inquire. 208pp; 8½×11, 5½×8½; of. Reporting time: 4 weeks. Payment: royalties semi-annually. Copyrights for author.

DOOR COUNTY ALMANAK, The Dragonsbreath Press, Fred Johnson, 10905 Bay Shore Drive, Sister Bay, WI 54234, 414-854-2742. 1982. Poetry, fiction, articles, art, photos, cartoons, interviews, parts-of-novels, long-poems, non-fiction. "*The Door County Almanak* is an occasional regional magazine/book covering a different topic each issue. It covers history, people, and events in N.E. Wisconsin, especially Door County. Open to writers from any area. Guidelines available with SASE" Irregular. Expects 1 issue 1991, 1 issue 1992. price per copy: $9.95; sample: $9.95. Back issues: #1-$4.95, #2-#4 $9.95 each. Discounts: 40% to trade. 300pp; 6×9; of. Reporting time: 2-8 weeks. Payment: copies, plus payment. Copyrighted, reverts to author. Pub's reviews. Ads: rate sheet available.

Dooryard Press, Tom Rea, Barbara Rea, 3645 Navarre Road, Casper, WY 82604, 307-235-9021. 1979. Poetry, art. "Please send a query with 5 sample poems. We publish 2 to 4 letterpress chapbooks and 1 to 2 full length books a year. Authors include Richard Hugo, Alberto Rios, Stefanie Marlis, Ed Harkness, Charles Levendosky, Stephen Knauth, William Kloefkorn, Samuel Hazo" avg. press run 500. Pub'd 4 titles 1990; expects 3 titles 1991, 3 titles 1992. 7 titles listed in the *Small Press Record of Books in Print* (20th Edition, 1991-92). avg. price, cloth: $10-$40; paper: $8. Discounts: bookstores: 1-4 copies, 35%; 5 or more, 40%. Jobbers, wholesalers, distributors: negotiable, special editions have short discount. 30pp; †of, lp. Reporting time: 1 month. Payment: 10% of run. Copyrights for author. COSMEP.

Doral Publishing, Luana Luther, Editor; Beverly Black, Editor; Jill Reges, Design, Layout, Production; Alvin Grossman, Publisher; Lynn Grey, Marketing Coordinator, PO Box 596, Wilsonville, OR 97070, 503-694-5707. 1986. Non-fiction. "Doral publishes books for the pure bred dog market. We specialize in breed books and those pertaining to pure bred dogs in general. Hardback books average some 300 pages in length" avg. press run 3M. Pub'd 3 titles 1990; expects 4 titles 1991, 4 titles 1992. 8 titles listed in the *Small Press Record of Books in Print* (20th Edition, 1991-92). avg. price, cloth: $24.95; paper: $14.95. 285pp; 6×9; of. Reporting time: 3-4 weeks. Payment: 10% 1st book - paid January & July. Copyrights for author. Publishers Marketing

Association, Dog Writer's Assoc. of America, Northwest Assoc. of Book Publishers.

Dormant Brain Research and Development Laboratory, T.D. Lingo, Director, PO Box 10, Black Hawk, CO 80422. 1957. "Published *Self Transcendence Workbook, Revised edition* by T.D. Lingo. Fundamental neurology to method of brain self-control, backward self-therapy and forward self-circuiting into the 1/3 bulk of dormant frontal lobes. Since 1957, a new order of advanced problem-solving intelligence, multiple orgasm and species conferencing telepathy to consensus democratic action has been observed to emerge automatically" avg. press run 1M. Pub'd 20 titles 1990; expects 20 titles 1991, 20 titles 1992. 1 title listed in the *Small Press Record of Books in Print* (20th Edition, 1991-92). avg. price, cloth: $25. 533pp; 6×9; †of. Copyrights for author.

DorPete Press, PO Box 238, Briarcliff Manor, NY 10510, 914-941-7029. Non-fiction. avg. press run 1.4M. Pub'd 3 titles 1990. 1 title listed in the *Small Press Record of Books in Print* (20th Edition, 1991-92). avg. price, cloth: $14.95; paper: $6.95. Discounts: 1 10%, 2-4 20%, 5-24 40%, 25+ 50%. 300pp; 5½×8½; of. Reporting time: 3 months. Payment: 10% on invoice price. Copyrights for author.

Dos Tejedoras Fiber Arts Publications, Karen Searle, PO Box 14238, St. Paul, MN 55114-0238, 612-646-7445. 1976. Non-fiction. "Monographs specializing in ethnographic textile techniques" avg. press run 5M. Pub'd 4 titles 1990. 10 titles listed in the *Small Press Record of Books in Print* (20th Edition, 1991-92). avg. price, cloth: $30; paper: $15. Discounts: 40% wholesale. 120pp; 8½×11; of. Reporting time: 6 weeks. Payment: semi-annually; negotiable for each title. Copyrights for author. COSMEP, Midwest Booksellers Association, Minn. Independent Publishers Association, Publishers Marketing Assn.

DOUBLE HARNESS, Andrew Cozens, 74 Huntington Road, York, Y03 7RN, England. 1978. Poetry, fiction, articles, art, photos, cartoons, interviews, criticism, reviews, music, letters, long-poems, news items. "*Double Harness* is a magazine combining modern literature, poetry, music, reviews, etc. with social/community issues, particularly lifestyle dicisions. All genuine letters receive personal attention. Not currently publishing" circ. 500-1M. Irregular. sub. price: 4 issues £3.00 UK, £3.50 USA, I.M.O.S. preferred; per copy: 75p - £1; sample: postage. Back issues: free for postage. Discounts: by arrangement. 64pp; 8×5; †of. Reporting time: varies but immediate ackowledgement. Payment: none as yet. Not copyrighted. Pub's reviews: 10 in 1990. §Poetry, contemporary fiction, literary criticism, records, lifestyle, social/community issues. Ads: aill by arrangement. ALP, ALMS.

Double M Press, Charlotte M. Stein, 16455 Tuba Street, Sepulveda, CA 91343, 818-360-3166. 1975. Poetry, fiction, photos, non-fiction. "Graphics" avg. press run 1M. Expects 2 titles 1991, 4 titles 1992. 3 titles listed in the *Small Press Record of Books in Print* (20th Edition, 1991-92). avg. price, paper: $9.50. Discounts: trade 40%, jobber 50%, agent 10%. 200+pp; 5½×8½, 8½×11½; of. Reporting time: 1 month. Payment: 8% softcover, paid semi-annually. Copyrights for author.

DoubLeo Publications, Jeri Blake, 227 East 11th St, New York, NY 10003, 212-473-2739. 1979. Articles, art, photos, news items, non-fiction. "We started for specific purpose of publishing important research works in *Sidereal* Astrology. Expanding cautiously into other subject areas. Query with SASE only" avg. press run 450. Pub'd 3 titles 1990; expects 1 title 1991. 2 titles listed in the *Small Press Record of Books in Print* (20th Edition, 1991-92). avg. price, paper: $7.50. Pages vary; 5¼×8½; †xerography or photo offset. Reporting time: as fast as time permits. Payment: arrangement.

Dovehaven Press, Ltd., Joseph R. Brockett, PO Box 4578, Riverside, CA 92514, 714-787-0971. 1986. "At this time, we are interested in seeing only book-length (100 pp.+) manuscripts on arts in education." avg. press run 5-10M. Expects 3 titles 1991, 3 titles 1992. avg. price, paper: $20. 150pp. Reporting time: 6 weeks. Payment: determined individually. Does not copyright for author. PMA.

Down There Press, Joani Blank, PO Box 2086, Burlingame, CA 94011-2086, 415-342-2536; 550-0912. 1975. Fiction, non-fiction. "The only small press in the country publishing exclusively sex education & sexual enhancement books. New titles in 1983 were *A Kid's First Book About Sex*, and *Let's Talk About Sex & Loving*. New imprint in 1983 *Yes Press*. New title in 1984 *Aural Sex and Verbal Intercourse*. In 1986, Revised edition of *Anal Pleasure and Health*. In 1988 *Herotica; A Collection of Women's Erotic Fiction*; 1989 revised edition of *Good Vibrations: The Complete Guide to Vibrators*; 1991 *Erotic by Nature*" avg. press run 5M. Pub'd 1 title 1990; expects 1 title 1991, 1 title 1992. 10 titles listed in the *Small Press Record of Books in Print* (20th Edition, 1991-92). avg. price, cloth: $35; paper: $5, $10. Discounts: booksellers—1 copy 20%, 2-9 35%, 10+ 40%; by arrangement to therapists and educators; 20% text adoptions. 48-144pp; 8½×11, 5½×8½, 6×9; of. Reporting time: 2 months. Payment: varies, average 10% cover price. Copyrights for author. COSMEP, Northern California Book Publicists Assn. (NCBPA), Bay Area Publishers Network (BAPN).

Downey Place Publishing House, Inc., Robert D. San Souci, PO Box 1352, El Cerrito, CA 94530, 415-529-1012. 1982. Fiction, interviews, non-fiction. "Now accepting manuscripts" avg. press run 10M. Expects 1 title 1991, 2 titles 1992. 3 titles listed in the *Small Press Record of Books in Print* (20th Edition,

1991-92). avg. price, cloth: $10.95. Discounts: 40%. 154pp; 6×9; of, varies. Reporting time: 6-8 weeks. Payment: will vary. Copyrights for author. Bookbuilders West, Northern California Book Publicists.

Dragon Cloud Books (see also SO & SO), John Marron, 232 Volkert Street, Highland Park, NJ 08904-3119, (201) 985-5565. 1973. Poetry, fiction, art, photos, interviews, long-poems, collages, concrete art, non-fiction. "Additional address: 1625 Curtis, Berkeley, CA 94702. *And It Still Moves*, Mulitcultural Poetry Calendar—Year of the Hare (1987)" avg. press run 500-1M. Pub'd 4 titles 1990; expects 4 titles 1991, 4 titles 1992. avg. price, cloth: $16; paper: $8; other: $8 calendar (stapled). Discounts: direct mail (add $1.50); trade 40/60; Small Press Distribution 50/50. 80-150pp; 5×8; of. Reporting time: 2 months. Payment: 10% of print run in contributors copies; 5% of production costs; combination thereof. Copyrights for author. Small Press Distribution, COSMEP, CCLM, Before Columbus, Poets & Writers, PEN, CPITS, CAC, St. Mark's Newsletter, Poetry Flash, Dustbooks.

Dragon Disks, Louie Crew, PO Box 30, Newark, NJ 07101-1545. 1985. "Publishes software for writers. Uses MS-DOS format, for all IBM compatibles. Requires clear manuals for each, on disk. Recent publications include *Apply* (manages applications for grants, jobs...), *Engbasic* (for those who write for foreign readers; flags words not in the 850-word vocabulary of Basic English); *Invent* (helps writers discover fresh metaphors), *My Agent*(formerly *Muses*) (which circulates manuscripts, builds bibliographies...), *Poetease* (which helps with assonance, consonance, and rhyme), *Styled* (monitors prose for clarity and grace). Copyrights and circulates programs as shareware" Pub'd 8 titles 1990; expects 1 title 1991, 2 titles 1992. avg. price, other: $7.50 per disk. electronic only. Reporting time: 2 months. Payment: split half of each order. Copyrights for author. Association of Shareware Professionals.

Dragon Gate, Inc., Gwen Head, Editor and Publisher; Marlene Blessing, Editor-in-Chief, 508 Lincoln Street, Townsend, WA 98368. 1980. Poetry, fiction. "We don't accept unsolicited mss." avg. press run 3M. Pub'd 5 titles 1990; expects 3 titles 1991, 3 titles 1992. 15 titles listed in the *Small Press Record of Books in Print* (20th Edition, 1991-92). avg. price, cloth: $14 poetry, $16 fiction; paper: $7 poetry, $8 fiction. Discounts: Trade: 1-5, 20%; 6+, 40%. Textbooks, 20%. Library jobbers: 1-5, 20%; 6-49, 40%; 50+, 42%. Libraries: 1 cloth, 10%. Poetry 72pp, fiction 175pp; 5½×9; of. Payment: varies. Copyrights for author. COSMEP.

THE DRAGONFANG, PRS Schwartz, Editor-in-Chief; Stephen Schwartz, Art Editor; Donna Bocian, Reviews, 9047 South River Rd., Waterville, OH 43566, 419-878-7246. 1990. Poetry, fiction, art, reviews, letters. "*I consider only fantasy and horror material.* Consider fiction to 6000 words, poetry to 2 pages, art. Recent contributers include: David Lunde, Russ Miller, Marge Simon, John Grey, Michael While, Janet R. DuPuy, Janet Reedman" circ. 100-200. 2/yr. Expects 1 issue 1991, 2 issues 1992. sub. price: $8 for 3 issues; per copy: $3; sample: $3. Back issues: $2.50 for a copy of #1 only. 50pp; 5½×8½; †of. Reporting time: 1-2 months. Payment: copies. Copyrighted, reverts to author. Pub's reviews. §All small press magazines. Ads: $10; 1/2 $5; 1/4 $3. SPWAO.

DRAGONFLY: East/West Haiku Quarterly, Middlewood Press, Richard Tice, Editor and Publisher; Jack Lyon, Editor; Lorraine Ellis Harr, Consulting Editor, PO Box 11236, Salt Lake City, UT 84147. 1965. Poetry. "Classical/traditional haiku, short renku (linked verse). Also prints translations of contemporary Japanese haiku. Short articles about haiku. Must be concise. Have published Paul O. Williams, Geri Barton, Lorraine Ellis Harr, Frederick Gasser, Kawano Akira, Helen Sherry, Emily Romano" circ. 400. 4/yr. Pub'd 4 issues 1990; expects 4 issues 1991, 4 issues 1992. sub. price: $12, $14 Canada, $22.60 foreign airmail, $16 foreign seamail; per copy: $3.50; sample: $3.50. Back issues: $3.00 for issues before 1985. Discounts: none. 64pp; 5½×8½; of. Reporting time: usually by return mail within 120 days. Payment: contests with cash awards, students 18 and younger receive contributor copies. Copyrighted. §Anything relating to haiku, haibun, or renku. No ads.

Dragon's Teeth Press, Cornel Lengyel, 7700 Wentworth Springs Road, El Dorado Nat. Forest, Georgetown, CA 95634. 1970. Poetry, music, long-poems, plays. avg. press run 1M. Pub'd 4 titles 1990. 23 titles listed in the *Small Press Record of Books in Print* (20th Edition, 1991-92). avg. price, paper: $3.50. Discounts: 30-40%. 64-128pp; 5½×8½, 8½×11; of. Reporting time: 6 weeks. Payment: 10% royalty. Copyrights for author.

The Dragonsbreath Press (see also DOOR COUNTY ALMANAK), Fred Johnson, 10905 Bay Shore Drive, Sister Bay, WI 54234, 414-854-2742. 1973. Poetry, fiction, art, photos, long-poems. "The press is mainly concerned with limited edition handmade books. Working mainly with handset type and illustrated with original artwork. The subject matter is completely open, but more partial to short fiction than poetry. Prices depend on the book. *We are not currently looking for any manuscripts. We do not publish novels*" Expects 1 title 1991, 1 title 1992. 8 titles listed in the *Small Press Record of Books in Print* (20th Edition, 1991-92). †lp. Reporting time: 1-3 months, should write before sending ms. include SASE. Payment: usually a sharing of costs and profits/a cooperative arrangment. Does not copyright for author.

Drama Book Publishers, Ralph Pine, Judith Holmes, 260 Fifth Avenue, New York, NY 10001, 212-725-5377; fax 212-725-8506. 1967. "In addition to the texts we publish, we have published such plays as *The Fantasticks*,

Hello Dolly, The Shadow Box, Evita, The Gin Game, etc. and really only publish plays if they are Broadway successes. Mostly we are a nuts & bolts publishing house and have recently dropped over 150 titles from out backlist. We do quite a lot of co-publishing in the UK with houses like Macmillan, Batsford, etc" avg. press run 3M. Pub'd 8 titles 1990; expects 6 titles 1991, 10 titles 1992. avg. price, cloth: $15; paper: $8.95. Discounts: varies; make inquiry for schedule. 200pp. Reporting time: depends on how busy we are. Payment: usually 10% with advance. Copyrights for author. ABA.

THE DRAMA REVIEW, Richard Schechner, Editor; Ann Daly, Managing Editor, MIT Press Journals, 55 Hayward, Cambridge, MA 02142, 617-253-2889. 1955. Articles, photos, interviews, reviews, plays. *"TDR* documents new trends in contemporary avant-garde performance (plays are published only as partial documentation of historically significant productions). *TDR* is interested in performance analysis, not dramatic evaluation, interpretation or criticism" circ. 5M. 4/yr. Pub'd 4 issues 1990; expects 4 issues 1991, 4 issues 1992. sub. price: $20; per copy: $6.00; sample: $6.00. Back issues: $12. Discounts: 40 percent bookstores; 10 percent subscription agencies. 144pp; 7×10; of. Reporting time: 2 weeks. Copyrighted, held for clearance by publisher. Pub's reviews: 20 in 1990. §Theatre, drama, art performance, avant-garde performance, indigenous drama. Ads: $350/$220. CCLM, COSMEP, ASME.

Dramaline Publications, Courtney Marsh, SAN 285-239X, 10470 Riverside Drive, Suite #201, Toluca Lake, CA 91602, 818-985-9148. 1983. Plays. "We publish 'how to' books for actors. Monologues and scenes. Occasionally plays. The monologues and scenes must be of no longer than a three minute duration, must embrace contemporary points of view, be written in modern language. The plays should be of unusual composition and structure and deal with current, relevant issues" avg. press run 2M. Pub'd 3 titles 1990; expects 3 titles 1991, 3 titles 1992. 23 titles listed in the *Small Press Record of Books in Print* (20th Edition, 1991-92). avg. price, paper: $5.95. Discounts: 40% to retailers only. 64pp; 5½×8½; of. Reporting time: 1 month. Payment: 10% of cover price paid yearly. Copyrights for author.

DRAMATIKA, Dramatika Press, John Pyros, Ellen Haasch-Pyros, Assistant Editor; Andrea Pyros, Associate Editor, 429 Hope Street, Tarpon Springs, FL 34689, 813-937-0109. 1968. Art, plays, concrete art. *"Performable pieces and mail art only*—must be easily photocopied. Minimum size: postcard. Maximum size: 8½ X 11. Mail art work, mail art essays, perf. piece art, perf. piece essays" 2/yr. Pub'd 2 issues 1990; expects 2 issues 1992. sub. price: $10; per copy: $5; sample: $3. Back issues: $5. Discounts: none. 25pp; 8×11; photocopy. Reporting time: 2 months. Payment: copies only. Copyrighted, reverts to author.

Dramatika Press (see also DRAMATIKA), John Pyros, Andrea Pyros, Ellen Haasch-Pyros, Assistant Editor, 429 Hope Street, Tarpon Springs, FL 34689, 813-937-0109. 1968. Photos, long-poems, plays, concrete art. "Solicit biographies of performing arts, avant-garde figures, especially from previously unpublished M.A. or PH.D. theses" avg. press run varies. Expects 2 titles 1991. 2 titles listed in the *Small Press Record of Books in Print* (20th Edition, 1991-92). 25pp; 8×11; photocopy. Reporting time: 2 months. Does not copyright for author.

DRAMATISTS GUILD NEWSLETTER, Jason Milligan, 234 West 44th Street, New York, NY 10036. News items. circ. 7.5M. 10/yr. Pub'd 10 issues 1990; expects 10 issues 1991, 10 issues 1992. sample price: $1.50. 10pp; 8½×11; of. Reporting time: 1 month. Copyrighted. Ads: $25 for 30 words or less, 25¢ for each add'l word, 55 word max.

DREAM INTERNATIONAL QUARTERLY, Dr. Les Jones, World Editor (E. Hemisphere); Chuck Jones, U.S. Editor (W. Hemisphere), 121 North Ramona Street #27, Ramona, CA 92065-6206, 619-789-3258. 1980. Poetry, fiction, articles, art, cartoons, reviews, letters, non-fiction. "Length of material accepted: 1,000-1,500 words. *Not accepted*: sexually explicit material or use of vulgar or 'four-letter' words. Basic type of subject accepted: anything relating to dreams; dream fragments, fiction, poetry, non-fiction, haiku, etc. Articles on precognition, astral projection, etc. 'Kidz Korner': contributions accepted from children, 6-16 years of age. Mss will not be returned unless so requested at time of submission. Also, fantasy pieces, fiction, prose and poetry. Checks/money orders and overseas drafts must be made payable to Charles Jones rather than DIQ" circ. 65-80. 4/yr. Pub'd 3 issues 1990; expects 3-4 issues 1991, 4 issues 1992. sub. price: $15 (+ $4.50 p/h); + $2 for deluxe binding; per copy: $4 (+ $1.50 p/h), $2 for deluxe binding; sample: $4, $5 outside Canada & US (+ $2 mailing), add $2 for 'deluxe' binding and $1.50 for p/h. Back issues: $5, $6 outside Canada & US (+ $2 mailing), add $2 for 'deluxe' binding. Discounts: 15% for 10 or more issues to same address. Contributors' guidelines, $1.00 each, writer's guidelines—$1.00 per copy. 70pp; 8½×11; †prof. xerox reproductions. Reporting time: 4-6 weeks. Payment: in the form of complimentary copie(s) upon receipt of $1.50 for p/h. Copyrighted, reverts to author. Pub's reviews: 2 in 1990. §Fiction—dream related and fantasy. Ads: $57/$12. Society of Ethical and Professional Publishers of Literature.

THE DREAMWEAVER, Ladyhawk (L. Tilton), PO Box 150692, Fort Worth, TX 76108, 817-332-1412. 1990. Poetry, fiction, articles, art, cartoons, interviews, reviews, letters, news items, non-fiction. circ. 150. 12/yr. Pub'd 3 issues 1990; expects 12 issues 1991, 12 issues 1992. sub. price: $10; per copy: $1; sample: $1.

Back issues: $1 if available. Discounts: will trade, accept stamps, donations, etc. 30-40pp; 5×7½; †laser. Payment: none. Pub's reviews: approx. 5 in 1990. §Metaphysical, Wicca, natural magick, etc. Ads: no charge on advertising at this time. WPPA.

DREAMS AND NIGHTMARES, David C. Kopaska-Merkel, 4801 Cypress Creek, #1004, Tuscaloosa, AL 35405, 205-553-2284. 1986. Poetry, art, cartoons. "Contributors: Ree Young, Bruce Boston, Robert Frazier, David Lunde, Lisa Kucharski, Lisa Lepovetsky. Generally poems should fit, single-spaced, on 8½ X 11 paper. I print some larger ones. Don't like gory or trite poems, but gore and sex ok if not gratuitous. *Any* format is fine" circ. 200. 4/yr. Pub'd 4 issues 1990; expects 4 issues 1991, 4 issues 1992. 5 titles listed in the *Small Press Record of Books in Print* (20th Edition, 1991-92). sub. price: $5/4 issues; sample: $1.25 in stamps. Discounts: on a case-by-case basis. 20pp; 5½×8½; photocopied. Reporting time: 2-8 weeks, average 4 weeks. Payment: $3 per contribution on acceptance plus 2 contributor's copies. Copyrighted, reverts to author. Ads: $4 for 8½ X 11 insert, $7 for 2. Science Fiction Poetry Assn.

DREAMS & VISIONS, Steve Stanton, Wendy Stanton, Skysong Press, RR #1, Washago, Ontario L0K 2B0, Canada. 1988. Fiction, art. "*Dreams & Visions* is a literary journal of contemporary Christian fiction. All stories should portray a Christian worldview or expand upon Biblical themes or ethics in an entertaining or enlightening manner. We are interested in fantasy, fables, humor, ethical and inspirational stories 2,000 to 8,000 words in length. Also cover art (b&w line drawings, five inches square or reducible.) U.S. residents may purchase Canadian stamps by mail from the National Philatelic Centre, Canada Post, Antigonish, N.S. B2G 2R8" circ. 400. 4/yr. Pub'd 3 issues 1990; expects 4 issues 1991, 4 issues 1992. sub. price: $12 (in U.S. funds outside of Canada); per copy: $3.95; sample: $3. Back issues: $10 for a package of 4 issues. Discounts: 50% bulk trade (minimum 10 @ $2), prepaid; in U.S. funds outside of Canada. 48pp; 5½×8½; of. Reporting time: 4-6 weeks. Payment: copies ($100 cash for Best Story of the Year as chosen by subscribers). Copyrighted, reserve one non-exclusive reprint. No ads. Canadian Magazine Publishers Association (CMPA).

Drift Creek Press, Craig J. Battrick, 1020 NW 34th, Corvallis, OR 97330, 503-754-6303. 1989. Non-fiction. "Additional address: PO Box 511, Philomath, OR 97370." avg. press run 2M. Pub'd 1 title 1990; expects 1 title 1991, 2 titles 1992. 1 title listed in the *Small Press Record of Books in Print* (20th Edition, 1991-92). avg. price, paper: $15.95. Discounts: 40% bookstores, 55% wholesalers. 200pp; 8½×10; of. Reporting time: 1 month. Payment: negotiable. Copyrights for author. PMA.

THE DROOD REVIEW OF MYSTERY, J. Huang, Editor & Publisher; B. Thoenen, Managing Editor; J. Jacobson, Managing Editor; E. Blachman, Managing Editor, Box 8872, Boston, MA 02114, 617-232-0411. 1982. Articles, art, cartoons, interviews, criticism, reviews, news items, non-fiction. "Short reviews 50-500 words. Articles 1.5M-5M words" circ. 1.5M. 12/yr. Pub'd 12 issues 1990; expects 12 issues 1991, 12 issues 1992. sub. price: $20; per copy: $2; sample: same. 18pp; 8½×11; of. Reporting time: 2-6 weeks. Payment: none. Copyrighted, reverts to author. Pub's reviews: 500 in 1990. §Mystery & detective fiction. Ads: $150/$75.

Dropzone Press, Roy T. Maloney, PO Box 882222, San Francisco, CA 94188, 415-776-7164; FAX 415-921-6776. 1980. Cartoons, interviews, non-fiction. "*Real Estate Quick & Easy* is main book. Also have travel video cassettes and posters on universe and USA History" avg. press run 5M. Pub'd 1 title 1990; expects 3 titles 1991, 3 titles 1992. 4 titles listed in the *Small Press Record of Books in Print* (20th Edition, 1991-92). avg. price, paper: $16.95. Discounts: distributed by Publishers Group West. 384pp; 8½×11; of. Reporting time: 60 days. Payment: negotiable. Copyrights for author. NWU.

DRUG INTERACTIONS AND UPDATES, Philip D. Hansten, John R. Horn, Lloyd Y. Young, Mary Anne Koda-Kimble, PO Box 5077, Vancouver, WA 98668, 206-253-7123; FAX 206-253-8475. 1972. "Joint publication with Lea & Febiger. Product includes text in a looseleaf, 3-ring binder and quarterly update mailings" 4/yr. Pub'd 4 issues 1990; expects 4 issues 1991, 4 issues 1992. sub. price: $70; per copy: $10. Back issues: $10. Discounts: subscription agencies 10%. 20pp; 8½×11. Copyrighted, does not revert to author. No ads. PNW Book Publishers Association, COSMEP, AAP.

Druid Books, Jon Reilly, PO Box 231, Ephraim, WI 54211. 1969. Poetry, fiction, photos. avg. press run 1M. Expects 1 title 1991, 1 title 1992. 9 titles listed in the *Small Press Record of Books in Print* (20th Edition, 1991-92). avg. price, paper: $7. Discounts: 40% retail, 45% distributors. 50pp; 5½×8½ usually; of. Reporting time: ASAP. Payment: author's royalties 10% of retail price, plus copies.

Druid Press, Anne George, Jerri Beck, 2724 Shades Crest Road, Birmingham, AL 35216, 205-967-6580. 1982. Poetry, non-fiction. "Our first 2 books are a book of poetry and a linguistic study of Southern Indian tribes" avg. press run 1M. Expects 2 titles 1991. 11 titles listed in the *Small Press Record of Books in Print* (20th Edition, 1991-92). avg. price, paper: $8-$10. Discounts: 20%. 50-100pp; of. Reporting time: 3 weeks. Payment: negotiable. Copyrights for author. Southern Publishers' Group.

Chris Drumm Books, Chris Drumm, PO Box 445, Polk City, IA 50226, 515-984-6749. 1983. Poetry, fiction, articles, interviews, satire, criticism, parts-of-novels, long-poems, plays, non-fiction. "I publish single-author

167

booklets using previously unpublished work by established science fiction/horror/fantasy authors. I've published works by R.A. Lafferty, Algis Budrys, John Sladek, James Gunn, Carter Scholz and Brian Stableford, all of whom are well-known science fiction authors. I'm only able to produce two or three titles a year, so I have to be pretty choosy about material I can accept. Still, I would be willing to consider work by talented newcomers to the field" avg. press run 500-1M. Pub'd 4 titles 1990; expects 6 titles 1991, 6-8 titles 1992. 28 titles listed in the *Small Press Record of Books in Print* (20th Edition, 1991-92). avg. price, other: booklet $2; $5 signed (100 copies). Discounts: less 40% for 5 or more titles (may be mixed); less 50% for 50 or more copies and less 60% for over 100 copies (titles may be mixed). 44pp; 4¼×7; of. Reporting time: 2 weeks-1 month. Payment: 25% of gross sales (40% on signed copies). Copyrights for author.

DRY CRIK REVIEW, John C. Dofflemyer, PO Box 51, Lemon Cove, CA 93244, 209-597-2512. 1990. Poetry, art, cartoons, reviews, parts-of-novels. "Less than 4,000 words. Recent contributors include Wallace McRae, Paul Zarzyski, Rod McQueary, Vess Quinlan, Buck Ramsey. Biases: prefer shorter works, 44 lines" circ. 250. 4/yr. Expects 4 issues 1991, 4 issues 1992. sub. price: $20; per copy: $6; sample: $6. Discounts: singles, amounts of 10 or more 1/3 off ($4). 44pp; 5×8; of. Reporting time: 60 days max, most 30. Payment: in copy. Copyrighted, reverts to author. Pub's reviews. §Books of cowboy poetry limited to past contributors. Ads: none.

Duck Down Press (see also SCREE), Kirk Robertson, PO Box 1047, Fallon, NV 89406. 1973. Poetry, art, photos, interviews, collages, concrete art. "Query with sample of work. Titles in print: *Chase* - Gerald Locklin; *Red Work Black Widow* - Steve Richmond; *Men Under Fire* - Ronald Koertge; *The Kid Comes Home* - Leo Mailman; *The Man In The Black Chevrolet* - Todd Moore; *Diet Pepsi & Nacho Cheese* - Nila Northsun; *Whiplash On The Couch* - John Bennett; *Asylum Picnic* - Robert Matte, Jr. *The Wages Of Sin* stories by Gerald Haslam; *None Such Creek*. New & selected poems by Al Masarik. *The Broken Face Of Summer* poems by Michael Hogan; *New Works* (anthology), *Small Bones, Little Eyes* poems by Nila North Sun + Jim Sagel; *21 & Over* Poems by William L Fox; *Cruisin At The Limit*-selected poems by Dr. Wagner; *Reasons & Methods*, poems by Kirk Robertson; *Cheek To Cheek*, poems & excerpts from interviews by Jo Harvey Allen; *Looking Past Today*, poems by Gary Short; *Time By Distance*, poems by William L. Fox; *East of New York City* - Norbert Krapf; *Excuses to be Outside* - A. Masarik; *Second Wind* - Phil Weidman, etc." avg. press run 500-1M. Pub'd 2 titles 1990; expects 3 titles 1991, 2-4 titles 1992. 25 titles listed in the *Small Press Record of Books in Print* (20th Edition, 1991-92). avg. price, paper: $2-$15; other: signed lettered editions - varies (no discount). Discounts: 5 or more, 40%. 24-120pp; size varies; of. Payment: copies plus share of money above expenses. Copyrights for author. CCLM.

THE DUCKBURG TIMES, Dana Gabbard, Editor, 3010 Wilshire Blvd., #362, Los Angeles, CA 90010-1146, 213-388-2364. 1977. Articles, art, photos, cartoons, interviews, criticism, reviews, letters, news items, non-fiction. "Our sole criterion for the acceptance of material is that in some way it relate to the works of Walt Disney and associates. We run quite a lot on famed comic book artist Carl Barks, but are also interested in material on other Disney artists, the studio, Disney animation, the theme parks, etc. If in doubt, contact us first. Especially on the look out for material from overseas fans. We have special guidelines to follow when running Disney copyrighted art available upon request. Always open to the unusual and critical. America's only magazine devoted solely to Walt Disney Comic books" circ. 750. 1/yr. Expects 1 issue 1991, 1 issue 1992. 2 titles listed in the *Small Press Record of Books in Print* (20th Edition, 1991-92). sub. price: $6; per copy: $1.50; sample: $1.50. Back issues: inquire. 28pp; 7×8½; of. Reporting time: ASAP. Payment: copy of issue material appears in. Copyrighted, reverts to author upon written request. Pub's reviews. §Walt Disney, animation, Carl Barks, comics, theme parks, and related. Ads: $25/free to subscriber if under 50 words, Disney related.

Duende Press, Larry Goodell, Box 571, Placitas, NM 87043, 505-867-5877. 1964. Poetry. "Performance poetry only" avg. press run 500. 4 titles listed in the *Small Press Record of Books in Print* (20th Edition, 1991-92). avg. price, paper: $5 up. Discounts: 40% plus mailing. †of. RGWA.

Dufour Editions Inc., Kristin Dufour, President; Christopher May, Operations Manager; Jeanne Dufour, Publicity Director; Sharon Donovan, Art Director, PO Box 449, Chester Springs, PA 19425-0449, 215-458-5005. 1949. Poetry, fiction, articles, criticism, reviews, long-poems, plays, non-fiction. "Dufour Editions publishes, co-publishes, and exclusively distributes selected titles of British or Irish origin. We also publish some work of American origin" avg. press run 500-5M. Pub'd 10 titles 1990; expects 15 titles 1991. 25 titles listed in the *Small Press Record of Books in Print* (20th Edition, 1991-92). avg. price, cloth: $18; paper: $8.54; other: $14.22. Discounts: trade 1-4 20%, 5-14 40%, 15-24 41%, 25-49 42%, 50-99 43%, 100+ 44%; short discounted titles: 20% any quantity. SCOP & STOP 30%; libraries 10%. Pages vary; size varies; of. Reporting time: 1-6 months. Payment: negotiated. Copyrights for author.

DUMARS REVIEWS, Denise Dumars, PO Box 810, Hawthorne, CA 90251. 1987. Poetry, reviews. circ. 100. 4/yr. Pub'd 4 issues 1990; expects 4 issues 1991, 4 issues 1992. sub. price: $7.50; per copy: $2; sample: $2. Discounts: bookstore rate 60/40. 30pp; 5½×8½; photocopy. Reporting time: 2 weeks. Payment: $2 plus 2 copies on publication. Copyrighted, reverts to author. Pub's reviews. §We do not accept unsolicited items for review.

Ads: $7/$4/$2 classified. Wiccan Pagan Press Association.

Dumpster Press (see also DUMPSTER TIMES), Wendy S. Duke, (AKA Wanda S. Duck), PO Box 80044, Akron, OH 44308, 216-762-1279. 1987. Poetry, fiction, art, cartoons, satire, criticism, plays. "At this time I am actively seeking essays on the following: anarchism, atheism, theatre and art. No poetry please! Would be interested in play scripts with an anarchist point of view" avg. press run 200+. Pub'd 1 title 1990; expects 4 titles 1991, 6 titles 1992. avg. price, other: $2. Discounts: none. Pages vary; size varies; †Gestetner duplicator. Reporting time: 2 weeks. Payment: complimentary copies/subscriptions. Will copyright if requested.

DUMPSTER TIMES, Dumpster Press, Wendy S. Duke, (AKA Wanda S. Duck), PO Box 80044, Akron, OH 44308, 216-762-1279. 1989. Poetry, fiction, articles, art, photos, cartoons, satire, criticism, letters, plays. "The *DT* is essentially an anarchist/atheist publication looking for well-written material from these points of view. Contributors have included Robert Nagler (poetry), Paul Weinman (White Boy), and Allen Thornton (essay). Logic, humor, and sharp thinking are essential ingredients. Six print issues, two cassettezines" circ. 200+. 6-8/yr. Pub'd 4 issues 1990; expects 8 issues 1991, 8 issues 1992. price per copy: $2; sample: $2. Discounts: none. 40pp; 7×8½; †gastetner duplicator. Reporting time: 2 weeks. Payment: contributor's copies. Not copyrighted. Pub's reviews: 2 in 1990. §Anarchism, atheism, theatre, art, Kinks. Ads: free to those who are worthy.

Dundurn Press Ltd, J. Kirk Howard, 2181 Queen Street East #301, Toronto, Ontario M4E 1E5, Canada, 416-698-0454; FAX 416-698-1102. 1973. avg. press run 2M. Pub'd 20 titles 1990; expects 20 titles 1991. avg. price, cloth: $24.95; paper: $14.95. Discounts: usual 40% for wholesalers and store-to begin. Biographies 250pp picture book, larger format 128pp; 6×9, 8½×11; of. Reporting time: 2-4 months. Payment: twice first year, then annually-10% of list price. Copyrights for author. ACP, CBIC.

Dunstan Press, Paul Zomberg, Joan Zomberg, 30 Linden Street, Rockland, ME 04841, 207-596-0064. 1984. "All titles developed in-house" avg. press run 5M. Pub'd 1 title 1990; expects 1 title 1991, 1 title 1992. avg. price, cloth: $12; paper: $5. Discounts: 1-4 copies, 30%; 5-9 copies 35%; 10+ copies 40%; bonus 5% on prepaid orders; free shipping on prepaid orders. 250pp; 4¼×7; phototypesetting.

THE DUPLEX PLANET, David B. Greenberger, PO Box 1230, Saratoga Springs, NY 12866, 518-587-5356. 1979. Interviews. "ISSN# 0882-2549" circ. 600+. 10/yr. Pub'd 10 issues 1990; expects 10 issues 1991, 10 issues 1992. 25 titles listed in the *Small Press Record of Books in Print* (20th Edition, 1991-92). sub. price: $12; per copy: $1.50; sample: $1.50. Back issues: 10 or more issues - $1.25 each; less than 10 - $1.50 each. Discounts: on request. 16pp; 5½×8½; of. Copyrighted.

DuReve Publications, Judith Lehman, PO Box 7772, Ann Arbor, MI 48107, 313-662-3801. 1987. Fiction, non-fiction. "New Age, healing, feminist, 'how-to' subject matter by women authors. Full-length books only, fiction and nonfiction" avg. press run 3M. Pub'd 1 title 1990; expects 2 titles 1991, 4 titles 1992. 1 title listed in the *Small Press Record of Books in Print* (20th Edition, 1991-92). avg. price, paper: $12.50. 200pp; 6×9. Reporting time: 12 weeks. Payment: negotiable. Copyrights for author.

THE DURHAM UNIVERSITY JOURNAL, J.W. Blench, School of English/University of Durham, Elvet Riverside, New Elvet, Durham, DH1 3JT, England, 091-374 2000 Ext. 2744. 1876. Articles, criticism, reviews. "Mss. and books for review should be sent to the editor. All correspondence on other matters relating to the journal should be sent to the Secretary, Durham University Journal, School of English, Elvet Riverside, New Elvet, Durham DH1 3JT, England. Subscriptions should be made payable to University of Durham. Articles are about 6,000 words long on average. Slightly longer or shorter articles are acceptable. The articles are of the usual academic standard for a learned journal. Recent contributors: J.W. Blench, Isobel Murray, Brocard Sewell" circ. 500. 2/yr. Pub'd 2 issues 1990; expects 2 issues 1991, 2 issues 1992. sub. price: U.K. £19, overseas £22, £14, (£15 by post) to members of staff and students of the Univ of Durham and Newcastle-upon-Tyne; per copy: £9; sample: £9. Back issues: variable, according to price on cover plus postage. Discounts: none. 150pp; 17×24.5cm; of. Reporting time: 6 weeks. Payment: none. Copyrighted, reverts to author according to current British Law. Pub's reviews: 66 in 1990. §Art, literature, history, philosophy, classical studies, theology, archaeology, economics, film and television. Ads: £45/£28 (15% discount if ad appears in both numbers of a volume).

DUST (From the Ego Trip), Camel Press, James Hedges, Editor, HC 80, Box 160, Big Cove Tannery, PA 17212, 717-573-4526. 1985. Articles, non-fiction. "Contributions of good literary quality are welcome; manuscripts should be between 1M and 2.5M words in length. Authors of unsolicited manuscripts will be expected to pay the cost of materials and shipping, plus $5/1M impressions for press time. There is no charge for typesetting. 500 copies of a 12-page issue would cost the author about $65." circ. 500. Irregular. Expects 3 issues 1991, 2 issues 1992. sub. price: $1-3 per issue on standing order; per copy: $1-3; sample: $1. Discounts: on request. 20pp; 4¼×5¾; †lp. Reporting time: 1 week. Payment: 50 free copies. Copyrighted, rights revert to author if requested. No ads. Amalgamated Printers Assn. (APA), American Amateur Press Assn. (AAPA).

Dustbooks (see also THE SMALL PRESS REVIEW), Len Fulton, PO Box 100, Paradise, CA 95967, 916-877-6110; 800-477-6110; fax 916-877-0222. 1963. "We have a small general trade list: poetry, novels, anthologies, non-fiction prose, how-to, etc. But it should be remembered that our real expertise & commitment is small press-mag info. On January 1st of every year we face a full year of publishing without looking at one new manuscript. We do four annuals: this Directory you're holding (now in its Twenty-Seventh annual edition!) which takes 5 months from start to finish; its companion volume, the *Directory of Small Magazine/Press Editors and Publishers*, and the *Small Press Record of Books in Print* (latest edition - over 1400pp). In 1990 we published the sixth edition of *Directory of Poetry Publishers* as a supplement to these information volumes. Write to us about it! We do a monthly, the *Small Press Review* (see separate listing). We've done a nice string of general trade books, but our capacity is severely modified by our mainstay titles above. In 1975 Dustbooks initiated The 'American Dust' Series, which seeks to chronicle the geographical, stylistic, ethnic, and genre diversity and richness of writing in the Contemporary Americas. Currently the series has fifteen volumes. The latest volumes in this series are *Women With And Without* by Carol Murray, and *Those Who Were There*, a bibliography of work about the war in Southeast Asia by 'those who were there,' edited by Merritt Clifton and others. In 1986 we brought out *Words In Our Pockets* edited by Celeste West - a survival kit for women writers. In 1987 we published Robert Peters' *Third Black & Blue Guide To Literary Periodicals*. Best to query before sending a manuscript for this series. NOTE: Canadian and foreign please remit in US funds only when ordering." avg. press run 1M-2M. Pub'd 5 titles 1990; expects 5 titles 1991, 5 titles 1992. 25 titles listed in the *Small Press Record of Books in Print* (20th Edition, 1991-92). avg. price, paper: $15. Discounts: 2-10 25%, 11-25 40%, 26+ 50% (bookstores), distributors by arrangement, jobbers 20-25%. Returns only after six months but before one year; returns are for credit ONLY. 300-1000pp; 5½x8½, 6x9; of. Reporting time: 3-6 months. Payment: royalty (15%). Copyrights for author.

DUSTY DOG, Dusty Dog Press, John Pierce, PO Box 1103, Zuni, NM 87327, 505-782-4958. 1990. Poetry, art, photos, reviews, collages. "Interested in high caliber well-crafted poetry from new and established talent. No haiku, light verse, or rhyme poetry. Avoid religious themes. Submit in batches of 3-10 poems, up to 60 lines. Always include SASE with proper return postage. Also interested in pen and ink drawings, black and white photography, and collage artwork" circ. 300. 3/yr. Pub'd 2 issues 1990; expects 3 issues 1991. sub. price: $7; per copy: $4; sample: $4. Back issues: $4. Discounts: none. 28pp; 5½x8½; †desktop. Reporting time: 2 weeks max. Payment: 1 copy. Copyrighted, reverts to author.

Dusty Dog Press (see also DUSTY DOG; DUSTY DOG REVIEWS), John Pierce, PO Box 1103, Zuni, NM 87327, 505-782-4958. 1991. Poetry. "Beginning in June 1991, the Dusty Dog Chapbook Series will publish its first chapbook: *Redeeming The Wings* by Simon Perchik. The Dusty Dog Chapbook Series publishes poetry chapbooks by invitation only. Subscription to the Chapbook Series is $8/yr for 3 titles." avg. press run 300. Expects 2-3 titles 1991, 3 titles 1992. 4 titles listed in the *Small Press Record of Books in Print* (20th Edition, 1991-92). avg. price, paper: $3. Discounts: none. 24pp; 5½x8½; †desktop. Reporting time: 5 weeks. Payment: varies, but usually author receives $10 cash payment and 10 copies of book upon publication. Author has option to buy additional copies at 25% off cover price. Copyrights for author.

DUSTY DOG REVIEWS, Dusty Dog Press, John Pierce, PO Box 1103, Zuni, NM 87327, 505-782-4958. 1990. Reviews. "*Dusty Dog Reviews* is a quarterly publication publishing reviews of small and midrange press poetry magazines and poetry chapbooks. Editors and publishers of poetry are invited to submit one copy of each issue published for review consideration. Each press will receive one copy of the issue your review appears in." circ. 350-450. 4/yr. Pub'd 1 issue 1990; expects 4 issues 1991, 4 issues 1992. sub. price: $10; per copy: $4; sample: $4. Back issues: $4. 30-50pp; 5½x8½; desktop. Reporting time: 2-4 weeks. Payment: 1 copy. Pub's reviews: 20-75 per issue in 1990. §Poetry magazines, poetry chapbooks.

Dyad Services (see also EMERGENCY LIBRARIAN), Ken Haycock, Dept. 284, Box C34069, Seattle, WA 98124-1069, 604-734-0255. 1973. Articles, art, criticism, reviews, letters, news items. "Emphasis on library service to children and young adults" avg. press run 7.5M. Pub'd 5 titles 1990; expects 5 titles 1991, 5 titles 1992. avg. price, paper: $45 billed, $40 prepaid; other: $9. Discounts: on request. 80pp; 8½x11. Reporting time: 2 months. Payment: $50 per article. Does not copyright for author. CMPA, Edpress, COSMEP.

Dynamic Information Publishing, Laurent E. Colon, PO Box 1172, McLean, VA 22101-1172. 1981. Non-fiction. "We especially publish books in the following subjects: How-to-do-it books + Business and Money-Making Books + Health Books + Self-help books + Craft & Hobbies + Consumer" avg. press run 10M. Expects 20 titles 1991, 30 titles 1992. 14 titles listed in the *Small Press Record of Books in Print* (20th Edition, 1991-92). avg. price, cloth: $12.95; paper: $7.95. Discounts: (2-4) 20%; (5-24) 40%; (25-49) 43%; (50-99) 46% (100-up) 50%. 250pp; 5½x8½; of. Reporting time: 6 months. Payment: to be arranged depending on the subject and the profitability of the book. Copyrights for author.

170

E

E Publications, Eunice J. Lockhart-Moss, PO Box 19033, Washington, DC 20036, 202-223-4060. 1987. Poetry, fiction, plays. avg. press run 2M. Pub'd 1 title 1990; expects 2 titles 1991, 2 titles 1992. 1 title listed in the *Small Press Record of Books in Print* (20th Edition, 1991-92). avg. price, paper: $9.95; other: $14.95. Discounts: to be negotiated. 120pp; 8½×5½; of. Reporting time: 6 months. Payment: author receives 10% of all copies of book sold, with payment made during July and January. Copyrights for author. American Bookdealers Exchange (ABE), PO Box 2525, La Mesa, CA 92041.

The E.G. Van Press, Inc., Engbert Vander Werff, PO Box 6053, London ON N5V 2Y3, Canada, 519-453-4529. 1977. Non-fiction. "We also publish a quarterly *Issues*" avg. press run 250. Pub'd 1 title 1990; expects 11 titles 1991. 4 titles listed in the *Small Press Record of Books in Print* (20th Edition, 1991-92). avg. price, paper: $5-$10. Discounts: 30%. 50pp; 8½×11; of. Reporting time: 1 month. Copyrights for author.

E.T.M. Publishing, Robert Owen Robbins, 305-B East 7th Street, Winfield, KS 67156, 316-221-4743. 1981. Fiction, collages, news items, non-fiction. "All material must be relevant to the doctrines set forth in the book, *What The Righteous Desire To See.* Write for the writer's guidelines before submitting. This program is primarily for the unknown or unpublished writer who is involved with one of the Eternal Truth Ministries Koinonia groups." avg. press run on ordered basis. Expects 1 title 1992. 2 titles listed in the *Small Press Record of Books in Print* (20th Edition, 1991-92). avg. price, paper: $3.95-$29.95; other: $39.95 expandable looseleaf. Discounts: please write for schedule. 400pp; 8½×11; of. Reporting time: 30-60 days. Payment: subsidy arrangements made with author, 15%-25% royalty and profits retrospect. Copyrights for author.

THE EAGLE, Jim Roaix, Managing Editor; Karen Cooper, Poetry Editor, PO Box 579MO, Naugatuck, CT 06770, 203-274-7853. 1981. Poetry, fiction, articles, art, photos, cartoons, interviews, reviews, music, letters, long-poems, news items, non-fiction. "Articles are usually preferred to be 6 typewritten 8½ X 11, double-spaced in length. Longer pieces are serialized for up to 6 issues (35-40 8½ X 11's). Prefer photos and/or illustrations whenever possible. Subject matter should be about American Indians or on issues of importance to Indians, i.e. environment, diabetes, alcoholism, etc" circ. 5M+. 6/yr. Pub'd 6 issues 1990; expects 6 issues 1991, 6 issues 1992. sub. price: $10; per copy: $2; sample: $2. Back issues: $27 complete set of available back issues. Discounts: classroom 20% postpaid, resale 40% postpaid. 28pp; 10¼×15; web offset. Reporting time: 30 days w/SASE. Payment: free subscription (we are all volunteers with no salaried employees). Copyrighted, reverts to author. Pub's reviews: 25-30 in 1990. §American Indian, nature. Ads: $378/$210/$16 column inch (3¼").

Eagle Publishing, PO Box 403, Red Bluff, CA 96080, 916-520-1126. 1989. Fiction, non-fiction. "Eagle Publishing began operation in August, 1989. Shortly thereafter released its first book regarding assault weapons permits. Its first major work, *Dead Man Walking,* is scheduled for a January, 1991 release. During the year 1991 Eagle Publishing has contracts for an audio version of *Dead Man Walking* and two books; one book relating to a small suburban fire department and the other a touching remembrance of a mother's son. Still a neophyte, Eagle Publishing plans 1-3 releases a year. We are confident that this number will steadily increase." Expects 1 title 1991, 2 titles 1992. 1 title listed in the *Small Press Record of Books in Print* (20th Edition, 1991-92). avg. price, paper: $9.95. 200-300pp; 5½×8½. Reporting time: 30 days. Payment: varies. Copyrights for author. MSPA, COSMEP, PMA.

Eagle Publishing Company, James Gray, 7283 Kolb Place, Dublin, CA 94568, 415-828-1350. 1980. Non-fiction. avg. press run 1.1M. Pub'd 1 title 1990; expects 1 title 1992. 1 title listed in the *Small Press Record of Books in Print* (20th Edition, 1991-92). avg. price, cloth: $20. Discounts: 50%. 350pp; of. Reporting time: 6 months. Payment: 5% of list price. Copyrights for author.

Eagle's View Publishing, Monte Smith, Publisher-Editor; Denise Knight, Editor, 6756 North Fork Road, Liberty, UT 84310, 801-393-4555 (orders); business phone 801-745-0903. 1982. Fiction, art, non-fiction. avg. press run 10M. Pub'd 4 titles 1990; expects 4 titles 1991, 4 titles 1992. 22 titles listed in the *Small Press Record of Books in Print* (20th Edition, 1991-92). avg. price, cloth: $14.95; paper: $8.95. Discounts: standard for trade and jobber. 80pp; size varies. Payment: varies. Copyrights for author. RMBPA, ABA, PMA, COSMEP.

EAP DIGEST, George Watkins, Performance Resource Press, Inc., 1863 Technology Drive, Suite 200, Troy, MI 48083-4244, 313-588-7733; fax 313-588-6633. 1979. Articles, art, photos, cartoons, interviews, news items. circ. 20M. 6/yr. Pub'd 6 issues 1990; expects 6 issues 1991, 6 issues 1992. 16 titles listed in the *Small Press Record of Books in Print* (20th Edition, 1991-92). sub. price: $36; per copy: $6. Back issues: $6. 92pp; 8½×11;

of, web. Reporting time: 10 days. Payment: one-year subscription. Copyrighted, does not revert to author. Pub's reviews: 67 in 1990. §Alcohol and drug—Employee Assistance Programs. Ads: $1550/$900/$2 per word.

EAR MAGAZINE, Carol E. Tuynman, Publisher; David L Laskin, Editor, 131 Varick Street #905, New York City, NY 10013-1323, 212-807-7944. 1973. Articles, art, photos, interviews, reviews, music, letters. *"Ear publishes New Music, reviews, calendar articles and information. We vary themes with each issue."* circ. 20M. 10/yr. Pub'd 10 issues 1990; expects 10 issues 1991, 10 issues 1992. sub. price: $25 indiv U.S., Canada, Mexico; $45 indiv. all other countries and all institutions; per copy: $2.95; sample: $3. Back issues: approx: $3 incl. handling/shipping (some rare issues up to $10). Discounts: available on request. 68pp; 8⅜×10¾; web off. Reporting time: 6 months. Payment: 1 year subscription, possible honorarium. Copyrighted, reverts to author. Pub's reviews: 10 in 1990. §New music, sound/text, performance art, topics relating to themes of new music developments. Ads: $1,250/$687/$375 1/4 page/$20 first 30 words, 10¢ each add'l word. AIO, CCLM, MPWA.

Earth Star Publications (see also THE STAR BEACON), Ann Ulrich, PO Box 117, Paonia, CO 81428, 303-527-3257. 1987. Fiction, non-fiction. "Open to any subject matter and length. Recent titles have included metaphysical and New Age subjects. In 1987 published *Thought* by Julian Joyce (collection of metaphysical essays dealing with every aspect of life); in 1988 published *Intimate Abduction*, a sci-fi/romance novel by Ann Carol Ulrich, covering aspects of true-to-life UFO abduction experiences." avg. press run 500. Pub'd 2 titles 1990; expects 2 titles 1991, 2 titles 1992. 4 titles listed in the *Small Press Record of Books in Print* (20th Edition, 1991-92). avg. price, paper: $7. 180pp; 5½×8½; of. Reporting time: 6 weeks. Payment: 100% to author; publisher collects one-time fee; open to other arrangements. Copyrights for author.

Earth-Love Publishing House, R. R. Jackson, Laodeciae Augustine, Senior Editor, 302 Torbett, Suite 100, Richland, WA 99352, 509-943-9567. 1990. Fiction, non-fiction. "Interested in New Age, self-help, spiritual development themes. Some fiction is acceptable if slanted toward spiritual development and/or earth healing/brotherhood. Publishes book an average of 8 months after acceptance." avg. press run 5M. Pub'd 1 title 1990; expects 1 title 1991, 2 titles 1992. 1 title listed in the *Small Press Record of Books in Print* (20th Edition, 1991-92). avg. price, paper: $16.95. Discounts: 2-5 20%, 6-10 30%, 11-99 40%, 100+ 50%; 5+ books with cash in advance additional 5% on discounted price; 5+ books with returns waived additional 5% on discounted price. 500+pp; 6×9; of. Reporting time: 3-4 months. Payment: 15% royalty on retail sales, 10% royalty on wholesale sales. NABE (North American Bookdealers Exchange), PO Box 606, Cottage Grove, OR, 97424.

EARTH'S DAUGHTERS: Feminist Arts Periodical, Kastle Brill, Co-Editor; Bonnie Johnson, Co-Editor; Robin Willoughby, Co-Editor; Ryki Zuckerman, Co-Editor, Box 622, Station C, Buffalo, NY 14209, 716-837-7778. 1971. Poetry, fiction, art, photos, satire, parts-of-novels, long-poems, collages, plays. "We are a feminist arts periodical." circ. 1M. 2-4/yr. Pub'd 4 issues 1990; expects 3 issues 1991, 3 issues 1992. sub. price: $12/3 issues, instit. $20/3 issues; per copy: varies; sample: $4. Back issues: available upon inquiry. Discounts: trade 30-35%; bulk 35%; jobber-straight rates. 50pp; size varies; of. Reporting time: atrociously long if mss is being seriously considered for publication, otherwise within 2 months. Payment: 2 issues complimentary and reduced prices on further copies. Copyrighted, reverts to author. §Work by women or in feminist themes. Not presently accepting ads. CCLM, NYSSPA, COSMEP, Arts Council, Inc.

Earth-Song Press, Marilyn J. Gillies, Publisher, 6553 Shadow Hawk Drive, Citrus Heights, CA 95621, 916-721-8719. 1980. Long-poems, non-fiction. avg. press run 100-500. Pub'd 3 titles 1990; expects 3 titles 1991, 3 titles 1992. 38 titles listed in the *Small Press Record of Books in Print* (20th Edition, 1991-92). avg. price, paper: $7.95. Discounts: 1-5 10%; 6-25 20%; 26-50 30%; 51-100 40%. 50-100pp; 5×8, 8×11; of, mi. Copyrights for author.

EARTHTREKS DIGEST, Five Corners Publications, Ltd., Deborah Smith-Gingras, Route 100, HCR 70, Box 7A, Plymouth, VT 05056, 802-672-3868. 1990. Photos, non-fiction. *"Earthtreks Digest* focuses on ecotravel, travel exploring the relationship between human beings and their environment through photography. Photo essays are 1/3 text and 2/3 photography. Any writing must be accompanied by photography. *Earthtreks Digest* features work from members of the International Network of Publishing Photographers (INPP). Subscription includes INPP membership." circ. 10M. 4/yr. Expects 4 issues 1991, 4 issues 1992. sub. price: $16.95; per copy: $6.95; sample: $4.25. Back issues: $4.25. Discounts: 2-4 20%, 5-19 30%, 20-49 40%, 50-99 45%, 100-199 48%, 200+ 50%, 5% additional for nonreturnables. 80pp; 8⅛×10⅞; of. Reporting time: 1 month. Payment: $10 cover photo, $5 photograph, $25 accompanying article. Copyrighted, reverts to author. Ads: Full page: 4c $1500, 1c $1050; half page: 4c $990, 1c $693; 1/4 page: 4c $675, 1c $475.

EARTHWISE LITERARY CALENDAR, Earthwise Publications, Barbara Holley, Editor, Publisher; Ted Wezyk, Art Editor; Chris Wezyk, Jr., Art Editor; Kaye Edwards Carter, Fiction Editor; Sally Volkell Newhouse, Editor's Assistant, PO Box 680-536, Miami, FL 33168. 1980. "We are always open to applicable suggestions. We do not solicit material for *Earthwise Literary Calendar*, but offer those accepted the option of joining the National Poetry Society (NFSPS) by joining our Miami Earth Chapter, a chapter of the Florida State Poets Assn., Inc. We do publish non-member poems as space permits, a fact that poets and artists are made aware of with literature furnished on acceptance. We are particularly anxious to bring new members into our state and national societies which provide many benefits for the poet. Membership in our local chapter, brings free subscription to our *Earthwise Review*, inclusion in the annual *Earthwise Literary Calendar* (since 1979), free Critique Service and more. SASE for more information" circ. 200-400. 1/yr. Pub'd 1 issue 1990; expects 1 issue 1991, 1 issue 1992. sub. price: free members, $8.95 non-members; per copy: same; sample: $1.50 calendars of previous years, when available, for 9 X 12 SASE while they last (indicate year preferred in available). Back issues: after 6/1 each year, current available calendar $3.00 plus 9 X 12 SASE. Discounts: will make available. 24-32pp; 9×12, 8½×11; of. Reporting time: 30-60 days. Payment: copy. Copyrighted, reverts to author. National Federation State Poetry Societies, Florida State Poets Assn., Inc.-Earth Chapter.

Earthwise Publications (see also EARTHWISE LITERARY CALENDAR; EARTHWISE REVIEW), Barbara Holley, Editor, Publisher; Kaye Edwards Carter, Fiction Editor; Ted Wezyk, Art Editor; Chris Wezyk, Art Editor (youth); Frank S. Fitzgerald-Bush, Poetry Contest Editor; Florence Kahn, Review Editor; Sarah Volkell Newhouse, Assistant Editor (submissions); Bob Raynor, Cartoon-Caricature Editor; Barbara Weston, Kaye Edwards Carter, Fiction; Short Story Editors, PO Box 680-536, Miami, FL 33168, 305-940-7157 (S. Newhouse/Asst. Editor); FAX 305-687-8387. 1978. Poetry, fiction, articles, art, interviews, satire, criticism, reviews, letters, long-poems, collages, concrete art, news items. "Last year *Earthwise Review* returned to its quarterly format. The review began originally in 1979 as the *Earthwise Newsletter* and we have published at least 2 issues each year, usually 3 or 4. We are currently attempting to stabilize our publishing schedule. We are committed to publishing six individual chapbooks each year. payment for material is on publication. We do accept interviews and pay $25 for each, more if accompanied by a photo or example of the writer's work. We conduct again quarterly competitions with cash prizes. Always use SASE. It brings you a wealth of information regarding our organization, its beginnings and how we work. Earthwise sponsors a chapter of the Florida State Poets Assn., Inc. This chapter in turn supports the annual *Earthwise Literary Calendar.*" avg. press run 500. Pub'd 2 titles 1990; expects 3-6 titles 1991. 13 titles listed in the *Small Press Record of Books in Print* (20th Edition, 1991-92). avg. price, paper: $5.00 Review, $5 to members, sscr 4 issues $18 incl. post. Discounts: on consignment, negotiable. 40-60pp; 5½×8½; of. Reporting time: 3-5 months (not during 6/15 - 8/15). Payment: $25 for interviews (query), articles, short stories, $5 for photos, $10 plus for cover art + royalty, $2 each for blk and whites, woodcuts a bit more, $30 for interview which include a picture of author/poem to print or reprint with appropriate credits, of course—poetry varies. Copyrights for author. COSMEP, CODA, CCLM.

EARTHWISE REVIEW, Earthwise Publications, Barbara Holley, Chief Editor; Sally Newhouse, Co-Editor; Kaye Carter, Fiction Editor; Barbara Weston, Short Story Editor; Teresa Baruksen, Articles Editor; Robert Raynor, Jr., Cartoons-Caricatures; Florence Kahn, Review Editor; Frank F. Fitzgerald-Bush, Poetry Editor; Edward Portnoy, Staff Artist, PO Box 680-536, Miami, FL 33168, 305-688-8558. 1979. Poetry, articles, art, interviews, criticism, reviews, letters, concrete art, news items. *"Earthwise Review* is issued bimonthly, contains a variety of themes of earthwise significance. Issues this year include: Rita Dove, Alice Walker, Mikki Giovanni in issue #1 (The Universal Black Word); also William Stafford and Marge Piercy in Poets & Writers of the Northestern U.S.A., Midwestern USA, Poets International, Science/Fantasy and the War Songs (*Tempest*)" circ. 5M. 4/yr. Pub'd 3 issues 1990; expects 4 issues 1991, 4 issues 1992. sub. price: $20; per copy: $5; sample: $3. Back issues: $3 when available. Discounts: negotiable. 12-16pp; 8½×11½ folded for mailing; of. Reporting time: 30-60 days. Payment: interviews ($30 with poem picture), sometimes small fee paid, always contributors copies. Copyrighted, reverts to author. Pub's reviews: 20-30 in 1990. §Poetry, fiction, ecology, crafts, art, music, the dance. Ads: $20/$10/$1.50. COSMEP, CODA.

East African Publishing House, Gacheche Warving, D. Nyoike Waiyaki, Khalfan E. Kasu, PO Box 30571, Nairobi, Kenya, 557417, 557788. 1965. avg. press run 7.5M. Pub'd 25 titles 1990; expects 35 titles 1991, 35 titles 1992. 3 titles listed in the *Small Press Record of Books in Print* (20th Edition, 1991-92). avg. price, cloth: Ksh. 60; paper: Ksh. 30.00. Discounts: 25%, 30%, 35%. size A4, A5, B6, B5; lp, of. Reporting time: 6 weeks. Payment: annually four months after closing date of financial year. Copyrights by special arrangement.

East Eagle Press, Patrick Haley, PO Box 812, Huron, SD 57350, 605-352-5875. 1981. Fiction, non-fiction. "Childrens literature, *The Little Person,* written by Patrick Haley, illustrated by Jonna Kool" avg. press run 2M. Pub'd 1 title 1990; expects 2 titles 1991, 2 titles 1992. 4 titles listed in the *Small Press Record of Books in Print* (20th Edition, 1991-92). avg. price, cloth: $9-$14; paper: $6. Discounts: library 25%, bookseller 40%, distributor 40%. 64pp; 6×9; of. Reporting time: 8-12 weeks. Payment: 10%, no advance. Copyrights for author.

EAST EUROPEAN QUARTERLY, Stephen Fischer-Galati, Box 29 Regent Hall, University of Colorado, Boulder, CO 80309, 303-492-6157. 1967. Articles. "Articles ranging from 8 to 48 printed pages; reviews. All articles dealing with Eastern European problems in historical perspective. Contributors from US and foreign academic institutions." circ. 900. 4/yr. Pub'd 4 issues 1990; expects 4 issues 1991, 4 issues 1992. sub. price: $12, $15 institutions; per copy: $4; sample: free. Back issues: same as regular rates. Discounts: agencies 12.5%. 128pp; 5½×8½; of. Reporting time: 6-8 weeks. Payment: none. Not copyrighted. Pub's reviews: 32 in 1990.

§East European history, civilization, economics, society, politics. Ads: $100/$60.

Eastern Caribbean Institute, S.B. Jones-Hendrickson, Editor & President, PO Box 1338, Frederiksted, VI 00841, 809-772-1011. 1982. Poetry, fiction, non-fiction. "Minimum Length: 60 pages. Bias: Eastern Caribbean Material. Recent Contribution: *Christmas Sports in St. Kitts-Nevis, Our Neglected Cultural Tradition, Sonny Jim of Sandy Point* (Aug. 1988)" avg. press run 1M. Pub'd 1 title 1990; expects 1 title 1991, 2 titles 1992. 3 titles listed in the *Small Press Record of Books in Print* (20th Edition, 1991-92). avg. price, cloth: $9.95; paper: $6. Discounts: 1-5, 20%; 6-24, 30%; 24-49, 40%; 50 + 50%. 100pp; 13.5×21.1mm; of. Reporting time: 1 month. Payment: negotiable. Copyrights for author.

EASTERN EUROPEAN POLITICS & SOCIETIES, University of California Press, Ivo Banac, University of California Press, 2120 Berkeley Way, Berkeley, CA 94720, 415-642-4191. 1987. Articles, reviews. "Editorial address: History Dept, Pierson College, Yale University, 2105A Yale Stn., New Haven, CT 06520. Copyrighted by American Council of Learned Societies." circ. 650. 3/yr. Expects 3 issues 1991, 3 issues 1992. sub. price: $25 indiv., $43 instit., $20 students ($4 foreign postage); per copy: $8.50 indiv., $14.50 instit., $6.75 students; sample: free. Back issues: same as single copy price. Discounts: foreign subs. agent 10%, one-time orders 10+ 30%, standing orders (bookstores): 1-99 40%, 100+ 50%. 140pp; 6×9; of. Copyrighted, does not revert to author. Pub's reviews. Ads: $200/$120.

ECA Associates, Dr. E. Curtis Alexander, PO Box 15004, Great Bridge Station, Chesapeake, VA 23320, 804-547-5542. 1979. Non-fiction. "We publish books written about Africa by African and African American writers" avg. press run 5M. Pub'd 2 titles 1990; expects 3 titles 1991, 4 titles 1992. 11 titles listed in the *Small Press Record of Books in Print* (20th Edition, 1991-92). avg. price, paper: $6.95. Discounts: 42% on orders of 20 or more books. 140pp; 5½×8½; of. Reporting time: 1 month. Payment: 10% of net quarterly. Copyrights for author. AAP.

The Ecco Press (see also ANTAEUS), Daniel Halpern, Editor-in-Chief; Chris Kingsley, Administrative Director; Cathy Jewell, Managing Editor; Stephen Morrow, Assistant Editor, 26 West 17th Street, New York City, NY 10011, 212-645-2214. 1971. Poetry, fiction, criticism, non-fiction. avg. press run 4M. Pub'd 25 titles 1990; expects 25 titles 1991, 25 titles 1992. 204 titles listed in the *Small Press Record of Books in Print* (20th Edition, 1991-92). avg. price, cloth: $14.95; paper: $9.95. Distributed by Norton - their discount schedule. Catalogue Sales—50-55% discount through Ecco Press. Pages vary; size varies; of. Reporting time: 8-12 weeks. Payment: advance and royalties. Copyrights for author.

ECHOS DU MONDE CLASSIQUE/CLASSICAL VIEWS, University of Calgary Press, K. Bradley, J. Oleson, S. Scully, Department of Classics, University of Calgary, Calgary, Alberta T2N 1N4, Canada, 403-220-5537. 1957. Articles, reviews, news items. "Reports on activities of Canadian classical archaeologists and articles on archaeological subjects, as well as articles and book reviews on classical history and literature." circ. 920. 3/yr. Pub'd 3 issues 1990; expects 3 issues 1991, 3 issues 1992. price per copy: $12.50 US, + GST Canada. Back issues: 1968-1981 $10 each or $125 together, then current prices. 128pp; 6×9; of. Reporting time: 6 weeks. Copyrighted, does not revert to author. Pub's reviews: 30 in 1990. §Classical studies. Ads: write for information.

THE ECLECTIC MUSE, Joe M. Ruggier, Managing Editor-Publisher; Jeffrey Woodward, Contributing Editor; Paul H. St. Pierre, Associate Editor, 340 West 3rd Street #107, North Vancouver, B.C. V7M 1G4, Canada, 604-984-7834. 1989. Poetry, fiction, articles, reviews, long-poems. "We are a traditionalist magazine seeking to introduce far more disciplined techniques than those which obtain in the so-called Modernist poetry of the post-Elio-Pound era. We shall always welcome well-crafted free verse and would positively like free verse to stay but we regard Eliot imitation to be as bad as Milton imitation at its worst and most hideous. We welcome short and long poems as well as poem cycles. Recent contributors have been Philip Higson, Warren Stevenson, Len McCarthy, Robert Darling, Freda Howell, Arnold Lipkind, Maria deGuzman, Geraldine Black, Catherine Linley, Jan Bono, John Laycock, and many others. We always make it a point to publish some women poets." circ. 200. 3/yr. Pub'd 3 issues 1990; expects 3 issues 1991, 3 issues 1992. sub. price: $20; per copy: $7; sample: $7. Back issues: $7 if available. Discounts: 20% for bulk wholesale. 40pp; 5½×8½; †of. Reporting time: 4 months. Payment: free author's copies. Copyrighted, reverts to author. Pub's reviews: 7 in 1990. §Traditionalist poetry of the late 20th century (contemporary). Ads: $60/$30/$15 business card. National Library.

ECOLOGY LAW QUARTERLY, University of California Press, Students of Boalt Hall School of Law, University of California Press, 2120 Berkeley Way, Berkeley, CA 94720, 415-642-4191. 1970. Articles, reviews, non-fiction. "Editorial address: 20 Boalt Hall School of Law, Univ. of CA, Berkeley, CA 94703. Copyrighted by Ecology Law Quarterly." circ. 1.3M. 4/yr. Pub'd 4 issues 1990; expects 4 issues 1991, 4 issues 1992. sub. price: $27.50 indiv., $45 instit., $20 students (+ $4 foreign postage); per copy: $7 indiv., $12 instit., $6.75 students (+ $4 foreign postage); sample: free. Back issues: $7 indiv., $12 instit. Discounts: foreign subs. agent 10%, one-time order 10+ 30%, standing orders (bookstores): 1-99 40%, 100+ 50%. 200pp; 6¾×10; of.

Reporting time: 1-2 months. Payment: varies. Copyrighted, does not revert to author. Pub's reviews: 6 in 1990. Ads: $200/$120.

ECONOMIC AFFAIRS, City Publications Ltd., Robert Miller, Editor, 2 Lord North Street, London SW1P 3LB, United Kingdom. 1980. Non-fiction. "Articles examine role of markets and state, developments in economic theory and political science. Emphasis on market as disseminator of information among participants in market process; price; government failure" circ. 4M. 6/yr. Pub'd 6 issues 1990; expects 6 issues 1991, 6 issues 1992. sub. price: $24; per copy: $4; sample: free. Back issues: $2. Discounts: details from City Publications, 3-4 St. Andrews Hill, London EC4V 5BY, on request. 48pp; size A4; of. Reporting time: 3-4 weeks or less. Payment: straight fee. Copyrighted, reverts to author if so desired. Pub's reviews: 20 in 1990. §Economics, government policy, etc. Anything with an economic aspect. Ads: details from City Publications.

ECOS: A Journal of Latino People's Culture, Abrazo Press, Carlos Cumpian, PO Box 2890, Chicago, IL 60690-2890, 312-935-6188. 1980. Poetry, photos, interviews, criticism, reviews, plays. "Recent contributors include Cecilio Garcia-Camarillo, Abelardo 'lalo' Delgado, Inez Hernandez, Deborah Pintonelli, Achy Obejas, Cynthia Gallaher, Sandra Cisneros, Carlos Cortez. We are looking for Chicano-Mexican, Latino, Puerto Rican, Cuban, American Indian, mixed heritage writers & poets. We publish when there are funds" circ. 500-1M. 1/yr. Expects 1 issue 1992. price per copy: $2-$3; sample: $3. Back issues: $5. Discounts: 20-50 10%, 50-100 20% for classroom use. 52pp; 8½x5; of, or laser printer. Reporting time: 8-9 weeks. Payment: 3-5 copies. Copyrighted, reverts to author. Pub's reviews. §Books by Latinos of poetry, short story, novels, prose. Exchange ads with small presses.

ECOSOCIALIST REVIEW, Chicago Democratic Socialists Of America, J. Hughes, Chicago DSA, 1608 N. Milwaukee, 4th Floor, Chicago, IL 60647, 312-752-3562. 1987. Articles, art, photos, cartoons, satire, criticism, reviews, letters, news items. "Articles should be submitted on Dos or Mac disk, no longer than 1000 words. We accept all news and analysis from an ecosocialist perspective." circ. 3M. 4/yr. Pub'd 4 issues 1990; expects 4 issues 1991, 4 issues 1992. sub. price: $8; per copy: $1; sample: $1. Back issues: $1. 16pp; 8½x11. Reporting time: submissions responded to within several months. Payment: none. Not copyrighted. Pub's reviews: several dozen in 1990. §Ecology, toxics, transportation, electoral politics, socialism, military policy, worker safety, Canada and Mexico, Third World development. Ads: 2x2 $20/2x3 $30/3x3 $45.

ECW Press (see also ESSAYS ON CANADIAN WRITING), Jack David, Robert Lecker, 307 Coxwell Avenue, Toronto, Ontario M4L 3B5, Canada, 416-694-3348. 1979. Poetry, articles, art, photos, cartoons, interviews, criticism, reviews, letters, collages, news items. "As a press, we specialize in books of literary criticism, especially of Canadian writers and issues. We also specialize in bibliographies, including the *Annotated Bibliography of Canada's Major Authors*" avg. press run 1M. Pub'd 18 titles 1990; expects 20 titles 1991, 20 titles 1992. 19 titles listed in the *Small Press Record of Books in Print* (20th Edition, 1991-92). avg. price, cloth: $40; paper: $16. Discounts: varies. 240pp; 6x9; of. Reporting time: 1 month. Payment: 10% paid yearly. Copyrights for author. ACP, CPPA.

Edge Publishing, George Fencl, Publisher, PO Box 3621, Longwood, FL 32779, 407-788-6357. 1986. "Trade publisher of hardcover and paperback nonfiction originals. Will act as a subsidy publisher and assist the author with editing, proofreading, promotion and distribution. Computer printout submissions acceptable. Recent nonfiction titles: *The Central Florida Career Guide* and *The Tampa Bay Career Guide*" avg. press run 3M. Pub'd 2 titles 1990; expects 2 titles 1991, 4 titles 1992. 4 titles listed in the *Small Press Record of Books in Print* (20th Edition, 1991-92). avg. price, paper: $18.95 spiral. Discounts: 50% wholesale. 100+pp; 8½x11; spiral binding, perfect-bound. Reporting time: 60 days. Payment: 10%-15% royalty on retail price with generally no advance given. Copyrights for author.

Edgeworth & North Books, Marion M. Stuart, V.P. Sales, Marketing, PO Box 812 West Side Station, Worcester, MA 01602-0812. 1989. Pub'd 1 title 1990. 1 title listed in the *Small Press Record of Books in Print* (20th Edition, 1991-92). avg. price, cloth: $24.95; paper: $19.95. Discounts: 2-4 copies 20%, 5-9 30%, 10-49 40%, 50-99 45%, 100+ 50%. 467pp; 7x10. COSMEP, PMA.

Ediciones El Gato Tuerto (see also EL GATO TUERTO), Carlota Caulfield, PO Box 210277, San Francisco, CA 94121. 1984. Poetry, fiction, articles, plays, non-fiction. "We request a clean typed manuscript. Interested in new or unpublished Spanish and Latin American poets and writers. No simultaneous submissions accepted" avg. press run 500-3M. Pub'd 1 title 1990; expects 1 title 1991. 3 titles listed in the *Small Press Record of Books in Print* (20th Edition, 1991-92). avg. price, paper: $7.95. Discounts: 5-25 copies 40%, 26+ copies 50%. 120pp; 5¼x8¼; of. Reporting time: 3 months. Payment: each negotiated individually; no advance. Does not copyright for author.

EDINBURGH REVIEW, Peter Kravitz, 22 George Square, Edinburgh EH8 9LF, Scotland, 0315581117/8. 1969. Poetry, fiction, articles, art, photos, interviews, criticism, reviews, long-poems. "Contributors, recent & future include: Henry Miller, James Baldwin, Douglas Dunn, George MacKay Brown, David Daiches, Neal Ascherson." circ. 2.5M. 4/yr. Pub'd 4 issues 1990; expects 4 issues 1991, 4 issues 1992. sub. price: UK £12, o/seas £18; per copy: £2.95; sample: £2.95. Back issues: £2.95. Discounts: 35% to trade. 160pp; size A5 paperback; of. Reporting time: 1 month. Payment: by negotiation. Copyrighted. Pub's reviews: 32 in 1990. §Arts, history, politics, general literary. Ads: £75/£45. SPA.

Edition Gemini, Gernot U. Gabel, Juelichstrasse 7, Huerth-Efferen D-5030, Germany, 02233/63550. 1979. Criticism, letters, non-fiction. avg. press run 150-300. Pub'd 3 titles 1990; expects 3 titles 1991. 1 title listed in the *Small Press Record of Books in Print* (20th Edition, 1991-92). avg. price, paper: DM20. Discounts: trade 30%. 70pp; 6×8½; of. Reporting time: 1 month. Payment: yes. Copyrights for author.

Edition Stencil (see also C.S.P. WORLD NEWS), Guy F. Claude Hamel, Editor, Publisher, c/o Guy F. Claude Hamel, 1307 Bethamy Lane, Gloucester, Ont. K1J 8P3, Canada, 741-8675. 1962. Fiction, criticism, long-poems, collages, plays, concrete art. "Monthly literary magazine" avg. press run varies. 36 titles listed in the *Small Press Record of Books in Print* (20th Edition, 1991-92). 8½×14; †mi, lp. Reporting time: by return mail, 1 month. Payment: negotiable. Copyrights for author.

Editions Ex Libris, C.P. 294, Sherbrooke, Quebec J1H 5J1, Canada, 819-565-7093. 1987. Non-fiction. Expects 3 titles 1991, 1 title 1992. avg. price, other: $19.95 Can. thermo-binding. Discounts: bookseller 25%. 200pp; 5½×8½; of.

Editorial Experts, Inc. (see also THE EDITORIAL EYE), Ann R. Molpus, 66 Canal Center Plaza #200, Alexandria, VA 22314, 703-683-0683. 1972. Articles, reviews. "We publish *The Editorial Eye* and 7 titles for professional publications people" avg. press run 5M. Pub'd 1 title 1990; expects 1 title 1991. 7 titles listed in the *Small Press Record of Books in Print* (20th Edition, 1991-92). avg. price, paper: $12-$28. Discounts: inquire. 60-342pp; size varies; of. Reporting time: 2 months. Payment: inquire. Copyrights for author. Soc. Schol. Pub., Women's Nat'l Book Club, Amer Soc. Indexers, Washington Book Pub., Pub Marketing Assn., Edpress, Council of Biology Editors, American Medical Writers Assn., COSMEP, Bookbuilders.

THE EDITORIAL EYE, Editorial Experts, Inc., Ann R. Molpus, 66 Canal Center Plaza, Suite 200, Alexandria, VA 22314, 703-683-0683. 1978. Articles, reviews. "*The Editorial Eye* focuses on editorial standards and practices. Its purpose is to help its readers produce high quality publications. Information on content, usage, style, language, software, and production tips" circ. 2.5M. 12/yr. Pub'd 12 issues 1990; expects 12 issues 1991, 12 issues 1992. sub. price: $87 for 12 issues, Canadian subs add $5 per year, overseas $94 year prepaid, US funds; per copy: $6; sample: free. Back issues: $6. Discounts: 10% to subscription agencies. 12pp; 8½×11; of. Reporting time: 30 days, query. Payment: $25-$100. Copyrighted, does not revert to author. Pub's reviews: 25 in 1990. §Editorial matters, style guides, proofreading, editing, software, production info. Ads: inquire. ASI, SSP, Washington Book Publishers, Publishers Marketing Assn., Washington Edpress, Council of Biology Editors, American Medical Writers Assn., COSMEP, Women's Nat'l Book Assn., Bookbuilders.

Editorial Research Service, Laird M. Wilcox, P.O.Box 2047, Olathe, KS 66061, 913-829-0609. 1978. Articles, interviews, reviews, letters, news items. "Publications include: *Guide to the Occult and Paranormal* 1991, 2,000 listings; *Guide to the American Right* 1991, 2,000 entries; *Guide to the American Left* 1991, 2,000 entries; *Master Bibliography on Political Psychology, Propoganda, Espionage, Intelligence, Terrorism and Assassination*, 1989, 3,200 entries" avg. press run 410. Pub'd 3 titles 1990; expects 8 titles 1991. 4 titles listed in the *Small Press Record of Books in Print* (20th Edition, 1991-92). avg. price, paper: $24.95. Discounts: 10% single copies, 25% 5 or more copies; prepayment required. 108pp; 8½×11; of. Reporting time: 30 days. Payment: flat fee. Does not copyright for author.

Editorial Review, William R. Taylor, Robert T. Taylor, 1009 Placer Street, Butte, MT 59701, 406-782-2546. 1983. "Not printing any more books in the near future" avg. press run 1M. Expects 2 titles 1991, 2 titles 1992. 3 titles listed in the *Small Press Record of Books in Print* (20th Edition, 1991-92). avg. price, paper: $11.95. Discounts: bookstore 40%, flexible for distributors, etc. 100pp; 6×9; of. Reporting time: 1 month. Payment: profit-sharing plan. Copyrights for author.

Editor's Desk (see also EDITOR'S DESK; JUNIOR EDITOR), Florence F. Bradley, Editor-in-Chief; Susie Pettrey, Senior Editor; Florence Ryan, Editor, 709 Southeast 52nd Avenue, Ocala, FL 32671, 904-694-2303; 694-2289. 1982. "We have had one perfect bound anthology, *The Best Of The Editor's Desk* published in 1984 by Rainbow Books of Moore Haven, FL. We have put together nine anthologies on our own, printed locally + sold to the poets included in Anthologies for about $5. We started this because we heard so many complaints of, 'I'd like to see my work in print, but everyone charges from $19.95-$35!' We only make expenses. We did a free chapbook as Christmas gift to 300 poets 1984 & 1985 & 1986" avg. press run 500. Pub'd 6 titles 1990; expects 10 titles 1991, 15 titles 1992. avg. price, paper: $5. Discounts: anything over 5 is discounted. 108pp; 5×8½; †photocopied on Sharp 9500. Reporting time: within 3 weeks. Payment: negotiable. Copyrights for author.

EDITOR'S DESK, Editor's Desk, Florence F. Bradley, Editor-in-Chief; Susie Pettrey, Senior Editor; Florence Ryan, Editor, 709 Southeast 52nd Avenue, Ocala, FL 32671, 904-694-2303; 694-2289. 1982. Poetry, articles, photos, news items. "We put out an informative magazine in a chatty, friendly format. We do constructive criticism on a limited basis because of small staff + do not charge a fee. We print markets, contests, rip-offs, poems, 'Good News' of what our 'family of poets' has won or where they've been published. We've helped many poets get started and have many letters thanking us for the encouragement to try their wings and get published elsewhere. We held a writers conference last Sept. in Ocala FL (Sloan Wilson, Banquet speaker) and one near Atlantic City, NJ. And will do so again this year. Brochure for #10 SASE. 1987—4th annual conferences: Speakers include Judson Jerome (in FL & NJ)" circ. 500. 12/yr. Pub'd 13 issues 1990; expects 12 issues 1991, 12 issues 1992. sub. price: $16 ($14/yr renewal); per copy: $2; sample: $1 for postage. Back issues: we give them away. Almost none available. Current one is always available. Free for list of names + addresses to Writer's Group Members in any amount. No discounts except to Groups (5 or more from one group at same time - sub is $16/yr). 36pp; 8½×11; †typed, Sharp 9500. Reporting time: 1 month from receipt, usually. Payment: $1 poem, $5-$10 articles, 1pg or 1/2 pg - single spaced & typed, $5 cover poems. Copyrighted, reverts to author. Pub's reviews: 24-30 books, 100 mags in 1990. §Poetry, juvenile writing, articles. Ads: $5-10 an inch, classified. National and Florida Poetry Societies, CODA (Poets + Writers), International Women's Writing Guild (IWWG), Florida Freelance Writers Association (FFWA), Small Printers Assn.

EDITOR'S DIGEST, Rio Grande Press, Rosalie Avara, Editor, PO Box 371371, El Paso, TX 79937, 915-595-2625. 1989. Poetry, articles, art, cartoons, interviews, satire, criticism, reviews, letters, news items, non-fiction. "Non-fiction articles are limited to 500 words; news briefs and humorous fillers are limited to 150 words. Articles that help, inform or entertain editors are welcome. *ED* is *for* editors *by* editors. Recent contributions include: "Advice to Aspiring Editors"; "Editors as Artists/Cartoonists"; "The New Tax Code"; "Crossfire"; "Networking Really Works"; "Today's Problems"; and several editor profiles. Now in third year, and going strong. Annual contest for subscribers." circ. 50-75. 4/yr. Pub'd 4 issues 1990; expects 4 issues 1991, 4 issues 1992. sub. price: $15, $18 Canadian, $20 foreign (US funds); per copy: $4, $5 foreign (US funds); sample: $4, $5 foreign. 56pp; 5½×8½; photocopy, saddle stapled. Reporting time: 4-6 weeks. Payment: 1 copy. Copyrighted, reverts to author. Pub's reviews: 2 in 1990. §Small press operations, editor profiles, how-to books for editors. Ads: $35/$20/50¢ per word (10 word min.). El Paso Writers League, TX Freelance Writer's Assoc., El Paso MS Club.

Ed-U Press, Inc., Kathleen Everly, Ph.D., 7174 Mott Road, Fayetteville, NY 13066. 1973. "Books, pamphlets, audio-visual materials in the area of family life education. Primarily distribute to state agencies, libraries, schools, and bookstores" avg. press run 10M. Expects 3 titles 1991. 4 titles listed in the *Small Press Record of Books in Print* (20th Edition, 1991-92). avg. price, paper: $6.50. Discounts: 20-40% bookstores; 20-40% jobbers. 75pp; 6×9. Copyrights for author.

Educare Press, Shane O'Mahony, PO Box 31511, Seattle, WA 98103, 206-781-2665. 1988. Poetry, fiction, music, letters, non-fiction. avg. press run 2M. Pub'd 2 titles 1990; expects 3 titles 1991, 2 titles 1992. 3 titles listed in the *Small Press Record of Books in Print* (20th Edition, 1991-92). avg. price, cloth: $19.95; paper: $9.95. Discounts: usual. 200pp; 5½×8; of. Copyrights for author. PMA.

EDUCATION DIGEST, Prakken Publications, Kenneth Schroeder, Managing Editor, PO Box 8623, Ann Arbor, MI 48107, 313-769-1211. 1934. Articles, reviews, news items. "*Education Digest* does not accept original manuscripts, prior publication required. Selected by editorial board" circ. 28M. 9/yr. Pub'd 9 issues 1990; expects 9 issues 1991, 9 issues 1992. sub. price: $27; per copy: $4; sample: free on request. Back issues: $4. Discounts: agent 10%, individual multi-year rates= 2 yr $48, 3 yr $69. 80pp; 5½×8; of. Payment: honorarium possible for rights. Copyrighted, reverts to author. Pub's reviews: 40-45 in 1990. §Education. Ads: $1000/$650. Ed Press.

EDUCATION IN FOCUS, Books for All Times, Inc., Joe David, Editor, PO Box 2, Alexandria, VA 22313, 703-548-0457. "A quarterly newsletter which provides an *in focus* look at education from a rational and humane viewpoint" 4/yr. Pub'd 4 issues 1990; expects 4 issues 1991, 4 issues 1992. 6pp; 8½×11.

EDUCATIONAL FOUNDATIONS, Caddo Gap Press, Kathryn M. Borman, Co-Editor; Patricia O'Reilly, Co-Editor, 915 L Street, Suite C-414, Sacramento, CA 95814. 1986. Articles. "*Educational Foundations* seeks manuscripts of 20-25 double-spaced typewritten pages on issues, themes, research, and practice in the social foundations of education. Most contributors are scholars in the various social foundations disciplines." circ. 700. 4/yr. Pub'd 4 issues 1990; expects 4 issues 1991, 4 issues 1992. sub. price: $30; per copy: $7.50. Discounts: agency 10%. 96pp; 6×9; of. Reporting time: 1-2 months. Payment: none. Copyrighted, rights revert to author if desired. §§$100 full page. COSMEP, EDPRESS.

The Edwin Mellen Press, Herbert Richardson, PO Box 450, Lewiston, NY 14092, 716-754-2266. 1974. "United Kingdom Division: The Edwin Mellen Press, Ltd., Lampeter, Dufed, Wales SA48 7DY. Canadian Division: The Edwin Mellen Press-Canada, PO Box 67, Queenston, Ontario L0S 1L0, 416-533-4787. We now have a poetry series (The Lewiston Poetry Series). These are small hardbound books including works by first published poets. The price range is $10-$20. By the way, we pay NO royalties at all on ANY books, but also require NO subsidies. We also require camera-ready copy to our specifications" avg. press run 500. Pub'd 40 titles 1990; expects 60 titles 1991, 80 titles 1992. 29 titles listed in the *Small Press Record of Books in Print* (20th Edition, 1991-92). avg. price, cloth: $49.95; paper: $19.95. Discounts: 20% to resellers, special discounts for quantity orders, text prices for all books. 300pp; 6×9; †of. Reporting time: 2 weeks. Payment: none. Copyrights for author optional.

Wm.B. Eerdmans Publishing Co., Anita Eerdmans, Publicity Manager, 255 Jefferson Avenue, S.E., Grand Rapids, MI 49503, 616-459-4591. 1911.

EFQ Publications (see also EROTIC FICTION QUARTERLY), Richard Hiller, PO Box 4958, San Francisco, CA 94101. 1983. Fiction. "We publish an irregular serial *book/magazine* which is an anthology of literary-quality short stories with a variety of sexual and/or erotic themes. We do NOT publish book-length mss. at this time" avg. press run 1M. Pub'd 1 title 1990; expects 1 title 1991. avg. price, paper: $9.95. Discounts: 20% to the trade up to 10 copies, postpaid, dropshipped if requested. *Payment with order only.* 186pp; 5×8; of. Reporting time: 1 week to 1 month, usually. Payment: $50 for short fiction, all rights revert to author (after publication). We print an individual notice.

EFRYDIAU ATHRONYDDOL, University Of Wales Press, J.I. Daniel, W. Gealey, 6 Gwennyth St., Cathays, Cardiff CF2 4YD, Wales, Cardiff 231919. Articles. "Philosphical material." circ. 350. 1/yr. Pub'd 1 issue 1990; expects 1 issue 1991, 1 issue 1992. sub. price: £1.50; per copy: £1.50; sample: £1.50. Back issues: £1.50. Discounts: trade 10%. 80pp; 9½×6; of. Payment: none. Copyrighted, does not revert to author. Pub's reviews: 1 in 1990. §Philosophical. UWP.

e.g. (see also STIFLED YAWN: A Magazine Of Contemporary Writing), Marta Deike, Gary Sullivan, 3232 Taraval St. #7, San Francisco, CA 94116, 415-661-0851. 1983. Poetry, fiction, satire, long-poems, collages, plays, concrete art. "20-page mss max. Humor/satire given priority. Recent books by Richard Morris, George Albon, Daniel Davidson, Jamei Paul. Mostly chapbook material. Press previously owned by David Highsmith. We took over in January, 1990." avg. press run 350-500. Expects 5 titles 1991, 3 titles 1992. avg. price, paper: $3.50. Discounts: negotiable. 25pp; 5½×8½; laser press. Reporting time: 3 months. Payment: negotiate. Copyrights for author. COSMEP.

EGW Publishing Company (see also POPULAR WOODWORKING; CHILDREN'S ALBUM; NEEDLEPOINT PLUS; TOLE WORLD), 1320 Galaxy Way, Concord, CA 94520. 1979. 8⅛×10⅞.

E-Heart Press, Inc., Frances B. Vick, Lucille Enix, Judyth Rigler, 3700 Mockingbird Lane, Dallas, TX 75205, 214-741-6915. 1979. avg. press run 3M-5M. Pub'd 2 titles 1990; expects 2-3 titles 1991, 2-3 titles 1992. avg. price, cloth: $19.95; paper: $12.95. Discounts: 1-4 20%, 5-24 40%, 25-99 42%, 100+ 45%. 225pp; 6×9; of. Reporting time: depends on # of mss in house. Payment: different arrangements with different authors and projects. Copyrights for author. Texas Publishers Assoc. (TPA), Publishers Market Assoc. (PMA).

Eidos (see also EIDOS: Erotic Entertainment for Women, Men, & Couples), Brenda L. Tatelbaum, PO Box 96, Boston, MA 02137, 617-262-0096. 1982. Poetry, fiction, articles, art, photos, cartoons, interviews, satire, criticism, reviews, letters, parts-of-novels, long-poems, plays, non-fiction. "In addition to our quarterly journal for women, *Eidos*, we have published three poetry chapbooks/collections. Our *Boston Collection of Women's Poetry, Volume 1* is comprised of material submitted to our poetry contest of 1983. We are constantly looking for material to publish. We read everything. Our editorial bias is to present work on the subject of erotica for women. Material submitted to us is automatically considered for publication in *Eidos: Erotic Entertainment For Women, Men, & Couples*" avg. press run 10M. Pub'd 1 title 1990; expects 2 titles 1991, 1+ titles 1992. 3 titles listed in the *Small Press Record of Books in Print* (20th Edition, 1991-92). avg. price, paper: $10. Discounts: 5+ 50%. 11×17; †of. Reporting time: 4-6 weeks. Payment: contributor's copies.

EIDOS: Erotic Entertainment for Women, Men, & Couples, Eidos, Brenda L. Tatelbaum, PO Box 96, Boston, MA 02137, 617-262-0096. 1982. Poetry, fiction, articles, art, photos, cartoons, interviews, satire, criticism, reviews, letters, parts-of-novels, long-poems, plays, non-fiction. "*Eidos* is a quarterly journal for women, men, and couples regardless of sexual orientation, preference or lifestyle. *Eidos* is a forum for the discussion and examination of two highly personalized dimensions on human sexuality: desire and satisfaction. Both new and established poets, writers, and visual artists are invited to submit. Artwork/photography may or may not be used with accompanying mss. Copyrighted. Computer printout, simultaneous, and photocopied submissions OK. Phone queries OK or submit complete ms. 100% of material is freelance written. We especially look for explicit erotic fiction. Submit short bio" circ. 10M+. 4/yr. Expects 4 issues 1991, 4 issues 1992. sub. price: $30; per copy: $10; sample: $10. Back issues: $10. Discounts: 5+ 50%. 48pp; 11×17; †of TAB newspaper. Reporting time: 4-6 weeks. Payment: contributor copies. Copyrighted, reverts to author. Pub's reviews: 6 in 1990. §All dimensions of human sexuality, especially women and sexuality, women and pornography, women's images, etc. Ads: $375-$504/$200-$274/$20 -50 words.

Eight Miles High Home Entertainment, Andrew Darlington, 44 Spa Croft Road, Teall Street, Ossett, W. Yorks WF5 0HE, England. 1971. "We also do cassettes now."

El Camino Publishers, Bradley Stone, 340 Old Mill Road #225, Santa Barbara, CA 93110, 805-687-2959; 682-9340. 1981. "This is our first title: *Persuasion* was officially released May 1, 1982, and the book is available now" Expects 3 titles 1991, 3-5 titles 1992. 1 title listed in the *Small Press Record of Books in Print* (20th Edition, 1991-92). Discounts: standard. 189pp; 6½×9. Reporting time: 6 months. Copyrights for author.

EL GATO TUERTO, Ediciones El Gato Tuerto, Carlota Caulfield, PO Box 210277, San Francisco, CA 94121, 504-866-8598. 1984. Poetry, fiction, articles, art, interviews, criticism, reviews, parts-of-novels, plays. "We publish poetry only. Submit double-spaced, typewritten pages, 3-5 poems and bio information. SASE always. Interested in new or unpublished poets. We also accept 2 pages poetry book reviews. We publish in Spanish and English. Among our recent contributors are Soledad Farina, Jesus J. Barquet, Rolando H. Morelli, Luisa Futoransky, Miguel Angel Zapata, Gregory McNamee and Linda McFerrin" circ. 1M. 2-3/yr. Pub'd 2 issues 1990; expects 2 issues 1991, 2 issues 1992. sub. price: $8 individuals, $12 institutions; per copy: $1.50; sample: $2. Back issues: $2.00. Discounts: none. 10pp; 8½×11; of. Reporting time: 7-10 weeks. Payment: 2 copies. Not copyrighted. Pub's reviews. §Spanish & Latin American poetry. No ads.

El Montecito Oaks Press, Inc., Joseph E. Ross, 135 Santa Isabel Lane, Santa Barbara, CA 93108-2514, 805-969-5698. 1989. Non-fiction. avg. press run 3M. Pub'd 1 title 1990; expects 2 titles 1991, 2 titles 1992. 1 title listed in the *Small Press Record of Books in Print* (20th Edition, 1991-92). avg. price, cloth: $20. Discounts: 40%. 250-300pp; 6×9; of. Reporting time: 4 weeks. Does not copyright for author. ABA, PMA, Book Publicists of So. CA.

ELAN POETIQUE LITTERAIRE ET PACIFISTE, Louis Lippens, 31 Rue Foch, Linselles 59126, France, 20.03.48.59. 1955. "Poesie et temoignages au service du pacifisme integral, de la non-violence active et de l'objection de conscience permanente." circ. 2M. 3/yr. sub. price: 50f (environ $6); sample: free. 12pp; of. Not copyrighted. §Pacifism. APS.

ELDRITCH SCIENCE, George Phillies, 87-6 Park, Worcester, MA 01605. 1987. Poetry, fiction, art, reviews, long-poems. "Stories 5-15,000 words. Science fiction or fantasy poems must rhyme and have meter" circ. 250. 1-2/yr. Pub'd 2 issues 1990; expects 2-3 issues 1991, 3 issues 1992. sub. price: $10; per copy: $3. 36pp; 8½×11; of. Reporting time: 2-6 weeks. Payment: copies. Not copyrighted. Pub's reviews: 30-40 in 1990. §Science fiction fanzines primarily. SPWAO.

The Electric Bank, Inc., 4225 University, Des Moines, IA 50311, 515-255-3552. 1982. Art, photos. avg. press run 150. Pub'd 2 titles 1990; expects 2 titles 1992. 4 titles listed in the *Small Press Record of Books in Print* (20th Edition, 1991-92). Discounts: 30% jobbers. †computer printout. Payment: split edition. Does not copyright for author.

THE ELECTRONIC PUBLISHING FORUM, Serendipity Systems, John Galuszka, PO Box 140, San Simeon, CA 93452. 1990. Articles, criticism, reviews, news items. "This publication is 'printed' on IBM-PC computer disks and is distributed by shareware vendors." 4/yr. Pub'd 2 issues 1990; expects 4 issues 1991, 4 issues 1992. sub. price: $12; per copy: $4; sample: $4. Back issues: $4. Discounts: discounts to 45%. †IBM-PC computer disks. Reporting time: 4 weeks. Payment: 25% royalty, pro rated. Copyrighted, reverts to author. Pub's reviews. §Related to writing, electronic publishing, or similar topics. COSMEP.

THE ELEPHANT-EAR, Linda Thomas, Managing Editor, Irvine Valley Coll., School of Humanities, 5500 Irvine Center Drive, Irvine, CA 92720, (714) 559-9300. 1983. Poetry, fiction, articles, art, photos, interviews, criticism, reviews, parts-of-novels, non-fiction. "*The Ear* is primarily a journal of Orange County writers and artists. We have published work from writers outside the county, but our purpose is to provide a forum for local work. Work must be submitted in duplicate; the writer's name should not appear on the work, but should be attached on a cover letter with address, phone number, and brief bio" circ. 2.5M. 1/yr. Pub'd 1 issue 1990; expects 1 issue 1991, 1 issue 1992. 150pp; 6×9; of. Reporting time: 1-5 months. Payment: copies only. Copyrighted, reverts to author. Pub's reviews. §Contemporary poetry and fiction, art, film.

Elephas Books, Michael Woodhouse, Gail White, Alison White, 361 Orrong Road, Kewdalee WA 6105, Australia, 09 470 1080. 1988. Non-fiction. "Mostly how-to and information books, some novels, one poetry anthology per year" avg. press run 5M. Pub'd 9 titles 1990; expects 15 titles 1991, 20 titles 1992. 1 title listed in the *Small Press Record of Books in Print* (20th Edition, 1991-92). avg. price, paper: $10. Discounts: trade 40%, agent 60%. 200pp; 5¼×8; of. Reporting time: 6 weeks. Payment: 10% of recommended retail price. Copyrights for author.

11 X 13 - BROADSIDE, Toledo Poets Center Press, Joel Lipman, Editor, 32 Scott House, University of Toledo, Toledo, OH 43606. "A quality broadside devoted to poetry, commentary, literary gossip and announcements. Visual language, typography and paper featured." circ. 1M. 4/yr. Pub'd 4 issues 1990; expects 3 issues 1991, 4 issues 1992. sub. price: $5; per copy: $2; sample: $2. 1pp; 11×13; of. Not copyrighted.

THE ELEVENTH MUSE, Diane Robinson, PO Box 2413, Colorado Springs, CO 80901. 1982. Poetry. circ. 300. 2/yr. Pub'd 2 issues 1990; expects 2 issues 1991, 2 issues 1992. sub. price: $7 for 2 issues; per copy: $3.50 as bookstores; sample: $3.85. Back issues: $3. 48-56pp; 8½x11; of. Reporting time: 1 month. Payment: 1 copy. Copyrighted, reverts to author. Pub's reviews. §Poetry, the writing of, etc. Ads: $100/$50/$25/must be camera ready. Poetry West - 60.

ELF: ECLECTIC LITERARY FORUM (ELF MAGAZINE), Cynthia K. Erbes, PO Box 392, Tonawanda, NY 14150, 716-695-7669. 1990. Poetry, fiction, articles, non-fiction. "Fiction (maximum 2500 words); poetry (not to exceed 30 lines, but ELF will consider longer poems); essays (maximum 2500 words), subject matter limited to literary concerns, e.g.: creative process, various genres, critiques, etc. Not academic or scholarly. Premier issue Spring 1991 will feature poet Olga Mendel, a nationally published poet and Judson Jerome, editor of *Poet's Market*. Our focus, generally, is unpublished authors." circ. 600-700. 4/yr. Expects 4 issues 1992. sub. price: $16; per copy: $4; sample: $4. Back issues: $4 + 50¢ s&h (if available). Discounts: 25% negotiable. 52pp; 8½x11; of. Reporting time: 3-4 weeks. Payment: 2 sample copies. Copyrighted, reverts to author. Ads: $100/$50.

ELLIPSE, Charly Bouchara, Patricia Godbout, Univ. de Sherbrooke, Box 10, Faculte des Lettres et Sciences Humaines, Sherbrooke, Quebec J1K 2R1, Canada, 819-821-7277. 1969. Poetry. "Poetry in translation" circ. 750. 2/yr. Pub'd 2 issues 1990; expects 2 issues 1991, 2 issues 1992. sub. price: $10; per copy: $5; sample: $5. Back issues: $4-$5. 90pp; 5½x8½. Copyrighted. CPPA.

The Ellis Press, David Pichaske, PO Box 1443, Peoria, IL 61655, 507-537-6463. 1980. "We are primarily a non-fiction press, publishing whatever strikes our fancy. We are looking for the book that will sell 2-3M copies to an easily identifiable target audience, one that can be reached by direct mailings. We want the book, in other words, that is too small for New York to bother with, but the book with definite appeal to a specific region, interest group, etc. We are *not* interested in first novels, collections of poetry, literature with the capital L, experimental work, books that will depend upon reviews and/or bookstores to generate sales. Our standard arrangement is 50-50 with authors after publishing costs have been met, said costs to induce typesetting, printing, binding, and initial *but not subsequent* promotion." avg. press run 2M. Pub'd 1 title 1990; expects 3 titles 1991, 5 titles 1992. 14 titles listed in the *Small Press Record of Books in Print* (20th Edition, 1991-92). avg. price, cloth: $14.95; paper: $5.95. Discounts: large wholesalers/jobbers/bookstores: 2-5 books 20%, 6-25 40%, 26+ 40%; classroom 20%; independent bookstores, 5+ books 40%. 250pp; 8½x5½; of. Reporting time: rejections in 1 month; acceptances take time, depend on availability of $. Payment: 50% of sales after costs, costs to include typesetting, printing, binding, initial promo. Copyrights for author.

Elm House Christian Communications Ltd (see also CHRISTIAN FAMILY; TODAY; 21ST CENTURY CHRISTIAN MAGAZINE), 37 Elm Road, New Malden, Surrey KT3 3HB, England, 01-942-9761. 1966. Articles, photos, interviews, reviews, letters, news items. avg. press run 18M. Pub'd 3 titles 1990; expects 3 titles 1991, 3 titles 1992. avg. price, other: £1.20. Discounts: varies. 52pp; size A4, varies; of, web. Reporting time: varies. Payment: varies.

Elm Publications, Elaine Mynatt, PO Box 23192, Knoxville, TN 37933, 615-966-5703. Non-fiction. avg. press run 2M. Pub'd 1 title 1990; expects 1 title 1992. 2 titles listed in the *Small Press Record of Books in Print* (20th Edition, 1991-92). avg. price, paper: $10. Discounts: 1-5 books 25%, 6-99 books 40%, 100+ 42%. 210pp; 5½x8½. Reporting time: 2 weeks. Payment: 10% paid quarterly, no advance. Copyrights for author. COSMEP.

ELT Press (see also ENGLISH LITERATURE IN TRANSITION, 1880-1920), Robert Langenfeld, Department of English, University of North Carolina, Greensboro, NC 27412-5001, 919-334-5446. 1988. Criticism. "ELT Press publishes the 1880-1920 British Author Series. We print books which make available new critical, biographical, bibliographical and primary works on 1880-1920 British authors. Cloth-bound books on acid-free paper, dust jackets, end sheets." avg. press run 500. Pub'd 2 titles 1990; expects 2 titles 1991, 2 titles 1992. 6 titles listed in the *Small Press Record of Books in Print* (20th Edition, 1991-92). avg. price, cloth: $30. Discounts: 30% to jobbers, agents. 300pp; 6x9. Reporting time: 3-5 months. Payment: negotiable. Copyrights for author.

The Elvendon Press, Bernice Hurst, Director; Ray Hurst, Director, 33 Elvendon Road, Goring-on-Thames, Reading, Berkshire RG8 0DP, England, (0491) 873227. 1978. "Hardback and trade paperback cookery and food related books, general, reference book and magazine packaging" avg. press run 10M. Pub'd 4 titles 1990; expects 6 titles 1991, 10 titles 1992. Discounts: 35% shop, 45-50% on bulk orders (shipping not included). of. Reporting time: 4-6 weeks. Payment: individually arranged. Copyrights for author. IPG.

Elysium Growth Press (see also JOTS (Journal of the Senses)), Ed Lange, Publisher, 700 Robinson Road, Topanga, CA 90290, 213-455-1000. 1961. avg. press run 10M-15M. Pub'd 6 titles 1990; expects 4 titles 1991, 4 titles 1992. 17 titles listed in the *Small Press Record of Books in Print* (20th Edition, 1991-92). avg. price, cloth: $12.95; paper: $9.95. Discounts: 40%. 106pp; 8½x11; of. Reporting time: 30 days. Payment: yes. Copyrights for author. PMA.

180

Embassy Hall Editions (see also THE GALLEY SAIL REVIEW), Stanley McNail, 1630 University Avenue, Suite 42, Berkeley, CA 94703, 415-486-0187. 1985. Poetry. "For the present unsolicited mss. are not being accepted. If interested in having work published over this imprint, poets should query first. Paperbacks are principal if not entire output. Some chapbooks in future" avg. press run 500. Pub'd 2 titles 1990; expects 2 titles 1991, 2 titles 1992. 6 titles listed in the *Small Press Record of Books in Print* (20th Edition, 1991-92). avg. price, paper: $6 ($3 chapbooks). Discounts: 40% to retail book dealers on consignment orders. 24-50pp; 5½×8½; of. Reporting time: 3 weeks to 30 days. Payment: subject to negotiation with individual author. Copyrights for author. CCLM, COSMEP.

EMBERS, Katrina Van Tassel, Mark Johnston, Charlotte Garrett, Box 404, Guilford, CT 06437, 453-2328. 1979. Poetry. "Some recent contributors: Walter McDonald, Marilyn Waniek, Brendon Galvin. Strong, clear, resonant poetry on any subject. Accept/reject continuously. No deadlines" circ. 500. 2/yr. Pub'd 2 issues 1990; expects 2 issues 1991, 2 issues 1992. sub. price: $11; per copy: $6; sample: $3. Back issues: $5-The Poetry of Women. 58-64pp; 5×8 (varies); lp. Reporting time: up to 2 months after deadline. Payment: 2 copies, contest payments occasionally. Copyrighted, reverts to author. No ads. CCLM.

Embers Press, Rebecca Newsom, 2150 Portola Drive, Santa Cruz, CA 95062, 408-476-6164. 1975. Poetry. "Books of Santa Cruz women poets *published bi-yearly*. We are a collective and use any profit to publish future issues" avg. press run 1M. Expects 1 title 1991. 2 titles listed in the *Small Press Record of Books in Print* (20th Edition, 1991-92). avg. price, paper: $4-$10.95; other: $10.95 for coming anthology. 120pp; 6×8½; of, lp. Reporting time: 1 month. Payment: varies. Copyrights for author.

EMERALD CITY COMIX & STORIES, Wonder Comix, Nils Osmar, PO Box 95402, Seattle, WA 98145, 206-527-2598. 1985. Poetry, fiction, articles, art, cartoons, interviews, satire, reviews, letters, long-poems, news items. circ. 10M. 6/yr. Pub'd 5 issues 1990; expects 6 issues 1991, 6 issues 1992. sub. price: $5.25; per copy: $1; sample: $1.25. Back issues: $1 each (issues 2-7 available). 12pp; 11×17; web press—newsprint. Reporting time: 2-3 months. Payment: 2 contributor's copies. Copyrighted, reverts to author. Pub's reviews: 7 in 1990. §Fiction, poetry, graphics, cartooning, humor, regional books. Ads: $210/$110/$20 business card.

EMERGENCY LIBRARIAN, Dyad Services, Ken Haycock, Dept. 284, PO Box C34069, Seattle, WA 98124-1069, 604-734-0255. 1973. Articles, art, criticism, reviews, letters, news items. "Emphasis on library service to children and young adults." circ. 7.5M. 5/yr. Pub'd 5 issues 1990; expects 5 issues 1991, 5 issues 1992. sub. price: $45 billed, $40 prepaid; per copy: $9; sample: free on request. Back issues: on request. Discounts: on request. 80pp; 8½×11. Reporting time: 2 months. Payment: $50/article. Not copyrighted. Pub's reviews: 250 in 1990. §Professional materials for librarians, magazines for young people, new paperbacks for children, new paperbacks for young adults. Ads: $720/$400. COSMEP, Edpress, CMPA.

EMERGING, LP Publications (Teleos Institute), Diane K. Pike, PO Box 7601, San Diego, CA 92167-0601, 619-225-0133. 1972. Articles, photos, cartoons, letters. circ. 500. 2/yr. Pub'd 2 issues 1990; expects 2 issues 1991, 2 issues 1992. sub. price: $25 or more; per copy: $12.50; sample: free. Discounts: none. 54pp; 8½×11; of. Reporting time: 1 month. Payment: none. Not copyrighted. No ads. Teleos Institute (aka The Love Project).

Emily Press, Llewellyn McKernan, 4639B Route 10, Barboursville, WV 25504-9650. 1981. Poetry. avg. press run 500. 1 title listed in the *Small Press Record of Books in Print* (20th Edition, 1991-92). avg. price, cloth: $8; paper: $4. Discounts: 25% libraries. 51pp; 5½×8½; of, hire printing and publishing company to do printing of book. Reporting time: 6 months. Payment: 10% for author. Copyrights for author.

EMPIRE! The NYS Inmate Literary Arts Magazine, Paul Gordon, Arthur Kill Correctional Facility, 2911 Arthur Kill Road, Staten Island, NY 10309, 718-356-7333 ext 406. 1984. Poetry, fiction, articles, art, satire, reviews, music, letters, parts-of-novels, long-poems, non-fiction. "Open *only* to New York State writers incarcerated in a state prision" circ. 5M. 1/yr. Pub'd 1 issue 1990; expects 1 issue 1991, 1 issue 1992. sub. price: free. Back issues: free. 48-60pp; †of. Reporting time: depends, usually 1 month. Payment: in copies. Copyrighted, reverts to author. Pub's reviews: 1 in 1990. §Any literature related to prison & prison writing.

Empire Publishing Service, PO Box 1344, Studio City, CA 91614-0344. 28 titles listed in the *Small Press Record of Books in Print* (20th Edition, 1991-92).

Empty Closet Enterprises (see also HOT WIRE: Journal of Women's Music & Culture), Toni L. Armstrong, 5210 N. Wayne, Chicago, IL 60640, 312-769-9009. 1984. "*Women's Music Plus* is the annual directory of the feminist women's music and culture industry. Names/addresses/phone #s/descriptions—performers, writers, producers, distributors, festivals, publications, publishers, editors, organizations, coffeehouses, artisans, film/video, photographers, more; first directory published 1977" avg. press run 2.5M. Pub'd 3 titles 1990; expects 3 titles 1991, 3 titles 1992. avg. price, paper: $6. Discounts: 40% for order of 5 or more. 64pp; 8½×11; of. Payment: copies, cash, ad space, subscriptions. COSMEP, Chicago Women in Publishing (CWIP), Feminist Writers Guild.

THE EMSHOCK LETTER, Steve Erickson, Randall Flat Road, PO Box 411, Troy, ID 83871, 208-835-4902.

1977. Poetry, fiction, art, satire, criticism, letters, non-fiction. *"The Emshock Letter* is a philosophical, metaphysical, sometimes poetic expression of ideas and events. It covers a wide range of subjects and represents a free-style form of expressive relation. It is a newsletter quite unlike any other. (We are taking steps to expand our circulation). 'The writings range from down-to-earth, poignant, wise observations about dreams, love, suffering, and the ups and downs of the spiritual path to far-flung adventure tales...a mind-expanding journey to places you haven't been and may not even have known existed...' (The SUN Issue #123). Submissions accepted from subscribers only" circ. 20. 3-12/yr. Pub'd 12 issues 1990; expects 8-10 issues 1991, 8-10 issues 1992. sub. price: $25; sample: none, *one issue cannot adequately depict a publication of this nature.* Back issues: in yearly groups only, $25. Discounts: none. 5-7pp; 8½×11; high quality xerox on colored paper. Reporting time: variable. Payment: copies. Copyrighted, reverts to author. Pub's reviews: 1 in 1990. §Poetry, philosophy, metaphysics, spirituality. No ads.

EN PASSANT, Chess Enterprises, Inc., B.G. Dudley, 107 Crosstree Road, Coraopolis, PA 15108. Non-fiction. circ. 400. 6/yr. Pub'd 6 issues 1990; expects 6 issues 1991, 6 issues 1992. sub. price: $7. 16pp; 8½×11; of. Not copyrighted. Pub's reviews: 8 in 1990. §Chess only. no ads.

En Passant Poetry Press (see also EN PASSANT/POETRY), James A. Costello, 4612 Sylvanus Drive, Wilmington, DE 19803. 1981. "Not interested in dazzle or schlock or mean street ravings" 1 title listed in the *Small Press Record of Books in Print* (20th Edition, 1991-92). avg. price, paper: $4. 48pp; 5½×8½; of. Reporting time: immediate to 2 weeks. Copyrights for author.

EN PASSANT/POETRY, En Passant Poetry Press, James A. Costello, 4612 Sylvanus Drive, Wilmington, DE 19803. 1975. Poetry, art, reviews. "We prefer stylistic chastity (not desperation) that sacrifices everything to the poem" circ. 300. Irregular. price per copy: $3; sample: $3. 40pp; 5½×8½; of. Reporting time: 1-3 weeks. Payment: 2 copies, book reviews are paid for at the rate of $10 per printed page. Copyrighted, publisher takes first rights, shares remaining rights with author. Pub's reviews. §Books of poetry especially those published by small presses. Query first. No ads.

ENCYCLOPEDIA BANANICA, Banana Productions, Anna Banana, PO Box 3655, Vancouver, B.C., V6B 3Y8, Canada, 604-876-6764. 1990. Articles, art, photos, cartoons, satire, reviews, music, letters. "ISSN: 1180-5331. Any type of material with one important criteria, must be about or contain significant references to Bananas: newstories, information, facts, fantasies, poems, photos, cartoons, artworks, slang usage, such as 'going bananas', 'top banana', 'banana nose'. Also info about mail art publications" circ. 500. 2/yr. Pub'd 1 issue 1990; expects 2 issues 1991, 2 issues 1992. sub. price: $12/3 issues; per copy: $4; sample: $4. 4pp; 11×17 folded to 8½×11; of. Reporting time: 6 months. Payment: copies only. Not copyrighted. Pub's reviews. §Publications relating to mail-art shows, projects.

Endeavor Publishing, Hardie W. Daniel, 30064 Annapolis Circle, Inkster, MI 48141, 313-729-7836. 1967. Poetry, fiction, non-fiction. *"Magnificent Poet* by Hardie W. Daniel, an attractive navy blue hardcover book with title stamped in gold and colorful, sky blue jacket. 112 pages, printed in royal blue ink. Size: 5½ X 8½. *Magnificent Poet* is a meaningfully beautiful book of poems, lyrics, maxims and reflections—yet more than merely another book. It is a lovely masterpiece—a monument of love, beauty, wisdom, truth, and health. *Magnificent Poet* is an exciting journey in verse and is like no other book. 'A credit to all mankind.' -Tex Clark, President, Brite Star, Nashville. 'Exciting and rewarding.' -Marie Teasley, The Michigan Chronicle. 'A fancy, enchanting delight.' -Helen S. Lee, The Songwriter's Review. 'Uplifting and compassionate.' -Marsha A. Perkins, Uniquely Yours Review. 'A beautifully written book.' -Dr. Charles D. Miller, School District, City of Highland Park, Michigan. 'Superb thoughts conveyed through their best media, poetry.' -Barbara Fischer, Pennman Publications" avg. press run 1M. 1 title listed in the *Small Press Record of Books in Print* (20th Edition, 1991-92). avg. price, cloth: $10. Discounts: 20% to libraries; 40% to bookstores; 50% to book distributors and jobbers. 5½×8½; of. COSMEP, PASCAL, NAIP, SPEX, ASCAP.

Energeia Publishing, Inc., Laureal Williams, Janet Lockhart, PO Box 985, Salem, OR 97308, 503-588-2926. 1990. Non-fiction. "Paperback 150-250+. Personal and business self-help. Recent contributor: Norman C. Tognazzini" avg. press run 5M-10M. Expects 2 titles 1991, 4 titles 1992. avg. price, cloth: $8. 200pp; 5½×8½; full web. Reporting time: 2-3 months with SASE. Payment: per agreement. Copyrights for author.

ENERGY ASIA, Petroleum News Southeast Asia Ltd., Michael Morrow, Publisher, Managing Editor, 146 Prince Edward Road, West, 6th Floor, Kowloon, Hong Kong, 3-805294, 3-803029, 3-805794. 1979. circ. 300. 49/yr. Pub'd 49 issues 1990; expects 49 issues 1991, 49-50 issues 1992. sub. price: US $100; per copy: US $2; sample: free. Discounts: 10%-agency. 4pp; 6¾×8½.

ENERGY UNLIMITED, Rhetta Jacobson, PO Box 493, Magdalena, NM 87825-0493. 1978. Articles, photos, cartoons, interviews, reviews, letters, news items. "Non-conventional technology for the researcher, inventor and layman" circ. 500. 4/yr. Pub'd 2 issues 1990; expects 4 issues 1991, 4 issues 1992. sub. price: $125; per copy: $6. Back issues: non-subscribers sets only #5-#20: $125. Subscribers sets: $96. 48pp; 8½×11; of. Payment: none. Copyrighted, does not revert to author. Pub's reviews: 2 in 1990. §Energy, unorthodox research, inventors work. Ads: $500/$350/$200 1/4 page/$15 25 words/50¢ per word.

ENFANTAISIE: La Revue des Jeunes, Viviane Gould, Editor-Publisher; Michael Gould, Story Editor, 2603 S.E. 32nd Avenue, Portland, OR 97202, (503) 235-5304. 1983. Fiction. "Need short stories, maximum approx. 1,000 words, for youngsters ages 12 thru 16. Submit preferably in French, or we will translate. We pay $20 per feature needing translation, plus 3 free copies. Reprint submissions ok. Prefer fiction relating realistically to youngsters. Humor, dialogue preferred. No lengthy introspection. No complex imagery or vocabulary. No religious or inspirational. Include SASE for manuscript return" circ. 2M. 4/yr. Pub'd 6 issues 1990; expects 6 issues 1991, 4 issues 1992. sub. price: $16; per copy: $4; sample: same. Back issues: $4 apiece, 3 for $10, 6 for $18. Discounts: agent 10%, classroom orders (min. 5): available; please inquire. 28pp; 8½×11; of. Reporting time: 30 days. Payment: $20 plus 3 free copies. Copyrighted, reverts to author. Ads: $240/$120/$60 1/4 page/$30 1/8 page. Edpress.

English Language Literature Association (see also LINQ), Cheryl Taylor, Co-ordinating Editor; E. Perkins, Co-ordinating Editor, English Department, James Cook Univ-North Quensland, Townsville 4811, Australia. 1971. Poetry, fiction, articles, interviews, criticism, reviews, parts-of-novels, long-poems, plays. "Critical articles about 3,000 words, reviews 1,000 words" avg. press run 350. Pub'd 2 titles 1990. 100pp; 5½×8½; of. Reporting time: 2-3 months. Payment: small first publication fee paid; no further fees payable or royalties taken; contributors notified of requests for further publication and xerox by other bodies. Copyrights for author.

ENGLISH LITERATURE IN TRANSITION, 1880-1920, ELT Press, Robert Langenfeld, Department of English, University of North Carolina, Greensboro, NC 27412-5001, 919-334-5446. 1957. Articles, criticism, reviews. "ELT publishes essays on fiction, poetry, drama, or subjects of cultural interest in the 1880-1920 period of British literature. We do not print essays on Joyce, Lawrence, Yeats, Virginia Woolf, or Henry James unless these authors are linked with minor figures in the period. 7,000 words is usually the maximum length for an essay." circ. 800. 4/yr. Pub'd 4 issues 1990; expects 4 issues 1991, 4 issues 1992. sub. price: $13; per copy: $4; sample: free. Back issues: single-copy rate, discounts for run of 5 years or more. No discounts on regular issues. of. Reporting time: 3 months. Payment: none. Copyrighted, does not revert to author. Pub's reviews: 90 in 1990. §Those related to the 1880-1920 period of British literature. Ads: $75.

ENGLISH STUDIES IN AFRICA-A Journal of the Humanities, Witwatersrand University Press, G.I. Hughes, Witwatersrand University Press, WITS, 2050 Johannesburg, Republic of South Africa, 011-716-2029. 1958. Criticism. "English literary studies." circ. 350. 2/yr. Pub'd 2 issues 1990; expects 2 issues 1991, 2 issues 1992. sub. price: R10 (indiv), R20 (instit); per copy: R6 individuals, R11 institutions; sample: on application. Back issues: available on request. Discounts: 10% agents. 65pp; 21×15cm (A5); of. Reporting time: 3 months. Payment: none. Copyrighted, does not revert to author. Ads: R100/R50.

Enitharmon Press, Alan Clodd, 22 Huntingdon Rd, East Finchley, London N2 9DU, England, 01 883 8764. 1969. Poetry, criticism. avg. press run 400. Pub'd 3 titles 1990; expects 5 titles 1991, 4 titles 1992. 52 titles listed in the *Small Press Record of Books in Print* (20th Edition, 1991-92). avg. price, cloth: £8; paper: £4; other: £15 signed, numbered issue. Discounts: 33% on wrapped and hardbound issues, 25% on signed, numbered. 8V0; lp, of. Reporting time: 2 months. Payment: royalty.

ENSEMBLE, THE NEW VARIETY ARTS REVIEW, Corporeal Studio Ltd., J.R. Moore, Editor, One Hudson Street, New York, NY 10013. 1986. Articles, art, interviews, criticism, reviews, letters, news items, non-fiction. "A quarterly newsletter that covers variety arts, magic, mime, clown, juggling and the history of these and related art forms. The readers are performers, students, collectors, and performing arts libraries" circ. 10M. 4/yr. Pub'd 4 issues 1990; expects 4 issues 1991, 4 issues 1992. sub. price: $12; per copy: $5; sample: same. Discounts: $18 subscription. 16pp; 8½×11; †of. Reporting time: 2 weeks. Copyrighted, reverts to author. Pub's reviews: 10 in 1990. §Clown, mime, theater history, magic, cabaret, eccentric vaudeville acts. Ads: $500/$250/$125 1/4 page/$65 1/8/display ads.

Entrepreneurial Workshops Publications, 4000 Aurora Building, Seattle, WA 98103, 206-633-5350. 1985. Non-fiction. Expects 1 title 1991, 2 titles 1992. 2 titles listed in the *Small Press Record of Books in Print* (20th Edition, 1991-92). avg. price, paper: $7.95. 152pp; 6×9. Copyrights for author.

ENTROPY NEGATIVE, Les Recherches Daniel Say Cie., Daniel Say, Box 65583, Vancouver 12, B.C. V5N 5K5, Canada. 1970. Articles, art, interviews, criticism. "Articles related to SF or fantasy, 1000 to 10,000 words usually of a serious mean. We cannot use U.S. stamps. Use i reply coupons for return postage" circ. 500. 4/yr. Pub'd 4 issues 1990; expects 4 issues 1991, 4 issues 1992. sub. price: $2; per copy: 75¢; sample: 75¢. 40pp; 28×21cm; †mi, of. Reporting time: 1 month. Payment: copies. Copyrighted. Pub's reviews: 50 in 1990.

ENTRY, Jennifer Hill, Publisher & Editor, PO Box 7648, Ann Arbor, MI 48107, 313-663-4686. 1984. Photos, non-fiction. "*Entry* is a newsletter listing photographic, film, and video competitions and juried exhibitions, workshops, awards and grants, publications of note (not reviewed) and news of interest to photographers. Photographs and occasional articles are also published" circ. 2.5M. 10/yr. Pub'd 10 issues 1990; expects 10 issues 1991, 10 issues 1992. sub. price: $18, $30/2 years, foreign first-class air $30/year, $45/2 years; sample: $2. 6-8pp; 8×11; of. Reporting time: 2 months. Copyrighted, reverts to author. §Fine art, photography and anything pertaining to areas listed above under additional comments. Ads: $300/$180/$100 1/4/$60 1/8.

Envirographics, Sharon L. Basiewicz, Editor-in-Chief; John A. Harant, Editor & Publisher, Box 334, Hiram, OH 44234, (216) 527-5207. 1986. Non-fiction. avg. press run 10M. Pub'd 1 title 1990; expects 1 title 1991, 1 title 1992. 1 title listed in the *Small Press Record of Books in Print* (20th Edition, 1991-92). avg. price, cloth: $21.95; paper: $14.95. Discounts: dealers 5-40%, 100-45%, 200-50%, 500+ 55%. 250pp; 8½x5½; of. Does not copyright for author. Publishers Marketing Association (PMA).

ENVIRONMENTAL NEWS DIGEST, Sahabat Alam Malaysia (Friends of the Earth Malayasia), 43 Salween Road, 10050 Penang, Malaysia. 1983. "A collection of over 200 newsbriefs which is summarised from over 300 major magazines/periodicals on 3rd world development and environment. Very useful as reference and documentation source. Useful for people who like to know more on environment but do not have the time or money to read or subscribe to all the magazines available as this Digest is a collection of news taken from other magazines" circ. 500. 3/yr. Pub'd 3 issues 1990; expects 3 issues 1991, 3 issues 1992. sub. price: $40/airmail or $30/seamail for 2 years (6 issues); per copy: US$7; sample: same. Back issues: $3. Discounts: 20-25%. 60pp; 8¾x11¾; of. Reporting time: 3 months. Payment: none, as we are a non-profit voluntary group. Not copyrighted. Pub's reviews: 30 in 1990.

ENVIRONMENTAL OPPORTUNITIES, Sanford Berry, PO Box 4957, Arcata, CA 95521, 707-839-4640. 1982. News items. circ. 4.1M. 12/yr. Pub'd 11 issues 1990; expects 13 issues 1991, 13 issues 1992. sub. price: $44; per copy: $4.50 (latest); sample: free. Discounts: none. 12pp; 8½x11; of. Copyrighted.

Eon Publications (see also ISSUE ONE), Ian Brocklebank, 2 Tewkesbury Drive, Grimsby, South Humberside DN34 4TL, England.

EOTU, Magazine of Experimental Fiction, Larry D. Dennis, Editor, 1810 W. State, #115, Boise, ID 83702, FAX 208-342-4996. 1987. Fiction, art. "Fiction: Experimental. Try to stretch the boundaries of creative expression, in style, story content, or story structure. Preferably all three. Stretch the boundaries of your imagination and talent. Write beyond where you are now. Write something better, something different, something new. Break from the realm of the ordinary. If you aren't sure your work is right for *Eotu*, send it anyway. Let us decide. Artwork: Black ink on white. Any subject matter, any style. Mechanics: Manuscripts should be typed, double-spaced, on white 8½ X 11 paper. Your name, address, and word count should appear on the title page. Your name and story's name should also appear on each page of your manuscript. Please respect a word limit of 5,000 words. Please, no simultaneous submissions. Submit the manuscript with a SASE. Illustrations must be black ink on white. Reproductions are okay if the lines are clear. We prefer size between 3 x 4 inches to 8½ x 11 inches. Submit as many as you wish, just include your name, address, and title of work on each piece of art. Submit with SASE" circ. 500. 6/yr. Pub'd 6 issues 1990; expects 6 issues 1991, 6 issues 1992. 4 titles listed in the *Small Press Record of Books in Print* (20th Edition, 1991-92). sub. price: $18; per copy: $4; sample: same. Back issues: $4. Discounts: negotiated individually. 68pp; 5½x8½; †some offset, rest is photocopied. Reporting time: 6-8 weeks. Payment: $5-$25 for fiction, $5 for artwork. Copyrighted, reverts depending on what I bought. Ads: none. SPWAO.

L'Epervier Press, Bob McNamara, Editor; Bridget Culligan, Managing Editor, 5419 Kensington Place North, Seattle, WA 98103, 206-547-8306. 1977. Poetry. "We are not reading at this time. Full length books only. Books by: Paul Nelson, Lynn Strongin, Pamela Stewart, Jack Myers, Bob Herz, Michael Burkard, Christopher Howell, Carolyn Maisel, Robert Morgan, Bruce Renner, Sam Pereira, Robert Lietz, Paul Jenkins, David Lenson, Barry Seiler, Mary Burritt, Bill Nelson, James Crenner, Albert Goldbarth, Linda Orr, Floyce Alexander" avg. press run 500-1M. Pub'd 4 titles 1990; expects 4 titles 1991. 35 titles listed in the *Small Press Record of Books in Print* (20th Edition, 1991-92). avg. price, cloth: $20; paper: $8. Distributed by Small Press Distribution/Book Slinger. 64pp; 5½x8½; of. Payment: copies (10% of press run). Copyrights for author.

Epica (see also CHALLENGE: A Journal of Faith and Action in Central America), Minor Sinclair, Catherine Collins, 1470 Irving Street NW, Washington, DC 20010, 202-332-0292. 1968. Articles, interviews, reviews, news items, non-fiction. "Epica is a small press which specializes in titles on Central America and the Caribbean, focusing on U.S. policy and movements for social justice within the region. We have published 'primers' on six countries in the region, two editions of college textbooks on the Caribbean, two books on theoloical reflections within Central America, and several books on political analysis on Central America. We often combine theological reflection with political analysis. In addition, Epica publishes periodic reports on issues of current interest in the region. Our authors are predominantly Epica staff, though we will consider and occasionally publish outside authors' work." avg. press run 8M. Pub'd 2 titles 1990; expects 2 titles 1991, 1 title 1992. 6 titles listed in the *Small Press Record of Books in Print* (20th Edition, 1991-92). avg. price, paper: $8. Discounts: 20% for bulk (10 or more) or course adoptions; commercial bookstores 2-4 copies 20%, 5-9 30%, 10+ 40%. 250pp; 8½x11; of. Payment: to be arranged. Does not copyright for author.

Epicenter Press Inc., Kent Sturgis, Morgan Lael, 18821 64th Ave NE, Seattle, WA 98155, 206-485-6822. 1989. Art, photos, non-fiction. avg. press run 6M. Pub'd 3 titles 1990; expects 3 titles 1991, 4 titles 1992. avg. price, cloth: $24; paper: $16. Discounts: 40% retail; 50% wholesale; 20% libraries. 176pp; 8½x5½; of. Reporting time: 3 months. Payment: 10% of receipts. Copyrights for author. ABA, PMA, BPNW.

EPIPHANY: A JOURNAL OF LITERATURE, Sandra Reyes, Editor; Dora Rainey, Co-Editor; George Rainey, Sr. Technical Editor, PO Box 2699, University of Arkansas, Fayetteville, AR 72701. 1990. Poetry, fiction, satire, criticism, reviews, parts-of-novels, long-poems, plays. "We do not limit length except any piece should not be over 35 pages. We usually reserve this length for stories. For poems we prefer that a poem be no longer than 5 pages but will consider poems up to 10 pages. The above address is for manuscripts only. Send subscription fees and contest fees to *Epiphany*, PO Box 547, Fayetteville, AR 72701. *Epiphany* will be giving the Miller Williams poetry award annually beginning in 1992. Entrance fee $2 per poem. First prize $250." circ. 350. 4/yr. Pub'd 4 issues 1990; expects 4 issues 1991, 4 issues 1992. sub. price: $12; per copy: $4; sample: $4. Discounts: none. 80-120pp; 5½x8½; †lazer. Reporting time: 2-4 months. Payment: $2 per poem, $5 per story, varies with length; also 2 copies; $10-$15 for critical essay with bibliography. Copyrighted, reverts to author. Pub's reviews. §Literary criticism—20th century including post-modernism. Ads: $75/$50/$25 1/4 page/camera ready.

EPIPHANY JOURNAL, Stephen Muratore, PO Box 14727, San Francisco, CA 94114, 415-431-4388. 1980. Poetry, fiction, articles, interviews, criticism, reviews, non-fiction. circ. 1M. 4/yr. Pub'd 4 issues 1990; expects 4 issues 1991, 4 issues 1992. sub. price: $18.50; per copy: $7; sample: $7. Discounts: subs. agencies $16.50 per year, bookstores $14 per year (In USA). 80pp; 8x10¾; †of. Reporting time: 3 months. Payment: negotiable, 2¢ per word maximum. Copyrighted. Pub's reviews: 15 in 1990. §Religion, social criticism, ecology, psychology. Associated Church Press.

EPM Publications, Inc., 1003 Turkey Run Road, McLean, VA 22101, 703-442-7810. 1973. Non-fiction. "Non-fiction books about Washington, D.C., and the Mid-Atlantic region, plus a high-quality line of quilt books—mostly paperback, 8½ X 11, with color. We do not encourage submissions, prefer query letters first" avg. press run 5M. Pub'd 11 titles 1990; expects 12 titles 1991, 12 titles 1992. 56 titles listed in the *Small Press Record of Books in Print* (20th Edition, 1991-92). 250pp. Payment: competitive with big NY houses. Copyrights for author.

EPOCH, Michael Koch, Editor, 251 Goldwin Smith Hall, Cornell Univ., Ithaca, NY 14853, 607-255-3385. 1947. Poetry, fiction, reviews. "We are interested in the work of both new and established writers. Recent contributors include: William Kennedy, Michael Ondaatje, Bobbie Ann Mason, Robert Kelly, Wanda Coleman, Austin Wright, Marie-Claire Blais, Clayton Eshleman, Colleen McElroy, Joseph Langland, Josephine Miles, many other fine writers, some of whom are not yet well known. Submissions received between May 15 and Sept. 1 will be returned unread" circ. 1M+. 3/yr. Pub'd 3 issues 1990; expects 3 issues 1991, 3 issues 1992. sub. price: $11; per copy: $4; sample: $4. Back issues: varies. Discounts: 40% dealers, bookstores, etc. 100pp; 6x9; of. Reporting time: 2 months. Payment: copies, 2 subscriptions, $1/line poetry, $10 magazine page prose. Copyrighted, reverts to author. Ads: $180 (full cover); $160 (full page); $90 (half-page). CCLM.

Equality Press, Gayle Kimball, 420-CSUC, Chico, CA 95929, 916-895-5605. 1986. Non-fiction. "Booklets, videotapes, books on equality, issues between genders and ethnic groups" avg. press run 500. Expects 2 titles 1991, 3 titles 1992.

THE EQUATOR, Authony A. Aiya-oba, 509 Cultural Center, 509 Ellis Street, San Francisco, CA 94109, 415-561-0502. 1991. Poetry, articles, long-poems. "We are basically a magazine of *Nuclear Thinking: the principle of reconciliation of irreconcilables*, and therefore welcome all kinds of creative works, especially those that express unity in diversity among humanity, and seek the protection and preservation of our planet." circ. 10M. 4/yr. Expects 3 issues 1991, 3 issues 1992. sub. price: donation; per copy: free; sample: free. 5-14pp; 11x17. Reporting time: 1 month. Payment: negotiable. Copyrighted, reverts to author. Pub's reviews. §Books that promote cosmic consciousness, and unity in diversity. Ads: $500/$300/$175 1/4 page/$70 business card.

EQUOFINALITY, Rod Mengham, John Wilkinson, 147 Selly Oak Road, Birmingham B30 1HN, England. 1982. Poetry, fiction, criticism, long-poems. "Distributed in the U.S. by Segue. #1: John Wieners, Andrew Duncan, Out To Lunch, Barry Macsweeney, Andy Johnson, Geoffrey Ward, Nigel Wheale. #2: Mark Hyatt, Anonymous, Khaled, John Wilkinson, Letitia Matiza, Out To Lunch, John James, Nick Totton, R.F. Langley, Hugh Sykes Davies. #3: Andrew Duncan, Duncan McNaughton, J.H. Prynne, Stephen Rodefer, Denise Riley, Geoffrey Ward, Andy Johnson, John Wilkinson, R.F. Walker, and Edward Mycue" circ. 300. Published every other year. Pub'd 1 issue 1990; expects 1 issue 1992. 1 title listed in the *Small Press Record of Books in Print* (20th Edition, 1991-92). No subscriptions available; price per copy: £1.75 (1 & 2), £2.50 (3); sample: £1.75 (1 & 2), £2.50 (3). Back issues: same. Discounts: 33%. 60pp; size A4; of. Reporting time: 1 month. Payment: none. Copyrighted, reverts to author. ALP.

Robert Erdmann Publishing, Dr. Glenn Austin, Bob Erdmann, 28629 Meadow Glen Way West, Escondido,

CA 92026-9503. 1978. Non-fiction. avg. press run 12M-15M. Pub'd 7 titles 1990; expects 12 titles 1991, 12 titles 1992. 12 titles listed in the *Small Press Record of Books in Print* (20th Edition, 1991-92). avg. price, cloth: $18.95; paper: $12.95. Discounts: trade 40-50%. 250pp; 6×9; of. Reporting time: 60 days. Payment: negotiated individually. Copyrights for author. ABA, PMA, COSMEP.

Erespin Press, Carol Kent, Managing Editor; David L. Kent, Copy Editor, 1705 Raven Drive, Austin, TX 78752. 1980. Poetry, satire, non-fiction. "Particularly interested in historical translations" avg. press run 200. Pub'd 1 title 1990; expects 4 titles 1991, 4 titles 1992. 11 titles listed in the *Small Press Record of Books in Print* (20th Edition, 1991-92). avg. price, cloth: $25; paper: $15. 50pp; 6×9; †lp. Reporting time: 1 week. Payment: by arrangement. Copyrights for author. APA (Amalgamated Printers' Association), MBS (Miniature Book Society).

ERGO! THE BUMBERSHOOT LITERARY MAGAZINE, Louise DiLenge, Producing Editor; Judith Roche, Editor, One Reel/Bumbershoot, PO Box 9750, Seattle, WA 98109-0750, 206-622-5123. 1986. Poetry, fiction, articles, art, photos, interviews, criticism, reviews, parts-of-novels, long-poems, news items. "Office address: 414 Ponitus Avenue North, Suite B, Seattle, WA 98109. Recent contributors: Louise Erdrich, Andrei Codrescu, Susàn Griffin, Robert Creeley, Sonia Sanchez, Tama Janowitz, James Dickey. No unsolicited manuscripts. Write for contest rules" circ. 1.5M. 1/yr. Pub'd 1 issue 1990; expects 1 issue 1991, 1 issue 1992. price per copy: $6; sample: $6 + $1 postage. Back issues: $5 + $1 postage. Discounts: none. 96pp; 5¼×8½; of, layout. Reporting time: 2 months. Payment: inclusive in residency honorarium for most/others receive a fee. Copyrighted, reverts to author. Pub's reviews: 2 in 1990. §New literary works; only winners of Bumbershoot competition printed. Ads: call or write for current information.

The Erie Street Press, Henry Kranz, 221 S. Clinton Avenue, Oak Park, IL 60302-3113, 708-848-5716. 1976. Poetry, reviews, letters, news items. "Unsolicited manuscripts need not be sent. Will not consider unsolicited materials" avg. press run 1M. Pub'd 1 title 1990; expects 2 titles 1991, 2 titles 1992. 13 titles listed in the *Small Press Record of Books in Print* (20th Edition, 1991-92). avg. price, paper: $7. Discounts: 40% to all buyers of 5+ copies. 72pp; 5¼×8½; of, photocopy. Payment: cooperative contract, terms vary. Copyrights for author. Independent Literary Publishers Association.

Paul S. Eriksson, Publisher, Paul S. Eriksson, Peggy Eriksson, 208 Battell Building, Middlebury, VT 05753, 802-388-7303. 1960. "Summer address: Forest Dale, VT 05745, (802) 247-8415" avg. press run 4M. Pub'd 5 titles 1990; expects 6 titles 1991, 6 titles 1992. 21 titles listed in the *Small Press Record of Books in Print* (20th Edition, 1991-92). avg. price, cloth: $17.95; paper: $9.95. Discounts: trade distributions through Independent Publishers Group. of. Reporting time: 3 weeks. Payment: 10%, 12½%, 15%, standard contract. Copyrights for author. Oblivion Press.

EROTIC FICTION QUARTERLY, EFQ Publications, Richard Hiller, PO Box 4958, San Francisco, CA 94101. 1983. Fiction. "We use only short fiction 500-5,000 words (preferably around 2,500). Nothing else. Mostly non-commercial, highest quality creative work with sexual themes. No 'men's magazine'-type stories" circ. 500-1M. Irregular. Expects 1 issue 1991. No subscriptions available; price per copy: $9.95 (cover price). Discounts: 20% to the trade up to 10 copies, postpaid, dropshipped if requested. *Payment with order only.* 186pp; 5×8; of. Reporting time: 1 week to 1 month, usually. Payment: $50 for most lengths. Copyrighted, reverts to author. No ads.

ESCAPE, Paul Gravett, Publisher and Co-Editor; Peter Stanbury, Co-Editor, Escape Publishing, 156 Munster Road, London SW6 5RA, England, 01-731 1372. 1983. Fiction, articles, art, photos, cartoons, interviews, satire, reviews. circ. 12M. 6/yr. Pub'd 6 issues 1990; expects 6 issues 1991, 6 issues 1992. sub. price: US/Canada £22; per copy: £1.95/$4.95; sample: £2.55/$6. Back issues: £2.55/$6. 68pp; 8×11; of. Reporting time: minimum 2 months. Payment: minimum $35 per page for comic strips. Copyrighted, reverts to author. Pub's reviews: 80 in 1990. §Comics, illustrated books, cartoons, graphics. Ads: $300/$165.

Escart Press, Gary Brannon, Don Bonner, Environmental Studies, University of Waterloo, Waterloo, Ontario N2L 3G1, Canada, 519-885-1211 X3110. 1990. Non-fiction. "Softcover non-fiction 75-200 pages; biography of explorers; popular exploration (historical); geographical sciences; general trade books and academic." avg. press run 500-1M. Pub'd 2 titles 1990; expects 2 titles 1991, 2 titles 1992. 1 title listed in the *Small Press Record of Books in Print* (20th Edition, 1991-92). avg. price, paper: $10. 100pp; †of. Reporting time: 2-4 weeks. Payment: negotiable. Copyrights for author.

THE ESCHEW OBFUSCATION REVIEW, Pen-Dec Press, Jim DeWitt, 3922 Monte Carlo, Kentwood, MI 49512, 616-942-0056. "I shun the MFA/Academic/Literary "weightness." Show me real-world high-energy expressions, new-generation poetry with a flow shot-full of live language and originality. Astonish me! Special interests: eye-opening b&w art, wildly far-out avant garde, heavy-breathing erotica, untested experimental, goofy humor, slashing satire, total-freedom women's, micro-short narrative." price per copy: $2.95. Discounts: to be arranged. 36pp; 6×8½; †copier. Reporting time: 1 month. Payment: to be arranged. Not copyrighted.

Esoterica Press (see also NOTEBOOK/CUADERNO: A LITERARY JOURNAL), Ms. Yoly Zentella, PO Box 15607, Albuquerque, NM 87174-0607. 1983. Poetry, fiction, articles, art, interviews, criticism, reviews, music, non-fiction. "We encourage submission of manuscripts on cultural, literary and historical themes, fiction, non-fiction, and poetry. We emphasize Latino literature" avg. press run 200. Pub'd 2 titles 1990; expects 1 title 1991, 1 title 1992. 4 titles listed in the *Small Press Record of Books in Print* (20th Edition, 1991-92). avg. price, paper: $5.50-$8.50. Discounts: 20% subscription agents, distributors, wholesalers 45%, bookstores 30%. 80-100pp; 5½×8½; xerox of. Reporting time: 8-16 weeks. Payment: expenses paid first, profits—60% author, 40% publisher. Copyrights for author. CCLM.

Esquire Books, Inc., S. Jim Rahman, 50 Sand Street, Garnerville, NY 10923-1430. 1987. "We are a publisher of consumer health books. Our books deal with scientific and medical facts about human health. The information is presented in easy-to-understand language" Expects 2 titles 1991, 6 titles 1992. avg. price, cloth: $15. Discounts: 45-55%. 250pp; 6×9. Payment: 10%. COSMEP, Book Marketing Update, ABE.

ESSAYS ON CANADIAN WRITING, ECW Press, Jack David, Robert Lecker, Lorraine York, 307 Coxwell Avenue, Toronto, Ontario M4L 3B5, Canada, 416-694-3348. 1974. Articles, art, photos, interviews, criticism, reviews, letters. "We prefer intelligent, well-written criticism of Canadian writing from any period or genre. We lean towards formalist criticism, and specialize in bibliographies, small press reviews, and French-Canadian literature." circ. 1.3M. 3/yr. Pub'd 3 issues 1990; expects 3 issues 1991, 3 issues 1992. sub. price: $20 individuals, $40 institutions; per copy: $7; sample: free. Back issues: $7. Discounts: 40% trade. 250pp; 5×7½; of. Reporting time: 1 month. Payment: depends on need. Copyrighted, reverts to author. Pub's reviews: 20 in 1990. §Canadian writing or criticism. Ads: query. CPPA.

ETC Publications, Dr. Richard W. Hostrop, 700 East Vereda Sur, Palm Springs, CA 92262-1608, 619-325-5352. 1972. "Considers timely topics in all non-fiction areas" avg. press run 2.5M. Pub'd 10 titles 1990; expects 12 titles 1991. 19 titles listed in the *Small Press Record of Books in Print* (20th Edition, 1991-92). avg. price, cloth: $19.95; paper: $9.95. Discounts: usual trade. 256pp; 6×9; of. Reporting time: 4 weeks. Payment: standard book royalties. Copyrights for author. COSMEP.

ETICA & CIENCIA, Zagier & Urruty Publicaciones, Patricia Morales, PO Box 94 Suc. 19, Buenos Aires 1419, Argentina, 541-572-1050. 1987. Articles, reviews, non-fiction. "U.S.A. adress: 6630 Indian Creek Drive #223, Miami Beach, FL 33141. We receive articles about scientific ethics and moral questions of scientists. Maximum 20 letter pages. Spanish or English." circ. 1.5M. 2/yr. Pub'd 2 issues 1990; expects 2 issues 1991, 2 issues 1992. sub. price: $8; per copy: $4; sample: $4. Back issues: $4. Discounts: 50% distributors, 30% bookstores. 36pp; 8½×11; of. Reporting time: 3 months. Payment: none. Copyrighted, reverts to author. Pub's reviews: 16 in 1990. §Science, philosophy, history, biographies, ethics. Ads: $400/$200.

THE EUGENE O'NEILL REVIEW, Frederick C. Wilkins, Department of English, Suffolk University, Boston, MA 02114, 617-573-8272. 1977. Articles, art, photos, cartoons, interviews, criticism, reviews, letters, plays, news items, non-fiction. *"The Review's* aim is to serve as a meeting ground for O'Neill enthusiasts of academe and those of the Theatre. So it tries to blend critical articles of a scholarly sort, with news and reviews of current productions and publications. Articles of all sizes - from pithy notes to lengthy analysis—are welcome. Over-long articles are serialized. ISSN 1040-9483" circ. 400. 2/yr. Pub'd 2 issues 1990; expects 2 issues 1991, 2 issues 1992. sub. price: $10 for individuals in US + Canada, all others $15; per copy: $8; sample: free. Back issues: $8 per copy. Discounts: none. 120pp; 6×9; of. Reporting time: 2-6 months, frequently sooner. Payment: none. Copyrighted, permissions to reprint (with acknowledgement) are never refused. Pub's reviews: 8 in 1990. §Any books or magazines devoted to Eugene O'Neill (in whole or in part) or to 20th century drama and any film or stage performance of O'Neill's work. Ads: $400/$200. Eugene O'Neill Society.

Euroeditor (see also NEW EUROPE), P.M. Oostveen, PO Box 212, Luxemburg, Luxembourg. 1972. Poetry, fiction, articles, art, photos, interviews, satire, criticism, reviews, music, letters, parts-of-novels, long-poems, plays. "Eugene Guillevic (France), De Andrade (Portugal), Sjostrand (Sweden), Jorge Guillen (Spain), Humberto Diaz-Casanueva (Chile)" of. Reporting time: 4 months. Copyrights for author.

EUROPA 1992, Robert Wolfgang, Jayme Simoes, Peter Kobs, Wolfe Publishing, PO Box 7599, S. Station, Nashua, NH 03060, 603-888-0338. 1989. Articles, photos, interviews, criticism, letters. *"Europa 1992* is a monthly American business report on Europe. We bring the political, economic, social and geopolitical events of Europe to our readers, helping them see both opportunities and pitfalls" circ. 3M. 12/yr. Pub'd 12 issues 1990; expects 12 issues 1991, 12 issues 1992. sub. price: $119; per copy: $20; sample: free. Back issues: $20. Discounts: 10% bulk, 6 months free or 1 year subscriptions to schools. 40-50pp; 8½×11; of. Reporting time: 2-3 weeks. Payment: $300-$600. Copyrighted, reverts to author. Pub's reviews: 2 in 1990. §European affairs, international business and financial markets, international trade. Ads: $2,500/$1,500/$995 1/3 page/$750 1/4 page.

EUROPEAN JUDAISM, Albert H. Friedlander, Kent House,, Rutland Gardens,, London SW7 1BX, England, 071-584-2754. 1966. Poetry, fiction, articles, interviews, criticism, reviews, letters. "Recent contributors include Alan Sillitoe, Antonia Fraser, Elaine Feinstein, Jakov Lind, Edouard Roditi, Dannie Abse, F. T. Prince, Jean Starobinski. The name of the magazine describes its orientation" circ. 1M. 2/yr. Pub'd 2 issues 1990; expects 2 issues 1991. sub. price: £9 ($18); per copy: £4.50 ($9); sample: gratis from Pergamon Press. Back issues: as single copies. Discounts: 20% to agencies. 52pp; 9½×7; lp. Reporting time: 6 weeks. Payment: 1 free copy. Copyrighted, reverts to author. Pub's reviews: 20 in 1990. §Judaism spec. plus religion, philosophy plus history in general. Literary expression by Jews (poems, short stories), novels.

EUTHANASIA ROSES, Yehudi Niemand, Serendipity, 759 Cranberry Ridge, Fairbanks, AK 99712, 907-457-8691. 1990. Poetry, articles, art, cartoons, satire, criticism, reviews, letters, long-poems, collages, news items, non-fiction. "Any art must be xeroxable. *E.R* exists to get out anything I think noteworthy, whatever the category" circ. 75. 2-4/yr. Pub'd 2 issues 1990; expects 2-4 issues 1991, 2-4 issues 1992. price per copy: $1; sample: $1. Back issues: $1. 18pp; 9.5×11; †xerox. Payment: none. Not copyrighted. Pub's reviews: 7 in 1990. §Music (esp. alternative), murder, creative politics, fiction. Ads: $50/$30/$20 1/4 page.

Evans Publications Inc., Robert L. Evans, Publisher; Yvonne M. Evans, Managing Editor, 133 S. Main, PO Box 665, Perkins, OK 74059, 405-547-2144. 1969. Fiction, non-fiction. "Until recently have been publishers of specialized monthly tab newspapers, such as *Horse Country, Motor Sports Forum,* and other publications geared to local and regional readership. Have now entered book publishing field with three historical books, *Cimarron Family Legends,* Vols. I (1978) and II (1980) and *Kicking Bird and the Birth of Oklahoma* (1983) by D.E. Newsom; four reprints, *Stillwater: Where Oklahoma Began* (1969), *Stillwater: Through the Years* (1974) both by Robert E. Cunningham; *Manual of Formulas* (1932); and *Pistol Pete: Veteran of the Old West* (1980) by Frank Eaton; one historical novel, *Come in This House* (1982) by Helen Dutton Russell; one biography, *Echoes From The Hills* (1981) by Winnie Corley; and one cookbook, *Journal Visits: Recipes and Cooks* (1979). Purchased rights in 1984 to a history of Carney, Oklahoma, titled *The Tie That Binds* by Winnie Corley. Most recent publications include *Oklahoma's First Ladies* (1983) and *Oklahoma' First Ladies: Activity Coloring Book* (1983) by Lu Celia Wise" avg. press run 1M-5M. Pub'd 4 titles 1990; expects 3 titles 1991, 4 titles 1992. 9 titles listed in the *Small Press Record of Books in Print* (20th Edition, 1991-92). avg. price, cloth: $14.95; paper: $7.00. Discounts: 30% to 40% off list or cover price. 200pp; size varies; of. Reporting time: 90-160 days. Payment: we will pay royalty or purchase all rights. Does not copyright for author.

EVENT, Dale Zieroth, Douglas College, PO Box 2503, New Westminster, B.C. V3L 5B2, Canada, 604-527-5293. 1970. Poetry, fiction, art, photos, reviews, long-poems, plays. "Although we are devoted to those who are writing high-quality work but are not yet established, we feature prominent authors as well. Previous contributors include Lorna Crozier, Carol Shields, Tom Wayman, and George Woodcock" circ. 1M. 3/yr. Pub'd 3 issues 1990; expects 3 issues 1991, 3 issues 1992. sub. price: $13/yr (+ 91¢ GST), $22/2yr (+ $1.54 GST); per copy: $5.50 (+ 39¢ GST); sample: current $5.50 + 39¢ GST. Back issues: $4 + 28¢ GST. Discounts: 20%. 120pp; 6×9; of. Reporting time: 3-4 months. Payment: honorarium. Copyrighted, reverts to author. Pub's reviews: 22 in 1990. §Poetry, short fiction, photography, drama. Ads: $100/$50. CMPA.

The Everett Companies, Publishing Division, PO Box 5376, 813 Whittington Street, Bossier City, LA 71171, 318-742-6240; 800-423-7033. 1988. Non-fiction. "Our major publishing is in the area of geneology, history and children's nonfiction. We are beginning a series 'Jewels of the Past' and another, 'Jewels of Black History.' The editor of the series is journalist and historian Sue Eakin, retired professor of LSU. The books published and scheduled for publication are based on her original research" 23 titles listed in the *Small Press Record of Books in Print* (20th Edition, 1991-92). Discounts: most of our schedules are less than 20%; this will be subject to revision as sales increase. †of. Reporting time: 1 month. Payment: standard. Copyrights for author.

Esoterica, The Craft Press, M. Lawton, P. Lawton, 4545 San Juan Avenue, Port Townsend, WA 98368, 206-385-2318. 1985. "Esoterica Press is *primarily* interested in the Dianic tradition of the Craft of the Wise and Dedicated—commonly but inaccurately called Witchcraft—but will review any MS concerned with a related subject, including well reasoned arguments against the Craft. Any religious viewpoint is welcome. Most material should be under 20k words. Material of a speculative nature such as new (or reworked) theories is welcome as long as it is so marked by the author(s). No material will be considered if it is denigratory toward any religious belief, practice, or group. Prospective contributors should note that circulation of this type of material is very limited and could result in controversy; many groups are active in opposing the Craft and anyone who practices it! For this reason, Esoterica, The Craft Press, will respect an author's request to remain anonymous." Pub'd 3 titles 1990; expects 5 titles 1991, 5+ titles 1992. 6 titles listed in the *Small Press Record of Books in Print* (20th Edition, 1991-92). avg. price, other: $10 pamphlet/looseleaf. Discounts: trade and classroom 20%. 30pp; 8½×11; †mi, of. Reporting time: immediate (1 week or less). Payment: individual arrangement depends on copy. Does not copyright for author.

THE EVERGREEN CHRONICLES, Lisa Albrecht, Managing Editor, PO Box 8939, Minneapolis, MN 55408-8939. 1985. Poetry, fiction, art, photos, cartoons, satire, criticism, reviews, letters, parts-of-novels, long-poems, plays, non-fiction. *"The Evergreen Chronicles* has represented the literary and artistic talent of gay men and lesbian women from the Midwest region during the 1st two years of its publishing history. September

188

1987 marks the acceptance of nationwide submissions, while retaining a Midwest literary voice. We publish a wide spectrum of poetry, prose and artwork: writers may submit up to 10 pages of poetry, and up to one 25-page story; artwork should be 5 X 7 minimum and up to 8½ X 11. Send 4 copies of written work and include a short bio" circ. 450. 2/yr. Pub'd 4 issues 1990; expects 2 issues 1991, 2 issues 1992. sub. price: $15 individual, $25 institution or supporting member; per copy: $4; sample: $4. Back issues: $4. Discounts: 60% wholesale. 70pp; 5½x8½; high-quality Xerographic. Reporting time: 3-6 months. Payment: in copies. Copyrighted, reverts to author. Pub's reviews. §Gay and lesbian literature. No ads.

The Evergreen Press, Charles L. Lewis, PO Box 83, 1900 Brooklane Village #C-12, Ellensburg, WA 98926-0083, 509-962-3078. 1990. Articles, art, photos, cartoons, interviews, non-fiction. avg. press run 3M. Pub'd 2-4 titles 1990. 2 titles listed in the *Small Press Record of Books in Print* (20th Edition, 1991-92). avg. price, cloth: $25; paper: $18. Discounts: 1-4 books 20%, 4-10 30%, 11-50 40%, 51-75 42%, 76-200 46%, 201+ 50%. 300pp; 6x9; of. Reporting time: 1 month. Payment: 8 to 10%. Does not copyright for author. Publishers Marketing Association.

Evon Publishing, Evyonne Bickler, RT #1, Box 658, Elcho, WI 54428, 275-3887. 1987. Non-fiction. avg. press run 1M. Pub'd 3 titles 1990; expects 10 titles 1991, 25 titles 1992. 1 title listed in the *Small Press Record of Books in Print* (20th Edition, 1991-92). avg. price, paper: $12.50. Discounts: jobber. 150pp; 5½x8½; of. Reporting time: 6-8 weeks. Payment: negotiable. Copyrights for author. PMA.

EWING EXCHANGE, Kinseeker Publications, Victoria Wilson, PO Box 184, Grawn, MI 49637. 1987. Articles, reviews, news items, non-fiction. circ. 40. 4/yr. Pub'd 4 issues 1990; expects 4 issues 1991, 4 issues 1992. sub. price: $10; per copy: $2.50; sample: same. Back issues: $2.50. 10pp; 8½x11; †photocopy. Reporting time: 2 weeks. Payment: varies. Not copyrighted. Pub's reviews: 3 in 1990. §Genealogy.

Ex Machina Publishing Company, Margaret R. Robinson, Owner; Ronald L. Robinson, Editor, Box 448, Sioux Falls, SD 57103. 1986. avg. press run 2M. Pub'd 1 title 1990; expects 2 titles 1991. 3 titles listed in the *Small Press Record of Books in Print* (20th Edition, 1991-92). avg. price, cloth: $15-$25; paper: $10-$20. Discounts: 2 20%, 40% bookstores, 50%+ distributors. 200-250pp; 5½x8½. Reporting time: varies. Payment: 10%. Copyrights for author.

Exanimo Press, Dean Miller, PO Box 967, Cedar Park, TX 78613. 1964. Non-fiction. "40M words. Recent authors we published: Warren Mkeritch, *Beachcomber's Handbook*; Deek Gladson, *Owlhooter's Manual - The Poor Man's Guide to Financial Independence*; Tron Miller, *Gold Rocker Handbook*; Karl von Mueller, *Coinshooter's Handbook*. We are always alert for how-to-do-it material for the mass market, particularly material that will help readers become free of the time-clock and become independent. How to operate small businesses like fleamarkets, garage or yard sales, pawnshops, swap & rummage shops, itinerant services for retired people, etc. We prefer to buy acceptable manuscripts outright. *All books are available in 24X microfiches, including our out-of-print titles*" avg. press run 5M. Pub'd 10 titles 1990; expects 10 titles 1991, 5 titles 1992. 6 titles listed in the *Small Press Record of Books in Print* (20th Edition, 1991-92). avg. price, paper: $5. Discounts: 40% to dealers, 50% to jobbers. 48pp; 7x10; of. Reporting time: usually within 30 days; often 3 or 4 days. Payment: 10% quarterly, but prefer to buy manuscript outright to alleviate problems. Copyrights for author.

Excalibur Publishing, 434 Avenue of Americas, #790, New York, NY 10011, 212-777-1790. 1990. Fiction, non-fiction. "First book is a novel, *Bloomin* by Maria Ciaccia; second, a children's book, *Alpha Beta and Gamma*; third, *Auditioning for Opera* by Joan Dornemann of Metropolitan Opera; fourth, *By Actors For Actors*, a compilation of scenes and monologues, in 1991. We are interested in books targeting the performing artist as well as children's books and books of a light, entertaining nature. One of our projects for 1992 is *The Dumpy Handbook*, a humorous answer to *The Preppy Handbook*. Another 1992 project is *Hollywood Hunks of the 50's*, a photo-essay book about matinee idols of the 50's." avg. press run 2-3M. Expects 4 titles 1992. 2 titles listed in the *Small Press Record of Books in Print* (20th Edition, 1991-92). avg. price, cloth: $18.95. Discounts: 1-4 20%; 5-9 30%; 10-24 40%; 25-49 42%; 50-74 44%; 75-99 46%; 100-199 48%; 200+50%. 6x9. Reporting time: please query first, then 6 weeks. Payment: 10% of sales. Copyrights vary. COSMEP, PMA.

Excellence Enterprises, LaVonne Taylor-Pickell, 15831 Olden Street #71, Sylmar, CA 91342, 818-367-8085. 1980. Poetry, fiction, non-fiction. "No unsolicited mss." avg. press run 2M. Pub'd 1 title 1990; expects 1 title 1991. 1 title listed in the *Small Press Record of Books in Print* (20th Edition, 1991-92). avg. price, paper: $10. 224pp; 6x9; of. Payment: negotiated. Copyrights for author. COSMEP, PMA.

EXETER STUDIES IN AMERICAN & COMMONWEALTH ARTS, Richard Maltby, Queens Bldg., Univ. of Exeter, Exeter EX4 4QH, England. 1970. Articles. 1-2/yr. Expects 1 issue 1991, 1 issue 1992. price per copy: $10. Back issues: $3.50. 120pp; 6x8¼; of. Payment: none. Copyrighted.

Exile Press, Leslie Woolf Hedley, Guy Daniels, 241 South Temelec Circle, Sonoma, CA 95476, 707-996-8684. 1983. Fiction, articles, satire. "Innovative stories. Meaning an individual way of seeing, thinking and expressing one's fictive art with substance. No academic kitsch, Third World PR, pop-commercial or folksy mss. Have published over 96 different authors to date. Also publishers of *Fiction 83*, *Fiction 84*, *Fiction 86*, anthologies" avg. press run 500-1.5M. Pub'd 5 titles 1990; expects 3 titles 1991, 2 titles 1992. 11 titles listed in the *Small Press Record of Books in Print* (20th Edition, 1991-92). avg. price, paper: $7.95; other: $12.95 and up. Discounts: 30-40%. 116-248pp; 5½×8; †of. Reporting time: under 6 weeks. Payment: in copies. Copyrights for author.

EXIT, Center Press, Frank Judge, Poetry, Editor & Publisher; Mary Whitney, Art Director, 232 Post Avenue, Rochester, NY 14619-1313, FAX 716-328-7016. 1976. Poetry, fiction, art, photos, interviews, reviews, concrete art. *"Exit* publishes poetry, fiction, translations, interviews, and art work. We are interested primarily in *quality* and prefer shorter pieces. Past numbers have included Cimatti, Bonazzi, Lifshin, Johnson, Langlois, Salzmann, Glen, Rahmmings, and Shoemaker. *Please furnish brief bio-bibliographical blurb for use with accepted material."* circ. 600. Irregular. sub. price: $15/3 issues; per copy: $6; sample: $6 when available. Back issues: out of print/stock. 48pp; 5½×8½; of, xerox. Reporting time: 2 months. Payment: 3 copies. Copyrighted, reverts to author. Pub's reviews. Ads: $75 full page. COSMEP.

EXIT 13 MAGAZINE, Tom Plante, Editor, 22 Oakwood Court, Fanwood, NJ 07023. 1987. Poetry, fiction, art, parts-of-novels. "Previously published *Berkeley Works* Magazine (1981-1985). I seek manuscripts of poetry and short prose, most with a poetic view of the terrain familiar to the writer. *Exit 13* prefers a geographic bent and uses work from all over the U.S. and occasional contributions from outside these borders. Fresh faces and views are welcome. Back issues are available; checks should be made payable to Tom Plante." circ. 400. 1/yr. Pub'd 1 issue 1990; expects 1 issue 1991, 1 issue 1992. sub. price: $5; per copy: $5; sample: $5. Back issues: $3 *Berkeley Works*. Discounts: 40% for 5 or more copies of any one issue, prepaid. 50pp; 5½×8½; of. Reporting time: 2 months. Payment: copy of issue containing author's work. Copyrighted, rights revert to author but *Exit 13* keeps anthology rights. Pub's reviews: 5 in 1990. §Small press poetry and anthologies. Ads: $30 camera ready/$7 1/4 page camera ready.

Expanded Media Editions, Pociao, PO Box 190136, Prinz Albert Str. 65, 5300 Bonn 1, Germany, 0228/22 95 83. 1969. Poetry, fiction, art, photos, interviews, criticism, music, collages. "Recent contributors: W. S. Burroughs, Jurgen Ploog, Claude Pelieu-Washburn, Allen Ginsberg, Gerard Malanga, Paul Bowles" avg. press run 2M. Pub'd 3 titles 1990; expects 2 titles 1991, 4 titles 1992. 13 titles listed in the *Small Press Record of Books in Print* (20th Edition, 1991-92). avg. price, paper: DM 15. Discounts: 1-5 copies 25%, 6-20 30%, 21-50 40%, 50+ 50%. 100pp; 21×14; lp. Payment: 10% per sold book. Copyrights for author.

EXPERIMENT IN WORDS, Robert W. Howington, PO Box 470186, Fort Worth, TX 76147, 817-763-0158. 1990. Poetry, fiction, art, reviews. "I dont want stories or poetry that falls into a so-called category. I want original pieces that create new categories. Dont get your ideas from the newspaper or TV or movies. Originality is attainable. Try to keep it at 1,500 words or less. Publishes short shorts. Each story, poem and drawing published is eligible for the Writer, Poet and Artist of the year Awards. The story, poem and drawing judged best (by me) for that calendar year will garner a monetary prize for its creator. The award winners and monetary amounts will be announced in the year's final issue. For 1990, Chris Sumberg won Writer of the Year with his short story *Lambrusco Salvato-Dega, The Author of Aghast...*in Issue No. 5. Charles Bukowski won Poet of the Year for his poem *spark* in Issue No. 4. Howard Musick won Artist of the Year for his b&w drawings in Issue Nos. 1 and 4." circ. 200. 1/yr. Pub'd 5 issues 1990; expects 3 issues 1991, 1 issue 1992. sub. price: $5; per copy: $5; sample: $5. Back issues: #4 and #5 $2 each. Discounts: none. 50-60pp; 8½×11; †mimeo. Reporting time: 1-3 months. Payment: 1 copy. Copyrighted, reverts to author. Pub's reviews: 5 in 1990. §Experimental, literary. Ads: $10/$5/10¢.

EXPERIMENTAL BASEMENT, eXpEriMenTal presS, cl champiOn, 3740 N. Romero Road #A-191, Tucson, AZ 85705, 602-293-3287. 1991. Poetry, fiction, art, photos, reviews, concrete art, news items. "Varied magazine size and format. Sometimes triangular, on t-shirts, etc. Issues of 5 mags (little) in an envelope. 13 lines max. Uses experimental to the highest level and language and visual poetry." circ. 150. 3/yr. Expects 1 issue 1991, 3 issues 1992. sub. price: $8; per copy: $3; sample: $3, $5 for sampling of a variety of products. Back issues: $3. Discounts: 40% to libraries and for resale. 65pp; size varies; xerox. Reporting time: next day. Payment: 1 copy. Copyrighted, reverts to author. Pub's reviews. §Will review anything sent, from traditional to experimental, music, comics, video, anything! Ads: free to subscribers, otherwise inquire.

eXpEriMenTal presS (see also EXPERIMENTAL BASEMENT), cl champiOn, 3740 N. Romero Road #A-191, Tucson, AZ 85705, 602-292-3287. 1991. Poetry, art, photos, reviews, concrete art, news items. "Each product varies in size and format—such as poetry printed on a book of napkins, mini-books packaged in ice cubes, large pieces of paper folded about 50 times containing 100 poems, etc. Mainly publish poems no longer than 13 lines, some exceptions. Uses only the uttermost pioneering and experimental poetry being made today. Some language and visual poetry too." avg. press run 200. Expects 12 titles 1991, 24 titles 1992. avg. price, other: $2. Discounts: 40% for resale and libraries. 40pp; xerox. Reporting time: next day. Payment: average of 8 copies, depending on funds/sales. Copyrights for author.

EXPLORATIONS, Art Petersen, Editor, English Dept., Alaska Univ. Southeast, 11120 Glacier Highway, Juneau, AK 99801. 1980. Poetry, fiction. "A literary publication. Subject matter less important than quality. Poetry, fiction, fine arts. Best for submitters to purchase a copy first. Except for students, faculty, and staff of UAS, a reading fee is required: $2 per poem up to (10, 60 lines maximum) and $4 for each short story (up to 2, 2500 words maximum); those paying reader's fees in the amount of $4 or more will receive a copy of the publication" circ. 250. 1/yr. Pub'd 1 issue 1990; expects 1 issue 1991, 1 issue 1992. sub. price: $4/1 issue, $7.50/2 issues, $11/3 issues; per copy: $4; sample: $4. Back issues: $3. 52pp; 5½x8½; of. Reporting time: 6 months, December through April. Payment: copies, $100 best poem, $100 best short story. Copyrighted. No ads.

Explorer's Guide Publishing, 4843 Apperson Drive, Rhinelander, WI 54501, 715-362-6029. 1984. Non-fiction. avg. press run 2M-3M. Pub'd 2 titles 1990; expects 4 titles 1991, 4 titles 1992. 6 titles listed in the *Small Press Record of Books in Print* (20th Edition, 1991-92). avg. price, paper: $4.95-$8.95. Discounts: 40% bookstores, distributor rates on request. 112pp; 8½x11, 6×9; of. Payment: negotiable contract. Copyrights for author. Minnesota Independent Publishers Association (MIPA), Mid-America Publishers (MAP), Upper Midwest Booksellers Association (UMBA), Publishers Marketing Association (PMA), COSMEP.

EXQUISITE CORPSE: A Monthly of Books and Ideas, Andrei Codrescu, English Department, Louisiana State University, Baton Rouge, LA 70803-5001, 504-388-2982; -2823. 1983. Articles, art, photos, cartoons, interviews, criticism, reviews, letters, long-poems, non-fiction. "We are violent partisans of fresh air. Material should be opinionated, passionate, occasionally vicious & terminally beautiful. We prefer mostly short pieces but will publish rambles, diatribes, etc. Recent contributors include Nadia Marin, John Cage, Jean-Jacques Passera, Lawrence Ferlinghetti, Jonathan Williams, Ronald Sukenick, Richard Kostelanetz and Nanos Valaoritis. We solicit reports from abroad and from weird American cities like Denver" circ. 2.5M. 4/yr. Pub'd 4 issues 1990; expects 4 issues 1991, 4 issues 1992. sub. price: $15; per copy: $2.50; sample: $2.50. Back issues: $2.50. Discounts: 40%. 24pp; 6×16; of. Reporting time: 4 weeks. Payment: zilch/nada. Copyrighted, reverts to author. Pub's reviews: 6 in 1990. §Fiction, poetry, cultural criticism, film, music, art, architecture, political theory, philosophy. No ads.

EXUM Publishing, David Exum, Publisher, 5705 Cochiti Drive NW, Albuquerque, NM 87120, 505-881-4413. 1988. Non-fiction. "Practical nonfiction" avg. press run 1M. Expects 8 titles 1991, 4 titles 1992. avg. price, paper: $10. 100-150pp; 8½x11. Payment: negotiable.

EyeDEA Books, Emily Odza, Editor; Jeff Norman, Editor, 477 Rich Street, Oakland, CA 94609, 415-653-7190. 1990. Fiction, art, photos. "EyeDEA Books is dedicated to the publication of artists' books. We're specifically interested in books that explore the relationship between visual images and text, or that combine images and text in new, interesting ways. Only work that is appropriate for printing in black and white will be considered. SASE required for return of materials." avg. press run 1M. Expects 2 titles 1991, 2 titles 1992. 2 titles listed in the *Small Press Record of Books in Print* (20th Edition, 1991-92). avg. price, paper: $8.95. Discounts: trade 1-4 20%, 1-4 prepaid 40%, 5-24 40%, 25-49 42%, 50-99 45%, 100+ 47%; add 3% additional discount for prepaid order. 56pp; 5½x8½; of. Reporting time: 30 days. Payment: not established. Copyrights for author.

F

FACES: The Magazine About People, Cobblestone Publishing, Inc., Carolyn Yoder, Editor-in-Chief; Sarah E. Hale, Assistant Editor, 30 Grove Street, Peterborough, NH 03458. 1984. Articles, non-fiction. "*Faces* is designed to expose young people to other peoples and cultures of the world; to help them realize that no country is any better than any other; to learn and understand how other people live and do things; to see the world in new ways and to help them reflect on how they assign importance to things, ideas and people in their own lives." circ. 12M. 9/yr. Pub'd 10 issues 1990; expects 9 issues 1991, 9 issues 1992. sub. price: $21.95; add $6 for foreign mail; per copy: $3.95; sample: $3.95. Back issues: $3.95. Discounts: 20% for sub. agencies; schools, 5 or more $12.95 year sub. 40pp; 7×9. Reporting time: 6 weeks before publication. Payment: on publication. Copyrighted, Cobblestone Publishing buys all rights. Pub's reviews: 20 in 1990. §Books for children, age 8-14, related to themes covered. No ads. Classroom Publishing Assoc./Ed Press.

FACTSHEET FIVE, Mike Gunderloy, 6 Arizona Avenue, Rensselaer, NY 12144-4502, 518-479-3707. 1982. Articles, art, cartoons, interviews, criticism, reviews, letters, news items, non-fiction. "Typical issue contains reviews of 1,000 or more amateur publications, together with review columns on music, books, movies & misc. short pieces. Available for trade with any interested magazine. Not looking for columnists or reviewers" circ.

10M. 8/yr. Pub'd 6 issues 1990; expects 8 issues 1991, 8 issues 1992. sub. price: $23; per copy: $3.50; sample: $3.50. Back issues: varies; complete set now $100. Discounts: none. 144pp; 8½×11; of. Payment: none. Copyrighted, reverts to author. Pub's reviews: 3,000 mags, 150 books in 1990. §Everything: anarchy, humor, new science, fiction, poetry, local interest, natural living. Ads: $145/$80/25¢ per word.

FAG RAG, Good Gay Poets Press, Fag Rag Collective, Box 15331, Kenmore Station, Boston, MA 02215, 617-426-4469. 1970. Poetry, fiction, articles, art, photos, cartoons, interviews, satire, criticism, reviews, music, letters, parts-of-novels, long-poems, collages, plays, concrete art, non-fiction. "prefer short contributions; need new b & w art always" circ. 5M, readership 20M. 1/yr. Pub'd 1 issue 1990; expects 2 issues 1991, 2 issues 1992. sub. price: US $10 for 4 issues, international $15 for 2 issues; per copy: $5; sample: $5. Back issues: $2.50. Discounts: $3 retail; 40% to retailers, 50% to distributors. 32pp; 11×17; web. Reporting time: max. 3 months. Payment: copies. Copyrighted, reverts to author. Pub's reviews: 10 in 1990. §Politics, gay lit., poetry, essays, culture. No ads. CCLM, COSMEP, NESPA.

The Fair Press (see also SNOWY EGRET), Karl Barnebey, PO Box 9, Bowling Green, IN 47833, 812-331-8529; 237-3213. 1966. †of, lp.

Fairfield Press, Denise Denniston, Editor-in-Chief, PO Box 773, Fairfield, IA 52556, 515-472-7231. 1985. Non-fiction. "Interested in manuscripts related to the TM (Transcendental Meditation) program" avg. press run 10-15M. Pub'd 1 title 1990; expects 3 titles 1991. avg. price, paper: $9.95. Discounts: 30-50% depending on quantity. 300pp; of. Payment: 10-15%. Copyrights for author.

The Fairfield Street Press, Marian Nicely, 308 North Fairfield Street, Ligonier, PA 15658, 412-238-0109. "Although *The Ladies First Army,* the first book issued by the FFSP, is a self-publishing effort, the FFSP is a service company providing copy and photographs to newspapers, magazines, businesses and individuals. Editorial, desktop publishing, mailing and marketing assistance are also offered" 1 title listed in the *Small Press Record of Books in Print* (20th Edition, 1991-92).

Falcon Press Publishing Company, William Schneider, PO Box 1718, Helena, MT 59624, 406-942-6597; 800-582-2665. 1978. Poetry, photos, non-fiction. avg. press run 10M. Pub'd 15 titles 1990; expects 20 titles 1991, 30 titles 1992. 65 titles listed in the *Small Press Record of Books in Print* (20th Edition, 1991-92). avg. price, cloth: $23; paper: $9.95. Discounts: 40% retail accounts; 50% wholesale; 20% library; discounts increase with quantity. 200pp; 6×9, 8½×11, 10×13½; of. Reporting time: 4-6 weeks. Payment: royalty, payable every month. Copyrights for author. Rocky Mtn. Booksellers Assn., Mtns. and Plains, PMA, Intermountain Booksellers Assn., So. Cal Booksellers Assn., No. Cal Booksellers Assn., Pac. NW Booksellers Assn., UMBA, SEBA, MEBA.

Fallen Leaf Press, Ann Basart, PO Box 10034, Berkeley, CA 94709, 415-848-7805. 1984. Music, non-fiction. "We publish reference books in music and scores of contemporary American music. We do not accept unsolicited musical scores" avg. press run music 150, books 500. Pub'd 2 titles 1990; expects 3 titles 1991, 3 titles 1992. 8 titles listed in the *Small Press Record of Books in Print* (20th Edition, 1991-92). avg. price, cloth: $25; paper: music $18, books $24. Discounts: 1-5 20%, 6-10 25%, 11-20 30%, 21-29 35%, 30+ 40%. Music varies, books 200-400pp; size varies; of. Reporting time: 1-2 months. Payment: varies. We sometimes copyright for author. COSMEP.

Falling Water Press, 213 South Main, Ann Arbor, MI 48104, 313-747-9810. 1984. avg. press run 1M. Pub'd 1 title 1990; expects 2 titles 1991, 1 title 1992. 3 titles listed in the *Small Press Record of Books in Print* (20th Edition, 1991-92). avg. price, cloth: $10.95; paper: $4.95. Discounts: 40% (no minimum order). 5½×8½. Reporting time: 1-2 months. Copyrights for author.

FAMILY LIFE EDUCATOR, Network Publications, a division of ETR Associates, Kay Clark, PO Box 1830, Santa Cruz, CA 95061, 408-438-4060. 1982. Non-fiction. circ. 3.8M. 4/yr. Pub'd 4 issues 1990; expects 4 issues 1991, 4 issues 1992. sub. price: $35 indiv, $55 instit; per copy: $12. Back issues: $10. Discounts: $35 individual, $55 Agency/Institution. 40pp; 8½×11. Copyrighted. Pub's reviews: 20 in 1990. §Health, education, sexuality, family life. PMA, PGW.

The Family of God, Susann Flammang, Poetry Editor, PO Box 19571, Las Vegas, NV 89132, 702-795-8511. 1985. Poetry, art. "The Family of God is publishing *The World Harvest* series of international anthologies to benefit world hunger. The first of the series is *Poet's For Africa.* All the proceeds from the book will go toward the relief and recover of famine in Africa. Prefer short, inspirational poems on love, brotherhood, sisterhood, peace and world hunger. (Religious poems will be accepted.) We will be including art in future volumes. Send up to 6 poems or art work with a SASE. We also publish a bimonthly newsletter that includes poetry, art, and inspirational messages. We sponsor many poetry contests & awards throughout the year. We are always looking for inspirational and religious poetry to read on our "Good News" radio broadcast" Pub'd 1 title 1990; expects 1 title 1991, 1 title 1992. 2 titles listed in the *Small Press Record of Books in Print* (20th Edition, 1991-92). avg. price, cloth: $19.95; paper: $8.95. Discounts: 30%-40%. 5½×8½. Reporting time: 2-3 weeks. Payment: none;

The World Harvest series of anthologies are published to alleviate world hunger. Copyrights for author.

FAMILY THERAPY, Libra Publishers, Inc., Martin Blinder, Editor, 3089C Clairemont Dr., Suite 383, San Diego, CA 92117, 619-581-9449. 1960. Articles. circ. 1.5M. 3/yr. Pub'd 3 issues 1990; expects 3 issues 1991, 3 issues 1992. sub. price: $40/$35; per copy: $13; sample: $13. Back issues: $13. Discounts: 10% to subscriber agents. 128pp; 6×9; of. Reporting time: 3 weeks. Payment: none. Copyrighted. Pub's reviews. §Behavioral sciences. Ads: $150/$85.

THE FAMOUS REPORTER, Leah Nischler, Ralph Wessman, PO Box 319, Kingston, Tasmania 7051, Australia. 1987. Fiction, articles, interviews, letters, parts-of-novels, plays, news items. "We are interested in good writing in a variety of styles. Recent contributors have been Anna Bianke, Stephen Radic, Yve Louis, Kevin Brophy, Graeme Harper, Jenny Boult, Chris Mansell, Giles Hugo and Knute Skinner; interviews have featured John Tranter, Mary Blackwood and Georgia Savage. Contributions from outside Australia are welcome" circ. 200. 1/yr. Pub'd 1 issue 1990; expects 1 issue 1991, 2 issues 1992. sub. price: (AUS) $10/2 issues; per copy: (AUS) $5.50; sample: (AUS) $2 plus postage. Back issues: issues #3 $AUS2 plus postage. Discounts: AUS$3 each for orders of 5+ copies plus postage. 76pp; 5½×8; mi. Reporting time: 4 weeks. Payment: complimentary copy of magazine. Copyrighted, reverts to author.

FANS OF HORROR, Joseph Olszewski, Jr., 2802 Shelley Road, Philadelphia, PA 19152, 215-677-8146. 1988. Articles, art, cartoons, interviews, reviews, letters, news items. "Heavy emphasis on horror articles. Censorship articles or newspaper clippings. Obscure horror film reviews/underground films" circ. 220+. 4/yr. Pub'd 4 issues 1990; expects 3 issues 1991, 4 issues 1992. sub. price: $8; per copy: $2; sample: $2. Discounts: trade for other fanzines, magazines, books, etc. 36pp; 8×11. Reporting time: immediately. Payment: copies. Not copyrighted. Pub's reviews: 20 in 1990. §Anything pertaining to the horror genre (film, books, comics, magazines, etc.). Ads: $10/$5/inquire.

Fantagraphics Books (see also AMAZING HEROES; THE COMICS JOURNAL; LOVE & ROCKETS), Gary Groth, (Comics Journal); Kim Thompson, (Amazing Heroes), 7563 Lake City Way, Seattle, WA 98115. Articles, art, cartoons, interviews, criticism, reviews, news items. "Fantagraphics publishes the widest variety of classic and contemporary comics and cartoons of any publisher, including the works of Robert Crumb, Jules Feiffer, E.C. Segar, Winsor McCay, Harold Gray, Hal Foster, Gilbert and Jaime Hernandez, Peter Bagge, Dan Clowes, Ralph Steadman, Spain Rodriguez, Kim Deitch, Rick Geary, Jose Munoz, and Carlos Sampayo" avg. press run 6M. Pub'd 30 titles 1990; expects 35 titles 1991, 35 titles 1992. 54 titles listed in the *Small Press Record of Books in Print* (20th Edition, 1991-92). Comics 32pp, magazines 75pp; 8½×11; of. Reporting time: 1-2 months. Payment: royalties vary; payment on publication. Copyrights for author. COSMEP.

FARCE, Raleigh's Review of Alternative Arts, The Paper Plant, John Dancy-Jones, PO Box 543, Raleigh, NC 27602, 919-834-9203. 1988. Poetry, fiction, articles, art, photos, cartoons, interviews, satire, criticism, reviews, letters, news items, non-fiction. "Short reviews and news of local culture, documentation and criticism of work by emerging artists, listings of Paper Plant community events, each issue contains one non-fiction article on local or N.C. cultural arts (#1 ran a descriptive review of over 30 N.C. self-published magazines, past and present). Recent poetry by Bob Rogers, art by David Larson, essay by the editor. Poems under 100 lines, essays and letters under 400 words, reviews under 100 words, are accepted for consideration. We attempt to nurture and promote artistic efforts in non-established channels and forums" circ. 1M. 4/yr. Expects 4 issues 1991, 4 issues 1992. sub. price: $20, $12 student, subscribers receive special benefits; sample: $2. 24pp; 5½×10½; of, lp portfolio to subscribers. Reporting time: 6 weeks. Payment: copies and a subscription. Copyrighted, reverts to author. Pub's reviews. §Poetry, performance art, anarchic politics, situationist theory, William Blake, 'zines and comix. Ads: $12 per 1½ X 2½" unit (up to 3). N.C. Writer's Network, PO Box 954, Carrboro, NC 27510.

FARMER'S DIGEST, Farmer's Digest Publishing Co., Frank Lessiter, PO Box 624, Brookfield, WI 53008-0624, 414-782-4480. 1972. Articles, photos, cartoons, interviews, letters, news items, non-fiction. circ. 18M. 10/yr. Pub'd 10 issues 1990; expects 10 issues 1991, 10 issues 1992. sub. price: $15; per copy: $3; sample: $3. Back issues: $3. 100pp; 6×9; of. Reporting time: none. Payment: none. Copyrighted, does not revert to author. Pub's reviews: 15 in 1990.

Farmer's Digest Publishing Co. (see also FARMER'S DIGEST), Frank Lessiter, PO Box 624, Brookfield, WI 53008-0624, 414-782-4480. 1938. Photos, cartoons, interviews. avg. press run 2.5M. Pub'd 2 titles 1990; expects 3 titles 1991, 5 titles 1992. avg. price, cloth: $20.95; paper: $8.95. Discounts: trade, bulk. 150pp; 6×9; of. Reporting time: 45 days. Payment: yes. Copyrights for author.

FARMER'S MARKET, John E. Hughes, Lisa Ress, Jean C. Lee, Jim McCurry, PO Box 1272, Galesburg, IL 61402. 1981. Poetry, fiction, art, photos, interviews, satire, parts-of-novels, long-poems, plays, non-fiction. "We are looking for serious, high-quality work" circ. 500. 2/yr. Pub'd 2 issues 1990; expects 2 issues 1991, 2 issues 1992. sub. price: $8; per copy: $4.50 + $1 p/h; sample: $3.50 + $1 p/h. Discounts: negotiable. 100pp; 5½×8½; of. Reporting time: 6-10 weeks. Payment: 1 copy. Not copyrighted. CLMP.

Farragut Publishing Co., Daniel Rapoport, Publisher; Elizabeth Webber, Senior Editor, 2033 M Street N.W., Washington, DC 20036, 202-872-4009; fax 202-872-4703. 1984. Non-fiction. "We publish quality trade non-fiction" avg. press run varies. Pub'd 3 titles 1990; expects 3 titles 1991, 3 titles 1992. 12 titles listed in the *Small Press Record of Books in Print* (20th Edition, 1991-92). avg. price, cloth: $21.95; paper: $10.95. Discounts: trade 1-4 copies 20%, 5-19 43%, 20+ 50%; wholesale/non-returnable 50%; schools and libraries 25%. Pages vary; 6×9; of. Reporting time: usually within 1 month. Payment: partnership agreement. Copyrights for author. COSMEP, PMA.

Fast Forward Publishing, R. Wayne Parker, PO Box 45153, Seattle, WA 98145-0153, 206-527-3112; fax 206-523-4829. 1989. "Other address (for shipping): 5556 35th Avenue NE, Seattle, WA, 98105-2312, (206) 527-0914. Although our first title, *The Computer Buyer's Handbook*, is self-published, our intention is to solicit and publish works from other writers as well. For the time being, our focus is on how-to books relating to popular consumer commodities, especially computers and consumer electronics. Later, we hope to expand into other non-fiction areas.' avg. press run 3M. Expects 3-5 titles 1991, 5-8 titles 1992. 1 title listed in the *Small Press Record of Books in Print* (20th Edition, 1991-92). avg. price, paper: $16.95. 256pp; 5¼×8¼; of. Reporting time: 30 days. Payment: negotiable. Copyrights negotiable. COSMEP.

FAT TUESDAY, F.M. Cotolo, Editor-in-Chief; B. Lyle Tabor, Associate Editor; Thom Savion, Associate Editor; Lionel Stevroid, Associate Editor; Kristen Vonoehrke, Managing Editor, 8125 Jonestown Road, Harrisburg, PA 17112, 717-469-7159. 1981. Poetry, fiction, art, satire, parts-of-novels, collages. "As *Fat Tuesday* enters its second decade, we find that publishing small press editions is more difficult than ever. Money remains a problem, mostly because small press seems to play to the very people who wish to be published in it. In other words, the cast is the audience, and more people want to be in *Fat Tuesday* than want to buy it. Unfortunately, sales are important even for renegade presses. It is through sales that our magazine supports itself. This is why we emphasize buying a sample issue ($5) before submitting. We have calculated that if only 25 percent of the submissions we received in the last year had bought sample issues, we could have published four or five issues in 1990 as opposed to the one we struggled to release. Four more issues would have meant many more acceptances. As far as what we want to publish—send us shorter works. *Crystals of thought and emotion which reflect your individual experiences. As long as you dig into your guts and pull out pieces of yourself. Your work is your signature...Like time itself, it should emerge from the penetralia of your being and recede into the infinite region of the cosmos,* to coin a phrase. Certainly, perusing any of the seven issues we have published ($5 each) in the last decade will let you know what we admire in an author's work, an artist's stroke. We often answer submissions with personal comments, opinions, howdayados and the like. So, write to us, send us pieces of your self, buy sample issues (and keep this in mind for all other small presses, too), please use SASEs and remember *Fat Tuesday* is mardi gras—so fill up before you fast. Bon soir." circ. 350-500. 1+. Expects 2 issues 1991, 3 issues 1992. price per copy: $5; sample: $5. Discounts: inquire. 36pp; 5½×8½, 8½×11; of. Reporting time: have patience, but usually quick! Payment: 1 complementary copy in which work appears. Copyrighted, reverts to author. Ads: $100/$50/25¢ per classified word.

Fathom Publishing Co. (see also **ALASKA ASSOCIATION OF SMALL PRESSES**), Constance Taylor, Box 1690, Cordova, AK 99574, 907-424-3116. 1978. Articles, photos, cartoons, interviews, letters, long-poems, news items, non-fiction. avg. press run 3M-5M. Pub'd 2 titles 1990; expects 3 titles 1991, 2 titles 1992. 8 titles listed in the *Small Press Record of Books in Print* (20th Edition, 1991-92). avg. price, paper: $3.50-$15.00. Discounts: libraries 25%, bookstores 40% over 10 copies, 25% 5-10 copies, 10% less than 5. 200pp; †of. Reporting time: 1 month. Payment: varies. Copyrights for author. COSMEP, AASP - Alaska Assn of Small Presses.

FATHOMS BELOW, Daniel M. Wright, 1320 N.W. 76th Avenue, Plantation, FL 33322-4740. 1990. Poetry, fiction, photos, cartoons, interviews, reviews, letters, collages, non-fiction. "Strange stuff. Contains music & zine reviews, comics, collages, stories both fiction and nonfiction, quotes, and this and that" circ. 50-100. 1-2/yr. Pub'd 1 issue 1990; expects 2 issues 1991, 2 issues 1992. price per copy: $1; sample: 3 stamps. Back issues: none. Discounts: willing to trade, contact for other 'specials' 40pp; 5½×8½; †photocopy. Reporting time: submissions make next available copy. Payment: only thanks and a copy of the issue. Not copyrighted. Pub's reviews: 30 in 1990. §Weird stuff, anything bizarre, printing/publishing, engineering, comics/cartoons, etc. Ads: none.

FEELINGS, Carole J. Frew, PO Box 2625, Lehigh Valley, PA 18001, 215-264-7594. 1989. Poetry. "*Feelings* prints poems of joy and life. Max. length 20 lines. No pornography, political. Prefers upbeat, humorous, inspirational. Send self-addressed stamped envelope for free guidelines" circ. 500-700. 4/yr. Pub'd 4 issues 1990; expects 4 issues 1991, 4 issues 1992. sub. price: $18; per copy: $5.50; sample: current $5.50. Back issues: $3.50. Discounts: none. 52pp; 8½×11; †sheet-fed. Reporting time: 2-4 weeks. Payment: none, except 3 cash awards ($10) each issue. Copyrighted, reverts to author. Pub's reviews: 6 in 1990. §Poetry only. Ads: $25/$15/classified: 50 words for $10.

FELICITY, Weems Concepts, Kay Weems, Star Route, Box 21AA, Artemas, PA 17211, 814-458-3102. 1988. Poetry, fiction, articles, art. "Poetry to 36 lines, short stories to 2,500 words. No erotica—work must be in good taste. Recent contributors: Angie Monnens, Andria Watson, John Grey." circ. 150-200. 12/yr. Pub'd 12 issues 1990; expects 12 issues 1991, 12 issues 1992. sub. price: $15; per copy: $2; sample: $2. Back issues: $2. 30-40pp; 8½×11; †Sharp copier. Reporting time: approximately 2-3 months with copy of publication which shows winners of contest entered. Payment: cash awards for 1st, 2nd & 3rd place contest winners, copies to contributors. Copyrighted, reverts to author. Ads: info furnished upon request. PA Poetry Society, Walt Whitman Guild, UAPAA, National Arts Society, National Federation of State Poetry Societies Inc., New Horizons Poetry Club, Southern Poetry Assoc.

Fell Publishers, Inc. (see also COOKBOOK SERIES; DIET & HEALTH SERIES; FELL'S HEALTH SERIES; FINANCIAL PLANNING SERIES; GOOD COOKING SERIES), Elizabeth Wyatt, Sherri Adelman, Assistant Editor, 2131 Hollywood Boulevard, Hollywood, FL 33020, 305-925-5242. 1943. Non-fiction. "Fell Publishers, Inc. was founded in 1943, and is today one of the leading publishers in the United States. We currently publish 10 new titles each season, and look for titles that compliment our existing list of 175 backlist titles. The following are recent books just published: *White Collar Stress*, *American Recipe Collection*, and *How to Improve Your Odds Against Cancer*" avg. press run 5M. Pub'd 20 titles 1990; expects 20 titles 1991, 20 titles 1992. 29 titles listed in the *Small Press Record of Books in Print* (20th Edition, 1991-92). avg. price, cloth: $14.95; paper: $9.95. 212pp; 5½×8½; of. Reporting time: 3 months. Payment: 10% for cloth and 7% for paperback. Copyrights for author.

FELL SWOOP, Acre Press, X.J. Dailey, 1521 N. Lopez Street, New Orleans, LA 70119. 1983. Poetry, fiction, articles, art, cartoons, interviews, satire, letters, collages, plays, news items. "Recent contribs: Richard Martin, John Miller, Ronald Reagan, s. Zivvit 57, Andrei Codrescu, James Haug, Normandi Ellis, Randall Schroth, Ed Dorn, Flung Hy, Elizabeth Thomas, Gordon Anderson. Please remember *Fell Swoop* is a gorilla/guerilla venture. Our writers use language rather than ape suits or bullets..." circ. 300. 2-3/yr. Pub'd 3 issues 1990; expects 2 issues 1991, 3 issues 1992. sub. price: $6; per copy: $3; sample: $3. Back issues: all issues $3. Discounts: none. 20pp; 8½×11; †xerox. Reporting time: quick as can be. Payment: copies and immortality on demand. Not copyrighted.

FELL'S HEALTH SERIES, Fell Publishers, Inc., Sherri Adelman, Elizabeth Wyatt, 2131 Hollywood Boulevard, Hollywood, FL 33020, 305-925-5242. 1943. Non-fiction. "We are the leading publisher of one-shot magazines in the United States. We have four categories in which we publish. These are diet & health, health, cookbook series and financial planning series. We are looking for full manuscripts that would lend itself to these areas" circ. 50M. 8/yr. Pub'd 8 issues 1990; expects 8 issues 1991, 8 issues 1992. price per copy: $2.95. Back issues: cover price. 128pp; 5-3/16×7⅝; of. Reporting time: 3 months. Payment: negotiated. Copyrighted, reverts to author. Ads: $2,000. PBAA, ACIDA.

Fels and Firn Press, John M. Montgomery, Editor and Publisher, 33 Scenic Ave., San Anselmo, CA 94960, 415-457-4361. 1961. Criticism, letters. "I published (1977) my own essay about Kerouac whom I knew. This is a more than doubling of a 1970 pamphlet of mine published elsewhere. 2,500 - 2,600 copies. Distribution in U.K. as well" avg. press run 1.5M. Pub'd 1 title 1990; expects 1 title 1991, 1 title 1992. 2 titles listed in the *Small Press Record of Books in Print* (20th Edition, 1991-92). Discounts: trade 30-40%, bulk 50%, jobber various. 150pp; 5½×9½, 5½×8½; of, lp. Reporting time: 30 days. Payment: conventional. Copyrights for author.

THE FEMINIST BOOKSTORE NEWS, Carol Seajay, PO Box 882554, San Francisco, CA 94188, 415-626-1556. 1976. Articles, art, photos, cartoons, interviews, criticism, reviews, letters, news items. "*FBN* is the trade magazine for feminist bookstores and the Women-in-Print movement. It reviews over 250 books per issue. Articles focus on feminist book selling and the Women-in-Print movement" circ. 600. 6/yr. Pub'd 6 issues 1990; expects 6 issues 1991, 6 issues 1992. sub. price: $60; per copy: $6; sample: $6. Back issues: $6. Discounts: 10% jobber. 100pp; 7×8½; of. Reporting time: 3 weeks. Payment: copies. Copyrighted, reverts to author. Pub's reviews: 1,500+ in 1990. §Books by, for, and about women—of interest to feminist bookstores and libraries. Ads: $660/$385/$2 per 25 characters. COSMEP.

FEMINIST COLLECTIONS: A QUARTERLY OF WOMEN'S STUDIES RESOURCES, Women's Studies Librarian, University of Wisconsin System, Susan Searing, Linda Shult, 112A Memorial Library, 728 State Street, Madison, WI 53706, 608-263-5754. 1980. Articles, interviews, criticism, reviews, non-fiction. "Publishes on topics such as feminist publishing, bookselling and distribution; feminist issues in librarianship; and resources for feminist research. Contributors are drawn mostly from the University of Wisconsin System." circ. 1.1M. 4/yr. Pub'd 4 issues 1990; expects 4 issues 1991, 4 issues 1992. sub. price: $23 individuals and women's programs, $43 institutions (includes subscriptions to *Feminist Collections*, *Feminist Periodicals*, and *New Books On Women & Feminism*); sample: $2.75. 30pp; 8½×11; desktop publishing; offset printing. Reporting time: 1-2 weeks. Payment: we are unfortunately unable to pay contributors. Not copyrighted. Pub's reviews: 84 in 1990. §Any feminist or women-related books or magazines are of interest and help us stay current; we particularly note feminist reference works.

Feminist Mens' Publications (see also CHANGING MEN), Peter Bresnick, Business Manager; Michael Biernbaum, Editor; Rick Cote, Editor, 306 N. Brooks #305, Madison, WI 53715, 608-256-2565. 1979. Poetry, fiction, articles, art, photos, cartoons, reviews, letters, news items, non-fiction. *"Changing Men, The National Journal of the Anti-Sexist Men's Movement*, represents a new vision of masculinity, perfectly compatible with feminism and gay rights. Emphasis is given to aspects of manhood not covered in the patriarchal, competitive mainstream. *Changing Men* explores non-violence, spirituality, men's history, family, etc. towards a better understanding of what men expect and what may be expected of them, in a sometimes painfully changing world. *Changing Men* is our only publication at present. We may be seeking to expand in the future." avg. press run 5M. Pub'd 2 titles 1990; expects 2 titles 1991, 3 titles 1992. avg. price, other: $6. Discounts: see *Changing Men*. 52pp; 8½×10½; of, we have occasionally used elves. Reporting time: 3 months.

FEMINIST PERIODICALS: A CURRENT LISTING OF CONTENTS, Women's Studies Librarian, University of Wisconsin System, Susan Searing, Ingrid Markhardt, 112A Memorial Library, 728 State Street, Madison, WI 53706, 608-263-5754. 1981. "Designed to increase public awareness of feminist periodicals, this publication reproduces table of contents pages from over 100 periodicals on a quarterly basis. An introductory section provides bibliographic background on each periodical." circ. 1.1M. 4/yr. Pub'd 4 issues 1990; expects 4 issues 1991, 4 issues 1992. sub. price: $23 individuals and women's programs, $43 institutions (includes subscriptions to *Feminist Periodicals*, *Feminist Collections*, and *New Books On Women & Feminism*); sample: $2.75. 136pp; 8½×11; of. Not copyrighted.

The Feminist Press at the City University of New York (see also WOMEN'S STUDIES QUARTERLY), Florence Howe, Publisher; Susannah Driver, Senior Editor, 311 East 94 Street, New York, NY 10128, 212-360-5790. 1970. Fiction, non-fiction. "The Feminist Press is a non-profit, tax-exempt publishing house, engaged in educational change. We publish reprints of neglected women's writing, biographies, & materials for nonsexist curriculum at every educational level." avg. press run 3M-5M. Pub'd 10 titles 1990; expects 12 titles 1991, 12 titles 1992. 112 titles listed in the *Small Press Record of Books in Print* (20th Edition, 1991-92). Discounts: inquire (retail, wholesale, institutional). lp, of. Reporting time: minimum of 2 months. Payment: 10% of net. Copyrights for author.

FEMINIST REVIEW, Collective, 11 Carleton Gardens, Brecknock Road, London N19 5AQ, United Kingdom. 1979. Articles, criticism, reviews. "A socialist *feminist* journal aiming to develop both theory and political strategy of the women's liberation movement, and women's position worldwide" circ. 4M. 3/yr. Pub'd 3 issues 1990; expects 3 issues 1991, 3 issues 1992. sub. price: (institutions) £45 UK, $86 U.S., £50 rest of world, (individuals) £19.50 U.K., £24 overseas, $38 U.S.; per copy: £8.50. 128pp; 240×170mm. Reporting time: 2 months. Payment: none. Copyrighted, reverts to author. Pub's reviews: 4-8 per issue in 1990. §Women: theory, politics, fiction, research. Ads: £110/£70/£55 1/3 page/£45 1/4 page.

FEMINIST STUDIES, Claire Moses, Editor & Manager, c/o Women's Studies Program, University of Maryland, College Park, MD 20742, 301-405-7413. 1972. Poetry, fiction, articles, art, photos, cartoons, interviews, criticism, reviews, parts-of-novels. "Sonia Alvarez, 'Women's Participation in the People's Church.' Amrita Basu, 'The Challenge of Difference in the Women's Movement in India.' Ruth Behar, 'Reading the Life Story of a Mexican Marketing Woman.' Susan Groag Bell, 'Women Create Gardens in Male Landscapes: A Revolutionist Approach to Eighteenth-Century English Garden History.' Kathleen M. Blee, 'Women in the 1920s Ku Klux Klan Movement.' Victoria Brown, 'Los Angeles High Schools in the 1920s and 1930s.' Dorothy Sue Cobble, 'Rethinking Troubled Relations between Women and Unions: The Exceptional Case of Waitress Activism.' Christine Cone, 'Navaho Women's Networks and Sex-Gender Values in Transition.' Penelope Engelbracht, 'The Postmodern Lesbian Subject.' P. Gabrielle Forman, 'A Reading of the House of the Spirits and Song of Solomon.' Anne Goldman, '(Literary) Production and Reproduction in Dessa Rose and Beloved.' Marion Kaplan, 'Jewish Women in Nazi Germany.' Teresa de Lauretis, 'Feminist Theory and Historical Consciousness.' Patricia Moran, 'Unholy Meanings: (S)mothering and the Production(s) of Katherine Mansfield.' Molly Mullin, 'Representations of History, Irish Feminism, and the Politics of Difference.' Veena Oldenburg, 'Lifestyle as Resistance: The Case of the Courtesans of Lucknow, India.' Margarete Sandelowski, 'Infertility and Imperiled Sisterhood.' Ailbhe Smyth, 'The Floozi in the Jacuzzi.' Margaret Talbot, 'Flora Tristan and Utopian Allegory.' Paul Thomas, 'Jean-Jaques Rousseau, Sexist?' Lisa Vogel, 'Debating Difference: Feminism, Pregnancy, and the Workplace.'" circ. 7M. 3/yr. Pub'd 3 issues 1990; expects 3 issues 1991, 3 issues 1992. sub. price: $48 institutions, $24 individuals; per copy: $20 inst., $10 indiv.; sample: $20 inst., $10 indiv. Back issues: $10 indiv., $20 instit. Discounts: none. 200-250pp; 6×9; of. Reporting time: 3-4 months. Payment: none. Copyrighted, does not revert to author. Pub's reviews: 6 in 1990. §In all fields of women's studies, on feminism, on sexuality, on family, on human relations, on psychology, significant works by women authors. Ads: $250/$125.

FERGUSON FILES, Kinseeker Publications, Victoria Wilson, PO Box 184, Grawn, MI 49637, 616-276-6745. 1987. Articles, reviews, news items, non-fiction. circ. 40. 4/yr. Pub'd 4 issues 1990; expects 4 issues 1991, 4 issues 1992. sub. price: $10; per copy: $2.50; sample: same. Back issues: $2.50. 10pp; 8½×11; †photocopy. Reporting time: 2 weeks. Payment: varies. Not copyrighted. Pub's reviews: 2 in 1990. §Genealogy.

Feris-Lee, Press, John Santo, PO Box 560, Lodi, NJ 07644, 201-778-4163. 1987. Non-fiction. avg. press run 5M. Expects 3 titles 1991, 10 titles 1992. avg. price, cloth: $21; paper: $16. Discounts: wholesalers 50%. 200pp; 6×9; of. Reporting time: 6 weeks. Payment: royalty vary from 7% to 10% and payment advance from $100 to $5,000. Copyrights for author.

THE FESSENDEN REVIEW, Mho & Mho Works, Douglas Cruickshank, Editor; Max L. Dunseath, Literary Editor, The Reginald A. Fessenden Educational Fund, Inc., Box 7272, San Diego, CA 92107, 619-488-4991. Poetry, articles, photos, satire, criticism, reviews, letters, non-fiction. "Contributors should read magazine before submissions. Uninformed submissions are driving us to distraction!" circ. 12M. 4/yr. Pub'd 4 issues 1990; expects 4 issues 1991, 4 issues 1992. sub. price: $22/2 years, $44/5 years; per copy: $3; sample: $1.18 in stamps. Back issues: $3 when available. Discounts: 25% for than 10 copies of single issue. 80pp; 8½×11; of. Reporting time: 60 days. Payment: token — $15 up to 500 words; $30 thereafter. Copyrighted, reverts to author. Pub's reviews: 600 in 1990. §All areas, especially the world of small presses. Ads: $1000/$500/-1/4 page $250. COSMEP.

Festival Publications, Alan Gadney, Editor, 7944 Capistrano Avenue, West Hills, CA 91304. 1976. "Current books are *Gadney's Guide To 1,800 International Contests, Festivals, And Grants In Film And Video, Photography, TV-Radio Broadcasting, Writing, Poetry, Playwriting And Journalism, Updated Address Edition* awarded 'Outstanding Reference Book of the Year' by the American Library Association (5½ x 8½, 610 pages, $15.95 for softbound, $23.95 for hardbound, plus $1.75 each postage & handling)" avg. press run 5M. Pub'd 1 title 1990; expects 4 titles 1991, 8 titles 1992. 1 title listed in the *Small Press Record of Books in Print* (20th Edition, 1991-92). avg. price, cloth: $24.95; paper: $15.95. Discounts: bookstores 1-5 assorted copies 20%, 6+ 40%; wholesale up to 50%. 300pp; 8½×11. Reporting time: 6 weeks. Payment: trade standard. Copyrights for author. COSMEP, PMA, BPSC.

FESTIVAL QUARTERLY, Phyllis Pellman Good, PO Box 419, Intercourse, PA 17534, 717-768-7171. 1974. Poetry, articles, photos, interviews, reviews, letters, news items. circ. 5M. 4/yr. Pub'd 4 issues 1990; expects 4 issues 1991, 4 issues 1992. sub. price: $9.90; per copy: $3. 40pp; 8½×11. Reporting time: 6 weeks. Payment: 4¢ word. Copyrighted, reverts to author on request. Pub's reviews: 32 in 1990. Ads: $275/$165/$210 2/3 page/$125 1/3 page/$75 1/6 page.

FIBERARTS, Altamont Press, Inc., Ann Batchelder, 50 College Street, Asheville, NC 28801, 704-253-0468. 1973. Articles, art, interviews, criticism, reviews, news items, non-fiction. circ. 22M. 5/yr. Pub'd 5 issues 1990; expects 5 issues 1991, 5 issues 1992. sub. price: $21; per copy: $4.50; sample: $4.50. Back issues: $4.50. Discounts: shops 35% US, 35% Canadian + postage, 50% foreign + postage. 80pp; 8⅜×10⅞; of. Reporting time: 3 weeks. Payment: yes, depends on length, content, etc. Copyrighted, reverts to author. Pub's reviews: 20-30 in 1990. §Arts, textiles. Ads: $795/$440/90¢. SMPG.

FIBERWORKS QUARTERLY, Bobbi A. McRae, PO Box 49770, Austin, TX 78765, 512-343-6112. 1984. Articles, interviews, reviews, news items, non-fiction. circ. 1M. 4/yr. Expects 4 issues 1991, 4 issues 1992. sub. price: $14; per copy: $4; sample: same. Back issues: $4. 12-16pp; 8½×11; of. Payment: none. Pub's reviews: 16-22 in 1990. §Fiber arts, textile design, small business, publishing, writing, trends in the textile areas.

FICTION, Mark Jay Mirsky, Editor, c/o Dept. of English, City College, 138th Street & Convent Ave., New York, NY 10031, 212-690-8170. 1972. Fiction, parts-of-novels. "We are a journal of new directions for the novel and short story. *Fiction* has brought the unknown and famous together in handsome pages to an international and discriminating audience of readers for over 15 years. We represent no particular school of fiction, except the innovative and in that sense our pages have been a harbor for many writers often at odds with each other. As a result of our willingness to publish the difficult and experimental to look at the unusual and obscure, while not excluding the well known, *Fiction* has won a unique reputation in the U.S. and abroad" circ. 4M. 2/yr. Pub'd 1 issue 1990; expects 2 issues 1991, 2 issues 1992. sub. price: $20/3 issues; per copy: $6.95 single, $8.95 double; sample: same. Back issues: $8. Discounts: limited specials on selected back issues. 175pp; 6×9; of. Reporting time: 1-3 months. Payment: $50 or copies. Copyrighted, reverts to author.

Fiction Collective Two, Inc., Curtis White, Co-Director; Ronald Sukenick, Co-Director; Donald Laing, Managing Editor, Publications Center, Campus Box 494, Colorado Univ., Boulder, CO 80309-0494, 303-492-8947. 1974. Fiction. "Novels and collections of short stories. Members are authors we have published or are about to publish. Distribution through The Talman Co., 150 Fifth Avenue, New York, NY 10011, (800) 537-8894. Manuscript queries to Fiction Collective Manuscript Central, Dept. of English, Campus Box 494, University of Colorado, Boulder, CO 80309-0494" avg. press run 2.2M. Pub'd 6 titles 1990. 74 titles listed in the *Small Press Record of Books in Print* (20th Edition, 1991-92). avg. price, cloth: $18.95; paper: $8.95. Discounts: 1-4 books 20%, 5-19 40%, 20-34 41%, 35-49 42%, 50-99 43%, 100-149 44%, 150-299 45%, 300+

46%. 200pp; 5½×8½; of. Reporting time: 6 months to 1 year. Payment: 10% royalties, 75% of subsidiary rights sales. Copyrights for author.

FICTION FORUM, CHIPS OFF THE WRITER'S BLOCK, Wanda Windham, PO Box 83371, Los Angeles, CA 90083. 1989. Fiction. "Fiction to 1200 words published" circ. 500+. 4/yr. Pub'd 4 issues 1990; expects 4 issues 1991, 4 issues 1992. sub. price: $12; per copy: $3; sample: $3. Back issues: none. Discounts: to be arranged. 40pp; 5×7; †photocopy. Reporting time: 2-3 weeks. Payment: copy only. Copyrighted, reverts to author.

FICTION FORUM, The Dayspring Press, Inc., John C. Brainerd, 18600 West 58 Avenue, Golden, CO 80403-1070, 303-279-2462. Fiction. Discounts: 1/3 over 15 copies.

FICTION INTERNATIONAL, San Diego State University Press, Harold Jaffe, Larry McCaffery, San Diego State University, San Diego, CA 92182, 619-594-5443, 594-6220. 1973. Poetry, fiction, articles, art, photos, interviews, satire, criticism, reviews, parts-of-novels, non-fiction. "Direct editorial correspondence to Harold Jaffe & Larry McCaffery at the Dept. of English at the above address. Business correspondence should be directed to Harry Polkinhorn, Managing Editor, San Diego State University Press, San Diego, CA 92182. Note: Manuscripts will be considered for publication only if they are received between September 1 and January 15. Our twin biases are politics and technical innovation—either integrated in a particular fiction, or apart. Interested in fiction & theory. *Fiction International* does not regularly publish poetry—only occasionally in special issues." circ. 1M. 2/yr. Pub'd 1 issue 1990; expects 2 issues 1991, 2 issues 1992. sub. price: $12/individual, $24/institution; per copy: $6/individual, $12/institution; sample: $6. Back issues: Vol. 2-11, $3; Vol. 13-14, $5. Discounts: text 20%, library jobbers 30%, trade distributors 50%, trade 40%. No discount on single copy orders. 288pp; 6×9; of. Reporting time: 1-2 months. Payment: varies. Copyrighted, reverts to author. Pub's reviews: 5 in 1990. §Fiction, aesthetics, politics. Ads: $300/$160/$85 1/4 page.

THE FICTION REVIEW, Robert Spryszak, Editor, PO Box 72939, Roselle, IL 60172. 1987. Fiction, interviews, satire, reviews, parts-of-novels. "*The Fiction Review* will consider everything from the wildly bizarre to the more-or-less standard so long as it is memorable. Don't let ceremony stand in your way. Social content a plus but come ready with fiction, not a manifesto. Will use everything from sketches to short stories to things unknown. *No poetry*. Just bust a move. Thomas Wiloch, Rupert Wondolowski, Hugh Fox, Lorri Jackson and such" circ. 300. 2/yr. Pub'd 1 issue 1990; expects 2 issues 1991, 2 issues 1992. sub. price: $15 individuals, $20 institutions for 2 yr. sub. (4 issues); per copy: $4 (postage paid); sample: same. Discounts: 30% to bookstores. 30-50pp; 8½×5½; of. Reporting time: 2-3 months. Payment: 2 contributor's copies. Copyrighted, reverts to author. Ads: inquire.

THE FIDDLEHEAD, Don MacKay, Managing Editor; Robert Gibbs, Poetry Editor; Robert Hawkes, Poetry Editor; Diana Austin, Fiction Editor; Anthony Boxill, Fiction Editor, Campus House, PO Box 4400, University of New Brunswick, Fredericton, NB E3B 5A3, Canada, 506-453-3501. 1945. Poetry, fiction, art, reviews, parts-of-novels, long-poems, plays. circ. 1.1M. 4/yr. Pub'd 4 issues 1990; expects 4 issues 1991, 4 issues 1992. sub. price: $18 Canada, U.S. $18US; per copy: $5.50 Can., $6 U.S.; sample: $5.50 + postage Canada; U.S. $6. Back issues: $3-$6.50. Discounts: 10% on purchases of 10 copies or more; bookstores 33⅓%. 114-130pp; 5¼×8½; of. Reporting time: 6-10 weeks. Payment: $10 printed page. Copyrighted. Pub's reviews: 30-40 in 1990. §Canadian literature. Ads: $100/$52. CMPA.

FIDELIS ET VERUS, Children Of Mary, John R. Walsh, PO Box 2421, Tallahassee, FL 32316. 1985. News items. "Traditional/Orthodox Roman Catholic items that are news plus doctrine (Catholic)" circ. 6M. 12/yr. Pub'd 6 issues 1990; expects 6 issues 1991, 6 issues 1992. sub. price: $10 for 12 issues; per copy: $1; sample: $1. Back issues: $1. Discounts: 10¢ per copy in bulk. 8pp; 10×15; computer, laser printer, web press, typesetter. Reporting time: monthly. Payment: submit cost of article. Not copyrighted. Pub's reviews: 2 in 1990. §Only traditional Roman Catholic books/magazines. Ads: $200/$110/$4 per column inch (4 column page); columns 14 picas printed.

FIELD, David Young, Stuart Friebert, Rice Hall, Oberlin College, Oberlin, OH 44074. 1969. Poetry, long-poems. "Also essays on poetry and translations of poetry" circ. 2.5M. 2/yr. Pub'd 2 issues 1990; expects 2 issues 1991. 13 titles listed in the *Small Press Record of Books in Print* (20th Edition, 1991-92). sub. price: $12, $20/2 years; per copy: $6 postpaid; sample: $6 postpaid. Back issues: $15, all backs/except current iussue. Discounts: 40% bookstores, 30% agencies. 100pp; 5¼×8½. Reporting time: 2-3 weeks. Payment: $15-$25 a page. Copyrighted, reverts to author. Pub's reviews: 7 in 1990. §New books of poetry. No ads. CCLM, COSMEP.

Fiesta Books Inc., PO Box 51234, Phoenix, AZ 85076-1234, 602-759-4555. 1987. Non-fiction. "Limited use of outside authors, query first. Topics: Arizona, Southwest, Southern California, family health and safety, business" avg. press run 5M. Pub'd 2 titles 1990; expects 2 titles 1991, 2 titles 1992. 4 titles listed in the *Small Press Record of Books in Print* (20th Edition, 1991-92). avg. price, paper: $9.95. Discounts: 40% bookstore, 55% distributor. Pages vary; 5½×8½; of. Reporting time: 90 days. Payment: varies. Copyrights for author.

198

COSMEP, PMA, Arizona Authors Association.

FIFTH ESTATE, Collective Staff, 4632 Second Avenue, Detroit, MI 48201, 313-831-6800. 1965. Articles, photos, criticism, reviews, letters, non-fiction. circ. 5M. 4/yr. Pub'd 4 issues 1990; expects 4 issues 1991, 4 issues 1992. sub. price: $6, $8 foreign, $10 institutions; per copy: $1.50; sample: $1.50. Back issues: $2. Discounts: none. 32pp; 10×14. Reporting time: we don't encourage unsolicited ms. Payment: none. Not copyrighted. Pub's reviews: 25 in 1990. §Ecology, politics, anarchism, feminism. Ads: not accepted.

FIGHTING WOMAN NEWS, Frances Steinberg, 11438 Z Cronridge Drive, Owings Mills, MD 21117, 301-363-4919. 1975. Articles, art, photos, cartoons, interviews, reviews, letters, news items, non-fiction. *"FWN* is a communications medium for women martial artists. We need articles to 2M words, with photos, on martial arts, self defense & combative sports. Our readership is knowledgeable & critical. Also feminist. We have published men including artists Rick Bryant, Val Mayerik & Sergio Aragones, but we strongly suggest that all would-be contributors, especially men, read a few issues first" circ. 4M. 4/yr. Pub'd 4 issues 1990; expects 4 issues 1991, 4 issues 1992. sub. price: $10 individuals or prepaid institutional, $15 institutional and foreign; per copy: $3; sample: $3.50. Back issues: #21-current $3.50; oldies #1,2,18 $2.50 the set. Discounts: 40% consignment, 50% no returns. 16-24pp; 8½×11; of. Reporting time: asap. Payment: from contributors' copies to honorarium, cover photo $20. Copyrighted, reverts to author. Pub's reviews: 16 in 1990. §Martial arts, self defense, combative sports, women's history in these areas, women's adventure fiction, sports medicine and conditioning, feminism. Ads: $125/$65. COSMEP.

The Figures, Geoffrey Young, 5 Castle Hill Avenue, Great Barrington, MA 01230-1552, 413-528-2552. 1975. Poetry, fiction. "Summer Brenner, prose, *The Soft Room*; Christopher Dewdney, prose, *Spring Trances In The Control Emerald Night*; Laura Chester, a novella, *Watermark*; Bob Perelman; Rae Armantrout, poems, *Extremities*; Barbara Einzig, prose, Disappearing Work, A Recounting, Stephen Rodefer, poems, *The Bell Clerk's Tears Keep Flowing*; Kit Robinson, poems, *Down And Back*; Lyn Hejinian, poetry, *Writing Is An Aid To Memory*; Steve Benson, poems, *As Is*; John Brandi, *Diary From A Journey To The Center Of The World*; Alan Bernheimer, poems *Cafe Isotope*; David Bromige, prose & poems *My Poetry*; Laura Chester, poems *My Pleasure*; Kathleen Fraser,prose *Each Next*; Geoffrey Young, poems & prose *Subject To Fits*; Johanna Drucker, prose, *Italy*; 1980; Michael Davidson, poetry, *The Prose of Fact*; 1981; Ron Silliman, long poem in prose, *Tjanting*, 1981; Paul Auster, poems, *Wall Writing*; David Benedetti, prose poetry, *Nictitating Membrane*; Tom Clark, prose and painting, *Baseball*; Julia Vose, *Moved Out On the Inside."* avg. press run 1M. Expects 3 titles 1991, 2 titles 1992. 46 titles listed in the *Small Press Record of Books in Print* (20th Edition, 1991-92). avg. price, cloth: $10; paper: $7.50. 75pp; 5½×8½; of. Reporting time: 1 month. Payment: 10% edition, 40% off on extra sales. Copyrights for author.

FIJACTIVIST, Larry Dodge, Don Doig, PO Box 59, Helmville, MT 59843, 406-793-5550. 1989. Articles, photos. "Mostly in-house, but we have arranged to publish relevant articles, i.e., Judy Huston on the Span Trial" circ. 10M. 4/yr. Pub'd 4 issues 1990; expects 4 issues 1991, 4 issues 1992. sub. price: $15; sample: free. Discounts: 25¢ each. 16pp; 11½×15; newsprint. Payment: none. Not copyrighted. Ads: none.

FILM, Peter Cargin, 21 Stephen Street, London W1P 1PL, England, 01-255 1444. 1954. Articles, photos, interviews, criticism, reviews, letters, news items. "Film news, film society news, criticisms, etc. advertising managers: address as above" circ. 2M. 10/yr. Pub'd 10 issues 1990; expects 10 issues 1991. sub. price: £18 sterling UK, £19 overseas; per copy: £1.50; sample: usually free. Back issues: £1.80. 12pp; size A4; of. Reporting time: 2 weeks. Payment: by arrangement. Copyrighted, reverts to author. Pub's reviews: 50 in 1990. §Cinema, television, video, social and critical uses of film. Ads: £120/£70.

FILM QUARTERLY, University of California Press, Ernest Callenbach, University of California Press, 2120 Berkeley Way, Berkeley, CA 94720, 415-642-4191. 1945. Interviews, criticism, reviews. circ. 6.9M. 4/yr. Pub'd 4 issues 1990; expects 4 issues 1991, 4 issues 1992. sub. price: $16 indiv., $34 instit. (+ $5 for postage); per copy: $4 indiv., $7.50 instit.; sample: free. Back issues: $4.50 indiv., $9 instit. Discounts: foreign subs. agents 10%, 10+ one-time orders 30%, standing orders (bookstores): 1-99 40%, 100+ 50%. 64pp; 8½×11; of. Reporting time: 2-3 weeks. Payment: 2¢ per word. Copyrighted, does not revert to author. Pub's reviews: about 100 in 1990. §Film. Ads: $300/$175.

FILM THREAT VIDEO GUIDE, DAvid E. Williams, Editor; Christian Gore, Publisher, PO Box 3170, Los Angeles, CA 90078-3170, 818-848-8971; FAX 818-848-5956. 1990. Poetry, fiction, articles, art, photos, cartoons, interviews, satire, criticism, reviews, music, letters, news items, non-fiction. "We are very flexible in relation to length—completely negotiable in all regards but are specifically interested in new films made by independent means—shorts, feature length, but with focus on filmmakers themselves. We also indulge in humor—oriented spoofs/interviews/features. Currently, we are offering a distribution service for hard-to-find films." circ. 20M. 4/yr. Pub'd 4 issues 1990; expects 4 issues 1991, 4 issues 1992. price per copy: $2.50; sample: $2.50. Discounts: bulk 40%, trade 40%, classroom/schools 50%. 75pp; 8½×11; †of. Payment: negotiable. Copyrighted, reverts to author. Pub's reviews: 20 in 1990. §Film, television, poetry, acting, media in general, sex. Ads: $275/$150/$500 color full.

THE FINAL PAGE, Matt Pierard, 1806 South Kings Avenue, Brandon, FL 33511. 1984. Poetry, fiction, articles, art, photos, cartoons, interviews, satire, criticism, reviews, music, collages, news items, non-fiction. *"Final Page* is a very open-ended publication. No set formats, page size, etc. Mod—liberal, underground, new/old wave music, mass media, regional reviews and critiques. Sort of a mixed homage to early *Creem, Nat'l Lampoon* and *New York Rocker* mags. A 'personal zine.' Paul 'Whiteboy' Weinman and (artist) Kevin Mitchell are recent contributors." circ. under 100. 4/yr. Pub'd 4 issues 1990; expects 4 issues 1991, 4 issues 1992. price per copy: 50¢-$1; sample: 50¢. Back issues: depends on size of issue 50¢-$1 each. 8-24pp; 5½×8½ to 8½×11; of. Reporting time: within a month. Payment: not currently, free issues (up to 5). Pub's reviews: 2 in 1990. §Old wave music, alternative lifestyles, experimental anything, short fiction. Ads: $30/$15.

Financial Awareness Corporation, PO Box 430, Buena Vista, CO 81211, 519-749-2164. 1 title listed in the *Small Press Record of Books in Print* (20th Edition, 1991-92).

FINANCIAL PLANNING SERIES, Fell Publishers, Inc., Sherri Adelman, Elizabeth Wyatt, 2131 Hollywood Boulevard, Hollywood, FL 33020, 305-925-5242. 1943. Non-fiction. "We are the leading publisher of one-shot magazines in the United States. We have four categories in which we publish. These are diet & health, health, cookbook series and financial planning series. We are looking for full manuscripts that would lend itself to these areas" circ. 50M. 8/yr. Pub'd 8 issues 1990; expects 8 issues 1991, 8 issues 1992. price per copy: $2.95. Back issues: cover price. 128pp; 5-3/16×7⅞; of. Reporting time: 3 months. Payment: negotiated. Copyrighted, reverts to author. Ads: $2,000. PBAA, ACIDA.

The Findhorn Press (see also ONE EARTH), Andrew Murray, Rhiannon Hanfmann, The Park, Findhorn, Forres, Morayshire IV360TZ, Scotland, 0309-30582. 1966. Articles, art, photos, cartoons, interviews, reviews, letters, non-fiction. "*The Findhorn Press* is one department of the Findhorn Foundation, a community of more than 200 members, founded twenty-seven years ago on the coast of the Moray Firth in northern Scotland. We specialise in books about alternative lifestyles, community living, holistic health and spirituality, psychology and philosophy and ecology" avg. press run 5M. Pub'd 2 titles 1990; expects 5 titles 1991, 3 titles 1992. 16 titles listed in the *Small Press Record of Books in Print* (20th Edition, 1991-92). avg. price, cloth: £9.50, $16.95; paper: £8, $14. Discounts: UK: single copy 25%, 2+ 35%, under £15 plus postage/packing. Overseas: 35% plus carriage. 200pp; 210×148mm, 215×185mm; of. Reporting time: 1-2 months. Payment: by arrangement, in line with normal trade practice. IPG, SPA.

Fine Arts Press, Lincoln B. Young, PO Box 3491, Knoxville, TN 37927, 615-637-9243. 1957. Poetry. "Any length, any style, any subject except pornography or racist material" avg. press run 2M. Pub'd 2 titles 1990; expects 2 titles 1991, 2 titles 1992. 32 titles listed in the *Small Press Record of Books in Print* (20th Edition, 1991-92). avg. price, cloth: $22.95; paper: $10. Discounts: to booksellers and contributors only. 300pp; 5½×8½; †of. Reporting time: up to 4 months. Payment: none for anthology submissions. Copyrights for author.

FINE MADNESS, Sean Bentley, Louis Bergsagel, Christine Deavel, John Malek, John Marshall, PO Box 31138, Seattle, WA 98103-1138. 1980. Poetry, fiction, articles, letters, long-poems, non-fiction. "Writers we have recently published include Naomi Shihab-Nye, David Kirby, Andrei Codrescu, Peter Wild, Paul Zimmer, Pattiann Rogers, Stuart Friebert, Elton Glaser, William Stafford, Barbara Molloy-Olund, Beth Bentley, Leslie Norris, Marc Hudson, and Melinda Mueller. We want to see evidence of minds at work. As T.S. Eliot wrote, *'The poet must become more and more comprehensive, more allusive, more indirect, in order to force, to dislocate if necessary, language into its meaning'*" circ. 800. 2/yr. Pub'd 2 issues 1990; expects 2 issues 1991, 2 issues 1992. sub. price: $9; per copy: $5; sample: $4. Back issues: Volume 1 Number 1 $10. Discounts: 40% trade. 80pp; 5½×8; of. Reporting time: 3 months. Payment: 1 copy of their issue plus a one-year subscription to *Fine Madness*. Copyrighted, reverts to author. Pub's reviews. §Poetry. No ads. CCLM.

FINE PRINT: The Review for the Arts of the Book, Sandra Kirshenbaum, Editor and Publisher; Elaine Ginger, Managing Editor, PO Box 193394, San Francisco, CA 94119, 415-543-4455. 1975. Articles, art, photos, interviews, criticism, reviews, letters, news items. "The first review medium devoted to the arts of the book, including printing, typography, papermaking, calligraphy, bookbinding, and illustration. Send all mail to: Box 3394, San Francisco, California 94119" circ. 3M. 4/yr. Pub'd 4 issues 1990; expects 4 issues 1991, 4 issues 1992. 1 title listed in the *Small Press Record of Books in Print* (20th Edition, 1991-92). sub. price: $45, $57 inst.; per copy: $12.50, except January '85 double issue - $25; sample: $12.50. Back issues: January 1985 Anniversary double issue, $25. Inquire as to issues currently available. Stock changes quickly. Discounts: bookstores may buy at 30% discount for 3 copies minimum. No returns. $4 off institutional orders from agents. 56pp; 9×12; lp, of. Reporting time: 4-6 weeks. Payment: 1 year free subscription plus author's copies; $150 for major articles. Copyrighted, reverts to author under new laws; we reserve right to reprint in a collection. Pub's reviews: 100 in 1990. §Book arts: history, printing, calligraphy, binding, typography. Ads: $900/$500/80¢.

Finesse Publishing Company, Linda Doran, PO Box 657, Broomfield, CO 80038, 303-466-4734. 1986. Non-fiction. avg. press run 1M. Expects 3 titles 1991, 3 titles 1992. 3 titles listed in the *Small Press Record of*

Books in Print (20th Edition, 1991-92). avg. price, paper: $20. 300pp; 8½×11. Reporting time: 6 weeks. Payment: 15% of all monies actually received, royalty payments every 6 months. Copyrights for author.

Fir Publishing Company, Angie Forest, PO Box 78436, Indianapolis, IN 46278, 317-872-4059. 1991. Fiction, non-fiction. "Street address: 7215 Normandy Way. We will only accept material that is solidly based in science or well-researched, has a critical but positive viewpoint on people, politics, and/or human institutions; and is easy is to read and entertaining. We have sufficient material to keep us through 1992." avg. press run 50M. Expects 2 titles 1991, 3 titles 1992. 1 title listed in the *Small Press Record of Books in Print* (20th Edition, 1991-92). avg. price, cloth: $25; paper: $15. Discounts: 55% by carton (usually about 38 books); 10 through carton 50%, 2-9 40%, single books 20% if payment accompanies order, for orders of 2 or more books, additional 6% if payment accompanies order and 4% if paid within 30 days. 350pp; lp. Reporting time: 3 months. Payment: 10%, plus an additional 2% to agents. Copyrights for author. PMA, PO Box 299, Hermosa Beach, CA 90254.

Fire Buff House, W. Fred Conway, PO Drawer 709, New Albany, IN 47150, 812-945-2617. 1987. Non-fiction. "Books, 125pp-250pp, heavily illustrated, on various facets of fire fighting history. Authors published 1987/88-Paul Ditzel" avg. press run 2.2M-3.3M. Pub'd 2 titles 1990; expects 2 titles 1991, 2-4 titles 1992. avg. price, cloth: $24.95. Discounts: 2-4 books 20%, 5-9 30%, 10-24 40%, 25-49 42%, 50-74 44%, 79-99 46%, 100-199 48%, 200+ 50%. 125-250pp; 8½×11; of. Reporting time: prompt. Payment: advance royalty on acceptance. We can copyright for author.

Firebrand Books, Nancy K. Bereano, 141 The Commons, Ithaca, NY 14850, 607-272-0000. 1985. Poetry, fiction, non-fiction. "*Firebrand Books* is a feminist and lesbian publishing company committed to making quality books in a variety of genres available to a wide audience" avg. press run 4M. Pub'd 6 titles 1990; expects 7 titles 1991, 8 titles 1992. 16 titles listed in the *Small Press Record of Books in Print* (20th Edition, 1991-92). Discounts: Bookpeople and Inland. Reporting time: 1 month except as otherwise specified. Payment: royalties. Copyrights for author.

Fireweed Press, PO Box 75418, Fairbanks, AK 99707-2136. 1976. "Publishes anthologies and prize-winning works by contemporary Alaskan authors. Submissions accepted only for projects in progress; no unsolicited manuscripts read. 1983: "Hunger and Dreams, The Alaskan Women's Anthology", 22 contributors including Sheila Nickerson, Mary TallMountain, Donna Mack, Jean Anderson; edited by Pat Monaghan. 1984: "A Good Crew" Anthology of men's writings about relationships in the north, edited by Larry Laraby and Roland Wulbert; "The Compass Inside Ourselves" by Nany Lord, winning short-story collection chosen by Stanley Elkin" avg. press run 1M. Pub'd 2 titles 1990; expects 2 titles 1991, 3 titles 1992. 6 titles listed in the *Small Press Record of Books in Print* (20th Edition, 1991-92). avg. price, cloth: $10.95; paper: $7.95. Discounts: 40% to bookstores, orders of 5 or more. 130pp; 6×9. Reporting time: 1 month. Payment: varies. Copyrights for author. COSMEP, AASP (Alaska Association of Small Presses).

The First East Coast Theatre and Publishing Company, Inc., Paul Boccio, President; Karen Boccio, Secretary, PO Box 32, Westtown, NY 10992, 914-726-4289. 1979. Poetry, fiction, long-poems, plays, non-fiction. avg. press run 500. Pub'd 1 title 1990; expects 1 title 1991, 3 titles 1992. 6 titles listed in the *Small Press Record of Books in Print* (20th Edition, 1991-92). avg. price, cloth: $10; paper: $3.95. Discounts: bookstores 40%; bulk orders 10%. 40-200pp; 5½×8½; lp. Reporting time: 6 weeks. Payment: 10% of retail. Copyrights for author.

FIRSTHAND, Bob Harris, Editor, PO Box 1314, Teaneck, NJ 07666, 201-836-9177. 1980. Poetry, fiction, articles, art, photos, cartoons, reviews, letters, parts-of-novels, news items, non-fiction. "Must appeal to a male homosexual audience" circ. 60M. 12/yr. Pub'd 12 issues 1990; expects 12 issues 1991, 12 issues 1992. sub. price: $48; per copy: $4.50; sample: $5. Back issues: $5. 132pp; 5×8; web-of. Reporting time: 4-6 weeks. Payment: $150 for 10-20 pages typed doublespaced. Copyrighted, rights can be discussed. Pub's reviews: 16 in 1990. §Homosexual-related items. Ads: $600/$300/no classified. Gay And Lesbian Press Association.

FISH DRUM MAGAZINE, Robert Winson, 626 Kathryn Avenue, Santa Fe, NM 87501. 1988. Poetry, fiction, articles, art, cartoons, interviews, criticism, reviews, music, letters, parts-of-novels, long-poems, collages, plays, concrete art, non-fiction. "I love West Coast poetry, the exuberant, talky, often elliptical and abstract 'continuous nerve movie' that follows the working of the mind and has a relationship to the world and the reader. Philip Whalen's work, for example, and much of *Calafia, The California Poetry*, edited by Ishmael Reed. Also magical-tribal-incantatory poems, exemplified by the future/primitive *Technicians of the Sacred*, ed. Rothenberg. *Fish Drum* has a soft spot for schmoozy, emotional, imagistic stuff. Literature, personal material that sings and surprises, OK? We've published poetry by Philip Whalen, Miriam Sagan, Joy Harjo, Arthur Sze, Nathaniel Tarn, Alice Notley, John Brandi, Steve Richmond, Jessica Hagedorn, Leo Romero, and Leslie Scalapino, all of whom have books around worth finding and reading. We're looking for New Mexico authors, also prose: fiction, essays, what-have-you, and artwork, scores, cartoons, etc. - just send it along." circ. 500. 2-4/yr. Pub'd 3 issues 1990; expects 4 issues 1991, 4 issues 1992. sub. price: $10/4 issues; per copy: $3;

sample: $3. Back issues: not available. Discounts: 40%. 40pp; 5½x8½; xerox with offset covers. Reporting time: 1 month. Payment: 2 or more copies. Copyrighted, reverts to author. Pub's reviews. §Poetry and fiction, natural history of the Southwest, Zen. No ads.

FISICA, Zagier & Urruty Publicaciones, Sergio Zagier, PO Box 94 Sucursal 19, Buenos Aires 1419, Argentina, 541-572-1050. 1985. Articles, reviews, non-fiction. "U.S.A. address: 6630 Indian Creek Drive #223, Miami Beach, FL 33141. Scientific contributions about physics, its philosophy and its teaching are welcomed, in Spanish or English. Maximum 25 letter pages." circ. 1.5M. 2/yr. Pub'd 2 issues 1990; expects 2 issues 1991, 2 issues 1992. sub. price: $8; per copy: $4; sample: $4. Back issues: $4. Discounts: 50% distributors, 30% bookstores. 64pp; 6½x8; of. Reporting time: 3 months. Payment: none. Copyrighted, reverts to author. Pub's reviews: 20 in 1990. §Physics, philosophy, mathematics, computation, history of science. Ads: $200/$100/$500 back cover.

Fithian Press, John Daniel, Editor, PO Box 1525, Santa Barbara, CA 93102, 805-962-1780. 1985. Poetry, fiction, non-fiction. avg. press run 1M. Pub'd 10 titles 1990; expects 20 titles 1991, 20 titles 1992. 57 titles listed in the *Small Press Record of Books in Print* (20th Edition, 1991-92). avg. price, cloth: $17.95; paper: $8.95. Discounts: trade 1-4 20%, 5+ 40%; wholesale 1-9 20%, 10+ 50%; library 10%. 128pp; 5½x8½; of. Reporting time: 6-8 weeks. Payment: flexible, author pays production costs and receives 50% net royalty. Copyrights for author. Publishers Marketing Assn. (PMA).

5 AM, Patricia Dobler, Lynn Emanuel, Ed Ochester, Judith Vollmer, 1109 Milton Avenue, Pittsburgh, PA 15218. 1987. Poetry. "Open to poems in any style, but particularly interested in content ignored by many literary magazines: poems about work, political poems, poems by and about gays, poems by and about ethnic minorities, comic and satire poems, poems dealing with rural experience. We want to avoid the sameness of many poetry magazines. Recent contributors: Jack Anderson, Robin Becker, Gar Bethel, Ellen Bishop, Victor Contoski, Jane Todd Cooper, Edward Field, Elton Glaser, Ron Koertge, Wendy Larsen, Alicia Ostriker, Rita Dove, Alberto Rios, and many others" circ. 750+. 2/yr. Expects 2 issues 1991, 2 issues 1992. sub. price: $6; per copy: $3; sample: $3. Back issues: $2. Discounts: 40% negotiable. 28pp; 11½x16; of. Reporting time: 1-2 months. Payment: copies. Copyrighted, reverts to author. Ads: $90 1/2 page/$50 1/4.

Five Corners Publications, Ltd. (see also EARTHTREKS DIGEST), Deborah Smith-Gingras, Route 100, HCR 70, Box 7A, Plymouth, VT 05056, 802-672-3868. 1990. Photos, non-fiction. "*Earthtreks Digest* focuses on ecotravel, travel exploring the relationship between human beings and their environment through photography. Photo-essays are 1/3 text and 2/3 photography. Any writing must be accompanied by photography. *Earthtreks Digest* features work from members of INPP." avg. press run 3M. Expects 3 titles 1991, 5 titles 1992. 3 titles listed in the *Small Press Record of Books in Print* (20th Edition, 1991-92). avg. price, cloth: $29.95. Discounts: 2-4 20%, 5-19 30%, 20-49 40%, 100-199 48%, 200+ 50%, 5% additional discount for nonreturnables. 120pp; 12x9; of. Reporting time: 1 month. Payment: one-time use, photos: cover $10, inside $5. Copyrights for author.

Five Fingers Press (see also FIVE FINGERS REVIEW), Aleka Chase, John High, Julia Ward, Thoreau Lovell, PO Box 15426, San Francisco, CA 94115. 1984. Fiction, interviews, non-fiction. "May begin running reviews" avg. press run 1M. Pub'd 2 titles 1990; expects 1-2 titles 1991. 5 titles listed in the *Small Press Record of Books in Print* (20th Edition, 1991-92). avg. price, paper: $6 + $1 postage. Discounts: subs. $12/2 issues; 40% consignment; 50% outright sale. 150pp; 6x9; of. Reporting time: 3 months. Payment: 2 copies of magazine. Does not copyright for author. CCLM.

FIVE FINGERS REVIEW, Five Fingers Press, Aleka Chase, Thoreau Lovell, John High, Julie Ward, PO Box 15426, San Francisco, CA 94115-0426. 1984. Poetry, fiction, interviews, non-fiction. "Diverse, innovative writing by socially committed writers with a variety of aesthetics, from narrative to language-centered. C.D. Wright, Stan Rice, Susan Griffin, Fernando Alegria, Robert Bly, Angela Jackson, Ron Silliman" circ. 1M. 2/yr. Pub'd 2 issues 1990; expects 2 issues 1991, 2 issues 1992. sub. price: $12; per copy: $6 + $1 postage; sample: $6 + $1 postage. Back issues: $3 + $1 postage. Discounts: 40% consignment, 50% outright sale, negotiable. 150pp; 6x9; of. Reporting time: 3-6 months. Payment: 2 copies. Copyrighted, reverts to author. Ads: $100 (4½ X 7½)/$70 (4½ X 3½)/$45 1/4 page (2 X 3). CCLM.

Five Islands Press Cooperative Ltd. (see also SCARP), R.K. Pretty, Deborah Westbury, Robert Hood, PO Box 1946, Wollongong, NSW 2500, Australia, 042-272875. 1987. Poetry, fiction. "Recent titles: *Redshift/Blueshift* by Chris Mansell, poetry, 64pp; *The Habit of Balance* by Ron Pretty, poetry, 64pp; *Daydreaming on Company Time* by Robert Hood, short prose fiction, 96pp; Steven Herrick, *Caboolture*; Walter Tonetto (Ed), *Earth Against Heaven*" avg. press run 1M. Pub'd 5 titles 1990; expects 4 titles 1991, 4 titles 1992. 9 titles listed in the *Small Press Record of Books in Print* (20th Edition, 1991-92). avg. price, paper: $10.95. Discounts: between 33⅓% and 40% to bookshops. 80pp; size A5; laser printer. Reporting time: 1-3 months. Payment: 10%. Copyrights for author.

FIVE LEAVES LEFT, Purple Heather Publications, Richard Mason, 12 Colne Road, Cowling, Keighley,

West Yorkshire, BD22 OBZ, England. 1983. Poetry, art, reviews, music, news items. "Do not send more than five poems. Prose should not exceed more than 2000 words. Unsolicited manuscripts that fail to include sufficient I.R.C.s or cash to cover, return postage will not be considered" circ. 500. 3/yr. Pub'd 3 issues 1990; expects 3 issues 1991, 3 issues 1992. sub. price: $10 *no* cheques; sample: $2 *No* cheques. Discounts: Send $5 for 3 assorted samples *No* cheques. 60pp; 5¾×8¼; of. Reporting time: 1 month. Payment: copy of magazine. Copyrighted, reverts to author. Pub's reviews: 40 in 1990. §Poetry "Across the Boardd" Ads: $10/$6 *no* cheques. YFSP (The Yorkshire Federation of Small Presses).

Five Star Publications, Linda F. Radke, Publisher, PO Box 3142, Scottsdale, AZ 85271-3142, 602-941-0770. 1985. "Submissions not being accepted at this time. Recent contributors: *Shakespeare for Children: The Story of Romeo & Juliet* by Cass Foster, *Nannies, Maids & More: The Complete Guide for Hiring Household Help* by Linda F. Radke, *The Sixty-Minute Shakespeare: Romeo and Juliet* by Cass Foster" Expects 4 titles 1991. 6 titles listed in the *Small Press Record of Books in Print* (20th Edition, 1991-92). avg. price, paper: $9.95-$14.95; other: $24.95 kit. Discounts: write for schedule. 100pp; 5½×8½, 8½×11. Reporting time: 90 days. Payment: to be arranged. Does not copyright for author. PMA, Arizona Authors' Association, COSMEP, Society of Children's Book Writers.

Fjord Press, Steven T. Murray, PO Box 16501, Seattle, WA 98116, 206-625-9363. 1981. Fiction, non-fiction. "*Translations of prose only*; please submit photocopies of original language text with translation sample. Also Western Americana" avg. press run 1.5M-5M. Pub'd 5 titles 1990; expects 10 titles 1991, 10 titles 1992. 23 titles listed in the *Small Press Record of Books in Print* (20th Edition, 1991-92). avg. price, cloth: $19.95; paper: $9.95. Discounts: bookstores Stop 40%; other, order from Publishers Services, PO Box 2510, Novato, CA 94948. 140-300pp; 5½×8½, 5×8; of. Reporting time: 12 weeks, query first. Payment: in copies. Copyrights for author. Book Publishers Northwest, PEN American Center, PEN Northwest.

Flax Press, Inc., Linda L. Holup, PO Box 2395, Huntington, WV 25724, 304-525-1109. 1988. Poetry, fiction, photos, music, non-fiction. "T.S. Innocenti *Song of Meditation*, published 11/88." avg. press run 5M-7M. Expects 1 title 1991, 1 title 1992. 1 title listed in the *Small Press Record of Books in Print* (20th Edition, 1991-92). avg. price, paper: $10.95. Discounts: 40% bookstores. Payment: negotiated individually. Copyrights for author.

FLIPSIDE, Kathleen Vail, Editor; George Swaney, Poetry Editor, Dixon Hall, California University of PA, California, PA 15419, 412-938-5946. 1987. Poetry, fiction, articles, art, photos, cartoons, non-fiction. "We prefer non-fiction articles written in New Journalism style—strong person voice, strong point of view, *subject not important*, just so the article is *well-written*. Photos or art helpful. Poetry must have narrative line" circ. 5M. 2/yr. Pub'd 2 issues 1990; expects 2 issues 1991, 2 issues 1992. sample price: $1. 48pp; of. Reporting time: 1 month. Payment: copies. Not copyrighted. Ads: $145/$80.

FLOATING ISLAND, Floating Island Publications, Michael Sykes, PO Box 516, Point Reyes Station, CA 94956. 1976. Poetry, fiction, articles, art, photos, cartoons, parts-of-novels, long-poems, collages. "No unsolicited manuscripts currently being accepted. Floating Island pubs. 1 every 3-4 years approx. 8½ X 11, 160pp, perfectbound cover in color, text B/W, 24pp of photographs (full-page) on coated stock, approx. 50 percent of text is poetry, 25 percent fiction & prose, 25 percent graphics-poetry fiction & prose is frequently illustrated, engravings, woodblocks, pen & pencil etc.-some artwork halftoned to retain fidelity, most is line-shot. Contributors include well-known poets & writers as well as previous unpublished artists. Editorial policy is determined solely by whim and is akin to a celebration which various persons have been invited to attend in the belief they may enjoy one another's company and perhaps find a small and appreciative audience as well. *Floating Island IV* (1989) ends First Series. No date set for start of Second Series" circ. 1M. 1 every 3-4 years. Pub'd 1 issue 1990. Standing orders only - full price; price per copy: $15; sample: full-price. Back issues: full-price - all issues. Discounts: 50% to dist.; 40% to retail outlets. 160pp; 8½×11; of. Reporting time: 2 months. Payment: copies. Copyrighted, reverts to author upon request. no ads. CLMP.

Floating Island Publications (see also FLOATING ISLAND), Michael Sykes, PO Box 516, Pt Reyes Sta, CA 94956. 1976. Poetry, fiction, articles, art, photos, parts-of-novels, long-poems. "No unsolicited manuscripts currently being accepted. I'll do 1 or 2 books a year, more if possible. I'm interested as much in the design and production of a book as its content and choose to work with manuscripts that offer me an interesting possibility of balancing these two areas of concern. Consequently the work is slow and deliberate. Authors must be patient. *Sleeping With The Enemy* by Christine Zawadiwsky, *Barn Fires* by Peter Wild. *Desemboque* by Frank Graziano, *Penguins* by David Hilton. *Up My Coast* by Joanne Kyger, *The Open Water* by Frank Stewart, *Dazzled* by Arthur Sze, *The Cowboy From Phantom Banks And Other Stories From Southeastern New Mexico* by John Brandi, *Two Weeks Off* by Kirk Robertson, *It's Alive She Says* by Cole Swensen, *Drug Abuse in Marin County* by Eugene Lesser, *Black Ash, Orange Fire* by William Witherup" avg. press run 1M. Pub'd 2 titles 1990; expects 7 titles 1991, 4 titles 1992. 30 titles listed in the *Small Press Record of Books in Print* (20th Edition, 1991-92). avg. price, paper: $8. Discounts: 50% jobbers, 40% bookstores. 64pp; 6×9, 5½×8½; of. Reporting time: 6-8 weeks. Payment: 10% of the press run. Does not copyright for author. CLMP.

J. Flores Publications (see also ACTION DIGEST), Eli Flores, PO Box 163001, Miami, FL 33116, 305-559-4652. 1981. Photos, non-fiction. "J. Flores Publications primarily publishes original non-fiction manuscripts on military science, weaponry, improvised weaponry, self-defense, survival, police science, and current events. How-to manuscripts are given priority. Query or submit outline/synopsis and sample chapters" avg. press run 3M. Pub'd 10 titles 1990; expects 10 titles 1991, 13 titles 1992. 16 titles listed in the *Small Press Record of Books in Print* (20th Edition, 1991-92). avg. price, paper: $12. Discounts: 50% of retail price (3-9 comes 40% off, 10-99 50% off, over 100 comes 55%). 150pp; 5½x8½; of. Reporting time: 30 days. Payment: 10% (copies 1-4,999), 12% (copies 5,000-10,000), 15% (over) based on NET receipts. Copyrights for author.

The Florian Group, F. Michael Sisavic, 5620 SW Riverside Lane #8, Portland, OR 97201. 1986. Non-fiction. "Other address: Astoria Building, PO Box 1423, Lake Oswego, OR 97035. Organizing, planning and recording charts, forms, logs for travel" avg. press run 10M. Expects 1 title 1991, 2 titles 1992. 1 title listed in the *Small Press Record of Books in Print* (20th Edition, 1991-92). avg. price, cloth: $21.95; paper: $9.95; other: leather bound $39.95. Discounts: 40%-60%. 128pp; 5¾x8; †of. Reporting time: 2 weeks. Payment: open. Copyrights for author. COSMEP, PMA, NWABP.

Floricanto Press (see also LECTOR), Roberto Cabello-Argardona, 16161 Ventura Blvd, Ste 830, Encino, CA 91436, 818-990-1885. 1978. avg. press run 2M. Expects 7 titles 1992. avg. price, cloth: $32; paper: $23. Discounts: 40% to trade for bulk orders 40+. 300pp; 6x9; of. Reporting time: 3 weeks. Payment: negotiable. Copyrights for author.

THE FLORIDA REVIEW, Russ Kesler, Editor; Kimberley Daniels, Managing Editor, PO Box 25000, Eng. Dept., Central Florida Univ., Orlando, FL 32816, 305-823-2038. 1972. Poetry, fiction, reviews. "We look for fiction (up to 7,500 words) and poetry (any length). We are especially interested in new writers. We publish fiction of high quality—stories that delight, instruct, and aren't afraid to take risks, and we welcome experimental fiction, so long as it doesn't make us feel lost or stupid. Also, we look for clear, strong poems—poems filled with real things, real people, real emotions, poems that might conceivably advance our knowledge of the human heart. Some of our recent contributors include Philip F. Deaver, Stephen Dixon, Gary Fincke, Karen Fish, Ruthann Robson, William Stafford, and Tom Whalen" circ. 1M. 2/yr. Pub'd 2 issues 1990; expects 2 issues 1991, 2 issues 1992. sub. price: $7; per copy: $4.50; sample: $4.50. Back issues: $4. Discounts: 20%. 128pp; 5½x8½; of. Reporting time: 8 weeks. Payment: occasional honoraria. Copyrighted, reverts to author. Pub's reviews: 6 in 1990. EBSCO, CCLM.

FLORIDA VOCATIONAL JOURNAL, Donald Caswell, 2003 Apalachee Parkway, Tallahassee, FL 32301, 904-487-2054. 1975. Articles, photos, interviews, news items, non-fiction. "*The Journal* is a forum for vocational educators that allows open discussion of current issues in vocational education and career development. We are especially interested in stories that affect Florida. Items under 1000 words especially appreciated" circ. 18M. 4/yr. Pub'd 6 issues 1990; expects 4 issues 1991, 4 issues 1992. sub. price: $10; per copy: $2; sample: $1. Back issues: $1 each, when available. Discounts: free to Florida educators, 40% for everybody else. 12-20pp; 8x11; of. Reporting time: 1-3 months. Payment: copies only. Copyrighted, rights don't revert unless negotiated prior to publication. Pub's reviews: 1 in 1990. §Education, vocational education, career development, labor trends. Ads: $1090/$600. NAVTEC, EPRESS.

Flower Press, Mary Appelhof, 10332 Shaver Road, Kalamazoo, MI 49002, 616-327-0108. 1976. "Flower Press celebrates the energizing power of self-sufficiency by publishing books, primarily written by Mary Appelhof, which help people regain control over their own lives. Although publications have included a family history (*Finding Back Your Family*, by Gilbert and Hilda Appelhof), poetry by Susie Clemens *Green Paisley*, and the *Ms. Fortune 500 Directory* ed. by Mary Appelhof, I am currently concentrating on studies about earthworms. *Worms Eat My Garbage*, with illustrations by Mary Frances Fenton (paper, 100 pp, 5¼ X 8½, $10.50 postpaid) has sold over 17,000 copies to date. I am not seeking manuscripts" avg. press run 5M. Expects 1 title 1991, 1 title 1992. 5 titles listed in the *Small Press Record of Books in Print* (20th Edition, 1991-92). avg. price, paper: $10. Discounts: 1-9 copies 20%, 10+ 40%. 110pp; 5¼x8¼; of. Payment: author defrays publishing cost. Copyrights for author. COSMEP.

Flume Press, Casey Huff, Elizabeth Renfro, 4 Casita, Chico, CA 95926-2412, 916-342-1583. 1984. Poetry. "We are—and intend to remain—a small not-for-profit press devoted to publishing the work of newer poets. We are interested in poetry with clear, strong images, a freshness, and an ability to excite in us a definite and strong reaction. We have few biases about form, although we do appreciate writing that shows crafting and control in its form. All submissions should be made through our annual Chapbook Contest. Look for ads or write us for guidelines. Deadlines always end of June. Reading fee: $6" avg. press run 300. Pub'd 1 title 1990; expects 1 title 1991, 1 title 1992. 7 titles listed in the *Small Press Record of Books in Print* (20th Edition, 1991-92). avg. price, paper: $5 + $1 p/h. Discounts: 2-10 25%, 11+ 40%. 30pp; 6x9; of. Reporting time: 6 weeks after contest deadline. Payment: $100 + 25 copies. Copyrights for author. COSMEP.

The Flying Pencil Press, Charlotte Towner Graeber, PO Box 7667, Elgin, IL 60121. 1986. Poetry, fiction, art, cartoons, non-fiction. "Books compiled of material written and illustrated by children 8-14, each book having a central theme. Send SASE for guidelines and information about upcoming projects" avg. press run 750-1M. Pub'd 1 title 1990; expects 2 titles 1991, 2 titles 1992. avg. price, paper: $8. Discounts: none at this time. 60-140pp; size varies. Reporting time: 4-6 weeks. Payment: copies, nominal payment. Copyrights for author.

Flying Pencil Publications, Madelynne Diness, PO Box 19062, Portland, OR 97219, 503-245-2314. 1983. Non-fiction. "Books related to outdoor adventuring, including non-fiction, fiction, how-to's, and guidebooks. Fishing is our subject-specialty" avg. press run 5M. Pub'd 2 titles 1990. 5 titles listed in the *Small Press Record of Books in Print* (20th Edition, 1991-92). avg. price, paper: $10.95. Discounts: 40% to retailers, 55% to distributors. 200pp; of. Payment: variable. NW Book Publishers Assoc./PMA/COSMEP.

FOCUS, World Wildlife Fund & The Conservation Foundation, Anne Hummer, World Wildlife Fund, 1250 24th street, NW, Washington, DC 20037, 202-293-4800. 1979. Articles, photos, interviews, reviews, news items, non-fiction. "Our newsletter is sent to WWF members." circ. 1,000,000. 6/yr. Pub'd 6 issues 1990; expects 6 issues 1991, 6 issues 1992. sub. price: $15; per copy: free; sample: free. Back issues: free. 8pp; 11×16⅝. Payment: nonprofit organization, therefore no payment. Copyrighted. Pub's reviews: 6 in 1990. §International conservation, wildlife around the world.

FOCUS, Ontario Library Association, Jefferson A.R. Gilbert, 100 Richmond St., E, Suite 300, Toronto, Ontario M5C 2P9, Canada, 416-363-3388. 1900. Articles, photos, interviews, criticism, reviews, letters, news items. circ. 4M. 4/yr. Expects 2 issues 1991, 4 issues 1992. sub. price: $48; per copy: $10. Back issues: N.A. Discounts: 15% to reconized agencies. 48-60pp; 8½×11; of. Reporting time: 2-4 months. Payment: 5 copies. Copyrighted, does not revert to author. Pub's reviews: 29 in 1990. §Anything of interest in librarianship: public, school, special, college & university. Ads: $360/$200/10¢ word, min. $15.

FOCUS: Library Service to Older Adults, People with Disabilities, Eunice G. Lovejoy, 2255 Pine Drive, Prescott, AZ 86301, 602-778-3821. 1983. Articles, reviews, news items. "This is a monthly newsletter for librarians and other persons concerned with library service to persons with disabilities and older adults" circ. 150-734. 12/yr. Pub'd 12 issues 1990; expects 12 issues 1991, 12 issues 1992. sub. price: $6.60; per copy: 55¢; sample: free. Back issues: same as subscription. 2pp; 8½×11; of. Copyrighted. Pub's reviews: 16 in 1990. §Aging, books by and about people with disabilities, library service to these groups. No ads.

Foghorn Press, Sara Shopkow, Vicki K. Morgan, Publisher, PO Box 77845, San Francisco, CA 94107, 415-641-5777. 1985. Photos, non-fiction. avg. press run 7.5M-12M. Pub'd 4 titles 1990; expects 6 titles 1991. 9 titles listed in the *Small Press Record of Books in Print* (20th Edition, 1991-92). avg. price, paper: $15.95. Discounts: trade. 500pp; 8½×11, 6½×9; lp. Reporting time: 2 months. Payment: 12% net. Does not copyright for author. Publishers Marketing Association (PMA).

Folder Editions, Daisy Aldan, Director; Diana Cohen, Associate Editor, 260 West 52 Street #5L, New York, NY 10019, 212-459-9086. 1959. Poetry, fiction, plays. "Recent Publications: *I Wanted to See Something Flying* poems by Harriet Zinnes, *The Fall of Antichrist* play in verse by Swiss poet, Albert Steffen translated from German by Dora Baxter, *The Breaking Which Brings Us Anew* poems by Charles Taylor, *Stones* by Daisy Aldan, *Verses For the Zodiac* by Daisy Aldan. *Between High Tides* poems by Daisy Aldan, *A Golden Story* novella, (pub. with NEA grant). Reprint: *Calendar of the Soul* by Rudolf Steiner, translated from gm. by Daisy Aldan. *In Passage,* poems by Daisy Aldan, *The Radiant Tree,* poems by Sylvia Spencer, *Somewhere,* poems and drawings by Diana Cohen" avg. press run 800-1M. Pub'd 5 titles 1990. 18 titles listed in the *Small Press Record of Books in Print* (20th Edition, 1991-92). avg. price, cloth: $9.95; paper: $5.95; other: $19.95 limited, signed. Discounts: up to 3 copies 20%, 3-5 30%, 40% for 5 copies or more to bookstores, dealers. 65-130pp; 6×9; of, lp, occasional linotype, word processing. Reporting time: 2 weeks. Payment: individual. Does not copyright for author. Small Press Center, NYC.

FOLIO: A LITERARY JOURNAL, Dept. of Literature, American University, Washington, DC 20016, 202-885-2971. 1984. Poetry, fiction, art, photos, interviews, parts-of-novels, non-fiction. "Recent contributors include: Robert Bausch, Colette Inez, Barbara Goldberg, Linda Pustan, Jean Valentine, Chitra Divakaruni, Henry Taylor. Quality fiction, poetry, translations, essays, and art. We like to comment on pieces when time permits. We sponsor a fiction/poetry contest with each spring issue. Please limit all poetry submissions to batches of five; fiction to 4,000 words. We don't read during the summer" circ. 400. 2/yr. Pub'd 2 issues 1990; expects 2 issues 1991, 2 issues 1992. sub. price: $10; per copy: $5 (includes postage); sample: $5. Back issues: $2. Discounts: 33%. 70pp; 6×9; of. Reporting time: 6-8 weeks. Payment: 2 contributors copies. Copyrighted, reverts to author.

FOLK ART MESSENGER, Ann Oppenhimer, PO Box 17041, Richmond, VA 23226, 804-355-6709. 1987. Articles, art, photos, interviews, criticism, reviews, news items. "2000 words or less. Subject: contemporary folk art. Contributors: Roger Cardinal, Roger Brown, John Turner, Norman Girardot" circ. 700. 4/yr. Pub'd 4 issues 1990; expects 4 issues 1991, 4 issues 1992. sub. price: $20; per copy: $5; sample: $5. Back issues: $5. Discounts: none. 12pp; 8½×11; lp. Reporting time: 30 days. Payment: none. Copyrighted, reverts to author.

Pub's reviews: 4 in 1990. §Folk art, quilts, crafts, Appalachia. Ads: none.

FOLK ERA TODAY, Allan Shaw, 6 South 230 Cohasset Road, Naperville, IL 60540, 708-961-3559. 1985. Articles, art, photos, cartoons, interviews, criticism, reviews, music, letters, news items, non-fiction. "Magazine devoted to popular folk music exclusively" circ. 15M. 4/yr. Pub'd 4 issues 1990; expects 3 issues 1991, 4 issues 1992. sub. price: $8; per copy: $2.50; sample: free (SASE requested). Back issues: $2 if available. Discounts: will be given, no set discounts, depends on quantity and purpose. 40pp; 8½×11; of. Reporting time: immediate. Payment: individual agreements. Not copyrighted. Pub's reviews: 3-4 in 1990. §Popular music, folk music. Ads: $350/$200/$140 1/3/$80 1/6.

The Folks Upstairs Press, Ben Phillips, Julie Phillips, 827A Bloor Street West, Toronto, Ontario M6G 1M1, Canada. 1969. Poetry. avg. press run 500. Expects 4 titles 1991, 4 titles 1992. avg. price, other: chap book $2.00. Discounts: straight 50%. 40-50pp; †of. Reporting time: 30-60 days. Payment: scant & individual.

Food For Thought Publications, Dick McLeester, PO Box 331, Amherst, MA 01004, 413-549-1114. 1976. "Special focus: dreams, bookstores" Discounts: trade 3-4 copies—30 percent; 5 or more copies—40 percent. 30 day billing. of.

FOOLSCAP, Judi Benson, 78 Friars Road, East Ham, London E6 1LL, England. 1987. Poetry, fiction, art, photos, parts-of-novels, long-poems, non-fiction. "Approx. 6 pages for fiction. Recent contributors include: Ken Smith, Nicki Jackowska, Libby Houston, Michael Blackburn, Brendon Cleary, Ian Duhig, Wendy McCormick, Matthew Caley (Br, Am, Irish, Scottish) etc. also Carol Ann Duffy, Sean O'Brien, Frances Wilson" circ. 200. 3/yr. Pub'd 3 issues 1990; expects 3 issues 1991, 3 issues 1992. sub. price: $15, £5; per copy: $2+$2 postage, $5/£2+.35 postage; sample: $2+$2 postage, $5/£2+.35 postage. Back issues: £1 + .35p or $4. 50pp; 6½×8; †of. Reporting time: 1-3 months. Payment: 1 complimentary copies. Copyrighted, reverts to author. Iolaire Association.

FOOTBALL: OUR WAY, Our Way Publications, Dale Jellings, 5014 Starker Avenue, Madison, WI 53716, 608-241-0549. 1984. Poetry, fiction, articles, art, cartoons, interviews, satire, news items, non-fiction. "We're interested in seeing any type, form or variety of sports talk. Picture, if you will, a nation-wide network of sports buffs spouting off, discussing, arguing, concuring, and generally dispensing information unique to each contributer. Background articles on players, stats, updates; articles on favorite players and teams, histories, ratings, systems. We also accept short poetry and fiction dealing with baseball or football." circ. 20-100. 5/yr. Pub'd 5 issues 1990; expects 5 issues 1991, 5 issues 1992. sub. price: $5; per copy: $1; sample: $1. Back issues: scarce, but $1 a copy for any we have left. 8pp; 8½×11; †photocopy. Reporting time: 1 month (may hold longer). Payment: copies. Copyrighted, reverts to author. Pub's reviews: 3 in 1990. §Sports, sports biography, sports reference, etc. Ads: $20/$15/$10 quarter page.

THE FOOTLOOSE LIBRARIAN, Balmy Press, William J. Cutts, Box 972, Minneapolis, MN 55458, 612-874-8108. 1981. Articles, reviews, news items. "Travel news, travel book reviews, membership news. Submissions by subscribers only" circ. 500. 6/yr. Pub'd 6 issues 1990; expects 6 issues 1991, 6 issues 1992. sub. price: $23; per copy: $2; sample: free. Back issues: $2. Discounts: 15% to agents, 10% libraries. 6pp; 8½×11; of. Payment: none. Copyrighted. Pub's reviews: 18 in 1990. §Travel. Ads: $150/$75/$2 per line.

FOOTSTEPS, Footsteps Press, Bill Munster, Box 75, Round Top, NY 12473. 1983. Poetry, fiction, articles, art, interviews, criticism, reviews, letters, parts-of-novels, long-poems, non-fiction. "Recent contributors: Ramsey Campbell, Dean R. Koontz, T.E.D. Klein, J.N. Williamson. Story limit 3500 words, likewise on non-fiction" circ. 1.5M. 2/yr. Pub'd 2 issues 1990; expects 2 issues 1991, 2 issues 1992. price per copy: $4.00; sample: $6.00 ppd. Back issues: $6.00-includes postage. Discounts: 20% discount to dealers on 10 or more. 80pp; 5½×8; of. Reporting time: 4-8 weeks. Payment: 2 copies or 1¢ a words-editor's choice. Copyrighted, reverts to author. Pub's reviews: 5 in 1990. §Horror only—fiction/non-fiction. Ads: trade.

Footsteps Press (see also FOOTSTEPS), Bill Munster, Box 75, Round Top, NY 12473. 1983. "Horror stories" avg. press run 300-1M. Pub'd 1 title 1990; expects 1 title 1991. 1 title listed in the *Small Press Record of Books in Print* (20th Edition, 1991-92). Discounts: varies. 64pp; 5½×8; of. Reporting time: 4-8 weeks. Payment: individual contracts. Copyrights for author.

FOOTWORK: THE PATERSON LITERARY REVIEW, Maria Mazziotti Gillan, Editor, Passaic County Community College, College Boulevard, Paterson, NJ 07509, 201-684-6555. 1979. Poetry, fiction, art. "Stories should be short. Poems: under 60 lines preferred. Poetry, fiction, reviews. 8½ X 11 size for art work. Clear photocopies acceptable. *No unsolicited reviews" circ. 1M. 1/yr. Pub'd 1 issue 1990; expects 1 issue 1991, 1 issue 1992. sub. price: $5; per copy: $5; sample: $5. Back issues: $5. Discounts: 40% for orders of 10 or more. 88-120pp; 8½×11; †of. Reporting time: 3 months. Payment: contributor's copies. Copyrighted, reverts to author. Pub's reviews: 3 in 1990. §Poetry, short stories. Ads: $160/$80/$40 1/4 page. CCLM.

FOR PARENTS, Carolyn Shadle, Interpersonal Communication Services, Inc., 7052 West Lane, Suite #090163, Eden, NY 14057, 716-992-3316. 1977. Poetry, articles, photos, cartoons, reviews, non-fiction. "Brief articles of inspiration, practical tips, and resources to help parents improve their communication with their children and become effective in guiding their moral development. Features: *Together Time, Put-Down-of-The-Month, Communication-on-the-Run, Helps For Church And Organization Leaders, Resources, TV-Use And Abuse"* circ. 4M. 5/yr. Pub'd 5 issues 1990; expects 5 issues 1991, 5 issues 1992. sub. price: $14.95; per copy: $3; sample: 50¢ in bulk. Back issues: $1.50. Discounts: 10+, $9.95; 50+$7.95. 8pp; 8½×11; of. Payment: small honorarium. Copyrighted, does not revert to author. Pub's reviews: 10 in 1990. §Parenting, TV, Family Enrichment, Moral Development, Communication, Children's book which encourage moral development or expression of feelings.

FOR POETS ONLY, L.M. Walsh, PO Box 4855, Schenectady, NY 12304. 1985. Poetry. "Quality poetry, any subject, no pornography. Recent contributors: J. Frazeur, A.M. Swaim, C. Weirich, R. Mehr, G. Labocetta" circ. 200. 4/yr. Pub'd 4 issues 1990; expects 4 issues 1991, 4 issues 1992. price per copy: $3; sample: $3.50. Back issues: $3.50. Discounts: libraries 30%. 30pp; 5½×8½. Reporting time: up to 4 months, often sooner. Payment: cash prizes quarterly, plus copies. Copyrighted, reverts to author. CLMP, Poets House.

Forbes/Wittenburg & Brown, Patricia Wood, 250 West 57th Street, Suite 1527, New York, NY 10107, 212-969-0969. 1988. Non-fiction. avg. press run 5M. Pub'd 1 title 1990; expects 1 title 1991, 1 title 1992. 3 titles listed in the *Small Press Record of Books in Print* (20th Edition, 1991-92). avg. price, paper: $9.95-$14.95. Discounts: 40-50%. 300pp; 5½×8½; of. Does not copyright for author.

FORBIDDEN LINES, Charles Overbeck, Managing Editor, PO Box 23, Chapel Hill, NC 27514, 942-5386. 1989. Poetry, fiction, articles, art, photos, cartoons, interviews, satire, criticism, reviews, letters, parts-of-novels, collages, plays, concrete art, news items, non-fiction. "Any length for stories is fine, but preferred length is 3,000-10,000 words. I have a strong bias towards good xerox collages, but all art is welcome." circ. 500. 6/yr. Pub'd 3 issues 1990; expects 5 issues 1991, 5 issues 1992. sub. price: $14; per copy: $2; sample: $2.50. Back issues: $1.50. Discounts: $1 off every 5 copies ordered in bulk. 64pp; 8×11; of. Reporting time: 1 month. Payment: contributor's copies, discounts on subscriptions. Copyrighted, reverts to author. Pub's reviews: none in 1990. §Science fiction, fantasy, horror, experimental, art, photography. Ads: $35/$25/$15 1/4 page.

FORCED EXPOSURE, Jimmy Johnson, Byron Coley, PO Box 1611, Waltham, MA 02254, 617-924-3923. 1982. Fiction, articles, art, photos, cartoons, interviews, satire, criticism, reviews, music, letters, plays. circ. 10M. 4/yr. Pub'd 4 issues 1990; expects 4 issues 1991, 4 issues 1992. sub. price: $9; per copy: $2.50; sample: same. Back issues: list available for SASE. Discounts: 30-50% discount available depending on # ordered—list with complete information available. 100pp; 8½×11; of. Reporting time: 4-6 weeks. Payment: varies. Copyrighted, reverts to author. Pub's reviews: 100 in 1990. §Music, science fiction, fiction (non-mainstream). Ads: $400/$250.

The Forces of Magic (see also The Broken Stone), D. Steven Conkle, Annabel Conkle, PO Box 246, Reynoldsburg, OH 43068. 1984. Poetry. "We are an imprint of *The Broken Stone*, and potential contributors should read the information under that listing. Our only bias is one in favor of high quality. Material submitted should be designed to fit a broadside or folio format since that's what we publish. Recent contributors include Taelen Thomas, d steven conkle, and Arthur Winfield Knight" avg. press run 300-500. Pub'd 1 title 1990; expects 5 titles 1991, 5 titles 1992. avg. price, other: $3 broadsides. Discounts: negotiable. 1 page; size varies; of. Reporting time: fast. Payment: percentage of copies. Copyrights for author. COSMEP.

Ford-Brown & Co., Publishers, Steven Ford Brown, PO Box 2764, Boston, MA 02208-2764. 1983. Poetry, articles, photos, interviews, criticism. "Profiles of American poets. Each limited edition volume includes selected poems, essays, interveiws, biographical and bibliographic information. Published volumes include *The Giver of Morning: On The Poetry of Dave Smith; Dissolve To Island: On The Poetry of John Logan; Earth That Sings: On The Poetry of Andrew Glaze; Poet As Zimmer, Zimmer As Poet: On The Poetry of Paul Zimmer; An Answering Music: On The poetry of Carolyn Kizer; Heart's Invention: On The Poetry of Vassar Miller; On The Poetry of Fred Chappell*. Also published titles of original poetry: *We, The Generation in the Wilderness*, Ricardo Feierstein, tr. J. Kates and Stephen Sadow" avg. press run 1.5M-3M. Pub'd 1 title 1990; expects 2 titles 1991, 3 titles 1992. 6 titles listed in the *Small Press Record of Books in Print* (20th Edition, 1991-92). avg. price, paper: $15.95; other: $75 signed edition. Discounts: standard 40% for 5+ copies, 20% 1-4 copies. 256-300pp; 5½×8½; of. Reporting time: 1 month. Payment: copies, percentages. Copyrights for author.

FOREFRONT—HEALTH INVESTIGATIONS, Steven W. Fowkes, John A. Mann, PO Box 60637, Palo Alto, CA 94306, 408-733-2010; 415-949-0919. 1983. Articles, interviews, reviews, news items. circ. 500. 6/yr. Pub'd 5 issues 1990; expects 6 issues 1991, 6 issues 1992. sub. price: $18; per copy: $3.50; sample: free. Back issues: $3/4 issues, $2.50/10 issues, $2/20 issues. 8pp; 8½×11; of. Reporting time: variable. Payment: tba. Copyrighted, does not revert to author. Pub's reviews: 2 in 1990. §Health, medicine, nutrition. Ads: none.

FOREHEAD: Writing & Art Journal, Beyond Baroque Foundation Publications, Benjamin Weissman, Editor, PO Box 2727, Venice, CA 90291, 213-822-3006. 1987. Poetry, fiction, art, criticism, reviews, non-fiction. *"Forehead: Writing & Arts Journal* is distributed by Sun & Moon Press in Los Angeles. Calendar

Of Events, and membership in Beyond Baroque Foundation available for $30 a year. A $30 membership does *not* include a subscription to *Forehead."* circ. 1M. 1/yr. Pub'd 1 issue 1990; expects 1 issue 1991, 1 issue 1992. sub. price: $15 institutions, $10 individuals; per copy: $6.50; sample: $6.50. Back issues: query. Discounts: none. 150pp; 6×8; of. Reporting time: 4-6 weeks. Payment: copies only. Copyrighted. Pub's reviews: 3 in 1990. Ads: $325/$175/$95 1/4 page. CCLM.

FORESIGHT MAGAZINE, John W.B. Barklam, Judy Barklam, 44 Brockhurst Road, Hodge Hill, Birmingham B36 8JB, England, 021-783-0587. 1970. Articles, reviews, letters, news items. "Articles of approx. 1000 words welcomed. A bias towards philosophy as related to life. Dealing also in mysticism, occultism, U.F.O.S and allied subjects. Aims are to help create peace and encourage spiritual awareness and evolution in the world" circ. 1.1M. 4/yr. Pub'd 4 issues 1990; expects 4 issues 1991, 4 issues 1992. sub. price: £2.50 - $4.50; per copy: 50p, $1; sample: 55p, $1.10. Back issues: 30p - 60¢. Discounts: none. 12pp; 14×10; †dupl, photocopying. Reporting time: immediate. Payment: none. Copyrighted, rights revert to author if requested. Pub's reviews: 40 in 1990. §Health, philosophy, psychic phenomena, UFOs, prediction, occult, spiritualism, and allied fiction. Ads: £9 ($16.25)/£5 ($9)/4p (8¢).

THE FORMALIST, William Baer, Editor, 525 S. Rotherwood, Evansville, IN 47714. 1990. Poetry. *"The Formalist* publishes only *metrical* poetry. Recent issues contained poetry by Howard Nemerov, Richard Wilbur, Elizabeth Jennings, Donald Justice, Robert Conquest, James Merrill, John Updike, X.J. Kennedy, May Swenson, Fred Chappell, John Hollander, Molly Peacock, Dana Gioia, Rachel Hadas and Elizabeth Spires. We are particularly interested in metrical poetry written in the traditional forms, including ballads, sonnets, couplets, the Greek forms, the French forms, etc. We will also consider metrical translations of major formalist non-English poets—from the Ancient Greeks to the present. We are not, however, interested in haiku (or syllabic verse of any kind) or sestinas. Only rarely do we accept a poem over 2 pages, and we do not publish any type of erotica, blasphemy, vulgarity, or racism. *The Formalist* considers submissions throughout the year, 3-5 poems at one time. We do not consider simultaneous submissions, previously published work, or disk submissions. A brief cover letter is recommended, and a SASE is necessary for the return of the MSS." 2/yr. Pub'd 2 issues 1990; expects 2 issues 1991, 2 issues 1992. sub. price: $12; per copy: $6.50; sample: $6.50. 128pp; 6×9; of. Reporting time: 4-8 weeks. Payment: 2 copies. Copyrighted, reverts to author.

FORMATIONS, Jonathan Brent, Frances Padorr Brent, 625 Colfax Street, Evanston, IL 60201. 1984. Fiction, photos. *"Formations* publishes recent American fiction, fiction in translation, essays on the arts, and photographs. Contributors include Milan Kundera, Primo Levi, Edna O'Brian, Luisa Valenzuela, Jan Kott, Robert Creeley, Arturo Vivante" circ. 1.2M. 3/yr. Pub'd 3 issues 1990; expects 3 issues 1991, 3 issues 1992. 1 title listed in the *Small Press Record of Books in Print* (20th Edition, 1991-92). sub. price: $16; per copy: $6.95; sample: same. Back issues: $6.95. Discounts: library rates: 1 yr. $32, 2 yr. $55; bookstore discounts upon request. 135pp; 8×11; lp. Reporting time: 1-3 months. Payment: varies. Copyrighted, reverts to author. Ads: $200/$125.

44 Press, Inc. (see also THE BAD HENRY REVIEW), Michael Malinowitz, Evelyn Horowitz, Mary du Passage, Box 150045, Van Brant Station, Brooklyn, NY 11215-0001. 1981. Poetry, long-poems. "Query first for books. Unsolicited ms will not be read. Plans 1 title per year: books of poetry, does collaboratives, chapbooks. No biases. First title scheduled for spring, 1990. Dues not expected to accept unsolicited ms, except for magazine, *The Bad Henry Review"* avg. press run 1M. Discounts: query. 64pp; 5½×8½; of. Payment: arranged with author. Copyrights for author. COSMEP, CODA.

Forty-Seven Books, Greg Bachar, c/o MFA Creative Writing Program, 452 Bartlett Hall, MA University, Amherst, MA 01002. 1991. Poetry, fiction, long-poems, non-fiction. "Will put together xerox books, one of poetry, one of fiction, one of something else or both. Surreal bent writing for initiates and diabolicals" avg. press run 47. Expects 3 titles 1991, 3 titles 1992. avg. price, paper: $4.70. 47pp; size varies; †mi, xerox. Reporting time: 4 weeks. Payment: copies (12), profits from book pay for its production and distribution. Copyrights for author.

Fotofolio, Inc., Martin Bondell, Juliette Galant, Ron Schick, 536 Broadway, 2nd Floor, New York, NY 10012, 212-226-0923. 1975. Art, photos. "Publishers of art and photographs in poster, postcard and notecard format and folios by artist or photographers. Recent contributors: Ralph Gibson, Lisette Model, Robert Mapplethorpe, Duane Michals, Man Ray, Brassal, Keith Haring, Cindy Sherman, Andre Kertesz, Bruce Weber, Bernice Abbott, Herb Ritts, Herri Cartier-Bresson, Neil Slavin, Alexander Rodchenko, Arnold Newman, Margaret Bourke-White, Annie Leibovitz" avg. press run 7.5M. Pub'd 300 titles 1990; expects 400 titles 1991. Discounts: 50%. duotone process, & four-color offset. COSMEP, ABA.

Foundation Books, Duane Hutchinson, Stephen K. Hutchinson, PO Box 29229, Lincoln, NE 68529, 402-466-4988. 1970. Poetry, non-fiction. "History, biography and storytelling are our main areas of interest. The format of the paperback books is 5½ X 8½. The binding is Smythe-sewn for added strength and alkaline-based paper stock is used which meets the requirements of the American National Standard for

Information Sciences - Permanence of Paper for Printed Library Materials, ANSI Z39.48-1984. The books are copyrighted by Foundation Books and Library of Congress Cataloging-in-Publication Data is included. Expanded bar codes are used on the back covers." avg. press run 1M-3M. Pub'd 4 titles 1990; expects 3 titles 1991, 4 titles 1992. avg. price, cloth: $19.95; paper: $6.95. Discounts: booksellers: 1 20%, 2-4 33%, 5-49 40%, 50-99 41%, 100-249 42%, 250+ 43%. 125-200pp; 5½x8½. Reporting time: acknowledge receipt, 1 week; reading 2-6 months. Payment: to be arranged with individual author. Does not copyright for author.

The Foundation Center, Thomas Buckman, President; Sara L. Engelhardt, 79 Fifth Avenue, New York, NY 10003, 212-620-4230. 1956. "The Foundation Center publishes and disseminates through its national library network of over 180 locations materials on foundation and corporate philanthropy. Reference. Production method: Primarily computer photocomposition, some in-house design and paste-up with additional freelance support" avg. press run 2M-18M. 59 titles listed in the *Small Press Record of Books in Print* (20th Edition, 1991-92). avg. price, other: $7.50-$350. Discounts: 5-24 copies 20%, 25-49 25%, 50-99 30%, 100+ 35%. Reporting time: 1-3 months. Payment: 10% royalty. Copyrights for author.

Four Walls Eight Windows, John Oakes, Daniel Simon, PO Box 548, Village Station, New York, NY 10014, 212-226-4998. 1987. Poetry, fiction, non-fiction. avg. press run 4M. Pub'd 16 titles 1990; expects 18 titles 1991, 18 titles 1992. 17 titles listed in the *Small Press Record of Books in Print* (20th Edition, 1991-92). avg. price, cloth: $19.95; paper: $9.95. Discounts: write for details. 300pp; 6x9, 5½x8¼; of. Reporting time: 3 months. Payment: varies. Copyrights for author. Publishers Group West, 4065 Hollis, Emeryville, CA 94608.

FOURTH WORLD REVIEW, John Papworth, 24 Abercorn Place, London, N.W.8, England. 1966. Articles, interviews, criticism, reviews, letters, news items, non-fiction. "Any material bearing on human scale concepts—politics and economics" circ. 2M. 5/yr. Pub'd 5 issues 1990; expects 5 issues 1991, 5 issues 1992. sub. price: according to self-assessed income status; per copy: £1; sample: £1. Back issues: £2. Discounts: 50%. 32pp; size A5. Payment: none. Pub's reviews: 18 in 1990. §Economics, politics, ecology. Ads: on application.

FOX VALLEY LIVING, Francie Graham Smith, Editor; Becky Moorehead Hoag, Associate Editor, 707 Kautz Road, St. Charles, IL 60174, 708-377-7570. 1989. Poetry, fiction, articles, art, photos, cartoons, interviews, satire, letters, news items, non-fiction. "'Almanac' uses short (200 words or less) 'newsy bites,' trivia, etc. Feature sections use articles in two sizes: 750 words, and 1,000 words. *All material must pertain to or have specific interest for the Fox River Valley Region of Illinois.*" circ. 30M. 6/yr. Pub'd 9 issues 1990; expects 6 issues 1991, 6 issues 1992. sub. price: $10.95; per copy: $2; sample: $2. Back issues: cover price, when available. Discounts: minimum of 5, $1 per issue + shipping. 96pp; 8x10¾; of. Reporting time: prefer written queries. Payment: upon publication. Copyrighted, rights restricted. Pub's reviews: 6 in 1990. §Anything by authors from our region, or about people, places or issues of regional interest. Ads: $1,900/$1,290/classifieds are 1/12 page $180. ABC.

FOXFIRE, Foxfire Press, Eliot Wigginton, Supervisor, Box B, Rabun Gap, GA 30568, 404-746-5828. 1966. Articles, interviews, non-fiction. "*Foxfire* is edited by high school students as educational project" circ. 4M. 4/yr. Pub'd 4 issues 1990; expects 4 issues 1991, 4 issues 1992. sub. price: $9; per copy: $2.25. Back issues: available upon request. Discounts: 40% trade. 64pp; 7x10; lp. Copyrighted, reverts to author.

Foxfire Press (see also FOXFIRE), Eliot Wigginton, Hilton Smith, Box B, Rabun Gap, GA 30568, 404-746-5828. 1981. Articles, photos, interviews, plays. "Student authors - high school education project" avg. press run 30M. Pub'd 2 titles 1990; expects 2 titles 1991, 3 titles 1992. avg. price, paper: $16. Discounts: 40% trade. 300pp; lp. Copyrights for author.

FPMI Communications, Inc., Ralph R. Smith, President, 3322 South Memorial Parkway, #40, Huntsville, AL 35801, 205-882-3042. 1985. Articles, interviews, non-fiction. "Formerly WordSmith, Inc. We normally publish short books of interest to Federal Government Employees, Federal Management issues, and other books of interest to public sector Gov't. employees" avg. press run 5M. Pub'd 4 titles 1990; expects 6 titles 1991, 6 titles 1992. 10 titles listed in the *Small Press Record of Books in Print* (20th Edition, 1991-92). avg. price, paper: $8.95. 75pp; 5½x8½; of. Reporting time: 60 days. Payment: varies depending upon nature of submission and subject matter. Does not copyright for author.

FRAGMENTS, Alchemy Press, Fred Calero, Publisher Editor, 1789 Macdonald Avenue, Brooklyn, NY 11230, 718-339-0184. 1988. Poetry, fiction, articles, art, photos, criticism, collages, news items, non-fiction. "Recent contributors: Jim Feast, Eve Teitebaum" circ. 1M. 4/yr. Pub'd 1 issue 1990; expects 3 issues 1991, 4 issues 1992. sub. price: $8; per copy: $2; sample: $2. Back issues: $2. Discounts: $1.50. 40pp; 5½x8½; †xerox. Reporting time: 60 days at least. Payment: 10 free issues. Copyrighted, reverts to author. Pub's reviews: 2 in 1990. §Poetry, art. Ads: $20/$15.

FRANK: AN INTERNATIONAL JOURNAL OF CONTEMPORARY WRITING AND ART, David Applefield, Editor-Publisher, BP 29, 94301 Vincennes Cedex, France, (1) 43-65-64-05. 1983. Poetry, fiction, art, photos, interviews, parts-of-novels, collages, plays. "All texts should be under 20 double spaced typed pages—absolutely open to all styles, techniques, visions, genres, languages. Recent contributors include: Vaclav Havel, W.S. Merwin, Gennadi Aigi, Maurice Girodias, Rita Dove, Maris Gallant, Duo Duo, Stephen Dixon, A.I. Bezzerides, Dennis Hopper, John Sanford, Bukowski, Hubert Selby, Italo Calvino, Breyten Breytenbach, Paul Bowles, Derek Walcott, Tom Waits, John Berger, Edmond Jabes, E.M. Cioran, Robert Coover, 40 Philippino protest poets, and plenty of lesser known talent. Additional address: Box 1190, Boston, MA 02205-1190'' circ. 4M. 2/yr. Pub'd 2 issues 1990; expects 2 issues 1991, 2 issues 1992. sub. price: $30 (4 issues), $60 instit.; per copy: $8; sample: $8. Back issues: issues 1-13 pack for $55. Discounts: 35% for bookstores and orders over 6 copies. 224pp; 8×5; of. Reporting time: 10 weeks. Payment: 2 copies plus $5/printed page. Copyrighted, reverts to author. Pub's reviews. §Literature, poetry, politics, art, translation. Ads: $1,000/$500/$3500 back cover. CCLM.

The Chas. Franklin Press, Linda D. Meyer, 7821 175th Street SW, Edmonds, WA 98020-1835, 206-774-6979. 1979. Non-fiction. avg. press run 5M. Expects 1 title 1991. 11 titles listed in the *Small Press Record of Books in Print* (20th Edition, 1991-92). avg. price, cloth: $9; paper: $3.95. Discounts: 40% to regular bookstores on 5 or more; 20% 2-4. 40pp; 5¼×8½. Reporting time: 2 months. Payment: average 8%. Copyrights for author.

FRASER FORUM, The Fraser Institute, Kristin McCahon, Production Editor, 626 Bute Street, 2nd Floor, Vancouver, BC V6E 3M1, Canada, 604-688-0221, FAX 604-688-8539. 1974. circ. 3M. 12/yr. Pub'd 12 issues 1990; expects 12 issues 1991, 12 issues 1992. sub. price: $48 + 7% GST Canadian subs.; per copy: $4 + 7% GST Canadian residents; sample: free. Back issues: $4 + 7% GST Canadian residents. Discounts: negotiable depending on quantity ordered. 36pp; 5½×8½; of. Copyrighted, does not revert to author. Association of Book Publishers of B.C. and Canada, Canadian Book Sellers Association.

The Fraser Institute (see also FRASER FORUM; ON BALANCE: MEDIA TREATMENT OF PUBLIC POLICY ISSUES), Kristin McCahon, Production Editor, 626 Bute Street, 2nd Floor, Vancouver, BC V6E 3M1, Canada, 604-688-0221, FAX 604-688-8539. 1974. News items, non-fiction. avg. press run 3M. Pub'd 6 titles 1990; expects 8 titles 1991, 8 titles 1992. avg. price, cloth: $29.95; paper: $19.95. Discounts: trade, quantity and jobber discounts available. 250pp; 5½×8½; of. Does not copyright for author. Association of Book Publishers of B.C. and Canada, Canadian Book Sellers Association.

‡**Free Association Books (FAB) (see also FREE ASSOCIATIONS: PSYCHOANALYSIS, GROUPS, POLITICS, CULTURE; RADICAL SCIENCE SERIES),** Les Levidow, Bob Young, Karl Figlio, 26 Freegrove Road, London N7 9RQ, United Kingdom, 01-609-5646-0507. 1983. Articles, art, photos, cartoons, interviews, criticism, reviews, letters, non-fiction. "Social critique of science, technology and medicine, especially from Marxist and psychoanalytic approaches" avg. press run 2.5M. Pub'd 4 titles 1990; expects 16 titles 1991. 23 titles listed in the *Small Press Record of Books in Print* (20th Edition, 1991-92). avg. price, cloth: £15; paper: £6. Discounts: 1/3 discount to bookshops. 192pp; size variable; of. Reporting time: 3 months. Payment: variable, to be negotiated. Copyrights for author. Association of Little Presses, Small Publishers Guild, PA.

FREE ASSOCIATIONS: PSYCHOANALYSIS, GROUPS, POLITICS, CULTURE, Free Association Books (FAB), Free Associations Editorial Board, 26 Freegrove Road, London N7 9RQ, United Kingdom, 01-609-5646. 1984. Articles, photos, cartoons, interviews, criticism, reviews, letters, non-fiction. "Themes being developed for future issues include: masculinity, fatherhood, children's fiction, women's depression and therapy, psychoanalysis in France, trainings in psychoanalysis, psychoanalysis and art, psychoanalysis and literature, psychoanalysis and anthropology, psychoanalysis and history, critical social psychology, anorexia, Freudian biologism, the politics and sociology of psychotherapy, the psychodynamics of racism" circ. 2.5M. 4/yr. Pub'd 1 issue 1990; expects 4 issues 1991, 4 issues 1992. sub. price: £20/$25 individuals, £35/$55 institutions; per copy: £5.50 individuals; £9 institutions. Back issues: £5-institutions; £2/$5-individuals. Discounts: 1/3 to bookshops. 160pp; size A5. Reporting time: 3 months. Payment: none. Not copyrighted. Pub's reviews. §Social and cultural aspects of psychoanalysis, psychotherapy, psychology of groups and personality. Ads taken on exchange basis only.

FREE FOCUS, Patricia D. Coscia, Editor; Nancy A. Jensen, Co-Editor, Wagner Press, 224 82nd Street, #1, Brooklyn, NY 11209, (718) 680-3899. 1985. Poetry, long-poems, collages. "We want all types except X-rated. The poems can be as long as 2 pages or as short as 3 lines. The subject matter is of all types and styles. The purpose of the magazine is to give women writers a place in literature, that women have a will to succeed and earn respect for their achievements. For guidelines, send SASE. Poetry contest deadline May 3rd, send for guidelines with SASE" circ. 100-150. 2/yr. Pub'd 2 issues 1990; expects 2 issues 1991, 2 issues 1992. sub. price: $3; per copy: $2; sample: $2. Back issues: $2. Discounts: none. 10pp; 8×14; †mi. Reporting time: as soon as possible. Payment: up to 2-4 copies of magazine. Copyrighted, reverts to author. Pub's reviews: 1 in 1990. §Poetry, writing. Ads: $1 full page. Brooklyn Writer's Club, 73rd Street & Ridge Blvd., Brooklyn, NY 11209.

FREE INQUIRY, Paul Kurtz, Council For Democratic & Secular Humanism, PO Box 5, Buffalo, NY 14215,

716-834-2921. 1981. Articles, cartoons, interviews, criticism, reviews, letters, non-fiction. "Recent contributors: Martin Gardner, B.F. Skinner, Albert Ellis, Steve Allen" circ. 20M. 4/yr. Pub'd 4 issues 1990; expects 4 issues 1991, 4 issues 1992. sub. price: $25; per copy: $5; sample: same. Back issues: 20% discount on 5 or more copies, 40% for 10 or more. Discounts: agency remits—40% 1st year, 20% 2nd year and after. 64pp; 8½x11; †of. Reporting time: varies. Payment: varies. Copyrighted. Pub's reviews: 12 in 1990. §Philosophy, religion, morality, humanism. Ads: varies.

FREE LIFE, Libertarian Books and the Libertarian Alliance, Chris R. Tame, Brian Micklethwait, 1 Russell Chambers, The Piazza, Covent Garden, London WC2E 8AA, England, 01-836-6913. 1979. Articles, interviews, criticism, news items. "Political, economical, cultural articles from a libertarian perspective" circ. 1M. 4/yr. Pub'd 4 issues 1990; expects 4 issues 1991, 4 issues 1992. sub. price: £10.00. †of. Reporting time: immediate. Payment: none. Copyrighted, does not revert to author. Pub's reviews. §Politics, economics, psychology, sociology.

FREE LUNCH, Ron Offen, PO Box 7647, Laguna Niguel, CA 92607-7647. 1988. Poetry, news items. "Please limit to three poems per submission. Do not want ponderous, abstract, philosophic work with pithy observations, nicey-nice religious poems with tacked-on morals, greeting card love, nature, or animal verse. Sympathetic to new poets, experimental work. No opposed to form per se. Want to give all 'serious' U.S. poets a free subscription (based on submissions). Recent contributors: James Reiss, Billy Collins, Frank Polite, Paul Weinman, Gerald Locklin, Malcolm Glass, Philip Dacey, Neal Bowers, Kendra Kopelke, Bill Zavatsky. Always try to comment on submissions. Must have SASE with *all* submissions, inquiries, etc" circ. 850. 3/yr. Pub'd 3 issues 1990; expects 3 issues 1991, 3 issues 1992. sub. price: $10; per copy: $4; sample: $4. 32pp; 5½x8½; of. Reporting time: 1-3 months. Payment: 1 copy of appearance issue and free subscription. Copyrighted, reverts to author.

Free People Press (see also BOTH SIDES NOW), Elihu Edelson, Route 6, Box 28, Tyler, TX 75704. 1974. "Free People Press is concentrating on getting *Both Sides Now* back in print for 1991" 3 titles listed in the *Small Press Record of Books in Print* (20th Edition, 1991-92). 8½x11; web of.

FREE PRESS, Campaign For Press & Broadcasting Freedom, Simon Collings, 9 Poland Street, London W1V 3DG, England, 01-437-2795; 01-437-0189. 1979. Articles, photos, cartoons, interviews, criticism, reviews, letters, news items, non-fiction. "Acts as a newsletter for members of the CPBF, with pages devoted to international media issues, right of reply, reviews, letters etc., plus special supplements on topical, ethical, political, and industrial issues related to the media; i.e. photo journalism, censorship, sexism, racism, peace, etc. Contributors include politicians, trades union activists, journalists in all media, etc" circ. 11.5M. 6/yr. Pub'd 6 issues 1990; expects 6 issues 1991, 6 issues 1992. price per copy: 30p. Back issues: 15p plus postage (50p to USA). Discounts: by arrangement—*Free Press* has largely a subscription sales market to CPBF members (£10pa. UK). 12pp; size A4; of. Reporting time: for Feb. 1 issue, its Jan. 8, April 1 its March 8, etc. Payment: commissioned photography only. Pub's reviews: 28 in 1990. §All aspects of the media—industrial, political, ethical, technical. Ads: £275/£150/£15-£100 display style.

FREE PRESS NETWORK, Michael Grossberg, Paula Brookmire, Steve Stephens, PO Box 15548, Columbus, OH 43215, 614-236-1908. 1981. Articles, interviews, criticism, reviews, letters, news items. "*Free Press Network* is the Free Press Association's newsletter for journalists committed to the defense—and expansion—of First Amendment rights. We're looking for articles, news items and editorials/essays analyzing the frontiers of freedom of communication: how the First Amendment can be extended to the electronic media, ways in which journalists can take the offensive in human rights/Bill of Rights issues as they affect the media and also as they affect the issues and problems journalists confront daily" circ. 500. 6/yr. Pub'd 6 issues 1990; expects 6 issues 1991, 6 issues 1992. sub. price: $20; per copy: $4; sample: $3. Back issues: $3. Discounts: none. 8-12pp; 8½x11; †of. Reporting time: 2 months. Payment: 1 year subscription to *Free Press Network*; book discounts. Not copyrighted. Pub's reviews: 18 in 1990. §Freedom of the press issues, media industry, human rights journalism, freelancing. Ads: $100/$60/20¢ per word. FPA.

FREE SPIRIT: NEWS AND VIEWS ON GROWING UP, Free Spirit Publishing Inc., Judy Galbraith, Editor-in-Chief; Pamela Espeland, Editor, 400 First Avenue North, Suite 616, Minneapolis, MN 55401, 612-338-2068. 1987. Articles, cartoons, interviews, non-fiction. "A newsletter that comes out five times during the school year (Sept.-May). Primary focus is the experience of growing up gifted/creative/talented. Also runs numerous surveys. Regular features include: 'Dear Judy Q & A' column, an interview by or about a unique person, articles by leading authorities in the field of psychology or education. The most recent issue focused on tests and test-taking. Also printed winning pieces from our writing contest. Request query before submissions, prefer articles under 1,500 words" circ. 3M. 5/yr. Pub'd 3 issues 1990; expects 5 issues 1991, 5 issues 1992. sub. price: $10; per copy: $2; sample: $2. Back issues: $3. Discounts: teacher's classroom supplement with orders of 10 or more to same address, 10-30 10%, 31+ 15%. 8pp; 11x17; of. Reporting time: 1 month. Payment: negotiable. Copyrighted, does not revert to author. Pub's reviews: 10 in 1990. §Non fiction books and computer software. Ads: 1/4 $210/1/2 $110/1/6 $70/classified $25 up to 40 words. PMA, MAP, Publisher's

Roundtable.

Free Spirit Publishing Inc. (see also FREE SPIRIT: NEWS AND VIEWS ON GROWING UP), Judy Galbraith, Pamela Espeland, 400 First Avenue North, Suite 616, Minneapolis, MN 55401, 612-338-2068. 1983. Non-fiction. "Specializes in non-fiction learning materials for teens. Includes books in gifted education and psychology/self-help with some parenting and teaching materials. *Please* query before sending unsolicited materials—submit only outline and sample chapter" avg. press run 5M. Pub'd 3 titles 1990; expects 6 titles 1991, 6 titles 1992. 26 titles listed in the *Small Press Record of Books in Print* (20th Edition, 1991-92). avg. price, paper: $10.95. Discounts: 10-24 books 20%, 25-49 25%, 50-99 30%, 100+ 40%. 150pp; 6×9, 8½×11; of. Reporting time: 1-3 months. Payment: individually negotiated. Copyrights for author. PMA, MAP, Publisher's Roundtable.

FREEBIES MAGAZINE, Linda Cook, Editor; Gene Zannon, Publisher, PO Box 20283, Santa Barbara, CA 93120, 805-962-9135. 1977. "All materials produced by in-house staff. We do not solicit or accept freelance materials. No submissions accepted" circ. 450M. 5/yr. Pub'd 6 issues 1990; expects 5 issues 1991, 5 issues 1992. sub. price: $8.95; per copy: $2.50; sample: $2.50. Back issues: not available. Discounts: 20% off on bulk/agency purchases. 32pp; 8¼×11. Copyrighted. Ads: classified $5.50/word ($15 minimum). COSMEP.

FREEDOM FORTNIGHTLY, Freedom Press, Collective, In Angel Alley, 84B Whitechapel High St, London E1 7QX, England, 071 247 9249. 1886. Articles, cartoons, criticism, reviews, letters, news items. circ. 1.7M. 24/yr. Pub'd 24 issues 1990; expects 24 issues 1991, 24 issues 1992. sub. price: £14 inland, £18 surface mail; per copy: 50p; sample: SAE. Back issues: available at price of current issue (or of sub. for year sets). Discounts: 25% to indiv/bulk order, 33% to shops. 8pp; size A3; †of. Reporting time: normally by return. Payment: none. Copyrighted, reverts to author. Pub's reviews: 30-35 in 1990. §Anarchism. No ads.

Freedom Press (see also FREEDOM FORTNIGHTLY; RAVEN ANARCHIST QUARTERLY), Collective, In Angel Alley, 84B Whitechapel High Street, London E1 7QX, England, 01-247-9249. 1886. avg. press run 2M. Pub'd 5 titles 1990; expects 5 titles 1991. 40 titles listed in the *Small Press Record of Books in Print* (20th Edition, 1991-92). avg. price, cloth: £6.00; paper: £2.37. Discounts: 33⅓% singles, 35% 2+ copies. 155pp; 8×5; †of. Reporting time: by return. Payment: by negotiation. Copyrights for author if required.

THE FREEDONIA GAZETTE, Paul G. Wesolowski, Editor-in-Chief; Raymond D. White, U.K. Editor; Neal E. Gorman, Graphics Editor, Darien B-28, New Hope, PA 18938, 215-862-9734. 1978. Articles, art, photos, cartoons, interviews, criticism, reviews, letters, news items, non-fiction. "Articles range from 1 typewritten page (double-spaced) to fifteen pages. We deal mainly with articles on the Marx Brothers and people associated with them, reviews of books on these topics, reviews of stage shows impersonating them, interviews with people who worked with the Marxes and with impersonators. We're especially in need of artwork, either drawings or caricatures of the Marxes. We have a strong reputation for well-researched articles which turn up facts not known to most fans and fanatics. U.K. subscriptions/submissions: Dr. Raymond D. White, 137 Easterly Road, Leeds LS8 2RY England" circ. 400. 2/yr. Pub'd 2 issues 1990; expects 2 issues 1991, 2 issues 1992. sub. price: $10; per copy: $5; sample: $5. Back issues: $5 when available (#1-#4,#8 currently sold-out). Discounts: 10 or more of the same issue (current or back issues) $4.50 each; 50 or more (mix and match current and/or back issues) $4 each. 20pp; 8½×11; of. Reporting time: maximum 1 month. Payment: sample copy. Copyrighted, rights generally don't revert to author, but open to negotiation. Pub's reviews: 4 in 1990. §Marx Brothers, humor, people associated with Marxes in any way. Ads: $60/$34.

FREELANCE, Saskatchewan Writers Guild, April Davies, Editor, Box 3986, Regina, Saskatchewan S4P 3R9, Canada, 306-757-6310. 1970. Poetry, fiction, articles, cartoons, interviews, reviews, letters, news items, non-fiction. "Our membership newsmagazine." circ. 750+. 10/yr. Pub'd 10 issues 1990; expects 10 issues 1991, 10 issues 1992. sub. price: $40/$20 for students & seniors (SWG membership rate); sample: free. 44pp; 8½×5½; of. Reporting time: varies. Payment: $15/published page. Copyrighted. Pub's reviews: 40 in 1990. §Canadian, esp. Sask-authored or published, literary works. Ads: $150/$100/20¢ per word.

Freelance Communications, Randy Cassingham, P.O. Box 1895, Upland, CA 91785, 714-985-3465. 1985. Non-fiction. avg. press run 3M-5M. Pub'd 1 title 1990; expects 2 titles 1991, 2 titles 1992. 2 titles listed in the *Small Press Record of Books in Print* (20th Edition, 1991-92). avg. price, paper: $12.95. Discounts: 1-4 20%, 5-24 40%, 25-49 43%, 50-99 46%, 100+ 50%, 500+ 55%. 96pp; 6×9; of. Reporting time: 1-2 weeks on queries. Payment: negotiable. Copyrights for author.

FREELANCE MARKET NEWS, Freelance Press Services, Saundrea Williams, Editor, Cumberland House, Lissadell Street, Salford, Manchester M6 6GG, England. 1962. "Provides market information telling writers and photographers where to sell. World-wide circulation" 11/yr. Pub'd 11 issues 1990; expects 11 issues 1991, 11 issues 1992. sub. price: overseas £22 ($36). 12pp; size A4. Reporting time: 1 week.

Freelance Press Services (see also FREELANCE MARKET NEWS), S.E. Williams, Arthur Waite, Cumberland House, Lissadell Street, Salford, Manchester M6 6GG, England, 061 832-5079. 1960. "We use articles of interest to freelance writers" avg. press run 2M. 12-32pp. Reporting time: 1 week. Does not copyright for author.

FREELANCE WRITER'S REPORT, Cassell Communications Inc., Dana K. Cassell, PO Box 9844, Ft. Lauderdale, FL 33310, 305-485-0795; 800-351-9278. 1977. Articles, interviews, news items, non-fiction. circ. 2.2M. 12/yr. Pub'd 12 issues 1990; expects 12 issues 1991, 12 issues 1992. sub. price: $40; per copy: $4; sample: $4. Back issues: $4. 8pp; 8½×11; of and desktop publishing. Reporting time: 1 month. Payment: 10¢ word. Copyrighted, reverts to author except for right to reprint. Pub's reviews: 36 in 1990. §Freelance writing and freelance photography. Ads: 30¢ per word with discount for multiple insertions. Florida Magazine Association.

The FreeSolo Press (see also THE CLIMBING ART), David Mazel, PO Box 816, Alamosa, CO 81101, 719-589-5579. 1987. Poetry, fiction, articles, art, photos, cartoons, interviews, satire, criticism, reviews, letters, parts-of-novels, long-poems, collages, news items, non-fiction. "We will consider any material pertaining to the mountains, mountaineering, wilderness exploration, mountain-area guides, or biographies of figures associated with the mountains. Last title: *The Colorado Trail* by Randy Jacobs" avg. press run 2M. Pub'd 1 title 1990; expects 1-2 titles 1991, 1-2 titles 1992. 1 title listed in the *Small Press Record of Books in Print* (20th Edition, 1991-92). avg. price, paper: $12.95. Discounts: 1-4 copies 20%, 5-24 40%, 25-49 43%, 50-99 46%, 100+ 50%; jobbers up to 55%. 192pp; 5¼×8½; of. Reporting time: 2 months. Payment: 8-12%, semi-annual. Copyrights for author.

French Broad Press, Jessica Bayer, J.W. Bonner, The Asheville School, Asheville, NC 28806, 704-255-7909. 1989. Poetry, fiction, criticism, parts-of-novels. "First two titles: Thomas Meyer's *Fourteen Poems* (24pp) and Jeffery Beam's *Midwinter Fires* (20pp). Forthcoming titles include Jonathan Greene's *Les Chambres des Poetes* (40pp), Jonathan Williams' *Quantulumcumque* (36pp), and Elizabeth Robinson's *String*" avg. press run 300. Pub'd 1 title 1990; expects 2 titles 1991, 2 titles 1992. 4 titles listed in the *Small Press Record of Books in Print* (20th Edition, 1991-92). avg. price, paper: $8-$15; other: $25-$75 limited edition. Discounts: 30%. 20-24pp; 5½×8½ (generally); of. Reporting time: several months to a year. Payment: copies (10% of run plus limiteds). Does not copyright for author.

Fresh Press, Sharon Elliot, 3712 Ortega Court, Palo Alto, CA 94303, 415-493-3596. 1977. Art. "Tasty, creative, natural foods recipes. *The Busy People's Fast Foodbook*, *Tofu Goes West* tofu in American style main dishes, breads and desserts *Tofu at Center Stage*, *The Busy People's Delightful Dinner Book* meatless main meal recipes-economical and flexible. Fun to make and to eat" avg. press run 20M. 4 titles listed in the *Small Press Record of Books in Print* (20th Edition, 1991-92). avg. price, paper: $5.95. Discounts: 50% jobbers, 10-50% trade, depending on number of books purchased. 120pp; 8×8; of. Reporting time: immediate reply on receipt, 1 month determination time. Payment: standard royalty. Copyrights for author. WBPA, PP.

FRIENDS OF PEACE PILGRIM, John Rush, Ann Rush, 43480 Cedar Avenue, Hemet, CA 92344, 714-927-7678. 1987. Poetry, articles, interviews, letters, non-fiction. "We do not pay for articles" circ. 10.5M. 3/yr. Pub'd 3 issues 1990; expects 3 issues 1991, 3 issues 1992. sub. price: free; per copy: free; sample: free. Back issues: free. Discounts: our printing cost. 8pp; 8½×11; of. Reporting time: 2 weeks. Payment: none. Not copyrighted. Pub's reviews: 3-4 in 1990. §World peace, inner peace. Ads: none.

Friends Of Tucson Pub Lib/The Maguey Press, Rolly Kent, c/o Tucson Public Library, PO Box 27470, Tucson, AZ 85726, 602-791-4391. 1976. Letters, parts-of-novels, long-poems. "*The Maguey Press* is now the publishing venture of Friends of the Tucson Public Library. The Maguey Press Poetry Chapbook Series is still available. New Maguey/community arts program for all people of the southern Arizona region. All proceeds from book sales help fund the Tucson Writers' Project. Contact Rolly Kent. Office address: Writers' Project, Tucson Public Library, PO Box 27470, Tucson, AZ 85726" avg. press run 1M. Expects 1 title 1991. avg. price, paper: $3.00 (Maguey Chapbooks); $6.00 (Writers' Project). Discounts: trade 40% discount; poets & writers listed professionals 40% off; others by arrangement. Chapbooks 32pp, Writers' Project 48pp; 5×7½, 8×12; of. Payment: copies (10% of run). Does not copyright for author.

Friends United Press, Ardith Talbot, 101 Quaker Hill Drive, Richmond, IN 47374, 317-962-7573. 1969. Non-fiction. "Non-fiction books (average length 100-180 pages) relating to Quaker (Society of Friends) history, biography, faith experience, and religious practice" avg. press run 1M. Pub'd 4 titles 1990; expects 4 titles 1991, 4 titles 1992. 26 titles listed in the *Small Press Record of Books in Print* (20th Edition, 1991-92). avg. price, paper: $8.95. Discounts: 40% to bookstores on orders over 5 copies. 150pp; 5½×8½; of. Reporting time: 6 months to 1 year. Payment: 7½% of our income on each title after production costs are met. Copyrights for author. PCPA (Protestand Church-Owned Publishing Association); QUIP (Quakers Uniting in Publishing).

FROG GONE REVIEW, Greg Schindler, PO Box 46308, Mt. Clemens, MI 48046, 313-263-3399. 1989. Poetry. "Only accept poetry Sept. 1-Jan. 15. Request poets send SASE for info first" circ. 500. 1/yr. Pub'd 1 issue 1990; expects 1 issue 1991, 1 issue 1992. sub. price: $4; per copy: $4; sample: $4. Back issues: $4. Discounts: $1.80 (10 or more) plus postage. 20pp; 8½×7; of. Reporting time: February or early March.

Payment: $10 each to five best poems. Copyrighted, reverts to author.

FROGPOND: Quarterly Haiku Journal, Sylvia Forges-Ryan, 87 Bayard Avenue, North Haven, CT 06473, 203-281-9653. 1978. Poetry, articles, reviews, news items. "Publish haiku, some tanka, renga (linked-verse) and very rarely a poem in another form relevant to haiku, some translations; brief essays and book reviews. Material should show familiarity with modern developments in haiku and senryu; not interested in 'pretty nature pictures.' Recent contributors: William J. Higginson, Penny Harter, Cor van den Heuvel, Alexis Rotella, Paul O. Williams, Johnny Baranski, Alvaro Cardona-Hine, Miriam Sagan. One-line haiku as well as the more traditional 3-line haiku and senryu are used, occasionally a 2-liner" circ. 700. 4/yr. Pub'd 4 issues 1990; expects 4 issues 1991, 4 issues 1992. sub. price: $20 USA & Canada, $28 overseas (airmail); per copy: $5 USA & Canada, $6 overseas; sample: $5 USA & Canada, $6 overseas. Back issues: same. Discounts: none. 48pp; 5½×9; of. Reporting time: 4-6 weeks. Payment: 1 copy. Copyrighted, reverts to author. Pub's reviews: 13 in 1990. §Books and chapbooks of contemporary haiku, senryu, new translations of Japanese haiku. No ads.

From Here Press (see also XTRAS), William J. Higginson, Penny Harter, Box 219, Fanwood, NJ 07023. 1975. Poetry, fiction, criticism, parts-of-novels, long-poems, plays, non-fiction. "In addition to *XTRAS* we publish regional (NJ) anthologies, and distribute some other small presses and self-published books." avg. press run 500-1M. Pub'd 3 titles 1990; expects 3 titles 1991, 3 titles 1992. 22 titles listed in the *Small Press Record of Books in Print* (20th Edition, 1991-92). avg. price, paper: $3-$4.95. Discounts: 40% to trade (5 mixed titles). 40-120pp; 5½×8½; of. Reporting time: 1 month. Payment: varies. Copyrights for author.

Fromm International Publishing Corporation, Thomas Thornton, Managing Editor, 560 Lexington Avenue, 21st Floor, New York, NY 10022, 212-308-4010. 1982. Fiction, art, music, letters, non-fiction. avg. press run 5M. Pub'd 5 titles 1990; expects 9 titles 1991, 13 titles 1992. avg. price, cloth: $16.95; paper: $11.95. Discounts: retail 1-4 copies 30%, 5-9 40%, 10-24 41%, 25-49 42%, 50-99 43%; libraries 10% any quantity; jobbers 1-5 25%, 6+ 50%. 250pp; 5½×8¼; of. Reporting time: 2 months. Payment: bi-annually, 7.5%. Copyrights for author.

Front Row Experience, Frank Alexander, 540 Discovery Bay Boulevard, Byron, CA 94514, 510-634-5710. 1974. Art, cartoons, non-fiction. "One page letter of inquiry first, submit manuscript only when requested. Submitted manuscripts should include self-addressed-stamped-return envelopes and should be typed double space of about 200 8½ X 11 size pages. They should be lesson plans or guidebooks for *teachers* from preschool to Jr. High. We are not interested in areas other than 'perceptual-motor development', 'movement education', 'special education', and 'educational games'. Some recently published books are: *Parachute Movement Activities, Step By Step, Holiday Movement Activities, Games We Should Play In School, Sticky Icky Movement Activities, The 'What Do You Mean I'm In Charge Of The School Pageant?' Handbook* and *Managing And Understanding Overactive Children, Fun Stunts and Tumbling Stunts"* avg. press run 500. Pub'd 1 title 1990; expects 1 title 1991, 2 titles 1992. 13 titles listed in the *Small Press Record of Books in Print* (20th Edition, 1991-92). avg. price, paper: $9.95. Discounts: 1+ 20%, 5+ 40%, 20+ 41%, 40+ 42%, 60+ 43%, 80+ 44%, 90+ 45%, further quantity discounts possible. 100pp; 8½×11; of. Reporting time: 1 week for letter of inquiry, 1 month for manuscript (include SASE). Payment: new author = 5% first 2,000 copies sold and 10% thereafter. New author who does workshops and other self-promotional activities = 8% first 2,000 copies sold and 10% thereafter. Established author = flat 10%. Royalties paid to authors every 6 months. Copyrights for author. Pacific Marketing Association.

Front Street Publishers, Martin K.M. Bruce, 22A Sheldon Drive, Poughkeepsie, NY 12603. 1978. Poetry, fiction, art, photos. "Primarily poetry but open to original ideas. 1981-82 Poetry Competition won by Margaret Ryan's *Filling out a Life* published in late 1982 (judge Mary Gordon, author of *The Company of Women.*) 1982-83 competition closed with publication in late 1983 of *Not the Fairy Tale* by Olive Bridge. Judge Howard Winn, Author of *Four Picture Sequence.* Poetry competitions suspended until further notice. Publication address is; 232 Elizabeth Street, New York, NY 10012" avg. press run 500-1M. 2 titles listed in the *Small Press Record of Books in Print* (20th Edition, 1991-92). avg. price, cloth: $12.95; paper: $10.95. Discounts: negotiable. 96pp; 5½×8; of. Reporting time: irregular. Payment: negotiable. Copyrights for author.

THE FRONT STRIKER BULLETIN, Bill Retskin, The Retskin Report, 3417 Clayborne Avenue, Alexandria, VA 22306-1410, 703-768-3932; FAX 703-768-4719. 1986. Non-fiction. "Articles relating to matchcover collecting in America, and the matchbook industry in America, only" circ. 600. 4/yr. Pub'd 4 issues 1990; expects 4 issues 1991, 4 issues 1992. sub. price: $10 bulk, $15 first class; sample: $2. Back issues: $2. 16pp; 8½×11; †of. Reporting time: 30 days. Copyrighted, reverts to author. §Matchcover collecting-hobbies. Ads: $35/$10 1/4 page.

Frontier Publishing, Jervis F. Russell, 322 Queen Anne Avenue North, Seattle, WA 98109. 1979. Fiction, cartoons, non-fiction. "60M to 120M words; Northwest USA fiction and non-fiction" avg. press run 3M. Pub'd 13 titles 1990; expects 10 titles 1991, 12 titles 1992. 1 title listed in the *Small Press Record of Books in Print* (20th Edition, 1991-92). avg. price, paper: $9.95. Discounts: bookstores 6-12 books 40%, 12+ 42%; jobbers

55%. 200pp; 6×9, 8½×11; of. Reporting time: 1 month. Payment: 6% to 10%, royalties paid monthly. Copyrights for author. Pacific Northwest Book Publishers Association.

FRONTIERS: A Journal of Women Studies, Louise Lamphere, Editor; Margaret Randall, Managing Editor; Jane Slaughter, Associate Editor, Mesa Vista Hall 2142, University of New Mexico, Albuquerque, NM 87131-1586, 505-277-1198. 1975. Poetry, fiction, articles, art, photos, interviews, criticism, reviews, letters, plays, news items, non-fiction. *"Frontiers* bridges the gap between academic and community women by publishing a journal that is substantive and accessible to all people interested in feminist issues. We seek both traditional and innovative work, collaborative and interdisciplinary manuscripts. Most issues have a theme, and articles and personal essays are included that express different viewpoints; also in each issue are a variety of other articles on nontheme topics plus creative work. We have no 'political bias' except feminism — in all its manifestations. We prefer to publish manuscripts under 40 pages. We also consider poetry, short stories, photographs, graphics, and book reviews" circ. 1.5M. 3/yr. Pub'd 3 issues 1990; expects 3 issues 1991, 3 issues 1992. sub. price: $20 indiv., $33 instit.; per copy: $8 indiv., $11 instit.; sample: $8. Back issues: same as single copy. Discounts: bookstores 40%, bulk rate 10% if 10 (ten) or more copies of the same issue are purchased/ordered together; no other discounts. 260pp; 6×9; of. Reporting time: 3-6 months for articles, 2-4 months for poetry. Payment: 2 copies of issue. Copyrighted, reverts to author if requested by author in advance. Pub's reviews: 10 in 1990. §All books of interest to women, on all subjects, especially feminist and women's studies topics. Ads: $250/$150/$80 1/4 page/no classified. COSMEP.

Frontline Publications, Ernie Hernandez, PO Box 1104, El Toro, CA 92630. 1982. Articles, non-fiction. "Books about management, science, and computers. Am seeking manuscripts on computer technology— particularly 'how-to' guidebooks geared toward unsophisticated (non-programmer oriented) end-users i.e. applications software, systems development, language examples" avg. press run 5M. Expects 1 title 1991, 2 titles 1992. 4 titles listed in the *Small Press Record of Books in Print* (20th Edition, 1991-92). avg. price, cloth: $26.95; paper: $19.95. Discounts: trade-none, wholesaler-50%, college classrooms-10% (on verified orders: instructor desk copies-free). 231pp; 5⅜×8½; †of. Reporting time: no info as yet. Payment: 10-15% of net. Copyrights for author.

Frozen Waffles Press/Shattered Sidewalks Press; 25th Century Chapbooks, David Wade, Bro. Dimitrios, Rick Fox, The Writer's Group, 329 West 1st Street #5, Bloomington, IN 47401, 812-333-6304 c/o Rocky. 1980. Poetry, art, cartoons, interviews, reviews, parts-of-novels, long-poems. "Poetry, prose poems; almost any kind of short work (plays, aphorisms, parables [modern], fantasy, Si Fi, futureworlds, etc.). Oral & visual qualities to be expressed in cassettes, post cards, poster poems, etc. Please NO more unsolicited material until notified in this directory! 'Poetry videos' in the future are a possibility! Would like *input* on this" avg. press run varies. 4 titles listed in the *Small Press Record of Books in Print* (20th Edition, 1991-92). avg. price, paper: $12; other: $25-$35 deluxe. Discounts: hope to give breaks to people over 40; mental institutions, prisons, etc. 22-45pp, 85-125pp; size varies; of. Reporting time: 5 seconds to 5 days; if you don't hear from us, we probably never got your material. Payment: at least one free copy of your work(s); money later, much money much later; inflation has bloated our poverty. Copyrights for author.

Fry's Incredible Inquirys (see also INCREDIBLE INQUIRY REPORTS), A. Fry, HC76, Box 2207, Garden Valley, ID 83622. 1982. Criticism, non-fiction. "Use very exotic 'how to' data on interdimensional machines, methods, conspiracy concepts, mind power and super human abilities" avg. press run 100. Pub'd 3 titles 1990; expects 3 titles 1991, 20 titles 1992. avg. price, cloth: $8. Discounts: 40%. 30pp; 8½×11; xerox. Reporting time: query first. Payment: 15% royalty. Does not copyright for author.

FUGITIVE POPE, Raleigh Clayton Muns, Anne L. Wagner, 3338 Sawtelle Drive, Apt. 20, Los Angeles, CA 90066, 213-398-3161. 1990. Articles, cartoons, satire, letters, collages. "Focus is on 'detritus from the information age' and library bizarrities" circ. 92. 6/yr. Pub'd 6 issues 1990; expects 6 issues 1991, 6 issues 1992. sub. price: $6; per copy: $1; sample: $1. Back issues: on request. 32pp; 5½×4¼; †photocopy, laser print. Reporting time: within 1 month. Payment: none. Copyrighted, reverts to author. Ads: $30/$15/free to interesting pubs.

Fulcrum, Inc., Robert C. Baron, Publisher, 350 Indiana Street, Suite 350, Golden, CO 80401, 303-277-1623. 1985. Non-fiction. "Nature narratives, American history, climbing and hiking guidebooks, river guidebooks, self-help, science, biography, travel, outdoor adventure, gardening" avg. press run 4-6M. Pub'd 12 titles 1990; expects 17 titles 1991, 20 titles 1992. avg. price, cloth: $20; paper: $13.95. Discounts: bookstore 42% for 5, 43% for 10; jobbers 50%, libraries 20%. 230pp; size varies; lp, desktop. Reporting time: 12 weeks. Payment: negotiable. Copyrights for author. Rocky Mountain Book Publisher's Association.

FULL DISCLOSURE, Glen Roberts, Box 903, Libertyville, IL 60048, 708-395-6200. Articles, photos, cartoons, interviews, reviews, letters, non-fiction. "Fax: 708-395-6022. Focus on privacy, electronic surveillance, government wrong-doing." circ. 7M. 6/yr. sub. price: $18; per copy: $2. 12pp; 11×17; Webb press. Copyrighted. Pub's reviews. §privacy, electronic surveillance, government wrong-doing. Ads:

$450/$285/20¢.

FUSE MAGAZINE, Editorial Board, 183 Bathurst Street, Main Floor, Toronto, Ont. M5T 2R7, Canada, 416-367-0159. 1974. Articles, art, interviews, criticism, reviews, music, news items. "Progressive, multi-sexual, multi-cultural, multi-dimensional criticism on and about cultural production and the social dynamics that influence it." circ. 6M. 5/yr. Pub'd 5 issues 1990; expects 5 issues 1991, 5 issues 1992. sub. price: $16 Canada; per copy: $3.50; sample: $3.50. Back issues: as on cover plus postage. Discounts: none. 56pp; 8¼×10¾; web. Payment: 7¢ (Cdn) per word. Copyrighted, does not revert to author. Pub's reviews: quite a few in 1990. §Arts, politics, cultural politics, sexual politics, government policy. Ads: $320/$200/$525-$75 (back cover to 1/4 page). CMPA.

The Future Press (see also PRECISELY), Richard Kostelanetz, Literature Director, PO Box 73, Canal Street, New York, NY 10013. 1976. Poetry, fiction, articles, art, music, parts-of-novels, long-poems, concrete art. "Committed exclusively to radically alternative materials for books and radically alternative forms of books. Have so far done a ladderbook, a cut-out book, a collection of cards containing numerals, a looseleaf book, a fold-out book, a book exclusively of numbers, another entirely of photographs, the same verbal text in two radically different book formats. What we can do depends, alas, largely on grants; and since U.S. funding agencies have been notoriously ungenerous toward experimental work and its practitioners, The Future Press is scarcely sanguine. The artists are there; the audience is there; the trouble still lies in the middle. We can't encourage submissions until the funding jam is busted." avg. press run 600-1M. Expects 1 title 1991, 2 titles 1992. 11 titles listed in the *Small Press Record of Books in Print* (20th Edition, 1991-92). avg. price, cloth: $10; paper: $3; other: $1 newsprint. Discounts: 40% to legitimate retailers paying in advance, and adding $1.50 for postage. 1-48pp; size varies; of. Payment: generous percentage of edition. Copyrights for author.

THE FUTURIST, Edward S. Cornish, World Future Society, 4916 St. Elmo Avenue, Bethesda, MD 20814, 301-656-8274. 1966. Articles, art, photos, reviews, news items, non-fiction. "A journal of forecasts, trends, and ideas about the future." circ. 31M. 6/yr. Pub'd 6 issues 1990; expects 6 issues 1991, 6 issues 1992. 3 titles listed in the *Small Press Record of Books in Print* (20th Edition, 1991-92). sub. price: $30; per copy: $6. 60pp; 8¼×10⅞; webb of. Reporting time: 8 weeks. Payment: author's copies (10). Copyrighted, reverts to author. Pub's reviews: 9 in 1990. §Future studies. Ads: $795/$475/$1.

Futurum Forlag (see also GATEAVISA), Engh, Hjelmsgt. 3, 0355 Oslo 3, Norway, +47 2 69 12 84. 1970. Articles, photos, cartoons, interviews, satire, criticism, reviews, music, letters, collages, news items, non-fiction. "Biases; Anarchistic/cultural" avg. press run 1.5M. Pub'd 3 titles 1990; expects 1 title 1991, 3 titles 1992. 3 titles listed in the *Small Press Record of Books in Print* (20th Edition, 1991-92). avg. price, paper: 50 NOK (US$7). Discounts: for bookshops and distributors. 150pp; size varies; of. Reporting time: inquire. Payment: inquire. Copyrights for author. APS.

FYI, Sarah Montague, 1285 Avenue of the Americas, 3rd Floor, New York, NY 10019, 212-977-2544. 1985. Non-fiction. "One 800-1,000 word article per issue" circ. 27M. 4/yr. Pub'd 4 issues 1990; expects 4 issues 1991, 4 issues 1992. sub. price: $5; per copy: $1.25; sample: free. Back issues: $2. Discounts: none. 16pp; 8½×11; web press. Reporting time: 1 month. Payment: $50. Copyrighted, reverts to author. Pub's reviews: 5 in 1990. §Arts, arts management, funding, legislation, production. No ads.

G

GAFF PRESS, John Paul Barrett, Publisher; Nancy Butterfield, Senior Editor; Mary Cvitanovitch, Editor, PO Box 1024, 114 SW Willow Lane, Astoria, OR 97103, 503-325-8288. 1987. Art, photos, cartoons, interviews, non-fiction. *"Sea Stories—Of Dolphins and Dead Sailors* by John Paul Barrett. True, harrowing tales of mystery, death, hardship and humor from the North Pacific Fishing Grounds. 128 pages, silkscreened sailcloth hardback. Handbound. ISBN 0-9619629-0-9. 1987. *Sea Stories—Book II: Seagods and Sundogs.* Interested in seeing true and extraordinary ocean-related adventure stories with a point. Published in 1990 *Nine Wednesday Nights,* an anthology of eleven Northwest writers' stories and poems, limited printing 250 copies; also planned for Spring 1990 *How I Make Books (and Why)"* avg. press run 5M-10M. Pub'd 1 title 1990; expects 2 titles 1992. 1 title listed in the *Small Press Record of Books in Print* (20th Edition, 1991-92). avg. price, cloth: $10-$15; paper: $12.50. Discounts: standard quantity to booksellers and distributors. 128-160pp; 4¼×5½; of. Reporting time: 1 month. Payment: negotiable—usually 1/2 and 1/2 payment and sales bonus. Copyrights for author.

Gahmken Press, Range D. Bayer, PO Box 1467, Newport, OR 97365. 1986. Non-fiction. avg. press run 150. Expects 2 titles 1991, 2 titles 1992. 7 titles listed in the *Small Press Record of Books in Print* (20th Edition,

216

1991-92). avg. price, paper: $14. Discounts: prepaid STOP order for 1 book 30% + $2 shipping, 2-5 30% + shipping, 6+ 30% + shipping. Shipping charges: $2 for first book, $1 for each add'l book. 70pp; 8½×11; photocopying. Reporting time: 3 weeks. Payment: open to negotiation. Does not copyright for author. COSMEP, Northwest Association of Book Publishers.

Gai Saber Monographs, Wayne Dynes, c/o GAU, Box 480, Lenox Hill Station, New York, NY 10021-0033, 212-864-0361. 1980. Non-fiction. "Stephen O. Murray, editor, *Male Homosexuality in Central and South America*; 1987, $7.95'' avg. press run 1M. Pub'd 1 title 1990; expects 1 title 1991, 1 title 1992. 4 titles listed in the *Small Press Record of Books in Print* (20th Edition, 1991-92). avg. price, paper: $7.95. Discounts: 40%. 200pp; 6½×8; of. Reporting time: 2 months. Copyrights for author.

Gain Publications (see also NATIONAL MASTERS NEWS), Al Sheahen, Editor, PO Box 2204, Van Nuys, CA 91404, 818-785-1895. 1982. Non-fiction. avg. press run 5M. Expects 1 title 1991, 3 titles 1992. 3 titles listed in the *Small Press Record of Books in Print* (20th Edition, 1991-92). avg. price, paper: $9.95. Discounts: 40%. 240pp; 5½×8½; of.

The P. Gaines Co., Publishers, Phillip Williams, PO Box 2253, Oak Park, IL 60303, 312-524-1073. 1979. Non-fiction. "We are now concentrating on self-help, business and legal guidebooks. Current publications: *How to Form Your Own Illinois Corporation Before the Inc. Dries!*, *The Living Will and the Durable Power of Attorney Book, With Forms*, and *Naming Your Business and Its Products and Services''* avg. press run 1M-5M. Expects 3 titles 1991. 8 titles listed in the *Small Press Record of Books in Print* (20th Edition, 1991-92). avg. price, paper: $7.95-$19.95. Discounts: standard. 150-200pp; 8½×11; of. Reporting time: 4 weeks. Payment: advances negotiable. Copyrights for author. COSMEP, PMA.

GALAXY CLASS, Christopher Simmons, PO Box 7000-822, Redondo Beach, CA 90277, 213-529-8573. 1987. Fiction, art, photos, criticism. "Star Trek Next Generation (TV show) fan magazine. Fiction, art, commentary. Stories any length to 30,000 words. Prefer 10,000-15,000 max. Will pay for convention photos, and rare material.'' circ. 1.2M. 3/yr. Pub'd 3 issues 1990; expects 4 issues 1991, 3 issues 1992. price per copy: $4.50 incl. 1st class p/h. Back issues: any 4 issues $16.25 ppd. Discounts: 10+ 40%, 50+ 50%, 100+ 60% (200+, may mix in quantities of 50 each for 60%). 32pp; 8½×11; of, xerox. Reporting time: 2-4 weeks. Payment: writers—subscription plus copies; artists—nominal payment. Copyrighted, reverts to author. Ads: none.

The Galileo Press Ltd., Julia Wendell, Editor-in-Chief; Andrew Ciofalo, Executive Editor; Jack Stephens, Senior Editor, 7215 York Road, Suite 210, Baltimore, MD 21212. 1980. Poetry, fiction, long-poems, non-fiction. "Prints collections of poetry, short fiction, novellas, non-fiction and children's literature. It is best to query first before submitting'' avg. press run 1M. Pub'd 3 titles 1990; expects 6 titles 1991, 5 titles 1992. 24 titles listed in the *Small Press Record of Books in Print* (20th Edition, 1991-92). avg. price, cloth: $15.95; paper: $9.95. Discounts: 40% to all bookstores; 40% to all classroom orders of 8 or more; 20%-55% wholesale; 10% courtesy library. 80pp; size varies; of. Reporting time: 3-6 months. Payment: 10% royalties plus author's copies. Copyrights for author. COSMEP, CODA, AWP, CCLM, PSA.

Gallaudet University Press, Dr. Elaine Costello, Editor-in-Chief, 800 Florida Avenue NE, Washington, DC 20002, 202-651-5488. 1980. Fiction, non-fiction. "Gallaudet University Press is a scholarly publisher specializing in work related to deafness, speech pathology, audiology, and related fields. The Press has a children's imprint called Kendall Green Publications that publishes children's texts and literature with a relation to hearing impairment, and an imprint called Clark Books for instructional materials'' avg. press run 3M-5M. Pub'd 15 titles 1990; expects 10 titles 1991, 15 titles 1992. 22 titles listed in the *Small Press Record of Books in Print* (20th Edition, 1991-92). avg. price, cloth: $19.95; paper: $7.50. Discounts: trade 40%, text 25%. 250pp; 6×9; of. Reporting time: 2 months. Payment: 10-15% of net. Copyrights for author. AAP, AAUP, Society of Scholarly Publishing.

The Gallery Press International, Inc., Lucian Coleman, PO Box 56175, New Orleans, LA 70156, 504-246-7379. 1989. avg. press run 5M. Expects 3 titles 1991, 4 titles 1992. avg. price, paper: $5.95. Discounts: 50% distributors; 10% libraries and educational institutes. 5½×8½. Reporting time: 3-4 weeks. Payment: negotiable. Copyrights for author.

Gallery West Associates, James Parsons, Philip Bareiss, PO Box 1238, Ranchos de Taos, NM 87557, 505-751-0073. 1980. Articles, art, non-fiction. "Writers must query. We are a very small art gallery press. *The Art Fever* is our first book publication. *The Creative West* is an annual magazine'' avg. press run varies. Pub'd 1 title 1990; expects 1 title 1991, 1 title 1992. 1 title listed in the *Small Press Record of Books in Print* (20th Edition, 1991-92). avg. price, cloth: $29.95 *The Art Fever*. Discounts: regular trade. of. Payment: by agreement. Usually copyrights for author.

GALLERY WORKS, Peter Holland, Jeanne Lance, 218 Appleton Drive, Aptos, CA 95003. 1973. Poetry, fiction, art, photos. "Recent contributors: David Bromige, Julia Blumenreich, James Sherry, Hannah Weiner,

Norman Fishcher, Nick Piombino. Art: Beverly Richey. Photos: Harry Dahlgren. Potential contributors are required to buy and read a copy before submitting. We never review" circ. 500. Expects 1 issue 1991. sub. price: $5/current issue (Gallery Works 8); per copy: $5; sample: $5. Back issues: $5 per issue #1-8, $30/set. Discounts: 40% to bookstores. 64pp; 5×7; of. Reporting time: from 2 months to a year. Payment: 2 free copies only. Copyrighted, reverts to author.

THE GALLEY SAIL REVIEW, Embassy Hall Editions, Stanley McNail, 1630 University Avenue, Suite 42, Berkeley, CA 94703, 415-486-0187. 1958. Poetry, criticism, reviews, news items. "GSR was founded in 1958 and published in San Francisco from 1958 through 1971. It has been revived for a second series. It has always been rather eclectic, but leaning toward modern romantic styles. We occasionally publish longer poems, but prefer shorter work because of space limitations. We are hospitable to new poets as well as established writers. Among contributors to our first series: Robert Hillyer, William Carlos Williams, Irving Layton, William Pillin, John Stevens Wade. Among recent contributors: James Broughton, Diane Wakoski, Lewis Turco, James Schevill, Thom Gunn, Ursula LeGuin. No particular biases; we prize sincerity and value craftsmanship" circ. 500. 3/yr. Pub'd 3 issues 1990; expects 3 issues 1991, 3 issues 1992. sub. price: 2-year $15 (add $2 outside US & CAN); per copy: $3; sample: $3. Back issues: none available at present. Discounts: sub rates are discounted-i.e., 1 yr., $8.00; 2 yrs., $15.00. 40% to retail book dealers on consignments. 40-44pp; 5½×8½; of. Reporting time: 3 weeks to 1 month. Payment: contributors are usually furnished 2-3 copies. Copyrighted, reverts to author. Pub's reviews. §Poetry collections, poetry journals, lit. criticism, biographies of poets, books concerning the craft of poetry or on the arts in relation to poetry. Ads: not available at present. CCLM, COSMEP.

Gallopade Publishing Group, Carole Marsh, Bob Longmeyer, 235 E. Ponce de Leon Avenue, Ste. 100, Decatur, GA 30030. 1979. Poetry, fiction, articles, long-poems, plays, non-fiction. "We are not seeking submissions; do welcome inquires about our writing/publishing books and workshops" We print on demand. Pub'd 25 titles 1990; expects 30 titles 1991, 40 titles 1992. 53 titles listed in the *Small Press Record of Books in Print* (20th Edition, 1991-92). avg. price, cloth: $17.95; paper: $14.95. Discounts: 2-4 20%, 5-9 40%, or 10+ 50% non-returnable, all pre-paid. 25-200pp; 8½×11, 5½×8½; †of. Publisher Assn. of the South.

Galloping Dog Press, Peter Hodgkiss, 45 Salisbury Gardens, Newcastle upon Tyne, London, NE2 1HP, England. 1976. Poetry, fiction, criticism, long-poems, concrete art, non-fiction. "Mimeo mostly—own printing and binding. Books perfect bound with lettered spines. Recent and forthcoming books mostly printed litho. Unsolicited mss not considered" avg. press run 200-1M. Pub'd 6 titles 1990; expects 8 titles 1991, 6 titles 1992. 35 titles listed in the *Small Press Record of Books in Print* (20th Edition, 1991-92). avg. price, cloth: varies; paper: from £1 - £4. $2.50 - $7.50; other: varies. Discounts: 20% single copy, 40% otherwise. 40-60pp; size A5, A4; of, mi. Payment: copies. Copyrights for author. ALP.

THE GAME'S AFOOT, Zirlinson Publishing, Shawn Tomlinson, 1036 Glacier Avenue, Pacifica, CA 94044. 1989. Articles, cartoons, reviews, letters. *"The Game's Afoot* is a progressive roleplaying newsletter with room for all types of ideas. We aren't owned by or owe allegiance to any game company or organization and are a free voice in this sufficating genre. Writers include Eileen Anderson, Andy Gore, J.D. Canell, Charles Barouch and others. Some of our contributors are professional writers, others talented beginners. We welcome all types." 6/yr. Pub'd 3 issues 1990; expects 6 issues 1991, 6 issues 1992. sub. price: $10; per copy: $1.50; sample: 2 1st class stamps. Back issues: $2 each. 20pp; 4¼×11; †desktop publishing, laser printed. Reporting time: 2 weeks. Payment: 5 copies of issue work appears in. Copyrighted. Pub's reviews: 1 in 1990. §Roleplaying games, supplements, adventures, anything to do with roleplaying games. Ads: $40/$25.

THE GAMUT, Louis T. Milic, Editor; Leonard Trawick, Co-Editor, Cleveland State University, 1983 E. 24th Street, #FT1218, Cleveland, OH 44115-2440, 216-687-4679. 1980. Poetry, fiction, articles, art, photos, cartoons, interviews, satire, criticism, music, letters, concrete art, non-fiction. "We are not exclusively an arts and letters medium, but as our name implies, one that covers all topics of interest to educated readers. Well-researched articles are of particular interest" circ. 1M+. 3/yr. Pub'd 3 issues 1990; expects 3 issues 1991, 3 issues 1992. sub. price: $15; per copy: $6; sample: $3. Back issues: $7. Discounts: yes. 96pp; 7×10; of. Reporting time: 1-3 months. Payment: $25-$250. Copyrighted, reverts to author. Ads: none.

GANDHABBA, Tom Savage, Nalanda University Press, c/o Savage, 622 East 11th Street, New York, NY 10009. 1983. Poetry. "Make checks payable to Tom Savage. Some recent contributors: Allen Ginsberg, Ted Berrigan, Anne Waldman, Jackson MacLow, Bernadette Mayer, Norman Fischer, Norman MacAfee, Alice Notley, Bruce Andrews, Charles Bernstein, Barrett Watten, Jack Anderson, Bru Dye, Sparrow, John Godfrey, Hannah Weiner, Tom Weatherly, Ron Padgett, Roland Legiardi-Laura. Biases: Each issue has a theme, i.e. political poetry (#4), poems longer than a page (#2). My biases are against "academic" verse. I publish unknowns with knowns but rarely publish beginners. Most poetry I publish I've heard read at readings but am open to learning about works in other ways. Although I have a non-egotistical bias, I do not publish "religious" poetry. Also: no poems longer than several pages will be considered unless solicited beforehand by myself" circ. 300. 1/yr. Pub'd 1 issue 1990; expects 1 issue 1991, 1 issue 1992. sub. price: $3.50; per copy: $3.50;

sample: $3.50. Back issues: for xerox facsimile of #1 (no for sale copies left of mimeo original) $50. Discounts: 60/40% consignment to bookstores. 100pp; 8½×11; †mi. Reporting time: 6-9 months. Payment: 2 copies. Copyrighted, reverts to author. CCLM.

W. Paul Ganley: Publisher (see also AMANITA BRANDY; WEIRDBOOK), W. Paul Ganley, P.O. Box 149, Amherst Branch, Buffalo, NY 14226, 716-839-2415. 1968. Poetry, fiction, articles, art. "We are overstocked with book manuscripts. Recent book contributors: Joseph Payne Brennan, J.N. Williamson, Brian Lumley. Books I most want are fantasy/horror (no crime) novels or collections of short stories by outstanding writers in the field. No beginners. Also novelty items (perhaps shorter than novel length): examples are *The New Devil's Dictionary* (just published) and *Pulptime* (published 1985: novella featuring Sherlock Holmes and the horror writer H.P. Lovecraft in a mystery. (That was an exception to the 'no crime' stipulation, because what I meant by that was the nature of the horror - supernatural, not Jack-the-Ripper kind of horror.) I am currently overstocked with book manuscripts. Authors should query first" avg. press run 1.5M. Pub'd 2 titles 1990; expects 3 titles 1991, 3 titles 1992. 7 titles listed in the *Small Press Record of Books in Print* (20th Edition, 1991-92). avg. price, cloth: $15-$25; paper: $5-$8.50; other: (deluxe signed edition) $30-$40. Discounts: depends on size of order. 40% postpaid on regular orders over $20 retail value. 20% discount for libraries. 64-192pp; 5½×8½; of. Reporting time: up to 3 months. Payment: depends on author, usually 10% if author is not well known (I try to pair him with a well known illustrator) or otherwise 15%. Copyrights for author.

William Gannon, Publisher, 2887 Cooks Road, Santa Fe, NM 87501, 505-438-3430. 1973. Fiction, articles, photos, non-fiction. "Our focus is books about New Mexico" avg. press run 2M. Pub'd 1 title 1990. avg. price, paper: $15. Discounts: regular trade terms to retail bookstores. 200pp; of. Payment: negotiable. Copyrights for author. Rocky Mountain Publishers Association.

Garret Press, Neil G. Tarvin, 4991 South Union Avenue, Tulsa, OK 74107-7839, 918-592-0729, 800-726-6265. 1989. Fiction, non-fiction. "We are a new press actively looking for authors, particularly those who want to get involved in the production and promotion of their book. We are interested in virtually any area of non-fiction, but especially graphic arts, self-help, psychology, business, and alternative medicine. We're looking for books that trip our triggers. We do not attempt to fit books into a production formula—every aspect of every book is treated individually and with as much care as if it were our own, and the author's input is welcome. We also treat each book individually as far as advances, royalties, etc. We will also purchase manuscripts outright, co-op with the author, or help the author self-publish." avg. press run varies. Expects 7 titles 1991, 12 titles 1992. Discounts: bookstores 40%; distributors 50-60%; bulk (over 500) 50%; libraries 20%. Pages vary; size varies; †of. Reporting time: 3 weeks. Payment: individually determined. Copyrights for author. COSMEP.

Garrett Park Press, Robert Calvert Jr., PO Box 190, Garrett Park, MD 20896, 301-946-2553. 1968. avg. press run 4M. Pub'd 4 titles 1990; expects 8 titles 1991, 5 titles 1992. 15 titles listed in the *Small Press Record of Books in Print* (20th Edition, 1991-92). avg. price, cloth: $20; paper: $12. Discounts: 30%. 400pp; 8½×11; of. Reporting time: 1 month. Payment: 10%. Copyrights for author.

Gaslight Publications, Jack W. Tracy, 626 N. College Avenue, Bloomington, IN 47404, 812-332-5169. 1978. Criticism, non-fiction. "Specialized studies of the mystery genre and related fields: biography, criticism, analysis, reference, film" avg. press run 3M. Pub'd 2 titles 1990; expects 6 titles 1991, 6 titles 1992. 16 titles listed in the *Small Press Record of Books in Print* (20th Edition, 1991-92). avg. price, cloth: $18. Discounts: 1 copy 20%, 2+ 40%. 150pp; 5½×8½; of. Reporting time: 30 days. Payment: 10% royalty, no advance. Copyrights for author.

THE GATE, Beth Robbins, PO Box 43518, Richmond Heights, OH 44143. 1984. Fiction, articles, art, cartoons, letters, news items, non-fiction. "No longer using fiction. Need occult and paranormal related articles up to 1,500 words. Write me with ideas or I'll supply a list of suggested topics" circ. 200. 4/yr. Pub'd 4 issues 1990; expects 4 issues 1991, 4 issues 1992. sub. price: $8; per copy: $2; sample: $2. Back issues: write for prices. 15pp; 8½×11; †of. Reporting time: 1 month. Payment: 1 copy. Copyrighted, reverts to author. Pub's reviews: 4 in 1990. §True occult literature. Ads: $10 business card size.

GATEAVISA, Futurum Forlag, Engh, Seifert, Axelsson, Stenseth, Granberg, Hjelmsgt 3, 0355 Oslo 3, Norway, +47 2 69 12 84. 1970. Poetry, fiction, articles, photos, cartoons, interviews, satire, criticism, reviews, music, letters, collages, news items, non-fiction. "Biases: Anarchistic" circ. 8M. 6/yr. Pub'd 5 issues 1990; expects 6 issues 1991, 6 issues 1992. sub. price: NOK120, US$17.50; per copy: NOK 25, US$3.50; sample: NOK 25, , US$3.50 (surface); NOK 50, US$7 (air). Back issues: same. Discounts: for bookshops and street vendors. 56pp; size A4, 30×21cm; of. Reporting time: inquire. Payment: rarely. Not copyrighted. Pub's reviews: 30 in 1990. §Political, counter-culture, arts, rock music, lifestyle, meaning of life. Ads: 3960 NOK/2400 NOK/12 NOK 50% discount/non-profit. APS, Norsk Tidsskriftforum.

GATES OF PANDRAGON, Ianus Publications, Inc., Claude J. Pelletier, Writer; Michel Gareau, Artist;

Alain Villeneuve, Letterer; Jean Carrieres, Editor, 33, Prince Street #243, Montreal, Quebec H3C 2M7, Canada, 514-397-0342. 1990. Articles, art. "Comic book of science fiction in Japanese comic-style." circ. 5M. 4/yr. Expects 4 issues 1991, 4 issues 1992. price per copy: $2.25; sample: $2.75 US. 36pp; 6¾×10; of. Payment: 10% cover price separate between artist, writer, and letterer/inker. Copyrighted, reverts after 2 years. Ads: $175/$150/$75 1/4 page/$300 back cover/$200 inside cover.

Gateway Books, 13 Bedford Cove, San Rafael, CA 94901-4472, 415-454-5215. 1985. avg. press run 5M. Pub'd 3 titles 1990; expects 2 titles 1991, 2 titles 1992. 5 titles listed in the *Small Press Record of Books in Print* (20th Edition, 1991-92). avg. price, paper: $11.95. 250pp; 6×9; of. Reporting time: 90 days. Payment: negotiable. Copyrights for author. Northern California Book Publicists Assn.

Gateways Books And Tapes (see also INNER JOURNEYS), Iven Lourie, Senior Editor; Linda Corriveau, Associate Editor; Della Heywood, Associate Editor, Box 370, Nevada City, CA 95959, 916-477-1116. 1972. "Length-varied, spiritual, metaphysical bias. E.J. Gold. Labyrinth trilogy" avg. press run 1M-5M. Pub'd 5 titles 1990; expects 4 titles 1991, 4 titles 1992. 13 titles listed in the *Small Press Record of Books in Print* (20th Edition, 1991-92). avg. price, paper: $12.50; other: $11.98 music cassettes. Discounts: 25/40% trade, 50% wholesalers (negotiable). 200pp; 5½×8½, 8½×11; of. Reporting time: 3 months maximum. Payment: negotiable. ABA.

GATHERING GIBSONS, Kinseeker Publications, Victoria Wilson, PO Box 184, Grawn, MI 49637, 616-276-6745. 1987. Articles, reviews, news items, non-fiction. circ. 40. 4/yr. Pub'd 4 issues 1990; expects 4 issues 1991, 4 issues 1992. sub. price: $10; per copy: $2.50; sample: same. Back issues: $2.50. 10pp; 8½×11; †photocopy. Reporting time: 2 weeks. Payment: varies. Not copyrighted. Pub's reviews: 2 in 1990. §Genealogy.

GAUNTLET: Exploring the Limits of Free Expression, Barry Huffner, 309 Powell Road, Springfield, PA 19064, 215-328-5476. 1990. Fiction, articles, art, photos, cartoons, interviews, satire, reviews, letters, news items, non-fiction. "Looking for material dealing with censorship - prints both sides of the issue. Also looking for censored work (with history of censorship), and censored art. Length 1000-2500 words. *No taboos.* Contributors include Ray Bradbury, Isaac Asimov, George Carlin, artist Rubert Williams, Douglas Winter, William F. Nolan, Henry Slesar and Harlan Ellison" circ. 8M. 1/yr. Expects 1 issue 1991, 1 issue 1992. sub. price: $7.95; per copy: $8.95; sample: $8.95. Discounts: 40-50% bookstores, 20% libraries, 55-60% distributors, 20-30% for bulk purchases for classroom (10 or more). 112pp; 8½×11; of. Reporting time: 3 weeks. Payment: 1/4¢ a word for text (up to 1¢), $2-$5 for art. Copyrighted, reverts to author. Pub's reviews: 4 in 1990. §Censored or controversial material, horror, fantasy or mystery. Ads: $100/$50/$25 1/4 page. Horror Writers of America (HWA), Small Press Writers & Artists Org. (SPWAO).

GAVEA-BROWN, Gavea-Brown Publications, Onesimo Teotonio Almeida, George Monteiro, Center For Portuguese and Brazilian Studies, Brown University, Providence, RI 02912, 401-863-3042. 1980. Poetry, fiction, articles, interviews, criticism, reviews, parts-of-novels, long-poems, plays, non-fiction. "Letters (fiction, poetry, plays) reflecting the Portuguese experience in the U.S. and Canada as well as studies on that experience. We accept both social sciences as well as humanistic approaches, as well as literary works. The journal accepts all the above in English and Portuguese" circ. 600. 1/yr. Pub'd 1 issue 1990; expects 1 issue 1991, 1 issue 1992. sub. price: $10, $15 institutions. 75pp; 6×9; of. Reporting time: 3 months. Not copyrighted. Pub's reviews: 10 in 1990. §Portuguese, American Studies, Portuguese studies, Portuguese-American creative works. Ads: $100/$75.

Gavea-Brown Publications (see also GAVEA-BROWN), Onesimo Teotonio Almeida, George Monteiro, Center For Portuguese and Brazilian Studies, Box 0, Brown University, Providence, RI 02912, 401-863-3042. 1980. Poetry, fiction, criticism, letters, long-poems, plays, non-fiction. "Publishes books of fiction, poetry, or plays related to the Portuguese experience in the U.S. and Canada in English or in Portuguese; studies on the Portuguese in the U.S. and Canada; studies on Portuguese Language and Culture; translation from Portuguese Literature" avg. press run 1M. Pub'd 3 titles 1990; expects 3 titles 1991, 3 titles 1992. 13 titles listed in the *Small Press Record of Books in Print* (20th Edition, 1991-92). avg. price, cloth: $15; paper: $6. 180pp; of. Reporting time: 3 months. Copyrights for author.

GAY CHICAGO MAGAZINE, Jerry Williams, General Manager; Ralph Paul Geinheidr, Publisher, 3121 North Broadway, Chicago, IL 60657, 312-327-7271. 1976. Fiction, articles, news items. "Fiction: 1,000-2,000 words" circ. 20M. 52/yr. Pub'd 53 issues 1990; expects 52 issues 1991, 52 issues 1992. sub. price: $80; per copy: $2; sample: $2. Back issues: $2. 112pp; 6¾×9¼; of. Reporting time: 30-90 days. Payment: minimal. Copyrighted, reverts to author. Pub's reviews: 20-25 in 1990. §Anything that would be of interest to the gay/lesbian community. Ads: $340/$190/$8 for 25 words. GLPA (Gay/Lesbian Press Association).

GAY SUNSHINE JOURNAL, Gay Sunshine Press, Inc., PO Box 40397, San Francisco, CA 94140, 415-824-3184.

220

Gay Sunshine Press, Inc. (see also GAY SUNSHINE JOURNAL; Leyland Publications), Winston Leyland, PO Box 40397, San Francisco, CA 94140, 415-824-3184. 1970. Poetry, fiction, interviews, criticism, letters, non-fiction. *"Gay Sunshine* was founded in 1970 to publish cultural, literary, political material by Gay people. During the first five years of its existence it published only the tabloid cultural journal, *Gay Sunshine.* Since 1975 it has been publishing chapbooks and books. A new imprint, Leyland Publications, started in 1984" avg. press run 5M. Pub'd 10 titles 1990; expects 10 titles 1991, 10 titles 1992. 59 titles listed in the *Small Press Record of Books in Print* (20th Edition, 1991-92). avg. price, cloth: $15; paper: $10; other: $5.95. Discounts: distributors to the Book Trade: Book People Distributors and Inland Dist. (at 40% discount) No discounts to individuals or libraries. Discounts to book jobbers & specialty shops. 192pp; 6×9, 5½×8½; sheet fed. Reporting time: 1 month. Payment: royalties. Copyrights for author.

GAYELLOW PAGES, Frances Green, Box 292 Village Station, New York, NY 10014, 212-674-0120. 1973. "Directory of organizations, businesses, publications, bars, AIDS resources, churches etc. of interest to gay women and men in USA & Canada. No charge to be listed; self-addressed stamped #10 envelope for details" circ. 50M. 1/yr. Pub'd 1 issue 1990; expects 1 issue 1991, 1 issue 1992. price per copy: $8.95; sample: $10 by mail. Discounts: 40% consigned, 50% prepaid. 256pp; 5×8; of. §Gay-related topics, gay-supportive feminist. Ads: $600/$375. GPA.

Gazelle Publications, T.E. Wade, Jr., 5580 Stanley Drive, Auburn, CA 95603, 916-878-1223. 1976. Poetry, non-fiction. "We consider juvenile material that is not fantasy, material suitable for classroom use, or how-to material. Brochure available showing current titles. Query first. We are not currently using unsolicited material" avg. press run 4M. Pub'd 2 titles 1990; expects 2 titles 1991, 2 titles 1992. 6 titles listed in the *Small Press Record of Books in Print* (20th Edition, 1991-92). avg. price, cloth: $9; paper: $8. Discounts: trade and library 30% to 40%. 150pp; 5½×8½; of. Reporting time: 1 week. Payment: open, depends on market potential. Copyrights for author. COSMEP.

GCBA Publishing, Michael J. Ebersole, Senior Editor; Daniel J. O'Connor, PO Box 292, Grand Canyon, AZ 86023, 602-638-2597. 1980. 5 titles listed in the *Small Press Record of Books in Print* (20th Edition, 1991-92). Copyrights for author. COSMEP, PMA, CNPCA.

GCT Inc. (see also CREATIVE KIDS; THE GIFTED CHILD TODAY), Fay L. Gold, Editor-Publisher; Marvin Gold, Editor, PO Box 6448, Mobile, AL 36660, 205-478-4700. 1978. avg. press run 2M. 17 titles listed in the *Small Press Record of Books in Print* (20th Edition, 1991-92).

GDE Publications (see also SOFTBALL ILLUSTRATED; SLOWPITCH TIPS; COACHING SLO'PITCH SOFTBALL), Glen D. Eley, PO Box 304, Lima, OH 45802. 1978. "line drawings" avg. press run 2M. Pub'd 2 titles 1990; expects 1 title 1991, 1 title 1992. 4 titles listed in the *Small Press Record of Books in Print* (20th Edition, 1991-92). Discounts: available to booksellers/will dropship. 75pp; 4¼×5½.

Gearhead Press, Bruce Rizzon, Co-Editor; Barbara Rizzon, Co-Editor, 565 Lincoln, Northwest, Grand Rapids, MI 49504, 459-7861 or 459-4577. 1975. Poetry, long-poems. "Our favorite poet right now is Bruce Rizzon. Write for free list of our titles. *A Walk in the Spring Rain, Vol. 2* will be out Fall, 1981, $1.00. Also expect *A Desolate Angel. Blood on the Moon* $2.00 and *Ninth Street, Five Raindrops* in 82 or 83, *Diamonds And Rust Poems, For Sale Poems, Dean Lake Poems* $1.00, *Asphalt Shadows Poems* $1.50, *Osiris Rising Poems, I Am The Lonely Sea* $6.00, *Dago Red, The Road* $2.50, and *The Blues,* all by Bruce Rizzon. Make all checks/money orders payable to Bruce Rizzon." avg. press run 10M. Pub'd 3 titles 1990; expects 5 titles 1991, 5 titles 1992. 47 titles listed in the *Small Press Record of Books in Print* (20th Edition, 1991-92). avg. price, cloth: $6; paper: $2.50; other: $1. Discounts: none. 26-60pp; 5½×8½; of. Reporting time: 4 minutes to 4 years? maybe. SASE on all submissions. We will read all manuscripts sent to us. Give us time before we return any unused mss or unwanted mss. Copyrights for author. PRCM, PSM, NFSPS, Peninsulapoets.

THE GELOSOPHIST, Humor News & Views From Around The World, Lone Star Publications of Humor, Lauren I. Barnett, Editor; Ash N.M. Lynby, Assistant Editor, PO Box 29000, Suite 103, San Antonio, TX 78229. Articles, photos, cartoons, interviews, satire, criticism, reviews, letters, news items. *"The Gelosophist* is a newsletter supplement to *The Lone Star Humor Digest* (formerly *Lone Star: A Magazine of Humor).* See also listings for *The Lone Star Humor Digest & Lone Star Comedy Monthly"* 3-6/yr. Expects 3 issues 1991, 3-6 issues 1992. sub. price: inquire; per copy: inquire; sample: inquire. Discounts: please inquire. 4pp; 8½×11; of. Reporting time: 2-3 months. Payment: send SASE for guidelines & pay scale. Copyrighted, reverts to author. Pub's reviews. §Humorous and humor-related books and periodicals. Ads: please inquire. COSMEP, AHHA (American Humorists and Their Happy Associates), SOCW (Society of Objectivist Comedy Writers).

Gemini Publishing Company, Don Diebel, 11543 Gullwood Drive, Houston, TX 77089, 713-484-2424. 1978. Non-fiction. avg. press run 2M-3M. Expects 1 title 1992. 3 titles listed in the *Small Press Record of Books in Print* (20th Edition, 1991-92). avg. price, paper: $8.95. Discounts: 1-24 50%; 25-49 55%; 50-99 60%; 100-199 65%; 200 or more books 70%. 200pp; 8½×5½; †of. Reporting time: 1 month. Payment: 5-10%. Copyrights for author. COSMEP, American Booksellers Exchange, Mailorder Associates, Texas Publishers Association, Publishers Marketing Association.

GemStone Press, Stuart M. Matlins, LongHill Partners, Inc., PO Bcx 237, Woodstock, VT 05091, 802-457-4000. 1987. Non-fiction. "Gemology, jewelry, fashion. Distributed to bookstores and libraries by Van Nostrand Reinhold" avg. press run 15M. Pub'd 1 title 1990; expects 2 titles 1991, 2 titles 1992. 3 titles listed in the *Small Press Record of Books in Print* (20th Edition, 1991-92). avg. price, cloth: $29.95; paper: $14.95. Discounts: 5-10 copies 30%, 11-39 40%, 40-79 45%, 80-119 48%. 304pp; 6×9; web. Reporting time: 1 month. Payment: depends on title and author. Copyrights for author. PMA, COSMEP.

GENEALOGICAL COMPUTING, Ancestry Publishing, Robert Passaro, Editor, PO Box 476, Salt Lake City, UT 84110, 801-531-1790. 1981. Reviews, news items, non-fiction. "All articles pertain in some way to both computers and genealogy. We cover all types of microcomputers: Macintosh, PC, Apple II, etc. Reviews are mostly software reviews although we do publish occasional book reviews" circ. 2.5M. 4/yr. Pub'd 4 issues 1990; expects 4 issues 1991, 4 issues 1992. sub. price: $25 US, $30 Canada & Mexico, $35 all other foreign countries via air mail; per copy: $8.50. Back issues: full volumes (1 year) $22.50; Volumes 1-5 $99. 48pp; 8½×11; of. Reporting time: 1 month. Payment: $75 to $100 on publication. Copyrighted, does not revert to author. Pub's reviews: 2 in 1990. §Computer applications to genealogy. Ads: $150/$75/$50 1/3 page/$35 1/4.

Genealogical Publishing Co., Inc., Michael Tepper, Sr. Vice President & Editor-in-Chief, 1001 North Calvert Street, Baltimore, MD 21202, 301-837-8271; 301-752-8492 fax. 1933. "We publish reference books (source records and how-to books) in the field of geneology, family history, and immigration" avg. press run 1M. Pub'd 50 titles 1990; expects 50 titles 1991, 50 titles 1992. avg. price, cloth: $25; paper: $12.95. Discounts: 25-50%. 300pp; 5×8; of. Reporting time: 1 week. Payment: negotiable. Does not copyright for author.

General Hall, Inc., Ravi Mehra, 5 Talon Way, Dix Hills, NY 11746-6238, (516) 243-0155. 1975. "College texts" avg. press run 3.5M. Pub'd 3 titles 1990; expects 3 titles 1991, 3-5 titles 1992. 33 titles listed in the *Small Press Record of Books in Print* (20th Edition, 1991-92). avg. price, cloth: $34.95; paper: $15.95. Discounts: 20%. 200-250pp; 6×9; of. Reporting time: 4-8 weeks. Payment: 10%. Copyrights for author. PA.

GENERATIONS SANPETE: INDEX OF ORAL HISTORIES OF RURAL UTAH, Dixie Dorius Bond, PO Box 555, Fayette, UT 84630. 1979. Articles, interviews, non-fiction. circ. 1M. 1-3/yr. Pub'd 2 issues 1990; expects 2 issues 1991, 2-4 issues 1992. price per copy: $25. Back issues: $3-$25. 60-100pp; 8½×11; laser, photo. Copyrighted, does not revert to author.

GENERATOR, Generator Press, John Byrum, Editor-Publisher, 8139 Midland Road, Mentor, OH 44060, 216-951-3209. 1986. Poetry, art, photos, criticism, reviews, collages, concrete art. "*Generator* is a yearly journal of visual and language poetries. Recent contributors include: Fernando Aguiar, Bruce Andrews, Dennis Barone, Tom Beckett, Charles Bernstein, Richard Kostelanetz, Sheila E. Murphy, Nick Piombino, and Ron Silliman. Maximum length for inclusion in any issue is 5 pages" circ. 200. 1/yr. Pub'd 1 issue 1990; expects 1 issue 1991, 1 issue 1992. sub. price: $5; per copy: $5; sample: $5. Discounts: 40% trade. 100pp; 8½×7; photocopy. Reporting time: 1 week to 1 month. Payment: contributor's copies. Copyrighted, reverts to author. Pub's reviews: 2 in 1990. §Language poetry, visual and concrete poetry, literary and art criticism, philosophy, and political philosophy.

Generator Press (see also **GENERATOR**), John Byrum, 8139 Midland Road, Mentor, OH 44060, 216-951-3209. 1986. Poetry, criticism, long-poems, collages, concrete art. "Not currently accepting unsolicited mss. May do so in future" avg. press run 200. Pub'd 5 titles 1990; expects 4 titles 1991, 4 titles 1992. 9 titles listed in the *Small Press Record of Books in Print* (20th Edition, 1991-92). avg. price, paper: $4. Discounts: 40% trade. 25pp; 7×8½; photocopy. Reporting time: 1 month. Payment: individually negotiated, % after publishing costs are met. Does not copyright for author.

GENII, Dante Larsen, PO Box 36068, Los Angeles, CA 90036. 1936. Poetry, fiction, articles, photos, cartoons, interviews, satire, criticism, reviews, letters, news items, non-fiction. circ. 6.5M. 12/yr. Pub'd 12 issues 1990; expects 12 issues 1991, 12 issues 1992. sub. price: $30; per copy: $3; sample: $3. 68pp; 8×11; of. Reporting time: open. Payment: none. Copyrighted, rights revert if requested. Pub's reviews: 100+ in 1990. §Magic. Ads: $300/$150/$100 1/4 page/$20 per inch.

THE GEORGIA REVIEW, Stanley W. Lindberg, Editor; Stephen Corey, Associate Editor, Univ. of Georgia, Athens, GA 30602, 404-542-3481. 1947. Poetry, fiction, art, photos, interviews, criticism, reviews, letters, plays, non-fiction. "An international journal of arts and letters, winner of the National Magazine Award in Fiction. Contributors range from previously unpublished to the already famous. Nonfiction preferences: thesis-oriented essays, *not* scholarly articles. Fiction and poetry selections are especially competitive. Translations and novel excerpts are *not* desired. During the months of June, July, and August unsolicited manuscripts are not considered (and will be returned unread)." circ. 5.3M. 4/yr. Pub'd 4 issues 1990; expects 4 issues 1991, 4 issues 1992. sub. price: $12 in US, $15 outside US; per copy: $5; sample: $4. Back issues: $5.

222

Discounts: agency sub. 10% ads 15%. 216pp; 7×10; lp. Reporting time: 1-3 months. Payment: $25 minimum page prose; $2 line poetry; plus copies. Copyrighted, reverts to author. Pub's reviews: 64 in 1990. §General humanities, poetry, fiction, the South, interdisciplinary studies. Ads: $275/$175. CCLM, CELJ, ASME.

Geoscience Press, Inc., Charles Hutchinson, Publisher, 1040 Hyland Circle, Prescott, AZ 86303, 602-445-8058. 1988. Cartoons, non-fiction. "Seeking book length mss of interest to gem, mineral, rock, and fossil collectors or hobbyists." avg. press run 2M-4M. Pub'd 4 titles 1990; expects 2 titles 1991, 2 titles 1992. 7 titles listed in the *Small Press Record of Books in Print* (20th Edition, 1991-92). avg. price, cloth: $40; paper: $19.95. Discounts: 1-4 20%, 5-24 40%, 25-49 42%, 50-99 43%, 100 or more 44%. Dist. to the trade by Gem Guides Book Co., 315 Cloverleaf Drive, Suite F, Baldwin Park, CA 91706. 250-350pp; 6×9; of. Reporting time: 2-3 months. Payment: 10% of net sales paid 2x a year. Copyrights for author. RMBPA.

GESAR-Buddhism in the West, Dharma Publishing, Iris Maitland, Managing Editor, 2425 Hillside Avenue, Berkeley, CA 94704, 415-548-5407. 1973. Poetry, art, photos, interviews, reviews, news items. "News from Buddhist organizations accepted" circ. 3.5M. 4/yr. Expects 4 issues 1991, 4 issues 1992. sub. price: $12; per copy: $3.50; sample: $2. Back issues: $2/copy. No discount for subscription. 48pp; 7×9¼; †of. Reporting time: 2 months. Payment: none. Copyrighted, does not revert to author. Pub's reviews. §Buddhist, human development, philosophy. No ads accepted. LPS.

Gesture Press, Nicholas Power, 68 Tyrrel Avenue, Toronto M6G 2G4, Canada. 1983. Poetry, art, photos, long-poems, collages, concrete art. "We're interested in expansive poems with new formal concepts or unique lexicons. The content will determine the form of publication, completing the gesture." avg. press run 100-250. Pub'd 3 titles 1990; expects 6 titles 1991, 5 titles 1992. 12 titles listed in the *Small Press Record of Books in Print* (20th Edition, 1991-92). avg. price, paper: $2-$6; other: $1 postcards, 1¢-$1.75 emphemera. Discounts: trade-40%, short-30%, agents-10%, libraries-full price. 1-40pp; size varies; of, hand-turned gestetner, xerox. Reporting time: 3 months. Payment: percentage of print run (usually 10%). Copyrights for author. Meet the Presses, Toronto Small Press Book Fair.

GET STUPID, Dr. Ahmed Fishmonger, 25 Grant Street, Cambridge, MA 02138, 617-661-1738. 1982. Art, cartoons, collages. "*Get Stupid* is an unusual art and humor mag for those who are not normal and like it that way. Recent contributors have been Kim Deitch, Ken DeVries, Carol Lay, Ruggles Smadbeck, Ahmed Fishmonger, Donna Kossy, Ivan Stang, Byron Werner, Tony Fitzgerald, Avion Outfox, Norton Bizango, and many others. As for bias, I print only good stuff. I accept no unsolicited submissions" circ. 300-450. 3/yr. Pub'd 3 issues 1990; expects 2-4 issues 1991. price per copy: $2; sample: $2. Back issues: $3. Discounts: 60/40 split my favor. 26pp; 8½×11; †xerox. Payment: $10-$30 per page depending on who you are. Copyrighted, reverts to author. Ads: no cost for products and publications I personally endorse. SPA, PO Box 471, Cambridge, MA 02142.

THE GETTYSBURG REVIEW, Peter Stitt, Editor, Gettysburg College, Gettysburg, PA 17325, 717-337-6770. 1988. Poetry, fiction, articles, art, photos, satire, criticism, parts-of-novels, long-poems, collages, non-fiction. "Suggested length for essays and fiction: 3,000-7,000 words. Recent contributors include: Joyce Carol Oates, Kelly Cherry, Stephen Dobyns, Marly Swick, Patiann Rogers, Debora Greger, Paul Zimmer, Diane Ackerman, E.L. Doctorow. We publish essay-reviews that treat books in broader context" circ. 2M. 4/yr. Pub'd 4 issues 1990; expects 4 issues 1991, 4 issues 1992. sub. price: $15, $20 foreign; per copy: $5 + $1 p/h; sample: $5 + $1 p/h. Back issues: $5 + $1 p/h. Discounts: bookstores 40% with option to return unsold copies. 176pp; 6×9½; lp. Reporting time: 1-3 months. Payment: $2 per line for poetry, $25 per page for prose. Copyrighted, reverts to author. Ads: $150/$225 cover. MLA, CLMP, CELJ.

GGL Educational Press, William W. Lau, 1501 East Chapman, Suite 346, Fullerton, CA 92631, 714-860-1088. 1983. avg. press run 3M. Expects 1 title 1991, 2 titles 1992. 1 title listed in the *Small Press Record of Books in Print* (20th Edition, 1991-92). avg. price, cloth: $27. Discounts: wholesaler and jobbers 45% for bulk purchase with prepayment, and 20% single copies. Return with full refund 6 months-1 year after purchase. 220pp; 6×9.

GHOST DANCE: The International Quarterly of Experimental Poetry, Ghost Dance Press, Hugh Fox, 526 Forest, E. Lansing, MI 48823. 1968. Poetry. "*Ghost Dance* experiencing a renaissance with the publication of Wicklund's *Moving Paper* and a little injection of cash into production-system. Still looking for the hitherto undone, unspoken, undreamed of." circ. 300. 4/yr. Expects 2 issues 1991. sub. price: $3.50; per copy: $1; sample: $1. Back issues: $1. Discounts: none. 32pp; 5½×8½; †of. Reporting time: 1 hour. Payment: copies. Not copyrighted. No ads.

Ghost Dance Press (see also GHOST DANCE: The International Quarterly of Experimental Poetry), Hugh Fox, 526 Forest, E. Lansing, MI 48823. 1968. Poetry. "Looking for the unheard of, undreamt of, like hearing Stravinsky for the first time—not 100 years after debut" avg. press run 200-500. Pub'd 1 title 1990; expects 2 titles 1991. 30 titles listed in the *Small Press Record of Books in Print* (20th Edition, 1991-92). avg. price, paper: $1; other: $1. Discounts: 50% to trade. 32-36pp; 5½×8½; †of. Reporting time: 1 day. Payment:

copies. Common law copyright.

Ghost Pony Press, Ingrid Swanberg, Editor, 2518 Gregory Street, Madison, WI 53711, 608-238-0175. 1980. Poetry, art, photos, interviews, long-poems, collages, concrete art. "We are interested in poetry and prose-poems. Open to all forms. Emphasis on lyric modes. Books, chapbooks, pamphlets, broadsides. Recent & upcoming contributors: Jonathan Moore, Stephen M. Miller, Peter Wild, d.a. levy, Ivan Arguelles, Connie Fox, W.R. Rodriguez, Gerald Locklin, prospero saiz" avg. press run 500. Expects 1 title 1991, 1 title 1992. 11 titles listed in the *Small Press Record of Books in Print* (20th Edition, 1991-92). avg. price, paper: $9; other: $1 broadsides. Discounts: 20% 1-5 copies; 40% trade on orders of more than 5 copies. 70pp; 6×9; of. Reporting time: 3-12 weeks. Payment: copies. Copyrights for author.

GHOST TOWN QUARTERLY, Donna B. McLean, PO Box 714, Philipsburg, MT 59858, 406-859-3365. 1988. Poetry, articles, photos, cartoons, interviews, non-fiction. "Articles must be factual. Prefer materials to be original and unpublished at time of submission. Not just statistics—like to be able to furnish to our readers the opportunity to learn something new, interesting & perhaps unusual that they wouldn't have known had they not read our magazine. Like to have photographs, both current and historical, submitted with articles. We need more cartoon submissions, to be related to the themes of the magazine." circ. 6M. 4/yr. Pub'd 4 issues 1990; expects 4 issues 1991, 4 issues 1992. sub. price: $11.50; per copy: $3.50; sample: $3.50. Back issues: $3.50. Discounts: 3+ issues $3 each. 52pp; 8½×11; of. Reporting time: 1-6 months. Payment: send note & SASE for info sheet. Copyrighted, reverts to author. Ads: $1,070 color, $720 b&w/$855 color, $370 b&w/display classified $62.50 per col. inch + $5 set-up fee/classified $1 per word. Towers Club USA (The original writers Entrepreneurial Research Service) PO Box 2038, Vancouver, WA 98668-2038.

GIANTS PLAY WELL IN THE DRIZZLE, Martha King, 326-A 4th Street, Brooklyn, NY 11215, 718-788-7927. 1983. Poetry, fiction, articles, art, cartoons, satire, criticism, letters, non-fiction. "Very compact publication—restricted in regards to prose or long poems: no ms longer than 8 double-spaced pages. Recent contributors: Bill Berkson, Guy Birchard, Robert Peters, Sheila Murphy, Ted Enslin, Larry Fixel, Laurie Price" circ. 600. 3-6/yr. Pub'd 2 issues 1990; expects 4 issues 1991, 4 issues 1992. sub. price: free, but editor exercises discretion; per copy: same; sample: free. Back issues: negotiable. 6pp; 8½×11; of. Reporting time: 10 minutes to 10 weeks. Payment: copies. Copyrighted, reverts to author. Pub's reviews. §Anything that merits notice. CCLM.

THE GIFTED CHILD TODAY, GCT Inc., Marvin Gold, PO Box 6448, Mobile, AL 36660, 205-478-4700. 1978. Poetry, fiction, articles, art, photos, cartoons, interviews, satire, criticism, reviews, letters, plays, news items, non-fiction. "By and for parents and teachers of gifted, creative, and talented children and youth" circ. 10M. 6/yr. Pub'd 6 issues 1990; expects 6 issues 1991, 6 issues 1992. sub. price: $29.97 (foreign postage add $6); per copy: $5; sample: $5. 64pp; 8½×11; of. Reporting time: 1 month. Payment: none. Copyrighted, reverts to author. Pub's reviews: 100 in 1990. §Any materials (including software, books, ed. material) dealing with gifted, creative, talented children and youth. Ads: $500/$275/$25 per col. inch. Edpress.

Gifted Education Press/The Reading Tutorium, Maurice D. Fisher, PO Box 1586, 10201 Yuma Court, Manassas, VA 22110-1586, 703-369-5017. 1981. Non-fiction. "Our books present clear and rigorous techniques for teaching gifted, average and handicapped children in grades K-12 based upon using educational theory and practice. We are also interested in books on how to parent the gifted, how to teach adults to read. They are sold primarily to school districts, libraries and universities across the nation. Some of our most recent books are: (1) *How to Use Computers with Gifted Students* by P. Terry; (2) *The Philosophy of Ethics Applied to Everyday Life* by James Logiudice & Michael E. Walters; (3) *Humanities Education for Gifted Children* by M. Walters; (4) *How to Increase Gifted Students' Creative Thinking and Imagination* by W. Wenger; and *Teaching Shakespeare to Gifted Children* by M. Walters. We are actively seeking manuscripts of 50 to 70 pages on educating gifted students, teaching adults how to read, creativity training, parenting the gifted, and how to use computers with the gifted. We are also actively searching for field representatives to sell our books across the USA through workshops and inservice training. Will not accept unsolicited manuscripts. Send 1 page letter of inquiry first" avg. press run 500. Pub'd 3 titles 1990; expects 5 titles 1991, 7 titles 1992. 20 titles listed in the *Small Press Record of Books in Print* (20th Edition, 1991-92). avg. price, paper: $12. Discounts: 20% to jobbers & bookstores. 50pp; 8½×11; xerography. Reporting time: 3-4 months. Payment: $1 per book sold by us; 80¢ per book sold to jobbers & bookstores. Copyrights for author. COSMEP.

Gild of Saint George (see also LIVERPOOL NEWSLETTER), Anthony Cooney, Rose Cottage, 17 Hadassah Grove, Lark Lane, Liverpool L17 8XH, England, 051-728-9176. 1982. Poetry, letters, non-fiction. "By 'letters' and 'non-fiction' is meant 'essays'. Essays of social credit/decentralist/Catholic interest." avg. press run 200. Pub'd 1 title 1990; expects 3 titles 1991, 3 titles 1992. avg. price, paper: $1; other: $2. 32pp; 5½×8, 8×12; †mi, photocopy. Reporting time: poetry 3 months, prose 1 month. Payment: none. Copyrights for author.

Gilgal Publications, Judy Osgood, Executive Editor, PO Box 3386, Sunriver, OR 97707, 503-593-8639. 1983.

Non-fiction. "We are currently publishing a series of 12 books on coping with stress and resolving grief. This is our Gilgal Meditation series. The contributors to each book are individuals who have lived through the experience they are talking about. For example, our first book was *Meditations For Bereaved Parents*. Some of the contributors to it were Paula D'Arcy, Meg Woodson & Joyce Landorf. The meditations are all 1 to 2 pages long and are written in what we call a "sharing tone". The authors aren't claiming to have all the answers. They are saying, "this is what helped me; maybe it will help you too". Our latest book released in May 1989 was *Meditations for the Terminally Ill and Their Families*. We ask that all potential contributors get our guidelines before they write a word for us" avg. press run 5M+. Pub'd 1 title 1990; expects 2 titles 1991, 2-3 titles 1992. 4 titles listed in the *Small Press Record of Books in Print* (20th Edition, 1991-92). avg. price, paper: $5.95. Discounts: for resale—40% off list. 72pp; 5¼×7½; of. Reporting time: 2 weeks - 2 months. Payment: on acceptance plus royalties. Copyrights for author.

Gilgamesh Press Ltd., K.A. Mooradian, V.A. Mooradian, 205 6th Street, Racine, WI 53403-1255. 1978. Art, photos, interviews, criticism, reviews, letters, news items, non-fiction. avg. press run 5M. Pub'd 2 titles 1990; expects 2 titles 1991. 5 titles listed in the *Small Press Record of Books in Print* (20th Edition, 1991-92). avg. price, cloth: $33; paper: $9.95. Discounts: universal schedule. 300pp; 6×9; †of.

Giorno Poetry Systems Records (see also DIAL-A-POEM POETS LP'S), John Giorno, 222 Bowery, New York City, NY 10012. 1967. Poetry, photos, cartoons, music. avg. press run 7M-10M. Pub'd 4 titles 1990; expects 4 titles 1991, 4 titles 1992. 23 titles listed in the *Small Press Record of Books in Print* (20th Edition, 1991-92). avg. price, other: $8.98 single album or cassette, $12.98 double album, $13.98 for double cassette or compact disc, $39.95 videopak. Discounts: 40% to book & record stores. Payment: $400 to each poet. Copyrights for author.

Giro Press, Y Salomon, PO Box 203, Croton-on-Hudson, NY 10520, 914-271-8924. 1 title listed in the *Small Press Record of Books in Print* (20th Edition, 1991-92).

Glacier House Publications, Dave Thorp, Box 201901, Anchorage, AK 99520, 907-272-3286. 1987. Non-fiction. avg. press run 5M. Pub'd 3 titles 1990; expects 5 titles 1991, 5 titles 1992. 1 title listed in the *Small Press Record of Books in Print* (20th Edition, 1991-92). avg. price, paper: $12.95; other: $90, 1100pp dictionary. Discounts: retail 40%, wholesale 50%. 96pp; 8½×11; †of. Payment: negotiable. Copyrights for author.

GLASS ART, Shawn Waggoner, PO Box 1507, Broomfield, CO 80038-1507, 303-465-4965. 1985. Articles, art, photos, letters. circ. 7M. 6/yr. Pub'd 6 issues 1990; expects 6 issues 1991, 6 issues 1992. sub. price: $20; per copy: $4; sample: free. Back issues: $4. 64-80pp; of. Copyrighted. Pub's reviews.

GLASS WILL, Toledo Poets Center Press, Joel Lipman, Department of English, University of Toledo, Toledo, OH 43606. 1976. "No unsolicited submissions." circ. 400. Alternate years. Pub'd 1 issue 1990. price per copy: $7.50; sample: $5. 250pp; 6¼×9¼; of. Payment: copies. Copyrighted, reverts to author.

GLB Publishers, W.L Warner, Editor & Publisher; John Hanley, Associate Editor, 935 Howard St., Suite B, San Francisco, CA 94103, 415-243-0229. 1990. Poetry, fiction, long-poems. "A contributory press for books of fiction and poetry by gay, lesbian, and bisexual authors. Both explicit and non-explicit. Also PO Box 78212, San Francisco, CA 94107." avg. press run 2M. Expects 4 titles 1991, 3 titles 1992. 2 titles listed in the *Small Press Record of Books in Print* (20th Edition, 1991-92). avg. price, cloth: $20; paper: $10.95. Discounts: 55%. 176pp; 5½×8½; of. Reporting time: 2 months. Payment: variable. Copyrights for author. PMA, COSMEP.

Glen Abbey Books, Inc., Bill Pittman, Editor-in-Chief, PO Box 31329, Seattle, WA 98109, 206-548-9360; 800-782-2239. 1986. Non-fiction. "Glen Abbey Books, Inc. publishes self-help and meditation books for persons of all ages who are involved in 12 Step recovery programs. We have also published two books on the history of Alcoholics Anonymous: *AA The Way It Began* and *Beware the First Drink!*, a comparison between AA and the Washingtonian Societies of the 1800s. Recent titles include: *Dealing with Depression in 12 Step Recovery; Easy Does It* and *12 Step Prayer Book* (a meditation set); and three titles in the Stepping Stones to Recovery series: *Stepping Stones to Recovery: For Women; Stepping Stones to Recovery: From Cocaine/Crack Addiction;* and *Stepping Stones to Recover: For Young People.* We welcome nonfiction submissions (no 'My Story,' fiction, or poetry, please). The best way to study our styles is to read our books." avg. press run 5M. Pub'd 4 titles 1990; expects 4 titles 1991, 4 titles 1992. 12 titles listed in the *Small Press Record of Books in Print* (20th Edition, 1991-92). avg. price, paper: $9. Discounts: jobbers usual. 200pp; 5½×8, 4×6; of. Reporting time: 1 month. Payment: per usual contract. Copyrights for author. ABA, PMA, Pac. NW Booksellers' Assoc., Book Publishers Northwest, Nat'l Assoc. of Desktop Publishers.

Glenbridge Publishing Ltd., James A. Keene, Editor-in-Chief & Vice-President, 4 Woodland Lane, Macomb, IL 61455, 309-833-5104. 1986. Non-fiction. "Currently have 7 additional titles in process, all of which are appropriate for all types of libraries (university, historical, college, community college, public, reference etc.), the trade market and use as auxiliary text/text material for college, university, and community college" avg.

press run 2.5M. Pub'd 4 titles 1990; expects 6 titles 1991, 4-6 titles 1992. 12 titles listed in the *Small Press Record of Books in Print* (20th Edition, 1991-92). avg. price, cloth: $18.95-$24.95; paper: $9.95-$14.95. Discounts: jobber 20%, trade: 1-2 books 20%, 3-9 30%, 10-49 40%, 50-99 42%, 100-299 44%, 300-499 46%, 500-999 48%, 1000 50%. 200-300pp; 6×9; professionally manufactured by major book company. Reporting time: 2-6 weeks. Payment: hard cover, 10%, pay once yearly. Copyrights for author.

Glendale House Publishing, B.J. Baker, Dan A. Kessel, 249 N. Brand Blvd., Suite 440, Glendale, CA 91203, 818-507-7475. 1987. Non-fiction. avg. press run 5M. Expects 1 title 1991, 2-3 titles 1992. 1 title listed in the *Small Press Record of Books in Print* (20th Edition, 1991-92). avg. price, paper: $12.95; other: $19.95. Discounts: trade 10%-40% Stop-33%; distributors 50%. Pages vary; 6×9, 8×11; of. Reporting time: 60 days. Payment: 20% net income. Copyrights for author. Publishers Marketing Association (PMA), 2401 Pacific Coast Hwy., Suite 206, Hermosa Beach, CA 90254.

GlenHill Productions, Ronald E. Pickup, PO Box 62, Soulsbyville, CA 95372, 209-532-7045. 1986. Poetry, fiction, art, photos, satire, criticism, parts-of-novels, long-poems, plays, non-fiction. "Additional address: 20150 Blackberry Lane, Soulsbyville, CA 95372. Length of material open. We seek prose and poetry which is of high quality and interest. A current title is *Not of Our Time*, a book of poetry by Tom Morgan. Bonnie Lind's novel, *Gypsies In the Wood*, will be published in late 1991 or 1992." avg. press run 1.5M-3M. Pub'd 2 titles 1990; expects 2 titles 1991, 2 titles 1992. 2 titles listed in the *Small Press Record of Books in Print* (20th Edition, 1991-92). avg. price, paper: $7. Discounts: 40% on 10 or more copies. Pages vary; 5½×8¼; of. Reporting time: 3 months. Payment: each author is worked with individually. Copyrights for author. CCLM.

Glenhurst Publications, Inc., Janet M. Donaldson, Central Community Center, 6300 Walker Street, St. Louis Park, MN 55416, 612-925-3632. 1982. Non-fiction. "Glenhurst publishes a series of global women's history and culture curriculum, and women in development materials, books, manuals, videos and film strips, to be taught in regular history and social studies courses. Our materials are appropriate for the high school and university levels. Average book length, 175 pp. Teacher's guides are also published" avg. press run 5M. Expects 2 titles 1991, 2 titles 1992. 13 titles listed in the *Small Press Record of Books in Print* (20th Edition, 1991-92). avg. price, paper: $9.95; other: film strips $35, videos $40. Discounts: 25% discount per class set. 175pp; 6½×9½. Reporting time: 1 month. Payment: 7%. Does not copyright for author. COSMEP.

The Gleniffer Press, Ian Macdonald, 11 Low Road, Castlehead, Paisley PA2 6AQ, Scotland, 041-889-9579. 1968. Poetry, art, photos, letters, long-poems, plays, news items. "Specialist in miniature books, limited editions. Mailing list of private buyers now established. Recently published '*Smallest Book In The World*'. Commission work" avg. press run 250-1M. Pub'd 1 title 1990; expects 4 titles 1991, 4 titles 1992. 4 titles listed in the *Small Press Record of Books in Print* (20th Edition, 1991-92). avg. price, cloth: $30; other: price varies. Discounts: 33⅓%. 30pp; †of, lp. Payment: single fees. Copyrights for author. MBS, BPS.

THE GLOBAL FORUM MAGAZINE, Adam A. Budzan, Jack J. Zuraw, Maria K. Kuczynska, Mathew Ustasz, International Relief Agency, Inc., 178 Jarvis Street, Suite 804, Toronto, Ontario M5B 2K7, Canada, 416-364-0124. 1988. Art, cartoons, interviews, reviews, letters, news items. "Under 4000 words. Main subjects: Articles related to nationalities and their right to freedom, historical perspectives, analysis of international events, third world events and development, international trade and investment, ecology, population health and nutrition, foreign aid, travel, ethnic cooking, international business, international arts and literature reviews, film and theatre, religion and politics, science, international job mart—classified, pen-pal, sports, geo-political crosswords." circ. 10M. 12/yr. Expects 2 issues 1991, 12 issues 1992. sub. price: $20 in Canada (US + 10%, overseas + 50%); per copy: $2.50; sample: same. Discounts: retail only. 60pp; 8½×11; †of. Reporting time: 2 months in advance. Payment: none. Copyrighted, reverts to author. Pub's reviews: 12 in 1990. §As indicated above. Ads: $600/$300/$200 1/4 page/60¢ per line Agency commission 15%.

The Global Press, John Wharton, 1510 York Street #204, Denver, CO 80206, 303-899-4918. 1982. Non-fiction. "Focuses primarily on employment opportunities in Japan." avg. press run 5M. Expects 1 title 1991, 1 title 1992. 2 titles listed in the *Small Press Record of Books in Print* (20th Edition, 1991-92). avg. price, paper: $12.95. Discounts: 0-50%. 264pp; 5½×8½; of. Reporting time: undetermined. Payment: undetermined. Copyrights for author.

Global Publishing Company, Charles Prosper, PO Box 35357, Los Angeles, CA 90035, 937-4356. 1987. Photos, concrete art, non-fiction. "Global Publishing Company is a subsidiary of Balloons by Prosper. I specialize and I am interested in *any* book-length treatise on *quality* balloon artistry. I wrote the first book on this subject entitled *How To Become a Balloon Artist And Make Up To $100,000 a Year*. I am only accepting books at the present time on balloon artistry." Expects 3 titles 1991, 5 titles 1992. 1 title listed in the *Small Press Record of Books in Print* (20th Edition, 1991-92). avg. price, paper: $35. Discounts: 3-200 40%, 200-500 50%, 500+ 55%. 150pp; 8½×11; of. Reporting time: 30 days. Payment: 7% of list price on softcover for the first 12,000 sold, and 9% above that number. Copyrights for author.

Global Sports Productions, Ltd., Ed Kobak, 1223 Broadway Street #101, Santa Monica, CA 90404-2707.

1980. avg. press run 15M. 2 titles listed in the *Small Press Record of Books in Print* (20th Edition, 1991-92). avg. price, paper: $19.95 (foreign add $7 surface or $13 airmail). Discounts: 20%. 350pp; 5½×8½.

GLOBAL TAPESTRY JOURNAL, BB Books, Dave Cunliffe, 1 Spring Bank, Salesbury, Blackburn, Lancs BB1 9EU, England, 0254 249128. 1971. Poetry, fiction, articles, art, interviews, reviews, letters, parts-of-novels, long-poems, collages, concrete art. "Mainly concerned with creative poetry & prose. Also those energy communications networks which liberate human animal beast mind. Be it psychedelics, mutant vampires or dead history memory recall. PM Newsletter is now incorporated, printing reviews, notices and listings." circ. 1,050. 4/yr. Pub'd 4 issues 1990; expects 4 issues 1991, 4 issues 1992. sub. price: $20/4 issues; per copy: $5; sample: $3. Back issues: $2. Discounts: one third trade. 72pp; size A5; †of. Reporting time: soon. Payment: one copy. Pub's reviews: 150 in 1990. §Poetry, creative prose. Ads: £20/£10/10p per word. NWASP.

GLOBE LITERARY, 3625 Greenwood North, Seattle, WA 98103. 1990. Long-poems. "Mythic prose-poetry only" †of.

The Globe Pequot Press, Charles Everitt, President; Linda Kennedy, VP-Publications Director; Kevin Lynch, Production Director; Bruce Markot, Managing Editor; Cleve Gardner, Sales Manager, 138 W. Main Street, Box Q, Chester, CT 06412, 203-526-9571. 1947. Art, photos, non-fiction. "We publish domestic and international travel guides, nature, outdoor recreation, gardening, home how-to, biography, regional history, and regional cookbooks. No poetry, fiction, or children's stories. Query letters are preferred. Standard submissions consist of one sample chapter, a table of contents, a one-page precis detailing the book and its saleability plus cover letter with some information about the author's credentials. We extend some advances. A free catalogue of all Globe Pequot Press books is available." avg. press run 5M. Pub'd 69 titles 1990; expects 63 titles 1991, 63 titles 1992. 245 titles listed in the *Small Press Record of Books in Print* (20th Edition, 1991-92). avg. price, cloth: $18.95; paper: $9.95. Discounts: trade 20% and ascending, contingent upon quantity. 192pp; 5½×8½, 7×10, 8½×11; of. Reporting time: 4-8 weeks. Payment: 8-12% of net. Copyrights for author. American Bookseller Association.

Globe Press Books, Joel Friedlander, PO Box 2045, Madison Square Station, New York, NY 10159-2045, 914-962-4614. 1985. Non-fiction. "Imprint: Fourth Way Books" avg. press run 5M. Pub'd 3 titles 1990; expects 4 titles 1991, 8 titles 1992. 8 titles listed in the *Small Press Record of Books in Print* (20th Edition, 1991-92). avg. price, cloth: $16; paper: $10. Discounts: 40%. 200pp; 6×9; of. Reporting time: 60 days. Payment: negotiable. Copyrights for author. NAPRA, PMA.

GO MAGAZINE, Bill Cushing, Editor; Michele Hope, Assistant Editor, 1139 N. Laura Street, Jacksonville, FL 32206, 904-354-4382. 1988. Poetry, fiction, articles, art, photos, cartoons, interviews, reviews, music. "Original poetry and artwork by Charles Bukowski. Interview and poetry by *Gargoyle* publisher Richard Peabody. Interviews with Living Colour, They Might Be Giants, Sonic Youth. Interview with zen poet Phillip Whalen" circ. 10M. 26/yr. Pub'd 7 issues 1990; expects 26 issues 1991, 26 issues 1992. sub. price: free. 16pp; 10×17; laser printer. Reporting time: 2 weeks. Payment: so far contributions have been free, will be paying eventually. Copyrighted. Pub's reviews. §Poetry, literary criticism, fiction, biographies. Ads: $640/$320/$160 1/4 page/$80 1/8.

GOING GAGA, Gareth Branwyn, 2630 Robert Walker Place, Arlington, VA 22207, 703-527-6032. 1988. Poetry, fiction, articles, art, photos, cartoons, interviews, satire, criticism, reviews, music, letters, collages, concrete art, non-fiction. "*Going Gaga* is a quarterly journal of experimental conversations and oblique strategies for personal and cultural change. Each issue has a theme. For instance, #2-Dead Dadaist Defiled, #3-Notebooks of the Mind, #4-Marginalia, #5-Self-Destructing Manifestoes. Recent contributors have included: Geof Huth, Andrew Gaze, Philip Hughes, Art Nahpro, Katherine Gekker & Dr. Patch Adams." circ. 300. 4/yr. Pub'd 4 issues 1990; expects 4 issues 1991, 4 issues 1992. sub. price: $12; per copy: $4; sample: $4. Back issues: $4. Discounts: negotiable. 40pp; 7×8½; †xerox, of. Reporting time: within 3 weeks. Payment: copies. Not copyrighted. Pub's reviews: 12 in 1990. §Experimental art, comics, poetry, cultural criticism, the audio & print underground. Trade ad for ad only.

GOKOOMA, I. Raty, PO Box 63, 83501 Outokumpu, Finland. 1990. Poetry, articles, art, cartoons, interviews, reviews, music, letters, news items. 1-4/yr. Pub'd 3 issues 1990; expects 3 issues 1991. price per copy: $2; sample: $2. Discounts: take contact. 48pp; size A5; of. Payment: cash. Not copyrighted. Pub's reviews: 50 in 1990. §Music, anarchy, art. Ads: $25/$13.

GOLD, SILVER AND URANIUM FROM SEAS AND OCEANS PROGRESS UPDATE, 7804 Vicksburg Avenue, Los Angeles, CA 90045, 213-645-7571. 1989. Reviews, non-fiction. 2/yr. Pub'd 4 issues 1990; expects 2 issues 1991, 2 issues 1992. price per copy: $5; sample: $5. Back issues: $3. 10-12pp; 8½×11; mi, of. Copyrighted. Pub's reviews: 2 in 1990. §Precious and valuable metals from seas, oceans and sediments.

GOLDEN ISIS, Gerina Dunwich, 23233 Saticoy Street, Building 105, Box 137, West Hills, CA 91304. 1980. Poetry, fiction, articles, art, cartoons, interviews, satire, reviews, letters, non-fiction. "Recent contributors include Don Blondeau, Lady Jenny, Vashti, J.C. Fiore. *Golden Isis* is a neo-pagan literary journal of mystical poetry, artwork, reviews, news and ads. Occult, Egyptian, cosmic and goddess-inspired poetry is published. All styles considered. *Under 60 lines preferred.* We occasionally use short stories: fantasy, mystery, sci-fi, occult & bizarre humor. Maximum length is 1500 words. Non-fiction articles should be interesting & off-beat. We are always interested in true encounters with the supernatural, astrology, E.S.P., psi phenomena, etc. *No pornographic, religious, sexist, racist or Satanic cult material, please.* Send SASE for free guidelines." circ. 3.6M. 4/yr. Pub'd 4 issues 1990; expects 4 issues 1991, 4 issues 1992. sub. price: $10 (overseas/$15.50), cash only; per copy: $3 cash only; sample: $3 cash only. Back issues: $3 cash only. 30pp; 5½×8¼; †Canon PC system. Reporting time: 1 month or sooner. Payment: 1 free copy. Copyrighted, reverts to author. Pub's reviews: 10 in 1990. §Poetry and occult books. Ads: $50/$25/$13 business card/50¢ word classified. WPPA.

Golden Sceptre, C. de Montet, 45911 Silver Avenue, Sardis, British Columbia V2R 1V8, Canada, 604-858-6934; fax 604-858-0870. 1983. Non-fiction. "No unsolicited material." avg. press run 5M. Pub'd 1 title 1990; expects 2 titles 1991, 2 titles 1992. 1 title listed in the *Small Press Record of Books in Print* (20th Edition, 1991-92). avg. price, paper: $13.95. Discounts: 40% to bookstores, 30% to libraries. 175pp; 7×10; of, lp. Payment: will vary depending on a particular author. Copyrights for author.

Golden West Books, Donald Duke, PO Box 80250, San Marino, CA 91118-8250, 213-283-3446. 1963. Photos. avg. press run 4M-5M. Pub'd 2 titles 1990; expects 3 titles 1991, 3 titles 1992. avg. price, cloth: $20-$57.95; paper: $5.95. Discounts: 40%. 265pp; 8½×11; of. Reporting time: 3 weeks. Payment: 10% royalties. Copyrights for author.

Golden West Historical Publications, William O'Shaunnessay, Dir. of Publ.; Albert Cummings, PO Box 1906, Ventura, CA 93002. 1977. Articles. "Generally between 50-80 pages in length in monograph set - only real bias is for historical/politically scientific accurate analyses - revisionist historian Daniel Patrick Brown *The Protectorate and The Northumberland Conspiracy: Political Intrigue in the Reigh of Edward VI (1547-1553)*; Daniel Patrick Brown's *The Tragedy of Libby & Andersonville Prison Camps*; & political analyst Bruce Jennings *The Brest-Litovsk Controversy* (an examination of the Russian surrender to Wilhelmine Germany in November-December, 1917), et al." avg. press run 3.5M-5M. Expects 2 titles 1991, 4 titles 1992. 3 titles listed in the *Small Press Record of Books in Print* (20th Edition, 1991-92). avg. price, paper: $3.45. Discounts: in multiples of ten, 10%, for classroom, college bookstore purchases (regardless of quantity) $2.75. 65-90pp; 6×9; of. Reporting time: 2 months. Payment: due to the fact that this firm is principally an outgrowth of the Valley Historical Alliance, only 3% per book. Copyrights for author.

Golden West Publishers, Hal Mitchell, 4113 North Longview, Phoenix, AZ 85014, 602-265-4392. 1973. *"Arizona Cook Book, Chili-Lovers' Cook Book* edited by Al Fischer & Mildred Fischer" avg. press run 10M. Pub'd 5 titles 1990; expects 6 titles 1991, 7 titles 1992. 44 titles listed in the *Small Press Record of Books in Print* (20th Edition, 1991-92). avg. price, paper: $5. Discounts: 5-99, 40%; 100 or more, 50%. 144pp; 5½×8½; of. Reporting time: 2-3 weeks. Payment: buy mscp. outright or royalties. Copyrights for author. AAA, Rocky Mtn., PMA.

Goldfish Press (see also CHRYSANTHEMUM), Koon Woon, 416-1/2 7th Avenue South, Seattle, WA 98104. 1989. Poetry, fiction, articles, satire, criticism, parts-of-novels, non-fiction. "Interested in works that combine literature with philosophy and socially-conscious." avg. press run 500. Expects 1 title 1991, 2 titles 1992. avg. price, paper: $10. Discounts: negotiable. 200pp; 6×9; of. Reporting time: 3 months. Payment: negotiable. Copyrights for author.

Goldstein & Blair, Arthur Naiman, President, PO Box 7635, Berkeley, CA 94707, (415) 524-4000. 1986. "First book, *The Macintosh Bible,* a tips and tricks book, and the best-selling book on the Macintosh computer, with 263,000 copies in print (not including five translations). Very favorably reviewed in *The New York Times* and other publications of note" avg. press run 20M. Pub'd 2 titles 1990; expects 8 titles 1991, 8 titles 1992. 1 title listed in the *Small Press Record of Books in Print* (20th Edition, 1991-92). avg. price, paper: $28. 1024pp; 7×9. Copyrights for author.

Gong Enterprises, Inc., Gwendolyn Gong, PO Box 1753, Bristol, VA 24203, 703-466-4672. Non-fiction. avg. press run 1M. Pub'd 1 title 1990; expects 1 title 1991. 3 titles listed in the *Small Press Record of Books in Print* (20th Edition, 1991-92). avg. price, cloth: $35; paper: $25. Discounts: 50%. 150pp; 6×9; typeset. Reporting time: 2 months. Payment: 20%. Copyrights for author.

GOOD CLEAN FUN, Gene Mahoney, 1190 Maria Privada, Mountain View, CA 94040. 1988. Poetry, fiction, articles, art, cartoons, interviews, satire, criticism, reviews, music, letters, non-fiction. "The magazine is primarily a quarterly collection of Gene Mahoney's comic strip 'Good Clean Fun,' which appears in various publications across the U.S. Also included are music reviews, poetry, and the comix of fellow Bay Area cartoonists Ace Backwords, Granger Davis, and Shannon Wheeler" circ. varies by request. 4/yr. Pub'd 2 issues 1990; expects 4 issues 1991, 4 issues 1992. sub. price: $8; per copy: $2; sample: $2. Back issues: $2. Discounts: not available. 8½×11; †copier. Reporting time: 1 month, send SASE. Payment: none. Copyrighted. Pub's reviews. §Comics, news, music, entertainment, politics. No ads.

228

GOOD COOKING SERIES, Fell Publishers, Inc., Sherri Adelman, Elizabeth Wyatt, 2131 Hollywood Boulevard, Hollywood, FL 33020, 305-925-5242. 1943. Non-fiction. "We are the leading publisher of one-shot magazines in the United States. We have four categories in which we publish. These are diet and health, health, cookbook series and financial planning series. We are looking for full manuscripts that would lend itself to these areas" circ. 50M. 8/yr. Pub'd 8 issues 1990; expects 8 issues 1991, 8 issues 1992. price per copy: $2.95. Back issues: cover price. 128pp; 5-3/16×7⅝; of. Reporting time: 3 months. Payment: negotiated. Copyrighted, reverts to author. Ads: $2,000. PBAA, ACIDA.

Good Gay Poets Press (see also FAG RAG), Good Gay Poets Collective, Box 277, Astor Station, Boston, MA 02123. 1973. Poetry. "Unsolicited ms. not requested" avg. press run 500. Pub'd 2 titles 1990; expects 1 title 1991. 13 titles listed in the *Small Press Record of Books in Print* (20th Edition, 1991-92). avg. price, cloth: $15; paper: $3-$5; other: $3-$5. Discounts: 40% to retailers, 50% to distributors. 64pp; 5½×8½; of. Payment: 10% of run to author; payment only after costs have been returned. Copyrights for author. CCLM.

Good Hope Enterprises, Inc., Richard O. Nwachukwu, PO Box 2394, Dallas, TX 75221, 214-823-7666; fax 214-823-7373. 1987. Non-fiction. "The company recently published *The Dark and Bright Continent: Africa in the Changing World, The Agony: The Untold Story of the Nigerian Society.*" avg. press run 5M. Pub'd 1 title 1990; expects 2 titles 1991, 2 titles 1992. 2 titles listed in the *Small Press Record of Books in Print* (20th Edition, 1991-92). avg. price, cloth: $17.95; paper: $9.25. Discounts: 35% to 55%. 200pp; 5½×8½; of. Reporting time: 3 months. Payment: based on sales. Copyrights for author. COSMEP.

Good Life Products, Inc., Maria V. Vila, 7709 NW 178th Street, Hialeah, FL 33015, 305-362-6998. 1986. Non-fiction. "We specialize in the field of Cosmetology. We publish books on haircutting, coloring and permanent waving. Also produce videotapes. We also publish in Spanish." avg. press run 5M. Pub'd 2 titles 1990; expects 2 titles 1991, 4 titles 1992. 7 titles listed in the *Small Press Record of Books in Print* (20th Edition, 1991-92). avg. price, cloth: $24.95; paper: $16.95; other: $27.95. Discounts: 4-9 20%, 10-19 30%, 20-39 40%, 40+ 50%. 200pp; 8½×11; of. Reporting time: 6 months. Payment: 5% of sales first 5,000, 6% after 5,000; bi-annual payments, advances. Copyrights for author. PMA, COSMEP.

GOOD READING MAGAZINE, Sunshine Press, Peggy Kuethe, Associate Editor, PO Box 40, Litchfield, IL 62056, 217-324-3425. 1964. Poetry, articles, photos, cartoons, non-fiction. circ. 7.5M. 12/yr. Pub'd 12 issues 1990; expects 12 issues 1991, 12 issues 1992. sub. price: $9; per copy: 90¢; sample: 50¢. 32pp; 5¼×7¼; of. Reporting time: 6-8 weeks. Payment: $10-$100. Copyrighted, reverts to author. No ads.

Good Times Publishing Co., Dorothy Miller, PO Box 8071-107, Blaine, WA 98230, 604-736-1045. 1989. Non-fiction. "Most recent publication: Food For Success, by Dr. Barbarah Tinskamper. At present we limit ourselves to self-help books only. In particular, nutrition and psychology. The author should have a university education of a reputable institution and have several years of experience in the field that he/she is writing about. The book should be geared to the general public; the style and format should be easy and fun to read." avg. press run 5M. Pub'd 3 titles 1990; expects 1 title 1991, 2 titles 1992. avg. price, paper: $8.95. Discounts: 55% wholesale, 40% bookstores. 140pp; 5½×8½; of. Reporting time: 2 months. Payment: 2-4%. Copyrights for author. PMA.

Goodheart-Willcox Company, 123 W. Taft Drive, South Holland, IL 60473, (312) 333-7200. 1921. Art, photos, interviews, reviews. Pub'd 30 titles 1990; expects 30+ titles 1991, 30+ titles 1992. 36 titles listed in the *Small Press Record of Books in Print* (20th Edition, 1991-92). avg. price, cloth: $15. Discounts: trade and school. 400pp; 8×11; compugraphic type setter. Reporting time: 1 month to 1 year. Payment: 10% net sales. Copyrights for author.

THE GOOFUS OFFICE GAZETTE, Samuel T. Godfrey, Chief-of-Stuff, The Goofus Office, PO Box 259, Pearl River, NY 10965, 914-620-1416. 1983. Poetry, fiction, articles, art, cartoons, interviews, satire, criticism, reviews, music, letters, news items, non-fiction. *The Gazette* promotes music, the arts. Demotes television and the deadly serious" circ. 350+. 2-4/yr. Expects 2 issues 1991, 6 issues 1992. sub. price: $15; per copy: $2; sample: $2. Back issues: $2. 6pp; 8½×14, 8½×11; †of. Reporting time: ASAP (1 month-2 years). Payment: free dinner. Not copyrighted. Pub's reviews. §Humor, cartoon, music, art, film. Ads: $10/$5/free. COSMEP.

THE GOPHERWOOD REVIEW, Sandra Reiff, Sharron Crowson, Box 58784, Houston, TX 77258, 713-532-1622. 1990. Poetry, fiction, articles, art, interviews, criticism, reviews, plays. "Biased toward experimental and surreal. Poetry under 40 lines. Fiction to 1,500 words. Highest quality literary work. No previously published. No simultaneous submissions" circ. 200. 2/yr. Expects 2 issues 1991, 2 issues 1992. sub. price: $7; per copy: $3.50; sample: $3.50. Back issues: $3. 52pp; 8×11½; of. Reporting time: 3 weeks. Payment: 1 copy. Copyrighted, reverts to author. Pub's reviews: 4 in 1990. §Experimental poetry and fiction. Ads: $80/$40/$20 business card, will exchange ads.

Teri Gordon, Publisher, Teri Gordon, 10901 Rustic Manor Lane, Austin, TX 78750-1133, 512-258-8309.

1987. Non-fiction. avg. press run 2M. Pub'd 1 title 1990; expects 2 titles 1991, 2 titles 1992. 2 titles listed in the *Small Press Record of Books in Print* (20th Edition, 1991-92). avg. price, paper: $6.95. Discounts: 10-99 copies 40%, 100+ 50%. 128pp; 8½×11, 4½×6½; word processor and Printing Press. Reporting time: 1 month. Payment: individually arranged. Does not copyright for author. Business Publishers of Texas (BPT), 3208 Amberway Drive, Arlington, TX 76014; COSMEP, PO Box 703, San Francisco, CA 94101; Austin Writers' League, 1501 West Fifth Street, Austin, TX 78703.

GORHAM, Axios Newletter, Inc., David Gorham, 800 South Euclid Street, Fullerton, CA 92632, 714-526-4952. 1981. Poetry, articles, art, photos, interviews, reviews, letters, parts-of-novels, news items, non-fiction. "A continuing journal of genealogy and history of all the various branches of the Gorham family. Need historical articles, on places named after the Gorhams, obscure Gorham pioneers, how to trace your ancestors, interviews of well-known persons involved in genealogy; new products about innovations in capturing, storing, indexing and retrieving data-personal opinion (must be in-depth and scholarly dealing with the Gorham genealogy and history); *Profiles of Present Day Gorham's.*" circ. 3M. 4/yr. Pub'd 4 issues 1990; expects 4 issues 1991. sub. price: $15; per copy: $2; sample: $2. Back issues: $2. Discounts: 40%, write for further information. 24pp; 8½×11; †of. Reporting time: 6-8 weeks. Payment: $10 to $100 depending on article (sometimes 2¢ a word). Copyrighted, reverts to author. Pub's reviews: 25 in 1990. §Genealogy and history. Ads: $320/$175/30¢. COSMEP.

Bruce Gould Publications, Bruce Gould, PO Box 16, Seattle, WA 98111. 1976. Non-fiction. "Publish books in the field of finance (business, stock and commodity markets)." avg. press run 10M. Expects 2 titles 1991. 12 titles listed in the *Small Press Record of Books in Print* (20th Edition, 1991-92). avg. price, cloth: $10.95; paper: $7.95. Discounts: 40% to bookstores, 55% to wholesalers. 200pp; 6×8½; †lp. Reporting time: 30 days. Payment: 10-20%. Copyrights for author. COSMEP.

Grace and Goddess Unlimited, Cindee Grace, PO Box 4367, Boulder, CO 80306. 1983. Non-fiction. "Books and audio tapes about holistic health and feminist spirituality. No unsolicited submissions wanted." avg. press run varies. Expects 2 titles 1991, 2 titles 1992. 2 titles listed in the *Small Press Record of Books in Print* (20th Edition, 1991-92). avg. price, paper: $35. Discounts: wholesale prices available through our distributor: New Leaf Distribution, 5425 Tulane Drive SW, Atlanta, GA, 30336. 250pp; 8½×11; mi. Payment: varies. Copyrights for author. The Wiccan/Pagan Press Alliance (WPPA), PO Box 1392, Mechanicsburg, PA, 17055.

Grade School Press, J. Lastman, L. Cohen, 3266 Yonge Street #1829, Toronto, Ontario M4N 3P6, Canada, 416-487-2883. 1989. Fiction, articles, reviews, non-fiction. "Focus: Education 'self-help' books for parents/teachers, directory & curriculum guides and training manuals, children/parenting" avg. press run 5M-7M. Expects 4-6 titles 1991, 6-8 titles 1992. 1 title listed in the *Small Press Record of Books in Print* (20th Edition, 1991-92). avg. price, paper: $14.95-$19.95; other: $65 reference (looseleaf) updating publication. Discounts: 40% bookstores, bulk (10+ copies same book) to individuals. 120-150pp; 5½×8½, 8½×11; of, desktop & pasteup. Reporting time: 2-4 months. Payment: individual arrangements. Copyrights for author. Association of Canadian Publishers (ACP).

GRAHAM HOUSE REVIEW, Peter Balakian, Bruce Smith, Box 5000, Colgate University, Hamilton, NY 13346. 1976. Poetry. "Our aim is to publish good poetry wherever we find it, poetry from the unknown and the well-established. We believe the best poetry struggles with language for music, image, and voice; is well made and attached with integrity to experience. Our contributors include: Hugo, Goldbarth, Soto, Wheatcroft, Seamus Heaney, Derek Walcott, Michael Harper, Defrees, Maxine Kumin, Carolyn Forche, Marilyn Hockyr, Cleopatra Mathis, and others. Also publish interviews, essays, and translations" circ. 500. 1/yr. Pub'd 1 issue 1990; expects 1 issue 1991, 2 issues 1992. sub. price: $7.50; per copy: $7.50; sample: $7.50. Back issues: $7.50 subject to availability. Discounts: trade 20-40%, negotiable. 120pp; 5½×8½; of. Reporting time: 4-8 weeks. Payment: copies only. Copyrighted, reverts to author. CCLM, COSMEP.

Graham-Conley Press, Ellen Conley, 1936 E. Belmont Drive, Tempe, AZ 85284, 602-491-1177. 1982. Non-fiction. "Our primary market is libraries. We are publishers of reference books, guides, directories, handbooks and computer software. Our most recent publication is a microcomputer indexing program and manual" avg. press run 1M. Expects 1 title 1991, 1 title 1992. 1 title listed in the *Small Press Record of Books in Print* (20th Edition, 1991-92). avg. price, paper: $20; other: $50 (software). Discounts: 2-4 20%, 5-9 30%, 10-24 40%, 25-49 42%, 50-74 44%, 75-99 46%, 100-199 48%, 200+ 50%. Pages vary; 8½×11; of. Reporting time: 1 month. Payment: 10% and up based on number of copies. COSMEP.

GRAIN, Saskatchewan Writers Guild, Box 1154, Regina, Sask. S4P 3B4, Canada, 306-757-6310. 1973. Poetry, fiction, art, parts-of-novels, long-poems, plays. "We publish only the best literary art. Length—flexible, though submissions preferably should not be more than 8 pages of poetry and 30 pages of prose or drama. Fiction and poetry are the main focus but we also consider creative non-fiction, songs, and produced one-act plays or excerpts from produced full-length plays." circ. 1M. 4/yr. Pub'd 4 issues 1990; expects 4 issues 1991, 4 issues 1992. sub. price: $15 (plus $1.05 GST); per copy: $5 (plus 35¢ GST); sample: $6 (plus 42¢ GST). Back issues: $5 each (plus 35¢ GST). Discounts: 25% for CPPA subscriptions. 80pp; 5½×8; of. Reporting time: 3 months. Payment: $30 poems, $40-$100 prose, $85 art cover, $30 inside art. Copyrighted, reverts to author. CPPA (2 Stewart Street, Toronto, M5V 1H6).

Grand River Press, Michael Maran, PO Box 1342, East Lansing, MI 48826, (517) 332-8181. 1986. Non-fiction. "We specialize in legal self-help publications for use in Michigan." avg. press run 1.5M. Pub'd 2 titles 1990; expects 2 titles 1991, 2 titles 1992. 3 titles listed in the *Small Press Record of Books in Print* (20th Edition, 1991-92). avg. price, paper: $18. Discounts: 40% trade. 150pp; 8½×11; of. Reporting time: 3 months. Payment: negotiable. Copyrights for author.

GRAND STREET, Ben Sonnenberg, Grand Street Publications, Inc., 50 Riverside Drive, New York, NY 10024, 212-496-6088. 1981. Poetry, fiction, articles. "No writers' guidelines" circ. 4M. 4/yr. Pub'd 4 issues 1990; expects 4 issues 1991, 4 issues 1992. sub. price: $24/$28 institutions & foreign; per copy: $6; sample: $6. Back issues: $8. Discounts: on request. 224pp; 6×9; lp. Reporting time: 6 weeks. Payment: yes. Copyrighted, reverts to author. Pub's reviews: 4 in 1990. §Biography, politics. Ads: $250. Coordinating Council of Literary Magazines.

GRANTA, Granta Publications Ltd, Bill Buford, 2-3 Hanover Yard, Noel Rd, London N1 88E, England, 071 704 9776, FAX: 071 704 0474. 1979 (New Series). Fiction, articles, photos, interviews, satire, reviews, letters, parts-of-novels, non-fiction. "Additional address: 250 West 57th Street, Suite 1203, New York, NY 10107, (212) 246-1313. *Granta* is a mass-marketed paperback magazine co-published with Penquin Books, devoted to contemporary literature and political discussion. *Granta* publishes fiction, cultural and political journalism, and photography. Recent contributors include John Berger, Susan Sontag, George Steiner, Gabriel Garcia Marquez, Salman Rushdie, Angela Carter, Ian McEwan, Jean Mohr, Don McCullin, Carolyn Forche, Russell Hoban, Bruce Chatwin, Walter Abish, Jonathan Schell, Milan Kundera, Mario Vargas Llosa, Nadine Gordimer, Raymond Carver, Fay Weldon, and many others. There are no restrictions of length. *Granta* does not publish poetry. In the United States, *Granta* is published by Granta USA, Ltd., a joint company with the New York Review of Books, and distributed by Viking Penguin, Inc" circ. 100M. 4/yr. Pub'd 4 issues 1990; expects 4 issues 1991, 6 issues 1992. sub. price: £19.95 ($28); per copy: £5.99 (or $8.95); sample: £5.99 (or $8.95). Back issues: £5 each with the purchase of 4 or more issues. Discounts: trade: 35%; bulk or classroom orders by arrangement (10% to 50% depending on order); agent 10%. 256pp; 5¾×8; of. Reporting time: 4-8 weeks. Payment: £75-£5,000 depending on length, topicality, etc. Copyrighted, reverts to author. Ads: £750/£400/special US rates available.

Granta Publications Ltd (see also GRANTA), Bill Buford, 2-3 Hanover Yard, Noel Rd, London N1 8RE, England, (071) 704 9776.

Grapetree Productions, Inc., Joan E. Gill, President, Box 10CN, 600 Grapetree Drive, Key Biscayne, FL 33149, 361-2060. 1981. Satire, letters. avg. press run 1M-2.5M. Pub'd 1 title 1990. 3 titles listed in the *Small Press Record of Books in Print* (20th Edition, 1991-92). avg. price, paper: $4.95, $5.95. Discounts: 40-60%. 96pp + covers; 5×8; of. Does not copyright for author. COSMEP, Florida Publishing, National Press Club.

Grapevine Publications, Inc., Christopher M. Coffin, Managing Editor; Daniel R. Coffin, Developmental Editor, PO Box 2449, Corvallis, OR 97339-2449, 503-754-0583; fax 503-754-6508. 1983. Non-fiction. "Grapevine Publications, Inc. welcomes all book ideas. Emphasis is on friendly how-to in the technical fields, but publishing is not limited to this. Future will include expanding into the textbook, with the emphasis on extremely high-quality teaching in a straight-forward, easily understood style. The long-term emphasis is on diversification, with a careful eye incessantly trained on high-quality, friendly alternative approaches to teaching, learning and literature. A query letter with several chapters excerpted from the manuscript is the best approach. Computer printouts OK. We will look seriously at all outstanding ideas." avg. press run 3M-10M. Pub'd 4 titles 1990; expects 11 titles 1991, 16 titles 1992. 15 titles listed in the *Small Press Record of Books in Print* (20th Edition, 1991-92). avg. price, paper: $20. Discounts: for resale: 25-40% off (volume based); distributor discounts negotiable upon request and qualifications. 250pp; 5⅛×7¼; of. Reporting time: 4-6 weeks. Payment: negotiable, 6-9% of retail. Copyrights for author. Publishers Marketing Association (PMA), 2401 Pacific Coast Hwy, Ste. 102, Hermosa Beach, CA 90254.

G'RAPH, Henry Roll, 2419 Greensburg Pike, Pittsburgh, PA 15221. 1980. Articles, art, photos, cartoons, reviews, letters. circ. 70. 4/yr. Pub'd 4 issues 1990; expects 4 issues 1991, 4 issues 1992. sub. price: $5; per copy: $1; sample: $1. Back issues: $1. 8pp; 8½×11; †Mita copier. Reporting time: 1 month. Payment: copies. Copyrighted, reverts to author. Pub's reviews: 4 in 1990. §Cartoons, graphics, arts, book arts, visual arts, media. Ads: $25/$15/$5 classified.

GRASS ROOTS, Night Owl Publishers, Megg Miller, Kath Harper, PO Box 242, Euroa, Victoria 3666, Australia. 1973. Poetry, articles, photos, letters, non-fiction. "Similar to *Mother Earth News*" circ. 25M. 6/yr. Pub'd 6 issues 1990; expects 6 issues 1991, 6 issues 1992. sub. price: $A22, overseas $A30; per copy: $A4; sample: $A4. Back issues: $A3.50. 80pp; size quarto; of. Reporting time: 3 months. Payment: $20 per page.

231

Not copyrighted. Pub's reviews: 50 in 1990. §Alternatives, gardening, technology, horticulture, agriculture, craft, food, community, health, natural lifestyles. Ads: $A575/$A310/30-40¢ per word. ABPA.

GRASSLANDS REVIEW, Laura B. Kennelly, PO Box 13706, Denton, TX 76203, 817-565-2025/2127. 1989. Poetry, fiction, photos. "Shorter pieces of fiction fare better, issue #4 (1991) was cited by *Factsheet Five* as a 'Publisher's Choice' selection. In *FF5* #43 we are described as 'a litmag which consistently publishes an interesting mix of work, some good old-fashioned stories plus stuff from the more experimental (but still solid) edge.' Authors published include Annie Dawid, James Hoggard, Jendi Reiter, Edward Mycue, Laurel Speer and Jonathan Bracker. Only material postmarked in October or March will be considered." circ. 200. 2/yr. Pub'd 2 issues 1990; expects 2 issues 1991, 2 issues 1992. sub. price: $4 individual; per copy: $2; sample: $2. Back issues: issues 1-3 $1, #4 $2. Discounts: none. 75pp; 6×8; †pagemaker plus xerox. Reporting time: can be as long as 3 months, depends due to limited reading period. Payment: 2 copies with special rate for extra copies. Copyrighted, reverts to author.

Gravity Publishing, Linda Foust, Publisher; Tony Husch, Publisher, 6324 Heather Ridge, Oakland, CA 94611, 415-339-3774. 1985. Non-fiction. "Additional address: 6116 Merced, Suite 233D, Oakland, CA 94611" avg. press run 5M. Pub'd 1 title 1990; expects 2 titles 1991, 3-5 titles 1992. 2 titles listed in the *Small Press Record of Books in Print* (20th Edition, 1991-92). avg. price, paper: $9.95. Discounts: standard to industry. 200pp; 6×9, 8½×8½; of. Reporting time: 4-6 weeks. Payment: standard, subject to negotiation. Copyrights for author. COSMEP, PMA, NCBPA.

Grayson Bernard Publishers, Inc., Susan T. Yerolemou, Director, 223 S. Pete Ellis Drive, Suite 12, Bloomington, IN 47408, 812-331-8182. 1990. Non-fiction. "Additional address: PO Box 5247, Bloomington, IN, 47407. Emphasis on materials for parents who wish to be actively involved in their children's education." avg. press run 3.5M. Pub'd 2 titles 1990; expects 6 titles 1991, 12 titles 1992. 1 title listed in the *Small Press Record of Books in Print* (20th Edition, 1991-92). avg. price, paper: varies. 100-250pp; 5½×8½; of. Reporting time: 4-6 weeks. Payment: negotiable, usually royalty of 8-15% of money received. COSMEP, PMA, MAP.

The Graywolf Press, Scott Walker, 2402 University Avenue #203, St. Paul, MN 55114, 612-641-0077. 1974. Poetry, fiction, criticism, long-poems, non-fiction. "No unsolicited manuscripts." avg. press run 3.5M-15M. Pub'd 12 titles 1990; expects 14 titles 1991, 16 titles 1992. 76 titles listed in the *Small Press Record of Books in Print* (20th Edition, 1991-92). avg. price, cloth: $18; paper: $10. Discounts: 1-4, 20%, 5-24 40%, 25-99 43%, 100-249 45%, 250-499 46%, 500+ 47%. 100-300pp; size varies; of. Reporting time: 8 weeks. Payment: negotiable. Copyrights for author.

GRDA Publications, Alfred Goldberg, PO Box 1407, Mill Valley, CA 94942. 1985. "Additional address: 110 Tiburon Blvd, Mill Valley, CA 94941" avg. press run 5M. Pub'd 1 title 1990; expects 3 titles 1991, 2 titles 1992. 9 titles listed in the *Small Press Record of Books in Print* (20th Edition, 1991-92). avg. price, cloth: $60; paper: $50. Discounts: based on volume, min. 6+ 10%, 16+ 20%, 50+ 30%. 6×9, 8½×11; of. Copyrights for author.

Great Blue Graphics, 312 Clarke, Helena, MT 59601. 1987. Expects 1 title 1991. 2 titles listed in the *Small Press Record of Books in Print* (20th Edition, 1991-92). avg. price, paper: $9.95. 160pp; 11×8½.

Great Elm Press, Walt Franklin, 1205 County Route 60, Rexville, NY 14877. 1984. avg. press run 300. Pub'd 5 titles 1990; expects 5 titles 1991. 16 titles listed in the *Small Press Record of Books in Print* (20th Edition, 1991-92). avg. price, paper: $4. 40pp; 5½×8½. Reporting time: 1 week.

GREAT EXPEDITIONS MAGAZINE, Craig Henderson, Box 8000-411, Sumas, WA 98295, 604-852-6170. 1978. Articles. "Additional address: Box 8000-411, Abbotsford, BC, Canada V2S 6H1" circ. 11M. 5/yr. Pub'd 4 issues 1990; expects 5 issues 1991, 5 issues 1992. sub. price: $18; per copy: $4; sample: free. Back issues: $4. Discounts: none. 48pp; 8×10½; of, web press. Reporting time: 60 days. Payment: $30-$80. Copyrighted, reverts to author. Pub's reviews: 20 in 1990. §Travel outside of North America. Ads: $700/$370. Canadian Magazine Publishers Association (CMPA).

Great Lakes Poetry Press, Chuck Kramer, Box 56703, Harwood Heights, IL 60656, 312-631-3697. 1987. Poetry. "We are interested in poetry and publish it in anthologies, single-author collections and in chapbooks. Poets may send us up to 10 poems (but no more than 10 pages of manuscript) and we'll be glad to take a look at them. If a poet has more than 10 poems, then we should be queried before the poems are sent along. Query should describe material in terms of theme, length, etc. One sample poem may be included with query." avg. press run varies. Pub'd 4 titles 1990; expects 3 titles 1991, 3 titles 1992. 11 titles listed in the *Small Press Record of Books in Print* (20th Edition, 1991-92). avg. price, paper: $24.99. Discounts: 40 to 60%. 400pp; 6×9; of. Reporting time: 4 weeks. Payment: to be negotiated. Copyrights for author. COSMEP, PMA, Chicago Book Clinic.

Great Point Press, A.L. Flanders III, William Sherry, Mary Barlow, West Coast; Advisory Board, Commercial Wharf, Nantucket Island, MA 02554, (617) 228-6566. 1985. Fiction, non-fiction. "We want only work of the

232

highest quality: we're not a publisher of last resort! We will take a chance on work if the author can show a 'pocket market'—it could be regional, special interest, whatever—which could find a general audience. If *fiction*, it should have a stickiness, a hook: we want work that will endure. *Reprints*: we are always on the lookout for books previously brought out, then neglected, by the major trade houses. When submitting, send the book along with rights status, and a brief history of sales, promotion (or lack of), etc. The third area, for which we are starting a new imprint, is *informational non-fiction for a specific market*. The author must know that market, how to reach it directly; the work should be, in short, 'the last word' on the subject. Query us first: if fiction, a precis and a sample chapter at most; if non-fiction, explain book in one page; if specific market, prove to us you know what you're talking about and sell us on the market—your book must be worth in excess of $20. Dot matrix OK. No poetry except by invitation. SASE always" avg. press run 3M+. Pub'd 1 title 1990; expects 2 titles 1991, 4+ titles 1992. 1 title listed in the *Small Press Record of Books in Print* (20th Edition, 1991-92). avg. price, cloth: $17.50; paper: $9.50; other: deluxe limited; varies. Discounts: trade: 2-4 20%, 5-24 40%, 25-49 42%, 50+ 45%. 180pp; 5½×8¼; of. Reporting time: 2-6 weeks. Payment: varies. Copyrights for author. COSMEP.

GREAT RIVER REVIEW, Orval A. Lund, Editor; Monica Drealan DeGrazia, Managing Editor; Gary Eddy, Reviews Editor; Emilio DeGrazia, Fiction Editor, 211 W 7th, Winona, MN 55987. 1977. Poetry, fiction, articles. "Poetry, fiction, articles on Midwestern writers, particularly contemporary authors. We are esp interested in material from and about the Midwest. We now publish translations of poetry. List of some of the authors whom we have published: Philip Dacey, Marisha Chamberlain, Eugene McCarthy, Meriddel LeSueur, Susan Toth, Jill Breckenridge, Mark Vinz, Frederick Manfred, Thom Tammaro" circ. 800. 3 every 2 years. Pub'd 3 issues 1990. sub. price: $9; per copy: $4.50; sample: $4.50. Back issues: $4.50. Discounts: 20% with orders of 5 or more. 145pp; 6×8; of. Reporting time: 1-4 months. Payment: copies. Copyrighted. Pub's reviews: 12 in 1990. §Arts, humanities, poetry, fiction. No ads. CCLM.

Great Western Publishing Company, John M. Cali, Jr., John M. Cali III, 1601 11th Street, Cody, WY 82414, 307-527-7480. 1987. News items, non-fiction. "Additional address: PO Box 98, Westfield, NY 14787" avg. press run 2M+. Pub'd 3 titles 1990; expects 3-4 titles 1991, 4-5 titles 1992. 6 titles listed in the *Small Press Record of Books in Print* (20th Edition, 1991-92). avg. price, paper: $15. Discounts: 1-99 50%, 100+ 60%. 128-224pp; 5½×8½, 8½×11. PMA, COSMEP.

GREATER PORTLAND, Shirley Jacks, Editor & Publisher, PO Box 15490, Portland, ME 04101-7490, 207-772-2811. 1965. Articles, art, interviews, non-fiction. "We are interested in features about the people, places, events, institutions, arts, trends, and issues of greater Portland, Maine, including the Casco Bay Islands. We need well-researched, highly-literate, engrossing features (first-person OK) only—writing that is shallow, simply descriptive, or tourist-oriented won't do. We are completely freelance written and buy 5 mss/issue. Send detailed query with clips and SASE." circ. 7M. 6/yr. Pub'd 4 issues 1990; expects 6 issues 1991, 6 issues 1992. sub. price: $9.97; per copy: $2.50; sample: $2.50 + $1.25 postage. Back issues: $2.50 + $1.25 postage. 64-80pp; 8½×11; web of. Reporting time: query - 1 week, ms - 2 weeks. Payment: 10¢/word. Copyrighted, we buy first N. Amer. serial rights. 1-time rates: $1,110 full-page color, $850 b/w. Regional Publishers Association.

GREEN ANARCHIST, P.N. Rogers, Box H, 34 Cowley Road, Oxford, Oxfordshire, United Kingdom, 0895-249406. 1984. Poetry, articles, cartoons, interviews, reviews, music, letters, news items. circ. 2.2M. 4/yr. Pub'd 4 issues 1990; expects 4 issues 1991, 4 issues 1992. sub. price: £2; per copy: 60p; sample: free. Back issues: 30p/issue. Discounts: 33% for s/r, streetsell is £4 for a bundle of 10, £12 for a 50-issue bulk order, no s/r. 24pp; 8×12 (A4); †photocopier. Reporting time: deadline approx. 1 month before publication. Payment: none. Not copyrighted. Pub's reviews: 24 in 1990. §Green/anarchist. Ads: £40/£20/6p per word for small ads.

GREEN EGG, Otter G'Zell, Diane Darling, PO Box 1542, Ukiah, CA 95482, 707-485-7787. 1968. Poetry, fiction, articles, art, photos, cartoons, interviews, satire, criticism, reviews, letters, news items, non-fiction. "*Green Egg* is a magazine of Paganism (i.e. Nature worship) and Goddess religion. Eco-Feminism, Mythology, Folklore are continuing themes. Articles: 1,000-3,000 words; fiction 1,000-3,000 words; reviews to 300 words; others varied. Contributors include Merlin Stone, Marion Zimmer Bradley, Antero Alli, Robert Anton Wilson, Anodea Judith, Ralph Metzner, Nybor, Phoenix & Arabeth, Kenny Klein, and many others. Send SASE for contributor's guide." circ. 5M. 4/yr. Pub'd 4 issues 1990; expects 4 issues 1991, 4 issues 1992. sub. price: $13; per copy: $3.95; sample: $5 (includes p/h). Back issues: $5 each, incl. postage (#81, 86-92). Discounts: 50% for distributors (over 100 copies); 40% for retailers (lots of 10). 52pp; 8½×11. Reporting time: 1 month. Payment: copy, sometimes free ad space—cover art='About Artist' Copyrighted, reverts to author. Pub's reviews: 21 in 1990. §Fantasy, Paganism, science fiction, mythology, history, nature, goddesses, feminist, ecology, Wicca. Ads: $385/$210/$150 1/3 page/$85 1/6 page/$55 business card. WPPA, PO Box 1392, Mechanicsburg, PA 17055.

The Green Hut Press, Janet Wullner Faiss, Publisher & Editor, 1015 Jardin Street East, Appleton, WI 54911, 414-734-9728. 1972. Poetry, fiction, art, non-fiction. "We publish the writing and artistic work of the late Fritz Faiss (1905-1981) *exclusively*. Limited editions. Thus far we work by mail order only, except for a few selected

233

bookstores. Enquiries welcome. We have prices ranging between $9 and, for a hand-colored-by-artist edition, $200. We do not accept manuscripts, unless they are suitable for Faiss artwork. Include postage please." avg. press run 200. 6 titles listed in the *Small Press Record of Books in Print* (20th Edition, 1991-92). Discounts: libraries 10%. 75pp; size varies; †of. COSMEP.

Green Key Press, Thorsten Wycliffe, Eva Ethel, Box 3801, Seminole, FL 34642, 813-596-0215. 1983. Fiction, non-fiction. "Contributors: Andrew Lytle, Alan Frederiksen. Novels of high literary merit *only*. 300-500 pages." avg. press run 2M. Pub'd 1 title 1990; expects 2 titles 1991, 4 titles 1992. 3 titles listed in the *Small Press Record of Books in Print* (20th Edition, 1991-92). avg. price, cloth: $15.95. Discounts: 40% for 5 copies or more. 325pp; 6×9; of. Reporting time: 3 months. Payment: 10% on the net price not list. Copyrights for author.

GREEN MOUNTAINS REVIEW, Neil Shepard, Tony Whedon, Johnson State College, Box A-58, Johnson, VT 05656, 802-635-2356. 1987. Poetry, fiction, articles, art, criticism, parts-of-novels, long-poems. circ. 1.5M. 2/yr. Expects 2 issues 1991, 2 issues 1992. sub. price: $5; per copy: $3; sample: $3. Discounts: 40% off for store buyers. 100pp; 6×9; lp. Reporting time: 2 months. Payment: copies. Copyrighted, reverts to author.

GREEN MULTILOGUE, Michael Tegtmeyer, 390 Jones Avenue, Toronto, Ont. M4J 3G3, Canada, 416-461-8467. 1986. Poetry, articles, art, photos, cartoons, interviews, satire, criticism, reviews, letters, non-fiction. "No censorship. Global, interactive. One page free for subscribers. For *green* thinkers." 6/yr. Pub'd 6 issues 1990; expects 6 issues 1991, 6 issues 1992. 2pp; 8½×11; †xerox. Reporting time: 1 month. Payment: authors pay yearly sub rate. Not copyrighted.

Green Stone Publications, PO Box 15623, Seattle, WA 98115-0623, 206-524-4744. 1987. Fiction. avg. press run 2M. Pub'd 1 title 1990; expects 1 title 1992. 1 title listed in the *Small Press Record of Books in Print* (20th Edition, 1991-92). avg. price, paper: $11.95. Discounts: 2-4 20%, 5-9 30%, 10-24 40%, 25-49 42%, 50-74 44%, 75-99 46%, 100-199 48%, 200+ 50%. 280pp; 5½×8½; of. COSMEP, Northwest Assn. of Book Publishers, Book Publishers Northwest.

The Green Street Press, Michael Hutcheson, PO Box 8119, Brattleboro, VT 05304-8119, 617-374-9923. 1984. Poetry, fiction, non-fiction. "We are especially interested in publishing new fiction of exceptional merit, and fiction reprints of neglected classics. Short story collections also welcome. All SASE will receive a response" avg. press run 5M. Pub'd 2 titles 1990; expects 5 titles 1991, 10 titles 1992. 6 titles listed in the *Small Press Record of Books in Print* (20th Edition, 1991-92). avg. price, cloth: $15.95; paper: $8.95. Discounts: inquire. 250pp; 4¾×7¼; of. Reporting time: 4 months. Payment: standard or collective. Copyrights for author.

GREEN SYNTHESIS-A NEWSLETTER AND JOURNAL FOR SOCIAL ECOLOGY, DEEP ECOLOGY, BIOREGIONALISM, ECOFEMINISM, AND THE GREEN MOVEMENT, Box 1858, San Pedro, CA 90733, 213-833-2633. 1975. Poetry, articles, art, cartoons, interviews, criticism, reviews, letters, news items, non-fiction. "No poetry" circ. 7M. 4/yr. Pub'd 3 issues 1990; expects 4 issues 1991, 4 issues 1992. sub. price: $5; per copy: $1.25; sample: $1.25. Back issues: $1.25. Discounts: 40% on bundle orders. 22pp; 8½×11; of. Payment: none. Not copyrighted. Pub's reviews: 6 in 1990. §Social ecology, deep ecology, bioregionalism, ecofeminism, green politics, green movement. No ads.

Green Tiger Press, Inc., 200 Old Tappan Road #BLDG, Old Tappan, NJ 07675-7005. 1970. Poetry, fiction, art, photos, criticism. "We specialize in illustrated children's books, and lean toward books of subtle fantasy & wonder." avg. press run 5M-10M. Pub'd 12 titles 1990; expects 12 titles 1991, 12 titles 1992. 8 titles listed in the *Small Press Record of Books in Print* (20th Edition, 1991-92). avg. price, cloth: $12.95; paper: $7.95; other: deluxe books from $17.95-$29.95. Discounts: from 40% to 48% depending on quantity; 50% on stationery products. 40pp; of. Reporting time: 8-16 weeks. Payment: varies. Copyrights for author. ABA, CBC.

Green Timber Publications, Tirrell H. Kimball, PO Box 3884, Portland, ME 04104, 207-797-4180. 1987. Poetry, fiction, non-fiction. "Children's books of all types" avg. press run 2.5M. Expects 2 titles 1991, 6 titles 1992. avg. price, paper: $7.95. Discounts: retail and wholesalers 2-4 books 20%, 5-9 30%, 10-24 40%, 25-49 42%, 50-74 44%, 75-99 46%, 100-199 48%, 200+ 50%. 60pp; 6×9. Reporting time: 6 weeks. Payment: 15% for author and illustrator combined. Copyrights for author. Maine Writers & Publishers Alliance, 19D Mason St., Brunswick, ME 04011.

GREEN ZERO, Jeff Vetock, PO Box 3104, Shiremanstown, PA 17011, 717-732-7191. 1990. Poetry, art, photos, criticism, collages. "*Green Zero* is a digest-sized quarterly dedicated to the presentation and ongoing discussion of poetry as it has evolved in the twentieth century. It is hoped that the magazine will serve as a catalyst for discussion and interaction among a growing circle of readers and writers. Recent contributors include Pam Rehm, Mark Scroggins, E.A. Miller, and Ed Webster. The editor is especially interested in work that exhibits an awareness of recent developments in art and literature (critical theory and otherwise)" circ. 150. 4/yr. Pub'd 4 issues 1990; expects 4 issues 1991, 4 issues 1992. sub. price: $2; per copy: 55¢; sample: 55¢

(payment in stamps O.K.). Back issues: 55¢. Discounts: direct inquiries to editor. 26-30pp; 5½x8½; †photocopy. Reporting time: 2-3 weeks. Payment: 2 copies. Copyrighted, reverts to author. Pub's reviews.

Greencrest Press Inc., Philippe R. Falkenberg, Box 7745, Winston-Salem, NC 27109, 919-722-6463. 1980. "We specialize in study skills." avg. press run 2M. Expects 1 title 1991. 1 title listed in the *Small Press Record of Books in Print* (20th Edition, 1991-92). avg. price, paper: $12.95. Discounts: 1-5, 20%; 6-49, 40%; 50-99,41%; 100+ 42%. of. Reporting time: 60 days. Payment: 10%.

The Greenfield Review Press/Ithaca House, Joseph Bruchac III, Editor; Carol Worthen Bruchac, Editor, PO Box 308, Greenfield Center, NY 12833-0308, 518-584-1728. 1970. Poetry. "Our main interest is contemporary poetry in general. Although we have been particularly open to work by writers not usually published by American small presses — writers from the '3rd World' women, prison writers. Some of our recent publications include major anthologies of Native American poetry, Asian American poets, a regional anthology from northern New York State and an anthology of short stories by women, *The Stories We Hold Secret,* as well as individual volumes of poetry by Lance Henson, Tanure Ojaide, Marilyn Chin, Kofi Awoonor, and Nia Francisco. We are also now the publishers of the *Ithaca House* series, which was acquired in 1986. No reading period in 1991." avg. press run 1M. Pub'd 2 titles 1990; expects 4 titles 1991, 4 titles 1992. 145 titles listed in the *Small Press Record of Books in Print* (20th Edition, 1991-92). avg. price, paper: $7.95 single author, $12.95 anthologies. Discounts: trade: 1-5 copies, 25%; 5 or more copies, 40%. 80pp single author, anthologies 300pp; 5½x8½; of. Reporting time: 2 weeks to 2 months. Payment: 2% of press run, $50 advance on royalties of 10% retail price on each copy sold. Copyrights for author. CCLM, COSMEP.

Greenhouse Review Press, Gary Young, 3965 Bonny Doon Road, Santa Cruz, CA 95060, 408-426-4355. 1975. Poetry, parts-of-novels, long-poems. "Greenhouse Review Press publishes a chapbook and broadside series. We are interested in manuscripts of up to 20 pages. Titles: *The Fugitive Vowels* by D.J. Waldie; *The Dreams of Mercurius* by John Hall; *House Fires* by Peter Wild; *Thirteen Ways of Deranging An Angel* by Stephen Kessler; *Looking Up* by Christopher Budkley; *Any Minute* by Laurel Blossom; *Yes* by Timothy Sheehan; *By Me By Any Can and Can't Be Done* by Killarney Clary; *Begin, Distance* by Sherod Santos; *Jack the Ripper* by John Hall." avg. press run 250. Pub'd 3 titles 1990; expects 4 titles 1991. 43 titles listed in the *Small Press Record of Books in Print* (20th Edition, 1991-92). avg. price, cloth: $50; paper: $20; other: $30 broadside. Discounts: 40% to bookstores. 16-32pp; size varies; †lp. Reporting time: 4 weeks. Payment: copies. Copyrights for author.

Greenlawn Press (see also NEW HEAVEN/NEW EARTH), Dan DeCelles, Publisher; Tom Noe, Editor, 107 S. Greenlawn Avenue, South Bend, IN 46617, 219-234-5088. 1982. Non-fiction. "We are a Christian publisher. Our primary sales come from charismatic Catholics, Pentecostal/charismatic Christians from other churches. We carry devotional/inspirational books of a general Christian nature, others primarily for Catholics. Books have been in the range of 100-150 pages. Publishing began under the auspices of a distributor of religious books and goods (Charismatic Renewal Services) in 1982. We published our first title with the Greenlawn Press imprint in 1985. We may also carry books of Christian-oriented political commentary and analysis." avg. press run 3M-5M. Pub'd 3 titles 1990; expects 2 titles 1991, 4 titles 1992. 15 titles listed in the *Small Press Record of Books in Print* (20th Edition, 1991-92). avg. price, paper: $4.95-$6.95; other: $2.50 pamphlets-saddle stitched. Discounts: trade 40% on orders of $25 or more; distributors 40% 10-99 units, 55% 100+ units. 100-150pp; 5½x8½; of. Reporting time: variable. Payment: negotiable, variable. Only copyright by specific arrangement.

Greenridge Press, Lorna C. Mason, 5869 Greenridge Road, Castro Valley, CA 94552, 415-881-4432. 1987. Non-fiction. "I am not a self-publisher, but, at least this year, I do not want unsolicited manuscripts" Pub'd 1 title 1990; expects 1 title 1991, 1 title 1992. 1 title listed in the *Small Press Record of Books in Print* (20th Edition, 1991-92). Copyrights for author. Bookbuilders West.

GREEN'S MAGAZINE, Clover Press, David Green, Box 3236, Regina, Saskatchewan S4P 3H1, Canada. 1972. Poetry, fiction. "Non-Canadian Mss. must be accompanied by International Reply Coupons. Stories to approx 3.5M poems to 40 lines. Want deep characterization in complex conflicts. Prefer to avoid profanity, explicit sexuality. Recents: Helene Scheffler-Mason, Solomon Pogarsky, Sheila Murphy, David Chorlton, Robert L. Tener. Prefer originals. No simultaneous submissions. (ISSN 0824-2992)." circ. 400. 4/yr. Pub'd 4 issues 1990; expects 4 issues 1991. sub. price: $12; per copy: $4; sample: $4. Discounts: negotiable. 100pp; 5¼x8½; †of. Reporting time: 8 weeks. Payment: copies. Copyrighted, reverts to author. Pub's reviews: 4 in 1990. §General. Ads: $100/$60.

THE GREENSBORO REVIEW, Jim Clark, Editor, Dept. of English, Univ. of North Carolina-Greensboro, Greensboro, NC 27412, 919-334-5459. 1966. Poetry, fiction. "We like to see the best being written regardless of subject or theme. We publish new talent beside established writers, depending on quality. No restrictions on length of poetry; short stories should be shorter than 7,500 words. Recent contributors include Jerry Bumpus, Catherine Petroski, Madison Smartt Bell, Julia Alvarez, Kelly Cherry, Michael McFee, Jeanne Schinto, and Larry Brown. Submissions accepted between August 15 and February 15 (deadlines for the two issues:

September 15 and February 15 each year). Literary Awards guidelines for SASE. No simultaneous submissions. SASE with mss. Recent stories anthologized in the 1989 editions of *The Best American Short Stories*, *Prize Stories: The O. Henry Awards*, and *Best of the West*, and forthcoming in *New Stories from the South"* circ. 500. 2/yr. Pub'd 2 issues 1990; expects 2 issues 1991, 2 issues 1992. sub. price: $8; per copy: $4; sample: $4. Back issues: $1.50/according to price on cover. Discounts: none. 124pp; 6×9; of. Reporting time: 2-4 months. Payment: 3 copies. Copyrighted, rights revert to author upon request.

Greensleeves Publishing, Ken Albertsen, PO Box 339, Nevada City, CA 95959, 916-273-4646. 1990. Non-fiction. *"U.S. and Foreign Diplomatic Contacts* is a comprehensive directory guide to U.S. embassies and consulates worldwide, foreign embassies and consulates in the U.S., all U.N. Mission addresses, and more." 2 titles listed in the *Small Press Record of Books in Print* (20th Edition, 1991-92). avg. price, paper: $15 postpaid. 50pp; 8½×11. Copyrights for author.

GreenTree Press, Richard Jones, Robert Salanski, Chuck Giliand, 3715 Beck Road, Bldg. C, St. Joseph, MO 64506, 816-233-4765; FAX 816-279-8787. 1 title listed in the *Small Press Record of Books in Print* (20th Edition, 1991-92).

GREY CITY JOURNAL, J. Hughes, 5627 S. Drexel, Chicago, IL 60637, 312-752-3562. 1958. Poetry, fiction, articles, art, photos, cartoons, interviews, satire, criticism, reviews, music, letters, collages, news items. "We are an independent newspaper, printed as part of the Friday issue of the University of Chicago newspaper, *The Maroon*. We generally accept copy only from University community writers, but would be interested in printing progressive cartoon strips from contributors." circ. 35M. 40/yr. Pub'd 40 issues 1990; expects 40 issues 1991, 40 issues 1992. sub. price: $30; per copy: $1; sample: $1. Back issues: $1. 5pp; 11×17. Reporting time: within several weeks. Payment: none. Copyrighted. Pub's reviews: several dozen in 1990. §Arts, culture and politics, we are very broad. Ads: write for rates.

Griffon House Publications/Bagehot Council (see also CNL/WORLD REPORT), Frank D. Grande, PO Box 81, Whitestone, NY 11357. 1970. "Publishers for Council on National Literatures - *Review of National Literatures* (annual); The Bagehot Research Council - (books on politics and foreign policy). No unsolicited mss for *RNL*; but articles for *WR*; articles on foreign policy for annual publication. *Review of National Literatures* (annual volume); publication of the Council on National Literatures (President and Exec. Dir. Anne Paolucci) Ed. Anne Paolucci. *Council on National Literatures World Report* (annual) Ed. Anne Paolucci. Other books: fiction, poetry, translation, politics and government, etc. *PSA: The Official Publication of the Pirandello Society of America* (annual)." avg. press run 1.5M. Pub'd 9 titles 1990; expects 7-8 titles 1991. 23 titles listed in the *Small Press Record of Books in Print* (20th Edition, 1991-92). avg. price, paper: $2.50-$21. Discounts: 10% for all agencies (only on membership dues: CNL= $35 USA, $45 other). 160-200pp; 5½×8½ WR, 6×9 CNL; †of. Reporting time: 1-4 weeks except RNL, by invitation only. Payment: copies only. Does not copyright for author.

Grimm Press & Publishing Co., Inc. (see also MASTERSTREAM; THE WASHINGTON TROOPER), Bruce D. Grimm, PO Box 1523, Longview, WA 98632, (206) 577-8598.

Gringo Guides, Inc., Richard Campagna, PO Box 7050, Grand Central Station, NY 10116. 1972. Poetry, articles, letters, parts-of-novels, long-poems, plays. "Prefer books for intellectuals with pragmatic, colloquial twist. Bi-coastal life styles, a favorite theme." avg. press run 2.5M. Pub'd 2 titles 1990; expects 4 titles 1991, 6 titles 1992. 2 titles listed in the *Small Press Record of Books in Print* (20th Edition, 1991-92). avg. price, cloth: $15.95; paper: $12.95. 125-160pp; 5×8; lp. Reporting time: 2 months. Payment: negotiable, favorable to authors. Copyrights for author for a fee. COSMEP.

Gross Advertising Service, Edmand J. Gross, Owner, 3445 Leora Avenue, Simi Valley, CA 93063, 805-527-0525. 1968. avg. press run 3M. Pub'd 1 title 1990; expects 1 title 1991, 2 titles 1992. 7 titles listed in the *Small Press Record of Books in Print* (20th Edition, 1991-92). avg. price, paper: $10. Discounts: trade varies to 40%, schools 20%, jobbers 20%-40%. 120pp; 8½×11; of. Payment: 10% of net sales. Copyrights for author.

Grosvenor USA, J. Terence Blair, Director, PO Box 7084, Salem, OR 97303-0084, 503-393-2962. 1981. Plays, non-fiction. "Previously MRA Books. Linked with Grosvenor Books, 54 Lyford Road, London SW18 3JJ, England. Primarily concerned with books which strengthen the moral and spiritual foundations of individuals, families, communities and nations; and which promote real understanding and reconciliation between conflicting groups; and which generally contribute to God's will being done on earth rather than the will of self-centered pressure groups. Generally not interested in unsolicited mss." avg. press run 3M-5M. Pub'd 3 titles 1990; expects 3 titles 1991, 4 titles 1992. 17 titles listed in the *Small Press Record of Books in Print* (20th Edition, 1991-92). avg. price, cloth: $12-$25; paper: $3-$9; other: brochures and pamphlets $1-$2.50. Discounts: bookstores 40%. 100-300pp; size varies; of. Payment: varies. Copyrights for author. COSMEP.

236

GROUND WATER REVIEW, Talking Leaves Press, George Kalamaras, Poetry Editor; Mary Ann Cain, Fiction Editor, 730 East Smith Street, Warsaw, IN 46580, 219-269-7680. 1984. Poetry, fiction, interviews, criticism, reviews, parts-of-novels, long-poems, collages. "GWR publishes irregularly. Currently not reading submissions. We hope to publish again in 1992, depending on funds. Do not send submissions then, but query first. Open to all forms of poetry and fiction by both new and established writers, but we stress high quality. We are particularly interested in poems which explore imaginative and emotive terrains, rich in association, with an expansive gesture. We encourage associative techniques, surrealism and "language" poetry. We also print translations. Emphasis on Greek, Italian, and Hispanic writers, but open to all cultures. Have printed translations of Ritsos, Scotellaro, Guidacci, Jimeno, Sologuren, Teillier, by Keeley, Feldman, Swann, and Crow. National contributors: John Bradley, James Grabill, Christopher Howell, Howard McCord, William Stafford, Bill Tremblay, William Michael Ryan, and others." circ. 200. Irregular. price per copy: $4.50, plus 75¢ postage/handling; sample: $4.50 plus 75¢ p/h. 70pp; 7×8½; of. Reporting time: 2-3 months. Payment: copy of issue work appears in. Copyrighted, rights revert to author, with written permission of our magazine. Pub's reviews.

GROUNDSWELL, Kristen Murray, General Editor; F.R. Lewis, Fiction Editor; Jim Flosdorf, Poetry Editor, PO Box 12093, Albany, NY 12212-2093, 518-449-8069. 1984. Poetry, fiction, interviews, satire, criticism, reviews, parts-of-novels, long-poems, plays. "Each issue focuses on interview with, critical essay on and new work by prominent writers (recently Judith Johnson, Eugene Garber, Alan Sillitoe, Louis Hammer); query first. Short stories to 7,500 words, including short shorts. Submit poems in groups of 3-7. Our only bias quality. Recent contributors: Janice Eidus, Elizabeth Adams, Lisa Koger. Read between September and May. Send SASE and brief bio note." 1/yr. Pub'd 2 issues 1990; expects 1 issue 1991, 1 issue 1992. sub. price: $16 institutions, $11 individuals; per copy: $11; sample: $11 (new; $6 older). Back issues: $6. Discounts: by request. 150pp; 5½×8½; of. Reporting time: 3 months maximum. Payment: depends on funding and copies. Copyrighted, reverts to author. Pub's reviews: 5 in 1990. §Of regional (Hudson Valley/upstate NY) interest or by regional authors. Ads: $125/$75. CCLM.

The Groundwater Press, E. Daniel Richie, Managing Editor; F.B. Claire, Consulting Editor; Rosanne Wasserman, Executive Editor; Arkady Rovner, Consulting Editor, 151 Ridge Street, 1B, New York, NY 10002, 212-228-5750. 1976. Poetry, fiction, art. "*GWP* does not accept unsolicited manuscripts. Review copies and examination or desk copies will be mailed upon request on organizational letterhead" avg. press run 100-500. Pub'd 5 titles 1990; expects 2 titles 1991, 2 titles 1992. 17 titles listed in the *Small Press Record of Books in Print* (20th Edition, 1991-92). avg. price, paper: $10. Discounts: wholesale 20%, retail 40%, distributors 50%. Chapbook 16-32pp, anthology 150-300pp; 5½×8½; of. Payment: yes, but based on grants. Copyrights for author, but not for anthologies which are only copyrighted as compilations.

THE GROVE, Naturist Foundation, Editorial Committee, Naturist Headquarters, Sheepcote, Orpington, BR5 4ET, England, 0689-871200. 1950. Articles, photos, cartoons, letters, news items, non-fiction. "House journal of Naturist Foundation & Sun Societies, circulating internationally to naturists. Contributions on subjects of interest to naturists welcome-with or without illustrations. But no payment offered!" circ. 800. 3/yr. Pub'd 3 issues 1990; expects 3 issues 1991, 3 issues 1992. sub. price: £10 ($20); per copy: £3-50 ($7); sample: £3-50 ($7). Back issues: $5. 24pp; 9½×7½; lp. Payment: none. Copyrighted. Pub's reviews: 3 in 1990. §Naturism, outdoor recreation. Ads: £80 ($160)/£40 ($80).

THE GROWING EDGE MAGAZINE, Tom Alexander, PO Box 1027, Corvallis, OR 97339, 503-757-0027; FAX 503-757-0028. "Indoor and outdoor gardening for today's high-tech grower. Covers hydroponics, controlled environments, drip irrigation, organic gardening, water conservation and more" price per copy: $4.95 + $1.50 p/h; sample: $4.95. 72pp; 8½×11.

Growing Room Collective (see also ROOM OF ONE'S OWN), Box 46160, Station G, Vancouver BC V6R 4G5, Canada, 604-321-1423. 1975. Poetry, fiction, art, photos, cartoons, interviews, criticism, reviews, parts-of-novels, long-poems, plays. "Good quality literary material by & about women, written from a feminist perspective" avg. press run 1.5M. Expects 4 titles 1991. avg. price, paper: $4. Discounts: 30% retail, trade; bulk negotiable; agent 15% off institutional orders only. 80pp; 5½×8½; of. Reporting time: 3 months. Payment: $10-$50 upon publication. Copyrights for author. CPPA.

GROWING WITHOUT SCHOOLING, Holt Associates, Inc., Susannah Sheffer, 2269 Massachusetts Avenue, Cambridge, MA 02140, 617-864-3100. 1977. Articles, interviews, reviews, news items, non-fiction. "Articles and stories about home education and learning outside or without schools" circ. 10M. 6/yr. Pub'd 6 issues 1990; expects 6 issues 1991, 6 issues 1992. sub. price: $25; per copy: $4.50; sample: $2 upon request. Back issues: $130 set of all back issues (82 issues). Discounts: standard on quantities over 10. 32pp; 8½×11; of. Reporting time: 2 months. Payment: none. Copyrighted, reverts to author. Pub's reviews: 40-60 in 1990. §Education, parenting, community. Ads: $700/$350/write for rates.

GRUE MAGAZINE, Peggy Nadramia, Hell's Kitchen Productions, PO Box 370, Times Square Station, New

York, NY 10108. 1985. Poetry, fiction, art, criticism, long-poems. "5000 word maximum for fiction; no minimum length. We're seeking something different in the way of horror, new, experimental, rude, disturbing. We have no taboos or restrictions; send us your hard-to-place stuff, what editors may have told you is too 'weird' or 'explicit', as long as it's horror. No sword and sorcery or SF. Recent contributors include Ramsey Campbell, Jessica Amanda Salmonson, Steve Rasnic Tem, Joseph Payne Brennan, Joe R. Lansdale, t. Winter-Damon, Don Webb, G. Sutton Breiding" circ. 3M. 3/yr. Pub'd 3 issues 1990; expects 3 issues 1991, 3 issues 1992. sub. price: $13; per copy: $4.50; sample: $4.50. Discounts: negotiable. 96pp; 5½×8½; of. Reporting time: 3 months from receiving mss. Payment: 2 copies plus 1/2¢ per word for fiction, upon publication, $5 per poem. Copyrighted, reverts to author. Ads: $50/$35/$25 per 1/4 page. SPWAO (Small Press Writers & Artists Organization), 13 Southwood Drive, Woodland, CA 95695; HWA (Horror Writers of America), 25971 Serenata Drive, Mission Viejo, CA 92691.

Gryphon House, Inc., Larry Rood, PO Box 275, 3706 Otis Street, Mt. Ranier, MD 20712, 301-779-6200. 1971. Non-fiction. "We publish books of activities for use by pre-school teachers and parents" avg. press run 6M. Pub'd 2 titles 1990; expects 3 titles 1991, 3 titles 1992. avg. price, paper: $12.95. Discounts: available upon request. 256pp; 8½×11; of. Reporting time: 3 weeks. Copyrights for author. COSMEP.

Gryphon Publications (see also HARDBOILED DETECTIVE; PAPERBACK PARADE), Gary Lovisi, PO Box 209, Brooklyn, NY 11228. 1983. Fiction, articles, art, interviews, satire, criticism, reviews, parts-of-novels, non-fiction. "We are a small press publisher that (in addition to publishing the magazines *Hardboiled Detective* and *Paperback Parade*) publish numerous books and chapbooks on a variety of subjects dealing with paperback collecting, pulp magazines, detective fiction, science fiction and fantasy, Sherlock Holmes—in fiction and non-fiction" avg. press run 500-1M. Pub'd 5 titles 1990; expects 4 titles 1991, 5 titles 1992. avg. price, cloth: $19.95; paper: $9.95; other: $5-$6.95 stapled booklet. Discounts: 40% on 5 or more per item/issue ordered. 50-200pp; 5×8; of. Reporting time: 3-6 weeks. Payment: varies. Copyrights for author.

GUARD THE NORTH, Les Recherches Daniel Say Cie., Daniel Say, Box 65583, Vancouver 12, B. C. V5N 5K5, Canada. 1971. Articles, art, interviews, criticism, reviews, letters. "500 to 3000 word light writing of science, writing, SF, fantasy etc." circ. 300. 8/yr. Pub'd 8 issues 1990; expects 8 issues 1991, 8 issues 1992. sub. price: $4; per copy: $.50; sample: $.25. 20pp; 21×28cm; †mi. Reporting time: 1 month. Payment: copies. Copyrighted. Pub's reviews: 100 in 1990. §Science or science fiction.

GUARDIAN, Karen Gellen, Editor; William Ryan, Editor, 33 W 17th St, New York, NY 10011, 212-691-0404. 1948. Articles, photos, cartoons, interviews, criticism, reviews, letters, news items. "Independent left newsweekly" circ. 15M. 46/yr. Pub'd 46 issues 1990; expects 46 issues 1991, 46 issues 1992. sub. price: $33.50; per copy: $1.25; sample: free. Back issues: $1.85. Discounts: 40% for resale. 20pp; 10¼×15; of. Reporting time: up to 1 month. Payment: yes. Not copyrighted. Pub's reviews: 50 in 1990. §Politics, history, current events, social trends, international affairs. Ads: $780/$430/42¢ a word.

Guarionex Press Ltd., William E. Zimmerman, Chief Editor & Publisher, 201 West 77th Street, New York, NY 10024, 212-724-5259. 1979. Non-fiction. "The goal of *Guarionex Press* is to publish books that help people articulate their thoughts and feelings. Our books affirm the power of the human spirit and imagination to overcome life's problems. Our first book is *How to Tape Instant Oral Biographies*. The book teaches youngsters and grownups how to interview family members and friends and use the tape or video recorder to capture their life stories, memories and traditions on tape. Great family, school and vacation activity. Its second is a new form of diary/journal called *A Book of Questions to Keep Thoughts and Feelings*; it helps people keep a diary. The third book is *Make Beliefs*, a gift book to spark the imagination. A new activity both for youngsters and adults. Our fourth is *Lifelines*; a book of hope to get you through the tough times of life" avg. press run 5M. Expects 1-2 titles 1991, 1-2 titles 1992. 4 titles listed in the *Small Press Record of Books in Print* (20th Edition, 1991-92). avg. price, paper: $5.95. Discounts: 10-50% depending on volume. 112pp; 4⅛×7⅛; of, lp. Reporting time: 3 months. Payment: fair arrangement-negotiable. Copyrights for author. COSMEP, COSMEP-New York Chapter.

Guernica Editions, Inc., Antonio D'Alfonso, PO Box 633, Station N.D.G., Montreal, Quebec H4A 3R1, Canada, 514-987-7411; FAX 514-982-9793. 1978. Poetry, fiction, photos, criticism, long-poems, plays, non-fiction. "Guernica Editions publish any fine work dealing with literature, criticism or politics. What we desire is serious thinking from conscientious persons. USA distributor: Small Press Distribution. Inland, Bookslinger." avg. press run 2M. Expects 12 titles 1991. 87 titles listed in the *Small Press Record of Books in Print* (20th Edition, 1991-92). avg. price, cloth: $26-$30; paper: $8-$15. Discounts: 40% to libraries for 10 and over, 40% to jobbers. 96pp; 4½×7½; of. Reporting time: we usually take 6 months before answering. Payment: authors receive about 10 copies and 10% royalty; copyright is shared by authors and publisher. Does not copyright for author. Association of Canadian Publishers, Literary Press Group, Association des editeur.

The Guild Bindery Press, Inc. (see also SOUTHERN READER), R.J. Bedwell, PO Box 1827, Oxford, MS 38655, 601-234-2596. 1986. Fiction, articles, interviews, criticism, reviews. avg. press run 2M-3M. Pub'd 12 titles 1990; expects 15 titles 1991, 18 titles 1992. avg. price, cloth: $28; paper: $11. Discounts: trade 40%. 250pp; 6×9; of. Reporting time: prompt. Payment: negotiated. Copyrights for author. Publishers Association of the South.

Guildford Poets Press (see also WEYFARERS), Jeffery Wheatley, Margaret Pain, Susan James, Martin Jones, 9 White Rose Lane, Woking, Surrey, GU22 7JA, England. 1972. Poetry. "Production of boklets temporarily suspended; concentrating on *Weyfarers* poetry magazine" avg. press run 200. 10 titles listed in the *Small Press Record of Books in Print* (20th Edition, 1991-92). avg. price, paper: £1 (overseas, £1.75 sterling or equivalent). 28pp; 8×6; of. Reporting time: 3 months. Payment: free copy of issue sent (mag), booklets co-operative arrangement. Required copyright copies of all publications are dispatched.

Guilt & Gardenias Press, Carlos Steward, Executive Director; Deborah Hill, Rona Britt, PO Box 318, Fayetteville, NC 28302, 919-323-1776. 1991. Poetry, fiction, articles, art, photos, cartoons, interviews, satire, criticism, reviews, music, parts-of-novels, long-poems, collages, plays, concrete art, news items, non-fiction. avg. press run 10M. Pub'd 3 titles 1990; expects 4 titles 1991, 6 titles 1992. avg. price, paper: $2. 24-36pp; tabloid.

Gulf Publishing Company, William J. Lowe, Editor-in-Chief, PO Box 2608, Houston, TX 77252-2608, 713-529-4301. 1916. Non-fiction.

Gull Books, Carolyn Bennett, Box 273 A, Prattsville, NY 12468, 518-299-3171. 1980. Poetry, fiction. "The only things we've been publishing lately are magazines featuring work by children, seniors, clients in psychiatric facilities and those in correctional facilities across New York State. All of the work is usually an outgrowth of my work as creative writing workshop leader/consultant." avg. press run 300. Pub'd 2 titles 1990; expects 3 titles 1991, 2 titles 1992. avg. price, paper: $6. Discounts: inquire. Poetry 64pp; fiction 124pp; 5½×8½; of. Payment: 10% on all books sold. Copyrights for author. NYSSPA.

Gumbs & Thomas Publishers, Inc., Bob Gumbs, Verl Thomas, 142 West 72nd Street, Suite #9, New York, NY 10023, 212-769-8022. 1985. Art, photos, non-fiction. "Specializing in books on black culture and history around the world" avg. press run 10M-25M. Pub'd 1 title 1990; expects 3 titles 1991, 5 titles 1992. 4 titles listed in the *Small Press Record of Books in Print* (20th Edition, 1991-92). avg. price, cloth: $15-$25; paper: $6-$15. Discounts: 1-10 books 30%, 11-24 35%, 25-49 40%, 50+ 45%. 104pp; of, lp. Reporting time: 2-4 weeks. Payment: 5% to 10% annual. Copyrights for author. COSMEP, PMA.

Gurze Books, Lindsey Hall, Box 2238, Carlsbad, CA 92008, 619-434-7533. 1980. Non-fiction. "Self-help, health/psychology." avg. press run 2M-4M. Pub'd 2 titles 1990; expects 2 titles 1991, 3 titles 1992. 6 titles listed in the *Small Press Record of Books in Print* (20th Edition, 1991-92). avg. price, cloth: $19.95; paper: $10.95. Discounts: trade distribution through PGW, B&T, Ingram. 176pp; 5¼×8¼. Reporting time: 4 weeks. Payment: varies. Copyrights for author. PMA.

Gut Punch Press, Derrick Hsu, PO Box 105, Cabin John, MD 20818. 1988. Poetry, fiction. "Looking for material to excite and interest; an innovative edge. Most recent title: *Sad Fashions* by Richard Peabody" avg. press run 1M. Pub'd 1 title 1990; expects 2 titles 1991, 2 titles 1992. 2 titles listed in the *Small Press Record of Books in Print* (20th Edition, 1991-92). avg. price, paper: $7.95. Discounts: write for schedule. 64pp; 5½×8½; of. Reporting time: 2 months. Payment: 50 copies of first printing plus a % of net profits to be determined on an individual basis. Copyrights for author.

The Gutenberg Press, Fred Foldvary, Sandra Fulmer, c/o Fred Foldvary, 101 Mt. Vernon, Alexandria, VA 22301, 703-683-7769. 1980. Non-fiction. "Recent authors: Tertius Chandler, Fred Foldvary, John Hospers. Mostly publish books on social issues, social philosophy, and ancient history. Titles include: *The Soul of Liberty*, by Fred Foldvary. *The Tax We Need*, by Tertius Chandler. *Remote Kingdoms* and *Godly Kings and Early Ethics* by Tertius Chandler, *Anarchy or Limited Government?* by John Hospers. One art book also published." avg. press run 600. Pub'd 2 titles 1990; expects 2 titles 1991, 2 titles 1992. 1 title listed in the *Small Press Record of Books in Print* (20th Edition, 1991-92). avg. price, paper: $10. Discounts: 40% bookstores and 52% jobbers. 300pp; 6×9; lp. Reporting time: within 1 month. Payment: after costs are met, profits are split 50/50. Copyrights for author. COSMEP.

GUTS, Keith A. Dodson, PO Box 2730, Long Beach, CA 90801. 1988. Poetry. "Looking for poetry that cuts to the bone. It is rare when a poem longer than one type-written page merits publication. Recent contributors: Steve Richmond, Bill Shields, Fred Voss, Al Masarik, Lisa Glatt, Star Bowers, Cheryl Townsend, Judson Crews." circ. 300-400. irregular. Pub'd 9 issues 1990; expects 1 issue 1991, unknown issues 1992. price per copy: $3; sample: $3. Back issues: GUTS #1 $125. Discounts: none. 22-44pp; 5½×8½; †of. Reporting time: 1-8 weeks. Payment: 2 copies. Not copyrighted.

Guyasuta Publishers, 1687 Washington Road, Pittsburgh, PA 15228. 1 title listed in the *Small Press Record of Books in Print* (20th Edition, 1991-92).

239

Gwasg Gwalia (see also LOL), 14a Stryd Y Porth Mawr, Caernarfon, Gwynedd, Wales, United Kingdom, 0970 86 304. 1965. "Director: Robat Gruffudd, Printers and publishers interested in anything that will help the Welsh Revolution (Free Wales-Welsh Wales!): posters, paperbacks, funny cards, music, poetry, plays, 'Cymraeg' stickers and of course that awful magazine *LOL*. Send for free 48pp catalogue!" avg. press run 2M. Expects 24 titles 1991. 15 titles listed in the *Small Press Record of Books in Print* (20th Edition, 1991-92). avg. price, cloth: £5; paper: £3. Discounts: 33⅓% Trade. 150pp; size C8; †of. Payment: 10%.

Gweetna Press (see also HOOFSTRIKES NEWSLETTER), Cathy Ford, PO Box 106, Mt. Pleasant, MI 48858, 517-772-0139. 1983. Poetry, fiction, articles, art, cartoons, long-poems. "Material may be equine related, i.e. horse, zebra, donkey, centaur, pegasus, etc. Also may be related to other animals. Distributed free as a service to animal welfare. Donations accepted." avg. press run 300. Pub'd 1 title 1990; expects 1 title 1991, 1 title 1992. 8-10pp; 8½×11; of. Reporting time: varies. Payment: in copies. Does not copyright for author.

GYPSY, Vergin Press, Belinda Subraman, S. Ramnath, c/o Belinda Subraman, 10708 Gay Brewer Drive, El Paso, TX 79935. 1984. Poetry, fiction, articles, art, photos, cartoons, interviews, satire, criticism, reviews, music, letters, parts-of-novels, long-poems, collages, plays, concrete art, news items, non-fiction. "No bias, eclectic, would like the best in art, fiction, essays, interviews, letters, memoirs—anything that relates to our new focus on humanism, political science and global environmental concerns." circ. 1M. 2/yr. Expects 2 issues 1991, 2 issues 1992. sub. price: $12 includes two issues of *Gypsy*; per copy: $7; sample: $7 (large format magazine, perfectbound). Back issues: $5-$20 for rare issues. Discounts: 1 copy, 20%; 2-4, 30%; 5-9, 40%; 10-49, 45%; 50+, 50%. 75-100pp; 8½×11½; of. Reporting time: 6 weeks to 3 months. Payment: one copy of mag. Copyrighted, reverts to author. Pub's reviews: 10 in 1990. §Political science, the environment, humanism, art, fiction, travel, letters, interviews, biographies and autobiographies—very little poetry. Ads: $50/$30/$20¼ page/$5 for 25 words of classifieds. COSMEP, CLMP.

H

The Hague Press (see also THE HAGUE REVIEW), Roger Hunt Carroll, Allan Mason-Smith, PO Box 385, Norfolk, VA 23501, 804-640-1694. 1980. Poetry. "We will look at any manuscripts sent to us, but rarely use anything unsolicited. See our listing in the 1988 Poet's Market edited by Judson Jerome. We tend toward the basic 'cooperative' type of publishing endeavor. Recent titles presented: Ruth Sherman, Robert Authur, Ann Hester." avg. press run 500. Pub'd 2 titles 1990; expects 1 title 1991, 1 title 1992. avg. price, paper: $4. Discounts: various. 32+pp; size varies. Reporting time: almost immediate. Payment: Individual arrangements. Does not copyright for author. none yet.

THE HAGUE REVIEW, The Hague Press, Roger Hunt Carroll, Allan Mason-Smith, PO Box 385, Norfolk, VA 23501, 804-640-1694.

HAIGHT ASHBURY LITERARY JOURNAL, Alice Rogoff, Joanne Hotchkiss, William Walker, 558 Joost Avenue, San Francisco, CA 94127. 1979. Poetry, fiction, art, photos, reviews, non-fiction. "Recent contributors: Eugene Ruggles, Steve Abott, Pancho Aguila, Jack Micheline, Beau Beausoleil, David Meltzer, Leslie Simon, Mona Lisa Saloy, Lorna Dee Cervantes, Merle Woo. Biases: culture and counter culture themes; street life, prison, and other institutions; feminist issues; political issues; family, crime, children, love and other visions." circ. 3M. 1½/yr. Pub'd 2 issues 1990; expects 2 issues 1991, 2 issues 1992. sub. price: $25 lifetime, includes 7 back issues, $5 for 2 issues; per copy: $1.50; sample: $2.50 (with postage). Discounts: $10 for 10. 16pp; 11½×17½; of. Reporting time: 3-5 months. Payment: 3 copies if mailed—more copies per poem if picked up in person. Copyrighted. Pub's reviews. Ads: $40 large/$30+/$20.

Haight-Ashbury Publications (see also JOURNAL OF PSYCHOACTIVE DRUGS), E. Leif Zerkin, Jeffrey H. Novey, 409 Clayton Street, San Francisco, CA 94117, 415-565-1904. 1967. Articles, art, photos, reviews, non-fiction. avg. press run 1.5M. Pub'd 1 title 1990; expects 1 title 1991, 1 title 1992. 4 titles listed in the *Small Press Record of Books in Print* (20th Edition, 1991-92). avg. price, paper: $30. We provide quantity discounts for our books; price list available. 100pp; 8½×11; of. Reporting time: 30 days. Does not copyright for author.

HAIKU ZASSHI ZO, George Klacsanzky, PO Box 17056, Seattle, WA 98107-0756. 1983. Articles, art, reviews, plays, non-fiction. "All materials accepted have some relation to haiku poetry, or other Japanese practices/arts that influence the writing of haiku (i.e. Zen, Noh drama, tea ceremony, etc.)" circ. 500-800. 2/yr. Pub'd 2 issues 1990; expects 2 issues 1991, 2 issues 1992. sub. price: $6; per copy: $3; sample: $3. Back issues: $3.50 semi-annual; $1.25 bi-monthly. 48-65pp; 5½×8½; †of. Reporting time: 1-3 months. Payment: none. Copyrighted, reverts to author. Pub's reviews: 5 in 1990. §Haiku, Tea Ceremony, Go & Shogi books, Sumi painting, Noh theatre. Ads: $25/$15/$7 business card size.

HALF TONES TO JUBILEE, Walter F. Spara, Faculty Editor; Allan Peterson, Faculty Editor; Patrick Cornelius, Student Co-Editor; Phil Bailey, Student Co-Editor, English Dept., 1000 College Blvd., Pensacola Jr. College, Pensacola, FL 32504, 904-484-1000 ext. 1400. 1986. Poetry, fiction, long-poems. "3-5 poem entries, SASE must accompany all submissions. Typed pages, clear photo copies or dot matrix accepted. No biases, 1,500 words short story length for fiction. Deadline: April 30/open. Recent contributors: Gayle Ellen Harvey, Larry Rubin, Peter Wild, R.T. Smith. Annual poetry contest $300 first, $200 second, 2 $50 prizes. Entry fee 2 per poem, 3 for $5. Deadline: April 30." circ. 500. 1/yr. Pub'd 1 issue 1990; expects 1 issue 1991, 1 issue 1992. sub. price: $4; per copy: $4; sample: $4. Back issues: $2. 100pp; 6×9; †of. Reporting time: 8-10 weeks. Payment: copies. Copyrighted, reverts to author. Pub's reviews: 1 in 1990. §Books of poetry and short stories. No ads.

Hallelujah Press Publishing Company, PO Box 496, Gilbert, AZ 85234-0496, 602-821-2287; 892-4309. 1980. Fiction. Pub'd 1 title 1990. 1 title listed in the *Small Press Record of Books in Print* (20th Edition, 1991-92). avg. price, paper: $9. Discounts: 2-4 books 20%, 5-24 40%, 25-49 43%, 50-99 46%, 100+ 50%; libraries no discount, schools 20%. 75pp; 5½×8½; of. Does not copyright for author.

HAMMERS, Nat David, 1718 Sherman #205, Evanston, IL 60201. 1990. Poetry, reviews. "*Hammers* is an end-of-the-millenium irregular poetry magazine. The first issue published this year includes mostly Chicago-area poets. Future issues will continue to stress Chicago-area poets. However, there will be a broader geographical emphasis as well. I am looking for clear, well-stated, vibrant, honest poetry." circ. 500. Irregular. Pub'd 2 issues 1990; expects 2 issues 1991, 2 issues 1992. sub. price: $10, become a pledgehammer, receive back issues #1, #2 and prospective issues #3 and #4; per copy: $3; sample: $3 + $1 postage/handling. 40pp; 8½×11; of. Reporting time: asap. Payment: 1 copy. Copyrighted, reverts to author. Pub's reviews. §Poetry.

Hampshire Books, Bruce Blackie, Publisher, 1660 Akron Peninsula Road #103, Akron, OH 44313-5156, 216-867-6868. 1989. Non-fiction. avg. press run 2.5M. Pub'd 4 titles 1990; expects 1 title 1991, 1 title 1992. avg. price, paper: $9.95. Discounts: bookstores and wholesalers. 200pp; 5½×8½. Copyrights for author.

HANDICAP NEWS, Phyllis A. Burns, Editor & Publisher, 3060 East Bridge Street, #342, Brighton, CO 80601-2724, 303-659-4463. 1984. Poetry, fiction, articles, criticism, news items, non-fiction. "*Handicap News* is for all people with disbilities, handicaps, and for those working with them. Rights, products, travel, etc. are covered each month. Writers are needed for *Handicap News*. Poems, inspirational pieces, tips, experiences, etc. are need from handicapped people and their families. For a sample copy, send $2 plus a SASE" circ. 500. 12/yr. Pub'd 12 issues 1990; expects 12 issues 1991, 12 issues 1992. sub. price: US $12.50; Canada $23; foreign $35; per copy: $2 plus a SASE; sample: $2 plus a SASE. 8pp; 8½×11. Reporting time: 1 month. Payment: 2 copies. Not copyrighted. Pub's reviews: 2 in 1990. §Books on handicapped subjects. Ads: classified 20¢ per word.

Handshake Editions (see also 'THE CASSETTE GAZETTE', An Audio Magazine), Jim Haynes, Atelier A2, 83 rue de la Tombe-Issoire, Paris 75014, France, 4327-1767. 1971. Poetry, fiction, articles, photos, cartoons, parts-of-novels. "Only personal face-to-face submissions solicited. Handshake mainly publishes Paris-based writers. Small print-runs, but we attempt to keep everything in print (i.e., frequent re-prints). Libertarian bias. Writers recently published include Ted Joans, Sarah Bean, Michael Zwerin, Jim Haynes, Elaine J. Cohen, Ken Timmerman, Judith Malina, Lynne Tillman, Samuel Brecher, Suzanne Brogger, Jayne Cortez, Amanda P. Hoover, Echnaton, Yianna Katsoulos, William Levy, and Barry Gifford." avg. press run 1M. Pub'd 12 titles 1990; expects 12 titles 1991. 7 titles listed in the *Small Press Record of Books in Print* (20th Edition, 1991-92). avg. price, paper: $10. Discounts: 1/3 prepaid; all cheques payable to Jim Haynes. Payment: by copies of the book. Copyrights for author.

HANG GLIDING, Gil Dodgen, U.S. Hang Gliding Assoc., Inc., PO Box 8300, Colorado Springs, CO 80933, (805) 944-5333. 1974. Articles, photos, cartoons, interviews, reviews, letters, news items. "Information pertaining to hang gliding and soaring flight" circ. 9M. 12/yr. Pub'd 12 issues 1990; expects 12 issues 1991, 12 issues 1992. sub. price: $29; per copy: $2.50; sample: same. Back issues: prior 1982 $1.50, after 1982 $2. Discounts: newsstand 50%. 52pp; 8½×11; of. Payment: limited, cover photo $40. Copyrighted. Pub's reviews: 3-5 in 1990. §Aviation, outdoor recreation. Ads: b/w: $385/$220/40¢ per word classified.

HANGING LOOSE, Hanging Loose Press, Robert Hershon, Dick Lourie, Mark Pawlak, Ron Schreiber, Emmett Jarrett, Contributing Editor, 231 Wyckoff Street, Brooklyn, NY 11217. 1966. Poetry, fiction. "Emphasis remains on the work of new writers-and when we find people we like, we stay with them. Among recent contributors: Kimiko Hahn, Paul Violi, Donna Brook, D. Nurkse, Steven Schrader, Kathleen Aguero, Ron Overton, Michael Lassell, Charles North. We welcome submissions to the magazine, but artwork & book mss. are by invitation only. We suggest strongly that people read the magazine before sending work." circ. 1.2M. 3/yr. Pub'd 3 issues 1990; expects 3 issues 1991. sub. price: $12.50/3 issues (individuals); per copy: $5; sample: $6.50 (incl. postage). Back issues: prices on request, including complete sets. Discounts: 40% to bookstores, 20% to jobbers. 96pp; 7×8½; of. Reporting time: 2-3 months. Payment: 3 copies. Copyrighted, does

241

not revert to author. Pub's reviews. §Poetry. No ads. CCLM, COSMEP.

Hanging Loose Press (see also HANGING LOOSE), Robert Hershon, Dick Lourie, Mark Pawlak, Ron Schreiber, Emmett Jarrett, Contributing Editor, 231 Wyckoff Street, Brooklyn, NY 11217. 1966. Poetry, fiction. "Book mss by invitation only." avg. press run 1M-2M. Pub'd 6 titles 1990; expects 6 titles 1991, 6 titles 1992. 54 titles listed in the *Small Press Record of Books in Print* (20th Edition, 1991-92). avg. price, cloth: $15; paper: $8. Discounts: bookstores, 40% (more than 4 copies), 20%, 1-4 copies; jobbers, 20%. 80-96pp; 5½×8½, varies; of. Payment: yes. Copyrights for author. CCLM, COSMEP.

Hans Zell Publishers (see also THE AFRICAN BOOK PUBLISHING RECORD; THE JOURNAL OF COMMONWEALTH LITERATURE), Hans M. Zell, Mary Jay, Alastair Niven, Caroline Bundy, PO Box 56, Oxford OX1 3EL, England, 0865-511428. 1975. Articles, interviews, criticism, reviews, non-fiction. "We are an imprint of Bowker-Saur Ltd." avg. press run 800. Expects 6 titles 1991. avg. price, cloth: £22.50; paper: £12. Discounts: 10% to subs. agents. 80-176pp; size A4, A5 or 240×160mm; of. Reporting time: 2-3 months. Payment: negotiable. Copyrights for author.

HAPPINESS HOLDING TANK, Stone Press, Albert Drake, Editor, 9727 SE Reedway Street, Portland, OR 97266-3738, 503-771-6779. 1970. Poetry, articles, criticism, reviews, letters, news items. "We've emphasized poetry, information, printing processes, & people. Any information of a literary nature will be passed along. The Mag lists dozens of new mags, dead mags, contests, etc. (in addition to poetry, commentary, essays, etc.) only $1.25. Philip Whalen, Earle Birney, Wm. Matthews, Wm. Stafford, Anselm Hollo, and more than 300 known/unknown poets. Magazine is in limbo at present." circ. 300-500. 1-2/yr. Pub'd 4 issues 1990; expects 2 issues 1991, 1 issue 1992. sub. price: $4; per copy: $1.50; sample: $1.50. Back issues: limited sets: 1-20 for $50 to libraries. Discounts: 40%. 50pp; 8½×11; †mi, of. Reporting time: 1-3 weeks. Payment: copies. Copyrighted. Pub's reviews: 20 in 1990. §Poetry & fiction. Ads: $15/$8.

Happy Rock Press, Philip R. Nurenberg, Phil Nurenberg, c/o: PO Box 24453, Los Angeles, CA 90024-0453. 1980. Poetry, articles, art, photos, interviews, reviews, letters, collages, non-fiction. "Address all correspondence *directly* to Phil Nurenberg. We solicit *interviewees* for *collaborative* ongoing works. Devoted to self-published-photostat-books of a *photo/interview* nature. Also manuscript consulting and editing. Designed to fill *any* size order in 6 to 8 weeks *with* pre-payment; within 2 weeks to 1 month for small orders; one copy orders fine too." Pub'd 1 title 1990; expects 2 titles 1991. 1 title listed in the *Small Press Record of Books in Print* (20th Edition, 1991-92). avg. price, paper: $4; other: $4 photostat. Discounts: contact Phil Nurenberg. 10-20pp; 8×10; †mi, photostat/xerox. Reporting time: 6-8 weeks or sooner. Payment: only if net profit—but always 2 free copies of work they appear in; basically a non-profit enterprise for author publicity and publication. Does not copyright for author. Maine Writers & Publishers Alliance.

THE HAPPY THRASHER, Tin-ear, PO Box 2246, Anaheim, CA 92814, 714-647-2307. 1987. Fiction, articles, art, photos, cartoons, interviews, satire, criticism, reviews, music, letters, collages, news items, non-fiction. "I basically want to expose as much information, *real* information, to people so that they can empower themselves in order to take control of their lives & bodies. Nothing is taboo and nothing is perpetual. Sex, abortion, cooking, love, soul mates, psychoanalysis, home brewing, botany, life, spirituality, karma, music, writing, reading, intelligence, and love is what I advocate." circ. 200-400. 6/yr. Pub'd 2 issues 1990; expects 6 issues 1991, 6 issues 1992. price per copy: $1.50; sample: $1.50. Back issues: #10 $2.25, #11 $1.75, #12 $1.50. Discounts: will trade to review other zines, plus 7"es and 12"es, tapes. 20pp; 8½×11; †mi. Payment: copy for them. Not copyrighted. Pub's reviews: a very lot in 1990. §Alternative and underground music, sex, art, literature, counter-culture, death, gore, subgenius. Ads: $10 1/2 page/$5 1/4 page/$3 1/8 and business card.

Harbinger House, Lisa Cooper, 2802 N. Alvernon Way, Tucson, AZ 85712, 602-326-9595. 1987. Interviews, criticism, non-fiction. "Harbinger House publishes books about contemporary social issues and personal growth and children's books that expand awareness and foster a love of reading. We strive to maintain a connecting thread of moral integrity and human concern through our diverse list. (Not to be confused with New Harbinger or Harbinger of a New Age)." avg. press run 5M. Pub'd 18 titles 1990; expects 5 titles 1991, 10 titles 1992. avg. price, cloth: $17.95; paper: $9.95. Discounts: trade 40%-46% DOQ, 50% wholesale, 20% library-school. 160pp; 5½×8½; of. Reporting time: 6 weeks. Payment: 10%-12% net. Copyrights for author. Publishers Marketing Association (PMA), Tucson Book Publishing Association (TBPA).

Harbor Publishing Company (see also JOURNAL OF THEORETICAL PSYCHOLOGY), Laura M. Morrison, 80 N. Moore Street, Suite 4J, New York, NY 10013, 212-349-1818. 1979. Non-fiction. "Harbor will publish selected applications of Integration Theory, not necessarily by professional social scientists or professional writers but well thought out and original material reflecting its author's own area of expertise or experience" avg. press run 5M. Pub'd 1 title 1990; expects 1 title 1991, 2 titles 1992. 1 title listed in the *Small Press Record of Books in Print* (20th Edition, 1991-92). avg. price, cloth: $29.95; paper: $24.95. Discounts: 10+ copies, 20%; No returns, no consignment, prepayment please. 350pp; 6×9; of. Reporting time: 2 weeks. Payment: depends on the state of the manuscript and on size of its potential market. Copyrights for author.

none.

HarCroft Publishing Company, Harrison B. Bell, Star Route Box 179, Hancock, ME 04640, 207-422-3383. 1988. Poetry, fiction, non-fiction. "Regional books only; quality paper back; Maine authors and illustrators; no determination on number of books published in a given year; no hard or fast rules about the above or anything else" avg. press run 500-2.5M. Pub'd 2 titles 1990; expects 2 titles 1991, 2 titles 1992. 2 titles listed in the *Small Press Record of Books in Print* (20th Edition, 1991-92). avg. price, paper: $9.95. Discounts: 30% 1-4 books (prepaid only), 5-9 40%, 10+ 45%, 50 days net; no returns on 1-4 books. 168pp; 5½×8¼; of. Reporting time: 3 months. Payment: no advances, 12-15% depending on material, semi-annual accounting. Copyrights for author. COSMEP, PMA.

Hard Press, Jeff Wright, 632 East 14th Street, #10, New York, NY 10009. 1976. Poetry, art, photos, cartoons, music, letters, collages. "To date *Hard Press* has published 76 different *post cards*, generally poetry of two to twenty lines, sometimes accompanied by art-work, but sometimes just original art work, cartoons, collages, photos, by themselves. Contributors include: Kathy Acker, Amiri Baraka, Ted Berrigan, Robert Creeley, Allen Ginsberg, Anselm Hollo, Bob Holman, Allan Kornblum, Phillip Lopate, Alice Notley, Maureen Owen, Pedro Pietri, Jayne Anne Phillips, Jeff Wright, Paul Zinkievich. Also three books to date" avg. press run 500. Pub'd 12 titles 1990; expects 16 titles 1991, 16 titles 1992. avg. price, paper: 50¢; other: postage. Discounts: 40%. 1 page; 5½×4¼; of. Reporting time: 8 weeks. Payment: 10% of copy. Copyrights for author. CCLM.

HARDBOILED DETECTIVE, Gryphon Publications, Gary Lovisi, PO Box 209, Brooklyn, NY 11228. 1988. Fiction, articles, interviews, letters, non-fiction. "Previously *Detective Story Magazine.* Publish the hardest, cutting-edge crime fiction, stories full of impact, action, violence. Also reviews, articles, interviews on hardboiled topics." circ. 400. 4/yr. Pub'd 4 issues 1990; expects 4 issues 1991, 4 issues 1992. sub. price: $20/6 issues; per copy: $5; sample: $5. Back issues: #1-9 $29, or $5 each. Discounts: 40% on 5 or more of each issue. 50-80pp; 5×8; of. Reporting time: 2-4 weeks. Payment: $5-$25 depending on quality and length, and 2 free copies on publication. Copyrighted, reverts to author. Pub's reviews: 3-4 in 1990. §Hardboiled, crime-fiction, mystery, suspense. Ads: $50/$25.

HARDWARE, The Magazine of SF Technophilia, Jimm Gall, Editor, 710 Adeline Street, Trenton, NJ 08611. 1988. Poetry, fiction, art, long-poems. "*Hardware* is dedicated to the obsessive and abnormal relationships between man and machine. Contributors include Bruce Boston, David Bunch, Paul Di Filippo, Robert Frazier, Felix Gotschalk and t. Winter-Damon" circ. 1.5M+. 2-3/yr. Pub'd 1 issue 1990; expects 3 issues 1991, 3 issues 1992. sub. price: $11; per copy: $4; sample: $4. Discounts: wholesalers/retailers 50%. 44pp; 8½×11; of. Reporting time: 2-6 months. Payment: $10-$50. Copyrighted, reverts to author. Ads: $80/$50/$30 1/4 page.

Holger Harfst, Publisher, Holger Harfst, Gerold Harfst, Postfach 5741, D8700 Wurzburg, Germany, 01149 931 411575. 1987. avg. press run 1M. Pub'd 2 titles 1990; expects 1 title 1991. 4 titles listed in the *Small Press Record of Books in Print* (20th Edition, 1991-92). avg. price, cloth: $19; paper: $14. 455pp; 5¾×8-2/5. Does not copyright for author.

Harlo Press, David Broughton, Manager, 50 Victor, Detroit, MI 48203. 1946. "We are primarily book printers although we publish a few titles" avg. press run 1-5M. Expects 3-4 titles 1991. 48 titles listed in the *Small Press Record of Books in Print* (20th Edition, 1991-92). avg. price, cloth: $10; paper: $6. Discounts: 1-4, 20%; 5-24, 40%; 25-49, 43%; 50-99, 46%; 100 or more, 50%. 200pp; 5½×8½; †of. Payment: yes. Copyrights for author.

HARMONY: VOICES FOR A JUST FUTURE, Sea Fog Press, Inc., Rose Evans, Managing Editor, PO Box 210056, San Francisco, CA 94121-0056, 415-221-8527. 1987. Poetry, articles, cartoons, interviews, criticism, reviews. "Harmony Magazine publishes articles on reverence for life—for animal rights, disabled, rights, gay rights, peace, justice, ecology—against war, capital punishment, abortion, euthanasia, covert action, etc." circ. 1.4M. 6/yr. Pub'd 6 issues 1990; expects 6 issues 1991, 6 issues 1992. sub. price: $12; per copy: $2; sample: $2. Back issues: $2. Discounts: 10+ copies 40%. 28pp; 8½×11; of. Reporting time: 3-8 weeks. Copyrighted, reverts to author. Pub's reviews: 3 in 1990. §War & peace, social justice, hunger. Ads: $100/$50/10¢ per word.

Harper Square Press, Phyllis Ford-Choyke, Arthur Choyke, 29 East Division Street, Chicago, IL 60610-2316, 312-337-1482. 1967. Poetry. "Temporarily inactive but expect 1 title in 1991" avg. press run 1M. 7 titles listed in the *Small Press Record of Books in Print* (20th Edition, 1991-92). Discounts: to be arranged. 104pp; 5½×8½. COSMEP.

HARP-STRINGS, Madelyn Eastlund, 310 S. Adams Street, Beverly Hills, FL 32265. 1989. Poetry. "Recent contributors: Ralph Hammond, Grace Haynes Smith, Charles Dickson. No short poems (under 16 lines), maximum lines 72. Looking for 'poems to remember.' Looking for narratives 'good story poems' ballads, patterned poetry. Annual contest: The Edna St. Vincent Millay Harp-Weaver Poetry Contest. Read only January 1 through February 28; May 1 through June 30; October 1 through November 30. Each reading is to plan the

243

following issue—no files are kept. Poems kept only for current issue." circ. 100. 3/yr. Pub'd 2 issues 1990; expects 3 issues 1991, 3 issues 1992. sub. price: $20; per copy: $8; sample: $8. Back issues: $5. 32pp; 5½x8½. Reporting time: 1-2 weeks during reading time. Payment: copy. Copyrighted, reverts to author.

Harris Stonehouse Press (see also THE DILETTANTE FORUM), Joan Elford Stone, 142 Woodlawn Drive, Marietta, GA 30067-4016. 1987. Poetry, fiction, music, plays. "We are promoting *Sex, Sin & Salvation* CIP 87-92182, ISBN 0-945340-15X. This is a collection of short stories and poems, 208 pages, soft cover, 5½ X 8½. The lead story, 'Snakebox Dance', is about a snake handling preacher in Appalachia and three sisters he has rescued. The story ends with a surprising twist. 'Boblo Riverboat Tragedy', tells how Mike O'Hanihey boarded the boat drunk and two hours later saved the lives of 1,200 passengers. 'Angel Lost', is a story about a little girl who disappears from her front porch and brings the whole town alive in its efforts to find her. 'Sex Makes You Blind' is a poem that will make you laugh about wearing glasses. There is more!" avg. press run 3M. Expects 3 titles 1991, 5 titles 1992. 1 title listed in the *Small Press Record of Books in Print* (20th Edition, 1991-92). avg. price, cloth: $16.95; paper: $11.95. Discounts: 2-5 books 20%, 15-24 35%, 25-34 40%, 35-50 42%, 51-99 45%, 100-199 50%, 200+ 55%. 224pp. Reporting time: usually 30 days. Payment: to be negotiated. Copyrights for author. COSMEP, PMA.

Harrison House Publishers, Paula Orriols, Publicist; Cris Bolley, Jimmy Peacock, PO Box 35035, Tulsa, OK 74153, 918-582-2126. 1975. Non-fiction. "Address #2: 1029 North Utica, Tulsa, OK 74110" avg. press run 15M. Pub'd 35 titles 1990; expects 40 titles 1991, 45 titles 1992. avg. price, cloth: $12.95; paper: $4.95; other: $3.98 children's books. Discounts: 1-4 books 20%, 5-49 40%, 50-99 41%, 100-249 42%, 500+ 45%. of, lp. Reporting time: 2 months. Copyrights for author.

Harrow and Heston, Publishers, Graeme Newman, Editor-in-Chief, Stuyvesant Plaza, P.O. Box 3934, Albany, NY 12203. 1983. Non-fiction. "Criminal justice texts and monographs" avg. press run 1M-2M. Pub'd 1 title 1990; expects 4 titles 1991, 4 titles 1992. 8 titles listed in the *Small Press Record of Books in Print* (20th Edition, 1991-92). avg. price, cloth: $27; paper: $12. Discounts: varies by title and number ordered: from 10%-50%. 200pp; 5½x8½, 6x9; of, lp. Reporting time: 6 weeks. Payment: negotiable. Copyrights for author.

Hartford Press, Robert Serling, 3960 Laurel Canyon Blvd, Suite 380, Studio City, CA 91604, 818-761-2952. 1987. Non-fiction. "Business and technical material. Primary audience is small business, entrepreneurs, middle to upper level management. We do not accept unsolicited manuscripts. What we do accept is a well written query letter with an overview, outline, and SASE. This should be no more than 3 pages" avg. press run 3M. Pub'd 1 title 1990; expects 2-4 titles 1991, 2-4 titles 1992. 3 titles listed in the *Small Press Record of Books in Print* (20th Edition, 1991-92). Discounts: 40-55%. lp. Reporting time: 4-6 weeks. Payment: negotiable. Copyrights for author. PMA, ABE, COSMEP.

THE HARVARD ADVOCATE, 21 South St., Cambridge, MA 02138, 617-495-0737. 1866. Poetry, fiction, articles, art, photos, cartoons, interviews, criticism, reviews, long-poems, collages, plays, non-fiction. "*The Harvard Advocate* publishes work from Harvard undergraduates, affiliates, and alumni. We regret that we cannot read manuscripts from other sources" circ. 4M. 4/yr. Pub'd 4 issues 1990; expects 5 issues 1991, 5 issues 1992. sub. price: $15 for 4 issues; per copy: $4; sample: $4. Back issues: price varies. Discounts: none. 40pp; 8½x11; lp. Reporting time: 4-6 weeks. Payment: none. Copyrighted, does not revert to author. Pub's reviews: 10 in 1990. §Literature and art. Ads: $275/$165. ALL.

Harvard Common Press, Bruce Shaw, 535 Albany Street, Boston, MA 02118, 617-423-5803. 1976. Photos, non-fiction. avg. press run 7.5-10M. Pub'd 6 titles 1990; expects 8 titles 1991, 8 titles 1992. 41 titles listed in the *Small Press Record of Books in Print* (20th Edition, 1991-92). avg. price, cloth: $17.95; paper: $9.95. Discounts: 10-49 40%, 50-99 45%, 100-299 50%. 220pp; 6x9; of. Copyrights for author.

HARVARD WOMEN'S LAW JOURNAL, Christina Scobey, Editor-in-Chief; Marie Arnold, Editor-in-Chief, Publications Center, Harvard Law School, Cambridge, MA 02138, (617) 495-3726. 1978. Articles, reviews. "We are a law review; all submissions are generally law related; however, legal histories, literary and sociological perspectives on the law as it affects women and feminism are welcomed." circ. 900. 1/yr. Pub'd 1 issue 1990; expects 1 issue 1991, 1 issue 1992. sub. price: $15 domestic (US), $20 foreign; per copy: $15. 350pp. Reporting time: varies. Copyrighted, does not revert to author. Pub's reviews: 5 in 1990. §Law related, legal histories and sociological literary perspectives on the law as it affects women and feminism.

Harvestman and Associates, Sheila Tangiers, Sales Director, PO Box 271, Menlo Park, CA 94026-0271, 415-326-6997 x1511. 1978. Photos. "Exciting, rare insider's view of a motorcycle run, poetry and pictorial essay give candid view of bikers in California and information on the US Motorcycle Jamboree" avg. press run 5M. Expects 1 title 1991. avg. price, paper: $48. Discounts: 60/40. 92pp; 8½x8; of. Copyrights for author.

THE HAUNTED JOURNAL, Baker Street Publications, Sharida Rizzuto, Sidney J. Dragon, Thomas Schellenberger, PO Box 994, Metairie, LA 70004, 504-734-8414. 1983. Poetry, fiction, articles, art, photos, cartoons, interviews, satire, criticism, reviews, letters, long-poems, collages, plays, news items, non-fiction.

circ. under 10M. 2-4/yr. Pub'd 4 issues 1990; expects 2-4 issues 1991, 2-4 issues 1992. sub. price: $28 for 4 issues; per copy: $7.90; sample: $7.90. Back issues: $7.90. 120pp; digest size; of, photo copy, excellent offset covers. Reporting time: 2-6 weeks. Payment: free copies, fees paid for articles, reviews and artwork negotiable. Copyrighted, reverts to author. Pub's reviews: 16 in 1990. §Horror in film and literature, the occult, new age, supernatural, poetry. Ads: free. NWC, SPWAO, HWA, Literary Markets, Mystery Writers of America (MWA), Western Writers of America (WWA), Arizona Authors Associaiton (AAA).

HAUNTS, Joseph K Cherkes, Nightshade Publications, PO Box 3342, Providence, RI 02906, 401-781-9438. 1984. Poetry, fiction, art, interviews, reviews. "*Haunts* is a publication for people who enjoy reading horror, science-fantasy, and supernatural tales in the same vein as the famous *Weird Tales* We are looking for those stories that will make people think twice before turning out the lights or going to the basement to change a blown fuse. Our market will be open to review of material from June 1st to December 1st, inclusively. Strong characters and strong fantasy/supernatural elements combined with plausibility and continuity of storyline will go a long way in the consideration of your work. We *do not want* explicit sexual scences, famous rewrites, blow by blow dismemberments, or pure adventure. Stories should be between 1,500 and 8,000 words. Manuscripts should be double-spaced and typed as clearly as possible. Photocopies that are clearly legible are preferred as this leaves the original in your care in the event of lost mail. Place your name and address in the upper left hand corner of the first page and your name and story title on each succeeding page. Send SASE if you wish the return of your manuscript. We cannot be held responsible for the return of manuscripts unless this policy is strictly adhered to. Past contributors: Mike Hurley, Colleen Drippe, Wayne Allen Sallee, Kathleen Jurgens, Scott Edelman, and Tom Elliott." circ. 1M. 4/yr. Pub'd 3 issues 1990; expects 4 issues 1991, 4 issues 1992. sub. price: $13; per copy: $3.95 + $1 p/h; sample: $3.95 + $1.25 for 1st class postage (optional). Back issues: limited copies of #1 $8.95, and #2 $7.95 + $1.25 p/h; write for our complete list. Discounts: 35-40% trade, 45-55% bulk (orders of 90 or more). 100pp; 6×9; of. Reporting time: 6-8 weeks. Payment: 1/4¢ up to 1¢ per word. Copyrighted, reverts to author. Pub's reviews. §Horror, fantasy, science fiction. Ads: $100 body copy ad/$200 inside covers/$250 back cover/$225 page 1. SPWAO, 13 Southwood Drive, Woodland, CA 95695.

HAWAI'I REVIEW, Jeanne Tsutsui, Fiction Editor; Teya Maman, Editor-in-Chief; Lani Kwon, Poetry Editor; Robin Shaffer, Non-Fiction Editor, c/o Dept. of English, 1733 Donaghho Road, Honolulu, HI 96822, 808-956-8548. 1973. Poetry, fiction, articles, art, photos, cartoons, interviews, satire, criticism, reviews, music, parts-of-novels, long-poems, plays, non-fiction. "Accept works of poetry, fiction, and non-fiction, including plays, short-short stories, reviews, essays, humor, songs and chants. Publish all forms of literature including works which focus on Hawai'i and the Pacific." circ. 2M. 3/yr. Pub'd 3 issues 1990; expects 3 issues 1991, 3 issues 1992. sub. price: $12; per copy: $5; sample: $5. Back issues: $4. 150-200pp; 6×9; of. Reporting time: 1-4 months. Payment: $25 inside art, $75 cover art, $10 short-short, $15 poetry, $5/page $10 minimum prose. Copyrighted, reverts to author. Pub's reviews: 1 in 1990. §Contemporary fiction, non-fiction on contemporary issues. Ads: $75/$50.

HAYDEN'S FERRY REVIEW, Salima Keegan, Managing Editor, Matthews Center, Arizona State University, Tempe, AZ 85287-1502, 602-965-1243. 1986. Poetry, fiction, art, photos, interviews. "Publishes approximately 25 poems, 5 short stories. Past contributors: Raymond Carver, Rick Bass, Joy Williams, John Updike, T.C. Boyle, Rita Dove, Maura Stanton and Joseph Heller." circ. 1M. 2/yr. Pub'd 2 issues 1990; expects 2 issues 1991, 2 issues 1992. sub. price: $10; per copy: $6; sample: $6. Back issues: Issues 1-4 $2.50 each. 128pp; 6×9. Reporting time: 8-10 weeks after deadline. Payment: in copies (2). Copyrighted, reverts to author. COSMEP.

Haypenny Press, Dawn Conti, 211 New Street, West Paterson, NJ 07424. 1988. Fiction, non-fiction. "Novellas and story collections, any genre except pornography. Editors are also interested in works for the Young Adult market, particularly when the author has a specific audience and purpose (ie: teachers of literacy programs; counsellors at runaway shelters, etc.). Y/A material must project something useful to its audience without preaching. Nonfiction: Exceptional and/or unusual how-to or self-help. General Info: Contracts/ payment varies with each situation. Prefer writers who can participate in the promotion and sales of their work.*Always* query first with SASE." avg. press run varies, can be as low as 200. Pub'd 1 title 1990; expects 3 titles 1991, 3 titles 1992. 2 titles listed in the *Small Press Record of Books in Print* (20th Edition, 1991-92). avg. price, paper: varies. 150pp; 5½×8½; †mi, of. Reporting time: generally a month or less. Payment: varies according to work and situation. Copyrights for author.

THE HEADWATERS REVIEW, Frank Laurich, PO Box 13682, Dinkytown Station, Minneapolis, MN 55414. "Accept poetry, prose, essays, translations, interviews and one-act plays. Each submission must include a SASE with sufficient postage (international postage coupon where applicable) for materials to be returned." 2/yr. sub. price: $15 (3 issues); per copy: $5; sample: $6.50. Reporting time: 3-6 months. Payment: copies. Copyrighted, reverts to author.

HEALING PATH, Mary Barker, Publisher; Artemis, Editor, PO Box 599-DB, Coos Bay, OR 97420, 0114. 1990. Poetry, articles, art, photos, cartoons, interviews, reviews, music, letters, collages, news items, non-fiction. *"Healing Paths* journal is dedicated to promoting healing for adult survivors of childhood sexual abuse. Contributions are welcome from anyone involved in the recovery/healing of a survivor(s), especially from survivors themselves." 6/yr. Expects 3 issues 1991, 6 issues 1992. sub. price: $18. 8½×11; of. Payment: copies. Copyrighted, reverts to author. Pub's reviews. §Childhood sexual abuse, incest, healing, recovery, dysfunctional families-of-origin. Ads: request ad rate card.

Health Alert Press, PO Box 2060, Cambridge, MA 02238, 617-497-4190. 1985. Non-fiction. "Education about health. Recent book on AIDS, 240 pages, educational, easy to read. Bought by individuals, hospitals, nursing organizations, school systems, city and state health departments." avg. press run 5M. Expects 1 title 1991, 1 title 1992. 1 title listed in the *Small Press Record of Books in Print* (20th Edition, 1991-92). avg. price, paper: $24.95. Discounts: varied according to quantity. 240pp; 7×10; of. Reporting time: 3 months. Payment: negotiable. PMA.

Health Educator Publications, Inc., Dana F. Oakes, 1580 Kirkland Road, Old Town, ME 04468, 207-827-3633. 1984. Non-fiction. avg. press run 10M. Pub'd 2 titles 1990; expects 4 titles 1991, 6 titles 1992. 4 titles listed in the *Small Press Record of Books in Print* (20th Edition, 1991-92). avg. price, paper: $12.95; other: $16.95 6-ring binder. Discounts: 20-40%. 250pp; 5×7; of. Reporting time: 1 month. Payment: 10-25%. Copyrights for author.

Health Plus Publishers, Paula E. Clure, PO Box 1027, Sherwood, OR 97140, 503-625-0589. 1965. Non-fiction. "We publish books on health, particularly holistic health, nutrition, and fitness. We are publishers of Dr. Paavo Airola's books, including *How to Get Well, Everywoman's Book*, and *Are You Confused?* Recent publications include: *Change Your Mind/Change Your Weight*, by Dr. James McClernan; *Exercise For Life*, by Mark L. Hendrickson and Gary J. Greene; *The Directory of Holistic Medicine and Alternate Health Care Services In The U.S.*, edited by Shirley Linde and Donald J. Carrow, M.D. We will consider material of any length. Prefer query first." avg. press run 7.5M-10M. Pub'd 4 titles 1990; expects 3 titles 1991, 4 titles 1992. 11 titles listed in the *Small Press Record of Books in Print* (20th Edition, 1991-92). avg. price, cloth: $15.95; paper: $8.95. Discounts: all trade accounts sold through Contemporary Books, Inc., Chicago, IL. For other accounts, inquire. 250pp; 5½×8½; of. Reporting time: acknowledge receipt immediately; max 3 months on decision. Payment: no advance, royalties negotiable. Copyrights for author.

Health Press, Kriszti Fehervary, Box 1388, Santa Fe, NM 87504, 505-982-9373. 1988. Non-fiction. "Books related to cutting-edge health topics, well-researched, geared to general public. Require outline with 3 chapters for submission—prefer complete manuscript. Authors must be credentialed (MD, PhD) or have credentialed professional write intro/preface. Controversial topics desired." avg. press run 5M. Pub'd 2 titles 1990; expects 8 titles 1991, 8 titles 1992. avg. price, cloth: $19.95; paper: $14.95. Discounts: bookstore 40%+, library 20%, (depending on quantity). 250pp; 6×9; of. Reporting time: 8-10 weeks. Payment: standard royalty, small advance. Copyrights for author. Rocky Mountain Book Publishers Association, Small Press Center.

Healthmere Press, Inc. (see also SPORTS-NUTRITION NEWS), Jacqueline B. Marcus, PO Box 986, Evanston, IL 60204, 312-251-5950. 1982. Non-fiction. "We publish books relating to health, fitness, diet, exercise, and cooking." avg. press run 2.5-5M. Pub'd 1 title 1990; expects 2 titles 1991, 4 titles 1992. avg. price, paper: $8.95. Discounts: 2 list; 3-12 25%; 12+ 40%. 150pp; of. Reporting time: 60 days. Payment: negotiable. Copyrights for author. COSMEP.

HEALTH/PAC BULLETIN, Nancy McKenzie, Executive Director; Ellen Bilofsky, Editor, 17 Murray Street, New York, NY 10007, 212-767-8890. 1968. Articles, art, photos, cartoons, interviews, criticism, reviews, letters, news items, non-fiction. circ. 2M. 4/yr. Pub'd 4 issues 1990; expects 4 issues 1991, 4 issues 1992. sub. price: $22.50 (student, low-income), $45 (instit), $35 (membership); per copy: $5; sample: same. Back issues: $5 indiv., $12 instit., $4 for members. Discounts: 2 yrs $70 (instit). 36pp; 8½×11; lp. Reporting time: 2 months. Payment: copies. Copyrighted, rights revert to author on request. Pub's reviews: 6 in 1990. §Health & health policy. Ads: $850/$500. HPAC.

HEALTHSHARING: A Canadian Women's Health Quarterly, Amy Gottlieb, Managing Editor; Susan Elliott, Production Coordinator, 14 Skey Lane, Toronto, Ontario M6J 3S4, Canada, 416-532-0812. 1979. Poetry, fiction, articles, photos, cartoons, interviews, reviews, letters, news items, non-fiction. circ. 5M. 4/yr. Pub'd 4 issues 1990; expects 4 issues 1991, 4 issues 1992. sub. price: $15 indiv., $28 groups/instit. (add $3 for US, $4 outside North America, Int'l money orders only); per copy: $3.50 + postage; sample: $3.50 + postage. 36pp; 8⅛×10-11/16; of. Copyrighted, reverts to author. Pub's reviews: 6 in 1990. §Women and women's health issues. Ads: $350/$200/$140 1/3 page/$120 1/4/$70 1/6/$60 1/8/inside cover, 2 color ads: $400/$225/$150 1/4. CMPA.

HearSay Press TM (see also BookNotes :(TM) Resources for Small & Self-Publishers), Cliff Martin, Box 555, West Linn, OR 97068-2706, 503-655-5010. 1986. Poetry, fiction, art, music, non-fiction. "Primary interests: SOCIAL SCIENCE, particularly Oral History, Sociology, Anthropology. MUSIC, Contemporary, Critical, Reference Works. LITERATURE, LOCAL ONLY (Pacific Northwest), novellas, short fiction, poetry" avg. press run 3M-5M. Expects 1 title 1991, 4 titles 1992. avg. price, cloth: $14.95; paper: $10.00; other: $1 broadsides unsigned, $10 signed. Discounts: 20% library jobber. 150pp; 5×8; silkscreen. Reporting time: 2 weeks on queries, 4-6 weeks on mss. Payment: varies, but usually small advance and 10% royalty. Copyrights for author. COSMEP, NW Assn. Book Pubs, ABA, PMA.

HEART BREAK HOTELVIS, Brian 'Memphis' Pea, c/o 16 Powis Road, Brighton, Sussex BN7 3HJ, England. 1991. circ. 1M. 4/yr. Expects 4 issues 1991, 4 issues 1992. price per copy: £1; sample: free (include return envelope). 20-30pp; †of. Payment: nil. Copyrighted, reverts to author. Pub's reviews: 3 in 1990. §Elvis Presley. Ads: free small ads in classified section.

Heart of the Lakes Publishing, Walt Steesy, Owner & Partner; Mary Steesy, Owner & Partner, PO Box 299, Interlaken, NY 14847-0299, 607-532-4997. 1976. Non-fiction. "We specialize in New York local history & genealogical source materials. In house typesetting, layout, mechanicals available to help 'self-publishers'. We strive for 10+ titles per year of our own plus a few for other societies, groups, etc. Prefer advance contact to see if we are interested in reviewing manuscript." avg. press run 500-2M. Pub'd 25 titles 1990; expects 25+ titles 1991, 25+ titles 1992. 21 titles listed in the *Small Press Record of Books in Print* (20th Edition, 1991-92). avg. price, cloth: $10-$50; paper: $5-$25. Discounts: trade—see ABA Bookbuyers Handbook. 200-500pp; 6×9, 8½×11, others available; of. Payment: various. Copyrights for author.

Heart Publishing & Production, PO Box 82037, Portland, OR 97282, 503-221-3989; 800-777-5458; FAX 503-774-4457. 1 title listed in the *Small Press Record of Books in Print* (20th Edition, 1991-92).

HEARTSONG REVIEW, Wahaba Heartsun, Editor, PO Box 1084, Cottage Grove, OR 97424. 1986. Articles, art, photos, cartoons, interviews, reviews, music, letters, news items. "We are a consumer's resource guide for New Age music of the Spirit, reviewing vocal and instrumental music of all positive spiritual paths. We welcome contributions relating to consciousness expansion and music. Short articles only, on new age music, sound and consciousness. We have *very* little room for unsolicited written material - don't send it. We accept musical audio tapes of a new age spiritual orientation for review. Reviews have a specific format - do not send unsolicited reviews. News items relating to new age music, etc., are welcome, as are cartoons and art." circ. 9M. 2/yr. Pub'd 2 issues 1990; expects 2 issues 1991, 2 issues 1992. sub. price: $8; per copy: $4 includes postage; sample: same. Back issues: $2 each. Discounts: $2/copy for 5 or more, $1.80/copy for 10+, $1.50/copy for 50+. 56pp; 8×10½; of. Reporting time: 1 month. Payment: none. Copyrighted, rights revert to author on articles, not reviews. Pub's reviews: 10 in 1990. §New age music, music therapy. Ads: $350/$225/$115 1/4 page/classified: $20 for 1st 30 words, + 30¢ each add. word.

HEATHENZINE, Split Personality Press, Ken Wagner, 511 West Sullivan Street, Olean, NY 14760. 1989. Poetry, fiction, articles, art, photos, cartoons, interviews, satire, criticism, reviews, music, letters, parts-of-novels, long-poems, collages, plays, concrete art, news items, non-fiction. "A raw literary and magazine review attempting to provide an 'overview' vision of what is happening in the micropress and more." circ. 150. 6/yr. Pub'd 1 issue 1990; expects 6 issues 1991, 6 issues 1992. sub. price: $12; per copy: $2.25; sample: $2.25. 60pp; 4¼×7; †photocopier. Reporting time: 2 weeks to 3 months. Payment: 1 copy. Not copyrighted. Pub's reviews. §All small pressmaterial, especially sexual and political, and humor. Ads: $30/$20/$15 1/4 page/$10 a notice.

The Heather Foundation, Spencer H. MacCallum, Box 4, Waterford, VA 22190, 301-695-5276. 1973. Non-fiction. "The Heather Foundation is dedicated to furthering understanding of society as an evolving natural phenomenon of spontaneously patterned cooperation among freely-acting individuals. Taxation and other institutionalized coercions are viewed as evidence of insufficient development of social organization, a condition to be outgrown. The Foundation sponsors research, lectures and publications. It also preserves and administers the intellectual estates of persons who contributed notably to the humane studies. Areas of focus include philosophy of science; the inspirational aspect of religion and the aesthetic arts; monetary theory and alternative money systems; and the institution of property-in-land relative to community organization. Interested persons are invited to request the Foundation's booklist, *"Creative Alternatives in Social Thought."* Write to The Heather Foundation" avg. press run 2M. Pub'd 1 title 1990; expects 1 title 1991, 1 title 1992. avg. price, cloth: $12.50; paper: $7. Discounts: universal schedule. 175pp; 6×9; of. Reporting time: 30 days. Copyrights for author.

HEAVEN BONE, Steven Hirsch, Donna Hirsch, Gordon Kirpal, Contributing Editor, PO Box 486, Chester, NY 10918, (914) 469-9018. 1986. Poetry, fiction, articles, art, photos, cartoons, interviews, satire, criticism, reviews, letters, parts-of-novels, long-poems, collages, non-fiction. "Recent contributors: Kirpal Gordon, David Memmott, Stephen-Paul Martin, Richard Paul Schmonsees, Fielding Dawson, Jack Collom. We love poems of transcendant spiritual ecstasy deeply rooted in nature, revelation and awakening to self, psychic insight, channelled wisdom, occult ritual (NO Satanism). Deep thought *can* be linked to a direct heart experience. I want to read poems that Ralph Waldo Emerson would have written in the eighties had he been a better poet than he was. Editor loves work of Rilke. "Where are his followers?" Nothing turns us off more than artificially forced end-line rhyming; however, rhymed verse will be considered if obviously excellent and showing careful work. We would like to see more short stories and essays on various literary and esoteric topics. Reviews also being considered, but query first. SASE please." circ. 1M. 2/yr. Pub'd 2 issues 1990; expects 2 issues 1991, 2 issues 1992. sub. price: $14.95/4 issues; per copy: $5; sample: $5. Discounts: 40% to bookstores, 55% to distributors. 48-70pp; 8½×11; desktop image-set, offset (saddle stapled). Reporting time: 1 week to 6 months. Payment: 2 free copies, 30% off additional copies. Copyrighted, reverts to author. Pub's reviews: 7 in 1990. §Psychic, occult, crystals, magic, transformational philosophy, poetry, fiction. Ads: $175/$125/$75 1/4 page. COSMEP.

Heavy Bro Publishing Company, Jack Tyler, 2021 L Street NW, Suite 250, Washington, DC 20036, 202-966-4276. 1988. Cartoons, satire, non-fiction. "Heavy Bro Publishing Company illustrated humor books and 'how-to' humor books" avg. press run 20M. Pub'd 2 titles 1990; expects 2 titles 1991, 4 titles 1992. 2 titles listed in the *Small Press Record of Books in Print* (20th Edition, 1991-92). avg. price, paper: $7.95-$9.95. Discounts: wholesalers 1-4 books 50%, 5-9 51%, 10-24 52%, 25-99 55%, 100-249 56%, 250-999 57%, 1000+ 58%. 128-160pp; 8½×9; typesetting. Reporting time: 30 days. Payment: to be negotiated, generally industry rates apply. Copyrights for author. ABA, PMA, Washington Bookbuilders.

HECATE, Hecate Press, Carole Ferrier, Editor, P.O. Box 99, St. Lucia, Queensland 4067, Australia. 1975. Poetry, fiction, articles, art, criticism, plays. "Articles on historical, sociological, literary, etc. topics. Aspects of women's oppression and resistance. Some interviews and reviews. Some creative writing. Please make all payments in equivalent in Australian currency if possible" circ. 2M. 2/yr. Pub'd 2 issues 1990; expects 4 issues 1991, 2 issues 1992. sub. price: $10/yr (ind), $25 (inst), please pay in Australian $; per copy: $4 (Ind); $10 (Inst); sample: $4 (ind); $7.50 (inst). Back issues: $8 volume (Ind); $15 (Inst). Discounts: 33% for bookshops. 112pp; 4×6½. Reporting time: varies. Payment: $5 page. Copyrighted. Pub's reviews: 15 in 1990. §Socialist, feminist. Ads: negotiable, exchange.

Hecate Press (see also HECATE), C. Ferrier, PO Box 99, St. Lucia, QLD 4067, Australia. 1975. avg. press run 2.5M. Pub'd 2 titles 1990; expects 2 titles 1991, 2 titles 1992. 3 titles listed in the *Small Press Record of Books in Print* (20th Edition, 1991-92). avg. price, paper: $5. Discounts: 33⅓% for bookshops. 112pp; 4×6½; of. Reporting time: varies. Payment: $5 page. Copyrights for author.

The Hegeler Institute (see also THE MONIST: An International Quarterly Journal of General Philosophical Inquiry.), John Hospers, Editor; Sherwood Sugden, Managing Editor, Box 600, La Salle, IL 61301, 815-223-1231. 1888. "Papers on metaphysics, epistemology, ethics, aesthetics. Write editor for topics (which are stated in advance.) Books in the Series: *Monist Library of Philosophy*." avg. press run 2M. Pub'd 4 titles 1990; expects 5 titles 1991, 5 titles 1992. 2 titles listed in the *Small Press Record of Books in Print* (20th Edition, 1991-92). avg. price, cloth: $29.95; paper: $9.95; other: $4.95 monographs. Discounts: 20% to agencies, 25% to bookstores. 160pp for quarterly, 360pp per Monist Library Book; 6×9; typeset, of. Reporting time: 3-4 months. Payment: reprints. APA.

Heidelberg Graphics, Larry S. Jackson, 1116D Wendy Way, Chico, CA 95926, 916-342-6582. 1972. "Heidelberg Graphics publishes manuscripts by invitation only. For all others we offer complete services for self-publishing. We seek manuscripts for nonfiction books. Recent titles include *The Middle Aged Princess and the Frog* (Alison Zier), *Focus 101* (LaVerne Harrell Clark), *The Face of Poetry* (ed. by Clark and Mary MacArthur), *Back in Town* (ed. by Susan Bent), *After the War* by H.R. Coursen, *Greyhounding This America* by Maurice Kenny, and our annual *Year of the Native American* calendar" avg. press run 600-6M. Pub'd 2 titles 1990; expects 2 titles 1991, 2 titles 1992. 8 titles listed in the *Small Press Record of Books in Print* (20th Edition, 1991-92). avg. price, cloth: $13.95; paper: $8.50; other: $8. Discounts: write for prices, wholesale, retail, distributor's. 200pp; 6×9; of, lp. Reporting time: 8-16 weeks. Payment: negotiable. Does not copyright for author. COSMEP, CCLM, SCCIPHC, GATF.

Heirloom Publications, Elizabeth Strayer, 4340 Hideaway Lane, PO Box 183, Mills, WY 82644, 307-235-3561. 1984. Poetry, art, photos, music, parts-of-novels. "We also offer professional writing and consulting services" avg. press run 1M. Pub'd 3 titles 1990; expects 3 titles 1991, 3 titles 1992. 4 titles listed in the *Small Press Record of Books in Print* (20th Edition, 1991-92). avg. price, cloth: $29; paper: $12. Discounts: 2-4 20%, 5-24 40%, 25-49 43%, 50-99 46%, 100+ 50%. 100pp; size varies; of, lp. Reporting time: 2-3 weeks. Payment: none. Copyrights for author.

Helicon Nine Editions, Gloria Vando Hickok, Editor-in-Chief, Box 22412, Kansas City, MO 64113, 913-722-2999. 1977. Poetry, fiction. "We are publishing high quality small volumes of fiction, poetry and/or essays" avg. press run 1M. Pub'd 1 title 1990; expects 3 titles 1991, 5 titles 1992. 1 title listed in the *Small Press Record of Books in Print* (20th Edition, 1991-92). avg. price, paper: varies. Discounts: 60/40 bookstores, distributors-negotiable. Pages vary; size varies; of. Payment: varies with individual writers. Copyrights for author. CLMP, COSMEP.

Helikon Press, Robin Prising, William Leo Coakley, 120 West 71st Street, New York City, NY 10023. 1972.

248

Poetry, art, long-poems. "We try to publish the most vital contemporary poetry in the tradition of English verse—using the work of the finest artists, designers, and printers and the best materials possible. We cannot now encourage submissions—we read a wide variety of magazines and ask poets to build a collection around particular poems we have selected. We hope to continue without government subsidy. Poets: Helen Adam, George Barker, Thom Gunn, John Heath-Stubbs, and Michael Miller." avg. press run 100 for limited editions, 500 for 1st printing of trade editions. Pub'd 1 title 1990; expects 1 title 1992. 4 titles listed in the *Small Press Record of Books in Print* (20th Edition, 1991-92). avg. price, cloth: $10-$20; paper: $5; other: limited eds. $20. Discount to the book trade: 30% for limited editions and 1-4 of trade edition; 40% for 5 or more of trade edition. 16pp limited editions, 60pp trade edition; no standard size (each book is designed to suit the particular poems & poet); of, lp. Reporting time: 2 weeks. Payment: yes. Copyrights for author.

Helios House, Ariel Tomioka, Ron Turner, 4905 Foster Way, PO Box 864, Carmichael, CA 95609-0864, 916-485-9588. 1988. Fiction, non-fiction. "We publish spiritually-oriented fiction and non-fiction. First title was *On the Breath of the Gods* by Ariel Tomioka. We will be publishing more titles by Ms. Tomioka and are reviewing manuscripts at present by others writing in a similar vein." avg. press run 4M. Pub'd 2 titles 1990; expects 3 titles 1991, 3 titles 1992. 4 titles listed in the *Small Press Record of Books in Print* (1991-92). avg. price, paper: $9.95. Discounts: bookstores 40%, jobbers 30%, distributors 55%. 240pp; 5½x8½; web. Reporting time: 1 month. Payment: 8% of cover price first 3,000 sold, 10% thereafter. Copyrights if author requests. NAPRA, PMA.

Helix Press, Aubrey R. McKinney, 4410 Hickey, Corpus Christi, TX 78413, 512-852-8834. 1984. Non-fiction. "Will consider limited no. manuscripts. Send inquiry/outline before submission" avg. press run 5M-10M. Pub'd 1 title 1990; expects 2 titles 1991, 4 titles 1992. 4 titles listed in the *Small Press Record of Books in Print* (20th Edition, 1991-92). avg. price, cloth: $25; paper: $19.95. Discounts: on request. 250pp; 6x9; of. Reporting time: 3 months. Payment: by arrangement. Copyrights for author. COSMEP.

Hellas (see also HELLAS: A Journal of Poetry & the Humanities), Gerald Harnett, Erika Harnett, 304 South Tyson Avenue, Glenside, PA 19038. 1988. Poetry. "See the entry for *Hellas*, the quarterly." avg. press run 2M. Expects 1 title 1991, 2 titles 1992. 1 title listed in the *Small Press Record of Books in Print* (20th Edition, 1991-92). avg. price, cloth: $10.95; paper: $6.95. Discounts: 10 or more 40%. 65-85pp; 6x9; of. Reporting time: 2 months. Payment: variable. Copyrights for author.

HELLAS: A Journal of Poetry & the Humanities, Hellas, Gerald Harnett, Erika Harnett, 304 South Tyson Avenue, Glenside, PA 19038, 215-884-1086. 1988. Poetry, articles, art, interviews, criticism, reviews, music, letters. "*Hellas* is a lively and provocative assault on a century of modernist barbarism in the arts. A unique, Miltonic wedding of *paideia* and *poiesis*, engaging scholarship and original poetry, *Hellas* has become the forum of a remarkable new generation of poets, critics and theorists dedicated to the renovation of the art of our time. We welcome: elegant verse, especially metrical, which avoids obscurantism and prosaism; essays on ancient, Renaissance and modern poetry, and on literatures of other eras and traditions, particularly relating to the role of classicism and Hellenism in literary history; short (1000-2000 words) essays for our 'ARS POETICA' section on such technical matters as meter and diction, particularly as they relate to the 'New Formalism'; and short, highly literate and entertaining essays on any subject for our 'Divertimenti' section." 2/yr. Expects 2-4 issues 1992. sub. price: $12; per copy: $6.50; sample: $7.75 postpaid. 170pp; 6x9; of. Reporting time: 6-8 weeks. Payment: copies. Copyrighted, reverts to author. Pub's reviews. §Poetry, criticism. Ads: by exchange.

HELTER SKELTER, Anthony Boyd, 979 Golf Course Drive, Suite 223, Rohnert Park, CA 94928, 408-624-7066. 1987. Poetry, fiction, art, photos, cartoons, interviews, reviews, music, letters. "This press also publishes broadsheets and an occasional pocketbook. A four year subscription is $10 and includes everything we print up. Recent contributors have been Cheryl Townsend, Susan Dodrill, and Steve Jackson. Each author is given a page to 'showcase' their stuff—a photo, a biography, and usually a couple poems." circ. 400. 1/yr. Pub'd 1 issue 1990; expects 1 issue 1991, 1 issue 1992. sub. price: $10/4 years; per copy: $2; sample: $2. Back issues: none available. Discounts: do trade issues for other presses' issue. 10pp; 8½x11; †photocopier. Reporting time: 1-2 weeks. Payment: 2 copies. Copyrighted, reverts to author. Pub's reviews: 5 in 1990. §Poetry, general interest, music, fiction, short story. Ads: $50/$25.

HEMLOCK QUARTERLY, Hemlock Society, Derek Humphry, PO Box 11830, Eugene, OR 97440. 1980. Non-fiction. "Only articles on voluntary euthanasia are used. Will consider thoughtful submissions." circ. 50M. 4/yr. Pub'd 4 issues 1990; expects 4 issues 1991, 4 issues 1992. sub. price: $20; sample: free. Back issues: first 14 newsletters, bound, $10. Discounts: none. 16pp; 8½x11; web offset. Reporting time: 3 weeks. Payment: none, a non-profit educational group. Not copyrighted. Pub's reviews: 6 in 1990. §Voluntary euthanasia, suicide. No ads. PMA, ABA.

Hemlock Society (see also HEMLOCK QUARTERLY), Derek Humphry, PO Box 11830, Eugene, OR 97440. 1980. Non-fiction. "Magazine is concerned exclusively with right-to-die issues, particularly active voluntary euthanasia for the terminally ill or seriously incurable ill. *Hemlock* has published *Let Me Die Before I Wake*, a guidebook to self-deliverance, and *Assisted Suicide: The Compassionate Crime*. The *Hemlock Society* is a non-profit corporation seeking to raise public, medical, and legal consciousness about euthanasia." avg. press run 10M. Pub'd 1 title 1990; expects 2 titles 1991, 1 title 1992. 7 titles listed in the *Small Press Record of Books in Print* (20th Edition, 1991-92). avg. price, paper: $10; other: $3 saddleback. Discounts: usual trade discounts, distribution by Carol Publishing, Secaucus, New Jersey. 180pp; 5½×8½; 1p. Reporting time: 1 month. Payment: by mutual agreement. Copyrights for author. PMA, ABA.

HEMLOCKS AND BALSAMS, Allen Speer, Box 128, Lees-McRae College, Banner Elk, NC 28604, 704-898-4284. 1980. Poetry, fiction, art, interviews, criticism, reviews, non-fiction. circ. 500. 1/yr. Pub'd 1 issue 1990; expects 1 issue 1991, 1 issue 1992. sub. price: $3; per copy: $3; sample: $3. Back issues: $1.50. 50-60pp; 6×9; of. Payment: none. Copyrighted, reverts to author. Pub's reviews: 2 in 1990. §Fiction, poetry, Appalachian studies, southern literature. COSMEP.

HENNEPIN COUNTY LIBRARY CATALOGING BULLETIN, 12601 Ridgedale Drive, Secretary, Technical Services Division, Hennepin County Library, Minnetonka, MN 55343-5648, 612-541-8562. 1973. "Purpose of publication: to announce changes in the Hennepin County Library Catalog (e.g., new or altered cross-references, DDC-numbers, and subject descriptors, citing authorities, precedents, & applications)." circ. 200. 6/yr. Pub'd 6 issues 1990; expects 6 issues 1991, 6 issues 1992. sub. price: $6 indiv., $12 instit.; per copy: $2; sample: free. Back issues: #99-109 (1989-90) still $1.50 each. Discounts: none. 30+pp; 8½×11; †of. Copyrighted. No ads.

Herald Press, S. David Garber, Book Editor; Michael A. King, Book Editor, 616 Walnut Avenue, Scottdale, PA 15683, 412-887-8500. 1941. Fiction, non-fiction. "Herald Press, which is a division of the Mennonite Publishing House, Inc. which is owned by the Mennonite Church, each year releases a wide variety of new books for adults, young people, and children (primarily for ages 9 and up). We invite book proposals from Christian authors in the areas of current issues, peace and justice, missions and evangelism, family life, personal experience, juvenile fiction, adult fiction, Bible study, inspiration, devotional, church history, and Christian ethics and theory." avg. press run 3.5M. Pub'd 30 titles 1990; expects 30 titles 1991, 30 titles 1992. avg. price, cloth: $14.95; paper: $9.95. Discounts: Trade, text, jobber. 160pp; 5½×8¼; †of. Reporting time: 3 months. Payment: 10% of retail price up to 25,000 copies, going to 11% for the next 25,000, and 12% thereafter. Copyrights for author. ABA, CBA, International Christian Booksellers Association.

HerBooks, Irene Reti, PO Box 7467, Santa Cruz, CA 95061. 1984. Poetry, fiction, articles, art, photos, cartoons, interviews, satire, letters, parts-of-novels, long-poems, non-fiction. "Primarily lesbian press, will not consider work by men. Our purpose is to publish radical, unassimilated, strong lesbian and feminist books." avg. press run 1.5M. Pub'd 2 titles 1990; expects 2 titles 1991, 2 titles 1992. 11 titles listed in the *Small Press Record of Books in Print* (20th Edition, 1991-92). avg. price, paper: $7. Discounts: 40% to bookstores, no minimum order; 40% to contributors. 100pp; 5½×8½; of. Reporting time: 1 month. Payment: negotiable, primarily co-publishing. Copyrights for author.

HERESIES: A FEMINIST PUBLICATION ON ART AND POLITICS, Collectively edited, Box 1306, Canal St. Station, New York, NY 10013, 212-227-2108. 1976. Poetry, fiction, articles, art, photos, cartoons, interviews, satire, criticism, music, letters, parts-of-novels, long-poems, collages, plays, concrete art. "Send SASE for brochure and/or guidelines to contributors; *all issues are thematic. Submissions are welcome but often returned unless marked specifically for a certain issue.* #15 *Racism Is The Issue*: 'Since racism comes up everywhere, every day, in all kinds of situations, [this issue can be] used and discussed by everyone, everywhere' (Issue Editorial). #16 *Media: Film & Video*: close focus on media images and feminist filmmakers and video artists. #17 *Acting Up! Women In Theater & Performance Art*: explores diverse political/cultural issues in the performing avant garde (Summer 1984). #18/19 *Mothers, Mags & Movie Stars: Feminism & Class*: the mother-daughter relationship as a vehicle to analyzing family, culture and class (Winter 1985)and *Satire*: a humorous remedy to conventional media presentations of women (Winter). #20 *Women's Activism* (1985). #21 *Food is a Feminist Issue* (Spring 87). #22 *Art 1985 Unestablished Channels* (Winter 1987), #23 *Coming of Age* (Summer 1988), #24 *12 Years*: Anniversary issue (Fall 1989). #25 *The Art of Education* (Fall 1990). Upcoming Themes: *Women on Men, Viva Latina*, and *Crime and Transgression*." circ. 8M. 2/yr. Pub'd 1 issue 1990; expects 2 issues 1991, 2 issues 1992. sub. price: $23 individuals, $33 institutions, add $6 for o'seas; per copy: $6.75 current issue; sample: $6. Back issues: $6 or 3/$15 for most. Discounts: 10 issues or more: 40%. 96pp; 8½×11; of. Reporting time: depends on process for individual issues; 6-12 months. Payment: $5-$15 so far. Copyrighted, reverts to author. Pub's reviews. Ads: on request.

Heresy Press, George Beahm, 713 Paul Street, Newport News, VA 23605, 804-380-6595. 1975. "Checklists on current fantasy artists. The first of these, *The Vaughn Bode Index*, appeared in 1975 and. The second, *Kirk's Works*, on the artist Tim Kirk, was published in Oct. 1980. These books are done in cooperation with, and annotated by, the artist involved; they are extensively illustrated, with an original color cover and photos of the artist besides examples of his work." avg. press run 2M. 2 titles listed in the *Small Press Record of Books in*

Print (20th Edition, 1991-92). avg. price, cloth: $20; paper: $9. Discounts: wholesale 40% for 10 or more, 50% for 100 or more. 90pp; 8½×11, 9×12. Copyrights for author.

Heritage Books, Inc., Laird C. Towle, 1540-E Pointer Ridge Place, Bowie, MD 20716, 301-390-7708. 1978. Non-fiction. "Subject matter of interest includes local and regional histories pertaining to eastern U.S. and source records of interest to historians and genealogists." avg. press run 200-300. Pub'd 60 titles 1990; expects 100 titles 1991, 120 titles 1992. avg. price, cloth: $30; paper: $20. Discounts: 1-5 assorted titles 20%, 6+ 40%; free shipping on both. 250pp; 5½×8½; of. Reporting time: 1 month. Payment: 10% of retail price, paid semi-annually. Does not copyright for author. PMA.

Heritage Press WI, Pat Middleton, Rt 1, 89 SPR, Stoddard, WI 54658, 608-457-2734. 1987. Non-fiction. "Comprehensive, well-researched travel guides for the Mississippi River Valley. Interest area: Mississippi River-travel, Great River Road" avg. press run 6.5M. Pub'd 1 title 1990; expects 2 titles 1991. 2 titles listed in the *Small Press Record of Books in Print* (20th Edition, 1991-92). avg. price, cloth: $10; paper: $10. Discounts: trade 40%; wholesalers 50%. 250pp; 5½×8½; lp. Reporting time: not looking for submissions. WAPA/MAP/PMA/MIP.

Heritage West Books, Sylvia Sun Minnick, 306 Regent Court, Stockton, CA 95204-4435, 209-464-8818. 1989. Non-fiction. "History, ethnography, biography" avg. press run 1M-1.5M. Pub'd 2 titles 1990; expects 3 titles 1991, 3 titles 1992. 6 titles listed in the *Small Press Record of Books in Print* (20th Edition, 1991-92). avg. price, cloth: $25; paper: $15. Discounts: trade-jobber, classroom: 2-4 20%, 5-24 40%. 6×9 to 9×13. Reporting time: 3 weeks. Payment: yes. Copyrights for author. PMA.

Hermes House Press, Inc. (see also KAIROS, A Journal of Contemporary Thought and Criticism), Richard Mandell, Alan Mandell, 52 Lanark Rd, Brookline, MA 02146-1844, 617-566-9766. 1980. Poetry, fiction, parts-of-novels, long-poems, plays. "Unsolicited manuscripts currently not being read; experimental works, translations, and artwork are encouraged; copy price, and number of pages vary. Recent work: *The Deadly Swarm*, short stories by LaVerne Harrell Clark; *The Bats*, a novel by Richard Mandell; *Three Stories*, by R.V. Cassill; *Going West*, poetry by Stanley Diamond; *Bella B.'s Fantasy*, short stories by Raymond Jean; *Crossings*, a novel by Marie Diamond. Upcoming work: *O Loma! Constituting a Self* (1977-1984), writings by sociologist Kurt H. Wolff." avg. press run 1M. Pub'd 1 title 1990; expects 3 titles 1991, 3 titles 1992. 7 titles listed in the *Small Press Record of Books in Print* (20th Edition, 1991-92). avg. price, paper: $6. Discounts: available upon request. Pages vary; 5½×8½, 4¼×7; of. Reporting time: 4-8 weeks. Payment: copies plus an agreed percentage after cost. Copyrights for author. COSMEP.

Hermetician Press, James Braha, Emmett Walz, PO Box 1961, Hollywood, FL 33022-1381, 305-922-6726. Non-fiction. "Looking for innovative astrological or occult mss. Must be practical and understandable to the reader" avg. press run 5M. Expects 2 titles 1991, 5 titles 1992. 2 titles listed in the *Small Press Record of Books in Print* (20th Edition, 1991-92). avg. price, cloth: $15; paper: $10. Discounts: 40% trade. 200-300pp; 7×10; of. Reporting time: 1-3 months. Payment: 10% average. Copyrights for author. P.W., COSMEP.

Hermitage (Ermitazh), Igor Yefimov, Marina Yefimov, PO Box 410, Tenafly, NJ 07670-0410, 201-894-8247. 1981. Poetry, fiction, articles, art, criticism, non-fiction. "We publish mostly books in Russian language or books in English dealing with Russian topics: literary criticism, history, translations from Russian, Russian culture, travel into Russia" avg. press run 1M. Pub'd 15 titles 1990; expects 15 titles 1991, 16 titles 1992. 7 titles listed in the *Small Press Record of Books in Print* (20th Edition, 1991-92). avg. price, cloth: $15; paper: $8.50. Discounts: 40% with 10 copies or more; 30% for jobbers if less than 10; no returns; no discount for libraries. 200pp; 5½×8½; of. Reporting time: 2 months. Payment: negotiable.

Heyday Books (see also NEWS FROM NATIVE CALIFORNIA), Malcolm Margolin, Box 9145, Berkeley, CA 94709, 415-549-3564. 1973. Non-fiction. "Books on California Indians, history, and natural history primarily. Also Northern California guides. Recent authors include Ivan Illich, Randall Gray Brown, Malcolm Margolin, John Steinbeck." avg. press run 5M. Pub'd 3 titles 1990; expects 5 titles 1991, 4 titles 1992. 30 titles listed in the *Small Press Record of Books in Print* (20th Edition, 1991-92). avg. price, cloth: $17.95; paper: $8.95. Discounts: 40% trade on orders of 5 copies or more. 150pp; 6×9; of. Reporting time: 3 weeks. Payment: comparable to what's offered by major publishers, in fact modeled on their contracts. Copyrights for author.

HFH Publications, Deborah Duquette, PO Box 81, LaGrande, OR 97850, 503-963-6410. 1987. Non-fiction. "Publish new material on animal husbandry." avg. press run 2.5M. Pub'd 1 title 1990; expects 1 title 1991, 1 title 1992. 1 title listed in the *Small Press Record of Books in Print* (20th Edition, 1991-92). avg. price, paper: $15. Discounts: 20%. 70pp; 6×9; of. Reporting time: 60 days. Payment: negotiable. Copyrights for author.

Hibiscus Press, Margaret Wensrich, Fiction; Joyce Odam, Poetry, P.O. Box 22248, Sacramento, CA 95822. 1972. Poetry, fiction, non-fiction. avg. press run 500-1M. Expects 1 title 1991, 2 titles 1992. 5 titles listed in the *Small Press Record of Books in Print* (20th Edition, 1991-92). avg. price, cloth: $14.95; paper: $9.95. Discounts: 40% 5+ copies. 112-144pp; 5⅜×8⅜; of. Reporting time: 2-4 months. Copyrights for author.

Hickman Systems - New Age Books, Jack Hickman, Irene Hickman, Manager, 4 Woodland Lane, Kirksville, MO 63501, 816-665-1836. 1983. Non-fiction. "We plan to republish choice out-of-print books that we feel should be preserved. 3-4 per year. Will also consider original non-fiction manuscripts" avg. press run 2.5M. Expects 1 title 1991. 4 titles listed in the *Small Press Record of Books in Print* (20th Edition, 1991-92). avg. price, cloth: $10.95; paper: $5.95-$6.95. Discounts: 1 copy 25%; 5-40%; 25-50%-or more. 200pp; 5½x8½; of. Reporting time: 1-2 months. Payment: negotiated. Copyrights for author on request.

HIDDEN SPRINGS REVIEW, Lisa Hezel, PO Box 29613, Los Angeles, CA 90029, 213-664-0007. 1985. Poetry. "Interested in poetry of all subjects, any length, rhymed or free verse. We sponsor an annual poetry contest. If interested, send for contest rules and enclose SASE" circ. 1M. 4/yr. Pub'd 2 issues 1990; expects 2 issues 1991, 4 issues 1992. sub. price: $10; per copy: $2.50; sample: $2.50. 50pp; 5½x8½; of. Reporting time: varies. Payment: 3 free copies and 1 year's subscription. Not copyrighted. Pub's reviews. §Poetry, arts and environment.

HIGH COUNTRY NEWS, Ed Marston, Publisher; Betsy Marston, Editor; C.L. Rawlins, Poetry Editor, PO Box 1090, Paonia, CO 81428, 303-527-4898. 1970. Poetry, articles, art, photos, cartoons, interviews, criticism, reviews, letters, news items. "We're after hard-hitting, but fairly-reported environmental journalism with a regional slant. We cover Montana, Wyoming, Colorado, Utah, Idaho and, occasionally, the Dakotas, and Arizona, New Mexico, Oregon and Washington. Poetry center spreads four times a year." circ. 10M. 24/yr. Pub'd 24 issues 1990; expects 24 issues 1991, 24 issues 1992. sub. price: $24 indiv., $34 instit.; per copy: $1; sample: free. Back issues: $2 single copy; bulk rates available on request. Discounts: sell in bulk to schools, libraries, organizations. 16pp; 10x16; of. Reporting time: 4 weeks. Payment: 5-10¢ per word, $10-$40 per published B & W photo. Copyrighted, reverts to author. Pub's reviews: 50 short blurbs in 1990. §Conservation, wildlife, energy, land use, and other natural resources issues. $10/inch camera ready under 4 column inches, $30/inch over 4 column inches.

HIGH PERFORMANCE, Astro Artz, Steven Durland, Editor, 1641 18th Street, Santa Monica, CA 90404-3807, 213-315-9383. 1977. Articles, art, photos, interviews, criticism, reviews. *"High Performance* is a magazine about contemporary art (performance, video, experimental theater/dance/music, multi-media). Contains news, features, interviews, profiles, reviews, criticism. Recent features and contributors: Philip Glass, Laurie Anderson, Lucinda Childs, Lewis MacAdams, Michael Ventura." circ. 25M. 4/yr. Pub'd 4 issues 1990; expects 4 issues 1991, 4 issues 1992. sub. price: $20 USA, $24 Canada, Mexico, $28 other countries ($55 air mail), $24 institutions; per copy: $6 including postage; sample: same. Back issues: $5. Discounts: 25-50%. 88pp; 8½x11; of. Reporting time: 3 months. Payment: $50-500. Copyrighted, reverts to author. Pub's reviews: 15 in 1990. §Performance art, video, records, art books, theater, dance, music. Ads: $750/$450.

HIGH PLAINS LITERARY REVIEW, Robert O. Greer, Jr., Editor-in-Chief, 180 Adams Street, Suite 250, Denver, CO 80206, (303) 320-6828. 1986. Poetry, fiction, articles, interviews, reviews, long-poems, non-fiction. "The *High Plains Literary Review* seeks to bridge the gap between academic quarterlies and commercial reviews. Prefer material 3,000-8,000 words in length." circ. 850. 3/yr. Pub'd 3 issues 1990; expects 3 issues 1991, 3 issues 1992. sub. price: $20; per copy: $7; sample: $3. Back issues: $3. Discounts: 20% to agent. 140pp; 6x9; of. Reporting time: 8 weeks. Payment: $5/page for prose, $10/page for poetry. Copyrighted, reverts to author. Pub's reviews: 9 in 1990. §Short story and poetry collections. Ads: $100/$60/$40 1/4 page. CCLM.

High Plains Press, Nancy Curtis, Box 123, Glendo, WY 82213, 307-735-4370. 1984. Poetry, non-fiction. "Specializes in Wyoming and the West." avg. press run 1M. Pub'd 4 titles 1990; expects 3 titles 1991, 2 titles 1992. 11 titles listed in the *Small Press Record of Books in Print* (20th Edition, 1991-92). avg. price, cloth: $19.95; paper: $8. Discounts: bookstores 1-4 20%, 5+ 40%. 200pp; 5½x8½; of. Reporting time: 2 months. Payment: based on material. Copyrights for author. PMA, Rocky Mtn. Publishers Assoc.

HIGH TECHNOLOGY LAW JOURNAL, University of California Press, Students of Boalt Hall School of Law, University of California Press, 2120 Berkeley Way, Berkeley, CA 94720, 415-642-4191. 1986. Articles. "Editorial address: 182 Boalt Hall School of Law, University of CA, Berkeley, Ca 94720. Copyrighted by High Technology Law Journal." circ. 800. 2/yr. Pub'd 2 issues 1990; expects 2 issues 1991, 2 issues 1992. sub. price: $45 (+ $3 foreign postage); per copy: $25 (+ $3 foreign postage); sample: free. Back issues: $25. Discounts: foreign subs. agent 10%, one-time order 10+ 30%, standing orders (bookstores): 1-99 40%, 100+ 50%. 250pp; 7x10; of. Copyrighted, does not revert to author. Pub's reviews: 8 in 1990. Ads: $200/$120.

High/Coo Press (see also MAYFLY), Randy Brooks, Shirley Brooks, 4634 Hale Dr, Decatur, IL 62526-1117, 317-567-2596. 1976. Poetry, articles, reviews, concrete art. "High/Coo Press chapbooks are published on an irregular basis by invitation only. Indiv. prices are $3.50 for chapbooks and $2.00 for mini-chapbooks (hd editions are $10.00 and $7.00 respectively). High/Coo Press publishes manuscripts of short poetry including haiku, tanka, senryu, epigrams, visual poetry, and others. Include a SASE for each submission. Sample our publications before submitting. Catalog 50¢ or first class stamp" avg. press run 350. Pub'd 2 titles 1990;

expects 2 titles 1991, 2 titles 1992. 41 titles listed in the *Small Press Record of Books in Print* (20th Edition, 1991-92). avg. price, cloth: $10; paper: $3.50 postpaid (chapbooks); other: $2 postpaid (mini-chapbooks). Discounts: 40% to authors of our titles; 40% to bookstores (minimum order 5 books). 24-48pp; 4¼×5½; †of, lp, laser. Reporting time: 2 months. Payment: copies and 15% after costs are met. Does not copyright for author.

HILL AND HOLLER, Seven Buffaloes Press, Art Cuelho, Box 249, Big Timber, MT 59011. price per copy: $6.75; sample: $6.

Hilltop Press, Robert E. Smithson, PO Box 4091, Virginia Beach, VA 23454. 1990. Interviews, non-fiction. "Unsolicited manuscripts not returned but may be read. Emphasis on religion and who's-who type books." avg. press run 1M. Expects 1 title 1991, 2 titles 1992. 1 title listed in the *Small Press Record of Books in Print* (20th Edition, 1991-92). avg. price, paper: $17.95. Discounts: College and public libraries 40%, wholesale 50%. 200pp; 5½×8½; of. Payment: individual arrangements. Does not copyright for author.

Hilton Thomas Publishers, Inc., Marshall T. Mattingly, President, 2035 Northside Drive, Atlanta, GA 30305-3927, 404-390-9546. 1987. Non-fiction. "Hilton Thomas Publishers, Inc. is a publishing company specializing in self-help educational materials for secondary school students, their parents, teachers and counselors. Products being considered for publication inclue books, audio and video tapes, and related items." avg. press run 5M. Pub'd 1 title 1990; expects 5 titles 1991, 11 titles 1992. 1 title listed in the *Small Press Record of Books in Print* (20th Edition, 1991-92). avg. price, cloth: $8.95; paper: $7.95. Discounts: 1-2 books 20%, 3-9 30%, 10-49 40%, 50-99 42%, 100-299 44%, 300-499 46%, 500-999 48%, 1000+ 50%. 40pp; 8½×11; of. Reporting time: 2-3 weeks. Payment: negotiated royalty, will consider buyout. Copyrights for author.

Himalayan Publishers, Rudolph Ballentine, M.D., Director; Lawrence Clark, Editor, RD 1, Box 400, Honesdale, PA 18431, 717-253-5551. 1971. Non-fiction. "*The Himalayan Publishers* has long been regarded as "The Resource for Holistic Living" by providing bestselling perennials on yoga, meditation, psychology, diet, exercise, preventive medicine, holistic health, and self-develoment. We believe that every person has the power to improve his life. Self-awareness and self-directed change is the theme of our publications. We believe the complex problems of modern life can be solved in natural ways. Our books provide unique synthesis of Eastern and Western disciplines, offering practical methods of living that foster inner balance and outer harmony. Our approach addresses the whole person—body, mind, and spirit—integrating the latest scientific knowledge with ancient healing and self-development techniques. Thus our publications, in addition to making sound holistic health principles and practices available to the public, are designed to help build a bridge between the timeless truths of the East and the modern discoveries of the West, and are meant to aid in the integration of science and spirituality" avg. press run 10M. Pub'd 4 titles 1990; expects 5 titles 1991, 5 titles 1992. 51 titles listed in the *Small Press Record of Books in Print* (20th Edition, 1991-92). avg. price, cloth: $19.95; paper: $8.95. Discounts: conventional trade. 250pp; 8½×5½; †of. Reporting time: 3 months. Payment: individual. Copyrights for author.

HIPPO, Karl Heiss, Chautauqua Press, 28834 Boniface Drive, Malibu, CA 90265-4206. 1988. Poetry, fiction, articles, art, satire. "3,000 words maximum. Focusing mainly upon fiction of any type imaginable. Would like to include anecdotal, semi-narrative, essays of a humanitarian and philosophical nature (nothing stuffy). All art must be uniquely compatible to the 'Xerox' medium. Letters, exchanges, and advertisements are welcome" circ. 150. 2/yr. Expects 2 issues 1991, 2 issues 1992. sub. price: $6, foreign add 50¢; per copy: $3.50, foreign add 50¢; sample: $3.50, foreign add 50¢. Back issues: #1, #2, #5 $2.50 each, #3 + #4 $4 each. Discounts: available for $3/copy in orders of five or more (sent book rate). 40-50pp; 5½×8½; xerox, innertube stamp. Reporting time: twice yearly; 'reading vacations' create delays up to, but not more than, 6 months. Payment: copy. Copyrighted, reverts to author. Ads: $10/$6/query on ad exchanges.

Hippopotamus Press (see also OUTPOSTS POETRY QUARTERLY), Roland John, B.A. Martin, Business Manager; Mansell Pargitter, S22, Whitewell Road, Frome, Somerset BA11 4EL, England, 0373-66653. 1974. Poetry, long-poems. "Size, number of pages, cost will vary with the material. Against: concrete, typewriter, neo-surrealism and experimental work. For: competent poetry in recognisable English, a knowledge of syntax and construction, finished work and not glimpses into the workshop, also translations. Recent pamphlets and books include G.S. Sharat Chandra (U.S.A.), Edward Lowbury (Canada), Stan Trevor (S. Africa) Shaun McCarthy, Peter Dale, William Bedford, Humphrey Clucas, Debjani Chatterjee, Peter Dent." avg. press run 750 paper, 250 cloth. Pub'd 3 titles 1990; expects 7 titles 1991. 18 titles listed in the *Small Press Record of Books in Print* (20th Edition, 1991-92). avg. price, cloth: £12, $24; paper: £6, $12. Discounts: 35% off singles, 45% off bulk orders. 80pp; size varies; of, lp. Reporting time: 1 month. Payment: by arrangement/royalty. Standard UK copyright, remaining with author. ALP, Password (Books) Ltd.

HIRAM POETRY REVIEW, Hale Chatfield, Carol Donley, Box 162, Hiram, OH 44234, 216-569-5331. 1967. Poetry, articles, art, photos, interviews, satire, criticism, reviews, letters, long-poems, collages, plays, concrete art. "We seek to discover new poets. Except for special features, ALL poems in HPR are selected from manuscripts submitted without specific invitation. (Reviews, plays, fiction, and supplements are by invitation only. Carbon, ditto, mimeograph, and electrostastic copies will not be read)" circ. 500. 2/yr. Pub'd 2 issues 1990; expects 2 issues 1991, 2 issues 1992. sub. price: $4, $10 for 3 yrs; per copy: $2; sample: free. Back issues: No. 1 unavail.; others vary; send for info. Discounts: 60-40 to subscription agencies; 60-40 to retail bookstores. 52pp; 9×6; of. Reporting time: 8-16 weeks. Payment: 2 copies plus 1 year subscription. Copyrighted, rights revert to author by request. Pub's reviews: 3 in 1990. §Poetry, books, some little magazines. No ads. CCLM, COSMEP.

Historical Society of Alberta (see also ALBERTA HISTORY), Hugh A. Dempsey, 95 Holmwood Ave. NW, Calgary, Alberta T2K 2G7, Canada. 1907. avg. press run 2.2M. Pub'd 1 title 1990; expects 1 title 1991, 1 title 1992. 7 titles listed in the *Small Press Record of Books in Print* (20th Edition, 1991-92). avg. price, paper: $4. Discounts: 33%. 32pp; 7×10; of. Reporting time: 3 months. Payment: none. Does not copyright for author.

HISTORICAL STUDIES IN THE PHYSICAL & BIOLOGICAL SCIENCES, University of California Press, J.L. Heilbron, University of California Press, 2120 Berkeley Way, Berkeley, CA 94720, 415-642-4191. 1970. Non-fiction. "Editorial address: Office for History of Science & Technology, 470 Stephens Hall, Univ. of CA, Berkeley, CA 94720." circ. 800. 2/yr. Pub'd 2 issues 1990; expects 2 issues 1991, 2 issues 1992. sub. price: $20 indiv., $36 instit. (+ $3 foreign postage); per copy: $10 indiv.; $18 instit. (+ $3 foreign postage); sample: free. Back issues: $10 indiv., $18 instit. Discounts: foreign subs. agent 10%, one-time orders 10+ 30%, standing orders (bookstores): 1-99 40%, 100+ 50%. 200pp; 6×9; of. Reporting time: 1-2 months. Copyrighted, does not revert to author. Ads: $200/$120.

HISTORY NEWS, AASLH Press, Joy B. Dunn, 172 Second Avenue N., Suite 102, Nashville, TN 37201, (615) 255-2971. 1941. Articles, reviews. *"History News* welcomes articles of interest to readers who work at historic sites, history museums, or educational agencies that advance knowledge, understanding, and appreciation of state, local, and regional history in the United States and Canada. We favor articles that tell how better to manage and administer such institutions and thus to serve the public. We cannot consider work that is primarily about historical events or persons" circ. 6.2M. 6/yr. Pub'd 6 issues 1990; expects 6 issues 1991, 6 issues 1992. sub. price: $40; per copy: $4. 36pp; 8⅜×10-13/16; of. Reporting time: 2 months. Payment: 3-5 copies. Copyrighted, does not revert to author. Pub's reviews: 16 in 1990. §"How-to" books telling history agency administrators how to do their jobs better, and general interest to state and local history fields. Ads: $750/$550/available in 1-time, 3-times, 6-times discount.

History West Publishing Company, PO Box 612066, San Jose, CA 95161, 408-259-8060. 2 titles listed in the *Small Press Record of Books in Print* (20th Edition, 1991-92). Discounts: 40% trade discount 1-99; 50% on 100 or more.

HMS Press, Wayne Ray, Box 340, Station B, London, Ont. N6A 4W1, Canada, 519-434-4740. 1983. Poetry, fiction, articles. avg. press run 400. Pub'd 4 titles 1990. 32 titles listed in the *Small Press Record of Books in Print* (20th Edition, 1991-92). avg. price, paper: $3.95/$8.95. 32pp; 5×7, 8×10; of. Reporting time: 30 days. Payment: 10%. SPAN (Small Press Action Network), SOWESTO (SouthWEST Ontario Publishers Assn.).

W.D. Hoard & Sons Company (see also HOARD'S DAIRYMAN), Elvira Kau, Book Editor, 28 Milwaukee Avenue West, Fort Atkinson, WI 53538, 414-563-5551. 1870. Articles, non-fiction. avg. press run 4M. Pub'd 3 titles 1990; expects 4 titles 1991, 3 titles 1992. 13 titles listed in the *Small Press Record of Books in Print* (20th Edition, 1991-92). avg. price, paper: $3; other: $20. Discounts: college bookstore 20%, other retail 40%. 100pp; 8¼×10½, 6×9; †of. Payment: varies. Does not copyright for author. COSMEP, PMA, WAPA.

HOARD'S DAIRYMAN, W.D. Hoard & Sons Company, Ewing Row, 28 Milwaukee Avenue West, Fort Atkinson, WI 53538, 414-563-5551. 1885. Articles, photos, cartoons, interviews, letters, news items, non-fiction. circ. 130M. 20/yr. Pub'd 20 issues 1990; expects 20 issues 1991, 20 issues 1992. sub. price: $10. Back issues: $1. 50pp; 10¼×14¼; †of. Payment: varies. Copyrighted, does not revert to author. Ads: $9100/$4550.

HOBBY BOOKWATCH (MILITARY, GUN & HOBBY BOOK REVIEW), Jack Britton, PO Box 52033, Tulsa, OK 74152, 918-743-7048. 1984. "Book reviews on all type military - i.e.: medals, decorations, insignia, patches, etc., history & science. Gun collecting, gun values, shooting, etc. All hobbies from art to zeppelin." circ. 10M+. 6/yr. Expects 6 issues 1991, 6 issues 1992. sub. price: $2; per copy: $1; sample: $1. Back issues: none. Discounts: none. 16pp; 8½×11; †of. Copyrighted. Pub's reviews: 200 in 1990. §Military, Gun & Hobby. Ads: $500/$300/1/4 = $180/1/8 = $100.

HOB-NOB, Mildred K. Henderson, 994 Nissley Road, Lancaster, PA 17601. 1969. Poetry, fiction, articles, art, cartoons, satire, criticism, reviews, letters, parts-of-novels, long-poems, news items, non-fiction. "Published Spring-Summer and Fall-Winter. Prose, poetry, reviews, letters, features. Usual maximum, 2M words. No new material accepted between 3/1 and 9/1. *No risque material.* Material from new contributors will be accepted *only during January and February*. No space available for new contributors till 1993" circ. 450-500. 2/yr. Pub'd 2 issues 1990; expects 2 issues 1991, 2 issues 1992. sub. price: $5; per copy: $3.50; sample: $3.

254

Discounts: $3 to libraries only. 60+pp; 8½×11; of. Reporting time: up to several months, less for rejections. Payment: free copy, first appearance only. Copyrighted, reverts to author. Pub's reviews: 6 (plus 3 reviews sent by contributors) in 1990. §Poetry, short fiction or non-fiction. No novels. Ads: $3.50 per paragraph (includes checking copy).

HOBO JUNGLE, Marc Erdrich, Ruth Boerger, Rucum Road, Roxbury, CT 06783, 203-354-4359. 1987. Poetry, fiction, art, cartoons, satire, music, parts-of-novels, long-poems, plays, non-fiction. "We serialize novels. We publish original music scores, line art" circ. 11M. 4/yr. Pub'd 2 issues 1990; expects 4 issues 1991, 4 issues 1992. sub. price: $12 (Free where available: New York City, and Connecticut); per copy: free; sample: $3 (for p/h). Back issues: $3 (for p/h). 64pp; 8×10½; of. Reporting time: 12-14 weeks. Payment: $10 honorarium. Copyrighted, reverts to author. Ads: $217 1/2 page/$115 1/4 page/$80 1/6 page/$61 1/8 page/no full page ads available. CLMP.

HOBO STEW REVIEW, Hobo Stew, 2 Eliot Street #1, Somerville, MA 02143. 1984. Poetry, fiction, articles, art, cartoons, satire, letters, collages, non-fiction. "Try tackling the heavy issues of the day; then try taking a nap. Fly a kite. Remember a really good cry and smile with the pain. Roll to the left and hold your breath. But keep at something. Hobo does *HSR* for the fun of it; and sometimes he does not appreciate a particular approach to funning. He will tell you so. Do not burst a blood vessel; merely look toward the thousands of other places that you might share your thoughts with. Keep it honest and keep at it." circ. 45. 4/yr. Pub'd 4 issues 1990; expects 4 issues 1991, 4 issues 1992. sub. price: $5; per copy: $2; sample: $2. Back issues: negotiable. 10pp; 8½×11; †photocopy. Reporting time: 2-4 weeks. Payment: 1 copy. Not copyrighted. Pub's reviews: 2 in 1990. §Currently receive magazines in trade—this seems to work well. Ads: none.

Hoffman Press, Robert P. Hoffman, Co-Editor; Virginia M. Hoffman, Co-Editor, PO Box 2996, Santa Rosa, CA 95405-0996, 707-538-5527. 1989. Articles, satire, criticism, non-fiction. "Primarily 'how-to' such as cookbooks, medicine/health" avg. press run 3M. Pub'd 2 titles 1990; expects 4 titles 1991, 7 titles 1992. 1 title listed in the *Small Press Record of Books in Print* (20th Edition, 1991-92). avg. price, paper: $12.95. Discounts: 50% to retailer, less 20% of wholesale to rep or distributor. 200pp; 7×10; of. Reporting time: a week or 2. Payment: royalty paid upon publication, advances in special situations. Copyrights for author.

Hohm Press, Anthony Zuccarello, Debra Hogeland, PO Box 2501, Prescott, AZ 86302, 602-778-9189. 1975. Poetry, satire, criticism, non-fiction. avg. press run 10M. Pub'd 2 titles 1990; expects 1 title 1991, 3 titles 1992. 16 titles listed in the *Small Press Record of Books in Print* (20th Edition, 1991-92). avg. price, paper: $9.95. Discounts: standard, 40% trade; distributors inquiry welcomed. 150pp; 5½×8½. Payment: upon request. Copyrights for author. Rocky Mountain Publishers Group.

Holistic Education Press (see also HOLISTIC EDUCATION REVIEW), Ron Miller, 39 Pearl Street, Brandon, VT 05733-1007, 802-247-8312. 1988. Articles, photos, reviews. "Topics relating to holistic education." avg. press run 3M. Expects 2 titles 1991, 2 titles 1992. avg. price, paper: $21. 300pp; 6×9; of. Reporting time: 4 months. Payment: variable.

HOLISTIC EDUCATION REVIEW, Holistic Education Press, Ron Miller, 39 Pearl Street, Brandon, VT 05733-1007, 802-247-8312. 1988. Articles, photos, interviews, reviews. "Interested in articles on holistic education, learning styles, global education, whole language, etc." circ. 2M. 4/yr. Pub'd 4 issues 1990; expects 4 issues 1991, 4 issues 1992. sub. price: $40 instit., $26 indiv.; per copy: $7.50. Discounts: 10%. 72pp; 8½×11; of. Reporting time: 3 months. Payment: none. Copyrighted. Pub's reviews: 12 in 1990. §Holistic education, learning styles, global education, whole language, etc.

THE HOLLINS CRITIC, John Rees Moore, P.O. Box 9538, Hollins College, VA 24020. 1964. Poetry, criticism, reviews. "Essay on particular work of one author; several poems. Essay approximately 5000 words, no footnotes. No unsolicited essay mss. Essays by prior commitment only. Short poems are published in every issue. Other features are a front picture of the author under discussion, a checklist of author's writing and a brief sketch of career, plus book reviews. Recent essayists: Mark Royal Winchell, James Robert Saunders, Henry Taylor, Michael Pearson, and Ed Weyhing." circ. 490. 5/yr. Pub'd 5 issues 1990; expects 5 issues 1991, 5 issues 1992. sub. price: $6 U.S.; per copy: $2 U.S.; sample: $2 U.S. Back issues: $2 U.S.; ($3 elsewhere). 20pp; 7½×10; lp. Payment: $25 for poems. Copyrighted, does not revert to author. Pub's reviews: 25 in 1990. §Mainly current fiction and poetry. CCLM, COSMEP.

THE HOLLYWOOD ACTING COACHES AND TEACHERS DIRECTORY, Acting World Books, Lawrence Parke, PO Box 3044, Hollywood, CA 90078, 213-466-4297. 1981. "Occasional articles by and or about subject material people, orgns, currently recommended procedures, etc" circ. 1.2M. 4/yr. Pub'd 4 issues 1990; expects 4 issues 1991, 4 issues 1992. No subscriptions available; price per copy: $12.50. Back issues: not available. Discounts: none except to bookstores (40%). 55pp; 8½×11; †of. Copyrighted, reverts to author. Ads: $400 1/2 page/special 6 months in both pub's, rate $800. COSMEP.

Hollywood Film Archive, D. Richard Baer, Editor, 8344 Melrose Ave., Hollywood, CA 90069, 213-933-3345.

1972. "HFA compiles and publishes film reference information. In addition to our own books, we are interested in high-quality comprehensive reference information on film or television. Please inquire before submitting material. Those submitting unsolicited material must include a self-addressed stamped envelope in order to have it returned. Our Cinema Book Society book club considers books of other publishers for sale to members, libraries, the film and TV industries, and the general public. We distribute motion picture reference books for other publishers, including the complete reprint of *Variety Film Reviews 1907-1990*, *Variety Obituaries 1905-1990*, and *Variety Television Reviews 1923-1988*" avg. press run 5M. Expects 7 titles 1991, 8 titles 1992. 3 titles listed in the *Small Press Record of Books in Print* (20th Edition, 1991-92). avg. price, cloth: $95; paper: $19. Discounts: 1-4 copies, 20% to bona fide booksellers, wholesalers, jobbers, etc., 5 or more 40%; large quantities, inquire. 8½x11; of. Reporting time: 3-4 weeks.

Holmgangers Press, Gary Elder, Editor; Jeane Elder, Editor, 95 Carson Court Shelter Cove, Whitethorn, CA 95489, 707-986-7700. 1974. Poetry, fiction, long-poems, plays. "We are no longer considering unsolicited ms." avg. press run 500. Pub'd 2 titles 1990; expects 2 titles 1991, 3 titles 1992. 47 titles listed in the *Small Press Record of Books in Print* (20th Edition, 1991-92). avg. price, paper: $3.95. Discounts: 1-4 20%; 5+ 40% off; pre-paid orders shipped post-free. 36pp; 5½x8½; of. Reporting time: 1-4 weeks. Payment: 10% net-after recovery. Copyrights for author.

Holt Associates, Inc. (see also **GROWING WITHOUT SCHOOLING**), Susannah Sheffer, Editor; Patrick Farenga, Publisher, 2269 Massachusetts Avenue, Cambridge, MA 02140, 617-864-3100. 1977. Reviews, non-fiction. "We have recently published *Child's Work: Taking Children's Choices Seriously* by Nancy Wallace and *Sharing Treasures: Book Reviews* by John Holt. Books about learning without school are our focus." avg. press run 1.5M. Pub'd 2 titles 1990; expects 2 titles 1991, 2 titles 1992. 3 titles listed in the *Small Press Record of Books in Print* (20th Edition, 1991-92). avg. price, paper: $12.95. Discounts: standard discounts apply; 4 national distributors currently handle our books. 150pp; 6x9; of. Reporting time: 2 months. Payment: negotiable. Copyrights for author.

Holy Cow! Press, Jim Perlman, PO Box 3170, Mount Royal Station, Duluth, MN 55803. 1977. Poetry, fiction, articles, parts-of-novels, long-poems. "Holy Cow! Press is a Midwestern independent publisher that features new work by both well-known and younger writers. Besides single author collections, we try to tastefully assemble anthologies centered around important themes. We are supportive of first books by younger writers; PLEASE query before submitting manuscripts." avg. press run 1.25M. Pub'd 3 titles 1990; expects 6 titles 1991, 4 titles 1992. 22 titles listed in the *Small Press Record of Books in Print* (20th Edition, 1991-92). avg. price, cloth: $13; paper: $6.95. Discounts: 40% off to classrooms, bulk, institutions, bookstores. 72pp; 6x9; of. Reporting time: 2-3 months. Payment: negotiable with each author. Copyrights for author. UMBA.

HOME EDUCATION MAGAZINE, Mark Hegener, Editor; Helen Hegener, Editor, PO Box 1083, Tonasket, WA 98855, 509-486-1351. 1984. Poetry, articles, art, photos, cartoons, interviews, satire, criticism, reviews, letters, news items. "*Home Education Magazine* is for families who choose to teach their children at home. Please write for editorial guidelines, include SASE." circ. 3.5M. 6/yr. Pub'd 6 issues 1990; expects 6 issues 1991, 6 issues 1992. sub. price: $24; per copy: $4.50; sample: $4.50. Back issues: please inquire. Discounts: write for info, include SASE. 56pp; 8½x11; web of. Reporting time: 6 weeks. Payment: $10 per typeset page (about 750 words). Copyrighted, reverts to author. Pub's reviews: 20 in 1990. §Homeschooling, education, child development, alternative education, family. Ads: $500/$250/$100 1/4 page /25¢ classified per word (min. $5/issue). PMA, NAPRA, AFFIRMS, COSMEP.

HOME PLANET NEWS, Home Planet Publications, Enid Dame, Donald Lev, P.O. Box 415 Stuyvesant Station, New York, NY 10009, 718-769-2854. 1979. Poetry, fiction, articles, art, photos, cartoons, interviews, criticism, reviews, letters, parts-of-novels, long-poems, news items. "We like lively work of all types and schools. Poetry should run about a page. (Need shorter ones right now.) For articles, reviews, etc., please query first. Some recent contributors include: Steve and Gloria Tropp, Richard Kostelanetz, Jan Clausen, Barbara Holland, Andrew Glaze, Daniel Berrigan, Toi Derricotte, Mary Mackey, William Packard, Richard Grayson, Nellie Wong, Will Inman, Virginia Scott, Leo Connellan, Hayden Carruth, Cornelius Eady, Wanda Coleman, Norman Rosten, Tuli Kupferberg, Dorothy Friedman, D. Nurkse, Gerald Locklin" circ. 3M. 3-4/yr. Pub'd 2 issues 1990; expects 3 issues 1991, 3 issues 1992. sub. price: $8; per copy: $2; sample: $2. Back issues: $2. Discounts: 40% consignment, 50% cash, 25% agents. 24pp; 10x15; of. Reporting time: 3 months. Payment: copies & 1 yr gift subscription. Copyrighted, reverts to author. Pub's reviews: 18 books, 10 magazines in 1990. §Poetry, fiction. Ads: $150/$75.

Home Planet Publications (see also **HOME PLANET NEWS**), Donald Lev, Enid Dame, PO Box 415 Stuyvesant Station, New York, NY 10009, 718-769-2854. 1971. Poetry. "Home Planet Publications publishes occasional books of poetry, but does not consider unsolicited manuscripts. For our magazine, *Home Planet News*, see listing above." avg. press run 400. avg. price, paper: $1.50. Discounts: 50% cash to stores; 40% consignment; 25% agents. 60pp; 5x8; of. Payment: negotiable. Copyrights for author.

Home Power, Inc. (see also HOME POWER MAGAZINE), Richard Perez, PO Box 275, Ashland, OR 97520, 916-475-3179. 1987. Non-fiction. "Our first book went to press May 1991, *Heaven's Flame: A Guide Book to Solar Cookers*. Proposed for late 1991: *The Battery Book* and *Compendium of Home Power Magazine*" avg. press run 5K. Expects 2 titles 1991. 1 title listed in the *Small Press Record of Books in Print* (20th Edition, 1991-92). Discounts: 40%. 100-400pp; size varies; of. Reporting time: 3-4 months. Payment: small advance, 16% of net sales 0-10K, 20% of net sales 10K+ - contract. Copyrights for author if so desired.

HOME POWER MAGAZINE, Home Power, Inc., Richard Perez, PO Box 130, Hornbrook, CA 96044, 916-475-3179. 1987. Articles, photos, reviews, letters, news items, non-fiction. "Length of material 1,000 to 8,000 words. All articles must contain hard, hands-on information about the use of renewable energy in home settings" circ. 10M. 6/yr. Pub'd 6 issues 1990; expects 6 issues 1991, 6 issues 1992. sub. price: $10; per copy: $3.50; sample: free. Back issues: #1-20 $2, #21 on $3.50 each. Discounts: bulk, agent 50% of cover. 100pp; 8½x11; of. Reporting time: 8 weeks. Payment: none. Copyrighted, rights revert if author so desires. Pub's reviews: 12 in 1990. §Renewable energy, ecology. Ads: $1200/$672/$337 1/4 page/multiple insertion discounts.

HOME RESOURCE MAGAZINE, Maureen McIntyre, PO Box 12061, Boulder, CO 80303, 303-449-6126. 1984. Articles, photos, interviews, satire. circ. 30M. 6/yr. Pub'd 3 issues 1990; expects 6 issues 1991, 6 issues 1992. sub. price: $22; per copy: $3.75; sample: no charge. Back issues: $3/copy. 80pp; of. Reporting time: 2 months. Payment: negotiable. Copyrighted, reverts to author. Pub's reviews: 0 in 1990. §House-building, solar, energy conservation, gardening. Ads: rate card on request.

Homestead Publishing, Carl Schreier, Box 193, Moose, WY 83012. 1980. Art, photos, non-fiction. "Our specialty is natural history of the Rocky Mountains, either children or adult, pictorial or literature." avg. press run 10M-25M. Pub'd 3 titles 1990; expects 3 titles 1991, 4 titles 1992. 3 titles listed in the *Small Press Record of Books in Print* (20th Edition, 1991-92). avg. price, cloth: $12-$25; paper: $5-$20. Discounts: 40% bookstores, 33% libraries, 50% jobbers. 90-250pp; 7x9; of. Reporting time: 2 months. Payment: depending on the work. Copyrights for author.

Homeward Press, John Curl, PO Box 2307, Berkeley, CA 94702, 412-526-3254. 1980. Poetry, non-fiction. "No unsolicited manuscripts" avg. press run 500. Expects 6 titles 1991, 1 title 1992. 9 titles listed in the *Small Press Record of Books in Print* (20th Edition, 1991-92). avg. price, paper: $5. 56pp; 5½x8½; of. Copyrights for author.

Honeybrook Press, Donnell Hunter, PO Box 883, Rexburg, ID 83440, 208-356-5133. 1984. Poetry. "Not soliciting manuscripts, have done some subsidy work and some speculative. Chapbooks by William Stafford, Nina Wicker, Leslie Norris, Donnell Hunter." avg. press run 150. Pub'd 1 title 1990; expects 4 titles 1991, 3 titles 1992. 10 titles listed in the *Small Press Record of Books in Print* (20th Edition, 1991-92). avg. price, paper: $10. Discounts: 20% to bookstores. 24pp; 6x9; †lp. Reporting time: 2 weeks. Payment: arranged. Copyrights for author.

Hong Kong Publishing Co., Ltd., Dean Barrett, 1801 World Trade Centre, Causeway Bay, Hong Kong, 5-8903067. 1975. Poetry, fiction, non-fiction. avg. press run 5M. Pub'd 3 titles 1990; expects 3-4 titles 1991, 3-4 titles 1992. 14 titles listed in the *Small Press Record of Books in Print* (20th Edition, 1991-92). avg. price, paper: $8 U.S. Discounts: 50% to distributors. 144pp; 7¼x10¼; †of. Payment: flat fee for commissioned work. Copyrights for author. SHKP.

HOOFSTRIKES NEWSLETTER, Gweetna Press, Cathy Ford, PO Box 106, Mt. Pleasant, MI 48858. 1983. Poetry, fiction, articles, art, cartoons, long-poems, non-fiction. "All material must be animal related, can be fantasy animals. Poetry can be any style. Fiction/non-fiction 2,000 word limit." circ. 400. 6/yr. Pub'd 4 issues 1990; expects 6 issues 1991, 6 issues 1992. 8-10pp; 8½x11; of. Reporting time: varies. Payment: copies. Copyrighted, reverts to author. Pub's reviews: 2-3 in 1990. §animal welfare & issues. SPWAO.

Hoover Institution Press, Pat A. Baker, Executive Editor, Stanford University, Stanford, CA 94305-6010, 415-723-3373. Non-fiction. "Manuscripts submitted are usually 200 to 600 pages. Subjects usually published are: economics, political science, public policy, U.S.-Soviet affairs, international studies, and reference books" avg. press run 1M. Pub'd 18 titles 1990; expects 13 titles 1991, 17 titles 1992. 26 titles listed in the *Small Press Record of Books in Print* (20th Edition, 1991-92). avg. price, cloth: $32.95; paper: $17.95. Discounts: wholesale: 1-3 copies 20%, 4-24 42%, 25-49 45%, 50-99 50%, 100-249 52%, 250+ 55%, retail 1-3 copies 20%, 4-24 42%, 25-49 43%, 50-99 44%, 100+ 45%. 300pp; 6x9; of. Reporting time: varies, 2-4 months. Payment: individually arranged. Copyrights for author. Bookbuilders West.

Hope Publishing House, Faith Annette Sand, Publisher, PO Box 60008, Pasadena, CA 91116, 818-792-6123; fax 818-792-2121. 1983. Criticism, non-fiction. "We deal with religious and educational topics and like to facilitate getting women and minorities into print, although we publish men, too. We are a nonprofit publishing venture, a program unit of the So. Calif. Ecumenical Council. We have published a Spanish/English side-by-side children's book, as well as the Spanish edition of Steve Biko's last book. We are currently interested in ecology, health and justice issues" avg. press run 3M-5M. Pub'd 6 titles 1990; expects 6 titles 1991, 6 titles 1992. 17 titles listed in the *Small Press Record of Books in Print* (20th Edition, 1991-92). avg. price, cloth: $14.95; paper: $8.95. Discounts: as required to trade and bulk buyers. 228pp; 6×9, 5½×8½, 8½×11; lp. Reporting time: 2 months. Payment: royalties are arranged, payments are made biannually. Copyrights for author. PMA, COSMEP.

HORIZONS BEYOND, Baker Street Publications, Sharida Rizzuto, Sidney J. Dragon, Thomas Schellenberger, PO Box 994, Metairie, LA 70004, 504-734-8414. 1983. Poetry, fiction, articles, art, photos, cartoons, interviews, satire, criticism, reviews, letters, long-poems, collages, plays, news items, non-fiction. circ. under 10M. 2/yr. Pub'd 4 issues 1990; expects 2 issues 1991, 2 issues 1992. sub. price: $18 for 2 issues; per copy: $7.90; sample: $7.90. Back issues: $7.90. Discounts: trade with other like publication. 80-100pp; digest size; of, photo copy, excellent quality offset covers. Reporting time: 2-6 weeks. Payment: free copies, fees paid for articles, reviews, and artwork negotiable. Copyrighted, reverts to author. Pub's reviews: 16 in 1990. §Science fiction and fantasy, adventure in film and literature, new age. Ads: free. NWC, SPWAO, HWA, Literary Markets, MWA, Western Writers of America (WWA), Arizona Authors Association (AAA).

HORIZONS INTERCULTURELS, INTERCULTURE, Maryse Bouchard, Coordinator and Editor, Intercultural Institute of Montreal, 4917 St. Urbain, Montreal, Quebec H2T 2W1, Canada, 514-288-7229. 1985. Articles, reviews, non-fiction. "Bilingual publication, French and English (ISSN 0827-1569). Length of material: 20M words average. Material: Reports on ethnocultural communities and reviews of cross-cultural events. Monchanin Cross-Cultural Centre News bulletin. Dossiers on specific themes: youth and delinquency, work and cultural pluralism." circ. 3M. 4/yr. Pub'd 4 issues 1990; expects 4 issues 1991, 4 issues 1992. sub. price: Can$12, outside Canada $17; sample: free. Discounts: subscription agencies receive 15%. 32pp; 8×10½; of. Reporting time: 3 months. Not copyrighted. Pub's reviews: 25 in 1990. §Cross-cultural issues. Ads: $350/$250.

HORIZONS WEST, Baker Street Publications, Sharida Rizzuto, Robert Dyer, Jr., PO Box 994, Metailie, LA 70004, 504-734-8414. 1983. Poetry, fiction, articles, art, photos, cartoons, interviews, satire, criticism, reviews, letters, long-poems, collages, plays, news items, non-fiction. circ. under 10M. 2/yr. Pub'd 2 issues 1990; expects 2 issues 1991, 2 issues 1992. sub. price: $18.60/2 issues; per copy: $7.90; sample: $7.90. Back issues: $7.90. Discounts: trade with other like publications. 100pp; digest size; of, photo copy, excellent quality offset covers. Reporting time: 2-6 weeks. Payment: free copies, fees paid to all contributors negotiable. Copyrighted, reverts to author. Pub's reviews: 16 in 1990. §The Old West, history, bios, autobios, stories, legends. Ads: Free. NWC, SPWAO, HWA, Literary Markets, MWA, Western Writers of America (WWA), Arizona Author Associaition (AA).

HORIZONTES, Jose Angel Villalongo Sr., P.C.C.C.-Cultural Affairs Dept., 1 College Boulevard, Paterson, NJ 07509, 201-684-6555. 1983. Poetry, art, photos. "Recent contributors are Jose Kozer, Maria Gillan, Rafael Bordao, Nelson Calderon, Antonio de Acosta, Miguel Angel Zapata, and Julio Cesar Mosches. All literary works must be in Spanish. Will accept English works but *must* be accompanied by the *Spanish version*. There is no restriction on subject matter, form, style, or purpose." circ. 1M. 1/yr. Pub'd 1 issue 1990; expects 1 issue 1991, 1 issue 1992. sub. price: $5; per copy: $5; sample: $5. Back issues: $5. Discounts: 40% for 5+ issues. 40-80pp; 8½×11. Reporting time: 4 months. Payment: 1 copy. Copyrighted, reverts to author. none.

THE HORROR SHOW, David B. Silva, Phantasm Press, 14848 Misty Springs Lane, Oak Run, CA 96069, 916-472-3540. 1982. Fiction, articles, cartoons, interviews, reviews, parts-of-novels. "Fiction: We're looking for solid horror fiction, not overly graphic nor overly violent, always set in a contemporary setting, and original in its premise. We are not interested in science fiction, sword and sorcery, or other genres which can easily be found in numerous other publications. A logical twist or surprise at the end is generally appreciated, but not necessary. More important is originality, strong characterization, a sense of mood. Try to avoid insect, dog, cat, mad slasher, and simplistic ghost stories. Maximum length is a firm 6,000 words. Non-fiction: Generally runs 1600-1800 words and is on assignment. If you have an idea, please make a proposal. We're looking for informative articles that have insight into the horror field, horror writers, etc. Must be well done, and keep in mind we already have a regular book reviewer, movie reviewer and interviewer" circ. 44M. 4/yr. Pub'd 4 issues 1990; expects 4 issues 1991, 4 issues 1992. sub. price: $14; per copy: $3.95; sample: $4.95. Back issues: $4.95. Discounts: 40% to stores, 50% to distributors. 72pp; 8½×11; of. Reporting time: 3 weeks. Payment: 1¢-2¢ per word, 1 copy. Copyrighted, reverts to author. Pub's reviews: 25-35 in 1990. §Horror. Ads: $1,000/$850.

HOR-TASY, Ansuda Publications, Daniel Betz, PO Box 158, Harris, IA 51345. 1980. Fiction. "We are looking for psychological horror & pure fantasy (eg: faeries, trolls, sword & sorcery, myths, legends). The horror we want is based on or in the mind, so we don't really want the over-used haunted houses, monsters, hexes, ghosts, etc. We'd like to get one issue out each year. We are not interested in science fiction" circ. 400. Expects 1 issue 1991, 1 issue 1992. price per copy: $2.95. 72pp; 5½×8½; †mi, with offset covers. Reporting time: immediately to 3 months. Payment: copies. Copyrighted, reverts to author.

258

HORTICULTURA MODERNA, Saul E. Camacho, Apartado 20236, Cali, Valle, Colombia, 93-396206. 1985. Articles, photos, reviews, letters, news items. circ. 7M. 4/yr. Pub'd 3 issues 1990; expects 4 issues 1991, 4 issues 1992. sub. price: $15; per copy: $5; sample: same. Back issues: $5. 36pp; 20.5×27.5cm; of. Payment: occasionally to some contributors. Copyrighted, does not revert to author. Pub's reviews: 12 in 1990. §Horticulture, general agriculture, life in agricultural rural areas. Ads: us$300/us$150.

HORTIDEAS, Greg Williams, Pat Williams, Route 1, Box 302, Gravel Switch, KY 40328, 606-332-7606. 1984. Articles, reviews, news items, non-fiction. "Short articles on vegetable, flower, and fruit growing, directed to amateur gardeners; including abstracts from the technical horticultural literature, new product reviews, and book reviews." circ. 1.6M. 12/yr. Pub'd 12 issues 1990; expects 12 issues 1991, 12 issues 1992. sub. price: $15; per copy: $1.50; sample: same. Back issues: $1.50. Discounts: none, mailorder only. 12pp; 8½×11; of. Reporting time: 1 month. Payment: free issue. Copyrighted, does not revert to author. Pub's reviews: 35 in 1990. §Gardening, horticulture, agriculture, botany, forestry. No ads.

The Hosanna Press, Cathie Ruggie Saunders, 215 Gale, River Forest, IL 60305, 708-771-8259. 1974. Poetry, fiction, art, concrete art. "Limited edition fine printings from foundry type on rag & unique handmade papers, w/ original graphics. Innovative concepts of book, paper, and print pursued." avg. press run 25-100. Expects 1 title 1991, 1 title 1992. 9 titles listed in the *Small Press Record of Books in Print* (20th Edition, 1991-92). avg. price, cloth: varies; paper: price varies; other: varies. Pages vary; size varies; †lp. Reporting time: 3-6 weeks. Payment: 10% of edition. Copyrights for author. APHA, American Center for Design.

HOT FLASHES, Robert Trammell, 5926 Marquita Avenue, Dallas, TX 75206-6116, 821-1308. 1985. Poetry, fiction, articles, art, photos, cartoons, satire, criticism, reviews, music, letters, long-poems, collages, concrete art, news items. "There is an emphasis on poetry, xerox and other kinds of photo art. Recent contributors include: Gerald Burns, Blaster Al, Robert Bly, Robert Creeley, Terry Allen, Randy Twaddle, Queen Octoroon, John M. Bennett, Roxy Gordon, James Hillman, Barry Silesky, Norman Weinstein, David Searey, LeAnne Howe and Martha King" circ. 200. 10/yr. Pub'd 9 issues 1990; expects 10 issues 1991, 10 issues 1992. 1 title listed in the *Small Press Record of Books in Print* (20th Edition, 1991-92). sub. price: $15; per copy: $2; sample: $2. Discounts: 40% off. 16pp; 8½×11; †of, and other photo processes. Reporting time: 6 weeks. Payment: 2 copies. Copyrighted, reverts to author. Pub's reviews: 5 in 1990. §Poetry, criticism, music, art. Ads: $110/$60/$35 1/4 page/$20 1/8.

Hot Off the Press, Paulette Jarvey, 7212 S Seven Oaks, Canby, OR 97013. 33 titles listed in the *Small Press Record of Books in Print* (20th Edition, 1991-92).

HOT WIRE: Journal of Women's Music & Culture, Empty Closet Enterprises, Toni Armstrong, Jr., Managing Editor; Lynn Siniscalchi, Business Manager; Katie Davis, Production Coordinator, 5210 North Wayne, Chicago, IL 60640, 312-769-9009. 1984. Articles, photos, cartoons, interviews, music, letters, news items, non-fiction. "Each 64 page issue includes stereo recording; women's music and comedy festival coverage; essays; 10 regular columns. *Hot Wire* is the only periodical devoted to feminist and lesbian-feminist women's music and culture scene. Accepts unsolicited ms" circ. 8M. 3/yr. Pub'd 3 issues 1990; expects 3 issues 1991, 3 issues 1992. sub. price: $16 U.S., $20 foreign; per copy: $7 includes p/h; sample: same. Back issues: $7. Discounts: 40% on orders of 5 or more. 64pp; 8½×11; of. Reporting time: 2 months. Payment: ad space, subscriptions, copies, possible cash. Copyrighted, reverts to author. Ads: $150/$85/$9 per col. inch/$65 1/3 page. COSMEP, CWIP (Chicago Women in Publishing), Feminist Writers Guild.

Hound Dog Press, Lena F. Reed, 10705 Woodland Avenue, Puyallup, WA 98373, (206) 845-8039. 1985. Non-fiction. 1 title listed in the *Small Press Record of Books in Print* (20th Edition, 1991-92). avg. price, cloth: $16. Discounts: for wholesale orders, 20% to 40%. 284pp; 5¼×8½.

House of Fire Press, Charles Allen, Mary Allen, 1019 Agate Street, Suite D, San Diego, CA 92109, 619-488-1208. 1988. Fiction, non-fiction. "We are primarily concerned with reprinting out-of-print titles, and are not actively seeking new titles at this time. We do plan, however, to begin publishing original works in two or three years. All our titles are printed with sewn bindings and acid-free paper" avg. press run 2M. Pub'd 2 titles 1990; expects 4 titles 1991, 6 titles 1992. avg. price, paper: $10. Discounts: 40% to bookstores; STOP orders appreciated; wholesale or bulk orders are negotiable; call or write. 300pp; 5½×8½; of. Payment: reprints made through arrangement with original publisher. Does not copyright for author.

House of Hits, Inc., Dan McKinnon, North American Airlines Bldg 75, Suite 250, JFK International Airport, Jamaica, NY 11430, 718-656-2650. 1973. "We're basically interested in aviation and history involving the Middle East. Current history" avg. press run 2M-10M. Pub'd 2 titles 1990; expects 3 titles 1991, 4 titles 1992. 2 titles listed in the *Small Press Record of Books in Print* (20th Edition, 1991-92). avg. price, cloth: $16.95; paper: $4.95. Discounts: libraries 20%, retailers 40%, wholesalers 50%. 200pp; 6×9; lp. Reporting time: 12 months. Payment: negotiated. Copyrights for author. BMF.

HOUSEWIFE-WRITER'S FORUM, Diane Wolverton, PO Box 780, Lyman, WY 82937, 307-786-4513.

1988. Poetry, fiction, articles, art, cartoons, interviews, satire, reviews, letters, news items, non-fiction. "Maximum 2,000 words, average 500-750 words. Preference for humorous slant or pathos. Non-fiction centers on writing and finding time to write. Special affinity for women's humor, especially domestic 'housewives' humor.'. Inquire for inclusion in conferences & workshops (happy to send copies if available)." circ. 1.2M. 6/yr. Pub'd 6 issues 1990; expects 6 issues 1991, 6 issues 1992. sub. price: $15; per copy: $4; sample: $4. Back issues: $3. Discounts: 50% to distributors. 40pp; 6½×10; Web. Reporting time: 1-3 months. Payment: 1¢ per word. Copyrighted, reverts to author. Pub's reviews: 2 in 1990. §Books and periodicals on writing. Ads: $75/$45/$25 1/4 page/25¢ classified word. Deneb Publishing.

HOWLING DOG, Mark Donovan, Parkville Publishing, 8419 Rhode Drive, Utica, MI 48317. 1985. Poetry, fiction, art, satire, criticism, music, letters. "Our purpose is to have an effect similar to the howl of a dog with its foot caught in the fence. We desire something that may not be pleasant or permanent, but will still be heard by everyone in the neighborhood until the time comes to unleash the poor beast to whatever other endeavors it may become involved in. Howling Dog contains found poetry, new-age fiction, and bizarre graphics. We generally choose pieces with an intense emotional expression, regardless of the social implications. Name and address on *each* page. Fiction 1000 words or less *only*. No poems less than 10 lines." circ. 500. 2/yr. Pub'd 2 issues 1990; expects 2 issues 1991, 2 issues 1992. sub. price: $20/4 issues; per copy: $5; sample: $4. Discounts: ask for info. 64pp; 6×9; of. Reporting time: varies, none without SASE. Payment: copies. Copyrighted, reverts to author. Pub's reviews: 1 in 1990. §Poetry, fiction, essays. Ads: full page $80; 1/2 page $40; 1/4 page $20. CCLM.

Howling Dog Press (see also ASHES; THE BEAST; STILETTO), Michael Annis, PO Box 5987, Westport Station, Kansas City, MO 64111. 1980. Poetry, fiction, art, photos, cartoons, interviews, satire, parts-of-novels, long-poems, collages, plays, concrete art. "*Stiletto* is a book series featuring 8 primary writers per issue (with secondary/shorter pieces by others) and 2 main artists. Average 200 pages. *The Beast* is a magazine featuring up to 100 writers per issue. It is social/political protest work. Average 216 pages. *Ashes* is a chapbook series featuring one writer per issue. Average 56 pages. Howling Dog also publishes books and broadsides." avg. press run 500. Pub'd 2 titles 1990; expects 3 titles 1991. Discounts: 30-40% trade, 20% classroom. †of, lp. Reporting time: up to 1 year. Payment: By publication, no standard. Copyrights for author.

THE HOWLING MANTRA, Daniel Marcou, PO Box 1821, LaCrosse, WI 54602, 608-785-0810. 1988. Poetry, art. "*The Howling Mantra* is an annual publication dedicated to exploring the regions of minimal and experimental poetry. Poems should be no longer than 20 lines. Less is more! Illustrations and b/w photos are also sought - please send only a photocopy or photo of all art. Past issues have included Bukowski, John Judson, Ellen Bryant Voight, Robert Schuller, and Felix Bundy. All submissions should include a SASE." circ. 150. 1/yr. Pub'd 3 issues 1990; expects 1 issue 1991, 1 issue 1992. sub. price: $5 (inc. 1 mag, 1 book); per copy: $2. Discounts: will trade with other publications. 52pp; 4¼×5½; of/lp. Reporting time: 4-6 weeks. Payment: one copy. Copyrighted, reverts to author. Ads: $50/$25/barter with me.

HOWLING WIND, Phil Mershon, Strangelove Press, 6202 N. 16 Street #43, Phoenix, AZ 85016, 602-279-0462. 1989. Interviews, criticism, reviews, music. "Interested mostly in record reviews (500 words), insights into popular music, the occasional interview of music personalities" circ. 300. 12/yr. Expects 12 issues 1991, 12 issues 1992. sub. price: $12; per copy: $1; sample: free. Back issues: $1.50. 24pp; 8½×11. Reporting time: 2-4 weeks. Payment: $75-$100 for record or book reviews. Copyrighted, reverts to author. Pub's reviews. §Popular music. No ads.

HUBBUB, Lisa Steinman, Jim Shugrue, 5344 S.E. 38th Avenue, Portland, OR 97202, 503-775-0370. 1983. Poetry. "*Hubbub* publishes poetry reviews by invitation only, but accepts submissions of all kinds of poetry: excellence is our only criterion." circ. 350. 2/yr. Pub'd 2 issues 1990; expects 2 issues 1991, 2 issues 1992. sub. price: $4; per copy: $2.85; sample: $2.85. Back issues: $2.85. Discounts: 40%. 35pp; 5½×8½; †of. Reporting time: 1-3 months. Payment: 2 contributor copies plus a small honorarium when we have grant funding. Copyrighted, reverts to author. Pub's reviews: 3 in 1990. §Poetry. Ads: $50/$25/will swap with other literary magazines in some cases.

HUBRIS, Tom Long, 1122-1/2 North 13th, Dekalb, IL 60115. 1991. Fiction, articles, art, photos, cartoons, satire, collages, concrete art, non-fiction. "The umbrella theme of *Hubris* is human arrogance and folly of all types—sexual, political, artistic, etc. Fiction up to 1,000 words, non-fiction up to 2,000 words. (No poetry will be considered.)" circ. 300. 6/yr. Expects 6 issues 1991, 6 issues 1992. sub. price: $10; per copy: $2; sample: $2. 20pp; 8½×11; mi. Reporting time: 1-2 weeks. Payment: copies. Not copyrighted. Ads: none.

THE HUDSON REVIEW, Paula Deitz, Co-editor; Frederick Morgan, Co-editor, 684 Park Avenue, New York, NY 10021, 212-650-0020. 1948. Poetry, fiction, articles, criticism, reviews, parts-of-novels, long-poems. "Although we have developed a recognizable group of contributors who are identified with the magazine, we are always open to new writers and publish them in every issue. We have no university affiliation and are not committed to any narrow academic aim; nor to any particular political perspective." circ. 4.5M. 4/yr. Pub'd 4 issues 1990; expects 4 issues 1991, 4 issues 1992. 3 titles listed in the *Small Press Record of Books in Print* (20th Edition, 1991-92). sub. price: $20 domestic, $24 foreign; per copy: $6; sample: $6. Back issues: varies. Bulk rates and discount schedules on request. 160pp; 4½×7½; of. Reporting time: 12 weeks maximum. Payment: 2½¢ per word for prose, 50¢ per line for poetry. Copyrighted, rights revert under 1978 law on request. Pub's reviews: 80 in 1990. §Literature, fine and performing arts, sociology and cultural anthropology. Ads: $300/$200. CCLM.

HUG THE EARTH, A Journal of Land and Life, Hug The Earth Publications, Kenneth Lumpkin, 42 Greenwood Avenue, Pequannock, NJ 07440. "Features Charles Olson, Gary Snyder, Flavia Alaya, Ken Lumpkin, E. Durling Merrill, et al. Poems and prose on environment and place in literature" 24pp; 8½×11.

Hug The Earth Publications (see also HUG THE EARTH, A Journal of Land and Life), Kenneth Lumpkin, 42 Greenwood Ave., Pequannock, NJ 07440. 1980. Poetry, art, criticism, reviews, letters, long-poems. "We publish broadsides, and a one-time only journal on land & life" avg. press run 500-1M. Pub'd 2 titles 1990; expects 1 title 1991. 1 title listed in the *Small Press Record of Books in Print* (20th Edition, 1991-92). avg. price, paper: $5; other: $2.50. 40pp; 4¼×5½; MacIntosh Model SE, with pagemaker 3.0 software. Reporting time: 6-8 weeks. Copyrights for author.

THE HUMAN ECOLOGY AND ENERGY BALANCING SCIENTIST, Human Ecology Balancing Sciences, Inc., Steven Rochlitz, Irene Yaychuk, PO Box 737, Mahopac, NY 10541, 516-751-3105. 1987. Articles, interviews, reviews, letters, news items, non-fiction. circ. 500. 4/yr. Pub'd 2 issues 1990; expects 4 issues 1991, 4 issues 1992. sub. price: $14.95; per copy: $3; sample: same. Back issues: $3. 10-12pp; 8½×11; of. Reporting time: 4 months. Payment: none. Copyrighted, does not revert to author. Pub's reviews: 2 in 1990. §Nutrition, health, alternative healing, medicine. Ads: $250/$150. COSMEP.

Human Ecology Balancing Sciences, Inc. (see also THE HUMAN ECOLOGY AND ENERGY BALANCING SCIENTIST), Steven Rochlitz, Irene Yaychuk, PO Box 737, Mahopac, NY 10541. 1986. Articles, photos, interviews, news items, non-fiction. avg. press run 5M. Pub'd 3 titles 1990; expects 1 title 1991, 3 titles 1992. 1 title listed in the *Small Press Record of Books in Print* (20th Edition, 1991-92). avg. price, paper: $19.95; other: $9.95 audio tapes. Discounts: trade 10-19 30%, 30-39 40%, over 40 50%. 272pp; 5½×8; of. Reporting time: 3 months. Payment: individually arranged. Copyrights for author. PMA.

Human Futures, PO Box 893, Hermosa Beach, CA 90254.

Human Kinetics Pub. Inc. (see also ADAPTED PHYSICAL ACTIVITY QUARTERLY (APAQ); COACHING VOLLEYBALL; COACHING WOMEN'S BASKETBALL; INTERNATIONAL JOURNAL OF SPORT BIOMECHANICS; JOURNAL OF THE PHILOSOPHY OF SPORT; JOURNAL OF SPORT MANAGEMENT; JOURNAL OF SPORT AND EXERCISE PSYCHOLOGY; JOURNAL OF TEACHING IN PHYSICAL EDUCATION; Leisure Press; Life Enhancement; PLAY & CULTURE; QUEST; SOCIOLOGY OF SPORT JOURNAL; THE SPORT PSYCHOLOGIST), Rainer Martens, President; Julie Simon, Publications Director, Box 5076, Champaign, IL 61820, 217-351-5076. 1974. Non-fiction. "Scholarly books and journals in sports medicine and science and physical education and professional journals in coaching issues & techniques" avg. press run 3M. Pub'd 30 titles 1990; expects 30 titles 1991, 30 titles 1992. 235 titles listed in the *Small Press Record of Books in Print* (20th Edition, 1991-92). avg. price, cloth: $32; paper: $16. Discounts: text 1-4 10%, 5+ 20%. 286pp; 6×9, 8½×11, 7¼×9½; of. Reporting time: 1-2 months. Payment: negotiable (7-18%). Copyrights for author. Society for Scholarly Publishing.

Humana Press, Thomas Lanigan, PO Box 2148, Clifton, NJ 07015, 201-773-4389. 1977. Poetry, fiction, articles, art, photos, non-fiction. "Material accepted as the spirit moves." avg. press run 1.5M. Pub'd 24 titles 1990; expects 30 titles 1991, 30 titles 1992. 35 titles listed in the *Small Press Record of Books in Print* (20th Edition, 1991-92). avg. price, cloth: $19.95; paper: $12.95. Discounts: varies with quantity. 300pp; 5¾×8½; of. Reporting time: 2-3 months. Payment: variable to no royalties; 10 copies of book to author, annual royalty report. COSMEP, PMA.

THE HUMANIST, Lloyd L. Morian, Editor; Frederick Edwords, Managing Editor; Rick Szykowny, Editorial Associate; Karen Ann Gajewski, Editorial Assistant, 7 Harwood Drive, PO Box 146, Amherst, NY 14226-0146, 716-839-5080. 1941. Articles, art, photos, cartoons, interviews, criticism, reviews, letters, non-fiction. "Nonfiction addressing ethical, social, or political concerns from a humanist perspective is most likely to be published" circ. 15M. 6/yr. Pub'd 6 issues 1990; expects 6 issues 1991, 6 issues 1992. sub. price: $19.75; per copy: $3.75; sample: same. Back issues: $4.25. Discounts: 40% bulk. 48pp; 8½×11; of, lp. Reporting time: 1-2 months. Payment: 10 free issues. Copyrighted, does not revert to author. Pub's reviews: 42 in 1990. §Church-state separation, feminism, ethics, science, humanism, education, politics. Ads: $595/$305/75¢.

HUMERUS, William Stanley Wyatt, PO Box 222, Piermont, NY 10986, 914-358-2371. 1988. Poetry, fiction, articles, art, photos, cartoons, satire, letters, parts-of-novels, collages, plays, non-fiction. circ. 1.5M. 3/yr. Pub'd 1 issue 1990; expects 3 issues 1991, 3 issues 1992. sub. price: $14; per copy: $5. Back issues: $5. 76pp; 8½×11;

of. Reporting time: 3-6 months. Payment: barter. Copyrighted, reverts to author. Ads: $400/$200/$50 card size/$75 1/6 page. WLWH.

Hundman Publishing (see also MAINLINE MODELER), Robert L. Hundman, 5115 Montecello Drive, Edmonds, WA 98020, 206-743-2607. 1979. Articles, photos, reviews, letters, non-fiction. "Books are railroad history, modeling and photography in nature" avg. press run 3.5M-5M. Pub'd 2 titles 1990; expects 6 titles 1991, 8 titles 1992. 2 titles listed in the *Small Press Record of Books in Print* (20th Edition, 1991-92). Discounts: dealer terms—20% for 1 book, 30% 2-3, 40% 4+, 10+ and we pay s/h. 100-350pp; 8½x11; of. Reporting time: 6-9 months. Payment: individual. Does not copyright for author.

HUNGRY ZIPPER, Sober Minute Press, brian david j(o(h)n)ston, PO Box 3576, Cambridge, Ont. N3H 5C6, Canada. 1989. Poetry, art, satire, collages, concrete art. *"If you've ever been caught napping while zipping, you'll know exactly where we are coming from.* Recent contributors: Guy R. Beining, John M. Bennett, Joe Blades, Greg Evason, brian david j(o(h)n)ston, M. Kettner, and David UU." circ. 50-100. 4/yr. Pub'd 4 issues 1990; expects 4 issues 1991, 4 issues 1992. sub. price: $6; per copy: $1.50; sample: $1.50. Back issues: $1.50. Discounts: 40% trade. 4-10pp; 8½x11; †rubber stamp, typewriter, photocopy, etc. Reporting time: immediate. Payment: 5 copies. Not copyrighted.

Hunter House Inc., Publishers, PO Box 847, Claremont, CA 91711, 714-624-2277. 1978. Non-fiction. "Ordering address: c/o Publishers Services, PO Box 2510, Novato, CA 94948, phone—415-883-3140" avg. press run 5M. Pub'd 8 titles 1990; expects 10 titles 1991, 12 titles 1992. 49 titles listed in the *Small Press Record of Books in Print* (20th Edition, 1991-92). avg. price, cloth: $24.95; paper: $11.95. Discounts: retailers 2-5 books 20%, 6-99 40%, 100-499 45%, 500+ 50%; wholesalers 2-5 20%, 6-49 40%, 50-99 45%, 100+ 50%; libraries 2-4 10%, 5+ 20%. 192pp; 6x9, 5½x8½; of. Reporting time: 3-6 months. Payment: 7½%-10% on pa, 10%-12½% on hb, report and pay once a year. Copyrights for author. PMA (Publishers Marketing Association), BISG (Book Industry Study Group).

Hunter Publishing, Co., Diane Thomas, P.O. Box 9533, Phoenix, AZ 85068, 602-943-1022. 1975. "We publish creative Ojo books—5 separate titles now. Interested in undertaking publishing venture for good craft-oriented ideas—resale to craft & hobby shops, book stores, museum gift stores, etc. Also one book pub. on Japanese silk flower making. Southwestern Indian Detours, handcover, ISBN 0-918126-12-6, $8.95. The above book encompasses 332+ pages, together with some 300+ photographs of the original Fred Harvey Co. & The Atchison, Topeka, and Santa Fe R.R. files of the tourist trips run in the Southwest, mainly in New Mexico, Arizona, Colorado, and California." avg. press run 10M-20M+. Pub'd 2 titles 1990. 9 titles listed in the *Small Press Record of Books in Print* (20th Edition, 1991-92). avg. price, cloth: $8.95; paper: $2.95-$5.95. Discounts: 40-50% retail; higher disc. to distributors. 24-52pp; 8½x11. Reporting time: 4 weeks. Payment: negotiable. Copyrights for author.

Huntsville Literary Association (see also POEM), Nancy Frey Dillard, Editor, c/o English Department, University of Alabama, Huntsville, AL 35899. 1967. Poetry. "Poems copyrighted by *Poem*, reprinting permission given on request." avg. press run 500. Pub'd 2 titles 1990; expects 2 titles 1991, 2 titles 1992. avg. price, paper: $5 a copy. 70pp; 4½x7⅓; lp. Reporting time: 30 days. Payment: copy. Copyrights for author. CCLM.

HURRICANE ALICE, Martha Roth, Shirley Nelson Garner, Toni A.H. McNaron, Janet Tripp, 207 Church St. S.E., Minneapolis, MN 55455. 1983. Poetry, fiction, articles, art, photos, cartoons, interviews, satire, criticism, reviews, letters, parts-of-novels, collages, non-fiction. "Emphasis on Feminist re-view of 1)books 2)performance 3)visual art 4)everything. Recent contributors include Meridel Le Sueur, Celia Eckhart, Enid Dame, Elizabeth Hampsten, Susan Griffin, Beth Brant." circ. 1M. 4/yr. Pub'd 4 issues 1990; expects 4 issues 1991, 4 issues 1992. sub. price: $10; per copy: $2.50; sample: $2.50. 12pp; 11x17; of. Reporting time: 2-3 months. Payment: in issues. Copyrighted, reverts to author. Pub's reviews: 20-25 in 1990. §Gender, performance. Ads: /$200/$30 for business-card (camera-ready). CCLM.

ZORA NEALE HURSTON FORUM, The Zora Neale Hurston Society, Ruthe T. Sheffey, Editor, PO Box 550, Morgan State University, Baltimore, MD 21239. 1986. "The official journal of the Society, appears bi-annually, with published essays and creative writing which will promote the appreciation of the life, works, and legacy of Zora Neale Hurston, and of the creative circles in which she moved in the first half of the twentieth century" 2/yr. Pub'd 1 issue 1990; expects 2 issues 1991, 2 issues 1992. sub. price: $15 + $2 p/h for 2 issues in the US, $21 in foreign countries; per copy: $9 in US, $15 in foreign countries. 45pp; 5½x8½. Reporting time: 3 months. Payment: none. Copyrighted, reverts to author. Pub's reviews: 2 in 1990. §African-American, female studies, Harlem Renaissant. Ads: $250/$175/$100 1/4 page/$50 1/8.

The Zora Neale Hurston Society (see also ZORA NEALE HURSTON FORUM), Ruthe T. Sheffey, Editor, PO Box 550, Morgan State University, Baltimore, MD 21239. "The Zora Neale Hurston Society was organized by a group of scholars, journalists, educators, folklorists, historians, students and other interested persons who wished to promote appreciation of the life, works, and legacy of Zora Neale Hurston, a multi-talented Black female anthropologist and novelist, and to preserve the heritage of Afro-American letters, particularly of the first half of the twentieth century" avg. press run 500. Pub'd 2 titles 1990; expects 2 titles 1991, 2 titles 1992. avg. price, paper: $9. Discounts: 15%. 55pp; 5½x8½. Reporting time: 3 months. Payment: none. Does not copyright for author.

Hutton Publications (see also MYSTERY TIME ANTHOLOGY; WRITER'S INFO; RHYME TIME POETRY NEWSLETTER), Linda Hutton, PO Box 1870, Hayden, ID 83835, 208-772-6184. 1983. Poetry, fiction, art. avg. press run 100. Pub'd 1 title 1990; expects 1 title 1991, 1 title 1992. avg. price, paper: $5. Discounts: half price to authors. 44pp; 8½x11; of. Reporting time: 1 month. Payment: 1/4¢ to 1¢ per word for fiction, 5¢ to 25¢ per line for poetry. Copyrights for author.

Hyde Park Publishing House, Inc., 3908 Avenue G, Austin, TX 78751, 512-467-9893. 1991. Non-fiction. avg. press run 1M. Expects 1 title 1991. avg. price, paper: $10. 250pp; 5½x8.

HYPATIA: A Journal of Feminist Philosophy, Linda Lopez McAlister, University of South Florida, SOC 107, Tampa, FL 33620-8100, 904-974-5531. 1986. Articles, reviews, non-fiction. "Address business and subscription correspondence to: Journals Manager, Indiana University Press, 10th & Morton Streets, Bloomington, IN 47401." circ. 1M. 3/yr. Pub'd 3 issues 1990; expects 3 issues 1991, 3 issues 1992. sub. price: $25 individual, $40 institution; per copy: $10 indiv., $20 inst.; sample: $10 indiv., free to institutions. Discounts: bulk 40% for 5 or more. 200-250pp. Reporting time: 6 months. Payment: none. Copyrighted, reverts to author. Pub's reviews. §Feminist philosophy. Ads: $200/$100/$50 1/4 page.

THE HYPERBOREAN, Hyperborean Micropublications, Richard Gaska, 2024 North Manor Drive, Erie, PA 16505, 814-456-6819. 1990. Articles, interviews, letters, news items, non-fiction. "Typical issue contains aphorisms and essays on freethought and anarchism. Special focus on freethought and anarchist history and bibliography" circ. 100. 6/yr. Pub'd 1 issue 1990; expects 6 issues 1991, 6 issues 1992. sub. price: $11; per copy: $2; sample: $1. Back issues: $2 each. Discounts: 5 or more copies 40%. 30pp; 8½x11; †photocopy. Reporting time: 2 months. Payment: none. Not copyrighted.

Hyperborean Micropublications (see also THE HYPERBOREAN), Richard Gaska, 2024 North Manor Drive, Erie, PA 16505, 814-456-6819. 1988. Articles, news items, non-fiction. "We specialize in reprinting freethought, anarchist and anti-slavery books and periodicals. We are always interested in new articles, books and bibliographies in these areas to micropublish. Also, will pay for photocopies or originals of rare freethought, anarchist and anti-slavery books and periodicals which are in the public domain" avg. press run 60. Pub'd 12 titles 1990; expects 20 titles 1991, 20 titles 1992. 4 titles listed in the *Small Press Record of Books in Print* (20th Edition, 1991-92). avg. price, paper: $1.50; other: $1.50-$5 per microfiche, $19 16mm microfilm. Discounts: 5 or more of one title 40%. 300pp; 5½x7; microfiche and 16mm microfilm, photocopy. Reporting time: 1-2 weeks. Payment: negotiable. Does not copyright for author.

I

I WANT TO EAT YOUR STOMACH, Lovely Publications, 81 Castlerigg Drive, Burnley, Lancashire BB12 8AT, England, U.K. 0282 74321. 1985. Poetry, fiction, articles, art, photos, cartoons, interviews, satire, criticism, reviews, letters, parts-of-novels, collages, plays, non-fiction. "We are weird. No specific lengths for poems. Sex-comedy, crass and kinky subjects only. Nothing serious. Contributors include: Andy Darlington, George Melly, Dave Cunliffe, Andrew Savage, Andy Robson, Val Kirkham, Ian Thorpe, Les Tate, Jon Daunt, Tom House, Pat McKinnon, Terry Cuthbert, Max Noiprox" circ. 250. 1-4/yr. Pub'd 2 issues 1990; expects 1 issue 1991, 4 issues 1992. sub. price: £5; per copy: 4 x IRC; sample: 4 x IRC. Discounts: rates by arrangement. 24pp; 4¼x11¾; of. Reporting time: maximum 3 weeks. Payment: a copy of the magazine & a grilled sausage. Copyrighted, reverts to author. Pub's reviews: 70 in 1990. §Sex-comedy, occult, crass, obscure little mags. Ads: £12/£7/1/4 page, £4/small box, £2. The Order of the Black Cabbage.

I. S. C. Press, Keith A. Whitmore, 4450 Ridgemont Drive #1311, Abilene, TX 79606-2745. 1982. "Although we intend to publish in a variety of formats, all of our books will be aimed at those pursuing inner knowledge and the growth of consciousness. Unsolicited submissions not encouraged" avg. press run 1M-2M. Expects 2 titles 1991, 3 titles 1992. 2 titles listed in the *Small Press Record of Books in Print* (20th Edition, 1991-92). avg. price, paper: $5.00. Discounts: 1 copy-less 25%; 2-4 copies-less 33%; 5-25 copies-less 40%; 26 of more-less 45%. 200pp; 5¼x8; †of. Payment: negotiable. Does not copyright for author.

Ianus Publications, Inc. (see also ANIME SHOWER SPECIAL; GATES OF PANDRAGON; POSTER-ZINE; PROTOCULTURE ADDICTS; SAMIZDAT), Claude J. Pelletier, 33, Prince Street #243,

Montreal, Quebec H3C 2M7, Canada, 514-397-0342. 1988. Fiction, articles, cartoons, interviews, reviews, letters, news items. Pub'd 2 titles 1990; expects 3 titles 1991, 4 titles 1992. 5 titles listed in the *Small Press Record of Books in Print* (20th Edition, 1991-92). avg. price, paper: $3.50. 36pp; 6¾×10¼; of. Reporting time: 3 months. Payment: 10% of cover price, keep rights 2-5 years. Copyrights for author. SWAC.

IASP NEWSLETTER, Edvard Aslaksen, International Association of Scholarly Publishers, PO Box 2959 Toyen, Universitets forlaget, 0608 Oslo 6, Norway. 1980. Letters, news items. circ. 600. 6/yr. Pub'd 6 issues 1990; expects 6 issues 1991, 6 issues 1992. sub. price: $55; per copy: $10; sample: free. Discounts: 10%. 12pp; 7×10; of. Payment: none. Copyrighted. Pub's reviews. §Scholarly publishing, University presses—world-wide.

IATROFON, R.S. Jaggard, 10 East Charles, Oelwein, IA 50662, 319-283-3491. 1981. Articles, reviews, letters, news items. *"Iatrofon* is the newsletter of IATROS, a group of private and independent doctors from around the world (Australia, Canada, United Kingdom, Norway, Finland, Switzerland, France, Ghana, Tanzania, and USA). We want to practice private medicine, devoting our efforts to serving the best interests of the patient. For that reason, we are not paid by government, and want government to get out of the way and let patients and doctors have freedom to choose." circ. 500. 4/yr. Pub'd 4 issues 1990; expects 4 issues 1991, 4 issues 1992. sub. price: $5; sample: free. Back issues: contribution. 8pp; 8½×11; of. Payment: none. Not copyrighted. Pub's reviews: 1 in 1990. No paid advertising. 803.

IBS Press, Betty Clare Moffatt, 744 Pier Avenue, #1, Santa Monica, CA 90405, (213) 450-6485. avg. press run 10M. Pub'd 5 titles 1990; expects 6 titles 1991, 6 titles 1992. 11 titles listed in the *Small Press Record of Books in Print* (20th Edition, 1991-92). avg. price, paper: $9.95-$14.95. 200-400pp; size varies. Reporting time: 1 month. Copyrights for author. PMA.

Icarus Books, Margaret Diorio, Poetry Editor; David Diorio, Non-fiction Editor, 1015 Kenilworth Drive, Baltimore, MD 21204, 301-821-7807. 1980. Poetry, non-fiction. "Last book published-*At Home In The Universe* by Oscar Bonny. This unique autobiography provides an intriguing personal account of the collapse of Tsarist Russian and early Soviet rule. Kenneth Boulding called it a remarkable tribute to the sheer resilience of the human race. In prior years we have published poetry chapbooks and a poetry collection. In the future, we expect to focus on non-fiction." avg. press run 1M. Pub'd 1 title 1990; expects 1 title 1991, 2 titles 1992. 2 titles listed in the *Small Press Record of Books in Print* (20th Edition, 1991-92). avg. price, paper: $11.95. Discounts: 20-40%. 250pp; 6×9. Payment: will vary depending on type. Baltimore Publishers Association (BPA), PO Box 5584, Balt., MD 21285-5584.

THE ICARUS REVIEW, McOne Press, Mark Lawrence, PO Box 50174, Austin, TX 78763, 512-477-2269. 1989. Poetry, fiction, articles, art, criticism, reviews, letters, parts-of-novels, long-poems, non-fiction. "Looking for short short stories, poems, myths and personal essays concerning men's issues in relationships and recovery. High literary standards. SASE for guidelines. Recent contributors include David Jewell, Lyman Grant, John McElhenney" circ. 300-500. 2/yr. Pub'd 1 issue 1990; expects 2 issues 1991, 2 issues 1992. sub. price: $6; per copy: $3; sample: $3. Discounts: 40% distributor. 50pp; 5½×8½; of. Reporting time: 3 weeks. Payment: 2 copies and half price on extra copies. Copyrighted, reverts to author. Pub's reviews: 2 in 1990. §Men's issues, recovery, father and son, relationships, mythology. Ads: $100/$60.

Ide House, Inc., Ruby B'orlaug, Executive Vice President; Antoinette Thorsgood, PO Box 160361, Las Colinas, TX 75016, 214-686-5332. 1979. Criticism, non-fiction. "Our woman's history books run approximately 100 pages, no less than 80, no limit above. Woman's history by Melinda K. Blade (San Diego, CA); Callie Foster Sturggs (Dallas, TX); Arthur Ide (Mesquite, TX); Darlene Tempelton (Springfield, OH); Esther Yao (Houston TX); Marion Cohen (Philadelphia, PA); other authors sought. Energy series: two volumes by Robert Vaughn Nelson; no limit on pages, usually 65+. We solicit new authors on this series! Ide House is a liberal press emphasising equality; pro woman's rights and dignity. We are seeking now primarily 1) books on woman's history; 2) gay rights and 1st Amendment. Will begin a hardback series on 042 - book length only, preference given to historical studies. *No Diaries. No poetry.* Will pay top royalty. All books under contract with author. We are *not* a vanity press. We will resume publishing in 1991. We are seeking books on censorship & First Amendment rights." avg. press run 1M-2M. Pub'd 8 titles 1990; expects 20 titles 1991, 45 titles 1992. 15 titles listed in the *Small Press Record of Books in Print* (20th Edition, 1991-92). avg. price, cloth: $15.95; paper: $10.95; other: $20 Buckram. Discounts: 40%; 50% over 20 copies. 80pp; 5×8; of, lp. Reporting time: 5 months, mss. must come with return postage. Payment: up to 10% royalty on net sales average. Copyrights for author.

Idea House Publishing Company, M.J. Breton, Publisher & Executive Editor; D.C. Breton, Senior Editor; C.L. Largent, Senior Editor, 2019 Delaware Avenue, Wilmington, DE 19806, 302-571-9570. 1990. Fiction, non-fiction. "Specialize in historical fiction with philosophical themes, reprints of classics in philosophy and religion, and non-fiction focused on religion and philosophy, Eastern and Western, applied to practical issues and social problems. Premier title: *The Soul Of Economies: Spiritual Evolution Goes To The Marketplace,* by Denise Breton and Christopher Largent" avg. press run 10M. Pub'd 1 title 1990; expects 1 title 1991, 1 title

1992. 1 title listed in the *Small Press Record of Books in Print* (20th Edition, 1991-92). avg. price, cloth: $25; paper: $15. Discounts: 20% libraries, schools; 1-24 44%, 25-49 47%, 50+ 50%. 350pp; 6×9; of. Reporting time: 1 month. Payment: arranged. Does not copyright for author. ABA, ALA, COSMPEP, PMA, MAP, NAPRA.

IDEAS IN INVESTING, Independent Research Services of Irvine (IRIS/I), Eva Rosenberg, Robert Miller, 4525 Hazeltine Avenue #3, Van Nuys, CA 91423-2832. 52/yr. Pub'd 52 issues 1990; expects 52 issues 1991, 52 issues 1992. 1-2pp; 8½×11.

THE IDEOLOGY OF MADNESS, Dr. Don Prescott, PO Box 1742, Arlington, TX 76012. 1985. Poetry, fiction, articles, art, cartoons, interviews, satire, criticism, reviews, letters, news items, non-fiction. "We pride ourselves as being a 'Stangian-Hate' 'zine (that is a publication dedicated to harassing the sub-genius foundation). Bob Black, Wade Poul, and Sid Nicely number among our most recent contributors. Recent issues have focused on vampires, time travel, and roadkills" circ. 300. 4/yr. Pub'd 2 issues 1990; expects 4 issues 1991, 4 issues 1992. sub. price: $5 for 5 issues; per copy: $1; sample: $1. Back issues: $1 if available. 20pp; †xerox. Payment: unfortunately we are a volunteer 'zine at the moment. Copyrighted, reverts to author. Pub's reviews: 20+ in 1990. §Science fiction, fantasy, horror, mystery, erotica. Ads: $5/$3/$2 1/4 page.

IDIOM 23, Professor David Myers, Liz Huf, University College of Central Queensland, Rockhampton, Queensland, 4702, Australia, 0011-079-360655. 1988. Poetry, fiction, art, photos, cartoons, satire, criticism, reviews, plays, non-fiction. "Length: ss to 2000 words; poetry: three double-spaced typed pages; book reviews: 600 words." 2/yr. Pub'd 2 issues 1990; expects 1 issue 1991, 2 issues 1992. sub. price: Aus $10; per copy: Aus $5. Back issues: Aus $3/issue. Discounts: current Aus $4. 50pp; 8¾×11¾. Reporting time: 4 weeks (outside). Not copyrighted. §Anything pertaining to, or on sale in Australia. Ads: $160/$85/$45 1/4 page.

IDO-VIVO, International Language (IDO) Society of Great Britain, Tom Lang, Nic Apglyn, International Language (IDO) Society of GB, 10 Heol Salop, Penarth, De Morgannwg CF6 1HG, Wales, 0222-483545. 1950. Poetry, fiction, articles, photos, cartoons, interviews, reviews, music, letters, parts-of-novels, news items, non-fiction. "Official bulletin of *International Language (IDO) Society*. Informal style, non-commercial, international outlook, circulates world-wide. Additional address: 2 Bentham Way, Staincross, Barnsley, South Yorkshire, England. Material: in IDO & in English on IDO & other constructed languages" circ. 200. 3/yr. Pub'd 4 issues 1990; expects 3 issues 1991, 3 issues 1992. sub. price: £3; sample: free. Back issues: free. Discounts: none. 24pp; 5¾×8¼; †of/li. Payment: none. Not copyrighted. No ads.

Igneus Press, Peter Kidd, 310 N. Amherst Road, Bedford, NH 03110, 603-472-3466. 1990. Poetry. "Poetry books 50-150 pages. Recent authors: W.E. Butts, P.J. Laska, William Kemmett" avg. press run 500. Pub'd 1 title 1990; expects 4 titles 1991, 2-4 titles 1992. 3 titles listed in the *Small Press Record of Books in Print* (20th Edition, 1991-92). avg. price, paper: $8. Discounts: 40%. 75pp; 5½×8; of. Reporting time: 1 month. Payment: 10% of run to author. Copyrights for author.

IKON, IKON, Inc., Susan Sherman, PO Box 1355, Stuyvesant Station, New York, NY 10009. 1981. Poetry, fiction, articles, art, photos, interviews, music, parts-of-novels, long-poems, collages, plays, non-fiction. "Feminist political cultural magazine emphasizing experience of Third World women, lesbian and working women, etc. We are interested in all kinds of material, particularly drawings, photos. Nothing over 10-15 pages please. Recent contributors have included Beth Brant, Adrienne Rich, Audre Lorde, Margaret Randall, Irena Klepfisz, Linda Hogan, Kimiko Hahn, Marian Roth, Michelle Cliff." circ. 2M. 2/yr. Pub'd 1 issue 1990; expects 2 issues 1991, 2 issues 1992. sub. price: $10 (2 issues); per copy: $6; sample: $4. Back issues: $5. Discounts: 40% to bookstores with 5 issue order. 128pp; 7×9; of. Reporting time: 90 days or less (try). Payment: $15 and 2 copies. Copyrighted, reverts to author. Women-In-Print.

IKON, Inc. (see also IKON), Susan Sherman, Editor; Kimiko Hahn, Poetry Editor; Beth Brant, Contributing Editor; Rachel deVries, Contributing Editor; Margaret Randall, Contributing Editor, PO Box 1355, Stuyvesant Station, New York, NY 10009. 1981. Poetry, fiction, articles, art, interviews, music, parts-of-novels, long-poems, collages, plays, non-fiction. "Rights revert to author on publication" avg. press run 2M. Pub'd 1 title 1990; expects 2 titles 1991, 2 titles 1992. 1 title listed in the *Small Press Record of Books in Print* (20th Edition, 1991-92). avg. price, paper: $6. Discounts: 5/40% (bookstores). 128pp; 7×9; of. Reporting time: 90 days. Payment: $15 + 2 copies. Does not copyright for author.

Illinois Heritage Press, John E. Hallwas, PO Box 25, Macomb, IL 61455, 309-836-8916. 1983. Non-fiction. "The press publishes books of popular history relating to Illinois. The books have a broad focus—as opposed to community histories, biographies, and narrow studies." avg. press run 2M. Pub'd 1 title 1990; expects 1 title 1991. 3 titles listed in the *Small Press Record of Books in Print* (20th Edition, 1991-92). avg. price, paper: $9-$15. 200-300pp; 6×9, 8×10; of. Reporting time: 90 days. Copyrights for author.

ILLINOIS LIBERTARIAN, Ken Drazak, 1111 Church Street, #405, Evanston, IL 60201, 708-475-0391. 1975. Articles, cartoons, interviews, reviews, letters, news items, non-fiction. "2M words max; Libertarian Party news, Libertarian activities, news analysis, opinion, informative articles, etc. Bias: Libertarian." circ. 1M.

12/yr. sub. price: $15; per copy: gratis; sample: gratis. 6pp; 8½×11; of. Reporting time: 2 weeks. Payment: none. Not copyrighted. Pub's reviews: 0 in 1990. Ads: $60/$40/business card $15.

ILLINOIS MAGAZINE, Sunshine Press, Peggy Kuethe, Editor, PO Box 40, Litchfield, IL 62056. 1961. Articles, photos, letters, news items, non-fiction. circ. 10M. 6/yr. Pub'd 6 issues 1990; expects 6 issues 1991, 6 issues 1992. sub. price: $12.50; per copy: $2.25; sample: $1.50. Back issues: $2.50. 48pp; 8¼×11; of. Reporting time: 8-10 weeks. Payment: $10-$200. Copyrighted, reverts to author. Pub's reviews: 6 in 1990. §Illinois books.

Illinois Writers, Inc. (see also ILLINOIS WRITERS NEWSLETTER; ILLINOIS WRITERS REVIEW), Lynn DeVore, PO Box 1087, Champaign, IL 61820, (217) 429-0117. 1975. "We publish 750-2,500 word reviews and critical essays. We also feature provocative commentary by authors and editors on the state of contemporary writing. Though our focus is upon Illinois presses, journals, and publications, we welcome essays about and reviews of books by nationally prominent writers. Recent contributors include Neal Bowers, Roger Mitchell, John Knoepfle, Lynda Hull, and David Wojahn. A one-year subscription includes 2 issues of *Illinois Writers Review*, 6 issues of our *Newsletter*, membership in Illinois Writers, Inc., and opportunity to enter our yearly poetry or fiction chapbook competition." avg. press run 500. 2 titles listed in the *Small Press Record of Books in Print* (20th Edition, 1991-92). 4pp; 8½×11; of. CCLM.

ILLINOIS WRITERS NEWSLETTER, Illinois Writers, Inc., Lynn DeVore, PO Box 1087, Champaign, IL 61820, 217-429-0117. 1976. "A bi-monthly newsletter which informs our membership of submissions, conferences, competitions, etc. We print most announcements we receive." circ. 400. 6/yr. Pub'd 6 issues 1990; expects 6 issues 1991, 6 issues 1992. sub. price: $15 (incl. *IWI Review* & membership); sample: free. Back issues: free. 4pp; 8½×11; of. Reporting time: announcements appear in the following issue. Copyrighted, reverts to author. Ads: $100/$50/$25 quarter-page. CCLM.

ILLINOIS WRITERS REVIEW, Illinois Writers, Inc., Kevin Stein, Editor; Jim Elledge, Associate Editor, PO Box 1087, Champaign, IL 61820, 217-429-0117. 1975. Poetry, articles, art, photos, criticism, reviews, parts-of-novels, long-poems. "We publish 750-2,500 word reviews and critical essays. We also feature provocative commentary by authors and editors on the state of contemporary writing. Though our focus is upon Illinois presses, journals, and publications, we welcome essays about and reviews of books by nationally prominent writers. Recent contributors include Neal Bowers, Roger Mitchell, John Knoepfle, Lynda Hull, and David Wojahn. A one-year subscription includes 2 issues of *Illinois Writers Review*, 6 issues of our *Newsletter*, membership in Illinois Writers, Inc., and opportunity to enter our yearly poetry or fiction chapbook competition." circ. 500. 2/yr. Pub'd 2 issues 1990; expects 2 issues 1991, 2 issues 1992. sub. price: $10 students, $15 regular, $20 institution; per copy: $4; sample: $2, if back issues are available. 48pp; 5½×8½; of. Reporting time: 6-8 weeks. Payment: varies with availability of funds; when we can, $25/review. Copyrighted. Pub's reviews: 20 in 1990. §Books of poetry or fiction authored or published in Illinois; Illinois literary magazines; some emphasis on small press work; books by nationally prominent authors. Ads: $100/$50/$25 quarter-page. CCLM.

Illuminati (see also ORPHEUS), P. Schneidre, PO Box 67e07, Los Angeles, CA 90067. 1978. Poetry, art, photos, cartoons, long-poems, plays. "Sales address: SPD, 1814 San Paldo Avenue, Berkeley, CA 94702. Interested in seeing submissions of all kinds. Include return postage." avg. press run 1M. Pub'd 15 titles 1990; expects 15 titles 1991, 15 titles 1992. 49 titles listed in the *Small Press Record of Books in Print* (20th Edition, 1991-92). avg. price, cloth: $15; paper: $7.95. Discounts: on request. 60pp; 9¼×5; of. Reporting time: 3 weeks. Payment: 10%-20% royalty, advance 1/3 of royalties of each edition average. Copyrights for author.

ILLUMINATIONS, Simon Lewis, Stephen Walsh, Bernard O'Keeffe, Ryde School, Queens Road, Ryde, Isle of Wight, PO33 3BE, England. 1982. Poetry, fiction, cartoons, interviews, reviews, letters, parts-of-novels, long-poems. "Additional address: Tom Dabbs, University of South Carolina, Box 11, Department of English, Columbia, SC 29208. *Illuminations* is devoted to promoting the work of new writers by publishing their work within the context of the work of established figures. Bias: Serious writers; we mostly publish poetry—will consider short fiction or short extracts. Recent contributors: Stephen Spender, James Dickey, Susan Sontag, Joseph Brodsky, Tom Stoppard, W.H. Auden, Seamus Heaney, Flannery O'Connor, Christopher Isherwood, Thomas Kinsella, Ezra Pound letters. Now looking to promote new fiction writers by reviewing first novels, and extracts of first novels" circ. 750. 1/yr. Pub'd 1 issue 1990; expects 1 issue 1991, 1 issue 1992. sub. price: $20 3 issues; per copy: $5; sample: $5. Back issues: negotiable. Discounts: 33⅓ commission. 60pp; 6½×9; of. Reporting time: 2-3 months minimum. Payment: none. Copyrighted, reverts to author. Pub's reviews. §New poetry, first novels. Ads: $150/$75/$40¼ page.

Illuminations Press, N. Moser, Chief Editor; Randy Fingland, Prose Editor, 2110 9th Street, Apt B, Berkeley, CA 94710, 415-849-2102. 1965. Poetry, fiction, art, photos, reviews, letters, long-poems, plays, non-fiction. "Via CCLM funds, and sales of mag., etc, 1 or more titles a year. *Illuminations Reader* anthology. ($25 paperback; $35 cloth). (Series by invitation only at present) - May send 5-10 pp. fiction or poetry sans fee;

266

above that $1/page reading fee (payable in advance, naturally)'' avg. press run 1M-2M. Pub'd 1 title 1990; expects 1 title 1991. 6 titles listed in the *Small Press Record of Books in Print* (20th Edition, 1991-92). avg. price, cloth: $25-$35; paper: $2.25-$4. 1/3 discount to retail outlets, 4 or less, 60/40 on 5 or more. No other discounts. 172-732pp; 5×8 or larger; of. Reporting time: 3-6 months. Payment: agreed percentage of profits. Copyrights for author.

IllumiNet Press, Nancy Kratzer, Co-Owner; Ron Bonds, Co-Owner, PO Box 746, Avondale Estates, GA 30002, 404-377-2590. 1990. Fiction, non-fiction. "Interested in paranormal, UFO, avant-garde, conspiracy theory, magick, anarchist philosophy" avg. press run 1.2M. Pub'd 2 titles 1990; expects 6 titles 1991, 8 titles 1992. 2 titles listed in the *Small Press Record of Books in Print* (20th Edition, 1991-92). avg. price, cloth: $24.95; paper: $10.95. Discounts: 50% 10 or more copies, 20% libraries. 220pp; 6×9; of. Reporting time: 60 days. Payment: 10-15%. Does not copyright for author.

ILR Press, Frances Benson, Director; Erica Fox, Managing Editor; Andrea Fleck Clardy, Special Projects, Cornell University, School of Indust. & Labor Relations, Ithaca, NY 14851-0952, 607-255-3061. 1945. "Our books deal with all aspects of work and working life, including economics, history, labor-management relations, law organizational theory, personnel management, and social policy. Manuscripts are accepted for publication only after favorable review by outside authorities and recommendation by the School's Research and Publications Committee" avg. press run 2M. Pub'd 10 titles 1990; expects 10 titles 1991, 12 titles 1992. 14 titles listed in the *Small Press Record of Books in Print* (20th Edition, 1991-92). avg. price, cloth: $26; paper: $10.95; other: $6 key issues. Discounts: 25% to the trade, quantity discounts. 200pp; 6×9; of. Reporting time: within 6 weeks to initial query. Payment: varies. Copyrights for author.

Image Industry Publications, Jacqueline Thompson, 10 Bay Street Landing, #7F, Staten Island, NY 10301-2511, 718-273-3229. 1978. Satire. avg. press run 3M. Expects 1 title 1992. avg. price, paper: $35. Discounts: available on request; only for purchases of 5 or more copies. 288pp; 6×9; of.

IMAGE MAGAZINE, Cornerstone Press, Anthony J. Summers, James J. Finnegan, Editor at large; Steve Lorenz, Assistant Editor, PO Box 388, Arnold, MO 63010-0388. 1972. Poetry, fiction, articles, art, photos, cartoons, interviews, satire, reviews, letters, parts-of-novels, long-poems, plays, concrete art. "We want stuff that will make us scream or otherwise perform unnatural acts. It must be good, and daring. Some recent contributors: check back issues. No sloppy attempts at creativity. Failure to send SASE results in a pair of dirty underwear and/or socks returned to sender. Submissions must be tight, well-written. You gotta be good to get in. We are always in need of good artwork and photography" circ. 400-600. 3/yr. Pub'd 3 issues 1990; expects 3 issues 1991. sub. price: $6; per copy: $3; sample: $3. Back issues: $5.00 per copy if I can find them. They are collectors items. Discounts: 1 free copy to any prisoner requesting. 40-60pp, special issues 80-175pp; 5½×8½; of. Reporting time: 6 weeks to infinity. Payment: 1 copy to contr. plus cash for best poem/s. story per issue. Copyrighted, reverts to author. Pub's reviews: 2 in 1990. §Anything. No ads. CCLM.

IMAGINATION MAGAZINE, Lisa Hake, PO Box 781, Dolton, IL 60419. 1990. Poetry, fiction, articles, art, photos, cartoons, interviews, satire, criticism, reviews, music, letters, parts-of-novels, collages, plays, concrete art, news items, non-fiction. "Recent contributors include Sheila Murphy, Michael Colin Murphy, H. Ray Nail. No porno or racism. Limit length to 24 lines-will consider longer poems." circ. 100. 13/yr (includes special year-end issue). Expects 12 issues 1991, 12 issues 1992. sub. price: $21; per copy: $2; sample: $3. Back issues: $1.50 June 1990-September 1990, $2.50 October 1990- on, May (premiere issue) not available. 32pp; 8½×7; †photo copied. Reporting time: 2-4 months. Payment: 1 copy. Copyrighted, reverts to author. Pub's reviews: will begin reviewing March 1991 in 1990. §Poetry, general, literary criticism, fiction and non-fiction. Ads: $13.50/$8.50/$4.50 1/4 page/$2.50 1/8 page/50¢ per word, 15 word minimum/$35 front inside cover/$25 back inside or outside cover.

Imaginative Solutions, Joyce A. Johnson, Box 3553, Merrifield, VA 22116-3553, 703-560-1013. 1990. "This is a company to support creative authors who are contributing to solutions to the challenges of the 90's. I want to publish books that address society's issues in a way that will assist us to understand these issues." 2 titles listed in the *Small Press Record of Books in Print* (20th Edition, 1991-92). avg. price, paper: $10. Discounts: 5+ books 40%, non-returnable 50%. 120pp; 6×9. Reporting time: 30 days. Payment: creative. Copyrights for author.

IMAGO, Philip Neilsen, Queensland Univ Technology, School of Communication, PO Box 2434, Brisbane Q1D 4001, Australia, (07)223 2111, FAX (07)229 1510. 1988. "Short stories and articles under 3000 words; poems preferably short; reviews 500 words." circ. 500. 2/yr. Pub'd 2 issues 1990; expects 2 issues 1991, 2 issues 1992. sub. price: $A12.50; per copy: $A7.50. 90pp; 5¾×8¼; of. Reporting time: 3 months. Copyrighted, reverts to author. Pub's reviews: 15 in 1990. §Novels, poetry, non-fiction, but such books need to be relevant to the Australian literary scene.

IMMANENT FACE, Carl Quesnel, Editor-in-Chief, PO Box 492 New Town Branch, Boston, MA 02258. 1987. Poetry, fiction, articles, art, photos, reviews, letters. "*IF* was created as a forum for people to express what they feel to be important. We prefer writing based on personal experience, reflection, and speculation. Essentially, if you've been working something out in your head, we'd like to see it on paper. We also encourage general fiction and poetry submissions as well as artwork—each issue features a variety." circ. 200+. 6/yr. Pub'd 2 issues 1990; expects 6 issues 1991, 6 issues 1992. sub. price: $10; per copy: $2; sample: $1. 25pp; 8½×11; duplicator/copier. Reporting time: 1 month maximum. Payment: $25 for cover artwork (please inquire). Not copyrighted. Pub's reviews: 1 in 1990. please inquire.

THE IMMIGRANT, Walter Vojislav Medenica, 4601 Barbara Drive, Beltsville, MD 20705. 1987. Poetry, fiction, articles, cartoons, satire, criticism, parts-of-novels, plays, non-fiction. 12/yr. sub. price: $18. 24pp; 11×15. No report prior to publication. Payment: free subscription. Copyrighted, reverts to author. Ads: //$7.50 per column inch.

Impact Publications, Mark Keller, Publisher; Caryl Rae Krannich, 10655 Big Oak Circle, Manassas, VA 22111, 703-361-7300. 1982. avg. press run 8M. Pub'd 3 titles 1990; expects 6 titles 1991, 6 titles 1992. 5 titles listed in the *Small Press Record of Books in Print* (20th Edition, 1991-92). avg. price, paper: $11.95. Discounts: 40% to bookstores; 50% to distributors (minimum orders). 300pp; 8½×11, 6×9; lp. Reporting time: 6 weeks. Payment: flexible. Copyrights for author.

Impact Publishers, Inc., Robert E. Alberti, President, PO Box 1094, San Luis Obispo, CA 93406, 805-543-5911. 1970. Photos, cartoons, non-fiction. "Personal development, relationships, families" avg. press run 5M-10M. Pub'd 5 titles 1990; expects 4 titles 1991, 4 titles 1992. 28 titles listed in the *Small Press Record of Books in Print* (20th Edition, 1991-92). avg. price, cloth: $11.95; paper: $8.95. Discounts: bookstores: up to 4 copies, 25% prepaid; 5-49 copies 40%; 50 plus copies, contact Impact re terms; libraries paper 10%; cloth 15%; wholesale distributors: contact Impact re terms. 200-300pp; 5⅜×8; of. Reporting time: 6-8 weeks. Payment: standard royalty contract. Copyrights for author. PMA, ABA.

IMPETUS, Implosion Press, Cheryl A. Townsend, 4975 Comanche Trail, Stow, OH 44224, 216-688-5210. 1984. Poetry, articles, art, cartoons, interviews, reviews, letters, collages, news items. "Into social/political protest work. Recent contributors include Gerald Locklin, Andrew Gettler, Steve Richmond." circ. 350. 4/yr. Pub'd 6 issues 1990; expects 4 issues 1991, 4 issues 1992. sub. price: $12, $18; per copy: $3; sample: $3. Back issues: $3. Discounts: free to prisoners/restricted income persons; trade with other publications. 55pp; 7×8½; †mi. Reporting time: within a month, usually same week. Payment: copy of issue appearing in. Copyrighted, reverts to author. Pub's reviews: 200+ in 1990. §Poetry. Ads: free to magazines I exchange with.

Implosion Press (see also IMPETUS), Cheryl A. Townsend, 4975 Comanche Trail, Stow, OH 44224, 216-688-5210. 1984. Poetry, art, cartoons, interviews, reviews, letters, collages, news items. "Quarterly magazines takes in above listed items. Annual All Female issues take above items pertaining only to the gender of issue. Chapbooks series (usually 4-6 per year) is by invitation only, but will look at material sent in. Broadsides are also printed. Have published chapbooks by Gerald Locklin, Lyn Lifshin/Belinda Subraman, Ron Androla, amongst others" avg. press run 400. Pub'd 4 titles 1990; expects 5 titles 1991, 6 titles 1992. 1 title listed in the *Small Press Record of Books in Print* (20th Edition, 1991-92). avg. price, paper: $2. Discounts: free for review. 24pp; 5½×8½. Reporting time: within a month, usually within same week. Payment: 20 copies of title. Copyrights for author.

IM-Press, Thomas Wnorowski, 3030 Chelsea Circle, Ann Arbor, MI 48108, (313) 973-7338. 1984. Non-fiction. "Interested in the following areas: self-improvement, 'How-to' topics, and 'technology-related on introductory level'" avg. press run 5M. Pub'd 2 titles 1990; expects 3 titles 1991, 4 titles 1992. 2 titles listed in the *Small Press Record of Books in Print* (20th Edition, 1991-92). avg. price, paper: $7.95. Discounts: 20% school, library, government; 40% store; 55% wholesaler, jobber. 70-90pp; 6×9; of. Reporting time: 30 days or less. Payment: by contract 7.5-12%. Copyrights for author.

IMPULSE, Eldon Garnet, Executive Editor; C. White, Art Director; B. Bolgon, Editor; J. Doyle, Editor; D. Lypchuk, Editor, 16 Skey Lane, Toronto, Ontario M6J 3S4, Canada, 1-416-537-9551. 1971. Fiction, articles, art, photos, interviews, music, parts-of-novels, non-fiction. "Unpublished material" circ. 5M. 4/yr. Pub'd 4 issues 1990; expects 3 issues 1991, 3 issues 1992. sub. price: $24 Can. & US; per copy: $10; sample: $10. Back issues: available upon request. Discounts: bookstores 40%, distributors 50%. 100pp; 8½×11; of. Reporting time: 4 months. Payment: yes. Copyrighted, does not revert to author. Ads: $700/$400/$250 1/4 page. CPPA, 2 Stewart Street, Toronto, Ontario M5V 1H6.

In Between Books, Karla Andersdatter, PO Box 790, Sausalito, CA 94966, 383-8447. Poetry. "I *do not* want unsolicited ms. I edit for Plain View Press, Austin, TX." avg. press run 1M. Pub'd 1 title 1990. 1 title listed in the *Small Press Record of Books in Print* (20th Edition, 1991-92). avg. price, paper: $4-$10. Discounts: 40% to stores, 20% to libraries. 8×5; varies. Copyrights for author.

In One Ear Press, Elizabeth Reid, 3527 Voltaire Street, San Diego, CA 92106, 619-223-1871. 1989. Poetry, articles, non-fiction. "Additional phone: 011-52-661-0369. In addition to books, we publish educational games,

268

greeting cards and a magazine." avg. press run 2M. Pub'd 1 title 1990; expects 4 titles 1991, 4 titles 1992. 4 titles listed in the *Small Press Record of Books in Print* (20th Edition, 1991-92). avg. price, paper: $12.95; other: comb $12.95. Discounts: bulk 40%. 224pp; 5×8½. Reporting time: 3 months. Payment: negotiated. Copyrights for author. COSMEP/PMA/San Diego Book Publicists.

INCITE INFORMATION, Mark Hand, 1507 E. Franklin Street #530, Chapel Hill, NC 27514. 1990. Articles, art, cartoons, reviews, letters, news items. "Length of material: 250-2,500 words. Biases: political free-for-all. Recent contributors: Mumia Abu-Jamal, Todd Mason, Joe Peacott, Ann Misch" circ. 300. 6/yr. Pub'd 9 issues 1990; expects 6 issues 1991, 6 issues 1992. sub. price: $10; per copy: $2; sample: $1. Back issues: $2 single, $10 volume. Discounts: 30% 5 or more. 20-24pp; 5½×8½; of. Reporting time: 1 month. Payment: none. Copyrighted, reverts to author. Pub's reviews: 25 in 1990. §History, political affairs, current affairs, regional (world), libertarianism. Ads: $25/$15/$10 1/4 page.

INCREDIBLE INQUIRY REPORTS, Fry's Incredible Inquirys, A. Fry, HC76, Box 2207, Garden Valley, ID 83622. 1987. Criticism, non-fiction. "Strange events, conspiracies, mental control methodology" circ. 5M. Spasmodic. Pub'd 1 issue 1990; expects 1 issue 1992. price per copy: $1; sample: same. Back issues: $1. Discounts: none. 4pp. Not copyrighted. No ads.

Indelible Inc. (see also MASSACRE), Roberta McKeown, BCM 1698, London WC1N 3XX, England, 0924-892-661. 1988. Poetry, fiction, photos, cartoons, satire, criticism, collages. "Indelible Inc. was founded to publish children's books, but has now branched out. Although the first 2 titles were hardcover picture books, later children's books (and those now being considered) are small chapbooks, published in 'The Black & White & Read All Over' Series. Submissions welcome but must be bizarre and charming and able to be illustrated in black & white. Indelible Inc. publishes *massacre*, an annual anthology of anti-naturalistic fiction and reprints neglected or out of print books of general interest with notes (titles include a 16th century poem about the Gout). Suitable submissions welcome: novellas (no long novels), criticism, suggestions for reprints from editors, short stories. No poetry (unless suggestions for out of print—and copyright—reprints). Indelible Inc. publishes the whimsical, odd, neglected and unusual. Its best-selling children's book, for example, is called *Derek the Dust-Particle* and has probably never been bought for a child." avg. press run 300. Pub'd 6 titles 1990; expects 4 titles 1991, 5 titles 1992. 8 titles listed in the *Small Press Record of Books in Print* (20th Edition, 1991-92). avg. price, cloth: £6.25-£15; paper: £2-£5. Discounts: libraries 10%, trade 35%. 40-88pp; 5½×8½; of. Reporting time: 1-2 months. Payment: 7% per net price of each book sold, 5 comp. copies; royalties do not amount to much since runs are so small. Copyrights for author. Small Press Group of Britain (SPG), BM Bozo, London WC1N 3XX, UK; Women in Publishing.

Independence Publishers Inc., Stanley Beitler, Editorial Director, Associate Publisher, PO Box 29905, Atlanta, GA 30359, 404-636-7092. 1987. Fiction, interviews, satire, criticism, letters, parts-of-novels, non-fiction. "We seek fiction and nonfiction (of social issues) manuscripts. We read all manuscripts submitted to us and accept either a complete manuscript or an outline with a few sample chapters." Expects 1 title 1991, 3 titles 1992. 2 titles listed in the *Small Press Record of Books in Print* (20th Edition, 1991-92). of. Reporting time: 4 weeks. Payment: royalty. Copyrights for author. Publishing Assoc. of the South (PAS), COSMEP.

Independent Publishing Co. (see also NEW WRITER'S MAGAZINE; YESTERDAY'S MAGAZETTE), Ned Burke, PO Box 15126, Sarasota, FL 34277, 922-7080. 1971. Poetry, fiction, articles, photos, interviews, reviews, letters, news items, non-fiction. "We specialize in meeting the printing needs of the desktop publisher & writer. We do first class books on 60# paper with glossy covers. Size & amount of copies needed can be small or large." avg. press run 500. Pub'd 6 titles 1990; expects 12 titles 1991, 20 titles 1992. 2 titles listed in the *Small Press Record of Books in Print* (20th Edition, 1991-92). avg. price, paper: $5. 60pp; 5½×8½; †of. Reporting time: 2 weeks. Payment: none. Copyrights for author.

Independent Research Services of Irvine (IRIS/I) (see also IDEAS IN INVESTING), Eva Rosenberg, 4525 Hazeltine Avenue #3, Van Nuys, CA 91423-2832. 2 titles listed in the *Small Press Record of Books in Print* (20th Edition, 1991-92). 8½×11.

Index House, Arne Jon Arneson, PO Box 716, Stevens Point, WI 54481-6892, 715-341-2604. 1985. avg. press run 500. Expects 2 titles 1991, 3 titles 1992. 4 titles listed in the *Small Press Record of Books in Print* (20th Edition, 1991-92). avg. price, paper: $45. Discounts: quantity only. 300pp; 6×9; lp. Payment: 50% of profits after production costs. Copyrights for author.

INDEX ON CENSORSHIP, Writers & Scholars International Ltd., Andrew Graham-Vooll, Editor; Philip Spender, Director & Pubisher, 39c Highbury Place, London N5 1QP, England, 071-359-0161. 1972. Poetry, fiction, articles, cartoons, interviews, satire, criticism, reviews, letters, parts-of-novels, plays, news items, non-fiction. "US sub price includes air-surface postage. Magazine is an outlet for manuscripts by authors who cannot be published in their own countries; and publishes reports on threats to freedom of expression-such as the censorship or persecution or torture of writers, scholars, journalists, artists, film-makers etc. Also publishes interviews, discussions and questionnaires. Scope is international-West and East, North and South. Contributors include: Vaclav Havel, Nadine Gordimer, Eduardo Galeano, Ernesto Cardenal, Georgi Vladimov, Sipho Sepamla, Don Mattera, Mario Vargas Llosa, Ivan Klima, Manlio Argueta, Manuel Puig, Lutz Rathenow, Naji al-Ali, Modhaffar al-Nawab, Hadi Khorsandi, Nawal el Saadawi, Mustafa Amin, Xu Wenli, Pramoedya Ananta Toer, Aziz Nesin. US address: c/o Fund for Free Expression, 485 Fifth Avenue, New York, NY 10017" circ. 5.5M. 10/yr. Pub'd 10 issues 1990; expects 10 issues 1991, 10 issues 1992. sub. price: $38, £24, students $22, £13; per copy: $3.60, £2.10; sample: free. Back issues: $4.25; £3. Discounts: agent 10%, bookshops variable (supplied via FFE, 485 Fifth Avenue, New York, NY 10017, or direct from London, or via local US distributor). 42pp; 275×213mm; of. Reporting time: variable. Payment: £50 per thou to authors. Authors' copyrights by arrangement. Pub's reviews: 29 in 1990. §Censorship, human rights, books by or about banned writers. Ads: £330 ($500)/£165 ($250).

INDEX TO FOREIGN LEGAL PERIODICALS, University of California Press, Thomas H. Reynolds, University of California Press, 2120 Berkeley Way, Berkeley, CA 94720, 415-642-4191. 1960. Articles, reviews, non-fiction. "Editorial address: The Law Library, Boalt Hall School of Law, Berkeley, CA 94720. Copyrighted by The American Association of Law Libraries." circ. 600. 3/yr. Pub'd 4 issues 1990; expects 4 issues 1991, 4 issues 1992. sub. price: $450 (+ $12 foreign postage). 250pp; 7×10; of. Copyrighted, does not revert to author. No ads accepted.

INDIA CURRENTS, Arvind Kumar, Box 21285, San Jose, CA 95151, 408-274-6966. 1987. Poetry, fiction, articles, art, photos, cartoons, interviews, satire, criticism, reviews, music, letters, parts-of-novels, collages, non-fiction. "Between 300-3,000 words. We look for insightful approach to India, its arts, culture, people. Recent contributors: Mandira Sen, Norman Weinstein, Ashok Jethanandani, Raphael Ardeo." circ. 15M. 12/yr. Pub'd 12 issues 1990; expects 12 issues 1991, 12 issues 1992. sub. price: $16; per copy: $2; sample: same. Back issues: $2. 72pp; 8½×11; of. Reporting time: 1 month. Payment: $20 per 1,000 words. Copyrighted, reverts to author. Pub's reviews: 12 in 1990. §India and Indians, colonialism, immigration. Ads: $300/$165/25¢. COSMEP.

THE INDIAN WRITER, Dr. P.K. Joy, C-23, Anna Nagar East, Madras-600 102, Tamil Nadu, India, 615370. 1986. Poetry, reviews, news items, non-fiction. "We publish short poems, book reviews, scholarly notes on mechanics of writings and news about national and international literary activities." circ. 750. 4/yr. Pub'd 4 issues 1990; expects 4 issues 1991, 4 issues 1992. sub. price: $20; per copy: free; sample: free. 16pp; †lp. Reporting time: 1 month. Payment: copy. Not copyrighted. Pub's reviews: over 40 in 1990. §Poetry. Ads: $50/$30. Writers Club of India.

Indiana Publications, Inc., David E. Salisbury, Melissa Ann Salisbury, PO Box 1213, Seymour, IN 47274, 812-523-8889. 1986. "The Great American Editions Series consist of 20 books on cities in America to be released on a time schedule over the next 5 years. The first volume on Indianapolis will be released in January of 1988, with Louisville, Cincinnati to be released in 1988. For the complete listing of releases, write to Indiana Publications, Inc." avg. press run 25M. Pub'd 1 title 1990; expects 3 titles 1991, 4 titles 1992. avg. price, cloth: $33. Discounts: 1-5 copies 30%, 6-20 35%, 21-49 40%, 50-99 45%, 99+ 50%. 280pp; 9×12. Reporting time: 4 months. Payment: none. Does not copyright for author. International Independent Publishers, Mid America Publishing Group.

INDIANA REVIEW, Allison Joseph, Editor; Dorian Gossy, Associate Editor, 316 North Jordan Avenue, Indiana University, Bloomington, IN 47405, 812-855-3439. 1982. Poetry, fiction, art, parts-of-novels, long-poems. "*Indiana Review* is a magazine of poetry, fiction, and essays. We prefer writing that shows both an awareness of language and of the world outside. We publish 6-8 stories and about 30 pages of poetry per issue. We like writers who take risks and handle material almost perfectly more than we like writers who take no risks and handle the material flawlessly. We're not beholden to any one genre, though stock science fiction, porn and the like finds its way home quite swiftly. All submissions are read start to finish. Recent contributors have included Charles Baxter, Pam Durban, Abby Frucht, Andre Dubus, Mark Jarman, Maria Flook, Richard Katrovas, David Mura." circ. 1M. 3/yr. Pub'd 3 issues 1990; expects 3 issues 1991, 3 issues 1992. sub. price: $12, institutions $15, please add $2 for overseas; per copy: $5; sample: $5. Back issues: $5. Discounts: trade 60/40% split; 50-50 to distributors. 124pp; 9×6; of. Reporting time: 2 weeks-4 months. Payment: $5 per page poem, $5 per page story. Copyrighted, reverts to author. Ads: $100/$60. CLMP.

INDIGENOUS WORLD/EL MUNDO INDIGENA, Roxanne Dunbar Ortiz, Chockie Cottier, 275 Grand View Avenue, No. 103, San Francisco, CA 94114, 415-647-1966. 1982. Poetry, articles, art, photos, cartoons, interviews, news items, non-fiction. "Bilingual, documentation of international, especially United Nations, activities of indigenous peoples all over the world, especially Indians of the Americas, with focus on Central America. No submissions accepted, all solicited" circ. 10M. 2/yr. Pub'd 2 issues 1990; expects 2 issues 1991, 2 issues 1992. sub. price: $20; per copy: $10; sample: $5. Back issues: $20. Discounts: 40%. 28pp; 12×17; web. Payment: none. Not copyrighted. Pub's reviews: 1 in 1990. No ads.

INDIVIDUAL LIBERTY, Society for Individual Liberty, Donald Ernsberger, PO Box 338, Warminster, PA

18974, 215-675-6830. 1969. ""'A newsletter dedicated to Individual Rights, Free Markets and Reason'"" circ. 1.7M. 12/yr. Pub'd 12 issues 1990; expects 12 issues 1991, 12 issues 1992. sub. price: $10; per copy: $1; sample: $1. Back issues: $1 per issue. Discounts: none. 8pp; 8½x11; †of. Reporting time: due date last Thursday before last Saturday of the month. Payment: none. Copyrighted, reverts to author. Pub's reviews: 8 in 1990. §Politics, philosophy, economics. Ads: $40/$25.

INDUSTRIAL RELATIONS LAW JOURNAL, University of California Press, Students of Boalt Hall School of Law, University of California Press, 2120 Berkeley Way, Berkeley, CA 94720, 415-642-4191. Articles, reviews, non-fiction. "Editorial address: 1 Boalt Hall School of Law, University of CA, Berkeley, CA 94720. Copyrighted by Industrial Relations Law Journal." circ. 850. 2/yr. Pub'd 4 issues 1990; expects 4 issues 1991, 4 issues 1992. sub. price: $32 indiv., $38 instit. (+ $4 foreign postage); per copy: $16 indiv.; $19 instit. (+ $4 foreign postage); sample: free. Back issues: $16 indiv.; $19 instit. Discounts: foreign subs. agent 10%, one-time order 10+ 30%, standing orders (bookstores): 1-99 40%, 100+ 50%. 250pp; 7x10; of. Reporting time: 1-2 months. Payment: varies. Copyrighted, does not revert to author. Ads: $200/$120.

INFINITE ONION, Dave Fischer, PO Box 263, Colorado Springs, CO 80901, 719-473-2647. 1989. Poetry, fiction, articles, art, photos, cartoons, interviews, satire, criticism, reviews, collages, news items, non-fiction. "Anarchist zine with bits and pieces on pot, racism, war, being free, bisexuality, cars, entropy, nazis, art, poetry, government, cops, anger, punk, reviews and more. Please don't send checks. If you must send a money order, please make it out to *David Fischer*; anything else will be sent back." circ. 1M. 5/yr. Pub'd 5 issues 1990; expects 4-5 issues 1991. sub. price: $5/5 issues; per copy: $1; sample: $1. Back issues: $1 for issue 5, 75¢ with other order. Discounts: will trade for similar anarchist zines, 50¢ a copy post paid for bulk (10 or more), can arrange barter. 24pp; 8½x11. Payment: none. Not copyrighted. Pub's reviews: 150+ in 1990. §Anarchist in orientation, punk rock magazines, or in relation to revolutionary struggle, anti-sexist, anti-racist. Ads: $70/$30/free for trade with other magazines.

Infinite Savant Publishing, PO Box 2321, Van Nuys, CA 91404, 213-293-7767. 1990. Fiction, non-fiction. avg. press run 500-1M. Expects 3 titles 1991, 4 titles 1992. 3 titles listed in the *Small Press Record of Books in Print* (20th Edition, 1991-92). avg. price, paper: $6.95. 160pp; 5½x8½; of. Reporting time: 3 weeks. Copyrights for author.

INFINITY LIMITED, A Journal for the Somewhat Eccentric, Genie Lester, PO Box 2713, Castro Valley, CA 94546, 415-581-8172. 1988. Poetry, fiction, articles, art, photos, cartoons, satire, reviews, long-poems, plays, non-fiction. "Until we expand we are limited to 40 pages including cover. We are dedicated to publishing emerging writers, artists, and philosophers who can present their ideas in interesting and/or entertaining format. Our goal is to present visually pleasing material that makes one think but that doesn't preach. Zany or romantic, we can accommodate both. Our subtitle is 'A journal for the somewhat eccentric'" circ. 1M. 4/yr. Pub'd 1 issue 1990; expects 4 issues 1991, 4 issues 1992. sub. price: $10; per copy: $3.95; sample: $3.95. 40pp; 8½x11; of. Reporting time: 5-6 weeks. Payment: 2 copies. Copyrighted, reverts to author. Pub's reviews: 1 in 1990. §Fiction, art, poetry. Ads: $100/$50/$10 business card.

Info Net Publishing (see also RACE ACROSS AMERICA PROGRAM), Herb Wetenkamp, JoAnn Byrne, PO Box 3789, San Clemente, CA 92674, 714-489-9267. 1986. Articles, art, photos, interviews, reviews, news items, non-fiction. "24-32 pages of facts, figures and bicycle rider profiles of competitors in the annual 3,000-plus-miles Race Across America (RAAM); route maps and descriptions, training techniques, history and other vital info." avg. press run 10M-20M. Pub'd 1 title 1990; expects 1 title 1991, 3 titles 1992. 3 titles listed in the *Small Press Record of Books in Print* (20th Edition, 1991-92). avg. price, cloth: $1. Discounts: 50%. 28pp; 8½x11; of. Reporting time: 1-2 months. Payment: please inquire. Copyrights for author.

INFOCUS, William Urban, 519 SW 3rd Avenue, #712, Portland, OR 97204-2519, 503-227-3393. Articles, art, photos, interviews, reviews, news items, non-fiction. "Articles should be a maximum of 1M words. Especially interested in new technology and its impact on business and paperwork. Enclose SASE. Simultaneous submissions ok. Query or send manuscript. Recent titles: *Laser Forms Make Mark at AAL*; *Knowing When to Automate Forms Inventory Management*; *Integrating Office Technologies*; *Promoting Forms Management In Smaller Federal Agencies.*" circ. 2.5M. 10/yr. Pub'd 4 issues 1990; expects 3 issues 1991. sub. price: $50 (US, US Possession, Canada, Mexico), all others $65, library rate $35; per copy: $10; sample: free. Back issues: $10 as available. Discounts: call publisher for quote. 8pp; 8½x11; of. Reporting time: 2 months. Payment: negotiable. Copyrighted, reverts to author negotiable. Pub's reviews: 5 in 1990. §Office automation, management techniques, paperwork simplification, forms and procedures. Ads: write for rate card.

Infolib Resources, Alex Spence, Editor, 469 Spadina Road, Suite 15, Toronto, Ontario M5P 2W6, Canada. 1982. Fiction, non-fiction. avg. press run 200. Pub'd 1 title 1990; expects 1 title 1991, 1 title 1992. 8 titles listed in the *Small Press Record of Books in Print* (20th Edition, 1991-92). avg. price, paper: $20. 125pp; 8½x11; professional photocopy (mi). Reporting time: 6 weeks. Payment: royalties 10-25%, negotiable. Does not copyright for author.

Information Requirements Clearinghouse, Donald Skupsky, 3801 E. Florida Avenue, Suite 400, Denver, CO 80201, 303-691-3600. 1984. Non-fiction. avg. press run 10M. Pub'd 1 title 1990; expects 2 titles 1991, 2 titles 1992. 2 titles listed in the *Small Press Record of Books in Print* (20th Edition, 1991-92). avg. price, cloth: $25; paper: $39. 344pp; 6×9, 8½×11; lp.

INFORMATION RETRIEVAL AND LIBRARY AUTOMATION, Lomond Publications Inc., Susan W. Johnson, Editor; Maxine Hattery, Managing Editor, PO Box 88, Mt. Airy, MD 21771, 301-829-1496. 1965. News items, non-fiction. "Topical coverage of new technologies, products/equipment, which improve information systems and library functions." circ. 1.2M. 12/yr. Pub'd 12 issues 1990; expects 12 issues 1991, 12 issues 1992. sub. price: $66; per copy: $5.50; sample: free. 12pp; 8½×11; of. Reporting time: 1 month. Copyrighted. Pub's reviews: 100 in 1990. §Any items appropriate to the above-defined scope. Ads: No Advertising. PMA (formerly PASCAL), Baltimore Publishers Association.

INITIATIV, Tryckeriforlaget, Leif Lindberg, Tumstocksvagen 19, Taby S-18304, Sweden, 08-7567445. 1983. Non-fiction. "Small business" circ. 15M. 6/yr. Pub'd 6 issues 1990; expects 6 issues 1991, 6 issues 1992. sub. price: SEK 215; per copy: SEK 52; sample: free. Back issues: SEK 25. 64pp; 210×297mm; of. Pub's reviews: 20 in 1990. §Business, especially small business. Ads: SEK 7.900.

INKBLOT, Inkblot Publications, Theo Green, 439 49th Street #11, Oakland, CA 94609-2158. 1983. Poetry, fiction, photos, parts-of-novels, long-poems, collages, concrete art. "Pieces may be any length, usually we publish items 2-4 pages long. We feature modern, avante-garde fiction and poetry from International writers. Issue 2 was dedicated to cut-up writing featuring: Jurgen Ploog, Claude Pelieu, F.A. Nettelbeck, Udo Breger, Bob Cobbing, etc" circ. 1M. 4/yr. Pub'd 4 issues 1990; expects 4 issues 1991, 4 issues 1992. sub. price: $12; per copy: $5; sample: $5. Back issues: $3.00 each. Discounts: 40-50%. 60-70pp; 8½×11; mi, of. Reporting time: 3-6 months. Payment: copies. Copyrighted, reverts to author. Pub's reviews: 0 in 1990. §Literature, art, colour, the 60s, etc. Ads: $50 -1/4 pg/$100 -1/2 pg etc. COSMEP.

Inkblot Publications (see also INKBLOT), Theo Green, Seamus O'Rourke, 439 49th Street #11, Oakland, CA 94609-2158. 1982. Poetry, fiction, articles, art, photos, interviews, reviews, parts-of-novels, long-poems, concrete art, non-fiction. "Recent books by Theo Green & Brion Gysin. Upcoming books, which will be smaller than the 8½ X 11 listed below, include titles from: Brion Gysin, F.A. Nettelbeck, Janine Brooks, Wanda Lucente, & Theo Green. Material is alternative—avante garde poetry & fiction. Terry Wilson, Bob Cobbing, Gellu Naum" avg. press run 500. Pub'd 2 titles 1990; expects 3 titles 1991, 5 titles 1992. 11 titles listed in the *Small Press Record of Books in Print* (20th Edition, 1991-92). avg. price, paper: $6. Discounts: 40-50%. 30-120pp; 5¼×8; mi, of. Reporting time: 1-3 months. Payment: flat advance plus percentage of sales. Copyrights for author. COSMEP.

Inkling Publications, Inc., Marilyn Bailey, John Hall, 824 Winnetka Avenue South, Minneapolis, MN 55426. 1980. Poetry, fiction, articles, interviews, non-fiction. "How-to manuscripts 40M—on" avg. press run 3M. Pub'd 1 title 1990; expects 2 titles 1991, 4 titles 1992. 2 titles listed in the *Small Press Record of Books in Print* (20th Edition, 1991-92). avg. price, cloth: varies; paper: price varies. Discounts: 2-5 20%; 6-9 25%; 10-20 30%; 21+ 40%. 112-176pp; 5½×8½, 8½×11 (directories); of. Reporting time: 6-8 weeks. Payment: 10% royalty. Copyrights for author.

INKSTONE, Inkstone Press, Keith Southward, Marshall Hryciuk, J. Louise Fletcher, PO Box 67, Station H, Toronto, Ontario M4C 5H7, Canada, 962-6051. 1982. Poetry, articles, reviews. "*Inkstone* is a magazine of Haiku which draws on the full spectrum of the genre" Irregular. Pub'd 4 issues 1990; expects 4 issues 1991, 4 issues 1992. sub. price: $15; per copy: $5; sample: $5. Back issues: $5. Discounts: none. 40pp; 5½×8½; of. Reporting time: 8 weeks. Payment: copies. Copyrighted, reverts to author. Pub's reviews: 10 in 1990. §Haiku and related.

Inkstone Press (see also INKSTONE), Keith Southward, Marshall Hryciak, J. Louise Fletcher, PO Box 67, Station H, Toronto, Ontario M4C 5H7, Canada. 1982. Poetry, articles, reviews. avg. press run 100. Pub'd 1 title 1990; expects 1 title 1991, 1 title 1992. avg. price, cloth: $15; paper: $5. Discounts: none. 40pp; 5½×8½; of. Reporting time: 8 weeks. Payment: copies. Copyrights for author.

INLET, Joseph Harkey, Editor; Kathleen Bogan Thomason, Assistant Editor, Virginia Wesleyan College, Norfolk, VA 23502. 1971. Poetry, fiction. "Published in Spring of every year. Poems: prefer under 30 lines; poems over 40 lines must be especially good. Open on style, subject, form. Short fiction: 700-3M words prefer under 1.5M words. We seek as much diversity as possible in the writing we publish. Submissions accepted September 1, through March 1. Send fiction and poetry to editor." circ. 700. 1/yr. Pub'd 1 issue 1990; expects 1 issue 1991, 1 issue 1992. sub. price: free with $1 in stamps—checks for such small amounts not accepted; per copy: same; sample: same. Back issues: same. 33pp; 8½×7½; of. Reporting time: 2 weeks-3 months, sometimes longer, no dual submissions. Payment: copies. Copyrighted.

INNER JOURNEYS, Gateways Books And Tapes, Iven Lourie, Nancy Christie, PO Box 370, Nevada City,

CA 95959. 1987. Reviews, news items. "This is a *newsletter* with capsule reviews in the *spiritual and consciousness* field only. We do not solicit authors, only review books in our own field" circ. 1M+. 4/yr. Expects 3-4 issues 1991, 3-4 issues 1992. sub. price: $5; per copy: $1; sample: free. 4-6pp; 8½×11; †of. Copyrighted, reverts to author. Pub's reviews: 4-6 per issue in 1990. §Sprituality, consciousness research, esotericism. No ads. American Booksellers Assn.

INNER SEARCH, Bruce Brown, Joan Brown, PO Box 3577, Station C, Ottawa, Ontario K1Y 4J7, Canada. 1990. Poetry, fiction, articles, art, interviews, reviews, letters, news items, non-fiction. "*Inner Search* is an informal newsletter—a Forum exploring soul, mind & body. We put emphasis on Forum: we look for input from our readers in the form of researched articles, opinioned essays, book reviews, etc. Focus is on exchanging ideas on subjects such as mysticism, comparative religion, reincarnation, etc. This is almost a magazine but in newsletter format. Keep articles under 3,000 words. Also open to fiction (under 2,000 words) and poetry (under 20 lines) as long as material pertains to mysticism, etc." circ. under 200. 4/yr. Expects 2 issues 1991, 4 issues 1992. sub. price: $9; per copy: $2.50; sample: $1. Back issues: $2. Discounts: over 10 copies 20%/over 5 copies 15%. 20pp; 8½×11. Reporting time: 3 weeks. Payment: copy only. Copyrighted, reverts to author. Pub's reviews. §Mysticism, occult, New Age, comparative religion. Ads: Query.

Inner Traditions International, Ehud C. Sperling, President & Publisher; Leslie Colket, Managing Editor, One Park Street, Rochester, VT 05767, 802-767-3174. 1975. Fiction, art, non-fiction. "Esoteric philosophy, occult and hermetic sciences, astrology, holistic health, mysticism, diet, nutrition, cookbooks" avg. press run 5M. Pub'd 50 titles 1990; expects 50 titles 1991, 50 titles 1992. 221 titles listed in the *Small Press Record of Books in Print* (20th Edition, 1991-92). avg. price, cloth: $24.95; paper: $10.95. 350pp; 6×9; of. Reporting time: 5 weeks. Payment: standard for industry. Copyrights for author. A.B.A.

Inner Vision Publishing Company, John Van Auken, Doris Dean, Henry Reed, PO Box 1117, Virginia Beach, VA 23451-0117. 1984. Non-fiction. "Spiritual/metaphysical self-help is our primary focus" avg. press run 3M. Pub'd 2 titles 1990; expects 2 titles 1991, 2 titles 1992. 10 titles listed in the *Small Press Record of Books in Print* (20th Edition, 1991-92). avg. price, paper: $10.95. Discounts: 30%, 40%, and 50%, depends on the specific book and arrangements. 185pp; 5½×8½; of. Reporting time: 3 months. Payment: 10 to 15%, depending on the arrangement. Copyrights for author. ABA, NAPRA.

Inner Wealth Press, Roy Carlisle, Don Child, Wyn Child, PO Box 487, Forest Knolls, CA 94933, 415-488-0771. 1987. Non-fiction. "Not soliciting at this time" avg. press run 3M. Pub'd 1 title 1990; expects 1 title 1992. 1 title listed in the *Small Press Record of Books in Print* (20th Edition, 1991-92). avg. price, paper: $12.95. 200pp; 5½×8½. COSMEP.

Innerer Klang, 7 Sherman Street, Charlestown, MA 02129. 1983. Poetry, fiction. Pub'd 1 title 1990; expects 2 titles 1991, 2 titles 1992. 6 titles listed in the *Small Press Record of Books in Print* (20th Edition, 1991-92). †lp.

INNOVATING, Harold S. Williams, The Rensselaerville Institute, Rensselaerville, NY 12147, 518-797-3783. 1963. Articles, cartoons, interviews, non-fiction. "Publication is dedicated to enabling people to lead change by example. The quarterly includes innovation assumptions, paradigms, research and examples. While the focus is on the public and voluntary sector, the content is also relevant to business and other kinds of organizations." circ. 1M. 4/yr. sub. price: $24; per copy: $7; sample: free. Back issues: $4. Discounts: according to volume. 70pp; 5½×8½; of. Reporting time: 6 weeks prior to publication date. Copyrighted, reverts to author. Pub's reviews: 2 in 1990. §Innovation/creativity, entrepreneur, management, education.

INQ Publishing Co., JanaSue Fitting, PO Box 10, N. Aurora, IL 60542, 708-801-0607. 1988. Fiction, articles, cartoons, news items, non-fiction. "Shipping address: 122 Juniper Dr., North Aurora, IL 60542" avg. press run varies. Pub'd 2 titles 1990; expects 1 title 1991, 5 titles 1992. 2 titles listed in the *Small Press Record of Books in Print* (20th Edition, 1991-92). avg. price, paper: $9.95; other: spirals $10.95. Pages vary; size varies; of. Reporting time: 6 weeks. COSMEP, MAPA.

THE INQUIRER, Keith Gilley, 1-6 Essex Street, London WC2R 3HY, England. 1842. Poetry, articles, cartoons. 26/yr. Pub'd 26 issues 1990; expects 26 issues 1991, 26 issues 1992. sub. price: $25; per copy: 25p; sample: free. 10pp; size A4 (297×210mm); of. Reporting time: 1 month. Copyrighted. Pub's reviews: 30 in 1990. §Religion, social matters. Ads: £3 + VAT @ 15%.

Inquiry Press, 1880 North Eastman, Midland, MI 48640-8838, 517-631-3350. 1975. "A division of Wysong Medical" 2 titles listed in the *Small Press Record of Books in Print* (20th Edition, 1991-92). avg. price, cloth: $15.95; paper: $8.95. Discounts: 4-10 15%, 11-25 20%, 26-50 30%, 51-100 40%, 100+ request quote. 450pp; 6×9; of, lp. Reporting time: 30 days.

INSECTS ARE PEOPLE TOO, H.R. Felgenhauer, PO Box 146486, Chicago, iL 60614, 312-772-8686. 1989. "Looking for insects doing people things and especially people doing insect things. Prospective contributors should send $3 for sample copy to get perspective." circ. 1M+. Erratic. Pub'd 1 issue 1990; expects 1 issue 1992. sub. price: $3; per copy: $3; sample: $3. Back issues: $3. 30pp; 8½×11; commercial printers. Reporting time: 1-3 weeks. Payment: liberal contributor's copies and/or modest honorarium. Copyrighted, reverts to author. Ads: $25/$15/inquire.

THE INSIDER GUNNEWS, John Aqualino, George Petersen, PO Box 2441, Merrifield, VA 22116, 202-832-0838. 1986. Non-fiction. "This publication deals exclusively with gun related issues: gun media, gun publications, associations connected with the gun issue, personalities, books, etc." circ. 1256. 12/yr. Pub'd 14 issues 1990; expects 12 issues 1991. sub. price: $50; per copy: $5. Back issues: $5. Discounts: 20%. 4pp; 8½×11; †of. Reporting time: depends, usually 1 month. Payment: every 30 days. Copyrighted, rights reverting depends. Pub's reviews: 3 in 1990. §Gun related issues or gun magazines, etc. Ads: none. DMMA, ESSA.

Insight Press, Merry Harris, Publisher; John Harris, Co-Publisher, PO Box 25, Ocotillo, CA 92259. Poetry, cartoons. *"Absolutely NO unsolicited manuscripts accepted!* Submissions are by invitation only. Otherwise we would be swamped. John is legally blind - Merry totally disabled. So we can't handle hundreds of unsolicited mss. Our books are published to creat a readership for good poetry at the non-academic level. We use only verses writtin in simple language which everyone can understand. We publish 15-20 poet's work each year. We also publish 3 newsletters:*Merry-Go-Round, Contest Carousel,* and Roadrunner. Artwork by Merry. We also use 1/4 of each printing to promote the individual author's work. Our selections of the contributors' work is widely reprinted. Our current plan is to convert to publishing fewer anthologies and featuring the work of individual poets. We are currently planning to publish two books of Indian poetry, by Falling Blossom and Malee Ridge, and a book of wild west poems by Little Buckaroo" avg. press run varies. Pub'd 1 title 1990; expects 1 title 1991, 1 title 1992. 1 title listed in the *Small Press Record of Books in Print* (20th Edition, 1991-92). avg. price, paper: $3. 40pp; 5½×4½; insta-print. Payment: one free copy. Copyrights for author. UAP (United Amateur Press), NAP (National Amateur Press), BAP (British Amateur Press).

Inspirational Publisher, Arthur C. Theimer, 2500 So. 370th St., Suite 134, Federal Way, WA 98003, 206-874-2310. 1989. Non-fiction. avg. press run 1M. Expects 1 title 1991. 1 title listed in the *Small Press Record of Books in Print* (20th Edition, 1991-92). avg. price, paper: $7.90. Discounts: 40%. 140pp; 5½×8½; lp. Copyrights for author.

Institute For Community Economics (see also COMMUNITY ECONOMICS), Kirby White, Lisa Berger, 151 Montague City Road, Greenfield, MA 01301, 413-774-7956. 1967. Non-fiction. "No unsolicited articles. In addition to our quarterly newsletter/magazine, we prepare booklets and books or manuals at times, such as our *Community Land Trust Handbook,* published for us by Rodale; the new *Community Loan Fund Manual* published by us; a *Legal Handbook for Community Land Trusts* to be published by us this year; a *National Directory of Community Development Loan Funds* prepared by ICE staff for the National Association of Community Development Loan Funds. While we did not actually publish the *CLT Handbook,* Rodale has turned over to us all the copies and we are now the sole source of the handbook" avg. press run 200-10M. Pub'd 2 titles 1990; expects 1 title 1991, 1 title 1992. avg. price, other: *CLT Handbook* $10; *Loan Fund Manual* in looseleaf form at $45. Discounts: available to related groups. lp.

Institute for Contemporary Studies/International Center for Economic Growth, A. Lawrence Chickering, Executive Editor; Janet Schilling Mowery, Managing Editor; Robert Davis, Editor; Heidi Fritschel, Editor; Tracy Clagett, Editor; Ysbrand Van der Werf, Assistant Editor, 243 Kearny Street, San Francisco, CA 94108, 415-981-5353; 800-326-0236. 1972. Articles, news items. "Books on domestic and international public policy issues. Books on international economics focus on developing countries." avg. press run 3M. Pub'd 8-10 titles 1990; expects 8-10 titles 1991, 12 titles 1992. 22 titles listed in the *Small Press Record of Books in Print* (20th Edition, 1991-92). avg. price, cloth: $25.95; paper: $12.95; other: $5 occasional papers, country studies. Discounts: bookstores 1-4 copies 20%; 5-49 40%; 50-99 44%; 100+ 46%; university bookstores 20% text orders; same as bookstores for trade books. 300pp; 6×9; of. Reporting time: 1-3 months. Payment: works for hire and royalty arrangements. Copyrights for author. COSMEP.

Institute for Palestine Studies (see also JOURNAL OF PALESTINE STUDIES), Hisham Sharabi, Philip Mattar, Linda Butler, PO Box 25697 Georgetown Station, Washington, DC 20007, 202-342-3990; 800-874-3614; FAX 202-342-3927. 1963. Non-fiction. avg. press run 2M-4M. Pub'd 4 titles 1990; expects 4 titles 1991, 4 titles 1992. avg. price, cloth: $17.95-$29.95; paper: $3.95-$19.95. Discounts: 30% booksellers, $20 libraries, bulk 11-30 35%, 31+ 40%. 55-1,312pp; 9×12¼ to 5½×8½. Payment: awards/grants. Copyrights for author.

Institute for Southern Studies (see also SOUTHERN EXPOSURE), Eric Bates, Editor, PO Box 531, Durham, NC 27702. 1973. Poetry, fiction, articles, art, photos, cartoons, interviews, reviews, plays, news items, non-fiction. avg. press run 8M. Pub'd 4 titles 1990; expects 4 titles 1991, 4 titles 1992. 27 titles listed in the *Small Press Record of Books in Print* (20th Edition, 1991-92). avg. price, paper: $5. Discounts: 5 or more copies 40%. 64pp; 8½×11; of. Reporting time: 4-6 weeks. Payment: on publication, no royalties. Copyrights for author. COSMEP.

Institute for the Study of Traditional American Indian Arts Press (see also AMERICAN INDIAN

BASKETRY), John M. Gogol, PO Box 66124, Portland, OR 97266, 503-233-8131. 1979. Articles, photos, interviews, criticism, non-fiction. "We are publishing a series of books on traditional American Indian arts, including: Basketry, beadwork, quillwork, blanket weaving, hide painting, feather work, stone and woodcarving, and medicine. Authors must have expertise in their subject. Material must be well illustrated. Length of publications from 16 to 160 pages." avg. press run 5M. Expects 2 titles 1991, 4 titles 1992. avg. price, paper: $10. Discounts: 40%. 80pp; 5½x8½; of. Reporting time: 1 month. Payment: varies, inquire.

Institute of Archaeology Publications, Ernestine Elster, Director of Publications; Carol Leyba, Senior Editor, University of California-Los Angeles, 405 Hilgard Avenue, Los Angeles, CA 90024-1510, 213-825-7411. 1975. Non-fiction. avg. press run 500. Pub'd 4 titles 1990; expects 4 titles 1991, 4 titles 1992. 19 titles listed in the *Small Press Record of Books in Print* (20th Edition, 1991-92). avg. price, cloth: $27.50; paper: $10.40. Discounts: 20% to agencies. 200pp; 8½x11; of. Reporting time: 60 days. Payment: none. Does not copyright for author.

Institute of Lesbian Studies, Ann Seawall, PO Box 60242, Palo Alto, CA 94306. 1985. Non-fiction. "Non-fiction lesbian and feminist theory" avg. press run 5M. Pub'd 1 title 1990; expects 1 title 1991, 3 titles 1992. 3 titles listed in the *Small Press Record of Books in Print* (20th Edition, 1991-92). avg. price, paper: $11.95. Discounts: bookstores 5+ books-40%; libraries 10%; distributors 50-55%; classroom orders 20%; payment net 90 days. 150pp; 5¼x8¼. Reporting time: 3 months. Does not copyright for author.

The Institute of Mind and Behavior Press (see also THE JOURNAL OF MIND AND BEHAVIOR), Raymond Russ, Ph.D., PO Box 522, Village Station, New York, NY 10014, 212-595-4853. 1980. Criticism, reviews, non-fiction. "Send manuscripts to Raymond Russ, Ph.D., Department of Psychology, University of Maine, Orono, Maine 04469. We are interested in scholarly manuscripts, with interdisciplinary thrust, in the areas of: the mind/body problem in the social sciences; the philosophy of experimentalism and theory construction; historical perspectives on the course and nature of scientific investigation; and mind/body interactions and medical implications." avg. press run 2M. Pub'd 1 title 1990; expects 2 titles 1991, 2 titles 1992. 5 titles listed in the *Small Press Record of Books in Print* (20th Edition, 1991-92). avg. price, paper: $18. Discounts: 18% on orders of 10 copies or more. 350pp; 5½x8½; of. Reporting time: 5-10 weeks. Payment: no fees to authors. Does not copyright for author.

J.P.R. Instone Publications, Jeff Instone, 7 Winkley Street, London E2 6P4, United Kingdom. 1990. Concrete art. "Computer generated artists' books" avg. press run 1M. Expects 2 titles 1991, 2 titles 1992. avg. price, paper: $13. Discounts: 30% trade, 40% education. 30pp; size A4 (210x297mm); lp. Copyrights for author. SLP, Cirque Divers, Paul Green.

Integral Publishing (see also SPECTRUM REVIEW), Georg Feuerstein, PO Box 1030, Lower Lake, CA 95457, 707-928-5751. 1986. Non-fiction. "Ideal length: 160-180 book pages (c. 64-72,000 words). Materials must be well researched and sophisticated but not aridly academic. General orientation: alternative thought. Lee Sannella, *The Kundalini Experience*; Howard S. Levi and Akira Ishihara, *The Tao of Sex*; Jean Lanier, *The Wisdom of Being Human*" avg. press run 4M. Expects 2 titles 1991, 2 titles 1992. 1 title listed in the *Small Press Record of Books in Print* (20th Edition, 1991-92). avg. price, cloth: $18; paper: $10. Discounts: 20% STOP orders; otherwise order through Bookpeople, New Leaf, Great Tradition. 160pp; 6x9; of. Reporting time: 2 weeks, preliminary letter essential. Payment: by arrangement. Copyrights for author. COSMEP.

INTEGRAL YOGA MAGAZINE, Swami Prakashananda, Route 1, Box 172, Buckingham, VA 23921, 804-969-4801. 1969. Poetry, fiction, articles, interviews, letters, non-fiction. circ. 1.2M. 4/yr. Pub'd 6 issues 1990; expects 4 issues 1991, 4 issues 1992. sub. price: $15; per copy: $2.50; sample: $2.50. Back issues: $1-$1.50. 32pp; 6x9. Copyrighted, reverts to author. §Spiritual, health, ecumenical, wholistic medicine, yoga.

Interalia/Design Books, G. Brown, S. Ewing, PO Box 404, Oxford, OH 45056-0404, 513-523-6880. 1989. Art, non-fiction. "It is the goal of Interalia/Design Books to make meaningful contributions to the art of the book as a container of knowledge—the textual manifestation of a culture's evolution—and to the book as an object by promoting the dissemination of quality design through an editorial focus on architecture, design/crafts, art criticism, art of the book, facsimiles of out-of-print primary sources on architecture, design/crafts and art criticism. Also by promoting quality in the art of bookmaking by experimenting with alternative structures for the production of books as objects, including alternative printing and binding methods, encouraging limited editions of experimental books and of books for the bibliophile, encouraging artist/writer/printer/binder collaborations." avg. press run 125+. Pub'd 1 title 1990; expects 1 title 1991, 4 titles 1992. 2 titles listed in the *Small Press Record of Books in Print* (20th Edition, 1991-92). avg. price, paper: $16. Discounts: 40% for orders of 10+. 100pp; 5½x8½; of. Reporting time: 4-6 weeks. Payment: varies. Copyrights for author.

Intercultural Press, Inc., Margaret D. Pusch, David S. Hoopes, Editor-in-Chief, PO Box 700, Yarmouth, ME 04096, 207-846-5168. 1980. Non-fiction. "Office of David S. Hoopes: 130 North Rd., Vershire, VT 05079. Books on intercultural communication, intercultural education and cross-cultural training, especially practical materials for use in teaching and training; other areas: multicultural education, orientation for living abroad. Shipping address: #16 U.S. Route One, Yarmouth, ME 04096'' avg. press run 5M. Pub'd 6 titles 1990; expects 8 titles 1991, 10 titles 1992. 50 titles listed in the *Small Press Record of Books in Print* (20th Edition, 1991-92). avg. price, cloth: $19.95; paper: $9; other: 8½ X 11 books $27.50. Discounts: 20% educational, 10 or more copies; 40% trade. 150pp; 6×9, 8½×11, 5½×8½; of. Reporting time: 2-8 weeks. Payment: royalty. Copyrights for author. COSMEP.

INTERCULTURE, HORIZONS INTERCULTURELS, Jacques Langlais, Associate Editor; Robert Vachon, Associate Editor, Intercultural Institute of Montreal, 4917 St-Urbain, Montreal, Quebec H2T 2W1, Canada, 514-288-7229. 1968. Articles, reviews, non-fiction. ''Printed in 2 separate editions: *Interculture* (English edition ISSN 0828-797X); *Interculture* (French edition ISSN 0712-1571). Length of Material: 20M words average (each issue devoted to a particular theme) Material: cross-cultural understanding - themes include education, medicine, spirituality, communication, politics and law in an intercultural perspective. Recent titles: *The Autonomous Economy, The Religion of the Future, The Archaeology of Development*. Recent contributors: Jacques Langlais, Robert Vachon, John W. Spellman, Merrill H. Jackson, Scott Eastham, Raimon Panikkar, Gustavo Esteva, Wolfgang Sachs.'' circ. 1M. 4/yr. 2 titles listed in the *Small Press Record of Books in Print* (20th Edition, 1991-92). sub. price: $17 individuals, $30 institutions in Canada (+ GST 7%), outside Canada add $5; per copy: $4, instit. $8 + GST in Canada and TVQ (8%) in Quebec; sample: $4.25. Back issues: all $4.25. Discounts: subscription agencies receive 15%. 40pp; 6¼×9½; of. Reporting time: 3 months. Copyrighted. §Cross-cultural issues. Canadian Periodical Publishers' Association/Association des Editeurs de periodiques culturels quebecois.

Interface Press (see also BRAIN/MIND BULLETIN), Marilyn Ferguson, Publisher, Editor, PO Box 42211, Los Angeles, CA 90042, 213-223-2500; 800-553-MIND. 1975. Articles, interviews, reviews, news items, non-fiction. avg. press run 10M. Pub'd 1 title 1990; expects 1 title 1991, 1 title 1992. avg. price, other: $3. Discounts: inquire. 8pp; 8½×11; of. Payment: none.

INTERIM, A. Wilber Stevens, Editor & Founder; James Hazen, Associate Editor; Joe McCullough, Associate Editor; John Heath-Stubbs, English Editor, Department of English, University of Nevada, Las Vegas, Las Vegas, NV 89154, 702-739-3172. 1944 (now revived 1986 with Vol. 5, No. 1). Poetry, fiction, long-poems. ''Will be limited to poetry and exceptionally good fiction. All issues of *Interim* (1944-55) have been reprinted by Kraus and Co. Now receiving fiction, 5,000 word limit.'' circ. 700. 2/yr. Pub'd 2 issues 1990; expects 2 issues 1991, 2 issues 1992. sub. price: $10/3 yrs; per copy: $3; $5 international; sample: $3. Back issues: a few original copies available $10 each. Discounts: 40% to bookstores on consignment, 5+ copies. 48pp; 6×9; †of. Reporting time: 1 month. Payment: contributor copies plus 3-year subscription. Copyrighted, rights revert on request. Pub's reviews: 2 in 1990. §Poetry, criticism. Ads: please write editor. CLMP.

Interim Press, Peter Dent, 3 Thornton Close, Budleigh Salterton, Devon EX9 6PJ, England, 5231. 1975. Poetry, art, criticism, letters, long-poems, plays. ''Books include *Candid Fields: Essays and Reflections on the Work of Thomas A. Clark, The Blue Wind: Poems in English from Pakistan. Not Comforts But Vision: Essays on the Poetry of George Oppen , A Remote Beginning* by Daud Kamal and *Royal Murdoch: Chills and Fevers: Poems and Letters, Journal* by Ian Robinson, *Scented Leaves from a Chinese Jar* by Allen Upward and *The Wreck of the Deutschland: an Historical Note* by Sean Street.'' avg. press run 250. Expects 1 title 1991. 14 titles listed in the *Small Press Record of Books in Print* (20th Edition, 1991-92). avg. price, paper: £2.40. Discounts: 33% to trade; 10% libraries. 24-40pp; 5¾×8¾; of. Reporting time: 2 weeks. Payment: copies only. Copyrights for author.

Interlink Press, Inc., 908 Kenfield Avenue, Los Angeles, CA 90049, (213) 472-2908. 1986. Non-fiction. avg. press run 6M. Pub'd 1 title 1990; expects 1 title 1991, 1 title 1992. 1 title listed in the *Small Press Record of Books in Print* (20th Edition, 1991-92). avg. price, cloth: $25; paper: $15. 200pp; 5½×8½; of. Payment: 8% - 12%. Copyrights for author. COSMEP, PMA.

Interlink Publishing Group, Inc., Michel Moushabeck, Phyllis Bennis, 99 Seventh Avenue, Brooklyn, NY 11215, 718-797-4292. 1987. Art, photos, non-fiction. avg. press run 10M. Pub'd 4 titles 1990; expects 20 titles 1991, 20 titles 1992. avg. price, cloth: $19.95; paper: $9.95. Discounts: Trade 40% & up. 160pp; of. Reporting time: 2 months. Payment: semi-annually, royalty varies. Copyrights for author. AAP, ABA.

INTERLIT, Tim Bascom, Editor; C. Lawrence Brook, Managing Editor, 850 North Grove, Elgin, IL 60120, 708-741-2400. ''Trade journal for editors, writers, and publishers in third world countries'' circ. 6M. 4/yr. Pub'd 4 issues 1990; expects 4 issues 1991, 4 issues 1992. $10 student, $15 indiv., $30 instit.—includes lifetime membership & discounts on our monographs & manuals. Back issues: $1.50 each. 24pp; 8½×10¾. Reporting time: 1 month. Payment: varies. Copyrighted. no ads. COSMEP, ACP (Assoc. Church Press), Evangelical Press Assoc.

Intermountain Publishing, Walter J. Polt, 1713 Harzman Road SW, Albuquerque, NM 87105, 505-242-3333. 2 titles listed in the *Small Press Record of Books in Print* (20th Edition, 1991-92).

276

INTERNATIONAL ART POST, Banana Productions, Anna Banana, PO Box 3655, Vancouver, B.C. V6B 3Y8, Canada. 1988. Art, photos. "ISSN 0843-6312. *IAP* is a cooperatively published periodical of stamps by artists (Artistamps), printed in an edition of 1500 copies in full color on gummed, glossy paper. Editions go to press as sufficient art and money accumulate to cover costs. After payment to participants, Banana Productions distributes the rest of the edition (approx. 700 sheets) through gallery and stationery shops, or uses them in promotional mailings" circ. 700. 2-4/yr. Pub'd 3 issues 1990; expects 3 issues 1991, 4 issues 1992. sub. price: $120/year packaged in bindersleeve, $95/year not packaged; per copy: $20/edition packaged, $16/edition unpackaged; sample: $10. Back issues: write for order form. Discounts: 50% wholesale. Pages vary; 9½×11 full sheet, 6¼×8½ 1/2 sheet, 5¾×5⅜ 1/4 sheet; of, full color on gummed stock, then perforated. Reporting time: 3-6 months, depending on how quickly an edition is sold. Payment: 500 copies their own stamp(s), 3 copies of the sheet on which it is printed, and 1 copy of any other sheet(s) in the edition. Copyrighted. Ads: none. SPAN (Small Press Action Network, Vancouver).

INTERNATIONAL BRAIN DOMINANCE REVIEW, Margaret Herrmann, Laura Herrmann, 2075 Buffalo Creek Road, Lake Lure, NC 28746, 704-625-9153. 1984. Poetry, articles, non-fiction. circ. 500. 2/yr. Pub'd 2 issues 1990; expects 2 issues 1991, 4 issues 1992. sub. price: $15; per copy: $7.50. Back issues: $7.50. 48pp; 8½×11; of. Copyrighted, reverts to author. Pub's reviews: 1 in 1990. §Any books on brain dominance, measuring thinking styles, whole brain thinking. Ads: none. COSMEP.

International Childbirth Education Association, Inc., Winnie Hunsburger, Director of Publications, PO Box 20048, Minneapolis, MN 55420-0048. 1960. Non-fiction. avg. press run 1M-15M. Pub'd 6 titles 1990; expects 6 titles 1991, 4 titles 1992. 4 titles listed in the *Small Press Record of Books in Print* (20th Edition, 1991-92). avg. price, paper: $3; other: pamphlets 20¢ each. Discounts: 2-4 copies, 25%; 5-50, 40%; 51-100, 45%; 100+ 50%. 68pp; 8½×11; of. Reporting time: 3-6 months. Payment: all authors contribute, no royalties. We hold copyright.

International Consulting Associates, Inc., Carlos A. Bonilla, Jana L. Brazda, 1020 N. Commerce, Stockton, CA 95202, 209-466-7678. 1988. News items. "Our first title, just released is *Quick Reference Guide to School Dropouts*. Books is distributed through Avenue Books in Stockton. We will be expanding to consider other author's manuscripts." avg. press run 2.5M. Expects 3-4 titles 1991, 3 titles 1992. 3 titles listed in the *Small Press Record of Books in Print* (20th Edition, 1991-92). avg. price, paper: $10. Discounts: classroom, 10% on orders of 20 or more. 55-300pp; 5×11; lp. Copyrights for author.

THE INTERNATIONAL FICTION REVIEW, Saad Elkhadem, Dept. of German & Russian, UNB, Fredericton, N.B. E3B 5A3, Canada, 506-453-4636. 1973. "The *IFR* is a biannual periodical devoted to international fiction. Mss are accepted in English and should be prepared in conformity with the *York Press Style Manual*; articles: 10-20 typewritten pages; reviews: 2-6 pp.; spelling, hyphenation, and capitalization according to *Webster*." circ. 600. 2/yr. Pub'd 2 issues 1990; expects 2 issues 1991. sub. price: $15 instit., $12 indiv.; per copy: $8; sample: $8. Back issues: same. Discounts: 20% for agents and jobbers. 90pp; 6×9; of. Reporting time: 6 weeks. Payment: none. Copyrighted. Pub's reviews: 35 in 1990. §Fiction and scholarly works on fiction. IFA.

International Information Associates, Richard Bradley, PO Box 773, Morrisville, PA 19067, 215-493-9214. 1988. Non-fiction. "Street address: 172 Hyde Park Place, Yardley, PA 19067. Materials should be all nonfiction in technical, business, or medical areas. Authors should be qualified in the field they are writing, e.g., our 2 most recent books—one about working with the Japanese was written by Alison R. Lanier who teaches at AMA, the Foreign Service Institute and NY's New School for Social Research; the other about 'recruiting' was written by Arthur Sharp who is a member of the business faculty at Central CT State U." avg. press run 4M. Pub'd 5 titles 1990; expects 6 titles 1991, 6 titles 1992. avg. price, paper: $17.95. Discounts: 1-5 books 25%, 6-24 30%, 25+ 42%. 250pp; 5⅜×8½; of. Reporting time: 3 weeks. Payment: 12% on first 3,000; 17% thereafter by contract. Copyrights for author. COSMEP, PMA.

International Jewelry Publications, Patricia Esparza, Beverly Newton, PO Box 13384, Los Angeles, CA 90013, 818-282-3781. 1987. Photos, interviews, non-fiction. "*The Diamond Ring Buying Guide: How to Spot Value & Avoid Ripoffs, The Ruby & Sapphire Buying Guide: How to Spot Value & Avoid Ripoffs* by Renee Newman." avg. press run 5M. Expects 1 title 1991, 13 titles 1992. 2 titles listed in the *Small Press Record of Books in Print* (20th Edition, 1991-92). avg. price, paper: $13. Discounts: 2-4 copies 30%, 5-24 40%, 25-49 43%, 50+ 45%. 150pp; 7×9; of. Reporting time: 1 month, but call first before submitting manuscript. Copyrights for author. PMA.

INTERNATIONAL JOURNAL FOR THE SEMIOTICS OF LAW, Deborah Charles Publications, E. Landowski, 173 Mather Avenue, Liverpool L18 6JZ, United Kingdom. 1988. Non-fiction. "English and French articles on semiotics of law" circ. 300. 3/yr. Pub'd 3 issues 1990. sub. price: £54 (incl. postage); per copy: £18; sample: £10. Back issues: on application. Discounts: 10% subscription agents. 112pp; royal 80; DTP Macintosh. Reporting time: 3 months. Payment: none. Copyrighted, does not revert to author. Pub's reviews: 7

in 1990. §Linguistics, philosophy, semiotics of law. exchange basis.

INTERNATIONAL JOURNAL OF SPORT BIOMECHANICS, Human Kinetics Pub. Inc., Richard C. Nelson, Box 5076, Champaign, IL 61825-5076, 217-351-5076. 1985. Articles, reviews. "Research articles on forces affecting human movement in sport and exercise" circ. 820. 4/yr. Pub'd 4 issues 1990; expects 4 issues 1991, 4 issues 1992. sub. price: $28 individual, $56 institution; per copy: $7 indiv., $15 instit.; sample: free. Back issues: $7 indiv., $15 instit. Discounts: 5% agency. 102pp; 6×9; of. Reporting time: 2 months. Payment: none. Not copyrighted. Pub's reviews: 1 in 1990. §Sport, Sport science, and physical education related to biomechanics. Ads: $170/$102 (4X rate).

International Language (IDO) Society of Great Britain (see also IDO-VIVO), Tom Lang, Nic Apglyn, 10 Heol Salop, Penarth, De Morgonnwg CF6 1HG, Wales, 0222-497414. 1930. "We publish Ido books and leaflets from time to time as needed." 1 title listed in the *Small Press Record of Books in Print* (20th Edition, 1991-92).

International Marine Publishing Co., Jonathan Eaton, V.P., Editor, Box 220, Camden, ME 04843, 207-236-4837. 1969. Non-fiction. "We publish non-fiction marine books" avg. press run 3M. Pub'd 28 titles 1990; expects 24 titles 1991, 24 titles 1992. 104 titles listed in the *Small Press Record of Books in Print* (20th Edition, 1991-92). avg. price, cloth: $20; paper: $13.95. Discounts: trade and wholesale, 40-50% depending on quantity. 225pp; 6×9, 7×10, 8½×11; of. Reporting time: 6 weeks. Payment: 10-15% of NET graduated royalty breaks. Copyrights for author. DMA, ABA.

INTERNATIONAL OLYMPIC LIFTER, PO Box 65855, Los Angeles, CA 90065, 213-257-8762. 1973. Poetry. circ. 3M. 6/yr. Pub'd 5 issues 1990; expects 6 issues 1991, 6 issues 1992. sub. price: $25 1st class, $36 foreign air; sample: $4. 36pp; 8½×11.

International Partners In Prayer, A.C. Doyle, Founder, Publishing Division, Box 570122, Houston, TX 77257. 1983. 5 titles listed in the *Small Press Record of Books in Print* (20th Edition, 1991-92). avg. price, cloth: $3.95; paper: $1.95. 17pp; 5½×8½. Reporting time: 6 weeks.

INTERNATIONAL POETRY REVIEW, Evalyn P. Gill, PO Box 2047, Greensboro, NC 27402, 919-273-1711. 1975. Poetry, art. "Fred Chappell, William Stafford, Willis Barnstone, Charles Edward Eaton." circ. 400. 2/yr. Pub'd 2 issues 1990; expects 2 issues 1991, 2 issues 1992. sub. price: $8; per copy: $4; sample: $4. 120pp; 6×9; of. Reporting time: 3 months. Payment: copies. Copyrighted, reverts to author. Ads: $100/$60/$35. CCLM.

International Printing, G & S Enterprises, 1127 Watkins Street #303, Philadelphia, PA 19148, 215-463-0463. avg. press run 1M. 2 titles listed in the *Small Press Record of Books in Print* (20th Edition, 1991-92). avg. price, other: leatherette $4.00. Discounts: 50 books, $3.00; 100+ $2.00 each. 1,000pp; of.

International Publications (see also AMERICAN COLLEGIATE POETS), Val M. Churillo, Editor, Manager, Owner, PO Box 44044-L, Los Angeles, CA 90044, 213-755-1814. 1975. Poetry. "We publish twice a year, Spring and Fall, a compilation of *student poetry* entered in "National College Poetry Contest". Five cash prizes with literary comments by Editor; about 50 Honorable mentions, the rest Special Awards. Please write for copy of rules. Published in English. Foreign language poems accepted. Maximum length of submissions: 14-16 lines" avg. press run 500. Pub'd 2 titles 1990; expects 2 titles 1991, 2 titles 1992. avg. price, paper: $12.50. 130pp; 5½×8½; of. Reporting time: 2-3 weeks following contest deadline. Payment: five cash prizes paid each title (see copy of rules for breakdown). Copyrights for author.

International Publishers Co. Inc., Betty Smith, PO Box 3042, New York, NY 10116, 212-366-9816; fax 212-366-9820. 1924. Non-fiction. avg. press run 5M. Pub'd 15 titles 1990; expects 15 titles 1991, 10 titles 1992. avg. price, cloth: $14-$19; paper: $5-$9. Discounts: text 20%. 200-400pp, some 96-150pp; 5×8, 5½×8½. Reporting time: 1 week to 2 months. Payment: pays royalties. Copyrights for author. NACS Association, ABA Association.

The International Society of Dramatists, Andrew Delaplaine, Box 1310, Miami, FL 33153, 305-531-1530. 1978. avg. press run 10M. Pub'd 5 titles 1990. 1 title listed in the *Small Press Record of Books in Print* (20th Edition, 1991-92). avg. price, cloth: $45; paper: $30. Discounts: 50% wholesalers, 45% booksellers. 250pp; 8½×11; of.

INTERNATIONAL TAX AND BUSINESS LAWYER, University of California Press, Students of Boalt Hall School of Law, University of California Press, 2120 Berkeley Way, Berkeley, CA 94720, 415-642-4191. Articles, reviews, non-fiction. "Editorial address: 126 Boalt Hall School of Law, Berkeley, CA 94720. Copyrighted by International Tax and Business Lawyer." circ. 500. 2/yr. Pub'd 2 issues 1990; expects 2 issues 1991, 2 issues 1992. sub. price: $40 (+ $3 foreign postage); per copy: $20; sample: free. Back issues: $20. Discounts: foreign subs. agent 10%, one-time order 10+ 30%, standing orders (bookstores): 1-99 40%, 100+ 50%. 200pp; 6¼×9½; of. Reporting time: 1-2 months. Payment: varies. Copyrighted, does not revert to author.

Pub's reviews: 5 in 1990. Ads: $200/$120.

THE INTERNATIONAL UNIVERSITY POETRY QUARTERLY, The International University Press, John Wayne Johnston, Editor, 1301 S. Noland Road, Independence, MO 64055, 816-461-3633. 1974. Poetry, criticism, reviews. "We prefer short, personal poetry, constructive criticism, and sprightly reviews. Emphasis is at all times upon creativity and insightfulness." circ. 325. 4/yr. Pub'd 4 issues 1990; expects 4 issues 1991, 4 issues 1992. sub. price: $200; per copy: $50; sample: $50. Back issues: $50. 15-30pp; 8½×11; †mi. Reporting time: 2-4 weeks. Payment: copies. Copyrighted, reverts to author. Pub's reviews. Ads: $50/$30/$1. COSMEP.

The International University Press (see also **THE INTERNATIONAL UNIVERSITY POETRY QUARTERLY**), John Wayne Johnston, Editor, 1301 S. Noland Rd., Independence, MO 64055, 816-461-3633. 1973. Poetry, criticism, reviews. "In addition to *The International University Poetry Quarterly*, TIU Press also prints TIU Annual Report, TIU Newsletter, and TIU Collegiate Sports Report. We print several academic books with a growing list of such works each year." avg. press run 250. Pub'd 30 titles 1990; expects 30 titles 1991, 30 titles 1992. 12 titles listed in the *Small Press Record of Books in Print* (20th Edition, 1991-92). avg. price, cloth: $20; paper: $10. Discounts: 25%-40% to distributors. 150pp; 8½×11; †mi. Reporting time: 8-10 weeks. Payment: copies. Copyrights for author. COSMEP.

INTERRACIAL BOOKS FOR CHILDREN BULLETIN, Council on Interracial Books For Children, Melba Kgositsile, Executive Director, 1841 Broadway, New York, NY 10023, 212-757-5339. 1967. Articles, art, photos, cartoons, reviews. circ. 5M. 8/yr. Expects 8 issues 1991. sub. price: $20 indiv, $28 instit; per copy: $2.95 single issue, $3.95 double issue; sample: same. Back issues: $2.95 single issue, $3.95 double issue. Discounts: single issues: $2 each for 10 or more; double issue: $2.50 each for 10 or more. 24pp; 8½×11; of. Reporting time: 2 months. Payment: minimal. Copyrighted, reverts to author. Pub's reviews: 100 in 1990. §Children's books 1-11 yrs., educational-human value, anti-racism, anti-sexism, Third World, feminist, children's books, school textbooks. No ads. COSMEP, LPS.

Intertext, Sharon Ann Jaeger, Editor; C.E. Simon, Managing Editor, 2633 East 17th Avenue, Anchorage, AK 99508. 1982. Poetry, criticism. "Our most noted titles have been *17 Toutle River Haiku,* by James Hanlen, done in calligraphy with full-color illustrations and Louis Hammer's *The Mirror Dances.* Writers please note: query first, sending three poems in a legal-size (#10) envelope by *first-class mail.* Please do not send an entire manuscript unless we ask to see it; do not send material by manuscript rate, either. We cannot return anything sent without SASE or IRC. We consider only strong full-length collections by writers of demonstrated achievement. As we have several projects in progress, we will not be considering unsolicited material until 1994." avg. press run 500-1M. Pub'd 3 titles 1990; expects 1 title 1991, 1 title 1992. 3 titles listed in the *Small Press Record of Books in Print* (20th Edition, 1991-92). avg. price, cloth: varies; paper: varies. Discounts: 1-4, 20%; 5-24, 40%; 25-49, 43%; 50-99, 46%; over 100, 50%. 64-96pp; size varies; of. Reporting time: 3-6 months on average. Payment: 10% royalty after all costs of production, promotion, and distribution have been met. No advances. Does not copyright for author. AASP (Alaska Association of Small Presses).

INTERVENTION IN SCHOOL AND CLINIC, Gerald Wallace, Editor, 8700 Shoal Creek, Austin, TX 78758-6897, 512-451-3246. 1965. Poetry, articles, cartoons, interviews, letters. *"Intervention in School and Clinic* (formerly Academic Therapy) deals with the day-to-day aspects of special and remedial education. It's articles and instructional ideas provide practical and useful information appropriate for immediate implementation. Topics include, but are not limited to, assessment, curriculum, instructional practices, and school and family management of students experiencing problem or behavior problems." circ. 5M. 5/yr. Pub'd 5 issues 1990; expects 5 issues 1991, 5 issues 1992. sub. price: North America: indiv. $35, instit. $80; foreign: $95; per copy: $10. Back issues: $10. Discounts: agencies receive 15% discount. 64pp; 8½×11; sheet fed. Reporting time: 2 weeks. Payment: none. Copyrighted, rights revert upon request. Pub's reviews: 8 in 1990. §Any books appropriate for the above stated aims and scope of the journal. Ads: $400/$200/$20 for 25 words or less (each add'l word 5¢). Ed Press.

INTUITIVE EXPLORATIONS, Gloria Reiser, PO Box 561, Quincy, IL 62306-0561, 217-222-9082. 1987. Poetry, articles, art, photos, cartoons, interviews, reviews, letters, news items, non-fiction. "Metaphysical/new age publication. Prefer articles under 1500 words. Encourage submissions. Products/books for review welcome." circ. 1M+. 12/yr. Pub'd 12 issues 1990; expects 12 issues 1991, 12 issues 1992. sub. price: $15; per copy: $2; sample: $2. Back issues: $2. Discounts: distributor price 50¢ per copy on minimum of 10 copies. 24pp; 8½×11; professional printer. Reporting time: 6 weeks or less. Payment: copies or advertising. Copyrighted, reverts to author. Pub's reviews: 50+ in 1990. §New Age metaphysics, self-help, occult sciences such as Tarot, philosophy, psychology, personal growth, mind potential. Ads: $35/$20/$10 1/4 page/line ads 35¢ per word, minimum of $7.

INVERTED-A HORN, Inverted-A, Inc., Amnon Katz, Aya Katz, 401 Forrest Hill, Grand Prairie, TX 75051, 214-264-0066. 1984. Poetry, articles, reviews, non-fiction. "First issue was a newsletter for buyers of Inverted-A equipment dealing in same and in aviation. Second issue deals with book reviews, filk, and science fiction. Third and fourth issues deal in politics and poetry." circ. 200. Irregular. Pub'd 1 issue 1990; expects 2 issues 1991, 2 issues 1992. sub. price: free; sample: free. 5pp; 8.5×11; †of. Reporting time: 6 weeks. Copyrighted, reverts to author. Pub's reviews: 1 in 1990. §Freedom, the Constitution, the right to bear arms, free enterprise, capitalism, aviation, poetry of classical form. Ads: $24/$12.

Inverted-A, Inc. (see also INVERTED-A HORN), Amnon Katz, Aya Katz, 401 Forrest HIll, Grand Prairie, TX 75051, 214-264-0066. 1977. Poetry, fiction, articles, reviews, letters, non-fiction. "Early publications were technical manuals for Inverted-A products. However, since then expanded into politics, literature, and poetry. Interested in personal rights and freedom and government interference with same and in free enterprise vs. capitalism. Recent titles: *The Blake Bunch* (poetry), *There Can Be Gods* (poetry)." avg. press run 500. Pub'd 2 titles 1990; expects 2 titles 1991, 2 titles 1992. 11 titles listed in the *Small Press Record of Books in Print* (20th Edition, 1991-92). avg. price, paper: $10. Discounts: 40% in quantities of 10 or more. 120pp; 5½×8½, 8½×11; †of. Reporting time: 6 weeks. Payment: one free copy and 40% discount on further copies. Copyrights for author.

INVESTMENT COLUMN QUARTERLY (newsletter), NAR Publications, Nicholas A. Roes, PO Box 233, Barryville, NY 12719, 914-557-8713. 1977. Articles, criticism, reviews, news items. 4/yr. Pub'd 10 issues 1990; expects 10 issues 1991, 4 issues 1992. sub. price: $75; per copy: $20; sample: $20. Back issues: $20. 2-4pp; 8½×11; †of. Copyrighted. Pub's reviews: 2 in 1990. §investments.

INVISIBLE CITY, Red Hill Press, San Francisco + Los Angeles, John McBride, Paul Vangelisti, PO Box 2853, San Francisco, CA 94126. 1971. Poetry, criticism, concrete art. "An eclectic gathering of poetry, translations, essays & visuals, published whenever enough good material is available. A tabloid (1971-81, 28 numbers),*Invisible City* is now in book-format with set themes. Forthcoming in 1991: *Daybook* by Robert Crosson, with *Division*, notes on American poetry edited by Paul Cuneo et al. 'Perhaps *the* orchestra of the eighth day.' Obviously experimental, *Invisible City* cherishes Samuel Johnson's phrase, "the reek of the human", and still observes E.P.'s precept, "OK, send 'em along: subject verb object". But please sample our wares ($3 postpaid) before submitting bundles of poetry" circ. 1M. 1-2/yr. Pub'd 1-2 issues 1990; expects 2+ issues 1991. sub. price: $10 postpaid (indiv.) $10 (libraries). 64pp; 5½×9; of. Copyrighted, reverts to author. Pub's reviews: 2 in 1990. §Poetry, translations, visuals. No ads. CLMP, COSMEP.

Ion Books (see also RACCOON), David Spicer, Senior Editor, PO Box 111327, Memphis, TN 38111-1327, 901-323-8858. 1980. Poetry, fiction, criticism, long-poems. avg. press run 1M. Pub'd 6 titles 1990; expects 6 titles 1991, 6 titles 1992. 16 titles listed in the *Small Press Record of Books in Print* (20th Edition, 1991-92). avg. price, cloth: $12.95; paper: $9.95. Discounts: 40% trade; bulk, negotiable; wholesalers, 40%. Pages vary; 6×9; of. Reporting time: 1-2 months. Payment: variable. Copyrights for author.

IOTA, David Holliday, 67 Hady Crescent, Chesterfield, Derbyshire S41 0EB, Great Britain, 0246-276532. 1988. Poetry, reviews. "Poetry: all subjects and styles, bar concrete (no facilities or expertise). Space being limited, shorter poems have the edge. Recent contributors include Alun Rees, Daniel B. Trinkle, Mary Rudbeck Stanko, Michael Cunningham, Harry Guest, Anne Clarke, Robert Lumsden" circ. 300. 4/yr. Pub'd 4 issues 1990; expects 4 issues 1991, 4 issues 1992. sub. price: $8 (add $10 if by cheque); per copy: $2; sample: $2. Back issues: $2. Discounts: shops 33%. 32pp; 5¾×8¼ (A5); †mi. Reporting time: first assessment, usually a couple of weeks; but a firm decision on inclusion or rejection may take months. Payment: 2 complimentary copies. Copyrighted, reverts to author. Pub's reviews: 27 in 1990. §poetry. No ads.

THE IOWA REVIEW, David Hamilton, Editor, 308 EPB, Univ. Of Iowa, Iowa City, IA 52242, 319-335-0462. 1970. Poetry, fiction, articles, interviews, criticism, reviews, parts-of-novels, long-poems, non-fiction. "We publish quality contemporary fiction, poetry, criticism, and book reviews. Recent contributors include Marianne Boruch, Rita Dove, Alln Gurganus, Donald Hall" circ. 1M. 3/yr. Pub'd 3 issues 1990; expects 3 issues 1991, 3 issues 1992. sub. price: instit. $20 (+$3 outside US), indiv. $15 (+$3 outside US); per copy: $6.95; sample: $5. Discounts: 10% agency, 30% trade. 192pp; 6×9; of. Reporting time: 2-4 months. Payment: $10 per page fiction, $1 per line poetry. Copyrighted, reverts to author. Pub's reviews: 10 in 1990. §Poetry, fiction, literary culture. Ads: $150/$80. CCLM.

Iowa State University Press (see also POET & CRITIC), Neal Bowers, English Department, ISU, 203 Ross Hall, Ames, IA 50011.

IOWA WOMAN, Marianne Abel, Editor; Sandra Witt, Poetry Editor, PO Box 680, Iowa City, IA 52244, 319-987-2879. 1979. Poetry, fiction, articles, art, photos, cartoons, interviews, criticism, reviews, letters, parts-of-novels, long-poems, collages, news items, non-fiction. "*Iowa Woman*, an award-winning quarterly, which publishes artwork and photography portfolios, fiction, poetry, essays, book reviews, and articles on the history, education, politics, and activities of interest to midwestern women. Freelancers who wish to address any of the above concerns are encouraged to submit materials or ideas. Annual fiction, essay & poetry contest." circ. 2.5M. 4/yr. Pub'd 4 issues 1990; expects 4 issues 1991, 4 issues 1992. sub. price: $15, Canadian and Pan-American $15, foreign $20; per copy: $4; sample: $5. Back issues: $3. Discounts: none. 48pp; 8⅛×10⅞;

280

of. Reporting time: 6-8 weeks; reads multiple submissions for fiction and essays. Payment: 2 copies, biographical note, indexing and 1-year subscription. Copyrighted, reverts to author. Pub's reviews: 17 in 1990. §Recent books by or of interest to women, small press preferred, regional, poetry, essays. Ads: $200/$120/$70 1/4 page/$10 per inch. CLMP.

Iranbooks, Inc., Farhad Shirzad, 8014 Old Georgetown Road, Bethesda, MD 20814, 301-986-0079. 1979. Poetry, fiction, news items, non-fiction. "We publish books about Iran and in Persian." avg. press run 3M. Pub'd 5 titles 1990; expects 5 titles 1991, 5 titles 1992. 6 titles listed in the *Small Press Record of Books in Print* (20th Edition, 1991-92). Discounts: 30%. of. Copyrights for author.

IRIS: A Journal About Women, Jennifer Gennari Shepherd, Box 323, HSC, University of Virginia, Charlottesville, VA 22908, 804-924-4500. 1980. Poetry, fiction, articles, art, photos, interviews, reviews, news items, non-fiction. "We welcome high-quality submissions of poetry, fiction, art and non-fiction. Our aim is to publish material on subjects that are of concern to women. Please send for a sample copy of our journal before submitting nonfiction. Recent contributors: Leslie Gossage, James Foster, Elizabeth Denton." circ. 2M. 2/yr. Pub'd 2 issues 1990; expects 2 issues 1991, 2 issues 1992. sub. price: $8; per copy: $4; sample: $5. Discounts: 20% for trade or bulk. 72pp; 8½x11. Reporting time: about 2 months. Payment: none. Copyrighted, reverts to author. Pub's reviews: 14 in 1990. §Books about women or that are written by women. Ads: $190/$120/$85 1/4 page.

Iris Communication Group, Marlene Miller, 1278 Glenneyre, Suite 138, Laguna Beach, CA 92651, 714-497-2101. 1987. Non-fiction. "Book length material on business and practical communication arts" avg. press run 3M. Pub'd 1 title 1990; expects 3 titles 1991, 5 titles 1992. 1 title listed in the *Small Press Record of Books in Print* (20th Edition, 1991-92). avg. price, paper: $20. Discounts: 2-9 books 40%, 10-99 50%, 100-499 60%. 225pp; 6x9; of. Reporting time: 2 weeks. Payment: negotiable. Copyrights for author. COSMEP, PMA.

IRISH FAMILY JOURNAL, O'Laughlin Press (Irish Genealogical Foundation), Michael C. O'Laughlin, Box 7575, Kansas City, MO 64116, 816-454-2410. 1978. Articles, art, photos, interviews, letters, news items, non-fiction. "Short articles, highlights, Irish American personalities, informal, tradition/history oriented. Time period: A) 1800's, B) current time for genealogy. Photos of Irish family castles, immigrants, lifestyle—1800's. Family names." circ. 2.5M+. 6/yr. Pub'd 6 issues 1990; expects 6 issues 1991, 6 issues 1992. sub. price: $45; per copy: $9; sample: $5. Back issues: $25 per year (6 issues). Discounts: bulk purchases: 40%-60% discount. 16pp; 8½x11; of. Reporting time: 2 weeks. Payment: inquire. Copyrighted, reverts to author. Pub's reviews: 24 in 1990. §Irish genealogy, history, folklore, tradition. Ads: $1,000/$550.

IRISH LITERARY SUPPLEMENT, Irish Studies, Robert G. Lowery, Editor-Publisher; Maureen Murphy, Features Editor, 114 Paula Boulevard, Selden, NY 11784, 516-698-8243. 1982. Interviews, criticism, reviews, parts-of-novels, non-fiction. "Published in association with Boston College. All work assigned." circ. 4.5M. 2/yr. Pub'd 2 issues 1990; expects 2 issues 1991, 2 issues 1992. sub. price: $5 ($6 libraries and foreign); per copy: $2.50; sample: $2.50. Back issues: $3. Discounts: only with subscription agencies. 46pp; 11x16; web. Reporting time: varies. Payment: copies and book for review. Copyrighted, reverts to author. Pub's reviews: 140 in 1990. §Irish material. Ads: $500/$300.

Irish Studies (see also IRISH LITERARY SUPPLEMENT), 114 Paula Boulevard, Selden, NY 11784, 516-698-8243.

IRON, Iron Press, Peter Mortimer, Editor; Jack Lithgow, Art Editor; Kitty Fitzgerald, Assist. Editor; David Stephenson, Assist. Editor, 5 Marden Terrace, Cullercoats, North Shields, Tyne & Wear NE30 4PD, England, 091-2531901. 1973. Poetry, fiction, art, letters, long-poems, plays. "*Iron*, by the end of 1991 will have reached the 65th edition, and will have featured more than 1,200 writers from five continents, as well as displaying the work of many graphic artists and photographers. It is an active encourager of new poetry, but also - just as important - the short story, a form it can publish up to 6M words. All material submitted gets an honest hearing, even if not accepted. Rejection slips form no part of *Iron's* philosophy. No more than five poems or two stories at any one time for submission please. IRC's are essential." circ. 800. 3/yr. Pub'd 4 issues 1990; expects 3 issues 1991, 3 issues 1992. sub. price: $25, £8; per copy: $8, £2 (no cheques please); sample: $8, £2 (no cheques please). Discounts: trade 33%, bulk negotiable. 72pp; size A5; of. Reporting time: 2 weeks. Payment: $10 per page/poem, $10 per page/prose. Copyrighted, rights remain with author. Pub's reviews: 30 in 1990. §Poetry, all small press publications. Ads: $60 (£30)/$40 (£20). ALP, ASM.

Iron Gate Publishing, Dina C. Carson, Risa J. Johnson, PO Box 999, Niwot, CO 80544, 303-530-2551. 1990. Non-fiction. avg. press run 1.5M. Pub'd 3 titles 1990; expects 5 titles 1991, 5 titles 1992. 1 title listed in the *Small Press Record of Books in Print* (20th Edition, 1991-92). avg. price, paper: $16. Discounts: based upon volume. 120pp; of. Reporting time: 3-6 weeks. Payment: 7-15%, payment quarterly. Copyrights for author.

Iron Press (see also IRON), Peter Mortimer, Editor, 5 Marden Terrace, Cullercoats, North Shields, Tyne & Near NE30 4PD, England. 1973. Poetry, fiction, art, reviews, letters, long-poems. "Unsolicited sets of manuscripts not encouraged." avg. press run 600. Pub'd 4 titles 1990; expects 4 titles 1991, 4 titles 1992. 25 titles listed in the *Small Press Record of Books in Print* (20th Edition, 1991-92). avg. price, paper: £3.50, $7. Discounts: trade 33%, bulk on negotiation. 52pp; size A5; of. Reporting time: 2 weeks. Payment: one off payment-repeated in case of reprint. Copyright remains with author. ASM.

IRONWOOD, Ironwood Press, Michael Cuddihy, P.O. Box 40907, Tucson, AZ 85717. 1972. Poetry, articles, art, photos, interviews, criticism, reviews, letters, long-poems. "Michael Cuddihy, editor. Prints poetry, including long poem, poetry reviews, interviews, translations, essays, and memoirs. Every 2nd or 3rd issue is a special issue on a single poet or aspect of poetry. Special issues so far: Oppen, James Wright, Transtromer. Linda Gregg/Vallejo, Language Poets, Milosz, Duncan, Dickinson/Spicer poetics. *Ironwood* stresses quality materials, design, and content" circ. 1.25M. 2/yr. Pub'd 2 issues 1990; expects 2 issues 1991, 2 issues 1992. sub. price: $9 indiv., $9.50 instit; per copy: $4.50; sample: $4 + .75 postage. Back issues: list available on request; full list in #21, with updated special issue prices. Discounts: 40% to bookstores, except universities. 200pp; 6×9; of. Reporting time: 2-7 weeks. Payment: when possible, $10 per page for poems (often less for longer poems). Pub's reviews: 6 in 1990. §Poetry, criticism, books of essays, autobiographies. Ads: $60/$35/$25 camera ready, $100/$60 7¼ X 4½. CCLM.

Ironwood Press (see also IRONWOOD), Michael Cuddihy, PO Box 40907, Tucson, AZ 85717. 1972. Poetry. avg. press run 500. Pub'd 1 title 1990. 12 titles listed in the *Small Press Record of Books in Print* (20th Edition, 1991-92). avg. price, paper: $2.50-$3.50. Discounts: 40% off for bookstores who order 5 or more. 32pp; 6×9; of. Reporting time: 2-6 months. Payment: 10% of press run to author. Copyrights for author if requested. CCLM.

Ironwood Publishing Company, Alison L. Grinder, Publisher; Timothy W. Grinder, PO Box 8464, Scottsdale, AZ 85252, 602-443-1390. 1984. Non-fiction. avg. press run 3.5M. Pub'd 2 titles 1990; expects 2-3 titles 1991. 1 title listed in the *Small Press Record of Books in Print* (20th Edition, 1991-92). avg. price, paper: $14.95. 200pp; 6×9; of. Payment: usually 10% net; bi-annually. Copyrights for author. COSMEP, PMA.

Ishtar Press, Inc. (see also PAINTBRUSH: A Journal of Poetry, Translations & Letters), Ben Bennani, Lang. & Lit. Division, Northeast Missouri State Univ., Kirksville, MO 63501, 816-785-4185. 1974. Poetry. "Richard Eberhart, Denise Levertov, David Ignatow, George Keithley, Joseph Bruchac, Douglas Blazek, Charles Levendosky, Sam Hamill, G. Wilson Knight, and others." avg. press run 500. Expects 1 title 1991. avg. price, paper: $5. Discounts: 20-40%. 65pp; 5½×8½; of, lp. Reporting time: 1-2 weeks. Payment: 10% of sales. Copyright is author's. CCLM, COSMEP, Associated Writing Programs.

ISI Press, Robert A. Day, 3501 Market Street, Philadelphia, PA 19104, 215-386-0100. 1977. Non-fiction. "Scholarly and professional books, especially those relating to communication (writing, editing, publishing, etc.)" avg. press run 5M. Pub'd 8 titles 1990; expects 17 titles 1991, 20 titles 1992. 46 titles listed in the *Small Press Record of Books in Print* (20th Edition, 1991-92). avg. price, cloth: $21.95; paper: $14.95. Discounts: retail trade: 1-4 copies, 20%; 5-24, 40%; 25-49, 42%; 50-99, 44%; 100-499, 46%; 500+, 48%. Textbooks: 20%. 175pp; 6×9; of. Reporting time: 30 days. Payment: 10% of list price. Copyrights for author. AAP, SSP, ABA.

THE ISLAND, Cottage Books, Eddie Stack, 731 Treat Avenue, San Francisco, CA 94110, 415-826-7113. 1987. Fiction, articles, interviews, reviews, news items, non-fiction. "Material is mainly of Irish interest. 2,000 words or so. Recent contributors - Peter O'Neill, Pat Healy, Carmel Sheridan, Eddie Stack" circ. 2M+. 4/yr. Expects 4 issues 1991, 6 issues 1992. sub. price: $8; per copy: $2.25; sample: $1. Back issues: $1.50. Discounts: 60/40. 24pp; 8½×11; of. Reporting time: 6 weeks. Payment: $50 max (under review). Not copyrighted. Pub's reviews: 6 in 1990. §Anything of Irish or Celtic bias-fiction, non-fiction. Ads: $600/$350/small ads $40. COSMEP, PMA.

Island Press, Barbara Dean, Joseph Ingram, 1718 Connecticut Avenue NW #300, Washington, DC 20009, 202-232-7933. 1978. Non-fiction. "Additional address: Box 7, Covelo, CA 95428" avg. press run 7M. Pub'd 28 titles 1990; expects 30 titles 1991. avg. price, cloth: $34.95; paper: $19.95. Discounts: trade 1-9 40%, 10-49 43%, 50-99 44%, 100-249 45%, 250+ 46%. 275pp; 6×9; of.

Island Publishers, Thelma Palmer, Co-Publisher; Delphine Haley, Co-Publisher, Box 201, Anacortes, WA 98221-0201, 206-293-3285/293-5398. 1985. Poetry, non-fiction. avg. press run 5M. Expects 2 titles 1991. 3 titles listed in the *Small Press Record of Books in Print* (20th Edition, 1991-92). avg. price, paper: $11.95. Discounts: 1-4 20%, 5-49 40%, 50+ 41%. 200pp; of. Reporting time: 1 month. Payment: inquire. Copyrights for author.

Islands (see also ISLANDS, A New Zealand Quarterly of Arts & Letters), Robin Dudding, 4 Sealy Road, Torbay, Auckland 10, New Zealand, 4039007. 1972. Poetry, fiction. "Book publishing only an occasional offshoot. *Islands* quarterly main function" avg. press run 2M. Pub'd 1 title 1990; expects 1 title 1991. 1 title listed in the *Small Press Record of Books in Print* (20th Edition, 1991-92). avg. price, paper: $9.50 (NZ). Discounts: 33⅓%, 2 or more; 25% single copies to retailers. 112pp; of, lp. Reporting time: ASAP. Payment: by arrangement. Copyrights for author.

ISLANDS, A New Zealand Quarterly of Arts & Letters, Islands, Robin Dudding, 4 Sealy Road, Torbay, Auckland 10, New Zealand, 4039007. 1972. Poetry, fiction, articles, art, photos, cartoons, interviews, satire, criticism, reviews, music, letters, parts-of-novels, long-poems, collages, plays, concrete art. "Basically New Zealand-related material. Copyrights revert to author but acknowledgement for future printings required, and notification. *Islands* faded into recess in 1981, basically from lack of money. Some hard saving and finangling saw a rebirth in July/August/September 1984, with a recosting, re-pricing and a New Series, but retaining the consecutive numbering. So *Islands* 34 (July '84) and *Islands* 35 (November '84) were published last year as New Series Vol. 1 Nos. 1 & 2. This year *Islands* 35 (April '85) as New Series Vol. 2 No 1. and Nov. 85 - 36 Vol. 2 No. 2, N.S. Vol. 3 Nos 1-4 (1986-87)" circ. 1.5M. 4/yr. Pub'd 1 issue 1990; expects 3 issues 1991, 4 issues 1992. sub. price: $33 (NZ), $39.60 (NZ) overseas (inc. GST); per copy: $11 (NZ)- $16.50 (NZ) overseas (inc. GST); sample: same. Back issues: first 8 vols available, at subscription price. Discounts: 33⅓% trade 2 or more copies 25% single copies, $5 discount on subsc. rate in NZ; $6 (NZ) overseas for subsc. agencies. 88pp; 8½×6; of, lp. Reporting time: asap. Payment: no set rate. Copyrighted, reverts to author. Pub's reviews: 26 in 1990. §Basically NZ fiction, verse, criticism. Ads: $96(NZ)/$52(o/s).

ISRAEL HORIZONS, Ralph Seliger, Editor; Arieh Lebowitz, Consulting Editor, 27 West 20th Street, Suite 902, New York, NY 10011, 212-255-8760, FAX 212-627-1287. 1952. Poetry, articles, art, photos, cartoons, interviews, reviews, letters, news items, non-fiction. "Most of our articles are about 1.5M-3M words in length. The magazine is a progressive/Socialist Zionist periodical, dealing with: progressive forces in Israel, specifically *Mapam* and the Kibbutz Artzi Federation—but not *exclusively* these groups—and general articles about Israeli life and culture. We also deal with problems facing Jewish communities around the world, from a progressive/Socialist Zionist perspective. Finally, we are also interested in bringing our readers general info that wouldn't make space in 'non-progressive' Jewish periodicals" circ. 2M. 4/yr. Pub'd 4 issues 1990; expects 4 issues 1991, 4 issues 1992. sub. price: $10; per copy: $2.50; sample: $2.50. Back issues: $2.50, depending on availability. 24-32pp; 8½×11; of. Reporting time: varies. Payment: $50 for articles, $25 for reviews, $25 for poems. Copyrighted, does not revert to author. Pub's reviews: 7 in 1990. §All Judaica, Middle East affairs, Arab-Jewish relations, socialist and other progressive political material, non- and fiction and other like material. Ads: $300/$150.

ISSUE ONE, Eon Publications, Ian Brocklebank, 2 Tewkesbury Drive, Grimsby, South Humberside DN34 4TL, England. 1983. Poetry, art, news items. "We provide contact panels for magazines we recieve that seem to be quality products, our format does not allow space for fuller review. We will not publish or support Facist, Racist, or Sexist material. Submissions of shorter material, e.g. below sonnet length proportionally stand a better chance of publication. Recent contributors: Dawne Anderson, Lisa Kucharski, Sheila G. Murphy, Arnold Lipkin" circ. 200. 4/yr. Pub'd 3 issues 1990; expects 4 issues 1991, 4 issues 1992. sub. price: £1 + 4 SAE; per copy: 25p; sample: free for postage. 6pp; of. Reporting time: within 2 months. Payment: free issue of the edition in which their piece appears. Copyrighted, reverts to author. CPA, Yorkshire Federation of Small Presses.

ISSUES, Sue Perlman, PO Box 11250, San Francisco, CA 94101, 415-864-4800 X136. 1978. Poetry, fiction, articles, art, photos, interviews, satire, reviews, non-fiction. "Messianic." circ. 40M. 6/yr. Pub'd 6 issues 1990; expects 6 issues 1991, 6 issues 1992. sub. price: free; per copy: free; sample: 50¢. Back issues: 75¢ each. 8-12pp; 8½×11; †of. Reporting time: 3-5 weeks. Payment: 10¢/word, minimum $25. Copyrighted, rights reverting is decided by contract. Pub's reviews: 5 in 1990. §Religion, Judaica, philosophy, Christianity. Ads: none.

IT GOES ON THE SHELF, Purple Mouth Press, Ned Brooks, 713 Paul Street, Newport News, VA 23605. 1984. Art, reviews. "Art only, I write the text myself" circ. 350. 1/yr. Pub'd 1 issue 1990; expects 1 issue 1991, 1 issue 1992. Discounts: trade, etc. 13pp; 8½×11; photocopy. Reporting time: 1 week. Payment: copy. Not copyrighted. Pub's reviews: 12+ in 1990. §Science fiction, fantasy, typewriters, oddities. SFPA, Slanapa.

Italica Press, Inc., Ronald G. Musto, Eileen Gardiner, 595 Main Street, #605, New York, NY 10044, 212-935-4230. 1985. Poetry, fiction, art, letters, long-poems, plays, non-fiction. "We specialize in English translations of Italian and Latin works from the Middle Ages to the present. Primary interests are in history, literature, travel, and art. Published titles include Petrarch, *The Revolution of Cola di Rienzo*, the poet's letters to the revolutionary; *The Marvels of Rome*, a medieval guidebook to the city; and Theodorich's *Guide to the Holy Land*, written c. 1172; *The Fat Woodworker* by Antonio Manetti, a comic Renaissance tale about Brunelleschi and his circle; and new translations from Italian of twentieth-century novels, *Cosima* by Grazia Deledda and *Family Chronicle* by Vasco Pratolini; *The Wooden Throne* by Carlo Sgorlon, *Dolcissimo* by Guiseppe Bonaviri, and *Woman at War* by Dacia Maraina. Our audience is the general reader interested in works of lasting merit." avg. press run 1M. Pub'd 6 titles 1990; expects 6 titles 1991, 6 titles 1992. 20 titles listed in the *Small Press Record of Books in Print* (20th Edition, 1991-92). avg. price, paper: $12.50. Discounts: trade single copy 20%, 25% 2 copies, 30% 3-4, 40% 5-25, 45% 26-50, 50% 51+; classroom 25% on adoptions of 5 or more; others are negotiable. 200pp; 5½×8½; of. Reporting time: 6 weeks. Payment: approx. 10% of net sales. Copyrights for author. COSMEP.

Ithaca Press, Charles E. Jarvis, Paul Jarvis, PO Box 853, Lowell, MA 01853. 1974. Fiction, criticism. *"Visions of Kerouac; The Life of Jack Kerouac,* by Charles E. Jarvis. *Zeus Has Two Urns,* by Charles E. Jarvis. *The Tyrants* by Charles E. Jarvis, 1977, fiction, 5¼ x 8, 161 pp, SQPA, $2.95, The book is a socio-political novel of the United States in the era of the Great Depression." avg. press run 5M. Pub'd 1 title 1990. 7 titles listed in the *Small Press Record of Books in Print* (20th Edition, 1991-92). avg. price, cloth: $7.95; paper: $3.45. Discounts: 40%. 220pp; 5½×8½; of. Copyrights for author. COSMEP, NESPA.

J

J & T Publishing, John Frank, PO Box 6520, Ventura, CA 93006, 805-525-8533, FAX: 525-4033. 1988. avg. press run 10M. Pub'd 1 title 1990; expects 3 titles 1991, 1 title 1992. 1 title listed in the *Small Press Record of Books in Print* (20th Edition, 1991-92). avg. price, cloth: $19.95; paper: $9.95. 250pp; 6×9. Reporting time: 3-4 months unless exceptional. Copyrights for author. PMA.

J P Publications, Chris Paffrath, 2952 Grinnel, Davis, CA 95616, 916-758-9727. 1980. Art, photos, interviews, non-fiction. "We do not actively seek material." avg. press run 8M. Pub'd 1 title 1990; expects 6 titles 1991, 10 titles 1992. 3 titles listed in the *Small Press Record of Books in Print* (20th Edition, 1991-92). avg. price, cloth: $20; paper: $12.50. Discounts: 2-5 20%; 6-24 40%; 25-49 42%; 50-100 45%; 101-200 48%; 201+ 50%. 200pp; 8×11; of. Payment: on an individual basis. Copyrights for author. COSMEP.

J. Barnaby Distributors, 1709 Hawthorne Lane, Plano, TX 75074, (214) 422-2770. 1986. Fiction. Pub'd 2 titles 1990; expects 5 titles 1991, 14 titles 1992. 3 titles listed in the *Small Press Record of Books in Print* (20th Edition, 1991-92). avg. price, paper: $6.00; other: library bound $9.95. 60pp; 8½×11; of. Payment: flexible. Copyrights for author.

JABBERWOCKY, Jeff VanderMeer, Duane Bray, Penelope Miller, Chimera Connections, Inc., 502 NW 75th Street #197, Gainesville, FL 32607-1608, 904-332-6586. 1989. Poetry, fiction, art, interviews, satire, parts-of-novels, long-poems, plays. "Fiction to 5,000 words, poetry to 1,000 lines. We have a loose definition of 'fantasy' especially when it comes to poetry—most mainstream poets should consider us just as open a market as any other. The lines between literary and commercial speculative fiction are blurry at best and we are open to *anything*. Contributors to first issue: International Fantasy Award-Winner Meredith Ann Pierce, Wayne Allen Sallee, Cliff Burns, Dave Hoing, Joel Zeltzer, Homero Aridjis, as well as an exclusive interview with Richard Adams (*Watership Down*) by Dale A. White." circ. 1M. 2/yr. Expects 2 issues 1991, 2 issues 1992. sub. price: $10; per copy: $4.50; sample: $4.50. Discounts: individually negotiated. 60pp; 5×8½; of. Reporting time: 1-3 weeks. Payment: $10-$50 ($25 average) fiction, $5-$30 for art/poetry. Copyrighted, reverts to author. Ads: $135/$80/send for rates. SPWAO.

Jacar Press, Richard Krawiec, Carol Collier, Paul Jones, 612 Bon Air Avenue, Durham, NC 27704-3302, 919-365-4188. 1986. Poetry, fiction, art, photos, parts-of-novels. "Preference for, though not limited to, Southern writing. Particularly interested in North Carolina writers, past or present residents. We're willing to consider novellas. We're interested in contemporary, not regional, writing" avg. press run 2M. Pub'd 1 title 1990; expects 1 title 1991, 2 titles 1992. avg. price, other: prices vary. Discounts: 50%, 60 days net, or on consignment. Returnable. 5½×8½; of. Reporting time: 2 months. Payment: varies. Copyrights for author.

JACARANDA REVIEW, Katherine Swiggart, Editor; Julie Giese, Fiction Editor; Gregory Castle, Poetry Editor; Jenny Senft, Business Manager, English Department, Univ. of California-Los Angeles, Los Angeles, CA 90024, 213-825-4173. 1984. Poetry, fiction, articles, photos, interviews, reviews, parts-of-novels, long-poems. "Recent contributors include Jorge Luis Borges, Carolyn Forche, Alfred Corn, Daniel Mencker, Jascha Kessler, Barry Spacks. Contributors should look at the magazines to get an idea of our (eclectic) interests" circ. 1.5M. 2/yr. Pub'd 2 issues 1990; expects 2 issues 1991, 2 issues 1992. sub. price: $10; per copy: $4; sample: $4. Back issues: $2.50 each. 160pp; 5½×8; of. Reporting time: 2 months. Payment: 3 copies plus 20% discount on additional copies. Copyrighted, reverts to author. Pub's reviews: 8 in 1990. §Contemporary fiction and poetry from small presses as well as large ones. Ads: $75/$37.50/$20 1/4 page. CCLM, Index of American Periodical Verse.

Jack October, H. L. Prosser, 1313 South Jefferson Ave., Springfield, MO 65807. 1967. Poetry, fiction, non-fiction. "Preference given to vedanta and nature topics, some consideration given to well-written erotic poetry if done with sensitivity." avg. press run varies. Discounts: *short* discount only. Reporting time: 30 days;

SASE must accompany submissions and inquiries, query letter before any submissions. Payment: in copies only.

The Jackpine Press, Betty Leighton, Publisher, 1007 Paschal Drive, Winston-Salem, NC 27106, 919-759-0783. 1975. Poetry, fiction. "1st book: *Balancing On Stones*, poems by Emily Wilson. 2nd book: *Out In The Country, Back Home*, poems by Jeff Daniel Marion. *Orion*, poem by Jerald Bullis. *Sidetracks*, poems by Clint McCown. *A Walk With Raschid and Other Stories* by Josephine Jacobsen. 6th book: *Thirtieth Year to Heaven: New American Poets*. 7th book: *Adios, Mr. Moxley: Thirteen Stories* by Josephine Jacobsen" avg. press run 1M-2M. Pub'd 1 title 1990; expects 1 title 1991. 4 titles listed in the *Small Press Record of Books in Print* (20th Edition, 1991-92). avg. price, cloth: $6.95; paper: $3.95; other: TYTH - $12.95/160 pages. Discounts: 30% for 5 or more books/cash 60 days. 70-160pp; 6×9; of. Reporting time: 2-3 months. Payment: separate arrangements with each author. Copyright by author. COSMEP.

Jackson's Arm, Michael Blackburn, c/o Sunk Island Publishing, PO Box 74, Lincoln LN1 1QG, England. 1985. Poetry, fiction, articles, interviews, criticism, reviews, long-poems. avg. press run 400. Pub'd 1 title 1990; expects 1 title 1991, 1 title 1992. 7 titles listed in the *Small Press Record of Books in Print* (20th Edition, 1991-92). avg. price, paper: £1.50 ($3). Discounts: 1/3 to booksellers. 16+pp; size A5; of, mi. Reporting time: up to 2 months. Payment: 10% of print run. Copyrights for author. The Association of Little Presses.

JACOB'S LETTER, Bonnie Lawrence, 121 Steuart Street, #402, San Francisco, CA 94105, (415) 387-1004. 1979. Poetry, fiction, articles, art, photos, interviews, criticism, reviews, non-fiction. "*Jacob* is a nonprofit organization dedicated to the expression of Jewish identity, value and traditions in art. Articles of interest to Jewish visual artists, musicians, playwrights, writers and craftspeople are welcome for publication in *Jacob's Letter*. Please submit written query before sending article" circ. 500. 4/yr. Pub'd 4 issues 1990; expects 4 issues 1991, 4 issues 1992. sub. price: $20; per copy: $2; sample: same. Back issues: $2. 24pp; 8½×11; of. Payment: very minimal. Copyrighted, reverts to author. Ads: $250/$150/$85 1/4 page/$45 1/8 plus classified.

Jaffe Publishing Management Service (see also ASIAN LITERARY MARKET REVIEW), Nicy Punnoose, Kunnuparambil Buildings, Kurichy, Kottayam 686549, India, 91-4826-470. 1985. "Jaffe specializes in publishing reports, manuals, directories, group catalogs, etc. for the book and magazine publishing industry" avg. press run 1.1M. Pub'd 2 titles 1990; expects 2 titles 1991, 2 titles 1992. avg. price, cloth: $10; paper: $50. Discounts: 25%. 96pp; 8½×11; †lp. Reporting time: 3 months. Payment: 10% on the published price on copies sold, payment annually. Copyrights for author.

JAG, R.S. Jaggard, 10 East Charles, Oelwein, IA 50662, 319-283-3491. 1962. Articles. "Dedicated to establishment and implementation of a free enterprise system in a land with a legitimate government that defends all persons against the use of force or violence by anybody against anybody else at any time for any reason" circ. 1M. 9/yr. Pub'd 9 issues 1990; expects 9 issues 1991, 9 issues 1992. sub. price: available on request, no fee required. 1pp; 8½×14; mi. Not copyrighted. Pub's reviews: 1 in 1990. No paid ads.

Jalmar Press (see also WARM FUZZY NEWSLETTER), Bradley L. Winch, President, 45 Hitching Post Drive, Building 2, Rolling Hills Estates, CA 90274, 213-547-1240. 1973. Poetry, fiction, art, photos, cartoons, interviews, satire, non-fiction. "Affiliated with B.L. Winch & Associates. Primarily interested in works in the humanistic area of psychology and books of general how-to interest. Have five series: 1) *Transactional Analysis For Everybody, Warm Fuzzy Series*, 2) *Creative Parenting and Teaching Series*, 3) *Conflict Resolution Series*, 4) *Right-Brain/Whole-Brain Learning Series*, 5) *Positive Self-Esteem Series*. Titles in *TA for Everybody Series*: Freed, Alvyn M. *TA for Tots* (and other prinzes); Freed, Alvyn & Margaret *TA for Kids* (and Grown-ups, too) 3rd edition newly revised and illustrated. Freed, Alvyn M. *TA for Teens* (and other important people); Freed, Alvyn M. *TA for Tots Coloring Book. TA for Tots* Vol. II - Alvyn M. Freed. Steiner, Claude *Original Warm Fuzzy Tale; Songs of the Warm Fuzzy* cassette (all about your feelings)" avg. press run 3M. Pub'd 4 titles 1990; expects 4 titles 1991, 4 titles 1992. 33 titles listed in the *Small Press Record of Books in Print* (20th Edition, 1991-92). avg. price, cloth: $16.95; paper: $12.95. Discounts: trade 25-45%; agent/jobber 25-50%. 200pp; 8½×11, 6×9; of. Reporting time: 4 weeks. Payment: 7½%-12½% of net receipts. Copyrights for author. COSMEP, ABA, CBA, PMA (PASCAL), EDSA.

Jamenair Ltd., Annie Mangold, PO Box 241957, Los Angeles, CA 90024-9757, 213-470-6688. 1986. Non-fiction. "Books and software related to job search and career changing." avg. press run 10M. 2 titles listed in the *Small Press Record of Books in Print* (20th Edition, 1991-92). avg. price, paper: $22.95. Discounts: depends on quantity. 330pp; 8⅜×10⅞; of. Reporting time: 30 days. Payment: open, depends on material. Copyrights for author. PMA, IWOSC, Soc. des Gens de Lettres de France, Society of Authors (UK).

JAMES DICKEY NEWSLETTER, Joyce M. Pair, Editor, 2101 Womack Road, Dunwoody, GA 30338, 404-551-3162. 1984. Poetry, articles, interviews, reviews, long-poems. "Lengthy mss. considered but may be published in sequential issues. All material should concern James Dickey/his work and includes comparative studies. We publish a few poems of *very* high caliber. Recent: Fred Chappell, R.T. Smith, Ronald Baughman, Romana Heylen, Ken Autrey, and Gordon VanNess." circ. 200. 2/yr. Pub'd 2 issues 1990; expects 2 issues

1991, 2 issues 1992. sub. price: $5 USA individuals, $10 institutions; per copy: $3.50 indiv., $7.50 instit; sample: $3.50, $7.50. Back issues: $3.50, $7.50. 30pp; 8½×11; †of. Reporting time: 2 weeks. Payment: 5 copies. Copyrighted, reverts to author. Pub's reviews: 4 in 1990. §Modern American, work of or about James Dickey. Ads: full page flyer inserted $100. CELJ.

JAMES JOYCE BROADSHEET, Pieter Bekker, Richard Brown, Alistair Stead, School of English, University of Leeds, West Yorkshire LS2 9JT, England, 0532-459898. 1980. Poetry, articles, art, photos, cartoons, criticism, reviews, letters, news items. circ. 800. 3/yr. Pub'd 3 issues 1990; expects 3 issues 1991. sub. price: £6/$12 (including airmail postage); per copy: £2 plus 50p postage ($4 plus $1 postage); sample: £2/$4. Back issues: at current annual subscription rate. Discounts: 33⅓% to bookshops only. 4-6pp; 11.7×16.5; of. Reporting time: 6 months-1 year. Payment: none. Copyrighted. Pub's reviews: 15 in 1990. §Modern literature, James Joyce, contemporary criticism. Ads: £50/$100 (U.S.) per column.

JAMES JOYCE QUARTERLY, University of Tulsa, Robert Spoo, Editor, University of Tulsa, 600 S. College, Tulsa, OK 74104. 1963. Articles, criticism, reviews. "Academic criticism of Joyce's works and of his critics; book reviews, notes, bibliographies; material relating to Joyce and Irish Renaissance and Joyce's relationship to other writers of his time. Articles should not normally exceed 20 pp. Notes should not excceed 6 pp. Please consult MLA *Handbook* and 'Special Note to Contributors' which appears on inside back cover of each issue of the *JJQ* regarding style & preparation of manuscript." circ. 1.9M. 4/yr. Pub'd 4 issues 1990; expects 4 issues 1991, 4 issues 1992. sub. price: $14 U.S., $15 foreign; per copy: $5 U.S.; $5.50 foreign; sample: $5. Back issues: check price with reprint house- Swets & Zeitlinger, PO Box 517, Berwyn, Pa 19312. 150pp; 6×9; of. Reporting time: 6-12 weeks. Payment: contributors' copies & offprints. Copyrighted, does not revert to author. Pub's reviews: 11 in 1990. §Joyce studies. Ads: $125 ($160 includes copy of *JJQ* subscription list on set of self-adhesive address labels)/$75. CELJ.

JAMES WHITE REVIEW; A Gay Men's Literary Quarterly, Philip Willkie, Greg Baysans, PO Box 3356, Traffic Station, Minneapolis, MN 55403, 612-291-2913. 1983. Poetry, fiction, art, photos, interviews, satire, long-poems, non-fiction. "Submissions deadlines Aug. 1, Nov. 1, Feb. 1, May 1." circ. 3M. 4/yr. Pub'd 4 issues 1990; expects 4 issues 1991, 4 issues 1992. sub. price: $12 (institutions $12, foreign $17); per copy: $3; sample: $3. Back issues: 5 or more copies $1.50 a copy. Discounts: retailers get 40%t. 40pp; 13×18; of, web. Reporting time: by our publication date. Payment: $25 short story, $10 poem. Copyrighted, reverts to author. Pub's reviews: 20 in 1990. §Poetry, fiction, creative nonfiction, biography. Ads: $400/$200/$120 1/4 page/$75 1/5 page. CCLM.

Jamison Station Press, John M. Townley, 802 West Street, Winston-Salem, NC 27127-5116. 1977. Non-fiction. "Usually print 250-300pp works on local history of the Great Basin area, as well as shorter guidebooks to historic sites in the same area" avg. press run 1M. Pub'd 6 titles 1990; expects 6 titles 1991, 6 titles 1992. 7 titles listed in the *Small Press Record of Books in Print* (20th Edition, 1991-92). avg. price, paper: $20; other: $2-$5. Discounts: 40% + depending on volume. 24-300pp; 8½×11; †of. Reporting time: 14 days. Payment: individual.

JASON UNDERGROUND'S NOTES FROM THE TRASHCOMPACTOR, Jason Underground, 2795 Via Vela, Camarillo, CA 93010, 805-482-3220. 1990. Articles, satire, criticism, reviews, music, news items. "*Jason Underground's Notes From The Trashcompactor* is a 'personal 'zine' consisting entirely of articles written by Jason himself. He does react to mail received; however, no submissions are accepted or printed. Everything published by Jesus Freaks Ink, including Jason's chapbooks, are offered completely free of charge; however, we do accept and very much appreciate donations of stamps or money or checks payable to Jason Underground. Biases: Christianity, anarchy, ecology, vegetarianism, communal living, Judaism, folk & punk & reggae music. We will also review books and music. Some will be included in our top ten, and one or two spotlighted." circ. 250. 6/yr. Pub'd 1 issue 1990; expects 6 issues 1991, 6 issues 1992. sub. price: free. Back issues: free. 6pp; 8½×11; †photocopy. Payment: no such thing. Not copyrighted. Pub's reviews: 25 in 1990. §All areas, Christian and Jewish theological and apologetic works, subversive history, anarchy. Ads: $55/$30/$17.50 1/4 page.

Jayell Enterprises Inc., James L. Limbacher, PO Box 2616, Fort Dearborn Station, Dearborn, MI 48123, 313-565-9687. 1984. Fiction. avg. press run 1M. Pub'd 1 title 1990; expects 1 title 1991, 1 title 1992. 1 title listed in the *Small Press Record of Books in Print* (20th Edition, 1991-92). avg. price, paper: $7.95. Discounts: 40%. 200pp; 5½×8½; of. Reporting time: 1 month. Copyrights for author. Inland.

JB & Me Publishing (see also CLIENT MAGAZINE), Marilyn Elkind, Managing Editor; Jack Bernstein, Publisher, PO Box 3879, Manhattan Beach, CA 90266. 1985. News items, non-fiction. "Length of material is irrelevant. Material should be on the subjects of advertising, publishing, marketing and sales." avg. press run 5M. Pub'd 2 titles 1990; expects 3 titles 1991, 4 titles 1992. 3 titles listed in the *Small Press Record of Books in Print* (20th Edition, 1991-92). avg. price, paper: $35. Discounts: varies. Pages vary; 8×10; of. Reporting time: 1-2 months. Payment: individually negotiated. Copyrights for author.

286

J'ECRIS, Jean Guenot, 85, rue des Tennerolles, Saint-Cloud 92210, France, (1) 47-71-79-63. 1987. "Specialized on technical data concerning creative writing for French writers" circ. 2M. 4/yr. Pub'd 4 issues 1990; expects 4 issues 1991, 4 issues 1992. sub. price: $47; per copy: $10; sample: free. Back issues: $8. 16pp; 19×28cm; †of. Payment: yes. Copyrighted, reverts to author. Pub's reviews: 15 in 1990. §Only books dealing with creative writing techniques. No ads.

JENNINGS MAGAZINE, Philip Sidney Jennings, Paul Magrath, 336 Westbourne Park Road, London W.11 1EQ, United Kingdom, 01-521-4349; 727-7810. 1985. Poetry, fiction, articles, art, cartoons, interviews, satire, criticism, letters, non-fiction. "Each issue contains an interview with an established literary figure, a story competition with £300 in prizes. A literary crossword puzzle, short stories, poems and articles. We do not publish novel extracts. Writers interviewed to date: Ian Cochrane, Martin Amis, Piers Paul Read, Lain Banks, Jeanette Winterson, Gavin Ewart. Entry to competition is by purchase of magazine. We rarely publish fiction over 4,000 words" circ. 2M. 4/yr. Pub'd 3 issues 1990; expects 4 issues 1991, 4 issues 1992. sub. price: £7.50 UK, £12 US (sterling only); per copy: £2 UK, $3 US; sample: £2 UK, £3 overseas. Back issues: £2 UK, £3 overseas. 44pp; 8-2/5×11-4/5; of, floppy disc. Reporting time: 2-5 weeks. Payment: £40-£5. Copyrighted, reverts to author. Pub's reviews: 24 in 1990. §Short story collections, novels, essays, writing manuals. Ads: £150/£80/£45 1/4/£110 2/3/£60 1/3 (30p per word, classified).

JEOPARDY, Western Washington University, College Hall 132, Bellingham, WA 98225, 206-676-3118. 1964. Poetry, fiction, art, photos, criticism, long-poems, plays. "1) prefer poetry of no more than 3 single-spaced, legal-paper pages in length. 2) prefer stories of no more than 15 triple-spaced, legal-paper pages in length. 3) recent well-known contributors: William Stafford, James Bertolino, Ron Bayes, Daniel Halpern, Joyce Odam, Madeline DeFrees, Richard Hugo, R.H.W. Dillard, Al Young, Beth Bentley, Annie Dillard, Kelly Cherry." circ. 4M. 1/yr. Pub'd 1 issue 1990; expects 1 issue 1991, 1 issue 1992. sub. price: $4; per copy: $4; sample: $2. Back issues: $2. 108pp; size varies; †of. Reporting time: accept submissions Sept. thrugh Jan.; report back in February. Payment: 2 complimentary copies. Copyrighted. CCLM, COSMEP.

Jessee Poet Publications (see also POETS AT WORK), Jessee Poet, RD #1, Portersville, PA 16051. 1985. Poetry, long-poems. "Chapbook publisher, send SASE for price. National contests (poetry) sponsor, send SASE for details." avg. press run 350. Pub'd 75 titles 1990. 4 titles listed in the *Small Press Record of Books in Print* (20th Edition, 1991-92). 5½×8½, 7×8½; †copy machine. Reporting time: 1 week. Payment: none. Does not copyright for author.

JEWISH CURRENTS, Morris U. Schappes, 22 E 17th Street, Suite 601, New York, NY 10003, 212-924-5740. 1946. Poetry, fiction, articles, art, photos, interviews, satire, criticism, reviews, letters, news items, non-fiction. "Articles of Jewish interest, progressive politics, Black-Jewish relations, 2-4M words; reviews of books, records, plays, films, events, 1.8M-2.5M words; lively style, hard facts, secular p.o.v., pro-Israel/non-Zionist." circ. 2.7M. 11/yr. Pub'd 11 issues 1990; expects 11 issues 1991, 11 issues 1992. 3 titles listed in the *Small Press Record of Books in Print* (20th Edition, 1991-92). sub. price: $20; per copy: $2; sample: $2. Back issues: $2. Discounts: 40% retail. 48pp (except Dec.=80pp); 5½×8½; of. Reporting time: 2 months. Payment: 6 copies + sub. Copyrighted. Pub's reviews: 60 in 1990. §Jewish affairs, political & cultural, feminism, civil rights, labor history. Ads: $125/$75/$50 - for 2 col. inch (greetings and memorials); $200/$125/$25 1 col. inch (commercial ads).

JEWISH LINGUISTIC STUDIES, David L. Gold, 67-07 215 Street, Oakland Gardens, NY 11364-2523. 1981. Articles, criticism, reviews, letters, non-fiction. "Formerly *Jewish Language Review*. Out-of-print issues available from University Microfilms International, 300 North Zeeb Road, Ann Arbor, MI 48106-1346." circ. 400. 1/yr. Pub'd 1 issue 1990; expects 1 issue 1991, 1 issue 1992. price per copy: varies according to issue; sample: same. Back issues: same. Discounts: none. 400pp; 8½×11; of. Reporting time: 4 months maximum. Payment: none. Copyrighted, does not revert to author. Pub's reviews: 50-60 in 1990. §Anything of Jewish or linguistic interest. Ads: rates available on request.

JEWISH VEGETARIANS OF NORTH AMERICA, Charles Stahler, Debra Wasserman, Jewish Vegetarians, PO Box 1463, Baltimore, MD 21203, 301-366-VEGE. 1983. Poetry, articles, cartoons, interviews, reviews, letters, news items, non-fiction. circ. 800. 4/yr. Pub'd 4 issues 1990; expects 4 issues 1991, 4 issues 1992. sub. price: $12; sample: SASE two first-class stamps. Back issues: inquire. Discounts: inquire. 16pp; 8½×11; of. Reporting time: 1 month. Payment: copies. Pub's reviews: 4 in 1990. §Vegetarianism, animal rights, Judaism. Ads: inquire.

JH Press, Terry Helbing, PO Box 294, Village Station, New York, NY 10014, 255-4713. 1979. Plays. "JH Press is a gay theatre publishing company, specializing in acting editions of produced gay plays. JH Press also handles the leasing rights for amateur productions of the plays. We have already published the *Gay Theatre Alliance Directory of Gay Plays*, compiled and edited and with an introduction by Terry Helbing and play scripts by Doric Wilson, Arch Brown, Jane Chambers, Sidney Morris, C.D. Arnold, Terry Miller, and other playwrights. (Forever After) (News Boy), (My Blue Heaven)." avg. press run 1M-2M. Pub'd 1 title 1990;

expects 1 title 1991, 1 title 1992. 11 titles listed in the *Small Press Record of Books in Print* (20th Edition, 1991-92). avg. price, paper: $3-$8. Discounts: 40% trade, 5 or more copies mixed titles. 144pp; 6×9, 5¼×7⅝; of. Reporting time: 2 weeks. Payment: % of retail sales to be negotiated. Copyrights for author. GPNY.

Jigsaw Publishing House, Toni Spencer, V.L. Thomas, 6830 S. Delaware Avenue, Tulsa, OK 74136-4501, 918-492-5112. 1989. *"Arthritis Self-Preservation* is a 160 page book with over 50 illustrations. It is instructional, inspirational and humorous. 50% of revenue paid to Arthritis Foundation research" avg. press run 5M-20M. Expects 3 titles 1991, 5 titles 1992. avg. price, paper: $15. Discounts: 50% 100+ copies. 160pp; 5½×11½; lp. Payment: 25%. Copyrights for author.

JIMMY & LUCY'S HOUSE OF 'K', Benjamin Friedlander, Andrew Schelling, 3816 Piedmont #6, Oakland, CA 94611-5329, 415-848-8177. 1984. Poetry, articles, art, criticism, reviews, music, letters, non-fiction. "Short reviews of experimental poetry, music and art. Essays on art and politics. Feature issues on individual writers and presses. A stream lined eclecticism. Recent contributors: Larry Eigner, Robert Duncan, Rachel DuPlessis, Susan Howe, Ron Silliman, Charles Bernstein, Beverly Dahlen, Barrett Watten. Starting with issue #4, each issue contains a special poetry supplement under the imprint *Lucy Has More Fun"* circ. 200. 3/yr. Pub'd 3 issues 1990; expects 3 issues 1991, 3 issues 1992. sub. price: $15; per copy: $5; sample: $5. Back issues: issues 1-3 $12. Discounts: none. 100pp; 7×8½; †xerox. Reporting time: immediate. Payment: copies. Copyrighted, reverts to author. Pub's reviews: 25 in 1990. §Experimental poetry, criticism, music.

JKM Publishing Company, 1418 Meadowlark Street, PO Box 521547, Longwood, FL 32752-1547, 407-767-5633. 1 title listed in the *Small Press Record of Books in Print* (20th Edition, 1991-92).

JLA Publications, A Division Of Jeffrey Lant Associates, Inc., Jeffrey Lant, President, 50 Follen Street #507, Suite 507, Cambridge, MA 02138, 617-547-6372. 1979. Non-fiction. "We are interested in publishing books of particular interest to small businesses, entrepreneurs and independent professionals. To get an idea of what we publish, simply write us at the above address and request a current catalog. Up until now our titles have been all more than 100,000 words in length and are widely regarded as the most detailed books on their subjects. Recent books include Debra Ashton's *Complete Guide to Planned Giving,* Jeffrey Lant's Revised Second Edition of *Money Talks: The Complete Guide to Creating a Profitable Workshop or Seminar in any Field* and Lant's book *Cash Copy: How to Offer Your Products and Services So Your Prospects Buy Them...Now!* We are now open, however, to shorter (though still very specific and useful) books in the 50,000-75,000 word length and titles in human development as well as business development. We are different because we pay royalties *monthly* and get our authors very involved in the publicity process. We do not pay advances for material but do promote strenuously through our quarterly catalog and Dr. Lant's Sure-Fire Business Success Column" avg. press run 4M-5M. Pub'd 7 titles 1990; expects 2 titles 1991, 5 titles 1992. 9 titles listed in the *Small Press Record of Books in Print* (20th Edition, 1991-92). avg. price, paper: $30. Discounts: 1-9 copies 20%, 10-99 40% (you pay shipping); thence negotiable up to 60% discount on major orders. 300+pp; 9×12; †lp. Reporting time: 30-60 days. Payment: 10%, monthly. Copyrights for author. COSMEP, Publishers Marketing Assn, National Assn. of Independent Publishers, Marin Self-Publishers Assn.

joe soap's canoe (see also JOE SOAP'S CANOE), Martin Stannard, 30 Quilter Road, Felixstowe, Suffolk IP11 7JJ, England, 0394 275569. 1978. Poetry. "Postmodernist Bias. Length of material not important. Recent Publications: Paul Violi, Keith Dersley, Michael Blackburn and Rupert Mallin. Manuscripts by request only." avg. press run 150. Pub'd 1 title 1990; expects 4 titles 1991, 2 titles 1992. 4 titles listed in the *Small Press Record of Books in Print* (20th Edition, 1991-92). avg. price, paper: £2 ($6). Discounts: 1/3 off. Pages vary; 6×8; †of. Payment: copies. Copyrights for author.

JOE SOAP'S CANOE, joe soap's canoe, Martin Stannard, 30 Quilter Road, Felixstowe, Suffolk IP11 7JJ, England, 0394 275569. 1978. Poetry, fiction, articles, art, photos, interviews, reviews, parts-of-novels, long-poems, plays. "Length not important; postmodernist bias. Recent contributors include: John Ashbery, Ron Padgett, Paul Violi, Peter Sansom, Robert Hershon, Ian McMillan. Is also running series of interviews with, so far, Kenneth Koch and John Ashbery featured." circ. 400-500. 1/yr. Pub'd 1 issue 1990; expects 1 issue 1991, 1 issue 1992. sub. price: £3.50 ($10); per copy: £3.50 ($10); sample: £3 or $6 (plus postage costs). Back issues: 1/2 price. Discounts: 1/3 off to trade, and to orders of 3 or more copies. 100pp; 6×8; †of. Reporting time: 6-8 weeks. Payment: copies. Copyrighted, reverts to author. Ads: £30 ($100)/ £15 ($50).

Joelle Publishing, Inc., Dennis Rahilly, PO Box 91229, Santa Barbara, CA 93190, 805-962-9887. 1987. Non-fiction. avg. press run 5M. Pub'd 1 title 1990; expects 2 titles 1991, 3 titles 1992. 2 titles listed in the *Small Press Record of Books in Print* (20th Edition, 1991-92). avg. price, paper: $9.95. Discounts: trade 40%, jobber 55%, library 20%. 140pp; 6×9; of. Reporting time: 3 weeks. Payment: to be arranged. Copyrights for author. COSMEP, PMA.

Johnson Books, Barbara Mussil, Publisher; Rebecca Herr, Editorial Director; Richard Croog, Sales & Promotion Director, 1880 South 57th Court, Boulder, CO 80301, 303-443-1576. 1978. Non-fiction. "Primarily a publisher of Western history, natural history, archaeology, outdoor recreation, and travel books" avg. press run 4M. Pub'd 10 titles 1990; expects 12 titles 1991, 12 titles 1992. 15 titles listed in the *Small Press Record of Books in Print* (20th Edition, 1991-92). avg. price, cloth: $22.95; paper: $9.95. Discounts: trade 20-45%, distributors 50-55%. 250pp; 6×9; †of. Reporting time: 2 months. Payment: varies, 7½%-10%. Copyrights for author. Rocky Mountain Book Publishers Association (RMBPA), PO Box 15426, Rio Rancho, NM 87174, Mountains & Plains Booksellers Assn, American Booksellers Assn.

Johnson Institute, Lenore Franzen, 7151 Metro Boulevard #250, Minneapolis, MN 55435, 612-944-0511. 1966. Non-fiction. "Booklets (10-40 pages), books 100+ pages. Biases: chemical dependence prevention, intervention, treatment issues. Recent contributors: Dick Schaefer, Dr. Timmen Cermak, Shelly Freeman and Peter Cohen." avg. press run 5M-10M. Pub'd 6 titles 1990; expects 40 titles 1991, 40 titles 1992. avg. price, cloth: $19.95; paper: $8.95; other: $2.50. Discounts: trade, quantity according to schedule. 100pp; 5⅜x7¾; desktop, linotronic conversion, printer. Reporting time: 4 weeks. Payment: negotiated from standard contract. Copyrights for author. American Booksellers Assoc. (ABA), 137 W. 25th St., New York, NY 10001.

Jones River Press, Doris M. Johnson, 20 Middle Street, Plymouth, MA 02360, 508-747-3899. 1990. Photos, non-fiction. "First title, *On The Cutting Edge*, is a biography of a famous surgeon. Second title, *Plymouth Yacht Club 1890-1990: A Centennial History*, is just what its title says. Third and fourth titles will be related to maritime history, shipwrecks, etc." avg. press run 500. 1 title listed in the *Small Press Record of Books in Print* (20th Edition, 1991-92). avg. price, cloth: $30. Discounts: 40%. 250pp; 6×9; of. Payment: varies. Copyrights by arrangement. COSMEP.

Jorvik Press, Peter Stansill, PO Box 18, Marylhurst, OR 97036-0018, 503-636-9244. 1989. Fiction, interviews, non-fiction. "Jorvik Press's current focus is thematic anthologies of short fiction. Other areas of interest are history, world affairs, psychology, and travel. Future titles will also include translations of short fiction from Scandinavia, Europe, and Latin America" avg. press run 5M-10M. Expects 3 titles 1992. avg. price, cloth: $18; paper: $9. Discounts: standard. 250pp; 5×7¾; of. Reporting time: 3 months. Payment: by negotiation. Copyrights for author.

JOTS (Journal of the Senses), Elysium Growth Press, Ed Lange, Arthur Kunkin, 814 Robinson Road, Topanga, CA 90290. 1961. Interviews, reviews, letters, news items. circ. 15M. 4/yr. Pub'd 4 issues 1990; expects 4 issues 1991, 4 issues 1992. sub. price: $4; per copy: $1; sample: $1. 40pp; 8½×11; of. Reporting time: 3 weeks. Payment: limited. Copyrighted. Pub's reviews: 6 in 1990. §Massage, self-appreciation, holistic health, nudism and clothing optionality. Ads: $300/$160.

JOURNAL FOR ANTHROPOSOPHY, Arthur Zajonc, Editor; Linda Fleishman, Managing Editor, HC01, Box 24, Dripping Springs, TX 78620, 413-256-0655. 1965. Poetry, fiction, articles, art, photos, interviews, criticism, reviews, letters, long-poems, non-fiction. "*The Journal for Anthroposophy* is a low-profile periodical, presenting articles, interviews, book reviews and poetry that eminate from, reflect or harmonize with the philosophical indications of Rudolf Steiner, whose spiritual science has been applied since the turn of the century, both in the U.S. and abroad, to matters of the natural and physical sciences, health, education, agriculture, and the arts. Recent contributors have included William Hunt (on Paul Celan), Rene Quarido (on Chartres & other articles), Rex Raab (on architecture), Dieter Rudloff (on Josef Beuys); *The Journal* has also featured works by Albert Steffen, Rudolf Steiner, the writings of Goethe, Blake, etc. Occasionally an article may be presented in two parts, appearing in two consecutive issues; range 800-6,000 words" circ. 1.3M. 2/yr. Pub'd 2 issues 1990; expects 2 issues 1991, 2 issues 1992. sub. price: $12 US, $15 foreign and institution; per copy: $6 US, $7.50 foreign; sample: free. Back issues: $6 each in U.S./$7.50 each abroad. Discounts: 1/3 off on orders of 5 or more copies, 15% on orders of a complete set of *Journals* (iss. #1 to current). 84pp; 6×9; of. Reporting time: about 3 weeks. Payment: usually none, but negotiable. Copyrighted, does not revert to author. Pub's reviews: 6 long, 24 short in 1990. §Spiritual science, education, metaphysics, biodynamic agriculture, art, science, music, literature, poetry. Ads: $250/$150/$90 1/4 page/discount for non-profit orgs. UIPD, SPD, both directories of Bowker Serials Bibliographies, 245 West 17 Street, New York, NY 10011.

THE JOURNAL: The Literary Magazine of the Ohio State University, Kathy Fagan, Michelle Herman, OSU Dept. of English, 164 W. 17th Avenue, Columbus, OH 43210, 614-292-4076. 1973. Poetry, fiction, articles, art, photos, interviews, criticism, reviews, parts-of-novels, long-poems. "We are looking for quality poetry, fiction, essays and reviews." circ. 1.2M. 2/yr. Pub'd 2 issues 1990; expects 2 issues 1991, 2 issues 1992. sub. price: $8; per copy: $5; sample: $5. Back issues: $2, before Spring 1980, $1.50. Discounts: 20% to stores. 80-100pp; 6×9; lp. Reporting time: 2-8 weeks. Payment: 2 issues, and a small stipend, when funds are available. Copyrighted, reverts to author. Pub's reviews: 4 in 1990. §Poetry. Ads: $80 6 X 9/$50 6 X 4½/we exchange ads with other literary magazines.

JOURNAL OF AESTHETICS AND ART CRITICISM, Donald Crawford, Editor, University of Wisconsin Press, 114 North Murray Street, Madison, WI 53715, 608-262-5839. "*JAAC* is the journal of The American Society for Aesthetics, an interdisciplinary society which promotes study, research, discussion and publication in aesthetics" circ. 2.7M. 4/yr. Pub'd 4 issues 1990; expects 4 issues 1991, 4 issues 1992.

JOURNAL OF AFRICAN LANGUAGES AND LINGUISTICS, Weidner & Sons, Publishing, Box 2178, Cinnaminson, NJ 08077, 609-486-1755. "See comments for Weidner & Sons, Publishing." Pub's reviews.

JOURNAL OF BORDERLAND RESEARCH, Borderland Sciences Research Foundation, Thomas Joseph Brown, Director, Editor; Alison Davidson, Editor, P.O. Box 429, Gaberville, CA 95440, 724-2043. 1945. Articles, photos, reviews, news items. "ISSN: 0897-0394. Issued to members of BSRF only. We print articles of research on alternative energy, medicine and health, Fortean phenomena, earth mysteries, and other Borderland subjects." circ. 1.2M. 6/yr. Pub'd 6 issues 1990; expects 6 issues 1991, 6 issues 1992. sub. price: $25; per copy: $5; sample: $5. Back issues: $5 each. 32pp; 8½×11; Web. Reporting time: 30-60 days on solicited, none on non-solicited. Payment: none. Copyrighted, rights revert if author desires it. Pub's reviews: 10 in 1990. §Alternative scientific and medical research, subtle energies. No ads.

JOURNAL OF CANADIAN POETRY, Borealis Press Limited, Frank M. Tierney, Business Editor; W. Glenn Clever, Business Editor; David Staines, General Editor, 9 Ashburn Drive, Nepean Ontario K2E 6N4, Canada, (613) 224-6837. 1976. Criticism, reviews. "Concerned solely with criticism and reviews of Canadian poetry. Does *not* publish poetry per se; we are a critical journal." circ. 500. 1/yr. Pub'd 1 issue 1990; expects 1 issue 1991, 1 issue 1992. sub. price: $12.95, $25/2 yrs, $33/3 yrs; per copy: $12.95; sample: $5. Back issues: $5. Discounts: book wholesalers 20%. 150pp; 5½×8½; of. Reporting time: 4 months. Payment: none. Copyrighted, reverts to author. Pub's reviews: 40 in 1990. §Poetry only (Canadian). Ads: inquire.

JOURNAL OF CANADIAN STUDIES/Revue d'etudes canadiennes, Michael A. Peterman, Trent University, Peterborough, Ont. K9J 7B8, Canada. 1966. Articles, criticism, reviews. circ. 1.4M. 4/yr. Expects 4 issues 1991. sub. price: $25 indiv., $45 instit., $15 special student rate; per copy: $7/$8. Back issues: $7. Discounts: 15% agency. 176pp; 5¾×9; of. Reporting time: 6 months approx. Payment: none. Copyrighted, joint rights. Pub's reviews: 6 in 1990. Ads: $200/$125. CMPA, Toronto.

JOURNAL OF CELTIC LINGUISTICS, University Of Wales Press, Martin J. Ball, Editor, 6 Gwennyth Street, Cathays, Cardiff CF2 4YD, Wales, 231919. Articles, reviews. circ. 500. Pub'd 1 issue 1990. sub. price: £10. Discounts: 10%. 128pp; size A5; of. Payment: none. Copyrighted, reverts to author. Pub's reviews. §Linguistics. Ads: £75/£37.50.

JOURNAL OF CHILD AND YOUTH CARE, G. Fewster, C. Bagley, T. Garfat, 117 Woodpark Boulevard, S.W. Calgary, Alberta T2W 2Z8, Canada, 403-281-2266 X436. 1982. Articles, reviews. "The issues of child care are universal and the journal is committed to the dissemination of information and knowledge for all who assume responsibility for the well-being of children." circ. 464. 4/yr. Pub'd 4 issues 1990; expects 4 issues 1991, 4 issues 1992. sub. price: $49.50 indiv., $71.50 instit., add G.S.T. Canada; outside Canada, price in U.S. dollars; per copy: $10. Back issues: $10. 100pp; 6×9; of. Reporting time: 2 months. Payment: none. Copyrighted, does not revert to author. Pub's reviews: 5 in 1990. §Child and youth care. Ads: write for info.

THE JOURNAL OF COMMONWEALTH LITERATURE, Hans Zell Publishers, Alastair Niven, Caroline Bundy, PO Box 56, Oxford OX1 3EL, England, 0865-511428. 1965. Articles, interviews, non-fiction. "Maximum length for articles: 4M words. Oxford style. Style guide available on request. Published by: Hans Zell Publishers, an imprint of Bowker-Saur Ltd. division of Butterworths, PO Box 56, Oxford, OX1 3EL, England, United Kingdom." circ. 1M. 2/yr. Pub'd 2 issues 1990; expects 2 issues 1991, 2 issues 1992. sub. price: £30 ($52) instit., £22.00 ($38) indiv.; per copy: £10 ($20); sample: inquire, at publisher's discretion. Back issues: £10 ($20). Discounts: agents 10%. 176pp; 5½×8½; of/li. Reporting time: 2-3 months. Payment: £8 a page for bibliographers; no payment to other contributors. Copyrighted. Ads: £95 ($180)/£65 ($130)/£120 ($240) back cover.

JOURNAL OF COMPUTING IN HIGHER EDUCATION, Paideia Publishers, Carol MacKnight, PO Box 343, Ashfield, MA 01330, 413-628-3838. 1989. Non-fiction. "Articles, reviews, reports on instructional technology-management information systems in higher education." circ. 3M. 2/yr. Expects 2 issues 1991, 2 issues 1992. price per copy: $9-$17. 130pp; 6×9; typeset. Reporting time: 3 months. Payment: none. Copyrighted, reverts to author. NERCOMP, 439 Washington Street, Braintree, MA 02184.

JOURNAL OF ITALIAN LINGUISTICS, Weidner & Sons, Publishing, Box 2178, Cinnaminson, NJ 08077, 609-486-1755. "See comments for Weidner & Sons, Publishing." Pub's reviews.

JOURNAL OF MENTAL IMAGERY, Akhter Ahsen, Ph.D., PO Box 240, Bronx, NY 10471. 1977. Articles, reviews. circ. 5,134 in USA, 6,434 in foreign countries. 4/yr. Pub'd 4 issues 1990. sub. price: $40; per copy: $25; sample: free. Back issues: same as current prices. Discounts: none. 92pp; 6×9 trim; of. Reporting time: 2 months. Payment: none. Copyrighted, does not revert to author. Pub's reviews: 2 in 1990. §Mental imagery. International Imagery Association.

THE JOURNAL OF MIND AND BEHAVIOR, The Institute of Mind and Behavior Press, Raymond Russ, Editor, PO Box 522, Village Station, New York, NY 10014, 212-595-4853. 1980. Articles, criticism, reviews, letters, non-fiction. "*The Journal Of Mind And Behavior (JMB)* is an academic journal dedicated to the interdisciplinary approach within psychology and related fields — building upon the assumption of a unified science. The editors are particularly interested in scholarly work in the following areas: the psychology, philosophy, and sociology of experimentation and the scientific method; the relationship between methodology, operationism, and theory construction; the mind-body problem in the social sciences, literature, and art; mind-body interactions and medical implications; philosophical impact of a mind-body epistemology upon psychology; historical perspectives on the course and nature of science. All manuscripts *must* follow style and preparation of the Publication Manual of the American Psychological Association (third edition, 1983) and be submitted in quadruplicate for review to: Dr. Raymond Russ, Department of Psychology, University of Maine, Orono, ME 04469." circ. 1096. 4/yr. Pub'd 4 issues 1990; expects 4 issues 1991, 4 issues 1992. sub. price: individual $35/yr, $64/2 yrs, $93/3 yrs, institutional $55/yr, $100/2 yrs, $150/3 yrs; per copy: $10; sample: free. Back issues: $93/3 yrs. individual; $150/3 yrs. institution (special package available upon request). Discounts: 15% on order of 10 copies or more. 186pp; 5½x8½; of. Reporting time: 5-10 weeks. Payment: none. Copyrighted, does not revert to author. Pub's reviews: 15 in 1990. §Psychology (both thoeretical and experimental), philosophy, history of science, medicine, art. Ads: $230/$130/discounts on multiple runs.

JOURNAL OF MODERN LITERATURE, Morton P. Levitt, Editor-in-Chief, Temple Univ., Philadelphia, PA 19122, 215-787-8505. 1970. Articles, interviews, criticism, reviews. circ. 2.2M. 3/yr. Pub'd 3 issues 1990; expects 3 issues 1991, 3 issues 1992. sub. price: U.S.: $16 individuals, $20 institutions/foreign: $20 and $25; per copy: $5 reg, $10 annual review bibliography; sample: free. Back issues: $5 regular; $10 annual review. Discounts: 10% for agencies. 160pp; 7x10; desktop publishing. Reporting time: 10-12 weeks. Payment: 3 copies of the issue. Copyrighted, does not revert to author. Pub's reviews: 300 in 1990. §Critical and scholarly works only. Ads: $200/$125/$75 quarter-page. COSMEP.

JOURNAL OF MUSICOLOGY, University of California Press, Marian Green, University of California Press, 2120 Berkeley Way, Berkeley, CA 94720, 415-642-4191. 1972. Articles, reviews, non-fiction. "Editorial address: PO Box 4516, Louisville, KY 40204." circ. 1.4M. 4/yr. Pub'd 4 issues 1990; expects 4 issues 1991, 4 issues 1992. sub. price: $24 indiv., $46 instit., $18 students (+ $4 foreign postage); per copy: $6 indiv., $11.50 instit., $4.50 students (+ $4 foreign postage); sample: free. Back issues: same as single copy price. Discounts: foreign subs. agent 10%, one-time order 10+ 30%, standing orders (bookstores) 1-99 40%, 100+ 50%. 128pp; 6x9; of. Reporting time: 1-2 months. Payment: varies. Copyrighted, does not revert to author. Pub's reviews: 8-10 in 1990. Ads: $200/$120.

JOURNAL OF NARRATIVE TECHNIQUE, George Perkins, General Editor; Barbara Perkins, Managing Editor, Eastern Michigan University, Ypsilanti, MI 48197, 313-487-0151. 1970. Criticism. "JNT is a scholarly magazine with international circulation. Essays run generally from 15 to 30 typed pages. Contributors should follow MLA style. JNT is the official publication of the Society for the Study of Narrative Literature" circ. 1.1M. 3/yr. Pub'd 3 issues 1990; expects 3 issues 1991, 3 issues 1992. sub. price: $20, libraries and institutions outside the US have a $10 postal surcharge; per copy: $8; sample: free. Back issues: $8. Discounts: 20% to subscription agents. 96pp; 6x9; photo typesetting, offset printing. Reporting time: 1-4 months. Payment: copies only. Copyrighted, reverts to author. Pub's reviews: 50 in 1990. §Same subject matter as for submission of articles. No paid advertising. Conference of Editors of Learned Journals.

JOURNAL OF NEW JERSEY POETS, Sander Zulauf, Editor; Donna Burton, Managing Editor; North Peterson, Assoc. Editor; Sara Pfaffenroth, Assoc. Editor; Charles Luce, Art Editor, County College of Morris, Randolph, NJ 07869, 201-328-5460. 1976. Poetry, photos, reviews. "Open to submission of poetry from present and past residents of New Jersey; no biases concerning style or subject. Review of books by New Jersey poets" circ. 500. 2/yr. Pub'd 2 issues 1990; expects 2 issues 1991, 2 issues 1992. sub. price: $7/2 issues; per copy: $4; sample: $4. Back issues: available on request. Discounts: 25% booksellers; 50% contributors. 64pp; 8½x5½; †of. Reporting time: 3-6 months. Payment: 2 copies per published poem. Copyrighted, reverts to author. Pub's reviews. §Poetry, books about poetry. Ads: upon request.

JOURNAL OF PALESTINE STUDIES, Institute for Palestine Studies, Hisham Sharabi, Philip Mattar, PO Box 25697 Georgetown Station, Washington, DC 20007. "Copyrighted by the Institute for Palestine Studies." circ. 4.3M. 4/yr. Pub'd 4 issues 1990; expects 4 issues 1991, 4 issues 1992. sub. price: $24 indiv., $36 instit., $17 student ($6 foreign postage); per copy: $6 indiv. & student, $9 instit.; sample: free. Back issues: same as single copy price. Discounts: foreign subs. agent 10%, one-time orders 10+ 30%, standing orders (bookstores) 1-99 40%, 100+ 50%. 250pp; 6x9; of. Ads: $200/$120.

THE JOURNAL OF PAN AFRICAN STUDIES, Itibari M. Zulu, California Inst. of Pan African Studies, PO Box 13063, Fresno, CA 93794, 209-266-2550. 1987. Articles, art, photos, interviews, reviews. "*TJPAS* is an international Afro-centric medium of African culture and consciousness." circ. 1M. 4/yr. Pub'd 1 issue 1990; expects 2 issues 1991, 3-4 issues 1992. sub. price: $12; per copy: $3.75; sample: same. Back issues: $4.50. Discounts: 40% retailers. 24pp; 8½x11; of. Reporting time: 1 month. Payment: 3 copies. Copyrighted, reverts to author. Pub's reviews. §African studies, Black studies (Afro-American), Pan African studies (international). Ads: $200/$125/$75.

291

JOURNAL OF POLYMORPHOUS PERVERSITY, Glenn C. Ellenbogen, PO Box 1454, Madison Square Station, New York, NY 10159, 212-689-5473. 1983. Satire. *"The Wall Street Journal* (12/20/84) called *JPP* "...a social scientist's answer to Mad Magazine." *JPP* is a humorous and satirical journal of psychology (and psychiatry and the closely allied disciplines). Materials submitted should relate to psychology, psychiatry, mental health, or mental health research. First and foremost, the article *must* be humorous and/or satirical. Manuscripts should be no longer than 8 double-spaced (4 typeset) pages. Articles are reviewed for consideration by one or more of 18 Associate Editors, each representing a specialty area. Recent contributions include "Psychotherapy of the Dead," "New Improved Delusions," "A Modern Day Psychoanalytic Fable," "Nicholas Claus: A Case Study in Psychometrics," "Burdenism," and "The Nasal Complex," and "The Etiology and Treatment of Childhood". We do not ever consider poems or cartoons. The best way to get a clear idea of what we are looking for is read a real psychology or psychiatry journal. Then write a spoof of it." circ. 4.2M. 2/yr. Pub'd 2 issues 1990; expects 2 issues 1991, 2 issues 1992. sub. price: $12.50; per copy: $6; sample: $6 includes postage. Back issues: $6 per issue. 24pp; 6¾×10; of. Reporting time: 4-6 weeks. Payment: 2 free copies. Copyrighted, does not revert to author. §Psychology and psychiatry. Ads: $395; back cover: $550/.

JOURNAL OF PSYCHOACTIVE DRUGS, Haight-Ashbury Publications, E. Leif Zerkin, Jeffrey H. Novey, 409 Clayton Street, San Francisco, CA 94117, 415-565-1904. 1967. Articles, art, photos. "The *Journal of Psychoactive Drugs* is designed as a multidisciplinary forum for the study of drugs, every issue features a variety of articles by noted researchers and theorists. ISSN 0279-1072." circ. 1.2M. 4/yr. Pub'd 4 issues 1990; expects 4 issues 1991, 4 issues 1992. sub. price: $70 (indiv.), $120 (instit.), + $15/yr surface postage outside U.S., + $35/yr airmail postage outside U.S.; per copy: $30; sample: $25. Back issues: $150 while supplies last of Vol.3-21. Discounts: 5% subscription agency. 100pp; 8½×11; of. Reporting time: 60-90 days on articles; 30 days on art for cover or book reviews. Payment: $100 for cover photo/art. Copyrighted, reverts to author. Pub's reviews: 10 in 1990. §Alcohol and other drug-related topics. Ads: $150/$100.

THE JOURNAL OF PSYCHOHISTORY, Psychohistory Press, Lloyd deMause, 2315 Broadway, NY, NY 10024, 212-873-5900. 1973. Articles, reviews. "Psychohistory of individuals and groups, history of childhood and family." circ. 3M. 4/yr. Pub'd 4 issues 1990; expects 4 issues 1991. sub. price: $52 individual, $99 organization; per copy: $10; sample: $10. Back issues: $10. 150pp; 7×9; of. Reporting time: 2 weeks. Payment: none. Copyrighted, does not revert to author. Pub's reviews: 40 in 1990. §Psychology & history. Ads: $150/$90.

JOURNAL OF REGIONAL CRITICISM, Arjuna Library Press, Joseph A. Uphoff, Jr., Director, 1025 Garner Street, Box 18, Colorado Springs, CO 80905-1774. 1979. Poetry, art, photos, criticism, parts-of-novels, long-poems, plays, news items, non-fiction. "This journal is an ongoing development of mathematical theories in the Fine Arts and Surrealism, with illustrative material, published as a xerox manuscript copy. We cannot, at this time, pay contributors except by enhancing their reputations, but we have plans for the future. Previous contributors considered on a priority basis. We present criticism by quotation or annotation. We are working in the context of the thought that poems make the literary mind function the way equations make the logical mind function, comparing and contrasting the two methods of depiction" circ. open. 6-12/yr. Pub'd 12 issues 1990; expects 12 issues 1991, 12 issues 1992. sample price: at cost. Back issues: at current cost. 4pp; 8½×11; †xerography. Reporting time: indefinite. Payment: none. Copyrighted, reverts to author.

JOURNAL OF SOCIAL BEHAVIOR AND PERSONALITY, Select Press, Roderick P. Crandall, PO Box 37, Corte Madera, CA 94925, 415-924-1612. 1986. "Academic research, psychology, speech, business, sociology, etc." 4/yr. Pub'd 5 issues 1990; expects 7 issues 1991, 7 issues 1992. sub. price: $62; per copy: $15; sample: free. 200pp; 8½×5½. Copyrighted, does not revert to author.

JOURNAL OF SOUTH ASIAN LITERATURE, Asian Studies Center, Michigan State University, Carlo Coppola, Surjit Dulai, Center for International Programs, Oakland University, Rochester, MI 48063, 313-370-2154. 1963. Poetry, fiction, articles, interviews, satire, criticism, reviews, parts-of-novels, long-poems, plays. circ. 300. 2/yr. Expects 2 issues 1991. sub. price: $19-$24; per copy: $9.00-$11.00; sample: $13. Back issues: $5.00-$12.00. Discounts: none. 200-400pp; 6×9; of. Reporting time: 12 weeks. Payment: none. Copyrighted. Pub's reviews: 48 in 1990. §South Asian. Ads: $150/$75. CCLM.

JOURNAL OF SPORT AND EXERCISE PSYCHOLOGY, Human Kinetics Pub. Inc., Diane L. Gill, Box 5076, Champaign, IL 61825-5076, 217-351-5076. 1979. Articles, reviews. "Scholarly journal." circ. 1,670. 4/yr. Pub'd 4 issues 1990; expects 4 issues 1991, 4 issues 1992. sub. price: $30 indiv., $60 instit.; per copy: $7.50 indiv; $16 institution; sample: free. Back issues: $7.50 indiv; $16 instit. Discounts: 5%. 96pp; 6×9; of. Reporting time: 2 months. Payment: none. Copyrighted. Pub's reviews: 4 in 1990. §Sport, sport science, physical education. Ads: $255/$153 (4X rate).

JOURNAL OF SPORT MANAGEMENT, Human Kinetics Pub. Inc., Gordon Olafson, Janet B. Parks, Box 5076, Champaign, IL 61825-5076, 217-351-5076. 1987. Articles, reviews. "Applied journal" circ. 425. 2/yr. Pub'd 2 issues 1990; expects 2 issues 1991, 2 issues 1992. sub. price: $14 indiv., $28 instit.; per copy: $7 indiv.,

$15 instit.; sample: free. Back issues: $7 indiv., $15 instit. Discounts: 5%. 92pp; 6×9; of. Reporting time: 2 months. Payment: none. Copyrighted. Pub's reviews. §sport, sport science, and physical education related to management. Ads: $170/$102 (4X rate). North American Society of Sport Management.

JOURNAL OF TEACHING IN PHYSICAL EDUCATION, Human Kinetics Pub. Inc., David C. Griffey, Thomas J. Martinek, Box 5076, Champaign, IL 61825-5076, 217-351-5076. 1981. Articles, reviews. "The teaching process and teacher education in physical education" circ. 725. 4/yr. Pub'd 4 issues 1990; expects 4 issues 1991, 4 issues 1992. sub. price: $28 individual, $56 institution; per copy: $7 indiv., $15 instit.; sample: free. Back issues: $7 indiv., $15 instit. Discounts: 5%. 102pp; 6×9; of. Reporting time: 2 months. Payment: none. Copyrighted. Pub's reviews: 2 in 1990. §sport, sport science, and physical education. Ads: $170/$102 (4X rate).

JOURNAL OF THE HELLENIC DIASPORA, Pella Publishing Co, A. Kitroeff, 337 West 36th Street, New York, NY 10018, 212-279-9586. 1974. Poetry, fiction, articles, art, photos, cartoons, interviews, satire, criticism, reviews, music, parts-of-novels, long-poems, collages, plays. "The magazine is concerned with the entire spectrum of scholarly, critical, and artistic work that is based on contemporary Greece." circ. 1M. 4/yr. Pub'd 4 issues 1990; expects 4 issues 1991, 4 issues 1992. sub. price: $15; per copy: $9; sample: $9. Back issues: $9 single/$15 double. Discounts: jobbers & bookstores-20%. 96-112pp; 5½×8½; †lp. Reporting time: 12 weeks. Payment: 30 offprints for articles. Copyrighted, reverts to author. Pub's reviews: 8 in 1990. §Modern Greek studies and affairs. Ads: $125/$75.

THE JOURNAL OF THE ORDER OF BUDDHIST CONTEMPLATIVES, Rev. Kinzan Learman, PO Box 199, Mt. Shasta, CA 96067, 916-926-4208. 1970. Poetry, articles, art, photos, interviews, letters, news items. *"The Journal of the Order of Buddhist Contemplatives* contains articles on Buddhist meditation and training written by priests of the Order and lay members of the congregation." circ. 560. 4/yr. Pub'd 4 issues 1990; expects 4 issues 1991, 4 issues 1992. sub. price: $20; per copy: $5; sample: $1. Back issues: inquire for prices. 92pp; 5½×8½; of. Payment: none. Copyrighted, reverts to author. Ads: none accepted.

JOURNAL OF THE PHILOSOPHY OF SPORT, Human Kinetics Pub. Inc., Klaus Meier, Box 5076, Champaign, IL 61825-5076, 217-351-5076. 1974. Articles, reviews. "Scholarly journal" circ. 400. 1/yr. Pub'd 1 issue 1990; expects 1 issue 1991, 1 issue 1992. sub. price: $12 individuals, $18 institutions; per copy: $12 indiv., $18 instit.; sample: free. Back issues: $12 indiv., $18 instit. Discounts: 5%. 105pp; 6×9; of. Reporting time: 2 months. Payment: none. Copyrighted. Pub's reviews: 2 in 1990. §Sport, sport science, and physical education related to philosophy. no ads. Philosophic Society for the Study of Sport.

JOURNAL OF THE WEST, Sunflower University Press, Robin Higham, Editor & President; Homer Socolofsky, Book Review Editor; Carol A. Williams, Associate Publisher-Director of Marketing, 1531 Yuma (PO Box 1009), Manhattan, KS 66502, 913-539-1888. 1962. Articles, reviews. "We solicit our own articles for theme issues and reviews, but will consider articles submitted from outside for the *About the West* section" circ. 4.5M. 4/yr. Pub'd 4 issues 1990; expects 4 issues 1991, 4 issues 1992. sub. price: $30 individuals, $40 institutions; per copy: $10 prepaid; sample: free. Back issues: handled by Kraus if over 5 years old; otherwise $10 prepaid. 112pp; 8½×11; †of. Reporting time: 3 months. Payment: 10 copies of issue. Copyrighted, does not revert to author. Pub's reviews: 160 in 1990. §The West, all angles. Ads: $300/$200. SSP.

JOURNAL OF THEORETICAL PSYCHOLOGY, Harbor Publishing Company, Laura M. Morrison, 80 N. Moore Street, Suite 4J, New York, NY 10013, 212-349-1818. 1986. Articles, interviews, criticism, reviews, news items, non-fiction. *"The Journal* was founded to publish research results, etc., concerning non-structural-trace theories of neuropsychology (have no outlet elsewhere)" circ. 200. Irregular. Pub'd 1 issue 1990; expects 1 issue 1991. price per copy: $5; sample: free. Back issues: $5. 20pp; 15×11; †NEC spinwriter printer 2000. Reporting time: 2 weeks. Copyrighted, reverts to author. Pub's reviews. §Any "non-structural-trace" theory material. Ads: $5,000/$2,500/we prepare the advertisement.

JOURNAL OF VISION REHABILITATION, Media Periodicals, Mary Ann Keverline, Editor, 2440 'O' Street, Suite 202, Lincoln, NE 68510, 402-474-2676. 1987. Non-fiction. "Professional journal for law vision theoreticians and practitioners" circ. 400. 4/yr. Pub'd 4 issues 1990; expects 4 issues 1991, 4 issues 1992. sub. price: $45; per copy: $13; sample: free. Back issues: $12.50. Discounts: AOA low vision members, $30.00; Sub Services Co's, 10%, AER member, $34. 80pp; 5½×8½; of. Reporting time: 1-3 months. Payment: none. Not copyrighted. Pub's reviews. §Low vision treatment, diagnose, rehabilitation. Ads: $325/$175/$95 quarter/back cover $350/$375/50¢ per classified word ($10 min.). Midwest Assn. of Publishers.

JOURNAL OF WELSH EDUCATION, University Of Wales Press, Dr. David Allsobrook, 6 Gwennyth Street, Cathays, Cardiff CF2 4YD, Wales, 231919. Articles, reviews. circ. 500. Pub'd 2 issues 1990. sub. price: £10; per copy: £5. Discounts: 10%. 64pp; size A4; of. Payment: none. Copyrighted, reverts to author. Pub's reviews. §Education. Ads: £75/£37.50.

Journey Publications, Kent Babcock, PO Box 423, Woodstock, NY 12498, 914-657-8434. 1976. "We publish books on philosophy and meditation which we feel are important responses to the problems of modern life.'' avg. press run 3M-5M. Pub'd 1 title 1990; expects 1 title 1991, 1 title 1992. 7 titles listed in the *Small Press Record of Books in Print* (20th Edition, 1991-92). avg. price, cloth: $8.95; paper: $8.95. Discounts: 25% for 1-4 books; 40% 5+; 50% postpaid to distributors. 125pp; 5½×8½; †of. Payment: contract. Copyrights for author.

Jubilee Press (see also BLACK MULLET REVIEW), Gina Bergamino-Frey, Box 34, Det 10/ 7WS, APO New York, NY 09182-5000. 1986. Poetry, fiction, art, photos, long-poems, concrete art. ''Books are published as a result of competition-winning manuscripts. Send SASE for contest information. *Jubilee Press* holds an annual chapbook competition'' avg. press run 600-800. Pub'd 1 title 1990; expects 1 title 1991, 1-2 titles 1992. avg. price, paper: $4.50 postage paid. Discounts: bulk orders of 10+ receive 40% discount. 32pp; 5¼×8½; of. Reporting time: within 1 month of contest deadline. Payment: author receives publication, 50 copies, advertising and royalty. Copyrights for author.

Judah Magnes Museum Publications, Paula Friedman, Editor; Nelda Cassuto, Editor, 2911 Russell Street, Berkeley, CA 94705. 1966. Art, non-fiction. ''Primarily art, Judaica, Western Americana, and related.'' avg. press run 1M. Pub'd 3-4 titles 1990; expects 3-4 titles 1991, 3-4 titles 1992. 1 title listed in the *Small Press Record of Books in Print* (20th Edition, 1991-92). Discounts: upon request. 150-200pp; size varies; photo-offset. Reporting time: query first. Does not copyright for author.

JUDY, J.C. Davie, D.C. Thomson & Company Limited, Albert Square, Dundee, Tayside DD1 9QJ, Scotland, 0382 23131. 1960. Poetry, fiction, articles, photos, cartoons, reviews, letters, non-fiction. ''Mainly picture-stories weekly, to appeal to young schoolgirls, plus general interest features. The photolitho annual has more features'' circ. 40M. 52/yr. Pub'd 52 issues 1990; expects 52 issues 1991, 52 issues 1992. sub. price: £20.80 inland, £27.95 overseas; per copy: 26p plus postage; sample: postage only. Back issues: cover price plus postage, if issues available. Discounts: none. 32pp; 8¼×11¾; †lp, photolitho. Reporting time: we start make-up 8 weeks before publication dates. Payment: by agreement. Copyrighted, does not revert to author except where specially arranged. Ads: £280/pro rata.

Julian Associates (see also NIGHT OWL'S NEWSLETTER; OUR WRITE MIND), Debbie Jordan, 6831 Spencer Hwy, #203, Pasadena, TX 77505, 713-930-8551.

JUMP CUT, A Review of Contemporary Media, John Hess, Chuck Kleinhans, Julia Lesage, P.O. Box 865, Berkeley, CA 94701, 415-658-4482. 1974. Articles, art, photos, cartoons, interviews, criticism, reviews, letters. ''Interested in commercial and independent film since 1970. Length as needed to make points, but shorter preferred; we strive for clarity in style. Biased to radical criticism, esp. Marxist and feminist. No cute and superficial reviews. Strongly suggest reading an issue before submission. Send SASE for 'Notice to Writers'.'' circ. 5M-6M. Irregular. Pub'd 1 issue 1990; expects 2 issues 1991, 2 issues 1992. sub. price: $14, Canada & abroad $16, $20 & $22 instit.; per copy: $4; Canada & abroad $4.50; sample: $4; Canada & abroad $4.50. Back issues: Nos. 1 & 2,6,7,8,9,19 sold out. $2; Canada & abroad $2.50 (30-32 3/$3.50, 33+ 4/$4.50). Also they are available from [Xerox International Microfilm]. Discounts: institutional rate is $20, Canada & abroad $22, agency 10%, bookstores 30%. 128pp; 8½×11; of. Reporting time: 3 weeks-3 months. Payment: copies. Contributor may retain copyright. Pub's reviews: 3 in 1990. §On the subjects of film and marxist culture and criticism. Ads: $250/$125. COSMEP.

JUNIOR EDITOR, Editor's Desk, Florence Bradley, Editor, 709 S.E. 52nd Avenue, Ocala, FL 32671, 904-694-2303; 694-2289. ''Written and illustrated by and for students of all ages. We are especially interested in reaching teachers and school librarians who would get students interested in submitting their work to us'' 6/yr. Pub'd 6 issues 1990; expects 6 issues 1991, 6 issues 1992. sub. price: $10 to teachers and school personnel.

Juniper Press (see also NORTHEAST), John Judson, Editor, 1310 Shorewood Dr, La Crosse, WI 54601. 1962. Poetry, fiction, articles, art, photos, interviews, criticism, reviews, parts-of-novels, long-poems. ''No submissions accepted without query first. Please include SASE with query or we cannot respond.'' avg. press run 300-500. Pub'd 9 titles 1990; expects 7 titles 1991, 6 titles 1992. 72 titles listed in the *Small Press Record of Books in Print* (20th Edition, 1991-92). avg. price, cloth: $20; paper: $6-$12; other: $30 signed. Discounts: write for arrangements. Pages vary; size varies; †lp, of. Reporting time: 8-12 weeks. Payment: copies of book. Does not copyright for author.

K

K, G.J. McFarlane, 351 Dalhousie Street, Brantford, Ontario N3S 3V9, Canada, (416) 529-3125. 1985. Poetry, fiction, articles, art, satire, criticism, reviews, parts-of-novels. circ. 75. Published as funds allow. Pub'd 1 issue 1990; expects 2 issues 1991, 3 issues 1992. sub. price: $10 per 3; per copy: $4; sample: $4. 50pp; 8×11; mi. Reporting time: 4 weeks. Payment: copy. Not copyrighted. Pub's reviews: 3 in 1990. §Poetry, fiction.

KAIROS, A Journal of Contemporary Thought and Criticism, Hermes House Press, Inc., Alan Mandell, William Rasch, c/o Mandell, 450 E. 63rd Street, Apt. 4C, New York, NY 10021, 212-758-3257. 1981. Poetry, fiction, articles, art, photos, interviews, criticism, reviews, long-poems, concrete art, non-fiction. "Volume I, No 3 focused on the meaning and experience of learning. Vol. I, No 4 focused on German culture and society in America. Vol. II, No 1 focused on the writings of Ernest Becker. Vol. II, No 2 included materials on technology and poetry-in-translation. Poetry, fiction and artwork are encouraged. Please include SASE." circ. 500. 2/yr. Pub'd 2 issues 1990; expects 2 issues 1991, 2 issues 1992. sub. price: $11 individual, $15 institutions; per copy: $6 + $1 p/h; sample: $6 + $1 p/h. Discounts: available upon request. 120pp; 5½×8½; of. Reporting time: 4-8 weeks. Payment: copies. Copyrighted, reverts to author. Pub's reviews: 2 in 1990. §See past issues for tone, scope and direction. Ads: on exchange basis only. COSMEP.

KALDRON, An International Journal Of Visual Poetry and Language Art, Karl Kempton, PO Box 7164, Halcyon, CA 93421-7164, 805-489-2770. 1976. Poetry. "*Kaldron* is an international journal of visual poetry and language art publishing historical and contemporary work. A visual poem or language art work is a wedding of literature and art. The poet and artist take the stuff of language-word(s), text, note, code, phonic character, type, cypher, symbol, glyph, rhythm, grammar, cluster, stroke, density, etc.—and wed it to patterns, lists, diagrams, sculpture, photography, painting, drawing, collage, xerography, silkscreen, optical and or kinetic art, etc. the sum of the images is the poem or the work. The roots of this expression go back to ancient charms and amulets, the visualization of magic spells once cast during the tying of special knots. The contemporary roots are found in futurism and dada from the earlier part of this century and more recently in the first world wide poetry expression, concrete poetry. Over the years *Kaldron* has become a vital link in the international network of visual peotry and language art. More than 30 nations have been represented by more than 130 individuals to date, and *Kaldron* has appeared in a large number of exhibitions around the country and the world. NOTE: *Kaldron* does not publish verse. Submissions are encouraged but must be enclosed with a self addressed and stamped (correct postage) envelope for response" circ. 1M. Irregular. Pub'd 1 issue 1990; expects 1 issue 1991, 1 issue 1992. sub. price: donations accepted; per copy: $5 most recent issue, $10 recent double; sample: all back issues are $10 each, limit of 4 per order. Back issues: limited number of sets available, contact publisher. Pages vary; size varies; of. Reporting time: 2 weeks to a month. Payment: 2 copies. Copyrighted, reverts to author. Pub's reviews. §Visual poetry, language art publications, art and poetry. No ads. CCLM.

KALEIDOSCOPE: INTERNATIONAL MAGAZINE OF LITERATURE, FINE ARTS, AND DISABI-LITY, Darshan C. Perusek, Editor, UCPSH, 326 Locust Street, Akron, OH 44302, 216-762-9755; 216-379-3349 (TDD). 1979. Poetry, fiction, articles, art, photos, interviews, satire, reviews, parts-of-novels, non-fiction. "We publish fiction, poetry, and visual arts that capture and reflect the experience of disability. Also critical essays and book reviews, photo essays, interviews, personal experience narratives. Established writers/artists featured along with new promising writers. *Kaleidoscope* presents works that challenge stereotypical perceptions of people with disabilities by offering balanced realistic images." circ. 2M. 2/yr. Pub'd 2 issues 1990; expects 2 issues 1991, 2 issues 1992. sub. price: $9 indiv., $12 instit., add $8 Int'l and $5 Canada; per copy: $4.50 ($7 International, payable in US currency); sample: $2 to cover p/h. Back issues: $3. Discounts: 20%. 64pp; 8½×11; of. Reporting time: 6 months. Payment: contributors receive 2 complimentary copies plus $10-$150. Copyrighted, reverts to author. Pub's reviews: 2 in 1990. §Disability-related short story, poetry, visual art, books. CLMP, COSMEP.

Kalimat Press, Anthony A. Lee, Managing Editor, 1600 Sawtelle Blvd., #34, Los Angeles, CA 90025-3114, 213-479-5668. 1978. Non-fiction. "Scholarly and Baha'i books." avg. press run 2M. Pub'd 8 titles 1990; expects 4 titles 1991, 4 titles 1992. avg. price, cloth: $16; paper: $12; other: $3. 200pp; 5½×8½; of. Reporting time: 4 weeks. Payment: 7½% net. Copyrights for author. COSMEP, New Age, Soc. of Scholarly Publishers.

KALLIOPE, A Journal of Women's Art, Mary Sue Koeppel, Editor, 3939 Roosevelt Blvd, Florida Community College at Jacksonville, Jacksonville, FL 32205, 904-387-8211. 1979. Poetry, fiction, articles, art, photos, interviews, criticism, reviews, plays. "*Kalliope* devotes itself to women in the arts by publishing their work and providing a forum for their ideas and opinions. Besides introducing the work of many new writers, *Kalliope* has published the work of established writers such as Marge Piercy, Denise Levertov, Susan Fromberg Schaffer, Kathleen Spivak and Ruth Moon Kempher. Most issues include an interview with a prominent woman in the arts. Most recent interviewees with *Kalliope* are Ellen Gilchrist and Louise Fishman. We have featured the photographs of Diane Farris, Elizabeth Gilliland, Joanne Leonard, Layle Silbert, and Anna Tomczak; the sculpture of Margaret Koscielny and Ella Tulin; the ceramics of Marilyn Taylor and Patti Warashina; and paintings and drawings by a large number of artists including Renee Faure, Marcia Isaacson, Lyn Lazarus, Sharon McGinley-Nally, Susan Zukowsky, and Mary Joan Waid. Theme issues have been devoted to women over 60, women under 30, women with disabilities, translations, Florida writers and artists, humor, women portraying men, and the spiritual quest" circ. 1M. 3/yr. Pub'd 3 issues 1990; expects 3 issues 1991. sub. price: $10.50; per copy: $7 recent issues; sample: $4 pre-1987 issues, $7 recent issues. Back issues: $7. Discounts: 40% to bookstores and distributors. 80pp; 8¼x7¼; of. Reporting time: 3-6 months. Payment: copies or subscription. Copyrighted, does not revert to author, but may be requested for purposes of republication. Pub's reviews: 2 in 1990. §Women in the arts. No ads. COSMEP, CCLM.

KANSAS QUARTERLY, Jonathan Holden, Ben Nyberg, G.W. Clift, John Rees, English Department, Kansas State University, Manhattan, KS 66506, 913-532-6716. 1968. Poetry, fiction, art, criticism. "We prefer good fiction and poetry aimed at an adult audience. We have no preference between the traditional or experimental, but are not interested in either for its own sake. We do special numbers in literary criticism, art, and history, but contributors should note special announced topics before submitting. Recent contributors: Stephen Dixon, Rolaine Hockstein, H.E. Francis, Peter La Salle, Greg Johnson, David Kirby, Peter Cooley, Rick Bass, Pat Rushin, Barbara Leith, Alvin Greenberg, Ian MacMillan, Jerry Bumpus, Starkey Flythe Jr., Lewis Turco, David Citino, Anita Skeen, Sharon Sheehe Stark, George Blake, L.B. Jones, Kathleen Spivack, David H. Lynn, Kent Nelson, William Mooney" circ. 1M-1.3M. 4/yr. Pub'd 4 issues 1990; expects 4 issues 1991, 4 issues 1992. sub. price: $20, $21 foreign/1 yr, $35, $37 foreign/2 yrs, $45, $48 foreign/3 yrs; per copy: $6 (or $7.50 for a double number); sample: $6. Back issues: $3 each up to 1983 (Vol. 14) $4 1984-86, $5 1987-88, $6 hereafter. Discounts: 10% to subscription agencies, 40% to bookstores with regular accounts (on consignment until next number). 176pp; 6x9; of. Reporting time: 2-4 months on poetry, 6+ months on fiction. Payment: 2 subscription copies and yearly awards to short fiction & poetry; fiction $250/$150/$100/$50, poetry $200/$100/$50/$25 (3 or more). Copyrighted, rights revert to author on request. Ads: Cover $125/$100/$55. CCLM, KAC.

KARAMU, Peggy Brayfield, Department of English, Eastern Illinois Univ., Charleston, IL 61920, 217-581-6291. 1965. Poetry, fiction. "Poems should be no longer than a page; short stories no more than 25 pages. Submit no more than 5-6 poems or 1 story at a time. We are looking for material that will interest a sophisticated, college-educated audience. We advise aspiring contributors to purchase and examine a sample issue to see what kind of material we like. Specify on your order whether your interest is *poetry* or *fiction*. Some recent contributors, poetry: Marianne Andrea, Robert Cooperman, Mindy Kronenberg; fiction: F.R. Lewis, Carol Goodman, Robert Wegner." circ. 400. 1/yr. Pub'd 1 issue 1990; expects 1 issue 1991, 1 issue 1992. sub. price: $3 indiv., $5 library; per copy: $4; sample: $3, 2 for $4. Back issues: $3; complete sets avail. inquire. Discounts: $25 for 10 copies. 60-96pp; 6½x8; of. Reporting time: initial screening, 1 month-6 weeks; promising material may be held up to 4 months for final decisions. Payment: 1 contributor's copy, 50% discount on additional copies. Copyrighted, reverts to author. Ads: $100/$50.

Kar-Ben Copies, Inc., Judyth Groner, Madeline Wikler, 6800 Tildenwood Lane, Rockville, MD 20852, 301-984-8733; 800-4KARBEN (in USA). 1975. "Juveniles on Jewish themes—fiction, holiday stories and texts, preschool and primary level" avg. press run 5M. Pub'd 8 titles 1990; expects 8 titles 1991, 8-10 titles 1992. 29 titles listed in the *Small Press Record of Books in Print* (20th Edition, 1991-92). avg. price, cloth: $12.95; paper: $4.95; other: $4.95 board book. Discounts: 40% to trade; 25% on quantity orders to schools; up to 50% to major distributors. 32-48pp; 8x10; of. Reporting time: 4-6 weeks. Payment: royalty based on gross sales, split between author/illustrator. Sometimes small advance. Copyrights for author. Washington Book Publishers, Association of Children's Booksellers, Association of Jewish Publishers, Women's National Book Association, Society of Children's Book Writers, Jewish Book Council.

R. Karman, 6600 Boulevard East, West New York, NJ 07093. 1972. Poetry, fiction, interviews, satire, reviews, parts-of-novels, long-poems, plays. "Originality and ability in expression looked for. Recent titles: *Planet Dreams, Body Between a Rock: The Diary, Its Cultivation and Keep*" avg. press run 200-300. Pub'd 2 titles 1990; expects 2 titles 1991. 5 titles listed in the *Small Press Record of Books in Print* (20th Edition, 1991-92). avg. price, paper: $5.50. Discounts: usual 1/3. 40pp; of, lp, xerox. Reporting time: variable. Payment: variable. Copyrights for author.

Karunaratne & Sons Ltd., 647, Kularatne Mawatha, Colombo 10, Sri Lanka, 941-692295. 1971. "We are a small publisher and also a distributor for small publishers in Sri Lanka. Now we are in progress of printing a bibliography on 'Sri Lankan Books in Print' which will be out in January 1991. Most of our books are on Buddhism." avg. press run 3M. Pub'd 7 titles 1990; expects 10 titles 1991, 10 titles 1992. avg. price, paper: US $6. Discounts: trade 30%, bulk 50%. 140pp; 5½x8½. Reporting time: air mail 14 days, surface mail 60-90 days. Payment: 10% after sales. Copyrights for author. The International Association of Independent Publishers, PO Box 703, San Francisco, CA, 94101.

Katydid Books, Thomas Fitzsimmons, Karen Hargreaves Fitzsimmons, c/o English Dept, Oakland University, Rochester, MI 48309-4401. 1973. Poetry, criticism, long-poems. "We do not want submissions" avg. press run 1.5M. Pub'd 3 titles 1990; expects 3 titles 1991, 3 titles 1992. 17 titles listed in the *Small Press Record of Books in Print* (20th Edition, 1991-92). avg. price, cloth: $28; paper: $12. Discounts: bookstore 35%, library 10%, wholesaler 50%. 200-300pp; 5x8, 6x9, 7x9; typeset; of. Payment: various. Copyrights for author.

Kawabata Press (see also SEPIA), Colin David Webb, Editor, Knill Cross House, Higher Anderton Road, Millbrook, Nr Torpoint, Cornwall, England. 1977. Poetry, fiction, articles. "At present booklets (about 30 pages each)—poetry or prose (up to 10M words)" avg. press run 100. Pub'd 3 titles 1990; expects 3 titles 1991, 3 titles 1992. 14 titles listed in the *Small Press Record of Books in Print* (20th Edition, 1991-92). avg. price, paper: 50p. 35pp; 6×8½; of. Reporting time: 14 days. Payment: 4 free copies plus 50% of all profits (after print costs are covered). Copyrights for author.

Kay Productions, Jerry Kay, PO Box 1728, Sonoma, CA 95476, 707-935-1666. 1987. Non-fiction. avg. press run 3M-5M. Pub'd 3 titles 1990; expects 3 titles 1991, 3 titles 1992. 6 titles listed in the *Small Press Record of Books in Print* (20th Edition, 1991-92). avg. price, paper: $9.95. Discounts: trade 40-50%, jobber 50%, classroom (through Lerner Publications). 22pp; of, also audio tapes. Does not copyright for author.

Keel Publications, PO Box 160155, Austin, TX 78716-0155. 1980. avg. press run 5M. Pub'd 2 titles 1990; expects 2 titles 1991, 4 titles 1992. 7 titles listed in the *Small Press Record of Books in Print* (20th Edition, 1991-92). avg. price, paper: $14.95. Discounts: 3-11 books 10%, 12-24 25%, 25-199 40%, 200-499 45%, 500+ -40% -25%. 110pp; 5½×8½. Copyrights for author. COSMEP, Publishers Marketing Assoc. (PMA).

THE KELSEY REVIEW, G. Robin Schore, Humanities Division, Mercer County Community College, Trenton, NJ 08690, 609-586-4800 ext. 326. Poetry, fiction, articles, cartoons, interviews, satire, criticism, reviews, music, parts-of-novels, long-poems, plays, non-fiction. "2,000 words maximum. Annually for residents of, and people who work in, Mercer County, New Jersey." circ. 1.5M. 1/yr. Pub'd 1 issue 1990; expects 1 issue 1991, 1 issue 1992. sub. price: free. Back issues: free, if available. 64pp; 7×11; lp. Reporting time: 30 days. Payment: 5 copies of journal. Copyrighted, reverts to author. Pub's reviews: 1 in 1990. No ads.

Kelsey St. Press, Rena Rosenwasser, Director; Thalia Kitrilakis, Patricia Dientsfrey, Marian Chapman, PO Box 9235, Berkeley, CA 94709, 415-845-2260. 1975. Poetry, fiction, art, non-fiction. "We are soliciting mss this year." avg. press run 1M. Pub'd 2 titles 1990; expects 2 titles 1991, 3 titles 1992. 18 titles listed in the *Small Press Record of Books in Print* (20th Edition, 1991-92). avg. price, paper: $6.75; other: signed limited editions, hand-colored by the artist $35. Discounts: 40% to the trade. 48pp; 5½×8½; of, lp. Reporting time: 4 months. Payment: in copies or 10% of the gross price. Copyright retained by author unless otherwise agreed.

KELTIC FRINGE, Kittatinny Press, Maureen Williams, Box 251, RD #1, Uniondale, PA 18470, 717-679-2745. 1986. Poetry, fiction, articles, art, interviews, satire, criticism, reviews, music, letters, news items, non-fiction. "*Keltic Fringe* welcomes submissions from Kelts of the six nations: Scotland, Man, Ireland, Wales, Cornwall, Brittany, and from anyone in the world involved in Keltic creativity. We are looking for essays on Keltic matters, memories, mythology, history, literature & the other arts, personalities; work from poets, musicians, storytellers; interviews with Kelts in all fields; features on Keltic happenings; news items from the Keltic community of North America; calligraphy, artwork & illustrations accompanying written pieces or as separate items. Length 100-2,000; 200-1,000 preferred. Recent contributors: Laurel Speer, Jennifer Stone, David A. Wilson, June Sawyers, Simon Humphrey." circ. 350. 4/yr. Pub'd 4 issues 1990; expects 4 issues 1991, 4 issues 1992. sub. price: $10; per copy: $3; sample: $3. Back issues: $2-$3. Discounts: not established yet. 12pp; 8½×11; of. Reporting time: 1 month or sooner. Payment: copies. Copyrighted, reverts to author. Pub's reviews: 4 in 1990. §Keltic subjects, work of Kelts. Ads: classified $10 for 25 words/display $15 for 1/4 column. COSMEP.

‡**KELTICA: THE INTER-CELTIC JOURNAL,** Kevin Dixon Gilligan, 96 Marguerite Avenue, Waltham, MA 02154, 617-899-2204. 1980. "Articles, interviews, and essays up to 10,000 words; reviews 200-2,000 words; fiction, plays, and novel excerpts up to 20,000 words. Material submitted must pertain to Celtic culture, i.e., Brittany, Cape Breton Island, Cornwall, Ireland, Galicia, the Isle of Man, Scotland, Wales, ancient Celtic Europe, or Celtic emigrant communities. No topical restrictions. Illustrations and photographs are welcomed, especially for lengthy articles. Bias favors professional writers from the Celtic countries, or whose work deals primarily with the latter; e.g. from Nos. 1-4: Bryan MacMahon, Criostoir Donnan, Reun ar C'halan, Jack Clem, Tony Curtis, Barry Fell, Joseph Clancy, Robert Minhinnick, Bob Lima" circ. 2.2M. 1/yr. Expects 2 issues 1991, 1 issue 1992. sub. price: $5.95; per copy: $5.95; sample: $3.00. Back issues: 2 issues-$10.95; 3 issues-$15.95. Discounts: 1-5 copies $4.00; 6-10 copies $3.75; 11-20 $3.60; 21 or more $3.50. 100pp; 8½×11; of. Reporting time: 2-3 months. Payment: $10 per published page. Copyrighted, rights revert in most cases. Pub's reviews: 24 in 1990. §Anything Celtic. No ads to date.

KENNEBEC: A Portfolio of Maine Writing, Carol Kontos, Terry Plunkett, University of Maine at Augusta, Augusta, ME 04330, (207) 622-7131. 1976. Poetry, fiction, satire, criticism, reviews, parts-of-novels. "Writers must have a Maine connection" circ. 5M. Pub'd 1 issue 1990; expects 1 issue 1991, 1 issue 1992. sub. price: free. 64pp; 11×14. Reporting time: 2 months. Payment: in copies. Not copyrighted.

The Kennebec River Press, Inc., Thea Wheelwright, President, 36 Old Mill Road, Falmouth, ME 04105-1637, 207-781-3002. 1981. Non-fiction. "Books of interest primarily to Maine readers. Three important titles coming up will be of countrywide interest" avg. press run 2.5M-3M. Pub'd 2 titles 1990; expects 8 titles 1991, 2 titles

1992. 7 titles listed in the *Small Press Record of Books in Print* (20th Edition, 1991-92). avg. price, cloth: $25-$40; paper: $12.95-$14.95; other: $25-$45. Discounts: stores 1-4 20%, 5-14 40%, 15-24 42%, 25+ 45% (all single or assorted titles); wholesalers 1 book 40%, 2-4 42%, 5-24 45%; 25-99 50%; libraries, schools 20%. 300+pp; size varies; of, lp. Reporting time: 1-2 months. Payment: 12½ to 15%, usually quarterly. Copyrights for author, unless author requests otherwise.

KENNETH COLEMAN'S FED TRACKER/REALITY THEORY NEWSLETTER, Kenneth Coleman, 4805 Courageous Lane, Carlsbad, CA 92008, 619-720-0107. 1982. "Two newsletters marketed together. Nation's top Fed Watcher; hasn't missed calling major economic change and market fluctuations. ISSN: *Fed Tracker/Reality Theory* 0739-3563, *Fed Tracker Special Report* 0889-9223." 20/yr. sub. price: $96. 5pp; 8½×11.

Kent Publications, Inc. (see also SAN FERNANDO POETRY JOURNAL), Richard Cloke, General Manager; Lori C. Smith, Editor-in-Chief; Shirley J. Rodecker, Asst. Editor, 18301 Halsted Street, Northridge, CA 91325, 818-349-2080. 1976. Poetry, fiction. avg. press run 1M. Pub'd 2 titles 1990; expects 4 titles 1991, 4 titles 1992. 9 titles listed in the *Small Press Record of Books in Print* (20th Edition, 1991-92). avg. price, paper: $3.25-$4.25. Discounts: jobber, 40% for orders of 5 or more; trade, 20%. 300pp; 5½×8½, 6×9; †of. Reporting time: 2 days to 1 month. Payment: 50% to author as received; copies to authors in SFPJ. Copyrights for author. CLMP.

KENTUCKY POETRY REVIEW, Wade Hall, Bellarmine College, Louisville, KY 40205. 1964. Poetry. "Recent poets: Wendell Berry, Robert Penn Warren, Marion Montgomery, David Madden, James Still, Paul Engle, John Unterecker, Jane Stuart, Marge Piercy, Diane Wakoski...Prefer poems 20-40 lines in length on any subject, any form." circ. 400. 2/yr. Pub'd 2 issues 1990; expects 2 issues 1991, 2 issues 1992. sub. price: $8; per copy: $5; sample: $5. Back issues: $5, if available. 64pp; 6×9; of. Reporting time: 1 month or less. Payment: 1 copy of issue with poet's poem. Copyrighted, reverts to author. Pub's reviews: 1 in 1990. §Collections of poetry.

Kenyette Productions, Kenyette Adrine-Robinson, 16402 Cloverside Avenue, Cleveland, OH 44128-2120, 216-921-5029. 1976. Poetry. "Permanent address: 4209 E. 186th Street, Cleveland, OH 44122 (216) 752-4069. Past president, Urban Literary Arts Workshop (ULAW), Karamu House, 2355 East 89th Street, Cleveland, OH 44106 (216) 795-7070. Member, Verse Writers Guild of Ohio, Poetry Society of America, International Platform Association." avg. press run 750. Expects 1 title 1991, 2 titles 1992. 3 titles listed in the *Small Press Record of Books in Print* (20th Edition, 1991-92). avg. price, cloth: $7.50; paper: $5.75. Discounts: non-profit organizations, bookstores, vendors, public schools. 56pp; 5½×8½; of and desktop. Reporting time: 2 months. Payment: negotiable. Copyrights for author. COSMEP, PO Box 703, San Francisco, CA 94101; International Black Writers & Artists Inc., PO Box 43576, Los Angeles, CA 90043.

THE KENYON REVIEW, Martha Finan, Managing Editor; Marilyn Hacker, Editor; David Lynn, Associate Editor, Kenyon College, Gambier, OH 43022, 614-427-3339. 1978. Poetry, fiction, articles, satire, criticism, reviews, parts-of-novels, long-poems. "Joyce Carol Oates, Martin Esslin, Carolyn Heilbrun, Junzo Shono, George Steiner, William Gass, Charles Altieri. Bookstore distributor is Bernard DeBoer. Issue dates are Jan. 15 (winter), April 15 (spring), July 5 (summer), and October (fall)." circ. 3M-4M. 4/yr. Pub'd 4 issues 1990; expects 4 issues 1991, 4 issues 1992. sub. price: $20 individuals, $23 libraries; per copy: $6 + $1 postage; sample: $7 includes postage. Back issues: available on request. Discounts: agency 15%, university press 15%. 144+pp; 7×10; of. Reporting time: 2 months. Payment: $10 prose, $15 poetry (per page) $15 minimum per poem. Copyrighted, reverts to author. Pub's reviews. §Literature, criticism, and the arts. Ads: $250/$150/$75 quarter page/$400 inside or back cover, 15% discount on ads for agencies and university presses. COSMEP, CCLM.

THE KEROUAC CONNECTION, Dave Moore, 19 Worthing Road, Patchway, Bristol BS12 5HY, England. 1984. Poetry, fiction, articles, art, photos, cartoons, interviews, satire, criticism, reviews, letters, parts-of-novels, collages, news items, non-fiction. "ISSN 0954-2965" circ. 600+. 2/yr. Pub'd 2 issues 1990; expects 2 issues 1991, 2 issues 1992. sub. price: UK £2, Europe £3, Canada £4, USA $5 (including Air-Mail postage); per copy: UK £1, Europe £1.50, Canada £2, USA $2.50; sample: UK £1, Europe £1.50, Canada £2, USA $2.50. Back issues: same. Discounts: 1/3 off on 10 copies or more. 36pp; 5¾×8¼; of. Reporting time: 1 month. Payment: free copies. Copyrighted, reverts to author. Pub's reviews: 16 in 1990. §Beat literature and related work. Ads: £20/£10 (camera-ready artwork only)/small ads - free.

Michael Kesend, Publishing, Ltd., Michael Kesend, Publisher, 1025 Fifth Avenue, New York, NY 10028-0134, 212-249-5150. 1979. Fiction, non-fiction. avg. press run 3M-7M. Pub'd 4 titles 1990; expects 6 titles 1991, 6 titles 1992. 22 titles listed in the *Small Press Record of Books in Print* (20th Edition, 1991-92). avg. price, cloth: $16.95; paper: $10.95. Discounts: 40% to retailers, 50% to wholesalers. of. Reporting time: 6 weeks to 2 months. Copyrights for author. PMA.

Kettering Foundation (see also KETTERING REVIEW), Robert Kingston, Editor; Judson Jerome,

Associate Editor, 200 Commons Road, Dayton, OH 45459-2799, 513-434-7300. 1985. Articles. "Additional addresses: 6 East 39th Street, 9th Floor, New York, NY 10016, 212-686-7016; 444 North Capitol Street, N.W., Suite 408, Washington, DC 20001, 202-393-4478." avg. press run 10M. Pub'd 2 titles 1990; expects 3 titles 1991, 3 titles 1992. avg. price, paper: $3.50. 64pp; 7×10; of. Reporting time: 2 months. Copyrights for author.

KETTERING REVIEW, Kettering Foundation, Robert J. Kingston, Editor-in-Chief, 200 Commons Road, Dayton, OH 45459-2799, 513-434-7300. 1983. "Designed for the intelligent lay public with special interest in governing, educating, science, international affairs or interdisciplinary fields. Non-fiction only. Requirements: Manuscripts of 1.5-3M words from those working in the fields of governing, educating or science who can address ideas of national importance in an interdisciplinary and popular readable fashion. Read a sample before submitting. Articles must be exceptionally well-written; issues usually organized around a theme. Uses 5-6 articles per issue. No footnotes. Mss. must be accompanied by SASE. No responsibility is assumed for the return of unsolicited manuscripts. Additional addresses: 6 East 39th Street, 9th Floor, New York, NY 10016, 212-686-7016; 444 North Capitol Street, N.W., Suite 408, Washington, DC 20001, 202-393-4478." circ. 8M. 3/yr. Pub'd 2 issues 1990; expects 3 issues 1991, 3 issues 1992. sample price: $3. 64pp; 7×10. Payment: copies.

Key Curriculum Press, Steve Rasmussen, PO Box 2304, Berkeley, CA 94702, 415-548-2304. 1971. "We publish math workbooks and occasional math textbooks" avg. press run 10M. Pub'd 4 titles 1990; expects 7 titles 1991, 10 titles 1992. avg. price, cloth: $20; paper: $3. Discounts: 40% to dealers. 40pp; 8½×11. Reporting time: 2 weeks. Payment: varies. Copyrights for author. COSMEP.

Key Publications, PO Box 6375, Woodland Hills, CA 91365, 818-992-4657. 1990. Non-fiction. "First book: *Parenting Your Aging Parents - The Easiest and Best Approach, Based On Real Experience.*" avg. press run as needed. Expects 1 title 1991, 1 title 1992. avg. price, cloth: $20; paper: $15. Discounts: negotiable. 300pp; 6×9; †of, desktop. Reporting time: 4 weeks with SASE. Payment: negotiable. Copyrights for author.

KEY WEST REVIEW, William J. Schlicht, Jr., Marion H. Smith, 9 Avenue G, Key West, FL 33042, 305-296-1365. 1987. Poetry, fiction, articles, art, photos, interviews, criticism, reviews, letters, parts-of-novels. "Business address: PO Box 2082, Key West, FL 33045-2082. Recent contributors: Richard Wilbur, Richard Eberhart, John Williams, Peter Taylor, James Merrill, George Starbuck, Alice Adams, Hal Bennett." circ. 1M. 2/yr. Pub'd 2 issues 1990; expects 2 issues 1991, 2 issues 1992. sub. price: $17; per copy: $10; sample: $5. Back issues: $5. Discounts: 20%-40%. 200pp; 6×9; of. Reporting time: 2-3 months. Payment: copies. Copyrighted, reverts to author. Pub's reviews: 1 in 1990. §Books by writers living in the Florida Keys, or fiction and poetry in which the Keys figure prominently. Ads: $100/$50/$300 inside front cover/$200 inside back cover. CCLM.

Keyboard Workshop, Duane Shinn, PO Box 700, Medford, OR 97501, 664-2317. 1966. Music. "Most publications are house-produced. Very little free lance material accepted" avg. press run 5M-25M. Expects 12 titles 1991. avg. price, paper: $10. Discounts: 50% basic; single copy 25%-over gross 67%. 40pp; 8½×11; of. Reporting time: 4 weeks. Payment: flat rate. Copyrights for author.

KEYSTROKES, Kiel Stuart, Howard Austerlitz, PO Box 2014, Setauket, NY 11733, 516-751-7080. 1980. Poetry, articles, cartoons, interviews, satire, criticism, reviews, letters, news items, non-fiction. "Contributors need not be subscriber/members. *KEYSTROKES* is primarily a member forum accepting outside adverts, and notices are free to members. Applications available for SASE." circ. 300+. 4/yr. Pub'd 4 issues 1990; expects 4 issues 1991, 4 issues 1992. sub. price: $15; per copy: $4; sample: $4. 12pp; 8½×7; †Photocopy, desktop publishing. Reporting time: 3 months. Payment: copies. Copyrighted, reverts to author. Pub's reviews: 12 in 1990. §How-tos on fiction, nonfiction, for writers, poetry, criticism. Member ads free/full page $75/half page $50/classfied word 75¢. \

Ki2 Books,** KiKi Canniff, PO Box 13322, Portland, OR 97213, (503) 256-3485. 1981. Non-fiction. "I am ready to accept other authors' travel books for publication—am looking for books for USA vacationers-particularly 'family' books slanted toward budget conscious folks and books about the Pacific Northwest. No color photos except covers." avg. press run 5M. Pub'd 2 titles 1990; expects 2 titles 1991, 2 titles 1992. 3 titles listed in the *Small Press Record of Books in Print* (20th Edition, 1991-92). avg. price, paper: $9.95. Discounts: upon request. 180pp; 5½×8½. Payment: negotiated after approval of manuscript. Copyrights for author. Northwest Assoc. of Book Publishers, PMA, Book Publicists NW, COSMEP.

THE KIBBUTZ JOURNAL, Horovitz Avshalom, 27 West 20th Street, New York, NY 10011, 212-255-1338. 1984. Articles, art, photos, interviews, letters. "Material dedicated to the study of the Kibbutz society and its relation to Zionism, Israeli society, World Jewry-social implications as well as economic contributions" circ. 14M. 1/yr. Pub'd 2 issues 1990; expects 1 issue 1991, 1 issue 1992. sub. price: donations accepted. 8pp; 11½×17½; of. Copyrighted, reverts to author.

KICK IT OVER, Kick It Over Collective, PO Box 5811, Station A, Toronto, Ontario M5W 1P2, Canada. 1981. Poetry, articles, art, photos, cartoons, interviews, reviews, letters, news items, non-fiction. "Articles and news shorts dealing with social change, ecology, feminism and related issues from anarchist perspective. Submissions welcome; send SASE for return if desired (if in USA, send a few coins instead of stamping the envelope)." circ. 3.5M. 4/yr. sub. price: $9. Discounts: we trade selectively, 40% off cover for orders of more than 5 copies or to bookstore. Very lenient to our distributors in various cities. 24pp; 10¼×15¼; web. Reporting time: depends how bad/good it is—decisions by concensus take time; say 2 months from receipt. Payment: subscription and glory. Not copyrighted. Pub's reviews: 8+ in 1990. §Radical feminism, anarchism, peace, alternative institutions and 'counter-culture' neo-paganism, anti-racism, and ecology.

KIDS LIB NEWS, Oness Press, Mycall Sunanda, Editor, PO Box 1064, Kurtistown, HI 96760. 1985. Poetry, fiction, articles, art, photos, cartoons, interviews, satire, criticism, reviews, letters, collages, plays, news items, non-fiction. "We use short materials in *Kids Lib News*. Published on Equinox & Solstice. We aim mostly at and from natural spiritual family life, homeducation & radical healing, the garbage lies & addictions of modern society. Creative craziness, goofy Sufi, natural home birth, baby-massage, Kidsex Lib, networking with new age families & groups since 1972. Universing Center began Creative Parenting in Eugene in 1973" circ. 1M. 4/yr. Pub'd 4 issues 1990; expects 4 issues 1991, 4 issues 1992. sub. price: $12; per copy: $3; sample: $2. Back issues: $4. Discounts: we do info trades for mags, art, articles,, ads, subs, bklts, etc. 48pp; 8½×11; zerox. Reporting time: 2 weeks. Not copyrighted. Pub's reviews: 4 in 1990. §Radical therapy, kids liberation, wholistic family life, Sufi. Ads: $20/$15/1/4 page $10/1/8 page $7/1/16 page $5.

KIDSCIENCE, Dr. Catherine Reed, 2215 Doswell Avenue, St. Paul, MN 55108. 1987. Non-fiction. "Our content is science activities for elementary schools. The magazine is by and for elementary teachers" circ. 500. 5/yr. Pub'd 5 issues 1990; expects 5 issues 1991, 5 issues 1992. sub. price: $10; per copy: $2; sample: $2. Back issues: $2. Discounts: institutional sub with copying privileges $50/yr. 28pp; 8½×11; of. Reporting time: varies. Payment: free 1 year sub. to all contributors. Copyrighted, reverts to author. Pub's reviews: 5 in 1990. §Science, especially elementary science. Ads: none.

KINGFISHER, Barbara Schultz, Editor; Ruthie Singer, Editor; Lorraine Hilton-Gray, Editor; Andrea Beach, Editor, PO Box 9783, North Berkeley, CA 94709. 1986. Poetry, fiction, art. "Translations, as well as a calendar of events for writers" circ. 1M. 2/yr. Pub'd 2 issues 1990; expects 2 issues 1991. sub. price: $10; per copy: $5; sample: $5. 120pp; 6×9. Reporting time: within 3 months. Payment: copies. Copyrighted, reverts to author. Ads: $125/$75/quarter page $50.

The Kingston Press, Inc., P.O. Box 2759, Clifton, NJ 07015, 609-921-0609. 1982. "Fine scholarly and college level works; strong emphasis on the Middle East, Asia, Russia, the Soviet Union. One of the world's greatest medievalists, Prof. Serge A. Zenkovsky, is into the 4th volume of the *Nikonian Chronicle* (the most complete chronicle compilation of Russia). These titles are all available. Catalog of complete list will be sent upon query" avg. press run 500-1M. Pub'd 5 titles 1990; expects 5 titles 1991, 4 titles 1992. 19 titles listed in the *Small Press Record of Books in Print* (20th Edition, 1991-92). avg. price, cloth: $25. Discounts: 1-4 copies 20%; 5-25 copies 25%; over 25 copies 40% (+ prepayment). 250pp; 6×9; of. Reporting time: 1-2 months. Payment: varies with each title. Does not copyright for author.

Kinseeker Publications (see also WANDERING WOLFS; ZINGSHEIM TIMES; ARNOLD AN-CESTRY; EWING EXCHANGE; CARROLL CABLES; NORTON NOTES; FERGUSON FILES; GATHERING GIBSONS), Victoria Wilson, PO Box 184, Grawn, MI 49637, 616-276-6745. 1986. Articles, reviews, news items, non-fiction. avg. press run 50. Pub'd 13 titles 1990; expects 15 titles 1991, 15 titles 1992. 29 titles listed in the *Small Press Record of Books in Print* (20th Edition, 1991-92). avg. price, paper: $2.50/$10 per year. Discounts: none. 10pp; 8½×11; †of. Payment: on individual basis. Copyrights for author.

KIOSK, Adam Ward, Charles Ward, Attn: Charles Ward, 317 West 106th Street #2-C, New York, NY 10025-3648. 1987. Poetry, fiction, art, photos, cartoons, interviews, long-poems. "*Kiosk* is a magazine of new and alternative voices in poetry and fiction. We also accept photography and drawings" circ. 500. 3/yr. Pub'd 2 issues 1990; expects 3 issues 1991, 3 issues 1992. sub. price: $6; per copy: $2; sample: free. Back issues: free. 40pp; 5½×8½. Reporting time: 1 month. Payment: none. Copyrighted, reverts to author. No ads.

Kitchen Sink Press (see also STEVE CANYON MAGAZINE; THE SPIRIT), Denis Kitchen, No. 2 Swamp Road, Princeton, WI 54968, 414-295-6922. 1969. Articles, art, cartoons, interviews, satire, letters. "Interested primarily in comic art and/or articles, interviews, etc. relating to comics and cartoonists." avg. press run 5M-20M. Pub'd 10 titles 1990; expects 12 titles 1991, 15 titles 1992. 34 titles listed in the *Small Press Record of Books in Print* (20th Edition, 1991-92). avg. price, cloth: $18.95-$25; paper: $10.95; other: $2, $4.95, $5.95. Discounts: 40% off to stores, 50%-60% off to distributors. 36-72pp paper, 160pp cloth; 7×10 paper, 8½×11 cloth, 6×9 comic; of. Reporting time: often same day, 2 weeks at outside. Payment: royalty basis. From $40/page to $200/cover for artwork used. Copyrights for author.

Kitchen Table: Women of Color Press, Barbara Smith, Publisher; Wanda Carrion-Mejias, Office Manager; Sheilah Sable, Office Manager, PO Box 908, Latham, NY 12110-0908, 518-434-2057. 1981. Poetry, fiction, articles, criticism, long-poems, plays, non-fiction. "Kitchen Table: Women of Color Press is the only publisher in the U.S. committed to publishing and distributing the writing of Third World women of all racial/cultural heritages, sexualities, and classes that will further the cause of Third World women's personal and political freedom" avg. press run 6.5M. Pub'd 2 titles 1990; expects 2 titles 1991, 3 titles 1992. 13 titles listed in the *Small Press Record of Books in Print* (20th Edition, 1991-92). avg. price, cloth: $18.95; paper: $8.95; other: $3.50 pamphlets. Discounts: 40% to bookstores or individuals who order 5 or more of any single title; 55% to distributors. 25-250pp; 5½x8½; of. Reporting time: 6 months. Payment: in general, 7% of cover price on the first 5M sold, with increased percentages thereafter. Copyrights for author. COSMEP, American Booksellers Assn.

KITE LINES, Aeolus Press, Inc., Valerie Govig, Publisher & Editor, PO Box 466, Randallstown, MD 21133-0466, 301-922-1212; fax 301-922-4262. 1977. Articles, art, photos, interviews, reviews, letters, news items. "All material is about *kites*. Do rights revert: rights limited to reprint in magazine; all other rights revert to author." circ. 13M. 4/yr. Expects 4 issues 1991. sub. price: $14; per copy: $3.95; sample: $3.95. Back issues: $3.95 each. Discounts: to kite shops, 20 copies minimum, $2.55 each for resale. 64pp; 8⅜x10⅞; of, web. Reporting time: 2 weeks to 3 months (varies with workload). Payment: $0-$100 + copies. Copyrighted, reverts to author. Pub's reviews: 8-12 in 1990. §Kites. Ads: $719/$411/$1 ($10 minimum). BPA, Small Magazine Publishers Group.

Kittatinny Press (see also KELTIC FRINGE), Maureen Williams, Box 251, RD #1, Uniondale, PA 18470, 717-679-2745. 1989. Poetry, fiction, articles, art, interviews, satire, criticism, reviews, non-fiction. "Kittatinny Press has only just been founded, yet hopes to publish one or two books in 1991 and will be seeking other writers' work in 1992." avg. press run 1M. Expects 2 titles 1992. COSMEP.

Klutz Press, John Cassidy, 2121 Staunton Court, Palo Alto, CA 94306, 415-857-0888. 1977. Non-fiction. "Have published 19 titles, *Juggling for the Complete Klutz* and *The Hacky-Sack Book*, *The Unbelievable Bubble Book* and *Country and Blues Harmonica for the Musically Hopeless*, and others. Interested in publishing how-to trade paperbacks" avg. press run 50M. Pub'd 4 titles 1990; expects 4 titles 1991, 4 titles 1992. 24 titles listed in the *Small Press Record of Books in Print* (20th Edition, 1991-92). avg. price, paper: $9.95. Discounts: standard trade. 5x8½; webb. Reporting time: 60 days. Payment: negotiable. Copyrights for author.

KMT, A Modern Journal of Ancient Egypt, KMT Communications, Dennis Forbes, 1531 Golden Gate Avenue, San Francisco, CA 94115, 415-922-7263. 1990. Articles, art, photos, interviews, reviews, collages. "Focus is *Ancient Egypt*: history, art, archaeology and culture" circ. 4M-5M. 4/yr. Pub'd 4 issues 1990; expects 4 issues 1991, 4 issues 1992. sub. price: $32; per copy: $8; sample: $9.50 (incl. p/h). Back issues: same. Discounts: distributor 40%-50%. 72+pp; 8⅛x10⅞; of. Reporting time: 60 days. Payment: $50-$400. Copyrighted, reverts to author. Pub's reviews: 10 in 1990. §History, culture, archaeology and art of Egypt. Ads: $600/$350/$270 1/3 page/$150 1/6 page. BAPA.

KMT Communications (see also KMT, A Modern Journal of Ancient Egypt), Dennis Forbes, 1531 Golden Gate Avenue, San Francisco, CA 94115, 415-922-7263. 1990. Non-fiction. "Subject: *Ancient Egypt*, history, art, archaeology and culture of" avg. press run 1M. Pub'd 1 title 1990; expects 1+ titles 1991. avg. price, cloth: $59.95; paper: $39.95. Discounts: 40% to distributors. 120pp; 8½x11; of. Reporting time: 60 days. Payment: by agreement. Copyrights for author. BAPA.

Knights Press, Elizabeth G. Gershman, PO Box 6737, Stamford, CT 06901, 203-969-1699. 1983. Fiction. "Offices located at 190 Henry Street, Stamford, CT 06902. Gay male fiction only. Plot must show a positive gay relationship or gay lifestyle. Manuscripts run from 65M to 100M words. In submitting, write for guidelines, or send sample chapter and plot and character outlines. Recent books: *Boys in the Bars* by Christopher Davis, *Some Dance to Remember* by Jack Fritscher." avg. press run 3M. Pub'd 8 titles 1990; expects 8 titles 1991, 8 titles 1992. 37 titles listed in the *Small Press Record of Books in Print* (20th Edition, 1991-92). avg. price, paper: $9. Discounts: 46% 2-50 books mixed titles, other wholesale & retail discounts available on request. 224-256pp; 5½x8½; lp. Reporting time: 90 days. Payment: 10%, with advance. Copyrights for author. Connecticut Press Club, ABA.

Knollwood Publishing Company, 505 Monongalia Avenue SW, Willmar, MN 56201, 612-382-6276. 1973. "Currently a one-book, one-record publishing house—'*Silver Spurs*', *Santa's Smallest Brightest Elf*. Record, sheet music, 4 full color posters (scenes from book), t-shirt stencil (5 x 8-full color)" 1 title listed in the *Small Press Record of Books in Print* (20th Edition, 1991-92). avg. price, cloth: $4.95; other: $2 record. Discounts: libraries, schools 30%, bookstores-20% to 40%; fund raisers & distributors-50%. 39pp; 8½x11.

Knowledge, Ideas & Trends, Inc. (KIT), Rita I. McCullough, 1131-0 Tolland Turnpike, Ste. 175, Manchester, CT 06040, 203-646-1621. 1990. Non-fiction. "Editorial address: 400 Prospect Street, Glen Rock, NJ 07450" avg. press run 2M. Expects 4 titles 1991, 4 titles 1992. 3 titles listed in the *Small Press Record of Books in Print* (20th Edition, 1991-92). 250pp; 5½x8½; of. Payment: per contract. Copyrights for author. COSMEP, PMA, ABA.

Knowledge Systems, Inc., 7777 West Morris Street, Indianapolis, IN 46231, 317-241-0749; 317-248-1503 (FAX). 1986. Non-fiction. "Adult non-fiction resources for effecting personal and social change. Both established authors and new writers providing practical insights based on life experience into social change for personal and planetary well-being" avg. press run 5M. Pub'd 2 titles 1990; expects 4 titles 1991, 5-6 titles 1992. 13 titles listed in the *Small Press Record of Books in Print* (20th Edition, 1991-92). avg. price, cloth: $16.95; paper: $12.95; other: $19.95 study guides. Discounts: single title order plan 1-10%; 2-4 20%, 5-24 40%, 25-49 44%, 50+ 50. 210pp; 6×9; of. Reporting time: 4-6 weeks. Payment: flexible—author can increase royalty by performing certain prepress tasks. Copyrights for author. COSMEP, PMA, Mid-America Publishers Group.

Konocti Books (see also SIPAPU), Noel Peattie, 23311 County Road 88, Winters, CA 95694. 1973. Poetry. "We have done 4 poetry books and 5 broadsides. Broadsides now appear under the imprint of Cannonade Press, using a 6 X 10 Kelsey. Query before sending! Book publishing suspended for the present." avg. press run 300. Pub'd 2 titles 1990; expects 1 title 1991. 3 titles listed in the *Small Press Record of Books in Print* (20th Edition, 1991-92). avg. price, paper: $6; other: broadsides are free. Discounts: 40% booksellers. 40pp; lp. Reporting time: 3 weeks. Payment: author's copies only. Copyrights for author. COSMEP, CLMP.

Kontexts Publications, Michael Gibbs, Overtoom 444, 1054 JW Amsterdam, The Netherlands, 020-836665. 1969. Poetry, articles, art, photos, interviews, criticism, reviews, letters, collages, concrete art. "Concerned with visual/experimental poetry and language arts. The magazine *Kontexts* has now folded. Last number 9/10 Winter 76/77, but Kontexts Publications will be continuing with the production of books and book-objects by individual writers/artists." avg. press run 400. Pub'd 1 title 1990. 10 titles listed in the *Small Press Record of Books in Print* (20th Edition, 1991-92). avg. price, paper: $4. Discounts: 33⅓% on 6 or more. †mi, of, lp. Copyrights for author.

KOOKS MAGAZINE, Out-Of-Kontrol Data Institute, Donna Kossy, PO Box 953, Allston, MA 02134. 1988. Articles, art, photos, cartoons, interviews, satire, reviews, letters, collages, news items, non-fiction. "*Please no poetry submissions! No fiction!*, but please do send Kook and Crackpot flyers, reviews and articles about Kooks. Send SASE for writers' guidelines and suggestions." circ. 750. 2/yr. Pub'd 2 issues 1990; expects 2 issues 1991, 2 issues 1992. sub. price: $15/4 issues; per copy: $4 + $1 p/h per order; sample: same. Back issues: $3: #2-#5 each + $1 p/h. Discounts: 60/40 consignment for distributors. 36pp; 8½×11; of. Reporting time: 2-3 months. Payment: free issue(s) and $15/articles; $5/review. Copyrighted, reverts to author. Pub's reviews: 10 in 1990. §Conspiracies & occult, UFO's, "kooks", extremist and crackpot literature, weird science, fanatics, fringe ideas, cults, history of religion. Ads: $75/$40/$25 1/4 page/$15 1/8 page/classified 20¢ per word.

Kore, Skip Fox, 420 Orangewood Drive, Lafayette, LA 70503-5228. 1982. Poetry. "To present *Kore* has only printed broadsides of short poems but will, in the near future, print letterpress chapbooks" avg. press run 200-400. Pub'd 5 titles 1990; expects 10 titles 1991, 10 titles 1992. 8 titles listed in the *Small Press Record of Books in Print* (20th Edition, 1991-92). avg. price, other: free on request. 5×7; †lp. Payment: in copies; 1/4 to 1/2 of run.

Korn Kompany, Dave Korner, Hilda Korner, PO Box 7414, M, Menlo Park, CA 94026, 415-965-3524. 1986. Photos. "Always looking for sports or recreational material dealing only with children of elementary age. We would like photographs (B/W) to accompany stories" avg. press run 1M. Pub'd 2 titles 1990; expects 1 title 1991, 1 title 1992. 1 title listed in the *Small Press Record of Books in Print* (20th Edition, 1991-92). avg. price, paper: $9.95. 64pp; size varies; of. Reporting time: 2 weeks. Payment: TBA with author. Copyrights arranged with author.

KOSMOS, Kosrof Chantikian, 20 Millard Road, Larkspur, CA 94939. 1974. Poetry. "We have established a *Modern Poets in Translation Series* to introduce poets of other parts of this planet to the reading public in the United States. We are interested in publishing translations of contemporary works by poets from outside of the United States, as well as new interpretations of significant poetic works of the past. We are also interested in publishing works in the areas of mythology, philosophy, classics, the arts, fiction, essays, criticism and so on. A letter of inquiry (along with a SASE) giving an outline of your proposed project should be sent to the editor before submission of a manuscript" avg. press run 1.2M. Pub'd 2 titles 1990; expects 2 titles 1991. 7 titles listed in the *Small Press Record of Books in Print* (20th Edition, 1991-92). avg. price, cloth: $17; paper: $7.95. Discounts: 20% (1-4 copies); 40% (5+). 88-256pp; 6×9; of. Reporting time: 7 weeks. Payment: standard. Copyrights for author.

Kozmik Press, David Stuart Ryan, 134 Elsenham Street, London SW18 5NP, United Kingdom, 874-8218. 1975. Poetry, fiction. "Would like synopsis of any work before consideration. U.S. book orders to: Seven Hills Distributors, 49 Central Avenue, Cincinnati, OH 45202." avg. press run 1M. Pub'd 2 titles 1990; expects 2 titles 1991, 3 titles 1992. 10 titles listed in the *Small Press Record of Books in Print* (20th Edition, 1991-92). avg. price, cloth: $14; paper: $8. Discounts: 40% retail, 50% wholesale. 232pp. Payment: only after sales.

Copyrights for author. ALP, COSMEP, IPG.

HJ Kramer, Inc, PO Box 1082, Tiburon, CA 94920. 1983. Fiction, non-fiction. avg. press run 10M-50M. Pub'd 5 titles 1990; expects 4 titles 1991, 8 titles 1992. 27 titles listed in the *Small Press Record of Books in Print* (20th Edition, 1991-92). avg. price, paper: $10.95. Pages vary; 5½x8½; of. Reporting time: 60 days. Payment: usual. Copyrights for author.

KRAX, Andy Robson, 63 Dixon Lane, Leeds, Yorkshire LS12 4RR, England. 1971. Poetry, fiction, articles, art, photos, cartoons, interviews. "Prefer whimsical and amusing work by both writers and artists." 2/yr. Pub'd 1 issue 1990; expects 2 issues 1991, 2 issues 1992. 7 titles listed in the *Small Press Record of Books in Print* (20th Edition, 1991-92). sub. price: £2.50 ($5) inclusive; per copy: £1.25 incl. postage; sample: $1. Back issues: on request. 48pp; size A5; of. Reporting time: 6-8 weeks. Payment: cover design only-£10 ($20). Copyrighted, reverts to author. SPG.

KREATURE COMFORTS, Sherman Willmott, 1916 Madison Avenue, Memphis, TN 38104, 901-274-1916. 1988. Fiction, articles, photos, cartoons, interviews, non-fiction. "Live music reviews" circ. 2M. 6/yr. Pub'd 4 issues 1990; expects 4-6 issues 1991, 4-6 issues 1992. sub. price: $12; per copy: $1.52; sample: same. Back issues: $1.52. 20pp; 8½x11; †varies. Payment: none. Copyrighted, reverts to author. Pub's reviews: 40-50 in 1990. §Music, tattoos, bizarre pop culture, Jim Thompsonesque, Hunter Thompson. Ads: $150/$75/call.

KROKLOK, Writers Forum, Bob Cobbing, Peter Mayer, 89A Petherton Road, London N5 2QT, England, 01-226-2657. 1971. Concrete art. "No submissions wanted." circ. 500. Irregular. Expects 1 issue 1991, 1 issue 1992. price per copy: £1.50. Back issues: £1. Discounts: 1/3 off. 32pp; size A4; †photo-copy. Payment: copies. Not copyrighted. ALP, COLP.

The Krsna Institute, Kusakratha dasa, PO Box 281, Culver City, CA 90232, 213-838-3535. 1986. "We publish only translations of Caitanya Vaisnava devotional poetry and theology. No submissions requested." avg. press run 100. Expects 11 titles 1991, 30 titles 1992. 100 titles listed in the *Small Press Record of Books in Print* (20th Edition, 1991-92). avg. price, paper: $6. Discounts: 33½% off. 150pp; 5x8; of. Payment: none, translators are monks and take no money for their work. Does not copyright for author.

Kumarian Press, Inc., Sondhi Krishna, Publisher-President; Terrence Young, 630 Oakwood Avenue, Suite 119, West Hartford, CT 06110-1529, 203-953-0214. 1977. Non-fiction. "Academic and scholarly books, workbooks and monographs. Books in the area of international development, social science, management, business" avg. press run 200-2M. Pub'd 9 titles 1990; expects 10 titles 1991, 10 titles 1992. 52 titles listed in the *Small Press Record of Books in Print* (20th Edition, 1991-92). avg. price, cloth: $27.50; paper: $19.95. Discounts: bookstores 10% on 2-4 mixed titles, 20% on 5+; wholesale and jobber 10-30%. 200pp; 6x9, 8½x11; of. Reporting time: 30-60 days. Payment: based on net. Copyrights for author in exceptional circumstances. COSMEP, PMA.

KUMQUAT MERINGUE, Christian Nelson, PO Box 5144, Rockford, IL 61125, 815-968-0713. 1990. Poetry, fiction, art, photos, satire, reviews. "Recent contributors: Keith Abbott, Terry J. Fox, Cheryl Townsend, Antler, Gina Bergamino. Mostly use short poetry, some short prose. Looking for stuff that 'reminds' us of the same feeling we get from reading Richard Brautigan. Also like to read things 'about' Richard Brautigan." circ. 150. 2-3/yr. Expects 3 issues 1991, 3 issues 1992. sub. price: $5; per copy: $2.50; sample: $2.50. Back issues: no special prices. 28pp; 5½x8½ (digest size); xerox. Reporting time: 25-50 days. Payment: 1 copy for each issue they appear in. Copyrighted, reverts to author. Ads: none.

Kurios Press, Barbie Engstrom, Publisher, Box 946, Bryn Mawr, PA 19010, 215-527-4635. 1974. "We have begun a series of travel-photographic guides which feature a detailed text, along with over 200 photographs; our guides are large-format paperbacks (8½ X 11), printed on 80 lb. glossy stock. The first guide was *Paris to See and Enjoy, Kenya Safari* was next, then came *India, Nepal, & Sri Lanka,* followed by *Egypt and a Nile Cruise,* published in January of 1984, *Paris With 12 Walking Tours, Safaris in Kenya and Tanzania,* and the revised editions of *India, Nepal and 'Sri Lanka,* as well as *Egypt and Nile Cruise.* We do not solicit manuscripts as all titles are done on assignment. We also consult with authors on how they can self-publish their own books on a fee basis." avg. press run 2.5M-10M. Expects 2 titles 1991. 5 titles listed in the *Small Press Record of Books in Print* (20th Edition, 1991-92). avg. price, paper: $15.95-$24.95. Discounts: standard except when special offers are given. 200-450pp; 8½x11; of. Payment: none. Copyrights for author.

KYOCERA USER, John Noyce, Publisher, John Noyce, G.P.O. Box 2222T, Melbourne, Vic. 3001, Australia.

L

L D A Publishers, Margaret Riconda, 42-36 209 Street, Bayside, NY 11361, 212-224-9484. 1974. Non-fiction. avg. press run 1M. Pub'd 5 titles 1990; expects 6 titles 1991, 8 titles 1992. 6 titles listed in the *Small Press Record of Books in Print* (20th Edition, 1991-92). avg. price, paper: $59.95. Discounts: 10% over 12 copies. 300pp; 8½×11; of. Copyrights for author. LDA.

L.A. GANG BANG, Lee Wochner, 1212A N. San Fernando #244, Burbank, CA 91504. 1988. Cartoons, reviews, letters. "We get a lot of submissions and have only six pages into which we can fit them. We like and print short and pithy. We just don't have the space for much else. We are a personal newsletter with a style all its own. A sample copy is highly recommended." circ. 300. 12/yr. Pub'd 12 issues 1990; expects 12 issues 1991, 12 issues 1992. sub. price: $9; per copy: $1; sample: $1. 6pp; 8½×11; †xerox. Payment: copies. Copyrighted, does not revert to author. Pub's reviews. §The offbeat, and anything to do with pop culture.

L.A.N.D. (see also LIVING AMONG NATURE DARINGLY!), Bill Anderson, 4466 Ike Mooney Road, Silverton, OR 97381, 503-873-8829. 1986. Fiction, interviews, plays, non-fiction. "Strong bias toward books detailing how to trap or raise small stock, i.e. mink, fox, raccoon, rabbit, quail, pheasant, chickens, etc. Also looking for mystery books with trapping and farming back drop. May have interest in science-fiction and in interviews of lesser-known political activists. Also need texts on Africa, Latin America. Three books now under editing: *The Tracker*—a modern day trapper trying to solve murder of 60's President stumbles across secret group composed of CIA, Mafia, Christians, Jews, and Moslems; *Mink Farming*; and *Raccoon Trapping & Ranching*" avg. press run 6M. Expects 2-4 titles 1991, 4-8 titles 1992. avg. price, cloth: $20; paper: $5. Discounts: bulk 50%, all others 42½%. 150pp; 4½×6½; of. Reporting time: 60 days. Payment: 15% royalty, advances not expected. Copyrights for author.

L.G.L.C. NEWSLETTER, Libertarians for Gay and Lesbian Concerns (LGLC), James L. Hudler, PO Box 447, Chelsea, MI 48118, 313-475-9792. 1983. Poetry, fiction, articles, art, photos, cartoons, interviews, satire, criticism, reviews, music, letters, collages, news items, non-fiction. "Primary interest is in material relevant to gay libertarians - political and educational." circ. 300. 6/yr. Pub'd 5 issues 1990; expects 6 issues 1991, 6 issues 1992. sub. price: $15; per copy: $2; sample: free. Back issues: $2. Discounts: can be worked out - call. 12pp; 8 1/2×11; †high quality copies. Reporting time: 2 months. Payment: negotiable. Copyrighted. Pub's reviews: 1 in 1990. §Freedom-oriented, problems of government violations of people's rights, censorship, AIDS, war and drugs. Ads: $30/$15/$8 1/4 page. LGLC.

LA BELLA FIGURA, Rose Romano, PO Box 411223, San Francisco, CA 94141-1223. 1988. Poetry, fiction, reviews. "Contributors: Maria Gillan, Rina Ferrarelli, Rachel DeVries, Gigi Marino, Kathy Freeperson, Lucia Chiavola Birnbaum. We publish only the work of Italian-Americas, with a special welcome for lesbians and gay men." circ. 100. 4/yr. Pub'd 3 issues 1990; expects 4 issues 1991, 4 issues 1992. sub. price: $8; per copy: $2; sample: $2. 10pp; 8½×11; of. Reporting time: 1-2 months. Payment: 2 copies. Copyrighted, reverts to author. Pub's reviews: 2 in 1990. §Italian-American culture. Ads: please write for info.

La Jolla Poets Press, Kathleen Iddings, PO Box 8638, La Jolla, CA 92038, 619-457-1399. 1985. Poetry. "Shelley Memorial Award winner, Leo Connellan, said in *Small Press Review: Kathleen Iddings has done an international service for everyone who cares for poetry's survival by offering the best poetry...* With this press and her non-profit, San Diego Poets Press, Kathleen has sought to publish some of the best poetry being written today. Query with 5 poems, bio, and SASE." avg. press run 500. Pub'd 2 titles 1990; expects 3 titles 1991. 6 titles listed in the *Small Press Record of Books in Print* (20th Edition, 1991-92). avg. price, cloth: $18; paper: $9. Discounts: negotiable. 35-150pp; size varies. Reporting time: 1 month. Payment: negotiable, payment usually books. Copyrights for author.

LA NUEZ, Rafael Bordao, Editor; Celeste Ewers, Associate Editor, PO Box 1655, New York, NY 10276, 212-260-3130. 1988. Poetry, fiction, articles, art, photos, interviews, criticism, reviews, letters, parts-of-novels, plays, news items. "Our magazine is international and *entirely in Spanish*. We do not accept simultaneous submissions, previously published work or work with political themes. SASE and short biographical note are required. Recent contributors: Justo Jorge Padron, Frank Dauster, Clara Janes, Louis Bourne, Kathleen March, Reinaldo Arenas" circ. 1M. 4/yr. Pub'd 4 issues 1990; expects 4 issues 1991, 4 issues 1992. sub. price: $12; per copy: $3; sample: $3.50. Discounts: 40%. 32-40pp; 8½×11; of. Reporting time: 6-8 weeks. Payment: 2 copies. Copyrighted, reverts to author. Pub's reviews: 5 in 1990. §Poetry, fiction, art. Ads: $200/$115/$65 1/4 page/$40 1/8/$25 1/16. COSMEP, CLMP.

LA RAZA LAW JOURNAL, University of California Press, Boalt Hall Students of the Univ. of California, University of California Press, 2120 Berkeley Way, Berkeley, CA 94720. 1983. "Editorial address: 37 Boalt Hall, University of California, Berkeley, CA 94720. Copyrighted by the *La Raza Law Journal*." circ. 250. 1/yr. Pub'd 1 issue 1990; expects 1 issue 1991, 1 issue 1992. sub. price: $15 (+ $3 foreign postage); per copy: same; sample: free. Discounts: foreign subs. agent 10%, one-time orders 10+ 30%, standing orders (bookstores) 1-99 40%, 100+ 50%. of. Ads: $200/$120.

LABEL, Paul Beasley, Editor; Ruth Harrison, 57 Effingham Road, Lee Green, London SE128NT, England, 01-690-9368. 1981. Poetry, fiction, articles, art. "All material welcome up to 250 lines. Among recent contributors: British—Carol A. Burdett, Earle Birney, Jill Daliburd (Canadian), Christopher Cardale; American—William P. Robertson, Arthur Winfield-Knight. Review section begins with issue 5 Spring 1985. Publishes poetry of a social & innovative emphasis: including social/surrealism, postmodern, performance, jazz, dub poetry. Each issue of LABEL features the work of at least one visual artist. eg. #5 John Frankland, #6 Conrad Atkinson (silk screen designs), #8 Mark Fairnington" circ. 600. 2/yr. Pub'd 1 issue 1990; expects 2 issues 1991, 2 issues 1992. sub. price: £3 or $12 cash or IRC equiv. only-no checks; per copy: £1.50 or $6; sample: £1.50 or $6. Back issues: same. Discounts: negotiable; up to 1/3 discount on a number of magazines. 75pp; 8×5; †of, lp, screen print, typset/offset/hand-bound (flat spine). Reporting time: short. Payment: copies. Copyrighted, reverts to author. Pub's reviews. §Poetry collections, anthologies, cultural-political, polemical articles/books. Ads: £30 or $80/£15 or $40. ALP.

Labor Arts Books, Emanuel Fried, 1064 Amherst St., Buffalo, NY 14216, 716-873-4131. 1975. Fiction, plays. "For the moment not seeking submissions. Still working on distribution of present publications: *The Dodo Bird, Drop Hammer, Meshugah and Other Stories, Elegy for Stanley Gurski, Big Ben Hood.*" avg. press run 5M. Expects 1 title 1991. 5 titles listed in the *Small Press Record of Books in Print* (20th Edition, 1991-92). avg. price, paper: $2.50-$9.95. Discounts: write for information. 32-320pp; size varies; lp. Payment: individual arrangement. Copyrights for author. COSMEP.

LACTUCA, Michael Selender, PO Box 621, Suffern, NY 10901. 1986. Poetry, fiction, art, reviews, parts-of-novels, long-poems. "Our bias is toward work with a strong sense of place or experience. Writing with an honest emotional depth and writing that is dark or disturbing are preferred over safer material. Work with a quiet dignity is also desired. Subject matter is wide open and work can be urban or rural in character. We don't like poems that use the poem, the word or the page as images or writing about being a poet/writer (though work about dead poets/writers is o.k.)." circ. 400. 3/yr. Expects 3 issues 1991, 3 issues 1992. sub. price: $10; per copy: $4; sample: $4. Back issues: $3 each if ordering more than one, $3.50 if ordering only one. Discounts: 40% bookstores, 60% distributors, consignment is fine. 72pp; 8½×7; †laser printed and/or photocopy of. Reporting time: within 3 months, usually less than 6 weeks. Payment: 2-5 copies depending on length of material. Copyrighted, reverts to author. Pub's reviews: 0 in 1990. §Only collections of poetry and fiction also artwork (black and white). CLMP, COSMEP, SPWAO.

LADYSLIPPER CATALOG + RESOURCE GUIDE OF RECORDS, TAPES & VIDEOS BY WOMEN, Ladyslipper, Inc., Laurie Fuchs, PO Box 3124, Durham, NC 27715, 919-683-1570. 1976. Music. "Contains annotated listings of over 1.6M records and tapes by women artists" circ. 200M. 1/yr. Pub'd 1 issue 1990; expects 1 issue 1991, 1 issue 1992. sub. price: free on request; per copy: same; sample: same. Back issues: same. 64pp; 8½×11; web of. Copyrighted.

Ladyslipper, Inc. (see also LADYSLIPPER CATALOG + RESOURCE GUIDE OF RECORDS, TAPES & VIDEOS BY WOMEN), Laurie Fuchs, PO Box 3124, Durham, NC 27715, 919-683-1570.

Lahontan Images, Tim I. Purdy, PO Box 1093, Susanville, CA 96130, 916-257-6747. 1986. Non-fiction. "Primarily interested in the history and related topics of eastern California and Nevada. First title is Eric N. Moody's *Flanigan: Anatomy of a Railroad Ghost Town.*" avg. press run 2M. Expects 2 titles 1991, 4 titles 1992. 5 titles listed in the *Small Press Record of Books in Print* (20th Edition, 1991-92). avg. price, paper: $10. Discounts: 5 or more 40%. 150pp; 6×9; of. Reporting time: 1 month. Payment: percentage of sales. Copyrights for author.

LAKE EFFECT, Jean O'Connor Fuller, Managing Editor; Mary Kilmer, Fiction; Joan Hondros-Kolp, Fiction; C.S. Muth, Poetry; Joan Loveridge-Sanbonmatsu, Poetry, Lake County Writers Group, PO Box 59, Oswego, NY 13126, 315-342-3579. 1985. Poetry, fiction, articles, art, photos, cartoons, satire, reviews, music, parts-of-novels, non-fiction. "Nonfiction should be queried and of regional interest. We use humor, essay, music, as well. All submissions must be unpublished. We acquire first serial rights. We use black and white art and photography. Do not send us simultaneous submissions unless you tell us up front." circ. 9M. 4/yr. Pub'd 4 issues 1990; expects 4 issues 1991, 4 issues 1992. sub. price: $7; per copy: $2; sample: $2. 24-28pp; tabloid; web, of. Reporting time: 2 months. Payment: $5 poems, $25 short stories, $10 art, $25 reviews, $20-25 illustration (assigned). Copyrighted, reverts to author. Pub's reviews: 15 in 1990. Ads: $250/$150/3 X 5-18 $40. CLMP.

LAKE SUPERIOR MAGAZINE, Paul L. Hayden, Lake Superior Port Cities, Inc., PO Box 16417, Duluth, MN 55816-0417, 218-722-5002. 1979. Fiction, articles, photos, cartoons, letters, news items, non-fiction. "We are a high-quality, glossy consumer magazine. We prefer manuscripts, but well-researched queries are attended to. We actively seek queries from writers in Lake Superior communities. Provide enough information on why the subject is important to the region and our readers, or why and how something is unique. We want details. The writer must have a thorough knowledge of the subject and how it relates to our region. We prefer a fresh, unused approach to the subject which provides the reader with an emotional involvement. Average 800-1,500 words, graphics/photos important" circ. 17M. 7/yr. Pub'd 7 issues 1990; expects 7 issues 1991, 7 issues 1992. 2 titles listed in the *Small Press Record of Books in Print* (20th Edition, 1991-92). sub. price: $21; per copy: $3.95; sample: $4.95. Back issues: Volume 1 (except #3)-$10; all other $5. 80pp; 8⅛×11; of/lo. Reporting time: 3-5 months. Payment: up to $400, pix $20 (B&W), $30 (color). Copyrighted, 1st rights for 90 days after publication. Pub's reviews: 15 in 1990. §Must be regional (Lake Superior) in topics covered. Ads: $150 b&w + $300 4-color/$655.

Lake View Press, Paul Elitzik, Director, PO Box 578279, Chicago, IL 60657, 312-935-2694. 1982. Fiction, non-fiction. "Areas of interest: books on film, and social issues." avg. press run 3M. Expects 3 titles 1991, 6 titles 1992. 8 titles listed in the *Small Press Record of Books in Print* (20th Edition, 1991-92). avg. price, cloth: $25; paper: $10. Discounts: 20% 2-4 copies, 40% 5+ for trade titles. 250pp; 5½×8½. Reporting time: 2 weeks-2 months, send queries first. Payment: varies; percentage of selling price. Copyrights for author.

LAMBDA BOOK REPORT, Jane Troxell, Editor; L. Page Maccubbin, Publisher; Rose Fennell, Managing Editor; Michael Brickey, Assistant Editor, 1625 Connecticut Avenue NW, Washington, DC 20009, 202-462-7924. 1987. Articles, art, photos, cartoons, interviews, criticism, reviews, letters, news items. "Review of contemporary gay & lesbian literature. ISSN 1048-9487" circ. 20M. 6/yr. Pub'd 6 issues 1990; expects 6 issues 1991, 6 issues 1992. sub. price: $15; per copy: $3; sample: $3. Back issues: $4. Discounts: wholesale 40% guaranteed sales. 48pp; 8½×11; of. Reporting time: 6 weeks. Payment: negotiable. Copyrighted, reverts to author. Pub's reviews: 150 in 1990. §Any books of interest to gay men, lesbians, their families and friends. Ads: $800/$450/$1.50 per word. GLPA, Alternative Press Index, COSMEP.

THE LAME MONKEY MANIFESTO, Rev. Dr. Neon Fleshbiscuit, Box 8763, Knoxville, TN 37996-4800, 615-525-8243. Poetry, fiction, articles, photos, cartoons, interviews, satire, criticism, reviews, music, letters, collages, news items, non-fiction. "*The LMM* seeks to expose its readers to alternate viewpoints and ideas, and arouse the individual to reconsider their own beliefs (past topics have included sex roles, drug use, religion). Average material length is 2-3 pages, typed double-spaced or equivalent, but rule is 'economy of words.' Submissions on 3½ disk (Mac or MS-DOS format) are preferred." circ. 5K. 4/yr. Pub'd 4 issues 1990; expects 4 issues 1991, 4 issues 1992. price per copy: $1; sample: $1. Back issues: if by cash, issue requested and random issues up to postage=$ received; if check, $1/issue. Discounts: trade with other publishers on free-free basis. 12pp; 9⅜×12⅞; web. Reporting time: 2 weeks. Payment: none. Copyrighted, reverts to author. Ads: $250/$140/$75 1/4 page/$40 1/8 page/$25 1/16 page.

LANCASTER INDEPENDENT PRESS, Clark Bagel, PO Box 275, Lancaster, PA 17603, 717-394-8019. 1969. Articles, art, photos, cartoons, interviews, satire, criticism, reviews, music, letters, news items, non-fiction. "Member of APS — APS material, community news, national/international news" circ. 2M. 12/yr. Pub'd 12 issues 1990; expects 12 issues 1991, 12 issues 1992. sub. price: $10 (includes donation); per copy: 50¢; sample: free with SASE. Discounts: 25%. 12pp; 11×17; of, web. Reporting time: 1 month. Payment: volunteer work; payment for investigative reporting. Copyrighted, does not revert to author. Pub's reviews: 10 in 1990. §Non-fiction, political, fiction-contemporary progressive. Ads: $150/$85/$1 a line. APS, RECON NETWORK.

Lancer Militaria, Box 886, Mt. Ida, AR 71957, 501-867-2232. 1978. "Specialize in reference type material for military collectors/historians." avg. press run 3M. Pub'd 2 titles 1990; expects 3 titles 1991. 7 titles listed in the *Small Press Record of Books in Print* (20th Edition, 1991-92). avg. price, cloth: $22; paper: $13. Discounts: 40-50% depending on quantity. 112pp; 8½×11. Copyrights for author.

Landon Publications, 1061-C South High Street, Harrisonburg, VA 22801. Pub'd 1 title 1990; expects 2 titles 1991, 2 titles 1992. 1 title listed in the *Small Press Record of Books in Print* (20th Edition, 1991-92). avg. price, paper: $8.95. Discounts: 2-4 copies 20%, 5-24 copies 40%, 25-49 copies 43%, 50-99 copies 46%, 100+ copies 50%. Copyrights for author.

LANDSCAPE, Blair Boyd, Publisher, PO Box 7107, Berkeley, CA 94707, 415-549-3233. 1951. Articles, photos, reviews. "A scholarly journal addressed to cultural geography, architecture, planning, environmental design, landscape architecture." circ. 3M. 3/yr. Pub'd 3 issues 1990; expects 3 issues 1991, 3 issues 1992. sub. price: $22 indiv. US, $42 institutions; per copy: $6.95; sample: $6.95. Back issues: on request. Discounts: on request. 48pp; 8½×11; of. Reporting time: 8-10 weeks. Payment: 2 year subscription. Copyrighted, does not revert to author. Pub's reviews: 6 in 1990. §Geography, architecture, landscape architecture, planning. No ads.

306

THE LANGSTON HUGHES REVIEW, George Houston Bass, Box 1904, Brown University, Providence, RI 02912, 401-863-3137. 1982. Articles, interviews, criticism, reviews, news items. "Re: events on Hughes' work" circ. 275-300. 2/yr. Pub'd 2 issues 1990; expects 2 issues 1991, 2 issues 1992. sub. price: $10 ($14 foreign); per copy: $7. Back issues: $9. 40-60pp; 6×9; of. Reporting time: 6-8 weeks. Payment: none. Copyrighted, does not revert to author, but on request of author rights are assigned. Pub's reviews: 1 in 1990.

Langston Press, Owen Levy, PO Box 1615, Morningside Station, New York, NY 10026, 212-932-1607. 1989. Fiction, art, photos, non-fiction. "We are a startup business and as such our initial titles are social diaries and planners. In 1992 we will publish our first trade titles." avg. press run 5M-10M. Expects 1 title 1991, 3 titles 1992. 1 title listed in the *Small Press Record of Books in Print* (20th Edition, 1991-92). avg. price, cloth: $18.95. Discounts: bookstores 50% returnable; others (stationary, etc.) 30-45% non-returnable. 96pp; 7½×9¼. Reporting time: 6 weeks to 3 months. Payment: on a per contract basis. Copyrights for author.

LANGUAGE ARTS JOURNAL OF MICHIGAN, Robert Root, John Dinan, Department of English, Central Michigan University, Mt. Pleasant, MI 48859. 1985. Articles, interviews, criticism, reviews. "Articles which discuss issues, theory, theory-based practice, and research in teaching and learning language arts, kindergarten through college. Manuscripts should be 6-15 pages, double-spaced, using new MLA style for parenthetical documentation and NCTE guidelines on non-sexist use of language. Send three copies and SASE return envelope. Special focus issues published in Fall, general issues published in Spring. Subscription address: MCTE, PO Box 892, Rochester, MI 48307. Publishes 8-9 articles per issue." circ. 600-700. 2/yr. Pub'd 2 issues 1990; expects 2 issues 1991, 2 issues 1992. sub. price: $15. 70-80pp; 5½×8. Payment: 2 copies of issue in which article appears. Copyrighted, reverts to author.

LANGUAGE INTERNATIONAL: THE MAGAZINE FOR THE LANGUAGE PROFESSIONS, Geoffrey Kingscott, Praetorius Limited, 5 East Circus Street, Nottingham NG1 5AH, England, 0602-411087. 1989. Articles, photos, interviews, reviews, non-fiction. "International topical news magazine for the translation and language teaching professions. Additional address: John Benjamins B.V., Publisher & Bookseller, Amsteldijk 44, PO Box 52519, 1007 HA Amsterdam, Holland." circ. 2M. 6/yr. Pub'd 6 issues 1990; expects 6 issues 1991, 6 issues 1992. sub. price: $90 (private $57); per copy: $15; sample: free. Back issues: $7.50. 48pp; 21×27.9cm; of. Reporting time: 4 weeks. Copyrighted, does not revert to author. Pub's reviews: 32 in 1990. §Bilingual & multilingual dictionaries, books on translation, linguistics. Ads: $700/$400/$15 per line. KNUB (Dutch Publ. Assn.).

Laocoon Books (see also CATALYST), M Kettner, K Kettner, PO Box 20518, Seattle, WA 98102, 206-323-7268. 1980. Poetry, fiction, art, photos, collages, plays, non-fiction. "We are not seeking manuscripts currently. Writers and visual artists are encouraged to refer to *Catalyst.*" avg. press run 300. Pub'd 1 title 1990; expects 2 titles 1991, 2 titles 1992. avg. price, paper: $2; other: $4. Discounts: 40% to retailers, 50% to distributors. 20pp; size varies; of. Reporting time: 4-10 weeks.

Kent P. Larsen, Inc., 30252 Pacific Island Drive #198, Laguna Niguel, CA 92677, 714-661-8865. 1989. Non-fiction. avg. press run 3M. Expects 1 title 1991, 2 titles 1992. avg. price, paper: $14.95. Discounts: trade 35% 1-2 books, 40% 3+; wholesalers 45% 1-2 books, 50% 3+. 144pp; 8½×11. Reporting time: 2 months. Payment: varies. Copyrights for author.

THE LAS VEGAS INSIDER, Donald Currier, Good 'n' Lucky, PO Box 1185, Chino Valley, AZ 86323-1185. 1974. Articles, criticism, reviews, news items. circ. 5.1M. 12/yr. Pub'd 12 issues 1990; expects 12 issues 1991. sub. price: $36; sample: $3. Back issues: $42 per 12 issues (any) 52. 4pp; 8×11; of. Reporting time: 1 week. Payment: yes. Copyrighted, reverts to author. Ads: $150/$75/70¢.

Last Generation/Underground Editions (see also NOTES FROM THE UNDERGROUND), Mark DuCharme, 2965 13th Street, Boulder, CO 80304, 303-938-9346. 1990. Poetry, art, criticism, long-poems, collages, plays, concrete art. "last generation is an extension of the publishing activities that began with *Notes From the Underground* (a.k.a. *Break to Open*). The premise is to publish work (primarily collections of poems or longpoems, though we would consider other projects) in booklet form. For now all last generation publications are photocopied and stapled in editions of 200. Title(s) published to date: *Life Could Be a Dream,* poems by Mark DuCharme. Forthcoming title(s): *The Dances of Invention,* poems by Vince Kueter. Neither the resources nor the editorial inclination exist to publish a large roster of titles, but room will be made for the occasional unsolicited manuscript that truly excites or terrifies us. Enclose SASE with correct postage, a short "statement" and brief bio. Also include publication history, if any, of the works being submitted. Limit is roughly 100 pp. double spaced (50 pp. single spaced). Authors are encouraged to query before sending complete manuscripts." avg. press run 200. Pub'd 1 title 1990; expects 1 title 1991. 1 title listed in the *Small Press Record of Books in Print* (20th Edition, 1991-92). avg. price, paper: $2.50 in US dollars (free to reviewers), all checks payable to Mark DuCharme. Discounts: 20%-40% to bookstores and distributors. 50-70pp; 8½×11; †mi. Reporting time: 6-9 months. Payment: 2 copies (more upon request); author will receive 50% of whatever profit is earned after production and distribution costs are recouped. Copyrights for author.

307

LATEST JOKES NEWSLETTER, Robert Makinson, PO Box 023304, Brooklyn, NY 11202-0066, 718-855-5057. 1974. Satire. circ. 200. 12/yr. Pub'd 6 issues 1990; expects 12 issues 1991, 12 issues 1992. sub. price: $18; per copy: $3; sample: $2. Back issues: $2. 2pp; 8½×11; of. Reporting time: 2 weeks. Payment: $1-$3 ($1 outright purchase, plus $2 extra if it reappears in publication that pays me). Copyrighted, reverts to author. Pub's reviews. §Humor, brief comments. Ads: classified, $1/word.

THE LATEST NEWS, Jennifer A. Payne, 501 Durham Road, Madison, CT 06443. 1989. Poetry, articles, photos, cartoons, interviews, satire, reviews, letters. *"TLN* is a personal publication produced quarterly for friends, family and a growing list of national readers. It's pretty simple in nature, with travel articles, stories, letters from readers and pictures." circ. 100. 4/yr. Pub'd 4 issues 1990; expects 4 issues 1991, 4 issues 1992. price per copy: $1; sample: $1. Back issues: $1. 4pp; 8½×11; †mi. Reporting time: 1 month. Payment: none. Not copyrighted. Pub's reviews: 2 in 1990. §Homes, personal, literature. Ads: none.

Latham Foundation (see also THE LATHAM LETTER), Latham Plaza, 1826 Clement Avenue, Alameda, CA 94501-1397, 415-521-0920.

THE LATHAM LETTER, Latham Foundation, Madeleine C. Pitts, Latham Foundation, Latham Plaza, 1826 Clement Avenue, Alameda, CA 94501-1397, 415-521-0920. 1918. Poetry, articles, cartoons, interviews, reviews, letters, non-fiction. circ. 4M. 4/yr. Pub'd 4 issues 1990; expects 4 issues 1991, 4 issues 1992. sub. price: $10; per copy: $1.50. Back issues: special rates. Discounts: contact Latham Foundation. 24pp; 8½×10; of. Reporting time: 30 days next issue-if appropriate as to time frame. Copyrighted, rights revert, but authorization to republish is rarely withheld. Pub's reviews: 14 in 1990. §Human/companion animal bond, pet-facilitated therapy, humane welfare, child protection, utilization of older executives in second careers, promotion of respect for all life through education.

LATIN AMERICAN LITERARY REVIEW, Latin American Literary Review Press, Yvette E. Miller, 2300 Palmer Street, Pittsburgh, PA 15218, 412-351-1477. 1972. Poetry, fiction, articles, photos, interviews, criticism, reviews, music, parts-of-novels, long-poems, plays, non-fiction. "Length of article varies from 10-40 pages in special issues. Some recent contributors: Roberto Gonzales Echevarria, Jose J. Arrom, Guillermo Cabrera Infante, John Updike, Alistair Reid, Robert Coles, Jorge de Sena, Harold de Campos, Joaquin de Sousa Andrade et al" circ. 1M. 2/yr. Pub'd 2 issues 1990; expects 2 issues 1991, 2 issues 1992. sub. price: $32; per copy: $16; sample: $16. Back issues: $16. Discounts: negotiable. 150pp; 6×9; of. Reporting time: within 12 weeks. Payment: on special issues. Not copyrighted. Pub's reviews: 17 in 1990. §Recent Latin American Fiction, poetry, and theatre. Ads: $200/$120/$80 1/4 page. CCLM.

Latin American Literary Review Press (see also LATIN AMERICAN LITERARY REVIEW), Yvette E. Miller, 2300 Palmer Street, Pittsburgh, PA 15218, 412-351-1477. 1977. Poetry, fiction, photos, criticism, plays, non-fiction. "Books of poetry published in bi-lingual format, (i.e., Spanish/English). Publication is not limited to Spanish or English" avg. press run 1.5M. Pub'd 8 titles 1990; expects 10 titles 1991, 10 titles 1992. 41 titles listed in the *Small Press Record of Books in Print* (20th Edition, 1991-92). avg. price, cloth: $25; paper: $12; other: $10. Discounts: negotiable. 160pp; 5½×8½. Reporting time: within 12 weeks. Payment: 10%. Copyrights for author. CCLM.

LATIN AMERICAN PERSPECTIVES, Ronald H. Chilcote, Managing Editor, PO Box 5703, Riverside, CA 92517-5703, 714-787-5508. 1974. Articles, art, photos, interviews, reviews. "Obtain subscriptions through: Sage Publications, 2111 West Hillcrest Drive, Newbury Park, CA 91320." circ. 2M. 4/yr. Pub'd 4 issues 1990; expects 4 issues 1991, 4 issues 1992. sub. price: $35; per copy: $11; sample: $10. Back issues: single issues $10, double issues $11. Discounts: 20%, 10 or more copies; 20% classroom & university bookstores. 128pp; 5×8; of. Reporting time: 6-9 months. Payment: none. Copyrighted. Pub's reviews: 5 in 1990. §Latin America, radical theory, political economy. Ads: $225/$150.

Latin American Press, Dale Seppa, Carmen Arroyo, 103 Sixth Avenue North, Virginia, MN 55792. 1985. Non-fiction. "Soft cover pocket size books about coins, medals, tokens and paper money of Latin America and other areas" avg. press run 1M. 3 titles listed in the *Small Press Record of Books in Print* (20th Edition, 1991-92). avg. price, cloth: $25; paper: $10. Discounts: trade. 50-150+pp; 4½×7, 5½×8½, 6×9; of. Reporting time: 3-5 weeks. Payment: 10% of actual sales. Copyrights for author.

The Latona Press (see also BELOIT POETRY JOURNAL), Marion K. Stocking, RFD 2, Box 154, Ellsworth, ME 04605. 1978. Non-fiction. "We are not looking for further manuscripts at the present time." avg. press run 1.5M. Pub'd 1 title 1990. 1 title listed in the *Small Press Record of Books in Print* (20th Edition, 1991-92). avg. price, cloth: $25; paper: $12.95. Discounts: To bookstores and wholesalers: 1-4 copies 20%, 5 or more 40%. Postage and shipping extra. No discount on orders not paid for in 30 days. 200pp; 6×9; of. Payment: royalties. Copyrights for author.

LAUGHING BEAR NEWSLETTER, Laughing Bear Press, Tom Person, Editor, PO Box 36159, Bear Valley Station, Denver, CO 80236, 303-989-5614. 1976. Articles, letters, news items. "Uses short articles (approximately 400 words) on small press publishing; news releases; letters concerning small press issues. *LBN* is for small press writers and publishers. The emphasis is on limited budget literary publishing: how to use design and strategies to reach readers, rather than the 80's approach of throwing money at the challenge." circ. 150. 12/yr. Pub'd 12 issues 1990; expects 12 issues 1991, 12 issues 1992. sub. price: $8; per copy: $1; sample: free with SASE. Back issues: $2. Discounts: write for rates. 3pp; 8½×11; photocopy. Reporting time: 1 month. Payment: 1 year subscription for articles. Copyrighted, reverts to author. Pub's reviews: 30+ in 1990. §Small press publications of all kinds including audio; publishing how-to especially. Ads: insert ads, $30/page not including printing; write for rates. COSMEP.

Laughing Bear Press (see also LAUGHING BEAR NEWSLETTER), Tom Person, Editor, PO Box 36159, Bear Valley Station, Denver, CO 80236, 303-989-5614. 1976. Poetry. "Poetry submissions by invitation only. *Laughing Bear Newsletter* is a monthly publication of small press information. $8/year. Send SASE for sample issue." avg. press run 500. Pub'd 1 title 1990; expects 2 titles 1991, 2 titles 1992. 17 titles listed in the *Small Press Record of Books in Print* (20th Edition, 1991-92). avg. price, paper: $3.00. Discounts: trade 40%. 64pp; 6×9; of. Reporting time: 1 day to 2 months. Payment: percentage of run. Copyrights for author. COSMEP.

Laughing Dog Press, Melane Lohmann, Rayna Holtz, 12509 SW Cove Road, Vashon, WA 98070, (206) 463-3153. 1974. Poetry, art. "*Laughing Dog Press* is a small, letterpress only, "book-arts" press. We handset, print, and handbind fine poetry with graphics on high quality papers." avg. press run 500. Pub'd 1 title 1990. 6 titles listed in the *Small Press Record of Books in Print* (20th Edition, 1991-92). avg. price, cloth: $30; paper: $8. Discounts: 20% for 1-5 books, or consignment; 30% for 5 or more, or to libraries. 15-90pp; 5×9, 5½×9½; †lp. Reporting time: 2 months, but we only select one each year. Payment: books, quantities negotiable. Copyrights for author.

THE LAUGHING MAN: The Alternative to Scientific Materialism and Religious Provincialism, The Dawn Horse Press, Richard Schorske, Editor, PO Box 3680, Clearlake, CA 95422. 1976. Articles, art, photos, interviews, criticism, reviews, letters, non-fiction. circ. 8M. 2/yr. Pub'd 4 issues 1990; expects 2 issues 1991, 2 issues 1992. sub. price: $12.95; per copy: $6.95; sample: $5.00. Back issues: $5.00. Discounts: 40%. 64pp; 8½×11; of. Reporting time: 2 weeks. Payment: sometimes. Copyrighted. Pub's reviews: 8 in 1990. §Spirituality, health, sexuality. Ads: $300/$185/no classified.

Owen Laughlin Publishers, Owen Laughlin, PO Box 6313, Clearwater, FL 34618-6313, 813-797-0404. 1955. Art, cartoons, non-fiction. "Prefer books of not less than 32 pages, or maximum of 128 pages, 8¼ X 11¼. We are especially interested in cookbooks." avg. press run 10M. Expects 2 titles 1991, 2 titles 1992. 1 title listed in the *Small Press Record of Books in Print* (20th Edition, 1991-92). avg. price, paper: $5.00-$10.00. Discounts: 40% bookstores, 60% distributors, 80% mail order houses. 64pp; 8×11; †web. Reporting time: 30 days. Payment: per submission and acceptance, amount varies with title. Copyrights for author.

THE LAUREL REVIEW, Craig Goad, Editor; David Slater, Editor; William Trowbridge, Editor; Randall R. Freisinger, Associate Editor; Jim Simmerman, Associate Editor; Jeanette Lynes, Associate Editor, Department of English, Northwest Missouri State University, Maryville, MO 64468, 816-562-1265. 1960. Poetry, fiction, art, parts-of-novels, long-poems, non-fiction. "We read Sept through May. We have no regional, political, ethnic, or religious bias. We seek well-crafted poems with fresh, vigorous imagery, precise use of language, and an awareness that poetry should be accessible to a wide range of serious readers, not merely to the poet and his/her immediate family. We would be delighted to find poems capable of making a reader laugh; we do not especially want poems that seek to persuade a reader of much of anything. Good poems are more important to us than are impressive reputations. Recent contributors: David Citino, Collette Inez, Walter McDonald, Marcia Southwick, Carol Bly, Jim Barnes, Henry Carlile, Albert Goldbarth, Richard Jackson, Pattiann Rogers, George Starbuck." circ. 750. 2/yr. Pub'd 2 issues 1990; expects 2 issues 1991, 2 issues 1992. sub. price: $8; per copy: $5; sample: $3.50. Back issues: $3.50. Discounts: 40%. 128pp; 6×9; of. Reporting time: 1 week to 4 months. Payment: 2 copies, plus one free one-year subscription. Copyrighted, reverts to author. Ads: $80/$40. COSMEP, CCLM.

THE LAVENDER NETWORK, Ronald B. Zahn, Publisher; Martha Burdick, Editor, PO Box 5421, Eugene, OR 97405, 503-485-7285. 1986. Poetry, fiction, articles, art, photos, cartoons, letters, news items, non-fiction. "Material exceeding 2,500 words is likely to run in two parts. Submissions should be oriented to Gay or Lesbian community. *TLN* is a progressive feature-oriented newsmagazine and established community resource guide that is published monthly and is designed to meet the needs of gay men and lesbians throughout the state of Oregon and into parts of Washington and Idaho. *TLN* focuses on rural outreach where no other gay and lesbian press is available." circ. 10M. 12/yr. Pub'd 12 issues 1990; expects 12 issues 1991, 12 issues 1992. sub. price: $25; sample: $2. 88-96pp; 7¼×9¾; web press. Reporting time: 60-90 days. Payment: copies only. Copyrighted, rights revert on request. Pub's reviews: 20-30 in 1990. §Must have a gay or lesbian theme. Ads: write for rates. GLPA.

LAW AND CRITIQUE, Deborah Charles Publications, Peter Goodrich, Managing Editor, 173 Mather

Avenue, Liverpool L18 6JZ, United Kingdom. 1990. Non-fiction. 2/yr. Pub'd 2 issues 1990. sub. price: £12 individuals, £35 institutions + postage; per copy: £9 individuals, £18 institutions; sample: £9. Discounts: 10% subscription agents. 112pp; royal 80; Mac DTD. Reporting time: 3 months. Payment: none. Copyrighted, does not revert to author. exchange basis.

Law Forum Press, Don Berry, 2318 Second Avenue, Seattle, WA 98121, 206-622-8240. 1986. Non-fiction. "How-To books for professionals" avg. press run 3M. Pub'd 1 title 1990; expects 3 titles 1991. 3 titles listed in the *Small Press Record of Books in Print* (20th Edition, 1991-92). avg. price, paper: $15. Discounts: 1-0%, 2-10%, 11-50-30%, 51-100-40%, 101+-50%. 50pp; 8½×11; of. Reporting time: 6 weeks. Payment: 6½% gross revenues, quarterly report. Copyrights for author.

Lawco Ltd./Moneytree Publications, James R. Lawson, PO Box 2009, Manteca, CA 95336, 209-239-6006. 1980. Non-fiction. "Interested in material on career strategies—company/career politics for our Moneytree imprint. We are also interested in material for the small business/business at home market, for our business imprint. We also publish business software under the Lawco Ltd. name. Finally, we are interested in how-to books on country/western dancing and pocket billiards." avg. press run varies. Expects 2 titles 1991, 3 titles 1992. 2 titles listed in the *Small Press Record of Books in Print* (20th Edition, 1991-92). avg. price, paper: $20; other: $20-$200. Discounts: up to this point our sales have been strictly by direct mail. 5½×8½; of, lp. Reporting time: 90 days. Payment: negotiable. Copyrights for author. MSPA, COSMEP, PMA.

LEADERSHIP DIRECTIONS, North American Students of Cooperation, Renee Ordeneaux, Box 7715, Ann Arbor, MI 48107, 313-663-0889.

Leadership Education and Development, Inc., Donna Harrison, 1116 West 7th Street, Suite 175, Columbia, TN 38401, 901-794-2985; 615-388-6135. 1987. Non-fiction. "Biases: ethical management. Recent contributor: Fred A. Manske, Jr., CEO of Purolator Courier." avg. press run 5-10M. Pub'd 1 title 1990; expects 1-2 titles 1991, 2-3 titles 1992. 2 titles listed in the *Small Press Record of Books in Print* (20th Edition, 1991-92). avg. price, cloth: $18.95. Discounts: distributors 50%, bookstores 40-45%, quantity retail discounts up to 35%. 200pp; size varies. Reporting time: 2-3 months. Payment: negotiable. Copyright negotiable. Publishers Association of the South, PO Box 4042, Albany, GA 31706.

LEAGUE SENTINAL, Venture Press, John Harrison, 54 Hindes Road, Harrow, Middlesex HA1 1SL, England. 6/yr. Pub'd 6 issues 1990; expects 6 issues 1991, 6 issues 1992. 8pp; size A4.

Leaping Mountain Press, James Grabill, John Bradley, PO Box 14663, Portland, OR 97214. 1985. Poetry. "Presently we publish short books 28-32 pages in length and aesthetically encourage associative imagery, grounded surrealism, leaping, the deep image, impure poetry, duende, and other modes of the emotive imagination. We publish quality chapbooks using fine materials and hope to distribute through networks like this directory. Write for the list of what is available. We are not reading for at least a year." avg. press run 300. Pub'd 1 title 1990; expects 1 title 1991, 1 title 1992. 15 titles listed in the *Small Press Record of Books in Print* (20th Edition, 1991-92). avg. price, paper: $3 plus postage. 32pp; 5½×8½. Copyrights for author.

LECTOR, Floricanto Press, Roberto Cabello-Argandona, Editor-in-chief, 16161 Ventura Blvd., #830, Encino, CA 91436, 818-990-1882. 1982. Articles, photos, interviews, reviews, news items. "*Lector,* the Hispanic Review Journal, is a biannual (twice a year) magazine containing over 100 reviews of Spanish language, bilingual and U.S. Hispanic-related titles. It also contains articles about Hispanic culture, interviews with prominent artists and writers, and a new direction for *Lector,* selected short fiction and poetry by U.S. Hispanic and Latin American writers. Send for writers guidelines. Query. Contributors must be subscribers" circ. 1M. 2/yr. Pub'd 2 issues 1990; expects 2 issues 1991, 2 issues 1992. sub. price: $45; per copy: $25; sample: $6. Back issues: $25. Discounts: Reviewers' discount: 50% off. 64pp; 8½×11; of. Reporting time: 8 weeks. Payment: negotiable to $150. Copyrighted. Pub's reviews: 600 in 1990. §Spanish language, bilingual (English-Spanish), and Hispanic related, and Latin American books. Ads: $225/$150.

Ledero Press, Michael M. Warren, U. T. Box 99, Galveston, TX 77550-2783, 409-761-2091. 1990. "No special requirements. Recent contributor: *Deer Dad* A Hunter's Guide by Michael M. Warren." avg. press run 2-5M. Expects 1 title 1991, 1 title 1992. 1 title listed in the *Small Press Record of Books in Print* (20th Edition, 1991-92). avg. price, cloth: $15-$25; paper: $8-$15. Discounts: 2-5 10%; 5-25 40%; 26-50 43%; 51-100 46%; 100+ 50%. 200pp; 6×9. Reporting time: 4-6 weeks. Payment: negotiable. Copyright if needed.

THE LEDGE POETRY AND PROSE MAGAZINE, Timothy Monaghan, 64-65 Cooper Avenue, Glendale, NY 11385, 718-366-5169. 1988. Poetry, fiction, long-poems, plays. "Up to 3 pages for poetry, up to 6 pages for fiction, up to 5 pages for prose, up to 5 pages for longpoems. Open to all slants. Recent contributors: Les Bridges, Steven Hartman, Elizabeth Hansen, Jackie Maslowski." circ. 400. 2/yr. Pub'd 3 issues 1990; expects 2 issues 1991, 2 issues 1992. sub. price: $12 + $1.50 p/h for 1 volume (6 issues); $6.75 + $1 for 3 issues; per copy: $3; sample: $3.75 ppd. Discounts: 40% for contributing authors. 76pp; 5½×8½; †of. Reporting time: 4-8 weeks. Payment: copies of the issue. Copyrighted, reverts to author. Ads: $50/$25/$15 1/4 page.

310

Rikki Leeson (see also REVIEWS UNLIMITED; TALES OF THE DESIGNERREAL UNIVERSE; COSMIC KALUDO), PO Box 581, Seattle, WA 98111. 1988. Poetry, fiction, art, cartoons, reviews, non-fiction. "Write for guidelines before making submissions" avg. press run 100-150. Pub'd 3 titles 1990; expects 3 titles 1991, 3 titles 1992. avg. price, paper: $2. Discounts: inquire. 24-36pp; size varies; photo-copy, of. Reporting time: 2 weeks. Payment: token fees are sometimes made, but cannot be guaranteed. Authors retain copyrights.

Leete's Island Books, Peter Neill, Box 3131, Branford, CT 06405-1731, 203-481-2536. 1977. "Fiction, essays, interesting reprints; for the moment, because of time, no unsolicited manuscripts accepted" avg. press run 2.5M. Pub'd 2 titles 1990; expects 3 titles 1991, 4 titles 1992. 18 titles listed in the *Small Press Record of Books in Print* (20th Edition, 1991-92). avg. price, cloth: $12.95; paper: $7.95. Discounts: 40%, distributed by: Independent Publishers Group, Chicago Review Press, 814 N. Franklin, 2nd FL., Chicago, Illinois 60610, 312-337-0747. 250pp; 5½x8½; of. Payment: varies with title. Copyrights for author.

Left Bank Books, David Brown, Sue Letsinger, Deb Halsted, Box B, 92 Pike Street, Seattle, WA 98101, 206-522-8864. 1980. Fiction, non-fiction. "Primarily books of social/political relevance. Recent authors published include Raoul Vaneigem's *Revolution of Everyday Life*; Fredy Perlman's *Anti-Semitism & The Beirut Program*; O. MacDonald's (editor) *Polish August: Dcuments of the Worker's Rebellion*. Also, pamphlets, posters, postcards, and buttons. In conjunction with our publishing, we distribute over 100 titles from 30 other presses, many imported—anarchist, feminist, socialist. Not accepting submissions at this date" avg. press run 1M. Pub'd 3 titles 1990; expects 3 titles 1991, 4 titles 1992. 6 titles listed in the *Small Press Record of Books in Print* (20th Edition, 1991-92). avg. price, paper: $6.95; other: Calendar $4, Posters $3. Discounts: 40% trade; 20% University/College bookstores; 10% libraries. 350pp; 5½x8; of/lo. Payment: 10% of retail price or 10% of print run.

LEFT BUSINESS OBSERVER, Doug Henwood, 250 West 85 Street, New York, NY 10024. 1986. Articles, interviews, reviews, letters, news items, non-fiction. "Pieces range from 100-3,000 words. Most written by editor, but occasional outside contributions" circ. 2.5M. 11/yr. Pub'd 11 issues 1990; expects 11 issues 1991, 11 issues 1992. sub. price: $20 indiv., $50 instit.; per copy: $2; sample: $2. Back issues: 4/$7.50, complete set $1 per issue. Discounts: classroom up to 50%, bookstores 40%. 8pp; 8½x11; of. Reporting time: 1 week. Payment: varies, up to 10¢/word. Copyrighted, does not revert to author. Pub's reviews: 2 in 1990. §Economics, politics, feminism, social sciences. Ads: none.

LEFT CURVE, Csaba Polony, Editor; Jack Hirschman, P.J. Laska, Susan Schwartzenberg, Georg Pinter, Luis Talamantez, PO Box 472, Oakland, CA 94604. 1974. Poetry, fiction, articles, art, photos, cartoons, interviews, criticism, reviews, music, letters, long-poems, collages, concrete art. "*Left Curve* is an artist produced journal addressing the crises of modernity from an integrative social-historical context by publishing original visual and verbal art, as well as critical articles." circ. 1.2M. Irregular. Pub'd 2 issues 1990. sub. price: $18 indiv, $30 instit (3 issues); per copy: $7; sample: $7. Back issues: $5. Discounts: 30% trade. 112pp; 8½x11; of. Reporting time: max. 3 months. Payment: 5 copies. Copyrighted. Pub's reviews: 2 in 1990. §Contemporary art, poetry, cultural politics, literature, cultural. Ads: $200/$125.

Left Field Press (see also ACM (ANOTHER CHICAGO MAGAZINE)), Barry Silesky, 3709 North Kenmore, Chicago, IL 60613, 312-248-7665.

THE LEFT INDEX, Joan Nordquist, 511 Lincoln Street, Santa Cruz, CA 95060, 408-426-4479. 1982. "*The Left Index* is a quarterly author/subject index to the contents of articles in journals of a left perspective." 4/yr. Pub'd 4 issues 1990; expects 4 issues 1991, 4 issues 1992. sub. price: $60 institution, $30 individual; per copy: $15 institution; $10 individual; sample: same. Back issues: $60/volume; $15 each issue. 75pp; 7x8½; of. Copyrighted.

LEFTHANDER MAGAZINE, Suzan Ireland, Managing Editor, Lefthanders International, PO Box 8249, Topeka, KS 66608, (913) 234-2177. 1975. Articles, cartoons, interviews, reviews, news items, non-fiction. circ. 26M. 6/yr. Pub'd 6 issues 1990; expects 6 issues 1991, 6 issues 1992. sub. price: $15; per copy: $2; sample: same. Back issues: $3.50. Discounts: none. 32pp; 8¼x10¾; of. Reporting time: 3 weeks to 2 months. Payment: varying, payment on publication. Copyrighted, does not revert to author. Pub's reviews: 4 in 1990. §Anything dealing with handedness, brain dominance, teaching to the right brain. Ads: $1,200/$775.

LEGACIES IN TIME, Proving Grounds International, Inc., Carolyn A. Okerchiri, PO Box 1074, Jackson, MI 49204, 517-782-1075. 1989. Poetry, articles, art, photos, interviews, criticism, reviews, letters, news items. "Byline given. 4,000 words maximum, typewritten or letter-quality printed materials are only ones accepted. No returns without SASE. Photocopied submissions okay." circ. 600. 4/yr. Pub'd 4 issues 1990; expects 4 issues 1991, 4 issues 1992. sub. price: $18; per copy: $5; sample: $2.50. Back issues: $3. Discounts: bulk, classroom. 26pp; 8½x11; lp. Reporting time: 6-8 weeks. Payment: on publication. Copyrighted, reverts to author. Pub's reviews. §History, current African affairs, African history, general philosophy, culture.

LEGACY: A JOURNAL OF AMERICAN WOMEN WRITERS, Martha Ackmann, Karen Dandurand, Joanne Dobson, Univ. of Massachusetts, Dept. of English, Bartlett Hall, Amherst, MA 01003, 413-545-4270. 1984. Criticism, reviews. "Critical articles in biography, bibliography, pedagogy related to 17th, 18th, 19th and early 20th-century American women writers." circ. 500. 2/yr. Pub'd 2 issues 1990; expects 2 issues 1991, 2 issues 1992. sub. price: $15; per copy: $9; sample: same. Back issues: varies. 80pp; 7×10; of. Reporting time: 12-16 weeks. Payment: none. Copyrighted, does not revert to author. Pub's reviews: 10 in 1990. §17th, 18th, 19th and early 20th-century American women writers. Ads: $130/$70/$35 1/4 page. CELJ.

Legacy Books (formerly Folklore Associates) (see also COME-ALL-YE), Richard K. Burns, Lillian Krelove, PO Box 494, Hatboro, PA 19040, 215-675-6762. 1970. "We import (England, Australia, Wales, etc.) a number of book and pamphlet materials in the areas of ethnic music, folklore, social history and serve as U.S. distributor. We do not encourage unsolicited submissions." avg. press run 4.5M. Expects 2 titles 1991, 4 titles 1992. 26 titles listed in the *Small Press Record of Books in Print* (20th Edition, 1991-92). avg. price, cloth: $9.95; paper: $3. Discounts: standard. 205pp; 6×9; lp. Reporting time: 4 months. Payment: 10% on actual (adjusted for discounts) gross income. COSMEP/ABA.

LEGAL INFORMATION MANAGEMENT INDEX, Elyse H. Fox, Legal Information Services, P.O. Box 67, Newton Highlands, MA 02161-0067, 508-443-4798. 1984. Articles, reviews. "Indexes articles, and reviews appearing in periodicals relating to legal information management and law librarianship. Payments must be made in U.S. funds" 7/yr. Pub'd 7 issues 1990; expects 7 issues 1991, 7 issues 1992. sub. price: $108 U.S., Canada & Mexico, $130 others (air mail); sample: free on request. Back issues: $75 annual cumulation. 32pp; 8½×11; of. Copyrighted.

Leisure Press (see also Human Kinetics Pub. Inc.), Rainer Martens, President; Brian Holding, Imprint Director, PO Box 5076, Champaign, IL 61820. Non-fiction. avg. press run 5M. Pub'd 12 titles 1990; expects 44 titles 1991, 44 titles 1992. 138 titles listed in the *Small Press Record of Books in Print* (20th Edition, 1991-92). avg. price, cloth: $19.50; paper: $12.75. Discounts: text 1-4 10%, 5+ 20%; trade 1-4 20%, 5-9 40%, 10-24 42%, 25-49 43%, 50-99 44%, 100-249 45%, 250-499 46%, 500+ 47%. 250pp; 6×9, 8½×11; of. Reporting time: 1-2 months. Payment: 7%-18%. Copyrights for author. Society of Scholarly Publishers.

Hal Leonard Books, Glenda Herro, PO Box 13819, 8112 W. Bluemound Road, Milwaukee, WI 53213, 414-774-3630. 1947. Music. avg. press run 10M. Pub'd 10 titles 1990; expects 10 titles 1991, 15 titles 1992. avg. price, cloth: $17.95; paper: $5.95. Discounts: 40% retail, 50% wholesale. 128pp; 8½×11; †of. Reporting time: 4-6 weeks. Payment: 7½% paperback, 10% hardcover, advance negotiable. Copyrights for author.

LESBIAN CONTRADICTION-A Journal of Irreverent Feminism, Jan Adams, Rebecca Gordon, Betty Johanna, 584 Castro Street, Suite 263, San Francisco, CA 94114. 1982. Articles, art, photos, cartoons, interviews, satire, criticism, reviews, non-fiction. "Because *LESCON* seeks to be a conversation among women, we ask that men not request subscriptions or make submissions. Contributors guidelines on request - SASE appreciated." circ. 2M. 4/yr. Pub'd 4 issues 1990; expects 4 issues 1991, 4 issues 1992. sub. price: $6; per copy: $1.50; sample: $1.50. Back issues: $1.50. Discounts: bookstore price 90¢/copy. 20pp; 11×17; web press newsprint. Reporting time: ca. 2 months. Payment: none. Pub's reviews: 8 in 1990. §Anything of interest to women, or feminists, and lesbians. No ads.

The Philip Lesly Company, Philip Lesly, 155 Harbor Drive, Suite 2201, Chicago, IL 60601. 1986. Non-fiction. "Book length; no mysticism, no leftist views. Recent book: *Bonanzas and Fool's Gold*, by Philip Lesly" avg. press run 4M. Expects 2 titles 1991, 2 titles 1992. 1 title listed in the *Small Press Record of Books in Print* (20th Edition, 1991-92). avg. price, paper: $9.95. Discounts: trade 45%; wholesaler 50%. 200pp; 6×9; of. Reporting time: 2 weeks. Payment: 10%, 12 1/2%, and 15% of net. Copyrights for author.

Let's Go Travel Publications, Keith Evans, Theresa M. Evans, Assistant Editor, 135 W. Nuevo, Suite-B, Perris, CA 92370, 714-943-4459. 1988. Non-fiction. "Recent contributor: Tommy B. Chase" avg. press run 6M. Expects 3 titles 1991, 3 titles 1992. 2 titles listed in the *Small Press Record of Books in Print* (20th Edition, 1991-92). avg. price, cloth: $11; paper: $9.50. 160pp; 5½×8½. Reporting time: 30-60 days. Payment: buys books outright, royalty between 6½% and 10%. Copyrights for author. COSMEP, American Writer's Guild.

THE LETTER EXCHANGE, Stephen Sikora, Editor, The Readers' League, PO Box 6218, Albany, CA 94706, 415-526-7412. 1982. Articles, cartoons, criticism, reviews, letters. "Very short contributions of any material about letter-writing." circ. 3M. 3/yr. Pub'd 3 issues 1990; expects 3-4 issues 1991, 4 issues 1992. sub. price: $18; per copy: $8 postage included; sample: $8. Back issues: $4.50. Discounts: none. 36pp; 5¼×8¼; of. Reporting time: 1 week. Payment: none. Copyrighted, reverts to author. Pub's reviews: 2 in 1990. §Letter-writing only. Ads: listings for correspondence cost 50¢ per word, commercial ads 70¢ per word, display $15 per col. inch (2" wide).

THE LETTER PARADE, Bonnie Jo, PO Box 52, Comstock, MI 49041, 349-8817. 1985. Poetry, fiction, articles, art, photos, cartoons, interviews, satire, criticism, letters, collages, news items, non-fiction. "Humor!"

circ. 100 or so. 12/yr. Pub'd 12 issues 1990; expects 12 issues 1991, 12 issues 1992. sub. price: $10; per copy: $1; sample: $1. Back issues: $1. 6pp; 8½×14; †xerox. Reporting time: monthly. Payment: free subscriptions. Not copyrighted. Pub's reviews. §President Nixon, popular culture, mathematics, Eastern Europe. Ads: all negotiable.

Levite of Apache, Molly Levite Griffis, 1005 N. Flood, #105, Norman, OK 73069, 405-366-6442. 1987. Fiction, art, photos, non-fiction. "Levite's is now specializing in children's books. Our original 8 titles were regional history with the exception of *Remarkable Ride of the Abernathy Boys*, which was a children's book and our best seller. We've sold over 30,000 of our 9 titles in 3 years!" avg. press run 1M. Pub'd 2 titles 1990; expects 2 titles 1991, 2 titles 1992. 10 titles listed in the *Small Press Record of Books in Print* (20th Edition, 1991-92). avg. price, cloth: $15; paper: $5. Discounts: 40% for more than 25 copies. 70-200pp; 5½×8; of. Reporting time: 1-2 months. Payment: 10%. Copyrights for author.

Lexikos, Mike Witter, PO Box 296, Lagunitas, CA 94938, 415-488-0401. 1980. Non-fiction. "Last year *Lexikos* combined with Don't Call it Frisco Press. We will continue to publish under both imprints and pursue much the same editorial policies as before." avg. press run 7M. Pub'd 6 titles 1990; expects 4 titles 1991, 4 titles 1992. 34 titles listed in the *Small Press Record of Books in Print* (20th Edition, 1991-92). avg. price, cloth: $24.95; paper: $9.95. Discounts: 50-55% to wholesalers; retail 1-4 20%, 5-9 40%, 10-24 42%, 25-49, 43%; 50+, 45%. 200pp; size varies; of. Reporting time: 1 month or less. Payment: negotiable; innovative publishing programs are being developed. Copyrights for author. NCBPA, COSMEP, ABA.

Leyland Publications (see also Gay Sunshine Press, Inc.), Winston Leyland, PO Box 40397, San Francisco, CA 94140, 415-824-3184. 1984. 8 titles listed in the *Small Press Record of Books in Print* (20th Edition, 1991-92).

LIBERAL DEMOCRAT NEWS, Mike Harskin, Editor, 4 Cowley Street, London SW1P3NB, England, 071222 7999; fax 071222 7904. 1946. Articles, photos, cartoons, interviews, satire, reviews, letters, news items, non-fiction. "Newspaper" circ. 11M. 50/yr. Expects 50 issues 1991. sub. price: £25; per copy: 60p; sample: free. Discounts: 6 for price of 5 on advertisements: 15 percent agency commission on advertisements. Reduction on bulk orders of newspaper. 8pp; 17×11; cold web offset litho. Reporting time: 10 days average. Payment: nil. Not copyrighted. Pub's reviews: 40-50 in 1990. §Political. Ads: £650/£350/25p classified word (min. 20 words).

LIBERATION! Journal of Revolutionary Marxism, WW Publishers, Vince Copeland, 46 West 21 Street, New York, NY 10010, 212-255-0352. 1989. Articles, reviews, non-fiction. "Recent articles: How the US took Panama; Crucial questions in Nicaragua; New phase of struggle in South Africa; National Conflict in Soviet Asia; Communist officers in the U.S. Civil War; Gay Liberation and Marxism; Counterrevolution in Eastern Europe; U.S. division of Korea" circ. 2M. 6/yr. Pub'd 1 issue 1990; expects 6 issues 1991, 6 issues 1992. sub. price: $10; per copy: $2; sample: $2. Back issues: $2. Discounts: 62.5% for orders over 10 (75¢ a copy). 40pp; 8¼×11. Reporting time: 1 month. Payment: none. Not copyrighted. Pub's reviews: 1 in 1990. §Third World, labor, women, gay, history, minorities.

Liberation Publications, Inc. (see also THE ADVOCATE), Robert McQueen, PO Box 4371, Los Angeles, CA 90078-4371, 213-871-1225.

Libertarian Books and the Libertarian Alliance (see also FREE LIFE), Chris R. Tame, Brian Micklethwait, 1 Russell Chambers, The Piazza, Covent Garden, London WC2E 8AA, England, 01-836-6913. 1988. "Political, economical, cultural articles from a libertarian perspective" Expects 2 titles 1991, 5 titles 1992. †of.

THE (LIBERTARIAN) CONNECTION, Erwin S. Strauss, Box 3343, Fairfax, VA 22038, 703-273-3297. 1968. Poetry, fiction, articles, art, photos, cartoons, interviews, satire, criticism, reviews, music, letters, parts-of-novels, long-poems, collages, plays, concrete art, news items, non-fiction. "Each member can contribute one page per issue, which is run unedited. Additional pages run (unedited) for the cost of printing and mailing. Contributors you may have heard of include Bob ('The Abolition of Work') Black, Ace ('Twisted Image') Backwords, Robert ('Illuminatus!') Shea, Gerry ('Neutron Gun') Reith, Mike ('Loompanics') Hoy, Mike ('Factsheet Five') Gunderloy, Pat ('Salon') Hartman, Lev ('Anarchy') Chernyi, R.W. ('Liberty Magazine') Bradford" circ. 100. 8/yr. Pub'd 8 issues 1990; expects 8 issues 1991, 8 issues 1992. sub. price: $20; per copy: $2.50; sample: $2.50. Back issues: $2.50. Discounts: none. 100pp; 5½×8½; of. Payment: none. Copyrighted, reverts to author. Pub's reviews: about 2 dozen in 1990. §Each contributor makes his/her own choices; works of psychology and of evolutionary science have been popular recently. Ads: ads may be submitted by subscribers as their free page, or as paid extra pages (current charge: $7 per extra page).

Libertarian Press, Inc./American Book Distributors, Robert F. Sennholz, Lyn M. Sennholz, PO Box 137, Spring Mills, PA 16875, 814-422-8001. 1952. Non-fiction. "LP publishes books and booklets on free market economics and political science. ABD is more diversified." avg. press run 2.5M-5M. Pub'd 2 titles 1990; expects 2 titles 1991, 4 titles 1992. avg. price, cloth: $20; paper: $8; other: $3 booklets. Discounts: up to 60%, based on quantity, larger discounts available on booklets. 300pp; 5×8; †of. Reporting time: 30 days. Payment: negotiable. Copyrights depending on contract.

Libertarian Publishers, Lloyd Licher, PO Box 6022, San Rafael, CA 94903, 415-472-3294. 1975. 7 titles listed in the *Small Press Record of Books in Print* (20th Edition, 1991-92).

Libertarians for Gay and Lesbian Concerns (LGLC) (see also L.G.L.C. NEWSLETTER), James Hudler, National Coordinator, PO Box 447, Chelsea, MI 48118-0953, 313-475-9792. 1981.

LIBERTY, R.W. Bradford, Karl Hess, Stephen Cox, PO Box 1167, Port Townsend, WA 98368, 206-385-5097. 1987. Poetry, fiction, articles, cartoons, interviews, criticism, reviews, non-fiction. "Good quality writing of interest to political libertarians (ie. people who believe that the role of government should be radically reduced or even eliminated altogether)." circ. 4.5M. 6/yr. Pub'd 6 issues 1990; expects 6 issues 1991, 6 issues 1992. sub. price: $19.50; per copy: $4; sample: same. Back issues: $4 each. Discounts: 40%, minimum draw 5, fully returnable. 72pp; 8½×11; of/lo. Reporting time: 2 week. Payment: negotiable; usually nominal. Copyrighted, reverts to author. Pub's reviews: 10 per issue in 1990. §History, philosophy, current events, public policy, economic theory, political theory, psychology, literature, etc. Ads: $123.75/$72/25¢ + $1 per insertion.

Liberty Bell Press & Publishing Co., Ron Jorgensen, 4700 South 900 East, Suite 3-183, Salt Lake City, UT 84117, 801-943-8573. 1988. Articles, interviews, criticism, non-fiction. "Published *Men In The Shadows* by Jason Roberts in September, 1988." avg. press run 2M. Expects 2 titles 1991, 10 titles 1992. 2 titles listed in the *Small Press Record of Books in Print* (20th Edition, 1991-92). avg. price, paper: $17.95. 155pp; 8½×11; of. Reporting time: 90 days. Payment: to be arranged. Copyrights for author. COSMEP.

Liberty Publishing Company, Inc., Jeffrey B. Little, Publisher, 440 S. Federal Highway #202, Deerfield Beach, FL 33441, 305-360-9000. 1977. Non-fiction. "Nonfiction, horse racing, travel, consumer books, computer software, video." avg. press run 5M-20M. Pub'd 6 titles 1990; expects 7 titles 1991, 6 titles 1992. 36 titles listed in the *Small Press Record of Books in Print* (20th Edition, 1991-92). avg. price, cloth: $16.95; paper: $8.95; other: software $49.95, video $39.95. Discounts: 40% - 5 or more assorted titles. 180pp; 5½×8¼. Reporting time: 3-4 weeks. Payment: 6-12% semi-annual. Copyrights for author. ABA.

LIBIDO: The Journal of Sex and Sensibility, Mariann Beck, Jack Hafferkamp, PO Box 146721, Chicago, IL 60614, 312-281-0805; 312-728-5979. 1988. Poetry, fiction, articles, art, photos, cartoons, interviews, satire, criticism, reviews, letters, parts-of-novels, long-poems, news items, non-fiction. "To paraphrase Oscar Wilde, *Libido* is the literary answer to a horizontal urge. It is a journal of the erotic arts and uses fiction (1,000-3,000 words), wordplay, photography, essays and reviews dealing in sex and sensibility. Very little poetry. Four to five poems per issue." circ. 7M. 4/yr. Pub'd 4 issues 1990; expects 4 issues 1991, 4 issues 1992. sub. price: $26; per copy: $7; sample: $7. Back issues: #1 & #2 $25 each, #3-#5 $15 each. Discounts: contact publisher for group discounts. 72pp; 5½×8; of, sheetfed. Reporting time: 3 months. Payment: $25; poetry $10-$25. Copyrighted, reverts to author. Pub's reviews: 10-12 in 1990. §Any area having to do with sexuality. Ads: $250/$130/$70 1/4 page.

Libra Publishers, Inc. (see also ADOLESCENCE; FAMILY THERAPY), William Kroll, President, 3089C Clairemont Dr., Suite 383, San Diego, CA 92117, 619-581-9449. 1960. Poetry, fiction, articles, art, photos, cartoons, interviews, satire, criticism, reviews, music, letters, parts-of-novels, long-poems, collages, plays, concrete art, news items. "Most interested in books in the behavioral sciences." avg. press run 3M. Pub'd 15 titles 1990; expects 20 titles 1991, 22 titles 1992. 5 titles listed in the *Small Press Record of Books in Print* (20th Edition, 1991-92). avg. price, cloth: $10.95; paper: $4.95. Discounts: 1-4 copies, 33⅓%; 5 or more, 40%. 160pp; 5½×8½; of. Reporting time: 4 weeks. Payment: 10% of retail price. Copyrights for author.

Librairie Droz S.A. (see also BIBLIOTHEQUE D'HUMANISME ET RENAISSANCE), A. Dufour, 11r.Massot, 1211 Geneve 12, Switzerland. 1934. Articles, criticism, reviews. "History of the 16th century" Pub'd 3 titles 1990; expects 3 titles 1991. avg. price, paper: 80 sw.fr. ($60) yr. 16×24; typography.

LIBRARY CURRENTS, Nancy Taylor, Practical Perspectives, Inc., PO Box 4518, Austin, TX 78765-1349, 512-346-1426. 1984. Reviews. circ. 800+. 12/yr. Pub'd 12 issues 1990; expects 12 issues 1991, 12 issues 1992. sub. price: $40 US, $46 Canada, $55 other foreign; per copy: $4; sample: free. Back issues: $5. Discounts: none. 8pp; 8½×11; †of. Reporting time: varies. Payment: yes. Copyrighted. Pub's reviews: 12 in 1990. §Librarianship, management, personnel information technology. No ads.

THE LIBRARY IMAGINATION PAPER!, Carol Bryan Imagines, Carol Bryan, 1000 Byus Drive, Charleston, WV 25311, 304-345-2378. 1979. Articles, art, photos, cartoons, interviews, satire, reviews, concrete art, news items. "Consistently wins awards for creativity of graphics. Each issue features high-quality, reproducible art, copy and ideas for all types of library programs and promotions. Also included are in-depth articles on Library PR subjects written by field experts. Issues contain an abundance of tried and tested tips for practical librarians, and adventurous ideas for brave librarians. Valuable source listings for obtaining related help and materials are also featured. One issue featured 14 ready-to-go library activity sketches; another had 18 ready-to-go bookmarks." circ. 2M. 4/yr. Expects 4 issues 1991. sub. price: $20; per copy: $5; sample: $1. Back issues: $5 per back issue. Discounts: Baker's Dozen Special of 13 subscriptions for the price of 12 when bulk mailed to a single address. 4pp; 11×17; of. Reporting time: depends. Payment: usually a free subscription. Copyrighted, reverts to author.

LIBRARY OUTREACH REPORTER, Library Outreach Reporter Publications, Allan M. Kleiman, Editor-in-Chief, 1671 East 16th Street, Suite 226, Brooklyn, NY 11229, 718-645-2396. 1987. Articles, photos, interviews, reviews, letters, news items, non-fiction. circ. 1M. 4/yr. Pub'd 5 issues 1990; expects 4 issues 1991, 4 issues 1992. sub. price: $18; per copy: $5; sample: free. Back issues: $4. Discounts: agent/jobber 15% commission. 24pp; 8½×11; of. Reporting time: 1 month. Payment: copies of issue in lieu of payment. Copyrighted, does not revert to author. Pub's reviews: 12 in 1990. §Aging, disabilities, jail/prison service, multicultural resources. Ads: $175/$125/other available on request.

Library Outreach Reporter Publications (see also LIBRARY OUTREACH REPORTER; THE LIT PAGE: The Magazine for Library Literacy; ON THE ROAD: Mobile Ideas for Libraries), Allan Kleiman, Editor-in-Chief, 1671 East 16th Street, Suite 226, Brooklyn, NY 11229, 718-645-2396. 1987.

Library Research Associates, Inc., Matilda A. Gocek, RD #5, Box 41, Dunderberg Road, Monroe, NY 10950, 914-783-1144. 1968. Non-fiction. "I attempt to give authors of fiction and non-fiction American history (N.Y.) a chance to be published." avg. press run 3.5M. Pub'd 4 titles 1990; expects 5 titles 1991. 9 titles listed in the *Small Press Record of Books in Print* (20th Edition, 1991-92). avg. price, cloth: $20; paper: $9. Discounts: 40% to book sellers. 250pp; 5½×8½; of, lp. Reporting time: 3 months. Payment: 10% royalties. Copyrights for author.

LIBRARY TALK: The Magazine for Elementary School Librarians, Linworth Publishing, Inc., Carolyn Hamilton, Editor & Publisher; Marlene Woo-Lun, President; Jenifer Wilson, Marketing Manager, 5701 N. High Street, Suite 1, Worthington, OH 43085, 614-436-7107; fax 614-436-9490. 1988. Articles, reviews. "We publish article manuscripts only *about* the management of the school library *by* authors who have been or are elementary school librarians" circ. 7M. 5/yr. Pub'd 5 issues 1990; expects 5 issues 1991, 5 issues 1992. sub. price: $35 US, $39 Canada, $45 foreign; per copy: $9; sample: complimentary copies free. Back issues: $9. Discounts: 5% classroom and subscription agency. 40pp; 8½×11. Copyrighted, does not revert to author. Pub's reviews: 625 in 1990. §Materials suitable for elementary school libraries, grades 1-6. Ads: $812/$528 (1x b/w)/$1712 (1x) 4-color on 2nd, 3rd, & 4th covers. EDPress.

LIBRARY TIMES INTERNATIONAL, Dr. R.N. Sharma, Future World Publishing Company, 8128 Briarwood Drive, Evansville, IN 47715-8302, 812-473-2420. 1984. Articles, photos, interviews, reviews, letters, news items. "Our journal is a news digest of world news in the field of library and information science. In addition, our publication includes articles, interviews, editorials, list of new publications, calendar of national and international meetings, and a column on 'Information Science Update'. We have reporters in fifty-five countries and a Board of International Editors" circ. varies. 6/yr. Pub'd 6 issues 1990; expects 6 issues 1991, 6 issues 1992. sub. price: $25; per copy: $6; sample: free. Back issues: $5 per issue including p/h. Discounts: 15% to jobbers, agents and bulk orders. 16pp; 8½×11; of, lp. Reporting time: 2 weeks. Payment: none. Not copyrighted. Pub's reviews: 6 in 1990. §Any field with emphasis on library and information science. Ads: $600/$350/$800 inside cover and last page.

Life Energy Media, Annalea Bennett, 14755 Ventura Blvd, Suite 1908, Sherman Oaks, CA 91403, 818-905-2747. 1975. "Publishes and produces print, audio, and video materials on life energy concepts in the areas of organizations, massage, therapy, movement and dance, expressive arts, yoga, martial arts, spiritual evolution and other related areas" avg. press run 500-5M. Pub'd 3 titles 1990; expects 3 titles 1991, 3 titles 1992. 1 title listed in the *Small Press Record of Books in Print* (20th Edition, 1991-92). avg. price, cloth: $19.95; paper: $12.95; other: articles $3.00. Discounts: trade, quantity, conferences, classroom, jobbers. 20-350pp; 5½×8½. Reporting time: initial interest—1 month. Payment: negotiable. We can copyright for author. PMA.

Life Enhancement (see also Human Kinetics Pub. Inc.), Box 5076, Champaign, IL 61820. 19. avg. press run 5M. Pub'd 10 titles 1990; expects 11 titles 1991, 12 titles 1992. 29 titles listed in the *Small Press Record of Books in Print* (20th Edition, 1991-92). avg. price, cloth: $28.50; paper: $13.80. Discounts: returnable text 1-4 10%, 5+ 20%; trade 1-4 20%, 5-9 40%, 10-24 42%, 25-49 43%, 50-99 44%, 100-249 45%, 250-499 46%, 500+ 47%. 217pp; 6×9, 8½×11.

Life-Link Books, Henry Parmelee, Jr., 360 Center Road, Easton, CT 06612-1606. 1989. Poetry, fiction. avg. press run 10M. Expects 1 title 1991, 4 titles 1992. avg. price, cloth: $15.95. 150pp; of, lp. Reporting time: 4 months. Copyrights for author.

LIFTOUTS, Preludium Publishers, Barry Casselman, 1503 Washington Avenue South, Minneapolis, MN 55454, 612-333-0031. 1983. Poetry, fiction, criticism, reviews, parts-of-novels. "*Liftouts* is devoted primarily to reviews of new books and critical essays. Some short fiction and poetry is published, with an emphasis on translated works by foreign authors who have not previously been published in English. *Unsolicited submissions are not considered at this time.* Any inquiries should be accompanied by SASE. Translations of stories by Clarice Lispector, Luiz Vilela, Hans Christoph Buch, Sergio Sant'Anna and others have appeared in previous issues." circ. 5M. 1/yr. Expects 1 issue 1992. sub. price: $5; per copy: $5; sample: $5. Back issues: $5. Discounts: negotiable. 40-75pp; 5×8½; of. Payment: varies. Copyrighted, reverts to author. Pub's reviews: 35 in 1990. §Poetry, fiction, plays, literary criticism, all literature in translation. Ads: $495/$275/$7.50 per column inch.

LIGHTHOUSE, Tim Clinton, Lynne Trindl, Lorraine Clinton, Lighthouse Publications, PO Box 1377, Auburn, WA 98071-1377. 1986. Poetry, fiction. "Content must be of a family 'G-rated' nature. Stories up to 5,000 words. Poems up to 50 lines. Free writer's guidelines available with SASE with one first-class stamp, and submission should be accompanied by SASE with sufficient postage for return of ms. We also have a children's section" circ. 300. 6/yr. Pub'd 6 issues 1990; expects 6 issues 1991, 6 issues 1992. sub. price: $7.95; per copy: $3; sample: $3 (includes writers' guidelines, p/h). Discounts: $2 each for authors who order copies. 56pp; 5½×8½; †xerox. Reporting time: within 2-8 weeks. Payment: up to-$50 for story, up to-$5 for a poem, upon publication. Copyrighted, reverts to author. No ads.

Lighthouse Press, Nancy Sarles Katzman, 50 Evans Road, Marblehead, MA 01945, 617-631-6416. 1989. Articles, non-fiction. "Materials are approximately 230 pages of hard cover, illustrated format, books published are a variety of subjects. Non-fiction, medical self-help, color photography and other works that are in progress" avg. press run 5M. Expects 2 titles 1991, 4 titles 1992. 1 title listed in the *Small Press Record of Books in Print* (20th Edition, 1991-92). avg. price, cloth: $18.95. Discounts: 20% across the board. 235pp; 6×9; of. Reporting time: 3 months. Payment: negotiable. Copyrights for author.

LIGHTNING SWORD, APKL Publications, Stephen Mark Rafalsky, PO Box 371, Woodstock, NY 12498. 1986. Poetry, articles, interviews, criticism, reviews, letters, long-poems. *"Lightning Sword,* a journal of poetry, derives its name from 'that great Blade reposing in the heart/ of Zion's mystic Stone,' and is the 'last, pure, great weapon of the naked heart' of our beleaguered and imperiled humanity. *LS* is aligned with no earthly government, religion or enterprise, but issues forth from the kingdom and word not of this world, guided by the living intelligence of Christ...Modern poetry, it seems, has rejected the ancient faith and its Spirit, no doubt prompted in some measure by the madness, atrocities and hypocrisy of those who have named God's name, but also—and in greater measure—by virtue of the Death-Spell in whose thrall humanity (with it poets) lurches and reels in the fiery night on Apokalypse Field, eyes unseeing the source of deepening shadow falling across the globe, misperceiving the blazing light that fights it...Poetry is the samurai sword of the human spirit, as well its Diamond Shield against the terrible, cunning assault; it is also a great divining stone, every polished word-facet an opening into the archetypal deeps of being; likewise it is a jeweled psychic depth-charge exploding in the midst of collective consciousness. For what is poetry but the rarest and deepest mode of speech, channeling the immeasurable energies of the human heart in whatever form and focus it will?...Without apology we own ourselves warriors of spirit, on the offensive against the multifarious death manifest in every aspect of this zombie civilization descended from the ancient horror born in the dread sting of death. Poetry is the lightning in the nighttime sky of our hearts, illuminating the archetypal issues beneath everyday appearance...Many are the afflictions that beset us without and within, our poetry true to all: demonic powers and their human hosts sweep our planet in a poorly contrived illusory peace while blood increasingly soaks the ground and nuclear trigger-fingers itch; inwardly we are learning to heal the emptiness, addictions, compulsions and love-destroying codependencies that wither the gardens of our hearts, lethal infections inherited from our ancient lineage of monstrosities. And though we are poet-warriors, in the citadel of our sacred humanity nurturning grace and the mysteries of health-sustaining love are the rule of our king. At His touch we are transformed into archetypal new men and women. We call all to rally to Him, escaping the madness of these days. We bear witness to the living presence of Jesus Christ in the human condition, and His saving life in us, and in all who will come. This is the burden and genius of our poetry. His Lightning Sword is wielded for love of His captive, precious humanity." circ. 1M+. Irregular. Expects 1 issue 1992. price per copy: $2; sample: $1. Discounts: negotiable. 4-16pp; 8½×11; †photo offset. Reporting time: 2 months. Payment: copies. Contributors must be willing to release copyrights into the public domain. Pub's reviews. §Poetry, criticism, reviews, essays on poetics.

LIGHTWORKS MAGAZINE, Charlton Burch, Designer and Editor; Andrea Martin, Managing Editor; Gary S. Vasilash, Editor, PO Box 1202, Birmingham, MI 48012-1202, 313-626-8026. 1975. Articles, art, photos, interviews, collages, concrete art. "Illuminating new and experimental art." circ. 2M. Irregular. Pub'd 2 issues 1990; expects 2 issues 1991, 2 issues 1992. sub. price: $20 (4 issues) individuals, $25 institutions; per copy: price varies; sample: $5. Back issues: #10 $2, #14/15-#18 $4, #13 $3, #5-#6 $1, all orders must add $1 to cover postage costs, #19-#20/21 $5. Discounts: 40% on orders of 12 copies of one issue at least, 50% on orders of 50 or more. 56pp; 8½×11; of. Reporting time: usually quick. Payment: none, other than a couple copies. Copyrighted. Pub's reviews: 60 in 1990. §Books, periodicals, and records which explore alternative & visual artforms. No ads.

LILITH, Susan W. Schneider, Editor-in-Chief, 250 West 57th, #2432, New York, NY 10107, 212-757-0818. 1976. Poetry, fiction, articles, art, photos, interviews, criticism, reviews, letters, parts-of-poems, long-poems, plays, news items, non-fiction. "The 'Jewish Woman's Quarterly'." circ. 10M. 4/yr. Pub'd 4 issues 1990; expects 4 issues 1991, 4 issues 1992. sub. price: $14; per copy: $3.50; sample: $4.50. Back issues: $5 for in-print back issues. Out-of-print to libraries only. Discounts: 50% to retailers. 32pp; 8½×11; of. Reporting time: 3 months. Payment: negotiable. Copyrighted, rights reverting to author negotiable. Pub's reviews: 20 in 1990. §Pertaining to the Jewish, female experience, history, biography/autobio., feminist, fiction, poetry. Ads: on request. CCLM, COSMEP.

LILLIPUT REVIEW, Don Wentworth, Editor, 207 S. Millvale Ave. #3, Pittsburgh, PA 15224. 1989. Poetry. "All poems must be 10 lines or *less*. All styles and forms considered. SASE or in the trash, period. 3 poems maximum per submissions. Any submission beyond the maximum will be returned unread" circ. 150-200. Irregular. Pub'd 9 issues 1990; expects 12 issues 1991, 12 issues 1992. sub. price: $12; per copy: $1; sample: $1 or SASE. Back issues: $1. 12pp; 4¼×3.6; of. Reporting time: 1-8 weeks. Payment: 2 copies. Copyrighted, reverts to author.

THE LIMBERLOST REVIEW, Richard Ardinger, HC 33, Box 1113, Boise, ID 83706-9702. 1976. Poetry, fiction, interviews, reviews. "Although *The Limberlost Review* No. 19 was published as a collection of letterpressed poem postcards by 20 poets, most recent numbers have been devoted to Limberlost Press books and chapbooks in lieu of regular issues of the *Review*. Known contributors to the magazine include John Clellon Holmes, Edward Dorn, Lawrence Ferlinghetti, Charles Bukowski, Emily Warn, Greg Kuzma, William Stafford. Recent issues have been devoted to the following books: *Gone in October: Last Reflections of Jack Kerouac* essays by John Clellon Holmes (#14, 15 1985), *What Thou Lovest Well Remains: 100 Years of Ezra Pound* (#16 1986) featuring essays on Pound by poets, edited by Richard Ardinger, and letterpressed chapbooks *No Wild Dog Howled*, poems by Bruce Embree (#17 1987), *Dire Coasts* poems by John Clellon Holmes (#18 1988), *Highway Suite* poems by Emily Warn (#20 1988), and *from Abhorrences* a pamphlet selection of poems from a longer work-in-progress by Edward Dorn (#21 1989), other books by John Rember, Nancy Stringfellow, William Studebaker, Robert Creeley." circ. 350-1M. 2-3/yr. Pub'd 2 issues 1990; expects 2 issues 1991, 2-3 issues 1992. 12 titles listed in the *Small Press Record of Books in Print* (20th Edition, 1991-92). No subscriptions available; price per copy: $9-10; sample: $9. Back issues: inquire. Discounts: 30% 5 or more. 48pp; 5½×8½; †of, lp. Reporting time: 1-2 months. Payment: in copies. Copyrighted, reverts to author. CLMP.

LIME GREEN BULLDOZERS (AND OTHER RELATED SPECIES), Lainie Duro, 1003 Avenue X, Apt. A, Lubbock, TX 79401, 806-744-7412. 1986. Poetry, fiction, art, photos. "No longer than one double-spaced page. No contributions welcome without some communication." circ. 300. 2/yr. Pub'd 2 issues 1990; expects 2 issues 1991, 2 issues 1992. price per copy: $3; sample: $3. 50pp; 8½×11; †xerox. Payment: none. Not copyrighted. Ads: none.

Limelight Editions, Mel Zerman, Jan Lurie, 118 East 30th Street, New York, NY 10016, 212-532-5525. 1984. Non-fiction. "Almost all of our books are paperback reprints of previously published works on the performing arts. We do occasional original publishing." avg. press run 4M. Pub'd 14 titles 1990; expects 14 titles 1991, 14 titles 1992. 95 titles listed in the *Small Press Record of Books in Print* (20th Edition, 1991-92). avg. price, cloth: $22.95; paper: $11.95. Discounts: graduated schedule for retailers, 50% for wholesalers. 300pp; 6×9; of. Reporting time: 3-4 weeks. Payment: generally 7½% against a modest advance. Does not copyright for author. ABA associate member.

Limerick Publications, Stephen T. Holland, PO Box 1072, Muscatine, IA 52761. 1982. avg. press run 2.5M. Expects 2 titles 1991. avg. price, cloth: $7.95; paper: $2.95. Discounts: 60-40. 150pp; size varies. Reporting time: 1 month.

LIMESTONE: A LITERARY JOURNAL, Matthew J. Bond, Editor, c/o Univ. of Kentucky, English Dept., 1215 Patterson Office Tower, Lexington, KY 40506. 1979. Poetry, fiction, art, photos, interviews, criticism, reviews, parts-of-novels, long-poems, collages, non-fiction. "*Limestone: A Literary Journal*, ISSN 0899-5966, has published work by Gurney Norman, James Baker Hall, Wendell Berry, and Guy Davenport. We accept manuscripts from any interested contributors, September through April only" circ. 1M. 1/yr. Expects 1 issue 1991, 1 issue 1992. sub. price: $3; per copy: $3; sample: $3. Back issues: $3. 50-80pp; 5½×8½; of. Reporting time: 1 year. Payment: 2 copies. Copyrighted, reverts to author. Pub's reviews. §Contemporary aesthetics. Ads: $150/$80.

Lincoln Publishing Company, 3434 Janice Way, Palo Alto, CA 94303. 1974. "Publish books on small business; how to earn money at home, etc. Books were written to order. Only thing we might possibly be interested in are books along this line, or closely related. Books are designed to sell well by mail. Titles of Publications: *How to Make $1,000 Monthly With Classified Ads*; *The Millionaire Book of 1,236 Unusual, Successful Home Businesses, How to Get Rich in Multi-Level Marketing*." 3 titles listed in the *Small Press*

Record of Books in Print (20th Edition, 1991-92). avg. price, cloth: $9.95; paper: $5.95. Discounts: write us. 8¼×10¾; of. Reporting time: 1 week. Payment: arranged individually.

Lincoln Springs Press, PO Box 269, Franklin Lakes, NJ 07417. 1987. Poetry, fiction, photos. "Please send 5 sample poems & bio. or 5 pages of prose plus SASE." avg. press run 1M. Expects 4 titles 1991, 4 titles 1992. 7 titles listed in the *Small Press Record of Books in Print* (20th Edition, 1991-92). avg. price, paper: $8.95. Discounts: 1-5 20%, 5-10 30%, 10+ 40%. 80pp; 5½×8½; of. Reporting time: 6 months. Payment: 15% royalty. Copyrights for author.

Lindisfarne Press, Christopher Bamford, PO Box 778, 195 Main Street, Great Barrington, MA 01230, 413-232-4377. 1973. Non-fiction. "Lindisfarne Press publishes works of literature, philosophy, religion, science, psychology, in quality smythe-sewn trade editions. By publishing titles that contribute to cultural transformation and speak for a new harmony between humanity, nature, and the ground of being, Lindisfarne Press hopes to make it possible for readers everywhere to have access to these vital and important ideas. We see this enterprise as contributing to the resacralization of knowledge and the creation of a planetary culture of spiritual values—a fit place to live" avg. press run 3M. Pub'd 4 titles 1990; expects 8 titles 1991, 10 titles 1992. 20 titles listed in the *Small Press Record of Books in Print* (20th Edition, 1991-92). avg. price, cloth: $21; paper: $9.95. Discounts: 40% to the trade. 170pp; 6⅛×9; of. Reporting time: 2 months. Payment: worked out individually. Copyrights for author.

Lindsay Press Inc. of Florida, PO Box 6316, Clearwater, FL 34618-6316, 813-797-2512. 1989. 1 title listed in the *Small Press Record of Books in Print* (20th Edition, 1991-92).

LINGUISTIC REVIEW, Weidner & Sons, Publishing, Box 2178, Cinnaminson, NJ 08077, 609-486-1755. "See comments for Weidner & Sons, Publishing." 4/yr. Pub'd 4 issues 1990; expects 4 issues 1991, 4 issues 1992. Pages vary. Copyrighted, does not revert to author. Pub's reviews: 10 in 1990. §Linguistics only. Exchange ads with other linguistic journals.

LININGTON LINEUP, Rinehart S. Potts, 1223 Glen Terrace, Glassboro, NJ 08028-1315, 609-589-1571. 1984. Poetry, fiction, articles, art, photos, cartoons, interviews, satire, criticism, reviews, letters, news items, non-fiction. "Being devoted to the study of the writings of one person (Elizabeth Linington), the publication accepts any material relating to her, her books, the characters, etc. Her pen-names: Anne Blaisdell, Lesley Egan, Egan O'Neill, Dell Shannon. Types of writings: historical fiction, detective mysteries, political commentary." circ. 400. 6/yr. Pub'd 6 issues 1990; expects 6 issues 1991, 6 issues 1992. sub. price: $12, foreign $15; per copy: $3, foreign $4; sample: free. Back issues: same as current. Discounts: half-price to bookstores, teachers, etc. 16pp; 8½×11; of. Reporting time: 1 month. Payment: quantity of copies of issue. Copyrighted, does not revert to author. Pub's reviews: 20 in 1990. §Reference books in mystery/detective field. Ads: $40/$20. Elizabeth Linington Society.

LINKS, Third World First, 232 Cowley Road, Oxford OX4 1UH, England. 1969. Poetry, fiction, articles, art, photos, cartoons, interviews. "ISSN: 0261-4014. Magazine showing links between economics, racism, and underdevelopment internationally. No unsolicited articles, please" circ. 3M. 4/yr. Pub'd 4 issues 1990; expects 4 issues 1991, 4 issues 1992. sub. price: £15; per copy: £3.50. Back issues: £1.95 (1x double issue 29/30 £3.50). Discounts: bookshops 33%, libraries 20%. 64pp; 15×21cm (A5); of. Payment: £50 per article. Copyrighted, does not revert to author. Federation of Radical Booksellers (U.K.).

LINQ, English Language Literature Association, Cheryl Taylor, Co-ordinating Editor; E. Perkins, Co-ordinating Editor, English Dept., James Cook Univ.-North Queensland, Townsville 4811, Australia. 1971. Poetry, fiction, articles, interviews, criticism, reviews, parts-of-novels, long-poems, plays. "Critical articles about 3M words. Reviews 1M words." circ. 350. 2/yr. Pub'd 2 issues 1990; expects 2 issues 1991, 2 issues 1992. sub. price: $20 indiv.; $25 instit. including postage, Australian; per copy: $10, Australian; sample: $2. Back issues: $1.50. 180pp; 5½×8½; of. Reporting time: 2 months. Payment: minimum AUS $20 per article, short story; $10 per poem, review. Copyrighted. Pub's reviews: 20 in 1990. §Any area of contemporary interest, political, sociological, literary.

Lintel, Bonnie E. Nelson, Publisher; Walter James Miller, Editorial Director, Box 8609, Roanoke, VA 24014, 703-982-2265. 1978. Poetry, fiction, art, long-poems. "We have gotten some good back-cover blurbs from Kurt Vonnegut, David Ignatow, Anthony Burgess, Robert Bly, Menke Katz, et al. We finance a book through advance subscriptions." avg. press run 1.5M. Pub'd 2 titles 1990; expects 1 title 1991, 1 title 1992. 21 titles listed in the *Small Press Record of Books in Print* (20th Edition, 1991-92). avg. price, cloth: $15; paper: $6.95; other: $22.50 hardcover binder. Discounts: 40% to Bookstores; 45% on 25 copies or more; 55% to wholesalers. 100pp; 5¾×9, 5×8; photo of. Reporting time: 2 months. Payment: author gets 100 copies on publication, and shares in the profits, if any. Each contract is worked out individually. Copyrights for author.

Linwood Publishers, Bernard L. Chase, Managing Editor, 481 Hambrick Road, Suite 16, Stone Mountain, GA 30083, 404-296-3950. 1982. Poetry, long-poems. avg. press run 500. Pub'd 2 titles 1990; expects 3 titles 1991,

4 titles 1992. 8 titles listed in the *Small Press Record of Books in Print* (20th Edition, 1991-92). avg. price, cloth: $15.95; paper: $6.75. Discounts: (1-4) 10%; (5-14) 20%; (15-24) 30%; (25 or more) 40%. 64pp; 6×9; of, lp. Reporting time: 30-60 days. Payment: poetry - per agreement. Copyrights for author. COSMEP.

Linworth Publishing, Inc. (see also THE BOOK REPORT: Journal for Junior & Senior High School Librarians; LIBRARY TALK: The Magazine for Elementary School Librarians), Carolyn Hamilton, Publisher & Editor; Cheryl Abdullah, Book Review Editor; Marlene Woo-Lun, President; Jenifer Wilson, Marketing Manager, 5701 N. High Street, Suite 1, Worthington, OH 43085, 614-436-7107; FAX 614-436-9490.

THE LION AND THE UNICORN: A Critical Journal of Children's Literature, Geraldine DeLuca, Roni Natov, Dept of English, Brooklyn College, Brooklyn, NY 11210, 780-5195. 1977. Articles, interviews, reviews. "Articles are generally 10-20 pp. typed and focus on some aspect of a theme or genre in children's literature. Articles should be critical rather than appreciative or purely historical. MLA form required for manuscripts. Letters of inquiry are encouraged. Recent contributors: X J Kennedy, Robert Coles, Elizabeth Sewell; interviews of Ursula Nordstrom, Milton Meltzer, Robert Cormier, Arnold Lobel. For subs. write to The Lion & Unicorn, Journal Division, Johns Hopkins Univ. Press, 701 West 40th Street, Suite 275, Baltimore, MD 21211" circ. 1.5M. 2/yr. Pub'd 2 issues 1990; expects 2 issues 1991, 2 issues 1992. sub. price: $15 indiv., $26 instit.; per copy: $15; sample: $15. Back issues: write to Johns Hopkins Univ. Press, 701 West 40th Street, Suite 275, Baltimore, MD 21211. 150pp; 6½×9½; of. Reporting time: 2-6 months; receipt of articles acknowledged immediately. Payment: none. Copyrighted, does not revert to author. Pub's reviews: 4 in 1990. §Children's and young adult literature, critical works on children's & young adult literature including fiction, poetry, drama.

Lion Press, Norma L. Leone, PO Box 92541, Rochester, NY 14692, 716-381-6410. 1985. Non-fiction. avg. press run 1M-5M. Pub'd 1 title 1990; expects 2-3 titles 1991, 3-5 titles 1992. 4 titles listed in the *Small Press Record of Books in Print* (20th Edition, 1991-92). avg. price, paper: $8-$15. Discounts: 20-40%. 1-200pp; 5½×8½; of. Reporting time: 1 month. Payment: 5% of retail price; no advance. Copyrights for author. COSMEP, NAIP.

Lionhouse Publishing Company, Blair Howard, 804 25th Street, Suite 155, Cleveland, TN 37311, 615-339-5779. 1991. Fiction, articles, non-fiction. "Additional address: 1273 Brown Ave. NW, Cleveland, TN 37311. Non-Fiction: Length 30,000 to 50,000 words. Fiction: Length 25,000 to 75,000 words. Articles: Travel articles 1,000 to 2,500 words; profiles 1,000 to 3,000 words." avg. press run 2M. Expects 2 titles 1991, 4 titles 1992. 1 title listed in the *Small Press Record of Books in Print* (20th Edition, 1991-92). avg. price, paper: $14.95. Discounts: trade. 125pp; 8½×11, 5½×8½; of. Reporting time: 4 weeks. Payment: 10%-15% of retail price. Copyrights for author.

Lions Head Press, Zoe Suzanne LeCours, PO Box 5202, Klamath Falls, OR 97601, 503-883-2101. 1985. Fiction, photos, cartoons, non-fiction. "We have activity/workbooks, romance novels, and pictorials. Books of any length will be considered, but looking for timeless pieces. All materials must be Christian oriented, fiction as well as non-fiction. Recent contributors: Suzanne Hieronymus, *Exit Here Please*, an in depth activity book taking people through the Book of Exodus; Pat Tukey, *Tennie Runner Travels*, a pre-school 'read to' book which is about what a child's tennis shoes see which a child doesn't; G. Hankins, *Washington For Jesus*, a pictorial of the international gathering of Christians in Washington, D.C." avg. press run 3M. Pub'd 1 title 1990; expects 3 titles 1991, 4 titles 1992. 2 titles listed in the *Small Press Record of Books in Print* (20th Edition, 1991-92). avg. price, paper: $5.80. Discounts: standard 40% discount on all purchases of 10 or more books. 50pp; 8×11; of. Reporting time: 4-6 weeks. Payment: depending on the length, type, and style, we do both percentages and outright purchases. Copyrights for author. Northwest Association of Book Publishers.

LIPS, Laura Boss, PO Box 1345, Montclair, NJ 07042. 1981. Poetry. "*Lips* publishes the best contemporary poetry submitted. No biases. Recent Contributors: Allen Ginsberg, Richard Kostelanetz, Marge Piercy, Warren Woessner, Marie Gillan, Alice Notley, E. Ethelbert Miller, Lyn Lifshin, Gregory Corso, Ishmael Reed, Michael Benedikt, Robert Phillips, Nicholas Christopher, David Ignatow, Stanley H. Barkan, Dennis Brutus, Molly Peacock" circ. 1M. 2/yr. Pub'd 2 issues 1990; expects 2 issues 1991, 2 issues 1992. sub. price: $10 indiv, $12 instit; per copy: $5; sample: $5 + $1 p/h. 80pp; 5½×8½; of. Reporting time: 2 months. Payment: 2 copies. Copyrighted, reverts to author. Ads: $100. CCLM.

LISTEN, Lincoln Steed, Editor; Glen Robinson, Associate Editor, PO Box 7000, Boise, ID 83707, 208-465-2500. 1948. Articles, art, cartoons, interviews, non-fiction. circ. 100M. 12/yr. Pub'd 12 issues 1990; expects 12 issues 1991, 12 issues 1992. sub. price: $17.95/$20.95 foreign; per copy: $2; sample: $1. Back issues: 40¢. 32pp; 10½×8; †of. Reporting time: 60 days. Payment: 5¢-7¢/word. Copyrighted, reverts to author.

THE LIT PAGE: The Magazine for Library Literacy, Library Outreach Reporter Publications, Debra Wilcox Johnson, Editor-in-Chief; Carol L. Sheffer, Editor-in-Chief, 1671 East 16th Street, Suite 226, Brooklyn, NY 11229, 718-645-2396. 1990. Articles, photos, interviews, reviews, letters, news items, non-fiction. circ. 500. 4/yr. Expects 4 issues 1991, 4 issues 1992. sub. price: $15; per copy: $4; sample: free. Back issues: $4 each. Discounts: agent/jobber 15% commission. 20pp; 8½×11; of. Reporting time: 1 month. Payment: copies of issue. Copyrighted, does not revert to author. Pub's reviews. §Literacy, English as a second language. Ads: $175/$125/other available upon request.

LITERARY CENTER QUARTERLY, Lori Powell, Marilyn Stablein, Box 85116, Seattle, WA 98145, 206-547-2503. 1986. Interviews, criticism, reviews, letters, non-fiction. "Recent contributors: Keith Abbott, Sean Bentley, Clifford Burke, etc. Review copies welcome; reviews 3-4 pages double-spaced, typed or on computer disk with hard copy especially welcome. (Review copies also displayed in Resource Library.) Also, articles on the writing craft, interviews with publishers & writers in the west and northwest. No poetry or fiction" circ. 2.6M. 4/yr. Pub'd 4 issues 1990; expects 4 issues 1991, 4 issues 1992. sub. price: $10; per copy: $2; sample: same. Discounts: inquiries okay. 18pp; 8½×11. Reporting time: 2 months. Payment: varies. Copyrighted, reverts to author. Pub's reviews: 8 in 1990. §Poetry, fiction, literature especially from the west and northwest. Ads: $240/$120/$10-$15 column inch.

LITERARY MAGAZINE REVIEW, G.W. Clift, Charles W. Wright, Associate Editor; J.V. Roper, Editor; Robin Mosher, Associate Editor; Marcella Clark, Mark Jarvis, David Kirby, Contributing Editor, English Department, Kansas State University, Manhattan, KS 66506, 913-532-6716. 1981. Articles, criticism, reviews. "*LMR* is devoted to providing critical appraisals of the specific contents of small, predominantly literary periodicals for the benefit of readers and writers. We print reviews of about 1.5M words which comment on the magazines' physical characteristics, on particular articles, stories, and poems featured, and on editorial preferences as evidenced in the selections. Recent contributors include Fred Chappell, George Garrett, J.B. Hall, Jonathan Holden, D.E. Steward, Phil Miller, Ben Nyberg, Ben Reynolds, and Richard Peabody. We would be happy to entertain queries offering disinterested reviews and omnibus notices and pieces describing, explaining, or dissecting the current literary magazine scene. Subscription exchange inquiries are welcome." circ. 600. 4/yr. Pub'd 4 issues 1990; expects 4 issues 1991, 4 issues 1992. sub. price: $12.50; per copy: $4; sample: $4. Back issues: $5 an issue. Discounts: 10% to subscription agencies. 64pp; 5½×8½; of. Payment: copies. Copyrighted, rights revert on author's request. Pub's reviews: 70 in 1990. §Literary magazines. We are interested in magazines which publish at least some fiction or poetry or both. No ads.

LITERARY MARKETS, Bill Marles, 4340 Coldfall Road, Richmond, B.C. V7C 1P8, Canada, 604-277-4829. 1982. "Newsletter reports on publishing opportunities for poets and fiction writers in the United States and Canada. Additional mailing address: PO Drawer 1310, Point Roberts, WA 98281-1310." circ. 1M. 6/yr. Expects 6 issues 1991, 6 issues 1992. sub. price: $12; per copy: $2; sample: $2. Discounts: 20% to subscriptions agencies. 6pp; 8½×11; of. Reporting time: 2 months. Payment: subscription. Copyrighted. Pub's reviews. §Writing and publishing. Ads: 2¢ an enclosure.

Literary Publications Company, Patricia McDonald, PO Box 652, Manchester, CT 06040, 203-688-5496. 1986. Poetry, art, non-fiction. "*Anthology*—annual publication of prize-winning poems from *Golden Eagle* subscribers. *The Time We Drove All Night*—chapbook by Ulrich Troubetzkoy, competition winner, publication scheduled Spring 1988. *Patterns in Poetry* by Esther Leiper, a book of uncommon poetry patterns by the poetry columnist for Inkling Publications. Publication scheduled Fall 1988. Most publications are of winning manuscripts in our contests. Anthology is annual with first issue produced Dec. 1987. Others possible must be instructional manuals for writing skills and subjects. *No vanity publishing*" avg. press run 300. Pub'd 1 title 1990; expects 6 titles 1991, 6 titles 1992. avg. price, paper: $6. Discounts: under consideration, contact the publisher if interested. 100pp; 5½×8½; †cover litho/content litho or mimeo. Reporting time: 30 days. Payment: contests $25 + 25 copies + 10% royalty, anthology 1 copy, others negotiable. Copyrights for author.

LITERARY RESEARCH: A Journal of Scholarly Method & Technique, Aletha Hendrickson, Managing Editor; Michael Marcuse, Editor; Mary Ann O'Donnell, Associate Editor, Department of English and World Literature, University of Maryland, College Park, MD 20742, 301-454-6953. 1976. Articles, reviews, news items. "Oriented toward information on literary research projects and the teaching of courses in literary research." circ. 350. 4/yr. Pub'd 4 issues 1990; expects 4 issues 1991, 4 issues 1992. sub. price: $10, $15 foreign; per copy: $3.00; sample: free. Back issues: $3.00 single, $5.00 double issue. Discounts: none. 90pp; 5½×8½; †of. Reporting time: 4 months. Payment: none. Copyrighted, does not revert to author. Pub's reviews: 25 in 1990. §Bibliography, research guides, studies of the literary research course. No ads. CELJ.

THE LITERARY REVIEW, Walter Cummins, Editor-in-Chief; Martin Green, Co-Editor; Harry Keyishian, Co-Editor; William Zander, Associate Editor, Fairleigh Dickinson University, 285 Madison Avenue, Madison, NJ 07940, 201-593-8564. 1957. Poetry, fiction, articles, interviews, criticism, reviews, long-poems. "We consider fiction and poetry submissions of any type and of any length (within reason) from new and established writers. We welcome critical articles on contemporary American and international literature and are eager to have submissions of essays that are written for a general literary audience rather than the academic quarterly market. *TLR* has always had a special emphasis on contemporary writing abroad (in translation) and we welcome submissions from overseas, and new translations of contemporary foreign literature. We are particularly interested in receiving translations of and essays on ethnic writing abroad." circ. 1.8M-2M. 4/yr.

320

Pub'd 4 issues 1990; expects 4 issues 1991, 4 issues 1992. sub. price: $18 U.S., $21 foreign; per copy: $5 U.S., $6 foreign; sample: $5 recent issues. Back issues: varies. Discounts: negotiable. 128-152pp; 6×9; of. Reporting time: 2-3 months. Payment: 2 free copies, additional copies at discount. Copyrighted, reverts to author. Pub's reviews: 12 in 1990. §Contemporary fiction, poetry, literary theory, US and world literature (contemporary). No ads. CCLM.

LITERARY SKETCHES, Olivia Murray Nichols, PO Box 810571, Dallas, TX 75381-0571, 214-243-8776. 1961. Articles, interviews, reviews, letters. "1M word maximum." circ. 500. 11/yr. Expects 11 issues 1991. sub. price: $7-year, $12.50-2 yrs or 2 subscriptions; per copy: 75¢; sample: SASE (#10). Back issues: 75¢. 4pp; 11×8½; of. Reporting time: 1 month. Payment: 1/2¢ per word. Copyrighted, reverts to author. Pub's reviews: 15-20 in 1990. §Literary biographies only, books on books. Ads: $10 per inch.

Little Bayou Press, 1735 First Avenue North, St. Petersburg, FL 33713-8903, 813-822-3278. 1982. Expects 1 title 1991, 1 title 1992. 1 title listed in the *Small Press Record of Books in Print* (20th Edition, 1991-92). avg. price, cloth: $25. Discounts: 1-10 copies - 40%; 11 or more 45%. 200pp; 7½×5½; of. Reporting time: 6 months. Payment: 15% of sale price, or 10% of list price. Copyrights for author.

Little Buckaroo Press, Cynthia V. Nasta, Pat S. Zilka, PO Box 3016, West Sedona, AZ 86340, 602-282-6278. 1989. Fiction. "Publishes only children's material with predominantly Arizona/Southwest themes heavily oriented toward a tourist market. Payment & copyright depends on material, will provide details" avg. press run 10M. Pub'd 1 title 1990; expects 1 title 1991, 1 title 1992. 1 title listed in the *Small Press Record of Books in Print* (20th Edition, 1991-92). avg. price, paper: $6.95. Discounts: 40%. 32pp; 9½×8½; of. Reporting time: 6-8 weeks. Arizona Authors Association.

LITTLE FREE PRESS, Ernest Mann, Editor-Publisher, Route 1, Box 102, Cushing, MN 56443. 1969. Articles, reviews, letters, news items, non-fiction. "Articles, etc, to focus on a better economic system for the world and total freedom for each individual" circ. 2M. 6-9/yr. Pub'd 9 issues 1990; expects 9 issues 1991, 9 issues 1992. 1 title listed in the *Small Press Record of Books in Print* (20th Edition, 1991-92). sub. price: free for stamp; per copy: free for stamp; sample: free for stamp. Back issues: free for stamp. Discounts: none. 6pp; 8½×11; of. Reporting time: 1 month. Payment: gratis only. Not copyrighted. Pub's reviews: 11 in 1990. §Solutions to world problems. No ads.

THE LITTLE MAGAZINE, Jan Ramjerdi, Lori Anderson, English Department, State Univ. of New York at Albany, Albany, NY 12222. 1965. Poetry, fiction. *"The Little Magazine* is an old literary magazine that refuses to die, revived this year (1990) as an annual under the editorship of SUNY-Albany's faculty and graduate student writers. We have no set guidelines; we're open to both experimental and traditional work. About 70% of the magazine is fiction; 30% poetry. We like poetry and fiction that foregrounds language, is innovative in form, that pushes the limits of its genre. We'd like to see more work by minority writers. *We read from Sept. 15 to Dec. 15 only—work sent at other times will be returned unread.* Max. length 6,000 words fiction; 6pp. poetry. Some contributors to 1990 issue: Jim Daniels, Alan Friedman, Diane Glancy, Edward Kleinschmidt, Simon Perchik, William Roorbach, Stephanie Strickland, Tom Whalen, Susan Wheeler, Marilyn Zuckerman." circ. 1.5M. 1/yr. Expects 1 issue 1991, 1 issue 1992. sub. price: $6; per copy: $6; sample: $6. Back issues: $4. Discounts: please inquire. 250pp; 5½×8½; of. Reporting time: 2-8 weeks. Payment: 2 copies. Copyrighted, reverts to author. Ads: $100/$50/discounts for camera-ready copy.

Little People's Press, Lindsey Ramos, PO Box 7280, Santa Cruz, CA 95061, 408-429-9506. 1990. "Children's stories" avg. press run 2.5M. Pub'd 4 titles 1990; expects 4 titles 1992. 1 title listed in the *Small Press Record of Books in Print* (20th Edition, 1991-92). Discounts: trade. 36pp; 8×6; †of. Payment: royalty only. Copyrights for author. COSMEP.

Little Red Hen, Inc., T.J. McDevitt, PO Box 4260, Pocatello, ID 83205, 208-233-3755. 1978. Fiction, non-fiction. avg. press run 5M. Pub'd 1 title 1990; expects 2 titles 1991, 2 titles 1992. 5 titles listed in the *Small Press Record of Books in Print* (20th Edition, 1991-92). avg. price, cloth: $8.95; paper: $8.90. Discounts: Usual. 140pp; 5½×8½; of.

Little River Press, Ronald Edwards, 10 Lowell Avenue, Westfield, MA 01085, 413-568-5598. 1976. Poetry. "Little River Press does not read or return unsolicited mss. We do limited editions of poetry. *Anonyms,* prose poems by Stephen Sossaman (1978) is available from an edition of 25 signed and 75 other copies at $5 and $2 respectively, postpaid. *Arrangements and Transformations in 18 pt. Century Oldstyle Bold,* concrete poetry by R. Edwards, $1.50. *Tenerife Haiku, Islas Canarias* by Cliff Edwards, $5.00; *Messages* concrete poetry by R. Edwards, $2.50." avg. press run 50-100. Pub'd 2 titles 1990; expects 2 titles 1991, 2 titles 1992. 7 titles listed in the *Small Press Record of Books in Print* (20th Edition, 1991-92). avg. price, paper: $5. 16-20pp; 7½×6¼; †lp. Copyrights for author.

Little Sam & Co. Press, Sharon L. Woloz, 1415 Camden Avenue #403, Los Angeles, CA 90025, 213-473-3324. 1988. avg. press run 5M-10M. Pub'd 1 title 1990; expects 3 titles 1991, 3-5 titles 1992. 2 titles listed in the *Small Press Record of Books in Print* (20th Edition, 1991-92). avg. price, paper: $6.95. 96pp; 6×9, 5½×8⅜. Reporting time: max. 4 weeks. Payment: negotiable. Copyrights for author.

Littlebooks, Frederick L. Watts, PO Box 863065, Plano, TX 75086, 214-727-6297. 1990. Non-fiction. "Self-publisher: non-fiction. Very early American History (excellent reference material, exhibiting previously unpublished military, land grants, Church and civil records from 1700 to c.1898). Also (in work) two books showing retirees how to develop and pursue second careers. One seminar workbook. I am interested in seeing manuscripts, commencing this year: American history, how-to's, technical and other. Finished product: First Class." avg. press run 500-1M. Pub'd 1 title 1990; expects 3 titles 1991, 5 titles 1992. avg. price, cloth: $35; paper: $27.50. Discounts: 30%-40%. 200-300pp; 8½×11; of.

The Live Oak Press, David Mike Hamilton, Editor-In-Chief, PO Box 60036, Palo Alto, CA 94306, 415-853-0197. 1982. Fiction, non-fiction. "Only articles for the betterment of mankind. No restrictions on length, etc." avg. press run 1M. Pub'd 1 title 1990; expects 1 title 1991, 2 titles 1992. 4 titles listed in the *Small Press Record of Books in Print* (20th Edition, 1991-92). avg. price, cloth: $35; paper: $15. Discounts: 40% 10 or more. 32-128pp; 6×9; of. Reporting time: 3 months. Payment: free copies, 10% after expenses recovered. Copyrights for author. Bookbuilders West, COSMEP.

LIVELY ARTS, Kenzo, PO Box 4906, San Diego, CA 92104. 1985. Poetry, articles, art, photos, cartoons, interviews, criticism, reviews, music, letters, collages. "Have featured interviews with: Ed 'Big Daddy' Roth, The Dammed, Fuzztones, Captain Sensible, Mojo Nixon, Link Protrudi and the Jaymen, Screaming Tribesmen and G.G. Allin. Also featured artwork by Jouni Waarankangas, C.S. Works, Jeff Gaither, R.K. Sloane, Mick Bladder and Chuck Preble" circ. 1M. 4/yr. Pub'd 4 issues 1990; expects 4 issues 1991, 4 issues 1992. price per copy: $1; sample: $1. 40pp; 5½×8; high-quality xerox. Payment: none. Not copyrighted. §Underground music, horror movies, art. No ads.

LIVERPOOL LAW REVIEW, Deborah Charles Publications, J. Kirkbride, 173 Mather Avenue, Liverpool L18 6JZ, United Kingdom. 1979. Non-fiction. 2/yr. Pub'd 2 issues 1990. sub. price: £12 individuals, £35 institutions + postage; per copy: £9 individuals, £18 institutions; sample: £9. Discounts: 10% subscription agents. 112pp; royal 80; Mac DTD. Reporting time: 3 months. Payment: none. Copyrighted, does not revert to author. Pub's reviews: 2 in 1990. §Modern law. exchange.

LIVERPOOL NEWSLETTER, Gild of Saint George, Anthony Cooney, Rose Cottage, 17 Hadassah Grove, Lark Lane, Liverpool L17 8XH, England, 051-728-9176. 1960. Articles, art, criticism, reviews, music, letters. "750-1M words of Social Credit/Decentralist/Catholic interest." circ. 200. 4/yr. Pub'd 4 issues 1990; expects 5 issues 1991, 5 issues 1992. sub. price: $4; per copy: $1; sample: $1. Back issues: all issues sold out. 20pp; 8×12; †mi. Reporting time: 3 months. Payment: none. Copyrighted, reverts to author. Pub's reviews: 10 in 1990. §Politics, etc. Ads: $1.

Liverpool University Press (see also BULLETIN OF HISPANIC STUDIES), Dorothy Sherman Severin, Professor; Ann L. Mackenzie, Dept. of Hispanic Studies, The University, PO Box 147, Liverpool L69 3BX, England, 051 794 2774/5. 1923. Articles, reviews. "Specialist articles on the languages and literatures of Spain, Portugal and Latin America, in English, Spanish, Portuguese, and Catalan" avg. press run 1.2M. Expects 4 titles 1991. 11 titles listed in the *Small Press Record of Books in Print* (20th Edition, 1991-92). avg. price, paper: £10. 112pp; metric crown quarto; of. Reporting time: 3 months. Payment: none. Does not copyright for author. CELJ.

LIVING AMONG NATURE DARINGLY!, L.A.N.D., Bill Anderson, 4466 Ike Mooney Road, Silverton, OR 97381, 503-873-8829. 1986. Fiction, articles, photos, cartoons, interviews, reviews, letters, news items, non-fiction. "Accept how-to articles related to trapping, farming, construction, from 300 to 3,000 words. Prefer positive, inspiring nature related articles and short stories showing how people can make a difference. Liberal populist favored. Recent contributors: Judy Atchison, Larry Irons, Conrad Russell" circ. 1M. 5/yr. Pub'd 5 issues 1990; expects 5 issues 1991, 5 issues 1992. sub. price: $9; per copy: $2; sample: $2.50. Back issues: $2.50 for issue 1 & 2, $2 for #3 thru 8. Discounts: bulk (over 5,000) 50%, jobber 40%-50%, all others 33%. 44pp; 8½×11; of. Reporting time: 30 days. Payment: $20 to $100 currently, trying to double by Spring. Copyrighted, does not revert to author. Pub's reviews: 12 in 1990. §Trapping, nature, farming, nostalgia, wildlife, mystery, politics/economics, 3rd World development. Ads: $97/$49.50/classified 25¢/word.

LIVING FREE, Jim Stumm, Box 29, Hiler Branch, Buffalo, NY 14223. 1979. Articles, cartoons, reviews, letters, news items, non-fiction. "We are pro-individual, pro-private property. Discuss ways for individuals, families, and small groups to live freer, more self-reliant lives. Not interested in politics, or mass movements for social change. By publishing mostly unedited letters, we provide a forum for freedom-seekers, survivalists, libertarians, homesteaders, anarchists, and other outlaws." circ. 200. 4-6/yr. Pub'd 7 issues 1990; expects 6 issues 1991, 8 issues 1992. sub. price: $8 6 issues; per copy: $1.50; sample: $1. Back issues: #1-#30 50¢ each, all others $1.25 each. Discounts: 40% for 5 or more copies of 1 issue to 1 address, no returns, also applies to subscriptions. 8pp; 8½×11; of. Payment: none. Not copyrighted. Pub's reviews: 6 in 1990. §Non-fiction:

self-reliance, enhancing freedom, living cheap, avoiding govt. restrictions. No display advertising; 20¢/word, $3 minimum.

LIVING OFF THE LAND, Subtropic Newsletter, Pine & Palm Press, Marian Van Atta, Editor; F.W. Dr. Martin, Associate Editor, PO Box 2131, Melbourne, FL 32902-2131, 305-723-5554. 1975. Articles, letters. "Publishes short articles (500) words on edibles of the subtropics. *The Surinam Cherry* by Dr. George Webster. *Red Bay, The Southland's Edible Aristocrat* by Donald Ray Patterson. Has a seed exchange." circ. 500. 5/yr. Pub'd 6 issues 1990; expects 5 issues 1991, 5 issues 1992. sub. price: $14 U.S. ($15 overseas); per copy: $3; sample: $2. Back issues: $2. Discounts: none. 6pp; 8½×11; of. Reporting time: 60 days. Payment: yes. Copyrighted, does not revert to author. Pub's reviews: 8 in 1990. §Subtropic gardening, foraging. Ads: $10 per ad per subscriber; $25 others.

LivingQuest, PO Box 3306, Boulder, CO 80307, 303-444-1319. 1987. Non-fiction. avg. press run 5M. Expects 2 titles 1991, 3 titles 1992. 2 titles listed in the *Small Press Record of Books in Print* (20th Edition, 1991-92). avg. price, paper: $10.95. 150pp; 7×10, 5½×8½; lo. Reporting time: varies. Payment: negotiable. Does not copyright for author. PMA.

LIZZENGREASY, Mark Wilhelm, Christine Waldman, Liz Stumps, G. Fletcher, Dai Ni Kuroda Kopo #203, Funabashi 5-30-6, Setagaya-ku, Tokyo-to 156, Japan. 1989. Poetry, fiction, articles, cartoons, satire, reviews, music, letters, news items, non-fiction. "Chiba office: Misty House #203, 2-15-1 Fujiwara, Funabashi, Chiba 273, Japan. Length of material: 2,000 words maximum. Our 'zine's about everyday life in foreign countries. Since we life in Japan, it's on everyday life in Japan." circ. 150+. 12/yr. Pub'd 12 issues 1990; expects 12 issues 1991, 12 issues 1992. sub. price: US$24, Y3000; per copy: US$2, Y250; sample: US$2, Y250. Back issues: few available. Discounts: none. 20pp; size B5; †of. Reporting time: 6 weeks. Payment: copies. Copyrighted, rights revert on request. Pub's reviews: 50 in 1990. §Contemporary Japanese culture/expatriot.

LLAMAS MAGAZINE, Clay Press, Inc., Cheryl Dal Porto, PO Box 100, Herald, CA 95638, 916-448-1668. 1979. Fiction, articles, art, photos, cartoons, interviews, satire, reviews, letters, news items, non-fiction. "Length of material, varied. Recent contributors: Dr. Murray E. Fowler, Marty McGee, Susan Jones, Dr. LaRue Johnson, Dr. Brad Smith, Dr. Clare Hoffman." circ. 5.5M. 8/yr. Pub'd 8 issues 1990; expects 8 issues 1991, 8 issues 1992. sub. price: $25; per copy: $5.75; sample: $5.75. Back issues: separate publication-Best of 3L. Discounts: negotiated. 128pp; 8½×11; of, sheet fed press. Reporting time: 30 days. Payment: negotiated. Copyrighted, reverts to author. Pub's reviews: 10-12 in 1990. §Camelids, backpacking, camping equipment, barns. Ads: full pg color $1067, b/w $561/-1/2 pg color $693, b/w $400/classified ads 50¢ word $20 minimum. COSMEP, SMPG (Small Magazine Publishers Group).

LLEN CYMRU, University Of Wales Press, Ceri Lewis, 6 Gwennyth St., Cathays, Cardiff CF2 4YD, Wales, 0222-231919. 1950. Articles. "Journal of various aspects of Welsh literature, printed in the Welsh language." circ. 300. 1/yr. Pub'd 1 issue 1990; expects 1 issue 1991, 1 issue 1992. sub. price: £5 per double issue; per copy: £5; sample: £5. Back issues: £5. Discounts: 10%. 143pp; of. Payment: none. Not copyrighted. Pub's reviews: 4 in 1990. §Welsh literature. UWP.

THE LLEWELLYN NEW TIMES, Llewellyn Publications, Lisa Peschel, PO Box 64383, St. Paul, MN 55164, 612-291-1970. Articles, interviews, reviews, letters. "*The Llewellyn New Times* is a unique mix of magazine and catalog of New Age products and services. It features articles and reviews of new books, tapes and videotapes as well as a complete networking section to connect people with similar interests. *The New Times* is not limited to any particular area in the New Age. It is the most complete publication of its kind." circ. 40M. 6/yr. sub. price: free to all mail order buyers; per copy: $1; sample: free. Discounts: dealers stocking the full line of Llewellyn titles get 30 free copies to give away or charge. Cover price of $1.00. 80pp; 8¼×11; of. Reporting time: 1 month. Payment: inquire for details and submission guidelines. Copyrighted, reverts to author. Pub's reviews: 8 in 1990. §New Age spirituality, alternative lifestyle, religious philosophy. Ads: $473/$268/$131 1/4 page.

Llewellyn Publications (see also THE LLEWELLYN NEW TIMES), Lorrie Oswald, Production Manager, PO Box 64383, St. Paul, MN 55164, 612-291-1970. 1897. Non-fiction. "Llewellyn Publications is the oldest publisher of New Age books in the Western Hemisphere. We have been bringing literature on spirituality, healing, astrology and religious philosophy to readers worldwide since 1897. Other subjects include: crystals, chakra therapy and yoga, psychic development, hypnosis, past life regression and astral projection. All Llewellyn authors are specialists in their fields—and most of them have a fairly broad background in New Age thought. Some recent contributors include: Anodea Judith—bodyworker and psychic healer, William Hewitt—certified hypnotherapist, Diane Stein—leader in Women's Spirituality movement; prolific writer, speaker and teacher; Scott Cunningham—specialist with crystals, herbal remedies, earth lore." avg. press run 3M. Pub'd 19 titles 1990; expects 22 titles 1991, 24 titles 1992. 56 titles listed in the *Small Press Record of Books in Print* (20th Edition, 1991-92). avg. price, paper: $7.95. Dealer discounts: single copy 20%, 2-4 40%, 5-99 43%, 100-499 45%, 500+ 50%. 200pp; 6×9; varies with printer. Reporting time: within 2 weeks. Payment:

inquire for details. Copyrights for author. Minnesota Publishers Roundtable.

A LOAD OF BULL, David Worton, Rupert, Charlotte Rhodes, Box 277, 52 Call Lane, Leeds, W. Yorkshire LS1 6DT, England. 1989. Poetry, fiction, articles, art, photos, cartoons, interviews, satire, criticism, reviews, music, letters, collages, news items, non-fiction. "Anything from one-line jokes to cartoons to pages-long articles accepted. We are a fanzine written by Wolverhampton Wanderers fans" circ. 3M. 4/yr. Pub'd 4 issues 1990; expects 4 issues 1991, 4 issues 1992. sub. price: £2.80; per copy: 50p (+ 20p p/h), $3 US; sample: same. Back issues: same. Discounts: commission= 10p per copy. 44pp; 5⅞×8-3/10; of. Reporting time: 1 week. Payment: free copy of issue in which contribution appears. Not copyrighted. Pub's reviews: 3 in 1990. §Soccer/football. Ads: none.

LOBLOLLY: A LITERARY BIANNUAL OF THE VORTEX, Tom Braswell, Editor; David J. Kelly, Managing Editor; Karen Bartlett, Associate Editor, 1310 Raleigh Road, Wilson, NC 27893, 919-237-2642. 1984. Poetry, fiction, art, photos, interviews, criticism, reviews, music, letters, long-poems, collages. "First issue had poems from four lines to thirteen pages. Our interests include all well-crafted poems; however, we do have strong interests in ethnopoetics, biopoetics, the convergence of oral and written culture where all art is art-in-motion. The first two issues of *LOBLOLLY* include work by Gary Snyder, Jonathan Williams, Fred Chappell, Reg Saner, Robert Morgan, Anthony Piccione, David Wilk, John Hawkes, an interview with Lucien Stryk, translations of Jules Laforgue from the French, and translations from the Chinese" circ. 500. 2/yr. Pub'd 1 issue 1990; expects 1 issue 1991, 2 issues 1992. sub. price: $8; per copy: $4.50; sample: $4.50. Back issues: same as above. Discounts: 30% to the trade on consignment, 40% on outright purchase. 104pp; 6×8½; of. Reporting time: 3 months. Payment: 2 copies to contributors. Copyrighted, reverts to author. Pub's reviews: 3 in 1990. §Poetry, fiction, ecology, anthropology, fine arts. Only trade ads w/ others at present.

The Lockhart Press, Russell A. Lockhart, Franklyn B. Lockhart, Box 1207, Port Townsend, WA 98368, 206-385-6412. 1982. Poetry, fiction, long-poems, non-fiction. "Our aim is to publish books devoted to the direct expression of the psyche's restless search for place and value in our time. Our books will be crafted by hand in every particular: printing by handpress from hand set type on handmade paper and hand bound in limited editions. Inqiries invited. Inaugural Publication *Midnight's Daughter*, poems by Janet Dallett, winner of Letterpress Prize, Festival of the Arts, Seattle, 1983." avg. press run 120-200. Pub'd 1 title 1990; expects 1 title 1991, 1 title 1992. 3 titles listed in the *Small Press Record of Books in Print* (20th Edition, 1991-92). avg. price, cloth: $75-$125. Discounts: 20% to distributors & subscribers to the press. 80pp; 6×9, 9×12; †lp. Reporting time: 2 months. Payment: 15% after direct cost recovery. Does not copyright for author. BAG.

LOCUS: The Newspaper of the Science Fiction Field, Charles N. Brown, Editor & Publisher; Faren Miller, Associate Editor; Shelly Clift, Advertising Manager, Assistant Editor, Box 13305, Oakland, CA 94661, 415-339-9196, 9198. 1968. Articles, photos, interviews, criticism, reviews, letters, news items. "News stories, reports on SF events." circ. 9M. 12/yr. Pub'd 12 issues 1990; expects 12 issues 1991, 12 issues 1992. sub. price: $32 individual, $35 institution; per copy: $3.50; sample: $3.50. Back issues: $3.50. Discounts: 40% plus postage on 10 or more. 90pp; 8½×11; of. Reporting time: 3 weeks. Payment: yes. Copyrighted. Pub's reviews: 400 in 1990. §S.F., fantasy, horror, related non-fiction. Ads: $500/$275/$1.75 per line.

Log Cabin Publishers, Kitty Miller, Editor and Publisher; Kathy Miller Rindock, Assistant Editor, PO Box 1536, Allentown, PA 18105, 215-434-2448. 1978. Articles, non-fiction. avg. press run 1M. Pub'd 2 titles 1990. 22 titles listed in the *Small Press Record of Books in Print* (20th Edition, 1991-92). avg. price, paper: $1.50 + 45¢ postage; other: $1.75 + 50¢ postage. Discounts: 40% booksellers; 10% and upwards on 5 or more copies. 18-24pp; 3½×8½; of. Reporting time: 2 weeks. Payment: all rights. Copyrights for author. COSMEP.

Logbridge - Rhodes, Inc., Frank Graziano, Editor; Jeanne Fowler Porter, Business Manager, PO Box 4511, Gettysburg, PA 17325-4511. 1980. Poetry, fiction, criticism, long-poems, non-fiction. avg. press run 1.5M. Pub'd 6 titles 1990; expects 4 titles 1991, 4 titles 1992. 13 titles listed in the *Small Press Record of Books in Print* (20th Edition, 1991-92). avg. price, cloth: $15; paper: $5.00; other: $30 limited editions. Discounts: 25% 1-4 books; 5 or more 40% trade; others arranged. Pages vary; size varies; of. Reporting time: 1-2 weeks. Payment: in copies. Copyrights for author.

Loiry/Bonner Press, William S. Loiry, Executive Editor; Carol J. Loiry, Book Editor, 2320 J Apalachee Parkway, Suite #494, Tallahassee, FL 32301-4939, 904-681-0019. 1985. Non-fiction. "We publish books written by professionals for the consumer, emphasizing self-help and how-to. Categories include medical, legal, personal growth, and other areas. *Loiry/Bonner Press* has recently published *How To Raise A Brat*, by Dr. Kenneth N. Condrell and *Habit Breakthrough*, by Mitchell Bobrow, M.S.W. For manuscripts we cannot publish, we refer them to the Author Consulting Program of *Loiry Publishing House*. *Loiry/Bonner Press* is a subsidiary of *Loiry Publishing House and Bonner Communications*." circ. 3.5M. Expects 2 issues 1991, 10 issues 1992. 2 titles listed in the *Small Press Record of Books in Print* (20th Edition, 1991-92). sub. price: $14.95; per copy: $9.95. Discounts: 1-24, 45%; 25-500, 50%; distributors, 40%. 300pp; 6×9; of. Reporting time: 4 weeks on query only. Payment: negotiable. Copyrighted. FPG (Florida Publishers Group), PAS

(Publishers Association of the South), AAP (Association of American Publishers.

LOL, Gwasg Gwalia, Robat Gruffudd, 14a Stryd Y Porth Mawr, Caernarfon, Gwynedd, Wales, United Kingdom, 0970 86 304. 1965. Poetry, art, photos, cartoons, satire, news items. "Satire, cartoons, Twll Tin Pob Sais." circ. 5M. 1/yr. Expects 1 issue 1991. 2 titles listed in the *Small Press Record of Books in Print* (20th Edition, 1991-92). sub. price: £1; per copy: 70p. Back issues: 1£. 28pp; 15×10; †of. Payment: none. Ads: £30. ALP.

LOLA-FISH, Bruno Pommey, 36, Residence Jean Mace, 28300 Mainvilliers, France. 1989. Art, photos, cartoons, reviews, collages. 6/yr. Pub'd 4 issues 1990. sub. price: $6; per copy: 3 IRCs. 32pp; size A6; †xerox. Not copyrighted. Pub's reviews: 100 in 1990. §Visual art, mail art, copy art, graphics, music.

Lollipop Power Books, Elizabeth Core, Editor; Paulette Bracy, Minority Editor, PO Box 277, Carrboro, NC 27510, 919-560-2738. 1970. Fiction. "We publish non-sexist, multi-racial books for children. Our books show both girls and boys as adventurous and independent, emotional and expressive. We hope to expose children to the variety of choices open to them." avg. press run 3M. Pub'd 1 title 1990; expects 1 title 1991, 1 title 1992. 14 titles listed in the *Small Press Record of Books in Print* (20th Edition, 1991-92). avg. price, cloth: $6.75; paper: $5. Discounts: 40% bookstores, 5+ copies. 32pp; size varies greatly; of. Reporting time: 8-12 weeks. Payment: 10% bookrun. Copyrights for author. USUFLP.

Lomond Publications Inc. (see also INFORMATION RETRIEVAL AND LIBRARY AUTOMATION), Thomas Hattery, Vice President, PO Box 88, Mt. Airy, MD 21771, 301-829-1496. 1963. Non-fiction. "We publish quality professional books in the fields of public policy, technology, and management with a bias toward books that combine two or more of these disciplines." avg. press run 1M-2M. 28 titles listed in the *Small Press Record of Books in Print* (20th Edition, 1991-92). avg. price, cloth: $25; other: $12, microfiche. Discounts: 1-4 copies 20%, 5-9 30%, 10-99 40%, 100+ 50%; trade books—1-3 20%, 4-99 40%, 100+ 50%; text—any quantity 20%. 250pp; 6×9. Reporting time: 2 months. Payment: royalty only, no advance. PMA (formerly PASCAL), Baltimore Publishers Association.

LONDON REVIEW OF BOOKS, Karl Miller, Mary-Kay Wilmers, Tavistock House South, Tavistock Square, London WC1H 9JZ, England, 01-388-6751. 1979. Poetry, fiction, articles, art, photos, criticism, reviews, letters, non-fiction. circ. 17M. 24/yr. Pub'd 22 issues 1990; expects 24 issues 1991, 24 issues 1992. sub. price: $48; per copy: $2; sample: $2 + postage. Back issues: $2.50 + postage. Discounts: 20% agency. 24pp; 374×257mm; of. Payment: negotiable. Copyrighted. Pub's reviews: 679 in 1990. Ads: £985/£595/.50p.

Lone Eagle Publishing Co., Joan Vietor Singleton, Ralph S. Singleton, 2337 Roscomare Road #9, Los Angeles, CA 90077-1815, fax 213-471-4969; 800-FILMBKS. 1982. "Professionals in the motion picture industry who specialize in a certain field are encouraged to submit ideas for our "filmmakers library" series of books. Present titles are: *Film Scheduling, Filmmakers Dictionary, Film Scheduling/Film Budgeting Workbook.* We also publish several annual directories, including *Film Directors: A Complete Guide*—an annual directory of motion picture directors." avg. press run 2.5M-3M. Pub'd 9 titles 1990; expects 12 titles 1991, 16 titles 1992. 13 titles listed in the *Small Press Record of Books in Print* (20th Edition, 1991-92). avg. price, cloth: $44.95; paper: $16.95. Discounts: 1-4, 20%; 5-9, 30%; 10-24, 40%; 25-49, 42%; 50-74, 44%; 75-99, 46%; 100-199, 48%; 200+, 50%. Textbook adoptions, 20%. 250pp; 6×9, 8½×11; of. Reporting time: 8 weeks. Payment: 5-10% monthly payment. Copyrights for author. PMA.

LONE STAR COMEDY MONTHLY, Lone Star Publications of Humor, Lauren I. Barnett, PO Box 29000, Suite 103, San Antonio, TX 78229. 1983. Pub'd 9 issues 1990; expects 12 issues 1991, 12 issues 1992. sub. price: inquire; per copy: $15; sample: $15. Back issues: inquire. 6pp; 8½×11. Reporting time: 1-3 months. Payment: send SASE for current pay scale. Copyrighted, reverts to author. AHHA (American Humorists and their Happy Associates); SOCW (Society of Objectivist Comedy Writers).

LONE STAR HUMOR, Lone Star Publications of Humor, Lauren Barnett, Editor & Publisher; Ash Lynby, Assistant Editor, PO Box 29000 Suite #103, San Antonio, TX 78229. 1981. Poetry, fiction, articles, art, photos, cartoons, interviews, satire, criticism, reviews, letters, news items, non-fiction. "Our only interest is humor. This includes humor in the form of jokes, riddles, puzzles, poetry, short stories, comic strips, cartoons and photos. We are also interested in humor news and features (i.e. profiles of professional humorists of any genre, news of humor-related organizations and events, and reviews/critiques of anything concerned with comedy). Also publish *Lonestar Comedy Monthly* for professional humorists" circ. 1M+. Frequency varies. Pub'd 6 issues 1990; expects 6 issues 1991, 3 issues 1992. sub. price: inquire; per copy: inquire; sample: inquire. Back issues: inquire. Discounts: inquire. 30-80pp; 5½×8½; of. Reporting time: 2-3 months. Payment: inquire for current rates. Copyrighted, reverts to author. Pub's reviews: numerous in 1990. §Humorous and humor related products and services, periodicals and books that publish humor, also comics/comix. Ads: inquire. AHHA (American Humorists & their Happy Associates).

Lone Star Press, Carroll Faith, PO Box 165, Laconner, WA 98257, 206-466-3377. 1984. Non-fiction. "Book length non-fiction related to pleasure boating" avg. press run 2M. Pub'd 1 title 1990; expects 3 titles 1991, 6 titles 1992. 1 title listed in the *Small Press Record of Books in Print* (20th Edition, 1991-92). avg. price, paper: $10.95. 180pp; 5½×8½; of. Reporting time: 4 weeks. Copyrights for author.

Lone Star Publications of Humor (see also THE GELOSOPHIST, Humor News & Views From Around The World; LONE STAR HUMOR; LONE STAR COMEDY MONTHLY), Lauren I. Barnett, Editor & Publisher; Ash N.M. Lynby, Assistant Editor, PO Box 29000, Suite #103, San Antonio, TX 78229. 1981. Pub'd 3 titles 1990; expects 3 titles 1991. 4 titles listed in the *Small Press Record of Books in Print* (20th Edition, 1991-92). avg. price, paper: inquire. 60pp; 5½×8½; of. Reporting time: 2-3 months. Payment: send SASE for guidelines & pay scale. Copyrights for author. AHHA (American Humorists and their Happy Associates).

LONG SHOT, Daniel Shot, Jack Wiler, Jessica Chosid, Tom Pulhamus, PO Box 6231, Hoboken, NJ 07030. 1982. Poetry, fiction, articles, art, photos, cartoons, non-fiction. circ. 1.5M. 2/yr. Pub'd 2 issues 1990; expects 2 issues 1991, 2 issues 1992. sub. price: $10; per copy: $5; sample: $5 + $1 p&h. Back issues: $5. 128pp; 5×8; †of. Reporting time: 6-8 weeks. Payment: copies. Copyrighted, reverts to author. Ads: $125/$75. CCLM.

THE LONG STORY, R. Peter Burnham, Editor, 11 Kingston Street, North Andover, MA 01845, 508-686-7638. 1982. Fiction. "Stories of 8,000-20,000 words, for serious educated literary people. We have very specific tastes and look for stories about common folk and committed fiction. Although we are left-wing (democratic socialist) and therefore prefer stories that reflect our left-wing concerns, you may be sure that we are not interested in crude doctrine or inept propaganda—literature and the usual literary criteria are our main focus. Since we are the only journal devoted strictly to long stories, we do not close the door or anything completely (except detective fiction, sci-fi, romance and other forms of popular fiction). But the best way to save yourself time and postage is to be familiar with us. Sample copies are $5, and writers are strongly urged to buy a copy before submitting (orders are filled on the same day that they are received). No multiple submissions, please; we are not interested in going over the contents of the bottom drawer you just cleaned out. No parts of novels; please note that we are a journal devoted to long stories, a literary form with a beginning, middle, and an end. Best length is 8,000-12,000 words since we are very unlikely to print a 20,000 word story unless it conforms exactly to our literary tastes. We will (and do), however, routinely publish one or two or so shorter long stories each issue that we do not personally like but which we feel are excellent examples of other kinds of fiction and other visions of the world besides our own. We are not enamored of literary experimentation for its own sake but have no objections to experimentation that actually reflects a new way of thinking—new form for a new vision is fine, that is, but experimentation that is self-referential, merely dawdling with language, is absolutely of no interest to us. We find behind just about every example of this kind of literary experimentation that we run across the malodorous presence of blind egoism and self-love that we find very offensive. Nor are we particularly interested in the usual produce of the writing programs—stories that are merely about relationships without any reaching after higher significance, stories with a psychological core as opposed to a thematic, moral core, stories that are thinly disguised autobiography, stories about writers, stories that take their inspiration from that ridiculous quick-cut technique every director and his brother uses in the movies nowadays, stories about adolescents coming of age. All these kinds of stories do very little for us. But any story that is an honest treatment of human experience, any story that reflects genuine life-response, will get a close and fair reading here" circ. 500. 1/yr. Expects 1 issue 1991, 1 issue 1992. sub. price: $5; per copy: $5; sample: $5. Back issues: $4. Discounts: 40% to bookstores. 150-175pp; 5½×8½; of. Reporting time: 1-2 months, sometimes longer. Payment: 2 copies and gift subscription. Copyrighted, reverts to author. No ads. CLMP.

LONGHOUSE, Longhouse, Bob Arnold, Green River R.F.D., Brattleboro, VT 05301. 1973. Poetry, long-poems. "*Longhouse* takes on no grants, funding or subscription - rather supports itself thru the good hearts of poets & readers of the journal. We're a homespun publication on the lookout for poems from the serious working poet. Any region/any style. Recent contributors: Hayden Carruth, Barbara Moraff, Keith Wilson, James Koller, Janine Pommy-Vega, Mary Oliver, Mike O'Connor, Bobby Byrd, Paul Metcalf, Frank Samperi, David Budbill, Cid Corman, Clive Faust, Theodore Enslin, Jane Brakhage, Drummond Hadley, Bill Deemer, Doc Dachtler, M.J. Bender, John Perlman. One should be familiar with the magazine before submitting poems, send for sample issue." circ. 200. 1/yr. Pub'd 1 issue 1990; expects 1 issue 1991. sub. price: $12 (includes folder series of *Scout*); sample: $8. 35pp; 8½×14; †mi, of. Reporting time: 2 weeks. Payment: copies. Pub's reviews: 30 in 1990. §Poetry, literary history, rural essays, music, film.

Longhouse (see also LONGHOUSE), Bob Arnold, Green River R.F.D., Brattleboro, VT 05301. 1973. Poetry, long-poems, concrete art. "Under the Longhouse imprint we have published 4 books of poetry including: *3 poems* by Bob Arnold, David Giannini and John Levy. *Scout* imprint has published booklets and folders by Theodore Enslin, Gerald Hausman, George Evans, David Huddle, Cid Corman, Jean Pedrick, Lyle Glazier, James Koller, Barbara Moraff, Bill Bathurst, Ian Hamilton Finlay, Jane Brakhage. Mss. solicited." avg. press run 100-200. Pub'd 2 titles 1990. avg. price, paper: $5. 5-30pp; 8×11; †mi, of, lp. Payment: copies.

THE LOOGIE, Seedy Edgewick, Renea Frey, 435 Probasco #3, Cincinnati, OH 45220, 513-281-1353. 1990.

Poetry, fiction, articles, art, photos, cartoons, interviews, satire, letters, collages, news items, non-fiction. "We publish prose, poetry, prose poetry, drawn artwork, photographs, comic-style art, articles, opinion columns, etc. Reviews aren't accepted currently. 'Intelligent Thought' is defined as thought not controlled by outside forces. This translates into the radical fringe, which is what we want. Any length, any style. No restrictions on content, except for non-exploitation. All requests for information should include return postage. No restrictions on length. We've recently published poetry by Kenneth Deigh, former publisher of *Kallisti* and currently publishing *Mezlim*. Checks payable to Andrew Mullen." circ. 30-50. 6/yr. Pub'd 2 issues 1990; expects 6 issues 1991, 6 issues 1992. sub. price: $6; per copy: $1 + stamp; sample: $1 + stamp. Back issues: same. Discounts: 75¢/issue for retailers and distributors. 16pp; 5½×8; xerox. Reporting time: 2-3 weeks. Payment: sample copy and artistic license. Copyrighted, reverts to author. Ads: $10/$5/$2.50 1/4 page.

Loom Press, Paul Marion, Box 1394, Lowell, MA 01853. 1984. Poetry. avg. press run 1M books, 500 chapbooks, 300 broadsides. Expects 2 titles 1991, 2 titles 1992. 6 titles listed in the *Small Press Record of Books in Print* (20th Edition, 1991-92). avg. price, paper: $5 book, $4 chapbook; other: $2 broadside. Discounts: trade 40%, libraries 20%. 64pp; 6×9, broadsides vary; of, lp. Reporting time: 30-60 days. Payment: individual negotiations. Copyrights for author.

Loompanics Unlimited, Michael Hoy, PO Box 1197, Port Townsend, WA 98368. 1973. Non-fiction. "We specialize in "unusual, controversial" books—some on "How to beat the System" like *How To Buy Land Cheap, Methods of Disguise, The Complete Guide to Lockpicking, The Computer Underground, The Construction and Operation of Clandestine Drug Laboratories,* etc. Length we look for is about 120-160 ms pages." avg. press run 1M. Pub'd 18 titles 1990; expects 20 titles 1991, 24 titles 1992. 98 titles listed in the *Small Press Record of Books in Print* (20th Edition, 1991-92). avg. price, cloth: $21.95; paper: $12.95. Discounts: 1-9 20%, 10-49 40%, 50-99 45%, 100-199 50%, 200+ 55%. 120pp; 5½×8½, 8½×11; of. Reporting time: 4 months. Payment: negotiable. Copyrights for author.

LOONFEATHER: A magazine of poetry, short prose, and graphics, Loonfeather Press, Betty Rossi, Editor; Marsh Muirhead, Bemidji Community Arts Center, 426 Bemidji Avenue, Bemidji, MN 56601, 218-751-4869; 243-2402. 1979. Poetry, fiction, photos, non-fiction. "Short poems and fiction (1.5M words), 90% Minnesota writers. *Query* before submitting. Unsolicited submissions often unaccepted from out-of-state writers." circ. 300. 2/yr. Pub'd 2 issues 1990; expects 2 issues 1991, 2 issues 1992. sub. price: $7.50; per copy: $4.95 postpaid. Back issues: $2.50 through Summer '87, $4.95 Fall '87 to present. Discounts: write for rates on multiple copies. 48pp; 6×9; of. Reporting time: 1 month following publication date. Payment: 2 copies. Copyrighted, reverts to author. Ads: $450 2 issues/$225/2 X 5 for 2 issues $90. CLMP.

Loonfeather Press (see also LOONFEATHER: A magazine of poetry, short prose, and graphics), Betty Rossi, 426 Bemidji Avenue, Bemidji, MN 56601, 218-751-4869; 243-2402. 1979. Poetry, fiction, art, photos, parts-of-novels, non-fiction. "We are particularly interested in publishing the work of emerging regional writers (Minnesota, Wisconsin, North Dakota, Canada) and works with regional settings. We will consider children's literature, journals, memoirs, biography. No science fiction." avg. press run 1.5M. Pub'd 1 title 1990; expects 3 titles 1991, 3 titles 1992. 3 titles listed in the *Small Press Record of Books in Print* (20th Edition, 1991-92). avg. price, paper: $7.95. Discounts: 40% bookstores, 55% distributors. 100pp; 5½×8; of. Reporting time: within 3 months. Payment: 10% on first 1000. Copyrights for author. CLMP.

Lord John Press, Herb Yellin, 19073 Los Alimos Street, Northridge, CA 91326, 818-363-6621. 1977. "Work only with established authors - our primary market is collectors and universities. Do not want unsolicited manuscripts. Published authors: John Updike, Norman Mailer, Robert B. Parker, Ray Bradbury, Ursula K. Le Guin, John Barth, Raymond Carver....." avg. press run 300-500. Pub'd 12 titles 1990; expects 12 titles 1991, 9 titles 1992. avg. price, cloth: $50. Discounts: trade 40%. 50pp; 6×9; of, lp.

LORE AND LANGUAGE, J.D.A. Widdowson, The Centre for English Cultural Tradition and Language, The University, Sheffield S10 2TN, England, Sheffield 768555 ext 6296. 1969. Poetry, articles, reviews, letters. "Articles and items for those interested in language, folklore, cultural tradition and oral history." circ. 300. 2/yr. Pub'd 2 issues 1990; expects 2 issues 1991, 2 issues 1992. sub. price: £10 indiv, £25 institutions; per copy: £5; sample: free. Back issues: Price dependent on issue required. Apply to Sheffield Academic Press. Discounts: none. 128pp; 15×21cm (A5); of. Reporting time: 3 weeks. Payment: none. Copyrighted. Pub's reviews: 120 in 1990. §Language, folklore, cultural tradition, oral history. Ads: £95/£70/£40 1/4 page. Sheffield Academic Press, 343 Fulwood Road, Sheffield, S10 3BP, Tel. (0742)670043.

Lorien House (see also BLACK MOUNTAIN REVIEW), David A. Wilson, PO Box 1112, Black Mountain, NC 28711, 704-669-6211. 1969. Poetry, fiction, non-fiction. avg. press run 500-1M. Pub'd 2 titles 1990; expects 1 title 1991, 2 titles 1992. 19 titles listed in the *Small Press Record of Books in Print* (20th Edition, 1991-92). avg. price, paper: $4-$8. Discounts: 5 copies 40%. 100pp; 5½×8½; †of. Reporting time: 1 week to 1 month. Does not copyright for author.

‡LOS ANGELES REVIEW (OF LITERATURE & CURRENT AFFAIRS), J.F. Miglio, 7536 Circuit

Drive, Citrus Heights, CA 95610. 1986. Articles, photos, interviews, satire, criticism, news items. "Book Reviews: reviews of new fiction and nonfiction books. Written in literary style. High-quality only. Word length-1,000 words. Articles: high-quality articles or interviews dealing with book publishers, prominent writers, political figures. Word length—2,000 to 3,000 words" circ. 10M. 4-6/yr. Expects 4 issues 1991, 10 issues 1992. sub. price: $12; per copy: $1.50; sample: same. Back issues: $1.50. Discounts: call publisher. 12-24pp; 11×13; of. Reporting time: 2-4 weeks. Payment: on acceptance; reviews ($25-$50), articles ($50-$250). Pub's reviews: 15 in 1990. §All areas—except highly technical, regional or academic. Ads: $1,356/$784/$200 1/8 page.

Los Arboles Publications, Jean E Beckman, PO Box 7000-54, Rendondo Beach, CA 90277, 213-375-0759. 1981. Non-fiction. avg. press run 4M. Pub'd 3 titles 1990; expects 4 titles 1991, 3 titles 1992. 21 titles listed in the *Small Press Record of Books in Print* (20th Edition, 1991-92). avg. price, paper: $7.95. Discounts: 40% churches and bookstores, 20% libraries, 50% distributors, 20% single copies. 200pp; 5⅜×8⅜; of. Payment: no advance, 10% of retail on paid orders. Copyrights for author. COSMEP.

Los Hombres Press, James Kitchen, Co-Publisher; Marsh Cassady, Co-Publisher, PO Box 632279, San Diego, CA 92163-2729, 619-234-6710. 1989. Fiction, non-fiction. "Gay and lesbian fiction and nonfiction; haiku (gay & nongay)." avg. press run 2M. Pub'd 5 titles 1991, 4 titles 1992. 3 titles listed in the *Small Press Record of Books in Print* (20th Edition, 1991-92). avg. price, paper: $9.95. Discounts: 45% for 5 copies. 230pp; 5×8½; of. Reporting time: 6 weeks. Payment: 10% on gross, no advance. Copyrights for author. The Publishing Triangle, COSMEP.

LOST AND FOUND TIMES, Luna Bisonte Prods, John M. Bennett, 137 Leland Ave, Columbus, OH 43214. 1975. Poetry, fiction, articles, art, photos, cartoons, satire, reviews, letters, parts-of-novels, long-poems, collages, concrete art. "Format and content for each issue will vary considerably. I am interested in the experimental and the primitive, and in anything new or unusual. Would like to see collaborations. Spanish and/or English. See Luna Bisonte Prods for further information." circ. 300. Irregular. Pub'd 2 issues 1990; expects 2 issues 1991, 2 issues 1992. sub. price: $14/5 issues; per copy: $4; sample: $4 for sample packet. Back issues: #1-10, #21-25 $20, #11-20 $40, #21-25 $20. Discounts: 40% for resale. 40pp; size varies; of. Reporting time: 2 weeks. Payment: copies. Copyrighted, reverts to author. Pub's reviews. §Literature, art, reviews.

LOST GENERATION JOURNAL, Thomas W. Wood, Jr., Deloris Wood, Route 5 Box 134, Salem, MO 65560, 314-364-5900; 729-5669. 1973. Poetry, fiction, articles, art, photos, cartoons, interviews, criticism, reviews, letters, news items, non-fiction. "*LGJ* topics deal with Americans in Europe, chiefly Paris, between 1919 and 1939. Primary emphasis is placed on Americans who began making a name for themselves in literature, graphic and performing arts such as Pound, Stein and Hemingway. Article length can vary, but we prefer pieces between 800 and 2,500 words. Poetry should be 20 lines or less. Good photographs and art should relate to the theme in time and place as should the articles and poetry. Scholars must document their work with footnotes and bibliography. Lost Generation people (those who started in Paris) must state when they were abroad and supply evidence of their qualifications or cite references for confirmation. Authors should supply a passport-size photograph of themselves and a 200-word biographical blurb. Recent contributors: Mark Bassett, Robin Dormin, Mark Orwoll, John McCall, Jerry Rosco." circ. 400. 1/yr. Pub'd 1 issue 1990; expects 1 issue 1991, 1 issue 1992. 1 title listed in the *Small Press Record of Books in Print* (20th Edition, 1991-92). sub. price: $10; per copy: $10; sample: $10. Back issues: $10. Discounts: $9.50 per year to subscription agency. 32pp; 8½×11; of. Reporting time: 6 weeks, SASE earlier. Payment: 1¢ per word or 3 copies of issue article appears. Copyrighted. Pub's reviews: 4 in 1990. §Twentieth Century literature, bibliography, biography, Americans in Paris, Hemingway, Pound, Stein, Miller. Ads: $150/$125/$85/$5 an inch. COSMEP, Conferences of Editors of Learned Journals, Society to Scholarly Publishing, AEJNC, MLA.

THE LOST PERUKE, P.M. Kellermann, PO Box 1525, Highland Park, NJ 08904. 1988. Satire. "No unsolicited manuscripts accepted. *Will not* publish any outside contributors." circ. 200. 12/yr. Pub'd 10 issues 1990; expects 12 issues 1991, 12 issues 1992. sub. price: $15; per copy: $1.50; sample: $1.50. Back issues: package rates available. Discounts: specified upon request. 32pp; 5½×8½; †xerography. Copyrighted, does not revert to author. Ads: $45/$25/rates specified to advertiser's needs.

Lost Roads Publishers, C. D. Wright, Editor; Forrest Gander, Editor, PO Box 5848, Weybosset Hill Station, Providence, RI 02903, 401-245-8069. 1977. Poetry, fiction, photos, long-poems. "We recently published Keith Waldrop's selected poems and short fiction by Frank Stanford and Sharon Doubiago. Published *The Battlefield Where The Moon Says I Love You*, a 542 page poem by Frank Stanford in 1978 with *Mill Mountain Press* under a grant for experimental lit. awarded by the NEA. Published *Trouble in Paradise* in 1981, the narrative drawings of Zuleyka Benitez: 40 graphite images." avg. press run 1M. Pub'd 6 titles 1990; expects 2 titles 1991, 3 titles 1992. 25 titles listed in the *Small Press Record of Books in Print* (20th Edition, 1991-92). avg. price, paper: $8.95. Discounts: 1 copy, net; 2-4 copies, 30% discount; 5-24 copies, 40% discount; 25 or more, 50% discount. We pay postage and handling on prepaid orders.). 124pp; 6×9; of, lp. Reporting time: 1 month. Payment: $300 author's payment, 20 copies. Editor sends copyright forms to author to copyright in their name.

Lotus Press, Inc., Naomi Madgett, Editor, PO Box 21607, Detroit, MI 48221, 313-861-1280. 1972. Poetry. "We are not considering any new material at this time" avg. press run 500-2M. Pub'd 4 titles 1990; expects 3 titles 1991, 3 titles 1992. 66 titles listed in the *Small Press Record of Books in Print* (20th Edition, 1991-92). avg. price, cloth: $18; paper: $7; other: $2.50 set of 4 broadsides. Discounts: usually 30-40% depending on size of order. 80pp; 5½x8½; of/lo. Reporting time: 6-8 weeks. Payment: copies which author may sell. Does not copyright for author. COSMEP.

LOUDER THAN BOMBS, Seminal Life Press, Bryan Ha, 2313 Santa Anita Avenue, S. El Monte, CA 91733, 818-575-1887. 1990. Poetry, fiction, art, photos, long-poems. "Everything is welcome except the dull and the sentimental. Strong, fresh language and imagery is what I am looking for. Any length or form, inluding prose-poems, is fine. Recent contributors: Antler, Steve Abee, Michael C. Ford, Lyn Lifshin, Andrew Demcak, A. Razor, Nancy Ellis Taylor." circ. 200. Pub'd 4 issues 1990; expects 4 issues 1991, 4 issues 1992. sub. price: $10; per copy: $3; sample: $3. Discounts: will trade with other poetry/fiction magazines. 60pp; 8½x11; †Xerox. Reporting time: within 1 week. Payment: 1 copy. Copyrighted, reverts to author. §Poetry, fiction, art.

THE LOUISVILLE REVIEW, Sena Jeter Naslund, Faculty Editor; Karen Johns, Editor, Univ. of Louisville, English Dept., 315 Bingham Humanities, Louisville, KY 40292, 502-588-6801. 1976. Poetry, fiction, parts-of-novels, long-poems, plays. "Some recent contributors: Maura Stanton, Patricia Goedicke, Greg Pape, Janet Sisk, Paula Rankin, Maureen Morehead, Aleda Shirley, Leon Driskell, Ellen Lesser" circ. 850. 2/yr. Pub'd 1 issue 1990; expects 2 issues 1991, 2 issues 1992. sub. price: $7 (postpaid); per copy: $4 (postpaid); sample: $3. Back issues: $3 each (postpaid). 96pp; 6x9; lp. Reporting time: 6-12 weeks. Payment: 1 compl. copy. Copyrighted, reverts to author. Do not advertise.

LOVE AND RAGE, A Revolutionary Anarchist Newsmonthly, Box 3 Prince Street Station, New York, NY 10012. 1989. Poetry, articles, art, photos, cartoons, interviews, criticism, reviews, music, letters, collages, news items, non-fiction. circ. 3M. 12/yr. Pub'd 7 issues 1990; expects 11-12 issues 1991, 12 issues 1992. sub. price: $7 3rd class, $12 1st class, overseas; per copy: $1; sample: $1. 12pp; 11x17. Not copyrighted. Pub's reviews: 2 in 1990. Ads: none.

LOVE & ROCKETS, Fantagraphics Books, Gary Groth, 7563 Lake City Way, Seattle, WA 98115. 1976. Fiction, cartoons, letters. "*Love & Rockets* is the creation of Jaime Gilbert and mario Hernandez. Its two main storylines; 'Locas' and 'Palomar', explore the lives of their female protagonists in, respectively, the Los Angeles barrios and a small coastal town in Mexico. The book does not use outside contributors save for letters of comment" circ. 18M. 6/yr. Pub'd 5 issues 1990; expects 6 issues 1991, 6 issues 1992. sub. price: $12; per copy: $2.25; sample: same. Back issues: $3.50 reprint issue #1. Discounts: 10%-60%, it varies, libraries 10%, comics dist. 60%, retailers 40-50%, jobbers 10%. 30pp; 8½x11. Payment: royalties. Copyrighted, reverts to author. COSMEP.

Love Child Publishing, 6565 Sunset Blvd., Suite 318, Hollywood, CA 90028. 1990. Articles, photos, interviews, reviews, news items, non-fiction. "Nonfiction: books—texts, guides, manual, directories, reference—for and about the entertainment industry." avg. press run 3M. Expects 3 titles 1991, 3 titles 1992. 2 titles listed in the *Small Press Record of Books in Print* (20th Edition, 1991-92). avg. price, paper: $20. Discounts: wholesale 55%; booksellers: 2-4 20%, 5-99 40%, 100+ 44%. 230pp; 8½x11; of. Reporting time: 4 weeks on queries, 6 weeks on manuscripts. Payment: varies, negotiable. Copyrights for author. Minority Publishers Exchange, American Black Book Writers Association.

Lovely Publications (see also I WANT TO EAT YOUR STOMACH), Sir Tapeworm of the Big Hill O'er Yonder, 81 Castlerigg Drive, Burnley, Lancashire BB12 8AT, United Kingdom. 1476. Poetry, reviews, music, news items. "Hello. We're very weird" Expects 1 title 1991, 1 title 1992. avg. price, other: $5. Discounts: free to women who send naked pictures of themselves. page size quite big but not grotesquely so; †hi ho, hi ho, it's off to work we go. Reporting time: 1 second. Payment: 1 copy of it that hasn't already been eaten. We don't know how to copyright for author. 66/73/508/176/199/50/69/88.

Lowen Publishing, Tod J. Snodgrass, PO Box 6870-19, Torrance, CA 90504-0870, 213-831-2770. 2 titles listed in the *Small Press Record of Books in Print* (20th Edition, 1991-92).

LOWLANDS REVIEW, Tom Whalen, 6109 Magazine, New Orleans, LA 70118. 1974. Poetry, fiction, art, interviews, reviews, parts-of-novels, long-poems. "We like the experimental/surreal, but are not averse to good work in any vein. Recent contributors include George Garrett, Stuart Dybek, Brian Swann, Julia Randall, Christopher Middleton, Robert Walser, William Harrison, Dino Buzzati, Henri Michaux, JoAnn Monks, etc. After LR 10, special issues are planned. We will not be reading unsolicited material." circ. 400. 2/yr. sub. price: $6; per copy: $3; sample: $3. Back issues: 1-10 $3 each. 48pp; 6x9; of. Reporting time: 2 weeks to 2 months. Payment: 2 copies. Copyrighted, reverts to author. Pub's reviews. §Fiction, poetry (contemporary).

Low-Tech Press, Ron Kolm, 30-73 47th Street, Long Island City, NY 11103, 718-721-0946. 1981. Poetry, fiction, art, cartoons, interviews, satire, parts-of-novels, long-poems. "Low-Tech Press is currently publishing a revised edition of *Welcome to the Barbecue*, poems by Ron Kolm. Cover art by Drew Friedman, illust. by Edward Jacobus. We are not set up to receive any unsolicited mss at present." avg. press run 500. Pub'd 1 title 1990; expects 1 title 1991, 1 title 1992. 5 titles listed in the *Small Press Record of Books in Print* (20th Edition, 1991-92). avg. price, paper: $5. Discounts: 60/40% to bookstores + postage. 75-150pp; 5½×8½; of. Reporting time: 2-4 weeks. Payment: each arrangement differs - all profits to authors so far. Copyrights for author.

Lowy Publishing, David C. Lowy, President, Janitor, Sergeant-at-Arms, 5047 Wigton, Houston, TX 77096, 713-723-3209. 1979. Fiction, art, cartoons, satire, letters, plays, non-fiction. "Not reading mss. presently." avg. press run 600. Pub'd 1 title 1990. 1 title listed in the *Small Press Record of Books in Print* (20th Edition, 1991-92). avg. price, paper: $8.25, varies. Discounts: 40% to bookstores, 25% to libraries-not all titles. 112pp, varies; size varies; of, photocopying. Payment: 10% of gross based on monthly sales. Copyrights for author.

LP Publications (Teleos Institute) (see also EMERGING), Diane K. Pike, PO Box 7601, San Diego, CA 92167-0601, 619-225-0133. 1972. Articles, photos, cartoons, letters. avg. press run 1M. 9 titles listed in the *Small Press Record of Books in Print* (20th Edition, 1991-92). avg. price, paper: $8.95. Discounts: available upon request. 120pp; size varies; of. Reporting time: variable. Copyrights for author.

LUCHA/STRUGGLE, New York CIRCUS, Inc., New York CIRCUS Collective, PO Box 37, Times Square Station, New York, NY 10108, 212-928-7600; FAX 212-928-2757. 1976. Articles. "Material published in *Lucha/Struggle* includes reporting, analysis and theological reflection on the current situation in Latin America and the U.S. response (government and popular responses). Recent contributors are economists, theologians and activists. They write about third world struggles, theology of liberation and U.S. immigration questions. Mss. should be received by the 1st of the following months: January, March, May, July, September, and November" circ. 3M. 6/yr. Pub'd 6 issues 1990; expects 6 issues 1991, 6 issues 1992. sub. price: $10; per copy: $2; sample: gratis. Back issues: $1.50 per issue; bulk or package prices on request. Discounts: bulk rate 40%. 40pp; 8½×11; of. We are not able to provide payment for articles, and can only promise distribution of the article. Pub's reviews: 1 in 1990. §Latin American history, liberation theology, U.S. foreign policy viz a viz Latin America, U.S., immigration, labor, economic issues.

LUCIDITY, Bear House Publishing, Ted O. Badger, Route 2, Box 94, Eureka Springs, AR 72632-9505, 501-253-9351. 1985. Poetry. "Any subject or style of poetry but must be comprehensible: subtle, yes; obscure, no. Line length: 66 characters; number of lines 40, including title and spacing. We seek lucid verse dealing with the wide spectrum of human experience. Do not submit without requesting guidelines first. Include SASE." circ. 250. 4/yr. Pub'd 4 issues 1990; expects 4 issues 1991, 4 issues 1992. sub. price: $8; per copy: $2; sample: $2. Back issues: $2. Discounts: negotiable. 56pp; 5½×8½; of. Reporting time: 90 days or less. Payment: copies and cash. Copyrighted, reverts to author. Pub's reviews: 4 in 1990. §Straight-forward, understandable poetry. No ads.

LUCKY HEART BOOKS, Salt Lick Press, James Haining, 1909 Sunny Brook Drive, Austin, TX 78743-3449. 1939. Poetry, fiction, articles, art, photos, cartoons, interviews, satire, criticism, reviews, music, letters, parts-of-novels, long-poems, collages, plays, concrete art. *"Letters to Obscure Men*. Verse by Gerald Burns. *Catch My Breath*. Verse, prose, and fiction by Michael Lally. *George Washington Trammell*. Verse by Robert Trammell. *Two Kids & The Three Bears*. Prose narrative by John Dennis Brown. *A Quincy History*. Verse, journal record by James Haining. Three titles in 1979: *Next Services*, poetry by Michalea Moore. *Book of Spells* (first third), poetry by Gerald Burns. *New Icons* verse by Peggy Davis; *Next Services* verse by Michalea Moore; *A Book of Spells* (first & third) verse by Gerald Burns; *Lovers/Killers* verse by Robert Trammell. *Pose Poems* verse by Julie Siegel; *A Child's Garden* verse by James Haining" circ. 1M. Irregular. Pub'd 1 issue 1990; expects 4 issues 1991, 3 issues 1992. sub. price: $6 mag, $5 books, $2 samplers. Back issues: write for information. Discounts: 60%-40%. 68pp; 8×10½, 9×6; †of, lp. Reporting time: 10 days. Payment: copies and $ if available. Copyrighted, rights released. No ads.

Billy Jack Ludwig Holding Co., Billy Jack Ludwig, Rich Howard, Bill Dawson, Ted Gamberdella, Box 670954, Dallas, TX 75367, 214-980-7141; 980-8274; 502-7136 (mobile); 800-274-3011; fax 214-980-8517. 1955. "Imprints: Sunbelt, Sunburst, Sunnybelt, Sunny Belt, Sunny Burst. We buy book outright. We are in the market for how-to book year around. We do not work on royalty at all now. We did at one time but got out of this business. We are still paying for a few that are still selling in reprint. Send manuscripts to us with money for return to sender. Additional address: Box 671099, Dallas, TX 75367. No religious, witchcraft, technical, sex, poetry." avg. press run 500. Pub'd 100-150 titles 1990. avg. price, cloth: $19.95-$99.95; paper: $16.95-$49.95. Discounts: 60% to distributors. 250pp; 8½×11, 9×6. Reporting time: 30 days. Payment: no royalties. Copyrights for author.

Lumen Books, Inc. (see also SITES), Ronald Christ, Dennis L. Dollens, 446 West 20 Street, New York, NY 10011, 212-989-7944. 1984. Articles, non-fiction. "Edgardo Cozarinsky, Diane Ackerman, Severo Sarduy." avg. press run 1M. Pub'd 1 title 1990; expects 3 titles 1991, 2 titles 1992. avg. price, paper: $7.95-$10.95. Discounts: trade 40/60. 84-146pp; 5×8; of. Reporting time: 1-3 months. Payment: no advance, 10% royalty.

Copyrights for author.

Luna Bisonte Prods (see also LOST AND FOUND TIMES), John M. Bennett, 137 Leland Ave, Columbus, OH 43214, 614-846-4126. 1974. Poetry, art, cartoons, satire, letters, collages, concrete art. "Interested in exchanges. We print broadsides and labels, chapbooks, poetry products, and a magazine. Would like to see more material in Spanish. See *Lost & Found Times* for further info." avg. press run 350. Pub'd 4 titles 1990; expects 4 titles 1991, 4 titles 1992. 45 titles listed in the *Small Press Record of Books in Print* (20th Edition, 1991-92). avg. price, paper: $4. Discounts: 40% for resale. 40pp; size varies; of, rubber stamps. Reporting time: 2 weeks. Payment: copies. Author must do own registering for copyright.

LUNA TACK, Dog Hair Press, David Duer, Editor; Ken McCullough, Contributing Editor; Steven LaVoie, Contributing Editor; Stephen Gilson, Contributing Editor, PO Box 372, West Branch, IA 52358-0144, 319-643-7324. 1981. Poetry, fiction, art, photos, cartoons, satire, criticism, reviews, letters, long-poems, collages, plays. "Our bias is towards a writing 'in which there is no seam between the personal and political, lyrical and engaged.' (D. Levertov). We are seeking out the freshness of style and subject that can best be discovered among young writers, but we also publish those established writers who epitomize this: e.g. Jim Heynen, Anselm Hollo, Susan Howe, Nathaniel Tarn, Cid Corman, Lydia Davis..." circ. 500-300. 2/yr. Expects 2 issues 1991, 1 issue 1992. sub. price: $6; per copy: $3; sample: $3.50. Back issues: #2 (March 1982) $2.50. Discounts: 40% with order of 5 or more copies (may mix issue numbers). 64pp; 5½×8½; of. Reporting time: 2 months. Payment: 2 copies. Copyrighted, reverts to author. Pub's reviews. §Contemporary poetry and fiction. No ads. CCLM.

The Lunchroom Press (see also MENU), David Bianco, Director, PO Box 36027, Grosse Pointe Farms, MI 48236. 1980. Poetry, articles, art, photos, interviews, criticism, reviews, concrete art. "The Lunchroom Press is interested in publishing book-length works documenting the latest trends in all of the arts. We will consider proposals for directory-type publications, anthologies, collections of photographs, as well as individual pieces that may be gathered into an anthology of our own editing." avg. press run 1M. Pub'd 1 title 1990; expects 1 title 1991, 1 title 1992. 4 titles listed in the *Small Press Record of Books in Print* (20th Edition, 1991-92). avg. price, paper: $5-$6. Discounts: 40% trade, minimum order of 10 copies, same to jobbers; 20% for 2-9 copies. 96pp; of. Reporting time: 2 months for acceptability, longer for actual use. Payment: percentage of gross sales paid in quarterly installments. Copyrights for author. PP (Poetry Project), PRC (Poetry Resource Center) (Detroit).

THE LUNDIAN, Modern Media, M. Robinson, Managing Editor; Monique Fransen, General Manager, PO Box 722, 220 07 Lund, Sweden, fax: 046-138221. 1988. Poetry, fiction, articles, art, photos, cartoons, interviews, satire, criticism, reviews, music, letters, news items, non-fiction. circ. 3M. 10/yr. sub. price: $25; per copy: $3.50; sample: $4. Back issues: $6. 12pp; size A4; desktop. Reporting time: 60 days. Payment: none. Copyrighted, reverts to author. Pub's reviews: 2 in 1990. §Short stories, general material, travel, sports. Ads: $300/$200/$1.50 classifieds. The English International Association of Lund.

LuraMedia, Inc., Marcia Broucek, PO Box 261668, San Diego, CA 92126, 619-578-1948. 1982. Non-fiction. avg. press run 3.5M. Pub'd 4 titles 1990; expects 6 titles 1991, 6 titles 1992. 27 titles listed in the *Small Press Record of Books in Print* (20th Edition, 1991-92). avg. price, cloth: $14.95; paper: $10.95. Discounts: 2-4 20%, 5-24 40%, 25-49 43%, 50-99 46%, 100+ 50%. 220pp; 6×9; of. Reporting time: 6 weeks. Payment: 10% net receipts. Copyrights for author. PMA, COSMEP.

Luthers, Gary Luther, Alan Luther, 1009 North Dixie Freeway, New Smyrna Beach, FL 32168-6221, 904-423-1600; 423-9450. 1988. "We are private publishers; unless partnership arrangements are made, the author generally pays to publish his/her work. We offer expert editing/art/design/negative and halftone production/marketing support. Manuscripts can be typeset directly from the author's IBM compatible computer discs or optically scanned (OCR) from good quality typewritten sheets. Either method reduces the cost of typesetting by 1) not retyping a manuscript, and 2) not introducing new errors in the process. Offset printing is used for paperback or hardcover books of 500 copies or more. On small books, limited runs of 150 or less can be produced economically by laser printer, with printed cover (letterpress or foil stamped) and plastic comb binding. Limited run books allow the author to sample a market cost effectively or to produce a work for select circulation...even as gifts" avg. press run 1M. Pub'd 10 titles 1990; expects 15 titles 1991, 15+ titles 1992. 10 titles listed in the *Small Press Record of Books in Print* (20th Edition, 1991-92). avg. price, cloth: $50; paper: $7.95. Discounts: 40% trade. 100+pp; 5½×8½, 6×9, 8½×11; of, LaserJet. Reporting time: 10 working days. Copyrights for author.

Lyceum Books, Inc., Anita Samen, President, 59 E. Van Buren, Suite 703, Chicago, IL 60605, 312-922-1880. 1989. Non-fiction. avg. press run 2M. Pub'd 5 titles 1990; expects 8 titles 1991, 6 titles 1992. 18 titles listed in the *Small Press Record of Books in Print* (20th Edition, 1991-92). avg. price, cloth: $29.95; paper: $18.95. Discounts: bookstores, wholesalers 1 copy 20%, 5+ copies 40%; libraries 10%. 300pp; 5¾×8¼, 6×9; of. Reporting time: 2 months. Copyrights for author.

LYNX, Terri Lee Grell, PO Box 169, Toutle, WA 98649, 206-274-6661. 1985. Poetry, fiction, articles, art, photos, interviews, criticism, reviews, letters. *"Lynx*, is the only magazine in the Western Hemisphere devoted to renga (linked verse). Subscribers participate in linking haiku-like stanzas to form a renga 'chain.' The form dates back to 12th century Japan, and was elevated to an artform by Matsuo Basho in the 14th century. Contemporary renga writers are primarily from the West, and include Hiroaki Sato, Marlene Mountain, John Cage, Jane Reichhold and Lorraine Ellis Harr. *Lynx* publishes solo renga, avant garde poetry and prose, art, commentaries, book reviews, interviews, photos, haiku. The Participation Renga section of *Lynx* is for subscribers only, and continues the tradition of *APA-Renga* whereby poets add links to ongoing renga, issue by issue, one link at a time. 'The exciting thing about renga is that it connects people. It's a weaving from heart to heart.'—Tundra Wind." circ. 800. 43/yr. Pub'd 3 issues 1990; expects 4 issues 1991, 4 issues 1992. sub. price: $15 US, $20 outside US; per copy: $4 US, $6 outside US. Back issues: $2 US, $4 outside US. Discounts: inquire. 24pp; 14×5¾; laser printing, printingpress. Reporting time: 4 weeks. Payment: copies. Not copyrighted. Pub's reviews: 4 in 1990. §Haiku, renga, new and rare poetry forms, Eastern philosophy, Japanese poetry and culture, Zen, avant garde topics and perpetuators. Ads: $20 per column inch. Haiku Society of America, Canadian Haiku Society, American Assoc. of Haikuists, International Council of Literary Magazines and Presses.

Lynx House Press, Christopher Howell, Editor; Valerie Martin, Managing Editor, PO Box 640, Amherst, MA 01004, 316-342-0755. 1972. Poetry, fiction. "Alternative address: 1326 West Street, Emporia, KS 66801. Lynx House Press publishes books of uncompromising esthetic and political intensity. While most of our authors have been publishing in journals (and chapbooks, limited editions and the like) before coming to us, we are not closed to new writers and new writing. Our list includes titles by Floyce Alexander, Ray Amorosi, Don Hendrie Jr., Joyce Thompson, Vern Rutsala, Valerie Martin, Bill Tremblay, Yusef Komunyakaa, Fred Pfeil, Gillian Conoley, and Wayne Ude" avg. press run 1M. Pub'd 2 titles 1990; expects 5 titles 1991, 5 titles 1992. avg. price, cloth: $15; paper: $7. Discounts: library and bookdealer—1 copy 10%, 2-4 20%, 5+ 40%. 70pp; 6×9; of. Reporting time: 6 weeks. Payment: 10% of press run. Copyrights for author.

LYRA, Lourdes Gil, Iraida Iturralde, Lyra Society for the Arts, Inc., PO Box 3188, Guttenberg, NJ 07093, 201-861-1941. 1986. Poetry, fiction, art, photos, interviews, criticism, reviews, non-fiction. "No length or thematic restrictions. We are multilingual and accept material in French, Italian, Spanish, etc., besides English. Recent contributors: J. Kozer, Belkis Cuza Male, Tom Whalen, Tony Mendoza, Severo Sarduy" circ. 700. 4/yr. Pub'd 2 issues 1990; expects 4 issues 1991, 4 issues 1992. sub. price: $15; per copy: $4; sample: $4. Back issues: $3. Discounts: 10% agents, classroom, advertisers. 28pp; 10½×8¼; of. Reporting time: 4-6 weeks. Payment: 5 copies. Copyrighted, reverts to author. Pub's reviews: 2 in 1990. §Film, literature (American, English, French, Spanish, Italian), art, photography. Ads: $150/$80/$50 1/4 page. CCLM, COSMEP, American Periodical Verse.

THE LYRIC, Commonwealth Press Virginia, Leslie Mellichamp, Editor; Elizabeth D. Mellichamp, Managing Editor, 307 Dunton Drive, Southwest, Blacksburg, VA 24060, 703-552-3475. 1921. Poetry. "Rhymed verse in traditional forms preferred, about 36 lines. We print poetry only. No political or social problems; accessible on first or second reading. Poems must be original, unpublished, and not under consideration elsewhere. Send SASE for reply." circ. 850. 4/yr. Pub'd 4 issues 1990; expects 4 issues 1991, 4 issues 1992. sub. price: $10 a yr., $19 for 2 yrs., $27 for 3 yrs., Canada and other foreign add $2 per year; per copy: $3; sample: $3. Back issues: depends on availability. Discounts: 10% to agencies. 32pp; 5⅜×7½; cold type. Reporting time: 1 month. Payment: contributors receive complimentary copy of issue with their poem; quarterly and annual prizes for poetry published; $40 quarterly, $725 (total) annually. Copyrighted, reverts to author. No ads. Small Press.

M

M & T Publishing (see also DR. DOBB'S JOURNAL), Jonathan Erickson, Editor-in-Chief, 501 Galveston Drive, Redwood City, CA 94063-4728, 415-366-3600. 1976. Articles, interviews, criticism, reviews, letters, news items. "A journal of software tools for advanced microcomputer programmers" avg. press run 78M. Pub'd 14 titles 1990; expects 14 titles 1991, 14 titles 1992. Discounts: 40-50% off retail to resalers; other discounts in volumes. 130pp; 8½×11; web. Reporting time: 3 months. Payment: standard royalty for books, fee for articles varies. Copyrights for author on request.

M.A.F. Press (see also THIRTEEN), Ken Stone, Box 392, Portlandville, NY 13834. 1976. Poetry. "Chapbooks, poetry (only)" avg. press run 100. Pub'd 16 titles 1990; expects 16 titles 1991. 98 titles listed in the *Small Press Record of Books in Print* (20th Edition, 1991-92). avg. price, paper: $2.50. Discounts: none.

32pp; 5½×8½; lp. Reporting time: 2 weeks. Payment: 50 copies of run. Does not copyright for author. COSMEP, CLMP, NAPT.

MAAT, Katherine Flanagan, 1223 South Selva, Dallas, TX 75218, 214-324-3093. 1985. Poetry, fiction, art, photos, interviews, reviews, parts-of-novels, long-poems, plays. "No length restrictions or style restrictions. Strength of work is final requirement. Recent contributors include: Lyn Lifshin, Tony Moffeit, Harry Calhoun, Bruce Combs" circ. 200+. 4/yr. Expects 4 issues 1991, 4 issues 1992. sub. price: $9; per copy: $3; sample: $3. Back issues: special rates to renewing subscribers. Discounts: will trade publications at editor's discretion. 40-60pp; 5½×8½; mi. Reporting time: 6 weeks max., most within 7 days. Payment: one copy of issue in which writer's work appears. Not copyrighted. Pub's reviews: 8 in 1990. §Poetry, little or literary mags.

THE MAC GUFFIN, Arthur Lindenberg, Schoolcraft College, 18600 Haggerty Road, Livonia, MI 48152, 313-462-4400, ext. 5292. 1983. Poetry, fiction, articles, art, photos, parts-of-novels, long-poems. "*The MacGuffin* is whatever everybody is after...*The MacGuffin* is where you find it... we are eclectic and holistic. We will print the best of everything with no biases. Contributors include Arthur Winfield Knight, Wendy Bishop, Janet Krauss." circ. 500. 3/yr. Pub'd 3 issues 1990; expects 3 issues 1991, 3 issues 1992. sub. price: $10; per copy: $3.75; sample: $3. Back issues: varies. Discounts: 30%-40%. 128pp; 5½×8½; of. Reporting time: 6-8 weeks. Payment: 2 contributor's copies. Copyrighted, reverts to author. CLMP, CODA.

MACROBIOTICS TODAY, George Ohsawa Macrobiotic Foundation Press, Sandy Rothman, Carl Ferre, 1511 Robinson Street, Oroville, CA 95965, 916-533-7702. 1970. Poetry, articles, interviews, reviews, non-fiction. "Length: 5-12 pages; double-spaced. Articles on macrobiotics, health, and nutrition accepted. Recent contributors include Anne Scott, Mark Mead, Noboru Muramoto" circ. 1.6M. 6/yr. Pub'd 11 issues 1990; expects 6 issues 1991, 6 issues 1992. sub. price: $20; per copy: $3; sample: $1 ppd. Back issues: $3.25 ppd, $9 1 year. Discounts: 60% regardless of number. 40pp; 8⅛×10¾; lp. Reporting time: 6 weeks. Payment: up to $75. Copyrighted, does not revert to author. Pub's reviews: 4 in 1990. §Macrobiotics, health, nutrition. Ads: $315/$180/$95 1/3 page/$45 1/12 pg/classifieds 25¢/frequency discounts. ABA.

M.H. Macy & Company, Mark Macy, Managing Editor, PO Box 11036, Boulder, CO 80301, 303-666-8130. 1984. Articles, interviews, satire, long-poems. "Additional address: 845 W. Linden Street, Louisville, CO 80027. Current project is a series peace anthologies." avg. press run 4M pa, 500 cl. Pub'd 2 titles 1990; expects 2 titles 1991, 2 titles 1992. 1 title listed in the *Small Press Record of Books in Print* (20th Edition, 1991-92). avg. price, cloth: $12.95; paper: $9.95. Discounts: 3 books 40%, 200 50%, additional 5% if payment accompanies order; educator exam copies 40%. 276pp; 5½×8½. Reporting time: 8 weeks for solicited mss. Payment: authors of each title share 40% of profits for first 7 years of publication. Copyrights for author.

MAD RIVER: A Journal of Essays, Charles S. Taylor, Department of Philosophy, Wright State University, Dayton, OH 45435, 513-873-2173. 1990. Articles, art, photos, interviews, satire, criticism, reviews, letters, non-fiction. "*Mad River* invites contributions of essays for the educated, general reader in all fields from both new and established writers. Manuscripts should not normally exceed 5,000 words and should be submitted in printed form. Accepted essays will be requested on floppy disk. Footnotes should be kept to a minimum and be collected at the end of the essay. No mss. will be returned unless accompanied by SASE. No responsibility is issued for their loss or injury." circ. 600. 3/yr. Expects 3 issues 1991, 3 issues 1992. sub. price: $18; per copy: $6; sample: $6. Back issues: none available. Discounts: none. 100pp; 7×10; of. Reporting time: 1 month. Payment: none. Copyrighted, reverts to author. Pub's reviews: 30 in 1990. §Art, science, humanities, Ohio. Ads: none.

Mad River Press, Barry Sternlieb, State Road, Richmond, MA 01254, 413-698-3184. 1986. Poetry, long-poems. "Manuscripts usually solicited. Recent contributors: Bob Arnold, Gary Snyder, William Lane, Janine Pommy Vega, Paul Metcalf, John Haines, Ann Chandonnet." avg. press run 125-500. Pub'd 3 titles 1990; expects 3 titles 1991, 3 titles 1992. 6 titles listed in the *Small Press Record of Books in Print* (20th Edition, 1991-92). avg. price, paper: $7-$20; other: broadsides $5-$25. 20-24pp; 5½×8, 6×9; †lp, of. Reporting time: 1 month. Payment: 10%-20% of press run. Copyrights for author.

THE MADISON INSURGENT, Ken Brady, Kenneth Lau, Jan Levine Thal, Chip Mitchell, Kathie Rasmussen, Andrew Rawson, Andrew Thomas-Cramer, Gita Upreti, Tom Waters, PO Box 704, Madison, WI 53701-0704, 608-251-3967. 1987. Poetry, articles, art, photos, cartoons, interviews, satire, criticism, reviews, music, letters, collages, plays, news items. "Devoted to fundamental change in our patriarchal, capitalist, racist society. Primarily focused on local news and analysis (Madison, WI)" circ. 15M. 22/yr. Pub'd 22 issues 1990; expects 22+ issues 1991, 22+ issues 1992. sub. price: $15; per copy: free; sample: free. Back issues: $2. Discounts: exchange subscriptions with other progressive periodicals. 12pp; 11×17; web. Payment: none. Copyrighted, does not revert to author. Pub's reviews: 5 in 1990. §Politics (progressive, feminist, anti-racist, etc.). Ads: $320/$192/plus frequency discounts.

THE MADISON REVIEW, Jack Murray, Poetry Editor; Sarah Goldberg, Fiction Editor, Dept of English, H.C. White Hall, 600 N. Park Street, Madison, WI 53706, 263-3303. 1978. Poetry, fiction, art, photos, parts-of-novels, long-poems. "Short, short stories welcome" circ. 500. 2/yr. Pub'd 2 issues 1990; expects 2 issues 1991, 2 issues 1992. sub. price: $7; per copy: $4; sample: $2.50. Back issues: $2/issue. Discounts: $2/book for bulk orders be happy to trade copies. 80-150pp; 6×9; of. Reporting time: replies given by Nov 15th for Fall issue and by April 15th for Spring. Payment: 2 copies. Copyrighted, reverts to author. Ads: $50/$35.

Maelstrom Press (see also MAELSTROM REVIEW), Leo Mailman, Editor & Publisher, 8 Farm Hill Road, Cape Elizabeth, ME 04107. 1972. Poetry, fiction, art, photos, cartoons, criticism, reviews, long-poems, plays. "Not currently publishing. Distributor: Applezaba Press, PO Box 4134, Long Beach, CA 90804." avg. press run 500-700. 9 titles listed in the *Small Press Record of Books in Print* (20th Edition). avg. price, paper: $3.50. Discounts: 0% (1 copy); 25% (2-5 copies); 40% (6+ copies). 68pp; 5½×8½; †of. Reporting time: 4-8 weeks. Payment: 10-30 copies of books plus half price on add'l copies; 2-5 copies of magazine (write for details). Copyrights for author. NEA.

MAELSTROM REVIEW, Maelstrom Press, Leo Mailman, Gerald Locklin, Associate Editor; Ray Zepeda, David Barker, Clifton Snider, Judy Salinas, John Kay, 8 Farm Hill Road, Cape Elizabeth, ME 04107. 1972. Poetry, fiction, art, photos, cartoons, criticism, reviews, long-poems, plays. "Not currently publishing. Distributor: Applezaba Press, PO Box 4134, Long Beach, CA 90804." circ. 400-500. 1/yr. sub. price: $5 (2 issues) indiv., $8 (2 issues) instit.; per copy: $3.50; sample: $3.50 (issues #12/13-#24/25 all available). Back issues: *Nausea* #1-11: (ltd offer): $25.00; *MAELSTROM REVIEW* issues #12-#25 (write for details). Discounts: 40% to bookstores (2 or more copies). 48pp; 7×8½; †of. Reporting time: 4-8 weeks. Payment: 2-5 copies with additional copies at 1/2 price. Copyrighted, reverts to author. §Po/fi/small press efforts. CCLM.

Maeventec (see also COMPUTER BOOK REVIEW), C. Char, 735 Ekekela Place, Honolulu, HI 96817, 808-595-7089. 1983.

THE MAGAZINE OF SPECULATIVE POETRY, Mark Rich, Roger Dutcher, PO Box 564, Beloit, WI 53512. 1984. Poetry, criticism, reviews, letters, long-poems. "Looking for the best of the new poetry, utilizing the ideas, imagery anad approaches developed by speculative fiction, and will welcome experimental techniques as well as the fresh employment of traditional forms." circ. 200. 4/yr. Pub'd 3 issues 1990; expects 4 issues 1991, 4 issues 1992. sub. price: $11; per copy: $3.50; sample: $2.50. Back issues: $3.50. Discounts: inquire. 22pp; 5½×8½; of. Reporting time: 1 month or less. Payment: $2-$20, plus copies. Copyrighted, reverts to author. Pub's reviews: 3 in 1990. §Speculative poetry. Ads: $60.

THE MAGE, Richard Davis, Student Association, Colgate University, Hamilton, NY 13346, 315-824-1000 (ask for Student Publications). 1983. Poetry, fiction, articles, art, interviews, criticism, reviews, letters, non-fiction. "We're especially interested in articles on the work of well-known authors in the fields of fantasy and science fiction. Average fiction length is 10,000-15,000 words. Send SASE for guidelines" circ. 750. 2/yr. Pub'd 2 issues 1990; expects 2 issues 1991, 2 issues 1992. sub. price: $6; per copy: $3.50; sample: $3.50. Back issues: Issue #5 $2.50; #6, 7, 8 $3. Special: buy any 2 backissues & take $2 off total price, any 3 is $3 off and all 4 is $5 off. Discounts: 25 or more copies—$2 per copy. 68pp; 8½×11; lp. Reporting time: 3-5 weeks. Payment: contributors receive 2 free copies. Copyrighted, reverts to author. Pub's reviews: 16 in 1990. §Fantasy, science fiction, horror. Ads: $55/$30/$16 1/4 page.

Mage Publishers, Inc., M. Batmanglij, N. Batmanglij, 1032 29th Street, NW, Washington, DC 20007, 202-342-1642. 1985. Poetry, fiction, art. "Mage publishes words of wisdom from other, sometimes forgotten, cultures and philosophies" avg. press run 5M-7M. Expects 5 titles 1991, 6 titles 1992. 9 titles listed in the *Small Press Record of Books in Print* (20th Edition, 1991-92). avg. price, cloth: $25; paper: $15; other: $3. Discounts: 2-4 20% off list; 10 or more 40% off. UPS additional. Payment: to be arranged on a per job basis. Copyrights for author. American Booksellers Association (ABA) COSMEP.

MAGIC CHANGES, Celestial Otter Press, John Sennett, Editor, PO Box 658, Warrenville, IL 60555, 708-416-3111. 1978. Poetry, fiction, art, photos, cartoons, interviews, satire, criticism, reviews, music, long-poems, plays. "We invite you to submit poetry, short fiction, and drawings for our upcoming issue: 'Art: The Last Gasp of a Lost Grasp.' We are especially looking for cover art. *Magic Changes* is divided into sections such as 'The Order of the Celestial Otter,' 'State of the Arts,' 'Time,' 'Music,' and 'Skyscraper Rats.' A magical, musical theme pervades." circ. 500. 1 issue every 18 months. Pub'd 1 issue 1990; expects 1 issue 1992. sub. price: $5; per copy: $5; sample: $5. Back issues: $5. Discounts: inquire. 100pp; 8½×11; †lp. Reporting time: 2 months. Payment: 1 or 2 issues. Copyrighted, reverts to author. Pub's reviews: 2 in 1990. §Poetry, rock n roll, short fiction, photography, all music. Ads: $60/$30/10¢.

Magic Circle Press, Valerie Harms, 10 Hyde Ridge Rd, Weston, CT 06883. 1972. Fiction, art, photos, criticism, non-fiction. "Recent contributors are children's authors Ann McGovern and Ruth Krauss; Diarist and novelist Anais Nin, Erika Duncan, Susan Thompson, Sas Colby. Not soliciting any new material." avg. press run 2M. Expects 1 title 1991. 6 titles listed in the *Small Press Record of Books in Print* (20th Edition, 1991-92). avg. price, cloth: $8; paper: $5. Discounts: 40% trade, 15% library. 150pp; 6×9; of. Reporting time: 2 months. Payment: depends. Copyrights for author. PEN, SCBW.

334

MAGIC REALISM, Pyx Press, C. Darren Butler, PO Box 620, Orem, UT 84059-0620. 1990. Poetry, fiction, articles, interviews, criticism, reviews. "Prefer fiction under 5,000 words, but flexible. Uses exaggerated realism, magic realism, some genre fantasy and glib fantasy of the sort found in folktales and myths. Query on articles, interviews, criticism, reviews if unfamiliar with the mag." circ. 200. 3/yr. Pub'd 2 issues 1990; expects 3 issues 1991, 3 issues 1992. sub. price: $12; sample: $4.95. 60pp; 5½x8½; xerox. Reporting time: 3 months, occasionally longer. Payment: 1 copy. Not copyrighted. Pub's reviews: 10 in 1990. §Literary fantasy, magic realism, some literary, folktale, myth. Ads: query.

MAGICAL BLEND, Magical Blend, Jerry Snider, Michael Peter Langevin, PO Box 11303, San Francisco, CA 94101. 1980. Poetry, fiction, articles, art, photos, interviews, reviews, letters, parts-of-novels, non-fiction. "Dane Rudhyar, Michael Moorcock, Mays Angelou, Shakti Gawain, Gary Snyder, Carlos Castanada, Ruth Montgomery, Robert Anton Wilson. Length approx 1,500 words average. Bias we print material which is of a positive, uplifting, psychic or spiritual nature. We hope to make our readers feel better about themselves & the world and help them get a better grasp of their destiny." circ. 75M. 4/yr. Pub'd 4 issues 1990; expects 4 issues 1991. sub. price: $14; per copy: $4; sample: $4. Back issues: $39 for 4 back issues, $119 for 4 set. Discounts: 100 or more, 50% retail. 108pp; 8¼x10¾; of, web press. Reporting time: 3 months. Payment: copies. Copyrighted, reverts to author. Pub's reviews: 30 in 1990. §Psychic/spiritual, positive. Ads: $845/$645/$1.50 per word/$205 business cards.

Magical Blend (see also MAGICAL BLEND), Jerry Snyder, Michael Langevin, PO Box 11303, San Francisco, CA 94101. 1980. Fiction, articles, art, photos, interviews, reviews, letters, parts-of-novels, non-fiction. "We use work which brings a smile, invokes a sense of happiness, beauty, awe or reverence, or inspires one to create." avg. press run 75M. Pub'd 4 titles 1990; expects 4 titles 1991. 1 title listed in the *Small Press Record of Books in Print* (20th Edition, 1991-92). avg. price, paper: $4. Discounts: 100+ copies 50% & shipping, 5+ copies 33% & shipping. 108pp; 8½x11; of, web press. Reporting time: 3 months. Payment: copies. Copyrights for author.

Magical Music Express, Greta Pedersen, Pam Donkin, PO Box 417, Palo Alto, CA 94302, 415-856-0987. 1983. Music. "Our product package is a music cassette and songbook for children. Material (original and folk music) reinforces important subject matter (assertiveness, peer pressure, environmental awareness), encourages creativity. For ages 4-10." avg. press run 2M. Expects 1 title 1992. 2 titles listed in the *Small Press Record of Books in Print* (20th Edition, 1991-92). avg. price, other: cassette/songbook $9.95. Discounts: depends on quantity and type of buyer. 5½x8½; of. Reporting time: 4 weeks. Payment: royalties paid semi-annualy; contract neg. Copyrights for author. ASCAP.

Magnificat Press, Stephen Dunham, PO Box 365, Avon-By-The-Sea, NJ 07717, 908-988-8915. 1986. Non-fiction. "We are nonprofit religious publishers of Catholic and general Christian books. We publish no fiction. We publish only books; minimum manuscript length 120 pp. 1991: *A New York City Teacher Learns Love* by Alex La Perchia, *My 20 Years With the Chinese* by Nicholas Maestrini." avg. press run 2.5M. Pub'd 5 titles 1990; expects 6 titles 1991, 6 titles 1992. 21 titles listed in the *Small Press Record of Books in Print* (20th Edition, 1991-92). avg. price, cloth: $12.95; paper: $6.45. Discounts: based on volume - list price of order. $45 order gets 45% off; $500 order gets 50% off extra 5% off for caselots. 192pp; 5½x8; web or cameron. Reporting time: 2 months or less. Payment: royalties paid twice yearly. Copyrights for author. Catholic Book Publishers Assn.

MAIL ORDER SUCCESS NEWSLETTER, Bob E. Teague, PO Box 14689, Dayton, OH 45413. 1985. Articles, news items, non-fiction. "100-200-700 words ea. 100 on News Briefs, 200 to 700 articles. Send SASE with material. Recent contributors Dr. Jeffery Lant and Glenn G. Dahlem PHd" circ. 8.2M. 8/yr. Pub'd 6 issues 1990; expects 8 issues 1991, 8 issues 1992. sub. price: $49; per copy: $6; sample: $6. Back issues: $6 copy or 3 for $15. 12pp; 8½x11; of. Reporting time: 2-3 months. Payment: 1 yr subscription on articles only. Copyrighted, does not revert to author. Pub's reviews: 5 in 1990. §Brief reviews about marketing, mail order, tax laws, postal service, production, publishing, distribution. No ads.

Main Track Publications, Bob Vincent, 2119 Forestwood Court, Fullerton, CA 92633, 714-441-2041. 1979. Music. "One book out, *Show Business is Two Words*." avg. press run 5M. Expects 1 title 1991. avg. price, cloth: $12.50; other: $12.50. Discounts: libraries, colleges 30%; agents 40%; jobbers 50%.

MAINE IN PRINT, Alison Daley Stevenson, 19 Mason Street, Brunswick, ME 04011, 207-729-6333. Articles, interviews, reviews, letters, news items. "Published monthly, *Maine In Print* is the newsletter of Maine Writers & Publishers Alliance, a non-profit literary organization. Each issue contains feature articles about writers and their craft; a calendar of statewide literary events; submissions, contests and grant opportunities; profiles of Maine authors and publishers; reviews of new Maine books; and more." circ. 5M. 11/yr. Pub'd 11 issues 1990; expects 11 issues 1991, 11 issues 1992. sub. price: $20. 12pp; 11x16; of. Reporting time: 6 weeks. Payment: $50 lead article. Not copyrighted. Pub's reviews: 100 in 1990. §Writing craft, desktop and small press publishing, Maine literature. COSMEP.

MAINLINE MODELER, Hundman Publishing, Robert L. Hundman, 5115 Montecello Drive, Edmonds, WA 98020, 206-743-2607. 1979. Articles, photos, reviews, letters. circ. 14M. 12/yr. Pub'd 12 issues 1990; expects 12 issues 1991, 12 issues 1992. sub. price: $29.75; per copy: $3.50. Back issues: $2.75 or $2.95. Discounts: dealer price-$2.60 or 25.4% off. 96pp; 8½x11; of. Reporting time: 6-9 months. Payment: individual. Copyrighted, does not revert to author. Pub's reviews: 12-15 in 1990. §Railfan, railroad history or modeling. Ads: $450/$234/$162 1/3 pg/$128 1/4 pg/$96 1/6 pg/$62 1/12 pg.

Maisonneuve Press, Robert Merrill, Dennis Crow, Annette Bus, PO Drawer 2980, Washington, DC 20013-2980, 301-277-4579. 1987. Criticism, non-fiction. "We seek compact and hard-hitting analyses of current cultural and theoretical developments—or articulations of how present conditions relate to earlier tendencies. Manuscripts should be freshly written and ideally have a published length of about 80 to 200 pages (40,000 to 100,000 words). All manuscripts will be carefully and promptly reviewed by an editorial committee." avg. press run 1M-2M. Expects 4 titles 1991, 8 titles 1992. 7 titles listed in the *Small Press Record of Books in Print* (20th Edition, 1991-92). avg. price, cloth: $17; paper: $10. Discounts: 1-10 copies 20%, 11+ 40%. 200pp; 6x9; offset, sewn binding. Reporting time: 4-5 months. Payment: no advance, 5-10% of sales. Copyrights for author.

Maize Press, Al Urista, Xelina R. Urista, 961 Bakersfield, Pismo Beach, CA 93449, (805) 773-5977. 1977. Poetry, fiction. "Focusing on poetry chapbook series" avg. press run 1M. Pub'd 2 titles 1990; expects 2 titles 1992. 1 title listed in the *Small Press Record of Books in Print* (20th Edition, 1991-92). avg. price, paper: $5.00. Discounts: 1-5, 20%; over 5, 40%. 78-156pp; 5½x8½; lp. Reporting time: 6 weeks. Payment: 10% of total printed copies. Copyrights for author. CCLM, COSMEP.

Majority, Inc., Gordon C. Moosbrugger, PO Box 2037, Saint Paul, MN 55102-0037, 612-224-3879. 1989. Fiction, plays. avg. press run 2M. Expects 1 title 1991, 2 titles 1992. 1 title listed in the *Small Press Record of Books in Print* (20th Edition, 1991-92). avg. price, cloth: $16.95; paper: $8.95. Discounts: 40%. 250-300pp; 5¼x8½; of. Reporting time: 60 days. Payment: negotiable. Copyrights for author. Minnesota Independent Publishers Association.

Malafemmina Press, Rose Romano, PO Box 411223, San Francisco, CA 94141-1223. 1990. Poetry, plays. "Malafemmina Press will be publishing a series of poetry chapbooks by Italian-American women on Italian-American themes" avg. press run 200. Pub'd 1 title 1990; expects 3 titles 1991. avg. price, paper: $2. 20pp; 5½x8½; of. Reporting time: 3 months. Payment: 50 copies and 50% discount. Copyrights for author.

THE MALAHAT REVIEW, Constance Rooke, Editor, PO Box 3045, Victoria, British Columbia V8W 3P4, Canada. 1967. Poetry, fiction, art, photos, interviews, criticism, parts-of-novels, long-poems, plays. "Short works preferred. Index available 1967-1977, $3.95; $4.95 overseas" circ. 1.8M. 4/yr. Pub'd 4 issues 1990. sub. price: $15 in Canada, $20 other; per copy: $6, special issues $7; sample: $6. Back issues: $6. Discounts: 33⅓%, agents and bookstores only, no returns policy. 135pp; 9x6; of. Reporting time: 12-15 weeks. Payment: $20 per poem page, $40 per thousand words-prose. Copyrighted. Pub's reviews: 72 in 1990. §Poetry, fiction, literary criticism. Ads: full page: $150 single issue, $500 four consecutive issues, half page: $100 single issue, $300 four consecutive issues, quarter page: $50 single issue, $160 four consecutive issues.

MALEDICTA: The International Journal of Verbal Aggression, Maledicta Press, Reinhold A. Aman, Editor & Publisher, PO Box 14123, Santa Rosa, CA 95402-6123. 1975. Articles. "See any issue. 'Style Sheet' available." circ. 4M. 1/yr. Pub'd 2 issues 1990; expects 2 issues 1991, 2 issues 1992. sub. price: $19.50, institutions $25; No sample copies available. Back issues: $20 per volume a year. Discounts: members 20%, booksellers 20-40%, jobbers 20-40%. 320pp; 5½x8½; of. Reporting time: 1 week. Payment: 20 free offprints. Copyrighted, reverts to author. Pub's reviews: 164 in 1990. §Verbal aggression (insults, curses, slang, etc.). No ads.

Maledicta Press (see also MALEDICTA: The International Journal of Verbal Aggression), Reinhold A. Aman, Editor & Publisher, PO Box 14123, Santa Rosa, CA 95402-6123. 1975. Articles. "Material of 100 pp typed minimum for books, and 25 pp maximum for articles; must deal with verbal aggression. Glossaries monolingual or bilingual, are preferred to other material. Backlog of 4 years. No cloth binding available." avg. press run 4M. Pub'd 1 title 1990; expects 2 titles 1991, 2 titles 1992. 15 titles listed in the *Small Press Record of Books in Print* (20th Edition, 1991-92). avg. price, paper: $15. Discounts: members 20%, booksellers 20-40%, jobbers 20-40%. 250pp; 5½x8½; of. Reporting time: 1 week. Payment: 10% paid annually, no advance. Copyrights for author.

MALLIFE, Bomb Shelter Propaganda, Mike L. Miskowski, PO Box 17686, Phoenix, AZ 85011, 602-279-3531. 1981. Poetry, fiction, art, photos, cartoons, collages, news items. "Concise works focusing on the Consumerist Tradition, both in form and content. One audio tape issue per year (SASE for guidelines). Guy R. Beining, Jake Berry, Alien Perrier." circ. 300. 2-3/yr. Pub'd 3 issues 1990; expects 3 issues 1991, 3 issues 1992. sub. price: $10; per copy: varies; sample: $2.97. Back issues: inquire. Discounts: standard to dealers, distributors, and retail outlets. 60pp; 5½x8½; †of, photocopy. Reporting time: 3-8 weeks. Payment:

contributor's copies. Copyrighted, reverts to author. Pub's reviews: 50 in 1990. §Micropress literature and artwork. Ads: inquire.

The Mandeville Press, Peter Scupham, John Mole, 2 Taylor's Hill, Hitchin, Hertfordshire SG4 9AD, England. 1974. Poetry. "The Mandeville Press publishes pamphlet collections of poets both new and established, in runs of approximately 250. The pamphlets are printed in letterpress, by hand, and sewn into card-covers. Recent collections by John Mole, Patric Dickinson, Lawrence Sail, and anthologies of contemporary verse" avg. press run 200-250. Pub'd 5 titles 1990. 17 titles listed in the *Small Press Record of Books in Print* (20th Edition, 1991-92). avg. price, paper: £1. Discounts: 33⅓% to trade. 16pp; 8⅜×5½; †1p. Reporting time: 2-3 weeks. Payment: copies. Copyrights for author.

MANGAJIN, Vaughan P. Simmons, 2531 Briarcliff Road #121, Atlanta, GA 30329, 404-634-3874. 1990. Articles, cartoons, reviews. "An inside, in-depth view of Japanese pop culture, especially comics. Also included are feature stories about various aspects of Japanese pop culture." circ. 15M. 10/yr. Pub'd 6 issues 1990; expects 10 issues 1991, 10 issues 1992. sub. price: $30; per copy: $4.50; sample: $5 include s/h. Discounts: write for schedule. 88pp; 8¼×10¾; of. Copyrighted, does not revert to author. Pub's reviews: 15 in 1990. §Japanese language learning or Japanese pop culture. Ads: write for rates.

MANHATTAN POETRY REVIEW, Elaine Reiman Fenton, F.D.R. PO Box 8207, New York, NY 10150, 212-355-6634. 1982. Poetry. "*CHOICE* said, "One of the best new little magazines...Only poetry is featured; there is not one book review or advertisement. Besides established writers, new poets are allocated considerable space. This magazine deserves a long life." Recent contributors include: Marge Pericy, David Ignatow, Judith Farr, Diane Wakoski. Each issue contains 60 pages of contemporary American poetry, chosen from unsolicited manuscripts; please use 9 X 4 envelope for 5-6 pages of poetry plus cover letter and SASE" circ. 1M. 2/yr. Pub'd 2 issues 1990; expects 2 issues 1991, 2 issues 1992. sub. price: $12; per copy: $7; sample: $7. Back issues: $25 ea. 60pp; 5½×8½; of. Reporting time: allow 12-16 weeks (longer in September, December, and August). Payment: one copy of issue. Copyrighted, reverts to author. CCLM.

THE MANHATTAN REVIEW, Philip Fried, Founder and Editor, c/o Philip Fried, 440 Riverside Drive, #45, New York, NY 10027. 1980. Poetry, articles, interviews, criticism, long-poems. "'My only prejudice is against those who lack ambition, believing there is no more to writing than purveying superficial ironies, jokes, or shared sentiments; or those who dedicate themselves to the proposition that poetry of a word, by a word and for a word shall not perish from this earth. A poem is not purely a verbal artifact. It must speak to and for human concerns. I welcome experiments, but poetry must ultimately communicate to an audience. It is not an unobserved wave in the vast ocean of language.' (quoted from preface to 1st issue). ISSN 0275-6889. In recent issues: Christopher Bursk, Peter Redgrove, Penelope Shuttle, Thomas Kinsella, Shelby Stephenson, Ana Blandiana, D. Nurkse, Bei Dao, Edmond Jabes." circ. 500. 2/yr. Pub'd 2 issues 1990; expects 2 issues 1991, 2 issues 1992. sub. price: 1 volume (2 issues) $10 individuals (U.S. and Canada), $14 libraries (U.S. and Canada), $18 libraries elsewhere; per copy: $5 individuals, $7 libraries; sample: $5 individuals, $7 libraries. Back issues: same, with 6 X 9 envelope and $1.25 postage. 64pp; 5½×8½; of. Reporting time: 12-14 weeks. Payment: 2 copies. Copyrighted, reverts to author. Pub's reviews: 4 in 1990. §Poetry. Ads: $150/$75. CCLM.

manic d press, Jennifer Joseph, PO Box 410804, San Francisco, CA 94141. 1984. Poetry, fiction, art, cartoons, collages. "Primarily interested in new work by young unknowns looking for a non-establishment outlet. If your typewriter's mightier than a nuclear bomb and you worry about the government please send something." avg. press run 500. Pub'd 9 titles 1990; expects 10 titles 1991, 12 titles 1992. 19 titles listed in the *Small Press Record of Books in Print* (20th Edition, 1991-92). avg. price, paper: $6; other: $3 chapbooks. Discounts: bookstores 40%, single title orders 20%. Pages vary; 5½×8½; of, xerox. Reporting time: 3 months. Payment: copies. Does not copyright for author.

Manifest Press, PO Box 2103, S. Hamilton, MA 01982, 508-468-3815. 1989. Non-fiction. avg. press run 2M-5M. Pub'd 1 title 1990; expects 1 title 1991. 1 title listed in the *Small Press Record of Books in Print* (20th Edition, 1991-92). avg. price, paper: $11.95. Discounts: standard. 168pp; 5½×8½; of. Reporting time: 3 months. Payment: no advances, 5% royalties. Does not copyright for author. NAPRA, PMA.

MANKATO POETRY REVIEW, Roger Sheffer, Box 53, Mankato State University, Mankato, MN 56001, 507-389-5511. 1984. Poetry. "Up to 60 lines. Favor poems with strong sense of place—landscape or townscape. Have published Walter Griffin, Gary Fincke, Jane Varley, Judith Skillman." circ. 200. 2/yr. Pub'd 2 issues 1990; expects 2 issues 1991, 2 issues 1992. sub. price: $5; per copy: $2.50; sample: $2.50. Back issues: $2.50. 35pp; 7×8; of. Reporting time: 2 months. Payment: copies. Copyrighted, reverts to author. Pub's reviews: none in 1990. §Poetry books.

MANNA, Roger A. Ball, Editor; Robert Raleigh, Consultant; Nina A. Wicker, Consultant; Becky Bradley, Consultant, 2966 West Westcove Drive, West Valley City, UT 84119. 1978. Poetry. "Good clean poetry, short inspirational poems, homespun farm poems, humorous poems - if it's good, we'll consider it - if it's good and humorous, we'll publish it. All material will be read, but none returned unless accompanied by SASE. Please don't submit a lone poem. No simultaneous or previously published submissions please." circ. 100-500. 2/yr. Pub'd 2 issues 1990; expects 2 issues 1991, 2 issues 1992. sub. price: $5; per copy: $3; sample: $3. Back issues: $3 (when available). 88pp; 5½×8½; lp. Reporting time: 3 weeks. Payment: prizes. Copyrighted, reverts to author. No ads.

MANOA: A Pacific Journal of International Writing, Robert Shapard, Editor; Frank Stewart, Associate Editor, English Department, University of Hawaii, Honolulu, HI 96822, 956-0370. 1988. Poetry, fiction, articles, art, photos, interviews, criticism, reviews, parts-of-novels, non-fiction. "Contributors include Ann Beattie, John Updike, Joyce Carol Oates, James D. Houston, Ursule Molinaro, Jonathan Penner, Jack Marshall, Richard Shelton, Gene Frumkin, Alberto Rios, Tim O'Brien, John L'Heureux, Ian MacMillan, Ai, Norman Dubie. Half or more of each issue will be American poetry and fiction; up to half of each issue will feature original translations of recent work from a Pacific or Asian country (issue #2 Papua New Guinea, #3 Korea, #4 Indonesia, #5 Japan). Please note that in poetry, fiction, and articles we are *not* necessarily interested in Pacific subjects or topics, but are interested in high quality literary poetry and fiction of any subject. We want to bring outstanding work from Asian and Pacific countries to the general U.S. literary readership, and in turn present outstanding work from the U.S. at large to Asian/Pacific readers, as well as to U.S. mainland readers." circ. 1.9M. 2/yr. Pub'd 2 issues 1990; expects 2 issues 1991, 2 issues 1992. sub. price: $15; per copy: $10; sample: $10. Back issues: $8. Discounts: agency 10%, multiple orders: 10-19 20%, 20+ 30%. 200pp; 7×10; of. Reporting time: prompt. Payment: competitive, depends on material and length. Copyrighted, reverts to author. Pub's reviews: 25 in 1990. §Anything of literary or cultural interest—poetry, fiction, arts, humanities, as long as related in some way to Pacific/Asia/Hawaii, which includes West Coast writers, presses. Ads: $150/$95. CCLM,CELJ.

Manroot Books, Paul Mariah, Box 762, Boyes Hot Springs, CA 95416. 1969. Poetry, long-poems. "We solicit. *Please* do not send mss without inquiring first. Primary interest. *Poetics* not poems." avg. press run 1M. Pub'd 1 title 1990; expects 2 titles 1991, 2 titles 1992. 25 titles listed in the *Small Press Record of Books in Print* (20th Edition, 1991-92). avg. price, cloth: $15; paper: $2.95-$8.95. Discounts: 40% to stores for 5 or more. 18-200pp; 5½×8½; of, handset. Reporting time: 3 months. Payment: yes. Copyrights for author. COSMEP.

Manrovian Press (see also PABLO LENNIS), John Thiel, Fandom House, 30 N. 19th Street, Lafayette, IN 47904. 1976. Poetry, fiction, articles, art, photos, cartoons, interviews, letters. "Science fiction, fantasy and science only" avg. press run 100. Pub'd 5 titles 1990; expects 5 titles 1991, 5 titles 1992. avg. price, paper: $1. 30pp; 8½×11; of. Reporting time: 2 weeks or less. Payment: none. Does not copyright for author.

Manuscript Press, Rick Norwood, PO Box 336, Mountain Home, TN 37684-0336, 615-926-7495. 1976. avg. press run 2-3M. Pub'd 1 title 1990; expects 1 title 1991, 1 title 1992. 4 titles listed in the *Small Press Record of Books in Print* (20th Edition, 1991-92). avg. price, cloth: $15; paper: $15. Discounts: 40% on 5 or more, 60% on 100 or more. 100-200pp; size varies, up to 16×22; various. Reporting time: slow. Payment: by arrangement. Copyrights for author.

MANUSHI - a journal about women & society, Madhu Kishwar, C-202 Lajpat Nagar - I, New Delhi, New Delhi 110024, India, 6833022 or 6839158. 1979. Poetry, fiction, articles, art, photos, cartoons, interviews, reviews, letters, parts-of-novels, news items, non-fiction. "Living & working conditions, struggles for change, of women in the Indian subcontinent; occasional articles on other third world countries, poetry, short stories, film review, etc." 6/yr. Pub'd 6 issues 1990; expects 6 issues 1991, 6 issues 1992. sub. price: $24 (USA), Rs 60 (India), $36 Rs 85 (instit); per copy: $4; sample: $4 (includes airmail postage). Back issues: $4 each. Discounts: 25% to agents on sales, 10% on subs. 44pp; 7×9; of. Reporting time: a month (approximate). Payment: none. Copyrighted, copyright is author's (permission required to reprint). §Women, civil liberties, human rights, third world, art, literature, historical and sociological studies. Ads: Rs 4000/Rs 2000.

Maple Hill Press, Ltd., Peter Fleck, Julie Fleck, 174 Maple Hill Road, Huntington, NY 11743, 516-549-3748; fax 516-421-2550. 1984. Non-fiction. "Word processing and other computer-related how-to books." Pub'd 1 title 1990; expects 1 title 1991, 2 titles 1992. 4 titles listed in the *Small Press Record of Books in Print* (20th Edition, 1991-92). avg. price, cloth: $19.95; paper: $14.95. Discounts: jobbers 45%, bookstores 40%, retail outlets 45%, libraries 35%. 200pp; 5½×8½; of. Reporting time: 2-4 weeks. Payment: standard paperback royalties and schedules. Copyrights for author. none.

Mar Vista Publishing Company, Edythe M. McGovern, 11917 Westminster Place, Los Angeles, CA 90066, 213-391-1721. 1979. "Since this first book is meant to appeal to an audience of providers (for young children), teachers of courses in Child Development, and children's librarians, it is my intention to stay with books along this same line. My experience as a teacher of children's literature and the contacts I have for distribution are all in this area, so that when I branch out it will be by publishing books to appeal to the same potential audience." avg. press run 5M. avg. price, paper: $10. Discounts: purchase of 10 or more, 20%. 294pp; 6×9; †of. Reporting time: 2 months. Payment: standard contract. Copyrights for author. COSMEP.

338

Maradia Press, Peter A. Ciullo, 228 Evening Star Drive, Naugatuck, CT 06770, 203-723-0758. 1990. Non-fiction. "Looking for well researched, fresh, concise, entertaining approach to consumer related issues. Please query with outline and sample chapter. If we agree to publish, we will supply guidelines for camera-ready text." avg. press run 1M. Expects 1 title 1991, 2-3 titles 1992. 1 title listed in the *Small Press Record of Books in Print* (20th Edition, 1991-92). Discounts: book trade 1-9 40%, 10-499 50%, 500+ 55%, additional 5% per category for no-return basis; libraries 20% FOB press. 5½x8½. Reporting time: 1 month. Payment: we will buy manuscript outright or offer 10% of cover price as royalty. Copyrights for author.

Marathon International Book Company, Jim Wortham, Publisher, Deptartment SPR, PO Box 33008, Louisville, KY 40232-3008, 502-935-3147. 1969. "We are considering books on addictions, ecology, alternative fuels, alternative energy and finances. No poetry, please." avg. press run 2M-5M. Expects 3 titles 1991. 19 titles listed in the *Small Press Record of Books in Print* (20th Edition, 1991-92). avg. price, cloth: $12.95; paper: $6.95. Discounts: 40% to trade. 64-130pp; 5½x8½; of, lp. Reporting time: 2-3 weeks. Payment: 10% royalty. Copyright in author's name. COSMEP.

Paul Maravelas, 15155 Co. Rd. 32, Mayer, MN 55360, 612-657-2237. 1981. avg. press run 100. Pub'd 1 title 1990; expects 1 title 1991, 1 title 1992. 2 titles listed in the *Small Press Record of Books in Print* (20th Edition, 1991-92). †lp. Reporting time: 2 weeks. Payment: arranged. Copyrights for author.

Peter Marcan Publications, Peter Marcan, 31 Rowliff Road, High Wycombe, Bucks, HP12 3LD, England. 1978. Non-fiction. "Currently, I am producing information directories, catalogues and reprints. My directory publications are: *Directory of Specialist Bookdealers in the UK Handling mainly new books, Arts Address Book*: a classified guide to national (UK and Ireland) and international organizations...with details of their activities and publications. A new publication (to be published 1991) is: *Art Historians in the U.K., a Directory of Expertise and Research, Greater London Local History Directory and Bibliography*. I have two current specialist series: *The String Players Library Series* and a *London's Docklands and East End Series*. A series on British twentieth century artists working in black and white is planned with a reissue of Arthur Wragg's *The Lord's Prayer in Black and White* 1989." avg. press run 350-1M. Pub'd 1 title 1990; expects 2 titles 1991, 2 titles 1992. 14 titles listed in the *Small Press Record of Books in Print* (20th Edition, 1991-92). avg. price, paper: £5.95-£15. Discounts: 35% discount to book trade for two or more copies. 62-120pp; size A5, A4; of.

March Street Press (see also PARTING GIFTS), Robert Bixby, 3006 Stonecutter Terrace, Greensboro, NC 27405. 1988. Poetry, fiction. "Currently reading. I hope to publish 3 books of poetry and one book of short stories per year. Reading fee: $10." avg. press run 50. Pub'd 1 title 1990; expects 1 title 1991, 2 titles 1992. 2 titles listed in the *Small Press Record of Books in Print* (20th Edition, 1991-92). avg. price, cloth: $5-$7. Discounts: write. 40pp; 5½x8½; †Xerox. Reporting time: 2-3 months. Payment: free copies, 15% of sales. Copyrights for author.

Marilee Publications, Mary E. Foster, PO Box 2351, Bonita Springs, FL 33959, 813-992-1800. 1981. Poetry, fiction, photos, non-fiction. "So far have written, published, and marketed one title. Cannot now accept submissions but hope to in future" avg. press run 250. Expects 1 title 1991, 1 title 1992. 1 title listed in the *Small Press Record of Books in Print* (20th Edition, 1991-92). avg. price, paper: $5. Discounts: will work on individual basis. 5x8; photo offset. Copyrights for author.

MARION ZIMMER BRADLEY'S FANTASY MAGAZINE, Marion Zimmer Bradley, PO Box 249, Berkeley, CA 94701, 415-601-9000. 1988. Fiction. "*Marion Zimmer Bradley's Fantasy Magazine* buys well-plotted short stories, up to 7,500 words. Our preferred length is 3,500 to 4,000 words, but we also buy short-shorts (under 1,000 words). We buy fantasy with no particular objection to modern settings, but we want action and adventure. Stories should stand alone. This is not a primary market for series and shared world stories. We are not a market for poetry, nor for hard science fiction or gruesome horror. No metaphysics, folklore, science fiction, rewritten fairy tales, 'hearth-witches,' and no radical feminism. Please read a few issues before submitting so that you can see the kind of thing we do buy. Manuscripts are returned only if accompanied by SASE. No simultaneous submissions. MZB cannot read dot-matrix." 4/yr. Pub'd 4 issues 1990; expects 4 issues 1991, 4 issues 1992. sub. price: $14/4 issues, $20 Canada, $30 foreign, in U.S. funds; per copy: $4.95; sample: $4.95. Back issues: $4.95 + $1.50 p/h per order. 64pp; 8½x11. Reporting time: 90% of submissions are returned the next day, but some stories may be held up to 6 months. Payment: on acceptance. Copyrighted, reverts to author. Ads: $100/$60.

MARK, Kenneth J. Bindas, Rm. 2514, Student Union, University of Toledo, Toledo, OH 43606, 419-537-2373. 1967. Poetry, fiction, articles, art, photos, interviews, criticism, reviews, music, parts-of-novels, plays, non-fiction. "Our theme is eclectic. Fiction, poetry, non-fiction, graphics, interviews, reviews, translations have all appeared in our pages and are welcome. From ultra-conservative to ultra-strange, our editorial policy knows few bounds. Prefer articles in University of Chicago style, but not necessary" circ. 2M. 2-3/yr. Pub'd 2 issues 1990; expects 2 issues 1991, 2 issues 1992. sub. price: $6-$10; per copy: $3; sample: $3. Back issues: limited number available at $2. 56pp; 6x9; of. Reporting time: 1 month. Payment: in copies.

Copyrighted, reverts to author. Pub's reviews: 2 in 1990. §Fiction, music, poetry, topical non-fiction, history, pop culture, philosophy, science.

Mark Publishing, Bill Witcher, Al Strickland, 5400 Scotts Valley Drive, Scotts Valley, CA 95066-3439, 408-438-7668. 1987. Non-fiction. avg. press run 10M. Pub'd 1 title 1990; expects 6 titles 1991, 10 titles 1992. 3 titles listed in the *Small Press Record of Books in Print* (20th Edition, 1991-92). avg. price, paper: $20. Discounts: up to 50%. 224pp; 8½×11; lp. Reporting time: 2 weeks. Payment: varies. Copyrights for author. ABA, COSMEP.

MARKETS ABROAD, Michael H. Sedge, Strawberry Media, Inc., 2460 Lexington Drive, Owosso, MI 48867, 517-725-9027. 1986. Articles, reviews, news items. "European office: Strawberry Media, Via Venezia 14/B-80021 Afragola (NA), Italy. Marketing info for freelance writers and photographers" circ. 400. 4/yr. Pub'd 4 issues 1990; expects 4 issues 1991, 4 issues 1992. sub. price: $25; per copy: $10; sample: same. Back issues: $8. Discounts: $40/2-year. 12pp; 8½×11; of. Reporting time: 1 week. Payment: 5¢ per word. Copyrighted, reverts to author. Pub's reviews: 12 in 1990. §Marketing, writing, photography, directories, reference. Ads: $150/$80/$45 1/4 page. COSMEP, PMA.

Markgraf Publications Group, James Hall, PO Box 936, Menlo Park, CA 94025, 415-940-1299. 1987. Non-fiction. avg. press run 5M. Pub'd 2 titles 1990; expects 3 titles 1991. 6 titles listed in the *Small Press Record of Books in Print* (20th Edition, 1991-92). avg. price, cloth: $32.95; paper: $18.95; other: $7.95. 200pp; 5½×8½; of. Payment: percentage of profit. Copyrights for author. COSMEP, PMA, Society for Scholarly Publishing.

The Marlboro Press, Austryn Wainhouse, Director, Box 157, Marlboro, VT 05344, 802-257-0781. 1982. Poetry, fiction, criticism, non-fiction. "At the outset we have had—perforce—to emphasize reprints and translations; but intend, in time, to publish original texts as well. We hope that our books will be recognized for their intellectual rigor and honesty. To the extent they are today the least of the big publisher's concerns, maintaining high standards is the role of the small press" avg. press run 2.5M. Pub'd 7 titles 1990; expects 8 titles 1991, 8 titles 1992. 30 titles listed in the *Small Press Record of Books in Print* (20th Edition, 1991-92). avg. price, cloth: $15.95; paper: $10. Discounts: Libraries: 10%; booksellers (upon a single copy): 20%; 2-5 copies: 30%; 6 or more copies: 40%. 195pp; 6×9; of. Reporting time: 3 months. Payment: arrangements vary. Copyrights for author.

Marlborough Publications, Judy Rauner, PO Box 16406, San Diego, CA 92116, 619-280-8310. 1980. "Workbook format for volunteer program management and board development for human service organizations, schools, religious organizations. Supplemental materials for trainers. Collection of short stories." avg. press run 3M. Pub'd 1 title 1990; expects 2 titles 1991, 1 title 1992. 3 titles listed in the *Small Press Record of Books in Print* (20th Edition, 1991-92). avg. price, paper: $10. Discounts: 5-20 10%, 20+ 20%; distributors 40%. 100pp; 8¼×11. Payment: 10% - joint author - 5% each. Does not copyright for author. BPSD.

Maro Verlag, Benno Kaesmayr, Riedingerstr. 24/6f, Augsburg, Germany, 0821-41 60 33. 1969. Poetry, fiction. "German and American writers in German translation: e.g. Charles Bukowski, John Fante, Gerald Locklin and Anne Waldman, Gilbert Sorrentino." avg. press run 7M-15M. Pub'd 10 titles 1990; expects 10 titles 1991, 10 titles 1992. 5 titles listed in the *Small Press Record of Books in Print* (20th Edition, 1991-92). avg. price, cloth: dm 20 to 28; paper: dm 10 to dm 28. Discounts: 35-50%. 200pp; 20.5×13.5cm; †of. Reporting time: 6 months. Payment: 10-15% of retail price. Copyrights for author.

MARQUEE, Douglas Gomery, 624 Wynne Road, Springfield, PA 19064, 215-543-8378. 1969. Articles, photos, interviews, criticism. "Historical research on American Theatre buildings contributed by members. Recent article Metropolitan Opera House, Philadelphia, PA 01908 by Irvin R. Glazer and current article-history of Atlantic City theatres w/vintage pictures. Comprehensive study Chicago Theatre, Chicago, IL (Northtown, Chicago), (Fox, Brooklyn), (H.A.B.S. Study), (Erlanger, Phila.)=current. Theatre Draperies Issue—1983 - Color issue - Fifth Avenue Th. Seattle, Washington. Special issue - 1984 - Preservation of OLD Theatres. 1985 Theatre Acoustics. 1976 Mastbaum Th. - Phila Pa; Earle Theatre, Philadelphia issue-1986; Al Ringling Th. Baraboo, WI - 1991." circ. 1M. 5/yr. Pub'd 5 issues 1990; expects 5 issues 1991, 5 issues 1992. sub. price: $25; per copy: $4.50; sample: $6. Back issues: $4.50. Discounts: library rate $15. 25pp; 8½×11; lp. Reporting time: 3 months. Copyrighted, reverts to author. Pub's reviews: 10 in 1990. §Theatre architecture.

Marquette Books, David Pearce Demers, Mona Pearce Demers, 1037 Arbogast Street, Shoreview, MN 55126-8103. 1988. Non-fiction. "We're looking for advice/how-to manuscripts, 80 to 150 pages preferred on all topics. Must be informative and authoritative" avg. press run 2.5M-5M. Expects 1 title 1991, 2-5 titles 1992. 1 title listed in the *Small Press Record of Books in Print* (20th Edition, 1991-92). avg. price, cloth: $17.95; paper: $9.95. Discounts: schedules offered to wholesalers, distributors, bookstores and other book reps. 80-150pp; 5½×8½; of. Reporting time: 2-4 weeks. Payment: negotiable. Copyrights for author. Minnesota Independent Publishers Association, 1007 Greenbriar St., St. Paul, MN 55106.

340

MARTHA'S VINEYARD MAGAZINE, Richard F. Reston, PO Box 66, Edgartown, MA 02539, 508-627-4311. 1985. Poetry, fiction, articles, art, photos, cartoons, interviews, reviews, music, long-poems, collages, plays, news items, non-fiction. "All of our material focuses on the island of Martha's Vineyard. We feature many new writers as well as local talent such as Walter Cronkite, Mike Wallace, Art Buchwald, Marianne Wiggins. *Martha's Vineyard Magazine* is the Vineyard's only magazine. We place an emphasis on history, art, environment, lifestyles, poetry, culture and special island events." circ. 12M-15M. 4/yr. Pub'd 4 issues 1990; expects 4 issues 1991, 4 issues 1992. sub. price: $15; per copy: $3.95. Back issues: $3.95. Discounts: bulk purchase of any issue @ $3 each. 70pp; 8⅛×10⅞; of. Reporting time: 1-2 months. Payment: $50-$150. Copyrighted, reverts to author. Pub's reviews. §Related to Martha's Vineyard or Cape Cod areas. Ads: $995/$595/$125 directory listing.

Maryland Historical Press, Vera F. Rollo, 9205 Tuckerman St, Lanham, MD 20706, 301-577-2436 and 557-5308. 1965. Non-fiction. "We publish material for Maryland schools; and for colleges with Aviation courses on free-lance basis. U.S. Aviation Law; Aviation Insurance; Maryland. History, Govt., Geog., Biography, and Black History; Americana. Our books are mostly set in type, printed via off-set process, illustrated, and about 80 percent are casebound, 20 percent paperback. We buy almost nothing, sorry." avg. press run 2M on paperbacks, 5M on casebound. Pub'd 3 titles 1990; expects 3 titles 1991, 3 titles 1992. 18 titles listed in the *Small Press Record of Books in Print* (20th Edition, 1991-92). avg. price, cloth: $16.75; paper: $7. Discounts: 33% to jobbers/dealers. 100-400pp; 8½×11; of. Payment: 10%. Copyrights for author.

Masefield Books, K. Fermoyle, 7210 Jordan Avenue, Suite B54, Canoga Park, CA 91303. 1991. Non-fiction. "We have two titles in process: *How to Use a Library* by M. Bloomfield, 2nd edition; and *Man in Transition* by M. Bloomfield, 2nd edition." avg. press run 500-1M. Expects 3-5 titles 1991, 3-5 titles 1992. 2 titles listed in the *Small Press Record of Books in Print* (20th Edition, 1991-92). avg. price, cloth: $27. Discounts: dealers 2-10 books 20%, 10-50 30%, 50-200 40%, over 200 50%. 200pp; 5×9; of. Reporting time: within 1 month. Payment: 10% of gross price. Copyrights for author.

THE MASSACHUSETTS REVIEW, Mary Heath, Editor; Jules Chametzky, Editor; Paul Jenkins, Editor, Memorial Hall, Univ. of Mass, Amherst, MA 01003, 413-545-2689. 1959. Poetry, fiction, articles, art, photos, interviews, satire, criticism, reviews, letters, long-poems, plays. "A SASE must accompany each manuscript + query. No fiction mss considered June 1 - Oct 1" circ. 2M+. 4/yr. Pub'd 4 issues 1990; expects 4 issues 1991. sub. price: $14; per copy: $5; sample: $5 and 50¢ postage. Back issues: $4-$10. Discounts: 15% on ads for univ. presses, adv. agencies, small presses; 40% bookstores. 172pp; 6×9; lp. Reporting time: 4-6 weeks. Payment: $50 stories $10 min poetry 35¢ per line. Copyrighted, rights revert on request. Ads: $125/$75/$50 -1/4. CCLM.

MASSACRE, Indelible Inc., Roberta McKeown, BCM 1698, London WC1N 3XX, England, 0924-892-661. 1990. Fiction, art, photos, cartoons, satire, criticism, collages. "*massacre* is an annual magazine of 'improbable' or 'anti-naturalistic' fiction. It does not publish genre sci-fi or, in general, stories that are futuristic or technology based. *massacre* is about juxtaposition, plundering, originality, the outre, weird and unexpected. It takes its precedents from dream literature, surrealism, satire and dada—writers like Beckett, Edward Gorey, Flann O'Brien. Stories can be up to 3,000 words in length. Poetry is seldom appropriate. Critical essays are also welcome if relevant; in the past these have featured French anti-naturalist playwrights, The Third Policeman, and the Theatre of the Absurd." circ. 300. 1/yr. Pub'd 1 issue 1990; expects 1 issue 1991, 1 issue 1992. sub. price: £4; per copy: £4; sample: £4 ($8). Back issues: #1 £2, #1+#2 £5. Discounts: libraries 10%, trade 35%. 84pp; 5½×8½; of. Reporting time: 1 month. Payment: copy of magazine; 50% discount on further copies. Copyrighted, reverts to author. Ads: £45/£25. Small Press Group of Britain (SPG), BM Bozo, London WC1N 3XX, UK; Women in Publishing (WIP).

MASSEY COLLECTORS NEWS—WILD HARVEST, Keith Oltrogge, Box 529, Denver, IA 50622, 319-984-5292. 1981. Articles. "Newsletter for collectors of Wallis, Ferguson, Massey Harris and Massey Ferguson tractors and farm equipment." circ. 1M. 6/yr. Pub'd 6 issues 1990; expects 6 issues 1991, 6 issues 1992. sub. price: $16; per copy: $2.50; sample: same. Back issues: $2.50. 24pp; 8½×11; of. Reporting time: 30 days. Not copyrighted. Ads: $75/$40/$20 1/4 page/classifieds are free.

MASTER THOUGHTS, Dominion Press, Friend Stuart, Editor, PO Box 37, San Marcos, CA 92079-0037, 619-746-9430. 1972. Articles. "Advanced Christian metaphysics. Not recommended for beginners. Weekly, but published quarterly for 13 weeks ahead. Mailed 4 times per year. No mss. accepted" circ. 100. 52/yr. Pub'd 52 issues 1990; expects 52 issues 1991, 52 issues 1992. sub. price: $15. Back issues: 1972-76 complete, bound $19.95; 1977-80 complete, bound $19.95; 1981-86 complete, bound $19.95; 1987-91 complete, bound $19.95; full set $69.95. Discounts: 30% dealers and agencies only; 40% on bound volumes. 2pp; 5½×8½; of. No ads.

MASTERSTREAM, Grimm Press & Publishing Co., Inc., Bruce D. Grimm, PO Box 1523, Longview, WA 98632, (206) 577-8598. 1981. Articles, photos, cartoons, interviews, reviews, letters, news items, non-fiction. "500-700 words/and news items pertaining to fire service and/or law enforcement in Washington State and the

Pacific Northwest" circ. 3.5M-5M. 4/yr. Pub'd 4 issues 1990; expects 4 issues 1991, 4 issues 1992. sub. price: $9.97; per copy: $3.95; sample: $2.50. Discounts: 35% agency, trade. 64pp; 8½x11; of. Reporting time: 45 days. Payment: 3¢ to 6¢/word. Copyrighted, does not revert to author. Pub's reviews. §Fire service and law enforcement, state government issues. Ads: $600/$395/$100 1/8. COSMEP.

THE MATCH, Fred Woodworth, PO Box 3488, Tuscon, AZ 85722. 1969. Fiction, articles, cartoons, interviews, criticism, reviews, letters, parts-of-novels, news items. "Recent articles include an expose of American atheists; part of novel, 'The Two Sisters'; serialization of 'Dream World.' Not seeking contributions" circ. 1.9M. 4/yr. Pub'd 1 issue 1990; expects 3 issues 1991, 4 issues 1992. sub. price: $12/4 issues; per copy: $2.50; sample: $2. Discounts: 50%, payable on receipt of copies. 60pp; 6½x9½; †of, lp. Pub's reviews: 17 in 1990. §Anarchism, government. No ads.

MATHEMATICAL SPECTRUM, Applied Probability Trust, D.W. Sharpe, Dept of Probability and Statistics, The University, Sheffield S3 7RH, England. 1968. Articles, reviews, letters. circ. 1.8M. 4/yr. Pub'd 4 issues 1990; expects 4 issues 1991, 4 issues 1992. sub. price: £6 ($11 U.S.). Back issues: on request. 32pp; 21x14.5cm. Payment: none. Copyrighted, does not revert to author. Pub's reviews: 16 in 1990. §Books on mathematics suitable for senior students in schools and beginning undergraduates in colleges and universities.

MATI, Ommation Press, Effie Mihopoulos, 5548 N. Sawyer, Chicago, IL 60625. 1975. Poetry, articles, art, photos, interviews, reviews, letters, long-poems. "Very open to experimental poetry and especially poems by women. The magazine was established to provide another source where new poets can see their work in print. The work doesn't have to be perfect, but show potential. *Mati* wants to encourage young poets to see as much of their work in print as possible. Open to exchange (magazines and ads) with other magazines. *Mati* will also be doing a series of poem postcards as special issues (both letterpress and offset, $1.00 a set) for which short poems (3-4 lines) are welcome to be submitted for consideration. The magazine will be changing this year from quarterly to once-annually. Recent contributors: Lyn Lifshin, Rochelle Ratner." circ. 500. 1/yr. Pub'd 4 issues 1990; expects 1 issue 1991, 1 issue 1992. sub. price: $2; per copy: $1.50 + 90¢ postage + handling; sample: $1.50+ 90¢ postage + handling. Back issues: No. 1, $15; No. 2, $20; No. 3, $15; No. 6, $2. Discounts: 20% on 5 copies or more. 40pp; 8½x11; of. Reporting time: 2 weeks-1 month. Payment: 1 copy. Copyrighted, reverts to author. Ads: $80/$40/$15.

Matilda Publications, Fonda Zenofon, Advisory Editor; Albert Hayes, Editor, 7 Mountfield Street, Brunswick, Melbourne, Victoria, Australia, 03-386-5604. 1974. Fiction, cartoons, plays, non-fiction. "We now publish non-fiction, how-to information" avg. press run 3M. Pub'd 3 titles 1990; expects 4 titles 1991, 6 titles 1992. 2 titles listed in the *Small Press Record of Books in Print* (20th Edition, 1991-92). avg. price, paper: $8. Discounts: trade and bulk inquiries welcome; write for discount list. 50pp; 6x9; †of. Reporting time: 1 month. Payment: only if we cover costs; if the edition does not sell, then we are stuck with a loss; but profit does not determine quality! Copyrights for author. BPW.

MATRIX, Red Herring Press, Carmen M. Pursifull, Editor & Readings Coordinator; Ruth S. Walker, Editor & Director, c/o Channing-Murray Foundation, 1209 W Oregon, Urbana, IL 61801, 217-344-1176. 1976. Poetry. "We publish an anthology and high quality chapbooks by present members only. Not soliciting manuscripts at this time." circ. 300. 2/yr. Pub'd 3 issues 1990; expects 2 issues 1991, 2 issues 1992. Discounts: 40%. 5½x8½; of. Payment: none. Copyrighted.

Maupin House, PO Box 90148, Gainesville, FL 32607. 1988. avg. press run 2M. Pub'd 2 titles 1990; expects 4 titles 1991, 5 titles 1992. 9 titles listed in the *Small Press Record of Books in Print* (20th Edition, 1991-92). Discounts: industry standard. Pages vary. Reporting time: 1 month. Payment: negotiable. Copyrights for author. Publishers Association of the South, ABA, Florida Publishers Group-NAIP, COSMEP.

MAXINE'S PAGES, Elaine Long, Box 866, Manchester, GA 31816. 1987. Articles, interviews, reviews, news items, non-fiction. *"Maxine's Pages* means whatever Maxine wants to throw in there. Circulation includes public safety training centers and agencies" circ. 100. 6/yr. Pub'd 6 issues 1990; expects 6 issues 1991, 6 issues 1992. sub. price: $5; per copy: $1; sample: $1. Discounts: will trade for other publications or information. 4pp; 8½x11; copier. Reporting time: 2 months. Payment: copy. Not copyrighted. Pub's reviews: 15 in 1990. §Drugs, radical politics, botanicals, alternative religion, police. Ads: none. Southeastern Small Press, Columbus, GA.

Mayapple Press, Judith Kerman, PO Box 5473, Saginaw, MI 48603-0473. 1978. Poetry, fiction, art, parts-of-novels, long-poems. "We have a special interest in regional writing, particularly from the Great Lakes area, as well as contemporary poetry, art/crafts, and feminist literature. We are generally interested only in *chapbook* length poetry or fiction. Our first book was a how-to crafts book (soft sculpture); our first poetry chapbook was by Toni Ortner-Zimmerman; newest chapbook is by Judith Minty (1981)." avg. press run 500-1M. Expects 1 title 1991, 1-2 titles 1992. 3 titles listed in the *Small Press Record of Books in Print* (20th Edition, 1991-92). avg. price, paper: $4-$7. Discounts: 1-5 copies to bookstores, jobbers & libraries 20%; 6 or more (mixed or same title) 30% consignment; 40% cash/returns; 50% no returns. 16-40pp; 5½x8½, 7x8, 8½x11; of. Reporting time: up to 6 months. Payment: for poetry/fiction, 6 copies plus generous discount on purchase of copies; for other, negotiable. Copyrights for author.

MAYFLY, High/Coo Press, Randy Brooks, Shirley Brooks, 4634 Hale Drive, Decatur, IL 62526-1117. 1985. Poetry. *"Mayfly* is a haiku magazine from High/Coo Press. In our opinion, haiku is best savored in small servings. Too often they are crowded together on a page, and the reader is overwhelmed by hundreds of haiku in a single issue. The result is that the reader is forced to become a critic and editor wading through the heaps of haiku in search of a few gems. We feel it is the duty of the editors and writers to make careful selection of only the very best, the most evocative, the truly effective haiku. We now use laser printing production and offer Macintosh haiku software" circ. 250. 3/yr. Pub'd 3 issues 1990; expects 3 issues 1991. sub. price: $10/3 copies; per copy: $3.50; sample: $3.50. Back issues: none. Discounts: none. 16pp; 3½×5; of. Reporting time: 3 months. Payment: $5 per haiku published. Copyrighted, reverts to author.

Mayhaven Publishing, Doris R. Wenzel, 803 Buckthorn Circle, Mahomet, IL 61853, 217-586-4493. 1990. Fiction, art, photos, cartoons, interviews, letters. "Additional address: PO Box 509. Our books (we presently have 3 - with 4 more planned for release by Sept. 1991) are directed toward the general audience. New titles will include books on science fiction, trains, mystery, humor, animals, biography" avg. press run 1.5M-2M. Pub'd 1 title 1990; expects 8 titles 1991, 8-9 titles 1992. 3 titles listed in the *Small Press Record of Books in Print* (20th Edition, 1991-92). avg. price, cloth: $19.95; paper: $15.95. Discounts: 2-5 20%, 6-25 30%, 26-99 40%-50%, 100+ 55%-60%. 100-300pp; 5½×8, 8½×11; of. Reporting time: 3-6 weeks. Payment: small advance, 10% of regular sales, royalty varies in other categories. Copyrights for author.

Mazda Publishers, Ahmad Jabbari, PO Box 2603, 2991 Grace Lane, Costa Mesa, CA 92626-2603, 714-751-5252. 1980. Non-fiction. avg. press run 2M. Pub'd 5 titles 1990; expects 7 titles 1991. 41 titles listed in the *Small Press Record of Books in Print* (20th Edition, 1991-92). avg. price, cloth: $21.95; paper: $5.95. Discounts: depend upon the quantities ordered. 195pp; 5¼×8¼; of, 4-color press. Reporting time: 6-8 weeks. Payment: open to negotiations. Copyrights for author.

McBooks Press, Alexander G. Skutt, Owner, Publisher, 908 Steam Mill Road, Ithaca, NY 14850, 607-272-2114. 1979. Non-fiction. "We can accept *no* unsolicited manuscripts. Letters of inquiry are welcome. We publish a very few books and we make the decision to publish on the basis of both commercial potential and artistic merit. Although we would consider other purposeful, well-written non-fiction, we are mostly interested in seeing inquiries about books on vegetarianism and regional books on upstate New York." avg. press run 3.7M. Pub'd 1 title 1990; expects 1 title 1991, 1 title 1992. 11 titles listed in the *Small Press Record of Books in Print* (20th Edition, 1991-92). avg. price, cloth: $14.95; paper: $8.95. Discounts: standard terms are available to bookstores, wholesalers, etc. 134pp; size usually 5½×8½ or 8½×11; of. Reporting time: 1 month on query letters. Payment: usual royalty basis with an advance. Copyrights for author.

THE MCCALLUM OBSERVER, Lynda Mendoza, PO Box 165, Downers Grove, IL 60515-0165, 708-852-6518. 1985. Fiction, articles, art, interviews, reviews, news items. circ. 250. 5/yr. Pub'd 5 issues 1990; expects 5 issues 1991, 5 issues 1992. sub. price: $11 US/Canada, $13 all other countries; per copy: $2 US/Canada, $2.50 others; sample: same. Back issues: same. Discounts: trade 1 year subscription for 1 year subscription. 28pp; 5½×8; of. Reporting time: May 5, July 5, Sept. 5, Nov. 5, Feb. 5. Payment: none. Copyrighted, reverts to author. Ads: $20/$10/$5 5x4"

McDonald & Woodward Publishing Company, Jerry N. McDonald, PO Box 10308, Blacksburg, VA 24062, 703-951-9465. 1986. Non-fiction. "Interested in book-length material (75 or more printed pages) for adults primarily. Main interests are natural & cultural history topics. Interested in socially-responsible controversial subjects, environmental issues, history of science, and travel-related subjects. Publish 'Guides to the American Landscape', a series of specialty guides to the natural and cultural history of the Americas." avg. press run 3M. Pub'd 2 titles 1990; expects 5 titles 1991, 4-6 titles 1992. 9 titles listed in the *Small Press Record of Books in Print* (20th Edition, 1991-92). avg. price, cloth: $25; paper: $13. Discounts: 25-40%. 200pp; 6×9; of. Reporting time: 1 week initial response. Payment: 10% on copies sold at or above trade discount, payment semiannually. Copyrights for author.

McFarland & Company, Inc., Publishers (see also WLW JOURNAL: News/Views/Reviews for Women and Libraries), Robert Franklin, President; Rhonda Herman, Business Manager; Lisa Camp, Assistant Editor, Box 611, Jefferson, NC 28640, 919-246-4460. 1979. "We want book-length manuscripts only (at least 225 pp. double spaced) of scholarly or reference books on film, literature, women's studies, history, political affairs, music, theatre/drama, parapsychology (not 'occult'), chess, science, etc., etc. No fiction, poetry, children's books, memoirs, etc." avg. press run 1M. Pub'd 85 titles 1990; expects 92 titles 1991, 95 titles 1992. 299 titles listed in the *Small Press Record of Books in Print* (20th Edition, 1991-92). avg. price, cloth: $30; paper: $18. Discounts: short to wholesalers and booksellers. Special arrangement for specialty booksellers that promote our titles. 240pp; 6×9; of. Reporting time: 10 days. Payment: average 10% of gross income from sales on first 1M sold; stepped up thereafter. Copyrights for author. COSMEP, ALA,SSP.

Laurence McGilvery, PO Box 852, La Jolla, CA 92038. 1960. Letters, non-fiction. avg. press run 100-25M.

Pub'd 3 titles 1990. 7 titles listed in the *Small Press Record of Books in Print* (20th Edition, 1991-92). avg. price, cloth: $12.50-$40; paper: $9.95-$20; other: microfiche: $50-$57.50. Discounts: 10-50%. 28-3386pp; size varies. Payment: 10%. Copyrights for author.

McKinzie Publishing Company, Edward Torrey, 11000 Wilshire Boulevard, PO Box 241777, Los Angeles, CA 90024, 213-934-7685. 1981. avg. press run 4M. Pub'd 1 title 1990; expects 1 title 1991, 2 titles 1992. 7 titles listed in the *Small Press Record of Books in Print* (20th Edition, 1991-92). avg. price, paper: $16.95. 250pp; webb. Reporting time: 6 weeks. Copyrights for author. Assoc. of American Publishers, American Booksellers Assoc., Canadian Booksellers Association, Australian Booksellers Association.

MCN Press, PO Box 702073, Tulsa, OK 74170. 1962. avg. press run 1M-10M. Expects 3 titles 1991. 9 titles listed in the *Small Press Record of Books in Print* (20th Edition, 1991-92). avg. price, cloth: $21.95; paper: $14.95. Discounts: 10-50%. 100pp; 8½x11. Reporting time: 6 weeks. Payment: 10% of gross. Copyrights for author.

McNally & Loftin, Publishers, W.J. McNally, Carol Fletcher, 5390 Overpass Road, Santa Barbara, CA 93111, 805-964-5117. 1956. "Specialize in Santa Barbara Channel Islands; Southern California and environmental history. Other address: 5390 Overpass Road, Santa Barbara, CA 93111." avg. press run 2.5M. Pub'd 4 titles 1990; expects 6 titles 1991, 6 titles 1992. 5 titles listed in the *Small Press Record of Books in Print* (20th Edition, 1991-92). avg. price, cloth: $18.50; paper: $12. Discounts: trade 40%. 144pp; 6x9, 5½x8½, 7x10; †of. Reporting time: 4 weeks. Payment: 10% net. Does not copyright for author. PMA.

McOne Press (see also ALL AVAILABLE LIGHT; CITY RANT; THE ICARUS REVIEW), John McElhenney, Jason Freeman, Mark Lawrence, PO Box 50174, Austin, TX 78763, 512-477-2269. 1989. Poetry, fiction, non-fiction. "A small run press specializing in chapbooks and perfect bound paperbacks of high literary quality" avg. press run 500+. Pub'd 3 titles 1990; expects 12 titles 1991, 20 titles 1992. avg. price, paper: $5. 50-150pp; 5½x8½; of. Reporting time: 4-6 weeks. Payment: 50% after printing charges; negotiations vary. Copyrights for author.

McPherson & Company Publishers, Bruce R. McPherson, PO Box 1126, Kingston, NY 12401, 914-331-5807. 1973. Fiction, art, photos, criticism, non-fiction. "Other imprints: Documentext, Treacle Press. Distributor of Tanam Press; Raymond Saroff, Publisher; and *Fiction International*. No unsolicited mss. Query." avg. press run 2M. Pub'd 5 titles 1990; expects 9 titles 1991, 10 titles 1992. 51 titles listed in the *Small Press Record of Books in Print* (20th Edition, 1991-92). avg. price, cloth: $16; paper: $8. Discounts: single copy 20%, 2-4 30%, 5-99 40%, 100+ 43%; prepaid STOP, 30%. 200pp; size varies; of. Reporting time: 2 weeks-2 months. Payment: royalties and copies. Copyrights for author.

ME MAGAZINE, Pittore Euforico, Carlo Pittore, PO Box 1132, Peter Stuyvesant Station, New York, NY 10009, 212-673-2705. 1980. Poetry, art, criticism, reviews, collages, concrete art. "Important article on Maine's mighty artist, Bern Porter. Also, artwork-profusely illustrated. *An Artburst From Maine* by Carlo Pittore. ISSN 0272-5657." circ. 2M. Published at editor's discretion. Expects 5 issues 1991. sub. price: $20; per copy: $5; sample: $5. Back issues: $5, $7.50 for ME IV (Audio Cassette). Discounts: 40%. 8pp; 8½x11; of. Reporting time: 2 months. Payment: copies. Not copyrighted. §Art movements, art, mail art. Ads: $140/$75. MPWA.

M/E/A/N/I/N/G, Susan Bee, Mira Schor, 60 Lispenard Street, New York, NY 10013. 1986. Articles, criticism, reviews. "Art magazine of criticism and articles by visual artists." circ. 1M. 2/yr. Pub'd 2 issues 1990; expects 2 issues 1991, 2 issues 1992. sub. price: $10 individuals, $15 institutions; per copy: $5; sample: $5. Back issues: $10 for #1. 60pp; 8½x11; of. Reporting time: 2 months. Payment: none. Copyrighted, does not revert to author. Pub's reviews. §art publications.

Meckler Corporation (see also SMALL PRESS: The Magazine & Book Review of Independent Publishing), Brenda Mitchell-Powell, Editor-in-Chief, 11 Ferry Lane West, Westport, CT 06880, 203-226-6967; FAX 203-454-5840. 1983.

MEDIA HISTORY DIGEST, Hiley H. Ward, 11 West 19th Street, New York, NY 10011, 212-675-4380. 1979. Articles, interviews, criticism, reviews, news items. "This is a bi-annual 'digest' of material on media history, using primarily original manuscripts. Ms will be original, but digest (brief) format will be followed. Articles should not exceed 2,500. First issue — Summer 1980." circ. 1M paid, 2M distributed. 2/yr. Pub'd 2 issues 1990; expects 4 issues 1991, 2 issues 1992. sub. price: $5 U.S., $8 Canada & foreign; per copy: $3.75; sample: $2.50. Back issues: $2.50. Discounts: to be determined. 64pp; 5½x8½; of. Reporting time: 2-4 months. Payment: $25 puzzles, $100 articles. Copyrighted. Pub's reviews: 20 in 1990. §Newspaper, broadcast, film, magazine, book of media. Ads: $525/$315.

The Media Institute, Richard T. Kaplar, Vice President, 3017 M Street NW, Washington, DC 20007, 202-298-7512. 1975. avg. press run 1M+. Pub'd 3 titles 1990; expects 3 titles 1991, 3 titles 1992. 20 titles listed in the *Small Press Record of Books in Print* (20th Edition, 1991-92). avg. price, paper: $12.95. Discounts: bulk

344

rates begin at 10 copies or more. 100pp; 5½×8½; of. Payment: contract only. Does not copyright for author.

Media Periodicals (see also JOURNAL OF VISION REHABILITATION; TECHNICALITIES), Linda Messman, Editorial Director, 2440 'O' Street #202, Lincoln, NE 68510. "A division of Westport Publishers, Inc."

Media Publishing, 2440 'O' Street, Suite 202, Lincoln, NE 68510. 1979. Non-fiction. "A division of Westport Publishers, Inc." avg. press run 1.5M. Pub'd 10 titles 1990; expects 10 titles 1991, 15 titles 1992. 4 titles listed in the *Small Press Record of Books in Print* (20th Edition, 1991-92). avg. price, cloth: $15; paper: $10. Discounts: standard trade. 176pp; 6×9, 8½×11, 5½×8½; of. Reporting time: 30 days. Payment: negotiable. Copyrights for author. MAPA.

MEDIA REPORT TO WOMEN, Sheila Gibbons, Editor, Communication Research Associates, Inc., 10606 Mantz Road, Silver Spring, MD 20903, 301-445-3230. 1972. News items. 6/yr. Pub'd 6 issues 1990; expects 6 issues 1991, 6 issues 1992. sub. price: $30 indiv, $45 instit; per copy: $10. Back issues: price list available. 12pp; 8½×11. Copyrighted. Pub's reviews. §Women and media. Ads: 75¢ per classified word.

MEDIA SPOTLIGHT, Albert James Dager, Editor & Publisher, Po Box 290, Redmond, WA 98073. 1977. Articles, art, photos, cartoons, interviews, reviews, music, letters, news items, non-fiction. "Any unsolicited submissions might not be returned!" circ. 3M. 4/yr. Expects 4 issues 1991, 4 issues 1992. sub. price: any tax-deductible donation, preferably at least $20; per copy: any tax-deductible donation; sample: any tax-deductible donation. Back issues: for those available (some only by photocopy), any tax-deductible donation. 20pp; 8½×11; of. Reporting time: 4 weeks to 4 months. Payment: copies. Copyrighted, reverts to author. Pub's reviews: 3 in 1990. §Media, Culture, Christian Lifestyle, Biblical analysis of media.

Media Weavers (see also WRITER'S N.W.), Linny Stovall, Dennis Stovall, Route 3, Box 376, Hillsboro, OR 97124, 503-621-3911. 1985. "Biannual editions of *Writer's Northwest Handbook*." avg. press run 5M. Expects 3 titles 1991, 2 titles 1992. avg. price, paper: $16.95. 200pp; 8×11.

MEDICAL HISTORY, Wellcome Institute for the History of Medicine, W.F. Bynum, V. Nutton, 183 Euston Road, London NW1 2BN, England. 1957. Articles, reviews, news items. circ. 900. 4/yr. Pub'd 4 issues 1990; expects 4 issues 1991. 2 titles listed in the *Small Press Record of Books in Print* (20th Edition, 1991-92). sub. price: individuals UK/Eire £35, overseas £44, institutions UK/Eire £49, overseas £55; per copy: £9. Back issues: £9 if available. 140pp; 5×8; of. Reporting time: 2 months. Payment: none. Copyright Trustees of the Wellcowe Trust. Pub's reviews: 154 in 1990. §All aspects of history of medicine and allied sciences. Ads: £170/£95.

Medical Physics Publishing Corp., 1300 University Avenue, Suite 27B, Madison, WI 53706, 608-256-3300. 1985. Non-fiction. "We publish non-technical science and medical books for the general public, including a series called Popular Topics in Science. We also publish technical books for medical physicists and the medical community" avg. press run 2M. Pub'd 9 titles 1990; expects 12 titles 1991, 18 titles 1992. 3 titles listed in the *Small Press Record of Books in Print* (20th Edition, 1991-92). avg. price, cloth: $32; paper: $15. Discounts: 1-2 20%, 3-10 40%, 11-20 42%, 21-50 44%, 51+ 46%. 200pp; 8½×11, 6×9, 7×10; of/lo. Reporting time: 2 weeks to 1 month. Payment: 10-20%. Copyrights for author. WAPA, UMBA, APA, ABA, COSMEP.

MEDICAL REFORM, Medical Reform Group, Haresh Kirpalani, Ulli Diemer, PO Box 366, Station J, Toronto, Ontario M4J 4Y8, Canada, 416-588-9167. 1979. Articles, cartoons, reviews, news items. "The Medical Reform Group is an organization dedicated to the reform of the health care system, according to the following principles: 1. Health care is a right. The universal access of every person to high quality, appropriate health care must be guaranteed. The health care system must be administered in a manner which precludes any monetary or other deterrent to equal care. 2. Health is political and social in nature. Health care workers, including physicians, should seek out and recognize the social, economic, occupational, and environmental causes of disease. 3. The institutions of the health care system must be democratized. *Medical Reform* carries articles advancing these views" circ. 250. 6/yr. Pub'd 7 issues 1990; expects 6 issues 1991, 6 issues 1992. sub. price: $25; per copy: $4.25; sample: $1. Back issues: $35 for complete set of all back issues. Discounts: can be arranged. 32pp; 8½×11; of. Reporting time: 2 months. Payment: none. Not copyrighted. Pub's reviews: 10 in 1990. §Health & medicine, especially social, environmental, economic, political aspects. Ads: $200/$120/25¢ per word. COSMEP.

Medical Reform Group (see also MEDICAL REFORM), Haresh Kirpalani, Ulli Diemer, PO Box 366, Station J, Toronto, Ontario M4J 4Y8, Canada, 416-588-9167. 1979. Articles. "The MRG publishes booklets and research materials dealing with the social, political, and economic aspects of health, and with possible changes to the health care system" Pub'd 3 titles 1990; expects 3 titles 1991. avg. price, other: $10. 96pp; 8½×11; of. COSMEP.

MEDITATION MAGAZINE, Patrick Harbula, Executive Editor; Tricia Harbula, Managing Editor, 17211 Orozco Street, Granada Hills, CA 91344, 818-366-5441. 1985. Poetry, fiction, articles, art, photos, cartoons, interviews, satire, reviews, music, letters, parts-of-novels, news items, non-fiction. "900-3,000 words." circ. 30M. 6/yr. Pub'd 4 issues 1990; expects 5 issues 1991, 6 issues 1992. sub. price: $17.95; per copy: $4; sample: free. Back issues: varies from $5-$15. 96pp; 8½x11; Web press. Reporting time: 2 months. Payment: $50-$150. Copyrighted, reverts to author. Pub's reviews: 30 in 1990. §Any that would fall within our editorial purpose. Ads: $879/$576.

MedLife Communications, Inc., William H. Brady, 3107 W. Colorado Ave. Ste. 266, Colorado Springs, CO 80904, 719-473-9205. 1990. "MedLife Communications, Inc. is a publishing/film company that specializes in health/medical/safety/educational information for families, employers, child care providers, and children. Although most our projects are first selected by our editor, we will accept outside proposals and namuscripts." avg. press run 10M. Expects 2 titles 1991, 6 titles 1992. 1 title listed in the *Small Press Record of Books in Print* (20th Edition, 1991-92). avg. price, paper: $12.95. Discounts: 50-555. 256pp; 6x9. Reporting time: 2 months. Copyrights for author.

Melrose, Michael Walton, 14 Clinton Rise, Beer, E. Devon EX12 3DZ, England, 0297-20619. 1981. Poetry, fiction, articles, art, music, letters, parts-of-novels, long-poems, plays, non-fiction. "Manuscripts considered ONLY if applicable to the interpretation of life as set forth in the Teachings of John Todd Ferrier, Founder, The Order of the Cross, 10, DeVere Gardens, Kensington, London W8 5AE, England." avg. press run 2.5M. Pub'd 1 title 1990; expects 1 title 1992. 12 titles listed in the *Small Press Record of Books in Print* (20th Edition, 1991-92). avg. price, cloth: $14.75; paper: $1. Discounts: To bookstores 33%-40%; to distributors 50%-55%. 265pp; 5¾x8¼; †of. Reporting time: probably under 2 months. Payment: none, royalty halved. Does not copyright for author.

MEMES, Norman Jope, c/o 38 Molesworth Road, Plympton Plymouth, Devonshire PL7 4NT, United Kingdom. 1989. Poetry, fiction, articles, art, interviews, criticism, reviews, music, parts-of-novels, long-poems, collages, plays, concrete art, non-fiction. "Short material (under 2,500 words) preferred. Black/white graphics only please. Obtain a sample copy before contributing (if possible)." circ. 250. 2-3/yr. Pub'd 2 issues 1990; expects 3 issues 1991, 2 issues 1992. sub. price: $10 (cash only); per copy: $4 (cash only); sample: $4 (cash only). Discounts: trade 33⅓% (minimum order 10, sent surface mail). 44pp; 8½x6; copyprint. Reporting time: 4 weeks from date of receipt. Payment: contributor's copy. Copyrighted, reverts to author. Pub's reviews: 60-70 in 1990. §Mainly 'literary' (pref. visionary/modernist), occult, counter-culture (inc. politics).

Men & Women of Letters, John Yewell, 1672 Wellesley Avenue, St. Paul, MN 55105-2006, 612-699-1594. 1988. Fiction. avg. press run 2M. Pub'd 1 title 1990; expects 1 title 1991, 1 title 1992. 1 title listed in the *Small Press Record of Books in Print* (20th Edition, 1991-92). avg. price, paper: $9.95. Discounts: 40% to stores, others negotiable, STOP. 125pp; 5½x8½; lp. Reporting time: 3-6 months. Payment: 10% of gross, prorated by page count. Copyrights for author.

The Menard Press, Anthony Rudolf, 8 The Oaks, Woodside Avenue, London N12 8AR, England. 1969. Poetry. "No new manuscripts can be considered for time being. 1) Nuclear politics poetry, poetics, translated poetry. 2) 4 books were published in 1986. 3) The press's poetry books are distributed in the USA by Small Press Distribution Inc., Berkely CA." avg. press run 750-5M. Pub'd 3 titles 1990; expects 5 titles 1991. 25 titles listed in the *Small Press Record of Books in Print* (20th Edition, 1991-92). avg. price, paper: $10. Discounts: usual. Poetry 56pp, politics 24pp; demi octavo; of, lp. ALP.

MEN'S REPORT, Sam Julty, Executive Editor, Center For Men's Studies, 2600 Dwight Way, Berkeley, CA 94704, (415) 549-0537. 1985. Poetry, articles, photos, cartoons, interviews, satire, criticism, reviews, letters, news items, non-fiction. "M/r is a magazine *about* men, i.e. men's studies in a popular format. M/r is for men and women readers and welcomes men and women writers. Opinion essays *about* men, their lives, lifestyles, work, play, family life, etc. especially welcome. Criticism o.k., bashing not o.k. Subscriptions, send to PO Box 40355, Berkeley, CA 94704. We will accept contributions to Center for Men's Studies" circ. 10M. 4/yr. Pub'd 3 issues 1990; expects 4 issues 1991, 4 issues 1992. sub. price: $12.50; per copy: $3.50. Back issues: same. Discounts: 40%. 32pp; 8.5x11; pagemaker proofs, of. Reporting time: 1-3 weeks. Payment: $100 articles, $10 poems. Copyrighted, reverts to author. Pub's reviews: 3 in 1990. §About men. Ads: $500/$300/$250 1/3 page/$200 1/6 page/$150 1/12 page $80/classified 75¢ per word.

Mendocino Book Partnership, Georgia-Ann Gregory, PO Box 1414, Mendocino, CA 95460-1414. 1986. Art. "Only pictorial art wi text" avg. press run 5M. Pub'd 1 title 1990. avg. price, cloth: $35. Discounts: please inquire. 96pp; 8½x10⅝ horiz; †4 or 5 color press, of. Reporting time: by arrangement. Payment: yes. Copyrights for author.

MENSUEL 25, Atelier De L'Agneau, Francoise Favretto, Robert Varlez, 39 Rue Louis Demeuse, 4400 Herstal, Belgium, (41) 363722. 1977. Poetry, fiction, articles, art, photos, cartoons, interviews, criticism, reviews, letters, parts-of-novels, collages. circ. 500. 6/yr. Pub'd 7 issues 1990; expects 7 issues 1991, 7 issues 1992. sub. price: 1200 FB; per copy: 200 FB; sample: free. Back issues: from 70 FB to 200 FB. 72pp; 21.5x28.5cm; †of. Copyrighted. Pub's reviews: 150 in 1990. §Poetry, art, letters. Ads: 1500FB/700FB/350FB

346

for 1/4 page.

MENTERTAINMENT, Sophie Ben-Shitta, PO Box 9445, Elizabeth, NJ 07202, 908-558-9000. 1989. Articles, photos, cartoons, interviews, reviews, letters. "3 editions: North/Central Jersey, New York/CT, South Jersey/PA. Our monthly edition, *Pink,* inside *Mentertainment* is an erotic entertainment trade magazine for the industry only. Not available for people outside the industry" circ. 100M. 12/yr. Pub'd 12 issues 1990; expects 12 issues 1991, 12 issues 1992. sub. price: $15/edition for 1st edition, $12 for additional; per copy: $1.50; sample: $1.50. Back issues: $2. 50pp; 7½×11; of, newsprint, b/w. Reporting time: 10 days. Payment: none, or almost none. Copyrighted, does not revert to author. Pub's reviews: 10 in 1990. §Sex, sexual entertainment, X-rated video, erotic dancing. Ads: $480/$335/1x1-2" $15 per issue/edition.

MENU, The Lunchroom Press, George Myers, Editor-in-Chief, PO Box 36027, Grosse Pointe Farms, MI 48236. 1985. Articles, art, photos, interviews, criticism, reviews, collages, news items. "Focus on the new and experimental, in literature and other arts. Reviews and literary/cultural criticism. Contributors include Hugh Fox, Richard Kostelanetz, Kenneth Warren, Buzz Spector, Charles Brownson, Robert Peters, Loris Essary, Gretchen Johnsen, etc." 1/yr. sub. price: $8.95; per copy: $8.95. Discounts: 2-9 copies 20%, 10+ 40%. 64pp; 8½×11; of. Reporting time: varies. Payment: copies. Copyrighted, reverts to author. Pub's reviews. §Literary, 'small press,' poetry, art, criticism, Belles Lettres. Ads: $40/$25/$15 1/4 page. PRC/M, PP/NY.

Mercer House Press, William J. Hardy, Jr., Director, P.O. Box 681, Kennebunkport, ME 04046, 207-282-7116. 1971. Non-fiction. "Education, mass communication, journalism." avg. press run 1M. Pub'd 1 title 1990; expects 1 title 1991, 1 title 1992. 2 titles listed in the *Small Press Record of Books in Print* (20th Edition, 1991-92). avg. price, cloth: $30; paper: $15. Discounts: 40% to wholesalers, 20% to libraries and university college bookstores. 140pp; 6×9; of. Reporting time: 4 weeks. Payment: 10-15%. Copyrights for author.

Mercury House, Alev Lytle Croutner, Executive Editor, 201 Filbert Street, #400, San Francisco, CA 94133, 415-433-7042; 433-7080 (Editorial). 1984. Fiction, non-fiction. "Mercury House is a general trade house of quality works from all over the world. Some recent contributors are: Colin Wilson, Jacob Needleman, Todd Walton, Ellen Alexander Conley, Meto Jovanovski and Gabriella Mautner" avg. press run 5M. Pub'd 16 titles 1990; expects 16 titles 1991, 16 titles 1992. 18 titles listed in the *Small Press Record of Books in Print* (20th Edition, 1991-92). avg. price, cloth: $16.95; paper: $9.95. 300pp; 5½×8½; of. Reporting time: 2 months. Payment: industry standard. Copyrights for author. PASCAL (Publishing Association of Southern California), ABA (American Booksellers Association), Northern California Book Publicists Association.

Merging Media, Diane C. Erdmann, Publisher & Editor, 516 Gallows Hill Road, Cranford, NJ 07016, 276-9479. 1978. Poetry, fiction, articles, art, photos, cartoons, interviews, criticism, reviews, letters, news items. "Open to manuscripts by invitation although will discuss loaning logo to preferred authors on arrangement. Send for title sheet availability. Enclose stamp. 24 titles since 1978." avg. press run 250-500. Pub'd 5 titles 1990. 5 titles listed in the *Small Press Record of Books in Print* (20th Edition, 1991-92). avg. price, cloth: $5; paper: $4.95 plus 50¢ postage. Discounts: 40% no consignment. 48pp; 6×9, 5×8; of. Reporting time: 1 month. Payment: contributors copies. Does not copyright for author. CCLM, WIFT, AWP, IWWG, FWG.

Meridian Learning Systems, Charles Chickadel, Publisher, 665 Third Street, Ste. 340, San Francisco, CA 94107, 415-495-2300. 1984. Non-fiction. "Small business, entrepreneurial orientation." Pub'd 1 title 1990; expects 1 title 1991, 2 titles 1992. 3 titles listed in the *Small Press Record of Books in Print* (20th Edition, 1991-92). Discounts: 2-24 40%, 25-99 45%, 100-499 50%, 500-999 55%, 1000+ 60%. of. Reporting time: 1 month. COSMEP, PMA.

Meridional Publications (see also NORTH CAROLINA LIBRARIES), Robert Reckenbeil, Publisher, 7101 Winding Way, Wake Forest, NC 27587, 919-556-2940. 1977. "In the early years Meridional Publications started by publishing educational multi-media programs which are still in print today, but the company has now branched into scientific journals in addition to one or two books published each year in the company name and about forty each year produced for other organiations and published in their name." avg. press run 1M-6M. Pub'd 1 title 1990. 2 titles listed in the *Small Press Record of Books in Print* (20th Edition, 1991-92). avg. price, cloth: $15; paper: $7; other: multi-media $16 to $20. Discounts: 20%-40% to trade (bookstores), 50 to 55% to jobbers and distributors. Pages vary; size varies; of. Reporting time: less than 1 month. Payment: 10% to 15% of gross price. Copyrights negotiable.

Merlin Books Ltd., E. Edwards, 40, East Street, Braunton, Devon EX33 2EA, United Kingdom. 1981. Poetry, fiction, non-fiction. "We are subsidy publishers." avg. press run 1M-3M. Pub'd 60 titles 1990; expects 70 titles 1991, 70 titles 1992. avg. price, cloth: £9; paper: £3. 64pp; 110×148mm (A5); of. Reporting time: 14 days. Payment: by arrangement. Copyrights for author.

MERLYN'S PEN: The National Magazine of Student Writing, R. Jim Stahl, Merlyn's Pen, Inc., PO Box

1058, East Greenwich, RI 02818, (401) 885-5175. 1985. Poetry, fiction, articles, art, photos, cartoons, reviews, letters, plays, non-fiction. "Authors must be students in grades 7-10, or age 13-16 if not in school." circ. 20M. 4/yr. Pub'd 4 issues 1990; expects 4 issues 1991, 4 issues 1992. sub. price: $16.95 + $3 for foreign orders; per copy: $4; sample: free. Back issues: $3. Discounts: classroom rates: 1-10 $16.95, 11-20 $7.95, 21+ $5.95, + $3 each sub. for foreign orders. 40pp; 8⅛×10⅞; web, of. Reporting time: 12 weeks. Payment: 3 copies of mag plus *The Elements of Style*. Copyrighted, reverts to author. Pub's reviews: 4 in 1990. §Kids (grades 7-10) send unsolicited reviews of *current* books, magazines, movies or of material previously published in *Merlyn's Pen*. Ads: b/w $1,150/$585/$490 1/3 page. Edpress.

Mermaid Press, Allen Thornton, Susan Thornton, Box 183, Vermilion, OH 44089. 1983. Satire, non-fiction. "We are interested in any truly different prose works, particularly humor." avg. press run 1M. Pub'd 1 title 1990; expects 1 title 1991. 1 title listed in the *Small Press Record of Books in Print* (20th Edition, 1991-92). avg. price, paper: $3. Discounts: standard. 150pp; 4×7; of. Reporting time: 1 week. Payment: individual negotiation. COSMEP.

Merrill Court Press, Adam Wolfe, Pleasant DeSpain, PO Box 85785, Seattle, WA 98145-1785. 2 titles listed in the *Small Press Record of Books in Print* (20th Edition, 1991-92).

MESSAGE POST, Light Living Library, Po Box 190—DB, Philomath, OR 97370. 1980. Articles, reviews, letters. "Helpful suggestions about portable dwelling, long comfortable camping, low-cost light-weight living. How-to save money, energy, weight, space, land, live and travel more imaginatively. Simultaneous, photocopy submission recommended." circ. 2M. 3/yr. 1 title listed in the *Small Press Record of Books in Print* (20th Edition, 1991-92). sub. price: $5/6 issues; per copy: $1. 12pp; 5½×8½; of. Payment: subscriptions or ads. Pub's reviews: 63 in 1990. Ads: 20¢ per word.

Metacom Press, William Ferguson, Nancy Ferguson, 1 Tahanto Road, Worcester, MA 01602-2523, 617-757-1683. 1980. Poetry, fiction. "Booklets have ranged from 16 to 28 pages. Titles so far are by John Updike, William Heyen, Ann Beattie, James Tate, James Wright, Diane Wakoski, Raymond Carver, James Merrill, John McPhee, Edward Gorey. All titles to date have been published in a limited-edition format, using imported papers and hand-binding. Our intention is to establish ourselves financially with the limited editions and then to move to a more democratic, less exclusive type of publication. No unsolicited manuscripts" avg. press run 150-300. Pub'd 1 title 1990; expects 2 titles 1991, 3 titles 1992. 8 titles listed in the *Small Press Record of Books in Print* (20th Edition, 1991-92). avg. price, cloth: $75; paper: $25. Discounts: 30% to dealers, 10% to libraries. 20pp; 6×9; †lp. Payment: 10% of list value of the edition. Copyrights for author.

Metagnosis Publications, PO Box 2777, Estes Park, CO 80517, 303-586-5940. 1990. avg. press run 2M-3M. Pub'd 2 titles 1990; expects 2 titles 1991, 3 titles 1992. 4 titles listed in the *Small Press Record of Books in Print* (20th Edition, 1991-92). avg. price, paper: $16.95. Discounts: retail only 1-4 20%, 5-99 40%; 100+ 50%. 150pp; 6×9, 8½×11. Reporting time: 6 weeks. Payment: 10%. Does not copyright for author. COSMEP, Mountains & Plains Booksellers.

Metamorphous Press, David Balding, Publisher; Lori Stephens, Senior Editor; Nancy Wyatt-Kelsey, Acquisitions Editor, PO Box 10616, Portland, OR 97210, 503-228-4972. 1982. Poetry, fiction, art, photos, cartoons, satire, non-fiction. "We prefer submissions that give a brief outline of the book, table of contents, sample of the writing style, and potential market. We then decide whether to request a complete manuscript. We can return manuscripts but prefer not to. For acknowledgement of receipt of initial info, please include SASE." avg. press run 2M-5M. Pub'd 5 titles 1990; expects 4 titles 1991, 4 titles 1992. 26 titles listed in the *Small Press Record of Books in Print* (20th Edition, 1991-92). avg. price, cloth: $17; paper: $11; other: $8 cassettes. Discounts: trade 40%; bulk depends on quantity—write for rates; classroom 20%. 200pp; 5½×8½; of. Reporting time: 1-3 months. Payment: negotiable. Copyrights for author. COSMEP, PNWBPA.

METAPHOR, Rhapsody International, Dr. Juba, Rubi Whiteside, Piri Thomas, 109 Minna St., Suite 153, San Francisco, CA 94105, 415-641-7231. 1985. Poetry, fiction, art, photos, cartoons, satire, music, letters, collages, plays, non-fiction. "Well written, non-vulgar material dealing with art & culture, culinary, health, fashion (tips & design), graphic & visual communication, & especially: any material of a humorous or inspirational nature. Profiles of artists should accompany submissions. Also accept in French, Spanish, Native American, African, & Asian tongues with tranlations." circ. 250. 4/yr. 1 title listed in the *Small Press Record of Books in Print* (20th Edition, 1991-92). sub. price: $7; per copy: $2.50; sample: $2.50. Discounts: available upon request. 50pp; 5½×8½, 8½×11; of. Reporting time: 2-4 weeks. Payment: copies. Copyrighted, reverts to author. Pub's reviews: 6 in 1990. Ads: available upon request. COSMEP, CCLM, WOWW.

METROSPHERE, Robert J. Pugel, Director; Iris R. Porter, Editor, Campus Box 32, Metropolitan State College, Denver, CO 80204, 303-556-2495. 1983. Poetry, fiction, articles, art, photos, cartoons, interviews, satire, long-poems, plays, non-fiction. "Fiction—2,000 words or less. Poetry—any style, prefer 50 lines or less. Non-fiction—personal essays, profiles, please query. Readership—43,000" circ. 5M. 1/yr. Pub'd 1 issue 1990; expects 2 issues 1991, 2 issues 1992. price per copy: $2; sample: $2. Back issues: $2. 92pp; 8½×11; of.

Reporting time: 2 months Sept.-May. Payment: 2 copies. Copyrighted, reverts to author. Ads: $300/$175/$100 1/4/$50 1/8.

MEXICAN STUDIES/ESTUDIOS MEXICANOS, University of California Press, Jaime E. Rodriguez, University of California Press, 2120 Berkeley Way, Berkeley, CA 94720, 415-642-4191. 1985. Non-fiction. "Editorial address: 340 Humanities Office Bldg., Univ. of CA, Irvine, CA 92717." circ. 1.3M. 2/yr. Pub'd 2 issues 1990; expects 2 issues 1991, 2 issues 1992. sub. price: $17 indiv., $34 instit. (+ $3 foreign postage); per copy: $8.50 indiv. $17 instit. (+ $3 foreign postage); sample: free. Back issues: $8.50 indiv.; $17 instit. Discounts: foreign subs. agent 10%, one-time orders 10+ 30%, standing orders (bookstores): 1-99 40%, 100+ 50%. 200pp; 6×9; of. Copyrighted, does not revert to author. Ads: $200/$120.

!MEXICO WEST!, Mexico West Travel Club, Inc., Shirley Miller, Editor, PO Box 1646, Bonita, CA 91908, 619-585-3033. 1975. Articles, news items. "800-1200 words. Current travel and recreational information on Baja and west coast of Mexico-story style." circ. 5M. 12/yr. Pub'd 12 issues 1990; expects 12 issues 1991, 12 issues 1992. sub. price: $35 per year includes membership in Mexico West Travel; sample: upon request. Back issues: $2 each. Discounts: none. 8pp; 8½×11; of/web. Reporting time: anytime. Payment: $40-$50. Copyrighted, reverts to author. Pub's reviews: 3 in 1990. §Mexico, travel, Baja. Ads: classified 40¢ per word. COSMEP.

Mexico West Travel Club, Inc. (see also !MEXICO WEST!), Shirley Miller, Editor, PO Box 1646, Bonita, CA 91908, 619-585-3033. 1975. Articles, news items. "800-1200 words. Current travel & recreational information on Baja and west coast of Mexico." avg. press run 5M. Pub'd 12 titles 1990; expects 12 titles 1991. avg. price, cloth: $35 (membership only way to obtain publication). 8pp; 8½×11; of/web press. Payment: $40-$50. Copyrights for author.

Meyerbooks, Publisher, David Meyer, Irene Richardson, P.O. Box 427, Glenwood, IL 60425, 708-757-4950. 1976. Non-fiction. "We consider material suitable to any specialized market that we can identify and properly promote to." avg. press run 3M-5M. Pub'd 2 titles 1990; expects 2 titles 1991, 2 titles 1992. 22 titles listed in the *Small Press Record of Books in Print* (20th Edition, 1991-92). avg. price, cloth: $18.95; paper: $9.95. Discounts: 1 copy 25%, 4-24 40%, 25-49 42%, 50+ 45% to trade; jobber discounts on request. 200pp; 6×9. Reporting time: 3-6 months, outlines 1 month report. Payment: arranged. Copyrights for author.

Mho & Mho Works (see also THE FESSENDEN REVIEW), Douglas Cruickshank, Senior Editor; Lynn Luneau, Associate Editor; Cese McGowan, Assistant Editor, Box 33135, San Diego, CA 92103, 619-488-4991. 1969. Non-fiction. "We do books on communications arts, and on occult sexual practices. We are also interested in material having to do with the physically handicapped (our fall 1983 title was *The Cripple Liberation Front Marching Band Blues*) — not the usual miracle-cure , but real and honest essays and book-length reports on the affect and effect of being physically handicapped in a Pepsi Generation World. Most of our books are of normal length. We require that any submissions be accompanied by self addressed stamped envelope—otherwise, the manuscripts will go into our scratch paper file. We wouldn't discourage any submissions, but they must be honest and direct" avg. press run 5M-10M. Pub'd 3 titles 1990; expects 3 titles 1991, 3 titles 1992. 10 titles listed in the *Small Press Record of Books in Print* (20th Edition, 1991-92). avg. price, cloth: $14.95; paper: $9.95. Discounts: 55% to Bookpeople, Inland Books, and New Leaf. 200-400pp; 6×9; cold type. Reporting time: 6 weeks. Payment: we pay ourselves back for cost of publication out of earliest proceeds. Then, we split 50/50 with author. Copyrights for author. COSMEP.

Micah Publications, Robert Kalechofsky, Roberta Kalechofsky, 255 Humphrey St, Marblehead, MA 01945, 617-631-7601. 1975. Fiction, articles, criticism. "Micah Publications publishes prose: scholarly, fictional, lyrical; a prose that addresses itself to issues without offending esthetic sensibilities, a prose that is aware of the esthetics of language without succumbing to esthetic solipsism. Three books a year. No unsolicited mss." avg. press run 800. Pub'd 2 titles 1990; expects 4 titles 1991, 2-3 titles 1992. 24 titles listed in the *Small Press Record of Books in Print* (20th Edition, 1991-92). avg. price, cloth: $20; paper: $10. Discounts: 2-5 20%, 6-9 30%, 10-49 40%, 50+ 50%. 280pp; 5¼×8½; author must submit camera-ready copy of text—we'll do designs and illustrations. Reporting time: 3 months. Payment: 20% to authors; after primary expenses of printing and advertising book is met from sale of books. Copyrights for author. COSMEP, AJP.

THE MICHAEL CONNECTION, M.C. Clark, PO Box 1873, Orinda, CA 94563, 415-256-7639. 1985. Articles, interviews, reviews. "We are interested in articles about the Michael Teaching or about other topics from the point of view of someone interested in the Michael Teaching (the teaching channeled by the entity Michael)" circ. 1M. 4/yr. Pub'd 5 issues 1990; expects 4 issues 1991, 4 issues 1992. sub. price: $15; per copy: $4; sample: $2. Back issues: $4 ($3 for some earlier issues). Discounts: wholesale $2.40. 32pp; 8½×11. Payment: all contributions on a volunteer basis. Copyrighted, reverts to author. Pub's reviews. §New Age philosophies. Ads: $150/$95/$60 1/4 page. COSMEP.

MICHIGAN FEMINIST STUDIES, 234 W. Engineering, Women's Studies, University of Michigan, Ann Arbor, MI 48109. "A journal produced in conjunction with the Women's Studies Program at the University of

Michigan" 1/yr. Pub'd 2 issues 1990; expects 1 issue 1991, 1 issue 1992. 120pp; 6×9. Not copyrighted.

MICHIGAN QUARTERLY REVIEW, Laurence Goldstein, 3032 Rackham Bldg., University of Michigan, Ann Arbor, MI 48109, 313-764-9265. 1962. Poetry, fiction, articles, art, interviews, criticism, reviews, letters, parts-of-novels, long-poems. "We are no longer solely a literary magazine. In addition to poetry, fiction, and reviews, we now include essays on a variety of topics in the humanities, arts & sciences. Writers are advised to refer to a sample back issue before submitting ($2)." circ. 1.8M. 4/yr. Pub'd 4 issues 1990; expects 4 issues 1991, 4 issues 1992. sub. price: $13; per copy: $3.50; sample: $2. Back issues: $2. Discounts: agency rates - $15 for institution subscription; 15% for agent. 160pp; 6×9; of. Reporting time: 6 weeks. Payment: $8/page of poetry, $8/page essays. Copyrighted, reverts to author. Pub's reviews: 14 in 1990. §Humanities, sciences, arts, literature. Ads: $100/$50. CCLM.

Michigan Romance Studies, Floyd Gray, Department of Romance Language, MLB, University of MI, Ann Arbor, MI 48109, 313-764-5373. 1980. Articles. "We publish articles on literary criticism in the romance languages." avg. press run 500. Pub'd 1 title 1990; expects 2 titles 1991, 2 titles 1992. avg. price, paper: $8; other: Vol. X and following $10. Discounts: 20% off to book wholesalers. 250pp; of. Copyrights for author.

THE MICKLE STREET REVIEW, PO Box 1493, Camden, NJ 08101, 609-541-8280. 1979. Poetry, fiction, articles, art, photos, interviews, criticism, reviews. "A journal dedicated to celebrating the influence of Walt Whitman on American poetry, published from Whitman's last residence." circ. 500. 1/yr. Expects 1 issue 1991. sub. price: $15 (includes membership); per copy: $15; sample: $15 current. Back issues: $10. Discounts: none. 96pp; 6×9; of. Reporting time: 2 months. Payment: 2 copies. Copyrighted. Pub's reviews: 6 in 1990. §Material related to Whitman.

Micro Pro Litera Press, Harry Bernstein, Managing Editor; William Severson, PO Box 14045, San Fraicisco, CA 94114, (415) 863-3037. 1986. Fiction, cartoons, satire, music, plays, non-fiction. "We are starting our company in 1986 with the publication of Dean Goodman's *San Francisco Stages: A Concise History, 1849-1986.* We have a number of areas of interest, especially theatre, the arts, music and humor/satire. We also publish music—both music and books are typeset on a laser printer" avg. press run 1-2M. Pub'd 1 title 1990; expects 1 title 1992. 2 titles listed in the *Small Press Record of Books in Print* (20th Edition, 1991-92). avg. price, cloth: $19.95; paper: $10.95. Discounts: Distributors: 3-5 books 30%, 6+ 50%; Bookstores: 3-5 books 30%, 6+ books 40%; no library discounts. 200pp; 6×9, 4×7; of. Reporting time: 6-8 weeks. Payment: 10-15% royalty on publisher's gross sales from the book, payable twice a year. Copyrights for author.

MICROCOSM, Quixsilver Press, Robert Randolph Medcalf, Jr., PO Box 847, Hanover, PA 17331-0847. 1981. Poetry, art. "Want science fiction poetry, fantasy poetry, horror poetry, and speculative poetry. Past contributorstors: Janet Fox, Bruce Boston, Robert Frazier, Thomas M. Egan, Mel Spivak, Kathleen Taylor, and Doug W. Hiser, Jr." circ. 100. 1/yr. Expects 1 issue 1992. sub. price: $4; per copy: $4; sample: $4. Discounts: 40% to wholesalers. 24pp; 5½×8½; of. Reporting time: 6 months. Payment: 1 contributor copy for poetry, $10 for illustrations. Copyrighted, reverts to author. SPWAO, SFPA.

Microdex Bookshelf, Chris Brozek, Christopher Fara, 1212 N. Sawtelle, Suite 120, Tucson, AZ 85716, 602-326-3502. 1989. Non-fiction. "Microdex Bookshelf specializes in creating common-sense manuals, tutorials and reference books for computer users. Absolutely no tech-jargon, but no condescending either, concise: don't belabor the obvious, yet include all details. Unsolicited manuscripts not accepted; inquire by letter, include SASE." avg. press run 500-5M. Pub'd 2 titles 1990; expects 4 titles 1991, 6 titles 1992. 5 titles listed in the *Small Press Record of Books in Print* (20th Edition, 1991-92). avg. price, paper: $19.95. Discounts: retail 40%, bulk 50-55%, libraries, teachers and S.C.O.P. 25%. 150pp; 5½×8½; †of. Reporting time: 30 days, include SASE, no returns unless prepaid. Payment: negotiable but typical 10% of list price. Copyrights negotiable. COSMEP.

MICROSOLUTIONS, Paul Walhus, Joy Newcom, 5211 Meadow Creek Drive, Austin, TX 78745-3015, 512-416-1644; FAX 512-416-1677. 1991. Articles, art, photos, cartoons, interviews, reviews, letters, news items, non-fiction. circ. 5M. 12/yr. Expects 8 issues 1991, 12 issues 1992. sub. price: $20; per copy: $2; sample: $2. Back issues: $3.50 per issue if available. Trade discounts to computer resellers for customer distribution. 12pp; 8½×11; of. Reporting time: 2 weeks. Payment: negotiable. Copyrighted, reverts to author. Pub's reviews: 8 in 1990. §Computer and trade publications. Ads: $450/$250/$1650 4 full pages.

MICROWAVE NEWS, Louis Slesin, PO Box 1799, Grand Central Station, New York, NY 10163, 212-517-2802. 1981. Articles, reviews, news items. "A bimonthly report on non-ionizing radiation (from such sources as power lines, microwave transmitters, radio transmitters, cellular phones, VDTs etc...). Including the latest research, legislation, litigation, regulations" circ. 1M. 6/yr. Pub'd 6 issues 1990; expects 6 issues 1991, 6 issues 1992. sub. price: $250; per copy: $50; sample: $50. Back issues: $95 a calendar year; bound volumes available. Discounts: by arrangement with publisher. 16pp; 8½×11; lp. Copyrighted, does not revert to author. Pub's reviews: 25-30 in 1990. §Non-ionizing radiation, epidemiology, medical application. Ads: $1200/$750/$450 1/4 page/$275 1/8/$150 1/16/$85 1/32.

350

THE MID COASTER, Peter Blewett, 2750 North 45th Street, Milwaukee, WI 53210-2429. 1986. Poetry, fiction, articles, art, photos, cartoons, interviews, satire, criticism, reviews, letters, parts-of-novels, long-poems, collages, plays, non-fiction. "20 page limit on prose. Recent contributors: Edward Field, Jesse Glass, Jr., Antony Oldknow, Dona Hickey." circ. 500. 1/yr. Expects 3 issues 1991, 3 issues 1992. sub. price: $4; per copy: $4; sample: $4. Back issues: $4. Discounts: none. 32pp; 8½×11; laserjet. Reporting time: 2-10 weeks. Payment: 2 copies, plus discount for extra copies. Copyrighted, reverts to author. Pub's reviews: 2 in 1990. §literature, nonfiction, fiction, poetry. Ads: $50/$35.

MID-AMERICAN REVIEW, Ken Letko, Dept of English, Bowling Green State University, Bowling Green, OH 43403, 419-372-2725. 1976. Poetry, fiction, articles, criticism, reviews, parts-of-novels, long-poems. "Contributors: Lucien Stryk, Greg Kuzma, Rita J. Doucette, Russel Edson, Mary Crow, H. E. Francis, Joe David Bellamy, Andre Dubus, Philip Graham, Jonathan Holden." circ. 1M. 2/yr. Pub'd 2 issues 1990; expects 2 issues 1991, 2 issues 1992. sub. price: $8; per copy: $5; sample: $4. Back issues: $10 for rare issues. Discounts: 20%/40%. 200pp; 5½×8½; of. Reporting time: 1-4 months. Payment: $7 per page for fiction and poetry up to $50. Copyrighted, reverts to author. Pub's reviews: 14 in 1990. §Fiction, poetry and criticism of contemporary literature. Ads: $50/$25/$1.50 and exchange. AWP, CCLM, CELJ.

The Middle Atlantic Press, Norman Goldfind, Publisher, PO Box 945, Wilmington, DE 19899, 302-654-9922. 1968. "We are a trade book and educational materials publisher. Our material is oriented to the Middle Atlantic region, but all of our books are sold nation-wide." avg. press run varies. Pub'd 3 titles 1990; expects 6 titles 1991, 8 titles 1992. 18 titles listed in the *Small Press Record of Books in Print* (20th Edition, 1991-92). avg. price, cloth: $10.95; paper: $5.95. Discounts: 40% for 5 plus copies. Pages vary with title; size varies with title; of. Reporting time: 2 months. Payment: 10% royalty on hardcover books, 5% on paperbacks to author, paid annually. Copyrights for author. PPG, PA.

Middle Coast Publishing, Toby Feldman, Roland Henry, PO Box 2522, Iowa City, IA 52244, 319-335-4078; 354-8944. 1980. Poetry, fiction, non-fiction. "We look for niches the big publishers are blind to, or so small they're not worth their time and money. Most interested in books with long backlist lifespan. Query letters only. SASE or no reply" avg. press run 5M. Pub'd 2 titles 1990; expects 5 titles 1991, 5 titles 1992. avg. price, cloth: $14.95; paper: $4.95. 192pp; 6×9; of. Reporting time: as long as it takes. Payment: standard. Copyrights for author. PMA.

MIDDLE EAST REPORT, Joe Stork, 1500 Massachusetts Ave., NW, #119, Washington, DC 20005, 202-223-3677. 1971. Poetry, fiction, articles, art, photos, cartoons, interviews, reviews, letters, news items. circ. 7M. 6/yr. Pub'd 6 issues 1990; expects 6 issues 1991, 6 issues 1992. sub. price: $25 individual, $45 institutions; per copy: $4.50 individual; $6 institutions; sample: $6 individual; $7.50 institutions (includes postage). Discounts: 40% for dealers with standing orders, 30% for orders of 5 or more from dealers without standing orders; 30% for non-trade bulk orders of 25 or more. 48pp; 8½×11; of. Reporting time: 4-8 weeks. Payment: $100 per 1,000 words, $400 max. Copyrighted. Pub's reviews: 30 in 1990. §Middle East politics, economics, culture, society, international economics, oil, Middle East fiction. Ads: $275/$145. APS, COSMEP.

MIDDLE EASTERN DANCER, Karen Kuzsel, Executive Editor & Publisher; Jeanette Spencer, Managing Editor, PO Box 181572, Casselberry, FL 32718-1572, 407-831-3402. 1979. Poetry, fiction, articles, art, photos, cartoons, interviews, satire, criticism, reviews, music, letters, concrete art, news items, non-fiction. "We run material that *only* directly relates to Middle Eastern dance and culture. Our audience is mostly dancers, although many are just cultural enthusiasts. We do *not* delve into politics. We are *not* interested in anything that doesn't deal with this subject matter." circ. 2M+. 12/yr. Pub'd 12 issues 1990; expects 12 issues 1991, 12 issues 1992. sub. price: $24; per copy: $4 (inc. p/h); sample: $1. Back issues: irrelevant unless they are ordering quantities. 36pp; 8½×11; typesetting. Reporting time: 3-4 weeks. Payment: on acceptance; $10 for stories, $20 with pix; 2 copies for poems, we do sometimes work out some advertising in exchange and will send copy of printed material. Copyrighted, reverts to author. Pub's reviews: 12-15 in 1990. §Must relate to subject as earlier specified. Ads: $195/$105/45¢ per word ($9.45 min). Florida Magazine Association, Po Box 10523, Tallahassee, FL 32302.

The Middleburg Press, Carl Vandermeulen, Box 166, Orange City, IA 51041, 712-737-4198. 1978. Poetry, fiction, photos, letters. "We specialize in books and novels with a Reformed background and perspective; and in high school journalism/photography books." avg. press run 3M. Pub'd 1 title 1990; expects 1 title 1992. 5 titles listed in the *Small Press Record of Books in Print* (20th Edition, 1991-92). avg. price, cloth: $12.95; paper: $6.95. Discounts: jobbers & bookstores: 1 copy-20%; 2-3 copies 30%; 4-7 copies 35%; 8 or more 40%. 128pp; 6×9; of. Reporting time: 6 months. Payment: to be negotiated. Copyrights for author.

Middlebury College Publications (see also NEW ENGLAND REVIEW), T.R. Hummer, Editor; Maura High, Editor, Middlebury College, Middlebury, VT 05753, 802-388-3711 ext. 5075. 1978. Poetry, fiction, articles, interviews, criticism, reviews, parts-of-novels, long-poems. "Fiction, poetry, essays and reviews of the highest quality." avg. press run 2M. Pub'd 4 titles 1990; expects 4 titles 1991, 4 titles 1992. 2 titles listed in the

Small Press Record of Books in Print (20th Edition, 1991-92). avg. price, paper: $4. Discounts: 25% classroom. 124pp; 6×9; of. Reporting time: 8 weeks. Payment: competitive. Does not copyright for author. COSMEP, CLMP.

Middlewood Press (see also DRAGONFLY: East/West Haiku Quarterly), Richard Tice, PO Box 11236, Salt Lake City, UT 84147, 801-966-8034. 1985. Poetry. "Middlewood Press publishes only haiku in single-author collections of 300 or more, anthologies of haiku, or critical works about haiku" avg. press run 400-2.5M. Expects 1 title 1992. 2 titles listed in the *Small Press Record of Books in Print*, 1991-92). avg. price, paper: $5. Discounts: hb wholesale-60%; pb wholesale-70%. 70-80pp; 5½×8½, 6×9; of. Reporting time: 2-3 months. Payment: 10% of retail price. Copyrights for author.

MIDEAST MONITOR, AAUG Press, Naseer H. Aruri, 556 Trapelo Road, Belmont, MA 02178, (617) 484-5483. 1984. Articles, non-fiction. "Articles should run about 4,500 words, including footnotes" circ. 5M. 6/yr. Pub'd 4 issues 1990; expects 4 issues 1991, 4 issues 1992. sub. price: $10, $13 outside N. America; per copy: $2.50; sample: free. 4pp; 8½×11; of. Reporting time: 1 month. Payment: $200. Copyrighted, does not revert to author. No ads.

MIDLAND REVIEW, c/o English Department, Oklahoma State University, Stillwater, OK 74078. 1985. Poetry, fiction, art, photos, interviews, criticism, reviews, long-poems, plays. circ. 1M. 1/yr. Expects 1 issue 1991, 1 issue 1992. sub. price: $6 & $11/2-years; per copy: $5; sample: $5. 100-120pp; 5½×8½; of. Reporting time: 3-6 months. Payment: 1 copy. Copyrighted, reverts to author. Pub's reviews: 0 in 1990. §Poetry, fiction, contemporary feminist and linguistic criticism, drama, experimental writing, Oriental, Native American, Hispanic American, Black American, women's work, comparative literature, art, interviews (40% OSU student work). Ads: $100/$50/quarter page $25.

Midmarch Arts Press (see also WOMEN ARTISTS NEWS), Judy Seigel, Editor, 300 Riverside Drive, New York City, NY 10025, 212-666-6990. 1975. Articles, art, photos, interviews, news items, non-fiction. avg. press run 3M-5M. Expects 2 titles 1991, 4 titles 1992. 10 titles listed in the *Small Press Record of Books in Print* (20th Edition, 1991-92). avg. price, paper: $5-$12.50. Discounts: Institutional L.P, Jobber L.P. for single copies; appropriate disc. for quantity. 100-318pp; 5½×8½, 6×9; of. Reporting time: 4 weeks. Payment to authors, payment to essayists for books. Copyrights for author. CCLM, COSMEP, Small Press American Booksellers Assoc.

MIDNIGHT IN HELL (The Weirdest Tales of Fandom), George N. Houston, The Dark Editor, The Cottage, Smithy Brae, Kilmacolm, Renfrewshire PA134EN, Scotland. 1990. Fiction, articles, art, photos, cartoons, interviews, reviews, parts-of-novels, news items. "Fiction between 1,000 and 3,500 words. Fiction to be based in the horror, sci-fi and fantasy genres or any crossovers of these and reviews within the same genres." circ. 150-200. 4/yr. Pub'd 4 issues 1990; expects 4 issues 1991, 4 issues 1992. price per copy: £1 ($3US) will go up by at least 50p ($1). Back issues: £1.50 (issue #2 not available). Discounts: trade—1 issue £.85, 10 £8, 20 £15 (current issue only); #7 will go up to 1 issue £1, 10 £9, 20 £17. 24-28pp; 8¼×11½ (A4); †photocopy. Reporting time: 8 weeks. Payment: classified. Copyrighted, reverts to author. Pub's reviews: 14 in 1990. §Horror, sci-fi, fantasy and dark fantasy (and any crossover). Ads: upon request.

MIDNIGHT ZOO, Jon L. Herron, Editor-in-Chief; ElizaBeth Gilligan, Senior Editor, 544 Ygnacio Valley Road #A273, PO Box 8040, Walnut Creek, CA 94596, 415-942-5116. 1990. Poetry, fiction, articles, art, cartoons, interviews, reviews, long-poems, news items. "Stories up to 10,000 words. We have a special edition in December which is over 500 pages. Paul Anderson, Paul O. Williams, Devin O'Branagan, Tad Williams, Teresa Edgerton, Alis Rasmussen, Harlan Ellison, Heather Gladney, Lisa Mason, Kevin J. Anderson, Kevin O'Donnell, Jr., Mary Caraker." circ. 3M. 6/yr. Pub'd 5 issues 1990; expects 7 issues 1991, 7-10 issues 1992. sub. price: $29.95; per copy: $4.95; sample: $6 incl. postage. Back issues: $3.50 & $8.95 for Dec. 1990 special edition. Discounts: distributors 50/50, stores 35%, schools 40%. 150pp; 8½×11; †of. Reporting time: 8-10 weeks. Payment: 1/2 to 1¢ per word plus contributor copy; $2-$20 art and copy; poems $3-$10 or copy only. Copyrighted, reverts to author. Pub's reviews: 20+ in 1990. §Horror, science fiction, fantasy. Ads: $120/$66/$36 4x3/$20 2x3. SPWAO, HWA, SFWA, EUWAO, Fandata.

MIDWEST CHAPARRAL, Margaret Garland, Editor; Jill Lockey, Treasurer, 1309 2nd Avenue SW, Waverly, IA 50677, 319-352-1716. 1942. Poetry. "Haiku (3 lines) otherwise maximum 20 lines free, blank or rhymed. 4-8 line humorous verse-no juvenile verse." circ. 150. 2/yr. Pub'd 2 issues 1990. sub. price: $3 for members of MFCP, $4 non-members; per copy: $1.25 (including postage); sample: $1. Back issues: $1.25. 24-36pp; 5½×8½; of, computer and laser writer. Reporting time: varies. Payment: none. Not copyrighted. No ads.

MIDWEST POETRY REVIEW, Tom Tilford, Editor, PO Box 4776, Rock Island, IL 61201. 1980. Poetry. circ. 10M. 4/yr. Expects 4 issues 1991. sub. price: $17; per copy: $3 plus $1 postage; sample: $3. Back issues: $2.50 plus 50¢ postage (when available). 48-52pp; 5½×8½; of. Reporting time: 14 days. Payment: $5 to 500. Copyrighted. Pub's reviews: 4-8 in 1990. §Original poetry collections by one author. Ads: $120 full page to 240 (commercial) 20 inch classified.

THE MIDWEST QUARTERLY, James B.M. Schick, Editor; Stephen Meats, Poetry; Dudley T. Cornish, Book Reviews, Pittsburg State University, Pittsburg, KS 66762, 316-231-7000-4369. 1959. Poetry, articles, interviews, criticism, reviews, non-fiction. "Scholarly articles on history, literature, the social sciences (especially political), art, music, the natural sciences (in non-technical language). Most articles run 4M to 5M words. Can use a brief note of 1M to 2M words once in a while. Chief bias is an aversion to jargon and pedantry. Instead of footnotes we use a minimum of parenthetical documentation. Reviews and interviews are assigned. Contributors: Kuzma, Etter, Ruark, Gallagher, Bly, Dana, Goldbarth, Hathaway, Holden, Kooser, Ostriker, Sobin, Stafford, among others, have been represented in our pages. Will consider all poems submitted." circ. 1M. 4/yr. Pub'd 4 issues 1990; expects 4 issues 1991. sub. price: $10 within U.S., otherwise $13; per copy: $3; sample: $3. Back issues: $3. Discounts: 10% to agencies. 110pp; 6x9; of. Reporting time: 3-6 months. Payment: copies only, varies 3 usually. Copyrighted, reverts to author. Pub's reviews: 12 in 1990. §Poetry, non-fiction. No ads. CCLM.

Midwest Villages & Voices, Gayla Ellis, Pat Kaluza, Rachel Tilsen, 3220 Tenth Avenue South, Minneapolis, MN 55407, (612) 224-7687. 1981. "We are a publishing group and cultural organization for midwestern writers and visual artists. Submission by invitation only." avg. press run 1M-3M. Pub'd 1 title 1990; expects 1 title 1991, 1 title 1992. 6 titles listed in the *Small Press Record of Books in Print* (20th Edition, 1991-92). avg. price, paper: $5-7. Discounts: 30% (but prefer purchase at discount through Bookslinger, 2402 University Ave. W., #507, St. Paul, MN 55114, 612-649-0271 or 1-800-397-2613. 64-96pp; 5½x8½. Payment: negotiated. Copyrights negotiated.

MIDWIFERY TODAY, Jan Tritten, Box 2672, Eugene, OR 97402, 503-344-7438. 1985. "Birth information for midwives, childbirth educators and interested consumers. Photos, experiences, technical and non-technical articles." circ. 2.5M. 4/yr. Pub'd 4 issues 1990; expects 4 issues 1991, 4 issues 1992. 1 title listed in the *Small Press Record of Books in Print* (20th Edition, 1991-92). sub. price: $30; per copy: $7.50; sample: $7.50. Back issues: $7.50. Discounts: $4 each for 10 of one issue for resale. 52pp; 8½x11; web press. Reporting time: 6 weeks. Payment: subscription. Copyrighted, reverts to author. Pub's reviews: 15 in 1990. §Midwifery, pregnancy, birth, childbirth education. Ads: $345/$201/50¢ word classified, $5 minimum.

MILDRED, Ellen Biss, Kathryn Poppino, Mildred Publishing Company, Inc., 961 Birchwood Lane, Niskayuna, NY 12309, (518) 374-5410. 1986. Poetry, fiction, art, photos, interviews, reviews, letters. "The name 'Mildred' comes from two separate words meaning 'mild' and 'strength.' Through art will come the nourishment of our inner lives on the psychological and mythological planes and the continual renewal of our spirits, our relationships, our culture and our world. Recent contributors include Adrian Louis, Lewis Hyde, Robert Bly, Madeline Tiger, and Kore Loy Wildrekinde." circ. 400-700. 2/yr. Pub'd 1 issue 1990; expects 2 issues 1991, 2 issues 1992. sub. price: $12; per copy: $6; sample: $6. Discounts: 1-5 copies 25%; 6-19 40%; 20+ 60%. 130-150pp; 6x9; of. Reporting time: 2-3 months. Payment: 2 copies. Copyrighted, reverts to author. Pub's reviews: 4 in 1990. §Poetry, photography, art, women. CCLM.

R. & E. Miles, Robert Miles, Elaine Miles, PO Box 1916, San Pedro, CA 90733, 213-833-8856. 1979. Non-fiction. "Returns to: 1252 W. 23 St., San Pedro, Ca. 90731." avg. press run 3.2M. Pub'd 2 titles 1990; expects 4 titles 1991, 4 titles 1992. 10 titles listed in the *Small Press Record of Books in Print* (20th Edition, 1991-92). avg. price, cloth: $16.95; paper: $8.95. Discounts: normal trade. 168pp; of. Reporting time: 8 weeks. Payment: small advance against 10% royalty. Copyrights for author. PMA.

Miles River Press, Peg Paul, President, 1009 Duke Street, Alexandria, VA 22314, 703-683-1500. 1981. Non-fiction. "Interested in current management and leadership theory, materials for latchkey children" avg. press run 5M-10M. Pub'd 1 title 1990; expects 1 title 1991, 1 title 1992. 3 titles listed in the *Small Press Record of Books in Print* (20th Edition, 1991-92). avg. price, paper: $10.25; other: range $4.95-$21.95. Discounts: trade. 64-278pp; size varies; of, lp. Reporting time: 1 month. Payment: varies. Copyrights for author. AAP.

MILIM, Y. David Shulman, 324 Avenue F, Brooklyn, NY 11218. 1990. Poetry, fiction, articles, art, interviews, reviews, parts-of-novels, long-poems. "*Milim* is a literary & arts magazine within a Torah framework. Black & white line drawings only." circ. 500-1M. 3/yr. Expects 3 issues 1991, 3 issues 1992. sub. price: $8; per copy: $3; sample: $3. 40pp; 8½x7; of. Reporting time: 2 weeks. Payment: copies. Copyrighted, reverts to author. Pub's reviews. §Books with literary or aesthetic value that relate to Torah interests. Ads: $30/$20.

THE MILITANT, Doug Jenness, Editor, 410 West Street, New York, NY 10014, 212-243-6392. 1928. Articles, photos, interviews, satire, criticism, reviews, letters, news items, non-fiction. circ. 12M. 50/yr. Pub'd 47 issues 1990; expects 50 issues 1991, 50 issues 1992. sub. price: $37; per copy: $1.25; sample: free. Back issues: $1.25. 16pp; 11½x18; †of. Payment: none. Not copyrighted. Pub's reviews: 10 in 1990. §Labors, issues, war, politics, economics, black studies, women's studies. Ads: $400/$250/75¢.

THE MILITARY ADVISOR, R.J. Bender Publishing, R.J. Bender, J. Weiblen, PO Box 23456, San Jose, CA 95153, 408-225-5777. 1989. Articles, photos, reviews, news items, non-fiction. circ. 5M. 4/yr. Pub'd 1 issue 1990; expects 4 issues 1991, 4 issues 1992. sub. price: $15; per copy: $3.50; sample: $3.50. Back issues: $3.50 each plus postage. Discounts: 33%-55%. 40pp; 8½×11; of. Reporting time: approx. 1½ months. Payment: not at this time. Copyrighted, does not revert to author. Pub's reviews. §Military WW2, German WW2 subject matter. Ads: $275/$138/schedule available.

MILITARY IMAGES MAGAZINE, Harry Roach, RR 1, Box 99A, Henryville, PA 18332-9801. 1979. Articles, photos, interviews, reviews. "Up to 12M words. Emphasis on American military history, 1839-1900, with heavy use of period photos (50 to 75 per issue). Some recent contributors: (all military historians) Michael J. McAfee, Philip Katcher, John Stacey, Joseph G. Bilby, William Gladstone, William Frassanito" circ. 3M. 6/yr. Expects 6 issues 1991, 6 issues 1992. sub. price: $18; per copy: $3; sample: $3. Back issues: $5. Discounts: $2.50 per copy to retailers in lots of 10 or more, 20% to jobbers. 36pp; 8½×11; of. Reporting time: 2-4 weeks. Payment: currently 3¢ word. Copyrighted, reverts to author. Pub's reviews: 28 in 1990. §American military history, 1839-1900. Ads: $150/$85/50¢.

Milkweed Editions, Emilie Buchwald, Editor; Randall Scholes, Art Director, Box 3226, Minneapolis, MN 55403, 612-332-3192. 1984. Poetry, fiction, articles, art. avg. press run 3M-5M. Pub'd 10 titles 1990; expects 11 titles 1991, 12 titles 1992. 46 titles listed in the *Small Press Record of Books in Print* (20th Edition, 1991-92). avg. price, cloth: $14.95-$18.95; paper: $8.95. 144pp; 6×9; of. Reporting time: 1-3 months. Payment: advance against royalties + royalties payment-varies by author. Copyrights for author. COSMEP.

Millers River Publishing Co., Allen Young, Box 159, Athol, MA 01331, 617-249-7612. 1983. Fiction, non-fiction. "Currently, operations are suspended; no queries please" avg. press run 2M. Pub'd 2 titles 1990. 6 titles listed in the *Small Press Record of Books in Print* (20th Edition, 1991-92). avg. price, paper: $7.95. Discounts: 40% to trade; 50% to jobber/distributor. 200pp; 6×9; of. Reporting time: 2 months, return postage a must. Payment: negotiable. Copyrights for author.

Milner Press, 715 Miami Circle, Suite 220, Atlanta, GA 30324, 404-231-9107. 1989. Pub'd 1 title 1990; expects 1 title 1991, 1 title 1992. 1 title listed in the *Small Press Record of Books in Print* (20th Edition, 1991-92).

THE MILWAUKEE UNDERGRADUATE REVIEW, Dean Andrade, Editor, PO Box 71079, Milwaukee, WI 53211. 1989. Poetry, fiction, articles, art, satire, criticism, non-fiction. "Submissions of essays (formal or informal), fiction (traditional or experimental), and poetry (all forms) are invited from undergraduates at colleges or universities anywhere in the country. Be sure to include your school's name, your current standing (freshman, junior, etc.), and your home and school address. Works will not be returned unless accompanied by sufficient postage" circ. 600. 2/yr. Pub'd 1 issue 1990; expects 2 issues 1991, 2 issues 1992. sub. price: $5; per copy: $3; sample: $2.50. Discounts: available—write. 60pp; 7×9; of. Reporting time: 8-10 weeks. Payment: 2 copies. Copyrighted, reverts to author. No ads.

Mina Press, Mei Nakano, Adam David Miller, PO Box 854, Sebastopol, CA 95473, 707-829-0854. 1981. Poetry, fiction, plays, non-fiction. "Pays attention to unpublished and non-mainstream writers. Rejects manuscripts that glorify war, portray gratuitous violence, demean group of human beings like minorities, women, children, elderly, handicapped. Likes children's books of the variety which conveys some meaningful experience. Send inquiring letter first with SASE." avg. press run 2M. Expects 5 titles 1991. 4 titles listed in the *Small Press Record of Books in Print* (20th Edition, 1991-92). avg. price, cloth: $21.95; paper: $7.95. Discounts: 40% retail; 50% distributors. 150pp; of. Reporting time: 60-90 days. Payment: standard trade book contract. Copyrights for author. COSMEP,.

MINAS TIRITH EVENING-STAR, W.W. Publications, Philip W. Helms, PO Box 373, Highland, MI 48357-0373, 313-887-4703. 1967. Poetry, fiction, articles, art, cartoons, interviews, criticism, reviews, letters, long-poems, news items, non-fiction. "Only Tolkien related material excepted. Questions to: Paul S. Ritz, PO Box 901, Clearwater, FL 34617" circ. 350+. 4/yr. Pub'd 6 issues 1990; expects 6 issues 1991, 8 issues 1992. sub. price: $5 U.S., $10 foreign; per copy: $2; sample: $2. Back issues: $1 each. Discounts: over 10 copies 75¢ each. 25pp; 8½×11; †of. Reporting time: 2 months. Payment: 5 free issues. Copyrighted, reverts to author. Pub's reviews: 15 in 1990. §Any Tolkien related or fantasy work. Ads: $15/$10/$5¼ page.

MIND IN MOTION, A MAGAZINE OF POETRY AND SHORT PROSE, Celeste Goyer, Editor, P.O. Box 1118, Apple Valley, CA 92307, 619-248-6512. 1985. Poetry, fiction, satire, parts-of-novels. "Poetry of 15-60 lines, all forms. Emphasis on free association and use of images to convey meaning. Fiction of 500-2500 words. Figurative poetic prose that exhibits tangible philosophy. Allegory, surrealism, parody, satire, psychology. All works should have titles that summarize the essence of the effort." circ. 250. 4/yr. Expects 4 issues 1991, 4 issues 1992. sub. price: $14, overseas $18; per copy: $3.50, overseas $4.50; sample: $3.50, $4.50 overseas. Discounts: negotiable. 52pp; 5½×8½; mi. Reporting time: 2-6 weeks. Payment: in copies when financially possible. Copyrighted, reverts to author. No advertising.

354

MIND MATTERS REVIEW, Carrie L. Drake, 1438 Pacific Avenue, San Francisco, CA 94109. 1988. Poetry, articles, non-fiction. "The trend for *MMR* is to publish criticism of psychological and sociological theories that give greater power to mental health establishment as an enforcer of the status quo in education and science" circ. 1M-2M. 9/yr. Pub'd 4 issues 1990. sub. price: $10 US, $15 foreign; per copy: $3; sample: $2. Discounts: half price for librarians and institutions. 60pp; 8½×11; desktop. Reporting time: 4 weeks. Payment: copies. Copyrighted. Pub's reviews. §U.S.-Russian relations, cultural exchanges, comparison, science and education in U.S./Russia/Third World.

MIND YOUR OWN BUSINESS AT HOME, Coralee Smith Kern, Box 14850, Chicago, IL 60614, 312-472-8116. 1981. Articles, interviews, criticism, reviews, letters, news items, non-fiction. 6/yr. Pub'd 6 issues 1990; expects 6 issues 1991, 6-9 issues 1992. sub. price: $36; per copy: $5.00; sample: $5.00. Back issues: none. Discounts: inquire. 8-12pp; 8½×11; of. Reporting time: 6-12 weeks. Payment: none, but contributor receives copy of newsletter in which contribution is published. Copyrighted, reverts to author. Pub's reviews: 10 in 1990. §Tax info, legal, insurance, acct. info. pertinent to home-based businesses, home typing, word processing, secretarial, how-to start business, success home-based businesses, computers, motivational publications. Ads: $700.00/$350.00/$175.00¼pg./$90.00⅛pg./$10.00 Minimum $.50 Word thereafter. WIP/NAA.

THE MIND'S EYE, Gene Foreman, Box 656, Glenview, IL 60025. 1984. Poetry, fiction, art, photos, satire, parts-of-novels. "40 lines max for poetry - do not submit more than 5 at a time. 4000 wds max for fiction" circ. 500. 2-3/yr. Pub'd 2 issues 1990; expects 2 issues 1991, 2 issues 1992. sub. price: 4 issues $12, 8 issues $22; per copy: $3.50; sample: $3.50. Back issues: $3.50. 35-45pp; 5½×8. Reporting time: 1-2 months. Payment: 2 contributor's copies - annual contest with cash prizes for subscribors. Copyrighted.

MINERVA: Quarterly Report on Women and the Military, Linda Grant DePauw, 1101 S. Arlington Ridge Rd. #210, Arlington, VA 22202, 703-892-4388. 1983. Poetry, fiction, articles, art, cartoons, interviews, reviews, letters, parts-of-novels, news items, non-fiction. "Editorial policy emphasizes diversity." circ. 700. 4/yr. Pub'd 4 issues 1990; expects 4 issues 1991, 4 issues 1992. sub. price: $40; per copy: $10.95; sample: $10.95. Discounts: 20% on 10-25 books to same address. 94pp; 5½×8½; of. Reporting time: 2-3 weeks. Payment: none. Copyrighted, reverts to author. Pub's reviews: 12 in 1990. §Military women and veterans, military wives, non-traditional occupations. No ads.

MINNE HA! HA!, Minne Ha! Ha!, Lance Anger, Pete Wagner, PO Box 14009, Minneapolis, MN 55414, 612-729-7687. 1979. Poetry, fiction, art, photos, cartoons, interviews, satire, letters, collages, plays, non-fiction. "Cultural humor and satire, especially of a topical nature—short pieces preferred—recently did "lighter side of total global nuclear devastation"." circ. 25M. 4/yr. Pub'd 1 issue 1990; expects 4 issues 1991, 4 issues 1992. sub. price: $17.50; per copy: $1.50; sample: $3. Back issues: complete set $28.00, or per issue $7.50. Discounts: $1.50 minimum. 24pp; 10×14; of. Reporting time: 2 months. Payment: profit sharing. Copyrighted, reverts to author. Pub's reviews: 14 in 1990. §Humor publications only. Ads: $1,255/$715. COSMEP.

Minne Ha! Ha! (see also MINNE HA! HA!), Lance Anger, Editor-in-Chief; Pete Wagner, Designer, PO Box 14009, Minneapolis, MN 55414. 1979. Articles, art, photos, cartoons, interviews, satire, collages. avg. press run 4M. Expects 2 titles 1991, 3 titles 1992. avg. price, paper: $10.00. Discounts: 20% to libraries, co-ops, political organizations, student groups. 150pp; 6×9; of. Reporting time: 60 days. Payment: co-op/profit sharing. Copyrights for author. COSMEP.

Minnesota Ink, Inc. (see also WRITERS' JOURNAL), 27 Empire Drive, Saint Paul, MN 55103-1861, 612-225-1306.

MINNESOTA LITERATURE, Mary Bround Smith, 1 Nord Circle, St. Paul, MN 55127, 612-483-3904. 1973. Articles, news items. "All material is written by editor and staff—all is news-oriented (information about Minnesota literature—publications, events, opportunities, opinions, essays by other writers)." circ. 750. 10/yr. Pub'd 10 issues 1990; expects 10 issues 1991, 10 issues 1992. sub. price: $10; sample: $1. Back issues: $1 if available. Discounts: we will arrange special classroom and group rates. 8pp; 8½×11; of. Reporting time: 1-2 months. Payment: $50 for essays related to creative writing. Not copyrighted. Ads: $15 column inch (3½").

THE MINNESOTA REVIEW, Helen Cooper, Susan Squier, Michael Sprinker, Dept. of English, SUNY-Stony Brook, Stony Brook, NY 11794. 1960. Poetry, fiction, articles, art, photos, cartoons, interviews, satire, criticism, reviews, letters, parts-of-novels, long-poems, collages. "A journal of committed writing. We are especially interested in new marxist and/or feminist work. Recent and forthcoming contributors in poetry include Lyn Lifshin, Kathleen Spivak, James Scully, and Tom Wayman; in fiction Harold Jaffe, Joe Ashby Porter, and Lynda Schor; in criticism Jean Franco, Fredric Jameson, and Gayatri Spivak. At least one issue a year is set around a special emphasis or topic: our Fall 84 issue is set around the subject of the politics of postmodern culture, from the Soho art scene to comtemporary poetics and punk rock. In each issue, through the poetry, fiction, essays and reviews, our aim is to present new writing which is necessarily difficult and/or pointedly experimental, together with equally outstanding but more accessible work." circ. 1M. 2/yr. Pub'd 2 issues 1990; expects 2 issues 1991. sub. price: $8 individual, $16 institutions and/or overseas; per copy: $4.50; sample: $4.50. Back issues: available; price $1 more than single copy price. Discounts: 40%. 160pp; 8½×5½; of. Reporting time: 2-4 months. Payment: copies. Copyrighted, reverts to author. Pub's reviews: 23 in 1990. §Poetry, fiction, drama, very interested in Marxist literary & cultural criticism, very interested in feminist literary & cultural criticism. Ads: $60/$30. CLMP.

Minor Heron Press, Anne MacNaughton, Peter Douthit, Tracy McCallum, 117 East Plaza, Taos, NM 87571, 505-758-0081. 1982. Poetry, fiction, photos, criticism, long-poems, non-fiction. "Quality literature: focusing on fiction and poetry, regional Southwestern Hispanic, Native American, national and international, some non-fiction and art. Recent authors: Peter Rabbit. Recent videotape: Allen Ginsburg, Gregory Corso, Peter Orlovsky, *Taos Annual Poetry Circus '82*." avg. press run 500-1M. 1 title listed in the *Small Press Record of Books in Print* (20th Edition, 1991-92). avg. price, paper: $7.00; other: $29.95 video tape. Discounts: standard 40% for bookstores. 100pp; 5×8; of. Reporting time: 90 days. Payment: by contract. Copyrights for author.

MINORITY PUBLISHERS EXCHANGE, Charles Taylor, PO Box 9869, Madison, WI 53715, 608-244-5633. 1982. Articles, reviews, news items, non-fiction. circ. 3M. 6/yr. Pub'd 1 issue 1990; expects 6 issues 1991, 6 issues 1992. sub. price: $48; per copy: $3; sample: $2. Back issues: $48 for years supply. 10pp; 8½×11. Reporting time: 4 weeks. Payment: $25. Copyrighted. Pub's reviews: 12-20 in 1990. §Marketins, Minority issues. Ads: 1 per word and $250 full page. COSMEP, Multicultural Publishers Exchange.

MINORITY RIGHTS GROUP REPORTS, 379 Brixton Road, London SW9 7DE, England, 071-9789498. 1970. "Specially commissioned reports only. Over 80 reports already published including titles on refugees, the Basques, Mexican-Americans, Zimbabwe, the Amerinidians of South America, the two Irelands, the Namibians, Arab Women, etc. for complete list please contact M.R.G. Distributed in USA by Cultural Survival, Boston, MA." circ. 2M. 6/yr. Pub'd 5 issues 1990; expects 6 issues 1991, 6 issues 1992. 12 titles listed in the *Small Press Record of Books in Print* (20th Edition, 1991-92). sub. price: $55 institution, $37 individual, includes free newsletter "Outsider"; per copy: $6.60 incl. p/h; sample: $6.60 incl p/h. Back issues: $6.60 incl. p/h. Discounts: by negotiation. 30pp; size A4; of. Payment: variable. Copyrighted. §Minorities, human rights.

MinRef Press, Rick Lawler, Alice Tang, 8379 Langtree Way, Sacramento, CA 95823, 916-424-8465. 1989. Non-fiction. "We plan to publish small, targeted reference guides that fill empty spots on the shelves of libraries. Books should also have appeal outside of libraries. We don't want to see complete manuscripts, but are interested in considering proposals and ideas." avg. press run 2M. Expects 2 titles 1991, 2 titles 1992. avg. price, paper: $6.95. Discounts: industry standard. 96pp; 5¼×8½; of. Reporting time: 1-2 months. Payment: by arrangement. Copyrights for author. Authors Guild, National Writers Club, SPWAO.

MIORITA...A Journal of Romanian Studies, Norman Simms, Charles Carlton, Dept of F.L.L.L., Univ of Rochester, Dewey Hall 482, Rochester, NY 14627, 716-275-4258, 275-4251. 1973. Poetry, fiction, articles, criticism, reviews, non-fiction. "Scholarly." circ. 300. 1/yr. Pub'd 1 issue 1990; expects 1 issue 1991. sub. price: $10; per copy: $5. Back issues: $5 each number, or cost of xeroxing. Discounts: 1/3 to retail; 10 percent sub agents. 100pp; 8½×5½; xerox. Reporting time: 2 months. Payment: copies. Copyrighted, reverts to author. Pub's reviews: 5 in 1990. §Romania and related fields. No ads.

MIP Company, PO Box 27484, Minneapolis, MN 55427. 1984. Poetry, fiction, non-fiction. 6 titles listed in the *Small Press Record of Books in Print* (20th Edition, 1991-92). Discounts: 30% when 30 or more copies purchased. Copyrights for author.

MIRACLES MAGAZINE, Paul Ferrini, PO Box 8118, Brattleboro, VT 05304. Poetry, articles, art, photos, interviews, reviews, non-fiction. 4/yr. Pub'd 2 issues 1990; expects 4 issues 1991, 4 issues 1992. sub. price: $25. 48pp; 8½×11. Reporting time: 1 month. Payment: none. Pub's reviews. §Spiritual psychology, New Age.

MIRAGE, Karyn Flynn, Box 75, Clawson, MI 48017, 313-585-0006. 1990. Photos, interviews. 4-6/yr. Expects 2 issues 1991, 4-6 issues 1992. sub. price: $19.95; per copy: $4.95; sample: $3. Back issues: none available. 40pp; 8½×11. Copyrighted. COSMEP.

MIRKWOOD, Tunnel Publishing, Joe 'Kingfish' Lane, PO Box 4083, Terre Haute, IN 47804, 812-234-3133. 1990. Articles, interviews, criticism, letters, news items. "This is a guide to alternative and underground press publishers and editors. Interested in features on such press operations." circ. 100. 4/yr. Pub'd 2 issues 1990; expects 4 issues 1991, 4 issues 1992. sub. price: $6; per copy: $2; sample: $1. 8pp; 8½×11; †of. Reporting time: 2 weeks. Payment: 1 copy per article. Not copyrighted. Pub's reviews: 12 in 1990. §underground press, history of alternative press, books on periodical publishing.

MIRRORS - IN THE SPIRIT OF HAIKU, AHA Books, Jane Reichhold, PO Box 1250, Gualala, CA 95445, 707-882-2226. 1988. Poetry, articles, art, satire, reviews, letters, concrete art, news items. "All material *must* be haiku-related. Each subscriber receives a 7.5 X 11 page which they choose the haiku, do the artwork (if any), are responsible for content and copyrights. What the author sends is copied and collated along with articles, reviews, letters, contests. *Mirrors* also has free ads for books as we try to meet the haiku poet's needs." circ.

200. 4/yr. Pub'd 3 issues 1990; expects 4 issues 1991, 4 issues 1992. sub. price: $16; per copy: $5; sample: $3. Back issues: $3. 60-80pp; 8½×11; †copy machine. Reporting time: subscribers know their work will be in; 1 week, if not. Payment: none. Copyrighted, reverts to author. Pub's reviews. §Haiku-related means renga, tanka, haibun, and haikai. Classified ads free to subscribers. HSA, New York; HPNC, San Francisco.

MISSISSIPPI MUD, Mud Press, Joel Weinstein, 1336 SE Marion Street, Portland, OR 97202, 503-236-9962. 1973. Poetry, fiction, art, photos, cartoons, interviews, satire, criticism, reviews, parts-of-novels, collages, plays. "Elegant, lucid writing and art from the *ne plus ultra* of the American scene." circ. 1.5M. Irregular. Pub'd 1 issue 1990; expects 2 issues 1991, 3 issues 1992. sub. price: $19/4 issues; per copy: $6 ppd; sample: $6 ppd. Back issues: $5/copy plus $1 postage. 48pp; 11×17; of. Reporting time: 2-3 months. Payment: copies. Copyrighted, reverts to author. Ads: $800/$450/$235 1/4 page/$125 1/8 page/$360 3/8 page.

MISSISSIPPI REVIEW, Frederick Barthelme, Editor; Rie Fortenberry, Managing Editor, Box 5144, Southern Station, Hattiesburg, MS 39406-5144, 601-266-4321. 1971. Poetry, fiction, art, photos, interviews, satire, criticism, reviews, parts-of-novels, long-poems, plays. circ. 1.5M. 2/yr. Pub'd 3 issues 1990; expects 2 issues 1991, 3 issues 1992. sub. price: $15; per copy: $8; sample: $5.50. Back issues: $5.50 and as offered. Discounts: none. 125-200pp; 5½×8¾; †of. Reporting time: 2-3 months. Payment: copies and honoraria. Copyrighted, reverts to author. Pub's reviews: none in 1990. §Contemporary lit & criticism, intrerviews. Ads: $100/$50/ Will consider trade-out. CCLM.

MISSISSIPPI VALLEY REVIEW, Forrest Robinson, Editor; Loren Logsdon, Fiction; John Mann, Poetry, Dept. of English, Western Illinois University, Macomb, IL 61455, 309-298-1514. 1971. Poetry, fiction. "Little, if any, ms. reading during summer. No long poems and no novella-length stories. *MVR* has published work by Jack Matthews, Howard Nemerov, Lucien Stryk, Laurence Lieberman, Daniel Curley, Ralph Mills, Jr., James Ballowe, John Judson, Lester Goldberg, Paul Bartlett, Winston Weathers, & John Craig Stewart. We prefer that poets submit no more than five poems at one time; fiction writers: one story at a time. We will *NOT* return submissions not including a SASE. We solicit our reviews" circ. 400. 2/yr. Pub'd 2 issues 1990; expects 2 issues 1991, 2 issues 1992. sub. price: $6; per copy: $3; sample: $3 plus postage. 64pp; 6×9; lp. Reporting time: 3 months. Payment: 2 copies of issue in which work appears plus 1 copy of succeeding 2 issues. Copyrighted, reverts to author. Pub's reviews: 2 in 1990. §We solicit our reviews. No ads.

THE MISSOURI REVIEW, Speer Morgan, Editor; Greg Michalson, Managing Editor, 1507 Hillcrest Hall, University of Missouri-Columbia, Columbia, MO 65211, 314-882-4474. 1978. Poetry, fiction, articles, art, cartoons, interviews, criticism, reviews, parts-of-novels, non-fiction. circ. 2.5M. 3/yr. Pub'd 3 issues 1990; expects 3 issues 1991, 3 issues 1992. 1 title listed in the *Small Press Record of Books in Print* (20th Edition, 1991-92). sub. price: 1 yr (3 issues) $12, 2 yrs (6 issues) $21, foreign countries $16 yearly; per copy: $5; sample: $5. No discounts. 224pp; 6×9; of. Reporting time: 10-12 weeks. Payment: $15-$20 per page minimum to $600. Copyrighted, author can reprint material without charge if author acknowledges mag. Pub's reviews: 3 in 1990. §Omnibus reviews only of poetry, fiction, criticism, literary biography. Ads: $50/$25/or exchange. CLMP, COSMEP.

MR. COGITO, Mr. Cogito Press, Robert A. Davies, Co-Editor; John M. Gogol, Co-Editor, 2518 N.W. Savier Street, Portland, OR 97210, 503-233-8131, 226-4135. 1973. Poetry, art, photos, long-poems. "We will publish the best poetry from the most varied schools of poetry. We are particularly interested in good translations of modern foreign poetry. Special interests: graphics—image, conceits, wit, heightened language: *poems that move us*. Among recent poets in our pages were Elizabeth Woody, Dian Million, Tomasz Jastrun, Kevin Irie, Mark Osaki. 1991 Contests: World of Islam, Eastern Europe." circ. 400. 2-3/yr. Pub'd 2 issues 1990; expects 2-3 issues 1991, 2-3 issues 1992. sub. price: $9 for 3 issues; per copy: $3; sample: $3. Back issues: varies. Discounts: 40% for 5 or more copies, 20% otherwise, none for libraries. 28pp; 4½×11; of. Reporting time: 2 weeks to 3 months. Payment: copies, contest $50/$100. Copyrighted, we reserve rights for publication in an anthology. Ads: 1 pg @ $75, exchange. CCLM.

Mr. Cogito Press (see also MR. COGITO), Robert A. Davies, Co-Editor; John M. Gogol, Co-Editor, 2518 N.W. Savier, Portland, OR 97210, 503-233-8131, 226-4135. 1978. Poetry, art, photos. "Line graphics-poetry by invitation." avg. press run 500. Pub'd 1 title 1990; expects 1-2 titles 1991, 1-2 titles 1992. 10 titles listed in the *Small Press Record of Books in Print* (20th Edition, 1991-92). avg. price, paper: $10. Discounts: 40% bookstores for 5 or more copies, 20% otherwise. 35pp; 5½×8½; of. Reporting time: 1-2 months. Payment: copies. Usually press holds copyright. CCLM.

Mr. Information, John Durant, P.O. Box 955, Ganges, B.C. V1S 1E0, Canada, 604-653-9260. 1980. Articles, news items, non-fiction. avg. press run 1M. Pub'd 685 titles 1990; expects 300 titles 1991, 300 titles 1992. 10 titles listed in the *Small Press Record of Books in Print* (20th Edition, 1991-92). avg. price, other: $1 & up. Discounts: Agents & Jobbers. 8pp; 8½×11, 4½×9⅞; †photocopy equipment. Reporting time: 3 weeks. Payment: open. Does not copyright for author.

Misty Hill Press, Sally C. Karste, 5024 Turner Road, Sebastopol, CA 95472, 707-823-7437. 1984. Poetry, fiction, articles, criticism, letters, long-poems, non-fiction. avg. press run 2M. Pub'd 1 title 1990; expects 1 title 1991, 1 title 1992. 1 title listed in the *Small Press Record of Books in Print* (20th Edition, 1991-92). avg. price, paper: $7.95. Discounts: 40% to bookstores. 125pp; 6×9. Reporting time: 3 months. Payment: royalty negotiable terms. Copyrights for author. COSMEP.

Mocha Publishing Company, 8475 SW Morgan Drive, Beaverton, OR 97005, 503-643-7591. 1 title listed in the *Small Press Record of Books in Print* (20th Edition, 1991-92).

Mockingbird Press, Jim Stallings, Laurie Stallings, PO Box 776, Needham Heights, MA 02194, 617-455-8940. 1986. Fiction, non-fiction. "Our press also provides contract research, writing, editing, media production services through a network of freelancers. This funds book publishing projects of the press" Reporting time: 6 weeks, SASE. Payment: negotiable. Copyrights for author. COSMEP.

THE MODEL & TOY COLLECTOR, Bill Bruegman III, 330 Merriman Road, Akron, OH 44303, 216-769-2523. 1986. Articles, interviews, reviews, letters, news items, non-fiction. circ. 20M. 4/yr. Pub'd 6 issues 1990; expects 4 issues 1991, 4 issues 1992. sub. price: $15; per copy: $3.50; sample: $4. Back issues: $5. Discounts: 50% off cover price (FOB). 40-44pp; 8½×11; of. Reporting time: averaging 2 months. Payment: free subscriptions, sometimes ad space, sometimes payment. Copyrighted, reverts to author. Pub's reviews: 2 in 1990. §Toys from 1940-80, model kits, specifically baby-boom collectibles. Ads: 20¢/word. COSMEP, Box 703, SF, CA 94101.

Model-Peltex Association (see also PELTEX), Dominique LeBlanc, Zaza, 3 Rue Des Couples, 67000 Strasbourg, France. 1981. Art, reviews. Pub'd 3 titles 1990; expects 3 titles 1991. avg. price, other: 100FF Abonnement. 100pp; size A4 and others. Payment: none. Copyrights for author.

MODERN HAIKU, Robert Spiess, PO Box 1752, Madison, WI 53701. 1969. Poetry, articles, reviews. ""Best haiku magazine in North America"—Museum of Haiku Literature, Tokyo. International circulation. Good university and public library subscription list. Publishes haiku only, plus related book reviews and articles. No restrictions on article length. Contributors should enclose self-addressed, stamped return envelope." circ. 650. 3/yr. Pub'd 3 issues 1990; expects 3 issues 1991, 3 issues 1992. 3 titles listed in the *Small Press Record of Books in Print* (20th Edition, 1991-92). sub. price: $12.50; per copy: $4.50; sample: $4.50. Back issues: $4.50. 104-112pp; 5½×8½; of. Reporting time: 2 weeks. Payment: $1 for each haiku; $5 page for articles. Copyrighted, reverts to author. Pub's reviews: 65 in 1990. §Haiku only. No ads.

MODERN IMAGES, Sue A. Morgan, 1217 Champaign Avenue, Mattoon, IL 61938-3167. 1968. Poetry, art. circ. 150. 4/yr. Pub'd 4 issues 1990; expects 4 issues 1991, 4 issues 1992. sub. price: $9.95; per copy: $3; sample: $2. Back issues: $2. 48-52pp; 5½×8½; of. Reporting time: 2 weeks. Copyrighted, reverts to author. §Poetry. No ads.

MODERN INTERNATIONAL DRAMA, George E. Wellwarth, Anthony M. Pasquariello, c/o Theatre Dept., S.U.N.Y., Binghamton, NY 13901, 607-777-2704. 1967. Plays. "We are the only journal in the United States devoted exclusively to the publication of previously untranslated plays from any language. Literary quality and dramatic viability are the only criteria. Permission to translate must be obtained by the translator. Write to above address for copy of stylistic rules." circ. 500. 2/yr. Pub'd 2 issues 1990; expects 2 issues 1991, 2 issues 1992. sub. price: $12.50 institution, $7 individual; per copy: $3.25; sample: $2.50. Discounts: 10% to subscription agents. 70pp; 6¾×9½; of. Reporting time: 1 month. Payment: 3 copies. Copyrighted, reverts to author. Ads: $300/$150.

THE MODERN LANGUAGE JOURNAL, David P. Benseler, Editor, Department of German, Ohio State University, Columbus, OH 43210-1229, 614-292-3748. 1916. Articles, interviews, reviews, letters, news items. "David P. Benseler, Editor, *The Modern Language Journal* (1980-88)" circ. 7M. 4/yr. Pub'd 4 issues 1990; expects 4 issues 1991, 4 issues 1992. sub. price: $15 indiv, $30 instit; per copy: $5; sample: $5. Back issues: $5. 150pp; 7½×10; of. Reporting time: 1-3 months. Payment: 2 copies of issue in which article appears. Copyrighted, does not revert to author. Pub's reviews: 230 in 1990. §Subjects of interest to language teachers and researchers. Ads: $240/$140/quarter pg $75. National Federation of Modern Language Teachers Associations.

MODERN LANGUAGE QUARTERLY, John C. Coldewey, 4045 Brooklyn Ave. N.E., Seattle, WA 98105, 206-543-2992. 1940. Criticism, reviews. "No unsolicited reviews. Literary criticism by and for scholars." circ. 1,975. 4/yr. Expects 4 issues 1991. sub. price: $16 individual, $20 institution, add $5 for foreign; per copy: $5 domestic, $6 foreign; sample: $3.00. Discounts: 10%. 112pp; 6⅝×9⅝; of. Reporting time: 1-3 months. Payment: none. Copyrighted, does not revert to author. Pub's reviews: 29 in 1990. §Only literary criticism. No ads.

Modern Learning Press/Programs for Education, Bernard Shapiro, Managing Editor, PO Box 167, Rosemont, NJ 08530. 1965. avg. press run 4M. Pub'd 10 titles 1990. 26 titles listed in the *Small Press Record of Books in Print* (20th Edition, 1991-92). avg. price, paper: $9.95. of. Payment: semi-annual. Copyright for author if required.

MODERN LITURGY, Resource Publications, Inc., William Burns, Publisher; Kenneth Guentert, Editor, 160 East Virginia Street, #290, San Jose, CA 95112, 408-286-8505. 1973. Poetry, fiction, articles, art, photos, cartoons, criticism, reviews, music, letters, plays, concrete art. "In-house graphics and typography." circ. 16M. 10/yr. Pub'd 9 issues 1990; expects 10 issues 1991, 10 issues 1992. sub. price: $40; per copy: $4; sample: $4. Back issues: $4. Discounts: 40% trade & bulk, 10% for prepaid agency subscriptions. 48pp; 8⅜×10⅞; of. Reporting time: 6 weeks. Payment: $1 to $100. Copyrighted, does not revert to author. Pub's reviews: 187 in 1990. §Religious arts, music, religious education, worship resources. Ads: $816/$578/60¢ per word. COSMEP, CPA.

Modern Media (see also THE LUNDIAN), M. Robinson, Managing Editor; Monique Francsen, General Manager, PO Box 722, 220 07 Lund, Sweden, fax: 046-138221. 1988. Poetry, fiction, articles, art, photos, cartoons, interviews, satire, criticism, reviews, music, letters, news items, non-fiction. avg. press run 3M. 1 title listed in the *Small Press Record of Books in Print* (20th Edition, 1991-92). avg. price, paper: $3.50. 12pp; size A4; of. Reporting time: 60 days. Payment: none. Does not copyright for author.

Modular Information Systems, 2440 16th Street, Suite 221, San Francisco, CA 94103, 415-863-0493. 1986. Non-fiction. avg. press run 5M. Expects 2 titles 1991, 2 titles 1992. 2 titles listed in the *Small Press Record of Books in Print* (20th Edition, 1991-92). avg. price, paper: $25. Discounts: 55%. 350pp; 7½×9. Copyrights for author.

Mogul Book and FilmWorks, Vincent Risoli, PO Box 2773, Pittsburgh, PA 15230, 412-461-0705. 1982. Fiction. Pub'd 1 title 1990; expects 2 titles 1991, 3 titles 1992. 2 titles listed in the *Small Press Record of Books in Print* (20th Edition, 1991-92). avg. price, cloth: $9.95. Reporting time: 2 weeks on inquiry, 4 weeks on manuscript.

MOKSHA JOURNAL, Vajra of Yoga Anand Ashram, Yogi Ananda Viraj, Yogi Ananda Satyam, Steve Crimi, Rocco LoBosco, 49 Forrest Place, Amityville, NY 11701, 516-691-8475. 1984. Poetry, non-fiction. "Limited fiction/poetry. The editorial committee welcomes articles, poetry, fiction and line drawings pertaining to the *concept* of Moksha, defined by Monier-Williams as 'liberation, release' (A Sanskrit-English Dictionary, 1899). The paths to moksha are myriad, and it is hoped that this journal will reflect a multiplicity of perspectives, including works pertaining to Yoga, various schools of Buddhism, Sufism, Mystical Christianity, etc." circ. 300-500. 2/yr. Pub'd 2 issues 1990; expects 2 issues 1991, 2 issues 1992. sub. price: $8; per copy: $4; sample: $4. 40-50pp; 7¼×9½; †of. Reporting time: 4-6 weeks. Payment: 2 issues. Copyrighted, does not revert to author. No ads.

MOM...GUESS WHAT! NEWSPAPER & TYPESETTING, Linda D. Birner, 1725 L Street, Sacramento, CA 95814-4023, 916-441-6397. 1978. Articles, photos, interviews, satire, criticism, reviews, letters, news items. circ. 21M. 24/yr. Pub'd 24 issues 1990; expects 24 issues 1991, 24 issues 1992. sub. price: $25; per copy: $1; sample: $1. Back issues: $1. 24pp; 10×15; of. Reporting time: 1 week. Payment: mostly volunteer, depends on article. Copyrighted. Pub's reviews: 26 in 1990. §Politics, gay & human rights. Ads: $500/$250/50¢ a word/$10 col. inch. SPC.

MOMENTUM, Jeff Bell, Glan Llyn, Glyn Ceiriog, Liangollen, 31 Alexandra Road, Clwyd LL20 7AB, Wales, 069-172-320. 1985. Poetry, fiction, cartoons, satire. "Mostly original short stories up to 2,500 words in length. Short poems. Will include *limited* amount of information, promotion on writers' circles, competitions, etc. F.O.C. Limited market for satirical literary/political cartoons (A5 page or 1/2 page)" circ. 300. 3/yr. Pub'd 3 issues 1990; expects 3 issues 1991, 3 issues 1992. sub. price: £4; per copy: £1.40; sample: 80p. Back issues: same, limited availability. Discounts: 10% on sales of 20 or more, 15% on 30 or more. 50pp; 6×9½; of. Reporting time: 1 month (approx). Payment: complimentary issue. Copyright is pending, reverts to author. Pub's reviews: 4 in 1990. §Short stories, poetry. Cannot return submissions for review. Ads: £12/£7/20p a word/inside front and back cover display £3 extra, copy from advertiser.

MONADNOCK GAY MEN, Kenneth E. DeVoid, Jr., PO Box 1124, Keene, NH 03431, 603-357-5544. 1982. Articles, art, photos, cartoons, criticism, reviews, letters, news items, non-fiction. "A monthly newsletter format which carries news of the Gay Community in the tri-state area of NH, VT and MA." circ. 250. 12/yr. Pub'd 12 issues 1990; expects 12 issues 1991, 12 issues 1992. sub. price: $12; per copy: $1; sample: $1. Back issues: $1. 4pp; 8×11. Reporting time: 1 month. Payment: none. Not copyrighted. Pub's reviews: 4 in 1990. §Gay issues. Ads: $50/$25/$10 business card.

MONDO HUNKAMOOGA, Proper Tales Press, Stuart Ross, PO Box 789, Station F, Toronto, Ontario M4Y 2N7, Canada. 1983. Articles, cartoons, interviews, criticism, reviews, letters, news items. *"Mondo Hunkamooga* attempts to deal with all aspects of small press publishing. Each issue contains a feature interview (Kenward Elmslie, bp Nichol, and Randall Brock have been featured), plenty of book reviews and small mag reviews, and columns dealing with writing, publishing, etc. Recent contributors have included: M.B. Duggan,

Opal L. Nations, Crad Kilodney, Jim Smith. *Mondo* wants to separate the boring and the worst of small press from that which is truly interesting. We invite correspondence, articles, tirades, etc. from small press publishers and writers absolutely anywhere" circ. 500. Pub'd 1 issue 1990; expects 3 issues 1991, 6 issues 1992. sub. price: $5 (6 issues); per copy: $1; sample: $1. Discounts: jobbers 10%, trade 30%. 16pp; 7×8½; of. Reporting time: 2 days to 2 months. Payment: copies. Copyrighted, rights revert on request. Pub's reviews: 75 in 1990. §Small press poetry, fiction, small mags, self-publishing, small press publishing. Ads: half page: $20/quarter page: $12.

THE MONIST: An International Quarterly Journal of General Philosophical Inquiry., The Hegeler Institute, John Hospers, Editor; Sherwood J.B. Sugden, Managing Editor, Box 600, La Salle, IL 61301, 815-223-2520. 1888. Articles. "*The Monist* is a quarterly journal addressed to scholars in philosophy & related disciplines, and is dedicated to the expression of free philosophical inquiry. Each issue is limited to articles on a single general topic selected in advance by the Editorial Board. No paper can be considered which has been published elsewhere. Recent contributors: Maurice Mandelbaum; Sir Peter Strawson; Philippa Foot; Charles Hartshorne; Wilfrid Sellars; William Frankena; Rev. Joseph Owens; Max Fisch; W.V. Quine." circ. 1.5M. 4/yr. Pub'd 4 issues 1990; expects 4 issues 1991, 4 issues 1992. sub. price: institution $28, individual $18; per copy: $7. Back issues: $7 (1962-1989). Discounts: 20% to agencies. 160pp; 6×9; of, typeset. Reporting time: 4-6 months. Payment: 25 offprints to nonsubscribers; 50 offprints to subscribers. Copyrighted, rights do not revert, but we usually grant permission to reprint. Pub's reviews: 26 in 1990. §Philosophy, theology. Ads: $150/$80. APA.

THE MONOCACY VALLEY REVIEW, William Heath, Mount St. Mary's College, Emmitsburg, MD 21727, 301-447-6122 X4832. 1985. Poetry, fiction, articles, art, photos, interviews, reviews, collages, non-fiction. "Submissions deadlines: January 15" circ. 500. 1/yr. Pub'd 1 issue 1990; expects 1 issue 1991, 1 issue 1992. sub. price: $8/2 years; per copy: $5; sample: $5. Back issues: $3. 60pp; 8½×11; of. Reporting time: 8 weeks. Payment: $10-$25 per contribution. Copyrighted, reverts to author. Pub's reviews: 2 in 1990. §No restrictions. Ads: $150/$70/$30 1/4 page. CCLM.

Monographics Press, Susan Hauser, Route 1, Box 81, Puposky, MN 56667, 218-243-2402. 1984. Poetry, articles, art, satire, criticism, letters. "Formerly Rasberry Press; 1972-84. No unsolicited submissions-return of unsolicited mss. immediately. Focus of each issue determined by whim of editor. R.P. 3 is poetry by Rich Behm. Work by: Carol Heckman, Beth Copeland, Tina Matthews, Judith Dunaway. R.P. 4/5 - a double issue, anthology format. R.P. 6 Dec, 1980, 10pp. Raspberry #7, December 1981, 8pp. $2.00 #8, Fall 1982 'Chickadee Issue', $2.00 Back issues of RP #3, 3, & 7 still available...$2 each; Mimeo Magic, 68 pp. How-To Book, 1984, $3.95. 1990 *Pictures From A Visit*, 16 pp, poetry, $5." avg. press run 100. Pub'd 1 title 1990; expects 1 title 1991, 1 title 1992. 1 title listed in the *Small Press Record of Books in Print* (20th Edition, 1991-92). avg. price, paper: $5. Discounts: none. 50pp; size varies; †mi. Reporting time: 1 week. Payment: copy. Copyrights for author.

Monroe Press, Dorothy Towvim, 362 Maryville Avenue, Ventura, CA 93003-1912. 1985. Non-fiction. "Manuscripts relating to family issues, parenting, communication, relationships, adolescents and children. Recent contribution: *Why Can't Anyone Hear Me? - A Guide for Surviving Adolescence*, by Dr. Monte Elchoness" avg. press run 5M. Pub'd 1 title 1990; expects 3 titles 1991, 3 titles 1992. 4 titles listed in the *Small Press Record of Books in Print* (20th Edition, 1991-92). avg. price, cloth: $16.95; paper: $10.95. Discounts: available upon request. 200pp; 5½×8½; of. Reporting time: 4 weeks. Payment: industry standard. Copyrights for author. Publishers Marketing Association (PMA), National Association of Independent Publishers (NAIP), COSMEP, Pacific Educational Marketing Association (PEMA).

THE MONTANA REVIEW, Owl Creek Press, Rich Ives, 1620 N. 45th St., Seattle, WA 98103, 206-633-5929. 1979. Poetry, fiction, articles, criticism, parts-of-novels, long-poems. "We are interested in quality translations in both poetry and fiction. Some recent contributors include Richard Hugo, James Wright, David Wagoner, Mekeel McBride, Laura Jensen, William V. Davis, Stephen Dixon, John Haines and many others. We are open to unknown writers and to writers from beyond the Northwest area. We aren't affiliated with a school or university" circ. 500-1M. 2/yr. Pub'd 2 issues 1990; expects 2 issues 1991, 2 issues 1992. sub. price: $9 year (2 issues); per copy: $5; sample: $5. Back issues: $3 each for #1, #2, #3; $4 for #4. Discounts: standard. 100-150pp; 5½×8½; of. Reporting time: 2-4 weeks. Payment: copies. Copyrighted. Pub's reviews: 3 in 1990. §Poetry, fiction, translations and non-fiction (creative). Ads: $100/$75. NEA, CCLM.

Montebello Press, 3041 SW Montebello Place, Palm City, FL 34990. 1 title listed in the *Small Press Record of Books in Print* (20th Edition, 1991-92).

MOODY STREET IRREGULARS: A Jack Kerouac Magazine, Moody Street Irregulars, Inc., Joy Walsh, Tim Madigan, Lisa Jarnat, PO Box 157, Clarence Center, NY 14032, 716-741-3393. 1977. Poetry, articles, art, photos, cartoons, interviews, criticism, reviews, music, letters, plays, news items. "*Moody Street Irregulars* is a Kerouac newsletter. We are looking for material on Kerouac and other Beat writers. The

360

magazine will always retain the spirit of Jack Kerouac. Recent contributors: George Dardess, Joy Walsh, Ted Joans, John Clellon Holmes, Tetsuo Nakagami, Gerld Nicosia, Dennis McNally, Janet Kerouac, Jack Kerouac, George Montgomery, Bill Gargan, Ben Walters" circ. 500-1M. 2-3/yr. Pub'd 2 issues 1990; expects 3 issues 1991. sub. price: $10; per copy: $5; sample: $5. Back issues: $5. Discounts: 40% to bookstores. 50pp; 8½×11; of. Reporting time: 1-3 months. Payment: copies. Copyrighted, reverts to author. Pub's reviews: 3-9 in 1990. §Books on Kerouac and the Beats. Will accept contributions. Inquire as to ads; we now accept them. NEW, COSMEP.

Moody Street Irregulars, Inc. (see also MOODY STREET IRREGULARS: A Jack Kerouac Magazine), Joy Walsh, Tim Madigan, Lisa Jarnat, PO Box 157, Clarence Center, NY 14032, 716-741-3393. 1977. Poetry, articles, art, photos, cartoons, interviews, criticism, reviews, music, letters, plays, news items. "Moody Street Irregulars will print poetry, and material pertaining to Kerouac and the Beats." avg. press run 1M-2.5M. Pub'd 2 titles 1990; expects 3 titles 1991. 2 titles listed in the *Small Press Record of Books in Print* (20th Edition, 1991-92). avg. price, paper: $5; other: $10 per year, $15 libraries. Discounts: 40% to bookstores. 50pp; 8½×11; of. Reporting time: 1-3 months. Payment: copies. Copyrights for author. NEW, Hallwalk, Jack Kerouac Club in Quebec, Alpha Beat Press in Montreal.

Moon Publications, Inc., Bill Dalton, Publisher; Mark Morris, Editorial V.P., 722 Wall Street, Chico, CA 95928, 916-345-5473; FAX 916-345-6751. 1973. Art, photos, criticism, letters. "Moon Publications specializes in travel handbooks for independent travelers. Each guide contains an informative introduction to the history and culture of the region, up-to-date travel information, clear and concise maps, color and black and white photographs, and a comprehensive subject/place-name index. All Moon guides are tradepaper 5X7 inches with a smyth-sewn binding. The geographic regions we are interested in are: Asia, the Pacific, and the Americas" avg. press run 6M-12M. Pub'd 31 titles 1990; expects 7 titles 1991. 38 titles listed in the *Small Press Record of Books in Print* (20th Edition, 1991-92). avg. price, paper: $8.95-$19.95. Discounts: trade 40%, wholesalers 50%, libraries 20%, bulk 55%. 450pp; 5⅛×7⅜; desktop. Reporting time: query first. Payment: royalty to 18% of publishers net invoice. Copyrights for author. COSMEP, ABA, Association of Travel Marketing.

Moonbeam Publications, Inc., 18530 Mack Avenue, Grosse Pointe, MI 48236, 313-884-5255. 1984. Non-fiction. "Moonbeam Publications publishes and distributes reference books to the library market" 12 titles listed in the *Small Press Record of Books in Print* (20th Edition, 1991-92). Discounts: jobber 10% on most titles.

Moonlight Press, Carolyn S. Peterson, Ann D. Fenton, 3407 Crystal Lake Drive, Orlando, FL 32806. 1981. Non-fiction. avg. press run 1M. Pub'd 1 title 1990; expects 2 titles 1991. 9 titles listed in the *Small Press Record of Books in Print* (20th Edition, 1991-92). avg. price, paper: $3.50-$15. Discounts: 40 for bookstores and wholesales; others-10% over $25 and 20% over $100. 28-219pp; 5½×8½, 8½×11; of/lo. Payment: 10% first 1000, 15% thereafter. Copyrights for author.

Moonsquilt Press, Michael Hettich, Karen Osborne, Colleen Ahern, Design, 16401 NE 4th Avenue, North Miami Beach, FL 33162, 305-947-9534. 1979. Poetry, fiction, interviews, criticism, reviews, music, long-poems, non-fiction. "We are interested in poetry that comes out of an awareness of *tradition* but is not necessarily *traditional*. We like craft but not craftiness or excessive sheen. We want to be moved. Mss 10 plus pages w/SASE." avg. press run 200-500. Pub'd 3 titles 1990; expects 2-3 titles 1991, 3 titles 1992. 9 titles listed in the *Small Press Record of Books in Print* (20th Edition, 1991-92). avg. price, paper: $3.00. Free to schools. 20pp; 5½×8½; of. Reporting time: 1 week. Payment: copies. Copyrights for author. CCLM, COSMEP.

MOONSTONE BLUE, NIGHT ROSES, Allen T. Billy, Sandra Taylor, PO Box 393, Prospect Heights, IL 60070, 708-392-2435. 1986. Poetry. "All submissions should be sent to *Night Roses*. *Moonstone Blue* series is interested in science fiction, fantasy and *Night Roses* subjects. *Moonstone Blue* is published with *Night Roses* as a special from time to time, no set frequency. We would like to do an issue every 12-18 months. *Moonstone Blue* is published to provide an extra outlet for *Night Roses* submissions." circ. 250. Irregular. Expects 1 issue 1991, 1 issue 1992. price per copy: $3; sample: $3. 48pp; 5⅜×8½; mi, lp. Reporting time: 4-12 weeks. Payment: 1 contributor's copy. Not copyrighted.

The Moretus Press, Inc. (see also AMERICAN BOOK COLLECTOR), William Burton, Publisher, PO Box 1080, Ossining, NY 10562, 914-941-0409. 1977. Non-fiction. avg. press run 5M. Pub'd 2 titles 1990; expects 2 titles 1991, 2 titles 1992. 1 title listed in the *Small Press Record of Books in Print* (20th Edition, 1991-92). avg. price, cloth: $20. Discounts: 1-4 25%; 5-9 33⅓%; 10-99 40%; 100+ 42% (no discount 1 copy reference books). 250pp; 6×9; of. Reporting time: 2-6 weeks. Payment: varies with publication. Copyrights for author.

Morgan-Rand Publications, Inc., R. Perkins, M. Weakley, 2200 Sansom Street, Philadelphia, PA 19103-4350, 215-557-8200, 800-354-8673. 1982. Non-fiction. "We are interested in reviewing manuscripts on subjects dealing with electronic publishing, compact disks, the information industry, etc. We are also directory publishers" avg. press run 2.5M. Pub'd 3 titles 1990; expects 5 titles 1991, 5+ titles 1992. avg. price, paper: $25+. Discounts: 40%. 150pp; 6×9 or 8½×11; of. Reporting time: varies, every effort made to be prompt.

Payment: negotiable. Copyrights for author. COSMEP, AAP, Philadelphia Publishers Group, IIA.

Morning Glory Press, 6595 San Haroldo Way, Buena Park, CA 90620. 12 titles listed in the *Small Press Record of Books in Print* (20th Edition, 1991-92).

Morningstar, Inc. (see also MUTUAL FUND VALUES; MUTUAL FUND SOURCEBOOK), Joe Mansueto, Publisher; Don Phillips, Editor, 53 West Jackson Blvd., Chicago, IL 60604, 312-427-1985. 1984. Non-fiction. Pub'd 1 title 1990; expects 1 title 1991, 1 title 1992. avg. price, paper: $195. Discounts: varies. 600pp; 8½x11; of. Reporting time: varies. Payment: varies.

Mortal Press, Terry James Mohaupt, 2315 North Alpine Road, Rockford, IL 61107-1422, 815-399-8432. 1975. Poetry, fiction, art, parts-of-novels, long-poems. avg. press run 250. Pub'd 1 title 1990; expects 1 title 1992. 2 titles listed in the *Small Press Record of Books in Print* (20th Edition, 1991-92). avg. price, cloth: $10; paper: $5. 75pp; 5½x8½; photo offset. COSMEP.

Mosaic Press, Miriam Owen Irwin, 358 Oliver Road, Dept. 45, Cincinnati, OH 45215, 513-761-5977. 1977. Poetry, fiction, satire. "We publish fine, hard-bound miniature books on any subject we find fascinating. We also publish a $3.00 miniature book catalog." avg. press run 2M. Pub'd 1 title 1990; expects 3 titles 1991, 2 titles 1992. 57 titles listed in the *Small Press Record of Books in Print* (20th Edition, 1991-92). avg. price, cloth: $24. 64pp; 3/4x1; of, traditional bindings. Reporting time: 2 weeks. Payment: $50 & 5 copies of book. Copyrights for author. Miniature Book Society.

Moscow Publishing Enterprises, Satty Kinarthy, Secretary; David Kinarthy, President, 326 South Highland Avenue, Los Angeles, CA 90036-3025, 213-934-2453/735-9969. 1985. Fiction, plays. "We are not self-publishers, but at present we don't accept any submissions of manuscripts from authors not affiliated with the Moscow Publishing Enterprises. Our schedule for the coming 12 months is already set: two novels and two stage plays" avg. press run 5-10M. Pub'd 1 title 1990; expects 2 titles 1991, 5 titles 1992. 2 titles listed in the *Small Press Record of Books in Print* (20th Edition, 1991-92). avg. price, cloth: $16.95; paper: $8.95. Discounts: 25%. 250pp; 5½x8½; of. Copyrights for author.

Mosquito Press, 27 A, Old Gloucester Street, London WC1N 3XX, United Kingdom. 1981. Non-fiction. "Nora Connolly O'Brien. *We shall rise again.* 1981. 121pp. 8 plates. (Memoirs of the daughter of James Connolly, leader of the Easter Uprising in Dublin in 1916). Sole publication by Mosquito Press so far." avg. press run 3M. Expects 1 title 1992. 6 titles listed in the *Small Press Record of Books in Print* (20th Edition, 1991-92). avg. price, cloth: £4.95 sterling; paper: £1.95 sterling. Various discounts in various countries. 121pp; 12x18cm; of. Payment: individual.

Mother Courage Press, Barbara Lindquist, Jeanne Arnold, 1533 Illinois Street, Racine, WI 53405-3115, 414-634-1047. 1981. Non-fiction. "FAX: 414-637-2227. Books that are therapeutic, life preserving or enhancing from a feminist perspective. Two of our books, *Something Happened to Me* and *Why Me* are for victims of child sexual abuse. Interested in fiction and non-fiction books for adults on difficult subjects such as child abuse, sibling death, teenage pregnancy, lesbianism, world peace, etc." avg. press run 2M-5M. Pub'd 4 titles 1990; expects 9 titles 1991, 2 titles 1992. 18 titles listed in the *Small Press Record of Books in Print* (20th Edition, 1991-92). avg. price, cloth: $16.95; paper: $9.95. Discounts: bookstores 1-4 copies 20%, 5+ 40%; distributors 50%. 189pp; 8½x11, 5½x8½; of. Reporting time: 6 weeks. Payment: 10% first 3,000 ($250 advance), 12% to 6,000 and 15% in excess of 6,000. Copyrights for author. COSMEP, ABA, MAP.

Mother of Ashes Press (see also THE PRINTER'S DEVIL; THE VILLAGE IDIOT), Joe M. Singer, Poet-in-Residence, PO Box 66, Harrison, ID 83833-0066. 1980. Poetry, fiction, articles, art, photos, cartoons, interviews, satire, reviews, letters, collages, news items, non-fiction. "This press would like to see book-length (over 50 ms pages) manuscripts on graphic arts for the small press. These should emphasize a do-it-yourself approach to book and magazine printing. Book-length literary manuscripts are considered by invitation only. Please see their separate listings for magazine requirements. The press also does publication printing." Pub'd 1 title 1990; expects 1 title 1991, 1 title 1992. 5 titles listed in the *Small Press Record of Books in Print* (20th Edition, 1991-92). Discounts: on request. †mimeo, screen printing, of, photocopy. Reporting time: 3 months. Payment: 15% of pressrun. Copyrights for author. Amer. Amateur Press Assn., National Amateur Press Assn.

Motheroot Publications, Paulette Balogh, PO Box 8306, Pittsburgh, PA 15221-0306. 1977. Poetry, fiction, articles, long-poems, plays. "We are a women's press—our first chapbook by Adrienne Rich published in July 1977. 2nd book May 1978. Material for/about women. Eight books to date" avg. press run 1M. Expects 1 title 1991, 1 title 1992. 8 titles listed in the *Small Press Record of Books in Print* (20th Edition, 1991-92). avg. price, paper: $3. Discounts: 40% bookstores, 50% distributors. 25pp; 8½x5½; of. Reporting time: 6 weeks. Payment: 25% after costs. Copyrights for author. CCLM.

MOTORBOOTY MAGAZINE, Mark Dancey, Danny Plotnick, PO Box 7944, Ann Arbor, MI 48107. 1987. Fiction, articles, art, photos, cartoons, interviews, satire, criticism, reviews, music, parts-of-novels, non-fiction. "This magazine has an attitude" circ. 6M. Sporadic. Pub'd 1 issue 1990; expects 2 issues 1991, 3 issues 1992.

sub. price: $12; per copy: $3; sample: $3. Back issues: $3. Discounts: trade with other publishers. 64pp; 8½×11. Copyrighted, reverts to author. Pub's reviews. §Satire, comics, music. Ads: $200/$120.

Motorsport International Publishing Co. (MIPCO), James P. McCarthy, Publisher; James Grinnell, Editor, R3 Box 6181, Sparta, WI 54656, 608-269-5591. 1989. Non-fiction. "We publish mainly auto racing related subjects. We also publish any material that relates to automobiles." avg. press run varies. Expects 2 titles 1991, 2 titles 1992. 2 titles listed in the *Small Press Record of Books in Print* (20th Edition, 1991-92). Discounts: standard 40-50% off list (wholesale price). Pages vary; size varies; of, typeset. Reporting time: 2 weeks. Payment: negotiable. Copyrights for author.

MT. AUKUM REVIEW, Ben L. Hiatt, PO Box 483, Mt. Aukum, CA 95656, 209-245-4016. 1985. Poetry, fiction, articles, art, photos, cartoons, interviews, satire, criticism, letters, parts-of-novels, long-poems, collages, concrete art, news items, non-fiction. "Magazine is going to published monthly Jan-June, 1986. In June I will evaluate the project and decide whether or not to continue for another six months" circ. 1.5M. 12/yr. Expects 1 issue 1991, 12 issues 1992. sub. price: $15; per copy: $2; sample: 50¢ to writers. Discounts: 40% on 5 or more copies. 48pp; 4¼×7; †of. Reporting time: 2 weeks or less. Payment: contributors copies plus subscription. Copyrighted, reverts to author. Pub's reviews. §Modern poetry, arts education. Ads: $25/$15/classified 10¢ per word.

THE MOUNTAIN ASTROLOGER, Tem Tarriktar, PO Box 11292, Berkeley, CA 94701, 415-267-3274. 1987. Poetry, fiction, articles, art, photos, cartoons, interviews, satire, reviews, letters, news items. "Any length; must be related to astrology. Call first if possible, otherwise send SASE for return of materials" circ. 5M-6M. 6/yr. Pub'd 6 issues 1990; expects 6 issues 1991, 6 issues 1992. sub. price: $16.75 bulk rate, $22 1st class; per copy: $3.50; sample: $3.50. Back issues: $3.50. 56pp; 8½×11; of. Reporting time: varies/ad trade preferred. Copyrighted, reverts to author. Pub's reviews: 15 in 1990. Ads: $210/$120/subject to change.

Mountain Automation Corporation, Claude Wiatrowski, PO Box 6020, Woodland Park, CO 80866, 719-687-6647. 1976. Art, photos, non-fiction. "We currently publish promotional books and videos, especially tourist souvenirs for specific attractions. We will be expanding into a line of larger, photographically illustrated books especially in the areas of the west, history, transportation, and travel." avg. press run 10M. Pub'd 1 title 1990; expects 1 title 1991, 1 title 1992. 6 titles listed in the *Small Press Record of Books in Print* (20th Edition, 1991-92). avg. price, paper: $3. Discounts: sold only through wholesalers and directly to promotional buyers. 24pp; 8½×5½; of. Reporting time: 1 month. Payment: determined individually. Copyrights for author. RMBPA, COSMEP.

Mountain Press Publishing Co., David Flaccus, Publisher, Senior Editor; Rob Williams, Business Manager; John Rimel, Marketing Director & Production Coordinator; Dave Alt, Roadside Geology Series Editor; Don Hyndman, Roadside Geology Series Editor; Daniel Greer, Roadside History Series Editor; Kathleen Ort, Assistant Editor, P.O. Box 2399, Missoula, MT 59806, 406-728-1900. 1948 (became full time publisher in mid-70's - printing company prior to that). Non-fiction. "We publish primarily non-fiction. Besides our successful *Roadside Geology* series, we are publishing regional nature/outdoor guides such as *Birds of the Northern Rockies*. We also publish quality western history and western Americana. In addition, we have published several 'how-to' books on outdoor-oriented activities such as our book *Flytying* by John McKim, *Packin' In on Mules and Horses* by Smoke Elser and Bill Brown, and *The Backyard Horseman* by Ron Rude." avg. press run 5M. Pub'd 10 titles 1990; expects 10 titles 1991, 12 titles 1992. 81 titles listed in the *Small Press Record of Books in Print* (20th Edition, 1991-92). avg. price, cloth: $26.95; paper: $12.95. Discounts: 5 or more copies, assorted titles, to bookstores - 40%. 150-360pp; 6×9, 5×7, 8½×11; of. Reporting time: 2-6 months. Payment: usually 10-15%, payable twice a year. Copyrights for author. Rocky Mountain Book Publishers Association, Publisher's Marketing Association.

Mountain Publishing, PO Box 1747, Hillsboro, OR 97123, 503-628-3995. 1989. Non-fiction. "Street address: 16175 S.W. Holly Hill Road. Manuscripts: book-length dealing with business." avg. press run 5M. Expects 2 titles 1992. 1 title listed in the *Small Press Record of Books in Print* (20th Edition, 1991-92). avg. price, paper: $29.95. Discounts: 2-5 copies 20%, 6-10 30%, 11-25 40%, 26-74 45%, 75+ 55%. 304pp; 6×9; of. Reporting time: 60 days. Payment: negotiable. Copyrights for author. PMA, COSMEP.

MOUNTAIN RESEARCH & DEVELOPMENT, University of California Press, Pauline Ives, University of California Press, 2120 Berkeley Way, Berkeley, CA 94720. "Editorial address: Pauline Ives, International Mountain Society, PO Box 1978, Davis, CA 95616. Copyrighted by International Mountain Society." circ. 950. 4/yr. Pub'd 4 issues 1990; expects 4 issues 1991, 4 issues 1992. sub. price: $30 indiv., $60 instit., $20 students (+ $6 foreign postage); per copy: $8 indiv., $16 instit., $6 students (+ $6 foreign postage); sample: free. Discounts: foreign subs. agent 10%, one-time orders 10+ 30%, standing orders (bookstores) 1-99 40%, 100+ 50%. 88pp; 8½×11; of. Ads: $200/$120.

Mountain State Press, c/o University of Charleston, 2300 MacCorkle, Charleston, WV 25304, 304-9471 ext 210. 1978. Poetry, fiction, satire, criticism, plays. "We specialize in regional materials: Appalachian subjects and authors, primarily. We publish book-length mss. of fiction, nonfiction, and poetry. Recent authors: Davis Grubb, *A Tree Full of Stars*; Stanley Eskew, *As I Remember It*; Bonnie McKeown, *A Peaceful Patriot*; W.E.R. Byrne, *Tale of the Elk*. Founding memberships in the Press are available for $25.00." avg. press run 1M. Pub'd 4 titles 1990; expects 3 titles 1991. 15 titles listed in the *Small Press Record of Books in Print* (20th Edition, 1991-92). avg. price, cloth: $7; paper: $5. Discounts: 40% to bookstores and 10% to libraries. 250pp; 5½×8½; photo-offset. Reporting time: 2 months or more. Payment: negotiable. Copyrights for author.

The Mountaineers Books, Donna DeShazo, Director, 1101 SW Klickitat Way, Suite 107, Seattle, WA 98134, 206-285-2665. 1961. Non-fiction. "We have nearly 200 titles in print, all having to do with the outdoors - how to, where to, history-climbing, hiking, skiing, snowshoeing, bicycling, mountaineering & expeditions. Must relate to mountaineering or self-propelled, non-commercial, non-competitive outdoor activities; mountain and/or NW history; conservation of natural resources." avg. press run 3M-5M. Pub'd 28 titles 1990; expects 28 titles 1991, 29 titles 1992. 41 titles listed in the *Small Press Record of Books in Print* (20th Edition, 1991-92). avg. price, cloth: $16.95; paper: $10.95. Standard book trade discounts. 240pp; 5½×8½; of. Reporting time: 1-2 months. Payment: negotiated royalties on net sales paid twice yearly. Copyrights for author. ABA, Pacific NW Book Publishers, Book Publicists NW.

Mountaintop Books, Gerald E. Thompson, PO Box 24031, Gallows Bay Station, Christiansted, VI 00824-0031, 809-773-3412. 1989. Poetry, fiction, criticism, non-fiction. "Humanism, free thought, Biblical studies. Query only, SASE. Length about 30,000 words." avg. press run 1M-5M. Expects 1 title 1991, 2 titles 1992. 1 title listed in the *Small Press Record of Books in Print* (20th Edition, 1991-92). avg. price, cloth: $30; paper: $20. Discounts: 2-4 20%, 5-24 40%, 25-49 43%, 50-99 46%, 100+ 52%. 100pp; 6×9; of. Reporting time: 3 months. Payment: royalty, schedule negotiated individually. Does not copyright for author.

Mountainwest Publishers, Sue Mangum, 5295 S. 300 W., Suite 475, Murray, UT 84107, 801-268-3232. 1989. Non-fiction. 1 title listed in the *Small Press Record of Books in Print* (20th Edition, 1991-92).

Mouvement Publications, E. J. Burke, 109 Forest Glen Road, Longmeadow, MA 01106, 607-272-2157. 1977. Non-fiction. avg. press run 2M. Pub'd 5 titles 1990; expects 5 titles 1991, 5 titles 1992. avg. price, cloth: $15.00; paper: $10.00. Discounts: 20% to bookstores. 250pp; of. Payment: 10-12%. Copyrights for author.

MOVING OUT: A Feminist Literary & Arts Journal, Jan Mordenski, Margaret Kaminski, Joan Gartland, PO Box 21249, Detroit, MI 48221. 1970. Poetry, fiction, art, photos, interviews, criticism, reviews, parts-of-novels, long-poems. "We publish quality work by women. *Library Journal* recently described our journal as one with a 'well-defined aesthetic sense which considers all facets of women's lives and literature. . .first choice for librarians who must make such a choice.' Please do not double submit or send work which has been published elsewhere. Enclose SASE. Plan 1 double issue each for 1989 & 1990" circ. 500-1M. Irregular. Pub'd 1 issue 1990; expects 1 issue 1991, 1 issue 1992. 2 titles listed in the *Small Press Record of Books in Print* (20th Edition, 1991-92). sub. price: $6 ($9 libraries); per copy: $6; sample: $6. Back issues: $6 per issue. Discounts: none. 48-100pp; 8½×11; of. Reporting time: 6-12 months. Payment: copy only, $100 prose & poetry to contest winners. Copyrighted, we ask a $5 fee & acknowledgment if reprinted elsewhere. Pub's reviews. §Women's writings. Ads: $200/$100. CCLM, COSMEP.

Moving Parts Press, Felicia Rice, 220 Baldwin Street, Santa Cruz, CA 95060, 408-427-2271. 1977. Poetry, fiction, art, letters, parts-of-novels, long-poems, collages. "*For Earthly Survival,* poems by Ellen Bass, was winner of 1980 Elliston Book Award. 1981 publication: *In the World's Common Grasses Poems of a Son, Poems of a Father* by William Pitt Root." avg. press run 250. Pub'd 1 title 1990; expects 3 titles 1991, 2 titles 1992. 7 titles listed in the *Small Press Record of Books in Print* (20th Edition, 1991-92). avg. price, cloth: $75; paper: $25; other: $15. Discounts: 30%. 45pp; 6×9; †lp, of. Reporting time: 1-2 months. Payment: 10% copies. Copyrights for author. PCBA.

MSRRT NEWSLETTER, Christopher Dodge, 4645 Columbus Avenue South, Minneapolis, MN 55407, 612-541-8572; 823-1214. 1988. Articles, cartoons, interviews, reviews, letters, news items, non-fiction. "Publication of the Social Responsibilities Round Table of the Minnesota Library Association. Focus is on peace and justice news and commentary for library community with special emphasis on annotations of alternative periodicals. Also includes book/audio visual reviews and networking information." circ. 200-250. 10/yr. Pub'd 10 issues 1990; expects 10 issues 1991, 10 issues 1992. sub. price: $15 payable MLA/MSRRT; sample: 52¢ SASE. 16pp; 8½×11. Payment: copy. Not copyrighted. Pub's reviews: 250+ in 1990. §Peace, politics, counter-culture, libraries, human rights, arts, Native American, civil rights, feminism, Third World, global education, environment, labor, anarchist, Chicano, Black, communism, gay/lesbian, animal rights, socialist, seniors, disabled.

MSS/NEW MYTHS, Robert Mooney, Editor, SUNY, Binghamton, NY 13901. 1961. Poetry, fiction, art, photos, parts-of-novels, long-poems, plays, non-fiction. "Any length-New fiction writers; old and new poets." circ. 1M. 2/yr. Pub'd 3 issues 1990; expects 3 issues 1991, 2 issues 1992. sub. price: $8.50; per copy: $5; sample: $5. Back issues: $4. Discounts: 20% for bookstores on consignment, 40% + pre-paid. Free freight.

200pp; 6×9; †of. Reporting time: 2-8 weeks. Payment: contributor copies. Copyrighted, reverts to author. Pub's reviews: 1 in 1990. §Children, literary, art & photography. Ads: varies. COSMEP.

Mud Press (see also MISSISSIPPI MUD), Joel Weinstein, Lynn Darroch, 1336 S.E. Marion Street, Portland, OR 97202. 1973. Fiction, art, photos, cartoons, interviews, satire, criticism, reviews, parts-of-novels, collages, plays. *"Mala Noche* by Walt Curtis, Joel Weinstein, Editor. *Between Fire and Love, Contempry Peruvian Writing*; Lynn Darroch, Editor." avg. press run 1.5M. Expects 1 title 1991. 2 titles listed in the *Small Press Record of Books in Print* (20th Edition, 1991-92). avg. price, paper: $5. 132pp; 7×9¾; of. Copyrights for author.

MUDFISH, Box Turtle Press, Jill Hoffman, Poetry Editor; Vladimir Urban, Art Editor, 184 Franklin Street, New York, NY 10013, 212-219-9278. 1983. Poetry, art, photos. circ. 1.5M. 1/yr. Pub'd 2 issues 1990; expects 2 issues 1991, 2 issues 1992. sub. price: $16 for 2 year subscription; per copy: $8 + $1.50; sample: $8 + $1.50. Back issues: $7 for #2, $6 for #3, plus $1.50. 168pp; 6⅞×8¼; lp. Reporting time: immediately to 6 months. Payment: 2 copies of magazine. Copyrighted, reverts to author. §Poetry books. Ads: $120 per page.

John Muir Publications, Inc., Ken Luboff, PO Box 613, Santa Fe, NM 87504, 505-982-4078. 1969. Non-fiction. "Non-fiction, travel, auto repair, general trade, young readers (8 and up), nonfiction." avg. press run 5M-10M. Expects 47 titles 1991, 50 titles 1992. avg. price, paper: $9.95. Discounts: 25-50%. 300pp; 8½×11, 4½×8½, 5½×8½, 7×10, 7×9; of. Reporting time: 4-6 weeks. Payment: by individual contract. Copyrights for author. COSMEP, ABA, Rocky Mountain Booksellers Association.

Multi Media Arts, Jackie Mallis, Editorial Director, PO Box 14486, Austin, TX 78761, 512-837-5503. 1978. "Not in the market for submissions. Our instructional kits, tapes, and books are all painstakingly designed by professional educators with extensive, practical, classroom experience. We cover a wide range of subject areas and target markets that include traditional classrooms, independent study, home-schooling, in-service training for staff development, and university programs. But there are some unifying themes: materials that have been tested and have proved successful; well-organized formats constructed upon recognized instructional models; time-saving, self-directed, self-contained units that require minimal or no preparation by the teacher or student; relevant, activity-oriented structures that actually teach specific skills based on coherent objectives and stated goals. Terms for discount schedules—FOB Austin, plus UPS shipping: Net 30 day on approved credit, COD. No returns without advance authorization or after 90 days from purchase. 100% credit only for returns that arrive back in new, saleable condition." avg. press run 500-1M. Pub'd 4 titles 1990; expects 7 titles 1991, 12 titles 1992. 37 titles listed in the *Small Press Record of Books in Print* (20th Edition, 1991-92). avg. price, paper: $15-$30. Discounts: standard to qualified dealers and distributors; quantity 1-9 20%, 10-49 30%, 50-99 40%, 100-249 42%, 250-499 44%, 500-999 46%, 1000-2499 48%, 2500+ 50%. 100-450pp; 8½×11, 5½×8½; of. Copyrights for author.

MULTICULTURAL TEACHING FOR PRACTITIONERS IN SCHOOLS AND COMMUNITY, Trentham Books, Gillian Klein, Editor, Unit 13/14, Trent Trading Pack, Botteslow St., Hanley, Stoke-on-Trent, Staffordshire ST1 3LY, England, 0782-274227. 1982. "For professionals in schools and community. It is concerned with all aspects of teaching and learning in a multicultural society. It is equally concerned with the wide range of social work serving young people, their families, and communities. It is, therefore, an inter-professional journal that focuses on practices of teachers and social and community workers in their day to day work with young people of all ethnic groups. Each issue consists of case studies of professional practice, discussion of its aims and purposes and examples of its achievements. There are also reviews of important new books and resources and information about courses, conferences, and events of professional interest to readers." 3/yr. Pub'd 3 issues 1990; expects 3 issues 1991, 3 issues 1992. sub. price: £20; per copy: £7; sample: £7. Back issues: £7. Discounts: 10% series disc. w/ ads. 64pp; 30×21cm; of. Reporting time: max 1 month, usually 2 weeks. Copyrighted. Pub's reviews: 47 in 1990. §Multi ethnic education, anti racist education. Ads: £200/£100/£.50.

Multiple Dimensions, Caryn Goldberg, Managing Editor, 2305 Canyon Drive, Los Angeles, CA 90068-2411, 213-469-4454. 1990. Fiction, non-fiction. "Multiple Dimensions is a new gay and lesbian publishing house focusing primarily on non-fiction, including biographies and autobiographies by and about prominent contemporary and historical gay men and lesbians, including political activists, cultural figures and spiritual leaders" avg. press run 8M. Expects 2 titles 1991, 5 titles 1992. 1 title listed in the *Small Press Record of Books in Print* (20th Edition, 1991-92). avg. price, paper: $9.95. Discounts: 40% on 5+ copies. 256pp; 5⅜×8⅜; of.

Mundus Artium Press, University of Texas at Dallas, Box 688, Richardson, TX 75083-0688. 1968. Poetry. "Bilingual poetry." avg. press run 1M-1.5M. Expects 2 titles 1991. 4 titles listed in the *Small Press Record of Books in Print* (20th Edition, 1991-92). avg. price, paper: $8. Discounts: 20% libraries. 6×9. Reporting time: 6 months.

MurPubCo, 3820 Lakebriar Drive, Boulder, CO 80304. 1985. Poetry, fiction, articles, cartoons. "MurPubCo published 2 titles in 1986. They can be ordered from the publisher at the above address." Pub'd 2 titles 1990;

expects 3 titles 1991. 1 title listed in the *Small Press Record of Books in Print* (20th Edition, 1991-92). avg. price, paper: $5; other: $1. Reporting time: 3 months. Does not copyright for author. Stone Soup Poets (Boston, MA).

MUSCADINE, Melinda Sanborn, 909 Arapahoe, Boulder, CO 80302-4459, 303-443-9748. 1977. Poetry, fiction, non-fiction. "Writers must be at least 60 years old. Mss need not be typewritten. Priority given to unpublished authors, very brief items & the slightly unusual. Poetry 4-12 lines. Fiction 1,500 maximum. General writings, such as essays & memories 200-1M words" circ. 400. 4/yr. Pub'd 6 issues 1990; expects 6 issues 1991, 6 issues 1992. sub. price: $6, $7.50 in Canada; per copy: $1.25; sample: $1.25. 28pp; 8½x11; †of. Reporting time: 3 weeks. Payment: 1 copy, occasional token payment. Copyrighted, reverts to author. CODA.

MUSEUM & ARTS WASHINGTON, Mary Gabriel, Sarah Grosin, 1707 L Street NW #222, Washington, DC 20036-4201. 1985. Articles, art, photos, interviews, criticism, reviews, news items. "We are primarily a visual arts magazine, but we also cover local performing and literary arts. Inquiries are recommended" circ. 50M. 6/yr. Pub'd 6 issues 1990; expects 6 issues 1991, 6 issues 1992. sub. price: $12; per copy: $2.95; sample: $2.95. Back issues: call us for availability. Discounts: 10-100 $2 per copy, over 100 $1.50. 120pp; 8¼x11; lp. Reporting time: 3-5 weeks. Payment: $350 for 1-page stories, features-varies. Copyrighted. Pub's reviews: 1 in 1990. §Arts-related, artists' books, Washington or mid-Atlantic. Ads: $3625 b&w, $4295 color/$2295 b&w, $2595 color. BPA.

Museum of New Mexico Press, Mary Wachs, Editor-In-Chief; James Mafchir, Publisher, PO Box 2087, Santa Fe, NM 87503, 505-827-6454. 1913. Articles, art, photos, reviews. "Publishes general non-fiction books and catalogs of museum exhibitions within Museum of New Mexico system and general books for the trade, particularly relating to the Southwest" avg. press run 2.5M-5M. Pub'd 6-10 titles 1990; expects 6-10 titles 1991, 6-10 titles 1992. 58 titles listed in the *Small Press Record of Books in Print* (20th Edition, 1991-92). Discounts: 1 to 4, 30%; 5-99 40%; 100, 45%. of. Reporting time: 4 weeks. Royaties negotiated on per contract basis. Copyrights for author.

MUSIC AND LETTERS, Oxford University Press, Nigel Fortune, John Whenham, Journals Subscription Department, Pinkhill House, Southfield Road, Eynsham, Oxford OX8 1JJ, England. 1920. Articles, reviews, music, letters. "Not specialized in scope, being open to the discussion of anything from primitive music to the latest experiments in the laboratory. But preference is given to contributors who can write, who have a respect for the English language and are willing to take the trouble to use it effectively." circ. 1.4M. 4/yr. Pub'd 4 issues 1990; expects 4 issues 1991, 4 issues 1992. sub. price: $72; per copy: $22; sample: free. 120pp; 6x9¾; †of. Reporting time: 4 months. Payment: £1 per printed page. Copyrighted, reverts to author. Pub's reviews: 79 books, 95 pieces of music in 1990. §Music, musical criticism, musical history, etc. Ads: £40.00 & pro rata/£23.00.

MUSIC OF THE SPHERES, John Patrick Lamkin, Managing Editor, PO Box 1751, Taos, NM 87571, (505) 758-0405. 1986. Poetry, fiction, articles, art, photos, cartoons, interviews, reviews, music, letters, news items, non-fiction. "Slant: items of interest to a readership of people interested in "New Age" music and art (visionary). Items related to spirituality, world peace through art and music, future visions, spiritual sexuality, mediums of video, 2D art exhibits, books, radio and TV, telecommunications, concerts, etc. related to New Age art and music" circ. 10M. 4/yr. Expects 3 issues 1991, 4 issues 1992. sub. price: $14; per copy: $4; sample: $5. Discounts: wholesale 50% off cover. 50pp; 8½x11; of. Reporting time: 30 days. Payment: please call or write. Copyrighted, reverts to author. Pub's reviews. §New Age art and music (any publication that includes these subjects), how-to for the artist and musician. Ads: $725 b/w/$400/75¢ per word classified.

MUSIC PERCEPTION, University of California Press, Diana Deutsch, Univ of CA Press, 2120 Berkeley Way, Berkeley, CA 94720, 415-642-4191. 1983. Reviews, music, non-fiction. "Editorial address: Department of Psychology, C-009, Univ of CA-San Diego, La Jolla, CA 92093." circ. 800. 4/yr. Pub'd 2 issues 1990; expects 4 issues 1991, 4 issues 1992. sub. price: $35, $75 instit. (+ $5 foreign postage); per copy: $8.75; $18.75 instit.; sample: free. Back issues: same as single copy price. Discounts: foreign subs. agents 10%, one-time orders 10+ 30%, standing orders (bookstores): 1-99 40%, 100+ 50%. 128pp; 7x10; of. Copyrighted, does not revert to author. Pub's reviews: 20 in 1990. §Music, physical psychology, psychology of perception. Ads: $200/$120.

MUSICAL OPINION, Denby Richards, 2 Princes Road, St. Leonards-on-Sea, East Sussex TN37 6EL, England, 0424-715167; fax 0424-730052. 1877. Articles. "500-2M words of general musical interest, organ. No verse." circ. 4.5M. 12/yr. sub. price: £32 UK, £35/US $70 overseas; per copy: £1.50 + postage; sample: free. Back issues: from £3 + postage. Discounts: 10% for trade. 40pp; 8¼x11½; †of. Reporting time: by arrangement. Payment: on publication. Copyrighted, reverts to author. Pub's reviews: 40 in 1990. §General music, opera, organ, church music, musical instruments trade. Ads: £500 color, £300/£180/£100/40p per classified word. British Sov. of Magazine Editors.

MUSICWORKS: THE CANADIAN AUDIO-VISUAL JOURNAL OF SOUND EXPLORATIONS, Gayle

Young, Editor-in-Chief; Lauren Pratt, Managing Editor; Wende Bartley, Cassette Editor, 1087 Queen Street West, Toronto, Ontario, Canada, 416-533-0192. 1978. Poetry, fiction, articles, art, photos, cartoons, interviews, criticism, reviews, music, letters, collages, news items. "Please send proposals, not finished materials." circ. 3M. 3/yr. Pub'd 3 issues 1990; expects 3 issues 1991, 3 issues 1992. sub. price: paper only $14 Canada, $20 elsewhere, $25 institution, paper with cassette $30 Canada, $36 elsewhere, $47 institution; sample: $4.50/$11.50 with cassette. Back issues: varies. Discounts: retail outlets 55%. 64pp; 8½×11; web-offset. Reporting time: varies. Payment: varies. Copyrighted, reverts to author. Pub's reviews. §Contemporary music—lp's, cd's, cassettes (non commercial). Ads: $200/$130/$80 1/4 page/$50 1/8/$15 for 40 words classified. CPPA.

Muso Press, Frank Aoi, 33 Fonda Road, Santa Fe, NM 87505-0232. 1985. Poetry, articles, photos. "Art photography books with Zen poetry." avg. press run 2M. Pub'd 1 title 1990; expects 1 title 1991, 1 title 1992. 2 titles listed in the *Small Press Record of Books in Print* (20th Edition, 1991-92). 8½×11; of. Copyrights for author.

Mustang Publishing Co., Rollin Riggs, Editor-in-chief, PO Box 3004, Memphis, TN 38173, 901-521-1406. 1983. Non-fiction. "We're especially interested in books for the 18-40 year old crowd—travel, humor, how-to, etc. We want proposals! Please enclose an SASE with proposals. No phone calls, please." avg. press run 5M. Pub'd 5 titles 1990; expects 6 titles 1991, 8 titles 1992. 16 titles listed in the *Small Press Record of Books in Print* (20th Edition, 1991-92). avg. price, paper: $8.95. Discounts: contact our distributor, National Book Network, Lanham, MD (800-462-6420). 160pp; 5½×8¼; of. Reporting time: 2-3 weeks. Payment: around 6-8%. Copyrights for author.

MUTUAL FUND SOURCEBOOK, Morningstar, Inc., Joe Mansueto, 53 West Jackson Blvd., Chicago, IL 60604, 312-427-1985. 1984. Photos, interviews, news items, non-fiction. 1/yr. Pub'd 1 issue 1990; expects 1 issue 1991, 1 issue 1992. sub. price: $195; per copy: $195. Back issues: none. Discounts: 2 yrs $355. 2000pp; 8×11½; of, lp. Reporting time: varies. Payment: varies. Copyrighted. §Investments.

MUTUAL FUND VALUES, Morningstar, Inc., Don Phillips, 53 West Jackson Blvd., Chicago, IL 60604, 312-427-1985. 1986. 26/yr. Pub'd 26 issues 1990; expects 26 issues 1991, 26 issues 1992. sub. price: $395; per copy: $55/3 month trial. Discounts: 2 yr subscription $695. 112pp + summary section (36pp); 8½×11; of. Copyrighted.

Mutual Publishing of Honolulu, Bemett Hymer, Ronn Ronck, 2055 N. King, Honolulu, HI 96819. 1974. Fiction, photos, non-fiction. avg. press run 10M. Pub'd 15 titles 1990; expects 10 titles 1991, 20 titles 1992. 31 titles listed in the *Small Press Record of Books in Print* (20th Edition, 1991-92). avg. price, cloth: $29.95; paper: $3.95-$4.95. Discounts: 40% dealer, 50% distributor, 30% library. 300pp. Reporting time: 1 year. Payment: 10% of receipts. Sometimes copyrights for author.

MW PENPAL WORLD MAGAZINE, Dr. M.L. Webber, PO Box 3121, Hutchinson, KS 67501. Poetry, articles, photos, interviews, news items, non-fiction. circ. 5M. 4/yr. Pub'd 2 issues 1990; expects 4 issues 1991, 4 issues 1992. sub. price: $4; per copy: $1. Back issues: $1. Discounts: 25¢ per copy. 8pp; 9×12. Copyrighted, reverts to author. Pub's reviews. Ads: $40/$20/$10 1/4 page/$4 one inch.

MY LEGACY, Weems Concepts, Kay Weems, Star Route, Box 21AA, Artemas, PA 17211, 814-458-3102. 1990. Poetry. "Any form or theme on poetry to 36 lines (sometimes longer). Short stories to 2,500 words, sometimes longer. Will try to use several poems in an issue by some poets—if I really like their work." circ. 150+. 4/yr. Pub'd 3 issues 1990; expects 4 issues 1991, 4 issues 1992. sub. price: $12; per copy: $3.50; sample: $3.50. Back issues: $3.50. 60-70pp; digest; †Sharp copier. Reporting time: 2-3 months. Payment: Editor's Choice Award to editor's favorite writer and poet in each issue. Copyrighted, reverts to author. Ads: I try not to use ads, not much room. PA Poetry Society, Walt Whitman Guild, UAPAA, National Arts Society, National Federation of State Poetry Societies Inc., New Horizons Poetry Club, Southern Poetry Assoc.

MY LIFE DEPENDS ON YOU, Martti Koski, Kiilinpellont. 2, Rusko 21290, Finland. 1981. News items, non-fiction. "This magazine is made to report illegal human experimenting. Expecializes telemtric electromagnetic brain research andmanipulation such and R.H.I.C. (Radio Hypnotic Infracerebral Control) or E.D.O.M. (Electronic dissolution of memory)" circ. 6M. 1/yr. Pub'd 1 issue 1990; expects 1 issue 1991, 1 issue 1992. sample price: $1. Discounts: 1M for $500. 16pp; 6×9; of. Payment: none. Not copyrighted. Pub's reviews: 1 in 1990. §Human rights, human experiment, ELF-radiowaves, unpublished important and interesting news. No paid advertising.

My Mother's House - Aitini Talo, Arto Kytohonka, Villa Remedia, Uusikyla, SF-16100, Finland, 358-18-631 136. 1982. Poetry, art, long-poems, collages. avg. press run 1M. Pub'd 5 titles 1990; expects 4 titles 1991, 6 titles 1992. avg. price, paper: US $15. Discounts: up to 36%. 124pp; 4×5; of. Reporting time: 4 weeks. Payment: with individual arrangement. Copyrights for author. Finnish Small Press.

MYCOPHILATELY, Vernon W. Pickering-Laurel Publications International, Giorgio Migliavacca, PO

Box 704, Road Town-Tortola, British Virgin Islands. 1983. "Devoted to every aspect of philately and mushrooms - i.e.: stamps depicting mushrooms + fungi" circ. 300. 2/yr. Pub'd 2 issues 1990; expects 2 issues 1991, 2 issues 1992. sub. price: $6; per copy: $3; sample: $3. Back issues: $6. 30-40pp; 6×8. Payment: none. Not copyrighted. Pub's reviews: 6 in 1990. §Philatelic articles/books dealing with mycophilately. Ads: $60/$40.

MYRIAD, Wendy Yeck, 11564 Poema Place #101, Chatsworth, CA 91311-1121. 1989. Poetry, fiction, art, photos, cartoons, interviews, satire, criticism. 2/yr. Expects 2 issues 1991, 2 issues 1992. price per copy: $2; sample: $2. Pages vary; 5½×8½. Reporting time: 3 months or less. Payment: 1 contributor copy. Copyrighted, reverts to author. Ads: $10/$5. Small Press Action Network, c/o Petarade Press, Box 65746, Station F, Vancouver, BC Canada V5N 5K7.

Myriad Moods, M.S. Hundere, 202 Thoraine Boulevard, San Antonio, TX 78212-5243, 512-824-1185. 1982. Poetry, photos, cartoons, interviews. "Interested in autobiographies. Recent authors: O.T. Goldsmith, Edyth Harrell." avg. press run 3M. Expects 6 titles 1991, 6 titles 1992. 3 titles listed in the *Small Press Record of Books in Print* (20th Edition, 1991-92). avg. price, cloth: $4; paper: $3. Discounts: quantity only. 96pp; 6×9. Reporting time: 10 days. Payment: negotiable. Copyrights for author. MM.

THE MYSTERY FANCIER, Guy Townsend, Editor & Publisher, 2024 Clifty Drive, Madison, IN 47250-1632, 812-273-6908. 1976. Articles, art, photos, interviews, criticism, reviews, letters, non-fiction. "*TMF* is for mystery fans. The people who read it are the same people who write for it. It's a casual, friendly, unpretentious magazine. The articles tend to be short, but there's no page limit. Most contributions by subscribers are published. Contributions accepted only from subscribers. If you don't subscribe, don't submit." circ. 200. 4/yr. Pub'd 4 issues 1990; expects 4 issues 1991, 4 issues 1992. sub. price: $25 second class US & Canada, $30 first class US & Canada, $25 surface mail overseas, $35 airmail overseas; per copy: $7.50; sample: same. Back issues: Vol 4, 7, 8, 9, are available, complete, for $15/volume; Vol 10 & 11 $25/vol; other single issues are available at $3/issue through #9, $7.50/issue for Vol 10 & beyond; all volumes available in quality cloth library binding for $35 per volume (Vols 1-12). Discounts: to dealers, 25% on 1-4 copies, 40% for 5 or more copies. 104pp; 5½×8½; of. Reporting time: notice of rejection within 2 weeks, usually no notice if accepted. Payment: none. Copyrighted. Pub's reviews: 200 in 1990. §Anything in the mystery, suspense, espionage, thriller fields, fiction & non-fiction. No ads.

Mystery Notebook Editions, Stephen Wright, PO Box 1341, FDR Station, New York, NY 10150. 1986. Fiction, non-fiction. "First Title: *The Adventures of Sandy West, Private Eye* (novel) by Stephen Wright." avg. press run 1M. Pub'd 1 title 1990. 1 title listed in the *Small Press Record of Books in Print* (20th Edition, 1991-92). avg. price, paper: varies. Pages vary; size varies; varies. Reporting time: 1-3 months, *query first*. Payment: individually arranged. Copyrights for author.

MYSTERY READERS JOURNAL, Janet A. Rudolph, PO Box 8116, Berkeley, CA 94707-8116, 415-339-2800. 1985. Articles, art, interviews, criticism, reviews, news items. "Each issue deals primarily with specific themes in mystery. Fiction (reviews of) 1989: Theatrical mysteries, murder on the job, legal mysteries, and bibliomysteries. 1990: Musical mysteries, murder on holiday, political mysteries, and beastly murders. 1991: Food mysteries, murder in the plot, gardening mysteries, holiday mysteries, murder on screen." circ. 2M. 4/yr. Pub'd 4 issues 1990; expects 4 issues 1991, 4 issues 1992. sub. price: $22.50, $35 overseas/library; per copy: $6. Back issues: $6/issue. 64pp; 7×8; †of, on xerox. Reporting time: 2 months. Payment: free issue. Copyrighted, does not revert to author. Pub's reviews: 600 in 1990. §Mystery fiction, literary review magazines. No ads. Mystery Readers International.

MYSTERY TIME ANTHOLOGY, Hutton Publications, Linda Hutton, Editor, PO Box 1870, Hayden, ID 83835, 208-772-6184. 1983. Fiction. "We use only mystery/suspense stories up to 1.5M words, which must be well-plotted." circ. 100. 1/yr. Pub'd 1 issue 1990; expects 1 issue 1991. sub. price: $5; per copy: $5; sample: $3.50. Back issues: $3.50. 44pp; 8½×11. Reporting time: 1 month. Payment: 1/4¢ to 1¢ per word for fiction, 5¢ to 25¢ per line for poetry. Copyrighted, reverts to author.

Mystic Crystal Publications, John Vincent Milewski, Virginia L. Harford, PO Box 8029, Santa Fe, NM 87504, 505-984-1048. 1987. Fiction, articles, interviews, non-fiction. "Concentration for 1987 to 1990 will be on a broad range of New Age books specializing in crystal material that is well-researched, documented or experiential. Publication will be *cooperative* ventures. Correspondence/submissions—send to John V. Milewski at above address with SASE. Recent title: *The Crystal Sourcebook: From Science to Metaphysics*" avg. press run 5M. Expects 1 title 1991, 2 titles 1992. 1 title listed in the *Small Press Record of Books in Print* (20th Edition, 1991-92). avg. price, cloth: $34.95; paper: $24.95. Discounts: for distributors, special markets, bookstores, catalogs, etc. 351pp; 8½×11; of. Reporting time: 3 months. Payment: proportional to their contribution to the book as well as sliding royalties. Copyrights for author. COSMEP, PMA via First Editions.

N

THE N.A. WAY, Andy Mann, PO Box 9999, Van Nuys, CA 91409, 818-780-3951. 1982. Articles, cartoons, non-fiction. "Only prints articles written by members of Narcotics Anonymous. Magazine is focused on recovery from drug addiction." circ. 10M. 12/yr. Pub'd 12 issues 1990; expects 12 issues 1991, 12 issues 1992. sub. price: $15; sample: free. Back issues: inquire. Discounts: 20% for 10 or more subscriptions to the same address. 36pp; 5½×8½; of. Reporting time: 2 months. Payment: none. Copyrighted, does not revert to author. WSO.

N. Y. HABITAT, Carol J. Ott, Publisher & Editor-in-Chief, 928 Broadway, New York, NY 10010, 212-505-2030. 1980. Articles, art, photos, interviews, news items. "A lively & informative magazine for boards of directors of co-ops & condominiums, and real estate professionals. Covers co-op management, tenant's rights, legal & financial affairs, management, energy conservation, and real estate markets." circ. 10M. 8/yr. Pub'd 7 issues 1990; expects 8 issues 1991, 8 issues 1992. sub. price: $30; per copy: $3.95; sample: $5 (includes postage). Back issues: $5. 80pp; 8⅛×10⅞; of. Reporting time: 6-8 weeks. Payment: $100-$800/article. Copyrighted. Pub's reviews: 5 1990. Ads: $1565/$975. MPA, BPA.

Nada Press (see also BIG SCREAM), David Cope, 2782 Dixie S.W., Grandville, MI 49418, 616-531-1442. 1974. Poetry, fiction, art. "Poets and writers *must* include SASE with their submissions and make sure there's enough postage on the envelope." avg. press run 100. Pub'd 2 titles 1990; expects 1 title 1991, 1 title 1992. 1 title listed in the *Small Press Record of Books in Print* (20th Edition, 1991-92). avg. price, paper: $3-$7; other: $3. 35pp; 8½×11; photo offset. Reporting time: 1 week - 1 month. Payment: copies.

The Naiad Press, Inc., Barbara Grier, Publisher, PO Box 10543, Tallahassee, FL 32302, 904-539-9322. 1973. Poetry, fiction. "Small press publishing lesbian feminist materials only, emphasizing genre fiction, romances, gothics, mysteries, science fiction, serious fiction...all with lesbian theme. Also publishes self-help, biography, autobiography, history, bibliography and very rarely poetry." avg. press run 12M. Pub'd 13 titles 1990; expects 15 titles 1991, 15 titles 1992. 151 titles listed in the *Small Press Record of Books in Print* (20th Edition, 1991-92). avg. price, paper: $8.95. Discounts: 40% dealers - 5 or more copies - mixed titles. of. Reporting time: 8 weeks. Payment: 15%, varies. Copyrights for author. COSMEP, Women in Print, ABA.

NAKED MAN, Naked Man Press, Mike Smetzer, c/o Mike Smetzer, R. 1, Box 2315, Unity, ME 04988. 1981. Poetry, fiction, cartoons, satire, reviews, long-poems, non-fiction. "Do not submit without inquiry." Irregular. Expects 1 issue 1991, 2 issues 1992. sub. price: $9/4 issues for U.S., $10.50 for foreign; per copy: $2.50; sample: $2.25. Discounts: 40% for bookstores. 48pp; 5½×8½; photocopy, of cover. Reporting time: 3 weeks, sometimes longer over academic vacations. Payment: copies. Copyrighted, reverts to author. Pub's reviews. §Poetry and fiction. No ads.

Naked Man Press (see also NAKED MAN), Mike Smetzer, c/o Mike Smetzer, R. 1, Box 2315, Unity, ME 04988. 1981. Poetry, fiction, art, satire, long-poems, collages, plays, concrete art, non-fiction. "Inquire before submitting" avg. press run 300-500. Expects 2 titles 1991, 2 titles 1992. 1 title listed in the *Small Press Record of Books in Print* (20th Edition, 1991-92). avg. price, paper: $2.50. Discounts: 40% trade. 32pp; 5½×8½; of, photocopy. Reporting time: 3 weeks, sometimes longer during academic vacations. Payment: 25 copies. Copyrights for author.

NAMBLA BULLETIN, Bill Andriette, Renato Corazza, Box 174, Midtown Station, New York, NY 10018, 212-807-8578. 1980. Poetry, fiction, articles, art, photos, cartoons, interviews, satire, criticism, reviews, letters, parts-of-novels, collages, news items, non-fiction. circ. 1.4M. 10/yr. Pub'd 10 issues 1990; expects 10 issues 1991, 10 issues 1992. sub. price: $25; per copy: $3; sample: $1. Back issues: $2.50-$3. Discounts: 50%. 24pp; 8½×11; of. Payment: none. Not copyrighted. Pub's reviews: 5 in 1990. §Gay, youth liberation, Paedophilia. GLPA, IGLA.

Name That Team!, Mike Lessiter, PO Box 624, Brookfield, WI 53008-0624. 1981. avg. press run 3M-10M. Pub'd 3 titles 1990; expects 2 titles 1991, 2 titles 1992. 1 title listed in the *Small Press Record of Books in Print* (20th Edition, 1991-92). avg. price, paper: $5.95-$20.95. Discounts: 40%. 100-360pp; 5½×8, 8½×11; of. Reporting time: 30 days. Copyrights for author.

Nancy Renfro Studios, Inc., Nancy Renfro, PO Box 164226, Austin, TX 78716, 1-800-933-5512; 572-327-9588. 1978. Art. "Emphasis on puppet educational media books." avg. press run 1.5M. Pub'd 2 titles 1990. 10 titles listed in the *Small Press Record of Books in Print* (20th Edition, 1991-92). avg. price, cloth: $16.95; paper: $13.95. Discounts: 1-4 books 20%; 5+ 40%. 150pp; 8½×11; †of. Reporting time: 2 weeks.

Payment: 10%. Copyrights for author.

NANCY'S MAGAZINE, Nancy Bonnell-Kangas, N's M Publications, PO Box 02108, Columbus, OH 43202, 614-294-7935. 1983. Poetry, articles, art, photos, cartoons, interviews, criticism, reviews, music, letters, plays, non-fiction. "An exuberant variety magazine with an emphasis on literature and graphics. Issues are broadly thematic. Poetry, recipes, survey results, histories, scientific diagrams, and social advice included. ISSN 0895-7576" circ. 1M. 1/yr. Pub'd 1 issue 1990; expects 1 issue 1991, 2 issues 1992. sub. price: $2; per copy: $2; sample: $2. Back issues: no special price. 36pp; 7×8½; †of. Reporting time: 1 month. Payment: copies. Copyrighted, reverts to author. Pub's reviews: 1 in 1990. §Fiction, music, American studies, comics, film. Ads: $20/$10/$5 1/4 page.

Nanny Goat Productions, Joyce Farmer, Box 845, Laguna Beach, CA 92652, (714) 494-7930. 1972. Cartoons, satire. "*Tits & Clits* and *Pandora's Box* are comic books dealing primarily with female sexuality in a humorous way. *Tits & Clits* is a series of 7 books, *Abortion Eve* is an educational comic dealing with pros/cons of abortion - age 14 to adult." avg. press run 10M-20M. Pub'd 1 title 1990; expects 1 title 1991. 1 title listed in the *Small Press Record of Books in Print* (20th Edition, 1991-92). avg. price, paper: $2.50. Discounts: 10% sales over $25. 36pp; 7×10; of. Reporting time: 3 weeks. Payment: 10% of cover x print run divided by 40, print on publication. Does not copyright for author.

NAR Publications (see also INVESTMENT COLUMN QUARTERLY (newsletter)), Nicholas A. Roes, Ed Guild, PO Box 233, Barryville, NY 12719, 914-557-8713. 1977. Articles, criticism, reviews, news items. "We publish educational, consumer, and general interest books. Titles have been plugged on Nat'l (Network) TV, wire services, radio, etc. Only 5 titles chosen yearly but given well co-ordinated PR campaign." avg. press run 5M. Pub'd 2 titles 1990; expects 3 titles 1991, 5 titles 1992. 8 titles listed in the *Small Press Record of Books in Print* (20th Edition, 1991-92). avg. price, paper: $9.95. Discounts: 25% library, classroom; 40% bookstore; special requests considered. 125pp; 5×7; of. Reporting time: 3 months. Payment: by arrangement. Copyrights for author.

National Council for Research on Women (see also WOMEN'S RESEARCH NETWORK NEWS), Paulette Tulloch, Sara D. Roosevelt Memorial House, 47-49 East 65th Street, New York, NY 10021, 212-570-5001. 1981. "The National Council for Research on Women is a coalition of over sixty member centers and organizations that support and conduct feminist research, policy analysis, and educational programs. Formed in 1981 as a working alliance to bridge traditional distinctions among scholarship, policy, and action programs, the Council works to strengthen ties with other national and international organizations and coalitions. Through its member centers, affiliates, and sponsored projects, the Council links over 10,000 women and men scholars and practitioners in this country and abroad and serves constituencies that include the academic community, public policy makers, and the public." 5 titles listed in the *Small Press Record of Books in Print* (20th Edition, 1991-92). Discounts: 3-5 20%, 5-10 25%, over 10 30%.

National Council of Teachers of English (see also COLLEGE ENGLISH), James C. Raymond, Drawer AL, University of Alabama, University, AL 35486, 205-348-6488. 1939. Poetry, articles, criticism, reviews, letters. avg. press run 16M. Pub'd 8 titles 1990; expects 8 titles 1991, 8 titles 1992. avg. price, paper: $4. 100pp; 7½×9½; of. Reporting time: 12 weeks. Copyrights for author.

THE NATIONAL FARM DIRECTORY, Jefferson J. Quade, PO Box 1574, Fort Dodge, IA 50501, 515-955-2488. 1990. Articles, photos, news items, non-fiction. 12/yr. Expects 11 issues 1991, 12 issues 1992. sub. price: $18; per copy: $2.50; sample: free. Back issues: $2.50. Discounts: none. 30pp; 8½×11; †of. Copyrighted, does not revert to author. Ads: $405/$203/$20 classifieds (25 words or less).

NATIONAL HOME BUSINESS REPORT, Barbara Brabec, Editor & Publisher, PO Box 2137, Naperville, IL 60567. 1981. "Contributions of information and articles from readers. One year subscription and publicity 'tag line' offered for articles." circ. 2.5M. 4/yr. Pub'd 4 issues 1990; expects 4 issues 1991, 4 issues 1992. sub. price: $18 US, $22 foreign US funds; per copy: $5; sample: $5. Back issues: $5 for current year's issues only, while supplies last. 28pp; 6×9; of. Payment: none. Copyrighted, reverts to author. Pub's reviews: 36+ in 1990. §Home business, crafts marketing, time management, business management, etc. Ads: 30¢ classified.

National Lilac Publishing Co., Robert Perkins, 295 Sharpe Road, Anacortes, WA 98221-9729. 1985. "Non-Fiction - juvenile. National Lilac's slogan is, 'Dedicated to Children's Health, Success and Happiness' We publish positive nonfiction books for children on sports, nutrition, fitness, and positive thinking. Much is produced in-house. We will have Langley, WA address by 9-'87" avg. press run 10M. Expects 4 titles 1991, 4 titles 1992. 1 title listed in the *Small Press Record of Books in Print* (20th Edition, 1991-92). avg. price, cloth: $9; paper: $4.50. Discounts: 50% established wholesalers, up to 40% retail stores, up to 30% libraries. 100pp; 5½×8½; of. Reporting time: 6 weeks. Payment: varies. Copyrights for author. SCBW (Society of Children's Book Writers).

NATIONAL MASTERS NEWS, Gain Publications, Al Sheahen, Editor, PO Box 2372, Van Nuys, CA

91404, 818-785-1895. 1977. Articles, art, photos, interviews, satire, criticism, reviews, letters, news items, non-fiction. "The *National Masters News* is the bible of the Masters Athletics Program. It is the only national publication devoted exclusively to track & field, race walking and long distance running for men and women over age 30. An official publication of the Athletics Congress, each month it delivers 24-40 pages of results, schedules, entry blanks, age records, rankings, photos, articles, training tips. Columns are about 1M words; anything of interest to over-age-30 performer/individual. Recent contributors: Mike Tymn, Hal Higdon, Dr. John Pagliano." circ. 6M. 12/yr. Pub'd 12 issues 1990; expects 12 issues 1991, 12 issues 1992. sub. price: $22; per copy: $2.50. Back issues: $2.50 plus 50¢ for each order. 40pp; 10×13. Reporting time: 15-30 days. Payment: $0 to $25. Not copyrighted. Pub's reviews: 3 in 1990. §Athletics for over-age-30 performer. Ads: $460/$300/75¢. TAFWA.

National Poetry Association Publishers (see also POETRY: USA QUARTERLY), Herman Berlandt, Editor; Vernon Edgar, Publisher, Fort Mason Center, Building D, San Francisco, CA 94123, 415-776-6602. 1985. Poetry. "The National Poetry Association is primarily a literary presenting organization, with weekly programs and the annual National Poetry Week Festival and Poetry-Film Festival. We are, however, occasional book publishers. Our last title was *Peace or Perish: A Crisis Anthology* (1983) with over 80 poets represented, including Creeley, Bly, Everson, Levertov, Kaufman, McClure, Mueller, etc. The anthology was edited by Neeli Cherkovski and Herman Berlandt. A forthcoming new title will be *The Living Word: A Tribute Anthology* of poets, writers and artists who have died of AIDS. Edited by Jeffrey Lilly, this anthology is *still inviting submissions* of work by poets, writers, artists who have died of AIDS. Friends of poets who have died are encouraged to send 3-5 poems for this memorial anthology. Planned for 1990-91 are a series of limited edition chapbooks. No submissions please. The Chapbook series is by invitation only." avg. press run 1M. Expects 1 title 1991, 4 titles 1992. avg. price, cloth: $10; paper: $5. Discounts: 50%. 124pp; 5½×8½; of, perfect bound. Payment: 2 copies. Does not copyright for author. PEN.

National Poetry Foundation (see also PAUSE), Johnathon Clifford, Helen Robinson, 27 Mill Road, Fareham, Hampshire PO 16 OTH, England, 0329-822218. 1981. Poetry. "We publish books of high quality poetry at no charge to the poet. Resident in the U.K. Registered charity #283032. We also give grants to deserving causes." avg. press run 800. Pub'd 15 titles 1990; expects 25 titles 1991. 8 titles listed in the *Small Press Record of Books in Print* (20th Edition, 1991-92). avg. price, paper: $10. Discounts: 25%. 44pp; size A5; of. Reporting time: by return. Payment: none. Copyrights for author.

National Publishers (see also THE UNEXPLAINED), Hank Krastman, PO Box 16790, Encino, CA 91416. 1960. Articles, photos, non-fiction. avg. press run 10M. Pub'd 6 titles 1990; expects 4 titles 1991. Discounts: 40%. 350pp; 5×8; of. Reporting time: 30 days. Payment: open. Copyrights for author.

National Stereoscopic Association (see also STEREO WORLD), John Dennis, Box 14801, Columbus, OH 43214, 614-263-4296. 1974. Articles, art, photos, cartoons, interviews, criticism, reviews, letters, news items, non-fiction. avg. press run 2.9M. 1 title listed in the *Small Press Record of Books in Print* (20th Edition, 1991-92).

NATURALLY, Bernard J. Loibl, PO Box 203, Pequannock, NJ 07440. Poetry, fiction, articles, art, photos, cartoons, interviews, reviews, news items, non-fiction. "*Naturally* focuses principally on international nudism and naturism—it is a color magazine that includes many ideological articles on this subject." circ. 6M. 4/yr. Pub'd 4 issues 1990; expects 4 issues 1991, 4 issues 1992. sub. price: $18; per copy: $5; sample: $6.50. Back issues: $15 per 4 issues. Discounts: 50% for quantities over 50, 40% for 4-49. 40pp; 8½×11; of. Reporting time: 6 weeks. Payment: negotiable. Copyrighted, reverts to author. Pub's reviews: 12 in 1990. §Books that express or mention body awareness. Ads: $200/$130.

NATURALLY YOURS, Backwoods Books, Marci Cunningham, McClellan Lane, PO Box 9, Gibbon Glade, PA 15440, 412-329-4581. 4/yr. Pub'd 4 issues 1990; expects 4 issues 1991, 4 issues 1992. sub. price: $10. Reporting time: 2 weeks.

NATURE SOCIETY NEWS, Harry Wright, Purple Martin Junction, Griggsville, IL 62340, (217) 833-2323. 1966. 12/yr. Pub'd 12 issues 1990; expects 12 issues 1991, 12 issues 1992. sub. price: $12, $17 US funds in Canada; sample: no charge. Discounts: 40% to agencies and catalogs. 24pp; 61×15½. Payment: only to regular staff contributors. Copyrighted, reverts to author. Pub's reviews: 24 in 1990. §Birds, nature (special emphasis: home-related; easter North America). No ads.

Naturegraph Publishers, Inc., Barbara Brown, Editor, PO Box 1075, Happy Camp, CA 96039, 916-493-5353. 1946. Non-fiction. "Our list includes natural history, Native American studies, gardening, health, and new age publications. Now looking at mss. on holistic learning." avg. press run 4M. Pub'd 3 titles 1990; expects 6 titles 1991, 6 titles 1992. 97 titles listed in the *Small Press Record of Books in Print* (20th Edition, 1991-92). avg. price, cloth: $14.95; paper: $7.95. Discounts: 1-4 20%, 5-24 40%, 25-49 42%, 50-99 43%, 100-249 44%, 250-499 45%, 500 & up 46%. 160pp; 5½×8½, 4¼×7¼, 8½×11; †of. Reporting time: 1-8 weeks. Payment: royalties. Copyrights for author. COSMEP, HUENEFELD.

Naturist Foundation (see also THE GROVE), Editorial Committee, Naturist Headquarters, Sheepcote, Orpington, BR5 4ET, England. 1950. Articles, photos, cartoons, letters, news items, non-fiction. "House Journal of Naturist Foundation and Sun Societies; international circulation to naturists. News and reports of interest to naturists are welcome." avg. press run 800. 1 title listed in the *Small Press Record of Books in Print* (20th Edition, 1991-92). avg. price, paper: £3.50 ($7) for single copies. Discounts: none. 24pp; 9½×7½; lp. Reporting time: 1 month. Payment: none. Copyrights for author. none.

The Nautical & Aviation Publishing Co. of American, Inc., Jan Snouck-Hurgronje, Publisher, 101 W. Read St., Suite 314, Baltimore, MD 21201, 301-659-0220. 1979. Non-fiction. "N & A's publishing program makes available high quality books that are genuinely needed in the military market. The books must be significant contributions to the literature and have popular appeal to gain the widest possible audience, which consists of the military and other people professionally concerned with defense affairs as well as readers of aviation, nautical, and military books who possess no specialized knowledge." avg. press run 4M. Pub'd 6 titles 1990; expects 8 titles 1991, 10 titles 1992. 1 title listed in the *Small Press Record of Books in Print* (20th Edition, 1991-92). avg. price, cloth: $24.95; paper: $15.50. Discounts: wholesale: 2-10 of same title = 40%, 11 or more of same title = 50%; trade: 1=20%, 2-10=40%, 11-20=41%, 21-30=42%, 31-40=43%, 41-50=44%, 51+=45%. 200pp; 6×9; of. Reporting time: 1 month. Payment: 15% of net receipts. Copyrights for author. Baltimore Publisher's Assoc.

Nautical Brass (see also NAUTICAL BRASS), Bill Momsen, PO Box 3966, N. Fort Myers, FL 33918-3966. 1981.

NAUTICAL BRASS, Nautical Brass, Bill Momsen, PO Box 3966, Fort Myers, FL 33918-3966. 1981. Photos, interviews, non-fiction. "Covers maritime history, collecting, restoring & identifying nautical antiques and collectibles, anything of interest concerning ships, maritime disasters, how devices are used aboard ships, developmental history of the devices, treasure and salvage. Any length from short articles to serialized installments" circ. 1.5M. 6/yr. Pub'd 6 issues 1990; expects 6 issues 1991, 6 issues 1992. sub. price: $36 1st class, $30, $46 overseas air; per copy: $5; sample: free to prospective authors. Back issues: $5 each (subject to availability). Discounts: 40%. 24pp; 8½×11; of. Reporting time: 1 month. Payment: negotiable. Copyrighted, reverts to author. Pub's reviews: 13 in 1990. §Nautical antiques, maritime history, marine salvage, restoration. Ads: $250/$125/25¢.

THE NAUTILUS, M.G. Harasewych, PO Box 7279, Silver Spring, MD 20907-7279. 1886. Articles, non-fiction. "Original scientific research in malacology (mollusks). Now in volume 102 (1988)" circ. 800. 4/yr. Pub'd 4 issues 1990; expects 4 issues 1991, 4 issues 1992. sub. price: $25 (individuals), $35 (institutions), foreign postage $3; per copy: $5; sample: $5. Discounts: 10% to agents on institutional rate ($30 per year). Cost to agent $27. 50pp; 8½×11; of. Reporting time: 9 months. Payment: charge page-charges, $55/page. Not copyrighted. Pub's reviews: 4 in 1990. §Only on mollusks.

NBM Publishing Company, Terry Nantier, 185 Madison Avenue #1502, New York, NY 10016, 212-545-1223; fax 212-545-1227. 1976. Cartoons. "We publish *graphic novels* high-quality *comics* in book form." avg. press run 5M. Pub'd 17 titles 1990; expects 18 titles 1991, 20 titles 1992. 63 titles listed in the *Small Press Record of Books in Print* (20th Edition, 1991-92). avg. price, cloth: $32.50; paper: $8.95. Discounts: 50% returnable 1 year; 60% non-returnable. Retail: 45% returnable 1 year; 50% non-returnable. 80pp; 8½×11; of. Reporting time: 2-4 weeks. Payment: 8-12% of sales (retail). Copyrights for author.

N-B-T-V, D.B. Pitt, Narrow Bandwidth Television Association, 1 Burnwood Dr., Wollaton, Nottingham, Notts NG8 2DJ, England, 0602-282896. 1975. Articles, photos, cartoons, interviews, criticism, reviews, letters, news items, non-fiction. "Normal maximum length of article 1M words. Longer articles would be serialised. Bias is towards projects on a low budget which readers can carry out at home/school/college etc." circ. 200. 4/yr. Pub'd 4 issues 1990; expects 4 issues 1991, 4 issues 1992. sub. price: £4; per copy: £1; sample: 75p (Annual sub - £4 to non-earners). Back issues: bound volumes II + III (one book) £3. Discounts: under review, please inquire. 13pp; size A4; xerography. Reporting time: 1 week. Payment: none. Copyrighted, copyright normally held on behalf of author but negotiable. Pub's reviews: 3 in 1990. §Television, hobby electronics, history of television (in English, Dutch, German, or French). Ads: £10/£6/small ads free to subscribers, otherwise negotiable.

NEBO, B.C Hall, Fiction; Paul Lake, Poetry; M.K. Ritchie, Non-Fiction & Translations, Department of English, Arkansas Tech University, Russellville, AR 72801, 501-968-0256. 1982. Poetry, fiction, articles, art, criticism, reviews, long-poems, non-fiction. "We are interested in quality poetry and fiction by both new and established writers. In fiction we are open to a wide range of styles. We seek poems whose rhythms are as compelling and memorable as their diction and images, and as a result we print a large number of formal poems (poems using meter and rhyme). We have published poems by Howard Nemerov, Timothy Steele, Julia Randall, Dana Gioia, Brenda Hillman, Turner Cassity, R. L. Barth, and many other excellent poets, many previously unknown to us. In addition, we are interested in well-written reviews and criticism of English

372

language poetry. We encourage poetic translations from contemporary writers and personal essays about travel in other parts of the world." circ. 300. 1-2/yr. Pub'd 1 issue 1990; expects 2 issues 1991, 2 issues 1992. sub. price: $5; per copy: $5; sample: $5. Back issues: $2. 48-60pp; 5×8; of. Reporting time: 2 weeks to 4 months. Payment: 1 copy. Copyrighted, reverts to author. Pub's reviews: 6 in 1990. §Poetry, fiction, literature in translation. Ads: $75/$45.

THE NEBRASKA REVIEW, Art Homer, Richard Duggin, ASH 215, University of Nebraska-Omaha, Omaha, NE 68182-0324. 1972. Poetry, fiction, reviews. "Dedicated to the best contemporary fiction and poetry. Previous contributors include Malcolm Glass, Michelle Herman, David Hopes, Mindy Kronenberg, Richard Robbins, Stephen Dixon, Don Welch, Luke Whisnat, Peter Wild. Prefer fiction and poetry which shows control of form and an ear for language, and which transcends mere competence in technique. Closed April 1 - August 30." circ. 300-500. 2/yr. Pub'd 2 issues 1990; expects 2 issues 1991, 2 issues 1992. sub. price: $6, $10/2 yrs; per copy: $3.50; sample: $2.50. Discounts: bookstores 60/40, distributors 50/50. 64pp; 6×9; of. Reporting time: 3 months. Payment: 2 copies and 1 yr subscription. Copyrighted, reverts to author. §Poetry and fiction. Ads: $50/$30. CCLM.

NEEDLEPOINT PLUS, EGW Publishing Company, Judy Swager, PO Box 5967, Concord, CA 94524, 415-671-9852. 1974. Poetry, art, photos, interviews, reviews, letters, non-fiction. *"Needlepoint Plus* is geared to all levels of needlepointers. It is a collection of original projects by (often well-known) designers, with graphs, stitch diagrams, step-by-step instructions and photos. Technical articles of various needlepoint techniques and uses of fabrics and materials are included, along with book reviews, new products on the market, tips and gift ideas. Focus on developing one's skills, expanding options in the field of needlepoint, enhancing creativity. Recent contributors: Vima Michelli, Shay Pendray, Marnie Ritter. Maggie Lane project featured on July/Augst 1986 cover. Project article can run up to four pages" circ. 30M. 6/yr. Pub'd 6 issues 1990; expects 6 issues 1991, 6 issues 1992. sub. price: $15; per copy: $2.95; sample: $2.95. 40pp; 8⅛×10⅞; of, web. Reporting time: 2-8 weeks. Payment: upon publication; first serial rights. Ads: $825 b/w/95¢ word.

NEGATIVE, Dan Janssen, 4508 Stone Crest Drive, Ellicott, MD 21043. 1991. Poetry, articles, art, reviews. circ. 20. 6/yr. Expects 4 issues 1991, 6 issues 1992. sub. price: $6; per copy: $1; sample: $1. 13pp; 8½×11; †copied. Payment: none. Not copyrighted. Pub's reviews. §Anarchy, art, animal rights, ani-American government. Ads: 3x3" $1.

NEGATIVE CAPABILITY, Negative Capability Press, Sue Walker, Editor; Ron Walker, Assistant Editor, 62 Ridgelawn Drive East, Mobile, AL 36608, 205-460-6146. 1981. Poetry, fiction, articles, art, photos, cartoons, interviews, satire, criticism, reviews, letters, long-poems, collages, news items, non-fiction. "Our only qualification is excellence. We publish poets who are established and hope to help establish those who are less well known but deserve to be known better. We welcome new talent, have no particular biases, but want poems which communicate, poems that remain in readers' minds when the poem is no longer before them." circ. 1M. 3/yr. Pub'd 3 issues 1990; expects 3 issues 1991, 3 issues 1992. sub. price: $12; per copy: $4; sample: $5. Discounts: 40% jobber. 184pp; 5½×8½; of. Reporting time: 6 weeks. Payment: 2 copies of publication. Copyrighted, reverts to author. Pub's reviews: 8 in 1990. §Poetry, fiction, non-fiction. Ads: $50/$25/10¢ a word. COSMEP, CCLM.

Negative Capability Press (see also NEGATIVE CAPABILITY), Sue Walker, Chief Editor; Ron Walker, Assistant Editor, 62 Ridgelawn Drive East, Mobile, AL 36608, 205-460-6146. 1981. Poetry, criticism. avg. press run 1M. Expects 3 titles 1991, 3 titles 1992. 9 titles listed in the *Small Press Record of Books in Print* (20th Edition, 1991-92). avg. price, paper: $5; other: $12 hardcover. Discounts: 40% jobber. 100pp; 6×9; of. Reporting time: 6 weeks. Copyrights for author.

The Neither/Nor Press, Denis McBee, Jock Henderson, Box 7774, Ann Arbor, MI 48107. 1980. Fiction, articles, art, photos, cartoons, interviews, satire, criticism, reviews, letters, collages, non-fiction. "Recent contributors include Gerry Reith, Bob Black, Ed Lawrence, Gregory Altreuter, John Meyer, and Mike Kazaleh. We are publishers of *jackass outlaw intellectualism, reading our books is like taking grit from the grindstone and putting it upside your head"* avg. press run 1M. Pub'd 1 title 1990; expects 3 titles 1991, 3 titles 1992. 4 titles listed in the *Small Press Record of Books in Print* (20th Edition, 1991-92). avg. price, paper: $5; other: $2. Discounts: 40% dealer, 50% or more to distributors. 100pp; size varies; of, xerox. Reporting time: 3 months. Payment: copies and/or subscriptions. Copyrights for author. CCLM, PRC of Michigan, Sub-Genius Foundation.

Nemeton Publishing (see also X-CALIBRE), Juli Taylor, Ken Taylor, PO Box 780, Bristol, BS99 5BB, United Kingdom, +44-272-715144. 1985. Poetry, art. "Nemeton Publishing is a bridge linking authors and artists on the one side with as wide an appreciative audience as possible on the other. *X-Calibre* poetry anthology carries more than 60 creative people across that physical divide on an annual basis. Authors of longer works are advised to send synopsis + examples (+IRC) initially. We have recently completed a major review of policy resulting in a complete overhaul of our operations." avg. press run 500. Pub'd 1 title 1990; expects 1 title 1992. 4 titles listed in the *Small Press Record of Books in Print* (20th Edition, 1991-92). avg. price, paper: £3. Discounts: by negotiation. 112pp; 5¾x8¼; of. Reporting time: 1 month. Payment: minimum 7.5% cover price paid on sales per 6 months. Copyrights for author.

The Nemo Press, Todd Illig, Ken Keller, 5119 Leavenworth Street, Omaha, NE 68106, 402-342-1545. 1983. Fiction, art, satire, letters, non-fiction. "We prefer to see manuscripts or project proposals from writers familiar with our specialty, or who are published professionals within our field. Editorial inquiries should be sent to our Kansas City office: The Nemo Press, 1131 White Avenue, Kansas City, MO 64126. We have published both short and long manuscripts, so our manuscript guidelines are rather broad: 30,000 words to 500,000 words. In other words, no project is too small or too large. We will look at multiple submissions from unagented writers, but be aware that our publishing schedules are usually booked solid most of the time, being a low-volume small press" avg. press run 500-5M. Pub'd 1 title 1990; expects 3 titles 1991, 4 titles 1992. avg. price, cloth: $19.95; other: deluxe/signed—2x trade price. Discounts: 1-4 copies 20%, 5-99 40%, 100+ 50%, deluxe/signed copies 20%, 30% and 40% as noted. 256pp; 6x9; of. Reporting time: 6-8 weeks. Payment: 10% of retail cover price on first 5,000 copies; royalty payments twice yearly. Copyrights for author.

NET, Polymath Systems, Kevin Langdon, PO Box 795, Berkeley, CA 94701, 415-524-0345. 1979. Articles, art, reviews, letters, non-fiction. "Articles up to 10 manuscript pages (20 in exceptional cases, serialized). We are looking for serious, thoughtful, original work in our fields of interest. Absolutely no humor, poetry, fiction, politics, or positive thinking. In addition to the types of material listed above, we print games and psychological tests (I.Q., vocabulary, etc)" circ. 5M. 4/yr. Expects 3 issues 1991, 4 issues 1992. sub. price: $10; per copy: $3; sample: same. Back issues: $2 (#1 $3). Discounts: based on size of order only: $20-10%, $50-15%, $100-20%, $200-25%, $500-30%, $1000-35%, etc. 52pp; 5½x8½; of. Reporting time: variable. Payment: none. Copyrighted, copyright by author or assigned to author on request. Pub's reviews. §Philosophy, psychology, psychometrics, religion, astronomy and space, games, computers, drugs, cults. No ads.

NETWORK, Tatiana Stoumen, Editor, Box 810, Gracie Station, New York, NY 10028, 212-737-7536. 1976. Interviews, reviews, news items. circ. 3M. 6/yr. Pub'd 6 issues 1990; expects 6 issues 1991, 6 issues 1992. sub. price: $35 with membership in IWWG, $45 foreign; sample: free. 28pp; 8½x11; of. Pub's reviews: 3 in 1990. Ads: $150 1/2 page/$100 1/4 page/$50 1/8 page.

NETWORK AFRICA FOR TODAY'S WORLD CITIZEN, Shirley Ademu-John, Editor; Ekundayo Ademu-John, Associate Editor, Pratt Station, PO Box 81, Brooklyn, NY 11205. 1982. Poetry, fiction, articles, art, photos, cartoons, interviews, reviews, music, letters, plays, news items, non-fiction. "Length of articles should be 750 to 1500 words, typed doubled spaced and sent in duplicate with a stamped self-addressed envelope." circ. 10.5M. 4/yr. Pub'd 4 issues 1990; expects 4 issues 1991, 4 issues 1992. sub. price: $16; per copy: $2.50; sample: $2.50. Back issues: $3. Discounts: Price quotes given upon inquiry. 36pp; 8½x11; †of. Reporting time: 2 months before next publication date. Payment: $30 - $100 depending on length and type of work submitted. Copyrighted, reverts to author. Pub's reviews: 4 in 1990. §Cross-cultural experiences, African studies, Caribbean studies, Black America experiences, novels, works encouraging cross-cultural understanding and communication. Ads: $250/$175/inside cover $300, back cover $375.

Network Publications, a division of ETR Associates (see also FAMILY LIFE EDUCATOR), Mary Nelson, Editorial Director, PO Box 1830, Santa Cruz, CA 95061, 408-438-4060. 1981. Non-fiction. Pub'd 25 titles 1990; expects 25 titles 1991. PMA, PGW.

Nevada Publications, Stanley W. Paher, 4135 Badger Circle, Reno, NV 89509, 702-747-0800. 1970. Poetry, articles, art, photos, cartoons. "We generally seek out the author, and do not solicit manuscripts. We publish books on Nevada, California and Arizona, mostly historic guides to scenic areas and ghost towns. All are lavishly illustrated and are solidly based in orginal research and are substantially edited." avg. press run 4M. Pub'd 9 titles 1990; expects 13 titles 1991, 9 titles 1992. 19 titles listed in the *Small Press Record of Books in Print* (20th Edition, 1991-92). avg. price, cloth: $20; paper: $9. Discounts: please inquire. Cloth 196pp, paper 48pp; 9x12, 8½x11; of. Payment: 10% 1st edition; subsequent editions negotiable. Will possibly copyright for author.

NEW AGE DIGEST, New Age Press, Jim Butler, New Age Press, PO Box 1373, Keala Kekua, HI 96750, 808-328-8013. 1983. Poetry, articles, satire, news items, non-fiction. "Always open to exchange." circ. 300-500. Irregular. Pub'd 5 issues 1990; expects 1-2 issues 1991. sub. price: donation, exchange; per copy: gratis; sample: gratis. Back issues: donations and contribution and exchange; please specify. Discounts: by arrangement. 14pp; 5x8½; †mi, of. Reporting time: varies. Payment: in copies. Not copyrighted. No ads.

New Age Press (see also NEW AGE DIGEST), Jim Butler, Editor; Michele Navone, Poetry Editor, PO Box 2089, Keala Kekua, HI 96750, 808-328-8031. 1982. Poetry, fiction, articles, satire, letters, non-fiction. avg. press run 50-500. Pub'd 6 titles 1990; expects 6 titles 1991, 6 titles 1992. 2 titles listed in the *Small Press Record of Books in Print* (20th Edition, 1991-92). avg. price, cloth: by arrangement; paper: same; other: same. Discounts: by arrangement. 16-100pp; 6x8, 9x11; †of, photocopy. Reporting time: ASAP. Payment: by

374

arrangement. Does not copyright for author.

THE NEW AMERICAN, Gary Benoit, PO Box 8040, Appleton, WI 54913, 414-749-3784. 1985. Articles, photos, cartoons, interviews, criticism, reviews, news items, non-fiction. *"The New American* is a conservative, anti-Communist biweekly. Article lengths range from 1,000 to 10,000 words. Most articles are staff-written, but all freelance material is carefully considered. Queries recommended." circ. 35M. 26/yr. Pub'd 26 issues 1990; expects 26 issues 1991, 26 issues 1992. sub. price: $39; per copy: $2; sample: $2. Back issues: $2 each + 15% ($2 minimum) p&h. Discounts: 55% bulk, 47.5% agent. 48pp; 8⅛×10¾. Reporting time: 90 days. Payment: 10¢ a word. Copyrighted, rights reverting is negotiable. Pub's reviews: 15 in 1990. §Politics, diplomacy, history, sociology, literature and arts. Ads: $1,460/$900.

NEW AMERICAN WRITING, Paul Hoover, Maxine Chernoff, 2920 West Pratt, Chicago, IL 60645. 1971. Poetry, fiction, art, criticism, reviews. "Work by Ann Lauterbach, Kenward Elmslie, Robert Coover, John Ashbery, Charles Bernstein, Charles Simic, Lyn Hejinian, Clark Coolidge, James Laughlin, Ned Rorem, Robert Creeley and others. Special issues: #4 Australian poetry; #5, Censorship and the arts. Covers by prominent artists." circ. 2M. 2/yr. Pub'd 2 issues 1990; expects 2 issues 1991, 2 issues 1992. sub. price: $12 domestic, $16 foreign; per copy: $6 domestic, $8 foreign; sample: $6. Back issues: varies, please inquire. Discounts: 60/40 to bookstores. 150pp; 5½×8½; of. Reporting time: 1-3 months. Payment: 2 copies, $5-$10 page. Copyrighted, reverts to author. Pub's reviews: 1 in 1990. §Poetry. Ads: $100. CCLM.

NEW ANGLICAN REVIEW, The Dayspring Press, Inc., John C. Brainerd, 18600 West 58 Avenue, Golden, CO 80403-1070, 303-279-2462. 1983. Poetry, fiction, articles, art, photos, cartoons, interviews, satire, criticism, reviews, music, letters, parts-of-novels, long-poems, collages, plays, concrete art, non-fiction. circ. 980. 12/yr. Pub'd 12 issues 1990; expects 12 issues 1991, 12 issues 1992. sub. price: $12; per copy: $2; sample: $2. Back issues: $2. Discounts: 1/3 over 15 copies. 60pp; 5½×8½; †of. Reporting time: 1-4 weeks. Copyrighted, rights reverting is negotiable. Pub's reviews: 10 in 1990. §Theology, philosophy, history, education. Ads: $35/$15.

NEW ART EXAMINER, Derek Guthrie, Publisher, 1255 South Wabash Avenue #4, Chicago, IL 60605-2427, 312-836-0330. 1973. Articles, art, interviews, criticism, reviews, letters, news items. "Commentary on and analysis of the exhibition and making of the visual arts." circ. 20M. 11/yr. Pub'd 11 issues 1990; expects 11 issues 1991, 11 issues 1992. sub. price: $29, $50/2 years; per copy: $3.95. Back issues: $3.95 each. Discounts: 3x, 6x, 11x rates. 56pp; 8¼×10⅞; web. Reporting time: 2 months. Payment: $35 word reviews, $40-$300 article. Copyrighted, does not revert to author. Pub's reviews: 20 in 1990. §Visual arts and architecture. Ads: $735 b&w, $1285 4-color/$410 b&w, $960 4-color/45¢.

New Atlantis Press, Edward P. Stevenson, 473 Pavonia Avenue, Jersey City, NJ 07306, 201-653-8221. 1985. "NAP will remain in the one-title category for at least another year. When that status changes, we will keep the Record and the Directory informed. However, we are interested in reviewing mss. dealing with issues of social change (non-fiction) in anticipation of our expansion" avg. press run 2M. Pub'd 1 title 1990; expects 1 title 1992. avg. price, paper: $15. Discounts: 2-4 20%, 5-24 40%, 25-49 43%, 50-99 45%, 100+ 50%. 352pp; 6×9. Reporting time: 60 days. Copyrights for author.

NEW BOOKS ON WOMEN & FEMINISM, Women's Studies Librarian, University of Wisconsin System, Susan Searing, Carolyn Wilson, 112A Memorial Library, 728 State Street, Madison, WI 53706, 608-263-5754. 1979. "A subject-arranged, indexed bibliography of new titles in women's studies, listing books and periodicals." circ. 1.1M. 2/yr. Pub'd 2 issues 1990; expects 2 issues 1991, 2 issues 1992. sub. price: $23 individuals and women's programs, $43 institutions (includes subscriptions to *New Books On Women & Feminism, Feminist Collections,* and *Feminist Periodicals;* sample: $2.75. 75pp; 8½×11; desktop publishing; offset printing. Not copyrighted.

New Broom Private Press (see also PHOENIX BROADSHEETS), 78 Cambridge Street, Leicester, England. 1968. avg. press run 100-120. Pub'd 1 title 1990; expects 3 titles 1991. 2 titles listed in the *Small Press Record of Books in Print* (20th Edition, 1991-92). avg. price, paper: £6. 20pp; 8×5; †lp. Payment: 6 copies. Copyrights for author.

NEW CATHOLIC REVIEW, The Dayspring Press, Inc., John C. Brainerd, 18600 West 58 Avenue, Golden, CO 80403-1070, 303-279-2462. 1983. Poetry, fiction, articles, art, photos, cartoons, interviews, satire, criticism, reviews, music, letters, parts-of-novels, long-poems, collages, plays, concrete art, non-fiction. circ. 980. 12/yr. Pub'd 12 issues 1990; expects 12 issues 1991, 12 issues 1992. sub. price: $12; per copy: $2; sample: $2. Back issues: $2. Discounts: 1/3 over 15 copies. 60pp; 5½×8½; †photo offset. Reporting time: 1-4 weeks. Copyrighted, rights reverting is negotiable. Pub's reviews: 10 in 1990. §Theology, philosophy, history, education. Ads: $35//$5 per inch.

New Chapter Press, Wendy Reid Crisp, Old Pound Road, Pound Ridge, NY 10576, 914-764-4011. 1986. Non-fiction. avg. press run 3.5M-33M. Pub'd 3 titles 1990; expects 3 titles 1991, 3 titles 1992. avg. price, cloth:

$17.95; paper: $9.95; other: mass market $6.95. Discounts: varies. 290pp; size varies; offset standard. Reporting time: 60 days. Payment: contracts vary. Copyrights for author. Publisher's Marketing Assoc.

New Cicada (see also NEW CICADA), Tadao Okazaki, Eric W. Amann, Consulting Editor; Lilli Tanzer, Consulting Editor, 40-11 KUBO, Hobara, Fukushima 960-06, Japan. 1977. Poetry. "Publishes the first and only magazine proposing the universal definition of haiku that is applicable to all languages. The magazine also introduces pronunciation, recitation, metrical analysis, and translation of, and comments on, the poems of major Japanese haiku poets. Maintains that 1) the haiku, in any language, is a triplet poem of 3-4-3 beats, and 2) the 3-4-3 syllable verse is the shortest, and the trimeter-tetrameter-trimeter triplet in general is the longest classical haiku forms in English. Regrets that the editors and publisher are unable to respond to most of the inquiries because of the volume of editorial and production/shipping works, but greatly welcomes opinions, views and suggestions on their publications. Opposes the old definition of haiku as syllabic verse. The publisher has proposed that traditional Japanese haiku is a form of ballad consisting of iambic trimeter-tetrameter-trimeter triplet lines." Pub'd 1 title 1990; expects 1 title 1991. Discounts: 60% per copy for trade or bulk greater than 10 copies. 40pp; 5¾x8¼; of. Reporting time: approximately 6 months. Payment: none. Does not copyright for author.

NEW CICADA, New Cicada, Tadao Okazaki, Eric W. Amann, Consulting Editor; Lilli Tanzer, Consulting Editor, 40-11 KUBO, Hobara, Fukushima 960-06, Japan, 0245-75-4226. 1977. Poetry. "The first and only magazine proposing the universal definition of haiku that is applicable to all languages. Original haiku in English. Pronunciation, recitation, metrical analysis, translations and interpretation of the works of major Japanese haiku poets. Maintains that 1) the haiku, in any language, is a triplet poem of 3-4-3 beats, and 2) the 3-4-3 syllable verse is the shortest, and the trimeter-tetrameter-trimeter triplet in general is the longest classical haiku forms in English. The editor has proposed that haiku, in its classical Japanese form, has iambic rhythm, and should be considered a type of ballad." 2/yr. Pub'd 2 issues 1990; expects 2 issues 1991, 2 issues 1992. sub. price: $6; per copy: $4; sample: $4. Back issues: $4 (volume 2, number 1 no longer available). Discounts: 60% per copy for trade or bulk greater than 10 copies. 40pp; 5¾x8¼; of. Reporting time: approximately 6 months. Payment: none. Copyrighted, reverts to author.

NEW COLLAGE MAGAZINE, New Collage Press, A. McA. Miller, General Editor, 5700 N. Tamiami Trail, Sarasota, FL 34243-2197, 813-359-4360. 1970. Poetry. "We want poetry with clear focus and strong imagery. Would like to see fresh free verse and contemporary slants on traditional prosodies" circ. 500. 3/yr. Pub'd 3 issues 1990; expects 3 issues 1991. sub. price: $9, $17/2 years; per copy: $3; sample: $3. Back issues: all available, $3/issue or $9 volume. Discounts: 60%/40% to dealers. 32pp; 5½x8½; of. Reporting time: 6 weeks. Payment: 2 copies. Copyrighted, reverts to author. Pub's reviews: 2 in 1990. §Poetry, some interviews. No ads. CCLM, COSMEP.

New Collage Press (see also NEW COLLAGE MAGAZINE), A. McA Miller, General Editor, 5700 North Trail, Sarasota, FL 34234, 813-359-4360. 1970. Poetry, reviews. "Must query" avg. press run 500. Pub'd 1 title 1990; expects 1 title 1991. 10 titles listed in the *Small Press Record of Books in Print* (20th Edition, 1991-92). avg. price, paper: $3. Discounts: 60%/40% to dealers. 32pp; 5½x8½; of. Reporting time: 6 weeks. Payment: by negotiation. First N.A. serial rights purchased. CCLM, COSMEP.

NEW CONTRAST, Douglas Reid Skinner, S.A. Literary Journal Ltd, PO Box 3841, Cape Town, 8000, Republic of South Africa, 021-477468. 1960. Poetry, fiction, art, photos, interviews, criticism, reviews, letters, non-fiction. "Length: up to 8,000 words prose maximum. Poems: 200-400 lines maximum" circ. 2M. 4/yr. Pub'd 2 issues 1990; expects 4 issues 1991, 4 issues 1992. sub. price: $24; per copy: R7.50 + postage + FX cost; sample: R7.50 + postage + FX cost. Back issues: R7.50 + FX cost + postage. Discounts: 33% trade. 96pp; 136mm X 212mm; of. Reporting time: 1½ months. Payment: copy of magazine. Copyrighted, reverts to author. Pub's reviews: 15 in 1990. §Poetry, criticism, biography, philosophy, short fiction, cultural essays. Ads: R200.

THE NEW CRITERION, Hilton Kramer, 850 Seventh Avenue, New York, NY 10019. 1982. Poetry, articles, criticism, reviews. circ. 7M. 10/yr. Pub'd 10 issues 1990; expects 10 issues 1991, 10 issues 1992. sub. price: $32; per copy: $4; sample: $4. Back issues: $5. 90pp; 7x10; of. Reporting time: 1 month. Payment: 10¢ per word for articles, $2.50 per line for poetry. Copyrighted, reverts to author. Pub's reviews: approx. 40 in 1990. §Art, architecture, music, poetry, theater. Ads: $650/$350.

THE NEW DANCE REVIEW, Anita Finkel, 32 W. 82nd Street #2F, New York, NY 10024, 212-799-9057. 1988. Articles, interviews, satire, criticism, music. "Long articles: over 3,000 words, no limit." circ. 500. 4/yr. Pub'd 4 issues 1990; expects 4 issues 1991, 4 issues 1992. sub. price: $20; per copy: $5; sample: $5. 24pp; 8½x11; of. Payment: $25+. Copyrighted, reverts to author. Pub's reviews: 3 in 1990. §dance.

NEW DAY PUBLICATIONS, Brenda Davis, Route 4, Box 10, Eupora, MS 39744, 258-2935. 1987. Poetry, fiction, reviews. "Four different titles per year (chapbook form). Main focus is on contests. Entry fee: $3 poetry, $5 short story. Accepts submissions, no purchase required, no reading fee. Guidelines for contests, submissions fee for SASE. Cash prize for all contests: Submissions—payment is contributors copy. Recent contributors: Bob La Loge, Kay Weems, Patty Hoye Ashworth, Brenda Davis, Anthony W. Wilt, Betty Davis Bush'' 4/yr. Expects 4 issues 1991, 4 issues 1992. sub. price: $10; per copy: $3.50; sample: $3.50. Back issues: $3. 50-75pp; 5½×8½. Reporting time: 4-6 weeks. Payment: free contributor's copy. Copyrighted, reverts to author. Pub's reviews. §Would like to review other poetry/short story mags. Ads: $10/$5.

NEW DELTA REVIEW, Kathleen Fitzpatrick, c/o Dept. of English, Louisiana State University, Baton Rouge, LA 70803-5001, 504-388-4079. 1984. Poetry, fiction, art, interviews, non-fiction. "We at *New Delta Review* are most interested in promoting 'new' writers and exploring new directions in poetry and fiction. We have no thematic or stylistic biases; we simply want pieces with raw energy behind them, pieces that make our palms sweat." circ. 200. 2/yr. Pub'd 1 issue 1990; expects 2 issues 1991, 2 issues 1992. sub. price: $7; per copy: $4; sample: $4. Back issues: $3.50 for any issue prior to the current one. 90pp; 6×9; of. Reporting time: 2-4 months. Payment: 2 contributors' copies, 50% discount on extras. Copyrighted, reverts to author. Pub's reviews: 8 in 1990. §Contemporary poetry and fiction, popular culture, works on contemporary authors. CLMP.

NEW DEPARTURES, Michael Horovitz, Piedmont, Bisley, Stroud, Glos., England. 1959. Poetry, articles, art, photos, cartoons, reviews, music, collages, plays, concrete art. "A new issue of the magazine has always been an event readers found worth waiting for. Only issues in print are a bumper celebration double #7 & #8—containing poetry, drawings, photos, collages, music & prose by: David Hockney, Gregory Corso, Ivor Cutler, Heathcote Williams, Samuel Beckett, R. D. Laing, Ted Hughes, Roger McGough, John Cage, Michael Hamburger, Thom Gunn & many more; plus numbers 12, 13, 14, 15, and 16 incl. Burroughs, Ginsberg, John Lennon, Paul Weller et al reinforcing the Poetry Olympics." circ. 5M. Irregular. Expects 2-8 issues 1991. 5 titles listed in the *Small Press Record of Books in Print* (20th Edition, 1991-92). sub. price: £10 or $20 for 2 issues (payment to be made in cash only, no checks); per copy: £3+50 post or $9+$1 post; sample: £3+50 post or $9+$1 post (payment to be made in cash, no checks). Back issues: #7/8 $350, #12 and #14 $30. Discounts: 1/3 to booksellers, agents, distributors. 64pp; size A4; of. Reporting time: varies. Payment: by arrangement. Copyrighted, reverts to author. Pub's reviews: 25 in 1990. §Poetry, art, some music, songs, jazz, any living literature. Ads: £100/pro rata. ALP.

NEW DIRECTIONS FOR WOMEN, Phyllis Kriegel, Editor, 108 West Palisade Avenue, Englewood, NJ 07631, 201-568-0226. 1972. Articles, art, photos, cartoons, interviews, satire, criticism, reviews, letters, collages, news items, non-fiction. "Maximum length 1M words. Must be from a feminist perspective or to help women." circ. 60M. 6/yr. Pub'd 6 issues 1990; expects 6 issues 1991, 6 issues 1992. sub. price: $12 indiv, $20 instit; per copy: $2; sample: $2. Back issues: $3 each. Discounts: $1.15 2-25 copies; $1 each over 25 copies. 28pp; 10×16; of. Reporting time: 2 months. Payment: 3¢ per word. Copyrighted. Pub's reviews: 75 in 1990. §By, for and about women & feminism. Ads: $600/$420/40¢ per word ($9 min). COSMEP.

New Earth Publications, Clifton Ross, PO Box 4790, Berkeley, CA 94704. 1990. Poetry. "Publisher of Latin American poetry anthologies with progressive political slant in bilingual editions. Poets include Nicaraguan (Ernesto Cardenal, Daisy Zamora, etc.), also chapbooks of North American spiritual/political poets (Bob Rivera, William Ruddy, Eugene Warren, Laurie Zimmerman and others). Also some prose, such as the spiritual writings of A.C. Sandino, Nazim Hikmet'' avg. press run varies. Expects 2 titles 1991. 1 title listed in the *Small Press Record of Books in Print* (20th Edition, 1991-92). avg. price, paper: $9.95; other: $3 each or $10 for 4 (chapbooks). Discounts: 60/40. Chapbooks 28-48pp, anthologies 200pp; 8½×5½; †of. Reporting time: up to 3 months. Payment: negotiable. Copyrights for author.

NEW ENGLAND ANTIQUES JOURNAL, Roy Williamson, Turley Publications, 4 Church Street, Ware, MA 01082, 413-967-3505. 1982. Articles, photos, news items. "Feature articles, 1,000-2,000 words and 5-7 b/w photos on antiques. Know the subject you are writing about." circ. 20M. 12/yr. Pub'd 12 issues 1990; expects 12 issues 1991, 12 issues 1992. sub. price: $19.95; per copy: $1.50; sample: free. Discounts: by individual arrangement. 100-120pp; 11×16; †of. Reporting time: 2-6 weeks. Payment: by individual arrangement. Copyrighted, reverts to author. Pub's reviews: 25 in 1990. §Antiques. Ads: $550/$295/15¢ per word ($5 min).

THE NEW ENGLAND QUARTERLY, The New England Quarterly, Inc., William M. Fowler, Jr., Editor; Linda Smith Rhoads, Assoc. Editor, 243 Meserve Hall, Northeastern University, Boston, MA 02115, 617-437-2734. 1928. Articles, criticism, reviews. "*The New England Quarterly*, a Historical Review of New England Life and Letters, publishes articles in the fields of literature, history, art, and culture; short memoranda and documents; and book reviews." circ. 2.3M. 4/yr. Pub'd 4 issues 1990; expects 4 issues 1991, 4 issues 1992. sub. price: $20; per copy: $7. Back issues: $10. 160pp; 6×9; of. Reporting time: 6-8 weeks. Payment: 1-year free subscription. Copyrighted, does not revert to author. Pub's reviews: 50 in 1990. §American literature (with some connection to New England), New England history, art, culture, biography (all with some connection to New England). Ads: $150/$100.

The New England Quarterly, Inc. (see also THE NEW ENGLAND QUARTERLY), William M. Fowler, Jr., Editor; Linda Smith Rhoads, Assoc. Editor, 243 Meserve Hall, Northeastern University, Boston, MA 02115,

617-437-2734. 1928. Articles, criticism, reviews. avg. press run 2.3M. Pub'd 4 titles 1990; expects 4 titles 1991, 4 titles 1992. avg. price, paper: $7. 160pp; 6×9; of. Reporting time: 6-8 weeks. Does not copyright for author.

NEW ENGLAND REVIEW, Middlebury College Publications, T.R. Hummer, Editor; Devon Jersile, Associate Editor, Middlebury College, Middlebury, VT 05753, 802-388-3711 ext. 5075. 1978. Poetry, fiction, articles, photos, interviews, criticism, reviews, parts-of-novels, long-poems. "We publish 4 issues every year. Some are thematic (Writers in the Nuclear Age; On Science—upcoming: Class Consciousness and the American Writer)." circ. 2M. 4/yr. Pub'd 4 issues 1990; expects 4 issues 1991, 4 issues 1992. sub. price: $18 individual, $30 institution; per copy: $6; sample: $6. Back issues: $5 Vol. I, no. 1. $7 Vol V. nos. 1/2, Vol VII no. 4 $6, $4 all other back issues. Discounts: 2 years, $33; 3 years, $50; 25% classroom. 200pp; 7×10; of. Reporting time: 2 months. Payment: $10 per page. Copyrighted. Pub's reviews: 14 in 1990. §Contemporary fiction, poetry, biography, autobiography, non-fiction. Ads: $275/$125/discounts for featured authors. COSMEP, CLMP.

NEW EUROPE, Euroeditor, PO Box 212, Luxemburg, Luxembourg. 1972. Poetry, fiction, articles, art, photos, interviews, criticism, reviews, music, letters, long-poems, plays. 4/yr. 80pp; 13×20cm; of. Reporting time: 4 months. Copyrighted. Pub's reviews.

New Fantasy Publications, Thomas H. Traubitz, Publisher, PO Box 2655, Columbia, MD 21045-1655. 1991. Fiction, art. "New Fantasy Publications is devoted to printing original works of imaginative literature. Both novels and multi-author short fiction collections are published. Works of fiction from unpublished authors welcome. Unsolicited manuscripts must be accompanied by a SASE." avg. press run 500-1M. Expects 1-2 titles 1992. avg. price, cloth: $20; paper: $15. 200pp; 7½×9; of. Reporting time: novels—180 days, short—90 days. Payment: individually negotiated. Copyrights for author.

NEW FRONTIER, New Frontier Education Society, Swami Virato, Executive Editor & Founder; Alan Cohen, Assoc. Editor, 101 Cuthbert Street, Philadelphia, PA 19106, 215-627-5683. 1980. Art, photos, music, news items. "We print that which is transformative and positive in nature. Material should address itself to personal and social transformation, the new age, holistic health, etc. showing the interconnection or harmony of spirit, mind, and body. Articles on assignment 750 to 3.5M word length. Submissions welcome with SASE" circ. 60M. 11/yr. Pub'd 11 issues 1990; expects 11 issues 1991, 11 issues 1992. sub. price: $18; per copy: $1.95; sample: $2. Back issues: $2. Discounts: 50% for 100 copies ppd. 56pp; 8¼×10½; webb press. Reporting time: 60 days. Payment: 4-5¢ a word. Copyrighted, reverts to author. Pub's reviews: 35 in 1990. §New Age, spiritual, holistic health, psychology, ecology, alternative lifestyle, parapsychological, appropriate technology, vegeterianism. Ads: $1320/$745/75¢.

New Frontier Education Society (see also NEW FRONTIER), Swami Virato, 46 North Front Street Side, Philadelphia, PA 19106, 215-627-5683. 1980.

NEW GERMAN REVIEW: A Journal of Germanic Studies, Christa Johnson, Dept of Germanic Languages, University of CA, Los Angeles, Los Angeles, CA 90024, (213) 825-3955. 1985. Articles, interviews, criticism, reviews. "Manuscripts should be prepared in accordance with the 1984 *MLA Handbook* (paranthetical documentation) and not exceed 20 typed pages including documentation. Unsolicited book reviews are not accepted." circ. 250. 1/yr. Pub'd 1 issue 1990; expects 1 issue 1991, 1 issue 1992. sub. price: $5, institutions $8; per copy: $5; sample: free. 85pp; 6×9; of. Reporting time: 2 months after submission deadline. Payment: none. Copyrighted, does not revert to author. Pub's reviews: 1 in 1990. Ads on exchange basis. Graduate Students Association (GSA), University of California, Los Angeles.

New Harbinger Publications, Inc., Matthew McKay, 5674 Shattuck Avenue, Oakland, CA 94609, 415-652-0215. 1973. Non-fiction. avg. press run 10M. Pub'd 2 titles 1990; expects 4 titles 1991, 4 titles 1992. 8 titles listed in the *Small Press Record of Books in Print* (20th Edition, 1991-92). avg. price, cloth: $19.95; paper: $10.95. 220pp; 6×9; of. Reporting time: 3 months. Payment: 15% on actual cash receipts. Copyrights for author. COSMEP, ABA, PMA.

NEW HEAVEN/NEW EARTH, Greenlawn Press, Jeanne DeCelles, Editor, 107 S. Greenlawn Avenue, South Bend, IN 46617, 219-234-5088. 1983. Articles, photos, interviews, news items, non-fiction. "ISSN #: 0896-3150. Articles generally range from 750-1250 words. We focus on the development and nurturing of lay spirituality within the realm of progressively orthodox Christianity. Articles on Christians living in some form of community are especially welcome, as are political/social commentaries and analyses from a Christian perspective" circ. 2.2M. 11/yr. Pub'd 11 issues 1990; expects 11 issues 1991, 11 issues 1992. sub. price: $12.95; per copy: $2.25; sample: free. Back issues: $2.25. 24pp; 8½×11; of. Reporting time: 15-30 days. Payment: negotiable. Copyrighted, does not revert to author. Pub's reviews: 20 in 1990. §Family life, Church-State relations, Christian spiritual growth, cultural/political trends. Ads: $190/$110/back cover: $100 1/3 page/$180 2/3. COSMEP.

378

New Hope International (see also NEW HOPE INTERNATIONAL ZINE; NEW HOPE INTERNA-
TIONAL REVIEW), Gerald England, 20 Werneth Avenue, Gee Cross, Hyde SK14 5NL, United Kingdom,
061-351 1878. 1970. Poetry, fiction, articles, criticism, long-poems, concrete art, non-fiction. "Founded as
Headland in 1970. Onetime UK distributor of Dustbooks Directory. Partner stole the name Headland (and all
the money in the bank a/c) in 1980 so New Hope International started up. Potential authors should have a body
of work published in magazines before approaching. Have published "Hope of Peace" by Iranian concert
pianist Novin Afrouz, a tribute to the late Basil Bunting, a collection by B.Z. Niditch and Editor's Dilemma
which tells the story of 20 years of small press publishing." avg. press run 500-1M. Pub'd 6 titles 1990; expects
6 titles 1991, 6 titles 1992. 9 titles listed in the *Small Press Record of Books in Print* (20th Edition, 1991-92).
avg. price, paper: $5. Discounts: on application. 32-48pp; size A5; some mimeo, some offset/litho. Reporting
time: 3-6 months. Payment: varies - usually authors have a very generous discount on copies. Does not
copyright for author. Small Press Group of Great Britain, Association of Little Presses.

NEW HOPE INTERNATIONAL REVIEW, New Hope International, Gerald England, 20 Werneth
Avenue, Gee Cross, Hyde, Cheshire SK14 5NL, United Kingdom, 061-351 1878. 1986. Art, reviews, letters,
news items. "Issued with subscriptions to *New Hope International* but also available separately—short reviews
of a wide range of publications including records, cassettes & computer software but main emphasis on poetry.
Unsolicited reviews not required but U.K. subscribers who can write fluently are welcome to join the reviewing
team." circ. 1M. 2-3/yr. Pub'd 2 issues 1990; expects 2 issues 1991, 3 issues 1992. sub. price: $20 (6 issues,
including magazine & special chapbooks); per copy: $5 (includes postage); sample: $4. 36-48pp; 11×8; mi.
Reporting time: usually within 3 weeks-3 months. Payment: copies. Not copyrighted. Pub's reviews: 600 in
1990. §Poetry, fiction (inc. childrens), literary criticism, cassettes, videos, computer software (with literary
interest), records, cds; 90% of items received are reviewed. Ads: on application. Small Press Group of Great
Britain, Association of Little Presses.

NEW HOPE INTERNATIONAL ZINE, New Hope International, Gerald England, 20 Werneth Avenue,
Gee Cross, Hyde, Cheshire SK14 5NL, United Kingdom, 061-351 1878. 1970. Poetry, fiction, articles,
criticism, letters, long-poems, non-fiction. "Founded as Headland in 1970. Partner stole the name Headland
(and all the money in the bank a/c) in 1980 so New Hope International started up. Publish poetry (including
translations) and short fiction. Reviews published in separate supplement. Guidelines for contributors available
for IRC." circ. 500-1M. 6/yr. Pub'd 6 issues 1990; expects 6 issues 1991, 6 issues 1992. sub. price: $20 (6
issues, including *NHI Review* and special chapbooks); per copy: $5; sample: $4. Back issues: on application.
Discounts: 33% to shops (cash with order). 36pp; 8×5; mi. Reporting time: up to 6 months, but usually only 4-6
weeks. Payment: copies. Not copyrighted. Pub's reviews: 600 in 1990. §Poetry, fiction (inc. childrens), social
works (if forward-thinking), art, music, erotica, humour, PC software. Ads: $50/$30. Small Press Group of
Great Britain, Association of Little Presses.

New Horizons Publishers, Lewis Green, 737 Tenth Avenue East, Seattle, WA 98102, 206-323-1102. 1983.
"All submissions must be conducive to photography, large format and must appeal to both the book and gift
markets. We are particularly interested in guidebooks. Most of our books will be self-published. We no longer
accept unsolicited ms" avg. press run 10M. Expects 2 titles 1991, 3-4 titles 1992. 3 titles listed in the *Small
Press Record of Books in Print* (20th Edition, 1991-92). avg. price, paper: $8.95. Discounts: 50-60% to
wholesalers, 20-55% to retailers. 96pp; 8×10. Reporting time: 2-4 weeks. Payment: royalties only. Copyrights
for author. PNBP.

The New Humanity Press, PO Box 215, Berkeley, CA 94701. 1986. Fiction, articles, art, photos, cartoons,
interviews, satire, criticism, reviews, music, letters, parts-of-novels, news items, non-fiction. "All material
book-length. Our slant is looking for the 'truth,' however we find it, and looking to improve our uniquely
human condition, with a view to universal justice and peace-seeking harmony for all life everywhere." avg.
press run 3M-5M. Expects 1 title 1991, 3 titles 1992. 1 title listed in the *Small Press Record of Books in Print*
(20th Edition, 1991-92). avg. price, paper: $19.95. Discounts: bulk and trade. 350pp; 6×9; of. Reporting time:
2-4 weeks. Payment: under consideration. Copyrights for author.

New Idea Press, Inc., Martha Gorman, Editor, 532 West Lois Way, Louisville, CO 80027-9543. 1985.
"Publishes popular health, psychology, social change and self-help books aimed at paraprofessionals and
general readership. Marketing methods include sales through non-profit organizations. Innovative, unorthodox
and controversial approaches welcome. We are looking for manuscripts on the physiological bases of addiction
and for well done children's books on mental illness and on grieving. Publishes paperback originals.
Simultaneous and photocopied submissions OK. Computer print-out submissions accepted (letter quality
preferred) and authors are encouraged to have manuscript on disk. SASE" avg. press run 2.5M. Pub'd 2 titles
1990; expects 4 titles 1991, 6 titles 1992. 3 titles listed in the *Small Press Record of Books in Print* (20th
Edition, 1991-92). avg. price, paper: $12. 150pp; 6×9; desktop. Reporting time: 1 month. Payment: no advance,
5-10% royalty. Copyrights for author.

NEW JERSEY NATURALLY, City Spirit Publications, Jerome Rubin, Editor-in-Chief & Publisher; Kenny

379

Schiff, Managing Editor, 590 Pacific Street, Brooklyn, NY 11217, 718-857-1545. 1984. Poetry, articles, art, interviews, non-fiction. "Wide range of material relating to a natural life-style, focus on New York, New Jersey, and Connecticut. We publish 3 annual books in January (formerly 1)." circ. 25M. 1/yr. Pub'd 1 issue 1990; expects 1 issue 1991, 1 issue 1992. price per copy: $3.50; sample: $2.50. 96pp; 5×8; web press. Reporting time: 2 weeks. Payment: varies. Copyrighted, reverts to author. Pub's reviews. §Natural lifestyle, health, environmentalism, natural foods/cooking, new age.

THE NEW LAUREL REVIEW, Lee Meitzen Grue, Editor, 828 Lesseps Street, New Orleans, LA 70117, 504-947-6001. 1971. Poetry, fiction, articles, art, photos, reviews, non-fiction. "We want fresh work; shy away from dry academic articles with footnotes, and from poems with the guts cut out. Recently published: Julie Kane, P.B. Panis, James Nolan, Arthur Pfistes III, Len Roberts, Marilyn Coffey, and Billy Marshall Stoneking." circ. 500. 1/yr. Pub'd 1 issue 1990. 1 title listed in the *Small Press Record of Books in Print* (20th Edition, 1991-92). sub. price: $8; per copy: double issue $8; sample: $5. Back issues: $4. 125pp; 6×9; of. Reporting time: varies, longer time for interesting work; somewhat crowded with fiction & poetry—about 6 weeks. (Do not read in summer). Payment: 1 copy of the magazine in which their work appears. Copyrighted. Pub's reviews: 5 in 1990. §Poetry and books about poets and related matter, collections of short fiction. CCLM.

NEW LETTERS, James McKinley, University of Missouri, Kansas City, MO 64110, 816-235-1168. 1971 (Predecessor, *University Review,* 1934). Poetry, fiction, articles, art, photos, satire, parts-of-novels, long-poems. "The best in contemporary fiction, poetry, personal essay, art, and photography. Contributors include Bly, Ignatow, Stafford, Gildner, Oates, Price, Harrison, Levertov, Kumin. Special issues on Paul Goodman, E.L. Mayo, Indian Writing, 2-Volume anthology of best of magazine's first decade." circ. 2.5M. 4/yr. Pub'd 4 issues 1990; expects 4 issues 1991, 4 issues 1992. 5 titles listed in the *Small Press Record of Books in Print* (20th Edition, 1991-92). sub. price: $17; per copy: $5; sample: $5. Back issues: $5-$7.50, rare issues $20. Discounts: 25% on contract of 4 ads. 128pp; 6×9; of. Reporting time: 2 weeks to 2 months. Payment: small, upon publication. Copyrighted, reverts to author. Pub's reviews: approx. 25 in 1990. Ads: $150/$90. CCLM.

New Levee Press, William F. Rushton, 3915 South 100 East Avenue, Tulsa, OK 74146-2434. 1986. Fiction, art, long-poems, non-fiction. "Specialty Niche Publishing in high technology and underserved markets" avg. press run 500-5M. Pub'd 1 title 1990; expects 6 titles 1991. 3 titles listed in the *Small Press Record of Books in Print* (20th Edition, 1991-92). avg. price, paper: $3.95-$45. 36-350pp; 5×7, 8½×11; of. Reporting time: 1 month. Payment: negotiable. Copyrights for author (optional). COSMEP, PMA, NIP (New York Independent Publishers), NYACN (New York Advertising & Communications Network).

New Liberty Press, Fanny Semiglia, Box 6598, New York, NY 10150, 212-750-8410. 1990. avg. press run 2M. Pub'd 2 titles 1990. 1 title listed in the *Small Press Record of Books in Print* (20th Edition, 1991-92). avg. price, paper: $12.95. 350pp; 6×9.

NEW METHODS JOURNAL (VETERINARY), AHT Lippert, Editor & Publisher, PO Box 22605, San Francisco, CA 94122-0605, 415-664-3469. 1976. Poetry, articles, art, photos, cartoons, interviews, criticism, reviews, letters, news items, non-fiction. "Double-spaced with one inch margins; material should be relevant to Veterinary field (prefer staff related - animal health technicians); most contributors are in the veterinary field with some experience. *New Methods* has a list of other animal publications in the animal field for $20." circ. 5.6M. 12/yr. Pub'd 3 issues 1990. sub. price: $18 (additional cost outside of U.S.A., all monies must be in U.S. funds); per copy: $3.60-mention Dustbooks & sample copies are only $2; sample: $3.60-mention Dustbooks & sample copies are only $2. Back issues: $3.60 with 25% discount after the first $10-mention DUSTBOOKS & sample copies are only $2. Discounts: free copies to published person. 24pp; 9×11; sheetfed. Reporting time: 2-6 weeks. Payment: if published, $25 first time with increase with each publication; generally no payment! Possible in the future; perks & commission. Copyrighted, reverts to author. Pub's reviews: 144 in 1990. §Animal, veterinary, employee related. Ads: $225/$123/smaller ad space is available.

NEW MEXICO HUMANITIES REVIEW, John Rothfork, Jerry Bradley, Lou Thompson, New Mexico Tech, Humanities Department, Socorro, NM 87801, 505-835-5445. 1978. Poetry, fiction, articles, art, photos, criticism, reviews, parts-of-novels. "A Southwest regional journal with broad interests. Recently published work by Jim Corder, Walt MacDonald, Jim Thomas, Peter Wild, Paul Ruffin, Clay Reynolds, Charles Edward Eaton, David Sheskin. We encourage submissions from and about the Southwest, including Native American and Chicano material. We are also interested in essays on science/technology and society written for a general readership." circ. 800. 2/yr. Pub'd 2 issues 1990; expects 2 issues 1991, 2 issues 1992. sub. price: $11; per copy: $6; sample: $6. Back issues: $5. Discounts: 40%. 150pp; 6×9; of. Reporting time: 6 weeks. Payment: one year's subscription. Copyrighted, rights revert on request. Pub's reviews: 18 in 1990. §Southwest regional, small press, Native American. Ads: $30/$15.

NEW MOON, Janice Bogstad, PO Box 2056, Madison, WI 53701-2056, 608-251-3854. 1981. Poetry, fiction, articles, art, cartoons, interviews, criticism, reviews, long-poems, non-fiction. "Book reviews: 1-5 pages; Review articles and Critical articles 5-10 (double-spaced typed) pages-under 3M words; #1-introduct. issue;

380

reviews of SF and Feminist-Critical works-April 1981. #2-15 page biblio. of women SF writers-Winter 1981-1982. #3-Critical articles by and about Samuel R. Delany on his early work (*Fall of The Towers* through *Babel-17*)-Spring 1982. #4-April 1987-Sex and Gender, Delany fiction. #5-August 1987'' circ. 600. 3/yr. Expects 3 issues 1991, 3 issues 1992. sub. price: $10/4 issues; per copy: $3.00; sample: $3. Back issues: inquire. Discounts: 5-10 10%; 11-25 20%; 25-50 35%; 51+ 45%. 36pp; 8½×11; of. Reporting time: 2-4 months. Payment: 1 free copy of issue in which work appears. Copyrighted, reverts to author. Pub's reviews: 15 books/9 magazines in 1990. §Science fiction, feminism, mass-media, contemp. criticism. Ads: $100/$55/$35¼. SF 3.

NEW MOON RISING, Scot Rhoads, 8818 Troy Street, Spring Valley, CA 91977, 619-466-8064. 1989. Poetry, fiction, articles, art, photos, cartoons, interviews, reviews, music, letters, long-poems, news items, non-fiction. ''Length of material: 1-10 pages (normally). Recent contributors: Scott Cunningham, Donald Michael Kraig, Lazeris. Especially looking for material that includes practical work/application'' circ. 1M+. 6/yr. Pub'd 6 issues 1990; expects 6 issues 1991, 6 issues 1992. sub. price: $13; per copy: $2.95; sample: $3. Back issues: $3. Discounts: work out. 36pp; 8½×11; of. Reporting time: usually 2 weeks. Payment: trade. Copyrighted, rights revert when requested. Pub's reviews: 8 in 1990. §New Age, metaphysics, paganism, mythology, magick. Ads: $100/$60/$35 1/4 page/$20 1/8 page. WPPA.

NEW NORTH ARTSCAPE, David Skarjune, Editor, 420 North 5th Street #990, Minneapolis, MN 55401-1378, 338-4974. 1984. Poetry, fiction, articles, art, photos, cartoons, interviews, satire, criticism, reviews, letters, parts-of-novels, long-poems, collages, plays, concrete art, non-fiction. ''500-2,500 words average length. Some recent articles were reviews of gallery exhibits, theatre, performance art, books, and film/video. We prefer informative, provocative art criticism, essays on all aspects of culture, and some short stories—both fiction and creative nonfiction'' circ. 3M. 6/yr. Pub'd 6 issues 1990; expects 6 issues 1991, 6 issues 1992. sub. price: $10; per copy: $2; sample: $2. Back issues: $2.00. Discounts: we are in the process of determining these. 28pp; 5×30m; of, laser printing/electronic typesetting. Reporting time: 4 weeks. Payment: $25 minimum. Copyrighted, reverts to author. Pub's reviews: 27 in 1990. §All the arts in Minnesota and thereabouts, including books written by Minnesotans or published by Minnesota small presses. Ads: $600/$350 *all rates subject to change. St. Paul Art Collective.

NEW ORLEANS REVIEW, John Mosier, Loyola University, Box 195, New Orleans, LA 70118, 504-865-2294. 1968. Poetry, fiction, articles, art, photos, interviews, criticism, long-poems, non-fiction. ''Walker Percy, Norman Mailer, James Wright, Alain Robbe-Grillet, Amiri Baraka, Susan Fromberg Schaeffer, Peter Wild, Christopher Isherwood, David Madden, Annie Dillard, Rosemary Daniell, Natalie Petesch, Doris Betts, Larry Rubin, Greg Kuzma, John William Corrington, Murray Krieger.'' circ. 750. 4/yr. Pub'd 4 issues 1990; expects 4 issues 1991, 4 issues 1992. sub. price: 4 issues - domestic $25 indiv, $30 instit, foreign $35; per copy: $9 domestic, $11 foreign; sample: $9 domestic, $11 foreign. Discounts: none. 100pp; 8½×11; of. Reporting time: 3 months. Payment: to poets, artists & fiction writers. Reprint permission available on request. CCLM, COSMEP.

NEW PAGES: Access to Alternatives in Print, New Pages Press, Casey Hill, Grant Burns, Ruthann Robson, PO Box 438, Grand Blanc, MI 48439, 313-743-8055; 313-742-9583. 1979. Articles, art, photos, cartoons, satire, criticism, reviews, news items. ''News and reviews of the progressive book trade. Access to informational tools. We are concerned with the growth & survival of an independent, progressive book trade. Our review section focuses on the small press, but we do not ignore the more significant publications from the major presses. Publishers are requested to send two copies of a book or magazine to be reviewed. Book reviewers should write for our guidelines. We pay $5 per review. Unsolicited reviews will be considered; 150-300 word length with following, information provided: title, author, publisher, publisher's address, date of publication, no. of pages, ISBN or ISSN, LC#, price, paper or hardback. When writing for guidelines, list your areas of interest, send samples of past reviews, if any.'' 3/yr. sub. price: $12/6 issues; per copy: $3; sample: $3. 32pp; 10×14 tabloid; of. Reporting time: 3-4 weeks. Payment: $5 for book reviews. Copyrighted, reverts to author. Pub's reviews. §Consider all materials rec'd. Ads: inquire.

New Pages Press (see also NEW PAGES: Access to Alternatives in Print), PO Box 438, Grand Blanc, MI 48439. ''We are interested in publishing books of value to librarians, booksellers and publishers, including 'how-to', directories, bibliographies. Query first.''

NEW PATHWAYS, Michael G. Adkisson, Editor & Publisher; Chris Kelly, Fiction Editor, PO Box 475174, Garland, TX 75047-5174. 1986. Fiction, art, interviews, reviews, letters. ''We are looking for speculative, science fiction or fantasy-approximately 2,000-4,000 words. *New Pathways* focuses on the future, environment and the cutting edge in culture. Although we are a renegade press, we understand and appreciate traditional good elements of literature. We have published such authors as Brian Aldiss, Phillip K. Dick, Paul DiFilippo, John Shirley, and Don Webb. Please send intro letter and SASE with manuscripts to MGA Services at the above address'' circ. 1.5M. 6/yr. Pub'd 3 issues 1990; expects 4 issues 1991. sub. price: $18/6 issues; per copy: $4.50; sample: $5 (postage included). Discounts: 60%. 60pp; 8½×11; of, also typeset. Reporting time: 5-6 weeks. Payment: copies or fee by arrangement with publisher. Copyrighted, reverts to author. Pub's reviews.

381

Ads: $200/$100/request info.

The New Poets Series, Inc., Clarinda Harriss Raymond, Editor-in-Chief; Michael Raymond, Editor-in-Chief, 541 Piccadilly Rd., Baltimore, MD 21204, 301-321-2863. 1970. Poetry. "NPS chapbooks contain enough poems (or poems plus graphics) to make about 60 pp. of type. Editorial bias in favor of excellent material in an original voice" avg. press run 1M. Pub'd 3 titles 1990. 26 titles listed in the *Small Press Record of Books in Print* (20th Edition, 1991-92). avg. price, paper: $6.95. Discounts: 40% to bookstores; $5.95 retail. 64pp; 6×9; of. Reporting time: 2-6 months. Payment: none, all revenue from sales goes to publish the next issue. Author holds own copyright. CCLM, COSMEP, Maryland State Arts Council, The Writers' Center.

THE NEW PRESS, Robert Abramson, Publisher; David Gerard, Editor; Harry Ellison, Poetry Editor, 87-40 Francis Lewis Blvd #A-44, Queens Village, NY 11427, 718-217-1464. 1984. Poetry, fiction, articles, art, interviews, satire, criticism, parts-of-novels, long-poems, non-fiction. "We run stories up to 10-18 pages double-spaced about almost anything we feel is rewarding. We use illustrations. We run commentary and criticism as well." circ. 1M. 4/yr. Pub'd 4 issues 1990; expects 4 issues 1991, 4 issues 1992. sub. price: $12; per copy: $3; sample: $3. Back issues: not available. 32pp; 8½×11; of. Reporting time: 8 weeks. Payment: 2 copies; $50 to best prose contribution to each issue. Copyrighted, reverts to author. Ads: $100/$60/$20 business card.

THE NEW RAIN MAGAZINE, Paul Celmer, John Krege, PO Box 2087, Chapel Hill, NC 27515. 1988. Poetry, fiction, long-poems, plays, non-fiction. "*The New Rain Magazine* is an interdisciplinary forum for scientists, scholars, and creative writers. We are interested in works which explore the problems associated with our increasingly technologically advanced society." circ. 2M. 4/yr. Expects 1 issue 1991, 4 issues 1992. sub. price: $15; per copy: $3.75; sample: $3.75. 50pp; 8½×11; of. Reporting time: 1-2 months. Payment: $25-$100 per short story and essay (approx. 3000 words), $25-$50 per poem. Not copyrighted. §Science and technology, sci-fi, environment, general fiction, avant garde.

THE NEW RENAISSANCE, An International Magazine of Ideas & Opinions, Emphasizing Literature & The Arts, Louise T. Reynolds, Editor-in-Chief; Louise E. Reynolds, Manager; James Woodbury, Poetry; Harry Jackel, Associate Editor; Ruth Moose, Consulting Editor; Patricia J.D. Michaud, Senior Editor, 9 Heath Road, Arlington, MA 02174. 1968. Poetry, fiction, articles, art, photos, interviews, satire, criticism, reviews, music, letters, parts-of-novels, collages, plays. "We accept submissions only from January 2 thru June 30. We have a purchase requirement for submitters. *TNR* is in the classicist tradition, not the alternative press tradition, and although we are open to many styles and statements, etc., we do not have an 'anything goes' philosophy. Study *TNR* before submitting. We're looking for writers who have something to say, who say it with style or grace, and, above all, who speak in a highly personal voice." circ. 1.5M. 2/yr. Pub'd 1 issue 1990; expects 2 issues 1991, 2 issues 1992. sub. price: $12.50/3 issues USA, $14.50/3 issues Canada, Mexico, Europe, $15.50/3 issues all others; per copy: $6.80 USA; $6.95 Canada, Mexico, Europe; $7.15 all others; sample: $5.65 back 2 issues or $4.80 (1982 issue); $6.45 (1987 or 1988 issue); $7.40 current. Back issues: limited number of Complete Sets available (#1-#23) @ $90.50 US. Discounts: subscription agents, etc. 20%; 20 or more copies or classroom use 20%, 50+ 30%; bookstores 33⅓%, advance payment. 144-192pp; 6×9; of. Reporting time: poetry 12-18 weeks, prose 18-21 weeks. Payment: $13 to $30 poems, $30 to $65 fiction, $50 to $150 non-fiction, $27 to $75 essay/reviews, $25 per drawing and/or visual art. Copyrighted, does not revert to author. Pub's reviews: 2 in 1990. §Want to see Press Releases only (literature, arts). Ads: $150/$85. CCLM.

New Rivers Press, Inc., C. W. Truesdale, 420 North 5th Street #910, Minneapolis, MN 55401, 612-339-7114. 1968. Poetry, fiction, art, photos, long-poems, concrete art. "We publish new writing of merit and distinction—poetry, combinations of poetry and prose, short fiction, memoirs, and translations (mostly poetry). We like to use graphics in as many books as possible. We are also involved in publishing such regional programs as the Minnesota Voices Project and the Many Minnesotas Project (a series of ethnic anthologies)." avg. press run 1M-2.5M. Pub'd 8 titles 1990; expects 10 titles 1991, 11 titles 1992. 166 titles listed in the *Small Press Record of Books in Print* (20th Edition, 1991-92). avg. price, paper: $6 poetry, $8 prose, $14.95 anthologies; other: $2.00. Discounts: 1-5 copies 20%, 6+ 40% trade; 50% for outright purchases. 96-300pp; 6×9; of. Reporting time: 1-6 months. Payment: negotiable; for a standard *New Rivers* book, the author receives 100 free copies, plus 15% royalties on list for second and subsequent printings. Minnesota Voices Project competition authors receive a $500 initial stipend plus the 15% royalties on list for second and subsequent printings. Graphic artists' commissions are negotiated. Copyrights for author.

New Saga Publishers, James A. Warren, Senior Editor; Anne Hale, Business Manager; Margot Lisa Miglins, Ph.D., Consultant, PO Box 56415, Sherman Oaks, CA 91413, 818-988-0940. 1988. Fiction, non-fiction. "Full-length novels, generally 275 to 400 pages. No light romances. Recent contributors: A.R. Langer, D.D., Kurt B. Fischel, former Vice-Pres., General Electric Co., retired." avg. press run 1M. Pub'd 1 title 1990; expects 3 titles 1991, 4 titles 1992. 4 titles listed in the *Small Press Record of Books in Print* (20th Edition, 1991-92). avg. price, paper: $8. Discounts: libraries, 50%/30 days; bookstores-on consignment 180 days, 50% 30 days after sale. 300pp; 5⅜×8½; †of. Reporting time: 30 days. Payment: by special arrangement only.

382

Copyrights for author. COSMEP, Round Table West.

New Seed Press, PO Box 9488, Berkeley, CA 94709. 1972. Fiction, art. "We are a small feminist collective commited to publishing non-sexist, non-racist stories for children which actively confront issues of sexism, racism, classism. Do not send unsolicited manuscripts. Query first with return stamped envelope." avg. press run 4M. Pub'd 1 title 1990; expects 2 titles 1991, 1 title 1992. 12 titles listed in the *Small Press Record of Books in Print* (20th Edition, 1991-92). avg. price, paper: $7. Discounts: 40% to bookstores and 55% to distributors; pay in advance including 10% postage. Pages vary; size varies; of. Reporting time: 2 months. Payment: varies. Copyrights for author.

NEW SINS, New Sins Press, Rane Arroyo, Editor; Glenn Sheldon, Creative Director; J. Manning, Assistant Editor, PO Box 7157, Pittsburgh, PA 15213, 412-621-5611. 1985. Poetry. "Primarily a broadsheet of gay/lesbian/bisexual poetry, under 40 lines in length. We need camera-ready art 8 X 8½ B & W for cover. Unsolicited submissions considered with SASE. Recent contributors: Dennis Cooper, Louie Crew, Charles Henri Ford, Thom Gunn, Indra, Paul Mariah, Claude Peck, Robert Peters, Ron Schreiber, and Ian Young. Will exchange subscriptions with other magazines. Subscriptions and single copies must be made payable to Rane Arroyo, not *New Sins*. This is a broadsheet-type format. Overstocked indefinitely!! Published only as quality submissions warrant it." circ. 200. 2/yr. Pub'd 1 issue 1990; expects 2 issues 1991, 2 issues 1992. sub. price: $3; per copy: $2; sample: 1st class stamp. Back issues: varies $2-$10. 4pp; 8½x11; of. Reporting time: 1 month. Payment: 5 copies & 2 year's subscription. Copyrighted, reverts to author. Ads: none.

New Sins Press (see also NEW SINS; STAGE WHISPER; VIOLENT VIRGINS), Rane Arroyo, PO Box 7157, Pittsburgh, PA 15213. 1985. Poetry, art, photos, collages, plays. "New Sins Press poetry chapbooks by invitation only. Recent contributor: Paul Mariah." avg. press run 200. Pub'd 6 titles 1990; expects 6 titles 1991, 6 titles 1992. avg. price, paper: $2. 8pp; 5½x8½; of. Reporting time: 1 month. Payment: in copies. Does not copyright for author.

New Society Publishers, Albert, Bloom, Davis, Hill, Sawislak, Hirshkowitz, Peterson, Powell, 4527 Springfield Avenue, Philadelphia, PA 19143, 215-382-6543. 1981. Non-fiction. "Books and resources on nonviolence, peace, feminism, worker self-management, ecology" avg. press run 4M. Pub'd 15 titles 1990; expects 16 titles 1991, 16 titles 1992. 48 titles listed in the *Small Press Record of Books in Print* (20th Edition, 1991-92). avg. price, cloth: $34.95; paper: $12.95; other: $3.45 pamphlet. Discounts: 40% for bookstore orders of 5 or more of any one title or mixed; wholesalers-contact. 240pp; 5½x8½, 6x9, 8½x11, 5¼x8; of. Reporting time: negotiable. Payment: negotiable. Copyrights for author if required. NSEF, Co-op America, Quakers United in Publishing, Progressive Booksellers Association, Religious Booksellers Association.

The New South Company, Nancy Cooke, 236 East Davie Street, Raleigh, NC 27601-1808. 1976. Fiction, art. "Not publishing at this time. All titles are in print and are actively selling." 5 titles listed in the *Small Press Record of Books in Print* (20th Edition, 1991-92). avg. price, cloth: $12; paper: $7. Discounts: 1-2 copies 20%, 3+ copies 40% to booksellers. lp, of. Reporting time: 3-4 weeks. Payment: 10% of retail price. Copyrights for author.

NEW SPOKES, Donald Atkinson, The Orchard House, 45 Clophill Road, Upper Gravenhurst, Bedfordshire MK45 4JH, England, 0462-711195. 1985. Poetry, art, photos. "Contributors are urged to subscribe/buy single issues" circ. 300+. 2/yr. Pub'd 3 issues 1990; expects 3 issues 1991, 2 issues 1992. sub. price: £7.50 UK, £9 overseas; per copy: £3.75, £4.50 overseas; sample: £3 UK, overseas £4 (in each case, add £6 for bank exchange charge if in dollars—payment in sterling preferred). Discounts: wholesale @ 66% of retail price. 64pp; 7x10; perfect. Reporting time: 4 weeks. Payment: free copy of relevant issue. Copyrighted, reverts to author. Pub's reviews: 6 in 1990. §Poetry. Ads: By arrangement. Small Press Soc.

New Star Books Ltd., Rolf Maurer, Audrey McClellan, 2504 York Avenue, Vancouver, B.C. V6K 1E3, Canada, 604-738-9429. 1974. Non-fiction. "*New Star* is a socialist press specializing in history, social issues, Central American and feminist titles." avg. press run 2M-3M. Pub'd 8 titles 1990; expects 8 titles 1991, 10 titles 1992. 46 titles listed in the *Small Press Record of Books in Print* (20th Edition, 1991-92). avg. price, cloth: $20; paper: $13. Discounts: 40% trade (5+ books); 10% libraries. 200-250pp; 5½x8½; of. Reporting time: 6-8 weeks. Payment: varies with contract. Copyrights for author. ACP, ABPBC.

NEW THOUGHT, Blaine C. Mays, Editor-in-Chief, International New Thought Alliance, 5003 East Broadway Road, Mesa, AZ 85206, 602-945-0744. 1913. Articles, interviews, reviews, news items. "*New Thought* is a self-help, metaphysical publication with articles designed to increase the creative fulfilling, and healing energies in each one of us. Material written from a philosophical and religious point of view is used in the magazine. Emphasis is always upon the positive, constructive, and inspirational." circ. 5M. 4/yr. Pub'd 4 issues 1990; expects 4 issues 1991. sub. price: $8; per copy: $2.25; sample: $2.25. Back issues: not offered. 64pp; 8½x11; of. Reporting time: 3-4 weeks. Payment: contributors' copies only. Copyrighted, reverts to author. Pub's reviews: 20 in 1990. §Metaphysics, spiritual enlightenments, self help. Ads: $565.90/$282.85/$24 column inch.

NEW UNIONIST, Jeff Miller, 621 West Lake Street, Rm 210, Minneapolis, MN 55408, 612-823-2593. 1975. Articles, photos, cartoons, reviews, letters, news items. "No outside manuscripts" circ. 9M. 12/yr. Pub'd 12 issues 1990; expects 12 issues 1991, 12 issues 1992. sub. price: 10 issues $3; per copy: 30¢; sample: free. Discounts: 15¢ each. 4pp; 11×17; of. Payment: copies only. Not copyrighted. Pub's reviews: 4 in 1990. §Socialism, labor, politics, current affairs.

New Victoria Publishers, Claudia Lamperti, PO Box 27, Norwich, VT 05055, 802-649-5297. 1977. Poetry, fiction, art, photos. "Non-profit" avg. press run 5M. Pub'd 3 titles 1990; expects 5 titles 1991, 6 titles 1992. 25 titles listed in the *Small Press Record of Books in Print* (20th Edition, 1991-92). avg. price, paper: $8.95. Discounts: 40% bookstore, 50% wholesale. 200pp; 5½×8½, 8½×11, 5¼×8¼; of. Reporting time: 1 month. Payment: negotiable or in copies. Copyrights for author. COSMEP, VT Book Publishers Association, ABA.

New View Publications, PO Box 3021, Chapel Hill, NC 27515-3021. 1987. Poetry, fiction, non-fiction. avg. press run 5M. Pub'd 1 title 1990; expects 3 titles 1991, 5 titles 1992. 3 titles listed in the *Small Press Record of Books in Print* (20th Edition, 1991-92). avg. price, paper: $10. Discounts: 40% wholesale. 100-200pp; 6×9. Reporting time: 3-4 weeks. Payment: varies. Copyrights for author.

New Voyage Books, Karen D. Jbara, 415 Route 18, Suite 234, East Brunswick, NJ 08816, 800-345-0096 (orders only). 1988. Non-fiction. "We are a highly focused publisher concentrating on self-help, relationship enrichment. Our material is upbeat and focuses on improving interpersonal communication and personal development. It must be practical, useful to our audience and easily applicable. No New Age, heavy psychology, theory or way-out material, please. Always query first with SASE. No unsolicited mss." avg. press run 5M. Expects 1 title 1991, 1-2 titles 1992. 1 title listed in the *Small Press Record of Books in Print* (20th Edition, 1991-92). avg. price, paper: $7.95. 220pp; 5½×8½; of. Reporting time: 4-8 weeks. Payment: negotiable. Copyrights for author. COSMEP, Publishers Marketing Association (PMA).

New World Library, Carol La Russo, Editorial Director, 58 Paul Drive, San Rafael, CA 94903. 1978. Fiction, non-fiction. "We have a best-selling book *Living In The Light* that we print 50,000 each run" avg. press run 7.5M-50M. Pub'd 4 titles 1990; expects 9 titles 1991, 4 titles 1992. 18 titles listed in the *Small Press Record of Books in Print* (20th Edition, 1991-92). avg. price, paper: $8.95; other: $10.95 instructional cassettes. Discounts: 50-55% to distributors, 10% to individuals ordering 5 or more titles. 175pp; 5½×8½; of. Reporting time: 8 weeks. Payment: 6-8% royalty to authors, paid semi-annually. Copyrights for author.

New World Marketing, 12963 West Chenango Drive, Morrison, CO 80465, 303-979-3506. Non-fiction. 1 title listed in the *Small Press Record of Books in Print* (20th Edition, 1991-92).

A NEW WORLD RISING, Grateful Fred, Box 33, 77 Ives Street, Providence, RI 02906. 1986. Poetry, art, photos, cartoons, music, letters, collages, news items. "Generally print excerts of material submitted by correspondents with their address. Primary focus is networking" circ. 50M. 4/yr. Pub'd 3 issues 1990; expects 4 issues 1991. sub. price: donation. 8pp; 10×16; newsprint (webb). Payment: none. Not copyrighted. Pub's reviews. §Culture (music), New Age/cosmic.

New Worlds Press, Ralph Hansen, Executive Director, Box 1458, Kalispell, MT 59903, 406-756-7067. 1989. Non-fiction. "Progressive" avg. press run 7.2M. Pub'd 1 title 1990; expects 3 titles 1991, 6 titles 1992. 1 title listed in the *Small Press Record of Books in Print* (20th Edition, 1991-92). avg. price, cloth: $22.95; paper: $12.95. 280pp; 6×9. Reporting time: 60 days. Payment: negotiable. Copyrights for author.

NEW WRITER'S MAGAZINE, Independent Publishing Co., George Haborak, PO Box 5976, Sarasota, FL 34277. 1986. Articles, photos, interviews, reviews, letters, news items. "Short articles (500-1000 wd) on *writing + writers*, etc. 'Up Close + Personal' lead story looks for personal interview with a recognized, professional writer (w/pix)." circ. 5M. 6/yr. Pub'd 6 issues 1990; expects 6 issues 1991, 6 issues 1992. sub. price: $12, $18/2-years; per copy: $2; sample: $2. Back issues: $1.50. Discounts: none. 24pp; 8½×11; †of. Reporting time: 2 months. Payment: $10-$50 for "Up Close & Personal" interview piece. Copyrighted, reverts to author. Pub's reviews: 6 in 1990. §Any and all books, magazines on the craft of writing - also, books by new writers. Ads: $300/$180/$1 a word (10 word min.).

New York CIRCUS, Inc. (see also LUCHA/STRUGGLE; AMANECER IN ENGLISH), New york CIRCUS Collective, PO Box 37, Times Square Station, New York, NY 10108, 212-928-7600. 1975. avg. press run 3M. Pub'd 10 titles 1990. avg. price, paper: $2. 40pp; 8½×11. Reporting time: 2 months. Payment: none. Does not copyright for author.

NEW YORK NATURALLY, City Spirit Publications, Jerome Rubin, Editor-in-Chief & Publisher; Kenny Schiff, Managing Editor, 590 Pacific Street, Brooklyn, NY 11217, 718-857-1545. 1984. Poetry, articles, photos, interviews, non-fiction. "Wide range of material relating to a natural life-style, focus on New York, New Jersey, and Connecticut. We publish 3 annual books in January (formerly 1)." circ. 100M. 1/yr. Pub'd 1 issue 1990; expects 1 issue 1991, 1 issue 1992. price per copy: $3.50; sample: $2.50. Back issues: $2. Discounts:

40% to retailers. 160pp; 5×8; web press. Reporting time: 2 weeks. Payment: varies. Copyrighted, reverts to author. Pub's reviews. §Natural lifestyle, health, environmentalism, natural foods/cooking, new age. Ads: $1650/$960/$495¼/$290¼/$150-1/16/$50 3-line/$350 coupons.

New York Zoetrope Inc., James Monaco, President; Stephanie Biasi, Sales Manager, 838 Broadway, New York, NY 10003, 420-0590. 1975. Criticism, reviews, non-fiction. "Film & cinema" avg. press run 5M-10M. Expects 8 titles 1991, 10 titles 1992. avg. price, cloth: $25; paper: $8.95. Discounts: booksellers: 1-4 copies 10% if prepaid, 5-24 copies 40%, 25-99 copies 42%, 100-249 copies 44%, 250-499 copies 46%, 500+ 48%. Pages vary; size varies; typesetting. Payment: negotiable. Copyrights for author.

Newmark Publishing Company, PO Box 603, South Windsor, CT 06074, 203-282-7265. 1986. Fiction, non-fiction. "*Breast Care Options* by Paul Kuehn, M.D, published Sept. 1986. *Night Flying Avenger* by Pete Grant, published June 1990." avg. press run 7.5M. Expects 3 titles 1991, 5 titles 1992. 1 title listed in the *Small Press Record of Books in Print* (20th Edition, 1991-92). avg. price, cloth: $17.95. Discounts: on request. 200pp; 6×9; of, lp. Reporting time: 3 months. Payment: individual contracts, negotiable. Copyrights for author. American Booksellers Association, New England Booksellers Association, International Assoc. of Independent Publishers, Publishers Marketing Association.

Newport House, Alan Garner, 100-P Via Estrada, Laguna Hills, CA 92653, 714-770-8323. 1987. avg. press run 20M. Pub'd 1 title 1990; expects 2 titles 1991, 3 titles 1992. 2 titles listed in the *Small Press Record of Books in Print* (20th Edition, 1991-92). avg. price, paper: $3.50. Discounts: 50%. 168pp; 4×7. Reporting time: varies. Payment: varies. Copyrights for author.

NEWS FROM NATIVE CALIFORNIA, Heyday Books, Malcolm Margolin, David W. Peri, Jeannine Gendar, PO Box 9145, Berkeley, CA 94709, (415) 549-3564. 1987. Articles, art, photos, cartoons, reviews, music, letters, news items, non-fiction. "We are interested in material related to California Indians, past and present." circ. 2.3M. 4/yr. Pub'd 5 issues 1990; expects 4 issues 1991, 4 issues 1992. sub. price: $15.95; per copy: $3.95; sample: $3.95. Back issues: $4 Vol 1, No. 1-$15. Discounts: 40% trade. 45pp; 8½×11; of. Reporting time: 3 weeks. Payment: up to about $50/article. Copyrighted, reverts to author. Pub's reviews: 7 in 1990. §We are interested only in material relating to California Indians. Ads: $350/$180/50¢.

NEWS FROM THE WHITE HOUSE, Eric Lowe, Michael Aimmes, PO Box 6088, Harrisburg, PA 17112, 215-987-3014. 1990. Poetry, fiction, articles, art, photos, cartoons, interviews, criticism, reviews, letters, long-poems, collages, news items, non-fiction. "Most type is 10 pt. w/12 pt. titles. Contributors include David Lane, Clark Martell, Michael Newgent, Allen Kaiser, Russell Taylor, and Steven Kenly. This is a pro-white newsletter, which advocates support of racial P.O.W.s and mature thinking and action of racial activists. It promotes white unity." circ. 2,561. 6/yr. Pub'd 4 issues 1990; expects 6 issues 1991, 6 issues 1992. sub. price: free. Back issues: donation—any amount. Discounts: trade for other publications, bulk prices same as cost to print. 4pp; 8½×11; of. Payment: none. Copyrighted, does not revert to author. Pub's reviews: 2 in 1990. §History, race/eugenics, military, politics/government, media, art. Ads: $20/$10/by agreement.

NewSage Press, Maureen Michelson, Publisher, PO Box 41029, Pasadena, CA 91114, 213-641-8912. 1985. Art, photos, interviews, non-fiction. "We are interested in publishing quality tradebooks—in content as well as production. Our specialty is photo essay books" avg. press run 7.5M. Pub'd 2 titles 1990; expects 2 titles 1991, 3 titles 1992. 6 titles listed in the *Small Press Record of Books in Print* (20th Edition, 1991-92). avg. price, cloth: $30; paper: $20; other: $60 limited edition (collectors' edition with limited runs of 100 or 200 books). Discounts: 1-2 books 20%, 3-24 40%, 25-49 42%, 50-99 44%, 100-299 46%, 300-499 48%, 500+ 50%. 140pp; size varies; of, duotone photographs, laser scanned, also color. Reporting time: 3 months. Payment: royalties paid, depends on each book, usually standard. Copyrights for author. COSMEP, ABA, PMA.

NEWSLETTER, Pleasure Dome Press (Long Island Poetry Collective Inc.), Pat Nesbitt, Editor, PO Box 773, Huntington, NY 11743. 1974. Articles, criticism, reviews, news items. "Features include: calendar of regional literary events (Long Island-NY City), 1-2 reviews per issue, an extensive small press markets column, and other informational materials of use to readers/writers of poetry." circ. 100. 6/yr. Pub'd 6 issues 1990; expects 6 issues 1991. sub. price: available only as part of Long Island Poetry Collective, Inc. dues, which are $18; sample: $1. 4pp; 8½×11; of. Reporting time: none. Payment: none. Copyrighted, reverts to author. Pub's reviews: 10 in 1990. §Poetry. No ads.

NEWSLETTER (LEAGUE OF CANADIAN POETS), Dolores Ricketts, Newsletter Copy Editor; Jill Humphries, Newsletter Production Editor; Richard Lush, Museletter, 24 Ryerson Avenue, Toronto, Ontario M5T 2P3, Canada, 416-363-5047. 1970. Poetry, articles, art, photos, cartoons, news items. "Essentially an in-house review of the Canadian poetry scene. Some feature articles, mostly of interest to League members (published professional poets). Also publish a big issue twice-yearly titled *Museletter*." circ. 500. 8-10/yr. Pub'd 8-10 issues 1990; expects 8-10 issues 1991, 8-10 issues 1992. sub. price: $25; per copy: $5 Museletter, $2 Newsletter ppd; sample: $2. Back issues: $2.50 issue as available (complete runs do not exist). 32pp Museletter, 4-6pp Newsletter; 8½×11; of. Payment: none. Copyrighted, reverts to author. Write for ad rates.

NEWSLETTER INAGO, Del Reitz, Editor and Publisher, Inago Press, PO Box 26244, Tucson, AZ 85726-6244, 602-294-7031. 1979. Poetry. *"NI* is circulated internationally. Each issue features the writing of only one poet (except for filler guests) with biosketch and commentary. Submissions by invitation; however, all others will be read. MS size 10-15 poems of no more than 50 lines each with SASE. Periodic Inago anthologies of poetry in print and/or audio tape of Inago Poets. All checks or money orders *must be made payable to Del Reitz."* circ. 200. 12/yr. Pub'd 12 issues 1990; expects 12 issues 1991, 12 issues 1992. sub. price: $16, overseas $18; per copy: $2, overseas $3; sample: $2, overseas $3. Back issues: $2, overseas $3. Discounts: none. 4pp; 8×10½; photo copy. Reporting time: immediate. Payment: contributor's copies (4 or more). Copyrighted, rights retained by author. No ads.

NEXT EXIT, Eric Folsom, 92 Helen Street, Kingston, Ontario K7L 4P3, Canada, 613-549-6790. 1980. Poetry, art, cartoons, criticism, reviews, long-poems. "Short prose - 2 pages; poems up to 2 pages; reviews 1-2 pages. We are interested in new & experimental work. Some contributors: Lyn Lifshin, B.Z. Niditch, Brian Burke, Mary Ellen Csamer." circ. 200. 2/yr. Pub'd 2 issues 1990; expects 2 issues 1991, 2 issues 1992. sub. price: $6; per copy: $3; sample: $3. Back issues: single copy $2; sample copy $2. Discounts: negotiable. 28pp; 5×8½; xerox. Reporting time: 3 months. Payment: in copies. Copyrighted, reverts to author. Pub's reviews: 6 in 1990. §Poetry. Ads: $50/page or exchange with other periodicals.

Newton-Cline Press, Jessie Gunn Stephens, 421 Sam Rayburn Fwy, Sherman, TX 75090, 214-893-1818. 1988. Non-fiction. "We publish books, workbooks and manuals under two imprints: Management Training Services and Volunteer Management Services. The first focuses on communications training for business and industry, the second on training for managers of volunteers in church and business. We welcome queries only (no complete manuscripts) in these specific fields, but proposals must be for highmargin books, because we sell almost exclusively by mail. Proposal should include author resume or detailed summary of experience/credentials for writing the manuscript. We like practical, down-to-earth writing that is jargon-free and information intensive" avg. press run 1M-5M. Expects 3 titles 1991, 3 titles 1992. 3 titles listed in the *Small Press Record of Books in Print* (20th Edition, 1991-92). avg. price, paper: $15-$29.95; other: $35-50 manuals in 3-ring binder. Pages vary; size varies; of. Reporting time: 1 month. Payment: negotiable. Copyrights for author. COSMEP.

NiceTown, Ted Wing, 5201 Media Street, Philadelphia, PA 19131, 215-473-7575. 1983. Poetry, fiction, articles, cartoons, interviews, reviews, plays. avg. press run 1M-2M. Pub'd 12 titles 1990; expects 14 titles 1991, 16 titles 1992. avg. price, cloth: $16; paper: $7. Discounts: I.B.O./30 pay NET. 150-200pp; size varies; †of. Reporting time: 60 days. Copyrights for author. ABPA, ABA, NPA.

Nicolas-Hays, Inc., B. Lundsted, Box 612, York Beach, ME 03910, 207-363-4393. 1976. Music, non-fiction. "We publish philosophy, music, psychology, alternative healing. We have recently published *The Book of Lilith* by Dr. Barbara Black Koltuv, a Jungian analyst practicing in New York City. *Rudolf Steiner and Holistic Medicine* by Francis X. King was published August 1987. We have published *The Pythagorean Plato* by Prof. Ernest McClain, a philosophical treatise on the symbolism of music and number in Plato's writings." avg. press run 3M-5M. Pub'd 2 titles 1990; expects 2 titles 1991, 2 titles 1992. 4 titles listed in the *Small Press Record of Books in Print* (20th Edition, 1991-92). avg. price, cloth: $12.95; paper: $9.95. Discounts: Normal trade discounts apply. Write for account information. Distributed by Samuel Weiser, Inc. at same address. 300pp; 6×9; of. Reporting time: 3 months. Payment: we pay royalties, information available on request. Copyrights for author.

Nierika Editions (see also AMERICAN WRITING: A MAGAZINE), Alexandra Grilikhes, 4343 Manayunk Avenue, Philadelphia, PA 19128, 215-483-7051. 1990. Poetry, fiction, articles, interviews, criticism, letters, parts-of-novels, long-poems, collages, non-fiction. "We are new and haven't published any books yet." avg. press run 1.5M.

Night Horn Books, Robert Anbian, PO Box 11536, San Francisco, CA 94101-7536, 415-750-0660. 1978. Poetry, fiction, articles, art, photos, cartoons, interviews, satire, criticism, reviews, letters, parts-of-novels, long-poems, collages, plays, concrete art. avg. press run 2M. Expects 1 title 1991, 2 titles 1992. 3 titles listed in the *Small Press Record of Books in Print* (20th Edition, 1991-92). avg. price, paper: $6. Discounts: 40% to the trade direct or through distributions; 50% off for 9 or less copies, 55% off 10 or more to jobbers, wholesalers. 100-125pp; 5½×8; of. Reporting time: 8-12 weeks. Payment: negotiable. Copyrights for author.

Night Owl Publishers (see also GRASS ROOTS), Megg Miller, Kath Harper, PO Box 242, Euroa, Victoria 3666, Australia. 1973. Articles, photos, letters, non-fiction. avg. press run 3M. Pub'd 2 titles 1990; expects 1 title 1991, 1 title 1992. 18 titles listed in the *Small Press Record of Books in Print* (20th Edition, 1991-92). avg. price, paper: $11. 143pp; 20.5×27cm, 13.7×21.5cm; of. Reporting time: 4 months. Payment: negotiable. Copyrights for author. ABPA.

NIGHT OWL'S NEWSLETTER, Julian Associates, Debbie Jordan, 6831 Spencer Hwy, #203, Pasadena, TX 77505, 713-930-8551. 1990. Poetry, fiction, articles, cartoons, interviews, satire, reviews, letters, non-fiction. "This publication is for people who can't sleep at night and want to use those hours productively. We will publish *no pornography!* We want to give positive support to Owls (night people) who must live and work in a world run by Larks (day people)." 4/yr. Pub'd 2 issues 1990; expects 4 issues 1991, 4 issues 1992. sub. price: $12; per copy: $3.50; sample: $3.50. Back issues: $3.50. 16pp; 8½x11; †Xerox. Reporting time: 1 month average. Payment: $1 minimum + 1 copy. Copyrighted, reverts to author. Pub's reviews: 1 in 1990. §night people, sleep research.

NIGHT ROSES, MOONSTONE BLUE, Allen T. Billy, Editor; Sandy Taylor, Graphics Editor, PO Box 393, Prospect Heights, IL 60070, 708-392-2435. 1986. Poetry, art. "Interested in poems about bells, dance, clocks, romance, fashions, ghost images of past or future, nature, arts. General poems 6-20 lines, some longer. Some recent contributors: Ida Fasel, Ken Stone, Mary R. De Maine, Jean Cameron and Ana Pine. All poets are treated equal at *Night Roses.* Hopefully, each issue of *Night Roses* will take its own direction and speak for itself." circ. 250. 2-3/yr. Pub'd 2 issues 1990; expects 3 issues 1991, 2 issues 1992. sub. price: $8; per copy: $3; sample: $2.50. Back issues: $3. 44pp; 5⅜x8½; mi. Reporting time: 6-10 weeks. Payment: 1 contributor's copy. Not copyrighted. §Poetry, dance, and art publications.

Nightingale Music, John G. Potts, 11190 Black Forest Road, Colorado Springs, CO 80908, 719-495-3815. 1990. Music, non-fiction. "Music-based 'how-to' guides" avg. press run 2.5M-5M. Expects 2 titles 1991, 3 titles 1992. 1 title listed in the *Small Press Record of Books in Print* (20th Edition, 1991-92). avg. price, paper: $10. Discounts: bulk 10%-15%, trade 25%-55%. 60pp; 5½x8½. Reporting time: 28 days. Payment: no advance, agreed royalties on sales, prod. costs deducted from royalties. Copyrights for author.

NightinGale Resources, Lila Teich Gold, PO Box 322, Cold Spring, NY 10516, 212-753-5383. 1982. Non-fiction. "We publish facsimile editions of quality books. To date they have been food oriented. Also cookbooks, directories." avg. press run 10M. Expects 2 titles 1991, 2 titles 1992. 5 titles listed in the *Small Press Record of Books in Print* (20th Edition, 1991-92). avg. price, cloth: $19.95; paper: $11.95; other: $6.95 pocket guide. Discounts: on request. Does not copyright for author. COSMEP, Small Press Center, New York City.

Nightshade Press (see also POTATO EYES), Carolyn Page, Roy Zarucchi, PO Box 76, Ward Hill, Troy, ME 04987, 207-948-3427. 1988. Poetry, fiction, art. "We have published the following: *The Knitted Glove* by Jack Coulehan, M.D., *My Father's Harmonica* by Madeline Tiger, *Closing the Gate* by Beverly Merrick, *Martyrdom of the Onion* by Michael Chitwood, and *Naming the Trees* by R.T. Smith." avg. press run 500-750. Pub'd 12 titles 1990; expects 16 titles 1991, 16 titles 1992. avg. price, paper: $5. Discounts: 40% to bookstores. 36pp; 8½x5½; of. Reporting time: 6-8 weeks. Payment: 75% of run to author; author pays Nightshare royalties equal to 1/2 of sales incrementally as books are sold; promotion is shared. Copyrights for author. CLMP, Maine Writers & Publishers Alliance, The New Hampshire Writers & Publishers Project and North Carolina Writers Network.

NIGHTSUN, Douglas DeMars, Barbara Wilson, School of Arts-Humanities, Frostburg S. University, Frostburg, MD 21532. 1981. Poetry, fiction, articles, art, photos, cartoons, interviews, satire, collages. "We want highest quality poetry. Subject matter open. Prefer poems not much longer than 40 lines not interested in the extremes of the sentimental obvious poetry on the one hand and subjectless "great gossamer-winged gnat" school on the other. Have recently published work by William Stafford, Antler, and Marge Piercy, Diane Wakoski, and Linda Paston—and an interview with Carolyn Forche." circ. 500-1M. 1/yr. Pub'd 1 issue 1990; expects 1 issue 1991, 1 issue 1992. sub. price: $5+$1.50 p/h; per copy: $5+$1.50 p/h; sample: $5+$1.50 p/h. Back issues: inquire. Discounts: inquire. 80pp; 5½x8½; of. Reporting time: 3 months. Payment: free copies. Copyrighted, reverts to author. Ads: $100/$60.

Nightsun Books, Frank Fleckenstein, 520 Greene Street, Cumberland, MD 21502, 301-722-2127. 1987. Poetry, fiction, cartoons, plays, non-fiction. "Please inquire before submitting manuscripts!" avg. press run 200-1M. Pub'd 5 titles 1990; expects 5 titles 1991, 1 title 1992. 7 titles listed in the *Small Press Record of Books in Print* (20th Edition, 1991-92). avg. price, cloth: $3-$10. 30-200pp; 5½x8½; †of. Reporting time: varies. Payment: varies, inquire.

THE NIHILISTIC REVIEW, Pessimism Press, Inc., Maxwell Gaddis, Executive Editor; Camilla Danielson, Oregon, Poetry; Camilla Danielson, Oregon, PO Box 1074, S. Sioux City, NE 68776, 402-494-3110. 1990. Poetry, fiction, art, photos, cartoons, interviews, satire, criticism, reviews, parts-of-novels, plays, non-fiction. "We at *The Nihilistic Review* desire all types of anti-establishment, antisocial and/or slightly misogynistic material. The more bizarre the better. We check each piece within our multi-layer staff to ensure it's ability to offend someone, place, or thing. It is not beneath us to send gratis a copy of the *Review* to the offended. We will not accept any 'feel good, chick type' fluff, weepy lyrics or rhymes. In fact, they will not be returned even if accompanied by SASE. Our most famous contributor is Charles Bukowski. Others include Malone, Lifshin, Weinman, Nagler, Cotolo and Joy Walsh. Any readers of Stephen King novels need not waste your postage. We're not your mag. *We are a very flexible publication.*" circ. 1M. 4/yr. Pub'd 1 issue 1990; expects 4 issues

1991, 4 issues 1992. sub. price: $20; per copy: $6; sample: $6. Back issues: any back issue for single copy price. Discounts: newstands/agents 40%, U.S. Government outlets add 40% to cover and/or subscription rates. 40pp; 8×11; †xerox. Reporting time: no later than 3 days after receipt. Payment: copies. Copyrighted, reverts to author. Pub's reviews: 1 in 1990. §Avant-garde, Beat, anti-establishment. Ads: $20/$11.50/$6 1/4 page/20¢ per word.

NIMROD, Francine Ringold, Arts and Humanities Council of Tulsa, 2210 So. Main, Tulsa, OK 74114. 1956. Poetry, fiction, articles, art, photos, interviews, parts-of-novels, long-poems, plays. "Recent contributors: Amy Clampitt, Josephine Jacobson, Michael McBride, Pattiann Rogers, James Allen McPherson, Tess Gallagher, Ishmael Reed, Denise Levertov, Francois Camoin, Beckian Goldberg, Gish Jen, Alvin Greenberg, Mary La Chapelle, Sharon Sakson. Annual *Nimrod/Hardman* Awards: in poetry (Pable Neruda Prize), in fiction (Katherine Anne Porter Prize). 1st prize in each category $1000, 2nd prize $500. Submissions are accepted between January 1 and April 1 each year. Past judges include Marvin Bell, Richard Howard, Charles Johnson, Paul West, Mark Strand, William Stafford, Stanley Kunitz, Rosellen Brown, Gordon Lish, Carolyn Kizer, Stephen Dunn, George Garrett, W.D. Snodgrass, John Leonard. Please send business size SASE for awards and guidelines." circ. 3M. 2/yr. Pub'd 2 issues 1990; expects 2 issues 1991. 9 titles listed in the *Small Press Record of Books in Print* (20th Edition, 1991-92). sub. price: $10 + $1.50 p&h, $3 p&h outside USA; per copy: $6.95; sample: $4.50. Back issues: varies. List of back issues available from *Nimrod*. Discounts: 10% orders over 20. 160pp; 6×9; of. Reporting time: 1-12 weeks. Payment: copies of issue in which work is published. Copyrighted, reverts to author. Ads: $150/$75. CCLM, COSMEP, AWP.

9N-2N-8N NEWSLETTER, Gerard W. Rinaldi, 154 Blackwood Lane, Stamford, CT 06903, 203-322-7283. 1985. Articles, art, photos, cartoons, interviews, criticism, reviews, letters, news items. "Magazine consists of 20-24/2 col. several photos, column pages, small print, equal to 32-40 in larger print." circ. 3M. 4/yr. Pub'd 4 issues 1990; expects 4 issues 1991, 4 issues 1992. sub. price: $12 US, $14 Canada, $16 foreign; per copy: $5; sample: $5. Back issues: $10 for 1986, $10 for 1987 back issues, $12 for 1988. Discounts: none. 20-24pp; 8½×11; †of. Reporting time: 1 month. Payment: none. Copyrighted, does not revert to author. Pub's reviews: 6-8 in 1990. §Agriculture, old tractors, farm memorabilia, farm equipment, farm lifestyle. No advertising.

NINETEENTH-CENTURY LITERATURE, University of California Press, G.B. Tennyson, Thomas Wortham, University of California Press, 2120 Berkeley Way, Berkeley, CA 94720, 415-642-4191. 1946. Reviews, non-fiction. "Editorial address: Dept. of English, University of California, Los Angeles, CA 90024." circ. 2.5M. 4/yr. Pub'd 4 issues 1990; expects 4 issues 1991, 4 issues 1992. sub. price: $19 indiv., $33 instit., $14 students (+ $4 foreign postage); per copy: $9; sample: free. Back issues: $9. Discounts: foreign subs. agents 10%, one-time orders 10+, standing orders (bookstores): 1-99 40%, 100+ 50%. 144pp; 6×9; of. Reporting time: 1-2 months. Copyrighted, does not revert to author. Pub's reviews: 100 in 1990. §19th-century literature, American and English. Ads: $200/$120.

19TH-CENTURY MUSIC, University of California Press, Walter Frisch, D. Kern Holoman, University of California Press, 2120 Berkeley Way, Berkeley, CA 94720, 415-642-4191. 1977. Criticism, reviews, non-fiction. "Editorial address: Dept. of Music, University of California, Davis, CA 95616." circ. 1.3M. 3/yr. Pub'd 3 issues 1990; expects 3 issues 1991, 3 issues 1992. sub. price: $23 indiv., $47 instit. (+ $4 foreign postage); per copy: $8 indiv.; $16 instit.; sample: free. Back issues: same as single copy price. Discounts: foreign subs. agents 10%, one-time orders 10+ 30%, standing orders (bookstores): 1-99 40%, 100+ 50%. 96pp; 8½×10; of. Reporting time: 1-3 months. Copyrighted, does not revert to author. Pub's reviews: 50 in 1990. §19th-century music. Ads: $200/$120.

Nioba, Uitgevers, Peter De Greef, Marc Van Gasse, Maarschalk Gerardstraat 6, 2000 Antwerpen, Belgium, 03/232.38.62. 1985. Poetry, fiction, articles, art, photos, cartoons, interviews, criticism. "Unlimited - prose & poetry. Specialised in international *homoerotic literature*" avg. press run 1M. Pub'd 48 titles 1990; expects 48 titles 1991, 60 titles 1992. avg. price, paper: $5. Discounts: 30%. 150pp; 12×19; †of. Reporting time: unlimited. Payment: 10%. Copyrights for author. VBVB.

NNIDNID: SURREALITY, Tony Shiels, 3 Vale View, Ponsanooth, Truro, Cornwall, United Kingdom. 1986. Poetry, fiction, articles, art, photos, cartoons, interviews, criticism, reviews, letters, collages, plays, news items. "Material commissioned from adherents of international surrealist movement only." circ. 750+. 2-3/yr. Pub'd 2 issues 1990; expects 2 issues 1991, 3 issues 1992. 6 titles listed in the *Small Press Record of Books in Print* (20th Edition, 1991-92). sub. price: £10; per copy: £4; sample: £4. 40pp; size A4; of. Payment: none. Copyrighted, reverts to author. Pub's reviews: 4 books in 1990. §Surrealism, painting, writing, cinema. No ads.

The Noble Press, Inc., Mark Harris, Executive Editor; M.T. Cozzola, Associate Editor, 213 West Institute Place #508, Chicago, IL 60610, 312-642-1168. 1988. Non-fiction. avg. press run 9M. Expects 4 titles 1991, 8 titles 1992. 7 titles listed in the *Small Press Record of Books in Print* (20th Edition, 1991-92). avg. price, cloth: $18.95; paper: $11.95. Discounts: negotiable. 256pp; 6×9; lp. Reporting time: varies. Payment: negotiable. Copyrights for author. ABA, PMA, COSMEP.

388

THE NOCTURNAL LYRIC, Susan Moon, Box 2602, Pasadena, CA 91101. 1987. Poetry, fiction, art, satire. "No stories longer than 2,000 words" circ. 200. 6/yr. Pub'd 6 issues 1990; expects 6 issues 1991, 6 issues 1992. sub. price: $10; per copy: $1.25; sample: $1.25. Back issues: $1-$1.25, sometimes we have special blowout deals. Discounts: $10 for 10 copies of same issue. 22pp; 5½×8½; †photocopying. Reporting time: rejections within 3 weeks, acceptances 6 months. Payment: none, as we're completely non-profit. Not copyrighted. Ads: none.

NOCTURNAL NEWS, Baker Street Publications, Sharida Rizzuto, Sidney J. Dragon, Thomas Schellenberger, PO Box 994, Metairie, LA 70004, 504-734-8414. 1983. Poetry, fiction, articles, art, photos, cartoons, interviews, satire, criticism, reviews, letters, long-poems, collages, plays, news items, non-fiction. "This publication covers the horror genre. All submissions must be double-spaced & typewritten. We will not publish explicit sex. We also include some occult submissions" circ. under 10M. 3/yr. Pub'd 3 issues 1990; expects 3 issues 1991, 3 issues 1992. sub. price: $11/3 issues; per copy: $2.50; sample: $2.50. Back issues: $2.50. Discounts: trade with other like publications. 8-10pp; 8½×11; of, photo copy, excellent quality. Reporting time: 2-6 weeks. Payment: free copies. Copyrighted, reverts to author. Pub's reviews: 16 in 1990. §Horror in film and literature, occult, supernatural, new age. Ads: free. NWC, SPWAO, HWA, Literary Markets, MWA, Western Writers of America (WWA), Arizona Authors Association (AAA).

Nolo Press, Ralph Warner, Stephen Elias, Senior Editor, 950 Parker Street, Berkeley, CA 94710, 415-549-1976. 1971. Non-fiction. "Our books are of a special nature: they are how-to guides for laypeople, instructive in various legal procedures, and are frequently (at least every 12-14 months) revised/updated to keep current with law changes. This means that our backlist books are often among our bestsellers and are treated as new books, which is very different from the backlist of other publishers. It also makes our new-books-per-year a little harder to figure (#10). Anywhere from 10-150 pages might change during a revision and we often re-introduce a backlist title that has been significantly changed to the media, complete with a new press release." avg. press run 8M. Pub'd 15 titles 1990; expects 20 titles 1991, 25 titles 1992. 66 titles listed in the *Small Press Record of Books in Print* (20th Edition, 1991-92). avg. price, paper: $17.95. Discounts: 50% to distributors (and negot.); 40-46% bookstores. 240pp; 8½×11; of. Reporting time: 1-6 weeks. Payment: 7-10% of retail, quarterly payment. Copyrights for author. NCBPA, AALL, AAP, ALA, ABA.

Nolo Press - Occidental, Charles Sherman, Editor; Trudy H. Devine, Manager, PO Box 722, Occidental, CA 95465, 707-874-3105. 1971. Non-fiction. avg. press run 10M. Pub'd 1 title 1990; expects 3 titles 1991, 2 titles 1992. 5 titles listed in the *Small Press Record of Books in Print* (20th Edition, 1991-92). avg. price, paper: $12.95. Discounts: 1-4 25%, 5-99 40%, 100+ 50%. 200pp; 8½×11; lp. Reporting time: 1 month. Payment: 8% of retail paid quarterly. Copyrights for author. ABA, PMA.

NOMOS: Studies in Spontaneous Order, Carol B. Low, Editor; John Enright, Poetry Editor, 257 Chesterfield, Glen Ellyn, IL 60137, 708-858-7184. 1982. Poetry, fiction, articles, art, cartoons, interviews, criticism, reviews, letters, long-poems, news items, non-fiction. "Writer's guidelines, ad rate schedules available. Length of material varies, with features running 2,000+ words. *Nomos* is taken from a Greek word meaning 'law or custom'. The word captures the spontaneous or unplanned nature of a free society. Individual freedom and responsibility is our bias." circ. 1M. 4/yr. Pub'd 4 issues 1990; expects 4 issues 1991, 4 issues 1992. sub. price: $18; per copy: $4.50; sample: $3. Back issues: $3 single copy + $1 post/handling. 32pp; 8½×11; of. Reporting time: 6 months maximum. Payment: 10 comp copies for original feature-length articles, 5 copies for poetry and reprints. Not copyrighted. Pub's reviews: 4 in 1990. §Free-market economics, individual rights, libertarian sci-fi. Ads: $100/$50/1/4 $25. none.

NON COMPOS MENTIS, Scott K. Smith, Scott K. Smith #74481, AZ State Prison, 10,000 S. Wilmot, Tucson, AZ 85777. 1990. Poetry, fiction, art, letters, collages, plays, non-fiction. "I prefer material that is fairly short (within 500-1000 words), due to the small size of my magazine. Do *not* put the name of the mag on the envelope. Always send SASE if you want your material back. Recent contributors have been Will Inman, Albert Huffstickler, Chris Woods, Pat McKinnon, Sylvia Manning, Cheryl A. Townsend, Mychele and others. I do *not* want any essays or any other material without some type of letter or intro of some type. I cannot charge for the mag from inside so I depend on donations made in U.S. Mint stamps." circ. 150-200. 6/yr. Pub'd 2 issues 1990; expects 6 issues 1991, 6 issues 1992. sub. price: donate; per copy: same; sample: donate. 40pp; 4¼×5½; †mi. Reporting time: 4 weeks. Payment: 1 contributors copy. Not copyrighted. Ads: write.

Non-Stop Books, John Bailey, PO Box 1354, Minnetonka, MN 55345-0354. 1980. Non-fiction. "We look for literate, experiential (rather than scholarly) accounts of spiritual transformation written from a non-dualistic, awakened perspective. Not currently interested in material related to karma, chakras, channels, past-lives, religious sects, or Christian fundamentalism. See our recently published *Awakening From The Dream Of Me* for an idea of our focus" avg. press run 2M-3M. Pub'd 1 title 1990; expects 2 titles 1991, 2 titles 1992. 1 title listed in the *Small Press Record of Books in Print* (20th Edition, 1991-92). avg. price, paper: $10.95. Reporting time: 3-5 weeks. Payment: standard. Copyrights for author. MIPA, NAIP, COSMEP.

THE NONVIOLENT ACTIVIST, Ruth Benn, War Resisters League, 339 Lafayette Street, New York, NY 10012, 212-228-0450. 1984. Articles, cartoons, interviews, reviews, news items. "News of interest to the nonviolence movement; special focus on activities of the War Resisters League" circ. 18M. 8/yr. Pub'd 8 issues 1990; expects 8 issues 1991, 8 issues 1992. sub. price: $25 inst.; per copy: $1.50; sample: $1. 24pp; 8½×11; of. Pub's reviews: 16 in 1990. §Nonviolence, organizing ideas/skills, war/peace. Ads: $250/$150.

NONVIOLENT ANARCHIST NEWSLETTER, Slough Press, Emma Joe Berkzhill, Box 1385, Austin, TX 78767. 1983. Articles, art, photos, cartoons, interviews, satire, collages. "We have evolved into individualist anarchist position and now only publish the essays of Chuck Taylor. Our affinities are with the *Me Zines.* Glad to trade with other publications. Not interested in unsolicited manuscripts of any form or kind" circ. 500. Frequency varies. sub. price: $3, NOTE: subscriptions can be paid in work or barter/trade; per copy: $1; sample: $1. Back issues: $3. 12-16pp; 5½×8½; of. Reporting time: 2 weeks. Payment: copies only. Not copyrighted. Pub's reviews: 0 in 1990. §Anarchism only. Ads: $20/$10/10¢.

NOOK NEWS CONFERENCES AND KLATCHES BULLETIN, The Writers' Nook Press, Eugene Ortiz, Editor; Jan May, Contributing Editor, 38114 Third Street, Suite 181, Willoughby, OH 44094, 216-975-8965. 1988. News items. "If you would like to publicize an upcoming writers' conference, workshop, or regular meeting, send the information to Jan May, 525 NW 17th Street, Oklahoma City, OK 73103." circ. 1M. 4/yr. Pub'd 2 issues 1990; expects 4 issues 1991, 4 issues 1992. sub. price: $18; per copy: $5; sample: $5. 12-16pp; 5½×8½. Not copyrighted. Ads: $250/$150/$87.50 1/4 page/unclassifieds 25¢/word. COSMEP.

THE NOOK NEWS CONTESTS AND AWARDS BULLETIN, The Writers' Nook Press, Eugene Ortiz, Editor; Deborah Bouziden, Contributing Editor, 38114 Third Street, Suite 181, Willoughby, OH 44094, 216-975-8965. 1990. News items. "If you would like to publicize a contest or award for writers, send complete information to Deborah Bouziden, 8416 Huckleberry, Edmond, OK 73034." circ. 1M. 4/yr. Pub'd 2 issues 1990; expects 4 issues 1991, 4 issues 1992. sub. price: $18; per copy: $5; sample: $5. 12-16pp; 5½×8½. Not copyrighted. Ads: $250/$150/$87.50 1/4 page/unclassifieds 25¢/word. COSMEP.

THE NOOK NEWS MARKET BULLETIN, The Writers' Nook Press, Eugene Ortiz, 38114 3rd Street #181, Willoughby, OH 44094, 216-975-8965. 1989. "*The Nook News Market Bulletin* is written and edited by Eugene Ortiz. It is, as the name implies, a marketing tool published for writers of all genres. I do not accept freelance submissions." circ. 500. 4/yr. Expects 4 issues 1991, 4 issues 1992. sub. price: $14.40; per copy: $4; sample: $4. 12pp; 5½×8½; †photocopy. Ads: $66/$36. COSMEP.

NOOK NEWS REVIEW OF WRITERS' PUBLICATIONS, The Writers' Nook Press, Eugene Ortiz, Editor; Marcella Owens, Contributing Editor, 38114 Third Street, Suite 181, Willoughby, OH 44094, 216-975-8965. 1991. Reviews. "If you would like a copy of your writer's publication reviewed, send it to Marcella Owens, PO Box 413, Joaquin, TX 75954." circ. 1M. 4/yr. Expects 4 issues 1991, 4 issues 1992. sub. price: $18; per copy: $5; sample: $5. 12-16pp; 5½×8½. Not copyrighted. Pub's reviews. §Anything having to do with the business or experience of freelance writing. Ads: $250/$150/$87.50 1/4 page/unclassifieds 25¢/word. COSMEP.

NOOSPAPERS, Greg Ruggiero, Stuart Sahulka, Open Dialogues, Inc., 215 N. Avenue West, Suite 21, Westfield, NJ 07090, 201-249-0280. 1986. Poetry, fiction, art, cartoons, interviews, satire, long-poems, collages, plays, concrete art. "*Noospapers* is a xeroxed journal for readers on the verge. Loosely bound by theme, tightly bound by three industrial-strength staples. We warmly accept: writing, visuals, found reprintables, collages, rants, insurgencies, heavy petting, communiques, plight, reviews, change, trembling, awe, fieldreports, glyphs, recoveries, interviews, rubble, documentations, and illimitable visions. Alternative Communication Speaking Beyond This Millenium! Upcoming work by Miekal And, Philip Athens, Vittore Baroni, Charles Bernstein, Jake Berry, Hakim Bey, Bob Black, Loris Essary, Greg Evason, G. Huth, Stephen-Paul Martin, Mike Miskowski, Harry Polkinhorn, Joseph Richey, and Ivan Sladek." circ. 200. 3/yr. Pub'd 3 issues 1990; expects 3 issues 1991, 3 issues 1992. sub. price: $8; per copy: $3; sample: $3. Back issues: $3. Discounts: none. 70pp; 8½×11; †photocopy. Reporting time: less than 2 weeks. Payment: copies. Copyrighted, reverts to author. Pub's reviews: 30 in 1990. §Politics, art and culture. Ads: $100/$50/$25 classifieds. CCLM.

Nordic Books, Niels Malmquist, PO Box 1941, Philadelphia, PA 19105, 609-795-1887. 1978. Non-fiction. "Book production services available for self-publishers of books with a Scandinavian background. Prefer non-fiction, original manuscripts or translations." avg. press run 500-1.5M. Expects 1 title 1991, 2 titles 1992. 19 titles listed in the *Small Press Record of Books in Print* (20th Edition, 1991-92). avg. price, cloth: $9.95-$45; paper: $3.25-$15.95. Discounts: 20% on imports. 96-800pp; size varies; of. Reporting time: 2 weeks. Payment: on individual basis. Copyrights for author.

North American Bookdealers Exchange (see also BOOK DEALERS WORLD), Al Galasso, Editorial Director; Judy Wiggins, Senior Editor; Russ von Hoelscher, Associate Editor, PO Box 606, Cottage Grove, OR 97424-0026. 1979. Articles, interviews, news items, non-fiction. "Manuscripts should be about making or saving money, self-publishing, mail order or book marketing. Will also accept titles relating to sexual communication, new diets, and health. Recent titles are *Book Dealers Dropship Directory* and *7 Vital Steps to Writing & Publishing Reports*" avg. press run 1M. Pub'd 2 titles 1990; expects 2 titles 1991, 2 titles 1992. avg. price, paper: $5-$10. Discounts: 50% off to 75% on larger wholesale orders. 40pp; 5½×8, 8½×11; of. Reporting time: 2 weeks. Payment: outright purchase. Does not copyright for author.

THE NORTH AMERICAN REVIEW, Robley Wilson, Univ. Of Northern Iowa, Cedar Falls, IA 50614, 319-273-6455. 1815. Poetry, fiction, articles, reviews, long-poems, non-fiction. "Environmental focus." circ. 5M. 4/yr. Pub'd 4 issues 1990; expects 4 issues 1991, 4 issues 1992. sub. price: $14; per copy: $4; sample: $4. Back issues: face price. Discounts: Agent 20%; bulk (10 or more) 30%. 72pp; 8⅛×10⅞ (ABP Standard); of. Reporting time: 10 weeks. Payment: $10 per published page; 50¢ a line for poetry. Copyrighted, rights assigned on request of author. Pub's reviews: 20 in 1990. §Poetry & short fiction. Ads: $500/$275. CLMP.

North American Students of Cooperation (see also LEADERSHIP DIRECTIONS), Sharon Pedersen, Director of Publications, Box 7715, Ann Arbor, MI 48107, 313-663-0889. 1969. Articles, cartoons, interviews, satire, reviews, letters. "1M-4M words. Articles should be related to student cooperatives, such as meeting process, board/mgmt. issues, maintainance, etc. Double-spaced. Returned only if accompanied by stamped self-addressed envelope" avg. press run 600. Pub'd 4 titles 1990; expects 5 titles 1991, 6 titles 1992. 12 titles listed in the *Small Press Record of Books in Print* (20th Edition, 1991-92). avg. price, paper: $1.75-$5. Discounts: to 40%. 48pp; 8½×11; of. Reporting time: 2 weeks. Payment: by arrangement. Does not copyright for author.

The North Carolina Haiku Society Press, Rebecca B. Rust, PO Box 14247, Raleigh, NC 27620, 919-231-4531. 1984. Poetry, criticism, non-fiction. "The North Carolina Haiku Society Press publishes material only of, or about, haiku." avg. press run 350. Pub'd 1 title 1990. 2 titles listed in the *Small Press Record of Books in Print* (20th Edition, 1991-92). avg. price, paper: $6; other: $3. Discounts: 40%. 64pp; 5½×8½; of. Reporting time: approx. 1 month (submissions must come in the form of applications for the grant). Payment: negotiable. Copyrights for author.

NORTH CAROLINA LIBRARIES, Meridional Publications, Frances Bradburn, Editor-in-Chief, 7101 Winding Way, Wake Forest, NC 27587, 919-556-2940. Articles, art, news items. circ. 2.7M. 4/yr. Expects 4 issues 1991. sub. price: $32; per copy: $15; sample: $15. Back issues: none. Discounts: none. 64pp; 8½×11; of. Reporting time: 1 month. Payment: none. Not copyrighted. Pub's reviews: 52 in 1990. §North Carolina. Ads: please request rates. North Carolina Library Association.

NORTH CAROLINA LITERARY REVIEW, Alex Albright, English Department, East Carolina University, Greenville, NC 27858, 919-757-6041/6684. 1991. Articles, photos, interviews, criticism, reviews, letters, news items, non-fiction. "Recent contributors: Fred Chappell, Doris Betts, Gay Wilentz. Length: 1,000-6,000 words. Biases: critical and historical essays and scholarly articles about N.C. writers; interviews with N.C. writers; occasional essays by N.C. writers, but no regularly published contemporary creative work; comprehensive essay reviews of recent books by N.C. writers; essays and articles on bookselling and libraries in N.C. MLA style when appropriate; please query before submitting articles." circ. 1.2M. 2/yr. Expects 2 issues 1992. sub. price: $12; per copy: $7; sample: $7. Discounts: 40% non-returnable; 20% with full credit for returns. 154pp; 6¾×10; lp. Reporting time: 4-6 weeks on queries only. Payment: $50-$500 for all articles; kill fee for solicited articles not published. Copyrighted, rights revert on request. Pub's reviews. §North Carolina writers. Ads: $200/$110.

North Country Books, Inc., Robert B. Igoe, M. Sheila Orlin, 18 Irving Place, Utica, NY 13501, 315-735-4877. 1965. Non-fiction. "NY State, history, biography, nostalgia, heavy accent on Adirondacks & upstate." avg. press run 3M-5M. Pub'd 5 titles 1990; expects 5 titles 1991, 5 titles 1992. 34 titles listed in the *Small Press Record of Books in Print* (20th Edition, 1991-92). avg. price, cloth: $14.95; paper: $9.95. Discounts: 1-4, 20%; 5, 40%. 200pp; 6×9, 7×10; of. Reporting time: 1-3 months. Payment: 8% retail price, 20% withheld against returns. Copyrights for author. COSMEP.

North Country Press, William M. Johnson, Publisher; Linnea K. Johnson, Publisher, PO Box 641, Unity, ME 04988, 207-948-2208. 1977. Poetry, fiction, cartoons, satire, non-fiction. "Three lines: outdoors (hunting, fishing, backpacking, etc.); history, lore, humor; literary (fiction, poetry, biography/profiles). A regional press publishing works about Maine and Northern New England, primarily, and generally authored by local writers. Quality work not strictly meeting the aforementioned criteria will, on occasion, be considered" avg. press run 2M-4M. Pub'd 5 titles 1990; expects 4 titles 1991, 4 titles 1992. 40 titles listed in the *Small Press Record of Books in Print* (20th Edition, 1991-92). avg. price, cloth: $15.95; paper: $8.95. Discounts: 40-50% depending on quantity. 226pp; 6×9; of. Reporting time: 3-4 months. Payment: advance against royalties: 1/2 at contract, 1/2 acceptance. Copyrights for author. Maine writers and publishers alliance.

NORTH DAKOTA QUARTERLY, North Dakota Quarterly Press, Robert W. Lewis, Editor; William Borden, Fiction Editor; Jay Meek, Poetry Editor, University of North Dakota, PO Box 8237, Grand Forks, ND

58202, 701-777-3321. 1910. Poetry, fiction, articles, art, photos, interviews, satire, criticism, reviews, long-poems, non-fiction. "Thomas McGrath, Sherman Paul, Daniel Curley, Leo Hamalian, Amy Clampitt, Stuart Friebert, Gerald Vizenor, Duane Niatum, Bruce Mazlish, N. Scott Momaday, Paula Gunn Allen, Peter Nabokov, Page Stegner, and Marieve Rugo have been recent contributors." circ. 750. 4/yr. Pub'd 4 issues 1990; expects 4 issues 1991, 4 issues 1992. sub. price: $15; per copy: $5; sample: $5. Back issues: $5. Discounts: 20%. 200pp; 6×9; †of. Reporting time: 1-4 months. Payment: in copies. Copyrighted, reverts to author. Pub's reviews: 47 in 1990. §Native American studies, Canadian studies, women studies, northern plains literature. Ads: $150/$100. CODA, CELJ, MLA.

North Dakota Quarterly Press (see also NORTH DAKOTA QUARTERLY), Robert W. Lewis, Editor; William Borden, Fiction Editor; Jay Meek, Poetry Editor, University of North Dakota, PO Box 8237, Grand Forks, ND 58202, 701-777-3321. 1910. 4 titles listed in the *Small Press Record of Books in Print* (20th Edition, 1991-92). †of.

North Star Press of St. Cloud, Inc., Rita Dwyer, Editor; Corinne Dwyer, Editor, PO Box 451, St. Cloud, MN 56302, 612-253-1636. 1969. Poetry, fiction, non-fiction. "Books only. Main theme is middle western Americana. Prefer not over 50M word mss. Not presently soliciting mss." avg. press run 2.5M-3M. Pub'd 6 titles 1990; expects 6 titles 1991, 6 titles 1992. 26 titles listed in the *Small Press Record of Books in Print* (20th Edition, 1991-92). avg. price, cloth: $20; paper: $12. Discounts: regular trade 40%; large order single title will give 2½ to 3% additional. 160pp; 6×9, 5½×8½; of. Reporting time: 2 weeks. Payment: 10% of net sales. Copyrights for author. Minn Book Publ Roundtable; Minn. Snd. Publishers assn.

North Stone Press (see also THE NORTH STONE REVIEW), PO Box 14098, Minneapolis, MN 55414. 1971. Poetry, fiction, criticism, reviews, letters. "At this point, these are the genres we're working with. More genres later, perhaps." avg. press run 1M-2M. Pub'd 1 title 1990; expects 1 title 1991, 2 titles 1992. avg. price, cloth: $15; paper: $7.95; other: as priced. Discounts: query, please, with proposal. Poetry 60pp, fiction 200-250pp; 5½×8½; of. Reporting time: 1 month to 6 weeks. Payment: after costs, yes. Copyrights for author. CLMP, COSMEP.

THE NORTH STONE REVIEW, North Stone Press, James Naiden, PO Box 14098, Minneapolis, MN 55414. 1971. Poetry, fiction, articles, art, photos, interviews, reviews, long-poems, non-fiction. "David Ignatow, Ralph Mills Jr., John Rezmerski, Karyn Sproces, G.T. Wright, Sigrid Bergie, etc." circ. 1.5M. 2/yr. Expects 1 issue 1991, 2 issues 1992. sub. price: $15; per copy: $7.50; sample: $7.50. Back issues: query first. Discounts: depends—query first. 200-250pp. Reporting time: 2-6 weeks. Payment: 2 copies. Copyrighted, reprint permission on written request. Pub's reviews: 15 in 1990. §Poetry, fiction. Ads: $60/$35/$25 1/4 page.

NORTHCOAST VIEW MONTHLY MAGAZINE, Scott K. Ryan, Damon Maguire, Blarney Publishing, PO Box 1374, Eureka, CA 95502, (707) 443-4887. 1982. Poetry, fiction, articles, art, photos, cartoons, interviews, satire, reviews, music, letters, parts-of-novels, long-poems, news items, non-fiction. "Length: Review- 2-3 pages, Features- 6-8 pages. Poetry: Recent works by Diane Wakoski, John Ross, Jim Dodge, Judith Mindy, Morris Herman, Stephen Miller, Margaret Randall" circ. 22.5M. 12/yr. Pub'd 12 issues 1990; expects 12 issues 1991, 12 issues 1992. 1 title listed in the *Small Press Record of Books in Print* (20th Edition, 1991-92). sub. price: $12; per copy: free; sample: $2. Back issues: $2. Discounts: will do publication trades. 48pp; 11×14½; of. Reporting time: 4-6 months. Payment: $10-$150. Copyrighted, rights revert on request. Pub's reviews: 30 in 1990. §most all. Ads: 750/400/18.

NORTHEAST, Juniper Press, John Judson, Editor, 1310 Shorewood Dr., LaCrosse, WI 54601, 608-788-0096. 1962. Poetry, fiction, articles, art, photos, interviews, criticism, reviews, parts-of-novels, long-poems. "We solicit any work of quality that has a human being behind it whose words help shape his and our awareness of being human. This has always come before fashion, reputation or ambition in our eyes. *Juniper Books* are chapbooks. A subscription includes two NE's and 2 Juniper books per year, 2 WNJ's plus gifts." circ. 4-500. 2/yr. Pub'd 2 issues 1990; expects 2 issues 1991, 2 issues 1992. sub. price: $33 for complete sub. including 2 poetry books per year, plus NE and all Juniper Books, $38 for institutions; per copy: $3; sample: $2.50. Back issues: write for information/most are available but in very small quantities. Discounts: Dealer and bookstore 20% for one book; 30% for 2-4 books (no returns); 40% for 5 or more (no returns). 48-60pp; avg. size varies; of, lp. Reporting time: 6-8 weeks. Payment: copies. Copyrighted, reverts to author. Pub's reviews: 4 in 1990. §Poetry, crit., experimental fiction, fiction. No ads.

NORTHEAST JOURNAL, Dawne Anderson, Editor; Dennis Holt, Editor, PO Box 2321, Providence, RI 02906. 1969. Poetry, fiction, articles, interviews, reviews. "*Northeast Journal* was previously published under the name of *Harbinger*. The staff is open to any work of quality. Unknown writers are welcome to submit. *Northeast Journal* is presently funded by a matching grant from the Rhode Island Council for the Arts." circ. 600. 1/yr. sub. price: $5; per copy: $5; sample: $5 ppd. Back issues: $5 ppd. Discounts: 33% to bookstores. 100pp; 5½×8½; of. Reporting time: 2-4 months. Payment: 1 yr subscription. Copyrighted, does not revert to author. Pub's reviews. §Poetry. No ads. CLMP, COSMEP, CODA.

Northeast Sportsman's Press, Jim Capossela, Publisher, PO Box 188, Tarrytown, NY 10591. 1981. Non-fiction. avg. press run 4M. Pub'd 4 titles 1990; expects 4 titles 1991, 4 titles 1992. 9 titles listed in the *Small Press Record of Books in Print* (20th Edition, 1991-92). avg. price, cloth: $19.95; paper: $12.95. Discounts: Distributed by: Stackpole Books Cameron & Kelker sts. Harrisburg, PA 17105 they set prices & terms. 216pp; 5½x8¼, 6x9; of. Reporting time: 4-6 weeks. Payment: varies. Copyrights for author.

NORTHEASTARTS MAGAZINE, Leigh Donaldson, J.F.K. Station, PO Box 6061, Boston, MA 02114. 1990. Poetry, fiction, articles, art, photos, interviews, criticism, reviews, parts-of-novels, non-fiction. "We accept manuscripts: poetry, fiction, and non-fiction features, when accompanied by a SASE. Poetry under 30 lines, fiction and non-fiction between 750-1,500 words is preferred. Black and white camera-ready art and screened photos a 5x8" (full-page) or 5x4½" (half-page) format are also considered. *NorthEastARTS* is interested in material of all types and varied perspectives, but strongly discourages the submission of any work that reflects a lack of moral, social and political consciousness. Checks and money orders should be made to Boston Arts Organization, Inc." circ. 500-750. 4/yr. Pub'd 2 issues 1990; expects 4 issues 1991, 4 issues 1992. sub. price: $8; per copy: $3.50; sample: $3.50. Back issues: $3.50. Discounts: none. 32pp; 5x8; of. Reporting time: 1-2 months. Payment: 1 copy. Copyrighted, reverts to author. Pub's reviews: a few in 1990. Ads: $75/$45 1/2 (horizontal)/$50 1/2 (vertical)/classifieds 25¢ per word, 30 word limit, $1 add'l word. CLMP.

THE NORTHERN ENGINEER, Cynthia Owen, Stephanie Faussett, Institute of Northern Engineering, University of Alaska, Fairbanks, AK 99775, 907-474-6113. 1968. Articles, art, photos, reviews, letters, non-fiction. "Science and engineering in the north." circ. 1M. 4/yr. Pub'd 4 issues 1990; expects 4 issues 1991, 4 issues 1992. sub. price: $15 USA, $20 other; per copy: $4; sample: $4. Back issues: $4. Discounts: on subscriptions: $28 USA, $33 other 2yr., Agency: USA-$13 1yr, $26 2yr; other-$18 1yr, $31 2yr. 28pp; 8½x11; of. Reporting time: 3-6 months. Payment: none. Not copyrighted. Pub's reviews: 2 in 1990. §Cold Regions Engineering. No ads.

Northern House (see also STAND MAGAZINE), Jon Silkin, Jon Glover, Jeffrey Wainwright, 19 Haldane Terrace, Newcastle upon Tyne NE2 3AN, England, (0)91)2812614. 1964. Poetry. avg. press run 500-1M. Expects 2 titles 1991, 1-2 titles 1992. 16 titles listed in the *Small Press Record of Books in Print* (20th Edition, 1991-92). avg. price, paper: $3-$5. Discounts: 33⅓% on more than 3 copies. 20pp; of. Payment: 10%. Copyrights for author.

NORTHERN LIGHTS STUDIES IN CREATIVITY, Stanely J. Scott, Editor, University of Maine at Presque Isle, Presque Isle, ME 04769, 207-764-0311. 1984. Poetry, fiction, articles, photos, interviews, music, letters. "Essays. Journal focuses on original statements, documents, interviews, and articles by artists, poets musicians, filmmakers, dramatists, or commentators which deal specifically with the issue of creativity, the creative process, and/or the audience (viewer)'s response to works of art. Recent contributors: Maxine Green on arts education, Dwayne Huebner on 'Spirituality and Knowing,' Robert Creeley on teaching and poetry, and other articles on creativity and the process of education." circ. 1M. Irregular. Expects 1 issue 1991. price per copy: $8; sample: $8. Back issues: $8. Discounts: 40% trade. 100pp; 6x9; of. Reporting time: 3 weeks. Payment: none. Copyrighted, reverts to author. §Books on the arts and creativity. Ads: $25 1/2 page.

NORTHERN NEW ENGLAND REVIEW, Alexandra Fox, Editor; Alexis Raymond, Managing Editor, PO Box 825, Franklin Pierce College, Rindge, NH 03461, 603-899-5111. 1973. Poetry, fiction, articles, art, photos, satire, criticism, reviews, parts-of-novels, long-poems, non-fiction. "Only accept submissions from residents of the Northern New England area (Maine, New Hampshire, Vermont)" circ. 600. 1/yr. Pub'd 1 issue 1990; expects 1 issue 1991, 1 issue 1992. sub. price: $5; per copy: $5; sample: $3.50. Back issues: $5. Discounts: 20% off classrooms. 100pp; 8½x11; photo offset. Reporting time: 1 year. Payment: 1 free copy. Copyrighted, reverts to author. Pub's reviews. §Literature, art, scholarship. Ads: $30/$20/$15 1/4 page.

THE NORTHERN REVIEW, Richard Behm, Managing Editor, Academic Achievement Center, 2100 Main Street, Stevens Point, WI 54481, 715-346-3568. 1986. Poetry, fiction, articles, art, photos, interviews, criticism, reviews, letters, long-poems, non-fiction. "*The Northern Review* is a general interest journal of essays and articles, fiction, poetry, artwork and reviews. The journal focuses on northern themes and issues—economic, environmental, cultural, and political. Articles and essays should be between 1200 and 4000 words, and they should be written in a lively style accessible to a wide spectrum of educated readers. *The Northern Review* is published spring and fall. All manuscripts should include SASE for return of submissions. Submissions should be sent to the Managing Editor." circ. 1M. 2/yr. Pub'd 2 issues 1990; expects 2 issues 1991, 2 issues 1992. sub. price: $8; per copy: $4; sample: $4. 48pp; 8½x11; of. Reporting time: 4-8 weeks. Payment: in copies. Copyrighted, reverts to author. Pub's reviews. §Any books related to the northern states. Ads: $100/$50/exchange classifieds no charge.

Northern Star Press, PO Box 28814, San Jose, CA 95159. 1988. Expects 1 title 1991. 1 title listed in the *Small Press Record of Books in Print* (20th Edition, 1991-92). avg. price, paper: $10. Discounts: Booksellers: 40%. 175pp; 8½x5½. Copyrights for author.

Northland Publishing Company, Susan McDonald, Editor-in-Chief; Associate Publisher, Betti Albrecht, Associate Editor, PO Box N, Flagstaff, AZ 86002, 602-774-5251. 1958. Art, photos, non-fiction. "Founded in 1958 as commercial printer by Paul E. Weaver, Jr. First books published in 1962. Independently owned until 1973, when Justin Industries, Inc. of Fort Worth, Texas, became corporate owner. Company remains autonomous." avg. press run 3.5M, 5M, 7.5M. Pub'd 13 titles 1990; expects 20 titles 1991, 20 titles 1992. avg. price, cloth: $35; paper: $15.95. Discounts: 1-4 30% prepaid, S.T.O.P.; 5-9 42% returnable; 10+ 45% returns allowed, free freight; 5+ 50% non-returnable; 10+ 50% non-returnable, free freight. 144pp; of. Reporting time: 6 weeks. Payment: 10% net receipts first printing softcover. Copyrights for author. ABA.

THE NORTHLAND QUARTERLY, Northland Quarterly Publications, Inc., Jody Namio Wallace, Editor, 1522 E. Southern Avenue #2161, Tempe, AZ 85282-5678. 1988. Poetry, fiction, articles, art, interviews, satire, criticism, reviews, parts-of-novels, non-fiction. 4/yr. Pub'd 4 issues 1990; expects 4 issues 1991, 4 issues 1992. sub. price: $20; per copy: $4.95; sample: $4.95. Back issues: $3. Discounts: 20% colleges, 30% orders over 100 copies. 96-150pp; 8½x5½; †of. Reporting time: 4-8 weeks. Payment: in copies. Copyrighted. Pub's reviews: 1 in 1990. §General literature, progressive politics, film. Ads: $400/$200/$100 full/half/quarterly/yearly.

Northland Quarterly Publications, Inc. (see also THE NORTHLAND QUARTERLY), Jody Namio Wallace, Editor-in-Chief, 1522 E. Southern Avenue #2161, Tempe, AZ 85282-5678. 1988. Poetry, fiction, articles, art, interviews, satire, criticism, reviews, parts-of-novels, non-fiction. avg. press run 2M. Pub'd 40 titles 1990; expects 50 titles 1991. 10 titles listed in the *Small Press Record of Books in Print* (20th Edition, 1991-92). avg. price, cloth: $15; paper: $10. Discounts: 20% colleges, 30% orders over 100 copies; distributors and wholesalers up to 45%. 150-200pp; 5½x8½; †of. Reporting time: 6-8 weeks. Payment: varies. Copyrights for author.

NORTHWEST MAGAZINE, THE OREGONIAN'S SUNDAY MAGAZINE, Ellen Heltzel, 1320 SW Broadway, Portland, OR 97201. Poetry, fiction, articles, art, photos, satire, non-fiction. circ. 412M. 52/yr. Pub'd 52 issues 1990; expects 52 issues 1991, 52 issues 1992. sub. price: $72—for Sunday only; per copy: $1; sample: free. Back issues: free. 32pp; 9⅞x11¼; †of. Reporting time: 2 weeks. Payment: on acceptance. Copyrighted, reverts to author. Ads: $4,000-$7,000 (color).

NORTHWEST REVIEW, John Witte, Editor; Cecelia Hagen, Fiction Editor; John Witte, Poetry Editor; George Gessert, Art Editor, 369 P.L.C., University of Oregon, Eugene, OR 97403, 503-686-3957. 1957. Poetry, fiction, art, photos, reviews, parts-of-novels, long-poems, plays. "Recent contributors: Raymond Carver, Hans Magnus Enzensberger, Olga Broumas, Barry Lopez, Morris Grave, Joyce Carol Oates, Richard Kostelanetz. Bias: Quality in whatever form. No other predisposition." circ. 1.2M. 3/yr. Pub'd 3 issues 1990; expects 3 issues 1991. 5 titles listed in the *Small Press Record of Books in Print* (20th Edition, 1991-92). sub. price: $14; per copy: $5; sample: $3. Back issues: $5 all except double issues or specially priced issues. Discounts: bookstore/agencies 20% consignment & 40% wholesale. 130pp; 6x9; of. Reporting time: 8-10 weeks. Payment: 3 copies. Copyrighted, reassigned upon request for inclusion in a book. Pub's reviews: 15 in 1990. §Literature, poetry' fiction, small press publications. Ads: $160 full page only. CLMP.

Northwoods Press (see also Conservatory of American Letters), Robert W. Olmsted, Publisher, PO Box 88, Thomaston, ME 04861, 207-354-6550. 1972. Poetry, fiction, news items. "Request 15 point program. SASE 2 stamps. We don't charge a reading fee, but require a donation, whatever you can afford. If you can't afford anything, convince us and we'll read free" avg. press run 500-1M. Pub'd 2 titles 1990; expects 3 titles 1991, 4 titles 1992. 38 titles listed in the *Small Press Record of Books in Print* (20th Edition, 1991-92). avg. price, cloth: $19.95; paper: $7; other: $75 collector's. Discounts: no. of paperback copies ordered X2% to a maximum 50% for 25 or more copies. No discount on hardcovers or collectors. 120pp; 5½x8½; of. Reporting time: 1 day to 3 weeks, usually less than 1 week. Payment: minimum advance $250, payable on contracting; minimum royalty 10% from first sale. Copyrights for author.

Northword Press, Inc., Tom Klein, PO Box 1360, Minocqua, WI 54548, 715-356-9800. 1981. Non-fiction. avg. press run 10M. Pub'd 18 titles 1990; expects 27 titles 1991, 32 titles 1992. 19 titles listed in the *Small Press Record of Books in Print* (20th Edition, 1991-92). avg. price, cloth: $35; paper: $9-$10. Discounts: 1-4 20%; 5-9 40%; 10-99 43%; 100+ 46%. 200pp; 6x9, 8½x11, 9x12; of. Reporting time: 60 days. Payment: standard, 15% of cash receipts. Copyrights for author.

Norton Coker Press (see also TOOK), Edward Mycue, PO Box 640543, San Francisco, CA 94164-0543, 415-922-0395. 1988. Poetry, fiction, art, satire, criticism, reviews, music, letters, plays, news items. avg. press run 150. Pub'd 1 title 1990; expects 2 titles 1991, 22 titles 1992. 35 titles listed in the *Small Press Record of Books in Print* (20th Edition, 1991-92). avg. price, paper: $5. Discounts: 5+ copies 40%. 44pp; 5x7; †various. Reporting time: 1-4 weeks. Payment: in copies. Copyrights for author.

NORTON NOTES, Kinseeker Publications, Victoria Wilson, PO Box 184, Grawn, MI 49637, 616-276-6745. 1987. Articles, reviews, news items, non-fiction. circ. 40. 4/yr. Pub'd 4 issues 1990; expects 4 issues 1991, 4 issues 1992. sub. price: $10; per copy: $2.50; sample: same. Back issues: $2.50. 10pp; 8½x11; †photocopy.

Reporting time: 2 weeks. Payment: varies. Not copyrighted. Pub's reviews: 3 in 1990. §Genealogy.

NOSTALGIA, A Sentimental State of Mind, Connie Lakey Martin, PO Box 2224, Orangeburg, SC 29116. 1986. Poetry, art, photos, cartoons, interviews, non-fiction. "90% of material is selected through contest entries: Short Story & Poetry Cash Awards offered Spring & Fall. Short Stories: 500-1,000 words, nostalgic, true story from personal experience, unpublished; Poetry: any style, nostalgic content, unpublished. Entry fee reserves copy of next season's edition. Biographical sketch of selected writer each edition." circ. 1M. 2/yr. Pub'd 2 issues 1990; expects 2 issues 1991, 2 issues 1992. sub. price: $5; per copy: $2.50; sample: $2.50. Discounts: 50% to bookstores. 22pp; 5½x8½; of. Reporting time: 3 weeks (or less). Payment: cash awards for short stories and poetry (through contests Spring and Fall). Copyrighted, reverts to author. Pub's reviews: 4 in 1990. §Poetry and short stories (non-fiction). Ads: $25 1/2 page/$10 1/3. Poetry Society of S.C.

NOSTOC, Arts End Books, Marshall Brooks, Editor, Box 162, Newton, MA 02168. 1973. Poetry, fiction, articles, criticism, reviews, parts-of-novels. "We are always on the watch for good poetry and short fiction. Our tastes are varied and wide-ranging. Freshness of content a must. A copy of our catalogue - detailing our past publications and describing our subscription package program is available upon request (please enclose a SASE)." circ. 300. 2/yr. Pub'd 2 issues 1990; expects 2 issues 1991, 2 issues 1992. sub. price: $8 for 4 issues; per copy: $3.50; sample: $3.50. Back issues: rates on request. Discounts: on request. 30pp; size varies; lp, of. Reporting time: within a few weeks, usually. Payment: modest payment upon acceptance. Copyrighted, reverts to author. §Small press history, poetry, fiction & politics. Ads: rates on request.

NOTEBOOK/CUADERNO: A LITERARY JOURNAL, Esoterica Press, Yoly Zentella, PO Box 15607, Albuquerque, NM 87174-0607. 1985. Poetry, fiction, articles, art, photos, interviews, criticism, reviews, music, parts-of-novels, plays, non-fiction. "Second issue subtitled *La Raza Cosmica* is devoted to writing by and about Chicanos and Latinos, with the first issue devoted to writing in general. Asian, Native, Black and Arab Americans are encouraged to submit manuscripts and art" circ. 150. 1/yr. Pub'd 2 issues 1990; expects 1 issue 1991, 1 issue 1992. sub. price: $8 individuals, $10 institutions; per copy: $8 indiv., $10 instit.; sample: $8 indiv., $10 instit. Back issues: $8. Discounts: 20% to subscription agents, bookstores 30%. 100pp; 5½x8½; xerox, of. Reporting time: 8-16 weeks. Payment: 1 copy. Copyrighted, rights revert, we just ask for proper credit. Pub's reviews: 20 in 1990. §History, culture, literary. Chicano and Latino American writers are encouraged to submit books for possible review and/or inclusion in Book Notes. CCLM.

NOTES & QUERIES, Oxford University Press, E.G. Stanley, L.G. Black, Journals Subscription Department, Pinkhill House, Southfield Road, Eynsham, Oxford OX8 1JJ, England. 1849. Articles, reviews. circ. 1.4M. 4/yr. Pub'd 4 issues 1990; expects 4 issues 1991, 4 issues 1992. sub. price: $83; per copy: $25; sample: free. 96pp; 185×130mm. Reporting time: 1 week to 6 months. Payment: none. Copyrighted. Pub's reviews: 191 in 1990. §English literature, criticism, poetry, language. Ads: £225($405)/£140($250)/£95($170) 1/4 page.

NOTES FROM THE UNDERGROUND, Last Generation/Underground Editions, Mark DuCharme, 2965 13th Street, Boulder, CO 80304, 303-938-9346. 1987. Poetry, fiction, art, cartoons, interviews, criticism, reviews, collages, concrete art. "*NOTES FROM THE UNDERGROUND* will publish one more issue (#7) under its present name, then change its name to *BREAK TO OPEN*. This is a purely superficial change, as the gist of the magazine will remain the same. Still looking for poetry that connects on some level with the avant-garde/experimental literary traditions that have developed in the United States and Europe. Most interested in personism (N.Y. School), 'surrealism' &/or 'language'-oriented writings. I tend to publish a lot of unknowns; in fact the purpose of the magazine has been to provide a medium in which the next generation of literary artists can find an audience. Poets and artists published include: John M. Bennett, Sheila E. Murphy, Nico Vassilakis, Nathan Whiting, M. Kettner, Glen Armstrong, Errol Miller, Christopher Funkhouser, Dan Nielsen, John Wright, Vince Kueter, Richard Loranger, Jose L. Garza, Jean Prafke, Mike Myers, David Moser, Wolf Knight, Laurie Wechter and Mark DuCharme. Feel free to send a large selection of work—if I like it I'll publish it. All art submissions should be photocopiable (i.e. collages, black ink drawings, etc.)—please DON'T send originals! ALWAYS include SASE with submissions!" circ. 100. 1-2/yr. Pub'd 1 issue 1990; expects 2 issues 1991, 1 or 2 issues 1992. sub. price: $5/2 issues, $10/4 issues (U.S. & Canada); $10/2 issues (elsewhere); U.S. dollars only—make all checks payable to Mark DuCharme; per copy: $2.50; sample: $2.50. Back issues: $2.50. Discounts: 20%-40% to bookstores and distributors. 30pp; 8½x11; †mi. Reporting time: varies wildly, usually 2-9 months. Payment: 1 copy. Copyrighted, reverts to author. Pub's reviews: 3 in 1990. §Small press poetry, literary criticism, poetry performance events, videos and other poetry media. Ads: $30/$15.

Not-For-Sale-Press or NFS Press, Lew Thomas, 243 Grand View Ave., San Francisco, CA 94114, 415-282-5372. 1975. Articles, art, photos, interviews. "*Photography & Language 8 x 10*, 1975, compiled by Lew Thomas, 48 pgs. 21 photos. *Performances And Installations*, Kesa, 1976, 62 pages, 50 photos." avg. press run 1.5-2M. Pub'd 1 title 1990; expects 3 titles 1991, 3 titles 1992. 9 titles listed in the *Small Press Record of Books in Print* (20th Edition, 1991-92). avg. price, paper: $15.95. Discounts: 40% trade, 55% wholesale, 6 titles 40% proforma. 48-120pp; 8x10, 9x12; of.

NOTTINGHAM MEDIEVAL STUDIES, Professor Michael Jones, Dept. of History, The University, Nottingham NG7 2RD, England. 1957. Articles. "Articles on medieval language, literature, history, etc. concerning the whole of Europe making up to some 170 pp of print @ 550 words per page." circ. 500. 1/yr. Expects 1 issue 1991. sub. price: £10 or $20; per copy: £10 or $20; sample: £10 or $20. Back issues: £10 or $20. Discounts: £9.50 or $19. 170pp; 7×9½; †of. Reporting time: 2 months. Payment: none. Copyrighted. Pub's reviews: 3 in 1990. §Same as for articles. No ads.

NOTUS NEW WRITING, Otherwind, Pat Smith, OtherWind Press, Inc., 2420 Walter Drive, Ann Arbor, MI 48103, 313-665-0703. 1986. Poetry, fiction, art, interviews, criticism, reviews, long-poems. "*Notus* deals with work up to approximately 16 pages focusing on contemporary and experimental poetry and fiction and also features translations, interviews and reviews. Recent contributors include Robert Creeley, Robert Kelly, Clark Coolidge, Ann Waldman, Rosemarie Waldrop, Cid Corman, John Yau, Edmond Jabes, Clayton Eshleman, and Charles Stein. Produce a sound sheet in each issue (33⅓ rpm)" circ. 500. 2/yr. Pub'd 2 issues 1990; expects 2 issues 1991. sub. price: $10; per copy: $5; sample: $5. Back issues: $5. 96pp; 8½×11; of. Reporting time: 4 months. Payment: complimentary copies. Copyrighted, reverts to author. Pub's reviews: 9 in 1990. CCLM, 666 Broadway, New York, NY 10012.

NOW AND THEN, Pat Arnow, Editor; Jo Carson, Poetry Editor, P.O. Box 19, 180A, East Tennessee State Univ., Johnson City, TN 37614-0002, 615-929-5348. 1984. Poetry, fiction, articles, art, photos, interviews, criticism, reviews, letters. "*Now And Then* is the publication of the Center for Appalachian Studies and Service of East Tennessee State University, Richard Blaustein, Director. Each issue is divided between expository and imaginative material: studies of Appalachian nature and culture on the one hand, and visual art, imaginative writing on the other. Issues always have a thematic focus; for example, recent issues focused on urban Appalachian activism in Appalachia and tourism in Appalachia. Each issue features juxtaposed visuals of an Appalachian locale now (present) and then (past). Photos, graphics, critical studies of Appalachian nature and culture, personal essays, poetry, fiction are welcomed for consideration on a continuing basis. 'Appalachia' is considered to cover the mountain region from Maine to Georgia. We'd like people to send for a free listing of upcoming issues and writer's guidelines." circ. 1.2M. 3/yr. Pub'd 3 issues 1990; expects 3 issues 1991, 3 issues 1992. sub. price: $9 individuals, $12 libraries; per copy: $3.50; sample: $3.50. Back issues: $2.50. 40pp; 8½×11; of. Reporting time: 4 months. Payment: copies and subscription to magazine. Copyrighted, reverts to author. Pub's reviews: 12 in 1990. §Appalachian arts, history, culture, ecology.

Now It's Up To You Publications, Tom Parson, 157 S Logan, Denver, CO 80209, 303-777-8951. 1980. Poetry. "Interested in the intersection between poetry/fiction/the arts, & political & social reality/unreality - all the openings, all possibilities. The writer, the publisher take it this far, now it's up to you. Publishing poetry postcards, broadsides, and books on letterpress, since 1984. Using handset types, linoleum cuts, & printer's blocks, for multi-color graphics with poems." avg. press run 300-1M. Pub'd 7 titles 1990; expects 7 titles 1991, 7 titles 1992. 18 titles listed in the *Small Press Record of Books in Print* (20th Edition, 1991-92). avg. price, paper: 50¢ postcards, $2-$5 broadsides, $2-$3 chapbooks. Discounts: 40% booksellers; returns accepted anytime. †lp. Reporting time: since birth of son, now four, very slow to correspond. Payment: copies - arrangement will vary (approx. 10% of press run). Copyrights for author.

John Noyce, Publisher (see also KYOCERA USER; ATINDEX; SOCIAL CHANGE & INFORMATION SYSTEMS), G.P.O. Box 2222T, Melbourne, Vic. 3001, Australia. 4 titles listed in the *Small Press Record of Books in Print* (20th Edition, 1991-92).

NRG, Dan Raphael, 6735 S E 78th, Portland, OR 97206. 1975. Poetry, fiction, art, photos, interviews, criticism, reviews, music, letters, parts-of-novels, long-poems, collages, concrete art. "Send those deliberate, seamless works elsewhere. *NRG* wants works that create/are events, not those that re-create. Want to see a fusion of language dynamics, gut rythmn, and abstract human/enviro-mental energy. Past contribs—K. Kempton, J. Grabill, J.M. Bennett, F.A. Nettlebeck, P. Ganick, I. Arguelles, McKinnon, J Gray, H. Polkinhorn, S.P. Martin, J. Berry, G. Evason, M. Rosenberg, S. Alexie." circ. 1M. 2/yr. Pub'd 2 issues 1990; expects 1 issue 1992. sub. price: $4; per copy: $2; sample: $2. Back issues: most $1.50, more for rarer issues. Discounts: negotiable. 24pp; 11×17, other formats; of. Reporting time: 2 months. Payment: copies. Not copyrighted. Pub's reviews: 25 in 1990. §Visual, experimental, linguistic, surreal. No ads. CCLM.

NUCLEAR TIMES, John Tirman, Sonia Shah, 401 Commonwealth Avenue, Boston, MA 02215, 617-266-1193. 1982. Articles, art, photos, cartoons, interviews, reviews, letters, news items, non-fiction. "Subscriptions: PO Box 351, Kenmore Station, Boston, MA 02215." circ. 30M. 4/yr. Pub'd 3 issues 1990; expects 4 issues 1991, 4 issues 1992. sub. price: $18; per copy: $4.50; sample: $2. Back issues: none available. Discounts: distributors 50% of cover price; subscription agencies 10% of sub. price; bulk per inquiry. 56pp; 7-7/16×9⅞; web. Reporting time: 60 days. Payment: upon publication, varies. Copyrighted, does not revert to author. Pub's reviews: 6 in 1990. §Nuclear arms race, peace, alternative security, foreign policy, environment, global security. Ads: $700/$420/$1 per word. COSMEP.

Nuclear Trenchcoated Subway Prophets Publications (see also **DIAMOND HITCHHIKER COBWEBS**), Lake, Ellis Dee, 118 E. Goodheart Avenue, Lake Mary, FL 32746. 1986. Poetry, fiction, articles, art, photos, cartoons, interviews, reviews, music, letters, parts-of-novels, long-poems, collages, plays, concrete art, non-fiction. "(Occult, eastern studies, avant-garde, anarchist, dada, surreal, beat, erotica, horror, sf, fantasy, mythology, drugs, counter culture, music, art, underground, punk, gothic, vampyrs, s/m, tantra, angels, dreams, poetic terrorism, assault theatre, art sabotage, mind machines, children ov thee night...); psychedelic nightmares, erotic suicide notes, psychotic hallucinations, bizarre drugs/sex, morbid trance writings, punk requiems, long nocturnal ramblings, obscure meditations/chants/magick...TOPY" avg. press run 200. Pub'd 6 titles 1990; expects 10 titles 1991, 10 titles 1992. 4 titles listed in the *Small Press Record of Books in Print* (20th Edition, 1991-92). avg. price, cloth: $6; paper: $1-2. 10-200pp; size varies. Reporting time: w/SASE—2-3 weeks, w/o—your whole life. Copyrights for author. SM, MDMA, OTO, TOPY, LSD.

Nucleus Publications, Vimala McClure, Managing Editor, Route 2, Box 49, Willow Springs, MO 65793. 1988. "We publish New Age and how-to books, and carry the complete works of Indian philosopher P.R. Sarkar. We are interested in how-to books with a holistic spiritual perspective; vegetarian cookbooks which use no eggs, onions, garlic, or mushrooms; alternative consumer information; women's and family issues." avg. press run 10M. Pub'd 3 titles 1990; expects 1 title 1991, 3 titles 1992. 8 titles listed in the *Small Press Record of Books in Print* (20th Edition, 1991-92). avg. price, paper: $9.95. Discounts: prepaid STOP orders 30%, 2-24 40%, 25-49 50%. 150-200pp; 9¼×8, 6×9. Reporting time: 8 weeks. Payment: small advance with royalty; contract negotiated. Copyrights for author. New Age Publishers and Retailers Alliance, Publishers Marketing Association.

NUMBERS, John Alexander, Alison Rimmer, Peter Robinson, Clive Wilmer, 6 Kingston Street, Cambridge, Cambs. CB1 2NU, United Kingdom, 0223 353425. 1986. Poetry. "As much space as possible to contributing poets to give our readers a comprehensive idea of the writers' work. We occasionally publish prose—but only by poets—R.L. Barth, Thom Gunn, Seamus Heaney, Bill Manhire, Vittorio Sereni, Yves Bonnefoy, Lauris Edmond, Medbh McGuckian, Margueritte Yourcenar, E.J. Scovell, Janet Lewis, Fernando Pessoa." circ. 1.5M. 2/yr. Pub'd 2 issues 1990; expects 2 issues 1991, 2 issues 1992. sub. price: £9, USA $16.50; per copy: £4.50. Back issues: £3.95 *Numbers* 1, £4.50 #2 and #3. Discounts: trade discount to bookshops 33⅓ (10% to some libraries). 150pp; of. Reporting time: varies. Payment: yes. Copyrighted, reverts to author. Ads: £200/£100/£25 1/4 page.

Nunciata, A.C. Doyle, Publishing Division, Box 570122, Houston, TX 77257. "Formerly Assoc. Advertisers Services." avg. press run 1.5M. Pub'd 3 titles 1990; expects 10 titles 1991. 9 titles listed in the *Small Press Record of Books in Print* (20th Edition, 1991-92). avg. price, cloth: $8.95; paper: $4.95. Discounts: standard to libraries + bookstores. 60pp; 5½×8½. Reporting time: 10 weeks.

NUTRITION ACTION HEALTHLETTER, Stephen B. Schmidt, Editor-in-Chief, 1875 Connecticut Avenue NW #300, Washington, DC 20009, 202-332-9110. 1974. Articles, art, photos, cartoons, interviews, criticism, reviews, letters, news items. "No submissions" circ. 250M. 10/yr. Pub'd 10 issues 1990; expects 10 issues 1991, 10 issues 1992. sub. price: $19.95; per copy: $2; sample: free. Back issues: $2. Discounts: quantity discounts available. 16pp; 8½×11; offset. Payment: negotiable. Copyrighted, rights revert only if requested. Pub's reviews: 10 in 1990. §Food, health, nutrition, fitness, gardening, related areas. No advertising accepted.

NUTSHELL, Tom Roberts, Christopher Nankivell, Penny Grimley, 8 George Marston Road, Ernsford Grange, Coventry CV3 2HH, Great Britain. 1988. Poetry, fiction, reviews, letters, parts-of-novels, long-poems. "We do not want to set any restrictions on length other than we can fit a piece of writing in. We remain open to any interesting, well-crafted poems or stories. Recent contributions have come from the UK, Ireland, Canada and the USA." circ. 200. 4/yr. Pub'd 4 issues 1990; expects 4 issues 1991, 4 issues 1992. sub. price: £6; per copy: £1.50; sample: £1.50 (postage extra outside U.K.). Back issues: £1. 60pp; 5¾×8⅓ (A5); photocopy. Reporting time: 2-6 weeks. Payment: £1.50. Copyrighted, reverts to author. Pub's reviews: 12 in 1990. §Short stories, poetry. Ads: £40/£20/quarter page £12/eighth page £7.50.

Nuventures Publishing, Ellen K. McNamara, PO Box 2489, La Jolla, CA 92038-2489, 800-338-9768. 1990. "Any submissions should be precopyrighted. First, obtain a copyright number through the Library of Congress. Then send only a one or two page synopsis with a copy of both sides of the 'Certificate of Copyright Registration,' complete with registration number to Topic Review, above address. Do *not* send entire manuscript unless you are contacted." avg. press run 10M. Pub'd 1 title 1990; expects 3 titles 1991, 8 titles 1992. 4 titles listed in the *Small Press Record of Books in Print* (20th Edition, 1991-92). avg. price, cloth: $18.95; paper: $5.95-$12.95. Discounts: trade 40%-55%. 300pp; 5¼×8 (pa), 6×9 (cl); lp. Reporting time: 4 weeks. Payment: negotiated. Does not copyright for author. ABA.

NYCTICORAX, John A. Youril, 8420 Olivine Avenue, Citrus Heights, CA 95610-2721. 1985. Poetry, fiction, articles, art, criticism, reviews, long-poems, non-fiction. "We are looking for excellence in poetry, fiction, and criticism. No restrictions on theme, style, or length. We would like to save the world and regenerate literature;

however, those objectives being unlikely, our only coherent editorial policy is to publish the very best of the material that comes our way" circ. 650. 3/yr. Pub'd 2 issues 1990; expects 3 issues 1991, 3 issues 1992. sub. price: $10; per copy: $4; sample: $4. Back issues: $4. Discounts: 20%-40%. 64pp; 5½x8½; of. Reporting time: 1-2 months. Payment: 1 copy. Copyrighted, reverts to author. Pub's reviews: 4 in 1990. §Humanities, arts, sciences, literature, criticism. Ads: $100/$50.

O

O.ARS, O.ARS, Inc., Don Wellman, Cola Franzen, Irene Turner, 21 Rockland Road, Weare, NH 03281, 603-529-1060. 1981. Poetry, fiction, articles, interviews, criticism, letters, parts-of-novels, long-poems, collages, concrete art, non-fiction. "Editorial correspondence: 21 Rockland Road, Weare, NH 03281. *O.ARS* prints poetry, visual poetry, and experimental fiction; also statements and essays bearing on contemporary poetics. Each vol. is a book-length anthology treating a specific topic. *O.ARS* 2: PERCEPTION included work by Adam, Arias-Misson, Berstein, Byrd, Corman, Deguy, Eshleman, Federman, Hejinian, Howe, Kostelanetz, Kempton, Middleton, Ott, Silliman, Waldrop, Watson, Yurkievich. *O.ARS* 3: Translations: Experiments in Reading. *O.ARS* 617: Voicing, *O.ARS* 8: "magazine iss."." circ. 1M. 1/yr. Pub'd 1 issue 1990; expects 1 issue 1991, 1 issue 1992. sub. price: $10; per copy: varies; sample: $5. Back issues: complete set 1-7 $50. Discounts: 50-55% on 10 or more copies to 40% on 5 copies to retailers. 128pp; 7x10; of. Reporting time: 1 week to 1 month. Payment: 3 or more copies. Copyrighted, reverts to author. Pub's reviews: 4 in 1990. §Poetry, poetics. Ads: $100/$50.

O.ARS, Inc. (see also O.ARS), Don Wellman, Cola Franzen, Irene Turner, 21 Rockland Road, Weare, NH 03281, 603-529-1060. 1981. Poetry, fiction, articles, art, photos, interviews, criticism, letters, long-poems, collages, concrete art, non-fiction. "Editorial correspondence: 21 Rockland Road, Weare, NY 03281" avg. press run 1M. Pub'd 1 title 1990; expects 1 title 1991, 1 title 1992. avg. price, paper: $5. Discounts: 50-55% on 10 or more, 40% on 5 or more. 96pp; 7x10; of. Reporting time: 4-6 weeks. Does not copyright for author.

Oak Plantation Press, PO Box 640, Rockwall, TX 75087-0640, 214-722-BOOK. 1990. 2 titles listed in the *Small Press Record of Books in Print* (20th Edition, 1991-92). avg. price, paper: $11.95. Discounts: 10-50 books 40%, 51-99 50%, 100-200 55%. 6x9.

Oak Tree (see also THE CIVIL ABOLITIONIST), Bina Robinson, Box 26, Swain, NY 14884, 607-545-6213. 1983. "We are a special interest organization promoting human health and the abolition of vivisection. Only two titles so far, one in 5th printing of 15,000 copies—other printed in Italy and imported. Expect to add two English titles in 1989, which have already been chosen. One will probably be printed here, the other in Italy or Germany. We are not commercial in that we do not pay authors or solicit manuscripts because our chosen subject is one that does not turn a profit. We are actually a non-profit organization devoted to education." avg. press run 5M. Pub'd 2 titles 1990; expects 1 title 1991, 1 title 1992. 3 titles listed in the *Small Press Record of Books in Print* (20th Edition, 1991-92). avg. price, paper: $12.33. Discounts: up to 40%. 303pp; 6x8½; of.

Oakhill Press, Martin N. James, 7449 Oakhill Road, Cleveland, OH 44146-5901, 216-646-9999. 1987. Non-fiction. "Corporate address: 19 North Main Street, Rittman, OH 44270-1407" avg. press run 2M. Expects 3 titles 1991, 3 titles 1992. 2 titles listed in the *Small Press Record of Books in Print* (20th Edition, 1991-92). avg. price, cloth: $14.95; paper: $12.95. Discounts: 40% bookstores, 20% corporate, other programs negotiable. 200pp; 5½x8½; of, computerized typesetting, photo-offset printing. Reporting time: varies, solicited submissions only. Payment: negotiated. Copyrights for author. Publishers Marketing Assn.

Oasis Books, Ian Robinson, 12 Stevenage Road, London, SW6 6ES, United Kingdom. 1969. Poetry, long-poems. "Oasis Books publish high-quality poetry and prose from the UK, North America and from other languages in translation, by both established and less well known poets in the form of booklets or full-length volumes. Mostly solicited mss only. Some recent titles: *Six Modern Greek Poets* (tr. John Stathatos); *Snath*, Martin Booth; *Half a Century of Kingston History* F. Sommer Merryweather; *HMS Little Fox* Lee Harwood; *Boston Brighton* Lee Harwood; *37 Poems* Werner Aspenstrom; *Casino* John Ash; *The Manual for the Perfect Organization of Tourneys* Paul Evans; *Athens Blues* Yannis Goumas; *Snapshots* Antony Lopez; *Tracts of the Country* John Wilkinson; *White Flock* Anna Akhmatova; *A Night with Hamlet* Vladimir Holan; *Selected Poems* Jean Claude Renard; *Deathfeast* Takis Sinopoulos; *Window* Leon Stroinski; *The Water Spider* Marcel Bealu; *Fading into Brilliance* David Chaloner; *Stones* Takis Sinopoulos; *How the Snake Emerged from the Bamboo Pole but Man Emerged from Both* Marvin Cohen. Refer to the *Small Press Record of Books in Print* for further titles." avg. press run 500. Pub'd 5 titles 1990; expects 5 titles 1991. 51 titles listed in the *Small Press Record* *of Books in Print* (20th Edition, 1991-92). avg. price, paper: $3-$6. Discounts: 35% over 1 copy, 25% otherwise (trade only). 24-100pp; size A5; †of, lp. Reporting time: 1 month. Payment: by arrangement. Copyrights for author. ALP, IPD (Independent Press Distribution).

OBESITY & HEALTH: CURRENT RESEARCH AND RELATED ISSUES, Frances M. Berg, Editor-Publisher, Healthy Living Institute, RR 2, Box 905, Hettinger, ND 58639, 701-567-2845. 1987. "Editorial office: 402 South 14th Street, Hettinger, ND 58639, 701-567-2646." circ. 1.5M. 6/yr. Pub'd 12 issues 1990; expects 6 issues 1991. sub. price: US $59 individual, $89 institution; group rates available; Canada add $1 per year, other countries add $9 per year; per copy: $9; sample: $5. Back issues: $4.50 - October 1990; after Oct. '90 - $9 (bimonthly issues). Discounts: agents 10%. 20pp; 8½×11; desktop & print shop. Payment: none. Copyrighted. Pub's reviews: 8 in 1990. §Obesity, weight management. Ads: $900.

OBLATES, Jacqueline Lowery Corn, Managing Editor, 15 South 59th Street, 9978, Belleville, IL 62223-4694, 618-233-2238. 1943. Poetry, articles, non-fiction. "*Oblates* sent to members of Missionary Assn. of Mary Immaculate." circ. 750M. 6/yr. Pub'd 6 issues 1990; expects 6 issues 1991, 6 issues 1992. Sample copy and writer's guidelines sent free with 52¢ SASE. Back issues: 6 issues (if available) for $1.33 postage 3rd Class. 20pp; 8½×5¼; †of. Reporting time: 4-6 weeks. Payment: $25 for poems, $75 for articles on acceptance. No ads. Catholic Press Association, National Catholic Development Conference.

Obsessive Compulsive Anonymous, PO Box 215, New Hyde Park, NY 11040, 516-741-4901; FAX 212-768-4679. 1988. Non-fiction. "12-step program for obsessive compulsive disorder" avg. press run 5M. Pub'd 1 title 1990; expects 1 title 1991, 1 title 1992. avg. price, cloth: $14.95. Discounts: distributor—CompCare Publishers 800-328-3330. 125pp; 5½×8½; of. PMA.

OBSIDIAN II: BLACK LITERATURE IN REVIEW, Gerald Barrax, Editor; Doris Laryea, Assistant Editor; Karla Holloway, Associate Editor; Joyce Pettis, Criticism Editor; Susie R. Powell, Fiction Editor; Sandra Govan, Book Review Editor, Dept. of English, Box 8105, NC State University, Raleigh, NC 27695-8105, 919-737-3870. 1975. Poetry, fiction, articles, interviews, criticism, reviews, letters, parts-of-novels, long-poems, plays, news items. "Founded in 1975 by Alvin Aubert as *Obsidian: Black Literature in Review*, the journal was transferred to North Carolina State University in 1986 as *Obsidian II*. The journal publishes creative works in English by Black writers worldwide, with scholarly critical studies by all writers on Black literature in English. Contributors to *Obsidian* and *Obsidian II* (both creative and scholarly) have included Michael S. Harper, Jay Wright, Gayl Jones, Houston A. Baker, Jr., Eugenia Collier, Lloyd W. Brown, Gerald Early, Wanda Coleman, Jerry W. Ward, Nikki Grimes, Raymond R. Patterson, Akua Lezli Hope, Gary Smith, Bu-Buakei Jabbi, Yusef Komunyakaa, Jane Davis, Philip Royster." circ. 400. 3/yr. Pub'd 3 issues 1990; expects 3 issues 1991, 3 issues 1992. sub. price: $12; per copy: $5; sample: $5. Discounts: 40% bookstores, 10% subscription agencies. 130pp; 6×9; †desktop/Macintosh SE. Reporting time: 2-3 months. Payment: 2 copies. Copyrighted, reverts to author. Pub's reviews: 6 in 1990. §Creative works by Black writers (poetry, fiction, drama); scholarship and criticism on same. Ads: $200/$100. CCLM.

Occam Publishers, Albor Road, RR1 Box 187A, Marathon, NY 13803-9755, 607-849-3186. 1988. Non-fiction. "Religious and moral issues for thoughtful people; liberal or 'neoliberal' outlook." Expects 1 title 1991, 1 title 1992. 1 title listed in the *Small Press Record of Books in Print* (20th Edition, 1991-92). avg. price, cloth: $19.95. Discounts: standard. 6×9; of. Reporting time: variable. Payment: negotiable. Copyrights for author. PMA, COSMEP.

Occasional Productions, David D. Edwards, Editor & Publisher, 5653 Orchard Park Drive, San Jose, CA 95123. 1978. "We are not soliciting new material" avg. press run 3M. Expects 1-3 titles 1991. 1 title listed in the *Small Press Record of Books in Print* (20th Edition, 1991-92). avg. price, paper: $7.95. Discounts: 40% to book dealers; 20% classroom use. 128pp; 7×7; of. Copyrights for author.

THE OCCASIONAL TUESDAY-ART NEWS, Tuesday-Art Press, George Jeffus, 3808 Rosecrans Street #134, San Diego, CA 92110. 1986. Articles, art, cartoons, interviews, satire, criticism, reviews, letters, collages, concrete art, news items. "Primarily orientated to San Diego art community. It is currently provided free through schools and galleries or personal copies at 50¢ or SASE and 25¢." circ. 500-1M. 10/yr. Pub'd 15 issues 1990; expects 15-20 issues 1991, 20+ issues 1992. price per copy: 25¢ and SASE. 3-5pp; 8½×11; †of. Reporting time: next issue. Payment: copies. Not copyrighted. Pub's reviews: 10 in 1990. §Art, design, problem solving, performance art. Ads: special arrangement.

Ocean Star Publications, Keith Whitaker, 30200 North Highway 1, Fort Bragg, CA 95437, 707-964-7302. Poetry, art, music, non-fiction. "We publish mostly Jewish Mystical material. SAE if the author wants their material returned" avg. press run 1M. Pub'd 2 titles 1990; expects 2 titles 1991, 3 titles 1992. avg. price, paper: $8. Discounts: 1982. 100pp; 6×9; of, computer lazerjet. Reporting time: 30 days. Payment: negotiable. Copyrights for author.

Ocean Tree Books, Richard L. Polese, PO Box 1295, Santa Fe, NM 87504, 505-983-1412. 1983. Non-fiction.

"All of our titles are non-fiction, most with an inspirational yet practical emphasis. Most titles involve the principles of peacemaking in some way, especially personal pilgrimages. We also produce guidebooks to the South and West. Length of our biggest book, *Peace Pilgrim* is 214 pages, but typically our books run less than 120 pages. Besides *Peace Pilgrim*, other authors are Barbara Marx Hubbard, Mikhail S. Gorbachev, Mary Lou Cook, Sue Guist, Narayan Desai, Richard Louis Polese. Peacewatch Editions is our series concerning international relations and peace issues in general. 'Enduring books that touch the spirit' typifies our work; we look for material that will be as relevant a dozen years from now as it is today." avg. press run 1.5M-3M. Pub'd 2 titles 1990; expects 3 titles 1991, 4 titles 1992. 13 titles listed in the *Small Press Record of Books in Print* (20th Edition, 1991-92). avg. price, cloth: $14.95; paper: $8.50. Discounts: trade: 1 20%, 2-4 30%, 5+ 40%, wholesale 50% to 55%. 180pp; 5½x8½; of. Reporting time: 5 weeks. Payment: royalties are based on unit sales x list price, and are of course negotiable. Competitive and a bit above average for the industry; no advances. Copyrights for author. Rocky Mountain Book Publishers Association (RMBPA).

Ocean View Books, Lee Ballentine, Editor; Jennifer MacGregor, Editor, Box 4148, Mountain View, CA 94040. 1981. Long-poems. "We publish a variety of surrealist and speculative/science-fiction texts, poetry and fiction. Original material only. Nothing confessional, personal, modern or traditional. No rhyme. No blank verse, free verse, or couplets. No unsolicited manuscripts, but feel free to query for a description of current projects. Recent authors: Robert Frazier, Ray Bradbury, William Stafford, Tom Disch, Rudy Rucker, Janet Hamill, Anselm Hollo. Recent projects: *Co-Orbital Moons, Poly.*" avg. press run 500. Pub'd 4 titles 1990; expects 4 titles 1991, 4 titles 1992. 10 titles listed in the *Small Press Record of Books in Print* (20th Edition, 1991-92). avg. price, cloth: $35; paper: $9.95. Discounts: inquire. 200pp; size varies; of. Reporting time: 3 months. Payment: negotiable. Copyrights for author. SFPA (Science Fiction Poetry Association), Bookbuilders West, American Bookseller's Association.

Oceanides Press, Susan Gordon, Doris Treisman, 1320 Albina, Berkeley, CA 94706. 1989. Poetry, fiction, art, photos. avg. press run 2M. Pub'd 1 title 1990; expects 1 title 1991. 1 title listed in the *Small Press Record of Books in Print* (20th Edition, 1991-92). avg. price, paper: $8.95. Discounts: 40%. 100pp; 5x7; of. Reporting time: varies, 1-2 months. Payment: varies. Does not copyright for author.

Tom Ockerse Editions, Thomas Ockerse, 37 Woodbury Street, Providence, RI 02906, 401-331-0783. 1965. Poetry, fiction, articles, art, photos, collages, concrete art. "The intended purpose of T.O.E. is to publish monographs of works by artists whose work is structured by a primary commitment to concrete language, i.e., self-describing/self-referral." avg. press run 300-1M. Pub'd 1 title 1990; expects 2 titles 1991. 13 titles listed in the *Small Press Record of Books in Print* (20th Edition, 1991-92). avg. price, cloth: $20; paper: $4; other: $100. Pages vary, no limit; size varies; of, lp, silkscreen, xerox. Payment: varies. Copyrights for author.

Octavia Press, Diana Tittle, 3546 Edison Road, Cleveland, OH 44121, (216) 381-2853. 1986. Non-fiction. avg. press run 5M. Expects 1 title 1991, 1 title 1992. 4 titles listed in the *Small Press Record of Books in Print* (20th Edition, 1991-92). avg. price, cloth: $20. Discounts: 5-24 books 40%; 25-99 42%; 100-249 43%; 250-999 44%; 1000-2499 45%; 2500+ 46%. 224pp; size varies; of. Reporting time: 6 weeks. Payment: varies. Copyrights for author. PMA, 2401 Pacific Coast Hwy, Suite 206, Hermosa Beach, CA 90254, COSMEP, PO Box 703, San Francisco, CA 94101.

Oddo Publishing, Inc., PO Box 68, Fayetteville, GA 30214. 1964. avg. press run 3.5M. Pub'd 3 titles 1990; expects 1 title 1991, 3 titles 1992. 9 titles listed in the *Small Press Record of Books in Print* (20th Edition, 1991-92). avg. price, cloth: $12.95. Discounts: available on request. 32pp; 7½x9¼; of. Reporting time: approx. 4 months. Payment: varies. Does not copyright for author.

ODESSA POETRY REVIEW, Odessa Press, Jim Wyzard, Editor, Publisher, RR 1 Box 39, Odessa, MO 64076. 1984. Poetry, art, photos. "Sponsors four yearly poetry competitions: Spring, Summer, Fall, Winter. Deadlines are May 31, August 31, November 30, and February 28, in that order. We will read only those poems which have been entered in one of the four competitions. Entries must be accompanied by $1 per poem entry fee and SASE. We would like to see more poetry about the social and human situations which the modern world must deal with. We will accept no poetry which we feel is in some way, socially unacceptable. SASE for guidelines" circ. 1M. 4/yr. Pub'd 4 issues 1990; expects 4 issues 1991, 4 issues 1992. 1 title listed in the *Small Press Record of Books in Print* (20th Edition, 1991-92). sub. price: $16; per copy: $4; sample: $4. Back issues: $4. Discounts: None. 150pp; 5½x8½; of. Reporting time: 1 month following competition deadline. Payment: $100, $50, $25, + 5 $5 to the top 8 poems per issue. Copyrighted, reverts to author. Ads: $100/$50/25¢ classified word/Reading notice $25. CCLM.

Odessa Press (see also ODESSA POETRY REVIEW), Jim Wyzard, R.R. 1, Box 39, Odessa, MO 64076.

Odin Press, Pamela Lawrence, PO Box 536, New York, NY 10021, 212-744-2538. 1977. Non-fiction. "Terms are net 30 days, FOB New York, NY 10021. Orders up to 100 lbs will be shipped via United Parcel Service or USPS special fourth class rate. Shipments over 100 lbs will be shipped Motor Freight. Refunds, less the cost of shipping, will be made for books returned in saleable condition within nine months of purchase date. For

400

additional information contact Pamela Lawrence at above address." avg. press run 2.5M. Expects 1 title 1991. avg. price, cloth: $28; paper: $18. Discounts: 1-9, 25%; 10-24, 40%; 25-99, 43%; 100-299, 46%; 300 or more, 50%. 208pp; 4¼×5½; of. Reporting time: 3 months. Payment: advance up to $2,000; royalty 8-15%, depending on volume. Copyrights for author.

Odysseus Enterprises Ltd., Joseph H. Bain, E. Angelo, PO Box 1548, Port Washington, NY 11050-0306, 516-944-5330; fax 516-944-7540. 1984. avg. press run 50M. Pub'd 1 title 1990; expects 1 title 1991. 1 title listed in the *Small Press Record of Books in Print* (20th Edition, 1991-92). avg. price, paper: $18. Discounts: trade 40%, jobbers 50%, distributors 55%. 500pp; 5½×8½. Copyrights for author. GLPA.

OFF MAIN STREET, David Vinopal, John Caserta, Ferris State College, Languages & Literature Dept., Big Rapids, MI 49307, (616) 796-8762. 1986. Poetry, fiction, non-fiction. "Poetry, short fiction, and personal essays. We look for carefully structured, highly crafted literature that reflects authors' understanding of literary traditions, irony, and subtlety of language in all its forms. High-quality translations are sought. Short fiction and personal essays: 500-3,000 words" circ. 500. 1/yr. Pub'd 1 issue 1990; expects 1 issue 1991, 1 issue 1992. sub. price: $3.50; per copy: $3.50; sample: $2.50. Back issues: $2.50. 64pp; 5½×8½; of. Reporting time: 6 weeks. Payment: copies. Copyrighted, reverts to author. §Literary magazines that publish poetry, fiction, personal essays.

OFF OUR BACKS, Carol Anne Douglas, Tricia Lootens, Alice Henry, Lorraine Sorrel, Angela Johnson, Jennie Ruby, Elliot Farar, Joanne Stato, Cricket Keating, Julia Hyles, Cecile Latham, 2423 18th Street, NW, 2nd Floor, Washington, DC 20009-2003, 202-234-8072. 1970. Articles, art, photos, cartoons, interviews, criticism, reviews, letters, news items. "Consider ourselves a radical feminist *news* journal, with complete coverage of national and international news about women. Free to prisoners." circ. 22M. 11/yr. Pub'd 11 issues 1990; expects 11 issues 1991, 11 issues 1992. sub. price: $19 indiv., $30 institutions (inc. libraries), $20 Canadian, $28 foreign, contributing subscription $22; per copy: $2 newstand price; sample: $2 domestic, $3 foreign, free to prisoners. Back issues: $2. Discounts: 40% for 5 or more copies monthly; billed/paid quarterly. 36pp; 10½×13½; of. Reporting time: 3 months. Payment: copies. Copyrighted, reverts to author. Pub's reviews: 50 in 1990. §Women. Ads: $400/$210/40¢ (prepaid). COSMEP, NESPA.

OFFICE NUMBER ONE, Carlos B. Dingus, 1709 San Antonio Street, Austin, TX 78701, 512-320-8243. 1989. Poetry, fiction, articles, cartoons, satire, letters. "*Office Number One* is a zine of satire. I need short (500 words or so) satirical news items, strange essays, or fiction. Poetry is limericks or haiku. Get it right for limericks. Satire should have an upbeat point and make sense—any kind of sense. Once in a great while I print a few serious words—500 or less on philosophy or religion—but it's got to be good. We plan a larger format and more pages soon." circ. 2M. 6/yr. Pub'd 6 issues 1990; expects 6 issues 1991, 6 issues 1992. sub. price: $8.84/8 issues; per copy: $2; sample: $2. Discounts: 24 copies $12 postpaid (minimum order). 12pp; 7×8½; of. Reporting time: 3 weeks. Payment: negotiable, but not much. Copyrighted, reverts to author. Ads: $125/$75/$40 1/4 page. Austin Writer's League.

Ohio Chess Association, OHIO CHESS BULLETIN, Roger Blaine, President, 224 East Broadway, Apt. B, Granville, OH 43023. Ads: $35/$20.

OHIO CHESS BULLETIN, Ohio Chess Association, Gary A. Markette, Editor; Roger E. Blaine, News Editor, 128 Ertle Street Northeast, Massillon, OH 44646-3230, 216-832-8907. 1945. Articles, art, photos, cartoons, interviews, satire, criticism, reviews, letters, news items. "Membership costs $12 annually, magazine free with membership" circ. 450. 6/yr. Pub'd 6 issues 1990; expects 6 issues 1991, 6 issues 1992. sub. price: $10; per copy: $1.75; sample: $1. Back issues: on request. 32pp; 5½×8½; of. Reporting time: 3 weeks. Payment: none. Not copyrighted. Pub's reviews: 18 in 1990. §Chess, fiction, or non-fiction. Ads: $35/$20/no classifieds.

‡**OHIO RENAISSANCE REVIEW,** James R. Pack, Publisher & Editor; Ron Houchin, Poetry Editor; Ariyan, Graphics Editor, PO Box 804, Infinity Press and Publications, Ironton, OH 45638, 614-532-0846. 1984. Poetry, fiction, articles, art, photos, interviews, reviews, non-fiction. "Poetry: Concrete free verse, no length limits; Recent contributors: Lyn Lifshin, Edward Romano, Tammy Chapman, J.F. DaVanzo. Fiction: Science fiction, fantasy, mystery, shortstories: 400- 2,000 words; Recent contributors: Dave Witte, Kathleen Alcala, Gary Earl Ross, Avery Jenkins. Art & Photos: Black & White line drawings and photos that embrace the fantastic" circ. 1M. 4/yr. Pub'd 1 issue 1990; expects 4 issues 1991, 4 issues 1992. sub. price: $20; per copy: $10; sample: $4. Back issues: $10 1st Edition. Discounts: none at present; interested parties should make written inquiry. 64pp; 7×10; of. Reporting time: 4-6 weeks. Payment: poetry 25¢ per line ($5 minimum), fiction $2.50 per printed column, art & photos $10 per item; all payments upon publication. Copyrighted, reverts to author. Pub's reviews. §Magazines of all types containing literature, books of poetry, science fiction, fantasy, or mystery fiction. Ads: $125/$75/50¢ (10-word minimum); discounts: x2-10%; x3-20%; x4-30%. none at present.

THE OHIO REVIEW, Wayne Dodd, Ellis Hall, Ohio University, Athens, OH 45701, 614-593-1900. 1959. Poetry, fiction, articles, interviews, reviews. circ. 2M. 3/yr. Pub'd 3 issues 1990; expects 3 issues 1991. 6 titles listed in the *Small Press Record of Books in Print* (20th Edition, 1991-92). sub. price: $12; per copy: $4.25; sample: $4.25 (current issue will be sent). Back issues: varies. Discounts: vary, sent on request. 144pp; 6×9; of. Reporting time: 90 days. Payment: rates vary, copies plus min. $5 per page prose; $15 per poem. Copyrighted. Pub's reviews: 2 in 1990. §Poetry, fiction, books, including all chapbooks. Ads: $175/$100. CCLM.

OHIO WRITER, Linda Rome, PO Box 528, Willoughby, OH 44094-0528. 1987. Articles, interviews, reviews. "Only service pieces published: interviews of writers, focus on aspect of writing in Ohio, reviews of books, bookshops, writer's conferences. Major piece 2,000 words; focus piece 1,500 words; column 800 words; book review 400-500 words" circ. 600. 6/yr. Pub'd 6 issues 1990; expects 6 issues 1991, 6 issues 1992. sub. price: $12; per copy: $2; sample: $2. 16pp; 8½×11; desktop pub, laser printer, offset printer. Reporting time: 3 months. Payment: $5-$50 depending on what. Copyrighted, reverts to author. Pub's reviews: 30 in 1990. §Books or magazines published in Ohio or by Ohio writers. Ads: $25 1/2/$35 1/9 page. under stewardship of the Poets' League of Greater Cleveland.

OHIOANA QUARTERLY, Barbara Maslekoff, Editor, 1105 Ohio Dept Bldg., 65 S. Front St, Columbus, OH 43215, 614-466-3831. 1958. Articles, art, reviews. "Pub'd by the Ohioana Library Assn. Reviews by staff and guest reviewers. Length of review varies from 40 to 800 words. Ohio authors or books on Ohio only. Articles on Ohio authors, music, other arts in Ohio, up to 2M words." circ. 1.2M. 4/yr. Pub'd 4 issues 1990; expects 4 issues 1991, 4 issues 1992. sub. price: $20 (membership); per copy: $5; sample: gratis. Back issues: $6. Discounts: $20 to libraries. 88pp; 5½×8½; of. Reporting time: 2 weeks. Payment: copies only. Copyrighted, rights do not revert, but we grant permission for full use by author. Pub's reviews: 450 in 1990. §Books about Ohio or Ohioans, books by Ohioans or former Ohioans, new magazines pub'd in Ohio. No ads.

George Ohsawa Macrobiotic Foundation Press (see also MACROBIOTICS TODAY), Carl Ferre, Managing Editor; Sandy Rothman, Editor, 1511 Robinson Street, Oroville, CA 95965-4841, 916-533-7702. 1970. Articles, non-fiction. "Articles about macrobiotics and health. Books of at least 90 pages on macrobiotics, health, diet and nutrition. Special interest in cookbooks. Recent contributors include Noboru Muramoto, Julia Ferre, Rachel Albert, and Pam Henkel" avg. press run 3M-5M. Pub'd 1 title 1990; expects 3 titles 1991, 3 titles 1992. 19 titles listed in the *Small Press Record of Books in Print* (20th Edition, 1991-92). avg. price, paper: $7.95. Discounts: 1-99 single or mixed 40%, 100+ 45%; distributors discount available. 260pp; 5½×8½, 6×9; typeset, lp. Reporting time: 6 weeks. Payment: 5% of gross retail sales, or 10% of net sales. Copyrights for author. ABA.

OIKOS: A JOURNAL OF ECOLOGY AND COMMUNITY, Arne Jorgensen, 55 Magnolia Avenue, Denville, NJ 07834. 1980. Poetry, fiction, articles, art, photos, cartoons, interviews, satire, reviews, letters, parts-of-novels, collages, concrete art, news items, non-fiction. "Writings for *Oikos* should 1) express an ecological concept which sees that the reconstruction of our fragmented society must accompany a movement toward ecological sanity; 2) convey the bioregional perspective; 3) deal with local/regional ecological initiative as an alternative to corporate exploitation and easily corrupted federal environmental regulation; 4) focus on the conflict between current economics and preserving Earth's living systems; 5) mention ecological concern as a factor in art, religion, science, literature, economics, philosophy, architecture, and social systems from prehistoric to post-industrial times. *Oikos* needs practical tips for self-reliant ecological living - apartment gardening, do-it-yourself solar energy projects, etc. Will exchange subscriptions with other magazines. Will also exchange with book publishers. *Oikos* needs review copies of books and magazines which deal with topics mentioned in this listing. Please include editor's name when addressing correspondence." circ. 1.25M. 1/yr. Expects 1 issue 1991, 1-2 issues 1992. sub. price: $11.50/4 issues; per copy: $2.50 postage included; sample: $1 (sample will be back issue). Back issues: $2 for 3 issues. Discounts: dealer 40-50%, the same or standard for all others. 18pp; 8½×11; of/lo or xerox. Reporting time: 2 months. Payment: at least 2 copies; *Oikos* intends to pay writers money if ever possible. Copyrighted, reverts to author. Pub's reviews: 0 in 1990. §Ecology and politics, self-reliance through alternate technology, organic gardening, etc., philosophy of humanity/nature relations, philosophical/world view implications of biology as expressed in books like Hans Jonas' *The Phenmenon of Life*, deep ecology a la the work of philospher Arne Naess, spiritual/philosophical/practical implications of biotechnology, also want articles on topics in this review list. No issue in 1986. A book review appeared in 1987. Ads: $85/$50/25¢. none.

O'Laughlin Press (Irish Genealogical Foundation) (see also IRISH FAMILY JOURNAL), Michael C. O'Laughlin, Box 7575, Kansas City, MO 64116, 816-454-2410. 1969. Articles, art, photos, interviews, letters, non-fiction. avg. press run 1M. Pub'd 2 titles 1990; expects 2 titles 1991, 2 titles 1992. 5 titles listed in the *Small Press Record of Books in Print* (20th Edition, 1991-92). avg. price, cloth: $45. Discounts: bulk purchases 40%-60% discount. 300pp; 8½×11; of. Reporting time: 30 days. Payment: inquire. Does not copyright for author.

OLD ABE'S NEWS, David T. Erb, Route 2, Box 242, Vinton, OH 45686, 614-388-8895. 1985. Interviews. "Agricultural history—'Old Iron' collecting. J.I. Case equipment, people, and history" circ. 1M. 4/yr. Pub'd 4 issues 1990; expects 4 issues 1991, 4 issues 1992. sub. price: $15, includes 1 yr. membership to J.I Case

Collectors Assn., Inc.; per copy: $2.50; sample: free. Back issues: $2 each for 5 or more. 28pp; 8½×11; produce camera ready mechanicals with Macintosh—photo offset printing. Payment: $50 honorarium for collector of History Stories published. Copyrighted, does not revert to author. Pub's reviews: 1 in 1990. §Agricultural history, farm equipment, ag. people stories. Ads: $100/$65/$35.

Old Adobe Press, Rafael Cunin, PO Box 969, Penngrove, CA 94951. 1971. "Temporarily inactive." avg. press run 500-1M 1st printing, 2.5M 2nd printing. Pub'd 1 title 1990; expects 1 title 1991. 1 title listed in the *Small Press Record of Books in Print* (20th Edition, 1991-92). avg. price, cloth: $9.95-$19.95; paper: $4.95-$9.95. Discounts: 1 copy 20%, 2-3 30% 4 or more 40%. 150pp; 5×8; of, lp. Reporting time: 6 weeks. Payment: standard. All titles copyrighted in author's name. COSMEP, COSMEP-WEST.

The Old Army Press, Mike Koury, PO Box 2243, Fort Collins, CO 80522, 303-484-5535. 1968. Non-fiction. "Western Military History with an emphisis on Custer and the Indian Wars" avg. press run 250-1.5M. Pub'd 3 titles 1990; expects 6 titles 1991, 6 titles 1992. avg. price, cloth: $30; paper: $9; other: $30-videos. Discounts: order of 5 or more - 40%, 100 or more 45%, over 300 - 50%. 120pp; 7×10, 5½×8½, 8½×11; of. Reporting time: 6 weeks. Payment: per contract. Does not copyright for author. Rocky Mountain Book Publishers.

Old Harbor Press, Margaret Calvin, PO Box 97, Sitka, AK 99835, 907-747-3584. 1983. Poetry, fiction, art, non-fiction. avg. press run 3M. Expects 1 title 1991, 1 title 1992. 5 titles listed in the *Small Press Record of Books in Print* (20th Edition, 1991-92). avg. price, paper: $9.95; other: limited $47.50. Discounts: 40% retailers; 50% wholesalers; 20% schools and libraries. 40pp; 6×9; †lp. Payment: 5% paid semiannually. Copyrights for author. Alaska Association of Small Presses.

THE OLD RED KIMONO, Jon Hershey, Ken Anderson, Humanities, Floyd College, Box 1864, Rome, GA 30163, 404-295-6312. 1972. Poetry, fiction. "*ORK* is looking for submissions of 3-5 short poems or one very short story (2,500 words max). Both poems and stories should be very concise and imagistic. Nothing sentimental or didactic. Mss. read Sept. 1 - March 1." circ. 1.2M. 1/yr. Pub'd 1 issue 1990; expects 1 issue 1991. 64pp; 8×11; of. Reporting time: 3 months. Payment: 2 copies. Copyrighted, reverts to author.

OLD TYME BASEBALL NEWS, D. Scott McKinstry, 2447 Judd Road, Burton, MI 48529, 313-744-2102; 616-348-2967. 1988. "650 words or less, b/w photos" 4/yr. Pub'd 4 issues 1990; expects 4 issues 1991, 4 issues 1992. sub. price: $19.95. 16pp; 12×17; of. Reporting time: asap. Payment: varies with article. Copyrighted, reverts depending on arrangement. §Baseball books.

Old West Publishing Co., 1228 E. Colfax Avenue, Denver, CO 80218. 1940. "Not seeking new material." avg. press run 2M. Expects 1 title 1992. 12 titles listed in the *Small Press Record of Books in Print* (20th Edition, 1991-92). avg. price, cloth: $30. Discounts: 40% any quantity non-returnable. 300pp; 6×9.

Old World Travel Books, Inc., 2608 E. 74th, PO Box 700863, Tulsa, OK 74170, 918-493-2642. 1 title listed in the *Small Press Record of Books in Print* (20th Edition, 1991-92). COSMEP, PMA.

Olde & Oppenheim Publishers, Mike Gratz, PO Box 61203, Phoenix, AZ 85082, 602-839-0560. 1984. "No submissions accepted." avg. press run 5M. Pub'd 3 titles 1990; expects 3 titles 1991, 3 titles 1992. 1 title listed in the *Small Press Record of Books in Print* (20th Edition, 1991-92). avg. price, cloth: $14.95. Discounts: 2-4 books 40%, 5-41 43%, 42-83 46%, 84+50%. 128pp; 5⅜×8; sheet-fed.

OLD-HOUSE JOURNAL, Patricia Poore, 435 9th Street, Brooklyn, NY 11215, 718-636-4514. 1973. "Restoration and maintenance techniques for the pre-1939 house. Practical how-to information for restoring older houses." circ. 140M. 6/yr. Pub'd 6 issues 1990; expects 6 issues 1991, 6 issues 1992. sub. price: $21; per copy: $3.95. Back issues: $4.95 per issue—also available in yearbooks. 80pp; 8¼×10¾; web of. Reporting time: 4-6 weeks. Copyrighted, does not revert to author. Pub's reviews: 24 in 1990. §Victorian and early 20th century decorating and antiques, architecture and architectural styles 1750-1940, also technical/construction methods. Ads: 2650/1720/$32.

The Olive Press Publications, Addis Lynne Norris, PO Box 99, Los Olivos, CA 93441. 1978. Poetry, non-fiction. "Not accepting submissions at this time. Specialize in historical material." avg. press run 5M. Pub'd 1 title 1990; expects 5 titles 1991, 5 titles 1992. 12 titles listed in the *Small Press Record of Books in Print* (20th Edition, 1991-92). avg. price, cloth: $12.95; paper: $7.95. Discounts: 40% over 5 copies. 250pp; 6×9, 5½×8½; of. PMA.

The Olivia and Hill Press, Inc., Jacqueline Morton, Brian N. Morton, PO Box 7396, Ann Arbor, MI 48107, 313-663-0235; FAX 313-663-0235. 1979. Non-fiction. "We began with *English Grammar For Students Of French*, in 1979, and have added editions in Spanish, German, Italian, Latin, and Russian; the first three have now come out in second editions. The second editions are $8.95; first editions are $7.95. We distribute foreign language cassettes (novels, plays, and poetry) imported from France, Germany and Spain. We also distribute cassette + book packages (fairy tales and stories) for children in French, Spanish and German. We publish two anecdotal street guides: *Americans in Paris* and *Americans in London*. Both are paperback, 350 pages, 60 photos, $12.95 each. We are interested in receiving unsolicited manuscripts in our area of interest." avg. press run 10M. Pub'd 2 titles 1990; expects 1 title 1991, 1 title 1992. 3 titles listed in the *Small Press Record of Books in Print* (20th Edition, 1991-92). avg. price, paper: $8.95, $12.95. Discounts: 20% to bookstores. 250pp; 6×9; of. Payment: standard. Copyrights for author.

C. Olson & Company, C.L. Olson, PO Box 5100, Santa Cruz, CA 95063-5100, 408-458-3365. 1979. Poetry, fiction, articles, art, photos, cartoons, interviews, reviews, letters, parts-of-novels, news items, non-fiction. "Material length is usually 10-15M words.Seeking manuscripts on natural health, ecological improvement projects, stress reduction, natural hygiene. Manuscripts must be provided with SASE, but query first with SASE." avg. press run 3M. Pub'd 2 titles 1990; expects 3 titles 1991, 4 titles 1992. 2 titles listed in the *Small Press Record of Books in Print* (20th Edition, 1991-92). avg. price, paper: $5.95. Discounts: write for information. 64pp; 5⅜×8½; of. Reporting time: 2-4 weeks. Payment: each book negotiated.

Olympic Publishing, Inc. (see also OLYMPIC TRAVEL GUIDE: YOUR GUIDE TO WASHINGTON'S OLYMPIC PENINSULA), Dan Youra, Patricia Thompson, 7450 Oak Bay Road, Port Ludlow, WA 98365, 206-437-2277. 1980. Articles, photos, non-fiction. "We are generally self-publishers. We do publish on a co-operative basis with others. We work with a wide range of topics and cannot narrow subject matter down to a couple topics." avg. press run 50M. Expects 3 titles 1991, 3 titles 1992. avg. price, paper: $4.95; other: $1.95 magazines. Discounts: 3-12 40%, 13-50 45%, 51-150 50%, 151+ 55%. 128pp; 5½×8½; of. Reporting time: fast. Payment: varies, co-operative. Pacific NW Book Publishers, Northwest Magazine Publishers.

OLYMPIC TRAVEL GUIDE: YOUR GUIDE TO WASHINGTON'S OLYMPIC PENINSULA, Olympic Publishing, Inc., Dan Youra, Editor; Patricia Thompson, Managing Editor, PO Box 353, Port Ludlow, WA 98365, 206-437-2277. 1984. Articles, photos, non-fiction. "We purchase interesting articles and photos on Olympic Peninsula" circ. 60M. 3/yr. Pub'd 2 issues 1990; expects 3 issues 1991, 3 issues 1992. sub. price: $6, including shipping; per copy: $1.95; sample: $1. Back issues: $1.50 includes shipping. Discounts: 3-12 40%, 13-50 45%, 51-150 50%, 151+ 55%. 48pp; 8×10; of. Reporting time: fast. Copyrighted, reverts to author. Pub's reviews: 3 in 1990. §Olympic Peninsula travel. Ads: $1,000/$600/$10. Pacific NW Book Publishers; Northwest Magazine Publishers.

Omega Cat Press (see also XENOPHILIA), Joy Oestreicher, 904 Old Town Ct., Cupertino, CA 95014, 408-257-0462. 1990. Poetry, art, long-poems. "Will entertain chapbook submissions in the future (annual chapbook contest); query for details." avg. press run 100-200. Expects 1 title 1992. avg. price, paper: $3. 30pp; 5½×8½; of. Reporting time: up to 1 year for chapbook competition. Payment: to be arranged (50 copies of chapbook). Copyrights for author. SPWAO.

Omega Cottonwood Press, Marilyn Coffey, Editor & Publisher, PO Box 524, Alma, NE 68920-0524. 1976. Poetry, fiction, articles, art, photos, satire, criticism, reviews, long-poems, collages. "Publishes poetry (from broadsides to long poems and collage-poems), fiction, satire, articles, photographs, both originals and reprints. Dedicated to publishing the short works of Marilyn Coffey, her students, Amethyst and other contemporary writers of poetry and short prose. The Press likes clear, finely crafted writing, polished and professional but with a bit of bite in it, fiction and poetry grounded in experience but filtered through the imagination. We publish, in particular, women's writing, feminist writing (by women or men), Great Plains topics, erotica, satire, and addiction (especially cross-addition) recovery pieces. By invitation only." avg. press run 50-300. Pub'd 5 titles 1990; expects 3 titles 1991, 6 titles 1992. 13 titles listed in the *Small Press Record of Books in Print* (20th Edition, 1991-92). avg. price, paper: $5 per chapbook. 40pp; 8½×11; quality photocopy. Payment: use of imprint + free copies. Author retains copyright.

Omega Press (formerly Sufi Order Publications), Duane Sweeney, General Manager, RD #1, Box 1030 D, New Lebanon, NY 12125. 1977. "Omega Press publishes the teachings of Hazrat Inayat Inayat Khan, Pir Vilayat Khan and other spiritual teachers. The works chosen reflect the *Sufi* ideals of love, harmony, beauty." avg. press run 4M. Pub'd 3 titles 1990; expects 1 title 1991, 1 title 1992. 10 titles listed in the *Small Press Record of Books in Print* (20th Edition, 1991-92). avg. price, paper: $7.95. Discounts: 2-4 copies 20%, 5-14 40%, 15-24 43%, 25-49 46%, 50+ 50%. 240pp; 5½×8½; of. Copyrights for author.

Ommation Press (see also MATI; SALOME: A JOURNAL FOR THE PERFORMING ARTS), Effie Mihopoulos, 5548 North Sawyer, Chicago, IL 60625. 1975. Poetry, fiction, art, photos, long-poems, plays, non-fiction. "Ommation Press is no longer publishing *The Ditto Rations Chapbook Series* (the chapbooks already published are still available for purchase, send SASE for list of titles), which has completed its proposed 20 titles. *Offset Offshoots* now has titles by Lyn Lifshin, Christine Zawadiwsky, Rochelle Ratner, Douglas MacDonald. *Dialogues on Dance* has 8 titles to date and more are planned." avg. press run 500-1M. Pub'd 4 titles 1990; expects 6 titles 1991. 157 titles listed in the *Small Press Record of Books in Print* (20th Edition, 1991-92). avg. price, cloth: $18; paper: $5 *Offset Offshoot*, $1-$2 *Ditto Rations*, $6 *Dialogues*; other: $1.50-$3 *Mati*, $6 *Salome*. Discounts: 20% on purchase of 10 or more copies. 25-50pp; 8½×11, 5×9; of. Reporting time: 1 month. Payment: 50 copies of book. Copyrights for author.

OMNIFIC, Weems Concepts, Kay Weems, Star Route, Box 21AA, Artemas, PA 17211, 814-458-3102. 1989. Poetry. "In this publication, everyone writing in good taste will have 4 poems/year published. Readers then vote on their favorites and awards will be given to the 3 receiving most votes, the poem in the "Lucky 7" slot, and the Editor's Choice. Along with the standard awards mentioned above, some readers have set up awards in their name and will send "something" to the person(s) that touched them in a special way with their writing. In the past these gifts have been stamps, newsletters, small cash awards, chapbooks, small gifts, and letters showing appreciation for a certain poem—all of which are most welcomed by the poet." circ. 200+. 4/yr. Pub'd 4 issues 1990; expects 4 issues 1991, 4 issues 1992. sub. price: $12; per copy: $3.50; sample: $3.50. Back issues: $3.50. 70-80pp; digest; †Sharp copier. Reporting time: 2-3 months. Payment: Editor's Choice Award of $5 to one or two people + various other small awards from readers and editor to several people. Copyrighted. Ads: uses ads only as fillers. PA Poetry Society, Walt Whitman Guild, UAPAA, National Arts Society, National Federation of State Poetry Societies Inc., New Horizons Poetry Club, Southern Poetry Assoc.

ON BALANCE: MEDIA TREATMENT OF PUBLIC POLICY ISSUES, The Fraser Institute, Kristin McCahon, Production Editor, 626 Bute Street, 2nd Floor, Vancouver, BC V6E 3M1, Canada, 604-688-0221. 1988. circ. 2M. 10/yr. Pub'd 10 issues 1990; expects 10 issues 1991, 10 issues 1992. sub. price: $95 + 7% GST Canadian subscribers; per copy: $8 + 7% GST Canadian residents; sample: free. Back issues: $8 + 7% GST Canadian residents. Discounts: negotiable depending on quantity ordered. 8pp; 8½×11; of. Copyrighted, reverts to author. Association of Book Publishers of B.C. and Canada, Canadian Book Sellers Association.

ON COURSE, Jon Mundy, Diane Berke, 459 Carol Drive, Monroe, NY 10950. 1983. Poetry, articles, art, photos, cartoons, interviews, satire, reviews, letters, news items, non-fiction. "Short articles: 1 page preferred, inspirational, homespun American philosophy, self-help, transpersonal psychology, holistic health, body work, yoga, zen, etc. Most articles are in house. Emphasis on *A Course In Miracles*. Interfaith approach." circ. 3.5M. 42/yr. Pub'd 44 issues 1990; expects 42 issues 1991. sub. price: $90, $2 per week; per copy: $2; sample: free. 32pp; 5½×8; †of, small press. Reporting time: 3 weeks. Payment: copies only so far. Not copyrighted. Pub's reviews: 8 in 1990. §Inspirational, self-help. Ads: $175/$95/$60 1/4 page/$35 1/8. Small Magazine Publishers Group.

ON GOGOL BOULEVARD: Networking Bulletin for Dissidents from East and West, Bob McGlynn, William Falk, 151 1st Avenue #62, New York, NY 10003, 718-499-7720; 212-206-8463. 1987. Poetry, articles, art, photos, cartoons, interviews, satire, criticism, reviews, letters, collages, news items, non-fiction. "Length: *short*. Biases: humorous, irreverant, iconoclastic" circ. 1.2M-3M. 3-4/yr. Pub'd 2 issues 1990; expects 3-4 issues 1991, 3-4 issues 1992. sub. price: $5 US, $10 abroad; per copy: $1; sample: $1. Back issues: $1. Discounts: trades possible, more than 5, 50¢ apiece. 14-24pp; 8½×11. Payment: none, non-profit zine. Not copyrighted. Pub's reviews. §Soviet bloc issues. Ads: no standards, negotiable.

ON THE LINE, Mary Clemens Meyer, Editor, 616 Walnut Avenue, Scottdale, PA 15683. 1971. Poetry, fiction, articles, photos, cartoons, interviews, non-fiction. circ. 9M. 52/yr. sub. price: $15.50; sample: send SASE. 8pp; 7×10; †li. Reporting time: 1 month. Payment: from 2¢-4¢/word on acceptance. Pub's reviews: 3 in 1990. §Books of interest to readers ages 10-14. No ads.

ON THE ROAD: Mobile Ideas for Libraries, Library Outreach Reporter Publications, Cathi Suyak Alloway, Editor-in-Chief, 1671 East 16th Street, Suite 226, Brooklyn, NY 11229, 718-645-2396. 1989. Articles, photos, interviews, news items, non-fiction. circ. 500. 4/yr. Pub'd 1 issue 1990; expects 4 issues 1991, 4 issues 1992. sub. price: $12; per copy: $4; sample: free. Back issues: $4 each. Discounts: agent/jobber 15% commission. 20pp; 8½×11; of. Reporting time: 1 month. Payment: copies of issue. Copyrighted, does not revert to author. Ads: $175/$125/other available upon request.

ON THE SPOT, Jonn Emm, PO Box 70614, New Orleans, LA 70172, 504-947-5165. 1991. Poetry, fiction, articles, art, photos, cartoons, interviews, reviews, music, collages. circ. 1M. Frequent. Expects 4-6 issues 1991, 12 issues 1992. sub. price: $25/13 issues; per copy: $3. 48pp; 8½×11; of. Payment: nil (for now). Ads: $250/$150.

1 BIT SHOE, Dave Walbridge, Kevin Stroheim, 2760 Louisiana Court #9, St. Louis Park, MN 55426. 1990. Art, photos, reviews, letters, collages. "Primarily composed of drawings, photos, essays and reviews. Experimental fun. Looking for comments, humor, ideas, art and good banana jokes." circ. 50-100. 3-4/yr. Expects 3 issues 1991, 4 issues 1992. price per copy: $2; sample: $2. 14pp; 5×8; †photocopy. Reporting time: varies. Payment: trade/copies. Copyrighted, rights reverting varies. Pub's reviews. §Literary, humor, arts, experimental, photography, theater.

ONE EARTH, The Findhorn Press, Eve Ward, Findhorn Foundation, The Park, Forres, Morayshire 1V36 0TZ, Scotland, 0309-30010. 1979. Articles, art, photos, cartoons, interviews, reviews, letters, non-fiction. "The purpose of *One Earth* magazine is to offer perspectives on the emerging planetary culture and the application of holistic values in a variety of fields. Each issue has a different theme. Includes articles by Findhorn community members, and features speakers and artists from conferences and arts festival hosted by the Findhorn

Foundation.'' circ. 3.5M. 4/yr. Pub'd 4 issues 1990; expects 4 issues 1991, 4 issues 1992. sub. price: UK £9, US (surface) $19.50, (airmail) $25.50; per copy: £2, $5; sample: £2, US $5. Back issues: £1, $2. Discounts: 10-49, 35%; 50+ 45%. 44pp; 12¼×8¾; †of. Reporting time: 2 months. Payment: by arrangement, usually by free copies. Copyrighted. Pub's reviews: 20 in 1990. §Metaphysics, the spiritual life, communities, social and political issues. Ads: on request. IPG.

ONE SHOT, Steven Rosen, Contract Station 6, Box 145, 1525 Sherman Street, Denver, CO 80203. 1986. Articles, photos, cartoons, interviews, criticism, letters, news items, non-fiction. ''The motto is 'attentive writing about neglected rock 'n' roll', and I am very open to anything that fits that description, including artwork. *One Shot* is dedicated to rock's one-hit wonders; such as Norman Greenbaum, Rosie and the Originals, and John Fred And The Playboy Band; but really wants writing about any post-war recording artist who hasn't managed to stay powerful or popular.'' circ. 250. 1/yr. Pub'd 1 issue 1990; expects 2 issues 1991, 2 issues 1992. sub. price: $8 3 issues; per copy: $3; sample: $3. Back issues: $3. 24pp; 8×11; lp. Reporting time: no longer than 1 month. Payment: up to $100 for original journalism. Copyrighted, reverts to author. Pub's reviews: 1 in 1990. §Popular music, rock 'n' roll, R.B., blues, folk. Ads: $50/$30.

OneOff Publishing, 7578 Caloma Circle, Carlsbad, CA 92009-7714. 1987. Satire, non-fiction. ''Short (100 pages more-or-less) softcover books. Humorous social commentary heavy on truth and light on ridicule. Illustrations employed as counterpoint'' avg. press run 1M. Expects 1 title 1991, 2 titles 1992. avg. price, paper: $3.95. Discounts: quantity. 100pp; 5⅜×8⅜; of. Reporting time: 3 months. Payment: will publish for costs plus a fee to be arranged with authors. Copyrights for author.

Oness Press (see also KIDS LIB NEWS), Mycall Sunanda, Editor, PO Box 1064, Kurtistown, HI 96760. 1981. Poetry, fiction, articles, art, photos, cartoons, interviews, satire, criticism, reviews, letters, collages, plays, news items, non-fiction. ''We publish our radical natural spiritual info in 60 small booklets from 12-72 pages, with many original drawings. We use supporting info from all sources for family liberation. In the spirithat evolves we develop newords, dances, playoga, Bucky Fuller trips, Sunergetics, Tantralini orgonenergy, Goddess love, Wholistic Parenting, ECODOPIA, Sufi-circle awareness, newave music, outdoor living, group-marriage, self-healing barter & Polarity-Rebirthing—we lead groups, keep learning & writing about discoveries, intuition & feelings of instincts on love'' avg. press run 200. Pub'd 15 titles 1990; expects 15 titles 1991, 10+ titles 1992. avg. price, other: $3 staplebound. Discounts: we trade info, subs, etc. 48pp; 8½×5½; xerox. Reporting time: 2 weeks. Payment: none. Does not copyright for author.

Oneworld Publications Ltd., J. Doostdar, Managing and Editorial Director; N. Doostdar, Financial and Sales Director, 1C, Standbrook House, Old Bond Street, London, W1X 3TD, England, (0747) 51339. 1985. Non-fiction. ''Trade Enquiries & Orders: Alpha Book Distributors, Inc., 303 West 10th Street, New York, NY 10014 USA. ISBN: 1-85168'' avg. press run 3M. Pub'd 4 titles 1990; expects 5 titles 1991, 5 titles 1992. 8 titles listed in the *Small Press Record of Books in Print* (20th Edition, 1991-92). avg. price, cloth: £8-50, $13.50; paper: £4-50, $7.50. Discounts: 35% trade. 150pp; 198×129mm; of. Reporting time: 2 months. Payment: 10% of wholesale price for first 5,000 copies, 12% for second, 15% for third. Copyrights for author. Publishers Association, UK.

Ontario Library Association (see also FOCUS; THE TEACHING LIBRARIAN), Jefferson A.R. Gilbert, Judy Tye, 100 Richmond St., E., Suite 300, Toronto, Ontario M5C 2P9, Canada, 416-363-3388. 1900. avg. press run 1.2M-3M. Pub'd 1-4 titles 1990; expects 3-4 titles 1991, 3-6 titles 1992. 7 titles listed in the *Small Press Record of Books in Print* (20th Edition, 1991-92). avg. price, paper: $36-$25. Discounts: 20% (10 or more). 60pp; 8½×11; of. Reporting time: 4-6 months. Payment: 10% (1-500), 20% (all additional) quarterly. Does not copyright for author. Book + Periodical Development Council.

ONTHEBUS, Bombshelter Press, Jack Grapes, Bombshelter Press, 6421 1/2 Orange Street, Los Angeles, CA 90048. 1989. Poetry, fiction, art, reviews. circ. 2M. 2/yr. Pub'd 2 issues 1990; expects 2 issues 1991, 2 issues 1992. sub. price: $24 for 3 issues; per copy: $9; sample: $9. Back issues: $9. Discounts: 40% bookstores. 200pp; 8½×5½; of. Reporting time: 12-16 weeks. Payment: 1 copy. Copyrighted, reverts to author. Pub's reviews: 26 in 1990. §Books of poetry. Ads: $300/$200/$125 1/4 page. COSMEP.

Oolichan Books, Ron Smith, Stephen Guppy, Rhonda Bailey, P.O. Box 10, Lantzville, B.C., V0R 2H0, Canada, 604-390-4839. 1975. Poetry, fiction, plays, non-fiction. ''Oolichan Books publishes *full-length* manuscripts of poetry and fiction. We prefer letters of inquiry with sample writing and SASE (with sufficient Canadian postage stamps or international postal reply coupons). We attempt to maintain a balance between established and newer authors. Generally we are not interested in the mass market book, but rather in serious fiction and poetry which indicates how the writer sees through language. We produce books of excellent quality in content and design, and many of our authors have won prestigious awards. Recent contributors include: Robert Kroetsch, Ralph Gustafson, Sharon Thesen, Joe Rosenblatt, Edna Alford, Linda Rogers, Bill Gaston, Ven Begamudre, Leon Rooke. Apart from our main interest in poetry and fiction we are also interested in western Canadian history, leftist politics, autobiography, and statements on poetics or collections of letters which reveal something of the stance of the writer and his/her attitude to the language." avg. press run 750-2M. Pub'd 8 titles 1990; expects 10 titles 1991, 10 titles 1992. 40 titles listed in the *Small Press Record of Books in Print* (20th Edition, 1991-92). avg. price, cloth: $24.95; paper: $10.95; other: $25 special editions, signed & numbered. Discounts: Trade: 40% on all orders over 3 copies, fewer than 3 copies: 30%. 76-160pp; 5½x8½; lp. Reporting time: 1-3 months. Payment: 10%. Copyrights for author. ACP, LPG, ABPBC, CBIC, CBA.

Open Book Publications, A Division of Station Hill Press, George Quasha, Publisher, Editor; Susan Quasha, Co-Publisher, Designer, Station Hill Road, Barrytown, NY 12507. 1981. Poetry, fiction, art, photos, criticism, music, letters, long-poems, collages, plays, concrete art. avg. press run 1.5M. Pub'd 5 titles 1990; expects 2 titles 1991, 2 titles 1992. 12 titles listed in the *Small Press Record of Books in Print* (20th Edition, 1991-92). avg. price, cloth: $14.95; paper: $7.95; other: $20.00 and up. Discounts: 50% with distributor; 10% on single titles; escalation with quantity. 96pp; 5¾x8¾, 5½x8½, 6x9. Reporting time: no guarantee except by written arrangement. Payment: percentage of gross or net income. Copyrights for author.

Open Books, Susan Moon, 1631 Grant Street, Berkeley, CA 94703, 415-548-2208. avg. press run 1M. Expects 1 title 1992. 7 titles listed in the *Small Press Record of Books in Print* (20th Edition, 1991-92). avg. price, paper: $7. Discounts: 40% retailers; 15% distributors. 150pp; 5½x8½.

Open Chain Publishing, Robbie Fanning, PO Box 2634, Menlo Park, CA 94026, 415-323-2549. 1987. Non-fiction. "Publisher of *The Busy Woman's Sewing Book* by Nancy Zieman, star of public television's 'Sewing With Nancy'" avg. press run 8M. Expects 3 titles 1991, 4 titles 1992. 8 titles listed in the *Small Press Record of Books in Print* (20th Edition, 1991-92). avg. price, cloth: $15; paper: $10. 128pp; 7¼x9; of. Copyrights for author. COSMEP, PMA.

Open Dialogues (see also OPEN MAGAZINE), Paul Pinkman, 215 North Avenue West, Suite 21, Westfield, NJ 07090, 201-249-0280.

Open Hand Publishing Inc., P. Anna Johnson, PO Box 22048, Seattle, WA 98122, 206-323-3868. 1981. Non-fiction. "Open Hand is a literary/political press publishing books which will help to promote social change." avg. press run 4M. Pub'd 1 title 1990; expects 3 titles 1991, 5 titles 1992. 17 titles listed in the *Small Press Record of Books in Print* (20th Edition, 1991-92). avg. price, cloth: $22.35; paper: $11.45. Discounts: distributed by the Talman Co. Inc. 250pp; 5½x8½; of. Reporting time: 8 weeks. Payment: individual arrangement with each author. Copyrights for author. Multicultural Publishers Exchange (MPE), ABA, Book Publishers NW (BPNW).

Open Horizons Publishing Company (see also BOOK MARKETING UPDATE), John Kremer, PO Box 1102, Fairfield, IA 52556, 515-472-6130. 1983. Articles, art, photos, cartoons, interviews, reviews, letters, news items, non-fiction. "Books on marketing, publishing, publicity, and anything that strikes the publisher's fancy. Jay Frederick Editions is an imprint." avg. press run 3M-5M. Pub'd 3 titles 1990; expects 3 titles 1991, 4 titles 1992. avg. price, cloth: $19.95; paper: $14.95. Discounts: 40%. 288pp; 6x9; of. Reporting time: 2 weeks. Payment: 10% of list price. Copyrights for author. COSMEP, PMA, MAP, MSPA, MIPA, ABA, UMBA.

OPEN MAGAZINE, Open Dialogues, Greg Ruggiero, Stuart Sahulka, Paul Pinkman, Open Dialogues, Inc., 215 North Avenue West, Suite 21, Westfield, NJ 07090, 201-249-0280. 1984. Poetry, fiction, articles, art, photos, interviews, parts-of-novels, collages, plays, concrete art. *"Open* works with uninhibited forms of writing and art that inspire change—be they targeted at social processes or the consciousness of the individual. We are fast to accept work that pioneers form, questions the given, and risks either discussing the intimate or proposing the radical. We are constantly restructuring, constantly exploring new ways to connect with our readers, writers, and other counter-consensus publications. Future issues will be accepting more essays, graphic art, and fiction, and less poetry. Recent and upcoming work by: Margaret Randall, Amiri Baraka, John Stockwell, Sesshu Foster, Nancy Burson, Dennis Hopper, Patricia Eakins, Allen Ginsberg, Deena Metzger, Greg Boyd, Loris Essary, John Cage" circ. 1M. 2/yr. Expects 2 issues 1991, 2 issues 1992. sub. price: $15 for 3 issues; per copy: $5; sample: $5. Back issues: $4/issue. Discounts: issue swap. 60pp; 8½x11; of. Reporting time: 3 weeks. Payment: copies, depending on grant status up to $50. Copyrighted, reverts to author. Pub's reviews: 1 in 1990. §Alternative paradigms of consciousness and perception, science, art, cultural politics, theory, and the future. Ads: $200/$100. CCLM, distributed through DeBoer.

OPEN ROAD, Vancouver News Group, Box 6135, Station G, Vancouver, B.C. V6R 4G5, Canada. 1976. Articles, art, photos, cartoons, interviews, satire, criticism, reviews, music, letters, parts-of-novels, news items, non-fiction. circ. 6M. 4/yr. Pub'd 3 issues 1990; expects 3 issues 1991, 3 issues 1992. sub. price: instit. $25, others 2 hours pay; per copy: $1.50; sample: $1.50. Back issues: #2,3,5,6,7,11,12,14,15 - $2 ea; #8,9,10,10½,13 - $1 ea. Discounts: 40% off reg. issue price for retailers; 50% off for wholesale distributors. 20pp; 11½x16¾; of. Reporting time: 3 months. Payment: none. Not copyrighted. Pub's reviews: 0 in 1990. §Anarchism, ecology, anti-authoritarianism, feminism, prisons, community organizing, anything with an anti-authoritarian slant to it. All popular struggles. Exchange ads only with other publications. APS.

THE OPERA COMPANION, James Keolker, #40 Museum Way, San Francisco, CA 94114, 415-626-2741. 1978. Articles, art, interviews, criticism, reviews, music. "Each issue covers one opera in depth with musical analysis, updated synopsis, articles of current research, interviews, reviews of pertinent recordings and texts" circ. 8M. 15/yr. Pub'd 15 issues 1990; expects 15 issues 1991, 15 issues 1992. sub. price: $30; per copy: $2.25; sample: complimentary. Back issues: available from 1978, $2.50 each. Discounts: for music students and/or opera-going seniors, special rates available. 16pp; 8½×11; of. Reporting time: 3 months in advance. Payment: upon arrangement. Copyrighted, rights revert to author, unless by special arrangement. Pub's reviews: 30 in 1990. §'Classical' or serious music in general, opera in particular. Ads: upon request. COSMEP.

OPOSSUM HOLLER TAROT, Larry Blazek, RR 3 Box 109, Orleans, IN 47452-9649, 812-755-4788. 1982. Poetry, fiction, articles, art, photos, cartoons, interviews, satire, criticism, reviews, letters, long-poems, news items, non-fiction. "*OPOSSUM HOLLER TAROT* focuses upon the unusual, the bizzare, critisisms on society. It is an undrground publication in the strictest sense, we psycially look to the future, repress all repression, live free or die, don't tread on me, look out for ghoulies, etc. Please single-space submissions!" circ. 8. Sporadic. Expects 20 issues 1991. 2 titles listed in the *Small Press Record of Books in Print* (20th Edition, 1991-92). sample price: $1.25. Back issues: 10¢ page, plus postage. 8pp; 8×10; photocopies. Payment: copies. Not copyrighted. Pub's reviews. §Sci-fi, fantasy/horror, corrupt government, anti-facism. Ads: trade.

ORANGE COAST MAGAZINE, Palmer Thomason Jones, OCNL, Inc., 245-D Fischer Avenue, Suite 8, Costa Mesa, CA 92626, 714-545-1900. 1974. Fiction, articles, interviews, reviews, music, letters, parts-of-novels, non-fiction. "*Orange Coast* provides its affluent, educated readers with local insight. Articles range from in-depth investigations (local politics, crimes, etc) to consumer guides, calendar of events and personality profiles. Articles must have relevance to Orange County." circ. 40M. 12/yr. Pub'd 13 issues 1990; expects 13 issues 1991, 13 issues 1992. sub. price: $19.95; per copy: $2.95; sample: same. Back issues: $5 if available. Discounts: contact circulation manager. 260pp; 8⅜×10⅞; web inside, sheet-fed cover. Reporting time: 3 months. Payment: $100-$300. Copyrighted, reverts to author. Pub's reviews: 24 in 1990. §Film, music, restaurants, books. Ads: B/W $2320/$1770; color $3040/$2480, singles classified—$4/word. WPA.

ORBIS, Mike Shields, Publisher, 199 The Long Shoot, Nuneaton, Warwickshire CV11 6JQ, England, 0203-327440. 1968. Poetry, art, reviews, letters, long-poems. "Keep it short: not over 1M words in most cases. All types of material considered, but wildly experimental or excessively traditional work not likely to be accepted. IRC must be included with submissions overseas. I have been amazed and frustrated at the number of submissions received from the USA with US-stamped addressed envelopes enclosed!" circ. 1M. 4/yr. Pub'd 4 issues 1990; expects 4 issues 1991, 4 issues 1992. sub. price: $30; sample: $2. Discounts: 30% to trade. 64pp; 5¾×8¼; of. Reporting time: up to 3 months. Payment: $10 or choice of copies, etc., to greater volume, plus cash prizes totalling £75 per issue. Copyrighted, reverts to author. Pub's reviews: 70 in 1990. §Mainly collections of poetry; also reference books of interest to writers. Ads: $100/$50.

Orbis Books, Robert Ellsberg, Editorial Director; Susan Perry, Senior Editor; William Burrows, Managing Editor, ATTN: Renee Turcott, Walsh Building, Maryknoll, NY 10545, 914-941-7590. 1970. Non-fiction. "Specialize in Liberation Theology, inter religious dialogue, peace and justice issues" avg. press run 3M. Pub'd 40 titles 1990; expects 45 titles 1991, 50 titles 1992. 23 titles listed in the *Small Press Record of Books in Print* (20th Edition, 1991-92). avg. price, cloth: $29.95; paper: $14.95. Discounts: 1-4 25%, 5-24 40%, 25-49 41%, 50-99 42%, 100-249 43%, 250+ 44%. 224pp; 6×9¼, 5⅜×8¼; of. Reporting time: 4 weeks to 3 months. Payment: negotiable. Copyrights for author.

THE ORCADIAN, J.E. Miller, The Orcadian Limited, PO Box 18, Kirkwall, Orkney, Scotland. 1854. Articles, photos, interviews, criticism, reviews, letters, news items. circ. 10M. 52/yr. Expects 52 issues 1991. sub. price: £30.60 (surface mail); per copy: 52p; sample: 52p. Back issues: depends on availability. 24pp; 400×270mm; †web offset. Copyrighted. Pub's reviews: 50-100 in 1990. §Local interest. Ads: £396/£198 + VAT tax at 15%. NS/SPA.

Orchises Press, Roger Lathbury, PO Box 20602, Alexandria, VA 22320-1602, 703-683-1243. 1983. Poetry, fiction, articles, concrete art. avg. press run 1M. Pub'd 3 titles 1990; expects 5 titles 1991, 4 titles 1992. 21 titles listed in the *Small Press Record of Books in Print* (20th Edition, 1991-92). avg. price, cloth: $20; paper: $10. Discounts: 40% on no return items to bookstores, distributors and jobbers; 20% if a return privilege is wanted. Items under $20 shipped no return unless otherwise stipulated. 80pp; 5×8; of. Reporting time: 2 weeks. Payment: 25% royalty after costs recouped, generous free copy policy. Copyrights for author.

‡**OREGON HISTORICAL QUARTERLY, Oregon Historical Society Press,** Priscilla Knuth, Executive Editor; Thomas Vaughan, Editor-In-Chief, 1230 S.W. Park Ave., Portland, OR 97205, 503-222-1741. 1900. Articles, photos, reviews, non-fiction. circ. 8M. 4/yr. Expects 4 issues 1991. sub. price: $15; per copy: $2.50; sample: $2.50. Back issues: $2.50. Discounts: 1-4 40%; 5+ 50%. 112pp; 6×9; of. Reporting time: 6 weeks. Payment: 10 copies of publication. Copyrighted. Pub's reviews: 20 in 1990. §Regional history. No ads.

Oregon Historical Society Press (see also OREGON HISTORICAL QUARTERLY), Bruce T. Hamilton,

Director-Publications; Adair Law, Editor; Kim Carlson, Editor; Lori McEldowney, Editor, 1230 S.W. Park Avenue, Portland, OR 97205, 503-222-1741. 1873. Non-fiction. avg. press run 1.5M. Pub'd 10 titles 1990; expects 10 titles 1991, 12 titles 1992. 10 titles listed in the *Small Press Record of Books in Print* (20th Edition, 1991-92). avg. price, cloth: $24.95; paper: $12.95. Discounts: 40% trade, 20% library. 200pp (varies); size varies w/book; of. Reporting time: 1 year. Payment: 10% on net sales. Copyrights for author.

Oregon State University Press, Jo Alexander, 101 Waldo Hall, Corvallis, OR 97331, 503-737-3166. 1961. "We publish only book-length scholarly work, particularly of regional importance and especially in the fields of history and biography, American and especially regional literature, and natural resource management. No fiction, no poetry." avg. press run 1M-2M. Pub'd 6 titles 1990; expects 6 titles 1991, 6 titles 1992. avg. price, cloth: $20; paper: $12. Discounts: 20-44% depending on quantity. of. Reporting time: 1-3 months. Payment: varies. Copyrights for author.

ORGANICA, Aubrey Hampton, Publisher; Susan Hussey, Managing Editor; Silvia Curbelo, Poetry & Fiction Editor; Carol Glass, Art Director; Dionisio D. Martinez, Copy Editor, 4419 N. Manhattan Avenue, Tampa, FL 33614, 813-876-4879. 1982. Poetry, fiction, articles, art, photos, interviews, criticism, reviews, music. "Writings on social & ecological issues, science and the arts. *Organica* is distributed *free of charge* through healthfood stores and book stores. Because of space limitations and the amount of excellent material on hand, we don't encourage unsolicited manuscripts of poetry and fiction, but what you send us will not go unread - just realize that your chances are slim. Articles and essays: query first. Recent contributors include Andrei Codrescu, Stephen Dobyns, C.D. Wright, Leslie Ullman, W.S. Merwin, Len Roberts, Allen Ginsberg" circ. 300M. 4/yr. Pub'd 4 issues 1990; expects 4 issues 1991, 4 issues 1992. price per copy: free; sample: $1. 28pp; 11×14; of. Reporting time: 2-4 weeks. Payment: varies, but competitive. Copyrighted, rights revert, poetry and fiction only. Pub's reviews: 12 in 1990. §Ecology, science, poetry, fiction, art, music, film, social issues.

The Organization (see also POLITICALLY INCORRECT), Thomas Lucero, M.J. Lyle, Box 170, 400 N. High Street, Columbus, OH 43215, 614-447-8178. 1991. Poetry, fiction, articles, cartoons, interviews, satire, reviews, music, letters, long-poems, news items, non-fiction. "3,000 words or more, collections. Minarchist/anarchist, marginalia, Loompanics-type" avg. press run 80. Expects 5 titles 1991, 10 titles 1992. avg. price, cloth: $10; paper: $5; other: $1 pamphlet. Discounts: 50% to retailers. 24pp; 8½×11; †mi. Reporting time: 5-45 days. Payment: upon acceptance; negotiable. Copyrights for author.

Organization for Equal Education of the Sexes, Inc. (OEES), Lucy Picco Simpson, PO Box 438, Blue Hill, ME 04614, 207-374-5110. 1977. Articles, art, photos, interviews, non-fiction. "Classroom posters, biographies of women, teacher guidelines, data on women." avg. press run 1M. Pub'd 1 title 1990; expects 3 titles 1991, 2 titles 1992. 3 titles listed in the *Small Press Record of Books in Print* (20th Edition, 1991-92). avg. price, paper: $4. Biographies 4pp; 11×17 poster size; commercial printers. Reporting time: varies. Payment: varies.

Oriel, Peter Finch, The Friary, Cardiff, Wales CF1 4AA, Great Britain, 0222-395548. 1974. Poetry, art. "Publications are confined to Welsh and Anglo-Welsh authors together with material about Wales. Unsolicited mss. are not requested. In existence are a number of fine edition poster poems. Catalogues available." avg. press run 2M. Pub'd 4 titles 1990. 26 titles listed in the *Small Press Record of Books in Print* (20th Edition, 1991-92). avg. price, paper: £4.95; other: £2.50 poster poems. Discounts: 33⅓-50%. of, lp. Payment: by arrangement. Does not copyright for author.

Oriel Press, Jeannette Moses, 2020 SW Kanan, Portland, OR, 97201, 503-245-6696. 1981. Fiction. "*Young adult fiction; direct toward the bright and gifted child.*" avg. press run 1M. 1 title listed in the *Small Press Record of Books in Print* (20th Edition, 1991-92). avg. price, cloth: $14.95; paper: $8.95. Discounts: 40%. 100pp; 6×9.

THE ORIGINAL ART REPORT (TOAR), Frank Salantrie, P.O. Box 1641, Chicago, IL 60690. 1967. Criticism, letters, news items, non-fiction. "Exclusive interest in fine art condition as it affects individuals, society, and artists, and as they affect it. Material must take advocacy position, one side or another. Prefer controversial subject matter and originality of treatment. Also, artist's position on non-art topics." circ. 100-1M. Irregular. Expects 6 issues 1991, 12 issues 1992. sub. price: $15.50/12 issues; per copy: $1.50; sample: $1.50. Back issues: $3.50 each. Discounts: 10 minimum to same address-$11.75 each/special artist discount-pay $9.95 for individual subscription. 3-issue sub $3.95. 6-8pp; 8½×11; of. Reporting time: 1-2 weeks. Payment: 1¢/word; max 1000 words on publication. Not copyrighted. Pub's reviews. §Visual fine art, histories, philosophies, criticism, science of art, and business of art. No ads.

THE ORLANDO SPECTATOR, Benjamin B. Markeson, Editor-in-Chief, 2390 S. Orange Blossom Trail, Apopka, FL 32703-1870, 407-293-2722. 1989. Poetry, articles, interviews, satire, criticism, reviews, music, letters, news items, non-fiction. "We are a free left-wing alternative newspaper for central Florida. Articles of any sort are generally no more than 1000-1500 words. We subscribe to Pacific News Service and New Liberation News Service." circ. 4.3M. 6/yr. Pub'd 3 issues 1990; expects 6 issues 1991, 6-12 issues 1992. sub. price: $12/10 issues; per copy: 2 stamps (58¢); sample: 2 stamps (58¢). 16-20pp; 10¼×13; of. Reporting time:

1-2 weeks, generally will telephone. Payment: $10 for news, commentary and reviews, $5 poetry; all payments are after publication. Copyrighted, reverts to author. Pub's reviews: 3 in 1990. §Non-fiction and comic books. Ads: $150/$75/$37.50 1/4 page/$18.75 1/8 page/$10 business card/$3 per col. inch.

ORNAMENT, Ancient Contemporary Ethnic, Robert K. Liu, Co-Editor; Carolyn L.E. Benesh, Co-Editor; Anne L. Ross, Assistant Editor, PO Box 2349, San Marcos, CA 92079. 1974. Art, criticism, reviews, letters, collages, news items. "Formerly published under the name of *The Bead Journal* which terminated with Volume 3, No. 4. As of Volume 4, No. 1 published under the name of *Ornament.*" circ. 30M. 4/yr. Pub'd 4 issues 1990. sub. price: $25 domestic; per copy: $6.25; sample: $7.25. Back issues: write for information. Discounts: 40% on wholesale orders. 96pp; 8×11; of, web. Reporting time: 4-6 weeks. Payment: copies of the magazine in which article appears, number depends on length of article. Copyrighted, reverts to author. Pub's reviews: 110 in 1990. §Jewelry, ancient, ethnic, contemporary, forms of personal adornment, costume, clothing. Ads: write for rates. IGCJAP, ACC.

ORO MADRE, Ruddy Duck Press, Loss Glazier, 44 North Pearl Street #44, Buffalo, NY 14202. 1980. Poetry, fiction, articles, art, photos, cartoons, interviews, criticism, reviews, letters, long-poems, collages, news items, non-fiction. "We do not accept unsolicited manuscripts. *Oro Madre* seeks translations of Latin American poetry. A copy of the original must accompany submission. Translations from other languages/countries also considered. Also sought: envigorating political and socially-aware poems and art which speak to the human condition world wide. We look for styles that are innovative, crisp, and communicate through use of language as well as through narrative, though narrative is not requisite. Submissions should address a world that extends beyond the scope of the writer's immediate present. Socially & politically relevant themes are encouraged. We also seek bibliograhical and reference material on small press and/or alternatives in publishing, society, etc. Book Reviews should be constructed as *progressions* that explore a vein of thought or pursue a theme or question in the work. Recent contributors include: Ivan Arguelles, Charles Bukowski, Wilfredo Castano, James Drought, Jack Hirschman, Gerald Locklin, Tony Moffeit, Alejandro Murguia, Leslie Simon, Mike Weiss, and A.D. Winans." circ. 500. 4/yr. Pub'd 4 issues 1990; expects 4 issues 1991, 4 issues 1992. sub. price: $12; per copy: $3.50; sample: $3.50. Back issues: price list available upon request. Discounts: available upon request. 48pp; 5½×8½; of. Reporting time: 4 weeks. Payment: in copies. Copyrighted, reverts to author. Pub's reviews: 24 in 1990. §Fiction, poetry, literary criticism, non-fiction, novels, magazines, chapbooks, small press, poetics, library topics. Ads: available upon request.

ORPHEUS, Illuminati, P. Schneidre, c/o Illuminati, PO Box 67e07, Los Angeles, CA 90067. 1980. Poetry, long-poems. "Contributors have included James Merrill, Charles Bukowski, Jerry Ratch, Kate Braverman, F.A. Nettelbeck, Bert Meyers, Lyn Lifshin, R.S. Thomas" circ. 1.1M. 3/yr. Pub'd 3 issues 1990; expects 3 issues 1991, 3 issues 1992. sub. price: $12.50; per copy: $4; sample: $4. Back issues: unavailable. Discounts: 50% bookstores, all others on request. 48pp; 6¾×11; of. Reporting time: 2 weeks. Payment: by private arrangement. Copyrighted. No ads. CCLM, COSMEP.

ORPHIC LUTE, Patricia Doherty Hinnebusch, 526 Paul Place, Los Alamos, NM 87544. 1950. Poetry. "For 1991 a new focus for *Orphic Lute*: short forms (poems 11 lines or fewer) and short free-verse poems (11 lines or fewer). Traditional haiku, not avant garde varieties. Sequences of haiku, lanternes, and Adelaide Crapsey cinquains desirable." circ. 250. 4/yr. Pub'd 4 issues 1990; expects 4 issues 1991, 4 issues 1992. sub. price: $10; per copy: $2.50; sample: $2.50. Back issues: $2.50. 40pp; 8½×5½; xerox. Reporting time: 1-3 months. Payment: in copy only. Copyrighted, reverts to author. Pub's reviews: 4 in 1990. §I only review books of poetry by subscribers.

The Oryx Press, Susan Slesinger, Editorial Vice President, 4041 N. Central Avenue, Suite 700, Phoenix, AZ 85012-3330, 602-254-6156. 1975. Photos, interviews, reviews, letters, news items. Pub'd 35 titles 1990; expects 40 titles 1991, 45 titles 1992. 6×9 or 8½×11.

OSIRIS, Andrea Moorhead, Box 297, Deerfield, MA 01342. 1972. Poetry, interviews, long-poems. "*Osiris* is an international multi-lingual literary journal publishing contemporary poetry in the original language. English, French, Spanish poetry appears without translation. Poetry from other languages such as Polish, Danish & Hungarian appears with facing English translation. Recent contributors: Robert Marteau (France), Helene Dorion (Quebec), Robert Harris (USA), Gyula Illyes (Hungary), Owen Davis (England)." circ. 1M. 2/yr. Pub'd 2 issues 1990; expects 2 issues 1991, 2 issues 1992. sub. price: $8 individuals, $10 institutions; per copy: $4; sample: $3. 40pp; 6×9; of. Reporting time: 4 weeks. Payment: 5 copies. Copyrighted, rights revert to author, with credit line to *Osiris*. Ads: query. CPLM.

OSTENTATIOUS MIND, Patricia D. Coscia, Editor; Nick Coscia, Co-Editor, Thursday Press, 224 82nd Street, #1, Brooklyn, NY 11209, 718-680-3899. 1987. Poetry, satire, criticism, long-poems, collages. "This magazine is designed to encourage the intense writer—the cutting reality. The staff deals in the truth of life: political, social and psychological. Please send SASE for guidelines. Some recent contributors: Jeannie Marvis and Nick Coscia. Poetry contest deadline is August 20. For guidelines, send SASE." circ. 100-150. 2/yr.

410

Expects 2 issues 1991, 2 issues 1992. sub. price: $3; per copy: $2; sample: $2. Back issues: $2. Discounts: none. 10pp; 5½x8½; †mi. Reporting time: as soon as possible. Payment: 2-4 copies. Copyrighted, reverts to author. §Poetry, politics, and psychological magazines. Ads: $1 per page. Brooklyn Poetry Club, 224-82nd Street, Brooklyn, NY 11209.

THE OTHER ISRAEL, Adam Keller, PO Box 956, Tel Aviv 61008, Israel, 972-3-5565804 (also fax). 1983. Articles, interviews, reviews, letters, news items, non-fiction. circ. 3M. 6/yr. Pub'd 6 issues 1990; expects 6 issues 1991, 6 issues 1992. sub. price: $30 indiv., $50 instit.; sample: free on request. Back issues: $15 for bound copy of issues 1-33, including index. Discounts: 33%. 12pp; 7x9½. Reporting time: 3 weeks average. Payment: none. Not copyrighted. Pub's reviews: 1 in 1990. §Middle East politics. Ads: $100/$60.

THE OTHER SIDE, Mark Olson, Editor; Rod Jellema, Poetry Editor, 300 West Apsley Street, Philadelphia, PA 19144, 215-849-2178. 1965. Poetry, fiction, articles, art, photos, cartoons, interviews, reviews. circ. 13M. 6/yr. Expects 6 issues 1991, 6 issues 1992. sub. price: $29.50; per copy: $4.50; sample: $4.50. Discounts: 5 or more issues, 50% off. 64pp; 8¼x11; of. Reporting time: 2 months. Payment: $15-$20 per poem. Copyrighted, reverts to author. Pub's reviews: 40 in 1990. §Peace and social justice from a Christian perspective. Ads: $475/$350/50¢.

OTHER VOICES, Dolores Weinberg, Founding Editor, Publisher; Lois Hauselman, Executive Editor; Sharon Fiffer, Executive Editor; Fran Podulka, Advisory Editor; June Brindel, Advisory Editor; Edith Freund, Advisory Editor; Vesle Fenstermaker, Advisory Editor; Ellen Harwich, Advisory Editor; Mary Gray Hughes, Advisory Editor; John Jacob, Advisory Editor; Ted Schaeffer, Advisory Editor, 820 Ridge Road, Highland Park, IL 60035, 708-831-4684. 1985. Fiction, art, interviews, letters, parts-of-novels, plays. "A prize-winning, independent market for quality fiction, we are dedicated to original, fresh, diverse stories and novel-excerpts by new, as well as recognized, talent. No taboos, except ineptitude and murkiness. 5M wd. max. preferred, but not mandatory. SASE required. Winner of 11 Ill. Arts Council Literary Awards for first 10 issues." circ. 1.5M. 2/yr. Pub'd 2 issues 1990; expects 2 issues 1991, 2 issues 1992. sub. price: $16 for 4 issues (2 yrs), $26 foreign surface ($32 foreign air); per copy: $4.95; sample: $5.90 (inc. postage); institutions $18/4 issues, add $8 per sub. for foreign. Back issues: $5.90 (inc. postage) when available. Discounts: 20% classroom, 40% trade; 50% general distributor. 180-225pp; 6x9; typesetter, printer. Reporting time: 10-12 weeks. Payment: copies, small cash gratuity. Copyrighted, reverts to author. Ads: $100/$60/exchange with non-profit lit. mags. COSMEP, CCLM, ILPA.

Otherwind (see also NOTUS NEW WRITING), Pat Smith, 2420 Walter Drive, Ann Arbor, MI 48103, 313-665-0703. 1986. avg. press run 500. Pub'd 2 titles 1990; expects 2 titles 1991, 2 titles 1992. 4 titles listed in the *Small Press Record of Books in Print* (20th Edition, 1991-92). avg. price, paper: $5; other: $8. Discounts: bookstores 40%. 96pp; 8½x11; of. Reporting time: 3-4 months. Copyrights for author.

OTISIAN DIRECTORY, Jeff Stevens, PO Box 235, Williamstown, MA 01267-0235. 1988. Poetry, fiction, articles, art, interviews, satire, criticism, reviews, collages, news items, non-fiction. "Material of any length gladly accepted. We are very much a 'fringe'/Alternative publication, and are therefore somewhat biased towards politics, ideas, attitudes divorced from the mainstream. We are primarily a magazine of reviews of alternative publications. However, we still reprint a great deal of art and the occasional article/work of fiction/satire/poetry." circ. 500. 4/yr. Pub'd 4 issues 1990; expects 4 issues 1991, 4 issues 1992. sub. price: $8; per copy: $2.50; sample: $3. Discounts: we accept trade (1 for 1 basis), bulk of 10-40% (ask us), free subscriptions for prisoners, others with zero income. 30pp; 8½x11. Reporting time: asap. Payment: mostly exposure serves as 'payment,' some solicited material paid for. Not copyrighted. Pub's reviews: 160 in 1990. §Alternative literature, occult, alternative politics, neo-pagan, anything non-mainstream. Ads: $10/$5/$2 business card/$1 classifieds.

OTTER, C. Southgate, M. Beeson, R. Skinner, Parford Cottage, Chagford, Newton Abbot TL13 8JR, United Kingdom. 1988. Poetry, long-poems. "*Otter* exists to publish the poetry of those connected by birth, upbringing of 'adoption' with Devon, England. We seem to develop a heightened understanding of community through poetry as a medium. We believe the medium is often at its most effective when traditional elements of prosody such as rhyme and metre are employed." circ. 400. 3/yr. Pub'd 3 issues 1990; expects 3 issues 1991, 3 issues 1992. sub. price: £5; per copy: £1.80; sample: £1.80 (convert to dollars & add $2 for U.S.). Discounts: standard 33⅓% to trade. 48pp; 5¾x8; of. Reporting time: 6-8 weeks. Payment: £2 per poem. Copyrighted, reverts to author. Ads: £15/£8.

OTTERWISE, Cheryl Miller, Marianne Matte, PO Box 1374, Portland, ME 04104, 207-883-4426. 1988. Poetry, fiction, art, photos, non-fiction. "All material in *Otterwise* is donated, our staff is also volunteers" circ. 3M. 4/yr. Pub'd 4 issues 1990; expects 4 issues 1991, 4 issues 1992. sub. price: $8; per copy: $2; sample: $2. Back issues: $2. Discounts: half price for order of 10 or more subscriptions to same address. 16pp; 8½x11; of. Payment: none. Copyrighted, reverts to author. Pub's reviews: 4 in 1990. §Animals, and nature related themes for kids ages 5-14. Ads: none.

Our Child Press, Carol Hallenbeck, 800 Maple Glen Lane, Wayne, PA 19087, 215-964-0606. 1984. Fiction, non-fiction. avg. press run 1M-2M. Pub'd 2 titles 1990; expects 2 titles 1991, 2 titles 1992. 6 titles listed in the *Small Press Record of Books in Print* (20th Edition, 1991-92). avg. price, paper: $12.95. Reporting time: 2 months. COSMEP.

OUR GENERATION, Black Rose Books Ltd., Jacques Roux, 3981 St. Laurent Blvd., #444, Montreal, Quebec H2W 1Y5, Canada, 514-844-4076. 1961. Articles, criticism, non-fiction. "15 pages, double-space maximum. Anarchist or libertarian socialist. Deals with social issues. Murray Bookchin, Noam Chomsky, George Woodcook" circ. 3M. 2/yr. Pub'd 2 issues 1990. sub. price: $14; per copy: $7.95; sample: $7.95. Back issues: $7.95 each. Discounts: 20-35% discount. 128pp; 6×9; of. Reporting time: 4 months. Payment: none. Copyrighted, does not revert to author. Pub's reviews: 15 in 1990. §Public affairs-women-anarchist-social critique-international. Ads: $200/$150. CPPA (Canadian Periodicals Publishers Association).

Our Way Publications (see also BASEBALL: OUR WAY; FOOTBALL: OUR WAY), 5014 Starker Avenue, Madison, WI 53716.

OUR WRITE MIND, Julian Associates, Debbie Jordan, Editor; Robin Parker, Associate Editor; R.S. Cooper, Associate Editor, 6831 Spencer Hwy, #203, Pasadena, TX 77505. 1991. Poetry, fiction, articles, cartoons, reviews. "250-1000 words for articles, reviews and stories; up to one page single-spaced for poetry." Expects 2 issues 1991, 2 issues 1992. 60+pp; 8½×11; Xerox. Reporting time: average 1 month. Payment: at least $1 and 1 copy. Copyrighted, reverts to author. Pub's reviews. §Anything on the art and business of writing.

OUROBOROS, Erskine Carter, 3912 24th Street, Rock Island, IL 61201. 1985. Poetry, fiction, art, satire. "*Ouroboros* is always looking for subscribers and contributors. There are no specific genre requirements, though such an apparently wide-open criterion does not exclude the particular tastes of the editors. Each issue seems to have its own 'theme' when it finally comes together. Short stories shouldn't exceed 3,500 words. Poets should submit at least 7-10 poems so we can select a fair representation of their work. We feature one artist each issue who illustrates any number of stories or poems that capture his or her fancy; this usually works out to be 6-10 drawings, including front and back covers. To be considered, the artist should submit a design for the cover—his/her interprctation of the *Ouroboros* logo, a serpent or dragon swallowing its own tail—plus some sample art work. Submitters should purchase a sample copy" circ. 300. 1/yr. Pub'd 1 issue 1990; expects 1 issue 1991, 1 issue 1992. sub. price: $16/4 issues; per copy: $4.25; sample: $4.25. Back issues: $4.25. 72pp; 6×9; of. Reporting time: usually 1-2 weeks. Payment: copies. Copyrighted, reverts to author. No ads.

OUT WEST, Chuck Woodbury, 10522 Brunswick Road, Grass Valley, CA 95945, 916-477-9378. 1988. Articles, photos, cartoons, news items, non-fiction. "750 words maximum. Black and white photos only. We buy 1x rights and reprints. We like offbeat travel articles about rural American West." circ. 10M. 4/yr. Expects 4 issues 1991, 4 issues 1992. sub. price: $8; per copy: $2.50; sample: same. Back issues: $2.50. Discounts: check with publisher if interested. 40pp; 10×13; of, web press, tabloid on newsprint. Reporting time: 2 weeks to 1 month. Payment: $2—$100. Copyrighted, reverts to author. Pub's reviews: 12 in 1990. §Camping, western travel, western U.S. travel guides. Ads: classified: 60¢ per word.

Out West Publishing (see also THE WHOLE CHILE PEPPER), Dave DeWitt, Editor; Nancy Gerlach, Food Editor, PO Box 4278, Albuquerque, NM 87196, 505-266-8322. 1986. Articles, photos, non-fiction. "Cookbooks" avg. press run 15M-50M. Pub'd 1 title 1990; expects 4 titles 1991, 4 titles 1992. avg. price, paper: $6.95. Discounts: 40%. 128pp; 6×9; web/offset. Reporting time: depends. Payment: negotiable. COSMEP.

OUTERBRIDGE, Charlotte Alexander, English A324, College of Staten Island, 715 Ocean Terrace, Staten Island, NY 10301, 212-390-7654, 7779. 1975. Poetry, fiction, interviews, satire, reviews, parts-of-novels, plays. "Slight bias toward form, craft & against clearly socio-political statements. Among contributors: Mary Susannah Robbins, Philip Dacey, Christopher Parker, Walter McDonald, Candida Lawrence, John McEveety Woodruff, P. B. Newman, Henry Alley, Mary Elsie Robertson, Jim Kates, Ben Brooks, Marilyn Throne. Special themes. Double annual, 1986-88, features childhood, outsider, war, language." circ. 500-1M. 1/yr. Expects 3-4 issues 1991. sub. price: $5; per copy: $5 double, $8, 86-88; sample: $5, $8, 86-88. Back issues: $5 double, $8, 86-88. Discounts: 20% for 10 or more. 100-120pp; 5½×8½; of. Reporting time: 8 weeks, except July, August. Payment: 2 copies. Copyrighted, reverts to author. Pub's reviews. §Poetry, fiction, novels. COSMEP/CCLM/SPR/NESPA/AWP.

Outlaw Books, Jeri D. Walton, Joann Horner, Lisa Taylor, PO Box 4466, Bozeman, MT 59772, 406-586-7248. 1988. "Publisher and publishing consultant for regional tettes, cowboys poetry and children book" avg. press run 3M-5M. Pub'd 4 titles 1990; expects 10 titles 1991, 10 titles 1992. avg. price, cloth: $16.95; paper: $7.95; other: children $4.95. Discounts: 6+40%. 75-300pp; 5½×8½. Reporting time: 2-4 weeks. Payment: 10% of whole price every quarter. Copyrights for author.

Out-Of-Kontrol Data Institute (see also KOOKS MAGAZINE), Donna Kossy, PO Box 953, Allston, MA

02134. 1984. Articles, art, photos, cartoons, interviews, satire, reviews, collages, news items, non-fiction. "In addition to the magazine, I publish illustrated extremist books and pamphlets. Current title: *Am I Insane?* by Dan Scott Ashwander." avg. press run 500. Expects 1 title 1991, 1 title 1992. 1 title listed in the *Small Press Record of Books in Print* (20th Edition, 1991-92). avg. price, paper: $3.50. 35pp; 5½×8½; of. Reporting time: varies. Payment: free copies and percentage of net profit. Does not copyright for author.

OUTPOSTS POETRY QUARTERLY, Hippopotamus Press, Howard Sergeant, Founder, Editor; Roland John, Editor, 22, Whitewell Road, Frome, Somerset BA11 4EL, United Kingdom. 1943. Poetry, articles, criticism, reviews. "*Outposts* is the longest-lived independent poetry magazine in the UK. It was founded to provide a satisfactory medium for those poets, recognised or unrecognised, who are concerned with the potentialities of the human spirit, and who are able to visualize the dangers and opportunites which confront the individual and the whole of humanity. Although recent contributors have included famous poets like Ted Hughes, Peter Porter, Roy Fuller, Vernon Scannell, Blake Morrison, Seamus Heaney & etc the magazine makes a special point of introducing the work of new and unestablished poets to the public." circ. 2.5M. 4/yr. Pub'd 4 issues 1990; expects 4 issues 1991, 4 issues 1992. sub. price: £10 or $24 (postage paid) for 1 year, £18 or $40 (postage paid) for 2 years; per copy: £3.50, $7; sample: $7. Back issues: price varies from £2-£10. Discounts: 33⅓%. 80pp; size A5; litho. Reporting time: 2 weeks, 4 weeks non-U.K. Payment: depends on length of poem. Copyrighted, reverts to author. Pub's reviews: 30 in 1990. §Poetry, criticism of poetry. Ads: £75 $120/£35 $70. ALP, Password (Books) Ltd.

OUTRE, Jake Berry, 2251 Helton Drive #N7, Florence, AL 35630, (205) 767-3324. 1986. Poetry, art. "Material should be no more than 2 single space pages per piece. Prefer experimental work. Work that shows the poet, writer, artist to be stretching personal boundaries. Not looking for perfect craft or technique so much as artistic courage and daring. Recent contributors include Jack Foley, Mike Miskowski, DeVillo Sloan, Jake Berry, Ivan Arguelles, John M. Bennett, H.D. Moe, Bill Whizz, Larry Eigner, Malok" circ. 150. 2/yr. Expects 2 issues 1991, 2 issues 1992. No subscriptions available; price per copy: $1.50; sample: $1.50. Back issues: $2.50. Discounts: will trade for other mags, $1 ea. for classroom use, otherwise make me an offer. 32pp; 5½×8½; xerox. Reporting time: 2 weeks to 1 month. Payment: copy of the issue in which work appears. Copyrighted, reverts to author. Ads: $25/$13/$7 1/4 page.

Outrider Press, Phyllis I. Nelson, President, 1004 East Steger Road, Suite C-3, Crete, IL 60417-1362, 312-672-6630. 1988. Poetry, fiction, art. avg. press run 500. Pub'd 1 title 1990; expects 3 titles 1991, 4 titles 1992. 2 titles listed in the *Small Press Record of Books in Print* (20th Edition, 1991-92). avg. price, paper: $5. Discounts: Book stores: 60/40; others: up to 50% off, depending upon # ordered. Variable, but under 100pp; 5½×8½; Desktop publishing/offset. Reporting time: 1-2 months. Payment: negotiable. Copyrights for author.

OVERLAND, Barrett Reid, PO Box 14146, Melbourne 3000, Australia. 1954. Poetry, fiction, articles, art, photos, cartoons, interviews, satire, criticism, reviews, letters, parts-of-novels, long-poems, plays, concrete art, non-fiction. "Motto: 'Temper democratic, bias Australian'. Liberal/left in politics, Australian in content" circ. 2.4M. 4/yr. Pub'd 4 issues 1990; expects 4 issues 1991, 4 issues 1992. sub. price: $Aust 24 (local), $Aust 40 (foreign), $80 (airmail); per copy: $6, $12; sample: by arrangement. Back issues: by arrangement. Discounts: by arrangement. 96pp; 7¼×9¾; of. Reporting time: 2 months. Payment: by arrangement. Copyrighted. Pub's reviews: 50 in 1990. §Material of Australian interest. Ads: $Aust 320/300/250/180.

OVERLAND JOURNAL, Lois Daniel, Oregon-California Trails Association, PO Box 1019, Independence, MO 64051-0519, 816-252-2276. 1983. Articles, photos, criticism, reviews, news items, non-fiction. "Articles concerning the covered wagon migration to the American West in the 19th century." circ. 2M. 4/yr. Pub'd 4 issues 1990; expects 4 issues 1991, 4 issues 1992. sub. price: $25; per copy: $6.25; sample: free to public libraries. Back issues: $6.25. Discounts: none. 45pp; 8½×11; of. Reporting time: 30 days. Payment: none. Copyrighted, reverts to author. Pub's reviews: 25 in 1990. §Covered wagon migration to the American West in the 19th century. Ads: $200/$100/third page $90/quarter page $50/sixth page $30.

THE OVERLOOK CONNECTION, David Hinchberger, Laurie Hinchberger, PO Box 526, Woodstock, GA 30188, 404-926-1762. 1987. Fiction, articles, art, photos, cartoons, interviews, reviews, parts-of-novels, news items, non-fiction. circ. 8M. 3/yr. Pub'd 3 issues 1990; expects 4 issues 1991, 4 issues 1992. sub. price: $12; per copy: $2.50; sample: $2.50. 150-170pp; 7×10; of. Reporting time: 8 weeks. Payment: none. Copyrighted, reverts to author. Pub's reviews: over 50 in 1990. §Fiction and non-fiction in horror, science fiction, and fantasy. Ads: $100/$60. HWA.

The Overlook Press, Road 1, PO Box 496, Woodstock, NY 12498, 914-679-8571. 1971. "We are distributed by Viking Press, although special sales are based in Woodstock, NY. Our editorial offices are located at 149 Wooster Street, 4th Floor, New York, NY 10012. Phone: 212-477-7162. We specialize in art and design books, although we also publish general non-fiction, fiction, and poetry. We have published *Milton Glaser: Graphic Design, The Art of Natural History, Animal Illustrators and Their Work* by S. Peter Dance, and *Images From the Bible: The Paintings of Shalom of Safed, The Words of Elie Wiesel. Industrial Design* by Raymond Loewy.

413

For these last two titles we published a deluxe edition with a signed lithograph. Our most recent successful title is a *Book of Five Rings* (Miyamoto Musashi, translated by Victor Harris)." Pub'd 30 titles 1990; expects 40 titles 1992. avg. price, cloth: $22.50; paper: $9.95; other: $35. Discounts: 40% or as per Viking discount schedule. Reporting time: 4-6 weeks. Payment: royalty periods Jan-June & July-Dec. Copyrights for author. AAP.

OVERSIGHT, Franklin Odel, PO Box 29292, Los Angeles, CA 90029-0292. 1989. Poetry, fiction, art, photos, interviews, satire, criticism, reviews. "*Oversight* is a photography/art publication, with a particular interest in artists working with image and text. The first issues will use artists, either students, alumni, or faculty, who are associated with the California Institute of the Arts" circ. 2M. 2/yr. Expects 1 issue 1991, 2 issues 1992. price per copy: $10; sample: $10. Back issues: $25. 32pp; 11×14; of. Payment: none. Pub's reviews. §Photography, desktop publishing. Ads: $1000/$550/$300 1/4 page.

OVERVIEW LTD., Joseph Lanciotti, Box 211, Wood-Ridge, NJ 07075, 201-438-9069. 1991. Poetry. "*Overview Ltd.* is a new poetry publication expecting to publish talented poets not published before. Poems should be no more than 25-30 lines. Submit 3-5 poems. General topics from life to death. No poems returned without SASE. We expect to publish about 50 poems per issue twice a year to start. Established poets also welcome. Copyright to poet" circ. 4-500+. 2/yr. Expects 1 issue 1991, 2 issues 1992. sub. price: $8; per copy: $4; sample: $4. Back issues: $5. Discounts: 40%. 60pp; 5½×8; desktop/offset. Reporting time: 1-2 months. Payment: 2 free copies. Copyrighted, reverts to author. Ads: $50/$25. NJPC.

OWEN WISTER REVIEW, Erika L.S.C. Knudson, PO Box 4238, University Station, Laramie, WY 82071, 766-6190. 1978. Poetry, fiction, articles, art, photos, interviews, satire, criticism, reviews, letters, parts-of-novels, collages, non-fiction. "100% freelance written publication. Submissions are considered on a continuous basis—the deadline for the spring issue is October 31; the deadline for the fall issue is March 31. All submissions must be accompanied by a short biographical statement and SASE. Photocopied and computer-printout submissions will be accepted, but dot-matrix is discouraged. We will consider almost anything that is well-written—no hallmark card verse. Due to space limitations, submissions of prose should be no longer than 14 double-spaced pages; exceptions may be made in some cases. Artists must sign a one-time-only release form; black and white artworks and graphics in any media, any size will be considered." circ. 300-500. Pub'd 2 issues 1990; expects 2 issues 1991, 2 issues 1992. sub. price: $6; per copy: $3; sample: $3. Back issues: $1. Discounts: none. 86pp; 6×9; of. Reporting time: 1-2 months. Payment: 1-2 complementary copies. Copyrighted, reverts to author. Pub's reviews. §Works of literary fiction, critical theory books, art books, and magazines.

Owl Creek Press (see also THE MONTANA REVIEW), Rich Ives, 1620 N. 45th St., Seattle, WA 98103, 206-633-5929. 1979. Poetry, fiction, articles, long-poems. "Owl Creek Press sponsors two poetry contests each year. A contest for Chapbooks has a submission period of Jan.-June and requires an entry fee of $5. For manuscripts under 40 pages. A contest for full-length books has a submission period of July-Dec. and requires an entry fee of $8. For manuscripts over 50 pages. Both contests require an SASE and each entrant receives a copy of the winning title. Winners receive publication and 10% of the first edition press run with additional payment for any reprinting. Selections are made from unpublished poems included in the manuscripts for publication in *The Montana Review*" avg. press run 500-2M. Pub'd 6 titles 1990; expects 8 titles 1991, 8 titles 1992. 27 titles listed in the *Small Press Record of Books in Print* (20th Edition, 1991-92). avg. price, cloth: $15; paper: $7. Discounts: standard. 5½×8½; lp, photo-offset. Reporting time: 4-8 weeks. Payment: 10%. NEA, CCLM.

OWLFLIGHT MAGAZINE, Unique Graphics, c/o Unique Graphics, 1025 55th Street, Oakland, CA 94608. 1980. Poetry, fiction, articles, art, photos, cartoons, interviews, satire, long-poems, collages, plays. circ. 1.5M. 0-3/yr. Expects 1 issue 1991, 1-2 issues 1992. sub. price: 3 issues—$10 U.S., $12 other countries, payable to Unique Graphics; per copy: $4; sample: $4 current issue, $2.50 back issue payable to Unique Graphics. Back issues: $2.50. Discounts: 40%-50% to bookstores, bulk purchases. 64pp; 8½×11; of. Reporting time: 1-6 weeks. Payment: 1¢/word, $1 minimum, plus 1-3 contributors' copies. Copyrighted, reverts to author. Ads: $100/$60/10¢. SPWAO.

Owlswick Press (see also AMRA), George H. Scithers, Box 8243, Philadelphia, PA 19101, 215-EV2-5415. 1975. Fiction, criticism, non-fiction. "*Owlswick Press* publishes mostly deluxe editions of fantasy classics (Lord Dunsany and L. Sprague de Camp are two of our principal authors) and a few non-fiction titles of interest to the science fiction readership. We do not publish one-author poetry collections, short story collections, or original novels. Query first before submitting anything. Before you even query, become familiar with the books *Owlswick* has published (send for our free catalogue)." avg. press run 1.5M-2.5M. Expects 2 titles 1991. 1 title listed in the *Small Press Record of Books in Print* (20th Edition, 1991-92). avg. price, cloth: $15-$20; paper: $7.95. Discounts: available upon request for buyers-for-resale. 250pp; of. Reporting time: 2-3 weeks. Payment: by arrangement. Copyrights for author.

414

Ox Head Press, Don Olsen, Rt. 3, Box 136, Browerville, MN 56438, 612-594-2454. 1966. Poetry, art, satire, long-poems, non-fiction. "3-6 poems per pamphlet. Now starting a new series of essay pamphlets in a miniature format. A 1000 word limit." avg. press run 200-300. Pub'd 4 titles 1990; expects 4 titles 1991, 4 titles 1992. 8 titles listed in the *Small Press Record of Books in Print* (20th Edition, 1991-92). avg. price, cloth: $25; paper: $8. Discounts: varies; no discount on single copies. Pages vary; 4¼x6¼, 2½x3¼; †lp. Reporting time: a week to a month. Payment: royalty plus copies. Copyrights for author.

OXALIS, Shirley Powell, Editor; Mildred Barker, Assistant Editor & Art Editor, PO Box 3993, Kingston, NY 12401, 914-687-7942. 1988. Poetry, fiction, articles, art, cartoons, reviews, parts-of-novels, collages, plays, non-fiction. "Poems limited to 3 pages, shorter preferred. Stories and prose, 3000 word maximum. We like imagery and emotion without sentimentality. Some recent contributors: Emilie Glen, Enid Dame, Robert Cooperman, Marael Johnson, Kathleen Malley, Penelope Moffet, Harriet Brown, Donald Lev." circ. 300. 4/yr. Pub'd 4 issues 1990; expects 4 issues 1991, 4 issues 1992. sub. price: $18; per copy: $5; sample: $4. Back issues: $4. Discounts: members of Poetry Society and libraries, $14. 52-60pp; 8½x11; of. Reporting time: varies. Payment: 2 copies. Copyrighted, reverts to author. Pub's reviews: 5-6 in 1990. §poetry, short stories, particularly by contributors. Ads: $100/$50/$10 business card size.

The Oxalis Group, Shaun Higgins, PO Box 8051, Spokane, WA 99203, (509) 838-3295. 1977. Poetry, non-fiction. "We require a query letter on all poetry. Previous poetry is a must. Non-fiction: send outline, three chapters." avg. press run 2M-5M. Expects 1 title 1991, 3 titles 1992. avg. price, cloth: $10.95; paper: $5.95. Discounts: 40% trade; 55% jobber. 5½x8; of. Reporting time: 6 weeks. Payment: 10% on first edition. Copyrights for author.

Oxbridge Communications, Inc. (see also PUBLISHING TRENDS & TRENDSETTERS), Barry Lee, Editorial Director, 150 Fifth Avenue, Suite 636, New York, NY 10011, 212-741-0231; 800-955-0231. avg. press run 3M. Pub'd 4 titles 1990; expects 6 titles 1991, 8 titles 1992. 1 title listed in the *Small Press Record of Books in Print* (20th Edition, 1991-92). Discounts: 40-50% resellers. Directories Publishers Forum-Northeast (DPFN).

OXFORD MAGAZINE, 356 Bachelor Hall, Miami University, Oxford, OH 45056, 513-529-5221. 1984. Poetry, fiction. "New and established writers." circ. 500. 2/yr. Pub'd 2 issues 1990; expects 2 issues 1991, 2 issues 1992. sub. price: $7; per copy: $4; sample: $4. Back issues: $2. 100pp. Reporting time: 8 weeks. Copyrighted, reverts to author.

Oxford University Press (see also BRITISH JOURNAL OF AESTHETICS; COMMUNITY DEVELOPMENT JOURNAL; MUSIC AND LETTERS; NOTES & QUERIES), Journal Subscriptions Department, Pinkhill House, Southfield Road, Eynsham, Oxford OX8 1JJ, United Kingdom.

Oyez, Robert Hawley, PO Box 5134, Berkeley, CA 94705. 1964. Poetry, criticism. "Books usually designed by Graham McIntosh. Usually report promptly but not reading at this time." avg. press run 500-1M. Pub'd 1 title 1990; expects 3 titles 1991. avg. price, cloth: $8-$10; paper: $2-$6. 60-80pp; 5½x8½. Payment: 10% royalties and copies. Copyrights for author.

OYEZ REVIEW, Paula Bargiel, Editor; Susan Kusar, Editor; Patty Magierski, Editor; Susan Smith, Editor, Roosevelt University, 430 S. Michigan Avenue, Chicago, IL 60605, 312-341-2017. 1965. Poetry, fiction, art, photos, parts-of-novels, long-poems. "We are especially interested in experimental fiction and poetry." circ. 500. 1/yr. Pub'd 1 issue 1990; expects 1 issue 1991, 1 issue 1992. sub. price: $4; per copy: $4; sample: $3.50. Back issues: $4. Discounts: none. 100pp; 5½x8½; of. Reporting time: 2-3 months. Payment: 2 copies. Copyrighted, reverts to author. CCLM, COSMEP.

P

P E N American Center, John Morrone, 568 Broadway, New York, NY 10012. 1922. "We publish the *Grants and Awards available to American writers* (New ISBN for this edition - 0-934638-10-1). The booklet is a directory of financial assistance for the writer. The 1990 edition is considerably updated, and includes 106 new awards, as well as lists of writers' residences." avg. press run 4.5M. 2 titles listed in the *Small Press Record of Books in Print* (20th Edition, 1991-92). avg. price, paper: $7.50 (postpaid) for individuals, $12.50 (postpaid) for libraries and educators. Discounts: 25% off on orders of 5 or more copies. 7x9.

P.I.E. (Poetry Imagery and Expression), Daryl Wayne Hall, Bill Tibben, PO Box 739, Parramatta, NSW 2124, Australia, 02 683-2971. 1984. Poetry, art, photos. "One page, per contributor, per issue." 2/yr. Pub'd 2 issues 1990; expects 2 issues 1991, 2 issues 1992. 1 title listed in the *Small Press Record of Books in Print* (20th

Edition, 1991-92). price per copy: $1; sample: $1 + p/h. Back issues: on application. 28pp; 1/2 foolscap; †photocopier. Copyrighted, reverts to author.

P.O. Publishing Company, Suzanna Pinter, Joseph Nykiel, Box 3333, Skokie, IL 60076. 1987. "Seek non-fiction contributions from investigative reporters who are looking at turning their experiences—and series of articles that have appeared in newspapers and/or magazines—into books. Prefer political-related subject matter. First book, *88* (published in January, 1988), deals with right-wing extremists such as Ku Klux Klan. A handbook for reporters covering government is scheduled to come out later this year." avg. press run 1.2M-3M. Expects 1 title 1991, 1 title 1992. 1 title listed in the *Small Press Record of Books in Print* (20th Edition, 1991-92). avg. price, cloth: $20. 200pp; 6×9. Reporting time: 60-90 days. Payment: negotiated on an individual basis. Copyrights for author. COSMEP, American Book Council, Mid-America Publishers Association.

PABLO LENNIS, Manrovian Press, John Thiel, Fandom House, 30 N. 19th Street, Lafayette, IN 47904. 1976. Poetry, fiction, articles, art, satire, criticism, reviews, letters, non-fiction. "Material should be very short, due to space. Open policy. Material is most apt to be rejected if it would look more in place in some other publication, and the addresses of these are given the author when known. Recent well-known contributors include many directory responders. The contents of *Pablo Lennis* are extraordinarily reportative of modern life. Don't be surprised if the world of our writers in some way turns out to be yours." circ. 100. 12/yr. Pub'd 12 issues 1990; expects 12 issues 1991, 12 issues 1992. sub. price: $15; per copy: $2; sample: $1. Back issues: none available. 22pp; 8½×11; of. Reporting time: 2 weeks or less. Payment: 1 copy of the issue plus copies of any issues containing commentary on the work. Not copyrighted. Pub's reviews: 42 in 1990. §Science fiction, fantasy, science. Ads: micro-ads 10¢ a word.

PACIFIC HISTORICAL REVIEW, University of California Press, Norris Hundley Jr., Univ of California Press, 2120 Berkeley Way, Berkeley, CA 94720, 415-642-4191. 1931. Reviews, non-fiction. "Editorial address: Department of History, Univ. of California, Los Angeles, CA 90024. Copyrighted by Pacific Coast Branch, American Historical Assn." circ. 1.7M. 4/yr. Pub'd 4 issues 1990; expects 4 issues 1991, 4 issues 1992. sub. price: $17 indiv., $35 instit., $12 students (+ $4 foreign postage); per copy: $7.50 indiv., $9 instit., $7.50 students (+ $4 foreign postage); sample: free. Back issues: $7.50 indiv., $8.50 instit., $7.50 students. Discounts: foreign subs. agents 10%, one-time orders 10+ 30%, standing orders (bookstores): 1-99 40%, 100+ 50%. 128pp; 6×9; of. Reporting time: 3 months. Payment: none. Copyrighted, does not revert to author. Pub's reviews: 100 in 1990. §Asia, American West, history, diplomatic history. Ads: $200/$120.

Pacific Information Inc., Kenneth H. Plate, 979 Eaton Drive, Felton, CA 95018, 405-335-5599; fax 408-335-3327. 1973. Non-fiction. "We publish 'how-to' and professional development monographs for the information professional (librarians, records managers, etc.). We do not publish scholarly works. The subject orientation of our publications is information technology. Normally we commission manuscripts rather than rely on submissions. Best to write us with description before submitting." avg. press run 1M. Pub'd 4 titles 1990; expects 5 titles 1991, 7 titles 1992. 8 titles listed in the *Small Press Record of Books in Print* (20th Edition, 1991-92). avg. price, paper: $25. Discounts: 10-20% bookstores, jobbers, classrooms depending on volume. 150pp; 8½×11; of. Payment: 10%, once per year. Copyrights for author.

Pacific Research Institute, 177 Post Street #500, San Francisco, CA 94108, 415-989-0833. 1979. Non-fiction. Pub'd 3 titles 1990; expects 4 titles 1991, 4 titles 1992. avg. price, cloth: $29.95; paper: $14.95. 300pp; 6×9. PMA.

THE PACIFIC REVIEW, James Brown, Faculty Editor, Department of English, Calif State University, San Bernardino, CA 92407, 714-880-5824. 1982. Poetry, fiction, articles, art, photos, interviews, satire, criticism, reviews, letters, parts-of-novels, long-poems, plays, non-fiction. "While the *PR* attempts to reflect its unique geographic region—Southern California—material is not limited to the area; the *PR* invites excellence in poetry, fiction, drama and essay." circ. 1M. 1/yr. Pub'd 1 issue 1990; expects 1 issue 1991, 1 issue 1992. sub. price: $4; per copy: $4; sample: $4 (libraries $6.50). Back issues: $2. Discounts: 40%. 104pp; 6×9; of. Reporting time: 2 months (mss are not read April-Sept.). Payment: in copies. Copyrighted, reverts to author. Pub's reviews: 0 in 1990. §Poetry, fiction, drama. Ads: $150/$100. CCLM.

Packet Press, Eric Balkan, 14704 Seneca Castle Court, Gaithersburg, MD 20878, 301-762-7145. 1985. Non-fiction. "Publish computer software plus reference material (various subjects) on diskette, for 'any word' full-text retrieval; also plastic credit-card-size reference cards" Pub'd 2 titles 1990; expects 2 titles 1991, 2 titles 1992. avg. price, paper: $12; other: $19.95 diskette, $3 plastic. Discounts: 50% to dealer. 100pp; 5½×8½. Reporting time: varies, 1 month maximum. Payment: negotiable. Copyrights for author. COSMEP.

Padakami Press, 23 Dana Street, Forty Fort, PA 18704, 717-287-3668; 800-338-5531. 1 title listed in the *Small Press Record of Books in Print* (20th Edition, 1991-92).

Pagan Press, John Lauritsen, 26 St. Mark's Place, New York, NY 10003, 212-674-3321. 1982. Non-fiction. "Gay liberation publisher. Our orientation is classical, scholarly, and pro-male. We do not wish to receive

416

unsolicited manuscripts." avg. press run 1M. Pub'd 1 title 1990; expects 1 title 1991, 1 title 1992. 3 titles listed in the *Small Press Record of Books in Print* (20th Edition, 1991-92). avg. price, paper: $7.45. Discounts: 5-24 copies = 40%; 25-49 copies = 42%; 50 or more = 45%. 200pp; 5½×8½; of.

PAGES, 3610 Country Club, Wichita, KS 67208, 316-684-9487. 1980. Poetry, fiction, photos, cartoons. *"Pages* is a non-profit, do-it-yourself project. The printer is the only one who gets paid. Each contributor pays $8 for each page he or she wishes to publish. For each page published the contributor receives six copies of the book. All material must be sent print-ready—that means typed or drawn on a half-sheet of regular size white typing paper, typed with black ribbon and clean keys. Margins must be 3/4 inch at the top, bottom and both sides of the sheet, so nothing gets cut off in the trimming. *Proofread* your material before you send it. It will be printed exactly as it comes. We need to sell about 50 pages for each issue to be able to pay the printer and mail your copies to you. If we do not sell enough pages to go to print, your money and material will be returned to you. Recent contributors: Lily Angle, Mary Neary, Fern Ruth." circ. 300. 1/yr. Pub'd 1 issue 1990; expects 1 issue 1991, 1 issue 1992. price per copy: $3; sample: $1. Discounts: $1.00. 40-48pp; 5½×8½; of. Reporting time: 3 months. Payment: none. Copyrighted, reverts to author.

Paideia Publishers (see also JOURNAL OF COMPUTING IN HIGHER EDUCATION), Patricia A. Stroman, Managing Editor, PO Box 343, Ashfield, MA 01330. 1983. Fiction, non-fiction. avg. press run 1M-2M. Pub'd 1 title 1990; expects 2 titles 1991, 3 titles 1992. 2 titles listed in the *Small Press Record of Books in Print* (20th Edition, 1991-92). avg. price, cloth: $17. Discounts: 1-3 = 30%; 4-9 = 35%; 10-49 = 40%; 50+ = 50%. 250pp. Reporting time: 30 days. Payment: 10% by special arrangement. Copyrights for author.

PAINTBRUSH: A Journal of Poetry, Translations & Letters, Ishtar Press, Inc., Ben Bennani, Language & Literature Divison, Northeast Missouri State Univ., Kirksville, MO 63501, 816-785-4185/4481. 1974. Poetry, articles, interviews, criticism, reviews. "Richard Eberhart, Denise Levertov, David Ignatow, George Keithley, Joseph Bruchac, Douglas Blazek, Charles Levendosky, Sam Hamill, G. Wilson Knight, and others." circ. 500. 2/yr. Pub'd 2 issues 1990; expects 2 issues 1991, 2 issues 1992. sub. price: indiv. $9, instit. $12 in U.S., foreign please add $2/year; per copy: $4; sample: $5/current only. Back issues: $7 when available. Discounts: 20-40%. 65pp; 5½×8½; of, lp. Reporting time: 2-4 weeks. Payment: copies, also monies when available. Copyrighted, reverts to author. Pub's reviews: 15 in 1990. §Poetry & translations. Ads: $75/$35. CCLM, COSMEP, Associated Writing Programs.

PAINTED BRIDE QUARTERLY, Lee W. Potts, Co-Editor; Teresa Leo, Co-Editor, 230 Vine Street, Philadelphia, PA 19106, 215-925-9914. 1973. Poetry, fiction, articles, art, photos, interviews, criticism, reviews, music, long-poems. *"PBQ* is a literary journal of the arts: poetry, reviews, essays, fiction, performance, art work and photography. Publish eclectic material. Many different first-rate poets. Include SASE. New or younger poets especially welcome; quality is a must, though." circ. 1M. 4/yr. Pub'd 4 issues 1990; expects 4 issues 1991, 4 issues 1992. sub. price: $16 individual, $20 institution and library; per copy: $5; sample: $5. 80pp; 6×9; of. Reporting time: 2-6 months. Payment: 1 year subscription + half-priced contributor's copies. Copyrighted, reverts to author. Pub's reviews: 4 in 1990. §Literature, poetry. Ads: $50/$30. CCLM.

PAINTED HILLS REVIEW, Michael Ishii, Kara D. Kosmatka, PO Box 494, Davis, CA 95617-0494, 916-756-5987. 1990. Poetry, fiction, art, photos, reviews. circ. 200-300. 4/yr. Expects 4 issues 1991, 4 issues 1992. sub. price: $10/$12 institutions; per copy: $3; sample: $3. Discounts: none. 48pp; 5½×8½; of. Reporting time: 4-6 weeks. Payment: in copies. Copyrighted, reverts to author. Pub's reviews. §Poetry, fiction (short stories). Ads: $40/$20/inquire.

EL PALACIO, Karen Meadows, Editor, PO Box 2087, Santa Fe, NM 87504-2087, 505-827-6451. 1913. Articles, art, photos, reviews. "Issues planned yr in advance; several articles per year by commission. Enquiries required in advance on freelance. College-level semi-popular style; 2.5M-5 words, art supplied by author. Museum related topics, Southwestern slant; archaeology, folk art, anthropology, history, the arts, geography. Recent contributors: Marc Simmons, Ruth Armstrong, Al Ortiz, Rudolfo Anaya, John L. Kessell." circ. 4M. 3/yr. Pub'd 2 issues 1990; expects 3 issues 1991, 3 issues 1992. sub. price: $18; per copy: $6; sample: $6. Back issues: to be determined under review-query. 60pp; 8½×11; of. Reporting time: 2 weeks-2 months. Payment: $50. Copyrighted, rights revert upon request. No ads. Museum of New Mexico Foundation.

Paladin Enterprises, Inc., Peder C. Lund, President and Publisher; Jon Ford, Editorial Director, PO Box 1307, Boulder, CO 80306, 303-443-7250. 1970. Non-fiction. "Non-fiction manuscripts on military related subjects are given first consideration. These include weaponry technology, police science, military, martial arts, self-defense, survival, terrorism, political kidnapping. When accompanied with photos, mss are reviewed and returned within three weeks. Lenghth of material 25,000 to 35,000. SASE required." avg. press run 1M-2M. Pub'd 39 titles 1990; expects 36 titles 1991, 38 titles 1992. 283 titles listed in the *Small Press Record of Books in Print* (20th Edition, 1991-92). avg. price, cloth: $19.95; paper: $14; other: $10 (reprints of technical manuals). Discounts: $50-$100 retail value - 20% all titles except supplementary list; $100-$500 40% ; $500-$1000 45%; $1000-$5000, 50% both all titles except supplementary list. Over $5000 55% except supplementary list. 175pp; 5½×8½, 8½×11; of. Reporting time: 4 weeks. Payment: standard 10, 12 & 15%. Copyrights for author.

PALIMPSEST, Ginalie Swaim, State Historical Society of Iowa, 402 Iowa Avenue, Iowa City, IA 52240, 319-335-3916. 1920. Articles, art, photos, interviews, letters, non-fiction. *"The Palimpsest* is Iowa's popular history magazine. It publishes manuscripts and edited documents on the history of Iowa and the Midwest that may interest a general reading audience. Submissions that focus on visual materials (photographs, maps, drawings) or on material culture are also welcomed. Originality and significance of the topic, as well as quality of research and writing, will determine acceptance. Manuscripts should be double-spaced, footnoted, and roughly 10-25 pages. Photographs or illustrations (or suggestions) are encouraged." circ. 4.5M. 4/yr. Pub'd 4 issues 1990; expects 4 issues 1991, 4 issues 1992. sub. price: $15; per copy: $4.50; sample: free. Back issues: 1920-1972—50¢, 1973-June '84—$1, July '84-Dec. '86—$2.50, 1987—Summer '89 $3.50. Discounts: retailers get 40% off single issue cover price. 48pp; 7⅜×10; of. Reporting time: 2 months. Payment: none, except for 10 complimentary copies. Copyrighted, does not revert to author.

Pallas Communications, Douglas Bloch, 4226 NE 23rd Avenue, Portland, OR 97211, 503-284-2848. 1986. Non-fiction. "Our works have a distinct 'New Age' flavor. We are interested in subject matter that deals with personal or planetary transformation. We want to publish books that promote a positive and healing effect on the planet and its people" avg. press run 5M. Pub'd 1 title 1990; expects 2 titles 1991, 2 titles 1992. avg. price, paper: $14.95. Discounts: bookstores= 2-4 books 20%, 5+ 40%; jobber= 50%-55%. 282pp; 8½×11; of. Reporting time: 1 month. Payment: 7½% of cover price for 1st 10,000, 8% over 10,000. Copyrights for author. COSMEP, Publishers Marketing Association (PMA).

PalmTree Publishers, PO Box 3787, Omaha, NE 68105, 402-345-1617. 1988. "We publish books, booklets, chapbooks, etc. We will do layout, typesetting, editing, printing, and copyrighting. We help people to self-publish their own works. Prices are very reasonable for small saddle stitched paper backs. We publish essays, poetry, philosophy, psychology, or any subject of interest to the author. We give advice, but do not act as subsidy or vanity publishers. We return you books which you must market and sell as best you can. The most we do for marketing is to recommend specific titles to read. Write for a quote, but be sure to include specifics such as stock, weight, cover, size, length, binding, illustrations, pictues, etc. For example, the simplest and most cost effective format is 5½ X 8½ finished, slightly smaller after tripping, using a 50-60lb cover, 20lb text, saddle stitched, and 40 numbered pages can be produced in lots of at least 150 for as little as $3 per book depending on the amount of editing, typesetting, graphics, etc. Prices are subject to change without notice and depend on current paper prices." avg. press run 150. Pub'd 2 titles 1990; expects 6 titles 1991, 12 titles 1992. 8 titles listed in the *Small Press Record of Books in Print* (20th Edition, 1991-92). avg. price, paper: $4.95. Discounts: 2-4 20%, 5-99 40%, 100+ 50%. 50pp; 5½×8½; of, Xerox. Reporting time: 2 weeks. Payment: half up front, half when finished. Copyrights for author.

Pamlico Press, William Stephenson, 1611 Oaklawn Avenue, Greenville, NC 27858, (919) 756-5964. 1987. "North Carolina history, biography, travel" avg. press run 1M. Expects 1 title 1991, 2-3 titles 1992. 1 title listed in the *Small Press Record of Books in Print* (20th Edition, 1991-92). avg. price, cloth: $18.95; paper: $12.95. Discounts: inquire. 200pp; 6×9. Reporting time: 3 months. Payment: to be arranged. Copyrights for author.

Pancake Press, Patrick Smith, 163 Galewood Circle, San Francisco, CA 94131, 415-648-3573. 1973. Poetry, long-poems. "Our principle interest is in poetry books by writers with fairly long experience. We do small first editions of poetry books which are the product of several years writing, and which have value as an autobiographical account of a significant social role—workers in all fields, sufferers of various passions, role-changers, all the democratic atoms of our national life." avg. press run 1M. Expects 1 title 1991, 1 title 1992. 6 titles listed in the *Small Press Record of Books in Print* (20th Edition, 1991-92). avg. price, paper: $10. Discounts: 40%. 35-50pp; 5½×7, 7×8½; of. Reporting time: 1 month. Payment: arranged by mutual consent. Does not copyright for author.

Pandemic International Publishers Inc., POB 61849, Vancouver, WA 98666, 503-786-2949. 2 titles listed in the *Small Press Record of Books in Print* (20th Edition, 1991-92).

Pandit Press, Inc., Kent Welton, 24843 Del Prado, Suite 405, Dana Point, CA 92629, 714-240-7151. 2 titles listed in the *Small Press Record of Books in Print* (20th Edition, 1991-92).

Pando Publications, Andrew Bernstein, 540 Longleaf Drive, Roswell, GA 30075, 404-587-3363. 1987. Fiction, non-fiction. "New publisher. Specialize in books on the card game of bridge. Recently expanded to children's books. Willing to consider new, full-length fiction and nonfiction manuscripts." avg. press run 3M-9M. Expects 3 titles 1991, 6-12 titles 1992. 3 titles listed in the *Small Press Record of Books in Print* (20th Edition, 1991-92). avg. price, paper: $11. Discounts: wholesalers 50%, bookstores: 1-4 20%, 5-24 40%, 25-49 42%, 50-199 43%, 200-499 45%, 500-1499 46%, 1500+ 47%. 200pp; 8½×11; webb press. Reporting time: 2 months. Payment: varies with author. Copyrights for author. Georgia Book Publishers Association, PO Box

7447, Atlanta, GA 30309.

PANDORA, Meg MacDonald, Editor; Polly Vedder, Art Editor; Ruth Berman, Poetry Editor, 2844 Grayson, Ferndale, MI 48220. 1978. Poetry, fiction, articles, art, cartoons, interviews, reviews, parts-of-novels, long-poems, news items. "Stories should be under 5,000 words, longer stories must be of exceptional quality as competition is very keen. Articles under 1,000 words will be considered—inquire first. Reviews of books of special interest to SF and fantasy readers and writers 200-500 words. Poems *must* be related to science fiction or fantasy. *Pandora* avoids material that is non-sexist, non-racist, non-stereotyped. Reviews, interviews, and articles should take this editorial preference into account. Send fiction to main address; poetry to 2809 Drew Ave. S., Minneapolis, MN 55416." circ. 1M. 2/yr. Pub'd 2 issues 1990; expects 2 issues 1991, 4 issues 1992. sub. price: $10/2 issues, $15/2 issues Canada, $20/2 overseas; 2yr subs available: $18/4 issues, $28/4 issues Canada, $36/4 issues overseas; per copy: $5 US; sample: $5 US, $7 Canada, $10 Foreign; US funds *ONLY*. Back issues: pre-#17 samples $2 each US, $6 Canada, $12 overseas. Discounts: please contact. 72pp; 5½x8½ (digest); of. Reporting time: 8 weeks. Payment: 1¢-2¢ a word for stories, $5 articles; $2.50 and up for poems; $7 and up for art FNASR; some one-time rights; some all-rights. Copyrighted, all rights not purchased revert to author. Pub's reviews: 0 in 1990. §Science fiction, fantasy, writing, art. Ads: display: $40; $25; $16.50; $11/non-display; $10 for 25 words; we will consider trades!

THE PANHANDLER, Michael Yots, Editor; Stanton Millet, The Panhandler Press, English Dept., Univ. Of West Florida, Pensacola, FL 32514, 904-474-2923. 1976. Poetry, fiction, art, photos. *"The Panhandler* is a magazine of contemporary poetry and fiction. We want poetry and stories rooted in real experience of real people in language with a strong colloquial flavor. Works that are engaging and readable stand a better chance with us than works that are self-consciously literary. Recent contributors: Walter McDonald, Malcolm Glass, Enid Shomer, David Kirby, Joan Colby." circ. 500. 2/yr. Pub'd 2 issues 1990; expects 2 issues 1991, 2 issues 1992. sub. price: $5/$8 includes yearly chapbook; per copy: $3; sample: $2. Back issues: $2. Discounts: 10 or more 40%. 64pp; 6×9; †of. Reporting time: 2 weeks to 2 months. Payment: copies. Copyrighted, reverts to author. Ads: $50/$25. CCLM, AWP.

Panjandrum Books (see also PANJANDRUM POETRY JOURNAL), Dennis Koran, David Guss, 5428 Hermitage Avenue, North Hollywood, CA 91607, 818-985-7259. 1971. "Panjandrum Books publishes quality paperbacks on selected non-fiction subjects. Recently centering in the fields of health, diet, cooking, music, and literature. Panjandrum Press Inc. publishes poetry and occasionally fiction. Reading fee: $5." avg. press run 3M-5M, 1M poetry. Pub'd 5 titles 1990; expects 6 titles 1991, 6 titles 1992. 43 titles listed in the *Small Press Record of Books in Print* (20th Edition, 1991-92). avg. price, cloth: $10-$14.95; paper: $4.95-$9.95. Discounts: standard to bookstores and other retailers; wholesalers 50% & up. Non-fiction 150pp, poetry 64pp; size varies; of. Reporting time: 2 months. Payment: varies. Copyrights for author. CLMP.

PANJANDRUM POETRY JOURNAL, Panjandrum Books, Dennis Koran, Editor-in-Chief; David Guss, Associate Editor, 5428 Hermitage Avenue, North Hollywood, CA 91607, 818-985-7259. 1971. Poetry, fiction, art, photos, cartoons, reviews, collages. "Eclectic; Rothenberg, Einzig, de Angulo, Bly, Ferlinghetti, Norse, McClure, Doria, Beausoleil, Vose, Weiss, Fraser, Vinograd, etc." circ. 2M. Expects 1 issue 1991, 1 issue 1992. sub. price: $14 instit. (3 issues); per copy: $4.95-$7; sample: varies with issue ordered as sample, plus shipping. Back issues: PAN 1: $10; 2-3, cassette: $9; 4, $5.95; 6/7: $6.95. Discounts: Trade: 1, 20%; 2-3, 30%; 4-25, 40%; 25-up, 50%. Library disc. Jobbers: 1-3, 20%; 4-25, 40%; 26-up, 45%. 10% on orders of 5-up copies. 100-140pp; 5½x8½ usually; of, lp. Reporting time: 1 month. Payment: as grants are avail.; 2 copies of issue. Copyrighted, rights revert with written permission. Pub's reviews. §some areas. no ads. CLMP.

Panopticum Press London, C. Michael-Titus, 44, Howard Road, Upminster, England, (04022) 22100. 1974. Poetry, letters, long-poems. "Economics, translations of literature and politics. Co-production with authors." avg. press run 300-3M. Pub'd 1 title 1990; expects 3 titles 1991, 3 titles 1992. 3 titles listed in the *Small Press Record of Books in Print* (20th Edition, 1991-92). avg. price, cloth: £7.50; paper: £1.20; other: £2.20. Discounts: none. 80-300pp; 148×210mm; of. Reporting time: 6 months. Copyrights for author.

Panorama Publishing Company, Elyssa A. Harte, 18607 Ventura Boulevard #310, Tarzana, CA 91356. 1974. Non-fiction. "We have two subject biases: psychology/self-help and biographies of famous people. Within those broad categories, we are flexible with format, i.e., we will do scholarly, text, and trade self-help paperback, or autobiography, biography, biography/cookbook. Our next project is by Ms. Florence Henderson, and is a celebrity review/cookbook, describing numerous stars appearing on her show 'Country Kitchen', along with their recipes" avg. press run 5M. Pub'd 2 titles 1990; expects 2 titles 1991, 4 titles 1992. 1 title listed in the *Small Press Record of Books in Print* (20th Edition, 1991-92). avg. price, cloth: $23.95; paper: $14.95. Discounts: 2-4 20%, 5-24 40%, 25-99 42%, 100-249 44%, 250+ 46%, stop orders 20%, colleges and libraries 20%. 250pp; 6×9; of. Reporting time: 2-4 weeks. Payment: 7% of sales price; paid semi-annually. Copyrights for author. Publishers Marketing Assoc. (PMA), 2401 Pacific Coast Hwy, Suite 206, Hermosa Beach, CA 90254; COSMEP, PO Box 703, San Francisco, CA 94101.

Panorama West Publishing, David Katz, PO Box 2088, Davis, CA 95617-4638, 916-756-7177; FAX 916-756-7188. 1959. Non-fiction. "We help authors and many historical societies to self-publish." avg. press run 3M. Pub'd 10 titles 1990; expects 19 titles 1991, 25 titles 1992. 23 titles listed in the *Small Press Record of Books in Print* (20th Edition, 1991-92). avg. price, cloth: $11.95; paper: $8.95. Discounts: 40% to bookstores. 200pp; 6×9 to 9×13; of. Reporting time: immediately. Payment: 10% royalty. Copyrights for author. Book Builders West.

Panther Press Ltd., John Miller, PO Box A-44, Wantagh, NY 11793, 516-783-5673. 1980. Satire, criticism, news items, non-fiction. avg. press run 5M. Pub'd 3 titles 1990. avg. price, paper: $10. Discounts: 50% distributors, 40% bookstores. 200pp; 5×8. Payment: 10% 5,000, 12% over 5,000. Copyrights for author.

PANURGE, David Almond, PO Box 1QR, Newcastle-Upon-Tyne NE99 1QR, England, 091-232-7669. 1984. Fiction, letters. "Fiction by new and up-and-coming writers. Work that shows vitality of languages, command of form, individual approach." circ. 1.2M. 2/yr. Pub'd 2 issues 1990; expects 2 issues 1991, 2 issues 1992. sub. price: £9/$18; per copy: £5/$10; sample: same. Back issues: £3/$6. Discounts: 40%. 120pp; size A5 portrait; lp. Reporting time: 1 week to 2 months. Payment: £10/1,000 words. Copyrighted, reverts to author. Ads: £60/£35.

THE PAPER BAG, The Paper Bag Press, Michael H. Brownstein, PO Box 268805, Chicago, IL 60626-8805, 312-285-7972. 1988. Poetry, fiction, art, cartoons, satire, long-poems, plays. "We are accepting black and white drawings (send originals), poetry any style (including Japanese forms), and short, short fiction—under 500 words (anything longer than 500 words will be returned). We are interested in new poets, artists, and writers as well as individuals who are established. Our only bias is with poetry that would work better as short fiction. We would like to see strong images in poetry. We comment on all rejections and many times steer the poet to another publication." circ. 200. 4/yr. Pub'd 4 issues 1990; expects 4 issues 1991, 4 issues 1992. sub. price: $10; per copy: $2.50; sample: $2.50. Back issues: $2.50. 30pp; 8½×6; of. Reporting time: 2 minutes to 8 weeks. Payment: contributor's copy. Copyrighted, reverts to author.

The Paper Bag Press (see also THE PAPER BAG), Michael H. Brownstein, PO Box 268805, Chicago, IL 60626-8805, 312-285-7972. 1988. Poetry, fiction, art, cartoons, parts-of-novels, long-poems, plays. "We accept black and white drawings (please send originals), poetry (any style—this includes Japanese forms), and short, short fiction (under 500 words—anything longer than 500 words will be returned). We have no biases other than we seek good images and frown on poetry that would better as fiction. We definitely comment on all rejections and many times give other publications' addresses for work we reject. We are actively seeking both new and established poets, artists, and writers. We plan to publish four chapbooks each year and many broadsheets. We are also interested in publishing poetry in other forms to reach the widest possible audience." avg. press run 20-300. Pub'd 2 titles 1990; expects 4 titles 1991, 4 titles 1992. 20pp; 8½×6; mi, of, lp. Reporting time: 2 minutes to 8 weeks. Payment: free contributors copies, but we hope to be able to pay some token amount soon. Does not copyright for author.

The Paper Plant (see also FARCE, Raleigh's Review of Alternative Arts), John Dancy-Jones, PO Box 543, Raleigh, NC 27602, 919-834-9203. 1983. Poetry, fiction. "Bookstore address: 309 W. Martin Street, Raleigh, NC 27601. The Paper Plant publishes broadsides and chapbooks for emerging writers working at a radically local level; our techniques and editorial approach align with that level. Editions of a few hundred copies are letterpress printed (or the covers are with chapbooks) and hand bound with hand-laid paper not to display 'fine printing' but to create an environment of independence, control of physical production, and maximum involvement between writer, designer, and publisher. We aim for a non-academic (indeed non-literary) audience whose ideas of poetry we can change. The press sponsors a weekly open reading in downtown Raleigh; many of our writers emerge from that forum. Many of us believe that publishing poetry is a supplement to an essentially oral art" avg. press run 300. Pub'd 2 titles 1990; expects 3 titles 1991, 3 titles 1992. avg. price, paper: $4; other: $2 broadsides. Discounts: 40% prepaid any number. 24pp; 5½×8½; of, lp, hand-laid broadsides and covers which we produce. Payment: 10% of the edition, negotiable royalties on reprints. Copyrights for author. The N.C. Writer's Network, PO Box 954, Carrboro, NC 27510.

PAPER RADIO, Neil S. Kvern, Editor & Publisher; Dagmar Howard, Contributing Editor, PO Box 85302, Seattle, WA 98145-1302. 1986. Poetry, fiction, articles, art, photos, criticism, reviews, parts-of-novels, collages, concrete art. "We like experimental, off-beat, sexy, probing, funny, political, personal, literary or semi-illiterate, poetry and prose, black & white art, etc. Recent contributors: Judson Crews, Dagmar Howard, Richard Kostelanetz, Sheila E. Murphy, Tamara Sellman, Mike Miskowski." circ. 500. 2/yr. Pub'd 2 issues 1990; expects 2 issues 1991, 2 issues 1992. sub. price: $10; per copy: $4; sample: $4. Back issues: $3, varies per availability. Discounts: inquire. 60pp; 8½×11, varies; photocopy, of. Reporting time: 1-2 months. Payment: copy of issue. Copyrighted, reverts to author. Pub's reviews: 12 in 1990. §Just about anything, mainly poetry, fiction, art published by small presses. Ads: $28/$18.

PAPER TOADSTOOL, Duncan Hilton, Ruth Strebe, Brigham Fordham, Jen K., 4946 West Point Way, West Valley, UT 84120, 801-972-8236. 1989. Poetry, fiction, art, photos, parts-of-novels. "We like lengthy poems, and short stories, fiction, or non-fiction. And easily reproducible illustrations. Everything is considered with great care, because we are very limited with space and money (we fund it outselves)." circ. 500. 2-3/yr. Pub'd 2 issues 1990; expects 2 issues 1991. price per copy: postage; sample: postage. Back issues: postage only. Discounts: bulk send postage, will make deals. 26pp; 5½×8½; of. Reporting time: anytime, we're always collecting. Payment: 1 copy of the issue their piece is printed in. Copyrighted, reverts to author. Ads: none.

PAPERBACK PARADE, Gryphon Publications, Gary Lovisi, PO Box 209, Brooklyn, NY 11228. 1986. Articles, photos, interviews, criticism, reviews, letters, news items, non-fiction. "A bi-monthly digest magazine devoted to collectible vintage, rare paperbacks with articles, interviews, lists and dozens of cover reproductions of scarce/rare books" circ. 500. 6/yr. Pub'd 6 issues 1990; expects 6 issues 1991, 6 issues 1992. sub. price: $20; per copy: $5; sample: $5. Back issues: $5 per issue. Discounts: 40% on 5 or more of each issue. 60-80pp; 5×8; of. Reporting time: 2-4 weeks. Payment: copies. Copyrighted, reverts to author. Pub's reviews: dozens in 1990. §Non-fiction. Ads: $50/$25.

Paperweight Press, L. H. Selman, 761 Chestnut Street, Santa Cruz, CA 95060, 408-427-1177. 1975. Art. avg. press run 3M. Pub'd 1 title 1990; expects 2 titles 1991, 3 titles 1992. 14 titles listed in the *Small Press Record of Books in Print* (20th Edition, 1991-92). avg. price, cloth: $30; paper: $15; other: $40. Discounts: 6 or more copies, 40%; Jobber 200 or more, 60%. 200pp; 8½×11; of. Reporting time: 4-6 weeks. Payment: 5% cover price. Copyrights for author.

Papier-Mache Press, Sandra Martz, 795 Via Manzana, Watsonville, CA 95076. 1984. Poetry, fiction, photos, letters, parts-of-novels, plays. "We typically publish anthologies of poetry and short fiction on a special theme, e.g. women and sports, women and aging, women and work and a limited number of single author titles. We generally focus on material by, for and about midlife and older women but also include work by socially aware male authors and poets. We prefer short stories of 2500 words or less and poems of 70 lines or less; however, longer work is sometimes accepted. Contributors should query with SASE before submitting work. Recent contributors include Sue Saniel Elkind, Mary Anne Ashley, Ruthann Robson, Molly Martin, Ric Masten." avg. press run 1M-3M. Pub'd 3 titles 1990; expects 3 titles 1991, 3 titles 1992. 13 titles listed in the *Small Press Record of Books in Print* (20th Edition, 1991-92). avg. price, paper: $10. Discounts: 1-4 copies 20%, 5-35 40%, 36+ 50%. 180pp; 7×9; of. Reporting time: 8 weeks on queries, 6-18 weeks on submissions. Payment: negotiated on individual basis, modest advance. Copyrights for author. Publishing Marketing Association (PMA), 2401 Pacific Coast Hwy, Suite 206, Hermosa Beach, CA 90254.

Papyrus Publishers, Geoffrey Hutchison-Cleaves, Editor; Robert Clarges, Managing Director, PO Box 466, Yonkers, NY 10704, 914-664-0840. 1982. Non-fiction. "Not accepting right now. NO PHONE CALLS, PLEASE. Distributors: (USA) Papyrus Publishers, Box 466, Yonkers, NY 10704; (UK) Vera Trinder Ltd., 38 Bedford Street, Strand, London WC2E 9EU, England." avg. press run 1M. Pub'd 4 titles 1990; expects 4 titles 1991, 4 titles 1992. 3 titles listed in the *Small Press Record of Books in Print* (20th Edition, 1991-92). avg. price, cloth: $20-$50; other: varies. Discounts: 40%. 378pp; 6×9; †of, lp. Copyrights for author.

Para Publishing (see also PUBLISHING POYNTERS), Dan Poynter, Publisher, PO Box 4232-Q, Santa Barbara, CA 93140-4232, 805-968-7277; fax 805-968-1379. 1969. Photos, cartoons, news items, non-fiction. "Para Publishing specializes in non-fiction books on parachutes/skydiving and book publishing/marketing. The technical parachute books and popular skydiving books have always been sold through non-traditional outlets. Publisher Dan Poynter is the author of 68 books, 19 monographs and over 500 magazine articles, most of them on publishing. He serves as a consultant to the mail order and publishing industries and conducts workshops in Santa Barbara on book marketing, promotion and distribution. Poynter is a past direcor of COSMEP and a past director of the Publishers Marketing Association. No manuscripts, query first. Query regarding parachute and publishing books only. When offering a parachute manuscript, we want to know how many jumps you have made." avg. press run 5M-10M. Pub'd 8 titles 1990; expects 7 titles 1991, 8 titles 1992. 43 titles listed in the *Small Press Record of Books in Print* (20th Edition, 1991-92). avg. price, cloth: $29.95; paper: $19.95; other: $19.95 monographs. Discounts: 6-199 40%, 200-499 50%, 500+ 55%. 300pp; 5½×8½, 8½×11; of. Reporting time: 1 week. Payment: 8% of list price. Copyrights for author. COSMEP, PMA, ABA.

Parable Press, Bethany Strong, 136 Gray Street, Amherst, MA 01002, 413-253-5634. 1976. "Drama, fiction and non-fiction, graphics" avg. press run 1M. Pub'd 3 titles 1990; expects 2 titles 1992. 3 titles listed in the *Small Press Record of Books in Print* (20th Edition, 1991-92). avg. price, cloth: $10.95; paper: $5.95. Discounts: 40% trade discount over 100 copies by arrangement; 2-5 20%; 6-24 40%; 25-49 42%; 50-100 45%; 100-200 48%; 200-up 50%. 400pp; 6×8; of. Copyrights for author. COSMEP.

Parabola Books (see also PARABOLA MAGAZINE), Rob Baker, Co-Editor; Ellen Draper, Co-Editor, 656 Broadway, New York, NY 10012, 212-505-6200. 1975. Fiction, interviews, non-fiction. avg. press run 3M. Pub'd 2 titles 1990; expects 2 titles 1991, 4 titles 1992. 7 titles listed in the *Small Press Record of Books in Print* (20th Edition, 1991-92). avg. price, cloth: $13; paper: $9.20. Discounts: 2-5 books 25%, 6-10 30%, 11-25 40%, 26-74 45%, 75+ 50%. 190pp; 5½×8½; of. Reporting time: 1 month. Copyrights for author. CCLM.

PARABOLA MAGAZINE, Parabola Books, Rob Baker, Co-Editor; Joseph Kulin, Executive Publisher; Ellen Draper, Co-Editor, 656 Broadway, New York, NY 10012-2317, 212-505-6200. 1976. Poetry, fiction, articles, art, photos, interviews, criticism, reviews, letters, non-fiction. "*Parabola* publishes articles of 3M-5M words, reviews of 750 words on scholarly subjects but with a literate and lively style. Recent contributors are Huston Smith, Helen Luke, Seyyed Hossein Nasr, Robert Aitken, P.L. Travers, Joseph Campbell, Gertrude Stein. Issues are organized by theme: addiction, creative response, sense of humor, repetition and renewal, questions, etc" circ. 40M. 4/yr. Pub'd 4 issues 1990; expects 4 issues 1991, 4 issues 1992. sub. price: $20; per copy: $6; sample: $6. Back issues: $8. Discounts: 2-5 books 25%, 6-10 30%, 11-25 40%, 26-74 45%, 75+ 50%. 128pp; 6¾x10; of, web. Reporting time: 21 days. Payment: yes. Copyrighted, reverts to author. Pub's reviews: 35 in 1990. §Mythology, comparative religion, anthropology, folklore, children's books,. Ads: $775/$520. Publishers Marketing Assoc., Coordinating Council for Literary Mags.

PARACHUTIST, Kevin Gibson, Director of Publications, 1440 Duke Street, Alexandria, VA 22314, 703-836-3495. 1958. Articles, photos, reviews, letters, news items, non-fiction. "Photographs" circ. 19M. 12/yr. Pub'd 12 issues 1990; expects 12 issues 1991, 12 issues 1992. sub. price: $21.50; per copy: $2; sample: $2. Back issues: $1. 68pp; 8½x11; of. Reporting time: 6 weeks. Payment: $50 front cover, centerfold. Copyrighted, does not revert to author. Pub's reviews: 6 in 1990. §Aviation sports. Ads: $580/$349/75¢ ($10 min.).

Paradigm Press, Gale Nelson, 11 Slater Avenue, Providence, RI 02906. 1988. Poetry, fiction. avg. press run 400. Pub'd 8 titles 1990; expects 6 titles 1991, 6 titles 1992. 15 titles listed in the *Small Press Record of Books in Print* (20th Edition, 1991-92). avg. price, cloth: $13; paper: $7; other: pamphlets $4. Discounts: our books are distributed by Small Press Distribution. 20-96pp; 5½x8½, 7x11; of. Reporting time: 3-5 months. Payment: 10% of copies. Does not copyright for author.

Paradise Publications, Greg Stilson, Christie Stilson, 8110 SW Wareham, Portland, OR 97223, 503-246-1555. 1983. Non-fiction. avg. press run 10M. Pub'd 2 titles 1990; expects 3 titles 1991, 3 titles 1992. 4 titles listed in the *Small Press Record of Books in Print* (20th Edition, 1991-92). avg. price, cloth: $9.95. 256pp; 5½x8½. Reporting time: 2 months. Payment: negotiable. Copyrights for author. PMA, COSMEP, NWABP, IFW & TWA.

THE PARADOXIST MOVEMENT, Florentin Smarandache, PO Box 42561, Phoenix, AZ 85080, 602-436-2126. 1991. Poetry, art, interviews, reviews, letters, plays. "*The Paradoxist Movement* is an avant-garde and experimental journal of literature (in English, French and Romanian) to promote a new movement that Florentin Smarandache founded in Romania ten years ago and about he wrote in Morocco: *Les Sens du Non-Sens* (fr.: The Sense of the Non-sense), and in France: *Antichambres/Antipoesies/Bizarreries* (fr.: Anterooms/Antipoems/Oddities). The name (the paradoxist movement) was used on the book *Le Sens du Non-sens* as a manifesto of poetry (new ideas): 1983." 50-70pp; 5x8½; of.

Paragon House Publishers, Ken Stuart, Editor in Chief, 90 5th Avenue, New York, NY 10011, 212-620-2820. 1983. Non-fiction. "Louis Simpson: *Collected Poems*, Robert Herzstein: *Roosevelt and Hitler*, Nathan Miller: *Spying for America*, Anthony Seratini: *Linus Pauling*, Armchair Traveller Series-paperback reprints of travel classics from brand name authors such as Steinbeck, Maugham, Auden, Waugh. Literary translations from French and German. New Age titles. American History. Military" avg. press run 5M-10M. Pub'd 100 titles 1990; expects 120 titles 1991, 140 titles 1992. avg. price, cloth: $19.95; paper: $10.95. 256pp; 6x9. Reporting time: 6-8 weeks. Payment: standard. Copyrights for author.

PARAGRAPH, Walker Rumble, Karen Donovan, Oat City Press, 1423 Northampton Street, Holyoke, MA 01040-1915, 413-533-8767. 1985. Fiction, non-fiction. "We publish paragraphs under 200 words that represent brief bursts of 'ordered sensibility.' Innovation is welcome." circ. 500. 2/yr. Pub'd 2 issues 1990; expects 3 issues 1991, 3 issues 1992. sub. price: $8 for 3 issues; per copy: $3; sample: same. Back issues: same. 40pp; 4¼x5½; of. Reporting time: 3 months. Payment: copies. Copyrighted, reverts to author. CCLM.

Paragraph Publications, Beverly Gaines, PO Box 2954, Pompano Beach, FL 33062, 305-946-5230. 1991. Non-fiction. Expects 1 title 1991, 2 titles 1992. Discounts: pending. 5¼x8. COSMEP, PMA, National Writers Club.

Parallax Press, Arnold Kotler, PO Box 7355, Berkeley, CA 94707, (415) 525-0101. 1986. "Buddhist and related books-especially how Buddhism might become more engaged in peace and social justice work. Primary author: Thich Nhat Hanh" avg. press run 2M. Pub'd 2 titles 1990; expects 10 titles 1991, 10 titles 1992. 4 titles listed in the *Small Press Record of Books in Print* (20th Edition, 1991-92). avg. price, paper: $10. Discounts: standard. 200pp; 5¼x8; Macintosh. Reporting time: 1 month. Payment: no advance, modest royalty. Copyrights for author. PMA, COSMEP.

Parent Education for Infant Development (see also THE BABY CONNECTION NEWS JOURNAL), Gina G. Morris, Drawer 13320, San Antonio, TX 78213, 512-493-6278. 1986. Articles, photos, cartoons, interviews, news items, non-fiction. "Publish only materials directly related to the field of infant sensory development. Especially interested in collective works on family life experiences and heartwarming parenting histories. Develop all types of extensive brochures, transparencies, pamphlets, booklets, syllabi, manuals which promote family-support, service and education. Primarily distribute to Certified Infant Development Specialists, lactation consultants, midwives, Certified Childbirth Educators, labor and delivery nurses, ob/gyn's, etc. Ads accepted in all our pub's and books. Limited. Write for prices. We do advertise our pub's widely and plan to promote all works through a carefully planned catalog, called Baby's Mart Catalog." avg. press run 500. Pub'd 16 titles 1990; expects 16 titles 1991, 25 titles 1992. 5 titles listed in the *Small Press Record of Books in Print* (20th Edition, 1991-92). avg. price, paper: $10-$12. Discounts: 10-19 20%, 20+ 40%, special discounts to IDEA members and hospital libraries. 40-50pp; 8½×11; †lp. Reporting time: 4-6 weeks. Payment: individually arranged. Copyrights for author. La Leche League, International Montessori Society, National Infant Development Education, National Center for Clinical Infant Programs, NAEYC, Parent Action, Family Resource Coalition, National Association of Neonatal Nurses, International Childbirth Education Association.

Parent Tapes, Inc., Bob Meyer, Senior Editor, PO Box 1025, Commack, NY 11725, 516-543-7082. 1988. Photos, non-fiction. "Parent Tapes, Inc. is a company which publishes, produces, and markets child development audiocassettes for parents. We are not accepting unsolicited manuscripts at this time." avg. press run 5M. Pub'd 2 titles 1990; expects 3 titles 1991, 4 titles 1992. 2 titles listed in the *Small Press Record of Books in Print* (20th Edition, 1991-92). avg. price, other: $10.95 audiocassette. Discounts: 40% bookstores & return policy, 50% non-book retail outlets/no return policy. recording & tape duplication.

Parenting Press, Inc., Shari Steelsmith, 11065 5th Avenue, NE, #F, Seattle, WA 98125, 206-364-2900. 1979. Non-fiction. "Non-fiction; parent education." avg. press run 5M. Pub'd 3 titles 1990; expects 4 titles 1991, 4 titles 1992. 31 titles listed in the *Small Press Record of Books in Print* (20th Edition, 1991-92). avg. price, cloth: $9.95; paper: $5.95; other: $10.95. Discounts: contact publisher. 41pp; 8½×11, 5½×8½; of. Reporting time: 2 months. Payment: case-by-case. Copyrights for author. COSMEP, Pacific NorthWest Book Publishers Assoc., PMA.

Paris Press, 2040 Polk Street #291, San Francisco, CA 94109, 415-931-7603. 1 title listed in the *Small Press Record of Books in Print* (20th Edition, 1991-92).

PARIS REVIEW, George A. Plimpton, Editor, 45-39 171 Place, Flushing, NY 11358, 539-7085. 1952. Poetry, fiction, articles, photos, interviews, parts-of-novels, long-poems, collages. "Prose, fiction, poetry, interviews with eminent authors. Writing published tends to the contemporary modes. Manuscript submissions to 541 East 72nd Street, New York, NY 10021." circ. 10M. 4/yr. Pub'd 4 issues 1990; expects 4 issues 1991, 4 issues 1992. sub. price: $20/4 issues; per copy: $6 on stands; sample: $7 order from Flushing Office. Back issues: list available upon request. Discounts: 40% returnable, 50% non-returnable + shipping. 200pp; 8½×5¼; of. Reporting time: 6 weeks. Payment: poems $50-$170 depending on length, fiction $300-$500. Copyrighted, reverts to author. Ads: $500/$300. CCLM.

Park & Park Publishers, Inc., PO Box 71201, Chevy Chase, MD 20813, 301-656-6511. 1987. Non-fiction. Pub'd 1 title 1990; expects 1 title 1991, 3 titles 1992. 3 titles listed in the *Small Press Record of Books in Print* (20th Edition, 1991-92). avg. price, cloth: $19.95. 200pp; 6×9. Reporting time: 1 month. Payment: yes. Does not copyright for author. COSMEP.

Dr. Homer W. Parker, P.E., Homer W. Parker, Sr., Consuelo R. Parker, 1601 Woodrock Drive, Round Rock, TX 78681, 512-255-0702. 1988. Non-fiction. "Books 64-200 pages preferred, but not a rigid length. Monographs from 2 pages to 200 pages and booklets on variety of engineering, scientific, archeology, evolution, lawsuit defense steps, diabetic subjects, freelance travel, ancient history. Seek material that is on 5.25" floppy disks using a word processor that our equipment can convert, query. Interested in international contacts. Have ISBN numbers and obtain Library of Congress numbers on books that meet their criteria. Our computer is IBM XT compatible, PC-DOS or MS-DOS 2.X to 3.3, hard disk, Princeton HX-12 monitor, laser jet series II printer, Wordstar 2000 Rev. 3.5- Wordstar professional 5.5 are used. Variety of fonts" avg. press run varies. Expects 12 titles 1991, 12 titles 1992. 16 titles listed in the *Small Press Record of Books in Print* (20th Edition, 1991-92). avg. price, paper: varies. Discounts: standard terms and conditions. 112pp; 6×9 most common, 5½×8, 8½×11; web, sheet, flat. Reporting time: query first, send #10 SASE for information. Payment: varies. Copyrights for author. PMA, COSMEP, BPT.

Parkhurst Press, Lynne Thorpe, PO Box 143, Laguna Beach, CA 92652, 714-499-1032. 1981. Fiction. "First book: *Alida - An Erotic Novel*, 180 pages. The intent of our press is to deal with material that changes the mythology of women." avg. press run 2.5M. Expects 1 title 1991, 1 title 1992. 1 title listed in the *Small Press Record of Books in Print* (20th Edition, 1991-92). avg. price, paper: $9. Discounts: 50%. 180pp; 5½×8½; of. Reporting time: 3 weeks. Payment: open.

PARNASSUS: POETRY IN REVIEW, Herbert Leibowitz, 41 Union Square West, Room 804, New York, NY 10003, 212-463-0889. 1972. "Length varies from four pages to forty. Editorial policy is intentionally eclectic. Recent and forthcoming contributors: Adrienne Rich, Jonathan Williams, Guy Davenport, Judith Gleason, Ross Feld, Biqniew Herbert, Marjorie Perloff, R.W. Flint, Michael Harper, Octavio Paz, Hayden Carruth, William Harmon, Joseph Brodsky, Seamus Heaney, Richard Wilbur, Galway Kinnell, Helen Vendler. Do not publish unsolicited poetry." circ. 1.75M. 2/yr. Pub'd 2 issues 1990; expects 2 issues 1991, 2 issues 1992. sub. price: $18 individuals, $36 institutions; per copy: $7-$10; sample: $7-$10. Back issues: vary $7-$12. Discounts: 10% to magazine subscription agencies, 30% to bookstores. 350pp; 6×9¼; of. Reporting time: 3 weeks to 2 months. Payment: $150 average, more if essay is long. Copyrighted, rights revert on request. Pub's reviews: 60-80 in 1990. §Poetry. Ads: $250/$150. CCLM.

PARNASSUS LITERARY JOURNAL, Denver Stull, Kudzu Press, PO Box 1384, Forest Park, GA 30051. 1975. Poetry, articles, reviews. "We are open to all poets. Also open to any subject or style, but please keep it clean. Short poetry has a better chance. Will not accept over 24 lines unless exceptionally good. Recent contributors include: Louis Daniel Brodsky, Alice Mackenzie Swaim, T.K. Splake, Ruth Wildes Schuler. Make checks payable to Denver Stull." circ. 200+. 3/yr. Pub'd 3 issues 1990; expects 3 issues 1991, 3 issues 1992. sub. price: $12, make checks payable to Denver Stull; per copy: $4.25; sample: $3.50. Back issues: $3 (when available). Discounts: 20%. 84pp; 5½×8½; lp. Reporting time: immediately. Payment: copy. Copyrighted, reverts to author. Pub's reviews: 3 in 1990. §Only publishing reviews for subscribers at the moment. COSMEP, National wrtiers club Academy of American Poets American Haiku Soc.

Parrot Press, Jennifer Warshaw, 767 Schiele Avenue, Unit A, San Jose, CA 95126. 1990. Non-fiction. "Non-fiction, clear concise books on parrots; care, training, breeding" avg. press run 5M. Pub'd 2 titles 1990; expects 3 titles 1991. 1 title listed in the *Small Press Record of Books in Print* (20th Edition, 1991-92). avg. price, paper: $14.95. Discounts: 2-4 10%, 5-9 20%, 10-19 30%, 20-99 40%, 100+ 50%. 100pp; 5×8, 7×10. Reporting time: 60 days. Payment: 10% 1st 7500 copies, 12% 2nd 7500, and then 15%. Copyrights for author.

PARTING GIFTS, March Street Press, Robert Bixby, 3006 Stonecutter Terrace, Greensboro, NC 27405. 1988. Poetry, fiction. "Poems any length—prefer up to 20 lines. Fiction to 1,000 words, but stress is on highly imagistic language." circ. 100. 2/yr. Pub'd 2 issues 1990; expects 2 issues 1991, 2 issues 1992. sub. price: $6; per copy: $3; sample: $3. Back issues: $3 each. Discounts: write. 38pp; 5½×8½; †Xerox. Reporting time: usually within 24 hours. Payment: 1 copy. Copyrighted, reverts to author.

PARTISAN REVIEW, William Phillips, Editor; Edith Kurzweil, Executive Editor, 236 Bay State Road, Boston, MA 02215, 617-353-4260. 1934. Poetry, fiction, articles, interviews, criticism, reviews, letters, parts-of-novels, long-poems, plays, non-fiction. circ. 8.2M. 4/yr. Pub'd 4 issues 1990; expects 4 issues 1991, 4 issues 1992. sub. price: $18; per copy: $5; sample: $6 including postage. Back issues: $4. 160pp; 6×9; of. Reporting time: 3-4 months. Payment: 1½¢ word, prose; $50 per poem. Copyrighted. Pub's reviews: 25 in 1990. §Books literature, politics, art, general culture, have backlog now. Ads: $200/$120. CCLM.

Partners In Publishing (see also **PIP COLLEGE 'HELPS' NEWSLETTER**), P.M. Fielding, Box 50347, Tulsa, OK 74150, 918-584-5906. 1976. Articles, interviews, reviews, letters, news items. "We are only interested in material directed to persons who work with learning disabled youth or adults *or* material directed to the learning disabled young person or adult. Emphasis on college, vocational training or career information. Authors should have academic credentials or practical experience." avg. press run 2M. Pub'd 1 title 1990; expects 1 title 1991, 1 title 1992. 1 title listed in the *Small Press Record of Books in Print* (20th Edition, 1991-92). avg. price, paper: $33, per year for 1 year subcription. Discounts: bulk rate (over 5 copies). 6pp; 11×12; of. Reporting time: 1 month. Payment: varies. We own copyright. COSMEP, OSP.

THE PARTY'S OVER, PO Box 366, Williamstown, MA 01267. 1990. News items, non-fiction. "An autonomous/anarchist publication including coverage of major news items, reports of resistance and armed struggle from around the globe, anti-establishment humor, and tips for carrying out direct action." circ. 700. 6/yr. Expects 6 issues 1991, 6 issues 1992. sub. price: pay what you can afford. 4pp; 5½×8½; †of. Not copyrighted. Pub's reviews: 2 in 1990. §Autonomous, anarchist, leftist politics and humor. Autonome Forum, PO Box 366, Williamstown, MA 01267.

PASSAGER: A Journal of Remembrance and Discovery, Kendra Kopelke, Sally Darnowsky, 1420 N. Charles Street, Baltimore, MD 21202-5779, 301-625-3041. Poetry, fiction, interviews, non-fiction. "Fiction and essays: 3,000 words maximum. Poetry: 50 lines maximum. No reprints. *Passager* publishes fiction, poetry, essays, interviews that give voice to human experience. We provide exposure for older writers, with a special interest in those who have recently discovered their creative self. We also act as a literary community for writers of all ages who are not connected to academic institutions or other organized groups." circ. 500. 4/yr. Pub'd 4 issues 1990; expects 4 issues 1991, 4 issues 1992. sub. price: $10; per copy: $3; sample: $3. 32pp; 8×8; of. Reporting time: 6-8 weeks. Payment: 1 year subscription. Copyrighted, reverts to author.

PASSAGES NORTH, Ben Mitchell, Editor; Mark Cox, Poetry Editor; Mary La Chapelle, Fiction Editor; Leslie Roberts, Managing Editor, Kalamazoo College, 1200 Academy Street, Kalamazoo, MI 49007, 616-383-5700; 616-383-8473. 1979. Poetry, fiction, art, photos, interviews, parts-of-novels. *"Passages North's* primary interest is high quality poetry and short fiction, work in translation, essays, criticism, reviews, photography, and graphic art. Contributors: Established and emerging writers; encourages students in writing programs. Recently published Stephen Berg, Juanita Brunk, Tess Gallagher, Linda Gregerman, Mark Halliday, Tony Hoagland, Cynthia Huntington, Thomas Lux, Medbh McGuckian, Lawrence Raab, Richard Speakes. Send SASE for submission guidelines. Submit all prose double-spaced with ample margins; use paper clips, not staples. Name and address on top left corner of top page; submissions returned if a SASE (w/adequate postage) is included." circ. 2.6M. 2/yr. Pub'd 2 issues 1990; expects 2 issues 1991, 2 issues 1992. sub. price: $5, $8 overseas; $8/2 years, $11 overseas; per copy: $3; sample: $3. Back issues: $3. Discounts: 2 years $8. 32pp; 11×15½; of. Reporting time: 3-6 weeks. Payment: copies; some cash depending on grant resources. Copyrighted, reverts to author. Ads: $200/$100/$50 1/4 page. CLMP.

PASSAIC REVIEW, Richard P. Quatrone, Forstmann Library, 195 Gregory Avenue, Passaic, NJ 07055, 201-438-7118. 1979. Poetry, fiction, articles, art, photos, interviews, satire, criticism, reviews, long-poems. "We want clear, courageous, personal work from great men and women." circ. 500. 2/yr. Pub'd 1 issue 1990; expects 2 issues 1991, 2 issues 1992. per copy: $3 + 75¢ postage; sample: $3 + 75¢ postage. Back issues: $3. Discounts: inquire. 50pp; 5½×8½; of. Reporting time: immediately to 52 weeks. Payment: copies of magazine. Copyrighted, reverts to author. §Small press poetry. Ads: $80/$40/$20/$10. CCLM.

Passport Press, Jack Levesque, Miranda d'Hauteville, PO Box 1346, Champlain, NY 12919-1346, 514-937-3868. 1976. "Travel and children's items." avg. press run 5M. Pub'd 1 title 1990; expects 2 titles 1991, 2 titles 1992. 5 titles listed in the *Small Press Record of Books in Print* (20th Edition, 1991-92). avg. price, paper: $12.95. Discounts: 20% with payment (small orders); 6 copies, 40%. 250pp; 5½×8½; of. PMA.

PAST TIMES: THE NOSTALGIA ENTERTAINMENT NEWSLETTER, Randy Skretredt, Jordan R. Young, 7308 Fillmore Drive, Buena Park, CA 90620. 1990. Articles, reviews, news items. "News and reviews regarding movies and music of the '20s, '30s and '40s; also old-time radio and popular culture. Nothing contemporary. Nothing about history or events outside the entertainment field. Nothing on antiques." circ. 2M. 4/yr. Pub'd 3 issues 1990; expects 4 issues 1991, 4 issues 1992. sub. price: $8; per copy: $2; sample: $2. Back issues: $3. 16pp; 8½×11; of. Reporting time: varies. Payment: copies. Copyrighted, reverts to author. Pub's reviews: 60+ in 1990. §movies, music of '20s, '30s, '40s; old-time radio; early '50s TV; classic reissues strips/comic books. Ads: $100/$60 (CRC)/25¢ per word.

Path Press, Samanera Bodhesako, Wye Estate, Ambegoda, Bandarawela, Sri Lanka, 057-2480. 1987. Articles, non-fiction. "Alternate address: 102 Fife Road, Colombo 5, Sri Lanka. We publish books concerned with self-investigation as guided by the Buddha's Teaching. Shorter articles could be included as part of an anthology. Our last book was nearly 600 pages, the next will be about 150. We are oriented towards the Pali Canon but our interest is in making available texts that will be useful to those seriously interested in changing themselves. About half our books are given free to libraries, etc. and we are supported more by donations from those who agree that what we do is worthwhile than by sales" avg. press run 1M. Pub'd 1 title 1990; expects 1 title 1991, 1 title 1992. 1 title listed in the *Small Press Record of Books in Print* (20th Edition, 1991-92). avg. price, cloth: $16; paper: $6. Discounts: 25% to 50% depending on circumstances. 590pp; 6×9; of. Reporting time: 2-3 months. Payment: none, a reasonable number of free copies will be provided. Copyrights for author.

Path Press, Inc., Bennett J. Johnson, President; Herman C. Gilbert, Executive Vice President, 53 West Jackson Blvd Suite 724, Chicago, IL 60604-3701, 312-663-0167. 1969. Poetry, fiction, non-fiction. "Our books will be distributed by African-American Book Dist., Inc. 53 West Jackson Blvd., Chicago, IL 60604." avg. press run 5M. Expects 1 title 1991, 6-10 titles 1992. 6 titles listed in the *Small Press Record of Books in Print* (20th Edition, 1991-92). avg. price, cloth: $14; paper: $6. Usual trade discounts. 300pp; 5½×8½; varies. Reporting time: 60-90 days. Payment: no advance, 10% royalty for first 5M copies, staggered rate to 15% after that. Copyrights for author. ABA, ALA.

Pathway Books, James R. Sherman, 700 Parkview Terrace, Golden Valley, MN 55416, 612-377-1521. 1979. Fiction, non-fiction. "List of Books: *Stop Procrastinating—Do It!*, *Rejection*, and *Escape To The Gunflint*, *Middle Age is Not a Disease*." avg. press run 10M. Pub'd 1 title 1990; expects 1 title 1991, 2 titles 1992. 7 titles listed in the *Small Press Record of Books in Print* (20th Edition, 1991-92). avg. price, paper: $2.95. Discounts: 50%. 100pp; 5½×8½; of. Reporting time: 2-3 weeks. Payment: negotiated. Does not copyright for author. Publishers Marketing Association, Minnesota Independent Publishers Association, Minnesota Book Publishers Roundtable, Upper Midwest Booksellers Association.

The Patrice Press, Gregory M. Franzwa, 1701 South 8th Street, St. Louis, MO 63104-0519, 314-436-3242. 1967. Non-fiction. "Full-length books, usually on history, primary emphasis on emigration to the American West in the 19th century." avg. press run 2M. Pub'd 6 titles 1990; expects 8 titles 1991, 8 titles 1992. 7 titles listed in the *Small Press Record of Books in Print* (20th Edition, 1991-92). avg. price, cloth: $25.95; paper: $12.95. Discounts: 1-4 20%, 5-9 40%, 10-24 42%, 25+ 43%. 300pp; 6×9; of. Reporting time: 30 days. Payment: 12.5% net. Does not copyright for author. MAPA (Mid-American Pub. Assoc.).

THE PATRIOT, Runaway Publications, James L. Berkman, PO Box 1172, Ashland, OR 97520, 503-482-2578. 1984. Poetry, long-poems. "Hard line on the cutting edge of American poetry." circ. 100. 1/yr. Pub'd 1 issue 1990; expects 2 issues 1991, 1 issue 1992. sub. price: $10; per copy: $10; sample: $10. Back issues: same. Discounts: 50% to govt. agencies/federal employees. 8pp; 5½x8½; of. Payment: negotiable. Copyrighted, rights reverting to author negotiable. Ads: negotiable.

PAUNCH, Arthur Efron, Editor & Publisher, 123 Woodward Avenue, Buffalo, NY 14214, 716-836-7332. 1963. Poetry, fiction, articles, photos, criticism, reviews, letters, long-poems, non-fiction. "After another delay, *Paunch* has issued #63-64, and in a new format. Entitled *The Passional Secret Places of Life*, after D.H. Lawrence's last theory of the novel, which he described and fulfilled in *Lady Chatterley's Lover*, the issue contains a foreword by the editor and ten articles on Lawrence. 256 pages of text—the journal's largest yet. These essays would be unlikely to appear in the standard professional journals: their passional qualities would not fit there. Contributors: Anne Pluto, Dennis Hoerner (on Ursula in *The Rainbow*, a Reichian approach), Jay Gertzman, Barry J. Scherr (on Lawrence's struggle with Plato in *Women in Love*), Karyn Sproles, Donald Gutierrez (apocalyptic vision in 'New Heaven and Earth'), Arthur Efron, Mary Galbraith (the 'feeling moment' in Lawrence), Jennifer Swift (on Lawrence's counter-vision to Eliot's 'Wasteland' in *Lady Chatterley*), and Joseph Brennan on 'Male Power' in Lawrence. Price for this issue, $15. Next issue, on the body and sexuality in recent Latin American novels; guest editor: Ruth Gabriela Kirstein." circ. 250. 1/yr. Expects 2 issues 1991, 1 issue 1992. sub. price: $10 indiv., $13 libraries; per copy: $12 double, $6 single, $15 D.H. Lawrence issue; sample: none. Discounts: agents, $1 a year. Double 172pp, single 96pp; 5½x8½; of. Reporting time: 60 days. Payment: copies. Copyrighted, reverts to author. Pub's reviews. §Literary criticism, Reich (Wilhelm), Thomas Hardy, Virginia Woolf, D.H. Lawrence. No ads.

PAUSE, National Poetry Foundation, Johnathon Clifford, Helen Robinson, 27 Mill Road, Fareham, Hampshire PO 16 OTH, England, 0329-822218. 1969. Poetry. "U.K. residents only." circ. 600+. 2/yr. Pub'd 2 issues 1990; expects 2 issues 1991, 2 issues 1992. sub. price: $10; per copy: $5. Discounts: 25%. 44pp; size A5; of. Payment: none. Copyrighted, reverts to author. Pub's reviews: 12 in 1990. free adverts, *if accepted*.

Paycock Press, Richard Myers Peabody, Jr., Editor; Peggy Pfeiffer, Co-Editor; M. Maja Prausnitz, Overseas Editor, PO Box 30906, Bethesda, MD 20814, 301-656-5146. 1976. Poetry, fiction, art, photos, satire, reviews, long-poems. "Poetry titles: *Blank Like Me* by Harrison Fisher, *Jukebox* by Tina Fulker, *I'm in Love with the Morton Salt Girl/Echt & Ersatz* by Richard Peabody, *Fernparallelismus* by Carlo Parcelli. Fiction titles: *The Love Letter Hack* by Michael Brondoli, *Natural History* by George Myers Jr. Anthology: *D.C. Magazines: A Literary Retrospective* ed. by Richard Peabody. Nonfiction: *Mavericks: Nine Independent Publishers* ed. by Richard Peabody" avg. press run 1M. Expects 1 title 1991, 1 title 1992. 8 titles listed in the *Small Press Record of Books in Print* (20th Edition, 1991-92). avg. price, paper: $3-$7.95. Dealer discount available. 60-100pp; 5½x8½, varies; of. Reporting time: 1 month. Copyrights for author.

PC Press, Mark W. McBride, Barbara Marsh, 6 Nelson Street, Rockville, MD 20850-3130, 301-294-7450. 1989. Reviews, non-fiction. "PC Press is interested in books and materials relating to personal computers and the use of personal computers in business. We look for material with a wide appeal, especially that which complements our software products. Recent contributors include John C. Dvorak, Elizabeth Cohn, and Susan Kleimann. Our books average 150-200 pages." avg. press run 10M. Pub'd 2 titles 1990; expects 3 titles 1991, 5+ titles 1992. 2 titles listed in the *Small Press Record of Books in Print* (20th Edition, 1991-92). avg. price, paper: $20. Discounts: varies. 175pp; 7×9; †of. Reporting time: 30 days. Payment: varies. Copyrights for author.

PC PUBLISHING, Robert Mueller, Editor, 950 Lee Street, Des Plaines, IL 60016, 708-296-0770. 1986. Articles, interviews, reviews, news items, non-fiction. "Editorial focus-desktop publishing for IBM PC computer users" circ. 50M. 12/yr. Pub'd 12 issues 1990; expects 12 issues 1991, 12 issues 1992. sub. price: $36; per copy: $3.95; sample: $3.95. Back issues: $3.95. Discounts: Varies-contact publisher. 80pp; 8×10¾; of. Reporting time: 2 weeks. Payment: varies. Copyrighted, reverts to author. Pub's reviews: 15 in 1990. §Computers, publishing. Ads: $3250/$1995/None. MPA.

PEACE & DEMOCRACY NEWS, Joanne Landy, Gail Daneker, Editor; Steven Becker, Thomas Harrison, Judith Hempfling, Brian Morton, Andrea Imredy, PO Box 1640, Cathedral Station, New York, NY 10025, 212-666-5924. 1984. Poetry, articles, art, photos, cartoons, interviews, reviews, letters. "Published by the Campaign for Peace and Democracy. Their aim is to promote peace and human rights from below based on grass-roots democratic movements around the world. To this end, *Peace And Democracy News* carries articles on topics ranging from the implications of changes in Eastern Europe for the Third World to the state of reproductive rights in various countries around the world." circ. 4M. 2/yr. Pub'd 1 issue 1990; expects 2 issues 1991, 2 issues 1992. sub. price: $5; in 1992: $10 indiv., $15 instit./international; per copy: $3, $5 in 1992; sample: free. Back issues: $2.50. Discounts: 10 or more copies, $2 apiece. 48pp; 8½x10½; regular printer, of. Reporting time: 1 month - 6 weeks. Payment: none. Not copyrighted. Pub's reviews: 1 in 1990. §Political, social, and economic human rights, economic development, U.S. foreign policy, peace movement, international

426

environmental problems and policies. we solicit ads, often as an exchange.

PEACE NEWS "For Nonviolent Revolution", Peace News Ltd, Ken Simons, 55 Dawes Street, London SE17 1EL, England, 071-703 7189. 1936. Poetry, articles, art, photos, cartoons, interviews, criticism, reviews, letters, news items, non-fiction. "London office: 5 Caledonian Road, London N1,Great Britain, 01-837 9795." circ. 4M. 12/yr. Pub'd 17 issues 1990; expects 13 issues 1991, 12 issues 1992. sub. price: inland £6, seamail £8, airmail £9; per copy: 50p; sample: free. Back issues: 50p inc p&p. Discounts: 10% agencies, airmail subs; 15% agencies, surface subs; 33⅓% bookshops, surface mail. 12pp; size A3; of. Payment: material costs to graphic artists. Copyrighted, reverts to author. Pub's reviews: 60 in 1990. §Health, conservation, alternatives, feminism, third world, politics. Ads: £113/£56.52/7p(min. £1.60). UAPS(E).

Peace News Ltd (see also PEACE NEWS "For Nonviolent Revolution"), Ken Simons, 55 Dawes Street, London SE17 1EL, England, 071-703 7189. 1936. Poetry, articles, art, photos, cartoons, interviews, criticism, reviews, letters, news items, non-fiction. avg. press run 4.5M. Pub'd 1 title 1990; expects 1 title 1991, 1 title 1992. avg. price, paper: £1-50. Discounts: 33⅓% trade. 32pp; of. Payment: non-profit, no percentage.

THE PEACE NEWSLETTER, Syracuse Peace Council, JoAnn Stak, Coordinator, 924 Burnet Avenue, Syracuse, NY 13203, 315-472-5478. 1936. Poetry, articles, art, photos, cartoons, interviews, satire, criticism, reviews, music, letters, collages, news items, non-fiction. "For people in Central or Upstate NY *THE PEACE NEWSLETTER* is invaluable as a source for news and events of the movement for peace and justice. For others, it can provide continuing examples of how one community attempts to combine theory with practice. In other words, it is a 'journal of local activism' with a liberationist, nonviolent slant! *THE PEACE NEWSLETTER* is strident in its pursuit of truth and fact, but it is not an adherent to the myth of 'objective' journalism." circ. 5M. 12/yr. Pub'd 11 issues 1990; expects 11 issues 1991, 11 issues 1992. sub. price: $10; per copy: $.75; sample: 50¢. Back issues: $.75 each. Discounts: 10 or more $.25 each plus shipping. 20pp; 8×11; of. Payment: none. Not copyrighted. Pub's reviews: 10 in 1990. §Peace, social justice. Ads: $120/$65/free, mostly local. APS, API.

Peaceable Kingdom Press, Olivia Hurd, Thacher Hurd, 2980 College Avenue #2, Berkeley, CA 94705, (415) 654-9989. 1983. Art. "We publish quality posters: reproductions from great children's book illustrations; also, a line of greeting cards by top illustrators of children's books" avg. press run 5M-10M. Pub'd 8 titles 1990; expects 30 titles 1991, 35 titles 1992. 3 titles listed in the *Small Press Record of Books in Print* (20th Edition, 1991-92). avg. price, other: posters $8.95, cards $1.25. Discounts: 50% wholesale. 18×24; †photo lithography. Payment: 2x yearly. Copyrights for author. ABA, American Bookseller's for Children.

PEACEWORK, Pat Farren, 2161 Massachusetts Avenue, Cambridge, MA 02140, 617-661-6130. 1972. Articles, photos, cartoons. "*PEACEWORK* is a New England Peace and Social Justice Newsletter." circ. 2.5M. 11/yr. Pub'd 11 issues 1990; expects 11 issues 1991, 11 issues 1992. sub. price: $8 by third class mail, $12 by first class mail; per copy: 60¢; sample: free. 16pp; 8½×11; desktop. Reporting time: 2 weeks - 1 month. Payment: free subscription. Not copyrighted. Pub's reviews: 9 in 1990. §Peace and social justice. Paid advertising not accepted.

Peachpit Press, Inc., Ted Nace, 1085 Keith Avenue, Berkeley, CA 94708, 415-527-8555. 1987. Non-fiction. avg. press run 10M. Pub'd 2 titles 1990; expects 8 titles 1991. 14 titles listed in the *Small Press Record of Books in Print* (20th Edition, 1991-92). avg. price, paper: $22.95. 350pp; 7×9; web press. Copyrights for author. NADTP.

Peachtree Publishers, Ltd., Margaret Quinlin, Executive Editor, 494 Armour Circle NE, Atlanta, GA 30324, 404-876-8761. 1977. Non-fiction. "Peachtree Publishers, Ltd. is interested in quality non-fiction. To submit a manuscript, send an outline and sample chapters, along with biographical information on the author and a SASE large enough to hold the material. Please mark to the attention of the Editorial Dept." avg. press run 5M-25M. Pub'd 15 titles 1990; expects 17 titles 1991, 19 titles 1992. avg. price, cloth: $17.95; paper: $7.95. Discounts: retail: 1-4 20%, 5-10 40%, 11-24 42%, 25-49 43%, 50-199 44%, 200-499 45%, 500+ 46%; jobbers: 50% on 50 or more assorted. 250pp; size varies; of. Reporting time: 12-16 weeks. Payment: individual basis subject to contractual terms. Copyrights for author. Publishers Association of the South (PAS), Little Rock, AR; Southeastern Booksellers Assn. (SEBA), Nashville, TN; American Booksellers Assn. (ABA), New York, NY; Publishers Publicity Assn. (PPA), New York, NY; Georgia Publishers Assn. (GPA), Atlanta, GA.

Peacock Books, Bibhu Padhi, Minakshi Padhi, College Square, Cuttack , Orissa 753003, India, 0671-22733. 1988. Poetry, long-poems. "We are a non-profit publishing house dedicated to contemporary poetry in English and in translation. We intend to produce 3-4 titles per year—our first book, *Magic Places* by Margaret Cook, is scheduled to appear in January 1990. All our titles will be handset, printed on a hand-operated letterpress, and individually sewn and bound by hand, using low-acid-content paper for the text pages and (in most cases) handmade paper for the cover and inner pages. Since we do not receive assistance of any kind from a funding agency, we ask our authors to partially defray a part of the expenses by buying at least 100 copies (but no more than 150 copies) of their book at 30% of the list price (we pay for the postage-surface mail). We do not ask for a straight subsidy. We've published poemcards and broadsides (although for the time being, these are by invitation only), and would be interested in chapbooks of 16-32 pages (preferably, long poems and poem cycles). We've published Naomi Shihab Nye, William Stafford, Mike Shields, Jayanta Mahapatra, among others. At this time, we are interested in 2-3 good mss from writers who haven't had a book published yet, but who have had some magazine publication.'' avg. press run 400. Expects 3 titles 1991, 3 titles 1992. 1 title listed in the *Small Press Record of Books in Print* (20th Edition, 1991-92). avg. price, cloth: $18; paper: $12; other: $1 broadside, $3 pack of 10 poemcards. Discounts: trade 40% 10+ copies, bulk 60%, classroom 30%, in every case postpaid, surface mail. 64-80pp; 5½×8½; lp. Reporting time: 6 weeks. Payment: 10% of the edition in copies. Copyrights for author. Association of Little Presses (London).

Peak Output Unlimited (see also THE APPLE BLOSSOM CONNECTION), Mary M. Blake, Jacquelyn D. Scheneman, PO Box 325, Stacyville, IA 50476, 515-737-2269. 1987. Poetry, fiction, articles, art, cartoons, interviews, reviews, plays, news items, non-fiction. "Anthologies, genealogies, saddle-stapled or perfectbound. Individual co-op plan authors—different degrees of help in advertising, marketing, distribution according to author's budget desires. Poetry collections, fiction or non-fiction work considered; royalties.'' avg. press run 100-10M. Pub'd 1 title 1990; expects 3 titles 1991, 6 Books; Periodical 12 titles 1992. 7 titles listed in the *Small Press Record of Books in Print* (20th Edition, 1991-92). avg. price, other: prices vary. Discounts: available on request plus SASE. Poetry 44-96pp; 5½×8½; †of. Reporting time: 4-6 weeks. Payment: varies, advances to $1,000, royalties to 10% on retail price. Copyrights for author. Mid-America Publishers Association.

PEARL, Pearl Editions, Joan Jobe Smith, Marilyn Johnson, Barbara Hauk, 3030 E. Second Street, Long Beach, CA 90803, 213-434-4523. 1987. Poetry, fiction, art, cartoons. "We are interested in accessible, humanistic poetry and short fiction that communicates and is related to real life. Humor and wit are welcome, along with the ironic and serious. No taboos stylistically or subject-wise. Prefer poems up to 35 lines and short stories up to 1200 words. Our purpose is to provide a forum for lively, readable poetry and prose that reflects a wide variety of contemporary voices, viewpoints, and experiences and that speaks to *real* people about *real* life in direct, living language, from the profane to the sublime. Have recently published poetry by Michael C. Ford, Ann Menebroker, Robert Peters, Linda King, Bill Shields, Laurel Ann Bogen.'' circ. 500. 2/yr. Pub'd 3 issues 1990; expects 2 issues 1991, 2 issues 1992. sub. price: $10; per copy: $5; sample: $5. 72pp; 5½×8½; of. Reporting time: 6-8 weeks. Payment: 2 copies. Copyrighted, reverts to author.

Pearl Editions (see also PEARL), Joan Jobe Smith, Marilyn Johnson, Barbara Hauk, 3030 E. Second Street, Long Beach, CA 90803, 213-434-4523. 1989. "Currently only publish winner of our annual chapbook contest.'' avg. press run 300. Pub'd 1 title 1990; expects 1 title 1991, 1 title 1992. 2 titles listed in the *Small Press Record of Books in Print* (20th Edition, 1991-92). avg. price, paper: $5. 24pp; 5½×8½; of. Copyrights for author.

Pearl-Win Publishing Co., Barbara Fitz Vroman, PO Box 300, Hancock, WI 54943, 715-249-5407. 1980. Poetry, fiction, non-fiction. "We are not enouraging submissions at this time since we have a backlog of good material.'' avg. press run 3M. Pub'd 2 titles 1990; expects 2 titles 1991. 7 titles listed in the *Small Press Record of Books in Print* (20th Edition, 1991-92). avg. price, cloth: $13.95; paper: $9.95. Discounts: 40% trade; 20% libraries. Poetry 64pp, prose 250pp; 6×9; of. Reporting time: reasonable. Payment: 10% hard, 7½ paper. Copyrights for author. WAPA, Wis. Authors and Publishers Assoc, Wild Rose, WI.

Peavine Publications, William P. Lowry, Box 1264, McMinnville, OR 97128, 503-472-1933. 1987. Non-fiction. "Specialty: a) weather & climate from the ecological perspective—mostly textboks; b) 'philosophical' works concerning atmospheric ecology.'' avg. press run 1M. Pub'd 1 title 1990; expects 1 title 1991, 1 title 1992. 1 title listed in the *Small Press Record of Books in Print* (20th Edition, 1991-92). avg. price, paper: $26-$32. Discounts: 20% to academic bookstores and suppliers. 250-350pp; 6×9. Reporting time: 2 months, please write/call first. Payment: each project negotiated. Copyrights for author. NW Assoc. of Book Publishers (NWABP), Salem and Portland, OR.

‡**PEBBLE**, Greg Kuzma, Department of English, University of Nebraska-Lincoln, Lincoln, NE 68588, 402-826-4038. Poetry. circ. 400. 1 issue every 18 months. Pub'd 1 issue 1990. sub. price: $15/4 issues; per copy: $4; sample: available-free. Back issues: issues 1-10, complete, price on request. 150pp; 4×7; of. Reporting time: variable. Payment: 4 copies. Copyrighted. Pub's reviews.

Pebble Press, Robert Piepenburg, 1313 N. Main Street, Ann Arbor, MI 48104-1044, 313-665-7119. 1990. Art, photos. avg. press run 4M. Expects 1 title 1991, 1 title 1992. 1 title listed in the *Small Press Record of Books in Print* (20th Edition, 1991-92). avg. price, paper: $24.95. Discounts: 40%. 160pp; 8×11; †of. Reporting time: 2 months. Payment: t.b.a. Copyrights for author.

Pebbles (see also The Broken Stone), d steven conkle, annabel conkle, PO Box 246, Reynoldsburg, OH 43068. 1984. Poetry. "We are an imprint of *The Broken Stone*, and potential contributors should read the information under that listing. Our only bias is one in favor of high quality. Material submitted should fit attractively onto a 15¢ or 25¢ postcard since that's what we publish. Recent contributors include Taelen Thomas and Arthur Winfield Knight. We also do some contract advertising. One good way to approach us is to enter our poemcard contest. Send SASE for guidelines'' avg. press run 300. Pub'd 2 titles 1990; expects 5 titles 1991, 5 titles 1992. avg. price, other: $1 poemcards. Discounts: negotiable. 1 page; size varies; of. Reporting time: varies wildly. Payment: percentage of copies. Copyrights for author. COSMEP.

Peccary Press, W. David Laird, Editor; Mark Sanders, Editor, Box 40850 Sun Station, Tucson, AZ 85717. 1977. Fiction, non-fiction. avg. press run 200. Pub'd 1 title 1990; expects 1 title 1991, 1 title 1992. 3 titles listed in the *Small Press Record of Books in Print* (20th Edition, 1991-92). avg. price, cloth: $40; paper: $20. Discounts: 20% for 5 or more copies. 40pp; size varies; †of. Reporting time: 3 months. Payment: varies. Copyrights for author.

PECKERWOOD, Ernie Ourique, Ibi Kaslik, 1503-1465 Lawrence Avenue West, Toronto, Ont. M6L 1B2, Canada, 416-248-2675. 1987. Poetry, fiction, articles, art, cartoons, satire, criticism, letters, parts-of-novels, long-poems, collages, non-fiction. "Submissions can be any length and style. *Peckerwood* has no guidelines or deadlines for any submissions. It isn't, however, a forum for different points of view. If you choose to make political comments or allusions in your work then we have to agree with those views. The best poetry is always a-political and that's what we favour. *Peckerwood* hates pornography, ugly laughter, the boss, television house-wives. Lately we've published John Bennett, Chris Wood, Jonathan Levant, Ray Gam. We'd love to receive more artwork or writings from people who would rather express themselves through music. 'Everything is writing; that is to say a fable' Cortazar." circ. 200. 3/yr. Pub'd 3 issues 1990; expects 3 issues 1991, 3 issues 1992. sub. price: $2; per copy: 50¢; sample: $1. Back issues: $1. Discounts: none. 30pp; 7×8½; †mi. Reporting time: it all depends on your postal service, we're fast. Payment: 5 copies of mag and lots of praise. Copyrighted, reverts to author. Ads: none.

Pedagogic Press, 317 S. Division, Suite 92, Ann Arbor, MI 48104, 313-668-4948. 1988. Fiction, non-fiction. "Production and publishing of educational materials, training manuals, newsletters, conference packets and small run books. Primarily focus on the education market, although also do some work for governmental agencies. Most publications are manuals to accompany services rendered by educational consultants, and we are interested in talking with anyone who may have a manuscript of this type, although they must currently be actively engaged in a consulting practice that utilizes the materials. We are also interested in multicultural gender fair children's books. Prospective authors should send a letter of interest, *not* a manuscript, along with a SASE." avg. press run varies. Pub'd 2 titles 1990. avg. price, other: $20. Discounts: none. 150pp; 8½×11; of, photocopy/spiral. Reporting time: varies. Payment: negotiable. Does not copyright for author. National Association for Desktop Publishing (NADTP).

PEDESTRIAN RESEARCH, L. Wilensky, Century Village, Dorchester Bldg A, Apt. 12A, West Palm Beach, FL 33417. 1973. "Biased viewpoint serving the pedestrian needs, interests, planning, protection, mobility, image, and long range welfare and *pedestrian environmental* viewpoint." circ. 500. 4/yr. Pub'd 4 issues 1990; expects 4 issues 1991, 4 issues 1992. sub. price: $5 membership includes subscription, foreign $8; per copy: $1.50 specific; sample: $1. Back issues: $1.50 past year, $3 more than a year old (reproductions xerox). Discounts: 25% on more than 5 issues sent to one address. 4pp; 8½×11; of. Reporting time: 1 month. Payment: optional. Not copyrighted. Pub's reviews: optional in 1990. §Pedestrian environment, pedestrians, pedestrian ideas, ecology, pedestrian viewpoints, pedestrian needs, interests, pedestrianism & environment, pedestrian mobility, traffic, and planning for pedestrians, encroachments on pedestrians. No ads. APA.

PEDIATRIC MENTAL HEALTH, Pat Azarnoff, Editor, Pediatric Projects Inc., PO Box 571555, Tarzana, CA 91357, 818-705-3660. 1981. Articles, interviews, reviews, news items, non-fiction. "*Pediatric Mental Health* has brief articles about the uses of play therapy, psychological preparation, and parent support for children in health care. In each issue we publish a full page bibliography on a psychosocial theme. We also note new books in child mental health, pediatric psychology, and health education." circ. 1.5M. 6/yr. Pub'd 6 issues 1990; expects 6 issues 1991, 6 issues 1992. sub. price: $28 US, $32 all other countries; per copy: $5; sample: $5. Back issues: $3 (also by theme, Vol. 1 & 2: $8). Discounts: 10% to agent, 10% classroom bulk rate. 8pp; 8½×11; †of. Reporting time: 4 weeks. Payment: copies only. Copyrighted, reverts to author. Pub's reviews: 18 in 1990. §Pediatric psychology, child mental health, parenting of handicapped children, play therapy, child psychiatry. No ads. COSMEP, NAA.

Pedicard Press, Archer D. Crosley, 14305 Indian Woods, San Antonio, TX 78249-2047, 512-492-2045; FAX 800-443-9636. Discounts: 60% on all orders.

T.H. Peek, Publisher, T.H. Peek, PO Box 50123, Palo Alto, CA 94303, 415-962-1010. 1966. "Our market is primarily for college textbooks. These sometimes go into AP or 12th grade high school. Some of the anthropology/art history are suitable for the trade market but our marketing is all geared for the textbook market (including college and university libraries)" avg. press run 5M. Pub'd 2 titles 1990; expects 3-4 titles 1991. avg. price, paper: $12.95. Discounts: text-20% 20%; some titles are sold at Trade: 20%, 33⅓%, 40%. 240pp; 8×11 or 7¼×10. Reporting time: 1 month. Payment: twice yearly. Copyrights for author. Book Builders West.

Peel Productions, Susan Joyce, Doug DuBosque, PO Box 185, Molalla, OR 97038-0185, 503-829-6849. 5

titles listed in the *Small Press Record of Books in Print* (20th Edition, 1991-92).

PEGASUS, M.E. Hildebrand, Pegasus Publishing, 525 Avenue B, Boulder City, NV 89005. 1986. Poetry. circ. 200. 4/yr. Pub'd 4 issues 1990; expects 4 issues 1991, 4 issues 1992. sub. price: $12.50, int'l add $5 postage; per copy: $4.50 includes postage; sample: $4.50 includes postage. Back issues: $4.50 includes postage. 32pp; 5½x8½; of. Reporting time: 2 weeks. Payment: publication. Copyrighted, reverts to author. §Poetry publishing. COSMEP.

THE PEGASUS REVIEW, Art Bounds, PO Box 134, Flanders, NJ 07836, 201-927-0749. 1980. Poetry, fiction, art, cartoons, satire. "Magazine done in calligraphy, illustrated and each issue based on a specific theme. Projected themes for 1991-1992: January/February - Courage, March/April - Dreams, May/June - Friends, July/Aug - America, September/October - Autumn, November/December - Christmas. Themes may be approached by means of poetry (not more than 24 lines), fiction (short, short), essays and cartoons. A SASE a must! Submissions should not be limited to one. Generally, returned material will be commented on. Recommend purchasing a sample copy to understand format. Upon publication each contributor will receive two (2) copies. Occasional book awards throughout the year. Since the Directory runs from 1990-91 it might be suggested that contributors inquire as to our upcoming themes. However, for 1991 I have tentatively come up with the following: January/February-Beginnings, March/April-Language, May/June-Parents, July/August-Children, September/October-God, November/December-Memories." circ. 180. 6/yr. Pub'd 6 issues 1990; expects 6 issues 1991, 6 occasional special issue issues 1992. sub. price: $7; per copy: $2; sample: $2. Back issues: $2. 10-12pp; 6½x8½; of. Reporting time: 3-4 weeks. Payment: 2 copies and additional book awards (throughout year). Copyrighted, reverts to author.

Pella Publishing Co (see also THE CHARIOTEER; JOURNAL OF THE HELLENIC DIASPORA), Leandros Papathanasiou, Publisher, President, 337 West 36th Street, New York, NY 10018, 212-279-9586. 1976. Poetry, fiction, articles, art, criticism, reviews, letters, plays. "We are interested in Modern Greek studies and culture, but also have a general list composed of new fiction and poetry by young writers and books on contemporary society and politics. We also publish books on the work of young artists." avg. press run 3M. Pub'd 4 titles 1990; expects 10 titles 1991, 10 titles 1992. 26 titles listed in the *Small Press Record of Books in Print* (20th Edition, 1991-92). avg. price, cloth: $25; paper: $12; other: $12. Discounts: Jobbers-30%; Bookstores-20%. 176pp; 5½x8½; †lp. Reporting time: 4-6 weeks. Payment: standard royalty arrangements. Copyrights for author. COSMEP.

PELTEX, Model-Peltex Association, Dominique LeBlanc, 3 Rue Des Couples, 67000 Strasbourg, France. Articles, art, photos, interviews, criticism, reviews, music, letters. 12/yr. Pub'd 9 issues 1990; expects 12 issues 1991, 12 issues 1992. sub. price: 50FF; per copy: 4FF. 4pp; size A4; †xerox, of. Payment: none. Copyrighted, reverts to author. Pub's reviews. §Graphismes, art (clivers), all kinds of zines and videos. Ads: 400FF/250FF.

PEMBROKE MAGAZINE, Shelby Stephenson, Editor; Norman Macleod, Founding Editor, PO Box 60, PSU, Pembroke, NC 28372, 919-521-4214 ext 433. 1969. Poetry, fiction, articles, art, photos, criticism, reviews. "Felix Pollak, Fred Chappell, A.R. Ammons, Betty Adcock, Robert Morgan, Barbara Guest, Fleda Jackson, Judson Crews, Reinhold Grimm, Leo Romero, Ronald H. Bayes." circ. 500. 1/yr. Pub'd 2 issues 1990; expects 1 issue 1991. sub. price: $5/yr, another $3 for supplementary issue, if published; per copy: $5 (overseas $5.50); sample: $5. Discounts: 40% bookstores. 200pp; 6x9; of. Reporting time: 1-4 months. Payment: copy. Copyrighted, rights revert to author, except for right of editor to reprint the magazine and to issue a PM anthology. Pub's reviews: 6 in 1990. §Native American poetry and novels. Ads: $40/$25. CCLM, COSMEP.

Pen & Ink Press, PO Box 235, Wicomico Church, VA 22579. 1980. avg. press run 3M. Pub'd 1 title 1990; expects 1 title 1992. 3 titles listed in the *Small Press Record of Books in Print* (20th Edition, 1991-92). avg. price, paper: $10. Discounts: 50% to distributors taking 20 or more copies; 40%-19 copies or less. 9x6. Payment: author/publisher.

PENCOM Press, 511 16th Street, Suite 630, Denver, CO 80202, 303-595-3991. 1 title listed in the *Small Press Record of Books in Print* (20th Edition, 1991-92).

Pendaya Publications, Inc., Earl J. Mathes, Manager, 510 Woodvine Avenue, Metairie, LA 70005, 504-834-8151. 1987. Non-fiction. "Design, construction, criticism" avg. press run 2M-3M. Pub'd 1 title 1990; expects 2 titles 1991, 2 titles 1992. 1 title listed in the *Small Press Record of Books in Print* (20th Edition, 1991-92). avg. price, cloth: $50. Discounts: upon individual request. 175pp; 8½x11; of. Reporting time: varies 2-3 months. Payment: varies. Does not copyright for author.

Pen-Dec Press (see also THE ESCHEW OBFUSCATION REVIEW), Jim DeWitt, 3922 Monte Carlo, Kentwood, MI 49512, 616-942-0056. 1978. Poetry, art, photos, cartoons, satire, reviews. avg. press run 50. Pub'd 3 titles 1990; expects 3 titles 1991, 3 titles 1992. 19 titles listed in the *Small Press Record of Books in Print* (20th Edition, 1991-92). avg. price, paper: $2.95 both mag and chapbooks. Discounts: to be arranged.

430

36pp; 6×8½; †copier. Reporting time: 1 month. Payment: to be arranged. Does not copyright for author.

Penfield Press, Joan Liffring-Zug, 215 Brown Street, Iowa City, IA 52245-1358. 1979. Photos, non-fiction. avg. press run 5M-10M. Pub'd 5 titles 1990; expects 6 titles 1991, 4 titles 1992. 40 titles listed in the *Small Press Record of Books in Print* (20th Edition, 1991-92). avg. price, cloth: $18.50; paper: $6.50-$8.95. Discounts: trade 40%, jobbers 60%. 88pp; 6×9; of. Payment: varies, usually 5%. Copyrights for author.

PENGUIN DIP, Stephen H. Dorneman, 94 Eastern Avenue #1, Malden, MA 02148. 1987. Articles, art, cartoons, interviews, criticism, reviews, letters. "Science fiction and adventure gaming fanzine, with a section devoted to the play of postal diplomacy" circ. 125. 10/yr. Pub'd 10 issues 1990; expects 10 issues 1991, 10 issues 1992. sub. price: $15; per copy: $1.50; sample: $1.50. 16pp; 8½×11; photocopy of Laserprint originals. Reporting time: 2-4 weeks. Payment: subscription credit. Copyrighted, rights revert only if requested. Pub's reviews: 8 in 1990. §Science fiction and fantasy, science fact, adventure gaming books and games. Ads: $50/$35/$20 1/4 page.

PENINHAND, Peninhand Press, Tom Janisse, Tom Smario, Laura Winter, PO Box 82699, Portland, OR 97282. 1990. Poetry, art, interviews. "We publish only unpublished poems read at poetry readings in Portland, Oregon for a local and Northwest audience" circ. 500. 2/yr. Expects 2 issues 1991, 2 issues 1992. sub. price: $2; per copy: $1; sample: $1. Discounts: 1-4 25%, 5+ 40%. 30pp; 5½×8½; of. Reporting time: 2 weeks-2 months. Payment: copies. Copyrighted, reverts to author. CCLM.

Peninhand Press (see also THE VOLCANO REVIEW; PENINHAND), Thomas Janisse, 3665 Southeast Tolman, Portland, OR 97202. 1979. Poetry, fiction, art, interviews, parts-of-novels. "We publish poetry, fiction & art both national & international. No unsolicited manuscripts at this time" avg. press run 500. Expects 2 titles 1991, 2 titles 1992. 2 titles listed in the *Small Press Record of Books in Print* (20th Edition, 1991-92). avg. price, paper: $1-$6 single issue. Discounts: 1-4 25%, 5 and over 40%. 30-104pp; 5½×8½; of. Reporting time: 2 weeks to 2 months. Payment: copies. Does not copyright for author. CCLM.

PENNINE PLATFORM, Brian Merrikin Hill, Ingmanthorpe Hall Farm Cottage, Wetherby, West Yorks LS22 5EQ, England, 0937-584674. 1966. Poetry, articles, art, photos, criticism, reviews. "The magazine is supported by the Yorkshire Arts Association. Tries to keep a high standard, both in poetry & art. Copyrighted for contributors who retain copyright." circ. 450. 3/yr. Pub'd 3 issues 1990; expects 3 issues 1991. sub. price: £5.40 UK, £9 abroad if in sterling, £12 abroad if in currency, £20 if by check not in sterling; per copy: £1.50; sample: £1.50. Back issues: £1. Discounts: trade for books in bulk less 30%. 32-36pp; 6×8¼; of. Reporting time: varies. Payment: none. Copyrighted. Pub's reviews: 10 in 1990. §Poetry. Ads: £10.

PENNSYLVANIA PORTFOLIO, Anthony Arms, Dauphin County Library System, 101 Walnut Street, Harrisburg, PA 17101, 717-234-4961. 1983. Articles, cartoons, interviews, criticism, reviews. "All articles, etc., are limited to native Pennsylvania authors, books about Pennsylvania, Pennsylvania libraries and presses that are out of the ordinary; cartoons and verse generally are about libraries." 2/yr. Pub'd 2 issues 1990; expects 2 issues 1991, 2 issues 1992. sub. price: $9; per copy: $4.50; sample: $4.50. Back issues: #1-12 or after #1 is o.o.p., #2-13 offered for $30. Discounts: $3 per copy. 32pp; 8½×11; of. Reporting time: usually within 2 weeks. Payment: all contributors, which include professional writers, college professors and artists donate their work as a contribution to Dauphin County Library System. Copyrighted, permission given if credited. Pub's reviews: 17 in 1990. §Native Pennsylvania authors or books about Pennsylvania or some aspect of Pennsylvania. Ads: $250.

THE PENNSYLVANIA REVIEW, Ed Ochester, Executive Editor; Lori Jakiela, Editor, English Department, 526 C. L., University of Pittsburgh, Pittsburgh, PA 15260. 1984. Poetry, fiction, articles, interviews, criticism, reviews, parts-of-novels, long-poems, non-fiction. "Superb quality overrides any other consideration. Contributors have included Tracy Kidder, Walter McDonald, Gordon Lish, Maxine Kumin, Philip Dacey, Linda Pastan, Maggie Anderson, Leslie Adrienne Miller, William Heyen, Dorothy Barresi, Stuart Friebert, Carol Lee Lorenzo, Sharon Doubiago" circ. 1M. 2/yr. Pub'd 2 issues 1990; expects 1 issue 1991, 2 issues 1992. sub. price: $10; per copy: $5; sample: $5. Back issues: $2.50. Discounts: 40% off retail sales price. 128pp; 7×10; of. Reporting time: 3 months. Payment: copies. Copyrighted, reverts to author. Pub's reviews: 6 in 1990. §Poetry, fiction, nonfiction. Ads: $125/$70/$40. CCLM.

Pennsylvania State University Press (see also SHAW. THE ANNUAL OF BERNARD SHAW STUDIES), Fred D. Crawford, Department of English, Central Michigan University, Mt. Pleasant, MI 48858, 517-774-3171. 1951. Articles. avg. press run 2M. Pub'd 1 title 1990; expects 1 title 1991, 1 title 1992. avg. price, cloth: $35; other: $35. Discounts: short-20%. 265pp; 6×9; of. Reporting time: 2 months. Payment: direct, $25 or $50 depending on length. Copyrights for author in name of publisher. AAUP.

PENNSYLVANIA'S LITERARY NETWORK NEWSLETTER, 1204 Walnut Street, Philadelphia, PA 19107. 1988. Articles, interviews, news items. "All writers wishing to submit must contact the All Muse Coordinator first. Articles should be less than 1,000 words. Article topics include: profiles of Pennsylvania authors, small presses, literary magazines, writers and other literary organizations, and issues relevant to the Pennsylvania literary community. *The Newsletter* is one part of the All Muse Network and serves to promote Pennsylvania authors, literature and literary events in Pennsylvania. It is a free publication funded by the Pennsylvania Council on the Arts, with 140,000 copies distributed throughout the state at the following locations: public libraries, college and university libraries, English departments and creative writing programs, public schools, reading series, and literary conferences. Notable statewide literary events, grants information, a listing of Pennsylvania Journals and Magazines, and articles of interest to the literary community appear in each issue. Literary presenters wishing to be listed in the *Newsletter* should contact the All Muse Coordinator or Correspondent in their area. Please send for submission form and guidelines." circ. 140M. 2/yr. Pub'd 2 issues 1990; expects 2 issues 1991, 2 issues 1992. sub. price: free; per copy: free; sample: free. Back issues: free, limited to stock. 32pp; 11¼×17; †of. Reporting time: 6 months. Payment: none. Copyrighted, reverts to author. Pub's reviews: 70 in 1990. §Pennsylvania-born or -based authors of fiction or poetry, literary magazines and journals based in Pennsylvania. Ads: $500 1/2 page/$150 1/4/$50 business card.

Pennypress, Inc., Penny Simkin, 1100 23rd Avenue East, Seattle, WA 98112, 206-325-1419. 1977. Non-fiction. "Publisher of books and pamphlets on childbirth and parenting" avg. press run 3M books, 10M pamphlets. Pub'd 1-2 titles 1990; expects 1-3 titles 1991, 1-3 titles 1992. 6 titles listed in the *Small Press Record of Books in Print* (20th Edition, 1991-92). avg. price, paper: $8.95; other: pamphlets 25¢. Discounts: 1-4 20%, 5 or more 40%. 4-100pp; 5×8, 6×9, 8½×11 (books), 8½×11 (pamphlets); of. Reporting time: 0-6 months. Payment: 10% of net paid quarterly. Does not copyright for author. COSMEP.

PENNYWHISTLE PEOPLE PAPER, Pennywhistle Press, Victor di Suvero, Box 734, Tesuque, NM 87574, 505-982-2622. 1986. Poetry. circ. 3M. Pub'd 1 issue 1990. sub. price: free. 16pp; 11×17; of. Payment: none. Copyrighted, reverts to author. Pub's reviews: 12 in 1990. Rocky Mountain Publishers Association.

Pennywhistle Press (see also PENNYWHISTLE PEOPLE PAPER), Victor di Suvero, Box 734, Tesuque, NM 87574, 505-982-2622. 1986. Poetry, long-poems. "Pennywhistle Chapbook Series: This new series of perfect-bound chapbooks are 32 pages in length. Pennywhistle Chapbooks celebrate the diversity and excellence of contemporary poetry. Published in the first set of six chapbooks in 1989 are: Jerome Rothenberg, Richard Silberg, Sarah Blake, Viola Weinberg, Jorge H.-Aigla, and Phyllis Stowell. The Second Series, scheduled for publication in May, 1991, will feature Dennis Brutus, Jack Marshall, Francisco X. Alarcon, Edith Jenkins, Joyce Jenkins, Suzanne Lummis and Judyth Hill. The Chapbook Series prefers to publish *either* long poems or coherent *series* of poems suitable for the chapbook format. Other full-length Pennywhistle books include poetry by James Broughton and Victor diSuvero. Forthcoming titles include an *Alan Watts Miscellany* and various other titles in literature and health." avg. press run 1.5M. Pub'd 6 titles 1990; expects 12 titles 1991, 18 titles 1992. 11 titles listed in the *Small Press Record of Books in Print* (20th Edition, 1991-92). avg. price, paper: $4-$10. Discounts: 2-4 20%, 5-24 40%, 25-49 43%, 50-99 46%, 100+ 50%; bookstores 60/40; distributors 50-55%, schools 20%. 32-250pp; 5¼×8⅜; of. Reporting time: 8-12 weeks. Payment: chapbooks—$100 royalty paid, author gets 50 books; other books by arrangement/contract with author. Copyrights for author. NPA, NPW, Rocky Mountain Publishers Association.

Pentagram Press, Michael Tarachow, 212 North Second Street, Minneapolis, MN 55401, 612-340-9821. 1974. Poetry, fiction, art, long-poems. "No unsolicited manuscripts." avg. press run 3-223. Pub'd 1 title 1990; expects 2 titles 1991, 1 title 1992. 16 titles listed in the *Small Press Record of Books in Print* (20th Edition, 1991-92). avg. price, cloth: $95-$350; paper: $20-$85. 1-132pp; size varies; †lp. Payment: varies. Does not copyright for author. APHA, N.Y. Typophiles, Ampersand Club.

PEN:UMBRA, David Rushmer, 1 Beeches Close, Saffron Walden Essex CB11 4BU, England. 1989. Poetry, fiction, art, parts-of-novels, long-poems, collages, concrete art, non-fiction. "Particularly interested in contemporary french literature and its influence on British and American writers. Also eroticism, extreme works." 1-2/yr. Pub'd 2 issues 1990; expects 1 issue 1991. price per copy: $5; sample: $5. Discounts: standard at 33%. 32-52pp; size A5; photocopy. Reporting time: approximately 1 month. Payment: 1 copy of magazine. Copyrighted. ALP.

The Penumbra Press, Bonnie P. O'Connell, G.A. O'Connell, 920 S. 38th Street, Omaha, NE 68105, 402-346-7344. 1971. Poetry, fiction, art, photos, collages. "Editions usually number 200-250 copies. All releases are hand printed from hand-set type. Most editions are casebound, some come out in paperback. Recent: *Counting the Days* Jon Anderson, *Stepping Outside* by Tess Gallagher, *Sleeping On Doors* by Steven Orlen, *The Prayers Of The North American Martyrs* by Norman Dubie, *Anxiety And Ashes* by Laura Jensen, *Dear Anyone* by William Keens. We also publish *'The Manila Series',* pamphlets in which each release is housed in a manila envelope. Latest titles: *Keeping The Night* by Peter Everwine, *Ten Poems* by Rita Dove,which is Number 4 in the Manila Series. *Good Evening and other poems* by Abigail Luttinger, and *Cartography* by Debora Greger, *Coffee, 3 a.m.* by Brenda Hillman. *The Man In The Yellow Gloves* by David St. John. Forthcoming: *Hearts, Fourteen Works in the Spirit of the Valentine, Brittle Water* by Sam Pereira" avg. press run 200-300. Pub'd 1 title 1990; expects 3 titles 1991, 3 titles 1992. 6 titles listed in the *Small Press*

Record of Books in Print (20th Edition, 1991-92). avg. price, cloth: $25-$50; paper: $15-$25. Discounts: 30% on individual standing orders, 30% to dealers who place a standing order for 5 copies of each release. 25% on dealers' orders of 5 or more copies of a single title. 35pp; size varies; †lp. Reporting time: 2 weeks to 2 months. Payment: 10% of the edition. Copyrights for author.

Penumbra Publishing Co., Ruth Moore, Editor, PO Box 781681, Dallas, TX 75378-1681, 214-351-1726. 1986. Fiction, non-fiction. avg. press run 2M. Pub'd 1 title 1990; expects 1 title 1991, 1 title 1992. 1 title listed in the *Small Press Record of Books in Print* (20th Edition, 1991-92). avg. price, paper: $8.95. Discounts: usual. 200pp; 5¼×8¼; lp. Reporting time: 4-6 months. Payment: negotiable. Copyrights for author. Texas Publishers Association.

PEOPLE'S CULTURE, Fred Whitehead, Box 5224, Kansas City, KS 66119. 1991. "This is in newsletter format. A continuation of publication edited by John Crawford, same title, New Series, #1 (January-February 1991), etc. Recent contributors include Crawford, Meridel LeSueur, Lyle Daggett, Robert Day. Dedicated to excavating and developing progressive, radical, socialist and communist culture, in the U.S. and internationally. Each issue includes a feature on 'An American Place' usually a historic site, monument, mural painting, etc." circ. growing. 6/yr. Expects 6 issues 1991, 6 issues 1992. sub. price: $15; per copy: $3; sample: $3. Back issues: $3. 8-12pp; 8½×11; photocopy (good quality). Reporting time: 1 week. Payment: copies. Copyrighted, reverts to author. Pub's reviews. §Poetry, history (esp. documentation), cultural theory, art, music, etc.

People's Publishing Co., Inc. (see also WESTERN & EASTERN TREASURES), Rosemary Anderson, 5440 Ericson Way, PO Box 1095, Arcata, CA 95521, 707-822-8442. 1988. Non-fiction. "Treasure-related non-fiction, how-to, ghost towns." avg. press run 3M. Expects 2 titles 1991, 2 titles 1992. 2 titles listed in the *Small Press Record of Books in Print* (20th Edition, 1991-92). avg. price, paper: $7.95. Discounts: trade, bulk, wholesale, special sales—vary depending on quantity and terms. 160pp; 7×10; of. Reporting time: 2 months. Payment: by contract. Copyrights for author.

Pepper Publishing, Peggy Lockard, President, 433 North Tucson Boulevard, Tucson, AZ 85716, 602-881-0783. 1973. avg. press run 3M. Pub'd 1 title 1990; expects 3 titles 1991. 8 titles listed in the *Small Press Record of Books in Print* (20th Edition, 1991-92). avg. price, cloth: $19.95; paper: $17.35. Discounts: textbooks, videotapes 20%, tradebooks 1-4 20%, 5-99 49%, 100+ 45%. 210pp; 11×8½. Rocky Mountain Book Publishers, Tucson Book Publishing Association, Publishers Marketing Association.

Pequod Press, Rlene H. Dahlberg, 344 Third Ave, Apt 3A, New York, NY 10010, 212-686-4789. 1977. Poetry, fiction, criticism. "At this point, the pieces must be fairly short, 9-12 pp. I intend to do fine press work, limited editions with original illustrations (100 copies) & offset trade edition (250-300 copies). At this point, I have all submissions for the next few years." avg. press run 350-400. Pub'd 1 title 1990. 13 titles listed in the *Small Press Record of Books in Print* (20th Edition, 1991-92). avg. price, paper: $6; other: $15. Discounts: 40% to trade. 16pp; 5×8½; †of, lp. Payment: 25 copies (later, hopefully, 10%). Does not copyright for author.

PERCEPTIONS, Temi Rose, 1317 South Johnson Street, Missoula, MT 59801-4805, 406-543-5875. 1982. Poetry, art, cartoons. "We have international contributions. Primarily women's poetry: Doreen Cristo, Patricia Roth Schwartz, Bulbul, Zana." circ. 100. 3/yr. Pub'd 3 issues 1990; expects 3 issues 1991, 3 issues 1992. sub. price: $10; per copy: $3; sample: $3. Back issues: $5. Discounts: trade - 15% to seller. 28pp; 4¼×5½; xerox. Reporting time: 1-3 months. Payment: 1 copy. Copyrighted, reverts to author.

PEREGRINE, Amherst Writers & Artists Press, Inc., PO Box 1076, Amherst, MA 01004. 1983. Poetry, fiction. "We are looking for poetry and fiction that seems to us to be fresh, imaginative, and human. Recent contributors published in *Peregrine*: Robert Long, Margaret Robison, Doug Anderson, Barbara Van Noord, Carol Edelstein, Peggy Roggenbnck Gillespie. Our staff is volunteer and funds are limited, therefore only patient writers need send work. We encourage multiple submissions." circ. 500. 1-2/yr (occasional). Pub'd 2 issues 1990; expects 2 issues 1991, ? issues 1992. price per copy: $4.50; sample: $4.50 postpaid. Back issues: $3. Discounts: 40%. 70pp; 5½×8; of. Payment: copy. Copyrighted, reverts to author. Ads: $100 full. Amherst Writers and Artists Press Inc.

Pergot Press, Margot S. Biestman, Publisher, 1001 Bridgeway, Suite 227, Sausalito, CA 94965, 415-332-0279. 1986. Non-fiction. "No unsolicited manuscripts. We are interested in publishing works which demonstrate application of Creative Behavior Process in every day home and professional life; for professionals, para-professionals, lay persons, children. Recent contribution: *Travel for Two: The Art of Compromise*." avg. press run 2M. Expects 2 titles 1991, 3 titles 1992. 1 title listed in the *Small Press Record of Books in Print* (20th Edition, 1991-92). avg. price, paper: $10.95. Discounts: 2-4 20%, 5-9 30%, 10-24 40%, 200 50%. 180pp; 6×9; of. Reporting time: 4 weeks. Does not copyright for author. COSMEP, MSPA (Drawer 1346, Ross, CA 94957), PMA.

A PERIODIC JOURNAL OF 'PATAPHYSICAL SUCCULENTOSOPHY, Xexoxial Endarchy, Amendant Hardiker, Glim Pechulia, 1341 Williamson, Madison, WI 53703, 608-258-1305. 1987. "Combining the science of imaginary solutions with the cult of growing unusual plants; the sense of precision, observation and science combined with the absurd and the unknown. Seeking submissions of relevant material: articles, poems, reviews, photos, graphics, letters, diagrams, and contact info and resources" circ. 200. 2/yr. Pub'd 2 issues 1990; expects 2 issues 1991, 2 issues 1992. sample price: $3.50, $5 overseas + $1 p/h. Discounts: 20% bookstores if $100+ ordered. 36pp; 5½×8½; †xerox. Reporting time: 1 month. Payment: 2 copies. Not copyrighted. Pub's reviews. No ads.

Perivale Press, Lawrence P. Spingarn, 13830 Erwin Street, Van Nuys, CA 91401-2914, 818-785-4671. 1968. Poetry, fiction, criticism, non-fiction. "We specialize in translations from foreign poetry by individuals or regional-national groups and in anthologies. Small editions (750-1,000 copies) from 40 pp to 230 pp. Recently published: *Poets West,* edited by L.P. Spingarn. *The Epigrams Of Martial, Tr.* by Richard O'Connell. *Not-So-Simple Neil Simon* by Edythe M. McGovern. *Birds of Prey* by Joyce Mansour. *Tr.* by Albert Herzing" avg. press run 1M. Pub'd 3 titles 1990; expects 3 titles 1991, 2 titles 1992. 19 titles listed in the *Small Press Record of Books in Print* (20th Edition, 1991-92). avg. price, cloth: $10; paper: $5. Discounts: 40% trade, 10% institution, 10% student, 20% teachers. 100pp; 5½×8½; of. Reporting time: 3 months. Payment: 10%-15% royalty, sliding. Will copyright for author if author pays fee.

The Permanent Press/The Second Chance Press, Martin Shepard, Judith Shepard, RD 2, Noyac Road, Sag Harbor, NY 11963, 516-725-1101. 1979. Fiction, satire, news items. "We publish original material and specialize in quality fiction." avg. press run 2M. Expects 12 titles 1991, 12 titles 1992. 70 titles listed in the *Small Press Record of Books in Print* (20th Edition, 1991-92). avg. price, cloth: $21.95; paper: $15.95. Discounts: 20-50%. 250pp; 5½×8½; lp. Reporting time: 8-12 weeks. Payment: 10% net, small standard advances, for all writers. Copyrights for author. ABA.

Permeable Press (see also DIGIT; PUCK!), Brian Clark, Kurt Putnam, 47 Noe Street, Suite 6, San Francisco, CA 94114-1017, 415-978-9759. 1984. Poetry, fiction. "Currently publishing Hugh Fox's novel *Shaman.* Ongoing project: *Digit Magazine*" avg. press run 5M. Pub'd 1 title 1990; expects 1 title 1991, 3 titles 1992. avg. price, paper: $10. Discounts: 40%. 200pp; 6×9; †of. Reporting time: 2 months. Payment: varies. Copyrights for author.

Perseverance Press, Meredith Phillips, PO Box 384, Menlo Park, CA 94026, 415-323-5572. 1979. Fiction. "Perseverance Press is interested in seeing mystery manuscripts of the old-fashioned sort; e.g. whodunits, puzzlers, village cozies, others without excessive gore and gratuitous violence. No exploitive or violent sex. Think Christie, Tey, Sayers, Cross, James, Kallen, Radley, Brett, Yorke, Millar, Block's burglar series, etc. (If you're not familiar with their work, we're probably not on the same wave length). Manuscripts should be 50M-80M words. Sometimes comments on rejected manuscripts" avg. press run 2M. Pub'd 2 titles 1990; expects 2 titles 1991, 2 titles 1992. 9 titles listed in the *Small Press Record of Books in Print* (20th Edition, 1991-92). avg. price, paper: $8.95. Discounts: 20% library; 40% trade (more for bulk); 50% wholesale (10+). 200pp; 5½×8½; of. Reporting time: 3 months. Payment: 10% of net receipts. Copyrights for author. COSMEP, PP, MWA.

Persistence Press, Kurt W. Schlicht, 4734 Wentworth Blvd., Indianapolis, IN 46201, 317-357-9071. 1983. Fiction, non-fiction. "Prefer contemporary artists and writers; short stories, original graphic artwork and photography, statements on nature and the environment, historical notes, humor and personal reminiscences. I solicit manuscripts. All subjects considered." avg. press run 100-200. Expects 3 titles 1991, 5 titles 1992. 6 titles listed in the *Small Press Record of Books in Print* (20th Edition, 1991-92). avg. price, other: $15-$25. Discounts: 30% on ten or more copies. 20pp; 6×9; †lp. Reporting time: 10 days. Payment: share of the edition (usually 40%). Does not copyright for author.

Persona Publications, #1-3661 West 4th Avenue, Vancouver B.C., V6R 1P2, Canada, 604-731-9168. 1984. Music, non-fiction. Pub'd 1 title 1990; expects 2 titles 1991, 4 titles 1992. 2 titles listed in the *Small Press Record of Books in Print* (20th Edition, 1991-92). avg. price, paper: $15.95. Discounts: 3 or more 40%; 50% for orders in case lots (36) or more; wholesalers/distributors 60%. 294pp; 6×9.

Personabooks, Pat Shell, 2054 University Avenue, Suite 502, Berkeley, CA 94704. 1976. Plays. "I also use expository and descriptive material, appropriate for textbooks." avg. press run 1M. Expects 1 title 1991, 1 title 1992. 7 titles listed in the *Small Press Record of Books in Print* (20th Edition, 1991-92). avg. price, paper: $8.50. 100pp; 7×10, 6×9; of. Reporting time: 1 month. Payment: by agreement. Copyrights for author.

Personal Efficiency Programs, Inc., Frank L. Christ, President; Alice Amlin, Vice-President of Publications, PO Box 249, Sierra Vista, AZ 85636-0249, 213-596-5242. 1981. Non-fiction. avg. press run 5M. Expects 1 title 1991, 3 titles 1992. 1 title listed in the *Small Press Record of Books in Print* (20th Edition, 1991-92). avg. price, paper: $19.95. Discounts: net to education; varies according to distributor. 200pp; 8½×11; lp. Reporting time: 30 days. Payment: negotiable. Does not copyright for author. PMA.

THE PERSONAL MAGNETISM HOME STUDY COURSE ON ALL HUMAN POWERS, Gil Magno,

434

2870 Pine Tree Drive, Suite F2, Miami Beach, FL 33140, 305-538-8427. 1985. Non-fiction. "These lessons are published at the rate of two per month. They are revisions and expansions of the works of Webster Edgerly on self-improvement, personal magnetism and psychic practicalism. We accept no articles." circ. 603. 24/yr. Pub'd 24 issues 1990; expects 24 issues 1991, 24 issues 1992. sub. price: $120/1 yr, $60/6 months, $30/3 months; per copy: $5; sample: $5. Back issues: $5. 44pp; 8½×11; of. Copyrighted. Pub's reviews: 3 in 1990. §Self-improvement, how-to, occult, psychic, mysticism, magnetism. No ads yet.

PERSONAL PUBLISHING, Terry Ulick, 21W550 Geneva, Wheaton, IL 60188-2279, (312) 250-8900. 1983. "Cover desktop publishing area" circ. 30M. 12/yr. Pub'd 12 issues 1990; expects 12 issues 1991, 12 issues 1992. sub. price: $30; per copy: $3; sample: same. Back issues: $3. Discounts: 50%. 104pp; 8⅛×10⅞. Reporting time: 2 months. Copyrighted. Pub's reviews. Ads: $1180/$612/ b/w. COSMEP, BPA.

Perspectives Press, Patricia Irwin Johnston, PO Box 90318, Indianapolis, IN 46290-0318, 317-872-3055. 1982. Fiction, articles, plays, non-fiction. "Established to create materials related to adoption infertility, and foster care" avg. press run 2M-5M. Pub'd 2 titles 1990; expects 2 titles 1991, 2 titles 1992. 11 titles listed in the *Small Press Record of Books in Print* (20th Edition, 1991-92). avg. price, cloth: $14.95; paper: $8.95. Discounts: 0-50%, begins at 2 copies with 25%. Adult 144pp, children 32-160pp; 6×9, 5½×8½. Reporting time: query, 1 month. Payment: varies. Copyrights for author. PMA, ABA, MAPA, Assa Booksellers Children.

Pessimism Press, Inc. (see also THE NIHILISTIC REVIEW), Maxwell Gaddis, Executive Editor, PO Box 1074, S. Sioux City, NE 68776, 402-494-3110. 1990. Poetry, fiction, satire, criticism, reviews, parts-of-novels, plays, non-fiction. "Would like to see experimental erotica, poetry, short stories. Anything in the Kerouac, Bukowski or Burroughs vein. If we can't help you, there is a good chance we can refer your work to someone that can." avg. press run 1M. Expects 1 title 1991. avg. price, paper: $6. 160pp; 4×6½. Reporting time: 1 month. Payment: 10% to author. Copyrights for author.

Peter Lang Publishing, Inc., Brigitte D. McDonald, Managing Editor; Michael Flamini, Editor; Heidi Burns, Editor; Thomas Derdak, Editor, 62 West 45 Street, New York, NY 10036, 212-302-6740. 1982. "We publish highly specialized non-fiction monographs, critical editions, and reference books in the humanities and social sciences. Proposals and completed manuscripts are welcome (minimum 200 pages)." avg. press run 500. Pub'd 200 titles 1990; expects 250 titles 1991, 275 titles 1992. 38 titles listed in the *Small Press Record of Books in Print* (20th Edition, 1991-92). avg. price, cloth: $35; paper: $20. Discounts: upon request. 250pp; 6×9, 6×8¾; †typeset or laserset. Reporting time: 2 months. Payment: varies acc. to contrast. Copyrights for author. Society for Scholarly Publishing International Association of Scholarly Publsing.

Peter Pauper Press, Inc., Nick Beilenson, Evelyn Beilenson, 202 Mamaroneck Avenue, White Plains, NY 10601, 914-681-0144. 1928. Fiction, non-fiction. "64 pages. Interested in humor, holiday, inspirational, general gift. No fiction." avg. press run 7M. Pub'd 10 titles 1990; expects 12 titles 1991, 14 titles 1992. 27 titles listed in the *Small Press Record of Books in Print* (20th Edition, 1991-92). avg. price, cloth: $6.95. Discounts: trade 40-50%. 64pp; 4¼×7¼; of. Reporting time: 2 weeks. Payment: buy ms outright. Sometimes copyrights for author.

The Petrarch Press, Peter Bishop, 133 West 72nd Street #703, New York, NY 10023, 212-362-7668. 1985. Poetry, non-fiction. "The Petrarch Press specializes in publishing fine press books, using handpresses and quality papers. Literature that is deemed appropriate for the medium is considered. Our interests are diverse; the first two books from the press are 1800 years apart in the time of their writing, (the apostle Thomas and R.M. Rilke). Thus far I have not been looking at submitted mss." avg. press run 175. Pub'd 1 title 1990; expects 3 titles 1991, 5 titles 1992. 4 titles listed in the *Small Press Record of Books in Print* (20th Edition, 1991-92). avg. price, cloth: $150. Discounts: varies. 65pp; 6¼×9½; †lp. Payment: varies. Does not copyright for author. COSMEP, PO Box 703, San Francisco, CA 94101.

Petroglyph Press, Ltd., 201 Kinoole Street, Hilo, HI 96720, 808-935-6006. 1962. Non-fiction. avg. press run 2M. Expects 2 titles 1992. avg. price, paper: $4.95. Discounts: 40% trade, 50% jobber, 55% 500+ books. 90pp; 5½×8½; †of. Payment: 10% author, 5% illustrator; paid quarterly. Does not copyright for author.

PETROLEUM NEWS: Asia's Energy Journal, Petroleum News Southeast Asia Ltd., Michael Morrow, Publisher; Managing Editor, 146 Prince Edward Road, West, 6th Floor, Kowloon, Hong Kong, 3-805294, 3-803029, 3-805794. 1969. circ. 7.5M. 12/yr. Pub'd 12 issues 1990; expects 12 issues 1991, 12 issues 1992. sub. price: US $100 (Asia), US $175 (elsewhere); per copy: US $12; sample: same. Discounts: 10% agency. 60pp; 8×11; of. Ads: $1925 col $1455 B/W/$1010 col $840 B/W.

Petroleum News Southeast Asia Ltd. (see also PETROLEUM NEWS: Asia's Energy Journal; ENERGY ASIA), Michael Morrow, 146 Prince Edward Road, West, 6th Floor, Kowloon, Hong Kong, 3-805294, 3-803029, 3-805794. 1969. Articles, photos, interviews, news items, non-fiction.

Petronium Press, Frank Stewart, 1255 Nuuanu Avenue, #1813, Honolulu, HI 96817. 1975. Poetry, fiction, long-poems. "Publications to date include signed, limited-edition broadsides and portfolios of Gardner,

Stafford, Logan, Denney, Merwin; books by Schmitz, Hoge, Edel, Quagliano, McPherson, Hindley, Honma, Matsueda, Hawaii's Asian-American writers and others.'' avg. press run 1M. Pub'd 2 titles 1990; expects 2 titles 1991, 6 titles 1992. 20 titles listed in the *Small Press Record of Books in Print* (20th Edition, 1991-92). avg. price, cloth: $14; paper: $6; other: $4. Discounts: 40% to the trade. Pages vary; 5½×7½; of, lp. Reporting time: 1-6 weeks. Payment: copies.

PF Publications, Fay A. Daley, PO Box 6202, Lindenhurst, IL 60046, 708-356-0625. 1990. Poetry, art, non-fiction. "We publish materials primarily for women who choose to work in the home, home-based business women, who want to remain the primary caregivers for their children. We are conservative and do not deal with satire. Additional address: 21545 W. Brentwood, Lake Villa, IL 60046." avg. press run 5M. Expects 1 title 1991, 1 title 1992. 1 title listed in the *Small Press Record of Books in Print* (20th Edition, 1991-92). avg. price, paper: $12.95. 160pp; 8½×11; of. Reporting time: 2 months. Payment: negotiable. Copyrights for author.

Pfeifer-Hamilton, Donald A. Tubesing, Nancy Loving Tubesing, 1702 E. Jefferson Street, Duluth, MN 55812, (218) 728-6807. 1977. Non-fiction. "A division of Whole Person Press. *Regional books:* 'How-to', geography, guide books, essays and stories, field guide in upper Midwest USA." avg. press run 10M. Pub'd 3 titles 1990; expects 3 titles 1991. 6 titles listed in the *Small Press Record of Books in Print* (20th Edition, 1991-92). avg. price, cloth: $16.95; paper: $12.95. Discounts: normal book trade conventions. 192pp; 6×9; web. Reporting time: 2 weeks. Payment: varies. Copyrights for author. PMA, Mid America Publishers, ABA, Minnesota Independent Publishers.

P-FORM, D. Travers Scott, Managing Editor, 756 N. Milwaukee Avenue, Chicago, IL 60622, 312-666-7737. 1986. Poetry, fiction, articles, art, photos, interviews, satire, criticism, reviews, concrete art, news items, non-fiction. *"P-Form* is dedicated to exploration and discussion of performance art, in its many forms, as well as the culture that generates it. Recent contributors have included Frank Moore, Carole Tormollan, Gary Indiana, Joanna Frueh, Dominique Dibbell, Lonnette Stonitsch, Jennifer Fink... Reviews should be 500 words, features not over 2,400. Experimental critical forms are encouraged" circ. 1M. 4/yr. Pub'd 4 issues 1990; expects 4 issues 1991, 4 issues 1992. sub. price: $10; per copy: $2.50; sample: $2.50. Back issues: $3 for available issues. 32pp; 9×11. Reporting time: varies. Payment: none as yet. Copyrighted, reverts to author. Pub's reviews. §Performance art, experimental dance/theatre, alternative art forms. Ads: $110/$55.

PF$ Publications, PO Box 9852, Bakersfield, CA 93309-9852, 805-834-3901. 1989. 1 title listed in the *Small Press Record of Books in Print* (20th Edition, 1991-92).

Phanes Press, David R. Fideler, PO Box 6114, Grand Rapids, MI 49516, 616-281-1224. 1985. Non-fiction. "Phanes Press publishes reprints and contemporary studies relating to the Western spiritual traditions of Neoplatonism, Gnosticism, Alchemy and Traditional Cosmology. We are interested in receiving original studies as well as translations. If contributors want their material returned they should enclose a SASE." avg. press run 3M. Pub'd 7 titles 1990; expects 15 titles 1991, 15 titles 1992. 21 titles listed in the *Small Press Record of Books in Print* (20th Edition, 1991-92). avg. price, cloth: $25; paper: $12.50. Discounts: Trade: 5 copies or more, less 40%; colleges: less 30%. 125pp; 6×9, 5½×8½, 5×7; of. Reporting time: 4 weeks, enclose SASE. Copyrights for author. COSMEP.

PHASE AND CYCLE, Phase and Cycle Press, Loy Banks, 3537 East Prospect, Fort Collins, CO 80525, 303-482-7573. 1988. Poetry. "We prefer poems of moderate length. We are looking for quality poems of all kinds and especially those that set out 'the long perspectives open at each instance' (Larkin)." circ. 200. 2/yr. Pub'd 2 issues 1990; expects 2 issues 1991, 2 issues 1992. sub. price: $5; per copy: $2.50; sample: $2.50. 52pp; 5½×8½; †photocopy. Reporting time: 5-10 weeks. Payment: 2 copies. Copyrighted, reverts to author.

Phase and Cycle Press (see also PHASE AND CYCLE), Loy Banks, 3537 East Prospect, Fort Collins, CO 80525. 1989. Poetry. "We are accepting inquiries only at present. No manuscripts. Our first publication is a poetry chapbook, *Breathing In The World,* by Bruce Holland Rogers and Holly Arrow. Second chapbook is *Out of Darkness,* by Mary Balazs." avg. press run 300. Pub'd 1 title 1990; expects 1 title 1991, 1 or 2 titles 1992. 2 titles listed in the *Small Press Record of Books in Print* (20th Edition, 1991-92). avg. price, paper: $4. 32-56pp; 5½×8½, 6×8½; †photocopy. Copyrights for author.

PHILATELIC LITERATURE NEWS INTERNATIONAL, Corn Nieuwland, Brandespad 14, NL-3067 EB Rotterdam, Holland. 1991. Reviews, news items. circ. 300. 4/yr. Pub'd 5 issues 1990; expects 4 issues 1991, 4 issues 1992. sub. price: $6 surface, $10 air; sample: $2. 12-16pp; size A5; †photostat. Not copyrighted. Pub's reviews: 600 in 1990. §Exclusively philatelic publications, press releases, etc.

Phillips Publications, Inc., Jim Phillips, PO Box 168, Williamstown, NJ 08094, 609-567-0695. 1972. Photos, news items. "Information and items needed for forthcoming books on WW II U.S. Airborne uniforms and equipment book, and U.S. Special Forces book, espionage cameras book" avg. press run 500-5M. Pub'd 1 title 1990; expects 3 titles 1991, 3 titles 1992. 3 titles listed in the *Small Press Record of Books in Print* (20th Edition, 1991-92). avg. price, cloth: $19.95; paper: $7.95. Discounts: 40%, 3 or more 20% single title.

35-400pp; 6×9; †of. Reporting time: 1 month. Payment: 20% after publication & ad costs. Copyrights for author.

Philmar Press, Margaret W. Baeuder, PO Box 402, Diablo, CA 94528-0402, 415-837-3490. 1982. Fiction, cartoons. avg. press run 1M. avg. price, paper: $6. 53pp; 5×8½. Reporting time: 3 months. Copyrights for author. NWC.

Philomel Books, Patricia Lee Gauch, Editor-in-Chief; Paula Wiseman, Senior Editor, 200 Madison, New York, NY 10016. 1980. Poetry, fiction, non-fiction. "We are a hardcover children's trade book list. Our primary emphasis is on picturebooks, with a growing list of middle-grade and young adult novels. We publish a small amount of poetry. We look for fresh and innovative books imbued with a child's spirit and crafted with fine writing and art. Recent selections include *Anno's Math Games* by Mitsumasa Anno, *Owl Lake* by Tejima, *Redwall* by Brian Jacques, and *Miracle at Clement's Pond* by Patricia Pendergraft" avg. press run 5M-10M. Pub'd 25 titles 1990; expects 30 titles 1991, 30 titles 1992. avg. price, cloth: $13.95. Novels 200pp, picturebooks 32pp; size varies. Reporting time: 1 month on queries, 3 months on manuscripts. Payment: varies. Copyrights for author.

PHILOSOPHY AND THE ARTS, Philosophy and the Arts Press, Daniel Manesse, Editor, PO Box 431, Jerome Avenue Station, Bronx, NY 10468. 1975. Poetry, fiction, articles, reviews, parts-of-novels, news items, non-fiction. "We are interested in articles of a page or two in length on anything pertaining to the life and work of Bertrand Russell. We are also interested in articles on philosophy and religion, holocaust" 1/yr. Pub'd 1 issue 1990; expects 3 issues 1991. sub. price: $2.98; per copy: $2.98; sample: $2.98. Back issues: $2 per copy. Discounts: none. 25pp; 8½×11; of. Reporting time: 1 week. Payment: copies of the magazine. Copyrighted, reverts to author. Pub's reviews: 2 in 1990. §Books about Bertrand Russell, philosophy, religion. Ads: $100/$50.

Philosophy and the Arts Press (see also PHILOSOPHY AND THE ARTS), Daniel Manesse, Editor, PO Box 431, Jerome Avenue Station, Bronx, NY 10468. 1975. 3 titles listed in the *Small Press Record of Books in Print* (20th Edition, 1991-92). avg. price, paper: $2.98. Discounts: 50% stores. 40pp; 8½×11; of. Reporting time: 2 weeks. Payment: with copies. Copyrights for author.

The Phlebas Press, Roderick Muncey, 2 The Stables, High Park, Oxenholme, Kendal, Cumbria LA9 7RE, United Kingdom. 1990. Poetry. *"Please write first* before submitting any manuscripts (limited activity at present). 1 booklet published so far, *Tors* by Norman Jope" avg. press run flexible. Pub'd 1 title 1990; expects 2 titles 1991, 3 titles 1992. avg. price, other: chapbook, around $5. Discounts: trade 33½% (minimum order 10, sent surface mail). 40pp; 8½×6. Reporting time: 8 weeks from date of receipt. Payment: author purchases and distributes copies. Copyrights for author.

PHOEBE, THE GEORGE MASON REVIEW, Rex Batson, Editor, G.M.U. 4400 University Dr., Fairfax, VA 22030, 703-323-3730. 1970. Poetry, fiction, photos, plays. "We are interested in publishing a wide diversity of poetry and fiction. Additionally, we now accept non-fiction, preferably personal and/or experimental." circ. 3.5M. 2/yr. Pub'd 2 issues 1990; expects 2 issues 1991, 2 issues 1992. sub. price: $8; per copy: $4.50; sample: $3.25. Back issues: $2. 80pp; 6×9; of. Payment: copies only. Copyrighted, reverts to author. COSMEP.

PHOENIX BROADSHEETS, New Broom Private Press, Toni Savage, Esq., 78 Cambridge Street, Leicester LE3 0JP, England, 547419. 1972. Poetry, art, long-poems. "Sheets are free, from the above address S.A.E. New Broom Private Press has a series of poems-sheets-finely illustrated. S.A.E. for samples. Nos. 1-350 issues, some handcoloured. Poetry mainly, sometimes excerpts from plays. Poets include: Brian Patten, Spike Milligan, Sue Mackrell, Charles Causley, Arthur Caddick, Edward Murch. Artists: Rigby Graham, Hans Erni, Toni Savage, Robert Tilling. American Poets: Jane Lord Bradbury, Gina Bergamino, Paul Humphrey, C.J. Stevens. We publish 10-15 sheets a year." circ. 2-300. Pub'd 12 issues 1990; expects 12 issues 1991, 12-15 issues 1992. sub. price: free plus postage; per copy: free plus postage; sample: free plus postage. 1 page; 9×5 approx.; †lp. Payment: copies only. Copyrighted.

Phoenix Publishing, Carol A. Vanetta, 12811 52nd Place West, Mukilteo, WA 98275-3053. 1986. Non-fiction. avg. press run 3M. Expects 2 titles 1991, 2 titles 1992. 2 titles listed in the *Small Press Record of Books in Print* (20th Edition, 1991-92). avg. price, paper: $7.95. Discounts: 3-49 40%, 50-199 45%, 200-499 50%, 500+ 40%-25%. 150pp; 5½×8½; of. Reporting time: 30 days. Payment: special arrangement. Copyrights for author. Publishers Marketing Association, Sigma Delta Chi—Society for Professional Journalists, Women in Communications.

Phoenix Publishing Inc., Douglas A. Brown, PO Box 10, Custer, WA 98240, 206-467-8219. 1969. Non-fiction. "Authors must write first before submitting manuscripts" avg. press run 10M. Pub'd 3 titles 1990; expects 3 titles 1991, 3 titles 1992. avg. price, cloth: $16.95; paper: $9.95. Discounts: 1-4 20%; 5-49 40%; 50-99 42%; 100+ 44%. 275pp; 5½×8½; of. Reporting time: 10 days. Payment: usually 10%, quarterly.

Copyrights for author if desired. COSMEP, PASCAL.

PHOTOBULLETIN, PhotoSource International, Lori Johnson, Editor, PhotoSource International, Pine Lake Farm, Osceola, WI 54020, (715) 248-3800, Our Fax# 715-248-7394. 1985. Photos, reviews, news items. *"Photobulletin* lists major book publishers and magazines." circ. 172. 52/yr. Pub'd 50 issues 1990; expects 50 issues 1991, 50 issues 1992. sub. price: $510; per copy: $11 (facimile); sample: $3. 3pp; 8½×11; of. Reporting time: 1 week. Payment: 25¢ per word. Copyrighted. No ads.

The Photographic Arts Center, Ltd., Robert S. Persky, 163 Amsterdam Avenue, New York, NY 10023, 212-838-8640. 1983. "Our orientation is information concerning fine art photography and picture resources. We do not publish books of pictures. Titles of general interest to artists are also considered—e.g. *The Artist's Guide To Getting/Having A Successful Exhibition."* avg. press run 5M. Pub'd 3 titles 1990; expects 7 titles 1991, 7 titles 1992. 16 titles listed in the *Small Press Record of Books in Print* (20th Edition, 1991-92). avg. price, cloth: $29.95; paper: $24.95. Discounts: 40% all categories on multiple orders only, 35% on stop orders, 30% on single orders. 125-400pp; 5×8, 8½×11. Reporting time: 30 days. Payment: varies with estimated market for book and production costs. Copyrights for author. COSMEP, PMA, The Small Press Center.

PHOTOGRAPHY IN NEW YORK, Bill Mindlin, PO Box 20351, Park West Station, New York, NY 10025, 212-787-0401. 1988. Articles, photos, interviews, reviews, news items. *"Photography in New York* is a bimonthly pocket guide to current gallery and museum exhibitions, private dealers, booksellers, classes, workshops and events of interest to the photographic community." circ. 7M. 6/yr. Pub'd 6 issues 1990; expects 6 issues 1991, 6 issues 1992. sub. price: $2.95; sample: $2.95. Discounts: returnable: 40% (min. 10), nonreturnable: (min 10) 49%. 72pp; 3⅞×9; †of. Reporting time: 5 weeks. Payment: to be determined. Copyrighted, does not revert to author. Pub's reviews. §Photography. Ads: $495/$295/$175 1/4; discounts for contrasts.

Photography Research Institute Carson Endowment, Thomas I. Perrett, 21237 S. Moneta Avenue, Carson, CA 90745. 1970. Non-fiction. "Also publishes Blue Book of Photography Prices ISSN (0738-8322)." avg. press run 20M. Pub'd 2 titles 1990; expects 4 titles 1991, 6 titles 1992. 8 titles listed in the *Small Press Record of Books in Print* (20th Edition, 1991-92). avg. price, paper: $29.95; other: $39.95 deluxe edition. Discounts: 5-10 20%, 11-24 40%, 25-49 43%, 50-99 46%, 100+ 50%. 255pp; 5¼×8; †of. Reporting time: 2-3 months. Payment: 8% of net. Copyrights for author.

THE PHOTOLETTER, PhotoSource International, Lynette Layer, Editor, PhotoSource International, Pine Lake Farm, Osceola, WI 54020, (715) 248-3800, Our Fax # 715-248-7394. 1976. Photos, reviews, news items. *"The Photoletter* is a photo marketing newsletter (monthly) which pairs picture buyers with photographers." circ. 1.4M. 12/yr. Pub'd 12 issues 1990; expects 12 issues 1991, 12 issues 1992. sub. price: $90; per copy: $9; sample: $9. Back issues: $3 each; 4 for $10. 3pp; 8½×11; of. Reporting time: 1 week. Payment: 15¢ word. Copyrighted. Pub's reviews: 2-3 in 1990. §Photography. Ads: inserts 10¢ each. Newsletter Association of America.

PHOTOMARKET, PhotoSource International, Lori Johnson, Editor, PhotoSource International, Pine Lake Farm, Osceola, WI 54020, (715) 248-3800, Our Fax # 715-248-7394. 1984. Photos, reviews, news items. *"Photomarket* lists mid-size book and magazine publishers." circ. 523. 22/yr. Pub'd 22 issues 1990; expects 22 issues 1991, 22 issues 1992. sub. price: $330; per copy: $15 (facimile); sample: $3. 3pp; 8½×11; of. Reporting time: 1 week. Payment: 20¢ per word. Copyrighted. No ads.

PhotoSource International (see also THE PHOTOLETTER; PHOTOMARKET; PHOTOBULLETIN), Lori Johnson, Editor; Lynette Layer, Editor, Pine Lake Farm, Osceola, WI 54020, 715-248-3800, Fax 715-248-7394. 1976. "We list the photo needs of book publishers, magazines, ad agencies and audio visual firms, corporations." avg. price, other: $5. 8½×11; of. Reporting time: 1 week.

Phrygian Press (see also ZYX), Arnold Skemer, James Goldberg, 58-09 205th Street, Bayside, NY 11364. 1984. Fiction. "Our publications are chracterized by surrealism, satire, irony, misanthropy, black humor and a piquant nihilism. There is a strong political element, not neccessarily of the right, nor of the left, but reflecting fiction grounded in man's political nature and history. Our first publication is Arnold Skemer's *The Famine*, a nightmarish novel of an India rocked by natural disaster and swept inexorably towards social disintegration and thermonuclear annihilation. Those who savor black humor will find it enrapturing, filled as it is with brutal misanthropy and heartless ironies. "Reminds me of Desnos in his apocalyptic vein": J.H. Matthews, world authority on surrealism. "Remarkable for the pitch of awe, hopelessness and degradation it sustains. Like the paintings of Hieronymous Bosch and the Book of Revelation, Skemer's work is the product of an imagination affected by mythic and Christian symbolism of the end of the world": The Small Press Book Review. "A remarkable first novel for anyone interested in India or apocalyptic visions": Merritt Clifton, Small Press Review. Do no send any unsolicited manuscripts. Do not query. We are now totally committed to future projects and cannot contemplate taking on anything new." avg. press run 1M. Expects 2 titles 1992. 1 title listed in the *Small Press Record of Books in Print* (20th Edition, 1991-92). avg. price, paper: $6.95. Discounts:

libraries and institutions 20%; wholesalers and bookstores 1-4 20%, 5 or more 40%. No discount on orders not paid in 30 days. 108pp; 5½x8½; of. Reporting time: with blinding speed. Payment: negotiable. Copyrights for author.

Piccadilly Books, Bruce Fife, PO Box 25203, Colorado Springs, CO 80936, 719-548-1844. 1985. Photos, cartoons, reviews. avg. press run 3M. Pub'd 3 titles 1990; expects 3 titles 1991, 3 titles 1992. 8 titles listed in the *Small Press Record of Books in Print* (20th Edition, 1991-92). avg. price, paper: $11. Discounts: 2-5 20%, 6-49 40%, 50-99 45%, 100-99-50%, 200+ 55%. 150pp; 8½x5½, 8½x11; of. Reporting time: 6 weeks. Payment: negotiable. Copyrights for author. PMA, COSMEP.

Piccolo Press, Elizabeth Nichols, 6844 Raven Crest, Colorado Springs, CO 80919, 719-598-4587. 1982. Poetry, music. avg. press run 250. Expects 1 title 1991, 1 title 1992. 2 titles listed in the *Small Press Record of Books in Print* (20th Edition, 1991-92). avg. price, other: $4 broadsides. American Pen Women.

Vernon W. Pickering-Laurel Publications International (see also MYCOPHILATELY), Vernon W. Pickering, Giorgio Migliavacca, PO Box 704, Road Town-Tortola, British Virgin Islands. 1983. "Philately, Postal History, History of the Caribbean, Caribbeana in general, History" Pub'd 3 titles 1990; expects 4 titles 1991, 4 titles 1992. 9 titles listed in the *Small Press Record of Books in Print* (20th Edition, 1991-92). avg. price, cloth: $15; paper: $10. Discounts: 30-40%. 100pp; of. Reporting time: 1 month. Payment: yes. Copyrights for author.

Pickle Point Publishing, Bonnie Stewart Mickelson, PO Box 4107, Bellevue, WA 98009, 206-462-6105. 1988. "Cookbooks" avg. press run 15M. Expects 1 title 1991, 2 titles 1992. avg. price, cloth: $23.95; paper: $16.95. Discounts: retail 40%, schedule adjusted to quantity. 220pp. Reporting time: varies. Payment: negotiated. Copyrights for author. PMA—Hermosa Beach, CA; NWABP—Marylhurst, OR; BPNW—Seattle, WA.

PIEDMONT LITERARY REVIEW, Gail White, Poetry Editor; Olga Kronmeyer, Fiction Editor; Dorothy McLaughlin, Oriental Verse Editor; Evelyn Miles, Managing Editor, RD 1, Box 512, Forest, VA 24551. 1976. Poetry, fiction, articles, photos, satire, criticism, reviews, long-poems, non-fiction. "All poetry forms and some...short prose as short stories. Cater to good taste, no overt sex. s.s. to 2,500 words." circ. 400. 4/yr. Pub'd 4 issues 1990; expects 4 issues 1991, 4 issues 1992. sub. price: $12, includes Piedmont Literary Society Membership & Newsletter; per copy: $3; sample: $3. Back issues: $2 per(donation). 60pp; 5x8; of. Reporting time: 8-12 weeks. Payment: copies. Copyrighted, reverts to author. Pub's reviews: 12 in 1990. §Poetry. Piedmont Literary Society.

Pierian Press (see also REFERENCE SERVICES REVIEW; SERIALS REVIEW), PO Box 1808, Ann Arbor, MI 48106.

PIG IN A PAMPHLET, Pig In A Poke Press, Harry Calhoun, 331 Ridge Point Circle #14, Bridgeville, PA 15017-1530. 1982. Poetry, fiction, articles, art, interviews, satire, criticism. "Looking for poetry, short fiction, short articles, reviews and commentary. Striving for emotional intensity coupled with coherency. Prosepoems OK; clipped prose thinly disguised as poetry, no. Editor will not confuse disjointed wailing and babbling for 'emotional poetry.' Don't mind rhyme if done well; looking for artwork (easily reproducible) also. We publish reviews of books and magazines, but please query first. Contributors have included Ann Menebroker, Gerald Costanzo, Katharine Privett, Peter Oresick, Charles Bukowski, Naiomi Shihab Nye, Paul Fischer, Judson Jerome, and Judson Crews, Jim Daniels, Robert Gregory, A.D. Winans. *No chapbook submissions unless solicited by editor.* Editor often gives extensive comment/criricism on submissions. Have published 15 titles since 1982. Please make checks out to 'Pig In A Poke' or 'Harry Calhoun'" circ. 400-500. Frequency varies. Pub'd 8 issues 1990; expects 1 issue 1991. sub. price: $3, will buy a potpourri of pamphlets; per copy: $1; sample: 50¢-75¢. Back issues: 50¢ for any pamphlets other than #12 (special Bukowski issue: sold out). Discounts: none planned as yet. 8-16pp (varies), sometimes in foldover, 'religious tract' style; 4½x5½ or smaller; of. Reporting time: varies, 2 weeks to 1 month. Payment: 1-4 copies. Copyrighted, reverts to author. Pub's reviews: 3 in 1990. §Poetry, of course, biographies of those in the arts, good current prose. No ads.

Pig In A Poke Press (see also PIG IN A PAMPHLET), 331 Ridge Point Circle #14, Bridgeville, PA 15017, 412-521-1237. 1982.

PIG IRON, Pig Iron Press, Jim Villani, Editor; Rose Sayre, Editor; Nate Leslie, Editor, P.O. Box 237, Youngstown, OH 44501, 216-783-1269. 1974. Poetry, fiction, articles, art, photos, cartoons, letters, long-poems, collages, plays, concrete art. *"Pig Iron* is a unique, high-energy series for writers and readers on the cutting ege of popular culture. Length: open. Style/bias: open. Paper only. Recent contributors: Reg Saner, Eve Shelnutt, Grace Butcher, Laurel Speer, Antler, Kenneth Patchen, Rhona McAdam, Maia, Katherine Soniat, Lesle Lewis, Terri Jewell, Phaedra Greenwood. For your personal cultural evolution." circ. 1M. 1/yr. Pub'd 1 issue 1990; expects 1 issue 1991, 1 issue 1992. 1 title listed in the *Small Press Record of Books in Print* (20th Edition, 1991-92). sub. price: $8, $15 for 2 years; per copy: $9.95; sample: $3. Back issues: write for backlist. Discounts: booksellers/3 or more copies 40%. 96pp; 8½x11; of. Reporting time: 16 weeks. Payment: 2 copies,

$5 per page fiction, $5 per poem. Copyrighted, reverts to author. No ads. CCLM.

Pig Iron Press (see also PIG IRON), Jim Villani, Editor; Rose Sayre, Editor; Naton Leslie, Editor, P.O. Box 237, Youngstown, OH 44501. 1974. Poetry, fiction, art, photos, collages, non-fiction. "No freelance submissions accepted. Literary, alternative lifestyles." avg. press run 1M. 15 titles listed in the *Small Press Record of Books in Print* (20th Edition, 1991-92). avg. price, paper: $9.95. Discounts: 40%. Pages open; 5½x8½, 8½x11; of. Payment: 10%, no advance. Copyrights for author.

THE PIG PAPER, Gary Pig Gold, Pig Productions, 70 Cotton Drive, Mississauga, Ontario L5G 1Z9, Canada, (416) 278-6594. 1975. Poetry, fiction, articles, art, photos, cartoons, interviews, satire, criticism, reviews, music, letters, collages, news items, non-fiction. "Length: Usually short (200-500 words); longer works are serialised over severl consecutive issues. Biases: Any material and opinions unheard of elsewhere. Recent contributors include: Tuli Kupferberg (ex-Fug), Jack Stevenson (of *Pandemonium*), Ace Backwords (*Twisted Image*)" circ. 1M. 3/yr. Pub'd 1 issue 1990; expects 3 issues 1991, 5 issues 1992. Lifetime sub. price: one (preferrably high-quality, 90 or 100-minute) audio cassette of subscriber's favorite sounds and/or words; price per copy: SASE or IRC; sample: SASE or IRC. Back issues: $1 each. 2pp; 8½x11; †xerox. Reporting time: varies. Payment: free subscription. Copyrighted, reverts to author. Pub's reviews: 3 in 1990. §Music, satire news/sociology, art/cartoons, film/video. Usually an exchange of ads. COSMEP.

Pig Press, Richard Caddel, 7 Cross View Terrace, Durham DH1 4JY, United Kingdom, D. 3846914. 1972-3. Poetry, long-poems. "Recent Contributors: Lee Harwood, Elaine Randell, Robert Creeley, Carl Rakosi, Bill Corbett, Ken Edwards, George Evans" avg. press run 500-1M. Pub'd 2 titles 1990; expects 2 titles 1991, 2 titles 1992. avg. price, paper: $10.00. Discounts: Trade: single 25%, 2-9 35%, 10+ 40%. 40-90pp; size varies; of, lp. Reporting time: most unsolicited ms. returned by return post. Payment: in copies. Copyright remains with author. ALP (Association of Little Presses), Password Books (UK), Small Press Distribution (USA).

PIGEON CREEK CLARION, Don Rodgers, Box 1014, Greenville, GA 30222. 1989. "Social commentary. Not accepting contributions" circ. 75. 6/yr. Pub'd 6 issues 1990; expects 6 issues 1991, 6 issues 1992. sub. price: $2; per copy: 50¢; sample: 50¢. 1 page; 8½x11; xerox. Not copyrighted.

Pigwidgeon Press, John Mahoney, PO Box 706, Derby Line, VT 05830, 819-876-2538. 1985. Fiction, photos, non-fiction. "We are physically based on a small farm in a primarily English-speaking area of Southern Quebec, publish in Vermont and Quebec (as Les Editions Pigwidgeon, RR 2, Ayers Cliff, Quebec, J0B 1C0) and our interests are, at this time, *regional* works, old *and* new; Northern Vermont and Southern Quebec. Our first book was a facsimile edition of a 60-year-old work about Lake Memphremagog ("Beautiful Waters"), which is about the people and communities along this 30-mile long lake shared by Vermonters & Quebecers. Volume 2, Beautiful Waters - 1985, Don't Remember Getting Born - 1986, Voices on the Border - 1987, Horatio-The Duck Who Thought He Was A Dog - 1986, The Bread & Soup Book - 1988, Get Me A Nutty Pig - 1988, Beautiful Memphremagog - 1987" avg. press run 1M. Pub'd 2 titles 1990; expects 3-4 titles 1991, 3-4 titles 1992. 6 titles listed in the *Small Press Record of Books in Print* (20th Edition, 1991-92). avg. price, cloth: $16-$18; paper: $6-$8. Discounts: TBA. 128-275pp; 5½x8½, 8½x11; of, computer typesetting on site/commercial production. Reporting time: 1-2 months. Payment: TBA. COSMEP.

THE PIKESTAFF FORUM, The Pikestaff Press, Robert D. Sutherland, Editor; James R. Scrimgeour, Editor; James McGowan, Editor; Curtis White, Editor, PO Box 127, Normal, IL 61761, 309-452-4831. 1977. Poetry, fiction, articles, art, photos, satire, criticism, reviews, parts-of-novels, long-poems, plays. "Poetry, prose fiction, drama, writing by children and young adults, reviews, commentary on contemporary literature. A regular feature, the *Forum*, will provide space for anyone to sound off on issues of importance to contemporary literature and/or the small-press scene. We are interested in writing that is clear and concise, that contains vivid imagery and concrete detail, and has human experience at the core. Traditional and experimental writing, established and non-established writers are welcome. Manuscripts should be accompanied by SASE. We publish as we have sufficient quality material to warrant an issue." circ. 1M. 1-2/yr. Pub'd 1 issue 1990; expects 1 issue 1991, 1 issue 1992. sub. price: $10 for 6 issues; per copy: $2 (including postage); sample: $2. Discounts: contributors, 50%; bookstores, 40%. 32-40pp; tabloid; of. Reporting time: within 3 months. Payment: 3 copies. Copyrighted, reverts to author. Pub's reviews: 3 in 1990. §Small press literary publications. CLMP, Independent Literary Publishers Association (ILPA).

The Pikestaff Press (see also THE PIKESTAFF FORUM), Robert D. Sutherland, Editor; James R. Scrimgeour, Editor; James McGowan, Editor; Curtis White, Editor, PO Box 127, Normal, IL 61761, 309-452-4831. 1977. Poetry, fiction. "Projects include chapbooks and single-volume collections of individual authors; and books containing single works of considerable length. Query first." avg. press run 500-2M. Pub'd 1 title 1990; expects 1 title 1991. 5 titles listed in the *Small Press Record of Books in Print* (20th Edition, 1991-92). avg. price, cloth: varies; paper: varies; other: varies. Discounts: 25-40% to bookstores depending on title. Pages vary; size varies; of. Reporting time: within 3 months. Payment: percentage of press run (to be negotiated); authors may purchase additional copies at a 50% discount. Copyrights for author. CLMP,

Independent Literary Publishers Association (ILPA).

PIKEVILLE REVIEW, James Alan Riley, Humanities Department, Pikeville College, Pikeville, KY 41501, 606-437-4046. 1987. Poetry, fiction, articles, interviews, reviews. "We publish contemporary fiction and poetry, interviews, creative essays and book reviews. We offer a $50 fiction award with each issue and a $50 essay award." circ. 500. 1/yr. Pub'd 1 issue 1990; expects 1 issue 1991, 1 issue 1992. sub. price: $4; per copy: $4; sample: $3. Back issues: $2. 80pp; 5½x8½; of. Reporting time: 2 months. Payment: copies. Pub's reviews: 2 in 1990. Ads: $100/$50.

The Pilgrim Press/United Church Press, Barbara Withers, Senior Editor, 475 Riverside Drive, 10th floor, New York, NY 10115, 212-870-2200. 1957. Non-fiction. "The presses are the publishers of the United Church of Christ" avg. press run 3.5M. Pub'd 20 titles 1990; expects 22 titles 1991, 25 titles 1992. 5 titles listed in the *Small Press Record of Books in Print* (20th Edition, 1991-92). avg. price, cloth: $16.95; paper: $9.95. Discounts: trade: 1-4 copies 20%, 5-24 40%, 25-99 42%, 100-249 43%, 250-499 44%, 500-999 45%, 1000+ 46%; jobber: 100+ 50%. 165pp; 5½x8¼; of. Reporting time: 3 months. Payment: occasional small advance, royalty 7½ to 10% of net. Copyrights for author. CBA, ABA.

Pinched Nerves Press, Steven Hartman, 1610 Avenue P, Apt. 6-B, Brooklyn, NY 11229. 1989. Poetry. "Publish local poets in NYC area. Magazine *Make Room for Dada* is published irregularly" avg. press run 150. Pub'd 4 titles 1990; expects 2 titles 1991. 1 title listed in the *Small Press Record of Books in Print* (20th Edition, 1991-92). avg. price, other: 25¢ xerox. 2pp; 4¼x11; xerox. Payment: none. Does not copyright for author.

Pinchgut Press, Marjorie Pizer, 6 Oaks Avenue, Cremorne, Sydney, N.S.W. 2090, Australia, 02-908-2402. 1948. Poetry, fiction, non-fiction. "Australian poetry and fiction; in particular, fantasy and psychology (i.e., self help)." avg. press run 1.2M-3M. Pub'd 1 title 1990. 11 titles listed in the *Small Press Record of Books in Print* (20th Edition, 1991-92). avg. price, paper: $7-$14. Discounts: usual trade discounts. of. Reporting time: quite quickly. Payment: 10% retail price.

Pine & Palm Press (see also LIVING OFF THE LAND, Subtropic Newsletter), Marian Van Atta, PO Box 2131, Melbourne, FL 32902-2131, 305-723-5554. 1973. "Has published *Living Off The Land,* subtropic handbook by Marian Van Atta. 1st edition 1972, 2nd 1974, and 3rd 1977 and *Wild Edibles.* No plans at present for publishing other authors - but may be able to in the future." avg. press run 5M. Pub'd 1 title 1990; expects 1 title 1991, 2 titles 1992. 2 titles listed in the *Small Press Record of Books in Print* (20th Edition, 1991-92). avg. price, paper: $5.95. Discounts: 40%. 60pp; 8x5½; of. Reporting time: 4 weeks. Payment: yes. Copyrights for author.

Pine Cone Press, Don W. Martin, Betty Woo Martin, 11362 Yankee Hill Road, PO Box 1494, Columbia, CA 95310, 209-532-2699. 1986. "Primarily guidebooks." avg. press run 10M. Pub'd 1 title 1990; expects 3 titles 1991. 5 titles listed in the *Small Press Record of Books in Print* (20th Edition, 1991-92). avg. price, paper: $12.95. Discounts: 45% wholesale, 55% distributor (or negotiable). 260-300pp; 6x9; desktop Laserjet III. Reporting time: 2 weeks. Copyrights for author. none.

Pine Hall Press, Willine Hall, Hank Hillin, PO Box 150657, Nashville, TN 37215. 1985. Non-fiction. "Book length, non-fiction, local, Tennessee, southern history, biographies, crime stories, books, FBI, federal agency stories (books). Additional address: 114 Abbottsford Dr., Nashville, TN 37215" avg. press run 7M. Pub'd 1 title 1990; expects 1 title 1991. 2 titles listed in the *Small Press Record of Books in Print* (20th Edition, 1991-92). avg. price, cloth: $19.95; paper: $10.95. Discounts: 40% trade. 500pp; 6x9; of. Does not copyright for author.

Pineapple Press, Inc., June Cussen, PO Drawer 16008, Southside Station, Sarasota, FL 34239, 813-952-1085. 1982. Fiction, non-fiction. "We publish hard and soft cover adult trade fiction and nonfiction" avg. press run 3M+. Pub'd 12 titles 1990; expects 12 titles 1991, 12 titles 1992. 61 titles listed in the *Small Press Record of Books in Print* (20th Edition, 1991-92). avg. price, cloth: $18.95; paper: $10.95. Discounts: trade: 1-3 copies 20%; 4-15 copies 40%; 16-49 42%; 5099 43%; 100-199 44%; 200+ 46%. 300pp; 5½x8¼, 6x9, or 8½x11; of, lo. Reporting time: 6 weeks. Payment: negotiable. Copyrights for author. BISAC.

Pinery Press, Philip Kallas, P.O. Box 672, Stevens Point, WI 54481. Non-fiction. "All of our materials deal with Portage County, WI." avg. press run 500. Pub'd 1 title 1990; expects 1 title 1991, 1 title 1992. 3 titles listed in the *Small Press Record of Books in Print* (20th Edition, 1991-92). avg. price, paper: $2.50. Discounts: 40/60. 40pp; 6x8; of. Reporting time: 2-3 months. Payment: case by case basis. Copyrights for author.

Pioneer Books, Rogan H. Moore, PO Box 704, Conyngham, PA 18219, 717-455-0757. 1988. Non-fiction. "Will consider well written and well researched manuscripts that are marketable in the fields of Americana, history (including state and local), genealogy and folklore. Prefer author to query before sending manuscript. Collections of period verses of a historical nature will be considered." avg. press run 1M. Pub'd 5 titles 1990; expects 3 titles 1991. 1 title listed in the *Small Press Record of Books in Print* (20th Edition, 1991-92). avg.

price, cloth: $25; paper: $15. Discounts: available upon request. 200pp; size varies; of, lp. Reporting time: 30-60 days. Payment: 10% royalty on sales; no advances. Copyrights for author. COSMEP.

PIP COLLEGE 'HELPS' NEWSLETTER, Partners In Publishing, P. M. Fielding, Box 50347, Tulsa, OK 74150, 918-584-5906. 1976. Articles, interviews, reviews, letters, news items, non-fiction. "Very short, fewer than 150 words unless special enough to take several pages of the newsletter." circ. 500. 13/yr. Pub'd 13 issues 1990; expects 13 issues 1991, 13 issues 1992. sub. price: $33; per copy: $3; sample: free with stamp (29¢). Back issues: $3 for each back issue or $8 for bound copy for each year Vol 1 - 1976, Vol 2 - 1977, Vol 3 - 1978. Discounts: if more than 1 subscription to same address. 4-8pp; 11×12; of. Reporting time: 1 month. Payment: copies, by line. Not copyrighted. Pub's reviews: 24 in 1990. §Learning disabilities, college made easy, careers for LD adults, people in LD field. COSMEP, OSP.

THE PIPE SMOKER'S EPHEMERIS, Tom Dunn, 20-37 120th Street, College Point, NY 11356. 1964. Poetry, fiction, articles, art, photos, cartoons, interviews, satire, criticism, reviews, letters, parts-of-novels, collages, news items. circ. 5M. 1-2/yr. Pub'd 1 issue 1990; expects 1 issue 1991, 2 issues 1992. 40-50pp; 8½×11; of. Reporting time: immediately. Payment: none. Copyrighted. Pub's reviews: 12 in 1990. §Tobacco, pipe smoking, books about books, smoking tobacco collectibles. TUCOPS.

Pittore Euforico (see also ME MAGAZINE), Carlo Pittore, PO Box 182, Bowdoinham, ME 04008, 207-666-8453. 1978. Poetry, fiction, art, photos, satire, music, letters, parts-of-novels, collages, concrete art. "Contributors include: Bern Porter, Charlie Morrow, Richard Kostelanez, Bill Jacobson, Bob Holman, Jeff Wright, Rainer Wiens, Laura Dean, Katherine Bradford. Titles include: *Colleagues* edited by Carlo Pittore; *Maine Moments in New York* edited by Carlo Pittore; *Yurtyet* edited by Carlo Pittore; *The Adventures of Carlo Pittore* by Carlo Pittore." avg. press run 750. Pub'd 4 titles 1990; expects 5 titles 1991. 21 titles listed in the *Small Press Record of Books in Print* (20th Edition, 1991-92). avg. price, paper: $6. Discounts: trade 40%. 100pp; 8½×11; of. Reporting time: 2 months. Payment: not yet. Copyrights for author. MWPA.

THE PITTSBURGH QUARTERLY, Frank Correnti, Editor; James Deahl, Canadian Editor, 36 Haberman Avenue, Pittsburgh, PA 15211-2144, 412-431-8885. 1991. Poetry, fiction, art, interviews, reviews, non-fiction. "Canadian address: Box 340, London, Ontario N6A 4W1. *The Pittsburgh Quarterly* was founded as a community project to present a literary magazine which would adhere to similar standards of excellence and format as many of the established magazines which publish poetry, short short stories, reviews, and essays. We plan to include an interview with a prominent figure in the writing community in each issue. Primarily, the magazine is looking for previously unpublished work, especially new work. This is envisioned as a proving ground for writers of merit but little publication credits to have their writing seen alongside that of established writers. The first issue includes, among others: poetry by Karen Blomain, Linda Watkins, Dieter Weslowski, Dennis Brutus, Judy Meiksin, Richard Dillon and Lynn Conroy; fiction by Richard Krawiec. Additional writers included in the first issue are Michael Wurster, Bruce Hoffman, Yun Wang, John DeChancie, Sue Powers' interview with Konstantinos Lardas, Arthur Knight, Kit Knight and others." circ. 500. 4/yr. Expects 4 issues 1991, 4 issues 1992. sub. price: $12, $14 Canadian and overseas; per copy: $4 in 1992; sample: $4. Back issues: $4. 76pp; 5½×8½; †of. Reporting time: 8-10 weeks. Payment: 1 copy. Copyrighted, reverts to author. Pub's reviews: 8 in 1991 in 1990. §Would prefer to review books of poetry from small presses. Ads: $100/$50/$25 1/4 page. COSMEP.

PIVOT, Martin Mitchell, Editor-in-Chief; Jack McManis, Assist. Editor, 221 South Barnard Street, State College, PA 16801, 212-222-1408. 1951. Poetry. "Editorial address: Martin Mitchell, editor, 250 Riverside Drive #23, New York, NY 10025" circ. 1.5M. 1/yr. Pub'd 1 issue 1990; expects 1 issue 1991, 1 issue 1992. sub. price: $14 ($15 foreign)/3-year; per copy: $5 ($6 foreign); sample: $3. 70pp; 6×9; lp. Reporting time: under 1 month. Payment: none. Copyrighted, does not revert to author.

The Place In The Woods (see also READ, AMERICA!), Roger A. Hammer, Editor & Publisher, 3900 Glenwood Avenue, Golden Valley, MN 55422, 612-374-2120. 1980. Poetry, art, photos, news items, non-fiction. "SAN 689-058X. Primarily interested in short biographies (and art) on significant achievements by American minorities—Black, Women, Native People, Seniors, Handicapped/Disabled, Hispanic, War Vets, Gay/Lesbians, Young Achievers, Business Person, Asian/Pacific, other minority persons with significant but *little-known* contributions to the American culture. Well-documented personalities (such as Blacks in sports or entertainment) are unacceptable. Interested in developing role models for minorities (adults and children). Need talented illustrators at whatever level, age who speak for their minority. Bios can run 50 to 500 words. Pays for completed work or leads. Queries recommended. Also looking for new material with themes appealing to elementary through seconday educational levels. Should be creative and original—subjects not found in general textbooks, yet of interest to mainstream Americans, young and adult." avg. press run 1M. Expects 4 titles 1991, 4 titles 1992. 6 titles listed in the *Small Press Record of Books in Print* (20th Edition, 1991-92). avg. price, paper: $7.95. Discounts: 40% wholesaler/distributor; 40% to RIF programs; quantity rates on request. 30-50pp; 8½×11; †of. Reporting time: 1 week. Payment: varies with material, negotiated with each title and author for all rights. Does not copyright for author.

Placebo Press (see also WALKING-STICK NOTES), Cecil Curtis, 4051 East Olive Road, #231, Pensacola, FL 32514-6444, 904-477-3995. 1976. Articles, cartoons, satire, reviews, non-fiction. "Cannot read unsolicited MSS. We plan to concentrate our efforts on *Walking-Stick Notes* plus a series of "Walking-Stick Papers"-reprints of essays and stories, bibliography, plus any new material (fiction or non-fiction of interest to *Walking-Stick* buffs." avg. press run 100. Pub'd 2 titles 1990; expects 4 titles 1991, 4 titles 1992. avg. price, paper: free distribution only. Pages vary; 5½×8½; †mi, xerography. Reporting time: within a week on queries. Payment: in copies. Does not copyright for author.

Plain View Press, Inc., Susan Bright, PO Box 33311, Austin, TX 78764, (512) 441-2452. 1976. Poetry, art, photos, cartoons, long-poems. "We publish feminist literature by women and men. 50 books in 1975. We also do video production work and we publish limited editions of family histories. Most of our books are signed, numbered editions. Additional address: 1509 Dexter, Austin, TX 78704" avg. press run 1M. Pub'd 5 titles 1990; expects 7 titles 1991, 7 titles 1992. 22 titles listed in the *Small Press Record of Books in Print* (20th Edition, 1991-92). avg. price, paper: $10; other: hand made, $6. Discounts: standard terms. Pages vary; size varies; of. Reporting time: varies. Payment: varies. Does not copyright for author.

PLAINS POETRY JOURNAL (PPJ), Jane Greer, PO Box 2337, Bismarck, ND 58502. 1981. Poetry, criticism. "Eager for good long poems and essays on poetry. No 'broken prose.' *PPJ*'s aim is to show how poetic *form* (meter, rhyme—in short, *sound*) is vital to *content*. Criticism should be along these lines. We consider previously published pieces. No 'Hallmark' verse, no 'conversational' free verse. We do not publish reviews; write for essay guidelines." circ. 500. 4/yr. Expects 4 issues 1991, 4 issues 1992. sub. price: $18/year, $32/2 years; per copy: $4.50; sample: $4.50. 44pp; 5½×8½; of. Reporting time: 2-3 weeks. Payment: 2 contributor's copies. Copyrighted, reverts to author. §Poetry.

Plains Press, David R. Pichaske, Southwest State University, Marshall, MN 56258, 507-537-6463. 1984. "We focus on material from the Minnesota/Iowa/South Dakota region—poetry, fiction and prose/critism/scholarship" avg. press run 1M. Pub'd 2 titles 1990; expects 2 titles 1991, 2 titles 1992. 3 titles listed in the *Small Press Record of Books in Print* (20th Edition, 1991-92). avg. price, cloth: $11.95; paper: $5.95. Discounts: 2-5 20%, 6+ 40%, STOP 40% and add shipping. 176pp; 5¼×8¼.

PLAINSONG, Frank Steele, Peggy Steele, Elizabeth Oakes, Box 8245, Western Kentucky University, Bowling Green, KY 42101, 502-745-5708. 1979. Poetry, articles, art, photos, interviews, criticism, reviews, letters. "We want to affirm the awareness of place as a source for poetry, to print work in which written language comes within hearing of spoken language, to cherish and preserve what it means to be, in the best sense, human during the dangerous decade ahead. We are not academic, although we have an interest in poetic form and craft, especially when alive but invisible. We are bored by the obvious—by irony as a reflex, by hysteria as a motive, by formulaic poems that stop where the formula stops. We favor relatively short poems. Recent contributors: William Stafford, Del Marie Rogers, Robert Bly, Betty Adcock. We have a sense of humor." circ. 500. Occasional. Expects 1 issue 1991. sub. price: $7 for 2 issues; per copy: $3.50; sample: $3. Back issues: first issue out of print—other back issues $3 each. 48pp; 6×9; of. Reporting time: 6 weeks. Payment: copies. Copyrighted, reverts to author. Pub's reviews: 0 in 1990. §Contemporary poetry (books and magazines), poetry in translation, criticism of poetry. Advertising free to selected publishers and schools.

PLAINSWOMAN, Elizabeth Hampsten, Editor, PO Box 8027, Grand Forks, ND 58202, 701-777-8043. 1977. Poetry, fiction, articles, art, photos, interviews, reviews, letters, news items, non-fiction. "Reestablished monthly publication (except February/August) in 1981." circ. 600. 10/yr. Pub'd 10 issues 1990; expects 10 issues 1991, 10 issues 1992. sub. price: $15 or $20 supporter, $10 low income; per copy: $3; sample: $3. Back issues: $3. Discounts: 30%/issue. 16pp; 8½×11; of. Reporting time: 1 month. Payment: 2 copies of issue in which work appears. Copyrighted, rights revert to author 2 years after publication. Pub's reviews: 10 in 1990. §Women & the law, women in general, women's history, women & politics, women in the West and Great Plains, fiction, poetry. No ads.

PLANKTON, Wolfhound Press, Seamus Cashman, 68 Moungjoy Square, Dublin 1, Ireland, 740354. 1984. Fiction, photos. circ. 5M. Pub'd 1 issue 1990; expects 1 issue 1991, 2 issues 1992. price per copy: £1 (IR). Discounts: 33⅓ trade discount. 48pp; of. Reporting time: ages - c. 6 months. Payment: small. Copyrighted, reverts to author. Ads: £350/£180/on request.

Planning/Communications, Daniel Lauber, 7215 Oak Avenue, River Forest, IL 60305-1935. 1976. Non-fiction. "Interested in books, particularly dealing with government careers, careers in general, urban affairs, housing, planning, government in general. Particularly interested in manuscripts that cut through the B.S. and ideological biases to deal with causes and solutions to domestic policy problems. Interested in career books on subjects that have not already been exhausted by other authors. Length of material: no less than 120 pages final book; prefer around 200+ pages, but we can be flexible." avg. press run 4.5M. Expects 4 titles 1991, 5 titles 1992. 4 titles listed in the *Small Press Record of Books in Print* (20th Edition, 1991-92). avg. price, paper: $14.95; other: $17.95. Discounts: trade standards (40%; standard return policy); bulk 10-29 copies 20%,

30-50 25%, 51+ 30%; write for classroom, jobber discounts. 200pp; 6×9; of. Reporting time: 2 months. Payment: contact us, varies with author, but better than industry standards. PMA.

Plantagenet House, Inc., Dean Broome, PO Box 271, Blackshear, GA 31516, 912-449-6601. 1981. Fiction. "Interested in novels. Larry Parr 'Springwood'; James J. Thornton, Jr., "A Matter of Sweet Revenge"" avg. press run 2M. Expects 2 titles 1991, 4 titles 1992. avg. price, cloth: $12.95. Discounts: 40%. 200pp; 5½×8½; †of. Reporting time: 6 weeks. Payment: standard. Copyrights for author.

Plantagenet Productions (see also PLANTAGENET PRODUCTIONS, Libraries of Spoken Word Recordings and of Stagescripts), Westridge (Open Centre), Highclere, Nr. Newbury, Berkshire RG159PJ, England. Pub'd 1 title 1990; expects 1 title 1992. 38 titles listed in the *Small Press Record of Books in Print* (20th Edition, 1991-92). avg. price, paper: £1.50 plus postage.

PLANTAGENET PRODUCTIONS, Libraries of Spoken Word Recordings and of Stagescripts, Plantagenet Productions, Dorothy Rose Gribble, Director of Productions, Westridge (Open Centre), Highclere, Nr. Newbury, Royal Berkshire RG15 9PJ, England. 1964. "Recordings of poetry, philosophy, narrative and light work on cassette, tape, LP. New books: *Gribble Annals 1* by Charles Besly Gribble, Captain East India Company, Besly 1986, £2.25 plus postage; *Gribble Annals 2* by Henry Gribble, Captain, East India Company, 1988, £4.50. *Milton Traditions*, compiled by F.G.M. Milton and Dr. Gribble, £10.50 (direct sales), 1990." Erratic. Pub'd 1 issue 1990; expects 3 issues 1991. price per copy: LP-£2.25, £2, £1 cassette tape £2.25, £1.75 postage extra.

Plas Y Bryn Press, Wyn Powell, Box 97, West Hill, Ontario M1E 4R4, Canada, 416-282-1974. 1988. Non-fiction. "United States address: Box 1348, Lewiston, NY 14092-1348" avg. press run 3M. Expects 1 title 1991, 2 titles 1992. 1 title listed in the *Small Press Record of Books in Print* (20th Edition, 1991-92). avg. price, cloth: $20; paper: $15. Discounts: 40% returnable, 50% nonreturnable. 190pp; 8¼×8¼; of. Reporting time: 6 weeks. Payment: individually arranged. Does not copyright for author. COSMEP, Publishers Marketing Association.

PLAY & CULTURE, Human Kinetics Pub. Inc., Garry Chick, Box 5076, Champaign, IL 61825-5076, 217-351-5076. 1988. Articles. circ. 275. 4/yr. Pub'd 4 issues 1990; expects 4 issues 1991, 4 issues 1992. sub. price: $28 indiv., $56 instit.; per copy: $7 indiv., $15 instit.; sample: free. Back issues: $7 indiv., $15 instit. Discounts: 5%. 98pp; 6×9; of. Reporting time: 2 months. Payment: none. Copyrighted. The Association for the Study of Play.

Players Press, Inc., Robert W. Gordon, Vice President Editorial, PO Box 1132, Studio City, CA 91604, 818-789-4980. 1965. Plays, non-fiction. avg. press run 10M-50M. Pub'd 14 titles 1990; expects 16 titles 1991, 20 titles 1992. 112 titles listed in the *Small Press Record of Books in Print* (20th Edition, 1991-92). avg. price, cloth: $20; paper: $6. Discounts: 25-55% trade. 50pp; 5½×8½; †lp. Reporting time: 3-6 months. Payment: varies, dependent on material. Copyrights for author.

Pleasure Dome Press (Long Island Poetry Collective Inc.) (see also XANADU: A LITERARY JOURNAL; NEWSLETTER), Mildred Jeffrey, Editor; Lois V. Walker, Business Manager; Barbara Lucas, Editor; Pat Nesbitt, Editor, Box 773, Huntington, NY 11743. 1976. Poetry. "We are not open to unsolicited mss. at this time. PDP has not been able to bring out any titles for a long time. We consider it dormant, rather than dead" avg. press run varies. Discounts: 10% on orders of $20 or more (includes *Xanadu* and Newsletter subs.). Pages vary; size varies; †lp, of. Payment: varies. We buy all rights. none.

PLEIADES MAGAZINE, John L. Moravec, Editor-in-Chief; Elizabeth Whitlatch, Business Editor; Cyril Osmond, Assistant Editor; Frank Klicpery, Literary Editor, Box 357, 6677 W. Colfax Avenue, Suite D, Lakewood, CO 80214, 303-237-3398. 1983. Poetry, fiction, articles, music, plays, non-fiction. "Short-shorts from 500-800 words." circ. 1.2M. 2/yr. Pub'd 2 issues 1990. sub. price: $9; per copy: $3; sample: $3. Back issues: $2. 75pp; 8½×11; †of, lp. Reporting time: 2 weeks. Payment: copies or cash awards. Copyrighted, reverts to author. Pub's reviews: 2 in 1990. §General humanitarian and social. Ads: $1 per word/block ads 3 X 2½ $25 two issues/customer furnishes ad (illustrations) black + white.

Plenum Publishing Corporation (see also THE AMERICAN JOURNAL OF PSYCHOANALYSIS; CHILDREN'S LITERATURE IN EDUCATION; POLITICAL BEHAVIOR; RESEARCH IN HIGHER EDUCATION; THE URBAN REVIEW), 233 Spring Street, New York, NY 10013.

Plexus Publishing, Inc. (see also BIOLOGY DIGEST), Thomas H. Hogan, 143 Old Marlton Pike, Medford, NJ 08055, 609-654-6500. 1977. Non-fiction. "Publish a limited number of books on biology and natural history" avg. press run 2M. Expects 4 titles 1991, 4 titles 1992. 5 titles listed in the *Small Press Record of Books in Print* (20th Edition, 1991-92). avg. price, cloth: $19.95. Discounts: 40%. 200pp; 5½×8½; of. Reporting time: 60 days. Payment: $500 advance against royalty of 10-15%. Does not copyright for author.

PLOTS, Margi L. Washburn, PO Box 371, Kewanee, IL 61443, 309-852-0332. 1990. Poetry, fiction, art, photos, cartoons, interviews, reviews, letters. "Fiction up to 10,000 words. Poetry—free verse, traditional. Quiet, emotional, chilling horror. No excessive sex, violence, strong language. Recent contributors: Barry Hoffman, Anke Kriske, Gregory Norris" circ. 250+. 4/yr. Pub'd 4 issues 1990; expects 4 issues 1991, 4 issues 1992. sub. price: $15; per copy: $4; sample: $4. Back issues: $4.50. 60pp; 8½×11; lp. Reporting time: 6-8 weeks. Payment: 1/2¢ per word & 1 copy. Not copyrighted. Ads: $50/$25/barter.

THE PLOUGH, Davie Mow, Hutterian Brethren, Spring Valley, Route 381, N. Farmington, PA 15437-9506, 412-329-1100; fax 412-329-0942. 1983. Poetry, articles, art, photos, interviews, criticism, reviews, letters, long-poems, non-fiction. "700-1,500 words/article" circ. 15M. 4/yr or less. Pub'd 4 issues 1990; expects 2 issues 1991. sub. price: no subscription, donations accepted; per copy: free; sample: free. Back issues: free. 20pp; 6×8¾; desktop. Reporting time: 3 weeks. Payment: none. Copyrighted, rights reverting to author negotiable. Pub's reviews: 5 in 1990. §Religion—current events, non-fiction. No ads. Evangelical Press Association (EPA).

PLOUGHSHARES, DeWitt Henry, Executive Director; Don Lee, Managing Editor; Joyce Peseroff, Associate Editor, Emerson College, 100 Beacon Street, Boston, MA 02116, 617-578-8753. 1971. Poetry, fiction, parts-of-novels, long-poems. "Maximum length for prose 6M words. We're biased towards new writers,and towards 'rediscovery' of neglected writers. Because of our revolving editorship, status of issues in progress & contrast of emphasis from issue to issue, we suggest inquiry prior to submission. Recent contributors: Joseph Brodsky, Rita Dove, Garrett Kaoru Hongo, Seamus Heaney, Carol Frost, Sharon Olds, Joyce Carol Oates, Michael S. Harper, Mary Oliver, Phillip Lopate, Sue Miller, Gerald Stern." circ. 3.8M. 3/yr. Pub'd 3 issues 1990; expects 3 issues 1991, 3 issues 1992. 4 titles listed in the *Small Press Record of Books in Print* (20th Edition, 1991-92). sub. price: $15/3 issues (domestic), $19/3 issues (foreign); per copy: $7.95; sample: $6. Back issues: prices vary; full file vols I-XVI61 $300. Discounts: 40% trade (5 copies or more); 10% agent. 220pp; 5½×8½; of. Reporting time: 3-5 months. Payment: $10/p prose ($50 max); $10/poem minimum, $5/page per poem over 2 printed pages, $50 max. Copyrighted, rights released on request. Pub's reviews. §Quality poetry, fiction, non-fiction. Ads: $110 (non-profit); $225 (trade)/$65 (non-profit); $125 (trade). CLMP.

THE PLOVER (Chidori), Paul E. Truesdell, Jr., Thomas Heffernan, PO Box 122, Ginowan City, Okinawa 901-22, Japan, 1-011-81-098-897-5042. 1989. Poetry, articles. "Bilingual (Japanese to English/English to Japanese) haiku/senryu and related forms. Publish traditional, classical-traditional, and free-style haiku etc. No avant garde forms accepted. Also, obviously 'desk-top', contrived haiku will not be considered. We are a nonprofit magazine. Publish during Spring and Fall. Deadlines end of May and November. Contributor submissions: no more than 20 haiku/senryu on 8½ X 11 sheet of paper. Submit with SAE and 1 IRC's. Subscriptions should be paid by international money order only" circ. 500. 2/yr. Pub'd 1 issue 1990; expects 2 issues 1991, 2 issues 1992. sub. price: $16 all postpaid int'l mail; per copy: $8; sample: $8. 28-48pp; 6×8½; of. Reporting time: 2-4 weeks. Payment: none. Copyrighted, reverts to author. Pub's reviews: 4 in 1990. §Haiku/senryu related forms.

THE PLOWMAN, Tony Scavetta, Box 414, Whitby, Ontario L1N 5S4, Canada, 416-668-7803. 1988. Poetry, art, photos, cartoons, music, letters, collages. "We publish endless anthologies." circ. 15M. 4/yr. Pub'd 3 issues 1990; expects 12 issues 1991, 12 issues 1992. sub. price: $8; per copy: $7.50; sample: free. Back issues: $3/copy. Discounts: 10%. 112pp; tabloid; Web Press. Reporting time: 1 week. Payment: cash prizes. Copyrighted, reverts to author. Pub's reviews: 400 in 1990. §ACC. Ads: $80-40-20-8.

THE PLUM REVIEW, Christina Daub, M. Hammer, PO Box 3557, Washington, DC 20007. 1990. Poetry, interviews, reviews. "Recent contributors: Mark Strand, William Stafford, Jane Hirshfield, Linda Hogan, Roland Flint, Ales Debeljak, James McCorckle, Henri Cole, Michael Collier, Ann Knox..." 2/yr. Pub'd 1 issue 1990; expects 2 issues 1991, 2 issues 1992. sub. price: $10; per copy: $5; sample: $5. Back issues: $5. Discounts: negotiable. 100pp; 6×9. Reporting time: 2 months. Payment: contributor's copy. Copyrighted, reverts to author. Pub's reviews. §Poetry. Ads: $200/$125/exchange ads w/literary magazines.

PM (The Pedantic Monthly), Erik A. Johnson, Editor; Lydia Renay, Fiction & Articles Editor, Numedia, 912 North Bushnell Avenue, Alhambra, CA 91801-1206. 1985. Fiction, articles, cartoons, satire, reviews, letters, parts-of-novels, news items. "Creative writing (short fiction) should be a maximum of 1,500 words; humorous essays, criticism, satire, and reviews can range from 250-2,000 words. We are looking to include more cartoons and offbeat line art; should be b & w, 3½ X 3½ maximum. Recent contributors include F.R. Duplantier, Joseph Costanza, Jeffrey Angus, Daniel Wildhirt, W.J. Tobin" circ. 500-1M. 4/yr. Pub'd 10 issues 1990; expects 4 issues 1991, 4 with one Special Edition each year (10 issues 1992. sub. price: $20; per copy: $2.50; sample: $3 (covers 1st-class single mailing). Back issues: not available any farther back than Summer 1987. Discounts: To distributors by arrangement. 16-24pp; 8½×11; of. Reporting time: 3-6 weeks. Payment: subscription (1 year) and copies. Copyrighted, reverts to author. Pub's reviews: 3 in 1990. §Humor, satire, political commentary, experimental. Ads: $200/$125/$15 col-inch words or classified display.

Pocahontas Press, Inc., Mary C. Holliman, President, 2805 Wellesley Court, Blacksburg, VA 24060-4126,

703-951-0467. 1984. Poetry, fiction, non-fiction. "Our first trade book is the true story of the Golden Hill Indians of Connecticut told in the words of Chief Big Eagle. We have begun a series of books for middle-school age children and teen-agers, short story length, in both Spanish and English with black-and-white illustrations; these are historical and biographical topics and most will be in the series Tales of the Virginia Wilderness. We are also interested in memoirs, family histories, and poetry collections, and will consider others." avg. press run poetry 500, other 3M-5M. Pub'd 3 titles 1990; expects 5 titles 1991, 4 titles 1992. 22 titles listed in the *Small Press Record of Books in Print* (20th Edition, 1991-92). avg. price, cloth: $12.95; paper: $5.95-$8.95. Discounts: for prepayment 5%, wholesalers: 1-2 20%, 3-50 40%, 51+ 50%. 80-180pp; 5½×8½; of. Reporting time: 3 months. Payment: 10% royalty. Copyrights for author. COSMEP, (VPW) Virginia Press Women, (NFPW) National Federation of Press Women, Multicultural Publishers Association.

POCKET INSPIRATIONS, Janey Mitchell, Editor, PO Box 796, Weaverville, CA 96093. 1989. Poetry, articles, letters. "Short inspirational pieces. How-to articles, personal experiences, essays, anecdotes, humor, hints, fillers, poetry. (Maximum 500 words.) *Pocket Inspirations* is published for the purpose of uplifting the heart and nourishing the spirit. Offers something for everyone in every issue." circ. 1M. 6/yr. Expects 5 issues 1991, 6 issues 1992. sub. price: $12; per copy: $3; sample: $3. Back issues: $2 plus SASE for random back issues. 28pp; 7×8½. Reporting time: 2-3 weeks. Payment: in copies upon publication. Copyrighted, reverts to author. 10¢ per word per issue; minimum ad is $2; 10% discount if ad is run in 3 consecutive issues.

POCKETS (Devotional Magazine for Children), Janet R. McNish, 1908 Grand, PO Box 189, Nashville, TN 37212, 615-340-7333. 1981. Poetry, fiction, non-fiction. "I would strongly advise writers to ask for guidelines and themes before submitting mss. Include SASE (29¢)." circ. 70M. 11/yr. Pub'd 1111 issues 1990; expects 11 issues 1991. sub. price: $14.95; per copy: $1.95; sample: SASE ($1.05 postage). Back issues: 73¢ postage. 32pp; 7×9½; of. Reporting time: 1 month. Payment: on acceptance. Copyrighted, reverts to author. No ads. Associated Church Press, Educational Press Association of America.

POEM, Huntsville Literary Association, Nancy Frey Dillard, c/o English Department, University of Alabama, Huntsville, AL 35899. 1967. Poetry. circ. 500. 2/yr. Pub'd 2 issues 1990; expects 2 issues 1991, 2 issues 1992. sub. price: $10; per copy: $5; sample: $5. Back issues: $5. 70pp; 4½×7½; lp. Reporting time: 30 days. Payment: copy. Copyrighted; No advertisement. CCLM.

The Poet, Doris Nemeth, Editor; Wanda Bearden, Art Editor; Nelly Ann Buck, Associate Editor, 2314 West Sixth Street, Mishawaka, IN 46544-1594, 219-255-8606. 1963. Poetry, art. "For profession people, free-lance writers, students, etc. Anthology. Acquires first North American serial rights. Uses about 2,000 mss. a year. Will send sample copy to the writer for $4.50. Will consider photocopied and simultaneous submissions. Returns reject material immediately. Submit up to six poems. Enclose SASE. We accept all forms of poetry, no set rules. We prefer 16 lines more or less. We read all manuscripts. We prefer not to see religious material. We use some photos and art work." avg. press run 2.5M. Pub'd 1 title 1990; expects 1 title 1991, 1 title 1992. avg. price, paper: $11.50. Discounts: none. 300pp; 8½×11; of. Reporting time: 4-6 weeks. Payment: none. Copyrights for author.

POET & CRITIC, Iowa State University Press, Neal Bowers, 203 Ross Hall, Iowa State University, Ames, IA 50011. 1961. Poetry, criticism, reviews. "We are looking for poems that display a sense of sound and imagery. All styles are welcome, provided the work is good. Recent contributors: Elizabeth Dodd, Cortney Davis, Peter Makuck, Ann Struthers, Brendan Galvin." circ. 500. 3/yr. Pub'd 3 issues 1990; expects 3 issues 1991, 3 issues 1992. sub. price: $16; per copy: $6; sample: $6. Back issues: $6. 48pp; 6×9; of. Reporting time: 2 weeks or sooner. Payment: one copy, additional copies at half price. Copyrighted, reverts to author. Pub's reviews: 3 in 1990. §Any poetry-related areas, with an emphasis on the contemporary. Ads: Exchanges only. CCLM.

POET LORE, The Writer's Center, Sunil Freeman, Managing Editor; Roland Flint, Executive Editor; Philip K. Jason, Executive Editor; Barbara Goldberg, Executive Editor, The Writer's Center, 7815 Old Georgetown Road, Bethesda, MD 20814-2415, 301-654-8664. 1889. Poetry, reviews. "All material submitted for possible publication must include a stamped, self-addressed envelope. Translations of contemporary world poets." circ. 650. 4/yr. Pub'd 4 issues 1990; expects 4 issues 1991, 4 issues 1992. sub. price: $12 indiv., $20 instit.; per copy: $4.50, $5 foreign postage; sample: $4.50. Back issues: $4.50. Discounts: agency 5%. 64pp; 6×9; of. Reporting time: 2-4 months. Payment: 2 copies of issue. Copyrighted, reverts to author. Pub's reviews: 17 in 1990. §Small press poetry books, and poetry books published by major publishers & university presses. Ads: $100/$55. CLMP.

POET MAGAZINE, Cooper House Publishing Inc., Peggy Cooper, Michael Hall, Joy Hall, PO Box 54947, Oklahoma City, OK 73154, 405-949-2020. 1984. Poetry, art, photos, reviews, long-poems. "We look at all poetry, any form, any length, any subject. What we are looking for in all poetry is a successful marriage of content and form, meaning and language. Poets at all levels of writing are considered for publication. We are also looking for articles about poetry. Recent contributors: Lewis Turco, Judith Saunders, Lyn Lifshin, Rochelle

Lynn Holt, Tom McKeown, Louis Phillips, Lee Schultz, Brian Swann" circ. 6M+. 4/yr. Pub'd 4 issues 1990; expects 4 issues 1991, 4 issues 1992. sub. price: $20; per copy: $5; sample: $2.50 when available. Back issues: $2.50 when available. Discounts: distributors 50%. 56pp; 8¼×11; of. Reporting time: 3-6 months. Payment: promotion, publication, and 1 contributor copy. Copyrighted, reverts to author. Pub's reviews: 4-12 in 1990. §Poetry and anything related to poetry such as writing, reading, teaching, publishing, etc. Ads: $450/$200/$300 2/3 page/$150 1/3 page/$75 business card/write for additional rates. COSMEP.

POET NEWS, Patrick Grizzell, Luke Breit, Mary Zeppa, 1727 I Street, Sacramento, CA 95814, 916-448-6679. 1979. Poetry, fiction, articles, art, interviews, criticism, reviews, long-poems, news items, non-fiction. "Some recent contributors have been Simon Perchik, D.R. Wagner, Sharon Oubiago. We publish reviews and articles primarily by & about local poets and writers, but we have expanded our editorial content to include articles and interviews of national interest" circ. 1M. 10/yr. Pub'd 10 issues 1990; expects 10 issues 1991, 10 issues 1992. sub. price: $18; per copy: free with SASE; sample: free with SASE w/54¢ affixed. Back issues: free with SASE. 16pp; 8×10; webb. Reporting time: 1 month. Payment: copies. Copyrighted. Pub's reviews: 14 in 1990. §Poetry & fiction by local, national and international authors. Ads: $50/$25/$10 QTR/$2.50 per column inch. Special rates to non-profits. CCLM.

Poet Papers (see also THE RECORD SUN), Laimons Juris G, P.O. Box 528, Topanga, CA 90290. 1969. Poetry, art, photos, long-poems, collages. "Please: If sending materials for consideration enclose self-addressed stamped envelope! *NO SASE-NO reply*. Poet Papers is interested to receive all information regarding funding and grants to publish poetry, photo and art books. We wish to upgrade the quality of our books. Experimenting with handmaking. *American Refugee Poet* $3.50, *Walking Sheet* $2" avg. press run 10M. Pub'd 1 title 1990; expects 2 titles 1991, 3 titles 1992. 12 titles listed in the *Small Press Record of Books in Print* (20th Edition, 1991-92). avg. price, other: $6.10. Discounts: library-trade 20%. 150pp; 7×10; †of, lp, silkscreen, handmade. Reporting time: if unsolicited by us, 1-5 years. Payment: copies of book or magazine. Does not copyright for author. PAF (People's Antarctica Foundation).

POETALK, Bay Area Poets Coalition, Inc., Maggi H. Meyer, Editor, 1527 Virginia Street, Berkeley, CA 94703, 415-845-8409. 1974. Poetry. "Send 4 (20 lines, 3 X 4 max) with SASE. One may be used" circ. 400-475. 12/yr. sub. price: $4; sample: free. 3pp; 8½×14 (folded). Reporting time: 2 months. Payment: copy. Copyrighted.

POETIC JUSTICE, Alan C. Engebretsen, 8220 Rayford Drive, Los Angeles, CA 90045. 1982. Poetry. "Some recent contributors: Vesta Neuron, Tony Moffeit, Joan Ritty, Beverly Corben, Ken Stone, Robert N. Zimmerman, Pearl Bloch Segall, Michael Fraley, Charles B. Dickson, Charles Corry, Arthur Winfield Knight." circ. 200. Irregular, approx. 1/yr. Expects 1 issue 1991, 1 issue 1992. sub. price: $10 for four issues; per copy: $3; sample: $3. Back issues: $3 each. Discounts: none. 44pp; 5⅜×8½; xerox press. Reporting time: days to weeks. Payment: one contributor's copy. Not copyrighted.

POETIC LICENCE, Ann Wainwright, 18 Stokesley Cres., Billingham, Cleveland, England. 1981. Poetry, fiction, articles, art, cartoons, criticism, reviews, long-poems, collages, news items, non-fiction. "*POET LICENCE* is a "homely" mag." circ. 200. 6/yr. Pub'd 6 issues 1990; expects 6 issues 1991, 6 issues 1992. sub. price: £5; per copy: 50p; sample: free (IRC if outside U.K.). Back issues: not many available: 25p + postage. 24pp (sides); 6×8; mi. Reporting time: 2 weeks. Payment: complimentary copy. Not copyrighted. Pub's reviews: 10 in 1990. §Poetry (modern), fiction, humorous books. Ads: £10/£5/£2.50 - 1/4 page.

Poetic Page (see also POETIC PAGE), Denise Martinson, PO Box 71192, Madison Heights, MI 48071-0192, 313-548-0865. 1989. Poetry, fiction. "We are doing four chapbooks and short story book per year (invitation only)." avg. press run unlimited (by orders). Expects 5 titles 1991, 5 titles 1992. avg. price, other: $6 chapbooks. Discounts: none. 40pp. Reporting time: 1 week short stories; all chapbooks invitational. Payment: Author receives 2/3 profit, poetry books only. Copyrights for author.

POETIC PAGE, Poetic Page, Denise Martinson, PO Box 71192, Madison Heights, MI 48071-0192, 313-548-0865. 1989. Poetry, articles, art, reviews, plays. "We prefer to 24 lines. All styles are acceptable except for crude or strong sexual content. We only publish one-third of the entries we receive. ($1.00 per poem submitted.) Prizes are $25.00-$15.00-$10.00. We purchase articles. Some of our poets: Alice Mackenzie Swaim, Marian Ford Park, Glenna Holloway, Pearl Bloch Segall and Doris Benson." circ. 250-350. 6/yr. Pub'd 5 issues 1990; expects 6 issues 1991, 6 issues 1992. 2 titles listed in the *Small Press Record of Books in Print* (20th Edition, 1991-92). sub. price: $10; per copy: $2; sample: $2. Back issues: $1.50. Discounts: none. 32-36pp; 8½×11; photocopied. Reporting time: after our bimonthly deadlines (15th bimonthly). Payment: winners receive 1 copy. Copyrighted, reverts to author. Pub's reviews: 6 in 1990. §poetry magazines and poetry books.

POETIC SPACE: Poetry & Fiction, Don Hildenbrand, PO Box 11157, Eugene, OR 97440. 1983. Poetry, fiction, articles, art, interviews, reviews, news items. "Short to medium length poems, short fiction, short essays, articles, reviews. Artwork (line drawings, sketches), graphics. Prefer quality contemporary poetry but open to beginners. No traditional, romantic, rhymed. Open to experimental. Recent contributors: John Bennett, Lawson Fusao Inada, Albert Huffstickler, Arthur Winfield Knight, Sesslu Foster, Walt Phillips, B.D. Love, Walt Fraser, Barbara Henning, Tyione Williams, Joan Jobe Smith, Crawdad Nelson, Olga Broumas (drawings)." circ. 500-600. 2/yr. Pub'd 2 issues 1990; expects 2 issues 1991, 2 issues 1992. sub. price: $15 1 year; per copy: $3; sample: $2. Back issues: $5 per issue. 16pp; 8½×11; of. Reporting time: 1-4 months. Payment: in copies depending on budget (as to number). Copyrighted, rights revert, but reserve right to include in anthology. Pub's reviews: 6 in 1990. §Poetry, contemporary, short stories, novels. Ads: $150/$80/$40 1/4 page/$30 3 X 4/$25 business card.

Poetical Histories, Peter Riley, 27 Sturton Street, Cambridge CB1 2QG, United Kingdom, 0223-327455. 1986. Poetry. "We publish only new British poetry in craft-produced pamphlets of 4-8 pages. Anyone submitting is strongly advised to consult previously published texts with regard to style." avg. press run 150-200. Pub'd 3 titles 1990; expects 4 titles 1991, 4 titles 1992. 3 titles listed in the *Small Press Record of Books in Print* (20th Edition, 1991-92). avg. price, paper: £3.50. Discounts: 1/3 off—trade. 8pp; octavo; lp. Reporting time: 2 weeks. Payment: usually none. Copyrights for author.

POETICS JOURNAL, Lyn Hejinian, Barrett Watten, 2639 Russell Street, Berkeley, CA 94705, 415-548-1817. 1981. Articles, interviews, criticism, reviews. "*POETICS JOURNAL* is published once a year. It is a journal of contemporary poetics by poets and prose writers as well as by other artists, critics, linguists, and political theorists. Issues to date include #1 "Introduction," #2 "Close Reading,", #3 "Poetry & Philosophy," #4 "Women & Language," #5 "Non/Narrative," #6 "Public & Private Language," #7 "Postmodernism?" #8 "Elsewhere" Future issues are planned on "The Person" and "Poetry & Pleasure." Past contributors include Ron Silliman, Leslie Scalapino, Alice Notley, Charles Bernstein, Bev Dahlen, and others." circ. 700. 1/yr. Pub'd 1 issue 1990; expects 1 issue 1991, 1 issue 1992. sub. price: US and Canada $20, $24 elsewhere; per copy: $8; sample: $8. Back issues: $50 for set of 1-5. Discounts: usual. 144pp; 6×9; of. Reporting time: 2 weeks. Payment: $2/page. Copyrighted, reverts to author. Pub's reviews: 8 in 1990. §Poetics, poetry, linguistics. No ads. CCLM.

POETPOURRI, Comstock Writers' Group, Inc., Box 3737 Taft Road, Syracuse, NY 13220. 1987. Poetry. circ. 500. 2/yr. Pub'd 2 issues 1990; expects 2 issues 1991, 2 issues 1992. sub. price: $8/2 issues; per copy: $4; sample: $4. Back issues: $3. 100pp; 5½×8½. Reporting time: 1-2 months. Payment: contributor's copy only. Copyrighted, reverts to author. §Poetry only.

POETRY, Joseph Parisi, Editor, 60 West Walton Street, Chicago, IL 60610, 312-280-4870. 1912. Poetry, reviews, long-poems. circ. 7.3M. 12/yr. Pub'd 12 issues 1990; expects 12 issues 1991, 12 issues 1992. sub. price: individuals $25, $31 outside USA, institutions $27, $33 outside USA; per copy: $2.50 plus $1 post.; sample: $2.50 plus $1 postage. Back issues: $3 plus $1 post. 64pp; 5×9; of. Reporting time: 8-10 weeks. Payment: $20-page prose, $2-line verse. Copyrighted, does not revert to author. Pub's reviews: 60 in 1990. §Poetry. Ads: $280/$174. CLMP.

POETRY AND AUDIENCE, Dr. J. Goodby, School of English, Cavendish Road, University of Leeds, Leeds Yorkshire, LS2 9JT, England. 1953. Poetry, reviews. "A market for serious, well crafted poems and prose of no more than 25 lines. Has a reputation for publishing established poets alongside quality material from unknown writers" circ. 400+. 2/yr. Pub'd 1 issue 1990; expects 2 issues 1991, 2 issues 1992. 2 titles listed in the *Small Press Record of Books in Print* (20th Edition, 1991-92). sub. price: overseas £2 per issue + 25% p/p, inland £1/issue + 25% p/p; per copy: £1; sample: £2 + 25% p/p. Back issues: £1 + 25% p/p. 60-80pp; quarto; of/lo. Reporting time: 1 month. Payment: none. Not copyrighted. Pub's reviews. §Poetry. Ads: £15, £8, back page £20. Yorkshire Federation of Small Presses.

Poetry Around, Robin Schultz, 436 Elm, Norman, OK 73069, 405-329-9143. 1982. Poetry. "No subject restrictions; almost always local or regional authors. Have published Larry Griffin, Jvar Jvash, Madison Morrison, Evan Zwick" avg. press run 400. Pub'd 2 titles 1990; expects 3 titles 1991, 2 titles 1992. avg. price, paper: $3.50. Discounts: 60% to booksellers. 36pp; 5½×8½; of. Reporting time: asap. Payment: 10% of run to author, but author is required to buy some additional copies at 1/2 retail price. Does not copyright for author.

POETRY AUSTRALIA, South Head Press, John Millett, Editor, Market Place, Berrima, N.S.W. 2577, Australia. 1964. Poetry, reviews. circ. 1.6M. 4-6/yr. Pub'd 4 issues 1990; expects 4 issues 1991, 4 issues 1992. sub. price: $40(USA); per copy: $10; sample: $4. Back issues: $12. Discounts: usual trade, 1/3 off. 80pp; 15½×24cm. Reporting time: 1 week - 1 month. Payment: copy of magazine. Copyrighted, reverts to author. Pub's reviews. §Poetry & prose. Ads: will exchange with U.S. mags.

POETRY CANADA, Quarry Press, Linda Bussiere, Managing Editor; Barry Dempster, Reviews and New Voices Editor, PO Box 1061, Kingston, Ontario K7L 4Y5, Canada. 1979. Poetry, articles, art, photos, cartoons, interviews, satire, criticism, reviews, news items. "Features a major Canadian poet on each cover and center-spread. As of Summer 1985, reviews every poetry book published in Canada. Each issue includes: International Page, New Voices Page. Prints feature articles by and about Canadian poets, autobiographical extracts of Canadian poets. Each issue features 5-7 full-page features of the 'rising stars' of Canadian poetry. SASE essential; foreign contributors use IRC." circ. 2.4M. 4/yr. Pub'd 4 issues 1990; expects 4 issues 1991, 4 issues 1992. sub. price: $15 indiv, $30 instit; per copy: $3.95; sample: $5 (includes 1st class individual p&h). Back issues: please inquire. 36pp; 11×15; of. Reporting time: 4-6 weeks. Payment: copies, $20 per poem 30-60 days after publication. Copyrighted. Pub's reviews: 32 in 1990. §Poetry Canadian, English & French Canadian. Ads: $200/$110 1-4 page/$55 classifieds/free. COSMEP, CMPA.

The Poetry Connection (see also THE POETRY CONNECTION), Sylvia Shichman, Editor; Publisher & Director, 301 East 64 Street #6K, New York, NY 10021, 212-249-5494. 1988. Poetry. "The Poetry Connection is a new "poetry contest information grapevine service whereby poetry contest flyers are distributed to *poets and writers,* provides information on *poetry information books, chap-book publishing,* and mailing of poetry contests for poetry publications and literary organizations and other information about activities pertaining to poetry"; also publishes *The Poetry Connection Newsletter* listing poetry contests!" Offset Printing. IWWG, National Writers Club, Poets & Writers, Southern Poetry Association.

THE POETRY CONNECTION, The Poetry Connection, Sylvia Shichman, Editor; Publisher & Director, 301 East 64 Street #6K, New York, NY 10021, 212-249-5494. 1988. Poetry. "*The Poetry Connection* distributes poetry contest flyers from numerous poetry publications and poetry organizations; information on how to *sell your poetry/books & chap-book publishing;* also publishes *The Poetry Connection Newsletter* listing poetry contests!" 6/yr. Pub'd 6 issues 1990; expects 6 issues 1991, 6 issues 1992. sub. price: $25; per copy: (Mini Sample - $3.50) plus 2 SASE'S; sample: (Mini Sample - $3.50) plus 2 SASE'S. Back issues: $3.50, $15 (6 months), $25 (1 year). †Offset Printing. Ads: $85/$50/$30 1/4 page/$20 1/8 page. IWWC, National Writers Club, Poets & Writers, Southern Poetry Association.

POETRY DURHAM, David Hartnett, Michael O'Neill, Gareth Reeves, Dept. of English, Univ. of Durham, Elvet Riverside, New Elvet, Durham DH1 3JT, England, (091) 374-2730. 1982. Poetry. "Anna Adams, Fleur Adcock, Charles Boyle, David Constantine, C.B. Cox, Kevin Crossley-Holland, Peter Dale, Donald Davie, Dick Davis, Douglas Dunn, Alistair Elliot, Gavin Ewart, Ruth Fainlight, Vicki Feaver, Roy Fisher, Duncan Forbes, Reginald Gibbons, James Greene, Romesh Gunesekera, Rachel Hadas, Michael Hulse, Denise Catharine James, Kathleen Jamie, James Kirkup, Jean Hanff Korelitz, Grevel Lindop, John Lucas, E.A. Markham, Jamie McKendrick, Medbh McGuckian, Samuel Menashe, Evangeline Paterson, William Scammell, Michael Schmidt, Peter Scupham, Deirdre Shanahan, C.H. Sisson, Gerard Smyth, Anne Stevenson, Martin Stokes, Matthew Sweeney, John Ward, Val Warner, David Wright." circ. 600. 3/yr. Pub'd 3 issues 1990; expects 3 issues 1991, 3 issues 1992. sub. price: £4-50; per copy: £1-50; sample: £1-50/$6. Discounts: 33⅓% off cover price for bookstores. Other discount by arrangement. 42pp; 5¾×8¼; of. Reporting time: 1 month. Payment: £12 sterling per poem. Not copyrighted. Pub's reviews: 5 in 1990. §Books of contemporary poetry. Ads: £15.

POETRY EAST, Richard Jones, Dept. of English, DePaul Univ., 802 West Belden Avenue, Chicago, IL 60614, 312-341-5114. 1980. Poetry, fiction, articles, art, photos, interviews, criticism, reviews, letters, collages, concrete art, news items. "Contributors include Tomas Transtromer, Amiri Baraka, Robert Hass, Stanley Kunitz, Gloria Fuertes, Philip Levine, Sharon Olds, Robert Bly, Louis Simpson, Richard Shelton, Miklos Radnoti, W. H. Auden, Larry Levis, Donald Hall, David Ignatow, Wm. Stafford, Linda Gregg, Czeslaw Milosz, James Tate, Denise Levertov, Louis Jenkins, June Jordan, Simon Ortiz, and Galway Kinnell. *Poetry East* also publishes volumes dedicated to a particular topic or poet. Recent special issues have included "Surrealism and Recent American Poetry" (*PE #7*); Art & Guns: Political Poetry at Home And Abroad" (*PE #9/10*); "Poetry and the Visual Arts" (*PE #13/14*); a special issue devoted to Muriel Rukeyser (*PE #16/17*); a collection of essays on Poetic form (PE# 20/21); "The Poetry of Thomas McGrath" (*PE #23/24*); and "The Poetry of Gerald Stern" (*PE # 26*). *Poetry East* is interested in reading essays on poetics, the relationship between art and the world, etc. We are also interested in translations and ideas for feature/symposia." circ. 1.5M. 2/yr. Pub'd 2 issues 1990; expects 2 issues 1991, 2 issues 1992. sub. price: $12; per copy: $7; sample: $7. Back issues: #9/10 *Art & Guns: Political Poetry* $10; #19 *The Inward Eye: the Photographs of Ed Roseberry* $10. Discounts: bookstores 30%. 200pp for single issue, 300pp for double issue; 5½×8½; of. Reporting time: 3 months. Payment: copies, honorariums. Copyrighted, reverts to author. Pub's reviews: 4-5 in 1990. §Poetry, criticism, biography, literature, film, art, photography, etc. Ads: $100/$50. CCLM.

POETRY FLASH, Joyce Jenkins, Publisher & Editor; Richard Silberg, Associate Editor; Dawn Kolokithas, Contributing Editor, PO Box 4172, Berkeley, CA 94704, 415-525-5476. 1972. Poetry, articles, art, photos, cartoons, interviews, criticism, reviews, letters, collages, news items. "*Poetry Flash* is California's monthly review of poetry. We cover far beyond the nine Bay Area counties. Our book reviews and interviews arent limited to Bay Area-We list whatever we find out about in Los Angeles or anywhere in California. We list conferences all over the country. We use West Coast calendar items, information interesting or useful to poets (places to publish, prizes, workshops, etc.) and reviews of books and readings. Monthly feature articles" circ. 17M. 12/yr. Pub'd 12 issues 1990; expects 12 issues 1991. sub. price: $12 individuals, $14 institutions; per copy: $1 or free at bookstores, libraries, cafes in the bay area; sample: $1. Back issues: $1. 24pp; 11½×15, tabloid; of. Reporting time: 3 months. Payment: subscription, payment for longer articles by arrangement. Copyrighted, reverts to author. Pub's reviews: 150 in 1990. §Poetry, exploratory fiction, criticism or literary biography, especially poetry related. Ads: $400/$200/$10 column inch. CLMP.

The Poetry Group (see also POETRY HALIFAX DARTMOUTH), Mark Hamilton, Box 7074 North, Halifax, Nova Scotia B3K 4J5, Canada. 1986. Poetry, fiction, art, reviews. "We publish on whim- if we like it, it goes in!" avg. press run 200. Pub'd 6 titles 1990; expects 6 titles 1991, 6 titles 1992. avg. price, paper: $2. Discounts: 10% jobbers, 20% 6 copies or more. 20pp; 7×8½; of. Reporting time: 2 weeks. Payment: 2 copies + $5 Canadian. Does not copyright for author. Canadian Poetry Association, Atlantic Publishers Association, Small Press Action Network.

POETRY HALIFAX DARTMOUTH, The Poetry Group, Mark Hamilton, PO Box 7074 North, Halifax, Nova Scotia B3K 5J4, Canada. 1986. Poetry, fiction, articles, art, photos, cartoons, satire, collages, concrete art, news items, non-fiction. circ. 300. 6/yr. Pub'd 11 issues 1990; expects 6 issues 1992. sub. price: $15 Can, $20 US; per copy: $2; sample: $2. Discounts: Book jobbers 10% off. 24-36pp; 7×8½; of. Reporting time: up to 4 months. Payment: 2 copies. Copyrighted, reverts to author. Pub's reviews: 2 in 1990. §Canadian poetry, music, literature. Ads: on request. Atlantic Publishers Association, Small Press Action Network.

Poetry Ireland Press (see also POETRY IRELAND REVIEW), John Ennis, 44 Upper Mount, St. Dublin 2, Ireland. 1981. Poetry, reviews. avg. press run 1M. Pub'd 4 titles 1990; expects 4 titles 1991, 4 titles 1992. avg. price, paper: $6. 100pp; 6×8; photoset. Reporting time: 3 months. Payment: in copies. Copyrights for author.

POETRY IRELAND REVIEW, Poetry Ireland Press, John Ennis, 44 Upper Mount Street, Dublin 2, Ireland. 1981. Poetry, interviews, criticism. *"Poetry Ireland Review* accepts material from outside Ireland. The themes do not have to be necessarily Irish. We publish both established and lesser-known poets" circ. 1M. 4/yr. Pub'd 4 issues 1990; expects 4 issues 1991, 4 issues 1992. sub. price: $30; per copy: $6; sample: $6. Back issues: $6. 100pp; 6×8; Photoset. Reporting time: 3 months. Payment: only to reviewers, complimentary copies to poets. Copyrighted, reverts to author. Pub's reviews: 15 in 1990. §New major collections of international interest. Ads: $100/$50.

POETRY KANTO, William Elliott, Kazuo Kawamura, Hisao Kanaseki, Makoto Ooka, Shuntaro Tanikawa, Kanto Gakuin University, Kamariya, Kanazawa-Ku, Yokohama 236, Japan. 1984. Poetry. "Poems normally 30 lines or less. Bias against bathos, pornography, and 'woe is me!' Some recent contributors include (among Westerners); Denise Levertov, William Stafford, Kenneth Hanson, Vi Gale, Vern Rutsala, William Pitt Root, Harry Guest, Arthur Kimball, William Elliott, Eleanor Wilner, Seamus Heaney. Solicit poems in English or Japanese. Query before submitting, with SAE and reply coupons." circ. 700. 1/yr. Pub'd 1 issue 1990; expects 1 issue 1991, 1-2 issues 1992. 1 title listed in the *Small Press Record of Books in Print* (20th Edition, 1991-92). Back issues: send reply coupons to cover air mail or sea mail. 50-60pp; 7×10; lp. Reporting time: 2-4 weeks. Payment: 3 contributor's copies. Not copyrighted.

Poetry Magic Publications (see also WRITER'S VOICE), Lisa Roose-Church, 1630 Lake Drive, Haslett, MI 48840, 517-339-8754. 1987. Poetry, articles, art. "We accept work from all areas. A subscription does not guarantee publication of your work. An SASE must accompany all work or work will be discarded. All work should be original, unpublished work of author submitting it. We will consider previously published work if date and name of publication is noted at the time of submission. We do not accept pornographic material but will consider sexual themes if done in taste. Again, we don't promise anything. We reserve the right to edit your short story/article for grammar, punctuation, etc. If work is not legible it will be returned unread" Pub'd 3 titles 1990; expects 4 titles 1991, 4 titles 1992. 1 title listed in the *Small Press Record of Books in Print* (20th Edition, 1991-92). Discounts: work out at time of request. 168pp; 5½×8½; photocopy. Reporting time: 2-4 months, sometimes less. Copyrights for author. United Amateur Press, National Writers Club, WICI.

THE POETRY MISCELLANY, Richard Jackson, Michael Panori, English Dept. Univ of Tennessee, Chattanooga, TN 37403, 615-755-4213; 624-7279. 1971. Poetry, interviews, criticism, reviews, long-poems. "David Wagoner, Denise Levertov, Mark Strand, Laura Jensen, Richard Wilbur, Donald Justice, James Tate, Dara Wier, Carol Muske, Maxine Kumin,Marge Piercy, Robert Penn Warren, Dan Epstein, Marvin Bell, Jean Valentine, David St. John, A.R. Ammons, Stanley Kunitz, Charles Simic, John Hollander, Linda Pastan, William Stafford, John Haines, Pamela Stewart, Galway Kinnell, W. S. Merwin, William Meredith, Laurence Raab, Cynthia MacDonald, Robert Pack, Carolyn Forche, Anthony Hecht, John Ashbery, Donald Finkel, Michael Harper, Robert Creeley, David Ignatow, Donald Hall, Heather McHugh, Sharon Olds, Stanley Plumly, William Matthews. Review essays 3M words. We use translations too. Send translations with originals to John Duval, Translation Workshop, University of Arkansas, Fayetteville, AK 72701." circ. 650. 1/yr. Pub'd 2 issues 1990; expects 2 issues 1991. sub. price: $3; per copy: $2; sample: $2. Back issues: same price as current issues. Discounts: 30% for orders of ten or more to groups and individuals. 60pp; 6×9; of. Reporting time: 8-10 weeks. Payment: copies. Copyrighted, rights revert upon request as for re-publication. Pub's reviews: 1 in 1990.

§Poetry, poetics. Ads: $50 half page. CCLM.

POETRY MOTEL, Suburban Wilderness Press, Patrick McKinnon, Bud Backen, Jennifer Willis-Long, 1619 Jefferson, Duluth, MN 55812. 1984. Poetry, fiction, art, photos, interviews, satire, criticism, long-poems, collages. "We tend toward work that brings an interesting story. We prefer characters other than 'you' & 'me' & 'I.' We consider rhythm the element lacking in most of the work we pass up. We have published Ron Androla, Kathy Brady, Hugh Fox, Albert Huffstickler, and Jesse Glass recently." circ. 400-500. 1-2/yr. Pub'd 2 issues 1990; expects 1-2 issues 1991, 1-2 issues 1992. sub. price: $14 3 issues, $100 lifetime sub; per copy: $4.95; sample: $4.95. Back issues: $18.95 each. Discounts: inquire. 50-60pp; 7×8½; of. Reporting time: 1-4 weeks. Payment: contributor's copy. Copyrighted, reverts to author. Pub's reviews: 2 in 1990. §Poetry books, literary mags. No ads.

POETRY NEW YORK, Burt Kimmelman, Editor; Cheryl Fish, Associate Editor, Ph.D. Program in English, CUNY, 33 West 42 Street, New York, NY 10036, (212) 642-2206. 1985. Poetry. "Translations welcome." circ. 500. 1/yr. Pub'd 1 issue 1990; expects 1 issue 1991, 2 issues 1992. price per copy: $5; sample: $5. Back issues: $4. 50pp; 7×9; lp. Reporting time: 4 months. Payment: copies. Copyrighted, reverts to author.

POETRY NIPPON, The Poetry Nippon Press, Atsuo Nakagawa, 11-2, 5-chome, Nagaike-cho, Showa-ku, Nagoya 466, Japan. 1967. Poetry, articles, photos, interviews, criticism, reviews, letters, news items. "Translations of Japanese poems, poems on topical themes or Japan, Tanka, Haiku, one-line poems are solicited from non-members. Guest poems are also printed." circ. 500. 4/yr. Expects 4 issues 1991. sub. price: 44 Int'l Reply Coupons, or $27 (by Int'l Postal Money Order only); per copy: 18 IRC's; sample: 4 IRC's. Back issues: depends on issues. Discounts: 30% for bulk order. 45pp; size A5; of. Reporting time: 1 year. Payment: depends on ms. Copyrighted, reverts to author. Pub's reviews: 6 in 1990. §Poetry books and magazines. Ads: $83/$52.

The Poetry Nippon Press (see also POETRY NIPPON), Atsuo Nakagawa, 11-2, 5-Chome, Nagaike-cho, Showa-ku, Nagoya 466, Japan, 052-833-5724. 1967. Poetry, articles, art, photos, interviews, criticism, reviews, letters, collages, concrete art, news items. "Translations of Japanese poems, poems on topical themes or Japan, Tanka, Haiku, one-line poems are solicited." avg. press run 200-1M. Pub'd 2 titles 1990; expects 2 titles 1991. 3 titles listed in the *Small Press Record of Books in Print* (20th Edition, 1991-92). Discounts: 30% for bulk order. 60-200pp; size A5; of. Reporting time: 1 year. Payment: depends on ms. Copyrights for author.

POETRY NOTTINGHAM: The International Magazine of Today's Poetry, Poetry Nottingham Society Publications, Claire Piggott, Summer Cottage, West Street, Shelford, Notts, NG12 1EJ, England, 0602 334540. 1941. Poetry, articles, art, criticism, reviews, letters, concrete art, news items. "Poems in any form. Overseas contributions welcome. Rates on application." circ. 400. 4/yr. Pub'd 4 issues 1990; expects 4 issues 1991, 4 issues 1992. sub. price: £7; per copy: £1.75 includes postage & handling.; sample: half price + p.p. £1 in sterling; or $5 U.S. Back issues: half price and p.p. Discounts: 33½% to bookshops. 36pp; 8¼×6; of. Reporting time: 2 months. Payment: complimentary copy. Copyright remains with authors. Ads: £10/£5.

Poetry Nottingham Society Publications (see also POETRY NOTTINGHAM: The International Magazine of Today's Poetry), Claire Piggott, Summer Cottage, West Street, Shelford, Notts. NG12 1EJ, England. 1941. Poetry. "Poetry including graphics." avg. press run 250. Expects 2 titles 1991, 2 titles 1992. 2 titles listed in the *Small Press Record of Books in Print* (20th Edition, 1991-92). avg. price, paper: £1.75 sterling. 8¼×6; of, lp. Reporting time: 2 months. Payment: complimentary copy. Copyrights for author.

POETRY OF THE PEOPLE, Paul Cohen, PO Box 13077, Gainesville, FL 32604, 904-375-3324. 1986. Poetry, art, photos, satire. "Length of poems ranges from one line to a page and a half. No racist or ethnocentric literature accepted. Upcoming issues: February 1991 - Martin Luther King; March 1991 - Reverend Angel Dust; April 1991 - Local Poetry (Gainesville, FL); May 1991 - Che Guevara; June 1991 - Erotic Poetry; July 1991 - Sky; August 1991 - Wind; September 1991 - Autumn; October 1991 - Ocean. The editor seeks poems that fit into these themes. If you have good poems that don't fit, send them anyway since they may be published in pamphlets not yet planned. Or they may have indirect references to themes included above. Poems to be returned should have an accompanying SASE. For an optional in-depth critique send $3. CHEAP!" circ. 300-3M. 12/yr. Pub'd 12 issues 1990; expects 12 issues 1991, 12 issues 1992. sub. price: $8; per copy: $1.50; sample: $1.50. Back issues: 1 for $1.50, 3 for $2, 7 for $3. Discounts: 7-20 15¢, 20-500 12¢, 500-1000 10¢, 1000-2000 8¢, 2000-5000 7¢, 5000+ 5¢. 8pp; 4¼×5½; of. Reporting time: 4 months. Payment: 5 sample copies. Copyrighted, reverts to author. Ads: $40/$25.

THE POETRY PEDDLER, Snowbound Press, J.J. Snow, A.M. Ryant, PO Box 250, W. Monroe, NY 13167, 315-676-2050. 1988. Poetry, reviews. "Send for guidelines. Poems of one page length only. Nothing that *exalts* bigotry, war or violence accepted—eros yes, porno no. Recent contributors: Tom Delargey, Jack Karpan, Charlie Mehrhoff, John Marrs, A.D. Winans, Walt Phillips, A.W. Knight, Stan Proper, Susan Manchester, Judson Crews, Nika Helmer" circ. 150. 6/yr. Pub'd 1 issue 1990; expects 6 issues 1991, 6 issues 1992. sub. price: $10; per copy: $2; sample: $2. Back issues: $2. 26pp; 8½×11; †desktop. Reporting time: 4 weeks.

451

Payment: 1 contributor's copy. Not copyrighted. Pub's reviews: 1 in 1990. §Poetry.

POETRY QUARTERLY, The Curlew Press, P.J. Precious, Hare Cottage, Kettlesing, Harrogate, Yorkshire, England, Tel: Harrogate 770686. 1975. Poetry, fiction, articles, art, photos, cartoons, interviews, satire, criticism, reviews, letters, parts-of-novels, long-poems, collages, plays, concrete art, news items. "One author booklets and poemsheets published occasionally. Do *not* send American stamps with mss" circ. variable. Irregular. Pub'd 1 issue 1990; expects 1-2 issues 1991. sub. price: £5.75 U.K., $15 USA; per copy: $1.50/50P when available; sample: free when available. Back issues: some available on request. 5×8, 8×14; printing and xerox. Reporting time: by return of post when possible. Payment: none. Copyrighted, reverts to author. Pub's reviews: 1 in 1990. §Poetry, literature. Ads: £10/£5/10 words £1; 20 words £2, etc.(please count 1 dollar 50 cents per pound to cover bank charges in UK). YFSP (Yorkshire Federation of Small Presses).

POETRY RESOURCE CENTER OF MICHIGAN (PRC) NEWSLETTER & CALENDAR, Lee Schreiner, 111 East Kirby, Detroit, MI 48202, 313-399-6163. 1979. Articles, news items. "The *PRC Newsletter & Calendar* prints news items and lists recent books and forthcoming readings, workshops and other events. All material should pertain to poetry in and about the state of Michigan. Deadline for the receipt of material is the 15th of the preceding month. *The Poetry Resource Center of Michigan* is a nonprofit, tax exempt organization. Patronage includes subscription. We do not publish unsolicited poetry" circ. 3M. 10/yr. Pub'd 10 issues 1990; expects 10 issues 1991, 10 issues 1992. sub. price: $20; sample: free. Back issues: inquire. 4pp; 8½×11; of. Payment: none.

POETRY REVIEW, Peter Forbes, 21 Earls Court Square, London SW5 9DE, England, 071-373-7861; fax 071-244-7388. 1912. Poetry, articles, photos, interviews, criticism, reviews, letters, long-poems. circ. 5M. 4/yr. Pub'd 4 issues 1990; expects 4 issues 1991. sub. price: $40, $60 airmail; per copy: $10 surface; $15 airmail; sample: $10 surface, $15 airmail. Back issues: $10 surface, $15 airmail. Discounts: 1/3 to trade. 72pp; 240×170mm, copy size 198×147mm; of/lo. Reporting time: 3 months. Payment: £15 per poet for first poem, £20 for 2 poems. Copyrighted, reverts to author. Pub's reviews: 120 in 1990. §Poetry, criticism, relevant novels, biographies/autobiographies, belle-lettres, etc. Ads: £220/£150/£250 back page/£220 3,500 loose inserts. The Poetry Society.

POETRY: USA QUARTERLY, National Poetry Association Publishers, Jack Foley, Fort Mason Center, Building D, San Francisco, CA 94123, 415-776-6602. 1985. Poetry, reviews. "In the spirit of Dylan Thomas, *Poetry: USA* encourages 'bold and compassionate poetry'. Our scope of coverage includes seven distinct features, and hopes to embrace (in poetry) the multi-faceted experience of mankind. *Poetry: USA's* operating principle is to 'let the voice of the poet be heard throughout the land!' Some of our recent contributors include Adrienne Rich, Michael McClure, Rosario Murillo, Allen Ginsberg, Maya Angelou, Francisco Alarcon, Judy Grahn, & others" circ. 6M. 4/yr. Pub'd 4 issues 1990; expects 4 issues 1991, 4 issues 1992. sub. price: $7.50; per copy: $2; sample: $1.50 + 50¢ postage. Back issues: $2 (includes postage). Discounts: 50%. 24pp; 11×13; of. Reporting time: March 21, June 21, Sept. 21, Dec. 21. Payment: 2 copies. Copyrighted, reverts to author. Pub's reviews: 4 in 1990. §Poetry and poetry anthologies. Ads: $250/$150/$50 1/8 page/$25 card. P.E.N.

POETRY TODAY, Diane Chehab, 4950 Richard Street, Suite 60, Jacksonville, FL 32207. Poetry. "Accepting submissions of quality poetry. Send #10 SASE for guidelines or order a sample copy. Open to beginners as well as established poets." sample price: $3 make checks out to D. Chehab. Payment: 2 copies.

POETRY WALES, Poetry Wales Press, Ltd., Mike Jenkins, Andmar House, Tondu Road, Bridgend, Mid Glamorgan CF31 4LJ, Wales. 1965. Poetry, articles, criticism, reviews, letters, long-poems. "Articles of not less than 2M words. All types of poetry considered. Originally biased towards Welsh, Anglo-Welsh poetry, or poetry by persons living in Wales. Now wider approach encompasing all British and US poets, writers and translations of foreign poets and critiques of same." circ. 1M. 4/yr. Pub'd 4 issues 1990; expects 4 issues 1991, 4 issues 1992. sub. price: £10, $30; per copy: £1.95; sample: £1.95 + postage. Back issues: £1.95. Discounts: trade 33⅓. 72pp; 180×250mm; of. Reporting time: 3-4 weeks. Payment: by arrangement. Copyrighted, reverts to author. Pub's reviews: 50 in 1990. §Poetry, criticism, literary history. Ads: £75/£50/£25 quarter-page.

Poetry Wales Press, Ltd. (see also POETRY WALES), M.R. Felton, Andmar House, Tondu Road, Bridgend, Mid Glamorgan CF31 4LJ, Wales. 1981. "America distribution: Dufour Editions Inc., PO Box 449, Chester Springs, PA 19425." avg. press run varies greatly. Pub'd 15 titles 1990; expects 20 titles 1991, 24 titles 1992. 97 titles listed in the *Small Press Record of Books in Print* (20th Edition, 1991-92). avg. price, cloth: $25; paper: $14. Discounts: 35% UK, 35% export. 100pp; size varies; of. Reporting time: up to 6 weeks. Payment: by contract. Copyrights for author.

POETRY/LA, Helen Friedland, Editor; Barbara Strauss, Asst. Editor, PO Box 84271, Los Angeles, CA 90073, 213-472-6171. 1980. Poetry. "We publish poems with no prior restraint as to subject matter, style, or length by poets living in the Los Angeles area. Poems must be of high literary quality for a knowledgable sophisticated readership." circ. 500. 2/yr. Pub'd 2 issues 1990; expects 2 issues 1991, 2 issues 1992. sub. price: $8; per copy: $4.25; sample: $3.50. Back issues: $3.50 (nos. 1 and 2, $2). Discounts: trade-40% off plus shipping; agent-20%

452

off plus shipping. 125pp; 5½×8½; of. Reporting time: 1-6 months. Payment: copies only. Copyrighted, rights revert upon request. CLMP.

Poets & Writers, Inc. (see also POETS & WRITERS MAGAZINE), Daryln Brewer, Editor; Debby Mayer, Director of Publications, 72 Spring Street, New York, NY 10012, 212-226-3586. 1973. Articles, photos, interviews, letters, concrete art, news items, non-fiction. "Poets & Writers publishes *A Directory of Poets and Fiction Writers* a listing of those who publish in the US and pamphlets of practical information for writers on subjects such as reading series sponsors, copyright, literary bookstores, writers' conferences list, high school writers' resources list, California writers' resources list. Additional titles: *Literary Agents: A Writer's Guide, The Writing Business, A Poets and Writers Handbook, A Writer's Guide to Copyright, Literary Bookstores - A Cross-Country Guide, Author & Audience: A Readings and Workshops Guide.*" avg. press run 3M-5M. Pub'd 4 titles 1990; expects 2 titles 1991, 3 titles 1992. 5 titles listed in the *Small Press Record of Books in Print* (20th Edition, 1991-92). avg. price, paper: $21.95 directory; other: $5.95-$11.95. Discounts: For directories: 5 or more, 40%; also to listed writers, 20%. Pages vary; 8½×11, 5¼×8; of. Reporting time: 2 months (*P & W Magazine*). Payment: minimal. Does not copyright for author. CLMP.

POETS & WRITERS MAGAZINE, Poets & Writers, Inc., Daryln Brewer, Editor, 72 Spring Street, New York, NY 10012, 212-226-3586. 1973. Articles, photos, letters, concrete art, news items. "*Poets & Writers Magazine* publishes factual articles of interest to writers, editors, publishers, and all others interested in contemporary American literature. It also publishes essays, interviews with writers, and news and comments on publishing, political issues, grants and awards, and requests for submissions. Most articles are written by freelance writers. Always send a letter of inquiry to the editor prior to submitting a manuscript. *Poets & Writers Magazine* has a Letters column and encourages comment from readers. We publish occasional reviews of reference books, but do not review poetry or fiction." circ. 40M. 6/yr. Pub'd 6 issues 1990; expects 6 issues 1991, 6 issues 1992. sub. price: $18/1 yr, $32/2 yrs for individuals, $16/1 yr, $28/2 yrs for writers listed with Poets & Writers; per copy: $3.50; sample: $3.50. Back issues: $3.50. Discounts: bookstores, min. 10 copies, 40%; to distributors, min. 10 copies, 50%; to teachers, for bulk subscriptions, min. 20, 20% to one address. 64-88pp; 8½×11; webb of. Reporting time: 2 months. Payment: $100-$300. Copyrighted, does not revert to author. Ads: $935/$500/$280/$165 less 20% at 6x rate. Classifieds: $25, up to 50 words; over 50 words, 50¢ per additional word. COSMEP, CCLM.

POETS AT WORK, Jessee Poet Publications, Jessee Poet, R.D. #1, Portersville, PA 16051. 1985. Poetry. "Length—about 20 lines and under. I publish everyone who writes in good taste. Charles Dickson, Ralph Hammond, Glenna Halloway, Ann Gasser, and at least 300 other poets. I am a marvelous market for unpublished poets." circ. 300+. 6/yr. Pub'd 6 issues 1990; expects 6 issues 1991, 6 issues 1992. sub. price: $16; per copy: $3; sample: $3. Back issues: $3. 36-40pp; 8½×11; †Mita copying machine. Reporting time: 1 week. Payment: none. Copyrighted, reverts to author. Ads: negotiable.

POET'S FORUM, The Dayspring Press, Inc., John C. Brainerd, 18600 West 58 Avenue, Golden, CO 80403-1070, 303-279-2462. Poetry. Discounts: 1/3 over 15 copies.

POETS ON:, Ruth Daigon, 29 Loring Avenue, Mill Valley, CA 94941. 1976. Poetry. "*Poets On:* explores basic human concerns through crafted poetry. Each issue is theme-oriented, e.g., *Loving, Loss, Roots...* Some of our contributors are Marge Piercy, Sharon Olds, Eve Merriam, John Tagliabue, James Chevill." circ. 475. 2/yr. Pub'd 2 issues 1990; expects 2 issues 1991. 1 title listed in the *Small Press Record of Books in Print* (20th Edition, 1991-92). sub. price: $8; per copy: $4; sample: $4. Back issues: $4. 48pp; 5½×8½; lp. Reporting time: 2 months. Payment: 1 copy. Copyrighted, reverts to author. COSMEP, CCLM.

POETS. PAINTERS. COMPOSERS., Carl Diltz, Jim Andrews, (Canada); Joe Keppler, 10254 35th Avenue SW, Seattle, WA 98146, 206-937-8155. 1984. Poetry, articles, art, photos, interviews, criticism, reviews, music, letters, long-poems, collages, plays, concrete art. circ. 300. 1/yr. Pub'd 1 issue 1990; expects 1 issue 1991, 2 issues 1992. price per copy: varies due to artwork involved; sample: $10 for either poster issue or tape issue. Back issues: $20 for third issue, $50 for fifth issue. Pages vary; 8½×11 for odd numbered issues; mi, of, silkscreen, hand printed, xerox, tape (audio). Reporting time: immediately. Payment: copy. Copyrighted, reverts to author. Pub's reviews: 20 in 1990. §Poetry, criticism, philosophy, art, film, popular culture, politics, religion.

POETS' ROUNDTABLE, Esther Alman, 826 South Center Street, Terre Haute, IN 47807, 812-234-0819. 1939. Poetry, news items. "*Poets' Rountable* is a bulletin published bimonthly for members of Poets' Study Club. It is not an open market for poetry. Open contests: One annual open competition—The International Contest, with awards of $25 and $15 in three categories: serious poems, light verse, traditional haiku. No entry fees. Deadline is February 1st each year. Send entries to Annual International Contest, Esther Alman, 826 South Center Street, Terre Haute, IN 47807. We use *only* material by members for publication, but annual contest is open to everyone." circ. 2M. 6/yr. Pub'd 6 issues 1990; expects 6 issues 1991, 6 issues 1992. sub. price: $6-membership; sample: free. 10pp; 8½×11; †mi. Payment: none. Copyrighted, reverts to author. Pub's reviews: 25 in 1990. No ads.

Pogo Press, Incorporated, Moira F. Harris, 4 Cardinal Lane, St. Paul, MN 55127, 612-483-4692. 1986. Art, non-fiction. "Submission by prearrangement only." avg. press run 3M. Pub'd 2 titles 1990; expects 2 titles 1991, 2 titles 1992. 7 titles listed in the *Small Press Record of Books in Print* (20th Edition, 1991-92). avg. price, cloth: $39.95; paper: $16.95. Discounts: query. Pages vary; size varies; of. Reporting time: 60 days. Payment: negotiable. Copyrights for author. Minnesota Independent Publishers Association.

Point Loma Publications, Inc., Emmette Small, PO Box 6507, San Diego, CA 92106. 1 title listed in the *Small Press Record of Books in Print* (20th Edition, 1991-92).

Point Publications, 3701 Shoreline Drive, Wayzata, MN 55391. 1 title listed in the *Small Press Record of Books in Print* (20th Edition, 1991-92).

Point Riders Press (see also RENEGADE), Arn Henderson, Frank Parman, PO Box 2731, Norman, OK 73070. 1974. Poetry. "Publisher of books of poetry. Over 20 books in print. Unsolicited mss discouraged. Not impressed by academic letterhead or address." avg. press run 500-1M. Pub'd 1 title 1990; expects 3 titles 1991, 2 titles 1992. 33 titles listed in the *Small Press Record of Books in Print* (20th Edition, 1991-92). avg. price, paper: $5.95. Discounts: single copy 15%, 2 to 4 copies 25%, 5 or more 40%. 64pp; 6×9, 5½×8½; of. Reporting time: 3-6 months. Payment: in copies. Copyrights for author.

POISON PEN WRITERS NEWS, Baker Street Publications, Sharida Rizzuto, Sidney J. Dragon, Thomas Schellenberger, PO Box 994, Metairie, LA 70004, 504-734-8414. 1983. Poetry, fiction, articles, art, photos, cartoons, interviews, satire, criticism, reviews, letters, long-poems, collages, plays, news items, non-fiction. circ. under 10M. 3/yr. Pub'd 3 issues 1990; expects 3 issues 1991, 3 issues 1992. sub. price: $12/3 issues; per copy: $4; sample: $4. Back issues: $4. Discounts: trade with other like publications. 25-35pp; 8½×11; of, photo copy, excellent quality offset covers. Reporting time: 2-6 weeks. Payment: free copies, fees paid for articles, reviews, art work. Copyrighted, reverts to author. Pub's reviews: 16 in 1990. §Writers' craft and writers' market. Ads: free. NWC, SPWAO, HWA, Literary Markets, MWA, Western Writers of America (WWA), Arizona Authors Association (AAA).

THE POISONED PEN, Jeffrey Meyerson, 8801 Shore Road, 6A East, Brooklyn, NY 11209-5409, 718-833-8248. 1978. Articles, interviews, criticism, reviews, letters, news items, non-fiction. "Anything of interest or related to the mystery field might be published. Bias, if any, towards 'fannish' rather than very 'academic', though many of our contributors are academics themselves. Recent contributors include: R. Jeff Banks, Marvin Lachman, Robert Adey, Maryell Cleary, Barry Pike, Gary Warren Niebuhr, George Kelley" circ. 350. 2/yr. Pub'd 2 issues 1990; expects 2 issues 1991, 2 issues 1992. sub. price: $20/$36 (overseas airmail); per copy: $5; sample: $5. Back issues: Vol 4 #5/6 $4.00 per copy, Vol 5 #1-2-3-4 $4 per copy, Vol 6 #1-2-3-4 $4 per copy. Discounts: single issue: 33%, 5 copies; 40%, 10 or more copies. 76pp; 8½×11; of. Reporting time: 2 weeks. Payment: one free issue for articles/reviews. Not copyrighted. Pub's reviews: 97 in 1990. §Mystery, detective, fiction, non-fiction, criticism.

Polexii Press, J. Michael Dashiell, PO Box 14, Goldsmith, IN 46045-0014. 1989. Poetry. "Publishing firm liberal, college educated audience" avg. press run 1M. Expects 2 titles 1991, 1 title 1992. 1 title listed in the *Small Press Record of Books in Print* (20th Edition, 1991-92). avg. price, paper: $7.95. Discounts: 40% direct to bookstores, 50% for wholesalers. 125pp; 6×9; of. Reporting time: 1 year. Payment: 15%. Copyrights for author. COSMEP.

POLITICAL BEHAVIOR, Plenum Publishing Corporation, Heinz Eulau, 233 Spring Street, New York, NY 10013, (212) 741-3087. 1979. Articles, non-fiction. "Since 1979, *Political Behavior* has provided a forum for the interdisciplinary study of groups and individuals as they interact in and with the political process. Drawing from the fields of economics, psychology, sociology, and political science, *PB* has become a unique and authoritative source for students of political behavior. All correspondence concerning subscriptions should be addressed to: Political Behavior, Fulfillment Dept., Agathon Press, Inc., 49 Sheridan Avenue, Albany, NY 12210. All editorial correspondence should be addressed to the Editor, Heinz Eulau, Dept. of Political Science, Stanford University, Stanford, CA 94305" 4/yr. Pub'd 4 issues 1990; expects 4 issues 1991, 4 issues 1992. sub. price: indiv. $25, instit. $50; per copy: $14. Back issues: 1979-87 (Vols. 1-9, 4 issues ea.) $50 per vol. Discounts: 10% discount to subscription agents. 96pp; 6½×9½; of. Reporting time: 3 months. Payment: none. Copyrighted, does not revert to author. Ads: $150/$90. COSMEP.

Political Research Associates, Jean Hardisty, 678 Massachusetts Avenue, Suite 205, Cambridge, MA 02139, 671-661-9313. 6 titles listed in the *Small Press Record of Books in Print* (20th Edition, 1991-92).

POLITICALLY INCORRECT, The Organization, Thomas Lucero, M.J. Lyle, Box 170, 400 N. High Street, Columbus, OH 43215, 614-447-8178. 1991. Poetry, fiction, articles, cartoons, interviews, satire, reviews, music, letters, long-poems, news items, non-fiction. "3,000 words or less. Minarchist, marginalia" circ. 74. 16/yr. Expects 16 issues 1991, 16 issues 1992. sub. price: $12; per copy: $1; sample: $1. Back issues: $1. Discounts: 50% to retailers. 8pp; 8½×11; †mi. Reporting time: 5-45 days. Payment: on acceptance; negotiable.

454

Copyrighted, reverts to author. Pub's reviews. §Politics, science religion, sex, health, music, wine, drugs, science fiction.

Pollard Press, Louise Lum, Owner, RR 01, Box 201, Niota, IL 62358-9782. 1989. Non-fiction. "Want humor and how-to's." avg. press run 1.5M. Expects 2-4 titles 1991, 2 titles 1992. 2 titles listed in the *Small Press Record of Books in Print* (20th Edition, 1991-92). avg. price, paper: $7.95, $9.95. Discounts: 40% bookstores. 170pp; 6×9, 5½×8½. Reporting time: 2 weeks. Payment: $200, 50¢ a book on books sold for standard retail prices. Copyrights for author. ABA, FPG, FLA, PMA.

Poltroon Press, Alastair Johnston, PO Box 5476, Berkeley, CA 94705, 415-654-4745. 1974. Poetry, fiction, art, photos, interviews, satire, criticism, concrete art, non-fiction. "Do not read unsolicited work. Recent books: Lucia Berlin's *Safe & Sound,* short stories, 1988; Alastair Johnston's *Musings On The Vernacular,* illustrated essays, 1988; Robert Gregory's *Interferences,* poetry, 1987; Dawn Kolokithas' *A Week In The Life Of The Marines, America's Elite Fighting Team,* experimental fiction, 1988." avg. press run 200-500. Pub'd 4 titles 1990; expects 5 titles 1991, 4 titles 1992. 5 titles listed in the *Small Press Record of Books in Print* (20th Edition, 1991-92). avg. price, cloth: $30; paper: $12. Discounts: distributor: Anacapa, Berkeley; Small Press Distribution. 64pp; 6×9; †lp. Payment: 15%. Copyrights for author. PCBA.

Polygonal Publishing House, Michael Weinstein, PO Box 357, Washington, NJ 07882, 908-689-3894. 1976. Non-fiction. "We publish books on mathematics." avg. press run 1M. Pub'd 1 title 1990; expects 1 title 1991, 1 title 1992. 12 titles listed in the *Small Press Record of Books in Print* (20th Edition, 1991-92). avg. price, cloth: $14; paper: $5. Discounts: 20% trade & bulk. 200pp; of. Payment: 17%.

Polymath Systems (see also NET), Kevin Langdon, PO Box 795, Berkeley, CA 94701, 415-524-0345. 1978. Articles, cartoons, criticism, reviews, letters, non-fiction. "We publish books, psychological tests, and computer software. Our books are on philosophical, psychological, and religious topics. We publish intelligence, vocabulary, and other psychological tests. We publish entertainment and productivity software for the IBM PC and compatibles. There are no upper or lower length limits. We are looking for serious, thoughtful, original work in our fields of interest. We are not interested in humor, poetry, fiction, politics, or positive thinking." avg. press run 1M. Expects 3 titles 1991, 3 titles 1992. 5 titles listed in the *Small Press Record of Books in Print* (20th Edition, 1991-92). avg. price, paper: $10; other: software $20. Discounts: based on size of order only: $20-10%, $50-15%, $100-20%, $200-25%, $500-30%, $1000-35%, etc. 75pp; 5½×8½, 8½×11; of. Reporting time: variable. Payment: 15% of post-discount gross or we buy copies manufactured by author. Copyrights for author if not already copyrighted.

Poor Souls Press/Scaramouche Books, Paul Fericano, Editor; Roger Langton, Assoc. Editor; Al Jarry, Pataphysical Editor; Gary Ligi, Assoc. Editor; Katherine Fericano, Managing Editor, PO Box 236, Millbrae, CA 94030. 1974. Satire. "Sorry, but Poor Souls Press cannot accept unsolicited material. If you're a satirist, we encourage self-publishing and close contact with others involved in the genre. Poor Souls Press is the book publishing subsidiary of Yossarian Universal (YU) News Service, the world's only parody news and disinformation syndicate with bureaus in 37 cities worldwide. We publish broadsides, postcards, chapbooks, pamphlets, and dispatches." avg. press run 1M-2.5M. Pub'd 3 titles 1990; expects 3 titles 1991, 3 titles 1992. 64 titles listed in the *Small Press Record of Books in Print* (20th Edition, 1991-92). avg. price, paper: $6.95; other: 2¢, 5¢, 10¢ etc. 1-24pp; 8½×11, 5½×8½; †mi/of/lp. Payment: usually pay our authors with half the print run. Copyrights for author. (YU) Yossarian Universal News Service.

POP VOID, Pop Void Publications, Jim Morton, 109 Minna Street, Suite 583, San Francisco, CA 94105, 415-362-1157. COSMEP.

Pop Void Publications (see also POP VOID), Jim Morton, 109 Minna Street, Suite 583, San Francisco, CA 94105, 415-362-1157. 1986. Articles, photos, interviews, criticism, non-fiction. "Accept 1,500 to 3,000 word articles on a wide variety of subjects. Prefer submissions by those who are familiar with *Pop Void's* editorial stance. Query first" avg. press run 5M. Pub'd 2 titles 1990; expects 4 titles 1991, 6 titles 1992. 1 title listed in the *Small Press Record of Books in Print* (20th Edition, 1991-92). avg. price, paper: $9.95. 128pp; 8×10; †of. Reporting time: 6 weeks. Payment: $50-$150 depending on article. Does not copyright for author. COSMEP.

POPULAR FOLK MUSIC TODAY, Allan Shaw, 6 South 230 Cohasset Rd., Naperville, IL 60540-3535, 608-961-3559. 1990. Articles, photos, cartoons, interviews, reviews, music, letters, news items, non-fiction. "Generally short" circ. 3M. 4/yr. Pub'd 4 issues 1990; expects 4 issues 1991, 4 issues 1992. sub. price: $8; per copy: $2; sample: free. 16pp; of. Payment: none. Not copyrighted. Pub's reviews. §Popular Music, Especially folk music.

Popular Medicine Press, Jack Z. Yetiv, PO Box 1212, San Carlos, CA 94070, 415-594-1855. 1986. Non-fiction. "Current active title is *Popular Nutritional Practices: A Scientific Appraisal,* a hard-hitting, unbiased book written by a physician/scientist. This 320-page book dispassionately evaluates multiple popular nutritional practices, including megavitamins, weight-loss diets, herbal remedies, starch blockers, food allergy and cytotoxic testing, Life Extension ideas and regimens, fish oil and heart disease, hypoglycemia, diets for diabetics, high blood pressure, and many others. Similar book manuscripts will be considered, although we are currently devoting most of our attention to the above title. This book is $17.95 (ppb.), $23.95 (case), retail, pp." avg. press run 5M. Expects 1 title 1991, 1 title 1992. 1 title listed in the *Small Press Record of Books in Print* (20th Edition, 1991-92). Discounts: trade, 20% on STOP orders. 350pp; 6×9; of. Reporting time: 8 weeks. Payment: to be arranged. Copyrights for author.

Popular Reality Press, David Crowbar, PO Box 571, Greenwood Lake, NY 10925-0571. 1984. Fiction, satire, criticism, non-fiction. avg. press run 2M. Pub'd 2 titles 1990; expects 2 titles 1991, 2 titles 1992. 4 titles listed in the *Small Press Record of Books in Print* (20th Edition, 1991-92). avg. price, paper: $6.50; other: $3.50 final PopReal, 48 page tabloid. Discounts: 40% for 5-20, 50% for 21-100, 60% for over 100; 5% for advance payment for over 20. 160pp; 5½×8½; of. Reporting time: 1 month if accompanied by SASE. Does not copyright for author.

POPULAR WOODWORKING, EGW Publishing Company, David Camp, Editor, 1320 Galaxy Way, Concord, CA 94520, 415-671-6852. 1981. Articles, photos, cartoons, interviews, reviews, letters, news items, non-fiction. "An independent magazine on woodworking in the U.S. Emphasis on original woodworking plans and projects. We also do product reviews, book reviews, woodworking show reviews, shop tips, and interviews with prominent woodworkers" circ. 180M. 6/yr. Pub'd 6 issues 1990; expects 6 issues 1991, 6 issues 1992. sub. price: $17; per copy: $3.95; sample: $3.95. Back issues: $3.95. 92pp; 8⅛×10⅞; web of. Reporting time: within 6 weeks. Payment: $125-one time, $250-two times per published page, $5 per photo used, prefer 350-1.5M words. Copyrighted, rights revert, unless otherwise stated. Pub's reviews: 8 in 1990. §Any woodworking topic, business practices (sm. business), how-tos, etc. Ads: $3600/$2304/$1.95 word. COSMEP.

Porcepic Books, Guy Chadsey, Managing Editor, 4252 Commerce Circle, Victoria, B.C. V8Z 4M2, Canada, 604-727-6522. 1971. Poetry, fiction, non-fiction. "Publish poetry, children's literature, science fiction, other books of social and political relevance by Canadian authors. James Reaney, Dorothy Livesay, Judith Merril, Marilyn Bowering, David Godfrey, Robin Skelton, Eliszbeth Vonarburg, Candas Jane Dorsey." avg. press run 3M-5M. Pub'd 9 titles 1990; expects 11 titles 1991, 14 titles 1992. 43 titles listed in the *Small Press Record of Books in Print* (20th Edition, 1991-92). avg. price, cloth: $24.95; paper: $12.95. Discounts: 40% 5+. 200pp; 6×9; of. Reporting time: 12-14 weeks. Payment: varies. Copyrights for author. ACP, ABPBC, LPG, CBA.

The Porcupine's Quill, Inc., Tim Inkster, Elke Inkster, 68 Main Street, Erin, Ontario N0B 1T0, Canada, 519-833-9158. 1974. Poetry, fiction, art, criticism. avg. press run 500-1M. Pub'd 6 titles 1990; expects 7 titles 1991, 7 titles 1992. 73 titles listed in the *Small Press Record of Books in Print* (20th Edition, 1991-92). avg. price, cloth: $20; paper: $8.95; other: $40 limited editions. Discounts: 5 & over, 40%. 112pp; 6×9; †of. Reporting time: 2 months. Payment: per contract. Copyrights for author. LPG ACP LCP.

PORTABLE LOWER EAST SIDE, Kurt Hollander, Arthur Neusesian, Managing Editor, PO Box 30323, New York, NY 10011-0103. 1984. Poetry, fiction, art, photos, parts-of-novels, non-fiction. "*PLES* publishes fiction, poetry, photography, art + essays on the Lower East Side of New York City, past and present. Issue #8, Number Two, will feature gay and lesbian literature and subjects. Forthcoming issues will include New African material. Urban and humorous writing is preferred. We have a jury of guest editors picked from issue to issue." circ. 1M. 2/yr. Pub'd 2 issues 1990; expects 2 issues 1991, 2 issues 1992. sub. price: $10; per copy: $5. Back issues: $5. Discounts: 40%. 100pp; 7×8½; †of. Reporting time: 1-2 months. Payment: copies + hopefully a small amount of $. Copyrighted, reverts to author. Pub's reviews. §Literature, fiction, history, lit. criticism, sociology, photography. Ads: $100/$75.

PORTENTS, Deborah Rasmussen, 12 Fir Place, Hazlet, NJ 07730, (201) 888-0535. 1986. Fiction, art, photos, interviews, reviews. "3,000 word limit of contemporary horror, dark fantasy, gothic and supernatural horror" circ. 300. 3/yr. Pub'd 3 issues 1990; expects 3 issues 1991, 3 issues 1992. sub. price: $10 (3 issues); per copy: $3.50; sample: same. Back issues: $2. 60pp; 5½×8½. Reporting time: 8 weeks. Payment: 1/4¢ per word and one copy. Copyrighted, reverts to author. Pub's reviews: 3 in 1990. §Horror. Ads: on a trade basis.

Bern Porter Books (see also BERN PORTER INTERNATIONAL), Bern Porter, 22 Salmond Road, Belfast, ME 04915, 207-338-3763. 1911. "Type of material used vanguard, experimental and classic contempory. Arts, bibliography, short story, drama, poetry, contemporary classic literature." avg. press run 1.75M. Pub'd 467 titles 1990; expects 482 titles 1991, 493 titles 1992. 32 titles listed in the *Small Press Record of Books in Print* (20th Edition, 1991-92). avg. price, cloth: $8.50; paper: $2.10; other: $12.50. Discounts: normal or all current standard. 167pp; 5½×7, 8½×11; lp. Reporting time: 3 weeks. Payment: 10% royalty on all sales. Copyrights in author's name. COSMEP, NESPA, MPW, STWP.

BERN PORTER INTERNATIONAL, Bern Porter Books, 22 Salmond Road, Belfast, ME 04915. 1911. 12/yr. sub. price: $12.50; sample: $1.50. 72pp; 8½×11. Reporting time: 30 days. Payment: per wordage. Copyrighted. Pub's reviews: 68 in 1990. §World Literature Experimental.

456

Portland Entertainment Publishing, Denise Sanders, Dana Jones, 114 Southwest Second, Portland, OR 97204, 503-299-6155. 1987. Fiction, non-fiction. "We are primarily looking for books that could be published as hard cover fiction or non-fiction. Our first book is non-fiction workbook entitled *Uncharged Battery*. The next two are fiction" avg. press run 15M. Pub'd 1 title 1990; expects 3 titles 1991, 5 titles 1992. avg. price, cloth: $16.95. 256pp; 5¾x8¾; †webb. Reporting time: 6-8 weeks. Payment: per individual. Copyrights for author.

PORTLAND REVIEW, Max Provino, Editor, PO Box 751, Portland, OR 97207, 503-725-4533. 1955. Poetry, fiction, articles, art, photos, criticism, parts-of-novels, long-poems, plays. *"Portland Review* is an arts and literary publication that seeks the innovative. Send for rate sheet. ISSN #0360-3091. Published once a year" circ. 400. 3/yr. Pub'd 3 issues 1990; expects 3 issues 1991, 3 issues 1992. sub. price: $15; per copy: $5; sample: $5. Back issues: $5. 60pp; 9x12; of. Reporting time: 1-2 months. Payment: copies only. Copyrighted, reverts to author. Ads: $80/$50/$30 1/4 page. CCLM, COSMEP.

Portmanteau Editions, Harry H. Barlow, Jennifer M. Thornton, PO Box 159, Littleton, NH 03561. 1987. Poetry, fiction, satire, non-fiction. "Publishing schedule filled. The editors, in the depressive phase of their manic-depression, can't consider new manuscripts or proposals at present." Pub'd 2 titles 1990; expects 2 titles 1991, 3 titles 1992. 3 titles listed in the *Small Press Record of Books in Print* (20th Edition, 1991-92). Discounts: standard. of. Reporting time: 4 months. Payment: standard royalties. Copyrights for author.

PORTRAITS POETRY MAGAZINE, Jay L. Chambers, 8312 123rd Street East, Puyallup, WA 98373, 206-848-5827. 1989. Poetry, art, reviews, long-poems. "We prefer poetry which communicates dimensions of the human experience in uncommon language. We like to see balance between the intellectual, emotional and spiritual facets of man. We love a poem that leaves something mysterious behind. We love a poet that has his *own voice*. We have recently published Frank Sibley, Patricia Mees Armstrong, Joanne McCarthy, and Don Larsen." circ. 200. 3/yr. Pub'd 3 issues 1990; expects 3 issues 1991, 3 issues 1992. sub. price: $10; per copy: $4; sample: $3. Back issues: $2. Discounts: we would sell more than 3 copies to any purchaser at $3 per issue. 28pp; 8½x11; photocopy. Reporting time: 3 months. Payment: 1 copy per page of material accepted. Copyrighted, reverts to author. Pub's reviews: 1 in 1990. §Poetry. Ads: $10/$7.

POSKISNOLT PRESS, Richard B. Murray, Senior Editor; Patricia D. Coscia, Editor, 224-82nd Street, Apt. #2, Brooklyn, NY 11209. 1989. Poetry, long-poems. "(Long poetry magazine) *Poskisnolt Press* is a small press magazine which focuses on long poetry and long prose. All types of subject matter is accepted, expected & rated. The poems can be as long as 2 pages. The purpose of the magazine is to give the poet of today a place in the literary world." circ. 200. 4/yr. Pub'd 4 issues 1990; expects 4 issues 1991, 4 issues 1992. sub. price: $8; per copy: $4; sample: $4. Back issues: $4. No discounts. 20pp; 7x8½; mi. Reporting time: as soon as possible. Payment: 2 copies. Copyrighted, reverts to author. Pub's reviews: 2 in 1990. §Poetry and short stories. Ads: $1. The Tiggie Society of Poetry, 415 Central Park West, New York, NY 10025.

THE POST, Publishers Syndication Int'l (PSI), A.P. Samuels, Publishers Syndication Int'l, 1377 K Street NW, Suite 856, Washington, DC 20005. 1987. Fiction. "No explicit sex, gore, sadism or horror. Manuscripts must be for a general audience. Just good plain story telling with unique plot. Photocopies okay, no simultaneous submissions, please. Fiction: Mystery/suspense short stories 10,000 words, buy 12 a year. We also buy 30,000 word mystery/suspense, buy 12 a year. Romance: 10,000 word, buy 12 a year, 30,000 word, buy 12 a year. Will buy first time manuscripts if good enough. The type of mystery we are looking for is devoid of references which might offend. (Sherlock Holmes would be a good example of the type of stories we require). Show word count on your submission. If you use a computer, please specify kind, disk size, density and the name of the word processing program you are using. In some cases we may request disk copy of your story. Please be aware that PSI is opening new markets for stories of this length and exact publishing date is not always available. When the story is published, the author will be notified." 24/yr. Expects 12 issues 1991, 24 issues 1992. 32pp; 8½x11; of. Reporting time: 4-6 weeks. Payment: 1-4¢ per word on acceptance plus royalty. Copyrighted.

Post Point Press, Jack W. Bazhaw, PO Box 4393, Bellingham, WA 98227. 1988. "Organized to publish a non-fiction book on archaeology; looking for other material" avg. price, cloth: $17; paper: $12. 156pp; 8x10. Payment: negotiable. Copyrights for author.

POSTCARD ART/POSTCARD FICTION, Martha Rosler, Martha Rosler, 143 McGuinness Blvd., Brooklyn, NY 11222. 1974. Fiction, art, photos. "I do all the writing myself. I chose mail as a means of dissemination because of its directness and because I wanted to raise questions about 'personal' and 'first-personal' communications, fiction, and autobiography. All my work is meant to relate the private, often female, sphere to the public, often male, sphere. Focuses of work have included food production, consumption, art careerism, and violence." circ. 600. 1-2/yr. Pub'd 1 issue 1990. sub. price: $5; per copy: $5; sample: $5. 12pp; postcard size; †mi. §Arts, film/video, photography.

POSTCARD CLASSICS, Deltiologists of America, Dr. James Lewis Lowe, PO Box 8, Norwood, PA 19074,

215-485-8572. 1960. "Focuses on pre-1920 picture postcards including views, comics, greetings—all publishers, all countries, all types" circ. 1.2M. 6/yr. Pub'd 6 issues 1990; expects 6 issues 1991, 6 issues 1992. sub. price: $12; per copy: $2.50; sample: $2.50. Back issues: 60 back issues of *Deltiology* for $30 plus shipping. 16pp; 8½×11. Reporting time: 30 days. Payment: usually in copies. Not copyrighted. Pub's reviews: 6 in 1990. §Books about picture postcards only. Ads: $50/$27.50.

The Post-Apollo Press, Simone Fattal, 35 Marie Street, Sausalito, CA 94965, 415-332-1458. 1982. Poetry, fiction. avg. press run 1M. Pub'd 2 titles 1990; expects 4 titles 1991, 2 titles 1992. 1 title listed in the *Small Press Record of Books in Print* (20th Edition, 1991-92). avg. price, paper: $10.95. Discounts: trade 40%; distributors 55%; jobber, classroom 20%. of. Reporting time: 6 months. Payment: percentage after all expenses are met. Copyrights for author.

POSTER-ZINE, Ianus Publications, Inc., Claude J. Pelletier, Alain Dubreuil, Michel Gareau, 33, Prince Street #243, Montreal, Quebec H3C 2M7, Canada, 514-397-0342. 1990. Articles, art, photos, cartoons, interviews. "Color poster on Japanese animation folded to magazine size, with article on the back. Issue #1 on Katsukiro Otomo's *Akira*" circ. 5M. 6/yr. Expects 3 issues 1991, 6 issues 1992. price per copy: $3.95; sample: $4.50. Poster + 4pp; 8½×11; of. Reporting time: no submissions. Payment: none. Copyrighted, reverts to author. Pub's reviews. §Japanese animation. Ads: $500/$300/$200 1/4 page.

The Post-Industrial Press, Robert Richards, PO Box 265, Greensboro, PA 15338. 1989. Poetry, fiction, criticism. "Contributors: Georges Perec, Gilles Doleuze, Unica Zurn, Johannes Poethen, Fabrice Gravereaux. All submissions *must* include SASE." avg. press run 1M-2M. Expects 2 titles 1991, 3-5 titles 1992. avg. price, paper: $5-$12. Discounts: standard trade and library. 50-200pp; 6×9; of, lp. Reporting time: immediately. Payment: negotiable. Copyrights for author.

POSTMODERN CULTURE, Eyal Amiran, John Unsworth, Box 8105, Raleigh, NC 27695, 919-737-2687. 1990. Poetry, fiction, articles, interviews, satire, criticism, reviews, parts-of-novels, plays, non-fiction. "Electronic mail addresses: pmc@ncsuvm.ncsu.edu (Internet), pmc@ncsuvm (Bitnet). Works in progress (to 3000 words), essays (to 8000 words), book reviews (1000-3000 words). Recent contributors include Andrew Ross, bell hooks, Kathy Acker, Neil Larsen. *Postmodern Culture* is a peer-reviewed journal, distributed free via electronic mail; it provides an international and interdisciplinary forum for discussion of contemporary literature, theory, and culture." circ. 900. 3/yr. Pub'd 1 issue 1990; expects 3 issues 1991, 3 issues 1992. sub. price: $15; per copy: $5; sample: $5. Back issues: All current and back issues are free to electronic mail subscribers. 200pp; Electronic mail/disk/microfiche. Reporting time: 6 weeks. Payment: none. Copyrighted, reverts to author. Pub's reviews: 1 in 1990. §Contemporary literature, theory, culture. Ads: $50/$25.

POTATO EYES, Nightshade Press, Roy Zarucchi, Carolyn Page, Ted Holmes, Fiction Editor, PO Box 76, Troy, ME 04987, 207-948-3427. 1988. Poetry, fiction, art, reviews, long-poems. "Recent contributors: Jane Todd Cooper, Robert Morgan, Richard Lemm, Jim Wayne Miller, Mary De Maine. Short Fiction: to 3,000 words. Poetry: concrete visual imagery, blank verse, free verse, narrative. We like poetry and fiction that is rural, rebellious or thought-provoking, or all of the above. Especially encourage poet-artists. Artwork: pen and ink preferred, but other black on white ok. No photography. General: no haiku, 'religious', Hallmarkian, light verse or navel study. Submit anytime. Send SASE." circ. 800. 2/yr. Expects 2 issues 1991, 2 issues 1992. sub. price: $11; per copy: $6; sample: $5. Back issues: $5. Discounts: 40% to bookstores. 96pp; 6×9; of. Reporting time: 6-10 weeks. Payment: copies. Copyrighted, reverts to author. Pub's reviews: 8 in 1990. §Chapbooks, poetry and short story collections. no ads. MWPA, CLMP, NCWN, NHWP.

Potentials Development, Inc., Janet Elkins, Adm. Assoc., 775 Main Street, Suite 604, Buffalo, NY 14203, 716-842-2658. 1978. Non-fiction. "How-to books for workers in human service. Eliminate negativism about aging. General interest: books on aging." avg. press run 500. Pub'd 5 titles 1990; expects 4 titles 1991, 4 titles 1992. 22 titles listed in the *Small Press Record of Books in Print* (20th Edition, 1991-92). avg. price, paper: $8.95; other: games, quizzes $3.95. Discounts: 10% 2-25 comb.; 20% 26+ comb.; 20% 2-15 same title; 35% 16+ same title. 65pp; 5½×8; of. Reporting time: 6 weeks. Payment: 5% first 3M, 8% thereafter. Copyrights for author if desired.

Potes & Poets Press Inc (see also ABACUS), Peter Ganick, 181 Edgemont Avenue, Elmwood, CT 06110, 203-233-2023. 1980. Poetry. avg. press run 160. Pub'd 8 titles 1990; expects 8 titles 1991. 34 titles listed in the *Small Press Record of Books in Print* (20th Edition, 1991-92). avg. price, paper: $3. Discounts: retail 40%. 16pp; 8½×11; stapled newsletter. Reporting time: 3 months. Payment: 12 copies. Copyrights for author.

POTPOURRI PARTY-LINE, Dody Lyness, Editor, 7336 Berry Hill, Palos Verdes, CA 90274-4404, 213-377-7040. 1983. "How-to directions for dried floral/herbal fragrance crafts; recipes for scented potpurri. Length of material: 1 page maximum. Advertising accepted. No cooking recipes, no doggerel verse." circ. 1.8M. 4/yr. Pub'd 4 issues 1990; expects 4 issues 1991, 4 issues 1992. sub. price: $15; sample: $3.95. Back issues: 1983-84 Series $7.95, 1984-85 Series $7.95, 1985-86 Series $9.95, 1986-87 Series $9.95, 1987-88 Series $9.95, 1988-89 Series $9.95; 1989-90 Series $9.95; 1990-91 Series $9.95. Discounts: none. 20pp;

8½×11; of. Reporting time: 2 months. Payment: none. Copyrighted, reverts to author. Pub's reviews: 8 in 1990. §Gardening, herbal lore, dried herbal handcrafts, fragrance crafts, tips for home-based businesses (herb farms, dried herbal/floral crafts at exhibitions, fairs, shows). Ads: $167/$92/75¢.

THE POTTERSFIELD PORTFOLIO, Shari Andrews, Joe Blades, Raymond Fraser, Jo-Anne Elder, Margaret McLeod, PO Box 1135, Station A, Fredericton, New Brunswick E3B 5C2, Canada, 506-454-5127. 1979. Poetry, fiction, art, photos, parts-of-novels, plays. "Material only by people living in or having strong personal ties with Atlantic Canada. No sexist, racist, homophobic or classist material. No erotica. Accepts English and French writing. Include SASE and short bio note. No simultaneous submissions. Buys first Canadian serial rights." circ. 1M. 2/yr. Pub'd 2 issues 1990; expects 2 issues 1991, 2 issues 1992. sub. price: $12 Canadian, $15 US and overseas (in U.S. dollars); per copy: $6; sample: $6. Discounts: trade 40% on 5 copies or more. 52pp; 8½×11; of. Reporting time: 8-12 weeks. Payment: 2 copies and honorarium. Copyrighted, reverts to author. Ads: $640/$320/$160 1/4 page/$80 1/8 page. CMPA.

Pottersfield Press, Lesley Choyce, RR 2, Porters Lake, N.S. B0J 2S0, Canada. 1979. Fiction, photos, cartoons, satire, non-fiction. "Interest in Canadian, Nova Scotian material, especially non-fiction right now." avg. press run 1M-2M. Pub'd 6 titles 1990; expects 6 titles 1991, 6 titles 1992. avg. price, paper: $9.95. Discounts: 20% 1-5 books, 40% 6+ mixed titles. 192pp; 6½×9½; of. Reporting time: 3 months. Payment: 10% list. Copyrights for author. ACP, APA, COSMEP.

POULTRY - A MAGAZINE OF VOICE, Poultry, Inc., Brendan Galvin, Editor; George Garrett, Editor; Jack Flavin, Editor, Box 4413, Springfield, MA 01101, 413-20435. 1980. Poetry, fiction, articles, art, cartoons, interviews, satire, non-fiction. "Parodies of contemporary poems, fiction, styles, lit. biz, which spoof mannerisms, folly, etc., but not the persons or personalities of authors. Must be short enough to fit 12 page tabloid format. *Parodies only*. Newspaper tabloid" circ. 1M. 2-3/yr. Pub'd 2 issues 1990; expects 2 issues 1991, 2 issues 1992. sub. price: $5; per copy: $2; sample: $2. Back issues: $2. Discounts: $5 for 3 issues. 8pp; 8½×11; of. Reporting time: 1 week to 1 month. Payment: 10 copies. Copyrighted, reverts to author. §Parodies of reviews. Ads: $100/$50.

Poultry, Inc. (see also POULTRY - A MAGAZINE OF VOICE), Brendan Galvin, Editor; George Garrett, Editor; Jack Flavin, Editor, Box 4413, Springfield, MA 01101, 413-20435. 1980. Poetry, fiction, articles, art, cartoons, interviews, satire, non-fiction. "Parodies of contemporary poems, fiction, styles, lit. biz, which spoof mannerisms, folly, etc., but not the persons or personalities of authors. Must be short enough to fit 12 page tabloid format. *Parodies only*. Newspaper tabloid" avg. press run 1M. Pub'd 2 titles 1990; expects 2 titles 1991, 2 titles 1992. avg. price, paper: $2; other: $2. Discounts: $5 for 3 issues. 8pp; 8½×11; of. Reporting time: 1 week to 1 month. Payment: 10 copies. Copyrights for author.

Samuel Powell Publishing Company, 2201 I Street, Sacramento, CA 95816, 916-443-1161. 1978. Fiction. avg. press run 750. Expects 1-2 titles 1991, 1-2 titles 1992. 5 titles listed in the *Small Press Record of Books in Print* (20th Edition, 1991-92). avg. price, paper: $5. Discounts: 50% distributors, 40% bookstores. 105pp; 5½×8½; of. Copyrights for author.

Power Publishing, Barbara Mahoney, PO Box 1805, Elkins, WV 26241, 304-636-8488. "New orders will receive free 'Behind the Veil' badge" 1 title listed in the *Small Press Record of Books in Print* (20th Edition, 1991-92). avg. price, other: $4.75 postpaid; make checks payable to "Behind the Veil"

Power Publishing Group, 10943 E. Gary Road, Scottsdale, AZ 85259. 1 title listed in the *Small Press Record of Books in Print* (20th Edition, 1991-92).

The Power Within Institute, Inc., 130 West Tugalo Street, Toccoa, GA 30577-2360, 404-886-1220; 1-800-533-POWER. 1 title listed in the *Small Press Record of Books in Print* (20th Edition, 1991-92).

THE PRAGMATIST, Jorge E. Amador, Box 392, Forest Grove, PA 18922. 1983. Articles, satire, reviews, letters, news items, non-fiction. "*The Pragmatist* presents practical proposals for saving every person thousands in taxes by opening up government monopolies & services to competition. Examines beliefs and legislation that hinder individuals' lifestyle choices. Length of material 1,000-2,500 words; best to inquire about topic first. Purchases first or second serial rights; will run copyright notice for individual authors on request. Foreign subscription (one year): US $12." circ. 1.8M. 6/yr. Pub'd 6 issues 1990; expects 6 issues 1991, 6 issues 1992. sub. price: $10; per copy: $3; sample: $3. Back issues: $3 each, $10 for volume sets (6 issues). Discounts: 50% to bookstores or reselling agents (3+ copies of same issue). 16pp; 8½×11; of. Reporting time: 8 weeks. Payment: 1¢ per word + 5 copies of issue with article, and 4 issue subscription. Not copyrighted. Pub's reviews: 11 in 1990. §Economics, civil liberties issues. Ads: $60/$35/$20 quarter-page/$12 eighth-page.

PRAIRIE FIRE, Andris Taskans, Managing Editor; Di Brandt, Poetry Editor; Scott Ellis, Books Editor; Louise Jonasson, Art Editor; Ellen Smythe, Fiction Editor; Todd Bruce, Fiction Editor, 423-100 Arthur Street, Winnipeg MB R3B 1H3, Canada, 204-943-9066. 1978. Poetry, fiction, articles, art, photos, interviews, criticism, reviews, letters, parts-of-novels, long-poems. "Length: up to 6M words prose, up to 6 poems. Biases:

459

Manitoba or Canadian literature. Contributors: Alexandre Amprimoz, Douglas Barbour, Lorna Crozier, Paul Dutton, Sandra Birdsell, Cecelia Frey, Van Begamudre, Patrick Friesen, Elisabeth Harvor, Robert Hilles, Patricia Young, Tom Wayman, Rudy Wiebe.'' circ. 1.4M. 4/yr. Pub'd 4 issues 1990; expects 4 issues 1991, 4 issues 1992. sub. price: $22 Canada, $26 USA and $28 foreign, institutions add $6 per annum; per copy: $7.95; sample: $7.95. Back issues: send for price list. Discounts: negotiable. 128pp; 9×6; of. Reporting time: 2 months. Payment: 1 copy and contributor's fee. Copyrighted, reverts to author. Pub's reviews: 48 in 1990. §Poetry, fiction, criticism, authors' biography/memoir. Ads: $125/$65. CMPA, AMBP.

THE PRAIRIE GOLD RUSH, Roger Baumgartner, Route 1, Box 76, Walnut, IL 61376, 815-379-2061. 1982. Articles, photos, interviews, letters, news items. ''Product and company history of the Minneapolis-Moline Co. plus current news and activities for farm equipment fans. Collectors and enthusiasts'' circ. 643. 4/yr. Pub'd 4 issues 1990; expects 4 issues 1991, 4 issues 1992. sub. price: $15; per copy: $3; sample: same. Back issues: $3. 28pp; 8½×11; of.

THE PRAIRIE JOURNAL OF CANADIAN LITERATURE, Prairie Journal Press, A. Burke, PO Box 997, Station G, Calgary, Alberta T3A 3G2, Canada. 1983. Poetry, fiction, interviews, criticism, reviews, long-poems. ''Recent contributors: Fred Cogswell, interviews with poet Lorna Crozier, playwright James Reaney. Literary biases for reviews of Canadian prairie literature; also one act plays'' circ. 500+. 2/yr. Pub'd 2 issues 1990; expects 2 issues 1991, 2 issues 1992. sub. price: $6, $12 institutions; per copy: $6; sample: $3. Back issues: $5. Discounts: negotiable. 40-60pp; 7×8½; of. Reporting time: 2 weeks. Payment: copies and honoraria. Copyrighted. Pub's reviews: 6 in 1990. §Western, prairie, literary, Canadian. Ads: $50/$25/exchange. CMPA, 2 Stewart Street, Toronto Canada M5V 1H6.

Prairie Journal Press (see also THE PRAIRIE JOURNAL OF CANADIAN LITERATURE), A. Burke, PO Box G 997, Station G, Calgary, Alberta T3A 3G2, Canada. 1985. Poetry, fiction, interviews, criticism, reviews, long-poems, plays. ''Recent publication of an anthology of short fiction by six authors and a collection of poetry by one author. *Prairie Journal Fiction* $6 and for $6 *A Vision of Birds* by Ronald Kurt. Potential contributors please send samples of work with IRC and envelope for reply, covering letter'' avg. press run 500+. Pub'd 1 title 1990; expects 2 titles 1991, 1 title 1992. 10 titles listed in the *Small Press Record of Books in Print* (20th Edition, 1991-92). avg. price, paper: $6. Discounts: negotiable. 40-60pp; 7×8½; of. Reporting time: 2 weeks - 6 months. Payment: copies. Copyrights for author. CMPA, Celebration of Women and the Arts, Alberta Writers' Guild.

Prairie Publishing Company, Ralph E. Watkins, PO Box 2997, Winnipeg, MB R3C 4B5, Canada, 204-885-6496. 1969. avg. press run 2M. Expects 4 titles 1991. 13 titles listed in the *Small Press Record of Books in Print* (20th Edition, 1991-92). avg. price, paper: $5. Discounts: 40% bookstores, 20% libraries & schools. 165pp; 6×9; of. Reporting time: 6-8 weeks. Payment: 10%. Copyrights for author. AMBP.

THE PRAIRIE RAMBLER, Jerry B., PO Box 505, Claremont, CA 91711. 1978. circ. 300. 12/yr. Pub'd 12 issues 1990; expects 12 issues 1991, 12 issues 1992. sub. price: $12; per copy: $1.23; sample: $1.23. 8pp; 8½×11.

PRAIRIE SCHOONER, Hilda Raz, Editor-in-Chief; Pamela Weiner, Business Manager, 201 Andrews Hall, Univ. of Nebraska, Lincoln, NE 68588-0334. 1927. Poetry, fiction, articles, art, photos, interviews, reviews, parts-of-novels, long-poems. circ. 2M. 4/yr. Pub'd 4 issues 1990; expects 4 issues 1991, 4 issues 1992. sub. price: $15; per copy: $4; sample: $2. Write for information on back issue prices. Write for information on discounts. 144pp; 6×9; of/lo. Reporting time: 3 months. Payment: copies of magazine, and annual prizes; payments depend on grants rec'd. Copyrighted, rights revert upon request. Pub's reviews: 20 in 1990. §Current literature, general culture. Ads: $150/$75. CLMP, CELJ.

PRAIRIE WINDS, Joseph Ditta, Dakota Wesleyan University, Box 159, Mitchell, SD 57301. 1930. Poetry, fiction, art, photos. ''Annual literary review. All submissions must have SASE. Art and photos—black and white only'' circ. 700. 1/yr. Pub'd 1 issue 1990; expects 1 issue 1991, 1 issue 1992. sub. price: $2; per copy: $2; sample: $2. Back issues: $3. 58pp; of. Payment: copies. Copyrighted, reverts to author. Ads: none.

Prakalpana Literature (see also PRAKALPANA SAHITYA/PRAKALPANA LITERATURE), Vatta-charja Chandan, Dilip Gupta, P-40 Nandana Park, Calcutta-700034, West Bengal, India, 9137-77-7327. 1974. Poetry, articles. ''Biases: we invite in English or in Bengali: 1) only avant garde experimental poem, story having definitely visual, sonorous & mathematical dimensions—which we call Sarbangin poetry; 2) Prakalpana (=P for prose, poetry + R for story + A for art, essay + K for kinema, kinetic + L for play + N for song, novel...)—which is a composition using the above forms appropriately; 3) also articles on Prakalpana literature. If selected, at first we publish the work (if possible with translation) in our mags, then we include it in our future anthology. Submissions not returnable. Length of material: in any case within 2,400 words.'' avg. press run 500. 6 titles listed in the *Small Press Record of Books in Print* (20th Edition, 1991-92). avg. price, other: rupees 3/-. Discounts: 20%. 48pp; 5½×8½; lp. Reporting time: 6 months. Payment: none. Does not copyright for author. Kobisena, Prakalpana (P-40 Nandana Park, Calcutta-700034, India).

460

PRAKALPANA SAHITYA/PRAKALPANA LITERATURE, Prakalpana Literature, Vattacharja Chandan, P-40 Nandana Park, Calcutta-700034, West Bengal, India, 9137-77-7327. 1977. Poetry, articles, reviews, letters, news items. "Biases: we invite in English or in Bengali: 1) only avant garde experimental poem, story having definitely visual, sonorous & mathematical dimensions—which we call Sarbangin poetry/story; 2) Prakalpana (=P for prose, poetry + R for story + A for art, essay + K for kinema, kinetic + L for play + N for song, novel...)—which is a composition using the above forms appropriately; 3) also criticism, essay & letters on Prakalpana literature. Submissions not returnable. Length of material: in any case within 2,400 words. Some recent contributors: Dilip Gupta, Vattacharja Chandan, Samir Rakshit, J.J. King, Geof Huth, Gerald England, John Byrum, Shyamali Mukhopadhyay Bhattacharya." circ. 1M. 1/yr. Pub'd 1 issue 1990; expects 2 issues 1991, 2 issues 1992. sub. price: 6 rupees; per copy: 6 rupees. Overseas: 4 IRCs or exhcnage of little mags; sample: 6 rupees. Overseas: 4 IRCs or exchange of little mags. Back issues: 20 rupees. Discounts: 20%. 68pp; 5½x8½; lp. Reporting time: 6 months. Payment: none. Not copyrighted. Pub's reviews: 6 in 1990. §Experimental/avant garde/alternative literary & art books and magazines. Ads: 500 rupees/300 rupees/800 rupees (2nd, 3rd, 4th cover pages). Kobisena, Prakalpana (P-40 Nandana Park, Calcutta-700034, India).

Prakken Publications (see also EDUCATION DIGEST; SCHOOL SHOP), George F. Kennedy, Publisher, PO Box 8623, Ann Arbor, MI 48107, 313-769-1211. 1935. News items, non-fiction. *"Prakken Publications* publishes reference books, textbooks, magazines, and workbooks in the areas of general education reference, as well as vocational and technology education. Recently published works include: *Exploring Solar Energy, Voices in American Education,* and *Vocational Education in the 1990's* Major Issues. (Note: *Education Digest does not* accept original manuscripts, prior publication required. Selected by editorial board)." avg. press run 2M. Pub'd 2 titles 1990; expects 4 titles 1991, 3 titles 1992. 11 titles listed in the *Small Press Record of Books in Print* (20th Edition, 1991-92). avg. price, cloth: $20; paper: $10. Discounts: 20% educational discount; bookstores, jobbers call for pricing. 150pp; 5½x8½; of. Reporting time: 2-4 months. Payment: negotiable royalty; generally, 10% of receipts, payable June 30, Dec. 30. Copyrights for author. Edpress, BPA.

PRECISELY, The Future Press, Richard Kostelanetz, Paul Zelevansky, PO Box 73, Canal Street, New York, NY 10013. "Critical essays on experimental literature, expecially of the past thirty years in North America. $2.00 for one number, $10.00 for five numbers, $18.00 for nine numbers, $32 for all sixteen numbers." 2/yr. Expects 1 issue 1992. price per copy: $2; sample: $2. 64pp; 5½x8½; of. Reporting time: 1 month. Payment: depends upon growth. Copyrighted, reverts to author. Pub's reviews: 0 in 1990. §Experimental literature.

Preludium Publishers (see also LIFTOUTS), Barry Casselman, 1503 Washington Avenue South, Minneapolis, MN 55454, 612-333-0031. 1971. Poetry, fiction, criticism, plays. "Preludium Publishers is interested in experimental work in poetry and fiction, and in the translation of new writing which has not previously been published in English. *Unsolicited manuscripts are not considered at this time.* Translators should make inquiry before sending any manuscript, and must include an SASE for a reply." avg. press run 1M. Expects 2 titles 1992. of. Payment: negotiable; some payment to all authors. Copyrights for author.

Premier Publishers, Inc. (see also BOOK NEWS & BOOK BUSINESS MART), Neal Michaels, Owen Bates, PO Box 330309, Fort Worth, TX 76163, 817-293-7030. 1971. Non-fiction. "We reprint and publish books on success, self-help, how-to, business success and the mail order industry. Also carburetor vaporization theory and instructions as well as other energy titles" avg. press run 5M. Pub'd 6 titles 1990; expects 10 titles 1991. 9 titles listed in the *Small Press Record of Books in Print* (20th Edition, 1991-92). avg. price, paper: $10; other: variable. Discounts: sold primarily through mail order trade. 50% discount to mail order dealers with quantity discounts averaging 60% and 70%. 96pp; 8x11; of, web. Reporting time: 4-12 weeks. Payment: negotiable; small royalty advances possible; outright royalties generally percentage of retail; amount dependent upon author and subject matter. Copyrights for author.

Prescott Street Press, Vi Gale, Editor, Publisher, PO Box 40312, Portland, OR 97240-0312. 1974. "We plan to publish two books in 1987. These are already scheduled. Other than that, we will remain on hold until we have cleared out some of the inventory on hand." avg. press run 500 paper, 250 hardcover. Pub'd 1 title 1990; expects 2 titles 1991. 16 titles listed in the *Small Press Record of Books in Print* (20th Edition, 1991-92). avg. price, cloth: $20; paper: $8.50; other: $2.50 poetry postcards. Discounts: Salal Series Postcards: $2.50 per pakt. (8 cards) usual trade discounts. Usual trade on books, also. 50-60pp; 6½x8¼; of, lp. Reporting time: 2 weeks. Payment: by arrangement. Copyrights for author. COSMEP, PSA, PEN, WW, OSPA.

The Preservation Press, Buckley C. Jeppson, Director, 1785 Massachusetts Avenue, NW, Washington, DC 20036, 202-673-4057. 1975. Art, photos, non-fiction. "The Preservation Press is the book publisher of the National Trust for Historic Preservation, a nonprofit organization chartered by Congress in 1949 to encourage interest and participation in historic preservation. The Preservation Press publishes books for the general public on topics of historic preservation, architecture and American culture." avg. press run 7.5M-10M. Pub'd 7 titles 1990; expects 13 titles 1991, 16 titles 1992. 34 titles listed in the *Small Press Record of Books in Print* (20th Edition, 1991-92). avg. price, cloth: $30; paper: $10. Discounts: average to the trade - 40% 5-24 copies, libraries 10%, 20% standing order plan. 200-300pp; 7x10; of. Reporting time: 2 months. Payment: negotiable.

461

Copyrights for author. Washington Book Publishers.

THE PRESIDENTS' JOURNAL, Cottontail Publications, Ellyn R. Kern, R 1, Box 198, Bennington, IN 47011, (812) 427-3914. 1984. Articles, art, photos, news items, non-fiction. "This newsletter will endeavor to represent primarily the personal and not the political side of the presidents and their families. By doing so we can learn more about the times they represented and the roots of our past as individuals in this great United States of America. Looking for columnists interested in writing for future issues on related topics. Submit ideas and sample of writing and qualifications." circ. 100. 4/yr. Pub'd 4 issues 1990; expects 4 issues 1991, 4 issues 1992. sub. price: $12; per copy: $3; sample: free for stamp (29¢). Back issues: $2.50. Discounts: 2 year subscription for $2 off total. 6pp; 8½×11; of. Reporting time: 6 weeks. Payment: will pay $5 for articles accepted for publication on review of a presidentially related tourist site (not a home). Describe details of location, theme, cost, authenticity, and impressions. Enclose SASE for return of manuscript. Pay $50 for 750 word articles. (Query) Up to $10 for reprints. Copyrighted, reverts to author. Pub's reviews: 4 in 1990. §Related to presidents. Ads: upon request.

Press Gang Publishers, Barbara Kuhne, 603 Powell Street, Vancouver, B.C. V6A 1H2, Canada, 604-253-2537. 1972. Fiction, non-fiction. "We are interested in publishing analytical and/or historical works by and about women. We are feminists. Also interested in fiction, in writing by women of color, in lesbian material." avg. press run 3M. Pub'd 4 titles 1990; expects 4 titles 1991, 4 titles 1992. 16 titles listed in the *Small Press Record of Books in Print* (20th Edition, 1991-92). avg. price, paper: $12.95. Discounts: 40% to bookstores, 20% to libraries and schools for 1-9 copies, 25% for 10+. 160pp; 5½×8½; †of. Reporting time: 4-8 weeks. Payment: varies. Copyrights for author. ACP, ABCPC.

The Press of Appletree Alley, Barnard Taylor, Box 608 138 South Third Street, Lewisburg, PA 17837. 1982. avg. press run 150. Pub'd 3 titles 1990; expects 3 titles 1991, 3 titles 1992. 13 titles listed in the *Small Press Record of Books in Print* (20th Edition, 1991-92). avg. price, cloth: $150. Discounts: 30% dealers, 10% standing orders. 48-60pp; 6¼×9½; †letterpress. Payment: 10%. Copyrights for author.

The Press of MacDonald & Reinecke, Lachlan P. MacDonald, PO Box 840, Arroyo Grande, CA 93420-0840, 805-473-1947. 1974. avg. press run usually 3M paperback, 500 hardcover. Pub'd 4 titles 1990; expects 6 titles 1991, 8 titles 1992. 2 titles listed in the *Small Press Record of Books in Print* (20th Edition, 1991-92). avg. price, cloth: $12.95; paper: $7.95. Discounts: 2-11 copies 20 percent; 12-49 40 percent. Payment with order. Fully returnable 90 days to 1 year if resalable condition. Trade. 120pp; 5½×8, 6×9; of. Reporting time: 2 weeks-2 months. Payment: varies according to involvement, usually 10%. Copyrights for author.

The Press of the Third Mind, Bradley Lastname, 65 East Scott Street, Loft 6P, Chicago, IL 60610, 312-337-3122. 1985. Fiction, articles, letters. "Our 'bias' is that we prefer material that is the literary equivalent of Mike Tyson on PCP. If you have a manuscript that is as persuasive as an ad by Leon Trotsky for frost-free refrigerators, we are MUCHO interested. Most recent book is *Concave Buddha* by Tom Vaultonberg. Recent anthology contributors include Jon Levant, Crad Kilodney, Brian Kehr, Sutton Breiding, Gaston Price, and Pat McGrath." avg. press run 2M. Pub'd 1 title 1990; expects 1 title 1991, 1 title 1992. avg. price, paper: $5. Discounts: 40%. 100pp; of. Reporting time: 7 seconds. Payment: varies. Copyrights for author. COSMEP, CCLM, AAP.

The Press of Ward Schori, Ward Schori, 2716 Noyes Street, Evanston, IL 60201, 312-475-3241. 1961. "Primarily into miniature books-less than 3 inches high. Also publish sponsored books of poetry, local history. Print shop and former address: 1580 Maple Avenue, Evanston, IL 60201." avg. press run 500. Pub'd 3 titles 1990; expects 4 titles 1991, 2 titles 1992. 1 title listed in the *Small Press Record of Books in Print* (20th Edition, 1991-92). avg. price, cloth: $15-$20; other: leather $25-$50. Discounts: to dealers, 20% on 2, 33⅓% on 5, 40% on 10 or more. 80pp; †of, lp. Copyrights for author. APA, Miniature Book Society.

Press Pacifica, Ltd., Jane Pultz, Publisher, PO Box 47, Kailua, HI 96734, 808-261-6594. 1975. Poetry, fiction, non-fiction. "We are a trade publisher. We also provide publishing consultation for self-publishers. We are not accepting mss at this time." avg. press run 2.5M-5M. Pub'd 1 title 1990; expects 1 title 1991. 24 titles listed in the *Small Press Record of Books in Print* (20th Edition, 1991-92). avg. price, cloth: $6.95-$9.95; paper: $1.95-$7.95. Discounts: trade 25-44%, libraries 15-25%, no consignments. 64-250pp; 5½×8½, 6×9, 8×10; of. Payment: 10% first book. Copyrights for author. Hawaii Book Publisher's Association.

Pressed Curtains (see also CURTAINS), Paul Buck, 4 Bower Street, Maidstone, Kent ME16 8SD, England, 0622-63681. 1971. Poetry, fiction, articles, art, photos, long-poems, plays. "Publish contributors central to magazine" avg. press run 400. Pub'd 4 titles 1990; expects 6 titles 1991. 6 titles listed in the *Small Press Record of Books in Print* (20th Edition, 1991-92). avg. price, paper: $5; other: $12. 60pp; size A4; of. Reporting time: days. Payment: copies. Copyrights for author. ALP.

PREVIEW: Professional and Reference Literature Review, Christy J. Havens, Mountainside Publishing, Inc., PO Box 8330, Ann Arbor, MI 48107, 313-662-3925, FAX 313-662-4450. 1988. Reviews. "Shipping address: 321 S. Main #300, Ann Arbor, MI 48104. We publish only reviews, and summaries of reviews published elsewhere; would like to receive review copies of books, or catalogs from publishers, in subject areas listed below. In addition to full-length, signed reviews, we include 30-40 in-house prepared evaluations/ annotations per issue" circ. 2M. 11/yr. Pub'd 11 issues 1990; expects 11 issues 1991, 11 issues 1992. sub. price: $43; per copy: $4; sample: free upon request. Back issues: $4. 44pp; 8½x11; of. Payment: none. Copyrighted, does not revert to author. Pub's reviews: 380 in 1990. §General reference, library and information science, management, higher education. Ads: $400/$290/$350 2/3 page.

Prickly Pear Press, Dave Oliphant, Jim Jacobs, 1402 Mimosa Pass, Cedar Park, TX 78613, 512-331-8825. 1973. Poetry. "No unsolicited mss considered. Joseph Colin Murphey, Sandra Lynn, Rebecca Gonzales, James Hoggard." avg. press run 500. 8 titles listed in the *Small Press Record of Books in Print* (20th Edition, 1991-92). avg. price, cloth: $13.95; paper: $5. Discounts: 10% to jobbers. 60pp; 6x4; of. Payment: copies. Copyrights for author. TC (Texas Circuit).

Prima Facie, Bradley R. Smith, Director, PO Box 3267, Visalia, CA 93278, 209-627-8757; FAX 209-733-2653. 1984. Articles, photos, cartoons, interviews, satire, reviews, letters, news items, non-fiction. "Will consider publishing anything (anything) that critiques the orthodox Holocaust story from a Revisionist point of view, or that critiques Revisionist scholarship from any point of view whatever." avg. press run 3.5M. Expects 2 titles 1991, 2 titles 1992. 1 title listed in the *Small Press Record of Books in Print* (20th Edition, 1991-92). avg. price, cloth: $12; paper: $7. Discounts: the usual—inquire. 150pp; 5½x8½; of. Reporting time: 30 days. Payment: depends. Copyright for author depends.

Prima Publishing, Ben Dominitz, Nancy Dominitz, PO Box 1260, Rocklin, CA 95677, 916-624-5718. 1983. Non-fiction. "We are interested in business, self-help, information, and nutrition books. Please query before sending manuscript. Books are distributed by St. Martins Press." avg. press run 10M-75M. Pub'd 60 titles 1990; expects 75 titles 1991, 90 titles 1992. 30 titles listed in the *Small Press Record of Books in Print* (20th Edition, 1991-92). avg. price, cloth: $13.95-$19.95; paper: $9.95. 200-300pp; 5½x8½. Reporting time: queries only—will report in 6 weeks. Payment: negotiable, based on type of book, price, etc. Copyrights for author. P.M.A.

Primal Publishing, Michael McInnis, 107 Brighton Avenue, Allston, MA 02134, 617-787-0203. 1986. Poetry, fiction, art, photos, satire, letters, parts-of-novels, non-fiction. "Primitive literature for modern people." avg. press run 1M-2M. Pub'd 2 titles 1990; expects 10 titles 1991, 10 titles 1992. 10 titles listed in the *Small Press Record of Books in Print* (20th Edition, 1991-92). avg. price, paper: $6.95. Discounts: assorted 10 or more 40%. 50-150pp; 5½x8½; of. Reporting time: 3-6 months. Payment: 12.5% gross after returns. Copyrights for author.

PRIMAVERA, Editorial Board, 1448 E. 52nd St., Box 274, Chicago, IL 60615, 312-324-5920. 1974. Poetry, fiction, art, photos, satire. "*Primavera* publishes work expressing the perspectives and experiences of women. We are interested equally in established and in unknown writers and artists. We will be happy to comment on your work in a personal letter *if you ask us to*. Please do not ask unless you are genuinely receptive to constructive, candid criticism. All submissions must be typed (double-spaced) and accompanied by a SASE of sufficient size, bearing sufficient postage. Recent contributors: Martha Berghend, Susan Marie Swanson, Pamela Miller, Sally Satel, Chitra Divakaruni, Jeane Krinsley" circ. 1M. 1/yr. Pub'd 1 issue 1990; expects 1 issue 1991. 7 titles listed in the *Small Press Record of Books in Print* (20th Edition, 1991-92). sub. price: $6; per copy: $6; sample: $5. Back issues: #1-#10 $5. Discounts: 10% off for orders of 3 or more. 100pp; 8½x5½; of. Reporting time: up to 6 months, usually 2 weeks. Payment: 2 copies. Copyrighted, reverts to author. No ads. COSMEP, CCLM, ILPA.

Primer Publishers, Diane M. Fessler, 5738 North Central, Phoenix, AZ 85012, 602-234-1574. 1979. Non-fiction. "Publish books about Southwest." avg. press run 5M. Pub'd 4 titles 1990; expects 4 titles 1991, 4 titles 1992. 18 titles listed in the *Small Press Record of Books in Print* (20th Edition, 1991-92). avg. price, paper: $6.95. Discounts: 40%. 175pp; of. Reporting time: 90 days, write first. Payment: negotiable. Copyrights for author. Rocky Mountain Publishers Association.

Princess Publishing, Cecile Hammill, Editor; Cheryl A. Matschek, Publisher, PO Box 386, Beaverton, OR 97075, 503-646-1234. 1987. Poetry, non-fiction. avg. press run 5M. Pub'd 5 titles 1990; expects 5 titles 1991, 10 titles 1992. 4 titles listed in the *Small Press Record of Books in Print* (20th Edition, 1991-92). avg. price, cloth: $24.95; paper: $12.95. 150pp; 5½x8; of, lp. Reporting time: 1 month. Payment: variable. Copyrights for author. NWBPA, Portland, OR.

Princeton Architectural Press (see also THE PRINCETON JOURNAL: THEMATIC STUDIES IN ARCHITECTURE), Kevin Lippert, Publisher, 37 East 7th Street, New York, NY 10003, 212-995-9620. 1980. Articles, art, photos, interviews, criticism, reviews. avg. press run 3M. Pub'd 20 titles 1990; expects 20 titles 1991, 20 titles 1992. 54 titles listed in the *Small Press Record of Books in Print* (20th Edition, 1991-92). avg. price, cloth: $50; paper: $15. Discounts: bookstores, jobbers - 40%. 200pp; size varies; of. Payment: varies. Copyrights for author.

Princeton Book Company, Publishers, Charles H. Woodford, President; Debi Elfenbein, Managing Editor, PO Box 57, Pennington, NJ 08534, 609-737-8177. 1975. Music, non-fiction. "Princeton Book Company, Publishers is a publisher of books on dance, health, physical education, and general education. Most of our books have a text as well as a trade market." avg. press run 3M. Pub'd 8 titles 1990; expects 10 titles 1991, 15 titles 1992. 137 titles listed in the *Small Press Record of Books in Print* (20th Edition, 1991-92). avg. price, cloth: $20; paper: $12. Discounts: 40% trade, 20% text. 200pp; 6×9; of. Reporting time: 6-8 weeks. Payment: 10% on net receipts; usually no advance. Copyrights for author.

THE PRINCETON JOURNAL: THEMATIC STUDIES IN ARCHITECTURE, Princeton Architectural Press, Julia Bourke, Volume 1; Taisto Makela, Volume 3, 37 East 7th Street, New York, NY 10003, 212-995-9620. 1983. Interviews, criticism, reviews. circ. 3M. 1 issue every 2 years. Expects 1 issue 1991. price per copy: varies per issue: Volume 1: $17, Volume 2: $24.95. Discounts: jobbbers and bookstores, 40%. 196pp; 7½×11; †of. Reporting time: 3 months. Payment: none. Copyrighted, does not revert to author. §Architecture, art, art history. No ads.

The Printable Arts Society, Inc. (see also BOX 749 MAGAZINE; RE:PRINT (AN OCCASIONAL MAGAZINE)), David Ferguson, Editor-in-Chief, 411 West 22nd Street, New York, NY 10011, (212) 989-0519. 1974. Poetry, fiction, art, photos, cartoons, satire, music, parts-of-novels, long-poems, collages, plays. avg. press run 5M. of.

PRINTED MATTER (Japan), TELS PRESS, Matthew Zuckerman, Editor, 3-31-14-207 Ikebukuro Honcho, Toshima-ku, Tokyo 170, Japan. 1977. Poetry, fiction, satire, criticism, reviews, parts-of-novels, long-poems, collages, plays. "Prefer short fiction, 500-2.5M words, and poetry up to 50 lines. All forms of fiction and poetry acceptable. Children's contest held in Autumn—children up to 12 eligible. All inquiries/submissions should be accompanied by SAE with 3 IRCs to guarantee reply/return" circ. 200. 6-8/yr. Pub'd 6 issues 1990; expects 6 issues 1991, 6 issues 1992. sub. price: 3000 Yen (4000Y including 2 one-author issues); per copy: 500 Yen; sample: 3 IRCs. Back issues: Vol. I, II: 500 Yen per copy; Vol. III-X: 400 Yen per copy. Discounts: negotiable upon request. 40pp; 4½×7; of. Reporting time: 6 weeks for overseas submissions. Payment: 2 copies. Copyrighted, reverts to author. Pub's reviews: 6 in 1990. §Poetry, short fiction, novels. Ads: 10M Yen/6M Yen. COSMEP.

THE PRINTER, Michael Phillips, Sally Phillips, 337 Wilson Street, Findlay, OH 45840, 419-423-9184. 1985. Articles, interviews, criticism, reviews, letters, news items, non-fiction. "Length: 500-1,500 words. Book arts. Subject: printing history, especially letterpress. Also news of private and fine press doings and productions, as well as current commercial letterpress." circ. 1.2M. 12/yr. Pub'd 12 issues 1990; expects 12 issues 1991, 12 issues 1992. sub. price: $20; per copy: $2; sample: $1. Back issues: $3 as available. Discounts: 25%. 12pp; 12×14; lp. Reporting time: 2-4 weeks. Payment: depends, up to 10¢ a word. Not copyrighted. Pub's reviews: 20+ in 1990. §Printing, history, letterpress. Ads: $299/$160/20 picz column inch $7.50. APHA, NAPA, AAPA, APA, BPS, PHS.

THE PRINTER'S DEVIL, Mother of Ashes Press, Joe M. Singer, Poet-in-Residence, PO Box 66, Harrison, ID 83833. 1986. Articles, art, photos, cartoons, interviews, reviews, letters, news items, non-fiction. "Emphasizing a do-it-yourself approach to book and magazine printing, *The Printer's Devil* welcomes how-to articles, news items, letters, book, magazine, and product reviews on all aspects of graphic arts for the small press. Light verse, cartoons, jokes, crossword puzzles, and other filler-type, printing-related items are appreciated." circ. 250+. 3/yr. Pub'd 1 issue 1990; expects 3 issues 1991, 3 issues 1992. sub. price: $6.25; per copy: $2.10; sample: $2. Discounts: 10 or more 50%. 24pp; 8¾×11½; †of/mimeo. Reporting time: 3 months maximum. Payment: copies. Not copyrighted. Pub's reviews: 31 in 1990. §Graphic arts, publishing. classified: 23¢ per line, $2.07 minimum—other rates on request. AAPA, NAPA.

PRISM international, Patricia Gabin, Executive Editor; Rodger Cove, Editor, E455-1866 Main Mall, University of British Columbia, Vancouver BC V6T 1Z1, Canada, 604-822-2514. 1959. Poetry, fiction, photos, parts-of-novels, long-poems, plays, non-fiction. "Use translation of poetry and fiction from languages other than English (e.g., Spanish, French, Japanese). No reviews or scholarly essays." circ. 1.4M. 4/yr. Pub'd 4 issues 1990; expects 4 issues 1991, 4 issues 1992. sub. price: $12 indiv., $18 libraries; per copy: $4; sample: $4. Back issues: varies. Discounts: differs with the issue. 88pp; 6×9; of. Reporting time: 8-10 weeks. Payment: $30 per printed page. Copyrighted, reverts to author. Ads: $100. CMPA.

PRISONER'S LEGAL NEWS, Paul Wright, Ed Mead, PO Box 1684, Lake Worth, FL 33460, 407-582-2701. 1990. Satire, reviews, letters, news items, non-fiction. "Additional address for checks: PO Box 1684, Lake Worth, FL 33460. *PLN* is published by prisoners and is uncensored. We offer prison news and analysis from a working class perspective and seek to educate prisoners in the use of the law for change, to organize prisoners and their families and to educate free citizens on the realities of prisons. We have readers in some 20 countries and cover national and international events, with an emphasis on Washington State. The bulk of each issue of *PLN* is written by prisoners." circ. 500+. 12/yr. Pub'd 8 issues 1990; expects 12 issues 1991, 12 issues 1992.

sub. price: $10; sample: donation. Back issues: none available. Discounts: made as needed. 10pp; 8½x11; †mi. Reporting time: 6 weeks. Payment: none. Not copyrighted. Pub's reviews: 40-50 in 1990. §Anything to do with prisons, prison/civil rights/criminal litigation and revolutionary politics.

PRIVACY JOURNAL, Robert Ellis Smith, PO Box 28577, Providence, RI 02908. 1974. Articles, cartoons, reviews, letters, news items. 12/yr. Pub'd 12 issues 1990; expects 12 issues 1991, 12 issues 1992. 4 titles listed in the *Small Press Record of Books in Print* (20th Edition, 1991-92). sub. price: $98; per copy: $10; sample: free. Back issues: $70 per whole year. Discounts: $35 to individuals if paid in advance. 8pp; 8½x11; of. Reporting time: 1 month. Pub's reviews. §Privacy, computers and society, surveillance. No ads.

PRIVATE INVESTIGATOR'S CONNECTION: A Newsletter for Investigators, Thomas Publications, Ralph D. Thomas, PO Box 33244, Austin, TX 78764, 512-832-0355. 1984. Non-fiction. "We will buy rights on stories related to the investigative profession. Magazine is the official publication of The National Association of Investigative Specialists." circ. 5M. 6/yr. Pub'd 6 issues 1990; expects 4 issues 1991, 6 issues 1992. sub. price: $25; per copy: $5; sample: $5. Back issues: $5.50. Discounts: none at this time. 24-36pp; 8½x11; †of. Reporting time: 1 month. Payment: depends. Copyrighted, reverts to author. Pub's reviews: 6 in 1990. §Subjects on general business, investigation and security. Ads: $175/$125/$75 1/4 page/Business card $25.

ProActive Press, James Craig, Marguerite Craig, 64 Via La Cumbre, Greenbrae, CA 94904, 415-461-7854. 1973. Fiction, articles, non-fiction. "We established the ProActive Press to assist in the co-creation of a caring society through humanistic politics. We are eager to share what skills we have with anyone who has a good, readable manuscript that offers a promising humane, pro-active program for humanizing social change. (We're not interested in more re-actions to the horrors we see and sense all about us.) Our *Synergic Power: Beyond Domination and Permissiveness* shows one kind of manuscript we're looking for. Also Utopian fiction" avg. press run 2.5M. Pub'd 1 title 1990; expects 1 title 1991. 3 titles listed in the *Small Press Record of Books in Print* (20th Edition, 1991-92). avg. price, paper: $6.95. Discounts: 40% trade, 20% text—both for orders of 5 or more books. 144pp; 5½x8½, 8½x11; of. Reporting time: varies, query. Payment: varies, query. Copyright by author's choice.

Pro/Am Music Resources, Inc., Thomas P. Lewis, Denis Stevens, 63 Prospect Street, White Plains, NY 10606, 914-948-7436. 1982. Music. "We publish and import books in the field of music exclusively, of principal interest to colleges and universities." avg. press run 300-1M. Pub'd 10 titles 1990; expects 20 titles 1991, 20 titles 1992. 25 titles listed in the *Small Press Record of Books in Print* (20th Edition, 1991-92). avg. price, cloth: $35; paper: $16. Discounts: write for schedule. 300pp; of. Payment: 10%. Copyrights for author.

PROCEEDINGS OF THE SPANISH INQUISITION, Robert Trumble, 2419 Greensburg Pike, Pittsburgh, PA 15221. 1984. Art, interviews, satire, reviews, letters, news items. circ. 70. 6/yr. Pub'd 6 issues 1990; expects 6 issues 1991, 6 issues 1992. sub. price: $5; per copy: $1; sample: $1. Back issues: $1. 8pp; 5½x8½; †Mita copier. Reporting time: 1 month. Payment: copies. Copyrighted, reverts to author. Pub's reviews: 2 in 1990. §Monty Python, John Cleese, etc. Ads: $25/$15/$5 classified.

PROCESSED WORLD, Collective editorial, 41 Sutter Street, #1829, San Francisco, CA 94104, 415-626-2979. 1981. Poetry, fiction, articles, art, photos, cartoons, interviews, satire, criticism, reviews, letters, collages, news items, non-fiction. circ. 4M. 3/yr. Pub'd 3 issues 1990; expects 3 issues 1991, 3 issues 1992. sub. price: $12; per copy: $4; sample: $4. Back issues: $4. Discounts: bulk orders (5 or more) 40% discount. 48pp; 8½x11; of. Reporting time: 1-3 months. Payment: none. Not copyrighted. Pub's reviews: 2-3 in 1990. §Work, alienation, political satire, radical political economy, radical fiction, poetry, etc. No ads accepted.

PROEM CANADA, Chris Magwood, Julie Bowen, 47 Gower Street, St. John, Afld., Canada, 705-749-5686. 1986. Poetry, fiction. "*Proem* accepts work from Canadians between the ages of 16 and 26. It is the primary forum for emerging talent in the country" circ. 2M. 1/yr. Pub'd 2 issues 1990; expects 2 issues 1991, 2 issues 1992. sub. price: $10; per copy: $5; sample: $5. Back issues: $6. Discounts: classroom sets sell for $3/copy. 60pp; 8½x11; of. Reporting time: 2-4 months. Payment: $50 each. Copyrighted, reverts to author.

PROFANE EXISTENCE, Troll, Newt, PO Box 8722, Minneapolis, MN 55408, 612-377-5269. 1989. Articles, art, photos, interviews, criticism, reviews, music, letters, news items. "Regular features on alternative healthcare and radical history" circ. 10M. 12/yr. Pub'd 7 issues 1990; expects 11 issues 1991, 12 issues 1992. sub. price: $18; per copy: $1.50; sample: $1.50. Back issues: $1.50. Discounts: half price all bulk orders over 10, special discounts for extra large quantities. 20pp; 11x17; of. Reporting time: variable. Payment: all voluntary. Not copyrighted. Pub's reviews: 300 in 1990. §Music, industry, alternative health, vegetarianism, radical politics. Ads: $2 for 40 words/ads start at 1/4 page down.

Professional Counselor Books, Cliff Creager, Editor; Susan Carr, Copy Editor; Lance Kuykendall, Assoc. Editor, PO Box 2079, Redmond, WA 98073, 206-867-5024; 800-622-7762. 1988. Non-fiction. "A division of A/D Communications Corp. Primarily publish titles dealing with all types of addictions and related subjects" avg. press run 7.5M. Pub'd 2 titles 1990; expects 3 titles 1991, 6 titles 1992. 4 titles listed in the *Small Press*

Record of Books in Print (20th Edition, 1991-92). avg. price, paper: $10. Discounts: available upon request. 190pp; 5½x8½; of. Reporting time: 6 months. Payment: negotiated with each author. Does not copyright for author. PMA, ABA, COSMEP.

Professional Publications, Inc., Michael R. Lindeburg, President, 1250 Fifth Avenue, Belmont, CA 94002. 1975. Non-fiction. "Interested in technical reference and career manuscripts only. For example, engineering, architecture, technology and eng. career advancement." avg. press run 2M-10M. Pub'd 9 titles 1990; expects 3 titles 1991, 3 titles 1992. 9 titles listed in the *Small Press Record of Books in Print* (20th Edition, 1991-92). avg. price, cloth: $45; paper: $20. Discounts: 25%-48% to bookstores, universities, libraries, depending on quantity ordered. 400pp; 8½x11, 6x9; of. Reporting time: 1 month. Payment: 8% first 5M, 10% next 5M, 12% after. Copyrights for author. ABA.

Professional Resource Exchange, Inc., Lawrence G. Ritt, Box 15560, Sarasota, FL 34277-1560, 813-366-7913. 1979. Non-fiction. "Books for mental health practitioners. Topics of recent books include innovations in clinical practice, law and psychology, how to write psychology papers, computer use in clinical practice. Manuscripts only solicited from practicing mental health professionals on topics of professional interest (e.g., no "self-help" books)." avg. press run 2M-3M. Pub'd 4 titles 1990; expects 6 titles 1991, 8 titles 1992. 35 titles listed in the *Small Press Record of Books in Print* (20th Edition, 1991-92). avg. price, cloth: $40; paper: $19.95. Discounts: variable depending on quantity and return privilege options (0-40%). 450pp; 6x9, 8½x11; web. Reporting time: 6 months average. Payment: variable - percentage or fixed dollar amts. Copyrights for author. FPG, COSMEP.

Profile Press, 3004 S. Grant Street, Arlington, VA 22202, 703-684-6208. 1988. Non-fiction. avg. press run 5M. Pub'd 1 title 1990. 1 title listed in the *Small Press Record of Books in Print* (20th Edition, 1991-92). avg. price, paper: $12.50. Discounts: 5-20 copies, 40% - all over 50%. 100pp; 5½x8½; of. Reporting time: 3 months. Copyrights for author.

Programmed Press, Sarah Bookbinder, Publisher, 599 Arnold Road, West Hempstead, NY 11552-3918, 516-599-6527. 1967. Non-fiction. avg. press run 3M. Pub'd 3 titles 1990; expects 3 titles 1991, 3 titles 1992. 3 titles listed in the *Small Press Record of Books in Print* (20th Edition, 1991-92). avg. price, cloth: $15; paper: $19.95. Discounts: 20% and up to 55%. 220pp; 7x10; comuter typeset, lp. Payment: 15%. Copyrights for author.

Progresiv Publishr (see also CASE ANALYSIS), Kenneth H. Ives, 401 E. 32nd #1002, Chicago, IL 60616, 312-225-9181. 1977. Articles, reviews. "Pamphlet series *Studies in Quakerism. Bookkeeping for Small Organizations* ($3.00), Spelling reform book *Written Dialects N Spelling Reforms: History N Alternatives* (list $5.00). *Teaching Science as a Second Culture* ($4.00), lengths so far, 32 to 112 pages. *Recovering the Human Jesus,* 300 pages, 1990, $21." avg. press run 300. Pub'd 1 title 1990; expects 3 titles 1991, 4 titles 1992. 22 titles listed in the *Small Press Record of Books in Print* (20th Edition, 1991-92). avg. price, paper: $4. Discounts: 5 or more 20%; 10 or more 30%. 45-60pp; 5x8 (pamphlets), 6¾x8¼ (CA); xerox. Reporting time: about a month. Payment: 10 copies. Quakers Uniting In Publications (QUIP).

Progressive Education (see also PROGRESSIVE PERIODICALS DIRECTORY/UPDATE), Craig T. Canan, PO Box 120574, Nashville, TN 37212. 1980. Art, cartoons, reviews, concrete art. avg. press run 1.5M. 1 title listed in the *Small Press Record of Books in Print* (20th Edition, 1991-92). avg. price, paper: $16. Discounts: over 5 $5 each. 36pp; 8½x11; of. Reporting time: 1 month. Payment: none. Copyrights for author.

PROGRESSIVE PERIODICALS DIRECTORY/UPDATE, Progressive Education, Craig T. Canan, PO Box 120574, Nashville, TN 37212. 1980. Art, cartoons, reviews, concrete art. circ. 1.5M. Expects 1 issue 1991. sub. price: $16; per copy: $16; sample: $16. Back issues: $16. Discounts: over 5, $5 each. 36pp; 8½x11; of. Reporting time: 4 weeks. Payment: none. Copyrighted, reverts to author. Pub's reviews: 600 in 1990. §Progressive periodicals on social concerns in U.S. Ads: $200/$100.

ProLingua Associates, Arthur A. Burrows, Raymond C. Clark, Patrick R. Moran, 15 Elm Street, Brattleboro, VT 05301, 802-257-7779. 1980. "We specialize in texts and resource materials for language teachers, at present particularly for English as a second language teachers. Our materials fit in with our Interplay Approach to language learning and teaching-practical, flexible, stressing student centered activities." avg. press run 3M-6M. Expects 5 titles 1991. 4 titles listed in the *Small Press Record of Books in Print* (20th Edition, 1991-92). avg. price, paper: $8.50. Discounts: 20% for trade/jobber. 150pp; 8½x11; of. Reporting time: 1 month. Payment: standard. Copyrights for author. TESOL.

Promontory Publishing, Inc., PO Box 117213, Carrollton, TX 75011-7213, 214-394-6020. 1986. Non-fiction. avg. press run 3M-5M. Pub'd 1 title 1990; expects 1 title 1991, 1 title 1992. 1 title listed in the *Small Press Record of Books in Print* (20th Edition, 1991-92). avg. price, paper: $13. Discounts: 2-9 25%, 10-99 30%, 100-299 40%, 500+ 50%. 140pp; 5x8. Reporting time: queries only. Payment: varies. Copyrights for author. PMA.

466

PROMOTION, Geoff Stevens, 8 Beaconview House, Charlemont Farm, W. Bromwich, West Midlands, B71 3PL, England. 1988. Poetry, articles, interviews, reviews, news items. "5 or 6 poets (other writers may be considered later) are promoted in each issue. Photo, short biog., achievements and aims listed, poem(s) and extracts from poem(s) given. Featured poets pay for inclusion and copies are sent (free) to editors/publishers/arts bodies, etc. Intended includees should write in the first instance." circ. 50. 2/yr. Expects 1 issue 1991. sub. price: free to selected editors etc.; per copy: free to selected editors etc.; sample: free to selected editors etc. 14pp; 10×8; †mi. Reporting time: 1 month. Payment: none. Not copyrighted. Pub's reviews: 80 in 1990. §Poetry, short stories, biography of writers, art. Ads: £10 2 pages ($25).

PROOF ROCK, Don R. Conner, Editor; Serena Fusek, Poetry Editor, Proof Rock Press, PO Box 607, Halifax, VA 24558. 1982. Poetry, fiction, articles, art, interviews, reviews. "Poems: 32 lines or less. Fiction: 2M words or less. Few subjects considered taboo if they are well done." circ. 300. 2/yr. Expects 2 issues 1991, 2 issues 1992. 6 titles listed in the *Small Press Record of Books in Print* (20th Edition, 1991-92). sub. price: $5; per copy: $3; sample: $3. Back issues: $2.50. Discounts: none. 40pp; 5½×8½; of. Reporting time: 3 months. Payment: contributor's copy. Not copyrighted. Pub's reviews: 20 in 1990. §Poetry. Ads: $25/$15/not available.

PROPER DHARMA SEAL, Buddhist Text Translation Society, City of 10,000 Buddhas, Talmage, CA 95481-0217, 707-462-0939. 1984. Poetry, fiction, articles, art, photos, interviews, reviews, letters, non-fiction. circ. 20M. 3/yr. Pub'd 3 issues 1990; expects 3 issues 1991, 3 issues 1992. sub. price: free; per copy: free; sample: free. Back issues: free if available. 4pp; tabloid newspaper; of. Payment: none. Copyrighted, reverts to author. §Buddhism. No ads.

Proper Tales Press (see also MONDO HUNKAMOOGA), Stuart Ross, PO Box 789, Station F, Toronto, Ontario M4Y 2N7, Canada. 1979. Poetry, fiction, long-poems, plays. "Interested mainly in surrealist, fringe, and bizarro writing, or hard-boiled nun stories. None of that other boring stuff. Do let's be absurd. Recent titles include *Antpath* by John M. Bennett ($2), *Shadows of Seclusion* by Randall Brock ($1.50), *Father, The Cowboys Are Ready To Come Down From The Attic*, a 3-day novel by Stuart Ross ($3), and *The Hats and Stockings of Great Heroes Who Sang for Six Months* by Opal Louis Nations ($3). Send 6 X 9 SASE for catalog and freebie. Submissions without SASE will wrap fish" avg. press run 750. Pub'd 3 titles 1990; expects 5 titles 1991, 6 titles 1992. 16 titles listed in the *Small Press Record of Books in Print* (20th Edition, 1991-92). avg. price, paper: $3. Discounts: 20-40%. 40pp; 5½×8½; of, mi, xerox. Reporting time: 12 weeks, often longer. Payment: negotiated individually with each author. Copyrights for author.

PROPHETIC VOICES, Ruth Wildes Schuler, Goldie L. Morales, Jeanne Leigh Schuler, 94 Santa Maria Drive, Novato, CA 94947. 1982. Poetry, articles, art. "Seeking only poetry at this time. Open to all kinds, but lean towards free verse. Prefer poetry that has a message, either social or personal. Recent contributors: William Stafford, A.D. Winans, Norman Russell, Laurel Speer, Mary Rudge, Alta, Bruce Combs, Sharri Love, etc. We are especially seeking poetry by poets in other countries around the world since ours is an international journal. We are also interested in the stance of the poet as philosopher. Will exchange magazines with other small press editors." circ. 400. 2/yr. Expects 2 issues 1991, 2 issues 1992. sub. price: $12, $14 for institutions and foreign subscribers; per copy: $6; sample: $6. Back issues: $4.50. 144pp; 7×8½; of. Reporting time: 1 day to 1 month. Payment: contributors copy. Copyrighted, reverts to author.

Prospect Hill Press, Eleanor Heldrich, 216 Wendover Road, Baltimore, MD 21218, 301-889-0320. 1981. Fiction, non-fiction. "Do not accept manuscripts prior to query. No more juveniles." avg. press run 3M. Pub'd 1 title 1990; expects 2 titles 1991, 2 titles 1992. 8 titles listed in the *Small Press Record of Books in Print* (20th Edition, 1991-92). avg. price, cloth: $13; paper: $12.95. Discounts: 1 book—no discount, 2-5 25%, 6-49 40%, 50+ 50%. 96pp; 8½×11; perfect bound, or smyth-sewn case bound. Reporting time: 2 weeks. Payment: to be negotiated. Copyrights for author. BP, COSMEP.

THE PROSPECT REVIEW, Peter A. Koufos, 557 10th Street, Brooklyn, NY 11215. 1989. Poetry, fiction, art, parts-of-novels, plays, non-fiction. "Recent contributors: E. Ethelbert Miller, Tony D'Arpino, Richard Burgin, Jana Harris." 1/yr. Expects 1 issue 1991, 1 issue 1992. sub. price: $12; per copy: $6; sample: $6. Back issues: no special back issue price. Discounts: none. 90pp; 6×9; Desk-top publishing. Reporting time: all submissions will be reported on prior to the release date of an issue. Payment: 1 copy per contributor. Copyrighted, reverts to author. Ads: $150/$125.

Protea Publishing Company, Susan E. Brown, 604 South Canterbury Road, Canterbury, CT 06331, 203-546-9380. 1988. Pub'd 1 title 1990. 1 title listed in the *Small Press Record of Books in Print* (20th Edition, 1991-92). Discounts: 2-4 20%, 5-24 40%, 25-49 43%, 50-99 46%, 100+ 50%. of.

Protean Publications, Paul Lester, 34 Summerfield Crescent, Flat 4, Edgbaston, Birmingham B16 OER, England. 1980. Poetry, fiction, cartoons, satire, criticism, non-fiction. "Deals with poetry, graphics, short stories and cultural criticism." avg. press run 300. Pub'd 2 titles 1990; expects 3 titles 1991. 31 titles listed in the *Small Press Record of Books in Print* (20th Edition, 1991-92). avg. price, paper: 40p. Discounts: by arrangement. 16-24pp; 4×6; of. Reporting time: 6 weeks. Payment: by arrangement. Copyrights for author.

467

PROTOCULTURE ADDICTS, Ianus Publications, Inc., Claude J. Pelletier, Alain Dubreuil, Michel Gareau, 33 Prince Street #243, Montreal, Quebec H3C 2M7, Canada, 514-397-0342. 1988. Fiction, articles, art, photos, cartoons, interviews, reviews, letters, news items. "13 issues published to date. ISSN 0835-9563. The anime and manba fan magazine" circ. 7M. 6/yr. Pub'd 4 issues 1990; expects 6 issues 1991, 9 issues 1992. sub. price: $18US; per copy: $2.50; sample: $3. Back issues: $3 for issue #3, 8-12. 36pp; 6¾×10; of. Reporting time: 2 months before publication. Payment: none, free copy of publication. Copyrighted, reverts to author. Pub's reviews: 10 in 1990. §Science fiction, Japanese comics and animation. Ads: $175/$150/$75 1/4 page/$300 back cover/$200 inside cover. SWAC.

PROVINCETOWN ARTS, Christopher Busa, 650 Commercial Street, Provincetown, MA 02657, 508-487-3167. 1985. Poetry, fiction, articles, art, photos, cartoons, interviews, criticism, reviews, collages, non-fiction. "Published annually in July, *Provincetown Arts* focuses broadly on the artists and writers who inhabit or visit the tip of Cape Cod. Previous cover subjects have included Norman Mailer, Robert Motherwell, and Annie Dillard. Placing contemporary creative activity in a context that draws upon a 75-year tradition of literature, visual art, and theatre, *Provincetown Arts* seeks to consolidate the voices and images of the nations foremost summer art colony. Some recent contributors include Olga Broumas, Douglas Huebler, Justin Kaplan, Stanley Kunitz, Joel Meyerowitz, and Susan Mitchell." circ. 5M. 1/yr. Pub'd 1 issue 1990; expects 1 issue 1991, 1 issue 1992. sub. price: $6; per copy: $5; sample: $5. Back issues: $6. Discounts: 40% for resale. 184pp; 9×12; of. Reporting time: 2 months. Payment: prose $100-300, poetry $25-125, art $25-300. Copyrighted, reverts to author. Pub's reviews: 2 in 1990. §Biographies of artists, exhibition catalogues. Ads: $650/$400/color available. CCLM.

Proving Grounds International, Inc. (see also LEGACIES IN TIME), Carolyn A. Okerchiri, PO Box 1074, Jackson, MI 49204, 517-783-4243. 1989. Poetry, articles, criticism, reviews, non-fiction. "Typewritten or letter-quality printed materials are only ones accepted. No returns without SASE. Photocopied submissions accepted." avg. press run 1M-3M. Expects 1 title 1991, 4 titles 1992. avg. price, paper: $4. Discounts: bulk, classroom, agent, jobber. 150pp; 4¼×6¾; lp. Reporting time: 8 weeks queries, 4 months on mss. Payment: 5-7% on retail price, $150 average advance. Copyrights for author.

Prudhomme Press, Harrison Leonard, PO Box 11, Tavares, FL 32778, 904-589-0100. 1989. "Although we only publish complete books occasionally, we are not 'self publishers.' However, *we do not accept unsolicited manuscripts.*" avg. press run 5M. Expects 2 titles 1991, 2 titles 1992. 1 title listed in the *Small Press Record of Books in Print* (20th Edition, 1991-92). avg. price, cloth: $18.95; paper: $14.95. Discounts: trade and jobber. 300+pp; 6×9; of. Copyrights for author. COSMEP, International Assn. of Independent Publishers.

Pruett Publishing Company, Gerald Keenan, Managing Ed.; Jim Pruett, Publisher, 2928 Pearl, Boulder, CO 80301, 303-449-4919. 1959. Art, photos, criticism, non-fiction. "Publisher of books pertaining to outdoor travel and adventure, western Americana, and railroadiana. Examples are an extensive pictorial history of the California Zephyr, *Twilight Dwellers: The Ghosts, Ghouls, & Goblins of Colorado*, a history of the American Indian in Colorado, *A Climbing Guide to Colorado's Fourteeners, Trout Bum* and *The View From Rat Lake*, collections of fly-fishing essays" avg. press run varies per book. Expects 25-33 titles 1991. 113 titles listed in the *Small Press Record of Books in Print* (20th Edition, 1991-92). avg. price, cloth: $15-$40; paper: $6-$14. Discounts: write for a copy of our complete schedule. Pages vary; size varies. Reporting time: within a week or two, if we reject mss; within 30-60 days, if mss is under consideration. Payment: generally a royalty basis for authors. Copyrights for author. ABA, RMBPA.

PSI Research/The Oasis Press, Rosanno Alejandro, Editor; Scott Crawford, Editor; Virginia Grosso, Editor, 300 North Valley Drive, Grants Pass, OR 97526, 800-221-4089 (CA); 800-228-2275. 1975. "Small business-oriented. Successful Business Library is a series of how-to business guides designed for entrepreneurs and small businesspersons" Pub'd 11 titles 1990; expects 34 titles 1991, 30 titles 1992. 72 titles listed in the *Small Press Record of Books in Print* (20th Edition, 1991-92). avg. price, paper: $19.95; other: $39.95. Discounts: 20%-40% bookstores, 15% libraries. 200pp; 8½×11; †Desktop publishing system, laser printer, xerox copier, offset. Reporting time: 2 weeks for expression of interest. Payment: as per licensing agreement. Does not copyright for author.

PSYCH IT, Charlotte L. Babicky, 6507 Bimini Court, Apollo Beach, FL 33572. 1986. Poetry, articles, art, cartoons. "Poetry, articles, spot art, cartoons crossword puzzles, and fillers." 4/yr. Pub'd 4 issues 1990; expects 4 issues 1991, 4 issues 1992. sub. price: $8; per copy: $2 + 50¢ p/h; sample: $2 plus 50¢ p/h. Back issues: *Psych It* Contests: $2 each plus SASE. 10-12pp; 8½×11; xerox. Reporting time: 3-4 weeks or less. Payment: $1 for cartoons, spot art, puzzles, poems, fillers; up to $5 for articles. Copyrighted, reverts to author. Ads: $20/$3.25 for 2¾ X 4½.

Psyche Press, Robert Endleman, Director, PO Box 780, New York, NY 10024, 212-721-4466. 1989. Non-fiction. "Books, 150-300 pp. on psychoanalytic social science and related. Can include collection of articles." avg. press run 1M-2M. Expects 3 titles 1991, 4 titles 1992. 4 titles listed in the *Small Press Record of*

468

Books in Print (20th Edition, 1991-92). avg. price, cloth: $29-$32; paper: $15-$18. Discounts: dealers 1-3 copies 20%, 4+ 40%; libraries, cloth editions 20%. 160-200pp; 6x9, 5½x8½; of. Reporting time: ASAP. Payment: standard for academic books, annual royalty. Copyrights open to negotiation.

PSYCHOANALYTIC BOOKS, Joseph Reppen, Editor, 211 East 70th Street, New York, NY 10021, 212-628-8792. 1990. Reviews. "Book reviews of books in the *broad* field of psychoanalysis including clinical and theoretical psychoanalysis, Freud studies, history of psychoanalysis, psychobiography, psychohistory, and the psychoanalytic study of literature and the arts. News and notes on books and journals in psychoanalysis. ISSN 1044-2103" circ. 1M. 4/yr. Pub'd 4 issues 1990; expects 4 issues 1991, 4 issues 1992. sub. price: $50, $90 institutions; per copy: $15. Back issues: $15. 160pp; 6x9; of. Reporting time: by invitation only. Payment: none. Copyrighted, does not revert to author. Pub's reviews: 100 in 1990. §Psychoanalysis, Freud studies, history of psychoanalysis, psychobiography, psychohistory, psychoanalytic study of literature and the arts. Ads: $200/$125. CELJ.

Psychohistory Press (see also **THE JOURNAL OF PSYCHOHISTORY**), Lloyd deMause, Editor, 2315 Broadway, New York City, NY 10024, 212-873-5900. 1973. Articles. avg. press run 2M. Pub'd 2 titles 1990; expects 3 titles 1991. 10 titles listed in the *Small Press Record of Books in Print* (20th Edition, 1991-92). avg. price, cloth: $25; paper: $12. Discounts: 20%. 300pp; 7x9; of. Reporting time: 4 weeks. Copyrights for author.

PSYCHOLOGY OF WOMEN QUARTERLY, Judith Worell, Dept. of Educ. & Counseling Psychology, 237 Dickey Hall, Univ. of Kentucky, Lexington, KY 40506-0017. 1976. Articles, reviews. circ. 3.5M. 4/yr. Pub'd 4 issues 1990; expects 4 issues 1991, 4 issues 1992. sub. price: $32; per copy: $20. Discounts: included with membership in Division 35 of the American Psychological Association. 128pp; 6x9. Reporting time: 3 months. Payment: none. Not copyrighted. Pub's reviews: 8 in 1990. §Psychology of women. Ads: contact Cambridge Univ. Press.

PSYCHOPOETICA, Geoff Lowe, Department of Psychology, University of Hull, Hull HU6 7RX, United Kingdom. 1980. Poetry, reviews. "Psychologically-based poetry. Recent contributors: Belinda Subraman, and Sheila E. Murphy, Wes Magee, Charlie Mehrhoff." circ. 350. 3/yr. Pub'd 3 issues 1990; expects 3 issues 1991, 4 issues 1992. price per copy: $2 (plus postage); sample: $2. Back issues: $1 (plus postage). Discounts: 20% on 5 or more. 40pp; 8¼x11½ (A4); †mi. Reporting time: 4 weeks. Payment: none. Copyrighted. Pub's reviews: 24 brief in 1990. §Modern poetry, bizarre poetry, 'off-beat', psychology.

The Pterodactyl Press, Zachary Pearce, PO Box 205, Cumberland, IA 50843, 712-774-2244. 1980. Poetry. "Material should fit into fewer than 100 pages." avg. press run 300-1M. Pub'd 2 titles 1990; expects 6 titles 1991, 8 titles 1992. 15 titles listed in the *Small Press Record of Books in Print* (20th Edition, 1991-92). avg. price, cloth: $20; paper: $7.50. Discounts: on request. 70pp; 6x9; †lp. Reporting time: 3 months. Payment: standard, paid twice a year but will pay all immed. if possible. Copyrights for author.

PTOLEMY/BROWNS MILLS REVIEW, David C. Vajda, Box 908, Browns Mills, NJ 08015, 609-893-0896. 1979. Poetry, fiction, articles, satire, criticism, parts-of-novels, long-poems, concrete art. "Refer to the *Small Press Record of Books in Print* for book listings." circ. 100-250. 1-2/yr. Expects 3-4 issues 1991, 2 issues 1992. 9 titles listed in the *Small Press Record of Books in Print* (20th Edition, 1991-92). sub. price: $4; per copy: $2; sample: $1-$2. Back issues: $1-$2. No discounts per se. 16pp; 5½x8½; of. Reporting time: 1 week to 1 month. Payment: 5 copies per acceptance. Copyrighted, rights revert with permission. No ads.

THE PUB, Ansuda Publications, Daniel R. Betz, Box 158, Harris, IA 51345. 1979. Poetry, fiction, articles, parts-of-novels, long-poems, news items. "6M word maximum on fiction. No set limit on articles (query *first* on articles *only*). No set length on poetry but will not consider haiku or poetry with senseless rhyming. Canadians are welcome to send SASE with loose Canadian postage" circ. 350. 2/yr. Pub'd 1 issue 1990; expects 2 issues 1991, 2 issues 1992. sub. price: $7.25/3 issues; per copy: $3; sample: $3. Discounts: query. 72pp; 5½x8½; †mi. Reporting time: immediately to 2 weeks, 2 months maximum. Payment: copies. Copyrighted, reverts to author. Ads: $10/$5/10¢ - will gladly exchange.

THE PUBLIC HISTORIAN, University of California Press, Otis Graham, University of California Press, 2120 Berkeley Way, Berkeley, CA 94720, 415-642-4191. 1978. Articles, interviews, reviews, news items, non-fiction. "Editorial address: Dept. of History, Ellison Hall, University of California, Santa Barbara, CA 93106." circ. 1.2M. 4/yr. Pub'd 4 issues 1990; expects 4 issues 1991, 4 issues 1992. sub. price: $32 indiv., $45 instit., $15 students (+ $4 foreign postage); per copy: $8 indiv.; $11.25 instit., $4 students; sample: free. Back issues: same as single copy price. Discounts: foreign subs. agents 10%, one-time orders 10+ 30%, standing orders (bookstores): 1-99 40%, 100+ 50%. 128pp; 6x9; of. Reporting time: 2-3 months. Copyrighted, does not revert to author. Pub's reviews: 50 in 1990. §History. Ads: $200/$120.

PUBLIC LANDS ACTION NETWORK, Katherine Bueler, PO Box 5631, Santa Fe, NM 87502. 1990. Poetry, fiction, articles, art, photos, cartoons, interviews, satire, criticism, reviews, letters, news items, non-fiction. circ. 2M. 4/yr. Pub'd 1 issue 1990; expects 3 issues 1991, 4 issues 1992. sub. price: $20; per copy:

469

free; sample: free. Discounts: bulk. 8pp; 8½×11; of. Payment: none. Not copyrighted. Pub's reviews.

THE PUBLIC RELATIONS QUARTERLY, Howard Penn Hudson, Paul Swift, PO Box 311, Rhinebeck, NY 12572, 914-876-2081. 1955. Articles, interviews, reviews. 4/yr. Pub'd 4 issues 1990; expects 4 issues 1991, 4 issues 1992. sub. price: $30; per copy: $7.50. 32pp; 9×11. Reporting time: 1 month. Payment: in copies. Copyrighted, reverts to author. Pub's reviews: 6-8 in 1990. §Public relations, writing, management. Ads: $600/$300/$25-inch.

The Public Safety Press, Christine Bettencourt, Judy James, 1320 Trancas Street, Suite 211, Napa, CA 94558, 707-255-7597. 1986. Non-fiction. "Books and training manuals: *Women's Guide To Fighting Back: Don't Be A Victim*, self-help; *Campus Emergency Response Manual*, school emergency action plans; *Municipal Crime Prevention Manual*, city crime prevention." avg. press run 1M. Pub'd 1 title 1990; expects 1 title 1991, 1 title 1992. 1 title listed in the *Small Press Record of Books in Print* (20th Edition, 1991-92). avg. price, paper: $12. Discounts: 30% bookstore, 10% cash to libraries, no disc. to individuals, 30% commercial for promotionals. 100pp; size varies; press, perfect binding, spiral binding for manuals. Reporting time: 30 days minimum. Payment: 15%. Copyrights for author.

Publications of Arts (Art Resources for Teachers & Students), M. Scherbatskoy, M. Montanez, Y. Yung-Ching, 32 Market Street, New York, NY 10002, 212-962-8231. 1970. Non-fiction. "ARTS publishes materials on the Chinese & Hispanic communities, documenting their holidays, language, music, games and history. Twenty booklets and two major publications—*A Pictorial History of Chinatown, New York City* and *The Trictionary* are now in print. Not interested in unsolicited manuscripts at this time" avg. press run 2M. Pub'd 2 titles 1990; expects 2 titles 1991, 2 titles 1992. avg. price, paper: $3. Discounts: 25-75 30%, 75+ 40%. 30-40pp; 7×7; †of. Copyrights for author.

Publishers Syndication Int'l (PSI) (see also THE POST), Mary Staub, A.P. Samuels, 1377 K Street NW, Suite 856, Washington, DC 20005. 1987. Fiction. "30,000 word mysteries, 30,000 word romances." avg. press run varies. Expects 2 titles 1991, 7 titles 1992. avg. price, paper: $1.95. 96+pp; 4⅜×5⅞; of. Reporting time: 4 weeks. Payment: .5 to 3¢ per word. COSMEP.

PUBLISHING POYNTERS, Para Publishing, Dan Poynter, PO Box 4232-Q, Santa Barbara, CA 93140-4232, 805-968-7277; fax 805-968-1379. 1986. News items. "Book marketing news and ideas from Dan Poynter. *Publishing Poynters* is full of non-fiction book marketing, promotion and distribution leads." circ. 8M. 4/yr. Pub'd 4 issues 1990; expects 4 issues 1991, 4 issues 1992. sub. price: $9.95/2 years; sample: $1. Back issues: $1 each ppd. 2pp; 8½×11; of. Reporting time: 2 weeks. Payment: none. Copyrighted. Pub's reviews: 20 in 1990. §Non-fiction book marketing, promotion or distribution *only*. PMA, COSMEP, ABA.

PUBLISHING TRENDS & TRENDSETTERS, Oxbridge Communications, Inc., Jim Mann, 150 Fifth Avenue, New York, NY 10011, 800-955-0231. 1978. Interviews, non-fiction. "Outside contributions not accepted. Each isssue deals with a single subject or aspect of periodical management." circ. 300. 10/yr. Pub'd 10 issues 1990; expects 10 issues 1991, 10 issues 1992. sub. price: $177; per copy: $20; sample: $20. Back issues: 3 for $57. Discounts: write for information. 16pp; 5½×8½; of. Copyrighted. Pub's reviews: 1 in 1990. §Journalism, publishing, magazines. No ads. NAA.

Publitec Editions, Maggie Rowe, Owner, 271-A Lower Cliff Drive, PO Box 4342, Laguna Beach, CA 92652, 714-497-6100; FAX 714-581-6465. 1983. Non-fiction. avg. press run 3M. Expects 1 title 1991, 1 title 1992. 5 titles listed in the *Small Press Record of Books in Print* (20th Edition, 1991-92). avg. price, cloth: $16.95; paper: $8.95. Discounts: 1-9 books 35%, 10+ 40% retail; 1-9 books 45%, 10+ 50% wholesale. 200pp; 6×9, 5½×8½; of. Reporting time: 1 month. Payment: varies according to amount of writing/editorial assistance required. Copyrights for author. PMA.

PUCK!, Permeable Press, Brian Clark, Kurt Putnam, Barbara del Rio, 350 Townsend Street #409-A, San Francisco, CA 94107. 1984. Poetry, fiction, articles, art, photos, cartoons, interviews, satire, criticism, reviews, music, letters, parts-of-novels, collages, plays, news items, non-fiction. "Material should be double-spaced, typewritten, or submitted on high density Macintosh diskette. SASE for return. Extremely biased, but you'll never know until you try. Radical reinterpretations of the mundane and overlooked." circ. 1M. 2/yr. Pub'd 1 issue 1990; expects 2 issues 1991, 2 issues 1992. sub. price: $15; per copy: $8; sample: $8. Discounts: 40% trade. 32pp; 8½×11; †of. Reporting time: 2 weeks to 2 months. Payment: copies and honorarium. Copyrighted, reverts to author. Pub's reviews: 100 in 1990. §Small or independent publishing/printing, apocalypse/conspiracy, commodity aesthetics.

Puckerbrush Press (see also THE PUCKERBRUSH REVIEW), Constance Hunting, PO Box 39, Orono, ME 04473-0039, 207-866-4868. 1971. Poetry, fiction, criticism. "*Things That Surround Us*, by Muska Nagel. *Notes From Sickrooms* by Julia Stephen. No strictly polemical stuff, please." avg. press run 250-1M. Pub'd 2 titles 1990; expects 3 titles 1991, 3 titles 1992. 30 titles listed in the *Small Press Record of Books in Print* (20th Edition, 1991-92). avg. price, paper: $8.95-$10.95. Discounts: 40%. 60-200pp; 6×9; of. Reporting time: 2

months. Payment: 10% of each retail copy. Copyright to author. MWPA.

THE PUCKERBRUSH REVIEW, Puckerbrush Press, Constance Hunting, 76 Main St., Orono, ME 04473. 1978. Poetry, fiction, reviews. "Maine-oriented" circ. 250-300. 1-2/yr. Pub'd 1 issue 1990; expects 1 issue 1991, 2 issues 1992. sub. price: $8; per copy: $4; sample: $2. Back issues: $1. Discounts: 40%. 60-100pp; 8½×11; of, compuprint. Reporting time: 1 month. Payment: copies. Copyrighted, does not revert to author. Pub's reviews: 20 in 1990. §Maine small/larger press and authors. Ads: $40.

Pudding House Publications (see also PUDDING MAGAZINE: THE INTERNATIONAL JOURNAL OF APPLIED POETRY), Jennifer Welch Bosveld, Editor; Doug Swisher, Associate Editor, 60 North Main Street, Johnstown, OH 43031. 1979. Poetry, non-fiction. "Will not return manuscripts for which SASE is not enclosed. $5.00 reading fee." avg. press run 500. Pub'd 3 titles 1990; expects 1 title 1991, 3 titles 1992. 18 titles listed in the *Small Press Record of Books in Print* (20th Edition, 1991-92). avg. price, paper: $4.50; other: varies. Discounts: 30% to classrooms, teachers, non-profit or charity organizations. Pages vary; 5½×8½; of. Reporting time: 2 weeks except for competition submissions; sometimes overnight. Payment: 20 copies of the book. Copyrights for author, but we don't register the copyright. COSMEP.

PUDDING MAGAZINE: THE INTERNATIONAL JOURNAL OF APPLIED POETRY, Pudding House Publications, Jennifer Welch Bosveld, Editor; Steve Abbott, Associate Editor; Doug Swisher, Associate Editor, 60 North Main Street, Johnstown, OH 43031. 1979. Poetry, articles, art, photos, cartoons, interviews, criticism, reviews, letters, non-fiction. "All styles and forms considered. Looking for the wildly different and the subtly profound. We recommend: reflections of intense human situations; poems on popular culture, politics, social concern, and the contemporary scene; concrete images and specific detail; artful expressions of unique situations; or the shock of recognition in things perhaps felt before (or almost felt) but never spoken. No trite comparisons, please. No cliches. No strictly religious verse or sentimentality. Mini-Articles: by poets who share their craft in the human services; about applied poetry experiences either from clients/patients or from psychiatrists, teachers, or other professionals and paraprofesionals who put the art of poetry to use in helping others; reviews of poetry books, how-to-write-poetry books, methodology books, and other relevant publications that would be beneficial in group or one-to-one service, professional/paraprofessional/self continuing education." circ. 2M. Irregular. Pub'd 1 issue 1990; expects 2 issues 1991, 2 issues 1992. sub. price: $12.75/3 issues; per copy: $4.75; sample: $4.75. Back issues: $5-$75 depending on issue; they are almost all out of print, $185 for back set. Discounts: 30% on 10 or more copies to classrooms, teachers, non-profit or charity organizations. 65pp; 5½×8½; of. Reporting time: usually overnight; if held, it's being considered, or we're travelling. Payment: 1 copy, featured poets receive 4 copies and $10. Copyrighted, reverts to author. Pub's reviews: 12 in 1990. §Poetry, 'applied poetry' Ads: $39/$25. COSMEP.

Pueblo Poetry Project, Tony Moffeit, 1501 E. 7th Street, Pueblo, CO 81001. 1979. Poetry, art, photos, long-poems. "*The Poetry Project* publishes an annual anthology of Pueblo poets. We've also put out more than 20 chapbooks, including: *Mojo* by Tony Moffeit, *Why Did I Laugh Tonight?* by Beth Ann Bassein, *Tapping Some Roots* by Ron Whitsitt, *Experiment in A* by Helen Roberts, *Gibbous* by Kim Cass-Nolan, *Hoodoo Woman* by Robbie Rubinstein, *A New Book* by Henry Darner, *My Skin Has Turned to Gray* by Joel Scherzer, *Delirium Trains* by Diane Rabson, *Speak Sunlight to Me* by John Senatore, *It's For You* by Bob Cordova and *Management Does Not Guarantee This Machine to Work* by Rick Terlep. Submissions limited to Pueblo area." avg. press run 100. Pub'd 1 title 1990; expects 1 title 1991, 1 title 1992. 20 titles listed in the *Small Press Record of Books in Print* (20th Edition, 1991-92). avg. price, paper: $1. Discounts: 40%. 24pp; 5½×8½; of. Reporting time: 2 months. Payment: 1/3 of press run. Copyrights for author.

Pueblo Publishing Press, Charles Penoi, Publisher; Mary Penoi, PO Box 850508, Yukon, OK 73085-0508, 405-354-7825. 1980. Fiction, non-fiction. "Photography" avg. press run 2M. Pub'd 5 titles 1990. 12 titles listed in the *Small Press Record of Books in Print* (20th Edition, 1991-92). avg. price, cloth: $14.95; paper: $3.95. 200pp; 4×7, 8½×11, 5½×8½. Reporting time: 3 months. Payment: depends on contract. Copyrights for author.

PUERTO DEL SOL, Kevin McIlvoy, Joe Somoza, Box 3E, New Mexico State University, Las Cruces, NM 88003, 505-646-2345. 1961. Poetry, fiction, art, photos, interviews, reviews, parts-of-novels, long-poems, plays. "Emphasis on Southwestern Chicano, Nat. Am. The primary emphasis, however, is on *top quality writing,* wherever it comes from. Some Latin American with trans." circ. 1M. 2/yr. Pub'd 2 issues 1990; expects 2 issues 1991, 2 issues 1992. sub. price: $10; per copy: $7; sample: $6. Back issues: complete set $200 (vol 1 no. 1-vol 27 no. 2). Discounts: 40% general, 50% jobber. 200pp; 6×9; of. Reporting time: 9 weeks. Payment: copies. Copyrighted. Pub's reviews: 8 in 1990. §Chicano, Nat. Am., poetry, fiction, Southwestern, anthologies. Ads: $120/$75. CCLM.

PULPHOUSE: THE HARDBACK MAGAZINE, Pulphouse Publishing, Dean Wesley Smith, Publisher; Kristine Kathryn Rusch, Editor, PO Box 1227, Eugene, OR 97440, 503-344-6742. 1987. Fiction. "We only publish short fiction-7,500 max. Science fiction, fantasy, and horror." circ. 1.3M. 4/yr. Pub'd 4 issues 1990;

471

expects 4 issues 1991, 4 issues 1992. sub. price: $68; per copy: $20; sample: $20. Discounts: 40% trade, 30% limited; minimum 5 book orders. 300pp; 5×9; of. Reporting time: 3 weeks. Payment: 3-6¢ per word. Copyrighted, reverts to author. §Any SF, Fantasy and Horror Mazagine. SFWA, HWA.

Pulphouse Publishing (see also **PULPHOUSE: THE HARDBACK MAGAZINE**), Dean Wesley Smith, Publisher & Editor, PO Box 1227, Eugene, OR 97440, 503-344-6742. 1984. Fiction. "Novellas-SF, fantasy, horror—25,000 words. Invitation only." avg. press run 10M. Pub'd 35 titles 1990; expects 161 titles 1991. avg. price, cloth: varies; paper: $2.50/magazine. Discounts: 50% nonreturnable. 48pp; 8×10½; of. Payment: per word. Copyrights for author. SFWA, HWA.

Puma Publishing Company, William M. Alarid, 1670 Coral Drive, Santa Maria, CA 93454, 805-925-3216. 1986. Non-fiction. avg. press run 10M. Pub'd 1 title 1990; expects 1 title 1991, 1 title 1992. 2 titles listed in the *Small Press Record of Books in Print* (20th Edition, 1991-92). avg. price, paper: $11.95. Discounts: 3-10 20%, 11-20 30%, 21-100 40%, 101-200 50%, 200+ 60%. 208pp; 5½×8½; of. Reporting time: 1 month. Payment: 10% of revenues. Copyrights for author. PMA, COSMEP.

PUNCTURE, Katherine Spielmann, Editor; Steve Connell, Managing Editor, 1592 Union Street, #431, San Francisco, CA 94123, 415-771-5127. 1982. Articles, art, photos, cartoons, interviews, reviews, news items, non-fiction. "A magazine of alternative rock and other independent music. Also covers fiction, non-fiction, photography. We will respond to queries with SASE & samples but not unsolicited submissions." circ. 6M. 4/yr. Pub'd 4 issues 1990; expects 4 issues 1991, 4 issues 1992. sub. price: $10/4 issues; per copy: $2.50; sample: $2.50. Back issues: varies. Discounts: retail 35% (min. 5), wholesale 50% (min. 25). 68pp; 8¼×10¾; web press. Payment: copies. Copyrighted, reverts to author. Pub's reviews: 5-6 per issue in 1990. §Records, tapes, books on rock, alternative music, culture, politics, photography, and strong current fiction. Ads: $250/$180.

Royal Purcell, Publisher, Royal Purcell, 806 West Second Street, Bloomington, IN 47403, 812-336-4195. 1985. Non-fiction. "Submit query first, preferably with specific outline of nonfiction subject and SASE." avg. press run 1M. Pub'd 1 title 1990; expects 1 title 1991, 2 titles 1992. 3 titles listed in the *Small Press Record of Books in Print* (20th Edition, 1991-92). avg. price, paper: $9.95. Discounts: 2-5 20%; 6-24 30%; 25-49 40%; 50-99 45%; 100 up 50%. 150pp; 8½×11; word processor/photocopier. Reporting time: 2 weeks for query. Payment: 10-15%. Copyrights for author.

The Purchase Press, John Guenther, PO Box 5, Harrison, NY 10528, 212-645-4442. 1980. Poetry. "Specializing in poetry, including translation into English language. Recent contributor: *Sonnets to Orpheus*, Rilke, trans. by Kenneth Pitchford, 3rd printing 1983. Recent publication: *Quai Malaquais*, a novel 1984." avg. press run 300. Pub'd 1 title 1990; expects 1 title 1991. 3 titles listed in the *Small Press Record of Books in Print* (20th Edition, 1991-92). avg. price, paper: $7.50. Discounts: 40% on all orders at wholesale; full list price on retail mail-order sales. 110pp; 6×9; of. Reporting time: 30 days. Payment: negotiated on each title. Copyrights for author. PEN (Poets, Editors, Essayists, Novelists), New York City, 568 Broadway, New York.

PURNA YOGA, Auromere Books and Imports, 1291 Weber Street, Pomona, CA 91768, 714-629-8255.

Purple Heather Publications (see also **FIVE LEAVES LEFT; THE TOLL GATE JOURNAL**), Richard Mason, 12 Granby Terrace, Headingley, Leeds, West Yorkshire, LS6 3BB, England. 1982. Poetry, fiction, articles, art, photos, interviews, reviews, music, letters, parts-of-novels, collages, news items, non-fiction. "A small press publisher of litary booklets and audio cassettes. The editor consider spoetry of all persuasions so long as it is not sexist or racist or extreme right-wing thought. Purple Heather are also considering submissions of audio cassettes from both individual and compilation release. Backstage Promotions are concerned with promoting live poetry performance, via Leeds Alternative Cabaret and also hosting the 1990 Leeds International Poetry Festival which is to be staged over 23 days during June/July. Richard can also help organise tours for visiting poets throughout the U.K. He recently produced an album which made number one in the English Independant charts. Study of booklets and cassettes is advised before submission to avoid any confusions and sample packs can be recieved for $6 *Please note we only accept cash; personal cheques are not accepted and we will not respond to such*" avg. press run 500. Pub'd 12-24 titles 1990; expects 12-24 titles 1991, 12-24 titles 1992. 5 titles listed in the *Small Press Record of Books in Print* (20th Edition, 1991-92). avg. price, paper: $5. 20-80pp; size A5, A4; of. Reporting time: normally within 6 weeks and publication, on acceptance, is normally within 6 months. Payment: contributors copy. Copyrights for author. YFSP (Yorkshire Federation of Small Presses).

Purple Mouth Press (see also **IT GOES ON THE SHELF**), Ned Brooks, 713 Paul Street, Newport News, VA 23605. 1975. Poetry, fiction, art, satire. avg. press run 500. 1 title listed in the *Small Press Record of Books in Print* (20th Edition, 1991-92). avg. price, paper: $10. Discounts: 40% for 5 or more. 50pp; of. Reporting time: 1 week. Payment: yes. Copyrights for author.

PURPLE PATCH, Geoff Stevens, 8 Beaconview House, Charlemont Farm, West Bromwich, West Midlands,

England. 1976. Poetry, fiction, articles, art, reviews, news items. "Mainly poetry. Fiction should be short." circ. varies. 6/yr. Pub'd 6 issues 1990; expects 6 issues 1991, 6 issues 1992. sub. price: £2-50 for 3 (i.e. £5/yr); per copy: 85P; $5 bill or £2 sterling cheque (due to postage/exchange charges etc.); sample: 85p, $5 bill. 14pp; 8¼x11¾; †mi. Reporting time: 1 month. Payment: none. Copyrighted, reverts to author. Pub's reviews: 150 in 1990. §Poetry, short stories, biographies of writers, art. Ads: free on acceptance. none.

Pushcart Press, Bill Henderson, PO Box 380, Wainscott, NY 11975, 516-324-9300. 1973. "Pushcart publishes *The Publish-It-Yourself Handbook: Literary Tradition and How-To*, edited by Bill Henderson, a complete guide on publishing without assistance of vanity or commercial publishers, including essays by Anais Nin, Stewart Brand, Alan Swallow, Leonard Woolf, Richard Kostelanetz, Len Fulton, Gordon Lish (plus 20 others). Complete bibliography and how-to section. Each year we will publish *The Pushcart Prize: Best of the Small Presses*, with the help of our distinguished contributing editors. We also published *The Little Magazine in America: A Modern Documentary History* edited by Elliott Anderson and Mary Kinzie and *The Writers Quotation Book*, edited by James Charlton (300 quotes on the writer's craft). We also sponsor the annual Editors' Book Award for manuscripts overlooked by commercial publishers. (All manuscripts must be nominated by an editor.)" avg. press run varies. Pub'd 6 titles 1990; expects 7 titles 1991, 7 titles 1992. 26 titles listed in the *Small Press Record of Books in Print* (20th Edition, 1991-92). avg. price, cloth: $15; paper: price varies. Discounts: 1-9, 20%; 10+, 40%. 500pp; 5½x8½; of. Reporting time: varies. Payment: 10%. Copyrights for author.

Pussywillow Publishing House, Inc., Teresa Trombetta, PO Box 1806, Gilbert, AZ 85234. "We publish for authors if the book is good." avg. press run 2.5M. Expects 2 titles 1991. 4 titles listed in the *Small Press Record of Books in Print* (20th Edition, 1991-92). avg. price, cloth: $8.95. Discounts: 40% stores; 15-20% reps; distributors 60%. 36pp; 11x8½, 5½x8½. Copyrights for author. AAA Assoc.; Society of Children Book Writers in Calif.

Pygmy Forest Press, Leonard Cirino, PO Box 591, Albion, CA 95410-1036. 1987. Poetry, fiction, non-fiction. "Manuscripts should be between 32-64 pages. One contest yearly as well as open submission year around. Prefer poets such as Roethke, Stevens, Berryman, Carruth, Haines, and many others. Open to all styles well written. Published *Lathe* by Michael Hettich in 1987. Plan 4-6 books 1988, including *Oedipus Drowned* by Sharon Doubiago and *The Source of Precious Life* by Leonard Corino" avg. press run 200-750. Pub'd 1 title 1990; expects 4-6 titles 1991, 4-6 titles 1992. 9 titles listed in the *Small Press Record of Books in Print* (20th Edition, 1991-92). avg. price, cloth: $20; paper: $4-$8. Discounts: 1/3 off to retail and institutional prisoners; libraries full price. 20-80pp; 5½x8½; of. Reporting time: immediate to 1 month. Payment: 10% of run for author. Copyrights for author.

Pyx Press (see also MAGIC REALISM; A THEATER OF BLOOD), C. Darren Butler, Box 620, Orem, UT 84059-0620. 1990. Poetry. "Not currently publishing any unsolicited book-length material."

Q

Q.E.D. Press, Cynthia Frank, 155 Cypress Street, Fort Bragg, CA 95437, 707-964-9520. 1985. Poetry, fiction, non-fiction. "Q.E.D. Press is a small, Mendocino-based publishing house whose vision is to publish fiction and non-fiction that inspires readers to transcend national boundaries through appreciation of world literature. Each year Q.E.D. publishes selected titles (non-fiction) of uncommon interest and quality. Q.E.D. Press is a division of Comp-Type, Inc., a typesetting and graphics shop specializing in book production for self-publishers." avg. press run 3M. Pub'd 1 title 1990; expects 6 titles 1991, 8 titles 1992. 20 titles listed in the *Small Press Record of Books in Print* (20th Edition, 1991-92). avg. price, cloth: $20.95; paper: $12.95. Discounts: 40%. 325pp; 5½x8½; of. Reporting time: 2 months. Payment: varies. Copyrights for author. COSMEP, Marin Self-Publishers Assoc., Bookbuilders West, Mendocino-Ft. Bragg Chamber of Commerce, Northern California Book Publicists Association, Pacific Northwest Booksellers Association, Publishers Marketing Association (PMA).

QED, John Bibby, 1 Straylands Grove, York Y03 0EB, England, 904-424-381. 1982. Non-fiction. "Educational publisher and book supplier, specializing in science and maths" avg. press run 2M. Pub'd 20 titles 1990; expects 20 titles 1991, 20 titles 1992. avg. price, paper: £5. Discounts: 40% over £40. 100pp; size A5; of. Reporting time: 1-3 months. Payment: 20% after breakeven point. Copyright subject to agreement. SPG.

QP Publishing, Nancy Sue Mitchell, Box 18281, Pittsburgh, PA 15236-0281, 412-885-1982. 1990. Non-fiction. "Primary focus is quality/technical non-fiction. Will consider other works in the non-fiction field. Also interested in any business publications" avg. press run 1M. Expects 1 title 1991. 1 title listed in the *Small*

Press Record of Books in Print (20th Edition, 1991-92). avg. price, cloth: $39.95. Discounts: 2-4 books 20%, 5-9 30%, 10-24 40%, 25-49 42%, 50-74 44%, 75-99 46%, 100-199 48%, 200+ 50%. 184pp; 5½x8½. Reporting time: unknown, will try within 30-60 days. Payment: negotiable. Copyrights for author. COSMEP, PMA, TOWERS Club, Ad-Lib.

QRL POETRY SERIES, Quarterly Review of Literature Press, Theodore Weiss, Renee Weiss, Princeton University, 26 Haslet Avenue, Princeton, NJ 08540, 921-6976. 1943. Poetry, long-poems. "Announcing the 45th anniversary special $5,000 Awards winners: Reg Saner, Jeanne McGabey, Jarold Ramsey, Craig Powell. Submission May and October only: a book of miscellaneous poems, a poetic play, a long poem, poetry translations—60 to 100 pages. Manuscripts in English are also invited from outside the U.S.A. Only one manuscript with SASE per reading period. Rejected manuscripts may be revised and re-submitted. To encourage support, a subscription is required with submission. Send SASE for complete manuscript submitting details." circ. 3-5M. 4-5/yr. Pub'd 1 issue 1990; expects 1 issue 1991. sub. price: 2 volumes paper $20, single $10, $20 institutional & hardback per volume; per copy: $20/cl, $10/pa, anniversary double volume $15/pa, $25/cl; sample: $10. Back issues: roughly $20 per volume, cloth; $10 per volume paper; write for catalog for complete list. Discounts: Bookstores 10% on 1 copy, 20% on 3-4, 40% on 5+; agency 10%. 250-350pp; 5½x8½; of, typeset. Reporting time: 6 weeks-2 months. Payment: $1,000 for each accepted manuscript. Copyrighted, does not revert to author. Ads: $200/$125. CCLM, COSMEP.

QSKY Publishing/Independent Publishing, Jim Grubbs, P.O. Box 3042, Springfield, IL 62708, 217-528-0886. 1985. Non-fiction. avg. press run 5M. Pub'd 3 titles 1990; expects 5 titles 1991, 10 titles 1992. 4 titles listed in the Small Press Record of Books in Print (20th Edition, 1991-92). avg. price, paper: $15. Discounts: negotiable. 200pp; 5½x8½; of. Reporting time: 30 days. Payment: negotiable. Copyrights for author.

Quantal Publishing B, Bill Cox, PO Box 1598, Goleta, CA 93116-1598, 805-964-7293. 1979. "I am interested in receiving manuscripts on Gestalt theories and mystical manuals." avg. press run 5M. Pub'd 2 titles 1990; expects 1 title 1991, 1 title 1992. 5 titles listed in the Small Press Record of Books in Print (20th Edition, 1991-92). avg. price, paper: $9.95. Discounts: usual. 200pp; 6x9; of. Reporting time: 1 month. Copyrights for author. COSMEP, Assoc. Jewish Book Publishers, P.M.A.

QUANTUM: Science Fiction & Fantasy Review, D. Douglas Fratz, 8217 Langport Terrace, Gaithersburg, MD 20877, 301-948-2514. 1973. Articles, art, photos, cartoons, interviews, satire, criticism, reviews, letters, non-fiction. "Length: articles 2,000-4,000 words; interviews 3,000-6,000 words; reviews 100-1,000 words. Material must be aimed at a *highly* knowledgable readership of writers, editors, publishers and fans/critics of science fiction and fantasy literature." circ. 1.7M. 3/yr. Pub'd 3 issues 1990; expects 3 issues 1991, 3 issues 1992. sub. price: $7; per copy: $3 ($3.50 foreign); sample: $3 ($3.50 foreign). Back issues: issues #8-38 $3 each. Discounts: 4-9 copies 30%; 10-99 40%; 100+ 55%. 36pp; 8½x11; of. Reporting time: 2-6 weeks. Payment: 1¢-2¢ per word; art $15/pg interior, $25 cover. Copyrighted, reverts to author. Pub's reviews: 60-100 in 1990. §Science fiction, fantasy, horror. Ads: $150/$90/25¢.

QUARRY MAGAZINE, Quarry Press, Bob Hilderley, Publisher; Steven Heighton, General Editor, Box 1061, Kingston, Ontario K7L 4Y5, Canada, 613-548-8429. 1952. Poetry, fiction, photos, interviews, reviews, parts-of-novels. "Publishes best of new Canadian writing and some foreign contributors." circ. 1M. 4/yr. Pub'd 4 issues 1990; expects 4 issues 1991, 4 issues 1992. sub. price: $18 Can., $20 US, $24 Europe/Australia; per copy: $5; sample: $5. Back issues: list available. Discounts: 40% stores. 120pp; 13½x21cm; †of. Reporting time: 12 weeks. Payment: $5 per page plus subscription. Copyrighted, reverts to author. Pub's reviews: 34 in 1990. §Poetry, new fiction, short story anthologies. Ads: $260/$190/none. CPPA.

Quarry Press (see also POETRY CANADA; QUARRY MAGAZINE), Bob Hilderley, Box 1061, Kingston, Ontario K7L 4Y5, Canada. 1965. Poetry, fiction, criticism, long-poems. "Seeking *beginning* Canadian authors." avg. press run 1M. Pub'd 6 titles 1990; expects 8 titles 1991, 10 titles 1992. 70 titles listed in the Small Press Record of Books in Print (20th Edition, 1991-92). avg. price, paper: $10.95; other: A/V packages for schools $25-$35. Discounts: 40% for bookstores. Pages vary; size varies; of. Reporting time: 2-3 months. Payment: 10 copies plus 10% royalty. Copyrights for author. CPPA, Literary Press Group, Association of Canadian Publishers, Canadian Book Information Centre.

QUARRY WEST, Ken Weisner, c/o Porter College, University of Calif, Santa Cruz, CA 95064, 408-429-2155. 1971. Poetry, fiction, art, photos, interviews, reviews, long-poems. "Occasional symposia, new fiction contest; we love fine translation. Recent contributors: Sharon Doubiago, Lucille Clifton, Nate Mackey, Bill Knott, Bruce Weigl, Brenda Hillman, Dennis Schmitz, Paul Violi" circ. 750. 2/yr. Pub'd 2 issues 1990; expects 2 issues 1991, 2 issues 1992. sub. price: $10; per copy: $7; sample: $3.50. Back issues: $3.50. 112pp; 6¾x8¾; of. Reporting time: 10-12 weeks. Payment: copies. Copyrighted, rights revert with permission. Pub's reviews: 2 in 1990. §Good new poetry collections. CCLM, Ingram Distributors (Nashville).

Quarterly Committee of Queen's University (see also QUEEN'S QUARTERLY: A Canadian Review), Boris Castel, Martha J. Bailey, Queen's University, Kingston, Ontario K7L 3N6, Canada. 1893. Poetry, fiction, articles, interviews, satire, criticism, parts-of-novels, plays. "Articles: 20-25 double-spaced pages plus copy on disk in Wordperfect. Recent contributors: Marlene Brant Castellano, Jerry S. Grafstein, Sylvia Ostry, Janice Gross Stein." avg. press run 1.7M. Expects 1 title 1991. avg. price, paper: $5. 224pp; 6×9; of. Reporting time: 2-3 months. Payment: yes. Copyrights for author. CPPA, CELJ.

Quarterly Review of Literature Press (see also QRL POETRY SERIES), Theodore Weiss, Renee Weiss, Princeton University, 26 Haslet Avenue, Princeton, NJ 08540. 1943. Poetry. "Manuscripts should be sent for reading during the months of October and May only. The collection need not be a first book. It should be between 60 and 100 pages if it is a group of poems, a selection of miscellaneous poems, a poetic play, a work of poetry translation, or it can be a single long poem of more than 30 pages. Some of the poems may have had previous magazine publication. Manuscripts in English or translated into English are also invited from outside the U.S.A. Only one manuscript may be submitted per reading period and must include an SASE. $1000 is awarded to each winning manuscript. The editors are grateful for the enthusiasm of all of those who entered into the support of the Series. They continue to require that each manuscript submitted be accompanied by a $20 subscription to the series. Please send SASE to QRL for special details." avg. press run 3M-5M. Pub'd 4-5 titles 1990. 4 titles listed in the *Small Press Record of Books in Print* (20th Edition, 1991-92). avg. price, cloth: $20; paper: $10. 350pp; 5½×8½; lp. Reporting time: 1-3 months. Payment: $1000 for each manuscript printed. Copyright by QRL.

QUARTERLY WEST, Tom Hazuka, Editor; Bernard Wood, Editor; Janet Bianchi, Poetry Editor, 317 Olpin Union, U. of Utah, Salt Lake City, UT 84112, 801-581-3938. 1976. Poetry, fiction, interviews, criticism, reviews, parts-of-novels, long-poems, non-fiction. "We publish fiction, poetry, and reviews, and look for quality writing—anything from experimental to traditional by new or established writers. We solicit our reviews but do read unsolicited ones. Since 1982 we have sponsored a biennial novella competition with cash prizes for the two finalists. We read MSS year-round and accept multiple submissions (make this clear in your cover letter). Contributors: Will Baker, Ron Carlson, Ray Carver, Fern Chertkow, Andre Dubus, Barry Hannah, Chuck Rosenthal, Gordon Weaver, W.D. Wetherall, Ai, Marvin Bell, Stephen Dobyns, Stephen Dunn, Tess Gallagher, Patricia Goedicke, David Ignatow, Larry Levis, Dave Smith" circ. 1M. 2/yr. Pub'd 2 issues 1990; expects 2 issues 1991, 2 issues 1992. sub. price: $8.50; per copy: $4.50; sample: $4.50. Back issues: $4.50. Discounts: agents 25%. 140pp; 6×9; of. Reporting time: 1 week to 2 months. Payment: 2 copies; year's subscription; $25-$50 fiction, $1 per line poetry. Copyrighted, does not revert to author. Pub's reviews: 7 in 1990. §Fiction, poetry, and non-fiction. Ads: $150/$85. CCLM.

QUARTOS MAGAZINE, Suzanne Riley, BCM Writer, 27 Old Gloucester Street, London WC1N 3XX, United Kingdom, 0559-371108. 1987. Poetry, fiction, articles, reviews, letters, news items. "Accepts writing related articles approx. 800-1000 words. Publication not produced by in-house writers and the majority of contributions come from readers. Regular feature on literary agents/publishing in UK." circ. 1M. 6/yr. Pub'd 6 issues 1990; expects 6 issues 1991, 6 issues 1992. sub. price: £18 airmail; per copy: £2. 24pp; size A4; camera-ready. Reporting time: 6-8 weeks. Payment: £5 per article. Copyrighted, reverts to author. Pub's reviews: 6 in 1990. §any publications of interest to writers plus guidelines for freelance writers. Ads: £20/£10/£5 1/4 page/10p per line. Welsh Academy, Small Press Group, Assoc. of Little Presses.

THE QUAYLE QUARTERLY, Deborah Werksman, Jeff Yoder, PO Box 8593, Brewster Station, Bridgeport, CT 06605, 203-333-9399. 1990. Poetry, fiction, articles, photos, cartoons, satire, letters, news items, non-fiction. "'A Watchful Eye on the Vice Presidency.' *The Quayle Quarterly* is a political satire magazine dedicated to the life and times, wit and wisdom of J. Danforth Quayle, 44th Vice President of the United States. Recent contributors include Jefferson Morley, Ralph Nader, Linda Marx and David Shenk" circ. 15M. 4/yr. Pub'd 4 issues 1990; expects 4 issues 1991, 4 issues 1992. sub. price: $14.95; per copy: $3.95; sample: $3.95. Back issues: set of 1990 back issues (4) $14. 20pp; 8½×11; of. Payment: negotiated. Copyrighted, rights reverting depends. Pub's reviews: 3 in 1990. §Politics, satire, political fiction. Ads: $500/$280.

QUEEN OF ALL HEARTS, Gaffney J. Patrick, Editor; Roger M. Charest, Managing Editor, 26 South Saxon Avenue, Bay Shore, NY 11706, 516-665-0726. 1950. Poetry, fiction, articles, art, non-fiction. "*Queen of all Hearts* Magazine promotes knowledge of and devotion to the Mother of God, by explaining the Scriptural basis as well as the traditional teaching of the Church concerning the Mother of Jesus; her place in theology, the apostolate and spiritual life of the Roman Catholic Church; to make known her influence, over the centuries, in the fields of history, literature, art, music, poetry, etc., and to keep our readers informed of the happenings and recent developments in all fields of Marian endeavors around the world. Length of article: 1500 to 2500 words. Authors: Roman Ginn, o.c.s.o., Viola Ward, Joseph Tusiani, etc." circ. 5M. 6/yr. Pub'd 6 issues 1990; expects 6 issues 1991, 6 issues 1992. 1 title listed in the *Small Press Record of Books in Print* (20th Edition, 1991-92). sub. price: $15; per copy: $2; sample: $2.50. Back issues: 50% discount. Discounts: schedules upon request. 48pp; 7¾×10¾; of. Reporting time: less than a month. Payment: yes, most of the time. Not copyrighted. Pub's reviews: 12 in 1990. §Marian topics. We do not accept advertising. CPA-Catholic Press Assn., 119 North Park Ave., Rockville Centre, NY 11570.

QUEEN'S QUARTERLY: A Canadian Review, Quarterly Committee of Queen's University, Boris Castel, Martha J. Bailey, Queen's University, Kingston, Ontario K7L 3N6, Canada, 613-545-2667. 1893. Poetry, fiction, articles, interviews, satire, criticism, parts-of-novels, plays. "Articles: 20-25 double-spaced pages plus copy on disk in Wordperfect. Recent contributors: Marlene Brant Castellano, Jerry S. Grafstein, Sylvia Ostry, Janice Gross Stein." circ. 1.7M. 4/yr. Pub'd 4 issues 1990; expects 4 issues 1991, 4 issues 1992. sub. price: $20 Canada, $22 U.S.; per copy: $6; sample: $6. Back issues: depends on age, min. $4, max. $6. Discounts: none. 224pp; 6×9; of. Reporting time: 3 months. Payment: up to $150 (short stories), $25 per poem, 25 free offprints (articles), copies, subscriptions. Copyrighted, reverts to author. Pub's reviews: 280 in 1990. §Serious books only, history, science, politics, philosophy, social science, literary studies, music, art, etc. Not interested in unsolicited reviews. Ads: $150/$85/no classified. CPPA, CELJ.

QUEST, Human Kinetics Pub. Inc., Shirl J. Hoffman, Box 5076, Champaign, IL 61825-5076, 217-351-5076. 1964. Articles, reviews. "Scholarly journal." circ. 1,320. 3/yr. Pub'd 3 issues 1990; expects 3 issues 1991, 3 issues 1992. sub. price: $21 indiv., $30 instit.; per copy: $7 indiv; $11 instit.; sample: free. Back issues: $7 indiv; $11 instit. Discounts: 5%. 144pp; 6×9; of. Reporting time: 2 months. Payment: none. Copyrighted. Pub's reviews: 0 in 1990. §Sport, sport science, physical education. No ads. National Association of Physical Education in Higher Education.

THE QUEST, Theosophical Publishing House, William Metzger, PO Box 270, Wheaton, IL 60189, 312-668-1571. 1988. Articles, art, photos, interviews, reviews, non-fiction. *"The Quest* is a wholistic metaphysical magazine, with articles on philosophy, comparative religion, science, arts, and psychology" circ. 20M+. 4/yr. Pub'd 4 issues 1990; expects 4 issues 1991, 4 issues 1992. sub. price: $14; per copy: $3.95; sample: $3. Back issues: $4. Discounts: 40% non-returnable; 20% returns accepted. 96pp; 8¼×10¾; web offset. Reporting time: 3 months. Payment: on publication. Copyrighted, rights revert by special request. Pub's reviews. §Wholistic perspective, comparative philosophy, science, religion, and the arts. Ads: $500/$275/$15 first 20 words, 50¢ each add'l word/frequency discounts offered.

Quick Books, Joel Scherzer, Robbie Rubinstein, PO Box 222, Pueblo, CO 81002. 1975. Poetry, fiction, non-fiction. "In 1983 we published *La Nortenita* by Tony Moffeit. Arthur Winfield Knight's *The Mushroom Nightshirt* came out in 1984. Upcoming are Helen Wade Roberts' *Front-Page Dada* and Allen kouler's *Marlem River Baby* and *A Heart in the Anteroom.* Not soliciting manuscripts at this time." avg. press run 100. Pub'd 1 title 1990; expects 3 titles 1991, 3 titles 1992. 4 titles listed in the *Small Press Record of Books in Print* (20th Edition, 1991-92). avg. price, paper: $1.00. Discounts: 40% to bookstores. 16pp; 5½×8½, 4¼×7; of, photocopy. Reporting time: up to 3 months. Payment: varies. Copyrights for author. CCLM.

Quicksilver Productions, Jim Maynard, P.O.Box 340, Ashland, OR 97520, 503-482-5343. 1973. Articles, art, news items, non-fiction. "Not accepting manuscripts at this time" avg. press run 15M. 8 titles listed in the *Small Press Record of Books in Print* (20th Edition, 1991-92). avg. price, paper: $7. Discounts: trade and jobbers, (trade from 40% at 5 copies to 50%) at 1,000 mixed titles. 224pp; of. Payment: 7½ to 9% of retail, paid twice annually. Copyrights for author.

Quiet Tymes, Inc., Roger J. Wannell, Founder, 2121 S. Oneida Street, Ste. 521, Denver, CO 80224, 303-757-5545. 1979. "Founding company: Jaygee Cassettes, 19 Golf Links Road, Burnham-on-Sea, Somerset TA8 2PW, United Kingdom, telephone: (0278) 789352, registed in London under No. 2619113. Exclusive worldwide rights to distribute *The Baby Soother* are licensed to The British Technology Group, a government body specializing in exporting British products, *excluding* Quiet Tymes, Inc. exclusive territory of North America; and Europe which is maintained by Jaygee Cassettes." 2 titles listed in the *Small Press Record of Books in Print* (20th Edition, 1991-92). avg. price, other: $14.95 cassette. 4½×7; audio-cassette duplication. Does not copyright for author.

QuikRef Publishing, Diana Gregory, Editor & Publisher; Claudia O'Keefe, Senior Editor, Art Director, 913 N. Sanborn Avenue, Los Angeles, CA 90029, 213-913-1430; fax 213-913-1066. 1987. Fiction, art, non-fiction. "We are concentrating on two lines: (1) juveniles, fiction on endangered animals and animal rights, and (2) 'handy' reference books, normally considered 'desk reference' books. Please send sufficient postage to return the ms. *No returns will be made without SASE.*" avg. press run 10M. Expects 1 title 1991, 6-8 titles 1992. 1 title listed in the *Small Press Record of Books in Print* (20th Edition, 1991-92). avg. price, cloth: $12-$16.99; paper: $4.99. Discounts: 40% to bookstores, 50% wholesalers, plus STOP order plan. Pages vary; size varies; of. Reporting time: 6 weeks. Payment: all royalty with advances negotiable. Copyrights for author. PMA.

Quill Books, Shirley Mikkelson, Editor, PO Box 728-DB, Minot, ND 58702. 1980. Poetry. "We publish poetry anthologies written by non-professional writers. No fees or obligations are required for publication. We prefer poems of 20-30 lines but will accept longer poems. Any subject acceptable but prefer topics such as family, friends, nature, love, and positive attitudes about life." avg. press run 1.2M-1.5M. Pub'd 5 titles 1990; expects 5 titles 1991, 5 titles 1992. avg. price, paper: $24.95. Discounts: 40% retail trade, 20% library. 148pp; 5½×8; of. Reporting time: 6-8 weeks. Payment: $500 Reader's Choice Award yearly; discount on books to authors.

476

The Quilt Digest Press, Harold Nadel, PO Box 1331, Gualala, CA 95445-1331, 704-884-4100. 1983. Articles, art. "Unsolicited ms. must come from knowledgeable quilt makers and quilt/women's historians. We *are not* interested in ms. from writers who have just discovered quilts." avg. press run 15M-25M. Pub'd 5 titles 1990; expects 10 titles 1991, 6 titles 1992. 21 titles listed in the *Small Press Record of Books in Print* (20th Edition, 1991-92). avg. price, cloth: $29.95; paper: $14.95. Discounts: distributed by Publishers Group West, Emeryville, CA. 120pp; 8¾x11; of. Reporting time: 1 month. Payment: varies, % based on gross receipts. Copyrights for author.

QUIMBY, Quimby Archives, D.B. Velveeta, Tim Gallivan, PO Box 281, Astor Station, Boston, MA 02123, 617-723-5360. 1985. Art, photos, cartoons, satire, letters, collages, concrete art. "*Quimby* magazine's emphasis is on printing visual art and comix" circ. 1M. 1/yr. Pub'd 1 issue 1990; expects 1 issue 1991, 1 issue 1992. sub. price: $10; per copy: $10; sample: $10. Back issues: $3. Discounts: we trade with other small press publications, and provide usual bulk discounts. 60-100pp; 11x15; of. Reporting time: 4-6 weeks. Payment: $20 a page. Copyrighted, reverts to author. Ads: $300/$150.

Quimby Archives (see also QUIMBY), D.B. Velveeta, Tim Gallivan, S. Thomas Suymbersky, PO Box 281, Astor Station, Boston, MA 02123, 617-723-5360. 1985. Art, photos, cartoons, satire, letters, collages, concrete art. "Primarily print comix and visual arts" avg. press run 1M. Pub'd 6-10 titles 1990. avg. price, paper: $1-$3. Discounts: usual bulk schedule. 40-60pp; 8½x11; of. Reporting time: 4-6 weeks. Payment: contributor's copies plus percentage of any profits. Copyrights for author.

Quintessence Publications & Printing Museum, Linomarl Beilke, Irene Beilke, 356 Bunker Hill Mine Road, Amador City, CA 95601, 209-267-5470. 1976. Poetry, articles, art, photos, criticism, plays. "Quintessence Publications is one of the largest and best-equipped exclusively letter-press operations still operating. Our slug-casting service on the Ludlow and Linotype machines is a service many letter-press publishers and printers require to do first-quality work. Over 2,000 type faces available" avg. press run 1M. Expects 2 titles 1991. 9 titles listed in the *Small Press Record of Books in Print* (20th Edition, 1991-92). avg. price, cloth: $25; paper: $12.95; other: $100 (separate edition). Discounts: trade 5+ 40%, others by arrangement. 90pp; 8x6¼; †lp. Reporting time: 2 weeks. Payment: by arrangement. Copyrights for author. APA.

Quixote Press (see also QUIXOTE, QUIXOTL), Morris Edelson, Melissa Bondy, Pat McGilligan, Olga Edelson, Felix Greene, Dick Krooth, 1810 Marshall, Houston, TX 77098. 1896. Poetry, fiction, articles, art, photos, cartoons, interviews, satire, criticism, reviews, music, letters, parts-of-novels, long-poems, collages, plays, concrete art, news items, non-fiction. "Will examine mss-query. No weepy lyrics, no Lyn Lifshin, Warren Woessner" avg. press run 400. Expects 10 titles 1991, 5 titles 1992. 3 titles listed in the *Small Press Record of Books in Print* (20th Edition, 1991-92). avg. price, paper: $3. 80pp; 4½x5; †of, rubberstamp, xerox. Reporting time: 6 months to eternity. Payment: variable. Copyrights for author. CCLM, NRA.

QUIXOTE, QUIXOTL, Quixote Press, The Tianamen Square Hooligans and Two Germanys Support Group, 1810 Marshall, Houston, TX 77098. 1868. Art, photos, cartoons, music, letters. "We are an anti-capitalist publication, promoting and praising people's struggles when we can find them, otherwise showing the misery and crime created by outmoded notions of empire abroad and repression at home. We seek leftist political pro-union, pro-working group writings, whitecollar, pink collar, new collar, attacks on the bourgeoisie and the rotten culchachacha promoted by the National Enchowment for the Arts. Recent contributors include Pablo Neruda, d.a. levy, Karl Marx, Felix Greene, A.D. Winans, John Levin, Pat McGilligan, Donna Langston, Margaret Benbow, and Nicarguan poets. We are not Quixote Center, a radical Catholic Group, but are proud to have spun them off. Special attention to mss. from Poland, Wisconsin, Cleveland and Texas" circ. 500. 4/yr. Pub'd 6 issues 1990; expects 10 issues 1991, 12 issues 1992. sub. price: $20; per copy: $2; sample: 2600 zolty or $2 American. Discounts: .001% to Bowker agents. 80pp; size varies; †of/xerox. Reporting time: 4 months to 40 years. Payment: copies, kewpies, cowpies. Copyrighted, reverts to author. Pub's reviews: 31 in 1990. §Satire, humor, fiction, post-Marxist Leninist Maoist thought, revolution (major or minor). Ads: $3,000/$150/7¢. CCLM, APS, LPS, CIO-AFL, NFL, BBC, PTA, TACL, NRA.

Quixsilver Press (see also MICROCOSM), Robert Randolph Medcalf, Jr., PO Box 847, Hanover, PA 17331-0847. 1981. Poetry, art. "Publishes multi-author anthologies of science fiction poetry, fantasy poetry, horror poetry, and speculative poetry. Publishes *Poet's Showcase* single poet collections." avg. press run 100. Expects 1 title 1992. avg. price, other: $4 chapbook. Discounts: by special arrangement. 24pp; 5½x8½; of. Reporting time: 6 months. Payment: 1 copy for multi-author anthologies, 10 copies & 10% cover price in royalty for one author collections. Copyrights for author. SPWAO, SFPA.

Quotidian Publishers, Judy Knowlton, President, Box D, Delaware Water Gap, PA 18327, (717) 424-5505. 1985. Fiction, articles, art, photos, cartoons, non-fiction. avg. press run 3M. Pub'd 4 titles 1990; expects 4 titles 1991, 4 titles 1992. avg. price, cloth: $14; paper: $8; other: giftbooks $3. Discounts: 40% bookstores, 15% 20 mixed titles. 96pp; 5¼x8½, 4¼x5½; typeset & printed the old-fashioned way. Reporting time: 6 weeks. Payment: 10%. Copyrights for author. COSMEP.

R

R & E Publishers, PO Box 2008, Saratoga, CA 95070, 415-494-1112/408-866-6303. 1967. "Publishes non-fiction books only — submissions in letter with abstract of book and table of contents. With stamped, self-addressed envelope. Free to fly. Chiropractic first aid. Successful parenting, self esteem." avg. press run 1M-10M. Pub'd 50 titles 1990; expects 25 titles 1991, 25 titles 1992. 19 titles listed in the *Small Press Record of Books in Print* (20th Edition, 1991-92). avg. price, cloth: $13; paper: $10. Discounts: trade 40%; wholesaler 55%. 135pp; 6×9; of. Reporting time: 2 months. Payment: royalties paid. Does not copyright for author. Peninsula Publishers/Writers Connection.

R & M Publishing Company, Charlotte Orange, Senior Editor; William Harvey, Editor; Mack B. Morant, PO Box 1276, Holly Hill, SC 29059, 804-732-4094, 804-520-5211. 1978. "We publish all kinds of materials that are quality. However, we are most interested in socio-psychological materials in the form of proses and historical documentations, and educational, (how to materials)." avg. press run 1M-2M. Pub'd 3 titles 1990; expects 4 titles 1991, 3 titles 1992. 7 titles listed in the *Small Press Record of Books in Print* (20th Edition, 1991-92). avg. price, paper: $6.95; other: $7.95. Discounts: 20-55%. 95pp; 5¼×8¼; lp. Reporting time: 6-12 weeks or less. Payment: negotiable. Copyrights for author. COSMEP, Multicultural Publishers Exchange.

R & R Publishing, Dennis Stricker, PO Box 308, Hermosa Beach, CA 90254, 213-374-5894. 1979. Non-fiction. "Additional address: 16919-B Hawthorne Blvd., Lawndale, CA 90260. Newest title: *Locks & Lockpicking: A Basic Guide For: Law Enforcement, Security, Military*. This is a small reference manual for law enforcement, security, and other legal related professionals. It explains how-to open locks, without the keys, by the technique of lockpicking" avg. press run 2M. Pub'd 4 titles 1990; expects 3 titles 1991, 6 titles 1992. 2 titles listed in the *Small Press Record of Books in Print* (20th Edition, 1991-92). avg. price, paper: $10. 50pp; 5½×8½; mi, of. Reporting time: 4 weeks. Payment: not set, is different each time and negotiable. Copyrights for author.

R.G.E. Publishing (see also BLACKJACK FORUM), Arnold Snyder, Alison Finlay, 414 Santa Clara, Oakland, CA 94610. 1980. "Relating to Casino Blackjack: Strategies, math/computer analyses, etc" avg. press run 2.5M. Pub'd 1 title 1990; expects 1 title 1991, 1 title 1992. 4 titles listed in the *Small Press Record of Books in Print* (20th Edition, 1991-92). avg. price, paper: $12.95. Discounts: 40% off for 6 or more copies. 84-124pp; 8½×11; of. Reporting time: 2-6 weeks. Payment: royalty only. Copyrights for author. COSMEP.

"R"-Kids Publishing Co., Janet Jennerjohn, PO Box 05796, Milwaukee, WI 53205, 414-453-4852. 1989. "We publish full color illustrated children's books. As of yet we have no contributors" avg. press run 3M-10M. Expects 4 titles 1991, 4 titles 1992. avg. price, paper: $2.95. 26-28pp; 7¼×11¼. Reporting time: 6 weeks. Payment: contract agreement. Copyrights for author.

Rabeth Publishing Company, Raymond Quigley, Elizabeth Quigley, Box 171, Kirksville, MO 63501, 816-665-8209. 1990. Fiction. avg. press run 400-2M. Expects 3 titles 1991, 3-4 titles 1992. 2 titles listed in the *Small Press Record of Books in Print* (20th Edition, 1991-92). avg. price, cloth: $16.50; paper: $9.95. Discounts: jobber. 200pp; 5½×8; 3 weeks. Payment: negotiable. Copyrights for author.

RACCOON, Ion Books, David Spicer, Senior Editor, PO Box 111327, Memphis, TN 38111-1327, 901-323-8858. 1986. Poetry, criticism. "Dark image, surreal, affirmative, woodsy; 15-35 lines. Poetry that expresses a need to be written; no brilliantly clever tidbits. First issue; Bruchac, Rollings, Cooley, Wild, others" circ. 500. 3 or 4. Pub'd 2 issues 1990; expects 3 issues 1991, 3 issues 1992. sub. price: $15; per copy: $5; sample: $5. Back issues: $5, #1 & #3 & #6 temporarily out-of-print. Discounts: distributed nationally to the trade, by Ebsco, Inc., and Faxon, Inc. under their respective schedules. 48pp; 6×9; of. Reporting time: 3-6 months. Payment: copies. Copyrighted, reverts to author. Pub's reviews. §Poetry. No ads.

RACE ACROSS AMERICA PROGRAM, Info Net Publishing, Herb Wetenkamp, JoAnn Byrne, PO Box 3789, San Clemente, CA 92674, 714-489-9267. 1986. Articles, art, photos, interviews, reviews, news items, non-fiction. "24-32 pages of facts, figures and bicycle rider profiles of competitors in the annual 3,000-plus-miles Race Across America (RAAM). Route maps and descriptions, training techniques, history and other vital info." circ. 10M-20M. 1/yr. Pub'd 1 issue 1990; expects 1 issue 1991, 3 issues 1992. price per copy: $1; sample: $1. Back issues: $3. Discounts: 50%. 28pp; 8½×11; of. Reporting time: 1-2 months. Payment: please inquire. Copyrighted, does not revert to author. Pub's reviews: 1 in 1990. §Bicycling, particularly relating to long-distance cycling. Ads: $995/$575.

RACKHAM JOURNAL OF THE ARTS AND HUMANITIES (RaJAH), Elizabeth Young, Editor; Patricia Armstrong, Dan Goldberg, Juliette Grievell, Catharine Krieps, Thomas Mussio, Peter Olson, 411 Mason Hall, University of Michigan, Ann Arbor, MI 48109, 313-763-2351. 1972. Poetry, fiction, articles, art, photos, cartoons, satire, criticism, letters, parts-of-novels, long-poems, plays, non-fiction. "Our primary (though not exclusive) purpose is to publish the work of graduate students at the University of Michigan" circ. 400-500. 1/yr. Pub'd 1 issue 1990; expects 1 issue 1991, 1 issue 1992. sub. price: $3 individuals, $5 institutions + 50¢ S & H; per copy: $3.50; sample: $1.50. Back issues: $1.50 each. 130pp; 6×9; of. Reporting time: 4-6 months. Payment: 3 copies of issue. Copyrighted, does not revert to author. Ads: $50/$25.

RACONTEUR: A Journal of World History, RACONTEUR Publications, Karl J. Schmidt, 2020 W. Pensacola St., Unit 46, Suite 515, Tallahassee, FL 32304, 904-222-5029. 1990. Articles, photos, cartoons, interviews, criticism, reviews, news items, non-fiction. "Articles and essays: Must not exceed 6,000 words, exclusive of footnotes. Photoessays, audioessays: Photoessays must include B&W photography, audioessays a transcribed copy of audio track as well as a high-quality audio casette. Interviews; Should focus on notable historian, a history-maker, or other such personality within the field. Reviews of recent books, journals, films, videos, and software: Must not exceed 1,000 words. Should include discussion of both the scope of the work and the quality of the research (books & journals), presentation (film & video), significance (all)." circ. 200. Expects 200 issues 1991, 200+ issues 1992. sub. price: $10; per copy: $5; sample: $5. Discounts: varies. 90pp; 5½×8½. Reporting time: 2-3 months. Payment: Copies, articles, essays, interview: 2 copies. Reviews: 1 copy. Copyrighted, reverts to author. Pub's reviews: 3 in 1990. §All areas of history, especially focusing on the history of the Third World. COSMEP.

RACONTEUR Publications (see also RACONTEUR: A Journal of World History), Karl J. Schmidt, 2020 W. Pensacola St., Unit 46, Suite 515, Tallahassee, FL 32304, 904-222-5029. 1990. Articles, photos, cartoons, interviews, criticism, reviews, news items, non-fiction. "We have not yet received any manuscripts for publication due to the recent date of our establishment as a press. We would like to publish non-fiction, specifically historical works dealing with the Third World, women, and minorities." Expects 1-2 titles 1991, 2-3 titles 1992. avg. price, paper: $5. 5½×8½. Reporting time: 3-4 months. Payment: varies. Copyrights for author. COSMEP.

Racz Publishing Co., Jeanette G. Racz, Business Manager, PO Box 287, Oxnard, CA 93032, 805-642-1186. 1973. avg. press run 3M. Pub'd 2 titles 1990; expects 2 titles 1991, 5 titles 1992. 5 titles listed in the *Small Press Record of Books in Print* (20th Edition, 1991-92). avg. price, cloth: $10; paper: $7. Discounts: trade: cl-1 copy 30%, 2 copies 35%, 10 copies 40%, 100 copies 45%; pa-1 copy 30%, 10 copies 35%, 50 copies 40%, 100 copies 42%, 500 copies 45%, 1000 copies 48%, 5000 copies 50%. Text: 1 copy 20%, 2 copies 30%, 11 copies 35%, 20 copies 40%. 200pp; 6×9; of. Payment: annually. Copyrights for author.

RADIANCE, The Magazine For Large Women, Alice Ansfield, PO Box 31703, Oakland, CA 94604, (415) 482-0680. 1984. Poetry, fiction, articles, art, photos, cartoons, interviews, satire, reviews, letters, parts-of-novels, long-poems, collages, concrete art, news items, non-fiction. "We want all kinds of articles related to the empowerment of larger women; articles sensitively done, with warmth, an intimate tone, and good, strong profiles of large women in all areas of life, across the country. We do not take diet articles or articles on weight loss programs. We encourage women to live fully now, not waiting until they lose 10, 15, 100 pounds. Articles on health, cultural awareness, spirituality, fashion, interviews, general well-being." circ. 20M. 4/yr. Pub'd 4 issues 1990; expects 4 issues 1991, 4 issues 1992. sub. price: $15; per copy: $4; sample: $3.50. 60+pp; 8½×11; of. Reporting time: 1-2 months. Payment: $50-$75 per article. Copyrighted, reverts to author. Pub's reviews: 35 in 1990. §Women, health, growth/self-care, women's tools (financial info., home, family), fashion, self esteem, media, politics. Ads: $975 b/w/$546 b/w/color $2200.

RADICAL AMERICA, John P. Demeter, Cynthia Peters, 1 Summer Street, Somerville, MA 02143, 617-628-6585. 1967. Articles. circ. 5M. 4/yr. Pub'd 4 issues 1990; expects 4 issues 1991, 4 issues 1992. sub. price: $20; per copy: $4.95; sample: $2.50. Back issues: apply. Discounts: 40%. 84pp; 7×10; of. Reporting time: 6 weeks. Payment: none. Copyrighted, reverts to author. Pub's reviews: 10 in 1990. §Politics, history, film, sociology, feminism. Ads: $225/$130.

‡**RADICAL SCIENCE SERIES, Free Association Books (FAB),** RSJ Collective, 26 Freegrove Road, London N7 9RQ, United Kingdom, 01-609-5646. 1974. Articles, photos, cartoons, interviews, criticism, reviews, letters, non-fiction. "Discusses ideology and practice of science, technology, and medicine from a radical political perspective. (ISSN 0305-0963)" circ. 2.5M. 3/yr. Pub'd 2 issues 1990; expects 3 issues 1991, 3 issues 1992. sub. price: 3 issues £14/$22 individuals, £18/$28 institutions; per copy: £5 ($7) individuals; £6 ($9) institutions; sample: same. Back issues: £5.00-institutions; £2.00/$5.00-individuals. Discounts: 1/3 to bookshops. 160pp; size A5; of. Reporting time: 3 months. Payment: none. Not copyrighted. Pub's reviews: 10 in 1990. §Social analysis of science, technology and medicine. Ads taken on exchange basis only.

RADIUS/Resources for Local Arts, Rural Arts Services, Ken Larsen, c/o CCA, 1212 P Street, Sacramento,

CA 95814, 916-447-7811. 1985. Articles, photos, interviews, reviews, news items, non-fiction. *"Radius* is published to assist the citizens of California to develop cultural programs that are financially sound, organizationally effective, and community relevant. *Radius* is for anyone who sees the arts as an essential ingredient in creating a climate in which California communities can thrive. Readers include administrators, board members, artists, volunteers, and others working in a wide variety of settings such as local arts agencies; colleges, universities, elementary and secondary schools; visual, literary, performing arts, and multi-discipline organizations; health and correctional facilities; federal, state, county, and municipal government. Authors: write for guidelines" circ. 6M. 6/yr. Pub'd 4 issues 1990; expects 6 issues 1991, 6 issues 1992. sub. price: $25; per copy: $7.50; sample: same. Discounts: inquire. 16pp; 8½×11; of. Reporting time: 3 months. Payment: none. Copyrighted, reverts to author. Pub's reviews: 6 in 1990. §Community arts. Ads: classifieds 25¢/word.

RAFALE, Richard Belair, 126 College Avenue, Orono, ME 04469, (207) 581-3764. 1977. Poetry, fiction, articles, art, photos, cartoons, interviews, satire, criticism, reviews, music, letters, parts-of-novels, long-poems, collages, plays, concrete art, news items, non-fiction. *"Rafale* is a bilingual supplement with a Franco-American and Francophone readership, and it seeks to encourage their artistic expression. We return submissions that don't meet that focus." circ. 4.5M. 4/yr. Pub'd 4 issues 1990; expects 4 issues 1991, 4 issues 1992. sub. price: $10; sample: $1. Back issues: $1.50. 4pp; 10¼×15; of. Reporting time: immediate. Payment: $10 plus 5 copies. Copyrighted, reverts to author. Pub's reviews. Ads: $200/$100/$50 1/4 page/$25 1/8. Franco-American Resource Opportunity Group (FAROG).

RAG MAG, Black Hat Press, Beverly Voldseth, Box 12, Goodhue, MN 55027, 612-923-4590. 1982. Poetry, fiction, articles, art, photos, cartoons, interviews, satire, criticism, reviews, letters, long-poems, plays, non-fiction. "Our only bias is quality. We are looking for poetry, satire, fiction, plays, articles, book reviews, and art & photos from any point of view and in any style. Poetry should be under 50 lines. Fiction under 3M words. Reviews, satire, articles, and fiction under 1M words. Our first issue featured work by Alvin Greenberg, Karla Hammond, Philip Dacey and many known and totally unknown writers and poets. We publish reviews of books only." circ. 200. 2/yr. Pub'd 2 issues 1990; expects 2 issues 1991, 2 issues 1992. sub. price: $10; per copy: $6; sample: $6. Back issues: $6 when available. Discounts: 40% to stores. 80pp; 6×9; of. Reporting time: 1 week to 2 months. Payment: in copies. Copyrighted, reverts to author. Pub's reviews: 2 in 1990. §Poetry, short stories, novels, plays. Ads: $30/$15. CCLM, COSMEP.

Ragweed Press, Inc., Libby Oughton, Laurie Brinklow, Lynn Henry, Catherine Matthews, Box 2023, Charlottetown, Prince Edward Island C1A 7N7, Canada, 902-566-5750. 1974. Poetry, fiction. "Primarily interested in women's fiction & poetry, and books by women for children" avg. press run 500-1.5M. Pub'd 10 titles 1990; expects 10 titles 1991, 12 titles 1992. 44 titles listed in the *Small Press Record of Books in Print* (20th Edition, 1991-92). avg. price, paper: $9.95. Discounts: 5+ copies (mixed): 40% bookstores, 20% institutions, 43% jobbers. 32-200pp; 5½×8½; of. Reporting time: 6 months. Payment: usually 10% retail price for first printing. Copyrights for author. Atlantic Publishers Association (Dalhousie University, Halifax, N.S.), Association of Canadian Publishers & Literary Press Group (260 King Street East, Toronto, Ontario).

Rainfeather Press, Steven B. Rogers, Editor, 3201 Taylor Street, Mt. Rainier, MD 20712. 1978. *"Temporarily suspended operations*. We are not currently seeking submission of manuscripts or letters of query. Unsolicited manuscripts will be returned unread." avg. press run varies with the type of publication. avg. price, paper: price varies. No discounts. Pages vary depending on title; 4¼×5½, 8½×14; of, xerox. Reporting time: 1-2 months for queries, longer for manuscripts once solicited. Payment: copies. Does not copyright for author. none.

Rainforest Publishing, Duncan Frazier, PO Box 101251, Anchorage, AK 99510, 907-373-7277. 1982. Fiction, art, photos, non-fiction. avg. press run 3M. Pub'd 1 title 1990; expects 2 titles 1991, 2 titles 1992. avg. price, cloth: $20; paper: $10. Discounts: 40% trade, 50% jobber. 200pp; 6×9; of. Reporting time: 90 days. Payment: negotiated. Copyrights for author. Alaska Assoc. Small Presses (AASP), Pacific NW Booksellers Assn. (PNBA), COSMEP.

Rainier Books, Eva Westerlind, PO Box 2713, Kirkland, WA 98083-2713, 206-821-5676. 1989. Non-fiction. avg. press run 5M. Expects 1 title 1991, 2 titles 1992. 1 title listed in the *Small Press Record of Books in Print* (20th Edition, 1991-92). avg. price, paper: $14.95. 150pp; 1p. Reporting time: 2 months. Payment: negotiable. Does not copyright for author. Northwest Association of Book Publishers (NWABP), Book Publishers Northwest (BPN), COSMEP, Women's National Book Association.

Rainy Day Press, Mike Helm, 1147 East 26th, Eugene, OR 97403, 503-484-4626. 1978. "History and culture of the Pacific Northwest is the prime concern of Rainy Day Press. The Oregon Country Library is indicative of our emphasis. The first four volumes were written by Fred Lockley in the 1920's. They are conversations with Oregon Country pioneers, previously published in the *Oregon Journal*, an oral history of life on the Oregon Trail and in the civilization building at its western end. The fifth, by Mike Helm, is a collection of ghost stories and other local legends taken from towns throughout Oregon. The sixth, in the framework of a contemporary journal, tells of a search for the mythical and historical soul of Oregon. Though I refer to Rainy Day Press as

480

'we', it is still a one horse show, and I am the horse. As I have a million ideas of my own for writing and publishing projects, I am not yet seeking manuscript submissions. Instead, send money.'' avg. press run 4M. Expects 1 title 1991, 1 title 1992. 6 titles listed in the *Small Press Record of Books in Print* (20th Edition, 1991-92). avg. price, paper: $10.15. Discounts: 1 book 0%; 2-5, 10%; 6-24, 40%; 25-49, 42%; 50-74, 44%; 75-99, 46%; 100-149, 48%; 150 or more, 50%. 300+pp; 5½×8½; of.

Rakhamim Publications, Dov Ben-Khayyim, PO Box 7, Berkeley, CA 94701. 1983. Fiction, non-fiction. "We are aiming to bring women into full equality among the Jewish people, through any efforts that will accomplish the goal. An example is our non-sexist passover Hagadah that has brought women into equality linguistically, historically, and spiritually.'' avg. press run 10M. Pub'd 1 title 1990; expects 1 title 1991, 1 title 1992. 1 title listed in the *Small Press Record of Books in Print* (20th Edition, 1991-92). avg. price, paper: $5. Discounts: 50¢ off book for order of 8 or more, via mail to publisher; other discounts available to bookstores via distributors Bookpeople and Inland Books. 50-80pp; 5½×8½. Reporting time: 3 months. Copyrights for author. COSMEP.

Rama Publishing Co., Richard Aschwanden, Charles Aschwanden, PO Box 793, Carthage, MO 64836-0793, 417-358-1093. 1983. Fiction, articles, non-fiction. "In 30 years of married life Richard and Maria Aschwanden of Carthage, MO, have reared 10 healthy children and never have had a doctor's or dentist's bill because of illness. They attribute this to a philosophy of healthy living which includes preventative family nutrition. Rama Publishing Co. is interested in editing and publishing booklets and books dealing with regeneration of mankind in the physical, mental, and spiritual aspects.'' avg. press run 500-2M. Expects 3 titles 1991, 5 titles 1992. 9 titles listed in the *Small Press Record of Books in Print* (20th Edition, 1991-92). avg. price, paper: $5. Discounts: 5-25, 25%; 26-50, 40%; 51+, 50%. 150pp; 5½×8¼; of. Reporting time: 5 weeks. Payment: 10-15% on net receipts; no advance. Copyrights for author.

Ramalo Publications, 2107 N. Spokane Street, Post Falls, ID 83854. 1988. Poetry, fiction, articles, art. "Family oriented - no weird sex or unnecessary violence" Expects 3 titles 1991, 3 titles 1992. 3 titles listed in the *Small Press Record of Books in Print* (20th Edition, 1991-92). MacIntosh, laserprint. Reporting time: 2-6 months. Payment: negotiable. Copyrights for author. COSMEP.

RAMBUNCTIOUS REVIEW, Mary Dellutri, Co-Editor; Richard Goldman, Co-Editor; Nancy Lennon, Co-Editor; Elizabeth Hausler, Co-Editor, Rambunctious Press, Inc., 1221 West Pratt Blvd., Chicago, IL 60626. 1984. Poetry, fiction, art, photos, satire, long-poems, plays. "*Rambunctious Review* accepts submissions from September through May. Length of material: poems 100 lines, fiction 12 pages. No biases. Recent contributors: Pamela Miller, Achy Obejas, Richard Calisch, Sean Lawrence.'' circ. 600. 1/yr. Pub'd 1 issue 1990; expects 1 issue 1991, 1 issue 1992. sub. price: $10/3 issues; per copy: $3.50; sample: $4. Back issues: $3. Discounts: please inquire. 48pp; 7×10; of. Reporting time: 6-9 months. Payment: 2 free copies of the magazine. Copyrighted, reverts to author. CCLM.

Ramp Creek Publishing Inc, PO Box 3, Smithville, IN 47458, 812-334-1852. 1989. Non-fiction. "Metaphysical books primarily. Only 2 books by Gail Fairfield so far.'' avg. press run 5M. Expects 2 titles 1991, 1 title 1992. avg. price, paper: $8.95-$15.95. Discounts: 40% bookstore; 50-60% distributors. 160-370pp; 6×9; of. Reporting time: 1 month.

RAMPIKE, Karl E. Jirgens, Editor; Jim Francis, Assistant Editor, 95 Rivercrest Road, Toronto, Ontario M6S 4H7, Canada, 416-767-6713. 1979. "*Rampike* is a thematic journal feature articles by and on contemporary authors and artists. Average article length about 5M words. Favour fiction that displays post-modern tendencies. Documentation of installations, performance pieces, etc. is also welcome, as are interviews. Contact editors for information on future themes. Recent issues have featured; Vito Acconci, Lauri Anderson, Joseph Beuys, William Burroughs, Chris Burden, Dennis Oppenheim, Kathy Acker, b.p. Nichol, Frank Davey, and others'' circ. 2M. 2/yr. Pub'd 2 issues 1990; expects 2 issues 1991, 2 issues 1992. sub. price: $15; per copy: $6; sample: $6. Back issues: ask for schedule. Discounts: stores 40%; distributors 40%; bulk orders up to 50%; sometimes negotiable. 80pp; 6×15 vertical; of. Reporting time: a month or two. Payment: limited, contact editors. Copyrighted, rights remain with author. Pub's reviews: 10 in 1990. §Contemporary criticism and/or fiction. Ads: $300/$175. C.P.P.A.

Rand Editions/Tofua Press, Marvin L. Rand, President, Po Box 2610, Leucadia, CA 92024, 619-753-2500. 1973. Photos, letters, non-fiction. "We publish books on the South Pacific, cookbooks, real estate law, California history, and general travel.'' avg. press run 3M-10M. Pub'd 1 title 1990; expects 2 titles 1991, 2 titles 1992. 13 titles listed in the *Small Press Record of Books in Print* (20th Edition, 1991-92). avg. price, cloth: $19.95; paper: $5.95; other: $5.95 (plastic comb-bound). Discounts: trade. 120-450pp; 5½×8½; of. Reporting time: 1 month. Payment: 10% retail to 15M copies, 12% over 15M; paid 3 times a year. Copyrights for author. ABA, BPSC, SD Book Publishers.

Ranger International Productions, Martin J. Rosenblum, Editor, Lion Publishing/Roar Recording, PO Box 71231, Milwaukee, WI 53211-7331, 414-332-7474. 1970. Poetry, long-poems. "We only publish sporadically and want no submissions. We publish new music and experimental poetry only.'' avg. press run 200. Pub'd 2 titles 1990. 12 titles listed in the *Small Press Record of Books in Print* (20th Edition, 1991-92). avg. price, paper: $7. Discounts: none. 100pp; size varies considerably; of. Payment: varies, usually copies. Copyrights for author.

Rarach Press, Ladislav R. Hanka, 1005 Oakland Drive, Kalamazoo, MI 49008, 616-388-5631. 1981. Poetry, art, long-poems. "This is essentially a vehicle for my art and rather personal and idiosyncratic notions of what I wish to print: i.e. occasional small books, poems set into an etching, wood engravings, handbills, posters for exhibitions, and one substantial book of 100 pp. containing 5 long poems in Czech. This is labor-intensive hand-done bibliophilia. My bread and butter is printing my own artwork often as suites of etchings or wood engravings sometimes with a bit of type-set commentary, titles or description. The bibliophilia is an amusement appearing irregularly. I am essentially uninterested in unsolicited manuscripts, unless someone wants me to illustrate something I like." avg. press run 20-30. Pub'd 1 title 1990; expects 1 title 1991, 1 title 1992. 6 titles listed in the *Small Press Record of Books in Print* (20th Edition, 1991-92). avg. price, cloth: $50; other: $200 and up handbound. Discounts: 10% off for dealers. 10-100pp; size highly variable; †lp, itaglio, wood engraving. Payment: done individually, generally in copies of print. Does not copyright for author.

RARITAN: A Quarterly Review, Richard Poirier, Editor-in-Chief; Thomas R. Edwards, Exec. Editor; Suzanne K. Hyman, Managing Editor, 31 Mine Street, New Brunswick, NJ 08903, 201-932-7852. 1981. Poetry, fiction, articles, interviews, criticism, reviews, non-fiction. "*Raritan* is a cultural quarterly concerned with politics, literature, the arts, and social sciences. In particular, we are interested in the workings of cultural power, in how certain political, social, and artistic movements have won popular attention and become a part of our artistic heritage. In addition to essays, *Raritan* prints a *small* quantity of poetry and fiction. Contributors include Denis Donoghue, James Merrill, Vicki Hearne, Edward Said, Frank Kermode, Eve Kosofsky Sedgwick, John Hollander, and Harold Bloom." circ. 5M. 4/yr. Pub'd 4 issues 1990; expects 4 issues 1991. sub. price: $16 individuals, $20 institutions; per copy: $5; sample: $5 where applicable. Back issues: $6 per copy. Discounts: available for bookstores, distributors, and subscription agencies. 160pp; 6×9; of. Reporting time: 6 weeks. Payment: $100. Copyrighted. Pub's reviews: 7 in 1990. §Literary criticism, philosophy, pol. sci., arts, linguistics, sociology. Ads: $275/$180. CCLM.

THE RAT RACE RECORD, Conny Jasper, PO Box 1611, Union, NJ 07083. 1988. Poetry, articles, art, cartoons, interviews, criticism, reviews, music, letters, news items, non-fiction. circ. 250. 4/yr. Pub'd 4 issues 1990; expects 4 issues 1991, 4 issues 1992. sub. price: $4; per copy: $1; sample: $1. 18pp; 8½×11; photocopy. Payment: free issues. Not copyrighted. Pub's reviews: 2 in 1990. §Psychology, spirituality, environmentalism, food and nutrition, holistic health care. Ads: $80/$50/$30 1/4 page.

The Rateavers, Bargyla Rateaver, Gylver Rateaver, 9049 Covina Street, San Diego, CA 92126, 619-566-8994. 1973. Non-fiction. "Organic gardening and farming, conservation methods, reprints or abstracts, mostly." avg. press run 2.5M-3M. Expects 1 title 1991. 7 titles listed in the *Small Press Record of Books in Print* (20th Edition, 1991-92). avg. price, paper: $20. Discounts: none. 300pp; 5½×8½, 9×6; lithography. Payment: 10% to author. Copyrights for author.

THE RATIONAL FEMINIST, Molly Gill, Editor-Publisher, Box 28253, Kenneth City Station, St. Petersburg, FL 33709. 1984. "We seek guest editorials, letters to editor; media reviews (print & audio); feminist continuum and dissent; political, such as anarchist, Maoist, etc. factions; design and cartoons, black and white, 1x3"; all volunteer at this time; books to review. Journals and magazines of the feminist continuum to review plus the counter-culture. All relating to feminist cause. About 400 words, double-spaced, typed, no computer sht. Letters, 200 words, same. Reviews, 400 words tops. Essays same. Top quality poetry: 30-60 lines tops. Please add white loyalties." circ. 100. 6/yr. Pub'd 6 issues 1990; expects 6 issues 1991, 6 issues 1992. sub. price: $20; per copy: $3; sample: $3. Back issues: $5. Discounts: can discuss. 15pp; 8½×14; †duplicating machine. Reporting time: 3-4 weeks leeway, but often 1 week. Payment: none at this time, mostly staff written. Copyrighted, reverts to author. Pub's reviews: 6 in 1990. §Feminists, censorship, film comedies, humor, quality TV reviews, re conservative women, women's sex lives, families-children-youth, older women. $25 business card.

RAVEN ANARCHIST QUARTERLY, Freedom Press, In Angel Alley, 84B Whitechapel High Street, London E1 7QX, England. circ. 1.2M. 4/yr. Pub'd 4 issues 1990; expects 4 issues 1991, 4 issues 1992. sub. price: £11 inland, £12 surface mail; per copy: £2.50. Discounts: 33⅓% singles, 35% on 2 or more. 96pp; size A5; †of. Reporting time: normally by return. Payment: none. Copyrighted, reverts to author. Pub's reviews: very few in 1990. §Anarchism. No ads.

Raven Rocks Press, Warren Stetzel, 54118 Crum Road, Beallsville, OH 43716, 614-926-1705. 1972. Non-fiction. "Raven Rocks Press has published Warren Stetzel's book, *School for the Young* (explores some of our assumptions about our human nature and the nature of our world), and reprinted *Hollingsworth's Vision*, a first-person account by a 19th century Quaker. We expect to publish materials which touch on a variety of fields: education, economics and social organization, environmental issues, solar and underground construction.

Those involved in Raven Rocks Press are members of Raven Rocks, Inc., an organization which is engaged in these and other fields, and much of what we publish will be out of our own experience. We will hope, too, to publish relevant material from elsewhere. No exact price is set for *School for the Young*. Rather, contributions are accepted from those able to make them. With this policy, it has been possible for some to secure the book at little or no cost. Others have been able to contribute enough to make up the difference." avg. press run 1.5M. Expects 1 title 1992. 2 titles listed in the *Small Press Record of Books in Print* (20th Edition, 1991-92). avg. price, cloth: $14. Discounts: schools & libraries 10%, bookstores & jobbers 40%. 269pp; 6×9; †of. Copyrights for author.

Raw Dog Press, R. Gerry Fabian, 128 Harvey Avenue, Doylestown, PA 18901, 215-345-6838. 1977. Poetry, photos, long-poems, collages. "We are now doing only our Post Poem Series. We will try to publish in summer. Submit any time. The type of poetry that we are looking for is short (2-10) lines. We want 'people-oriented' work. We'll send samples for $1.00. You MUST enclose a short note and a SASE. Neatness and professionalism really count with us. We might also do chapbooks but the author had better be willing to take an active part both creatively and financially." avg. press run 300-500. Pub'd 1 title 1990; expects 2 titles 1991, 2 titles 1992. 17 titles listed in the *Small Press Record of Books in Print* (20th Edition, 1991-92). avg. price, paper: $3; other: $3. Discounts: will negotiate and haggle with anyone; will exchange. 10-12pp; 4×6; †of. Reporting time: 1 month. Payment: varies with the material but we will work something out (copies +). Copyright is agreed upon.

THE RAYSTOWN REVIEW, Mike Herncane, RD1, Box 205, Schellsburg, PA 15559. 1990. Poetry, fiction, photos, interviews, criticism, reviews. "Poetry up to 60 lines, short fiction up to 3,500 words. Send manuscripts with brief cover letter and SASE" circ. 500. 1/yr. Pub'd 1 issue 1990; expects 1 issue 1991, 1 issue 1992. price per copy: $3; sample: $3. 60+pp; 8×11; of. Reporting time: 1-2 months. Payment: sample copies. Copyrighted, reverts to author.

RE Publications, Cameron C. Nickels, Sue A. Nickels, 246 Campbell Street, Harrisonburg, VA 22801, 703-433-0382. 1984. Non-fiction. "Publish THE HOME INDEX, an annual index to do-it-yourself information in periodicals. Also interested in publishing other do-it-yourself titles. Perhaps Americana/American literature scholarehip as well" avg. press run 1M. Pub'd 1 title 1990; expects 1 title 1991, 2 titles 1992. 3 titles listed in the *Small Press Record of Books in Print* (20th Edition, 1991-92). avg. price, paper: $35. Discounts: to jobbers, 20%. 120pp; 7×9; †lp. Reporting time: 30 days. Payment: tba. COSMEP, Box 703, San Francisco, CA 94101.

REACHING OUT, Wellberry Press, Donald Caswell, 2022 East Forest Drive, Tallahassee, FL 32303, 904-386-5508. 1989. Poetry, articles, interviews, news items, non-fiction. "We are only interested in material dealing with child abuse and neglect, child abuse prevention techniques, stress control, lay counselling, motivating and training volunteers, and child development. Under 500 words" circ. 150. 4/yr. Pub'd 4 issues 1990; expects 4 issues 1991, 4 issues 1992. sub. price: $10; per copy: $3; sample: $1. Back issues: for postage if any on hand. Discounts: free to Family Enrichment volunteers and contributors and to child abuse prevention groups. 4pp; 8½×11; photocopy. Reporting time: 1-3 months. Payment: copies only. Not copyrighted. Pub's reviews. §Child abuse prevention, stress management, child welfare issues. Ads: $25/$15.

READ, AMERICA!, The Place In The Woods, Roger A. Hammer, Editor & Publisher, 3900 Glenwood Avenue, Golden Valley, MN 55422, 612-374-2120. 1983. Reviews. "A quarterly newsletter to Libraries Reading Is Fundamental, Head Start, and migrant education programs. ISSN-0891-4214. Looking for professional children's librarians to do regular reviews." circ. 5.5M. 4/yr. Pub'd 4 issues 1990; expects 4 issues 1991, 4 issues 1992. sub. price: $25; per copy: $7.50; sample: free. Back issues: $5. Discounts: 15% to qualified book suppliers & librarians. 8pp; 8½×11; †of. Reporting time: 1 week. Payment: $10 per review or article. Copyrighted, does not revert to author. Pub's reviews: 8 in 1990. §Children's books, P/K - 12. Ads: use flyer inserts—rates on request.

Readers International, Inc., S. Carroll, Executive Editor; D. Connell, Executive Editor, PO Box 959, (US Book Service Department), Columbia, LA 71418. 1982. Fiction. "*Only publish* fiction by authors from outside Western Europe, usually in English translation for the first time. U.K. Editorial Branch: 8 Strathray Gardens, London NW3 4NY England. US Distributor: Consortium, 287 East Sixth Street, Suite 365, St. Paul, MN 55101; 612-221-9035; orders only, (800)283-3572." avg. press run 5M. Pub'd 6 titles 1990; expects 6 titles 1991, 6-8 titles 1992. avg. price, cloth: $18.95; paper: $10.95. Discounts: contact distributor or US Book Service. 200pp; 5×8; web printing. Reporting time: 3 months; no unsolicited submissions. Payment: standard advances against 8% royalty (2% royalty to translator). Joint copyright.

Reading Matters, Anita Heitler, PO Box 300309, Denver, CO 80203, 303-757-3506. 1985. avg. press run 10M. Expects 1 title 1991, 1 title 1992. 1 title listed in the *Small Press Record of Books in Print* (20th Edition, 1991-92). avg. price, cloth: $17.95; paper: $9.95. Discounts: stores 1-4 20%, 5+ 40%. 52pp; 8×5. Reporting time: 4 weeks. Payment: negotiable. Does not copyright for author. PASCAL.

The Real Comet Press, Catherine Hillenbrand, 3131 Western Avenue #410, Seattle, WA 98121-1028,

206-283-7827. 1980. Art, photos, cartoons, criticism, concrete art, non-fiction. "Special interest in visual arts: artists books, art catalogs, criticism, issues in contemporary art, art and social change, and popular culture. Distributed to the trade by Consortium Book Sales and Distribution, 287 E. 6th Street, Suite 3651, Saint Paul, MN 55101, (800) 283-3572, FAX (212) 221-0124" avg. press run 5M-10M. Pub'd 7 titles 1990; expects 2 titles 1991. 34 titles listed in the *Small Press Record of Books in Print* (20th Edition, 1991-92). avg. price, paper: $5.95-$19.95. Discounts: 1-4 books, assorted titles 20%, 5+ $40%; library 20% (2 or more assorted titles). 100+pp; size varies; of. Reporting time: 2 months. Payment: varies. Copyrights for author. COSMEP, PNW-BPA American Booksellers Assn., Museum Store Assn., ABA.

REAL FICTION, Carol Tarlen, Co-Editor; Genevieve Belfiglio, Co-Editor; Owen Mould, Co-Editor, 298-9th Avenue, San Francisco, CA 94118. 1982. Fiction, interviews, reviews, parts-of-novels. "Interested in innovative, unabstruse writing—that is writing that takes chances without obscuring intent or meaning. We are more interested in form as a vehicle of expression than as a virtuoso routine. We publish a broad range of narrative styles and subjects. Include SASE." circ. 500. 1/yr. Pub'd 1 issue 1990; expects 1 issue 1991, 1 issue 1992. sub. price: $15/2 yrs, $30/2 yrs instit.; per copy: $4; sample: $4. Back issues: $4. Discounts: 60/40 bookstores; 10% agents. 85pp; 5×7; of. Reporting time: 1 week to 3 months. Payment: 3 contributor's copies. Copyrighted, reverts to author. Ads: negotiable.

REAL PEOPLE, Alex Polner, 950 Third Avenue, New York, NY 10022, 212-371-4932. 1988. Articles, photos, interviews, non-fiction. "1000-1500 words, articles about *celebrities and very interesting people*; articles about issues (e.g., true crime, people and their "interesting" occupations)." circ. 150M. 6/yr. Pub'd 6 issues 1990; expects 6 issues 1991, 6 issues 1992. sub. price: $21; per copy: $3.50; sample: $3.50. Back issues: $3. Discounts: negotiable. 80pp; 5⅛×7⅞; of. Reporting time: 4 weeks. Payment: $100-$200. Copyrighted, rights do not revert, except on special occasions. Pub's reviews: 25 in 1990. §Celebrities/biographies, autobiographies, memoirs, annual children's books roundtrip, photo/art books, cookbooks. Ads: color $2400, b&w $2000/color $1440, b&w $1200/75¢ per word (25 word minimum).

Real People Press, Steve Andreas, Editor and Owner, Box F, Moab, UT 84532, 801-259-7578. 1967. Non-fiction. "Do not send ms. Send inquiry and short sample: 1-10 pp only! Psychology + *closely* related topics only." avg. press run 30M. Pub'd 1 title 1990; expects 1 title 1991, 1 title 1992. 2 titles listed in the *Small Press Record of Books in Print* (20th Edition, 1991-92). avg. price, cloth: $10; paper: $6.50. Discounts: Postpaid: no handling charges 1-4, 20%; 5-24, 40%; 25-349, 41%; 350-up, 50% + freight; 1000+ 50% freight prepaid. 250pp; 6×9; belt press. Reporting time: ASAP. Payment: 12½% paid 6 months. Copyrights for author.

THE REALIST (NEWSLETTER), Paul Krassner, Box 1230, Venice, CA 90294, 213-392-5848. 1958. Cartoons, satire, non-fiction. circ. 3M. 6/yr. Pub'd 6 issues 1990; expects 6 issues 1991, 6 issues 1992. sub. price: $12; per copy: $2; sample: $2. Back issues: $2. Discounts: 50% on consignment. 8pp; 8½×11; of. Reporting time: 2-3 weeks. Payment: $25-$100. Not copyrighted. Ads: none.

Reality Studios, Ken Edwards, 4 Howard Court, Peckham Rye, London SE15 3PH, United Kingdom, 071-639-7297. 1978. Poetry, interviews, criticism, long-poems, concrete art. "Experimental poetry press. Books can be ordered from Small Press Distribution, Berkeley." Expects 2 titles 1991, 2 titles 1992. 3 titles listed in the *Small Press Record of Books in Print* (20th Edition, 1991-92). Discounts: negotiable. of. Reporting time: fairly quickly. Payment: copies and/or flat fee. Copyright remains with author. ALP, SPG.

THE REAPER, Story Line Press, Robert McDowell, Mark Jarman, Tom Wilhelmus, Fiction Editor, c/o Story Line Press, Three Oaks Farm, Brownsville, OR 97327-9718, 503-466-5352. 1981. Poetry, fiction, satire, criticism, reviews, letters, long-poems. "We are interested primarily in narrative poetry. Most essays are written by the editors, but we do consider essays by others" circ. 700. 1/yr. Pub'd 3 issues 1990; expects 3 issues 1991, 1 issue 1992. sub. price: $15; per copy: $15; sample: $15. Back issues: $5. Discounts: 40% to bookstores & classes orders of 5 or more; 20% orders under 5. 150pp; 5½×8; of, perfect. Reporting time: 2-4 weeks. Payment: copies. Copyrighted, reverts to author. Pub's reviews: 12 in 1990. §Poetry, fiction, criticism, biography. Ads: $100/$50. CLMP.

REASON MAGAZINE, Virginia I. Postrel, Editor, 2716 Ocean Park Blvd., Suite 1062, Santa Monica, CA 90405, 213-392-0443. 1968. Articles, art, photos, cartoons, interviews, reviews, letters, news items, non-fiction. "Recent contributors: Thomas Sowell, Aaron Wildavsky, Milton Friedman, Tom Bethell, George Gilder, Martha Bayles, John Fund, Larry Niven, Karl Hess. Length: Review—1,000 words, articles—1,500-6,000 words, interviews—4,000 words. Biases: Free market/limited government orientation, baby boom topics/audience" circ. 35M. 11/yr. Pub'd 11 issues 1990; expects 11 issues 1991, 11 issues 1992. sub. price: $24; per copy: $2.95; sample: $2. Back issues: $4. 58pp; 8½×11; of. Reporting time: 2 months. Payment: varies $150 for book review, $250-$2,000 articles. Copyrighted. Pub's reviews: 40 in 1990. §Public policy, politics, economics, science fiction, current affairs, social policy, fiction, history.

Rebis Press, Betsy Davids, Jim Petrillo, P.O. Box 2233, Berkeley, CA 94702, 415-527-3845. 1972. Poetry, fiction, art, parts-of-novels, long-poems, concrete art. "We're overloaded and are not encouraging unsolicited mss. at this time. Publish no more than 1 book a year" avg. press run 125. Pub'd 1 title 1990; expects 1 title 1991, 1 title 1992. 7 titles listed in the *Small Press Record of Books in Print* (20th Edition, 1991-92). avg. price, other: $35. Discounts: trade 40% on 2 or more copies. 45pp; size varies; †of, lp, xerography. Reporting time: 6 months or longer. Payment: royalties. Copyrights for author.

Les Recherches Daniel Say Cie. (see also GUARD THE NORTH; ENTROPY NEGATIVE), Box 65583, Vancouver 12, B.C. V5N 5K5, Canada.

RECON, Recon Publications, Chris Robinson, Editor; Lewis Bellis, Business Manager, P.O. Box 14602, Philadelphia, PA 19134. 1973. Articles, cartoons, interviews, reviews. "A publication dealing with revolutionary military affairs: expose Pentagon planning, revolutionary strategy & tactics, GI movement, Third World struggles, women in the military, last issue 4/91 now at printer." circ. 2M. 4/yr. Pub'd 4 issues 1990; expects 4 issues 1991, 6 issues 1992. sub. price: $15, $24/2 yrs, $36/3 yrs; sample: free. Back issues: $20/year. 16pp; 8½×11; of. Reporting time: within a week. Payment: copies only. Pub's reviews: 27 in 1990. §Politics, the military, history, geography. Ads: $40/$20/50¢-word. COSMEP.

Recon Publications (see also RECON), Chris Robinson, Editor; Lewis Bellis, Business Manager, PO Box 14602, Philadelphia, PA 19134. 1973. avg. press run 2M. 5 titles listed in the *Small Press Record of Books in Print* (20th Edition, 1991-92). of. COSMEP.

RECONSTRUCTIONIST, Reconstructionist Press, Joy D. Levitt, Federation of Reconstructionist Congregations and Havurot, Church Road & Greenwood Avenue, Wyncote, PA 19095, 215-887-1988. 1935. Poetry, fiction, articles, art, photos, reviews, letters, non-fiction. circ. 10M. 4/yr. Pub'd 6 issues 1990; expects 4 issues 1991, 4 issues 1992. sub. price: $20; per copy: $5. Back issues: $3. 32pp; 8½×11; lp. Reporting time: 1-3 months. Payment: $25-$36. Copyrighted, reverts to author. Pub's reviews: 20 in 1990. §Judaica, public policy, religious studies. Ads: $250/$150.

Reconstructionist Press (see also RECONSTRUCTIONIST), Church Road & Greenwood Avenue, Wyncote, PA 19095, 215-887-1988. 2 titles listed in the *Small Press Record of Books in Print* (20th Edition, 1991-92).

THE RECORD SUN, Poet Papers, Laimons Juris G, PO Box 528, Topanga, CA 90290. 1969. Poetry, articles, art, photos, cartoons, satire, criticism, reviews, music, letters, collages. "All work submitted *MUST* have self-addressed stamped envelopes - or we do *not* reply. Most of our contributors are subscribers (whom *The Record Sun* is printed for!)" circ. 8M. 4/yr. Pub'd 4 issues 1990; expects 4 issues 1991, 4 issues 1992. sub. price: $8; sample: $2. Back issues: first issue Anniversary Issue $4. Discounts: deal with retailers directly. 3-12pp; 8½×14; †of, photocopy. Reporting time: at least 2 years (editorship rotates-and our editors travel frequently). Payment: copies. Copyrighted, reverts to author. Pub's reviews: 7 in 1990. §Poetry, photography, graphics, cartoons, joy, fun, satire, statistics, information. Ads: $50/$1.

Recovery Publications, Valerie Deilgat, Ron Halvorson, 1201 Knoxville Street, San Diego, CA 92110, 619-275-1350. 1987. Non-fiction. "Publishes recovery-oriented material for adult children of alcoholic and other dysfunctional families." avg. press run 25M. Pub'd 2 titles 1990; expects 4 titles 1991, 6 titles 1992. 7 titles listed in the *Small Press Record of Books in Print* (20th Edition, 1991-92). avg. price, paper: $11.95. Discounts: bookstores and distributors. 190pp; size varies. Reporting time: 6-8 weeks. Payment: negotiable. Copyrights for author. COSMEP, PMA, ABA, CBA.

RECOVERY TODAY, Charles Martin, PO Box 754, Goldenrod, FL 32733, 407-679-5622. 1990. Poetry, fiction, articles, art, photos, cartoons, interviews, criticism, reviews, music, letters, news items, non-fiction. circ. 45M. 12/yr. Pub'd 12 issues 1990; expects 12 issues 1991, 12 issues 1992. sub. price: $15; per copy: $2; sample: free with writer's guidelines. Back issues: $5. 24pp; 10×13; †web. Reporting time: 10 days. Payment: none. Copyrighted, reverts to author. Pub's reviews: 12 in 1990. §Any area of addiction, 12 steps, etc. Ads: $1050/$550/$300 1/4 page/multi-discount.

Recreation Sales Publishing, Inc., Diane Dirksen, 150 E. Olive Avenue, Suite 110, Burbank, CA 91502, 818-843-3616. 1974. Non-fiction. "Non-fiction guidebooks on outdoor recreation." avg. press run 40M. Pub'd 3 titles 1990; expects 2 titles 1991, 2 titles 1992. 4 titles listed in the *Small Press Record of Books in Print* (20th Edition, 1991-92). avg. price, paper: $16.95. Discounts: 40% dealers, 55% distributors. 208pp; 8½×11; of. Outdoor Writer's of America.

Red Alder Books, David Steinberg, Box 2992, Santa Cruz, CA 95063, 408-426-7082. 1974. Poetry, fiction, art, photos, letters, long-poems, non-fiction. "Our present emphasis is on books dealing with male sex roles, and books of imaginative erotic writing and photography." avg. press run 3M. Pub'd 1 title 1990; expects 2 titles 1991, 2 titles 1992. 5 titles listed in the *Small Press Record of Books in Print* (20th Edition, 1991-92). avg. price, cloth: $35; paper: $6. Discounts: 40% (5 or more); 20% (2-4). 150pp; 6×9, 8½×11; of. Reporting time: 2-6 weeks. Payment: varies. Copyrights for author. COSMEP.

RED BASS, Jay Murphy, Editor, 2425 Burgundy Street, New Orleans, LA 70117, 504-949-5256. 1981. Poetry, fiction, articles, art, photos, cartoons, interviews, satire, criticism, reviews, music, letters, parts-of-novels, long-poems, collages, plays, concrete art, news items, non-fiction. *"Red Bass*—collage—the poetic principle applied to magazine production— seeks to present at least some of the most interesting events in the art and politics of our culture. We accept art, poetry, fiction, non-fiction, reviews. We want art that is committed to the transformation of society, and we want it to be good. Some recent contributors include Lucy Lippard, Mary Beth Edelson, Kathy Acker, Joseph Nechvatal, Elizam Escobar, Carolee Schneemann, James Purdy, Nancy Spero" circ. 3M. 2-3/yr. Pub'd 2 issues 1990; expects 2 issues 1991, 3 issues 1992. sub. price: $20 (3 issues); per copy: $7.50; sample: $5. Back issues: $4. Discounts: negotiable. 80-120pp; 8½x11; of. Reporting time: 4-5 months. Payment: copies plus one year subscription, sometimes in cash depending on issue and resources. Copyrighted, reverts to author. Pub's reviews: 8 in 1990. §Visual arts, poetry, fiction, film, performance, history, politics. We prefer works from small presses. Ads: $350/$175/$75 1/4 page. Council of Literary Magazines and Presses (CLMP).

Red Candle Press (see also CANDELABRUM POETRY MAGAZINE), M.L. McCarthy, 9 Milner Road, Wisbech, PE13 2LR, England, tel: 0945 581067. 1970. Poetry. "Poetry. The Red Candle Press provides a (free) service to poets and does not aim to make a profit. At present we are publishing saddle-stitched pamphlets of 16-20 pp, and the author, who retains copyright, gets a royalty-advance of £10, and five free copies. Contributors to *Candelabrum Poetry Magazine* and to anthologies receive one free copy but no cash payment at present" avg. press run 200. Pub'd 2 titles 1990; expects 2 titles 1991, 2 titles 1992. 7 titles listed in the *Small Press Record of Books in Print* (20th Edition, 1991-92). avg. price, paper: £1.80 for poetry. Discounts: 1/3 to booksellers. Poetry 16-20pp; 5½x8; of, lp. Reporting time: 1-3 months. Payment: free copy to magazine contributors; £10 royalty-advance, and 5 free copies to authors of poetry pamphlets. Copyrights for author.

Red Car Press, Michael Allen, 12228 Venice Boulevard #458, Los Angeles, CA 90066. 1989. avg. press run 10M. Expects 1 title 1991, 2 titles 1992. avg. price, paper: $14.95. Discounts: 53% to distributors. 200pp. Reporting time: 90 days. Does not copyright for author. COSMEP.

Red Cedar Press (see also RED CEDAR REVIEW), 325 Morrill Hall, Michigan State University, E. Lansing, MI 48824. 5 titles listed in the *Small Press Record of Books in Print* (20th Edition, 1991-92).

RED CEDAR REVIEW, Red Cedar Press, Carol Bracewell, Editor-in-Chief, 325 Morrill Hall, Dept. of English, Mich. State Univ., E. Lansing, MI 48824, 517-355-9656. 1963. Poetry, fiction, art, photos, interviews, criticism, reviews, parts-of-novels, long-poems. "We have no particular editorial bias-clarity is appreciated, sentimentality isn't. Some recent contributors: William Stafford, Diane Wakoski, Hugh Fox, Judith McCombs, Barbara Drake, Charles Edward Eaton, Dan Gerber, Herbert Scott, Lyn Lifshin. We're also open to new writers; we generally try to comment on promising work that we don't accept. In some cases, we ask for resubmissions-no guarantees, of course. In addition to poetry and fiction, we'd like to receive reviews, interviews, and graphic art for consideration. Our two annual issues come out around March/April and Oct/Nov, but submissions are considered year-round. Reporting time longer in summer. No simultaneous submissions, please" circ. 400. 2/yr. Pub'd 1 issue 1990; expects 2 issues 1991, 2 issues 1992. sub. price: $7; per copy: $3.50; sample: $2. Back issues: $1.00. 80pp; 8½x5½; of. Reporting time: 6-8 weeks. Payment: 2 copies. Copyrighted, reverts to author. Pub's reviews: 1 in 1990. §Poetry, fiction, translations, books, chapbooks, magazines, anthologies. No ads. CCLM.

Red Crane Books, 826 Camino de Monte Rey, Santa Fe, NM 87501, 505-988-7070. 1989. "Special interest in Southwestern subjects; general trade books." avg. press run 4M. Pub'd 5 titles 1990; expects 10 titles 1991, 10 titles 1992. 9 titles listed in the *Small Press Record of Books in Print* (20th Edition, 1991-92). avg. price, cloth: $18.95; paper: $9.95. Discounts: libraries 20%, bookstores 1-4 20%, 5-9 40%, 10-49 42%, 50-100 44%, 100+ 46%. 150pp; 6x9; of. Reporting time: 3 months. Payment: negotiable. Copyrights for author. Rocky Mountain Book Publishers Association (RMBPA).

RED DANCEFLOOR, David Goldschlag, PO Box 3051, Canoga Park, CA 91306, 818-785-7650. 1990. Poetry, fiction, articles, art, reviews. "Recent contributors: Gerald Locklin, Michael C. Ford, Sue Saniel Elkind" circ. 400-500. 4/yr. Pub'd 1 issue 1990; expects 4 issues 1991, 4 issues 1992. price per copy: $5; sample: $3.50. Discounts: send for information. 90-120pp; 5½x8½; †of. Reporting time: 4-6 weeks (usually sooner). Payment: 1 copy and 30% off additional copies. Copyrighted, reverts to author. Pub's reviews. §Literary, art, music. Ads: send SASE for info.

RED DIRT, Lorna Dee Cervantes, Jay Griswold, 1630 30th Street, Suite A-307, Boulder, CO 80301. 1991. Poetry, art, photos, reviews, long-poems, collages. "International crosscultural poetry rooted in the earth and rendered in blood: poems of significance, heart and craft; also translations, visual art, some short fiction and non-academic prose; bilingual, some untranslated Spanish. Editors are socially committed, serious poets looking for same. We read all, require SASE, and answer personally. Yusef Komunyakaa, Diane Glancy, Margaret Randall, Julio Cortazar, Laurel Speer, Victor Hernandez Cruz, Ray Gonzalez, Daisy Zamora, Gu

Cheng, William Stafford, Luis Rodriguez, Pamela Uschuk, Joseph Bruchac III, Sherman Alexie, Chitra Divakaruni, Maggie Jaffe, William Matthews alongside previously unpublished writers." circ. 1M-1.5M. 2/yr. Expects 2 issues 1991, 2 issues 1992. sub. price: $10, $20 institutions, $20 foreign, $50 special lifetime subscription; per copy: $7; sample: $7. Discounts: 40% over 10. 152pp; 7×8½; of, guest lp. Reporting time: 1 week to 4 months. Payment: 2 copies & discount on extra issues. Copyrighted, reverts to author. Pub's reviews: 1 in 1990. §Poetry and crosscultural literary magazines. Ads: $80/$50/$25 1/6 page (2x3).

Red Dust, Joanna Gunderson, PO Box 630, Gracie Station, New York, NY 10028, 212-348-4388. 1963. Poetry, fiction. "Short works, once accepted, must be sent on disc. In general, authors get 50 copies. There is no advance." avg. press run 1M. Pub'd 4 titles 1990; expects 4 titles 1991, 4 titles 1992. 53 titles listed in the *Small Press Record of Books in Print* (20th Edition, 1991-92). avg. price, cloth: $10; paper: $3. Discounts: libraries 20%; wholesalers & booksellers 1 copy-30%, 2 or more-40%, paperback 1-4 copies-20%, 5 or more-40%. 140pp, short works 14-32pp; 8½×5½; of. Reporting time: 2 months. Payment: $300 advance against royalty. Copyrights for author in most cases.

Red Eye Press, James Goodwin, Richard Kallan, 4238 Glenwood Avenue, Los Angeles, CA 90065, 213-225-3805. 1988. Art, photos, non-fiction. avg. press run 5M-10M. Pub'd 1 title 1990; expects 2 titles 1991, 2 titles 1992. 2 titles listed in the *Small Press Record of Books in Print* (20th Edition, 1991-92). avg. price, paper: $19.95. 360pp; 5½×8⅜; of. Reporting time: 8 weeks. Payment: 10%. Copyrights for author. PMA, NCBPA.

Red Hen Press, Joanne O'Roark, Hope Bryant, PO Box 3774, Santa Barbara, CA 93130, 805-682-1278. 1984. Fiction. "RED HEN is a children's press, producing two-three titles a year. We have published five picture books in the three-seven year old age range, three in full-color, and two in three-color. We are soon to launch RED HEN Pullet Books for beginning and middle grade readers. It is our aim to introduce promising new authors and illustrators, and we are enthusiastic about combining them in good children's books." avg. press run 2M. Pub'd 2 titles 1990; expects 4 titles 1991, 2-3 titles 1992. avg. price, cloth: $8.95; paper: $3.95. Discounts: 40-50%. 32pp pic.bk., 50pp older; size varies; of. Reporting time: 1 month. Payment: advance against royalties. Copyrights for author. Publishers Marketing Group.

Red Herring Press (see also MATRIX), Carmen M. Pursifull, Editor; Ruth S. Walker, Editor & Director, c/o Channing-Murray Foundation, 1209 W. Oregon, Urbana, IL 61801, 217-344-1176. 1976. Poetry. "*Matrix*, annual poetry anthology, not soliciting manuscripts at this time. We publish high-quality chapbooks (preferably first books), generally by present members of the Red Herring Poetry Workshop." avg. press run 300. Pub'd 3 titles 1990; expects 2 titles 1991, 2 titles 1992. 6 titles listed in the *Small Press Record of Books in Print* (20th Edition, 1991-92). avg. price, paper: $5 (chapbooks), $8 (anthologies). Discounts: Standard 40%. Chapbooks 30-50pp, anthologies 100-150pp; 5½×8½; of. Payment: 20% press run. Copyrights for author.

Red Hill Press, San Francisco + Los Angeles (see also INVISIBLE CITY), John McBride, Paul Vangelisti, PO Box 2853, San Francisco, CA 94126. 1969. Poetry, criticism, concrete art. "Primarily a poetry & translation press, with emphasis on Italian and California poetry. Immediately forthcoming, *Aphorisms* by Edouard Roditi (with a very brief note by Paul Goodman), and *alephs again* by Paul Vangelisti" avg. press run 1M. Expects 3 titles 1991. 62 titles listed in the *Small Press Record of Books in Print* (20th Edition, 1991-92). avg. price, cloth: $15; paper: $5. Discounts: consult Small Press Distribution (Berkeley). 48-80pp; size varies moving to 9x5½; of. Reporting time: extended. Payment: copies. Copyrights for author. COSMEP, CLMP.

RED HOT WORK-AT-HOME REPORT, Ed Durham, 15 Brunswick Lane, Willingboro, NJ 08046, 609-835-2347. 1986. News items, non-fiction. "Articles are 1000 words or less, about issues relevant to small home-based businesses." circ. 1.2M. 6/yr. Pub'd 6 issues 1990; expects 6 issues 1991, 6 issues 1992. sub. price: $39; sample: $3. Back issues: not sold, given to new subscribers. Discounts: 50% jobbers, agents. 12pp; 8½×11; of. Reporting time: 3 months. Payment: small payment for features. Copyrighted, reverts to author. Pub's reviews: 41 in 1990. §Business, motivational, money-making. Small Business Press.

Red Ink/Black Hole Productions (see also TAPJOE: The Anaprocrustean Poetry Journal of Enumclaw), Noah Farnsworth, PO Box 104, Grangeville, ID 83530-0104. 1987. Poetry. "Inquiries are welcome. Our interest is in poetry—nature, social justice, peace." avg. press run 100-300. Pub'd 2 titles 1990; expects 2 titles 1991, 2 titles 1992. avg. price, paper: $3. Discounts: by arrangement. 20-30pp; 5½×8½; of. Reporting time: 1-3 months for manuscripts. Copyrights for author.

Red Key Press, Margaret Key Biggs, Editor; Wayne S. Biggs, Art Editor, PO Box 551, Port St Joe, FL 32456, 904-227-1305. 1982. Poetry, art. "The main purpose of Red Key Press is to publish clothbound books, 80-100 pages. The first by the editor, *Magnolias and Such*, is available for $3 plus 50¢ for postage. Length of book is negotiable as is payment. Biases: the individual above all else. Strong environmental focus. I fully believe the poets of this continent have had a great deal to do with changing the tide of thinking about nuclear mistakes. Query before sending ms. A SASE is always required for queries and for mss. UPS address only: 214 Charles Avenue, White City, Florida at Port St. Joe, FL 32456" avg. press run 250-500. Pub'd 4 titles 1990; expects 2 titles 1991. 2 titles listed in the *Small Press Record of Books in Print* (20th Edition, 1991-92). avg. price, cloth: $14; paper: $14. Sorry, no discounts. 80-100pp; 5½×8; of. Payment: negotiable. Copyrights for author.

Red Letter Press, Helen Gilbert, Managing Editor, 409 Maynard Avenue South #201, Seattle, WA 98104, 206-682-0990. 1990. Non-fiction. avg. press run 3M. Pub'd 1 title 1990; expects 1 title 1991, 1-2 titles 1992. avg. price, paper: $8.95. Discounts: bookstores 1-5 20%, 6+ 40%; wholesalers/distributors negotiable; classes 20%. 150pp; 5½×8½; of. Small Press Center, Northwest Association of Book Publishers.

Red Oak Press, 2447 Redbud Trail Drive, Germantown, TN 38138. 1 title listed in the *Small Press Record of Books in Print* (20th Edition, 1991-92).

THE RED PAGODA, A JOURNAL OF HAIKU, Lewis Sanders, 125 Taylor Street, Jackson, TN 38301, 901-427-7714 (after 6 p.m.). 1982. "I use haiku, renga, tanka, senyru and some black and white artwork" circ. 130. 4/yr. Pub'd 4 issues 1990; expects 4 issues 1991, 4 issues 1992. sub. price: $12; per copy: $3; sample: $2 if available. Discounts: can be worked out. Poets should inquire. 36-50pp; digest size; mi. Reporting time: 3 weeks. Payment: none. Not copyrighted. Pub's reviews: 2-3 in 1990. §Books or magazine on haiku, etc.

RED POWER, Daryl A. Miller, Box 277, Battle Creek, IA 51006, 712-365-4873. 1986. Articles, letters, news items. "Magazine for people interested in International Harvester and its products" circ. 850. 6/yr. Pub'd 6 issues 1990; expects 6 issues 1991, 6 issues 1992. sub. price: $10; per copy: $1.50; sample: none. Back issues: $1.50 each. Discounts: none. 20pp; 8½×11; of. Payment: free subscription. Not copyrighted. Pub's reviews: 2 in 1990. §Farm equipment, trucks. Ads: $50/$30/$17 1/4 page.

Red Wheelbarrow Press (see also WORKING CLASSICS), David Joseph, Editor; Carol Tarlen, Assistant Editor, 298 9th Avenue, San Francisco, CA 94118, 415-387-3412. 1981. 6 titles listed in the *Small Press Record of Books in Print* (20th Edition, 1991-92).

Redbird Press, Inc., PO Box 11441, Memphis, TN 38111, 901-323-2233. 1981. Art, photos, reviews, music, non-fiction. avg. press run 5M. Expects 3 titles 1991, 3 titles 1992. 3 titles listed in the *Small Press Record of Books in Print* (20th Edition, 1991-92). avg. price, cloth: $15.95; paper: $11.95. 32pp; of. Copyrights for author.

RedBrick Press, Jack Erickson, PO Box 2184, Reston, VA 22090, 703-476-6420. 1987. Non-fiction. "Will begin publishing natural history/science in 1992." avg. press run 5M. Expects 2 titles 1991, 3 titles 1992. 4 titles listed in the *Small Press Record of Books in Print* (20th Edition, 1991-92). avg. price, cloth: $16.95; paper: $13.95. Discounts: 40% book stores. 160pp; 6×9; of. Reporting time: 4 weeks. Washington Independent Writers (WIW), Publishers Marketing Association, COSMEP.

Redeemer Resources, S. Balika, A. Palmer, J. Worrall, 4146 State Road, Medina, OH 44256-8408. 1985. Long-poems, plays, non-fiction. "Our material is religious in nature, directed at both adults and children. The length of the materials varies anywhere from several pages to one hundred pages in length. Our most recent contributors have been rectors in the Episcopal Church" avg. press run 100. Expects 15 titles 1991, 25 titles 1992. 11 titles listed in the *Small Press Record of Books in Print* (20th Edition, 1991-92). avg. price, cloth: $29.95; paper: $2.50; other: $1.50. 20pp; 8½×11, 5½×8½; lp. Reporting time: 1 month. Payment: 10½%.

THE REDNECK REVIEW OF LITERATURE, Penelope Reedy, PO Box 730, Twin Falls, ID 83301, 208-734-6653. 1975. Poetry, fiction, interviews, satire, criticism, reviews, letters, parts-of-novels. "2.5M word limit usually. We seek to contribute to the establishment and analysis of literature of the West. No hard history or gunfighter tales. Most material deals with contemporary themes with the past in the background. Seek native American work." circ. 500. 2/yr. Pub'd 1 issue 1990; expects 2 issues 1991, 2 issues 1992. sub. price: $14; per copy: $6 + $1 p/h; sample: $6 + $1 p+h. Back issues: few available. Discounts: wholesale for $4.50 + p+h. 80pp; 8½×11; †of, lp. Reporting time: couple of weeks. Payment: 1 copy and discount for more. Copyrighted, reverts to author. Pub's reviews: 30 in 1990. §Books about the west a la Abbey, Silko, Eastlake. Ads: $100/$50/$35 1/3 page.

Redpath Press, Elizabeth J. Atkinson, 420 North 5th Street, Ste. 710, Minneapolis, MN 55401, (612) 332-1278. 1985. Fiction. avg. press run 5M. Pub'd 12 titles 1990; expects 10 titles 1991, 12 titles 1992. avg. price, paper: $5.95. Discounts: 50% discount-trade. 32pp; 4×7½; of.

Redwood Press, Philip L. Fradkin, PO Box 817, Pt. Reyes, CA 94956, 415-663-8733. 1986. Non-fiction. "We specialize in books on San Francisco Bay Area, California, and western history and natural history subjects. Solid research and readable text are musts" avg. press run 2-5M. Pub'd 1 title 1990; expects 1 title 1991, 1 title 1992. 2 titles listed in the *Small Press Record of Books in Print* (20th Edition, 1991-92). avg. price, paper: $8.95. Discounts: 40% trade, 5 copies or more; 48% for over 100 copies. 200pp; 6×9; of. Reporting time: 1 month. Payment: negotiable. Copyrights for author.

I. Reed Books, Ishmael Reed, Steve Cannon, PO Box 3288, Berkeley, CA 94703. 1973. Poetry, fiction, plays. "No unsolicited manuscripts. Publishers of American multicultural authors, including recently: Quincy Troupe,

Mei-mei Berssenbrugge, Amiri Baraka, Joy Harjo, Shawn Wong, Colleen McElroy.'' avg. press run 2M. Pub'd 2 titles 1990; expects 2 titles 1991, 2 titles 1992. 19 titles listed in the *Small Press Record of Books in Print* (20th Edition, 1991-92). avg. price, cloth: $10; paper: $4.95-$5.95. Discounts: standard to the trade; 1 copy, 10%; 2-4, 20%; 5 plus, 40%. 100-120pp; 5½×8½; of. Payment: standard. Copyrights for author.

Reference Service Press, Eric Schlachter, Sandra Goldstein, 1100 Industrial Road, #9, San Carlos, CA 94070. 1975. Non-fiction. ''Reference Service Press is a library-oriented reference book publishing company. We specialize in the development of directories of financial aid for special needs groups (e.g. women, minorities, the disabled).'' avg. press run 3M. Pub'd 3 titles 1990; expects 4 titles 1991, 3 titles 1992. 6 titles listed in the *Small Press Record of Books in Print* (20th Edition, 1991-92). avg. price, cloth: $40. Discounts: up to 20%. 350pp; 8½×11, 6×9; lp. Reporting time: 60 days or less. Payment: 10% and up, depending upon sales; royalties paid annually. Copyrights for author. Publishers Marketing Association, COSMEP.

REFERENCE SERVICES REVIEW, Pierian Press, Ilene Rockman, Editor; Pamela Abston, Managing Editor, PO Box 1808, Ann Arbor, MI 48106, 313-434-5530. 1972. Reviews. ''Library/reference'' circ. 3M. 4/yr. Pub'd 4 issues 1990; expects 4 issues 1991. sub. price: $45; per copy: $13.50; sample: free. Back issues: available. Discounts: none. 100pp; 8½×11; of. Reporting time: 4 weeks. Payment: none. Pierian Press holds copyright. Pub's reviews: 500 in 1990. §All subjects in reference format. Ads: inquire.

REFLECT, William S. Kennedy, 3306 Argonne Avenue, Norfolk, VA 23509, 804-857-1097. 1979. Poetry, fiction, articles, art, cartoons, reviews, letters. ''We have become a vehicle for the presentation of poetry and prose representing the 1980's Spiral Back-to-Beauty Movement, the euphony-in-writing school showing 'an inner-directed concern with sound...' Spiral writing in the terminology of the movement's adherents. Beauty is the criterion here; all forms judged and accepted with that in mind. We use two or three short stories per issue, mostly short-shorts, but of the newly emerging Spiral Fiction genre. See a copy of the magazine for the four rules of Spiral Fiction'' 4/yr. Pub'd 4 issues 1990; expects 4 issues 1991, 4 issues 1992. 2 titles listed in the *Small Press Record of Books in Print* (20th Edition, 1991-92). sub. price: $8; per copy: $2; sample: $2. Back issues: $1 (if available). 48pp; 5½×8½; †zerox. Reporting time: 2 weeks to 2 months. Payment: 1 contributor's copy. Not copyrighted. Pub's reviews: 3 in 1990. §Literary, poetry, general small press. Ads: $5 1/3 page/10¢ per word.

REFLECTIONS, Dean Harper, PO Box 368, Duncan Falls, OH 43734, 614-674-5209; 796-2595. 1980. Poetry, fiction, articles, photos, interviews. ''We are always looking for good fresh articles on how to write poetry. We are always looking for interviews of poets.'' circ. 1M. 2/yr. Pub'd 2 issues 1990; expects 2 issues 1991, 2 issues 1992. sub. price: $5; per copy: $3; sample: $2. Back issues: $2. Discounts: $2 for 25+. 32pp; 8½×11. Reporting time: 2 weeks. Payment: contributors copy. Copyrighted, reverts to author. Ads: $100/$50/$25 1/4.

Regent Press, Mark B. Weiman, 2747 Regent Street, Berkeley, CA 94705, 415-548-8459. 1978. Fiction, non-fiction. avg. press run 1M-1.5M. Pub'd 3 titles 1990; expects 3 titles 1991, 3 titles 1992. 9 titles listed in the *Small Press Record of Books in Print* (20th Edition, 1991-92). avg. price, paper: $9.95. Discounts: 1 copy 20%, 2-3 30%, 4+ 40%. 125pp; 5½×8½; †of. Reporting time: varies. Payment: varies, % of gross. Copyrights for author. COSMEP.

Rehab Publications, 1237 28th Avenue, PO Box 22606, San Francisco, CA 94122. 1 title listed in the *Small Press Record of Books in Print* (20th Edition, 1991-92).

Relampago Books Press (see also CARTA ABIERTA), Juan Rodriguez, PO Box 307, Geronimo, TX 78115, 512-379-0797. 1985. Poetry, criticism. ''Chicano, exclusively'' avg. press run 500. Pub'd 3 titles 1990; expects 1 title 1991, 2 titles 1992. 3 titles listed in the *Small Press Record of Books in Print* (20th Edition, 1991-92). avg. price, paper: $8. Discounts: 40% off list. 50pp; 5½×8½. Reporting time: 6 weeks.

Reliant Marketing & Publishing, PO Box 17456, Portland, OR 97217, 257-0211. 1983. ''Will only view manuscripts of the *how to* nature, etc.'' 1 title listed in the *Small Press Record of Books in Print* (20th Edition, 1991-92). avg. price, paper: $4.95. Discounts: inquire. 64pp; 8½×11. Reporting time: 3 weeks. Copyrights for author.

RELIX, Toni Brown, Publisher & Managing Editor, PO Box 94, Brooklyn, NY 11229, 718-258-0009. 1972. Poetry, fiction, articles, art, photos, cartoons, interviews, satire, criticism, reviews, music, letters, news items. ''*Relix* covers rock music from the late 1960's to present. With accent on San Francisco groups. Focus of magazine on top groups, i.e. Zappa, Dylan, Blues, Grateful Dead and Reggae. Highlights on Grateful Dead, Robert Hunter, Kingfish, Dinosaurs, NRPS, Peter Rowan, and others.'' circ. 38M. 6/yr. Pub'd 6 issues 1990; expects 6 issues 1991. 1 title listed in the *Small Press Record of Books in Print* (20th Edition, 1991-92). sub. price: $23; per copy: $3.50; sample: $3.50. Back issues: $3 and up. Discounts: stores: 75% of cover C.O.D. per copy, min. order 25 (heads for returns) distributors: 50% + credit terms available. 60pp; 8½×11; of. Reporting time: 8 weeks before publication. Payment: photos min of $20 + up to $800 for cover photo/articles, minimum of $1.75 per col. inch, more for cover stories or major articles. Copyrighted, does not revert to author. Pub's reviews: 10 in 1990. §Rock music. Ads: $1500/$800/write for info.

Relocation Research/Emigrants, Bill Seavey, PO Box 1122, Sierra Madre, CA 91024, 818-568-8484. 1983. "Information to help urbanites move to rural 'Edens.' Newsletter available thru membership in Emigrants" avg. press run varies. Pub'd 2-3 titles 1990. Reporting time: 2-3 weeks. Payment: varies. Does not copyright for author.

REMARK, Again + Again Press, Laurel Speer, Editor; Maureen Williams, Contributing Editor, PO Box 20041, Cherokee Station, New York, NY 10028. 1990. *"Remark* is an essay/review journal, primarily staff-written. Editor will entertain queries for guest essays and guest reviews. Address all queries to Laurel Speer, Editor, PO Box 12220, Tucson, AZ 85732-2220." circ. 200. 4/yr. Pub'd 1 issue 1990; expects 4 issues 1991, 4 issues 1992. sub. price: $10 indiv., $12 instit., $15 Canada, $27 international (funds drawn on a U.S. bank for Canada and international); sample: $2.50, $4 Canada, $7 international. 40pp; 8½x11; †office quality xerox, stock cover. Reporting time: immediate to 2 weeks. Payment: $10 per essay, $25 per set of 5 reviews. Copyrighted, reverts to author. Pub's reviews: 80-100 in 1990. §Small, university, and mid-range presses. COSMEP.

Renaissance House Publishers (a division of Jende-Hagan, Inc.), Eleanor H. Ayer, PO Box 177, 541 Oak Street, Frederick, CO 80530, 303-833-2030. 1973. Non-fiction. "We are not currently accepting new manuscripts. We are focusing on our *American Traveler Guidebooks* series which currently includes 15 guides on Colorado, 8 on Arizona, and 8 forthcoming on California in 1992." avg. press run 3.5M. Pub'd 6 titles 1990; expects 6 titles 1991, 10 titles 1992. 47 titles listed in the *Small Press Record of Books in Print* (20th Edition, 1991-92). avg. price, cloth: $15.03; paper: $7.45; other: all *American Traveler* guides are $4.95. Discounts: 1 copy net; 2-4 20%; 5-24 40%, 25-49 41%, 50-99 42%, 100-249 43%, 250-499 44%, 500-999 45%, 1000 47%; add 5% for books ordered non-returnable. Adult 200pp, juvenile and *American Traveler* guides 48pp; 5½x8½, 8½x11, 6x9; of. Reporting time: 6-8 weeks. Payment: anywhere from 7-12% of net receipts on first printing; renegotiate on subsequent printings. Copyrights for author. COSMEP, Rocky Mr. Book Publishers Assn., Society for Children's Book Writers, Western Writers of America.

RENDITIONS, Renditions Paperbacks, Eva Hung, Editor; D.E. Pollard, Editor, Chinese University of Hong Kong, Shatin, NT, Hong Kong. 1973. "A Chinese-English translation magazine. Publishes translations only of Chinese poetry, prose and fiction, classical and contemporary. Also welcomes articles on related topics dealing with Chinese language, literature and arts, or on translation. All submitted translations must be accompanied by Chinese text; require *pinyin* romanization. Special issues include: Contemporary Women Writers; Hong Kong Writing; Middlebrow Fiction; Drama; Classical Prose; Taiwan literature." circ. 750. 2/yr. Pub'd 1 issue 1990. sub. price: US$20; per copy: US$10. Back issues: varies; write for prices. Discounts: trade discount for agents and bookstores. 160pp; 10¼x7½; of. Reporting time: 3 months. Payment: honoraria and offprints and 2 free copies to contributors. Copyrighted, does not revert to author. Ads: US$160/US$90.

Renditions Paperbacks (see also RENDITIONS), Eva Hung, General Editor; T.L. Tsim, General Editor, Research Centre for Translation, Chinese University of Hong Kong, Shatin, NT, Hong Kong, 852-6952297/2399. 1986. "Telex: 50301 CUHK HX. Fax: 852-6015149. Telegram: SINOVERSITY." avg. press run 1M. Pub'd 4 titles 1990; expects 3 titles 1992. 13 titles listed in the *Small Press Record of Books in Print* (20th Edition, 1991-92). avg. price, paper: US$8.50. 150pp; 5½x8½; of. Payment: 5-10% on sales.

RENEGADE, Point Riders Press, Frank Parman, Point Riders Press, PO Box 2731, Norman, OK 73070, 405-524-5733. 1984. Poetry, fiction, articles, art, photos, reviews. "Occasional publication usually in form of chapbook, but sometimes other formats; posterpoem with newsletter, sometimes double issue; not impressed by academic letterheads. Themes vary from avant guard poetry, to western history, including ethnic studies, (usually native American poetry)." circ. 300-700. 3-4/yr. Pub'd 2 issues 1990; expects 4 issues 1991, 4 issues 1992. sub. price: $11/4 numbers + newsletter format; per copy: $4; sample: $3-$8 for 4 numbers (our choice). Discounts: single copy 15%; 2-4 25%; 5 or more 40%. 32pp; 5½x8½; of. Reporting time: 4-6 weeks, send individual poems with query—also use book reviews. Payment: copies. Copyrighted, reverts to author. Pub's reviews: 2 in 1990. §Regional publications of all types but primarily poetry, ethnic studies, western history. No ads. none.

The Rensselaerville Systems Training Center, Barry Adkins, Dave Strock, PO Box 157, Rensselaerville, NY 12147-0157, 518-797-3954. 1989. Non-fiction. avg. press run 2M. Pub'd 1 title 1990; expects 4 titles 1991, 8 titles 1992. 1 title listed in the *Small Press Record of Books in Print* (20th Edition, 1991-92). avg. price, paper: $29.95. Discounts: 1-4 20%, 5-24 40%, 25-49 43%, 50-59 46%, 100+ 50%. 8½x11; †of. Payment: open. Copyrights for author.

Rental Business Press (see also RENT-TO-OWN ADVERTISING & PROMOTIONS PLANNER; RENT-TO-OWN COLLECTIONS MANAGER; RENT-TO-OWN LEGAL & FINANCIAL BULLETIN; AUSTIN SENIOR CITIZEN; TEXAS WINEMARKET NEWS), Elizabeth T. Winn, 5600 Cedro

Trail, Austin, TX 78731, 512-338-1712.

RENT-TO-OWN ADVERTISING & PROMOTIONS PLANNER, Rental Business Press, Elizabeth T. Winn, PO Box 26505, Austin, TX 78755-0505, 512-338-1712. 1987. Articles, interviews, news items, non-fiction. "A monthly report on rent-to-own advertising and promotion ideas, in-store promotions that bring in orders, getting supplier co-op advertising, stretching TV and radio ad dollars and *bonus* with each issue, samples of successful rent-to-own advertising and ready-to-use clip art for print and direct mail advertising." circ. 300. 12/yr. Expects 3 issues 1991, 12 issues 1992. sub. price: $35; per copy: $5; sample: free (when available). Discounts: occasional package subscription specials. 5pp; 8½×11; of. Reporting time: 3 weeks. Payment: none, by-line provided. Copyrighted, does not revert to author. Pub's reviews. §Electronics, appliance, furniture advertising samples or methods. Publishers Marketing Assoc. (PMA), 2401 Pacific Coast Hwy, Suite 206, Hermosa Beach, CA 90254; International Assoc. of Independent Publishers (COSMEP), PO Box 8703, San Francisco, CA 94101.

RENT-TO-OWN COLLECTIONS MANAGER, Rental Business Press, Elizabeth T. Winn, PO Box 26505, Austin, TX 78755-0505, 512-338-1712. 1987. Articles, interviews, news items, non-fiction. "A monthly report on collections management formulas, customer/employee collections situations with proposed solutions, collections lawsuits and damage results, preventing skips and retrieving stolen merchandise, determining lost rental income and monthly revenue potential per store" circ. 300. 12/yr. Expects 3 issues 1991, 12 issues 1992. sub. price: $35; per copy: $5; sample: free (when available). Discounts: occasional package subscription specials. 5pp; 8½×11; of. Reporting time: 3 weeks. Payment: none, by-line provided. Copyrighted, does not revert to author. Pub's reviews. §Effective collections management. PMA, COSMEP.

RENT-TO-OWN LEGAL & FINANCIAL BULLETIN, Rental Business Press, Elizabeth T. Winn, PO Box 26505, Austin, TX 78755-0505, 512-338-1712. 1987. Articles, interviews, news items, non-fiction. "A monthly report on rent-to-own lawsuits, state and federal legislative updates, rent-to-own business formulas and accounting methods, tax considerations for rent-to-own, legal and financial how-to in buying, selling, and franchising rental stores, rent-to-own insurance issues, payroll management, product sales statistics, and rental rate strategies" circ. 600. 12/yr. Expects 3 issues 1991, 12 issues 1992. sub. price: $35; per copy: $5; sample: free (when available). Discounts: occasional package subscription specials. 5pp; 8½×11; of. Reporting time: 3 weeks. Payment: none, by-line provided. Copyrighted, does not revert to author. Pub's reviews. §Electronics, appliance, furniture rental, collections management and consumer leasing issues. PMA, COSMEP.

REPRESENTATIONS, University of California Press, University of California Press, 2120 Berkeley Way, Berkeley, CA 94720, 415-642-4191. 1982. Art, photos, criticism, non-fiction. "Editorial address: *Representations*, 320 Wheeler Hall, University of California, Berkeley, CA 94720." circ. 2.4M. 4/yr. Pub'd 4 issues 1990; expects 4 issues 1991, 4 issues 1992. sub. price: $24 individual, $48 institution, $16 students (+ $5 foreign postage); per copy: $6.50 indiv + students; $13 instit (+ $5 foreign postage); sample: free. Back issues: $6.50 indiv. and students, $13 instit. Discounts: foreign subs. agent 10%, one-time orders 10+ 30%, standing orders (bookstores): 1-99 40%, 100+ 50%. 152pp; 7×10; of. Reporting time: 1 month. Copyrighted, does not revert to author. Ads: $200/$120.

RE:PRINT (AN OCCASIONAL MAGAZINE), The Printable Arts Society, Inc., David Ferguson, c/o BOX 749 Magazine, 411 West 22nd Street, New York, NY 10011. 1973. Poetry, fiction, satire, long-poems. "*RE:PRINT*, an occasional magazine, has been established to print and sell separately works of general interest that have been published in *BOX 749* (another publication of *Seven Square Press*) and other magazines. We run 5M of each issue and sell the copies until the print run is sold out. So far two stories have been published in the *RE:PRINT* series; we welcome the calling of our attention to other exceptional already-published work. Submissions only on request." circ. 5M. 1/yr. price per copy: $.75; sample: $.75. 8-16pp; 4¼×11; †of. Payment: copies. Copyrighted. COSMEP, NESPA.

RE/SEARCH, Re/Search Publications, V. Vale, Andrea Juno, 20 Romolo, Suite B, San Francisco, CA 94133, 415-362-1465. 1977. Fiction, articles, art, photos, cartoons, interviews, satire, criticism, reviews, music, letters, parts-of-novels, collages, news items, non-fiction. "Recent contributors: Brion Gysin, J G Ballard, William S Burroughs. No unsolicited contributions, please! Write first." circ. 10M. 1/yr. Pub'd 1 issue 1990; expects 2 issues 1991, 2 issues 1992. sub. price: $40/3 issues; per copy: $18; sample: $20. Back issues: varies with issue. Distributed by SUBCO, PO Box 168, Monroe, OR 97456, 1-800-274-7826. 200pp; 8½×11; of. Reporting time: 4 weeks. Payment: varies, mostly volunteer. Copyrighted, reverts to author. Pub's reviews: 20 in 1990. §Anything on beat generation, William S Burroughs, Brion Gysin, et al and innovative fiction. No ads.

Research & Discovery Publications (see also TREASURE HUNTING RESEARCH BULLETIN), John C. Davis, PO Box 761, Patterson, LA 70392. 1986. "We are interested only in manuscripts on treasure hunting, buried treasure, lost mines, shipwrecks, salvage, and sunken treasure." avg. press run 2.5M. Pub'd 4 titles 1990; expects 6 titles 1991, 8 titles 1992. 3 titles listed in the *Small Press Record of Books in Print* (20th Edition, 1991-92). avg. price, paper: $5.95. Discounts: send inquiry. 150pp; 8½×11. Reporting time: 30 days.

Payment: 20% on accepted works. Copyrights for author.

RESEARCH IN HIGHER EDUCATION, Plenum Publishing Corporation, Charles F. Elton, 233 Spring Street, New York, NY 10013, (212) 741-3087. 1973. Articles, non-fiction. *"Research in Higher Education* is directed to those concerned with the functioning of post-secondary educational institutions, including two-year and four-year colleges, universities, and graduate and professional schools. It is of primary interest to institutional researchers and planners, faculty, college and university administrators, student personnel specialists and behavioral scientists. All correspondence concerning subscriptions should be addressed to: Research in Higher Education, Fulfillment Dept., Agathon Press, Inc., 49 Sheridan Ave., Albany, NY 12210. All editorial correspondence should be addressed to the Editor, Charles F. Elton, Dept. of Higher Education, 111 Dickey Hall, University of Kentucky, Lexington, KY 40506'' circ. 1.1M. 8/yr. Pub'd 8 issues 1990; expects 8 issues 1991, 8 issues 1992. sub. price: indiv. $50, instit. $100; per copy: $14. Back issues: 1973-87 (Vols. 1-27, 4 issues ea.), $50 per vol. Discounts: 10% discount to subscription agents. 112pp; 6½×9½; of. Reporting time: 3 months. Payment: none. Copyrighted, does not revert to author. Ads: $225/$140. COSMEP.

Re/Search Publications (see also RE/SEARCH), V. Vale, Andrea Juno, 20 Romolo, Suite B, San Francisco, CA 94133, 415-362-1465. 1977. Fiction, articles, art, photos, cartoons, interviews, criticism, music, collages, non-fiction. "No unsolicited submissions, please! Write first." avg. press run 5M. Pub'd 3 titles 1990; expects 3 titles 1991, 3 titles 1992. 7 titles listed in the *Small Press Record of Books in Print* (20th Edition, 1991-92). avg. price, cloth: $50; paper: $18. Dist. by SUBCO, PO Box 10233, Eugene, OR 97440. 200+pp; 8½×11; of. Reporting time: 3 weeks. Copyrights for author.

Resolution Business Press, John Spilker, 11101 N.E. Eighth Street, #208, Bellevue, WA 98004, 206-455-4611. 1987. Articles, non-fiction. "Computer books. We have just published *Northwest High Tech 1991: A Guide to North America's Fastest Growing Computer Region, Northwest Computer Jobs 1991* and *Northwest High Tech 1991 Database"* avg. press run 3M. Pub'd 1 title 1990; expects 3 titles 1991, 4 titles 1992. 3 titles listed in the *Small Press Record of Books in Print* (20th Edition, 1991-92). avg. price, paper: $24.95; other: $69.95 disk package. Discounts: 40%. 448pp; 5½×8½; of. Reporting time: 2-3 months. Payment: varies. Copyrights for author. NW Booksellers, Book Publishers Northwest.

RESOLVE NEWSLETTER, World Wildlife Fund & The Conservation Foundation, Gail Bingham, 1250 24th Street, NW, Washington, DC 20037, 202-293-4800. 1948. Articles, non-fiction. "A newsletter about environmental dispute resolution. In addition to a lead article, the newsletter provides updates on mediation efforts and references to new literature. Complimentary subscriptions are available by writing to the editor, *Resolve,* World Wildlife Fund & The Conservation Foundation" circ. 6M. 4/yr. Pub'd 2 issues 1990; expects 4 issues 1991, 4 issues 1992. sub. price: free; per copy: free; sample: free. Back issues: free. 16pp; 9×12; of. Copyrighted. Pub's reviews: 5 in 1990. §Mediation, alternative dispute resolution, environmental disputes.

RESONANCE, Judy Wall, PO Box 69, Sumterville, FL 33585, (904) 793-8748. 1985. Articles, photos, cartoons, interviews, criticism, reviews, letters, news items, non-fiction. "The purpose of *Resonance* is to review the scientific literature in the field of bioelectromagnetics; that is, the interaction between electric and/or magnetic fields and living organisms. Camera-ready copy—1-12 pages, single spaced, *include references.* Topics may focus on medical applications; zoological adaptations; natural and artificial radiation; biological, physical and chemical structures involved. Original research or reviews of books or articles accepted. As a science-oriented journal, I use materials that frequently cite references. I published a supplemental issue that consists entirely of a listing of 200 books and articles in the field of bioelectromagnetics." circ. 100. 4/yr. Pub'd 4 issues 1990; expects 4 issues 1991, 4 issues 1992. sub. price: $8; per copy: $2; sample: $2. Back issues: price list available, usually $2 apiece. Discounts: 10% discount if ordering entire set of back issues. 24pp; 5½×8½; †copy machine. Reporting time: 2 weeks to 2 months. Payment: 1-10 copies depending on length of article. Copyrighted, reverts to author. Pub's reviews: 6 in 1990. §Bioelectromagnetics—scientific literature in the field. Ads: $25/$15/$10 1/3 page/$5 1/4.

RESONANCE, Evan T. Pritchard, PO Box 215, Beacon, NY 12508, 914-838-1217. 1986. Poetry, fiction, articles, art, photos, cartoons, interviews, satire, reviews, letters, non-fiction. "Length is variable, 1200 words preferred for articles and stories. Looking for articles/poems that either go into depth on one subject, or inter-relate several areas not usually linked. We seek the personal and the universal, unique yet accessible. Recent contributors: Coleman Barks, Aron Gandhi, Pete Seeger, Cris Williamson, Madeleine L'Engle (interviews). Also Ariel Tomioka, Susan Hanniford Crowley, Robert Bucher" circ. 2M. 3/yr. Pub'd 3 issues 1990; expects 3 issues 1991, 3 issues 1992. sub. price: $10; per copy: $3; sample: $3. Back issues: $2. Discounts: $1 each for 10 plus postage. 52pp; 8½×11; of. Reporting time: 6-8 weeks. Payment: 1 copy. Not copyrighted. Pub's reviews: 10+ in 1990. §Self-help, philosophy, religion (inter-denom), New Age. Ads: $200/$100/$50 1/4 page/$25 business card. CCLM.

Resource Publications, Inc. (see also MODERN LITURGY), William Burns, Publisher; Kenneth Guentert, Editorial Director, 160 East Virginia Street #290, San Jose, CA 95112, 408-286-8505. 1973. Poetry, fiction, articles, art, photos, cartoons, interviews, criticism, reviews, music, letters, plays, concrete art, news items. "Interested primarily in imaginative resources for worship, counseling, ministry, and education. In-house graphics and typography." avg. press run 2M-5M. Pub'd 20 titles 1990; expects 18 titles 1991, 18 titles 1992. 105 titles listed in the *Small Press Record of Books in Print* (20th Edition, 1991-92). avg. price, cloth: $14.95; paper: $9.95. Discounts: standard trade. 120pp; 5½×8½ to 8½×11; of. Reporting time: 8 weeks. Payment: editorial fee or royalty on sales. Copyrights for author. COSMEP, CPA, NPM, NCGA, CBA, IFRAA, CPCA, NPHA.

RESOURCE-MAG, FOR PUBLISHING PROFESSIONALS, Lynn McFadgen, 20 Tettenhall Road, Etobicoke, Ontario M9A 2C3, Canada, 416-231-7796. 1982. Articles, interviews, reviews. "A professional development newsletter for the magazine and newsletter industry in Canada and the U.S. Focuses on marketing (circulation, direct marketing, advertising, sales, promotion) topics with additional coverage on editorial, management and design." 10/yr. Pub'd 10 issues 1990; expects 10 issues 1991, 10 issues 1992. sub. price: $56; per copy: $6; sample: same. Back issues: 3 for $15. 8pp; 8½×11; of. Reporting time: 2 weeks. Payment: upon request. Copyrighted, reverts to author. Pub's reviews: 20 in 1990. §Publishing, journalism, direct mail, marketing, advertising, editing.

RESOURCES FOR FEMINIST RESEARCH/DOCUMENTATION SUR LA RECHERCHE FEMIN-ISTE, J. Wine, Editor; Melanie Randall, Editor; Mary Louise Adams, Editor; Philinda Masters, Editor, 252 Bloor Street W., Toronto, Ontario M5S 1V6, Canada, 416-923-6641, ext. 2278. 1972. Articles, interviews, reviews, news items, non-fiction. "Documentation sur la recherche feministe/abstracts, articles, bibliographies, resource guides. Thematic issues regularly. Bilingual (English and French)" circ. 1.2M. 4/yr. Pub'd 4 issues 1990; expects 4 issues 1991, 4 issues 1992. sub. price: $25 Canadian, $40 foreign, $50 institution (Canada), $65 institution (outside Canada); per copy: $6.50 individual; $10 institution; sample: free to institutions and libraries. Back issues: individuals: $6.50 each, $25 volume, $40 outside Canada/vol; institutions: $10 each, $50 vol./Canada, $65 outside Canada. Discounts: write for details. 80-100pp; 8½×11; †of. Reporting time: 8-16 weeks (mostly we solicit). Payment: none. Copyrighted, joint rights. Pub's reviews: 125 in 1990. §Women's studies, feminist research. Ads: $200/$100/$50 1/4 page.

RESPONSE: A Contemporary Jewish Review, Paul Lerner, 27 West 20th Street, 9th Floor, New York, NY 10011. 1966. Poetry, fiction, articles, art, photos, interviews, criticism, reviews, non-fiction. "Material: short stories up to 20 pages double-spaced. All material must have a Jewish theme." circ. 1.2M. 4/yr. Pub'd 1 issue 1990; expects 4 issues 1991, 4 issues 1992. sub. price: $16; per copy: $4. Back issues: $6. Discounts: distributor (DeBoer) 600 issues $2/issue. 96pp; 6×9. Reporting time: 8 weeks. Payment: 5 complimentary issues. Copyrighted, reverts to author. Pub's reviews. §Judaic studies, Jewish/Israeli history. Ads: $150/$90/$50 1/4 page, also exchanges.

Reunion Research, Tom Ninkovich, 3145 Geary Boulevard #14, San Francisco, CA 94118, 209-336-2345. 1981. Non-fiction. avg. press run 5M. Expects 2 titles 1991, 1 title 1992. 1 title listed in the *Small Press Record of Books in Print* (20th Edition, 1991-92). avg. price, paper: $13. Discounts: 3-8 books 20%, 9-25 books 40%. 240pp; 5½×8½; of.

REVIEW LA BOOCHE, Gerald Dethrow, Michel Jabbour, Brendan Straubel, 110 South Ninth, Columbia, MO 65201, 874-9519. 1976. Poetry, fiction, art, parts-of-novels, collages. "We are not interested in genre material (erotica, sci-fi, etc.), but are open to most styles, forms and themes. Recent contributors: Tom McAfee, George Garret, William Stafford, Jack Driscoll" circ. 500. 2/yr. Expects 2 issues 1991, 2 issues 1992. sub. price: $6; per copy: $3.50; sample: free. Back issues: $3 (very limited supply). Discounts: our first new issue (fall '89) will be free. 98pp. Reporting time: 45 days. Payment: 3 copies, $100 to best story and poem in each issue. Copyrighted, reverts to author.

REVIEW. LATIN AMERICAN LITERATURE & ARTS, Americas Society, Alfred Mac Adam, Editor; Daniel Shapiro, Managing & Poetry Editor, Americas Society, 680 Park Avenue, New York, NY 10021, 212-249-8950. 1968. Poetry, fiction, articles, art, interviews, criticism, reviews. "Latin American literature and arts." circ. 4.5M. 2/yr. Pub'd 2 issues 1990; expects 2 issues 1991, 2 issues 1992. sub. price: $14; per copy: $7; sample: free. Back issues: $6. Discounts: agency 15%. 88pp; 8½×11; lp. Reporting time: 4-6 weeks. Payment: $50 per review-translation, $100-$200 per article. Copyrighted, reverts to author. Pub's reviews: 30 in 1990. §Latin American literature in translation & interdisciplinary texts on Lat. Am. topics. Ads: $500/$300.

THE REVIEW OF CONTEMPORARY FICTION, Dalkey Archive Press, John O'Brien, Steven Moore, 5700 College Road, Lisle, IL 60532. 1980. Articles, interviews, criticism, reviews. "First twenty issues devoted to Gilbert Sorrentino, Paul Metcalf, Hubert Selby, Douglas Woolf, Wallace Markfield, William Gaddis, Coleman Dowell, Nicholas Mosley, Paul Bowles, William Eastlake, Aidan Higgins, Jack Kerouac, Robert Pinget, Julio Cortazar, John Hawkes, William S. Burroughs, Ishmael Reed, Juan Goytisolo, Camilo Jose Cela, Charles Bukowski. Recent contributors: Gilbert Sorrentino, Robert Creeley, William S. Burroughs, Carlos Fuentes, Paul Metcalf, Edward Dorn, Edmund White, Thom Gunn, Luisa Valenzuela, Juan Goytisolo, Samuel

Beckett, Gabriel Garcia Marquez." circ. 3.5M. 3/yr. Pub'd 3 issues 1990; expects 3 issues 1991, 3 issues 1992. sub. price: $15 indiv., $22 instit.; per copy: $8; sample: $8. Back issues: $30 back volumes. Discounts: 10% to agencies; 50% to bookstores when paid in advance. 240pp; 6×9; of. Reporting time: 2 weeks. Payment: copy. Copyrighted, reverts to author. Pub's reviews: 75 in 1990. §Fiction, criticism. Ads: $150/exchange. COSMEP, CCLM.

REVIEWS UNLIMITED, Rikki Leeson, Rikki Leeson, PO Box 581, Seattle, WA 98111. 1990. Reviews. "There are no annual subscriptions yes, yet, but this could change in the near future. Usually available on an issue-by-issue basis. Comics are my main interest, then fiction and non-fiction, poetry, and music. Zines, books, tapes and records may be submitted for review" circ. varies. 6-12/yr. Pub'd 6 issues 1990; expects 12 issues 1991, 12 issues 1992. price per copy: $1.50; sample: $1.50. Back issues: inquire. Discounts: inquire. 24pp; size currently 10×4¼, hopefully 8½×11 soon; photocopy, possibly offset soon. Copyrighted, reverts to author. Pub's reviews: about 150 in 1990. §Comics, art, music, fiction, non-fiction, poetry. Ads: inquire as to current rates.

REVUE CELFAN REVIEW, CELFAN Editions Monographs, Eric Sellin, Editor, Department of French and Italian, Tulane University, New Orleans, LA 70118. 1981. Articles, interviews, criticism, reviews. "Publishes only material pertaining to French-language literature of Northern Africa" circ. 150. 3/yr. Pub'd 3 issues 1990; expects 3 issues 1991, 3 issues 1992. sub. price: $7.50 for US and Canada, $10 elsewhere; per copy: $4.00. Back issues: prices on request. Discounts: on request for agencies. 40pp; 4½×7½; of. Reporting time: 1 month. Payment: copies only. Copyrighted, rights remain with journal, permissions on request. Pub's reviews: 20 in 1990. §French-language literature of Northern Africa and criticism of same. Occasional exchange ad, please query. Council of Editors of Learned Journals (CELJ).

RFD, Short Mountain Collective, PO Box 68, Liberty, TN 37095, 615-536-5176. 1974. Poetry, fiction, articles, art, photos, cartoons, interviews, reviews, letters, news items, non-fiction. "RFD is a country journal by gay men, for gay men. Any material relevant to building our community is considered." circ. 2.5M. 4/yr. Pub'd 4 issues 1990; expects 4 issues 1991, 4 issues 1992. sub. price: $18 2nd Class mailing, $25 1st Class, $20 foreign; per copy: $5.50; sample: $5. Back issues: $2 each when available over 1 year old. Discounts: bookstores 40%. 70pp; 8½×11; of. Reporting time: 3 months minimum. Payment: 1 copy of the issue in which their work appears. Not copyrighted. Pub's reviews: 33 in 1990. §Country concerns, spiritual realities, gay men, poetry, alternatives (new age). Ads: $350/$175. CCLM, COSMEP, GLPA, IGLA.

RGM Publications, Delores Valdez, PO Box 2432, Key West, FL 33045-2432, 305-294-5710; 296-0809. 1984. Reviews, non-fiction. "RGM Publications specializes in motion picture/entertainment subjects. Biographies of celebrities or star profiles, movie tie-ins are also considered. Anything to do with film, television, radio, music, or entertainment in general" avg. press run 10M-15M. Pub'd 1 title 1990; expects 1 title 1991, 4 titles 1992. 5 titles listed in the *Small Press Record of Books in Print* (20th Edition, 1991-92). avg. price, paper: $12.95. 160pp; 8½×11; of. Reporting time: 10 business days. Payment: advance plus 8% royalty off net sales for 1st 15,000 copies sold. Copyrights for author. Publisher's Marketing Association (PMA), 2401 Pacific Coast Highway, Hermosa Beach, CA 90254.

Rhapsody International (see also METAPHOR), 109 Minna Street, Suite 153, San Francisco, CA 94105.

RHETORICA: A Journal of the History of Rhetoric, University of California Press, Michael Leff, Univ of California Press, 2120 Berkeley Way, Berkeley, CA 94720, 415-642-4191. "Publication of and copyrighted by the International Society for the History of Rhetoric. Editorial address: Department of Communication Studies, Northwestern Univ., 1815 Chicago Ave, Evanston, IL 60208-1340." circ. 900. 4/yr. Pub'd 1 issue 1990; expects 4 issues 1991, 4 issues 1992. sub. price: $30 indiv., $50 instit., $15 students; per copy: $7.50 indiv., $12.50 instit., $7.50 students; sample: free. Back issues: same as single copy price. Discounts: foreign subs. agents 10%, one-time orders 10+ 30%, standing orders (bookstores): 1-99 40%, 100+ 50%. 112pp; 6×9; of. Reporting time: 2 months. Payment: none. Copyrighted, does not revert to author. Ads: $200/$120.

The Rheumatoid Disease Foundation, 5706 Old Harding Road, Franklin, TN 37064, 615-646-1030. 5 titles listed in the *Small Press Record of Books in Print* (20th Edition, 1991-92).

Rhiannon Press, Peg Carlson Lauber, 1105 Bradley Avenue, Eau Claire, WI 54701, 715-835-0598. 1977. Poetry, long-poems. "Concentration on midwest women's poetry. Line up chapbook authors on my own." avg. press run 200-250. Pub'd 1 title 1990; expects 1 title 1991, 1 title 1992. 6 titles listed in the *Small Press Record of Books in Print* (20th Edition, 1991-92). avg. price, paper: $5. 25-35pp; 5½×8½; of. Payment: copies of work or percentage of copies. Copyrights for author. COSMEP.

RHINO, Kay Meier, Co-Editor; Martha M. Vertreace, Co-Editor, c/o Kay Meier, 8403 West Normal Avenue, Niles, IL 60648. 1976. Poetry. "Additional address: Martha Vertreace, 1157 E. 56th Street, Chicago, IL 60637. We're looking for excellent poetry and one short story (not over 10 pages) well-crafted with fresh insights. Please supply SASE. We print on high-quality paper. Please submit material between Jan 1 and May 31." circ. 500. 1/yr. Pub'd 1 issue 1990. sub. price: $5; per copy: $5; sample: $5 + 90¢ p/h. Back issues: $3 + 90¢ p/h.

96pp; 5½×8½; of. Reporting time: 2 months. Payment: 1 contributor's copy. Copyrighted, reverts to author.

RHODODENDRON, Steven Jacobsen, Guerilla Poetics, Inc., 879 Bell Street, East Palo Alto, CA 94303. 1984. Poetry, fiction, criticism, reviews, parts-of-novels, long-poems. "Biases: we do not generally use confessional, first-person oatmeal writing. Nor do we publish well-polished, professionally crafted examples of the Anonymous American Voice. We *do* use material which is truthful to its own vision, regardless of style or technique. Recent contributors: Steve Richmond, Douglas Goodwin, Wanda Coleman, Joseph Pjerrou." circ. 500. 4/yr. Pub'd 1 issue 1990; expects 4 issues 1991, 4 issues 1992. sub. price: $15; per copy: $3.50; sample: $2.50. Back issues: $2.50. Discounts: none. 40+pp; 8½×5½; photo. Reporting time: 3 months maximum. Payment: 3 copies. Copyrighted, reverts to author. Pub's reviews: 26 in 1990. §Poetry, fiction, short-shorts, prose poems, novels, small presses. Ads: $100/$50. The Al Vasco Revolution.

RHYME TIME POETRY NEWSLETTER, Hutton Publications, Linda Hutton, PO Box 1870, Hayden, ID 83835, 208-772-6184. 1981. Poetry. "We prefer traditional rhymed poetry up to 16 lines, without pen names." circ. 200. 6/yr. Pub'd 6 issues 1990; expects 6 issues 1991. sub. price: $7.50; per copy: $1.25; sample: free for SASE (2 stamps). 6-8pp; 8½×11; of. Reporting time: 1 month. Payment: one publication copy. Copyrighted, reverts to author.

JEAN RHYS REVIEW, Nora Gaines, Box 568 Havemeyer Hall, Columbia University, New York, NY 10027, 212-854-2929. 1986. Criticism, reviews. circ. 65. 2/yr. Pub'd 2 issues 1990; expects 2 issues 1991, 2 issues 1992. sub. price: $14 indiv., $20 inst.; per copy: $8.50; sample: $8.50. Back issues: $10. Discounts: 30%. 45pp; 8½×11; †MacIntosh Computer. Reporting time: 6 weeks. Payment: complementary 1-year subscription. Copyrighted. Pub's reviews: one in 1990. §Jean Rhys studies, literary modernism, Commonwealth literature (West Indian), European/Commonwealth literature between 1915-1970, particularly women authors. MLA, CELJ.

THE RIALTO, Michael Mackmin, John Wakeman, 32 Grosvenor Road, Norwich, Norfolk, NR2 2PZ, England. 1984. Poetry. circ. 3M. 3/yr. Pub'd 3 issues 1990; expects 3 issues 1991, 3 issues 1992. sub. price: $24; per copy: $8.50; sample: $8.50. Back issues: $8.50. Discounts: U.K. trade at 1/3 off, other enquiries welcome. 48pp; size A4; of. Reporting time: up to 12 weeks. Payment: £5 sterling per poem. Copyrighted, reverts to author.

RIDGE REVIEW, Ridge Times Press, Jim Tarbell, Judith Tarbell, Lucie Marshall, Box 90, Mendocino, CA 95460, 707-964-8465. 1981. Poetry, fiction, articles, art, photos, cartoons, interviews, satire, criticism, reviews, music, letters, parts-of-novels, long-poems, collages, plays, concrete art, news items, non-fiction. "We would like to hold articles to 1.5M words. We are involved with an in-depth inspection of life on the Northern California Coastal Ridges and dedicate a large portion of each issue to one aspect of that life. Recent themes include sheep, horticulture, intentional communities, marijuana, timber, fishing, tourism, politics, land use, crafts, health, water, work and agriculture. Future issues will look at sports cultures, global view from the Ridges, fairs." circ. 3.5M. 4/yr. Pub'd 4 issues 1990; expects 4 issues 1991, 4 issues 1992. sub. price: $10; per copy: $3; sample: $3 for writers. Back issues: $1.80 each. Discounts: 40% off on bulk sales over 10. 64pp; 7×10; †of, lp. Reporting time: 2 months. Payment: $15. Copyrighted, reverts to author. Pub's reviews: 16 in 1990. §Locally published books & books on theme of issue. Ads: $330/$179/$88 1/4 page. COSMEP.

Ridge Row Press, Richard W. Rousseau, 10 South Main Street, Montrose, PA 18801, 717-278-1141. 1981. Non-fiction. "Editorial Office: University of Scranton, Scranton, PA 18510" avg. press run 500-1M. Pub'd 1 title 1990; expects 2 titles 1991. 7 titles listed in the *Small Press Record of Books in Print* (20th Edition, 1991-92). avg. price, paper: $17. Discounts: 1-5 books 20%, 6 books or more 30%. 225pp; 5½×8½; †of. Reporting time: brief. Payment: standard.

Ridge Times Press (see also RIDGE REVIEW), Jim Tarbell, Judy Tarbell, Box 90, Mendocino, CA 95460, 707-964-8465. 1981. "We are not currently accepting new titles." avg. press run 3.5M. 4 titles listed in the *Small Press Record of Books in Print* (20th Edition, 1991-92). avg. price, paper: $3. Discounts: 40% off cover price. 160pp; 7×10 for magazine; †of, lp. Reporting time: 2 months. Payment: $15 + 2 copies. Copyrights negotiable. COSMEP.

Ridgeway Press, M.L. Liebler, PO Box 120, Roseville, MI 48066. 1973. avg. press run 200-250. Pub'd 3 titles 1990; expects 10 titles 1991, 5 titles 1992. 7 titles listed in the *Small Press Record of Books in Print* (20th Edition, 1991-92). avg. price, paper: $3. 30-40pp; 5½×7½. Reporting time: up to 6 months. Payment: authors get 50 copies of book. Does not copyright for author.

Riegel Publishing, Martin Riegel, PO Box 3241, San Clemente, CA 92674, 714-498-5732. 1987. Non-fiction. avg. press run 500. Pub'd 8 titles 1990; expects 6 titles 1991, 10 titles 1992. 4 titles listed in the *Small Press Record of Books in Print* (20th Edition, 1991-92). avg. price, cloth: $12; paper: $8. Discounts: libraries 25%, bookstores: less than 4 copies 20%, 4-9 40%, 10+ 50%. 100pp; 5½×8½; of. Reporting time: 30 days. Payment: varies. Copyrights for author.

Right Here Publications (see also WRITE NOW!), Emily Jean Carroll, PO Box 1014, Huntington, IN 46750, 219-356-4223. 1984. Poetry. "Poetry anthologies, humor, cooking, self-help, how-to books." avg. press run 1M. Pub'd 2 titles 1990; expects 1 title 1991. 2 titles listed in the *Small Press Record of Books in Print* (20th Edition, 1991-92). avg. price, paper: $4.95. Discounts: please inquire. 58pp; 5½x8½; of. Reporting time: 2-3 months. Payment: varies. Copyrights for author.

RIGHTING WORDS—THE JOURNAL OF LANGUAGE AND EDITING, Michael S. Ward, Freedonna Communications, Drawer 9808, Knoxville, TN 37940. 1986. Articles, art, photos, cartoons, interviews, criticism, reviews, letters, news items. "Articles of about 3,000 words, well-written (without footnotes and professorial lingo) for audience of copy editors, book and magazine editors, and teachers of English and journalism—as well as language hobbyists. Practical advice and information on editing and language always welcome. Contributors include Willard Espy and Rudolf Flesch. Free-lance submissions are welcome" 4/yr. Pub'd 6 issues 1990; expects 4 issues 1991, 4 issues 1992. sub. price: $24; per copy: $5.95; sample: $5. Back issues: $6.50 plus $1 postage and handling. 52pp; 6⅞x9½; web, perfect bound. Reporting time: report only on accepted ms. Payment: have not been less than $50. Copyrighted, reverts to author. Pub's reviews: 20 in 1990. §Language, usage, editing, reference works, language history.

The Rights' Press, Joe Duval, PO Box 555, Coalinga, CA 93210, (209) 935-3772. 1986. Satire, criticism, non-fiction. "Submissions must show the relationship between contemporary social, political, economic problems and the U.S. revolutionary ideology as set forth in the Declaration of Independence. (All are created with equal, inalienable rights; the purpose of government is to secure individual rights; and the people have the right to change their government). Under 45,000 words" avg. press run 2M. Pub'd 1 title 1990; expects 2 titles 1991, 3 titles 1992. avg. price, paper: $8.00. Discounts: on request. 120pp; 5½x8-12; of. Reporting time: 90 days. Payment: open. Prefer not to copyright for author.

Roberts Rinehart, Inc. Publishers, Frederick R. Rinehart, President, PO Box 666, Niwot, CO 80544-0666. 1984. Non-fiction. "Roberts Rinehart publishes in two general categories: natural history for children and adults, and specialized limited editions. We do not publish fiction or poetry" avg. press run 5M. Pub'd 5 titles 1990; expects 6 titles 1991, 6 titles 1992. 13 titles listed in the *Small Press Record of Books in Print* (20th Edition, 1991-92). avg. price, cloth: $15; paper: $6.95. Discounts: trade 1-49 copies 40%; 50-99 copies 45%; 100+ 50%. 200pp; 6x9; of. Reporting time: 1 week. Payment: escalating 5% of net to 20%. Copyrights for author.

Rio Grande Press (see also EDITOR'S DIGEST; SE LA VIE WRITER'S JOURNAL), Rosalie Avara, Editor, Publisher, PO Box 371371, El Paso, TX 79937, 915-595-2625. 1989. Poetry, fiction, articles, art, cartoons, interviews, satire, criticism, reviews, letters, plays, news items, non-fiction. "We plan to publish chapbooks, and have published several poetry anthologies." avg. press run 150. Pub'd 9 titles 1990; expects 11 titles 1991, 12 titles 1992. 4 titles listed in the *Small Press Record of Books in Print* (20th Edition, 1991-92). avg. price, paper: $4, $5 foreign (US funds); other: $4.95, $5.95 foreign (US funds) for anthologies. 70pp; 5½x8½; photocopied, saddle stapled. Reporting time: 6-8 weeks. Payment: expect to pay $5-$25 on contests; 1 copy on articles, cartoons. Copyrights for author. El Paso Writer's League, TX Freelance Writers Assoc., El Paso MS Club.

RIP OFF COMIX, Kathe Todd, Gilbert Shelton, PO Box 4686, Auburn, CA 95604, 916-885-8183. 1977. Art, cartoons. "We prefer comic art stories 1-6 pages in length, compatible with vertical magazine format, black-and-white line art. Pieces are usually humorous, adult-'underground' oriented, anti-establishment slant. Contributors include Gilbert Shelton, Larry Todd, Trina Robbins, Spain Rodriguez and other 'underground' cartoonists." circ. 5M. 4/yr. Pub'd 4 issues 1990; expects 4 issues 1991, 4 issues 1992. price per copy: $3.50 add $1.25 p/h, CA add 6% sales tax; sample: same. Back issues: issues 14-20, 22 $2.95 plus p/h. Discounts: wholesalers (for resale to stores) 62% full case, 60% reg. (off cover). Store 40% off cover w/minimum order. Write for details. 52pp; 8¼x10¾; of. Reporting time: within 1 month; for best results enclose SASE. Payment: advance $75/pg (new), $50/pg (reprint); against a page credit royalty on copies sold. Copyrighted, we buy 1-time pub. rights only.

RIPPLES, Shining Waters Press, Karen Schaefer, Editor; Jim Schaefer, Publisher, 1426 Las Vegas, Ann Arbor, MI 48103. 1973. Poetry, fiction, reviews, long-poems, news items. "Unique publishing venture for developing poet and short fiction writer. Interested in natural, organic images of daily life around the perceiver. We will now publish reviews of unpublished works, including novels, novellas, plays, screenplays, send clear photocopies of work(s), with sufficient SASE and any additional background info, plus name, address, phone number so publishers can contact you. Also send 5 X 7 B/W glossy photo and short biography" circ. 1M. 4/yr. Expects 4 issues 1991. sub. price: $18.50; per copy: $4.75 plus SASE; sample: $4.75. Back issues: variable. Pages vary; 8½x11; of. Reporting time: 1 week. Payment: copy. Copyrighted, reverts to author. Pub's reviews: 10-12 in 1990. §Poetry, fiction, drama, novels. Ads: $40. CCLM, COSMEP.

RISING STAR, Scott E. Green, Star/Sword Publications, 47 Byledge Road, Manchester, NH 03104,

603-623-9796. 1980. Articles, reviews. "Basically I do a newsletter on markets for writers and artists in sf/fantasy/horror markets. All checks to be made out to Scott E. Green." circ. 150. 6/yr. Pub'd 6 issues 1990; expects 6 issues 1991, 6 issues 1992. sub. price: $7.50; per copy: $1.50; sample: same. Discounts: none. 3pp; 8½×11; mi. Reporting time: 3 weeks. Payment: $3 per piece. Not copyrighted. Pub's reviews: 8 in 1990. §Science fiction, fantasy, horror. Ads: $20/$12/$8 1/4 page.

Ritz Publishing, David A. Andersen, 202 West 5th Avenue, Ritzville, WA 99169-1722, 509-659-4336. 1990. Fiction, art, cartoons, parts-of-novels, non-fiction. "Short stories and novels about the Vietnam War experience" avg. press run 2M. Pub'd 1 title 1990; expects 1 title 1991, 1 title 1992. 1 title listed in the *Small Press Record of Books in Print* (20th Edition, 1991-92). avg. price, paper: $14. Discounts: distributors and bookstores nonstocked 35%, stocked 50%. 300pp; 5½×8½; of. Reporting time: 3 months. Payment: individual. Copyrights for author. PMA.

Rivelin Grapheme Press, Snowdon Barnett, The Annex Kennet House, 19 High Street, Hungerford, Berkshire RG17 0NL, England, 0488-83480. 1974. Poetry, long-poems. "Average length 52-84 pages. Recent books include poetry by Peter Redgrove, Elizabeth Bartlett, Nicki Jackowska, Alexis Lykiard, Peter Finch, and Philip Callow. No biases" avg. press run 600. Pub'd 6 titles 1990; expects 4 titles 1991, 4 titles 1992. 19 titles listed in the *Small Press Record of Books in Print* (20th Edition, 1991-92). avg. price, cloth: £9.95; paper: £4.95. Discounts: 35% trade, 25% on single copies. 52-84pp; size A5; lp. Reporting time: 2 months. Payment: by arrangement, usually in free copies. Copyrights for author. ALP, IPD.

River Basin Publishing Co., Robert A. Buntz Jr., President, 403 Laurel Avenue, St Paul, MN 55102, 612-291-0980. 1979. avg. press run 5M. Pub'd 1 title 1990; expects 1 title 1991, 1 title 1992. 1 title listed in the *Small Press Record of Books in Print* (20th Edition, 1991-92). avg. price, cloth: $8.95; paper: $5.95. Discounts: trade 20%, distributors 40%. 152pp; 5½×8½. Payment: variable. Copyrights for author.

RIVER CITY, Sharon Bryan, Editor, Department of English, Memphis State University, Memphis, TN 38152, 901-454-4438. 1980. Poetry, fiction, articles, interviews. "*River City* publishes fiction, poetry, interviews, and essays. Please do not send unsolicited manuscripts during the summer." circ. 1M. 2/yr. Expects 2 issues 1991, 2 issues 1992. sub. price: $6 individuals, $7 organizatons; per copy: $4; sample: $4. 100pp; 6×9; of. Reporting time: 2 weeks to 3 months. Payment: 2 copies & annual $100 Hohenberg Award for the best poem or fiction selection; cash when grant funds are available. Copyrighted, reverts to author. Ads: $100/$50. CCLM.

RIVER STYX, Lee Schreiner, Editor-in-Chief; Anne T. Makeever, Managing Editor; Quincy Troupe, Senior Editor; Castro Michael, Senior Editor, #14 South Euclid, St. Louis, MO 63108, 314-361-0043. 1975. Poetry, fiction, art, photos, cartoons, interviews, long-poems. "*River Styx* is an award-winning multi-cultural publication of literature and art. Recent issues have featured Toni Morrison, Nicholas Christopher, John Pinderhughes, Anthony Barboza, Carolyn Forche, Margaret Atwood, Derek Walcott, Amiri Baraka, Ansel Adams, Grace Paley, Antonio Machado, Luisa Valenzuela, June Jordan, Allen Ginsberg, Ishmael Reed, Gary Snyder, Olga Broumas, and Howard Nemerov. Art/photography by Michael Kenna, Marilyn Hacker, Wendy Rose, Elsa Dorfman. Submissions only in September and October." circ. 3M. 3/yr. Pub'd 3 issues 1990; expects 3 issues 1991, 3 issues 1992. sub. price: $20 individuals, $28 institutions; per copy: $7; sample: $7. Back issues: complete set, issues 2-24: $225. Discounts: 33% to stores, 40% with orders of 10 or more. 90pp; 5½×8½; of. Reporting time: 2 months. Payment: contributor's copy + $8/page. Copyrighted, reverts to author. Ads: $175/$90. CLMP.

Rivercross Publishing, Inc., Josh Furman, 127 East 59th Street, New York, NY 10022, 421-1950. 1945. avg. press run 1M. Expects 12 titles 1991, 30 titles 1992. 15 titles listed in the *Small Press Record of Books in Print* (20th Edition, 1991-92). avg. price, cloth: $12; paper: $9. Discounts: 1-4 books 25%, 5-49 33%, 50-250 40%, 250-500 46%. of. Reporting time: write first for information. Copyrights for author.

RIVERRUN, Harvey Gordon, Editor, Glen Oaks Community College, 62249 Shimmel Road, Centreville, MI 49032-9719, 616-467-9945 ext. 277. 1974. Poetry. "All forms of poetry" circ. 600. 2/yr. Pub'd 2 issues 1990; expects 2 issues 1991, 2 issues 1992. price per copy: $3; sample: $3. 35-40pp; 8½×11. Reporting time: immediate acknowledgement (except during summer months). Payment: 2 copies per contributor. Not copyrighted.

Riverside Productions, Martha C. Riley, PO Box 26, Delphi, IN 46923, 317-564-6180. 1987. Music. "We publish musicdance education materials for use by teachers of elementary and junior high age children. Materials include booklets with accompanying audio or video cassettes, original musical compositions for children, and arrangements for Orff instruments (collections only)" Expects 3 titles 1991, 3 titles 1992. avg. price, paper: $8; other: $16-$35 mixed media. 20pp; 5×8. Payment: 15%. Copyrights for author. COSMEP.

RIVERSIDE QUARTERLY, Leland Sapiro, Redd Boggs, Fiction; Sheryl Smith, Poetry; Mary Emerson, Art, 807 Walters St #107, Lake Charles, LA 70605-4665, 318-477-7943. 1964. Poetry, fiction, articles, art, satire, criticism, reviews, letters. "*RQ* prints reviews, essays on all aspects of science-fiction and fantasy, but emphasis is on current scenes rather than, e.g., gothic horror or fantasy in the Gilded Age. Some recent titles: Marilyn House, "Miller's Anti-Utopian Vision: *A Canticle for Leibowitz*"; Dennis Kratz, "Heroism in Science Fiction: Two Opposing Views"; Justin Leiber, "Fritz Leiber: Swordsman and Philosopher". No maximum word length for essays or review, but fiction is restricted to 3.5M words. Contributors are urged to read several copies of the *RQ* (available at any major public or university library) before submitting MSS. Send fiction to: Box 1111, Berkeley, CA 94701; poetry to: 515 Saratoga, Santa Clara, CA 95050; art to: 2521 SW Williston Road, Gainesville, FL 32608." circ. 1.1M. Irregular. Pub'd 1 issue 1990; expects 2 issues 1991, 3 issues 1992. sub. price: $6, 4 issues; per copy: $2; sample: $2. Back issues: $2. Discounts: 20% on orders of 5 or more. 68pp; 8½×5½; of. Reporting time: 10 days. Payment: copies. Copyrighted, reverts to author. Pub's reviews: 4 in 1990. §Science-fiction and fantasy. Ads: traded or donated. CCLM.

RIVERWIND, Audrey Naffziger, Editor; C.A. Dubielak, Associate Editor, General Studies, Hocking Technical College, Nelsonville, OH 45764, 614-753-3591. 1977. Poetry, fiction, art, reviews. "Open to new and established writers. No biases, but experimental fiction will have a harder time gaining acceptance here. Story length: not to exceed 15 manuscript pages, double-spaced. On poetry: batches of 3-6, any subject, but typed. We tend to favor a lean style—on the order of a Wright or a Maxine Kumin—but are open to an occasional *Howl*. Recent contributors include Nate Leslie, Gerry Smith, Larry Smith, Ken Letko, Lee Martin, John Haines, John Aber and Catherine Hammond." circ. 1M. 1/yr. Pub'd 1 issue 1990; expects 1 issue 1991, 1 issue 1992. sub. price: $2.50; per copy: $2.50; sample: $1. Back issues: appropriate-sized SASE will suffice. 80pp; 6×9; of. Reporting time: 1-3 months. Payment: 2 copies. Copyrighted, reverts to author. Pub's reviews: 2 in 1990. §Contemporary American poetry and fiction. Ads: open. OATYC.

THE ROANOKE REVIEW, Robert R. Walter, English Department, Roanoke College, Salem, VA 24153, 703-375-2367. 1968. Poetry, fiction. "Poems to 100 lines, fiction to 2500 words. Recent contributors include Ken Pobo, Norman Russell, and Mary Balazs." circ. 200-300. 2/yr. Pub'd 2 issues 1990; expects 2 issues 1991, 2 issues 1992. sub. price: $5.50; per copy: $3; sample: $3. Back issues: $3. Discounts: $5 to libraries and agencies. 48-60pp; 6×9; †of. Reporting time: 8-10 weeks. Payment: 3 copies. Copyrighted, reverts but acknowledgement of original pub. demanded.

Robinson Press, Inc., Marvin Fries, Owner; Carolyn S. Thomas, Director of Publishing, 1137 Riverside Drive, Ft. Collins, CO 80524, 303-482-5393. 1909. Fiction, non-fiction. "We particularly feature historical texts, Western books especially. We also include health titles. Our newest book is a bilingual (Japanese/English) children's work." avg. press run 1M. Expects 2 titles 1991, 5 titles 1992. 21 titles listed in the *Small Press Record of Books in Print* (20th Edition, 1991-92). avg. price, cloth: $20-$80; paper: $7.95. Discounts: 3-9 books 15%, 10+ 20%. 120pp; 6×9. Payment: receive 15% of retail orders, 7½% wholesale, one payment annually. Copyrights for author. Rocky Mtn. BPA 755 Brook Road, Boulder, CO 80302, Mtns & Plains Booksellers.

Roblin Press, PO Box 152, Yonkers, NY 10710, 914-337-4576. 1979. Non-fiction. "Looking for non-fiction—primarily "how-to" and self-help type book manuscripts." avg. press run 25M. Pub'd 1 title 1990; expects 3 titles 1991, 6 titles 1992. 2 titles listed in the *Small Press Record of Books in Print* (20th Edition, 1991-92). avg. price, paper: $3.50. Discounts: 4-10 copies—25% discount; 10-499 copies—40%; 500+—50%. 96pp; 8½×11. Reporting time: 30 days. Payment: flexible, prefer outright purchase. Does not copyright for author.

THE ROCK HALL REPORTER, Art Edwards, Big 'O' Publications, PO Box 24124, Cleveland, OH 44124. 1988. Articles, photos, cartoons, interviews, criticism, reviews, music, letters, news items, non-fiction. "Most of our material covers the past, present, and future of Rock 'n' Roll, as well as the people, events, and activities surrounding the Rock 'n' Roll Hall of Fame and Museum in Cleveland, OH." 6/yr. Expects 6 issues 1992. sub. price: $10.20, $12.20 in Canada; per copy: $1.75; sample: same. Back issues: $2.50 per issue. Discounts: libraries 10%, wholesalers schedule available upon request. 10pp; 8½×11. Reporting time: 6 weeks. Payment: varies. Copyrighted, does not revert to author. Ads: write for information.

Rock Steady Press, Craig Stockfleth, 2750 Market Street #102, San Francisco, CA 94114, 415-255-4518. 1988. Poetry, fiction, art, photos, cartoons, satire, parts-of-novels, collages, plays. "The editor, himself disabled, has a natural bias towards submissions by disabled authors/artists. All others are encouraged to apply, however, and this bias should *not* be interpreted as editorial policy. All materials will be considered—if I like it, it will be considered all the more seriously. (Hint: I like non-traditional forms of the written word—prison writing, cyberpunk stuff, and white trash novels—and things visual, and that may be considered in other circles to be 'controversial'.)" avg. press run 500. Pub'd 1 title 1990; expects 1 title 1992. 1 title listed in the *Small Press Record of Books in Print* (20th Edition, 1991-92). avg. price, paper: $35. Discounts: 40% to trade. 169pp; 8×10; of. Reporting time: depends. Payment: depends. Author's responsible for copyrights.

Rockwell Publishing, Doris Rockwell Gottilly, 7905 Breda Court, Raleigh, NC 27606. 1986. "Publish books on dolls, paperdolls and teddy bears" Pub'd 1 title 1990; expects 2 titles 1991, 2 titles 1992. 2 titles listed in the

498

Small Press Record of Books in Print (20th Edition, 1991-92). avg. price, paper: $8.95. Discounts: 3 books up 40%, 200+ 50%. 50+pp; 8×11; of. Copyrights for author.

Rocky Mountain Writers Guild, Inc., James Hutchinson, Executive Director, 837 15th Street, Boulder, CO 80302-7623. 1967. avg. press run 9M. avg. price, paper: $4.95. Discounts: 50/40%. 4½×7½; contract typesetting & printing. Payment: 10%. Copyrights for author.

Rocky Top Publications, Emerson Bach, General Editor; Joseph Gooze, Science Editor, Div. of Rocky Top Supply, PO Box 33, Stamford, NY 12167. 1982. Non-fiction. "No unsolicited manuscripts. Our press specializes in environmental, medical, and scientific material, which is controversial. All material must be well-written and researched. Especially interested in the interaction between the three groups." avg. press run 500-1M. Pub'd 4 titles 1990; expects 10 titles 1991, 2 titles 1992. 9 titles listed in the *Small Press Record of Books in Print* (20th Edition, 1991-92). avg. price, paper: $16.95. Discounts: 40% over 10 (minimum purchase). 120pp; 8½×11; †of. Payment: variable. Copyrights for author. LMP, BIP, WM.

Rodmell Press, Linda Cogozzo, Donald Moyer, 2550 Shattuck Avenue, #18, Berkeley, CA 94704, 415-841-3123. 1988. "Contributors: Jean Couch, Mary Pullig Schatz (M.D.), Dona Holleman. Length of material: 50,000 to 100,000 words. Emphasis: Hatha Yoga as it relates to health and fitness from professionals in the field; development of spiritual practice in contemporary American society; women in Buddhism; Buddhist philosophy; yoga philosophy." avg. press run 8M. Pub'd 1 title 1990; expects 2 titles 1991, 2 titles 1992. 1 title listed in the *Small Press Record of Books in Print* (20th Edition, 1991-92). avg. price, paper: $17.95. Discounts: 1-9 30%, 10-49 40%, 50+ 42%. 225pp; 8×10. Reporting time: 3 months. Payment: 8% for first 5,000 paper; 10% thereafter. Copyrights for author. PMA, NAPRA, COSMEP.

Rolling House Publications, Fred Reyes, Editor-in-Chief, PO Box 3865, Berkeley, CA 94703-0865, 415-548-4228. 1985. Poetry, fiction, art, photos, satire, criticism, music. avg. press run 3M. Expects 2 titles 1991. 1 title listed in the *Small Press Record of Books in Print* (20th Edition, 1991-92). avg. price, cloth: $10.95; paper: $5.95; other: $19.95 (talking book set of 4 cassettes). Discounts: 2-4 10%, 5-9 30%, 10+ 40%. 130pp; 5½×8½; of. Reporting time: 60 days. Copyrights for author. Publishers Marketing Association (PMA), COSMEP, New Age Publishers & Retailers Alliance (NAPRA).

ROMANCE PHILOLOGY, University of California Press, Jerry R. Craddock, University of California Press, 2120 Berkeley Way, Berkeley, CA 94720, 415-642-4191. 1947. Reviews, non-fiction. "Editorial address: Dept. of French, University of California, Berkeley, CA 94720." circ. 1.1M. 4/yr. Pub'd 4 issues 1990; expects 4 issues 1991, 4 issues 1992. sub. price: $25 indiv., $50 instit., $13 students (+ $5 foreign postage); per copy: $7.50 indiv., $12 instit., $7.50 students; sample: free. Back issues: same as single copy price. Discounts: foreign subs. agent 10%, one-time orders 10+ 30%, standing orders (bookstores): 1-99 40%, 100+ 50%. 128pp; 6×9; †of. Reporting time: 2-3 months. Payment: none. Copyrighted, does not revert to author. §Romance languages and literature. Ads: $200/$120.

ROMANIAN REVIEW, George G. Potra, Piata Presei Libere 1, Bucharest, Romania, 173836. 1946. Poetry, fiction, articles, art, photos, cartoons, interviews, satire, criticism, reviews, music, letters, parts-of-novels, long-poems, plays, concrete art, news items, non-fiction. "The *Review* is published in French, English, German and Russian language editions." circ. 6M. 6/yr. Pub'd 6 issues 1990; expects 6 issues 1991, 12 issues 1992. sub. price: $13.98; per copy: $2.33; sample: free. 96pp; 17×24cm; lp. Reporting time: 1 month. Payment: royalties according to Romanian law. Copyrighted, reverts to author. Pub's reviews: 80 in 1990. §Romanian literature, arts, culture, science.

THE ROMANTIST, The F. Marion Crawford Memorial Society, John C. Moran, Founder, Editor; Steve Eng, Co-Editor; Jesse F. Knight, Co-Editor; Don Herron, Contributing Editor; Richard Dalby, Contributing Editor, Saracinesca House, 3610 Meadowbrook Avenue, Nashville, TN 37205. 1977. Poetry, articles, art, photos, interviews, criticism, reviews, letters, long-poems, collages. "H. Warner Munn, Donald Sidney-Fryer, Clark Ashton Smith, Robert E. Howard, George Sterling, and kindred authors. Purview is Modern Romanticism, especially Imaginative Literature (emphasis upon Fantasy); contains a regular section on F. Marion Crawford (1854-1909). Publishes mostly traditional (rhymed) poetry, but some "free verse". No fiction" circ. 300 (limited and numbered). 1/yr. Pub'd 1 issue 1990; expects 1 issue 1991, 1 issue 1992. price per copy: $12.50 incl postage. Back issues: $12.50 (#1, #2 and #3 out of print). Discounts: 20% to 40% depending upon quantity. 100-120pp; 8½×11; of, lp. Reporting time: within 1 month. Payment: 1 copy (at present). Copyrighted, does not revert to author, but we permit repub. elsewhere without charge on condition that acknowledgement of *The Romantist* be made. Pub's reviews: 9 in 1990. §Fantasy, horror, weird, supernatural fiction, Romanticism, etc. Ads: $50/$25/$15.

ROMEO NEWSLETTER, Robert Franklin, 120 Village Square, Suite 148, Orinda, CA 94563, 415-254-7409. 1991. Articles, art, photos, cartoons, interviews, satire, letters, news items. circ. 1.5M. 4/yr. Expects 4 issues 1991, 4 issues 1992. sub. price: $150; per copy: $50; sample: $50. Back issues: $50. Discounts: none. 14pp; 8½×11; of. Reporting time: 2 months. Payment: upon acceptance. Copyrighted, reverts to author. Ads: $300 1/2 page/classified $5/word. PMA.

Ronin Publishing, Inc., J. Sebastian Orfali, Publisher, Box 1035, Berkeley, CA 94701, 415-540-6278. 1983. Non-fiction. "No unsolicited material." avg. press run 5M-10M. Pub'd 6 titles 1990; expects 6 titles 1991, 10 titles 1992. 21 titles listed in the *Small Press Record of Books in Print* (20th Edition, 1991-92). avg. price, cloth: $19.95; paper: $9.95. Discounts: up to 100 40%, 101+ 50%. Pages vary; 6×9 usually; desktop publishing, repackaging. Payment: 10% net, some advances. Copyrights for author. NCBPA, ABA, COSMEP, PMA.

ROOM, John Perlman, 29 Lynton Place, White Plains, NY 10606-2818. 1987. Poetry. *"Room* publishes 2 (or 3) poets per issue. Some recent pairings include: Perlman/McInerney, Sternlieb/Giannini, Young/Eigner, DiPalma/Watson, Taggart/Harrison. *Room* is distributed gratis. Mss. not sought this year, but will be read beginning '89 (Fall). Copies on request when available." circ. 150. 2/yr. Pub'd 2 issues 1990; expects 2 issues 1991, 2 issues 1992. sub. price: gratis. Pages vary; 5½×8; lp, xerox. Reporting time: ASAP. Payment: copies. Not copyrighted.

ROOM OF ONE'S OWN, Growing Room Collective, PO Box 46160, Station G, Vancouver, British Columbia V6R 4G5, Canada, 604-327-1423. 1975. Poetry, fiction, art, photos, cartoons, interviews, reviews, parts-of-novels, long-poems, plays. "Good quality literary material by & about women, written from a feminist perspective. Payment in Canadian funds only" circ. 1.5M. 4/yr. Pub'd 4 issues 1990. sub. price: $15 ($20 foreign) indiv, $20 ($25 foreign) instit; per copy: $4; sample: $5. Back issues: depends on availablility — query issues wanted. Discounts: trade 30%, bulk-negotiable. 80pp; 5½×8½; of. Reporting time: 3 months. Payment: $50. Copyrighted, reverts to author. Pub's reviews: 10 in 1990. §Literature, women. Ads: $90/$50. CPPA.

Roscher House, Linda Bowman, PO Box 201390, Austin, TX 78720, (512) 258-2288. 1987. Non-fiction. "Non-fiction for specific audiences" avg. press run 5.5M. Pub'd 1 title 1990; expects 2 titles 1991, 2 titles 1992. 1 title listed in the *Small Press Record of Books in Print* (20th Edition, 1991-92). avg. price, cloth: $24.95; paper: $14.95. 200+pp; 6×9; of. Reporting time: varies, 1-3 months. Payment: 10% royalty. Copyrights for author.

Rose Publishing Co., Walter Nunn, 2723 Foxcroft Road, #208, Little Rock, AR 72207-6513, 501-372-1666. 1973. Art, photos, cartoons. "Primarily books of nonfiction about Arkansas. Typical titles are 150-250 pp, usually cloth or trade paperback." avg. press run 1M. Pub'd 7 titles 1990; expects 6 titles 1991, 6 titles 1992. 19 titles listed in the *Small Press Record of Books in Print* (20th Edition, 1991-92). avg. price, cloth: $14.95; paper: $9.95. Discounts: trade, 5-24 copies, 40%; classroom, 10% for college and public schools. 200pp; 5½×8½; of. Reporting time: 6 weeks. Payment: 10% of gross. Copyrights for author. COSMEP, ABA.

Martha Rosler (see also POSTCARD ART/POSTCARD FICTION), 143 McGuinness Blvd., Brooklyn, NY 11222. 1974. Fiction, art, photos. "So far all works have been serial postcard 'novels' and other fiction, written by myself." avg. press run 1M. Pub'd 1 title 1990; expects 1 title 1991, 1 title 1992. 5 titles listed in the *Small Press Record of Books in Print* (20th Edition, 1991-92). avg. price, paper: $5.00. 12pp; 4½×6; †of, mi. Does not copyright for author.

Ross Books, Elizabeth Yerkes, Box 4340, Berkeley, CA 94704, 415-841-2474. 1977. "Bicycle books, popular science, holography, how-to books in general" avg. press run 3.5M-10M. Pub'd 2 titles 1990; expects 4 titles 1991, 6 titles 1992. 19 titles listed in the *Small Press Record of Books in Print* (20th Edition, 1991-92). avg. price, cloth: $14.95; paper: $8.95. Discounts: 40% stores. 192pp; 6×9, 8½×11; of. Reporting time: 2 months. Payment: 8-10% of net price. Copyrights for author. NCBPA.

Rossi, B. Simon, PO Box 2001, Beverly Hills, CA 90213, 213-556-0337. 1979. "Interested in material on self-help, non-fiction, super creative ideas for books. Useful informative manuscripts on the human behaviors, personal experiences and life are welcome. Interesting guides on how-to and useful information are also of interest. Titles relating to health, nutrition, sports, fitness, well being and the human mind and body are appreciated. Topics such as personal computing, real estate, publishing, and investing, etc., may also be submitted." 1 title listed in the *Small Press Record of Books in Print* (20th Edition, 1991-92). avg. price, paper: $5. Discounts: 40% to recognized dealers. Special larger rates for quantity orders. Write for more info. *Orders are FOB Beverly Hills, Ca.* 100pp; 8½×5½; of. Reporting time: 3-5 weeks (return postage paid envelope must be included for return of material & quick response). Payment: negotiable. Copyrights for author.

THE ROTKIN REVIEW, Charles E. Rotkin, Editor, Publisher, RR 4, Peekskill, NY 10566-9804. 1985. Articles, interviews, reviews. "Reviews & direct marketing of books related to photographic, art and communication books. No unsolicited ms!" circ. 10M. 4/yr. Pub'd 4 issues 1990; expects 4 issues 1991, 4 issues 1992. sub. price: $25; per copy: $7.50; sample: free to libraries or photo, art & book buyers. Back issues: free, if available, with new subscription. Discounts: 10%. 36pp; 8½×11; computer typeset, offset print. Payment: yes, negotiable. Copyrighted, reverts to author. Pub's reviews: 150 in 1990. §Only photography, art, and communication. Ads: $1250/$850/$500 1/4 page/agency discount granted. ASPP, ASMP, NPPA, PAI, NPC, OPC, PACA.

THE ROUND TABLE: A Journal of Poetry and Fiction, Alan Lupack, Barbara Tepa Lupack, PO Box 18673, Rochester, NY 14618. 1984. Poetry, fiction. "We look for quality and craftsmanship rather than any particular form. We read poetry and fiction Nov 1 - June 30. In 1987 we adopted an annual format, combining poetry & fiction. In 1989, we did another issue of the theme of King Arthur & the Knights of the Round Table. In 1990 we returned to general poetry and fiction. Now we alternate Arthurian and general issues." circ. 125. 1/yr. Pub'd 1 issue 1990; expects 1 issue 1991, 1 issue 1992. sub. price: $12.50 for Arthurian issues; $7.50 for general; sample: $5; $12.50 for special Arthurian issue. Back issues: same. 64pp; 8½×5½; of. Reporting time: we try for 2 months, usually longer. Payment: 2 copies. Copyrighted, reverts to author.

Routledge, William Germano, 29 West 35th Street, New York, NY 10001. 1978. Poetry, fiction, criticism, non-fiction. Pub'd 600 titles 1990; expects 1,000 titles 1991, 1,000 titles 1992. avg. price, cloth: $30; paper: $15. Discounts: T=40%, short= 30%. 250pp.

Rowan Mountain Press (see also SISTERS IN CRIME BOOKS IN PRINT), PO Box 10111, Blacksburg, VA 24062-0111, 703-961-3315. 1988. Poetry, non-fiction. "Appalachian poetry and short stories. Manuscript submission by invitation. Recent authors: R. Franklin Pate, Jim Wayne Miller, Sharyn McCrumb, Bennie Lee Sinclair, Harry Dean." avg. press run 300. Pub'd 4 titles 1990; expects 3 titles 1991, 3 titles 1992. 7 titles listed in the *Small Press Record of Books in Print* (20th Edition, 1991-92). avg. price, paper: $6. Discounts: 2-4 copies 20%, 5+ 40%. 50pp; 5½×8½; of. Reporting time: invited manuscripts only. Payment: 10% of press run. Copyrights for author.

(ROWBOAT), Greg Bachar, Stephen Healey, Paul Dickinson, Eric Forst, c/o MFA Creative Writing Program, 452 Bartlett Hall, MA University, Amherst, MA 01003. 1990. Poetry, fiction, articles, art, photos, cartoons, interviews, satire, criticism, reviews, music, letters, parts-of-novels, long-poems, collages, concrete art, non-fiction. "Art: black and white xerox ready. Prose: 8 pages maximum. Poetry: any length. Reviews: brief, giving the reader a *sensation* of the thing reviewed...not just synopsis." circ. 300-600. 6-8/yr. Pub'd 3 issues 1990; expects 6 issues 1991, 8 issues 1992. sub. price: $5; per copy: $1; sample: free w/2 stamp SASE. Back issues: $1 with 2-stamp SASE. Discounts: none. 8-10pp; 8½×14; †mi, xerox. Reporting time: 1 month. Payment: copies. Copyrighted, reverts to author. Pub's reviews: 12 in 1990. §Poetry, fiction, art, music, modern culture, writers, surrealism, boating. Ads: $50/$25/$10 3x3" block.

Royal Publishing (see also SHARING IDEAS FOR PROFESSIONAL SPEAKERS), Dottie (C.S.P.) Walters, 18825 Hicrest Road, PO Box 1120, Glendora, CA 91740, 818-335-8069. 1974. 20 titles listed in the *Small Press Record of Books in Print* (20th Edition, 1991-92).

Royce Baker Publishing, Inc., Nancy Skinner, 953 Mountain View Drive, Suite 511, Lafayette, CA 94549.

RUBBERSTAMPMADNESS, Roberta Sperling, PO Box 6585, Ithaca, NY 14851-6585. 1980. Articles, art, photos, interviews, reviews, letters. circ. 6M. 6/yr. Pub'd 6 issues 1990; expects 6 issues 1991, 6 issues 1992. sub. price: $18 for 6 issues; per copy: $4; sample: $4. Back issues: $5. 56pp; 10¼×16; of. Payment: $50-$150 depending on size of article. Not copyrighted. Ads: $570/$360/$1.75 per word.

Ruddy Duck Press (see also ORO MADRE), Loss Glazier, 44 North Pearl Street #44, Buffalo, NY 14202-1422. 1980. Poetry, fiction, articles, art, photos, interviews, criticism, long-poems, non-fiction. "Ruddy Duck Press does not accept unsolicited manuscripts. Styles are encouraged which are innovative, crisp, and communicate through use of language and form as well as through narrative. Collections are sought which explore aspects of a themes that address a variety of people, i.e. themes that extend beyond the writer's immediate surroundings & events. They must exhibit a *controlled*, thought-out use of language, style, and form. Non-fiction works are also sought: travel pieces, jazz music topics, small press, literary criticism, and discussions of regional literatures are especially welcome. Be sure to query before sending material." avg. press run 500. Pub'd 4 titles 1990; expects 4 titles 1991, 4 titles 1992. 5 titles listed in the *Small Press Record of Books in Print* (20th Edition, 1991-92). avg. price, cloth: available upon request; paper: $3-$12; other: available upon request. Discounts: available upon request. 48pp; 5½×8½; of. Reporting time: query first, 4-6 weeks. Payment: copies. Copyrights for author.

THE RUGGING ROOM BULLETIN, Jeanne H. Fallier, Editor & Publisher, 10 Sawmill Drive, PO Box 824, Westford, MA 01886. "History, instruction, information on traditional American hooking, and coming events, etc." 4/yr. sub. price: $8.75 ($10 Canadian); per copy: $2.50; sample: free. Back issues: $3.50. 12pp; 8½×11. Reporting time: 3 weeks. Payment: extra copies. Copyrighted, reverts to author. Pub's reviews. §Fiber arts, color, mainly traditional hooking. Ads: $35 1/2 page/$20 1/4/classified $10.

Runaway Publications (see also THE PATRIOT), James L. Berkman, PO Box 1172, Ashland, OR 97520, 503-482-2578. 1977. Poetry, long-poems. "No unsolicited submissions. Neoconservative." avg. press run 400. Pub'd 1 title 1990; expects 1 title 1991, 1 title 1992. 8 titles listed in the *Small Press Record of Books in Print* (20th Edition, 1991-92). avg. price, paper: $10. Discounts: 50% for govt. agencies/federal employees. 30pp; 5½×8½; of. Payment: negotiable. Copyrights for author.

The Runaway Spoon Press, Bob Grumman, Box 3621, Port Charlotte, FL 33949-3621, 813-629-8045. 1987. Poetry, art, cartoons, satire, criticism, reviews, long-poems, collages, plays, non-fiction. "Additional address: 1708 Hayworth Road, Port Charlotte, FL 33952. First 3 contributors: Bob Grumman, G. Huth, Karl Kempton. Bias against overt political content; especially interested in visual poetry. Hope to print comic books. I consider myself eclectic—in favor of avant garde work with roots in tradition & traditional literature that's technically adventurous." avg. press run 100. Pub'd 11 titles 1990; expects 10 titles 1991, 10 titles 1992. 42 titles listed in the *Small Press Record of Books in Print* (20th Edition, 1991-92). avg. price, paper: $3. Discounts: 40% off for purchase of 5 or more copies of a book. 48pp; 5½×4¼; †xerox. Reporting time: 1 week. Payment: author gets 25% of first printing, 10% royalty thereafter. Copyrights for author.

Running Press, Nancy Steele, Editorial Director, 125 South Twenty-Second Street, Philadelphia, PA 19103, 215-567-5080. 1973. Non-fiction. "We publish mainly quality trade paperbacks. We publish a number of children's books, including *The Kid's Book of Secret Codes, Signals, and Ciphers*, *Night Sky*, and *Crystals*. We publish collections of literary classics: *The Unabridged Mark Twain*, *The Unabridged Edgar Allan Poe*, *Robert W. Service Best Tales of the Yukon*, and medical guide: *The Running Press Edition of the American Classic Gray's Anatomy*, *The Diabetic's Brandname Food Exchange Handbook*, *Nursing A Loved One At Home*. Our line of reference books covers a wide range of expertise and includes our glossary series on the specific languages of banking, accounting, real estate and such, as well as *The Computor Dictionary* and *The Graphic Designer's Handbook*, and directories such as *Religious Writer's Marketplace* and *The Software Writer's Marketplace*. Running Press will consider manuscripts on all subjects, and will return submissions if they are accompanied by a self-addressed stamped envelope." avg. press run 30M. Pub'd 66 titles 1990; expects 90 titles 1991, 100 titles 1992. 200 titles listed in the *Small Press Record of Books in Print* (20th Edition, 1991-92). avg. price, cloth: $19.95; paper: $12.95. Discounts: 1-4 20%, 5-24 40%, 25-49 42%, 50-99 43%, 100-249 44%, 250-599 45%; 600-1499 46%, 1500+ 47%, 50% wholesale. of. Reporting time: 1 month. Payment: negotiable. Copyrights for author. AAP, ABA.

Rural Arts Services (see also RADIUS/Resources for Local Arts), Ken Larsen, 1212 P Street, Sacramento, CA 95814-5808. 1979. "We publish periodicals only"

RURAL NETWORK ADVOCATE, Lois Fields, 6236 Borden Road, Boscobel, WI 53805. 1980. Poetry, articles, art, photos, cartoons, satire, criticism, reviews, letters, non-fiction. "All items published must come from members of Rural Network (a social support group for country-oriented single adults) or from subscribers to the *Rural Network Advocate*. All items published are original works." circ. 500. 12/yr. Pub'd 12 issues 1990; expects 12 issues 1991, 12 issues 1992. sub. price: $10; per copy: $1; sample: $1. Back issues: not available. Discounts: none. 8pp; 8½×11; of. Reporting time: 7 days. Payment: none. Copyrighted, does not revert to author. Pub's reviews: 2 in 1990. §Single life, homesteading, rural life, sustainable agriculture, cottage industry. Ads: none.

The Russian Writers' Club Publishing House, Yevgeny Lubin, PO Box 579, East Hanover, NJ 07936. 1980. Poetry, fiction, non-fiction. "Books in Russian language or translated from Russian into English" avg. press run 1M. Pub'd 3 titles 1990; expects 3 titles 1991, 4 titles 1992. 4 titles listed in the *Small Press Record of Books in Print* (20th Edition, 1991-92). avg. price, paper: $10. Discounts: 40%. 200pp; 5½×8½; of. Reporting time: 4 weeks. Payment: negotiable. Copyrights for author.

RYAN'S REVIEW, Telstar Publishing, Kathleen Lee Mendel, 7810 Bertha Avenue, Parma, OH 44129-3110. 1990. Poetry. "Entire publication is poetry by school age children under 16 years of age" circ. 125. 4/yr. Expects 3 issues 1991, 4 issues 1992. sub. price: $4; per copy: $1; sample: $1. Discounts: none. 40pp; 5½×8½; of. Reporting time: 1 month. Payment: none. Copyrighted, reverts to author. No ads.

The Rydal Press, Clark Kimball, Publisher-Editor, PO Box 2247, Santa Fe, NM 87504-2247, 505-983-1680. 1985. Poetry, fiction, articles, art, plays, non-fiction. "Original literature, including short stories, bibliographies, novels, essays relevant to New Mexico and/or the Southwest, suitable for signed, limited, slipcased letterpress editions which can be resold to trade houses later" avg. press run 250. Pub'd 1 title 1990; expects 1 title 1991, 1 title 1992. 3 titles listed in the *Small Press Record of Books in Print* (20th Edition, 1991-92). avg. price, cloth: $100. Discounts: 1 copy 10%, 2 or more 20%. 125pp; 6×9; lp. Reporting time: 1 month. Payment: negotiable, but including copies and royalties for reprint editions. Copyrights for author.

S

S & S Press, D. W. Skrabanek, Anne R. Souby, PO Box 5931, Austin, TX 78763-5931. 1978. Non-fiction. "We are dedicated to the pursuit of whatever strikes our fancy. ISBN 0-934646" avg. press run 250. Pub'd 6 titles 1990; expects 3 titles 1991, 3 titles 1992. 14 titles listed in the *Small Press Record of Books in Print* (20th Edition, 1991-92). avg. price, paper: $2 to $10. Discounts: trade 20-50%; libraries 20%. 20-110pp; 5×8, 8×11; †of. Reporting time: 4-6 weeks (SASE). Payment: varies, average 5-10%. Copyrights for author.

S.E.T. FREE: The Newsletter Against Television, Steve Wagner, Box 10491, Oakland, CA 94610, 415-763-8712. 1982. Articles, cartoons, letters, news items, non-fiction. "Short items about the electronic media and related items from an anti-television viewpoint. Alena Smith and Charles Frink are recent contributors." circ. 1.2M. 4/yr. Pub'd 4 issues 1990; expects 4 issues 1991, 4 issues 1992. sub. price: $5 for 10 issues; sample: free. Back issues: not available. 4pp; 8½×14; of. Reporting time: by return mail if SASE included. Payment: none. Not copyrighted. Pub's reviews: 3 in 1990. §Anything related to television, propaganda, and the media. Ads: none.

S.I.R.S. Caravan Publications, Saadi Neil Klotz, Editor; Danya Veltfont, Editor, 65 Norwich Street, San Francisco, CA 94110, 415-285-0562. 1972. Long-poems, non-fiction. "We publish primarily works of Eastern philosophy and Sufism, generated from several established authors and musicians. Books include *Sufi Vision & Initiation* and *The Jerusalem Trilogy* by Samuel L. Lewis (Sufi Ahmed Murad Chisti) and musical recordings of the Dances of Universal Peace and the Sufi Choir" avg. press run 2M. Pub'd 2 titles 1990; expects 2 titles 1991, 2 titles 1992. 4 titles listed in the *Small Press Record of Books in Print* (20th Edition, 1991-92). avg. price, paper: 9.95; other: music tapes, $9-$11. Discounts: 45% to trade for payment with order; 40% on account; 55% to jobbers for orders of 10 or more. 101pp; 5½×8½; of. Reporting time: 2 months. Payment: varies. Copyrights for author. COSMEP, PMA.

Sachem Press, Louis Hammer, Editor, PO Box 9, Old Chatham, NY 12136, 518-794-8327. 1980. Poetry, fiction, art, photos, long-poems, collages. "No new submissions until Jan. 91. Statements of projects will be read before then. Prefer books of 60-150 pp. Translations, anthologies of poetry, collections of short fiction. Published: Louis Hammer's *Birth Sores/Bands*, 1980; *Selected Poems of Cesar Vallejo*, translated by H.R. Hays, June 1981; *Selected Poems of Miltos Sahtouris*, translated by Kimon Friar, Spring, 1982; Yannis Ritsos, *Erotica*, translated by Kimon Friar; *Recent Poetry of Spain*, translated & edited by Louis Hammer & Sara Schyfter, Dec. 1983; *The Danger & The Enemy* by Jos Vandeloo, 1986; *Remains: Stories of Vietnam* by William Crapser, 1988." avg. press run 1.2M-2M. Expects 2 titles 1991, 2 titles 1992. 9 titles listed in the *Small Press Record of Books in Print* (20th Edition, 1991-92). avg. price, cloth: $17; paper: $8.95. Discounts: 5-24 40%, 25-49 43%, 50-99 46%, over 100 50%. 150pp; 5½×8¼; of. Reporting time: 2-3 months. Payment: varies, individually negotiated. Copyrights for author.

Sackbut Press, Angela Peckenpaugh, 2513 E Webster Place, Milwaukee, WI 53211. 1978. Poetry, art, cartoons. "I am no longer publishing *Sackbut Review*. I only publish poem notecards now. Also distributing *New Roads, Old Towns*, an anthology of poetry by David Steingass, Gianfranco Pagnucci, Edna Meudt, published by Rountree Publications, Platteville, WI. Nov. 1988." avg. press run 150 cards. Pub'd 1 title 1990. 2 titles listed in the *Small Press Record of Books in Print* (20th Edition, 1991-92). avg. price, cloth: 40¢ a piece or 10 for $3.50 postcards; paper: 50¢ each for notecards. 1 page; of. Reporting time: 1 month. Payment: at least 25 copies. Copyrights for author.

SACRED FIRE, Robert Augustus Masters, PO Box 91980, West Vancouver, B.C. V7V 4S4, Canada, 604-922-8745. 1990. Poetry, articles, art, photos, cartoons, interviews, reviews, music. "3, words. Biases: Heartfelt, passionate depth writing. Turning away from *nothing* on the path to being Fully Human." circ. 20M. 4/yr. Pub'd 3 issues 1990; expects 4 issues 1991, 4 issues 1992. sub. price: $20; per copy: $6; sample: $6. 64-80pp; 8½×11; of, web. Reporting time: 2 months. Payment: from $15 to $100. Copyrighted, reverts to author. Pub's reviews: 6 in 1990. §Communities, spirituality, bodywork, awakening, healing, children. Ads: $450, see our schedule. PMA, COSMEP, SMPG.

Sa-De Publications Inc., Sam L. Vulgaris, PO Box 42607, Portland, OR 97242, 503-235-2759. 1987. Poetry. avg. press run 500-1M. Pub'd 1 title 1990; expects 2 titles 1991, 3 titles 1992. avg. price, paper: $14.95. Discounts: 1-2 books 20%, 3-6 30%, 7-15 40%, 16+ 50%. 200pp; 5×7; †of. Reporting time: continuous submissions. Payment: free publication at this time, maybe payments later. Does not copyright for author.

Sagapress, Inc., Ngaere Macray, Box 21, Sagaponack Road, Sagaponack, NY 11962, 516-537-3717. 1982. Non-fiction. "Distributed by Timber Press, 9999 SW Wilshire, Portland, OR 97225, 1-800-327-5680." avg. press run 5M. Pub'd 4 titles 1990; expects 5 titles 1991, 5 titles 1992. 17 titles listed in the *Small Press Record of Books in Print* (20th Edition, 1991-92). avg. price, cloth: $35; paper: $24. Discounts: trade. 300pp.

SAGE: A SCHOLARLY JOURNAL ON BLACK WOMEN, Patricia Bell Scott, Editor; Beverly Guy Sheftall, Co-Editor, PO Box 42741, Atlanta, GA 30311-0741, 404-681-3643 ext. 360. 1984. Articles, photos, interviews, criticism, reviews, news items. circ. 1M. 2/yr. Pub'd 2 issues 1990; expects 2 issues 1991, 2 issues 1992. sub. price: $15 (ind.), $25 (inst.); per copy: $8; sample: free to institutions only. Back issues: $5. Discounts: NWSA members and students $10 (indiv.), prisoners free. 72pp; 8½×11; of. Reporting time: 30 days. Payment: none. Copyrighted, reverts to author. Pub's reviews: 20 in 1990. §Black studies, women's

503

studies, Black women's studies, Afro-American and women's literature. Ads: $250/$125/$62.50 1/4 page.

Sahabat Alam Malaysia (Friends of the Earth Malayasia) (see also ASIA-PACIFIC ENVIRONMENT NEWSLETTER; ENVIRONMENTAL NEWS DIGEST; SUARA SAM), 43 Salween Road, 10050 Penang, Malaysia. 1977. 17 titles listed in the *Small Press Record of Books in Print* (20th Edition, 1991-92).

St. Andrew Press, Ray Buchanan, PO Box 329, Big Island, VA 24526, 804-299-5956. 1986. Poetry, non-fiction. avg. press run 1.5M. Expects 2 titles 1991, 3 titles 1992. 5 titles listed in the *Small Press Record of Books in Print* (20th Edition, 1991-92). avg. price, paper: $5.95; other: $9.95. Discounts: standard. 100pp; 5½x8½; of. Reporting time: 6 weeks. Payment: by individual arrangement. Copyrights for author. COSMEP.

Saint Andrews Press, Ron Bayes, Founding & General Editor; Grace Gibson, Associate Editor; William Morris, Assistant Editor, c/o Saint Andrews College, Laurinburg, NC 28352-5598, 919-276-3652. 1969-70. Poetry, fiction, criticism, reviews, long-poems, plays. "Unlike the *St. Andrews Review,* which welcomes unsolicited mss, the press solicits its mss—often from previous contributors to the magazine. Books average about 60 pp. Recent books: *Jouney into Morning,* Sam Ragan; *Names, Dates, & Places,* Joel Oppenheimer; *Leave Your Sugar For The Cold Morning,* Warren Carrier; *Here I Am!,* Dick Bakken; *Terra Amata,* Kathryn B. Gurkin; *Middle Creek Poems,* Shelby Stephenson; *The Medicine Woman,* Julie Suk; *Shanghai Creek Fire,* Rob Hollis Miller; *Town Clock Burning,* Charles Fort; *A Beast in View,* Ron Beyes. Currently not accepting manuscripts, query after Jan." avg. press run 750. Pub'd 10 titles 1990; expects 12 titles 1991, 10 titles 1992. 23 titles listed in the *Small Press Record of Books in Print* (20th Edition, 1991-92). avg. price, cloth: $19.95; paper: $9.95; other: $4.95 chapbooks. Discounts: 40%. 80pp; 6x9; lp. Payment: 10% of copies in lieu of royalty. Does not copyright for author. CLMP, COSMEP.

St. Bede's Publications, Sr. Scholastica Crilly, PO Box 545, Petersham, MA 01366, 508-724-3407. 1977. Poetry, fiction, articles, letters, non-fiction. "Prefer books on prayer/spirituality, theology, saints, etc. Prefer shorter books, under 200 pages. Recent contributors: Ronda Chervin, Basil Pennington, Louis Bouyer, John Schug" avg. press run 1.5M-3M. Pub'd 12 titles 1990; expects 10 titles 1991, 10 titles 1992. 6 titles listed in the *Small Press Record of Books in Print* (20th Edition, 1991-92). avg. price, cloth: $17.95; paper: $5.95; other: $6.95 cassettes. Discounts: 40% on 5 or more, other depends on quantity and customer. 125-200pp; 5½x8½; of, web press. Reporting time: 1-2 months. Payment: % of sales on retail price. Copyrights under author's name. Catholic Book Publishers Assoc.

ST. CROIX REVIEW, Angus MacDonald, Editor & Publisher; Barry Myles MacDonald, Editor; William F. Rickenbacher, Editor, Box 244, Stillwater, MN 55082, 612-439-7190. 1968. Articles, criticism, reviews, letters. "19th century liberalism." circ. 1.5M. 6/yr. Pub'd 6 issues 1990; expects 6 issues 1991, 6 issues 1992. sub. price: $25 1-year membership price; per copy: $4; sample: $4 postage & handling. Back issues: $4. Discounts: 50% for bulk orders, of 10. 64pp; 6x9; †of. Reporting time: 14 days. Payment: none. Copyrighted, does not revert to author. Pub's reviews: 25 in 1990. §Social commentary. No ads.

St. John's Publishing, Inc., Donald E. Montgomery, Editor-in-Chief; Donna L. Montgomery, President, 6824 Oaklawn Avenue, Edina, MN 55435, (612) 920-9044. 1986. Fiction, non-fiction. "Trade paperback publisher of quality nonfiction. No manuscripts accepted for review without prior approval based on query letter and synopsis with SASE." avg. press run 5M. Pub'd 1 title 1990; expects 3 titles 1991, 3 titles 1992. 6 titles listed in the *Small Press Record of Books in Print* (20th Edition, 1991-92). avg. price, paper: $9.95. Discounts: per quantity for individuals, schools, libraries, government agencies; up to 42% for bookstores; 50% for wholesalers and jobbers. 200pp; 5½x8½; of. Reporting time: 3 weeks or less. Payment: standard royalty; minimal advance; payments semi-annual. Copyrights for author. International Association of Independent Publishers (COSMEP), Publishers Marketing Association (PMA), Minnesota Independent Publishers Assoc. (MIPA), Upper Midwest Booksellers Assoc. (UMBA), Mid-America Publishers Assoc. (MAPA).

ST. JOSEPH MESSENGER, Sister Ursula Maphet, Editor, PO Box 288, Jersey City, NJ 07303, 201-798-4141. 1898. circ. 26M. 4/yr. sub. price: $5; sample: free. 16pp; 8½x11. Reporting time: 2 weeks.

ST. LOUIS JOURNALISM REVIEW, Charles L. Klotzer, Editor-Publisher, 8380 Olive Boulevard, St. Louis, MO 63132, 314-991-1699. 1970. Articles, photos, cartoons, interviews, satire, criticism, reviews, letters, news items. circ. 6.5M. 10/yr. Pub'd 12 issues 1990; expects 10 issues 1991, 10 issues 1992. sub. price: $25; per copy: $2; sample: $2. Back issues: $2. Discounts: 20% to sub agencies, 40% to stores & outlets. 24pp; 11x16½; of. Reporting time: 2-3 weeks. Payment: $40-$150 (or more). Copyrighted, does not revert to author. Pub's reviews: 20 in 1990. §Critique of print and broadcast media, journalism, particularly St Louis area, media, communications, press, broadcasting, cable, and items not covered by media. write for rates. SDX, Press Club of St. Louis, I.R.E.

ST. MAWR, John H. Kennedy, 496a Hudson Street, Suite K118, New York, NY 10014, 212-787-7155. 1973 (print) 1977 (tape) 1991 (computer disk/BASIC). Poetry, articles, art, interviews, music, long-poems, plays, news items. "*St. Mawr* (previously *VEINS,* in print and audiotape formats) is now a computer disk and on-line

504

biannual magazine publishing language poetry and multi-media works (primarily combinations of music, drama, poetry and graphic art). Traditional fiction forms are not accepted, and our bias is towards work which reflects the structures and intentions of jazz. At this time, all submissions must be on IBM formatted 5¼" disks in GWBASIC language to run disks. Formats will be more flexible in 1992." circ. varies. 2/yr. Expects 2 issues 1992. sub. price: $16.50; per copy: $3.50 or $3.00 plus SASE (3 oz.); sample: $5 (loose stamps, checks, cash). Back issues: print issues 3 1st-class stamps, tape issues $2.50 + pre-addressed mailer. Discounts: 40% bulk, min. 20. 5¼" disk. Reporting time: 3 weeks. Payment: copies. Copyrights: if you are concerned, secure your own; assign us one time rights. Pub's reviews. §poetry & music (also poetics). Preprinted insertions only ($.50 per 5 X 5 in. block of print). CLMP, NESPA, COSMEP.

SALAD, Elaine Liner, Caryl Herfort, Box 64980-306, Dallas, TX 75206. 1990. Poetry, fiction, letters, parts-of-novels, plays. "Prefer short-short stories, under 1500 words. Short poetry; no epics. Short plays welcomed but they must be very short. Scenes from plays all right. We routinely reject violent, profane and sexist material. We don't appreciate woman-bashing or use of words describing anatomy that begin with the letter "c". We like off-center humor and non-traditional uses of language. No whining about love or overuse of water images, please. Make us laugh. Give us a shove. We also like a Texas-Southwestern slant—no Texana. Recent contributors include poets Sheryl L. Nelms, Michael Helsem, and Michelle Rhea, all of whom have been published nationally. Singer Sara Hickman wrote a short oddity for our first edition." circ. 1M. 2/yr. Expects 1 issue 1992. sub. price: $12; per copy: $5; sample: $6 (includes postage). Back issues: $4. 80pp; 8¼x6¼. Reporting time: 1 month. Payment: 2 copies. Copyrighted, reverts to author.

SALISBURY REVIEW, Claridge Press, Roger Scruton, Jessica Douglas-Home, 33 Canonbury Park South, London N1 2JW, United Kingdom. 4/yr. Pub'd 4 issues 1990; expects 4 issues 1991, 4 issues 1992. sub. price: $35; per copy: $8. size A4. Payment: none. Pub's reviews.

SALMAGUNDI, Robert Boyers, Editor; Peggy Boyers, Executive Editor, Skidmore College, Saratoga Springs, NY 12866, 518-584-5000. 1965. Poetry, fiction, articles, photos, interviews, satire, criticism, reviews, letters, parts-of-novels, non-fiction. "Recent contributors: George Steiner, Conor Cruise O'Brien, Leszek Kolakowski, Christopher Lasch, Jean Elshtain, Renata Adler, Cynthia Ozick, Susan Sontag, Terry Eagleton, Carlos Fuentes, G. Cabrera Infante, John Bayley, Jacques Barzun, John Lukacs, Phyllis Grosskurth." circ. 5M-8M. 4/yr. Pub'd 4 issues 1990; expects 4 issues 1991, 4 issues 1992. sub. price: $12; per copy: $5; sample: $4. Back issues: send SASE for the list. Discounts: 40% to stores. 300pp; 5½x8½; cold type. Reporting time: 6 months. Payment: varies. Copyrighted, reverts to author. Pub's reviews: 12 in 1990. §Politics, social sciences, literary crit, poetry, fiction, essays. Ads: $150/$100/$200 cover. CCLM, PEN.

THE SALMON, Salmon Publishing, Jessie Lendennie, Editor, Bridge Mills, Galway, Ireland, tel: 62587. 1981. Poetry, photos. "Poetry, prose, graphics, photos, translations. We look for work of social relevance, but not necessarily overtly political, work with an individual spark, innovative; *all* work of quality is seriously considered. Send no more than 6 poems, with your name on each page and an International Reply Coupon for return postage. We have a slight bias toward Irish writers (there are not enough outlets for poetry here), but often publish Americans and British writers, and are very happy to get translations. Recent contributors include Eavan Boland, Nuala Archer, Knute Skinner, Beth Joselow, James Liddy, Nuala Ni Dhomhnaill, Michael Egan, Eva Bourke, Rita Ann Higgins and Fred Johnston." circ. 1M. 3/yr. Pub'd 2 issues 1990; expects 3 issues 1991, 3 issues 1992. sub. price: $20/airmail, $15/surface, £5 Ireland & U.K., £6.00 Europe; per copy: $5 (£2.00 Ireland & U.K.); sample: $5 (airmail). Back issues: vary from $2.50 (£1.10) to $1.50 (.75p). Discounts: trade 30-40%. 96pp; size A5 (6x8½); of. Reporting time: 1-3 months. Payment: depends on Arts Council funding. Copyrighted. Ads: £100 back cover ($150)/£75 inside page ($90)/£45 1/2 page ($60).

Salmon Publishing (see also THE SALMON), Jessie Lendennie, Director, Auburn, Upper Fairhill, Galway, Ireland, 62587. 1985. Satire. "Books in 1990: *Learning To Spell Zucchini* by Knute Skinner, *Song at the Edge of the World* by Fred Johnston. Current titles: *We Came Out Again to see the Stars* by Michael Egan, and *Gog and Magog* by Ciaran O'Driscoll. Earlier titles: *Goddess On The Mervue Bus* by Rita Ann Higgins, and *Gonella* by Eva Bourke with illustrations by Jay Murphy." avg. press run 1M. Pub'd 11 titles 1990; expects 9 titles 1991, 9 titles 1992. 27 titles listed in the *Small Press Record of Books in Print* (20th Edition, 1991-92). avg. price, cloth: £9.00 (approx. $15); paper: £4.50 (approx. $8). Discounts: trade 30-40%. 70pp; size A5—149mm X 213mm; of. Reporting time: 2-3 months. Payment: 10% of cover price. Copyrights for author. Cle-Irish Publishers' Association.

SALOME: A JOURNAL FOR THE PERFORMING ARTS, Ommation Press, Effie Mihopoulos, Editor, 5548 N. Sawyer, Chicago, IL 60625, 312-539-5745. 1975. Poetry, fiction, articles, art, photos, cartoons, interviews, satire, criticism, reviews, music, letters, long-poems, collages, plays, concrete art. "*Salome* is a journal that covers the performing arts in all aspects—theatre, dance, performance art, poetry, music, film. Poetry and fiction submitted should relate to these topics somehow." circ. 500. 2/yr. Pub'd 4 issues 1990; expects 8 issues 1991. sub. price: $12; per copy: $2 (poem postcard issues); $4 (double issues); $6 triple issue (specials on Martha Graham and Isadora Duncan); sample: $2 (postcards); $8 (current sample); $4 older issue.

Back issues: $4 each (double issue). Discounts: 40% 10 copies or more. 60-120pp; 8½×11; of. Reporting time: 2 weeks to 1 month. Payment: contributor's copy. Copyrighted, reverts to author. Pub's reviews: 50 books/5 magazines in 1990. §Everything concerning performing arts, (books, magazines, performances, films, video, etc.). Ads: $100/$60/$40.

SALON: A Journal of Aesthetics, Pat Hartman, 305 W. Magnolia, Suite 386, Ft. Collins, CO 80521, 303-224-3116. 1988. Articles, art, photos, cartoons, interviews, satire, criticism, reviews, music, letters, collages, news items, non-fiction. "Aesthetics is the relation between the arts and other areas of human endeavor. *Salon* has a libertarian focus. Recent contributors: L. Neil Smith, Richard Kostelanetz." circ. 150. 4/yr. Pub'd 4 issues 1990; expects 4 issues 1991, 4 issues 1992. sub. price: $20; per copy: $5; sample: $5. 60pp; 8½×11; xerox. Reporting time: asap. Payment: 1 complimentary copy. Copyrighted, reverts to author. Pub's reviews: 10 in 1990. §Arts. Ads: $40/$20/$3 business card size ad.

SALT LICK, Salt Lick Press, James Haining, 1909 Sunny Brook Drive, Austin, TX 78723-3449. 1939. Poetry, fiction, articles, art, photos, interviews, satire, criticism, reviews, letters, parts-of-novels, long-poems, collages, concrete art, non-fiction. circ. 1.5M. Irregular. Pub'd 1 issue 1990; expects 1 issue 1991, 1 issue 1992. price per copy: $6; sample: $6. Back issues: write for prices. Discounts: 40%. 64pp; 8½×11; †of. Reporting time: 2-4 weeks. Payment: copies. Copyrighted, reverts to author. Pub's reviews. §Open to all materials.

Salt Lick Press (see also LUCKY HEART BOOKS; SALT LICK), James Haining, 1909 Sunny Brook Drive, Austin, TX 78723-3449. 1969. Poetry, fiction, articles, art, photos, criticism, letters, parts-of-novels, long-poems, non-fiction. "Open. Published materials by Lally, Burns, Searcy, Trammell, Shuttleworth, Creeley, Slater, Dante, Hungry Coyote, Firer, Nelson, King, Hart, Ackerman, Murphy, Musicmaster, et al" avg. press run 1M. Pub'd 1 title 1990; expects 1 title 1991, 1 title 1992. 14 titles listed in the *Small Press Record of Books in Print* (20th Edition, 1991-92). avg. price, paper: $6. 68pp; 8½×11; †of/hand work. Reporting time: 2-3 weeks. Payment: copies and $ if available. Copyrights for author. CLMP.

Salt-Works Press, Tom Bridwell, Marilyn Kitchell, 18903 Spring Canyon Road, Montrose, CO 81401-7906. 1973. Poetry, fiction, articles, art, photos, criticism, long-poems, non-fiction. "Fine hand-set letterpress publications, hand-sewn, graphics, contemporary poetry & prose" avg. press run 300-700. Pub'd 4 titles 1990; expects 5 titles 1991, 4 titles 1992. 49 titles listed in the *Small Press Record of Books in Print* (20th Edition, 1991-92). avg. price, cloth: $17.50; paper: $4-$8. Discounts: Standard. 20-70pp; 6×9; †lp. Reporting time: 6 weeks. Payment: copies. Copyrights for author.

Salvo Books, Sidney Allinson, Suite 465, 7305 Woodbine Avenue, Markham, Toronto, Ontario L3R 3V7, Canada, 416-493-9627. 1985. Fiction, non-fiction. "Mss. welcomed on: military history, business, industrial security; crime prevention, literary reviews of genre fiction, illustrated books—aviation, military, social/sexual history" avg. press run 5M. Pub'd 1 title 1990; expects 2 titles 1991, 4 titles 1992. avg. price, cloth: $24; paper: $12.95. Discounts: 40%-50% trade/educ. 290-350pp; lp. Reporting time: 90 days. Payment: 10%, outright purchase. Copyrights for author. COSMEP.

SAMISDAT, Samisdat, Merritt Clifton, Editor-in-Chief, 456 Monroe Turnpike, Monroe, CT 06468, 203-452-0446. 1973. Poetry, fiction, art, satire, criticism, parts-of-novels, long-poems, plays, non-fiction. "Having hung tough for over 18 years and 225 numbers, we reckon we're good for more; but it's also time to cut back, take it easier, have a life away from the word-processor and printing press. Instead of publishing *Samisdat* regular issues on a quarterly basis, I anticipate publishing annually or semi-annually, as occasion demands and time permits. Send your stuff here if you're fighting the battle to save Planet Earth, on whatever front (pollution, patriarchy, animal rights, civil rights), if you know something about it we don't already know, if you're seeking an audience of hardworking, self-critical, committed fellow activists. No knee-jerk leftism *or* flag-waving neo-fascism, please. If you're looking to get famous, get tenure, get a grant, this isn't the place. No photocopies or multiple submissions. We treat all submissions as personal correspondence, expecting the same courtesy of would-be contributors. And yes, you will have a damned sight better chance of acceptance if you've read *Samisdat* before submitting. Blind submissions have a tendency to be absurdly irrelevant." circ. 300. 1-2/yr. Pub'd 2 issues 1990. sub. price: $15 for 250 pages; per copy: $3; sample: $3. Back issues: query, $150 brings all available back numbers. Discounts: 40% on prepaid orders totaling $20 or invoice orders totaling $20 or more. 40-60pp; 8½×5½; †photocopy. Reporting time: 2 seconds to 2 weeks. Payment: copies. Copyrighted, reverts to author. Pub's reviews: 50 in 1990. §Because our former policy of reviewing everything received was excessively abused, we are now reviewing only selected items. We no longer exchange with publications and publishers whose work does not interest us. Having to go this route is not our preference, but has become necessary as a matter of survival; through 1989 we were receiving over 20 books and mags each and every week, often in bundles of five or ten. Nobody can possibly conscientiously read that much drivel. Ads: $25/page.

Samisdat (see also SAMISDAT), Merritt Clifton, 456 Monroe Turnpike, Monroe, CT 06468. 1973. Poetry, fiction, criticism. "After 18 years and 230 publications, I have restructured Samisdat to accomodate my much increased workload as new father and as news editor of *The Animal's Agenda*, the international magazine of animal rights and ecology. I do not anticipate publishing more than three new poetry chapbooks per year, and am no longer publishing any novels or novellas. Chapbooks will be published, when I do them, under my standard arrangement only, whereby authors cover material costs in exchange for half the press run. Please query before submitting manuscripts." avg. press run 300. Pub'd 3 titles 1990. 52 titles listed in the *Small Press Record of Books in Print* (20th Edition, 1991-92). avg. price, paper: $2.50; other: $5 for 6 recent chapbooks. Discounts: 40%, prepaid, $20.00 or more total; 20% on invoice orders of $20.00 or more; 0% on smaller orders. 12-40pp; 8½×5½; †photocopy. Reporting time: 2 minutes to 2 weeks. Payment: yes. Copyrights for author.

SAMIZDAT, Ianus Publications, Inc., Claude J. Pelletier, Yves Meynard, 33, Prince Street #243, Montreal, Quebec H3C 2M7, Canada, 514-397-0342. 1986. Fiction, articles, interviews, criticism, reviews. "Quebec science fiction fanzine, it's a workbench for young authors. 18 issues published yet. In French. ISSN 0830-9647" circ. 100. Irregular. Pub'd 2 issues 1990; expects 3 issues 1991, 4 issues 1992. sub. price: $10; per copy: $2.50; sample: $3. Back issues: $3.50. 40pp; 5½×8½; polycopy. Reporting time: anytime. Payment: none. Copyrighted, reverts to author. Pub's reviews: 30 in 1990. §Science fiction. Ads: $10/$5/$3 1/4 page/$15 back cover. SWAC.

San Diego Poet's Press, Kathleen Iddings, Editor, Publisher, c/o Kathleen Iddings, PO Box 8638, La Jolla, CA 92038, (619) 457-1399. 1981. Poetry. "Shelley Memorial Award winner, Leo Connellan, said in the *Small Press Review*, *"Kathleen Iddings has done an international service for everyone who cares for poetry's survival by offering the best poetry..."* With this non-profit press, Kathleen has published six individual poets, four poetry magazines, and a poetry anthology of social/political poetry, *Poets Voices 1984*. The latter includes poets Allen Ginsberg, Galway Kinnell, Carolyn Kizer, Robert Pinsky, Tess Gallagher, Carolyn Forche, John Balaban, and others. In 1989, Kathleen established *The American Book Series*, a contest for publishing a winning poet's first book. Winners of the national contests are: 1989, Joan LaBombard's *The Counting of Grains*; 1990, Regina McBride's *Yarrow Fields*; 1991, Charles Atkinson's *The Only Cure I Know*. Individuals' books are $10 plus $2 postage/handling. Future winners will be selected from the best poetry received throughout the year. Query with six poems, bio and SASE. Contests are funded by donations. Donations are tax-deductible." avg. press run 500. Pub'd 2 titles 1990; expects 6 titles 1991. 7 titles listed in the *Small Press Record of Books in Print* (20th Edition, 1991-92). avg. price, cloth: $20; paper: $10. Discounts: negotiable. 75pp; 5½×8½; of. Reporting time: 1 month. Payment: negotiable. Copyrights for author.

San Diego State University Press (see also FICTION INTERNATIONAL), Hal Jaffe, Larry McCaffery, San Diego State University, San Diego, CA 92182, 619-594-6220. avg. press run 1M. Pub'd 2 titles 1990; expects 2 titles 1991, 2 titles 1992. avg. price, paper: $6. Discounts: 20% multiple copies. 288pp; 6×9; set, printed and bound out of house. Reporting time: 90 days. Payment: 2 copies of book. Copyrights for author.

SAN FERNANDO POETRY JOURNAL, Kent Publications, Inc., Cerulean Press (Subsidiary of Kent Publications), Richard Cloke, Editor-in-Chief; Shirley J. Rodecker, Associate Editor; Lori C. Smith, Associate Editor, 18301 Halstead Street, Northridge, CA 91325. 1978. Poetry. "Though published in San Fernando Valley & Los Angeles, it is not regional. Usual submission with SASE. Seeking peripheral, experimental, *social protest, activist* & frontiers-of-consciousness poetry keyed to our space in time. Free guidelines with SASE. Prefer themes with social consciousness, outward looking orientation—though we're not stubborn & will welcome good material on any theme or in any genre. (Our crystal ball, however, tells us of much trouble ahead). Among regular contributors to *SFPJ* are: C.J. Roner, Patrick O'Neill, Jack Bernier, Elsen Lubetsky, Sister Mary Ann Henn, Sue Saniel Elkind, Stan Proper, Joan Auer Kelly." circ. 500. 4+. Pub'd 6 issues 1990; expects 4 issues 1991, 4 issues 1992. sub. price: $10 for 4 issues (20% off to poets published); per copy: $3; sample: $2.50, will exchange with other poetry mags, no charge. Discounts: wholesale, 40%; bookstores, 20%; contributor's extra copies, 20%. 100pp; 5½×8½; †of, copier, electrostatic. Reporting time: 2 days to 1 month. Payment: copies of mag. to each author. Copyrighted, reverts to author. Pub's reviews: 2 in 1990. §Other magazines with a social orientation: anti-war, environmental, poverty, peace, women's liberation, unemployment, minority rights, etc. Ads: $50/$25/$10 col inch. CLMP.

THE SAN FRANCISCO ALMANAC, Walter Biller, 1657 Waller Street, San Francisco, CA 94117, 800-352-5268. 1990. Fiction, articles, art, reviews, plays, news items, non-fiction. "A compendium of San Francisco endeavors and activities, local fiction (some), histories, shops and non-profit events. Purchase of *Almanac* (annual) includes 2 biannual newsletters. (Fiction, San Francisco oriented *only*). We will also distribute SF/Bay Area 'small publisher' promo materials to our readers (small fee) with reader newsletter, *The Almanac News*. Inquire." 1/yr. Pub'd 1 issue 1990; expects 1 issue 1991, 1 issue 1992. sub. price: $12.95; per copy: $12.95 (include $3 per order/1st class mail); sample: $12.95. Discounts: distributed by The Almanac Press; call toll-free. 360pp; 4×6; of. Reporting time: 1 month, return with SASE. Payment: none. Copyrighted, reverts to author. Pub's reviews. §All things San Francisco-Historical & Present Day Life in "The City" Ads: $500/$280/$125 1/4 page.

SAN FRANCISCO REVIEW OF BOOKS, Elgy Gillespie, Editor, 1117 Geary, San Francisco, CA 94109,

415-771-1252. 1975. Articles, art, photos, interviews, criticism, reviews, letters, news items. "Book reviews of titles from both large and small presses; current titles, but not best sellers. Minimum no. words: 600; Max. 2M, with editor's ok. Recent contributors: M.F.K. Fisher, Lawrence Weschler, Terry Eagleton, James D. Houston." circ. 5M. 4/yr. Pub'd 4 issues 1990; expects 4 issues 1991, 4 issues 1992. 1 title listed in the *Small Press Record of Books in Print* (20th Edition, 1991-92). sub. price: $15; per copy: $4; sample: $4. Back issues: $1-$5. Discounts: usually 40% on consignments, 40% on outright purchases of 5 or more. 56pp; 8½×11; of. Reporting time: 6 weeks. Payment: varies to $150. Copyrighted, reverts to author. Pub's reviews: 300 in 1990. §Fiction, poetry, nonfiction, university presses. Ads: $950/$600/$75 per 40 words. CLMP, COSMEP, ABA, NCBA.

SAN JOSE STUDIES, Fauneil J. Rinn, c/o English, San Jose State University, San Jose, CA 95192, 408-924-4476. 1974. Poetry, fiction, articles, art, photos, criticism, non-fiction. "Length of essay material and fiction: 15-25 double spaced pages; 3-7 poems (from 7-12 pages per issue). Biases: scholarly and comprehensible to general audience. Recent contributors: David Citino, James Laughlin, Barbara La Porte, Adrienne Rich. We would be interested in good, original, scholarly but comprehensible essays on any subject; poetry of any type but interested in quality and verse that says something." circ. 400. 3/yr. Pub'd 3 issues 1990; expects 3 issues 1991, 3 issues 1992. sub. price: $12 individuals, $18 institutions; per copy: $5; sample: $3.50. Back issues: $3.50. Discounts: 15% to subscription agencies and booksellers. 128pp; Reader's Digest size; of. Reporting time: 6-8 weeks. Payment: 2 free copies. Copyrighted, reverts to author. Coordinating Council of Literary Magazines.

San Luis Quest Press, Albert Eglash, Box 666, Avila, CA 93424-5822, 805-543-8500. 1979. "Publishes books in the field of psychology. Current publications are in the field of communication: in these texts a humanistic alternative to assertion training is being offered. For nurses, teachers, parents, lovers." Pub'd 3 titles 1990; expects 5 titles 1991. 2 titles listed in the *Small Press Record of Books in Print* (20th Edition, 1991-92). avg. price, paper: $30. Discounts: 20-25%. 150pp; 8½×11; †of. Payment: none.

SAN MIGUEL REVIEW, John Brander, Charles Kuschinski, Michael Cramer, 1200 E. Ocean Boulevard #64, Long Beach, CA 90802, 213-495-0925. 1973. Poetry, fiction, articles, art, photos, parts-of-novels. "*San Miguel Review* will be the literary magazine of the American and English-speaking community of San Miguel de Allende, Gto., Mexico. Submissions in Spanish acceptable" circ. 500-1M. 1/yr. Expects 1 issue 1992. price per copy: $5. Discounts: 40%. 96pp. Reporting time: variable. Payment: 1 copy. Copyrighted, reverts to author. Pub's reviews. §Primarily poetry, fiction of interest to the American literary community in Mexico.

Sand River Press, Bruce W. Miller, 1319 14th Street, Los Osos, CA 93402, 805-543-3591. 1987. Non-fiction. avg. press run 3M. Pub'd 2 titles 1990; expects 2 titles 1991, 3 titles 1992. 6 titles listed in the *Small Press Record of Books in Print* (20th Edition, 1991-92). avg. price, cloth: $18.95; paper: $9.95. Discounts: 3+ 40%, 100+ 42%, 200+ 43%. 132pp; 6×9; of. Reporting time: 8 weeks, must send return postage. Payment: standard. Copyrights for author.

Sandberry Press, Pamela Mordecai, Managing Editor; Martin Mordecai, Associate Editor; Sonia Chin, Consulting Editor, PO Box 507, Kingston 10, Jamaica, West Indies, 809-92-76423. 1986. Poetry, fiction, photos, parts-of-novels. "Caribbean poetry series has five titles; includes poetry by Caribbean authors; focus is on first collections. Number four poet is Dennis Scott (He plays Lester, the father-in-law, on The Cosby Show). 2 titles planned for publication each year. Also plans for anthologies of fiction, poetry; for simultaneous publication of these collections on audio cassette; for publication of books for children and for publication of textbooks" avg. press run 1M. Pub'd 1 title 1990; expects 5 titles 1991, 5+ titles 1992. 3 titles listed in the *Small Press Record of Books in Print* (20th Edition, 1991-92). avg. price, cloth: $8; paper: $6. Discounts: graduated according to size of order; none lower than 25%. 56+pp; 5×9; of. Reporting time: 3 months. Payment: usually 10% of net receipts; payments once P.A. on 31st December. Copyrights for author. Univ. of the West Indies Publishing Assoc. (UWIPA), Book Industry Assoc. of Jamaica (BIAJ).

Sandhill Publications, Jeffrey M. Keller, 441 Woodland Place, Leonia, NJ 07605. 1977. Art, photos, non-fiction. "Primarily interested in regional books (NY city, NE U.S.). Nonfiction: walking guides, natural history, city activities" avg. press run 5M. Expects 1 title 1991, 2 titles 1992. 1 title listed in the *Small Press Record of Books in Print* (20th Edition, 1991-92). avg. price, paper: $8. Discounts: 10-24: 40%, 25-99: 45%, 100-199: 50 %, 200 and up 55%. of. Payment: negotiable. COSMEP.

Sandhills Press, Mark Sanders, 219 S 19th Street, Ord, NE 68862. 1979. Poetry, interviews, criticism, long-poems. "No unsolicited mss; will likely cease publication after 1990" avg. press run 500. Pub'd 3 titles 1990; expects 2 titles 1991, 3 titles 1992. 5 titles listed in the *Small Press Record of Books in Print* (20th Edition, 1991-92). avg. price, cloth: $13; paper: $7. Discounts: 1-4 at 20%; 5 or more 40% for bookstore and classroom orders; 50% tojobber or distributor. 64-276pp; 5½×8½, 6×9; of. Reporting time: 4 months. Payment: copies or by arrangement. Copyrights for author.

SANDHILLS/ST. ANDREWS REVIEW, Stephen E. Smith, 2200 Airport Road, Pinehurst, NC 28374, 919-692-6185. 1970. Poetry, fiction, articles, art, photos, interviews, criticism, reviews, parts-of-novels,

508

long-poems, collages, plays, non-fiction. "Pound Studies, Black Mountain Studies, Japanese Studies continue to be interests, but we are not exclusivist and eagerly seek new talent. Recent contributors have included Rex McGuinn, Sister Bernetta Quinn, Jon Johnson, Sizzo DeRachewiltz, Yukio Mishima translated by Hiroaki Sato, Joel Oppenheimer, E. Waverly Land, John Cage, Tom Patterson, Martin Robbins, and John Williamson. We try to run at least one outstanding long poem each issue (e.g.: Judith Johnson Sherwin's *How The Dead Count.*" circ. 300-500. 2/yr. Pub'd 2 issues 1990; expects 2 issues 1991, 2 issues 1992. sub. price: $12; per copy: $6; sample: $5. Back issues: on request. Discounts: 40%. 120pp; 7×10; of. Reporting time: average 1 month during academic year. Payment: copies. Copyrighted, reverts to author. Pub's reviews: 4 in 1990. §Books of poetry, fiction, no mags. Ads: $50/$25. CCLM, COSMEP.

Sandpiper Press, Marilyn Reed Riddle, PO Box 286, Brookings, OR 97415, 503-469-5588. 1979. Poetry, fiction, articles, art, photos, non-fiction. "Specialize in large print. Books about 64-84 pages. Native American authors only contact editor for needs." avg. press run 2M. Pub'd 1 title 1990; expects 1 title 1992. 7 titles listed in the *Small Press Record of Books in Print* (20th Edition, 1991-92). avg. price, paper: $4-$8. Discounts: libraries, schools, churches - 20% single copy, 10 or more per order 40% wholesale. 24-84pp; 5½×8½; of. Reporting time: 90 days. Payment: buy for cash. Does not copyright for author.

SANDSCRIPT, Cape Cod Writers Inc, Barbara Renkens Dunning, Editor; Jean Lunn, Poetry Editor, c/o Lunn, 25 Harvard Street, Hyannis, MA 02601, 617-362-6078. 1977. Poetry, fiction, photos, interviews, reviews, non-fiction. "Most contributors either live on Cape Cod or visit the Cape in the summer; however a limited amount of material is published by new writers from other areas." circ. 500. 2/yr. Pub'd 1 issue 1990; expects 2 issues 1991, 2 issues 1992. sub. price: $5; per copy: $3; sample: $2. Back issues: $2. Discounts: 40% discount to bookstores and in quanities of more than five. 50pp; 6×9; of. Reporting time: fiction up to 2 months, poetry up to 6 months. Payment: 1 free copy. Copyrighted, reverts to author. Pub's reviews: 4 in 1990. §Fiction, poetry, magazines. Ads: $25/$15. CCLM.

Sang Froid Press, Mark Stratman, PO Box 272, Excelsior, MN 55331, 612-470-9986. 1984. Art, photos, non-fiction. avg. press run 5M. Expects 2 titles 1991, 4 titles 1992. 2 titles listed in the *Small Press Record of Books in Print* (20th Edition, 1991-92). avg. price, paper: $8.95. So far, we have sold via direct mail at cover price, with some minor trade sales at discounted prices. 164pp; †of. Reporting time: 60 days or sooner. Payment: to be arranged per project. Copyrights for author.

Sanguinaria Publishing, Selma Miriam, Betsey Beaven, Noel Furie, 85 Ferris Street, Bridgeport, CT 06605, 203-576-9168. 1980. "We will publish material of interest to feminists." avg. press run 5M. Expects 1 title 1991. 3 titles listed in the *Small Press Record of Books in Print* (20th Edition, 1991-92). avg. price, paper: $12.95. Discounts: 40% for 5 or more copies; single copies, net. 348pp; 6×9. Payment: 10% royalty fees. Copyrights for author.

Santa Barbara Press, George Erikson, 223 Via Sevilla, Santa Barbara, CA 93109, 805-966-2060. 1983. Non-fiction. "We are leaning towards fictional reprints eg. Zane Grey. Do not expect to be publishing much contemporary fiction at present. Interested in non-fiction material mainly." avg. press run 10M. Pub'd 1 title 1990; expects 9 titles 1991, 12 titles 1992. 2 titles listed in the *Small Press Record of Books in Print* (20th Edition, 1991-92). avg. price, cloth: $12.95; paper: $9.95. Discounts: inquire. 120-340pp; 5½×8½; of. Reporting time: 3-4 months. Payment: 6-7%. Copyrights for author.

Santa Lucia Chapter - Sierra Club, PO Box 15755, San Luis Obispo, CA 93406, 805-473-1947. 1956. "Only San Luis Obispo County ecology subjects" Expects 1 title 1991. 1 title listed in the *Small Press Record of Books in Print* (20th Edition, 1991-92). avg. price, paper: $8.95. Discounts: 40% 10+. 6×9; of.

THE SANTA MONICA REVIEW, Jim Krusoe, 1900 Pico Boulevard, Santa Monica, CA 90405. 1988. Poetry, fiction, parts-of-novels, long-poems. "Recent contributors: Ann Beattie, Maxine Chernoff, Guy Davenport, Arturo Vivante, Alicia Ostriker, Tom Clark, Paul Hoover, Joyce Carol Oates, Maureen Owen." circ. 1M. 2/yr. Pub'd 1 issue 1990; expects 2 issues 1991, 2 issues 1992. sub. price: $10; per copy: $6; sample: $6. Back issues: $10. 132pp; 5½×8½; of. Reporting time: varies. Payment: copies. Copyrighted, reverts to author. Ads: $500.

Santa Susana Press, Norman E. Tanis, Editor, University Libraries, CSUN, 18111 Nordhoff Street, Northridge, CA 91330, 818-885-2271. 1976. Poetry, fiction, art, long-poems, plays, concrete art, non-fiction. "Recent contributors: Ray Bradbury, William Saroyan, Norman Corwin. Fine press, limited editions and facsimile series." avg. press run 200. Pub'd 3 titles 1990; expects 2-3 titles 1991, 2 titles 1992. avg. price, cloth: $100; paper: $8; other: $150+ special lettered editions. Discounts: to dealers only on multiple purchases only 40%. 50pp; size varies; of, lp. Reporting time: 1 month. Payment: purchase outright. Copyrights for author. COSMEP, Publishers Marketing Association.

Saqi Books Publisher, 26 Westbourne Grove, London W2 5RH, England, 071-221-9347; FAX 071-229-7692. 1983. "Main focus is on works dealing with the Middle East, Islam and the Third World. Saqi's authors include some of the major European experts on the Middle East, as well as writers from the region itself: Germaine Tillion, Jacques Berque, Maxime Rodinson." avg. press run 3.5M. Pub'd 8 titles 1990; expects 8 titles 1991, 10 titles 1992. 24 titles listed in the *Small Press Record of Books in Print* (20th Edition, 1991-92). avg. price, cloth: $25; paper: $6.95. Discounts: as arranged by U.S. distributors—Medialink International Inc. 224pp; 5¼×8; of. Reporting time: 8 weeks. Payment: annually (March). Copyrights for author.

Raymond Saroff, Publisher, Box 269, Acorn Hill Road, Olive Bridge, NY 12461. 1989. Fiction, non-fiction. "Raymond Saroff, Publisher was established initially to bring into print the complete works of the late Howard Rose. Our areas of interest are American art (including folk art), and fiction from, of, or about Chicago. No unsolicited manuscripts. Send query and 2-page sample." avg. press run 1.5M. Expects 5 titles 1991, 2 titles 1992. 4 titles listed in the *Small Press Record of Books in Print* (20th Edition, 1991-92). avg. price, cloth: $20; paper: $10. Discounts: Distributed by McPherson & Co. 300pp; 5½×8½. Reporting time: 1-3 months. Payment: standard royalties. Copyrights for author.

SARU Press International, Drew Stroud, 559 Jordan Road, Sedona, AZ 86336. 1980. Poetry. "I am primarily interested in accurate, imaginative translations of Japanese and Hispanic poetry and short fiction." avg. press run 500. Pub'd 8 titles 1990; expects 4 titles 1991, 2 titles 1992. 15 titles listed in the *Small Press Record of Books in Print* (20th Edition, 1991-92). avg. price, cloth: $10; paper: $8.95. Discounts: depends on size or order. On large orders, can supply at very close to cost. of. Reporting time: will read immediately upon receipt. Payment: depends how much of production cost is shared by author. Copyrights for author.

Saskatchewan Writers Guild (see also GRAIN; WINDSCRIPT; FREELANCE), Box 3986, Regina, Saskatchewan S4P 3R9, Canada, 306-757-6310. 1969. 1 title listed in the *Small Press Record of Books in Print* (20th Edition, 1991-92). of.

Sasquatch Books, David Brewster, 1931 2nd Avenue, Seattle, WA 98101, 206-623-3700. 1975. 11 titles listed in the *Small Press Record of Books in Print* (20th Edition, 1991-92).

SAT SANDESH: THE MESSAGE OF THE MASTERS, Art Stein, Vinod Sena, 680 Curtis Corner Road, Wakefield, RI 02879, (401) 783-0662. 1968. Articles, photos, interviews, reviews, letters, parts-of-novels, long-poems. "Subscription address: Route 1, Box 24, Bowling Green, VA 22427. *Sat Sandesh: The Message of The Masters* is published for the purpose of sharing the teachings of Sant Rajinder Singh, Sant Darshan Singh Ji, Param Sant Kirpal Singh Ji, and Hazur Baba Sawan Singh Ji, and earlier teachers of Surat Shabd Yoga (meditation on inner light and celestial sound). (Free distribution: 850)." circ. 938. 12/yr. Pub'd 12 issues 1990; expects 12 issues 1991, 12 issues 1992. sub. price: $16; per copy: $1.50; sample: free. Back issues: $1.50. Discounts: bookstores & libraries 40%; distributors, contact for information. 32pp; 6×9; of. Reporting time: 4-6 weeks. Payment: none. Not copyrighted. Pub's reviews: 2 in 1990. §Books of Sawan Kirpal Publications. No ads.

SATORI, Gary Green, Pat Sims, Hands Off The Press, Inc., PO Box 318, Tivoli, NY 12583, 914-757-4443. 1988. Poetry, fiction, articles, art, photos, cartoons, interviews, collages, non-fiction. "Fiction: 250-2000 words. Art: black and white or art that will reproduce well in black and white. Recent contributors: Dick Higgins, A.D. Coleman, Les Krims, John Carr, Laura Battle, Mikhail Horowitz, Janine Pommy Vega, Cynde Gregory, Alison Knowles, Robert Mezey" circ. 500. 4/yr. Pub'd 3 issues 1990; expects 4 issues 1991, 4 issues 1992. sub. price: $8; per copy: $2; sample: $2. Back issues: $2. Discounts: 40% retailers when returnable, 50% when non-returnable. 20pp; 8½×11; of. Reporting time: 1-2 months. Payment: in issues. Copyrighted, reverts to author. Ads: $100/$75/$50 1/4 page. CCLM.

Saturday Press, Inc., PO Box 884, Upper Montclair, NJ 07043, 201-256-5053. 1975. Poetry. "Sponsor of Eileen W. Barnes Award for women poets over forty. No uninvited submissions at this time." avg. press run 1M. Expects 2 titles 1991, 2 titles 1992. 10 titles listed in the *Small Press Record of Books in Print* (20th Edition, 1991-92). avg. price, paper: $5-$7. Discounts: 40% to bookstores; 20% to jobbers. 64-102pp; 5½×8½, 6×9; of. Reporting time: responds to queries in 2 weeks. Payment: individual arrangement. Copyrights for author. COSMEP.

SAUL BELLOW JOURNAL, Liela Goldman, 6533 Post Oak Drive, West Bloomfield, MI 48322. 1981. Articles, interviews, criticism, reviews, news items. "Publishes essays on the writings of Saul Bellow. Manuscripts should be approx. 4,000 words and should be sent, in duplicate accompanied by a SASE, to the editor. *SBJ* also publishes reviews of books on Bellow's works as well as news, information, queries, and summaries of articles published elswewhere on Bellow's writings. Recent contributors: Daniel Walden, Allan Chavkin, Gloria Cronin, Joseph Cohen, Mark Weinstein, S. Lillian Kremer, Daniel Fuchs, M. Gilbert Porter, et al." 2/yr. Pub'd 2 issues 1990; expects 2 issues 1991, 2 issues 1992. sub. price: $12 individuals, $20 library, institutions & foreign subs + $5 postage. Back issues: $8. 70pp; 6¼×9. Reporting time: 60 days. Payment: copy of journal. Copyrighted. Pub's reviews: 4 in 1990. §Anything on Saul Bellow and/or his works.

The Saunderstown Press, J.C. Patterson, PO Box 307, Saunderstown, RI 02874, 401-295-8810. 1985. Poetry,

510

fiction, satire, non-fiction. "We publish from 2-4 titles per year. Always interested in new authors but no unsolicited manuscripts. Current books in production include medicine, history, careers, children's book, religion and inspirational poetry" avg. press run 1M. Pub'd 3 titles 1990; expects 5 titles 1991, 7 titles 1992. avg. price, cloth: $7.95; paper: $5.95. Discounts: 50% trade, 20% educational and/or jobber. 100pp; 6×9. Reporting time: 2-3 weeks from receipt. Payment: 20% (25% for exceptional). Copyrights for author. COSMEP.

Sauvie Island Press, Susan L. Roberts, PO Box 751, Beaverton, OR 97075-0751, 503-626-4237. 1980. Poetry, fiction, articles, art, photos, cartoons, interviews, satire, criticism, reviews, music, letters, parts-of-novels, long-poems, collages, news items, non-fiction. avg. press run 25M-50M. Pub'd 6 titles 1990; expects 8 titles 1991, 12 titles 1992. 5 titles listed in the *Small Press Record of Books in Print* (20th Edition, 1991-92). avg. price, cloth: $24.95; paper: $16.95; other: $2.50-$4.50 mags. Discounts: none. 148-250pp; 8½×11, 8½×5½; †of, lp, high-speed repographics. Reporting time: 4 weeks with SASE. Payment: 25% on net retail sales. Copyrights for author. NW Association of Book Publishers, PO Box 633, Marylhurst, OR 97036.

Savant Garde Workshop, Vilna Jorgen II, Publisher & Editor-in-Chief, PO Box 1650, Sag Harbor, NY 11963-0060, 516-725-1414. 1964. Poetry, fiction, criticism, long-poems, plays, concrete art, non-fiction. "Please query before sending submissions with SASE. Focus on multinational intelligentsia. Looking for people who have eventual Nobel Prize potential. Publish limited signed editions and their overruns." avg. press run 1M. Pub'd 2 titles 1990; expects 3 titles 1991, 6 titles 1992. 2 titles listed in the *Small Press Record of Books in Print* (20th Edition, 1991-92). avg. price, cloth: $1000 (originals); paper: $75 (overruns); other: $25 bind-it-yourself teacher editions (no discount). Discounts: 25%-50% rare bookdealers, bookdealers, wholesalers, art galleries & print shops. 300pp; 7×10; †computer desktop, multicolor dot-matrix and/or laser printers. Reporting time: return mail. Payment: varies. Copyrights for author. COSMEP.

Saxifrage Books, E.M. Wallace, 387 South Bryant Street, Denver, CO 80219-3020, 756-3548. 1988. Poetry, art, photos. "80 to 100 page books of poetry with art illustrations. Only considering works of high literary quality written by Colorado authors" avg. press run 500-1M. Expects 3 titles 1991, 5 titles 1992. avg. price, paper: $9.95. Discounts: classroom $6.95, library $7.95. 80-100pp; 5½×8½. Reporting time: 3 months on books, single poems 2 weeks. Payment: 40% commission on total sales. Copyrights for author.

Say When Press, W.R. Tish, PO Box 942, Greenbelt, MD 20770, 301-474-0352. 1985. Poetry, fiction. "Say When Press specializes in multi-genre works. First title published: *Order and Chaos, Nothing at all* by W.R. Tish; a combination of fiction, poetry, philosophy, humor, and graphics." avg. press run 4M. Expects 1 title 1991, 1 title 1992. 1 title listed in the *Small Press Record of Books in Print* (20th Edition, 1991-92). avg. price, paper: $5.95. Discounts: determined on case-by-case basis. 128pp; 8½×11; of. Reporting time: 2 weeks, *query first!* Copyrights for author.

SCANDINAVIAN REVIEW, Lena Biorck Kaplan, Publisher; Adrienne Gyongy, Editor, 725 Park Avenue, New York, NY 10021, 212-879-9779. 1913. Poetry, fiction, articles, art, photos, interviews, satire, criticism, reviews, letters, parts-of-novels, long-poems, plays, non-fiction. "Suggested length of articles: 1500-2000 words. Include return postage and SAE. Recent contributors: Peter Cowie, Ingemar Lindahl, Robert Bly, Hans Dahl, Tove Ditlevsen, Anselm Hollo, Mauno Koivisto (Pres. of Finland), Vigdis Finnbogadottir (Pres. of Iceland), and others. Focus: Scandinavian culture and society." circ. 3.5M. 3/yr. Pub'd 3 issues 1990; expects 3 issues 1991, 3 issues 1992. sub. price: $15 ($20 foreign); per copy: $4; sample: $4. Back issues: 4/1985 ASF 75th Anniversary Issue, 4/1987 Finnish Independence issue, 1/88 Swedish issue, 2/1988 Norwegian issue. Discounts: negotiable. 96-104pp; 6×9¼; of. Reporting time: 3 months to publish. Payment: poetry $10 p.(a/t), articles $100-$200, fiction $75-$125 (a/t). Copyrighted, reverts to author. Pub's reviews: several in 1990. Ads: $400/$250/$150 1/4 page.

SCAREAPHANALIA, Michael Gingold, PO Box 489, Murray Hill Station, New York, NY 10156-0489. 1983. Photos, interviews, criticism, reviews, news items. "As *Scareaphanalia* is mainly a vehicle through which to express my views on the current horror film and video scene, I generally do not use outside reviewers or artists. Those interested in contributing a specific review or piece of art are welcome to write and query me, however. I frequently exchange plugs for other fanzines, but generally don't accept advertising." circ. approx. 175. 12/yr. Pub'd 12 issues 1990; expects 12 issues 1991, 12 issues 1992. sub. price: $7.50, $14 overseas; per copy: 60¢, $1 overseas; sample: same. Back issues: 60¢, list available upon request. 8pp; 7×8½; †mi. Not copyrighted. Pub's reviews: 10 in 1990. §Fanzines and books devoted to the horror cinema. Ads: none.

Scarecrow Press (see also VOYA (Voice of Youth Advocate)), Norman Horrocks, Vice President, Editorial; Barbara Lee, Senior Editor; Danielle Salti, Editor; Catherena Mescone, Associate Editor, PO Box 4167, Metuchen, NJ 08840, 201-548-8600. 1950. Poetry, criticism, music, non-fiction. "Very varied list. Emphasis on reference books, scholarly monographs, some professional textbooks. Dominant subject areas include: Cinema, women, minorities, music, literature, library science, social work, parapsychology." avg. press run 750. Expects 100 titles 1991. 12 titles listed in the *Small Press Record of Books in Print* (20th Edition, 1991-92).

avg. price, cloth: $20. Discounts: net to libraries, etc; 10% to trade (we pay post). 250pp; 5½×8½; of. Reporting time: 1 week. Payment: 10% first 1M copies; 15% thereafter. Copyrights for author. AAP, ALA.

Scareware (see also DARK TOME), Michelle Marr, PO Box 705, Salem, OR 97308, 503-371-8647. 1990. Fiction. "Horror novels published on 5¼" floppy disk for IBM and compatible" Expects 5-6 titles 1991, 10+ titles 1992. avg. price, other: $3 disk. Discounts: none. 200pp; †diskette copies. Reporting time: 2 months. Payment: 25% quarterly. Copyright for author if requested.

Scarf Press, Mark L. Levine, 58 E 83rd Street, New York, NY 10028, 212-744-3901. 1979. "Books available from Bloch Publishing. Publisher of M.C.Gaines *Picture Stories from the Bible: ...in Full Color Comic Strip Form* (old and new testament editions). No unsolicited manuscripts." avg. press run 50M. 2 titles listed in the *Small Press Record of Books in Print* (20th Edition, 1991-92). avg. price, cloth: $12.95. Discounts: order from wholesalers or Bloch Publishing, 37 W. 26 St. (9th floor), NYC 10010. 224pp (o.t.), 144pp (n.t.); 7¼×10; of. Copyrights for author.

SCARP, Five Islands Press Cooperative Ltd., R.K. Pretty, PO Box 1144, Wollongong, NSW 2500, Australia, (042) 270985. 1982. Poetry, fiction, articles, art, photos, interviews, criticism, reviews. "Prose to 3,000 words. Interviews and articles on contemporary arts and writing. *Scarp 17* features an article and prose pieces by Joanne Burns, graphics, poetry, prose fiction and reviews, plus an article on women's travel writing. Now in landscape format with improved reproduction of graphics. *Scarp 18* will feature Claud Raine." circ. 1M. 2/yr. Pub'd 2 issues 1990; expects 2 issues 1991, 2 issues 1992. sub. price: $12; per copy: $6; sample: $6. Back issues: #5-12 $2. Discounts: 40%. 80pp; size A4 landscape; laser printer. Reporting time: 2-8 weeks. Payment: poetry $20, prose $40-$100. Not copyrighted. Pub's reviews: 12 in 1990. §Poetry, fiction, interarts. Ads: $200/$130/$70 1/4 page.

SCAVENGER'S NEWSLETTER, Janet Fox, 519 Ellinwood, Osage City, KS 66523, 913-528-3538. 1984. Poetry, articles, art, cartoons, interviews, letters, news items. "*Scavenger's* is a newsletter listing markets for the sf/fantasy/horror writer or artist. Besides market news I use short (700-1000 wd.) articles of interest to the readership, poems under 10 lines as filler on sf/fantasy/horror. Art, covers 8½ X 5½" (digest) and small inside drawings no larger than 4 X 4, all art b & w. Recent contributors include Don Webb, Dan Crawford, James A. Lee, Shannon Riley." circ. 1M. 12/yr. Pub'd 12 issues 1990; expects 12 issues 1991, 12 issues 1992. sub. price: $11.50; per copy: $1.50; sample: $1.50. Back issues: none. 32pp; 8½×5½; quick print. Reporting time: 2 weeks to 1 month. Payment: $2 for poems/inside art, $4 for articles/covers on acceptance + 1 contributor's copy. Copyright not registered but symbol printed at time of publication, all rights revert to contributors. Pub's reviews: 12 in 1990. §Sf/fantasy/horror small press publications. No ads.

Scentouri, Publishing Division, A.C. Doyle, c/o Prosperity + Profits Unlimited, Distribution Services, Box 570213, Houston, TX 77257. 1982. avg. press run 1.5M. 12 titles listed in the *Small Press Record of Books in Print* (20th Edition, 1991-92). avg. price, cloth: $3.95; paper: $1.25; other: $2.50. Discounts: 25% to libraries, bookstores, etc. 35pp; 8½×11, 5½×8½. Reporting time: 6 weeks.

Art Paul Schlosser Books, Tapes, & Garbage Gazzette (see also ART'S GARBAGE GAZZETTE), Art Paul Schlosser, 214 Dunning, Madison, WI 53704, 608-249-0715. Poetry, fiction, art, cartoons, letters, news items, non-fiction. "I mostly just publish books I wrote, but am willing to look at other people's stuff. Two books released. *It's Jesus in Me*, released 1989 $6.50 and 1 year of *Art's Garbage Gazzette* $3.90 released 1991" avg. press run depends on how well they sell. Expects 1 title 1991, 1 title 1992. 8½×11. Payment: 1/2 of profits after printing cost is paid.

SCHMAGA, James E. Kern, 436 Indiana Street, Vallejo, CA 94590-4441. 1989. Poetry, fiction, articles, art, photos, cartoons, interviews, satire, criticism, reviews, music, letters, collages, news items, non-fiction. "We welcome the offbeat or controversial. Challenge us." circ. 100. 3/yr. Pub'd 3 issues 1990; expects 3 issues 1991, 3 issues 1992. sub. price: $3; per copy: $1; sample: $1. 30pp; 5½×8½; †mi. Reporting time: approx. 2 months (at most). Payment: copies only. Not copyrighted. Pub's reviews: 5 in 1990. §Music, history, politics, religion, film, just about anything.

Schneider Educational Products, Sharon Schneider, 2880 Green St., San Francisco, CA 94123, 415-567-4455. 1989. Poetry, plays, non-fiction. "We do books in series. Each series has to have a concept, be appropriate for children 6 mos-8 years old, have four beginning titles, and be expandable to 8-10 titles. Do not send original artwork or writing. 6 pics only. We cannot return submissions unless they are sent with a postage paid envelope." avg. press run 10-25M. Pub'd 4 titles 1990; expects 10 titles 1991, 10-12 titles 1992. avg. price, other: $5.95. Discounts: 50%/55% wholesalers. 12pp; 6×7⅓; †of. Reporting time: 30 days. Copyrights for author. PMA, ABA, NCBA, COSMEP, IPA.

SCHOOL MATES, U.S. Chess Federation, Jennie Simon, Bob Nasiff, 186 Route 9W, New Windsor, NY 12553, 914-562-8350. 1987. Poetry, fiction, articles, art, photos, cartoons, interviews, collages. "Length: 500-750 words; i.e., short articles for grades 3-6 about chess and chessplayers. Games, puzzles, artwork relating to chess also welcome." circ. 6M. 6/yr. Pub'd 4 issues 1990; expects 6 issues 1991, 6 issues 1992. sub. price: $7.50 ($7 to US Chess Federation 'Scholastic' members); per copy: $2.25; sample: free. Back issues: $2.25. 16pp; 8⅜×11; of. Reporting time: 2 months lead time. Payment: $40/1,000-word mss. Copyrighted. no ads.

SCHOOL SHOP, Prakken Publications, Susanne Peckham, Managing Editor, PO Box 8623, Ann Arbor, MI 48107, 313-769-1211. 1941. Articles, cartoons, news items, non-fiction. *"School Shop* serves the field of industrial education, which includes automotive, drafting, general shop, graphic arts, electronics, machine shop, welding, wood working, and other subjects of interest to teachers in junior highs, senior highs, vocational-technical schools, and community colleges" circ. 45M. 10/yr. Pub'd 10 issues 1990; expects 10 issues 1991, 10 issues 1992. sub. price: $25; per copy: $4; sample: free (note: qualified individuals receive the mag free on request). Back issues: $4. Discounts: agent= 10%, individual multi-year rates= 2 yr, $45, 3 yr $65. 80pp; 8½×11; of. Reporting time: 2 months. Payment: honorarium $25-$100, depends on length. Copyrighted, does not revert to author. Pub's reviews: 40 in 1990. §Technical/vocational education, technology, crafts. Ads: $3250/$1950/$720 1/6 page/$180 col. inch. Edpress, BPA, Educational Exhibitors Assn./ SHIP.

SCIENCE AND NATURE, The Annual of Marxist Philosophy for Natural Scientists, Lester (Hank) Talkington, Dialectics Workshop, 53 Hickory Hill, Tappan, NY 10983, 914-359-2283. 1978. Poetry, articles, art, cartoons, reviews, non-fiction. "Our primary purpose is to show how Marxist philosophy is useful to physicists, biologists and mathematicians. We negotiate on length, etc." circ. 1.5M. 1/yr. Pub'd 1 issue 1990; expects 1 issue 1991, 1 issue 1992. sub. price: $7.50; per copy: $7.50; sample: $7.50. Back issues: $5. Discounts: 40% trade, 20% classroom. 150pp; 5½×8½; of, desk top typography. Reporting time: 1-3 months. Payment: none. Copyrighted, reverts to author. Pub's reviews: 16 in 1990. §Philosophy and history of natural sciences. Ads: only exchanges.

SCIENCE AND TECHNOLOGY, Univelt, Inc., H. Jacobs, Series Editor, PO Box 28130, San Diego, CA 92128, 619-746-4005. 1964. "Space and related fields. An irregular serial. Publishers for the American Astronautical Society. Standing orders accepted. Vols 1-65 published." circ. 500-1M. Irregular. Pub'd 5 issues 1990; expects 5 issues 1991, 5 issues 1992. sub. price: no. Discounts: 20%, or more by arrangement; special prices for classroom use. 200-700pp; 7×9½; of. Reporting time: 60 days. Payment: 10% (if the volume author). Copyrighted, authors may republish material with appropriate credits given. No advertising.

SCIENCE BOOKS & FILMS, Nancy Van Gorden, Acting Editor, 1333 H Street, Northwest, Washington, DC 20005, 202-326-6463. 1965. Articles, interviews, reviews, news items. "Reviews books, films, videos and filmstrips in all the sciences for all ages" circ. 4.5M. 5/yr. Pub'd 5 issues 1990; expects 5 issues 1991, 5 issues 1992. sub. price: $35; per copy: $7 + $1.50 p/h; sample: free. Back issues: $7, plus $1.50 p/h. Discounts: agents 10%. 68pp; 8¼×11; of. Payment: none. Copyrighted, reverts to author. Pub's reviews: 1500 in 1990. §Sciences. Ads: $750/$525/$375 1/4 page.

SCIENCE FICTION CHRONICLE, Algol Press, Andrew Porter, Editor, Publisher; Don D'Ammassa, Book Critic; Vincent DiFate, Contributing Editor; Frederik Pohl, Contributing Editor; Robert Silverberg, Contributing Editor; Stephen Jones, Contributing Editor; Jo Fletcher, Contributing Editor; Jeff Rovin, Contributing Editor, PO Box 2730, Brooklyn, NY 11202-0056, 718-643-9011 (phone & fax). 1979. Articles, art, photos, reviews, letters, news items, non-fiction. *"SF Chronicle* is a monthly newsmagazine serving the SF fantasy and horror fields through current news, market reports, letters, comprehensive coverage of events, conventions and awards, columns, and reviews." circ. 5.6M. 12/yr. Pub'd 12 issues 1990; expects 12 issues 1991, 12 issues 1992. sub. price: $27 US, $33 Canada & US First class, $36 Europe, Australia, Africa, Asia; per copy: $2.75; sample: $2.75. Back issues: all issues $2.50. Discounts: 60% trade, write publisher; also distributed by Ingram Periodicals. 36-52pp; 8×11; of. Reporting time: 1 week. Payment: 3-5¢ word. Copyrighted, does not revert to author. Pub's reviews: 600 (400 book, 150 mag, 50 software) in 1990. §SF, fantasy, reference, horror, children's fantasy. Ads: $355/$182/20¢.

THE SCIENCE FICTION CONVENTION REGISTER, Erwin S. Strauss, Box 3343, Fairfax, VA 22038, 703-273-3297. 1974. "Lists upcoming science fiction and related conventions (several hundred per issue) in chronological order, indexed by place, name and participants." circ. 400. 4/yr. Pub'd 4 issues 1990; expects 4 issues 1991, 4 issues 1992. sub. price: $10; per copy: $2.50; sample: $2.50. Back issues: none available. 22pp; 8½×11; of. Copyrighted. Ads: none.

SCIENCE FOR PEOPLE, British Society For Social Responsibility In Science, 25 Horsell Road, London N5 1XL, United Kingdom, 01-607-9615. 1969. Articles, cartoons, interviews, reviews, letters, non-fiction. "Science critique. Social impact of science and scientific discovery." circ. 2M. Irregular. Pub'd 3 issues 1990; expects 4 issues 1991, 4 issues 1992. sub. price: 4 copies £5 individual, £12 institutions; per copy: £1; sample: £1. Back issues: Nos. 40-49 £5 (individual) £15 (institution). Discounts: 10%. 32pp; size A4; li. Payment: none. Copyrighted. Pub's reviews: 10 in 1990. §Suere, ecdos, food, hazards, third world, health. Ads: £120/£60.

SCIENCE/HEALTH ABSTRACTS, Phylis Austin, PO Box 319, Ft. Mitchell, AL 36856, 404-288-5495.

1980. News items, non-fiction. circ. 1M. 6/yr. Pub'd 6 issues 1990; expects 6 issues 1991, 7 issues 1992. sub. price: $6; per copy: $1; sample: $1. Back issues: $1/issue. 6pp; 8½×11; †of. Reporting time: 4-6 weeks. Payment: none. Copyrighted, reverts to author. Pub's reviews: 20 in 1990. §Health, computers, science, gardening, alternative medicine. No ads. COSMEP.

SCILLONIAN MAGAZINE, Clive Mumford, c/o T. Mumford, St. Mary's, Isles of Scilly, Cornwall, England. 1925. Poetry, fiction, articles, photos, interviews, reviews, letters, news items. "A voluntary local magazine run entirely for the islands." circ. 2.3M. 2/yr. Pub'd 2 issues 1990; expects 2 issues 1991, 2 issues 1992. sub. price: £7, £6 overseas; per copy: £1.75; sample: £3. Discounts: none. 125pp; 9×5. Reporting time: 3-4 weeks. Payment: nil. Copyrighted, reverts to author. Ads: £45/£35.

Scojtia Publishing Company, Patrique Quintahlen, Editor-in-Chief; Willard Jordan III, Business Manager & Senior Editor, 6457 Wilcox Station, PO Box 38002, Los Angeles, CA 90038, FAX 213-470-2667. 1986. "Scojtia Publishing Company publishes 5 titles a year, and plans to expand its operations in 1987; we are seeking primarily contemporary romance, historical, adventure, suspense, and science fiction in the area of fiction; we are seeking business, how to start your own business (along the lines of the *New Trends in Entrepreneuring*), how-to books related to *How To Publish Your Own Book, How To Be A Successful Self-Publisher*, health books such as *Building The Immune System through Enzymatic Vitamin Therapy*, and health related handbooks, also books on AIDS (Scholarly -related to treatment* and Vaccine Discovery and Procedures used toward Discovery of recent Vaccines,* we are seeking books on Psychology -Contemporary books like *Co-Dependent No More, How To Live With Someone* by Viscott, and *The Road Less Traveled* by M. Scott Peck, MD. We are also interested in books on Zen, and Zen books combining such disciplines as philosophy*psychology*history*and/or martial arts; we are seeking biographies from primarily scholarly, acting, science, and political backgrounds, and books on choreography and dance" avg. press run 2M-5M. Expects 5 titles 1991, 10 titles 1992. 2 titles listed in the *Small Press Record of Books in Print* (20th Edition, 1991-92). avg. price, cloth: $7.95; paper: $4.95; other: $17.95 hardback. Discounts: 1 25% prepaid, 2-9 copies 30%, 10-499 40%, 500+ 50%. 150-250pp; 6⅛×9¼; of. Reporting time: 2-9 months. Payment: standard royalty 7% to 10%. Copyrights for author. PMA.

Score (see also SCORE), Crag Hill, Bill DiMichele, Laurie Schneider, 491 Mandana Street #3, Oakland, CA 94610-2123, 415-268-9284. 1983. Poetry, fiction, art, photos, interviews, criticism, reviews, music, letters, parts-of-novels, long-poems, collages, plays, concrete art, non-fiction. "Presently, because of other publishing commitments (a magazine, a broadsize series, a color xerox series), we are only able to publish 1 book per year. Please query." avg. press run 200. Pub'd 1 title 1990; expects 1 title 1991, 1 title 1992. 9 titles listed in the *Small Press Record of Books in Print* (20th Edition, 1991-92). avg. price, paper: $5. 36pp; 8½×11; of. Reporting time: 2 months. Payment: 1/4 of first edition then copies at cost. Does not copyright for author.

SCORE, Score, Bill DiMichele, Crag Hill, Laurie Schneider, 491 Mandana Street #3, Oakland, CA 94610-2123, 415-268-9284. 1983. Articles, art, photos, interviews, criticism, reviews, letters, concrete art. "Our primary focus is the visual poem—creative, historical, theoretical—but we're also interested in any work pushing back boundaries, verse or prose. Subscription price includes 2 issues of *SCORE* plus occasional publications such as broadsides and postcards." circ. 150-250. 1/yr. Pub'd 1 issue 1990; expects 1 issue 1991, 1 issue 1992. sub. price: $6; per copy: $6; sample: $6. Back issues: query. 36pp; 8½×11; of. Reporting time: 2 weeks to 2 months. Payment: 2 copies. Not copyrighted. Pub's reviews: 6 in 1990. §We would be interested in books and magazines with a visual/literal basis. No ads.

Scots Plaid Press (Persephone Press), Mary Belle Campbell, Editor-Publisher, 22-B Pine Lake Drive, Whispering Pines, NC 28327-9388. 1987. Poetry, long-poems. "Aesthetic paperbacks. *Query first*; include bio/vita, SASE; ask for guidelines." avg. press run 500. Pub'd 4 titles 1990; expects 4 titles 1991, 4 titles 1992. avg. price, paper: $7.95. 32-64pp; size varies; of. Reporting time: 1 day to 1 month. Payment: by arrangement. Copyrights for author. NCWN, NCPS, NCHS, NCWC, P&W Inc., AWP.

Scottwall Associates, Publishers, James Heig, 95 Scott Street, San Francisco, CA 94117, 415-861-1956. 1982. Non-fiction. "We publish books on California history, biographies." avg. press run 5M-10M. Pub'd 2 titles 1990; expects 2 titles 1991, 2-3 titles 1992. 1 title listed in the *Small Press Record of Books in Print* (20th Edition, 1991-92). avg. price, cloth: $29.95; paper: $15. Discounts: 40% to bookstores in quantity orders; 40% to prepaid STOP orders; 30% single copy orders. 200pp; 8½×11; of. Reporting time: indefinite. Payment: 10% royalty on all books sold and paid for. Copyrights for author.

SCP NEWSLETTER, Tal Brooke, Brooks Alexander, PO Box 4308, Berkeley, CA 94704. 1975. Articles, interviews, reviews, letters. "*SCP* is a non-profit organization that researches and publishes information on new religious movements and spiritual trends." circ. 18M. 4/yr. Pub'd 4 issues 1990; expects 4 issues 1991, 4 issues 1992. sub. price: $25/year; per copy: $2; sample: free. Back issues: varies. Discounts: 40%. 20-30pp; 8½×11; desktop publishing. Reporting time: 3-6 weeks. Payment: varies. Copyrighted, does not revert to author. Pub's reviews: 4 in 1990. §Religion, metaphysics, theology, sociology and psychology of religion. Evangelical Press

Assocation (EPA), Box 4550, Overland Park, KS 66204, Evangelical Council on Financial Accountability.

SCREAM MAGAZINE, Alternating Crimes Publishing, Russell Judd Boone, Katherine E. Boone, PO Box 10363, Raleigh, NC 27605, 919-834-7542. 1985. Poetry, fiction, articles, art, photos, cartoons, interviews, reviews, parts-of-novels, long-poems, plays, non-fiction. "Recent contributors: Charles Bukowski, Michael S. Reynolds, Matt Feazell, William Nealy. Length: open Ace Backwords" circ. 1.5M. 2/yr. Pub'd 2 issues 1990; expects 2 issues 1991, 4 issues 1992. sub. price: $10/2 issues; per copy: $4; sample: $4 + $1 postage = $5. Back issues: Number 5 @ $5, Number 6 @ $5. Discounts: 40%, negotiate with distributors on individual basis. 64pp; 8½×11; of. Reporting time: 16 weeks. Payment: contributor's copies. Copyrighted, reverts to author. Pub's reviews: 12 in 1990. §fiction and non-fiction, graphic novel, comics, fiction, poetry, music, magazines. Ads: $300 inside covers/$200 full page/inquire for other sizes. COSMEP, N.C. Writer's Network.

THE SCREAM OF THE BUDDHA, Buddha Rose Publications, Dr. Scott Shaw, PO Box 902, Hermosa Beach, CA 90254, 213-318-6743. 1989. Poetry, fiction, art, photos, interviews, long-poems, plays. circ. 1,108. 4/yr. Pub'd 1 issue 1990; expects 4 issues 1991, 4 issues 1992. sub. price: $35; per copy: $12; sample: $12. Discounts: 100 or more per year 55%. 20pp; 5½×8½; of. Reporting time: 2 months. Payment: copy. Copyrighted, reverts to author. Pub's reviews. §Mysticism, spirituality, art, cultural studies, poetry. Ads: $1000/$500/$250 1/4 page.

SCREE, Duck Down Press, Kirk Robertson, PO Box 1047, Fallon, NV 89406, 702-423-6643. 1973. Poetry, fiction, articles, art, photos, interviews, satire, reviews, letters, long-poems, collages, concrete art. "Becoming irregular/thematic—when there is enough material and/or reason. Prospective contributors should send 5-7 poems, or a sampling of artwork/photos and *must* include a SASE if they want a reply. Interested in: work related to the visual arts - photography, collage, etc.; material from oral traditions; work that speaks strongly of the author's place - internal or external. Some contributors: Al Masarik, Charles Bukowski, Ted Kooser, Gerald Haslam, Bern Porter, Michael Hogan, Richard Shelton, Bill Fox, Dave Etter, Albert Drake, Tom Clark, Michael Hannon, Jo Harvey Allen, Ron Koetege, Gerald Locklin, etc., etc." circ. 1M. 1/yr. Expects 1 issue 1992. sub. price: $5 individuals, $17.50 institutions; per copy: #15/16 $3 + postage; #17/18 $5 + postage; #19-21 photo issue $12.95 + postage; #22/23 $3.50 + postage; sample: varies. Back issues: #1, #17/18 $5 + postage; 2-8 $2 + postage; 9/10, 11/12, 13/14, 15/16, $3 + postage, #19-21 $10. Discounts: 5 or more copies, 40%. 72-200pp; 11×17, varies; of. Reporting time: 2 weeks or so. Payment: copies and $ if possible. Copyrighted, rights revert, as long as acknowledgement to *Scree* is made upon publication elsewhere and we receive copy of the publication. Pub's reviews: 60-100 in 1990. §Poetry, contemporary fiction, collage, little mags, photography, art. Ads: inquire. CCLM.

Scribblers Publishing, Ltd., Gary Tunmore, Jean Newcomb, PO Box 90075-139, Houston, TX 77069, 713-440-5698. Poetry, fiction, art, parts-of-novels, long-poems, non-fiction. avg. press run 5M. Pub'd 3 titles 1990; expects 6 titles 1991, 12 titles 1992. avg. price, cloth: $16.95; paper: $19.95. Discounts: general. 250pp; 6×9; of. Reporting time: 6 weeks. Payment: royalties paid and negotiable. Copyrights for author. Alpha Omega Literary Agent, P.E.N., Austin Writers Guild, COSMEP.

SCRIPSI, Peter Craven, Michael Heyward, Ormond College, University of Melbourne, Parkville, Victoria 3052, Australia, (03) 3476360; 3474784. 1981. Poetry, fiction, articles, art, photos, interviews, criticism, reviews, parts-of-novels, long-poems. circ. 2M. 4/yr. Pub'd 4 issues 1990; expects 4 issues 1991, 4 issues 1992. 1 title listed in the *Small Press Record of Books in Print* (20th Edition, 1991-92). sub. price: $35; per copy: $10; sample: $10. Back issues: $10. Discounts: negotiable (25-40%). 250pp; 6¾×8¼; of. Reporting time: 8 weeks. Payment: variable. Copyrighted, reverts to author. Pub's reviews: 15 in 1990. §Poetry, fiction, criticism. Ads: $300/$150.

Script Humanistica, Bruno Diamini, Editor, 1383 Kersey Lane, Potomac, MD 20854, 301-294-7949; 614-340-1095. 1 title listed in the *Small Press Record of Books in Print* (20th Edition, 1991-92).

SCRIPT IDEAS, Gisela Hoschek, 449 Santa Fe Drive #239, Encinitas, CA 92024, 619-944-5182. 1990. Fiction, plays, non-fiction. "Publishes synopses of new screenplays for story ideas for authors' self promotion. Newsletter/tabloid format." circ. 4M. Published as filled. Expects 12 issues 1991, 12 issues 1992. 4pp; 8½×11; of. Reporting time: 7 days. Payment: none. Not copyrighted. Ads: $50 for 100 word synopsis; $40 each additional 100 words.

SCRIVENER, Sam Anson, Production; Thea Boyanowsky, Submissions; Peter Sampson, Managing, McGill University, 853 Sherbrooke Street W., Montreal, P.Q. H3A 2T6, Canada, 514-398-6588. 1980. Poetry, fiction, art, photos, interviews, satire, criticism, reviews, non-fiction. "Recent book reviews only. Prose less than 25 pages typed; creative shorts. Poetry 3-10 pages. Black & white photos and graphics. Please send international reply coupon (not U.S. stamps) + self-addressed envelopes. New material only—no reprints. Does not report from May to August." circ. 1.5M. 1/yr. Pub'd 1 issue 1990; expects 1 issue 1991, 1 issue 1992. sub. price: $4.50/yr; $4 multi-year; per copy: $5; sample: $3. Back issues: $2.50/issue. Discounts: 40% commission for 10 or more copies. 85pp; 7×9; of. Reporting time: 4-6 months. Payment: 6 free copies; limited cash payments.

Copyrighted, reverts to author. Pub's reviews: 14 in 1990. §Canadian and American fiction, poetry, criticism. Ads: $225/$165/$100 1/4 page/Business Card $65. CPPA.

Scroll Publishing Co., David W. Bercot, Rt 19, Box 890, Tyler, TX 75706, 214-597-8023. 1989. Non-fiction. "We publish primarily works pertaining to the early Christians and their writings (A.D. 100-325). Query letter must precede all submissions." avg. press run 10M. Pub'd 2 titles 1990; expects 3 titles 1991, 3 titles 1992. 5 titles listed in the *Small Press Record of Books in Print* (20th Edition, 1991-92). avg. price, paper: $7.95. Discounts: 40% to bookstores. 175pp; of. Reporting time: 60 days. Payment: negotiable. Does not copyright for author. CBA.

SE LA VIE WRITER'S JOURNAL, Rio Grande Press, Rosalie Avara, Editor, PO Box 371371, El Paso, TX 79937, 915-595-2625. 1987. Poetry, fiction, articles, art, cartoons, interviews, reviews, letters, plays, concrete art, news items, non-fiction. "'Life' theme (La Vie) through; poems to 30 lines; short stories, essays, limited to 500 words; fillers, anecdotes, limited to 150 words. Recently published poems by Marian Ford Park, Harry B. Sheftel, Alice Mackenzie Swaim, Marianne McNeil and Kenneth G. Geisert. Also accept b&w cartoons, cartoons, cover designs, short humor poems. Contests held each quarter in poetry, essays, short stories, with special monthly contests included. Subscribers receive free entry coupon." circ. 300. 4/yr. Pub'd 4 issues 1990; expects 4 issues 1991, 4 issues 1992. sub. price: $14, $16 Canada, $18 foreign (US funds); per copy: $4; sample: $4, $5 foreign (US funds). 80pp; 5½×8½; photocopied, saddle stapled. Reporting time: 6-8 weeks after contest ends. Payment: reg.-1 copy, contests pay from $5 to $25. Copyrighted, reverts to author. Pub's reviews: 12 in 1990. §Chapbooks of poetry, prose, short stories, and new small press publications. Ads: $50/$25/$5 per display/$3 for 3 lines. El Paso Writers League, TX Freelance Writers Assoc., El Paso MS Club.

Sea Challengers, Ken Hashagen, Editor, 4 Somerset Rise, Monterey, CA 93940, 408-373-6306. 1977. avg. press run 5M. Pub'd 1 title 1990; expects 2 titles 1991, 2 titles 1992. 9 titles listed in the *Small Press Record of Books in Print* (20th Edition, 1991-92). avg. price, cloth: $25; paper: $18.95. Discounts: STOP 25%; 2-9, 40%; 10-99, 45%; 100+ 50%. 112pp; 7×9, 8×10; lp. Reporting time: 30 days. Payment: 10% of retail on each book sold up to 49% & 7% of retail of books sold at 50% discount or below; no royalties on the first 300 copies, 4% on co-invested books. Copyrights for author.

Sea Fog Press, Inc. (see also HARMONY: VOICES FOR A JUST FUTURE), Rose Evans, 447 20th Avenue, San Francisco, CA 94121, 415-221-8527. 1982. Non-fiction. "2 children's books published, 1 bimonthly magazine." avg. press run 5M. Expects 1 title 1991. 2 titles listed in the *Small Press Record of Books in Print* (20th Edition, 1991-92). avg. price, cloth: $12.95; paper: $7.95. Discounts: bookstores 4+ copies, 40%. 200pp; 8½×11; of. Reporting time: 1 month. Payment: standard. Copyrights for author.

SEA KAYAKER, Christopher Cunningham, 6329 Seaview Avenue NW, Seattle, WA 98107, 206-789-1326. 1984. Fiction, articles, art, photos, cartoons, interviews, reviews, letters, non-fiction. "1M-3M words; specializing in sea kayaking; bias towards environmental." circ. 10M-12M. 4/yr. Pub'd 4 issues 1990; expects 4 issues 1991, 4 issues 1992. sub. price: $13; per copy: $3.50; sample: $4.60 postpaid. Discounts: 12 and up returnable, 40%; 12 and up non-returnable, 45%. 76pp; 7¼×10; sheet fed. Reporting time: 2 months. Payment: $50-$100 per publ. page, on publication. Copyrighted, reverts to author. Pub's reviews: 4 in 1990. §kayaking. Ads: $910/$695/$360 1/4/$265 1/6/$210 1/8.

Sea Otter Press, PO Box 4484, Rolling Bay, WA 98061, 206-842-8148. 1 title listed in the *Small Press Record of Books in Print* (20th Edition, 1991-92).

Sea Sports Publications, Robert J. Bachand, Editor; Mike Gachek, Associate Editor, PO Box 647, 10 Buckingham Place, Norwalk, CT 06852-0647, 203-866-5376. 1979. Photos, non-fiction. avg. press run 2M-3M. Pub'd 1 title 1990; expects 1 title 1991, 1 title 1992. avg. price, cloth: $19.95; paper: $11.95. Discounts: 1-2 30%, 3-49 40%, 50+ 50%. 110-400pp; 6×9; of, camera-ready from laser printer. Reporting time: 6 weeks. Payment: 7.5%-10% of retail. Copyrights for author.

Sea Urchin Press, Eileen J. Ostrow, PO Box 10503, Oakland, CA 94610-0503, 415-428-0178. 1977. Poetry, photos, plays, non-fiction. "Not soliciting new work at the current time." avg. press run varies. 2 titles listed in the *Small Press Record of Books in Print* (20th Edition, 1991-92). of. Payment: 10%. Copyrights for author. Pacific Center for Book Arts.

Seabird Publishing, Pat Nobles, PO Box 624, Broken Arrow, OK 74013, 918-258-6209. 1986. Expects 2 titles 1991, 4 titles 1992. 1 title listed in the *Small Press Record of Books in Print* (20th Edition, 1991-92). avg. price, paper: $2.95. Discounts: 20% 2-4 books; 40% 5-24; 43% 25-49; 46% 50-99; 50% 100+. 224pp; 4¼×6¾; of. Western Writers of America.

Seacoast Information Services, John Hacunda, 4446 South County Trail, Charlestown, RI 02813, 401-364-6419. 1990. Non-fiction. "*Computers and Visual Stress: How to Enhance Visual Comfort While Using Computers.*" avg. press run 5M. Pub'd 1 title 1990; expects 1 title 1991, 2 titles 1992. 1 title listed in the *Small Press Record of Books in Print* (20th Edition, 1991-92). avg. price, paper: $10. Discounts: 3 or more, 40%; 200

or more, 50%. 100-200pp; 5½×8½; of. Reporting time: 2 months. Payment: negotiable. Copyrights for author. COSMEP, Publishers Marketing Association.

The Seal Press, Barbara Wilson, Faith Conlon, 3131 Western Avenue, Suite 410, Seattle, WA 98121-1028, 206-283-7844. 1976. Fiction, non-fiction. "Feminist fiction and women's studies. New Leaf Series for women in abusive relationships. Translations." avg. press run 2M-8M. Pub'd 9 titles 1990; expects 10 titles 1991, 12 titles 1992. 51 titles listed in the *Small Press Record of Books in Print* (20th Edition, 1991-92). avg. price, cloth: $16.95; paper: $8.95. Discounts: standard. 5½×8½; of. Reporting time: 2 months. Payment: 7% (trade paperback); standard payment. Copyrights for author. COSMEP, PMA, Pacific NW Book Publishers' Association.

THE SEARCH - JOURNAL FOR ARAB AND ISLAMIC STUDIES, Center for Arab and Islamic Studies, Samir Abed-Rabbo, PO Box 543, Brattleboro, VT 05301, 802-257-0872. 1980. Articles, criticism, reviews. "A scholarly journal for Arab and Islamic Studies, including politics, economics, history, religion, sociology, art, etc." circ. 4M. 1/yr. Expects 1 issue 1991, 1 issue 1992. sub. price: $15 indiv., $25 org.; per copy: $15 indiv., $25 org.; sample: $15 indiv., $25 org. Back issues: $15 indiv., $25 org. Discounts: student $12. 120pp; 5½×8½; of. Reporting time: 1 month. Copyrighted, reverts to author. Pub's reviews. §Arab and Islamic Studies. Ads: $300/$175.

Seascape Enterprises, Patrica Blaszak, PO Box 176, Colonial Heights, VA 23834, 804-526-7119. 1984. Poetry, non-fiction. "Boating or marine themes only. Black and white or color. All work is illustrated. Book trade distribution by The Talman Co. Marine trade distribution by Plath, Ltd. All other distribution by Seascape Enterprises." avg. press run 5M. Pub'd 2 titles 1990; expects 4 titles 1991, 2-3 titles 1992. 6 titles listed in the *Small Press Record of Books in Print* (20th Edition, 1991-92). avg. price, cloth: $24.95; paper: $17.95; other: $7.95 kids. Discounts: 1-4 20%, 5-9 40%, 10-19 45%, 20+ 50%. Adult 360 pp, kids 32pp; size varies; of. Reporting time: up to 1 year. Payment: negotiable. Copyrights for author. Washington Book Publishers.

SEATTLE STAR, Michael Dowers, Starhead Comix, PO Box 30044, Seattle, WA 98103. 1982. Cartoons. circ. 8M. 6/yr. Pub'd 6 issues 1990; expects 6 issues 1991, 6 issues 1992. sub. price: $6.50; per copy: $1; sample: same. Back issues: $1. Discounts: will trade ad discount, bulk orders. 16-20pp; 9½×12½; web. Payment: none. Copyrighted, reverts to author. Pub's reviews: 4 in 1990. §Cartooning—alternative/ underground type publication. Ads: $200/$100/$50 1/4 page.

Second Aeon Publications, Peter Finch, 19 Southminster Road, Roath, Cardiff, Wales CF2 5AT, Great Britain, 0222-493093. 1967. Poetry, art, long-poems, collages, concrete art. avg. press run 300-1M. Pub'd 1 title 1990. 2 titles listed in the *Small Press Record of Books in Print* (20th Edition, 1991-92). avg. price, paper: £3. Discounts: by arrangement. 50pp; size A4; mi, of. Reporting time: 2 weeks. Payment: by arrangement. Does not copyright for author. ALP.

Second Coming Press, A.D. Winans, PO Box 31249, San Francisco, CA 94131, 415-991-2302. 1972. Poetry, fiction. avg. press run 1M-1.5M. Pub'd 1 title 1990; expects 1 title 1992. 41 titles listed in the *Small Press Record of Books in Print* (20th Edition, 1991-92). avg. price, cloth: $12.95; paper: $4.95. Discounts: 20% library only if this listed source is quoted. 40% Bookstores: 5 or more copies. 64-72pp, anthologies 200-240pp; 5½×8½, anthologies 6×9; of. Reporting time: 30 days. Payment: 10% of press run, 50% of any profit after expenses are met. Only copyrights for author upon arrangement. COSMEP, CLMP.

The Second Hand, Janice Stiefel, PO Box 204, Plymouth, WI 53073, 414-893-5226. 1980. avg. press run 500. avg. price, paper: $3.50. 50pp; 5½×8½; †mi. Does not copyright for author.

SECONDS MAGAZINE, S. Barrymore Blush, PO Box 2553, Stuyvesant Station, New York, NY 10009, 212-260-0481. 1987. Articles, art, photos, cartoons, interviews, music. "*Seconds* offers in-depth discussions with rock music's most intriguing personalities, regardless of genre or mass popular appeal. Contributors include top underground music/art writers like Steven Blush, Carlo McCormick, George Petros and artists/photogs like Robert Williams, Michael Lavine, R. Kern, and Mark Leialoha." circ. 10M. 6/yr. Pub'd 4 issues 1990; expects 6 issues 1991, 6 issues 1992. sub. price: $15; per copy: $2.50; sample: $2.50. Back issues: $3 each; 10 copies for $25; 15 copies for $31. Discounts: dependent on order. 40pp; 10½×14½. Reporting time: 60 days. Payment: $100 per interview. Copyrighted, reverts to author. Pub's reviews: 20 in 1990. §Music, art. Ads: $300 (b/w)/$150 (b/w)/$80 (b/w) 1/4 page; add $150 per color.

SECRETARIAL/OFFICE SERVICES QUARTERLY, Kay Young, 1421 Willow Brook Cove #4, St. Louis, MO 63146, 314-567-3636. 1991. Articles, cartoons, reviews. "Short articles related to secretarial services or other office support services" 4/yr. Expects 1 issue 1991, 4 issues 1992. sub. price: $25; per copy: $7; sample: $3. 12-14pp; 4¼×8½. Payment: free subscription. Copyrighted, reverts to author. Pub's reviews. §Secretarial services, small business, word processing, desktop publishing.

Security Seminars Press, David Y. Coverston, Martha C. Coverston, 5724 S.E. 4th Street, PO Box 70162, Ocala, FL 32670-0162, 904-694-6185. avg. press run 1.5M. Expects 3 titles 1991. 7 titles listed in the *Small*

Press Record of Books in Print (20th Edition, 1991-92). avg. price, cloth: $15; paper: $12. Discounts: STOP + TO 50%. 200pp; 5½×8½. FPA.

Sedna Press, Joanne Townsend, Co-Editor; Ann Chandonnet, Co-Editor, 5522 Cope Street, Anchorage, AK 99518, 333-8324. 1 title listed in the *Small Press Record of Books in Print* (20th Edition, 1991-92).

See Sharp Press, Charles Bufe, PO Box 6118, San Francisco, CA 94101, 415-626-2160; FAX 626-2685. 1984. Non-fiction. "Length is unimportant—quality is the deciding factor; our published works range from a 4,000 word pamphlet to a 100,000-plus word quotations book. Biases are towards works with anarchist and/or atheist views and toward works providing practical information. We value clear writing and dislike verbal exhibitionism and the use of academic and political jargon. We do all of our own pre-press work (design, typesetting, camera work, layout) and operate under the name Typesetting Etc. Much of our work involves producing materials for other small publishers." avg. press run 1M-3M. Pub'd 1 title 1990; expects 2 titles 1991, 2 titles 1992. 11 titles listed in the *Small Press Record of Books in Print* (20th Edition, 1991-92). avg. price, paper: $9.95; other: $1.50 pamphlets. Discounts: bookstores 40%, distributors 50%. 24-150pp; 5½×8½, vary; of. Reporting time: very quickly. Payment: varies according to material. Copyrights for author. COSMEP.

Seed Center, Norton DeRay, Director, PO Box 1700, Redway, CA 95560-1700, 707-923-2524. 1972. Fiction, non-fiction. "Generally oriented but not limited to self-awareness, self-discovery & metaphysical topics." avg. press run 2M. Expects 1 title 1991. 1 title listed in the *Small Press Record of Books in Print* (20th Edition, 1991-92). avg. price, paper: $8. Discounts: trade, jobber. 100-150pp; 4¼×7⅛, 6×9; of. Reporting time: varies, 1-4 months. Payment: 8 to 15% paid semi-annually. Copyrights for author.

SEED SAVERS EXCHANGE, Kent Whealy, RR 3, Box 239, Decorah, IA 52101, 319-382-5990. 1975. Articles, photos, interviews, letters, non-fiction. "Seed Exchange of Heirloom Vegetable & Fruit Varieties." circ. 5M. 3/yr. Pub'd 3 issues 1990; expects 3 issues 1991, 3 issues 1992. 4 titles listed in the *Small Press Record of Books in Print* (20th Edition, 1991-92). sub. price: $25. Back issues: not available. 180pp; 7½×10½; of. Payment: none. Copyrighted. §Heirloom vegetables and also seed saving and seed storage techniques. No ads accepted.

SEEMS, Karl Elder, Editor, c/o Lakeland College, Box 359, Sheboygan, WI 53082-0359. 1971. Poetry, fiction, articles, reviews, parts-of-novels, long-poems. "No. 14, *What Is the Future of Poetry?*, in its third printing, contains essays by Cutler, Dacey, Dunn, Evans, Elliott, Etter, Flaherty, Gildner, Hathaway, Heffernan, Hershon, Heyen, Hilton, Matthews, McKeowin, Morgan, Oliphant, Rice, Scott, Sobin, Stryk, and Zimmer. ($5)" circ. 350. Irregular. Pub'd 1 issue 1990; expects 1 issue 1991, 1 issue 1992. 3 titles listed in the *Small Press Record of Books in Print* (20th Edition, 1991-92). sub. price: $16/4 issues; per copy: $4; sample: $4. Discounts: 25%. 40pp; 8½×7; of. Reporting time: 1-3 months. Payment: copies. Copyrighted, reverts to author. CLMP.

The Segue Foundation, James Sherry, Editor, 303 East 8th Street, New York, NY 10009. 1977. Poetry, criticism. avg. press run 1M. Pub'd 4 titles 1990. 30 titles listed in the *Small Press Record of Books in Print* (20th Edition, 1991-92). avg. price, paper: $7.50. Discounts: bookstores 40%. 85pp; size varies; of. Reporting time: long. Payment: 10% of run. CLMP.

Seismograph Publications, Michael J. Mayo, PO Box 170127, San Francisco, CA 94117. 1985. Poetry, long-poems. "*Practising Angels: A Contemporary Anthology of San Francisco Bay Area Poetry* features recent work from 70 poets of the Bay Area, including: Alegria, Broughton, Corso, Cruz, DiPrima, Duncan, Ferlinghetti, Fraser, Grahn, Griffin, Gunn, Hirschman, Meltzer, Mirikitani, Norse, Palmer, Ronan, Walker, and Wong. Winner 1987 American Book Award. We solicit only. Please do not send mss. without inquiring first." avg. press run 1M-2M. Expects 1 title 1991, 3 titles 1992. 2 titles listed in the *Small Press Record of Books in Print* (20th Edition, 1991-92). avg. price, paper: $9.95. Discounts: 40% to the trade. 5½×8½; of. Copyrights for author.

Selah Publishing Co., David P. Schaap, John Worst, PO Box 103, Accord, NY 12404, 201-249-9849. 1988. Articles, criticism, music. "Publish primarily in the field of Church Music and Hymnology. Books vary in length from small to large publications." avg. press run 5M. Expects 2 titles 1991, 2-4 titles 1992. 1 title listed in the *Small Press Record of Books in Print* (20th Edition, 1991-92). avg. price, cloth: $12; paper: $9. Discounts: trade 1-2 copies 20%, 3-49 40%, 50-99 45%, 100+ 50%. 200pp; 6×9; of. Reporting time: 1-2 months. Payment: generally 10% of retail sales price. Copyrights for author.

Select Press (see also JOURNAL OF SOCIAL BEHAVIOR AND PERSONALITY), Roderick P. Crandall, Ph.D., PO Box 37, Corte Madera, CA 94925, 415-924-1612. 1986.

Selective Books, Inc., Lee Howard, Box 1140, Clearwater, FL 34617. 1970. "Business opportunity and moneymaking books related to business." avg. press run 5M. Expects 2 titles 1991. 5 titles listed in the *Small Press Record of Books in Print* (20th Edition, 1991-92). avg. price, paper: $10. Discounts: 40% to retail stores; 50% to wholesalers or mail order dealers. Quantity lot prices for 100 or more by quote. 100pp; web offset. Reporting time: immediate, query first. Payment: individual. Copyrights for author.

518

Selene Books, Robert Navon, PO Box 220-253, El Paso, TX 79913. 1983. Poetry. "We are a scholarly reprint publisher, reprinting serious books of literature and philosophy for scholars and libraries. Right now we are starting the 'Great Works of Philosophy Series' which will emphasize works in the Platonic/Pythagorean traditions. Accepting submissions in metaphysical/occult books of serious quality and well-written stories for our Selene Literary Series." avg. press run 500. Pub'd 3 titles 1990; expects 3 titles 1991, 3 titles 1992. 14 titles listed in the *Small Press Record of Books in Print* (20th Edition, 1991-92). avg. price, cloth: $15-35; paper: $5-15. Discounts: 20%. 100-250pp; 6×9; of.

SELF AND SOCIETY, Vivian Milroy, 62 Southward Bridge Road, London, England. 1973. Poetry, fiction, photos, cartoons, interviews, criticism, reviews, letters, news items. "Material within field of humanistic psychology; length from 500 to 5000 words: popular science approach, not too much jargon. Recent articles on Wilhelm Reich, Carl Rogers, Abraham Maslow. Psychodrama, sexual politics." circ. 3.5M. 6/yr. Pub'd 6 issues 1990; expects 6 issues 1991, 6 issues 1992. 7 titles listed in the *Small Press Record of Books in Print* (20th Edition, 1991-92). sub. price: £13; per copy: £2.00; sample: £1. Back issues: £2.50. Discounts: 33⅓%. 56pp; size A5; of. Reporting time: 1 month. Payment: nil. Copyrighted, reverts to author. Pub's reviews: 24 in 1990. §Psychology (humanistic, growth movement), human potential. Ads: £50/£30/10p. AHP.

Selous Foundation Press, 325 Pennsylvania Avenue, SE, Washington, DC 20001. 1987. "Agent: American Comnet, Inc., 2101 Wilson Blvd, Suite 523, Arlington, VA 22201. Contact: Fay S. Gold" avg. press run 3M. Pub'd 2 titles 1990; expects 4 titles 1991, 6 titles 1992. 4 titles listed in the *Small Press Record of Books in Print* (20th Edition, 1991-92). avg. price, cloth: $17.95. Discounts: bookstores-prorated by # of copies, discounters/sales reps—60%/60 days, 55%/90 days. 250pp. Reporting time: 90 days. Payment: negotiable. Copyrights for author. Publishers Marketing Assoc., American Booksellers Assoc.

Seminal Life Press (see also LOUDER THAN BOMBS), Bryan Ha, 2313 Santa Anita Avenue, S. El Monte, CA 91733, 818-575-1887. 1990. Poetry, fiction. "Plan to do 15-20 poems chapbooks, to be distributed free. Everything is welcome. Also would like to see short stories." avg. press run 200. Expects 4 titles 1991, 4 titles 1992. †Xerox. Reporting time: within 1 week. Copyrights for author.

Semiotext Foreign Agents Books Series (see also SEMIOTEXT(E)), Jim Fleming, Sylvere Lotringer, 522 Philosophy Hall, Columbia University, New York, NY 10027, 212-280-3956. 1983. "Small books under 250 pages; politics, philosophy and culture" avg. press run 5M. Pub'd 3 titles 1990; expects 5 titles 1991, 7 titles 1992. avg. price, paper: $4.95. Discounts: Trade, 40%; distributors, 50%. 200pp; 4½×7; of. Reporting time: 6 weeks. Payment: arranged per title. Copyrights for author.

SEMIOTEXT(E), Autonomedia, Inc., Semiotext Foreign Agents Books Series, Sylvere Lotringer, Jim Fleming, 522 Philosophy Hall, Columbia University, New York, NY 10027, 212-280-3956. 1974. "Do not solicit submissions" circ. 6M. 2/yr. Pub'd 1 issue 1990; expects 2 issues 1991, 2 issues 1992. sub. price: $12; per copy: $6; sample: $6. Discounts: Trade discount 40%; distributors, 50%. 350pp; 6×10; of. Copyrighted, reverts to author. Pub's reviews. Ads: $500/$250.

Senay Publishing Inc., James Senay, President, PO Box 397, Chesterland, OH 44026, 216-256-8519. 1979. avg. press run 20M. Expects 1 title 1991. 3 titles listed in the *Small Press Record of Books in Print* (20th Edition, 1991-92). avg. price, paper: $7.95. Discounts: on request. 200pp; 6×9; of. Copyrights for author.

SENECA REVIEW, Deborah Tall, Hobart & William Smith Colleges, Geneva, NY 14456, 315-781-3349. 1970. Poetry, articles, interviews, criticism, long-poems. circ. 600. 2/yr. Pub'd 2 issues 1990; expects 2 issues 1991, 2 issues 1992. sub. price: $8, $15 2 years; per copy: $5; sample: $5. Back issues: $5. Discounts: 40% trade for stores. 100pp; 8½×5½; lp. Reporting time: 3-10 weeks. Payment: copies. Copyrighted, reverts to author. Ads: $75/special small press rates/exchange. CLMP, NYSSPA.

SENSATIONS, David Messineo, International Poetry Editor, c/o 2 Radio Avenue, #A5, Secaucus, NJ 07094. 1987. Poetry, fiction, art, long-poems. circ. 250. 2/yr. Pub'd 1 issue 1990; expects 1 issue 1991, 2 issues 1992. sub. price: $12; sample: $7. Back issues: $7 4th issue. 50-70pp; 8½×11; combination of offset and high-quality copying (original done on Laser Writer). Reporting time: 2-6 weeks after deadline. Copyrighted, reverts to author. §Other small literary magazines, other internationally distributed literary magazines. Ads: $100/$50.

THE $ENSIBLE SOUND, Karl Nehring, 403 Darwin Drive, Snyder, NY 14226, 716-681-3513. 1976. Articles, art, photos, cartoons, interviews, satire, criticism, reviews, music, letters, news items, non-fiction. "We run mainly audio equipment reviews, musical recording reviews, audio semi-technical articles, and audio and music industry news" circ. 8M. 4/yr. Pub'd 4 issues 1990; expects 4 issues 1991, 4 issues 1992. sub. price: $18; per copy: $5.50; sample: $2. Back issues: $3 each after one year old. Discounts: 5 or more - $2 each. 60pp; 5½×8½; of. Reporting time: 2 weeks. Payment: yes. Copyrighted, reverts to author. Pub's reviews: 14 in 1990. §Technical, music related, audio related. Ads: $700/$420.

SENSOR, George Rawlins, Connie Rawlins, PO Box 16074, San Diego, CA 92116. 1976. Poetry, fiction, art, photos, cartoons, long-poems, collages, concrete art. "Recent contributors: Ivan Arguelles, Vern Rutsala, Judith

Rasco, William Virgil Davis, Robert Peters, Fred Moramarco, Karl Kempton, Richard Kostelanetz, Glenna Luschei, Madam X. Interested in both unknown and established writers'' circ. 700. 1/yr. Pub'd 1 issue 1990; expects 1 issue 1991, 1 issue 1992. sub. price: $5; per copy: $5; sample: $5. Back issues: $5. Discounts: 40%. 80pp; 8½×7; of. Reporting time: 2 months. Payment: 1 copy. Copyrighted, reverts to author. Pub's reviews. Ads: $40/$20. COSMEP.

Sentinel Books, George Biggers, Sentinel Communications Co., 633 North Orange Avenue, Orlando, FL 32801, 407-420-5588. 1987. Articles, reviews, news items, non-fiction. "General trade titles as well as titles of regional interest." avg. press run 20M. Pub'd 6 titles 1990; expects 8 titles 1991, 10 titles 1992. 20 titles listed in the *Small Press Record of Books in Print* (20th Edition, 1991-92). avg. price, cloth: $24.95; paper: $8.95. Full discount schedules apply. 192pp; 6×9; †of. Reporting time: 1 month. Payment: negotiable royalty. Copyrights for author. PAS, SEBA, ABA, BISAC.

SEPIA, Kawabata Press, Colin David Webb, Editor, Knill Cross House, Higher Anderton Road, Millbrook, Nr Torpoint, Cornwall, England. 1977. Poetry, fiction, articles, art, reviews. "Shorter prose (under about 2.5M words preferred), shorter poems (under 40 lines preferred), short reviews (under 2.5M words preferred). Recent contributors: Steve Walker, Jacques Du Lumiere, E. Wexler, B. Darldorf" circ. 150. 3/yr. Pub'd 3 issues 1990; expects 3 issues 1991, 3 issues 1992. sub. price: $3; per copy: 50p ($1); sample: 50p ($1). Back issues: as above, issues 35, 36, 37. 32pp; 6×8½; of. Reporting time: 14 days. Payment: free copy. Copyrighted, reverts to author. Pub's reviews: 19 in 1990. §Poetry, fiction.

SEQUOIA, Carlos Rodriguez, Poetry Editor; Marion Rust, Fiction Editor, Storke Publications Bldg., Stanford, CA 94305. 1897. Poetry, fiction, photos, interviews, criticism, reviews, long-poems, plays. "We publish innovative, beautiful language. Are not interested in flat 'realism', in fiction or in workshop poetry. (Formal verse welcome). Recent contributors: N. Scott Momaday, J. V. Cunningham, Al Young, Seamus Heaney, Rita Dove, Susan Howe, Clark Coolidge, Janet Lewis." circ. 1M. 2/yr. Pub'd 3 issues 1990; expects 2 issues 1991, 2 issues 1992. sub. price: $10; per copy: $5; sample: $5. Back issues: varies. Discounts: none. 80pp; 6×9; of. Reporting time: 2 months. Payment: multiple copies. Copyrighted, reverts to author. Pub's reviews: 4 in 1990. §Contemporary fiction, poetry, literary criticism, feminist issues. Ads: $100/$60.

Serendipity Systems (see also THE ELECTRONIC PUBLISHING FORUM), John Galuszka, PO Box 140, San Simeon, CA 93452. 1986. Fiction, non-fiction. "Serendipity Systems publishes BOOKS-ON-DISKS editions (fiction) and distributes BOOKWARE editions (any genre or type of book). All books are 'printed' on IBM-PC computer disks." avg. press run 'printed' to order. Pub'd 19 titles 1990. 14 titles listed in the *Small Press Record of Books in Print* (20th Edition, 1991-92). avg. price, other: BOOKS-ON-DISKS $6-$10; BOOKWARE $4. Discounts: discounts to 45%. †IBM-PC computer disks. Reporting time: 4 weeks. Payment: BOOKS-ON-DISKS 33%, BOOKWARE 25%. Copyrights for author. COSMEP.

SERIALS REVIEW, Pierian Press, Pamela Abston, Managing Editor; Will Hepfer, Co-Editor; Cindy Hepfer, Co-Editor, PO Box 1808, Ann Arbor, MI 48106, 313-434-5530. 1975. Articles, reviews. 4/yr. Pub'd 4 issues 1990; expects 4 issues 1991, 4 issues 1992. sub. price: $45; per copy: $13.50; sample: free. 110pp; 8½×11; of. Reporting time: 4 weeks. Payment: none. Pierian Press holds copyright. Pub's reviews: 400-500 in 1990. §All new serials, all books dealing with serials. Ads: inquire.

SERIE D'ECRITURE, Spectacular Diseases, Rosmarie Waldrop, 83(b) London Road, Peterborough, Cambs. PE2 9BS, England. 1980. Poetry, fiction, parts-of-novels, long-poems. "Translations of current French writing. No unsolicited submissions needed." circ. 500. 1/yr. Pub'd 1 issue 1990; expects 1 issue 1991, 1 issue 1992. sub. price: $9.50; per copy: $5.50; sample: $5.50 or $6.50. Back issues: $3.50 Issues #1-4, $5.50 Issues 5 on. Discounts: 40-50% dependent upon contract. 64pp; of. Payment: copies. Copyrighted, reverts to author. ALP.

Serpent & Eagle Press, Jo Mish, 273 Main Street, Oneonta, NY 13820, 607-432-5604. 1981. Poetry, fiction, art, photos, non-fiction. "I've shifted emphasis to short book-length work on historical & folk-lore oriented subjects. I'll put out an occasional book of poetry." avg. press run 200. Pub'd 2 titles 1990; expects 2 titles 1991, 2 titles 1992. avg. price, cloth: $15; paper: $5. Discounts: 40%. 30pp; 6×8; †1p. Reporting time: not accepting submissions during 1991. Payment: varies. Does not copyright for author.

Seven Buffaloes Press (see also BLACK JACK & VALLEY GRAPEVINE; THE AZOREAN EXPRESS; THE BREAD AND BUTTER CHRONICLES; HILL AND HOLLER; THE BADGER STONE CHRONICLES), Art Cuelho, Box 249, Big Timber, MT 59011. 1973. Poetry, fiction, art, photos, interviews, reviews, parts-of-novels, long-poems, collages. "Book-length manuscripts are not being accepted at this time. I do publish some books, even novels, but the authors are those that have had work in my magazines." avg. press run 750. Pub'd 8 titles 1990; expects 2 titles 1991. 63 titles listed in the *Small Press Record of Books in Print* (20th Edition, 1991-92). avg. price, paper: $6.75. Discounts: 1-4, 0%; 5 copies or over, 40%. 80pp; 5½×8½; †of. Reporting time: within a week; sometimes same day. Payment: negotiable. Copyrights for author. CLMP.

700 Elves Press (see also COLOR WHEEL), Frederick Moe, William Szostak, 4 Washington Court,

Concord, NH 03301. 1990. Poetry, fiction, art, photos, music. "700 Elves Press publishes literary magazine *Color Wheel*, anthologies, cassettes and chapbooks. SASE is essential for guidelines or current projects." avg. press run varies according to title. Expects 3 titles 1991, 3 titles 1992. avg. price, other: varies. of. Reporting time: 4-6 weeks. Payment: copies or contractual arrangements. Does not copyright for author.

Seven Locks Press, James A. Morris, P.O. Box 27, Cabin John, MD 20818, (301) 320-2130. 1978. avg. press run 5M. Pub'd 6 titles 1990; expects 8 titles 1991, 10 titles 1992. 28 titles listed in the *Small Press Record of Books in Print* (20th Edition, 1991-92). avg. price, cloth: $14.95; paper: $9.95. Discounts: usual. Pages vary; size varies. Reporting time: 1 month. Payment: normally 10% on receipts. Copyrights for author.

Seventh Son Press (see also BLIND ALLEYS), Glenford H. Cummings, Charles Lynch, Aissatou Mijiza, Michael S. Weaver, Rutgers Univ, Box 29, Camden, NJ 08102, 609-757-6117. 1982. Poetry, fiction, plays. "We are devoted mainly to *Blind Alleys*. Manuscripts of poetry and fiction are accepted only on invitation" avg. press run 500. Expects 1 title 1991, 2 titles 1992. Discounts: 40% to bookstores, libraries and jobbers. 70pp; 6×9. Reporting time: 3-6 months. Payment: varies with contract. Does not copyright for author. CCLM.

Seventh-Wing Publications, 515 East Washington Street, Colorado Springs, CO 80907, 719-471-2932. 1987. Fiction, non-fiction. "Ms should be sent with SASE only after an approved query. We want to firmly establish a list with a couple of 'strong' how-to's, philosophy/psychology, well-written literature, and maybe a few more children's books. Writers should be a cut above the rest and general first rough should be well over a hundred pages; children's work is an exception. Seventh-Wing is primarily interested in true literary work, not so much work that has a commercial slant. Any mss sent before query will be promptly returned to addressee" avg. press run 500-1M. Expects 3 titles 1991, 5 titles 1992. 4 titles listed in the *Small Press Record of Books in Print* (20th Edition, 1991-92). avg. price, cloth: $10.95; paper: $4.95; other: $1.95 children's books. Discounts: typical trade schedule. 120pp; 4×7; of, lp. Reporting time: 1 month—must query first. Payment: will vary with each book/contract. Copyrights for author. R.R. Bowker, Publisher's Weekly, H.W. Wilson, Baker & Taylor.

SEWANEE REVIEW, George Core, Editor, Univ. of the South, Sewanee, TN 37375, 615-598-1246. 1892. Poetry, fiction, articles, criticism, reviews, letters, parts-of-novels, non-fiction. "Publish book reviews, but books and reviewers are selected by editor." circ. 3.4M. 4/yr. Pub'd 4 issues 1990; expects 4 issues 1991, 4 issues 1992. sub. price: $20 instit., $15 indiv.; per copy: $5.75; sample: $5.75. Back issues: $6.75 for 1964 onward; $7.75 before 1964. Discounts: 15% to subscription agents. 192pp; 6×9; lp. Reporting time: 1-3 weeks after receipt. Payment: prose $11/page, poetry 60¢/line. Copyrighted, we request partial rights. Pub's reviews: 51 in 1990. Ads: $175/$110. CLMP.

‡**SEZ: A Multi-Racial Journal of Poetry & People's Culture, Shadow Press, U.S.A.,** Jim Dochniak, Editor, PO Box 8803, Minneapolis, MN 55408, 612-822-3488. 1978. Poetry, fiction, articles, art, photos, cartoons, interviews, criticism, reviews, letters, long-poems, news items, non-fiction. "*SEZ* is one of only a few literary journals dedicated to publishing class-conscious, Third World and issue-oriented writers and artists. Special attention is paid to upper midwest Third World writers and artists as well as writers and artists who, for one reason or another, are outside the cultural mainstream. Our motto is "Art for Humanity's Sake"; therefore, we are in opposition to elitist, "art for art's sake" work in any form. Each issue is thematic and includes hefty Resources, Recommended Reading, News & Notes sections. Theme for last issue: Labor, Literature and the Arts with special sections on new poems from El Salvador and upper midwest Chicano/Latino writers. Unsolicited mss. welcome (between Sept. and Apr.) *only from subscribers or with a check for a sample issue ($4.50).* SASE and short bio. (no publishing credits please must be included. Length: 2.5M words, prose; 10pps., poetry. Recent contributors: Thomas McGrath, Anya Achtenberg, Mary McAnally, Ruben Medina, Roque Dalton, Emanuel Fried, Claribel Alegria, etc. Note: *SEZ* comes out on an irregular basis; reporting time may take months" circ. 1-2M. Irregular. Expects 1 issue 1992. sub. price: $7 individuals, $8 libraries, institutions (4 consecutive numbers); per copy: $3.50; $4.50 double issues; sample: $4.50. Back issues: $3.50; $4.50. Discounts: 35% trade, 50% bulk, distrib. etc. 32pp, 90pp double; 8½×11; of. Reporting time: 1 week to 6 months. Payment: 2 copies. Copyrighted, reverts to author. Pub's reviews: 25 in 1990. §Midwest regional, 'minority', men's & women's issues, cultural and literary traditions, folklore, political, Third World, worker-writer. Ads: inquire. CCLM, MELUS, TCCWA.

SF3 (see also AURORA),** PO Box 1624, Madison, WI 53701-1624, 267-7483 (days); 255-9905 (evenings).

Shadetree Publishing Inc., Randy Farmer, Robert Ling, Fred McClendon, PO Box 110577, Carrollton, TX 75011, 214-341-3256. 1989. avg. press run 10M. Expects 4 titles 1991, 4 titles 1992. 1 title listed in the *Small Press Record of Books in Print* (20th Edition, 1991-92). avg. price, paper: $19.95. Discounts: trade wholesale 50% for cash in advance, plus freight. 200pp; 5½×8½. Reporting time: 1 month. Payment: negotiable. Copyrights for author. Publishers Marketing Association.

‡**Shadow Press, U.S.A. (see also SEZ: A Multi-Racial Journal of Poetry & People's Culture),** Jim Dochniak, Editor, PO Box 8803, Minneapolis, MN 55408, 612-822-3488. 1978. Poetry, fiction, art, photos, cartoons, interviews, criticism, reviews, letters, long-poems, news items, non-fiction. "*Shadow Press* aims to

publish and present writing and art work which is reflective of the struggle for New Human Images. Special attention given to writing and art work which is honest in its intention to add to the struggle for human dignity. NO ART FOR ARTS' SAKE, ESCAPIST, or DECADENT work, please. Attention given to 'minorities', worker-writers, the economically disadvantaged, and work which reflects a cultural heritage. No unsolicited mss, but inquiries welcomed w/a SASE. Length relative to project: broadsides/1-5 pps., chapbooks/20-40 pps., books/50-100 pps., etc. First book-length collection: *Songs From My Father's Pockets* by poet Ivory Giles." avg. press run 500-1M. Pub'd 2 titles 1990; expects 4 titles 1991, 4 titles 1992. 8 titles listed in the *Small Press Record of Books in Print* (20th Edition, 1991-92). avg. price, paper: $4.50; other: $1.50/pamphlets; $1.00/broadsides. Discounts: 40% trade, 50% distrib., bulk negot. 32-64pp; 5½×8½; of. Reporting time: 1 week to 6 months. Payment: inquire (usually percentage of print run). Copyrights for author. CCLM.

Kirit N. Shah, Kirit N. Shah, 980 Moraga Avenue, Piedmont, CA 94611, 415-653-2076. 1981. "Addresses in India: (1) 24 Sharda Society, Ahmedabad 7, Gujarat, 380007, India. (2) Aruna Prakashan, 1266 Shivam Society, Sector 27, Behind DSP Office, Gandhinagar, Gujarat, India. Other authors: Mr. K.J. Mehta and Miss Harsiddha K. Mehta. Books published in India are in Gujarati language." avg. press run 2.5M U.S., 1M India. Pub'd 1-4 titles 1990; expects 1-3 titles 1991, 2-4 titles 1992. 3 titles listed in the *Small Press Record of Books in Print* (20th Edition, 1991-92). avg. price, paper: $10; other: $5, books published in India - hardbound. Discounts: 5-9 copies 5%, 10-14 10%, 15-24 15%, 25+ 20%. 170pp; 8½×11; of. Reporting time: 1 month. Payment: negotiable. Copyrights for author.

THE SHAKESPEARE NEWSLETTER, Louis Marder, 1217 Ashland Ave., Chicago, Evanston, IL 60202, 312-475-7550. 1951. Poetry, articles, criticism, reviews, letters, news items. "Short pithy poems-dozen lines or so. For articles-send your conclusions & I will let you know if I can consider the article: brief, 750-1500 words, original, expository rather than critical, which show a knowledge of the previous scholarship" circ. 1.90M+. 4/yr. Pub'd 4 issues 1990; expects 4 issues 1991, 4 issues 1992. sub. price: indiv. $12, 2-yr $20, instit. $12; per copy: $3; sample: $3 + 50¢ postage. Back issues: $3 each $10 per yr plus $1 postage. Discounts: none. 12pp; 8½×11; of. Reporting time: less than a month usually. Payment: 3 copies. Not copyrighted. Pub's reviews: 30+ in 1990. §Scholarly and any interesting Shakespeareana and related material. Ads: $420/$230.

Shann Press, Yun-Pi Shann, PO Box 45, Germantown, MD 20875-0045, 301-972-3012. 1989. Fiction. Expects 1 title 1991, 3 titles 1992. avg. price, paper: $4.95. 250-300pp; 4-3/16×6⅞; lp. Reporting time: 8-12 weeks. Copyrights for author.

SHARING IDEAS FOR PROFESSIONAL SPEAKERS, Royal Publishing, Dorothy M. Walters, 18825 Hicrest Road, PO Box 1120, Glendora, CA 91740, 818-335-8069; fax 818-335-6127. 1979. "Our newsmagazine is to the world of paid speaking what variety is to show business. We feature stories, news, announcements about speakers, their books, cassette albums, meeting planners and all elements of the world of paid speaking. We restrict material: by and about speakers. Submissions by subscribers only." circ. 3M. 6/yr. Pub'd 6 issues 1990; expects 6 issues 1991, 6 issues 1992. sub. price: $95 2/yr, includes free *Speak and Grow Rich* paperback book; Canada and Mexico $124 2/yr (includes book in Mexico); all other foreign $179 2/yr, includes book; sample: $5 one time only. Back issues: varies as to availability. 40pp; 8½×11; web offset. Reporting time: 2 months. Payment: none. Copyrighted, reverts to author. Pub's reviews: 50 in 1990. §We are interested in anything on the subject of paid speaking. Must be advertiser or subscriber. Ads: $539/$350/$600 outside back cover/$570 inside cover. NSA, GVCNSA.

Sharp & Dunnigan Publications, Incorporated, Paul Drew Stevens, Editor, 2803 Gramercy Avenue, Torrance, CA 90501-5431, 916-891-6602. 1984. "Though interested in other material, we focus on U.S. military history" avg. press run 10M+. Pub'd 1 title 1990; expects 5 titles 1991, 3 titles 1992. 3 titles listed in the *Small Press Record of Books in Print* (20th Edition, 1991-92). avg. price, cloth: $18.95. Discounts: write for details. 360pp; 6×9. Reporting time: within 30 days. Payment: write for details. Publishers Marketing Association.

SHATTERED WIG REVIEW, Angus, Anne Bonafede, Nancy-Simone, Louise Spiegler, R. Wondolowski, 523 East 38th Street, Baltimore, MD 21218, 301-243-6888. 1988. Poetry, fiction, articles, art, photos, cartoons, interviews, satire, letters, parts-of-novels, collages, non-fiction. "Biased towards socially conscious pieces that also experiment with the medium they employ. Recent contributors include John Bennet, Al Ackerman, Jake Berry and Dan Raphael." circ. 500. 2/yr. Expects 4 issues 1991, 4 issues 1992. sub. price: $6; per copy: $3; sample: $3. 60pp; 8½×8½; of. Reporting time: 1-2 months. Payment: 1 copy. Not copyrighted. Pub's reviews: 3 in 1990. §Prose poetry, social commentary.

SHAW. THE ANNUAL OF BERNARD SHAW STUDIES, Pennsylvania State University Press, Fred D. Crawford, Department of English, Central Michigan University, Mt. Pleasant, MI 48859, 517-774-3171. 1951. Articles, interviews, criticism, reviews, letters. circ. 2M. 1/yr. Pub'd 1 issue 1990; expects 1 issue 1991, 1 issue 1992. sub. price: $35; per copy: $35. Back issues: Vol 1-13, $1.75; Vol. 14-21, $3; 1981 to 1990, $25; after 1991, $35. Discounts: $1 to agents. 265pp; 6×9; of. Reporting time: 2 months. Payment: $25 and $50 depending on length. Copyrighted, does not revert to author. Pub's reviews: 3 in 1990. §Shaw. No ads. AAUP.

Shearer Publishing, William H. Shearer, President, 406 Post Oak Road, Fredericksburg, TX 78624, 512-997-6529. 1981. Fiction, non-fiction. avg. press run 2M-40M. Pub'd 7 titles 1990; expects 6 titles 1991, 8 titles 1992. 40 titles listed in the *Small Press Record of Books in Print* (20th Edition, 1991-92). avg. price, cloth: $13.95; paper: $8.95. 250pp. Reporting time: average of 3 months. Payment: depends on book. Copyrights for author. American Booksellers Assn.

Shearsman Books, Tony Frazer, c/o IPD (Independent Press Distribution), 12 Stevenage Road, London SW6 6ES, United Kingdom, 0752-779682. 1981. Poetry. "Main interests are postmodernist poetry and poetry in translation, particularly contemporary French poetry. This year's books are by George Evans (*Wrecking*) and David Wevill (*Figure of Eight*). Distribution address: Independent Press Distribution, 12 Stevenage Road, London SW6 6ES, England." avg. press run 400. Pub'd 1 title 1990; expects 3 titles 1991, 3 titles 1992. 9 titles listed in the *Small Press Record of Books in Print* (20th Edition, 1991-92). avg. price, paper: £3.95. Discounts: on application to distributor. 40pp; 4½×6½; of. Reporting time: 1 month. Payment: negotiable number of copies of the book. Copyrights for author in UK only. ALP.

Sheed & Ward, Robert Heyer, PO Box 419492, Kansas City, MO 64141-6492, 800-444-8910. 1984. avg. press run 3.5M-5M. Pub'd 30 titles 1990; expects 30 titles 1991, 30 titles 1992. avg. price, cloth: $18; paper: $7.95. Discounts: books-1 copy 20%, 2-4 30%, 5-49 40%, 50-259 42%, 250-849 44%, 850+ 46%; booklets (single titles only)-1 copy $2 ea., 2-9 $1.75, 10-24 $1.50, 25-99 $1.30, 100+ $1.10; special bookseller discount-50+ copies, single or assorted titles, $1 ea. 150pp; 5⅜×8⅜. Reporting time: 3 months or sooner. Copyrights for author.

The Sheep Meadow Press, Stanley Moss, Publisher, Editor-in-Chief, PO Box 1345, Riverdale-on-Hudson, NY 10471, 212-549-3321. 1976. Poetry, fiction. avg. press run 2.5M. Pub'd 4 titles 1990; expects 14 titles 1991, 8 titles 1992. 64 titles listed in the *Small Press Record of Books in Print* (20th Edition, 1991-92). avg. price, cloth: $14.95; paper: $10.95. Discounts: 40%. 100pp; 8½×5½, 6×9; of. Reporting time: 3 months. Payment: 10%. Copyrights for author.

Sheer Joy! Press, Patricia Adams, Editor, PO Box 608, Pink Hill, NC 28572, 919-568-6101. 1986. Fiction, non-fiction. avg. press run 1M. Expects 2 titles 1991, 2 titles 1992. 4 titles listed in the *Small Press Record of Books in Print* (20th Edition, 1991-92). avg. price, paper: $9.95. 200pp; 5½×8½; of. Reporting time: 60 days. Copyrights for author.

SHENANDOAH, Dabney Stuart, Editor; Lynn L. Williams, Managing Editor, PO Box 722, Lexington, VA 24450, 703-463-8765. 1950. Poetry, fiction, interviews, reviews, parts-of-novels. "Literary quarterly publishing award-winning fiction, poetry, essays and interviews." circ. 1M. 4/yr. Pub'd 4 issues 1990; expects 4 issues 1991, 4 issues 1992. sub. price: $11; per copy: $3.50; sample: $3.50. Back issues: $6. Discounts: 50% bulk rate to bookstores. 100pp; 6×9; of. Reporting time: 3 weeks. Payment: $25/page prose, $2.50/line poetry + 1 year free subscription, 1 free copy of issue in which work appears. Copyrighted, rights revert by request. Ads: $200/$100. CLMP.

SHENANDOAH NEWSLETTER, Scan Doa, 736 West Oklahoma Street, Appleton, WI 54914. 1973. Poetry, articles, criticism, reviews, letters, news items, non-fiction. "All material must relate to American Indian by Indians. Editor holds strict rights on this." circ. 1M. 12/yr. Pub'd 12 issues 1990; expects 12 issues 1991, 12 issues 1992. sub. price: $13; per copy: $1.50; sample: $1.50. 21pp; 8½×11; †mi. Reporting time: material must be into office by 24th of previous month. Payment: none. Not copyrighted. Pub's reviews: 1 in 1990. §Material relating to Native Peoples and their struggles/history. Ads: none.

Shepherd Books, Nicholas Palmer, Barbara Aloia, Box 2290, Redmond, WA 98073, 206-882-4500. 1987. Fiction, cartoons, satire, non-fiction. "Novels of any length, cartoon books. Preferences: mature fiction dealing with modern life, satire. Recent contributor: Reverend Wing F. Fing." avg. press run 5M. Pub'd 1 title 1990; expects 2 titles 1991, 5 titles 1992. 1 title listed in the *Small Press Record of Books in Print* (20th Edition, 1991-92). avg. price, cloth: $17; paper: $10.95. Discounts: 40-55% depending on size of order. Pages vary widely; 8×5½; of. Reporting time: 1 month. Payment: varies. Copyrights for author.

Shepherd Publishers, James M. Shepherd, President, 118 Pinepoint Road, Williamsburg, VA 23185-4436, 804-229-0661. 1982. Non-fiction. "Publisher of books—at present in field of house construction only." avg. press run 3M. Pub'd 1 title 1990; expects 1 title 1991, 1 title 1992. 3 titles listed in the *Small Press Record of Books in Print* (20th Edition, 1991-92). avg. price, paper: $16. Discounts: 47% bookstores, 50% wholesalers. 260pp; 8½×11, 5½×8½; of. Reporting time: not established yet—we are interested, however. Payment: 5% to 15%. Copyrights for author.

SHERLOCKIAN TIDBITS, Arnold Korotkin, 12 Glenwood Rd., Upper Montclair, NJ 07043. 1987. Photos, cartoons, news items. "Our publication contains article, graphics, reviews, etc." circ. 221. 4/yr. Pub'd 4 issues 1990; expects 4 issues 1991, 4 issues 1992. sub. price: $8; per copy: $2; sample: $2. 13pp; 8½×11; †of. Not copyrighted. Pub's reviews: 4 in 1990. §Mystery books, magazines, etc.

Sherwood Sugden & Company, Publishers, Sherwood Sugden, 315 Fifth Street, Peru, IL 61354, 815-223-1231; 815-223-2520. 1975. Non-fiction. avg. press run 3M. Pub'd 2 titles 1990; expects 3 titles 1991, 4 titles 1992. 27 titles listed in the *Small Press Record of Books in Print* (20th Edition, 1991-92). avg. price, cloth: $19.95; paper: $7.95. Discounts: 40% STOP; otherwise 25%-1 copy, 35%-3 copies, 40%-5+ copies. 300pp; 5½×8½, 6×9; of, typeset. Reporting time: 2-3 months. Payment: 8%-12%. Copyrights for author.

Shield Publishing, Inc., 2940 Rue Renoir #111, South Bend, IN 46615. 1 title listed in the *Small Press Record of Books in Print* (20th Edition, 1991-92).

SHINING STAR, Becky Daniel, Shining Star Publications, PO Box 299, Carthage, IL 62321. 1980. Poetry, fiction, articles, art, cartoons, interviews, music, plays. circ. 22M. 4/yr. Pub'd 4 issues 1990; expects 4 issues 1991, 4 issues 1992. sub. price: $16.95; per copy: $2. Back issues: $4.50. Discounts: $29.95/2 yrs, $44.95/3 yrs (dealer prices for bookstores). 80pp; 8½×11; of. Reporting time: 4-6 weeks. Payment: $10-$50. Copyrighted, does not revert to author. Ads: Ryan Communications Group, PO Box 1606, Marysville, WA 98270, (206) 653-7199.

Shining Waters Press (see also RIPPLES), Karen Schaefer, Editor, 1426 Las Vegas, Ann Arbor, MI 48103. 1973. Poetry, fiction, reviews, long-poems, news items. 1 title listed in the *Small Press Record of Books in Print* (20th Edition, 1991-92). of. Reporting time: 2 weeks on manuscripts. Payment: negotiable.

SHIRIM, Marc Steven Dworkin, 2405 Hollister Terrace, Glendale, CA 91206. 1982. Poetry. "*Shirim* seeks poetry (original + translated) of Jewish reference. Such known poets as Yehuda Amichai, Robert Mezey, Deena Metzger, Karl Shapiro, Irving Layton, Jerome Rothenberg, and Howard Schwartz have had poetry appear in the magazine. All submissions are welcome." circ. 750. 2/yr. Expects 1 issue 1991, 2 issues 1992. sub. price: $7; per copy: $4; sample: $4. 44pp; 5¼×8½; †of. Reporting time: 2 months. Payment: copies. Copyrighted, reverts to author. Pub's reviews: 2 in 1990.

Shiro Publishers, 8680 West Rice Place, Littleton, CO 80123. 1988. "Additional address: 8680 W. Rice Place, Littleton, CO 80123" avg. press run 3M. Pub'd 1 title 1990; expects 3 titles 1991. 1 title listed in the *Small Press Record of Books in Print* (20th Edition, 1991-92). avg. price, paper: $12.95. Discounts: dependent on whether wholesale or bookstore or library. 130pp; 7×9. Reporting time: immediate. Copyrights for author.

SHMATE, Shmate Press, Steve Fankuchen, Box 4228, Berkeley, CA 94704. 1982. Poetry, fiction, articles, art, photos, cartoons, satire, criticism, reviews, music, letters, long-poems, news items, non-fiction. "A journal of politics, culture, and the arts, with emphasis of a progressive Jewish approach, literature, and action; special issues on single subjects e.g. humor, Holocaust resistance, gay and lesbian Jews, Jewish identity, the political and social right, the farm crisis, Gypsies/Roma, gays and the Holocaust, Israel and Palestine, pornography" circ. 2.5M-3M, issue on right 7M. 4/yr. Pub'd 4 issues 1990; expects 4 issues 1991, 4 issues 1992. sub. price: $15 for 4 issues, $25 instit.; per copy: $3, $5 #11-12, #21-22 double issues, $6.50/issue instit.; sample: $3. Back issues: 3.50 #1 only to libraries at $15. Discounts: 40%. 32-40pp; 8½×11; web offset. Reporting time: depends on subject- 1 week to 2 months for special issue confirmation. Payment: copies. Copyrighted, joint rights. Pub's reviews: 6 in 1990. §Native Americans, archaeology, indigenous peoples, science, history, politics, resistance, Holocaust, intellectual/ideas...anything... Ads: $300/$170/$22.50 per inch. APS.

Shmate Press (see also SHMATE), Steve Fankuchen, Box 4228, Berkeley, CA 94704. 1982. "A journal of progressive politics and culture with an emphasis on a Jewish perspective" avg. press run 3.5M. Expects 4 titles 1991. 8 titles listed in the *Small Press Record of Books in Print* (20th Edition, 1991-92). avg. price, paper: $3. Discounts: 40%. 40pp; 8½×11; web offset. Reporting time: 2 weeks to 2 months. Payment: copies. Copyrights jointly. APS.

Shoe Tree Press, Joyce McDonald, Editor-in-Chief, PO Box 219, Crozet, VA 22932-0219. 1984. Poetry, fiction, non-fiction. "We specialize in children's books. Our current needs are for juvenile nonfiction books for middle years (8-11) and early young adult (12-14). We do not accept unsolicited manuscripts. Please query with a proposal. Distributed by The Talman Company, 150 Fifth Avenue, New York, NY 10011" avg. press run 3M-5M. Pub'd 2 titles 1990; expects 3 titles 1991, 4 titles 1992. 11 titles listed in the *Small Press Record of Books in Print* (20th Edition, 1991-92). avg. price, cloth: $12.95; paper: $4.95. Discounts: 40% to 48% depending on quantity, 50% to wholesalers. 48-224pp; 5½×8½; of. Reporting time: 2-4 months. Payment: standard royalties. Copyrights for author.

SHOOTING STAR REVIEW, Jerry Ward, Poetry Chair; Valerie Lawrence, EllenKeita Mark, Nzadi, Romella Kitchens, Jane Todd Cooper, 7123 Race Street, Pittsburgh, PA 15208, 412-731-7039. 1986. Poetry, fiction, art, photos, reviews, parts-of-novels, non-fiction. "Include a cover letter and place artist's name with address and phone on every page. All text must be complete and typed (double space) on one side of plain, white 8.5x11" paper. Poems can be single spaced. Clear photocopies and computer printouts OK. Reprints and multiple submissions accepted. Return envelopes with proper postage (or post cards) are required for responses.

Fiction & Tales: Up to 3,000 words. Short short fiction under 1,000 words encouraged. Essays: Up to 2,000 words. Narrative (a first person, story-telling voice) preferred. Poetry: Maximum 50 lines per poem. Up to six poems per quarter. One poem per page. Submissions must be innovative and well structured." circ. 1.5M. 4/yr. Pub'd 4 issues 1990; expects 4 issues 1991, 4 issues 1992. sub. price: $10; per copy: $3; sample: $3. Back issues: $3. Discounts: 40% to writers published in an issue, 50% for 10+ copies. 32pp; 8½×11; of. Reporting time: 3 months. Payment: $5 poetry, $10 essay and folktales, $20 fiction and 2 magazine copies. Copyrighted, reverts to author. Ads: $750/$425/no classified/25% off to nonprofit organizations, small presses, artists and writers. Poets & Writers, CCLM, COSMEP, African American Writers Guild, UWAP.

Michael Shore Associates, Michael Shore, Publisher & Editor; Hollace Shore, Managing Editor, 26 Golden Hill Street, Milford, CT 06460, 203-324-0799. 1978. Non-fiction. avg. press run 1.5M. Pub'd 3 titles 1990; expects 3 titles 1991, 3 titles 1992. avg. price, paper: $7.99. Discounts: 20% across the board. 125pp; 5½×8½ (trim size); of. Reporting time: 2 months. Payment: 10% royalty on retail price. Does not copyright for author.

SHOTS, Daniel Price, Box 109, Joseph, OR 97846. 1986. Poetry, fiction, articles, art, photos, cartoons, reviews, letters, parts-of-novels, collages, non-fiction. "*Shots* is a journal about the art of fine photography" circ. 1.6M. 6/yr. Pub'd 6 issues 1990; expects 6 issues 1991, 6 issues 1992. sub. price: $15; per copy: $2.50; sample: $2.50. Back issues: $2.50. 72pp; 11×14; of. Reporting time: 1 month. Payment: none. Copyrighted, reverts to author. Pub's reviews: 6 in 1990. §Photography. Ads: $300.

Shy City Press (see also TABULA RASA), Lisa Nease Yeaga, 208 Reno St., #1, New Cumberland, PA 17070, 717-774-7627. 1990. Poetry, letters. "We are interested in publishing small poetry chapbooks and letters but have no plans to do so as yet. Open to submissions. Complete policies are not established as of this time."

SICILIA PARRA, Arba Sicula, Inc., Gaetano Cipolla, c/o Modern Foreign Languages, St. John's University, Jamaica, NY 11439-0002, 718-331-0613. 1979. Poetry, fiction, articles, art, photos, reviews, music, letters, long-poems, collages, plays, news items, non-fiction. "Bilingual ethnic oriented material in the Sicilian language with a lyrical English translation" circ. 1.5M. 2/yr. Pub'd 2 issues 1990; expects 2 issues 1991, 2 issues 1992. sub. price: $20; per copy: $10; sample: $10. Back issues: ask for quote. Discounts: ask for quote. 20pp; 8½×11; laser. Reporting time: flexible. Payment: none. Copyrighted, does not revert to author. Pub's reviews: several in 1990. §Sicilian ethnic worldwide. Ads: $150/$75/$6 column inch.

Sicilian Antigruppo/Cross-Cultural Communications (see also COOP. ANTIGRUPPO SICILIANO; TRAPANI NUOVA, TERZA PAGINA), Nat Scammacca, Villa Schammachanat, via Argenteria Km 4, Trapani, Sicily, Italy, 0923-38681. 1968. Poetry, fiction, articles, art, photos, interviews, satire, criticism, letters, parts-of-novels, collages, concrete art. "For our newspaper, a weekly, articles are usually up to 3½ typewritten pages. For our reviews any length. For books, essays, criticism on any subject no limit. Books of poetry, 64 pages. Languages: Italian, English and Sicilian. We are doing a series of 20 books of poetry of American poets completely in Italian and English, the languages face to face. Some writers and poets are: Crescenzio Cane, Ignazio Apolloni, Pietro Terminelli, Gianni Diecidue, Nat Scammacca, Franco DiMarco, Santo Cali, Carmelo Pirrera, L. Ferlinghetti, R. Bly, Guiseppe Zaggario, Ignazio Navarra, Cesare Zavattini, Laura Boss, Maria Gillan, Enzo Bonventre." avg. press run 1M-2M. Expects 12 titles 1991. 39 titles listed in the *Small Press Record of Books in Print* (20th Edition, 1991-92). avg. price, cloth: $5; paper: $10; other: $5. Discounts: 33%. 150pp; †mi, of, lp. Reporting time: 1 month. Payment: regular contract 10% etc. Copyrights for author.

Sierra Club Books, Jon Beckmann, 100 Bush Street, San Francisco, CA 94104, 415-291-1600. 1892. Fiction, non-fiction. "Natural history, science, environmental issues, and photographic works, literature." avg. press run 7.5M. Pub'd 35 titles 1990; expects 35 titles 1991, 35 titles 1992. avg. price, cloth: $18.95; paper: $12.95. Discounts: 40-50% trade/wholesalers. 200+pp; 6×9, 9×12; of. Reporting time: 4-6 weeks. Payment: customary—advance against royalties. Copyrights for author.

Sierra Oaks Publishing Company, Stephanie Morris, Managing Editor, 1370 Sierra Oaks Lane, Newcastle, CA 95658-9791. 1986. Articles, art, photos, non-fiction. "Length of material usually runs about 135 pages. Children's stories run approximately 50 pages. We are a small press specializing in the history and culture of the American West. American Indian culture, history, and legend is our main interest. We are also producing some children's stories based on Native American legends and mythology. Recent contributors include Dr. William Leckie, and award winning authors Clifford E. Trafzer and Richard Carrico." avg. press run 2.5M. Pub'd 5 titles 1990; expects 5 titles 1991, 10 titles 1992. 15 titles listed in the *Small Press Record of Books in Print* (20th Edition, 1991-92). avg. price, paper: $10.95 adult books, $6.95 children's books. Discounts: 40% if for resale, 50% for jobbers. 135pp; 8×8½; of. Reporting time: 2-6 weeks. Payment: 10% of sales after initial run. Copyrights for author. COSMEP, NCBA.

Sierra Trading Post, Joseph F. Petralia, PO Box 2497, San Francisco, CA 94126, 415-456-9378. 1979. Non-fiction. "*Publisher looking for additional manuscripts.*" avg. press run 8M-10M. Pub'd 2 titles 1990; expects 1 title 1991, 2 titles 1992. 2 titles listed in the *Small Press Record of Books in Print* (20th Edition,

1991-92). avg. price, cloth: $18.95; paper: $8.95. Discounts: 40-55%. 128pp; 6×9; of. Reporting time: 90 days. Payment: negotiable. Copyrights for author.

Siftsoft, 12950 SW 4th Street, #H-306, Pembroke Pine, FL 33027. "Additional address: 12950 S.W. 4th Court, H-306, Pembroke Pines, FL 33027" 1 title listed in the *Small Press Record of Books in Print* (20th Edition, 1991-92).

SIGN OF THE TIMES-A CHRONICLE OF DECADENCE IN THE ATOMIC AGE, Studio 403, Mark Stephen Souder, 3819 NE 15th, Portland, OR 97212, 206-323-6764. 1981. Fiction, art, photos, cartoons, satire, collages. circ. 750. 2/yr. Expects 2 issues 1991. sub. price: $7.50; per copy: $4; sample: $4.50. Back issues: $5+. Discounts: 5-20 copies $2.40 each. 32pp; 8×10; of. Reporting time: 6 weeks. Payment: by prior arrangement. Copyrighted, does not revert to author. No ads.

THE SIGNAL - Network International, Joan Silva, David Chorlton, PO Box 67, Emmett, ID 83617, 208-365-5812. 1987. Poetry, fiction, articles, art, interviews, criticism, reviews, letters. "Additional address: 118 West Palm Lane, Phoenix, AZ 85003. Length: no hard and fast rule, fiction under 3,000 words pref. Biases: no religious or tract material - we like translation(s), very broad range on style, subject matter." circ. 500. 2/yr. Pub'd 1 issue 1990; expects 2 issues 1991, 2 issues 1992. sub. price: $10; per copy: $5; sample: $6. Back issues: $3. 50-60pp; 8½×11; of. Reporting time: from 2 weeks to 2-3 months, no reading during June, July, August. Payment: in copies. Copyrighted, reverts to author. Pub's reviews: 7 in 1990. §Art, lit. criticism, women's issues, social commentary.

Signal Books, D. McMillan, A.R. Shuh, PO Box 940, Carrboro, NC 27510, 919-929-5985. 1985. Poetry, fiction, non-fiction. avg. press run 3.5M. Pub'd 2 titles 1990; expects 4 titles 1991, 6 titles 1992. avg. price, cloth: $16; paper: $15. Discounts: standard industry. 250pp. Reporting time: 6 weeks. Payment: standard industry contracts. Copyrights for author.

Signature Books, Gary James Bergera, 350 South 400 East, #G4, Salt Lake City, UT 84111, 801-531-1483. 1981. Poetry, fiction, articles, cartoons, non-fiction. "Western USA subjects—fiction/non-fiction." avg. press run 2M. Pub'd 10 titles 1990; expects 15 titles 1991, 12 titles 1992. 36 titles listed in the *Small Press Record of Books in Print* (20th Edition, 1991-92). avg. price, cloth: $19.95; paper: $9.95. Discounts: 20%-50%. 250pp; 6×9. Reporting time: 6-9 months. Payment: 8% semi-annual. Copyrights for author. Association of Utah Publishers.

SIGNPOST, Ann Marshall, Editor, 1305 Fourth Avenue #512, Seattle, WA 98101, 206-625-1367. 1966. Articles, art, photos, cartoons, reviews, letters, news items, non-fiction. "Editorial content is heavily weighted for Pacific Northwest backpackers, ski tourers, snow shoers, etc. We frequently purchase outside material, but usually pay not more than $25.00 a page." circ. 3.3M. 12/yr. Pub'd 12 issues 1990; expects 12 issues 1991, 12 issues 1992. sub. price: $25; per copy: $2.50; sample: n/c. Back issues: $2.50. 40pp; 8½×10¾; of. Payment: $5-$40. Copyrighted, reverts to author. Pub's reviews: 24 in 1990. §Hiking, backpacking, cross-country skiing, snowshoeing, nature study and related activities. Ads: $250/$125/40¢-wd. $10 min.

Signpost Press Inc. (see also THE BELLINGHAM REVIEW), Knute Skinner, Editor, 1007 Queen Street, Bellingham, WA 98226, 206-734-9781. 1975. Poetry, fiction, art, photos, reviews. "Query before submitting book ms." avg. press run 500. Pub'd 2 titles 1990; expects 3 titles 1991, 2 titles 1992. 13 titles listed in the *Small Press Record of Books in Print* (20th Edition, 1991-92). avg. price, cloth: $12; paper: $3 for chapbooks, $8 for books. Discounts: 40% on 5 or more copies. 24-68pp; 5½×8½; of. Reporting time: 1-3 months. Payment: varies. Copyrights for author.

SIGNS: JOURNAL OF WOMEN IN CULTURE AND SOCIETY, Jean O'Barr, Editor, Duke University, 207 East Duke Building, Durham, NC 27708, 919-684-2783. 1975. Articles, criticism, reviews, letters, non-fiction. circ. 7M. 4/yr. Pub'd 4 issues 1990; expects 4 issues 1991, 4 issues 1992. sub. price: $29 indiv., $58 instit., $21 students; per copy: $7.50 indiv.; $14.50 instit. Back issues: contact business office, University of Chicago Press, Journals Division, PO Box 37005, Chicago IL 60637, for this information. Discounts: standard agencies. 200pp; 6×9; of. Reporting time: 3-6 months, contact editorial office, address listed above, for this information. Payment: 10 copies of journal issue or 1/yr subscription. Copyrighted, does not revert to author. Pub's reviews: 18 in 1990. §Women. Ads: $180/$125.

Sigo Press, Sisa Sternback, PO Box 8748, Boston, MA 02114-0037, 617-523-2321. 1980. "Imprint: Coventure, Ltd." avg. press run 5M. Pub'd 3 titles 1990; expects 20 titles 1991, 15 titles 1992. 3 titles listed in the *Small Press Record of Books in Print* (20th Edition, 1991-92). avg. price, cloth: $35; paper: $13.95. Discounts: trade 1-4, 20%; 5-50, 40%; 51-150, 44%; 151+, 46%. 200pp; 6×9. Reporting time: 2-4 weeks. Payment: negotiable. Copyrights for author. ABA, Boston International.

Silver Apples Press, Geraldine Little, PO Box 292, Hainesport, NJ 08036. 1982. Poetry. "1st chapbook contest was held in 1987." avg. press run 500. Expects 1 title 1991, 2 titles 1992. 5 titles listed in the *Small Press Record of Books in Print* (20th Edition, 1991-92). avg. price, paper: $3 chapbooks, $7-$8 larger collections.

24-50pp; 5½×8½. Reporting time: 3 weeks. Payment: copies of title only. Sometimes copyrights for author.

Silver Dawn Media, Susan Strang, 1606 Arcane Street, Simi Valley, CA 93065. 1989. Fiction, non-fiction. "We are strictly a book publisher. We accept material only from authors we know, or from reputable agents. Our bias is towards books having appeal to intellectuals as well as the general public. Our slogan is, 'Intelligent books for intelligent people'" avg. press run 700. Pub'd 2 titles 1990. avg. price, cloth: $16.95; paper: $6.95. Discounts: send inquiry letter re a particular title. 160pp; size varies; of. Reporting time: 4 weeks. Payment: no advance, royalties based on gross receipts of company rate subject to negotiation. Copyrights for author.

Silver Dollar Press, Arthur W. Smith, Plaza Towers, Suite 8B, 6115 W. Markham Street, Little Rock, AR 72205-3151, 501-753-4181. 1984. "Uses illustrations. Second Edition" avg. press run 1M. Pub'd 1 title 1990; expects 2 titles 1991, 1 title 1992. 2 titles listed in the *Small Press Record of Books in Print* (20th Edition, 1991-92). avg. price, paper: $8.95 Second edition. Discounts: 25% to dealers, 40% to distributors. 70pp; 8½×11; †of.

Silver Forest Publishing, PO Box 3520, Evergreen, CO 80439, 303-674-5755. 1989. Fiction, non-fiction. "We basically have two lines of books, children's and New Age. We currently have one book in each line published. Our children's book was just released (*Heart Tales* by Jean-Marie Hamel)" avg. press run 10M. Pub'd 1 title 1990; expects 2 titles 1991, 3-5 titles 1992. 2 titles listed in the *Small Press Record of Books in Print* (20th Edition, 1991-92). avg. price, cloth: $12.95; paper: $9.95; other: $18.95 book and tape set. Discounts: 1-4 20%, 5+ 40%, distributors 50-55%. 48-160pp; size varies. Reporting time: 6-10 weeks. Payment: varies. Copyrights for author. NAPRA (New Age Publishing & Retail Alliance), COSMEP, ABA, ABC (Assoc. of Booksellers for Children).

Silver Skates Publishing, Carolyn Soto, 1020 Santa Fe Avenue, Albany, CA 94706, 415-528-1302. 1986. Poetry, fiction, non-fiction. avg. press run 1.5M. Pub'd 1 title 1990; expects 2 titles 1991, 3 titles 1992. avg. price, paper: $10. Discounts: 40% bookstores, 20-40% jobbers. 170pp; 6×9; of. Reporting time: 2 weeks. Payment: copies only, by arrangement. Copyrights for author.

SILVER WINGS, Jackson Wilcox, PO Box 1000, Pearblossom, CA 93553-1000, 805-264-3726. 1983. Poetry. "Poems with Christian foundation focusing on the realities of faith." circ. 500. 4/yr. Pub'd 4 issues 1990; expects 4 issues 1991, 4 issues 1992. sub. price: $7; per copy: $2; sample: $2. Back issues: $2 as available. Discounts: 20%. 32pp; 5½×8½; †mi. Reporting time: 4 weeks. Payment: 1-yr subscription and copy of issue with poem ($9 value). Not copyrighted. Pub's reviews: 6 in 1990. §Poems.

SILVERFISH REVIEW, Rodger Moody, Editor, PO Box 3541, Eugene, OR 97403, 503-344-5060. 1979. Poetry, fiction, interviews, reviews, long-poems, collages. "Also publishes translations." circ. 750. Irregular. Pub'd 2 issues 1990; expects 2 issues 1991, 2 issues 1992. 11 titles listed in the *Small Press Record of Books in Print* (20th Edition, 1991-92). sub. price: $9 individuals, $12 institutions; per copy: $3 regular issues, $4 poetry chapbooks; sample: $3 plus $1 for postage. Discounts: 20% consignment, 40% wholesale for bookstores. 48pp reg. issues, 28pp chapbooks; 5½×8½; of. Reporting time: 6-12 weeks. Payment: 5 copies regular issues and small payment when funding permits, $100 to winner of annual poetry chapbook contest plus 25 copies. Copyrighted, reverts to author. Pub's reviews: 4 in 1990. §Poetry, fiction. Ads: $50/$25. CLMP.

Silverleaf Press, Inc., Ann E. Larson, PO Box 70189, Seattle, WA 98107. 1986. Fiction. "We are looking for well-written feminist and lesbian fiction. Recent publications include a novel by Marian Michener, *Three Glasses of Wine Have Been Removed From This Story* an anthology, *Crossing The Mainstream: New Fiction By Women Writers*, and *Silverleaf's Choice: An Anthology of Lesbian Humor.*" avg. press run 1.5M-2M. Pub'd 1 title 1990; expects 1 title 1991, 1 title 1992. 2 titles listed in the *Small Press Record of Books in Print* (20th Edition, 1991-92). avg. price, paper: $8.95. Discounts: bookstores 40%. 150pp; 5½×8½; of. Reporting time: 1-3 months. Payment: individually negotiated. Copyrights for author.

Simon & Pierre Publishing Co. Ltd., Marian M. Wilson, Publisher & General Editor, Box 280, Adelaide St. P.O., Toronto, Ontario M5C2J4, Canada, 416-363-6767. 1972. Fiction, art, photos, plays, non-fiction. "Publish two illustrated drama series including one act and full length professionally performed plays, audition books, educational drama, theatre histories, and children's plays in cloth and paper binding, plus new fiction, Sherlockian books, biographies and non-fiction. Canadian authors only. Some children's poetry, haiku, educational poetry." avg. press run 2M. Pub'd 8 titles 1990; expects 14 titles 1991, 14 titles 1992. 76 titles listed in the *Small Press Record of Books in Print* (20th Edition, 1991-92). avg. price, cloth: $22.95 Canada; paper: $14.95 Canada. Discounts: trade 1-4, 20%, 5 or more 40%; wholesalers 1-24 20%, 25+ 46%; classroom & bulk discounts. 64-250pp; 6×9; of. Reporting time: 2 weeks if rejected; 3 months if being considered for publication. Payment: average 10% list price royalty plus escalation, trade; 8% of net, educational. Copyrights for author. COSMEP, ACP, CBPC, OLA, LPG, OPAO.

SINCERE SINGLES, Adrienne Schiff, PO Box 1719, Ann Arbor, MI 48106, 313-476-6110. 1984. Photos, non-fiction. "Once in a while a photo or a paid advertisement" circ. 6M. 12/yr. Pub'd 12 issues 1990; expects

12 issues 1991, 12 issues 1992. sub. price: $15; per copy: $2; sample: free. 32pp; 3½x8½; of. Ads: $250/$125/$24.95 20 words, 60¢/addition. SPA.

SING HEAVENLY MUSE! WOMEN'S POETRY AND PROSE, Sue Ann Martinson, Editor, PO Box 13320, Minneapolis, MN 55414. 1977. Poetry, fiction, art, photos. "We are interested in publishing a variety of fine writing by women. Contributors include: Meridel LeSueur, Patricia Hampl, Diane Glancy, Carol Bly, Celia Gilbert, and Linda Hogan. Please inquire about artwork." circ. 2M. 2/yr. Pub'd 1 issue 1990; expects 2 issues 1991, 2 issues 1992. sub. price: $19 (3 issues); per copy: $7 + $1.50 p/h; sample: $4. Back issues: $4. Discounts: 40% trade. 125pp; 6x9; of. Reporting time: 3-6 months. Payment: 2 copies, honorarium. Copyrighted, reverts to author. Ads: please inquire. COSMEP, CCLM.

SING OUT! The Folk Song Magazine, Mark Moss, Editor; Diane Petro, Managing Editor, PO Box 5253, Bethlehem, PA 18015-5253, 215-865-5366. 1950. Articles, art, photos, interviews, reviews, music, letters, news items. "We print music and lyrics of folk songs." circ. 8M. 4/yr. Pub'd 3 issues 1990; expects 4 issues 1991, 4 issues 1992. sub. price: $15 indiv., $17.50 instit.; per copy: $3.75; sample: $4.75. Back issues: $3 to $8 depending on the issue, write to Circulation Department for complete list. 112-130pp; 5½x8½; of. Reporting time: variable. Payment: copies or records. Copyrighted, reverts to author. Pub's reviews: 100 in 1990. §Music, folklore, politics, arts, third world, ethnic materials, etc., women history labor, Folk music records. Ads: $240/$150/50¢.

Singing Bone Press, Jerred Metz, Phil Sultz, Tom Lang, 2318 Albion Place, Saint Louis, MO 63104, 314-865-2789. 1975. Poetry, fiction, long-poems, non-fiction. "We solicit our material, do not take mailed offerings. Aside from *Halley's Comet, 1910, Fire in The Sky*, $9.95, which is done as a trade paperback, we specialize in books using unusual formats, frequently involving a mixture of papers including hand-made paper and publish authors and poets including Jerome Rothenberg, Don Willcox, Phil Sultz and Jerred Metz. Additional address 2318 Albion Place, Saint Louis, MO 63104" avg. press run 101. Pub'd 2 titles 1990; expects 1 title 1991, 1 title 1992. avg. price, cloth: $75; other: $75 packets. Discounts: our trade editions: 1-5 copies - 20%; 5-10 - 25%; 10-15 - 30%; 15-20 - 35%; 20+ - 40%. 40pp; size varies; †lp, proof press, silkscreen. Payment: worked out on individual basis. Copyrights for author.

Singing Horse Press, Gil Ott, Editor & Publisher, PO Box 40034, Philadelphia, PA 19106. 1976. Poetry, long-poems. "Currently available: *Unity* by David Miller ($3), *The End Befallen Edgar Allen Poe* by S.S. Kush ($2), *Differences for Four Hands* by Rosmarie Waldrop ($4), *Traffic* by Gil Ott ($2.50), and *Aural* by Vassilis Zambaras ($2.50). Solicited material only." avg. press run 500. Pub'd 2 titles 1990; expects 2 titles 1991, 2 titles 1992. 8 titles listed in the *Small Press Record of Books in Print* (20th Edition, 1991-92). avg. price, paper: $6. Discounts: 40% order 3 or more copies, no consignment. Chapbooks 24pp, books 48pp; of. Payment: 10% of press run. CLMP.

THE SINGLE HOUND, Andrew P. Leibs, Box 598, Newmarket, NH 03857, 603-659-2685. 1989. Criticism. "*The Single Hound* is a literary journal devoted to studying the poetry and image of Emily Dickinson. Recent contributors: Richard B. Sewall, Isaac Asimov, Robert Bly." circ. 100. 2/yr. Expects 2 issues 1991, 2 issues 1992. sub. price: $12; per copy: $7; sample: $5. Back issues: Vol. 1 #1+2 $10. Discounts: none as yet. 24pp; 5½x8; †of. Reporting time: 2-3 weeks. Payment: copies. Copyrighted, reverts to author. Pub's reviews: 1 in 1990. §Books on Emily Dickinson. No ads.

SINGLE SCENE, ARIZONA GREAT OUTDOORS, Janet L. Jacobsen, 7432 East Diamond, Scottsdale, AZ 85257, 602-945-6746. 1972. Poetry, articles, interviews, reviews, letters, news items, non-fiction. "Positive, helpful information on how to live a happy single life and how to improve relationships. Article length 600-1200 words." circ. 7M. 12/yr. Pub'd 12 issues 1990; expects 12 issues 1991, 12 issues 1992. sub. price: $8.50; per copy: 75¢; sample: $1. Discounts: contact editor. 28pp; 10¼x16; web press. Reporting time: up to 2 months. Payment: not currently paying for material. Copyrighted, reverts to author. Pub's reviews: 1 in 1990. §Single life, personal growth, self-improvement. Ads: $512/$262/$10 per column inch/40¢ word classified. Singles Press Association (SPA).

SINGLE TODAY, Paula M. Pederson, 2500 Mt. Moriah #185, Memphis, TN 38115, 901-365-3988. 1987. Poetry, articles, photos, interviews. "500-1000 words of interest to single adults, singles coping with divorce, etc." circ. 15M. 12/yr. Pub'd 6 issues 1990; expects 9 issues 1991, 12 issues 1992. sub. price: $25; per copy: $4; sample: $4. Back issues: $4. Discounts: bulk. 20-32pp; 8½x11, 7½x9½; of newsprint. Reporting time: 2 weeks. Payment: copies. Copyrighted, reverts to author. Pub's reviews: 10-12 in 1990. §Communication/relationships, single living. Ads: $420/$250/$50 1/6 page + typeset fee $15. SPA.

Singlejack Books, Stan Weir, Editor, PO Box 1916, San Pedro, CA 90733, 213-548-5964. 1977. Poetry, fiction, articles, non-fiction. "Currently soliciting work description and how-to book manuscripts for labor force audience. Query before submitting." avg. press run 3M. Expects 2 titles 1991, 2 titles 1992. 11 titles listed in the *Small Press Record of Books in Print* (20th Edition, 1991-92). avg. price, paper: $6. Discounts: normal trade, distributor, jobber, etc. Prepaid orders of any size with no invoice needed and customer supplies label gets 40% discount. 128pp; 5½×8½, 3½×5. Reporting time: 10 weeks. Payment: small advance against 8% royalty. Copyrights for author.

SINGLES ALMANAC, Dorothy Fishbein, 138 Brighton Avenue #209, Boston, MA 02134, 617-254-8810. 1981. Poetry, fiction, articles, art, photos, cartoons, interviews, satire, criticism, reviews, music, letters, parts-of-novels, long-poems, collages, plays, concrete art, news items, non-fiction. "We might use any of the above, as long as it has a singles slant. Length can be anywhere from 600-1500 words." circ. 75M. 12/yr. Pub'd 12 issues 1990; expects 12 issues 1991, 12 issues 1992. sub. price: $12; per copy: $2; sample: $1. Back issues: $3. Discounts: negotiable. 32pp; 8¼×10¾. Reporting time: about 2 months. Payment: the prestige of being associated with the finest singles publication in the country. Copyrighted, reverts to author. Pub's reviews: 2-3 in 1990. §Material directly related to singles. Ads: $800/$500/$1 per word. Singles Press Association (SPA).

Singular Speech Press, Don D. Wilson, Editor, Ten Hilltop Drive, Canton, CT 06019, 203-693-6059. 1976. Poetry. "No longer self-publishing; now seeking mss; published a book by a fine poet (in 1989), another forthcoming in mid-1990." avg. press run 200-300. Pub'd 1 title 1990; expects 3 titles 1991, 3 titles 1992. 11 titles listed in the *Small Press Record of Books in Print* (20th Edition, 1991-92). avg. price, paper: $6. Discounts: 40%. 24-48pp; 5½×8½; of. Reporting time: 1 month max. Payment: split press run. Copyrights for author.

SINISTER WISDOM, Elana Dykewomon, PO Box 3252, Berkeley, CA 94703. 1976. Poetry, fiction, articles, art, photos, cartoons, interviews, satire, criticism, reviews, letters, parts-of-novels, long-poems, collages, plays, concrete art, non-fiction. "*Sinister Wisdom* is a magazine for the lesbian imagination in the arts and politics. Contributors range from 'famous' writers to first-time submitters—quality and original voice are what count. Subject matter may be anything that expresses depth of vision. Multi-cultural: writing by 3rd world, Jewish, disabled, fat, ethnic, working class, older and younger lesbians encouraged." circ. 3M. 3/yr. Pub'd 3 issues 1990; expects 2 issues 1991, 3 issues 1992. sub. price: $17, $22 foreign; per copy: $6.50 (pp); sample: $6.50 (pp). Back issues: price as published, from $3-$5. Discounts: 40% to bookstores, 45-50% for bulk sales of 50 or more. 128-144pp; 5×8; of. Reporting time: 3-9 months. Payment: 2 copies. Copyrighted, reverts to author. Pub's reviews: 10 in 1990. §Lesbian and women's poetry, fiction, theatre, arts and non-fiction, especially with radical emphasis. Ads: $150/$75/$40 1/4/write for classified.

Sink Press, Spencer Selby, PO Box 590095, San Francisco, CA 94159-0095. 1986. Poetry. avg. press run 300. Pub'd 2 titles 1990; expects 2 titles 1991, 2 titles 1992. 2 titles listed in the *Small Press Record of Books in Print* (20th Edition, 1991-92). avg. price, paper: $5. Discounts: by arrangement. 35pp; 5½×8½; of. Reporting time: 1-2 months. Payment: copies. Copyrights for author.

SINSEMILLA TIPS (Domestic Marijuana Journal), Tom Alexander, PO Box 1027, Corvallis, OR 97339-1027, 503-757-0027; 757-8477; fax 503-757-0028. 1980. Poetry, fiction, articles, art, photos, cartoons, interviews, satire, criticism, reviews, music, parts-of-novels, news items, non-fiction. "Published by New Moon Publishing, Inc. We are the trade journal of the marijuana industry. I have been on numerous talk shows (Donahue, CBS Morning News)." circ. 15M. 4/yr. Pub'd 4 issues 1990; expects 4 issues 1991, 4 issues 1992. sub. price: $28; per copy: $7; sample: $8.50 (includes postage). Back issues: cover price plus $1 each postage. Discounts: distributor 55-60%; retail stores 30-40% (Depending COD, net 30 days or prepaid) Full credit on unsold copies. 100pp; 7×10; of, web. Reporting time: 2-3 months (sometimes 1 month). Payment: $20-$25 per printed page (around 2.5¢ word). Copyrighted, does not revert to author. Pub's reviews: 8 in 1990. §Anything relating to marijuana and/or its cultivation in America. Ads: $450/$275/Covers back-$1195, inside-$995. COSMEP, New Pages, NW Book Publishers, American Booksellers Association.

SIPAPU, Konocti Books, Noel Peattie, 23311 County Road 88, Winters, CA 95694, 916-662-3364; 916-752-1032. 1970. Articles, interviews, reviews. "A newsletter for librarians interested in third world studies, the counter-culture, peace & alternative and independent presses. Konocti Books publishes no poetry at present. Make all checks out to Noel Peattie, Editor and Publisher, *Sipapu*. No stamps accepted." circ. 400. 2/yr. Pub'd 2 issues 1990; expects 2 issues 1991. sub. price: $8; per copy: $4; sample: $4. Back issues: no special prices, but many back issues out of print. Complete file now microfilmed at University of Southern California. Discounts: books 40%, periodical 10%. 24pp; 8½×11; of. Reporting time: 3 weeks, *query before sending*. Payment: 5¢ per word. Copyrighted, rights revert on request. Pub's reviews: 40 in 1990. §3d world, regional, special items, poetry. *No ads!* COSMEP, CLMP.

SISTERS IN CRIME BOOKS IN PRINT, Rowan Mountain Press, Linda Grant, PO Box 10111, Blacksburg, VA 24062-0111, 703-961-3315. 1989. "Compendium of information on current mystery titles by women authors." circ. 5M+. 2/yr. Pub'd 2 issues 1990; expects 2 issues 1991, 2 issues 1992. price per copy: $2. Back issues: none available. Discounts: 2-4 20%, 5+ 40%. 45pp; 5½×8½; of. Payment: none. Not copyrighted. Ads: none.

SISYPHUS, Christopher Corbett-Fiacco, Editor; Michael Fiacco, Associate Editor, 8 Asticou Road, Boston, MA 02130, 617-983-5291. 1990. Poetry, fiction, art, satire, long-poems, plays. "*SISYPHUS* exists to provide another outlet for the expression of the vision of artists through poetry, prose and sketch or line art. *SISYPHUS* actively seeks submissions by new and as yet undiscovered artists and the more 'experienced' types. We're interested in work that has meaning, substance, and style. *SISYPHUS* is neither an amateur showcase nor a literati notepad at the hippest happening since Mapplethorpe. We're as uninterested in poetic popcorn as we are unimpressed by vaguely related strings of adjectives masquerading with pretension as intent. We seek work that speaks of and to humanity, human emotion, and life itself, whatever that is. Everyone alive is an artist, but not every artist is alive with vision or with truth. The editor seeks to promote through publication artwork that is alive, created by artists living real lives, who undertake to lift the ballast of their vision to the horizon of sight, and to pursue the realization of their understanding all the way to the summit of that most public public-ation: publication. Everyone submitting work or corresponding with the magazine is treated professionally, and with respect. Our motto: *SISYPHUS* may be small, but not insignificant'' 6/yr. Pub'd 4 issues 1990; expects 6 issues 1991, 6 issues 1992. sub. price: $12 US, $18 int'l; per copy: $2.50 US, $3.50 int'l; sample: $1.50 US, $2 int'l. 20pp; 8½×11; †photocopy. Reporting time: 1-2 weeks. Payment: 1 copy of issue in which work appears. Copyrighted, reverts to author. Ads: $20/$10/$6 1/4 page/$3 1/8 page/classified $1/100 character line; free for trade; free as space permits for non-fee contests.

SITES, Lumen Books, Inc., Dennis L. Dollens, 446 West 20 Street, New York, NY 10011. 1979. Fiction, art, photos, interviews, criticism. "Works dealing with specific architectural places, buildings, urban sculpture, etc." circ. 1.5M. 1/yr. Pub'd 1 issue 1990; expects 1 issue 1991, 1 issue 1992. price per copy: $6; sample: $6. Back issues: prices vary. Discounts: trade 40/60, subscription agents 20/80. 90pp; 6×11; of. Reporting time: 1-3 months. Payment: $50 articles, $35 reviews. Copyrighted, does not revert to author. Pub's reviews: 12 in 1990. §Architecture, urban sculpture, relation of literature and architecture. Ads: $300/$150.

Skidmore-Roth Publishing, 1001 Wall Street, El Paso, TX 79915-1012. 1987. Non-fiction. "Primarily a health-care publisher with strong emphasis on the trade market. Distributor in U.S.: Publishers Group West (Trade) medical wholesalers: J.A. Majors, Login Brothers, Mathews Medical Books, Rittenhouse Book Distributors." avg. press run 10M-20M. Pub'd 3 titles 1990; expects 10 titles 1991, 15 titles 1992. 25 titles listed in the *Small Press Record of Books in Print* (20th Edition, 1991-92). avg. price, paper: $12.95; other: $16.95. Discounts: 0-50% depending on quantity. 300pp; 5×7; mi, lp, web. Reporting time: 60-90 days. Payment: 15% on regular sales, 10% foreign, 5%-50% discount and over. Copyrights for author.

SKYDIVING, Michael Truffer, PO Box 1520, DeLand, FL 32721, 904-736-9779; fax 904-736-9786. 1979. Articles, photos, cartoons, interviews, news items, non-fiction. "Contributors must be knowledgeable about sport parachuting." circ. 8.6M. 12/yr. Pub'd 12 issues 1990; expects 12 issues 1991, 12 issues 1992. 1 title listed in the *Small Press Record of Books in Print* (20th Edition, 1991-92). sub. price: $15; per copy: $2; sample: $2. Back issues: $2.50. Discounts: depends, inquire. 32pp; 11×15; of. Reporting time: 3 weeks. Copyrighted, reverts to author, but depends. Pub's reviews: 10 in 1990. §Aviation, parachuting, skydiving. Ads: $574/$337/40¢ per word.

SKYLARK, Pamela Hunter, Editor-in-Chief, 2233 171st Street, Purdue University Calumet, Hammond, IN 46323, 219-844-0520. 1972. Poetry, fiction, articles, art, photos, interviews, satire, criticism, parts-of-novels, plays, non-fiction. "*Skylark* is the fine arts annual of Purdue University Calumet. We are equally interested in the works of known and unknown authors. All submissions must be typed double-spaced on 8½ X 11 paper and be accompanied by a S.A.S.E. of sufficient size bearing sufficient postage." circ. 500-1M. 1/yr. Pub'd 1 issue 1990; expects 1 issue 1991, 1 issue 1992. sub. price: $6; per copy: $6; sample: $3.50 back issues. Back issues: $3.50 each if available. 100pp; 8½×11; lp. Reporting time: 3-6 months (longer in summer). Payment: copy of publication. Copyrighted, reverts to author. Ads: $100/$60/$40 1/4 page (rates subject to change). CLMP.

Skyline West Press, Philip J. Roberts, PO Box 4281, University Station, Laramie, WY 82071, 307-742-4840. 1982. Non-fiction. "Submitted manuscripts should deal with history of the Rocky Mountain West or reference works on that geographic area" avg. press run 2M. Pub'd 1 title 1990; expects 1 title 1991, 2 titles 1992. 2 titles listed in the *Small Press Record of Books in Print* (20th Edition, 1991-92). avg. price, paper: $11.95. Discounts: 40% to recognized dealers. Pages vary (24-400pp); size varies with type of publication; of. Reporting time: 2-3 weeks. Payment: varies with author (negotiable). Copyrights for author.

SLANT, A Journal of Poetry, Richard Hudson, UCA PO Box 5063, Conway, AR 72032, 501-450-3180. 1986. Poetry. "We use traditional and 'modern' poetry, even experimental, moderate length, any subject on approval of Board of Readers. Our purpose is to publish a journal of fine poetry from all regions. No haiku, no translations. Simultaneous submissions ok, no previously published poems. No multiple submissions. Recent contributors include Dan Ford, Marge Piercy, Peter Wild, and Gwendolyn Brooks. Submission deadline is November 15 for annual spring publication." circ. 200. 1/yr. Pub'd 1 issue 1990; expects 1 issue 1991, 1 issue 1992. sub. price: $10; per copy: same; sample: $10. Back issues: $10. Discounts: negotiable. 145pp; 6×9; of. Reporting time: 3-4 months from deadline. Payment: 1 copy on publication. Copyrighted, reverts to author. No ads.

530

Slate Press, David Ebony, Box 1421, Cooper Station, New York, NY 10276. 1986. Fiction, criticism, non-fiction. "Recent books published by Slate Press include *Loop, 50 Ideas for Pictures*, a collection of 50 short prose condensations of the rhetoric of film by Peter Zabelskis; and *The Age of Oil*, essays on selected topics in psychoanalysis and popular culture by Duncan Smith. Although we are not actively seeking unsolicited manuscripts at the present time, this policy may change." avg. press run 1.5M. 2 titles listed in the *Small Press Record of Books in Print* (20th Edition, 1991-92). avg. price, paper: $4.95-$5.95. Discounts: 40%. 150pp; 5⅛×7¾; of, perfect binding, film lamination on covers. Reporting time: varies. Payment: varies. Copyrights for author, assist in obtaining author-held copyright.

THE SLEEPWALKER'S JOURNAL, Nick Barrett, Theodore Hattemer, 820 North Park Street, Columbus, OH 43215, 614-294-2922. 1989. Poetry, fiction, art, photos. "We are looking for unpublished young poets. We will publish poetry, short fiction, photos, art, and multimedia art. We published 7 poets in our last issue and expect to publish 10 in our next. The magazine is young, and the poets we are looking for should be just a bit older than that." Pub'd 1 issue 1990; expects 2 issues 1991, 3 issues 1992. sub. price: free, $2 outside Columbus. Back issues: $3.

Sleepy Hollow Press, Saverio Procario, 150 White Plains Road, Tarrytown, NY 10591, 914-631-8200. 1972. Non-fiction. "Historical Material. American history and literature, pre-1900." avg. press run 3M. Pub'd 1 title 1990; expects 2 titles 1991, 4 titles 1992. 27 titles listed in the *Small Press Record of Books in Print* (20th Edition, 1991-92). avg. price, cloth: $19; paper: $10; other: $3. Discounts: 40% trade, jobber. 300pp; 5⅜×8¾, 8½×11; of. Reporting time: 3 months. Payment: 5-10%. Copyrights for author.

SLEUTH JOURNAL, Baker Street Publications, Sharida Rizzuto, Sidney J. Dragon, Thomas Schellenberger, PO Box 994, Metairie, LA 70004, 504-734-8414. 1983. Poetry, fiction, articles, art, photos, cartoons, interviews, satire, criticism, reviews, letters, long-poems, collages, plays, news items, non-fiction. circ. under 10M. 2-4/yr. Pub'd 4 issues 1990; expects 2-4 issues 1991, 2-4 issues 1992. sub. price: $28 for 4 issues; per copy: $7.90; sample: $7.90. Back issues: $7.90. Discounts: trade with other like publications. 80-100pp; digest size; of, photo copy, excellent quality offset covers. Reporting time: 2-6 weeks. Payment: free copies, fees paid for articles, reviews, and artwork negotiable. Copyrighted, reverts to author. Pub's reviews: 16 in 1990. §Mystery in film and literature, true crime. Ads: free. NWC, SPWAO, HWA, Literary Markets, MWA, Arizona Authors Association (AAA), Western Writers of America (WWA).

SLIPSTREAM, Dan Sicoli, Robert Borgatti, Livio Farallo, Slipstream Productions, Box 2071, New Market Station, Niagara Falls, NY 14301, 716-282-2616 (after 5 p.m., E.S.T.). 1980. Poetry, art, photos, parts-of-novels, long-poems, collages, concrete art. "Submissions are completely open. Query for themes. Reading through 1991 for a general issue. Some recent contributors are Elliot Richman, Gerald Locklin, Suzy Flory, Lyn Lifshin, Kurt Nimmo, Beverly Silva, Joseph Semenovich, Frederick A. Raborg Jr., Alan Catlin, Charles Bukowski, Tom House, Richard Amidon. ISSN 0749-0771. Also produce an audio poetics cassette tape. Spoken word, songs, audio experiments, etc., all welcome on audio cassette." circ. 300. 1-2/yr. Pub'd 1 issue 1990; expects 1 issue 1991, 2 issues 1992. 6 titles listed in the *Small Press Record of Books in Print* (20th Edition, 1991-92). sub. price: $7.50; per copy: $4; sample: $4. Back issues: available upon request. 120pp; 7×8½; of. Reporting time: 2-8 weeks. Payment: presently only in copies. Copyrighted, reverts to author.

Slough Press (see also NONVIOLENT ANARCHIST NEWSLETTER), Jim Cole, Box 1385, Austin, TX 78767. 1973. "Slough Press publishes essay, poetry, nonfiction, and short story books. Quality is our only criteria. We dont consider work from writerw who are unfamiiar with our line of books. Read before you send" avg. press run 500. Pub'd 3 titles 1990; expects 4 titles 1991, 4 titles 1992. 5 titles listed in the *Small Press Record of Books in Print* (20th Edition, 1991-92). avg. price, cloth: $10.95; paper: $5.95. Discounts: vary. 80pp; 5½×8½; of. Reporting time: 2 weeks. Payment: varies. Copyrights for author.

SLOW DANCER, Slow Dancer, John Harvey, Editor; Alan Brooks, U.S. Editor, Alan Brooks, Box 3010, RFD 1, Lubec, ME 04652. 1977. Poetry, fiction. "Send poetry to Alan Brooks, UK poetry and *all* fiction to John Harvey, 58 Rutland Road, West Bridgford, Nottingham NG2 5DG, United Kingdom. Keep the fiction short." circ. 500. 2/yr. Pub'd 2 issues 1990; expects 2 issues 1991, 2 issues 1992. sub. price: $20 (£6) 2-years; $36 (£10) 4-years; per copy: $5 (£1.75); sample: $4 (£1). 48pp; 8½×5½; of. Reporting time: average 2 months. Payment: 3 copies. Copyrighted, reverts to author.

Slow Dancer (see also SLOW DANCER), John Harvey, 58 Rutland Road, W. Bridgford, Nottingham NG2 5DG, United Kingdom, 0602-821518. 1977. Poetry. "No unsolicited book manuscripts, we publish authors who have appeared in *Slow Dancer Magazine*." avg. press run 500. Pub'd 2 titles 1990; expects 2 titles 1991, 2 titles 1992. 9 titles listed in the *Small Press Record of Books in Print* (20th Edition, 1991-92). avg. price, paper: $5 (£3). 24-56pp; 5½×8½; of. Payment: copies. Copyright remains with author. Association of Little Presses.

SLOWPITCH TIPS, GDE Publications, PO Box 304, Lima, OH 45802. 1982. "Instructional Series; timely step-by-step tips covering all aspects of the game for coaches & players"

Small Helm Press, Pearl Evans, Jean Maston, Contact Person, 622 Baker Street, Petaluma, CA 94952, (707) 763-5757. 1986. Non-fiction. "Small Helm Press is not able to receive unsolicited contributions at this time." Pub'd 1 title 1990; expects 2 titles 1991, 2 titles 1992. 4 titles listed in the *Small Press Record of Books in Print* (20th Edition, 1991-92). avg. price, cloth: $17.95; paper: $12. Discounts: 3 up 40%, 200 up 50%, 500 up 40%-25%. 200pp; 5½×8½; of. Payment: individual basis. Does not copyright for author. PMA (Publishers Marketing Association), 2401 Pacific Coast Hwy, Ste. 206, Hermosa Beach, CA 90254; COSMEP The International Association of Ind. Pub., Box 703, San Francisco, CA 94101.

THE SMALL POND MAGAZINE OF LITERATURE aka SMALL POND, Napoleon St. Cyr, PO Box 664, Stratford, CT 06497, 203-378-4066. 1964. Poetry, fiction, articles, art, satire, reviews, concrete art, non-fiction. "Max: Fiction 2.5M words, poetry approx 100 lines, other prose 2.5M words. Recent contributors: some nobodies—some somebodies." circ. 300+. 3/yr. Pub'd 3 issues 1990; expects 3 issues 1991. sub. price: $7.50; per copy: $3; sample: $3, $2.50 random back issue. Back issues: inquire. Discounts: inquire. 40pp; 5½×8½; of. Reporting time: 7-45 days, longer in summer. Payment: 2 copies. Copyrighted, does not revert to author. Pub's reviews: 12 in 1990. §Only poetry (books). Ads: $35/$20/$10 1/4 pg. CLMP.

SMALL PRESS: The Magazine & Book Review of Independent Publishing, Meckler Corporation, Brenda Mitchel-Powell, Editor-in-Chief, 11 Ferry Lane West, Westport, CT 06880, 203-226-6967; FAX 203-454-5840. 1983. Articles, interviews, reviews, news items, non-fiction. circ. 5.2M. 6/yr. Pub'd 6 issues 1990; expects 6 issues 1991, 6 issues 1992. sub. price: $35; per copy: $6; sample: free. 68pp; 8¼×11¼; of. Reporting time: 6 weeks. Payment: per arrangement. Copyrighted, reverts to author. Pub's reviews: 600 in 1990. §Any publications published by small, independent publishers, regardless of subject matter. Ads: $725/$485/$325 1/4 page.

THE SMALL PRESS BOOK REVIEW, Henry Berry, Editor; David C. Parks, Travel-Nature Editor, PO Box 176, Southport, CT 06490, 203-268-4878. 1985. Articles, reviews, news items. "Reviews: 150-200 words, plus annotation books also received. Reviewers send SASE for guidelines. Articles—developments in the field of small presses; 300-800 words." circ. 2M. 6/yr. Pub'd 6 issues 1990; expects 6 issues 1991, 6 issues 1992. sub. price: $26; per copy: $5; sample: $5. Back issues: $4. Discounts: inquire with publisher. 24-28pp; 8½×11; of. Reporting time: 1 month. Payment: articles and reviews 2 copies. Copyrighted, does not revert to author. Pub's reviews: 800 in 1990. §Interested in all areas. Ads: $175/$135/$45 per 5 lines, 50 char. per line/$15 each additional line. COSMEP.

Small Press International (see also BARBIZON MAGAZINE), Don Elzer, General Secretary, PO Box 61, Lumby, B.C. V0E 2G0, Canada, (604) 547-6621. 1985. Poetry, fiction, articles, art, photos, cartoons, interviews, criticism, reviews, music, letters, parts-of-novels, concrete art, news items, non-fiction. "*SPI* specializes in small press runs for its publishing endeavours. We apply most of our energy to *whole earth* fields. *SPI* is owned by The Barbizon Foundation and operated as a collective" avg. press run 1.5M. Pub'd 3 titles 1990; expects 8 titles 1991, 16 titles 1992. avg. price, paper: $3.75. Discounts: 25% off cover price; bulk distributor (40 copies) 50% off. 52pp; 5×8; †of. Reporting time: varies. Payment: negotiable. Copyright negotiable.

SMALL PRESS MONTHLY, John Nicholson, Editor, Small Press Group of Britain, BM Bozo, London WC1N 3XX, England, 0234-211606. 1988. Articles, photos, interviews, letters, news items. "Full coverage of the small press scene in Britain-News, reports, advice, info, events. Also section on international news." circ. 500. 12/yr. Pub'd 12 issues 1990; expects 12 issues 1991, 12 issues 1992. sub. price: £15; per copy: £1; sample: £1.25. Back issues: £2. Discounts: normal trade rates. 12pp; 8¼×11¾; of. Copyrighted. Ads: £80/£50/1/4 £30/1/8 £20.

SMALL PRESS NEWS, Stony Hills Productions, Diane Kruchkow, Editor & Publisher, Weeks Mills, New Sharon, ME 04955. 1981. Articles, letters, news items. "*SPN* presents the lowdown on the small press scene nationwide—critical examinations of orgs. such as CCLM, NEA, etc., as well as editorials, commentary, mss. wanted, contests, conferences and fairs, "From The Bookshelf"—an annotated look at recent publications, plus guests and essays, and original poetry. Editor Diane Kruchkow has been actively involved in the small press for nearly 20 years." circ. 500. 10/yr. Pub'd 2 issues 1990; expects 10 issues 1991, 10 issues 1992. sub. price: $10/10 issues; per copy: $1.50; sample: $1.50. Back issues: $2. 8pp; 8½×11; †mi, of. Reporting time: immediate. Payment: copies. Copyrighted. Pub's reviews. §Poetry, fiction, criticism. Ads: $75/$50/$1 line-classified (ads are printed offset). COSMEP, MWPA, CCLM.

THE SMALL PRESS REVIEW, Dustbooks, Len Fulton, Editor-Publisher; Laurel Speer, Contributing Editor ('Speer'); Merritt Clifton, Contributing Editor ('Help'); Robert Peters, Contributing Editor (Magazine Reviews), PO Box 100, Paradise, CA 95967-9999, 916-877-6110. 1966. Articles, cartoons, interviews, reviews, letters, news items. "The *Small Press Review* seeks to study and promulgate the small press and little magazine (i.e. the *independent* publisher) worldwide. It was started in 1966 as part of an effort by its publisher to get a grip on small press/mag information since no one at the time (or for some years thereafter) seemed interested in doing it. It was also designed to promote the small press in a variety of ways. It links with other *Dustbooks* small-press info titles, updating the annual *International Directory of Little Magazines and Small Presses* and the annual *Small Press Record of Books in Print*. *SPR* is always on the lookout for competently written reviews (yes, we have a 'style sheet'—write for it), as long as they hold to a page in length and review a title published by a small press. *SPR* has a regular 'News Notes' section which gives info about small press activities, manuscript needs (*and there are many!*), contests, prizes and so on. We print full-info listings monthly on twenty or so new small presses and mags. In the case of these latter listings, we generally utilize data from *Int'l Directory* report forms which come in to us throughout the year (if your magazine or press is not listed in either the *Int'l Directory* or *Small Press Record of Books in Print* please write to us for a form. If you fill out a form for the *Directory* you will automatically receive a form for the *Record* later.) NOTE: Canadian and foreign please remit in US funds only when ordering.'' circ. 3.5M. 12/yr. Pub'd 12 issues 1990; expects 12 issues 1991, 12 issues 1992. sub. price: individuals $23/yr, $30/2 yrs, $33/3 yrs, $36/4 yrs; institutions $29/yr, $39/2 yrs, $47/3 yrs, $52/4 yrs; per copy: $2.50; sample: free. Back issues: inquire. Discounts: schedule available for agents. 16pp; 8½×11; of. Reporting time: 3 weeks. Not copyrighted. Pub's reviews: 100 in 1990. §Anything published by a small press. Ads: $150/$90/$75/$50/(display); $17 col. inch for SPR Mart, an unclassified display section on the back cover monthly.

Small-Small Press (see also WORKSHOP), Tom Fallon, 226 Linden Street, Rumford, ME 04276, 364-7237. 1982. Articles, interviews, satire, criticism, reviews, letters, collages, concrete art, news items. avg. press run 500. Pub'd 1 title 1990; expects 1 title 1992. 4 titles listed in the *Small Press Record of Books in Print* (20th Edition, 1991-92). avg. price, paper: $9. 100pp; 5½×8½; of. Reporting time: 1 month. Payment: 10 copies. Does not copyright for author. MWPA.

SMARANDACHE FUNCTION JOURNAL, R. Muller, PO Box 42561, Phoenix, AZ 85080. 1990. "Research papers in number theory about Smarandache Function: let n be an integer, then m(n) is the smallest integer m such that m! is divisible by n." 1/yr. Pub'd 1 issue 1990; expects 1 issue 1991, 1-2 issues 1992. Back issues: none available. 80pp; 8½×11; of. Reporting time: 1 month. Payment: free copies of the magazine. Pub's reviews. §Papers, books, etc. about Smarandache Function.

Smiling Dog Press, Dean Creighton, 9875 Fritz, Maple City, MI 49664, 616-334-3695. 1989. Poetry, fiction. "Recent contributors: Kurt Nimmo, Kell Robertson, Charlie Mehnhoff" avg. press run 300. Pub'd 2 titles 1990; expects 7 titles 1991. avg. price, paper: $4. 12pp; †lp. Reporting time: 2 months. Payment: in copies. All rights revert to author.

The Smith (The Generalist Assn., Inc.), Harry Smith, Editor, 69 Joralemon Street, Brooklyn, NY 11201. 1964. "Sometimes does own printing" avg. press run 1M. Pub'd 4 titles 1990; expects 4 titles 1991. 28 titles listed in the *Small Press Record of Books in Print* (20th Edition, 1991-92). avg. price, cloth: $16.95; paper: $9.95. Discounts: varies. 100pp; 6×9; of, lp. Reporting time: 8-10 weeks. Payment: $500 outright against royalties. Copyrights for author. CCLM, COSMEP.

Genny Smith Books, Genny Smith, 1304 Pitman Avenue, Palo Alto, CA 94301, 415-321-7247. 1976. Articles, photos, non-fiction. "I specialize in publications on the Eastern Sierra region of California — to date, guidebooks, natural history, regional history and sets of historic postcards. My guidebooks (I edit and coauthor them) to this mountain-and-desert vacation area include chapters on roads, trails, natural history and history. Best known localities in this region are Owens Valley and Mammoth Lakes. These guidebooks are for sightseers, campers, hikers, fishermen, nature lovers and history buffs. Alternate address: PO Box 1060, Mammoth Lakes, CA 93546'' avg. press run 7M. Pub'd 1 title 1990; expects 1 title 1991. 5 titles listed in the *Small Press Record of Books in Print* (20th Edition, 1991-92). avg. price, cloth: $17.50; paper: $10.95. Discounts: 40%. 224pp; 6×9, 7½×10; of. Payment: varies from sharing of royalties to flat payment for material. Copyrights for author. Bookbuilders West.

Gibbs Smith, Publisher, Madge Baird, Editorial Director; Steve Chapman, Fiction, 1877 East Gentile Street, PO Box 667, Layton, UT 84041, 801-544-9800. 1969. Poetry, fiction, art, criticism, non-fiction. "Trade imprint: Peregrine Smith Books. Books on architecture, arts, reprints, short stories, novels, guide books, natural environment, poetry, photography.'' avg. press run 5M. Pub'd 24 titles 1990; expects 30 titles 1991, 30 titles 1992. avg. price, cloth: $18.95-$49; paper: $9.95-$14.95. Discounts: 46% average discount. 200pp; 5½×8½, 8½×11; of. Reporting time: 10 weeks. Payment: 10% on net. Copyrights for author. AAP, ABA, Rocky Mountain Book Publishers.

Richard W. Smith Military Books, PO Box 2118, Hendersonville, TN 37077. avg. press run 1.5M. Pub'd 1 title 1990; expects 1 title 1991. 3 titles listed in the *Small Press Record of Books in Print* (20th Edition, 1991-92). avg. price, cloth: $20; paper: $15. 200pp; 8½×11. Payment: yes. Copyrights for author.

SMOKE, Dave Ward, 40 Canning Street, Liverpool L8 7NP, England. 1974. Poetry, fiction, art, photos, cartoons, long-poems, collages, concrete art. "Tom Pickard, Jim Burns, Dave Calder, Roger McGough, Frances Horovitz.'' circ. 1.5M. 2/yr. Pub'd 3 issues 1990; expects 3 issues 1991. sub. price: £2/3 issues incl. postage;

per copy: 50p plus post; sample: 50p plus post. 24pp; size A5; of. Reporting time: as quickly as possible. Payment: none. Not copyrighted. No ads.

SMS Publishing Corp., Sara M. Schreiner, Principal Editor, PO Box 2276, Glenview, IL 60025. 1981. Articles, non-fiction. avg. press run 2M-10M. Expects 1 title 1991, 1 title 1992. 3 titles listed in the *Small Press Record of Books in Print* (20th Edition, 1991-92). avg. price, cloth: $35; paper: $10. Discounts: 20% for orders of 2-5, 40%+ for orders of 6 and up. Special discounts to educators. 160+pp; 5½×8½; of. Reporting time: 1-3 months. Payment: to be negotiated. Copyrights for author. COSMEP.

Smyrna Press, Dan Georgakas, Jim Malick, Barbara Saltz, Box 1151, Union City, NJ 07087. 1964. Poetry, fiction, art, parts-of-novels, collages, plays, non-fiction. "We try to publish one-three books a year which combine the latest technical breakthroughs with a concern for social change that is essentially Marxist but undogmatic. Our current projects combine art and politics as well as themes of sexual liberation. We can use good line drawings or woodcuts. We publish art books. Query before sending any material. Sample copies of literary books, $2; sample copies of art books, $3." avg. press run 2M. Pub'd 2 titles 1990; expects 1 title 1991, 1 title 1992. 19 titles listed in the *Small Press Record of Books in Print* (20th Edition, 1991-92). avg. price, cloth: $25; paper: $10; other: $2. Discounts: 40% bookstores, 10% education, bulk by arrangement. 60-250pp; 6×9; lp. Reporting time: 2-3 weeks, query before submitting. Payment: copies and 10% net. Copyrights for author.

THE SNAIL'S PACE REVIEW, Darby Penney, Ken Denberg, RR#2, Box 363 Brownell Road, Cambridge, NY 12816, 518-692-9953. 1991. Poetry, reviews. "We are looking for excellent poetry of all genres, as well as translations and book reviews (poetry only). Submissions from members of ethnic and cultural minorities, people of color, and women are particularly encouraged. Recent contributors include Fred Chappell, Martha Collins, Judith Hemschemeyer, Shirley Kaufman, Maurice Kenny, Jerome Rothenberg and Lee Upton." circ. 250. 2/yr. Expects 2 issues 1991, 2 issues 1992. sub. price: $8; per copy: $4; sample: $4. Back issues: $3 each for Vol. 1 #1 & #2. Discounts: 40% trade. 36pp; 5½×8½; of. Reporting time: 2-10 weeks. Payment: 2 copies. Copyrighted, reverts to author. Pub's reviews. §Poetry. Ads: none.

SNAKE NATION REVIEW, Roberta George, Janice Daugharty, Pat Miller, 2920 North Oak, Valdosta, GA 31602, 912-242-1503. 1989. Poetry, fiction, art, photos. circ. 200. 2/yr. Pub'd 2 issues 1990; expects 2 issues 1991, 2 issues 1992. sub. price: $15; per copy: $6; sample: $5 (includes mailing). Back issues: $5 (includes mailing). Discounts: 40% to bookstores, jobbers. 110pp; 6×9; lp. Reporting time: 3 months. Payment: 2 copies or prize money. Copyrighted, reverts to author. Ads: $100/$50/$25.

Snow Lion Publications, Inc., Sidney Piburn, PO Box 6483, Ithaca, NY 14851, 607-273-8506; 607-273-8519; fax 607-273-8508. 1980. Non-fiction. avg. press run 10M. Pub'd 6 titles 1990; expects 15 titles 1991, 15 titles 1992. 14 titles listed in the *Small Press Record of Books in Print* (20th Edition, 1991-92). avg. price, cloth: $30; paper: $12. Discounts: 8% average. 250pp; 5½×8½. Payment: 10% average. Copyrights for author. ABA.

Snowbird Publishing Company, William H. Meyer, Editor & Publisher, PO Box 729, Tellico Plains, TN 37385, 615-546-7001; fax 615-524-8612. 1991. Poetry, fiction, non-fiction. "Additional address: 2313 Sutherland Avenue, Knoxville, TN 37919. Snowbird Enterprises, Inc., is owned by William and Joanna Meyer,-both American Indians. Both William and Joanna have many years of editorial and book production experience. Snowbird Publishing Co. will seek primarily American Indian authors and scholars with books in any subject area—poetry, fiction and non-fiction. There is no publisher at this time focusing on Native Americans as far as we are aware. It is our intention to fill that gap. Already at the beginning of this year, we are preparing to print a book on Advanced Calculus by Clyde Davenport, a cookbook, and a novel. A book of poetry and a pamphlet series are being considered. William Meyer, publisher, is author of the 1969 book, *Native Americans: The New Indian Resistance*." avg. press run depends on subject and pre-press feedback. Expects 3-4 titles 1991, 4-6 titles 1992. 1 title listed in the *Small Press Record of Books in Print* (20th Edition, 1991-92). avg. price, cloth: $16. Discounts: to be established, probably along standard industry guidelines. 200pp; 6×9; of. Reporting time: 3-4 weeks. Payment: per contract. Copyrights for author.

Snowbound Press (see also **THE POETRY PEDDLER**), J.J. Snow, A.M. Ryant, PO Box 250, W. Monroe, NY 13167, 315-676-2050. 1988. Poetry. "Nothing that *exalts* bigotry, war or violence accepted—eros yes, porno no. Recent contributors: Rob Allan, J.J. Snow. Send for details on publishing program. Submissions by invitation only" avg. press run 50. Expects 4 titles 1991, 6 titles 1992. avg. price, paper: $2. 18pp; 5½×8½; †desktop. Payment: subsidy by special arrangement. Does not copyright for author.

SNOWY EGRET, The Fair Press, Karl Barnebey, Editor; Michael Aycock, Editor; Humphrey A. Olsen, Reviewer, PO Box 9, Bowling Green, IN 47833, 812-331-8529. 1922. Poetry, fiction, articles, art, interviews, satire, criticism, reviews, letters, parts-of-novels, long-poems, non-fiction. "Emphasis on natural history and human beings in relation to nature from literary, artistic, philosophical, and historical points of view. Prose generally not more than 3M words but will consider up to 10M; poetry generally less than page although long poems will be considered. Interested in works that celebrate the abundance and beauty of nature and examine

534

the variety of ways, both positive and negative, through which human beings interact with the natural world and living things. Looking for nature-oriented original graphics (offset prints, lithographs, woodcuts, etc) that can be editioned as part of an issue. Review copies of books desired. Originality of material or originality of treatment and literary quality and readability important. Payment on publication plus 2 contributor's copies. Recent contributors: Stephen Lewandowski, Conrad Hilberry, Barry Greer, Jane Candia Coleman, Margarita Mondrus Engle, Linda Rabben. Submit review materials to Humphrey A. Olsen, Reviewer, 107 S. 8th Street, Williamsburg, KY 40769. Send 6 X 9 SASE for prospectus with examples of recently published works and writer's guidelines" circ. 500. 2/yr. Pub'd 2 issues 1990; expects 2 issues 1991, 2 issues 1992. sub. price: $12; per copy: $8; sample: $8. 60pp; 8½×11; †of. Reporting time: 2 months. Payment: prose, $2 mag page; poetry, $2/poem, $4 mag page. Copyrighted, reverts to author. Pub's reviews: 10 in 1990. §People in relation to natural surroundings, fresh nature poetry, fiction, essays, criticism, philosophy, biography. No ads.

SNUG, Geoffrey Brock, 1327 High Road #Y-6, Tallahassee, FL 32304, 904-224-9196. 1988. Poetry, fiction, art, photos, cartoons. "Biases: eclectic. Recent contributors: J. Allyn Rosser, Hank Heuler, Manolis Polentas, Mary Jane Ryals. Black and white photocopiable art only. Include SASE with all correspondence." circ. 100+. 2/yr. Pub'd 1 issue 1990; expects 2 issues 1991, 2 issues 1992. sub. price: $2/copy; per copy: $2; sample: $2. Back issues: $2. Discounts: available on request. 36pp; 4.25×3.67; †desktop pub./laser print/photocopy. Reporting time: as soon as possible (varies). Payment: contributors receive 3 copies and subscription. Not copyrighted. Ads: none.

SO & SO, Dragon Cloud Books, As Is/So & So Press, John Marron, 232 Volkert Street, Highland Park, NJ 08904-3119, (201) 985-5565. 1973. Poetry, art, photos, collages, concrete art, non-fiction. *"And It Still Moves*—Multicultural poetry calendar, published once a year" circ. 2M. Irregular. Pub'd 1 issue 1990; expects 1 issue 1991, 1 issue 1992. sub. price: $8; per copy: $8; sample: $4. Back issues: 1973-80 $4/issue. 32-150pp; 8½×11; of. Reporting time: 2 months. Payment: 1-5 contributor copies. Copyrighted, reverts to author. CCLM.

Sober Minute Press (see also HUNGRY ZIPPER), brian david j(o(h)n)ston, PO Box 3576, Cambridge, Ont. N3H 5C6, Canada, 519-740-8166. 1988. Poetry, art, collages, concrete art. "In 1989, Sober Minute Press published *bfp(h)aGe, An Anthology Of Visual Poetry And Collage.* Contributors to bfp(h)aGe (bu-fay-j) were as follows: bpNichol, jwcurry, Greg Evason, Daniel f. Bradley, brian david j(o(h)n)ston, and Sha(u)nt Basmajian. The purpose of SMP is to promote and publish concrete and visual poetry and collage. Please enclose a SASE with your correspondence." avg. press run 1M. Expects 1 title 1992. 1 title listed in the *Small Press Record of Books in Print* (20th Edition, 1991-92). avg. price, paper: $9.95. Discounts: 40% trade, 10% library. 64pp; 6×9; of. Reporting time: 3-6 months. Payment: copies. Copyrights for author.

SOCIAL ANARCHISM: A Journal of Practice And Theory, Howard J. Ehrlich, Mark Bevis, Chris Stadler, 2743 Maryland Avenue, Baltimore, MD 21218, 301-243-6987. 1980. Poetry, fiction, articles, art, photos, cartoons, interviews, satire, criticism, reviews, letters, non-fiction. "Essays should be between 1,000 and 3,000 words. Book reviews: 500-2,000 words. Recent contributors: Neala Schleuning, Ruthann Robson, Kingsley Widmer, Brian Martin, David Koven, Richard Kostelanetz, George Woodcock, David Wieck." circ. 1.2M. 2/yr. Pub'd 1 issue 1990; expects 2 issues 1991, 2 issues 1992. 7 titles listed in the *Small Press Record of Books in Print* (20th Edition, 1991-92). sub. price: $10 for 4 issues; per copy: $3.50; sample: $3.50. Back issues: $3.50. Discounts: 40% plus postage. 96pp; 6×9; of. Reporting time: 6 weeks. Payment: 5 copies. Not copyrighted. Pub's reviews: 9 in 1990. §Anarchism, feminism, ecology, Green politics and culture, communitarianism.

SOCIAL CHANGE & INFORMATION SYSTEMS, John Noyce, Publisher, John L. Noyce, G.P.O. Box 2222T, Melbourne, Vic. 3001, Australia. 1972. Poetry, fiction, articles, art, photos, cartoons, interviews, satire, news items. "Anything on librarianship and social change; sexism, racism, workers' control in librarianship and related areas such as info work, publishing, etc." circ. 200. 3/yr. Pub'd 3 issues 1990; expects 3 issues 1991, 3 issues 1992. sub. price: libraries £21 Sterling, individuals £10 Sterling. Discounts: 10 percent to trade. 32pp; size A5; †xerox. Reporting time: we try. Payment: free copy. Copyrighted, reverts to author. Pub's reviews: 30-40 in 1990. §Libraries, social change, alternative society/work/ideas. Ads: on application.

SOCIAL JUSTICE: A JOURNAL OF CRIME, CONFLICT, & WORLD ORDER, Crime and Social Justice Associates, Inc., Gregory Shank, PO Box 40601, San Francisco, CA 94610, 415-550-1703. 1974. Poetry, articles, interviews, satire, reviews, letters, news items, non-fiction. "Maximum length: 30 double-spaced ms pages, including footnotes. Recent authors: Lennox Hinds, Francis Boyle, Noam Chomsky, Eduardo Galiano, Richard Falk, Pablo Gonzales Casanova. A journal of progressive criminology and international law." circ. 3M. 4/yr. Pub'd 4 issues 1990; expects 4 issues 1991, 4 issues 1992. sub. price: $30 individual, $60 institution; per copy: $10 individual, $15 institutions; sample: $10. Back issues: same as single copy price or available from University Microfilms, Ann Arbor, MI. Discounts: agency 15%, trade discount to stores. 150-175pp; 6×9; of. Reporting time: 90 days. Payment: none. Copyrighted, does not revert to author. Pub's reviews: 6 in 1990. §Criminology, international law, civil liberties, minority issues, pedagogy, women, human rights. Ads: $125/$75.

Social Order Series, Robert Schutz, 7899 St. Helena Road, Santa Rosa, CA 95404, 707-539-0569. 1985. Articles, non-fiction. "10,000 to 12,000 words. Interested particularly in application of ethics to life. Hence, "Friendly Business," by Robert Schutz, "The Defense of the Peaceable Kingdom," by Marshall Massey. Has to be insightful and incisive, show how to improve the social order" circ. 1.2M. Expects 2 issues 1991, 3 issues 1992. price per copy: $3. Discounts: 40% FOB. 36pp; 5¼×7½; lp. Reporting time: 2 months. Payment: 6-10%. Copyrighted. QUIP.

SOCIAL POLICY, Audrey Gartner, Managing Editor; Frank Riessman, Editor-in-Chief; Alan Gartner, Editor, 25 West 43rd Street, Room 620, New York, NY 10036, 212-642-2929. 1970. Articles, art, photos, interviews, criticism, reviews, letters, non-fiction. "Articles run 2M-5M words, on contemporary social thought and policy analysis (environmental, economics, community development, education). Recent special issues dealt with 'self-help', 'women and health', 'Images of the disabled', 'effective schools'. Contributors include Richard Cloward, Frances Piven, S.M. Miller, Barbara Ehrenreich, Harry Boyte, Heather Booth, Stanley Aronowitz and community activists." circ. 3M. 4/yr. Pub'd 4 issues 1990; expects 4 issues 1991. sub. price: $20 individuals, $35 institutions; per copy: $5; sample: $3. Back issues: $4. Discounts: 10% agent. 64pp; 7×11; lp. Reporting time: 2-4 weeks. Payment: none. Copyrighted, does not revert to author. Pub's reviews: 2 in 1990. §Nonfiction, social policy materials, esp. in area of economics and human services, sociology. Ads: $300/$180. COSMEP.

SOCIAL PROBLEMS, University of California Press, Merry Morash, University of California Press, 2120 Berkeley Way, Berkeley, CA 94720, 415-642-4191. 1953. Articles, reviews, non-fiction. "Editorial address: Dept. Sociology, Drake University, Des Moines, IA 50311. Copyrighted by Society for the Study of Social Problems." circ. 3.9M. 5/yr. Pub'd 5 issues 1990; expects 5 issues 1991, 5 issues 1992. sub. price: $66 (+ $5 foreign postage); per copy: $16.50; sample: free. Back issues: same as single copy price. Discounts: foreign subs. agent 10%, one-time order 10+ 30%, standing orders (bookstores): 1-99 40%, 100+ 50%. 128pp; 7×10; of. Copyrighted, does not revert to author. Ads: $200/$120.

SOCIALISM AND DEMOCRACY, Michael E. Brown, Frank Rosengarten, 33 West 42nd Street, New York, NY 10036, 212-790-4300. 1985. "Average article runs 25-30 pages typescript; articles interpret historical and current developments primarily from a socialist point of view. Among recent contributors are: James Petras, Jean Franco, Andrew Levine, Stephen F. Cohen, Alem Habtu, Lynn Turgeon, John J. Neumaier" circ. 500. 2/yr. Pub'd 2 issues 1990; expects 2 issues 1991, 2 issues 1992. sub. price: $8/2 issues, $18/5 issues; per copy: $4; sample: free. Back issues: issue #1, $1; #2, $2; #3, $3. Discounts: 40% trade. 200pp; 6×9. Reporting time: 2 months. Payment: nominal fees of $100 upon agreement with author. Pub's reviews: 16 in 1990. §Marxist theory; socialist history, movements, thought; Soviet politics and society; problems in historical method; popular culture. COSMEP, Po Box 703, San Francisco, CA 94101.

SOCIALISM AND SEXUALITY, Chicago Democratic Socialists Of America, Robert Hinde, Chicago DSA, 1608 N. Milwaukee #403, Chicago, IL 60647. 1990. Articles, art, cartoons, interviews, criticism, reviews, collages, news items, non-fiction. "We are interested in contributions examining lesbian, gay, and bisexual politics from a democratic socialist perspective. Any artwork submitted should fall under this general heading and should be able to be reproduced via photocopying." circ. 100. 4/yr. Pub'd 3 issues 1990; expects 4 issues 1991, 4 issues 1992. sub. price: $8; per copy: $1; sample: $1. Back issues: $1. Discounts: $10 per 20 copies of any single issue. 8pp; 8½×11; †mi. Reporting time: 1 month. Payment: 1 copy. Not copyrighted. Pub's reviews: none in 1990. §Lesbian/gay politics, AIDS.

SOCIETE, Technicians of the Sacred, Courtney Willis, 1317 N. San Fernando Blvd, Suite 310, Burbank, CA 91504. 1983. Poetry, fiction, articles, art, photos, interviews, reviews, music, non-fiction. "Related to African, neo-African systems, religion, magic, hermetic, etc." circ. 500. 3/yr. Pub'd 3 issues 1990; expects 3 issues 1991, 3 issues 1992. sub. price: $15; per copy: $6; sample: $6. Back issues: $6. 50pp; 8½×11; †photocopy. Reporting time: 4 weeks. Payment: copy of issue. Copyrighted. Pub's reviews: 1 in 1990. §Voodoo-neo African, African religions, magic, occult, religion, gnosticism, hermetics.

SOCIETY, Irving Louis Horowitz, Editor-in-Chief, Transaction, Rutgers University, New Brunswick, NJ 08903, 201-932-2280. 1963. Articles, photos, interviews, reviews, non-fiction. "Most articles submitted are not more than 6000 words long. Subject matter is diversified, but confined to social science and public policy. Most authors are social scientists; most readers are generally informed about social science, but are not specialists." circ. 15M. 6/yr. Pub'd 6 issues 1990; expects 6 issues 1991, 6 issues 1992. sub. price: $36 individual, $15 students; per copy: $6. Back issues: $17. Discounts: agents 10%. 96pp; 8½×11; of. Reporting time: varies, often within 1 month. Payment: none. Copyrighted, does not revert to author. Pub's reviews: 30+ in 1990. §Books about social science, public policy. Ads: $750/$575.

Society for Individual Liberty (see also INDIVIDUAL LIBERTY), Donald C. Ernsberger, PO Box 338, Warminster, PA 18974, 215-675-6830. 1969. avg. press run 2M.

Society Of Authors (see also THE AUTHOR), Derek Parker, 84, Drayton Gardens, London, England SW10 9SB, United Kingdom, 01-373-6642. 1884. "Business renumeration & status of writers in all media. Author

536

keeps copyrights. We take first British serial rights.'' avg. press run 5M. Pub'd 4 titles 1990; expects 4 titles 1991, 4 titles 1992. avg. price, paper: £4.50. 32pp; size A4; of, lp. Reporting time: 6 weeks before publication (third week of March, June, Sept., Dec.). Payment: £50 per 1M words. Copyrights, author keeps copyright.

SOCIOLOGY OF SPORT JOURNAL, Human Kinetics Pub. Inc., Jay J. Coakley, Box 5076, Champaign, IL 61825-5076, 217-351-5076. 1984. Articles, reviews. "Human behavior in the context of sport and physical activity" circ. 725. 4/yr. Pub'd 4 issues 1990; expects 4 issues 1991, 4 issues 1992. sub. price: $28 individual, $56 institution; per copy: $7 indiv., $15 instit.; sample: free. Back issues: $7 indiv., $15 instit. Discounts: 5%. 102pp; 6×9; of. Reporting time: 2 months. Payment: none. Copyrighted. Pub's reviews: 12 in 1990. §Sport, sport science, and physical education related to sociology. Ads: $170/$102 (4X rate). North American Society of Sport Sociology.

SOCKS, DREGS AND ROCKING CHAIRS, dbqp, Ge(of Huth), editor, 317 Princetown Road, Schenectady, NY 12306-2022. 1982. Poetry, cartoons, collages, concrete art. *"Socks, Dregs & Rocking Chairs (SD&RC)* is an irregular comicbook (xeroxed). Subscriptions can be of any dollar amount—cost (which varies) per issue will be subtracted when mailed" circ. 100. 1/yr. Pub'd 1 issue 1990; expects 1 issue 1991, 1 issue 1992. sub. price: 75¢; per copy: 75¢; sample: 75¢. Back issues: 75¢. Discounts: none. 8pp; size varies; †photocopy. Reporting time: 2 weeks. Payment: at least 2 copies; 1/4 of press run is divided among contributors. Copyrighted, reverts to author.

SOFTBALL ILLUSTRATED, GDE Publications, Glen D. Eley, PO Box 304, Lima, OH 45802. 1980. Articles, interviews. "Instructional articles & drawings." circ. 1M. 2/yr. Pub'd 8 issues 1990; expects 6 issues 1991. sub. price: $15.95; per copy: $3.50. Back issues: all subscribers get each issue published in series. 32pp; 8½×11; of. Payment: none. Copyrighted, reverts to author. Ads: $250/$100/$1.50 per word (10 min).

SoftServe Press, 7000 Bianca Avenue, Van Nuys, CA 91406-3512, 818-996-7000; fax 818-996-0008. 1 title listed in the *Small Press Record of Books in Print* (20th Edition, 1991-92).

SOJOURNER, THE WOMEN'S FORUM, Karen Kahn, Editor, 42 Seaverns Avenue, Jamaica Plain, MA 02130-1109, 617-524-0415. 1975. Poetry, fiction, articles, photos, cartoons, interviews, criticism, reviews, letters, news items, non-fiction. *"Sojourner* has an open editorial policy—we attempt to present a forum for women, and we will consider anything for publication which is not racist, sexist, or homophobic." circ. 45M. 12/yr. Pub'd 12 issues 1990; expects 12 issues 1991, 12 issues 1992. sub. price: $17; per copy: $2; sample: $2. Back issues: $2. Discounts: 60% agent, 40% bookstore. 48pp; 11×17; of, web press. Reporting time: 2 months. Payment: 2 free copies, one-year subscription. Copyrighted, rights revert if requested. Pub's reviews: 100 in 1990. §Feminism, women's issues, any book, film, etc., by a woman or about women. Ads: $950/$500/$16 for 4 lines, 40 characters/line.

Soleil Press, Martha Blowen, RFD #1, Box 452, Lisbon Falls, ME 04252, 207-353-5454. 1988. Poetry, fiction. "Soleil Press publishes only material from/about/by Franco-Americans (people of French Canadian ancestry). We are not interested in material about the Continental French. Soleil Press also distributes books on or about or by Franco-Americans and welcomes inquiry by authors and presses about our carrying their Franco-content book in our catalog." avg. press run 1M-2M. Pub'd 1 title 1990; expects 1 title 1991, 1 title 1992. 3 titles listed in the *Small Press Record of Books in Print* (20th Edition, 1991-92). Discounts: 50% to jobbers, 40% cash to bookstores, 30% speculation to bookstores. 5½×8; of. Reporting time: 1-3 months. Payment: varies. Copyrights for author. Maine Writers & Publishers Alliance (MWPA).

SOLO FLYER, Spare Change Poetry Press, David B. McCoy, 2115 Clearview NW, Massillon, OH 44646. 1979. Poetry, long-poems. "*Solo Flyer* is a non-subscription publication. Three 4-page flyers will be published a year, each by an individual author. All styles of poetry using capitalization and punctuation will be considered, but *send only from May Day through Labor Day*." circ. 100. 3/yr. Pub'd 3 issues 1990; expects 3 issues 1991, 3 issues 1992. sample price: free with SASE. 4pp; 5¼×8½; †photocopy. Reporting time: 1-3 months. Payment: 20-25 copies. Copyrighted, reverts to author.

SOM Publishing, division of School of Metaphysics (see also THRESHOLDS JOURNAL), Dr. Barbara O'Guinn, CEO & Editor-in-Chief, HCR 1, Box 15, Windyville, MO 65783, 417-345-8411. 1973. avg. press run 3.5M. Pub'd 1 title 1990; expects 4 titles 1991, 4 titles 1992. 11 titles listed in the *Small Press Record of Books in Print* (20th Edition, 1991-92). avg. price, paper: $7.95. Discounts: 40% trade, 50% jobbers, 20% organizations, churches, groups without sales tax number. 180pp; 5½×8½, 4½×7.

Somesuch Press, Stanley Marcus, 4800 Tower II, First Rep Bank Center, Dallas, TX 75201, 214-922-0022. 1974. Fiction, articles, art, non-fiction. avg. press run 300. Pub'd 3 titles 1990; expects 2 titles 1991, 1 title 1992. 16 titles listed in the *Small Press Record of Books in Print* (20th Edition, 1991-92). avg. price, cloth: $40. Discounts: 40%, 10 or more copies, 33⅓%, 1-10 copies. 40pp; 2⅞×3; lp. Reporting time: 1 month. Payment: by negotiation. Copyrights for author.

SOMNIAL TIMES, Gloria Reiser, Judy Landaiche, Box 561, Quincy, IL 62306-0561, 217-222-4141. 1989.

Poetry, articles, interviews, reviews, letters, news items, non-fiction. "Anything relating to dreams and dreaming" circ. 75. 6/yr. Pub'd 6 issues 1990; expects 6 issues 1991, 6 issues 1992. sub. price: $8; per copy: $1.50; sample: $1.50. Back issues: $1.50. Discounts: 75¢ each for resale, $1 each for classroom or group use. 10pp; 8½×11; †photocopy. Reporting time: 4-8 weeks. Payment: none, advertising if desired. Not copyrighted. Pub's reviews: 3-4 in 1990. §Anything related to dreams and dreaming, reveries, daydreams, fantasy, etc. Ads: $20/$10/line ads 35¢ per word.

SONOMA MANDALA, Elizabeth Herron, Faculty Advisor, Department of English, Sonoma State University, Rohnert Park, CA 94928, 707-664-2140. 1973. Poetry, fiction, art, photos, satire. "Among recent contributors: Martha Elizabeth, Andrei Voznesensky, Jonah Raskin, Gerald Haslam, Claribel Alegria, P. Burningham, Simon Perchik, Ivan Arguelles. Student work is always supplemented by writing from off-campus. Reads off-campus material from 9/15-12/15 each year. We will consider up to 10 pages of fiction or 5 poems per contributor. Please identify simultaneous submissions. We must staple work and so encourage contributors to submit good-quality photocopies." circ. 500. 1/yr. Pub'd 1 issue 1990; expects 1 issue 1991, 1 issue 1992. sub. price: $5; per copy: $5; sample: $5. Back issues: $3. 110pp; 5×8½; †of. Reporting time: 3 month average during reading period. Payment: 2 copies. Copyrighted, reverts to author. CLMP.

SONORA REVIEW, Joan Marcus, Editor; Bruce Upbin, Managing Editor; Andrea Wesblin, Poetry Editor; Jennifer Rocco, Poetry Editor; Dianne Savers, Fiction Editor; Stacey Elmeer, Fiction Editor; Karen Falkenstrom, Nonfiction Editor, Dept. of English, University of Arizona, Tucson, AZ 85721, 602-621-8077; 621-1836. 1980. Poetry, fiction, articles, interviews, satire, criticism, reviews, letters, parts-of-novels, non-fiction. "We publish poetry, fiction, and literary non-fiction, as well as interviews and occasional special features. Fiction and poetry prizes ($150/$50) in fall and spring issues, respectively. Submissions should be accompanied by SASE. Any questions or forms should be addressed to Andy Robinson, Managing Editor." circ. 650. 2/yr. Pub'd 2 issues 1990; expects 2 issues 1991, 2 issues 1992. sub. price: $8; per copy: $5; sample: $4. Back issues: $3 (through #10). Discounts: 40% to bookstores. 120pp; 6×9; of. Reporting time: 3 months. Payment: 2 contributor's copies. Copyrighted, reverts to author. §Fiction, poetry, general interest books. CLMP.

SORE DOVE, Sore Dove Publishers, Soheyl Dahi, Editor, PO Box 6332, San Mateo, CA 94403. 1986. Poetry. "Women and minorities are most welcome" circ. 250. 3/yr. Pub'd 3 issues 1990; expects 3 issues 1991, 3 issues 1992. sub. price: $4.50; per copy: $3; sample: $3. 25pp; 11×16. Reporting time: 2 weeks. Payment: one copy. Copyrighted. Pub's reviews: 2 in 1990. Ads: $20/$12.

Sore Dove Publishers (see also SORE DOVE), Soheyl Dahi, Editor, PO Box 6332, San Mateo, CA 94403. 1986. Poetry. "Women and minorities are most welcome" avg. press run 250. Pub'd 3 titles 1990. 2 titles listed in the *Small Press Record of Books in Print* (20th Edition, 1991-92). avg. price, cloth: $3. 25pp; 11×16. Reporting time: 2 weeks. Payment: contributor's copy for the magazine. Copyrights for author.

Sororal Publishing, J. B. Reid, Box 2041, Winnipeg, MB, R3C 3R3, Canada, 204-774-9966. 1989. Fiction, articles. "Short stories: 1,000-5,000 words. Collection of essays: 2,000-8,000 words. Books: 40,000-60,000 words. Chapbooks: 1,000-10,000 words. Favor history and women's studies." avg. press run 1M. Pub'd 3 titles 1990; expects 6 titles 1991, 6 titles 1992. avg. price, paper: $12.95. Discounts: 40% bookstores, 20% bulk (organizational). 200pp; 6×9; of. Reporting time: 3 months. Payment: 10% of first 5,000; 12.5% 5,000+; token advance. Copyrights for author. AMBP-Association of Manitoba Book Publishers.

SOULLESS STRUCTURES, Michael McLellan, 550 Pinewood Drive, Pendleton, SC 29670, 803-646-9048. 1990. Poetry, fiction, articles, art, photos, interviews, criticism, reviews, music, letters, news items. "Left-wing slant on most articles, a strong punk/youth cultural attitude" circ. 70. Irregular. Pub'd 3 issues 1990; expects 3-4 issues 1991, 3-4 issues 1992. sub. price: not available; per copy: $1.50; sample: $1.50. Back issues: $1.50. Discounts: 75¢-$1 for bulk, depending on quantity. 40pp; 5½×8½; †xerox. Payment: none. Not copyrighted. Pub's reviews: 50 in 1990. §Anything at all. Ads: none.

SOUND CHOICE, David Ciaffardini, PO Box 1251, Ojai, CA 93023, 805-646-6814. 1984. Poetry, fiction, articles, art, photos, cartoons, interviews, satire, criticism, reviews, music, letters, parts-of-novels, long-poems, collages, plays, concrete art, news items, non-fiction. "Up to 12 pages, typed, double spaced. Contributors should subscribe and be familiar with the publictaion. Recent contributions include: Utilizing public access television, and interview with documentary film maker Les Blank, the music of Burundi, the Belgium music underground. We like 'gonzo' journalism although we find that few writers have the skill, tenacity and insight to do it right" circ. 6M. 6/yr. Pub'd 3 issues 1990; expects 4 issues 1991, 4 issues 1992. sub. price: $10/4 issues US, $15/4 issues foreign; per copy: $3; sample: $3. Back issues: varies. Discounts: variable. 96pp; 8¼×10¾; web press. Reporting time: 120 days. Payment: none. Copyrights sometimes. Pub's reviews: 50+ per issue in 1990. §Music, audio research and experimentation, radio, publishing, underground or non mainstream periodicals of all kinds. Ads: $300/$150/$75 1/4 page/$30 1/8 page/classifieds $15 per 40 words. Audio Evolution Network (A.E.N.), PO Box 1251, Ojai, CA 93023.

Sound View Press, Peter Hastings Falk, 170 Boston Post Road, Madison, CT 06443, 203-245-2246. 1985.

538

"Publisher of the 25,000-entry biographical dictionary, *Who Was Who In American Art*, and monographs on American artists in conjunction with museum or gallery exhibitions." avg. press run 2M. Pub'd 2 titles 1990; expects 6 titles 1991, 5 titles 1992. avg. price, cloth: $39-$149. Discounts: on orders of 3 or more copies 20%-40%. 250-1,200pp; 8½×11; we subcontract printing, binding, fulfillment, etc. Reporting time: 2 weeks. Payment: negotiable. Copyrights for author. COSMEP, PMA.

Soundboard Books, 1016 E. El Camino Real, Suite 124, Sunnyvale, CA 94087, 408-738-1705. 1990. Non-fiction. avg. press run 2M. Pub'd 1 title 1990; expects 2 titles 1991, 2 titles 1992. 2 titles listed in the *Small Press Record of Books in Print* (20th Edition, 1991-92). avg. price, paper: $6.95. Discounts: 2-15 20%, 16+ 40%. 48pp; 6×9; of. Copyrights for author. COSMEP.

SOUNDINGS EAST, Rod Kessler, Advisory Editor, English Dept., Salem State College, Salem, MA 01970, 508-741-6000. 1973. Poetry, fiction, art, photos, interviews. "Our primary interest is poetry and short fiction. We print several stories in each issue. Since 1980 we have presented a 'Feature Poet' section, usually a New England poet who has not yet published a book. These have included: Christopher Jane Corkery, Michelle Gillet, Don Johnson, Susan Donnelly, Jackie Crews, Guri Andermann, Carole Borges, Debra Allbery, Robert Cooperman, and Martha Ramsey" circ. 2M. 2/yr. Pub'd 2 issues 1990; expects 2 issues 1991, 2 issues 1992. sub. price: $6; per copy: $3; sample: $3. Back issues: usually $3 per copy. Discounts: we charge $16 for three years. (50¢ per issue deducted for subscription service, etc.). 64pp; 5½×8½; of. Reporting time: 1-6 months, we do *not* read during the summer. Payment: 2 free copies, more if wanted. Copyrighted, reverts to author.

SOUNDMAKERS, Lynn Donnell, PO Box 17999, Nashville, TN 37217, 615-834-0027. 1985. "Do not use unsolicited material. *SoundMakers* is an educational publication for aspiring songwriters, lyric writers, singers and poets who write poetry with commercial song potential. Articles by music industry experts advise readers on how to improve their craft and market their material to the music industry. *SoundMakers* is a free service of the Music City Song Festival music competition." circ. 200M. 1/yr. Pub'd 1 issue 1990; expects 1 issue 1991, 1 issue 1992. sub. price: free; per copy: free; sample: free. Back issues: free. 56+pp; 8⅜×10⅞. Copyrighted, does not revert to author.

THE SOUNDS OF POETRY, Jacquiline Sanchez, Publisher; Jousseline Sanchez, Editor, 8761 Avis, Detroit, MI 48209, 843-8478. 1983. Poetry, articles, art, reviews. "We would like to see more work by Hispanics. Recent contributors: The Sanchez sisters (Maria, Jousseline, Ericka, Jessica), Trino Sanchez, S.J., Jose Sanchez, Robert Tubridy, Ken Stone, Jacqueline Sanchez. Plays are printed in segments (one act plays only)" circ. 200. 4/yr. Pub'd 4 issues 1990; expects 4 issues 1991, 4 issues 1992. sub. price: $5; per copy: $1.50; sample: $1.50. Back issues: not available. Discounts: libraries 20%. 8-16pp; 8½×11; AB Dick 360. Reporting time: 2 weeks to 1 year. Payment: 1 copy in which work appears. Copyrighted, reverts to author. Pub's reviews: 2 in 1990. §Poetry, nothing obscene or political. Ads: $50/$25/$15 1/4 page/$10 1/8. Latino Poets Association.

SOURCE: NOTES IN THE HISTORY OF ART, Laurie Schneider, 1 East 87th Street, Suite 8A, New York, NY 10128, 212-369-1881. 1981. Art, letters. "*Source* publishes short articles, notes and reviews on art and archaeology from antiquity to the present. None exceed 2M words including footnotes, with accompanying illustrations limited to three. Some recent contributors include Michael Evans, Helmut Nickel, Helen S. Ettlinger, Reinhold Hohl, Oscar White Muscarella, Robert Rosenblum and Caroline Houser." circ. 1M. 4/yr. Pub'd 4 issues 1990; expects 4 issues 1991, 4 issues 1992. sub. price: $20; per copy: $5; sample: free. Back issues: same. Discounts: 10% to subscription agencies. 32pp; 7×9; of, compugraphic phototypesetting. Reporting time: 3 months. Payment: 20 free copies. Not copyrighted.

SOURCE OF WISDOM, Buddhist Text Translation Society, City of 10,000 Buddhas, Talmage, CA 95481-0217, 707-462-0939. circ. 20M. sub. price: free; per copy: free; sample: free. Back issues: free, if available. 4pp; tabloid newspaper; of. Payment: none. §Buddhism. No ads. 81.

SourceNet (see also WHOLE AGAIN RESOURCE GUIDE), Tim Ryan, PO Box 6767, Santa Barbara, CA 93160, 805-494-7123. 1980. "Directory of alternative and new age periodicals; books of fonts for the Macintosh" Expects 1 title 1991, 1 title 1992. avg. price, paper: $24.95 + $2 postage and handling. Discounts: 40% on 5+ copies. 300pp; 8½×11; of.

SOUTH AMERICAN EXPLORER, Don Montague, PO Box 18327, Denver, CO 80218-1425, 303-320-0388. 1977. Articles, photos, interviews, reviews, letters, news items, non-fiction. circ. 7M. 4/yr. Pub'd 4 issues 1990; expects 4 issues 1991, 4 issues 1992. sub. price: $15 4 issues; subs included in $25 Club membership; per copy: $4; sample: $2. Back issues: $4. Discounts: $1 per issue. 56pp; 8½×11; web of. Reporting time: 8 weeks. Payment: negotiable. Copyrighted, reverts to author. Pub's reviews: 16 in 1990. §Latin America, natural history, field sciences, adventure, folk art, outdoor sports, travel, South American history. Ads: $750/$375/25¢.

SOUTH CAROLINA REVIEW, Mark Royden Winchell, Managing Editor; Richard Calhoun, Executive Editor; Frank Day, Associate Editor; Carol Johnston, Associate Editor, English Dept, Clemson Univ, Clemson, SC 29634-1503, 803-656-3229. 1968. Poetry, fiction, articles, interviews, satire, criticism, reviews. "Joyce

Carol Oates, Mark Steadman, Leslie Fiedler, Cleanth Brooks." circ. 600. 2/yr. Pub'd 2 issues 1990. sub. price: $7; per copy: $5; sample: $5. Back issues: $5. 184pp; 9×6; †desktop, Ventura. Reporting time: 6-9 months. Payment: copies. Copyrighted. Pub's reviews: 30 in 1990. §Poetry, literary history, criticism. Ads: $125/$75. CLMP, CELJ.

SOUTH COAST POETRY JOURNAL, John J. Brugaletta, California State University, English Department, Fullerton, CA 92634. 1985. Poetry. "Prefer poems under 40 lines. At least 3 editors read every poem received." circ. 500. 2/yr. Pub'd 2 issues 1990; expects 2 issues 1991, 2 issues 1992. sub. price: $9; per copy: $5; sample: $3.50. Back issues: $5. Discounts: 40%. 60pp; 5½×8; of. Reporting time: 6-8 weeks. Payment: 1 copy. Copyrighted, reverts to author. Ads: $50/$25. COSMEP, CLMP.

SOUTH DAKOTA REVIEW, John R. Milton, Box 111, University Exchange, Vermillion, SD 57069, 605-677-5229/5966. 1963. Poetry, fiction, articles, art, interviews, criticism, parts-of-novels. "Issues vary in content; not every type of material will be in each issue. Occasional annotated listing of selected 'Books Received'." circ. 500. 4/yr. Pub'd 4 issues 1990; expects 4 issues 1991, 4 issues 1992. sub. price: $15; per copy: $5. Back issues: most are available, send for price list. Discounts: 40% to bookstores. 140+pp; 6×9; of. Reporting time: varies, average 2 weeks except during summer and occasional unforeseen busy periods; initial favorable reaction can lead to longer reporting time. Payment: 1-4 copies. We reserve our own reprint rights. No ads. CLMP.

South End Press, Karin A. San Juan, Todd Jailer, Cynthia Peters, Loie Hayes, Tanya McKinnon, Steve Chase, 116 St. Botolph Street, Boston, MA 02115, 617-266-0629. 1977. Poetry, fiction, articles, art, criticism, non-fiction. "At South End Press—a collectively managed, non-profit publisher of non-fiction—our goal is to provide books that encourage critical thinking and constructive action, thereby helping to create fundamental social change. Since 1977, we have released over 160 titles addressing the key issues of the day, focusing on political, econimic, cultural, gender, race, and ecological dimensions of life in the United States and the world." avg. press run 5M. Pub'd 15 titles 1990; expects 15 titles 1991, 15 titles 1992. 21 titles listed in the *Small Press Record of Books in Print* (20th Edition, 1991-92). avg. price, cloth: $25; paper: $10. Discounts: bookstores 20-50%. 250pp; 5½×8½; in-house typesetting, layout. Reporting time: 6-8 weeks. Payment: 10% of discount price. Copyrights for author.

THE SOUTH FLORIDA POETRY REVIEW, S.A. Stirnemann, Editor; Virginia Wells, Associate Editor; Shirley Blum, Business Editor; Carole Borges-Rosen, Associate Editor, 7190 N.W. 21 Street, Room 103, Ft. Lauderdale, FL 33313, 305-742-5624. 1983. Poetry, interviews, criticism, reviews. "No limitations on length or subject matter. Previously unpublished poetry of the highest literary quality. Recent contributors: Marvin Bell, Mark Jarman, Philip Levine, Lisel Mueller, William Stafford, Gerald Stern, Diane Wakowski." circ. 500-600. 3/yr. Pub'd 3 issues 1990; expects 3 issues 1991, 3 issues 1992. sub. price: $7.50 individual, $9 institutions; per copy: $3.50; sample: $3.50. Back issues: $3.50. 68-72pp; 6×9; of. Reporting time: 6-12 weeks. Payment: 2 copies. Copyrighted, reverts to author. Pub's reviews: 15 in 1990. §Poetry books published within the previous year. Ads: $100/$65. CLMP.

South Head Press (see also POETRY AUSTRALIA), John Millett, Editor, Market Place, Berrima, N.S.W. 2577, Australia. 1964. Poetry. avg. press run 6M. Pub'd 1 title 1990; expects 3 titles 1991, 3 titles 1992. 10 titles listed in the *Small Press Record of Books in Print* (20th Edition, 1991-92). avg. price, cloth: $15; paper: $9. Usual trade discount. 84pp; 6×14cm. Reporting time: 3-6 months. Payment: negotiated. Copyrights for author.

Southeastern FRONT, Robin Merritt, Curator, 565 17th Street, NW, Cleveland, TN 37311. 1985. Poetry, fiction, articles, art, photos, cartoons, interviews, criticism, reviews, music, letters, parts-of-novels, long-poems, collages, plays, concrete art, non-fiction. "*Southeastern FRONT* organization publishes *Southeastern FRONT* (or *FRONT*) magazine. It is a presentation of art, fiction, poetry, cultural events + cultural history. We are an artists/writers representation service. We aim to help new, young and/or isolated artists + writers get their works into public view. *A Magazine Gallery. Southeastern FRONT* also prints short edition books for individuals and companies." circ. approx. 1.5M. Irregular. Pub'd 1 issue 1990; expects 2 issues 1991. 1 title listed in the *Small Press Record of Books in Print* (20th Edition, 1991-92). sub. price: send SASE; per copy: send SASE; sample: send SASE. Back issues: send SASE. Discounts: send SASE. 50-80pp; 8½×11; †of. Reporting time: 2-6 weeks. Payment: exposure to select galleries, publishers. Copyrighted, reverts to author. Pub's reviews. §Brief ones; arts, philosophy, fiction. Ads: $160/$85/$45 1/4 page/$25 1/8 page/classifieds $5.

THE SOUTHERN CALIFORNIA ANTHOLOGY, Master of Professional Writing Program, WPH 404/Univ. of Southern Calif., Los Angeles, CA 90089-4034, 213-740-3252. 1983. Poetry, fiction, interviews. "Recent contributors include John Updike, James Merrill, Robert Bly, Joyce Carol Oates, James Ragan, Richard Yates, Doris Grumbach, Amiri Baraka, Peter Viereck, Andrei Voznesensky, Yevgeny Yevtushenko, Donald Hall, Denise Levertov, X.J. Kennedy." circ. 1.5M. 1/yr. Pub'd 1 issue 1990; expects 1 issue 1991, 1 issue 1992. sub. price: $7.95; per copy: $7.95; sample: $5.95. Back issues: $5.95. 140pp; 5½×8½; †lp.

540

Reporting time: 3-4 months. Payment: in copies. Copyrighted, reverts to author. COSMEP.

SOUTHERN EXPOSURE, Institute for Southern Studies, Eric Bates, Managing Editor, PO Box 531, Durham, NC 27702, 919-688-8167. 1973. Fiction, articles, art, photos, interviews, reviews, parts-of-novels, long-poems, collages, plays. "All material must be related to social change, cultural features, oral history, economic and political aspects of the South. A query letter can be helpful, but is not necessary. Very little fiction or poetry published. We publish four regular issues each year" circ. 10M. 4/yr. Pub'd 4 issues 1990; expects 4 issues 1991, 4 issues 1992. sub. price: $16 ($20 libraries); per copy: $5; sample: $4. Back issues: $2.50-$4.50. Discounts: 40% 5 or more. 64pp; 8½×11; of. Reporting time: 8 weeks. Payment: $75-$200. Copyrighted, does not revert to author. Pub's reviews: 32 in 1990. §Southern, related to the South. Ads: $600/$300. COSMEP.

SOUTHERN HUMANITIES REVIEW, Thomas L. Wright, Co-Editor; Dan R. Latimer, Co-Editor, 9088 Haley Center, Auburn Univ., Auburn, AL 36849, 205-844-9088. 1967. Poetry, fiction, articles, interviews, satire, criticism, reviews, parts-of-novels, non-fiction. "Peter Green, Christopher Norris, Lars Gustafsson, Donald Hall, Ann Deagon." circ. 750. 4/yr. Pub'd 4 issues 1990; expects 4 issues 1991, 4 issues 1992. sub. price: $12 U.S., $16 foreign; per copy: $4 U.S.; $5 foreign; sample: $4 U.S.; $5 foreign. Back issues: same as single copy price/or complete volumes, same as current 1-year subscription. Discounts: none. 100pp; 6×9; lp. Reporting time: 1-3 months. Payment: $100 best essay, $100 best story, $50 best poem *published* each volume. Copyrighted, does not revert to author. Pub's reviews: 57 in 1990. §Criticism, fiction, poetry. Ads: $100/$50. CELJ, CLMP.

SOUTHERN LIBERTARIAN MESSENGER, John T. Harllee, Rt. 10 Box 52 A, Florence, SC 29501. 1972. Articles, art, cartoons, interviews, satire, reviews, letters, news items, non-fiction. circ. 650. 12/yr. Pub'd 12 issues 1990; expects 12 issues 1991. sub. price: $6; per copy: 50¢; sample: free. Back issues: 50¢ if available. Discounts: 50% to dealers on orders of 10 copies or more; library subscriptions $3/year. 8pp; 8½×11; of. Reporting time: variable. Payment: complimentary subscriptions. Not copyrighted. Pub's reviews: 2 in 1990. §Libertarian, politics, economics, humor. Ads: $40/$20/25¢.

SOUTHERN POETRY REVIEW, Lucinda Grey, Co-Editor; Ken McLaurin, Co-Editor, Department of English, UNC Charlotte, Charlotte, NC 28223, 704-547-4309; 704-547-2633. 1958. Poetry. "*SPR* is not a regional mag, though we function naturally as an outlet for new Southern talent. We emphasize variety and intensity. No restrictions on style, content or length. (We do not consider poems during the summer months.)" circ. 1-1.2M. 2/yr. Pub'd 2 issues 1990; expects 2 issues 1991, 2 issues 1992. sub. price: $6; per copy: $3.50; sample: $2. Back issues: $2. Discounts: 30%. 80pp; 6×9; of. Reporting time: 4-6 weeks. Payment: contributor copy. Copyrighted, reverts to author. Pub's reviews: 6 in 1990. §Eclectic. No ads. CLMP, COSMEP.

SOUTHERN QUARTERLY: A Journal of the Arts in the South, Peggy W. Prenshaw, Editor; Noel Polk, Advisory Editor; Thomas J. Richardson, Advisory Editor; Stephen Flinn Young, Managing Editor; Lola Norris, Editorial Assistant, Box 5078, Southern Station, USM, Hattiesburg, MS 39406-5078, 601-266-4370. 1962. Articles, photos, interviews, criticism, reviews, music, letters. "The editor invites essays, articles and book reviews on both contemporary and earlier literature, music, art, architecture, popular and folk arts, theatre and dance in the South. Particularly sought are survey papers on the arts and arts criticism — achievements, trends, movements, colonies. Special issues are available on southern women playwrights, contemporary southern theatre, and on southern art and artists. Forthcoming are special issues on Erskine Caldwell, in the art South, Caroline Gordon. Inquiries and manuscripts should be addressed to *The Southern Quarterly* at the above address." circ. 700. 4/yr. Pub'd 4 issues 1990; expects 4 issues 1991, 4 issues 1992. sub. price: $9, $16/2 years; $20/year institutions; per copy: $5 (special issue prices may vary); sample: $5. Back issues: vary. Discounts: subscription agency $7.65/individual subscriptions; $17 institutional subscriptions. Discount applies *only* to domestic subscriptions—full rate outside US. 156pp; 6×9; of. Reporting time: 3-5 months. Payment: 2 copies of journal and 1 yr. subscription. Copyrighted, reverts to author. Pub's reviews: 34 books, 25 films in 1990. §Studies of the arts in the South: literature, music, art, architecture, popular and folk arts, theatre and dance. Ads: 100/$75. CELJ.

SOUTHERN READER, The Guild Bindery Press, Inc., R.J. Bedwell, PO Box 1827, Oxford, MS 38655, 601-234-2596. 1986. Fiction, articles, interviews, criticism, reviews. circ. 3M. 4/yr. Pub'd 2 issues 1990; expects 4 issues 1991, 4 issues 1992. sub. price: $12.95; per copy: $3.95; sample: $3.95. Discounts: trade 40%. 76pp; 8½×11; of. Copyrighted, reverts to author. Pub's reviews: 40 in 1990. §Southern literature, American and Southern history. Publishers Association of the South.

Southern Resources Unlimited, Ilene J. Cornwell, 5632 Meadowcrest Lane, Nashville, TN 37209-4631, 615-356-3211. 1981. Art, photos, non-fiction. "We are not soliciting mss at this time" avg. press run 5M-6.5M. Pub'd 2 titles 1990; expects 1 title 1991. avg. price, paper: $7.95. Discounts: 20% retail. 150pp; 8½×11; of. Payment: negotiable. Copyrights for author.

THE SOUTHERN REVIEW, James Olney, Dave Smith, 43 Allen Hall, Louisiana State University, Baton

Rouge, LA 70803, 504-388-5108. 1965 new series (1935 original series). Poetry, fiction, articles, interviews, criticism, reviews, letters, parts-of-novels. "We emphasize craftsmanship and intellectual content. We favor articles on contemporary literature and on the history and culture of the South. Recent contributors: Lewis P. Simpson, W.D. Snodgrass, Hayden Carruth, Reynolds Price, Lee Smith, Mary Oliver, Miriam Kuznets, Lewis Nordan, Emily Grosholz." circ. 3.1M. 4/yr. Pub'd 4 issues 1990; expects 4 issues 1991, 4 issues 1992. sub. price: $15 ind., $30 inst.; per copy: $5 ind., $10 inst.; sample: $5 ind., $10 inst. Back issues: $5 ind., $10 inst. 250pp; 6¾x10; lp. Reporting time: 2 months. Payment: poetry $20/page, prose $12/page. Copyrighted, reverts to author. Pub's reviews: 12 in 1990. §Contemporary literature, fiction, poetry, culture of the South. Ads: $150/$90. CLMP.

Southport Press, Travis DuPriest, Mabel DuPriest, Dept. of English, Carthage College, Kenosha, WI 53141, 414-551-8500 (252). 1977. Poetry, fiction, art, non-fiction. "We do hand printing of old and contemporary fiction and poetry. First imprint: portfolio of Wilma Tague's poetry. Currently accepting no unsolicited mss. New titles: *The Birth Narratives of Luke*, Trans. by David Rhoads, Carol Smith, John Spangler, woodcut by Tina Rasmussen. *A Child's Alphabet* (Broadside). In Press: *Gravestone Verses of Virginia*." avg. press run 100. Expects 2-3 titles 1991, 3 titles 1992. 6 titles listed in the *Small Press Record of Books in Print* (20th Edition, 1991-92). avg. price, cloth: $7.50; other: $1 broadsides (unbound). 10-25pp; 7x10; †lp. Reporting time: 2 weeks. Copyrights for author.

Southwest Research and Information Center (see also THE WORKBOOK), Kathy Newton, PO Box 4524, Albuquerque, NM 87106, 505-262-1862. 1974. Articles, reviews, news items. "Resource information for citizen action of all kinds." avg. press run 3M. Pub'd 4 titles 1990; expects 4 titles 1991, 4 titles 1992. 7 titles listed in the *Small Press Record of Books in Print* (20th Edition, 1991-92). avg. price, paper: $3.50. Discounts: 40% to distributors. 48pp; 8½x11; of. Reporting time: 1 month. Payment: none. Does not copyright for author. None.

SOUTHWEST REVIEW, Willard Spiegelman, Editor; Elizabeth Mills, Associate Editor and Director of Development, Southern Methodist University, 6410 Airline Road, Dallas, TX 75275, 214-373-7440. 1915. Poetry, fiction, articles, interviews, criticism, parts-of-novels, long-poems, non-fiction. "Poetry, fiction, essays, interviews. A quarterly that serves the interests of its region but is not bound by them. The *Southwest Review* has always striven to present the work of writers and scholars from the surrounding states and to offer analyses of problems and themes that are distinctly southwestern, and at the same time publish the works of good writers regardless of their locales." circ. 1.6M. 4/yr. Pub'd 4 issues 1990; expects 4 issues 1991, 4 issues 1992. sub. price: $20; per copy: $5; sample: $5. Back issues: available on request. Discounts: 15% to agencies. 144pp; 6x9; of. Reporting time: 3 months. Payment: yes. Copyrighted, reverts to author. Ads: $250 (1X), $700 (4X)/$150 (1X), $469 (4X). CLMP, CELJ, SSP.

SOUTHWESTERN DISCOVERIES, Todd G. Dickson, Managing Editor, 15 Calle Bienvenida, Tijeras, NM 87059, 505-247-8736. 1986. Poetry, fiction, articles, interviews, reviews, news items. circ. 500. 3/yr. Pub'd 3 issues 1990; expects 4 issues 1991, 4 issues 1992. 21 titles listed in the *Small Press Record of Books in Print* (20th Edition, 1991-92). sub. price: $8.10; per copy: $2.95; sample: $2.95 in US postage. Back issues: $2.50. Discounts: none. 52pp; 7x6; of. Reporting time: 4 months. Payment: 5 copies of magazine. Copyrighted, reverts to author. Pub's reviews: 25 in 1990. §Southwestern contemporary writing of all kinds. Ads: $125/$75.

SOU'WESTER, Fred W. Robbins, Editor, English Dept., Southern Illinois University, Edwardsville, IL 62026-1438. 1960. Poetry, fiction, satire, long-poems, plays. "We have no particular editorial biases or taboos. We publish the best poetry and fiction we can find." circ. 300. 3/yr. Pub'd 3 issues 1990; expects 3 issues 1991, 3 issues 1992. sub. price: $10, $18 2 years; per copy: $5; sample: $5. Back issues: price varies. 88pp; 6x9; of. Reporting time: 4-6 weeks. Payment: copies (also cash prizes). Copyrighted, reverts to author. No ads.

Sovereign Press, Kirk Dammon, Editor, 326 Harris Rd, Rochester, WA 98579. 1968. Fiction, articles, art, photos, plays. "We limit our publications to works oriented on individual sovereignty as a culture; within that field we are looking for fiction, non-fiction, and art works of lasting merit. Recent contributors: John Harland, Melvin Gorham, Jill Von Konen, Marguerite Pedersen." avg. press run 5M. Pub'd 4 titles 1990; expects 5 titles 1991, 6 titles 1992. 16 titles listed in the *Small Press Record of Books in Print* (20th Edition, 1991-92). avg. price, cloth: $9; paper: $5. Discounts: libraries and booksellers—single or assorted titles, 1-9 20%, 10-29 40%, 30-99 50%, 100+ 55%. 120pp; 5½x8½; of. Reporting time: 1 month. Payment: individually arranged. Copyrights for author.

SOVIET SPACEFLIGHT REPORT, Starwise Publications, Peter J. Kappesser, PO Box 25, Pulaski, NY 13142. 1987. Articles, art, photos, interviews, news items, non-fiction. "ISSN 0889-020X. Bimonthly newsletter reporting spaceflight activities of the U.S.S.R. Please query first; Enclose S.A.S.E. for guidelines" 6/yr. Pub'd 6 issues 1990; expects 6 issues 1991, 6 issues 1992. sub. price: individual rate—$15 for 6 issues (North America), $25 (overseas), institutional rate—add $10 to individual rate; per copy: $2.50; sample: $1. 12pp; 8½x11; †xerographic duplicator, of/lo for photos pages. Reporting time: 4 weeks. Payment: negotiable.

542

Copyrighted, does not revert to author. Pub's reviews: 1 in 1990. §U.S.S.R., astronomy, space, science. No ads.

THE SOW'S EAR POETRY JOURNAL, Errol Hess, Word Editor; Larry Richman, Word Editor; Mary Calhoun, Graphics Editor, 245 McDowell Street, Bristol, TN 37620, 615-764-1625. 1988. Poetry, art, photos, cartoons, interviews, criticism, reviews. "Accept poetry, reviews of poetry (books, magazines, etc.), interviews of poets. Recent contributors include: Lee Smith (interviewing a poet), David Huddle, Marge Piercy, Josephine Jacobsen, Jim Wayne Miller, John Grey, Eve Shelnutt, Fred Chappell. Open to any style or length of poetry. Pretty tough competition; we publish about 3% of work submitted. Offer free ads to poetry magazines which do not charge reading fees. Inquire for format." circ. 750. 4/yr. Pub'd 4 issues 1990; expects 4 issues 1991, 4 issues 1992. sub. price: $10; per copy: $3.50; sample: $3.50. Back issues: $3.50 when available. Discounts: standard. 32pp; 8½x11; of. Reporting time: 3-4 months. Payment: 1 copy. Copyrighted, reverts to author. Pub's reviews: 4 in 1990. §Any poetry. Ads: free to poetry mags which don't charge fees to read. CLMP.

SPACE AND TIME, Space and Time Press, Gordon Linzner, Editor; Jani Anderson, Assistant Editor, 138 West 70th Street 4-B, New York, NY 10023-4432. 1966. Poetry, fiction, art, cartoons. "*Space and Time* is a fantasy and science fiction magazine, we have a very broad definition of fantasy (which includes SF) and we aren't fussy about sub-genre barriers, but we want nothing that obviously falls outside of fantasy (i.e. straight mystery, mainstream, etc.). Prefer under 10M words. Overstocked on poetry (except narrative poems) through 1991. Not currently looking at new submissions of any kind." circ. 450. 2/yr. Pub'd 2 issues 1990; expects 2 issues 1991, 2 issues 1992. sub. price: $9.50; per copy: $5; sample: $5. Back issues: complete set available back issues $40. Discounts: 40% off on orders of 5 or more copies of an issue. 120pp; 5½x8½; of. Reporting time: 6-8 weeks maximum. Payment: 1/2¢ per word on acceptance. Copyrighted, reverts to author. Ads: $50/$30/$17.50 1/4 page/5¢ word. SPWAO.

Space and Time Press (see also SPACE AND TIME), Gordon Linzner, Co-Publisher; Jani Anderson, Co-Publisher & Book Editor, 138 West 70th Street 4-B, New York, NY 10023-4432. 1984. Fiction. "Fantasy and science fiction novels—preferably ones that don't fit neatly into a sub-genre. Interested in seeing borderline fantasy-mysteries, along lines of George Chesbro's *Mongo* series." avg. press run 1M. Pub'd 1 title 1990; expects 2 titles 1991, 1 title 1992. 8 titles listed in the *Small Press Record of Books in Print* (20th Edition, 1991-92). avg. price, cloth: $15.95; paper: $6.95. Discounts: 1 25%, 2-4 35%, 5-24 40%. 160pp; 5½x8½; of. Reporting time: several months if we're interested—therefore suggest authors continue circulating ms. until they hear from us. Payment: 10% of cover price, based on print run, within 3 months of publication. Copyrights for author. Small Press Writers and Artists Organization.

Space City Publications, Carolyn Blacknall, PO Box 890263, Houston, TX 77289, 713-480-9102. 1989. Articles, non-fiction. "We specialize in business 'how-to' books, especially dealing with advertising, mail order sales, desktop publishing, and writing and self-publishing" avg. press run 3M. Expects 1 title 1991, 6 titles 1992. 1 title listed in the *Small Press Record of Books in Print* (20th Edition, 1991-92). avg. price, paper: $12.95. 192pp; 5½x8½. Reporting time: 4-6 weeks. Copyrights for author. COSMEP.

THE SPACE PRESS, Frank V. Vernuccio Jr., Editor-in-Chief, Vernuccio Publications, 645 West End Avenue, New York, NY 10025, 212-724-5919. 1981. Articles, art, photos, interviews, reviews, news items, non-fiction. "*The Space Press* provides complete coverage of all outer space related news, affairs, topics and issues. Our readership consists of individuals and agencies with an interest or expertise in aerospace matters. Subject material used is objective in tone, and original.Only serious topics are used. *The Space Press* is read throughout North America, Western Europe, Asia, and Australia." circ. 1M. 12/yr. Pub'd 12 issues 1990; expects 12 issues 1991, 12 issues 1992. sub. price: $50; per copy: $1.25; sample: $1.25. Back issues: $1.25 per issue. Discounts: 10% on purchases of 10-30; 15% 31-50; 20% 51-75; 30% 76-100. Higher quantity rates available on request. 20pp; 8½x11; of. Reporting time: 1 month. Payment: by negotiation. Copyrighted, reverts to author by negotiation. Pub's reviews: 2 in 1990. §High technology, aerospace affairs, outer space affairs, military affairs. Ads: $250/$150/$15 flat rate per ad up to 50 words.

Spare Change Poetry Press (see also SOLO FLYER), David B. McCoy, 2115 Clearviw NE, Massillon, OH 44646. 1979. Poetry, long-poems. "Presently, Spare Change Poetry is publishing *Solo Flyer*." avg. press run 100. Pub'd 3 titles 1990; expects 3 titles 1991, 3 titles 1992. 1 title listed in the *Small Press Record of Books in Print* (20th Edition, 1991-92). 4pp; 5¼x8½; †photocopy. Reporting time: 1-3 months. Payment: 20-30 copies. Copyrights for author.

SPARE RIB, Editorial Collective, 27 Clerkenwell Close, London EC1 0AT, England. 1972. Articles, news items. "We print articles by women only on a wide range of subjects. For features, brief proposals (rather than finished article) should be submitted to Marcel Farry. We welcome unsolicited short items of news or for our regular columns. Contributors are usually also readers (but not always)." circ. 25M. 12/yr. Pub'd 12 issues 1990; expects 12 issues 1991, 12 issues 1992. sub. price: £27; per copy: £1.50; sample: £2.20 incl. postage airmail. Back issues: £2.20 incl. postage airmail. Discounts: trade discount by negotiation with distributor, Central Books, 14 Leathermarket, London SE1, Britain. 60pp; size A4; of. Reporting time: 3 weeks minimum.

Payment: low! Joint copyright, does not revert to author. Pub's reviews: 6 per month in 1990. §Books by women, about women, feminist writing. Ads: £675 + VAT/£345 + VAT/70p per word.

Sparkling Diamond Paperbacks, Eric Tobin, 66 St. Joseph's Place, Off Blessington Street, Dublin 7, Ireland. 1972. Non-fiction. "Non-fiction, dramatic, personal experience. Sent post-free, world-wide." avg. press run 5M. Pub'd 1 title 1990; expects 1 title 1992. 1 title listed in the *Small Press Record of Books in Print* (20th Edition, 1991-92). avg. price, paper: £5.50. Discounts: 50%. 136pp; 5½×8. Reporting time: no particular length of time. Payment: the usual. Copyrights for author.

Sparrow Hawk Press, Charles C. Harra, PO Box 1274, Tahlequah, OK 74465, 918-456-3421. 1987. Art, photos, non-fiction. "Sparrow Hawk Press is also available to do book design and production on a contract basis for other publishers. Full editorial, graphic design, and production services are available" avg. press run 4M. Pub'd 2 titles 1990; expects 3 titles 1991, 3 titles 1992. 5 titles listed in the *Small Press Record of Books in Print* (20th Edition, 1991-92). avg. price, paper: $9.95. Discounts: industry standard. 250pp; size varies; of. Reporting time: 3 weeks. Payment: negotiated for each project. Copyrights for author. COSMEP PO Box 703, San Francisco, CA 94101, NAPRA PO Box 9, Eastsound, WA 98245.

SPARROW POVERTY PAMPHLETS, Sparrow Press imprint, Sparrow Press, Felix Stefanile, Selma Stefanile, 103 Waldron Street, West Lafayette, IN 47906. 1954. Poetry. "By invitation only." circ. 900. 2 or 3. Pub'd 3 issues 1990; expects 3 issues 1991, 3 issues 1992. sub. price: $7.50; per copy: $2.50; sample: $2 (back issues). Back issues: if not a collector's item, $2. Discounts: 10% for classes. Only 20% on single orders from jobbers, agents, etc. 40% for two or more. 28-32pp; 5½×8½; of. Reporting time: about 6 weeks. Payment: $30, plus 20% after cost, occasional reprinting. Copyrighted, reverts to author on request. §No biases. No ads. CCLM.

Sparrow Press (see also SPARROW POVERTY PAMPHLETS, Sparrow Press imprint; Vagrom Chap Books, Sparrow Press imprint), Felix Stefanile, Editor; Selma Stefanile, Editor, 103 Waldron Street, West Lafayette, IN 47906. 1954. Poetry. "Sparrow Press considers manuscripts by invitation only. For those who want an idea of the kind of poetry we have been publishing for the past 38 years, since 1954, sample copies of our issues may be ordered: $2 for pamphlet, $3 for chapbook. We have recently published Ger Killeen, winner of the But Stem award for 1989. Also: Gray Burr, Alice Monks Mears, Ralph J. Milld Jr., Alice Monks Mears." avg. press run 500-1.5M. Pub'd we are occasional publishers titles 1990. 6 titles listed in the *Small Press Record of Books in Print* (20th Edition, 1991-92). CCLM.

Spear Shaker Press (see also SPEAR SHAKER REVIEW), Stephanie Carvana, PO Box 308, Napanoch, NY 12458, 914-647-3608. 1987. Poetry, fiction, articles, satire, reviews, plays. "Must be relevant to Shakespeare authorship question and/or Edward De Vere, 17th Earl of Oxford. Will look at anything that applies. Must be of high literary or artistic quality." avg. press run 500. Pub'd 1 title 1990; expects 1 title 1992. avg. price, paper: $12. Discounts: 40% to jobbers. 100pp; of. Reporting time: 1 month. Payment: negotiable. Copyrights for author.

SPEAR SHAKER REVIEW, Spear Shaker Press, Stephanie Carvana, PO Box 308, Napanoch, NY 12458, 914-647-3608. 1987. Poetry, fiction, articles, cartoons, satire, reviews, letters. "Must be relevant to Shakespeare authorship question and/or Edward de Vere, Earl of Oxford. Maximum size 15 pages, short articles and letters preferred, will stretch space available if you have something really good." circ. 600. 4/yr. Expects 4 issues 1991, 4 issues 1992. sub. price: $24; per copy: $6; sample: $6. Back issues: #1 & #2 $8, #3 $4. Discounts: 40% to bulk/jobbers, minimum order of 10 copies. 20pp; 8½×11; of. Reporting time: 2-3 weeks. Payment: none. Copyrighted, reverts to author. Pub's reviews: 4 in 1990. §Shakespeare, Shakespeare authorship, Earl of Oxford, Elizabethan era. Ads: $100/$60/$40 1/4 page.

SPECIALTY TRAVEL INDEX, C.S. Hansen, A.E. Alpine, 305 San Anselmo Avenue #313, San Anselmo, CA 94960-2660, 415-459-4900. 1980. Non-fiction. "Directory of special interest travel." circ. 43M. 2/yr. Pub'd 2 issues 1990; expects 2 issues 1991, 2 issues 1992. sub. price: $8; per copy: $5; sample: $5. Back issues: $10. Discounts: 1-10 copies 40%; 10+ 50%. 148pp; 8⅜×10⅞; of. Copyrighted. Pub's reviews: 6 in 1990. §Travel trade. Ads: $1,540 b&w, $1,840 4-c/100 words $250, extra words $25 for 25 word increment.

Spectacular Diseases (see also SERIE D'ECRITURE; SPECTACULAR DISEASES), Paul Green, 83(b) London Road, Peterborough, Cambs, England. 1975. Poetry, art, long-poems. "Bias toward the long poem, or material taken from work in progress. Eight issues of magazine produced so far. 17 books produced so far. Material usually solicited." avg. press run 150-350. Expects 2 titles 1991. 18 titles listed in the *Small Press Record of Books in Print* (20th Edition, 1991-92). avg. price, paper: 75p (ascending up to £2.50). Discounts: trade 33⅓%. 5-25pp; 5¾×8; of. Reporting time: 3-4 weeks. Payment: copies only. Copyrights for author. ALP.

SPECTACULAR DISEASES, Spectacular Diseases, Paul Green, Paul Buck, Robert Vas Dias, 83(b) London Road, Peterborough, Cambs, England. 1975. Poetry, art, long-poems. "Bias to the long poem or work in progress. Work usually solicited. Enquire before submitting." circ. 350-500. 1/yr. Pub'd 1 issue 1990; expects

544

1 issue 1991, 1 issue 1992. sub. price: £4.00/4 issues; per copy: £1.00; sample: as issued. Back issues: #1 £1, #2 & #3 50p, #4 75p, #5 & #7 £1.50, #6 £1, $8 £1.80. Discounts: 33%. 40-60pp; 5¾×8; of. Reporting time: 3-4 weeks. Payment: copies. Copyrighted, reverts to author. Ads: inquire first. ALP, Small Press Group of Britain.

SPECTRUM, A Guide to the Independent Press and Informative Organizations, Spectrum Publications, Bayliss ("Jim") Corbett, 762 Avenue 'N', S.E., Winter Haven, FL 33880, (813) 294-5555. 1973. "A unique, international directory for professionals and general readers" circ. 500. Irregular. Pub'd 1 issue 1990; expects 1 issue 1991, 1 issue 1992. No subscription service available; price per copy: $14.95 prepaid; sample: $14.95 prepaid (no back issues available). Back issues: none available. Discounts: for cash only, 2 for $28, 10 for $100 delivered book rate. 80pp; 8½×11; of. Payment: none. Copyrighted.

SPECTRUM—The Wholistic News Magazine, Roger G. Windsor, 61 Dutile Rd., Laconia, NH 03246, 603-528-4710. 1988. Articles, interviews. "We do not accept articles from outside our staff." circ. 3M+. 6/yr. Pub'd 6 issues 1990; expects 6 issues 1991, 6 issues 1992. sub. price: $15; per copy: $2.75; sample: $3. Back issues: $3.50. Discounts: 40% retailers; 50% distributors. 36pp; 8×11; web and sheet fed press. Copyrighted, reverts to author. §Health, diet, spiritual, environmental, lifestyle. Ads: $295; 1/2 $155; 1/3 $115; 1/6 $58.

Spectrum Productions, Nick Starbuck, 979 Casiano Rd., Los Angeles, CA 90049. Plays. "We are interested in receiving inquiries (not mss.) in the field of translations of European drama before the twentieth century." 6 titles listed in the *Small Press Record of Books in Print* (20th Edition, 1991-92). lp. Copyrights for author. COSMEP.

Spectrum Publications (see also SPECTRUM, A Guide to the Independent Press and Informative Organizations), Bayliss ("Jim") Corbett, 762 Avenue 'N', S.E., Winter Haven, FL 33880, 813-294-5555. 1973. "A unique, international directory for professionals and general readers" avg. press run 500. Pub'd 1 title 1990; expects 1 title 1991, 1 title 1992. 1 title listed in the *Small Press Record of Books in Print* (20th Edition, 1991-92). avg. price, paper: $14.95 prepaid. Discounts: for cash only, 2 for $28, 10 for $100 delivered book rate. 80pp; 8½×11; photo, of.

SPECTRUM REVIEW, Integral Publishing, Georg Feuerstein, PO Box 1030, Lower Lake, CA 95457, 707-928-5751. 1986. Articles, interviews, reviews, letters. "Seeks to promote the integration of knowledge. Has a spiritual orientation. Few outside contributions. Numerous book reviews" circ. 2M. 4/yr. Pub'd 4 issues 1990; expects 4 issues 1991, 4 issues 1992. sub. price: $12, overseas airmail charge $4.50 per year; per copy: $3; sample: $3. 10pp; 8½×11; of. Reporting time: most material is generated in-house. Payment: by arrangement. Copyrighted. Pub's reviews: 40 per issue in 1990. §Religion, spirituality, philosophy, social sciences, arts. No ads. COSMEP.

SPECTRUM STORIES, Wonder Press, Walter Gammons, Box 58367, Louisville, KY 40268-0367. 1982. Fiction, art, cartoons. "Primarily we are a magazine of science-fiction, fantasy, and horror short stories of 2M-7M words." circ. 2.5M-3M. 4/yr. Pub'd 4 issues 1990; expects 4 issues 1991, 4 issues 1992. sub. price: $26 US; per copy: $6.50; sample: $6.50. Back issues: $6.50. Discounts: 50% off cover price and often 55% for bulk jobber, agents. 95-100pp; 8½×11; †of. Reporting time: 2 weeks to 2 months. Payment: 2 contributor copies to 1/4¢ - 1¢ per word. Copyrighted, reverts to author with written request. Ads: query.

The Speech Bin, Inc., Jan J. Binney, Senior Editor, 1766 20th Avenue, Vero Beach, FL 32960, 407-770-0007, FAX 407-770-0006. 1984. "The Speech Bin publishes educational materials and books in special education, speech-language pathology, audiology, and treatment of communication disorders in children and adults. One publication is *Getting Through: Communicating When Someone You Care For Has Alzheimer's Disease*, a unique book written for caregivers (both family members and professionals) of Alzheimer's victims. Most Speech Bin authors are specialists in communication disorders or education although we are eager to receive queries for new books and materials from all authors who write for our specialized market. The Speech Bin also publishes educational card sets and games plus novelties." avg. press run 1M+. Pub'd 8-10 titles 1990; expects 10-12 titles 1991, 10-12 titles 1992. 29 titles listed in the *Small Press Record of Books in Print* (20th Edition, 1991-92). avg. price, paper: $10-$25; other: $4-$50. Discounts: 20%. 50-200pp; 8½×11; of. Reporting time: 6 weeks. Payment: varies. Copyrights for author.

Spelman Publishing, Inc., Philip O. Spelman, President, 26941 Pebblestone Road, Southfield, MI 48034-3333, FAX 313-355-3686. 1984. Photos, non-fiction. "HealthProInk & 33 Publishing are imprints. We publish books only. Automotive, sexual improvement and self-help, celebrity biography and autobiography." avg. press run 5M-10M. Pub'd 1 title 1990; expects 3 titles 1991, 3-4 titles 1992. 3 titles listed in the *Small Press Record of Books in Print* (20th Edition, 1991-92). avg. price, cloth: $19.95; paper: $12.95. Discounts: 3 copies 20%, 9 copies 40%, 200 copies 50%. 200pp; 6×9; of, laser typeset from Mac. Reporting time: varies, write first before ms. Payment: varies. Copyrights for author. COSMEP, PMA, Book Exchange.

SPENCER'S BOOK WORLD, Spencer's Int'l Enterprises Corp., PO Box 43822, Los Angeles, CA 90043, 213-937-3099. 1987. News items. circ. 30M. 4/yr. Expects 3 issues 1991, 4 issues 1992. sub. price: $16; per copy: $4; sample: $3. 16pp; †of. Reporting time: 3 months. Payment: upon acceptance of material. Copyrighted. Pub's reviews: 0 in 1990. Ads: $200/$110/1'' ads $12 ($36, 4 issues)/2'' ads $22 ($66, 4 issues)/3'' ad $32 ($96, 4 issues).

Spencer's Int'l Enterprises Corp. (see also SPENCER'S BOOK WORLD; ANCIENT CONTROVERSY; BLACK HERITAGE UNVEILED NEWSLETTER), Kay Guffey, PO Box 43822, Los Angeles, CA 90043, 213-937-3099. 1986. Poetry, news items. "Additional address: 2410 1/2 Hunt Street, Vicksburg, MS 39180, 601-634-0272'' avg. press run 5M. Pub'd 10 titles 1990; expects 10 titles 1991, 15 titles 1992. avg. price, cloth: $15; paper: $10. Discounts: 2-4 books 20%, 5-9 30%, 10-24 40%, 25-49 42%, 50-99 45%, 100+ 50%. 150-200pp; 8½×11; of. Reporting time: 3 months. Copyrights for author. American Book Exchange, PO Box 2525, La Mesa, CA 92041.

SPEX (Small Press Exchange), John Fremont, 155 Cypress Street, Fort Braggs, CA 95437, 707-964-9520. 1979. Articles, reviews, letters, news items. "Additional address: Box 1346, Ross, CA 94957, (415) 454-1771. This is the newsletter of the Marin Small Publishers Association, a non-profit.'' circ. 500. 6/yr. Pub'd 6 issues 1990; expects 6 issues 1991, 6 issues 1992. sub. price: $20. 12pp; 8½×11; lp. Payment: none. Copyrighted. Pub's reviews: 25-30 in 1990. §Self-publishing, book marketing, book production. Ads: $35 business card size/request ad rate card.

SPHINX—WOMEN'S INTERNATIONAL LITERARY/ART REVIEW (IN ENGLISH), Carol A. Pratl, 175 Avenue Ledru-Rollin, Paris 75011, France, 43.67.31.92. 1984. Poetry, fiction, art, photos, interviews, criticism, parts-of-novels, long-poems, plays. "Short stories (2000-3000 words), novel excerpts (2000-3000 words). Poetry: we print original version and English translation. Interviews with writers and artists, notes from abroad, and essays-query first. Experimental writing and art preferable on any theme. Recent contributors: Kathy Acker, Grace Paley, Julia Kristeva'' circ. 2M. 1/yr. Pub'd 1 issue 1990; expects 1 issue 1991, 1 issue 1992. sub. price: $15/3 years; per copy: $5.00; sample: $5.00 + $1 airmail. Back issues: $4.00 + $1 airmail. Discounts: 30% bookshops and libraries; 50% distributors. 78pp; 21×21cm; of. Reporting time: 4-6 months. Payment: in copies. Copyrighted, reverts to author. Pub's reviews: 2 in 1990. §Books written by women (fiction and non-fiction). Ads: $250/$175/$100 1/4 page.

Sphinx Publishing, Mark Warda, PO Box 2005, Clearwater, FL 34617, 813-446-6840. 1983. 20 titles listed in the *Small Press Record of Books in Print* (20th Edition, 1991-92).

The Spinning Star Press, Carl Tate, Bob Starr, 1065 E. Fairview Blvd., Inglewood, CA 90302, 213-962-3862. 1986. Music. "Length of material: 108 pages. Biases: cataloging and chronicle of recording artists from the South and West. Recent contributors: Bob Starr, Carl Tate, The All-Star Band, etc. We are inactive as of now on #18, 19, 20, 25.'' avg. press run 1M. Pub'd 1 title 1990; expects 1 title 1991, 2 titles 1992. 1 title listed in the *Small Press Record of Books in Print* (20th Edition, 1991-92). avg. price, paper: $10. Discounts: bulk, classroom, agents, jobbers, etc. 108pp; 5½×8½; †mi.

Spinster's Book Company (see also Aunt Lute Books), Sherry Thomas, Joan Pinkvoss, PO Box 410687, San Francisco, CA 94141, 415-558-9586. 1978. Fiction, criticism, plays, non-fiction. "We publish only feminist material. Recent authors: Barbara McDonald, Sandra Butler, Joann Loulan, Anne Cameron.'' avg. press run 3M-5M. Pub'd 6 titles 1990; expects 7 titles 1991, 10 titles 1992. 23 titles listed in the *Small Press Record of Books in Print* (20th Edition, 1991-92). avg. price, cloth: $18.95; paper: $9.95. Discounts: 40% to bookstores on orders of 5 or more books, 50+ mixed titles - 45%, 50-55% for distributors, 20% on classroom orders, no rate for single orders from library, jobbers, etc. 40% on STOP orders, 2-5 copies 20%. 185pp; 5½×8; of. Reporting time: 3 months. Payment: 7% on first 5M; increased thereafter. Copyrights for author. Bookbuilders West.

THE SPIRIT, Kitchen Sink Press, Denis Kitchen, Editor, No. 2 Swamp Road, Princeton, WI 54968. 1985. circ. 12M. 12/yr. Expects 12 issues 1991. sub. price: $24; per copy: $2; sample: $2. Back issues: $2. Discounts: 40% stores, 50-60% distributors. 36pp; 6×9; of. Payment: negotiable. Copyrighted. Ads: $110.

SPIRIT MAGAZINE, Cosmic Circus Productions, Rey King, 414 S. 41st Street, Richmond, CA 94804, 415-451-5818. 1984. Fiction, articles, photos, cartoons, parts-of-novels, collages, non-fiction. "We specialize in illustrated articles comics and audio cassettes'' circ. 2M. 2/yr. Pub'd 1 issue 1990; expects 1 issue 1991, 2 issues 1992. price per copy: $5 plus $1 postage; sample: $5 plus $1 postage. Back issues: $10. Discounts: send for rates. 80pp; 6¾×10; of. Reporting time: 6 months. Payment: copies plus $10 per page. Copyrighted. §UFO contacts, channeling. Ads: $75/$50/$25. Artists Network.

Spirit Press, Christy Polk, 1951 Branciforte Drive, Santa Cruz, CA 95065. 1986. Non-fiction. "Also books for non-profit'' avg. press run 5M. Pub'd 3 titles 1990; expects 1 title 1991, 2 titles 1992. 4 titles listed in the *Small Press Record of Books in Print* (20th Edition, 1991-92). avg. price, paper: $14.95. Discounts: 40% off to stores. 224pp; 5½×8, 7×9; of. Reporting time: 1 month. Payment: standard. Copyrights for author. Womens National Book Assn., NC Publicists Assoc.

THE SPIRIT THAT MOVES US, The Spirit That Moves Us Press, Inc., Morty Sklar, PO Box 820,

Jackson Heights, NY 11372, 718-426-8788. 1975. Poetry, fiction, art, photos, parts-of-novels, long-poems, collages, concrete art. "Please query for theme with SASE before sending work. My only prejudices are those of personal taste. Will publish anything that grabs me; prefer work that comes from feeling. I like translations from all languages." circ. 1.5M. Irregular. Pub'd 1 issue 1990; expects 1 issue 1991, 1 issue 1992. sub. price: $11.20 Vol. 9, $12.60 Vol. 10; also available in cloth and signed A-Z cloth; per copy: varies with issue; sample: $5 for *The Spirit That Moves Us Reader* or *Free Parking* (Vol. 10, #2); $3 for our choice. Back issues: 10-volume set, 1) with photocopies of Vol 1, #3 & Vol 2, #1: $92; 2) with original Vol 1, #3 & Vol 2, #1: $140, includes ten special issues. Discounts: 40% for 5 or more, 20% for 2-4; 10% for 1, (may mix issues or combine with books). Distributors query; bulk rates available, for classes, etc. 202pp; 5½×8½; of. Reporting time: 3 months after deadline date. Payment: clothbound or two paperbacks, money when possible, + 40% off paperback copies and 25% off extra clothbounds. Copyrighted, reverts to author. CLMP, Small Press Center in Manhattan.

The Spirit That Moves Us Press, Inc. (see also **THE SPIRIT THAT MOVES US**), Morty Sklar, Editor, Publisher; Mary Biggs, Co-Editor, PO Box 820, Jackson Heights, NY 11372, 718-426-8788. 1974. Poetry, fiction, art, photos, parts-of-novels, long-poems, collages, concrete art. "Please query with a SASE before sending work. Catalog available for the asking." avg. press run 1M-4.2M. Pub'd 1 title 1990; expects 1 title 1991, 1 title 1992. 19 titles listed in the *Small Press Record of Books in Print* (20th Edition, 1991-92). avg. price, cloth: $12-$17.50; paper: $2-$11.50. Discounts: 10% for 1; 20% for 2-4; 40% for 5 or more (may mix titles); Distributors query. Classroom orders (10 or more): 30% plus free desk copy. 16-504pp; 5½×8½ pa; 6×9 cl; of. Reporting time: 1 month. Payment: 10% of run for single author book; clothbound copy for anthologies, plus cash if sales are sufficient+ 40% off paperback copies and 25% off clothbounds. Copyrights for author. CLMP, The Small Press Center in Manhattan.

SPIT, Edited Collectively, 529 2nd Street, Brooklyn, NY 11215, 718-499-7343. 1990. Poetry, fiction, articles, art, photos, cartoons, interviews, satire, music, letters, parts-of-novels, long-poems, collages, plays, concrete art, non-fiction. "We are a consensus-run magazine for emerging artists. We are open to publishing any form an artist or writer might define as 'art' that will fit our format. We encourage both experimental and mainstream submissions and publish both. We encourage minority submissions. Our most established contributors have been comic artist Mark Newgarden, media artist Barbara Rosenthal, and Australian poet Warrick Wynne" circ. 400. 2/yr. Expects 2 issues 1991, 2 issues 1992. sub. price: $6; per copy: $3; sample: $3. Back issues: $2 for Issue #1. Discounts: complimentary copies available for publicity purposes, bulk discounts negotiable. 50-75pp; 8½×11; of. Reporting time: up to 6 months. Payment: 1 issue negotiable. Copyrighted. §For our listings section: small arts magazines, chapbooks, and small press publications of any kind.

SPITBALL: The Literary Baseball Magazine, Mike Shannon, Editor & Publisher; Virgil Smith, Poetry Editor; Larry Dickson, Fiction Editor; Kevin Grace, Book Review Editor; Greg Rhodes, Articles Editor, 6224 Collegevue, Cincinnati, OH 45224, 513-541-4296. 1981. Poetry, fiction, articles, art, cartoons, interviews, satire, criticism, reviews, parts-of-novels, long-poems, collages, plays, concrete art, non-fiction. "*Spitball* is a unique litarary magazine devoted to baseball. We publish primarily poetry & fiction, with no biases concerning style or technique or genre. We strive to publish only what we consider to be good work, however, and using baseball as subject matter does not guarantee acceptance. We have no big backlog of accepted material, nevertheless, and good baseball poetry and fiction submitted to us can be published reasonably quickly. If one has never written about baseball, it would probably help a great deal to read the magazine or our book, *The Best of Spitball*, an anthology, published by Pocket Books, March 1988. We welcome new contributors. We try to give considerate fair treatment to everything we receive and are happy to offer constructive criticism. It is possible that we may be able to make monetary payments soon for all accepted material, but no promises on that score. Regular contributors: Bob Harrison of East Meadow, NY; Tim Peeler of Conover, NC; & Robert Lord Keyes of Amherst, MA. We continue to publish special issues, usually 2 a year. First issue of 1989 was devoted entirely to David Martin's sequence of poems connecting one-time Milwaukee Brewers outfielder Gorman Thomas to Wisconsin lorre and mythology" circ. 1M. 4/yr. Pub'd 4 issues 1990; expects 4 issues 1991, 4 issues 1992. sub. price: $12; per copy: $5; sample: $5. Back issues: many sold out, write for prices and availability. Discounts: can be negotiated. 52pp; 5½×8½; of. Reporting time: from 1 week to 3 months. Payment: copies. Not copyrighted. Pub's reviews: 60 in 1990. §We would love to receive review copies of any small press publications dealing with baseball, especially baseball poetry and fiction. Ads: $100/$50.

SPL Publishing Group, 11777 Park Lane North, Granger, IN 46530-8649, 219-272-0389. 1987. "Publishing focus limited to business, financial, personal money management, investing, and Christian material." avg. press run 5M. Expects 1 title 1991, 2 titles 1992. 1 title listed in the *Small Press Record of Books in Print* (20th Edition, 1991-92). avg. price, paper: $15. Discounts: negotiable. 76pp; 8½×11. Reporting time: 30-60 days. Payment: negotiable. Copyrights for authors if requested. American Booksellers Exchange, COSMEP.

Split Personality Press (see also **HEATHENZINE; TEMM POETRY MAGAZINE**), Ken Wagner, 511 West Sullivan, Olean, NY 14760. 1989. Poetry, fiction, art, photos, collages. avg. press run 50-200. Pub'd 1 title 1990; expects 7-10 titles 1991, 6-15 titles 1992. 10-70pp; 4¼×7; †photocopier. Reporting time: 1-6 months. Payment: 20-50 copies. Does not copyright for author.

Spoon River Poetry Press (see also SPOON RIVER QUARTERLY), David R. Pichaske, PO Box 6, Granite Falls, MN 56241. 1976. Poetry. "We do not, as a rule, solicit book-length manuscripts. Mostly we favor Midwest writers working with Midwest subjects and themes" avg. press run 1.5M. Pub'd 6 titles 1990; expects 6 titles 1991, 6 titles 1992. avg. price, cloth: $15; paper: $6. Discounts: 2-5 20%, 6+ 40% to bookstores; textbook orders 20%; 20% if payment accompanies order to individuals and libraries. 32-400+pp; 5½×8½, 6×9; of. Payment: 50% of receipts over set, print, bind costs. Copyrights for author.

SPOON RIVER QUARTERLY, Spoon River Poetry Press, Lucia Getsi, Editor, PO Box 6, Granite Falls, MN 56241. 1976. Poetry. circ. 250. 4/yr. Pub'd 4 issues 1990; expects 4 issues 1991, 4 issues 1992. sub. price: $10; per copy: $3; sample: $3. 64pp; 5¼×8¼; of. Reporting time: 2 months. Payment: copies. Copyrighted, reverts to author.

THE SPORT PSYCHOLOGIST, Human Kinetics Pub. Inc., Daniel Gould, Glyn C. Roberts, Box 5076, Champaign, IL 61820, 217-351-5076. 1987. Articles, reviews. "Applied journal" circ. 650. 4/yr. Pub'd 4 issues 1990; expects 4 issues 1991, 4 issues 1992. sub. price: $30 indiv., $60 instit.; per copy: $7.50 indiv., $16 instit.; sample: free. Back issues: $7.50 indiv., $16 instit. Discounts: 5%. 102pp; 6×9; of. Reporting time: 2 months. Payment: none. Copyrighted. Pub's reviews. §Sport, sport science, and physical education related to psychology. Ads: $170/$102 (4X rate).

Sports Support Syndicate (see also STROKES), Mark Rauterkus, 1739 East Carson Street, Pittsburgh, PA 15203, 412-481-2497. 1988. Articles, art, photos, cartoons, reviews, news items, non-fiction. "Sports-specific titles for serious participants and coaches. Intelligence products and progressive publishing is our goal. We advertise and use catalogs as well as sales to trade and specialty-sport shops. Massive literacy campaign slated for 90's. We also co-publish and help with investors or major publishing houses." avg. press run 1M. Pub'd 5 titles 1990; expects 10 titles 1991, 10 titles 1992. 2 titles listed in the *Small Press Record of Books in Print* (20th Edition, 1991-92). avg. price, cloth: $21.95; paper: $15.95; other: software under $40. Discounts: 40%. 190pp; 6×9; desk-top. Reporting time: 2 weeks. Payment: percentage on sales of 5 up to 25% with one-year delayed payment. Copyrights for author.

SPORTS-NUTRITION NEWS, Healthmere Press, Inc., Jacqueline B. Marcus, PO Box 986, Evanston, IL 60204, 312-251-5950. 1982. Interviews, reviews, news items, non-fiction. "*SPORTS-NUTRITION NEWS* is a bimonthly publication in newsletter format. We report on the relationship between nutrition and exercise, with an emphasis on sports and endurance. Each issue features an indepth article of current interest, questions and comments from our readers, news briefs, regular columns by well known sports nutritionists, book reviews, and research abstracts. All articles are written by accredited professionals in their fields." 6/yr. Pub'd 6 issues 1990; expects 6 issues 1991, 6 issues 1992. sub. price: $43; per copy: $6.50; sample: free. Back issues: $6.50 per back copy—10 or more $6 each. Discounts: agency discount 10%. 8pp; 8½×11; of. Reporting time: 30 days. Payment: yes. Copyrighted, does not revert to author. Pub's reviews: 25 in 1990. §Fitness, diet, training, diet and training cookbooks. COSMEP.

Spredden Press, Gillian Dickinson, 55 Noel Road, London, England N1 8HE, England, 071-226-9098. 1988. Non-fiction. "Books of primarily north of England origin, with national/international interest." avg. press run 1.5M-2M. Pub'd 1 title 1990; expects 9 titles 1991, 6 titles 1992. 1 title listed in the *Small Press Record of Books in Print* (20th Edition, 1991-92). avg. price, cloth: £14.95; paper: £7.95. Discounts: 35% trade. 220pp; 5×8; of. Reporting time: 2 months. Payment: 10% payable every half year. Copyrights for author. Independent Publishers Guild (IPG).

SPRING: A Journal of Archetype and Culture, Spring Publications Inc, Charles Boer, Ross Miller, James Hillman, English Department, Box U-25, University of Connecticut, Storrs, CT 06268. 1941. Articles, interviews, criticism. "App. 200 pages, 20 page articles in magazine; James Hillman, Patricia Berry, Charles Boer, Edward Casey." circ. 1.8M. 1/yr. Pub'd 1 issue 1990; expects 1 issue 1991, 1 issue 1992. sub. price: $15 libraries + institutions + shipping if billed, no shipping charge if prepaid; per copy: $12.50 + shipping charges for individuals + bookstores + jobbers (less appropriate discount); $15 libraries + institutions (as above). Back issues: 1975-85 $15, 1985, 1984 and 1981, and 1977 o.p.; same distinction betw. libraries/instit. + indiv./resale. Discounts: classroom: 30%; jobbers & trade: 15% 1-4 copies; 40% 5 to 99; 42% 100-249; etc. 200pp; 6×9; of. Reporting time: 3 months. Payment: varies. Copyrighted, does not revert to author. Pub's reviews: 12 in 1990. Ads: $200/$150.

Spring Publications Inc (see also SPRING: A Journal of Archetype and Culture), James Hillman, Editor; Mary Helen Sullivan, Managing Editor, PO Box 222069, Dallas, TX 75222, 214-943-4093, 4094. 1941. Articles, interviews, criticism, non-fiction. "Jungian background but critical reflection on Jungian tradition; intellectual but neither academic nor new age." avg. press run 2M. Pub'd 9 titles 1990; expects 10 titles 1991, 10 titles 1992. 77 titles listed in the *Small Press Record of Books in Print* (20th Edition, 1991-92). avg. price,

548

paper: $12. Discounts: trade: 1-4 books, 15%; 5-99 books, 40%; 100+ 42%; 40% (same terms jobbers) classroom: 30%. 200pp; 5½×8½, 6×9; of. Reporting time: 3 months. Payment: varies. Copyrights for author. COSMEP.

Spring Street Press, Robert H. Romer, 104 Spring Street, Amherst, MA 01002, 413-253-7748. 1984. Non-fiction. avg. press run 3M. Pub'd 1 title 1990; expects 1 title 1991, 2 titles 1992. 2 titles listed in the *Small Press Record of Books in Print* (20th Edition, 1991-92). avg. price, paper: $8. Discounts: 25% to dealers, etc. 120pp; of. Payment: negotiable. Does not copyright for author.

SPROUTLETTER, Michael Linden, Box 62, Ashland, OR 97520, 503-488-2326 (9-5 M-F Pac. Time). 1980. Articles, interviews, reviews, letters, news items, non-fiction. *"Sproutletter* publishes articles, book reviews, recipes and news items relating to sprouting algae (blue-green), indoor gardening, live foods, vegetarianism, holistic health and nutrition. Query requested before submitting works. Articles should be no more than 1M words." circ. 3.1M. 6/yr. Pub'd 4 issues 1990; expects 6 issues 1991, 6 issues 1992. sub. price: $17 USA, $23 Canada and Mexico, $23 foreign surface, $30 foreign airmail; per copy: $3, $4.50 Can/Mex, $4.50 surf, $5.50 air; sample: same. Discounts: 10-50 40%, 51-100 45%, 101-200 50%. 12pp; 8½×11; of. Reporting time: 4 weeks. Payment: $25-$50. Copyrighted, reverts to author. Pub's reviews: 20 in 1990. §Sprouting, raw foods, indoor gardening, holistic health, nutrition. Ads: $160/$90/25¢.

SPSM&H, Amelia Press, Frederick A. Raborg, Jr., Editor, 329 'E' Street, Bakersfield, CA 93304, 805-323-4064. 1986. Poetry, fiction, articles, art, cartoons, criticism, reviews. "Sonnets, sonnet sequences, traditional or experimental, fiction to 3,000 words pertaining somehow to the sonnet; essays to 2,000 words about the form, history and/or technique; pen & ink sketches, line drawings and cartoons with romantic or Gothic themes. We welcome newcomers. Sponsors the annual Eugene Smith Sonnet Awards. Reviews collections of sonnets and books about the form. Contributors include: Margaret Ryan, Judson Jerome, Robert Wolfkill, Harold Witt and many others" circ. 600. 4/yr. Pub'd 4 issues 1990; expects 4 issues 1991, 4 issues 1992. sub. price: $14; per copy: $4.50; sample: $4.50. Back issues: $4.50 when available. Discounts: contributor's discount, 20% on five or more copies. 20pp; 5½×8½; of. Reporting time: 2 weeks. Payment: none, except two *best of issue* poets each receive $14 on publication, plus copy. Copyrighted. Pub's reviews: 5 in 1990. §Collections of sonnets, books which contain a substantial number of sonnets and books about the form. Will consider ads based on $60/$40/$25.

SPUR, Roz Penney, 25, Beehive Place, Brixton, London SW9 7QR, England. 1972. Articles, photos, cartoons, reviews, letters, news items. "Geared to needs of political lobbying and public awareness activists in Britain and its relation to the Third World" 10/yr. Pub'd 10 issues 1990. sub. price: £9; per copy: 20p; sample: S.A.E. Discounts: available on request. 8pp; size A3; of. Reporting time: 2 weeks. Payment: discretionary. Copyrighted. Pub's reviews: 20 in 1990. §World development, Third World, development education. No ads.

SPWAO SHOWCASE, Mike Olson, Director, 309 North Humphrey Circle, Shawano, WI 54166. 1977. Poetry, fiction, art, photos, cartoons, parts-of-novels, long-poems, collages. "Editor changes annually. Available for contribution only by *SPWAO* members. We are interested in new members to join *SPWAO*; once a member, contributions may be made to the biannual *Showcase*, which alternates with *The Best of the Small Press*—open to nonmembers." circ. 500. 1/yr. Pub'd 1 issue 1990; expects 1 issue 1991, 1 issue 1992. price per copy: $6.95; sample: $6.95. Back issues: $3. 76pp; 8½×11; of. Reporting time: 2-4 weeks. Payment: copies. Copyrighted, reverts to author. SPWAO (Small Press Writers & Artists Organization).

SQUARE ONE - A Magazine of Fiction, William D. Gagliani, PO Box 11921, Milwaukee, WI 53211-0921. 1984. Fiction, art, parts-of-novels. "500-7,500 words (3,500 words preferred). *Query for longer or novel excerpts.* No biases—only taboo is boredom. SASE for fiction guidelines. Recent contributors: Cheryl Sayre, D.W. Taylor." circ. 250. 1/yr. Pub'd 1 issue 1990; expects 1 issue 1991, 1-2 issues 1992. sub. price: currently $7.50 postpaid; 2-issue subscription $13.50 postpaid; V.4/5 $6.50 ppd; per copy: V.3: $3.50; V.4/5 (double): $5.50; sample: V.3: $3.50 + 9 X 12 SASE with $2.03 postage. Make checks payable to William D. Gagliani. Back issues: Volume I $1 plus postage (send 9 X 12 envelope with 5 first class stamps), Vol. II $2.50 + p/h (send 9 X 12 envelope w/7 1st class stamps). 70-85pp; 7×8½; DTP/commercial printer. Reporting time: currently 1-14 months, 65% receive critique (time permitting), do not read mss May-September unless clearly marked *"keep on file"* Payment: 2 copies (1 to artists). Copyrighted, reverts to author. Ads: $50/$30/$20 1/4 page/$10 1/8.

The Square-Rigger Press, Daniel Talbot von Koschembahr, 1201 North 46th Street, Seattle, WA 98103-6610, 206-548-9385. 1973. Poetry, fiction, articles, art, non-fiction. "There have been two miniatures published by the Square-Rigger Press. The first, *Moving With the Wind* (32 pp, 8 illustrations) oriental binding/blind embossed sup case and *An Italic Alphabet* (30 pp, bound in a similar manner)" avg. press run 150-200. Expects 1 title 1991, 2+ titles 1992. 1 title listed in the *Small Press Record of Books in Print* (20th Edition, 1991-92). avg. price, other: bound in boards: 1st miniature $15.00. 30pp; 1¾×1-3/16, 1¼×2⅜; †lp.

George Sroda, Publisher, George Sroda, Amherst Jct., WI 54407, 715-824-3868. Articles. "Has published two books, *Facts About Nightcrawlers*, and *The 'Life Story'—of—TV Star and Celebrity Herman The Worm."* avg. press run 30M. Pub'd 1 title 1990; expects 1 title 1991. 2 titles listed in the *Small Press Record of Books in Print* (20th Edition, 1991-92). avg. price, paper: $7.45 postpaid. Discounts: distributors, 40%. 8¼×5½.

ST Publications/Book Division, George B. Harper, Manager, Book Division, 407 Gilbert Avenue, Cincinnati, OH 45202, 513-421-2050; fax 513-421-5144. 1957. "We use material in the areas of sign painting and manufacture, lettering, craft techniques used in making signs: wood carving, gold leafing, sandblasting, etc. Also, material on silkscreen printing, either as an art or an industrial process, on any kind of surface, paper, garment, ceramic, etc. Will also consider material on store design and display or merchandising, retail promotion ideas, etc." avg. press run 2M-5M. Pub'd 2 titles 1990; expects 5 titles 1991, 7 titles 1992. 14 titles listed in the *Small Press Record of Books in Print* (20th Edition, 1991-92). avg. price, cloth: $24.38; paper: $18.61. Discounts: 1-4 copies 20%; 5-24 40%; 25-49 42%; 50-499 44%; 500-999 46%; 1000-2499 48%; 2500+ 50%. 200pp; 6×9. Reporting time: 6-8 weeks. Payment: monthly royalty checks; 10% to 12½% on net price or 20% on net price after production cost recovery. Does not copyright for author. Publishers Marketing Association (PMA); COSMEP.

Stabur Press, Inc., Paul Burke, 23301 Meadow Park, Redford, MI 48239, 313-535-0572. 1986. Art, cartoons, satire. avg. press run 15M. Expects 3 titles 1991, 3 titles 1992. 5 titles listed in the *Small Press Record of Books in Print* (20th Edition, 1991-92). avg. price, cloth: $18.95; paper: $9.95; other: $34.95 collector. Discounts: retailer 40%, distributor 55% (60% non-returnable). 144pp; 8½×11. Payment: 7½% - 12% neg. advance. Copyrights for author.

STAGE WHISPER, New Sins Press, Rane Arroyo, PO Box 7157, Pittsburgh, PA 15213. *"Stage Whisper* considers unsolicited one-act plays if accompanied by Vita and SASE. Recent contributors: B.Z. Niditch, Glenn Sheldon. See sample copy first! Checks/money orders must be payable to Rane Arroyo." sample price: $2.

STAND MAGAZINE, Northern House, Jon Silkin, Lorna Tracy, 179 Wingrove Road, Newcastle-on-Tyne NE49DA, England, 091-273-3280. 1952. Poetry, fiction, art, interviews, criticism, reviews, letters. circ. 4.5M. 4/yr. Pub'd 4 issues 1990; expects 4 issues 1991. sub. price: $22; per copy: $8; sample: $5. Back issues: $5. 80pp; 6-1/10×8; of. Reporting time: 1-2 months. Payment: $45/poem, $45/1,000 words prose. Copyrighted, reverts to author. Pub's reviews: 30 in 1990. §Literature, politics. Ads: $225/$112/$56 1/4 page. CCLM.

STAPLE, Donald Measham, Bob Windsor, Derbyshire College of HE, Mickleover, Derby, Derbyshire DE3 5GX, United Kingdom. 1983. Poetry, fiction, interviews, parts-of-novels. "One of the few magazines where the new writer can be first published side by side with the established, and the very well known: we have published Silkin, Redgrove, Fisher, Porter, Bartlett, Adcock. Runs biennial competition: 1986, 1988, 1990, 1992 (deadline 31 December). Launching Staple *First Editions* series of monographs July 1991—essential to send for conditions before submission." circ. 600. 3/yr. Pub'd 3 issues 1990; expects 3 issues 1991, 3 issues 1992. sub. price: £7 overseas (sterling only); per copy: £4; sample: £2 (sterling only). Back issues: £1. Discounts: 20%. 72pp; size A5; of. Reporting time: 3 months maximum. Payment: special issues only & competition (£500 in prizes). Not copyrighted. Ads: £50/£25/£12.50 1/4 page.

THE STAR BEACON, Earth Star Publications, Ann Ulrich, PO Box 117, Paonia, CO 81428, 303-527-3257. 1987. Poetry, articles, art, photos, cartoons, interviews, reviews, letters, long-poems, news items, non-fiction. *"Star Beacon* readers are looking for the latest information on UFOs and related phenomena, as most of them are UFO percipients of various degrees, searching for answers. Because science, for the most part, has rejected them, *Star Beacon* readers are turning to metaphysics (the science of higher mind) for such answers as why are we here, where are we going, how can we make our world and the universe better" circ. 500+. 12/yr. Pub'd 8 issues 1990; expects 12 issues 1991, 12 issues 1992. sub. price: $14; per copy: $1.25; sample: $1.25. Back issues: $1.25. 8pp; 8½×11; of. Reporting time: 2 weeks. Payment: copies. Not copyrighted. Pub's reviews: 3 in 1990. §UFOs, metaphysics, psychic phenomena, New Age living. Ads: $2 per column inch.

Star Books, Inc. (see also STARLIGHT), Irene Burk Harrell, President & Editor, 408 Pearson Street, Wilson, NC 27893, 919-237-1591. 1983. Poetry, fiction, articles, art, photos, cartoons, letters, long-poems, non-fiction. "Only material with strong Christian emphasis, lifting up the Light of the world, Jesus Christ. Specializing in testimonies, Bible study books, devotionals, poetry, novels, juvenilia. All material should be biblically sound, well written. Most recent publication, *Won't Somebody Help Me!,* by Janice Gravely. Bestsellers: *Healing Hidden Hurts,* by Kay Zibolsky; *He Hits: Hope for Battered Women,* by Janet Jonathon; *A Heart Set Free,* by Gloria Phillips; *How I Was Healed of Cancer,* by Cynthia Wilson. By mid-year 1991, we expect to have a total of 68 books, 3 tracts and 15 issues of our quarterly magazine, *StarLight."* avg. press run 500-10M. Pub'd 13 titles 1990; expects 21 titles 1991. 35 titles listed in the *Small Press Record of Books in Print* (20th Edition, 1991-92). avg. price, paper: $6. Discounts: 40% bookstores; 45-55% jobbers. 75-200+pp; 5½×8½, 4¼×7, 4¼×5½; of. Reporting time: 2 months or less. Payment: begins at 10%, with increased percentages for sales above 25,000 copies. Copyrights for author.

Star Publications, Dave Damon, Editor, PO Box 22534, Kansas City, MO 64113, 816-523-8228. 1977. Pub'd

1 title 1990; expects 2 titles 1991. 6 titles listed in the *Small Press Record of Books in Print* (20th Edition, 1991-92). avg. price, cloth: $12.95. Discounts: 40% w/approved credit.

STAR ROUTE JOURNAL, Mary Siler Anderson, PO Box 1451, Redway, CA 95560, 707-923-3351. 1978. Poetry, fiction, articles, art, photos, cartoons, interviews, satire, criticism, reviews, letters, non-fiction. "Recent contributors: Paul Encimer, Grimalda Montrose. Our bias is contemporary and historic counter-culture." circ. 800. 10/yr. Pub'd 10 issues 1990; expects 10 issues 1991, 10 issues 1992. sub. price: $12; per copy: $1.25; sample: $1.25. Back issues: not available. Discounts: by arrangement. 16-24pp; 9-17/18×13½; of. Reporting time: 3-4 weeks. Payment: rarely money, usually a subscription. Copyrighted, reverts to author. Pub's reviews: 20 in 1990. §Poetry, history, ecology, feminism, politics, the occasional short story. Ads: $170/$90/$4.25 col. inch.

Star Rover House, Robert Martens, 1914 Foothill Blvd., Oakland, CA 94606, 415-532-8408. 1978. Fiction. "Reprinting of all 56 books by Jack London. All orders to: Lexikos, PO Box 296, Lagunitas, CA 94938, (415) 488-0401" avg. press run 1,250. Pub'd 3 titles 1990; expects 5 titles 1991, 4 titles 1992. 22 titles listed in the *Small Press Record of Books in Print* (20th Edition, 1991-92). avg. price, paper: $6.95/$9.95. Discounts: 2-4 copies 20%, 5-14 40%, 15-49 42%, 50-99 43%, 100+ 44%. 250-300pp; 4×6½, 5¼×8; †of. Reporting time: 1 month. Payment: yes, inquire. Copyrights for author.

Starchand Press, Odeda Rosenthal, Box 468, Wainscott, NY 11975. 1979. Poetry, fiction, articles. avg. press run 1M. Expects 3 titles 1991. 4 titles listed in the *Small Press Record of Books in Print* (20th Edition, 1991-92). avg. price, paper: $5.00. Discounts: 40% over 100; 20% smaller order. 48pp; 5⅝×8⅞; of. Reporting time: 3 weeks. Payment: author subs. Copyrights for author.

Starfield Press, Frank Fara, 10603 N. Hayden Road, Suite 114, Scottsdale, AZ 85260, 602-951-3115. 1986. Music. 1 title listed in the *Small Press Record of Books in Print* (20th Edition, 1991-92). Discounts: 40% to wholesalers.

Starfish Press, David J.A. Shears, Publisher, 6525-32nd Street NW, PO Box 42467, Washington, DC 20015, 202-244-2178. 1989. Non-fiction. avg. press run 2.5M. Expects 1 title 1991. 1 title listed in the *Small Press Record of Books in Print* (20th Edition, 1991-92). avg. price, paper: $10.95. Discounts: 40% retail, 50% wholesale & orders over 100 copies. 192pp; 5⅜×8½. Reporting time: 2 months. Payment: royalties only. Copyrights for author.

THE STARK FIST OF REMOVAL, Rev. Ivan Stang, Church of the SubGenius, PO Box 140306, Dallas, TX 75214. 1979. Fiction, art, cartoons, satire, collages, news items. "*The Church of the SubGenius* is either the one true, brain-splittingly funny *Religion* for MUTANTS, or the most extensive art-stage-video-magazine-book project ever to seek collaborators. Probably both. We have 2 books published by McGraw-Hill and Simon and Schuster, but we publish the tapes, magazines, radio shows (in most major cities) and video tapes. It is a self-contained UNIVERSE of sick humor and many major artists in all media are now contributing. We publish once a week for radio" circ. 5M. 2/yr. Pub'd 2 issues 1990; expects 2 issues 1991, 2 issues 1992. sub. price: $20 2-year; per copy: $3.50; sample: same. Back issues: none available except Pamphlets 1 & 2 ($1 each). Discounts: 50% off cover price in quantities more than 10. 100pp; 8½×11; lp. Reporting time: 2 months. Payment: none for magazines; royalties for tapes. Copyrighted, rights sometimes revert to authors. Pub's reviews: 150 in 1990. §Occult, music, sci-fi, religion, science, extremist politics (either side), avant-garde art. NO POETRY. No ads.

StarLance Publications (see also VOYAGES SF), 50 Basin Drive, Mesa, WA 99343, 509-269-4497. 1987. Fiction, art, cartoons. "We published our first book in 1990 (previously periodicals only), and plan to maintain a regular publishing release schedule. All currently planned books are collections of cartoons, science fiction and fantasy illustration, illustrated science fiction and fantasy short fiction, and graphic novels. Desired art is black line and all mediums that reproduce well in b/w halftone. Books aimed at mainstream market, including young adults. Profanity and nudity are not desired." Pub'd 1 title 1990; expects 3 titles 1991, 4-6 titles 1992. 2 titles listed in the *Small Press Record of Books in Print* (20th Edition, 1991-92). avg. price, paper: $7.95. Discounts: 25-50% based on quantity. 96pp; 5½×8¼. Reporting time: 2-4 weeks. Payment: negotiable. COSMEP.

STARLIGHT, Star Books, Inc., Irene Burk Harrell, 408 Pearson Street, Wilson, NC 27893, 919-237-1591. 1987. Poetry, fiction, articles, art, photos, cartoons, letters, long-poems, non-fiction. "10-12 typewritten pages (double spaced) maximum; no minimum. All material must be strongly Christian, in line with biblical principles." circ. varies. 4/yr. Pub'd 4 issues 1990; expects 4 issues 1991, 4-6 issues 1992. sub. price: $15; per copy: $4; sample: $4. Back issues: $4 ($2.40 to contributors published therein). Discounts: 40% to contributors, bookstores. 64-68pp; 5½×7½; †Canon copier. Reporting time: 1 month or less. Payment: 3 contributors' copies. Copyrighted, reverts to author. No ads.

Starlight Press, Ira Rosenstein, Box 3102, Long Island City, NY 11103. 1980. Poetry. "Starlight Press is planning to publish an anthology of poetry, its second, within the next year and welcomes submissions. This anthology will be dedicated to the sonnet form. To submit for the anthology, send a maximum of 3 sonnets. While strictly metered, 14-line sonnets are welcome, Starlight is most open to expansions of the form: 16-line sonnets, sprung-metered sonnets, unmetered, half-rhymed, unrhymed, multi-stanza, use your creativity. Also: Starlight books are rectangular—your longest line can be unfurled (limit: 130 spaces). What matters is that all poems partake, however tenuous this description may seem, of sonnetness, and, beyond that, that they constitute a vivid experience for the reader." avg. press run 300. Pub'd 1 title 1990; expects 2 titles 1992. 5 titles listed in the *Small Press Record of Books in Print* (20th Edition, 1991-92). avg. price, paper: $4. Discounts: normal trade. 35pp; 8½×7; of. Reporting time: 2 months. Payment: 2 free copies & 50% discount on further Starlight copies (any title). Copyrights for author.

StarMist Books, Beth Boyd, President; Nila Joy, Editor, Box 12640, Rochester, NY 14612. 1986. Poetry, fiction. "StarMist Books publishes poetry with depth, sensitivity and power. Award-winning poet Jani Johe Webster is one of our authors. Our most recent poet is Virginia Johe." avg. press run 500. Expects 2 titles 1991, 2-4 titles 1992. 2 titles listed in the *Small Press Record of Books in Print* (20th Edition, 1991-92). avg. price, paper: $6. 75pp; 5½×8½; of. Reporting time: 2 weeks. Payment: negotiable. Copyrights for author. Jani Johe Webster: (Writers Organizations: UAPAA, WWA, Writers & Books), StarMist Books: (Nat'l Assoc. of Independent Publishers), COSMEP.

STAR-WEB PAPER, Thomas Michael Fisher, Tom Fisher, P.O. Box 40029, Berkeley, CA 94704, 505-523-7923. 1973. Poetry, fiction, articles, art, photos, cartoons, interviews, satire, criticism, reviews, music, letters, parts-of-novels, long-poems, collages, plays, concrete art, news items, non-fiction. "*Star-Web Paper* has changed location and priorities in the past, but we retained our original spirit of community energy; subscribed to by approximately fifteen major universities in the U.S. and Canada, *SWP* is available on microfilm, and is listed in numerous directories and indexes of periodicals. In past issues, *SWP* has presented the work of Ed Dorn, George Bowering, James Bertolino, Charles Olson, Robert Creeley, Jonathan Williams, John Cage, Hugh Fox, Lyn Lifshin, George Montgomery, Anselm Hollo, Len Fulton, David Meltzer, Peter Wild, Robert Kelly, and many others. Happily, a trademark of *SWP* is its encouragement of submissions by "unknown" writers; a great joy is to "discover" work of merit for the first time, and much of our best material in the magazine has comes from new folk. We do mutual flier-exchange programs — send us your fliers or announcements for our outgoing mail, and we'll send you ours. Books and magazines wanted for review and/or exchange. Recent issues include work by Jackson MacLow, Keith Wilson, John Brandi, Arlene Zekowski, Stanley Berne, Dick Bakken, Ron Bayes, F.A. Nettelbeck, Ken Saville, Loris Essary, Richard Kostelanetz, Carol Berge, George Montgomery, Lyn Lifshin, Judson Crews, Juam Arguelles" Irregular. Pub'd 1 issue 1990; expects 1 issue 1991, 1 issue 1992. sub. price: $10/2 issues individual, $25/2 issues institutions; per copy: $5 (includes postage); sample: $5 (includes postage). Back issues: 1,2,3,4,5,6,7,8,9: information sent upon request. Discounts: by arrangement. 80pp; 8½×11; of, xerox. Reporting time: 2 weeks. Payment: copies. Copyrighted, reverts to author. Pub's reviews: 15 in 1990. §Arts, photography, earth, primitive, music, magic, 'literature of conciousness' in all its forms. Ads: by arrangement. RGWA, RGD.

STARWIND, Starwind Press, David F. Powell, PO Box 98, Ripley, OH 45167, 513-392-4549. 1974. Fiction, articles, art, cartoons, interviews, satire, criticism, reviews, news items. "We look for science fiction (hard and soft), fantasy and non-fiction of scientific and technological interest. Length of fiction - 2,000-10,000 words. Length of non-fiction 2,000-5,000 words" circ. 2.5M. 4-6/yr. Expects 3 issues 1991, 4-6 issues 1992. sub. price: $14; per copy: $3.50; sample: same. Back issues: $3.50. Discounts: 20% on consignment minimum 10. 68pp; 8½×11; †of. Reporting time: 6-8 weeks. Payment: 1-4¢/word; copy of issue in which work appears. Copyrighted. Pub's reviews: 0 in 1990. §Science fiction, science, technology, computers. Ads: $100/$60/$4 column inch.

Starwind Press (see also STARWIND), PO Box 98, Ripley, OH 45167, 513-392-4549.

Starwise Publications (see also SOVIET SPACEFLIGHT REPORT), Peter J. Kappesser, PO Box 25, Pulaski, NY 13142. 1984. Articles, art, photos, interviews, news items, non-fiction. "(S.A.N. 685-9577) Please Query First; Enclose S.A.S.E. for guidelines. Sample issue $1. Bimonthly newsletter reporting spaceflight activities of the U.S.S.R." avg. price, other: $2.50 per issue; 6 issues $15. 12pp; 8½×11; †xerographic duplicator, of/lo for photos pages. Reporting time: 4 weeks. Payment: negotiable.

STATE AND LOCAL GOVERNMENT REVIEW, Richard W. Campbell, Jr., Carl Vinson Institute of Government, University of Georgia, Terrell Hall, Athens, GA 30602, 404-542-2736. 1968. "A journal of research and viewpoints on state and local government." circ. 900. 3/yr. Pub'd 3 issues 1990; expects 3 issues 1991, 3 issues 1992. sub. price: $12 individual, $18 library; per copy: $5. Back issues: volumes 1-7 $1/copy, all other $5/copy. 90pp; 8½×11. Copyrighted.

State of the Art Ltd., Carol Ayers, Harry M. Fleenor, Jr., 1625 South Broadway, Denver, CO 80210, 303-722-7177. 1983. Non-fiction. "12 titles in print. 50% subsidy press." avg. press run 3M. Pub'd 3 titles

1990; expects 8 titles 1991, 12 titles 1992. 10 titles listed in the *Small Press Record of Books in Print* (20th Edition, 1991-92). Discounts: trade. 200pp; size varies. Reporting time: 2-3 months. Payment: standard. Copyrights for author. COSMEP, PO Box 703, San Francisco, CA 94101.

State Street Press, Judith Kitchen, Stan Sanvel Rubin, Bruce Bennett, Linda Allardt, PO Box 278, Brockport, NY 14420, 716-637-0023. 1981. Poetry. "20-24 pages of poetry that works *as a collection*. We are looking for variety and excellence in many styles. We choose 3-5 chapbooks from an anonymous competition. Cost: $5 handling fee. Chapbook sent to each contestant. Authors include: Christopher Bursk, Stephen Corey, Stephanie Strickland, Marcia Falk, Nancy Simpson, Michael Cadnum, Judson Mitcham, David Weiss, Hilda Raz, Jerah Chadwick, Cornelius Eady." avg. press run 400. Pub'd 6 titles 1990; expects 6 titles 1991, 6 titles 1992. 44 titles listed in the *Small Press Record of Books in Print* (20th Edition, 1991-92). avg. price, paper: $5. Discounts: 40% to bookstores; $15 set of 5. 32pp; of. Reporting time: 4-5 months after contest deadline. Payment: 25 copies to the author, 25 review copies, author can buy at cost. Copyrights for author.

Station Hill Press, George Quasha, Publisher & Director; Susan Quasha, Associate Publisher & Co-Director; Cathy Lewis, Director of Marketing, Station Hill Road, Barrytown, NY 12507, 914-758-5840. 1978. Poetry, fiction, art, photos, satire, criticism, music, letters, long-poems, collages, plays, concrete art, non-fiction. "Publisher of international literature & visual and performing arts, emphasizing the contemporary & innovative, yet excluding neither the ancient nor the traditional, presented with a commitment to excellence in book design and production. Prose fiction by Maurice Blanchot, Rosemarie Waldrop, Franz Kamin, Lydia Davis, Spencer Holst; poetry by John Cage, Jackson Mac Low, Kenneth Irby, Robert Kelly, Paul Auster, Armand Schwerner, Charles Bernstein, Norman Weinstein, etc.; discourse by James Hillman, Ed Sanders, Blanchot, Porphyry, etc; visual arts by Russian avant-garde, Wolf Kahn, Thomas Dugan, etc. Other imprints and series include: *Artext, Contemporary Artist Series, Open Book,* and *P-U-L-S-E Books.*" avg. press run 1.5M-3M. Pub'd 12 titles 1990; expects 20 titles 1991, 20 titles 1992. 84 titles listed in the *Small Press Record of Books in Print* (20th Edition, 1991-92). avg. price, cloth: $18; paper: $6; other: $12-$100 special editions. Discounts: 50% distributor, 10% on single orders, escalating with qty. 64-200pp; 5¾x8¾, 5½x8½, 6x9, 7x10. Reporting time: no guarantee except by written arrangement. Payment: usually 10% of edition in copies or 10% of gross. Copyrights for author.

Steel Balls Press, John J. White, E.F. Bellevue, Box 807, Whittier, CA 90608, 213-693-0397. 1986. Non-fiction. "No unsolicited m/s! Query letters only. Specialize in controversial how-to/self help. *Absolutely no New Age, poetry, fiction.*" avg. press run 10M. Pub'd 2 titles 1990; expects 2 titles 1991, 2 titles 1992. 1 title listed in the *Small Press Record of Books in Print* (20th Edition, 1991-92). avg. price, paper: $15. Discounts: normal trade. 220pp; 8½x5½; web of. Reporting time: 6 weeks. Payment: 10% retail cover price after 500 copies. Does not copyright for author. ABA, PMA, COSMEP, SCBP, SDBP, SCBA, SDBA.

SteelDragon Press, Will Shetterly, Emma Bull, Box 7253, Minneapolis, MN 55407, 612-721-6076. 1984. Fiction. "Unsolicited manuscripts are submitted at the author's risk, and must include a SASE" avg. press run 1M-5M. Expects 2-4 titles 1991. 4 titles listed in the *Small Press Record of Books in Print* (20th Edition, 1991-92). avg. price, cloth: $17-$20. Discounts: 40% retailers, 50% distributors. 5½x8½, 7x10; of. Reporting time: 3 days to 3 months. Payment: $300-$1,000 advance on 10% royalty. Copyrights for author.

Stemmer House Publishers, Inc., Barbara Holdridge, 2627 Caves Road, Owings Mills, MD 21117. 1975. Fiction, non-fiction. avg. press run 5M. Pub'd 20 titles 1990; expects 15 titles 1991, 15 titles 1992. 13 titles listed in the *Small Press Record of Books in Print* (20th Edition, 1991-92). avg. price, cloth: $10.95-$24.95; paper: $3.50-$14.95. Discounts: 40% for 5 assorted titles or more. 170pp; 6x9, 7x10, 8½x11; of. Reporting time: 8 weeks. Payment: royalty and advance. Copyrights for author. CBC.

Step Ahead Press, A Heartlite Inc. Company, Karen Lohman, 6509 Brecksville Road, PO Box 31360, Cleveland, OH 44131, 216-526-6727. 1986. Non-fiction. "Book length 100+ pgs." Pub'd 2 titles 1990; expects 4 titles 1991, 4 titles 1992. 2 titles listed in the *Small Press Record of Books in Print* (20th Edition, 1991-92). avg. price, cloth: $23.95; paper: $17.95. Quantity discount schedule applies to libraries, bookstores & wholesalers; please inquire. 100+pp; 6x9. Reporting time: 30 days. Payment: 10% computed every 6 months on sales, less returns, discounts & bad sales. Copyrights for author.

Step-Over Toe-Hold Press, George Montgomery, Linda Karlson, PO Box 40, Rosendale, NY 12472, 914-658-8780. 1980. Poetry. "*Step-Over Toe-Hold Press* plans to make major changes in 1987. We plan to go from offset printing to photocopy. We plan to put out one or two anthologies. The first will be by invitation only, the second by open submissions. Our bias is originality" avg. press run 500. Expects 1-2 titles 1991. 2 titles listed in the *Small Press Record of Books in Print* (20th Edition, 1991-92). avg. price, paper: $3.50. 48pp; 5½x8½; of.

Stepping Stone Books, Art Lumbago, 17939 Chatsworth Street, Ste 102, Granada Hills, CA 91344, 818-368-4268. 1990. Non-fiction. "We publish self-help psychology books. Our first book is on memory-training and we are working on a speed reading book. We are also looking for books on right-brain thinking." avg. press run 5M. Expects 3 titles 1991, 4 titles 1992. 1 title listed in the *Small Press Record of Books in Print* (20th Edition, 1991-92). avg. price, cloth: $16.95; paper: $12.95. 180pp; 5½×8½. Copyrights for author. PMA, COSMEP, ABA.

STEREO WORLD, National Stereoscopic Association, John Dennis, Box 14801, Columbus, OH 43214, 614-263-4296. 1974. Articles, photos, criticism, reviews, letters, news items, non-fiction. "Short-to-medium length articles relating to the history of stereoscopic photography, and to current trends in collecting stereo photographs, as well as material on recent progress in the use of 3-D techniques in movies, television, and photography. Recent contributors include Peter Palmquist, Richard C. Ryder, William Brey, and David Starkman." circ. 2.7M. 6/yr. Pub'd 6 issues 1990; expects 6 issues 1991, 6 issues 1992. sub. price: $22; per copy: $3.50; sample: $3.50. Back issues: reduced prices for older issues. Discounts: none. 40-48pp; 8½×11; of. Reporting time: 1 month. Payment: none. Copyrighted, reverts to author. Pub's reviews. §Those relating to the history of photography, collecting photographica, photographic techniques, especially as they relate to stereo. Ads: $95/$55/20¢.

Stereopticon Press, Etta Ruth Weigl, Editor and Publisher, 534 Wahlmont Drive, Webster, NY 14580, 716-671-2342. 1982. Poetry. "Favors the well-made book of poems, with illustration if possible. Usually inspects invited manuscripts only; willing to examine unsolicited work with sufficient SASE for return. Very small output" avg. press run 500. Pub'd 1 title 1990; expects 1 title 1992. 2 titles listed in the *Small Press Record of Books in Print* (20th Edition, 1991-92). avg. price, cloth: $13.95; paper: $8.95. Discounts: the usual. 65-80pp; 6×9; of. Reporting time: 3 months. Payment: varies.

Sterling-Miller, Stuart A. Sandow, President, PO Box 2413, Staunton, VA 24401. 1978. Interviews, music, letters, non-fiction. "Sterling-Miller is a small publishing company specializing in books for the Museum market. We also package book properties for industry promotions and tie ins." avg. press run 5M. Expects 4-5 titles 1991. 1 title listed in the *Small Press Record of Books in Print* (20th Edition, 1991-92). avg. price, other: $14.95 (books on cassette). Discounts: short 25%, 40% to 50 units, 50+ to distributors. Reporting time: 3 weeks. Payment: varies. Copyrights for author. COSMEP.

STEVE CANYON MAGAZINE, Kitchen Sink Press, Peter Poplaski, No. 2 Swamp Road, Princeton, WI 54968, 414-295-6922. 1983. "Dedicated to in-depth study of the career of Milton Caniff, creator of *Terry & The Pirates*, and *Steve Canyon*. Examines also his related work, influences, the times, etc." circ. 5M. 4/yr. Pub'd 4 issues 1990; expects 6 issues 1991, 4 issues 1992. sub. price: $36; per copy: $5.95; sample: $5.95. Back issues: $4.95 + 50¢. Discounts: 40% to stores, 60% to distributors. 68pp; 8½×11; of. Reporting time: 2 weeks. Payment: $100 for average article. Copyrighted. Ads: $110.

THE WALLACE STEVENS JOURNAL, John N. Serio, Clarkson University, Potsdam, NY 13699-5750, 315-268-3987. 1977. Poetry, articles, criticism, reviews, letters, news items. "*The Wallace Stevens Journal* publishes criticism on the poetry of Wallace Stevens. It also publishes archival material, Stevensesque poems, a current bibliography, and book reviews. Recent contributors include: Ihab Hassan, Roy Harvey Pearce, Joseph N. Riddel, Peter Brazeau, Milton Bates." circ. 550. 2/yr. Pub'd 2 issues 1990; expects 2 issues 1991, 2 issues 1992. sub. price: $20 for individuals ($35 2-years), $25 for institutions, $30 for foreign; per copy: $10; sample: free. Back issues: $5 per number. 96pp; 6×9; desktop. Reporting time: 6 weeks. Payment: copies. Copyrighted, reverts to author. Pub's reviews: 5 in 1990. §Wallace Stevens. Ads: $125/$75. Wallace Stevens Society, Inc.

STICKY CARPET DIGEST, Thomas Deja, 38-27 147th Street, Apt. #3, Flushing, NY 11354, 718-463-7756. 1990. Cartoons, interviews, satire, criticism, reviews. "Please query first. We do mostly short video and record reviews of 2-300 words, at least one interview with a film or music celeb (recent interviewees include Paul Bartel and John Doe of X), some satire, and longish articles which look at film personalities, authors, etc. in depth. The writing style is outrageous, humorous and very fast—think of a cross between *Spy, Spin & Tales From the Crypt*. Our 1st consideration is to entertain!" circ. 4-600. 8/yr. Pub'd 8 issues 1990; expects 7 issues 1991, 8 issues 1992. sub. price: $9; per copy: $1; sample: $1. Back issues: $1.25. Discounts: 50% to retail outlets and distributors. 16pp; 8½×11; †laserprinter. Reporting time: within 1 month, query first—no unsolicited! Payment: 1 copy and profit-sharing at year-end. Copyrighted, reverts to author. Pub's reviews: 24 in 1990. §Other media 'zines, horror, sf, mystery books, film and video reference books. Ads: 1/2 page—$20, $25 back cover; 1/4 page—$15, $20 b.c.; business card—$5, $10 b.c.

STIFLED YAWN: A Magazine Of Contemporary Writing, e.g., Marta Deike, Gary Sullivan, 3232 Taraval #7, San Francisco, CA 94116, 415-661-0851. 1990. Poetry, fiction, articles, interviews, satire, criticism, reviews, parts-of-novels, long-poems, plays. "Strong emphasis on esperimental humor. Any length. Recent contributors include Tom Ahern, Mark Leyner, Dodie Bellamy, Kevin Killian, Richard Morris, Stephen-Paul Martin, Bradley Lastname, Spencer Selby" circ. 500. Expects 1 issue 1991, 2 issues 1992. sub. price: $9; per copy: $5.95; sample: $5. Discounts: negotiate. 120pp; 5¼×8½; †laser press. Reporting time: 1-2 months. Payment: 2 copies. Copyrighted, reverts to author. Pub's reviews. §Humor, satire, language, alternative.

COSMEP.

STILETTO, Howling Dog Press, Michael Annis, PO Box 5987, Westport Station, Kansas City, MO 64111. 1989. Poetry, fiction, art, photos, satire, parts-of-novels, long-poems, collages, plays, concrete art. "Recent contributors: Burroughs, Waldman, Codrescu, Leary, DiPrima, DeCormier-Shekerjian, Tavel, Ray, Vando, Bergt, Annis, Jaffe, Antler, Wakoski, DeClue, Heyen, Tarn, Low, Goldbarth. 'If you have a statement to make, make it here...'" circ. 2M. 1/yr. Pub'd 1 issue 1990; expects 1 issue 1991, 1 issue 1992. price per copy: $20; sample: $12.50. Discounts: 30% trade, 20% classroom. 200pp; 5×11¼; †of. Reporting time: up to 1 year. Payment: 20 copies writers (primary), 10 copies artists. Copyrighted, reverts to author.

Still Point Press, Charlotte T. Whaley, Editor, Publisher; Gould Whaley, Jr., Publisher, 4222 Willow Grove Road, Dallas, TX 75220, 214-352-8282. 1984. Fiction, non-fiction. "The Still Point Press has been established to publish books of merit and distinction in small limited editions. We are open to a broad range of subjects in the arts and humanities, particularly in the fields of history, biography, and the book arts. No unsolicited mss." avg. press run 300-500. Expects 1 title 1991, 1 title 1992. 6 titles listed in the *Small Press Record of Books in Print* (20th Edition, 1991-92). avg. price, cloth: $15-$30; other: $50-$200 for limited editions. Discounts: Retail trade: 1-4 copies, 20%; 5-49, 40%; 50-99, 42%; 100-249, 44%; 250+, 46%. Wholesale trade: 1-4 copies, 25%; 5-49, 45%. Discounts negotiable for limited editions. Trade edition 100-250pp, limited edition 50-100pp; 6×9, varies for limited editions; lp, of, photocomposition. Payment: negotiable. Copyrights for author. BPT, SWBA (Southwestern Booksellers Assoc.), TSHA (Texas State Historical Assoc.), TFS (Texas Folklore Society).

Still Waters Press, Shirley Warren, Editor, 112 W. Duerer Street, Galloway, NJ 08201, 609-652-1790. 1989. Poetry, fiction, non-fiction. "Chapbooks of poetry, short fiction, the essay. Dedicated to the discovery and cultivation of significant works by or about women. No lesbian themes. Some books on poetic craft, especially as practiced by women, are planned." avg. press run 300. Pub'd 5 titles 1990; expects 5 titles 1991, 5 titles 1992. 14 titles listed in the *Small Press Record of Books in Print* (20th Edition, 1991-92). avg. price, paper: $4.95. Discounts: 1-5 copies 20%, 6-10 30%, 11+ 40%—dealers only. 24-48pp; 5½×8½; of. Reporting time: 1 month, no report if SASE is not included with submission/correspondence. Payment: 10% of press run, discounts to author on additional copies, 10% of net profits, if any. Copyrights for author. COSMEP.

Stillpoint Publishing (see also TIMBERLINE/VISION ONE), Dorothy Z. Seymour, Editor, Box 640, Walpole, NH 03608, 603-756-9281. 1983. "Recent contributors: Carolyn M. Myss, C. Norman Shealy, Barry K. Weinhold, Janae B. Weinhold, Jerry Lynch, Dan Millman, Ramon Stevens, John Robbins, Naomi Stephan, Liah Kraft-Macoy. Book format, nonfiction publishing in the field of self-awareness and human consciousness." avg. press run 5M-15M. Expects 10 titles 1991, 10-15 titles 1992. 22 titles listed in the *Small Press Record of Books in Print* (20th Edition, 1991-92). avg. price, cloth: $15.95; paper: $9.95. Discounts: per Publishers' Group West, California. 275pp (adult); 5½×8¼. Reporting time: 4 weeks. Payment: varies. Copyrights for author.

THE STONE, Rich Jorgensen, c/o Greenpeace, 1112-B Ocean, Santa Cruz, CA 95060, 408-429-9988. 1967. Poetry, fiction, art, photos, cartoons. "Not currently accepting submissions. Mostly we publish poetry of the body's land, love. The Stone is elemental." circ. 500. Irregular. Pub'd 1 issue 1990; expects 1 issue 1992. sub. price: $5; per copy: $5; sample: $1. Back issues: $1 if avail. Discounts: 40% to the trade. 64pp; 5½×8½; of. Reporting time: 1-2 months. Payment: 2 contributor copies. Copyrighted.

Stone and Scott, Publishers, PO Box 56419, Sherman Oaks, CA 91413-1419, 818-904-9088. 1990. "We are over-committed for foreseeable future and are not seeking submissions." avg. press run 1M. Pub'd 1 title 1990; expects 3 titles 1991. 3 titles listed in the *Small Press Record of Books in Print* (20th Edition, 1991-92). avg. price, cloth: $20; paper: $10. 100pp; 6×9. PMA.

Stone Bridge Press, Peter Goodman, Publisher, PO Box 8208, Berkeley, CA 94707. 1989. Fiction, non-fiction. "Interested in material on Japan and Japanese culture: 1) Language—classroom texts and self-study, especially intermediate level. 2) Japanese fiction in translation—novels and short story collections, fine literature primarily, but will consider mysteries and science fiction. 3) Design—especially gardens and architecture. 4) Current affairs and business. Do *not* want cliched treatments of Japan, *haiku* diaries, or books based entirely on second sources and outdated studies/translations. Wish to present contemporary portrait of Japan of use to people who need to interact or deal with Japan." avg. press run 3M. Expects 3 titles 1992. 2 titles listed in the *Small Press Record of Books in Print* (20th Edition, 1991-92). avg. price, paper: $12.95. Discounts: available through distributor. †of. Reporting time: 1-2 months, 2 weeks if proposal only. Payment: advance vs. royalties. Copyrights for author. COSMEP, Marin Self-Publishers (Box 309, Mill Valley, CA 94942).

Stone Circle Press, Ken Ruffner, Barbara Donley, E. Randall Keeney, Len Irving, PO Box 44, Oakland, CA 94604, 415-658-1135; 893-2972. 1987. Poetry, fiction, art, non-fiction. "We are interested in material of Celtic history, general culture and mythology contemporary and ancient." avg. press run 1M. Pub'd 2 titles 1990; expects 1 title 1991, 1 title 1992. 4 titles listed in the *Small Press Record of Books in Print* (20th Edition, 1991-92). avg. price, paper: $8.50. Discounts: 60/40 stores, 50/50 distributor, trade practice. 94pp; 8½×5½; of.

Reporting time: 60 days. Payment: none, non-profit press. Copyrights for author.

STONE DRUM: An International Magazine of the Arts, Stone Drum Press, Joseph Colin Murphey, Poetry, Managing Editor; Dwight Fullingim, Fiction Editor, 3003 Riercrest Drive, Austin, TX 78746. 1972. Poetry, fiction, articles, art, photos, interviews, reviews, music. "Poems: 15-20 lines. Fiction: 4,000 words and under. Articles (no criticism) on the arts: limit 3,000 words. Reviews: 1,500-2,000 words. Graphics—as art—not illustrations. Recent contributors: Robert Bly, William Stafford, Richard Laubly, Earl Birney, William Barney, William Matthews, Jack Myers, David Ray, Sonia Sanchez, Vassar Miller, Judson Crews, Walter McDonald, Naomi Shihab-Nye. ISSN 1046-6475. Reading Period, September 1 to November 30; please do not submit at other times" circ. 500-1M. 1-2/yr. Pub'd 1 issue 1990; expects 2 issues 1991, 1 issue 1992. sub. price: 2 years $12; per copy: $7. Back issues: few available: #1-#3 (72,73,74) all 3 at $75, #3-#6 $7 each. Discounts: 60/40, 40% to bookstores, agents, jobbers. 85pp; 6×9; of. Reporting time: 3 weeks. Payment: copies only. Copyrighted, reverts to author. Pub's reviews: 3 in 1990. §Poetry, novels ("fine writing" so called). I'm not interested in "NY market" Ads: $100/$50/will support some lit mags free.

Stone Drum Press (see also STONE DRUM: An International Magazine of the Arts), PO Box 233, Valley View, TX 76240. 1972. Poetry. "Do not publish more than one or two per year. We are not looking for unsolicited material at this time" avg. press run 500. Pub'd 2 titles 1990. 2 titles listed in the *Small Press Record of Books in Print* (20th Edition, 1991-92). avg. price, paper: $7. Discounts: Bookstores: 60/40%. 60pp; 6×9; of. Payment: so far cost of printing comes first, after that by arrangement. Copyrights for author.

Graham Stone, Graham Stone, GPO Box 4440, Sydney 2001, Australia, 02-3009879. 1989. Fiction, criticism, non-fiction. "Initial program mainly reprints of old Australian science fiction works. Present plans will take several years. No submissions wanted yet. Production is by good quality photocopier, bound by hand in traditional cloth hard covers. First two are short items that might be called chapbooks. I am compiling a comprehensive bibliography of Australian science fiction for eventual publication, and collecting my numerous book reviews and historical notes on this field. But most books will be reprints of old books and magazine items by Australian authors." avg. press run 100. Expects 2 titles 1991. 2 titles listed in the *Small Press Record of Books in Print* (20th Edition, 1991-92). avg. price, cloth: $12. Discounts: 50%. 40pp; †photocopy. Payment: half share of proceeds. Copyrights for author.

Stone Man Press, Alan Brooks, Box 3010, RFD 1, Lubec, ME 04652, 207-733-2194. 1983. Poetry. avg. press run 500. Pub'd 1 title 1990; expects 1 title 1992. 6 titles listed in the *Small Press Record of Books in Print* (20th Edition, 1991-92). avg. price, paper: $4-$7. Discounts: 30-40% to booksellers, libraries. 20-50pp; 5½×8½; photo, of. Reporting time: 8 weeks. Payment: negotiable. Copyrights for author negotiable.

Stone Press (see also HAPPINESS HOLDING TANK), Albert Drake, 9727 SE Reedway Street, Portland, OR 97266-3738. 1968. Poetry. "Small books and pamphlets. Published Peter Nye, Judith Root, Barbara Drake, and Judith Goren: recent chapbooks are *Beer Garden*, Lee Upton, and *Returning To Blind Lake On Sunday*, Jim Kalmbach, book, Earle Birney's *The Mammoth Corridors*. Also publish posters: Richard Kostelanetz, Harley Elliott, William Stafford, Earle Birney, Anselm Hollo, etc. Six posters for $3. Poetry Pack ($5) includes 2 issues of the magazine, 2 chapbooks, pamphlet, 3 posters, postcards, etc." avg. press run 300-500. Pub'd 1 title 1990; expects 1 title 1992. 18 titles listed in the *Small Press Record of Books in Print* (20th Edition, 1991-92). avg. price, paper: $1. Discounts: 25%. 16-20pp; 8½×5½, 8½×7; of. Reporting time: 1-3 weeks. Copyrights for author.

STONE SOUP, The Magazine By Children, Gerry Mandel, William Rubel, Box 83, Santa Cruz, CA 95063, 408-426-5557. 1973. Poetry, fiction, art, photos, reviews, letters, parts-of-novels, long-poems, plays. "All material written & drawn by children 3-13." circ. 12M. 5/yr. Pub'd 5 issues 1990; expects 5 issues 1991. sub. price: $23; per copy: $4.75; sample: $4.75. Back issues: prices upon request. Discounts: schedule available upon request. 48pp; 6×8¾; of. Reporting time: 4 weeks. Payment: 2 copies plus $10. Copyrighted, does not revert to author. Pub's reviews: 10 in 1990. §Children's books. Ads: rates available upon request. Edpress.

STONE TALK, Toad Hiway Press, Doug Martin, Editor-in-Chief; Kevin Anderson, Assistant Editor; John Colvin, Assistant Editor; Brian Beatty, Assistant Editor, Box 44, Universal, IN 47884, 317-832-8918. Poetry, fiction, interviews, music, long-poems. "We would like to receive demo-tapes from musicians so as to release a cassette-series of alternative rock, country, jazz, and blues for our *Stone Talk* cassette series, which consists of recorded poetry, music, artistic noise" circ. 50. Pub'd 1 issue 1990; expects 1 issue 1991, 1 issue 1992. price per copy: $3. †basic cassette dubbing. Reporting time: 3 months. Payment: 1 free tape.

Stone Wall Press, Inc, Henry C. Wheelwright, 1241 30th Street NW, Washington, DC 20007, 202-333-1860. 1972. Non-fiction. "Non-fiction—Frontier or second tier national outdoor recreational material with photos or illustrations. Optimally combining pragmatic material with adventure, humor, and overriding sense of ecology. Environmental issues; endangered plants, animals, etc.. Distributed by Charles Tuttle Co., Box 410, Rutland, VT 05701. Telephone 1-800-526-2778." avg. press run 3M-4M. Pub'd 1 1990; expects 6 titles 1991, 3 titles 1992. 17 titles listed in the *Small Press Record of Books in Print* (20th Edition, 1991-92). avg. price, cloth:

556

$24.95; paper: $12.95. Discounts: standard. 240pp; 6×9; of. Reporting time: 2 weeks. Payment: tba. Copyrights for author. Washington Book Publishers Assoc.

Stonehouse Publications, Lewis Watson, Sharon Watson, Timber Butte Road, Box 390, Sweet, ID 83670, 208-584-3344. 1974. Photos. avg. press run 10M. Expects 1 title 1992. 1 title listed in the *Small Press Record of Books in Print* (20th Edition, 1991-92). avg. price, paper: $8.95. Discounts: trade 40% any quantity, fully refundable; mail order 46%, jobber & bulk 50%; library 40%. 100pp; 8½×11; of.

Stony Hills Productions (see also SMALL PRESS NEWS), Diane Kruchkow, Weeks Mills, New Sharon, ME 04955. 2 titles listed in the *Small Press Record of Books in Print* (20th Edition, 1991-92).

Stop Light Press, Gerry LaFemina, April Lindner, PO Box 970, Bronxville, NY 10708. 1989. Poetry. "Primarily poetry chapbooks" avg. press run 350. Pub'd 4 titles 1990; expects 3 titles 1991, 3 titles 1992. 7 titles listed in the *Small Press Record of Books in Print* (20th Edition, 1991-92). avg. price, paper: $3.50. 20pp; 5½×9; of. Reporting time: 2 months. Payment: percentage of print run. Copyrights for author.

Storey/Garden Way Publishing, M. John Storey, Publisher; Deborah Burns, Editor; Sarah May Clarkson, Editor; Gwen Steege, Editor; Constance Oxley, Editor, Schoolhouse Road, Pownal, VT 05261, 802-823-5811. 1971. "How-to books for self-sufficient living in the areas of energy conservation, home construction, gardening, food preparation, livestock care and country living, cooking, crafts" avg. press run 10M. Pub'd 15 titles 1990; expects 15 titles 1991, 15 titles 1992. 59 titles listed in the *Small Press Record of Books in Print* (20th Edition, 1991-92). avg. price, cloth: $16.95; paper: $7.95. Discounts: 5 - 40%; 25 - 41%; 50 - 42%; 100 - 43%; 250 - 44%; 500 - 46%; books distributed by Harper & Row, *GWP* books assort with H&R books for discount. 180pp; 8½×11, 6×9, 8×10, 8×7. Reporting time: 2-4 weeks. Payment: flexible. Copyrights for author. ABA.

STORIES, Amy R. Kaufman, PO Box 1467, Arlington, MA 02174-0022. 1982. "Exclusively short stories of enduring value; send s.a.s.e. for guidelines; guidelines must be read before submitting" circ. 5M. 4/yr. Pub'd 4 issues 1990; expects 4 issues 1991, 4 issues 1992. sub. price: $18; per copy: $4, 2 for $7; sample: $4, 2 for $7. Back issues: 2 for $7. Discounts: to be discussed. 44pp; 8½×11. Reporting time: 12 weeks. Payment: $50-$200, upon publication. Copyrighted, reverts to author. Ads: $275/$150.

Stormline Press, Inc., Raymond Bial, Linda LaPuma Bial, PO Box 593, Urbana, IL 61801, 217-328-2665. 1985. Poetry, fiction, art, photos. "Stormline Press publishes works of literary and artistic distinction with preference for work which deals sensitively with rural and small town life. All publications are professionally designed and printed to critical standards. *First Frost*, the debut publication of the press, was a "Writer's Choice" selection. No unsolicited manuscripts. Please query with SASE *during November and December only* for writers guidelines." avg. press run 1.5M. Pub'd 3 titles 1990; expects 3 titles 1991, 3 titles 1992. 6 titles listed in the *Small Press Record of Books in Print* (20th Edition, 1991-92). avg. price, cloth: $17.95; paper: $8.95; other: $14.95 *First Frost* which includes 18 duotones. Discounts: 40% bookstores; 55% jobbers; Bulk discounts to be negotiated. Poetry 40-80pp, fiction 80-200pp; 6×9. Payment: 15% on sale of first 1000 copies after production costs have been recouped. Copyrights for author. Illinois Writers, Inc.

STORY, Lois Rosenthal, Editor; Jack Heffron, Associate Editor, 1507 Dana Avenue, Cincinnati, OH 45207, 513-531-2222. 1989. Fiction, parts-of-novels. "*Story* publishes only fiction—short stories and novel excerpts. We're looking for well-told stories by established writers and by unknowns. Recent contributors include Norman Mailer, Max Apple, Rick Bass, Fred Chappell, E.S. Goldman, Melissa Pritchard, Maxine Chernoff. Minimum: 1,000 words, maximum 8,000 words. Average 3,000-5,000." circ. 30M. 4/yr. Pub'd 4 issues 1990; expects 4 issues 1991, 4 issues 1992. sub. price: $17; per copy: $5; sample: $5 and SASE $2.40 first class. Back issues: same as above. Discounts: 40% off cover, retailers only. 128pp; 6¼×9½; of. Reporting time: within 1 month. Payment: $250. Copyrighted, reverts to author. nonprofit rates: full page 1X $695, 2X $670, 4X $625, 8X $560; 1/2 page: 1X $400, 2X $390, 4X $360, 8X $325. General rates: full 1X $895, 2X $860, 4X $800, 8X $725; 1/2 page: 1X $520, 2X $495, 4X $465, 8X $420. Classified: $2/word 1X, $1.50/word 4X, 15 word minimum. MPA, CLMP.

Story County Books, Theresa Pappas, Co-Editor; Michael Martone, Co-Editor, 155 Winthrop Street #2, Medford, MA 02155. 1984. Fiction. "Story County Books is published in Story County, Iowa. We publish one story chapbooks in formats that vary with each story. We publish cheap chapbooks, and we try to keep the price under $1. Our first book was Michael Wilkerson's *Can This Story Be Saved?* a take-off of the *Ladies Home Journal* piece. We chose a Dell Purse Book format to complement the 'self-improvement' parody of the piece. We are interested in clever stories, regional stories, stories with a voice" avg. press run 500. Pub'd 1 title 1990; expects 1 title 1991, 1 title 1992. 3 titles listed in the *Small Press Record of Books in Print* (20th Edition, 1991-92). avg. price, paper: $1.50. Discounts: 50%. Pages vary; size varies. Reporting time: 1 month. Payment: by arrangement. Copyrights for author.

Story Line Press (see also THE REAPER), Robert McDowell, Mark Jarman, Three Oaks Farm, Brownsville,

OR 97327-9718, 503-466-5352. 1985. Poetry, fiction, criticism, long-poems, plays, non-fiction. avg. press run 2.5M. Pub'd 8 titles 1990; expects 9 titles 1991, 12 titles 1992. 22 titles listed in the *Small Press Record of Books in Print* (20th Edition, 1991-92). avg. price, cloth: $16; paper: $8. Discounts: bookstores 1-5 20%, 5-10 33%, 10+ 40%; 20% to libraries. 140pp; 6×9; of. Payment: standard author's contract. Copyrights for author. CLMP.

STORYQUARTERLY, Anne Brashler, Co-Editor; Diane Williams, Co-Editor, PO Box 1416, Northbrook, IL 60065. 1974. Fiction, art, interviews, satire, letters, parts-of-novels. "*StoryQuarterly* wishes to see great fiction. We publish many writers for the first time." circ. 2M. 2/yr. Pub'd 2 issues 1990; expects 2 issues 1991, 2 issues 1992. sub. price: 4 issues—$12, $14 library & institution, $13 Canada, $16 foreign, $24 air; per copy: $4; sample: $4. Back issues: $4 (SQ). Discounts: 40% bookstores; 20% distributors. 110pp; 5¾×8¾; of. Reporting time: up to 4 months. Payment: 5 copies, occassionally $. Copyrighted. Ads: $150/$100 or lit mag exchange. CCLM, COSMEP, IAC (Ill. Arts Council).

Storytime Ink International, Christine Petrell Kallevig, PO Box 813, Newburgh, IN 47629, 812-853-6797. 1991. "Looking for material that combines storytelling with a tangible art form, i.e. cutting stories, drawing stories, folding stories. Should be less than 1,000 words with an ironic twist at the end. No violence. Should be appropriate for children, but entertaining for adults." avg. press run 5M. Expects 4 titles 1991, 6 titles 1992. 1 title listed in the *Small Press Record of Books in Print* (20th Edition, 1991-92). avg. price, paper: $11.50. Discounts: usual trade. 100pp; 8½×11; of. Reporting time: 1 month. Payment: negotiable. Copyrights for author.

Straight Arrow Publishing, Jerry R. Schwartz, PO Box 1092, Boise, ID 83701-1092. 1984. Fiction, articles, satire, non-fiction. avg. press run 10M. Pub'd 1 title 1990; expects 2 titles 1991, 2 titles 1992. avg. price, paper: $5.95. Discounts: standard (40%+++) (inquire). 172pp; 4¼×7. Reporting time: 6 weeks or less. Payment: to be arranged. Copyrights for author. COSMEP, Northern California Books Publicists Association.

STRAIGHTEDGE, Stan Warshaw, 16 Chaplin Avenue, Rutland, VT 05701.

Stratton Press, Stephen S. Ashley, PO Box 22391, San Francisco, CA 94122, 415-759-5270. 1985. Non-fiction. Expects 1 title 1991, 1 title 1992. 1 title listed in the *Small Press Record of Books in Print* (20th Edition, 1991-92). avg. price, paper: $16. 200pp; 5×8; lp.

Strawberry Hill Press, Joseph Lubow, Carolyn Soto, Mary Burden Castiglione, Anne Ingram, 3848 SE Division St, Portland, OR 97202-1641, 415-664-8112. 1973. Non-fiction. "*NO* poetry or religion. No manuscripts under 300 pages. Primary interests: self-help, biography/autobiography, third world, health & nutrition, cookbooks, inspiration, history. Some fiction—mostly mysteries. Latest titles: *Diary of Courage* by Mary Woodward Priest, *Silent Menace* by Dorothy Senerchia, *Of Rhyme and Reason* by Bernard Spiro, *Dogheaded Death* by Ray Faraday Nelson, and *Jack Oakie's Oakridge* by Victoria Horne Oakie. We look at nothing, and return nothing, that is not accompanied by SASE with *proper* postage. We prefer receiving query letters first." avg. press run 5M. Pub'd 8 titles 1990; expects 12 titles 1991, 12 titles 1992. avg. price, cloth: $16.95; paper: $8.95. 240pp; 6×9. Reporting time: roughly 7 weeks. Payment: 10% of gross; no advances, ever; every 6 months. Copyrights for author.

Strawberry Patchworks, Susan A. McCreary, 11597 Southington Lane, Herndon, VA 22070-2417, 703-709-0751. 1982. Non-fiction. "We specialize in one subject cookbooks, softcover using 4 color process on cover. Emphasis on originality of subject and exploring every aspect of the subject. Poetry, art and history are incorporated throughout books." avg. press run 2M-4M. Pub'd 1 title 1990; expects 1 title 1991, 1 title 1992. 5 titles listed in the *Small Press Record of Books in Print* (20th Edition, 1991-92). avg. price, paper: $4-$6. Discounts: trade 40%, wholesaler 50%. 100-200pp; 6×9; of. Reporting time: 1 month or less. Payment: negotiable, no advances. Copyrights for author.

Strawn Studios Inc., John T. Strawn, 4663 Utah Street, San Diego, CA 92116-3147, 515-224-4760. 1981. Poetry, fiction, art, photos. avg. press run 1M. Pub'd 1 title 1990; expects 3 titles 1991, 6 titles 1992. 1 title listed in the *Small Press Record of Books in Print* (20th Edition, 1991-92). avg. price, paper: $5.95. Discounts: 50%. 75pp; size varies. Reporting time: 20 days. Payment: negotiable. Copyrights for author.

STREAM LINES, MN JOURNAL OF CREATIVE WRITING, Tracy Moral, Managing Editor, 207 Lind Hall, 207 Church Street, SE, Minneapolis, MN 55414, 612-625-6872. 1979. Poetry, fiction, art, photos, interviews, parts-of-novels, long-poems, plays, non-fiction. circ. 1M. 2/yr. Pub'd 1 issue 1990; expects 2 issues 1991, 2 issues 1992. sub. price: $4; per copy: $2.50; sample: $2. Back issues: $1.75. 50pp; 8½×11; of. Reporting time: 3 months. Payment: 3 complimentary copies. Not copyrighted.

Street Press, Graham Everett, Box 772, Sound Beach, NY 11789. 1974. Poetry. avg. press run 500. Pub'd 3 titles 1990; expects 4 titles 1991, 12 titles 1992. 7 titles listed in the *Small Press Record of Books in Print* (20th Edition, 1991-92). avg. price, paper: $3.00. Discounts: 60/40. 48pp; 5½×8½; †of. Reporting time: 3 months. Payment: to be arranged. Copyrights for author. CCLM, COSMEP.

STREET VOICE, Curtis Price, PO Box 22962, Baltimore, MD 21203, 301-332-1207. 1991. Poetry, articles, interviews, news items. "1 page broadsheet distributed directly to addicts and street people every month. Focus on 'barefoot doctor' medical survival tips, resource information, point of view articles and observations/ anecdotes from street corner community. A separate quarterly newsletter format publication is in planning stages for longer articles not appropriate to 1 sheet format." circ. 5M. 12/yr. Expects 12 issues 1991, 12-24 issues 1992. sub. price: $6; per copy: $1; sample: $1. Discounts: write for information. 1 page; 8½×11; xerox. Reporting time: outside submissions not encouraged, will consider on a case-by-case basis. Payment: none. Not copyrighted. Pub's reviews. §Drug/addiction issues, homelessness issues. Ads: none at present.

STRESS MASTER, Conscious Living, Dr. Tim Lowenstein, PO Box 9, Drain, OR 97435. 1976. Articles, music, non-fiction. circ. 320M. 4/yr. Pub'd 2 issues 1990; expects 2 issues 1991, 2 issues 1992. sub. price: $1; per copy: $1; sample: $1. Discounts: on request. 8pp; 17½×11; web-offset. Pub's reviews. §Self-improvement, self-help, health, psychology.

"STRICTLY NOTHING BUT" THE BLUES, Michael Dollins, PO Box 81383, San Diego, CA 92138, 619-222-0577. 1988. Articles, photos, interviews, reviews, music, letters, news items, non-fiction. "We call it *The Blues.* Anything on blues and related music, artists, radio, and record labels." circ. 1M. 12/yr. Pub'd 12 issues 1990; expects 12 issues 1991, 12 issues 1992. sub. price: $10; per copy: $1; sample: $1. Back issues: $1. 12pp; 8½×11; of, photocopy. Payment: subscriptions. Copyrighted, reverts to author. Pub's reviews: 2 in 1990. §Live interviews, historical. Ads: $40/$25/$16 1/4 page/$12 1/8 page. So. California Writers, ASCAP.

Stride Publications, Rupert M. Loydell, 37 Portland Street, Newtown, Exeter, Devon EX1 2EG, England. 1981. Poetry, fiction, art, photos, cartoons, interviews, criticism, reviews, music, parts-of-novels, long-poems, collages, concrete art. "Will *not* select from vast m/s. Expect m/s edited and 'shaped' by author." avg. press run 500. Pub'd 15 titles 1990; expects 18 titles 1991, 17 titles 1992. 31 titles listed in the *Small Press Record of Books in Print* (20th Edition, 1991-92). avg. price, cloth: £12.50; paper: £4.95. Discounts: 35%. 60-100pp; size A5; of. Reporting time: varies, maximum 6 months. Payment: agreed number free copies and trade price for furthur copies. Copyrights for author.

Stripes Publishers, USA, Rick Rahim, PO Box 2109, Falls Church, VA 22042, 703-271-9155. 1986. Articles, art, photos, cartoons, interviews, criticism, reviews, letters, news items, non-fiction. "Anything related to sports officiating" avg. press run 4M. Pub'd 3 titles 1990; expects 4 titles 1991, 5 titles 1992. avg. price, cloth: $20. 80pp; 8½×11; †of. Payment: negotiable. Copyrights for author.

STROKER, Irving Stettner, Editor; Thomas Birchard, Publisher, 129 2nd Ave. No. 3, New York, NY 10003. 1974. Poetry, fiction, articles, art, photos, interviews, collages. "An 'unliterary' literary review looking for beauty, Zen, humor, sincerity, etc. and/or good writing. Print stories, essays, ink drawings, few poems. Unsolicited manuscripts accepted. Already published: Henry Miller, Tommy Trantino, Seymour Krim, Mohammed Mrabet (translated by Paul Bowles) and others known and unknown. Pay in contributor copies; we're a financial failure but the best magazine in America!" circ. 600. 3-4/yr. Pub'd 3 issues 1990; expects 3 issues 1991, 3 issues 1992. 1 title listed in the *Small Press Record of Books in Print* (20th Edition, 1991-92). sub. price: $9 for 3 issues, $16 for 6 issues, $30 for 12 issues; per copy: $3.50; sample: $3.50 (postage included). Back issues: $10. 48pp; 5½×8½; of. Reporting time: 4-6 weeks. Payment: contributor copies. Not copyrighted. §Fiction, art. Ads: $100/$50/$25.

STROKES, Sports Support Syndicate, Mark Rauterkus, 1739 East Carson Street, Pittsburgh, PA 15203, 412-481-2497. 1989. Articles, reviews, non-fiction. "We promote sports reading materials and other media. Aggressive literacy campaign for 90's. Also cooperative efforts to review nd award authors/publishers in many specific specialty areas. Newsrelease reviews of sports titles most valuable." circ. 1M. 12/yr. Expects 4 issues 1991, 12 issues 1992. sub. price: $10; per copy: $2; sample: $2. Back issues: none. Discounts: none, subscription only. 8pp; 8×11; desk-top. Reporting time: 2 weeks. Payment: minimal amount. Not copyrighted. Pub's reviews: 100 in 1990. §Sports, outdoors, nautical, fitness, athletics, health. No ads.

STRUGGLE: A Magazine of Proletarian Revolutionary Literature, Tim Hall, PO Box 13261, Harper Station, Detroit, MI 48213-0261. 1985. Poetry, fiction, articles, art, cartoons, satire, criticism, reviews, music, letters, collages, plays. "We want literature and art of rebellion against the ruling class." 4/yr. Pub'd 4 issues 1990; expects 18 issues 1991, 4 issues 1992. sub. price: $6; per copy: $1; sample: $1.50 via mail. Back issues: by arrangement (vol. 1 available, photocopied at extra charge). Discounts: by arrangement. 36pp; 5½×8½; photo-offset. Reporting time: 3 months maximum; generally shorter, usually critique (time permitting). Payment: 2 copies. Not copyrighted. Pub's reviews: 0 in 1990. §Social protest poetry, fiction, drama, movies, TV, music, Marxist or anti-establishment literary criticism. No ads.

STUDENT LAWYER, Sarah Hoban, Editor; Miriam Krasno, Managing Editor, American Bar Association Press, 750 N. Lake Shore Drive, Chicago, IL 60611. 1972. Articles. "*Student Lawyer* is a monthly legal affairs magazine circulated to members of the ABA's Law Student Division. It is not a legal journal. It is a features magazine, competing for a share of law students' limited spare time, so the articles we publish must be informative, lively "good reads". We have no interest whatsoever in anything that resembles a footnoted, academic article. *Student Lawyer* has 4 feature articles in each issue, ranging from 2,500 to 4,000 words apiece. We also have 5 to 6 departments , 1200-1800 word articles covering innovative legal programs, commentary, and brief law school and legal world news items. Writers should write according to the amount of their material and not beyond. We are interested in professional and legal education issues, sociolegal phenomena, legal career features, profiles of lawyers who are making an impact on the profession, and the (very) occasional piece of fiction. We do not accept poetry." circ. 35M. 9/yr. Pub'd 9 issues 1990; expects 9 issues 1991, 9 issues 1992. sub. price: $19; per copy: $2 + $1 handling; sample: same. Discounts: included in membership to ABA's Law Student Division. 56pp; 8⅜×10⅞; of, web. Reporting time: 4 weeks. Payment: varies—$100 to $700. Copyrighted, reverts to author. Ads: $1,340/$810/$22.50 first 20 words, $1/word thereafter. BPA.

STUDENT LEADERSHIP JOURNAL, Jeff Yourison, Editor, PO Box 7895, Madison, WI 53707-7895, 608-274-4823 X425, 413. 1940. Poetry, articles, photos, cartoons, reviews. "For college students: A Christian approach to the needs and issues leaders face. Articles should be aimed at evangelical student leaders of college age." circ. 8M. 4/yr. Pub'd 4 issues 1990; expects 4 issues 1991, 4 issues 1992. sub. price: $12.50; per copy: $3; sample: $3. Discounts: none. 28pp; 8½×11. Reporting time: 3 months. Payment: $35-$100. Copyrighted, reverts to author. Pub's reviews: 4 in 1990. §Books on spiritual growth or other areas of interest to college students. Ads: none. InterVarsity Christian Fellowship.

Student Media Corporation (see also COLORADO NORTH REVIEW), L. Christopher Baxter, Editor, University Center, University of Northern Colorado, Greeley, CO 80639. 1964. Poetry, fiction, art, photos, plays. "On written request of author, copyright is assigned. Poetry, art, and fiction up to 20 pages." avg. press run 2.5M. Pub'd 2 titles 1990; expects 2 titles 1991, 2 titles 1992. avg. price, paper: $3.50; other: $2.50. Discounts: none. 120-180pp; 6×9; of. Reporting time: 4-8 weeks. Payment: copies. Copyrights for author on request. COSMEP, CLMP.

STUDIA CELTICA, University Of Wales Press, J.E. Caerwyn Williams, University of Wales Press, 6 Gwennyth St., Cathays, Cardiff CF2 4YD, Wales, Cardiff 231919. 1966. Articles. "Devoted mainly to philological and linguistic studies of the Celtic languages." circ. 300. 1 double volume every 2 years. sub. price: £20 per double volume; per copy: £20; sample: £20. Back issues: £10 per double issue. Discounts: 10%. 350pp; 9½×6; of. Payment: none. Pub's reviews: 9 in 1990. §Celtic. No ads. UWP.

Studia Hispanica Editors, Luis A. Ramos-Garcia, Dave Oliphant, Carol E. Klee, Luis Fernando Vidal, Attn: Luis Ramos-Garcia, 5626 W. Bavarian Pass, Fridley, MN 55432, 612-574-9460. 1978. Poetry, fiction, art, photos, criticism, letters. "Studia Hispanica Editors, along with Prickly Pear Press, has just published *From The Threshold/Desde el umbral*, Contemporary Peruvian fiction in translation. It is a bilingual edition featuring writers who wrote their works during the 1978-1985 period. The second edition of *Studia Hispanica I: Latin American & Spanish Literary Articles* (with an introduction of the Spanish poet Jorge Guillen and Juan Goytisolo) in honour of Rodolfo Cardona is available now. Forthcoming: *Bilingual Anthology of Contemporary Spanish Poetry: Circa 1970-1988*, edited and translated by Luis A. Ramos-Garcia and Dave Oliphant, and *Embers of Meaning/Pavesas de Sentido*, contemporary bilingual poetry from Spain by Jenaro Talens, edited by Luis Ramos-Garcia and Giulia Colaizzi, translated by G. Colaizzi." avg. press run 1M. Pub'd 1 title 1990; expects 1 title 1991, 2 titles 1992. 10 titles listed in the *Small Press Record of Books in Print* (20th Edition, 1991-92). avg. price, cloth: $25; paper: $9.95. Discounts: 20%-40%. 200pp; 8×5½; of, lp. Reporting time: 3 months. Payment: none. Does not copyright for author. Prickly Pear Press.

STUDIA MYSTICA, Mary E. Giles, Editor; Kathryn Hohlwein, Art & Poetry Editor, Calif. State Univ., 6000 J Street, Sacramento, CA 95819. 1978. Poetry, fiction, articles, art, photos, interviews, reviews, music, letters, parts-of-novels, long-poems, collages, plays, concrete art. "Primary focus is interrelationship of arts and mystical experience. Interdisciplinary and descriptive in approach. We do *not* welcome speculative theology." circ. 450. 4/yr. Expects 4 issues 1991, 4 issues 1992. 1 title listed in the *Small Press Record of Books in Print* (20th Edition, 1991-92). sub. price: $14 individual, $20 institution; per copy: $4.00; sample: free. Back issues: Vol. I, II, III $3.50 per issue. Discounts: can be arranged with agents. 80pp; 5½×8½; †of. Reporting time: 3 weeks. Payment: irregular, some payment available for fiction and graphics. Copyrighted. Pub's reviews: 12-16 in 1990. §Mysticism, arts and religion. Ads: $150/$80.

STUDIO - A Journal of Christians Writing, Paul Grover, Robert Leighton-Jones, Louise Potter, Dimity Fifer, Kate Lumley, 727 Peel Street, Albury, N.S.W. 2640, Australia. 1980. Poetry, fiction, articles, reviews, letters. "Published poets by reputable Australian publishing houses have been represented. Material varies from short poems to short stories of 2M to 5M words." circ. 300. 4/yr. Pub'd 4 issues 1990; expects 4 issues 1991, 4 issues 1992. sub. price: $AUD39; per copy: $AUD6; sample: $AUD6 (air mail). No back issues available. Discounts: order of 20 or more in advance of printing receives 10%. 32pp; 14.5×21cm; lp. Reporting time: 3 months. Payment: for contests $AUD75, no payment for ordinary submissions but free copy posted for submissions. Copyrighted, reverts to author. Pub's reviews: 30 in 1990. §Christian poetry, fiction. No ads permitted.

Studio 403 (see also SIGN OF THE TIMES-A CHRONICLE OF DECADENCE IN THE ATOMIC AGE), 3819 NE 15th, Portland, OR 97212, 206-323-6764. 1981. Fiction, art, photos, cartoons, satire, collages. avg. press run 750. Expects 2 titles 1992. 8×10; of. Reporting time: 6 weeks.

STUDIO NORTH, Daniel Buckley, 78 Fox Run, Barrie, Ontario L4N 5A8, Canada, 705-734-0682. 1988. Articles, art, photos, interviews, reviews, letters, news items, non-fiction. *"Studio North* is a magazine dedicated to taxidermy, carving and other wildlife arts. Emphasis is placed on instructional/educational/how-to articles on these and related subjects. Articles on nature, wildlife, wildlife conservation/legislation, book and seminar reviews and photo-essays of wildlife art, artists and shows/exhibitions are also welcome." circ. 250+. 4/yr. Pub'd 4 issues 1990; expects 4 issues 1991, 4 issues 1992. sub. price: $28 Cdn.; per copy: $7; sample: $4. Discounts: negotiable. 40pp; 8½×11; †of. Reporting time: 6 weeks. Payment: none at present, anticipated in future. Copyrighted, reverts to author. Pub's reviews: 4 in 1990. §Taxidermy, wildlife carving and art, nature, hunting, fishing, and related. Ads: $365/$255/$140 1/4 page/all Canadian $.

STUDIO ONE, Heather Fredrics, Timothy Fehl, College of St. Benedict, St. Joseph, MN 56374. 1976. Poetry, fiction, art, photos, satire, long-poems. "Short fiction should generally be fewer than 5,000 words. *Studio One* accepts submissions of literary and visual art from across the nation, but contributors from the Midwest are especially encouraged to submit. Art should reproduce well in black and white." circ. 900. 1/yr. Pub'd 1 issue 1990; expects 1 issue 1991, 1 issue 1992. sub. price: free, availability is extremely limited; all contributors receive one complimentary copy, all others are asked to send enough postage. 70-100pp; 7½×10; of. Reporting time: we try to send out acceptance/rejection letters within 1 month of the deadline. Payment: 1 copy. Copyrighted, reverts to author.

STYLUS, Michael Olson, PO Box 1716, Portland, OR 97207. 1989. Articles, interviews, criticism, reviews. circ. 2M. 6/yr. Expects 6 issues 1991, 6 issues 1992. sub. price: $5; sample: free. Back issues: $2. Discounts: none. 4pp; 17×11; †of. Reporting time: 2 weeks. Payment: none. Copyrighted, reverts to author. Pub's reviews. Ads: $30 for 4 column inches, good for 2 issues.

SUARA SAM, Sahabat Alam Malaysia (Friends of the Earth Malaysia), 43 Salween Road, 10050 Penang, Malaysia, 04-376930, 375705. 1981. "The official SAM newsletter. It contains up-to-date reporting on environment and development issues over the past two months. The articles are very accurate, detailed and informative since it is taken from indepth research, field survey, and interviews" circ. 1.5M. 6/yr. Pub'd 6 issues 1990; expects 6 issues 1991, 6 issues 1992. sub. price: US $25/airmail or US $18/seamail; per copy: US$3; sample: same. Back issues: US$2. Discounts: negotiable-about 20%. 16pp; 10½×15½; of. Reporting time: 2 months. Payment: none, as we are a non-profit group. Not copyrighted. Pub's reviews: 20 in 1990. §Community issues, agriculture, multinationals, workers issues, wildlife, forestry, conservation, energy, toxic chemicals and general environment issues. Ads: free. Friends Of The Earth International, PO Box 17170, 1001 JD Amsterdam, Holland.

SUB ROSA, Noemie Maxwell, Nico Vassilakis, 454 37th Street (Basement), Brooklyn, NY 11232. 1985. Poetry, fiction, art, photos, cartoons, interviews, collages, plays, non-fiction. "No restrictions on length. Looking for experiments with words. Recent contributors include: Archibald Henderson, Alan Atkinson, Juanita Tobin, Duane Locke, James Grabill" circ. 150+. 9/yr. Pub'd 9 issues 1990; expects 9 issues 1991, 9 issues 1992. 4 titles listed in the *Small Press Record of Books in Print* (20th Edition, 1991-92). sub. price: $15; per copy: $2; sample: $2. Back issues: $1 or anything that can be contributed. Discounts: taken on a case by case basis. 26-36pp; 5½×8½ (sometimes varies); xerox. Reporting time: 1-2 months, sometimes immediate. Payment: 1 copy. Not copyrighted. Ads: $25 considered a contribution. CCLM.

SUB STANDARD, Brian Paisley, PO Box 245, Willoughby, N.S.W. 2068, Australia, 6987071. 1987. Articles, art, cartoons, interviews, satire, criticism, collages. circ. 1M. 2/yr. Pub'd 2 issues 1990; expects 2 issues 1991, 2 issues 1992. price per copy: $2. Discounts: cheaper rates for bulk—variable. 36pp; size A4; †of, photocopy. Reporting time: no submissions. Payment: all material by me. Ads: none.

SUB-TERRAIN, Anvil Press, Brian Kaufman, Managing Editor; Paul Pitre, Poetry Editor; J.L. McCarthy, PO Box 1575, Station A, Vancouver, B.C. V6C 2P7, Canada, 604-876-8710. 1988. Poetry, fiction, photos, satire, criticism, long-poems, plays. circ. 500. 4/yr. Pub'd 2 issues 1990; expects 4 issues 1991, 4 issues 1992. sub. price: $8; per copy: $2; sample: $3 to cover post. Back issues: $3.50. 16-20pp; 7×10. Reporting time: 1-2 months. Payment: in copies, 2-5 depending on article/story/poem length used. Copyrighted, reverts to author. Small Press Action Network (SPAN).

SUBTEXT, Tresy Kilbourne, 1815 North 137th, Seattle, WA 98133, 206-782-4378. 1990. Articles, cartoons, reviews, news items. "Generally progressive newspaper that seeks to counter the U.S.-centered orientation of the major media. Focus is on the Third World" circ. 2M-4M. 26/yr. Pub'd 17 issues 1990; expects 26 issues 1991, 26 issues 1992. sub. price: $20; per copy: $2; sample: free. Back issues: $2 (when available). Discounts: 60/40. 8-12pp; 11×17; of. Reporting time: 2 weeks. Payment: none right now, except photos ($15), or cartoons ($15). Not copyrighted. Pub's reviews: 4-5 in 1990. §Fiction and nonfiction dealing with developing countries.

561

THE SUBTLE JOURNAL OF RAW COINAGE, dbqp, Ge(of Huth), editor, 317 Princetown Road, Schenectady, NY 12306-2022. 1987. Poetry, cartoons, collages, concrete art. *"The Subtle Journal of Raw Coinage (SJRC)* is a monthly magazine publishing undefined neologisms in poetic/expressive contexts and formats. Some poetry written *exclusively* with neologisms will be considered for publication. Pwoermds (one-word poems such as Aram Saroyan's 'eyeye') are especially welcome" circ. 50-500. 12/yr. Pub'd 12 issues 1990; expects 12 issues 1991, 12 issues 1992. sub. price: can be any dollar amount—cost (which varies) per issue will be subtracted when mailed; per copy: 50¢-$3; sample: $1. Discounts: none. 5pp; size varies; †photocopy, rubberstamp, mimeograph, handtyping, hectography, handwriting, spirit duplicating, dot-matrix, laser printing. Reporting time: 2 weeks. Payment: at least 2 copies; 1/4 of press run is divided among contributors. Not copyrighted.

Suburban Wilderness Press (see also POETRY MOTEL), Bud Backen, Patrick Mckinnon, Jennifer Willis-Long, 1619 Jefferson, Duluth, MN 55812. 1984. Poetry, fiction, art, photos, collages. "MLNA—Chapbooks, broadsides" avg. press run 150. Pub'd 20 titles 1990; expects 25 titles 1991, 30 titles 1992. avg. price, paper: $1-$5. Discounts: inquire. Pages vary; of. Reporting time: 1-3 weeks. Payment: various. Copyrights for author.

SUBWAY, Crystal Waters, PO Box 2001, New York, NY 10009. 1986. Poetry, fiction, articles, art, photos, cartoons, interviews, satire, criticism, reviews, music, letters, parts-of-novels, long-poems, collages, plays, concrete art, news items, non-fiction. *"subway* is a comprehensive literary visual, and performing arts portfolio and information exchange publication. The idea for *subway* originated with the realization of a definite need for a new magazine willing to publish works by, for, and about new artists. *subway* encourages innovation, diversity, and FREEDOM of EXPRESSION. We are committed to aiding quality artists in gaining publicity, with the hope that they will receive continued interest and support from our readers. A potential audience needs to know what's out there before they can want it. That's why *subway* is so diversified. We don't expect to "please all of the people all of the time"; our aim is to help connect the artist with their prospective audience—and perhaps along the way we will help to open eyes, ears, and minds to appreciate all forms of art" circ. 500-1M. 6-12/yr. Expects 6 issues 1991, 6-12 issues 1992. sub. price: $8/6 issues, $15/12 issues; per copy: $2.00; sample: $1.50; reviewers and interested distributors—free; also free to other mags if they send me a copy of their magazine in exchange. Back issues: $2.00. Discounts: negotiable; please write. 20pp; 8½×11; of. Reporting time: we only report if requested, send SASE. Payment: free copy, 30% discount on further copies of the issue in which their work appears. Copyrighted, reverts to author. Pub's reviews. §Everything, especially those that help with artists' networking, marketing, how-to, etc. Ads: $160/$80/classified: 10¢/word; $1 minimum; free to those seeking artistic services.

Success Publications, PO Box 4608, McAllen, TX 78502-4608, 512-687-8747. 1987. Non-fiction. Pub'd 1 title 1990; expects 1 title 1991, 1 title 1992. 1 title listed in the *Small Press Record of Books in Print* (20th Edition, 1991-92). avg. price, cloth: $19.95. Discounts: standard. 224pp; 6×9. Payment: varies. Copyrights for author. COSMEP.

Success Publishing, Allan H. Smith, 2812 Bayonne Drive, Palm Beach Gard., FL 33410-1432. 1978. Non-fiction. "How to make money. How to start in business. How to market your product. How to publish. Sewing, craft, business." avg. press run 2M-5M. Pub'd 6 titles 1990; expects 4 titles 1991, 6 titles 1992. 6 titles listed in the *Small Press Record of Books in Print* (20th Edition, 1991-92). avg. price, paper: $15. Discounts: 1-$10, 2-6 25%, 7-15 40%, 16-50 50%, 50-100 53%, library- 25%. 150pp; 8½×11; lp. Reporting time: 90-120 days. Payment: varies. Copyrights for author. NAIP, FPG.

Success Publishing Company, 9250 Greenback Lane, Suite 128, Orangevale, CA 95662. 1 title listed in the *Small Press Record of Books in Print* (20th Edition, 1991-92).

SULFUR, Clayton Eshleman, 210 Washtenaw, Ypsilanti, MI 48197-2526, 313-483-9787. 1981. Poetry, art, photos, interviews, criticism, reviews, long-poems. *"Sulfur* primarily solicited; concerned with explorative poetry & poetics, translations, reviews & essays; also archival materials." circ. 2M. 2/yr. Pub'd 3 issues 1990; expects 2 issues 1991, 2 issues 1992. sub. price: $13 indiv., $19 inst. (add $4 for out of US mailing); per copy: $8; sample: $6. Back issues: $6 each; Nos. 1, 15, 17 & 19 only available with purchase of complete sets (1-28 $240.00). Discounts: institution $19 a year; jobber or agent $15; double & triple for 2 & 3 year sub. 256pp; 6×9; of, lazer type. Reporting time: 2 weeks. Payment: $35. Copyrighted, reverts to author. Pub's reviews: 50 in 1990. §Current poetry, criticism, & translations. Ads: $150/$85. CLMP.

The Sulgrave Press, John S. Moremen, President; John R. Moremen, Secretary-Treasurer, 2005 Longest Avenue], Louisville, KY 40204, 502-459-9713. 1988. Poetry, fiction, non-fiction. "First: *Bo McMillin: Man & Legend*, C. Akers and J. Carter—biography. Second: *In a Yellow Room*, Maureen Morehead—poetry. Third: *The Jack Daniels Old Time Barbecue Cookbook*, V. Staten—cookbook. Fourth: co-publisher of *The Royal Military Academy at Sandhurst.*" avg. press run first book 5M, second book 500, third book 35M, fourth 10M.

Pub'd 2 titles 1990; expects 2 titles 1991. avg. price, cloth: $18.50. Discounts: 30% to trade, 50% to jobbers. 250pp. Payment: various. Copyrights for author.

Summer Stream Press, David Duane Frost, Co-Editor; Nancy E. Sartin, Co-Editor; Rae Jappinen, Production Editor, PO Box 6056, Santa Barbara, CA 93160-6056, 805-962-6540. 1978. Poetry, non-fiction. "This press is now producing and marketing a series of cassette tapes under the general title: Poetic Heritage. #102180 Elinor Wylie/Amy Lowell; #103010 Sara Teadsale/Margaret Widdemer; #103150 Edna St. Vincent Millay; #103290 Emily Dickinson/Lizette Woodworth Reese. 2/4/81 published *Broadsides* by David Duane Frost. Copy price $4.00. 8½ x 11, 22 pages, removable 'broadsides' of poetry. Paper cover, ISBN 0-932460-01-1." avg. press run 1.5M. Expects 1 title 1991, 1 title 1992. 6 titles listed in the *Small Press Record of Books in Print* (20th Edition, 1991-92). avg. price, cloth: $19.95; paper: $14.95; other: $8 (tapes). Discounts: 50% no returns. 200pp; 5½x8½; of. Reporting time: 6 months. Payment: 15% - paid annually January 1st. Copyrights for author.

Summerthought Ltd., Peter Steiner, PO Box 1420, Banff, Alberta T0L0C0, Canada, 762-3919; fax 403-762-4126. 1969. Poetry, photos. avg. press run 10M. Pub'd 2 titles 1990; expects 1 title 1991, 1 title 1992. 12 titles listed in the *Small Press Record of Books in Print* (20th Edition, 1991-92). avg. price, cloth: $14.95; paper: $6.95. Discounts: 40% trade, 20% classroom. 160pp; 6×9; lp. Reporting time: 2 weeks. Payment: 10%-12½% reprint. Copyrights for author. CBA.

THE SUN, A MAGAZINE OF IDEAS, Sy Safransky, 107 North Roberson Street, Chapel Hill, NC 27516, 919-942-5282. 1974. Poetry, fiction, articles, art, photos, cartoons, interviews, satire, criticism, letters, parts-of-novels, long-poems, collages, news items, non-fiction. "Interested in articles on any subject, of any length, that enrich our common space." circ. 15M. 12/yr. Pub'd 12 issues 1990; expects 12 issues 1991, 12 issues 1992. sub. price: $30; per copy: $3; sample: $3. Back issues: $3; complete set $100. Discounts: vary. 40pp; 8½x11; of. Reporting time: 3 months. Payment: copies and complimentary subscription and $100 for essays and stories, $25 for poetry. Copyrighted, reverts to author. Pub's reviews: 3 in 1990. §All areas.

Sun Books (see also THE TOWNSHIPS SUN), Patricia Ball, Editor, Box 28, Lennoxville, Quebec J1M 1Z3, Canada. "Books published only for clients to their specs. They hold all rights etc." 2 titles listed in the *Small Press Record of Books in Print* (20th Edition, 1991-92).

Sun Designs, PO Box 206, Delafield, WI 53018, 414-567-4255. 1979. Photos. "These are books of designs, with some plans, some books have a short history, toy book has children's story" avg. press run 20M. Pub'd 2 titles 1990; expects 1 title 1991, 1 title 1992. 1 title listed in the *Small Press Record of Books in Print* (20th Edition, 1991-92). 96pp; 8½x11; †of. Copyrights for author.

SUN DOG: The Southeast Review, Jamie Granger, 406 Williams Bldg., English Dept., F.S.U., Tallahassee, FL 32306-1036, 904-644-4230. 1979. Poetry, fiction, articles, art, photos, interviews, criticism, reviews, parts-of-novels, long-poems, plays, non-fiction. "We want stories and poems which are well-written, beautifully written, with striking images, incidents, and characters. Send us only your best work. We are interested more in quality than in style or genre. Send complete ms with SASE. Typed, double-spaced, on good bond. Clear photocopies are okay." circ. 2.5M. 2/yr. Pub'd 2 issues 1990; expects 1 issue 1991, 2 issues 1992. sub. price: $8; per copy: $4; sample: $4. Back issues: $4. 93pp; 6×9; of. Reporting time: 6-8 weeks. Payment: copies. Copyrighted, rights revert, but we do ask to be mentioned in later publications. Pub's reviews: 2 in 1990. §First novels, short story collections, poetry collections, anything of literary value. Ads: please write for rates. CLMP.

Sun Eagle Publishing, Dr. James F. Dorobiala, PO Box 33545, Granada Hills, CA 91394, 818-360-2224. 1987. Photos, cartoons, reviews, non-fiction. "We are soliciting manuscripts on health" avg. press run 5M. Expects 2 titles 1991, 1 title 1992. 1 title listed in the *Small Press Record of Books in Print* (20th Edition, 1991-92). avg. price, cloth: $24.95; paper: $9.95; other: $39.95 videotapes, VHS/BETA, $75 VHS pal version. Discounts: 1-4 net, 5-9 30%, 10-24 35%, 25-49 40%, 50-500 45%, 500+ 50%, no returns take an extra 5% per category. 168pp; 8⅜x5⅜; of, web press. Reporting time: 30 days. Payment: negotiable. Copyrights for author. COSMEP, PMA.

Sun Features Inc., Joyce Lain Kennedy, PO Box 368-D, Cardiff, CA 92007, 619-753-3489. 1973. avg. press run 10M. Pub'd 5 titles 1990; expects 3 titles 1991, 2 titles 1992. 7 titles listed in the *Small Press Record of Books in Print* (20th Edition, 1991-92). avg. price, paper: $5.50 prepaid ($4.95 per booklet plus 55¢ p & h). Discounts: available to schools, organizations, libraries and book dealers. 28-48pp; 3¾x8½; of. Payment: open. Copyrights for author.

Sun, Man, Moon Inc., Janice Baylis, Editor, PO Box 5084, Huntington Beach, CA 92615, 213-598-5342. 1976. Non-fiction. "So far I've only printed my own dream materials. Am interested in materials which relate Jungian psychology to other topics such as art, literature, life, etc. Interested in works about symbolism. Non-fiction only." avg. press run 3M. Expects 1 title 1991. 4 titles listed in the *Small Press Record of Books in Print* (20th Edition, 1991-92). avg. price, paper: $10. Discounts: trade 40%; bulk 45%; agent 10%; jobber 10%.

200pp; 5½×8½, 8½×11; of. Reporting time: 2 months. Payment: 12%. Copyrights for author. COSMEP.

Sunburst Press (see also AN SEANRUD), Rudi Holzapfel, Sean Day, 25 Newtown Avenue, Blackrock, Co. Dublin 882575, Ireland. 1974. Poetry, satire, criticism, long-poems. "Anything Ireland/Irish—mildly patriotic bias, mainly R.C., anti-Capitalist, anti-Communist—otherwise no hangups. We're always broke so be prepared to help out a bit unless you're a Dostoevsky. Particularly interested in the Irish poet James Clarence Mangan, and the English Catholic poets Francis Thompson, Coventry Patmore, etc. Also interested in the Catalan painter Mariano Andreu, 1888-1976" avg. press run 600-2M. Pub'd 1 title 1990; expects 1 title 1991, 1 title 1992. 7 titles listed in the *Small Press Record of Books in Print* (20th Edition, 1991-92). avg. price, paper: £5. Discounts: variable. 100-150pp; 8vo; †of, lp. Reporting time: 1 month to 1 year. Payment: royalty can arrange payments for our authors if they wish. Does not copyright for author.

SUNDOG, Gail Rixen, Route 1, Box 57, Chokio, MN 56221, 612-324-7456. 1979. Poetry, art, photos. "Most issues less than 25 pages, some short stories considered. We only read manuscripts in the spring" circ. 125. 1/yr. Pub'd 1 issue 1990; expects 1 issue 1991, 1 issue 1992. price per copy: $3.50; sample: $2 postpaid—back issues only. Back issues: $1.50-$3.25. Discounts: usually 20% for over 10 copies. 25pp; 5½×8½; of. Payment: 2 copies, artists and writers. Not copyrighted.

Sunflower University Press (see also JOURNAL OF THE WEST), Robin Higham, President; Carol A. Williams, Associate Publisher, Director of Marketing, 1531 Yuma, (Box 1009), Manhattan, KS 66502, 913-539-1888. 1977. Satire, reviews. "Aviation, military and Western American history; paper and hardback books." avg. press run 2M. Pub'd 2 titles 1990; expects 4-8 titles 1991, 10-15 titles 1992. 54 titles listed in the *Small Press Record of Books in Print* (20th Edition, 1991-92). avg. price, cloth: $20-$40; paper: $12-$20. Discounts: on a no-returns basis for wholesalers, paperbacks, 1-10 25%, 11-20 30%, 21-50 35%, 51+ 40%. 150pp; 8½×11, 5½×8½, 6×9; †of. Reporting time: 3 months. Copyrights for author.

Sunlight Publishers, Joseph Kent, Poetry Editor, PO Box 640545, San Francisco, CA 94109, 415-776-0372. 1989. Poetry. "Recently published *White Wind,* a collection of poems by Joseph Kent. Some bias toward poetic consciousness of an evolutionary nature and organic poetry in the modernist vein based on experience of the perceiver." avg. press run 700. Expects 2 titles 1991. 1 title listed in the *Small Press Record of Books in Print* (20th Edition, 1991-92). avg. price, paper: $6.95. Discounts: 2-4 30%, 5-100 40%. 64pp; 6×9; of. Reporting time: 1 month. Payment: 10% royalty on all sales, paid twice yearly. Copyrights for author. COSMEP.

SUNSHINE MAGAZINE, Sunshine Press, Peggy Kuethe, Associate Editor; Joyce Burch, Assistant Editor, PO Box 40, Litchfield, IL 62056, 217-324-3425. 1924. Poetry, fiction, letters. "No deviations from this type of material is accepted." circ. 60M. 12/yr. Pub'd 12 issues 1990; expects 12 issues 1991, 12 issues 1992. sub. price: $10; per copy: $1; sample: 50¢. Back issues: varies with cover price. Discounts: authors receive additional copies at half the cover price. 48pp; 5¼×7¼, digest size; of. Reporting time: 6-8 weeks. Payment: $10-$100. Copyrighted, reverts to author. No outside advertising.

Sunshine Press (see also GOOD READING MAGAZINE; ILLINOIS MAGAZINE; SUNSHINE MAGAZINE), Peggy Kuethe, Associate Editor; Joyce Burch, Assistant Editor, PO Box 40, Litchfield, IL 62056, 217-324-3425. 1924. Poetry, fiction, articles, photos, cartoons, letters, non-fiction. "*Illinois* is regional, *Sunshine* is fiction, *Good Reading* is general interest." avg. press run 6M-45M. avg. price, other: 90¢-$2.25. 32-48pp; 8¼×11, 5¼×7¼; of. Reporting time: 6-8 weeks. Payment: varies. Does not copyright for author.

Sunstone Press, James Clois Smith, Jr., President, PO Box 2321, Santa Fe, NM 87504-2321, 505-988-4418; fax 505-988-1025. 1971. Poetry, fiction, art, non-fiction. avg. press run 3M. Pub'd 16 titles 1990; expects 18 titles 1991, 15 titles 1992. 168 titles listed in the *Small Press Record of Books in Print* (20th Edition, 1991-92). avg. price, cloth: $18.95; paper: $8.95; other: $12.95. Discounts: standard. 128pp; 5½×8½, 8½×11; of. Reporting time: 90 days. Payment: royalty only. Copyrights for author. RMPG.

Sunstone Publications, Lori Solensten, RD 4, Box 700A, Cooperstown, NY 13326, 607-547-8207. 1982. Non-fiction. "Currently specialize in cut-and-assemble books with a science/space emphasis. First book published is *Astro-Dome—3-D Map of the Night Sky* (October 1983). Stars glow in the dark on this 20" dome. 24 page Constellation Handbook is included. Also published, *Astro-Dots* children's book. Also New Age titles including *The Essene Book of Days, The Earthstewards Handbook, Warriors of the Heart* and *Essene Engagement Calendar.*" avg. press run 10M. Expects 2 titles 1991. 5 titles listed in the *Small Press Record of Books in Print* (20th Edition, 1991-92). avg. price, paper: $3.95-$12.95. Discounts: varies—up to 55%. 200pp; 8¼×11⅝. Reporting time: 3 months. Payment: varies. Copyrights for author. ABA, DMMA, AAP.

Surrey Press, M. Roccia, 224 Surrey Road, Warminster, PA 18974, 215-675-4569. 1983. Fiction, non-fiction. avg. press run 5M. Expects 1 title 1991, 2 titles 1992. 1 title listed in the *Small Press Record of Books in Print* (20th Edition, 1991-92). Under 266pp; 6×9; †of. Reporting time: 6 weeks. Payment: 10%. Copyrights for author.

Survival News Service (see also BURWOOD JOURNAL), Christopher Nyerges, Box 41834, Los Angeles,

CA 90041, 213-255-9502. 1980. Non-fiction. "Topics: Wild foods, recycling, urban survival, plants, thinking, American Indians, practical applications of spiritual principles." avg. press run 1M. Expects 6 titles 1991, 6 titles 1992. avg. price, paper: $10. Discounts: 40% to dealers, 50% to jobbers (minimum order is set). 30-240pp; 5×8; of. Reporting time: 1 month, however we do *most* of our own material. Payment: TBA. Copyrights for author if applicable.

SURVIVE & WIN, John Williams, Laurie Williams, 2011 Crescent, PO Drawer 537, Alamogordo, NM 88310, 505-434-0234. 1987. Articles, art, photos, cartoons, interviews, reviews, letters, news items, non-fiction. "*Survive & Win* includes computer, communication, electronic, phone, weapon, security, surveillance, energy, financial, medical and legal survival. And how to survive and win *Now* and *The Day After* in urban, suburban, rural and wilderness areas. Chock full of hard-to-find survival info of all kinds. Includes no-holds-barred editorials, articles and columns. We need many more subscribers, feature and column writers, information contributors and advertisers." circ. 10M. 12/yr. Expects 6 issues 1991, 12 issues 1992. sub. price: $29; per copy: $3; sample: same. Back issues: $3. Discounts: 20% off 100+. 4pp; 8½×11; †of. Reporting time: 60 days. Payment: depends upon value of article, $200-$2,000. Copyrighted, does not revert to author. Pub's reviews: 6 in 1990. §Electronic, computer, energy, weapons, security, financial, medical, legal survival. Ads: $250/$150.

Sutherland Publishing, 16956-6 McGregor Boulevard, Fort Myers, FL 33908, 813-466-1626. 1981. Fiction, photos, non-fiction. avg. press run 5M. Pub'd 1 title 1990; expects 1 title 1991, 1 title 1992. 4 titles listed in the *Small Press Record of Books in Print* (20th Edition, 1991-92). avg. price, cloth: $15; paper: $10. Discounts: trade 40%; jobber 50%. 250-300pp; 6×9, 8½×11; †of. Reporting time: 4-6 weeks. Payment: 10-20 author copies and 10% retail. Copyrights for author. NAIP FPG.

Swallow's Tale Press, Joe Taylor, Editor, Route 2, Box 90D, Coatopa, AL 35470. 1983. Poetry, fiction. avg. press run 1M. Pub'd 3 titles 1990; expects 3 titles 1991, 3 titles 1992. 9 titles listed in the *Small Press Record of Books in Print* (20th Edition, 1991-92). avg. price, cloth: $14; paper: $8. Discounts: 20-50%. 88pp; 5½×8½; of. Reporting time: 4 months. Payment: standard. Copyrights for author.

Swamp Press (see also TIGHTROPE), Ed Rayher, 323 Pelham Road, Amherst, MA 01002. 1975. Poetry, fiction, art, photos, parts-of-novels, long-poems, collages. "We make limited edition books which live up to the standards of the fine-crafted poem. We're open to almost anything, as long as it's the best...to last 1,000 years. Recent contributors: Bonnie Gordon, Phil Cox, Robert Bensen." avg. press run 300. Pub'd 2 titles 1990; expects 2 titles 1991, 2 titles 1992. 17 titles listed in the *Small Press Record of Books in Print* (20th Edition, 1991-92). avg. price, cloth: $25; paper: $5. Discounts: dealers and booksellers 40%, continuing collectors 40%, libraries 20%. 36pp; size varies; †lp. Reporting time: 8 weeks. Payment: 10% press run. Does not copyright for author. CCLM, 666 Broadway, NYC 10112; LGNE, PO Box 788, Cambridge, MA 02238; MBS, 6128 St. Andrew's Lane, Richmond, VA 23226.

SWAMP ROOT, Al Masarik, Editor; Jill Andrea, Managing Editor, Box 1098, Route 2, Jacksboro, TN 37757, 615-562-7082. 1987. Poetry, articles, art, photos, interviews, reviews, letters, collages. "Biased toward clarity, brevity, and strong imagery. Contributors include: Naomi Shihab Nye, John Haines, Tina Barr, Vivian Shipley, Bert Meyers, Linda Hasselstrom, Kirk Robertson, Robert Sund, Ann Menebroker." circ. 1M. 3/yr. Pub'd 1 issue 1990; expects 2 issues 1991, 3 issues 1992. sub. price: $12, $15 libraries; per copy: $5; sample: $5. Discounts: usual. 64pp; 6½×8½; of. Reporting time: 1 week to 1 month. Payment: 3 copies of issue, plus a year's subscription. Copyrighted, reverts to author. Pub's reviews. §Poetry. COSMEP, CLMP.

Swan Publishing Company, Sharon Davis, Hal Davidson, 126 Live Oak, Alvin, TX 77511, 713-388-2547. 1987. Non-fiction. "Our first two books have been successful; *How Not To Be Lonely* is approaching 400,000 copies in print in 13 months. *A Guide To Putting Yourself In The Movies* has 10,000 first printing and 25,000 second printing and we anticipate doing an additional 25,000 in the weeks ahead. Our authors work with us to promote their books and we work under an unusual arrangement. We are not a vanity publisher but we sought investors for the authors and worked the arrangements to mutual satisfaction." avg. press run 10M. Pub'd 2 titles 1990; expects 3 titles 1991, 5 titles 1992. 3 titles listed in the *Small Press Record of Books in Print* (20th Edition, 1991-92). avg. price, paper: $9.95. Discounts: 1-10 copies 10%, 11-50 20%, 51-100 25%, 100+ 40-50%. 230pp; 5½×8½; of. Reporting time: 1 month maximum. Payment: 5-10% more with volume sales. Copyrights for author.

Swand Publications, Samuel Wolf, 120 N. Longcross Road, Linthicum Heights, MD 21090, 301-859-3725. 1971. Music, non-fiction. avg. press run 250-500. Expects 1 title 1991, 1 title 1992. 12 titles listed in the *Small Press Record of Books in Print* (20th Edition, 1991-92). avg. price, paper: $5; other: $5-$10 music. Discounts: 40% to dealers plus post plus small surcharge. 55-125pp; 8½×11; of. Payment: 10% after out-of-pocket costs are recovered.

Sweet Forever Publishing, Denise Shumway, Randall Weischedel, PO Box 1000, Eastsound, WA 98245, (206) 376-2809. 1986. Fiction. "We are looking for fiction of an unlimited nature, fiction that lifts the spirit and leaves the reader open to new possibilities for the human spirit, especially in the area of fantasy, science fiction or 'new age'" avg. press run 5M. Pub'd 1 title 1990; expects 2 titles 1991, 2 titles 1992. 1 title listed in the *Small Press Record of Books in Print* (20th Edition, 1991-92). avg. price, cloth: $15.95; paper: $10.95. Discounts: 40% trade. 300pp; 6×9. Reporting time: 3-4 weeks. Payment: no advances, 7-10% royalties. Copyrights for author. NAPRA (New Age Publishing and Retailing Alliance), PO Box 9, Eastsound, WA; PMA, 2401 E. Pacific Hwy #206, Hermosa Beach, CA.

SYBEX Computer Books, Rudolph Langer, Editor-in-Chief, 2021 Challenger Drive, Alameda, CA 94501. 1976. Non-fiction. *"SYBEX* is a press specializing in books about microcomputing for the personal, business and technical fields" Pub'd 80 titles 1990; expects 100 titles 1991, 120 titles 1992. avg. price, paper: $23.95. Discounts: query. 450pp; 7½×9; of. Payment: query. Copyrights for author. AAP.

SYCAMORE REVIEW, Michael Kiser, Department of English, Purdue University, West Lafayette, IN 47907, 317-494-3783. 1988. Poetry, fiction, photos, interviews, non-fiction. *"The Sycamore Review* accepts personal essays (25pp max.), short fiction (30pp max.), translations, and quality poetry in any form (6pp max.). We are a journal devoted to contemporary literature, publishing both traditional and experimental forms. There are no official restrictions as to subject matter. Both American and international authors will be represented" circ. 1M. 2/yr. Pub'd 2 issues 1990; expects 2 issues 1991, 2 issues 1992. sub. price: $9; per copy: $5; sample: $5. Back issues: $5. 100pp; 6×9; of. Reporting time: 4 months maximum. Payment: 2 copies. Copyrighted, reverts to author. Ads: $100/$65.

Sylvan Books, Thomas Duncan, PO Box 101, Maple City, MI 49664-0101, 616-228-6239. 1984. 2 titles listed in the *Small Press Record of Books in Print* (20th Edition, 1991-92).

Symbiosis Books, Rosanne Werges, 8 Midhill Drive, Mill Valley, CA 94941, 415-383-7722. 1985. avg. press run 4M. Pub'd 1 title 1990; expects 1 title 1991. 2 titles listed in the *Small Press Record of Books in Print* (20th Edition, 1991-92). avg. price, paper: $3.95. Discounts: 40% 3-11 books, 42% 12-24 books, 44% 25-49 books, 46% 50-75 books, 48% 76-99 books, 50% 100+ books. 32pp; 8½×11. Reporting time: 3 weeks. Payment: 15%. Copyrights for author. COSMEP.

SYNAESTHESIA, Tim Peeler, Route 3, Box 283, Hickory, NC 28602, (704) 327-9124. 1986. Poetry, fiction, art, photos, cartoons. "Should send inquiries before submitting / accept submissions only in September" circ. 500. 1/yr. Pub'd 1 issue 1990; expects 1 issue 1991, 1 issue 1992. price per copy: $4; sample: $2. 50pp; 8½×11; of. Reporting time: 1-2 months. Payment: none, but give prizes of $100 to top entries. Not copyrighted. No ads.

Synergetic Press Inc., Tango Parrish Snyder, Kathleen Dyhr, PO Box 689, Oracle, AZ 85623, 602-622-0641. 1971. Poetry, fiction, art, cartoons, long-poems, plays, non-fiction. "50-350 pages in length. New and classic works in biospherics, drama, management, fiction, culturology, and poetry" avg. press run 2M. Pub'd 4 titles 1990; expects 3 titles 1991, 3 titles 1992. 17 titles listed in the *Small Press Record of Books in Print* (20th Edition, 1991-92). avg. price, paper: £3.95, $5.95. Discounts: individuals: 5-9 20%, 10-24 40%, 25+ 45% (poetry books 35% max.); bookstores: 1-2 35% + p/h, 3-24 40% post-free, 24-49 45%, 50-99 48%, 100+ 50%. 200pp; 6×9; of. Reporting time: 1-3 months. Payment: 10% authors royalty. Sometimes copyrights for author. Tucson Book Publishing Association.

Synergetics Press (see also CHANGE: The Journal of the Synergetic Society), Art Coulter, 1825 North Lake Shore Drive, Chapel Hill, NC 27514, 919-942-2994. 4 titles listed in the *Small Press Record of Books in Print* (20th Edition, 1991-92). †of. Does not copyright for author.

Synergistic Press, Bud Johns, 3965 Sacramento St., San Francisco, CA 94118, 415-EV7-8180. 1968. Articles, art, letters, non-fiction. "Our non-fiction interests are wide ranging, which is best shown four titles in print: *My ABC Book of Cancer,* written and illustrated by a 10-year-old cancer patient with supplemental text about her and childhood cancer; *What Is This Madness?,* the story of a new sport's invention and its early years; *Last Look At The Old Met,* a personal portrait in drawings and text of the old Metropolitan Opera House, *Not a Station But a Place,* an art and text portrait of the Gare de Lyon in Paris and *Bastard In The Ragged Suit,* the published work of a leading protetarian writer of the '20s and '30s, with selections from manuscript fragments and drawings during the last two decades of his life when he didn't submit his work for publication, plus a biographical introduction. To date all of our titles have been developed internally and that will probably be true of a majority of our titles in the immediate future. Average $7.50 (high $12.50, low $2.50)." avg. press run 3M-5M. Expects 1 title 1991, 2 titles 1992. 10 titles listed in the *Small Press Record of Books in Print* (20th Edition, 1991-92). avg. price, cloth: $8.50; paper: $5. Discounts: trade: single copies, 20%; 2-5, 35%, 6-11, 37%; 12-49, 40%, 50 or more, 47%; wholesaler/jobber discounts upon request. Pages vary, have published from 52-216pp; of. Reporting time: 1 month. Payment: varies with title. Copyrights for author.

Synerjy (see also SYNERJY: A Directory of Renewable Energy), Jeff Twine, PO Box 1854/Cathedral Station, Cathedral Station, New York, NY 10025, 212-865-9595. 1974. "Bibliography directory of solar, wind, wood, energy, etc. Publications, products, facilities." avg. press run 400. Pub'd 2 titles 1990; expects 2 titles 1991. avg. price, paper: $30. Discounts: $50 for 1 yr subscription (institutions); $20 for 1 yr individuals. 70pp;

566

8½×11; of.

SYNERJY: A Directory of Renewable Energy, Synerjy, Jeff Twine, Box 1854/Cathedral Station, New York, NY 10025, 212-865-9595. 1974. "Bibliographic directory of solar, wind, wood, water, energy; heat transfer & storage of energy. Publications, products, facilities. July issues are yearly cumulations." circ. 400. 2/yr. Pub'd 2 issues 1990; expects 2 issues 1991, 2 issues 1992. sub. price: $50 institution, $20 individual; per copy: $25 winter issue; $35 summer cumulation. Back issues: $90 for 10 cumulative back issues. Discounts: $45/yr for standing order. 70pp; 8½×11; of. Copyrighted, reverts to author.

Synesis Press, Juliana Panchura, Editor-in-Chief, PO Box 1843-N, Bend, OR 97709, 503-382-6517, fax 503-382-0750. 1989. Articles, art, cartoons, interviews, reviews, letters, news items, non-fiction. Pub'd 1 title 1990; expects 6 titles 1991, 6 titles 1992. 1 title listed in the *Small Press Record of Books in Print* (20th Edition, 1991-92). avg. price, paper: $15. Discounts: trade 40%. 250pp; 6×9. Reporting time: 3 weeks. Payment: negotiable. Copyrights for author.

Synthetix, Catherine Jarett, PO Box 1080, Berkeley, CA 94701, 415-428-9009. 1982. Non-fiction. "Specialize in material on Hewlett-Packard calculators, including Series 10, all models of the HP-41, and the new HP-42" avg. press run 4M. Pub'd 1 title 1990; expects 2 titles 1991, 2 titles 1992. 10 titles listed in the *Small Press Record of Books in Print* (20th Edition, 1991-92). avg. price, paper: $17. Discounts: 30-40% to dealers. 200pp; 5⅝×8⅜. Reporting time: 6 weeks. Payment: 5-15% depending on length, quality, and marketability. Copyrights for author. PASCAL.

Syracuse Cultural Workers, Dik Cool, Director, PO Box 6367, Syracuse, NY 13217, 315-474-1132. 1982. Art, photos, cartoons, collages. "SCW publishes the annual Peace Calendar, posters, notecards, and postcards. We are primarily a visual arts publisher and distributor. Our images, in general, relate to peace and social justice, personal or social liberation and feminism. We distribute posters for 110 small publishers; sell wholesale and by direct mail" avg. press run 20M. Pub'd 3 titles 1990; expects 5 titles 1991, 6 titles 1992. avg. price, paper: $10.95 Peace Calendar; other: $6-$40. Discounts: 40% Bookpeople, Inland, New Leaf national distributors, etc. for calendar. 28pp; 14×11; of, silkscreen. Reporting time: 3-6 months. Payment: 4% of list price, one time calendar payment $100, cover $250. Does not copyright for author.

Syracuse Peace Council (see also THE PEACE NEWSLETTER), JoAnn Stak, Coordinator, 924 Burnet Avenue, Syracuse, NY 13203, 315-472-5478. 1936. Poetry, articles, art, photos, cartoons, interviews, satire, criticism, reviews, music, letters, collages, news items, non-fiction. avg. press run 5M. 3 titles listed in the *Small Press Record of Books in Print* (20th Edition, 1991-92). Discounts: standard 33-50% on most. of. Does not copyright for author.

Syzygy, Albert G. Choate, Box 428, Rush, NY 14543, 716-226-2127. 1981. Non-fiction. "Interested in fundamental studies, especially an interdisciplinary yet scientific approach to the foundations of existence and understanding. Recent title: *The Core of Creation* by Albert G Choate." avg. press run 1.2M. Pub'd 1 title 1990; expects 1 title 1991, 1 title 1992. 2 titles listed in the *Small Press Record of Books in Print* (20th Edition, 1991-92). avg. price, paper: $8. Discounts: 50%. 128pp; 5¼×8¼; of. Reporting time: 1 month. Payment: negotiable, also subsidy possible.

SZ/Press, Suzanne Zavrian, PO Box 20075, Cathedral Finance Station, New York, NY 10025, 212-749-5906. 1976. Poetry, art, non-fiction. "Primarily conceptual art and poetry experimenting with new use of language. Last published: Erika Rothenberg, Angus MacLise, Frank Kuenstler" avg. press run 500. 4 titles listed in the *Small Press Record of Books in Print* (20th Edition, 1991-92). avg. price, paper: $6. 48pp; size varies; of. Reporting time: 8 weeks. Payment: negotiable, usually 10% royalty. Copyrights for author.

T

THE T.E. LAWRENCE SOCIETY NEWSLETTER, Nicholas Adrian Birnie, 'Ambleside', 101 Hempstead Road, Kings Langley, Hertfordshire WD4 8BS, United Kingdom, 0923-263501. 1985. Poetry, articles, art, photos, interviews, criticism, reviews, letters, news items, non-fiction. circ. 600+. 4/yr. Pub'd 4 issues 1990; expects 4 issues 1991, 4 issues 1992. sub. price: £8-12; per copy: £1; sample: free. Back issues: 70p. 18-20pp; size A4; †of. Reporting time: varies. Payment: none. Copyrighted, reverts to author. Pub's reviews: 4 in 1990. §T.E. Lawrence. Ads: £25/£15.

Tabor Sarah Books, 2419 Jefferson Avenue, Berkeley, CA 94703. 1985. avg. press run 2M. Pub'd 1 title 1990; expects 2 titles 1991. 2 titles listed in the *Small Press Record of Books in Print* (20th Edition, 1991-92). avg. price, paper: $6. Discounts: 3/20%, 6/40%, 25/45%, 50/50%. 48pp; 7×10; of. COSMEP.

TABULA RASA, Shy City Press, Lisa Nease Yeager, 208 Reno St., #1, New Cumberland, PA 17070, 717-774-7627. 1990. Poetry, fiction, art, photos, interviews, reviews. "Length-preferably 1-2 pages. Will consider longer if exceptional. No restricions on content, style, school, form. Recent contributors: Kerry Shawn Keys, Liza Wielard, Bart Solarczyk, Palo, Miriam Kessler" circ. 150. 4/yr. Expects 3 issues 1991, 4 issues 1992. sub. price: $14; per copy: $3.50; sample: $4.50. 28pp; 7×8½; of. Reporting time: 2-8 weeks. Payment: 1 copy. Copyrighted, reverts to author. Pub's reviews: 0 in 1990. §Small press literary/poetry magazines, poetry chapbooks.

Tafford Publishing, Inc., Philip Jr. Gurlik, PO Box 271804, Houston, TX 77277, 713-529-3276. 1984. "Most of the books we publish are by established science fiction and fantasy writers, not necessarily in these genres however." avg. press run 3-4M. Pub'd 4 titles 1990; expects 3 titles 1991, 4 titles 1992. 5 titles listed in the *Small Press Record of Books in Print* (20th Edition, 1991-92). avg. price, cloth: $19.95. Discounts: 30-46% retail; 20% library; 50% wholesale. 250pp; 5½×8½. Reporting time: 1-2 months. Payment: flexible. Copyrights for author.

TAI CHI, Wayfarer Publications, Marvin Smalheiser, Editor, PO Box 26156, Los Angeles, CA 90026, 213-665-7773. 1977. Articles, interviews, reviews, letters, news items. "Articles about T'ai Chi Ch'uan, I Ching, Chi kung, meditation, health about 700-2.5M words each." 6/yr. Pub'd 6 issues 1990; expects 6 issues 1991, 6 issues 1992. sub. price: $20; per copy: $3.50; sample: $3.50. 48pp; 8½×11; of. Reporting time: 2 weeks. Copyrighted. Pub's reviews: 12 in 1990. Ads: $300/$200/$1 per word. COSMEP.

TAKAHE, Sandra Arnold, David Howard, Bernadette Hall, Ray Mutton, Tony Scanlan, PO Box 13-335, Christchurch 1, New Zealand, 03-517973. 1989. Poetry, fiction, art, cartoons, long-poems. "*Takahe* is a general literary quarterly which has no preconceived biases as to length or form. It aims to introduce young writers to a larger readership than they might otherwise enjoy by publishing them alongside established figures (e.g. Owen Marshall, Michael Harlow, Elizabeth Smither). *Takahe* is interested in translation in addition to original fiction/poetry." circ. 225. 4/yr. Pub'd 1 issue 1990; expects 4 issues 1991, 4 issues 1992. sub. price: $24NZ; per copy: $6NZ; sample: $7.50NZ. 56pp; 8×11¾; †mi. Reporting time: 4-6 weeks. Payment: complimentary copy, plus small increment at editor's discretion. Copyrighted, reverts to author. Ads: $80NZ/$40NZ.

TALES OF THE DESIGNERREAL UNIVERSE, Rikki Leeson, Rikki Leeson, PO Box 581, Seattle, WA 98111. 1989. Poetry, fiction, articles, art, cartoons, satire, criticism, reviews, letters, news items. "Comics are my main concern in publishing. Secondly, reviewing them. Thirdly, music reviews, then the poetry, articles, etc." circ. 100. Irregular. Pub'd 1 issue 1990; expects 2 issues 1991. price per copy: $2.50; sample: $2.50. Back issues: inquire. Discounts: inquire. 24pp; 6½×10; photocopy. Reporting time: 2 weeks. Token payments are made sometimes but not guaranteed; contributors copies are guaranteed. Copyrighted, reverts to author. Pub's reviews: about 150 in 1990. §Comics, art, music. Ads: inquire.

TALISMAN: A Journal of Contemporary Poetry and Poetics, Edward Foster, Box 1117, Hoboken, NJ 07030, 201-798-9093. 1988. Poetry, articles, interviews, criticism, reviews. "Each issue of *Talisman* is centered on the work of a major contemporary poet. We publish poetry, interviews with poets, reviews of poetry, articles on poetics, articles on poetry." circ. 650. 2/yr. Pub'd 2 issues 1990; expects 2 issues 1991, 2 issues 1992. sub. price: $9/2 issues individual, $13/2 issues institutions; per copy: $5; sample: $5. Discounts: negotiable. 152pp; 5½×8½; of. Reporting time: 1 month. Payment: copy. Copyrighted, reverts to author. Pub's reviews: 4 in 1990. §The best current poetry, poetic theory. Ads: $100/$50. COSMEP.

Talking Leaves Press (see also GROUND WATER REVIEW), George Kalamaras, Poetry Editor; Mary Ann Cain, Fiction Editor, 730 East Smith Street, Warsaw, IN 46580, 219-269-7680. 1986. Poetry. "Talking Leaves Press has grown out of our magazine, *Ground Water Review*, which is currently not seeking material. We have begun a broadside series to continue the work of the press, focusing on surrealist and "language" poetries. Broadsides of poetry by James Grabill, Jorge Teillier, Roberto Zingarello, Ray Gonzalez, Rita Repka, Jay Griswold, Nancy Weber, Phil Woods, Kenneth Rexroth, and others, with translations by Mary Crow. We are also open to all forms of poetry by both new and established writers, but we stress high quality. We are interested in translations, with an emphasis on Greek, Italian, and Spanish writers; however, we are open to all cultures. Send for catalog of current listings of Broadside Series. Broadsides sell for $1 each plus 75¢ postage per order." avg. press run 100. Expects 6 titles 1991, 6 titles 1992. 9 titles listed in the *Small Press Record of Books in Print* (20th Edition, 1991-92). avg. price, other: $1 per broadside, plus 75¢ postage per order. Discounts: write for schedule. 1 page; 8½×11; lp. Reporting time: 2-3 months. Payment: copies of broadside. Copyrights for author.

Talon Books Ltd, Karl Siegler, 201/1019 East Cordova Street, Vancouver, BC, Canada, 604-253-5261. 1967. Poetry, fiction, art, photos, criticism, letters, plays, non-fiction. "Talon Books, a leading Canadian literary press, specializes in fiction, drama, poetry, and ethnography, with a growing list of criticism and issues/ideas" avg. press run 3M. Pub'd 11 titles 1990; expects 12 titles 1991, 12 titles 1992. 146 titles listed in the *Small Press Record of Books in Print* (20th Edition, 1991-92). avg. price, cloth: $29.95; paper: $11.95. Discounts: 1

copy, 20%; 10 copies, 40%; - 1,000 copies, 46%; libraries, 10%. 128pp; 5½×8½, 6×9; of. Reporting time: 3-6 months. Payment: royalty % of retail sale price. Copyrights for author. ACP, COSMEP, CBA, ABPBC, LPG.

Tamal Vista Publications, Katherine deFremery, 222 Madrone Ave, Larkspur, CA 94939, 924-7289. 1976. Non-fiction. *"The Stripper's Guide to Canoe-Building."* 3 titles listed in the *Small Press Record of Books in Print* (20th Edition, 1991-92). Discounts: 1-4 copies 20%, must have CWO; 5+ 40%. 96pp; 9×12; of. Reporting time: 1 month. Copyrights for author. COSMEP.

Tambra Publishing, Tambra Campbell, Kathy Stevenson, PO Box 14161, Las Vegas, NV 89114-4161, 702-876-4232; FAX 702-876-5252. 1985. Photos, non-fiction. "Publishes books and audio cassettes dealing with self-help through the use of handwriting analysis. Reaches market through direct mail, reviews, and wholesales, including Baker & Taylor. In this literary and historical first edition, *The K.G. Stevens Slant on Celebrity Handwriting,* the author K.G. Stevens shows the reader how to tell what someone is like simply by looking at his handwriting. The reader acquires the basic skills of a handwriting analyst. Includes 85 analyses signed-off-as-accurate by celebrities such as Kenny Rogers, Johnny Carson, Linda Evans, and Henry Kissinger. The author was featured on Eyewitness News as '#1 in the world,' and 'the woman who can change your life by changing your handwriting.' She introduces the reader to her specialty: the concept of changing yourself by changing your writing—self-help. Author is a speaker, college teacher, and entertainer. Foreword by actor Robert Cummings" avg. press run 5M, 50M anticipated rerun. Pub'd 1 title 1990; expects 1 title 1991, 1 title 1992. 2 titles listed in the *Small Press Record of Books in Print* (20th Edition, 1991-92). avg. price, cloth: $36.95; paper: $21.95; other: $6.50 + $1 s/h audiocassette: Handwriting Reveals Personality. Discounts: bookstores 40%, distributors 50%, colleges, groups orders, and organizations 22%; libraries 20%; others inquire. 328pp; 8½×11; lp. Payment: negotiable. Copyrights for author. Publishers Marketing Assoc. (PMA), 2401 Pacific Coast Hwy, Ste. 206, Hermosa Beach, CA 90254; Book Publicist of So Cal (BPSC), 6430 Sunset, Ste. 503, Hollywood, CA 90028, COSMEP, NWC National Writers Club, Aurora, CO.

TAMPA REVIEW, Richard B. Mathews, Editor; Don Morrill, Poetry Editor; Andy Solomon, Fiction Editor; Kathryn Van Spanckeren, Poetry Editor, Box 19F, Tampa University, Tampa, FL 33606-1490, 813-253-3333 X621; 813-343-3633; FAX 813-251-0016 (use name, Richard Mathews). 1988. Poetry, fiction, art, photos, interviews, reviews, non-fiction. *"The Tampa Review* is the faculty-edited literary journal of the University of Tampa. It publishes new works of poetry, fiction, non-fiction and art. Each issue includes works from other countries in order to reflect the international flavor of the city of Tampa and its ties to the international cultural community. We would like to increase the amount of creative non-fiction in our contents and we are considering publishing two issues per year. Recent contributors: Tom Disch, David Ignatow, Elizabeth Jolley, Denise Levertov, William Stafford." circ. 500-800. 1/yr. Pub'd 1 issue 1990; expects 1 issue 1991, 1 issue 1992. sub. price: $7.50; per copy: $7.50. Discounts: 30% for cash payment, 15% on consignment. 96pp; 7½×10½. Reporting time: 12 weeks. Payment: $10 per page. Copyrighted, reverts to author. Ads: none.

TANDAVA, Tom Blessing, Leona Blessing, PO Box 689, East Detroit, MI 48021. 1982. Poetry, fiction. *"Tandava* has published poetry by William Doreski, Ivan Arguelles, Sheila Murphy, Tony Moffeit, and others. We are now accepting fiction set in India or the Great Lakes area. We are also interested in prose poems" circ. 100. 2-6/yr. Pub'd 4 issues 1990; expects 6 issues 1991, 6 issues 1992. sub. price: $4; per copy: $1-$2.50; sample: $1.25. 24pp; 8×11, 5½×8; of, xerox. Reporting time: 1-4 weeks. Payment: 1 copy. Not copyrighted.

Tangram Press, Dayna Fenker, PO Box 2249, 2063 Ravenswood, Granbury, TX 76048, 817-579-1777. Poetry, photos, cartoons, non-fiction. avg. press run 5M. Pub'd 1 title 1990; expects 3 titles 1991, 3 titles 1992. 5 titles listed in the *Small Press Record of Books in Print* (20th Edition, 1991-92). avg. price, cloth: $45; paper: $15. 120pp; 7½×9¼, 12×12; of.

Taos Bluewater Press, Paul Mallamo, PO Box 529, Taos, NM 87571, 505-758-5617. 1990. Fiction, non-fiction. *"Yo Money*—a very fast guide to car buying" Expects 1 title 1991. 1 title listed in the *Small Press Record of Books in Print* (20th Edition, 1991-92). avg. price, paper: $10. 50pp; 6×8; †mi. Reporting time: 2 weeks. Payment: standard. Does not copyright for author.

TAPAS, Richard Patel, 4017A Shenandoah, St. Louis, MO 63110, 314-772-8237. 1989. Poetry, fiction, articles, art, photos, cartoons, interviews, long-poems, collages, plays, non-fiction. "All works must be 5,000 words or less. SASE. We have no editorial biases or taboos. Like our title, we publish a wide variety of literary hors d'oeuvres." circ. 350. 3/yr. Pub'd 2 issues 1990; expects 3 issues 1991, 3 issues 1992. sub. price: $10; per copy: $4.50; sample: $4.50. 52pp; 8½×11; †mimeo. Reporting time: 1-3 months. Payment: copies. Copyrighted, reverts to author. Pub's reviews: 2 in 1990. §Fiction, non-fiction, art, poetry, anything. Ads: $30; 1/2 $15.

TAPJOE: The Anaprocrustean Poetry Journal of Enumclaw, Red Ink/Black Hole Productions, Noah Farnsworth, Lisa Therrell, PO Box 104, Grangeville, ID 83530. 1987. Poetry. "We prefer poems of 10-40 lines but do consider any length. We also prefer poems with an 'ecological' slant—in a very general sense. We will *not* consider previously published material. We publish occasional special issues and chapbooks which subscribers will receive free. Recent contributors include: Gary Cummisk, Sheryl Nelms, Douglas Campbell."

circ. 200-300. 2/yr. Pub'd 2 issues 1990; expects 2 issues 1991, 2 issues 1992. sub. price: $10/4 years; per copy: $3; sample: $3. Discounts: by arrangement. 20-30pp; 5½×8½; of. Reporting time: 4-12 weeks. Payment: copies only. Copyrighted, reverts to author.

TAPLIGHT NEWSLETTER, Ann M. Strong, Editor & Publisher, 1827 E. Mississippi Avenue, Denver, CO 80210, 303-744-2677. 1987. Poetry, articles, art, photos, cartoons, non-fiction. "Ideal length 800 words. Accept articles 650-1,300 words. All articles and stories written in personal, first-person, sharing format about healing emotional pain & celebrating spirit. SASE for writer's guidelines." circ. 750. 12/yr. Pub'd 12 issues 1990; expects 12 issues 1991, 12 issues 1992. sub. price: $17; per copy: $2; sample: $2. Back issues: $2. 8pp; 8½×11; †of. Reporting time: 2 months. Payment: articles 10 copies, poems 5 copies. Copyrighted, reverts to author. §Personal story in all areas of growth, spirituality, healing. Ads: $300-full/$160½/$35-business card no classifieds.

TAPROOT, a journal of elder writers, Philip W. Quigg, Editor; Enid Graf, Associate Editor, Fine Arts Center 4290, University at Stony Brook, Stony Brook, NY 11794-0001, 516-632-6635. 1974. Poetry, articles, art, photos, non-fiction. "Poetry, prose and art by elder writers. Publication limited to Taproot Workshop members." circ. 750-1M. 2/yr. Pub'd 2 issues 1990; expects 2 issues 1991, 2 issues 1992. sub. price: $8; per copy: $5; sample: $6. Back issues: $6. Discounts: please inquire. 80pp; 8½×11; of. Reporting time: 2 months. Payment: 1 copy. Copyrighted, reverts to author. Ads: $1,000/$500/negotiable.

TAPROOT LITERARY REVIEW, Tikvah Feinstein, 302 Park Road, Ambridge, PA 15003, 412-266-8476. 1987. Poetry, fiction, art, photos, long-poems, non-fiction. "Taproot Literary Review, a locally published anthology with growing national participation and audience, will offer money prizes, publication, promotion and public readings for winners and authors in its annual poetry and fiction writing contest. Poetry and short fiction will be accepted. First-place winners in fiction and poetry will win $30 prizes; the second-place winner in poetry, $15; and the third-place winner in poetry, $10. A university appointed panel will judge the entries. Deadline for entry is Dec. 31. For guidelines, send a self-addressed, stamped envelope to above address. Submissions accepted between September and December only. Also collection of Women's Shelter issues for survivors and healers—accepting poetry and essays, no fiction. For publication 1992." circ. 500. 1-2/yr. Pub'd 1 issue 1990; expects 1 issue 1991, 2 issues 1992. sub. price: $5.50 + $2 p/h; per copy: $5.50 + $2 p/h; sample: $4 + 98¢ stamps. Back issues: $4 + 98¢ stamps. Discounts: classroom, libraries or retailers $4. 72pp; 6×9; of. Reporting time: 3 months or less. Payment: copies or cash prizes on contest. Copyrighted.

TAR RIVER POETRY, Peter Makuck, Department of English, East Carolina University, Greenville, NC 27834, 919-752-6041. 1978. Poetry, reviews. "Among recent featured contributors have been William Stafford, A. Poulin, Jr., Frederick Morgan, Michael Mott, Ralph Mills, Jr., Laurence Lieberman, Teresa Svoboda, Paul Mariani, Jay Parini, Peter Cooley, William Pitt Root, Brenda Hillman, W. S. Di Piero, Bruce Weigl, Greg Kuzma, Peter Wild, Albert Goldbarth, Leslie Norris, John Logan, Louis Simpson, Stephen Dunn, Mark Jarman, David Wojahn, William Matthews, Brendan Galvin, Vern Rutsala, Jonathan Holden, Carolyn Kizer" circ. 1M. 2/yr. Expects 2 issues 1992. sub. price: $8, $14/2 yrs; per copy: $4.50; sample: $4.50. Back issues: $4.50. Discounts: 40% to bookstores. 64pp; 6×8¾; of. Reporting time: 6-8 weeks. Payment: contributor's copies. Rights reassigned to author upon request. Pub's reviews: 10 in 1990. §Poetry. We swap ads.

Targeted Communications, Gary Tartaglia, Editor & Publisher, PO Box 18002, Cleveland Heights, OH 44118-0002, 216-397-0268. 1984. Interviews, satire, news items, non-fiction. "Looking for authors who have a knack for taking complex or technical subjects and simplifying them easily so that the average person can understand them completely. Want people who write in a tell-it-like-it-is approach, who are blunt, honest, down-to-earth. Specialize in selling books by direct mail." avg. press run 1.5M. Pub'd 3 titles 1990; expects 5 titles 1991, 7 titles 1992. 2 titles listed in the *Small Press Record of Books in Print* (20th Edition, 1991-92). avg. price, paper: $19.95. Discounts: 25% to libraries and classrooms; 40% to bookstores; 50% to wholesalers. 155pp; 5½×8½, 8½×11; †of. Reporting time: 2 weeks. Payment: 5%-10% royalty to authors paid quarterly. Does not copyright for author. COSMEP, American Bookdealers Exchange, PMA.

TATTOO ADVOCATE JOURNAL, Shotsie Gorman, Editor & Publisher, PO Box 8390, Haledon, NJ 07538-0390, 201-790-0429. 1987. Fiction, non-fiction. "Jack Dann Sci Fi/William Barrett (from shorts to 2,000 words articles non-fiction). Fiction in 25 page maximum 1 1/2 spaced. Looking for cross over references from all sources to tattooing and body decoration. Anthropological, Rites of passage, Enthnographic articles, and healing thru meditation and alternative lifestyles for health. Articles on art especially the politics of... References to tattooing in religious writings and commentary. Social, medical Psychology, and pop culture. Political comedy left leaning. Social satire specifically on mores and prejudice" circ. 10M. 2/yr. Expects 2 issues 1991, 2 issues 1992. sub. price: $15; per copy: $8.50; sample: $5. Discounts: 1-10 20%, 11-25 23%, 26-40 35%, 40-55 40%, 55-100 45%, 100+ 50%. 64-100pp; 8½×11; of. Reporting time: 4 weeks. Payment: 300 word minimum $40, 1,000 words $200, 1,500-2,000 $100-$300. Copyrighted, rights revert according to negotiations. Pub's reviews. §Photography, arts, enthnological, sociological, self-help, New Age, how-to art books, comic art, science fiction illustrations. Send for ad rates. COSMEP.

Taurean Horn Press, Bill Vartnaw, 1355 California #2, San Francisco, CA 94109. 1974. Poetry. "Publications in print: *Blind Annie's Cellar* by Paul Vane. *The Neighborhood* by Bernard Gershenson *In Concern: for Angels* by Bill Vartnaw in conjunction with Out West Ltd. *Excerpts from A Mountian Climber's Handbook* by Carol Lee Sanchez in conjunction with Out West Ltd. *Amateur Blues* by Lynn Watson. No submissions accepted." avg. press run 500. Pub'd 1 title 1990. 3 titles listed in the *Small Press Record of Books in Print* (20th Edition, 1991-92). avg. price, paper: $4-10. Discounts: 40% to book trade. 80pp; of. Payment: copies and/or other arrangements agreed upon prior to publication. Copyrights for author.

Tax Property Investor, Inc., F. Marea, PO Box 4602, Winter Park, FL 32793, 407-671-0004. 1989. Non-fiction. "Publishing for real estate investors." avg. press run 5M. Expects 1 title 1991, 3 titles 1992. 1 title listed in the *Small Press Record of Books in Print* (20th Edition, 1991-92). avg. price, paper: $29.95. Discounts: trade 3-99 40%; 100-199 45%; 200499 50%, 500+ 55%. 160pp; 8½×11; of. Reporting time: 30 days. Payment: to be negotiated.

TBW Books, Inc., Lois Burns, c/o Lois Burns, Gurnet Road, Brunswick, ME 04011. 1978. Art, non-fiction. "Non-fiction: Books on calligraphy and related subjects and books of historical interest to Maine readers. I also run the TBW calligraphy book club. We also publish a few children's books" avg. press run 2.5M-3M. Pub'd 2 titles 1990; expects 2 titles 1991, 3 titles 1992. 15 titles listed in the *Small Press Record of Books in Print* (20th Edition, 1991-92). avg. price, cloth: $12-$35; paper: $4.95-$17.95; other: $5-$6 art posters. Discounts: library 20%, schools 20%. I also handle distribution to the trade through direct mail; stores 40% for 1-8 or mixed copies, 9-15 42%, 16+ 45% (subject to change). Pages vary; size varies. Reporting time: about a month. Payment: 10% up to 15%, arranged per title. Usually copyrights for author.

te Neues Publishing Company, Hendrik te Neues, Managing Director, Publisher; Glenda Galt, Editor, 15 East 76th Street, New York, NY 10021, 212-288-0265. 1982. Art, photos. "We publish fine art and photography calendars. Distribute Prestel Art Books" avg. press run 10M+. Pub'd 60 titles 1990; expects 60 titles 1991, 60 titles 1992. avg. price, cloth: $40; paper: $25; other: $9.95 calendars. †of. Reporting time: within 4 weeks. Payment: varies. ABA, MSA.

TEACHER EDUCATION QUARTERLY, Caddo Gap Press, Alan H. Jones, Editor & Publisher, 915 L Street, Suite C-414, Sacramento, CA 95814. 1974. Articles. "*Teacher Education Quarterly* welcomes manuscripts of any length on subjects related to teacher education, both theory and practice, from scholars and practitioners in the field and other interested persons." circ. 600. 4/yr. Pub'd 4 issues 1990; expects 4 issues 1991, 4 issues 1992. sub. price: $30; per copy: $7.50. Discounts: agencies 10%. 96pp; 6×9; of. Reporting time: 1-2 months. Payment: none. Copyrighted, rights revert if desired. Pub's reviews: 20 in 1990. §Anything in the education and teacher education fields. Ads: $100 full page. COSMEP, EDPRESS.

Teachers & Writers Collaborative (see also TEACHERS & WRITERS MAGAZINE), Ron Padgett, 5 Union Square West, New York, NY 10003, 212-691-6590. 1967. Articles, interviews, reviews. "No poetry." avg. press run 3M. Pub'd 3 titles 1990; expects 2 titles 1991. 28 titles listed in the *Small Press Record of Books in Print* (20th Edition, 1991-92). avg. price, cloth: $17.95; paper: $8.95. Discounts: varies. 160pp; 6×9, 8½×11; of. Reporting time: varies. Payment: varies. Copyrights for author. EPAA.

TEACHERS & WRITERS MAGAZINE, Teachers & Writers Collaborative, Ron Padgett, 5 Union Square West, New York, NY 10003, 212-691-6590. 1967. Articles, interviews, reviews, letters. circ. 2M. 5/yr. Pub'd 5 issues 1990; expects 5 issues 1991. sub. price: $15; per copy: $3 plus $1 shipping; sample: $3 plus $1 shipping. Back issues: $3-$5 plus $1 p+h. Discounts: none. 12pp; 8½×11; of. Reporting time: varies. Payment: varies. Copyrighted, reverts to author. Pub's reviews: 5 in 1990. §Education and writing. EPAA.

THE TEACHING LIBRARIAN, Ontario Library Association, Judy Tye, 100 Richmond Street, E, Suite 300, Toronto, Ontario M5C 2P9, Canada, 416-363-3388. 1974. Articles, reviews. circ. 1.2M. 4/yr. Pub'd 4 issues 1990; expects 4 issues 1991, 4 issues 1992. sub. price: $25; per copy: $7. Back issues: $7. Discounts: agent, jobber 20%. 48-60pp; 8½×11; of. Reporting time: 2-6 months. Payment: none, contributions voluntary. Copyrighted, does not revert to author. Pub's reviews: 650 in 1990. §Media for elem/sec school use (books, mags, govt. pubs., non-print, reference, professional). Ads: $200/$125/10¢ word, min. $15.

TeakWood Press, Robert Martin, 160 Fiesta Drive, Kissimmee, FL 34743. 1987. "We are a publisher of travel books and would be interested in seeing queries accompanied by a sample chapter for: travel guides, how to travel books and first-person adventure travel. Recent titles: *Fly There For Less: How to Save Money Flying Worldwide, Passage Through The Darien: Biking the Pan American Highway's Jungle Gap.*" avg. press run 3M-5M. Pub'd 2 titles 1990; expects 2 titles 1991, 2-3 titles 1992. avg. price, cloth: $18.95; paper: $9.95. Discounts: available to the trade on request. Pages vary; 5½×8½. Reporting time: 8-10 weeks. Payment: varies with author based on author's experience and quality of manuscript. Copyrights for author. PMA, COSMEP.

Teal Press, Robert D. Jebb, PO Box 4098, Santa Fe, NM 87502-4098. 1983. Poetry, fiction. "Interested in serious, quality fiction, poetry and literature that demands reflection on the human condition. Interested in receiving fiction of novella length. Not interested in prose over approximately 150 pages. No mss. returned without SASE" avg. press run 1M-1.5M. Pub'd 3 titles 1990; expects 3 titles 1991, 3 titles 1992. 11 titles listed in the *Small Press Record of Books in Print* (20th Edition, 1991-92). avg. price, paper: $7. of. Reporting time: 1 month. Copyrights for author. RMBPA.

TEC Publications, Timothy Edward Curley, PO Box 189601, Sacramento, CA 95818, 916-457-4937. 1980. avg. press run 60M. Expects 2 titles 1991, 3 titles 1992. 2 titles listed in the *Small Press Record of Books in Print* (20th Edition, 1991-92). avg. price, paper: $10. Discounts: 50%. 198pp; 8½×11; of. Reporting time: varied. Payment: 10% for first run. Does not copyright for author.

Technical Communications Associates, John A. Nelson, Jr., 1250 Oakmead Parkway, Suite 210, Sunnyvale, CA 94086. "Tutorials and training materials on structured concepts of documentation" avg. press run 20M. Pub'd 3 titles 1990; expects 6 titles 1991, 9 titles 1992. 20 titles listed in the *Small Press Record of Books in Print* (20th Edition, 1991-92). avg. price, paper: $39.95. Discounts: 30% avg. 150-200pp; 8½×11. Payment: 10%-15%. Copyrights for author.

TECHNICALITIES, Media Periodicals, Brian Alley, Editor, 2440 'O' Street, Suite 202, Lincoln, NE 68510-1125, 402-474-2676. 1980. Interviews, news items, non-fiction. "Professional newsletter for libraries and librarians working at or towards automation. Articles should be typed and double-spaced; no more than 8 pages in length." circ. 650. 12/yr. Pub'd 12 issues 1990; expects 12 issues 1991, 12 issues 1992. sub. price: $42; per copy: $4.50; sample: no charge. Back issues: $4.50. 16pp; 8½×11; of. Payment: varies. Not copyrighted. Pub's reviews: 2 in 1990. §Librarianship and microcomputers for library use. Ads: write for rate card information. MAPA.

Technicians of the Sacred (see also SOCIETE), Courtney Willis, 1317 N. San Fernando Blvd., Suite 310, Burbank, CA 91504. 1983. Non-fiction. avg. press run 500. Pub'd 3 titles 1990; expects 4 titles 1991. 3 titles listed in the *Small Press Record of Books in Print* (20th Edition, 1991-92). avg. price, paper: $25. 130pp; 10½×12; of. Reporting time: 4 weeks. Copyrights for author.

TechWest Publications, David I. Gourley, 560 South Hartz #447, Danville, CA 94526, 415-838-2670. 1986. Poetry, art, photos, non-fiction. avg. press run 4M. Expects 5 titles 1991, 8 titles 1992. avg. price, cloth: $16; paper: $14. Discounts: CWO= 1-9 40%, 10-49 50%, 50-up 60%; Invoice 1-9 25%, 10-49 35%, 50-up 45%. 300pp; 7⅛×9¼; of. Reporting time: 3-4 weeks. Payment: on publication - rates vary. Copyrights for author. PMA.

The Teitan Press, Inc., Martin P. Starr, Vice-President; Franklin C. Winston, President, 339 West Barry Avenue, Suite 16B, Chicago, IL 60657, 312-929-7892. 1985. Fiction, non-fiction. "At present we only use in-house material." avg. press run 2M. Pub'd 1 title 1990; expects 1 title 1991, 1 title 1992. 5 titles listed in the *Small Press Record of Books in Print* (20th Edition, 1991-92). avg. price, cloth: $24.95. Discounts: 50% to wholesalers, 20%-40% to retail outlets depending on quantity; 10% to libraries postpaid. 200pp; 5×7; of. Reporting time: 1 month. Payment: 10% royalty, reporting and payment twice. Copyrights for author. COSMEP.

Tejas Art Press, Robert Willson, 207 Terrell Road, San Antonio, TX 78209, 512-826-7803. 1979. "All of our books will be illustrated fully, by author or our staff. At present all books stay with the 100 page size, none smaller. Thus a poet must have that much material to submit. Our special interests are poetry and drama, and book art, with almost exclusive attention to Texas and the Southwest Indian. Present books printed, in stock. Poetry by Catherine E. Whitmav. Illustrated, ink. Translations of Aztec poetry, by John Cornyn. Illustrated. We use some small flat runs of color over line drawings." avg. press run 200. Pub'd 2 titles 1990; expects 2 titles 1991, 2 titles 1992. 4 titles listed in the *Small Press Record of Books in Print* (20th Edition, 1991-92). avg. price, cloth: $20; paper: $5. Discounts: ask/advance payment required. 100pp; 7×8½; of. Reporting time: prompt, but write first (Indian or Texan). Payment: write. Copyrights for author. TC.

Telephone Books, Maureen Owen, 109 Dunk Rock Rd., Guilford, CT 06437, 203-453-1921. 1971. Poetry, fiction, plays. "Press *temporarily* dormant, but titles remain available. Books: *The Amerindian Coastline Poem* by Fanny Howe; *Hot Footsteps* by Yuki Hartman; *Ciao Manhattan* by Rebecca Wright; *Delayed: Not Postponed* by Fielding Dawson; *The Secret History of the Dividing Line* by Susan Howe; *The Temple* by Janet Hamill; *No More Mr. Nice Guy* by Sam Kashner; *Audrey Hepburn's Symphonic Salad and the Coming of Autumn* by Tom Weigel; *The Telephone Book* by Ed Friedman; *3-Way Split* by Rebecca Brown; *Hot* by Joe Johnson; *The Celestial Splendor Shining Forth From Geometric Thought* and *On the Motion of the Apparently Fixed Stars* by Britt Wilkie. No unsolicited ms." avg. press run 750-1M. Pub'd 3 titles 1990. 18 titles listed in the *Small Press Record of Books in Print* (20th Edition, 1991-92). avg. price, paper: $3 (All cks made out to: Maureen Owen). 40pp; size varies; of. Reporting time: not accepting submissions. Payment: in copies. Copyrights for author. CCLM, NESPA, BC.

TELOS, Telos Press, Paul Piccone, 431 East 12th Street, New York, NY 10009, 212-228-6479. 1968. Articles, criticism, reviews. circ. 3.5M. 4/yr. Pub'd 4 issues 1990; expects 4 issues 1991, 4 issues 1992. sub. price: indiv. $28, instit. $70; per copy: indiv. $8.50; instit. $17; sample: same. Back issues: same. Discounts: 30% bulk orders; 10% agent. 240pp; 6×9; of. Reporting time: 6 months. Payment: none. Copyrighted. Pub's reviews: 40 books, 40 journals in 1990. §Left-wing philosophy, lit. criticism, politics. Ads: $400/$250.

Telos Press (see also TELOS), Paul Piccone, 431 East 12th Street, New York, NY 10009, 212-228-6479. 1968. Articles, criticism, reviews. avg. press run 4.5M. Expects 2 titles 1991, 2 titles 1992. 12 titles listed in the *Small Press Record of Books in Print* (20th Edition, 1991-92). avg. price, cloth: $18; paper: $9. Discounts: usual is 30%, other can be arranged. 200pp; size varies; of. Reporting time: 6 months. Payment: no set policy. Copyrights for author.

TELS PRESS (see also PRINTED MATTER (Japan)), Matthew Zuckerman, Editor & Fiction Editor; John Evans, Poetry Editor, c/o The Second Story, Nakijima Bldg, 2nd Floor, 1-26-7 Umegaoka, Setagaya-ku, Tokyo 154, Japan, 03-706-5055. 1977. Poetry, fiction, long-poems, non-fiction. "Recent authors: Joseph Simas, Eric Selland, Seija Kamefuchi, Cid Corman, Masaya Saito and others. Prefer that the writer(s) be living in Japan at time of publication" avg. press run 300-500. Pub'd 2 titles 1990; expects 2 titles 1991, 3 titles 1992. 11 titles listed in the *Small Press Record of Books in Print* (20th Edition, 1991-92). avg. price, paper: $7.50 postpaid. Discounts: negotiable upon request. 60pp; 6×8½; of. Reporting time: 8 weeks for overseas submissions. Payment: 10% of the copies. Does not copyright for author. COSMEP.

Telstar Publishing (see also RYAN'S REVIEW; THE YELLOW PAGES), Kathleen Lee Mendel, 7810 Bertha Avenue, Parma, OH 44129-3110. 1989. Poetry, long-poems. "Length of poetry, when written well, is not as important as the width. Have recently published Dolores Malaschak, Rayn Greenblatt, Kay Weems, Denise Martinson, Ana Pine, etc. All books are themed projects. Always request list of current themes" avg. press run 200-500. Pub'd 1 title 1990; expects 12 titles 1991, 16 titles 1992. 6 titles listed in the *Small Press Record of Books in Print* (20th Edition, 1991-92). avg. price, paper: $12. Discounts: 10 or more copies 45%. 140pp; 5½×8½; of. Reporting time: 2-3 months. Payment: 1-20%. Copyrights for author.

TEMBLOR: Contemporary Poets, Leland Hickman, 4624 Cahuenga Blvd. #307, North Hollywood, CA 91602, 818-761-6112. 1985. Poetry, criticism, long-poems. "Writers in most recent issue (#8): Barbara Guest, Ron Silliman, Leslie Scalapino, Steve McCaffery, Diane Ward, Robert Kelly, Duncan McNaughton, David C.D. Gasz, John Taggart, Nathanial Tarn, Hank Lazer, John Thomas, Mary Haynes, Andrew Levy, Charles O. Hartman, Stephen Ratcliffe, Benjamin Hollander" circ. 1M. 2/yr. Expects 2 issues 1991, 2 issues 1992. sub. price: $16/2 issues indiv., $20/2 issues instit., $30/4 issues indiv., $40/4 issues instit.; per copy: $7.50; sample: $8.50. Back issues: $8.50. Discounts: bookstores 40%, distributor negotiated. 180-200pp; 8½×11; of. Reporting time: 2 months. Payment: yes, plus copies. Copyrighted, reverts to author. Pub's reviews: 13 in 1990. §Poetry books and magazines. Ads: $125/$75/1-4 pg $40.

TEMM POETRY MAGAZINE, Split Personality Press, Ken Wagner, 511 West Sullivan Street, Olean, NY 14760. 1989. Poetry, art, photos, long-poems, collages. *"Temm Poetry Magazine* is attempting to provide an 'overview' forum for all poetic and visual arts voices/visions. All styles are welcome, from naive/primitive to lyrical/imaginal and *everything* in between." circ. 200. 12/yr. Pub'd 1 issue 1990; expects 11 issues 1991, 12 issues 1992. sub. price: $12; per copy: $1.25; sample: $1.25. Back issues: $2 each while supplies last. 28pp; 4¼×7; †photocopier. Reporting time: 2 weeks to 3 months. Payment: 1 copy. Not copyrighted. Pub's reviews: Literature, poetry, art, politics in 1990. No ads.

TEMPORARY CULTURE, Henry Walton Wessells, PO Box 8180, New York, NY 10116-4650. 1988. Poetry, fiction, art, photos, non-fiction. "Under 5 pages—fiction and journalism (spurious and/or factual). Looking for the new mythologies emerging from the decaying American ideological infrastructure. B&w artwork in 8½ X 11 format. Recent artists include M.J. Duffy, T. Saunders, D.R. Dowland, S. Dorfman." circ. 250. 2/yr. Pub'd 2 issues 1990; expects 2 issues 1991, 2 issues 1992. sub. price: $10; per copy: $5; sample: $5. Back issues: $5 as available. 28pp; 4¼×11; †high resolution photocopy. Reporting time: 2 months. Payment: contributors' copies only. Copyrighted, reverts to author. Pub's reviews: 5-8 in 1990. §Poetry, science fiction.

Ten Mile River Press, Duane BigEagle, William Bradd, 3809 Spring Hill Road, Petaluma, CA 94952-9637, 707-964-5579. 1979. Poetry, fiction. "Do to extremely limited funding, submission of material is by invitation only." avg. press run 500. Pub'd 3 titles 1990; expects 3 titles 1991. 11 titles listed in the *Small Press Record of Books in Print* (20th Edition, 1991-92). avg. price, paper: $3.50. Discounts: 40% trade. 35pp; 5½×8½; †of. Payment: 10% of run. Copyrights for author.

Ten Penny Players, Inc. (see also WATERWAYS: Poetry in the Mainstream), Barbara Fisher, Co-Editor; Richard Spiegel, Co-Editor, 393 St. Paul's Avenue, Staten Island, NY 10304-2127, 718-442-7429. 1975. Poetry, fiction, plays. "Books: Age range is child to adult. Varying lengths: 8pp-150pp. At present doing a series of read aloud and playscripts, fully illustrated and chapbooks of child poets/artists. We stress an integration of language and picture so that the material can be used either as a book to read or a book to perform. Also child + adult poets published monthly in magazine and 40 literary magazines from NYC high schools. No unsolicited manuscripts, please." avg. press run 200. Pub'd 2 titles 1990; expects 2 titles 1991, 3 titles 1992. 25 titles listed in the *Small Press Record of Books in Print* (20th Edition, 1991-92). avg. price, paper: $3.50; other: *Waterways*: $2 copy/$20 subscription. Discounts: standard 60/40. 60pp; 8½×5½; †of, lp, xerox. Payment: negotiable. Copyrights for author. WP.

Ten Speed Press, M.P. Bear, PO Box 7123, Berkeley, CA 94707, 415-845-8414. 1971. Satire, non-fiction. "We publish trade books." avg. press run 10M. Pub'd 30 titles 1990; expects 25 titles 1991, 25 titles 1992. avg. price, cloth: $17.95; paper: $9.95. Discounts: usual trade 40% to 50%. 288pp; 6×9; of. Reporting time: 3 months. Payment: standard. Copyrights for author. ABA.

Ten Star Press, D. Millhouse, PO Box 2325, Inglewood, CA 90305-0325, 213-758-2123. 1988. Poetry, fiction, criticism, reviews, parts-of-novels, plays, non-fiction. "Primarily fiction (novels and novellas), non-fiction and collections of various types of material. Radical left and socialist oriented. Distributor for bookstores: ILPA, PO Box 816, Oak Park, IL 60303; all other orders go to Ten Star." avg. press run 2M-3M. Pub'd 2 titles 1990; expects 1 title 1991. 3 titles listed in the *Small Press Record of Books in Print* (20th Edition, 1991-92). avg. price, cloth: $15; paper: $10. Discounts: can be arranged. 250-350pp; 5½×8½; of. Reporting time: 1 month. Payment: to be arranged. Does not copyright for author.

Tessera Publishing, Inc., P.J. Bell, Managing Editor; Donna Montgomery, Acquisitions Editor, 9561 Woodridge Circle, Eden Prairie, MN 55347, 612-941-5053. 1989. Non-fiction. "We are doing 2 books this year. *Dark Sky, Dark Land* is the collection of stories of Hmong refugee boys, how they escaped their war-torn homeland, eventually wound up in Minnesota and are managing to thrive. The other is a collection of cameo stories remembering the women of Viet Nam. These are fundamentally human interest stories—uncommon stories about ordinary people." avg. press run 4M. Pub'd 1 title 1990. 2 titles listed in the *Small Press Record of Books in Print* (20th Edition, 1991-92). avg. price, cloth: $19.95; paper: $14.95. 175-200pp; 6×9; of. Reporting time: 2 weeks. Copyrights for author. COSMEP.

Tesseract Publications, Janet Leih, 3001 West 57th Street, Sioux Falls, SD 57106-2652. 1981. Poetry, fiction, non-fiction. "Prefer feminist, non-fiction, poetry." avg. press run 300-500. Pub'd 1 title 1990; expects 3 titles 1991, 3 titles 1992. 12 titles listed in the *Small Press Record of Books in Print* (20th Edition, 1991-92). avg. price, paper: $5. Discounts: available on request. 60pp; 5½×8½; of. Reporting time: 3 months. Payment: subsidized publications only. Copyrights for author if asked. COSMEP.

Texas Monthly Press, Cathy Casey Hale, Director & Vice President, PO Box 1569, Austin, TX 78767, 512-476-7085. 1975. Fiction, photos. avg. press run 5M-10M. Pub'd 25 titles 1990; expects 25 titles 1991, 25 titles 1992. 9 titles listed in the *Small Press Record of Books in Print* (20th Edition, 1991-92). avg. price, cloth: $18.95; paper: $10.95. Discounts: 40% trade to booksellers, 50% nonreturnable. 275pp; 6×9; of. Reporting time: 3 weeks. Payment: advance against royalties paid and royalty percentages based on net sales. Copyrights for author.

THE TEXAS REVIEW, Texas Review Press, Paul Ruffin, English Department, Sam Houston State University, Huntsville, TX 77341. 1976. Poetry, fiction, articles, photos, interviews, reviews. "Because of the size of our magazine, we do not encourage the submission of long poems or exceptionally long short stories. Now accept photography, critical essays on literature and culture, etc. Each year we publish the *The Texas Review* Poetry Award Chapbook. We will no longer read during May through August." circ. 750-1M. 2/yr. Pub'd 2 issues 1990; expects 2 issues 1991. sub. price: $10; per copy: $5; sample: $5. Back issues: $5. Discounts: 40% to libraries. 148pp; 6×9; of. Reporting time: 8 weeks. Payment: copies, subscription (1 year). Copyrighted, rights revert on request. Pub's reviews: 24 in 1990. §Poetry, fiction, history, art, literary criticism, informal essays. Exchange ads only. COSMEP, CCLM.

Texas Review Press (see also THE TEXAS REVIEW), Paul Ruffin, English Department, Sam Houston State University, Huntsville, TX 77341. 1979. "We read only solicited manuscripts. We do not read May-August" avg. press run 500. 10 titles listed in the *Small Press Record of Books in Print* (20th Edition, 1991-92). avg. price, paper: $10. 160pp; 6×9; of. Copyrights for author.

TEXAS WINEMARKET NEWS, Rental Business Press, Elizabeth T. Winn, Cellar Press, 5600 Cedro Trail, Austin, TX 78731. 1987. Articles, art, photos, interviews, criticism, reviews, news items, non-fiction. "A newsletter designed to provide trade and consumer readers with current information regarding production, marketing, distribution, and tasting reviews of Texas wines (primarily), as well as other wines sold and consumed by the Texas market. Regular departments address owner profiles, new releases, product sales statistics, event publicity" circ. 5M. 12/yr. Expects 1 issue 1991, 12 issues 1992. sub. price: $14; per copy: $2; sample: free (when available). 5pp; 8½×11; of. Reporting time: 3 weeks. Payment: by-line provided. Copyrighted, does not revert to author. Pub's reviews. §Grape growing, wine making, and marketing and distribution of wine and related products. PMA, COSMEP.

Textile Bridge Press, Joy Walsh, PO Box 157, Clarence Center, NY 14032. 1978. Poetry, fiction, criticism, long-poems, non-fiction. avg. press run 500. Expects 3-4 titles 1991. 30 titles listed in the *Small Press Record of Books in Print* (20th Edition, 1991-92). avg. price, paper: $2-$10; other: $1 broadsides (there are now 30). Discounts: 40% to bookstores. 32-140pp; 5×8½; of. Reporting time: 1 month. Payment: copies of 50 for run of 500; 30 for run of 300. Copyrights for author. NEW, Hall Walls, Just Buffalo, Arts Council.

THALIA: Studies in Literary Humor, Jacqueline Tavernier-Courbin, Dept of English, Univ of Ottawa, Ottawa K1N 6N5, Canada, 613-230-9505. 1978. Articles, art, cartoons, interviews, satire, criticism, reviews, letters, collages, non-fiction. circ. 500. 2/yr. Pub'd 1 issue 1990; expects 2 issues 1991, 2 issues 1992. sub. price: $15 individuals, $18 libraries; per copy: $8; sample: $8. Back issues: $12 for most volumes. Discounts: by direct query only. 75pp; 7×8½; lp. Reporting time: varies with ms content. Payment: none. Copyrighted. Pub's reviews: 7 in 1990. §Any area connected to humor. Ads: $150/$75. Thalia: Association for the Study of Literary Humor.

Tharpa Publications Limited, 15 Bendemeer Road, London SW15 1JX, England, 081-788-7792. 1984. Non-fiction. "Publishers of Buddhist books and visual Dharma reproductions" avg. press run 5M. Pub'd 2 titles 1990; expects 5 titles 1991, 4 titles 1992. 13 titles listed in the *Small Press Record of Books in Print* (20th Edition, 1991-92). avg. price, cloth: $22.95; paper: $18.95. Discounts: 55-55% wholesale, 35-40% retail. 250-300pp; 5¼×8½; of. Reporting time: 1-2 months. Payment: 10% royalty paid bi-annually. Copyrights for author. Independent Publishers Guild.

THEATER, Joel Schechter, Editor, 222 York Street, New Haven, CT 06520, 203-436-1417. 1968. Articles, interviews, satire, criticism, reviews, letters, plays. *"Theater* is a critical journal of contemporary theatre. Each issue features texts of important new plays, as well as articles, interviews, and essays by prominent writers and practicing professionals. Specific issues offer retrospectives of artists or consider issues which impact on theatre throughout the world. Recent issues include a retrospective on Peter Brook, and topics such as dramaturgy, translation, clowning, and paratheatre. Contributors include August Wilson, Athol Fugard, JoAnne Akalaitis, Rustom Bharucha, Joseph Chaikin, Jan Kott, and Eric Bentley." circ. 2.3M. 3/yr. Pub'd 3 issues 1990; expects 3 issues 1991, 3 issues 1992. sub. price: $20 individuals, $24 libraries; per copy: $7; sample: $7. Back issues: $5/$7. Discounts: agents 15%; bookstores 25%-30%; bulk 10-15% (back issues only). 96pp; 9½×9½; of. Reporting time: 8 weeks. Payment: $25-$150. Copyrighted, does not revert to author. Pub's reviews: 3 in 1990. §New books on theater, new plays. Ads: $200/$100. CCLM.

A THEATER OF BLOOD, Pyx Press, C. Darren Butler, PO Box 620, Orem, UT 84059-0620. 1990. Poetry, fiction, articles, interviews, criticism, reviews. "Mostly poetry, fiction under 1,000 words. Intense literary material; no gore, pornography, vampires, etc." circ. 100-200. 1 every 9 months. Pub'd 2 issues 1990; expects 1 issue 1991, 1-2 issues 1992. sub. price: $7; sample: $2.50. 32pp; 5½×8½; xerox. Reporting time: 3 months, occasionally longer. Payment: 1 copy. Not copyrighted. Pub's reviews: 10 in 1990. Ads: query.

Theatre Arts, William P. Germano, 29 West 35th Street, New York, NY 10001, 212-244-3336. "Practical theatrebooks on acting, directing, lighting, and scenery" Pub'd 3 titles 1990; expects 3 titles 1991, 3 titles 1992. 3 titles listed in the *Small Press Record of Books in Print* (20th Edition, 1991-92). avg. price, cloth: $25; paper: $13.95. Reporting time: 3 months. Payment: regular terms. Copyrights for author. Division of Routledge, Chapman & Hall, Inc.

Theatre Communications Group (see also AMERICAN THEATRE MAGAZINE), M. Elizabeth Osborne, Jim O'Quinn, 355 Lexington Avenue, New York, NY 10017, 212-697-5230. 1961. Criticism, plays, non-fiction. avg. press run 5M. Pub'd 10 titles 1990; expects 10 titles 1991, 10 titles 1992. 4 titles listed in the *Small Press Record of Books in Print* (20th Edition, 1991-92). avg. price, cloth: $20; paper: $12.95. Discounts: standard. 250pp; 6×9; of. Payment: negotiated per title, advance against percent of royalty. Copyrights for author.

THEATRE DESIGN AND TECHNOLOGY, U.S. Institute for Theatre Technology, Inc., Eric Fielding, Editor; Cecelia Fielding, Editor, 10 West 19th Street #5A, New York, NY 10011-4206, 212-924-9088. 1965. Articles, photos, interviews, reviews, letters, news items. "The magazine covers the art and technology of producing live performance events. Articles discuss historical scene design as well as contemporary design. Pieces on lighting and sound focus on both the artistic effects of these elements and the newest, most effective ways to use these elements. Costume design and designers are often highlighted. Reports on newly created standards in the industry, health and safety issues, new facilities, and new products appear regularly. Interpretive articles as well as technical research findings all combine to make *TD&T* an important and one-of-a-kind source for practitioners of theatre design, theatre building, and theatre technology" circ. 4M. 4/yr. Pub'd 4 issues 1990; expects 4 issues 1991, 4 issues 1992. sub. price: $30 domestic, $35 foreign; per copy: $8. Back issues: $8. Discounts: none. 64pp; 8¼×11; web offset. Reporting time: 6 weeks. Payment: none. Copyrighted, held by magazine after publication unless author wishes separate copyright. Pub's reviews: 15 in 1990. §Books only, scenography, scene design, engineering, architecture, costume. Ads: $420/$250. COSMEP.

THEATRE NOTEBOOK, Katharine Worth, Michael Booth, Russell Jackson, Shakespeare Institute,

University of Birmingham, Birmingham, London B15 2RX, England. 1945. Articles, photos, reviews. "Scholarly articles on British theatre history & technique. Articles up to 5M words. Notes & queries on subject. Free to members of Society for Theatre Research." circ. 1.3M. 3/yr. Pub'd 3 issues 1990; expects 3 issues 1991, 3 issues 1992. sub. price: $26; per copy: $9. Back issues: $20. 48pp; 8½×5½; of. Reporting time: 4-6 weeks. Payment: none. Copyrighted. Pub's reviews: 20 in 1990. §Books on British Theatre History. Ads: £60/£40. STR (Society for Theatre Research).

THEMA, Virginia Howard, THEMA Literary Society, Box 74109, Metairie, LA 70033-4109. 1988. Poetry, fiction, art, cartoons. "Each issue related to a unique central premise. 1992 themes: (December 1991)—It's Got to be Here...Somewhere; March—When the Birds Stopped Singing; June—These Are Not the Best Shoes I Own; September—Unrecognized at the Airport; December—Tracks in the Snow. Manuscript submission deadlines: 4 months before month of publication." circ. 250. 4/yr. Pub'd 4 issues 1990; expects 4 issues 1991, 4 issues 1992. sub. price: $16; per copy: $5; sample: $5. Back issues: $6. Discounts: 10%. 200pp; 5½×8½; of. Reporting time: 1-2 months after manuscript submission deadline of specific issue. Payment: $25 short stories, $10 poetry, $10 b/w artwork, $25 b/w cover art, $10 short-short pieces. Copyrighted, reverts to author. §Fiction. Ads: $150/$100/$50 1/4 page. COSMEP, CLMP, CELJ.

THEMATIC POETRY QUARTERLY, W.I. Throssell, Audio-Visual Poetry Foundation, 400 Fish Hatchery Road, Marianna, FL 32446, 904-482-3890. 1971. Poetry. "Under 36 lines prefered" circ. 100. 4/yr. Pub'd 4 issues 1990; expects 4 issues 1991, 4 issues 1992. sub. price: $12; per copy: $3; sample: $3. Back issues: $3. 20pp; 8½×11; †mi. Reporting time: 1 week. Payment: none. Not copyrighted.

THEOLOGIA 21, Dominion Press, A. Stuart Otto, Editor, PO Box 37, San Marcos, CA 92079-0037, 619-746-9430. 1970. Articles, reviews, letters. "No mss accepted" circ. 100. 4/yr. Pub'd 4 issues 1990; expects 4 issues 1991, 4 issues 1992. sub. price: $15; per copy: not available; sample: not available. Back issues: 1976-80 complete, bound $24.95; 1981-86 complete, bound $24.95; 1987-90 complete, bound $24.95; full set $69.95. Discounts: 30% to dealers, agencies; 40% on bound volumes. 4pp; 8½×11; of. Pub's reviews: 1 in 1990. §Theology (Christian). No ads.

Theosophical Publishing House (see also THE QUEST), Shirley Nicholson, 306 West Geneva Road, Wheaton, IL 60187, 312-665-0130. 1968. Art, non-fiction. "Esoteric, comparative religion, psychology, philosophy, health, holistic healing, astrology, meditation, holistic living." avg. press run 5M. Pub'd 12 titles 1990; expects 12 titles 1991, 12 titles 1992. 13 titles listed in the *Small Press Record of Books in Print* (20th Edition, 1991-92). avg. price, cloth: $14.95; paper: $9.95; other: $6.95 miniatures. Discounts: 1-4 books 20%, 5+ 40% or more. 200pp; 5¼×8¼; sheetfed & web offset. Reporting time: 1-6 months. Payment: paid once a year. Copyrights for author. American Booksellers Association.

THEY WON'T STAY DEAD!, Brian Johnson, 11 Werner Road, Greenville, PA 16125, 412-588-3471. 1989. Articles, photos, cartoons, interviews, criticism, reviews, music, letters, news items. "16-20 pages of 'Psychotronic' film and culture, including horror and 'trash' film reviews and commentary. Also comments on anything oddball or shocking. Recent contributors include Greg Goodsell, Dave Szurek, D.Ho Grover and Webster Colcord. Biases include all the above." circ. 300. 6/yr. Pub'd 6 issues 1990; expects 6 issues 1991, 6 issues 1992. sub. price: $6; per copy: $1; sample: $1. Back issues: $1.50. Discounts: 50¢ each. 16-20pp; 5½×8½; †xerox. Payment: 1 copy of issue. Not copyrighted. Pub's reviews: 6 in 1990. §Horror, controversial or true crime. Ads: free sample of product(s).

Theytus Books Ltd., Greg Young-Ing, Manager, PO Box 218, Penticton, B.C. V2A 6K3, Canada, 604-493-7181. 1980. Poetry, fiction, photos, non-fiction. "Recent contributors: Jeannette Armstrong, Beth Cuthand, Douglas Cardinal, Ellen White." avg. press run 4M. Pub'd 4 titles 1990; expects 4 titles 1991, 4 titles 1992. 5 titles listed in the *Small Press Record of Books in Print* (20th Edition, 1991-92). avg. price, paper: $13.95; other: $49.95. Discounts: applicable to retail and wholesale dealers, cloth or paper, single or assorted titles: 1 copy 20%, 2-4 30%, 5-99 40%, 100-199 41%, 200-299 42%, 300-399 43%, 400-499 45%, 500+ 50%, wholesalers 55%. 150pp; 5½×8½; of. Reporting time: 6 months to 1 year. Payment: 8-10% 2 times a year. Copyrights for author. ACP, 260 King Street East, Toronto, Ont., CBIC (same), ABPBC 1622 W. 7th Ave., Vancouver, B.C. Canada V6J 1S5.

THE THIRD HALF, Kevin Troop, "Amikeco", 16, Fane Close, Stamford, Lincs., PE9 1HG, England. 1987. Poetry, fiction. "Length of stories: up to 1200 words. Poems: up to 30 lines. Recent contributors: Michael Newman, Margaret Munro Gibson, Rupert Loydell. Well-written stories or poems in good English is the aim!" 6/yr. Pub'd 6 issues 1990; expects 6 issues 1991, 6 issues 1992. sub. price: £3-60; per copy: 75p; sample: £1. Back issues: £1. Discounts: available on request. 20pp; size A5; †photocopies. Reporting time: as quickly as humanly possible. Payment: a magazine. Copyrighted, reverts to author.

Third Lung Press (see also THIRD LUNG REVIEW), Tim Peeler, PO Box 361, Conover, NC 28613, 704-465-1254. 1985. Poetry, art, photos. "All manuscripts are solicited" avg. press run 200-300. Pub'd 2 titles 1990; expects 3 titles 1991, 3 titles 1992. 7 titles listed in the *Small Press Record of Books in Print* (20th

Edition, 1991-92). avg. price, paper: $3. Discounts: bulk $2 per 25 or more. 20pp; 5½x8½; of. Payment: 40 copies of first 100. Does not copyright for author.

THIRD LUNG REVIEW, Third Lung Press, Tim Peeler, PO Box 361, Conover, NC 28613, 704-465-1254. 1985. Poetry, art, photos, reviews. "Tend to publish work that deals with social themes, although we have no conscious biases. Recent contributors include Arthur Knight, Harry Calhoun, Hal Daniel, Charles Bukowski" circ. 150. 1/yr. Pub'd 1 issue 1990; expects 1 issue 1991, 1 issue 1992. sub. price: $3; per copy: $3; sample: $3. 32pp; 11½x8½; of. Reporting time: 2 weeks. Payment: 1 copy of issue. Not copyrighted. Pub's reviews: 9 in 1990. §Mostly small press chapbooks, general subject matter.

THIRD RAIL, Third Rail Press, Uri Hertz, PO Box 46127, Los Angeles, CA 90046, 213-850-7548. 1975. Poetry, fiction, articles, art, photos, interviews, criticism, reviews. "*Third Rail* prints very little unsolicited material. No unsolicited submissions of poetry. The magazine is interested mainly in articles, interviews, essays, etc covering international literature and arts, most of which are solicited. Translations are printed regularly. Recent contributors include Philip Glass, Allen Ginsberg, Gary Snyder, Michael McClure, Edouard Roditi, Kazuko Shiraishi, George Herms, Robert Duncan, Jack Hirschman, David Meltzer, Fernando Alegria, Juan Epple, and Lucia Hwong" circ. 5M. 1/yr. Pub'd 1 issue 1990; expects 1 issue 1991, 1 issue 1992. sub. price: $30/4 issues (4 years); per copy: $7.95; sample: $7.95 plus postage. Back issues: inquire. Discounts: retailers 40%, inquire for others. 96pp; 8¾x11; of. Reporting time: 1-2 months. Payment: 2 copies of issue in which work appears. Copyrighted, reverts to author. Pub's reviews: 12 in 1990. §Literature, criticism, theater, film, translations. Ads: $800/$440/$240 for -1/4 page, $140 for -1/8 page, inquire.

Third Rail Press (see also THIRD RAIL), Uri Hertz, PO Box 46127, Los Angeles, CA 90046, 213-850-7548. 1975. Poetry, fiction, articles, art, photos, cartoons, interviews. "No unsolicited submissions of poetry" avg. press run 3M-5M. Pub'd 1 title 1990. avg. price, paper: $7.95. Discounts: bookstores & retailers 40%. 96pp; 8¾x11; of. Reporting time: 1-2 months. Payment: copies. Copyrights for author.

THIRD WAY, Third Way Ltd., Peter Cousins, Editor, 2 Chester House, Pages Lane, Muswell Hill, London NI0 1PR, England, 081-883-0372. 1977. Articles, photos, cartoons, interviews, criticism, reviews, letters, news items, non-fiction. circ. 3.5M. 10/yr. Pub'd 11 issues 1990; expects 10 issues 1991, 10 issues 1992. sub. price: UK £18, Europe £21.50, rest of world £23; per copy: £1.80. Back issues: cover price (min £1). 36pp; size A4; of, web. Reporting time: 6 weeks. Payment: £10-£30 (occasionally more). Copyrighted. Pub's reviews: 64 in 1990. §Christian analysis of social, political and cultural issues. Ads: £140/£75/£2 per column certn.

Third Way Ltd. (see also THIRD WAY), Peter Cousins, Editor, 2 Chester House, Pages Lane, Muswell Hill, London NI0 1PR, England, 081-883-0372. 1977. avg. press run 3.5M.

Third World First (see also LINKS), 232 Cowley Road, Oxford OX4 1UH, England. 1969. Poetry, fiction, articles, art, photos, cartoons, interviews. "ISSN: 0261-4014. Magazine showing links between economics, racism, and underdevelopment in the Third World. No unsolicited articles, please" avg. press run 3M. Pub'd 4 titles 1990; expects 4 titles 1991, 4 titles 1992. 19 titles listed in the *Small Press Record of Books in Print* (20th Edition, 1991-92). avg. price, paper: £3.50. Discounts: bookshops 33%, libraries 20%. 64pp; 15x21cm (A5); of. Payment: £50 per article. Does not copyright for author. Federation of Radical Booksellers (U.K.).

THIRD WORLD RESOURCES, Tom Fenton, Mary Heffron, 464 19 Street, Oakland, CA 94612, 415-835-4692; 536-1876; fax 415-835-3017. 1985. Reviews. "Available electronically through PeaceNet." circ. 2M. 4/yr. Pub'd 3 issues 1990; expects 4 issues 1991, 4 issues 1992. sub. price: North America: $35/2-yr indiv, $35/1-yr org.; Foreign: $50/2-yr indiv, $45/1-yr org.; per copy: $3.50; sample: North America-$2, Foreign-$3. Back issues: $30 per volume. Discounts: inquire. 24pp; 8½x11; of. Payment: none. Not copyrighted. Pub's reviews: 300 in 1990. §Political economy, U.S. foreign policy, Third World affairs. Ads: $450/$225/third page $150/5X5 $150. Alternative Press Syndicate, INTERDOC, ERIC.

THIRTEEN, M.A.F. Press, Ken Stone, Box 392, Portlandville, NY 13834-0392, 607-286-7500. 1982. Poetry, art. "We use only poetry of 13 lines; any subject as long as in good taste. Rochelle Holt, Barbara Crooker, Irving Weiss, Mary Ann Henn, Joyce Chandler, Guy Hamel, Sigmund Weiss, L. Cirino, Ida Fasel, John Ditsky, Sue Elkins, Ingrid Reti, David Transue, Esther Stockton, Harland Ristan, Virginia Smith, T.K. Splake, Ken Stone, Rod Farmer, Stan Proper. Art work: Esther Stockton, David Transue." circ. 350. 4/yr. Pub'd 4 issues 1990; expects 4 issues 1991, 4 issues 1992. sub. price: $5; per copy: $2.50; sample: $2.50. Back issues: none. Discounts: none; advance year payment discount available - two years $8; three years $10. 40pp; 8½x11½; lp. Reporting time: at most 2 weeks. Payment: one copy of issue; for special issues 2 to 6 copies. Not copyrighted. Pub's reviews: 24 in 1990. §Poetry. No ads. COSMEP, CLMP, NAPT.

Thirteen Colonies Press, John F. Millar, 710 South Henry Street, Williamsburg, VA 23185, 804-229-1775. 1986. Art, music, non-fiction. "We specialize in popular history (non-fiction) from the period of the Renaissance up to 1800." avg. press run 3M. Pub'd 2 titles 1990; expects 3 titles 1991, 3 titles 1992. 10 titles listed in the *Small Press Record of Books in Print* (20th Edition, 1991-92). avg. price, cloth: $30; paper: $20.

577

Discounts: retailer 40% up to 24 copies, 45% 24+ copies; wholesaler 20% up to 6 copies, 50% up to 24 copies, 60% 24+ copies; libraries 10% 1 book, 2+ books 30%. 200pp; 6×9 to 12×12; of. Payment: 10% gross sales, paid quarterly on previous quarter's sales. Copyrights for author. PMA, COSMEP, NAIP.

13th MOON, Judith E. Johnson, Editor, 1400 Washington Avenue, SUNY, English Department, Albany, NY 12222-0001, 212-678-1074. 1973. Poetry, fiction, articles, art, photos, interviews, criticism, reviews, letters, parts-of-novels, long-poems, collages, plays, concrete art, news items, non-fiction. *"13th Moon* is a literary magazine publishing quality work by women. Current issues include work by Marge Piercy, Cherrie Moraga, Marie Ponsot, Toi Derricotte, Judith Moffett, Cheryl Clarke, Judy Grahn, Carol Emshwiller. Vo. VII nos. 1&2 was a double issue on Working-Class Experience. In 1983-84, we have published or will publish translations of French novelist Jocelyne Francois, Brazilian writers Claric Lispector, Nelida Pinon and Myrim Campello, Hungarian poet Agnes Gergely. Artwork by Harmony Hammod, Affrekka Jefferson, May Stevens, Gina Gilmour. Issues on Narratives and formal poetry in preparation'' circ. 2.5M. 2/yr. Pub'd 1 issue 1990; expects 1 issue 1991. 1 title listed in the *Small Press Record of Books in Print* (20th Edition, 1991-92). sub. price: $13 for 2 issues; per copy: $6.50; sample: $6.50 plus 75¢ postage. Back issues: $5.95 plus $.75 postage. Discounts: the usual 40% discount on orders of 5 or more. 200pp; 6×9⅛; of. Reporting time: 2 weeks to 4 months. Payment: copies. Copyrighted, reverts to author. Pub's reviews: 17 in 1990. §Poetry by women small press books by women/literature by women/women's literary history by women. Ads: $200/$125. CCLM, NESPA,COSMEP.

THIS IS IMPORTANT, F.A. Nettelbeck, Editor, PO Box 323, Beatty, OR 97621, 503-533-2375. 1980. Poetry. "Patterned after a religious tract and features one poem from six different poets each issue. The pamphlets are distributed on buses, subways, toilet floors, in laundromats, bars, theaters, etc., with the aim being to get poetry out to non-literary types and others. Some of the featured poets have included: William S. Burroughs, Richard Kostelanetz, Wanda Coleman, Todd Moore, Tom Clark, John Giorno, Lyn Lifshin, David Fisher, James Bertolino, John M. Bennett, Jack Micheline, Ann Menebroker, Judson Crews, Anselm Hollo, Flora Durham, Charles Bernstein, Robin Holcomb, Douglas Blazek, James Grauerholz, Nila Northsun, Allen Ginsberg...as well as many others. Send poems. We want it *all* as long as it's *small*...but, *make me cry.* Make checks payable to F.A. Nettelbeck.'' circ. 1M. 4/yr. Pub'd 2 issues 1990; expects 2 issues 1991, 2 issues 1992. sub. price: $10; per copy: SASE; sample: $1. Back issues: individual issues vary in price, when available. Limited complete sets of Issues #1-#16 are available for $75 per set. Discounts: none. 8pp; 2¾×4¼; of. Reporting time: immediate. Payment: 50 copies. Copyrighted, reverts to author.

THIS MAGAZINE, Judy MacDonald, Managing Editor, 16 Skey Lane, Toronto, Ontario M6J 3S4, Canada, 416-588-6580. 1966. Poetry, fiction, articles, art, photos, cartoons, interviews, criticism, reviews, letters. "2,000-3,000 words. Canada's Independent Journal of Politics, culture, feminism and labour.'' circ. 8M. 8/yr. Pub'd 8 issues 1990; expects 8 issues 1991, 8 issues 1992. sub. price: $22.50 U.S., $19.50 Can.; per copy: $2.95; sample: $2.95. Back issues: $3. Discounts: 10% to agencies. 44pp; 8¼×11⅜; of. Reporting time: 6 weeks. Payment: 100%. Copyrighted, reverts to author. Pub's reviews: 8 in 1990. §Labour, education, politics, culture. Ads: $400/$185/$25. CMPA.

This Press, Barrett Watten, c/o Small Press Distribution, Inc., 1731 Stuart Street, Berkeley, CA 94703-1624. 1974. Poetry, fiction, long-poems. avg. press run 300-1M. Pub'd 1 title 1990; expects 1 title 1991, 1 title 1992. 8 titles listed in the *Small Press Record of Books in Print* (20th Edition, 1991-92). avg. price, cloth: $20 (Eigner); paper: $5. Discounts: see SPD, Inc. 96pp; 5×7 to 6×9; of.

Thistledown Press Ltd., Allan Forrie, Production Manager; Glen Sorestad, President; Sonia Sorestad, Treasurer; Patrick O'Rourke, Editor-in-Chief, 668 East Place, Saskatoon, Saskatchewan S7J 2Z5, Canada, 306-244-1722. 1975. Poetry, fiction. "Canadian authors only.'' avg. press run 750. Pub'd 11 titles 1990; expects 12 titles 1991, 12 titles 1992. 86 titles listed in the *Small Press Record of Books in Print* (20th Edition, 1991-92). avg. price, cloth: $20 poetry; $22 fiction; paper: $11 poetry; $16.50 fiction. Discounts: bookstores: 1-4 20%, 5+ 40% (with return privilege) 50% (non-returnable); jobbers (Canada): 30%; jobbers (outside Canada) 20%. 80-128pp; 5½×8½; of. Reporting time: 8-12 weeks. Payment: 10% of list. Copyrights for author. ACP, LPG, SPG.

Thomas Publications (see also PRIVATE INVESTIGATOR'S CONNECTION: A Newsletter for Investigators), Ralph D. Thomas, Barbara Thomas, PO Box 33244, Austin, TX 78764, 512-832-0355. 1983. Non-fiction. "Publisher of training manuals related to the private investigative profession and police trades.'' avg. press run 5M. Pub'd 2 titles 1990; expects 10 titles 1991, 20 titles 1992. 7 titles listed in the *Small Press Record of Books in Print* (20th Edition, 1991-92). avg. price, paper: $10. Discounts: 40-75%. 12pp; 8½×11; †of. Reporting time: 1 month, all answered. Payment: 5% to 15% depending on work. Copyrights for author.

THE THOMAS WOLFE REVIEW, John S. Phillipson, Editor; Aldo P. Magi, Associate Editor, Department of English, University of Akron, Akron, OH 44325, 216-972-7470. 1977. Poetry, fiction, articles, criticism. "Our chief interest is articles about Thomas Wolfe, either scholarly or at least of interest to an educated reader of Wolfe. Occasionally we publish poetry or fiction about him. Maximum length of articles, double-spaced, 25 pages, but we prefer shorter pieces." circ. 800. 2/yr. Pub'd 2 issues 1990; expects 2 issues 1991, 2 issues 1992. sub. price: $3; per copy: $1.50; sample: free. Back issues: $1.50. Discounts: none. 64pp; 5½x8½; †lp. Reporting time: 2 weeks. Payment: in copies. Copyrighted, does not revert to author.

Thompson and Co. Inc., Brad Thompson, Publisher, 4600 Longfellow Avenue South, Minneapolis, MN 55407-3638, 612-331-3963. 1981. Fiction, non-fiction. avg. press run 7M. Pub'd 1 title 1990; expects 6 titles 1991, 6 titles 1992. 1 title listed in the *Small Press Record of Books in Print* (20th Edition, 1991-92). avg. price, paper: $11.95; other: professional: $60. Discounts: available upon request to qualified customers. Reporting time: 2 months. Payment: between 5% and 15% royalty. Copyrights for author. I.P.A. (Independent Publishers Association).

Thorntree Press, Eloise Bradley Fink, John Dickson, 547 Hawthorn Lane, Winnetka, IL 60093, 708-446-8099. 1985. Poetry. "Thorntree Press accepts submissions in odd-numbered years for The Goodman Competition—January 1 - February 14. Poets are invited to mail a titled group of ten pages of unpublished poetry—with clear, crisp imagery. Any number of poems may be included, either single or double spaced. Xeroxes and printouts are preferred, along with a $4 entry fee. Mss will not be returned. Awards will be $400, $200, $100. In addition, from the top 15 finalists, a 30-page manuscript will be accepted for consideration for publication in *Troika*. Publications due 1992 include *Troika III* and *Troika IV*, plus two special editions." avg. press run 1M. 11 titles listed in the *Small Press Record of Books in Print* (20th Edition, 1991-92). avg. price, paper: $5.95. Discounts: to be arranged. 96pp; 6x9; mi. Reporting time: 2 months after contest. Payment: uncertain at this time. Copyrights for author.

Thornwood Book Publishers, A. Edward Foote, PO Box 1442, Florence, AL 35631, 205-766-6782. 1982. Photos, cartoons, non-fiction. "Also produce & market videos" avg. press run 500. Pub'd 1 title 1990; expects 1 title 1991, 2 titles 1992. 3 titles listed in the *Small Press Record of Books in Print* (20th Edition, 1991-92). avg. price, cloth: $19.95; paper: $5.95. Discounts: 6 or more 40%. 336pp; 5½x8½; of. Reporting time: 3 weeks. Payment: negotiable, usually subsidy by author. Copyrights for author.

Thorp Springs Press, Paul Foreman, Foster Robertson, 1002 Lorrain Street, Austin, TX 78703-4829. 1971. Poetry, fiction, plays. "Publication *Hyperion* indefinitely suspended-back issues through #16 (1980) available. No definite plans for continued publication at this time." avg. press run 1M. Pub'd 5 titles 1990. 27 titles listed in the *Small Press Record of Books in Print* (20th Edition, 1991-92). avg. price, cloth: $15; paper: $7; other: $2 pamphlet. Discounts: bookstores 40%, 10 or more copies; jobbers 10%, 3-10 copies; 20%, 11-50 copies. 150-200pp; 9x6, 5½x8½; of. Reporting time: 6 months. Payment: standard to above. Copyrights for author. COSMEP-SOUTH, COSMEP, Texas Circuit.

THOUGHT, A REVIEW OF CULTURE & IDEA, G. Richard Dimler, University Box L, Bronx, NY 10458, 212-579-2322. 1926. Articles, letters, non-fiction. "*Thought* publishes articles in the areas of philosophy, theology, literature and the arts within the context of the Judeo-Christian tradition. Occasionally *Thought* is devoted to an outstanding figure or a special topic: for example, Christianity and Post-Marxism, March 1987; The Church and Social Justice: Latin American Perspectives, June 1988; and Werner Stark's *The Social Bond*, March 1989. We do publish feature reviews." circ. 1.2M. 4/yr. Pub'd 4 issues 1990; expects 4 issues 1991, 4 issues 1992. sub. price: $17.50; per copy: $7.50; sample: $2. Back issues: $7.50. Discounts: agent 20%. 120pp; 6¾x10; of. Reporting time: 3 months. Payment: none. Copyrighted, does not revert to author. Pub's reviews: 6 in 1990. §Humanities, social sciences. Ads: $250/$150. CPA, Soc. for Scholarly Publishing.

THOUGHTS FOR ALL SEASONS: The Magazine of Epigrams, Michel Paul Richard, Editor-in-Chief; Roger Wescott, Ray Mizer, 11530 S.W. 99th Street, Miami, FL 33176, 305-598-8599. 1976. Articles, art, satire. "Form: One sentence or one paragraph original thoughts. Art work: Pen and ink." circ. 1M. Irregular, special issues. Expects 1 issue 1991. sub. price: $4.50; per copy: $4.50; sample: $4.50. Back issues: Vol. 2&3 available $3.75. Discounts: none. 84pp; 5½x8½; of. Reporting time: 30 days. Payment: none. Copyrighted, reverts to author. §Epigrams and aphorisms, as well as essays on the epigram as a literary form. Ads: $80/$45.

A Thousand Autumns Press, Chiaki Takeuchi, 760 Hermosa Palms, Las Vegas, NV 89123, 702-361-0676. 1988. Fiction, non-fiction. avg. press run 2M. Pub'd 1 title 1990; expects 1 title 1991, 1 title 1992. 3 titles listed in the *Small Press Record of Books in Print* (20th Edition, 1991-92). avg. price, cloth: $24.95; paper: $12.95; other: $19.95. Discounts: 20%-40%. 300pp; 5½x8½. Reporting time: 30 days (really not looking now). Payment: 10%, no advance. Copyrights for author. PMA, American Booksellers Association.

Three Continents Press, Inc., Donald Herdeck, Co-Editor and Publisher; Norman Ware, Int'l Editor; Lyndi Schrecengost, Assistant Editor, 1901 Pennsylvania Ave, NW, #407, Washington, DC 20006, 202-223-2554, 223-2604. 1973. Poetry, fiction, criticism, long-poems, plays. "Publishers of Third World literature (Africa, Caribbean, Middle East, Pacific, Asia), and the scholarship thereof" avg. press run 1M-2M. Pub'd 32 titles 1990; expects 32 titles 1991, 30 titles 1992. 82 titles listed in the *Small Press Record of Books in Print* (20th Edition, 1991-92). avg. price, cloth: $18; paper: $10. Discounts: 30% prepaid by retailers and wholsalers; 20% prepaid by libraries; 20% not prepaid, university bookstores. No discounts on single-copy orders. 175-250pp;

6×9, 5½×8½; of. Reporting time: 5-6 weeks, but often much longer. Payment: usually 10% with   advance. Copyrights for author.

III Publishing, Bill Meyers, PO Box 170363, San Francisco, CA 94117-0363, 415-221-1441. 1989. Fiction, satire. "Interested in short to medium length novels, especially satire from unusual viewpoints." avg. press run 2M. Pub'd 1 title 1990; expects 3-4 titles 1991, 5-6 titles 1992. 3 titles listed in the *Small Press Record of Books in Print* (20th Edition, 1991-92). avg. price, paper: $6. of. Reporting time: 2-4 weeks. Payment: negotiable. Copyrights for author.

THE THREEPENNY REVIEW, Wendy Lesser, Editor; Paul Bowles, Consulting Editor; John Berger, Consulting Editor; Elizabeth Hardwick, Consulting Editor; Robert Hass, Consulting Editor; Brenda Hillman, Consulting Editor; Gore Vidal, Consulting Editor, PO Box 9131, Berkeley, CA 94709, 415-849-4545. 1979. Poetry, fiction, art, interviews, criticism, reviews. "Length of material: Reviews should be 1M-3M words, covering several books or an author in depth, or dealing with a whole topic (e.g., the current theater season in one city, or the state of jazz clubs in another). Fiction should be under 5M words; poems should be under 100 lines. Special features: Though primarily a literary and performing arts review, *The Threepenny Review* will contain at least one essay on a topic of current social or political concern in each issue. Interested essayists should first submit a letter of inquiry. Recent Contributors: Czeslaw Milosz ,Thom Gunn, Susn Sontag. *SASE must accompany all manuscripts.*" circ. 8M. 4/yr. Expects 4 issues 1991. sub. price: $10, $16 for 2 years; per copy: $3; sample: $4. Back issues: variable (price list available). 36pp; 11×17; of. Reporting time: 2 weeks to 2 months. Payment: $50-$100. Copyrighted, reverts to author. Pub's reviews: 20 in 1990. §Fiction, poetry, essays, philosophy, social theory, visual arts and architecture, history, criticism. Ads: $600/$350. CCLM.

Threshold Books, Edmund Helminski, RR4 Box 600, Putney, VT 05346, 802-387-4586 or 245-8300. 1981. Poetry, fiction, non-fiction. "Most recent publications include translations of Rumi. Interested in World literature of high quality, spiritual and philosophical works from Eastern and Western traditions; books of cultural importance." avg. press run 2M. Pub'd 2 titles 1990; expects 3 titles 1991, 3 titles 1992. 13 titles listed in the *Small Press Record of Books in Print* (20th Edition, 1991-92). avg. price, cloth: $15; paper: $10. Discounts: 40% trade; 45% bulk. 60-160pp; 5½×8½; of, lp. Reporting time: 60 days. Payment: 10-15%. Copyrights for author. COSMEP/SSP.

THRESHOLDS JOURNAL, SOM Publishing, division of School of Metaphysics, Dr. Barbara O'Guinn, Editor-in-Chief; Laurel Fuller, Senior Editor, HCR 1, Box 15, Windyville, MO 65783, 417-345-8411. 1975. "Submissions in eight categories considered: Arts and Sciences, Business, Health, Creative Writing, Humor, Personal Insight, Education (Most Influential Teacher), Scholar's Report. Double-spaced, typed manuscripts 9-12 pages in length. Interview with well-known people who are successful in their fields. Recent interviews with Bernie Siegel, Diane Stein, Fred Pryor, Stella Parton, etc." circ. 5M+. 6/yr. Pub'd 6 issues 1990; expects 6 issues 1991, 6 issues 1992. sub. price: $13.40; per copy: $2.60; sample: on request. Back issues: $4 plus shipping. Discounts: 40% trade, 50% jobber, 20% organizations, churches, groups without sales tax number. 36pp; 7½×10; †of. Reporting time: 5 weeks. Payment: if accepted, exposure. Copyrighted, does not revert to author. Pub's reviews. §Self-development, personal insight, metaphysics, health, fiction, astrology. Ads: $250/$125/$25 business card.

THUNDER & HONEY, Akbar Imhotep, PO Box 11386, Atlanta, GA 30310. 1983. Poetry, fiction. "Poems should be less than 40 lines, fiction (up to 2500 words). Recent contributors: Charlie Braxton, Nia Damali, Frank Smith, Alan Sugar, Akbar Imhotep" circ. 1.5M. 4/yr. Pub'd 3 issues 1990; expects 2 issues 1991, 4 issues 1992. sub. price: $2.50; per copy: 75¢. 4pp; 11×17; of. Payment: copies. Copyrighted, reverts to author. Ads: $210/$120/$60 quarter page/$40 sixth page. Coordinating Council Literary Magazines (CCLM).

Thunder & Ink, Tim Burke, Writer & Editor; Ann Burke, Illustrator, PO Box 7014, Evanston, IL 60201, 708-492-1823. 1988. Fiction. "Children's fiction. Young and middle readers. No teen or toddler books. Not accepting submissions in 1991." avg. press run 1-2M. Pub'd 1 title 1990; expects 1 title 1992. 1 title listed in the *Small Press Record of Books in Print* (20th Edition, 1991-92). avg. price, paper: $5. Discounts: trade 30-40%, jobber 40-60%. 32pp; 8½×5½; of. Payment: tba. Copyrights for author. COSMEP.

Thunder City Press, Steven Ford Brown, Editor, PO Box 2764, Boston, MA 02208. 1975. Poetry, fiction, art, photos, interviews, criticism, reviews. "Books by Pier Giorgio Di Cicco, Peter Cooley, D.C. Berry, Emily Borenstein, Ed Ochester, Andrew Glaze, Georg Trakl, M.R. Doty, Enrique Anderson Imbert, Ofelia Castillo, Michael Waters, Tomas Transtromer, Theodore Haddin. Looking for work that ends the virtual necessity for the World. ***The American Poets ProFile series: a series of books profiling American poets and their work including profiles of Dave Smith, John Logan, Andrew Glaze, Paul Zimmer, Vassar Miller, Carolyn Kizer, Fred Chappell." avg. press run 500-1.5M. Pub'd 5 titles 1990; expects 5 titles 1991, 6 titles 1992. 2 titles listed in the *Small Press Record of Books in Print* (20th Edition, 1991-92). avg. price, paper: $12.95; other: $50 signed & numbered. Discounts: 1-4 copies 20%, 5+ 40%. 64-250pp; 5½×11; of. Reporting time: 1 month. Payment: copies, book promotion, reviews, cash. Copyrights for author.

Thunder Creek Publishing Co-operative (see also Coteau Books), Shelley Sopher, Managing Editor, 401-2206 Dewdney Avenue, Regina, Sask. S4R 1H3, Canada, 306-777-0170. 1975. Poetry, fiction, interviews, criticism, long-poems, plays, non-fiction. "Bookorders: University of Toronto Press, 5201 Dufferin St., Downsview, Ont. M3T 5T8, Canada. Primarily literary material accepted, although the press has recently expanded into areas other than adult poetry, prose and drama such as children's storybooks, anthologies of writing and songs for children, a Canadian women's desk calendar, literary criticism and reference books. *Only manuscripts by Canadian writers are considered.*" avg. press run 3M. Pub'd 8 titles 1990; expects 8 titles 1991, 9 titles 1992. 29 titles listed in the *Small Press Record of Books in Print* (20th Edition, 1991-92). avg. price, cloth: $21.95 Cdn.; paper: $10.95; other: $6.95 mass market format. Discounts: retail - 40%; libraries - 20% on standing orders of 9 or less; wholesale, jobbers 20% on 1-9 copies, 46% on 10+. 120-325pp; 6×9, 4¼×7, 8×8, 8½×11; of. Reporting time: 2-6 months. Payment: 10% unless otherwise arranged, & signing bonus & author copies. Copyrights for author. Assn. of Canadian Publishers (ACP), Can. Book Info Centre (CBIC), Can. Telebook Agency (CTA), Literary Press Group (LPG), Canadian Booksellers Association (CBA), Saskatchewan Publishers Group (SPG).

THUNDERMUG REPORT, Tiptoe Literary Service, Anne Grimm-Richardson, 110 Wildwood Drive, PO Box 206-876, Naselle, WA 98638, 206-484-7722. 1991. Poetry, articles, cartoons. "Business newsletter, local promotion and news, but with worldwide scope (especially The Americas) and interest in trade. Space limitations. *Everything* must be *brief.* A few short paragraphs at most. Short verse, humorous only. Promoting, retirement/tourism/relocation of small businesses." 4/yr. Expects 4 issues 1991, 4 issues 1992. sub. price: with a membership only; sample: $1. Back issues: $1 premier issue, mailed anywhere in the world. Discounts: none. 10pp; 8½×11. Reporting time: 45 days. Payment: copy. Pub's reviews. §Unlikely we could use - mainly local oriented. Ads: $100/$55/$20¢ per word, $2 minimum. COSMEP, Int'l Assn. of Publishers, PO Box 703, San Francisco, CA 94101.

Thunder's Mouth Press, Neil Ortenberg, 54 Greene Street, Suite 4S, New York, NY 10013. 1981. Poetry, fiction, articles, art, photos, cartoons, interviews, satire, criticism, reviews, long-poems, non-fiction. "Unsolicited manuscripts not accepted." avg. press run 7M-10M. Pub'd 6 titles 1990; expects 15 titles 1991, 20 titles 1992. 37 titles listed in the *Small Press Record of Books in Print* (20th Edition, 1991-92). avg. price, cloth: $21.95; paper: $11.95. Distributed by PAW, 4065 Hollis, PO Box 8843, Emeryville, CA 94608. 200-250pp; size varies; of. Reporting time: 10-12 weeks. Payment: on individual basis. Copyrights for author. COSMEP.

Tiare Publications, Gerry L. Dexter, President, PO Box 493, Lake Geneva, WI 53147, 414-248-4845. 1986. Non-fiction. "Publish radio communications and radio communications monitoring books." avg. press run 1M. Pub'd 10 titles 1990; expects 10 titles 1991, 10 titles 1992. 1 title listed in the *Small Press Record of Books in Print* (20th Edition, 1991-92). avg. price, paper: $12.95. Discounts: standard. 100pp; 5½×8½, 8½×11; of. Reporting time: 1 month. Payment: 15% royalty. Publisher holds copyright.

Tide Book Publishing Company, Rose Safran, Box 101, York Harbor, ME 03911-0101, 207-363-4534. 1979. Articles, art, interviews, news items, non-fiction. "Currently specializing in popular sociological issues. Most recent title is *Don't Go Dancing Mother* by Rose Safran; subject matter is social gerontology. All titles will be brief. Line drawings are used. Will produce only quality trade paperbacks." avg. press run 2M-5M. Expects 1 title 1991. 1 title listed in the *Small Press Record of Books in Print* (20th Edition, 1991-92). avg. price, paper: $6.95. Discounts: 20% single copy trade, 40% 5+ copies trade, jobber 50-55%, salesman 10% of the net sale, inquire about bulk. 100pp; 6×9; lp. Reporting time: ASAP. Payment: no fixed arrangements. Copyrights for author. NESPA, COSMEP.

TIDEPOOL, Herb Barrett, 4 East 23rd Street, Hamilton, Ontario L8V 2W6, Canada, 416-383-2857. 1983. Poetry, articles, art. "*Tidepool* will henceforth be using both haiku and short verse, maximum, 32 lines. Open to writers world-wide. Articles on haiku and modern poetry-maximum 1500 words." circ. 300. 1/yr. Pub'd 1 issue 1990; expects 1 issue 1991, 1 issue 1992. sub. price: $5; per copy: $5; sample: $3. Back issues: 2 for $5. Discounts: 40%. 70pp; 5¼×8½; of. Reporting time: 1 month. Payment: by copies. Copyrighted, reverts to author. IBIP.

TIERRA DEL FUEGO MAGAZINE, Zagier & Urruty Publicaciones, Sergio Zagier, Dario Urruty, PO Box 94 Sucursal 19, Buenos Aires 1419, Argentina, 541-572-1050. 1989. Articles, photos, reviews, non-fiction. "U.S.A. address: 6630 Indian Creek Drive #223, Miami Beach, FL 33141. We need manuscripts about travel subjects concerning southern South America and Antarctica. Also photos and drawings. Any language. Maximum 3 letter pages." circ. 7M. 1/yr. Pub'd 1 issue 1990; expects 1 issue 1991, 2 issues 1992. sub. price: $8; per copy: $8; sample: $8. Back issues: $8. Discounts: 50% distributors, 30% bookstores, 20% travel companies and institutions. 84pp; 8×11½; of. Reporting time: 6 weeks. Payment: Depending on the kind of work. Copyrighted, reverts to author. Pub's reviews: 3 in 1990. §Travel, South America, Antarctica, cruises, fishing, natural history, adventour. Ads: $1,150/$600/$2,500 back cover.

581

TIGER LILY MAGAZINE: The Magazine by Women of Colour, Williams-Wallace Publishers, Inc., Zanana Akande, Ann Wallace, PO Box 756, Stratford, Ontario, Canada, 519-271-7045. 1986. Poetry, fiction, articles, interviews, non-fiction. "Length of material maximum 3,000 words. Some contributors: Marjorie Agosin, Leah Creque-Harris, Margarita Papaendreau, Dr. Victoria Lee. We do *not* publish any anti-racial, anti-sexist, anti-class material" circ. 15M. 5/yr. Pub'd 1 issue 1990; expects 5 issues 1991, 5 issues 1992. sub. price: $14.95; per copy: $2.95; sample: $2.95. Back issues: $3. Discounts: 20%-40%. 40pp; 5×10. Reporting time: 7 weeks. Payment: 5¢ per word. Copyrighted, reverts to author. Pub's reviews. §Fiction, women, particularly by or about Women of Colour. Ads: $950/$635/$420 1/3/$380 1/4/$235 1/6. ACB, CBPC.

TIGER MOON, Tiger Moon, Terry Kennedy, Mark James Miller, 1850 Chester Lane, Cambria, CA 93428, 815-927-3920. 1991. Poetry, fiction, articles, interviews, non-fiction. "We are just getting started. We are compiling first-person narratives from survivors of incest right now. We will also publish one poetry collection and one short story collection this year. We are looking for very non-mainstream work that big houses simply can't risk running. We are not a vanity or subsidy press but we help the author raise funds because we don't have big marketing bucks or advertising dollars. We consider ourselves service oriented—serving *real* needs of readers." Discounts: our books are available free to prisons and we give discounts to people who will write to us directly. Reporting time: within 2 months. Payment: copies; but you can collect the cover price at readings or direct selling. §Women's issues, native American, spiritual, poetry, fiction, short fiction.

Tiger Moon (see also TIGER MOON), Terry Kennedy, Mark James Miller, 1850 Chester Lane, Cambria, CA 93428, 815-927-3920. 1991. Poetry, fiction, non-fiction. "We are just getting started. We are compiling first-person narratives from survivors of incest right now. We will also publish one poetry collection and one short story collection this year. We are looking for very non-mainstream work that big houses simply can't risk running. We are not a vanity or subsidy press but we help the author raise funds because we don't have big marketing bucks or advertising dollars. We consider ourselves service-oriented—serving *real* needs of readers." avg. press run 1M. Expects 2 titles 1991, 3 titles 1992. avg. price, cloth: $9.99. 100-200pp; size varies. Reporting time: 2 months. Payment: copies. Copyrights for author.

TIGHTROPE, Swamp Press, Ed Rayher, 323 Pelham Road, Amherst, MA 01002. 1975. Poetry, fiction, art, long-poems, collages. "Fine poetry, fiction and graphic art printed by letterpress in artistic and unconventional formats. Recent contributors: Julie Juarez, Alan Catlin." circ. 350. 2/yr. Pub'd 1 issue 1990; expects 2 issues 1991, 2 issues 1992. sub. price: $10; per copy: $6; sample: $6. Back issues: $6. Discounts: bookstores and dealers 40%. 36pp; size varies; †lp. Reporting time: 8 weeks. Payment: copies, cash sometimes, usually for fiction. Copyrighted, reverts to author. CCLM, 666 Broadway, NYC 10112-2301.

Tilbury House, Publishers, Mark Melnicove, 132 Water Street, Gardiner, ME 04345, 207-582-1899. 1990. Poetry, fiction, articles, art, photos, cartoons, interviews, satire, criticism, reviews, music, letters, parts-of-novels, long-poems, collages, plays, concrete art, news items, non-fiction. "Tilbury House, Publishers publishes poetry, fiction, children's books, essays and books about the environment, regional titles, and art books" avg. press run 500-5M. Pub'd 5 titles 1990; expects 8 titles 1991, 8 titles 1992. 34 titles listed in the *Small Press Record of Books in Print* (20th Edition, 1991-92). avg. price, cloth: $25.95; paper: $12.95. Discounts: 20% libraries, 40% bookstores. 200pp; 6×9, 8×9, 5×7, 5½×8½; of, lp. Reporting time: 2 months. Payment: 8-10% royalties. Copyrights for author. MWPA.

Tilton House, Kathleen Tilton, 255 East Street #1, Mountain View, CA 94043-3752. 1986. Poetry, long-poems. "Tilton House specializes in poetry and fiction." avg. press run 1M. Pub'd 4 titles 1990; expects 4 titles 1991, 4 titles 1992. 7 titles listed in the *Small Press Record of Books in Print* (20th Edition, 1991-92). avg. price, paper: $4.50-$5.50; other: $4.50 poetry. Discounts: libraries 10%. 40pp; 5½×8½; †typesetting. Reporting time: 3 months. Payment: copies. Does not copyright for author. SCBW, COSMEP, PMA.

Timber Press, Richard Abel, Senior Editor; Darcel Goetinck, Production Editor, 9999 S.W. Wilshire, Portland, OR 97225, 503-292-0745. 1976. Articles, art, photos. "Other imprints: Dioscorides Press, Amadeus Press, Areopagitica Press. Main emphasis is Northwestern subject matter, horticulture, forestry, botany, music and history" avg. press run 5M. Pub'd 38 titles 1990; expects 45 titles 1991, 50 titles 1992. 80 titles listed in the *Small Press Record of Books in Print* (20th Edition, 1991-92). avg. price, cloth: $32.95; paper: $22.95. Discounts: 1, 20%; 5, 40%; 25, 42%; 100, 43%; 250, 44%; 500, 46%. 275pp; 8×5, 8½×11; of. Reporting time: 21 days. Payment: by arrangement. Copyrights for author. PNWPA (Pacific Northwestern Publishers Assn.), COSMEP.

Timberline Press, Clarence Wolfshohl, Rt. 1, Box 1434, Fulton, MO 65251, 314-642-5035. 1975. Poetry, non-fiction. "Print chapbooks of 20-50 pages (prefer shorter 20-30 pp). We look at all poetry sent, but lean toward nature poetry with a sense of place or good lyrical, imagistic poetry. Actually, our taste is eclectic with quality being our primary criterion. We are branching out to publish short essays of natural history (under 20 pages) which will be printed in a reduced size format (not miniature). No set preference, but possible contributors should be familiar with better contemporary writers of natural history." avg. press run 200. Pub'd

1 title 1990; expects 2 titles 1991, 2 titles 1992. 6 titles listed in the *Small Press Record of Books in Print* (20th Edition, 1991-92). avg. price, paper: $5-$7.50. Discounts: 1-4 books 25%, 5+ 40%. 25-45pp; 5½×7, 6×9; †lp. Reporting time: 30 days. Payment: 50-50 split after expenses. Does not copyright for author.

TIMBERLINE/VISION ONE, Stillpoint Publishing, Dorothy Z. Seymour, Editor, Box 640, Walpole, NH 03608, 603-756-9281. 4/yr. Pub'd 4 issues 1990; expects 4 issues 1991, 4 issues 1992.

Timeless Books, Rita Foran, Editor; Julie McKay, Editor, PO Box 50905, Palo Alto, CA 94303-0673, 604-227-9224. 1977. Non-fiction. "Timeless publications are for those who seek a deeper meaning and purpose to their lives. Our focus is on the ancient teachings of yoga and Buddhism. Inspiration is combined with practical tools for living a life of quality to bring out the best in ourselves and others." avg. press run 3M books, 1M booklets. Pub'd 3 titles 1990; expects 3 titles 1991, 3 titles 1992. 8 titles listed in the *Small Press Record of Books in Print* (20th Edition, 1991-92). avg. price, cloth: $22.95; paper: $11.95; other: $5 booklets. Discounts: books and booklets, 40% over five copies. 250pp; 6×9; of. Copyrights for author. COSMEP, NAPRA, PMA.

Timely Books, Yvonne MacManus, Jo Anne Prather, 4040 Mountain Creek Road, Suite 1304, Chattanooga, TN 37415, 615-875-9447. 1978. Fiction, non-fiction. "We publish both fiction and non-fiction (in trade paperback format), primarily serious feminist or lesbian themes, but also interested in gay MSS. Will consider original MSS, not to exceed 70M words" avg. press run 2M-4M. Pub'd 1 title 1990; expects 1-2 titles 1991, 1-2 titles 1992. 9 titles listed in the *Small Press Record of Books in Print* (20th Edition, 1991-92). avg. price, paper: $8. Discounts: 3-5 copies, 20%; 6-10 copies, 30%; 11-19 copies, 35%; 20 and up, 40%. 200pp; 5½×8½; of. Reporting time: 6-8 weeks. Payment: varies - usual trade paperback; no advance. Copyrights for author.

Times Change Press, Lamar Hoover, Editor & Publisher, PO Box 1380, Ojai, CA 93024-1380, 805-646-8595. 1970. Criticism, non-fiction. "Times Change Press is a noncommercial publishing company producing books and posters on political and sexual his/herstory, personal liberation, feminism, and radical ecology. Book and poster orders: Publishers Services, Box 2510, Novato, CA 94948; 415-883-3530." avg. press run 4M. Pub'd 2 titles 1990; expects 3 titles 1991, 3 titles 1992. 27 titles listed in the *Small Press Record of Books in Print* (20th Edition, 1991-92). avg. price, cloth: $13; paper: $6. Discounts: 1-4 copies 20%, 5+ 40%, posters 50%. 94pp; 5½×7; of. Reporting time: 2 months. Payment: negotiable. Copyrights for author. PMA, COSMEP, MPE, Small Press Center.

TIN WREATH, David Gonsalves, PO Box 13401, Albany, NY 12212-3401. 1985. Poetry. "*Tin Wreath* appears quarterly with selected late 20th-century visions of the actual and the possible, and is available free upon request. We're looking for poetry that makes contact with the deeper forces at work in the world, and poetry that explores the musical and sculptural qualities inherent in the language; we'd prefer to see abstract, minimalist, and/or non-discursive poetry." circ. 250. 4/yr. Pub'd 4 issues 1990; expects 4 issues 1991, 4 issues 1992. sub. price: free; per copy: free; sample: free. Back issues: free. 28pp; 5½×8½; †xerographic reproduction. Reporting time: 13 days to 13 weeks. Payment: copies. Copyrighted, reverts to author.

Tioga Publishing Co., Karen Nilsson, 150 Coquito Way, Portola Valley, CA 94028, 415-854-2445. 1979. "Non-fiction-travel, journals. Focus on Western America - its natural and literary heritage." avg. press run 5M. Pub'd 2 titles 1990; expects 2 titles 1991, 2 titles 1992. 18 titles listed in the *Small Press Record of Books in Print* (20th Edition, 1991-92). avg. price, cloth: $35; paper: $12. Discounts: industry standard. 200-300pp; 6×9. Reporting time: 1 month, not solicited. Payment: negotiated depending upon marketing efforts of author. Copyrights for author. NCBP Assoc., PMA, COSMEP.

Tippy Reed Publishing, Megan Sue Whittaker, PO Box 260301, Lakewood, CO 80226, 303-797-6393. 1991. Fiction, art, photos, interviews, parts-of-novels, non-fiction. avg. press run 70M. Expects 3 titles 1991, 10 titles 1992. 3 titles listed in the *Small Press Record of Books in Print* (20th Edition, 1991-92). avg. price, cloth: $19; paper: $13.50. Discounts: 2-4 20%, 5-99 40%, 100+ 50%, bookstores 40%, wholesales and distributors 55%. 375pp; 6×9; of. Reporting time: 8-10 weeks. Payment: hardcover—10% on first 5,000 copies, 12½% on next 5,000, and 15% thereafter; trade paperbacks—10% on first 20,000 copies, 12½% up to 40,000 then thereafter. Copyrights for author.

Tiptoe Literary Service (see also THUNDERMUG REPORT), A. Grimm-Richardson, 110 Wildwood Drive, PO Box 206, Naselle, WA 98638, 206-484-7722. 1985. "We publish staff written how to pamphlets—others please query with SASE" avg. press run 1M. Pub'd 3 titles 1990; expects 3 titles 1991. 23 titles listed in the *Small Press Record of Books in Print* (20th Edition, 1991-92). avg. price, other: $4.95 saddle-stitched (pamphlets). 12pp; 5½×3½; computer typeset, commercially printed. Reporting time: 45 days. Does not copyright for author. COSMEP, SSA, WAHPACWA - CWI (Wahkiakum Pacific Writers Association - Crossroads Writers International), NASELLE-Gray's River Valley Chamber of Commerce.

T-J TODAY, Alice Leyland, Editor, Publisher, 732 Cynthia Court, Watsonville, CA 95076, 408-728-3948. 1981. Articles, art, photos, cartoons, interviews, criticism, reviews, music, letters. "Articles solicited that are of interest to followers of traditional jazz: biographies of artists, living or dead, festivals/jubilees, noteworthy bands, other items of interest to traditional musicians or listeners. NOTE: *T-J Today* is primarily a directory on the order of TV Guide, and lists on a nationwide basis where the jazz bands are playing, special events and one-day events, lists of bands and their leaders, and jazz societies." circ. 1M. 4/yr. Pub'd 4 issues 1990; expects 4 issues 1991, 4 issues 1992. sub. price: $13; per copy: $4. 82pp; 4½×6¼; of. Reporting time: 1 month. Payment: 10¢ per printed line (average 6 words), $5 per photo used. Copyrighted, does not revert to author. Ads: $115/$75/$45/$6 bus card/$150 inside front cover/$135 inside back cover.

TOAD HIWAY, Toad Hiway Press, Doug Martin, Editor-in-Chief; Kevin Anderson, Assistant Editor; John Colvin, Assistant Editor; Paul Bauer, Art Editor; Brian Beatty, Assistant Editor, Box 44, Universal, IN 47884, 317-832-8918. 1988. Poetry, fiction, art, photos, interviews, reviews, music, plays, non-fiction. "Our guidelines are as follows: 5 poems maximum (any style, although we lean toward mainstream and experimental work), 4 short stories, 4 drawings, photos, etc. Some recent contributors include Gayle Elen Harvey, Gene Fehler, and Ron Mitchell, Arthur Knight, Judson Crews, Glen Armstrong, Lyn Lishin" circ. 200. Irregular. Pub'd 2 issues 1990; expects 1 issue 1991, 1 issue 1992. sub. price: $4/3 issues; per copy: $2; sample: 25¢ first issue. Discounts: we are willing to trade with other small press publications. 20pp; 5½×8½; of. Reporting time: 3 months. Payment: 2 free copies. Copyrighted, reverts to author. Pub's reviews. §Poetry and fiction books, performance art, magazines. Ads: $50/$25/$10 1/4 page/$5 1/8 or trade.

Toad Hiway Press (see also TOAD HIWAY; STONE TALK), Doug Martin, Editor-in-Chief; Kevin Anderson, Assistant Editor; John Colvin, Assistant Editor; Brian Beatty, Assistant Editor, Box 44, Universal, IN 47884, 317-832-8918. 1989. Poetry, fiction, art, photos, interviews, reviews, music, plays, non-fiction. "We would like to print poetry and fiction chapbooks mostly. Still, we would like to print a book which consists of articles and interviews on performance artists like Laurie Anderson. Also, we would like to receive demo-tapes from musicians so as to release a cassette-series of Alternative Rock" avg. press run 200. Expects 1 title 1991, 1 title 1992. avg. price, paper: $2. Discounts: we are willing to trade with other publications. 20pp; 5½×8½; of. Reporting time: 3 months. Payment: by arrangement. Copyrights for author.

TODAY, Elm House Christian Communications Ltd, Dave Roberts, Editor, 37 Elm Road, New Malden, Surrey KT3 3HB, England, 01-942-9761. 1955. Articles, art, photos, interviews, reviews, letters, news items. circ. 7M. 12/yr. Pub'd 12 issues 1990; expects 12 issues 1991, 12 issues 1992. sub. price: £15.90; per copy: £1.20; sample: free. Back issues: by arrangement. Discounts: negotiable. 48pp; 273×255mm; of, web. Payment: yes. Copyrighted. Pub's reviews: 120 in 1990. §Christian doctrine, biography, living.

Todd Publications (see also DIRECTORY MARKETPLACE), Barry Klein, Nancy Rout, PO Box 301, West Nyack, NY 10994, 914-358-6213. 1973. "Directories and reference books" avg. press run 3M. Pub'd 3 titles 1990; expects 3 titles 1991, 5 titles 1992. 1 title listed in the *Small Press Record of Books in Print* (20th Edition, 1991-92). avg. price, cloth: $50; paper: $25. Discounts: 20% wholesalers, 20-40% bookstores. 400pp; 6×9; of. Reporting time: 4 weeks. Payment: 10-15%. Copyrights for author.

TOLE WORLD, EGW Publishing Company, Zach Shatz, PO Box 5986, Concord, CA 94524, 415-671-9852. 1977. Poetry, art, photos, interviews, reviews, letters, non-fiction. "*Tole World* is devoted to the traditions of Tole and decorative painting" circ. 55M. 6/yr. Pub'd 6 issues 1990; expects 6 issues 1991, 6 issues 1992. sub. price: $15; per copy: $3.50. 72pp; 8⅛×10⅞; of, web. Reporting time: 2-6 weeks. Payment: upon publication, first serial rights. Pub's reviews. Ads: $750 b/w/95¢ word.

Toledo Poets Center Press (see also GLASS WILL; 11 X 13 - BROADSIDE), Joel Lipman, Department of English, University of Toledo, Toledo, OH 43606. 1976. Poetry, articles, art, long-poems, concrete art. "Please no unsolicited work. Publishes area writers, area inmate writers." avg. press run 200-1M. Pub'd 1 title 1990; expects 2 titles 1991, 2 titles 1992. 3 titles listed in the *Small Press Record of Books in Print* (20th Edition, 1991-92). avg. price, paper: $1-$7.50. Discounts: 40% for bookstores. 9¼×6¼, 11×30; of. Payment: copies. Does not copyright for author.

THE TOLL GATE JOURNAL, Purple Heather Publications, Richard Mason, 12 Colne Road, Cowling, Keighley, West Yorkshire, BD22 0BZ, England. 1983. Poetry, fiction, articles, art, photos, interviews, reviews, music, letters, parts-of-novels, collages, news items, non-fiction. "Do not send more than five poems. Prose should not exceed 2000 words. Type only on one side of the paper. Double spacing is not necessary. Artwork, including cover designs are welcome. Camera ready copy is always appreciated. Our size is A5. Unsolicited manuscripts failing to include sufficient I.R.C.s or cash to cover return postage will not be considered. This rule applies to literary agents also" circ. 500. 2/yr. Expects 2 issues 1991, 2 issues 1992. sub. price: $10 cash (*no* cheques); per copy: $5 cash *No* cheques; sample: $2 cash *No* cheques. Discounts: details available on request. 68pp; 5¾×8¼; of. Reporting time: 1 month. Payment: copies of magazine. Copyrighted, reverts to author. Pub's reviews: 100 in 1990. §Poetry, Art, Music, Ecology, Conservation. Ads: $15/$7.50/$4¼ page, 10¢ a word, minimum 20 words *No* cheques. YFSP (The Yorkshire Federation of Small Presses).

Tomart Publications, Tom Tumbusch, Jack Wade, Customer Service; Bob Raymond, Editor, Disneyana

Series; Rebecca Trissel, Assistant to Publisher, PO Box 292102, Dayton, OH 45429, 513-294-2250. 1977. Non-fiction. "We are publishers of antique & collectible photo price guides for Disneyana (any Disney product), radio premiums, character glasses, space adventure collectibles, etc. Other non-fiction on related subjects. Books on musical theatre." avg. press run 6M-10M. Pub'd 2 titles 1990; expects 3 titles 1991, 5 titles 1992. 7 titles listed in the *Small Press Record of Books in Print* (20th Edition, 1991-92). avg. price, cloth: $29.95; paper: $24.95. Discounts: booksellers 40%, distributors up to 60%. 220pp; 8½×11, 7×10, 5½×8½; of. Reporting time: 30 days. Payment: 10% for camera ready, advance. Copyrights for author. COSMEP.

Tombouctou Books, Michael Wolfe, Box 265, Bolinas, CA 94924, 415-868-1082. 1975. Poetry, fiction, interviews, long-poems. "No unsolicited mss. Distributed to the trade by Subterranean Book Co., POB 10233, Eugene, OR 97410" avg. press run 500-2M. Pub'd 4 titles 1990; expects 4 titles 1991, 4 titles 1992. 21 titles listed in the *Small Press Record of Books in Print* (20th Edition, 1991-92). avg. price, cloth: $5-$10; paper: $7; other: signed hardback, limited edition, $35. Discounts: inquire publisher. 48-200pp; 5½×8½; †of. Payment: varies. Copyrights for author.

TOOK, Norton Coker Press, Edward Mycue, PO Box 640543, San Francisco, CA 94164-0543, 415-922-0395. 1988. Poetry, fiction, art, satire, criticism, reviews, music, letters, plays, news items. "We published 17 issues in 1988. We have not published any issues since. We plan to begin anew—but not so soon yet." circ. 150. Occasional. sub. price: $5; per copy: $1.50; sample: $1.50. 8-32pp; 5×8; †xerox. Payment: copy. Copyrighted, reverts to author. Pub's reviews.

Top Of The Mountain Publishing, Dr. Tag Powell, Dr. Judith L. Powell, 11701 Belcher Road South, Ste. 123, Largo, FL 34643-5117, 813-530-0110. 1979. Non-fiction. *"Contesting: The Name It And Claim It Game* by Helene Hadsell, 256 pages, trade paperback. *Numerology: A Number Of Your Friends Are Aniimals* by Jackie Suggs, 256 pages, tradepaper. *As You Thinketh* by Allen/Powell, 104 pages, hardcover/trade paperback. *Silva Method Of Mind Mastery* by Powell, 256 pages, hardcover/trade paperback." avg. press run 5M. Pub'd 6 titles 1990; expects 10 titles 1991, 15 titles 1992. 10 titles listed in the *Small Press Record of Books in Print* (20th Edition, 1991-92). avg. price, cloth: $22.95; paper: $12.95. Discounts: standard. 250pp; 5⅜×8½; of. Reporting time: varies. Payment: 7% to 10%. Copyrights for author. PMA, ABA, COSMO, NAPRA, International Publishers Alliance, Florida Publishers Group.

TOPICAL TIME, Glen Crago, Editor, 1633 Park Ridge Lane, Toledo, OH 43614, 419-382-2719. 1949. Articles, photos, cartoons. "A magazine for stamp collectors who are interested in the subjects shown on stamps." circ. 8M. 6/yr. Pub'd 6 issues 1990; expects 6 issues 1991, 6 issues 1992. sub. price: $12; per copy: $2.75; sample: $2.75. Discounts: inquire. 96pp; 5×8; of, lp. Reporting time: 2 weeks. Payment: tearsheets of articles, no money. Copyrighted, does not revert to author. Pub's reviews: 100 in 1990. §Stamp collecting books + periodicals. Ads: $170/$94/1/4 $52/classified word 30¢ a word.

Topping International Institute, Wayne W. Topping, 2622 Birchwood Ave, #7, Bellingham, WA 98225, 206-647-2703. 1984. Non-fiction. "Wholistic health area only. Alternative health care. Stress management." avg. press run 2M+. Expects 4 titles 1991, 2 titles 1992. 5 titles listed in the *Small Press Record of Books in Print* (20th Edition, 1991-92). avg. price, paper: $9.95. Discounts: 3+ 40%, 200+ 50%, 500+ 40%-25%. 150pp; 5½×8½, 8½×11; of. Reporting time: 3 months. Payment: 8-10% royalty. Copyrights for author. COSMEP (PO Box 703, San Francisco, CA 94101).

Torngat Books, David Belknap, Paul Duval, Lawrence Millman, PO Box 384, Dublin, NH 03444, 603-563-8338. 1987. Non-fiction. "We are searching for the springs of adventure. Especially welcome are any length manuscripts nonfiction on general wilderness travel, marine and terrestrial, any latitude—hair shirt stories of loss and redemption, contrast and the cult of danger, simple escape, the curious traveler, the scientific man, and the greater mystery. Additionally, Torngat Books is committed to the relaunching of adventure classics from the remote corners of the earth, bringing exciting tales by long-neglected writers back in the injoyent of contemporary readers. Subrights people and book finders please submit proposals. Reporting time immediate unless the editors are out in the wilderness (what's left of it), then allow two months" avg. press run 5M-10M. Pub'd 2 titles 1990; expects 5 titles 1991. avg. price, paper: $12. Discounts: standard trade. 150-300pp; size varies; of. Reporting time: immediate or ASAP. Payment: standard rates. Copyrights for author.

Tortilla Press, David L. Eppele, 8 Mulberry Lane, Bisbee, AZ 85603, 602-432-7040. 1988. Fiction, articles, art, photos, cartoons, parts-of-novels, news items. "We specialize in publishing books on cactus and succulents, arid land plants, deserts and southwestern essays on nature. IBM compatible disks accepted." avg. press run 8M-10M. Pub'd 3 titles 1990; expects 6 titles 1991, 8 titles 1992. 4 titles listed in the *Small Press Record of Books in Print* (20th Edition, 1991-92). avg. price, cloth: $30; paper: $17.95. Discounts: 20% classroom, 40% wholesale (trade, bulk, agents). 250pp; 6×8; of. Reporting time: 1 month. Payment: varies. Copyrights for author.

Tory Corner Editions, Alan Quincannon, Editor-in-Chief; Loretta Bolger, Jeanne Wilcox, PO Box 8100, Glen

Ridge, NJ 07028, 201-669-8367. 1990. avg. press run 2.5M. Expects 5 titles 1991, 5 titles 1992. 6 titles listed in the *Small Press Record of Books in Print* (20th Edition, 1991-92). Copyrights for author. COSMEP.

TOUCHSTONE LITERARY JOURNAL, William Laufer, Publisher; Guida Jackson, Managing Editor; Chris Woods, Contributing Editor, PO Box 8308, Spring, TX 77387-8308. 1976. Poetry, fiction, interviews, criticism, reviews, non-fiction. "Contributors strongly urged to subscribe. No line limit for good poetry, prose. SASE for details." circ. 1M. 1/yr. Pub'd 2 issues 1990; expects 1 issue 1991, 1 issue 1992. 4 titles listed in the *Small Press Record of Books in Print* (20th Edition, 1991-92). sub. price: $7; per copy: $7—$5 for extra copies for contributors; sample: $4. Back issues: $4. 80pp; 5½x8½; of, typeset, perfect bound. Reporting time: 6 weeks. Payment: 1 copy. Copyrighted, reverts to author. Pub's reviews: 6 in 1990. §Poetry, short story collections. Ads: send camera-ready sample for price quote (plus SASE). CCLM, The American Humanities Index.

Tough Dove Books, Denise Sheffield, PO Box 1999, Redway, CA 95560. 1985. Fiction. "No longer seeking submissions." avg. press run 5M-10M. Pub'd 1 title 1990; expects 1 title 1991. 4 titles listed in the *Small Press Record of Books in Print* (20th Edition, 1991-92). avg. price, paper: $8.95. Discounts: 40% or 5+, net 30. 260pp; 5½x8½; of. Payment: variable. Copyrights for author.

TOWARD FREEDOM, Kevin J. Kelley, 209 College Street, #202A, Burlington, VT 05401, 802-658-2523. 1952. Articles, photos, cartoons, interviews, criticism, reviews, letters, news items. "Third world and eastern Europe." circ. 3M. 8/yr. Pub'd 8 issues 1990; expects 8 issues 1991, 8 issues 1992. sub. price: $20; per copy: $3; sample: $3. Back issues: $3, Xerox $4. Discounts: 1-5 10%, 5-10 20%, 10+ 40%. 20pp; 8½x11; of. Reporting time: 30 days. Payment: $80-$125. Copyrighted, reverts to author. Pub's reviews: 5 in 1990. §Third World, politics, culture, non-alignment, eastern Europe. Ads: $400/$300/50¢.

TOWARDS, Clifford Monks, 3442 Grant Park Drive, Carmichael, CA 95608, 916-485-9274. 1977. Poetry, articles, photos, interviews, criticism, reviews, letters. "*Biases*: to make wider known the work of S.T. Coleridge, Rudolf Steiner, J.W. Von Goethe, Owen Barfield, and related authors. *Themes*: evolution of consciousness, imagination, polarity, metamorphoses, in all forms of writing. *Recent contributors*: O. Barfield, Kenneth Melia, G.B. Tennyson, Brian Stockwell, Georg Kuhlewind, Douglas Sloan, Norman Macbeth" circ. 750-1M. 2/yr. Pub'd 2 issues 1990; expects 2 issues 1991, 2 issues 1992. sub. price: $7; per copy: $4 (includes post.); sample: same. Back issues: $4 (available V 1 #3, 4, 5, 7; Vol II, #1, 2, 3, 4, 5), xerox avail on Vol I #1, 2, and 6 (available V3 #1, 2). Discounts: 40% retail, 50% wholesale. 44pp; 8½x11; of. Reporting time: 2-3 months. Payment: modest. Copyrighted, reverts to author. Pub's reviews: 6 in 1990. §Science (history and philosophy of), philosophy, literary criticism. Ads: $175/$90/50¢.

TOWER, Tower Press, Vincent Francis, Joanna Lawson, Dundas Public Library, 18 Ogilvie Street, Dundas, Ontario, L9H 2S2, Canada. 1950. Poetry. "Length of material should be up to 40 lines" circ. 200. 2/yr. Pub'd 2 issues 1990; expects 2 issues 1991, 2 issues 1992. sub. price: $6 Canada and US, $7.50 abroad (Can. funds); per copy: $2.75; sample: $1. Back issues: $1. Discounts: 40%. 44pp; 5½x8½; of. Reporting time: 1 month if submitted in February or August. Payment: none. Copyrighted, reverts to author.

Tower Press (see also TOWER), Joanna Lawson, Dundas Public Library, 18 Ogilvie Street, Dundas, Ontario, L9H 2S2, Canada. 1950. Poetry.

Tower Press, Ted Alleman, RR 2 Box 411, Duncansville, PA 16635-9512. 1985. "Tower Press is a social science based press which specializes in the publication of prison inmate material" Pub'd 1 title 1990; expects 2 titles 1991, 2 titles 1992. 1 title listed in the *Small Press Record of Books in Print* (20th Edition, 1991-92). avg. price, paper: $6.95. Discounts: 35%-bookstores, 20%-libraries. 200pp. Reporting time: 6-8 weeks. Copyrights for author. Prison Inmate Literature.

THE TOWNSHIPS SUN, Sun Books, Patricia Ball, Editor; Marion Greenlay, Business Manager; Ramona Garrett, Ad. Sales, Box 28, Lennoxville, Quebec J1M 1Z3, Canada. 1972. Articles, photos, interviews, letters, news items, non-fiction. "*The Townships Sun* is Quebec's only rural English-language alternative newspaper. We cover agriculture, ecology, folklore, arts & crafts, how-to, and anything else of importance or interest to the people of Quebec's Eastern Townships. Because the English speaking popluation of Quebec is declining, we are broadening our circulation to reach adjacent parts of New England, the Maritimes, and Ontario; thus articles pertaining to these regions may also be welcome. We do use reprints from other periodicals, providing that they do not have substantial circulation in the Eastern Townships." circ. 1.9M. 12/yr. Pub'd 12 issues 1990; expects 12 issues 1991, 12 issues 1992. sub. price: $15, $20 outside Canada; per copy: $1.50; sample: $1.50. Back issues: $2. 20pp; 10¼x13¾; of. Reporting time: 1 month. Payment: $1 per inch. Copyrighted, reverts to author. Pub's reviews: 12 in 1990. §Agriculture, back-to-earth alternative philosophy, folklore, Canadiana, ecology, regional history, topics current interest - drugs, travel, etc. Ads: 55¢ MAL or $15 CNU. AQREM.

TOWPATHS, Dr. A.F. Celley, 2121 Brookdale Road, Toledo, OH 43606, 419-531-9575. 1963. Articles, photos. "The Canal Society of Ohio, business address: 550 Copley Road, Akron, OH 44320." circ. 300. 4/yr.

Pub'd 4 issues 1990; expects 4 issues 1991, 4 issues 1992. sub. price: $18; per copy: $2.50; sample: same. Back issues: varies. Discounts: none. 12-16pp; 6×9; of. Reporting time: varies. Payment: none. Not copyrighted. No ads.

TQS NEWS, TQS Publications (Tonatiuh - Quinto Sol International Inc.), Octavio I. Romano, PO Box 9275, Berkeley, CA 94709, 415-655-8036. News items, non-fiction. "Our news sources come direct from university news releases and department reports. The original articles are editorial and satire authored by the editor. NO submissions." circ. 500. 4/yr. Pub'd 4 issues 1990; expects 4 issues 1991, 4 issues 1992. sub. price: $14; per copy: $4; sample: no charge. Back issues: $4. Discounts: none. 8pp; 8×11; of. Reporting time: no submissions. Payment: none. Copyrighted, does not revert to author. Ads: none. NCBPA, COSMEP.

TQS Publications (Tonatiuh - Quinto Sol International Inc.) (see also TQS NEWS), Octavio I. Romano, PO Box 9275, Berkeley, CA 94709, 415-655-8036; FAX 415-601-6938. 1967. Fiction, non-fiction. "We do not publish frequently. We do not actively encourage submissions" avg. press run 10M. Pub'd 1 title 1990; expects 1 title 1991, 2 titles 1992. 8 titles listed in the *Small Press Record of Books in Print* (20th Edition, 1991-92). avg. price, paper: $12; other: range from $2.50 to $12. Discounts: bookstores: 1 book 20%, 2-5 30%, 6+ 40%; college & university bookstores: 20% 1 book, 25% 2+; wholesale 50% on average. Applies only to prepaid orders. 256pp; 6×9; of. Reporting time: 3-4 months. Payment: negotiable, varies. Copyrights for author. NCBPA, COSMEP.

Trabarni Productions, Gail D. Whitter, 1531-550 Cottonwood Avenue, Coquitlam, BC V3J 2S1, Canada, 604-939-7910. 1989. Poetry, art, long-poems, non-fiction. "Tend to be *regional* when it comes to authors" avg. press run 250. Pub'd 4 titles 1990; expects 4 titles 1991, 4 titles 1992. 2 titles listed in the *Small Press Record of Books in Print* (20th Edition, 1991-92). avg. price, paper: $5.95. Discounts: 40% bookstores & bulk, 20% distributors. 48pp; 5½×8½; of, lp. Reporting time: not accepting unsolicited mss until 1992. Payment: 50 copies of book (usually). Does not copyright for author. Small Press Action Network (SPAN), Halifax, Nova Scotia.

Trackless Sands Press, Don Hausrath, 3790 El Camino Real, Suite 104, Palo Alto, CA 94306, 415-855-8086. 1988. Fiction, non-fiction. "Focusing on Asian studies, travel" avg. press run 4M. Expects 2 titles 1991, 4 titles 1992. 2 titles listed in the *Small Press Record of Books in Print* (20th Edition, 1991-92). avg. price, cloth: $19.95; paper: $12.95. Discounts: standard. of. Reporting time: 2 months. Payment: standard terms. Copyrights for author. COSMEP.

TRACKS, The Dedalus Press, John F. Deane, 24 The Heath, Cypress Downs, Dublin 6, Ireland. 1980. Poetry, long-poems. "Special issue on Thomas Kinsella, articles, interview, new poems, translations" circ. 700-1M. 2/yr. Pub'd 2 issues 1990; expects 2 issues 1991, 2 issues 1992. sub. price: £5; per copy: £3; sample: £3. Discounts: 33⅓% on orders of 3+. 64pp; size A5; of. Reporting time: 1 month. Payment: by arrangement, and commissioned work only. Copyrighted, reverts to author. Pub's reviews: 2 in 1990. §Poetry, original and in translation. 73.

TRADESWOMEN MAGAZINE, Molly Martin, Helen Vozenilek, Tradeswomen Inc., PO Box 40664, San Francisco, CA 94140, 415-821-7334. 1981. Poetry, fiction, articles, art, photos, cartoons, interviews, satire, reviews, letters, news items, non-fiction. "*Tradeswomen Magazine* is aimed at women working in non-traditional blue collar jobs. We prefer to have articles and other contributions come from tradeswomen. However, we do occassionally accept materials from individuals who have an interest in supporting tradeswomen but who are not tradeswomen themselves." circ. 2M. 4/yr. Pub'd 4 issues 1990; expects 4 issues 1991, 4 issues 1992. Individuals: free subscription with annual membership of $35, (instit.) $25; price per copy: $3.50; sample: $3. Back issues: $3, includes postage. Discounts: 25% to subscription agencies, 40% to bookstores. 40pp; 8¼×10¾; of. Reporting time: 2 months. Payment: issues. Copyrighted, reverts to author. Pub's reviews: 2 in 1990. §Tradeswomen, tradeswork, labor, networking, affirmative action, emloyment. Ads: $500/$275/$160¼ page/$100⅛ page/50¢ word, $10 minimum for classified. Tradeswomen, Inc.

TRADITION, Bob Everhart, Editor, PO Box 438, Walnut, IA 51577, 712-784-3001. 1976. "MUST deal with traditional country bluegrass and folk music." circ. 2.5M. 6/yr. Pub'd 6 issues 1990; expects 6 issues 1991, 6 issues 1992. sub. price: $10; per copy: $3; sample: $3. Back issues: $3. 44pp; 8½×11; †of. Reporting time: 6 weeks. Payment: yes, determined. Copyrighted, reverts to author. Pub's reviews: 10 in 1990. §Traditional country-bluegrass-faith music. Ads: $300/$160/$50.

Tradition Books, Hermene Terry, 614 Lenox Avenue, Westfield, NJ 07090, 201-232-8587. 1987. Fiction. "Tradition Books publishes translations into English of Yiddish fiction, poetry, non-fiction" avg. press run 1.5M. Expects 3 titles 1991, 3 titles 1992. 1 title listed in the *Small Press Record of Books in Print* (20th Edition, 1991-92). avg. price, paper: $12. Discounts: bookstores 40%, distributors 50%. 300pp; 6×9; lp. Reporting time: 8 weeks.

TRANET, William N. Ellis, Editor, Box 567, Rangeley, ME 04970, 207-864-2252. 1976. Reviews, news items. "Newsletter-directory." circ. 2M. 6/yr. Pub'd 6 issues 1990; expects 6 issues 1991, 6 issues 1992. sub.

price: $150 organizations, $30 subsidizing, $15 for third world and other individual A.T. workers, $50 libraries; per copy: $5; sample: $5. Back issues: $5. Discounts: to organizational members for bulk copies. 20pp; 8×11; of. Reporting time: 30 days. Payment: none. Not copyrighted. Pub's reviews: 150 in 1990. §Economic development, alternative/appropriate technology (especially hands-on how-to books). No ads. NPC.

TRANSITIONS ABROAD: The Guide to Living, Learning, and Working Overseas, Clayton A. Hubbs, Editor & Publisher, 18 Hulst Road, PO Box 334, Amherst, MA 01004, 413-256-0373. 1977. Articles, art, photos, letters, news items, non-fiction. "We like material with specific information on long-stay educational, low-budget, and socially responsible travel abroad." circ. 13M. 6/yr. Pub'd 6 issues 1990; expects 6 issues 1991, 6 issues 1992. sub. price: $18; per copy: $3.50 postpaid; sample: $4.50 postpaid. Back issues: 6 issues $20; all back issues $70. Discounts: 50%. 64pp; 7½×10; webb off. Reporting time: 1-2 months. Payment: 1 month after publication. Copyrighted, reverts to author. Pub's reviews: 50 in 1990. §Literary travel material, travel books, language study, resource material on work, study and travel abroad. Ads: $840/$630/$1 per word. Small Magazine Publishers.

TRANSLATION, Translation Center, Frank MacShane, Director, Translation Ctr./412 Dodge, Columbia University, New York, NY 10027, 212-854-2305. 1972. Poetry, fiction, articles, interviews, satire, letters, parts-of-novels, long-poems. "*Translation* publishes new translations of contemporary foreign literature. Submissions may be excerpts from novels, poetry, short stories, or literary essays (non-academic), and should include the following: a ten-line biographical sketch of the translator (co-translator), a ten-line biographical sketch of the author, the relevant foreign language text, and a note stating that copyright clearance has been obtained. Manuscripts can only be returned if an SASE is included. *Translation* is published in April and October each year" circ. 1.5M. 2/yr. Pub'd 1 issue 1990; expects 2 issues 1991, 2 issues 1992. sub. price: $17 domestic, $18 foreign; per copy: sample: $9. Back issues: Vols. 2-6: $3.50, Vol. 7: $7.00. Discounts: none. 220+pp; 6×9; lp. Reporting time: 3-6 months. Copyrighted. Ads: $200/$100. CCLM, COSMEP.

Translation Center (see also TRANSLATION), Frank MacShane, 412 Dodge, Columbia University, New York, NY 10027, 212-854-2305. 1972. Poetry, fiction, art, long-poems, plays. "*Translation* publishes new translations of contemporary foreign literature. Submissions may be excerpts from novels, poetry, short stories, or literary essays (non-academic), and should include the following: a ten-line biographical sketch of the translator (co-translator), a ten-line biographical sketch of the author, the relevant foreign language text, and a note stating that copyright clearance has been obtained. Manuscripts can only be returned if an SASE is included. *Translation* is published in April and October each year" avg. press run 1M-2M. Expects 2 titles 1991. avg. price, paper: $9. 250pp; 6×9; lp. Reporting time: up to 6 months. Payment: copies only (2). Copyrights for author. COSMEP, CCLM.

TRANSLATION REVIEW, Sheryl St. Germain, Managing Editor; Rainer Schulte, Editor; Dennis Kratz, Editor, Univ. of Texas-Dallas, Box 830688, Richardson, TX 75083-0688, 214-690-2093. 1978. Articles, interviews, criticism, reviews, news items, non-fiction. "The *Translation Review* is a publication of the American Literary Translator's Association and is distributed to members and subscribing libraries. The *Review* deals exclusively with the theory, application and evaluation of literary works in translation." circ. 1M. 3/yr. Pub'd 3 issues 1990; expects 3 issues 1991, 3 issues 1992. Subscription by membership to ALTA only, library subscription $15; price per copy: $5; sample: $5. Back issues: $5 each. Discounts: for classroom use 40%. 44pp; 8½×11; of. Reporting time: 8-12 weeks. Payment: copies. Copyrighted. Pub's reviews: 40 in 1990. §Any literary work in recent translation. Ads: $200/$125. Society for Scholarly Publishing.

TRANS-MISSOURI ART VIEW, Al Strong, Publisher; Marilyn Coffey, Editor, 1506 Harney Street, Omaha, NE 68102. 1990. Poetry. "Needs poems of moderate length. May use an occasional short or long poem (about 80 lines maximum). Form, style, content open. *Trans-Missouri Art View* is an affirmative action publisher, does not discriminate on the basis of race, sex, etc. Indeed welcomes a diversity of viewpoints." circ. 2.3M. 12/yr. 8-12pp; 11×16. Reporting time: 6 weeks. Payment: 5¢ per word, minimum $10 a poem, +3 copies with poem, + free subscription offer, + complimentary copies of poem. Copyrighted, reverts to author.

TRANSNATIONAL PERSPECTIVES, Rene Wadlow, CP 161, CH-1211 Geneva 16, Switzerland. 1974. Poetry, articles, art, reviews. "Basically a journal of world politics with an emphasis on conflict resolution, human rights, arms control. Poems on a wide range of topics. Book reviews on culture as well as politics." circ. 5M. 3/yr. Pub'd 3 issues 1990; expects 3 issues 1991, 3 issues 1992. sub. price: $15; per copy: $5; sample: free. Back issues: $3. 48pp; 29×20cm; of. Reporting time: 2 months. Payment: 5 or more copies of issue with poem. Not copyrighted. Pub's reviews: 30 in 1990. §World politics, culture, poetry. No ads.

Transport History Press, Alan R. Lind, Roy G. Benedict, Zenon R. Hansen, PO Box 201, Park Forest, IL 60466, 708-748-7855. 1973. Photos, non-fiction. "Use manuscripts on the operations, economics, history and future of all forms of transportation. Specialty is profusely illustrated books on railroad, light rail, street railway, and electric interurbans, including elevated and subway rapid transit lines. Often use tie-in with local and regional history to produce books of interest not only to students of transportation but also to urbanologists, regional planners, geographers, government officials, consulting engineers, transit executives, researchers, and economists. Books run about 55,000 words. Profusely illustrated, using large 8 1/2 x 11 format and highest quality dull coated paper stock for maximum fidelity in photo reproduction. Use about 400-500 large illustrations in each 400 to 480-page book. Prefer to consider only those manuscripts accompanied by hundreds of excellent photos. Also use detailed tables, charts, rosters and maps to trace corporate histories and particular railroad and transit car histories." avg. press run 4M-6M. Expects 1 title 1991, 1 title 1992. 4 titles listed in the *Small Press Record of Books in Print* (20th Edition, 1991-92). avg. price, cloth: $30; paper: $12.50. Discounts: 40% standard to retailers for any quantity. 50% to wholesalers and distributors. Actual postage paid for shipping added to invoice. 400pp; 8½x11; of. Reporting time: 6 months to 1 year. Payment: all royalty arrangements subject to agreement; we have a generous royalty arrangement. Does not copyright for author. COSMEP.

TRAPANI NUOVA, TERZA PAGINA, Sicilian Antigruppo/Cross-Cultural Communications, Rolando Certa, Nat Scammacca, Villa Schammachanat, Via Argentaria Km 4, Trapani, Sicily, Italy. 1968. Poetry, articles, interviews, satire, criticism, reviews, letters, collages, concrete art. "3 to 5 typewritten pages, cultural in every field. Recent contributors: Enrico Crespolti, Guiseppe Zagarrio, Nicolo Dalessandro, Nat Scammacca, Francesco Carbone, Gianni Diecedue, Franco DiMarco, *only* Italian." circ. 5M. 52/yr. Expects 3 issues 1991. sub. price: $25; per copy: $3.50; sample: free. Back issues: $2. Discounts: 33%. 12pp; 24×18; of. Reporting time: 1 month. Payment: none. Copyrighted, reverts to author. Pub's reviews. §All areas. Ads: $100/$50.

Travel Keys, Peter B. Manston, Publisher, PO Box 160691, Sacramento, CA 95816, 916-452-5200. 1984. Reviews, non-fiction. "Practical, succinct travel and antique guides. Distributed to bookstores by Bob Adams Inc., 260 Center Street, Holbrook, MA 02343 (617) 7C7-8100 or (800) 872-5627, fax 617-767-0994. Non-bookstores contact Travel Keys directly. Staff-written or sometimes work for hire." avg. press run 5M-12M. Pub'd 5 titles 1990; expects 4 titles 1991, 6 titles 1992. 9 titles listed in the *Small Press Record of Books in Print* (20th Edition, 1991-92). avg. price, cloth: $14.95; paper: $6.95-$15.95. Discounts: Bookstores: 50% and free freight; non-book 40-50%. 320pp; 3¾x7½, 5½x8½; of. Reporting time: 1 month maximum. Payment: variable. Usually copyrights for author, but fee charged against author's royalty account. PMA (Publishers Marketing Ass'n), ABA (associate member).

Traveler's Health Publications, Inc., Lawrence E. Pawl, PO Box 2737, Grand Rapids, MI 49501, 800-735-8941; 616-942-1271. 1989. Non-fiction. "Seeking book-length material on travel and health. Examples of recent material are *Sex and Travel*, *First Aid for Sportsmen*. Author should be health-care professional with substantial credentials. Books should be written for laymen-mass market." avg. press run 10M. Pub'd 1 title 1990; expects 1 title 1991. 1 title listed in the *Small Press Record of Books in Print* (20th Edition, 1991-92). avg. price, paper: $7.95. Discounts: 10-100 40%, 100-500 50%. 180pp; 4×6; of. Reporting time: 2-4 weeks. Payment: 7.5% 1-5000 copies, 10% over 5000. Copyrights for author. PMA, COSMEP.

TRAY FULL OF LAB MICE PUBLICATIONS, Melissa Jasper, Matt Jasper, PO Box 303, Durham, NH 03824. 1989. Poetry, fiction, art, photos. "Recent contributors: Ursula Hegi, Charles Simic, Nancy Krygowski, Mekeel McBride, Tymoteusz Karpowicz, Richard Moore, Jack Kelley, Dick Higgins, Elin O'Hara Slavick, Anthony McCann, Andrea Luna, Dan Leone, Joel Brouwer, Sylvia Dakessian, Charles Provenzano, Robert Dunn, Mikhail Iossel, Russell Edson. Submissions should, if possible, be accompanied by payment for a sample issue. As of 1991, mail will be forwarded to us from the following address: #43 Sherwood, Gilford, NH 03246" circ. 2.5M. 2/yr. Expects 1 issue 1991, 2 issues 1992. sub. price: $6; per copy: $3; sample: $3. Back issues: $3. Discounts: 50% off on quantities of 10 or more. 64pp; 5×7; lp. Reporting time: 1-8 weeks. Payment: Benedictine and Trappist wines or 7 copies of issue. Copyrighted, reverts to author. §Small Moorish kingdoms, pyrrhonian thought. Ads: $100/$50/will trade ads.

Treasure Chest Publications, Inc., Nancie Mahan, PO Box 5250, Tucson, AZ 85703, 602-623-9558. 1975. avg. press run 5M. Pub'd 5 titles 1990; expects 6 titles 1991, 6 titles 1992. avg. price, cloth: $24.95; paper: $9.95. 64pp; 8×11. Reporting time: 90 days. Payment: quarterly. Does not copyright for author. Publishers Marketing Assoc. (PMA), Tucson Book Publishing Assoc.

TREASURE HUNTING RESEARCH BULLETIN, Research & Discovery Publications, John C. Davis, PO Box 761, Patterson, LA 70392. 1986. circ. 300. Pub'd 4 issues 1990; expects 4 issues 1991, 4 issues 1992. sub. price: $10; per copy: $3; sample: same. Back issues: $3. 8pp; 8½x11; †4. Reporting time: 30 days. Payment: depends on length. Copyrighted, reverts to author. Pub's reviews: 6 in 1990. §Books on treasure hunting, buried treasure, lost mines, shipwrecks, salvage, and sunken treasure. No ads.

Tree Shrew Press, Richard M. Swiderski, PO Box 8036, North Brattleboro, VT 05304. 1979. Poetry, fiction, photos, collages, concrete art. "We are devoted to the publication of poetic constructions, that is objects assembled from printed sheets, and employ a wide range of processes and materials. We also publish short ficiton in booklet form, and are currently beginning to publish novels" avg. press run 250. Pub'd 2 titles 1990; expects 2 titles 1991, 1 title 1992. 1 title listed in the *Small Press Record of Books in Print* (20th Edition,

1991-92). avg. price, paper: $8. Discounts: 20%/30%. 150pp; size varies greatly; †lo, lp. Reporting time: 3 months, query first. Does not copyright for author.

TRENDS & PREDICTIONS ANALYST, Patrick O'Connell, 12628 Black Saddle Lane, Germantown, MD 20874, 301-972-1980. 1985. Reviews, news items, non-fiction. "Earthchanges, information-sources, safe-areas, social-economic trends, UFO's, innerearth, subterranean worlds, survival strategies, astrology, alternative healing techniques, alternative energy sources, and much more. Length varies." circ. 200. 2/yr. Pub'd 2 issues 1990; expects 2 issues 1991, 2 issues 1992. sub. price: $4, $5 foreign (U.S. funds only); per copy: $2, $3 foreign; sample: $1, $3 foreign. Back issues: $2 each. Discounts: negotiable, but usually $1/each issue. 10pp; 8½x11; †photocopy. Reporting time: 2 weeks. Payment: contributor's complimentary copies. Not copyrighted. Pub's reviews: 12-18 in 1990. §Social-economic items, New Age, UFO's, astrology, survival, dowsing, agriculture (farming/gardening). Ads: $100/$50/10¢ per word classified.

Trentham Books (see also MULTICULTURAL TEACHING FOR PRACTITIONERS IN SCHOOLS AND COMMUNITY; DESIGN AND TECHNOLOGY TEACHING), Unit 13/14, Trent Trading Pack, Botteslow St., Hanley, Stoke-on-Trent, Staffordshire ST1 3LY, England, 0782 274227; fax 0782 281755. 5 titles listed in the *Small Press Record of Books in Print* (20th Edition, 1991-92).

Trestletree Publications, Richard Steiner, PO Box 295, Albany, NY 12201, 518-452-2000. 1986. "Book length (200 pages +) emphasizing the improvement of the management and performance of organizations in the private, nonprofit and public sectors. Must have strong, activist, how-to prescriptions based on practical understanding of how these systems operate" avg. press run 2M. Pub'd 1 title 1990; expects 1 title 1991, 2 titles 1992. avg. price, paper: $17. Discounts: 1-5 20%, 6-50 30%, 51-100 40%, 101-150 50%, 151+ 55%. 220pp; 6x9. Reporting time: 60 days. Payment: negotiable. Copyrights for author.

Triad Press, Jane Segerstrom, PO Box 42006, Houston, TX 77242, 713-789-0424. 1980. Art, photos, non-fiction. avg. press run 5M-10M. Pub'd 1 title 1990; expects 1 title 1992. 2 titles listed in the *Small Press Record of Books in Print* (20th Edition, 1991-92). avg. price, paper: $14.95. Discounts: 1-10 40%, 11-99 40%pp, 100+ 50%. 168pp; 8½x11; of. Reporting time: 4 weeks. Payment: standard royalties, advance-on-completion. Copyrights for author. PMA, TPA.

Triad Publishing Co. Inc., Lorna Rubin, Lenore Freeman, 1110 NW 8th Avenue Suite C, Gainesville, FL 32601, 904-373-5800. 1978. Non-fiction. "Health and medical fields" avg. press run 10M. Pub'd 4 titles 1990; expects 3 titles 1991, 4 titles 1992. 21 titles listed in the *Small Press Record of Books in Print* (20th Edition, 1991-92). avg. price, cloth: $15; paper: $8.95; other: $11.95 spiralbound. Inquire for discount schedule. 224pp; 6x9; of. Reporting time: 3-6 months. Payment: 6%-10% cover price, once yearly. Copyrights for author. PAS, PMMA.

TRIBE: An American Gay Journal, Columbia Publishing Company, Inc., Bernard Rabb, 234 East 25th Street, Baltimore, MD 21218, 301-366-7070. 1989. Poetry, fiction, articles, interviews, criticism, parts-of-novels, long-poems, plays, non-fiction. "Length unlimited. Bias: writings for and by gay men. Recent contributors: Edmund White, Andrew Holleran, Paul Monette, Larry Duplechan, Richard Hall, David B. Feinberg, James Carroll Pickett, Philip Gambone, John Preston, Cary Alan Johnson, Rudy Kikel, David Bergman, Michael Lynch, among others" circ. 1.2M. 4/yr. Pub'd 1 issue 1990; expects 4 issues 1991, 4 issues 1992. sub. price: $22; per copy: $6; sample: $6. Discounts: distributed to the book trade by Inland Book Company and Bookpeople. 96pp; 6x9; of. Reporting time: 3-6 months. Payment: none at present. Copyrighted, reverts to author. Publishing Triangle (New York City).

THE TRIBUNE, Anne S. Walker, Executive Director + Editor, 777 United Nations Plaza, 3rd floor, New York, NY 10017, 212-687-8633. 1976. "Attached copy of a typical newsletter. International Women's Tribune Centre. We do not accept submissions." circ. 14M. Eng. & Span. 4/yr, French 3/yr. 12 titles listed in the *Small Press Record of Books in Print* (20th Edition, 1991-92). sub. price: free in developing countries, $12 U.S. & Canada, $16 Europe, Aust/New Zealand; per copy: $3; sample: same. 48pp; 8½x11; camera-ready copy prepared by IWTC. offset printing. Desk top publishing using macintosh computer, laser printer. Payment: none. Not copyrighted. No ads.

Tributary Press, Dudley Clark, Peggy DePalma, PO Box 3246, Idyllwild, CA 92349, 714-659-3278. 1986. Fiction, satire. "Currently we are in the main interested only in children's books, esp. ills., geared for early ages 3-8. Later on we plan to publish adult fiction, essentially satire or 'black' humor. As far as length is concerned, we want short to med. length, pithy, substantive material with a point—like our first book *Roxanne's Hands*, an amusing account of how an 8 year old girl stops chewing her nails. Focus efforts on specific areas or problems of growing up, such as fear of the dark, parents separating, dealing with siblings, and so forth. BUT keep it light and not overly didactic" avg. press run 5M. Pub'd 1 title 1990; expects 3 titles 1991. avg. price, paper: $5.95. Discounts: 40% bookstores, up to 45% for libraries (our big buyer). 25-60pp; of. Reporting time: 6 weeks average. Payment: arranged with author. COSMEP.

Trigon Press, Roger Sheppard, Judith Sheppard, 117 Kent House Road, Beckenham, Kent BR3 1JJ, England, 01-778-0534. 1975. Non-fiction. "No subs required at present. Publish books for the new and antiquarian book trade. Mostly edit our own material: hope to be able to publish more bibliographies and co-editions of book trade and library reference material. Now going to press with our 5th edition of the *International Directory of Book Collectors*" avg. press run 1.5M. Pub'd 2 titles 1990; expects 2 titles 1991, 2 titles 1992. 2 titles listed in the *Small Press Record of Books in Print* (20th Edition, 1991-92). avg. price, cloth: $18.50; paper: $12. Discounts: singles 25%, multiples 35%. Export postage extra. 280pp; 5×9; of. Payment: 10%. Copyrights for author. IPG(UK).

Trilogy Books, Marge Wood, 155 S. El Molino Avenue, Suite 103, Pasadena, CA 91101, 818-440-0669. 1990. Non-fiction. avg. press run 5M. Expects 2 titles 1991, 3 titles 1992. 1 title listed in the *Small Press Record of Books in Print* (20th Edition, 1991-92). avg. price, paper: $14.95. 6×9; of. Reporting time: 2 months. Payment: negotiable. Copyrights for author. PMA, 2401 Pacific Coast Hwy, Suite 102, Hermosa Beach, CA 90254.

TRIQUARTERLY, Reginald Gibbons, Editor; Kirstie Felland, Managing Editor; Bob Perlongo, Executive Editor; Susan Hahn, Associate Editor, Northwestern University, 2020 Ridge, Evanston, IL 60208, 708-491-7614. 1964. Poetry, fiction, art, photos, criticism, reviews, parts-of-novels. "Write for contributor's guidelines." circ. 5M. 3/yr. Pub'd 3 issues 1990; expects 3 issues 1991, 3 issues 1992. sub. price: $18; per copy: $9.95; sample: $4. Back issues: price list on request. Discounts: available on request. 256pp; 6×9; of. Reporting time: 8-12 weeks. Payment: varies. Copyrighted, rights revert upon request. Pub's reviews: 0 in 1990. §Literature, the arts, general culture. Ads: $250/$125 (quantity discount of 20% for three insertions). CLMP, IL Literary Publishers Association.

Triton Books + Gallery, 4409 Lowell Avenue, La Crescenta, CA 91214, 818-249-0793. 1982. Fiction, art, photos, interviews. "We publish Award Winning Science Fiction from 1926-1954. All editors are top notch well-known pros. Short, medium, long length stories. Illustrated. Do not accept submissions" avg. press run 2M. Pub'd 1 title 1990; expects 4 titles 1991, 4 titles 1992. avg. price, other: hardback $14.95. Discounts: 40% trade, 50% to distributors. 320pp; 5½×8¼; of. Payment: 10% first 5M, 12½% to 75, 15% over that, subject to change. Does not copyright for author. COSMEP.

Triumph Books, Mitch Rogatz, 644 S. Clark Street, Chicago, IL 60605, 939-3330. 1990. avg. press run 8M. Pub'd 2 titles 1990; expects 4 titles 1991, 4 titles 1992. avg. price, cloth: $25; paper: $15. Discounts: sliding. 300pp; 6×9; of. Payment: 10%-12%. Does not copyright for author. ABA.

TRIVIA, A JOURNAL OF IDEAS, Lise Weil, Editor, Box 606, North Amherst, MA 01059, 413-367-2254. 1982. Articles, interviews, criticism, reviews, non-fiction. "*Trivia* publishes feminist theory, critical essays, reviews, experimental prose, translations, and *Trivial Lives*, which brings to light neglected aspects in the lives of women writers and thinkers." circ. 2M. 2/yr. Pub'd 2 issues 1990; expects 3 issues 1991, 3 issues 1992. sub. price: $14 ($16 out of USA), $20 institutions/libraries ($22 out of USA); per copy: $5 ($6 out of U.S.A.); sample: $6 ($7 out of U.S.A.). Back issues: #3-6 $3, #7-12 $4. 116pp; 5½×8½; of. Reporting time: 2-3 months. Payment: 3 copies of issue where article appears. Copyrighted, reverts to author. Pub's reviews: 3 in 1990. §Lesbian/Feminist theory, scholarship, women's literature. Exchange, ask for ad rate sheet. CLMP.

TRIVIUM, Colin Clifford Eldridge, Dept. Of History, St. David's University College, Lampeter, Dyfed SA48 7ED, Great Britain, 0570-422351 ext 244. 1966. Articles, criticism, reviews. "Articles: av. length - 5M-7M words. Bias: towards the humanities." circ. 300. 1/yr. Pub'd 1 issue 1990; expects 1 issue 1991, 1 issue 1992. 2 titles listed in the *Small Press Record of Books in Print* (20th Edition, 1991-92). sub. price: £7 sterling; per copy: £7 sterling. Back issues: contact business editor. 180pp; size A5; †of. Reporting time: 6-8 weeks. Payment: none. Copyright vested in editor of *Trivium*. Pub's reviews: 0 in 1990. §Humanities. Ads: £25/£12.50.

TROPICAL AND GEOTROPICAL MEDICINE, Weidner & Sons, Publishing, Box 2178, Cinnaminson, NJ 08077, 609-486-1755. "See comments for Weidner & Sons, Publishing." Pub's reviews.

TROUBLE & STRIFE, The Collective, c/o Norwich Womens Centre, PO Box 8, Diss. Norfolk 1P22 3XG, England. 1983. Articles, art, photos, cartoons, interviews, criticism, reviews, music, letters, non-fiction. "To record and reflect on current feminist theory and practice—each issue contains an interview based on British feminist organizing "Writing Our Own History". Radical feminism. Contributors range from best-selling authors through to grass-roots activists" circ. 3.5M. 3/yr. Pub'd 2 issues 1990; expects 3 issues 1991, 3 issues 1992. sub. price: £9-50 Europe or seamail, £13 airmail U.S., institutions £30; per copy: £2.50; sample: same. Back issues: £3.50 for 3 + postage (issues 1/2/ not available). Discounts: agent 15%, trade via a distributor. 52-56pp; 8.3×9.8; lp. Reporting time: 1-3 months. Payment: none. Copyrighted, reverts to author. Pub's reviews: 12 in 1990. §Feminism internationally, women's lives and experiences. Ads: £75/£40/negotiable.

Trout Creek Press (see also DOG RIVER REVIEW), Laurence F. Hawkins, Jr., Editor, 5976 Billings Road, Parkdale, OR 97041, 503-352-6494. 1981. Poetry. avg. press run 500. Pub'd 2 titles 1990; expects 3 titles 1991, 4 titles 1992. 12 titles listed in the *Small Press Record of Books in Print* (20th Edition, 1991-92). avg. price, paper: $4. Discounts: 40% (order of 5 or more). 48pp; 5×8; †of. Reporting time: 3 months. Payment: negotiable. Copyrights for author. CCLM.

Trouvere Company (see also WRITERS GAZETTE NEWSLETTER), Brenda Williamson, Route 2, Box 290, Eclectic, AL 36024. 1980. Non-fiction. "Looking for manuscripts that deal with the horse industry, horse owners, showers, breeders, etc... Want well-written, explanatory information to show writer has knowledge in the field either by experience (preferred) or by study. Open to any new angles in marketing the particular manuscript. 5,000-30,000 words or 20-120 typed double-spaced pages. How-to, self-help, tech. are most sought. Examples: Horseshoeing, building feeders, fencing, feeding, breeding, showing, management training, etc. Publishes soft-bound, pamphlet and booklet originals. simultaneous and photocopy okay. SASE. Recent title: *50 Barn Designs*" avg. press run 500. Pub'd 1 title 1990; expects 1-2 titles 1991, 2-4 titles 1992. avg. price, paper: $5; other: $3-$10. Discounts: wholesale 25%-40%, library-institution 20% per copy. 20-200pp; 5½×8, 8½×11; custom printer. Reporting time: 4-6 weeks. Payment: 5% on retail or flat fee; no advance. Copyrights for author.

TRUE FOOD, Ceres Press, David Goldbeck, Editor; Nikki Goldbeck, Food Editor, PO Box 87, Woodstock, NY 12498. 1988. News items, non-fiction. "Recent contributor: M.F.K. Fisher, Robert Rodale." 4/yr. Expects 4 issues 1991, 4 issues 1992. sub. price: $14; per copy: $3.50; sample: same. Back issues: $3.50. 8pp; 8½×11; of. Reporting time: asap. Payment: negotiated. Copyrighted, reverts to author. Pub's reviews: 2 in 1990. §Cooking, nutrition, food, health, kitchen design, agriculture. No ads.

Truly Fine Press, Jerry Madson, PO Box 891, Bemidji, MN 56601. 1973. Poetry, fiction. "Truly Fine Press has in the past published a pamphlet series, and also published Minnesota's first tabloid novel. Must query first." avg. press run varies. Expects 1 title 1991. 12 titles listed in the *Small Press Record of Books in Print* (20th Edition, 1991-92). Pages vary; size varies; †of, mi. Reporting time: 2 weeks to 6 months. Copyrights for author.

Truth Center (see also AGAPE), W. Norman Cooper, Val Schorre, 6940 Oporto Drive, Los Angeles, CA 90068, 213-876-6295. 1970. Articles. avg. press run 3M-4M. Pub'd 1 title 1990; expects 1 title 1991, 1 title 1992. 9 titles listed in the *Small Press Record of Books in Print* (20th Edition, 1991-92). avg. price, cloth: $8.50; paper: $6.50. 120-300pp; 5¼×8¼. Payment: none. Copyrights for author.

Tryckeriforlaget (see also INITIATIV), Leif Lindberg, Tumstocksvagen 19, Taby S-18304, Sweden, 08-7567445. 1983. Fiction, non-fiction. avg. press run 3M. Pub'd 1 title 1990; expects 7 titles 1991, 4 titles 1992. avg. price, cloth: SEK 170; paper: SEK 90. 200pp; of. Swedish Association of Publishers.

TSUBUSHI, Kevin Starbard, 3-4-3-204 Togoshi, Shinagawa-ku, Tokyo 142, Japan, 03-3786-9782. 1990. Poetry, articles, art, photos, interviews, reviews. "Anything pertaining to Butoh Dance, or in the spirit of Butoh Dance (rituals, primitive music, theatre, and dance) will be considered for publication." circ. 600. 4/yr. Pub'd 1 issue 1990; expects 4 issues 1991, 4 issues 1992. sub. price: in US—Y2600 or $20; per copy: Y500, $3.50; sample: $2. Back issues: $2. Discounts: undecided at present. 20pp; 7×10; lp. Reporting time: 2 months. Payment: varies. Not copyrighted. Ads: $60/$30.

TSUNAMI, Lee Rossi, PO Box 1442, Venice, CA 90294, 213-453-6303. 1987. Poetry, art, photos, criticism, reviews. "We prefer poems and poets that aren't afraid to take risks. No limits on style or subject matter, but we prefer shorter poems (less than 2 pages). We enjoy narrative voice, concrete expressions of modern life, surrealism. Recent contributors: Fred Voss, Clayton Eshleman, Suzanne Lummis, William Witherup, Laurel Ann Bogen." circ. 600. 2/yr. Pub'd 2 issues 1990; expects 2 issues 1991, 2 issues 1992. sub. price: $10; per copy: $6; sample: $6. Back issues: $6 per copy. Discounts: 40% discount to retailers, 55% to distributors. 70pp; 5½×8½; of. Reporting time: 2 months. Payment: 1 copy per accepted piece. Copyrighted, reverts to author. Pub's reviews: 3 in 1990. §Recent books of poetry. Ads: $100/$75.

TUCSON MOTOR NEWS, Bean Avenue Publishing, Bruce A. Kaplan, PO Box 1055, Tucson, AZ 85702. 1990. Articles, news items. "How to articles on auto racing, car care, transportation issues, environmental issues. We need articles of interest to motorsport fans and participants" 26/yr. Pub'd 4 issues 1990; expects 40 issues 1991, 50 issues 1992. sub. price: $40; per copy: $1; sample: $1. Back issues: $1. Discounts: none. 16pp; 8½×11; of. Copyrighted, does not revert to author. Pub's reviews. §Automotive, technical, racing, motorcycles, boating. Ads: $333.20/$166.60/$83.30 1/4 page.

TUCUMCARI LITERARY REVIEW, Troxey Kemper, Editor; Neoma Reed, Assistant Editor, 3108 W. Bellevue Avenue, Los Angeles, CA 90026. 1988. Poetry, fiction, articles, cartoons, satire, criticism, reviews, letters, non-fiction. "We prefer familiar, rhyming poems in the standard forms, not rambling, disjointed fragments and words that are not tied together to *mean* anything." circ. 200. 6/yr. Pub'd 9 issues 1990; expects 7 issues 1991, 6 issues 1992. sub. price: $12; per copy: $2; sample: $2 (includes postage). Back issues: $2 postpaid. 40pp; 5½×8½; †xerox copier. Reporting time: 2 weeks, sooner if rejected, later if accepted and SASE is returned with copy of magazine. Payment: 1 copy. Not copyrighted. §Writing and publishing if the book is deemed of value to *TLR* readers. CLMP.

Tudor Publishers, Inc., Eugene Pfaff, Jr., 3007 Taliaferro Road, Greensboro, NC 27408-2628, 919-282-5907. 1985. Fiction, non-fiction. "Tudor is interested in the following types of material: commercial books of wide general interest, either fiction or non-fiction, which we will consider for a straight royalty contract; and quality manuscripts of almost any type which we occasionally offer to publish. We would prefer to see material from writers with at least some record of publication in mags and journals, but we will consider a well-done proposal or query from anyone. We try to be open and to respond promptly. Additional address: PO Box 38366, Greensboro, NC 27438." avg. press run 3M-5M. Pub'd 3 titles 1990; expects 4 titles 1991, 4 titles 1992. avg. price, cloth: $18.95; paper: $9.95. Discounts: write for schedules. 200pp; 5½x8½, 6x9; of. Reporting time: 2-4 weeks. Payment: standard; occasional moderate advance. Copyrights for author. COSMEP, PMA, Publishers Assoc. of the South (PAS).

Tuesday-Art Press (see also THE OCCASIONAL TUESDAY-ART NEWS), George Jeffus, 3808 Rosecrans Street #134, San Diego, CA 92110. 1985. Fiction, art, cartoons, satire, collages, non-fiction. "Publish mainly short small art books (avant-garde, experimental, illustration), calendars, art objects, cards, instructional, comics." avg. press run 500-1M. Pub'd 10 titles 1990; expects 10 titles 1991, 15 titles 1992. 5 titles listed in the *Small Press Record of Books in Print* (20th Edition, 1991-92). avg. price, cloth: $10-$15; paper: $5-$10. †of, lp. Reporting time: make arrangements. Payment: by contract, generally no reprints, payments made upon sales. Copyrights for author.

TULSA STUDIES IN WOMEN'S LITERATURE, Holly Laird, 600 S. College, Tulsa, OK 74104, 918-631-2503. 1982. Articles, criticism, reviews, letters. circ. 500. 2/yr. Pub'd 2 issues 1990; expects 2 issues 1991, 2 issues 1992. sub. price: U.S. individuals $12/1 yr, $23/2 yrs, $34/3 yrs, institutions $14/$27/$40, other individuals $15/$29/$43, institutions $16/$31/$46, U.S. students $10/$19/$28, elsewhere students $12/$23/$34, airmail surcharge $3; per copy: $7 US/$8 elsewhere; sample: $7US/$8 elsewhere. Back issues: $10. 150pp; 6x9; of. Reporting time: 6 months. Payment: none. Copyrighted, does not revert to author. Pub's reviews: 20 in 1990. §Women's literature—critical studies. Ads: $150/$75. CELJ.

Tunnel Publishing (see also MIRKWOOD), Joe 'Kingfish' Lane, PO Box 4083, Terre Haute, IN 47804, 812-234-3133. 1985. Criticism, reviews, non-fiction. "We like how-to or how-it's-been-done books on underground press and alternative publishing. Send for sample copy of *Mirkwood* ($1) and see what we are interested in." avg. press run 200. Expects 1 title 1991, 2 titles 1992. 1 title listed in the *Small Press Record of Books in Print* (20th Edition, 1991-92). avg. price, paper: $3. Discounts: 50% to distributors, 10 or more, payment must accompany order. 20pp; of. Reporting time: 2 days to 2 weeks. Payment: negotiable. Does not copyright for author. NLNS (New Liberation News Service).

TURN-OF-THE-CENTURY WOMEN, Margaret D. Stetz, c/o Department of English, Georgetown University, Washington, DC 20057. 1984. Articles, art, criticism, reviews. "Scholarly journal dealing with literature, art, social history, bibliography relating to or by women in the period 1880-1920. Short articles particularly welcome; also reviews of new books and exhibitions" circ. 350. 2/yr. Pub'd 2 issues 1990; expects 2 issues 1991, 2 issues 1992. sub. price: $15(US), $20 outside USA; per copy: $7; sample: $2. Back issues: $6/issue. Discounts: none. 56-72pp; 6x9; of, from typesetting. Reporting time: varies. Payment: none. Copyrighted. Pub's reviews: 1 in 1990. §Works by and about women (primarily British and American) 1880-1920. Ads: $40/$25/will accept reciprocal ads. CELJ.

TURNSTILE, 175 5th Avenue, Suite 2348, New York, NY 10010. 1986. Poetry, fiction, articles, art, photos, interviews, satire, criticism, parts-of-novels, long-poems, non-fiction. "Quality material in all categories listed above. 'Visual and literary landscapes.' Our average piece is about 10-15 typewritten pages. We have published stories by Fenton Johnson, David Shields, and Ann Copeland. Please query for submission guidelines." circ. 1.5M-2M. 2/yr. Pub'd 2 issues 1990; expects 2 issues 1991, 2 issues 1992. sub. price: $12; per copy: $6.50; sample: $6.50. Back issues: $8. Discounts: query for library rates. Contributors have reduced subscription rates. 128pp; 6x9; lp. Reporting time: 10-12 weeks. Payment: in issues. Copyrighted, reverts to author. Ads: one-time: $150/$100/$75; 2 time: $125/$80/$65. CLMP, COSMEP.

Turnstone Press, Marilyn Morton, Managing Editor, 607-100 Arthur Street, Winnipeg R3B 1H3, Canada, 204-947-1555. 1976. Poetry, fiction, criticism, long-poems. "Contemporary Canadian writing." avg. press run 1M. Pub'd 8 titles 1990; expects 8 titles 1991, 8 titles 1992. 95 titles listed in the *Small Press Record of Books in Print* (20th Edition, 1991-92). avg. price, paper: $10.95. Discounts: bookstores 1-4 copies 20%, 5+ 40%; schools & libraries 10%; wholesalers 45%. Poetry 80pp, fiction & criticism 220pp; 5½x8½; of. Reporting time: 2-3 months. Payment: 10% paid annually. Copyrights for author. LPG, ACP, AMBP, CBIC, CBA.

Twelvetrees Press/Twin Palms Publishers, Jack Woody, 2400 North Lake Avenue, Altadena, CA 91001. 1980. Poetry, art, photos. "Additional address: PO Box 188, Pasadena, CA 91102. 1988 books include work by: Herb Ritts, Herbert List, Norman Mauskopf, Duane Michals, Ken Schles. Previous work by: Duane Michals, Robert Mapplethorpe, Dennis Hopper, William Claxton, George Platt Lynes, among others. Total number published: 40." avg. press run 4M. Pub'd 7 titles 1990; expects 4 titles 1991. avg. price, cloth: $50. Discounts: bookstores 20% 1 title, 30% 2-4, 40% + free freight for 5+ titles; individuals receive 10% if order is over $100. 125pp; oversized; roto-grauvre, of. Reporting time: indefinite. Payment: dependent on individual agreement. Copyrights for author.

21st Century Books, Robert Kirkpatrick, Senior Editor, PO Box 5225, Lafayette, LA 70502, 318-233-6388. 1981. Poetry, fiction, satire, long-poems, plays, non-fiction. "We are primarily interested in outrageous satire, irreverent narrative verse like that of Edward Leer (lots of verbal virticosity and clever rhymes), as well as futuristic writing (what will the new religion of tomorrow be like?). We don't like the way that most poets stylize their work to be on the inside. Instead of dillitantes, we're interested in novelists or poets with big powerful personality who despise being 'in style.' We like writers who attack society, but are bored by trite, outdated philosophies like communism and socialism. We're interested in the counter-culture if it is original and not drug oriented" avg. press run 1M. Pub'd 1 title 1990; expects 6 titles 1991, 8 titles 1992. avg. price, paper: $15. Discounts: 50%. 150pp; 5½×7½; of. Reporting time: 3 months. Payment: 10%. Copyrights for author. 526/37/50/73/78/31/215.

21ST CENTURY CHRISTIAN MAGAZINE, Elm House Christian Communications Ltd, Hilary Saunders, Editor, 37 Elm Road, New Malden, Surrey KT3 3HB, England, 01-942-9761. 1968. circ. 16M. 12/yr. Pub'd 12 issues 1990; expects 12 issues 1991, 12 issues 1992. sub. price: £15.90; per copy: £1.20; sample: same. Back issues: £1.20. 60pp; 210×275mm. Pub's reviews: 50 in 1990. Ads: £4.90 + VAT/£285 + VAT/55p per word.

21st Century Publications, 401 N. 4th Street, PO Box 702, Fairfield, IA 52556, 515-472-5105. 1974. Articles, art, photos, interviews, letters, news items. "Books on Fruitarianism & Live Food related to Spirituality and Healing. We publish books on healing, vegetarianism, spiritual. Recently published books: V. Kulvinskas, M.S., N.D. *Survival Into 21st Century,* introduction by Dick Gregory, art: Peter Max. $14.95—*Nutritional Evaluation Of Sprouts,* $5.95—Abramowski, M.D., *Fruitarian Diet For Regeneration* $1.00. *Love Your Body-Poorman's Vegetarianism* $4.95." avg. press run 2M. 8 titles listed in the *Small Press Record of Books in Print* (20th Edition, 1991-92). avg. price, paper: $9.00; other: $2.50. Discounts: jobbers 60%, trade 40%, agent 10%, classroom 25%. 100-320pp; 8×11; of. Reporting time: 3 months. Payment: yes. Copyrights for author.

The Twickenham Press, Arnold Greissle-Schoenberg, Barbara Beesley, 31 Jane Street, New York, NY 10014, 212-741-2417. 1980. Fiction. "We are *not* reading any new submissions this year. In Oct. appeared our off-beat psycho-historical novel entitled *Klytaimnestra, Who Stayed At Home*; the author, Nancy Bogen is a professor of English literatue and a feminist. In 1981, we published the first English version of the celebrated Danish classic *Adam Homo* by Frederik Paludan-Muller, the translator of Prof. Stephen Klass." avg. press run 1M. 2 titles listed in the *Small Press Record of Books in Print* (20th Edition, 1991-92). avg. price, paper: $7. Discounts: 20% to libraries; 40% to dealers; returns to 99 years. 250pp; 5½×8¼; lp. Reporting time: long. Payment: 50% of net profits after recovery. Does not copyright for author. COSMEP.

Twin Peaks Press, Helen Hecker, PO Box 129, Vancouver, WA 98666, 206-694-2462 FAX 206-696-3210. 1984. "Query first, publish books." avg. press run 10M. Expects 6 titles 1991, 12 titles 1992. 5 titles listed in the *Small Press Record of Books in Print* (20th Edition, 1991-92). avg. price, paper: $9.95. Retail trade ordering information; 1 (None) 2-6 (20%) 6-up (40%), distributors write. 192pp; 5½×8½. Reporting time: varies. Payment: negotiable. Copyrights for author. COSMEP, Marin Small Publishers Assn., Northwest Assn of Book Publishers, Book Publishers Northwest.

TWISTED, Christine Hoard, Editor & Publisher, 22071 Pineview Drive, Antioch, IL 60002. 1985. Poetry, fiction, articles, art, photos, cartoons, interviews, satire, criticism, reviews, letters, parts-of-novels, long-poems, collages, non-fiction. "No sword and sorcery or hard science fiction. Lengths up to 5,000 words, no minimum on words. Prefers horror and dark fantasy (graphic or sexual in content okay). No sexism or racism. Make checks or money orders payable to Christine Hoard." circ. 200-300. Irregular. Expects 1 issue 1991, 1 issue 1992. price per copy: $6; sample: $6. Back issues: $6. Discounts: contact editor. 150pp; 8½×11; of. Reporting time: 1-3 months. Payment: currently in copies. Copyrighted, reverts to author. Pub's reviews: 0 in 1990. §Horror. Ads: $10/$5. SPWAO.

TWISTED IMAGE NEWSLETTER, Ace Backwords, 1630 University Avenue #26, Berkeley, CA 94703, 415-644-8035. 1982. Articles, cartoons, interviews, satire, reviews, music. "95% of the material is created by me, so I'm not particularly interested in unsolicited material" circ. 400. 12/yr. Pub'd 12 issues 1990; expects 12 issues 1991, 12 issues 1992. sub. price: $12; per copy: $1; sample: $1. Back issues: set of 7 back issues $10. 8pp; 8½×11; †xerox. Reporting time: within a week if accompanied by SASE. Payment: absolutely zero. Copyrighted, reverts to author. Pub's reviews: 4 in 1990. §I like comics, Bukowski, hate poetry, like humor and sex. Ads: none.

2AM MAGAZINE, 2AM Publications, Gretta M. Anderson, PO Box 6754, Rockford, IL 61125-1754, 815-397-5901. 1986. Poetry, fiction, articles, art, cartoons, interviews, reviews, letters. "Recent contributors:

J.N. Williamson, Leonard Carpenter, William Relling Jr., Wayne Allen Sallee, Donald Burkeson, Janet Loumer, Avram Davidson, John Coyne." circ. 1M. 4/yr. Pub'd 4 issues 1990; expects 4 issues 1991, 4 issues 1992. sub. price: $19; per copy: $4.95; sample: $5.95. Back issues: $5.95. Discounts: 40% trade. 68pp; 8½×11; of. Reporting time: 8-12 weeks. Payment: 1/2¢ per word minimum. Copyrighted, reverts to author. Pub's reviews: 100+ in 1990. §Horror fiction, science fiction, how to write. Ads: $200/$75/$50 1/4 page. COSMEP, SPWAO.

2AM Publications (see also 2AM MAGAZINE), Gretta McCombs Anderson, PO Box 6754, Rockford, IL 61125-1754, 815-397-5901. 1986. Fiction. "We publish annual anthologies of horror fiction, both original and reprint. Also publish how-to books on writing horror fiction, marketing genre fiction, and survival as a free-lance horror writer. *The 2AM Treasury of Terror* reprints the best horror fiction published in *2AM Magazine*, *The Horror Show Magazine*, and other small press genre publications." avg. press run 2M. Pub'd 1 title 1990; expects 1 title 1991, 2 titles 1992. 3 titles listed in the *Small Press Record of Books in Print* (20th Edition, 1991-92). avg. price, cloth: $19.95; paper: $9.95. Discounts: 40% trade. 150pp; 6×9; of. Reporting time: 2-4 months. Payment: negotiable, offer individual contract. Copyrights for author. COSMEP, SPWAO.

'2D' (DRAMA AND DANCE), 2D Publications, Ken Byron, Knighton Fields Drama Centre, Herrick Road, Leicester LE2 6DJ, England, 0533-700850-701525. 1981. Articles, reviews. "Since its first issue in October 1981 '2D' has established itself as a major forum for the exchange of ideas and information between Drama and Dance practitioners, many of whom have commented enthusiastically on both the range and the quality of the contributions. '2D' includes material by those individuals who are pushing forward the boundaries of our thinking and practice, as well as articles offering clear, practical guidance to the unsure or inexperienced, and a substantial book review section. It covers the whole field of Drama and Dance in Education—from infants to university students—and looks at Drama and Dance in the wider community beyond schools and colleges. If you want to tune in to the best thinking and practice across the world, then take out a subscription to '2D'." circ. 3M. 2/yr. Pub'd 2 issues 1990; expects 2 issues 1991, 2 issues 1992. sub. price: £5, $10 U.S., $12 Canada, $13 Australia; per copy: £2.50 (sterling only); sample: £2.50 (sterling only). 80pp; 5×7. Payment: £10 per 1,000 words. Copyrighted, reverts to author. Pub's reviews: 10 in 1990. §Drama and Dance in Education. Ads: £85/£70/£50 1/4 page.

2D Publications (see also '2D' (DRAMA AND DANCE)), Knighton Fields Drama Centre, Herrick Road, Leicester LE2 6DJ, England, 0533-700850-701525.

Two Rivers Press, Juan Romero, Fiction; Harrison Begay, Poetry; Anna Whitehorse, Art, Route 9, Box 56, Santa Fe, NM 87505. 1988. Poetry, fiction, art, photos, interviews, criticism, reviews, parts-of-novels. "Rights revert to author" avg. press run 250. Pub'd 2 titles 1990; expects 2 titles 1991. 3 titles listed in the *Small Press Record of Books in Print* (20th Edition, 1991-92). avg. price, cloth: $12; paper: $6. 60pp; size varies; †lp. Reporting time: 3 months. Does not copyright for author.

Tyger Press (see also ANGRY), Steven Marks, 325 Captain's Walk, Room 301, New London, CT 06320, 442-1835. 1989. Fiction, non-fiction. "Tyger Press is a publisher of books, monographs, etc. which are marketable and timeless (long 'shelf life'). All publications must make an important contribution to creative expression or to an area of intellectual inquiry. Tyger Press takes its name from the poem by William Blake." avg. press run 500. Pub'd 1 title 1990; expects 2 titles 1991, 5 titles 1992. 1 title listed in the *Small Press Record of Books in Print* (20th Edition, 1991-92). avg. price, paper: $8.95; other: $19.95 xerox. Discounts: standard, available upon request. Pages vary; size varies; of, xerox. Reporting time: 6 months. Payment: by arrangement. Does not copyright for author. COSMEP.

TYRO MAGAZINE, Tyro Publishing, Stan Gordon, 194 Carlbert Street, Sault St. Marie, Ontario P6A 5E1, Canada, 705-253-6402. 1984. Poetry, fiction, articles, art, cartoons, satire, reviews, parts-of-novels, long-poems, non-fiction. "*Tyro* is a practice and discussion medium for developing writers. Length: usually not more than 5000 words." circ. 500-700. 3/yr. Pub'd 6 issues 1990; expects 3 issues 1991, 3 issues 1992. sub. price: $27; per copy: $10; sample: $10. Discounts: 25%-40%. 210pp; 5½×8½. Reporting time: usually within 2 weeks (not more than 8). Payment: none. Authors retain all rights. Pub's reviews: 3 in 1990. Free ad space for writers' group members.

Tyro Publishing (see also TYRO MAGAZINE), Stan Gordon, 194 Carlbert Street, Sault St. Marie, Ontario P6A 5E1, Canada, 707-253-6402. 1984. Poetry, fiction, articles, art, cartoons, satire, reviews, parts-of-novels, long-poems, non-fiction. "We seriously consider work from previously unpublished authors." Pub'd 2 titles 1990; expects 2 titles 1991, 2 titles 1992. 2 titles listed in the *Small Press Record of Books in Print* (20th Edition, 1991-92). avg. price, paper: $10. Discounts: 25%-40%. 150pp; 5½×8½; depends on size and press run. Reporting time: 4-8 weeks. Payment: varies. Does not copyright for author.

U

U.S. Chess Federation (see also CHESS LIFE; SCHOOL MATES), Glenn Petersen, (CL); Jennie Simon, (SM), 186 Route 9W, New Windsor, NY 12553, 914-562-8350. 1939. Articles, photos, cartoons, news items, non-fiction.

U.S. Institute for Theatre Technology, Inc. (see also THEATRE DESIGN AND TECHNOLOGY), Eric Fielding, Editor; Cecelia Fielding, Editor, 10 West 19th Street #5A, New York, NY 10011-4206, 212-924-9088. 1965. Articles, interviews, criticism, reviews. avg. press run 5M. 72pp; 8¼×11; electronic. Reporting time: 6-10 weeks. Payment: none.

UCS Press, Jim Dobkins, 3531 W. Glendale Avenue, Suite 202, Phoenix, AZ 85051, 602-841-7176. 1987. Non-fiction. "Our publishing schedule is complete through 1990. We're interested in nonfiction manuscripts that lend themselves to wide-spread, rapid publicity, and can support minimum first printings of 10,000 books" avg. press run 10M. Expects 3 titles 1991, 5 titles 1992. 7 titles listed in the *Small Press Record of Books in Print* (20th Edition, 1991-92). avg. price, cloth: $16.95-$18.95; paper: $6.95-$8.95. Discounts: contact publisher for rates. 144-300pp; 5½×8½, 6×9; cameron belt press, of. Payment: 10% royalty; quarterly payment schedule. Copyrights for author. Publishers Marketing Asociation.

Ultimate Secrets, Box 43033, Upper Montclair, NJ 07043, 201-857-6283. 1991. Non-fiction. "We publish what we call 'hard core' how-to books, such as our current title *How to be Outrageously Successful With the Opposite Sex*. We are very interested in submissions of how-to books for our consideration. No diet, health, gardening or home repair." avg. press run 10M-50M. Expects 4 titles 1991, 4 titles 1992. avg. price, paper: $19.95. Discounts: 2-4 books 20%, 5-9 30%, 10-24 40%, 25-49 42%, 50-74 44%, 75-99 46%, 100-199 48%, 200+ 50%; STOP orders 40%. 150-200pp; 8½×11; of. Reporting time: 30 days. Payment: varies. Copyrights for author. PMA.

Ultralight Publications, Inc., Michael A. Markowski, 1 Oakglade Circle, Hummelstown, PA 17036-9525, 717-566-0468. 1981. Non-fiction. "NOTE: All books are perfect bound." avg. press run 5M-7M. Pub'd 3 titles 1990; expects 6 titles 1991, 6 titles 1992. 6 titles listed in the *Small Press Record of Books in Print* (20th Edition, 1991-92). avg. price, paper: $10.95-$17.95. Discounts: 2-20%; 5-40%; 25-40%; 50-43%; 100-44%; 250-45%; 500-48%; 750-50%. 144-352pp; 6×9, 7⅜×9¼, 6⅛×9¼; of. Reporting time: 3 weeks. Payment: 10% net and half advance on signing, 1/2 on completion of ms. *UP* holds copyrights.

Ultramarine Publishing Co., Inc., Christopher P. Stephens, PO Box 303, Hastings-on-Hudson, NY 10706, 914-478-2522. 1965. Poetry, fiction. "We rescue books. We primarily distribute titles for authors (a major publisher has remaindered). The author buys some of the stock and we sell it for the author and split the proceeds." avg. press run 500-2.5M. Pub'd 20 titles 1990; expects 25 titles 1991, 30 titles 1992. avg. price, cloth: $15; paper: $8. Discounts: 1-4 20%; 5-9 30%; 10+ 40%. 250pp; 6×9; of. Reporting time: 60 days. Payment: varies. Copyrights for author.

UMBRELLA, Judith A. Hoffberg, PO Box 40100, Pasadena, CA 91114, 818-797-0514. 1978. Articles, art, photos, cartoons, interviews, criticism, reviews, news items, non-fiction. "Short reviews of artists' books, artists' periodicals, microfiche, video, performance, Xerox art, news & reviews of artists' book conferences and exhibitions. Individuals: $15 US, $20 elsewhere abroad, Institutions: $25 US, $30 for surface airmail foreign." circ. 1M. 2/yr. Pub'd 2 issues 1990; expects 2 issues 1991, 2 issues 1992. sub. price: $15; per copy: $7.50; sample: $5. Back issues: $5 and above. Discounts: none. 24pp; 8½×11; of. Reporting time: immediate. Payment: none. Copyrighted, reverts to author. Pub's reviews: 200 in 1990. §Contemporary art, photography, bookworks by artists, new artists' publications like periodicals, pamphlets, audioworks by artists, records by artists, microfiche, copy art. Ads: /$100/25¢ - no full pages. APHA.

Umbrella Books (see also Copyright Information Services), Jerome K. Miller, Po Box 1460-A, Friday Harbor, WA 98250-1460. 1988. "One book available in the spring 1988. Six additional titles in preparation. Umbrella Books will specialize in travel guides to the Pacific Northwest. We are seeking manuscripts for travel guides" Expects 3 titles 1991, 6 titles 1992. avg. price, paper: $10.95. Discounts: In process. 150pp; 5½×8½.

UMI Research Press, Christine Hammes, Acquisitions Editor; Bradley Taylor, Managing Editor, 300 North Zeeb Road, Ann Arbor, MI 48106, 313-973-9821. 1978. "Original, scholarly monographs published in subject area series with manuscripts selected by series editors who are prominent scholars in that particular field" avg. press run 700. Pub'd 45 titles 1990; expects 58 titles 1991, 60 titles 1992. 45 titles listed in the *Small Press Record of Books in Print* (20th Edition, 1991-92). avg. price, cloth: $39.95; paper: $19.95. Discounts:

596

bookstores 1-4 copies 20%, 5-9 30%, 10-49 40%, 50+ 41%+. 250pp; 6×9; of. Reporting time: 2-3 months. Payment: 5% royalty to authors. Copyrights for author. University Microfilms International (UMI) 300 North Zeeb Road, Ann Arbor, MI 48106.

THE U*N*A*B*A*S*H*E*D LIBRARIAN, THE "HOW I RUN MY LIBRARY GOOD" LETTER, Marvin H. Scilken, Editor; Mary P. Scilken, Assoc. Editor, G.P.O. Box 2631, New York, NY 10116. 1971. Articles, cartoons, satire, criticism, reviews. "U*L seeks long (and especially short) articles on innovative procedures; forms used in libraries. Articles should be complete to enable the reader to 'do it' with little or no research. Single paragraph 'articles' are ok with U*L. We ask for non exclusive rights. Also humous library situations and library poetry." 4/yr. Pub'd 4 issues 1990; expects 4 issues 1991. sub. price: $30 foreign & Canadian postage add $6, payable in US funds on US bank; per copy: $7.50 foreign + Canadian postage add $1.25; sample: $7.50 foreign & Canadian postage add $1.25. Back issues: (most are in print) are $7.50 each, add $1.25 foreign + Canadian. 32pp; 8½×11; of. Payment: none. Copyrighted. Pub's reviews. §Library subjects only.

UNARIUS LIGHT, Ruth Norman, Publisher & Editor; Barbara Reynolds, Associate Editor, 145 S. Magnolia Avenue, El Cajon, CA 92020, 619-447-4170. 1954. Poetry, articles, art, photos, interviews, reviews, long-poems, non-fiction. "The materials is a summary of events that have taken place at the Unarius Academy of Science—an expository statement of the teachings of past life therapy. The key factors are dialogues or communications on all topics of life from intelligent minds of other more advanced people who once lived on Earth, incorporationg the interdimensional physics of energy." circ. 2M. 4/yr. Pub'd 4 issues 1990; expects 4 issues 1991, 4 issues 1992. sub. price: $20; per copy: $5; sample: free. Back issues: $3 single copy. Discounts: 40%. 45pp; 5½×8½; †of. Reporting time: 2 months. Payment: none. Copyrighted, does not revert to author.

UNBRIDLED LUST!, Unbridled Lust! Publishing, Matt LeClair, Bradly K. Finch, 8 Elm Street #2, Orono, ME 04473, 207-866-3535. 1990. Poetry, fiction, articles, art, photos, cartoons, interviews, satire, criticism, reviews, music, letters, parts-of-novels, long-poems, collages, plays, news items, non-fiction. "Things have been quiet, too quiet, for too damn long. A time for change has come. New legends must be written. New visions must be created. Challenges must be issued. Frontiers must be exploded. Be part of the revolution. No sexist or racist material will be accepted. Submissions should provoke an emotional and/or intellectual response. Send a SASE if you have questions, or would like a copy of guidelines. Fiction should get to the point fairly quickly; we don't have room to wait until chapter 47 when something happens. ANY subject(s) will be considered. Contributors include: Timothy Leary and Carolyn Forche, interviews with Joey Ramone and Rinde Eckert, G. Gordon Liddy and Timothy Leary, Samuel R. Delaney, Phillip Agee." circ. 500. 6/yr. Pub'd 2 issues 1990; expects 6 issues 1991, 6 issues 1992. sub. price: $15; per copy: $2.50; sample: 2.50. Back issues: Issues #1 and #2 can be purchased together for $4 ppd. Discounts: 75% of cover price for retailers and distributors. 45pp; 5½×8½; of. Reporting time: 4-6 months. Payment: 2 copies to contributors. Copyrighted, reverts to author. Pub's reviews: 1 in 1990. §Punk, religion, occult, industrial culture, contemporary music, erotica, pornography, film, video, art, cybernetics, technology, sex, comix, lovecraft, Crowley, post-modernism, drugs, terrorism, survivalism, vegetarianism, voodoo, deviance, horror, crime, tattoo, politics, conspiracy theory, mental illness, mysticism, feminism,... Ads: By insert only, price varies.

Unbridled Lust! Publishing (see also UNBRIDLED LUST!), Bradly K. Finch, Matt LeClair, 8 Elm Street #2, Orono, ME 04473, 207-866-3535. 1990. Poetry, fiction, articles, art, photos, cartoons, interviews, satire, criticism, reviews, music, letters, long-poems, collages, plays, news items, non-fiction. "Things have been quiet, too quiet, for too damn long. A time for change has come. New legends must be written. New visions must be created. Challenges must be issued. Frontiers must be exploded. Be part of the revolution. No sexist or racist material will be accepted. Submissions should provoke an emotional and/or intellectual response. Send a SASE if you have questions, or would like a copy of guidelines. Fiction shuld get to the point fairly quickly; we don't have room to wait until chapter 47 when something happens. ANY subject(s) will be considered. Contributors include: Timothy Leary and Carolyn Forche, interviews with Joey Ramone and Rinde Eckert, G. Gordon Liddy, Timothy Leary, Samuel R. Delaney, Phillip Agee." avg. press run 500. Pub'd 2 titles 1990; expects 6 titles 1991, 6 titles 1992. avg. price, other: $2.50 saddle. Discounts: Please contact publisher directly. 45pp; 5½×8½; of. Reporting time: 4-6 months. Payment: Please contact publisher directly. Does not copyright for author.

THE UNDERGROUND FOREST - LA SELVA SUBTERRANEA, Joseph Richey, Anne Becher, 1701 Bluebell Avenue, Boulder, CO 80302. 1986. Poetry, fiction, articles, cartoons, interviews, criticism, reviews, letters, long-poems, concrete art, news items, non-fiction. "Half of TUF material is reprinted with permission from other small press publications from North, South and Central Americas. Our emphasis is on creative non-fiction, be it poetry, song, investigative journalism. We are a bilingual hemispheric journal. We especially welcome translations to or from Spanish. Some recent contributors: Eduardo Galeano, Glenn Gant, Daisy Zamora, Diana Bellessi, Jack Collom, Tom Clark, Diane diPrima, William Burroughs, Anne Waldman, Allen Ginsberg, Barry Commoner, Ed Sanders, Ernesto Cardenal, Daniel Sheehan, Andre Gregory, Jose Arguelles,

Margaret Randall...'' circ. 5M. 3/yr. Pub'd 3 issues 1990; expects 3 issues 1991, 3 issues 1992. sub. price: $12/4 issues; per copy: $3; sample: $3. Discounts: 40% to bookstores. 48pp; 5½×17; †of. Reporting time: 90 days. Payment: in copies. Not copyrighted. Pub's reviews: 40 in 1990. §Art, Latin America, translations, non-fiction, poetry, creative journalist productions, ecology, sustainable development. Ads: $100/$50. MWPA, Maine Writers & Publishers Alliance, 19 Mason Street, Brunswick, ME 04011.

UNDERGROUND SURREALIST MAGAZINE, Mick Cusimano, Underground Surrealist Studio, PO Box 2565, Cambridge, MA 02238, 617-891-9569. 1987. Cartoons. "Comicstrips and cartoons on any subject. Pointless and pornographic material discouraged'' circ. 300. 1/yr. Pub'd 1 issue 1990. sub. price: $3; per copy: $3; sample: same. Discounts: inquire. 28pp; 8½×11; of. Reporting time: 1 month. Payment: contributor's copy. Copyrighted, reverts to author. Ads: $95/$50. Small Press Alliance.

UNDERPASS, Barry Hammond, Brian Schulze, #574-21, 10405 Jasper Avenue, Edmonton, Alberta T5J 3S2, Canada. 1986. Poetry, art. "Uses contemporary, urban, avant-garde, concrete or discursive prose poems, any length. No nature, religious poems or rhymers. Also needs b&w artwork suitable for reproduction 5½'' X 8½''. Has recently published poetry by B.Z. Niditch, Alice Major and Brian Burke." circ. 100-300. 1/yr. Pub'd 1 issue 1990; expects 1 issue 1991, 1 issue 1992. sub. price: $6.95; per copy: $6.95; sample: $3.50. Back issues: $3.50. Discounts: bookstores 40%. Pages vary; 5½×8½; of. Reporting time: 6 weeks. Payment: small honorarium plus 2 contributor copies. Copyrighted, reverts to author. Ads: $25/$15. Small Press Action Network.

Underwhich Editions, Paul Dutton, Beverly Daurio, Steven Smith, Frank Davey, Karl Jirgens, PO Box 262, Adelaide Street Station, Toronto, Ontario M5C 2J4, Canada, 536-9316. 1978. Poetry, fiction, art, interviews, music, long-poems, collages, plays, concrete art, non-fiction. "Dedicated to presenting, in diverse and appealing physical formats, new works by contemporary creators, focusing on formal invention and encompassing the expanded frontiers of literary and musical endeavor. Recent contributors include: Paul Dolden, Michael Chocholak, Victor Coleman, Mara Zibens, Kate Van Dusen." avg. press run 200-500. Pub'd 11 titles 1990; expects 5 titles 1991, 7 titles 1992. 46 titles listed in the *Small Press Record of Books in Print* (20th Edition, 1991-92). avg. price, cloth: $10; paper: $5; other: $2.50. Discounts: 40% to retailers, 20% to educational institutions and libraries, 40% to radio stations. 30-50pp; of, lp. Reporting time: 6-12 months. Payment: negotiable. Copyright remains with author.

Underwood-Miller, Inc. & Brandywyne Books, Chuck Miller, 708 Westover Drive, Lancaster, PA 17601-1231, 717-285-2255. 1976. Fiction, criticism. "Our fiction line consists of high quality limited editions designed for libraries and collectors. We use sewn signitures, library quality cloth and acid free paper on all our books. We publish only established authors such as Jack Vance, Roger Zelazny, Robert Silverberg. Underwood/Miller are the editors of several critical books on the works of living authors. *Jack Vance* was published in 1980 by Taplinger. *Fear Itself*—The Horror Fiction of Stephen King was published in 1982 by Underwood/Miller, paper edition available from NAL. *Kingdom of Fear: The World of Stephen King* was published by Underwood-Miller and NAL in 1986" avg. press run 1M-1.5M. Pub'd 8 titles 1990; expects 13 titles 1991, 15 titles 1992. 20 titles listed in the *Small Press Record of Books in Print* (20th Edition, 1991-92). avg. price, cloth: $20. Discounts: 5+ titles mixed 40%; 50+ mixed 50%. 250pp; 6½×9½; of. Reporting time: 2 weeks. Payment: 10%. Copyrights for author.

THE UNEXPLAINED, National Publishers, Hank Krastman, PO Box 16790, Encino, CA 91416. 1986. Articles, photos, non-fiction. "Only articles with photographs" circ. 30M. 4/yr. Expects 1 issue 1991, 4 issues 1992. sub. price: $10; per copy: $2.95; sample: same. Back issues: $2.95. Discounts: 40%. 32-40pp; 8½×11; of, full color. Reporting time: 30 days. Payment: upon publication. Copyrighted, does not revert to author. Pub's reviews. §Metaphysical.

Unicorn Press, Alan Brilliant, Editor, PO Box 3307, Greensboro, NC 27402. 1965. Poetry, fiction. "Most Unicorn books are printed on acid-free paper, bound between real Davey board by hand and editions sewn, not glued. We are not able to report on unsolicited manuscripts" avg. press run 500 chapbooks, 2M full-length books. Pub'd 10 titles 1990; expects 12 titles 1991. 79 titles listed in the *Small Press Record of Books in Print* (20th Edition, 1991-92). avg. price, cloth: $17.50; paper: $7; other: $8 chapbooks. Discounts: 40% bookstores, 10% libraries. 150pp; 5½×8½; †lp. Reporting time: varies. Payment: 10% of all sales. Copyrights for author. COSMEP.

The Unicorn Publishing House, Bill McGuire, Senior Editor; John Ingram, Editor; Heidi Corso, Art Director, 120 American Road, Morris Plains, NJ 07950. 1981. "We are no longer accepting original manuscripts" avg. press run 50M. Pub'd 7 titles 1990; expects 14 titles 1991, 28 titles 1992. avg. price, cloth: $9.95-$16.95; other: $6.95 Little Unicorn Series. Discounts: 43% up to 99 books, 45% up to 499 books, 50% above 500 books. 192pp; 8×10. Copyrights for author.

Unified Publications, 1050 University Avenue, Suite 103-203, San Diego, CA 92103, 619-497-0573. 1990. Non-fiction. avg. press run 5M. Pub'd 1 title 1990; expects 2 titles 1991, 3 titles 1992. 2 titles listed in the *Small*

Press Record of Books in Print (20th Edition, 1991-92). avg. price, paper: $9.95. Discounts: 40% for wholesale to bookstore. 160pp; 5¾×8⅜; of. COSMEP.

THE UNINTELLIGENCER, J.C. Coleman, PO Box 3194, Bellingham, WA 98227. 1983. Fiction, articles, art, photos, cartoons, satire, criticism, reviews. "A variety of offbeat material in every issue. Does not accept submissions or advertising. All payments must be in *cash*. Trade of similar publications is welcome" circ. 50-100. 4/yr. Pub'd 4 issues 1990; expects 4 issues 1991, 4 issues 1992. sub. price: $5; per copy: $1. Discounts: 80¢/ea for orders or 10 or more. 20pp; 5½×8½; photocopy. Copyrighted. Pub's reviews: 35 in 1990. §Non-mainstream, underground stuff. Ads: none.

Union Park Press, William A. Koelsch, PO Box 2737, Boston, MA 02208. 1978. Non-fiction. "At present the press confines itself to material on gay life and liberation. It has so far published two books, A. Nolder Gay's *The View From the Closet: Essays on Gay Life and Liberation*, (1978); and *Some of My Best Friends: Essays in Gay History and Biography*, (1990)." avg. press run 2M. Pub'd 1 title 1990. 2 titles listed in the *Small Press Record of Books in Print* (20th Edition, 1991-92). avg. price, paper: $7. Discounts: 1-4 copies, 20%; 5 or more, 40%. 140pp; 5¼×8¼; of. Reporting time: 1 month. Payment: none. Copyrights for author.

UNION SHOP BLUFF, A. Le Goaix, 205A Liverpool Street, Guelph, Ontario N1H 2L6, Canada, 519-767-1998. 1990. Poetry, art, photos, collages, concrete art, non-fiction. "Recent contributors: F.A. Nettlebeck, Greg Evason, Daniel F. Bradley, Philipe Grasman, Dan Nielsen, John M. Bennett, Jim Vallely. Leans towards experimental poetry" circ. 120. 6/yr. Pub'd 1 issue 1990; expects 6 issues 1991, 6 issues 1992. sub. price: $6; per copy: SASE; sample: SASE. 1 page; 8½×14; †xerox. Reporting time: 2 weeks. Payment: copies. Not copyrighted.

Union Square Press, Nathan J. Sambul, Publisher, 5 East 16th Street, New York, NY 10003, 212-924-2800. 1987. Non-fiction. "Subjects: business, media. Contributors: Mark Schubin, John Rice, Michael Dainard." avg. press run 5M. Pub'd 4 titles 1990; expects 4 titles 1991, 4 titles 1992. 4 titles listed in the *Small Press Record of Books in Print* (20th Edition, 1991-92). avg. price, cloth: $29.95; paper: $19.95. 250pp; 5½×8½; of. Reporting time: 90 days. Payment: 10% of list price. Copyrights for author. COSMEP, PMA.

UNION STREET REVIEW, Ellen Stone, Editor; Raymond C. Shilobod, Associate Editor, PO Box 19078, Alexandria, VA 22320, 703-836-4549. 1988. Fiction, articles, interviews, reviews, parts-of-novels. "Prefer fiction with memorable characters, strong story line. No poetry. Reviews, essays with strong personal voice. Interviews with writers. Special interest in memoirs. No simultaneous submissions." circ. 300-500. Irregular. Pub'd 1 issue 1990; expects 2 issues 1991, 2 issues 1992. price per copy: $6.50; sample: $6.50. Back issues: $9 first edition. Discounts: 30-35%. 110-128pp; 5½×8½; of. Reporting time: 5-8 weeks. Payment: none at present. Copyrighted, reverts to author. Pub's reviews: 1 in 1990. §Just about anything literary—no romances, spy novels, science fiction.

Unique Adventures Press, Doug & Barbara Luhmann, PO Box 185, San Juan Capistrano, CA 92693, 714-661-3991. 1990. Pub'd 1 title 1990; expects 2 titles 1991, 2 titles 1992. 1 title listed in the *Small Press Record of Books in Print* (20th Edition, 1991-92). avg. price, cloth: $19.95; paper: $14.95. Discounts: 2-4 20%, 5-9 40%, 10-99 50%, 100+ 55%. 70pp; 9×9; †of. Payment: flat fee, after sale. Copyrights for author.

Unique Graphics (see also OWLFLIGHT MAGAZINE), Millea Kenin, 1025 55th Street, Oakland, CA 94608, 415-655-3024. 1980. Poetry, fiction, articles, art, photos, cartoons, satire, interviews, long-poems, collages, plays. "In addition to magazines, Unique Graphics publishes Owlflight Books anthologies (produced in 1985: *Punnable Horror Stories* and *Sordid Sorcery - SF* humor). Write for information on current projects, before submitting." avg. press run 1.5M. 1 title listed in the *Small Press Record of Books in Print* (20th Edition, 1991-92). avg. price, paper: price widely variable (none over $10). Discounts: 50% pd, no returns (50-100 copies), 40% pd, no returns (over 100 copies). Pages vary; size varies; of. Reporting time: acknowledgement within 4 weeks, up to 6 months for final decision. Payment: flat fee for one-time publication rights, in most cases; occasionally, one-author collections, novellas, etc. on a profit & expense sharing basis (details negotiable). Copyrights in author's name. SPWAO.

UNIROD MAGAZINE, K.G. Bradley, 4214 B. Filbert Avenue, Atlantic City, NJ 08401. 1990. "Either William Burroughs or Henry Miller said that literature hasn't progressed nearly as far as art has, which I believe. I really thirst to run experimental writing in *Unirod*. But it's not limited to that—*Unirod* wants articles, essays, interviews, general fiction, poetry, comix, etc, etc. Artwork is also important to *Unirod*." circ. 100. 6/yr. Pub'd 2 issues 1990; expects 6 issues 1991, 6 issues 1992. sub. price: $12; per copy: $2; sample: $2. Back issues: inquire. Discounts: inquire. 24pp; 8½×11; †photocopy. Reporting time: 1-2 weeks. Payment: 1 copy and my hearty thanks and maybe worldwide fame. Copyrighted, reverts to author. Pub's reviews: 2 in 1990. §All areas, but especially experimental works or new ideas. Ads: inquire (will trade with other publications).

United Artists, Lewis Warsh, Box 2616, Peter Stuyvesant Station, New York, NY 10009. 1977. Poetry, interviews, long-poems. "Recent books by: Anne Waldman, Gary Lenhart, Bill Kushner, Liam O'Gallagher,

Bernadette Mayer, Lewis Warsh, Steve Carey." avg. press run 1.5M. Pub'd 4 titles 1990; expects 4 titles 1991, 4 titles 1992. 28 titles listed in the *Small Press Record of Books in Print* (20th Edition, 1991-92). avg. price, paper: $5. Discounts: 2-5 25%, 6+ 30%. 100pp; 5½×8; of.

United Lumbee Nation (see also UNITED LUMBEE NATION TIMES), Silver Star Reed, P.O. Box 512, Fall River Mills, CA 96028, 916-336-6701. 1977. Poetry, art. "We have two copyrighted books out: *United Lumbee Indian Ceremonies*; and an Indian cookbook, *Over The Cooking Fires*, the art of cooking and the art of Indian Ceremonies, both edited, and compiled by Princess Silver Star Reed." avg. press run 100. Pub'd 1 title 1990; expects 1 title 1992. 1 title listed in the *Small Press Record of Books in Print* (20th Edition, 1991-92). avg. price, paper: $3.75-$7.50. Discounts: $2.50 per copy. 20-25pp; 5½×8½. Payment: none. Does not copyright for author.

UNITED LUMBEE NATION TIMES, United Lumbee Nation, Silver Star Reed, P.O. Box 512, Fall River Mills, CA 96028, 916-336-6701. 1979. Poetry, articles, photos, interviews, reviews, letters, news items. circ. 650-1M. 3-4/yr. Pub'd 3 issues 1990; expects 4 issues 1991, 4 issues 1992. sub. price: $4; per copy: $1; sample: $1. Back issues: 4 issues /copies $3.50. Discounts: 75¢ per copy. 8pp; 11½×15. Reporting time: no set time, write for press time of next issue. Payment: none. Not copyrighted. Pub's reviews: 1 in 1990. §Native American Indian Heritage and Native American Indians today. Ads: $120/$60/Business card size $12/10% discount if put in four issues.

United Press Inc., Herman Levy, Editor; Phillip Partee, Author, PO Box 4064, Sarasota, FL 34230. 1979. "1 book thus far: *The Layman's Guide to Fasting and Losing Weight* by Phillip Partee. Introduction by Dick Gregory (comedian author)" avg. press run 25M. Expects 1 title 1991. avg. price, paper: $4.95. Discounts: 50% to distributors, 40% to retailers. 121pp; 5¼×8¼; of. Payment: none. Copyrights for author.

Univelt, Inc. (see also AAS HISTORY SERIES; ADVANCES IN THE ASTRONAUTICAL SCIENCES; SCIENCE AND TECHNOLOGY), H. Jacobs, PO Box 28130, San Diego, CA 92128, 619-746-4005. 1970. "We are publishing books on space, astronomy, veterinary medicine (esp. first aid for animals), and technical communication (writing, editing, word processing, publishing, etc.). *Realm of the Long Eyes* (astronomy); *General First Aid for Dogs* (veterinary medicine); *The Case for Mars, The Human Quest in Space* (space). Publishers for the American Astronautical Society." avg. press run 500-2M. Pub'd 10 titles 1990; expects 10 titles 1991, 10 titles 1992. 30 titles listed in the *Small Press Record of Books in Print* (20th Edition, 1991-92). avg. price, cloth: $25-$60; paper: $20-$50; other: some books at $7 to $15. Discounts: 20%; special discounts for classroom use; larger discounts by arrangement. 100-700pp; 7×9½ and others; of. Reporting time: 60 days. Payment: 10% for a volume author. Copyright held by Society or Univelt but obtained by Univelt.

University Editions, Inc., Ira Herman, Managing Editor, 59 Oak Lane, Spring Valley, Huntington, WV 25704, 304-429-7204. 1984. Poetry, fiction, non-fiction. "Open to new writers. Publishes book-length (45-400 page mss) fiction, poetry, and non-fiction works. Will read first novels. Open to Academic and creative writing. Recent authors include Robert Bowie, Dr. Paul Christensen, and Dr. Clifford C. Cawley. Publishes paperback originals and reprints. Presently reading unsolicited manuscripts in all categories. Enclose SASE for return of material. Simultaneous and photocopied submissions are acceptable. Will consider mss in areas not mentioned if quality is high. A brief synopsis (one or two pages) is helpful. During the next year, at least, we will be doing primarily subsidized publication, although we may be open to doing an occasional non-subsidized title. On subsidized books, author receives all sales proceeds until breakeven point, and royalty thereafter. Attempts to encourage and establish new writers." avg. press run 500-1M. Pub'd 15 titles 1990; expects 20 titles 1991, 25 titles 1992. 6 titles listed in the *Small Press Record of Books in Print* (20th Edition, 1991-92). avg. price, paper: $5-$9. Discounts: 40% bulk order; free examination copies to potential adopters and jobbers. 64-300pp; 5½×8½; of. Reporting time: 1 month. Payment: depends on author and subject matter; 15% royalty on nonsubsidized titles. Copyrights for author.

University of Calgary Press (see also ECHOS DU MONDE CLASSIQUE/CLASSICAL VIEWS; ARIEL—A Review of International English Literature; ARCTIC—Journal of the Arctic Institute of America; CANADIAN JOURNAL OF DRAMA AND THEATRE; CANADIAN JOURNAL OF PROGRAM EVALUATION/Le Revue canadienne d'evaluation de programme; CANADIAN JOURNAL OF PHILOSOPHY), Linda Cameron, Director; John King, Production Coordinator; Denise Szekrenyes, Journals Coordinator, 2500 University Drive NW, Calgary, Alberta T2N 1N4, Canada, 403-220-7578. 1982. Non-fiction. "The University of Calgary Press (UCP) was established in 1982 and since then has developed an active publishing program that includes up to 12 new scholarly titles each year and 8 journals. UCP publishes in a wide variety of subject areas and is willing to consider any innovative scholarly publication. The intention is not to restrict the publication list to specific areas. All prices and specifications are subject to change without notice. Prices are in US dollars outside of Canada. Postage & Handling (Canada and US) is $2 for the first book and $1 for each additional book. Books will be shipped at publishers' bookrate. Postage & Handling (outside North America) is $3 for the first book and $1.50 for each additional book. Books will be shipped at publishers' bookrate. Canadians please add 7% GST to book price." avg. press run 750. Pub'd 12 titles 1990; expects 14 titles 1991, 12 titles 1992. 135 titles listed in the *Small Press Record of Books in Print* (20th Edition, 1991-92). avg. price, paper: $29.95. Discounts: booksellers. 200pp; 6×9; of. Reporting time: 2-6 weeks. Payment: after all costs are covered, %. Copyrights for author. BPAA, ACUP, ACP, AAUP, CBIC, CMPA, IAPG, SSP.

University of California Press (see also AGRICULTURAL HISTORY; ASIAN SURVEY; BERKELEY WOMEN'S LAW JOURNAL; CALIFORNIA LAW REVIEW; CLASSICAL ANTIQUITY; COMPUTING SYSTEMS; EASTERN EUROPEAN POLITICS & SOCIETIES; ECOLOGY LAW QUARTERLY; FILM QUARTERLY; HIGH TECHNOLOGY LAW JOURNAL; HISTORICAL STUDIES IN THE PHYSICAL & BIOLOGICAL SCIENCES; INDEX TO FOREIGN LEGAL PERIODICALS; INDUSTRIAL RELATIONS LAW JOURNAL; INTERNATIONAL TAX AND BUSINESS LAWYER; JOURNAL OF MUSICOLOGY; LA RAZA LAW JOURNAL; MEXICAN STUDIES/ESTUDIOS MEXICANOS; MOUNTAIN RESEARCH & DEVELOPMENT; MUSIC PERCEPTION; NINETEENTH-CENTURY LITERATURE; 19TH-CENTURY MUSIC; PACIFIC HISTORICAL REVIEW; THE PUBLIC HISTORIAN; REPRESENTATIONS; RHETORICA: A Journal of the History of Rhetoric; ROMANCE PHILOLOGY; SOCIAL PROBLEMS; VIATOR: Medieval and Renaissance Studies), Sandra Whisler, Journals Manager, 2120 Berkeley Way, Berkeley, CA 94720, 415-642-4191. 1893. Articles, photos, interviews, criticism, reviews. avg. press run varies. Pub'd 28 titles 1990; expects 30 titles 1991, 32 titles 1992. avg. price, cloth: varies; paper: varies. Pages vary; 6×9, 7×10; of. Reporting time: varies widely. Payment: none. Copyrights in the name of Regents of the University of California (see individual listings). AAUP.

University of Massachusetts Press, Bruce Wilcox, Director; Clark Dougan, Senior Editor, Box 429, Amherst, MA 01004, 413-545-2217. 1964. Poetry, fiction, non-fiction. "Scholarly publications in the humanities and social sciences" avg. press run 1.25M-1.5M. Pub'd 42 titles 1990; expects 28 titles 1991, 35 titles 1992. 8 titles listed in the *Small Press Record of Books in Print* (20th Edition, 1991-92). avg. price, cloth: $31.60; paper: $14.70. Discounts: short 20-25%, trade 40-50%. 244pp; 5½×8½. Reporting time: 2-3 months. Payment: varies. Copyrights for author. AAUP.

University of Tulsa (see also JAMES JOYCE QUARTERLY), Robert Spoo, Editor, 600 South College, Tulsa, OK 74104. 1963. Articles, criticism, reviews. avg. press run 1.9M. Expects 4 titles 1992. 3 titles listed in the *Small Press Record of Books in Print* (20th Edition, 1991-92). avg. price, paper: $5. 150pp; 6×9; of. Reporting time: 6-12 weeks. Payment: contributor's copies and offprints. Copyrights for author. CELJ.

University Of Wales Press (see also BULLETIN OF THE BOARD OF CELTIC STUDIES; CONTEMPORARY WALES; EFRYDIAU ATHRONYDDOL; LLEN CYMRU; STUDIA CELTICA; WELSH HISTORY REVIEW; Y GWYDDONYDD; JOURNAL OF WELSH EDUCATION; JOURNAL OF CELTIC LINGUISTICS), 6 Gwennyth St., Cathays, Cardiff CF2 4YD, Wales, 231919. 1922. Articles, criticism, non-fiction. avg. press run 500. Pub'd 6 titles 1990; expects 4 titles 1991, 5 titles 1992. avg. price, paper: £8. Discounts: 10%. 100pp; lp, of. Payment: none. Does not copyright for author. UWP.

UNIVERSITY OF WINDSOR REVIEW, Joseph Quinn, c/o University of Windsor, Windsor, Ontario N9B3P4, Canada. 1966. Poetry, fiction, articles, art, criticism, reviews. "We try to offer a balance of fiction and poetry—we seem to have developed into a platform for some really excellent fiction and poetry: W.D. Valgardson, Joyce Carol Oates, Tom Wayman, etc." circ. 500. 2/yr. Pub'd 2 issues 1990; expects 2 issues 1991, 2 issues 1992. 1 title listed in the *Small Press Record of Books in Print* (20th Edition, 1991-92). sub. price: $12 Cdn. and $10 U.S. per year; per copy: $6 Cdn. and $5 U.S. per year; sample: $6 Cdn. and $5 U.S. per year. Back issues: please write. 100pp; 5¾×9; lp. Reporting time: 6 weeks. Payment: $25 for story or essay, $10 for poem. Copyrighted, reverts to author. No ads. COSMEP.

UNMUZZLED OX, ZerOX Books, Michael Andre, 105 Hudson Street #311, New York, NY 10013, 212-226-7170. 1971. Poetry, fiction, articles, art, photos, interviews, criticism, reviews, music, letters, parts-of-novels. "*Unmuzzled Ox* is a magazine of pre-anti-post-modernism. 'Our goal is the destruction of the State & the imposition of a Roman Catholic Thearchy.' It's helpful if contributors already understand pre-anti-post-modernism. Tabloid. Additional address: Box 550, Kingston, K7L 4W5 Ontario, Canada. We do not publish reviews, but we review books elsewhere and love to get them." circ. 20M. 2/yr. sub. price: $20; per copy: $5; sample: $7. Back issues: 1-6: $12 each 7-21 cover price. Discounts: 40%. 140pp; 8½×5½ or tabloid; of. Reporting time: 2 weeks. Payment: none. Copyrighted. §Art, literature, music, politics. Ads: $65/$35. CLMP.

UP AGAINST THE WALL, MOTHER..., Lee-Lee Schlegel, Editor-in-Chief; Jacki Warchol, Production Editor, 4114 Wood Spice Lane, Lorton, VA 22079. 1981. Poetry. "*Up Against The Wall, Mother...* is a poetry journal devoted to women in crisis; internal and external, expressing their feelings and needs through poetry. Our goal is to bring women's thoughts and feelings to light, explore them and accept them with new insights. Please submit four to six poems at a time, forty lines or less. No payment is given for accepted work (just exposure and a friendly ear). We are non-profit, our staff is volunteer and we deeply appreciate a SASE in all correspondence. ISSN 1041-9993." circ. 400. 4/yr. Pub'd 4 issues 1990; expects 4 issues 1991, 4 issues 1992. sub. price: $12; per copy: $3.50; sample: $3.50. Back issues: $3. Discounts: negotiable. 45pp; 5½x8½; laser. Reporting time: less than 2 weeks. Payment: none yet. Copyrighted, reverts to author. No ads.

UPDATE, American Council for the Arts/ACA Books, Sally Ahearn, 1285 Avenue of the Americas, 3rd Floor, Area M, New York, NY 10019, (212) 245-4510. 1975. Articles. circ. 2.5M. 12/yr. Pub'd 12 issues 1990; expects 12 issues 1991, 12 issues 1992. sub. price: with ACA membership only. 8pp; 8½x11.

Upper Access Inc., Thom Gray, Steve Carlson, Lisa Carlson, PO Box 457, 1 Upper Access Road, Hinesburg, VT 05461, 800-356-9315; 802-482-2988; fax 802-482-3125. 1987. Non-fiction. *"No* genre focus. We are looking for unique non-fiction to improve the quality of life. (We also have a mail order bookstore to market books of other small publishers. Wide range of topics considered. Annual circ. 100,000.) Our titles: *Caring For Your Own Dead: A Final Act of Love; Letters From the Other Side; Cheap Eating Handbook; Herbs of the Earth,* a self teaching guide to healing remedies; *Your Low-Tax Dream House,* a new approach to slashing the cost of home ownership. We offer 800 fulfillment service (Visa, American Express and MC) for retail sales for other small publishers. Marketing a low-cost software program that we developed for small presses, PIIGS: Publishers Invoice and Information Generating System." avg. press run 5M. Pub'd 2 titles 1990; expects 2 titles 1991, 2 titles 1992. 6 titles listed in the *Small Press Record of Books in Print* (20th Edition, 1991-92). avg. price, cloth: $17.95; paper: $12.95. Discounts: library 15%; 1-9 40%; 10+ 50%; we pay postage on prepaid orders. 195-343pp; 6x9; of. Reporting time: 2 weeks, usually. Payment: 10% of net sales to 5,000 books, 15% thereafter, modest advance for finished mss. Copyrights for author. COSMEP, PMA, Vermont Pub. Group, Nat'l Assoc. Indep. Publishers.

Upper West Side Publishing, Kevin Browne, PO Box 1512, New York, NY 10023, 212-289-7942. 1990. Fiction. "Fiction-novel, short story, any length. Also interested in comic book type art. Read *Nightales* to examine style. All submissions will be acknowledged." avg. press run 5M. Expects 1 title 1991, 2 titles 1992. 1 title listed in the *Small Press Record of Books in Print* (20th Edition, 1991-92). avg. price, paper: $14.95. Discounts: 1-2 0%; 3-199-40%; 200-499 50%. 320pp; 6x9; lp. Reporting time: 6 weeks. Copyrights for author. PMA, COSMEP.

Upstart Publishing Company, Inc., D.H. Bangs, Editor, 12 Portland Street, Dover, NH 03820, 607-749-5071. 1976. Articles, non-fiction. "Small business management books with an emphasis on practical, jargon-free how-to information for the owner/manager. We prefer information that is based on experience. We also like lots of examples, checklists and devices that involve the reader." avg. press run 5M. Pub'd 3 titles 1990; expects 3-4 titles 1991, 4-5 titles 1992. 8 titles listed in the *Small Press Record of Books in Print* (20th Edition, 1991-92). avg. price, paper: $18.95. Discounts: 5-9 copies 40% FOB publisher, 10-49 45% free freight, 50-99 46% free freight. 160pp; 8½x11, 6x9; of. Reporting time: 4-6 weeks. Payment: negotiable. PMA, COSMEP, ABA.

Upword Press, Lyn Evans, Warren Evans, PO Box 1106, Yelm, WA 98597, 206-458-3619. 1987. Fiction, non-fiction. "Full length non-poetry books only. Metaphysical—New Age." avg. press run 5M. Expects 2 titles 1991, 2 titles 1992. 3 titles listed in the *Small Press Record of Books in Print* (20th Edition, 1991-92). avg. price, cloth: $15.95; paper: $9. 250pp; 6x9; of. Reporting time: 2-4 weeks. Payment: varies, advance royalty. Copyrights for author. COSMEP.

THE URBAN REVIEW, Plenum Publishing Corporation, David E. Kapel, William T. Pink, 233 Spring Street, New York, NY 10013, (212) 741-3087. 1966. Articles, non-fiction. *"The Urban Review* provides a forum for communication among urban educators, scholars, administrators, and all others concerned with improving public education in urban communities. The journal publishes original reports on important empirical studies and theoretical essays that examine the basic issues confronting urban schools. All correspondence concerning subscriptions should be addressed to: The Urban Review, Fulfillment Dept., Agathon Press, Inc., 49 Sheridan Avenue, Albany, NY 12210. All editorial correspondence should be addressed to: David E. Kapel, Editor, College of Education, University of New Orleans, New Orleans, LA 70148" 4/yr. Pub'd 4 issues 1990; expects 4 issues 1991, 4 issues 1992. sub. price: indiv. $22, instit. $44; per copy: $12.50. Back issues: 1975-87 (Vols. 8-19, 4 issues ea.), $44 per vol. Discounts: 10% discount to subscription agents. 64pp; 6½x9½; of. Reporting time: 3 months. Payment: none. Copyrighted, does not revert to author. Ads: $160/$100. COSMEP.

The Urbana Free Library, Frederick A. Schlipf, 201 South Race Street, Urbana, IL 61801, 217-367-4057. 1874. Articles, photos, non-fiction. "Most of the library's publications are prepared by the Champaign County Historical Archives—the Library's local history and genealogy department—which publishes original and reprint material on the history and people of Champaign County and east central Illinois. The Archives' major publications series is its *Champaign County Historical Archives Historical Publications Series,* which now includes 9 titles in print: 1) *The 1858 Alexander Bowman Map of Urbana and West Urbana* (second edition, 1981); 2) *The 1863 Alexander Bowman Map of Champaign County* (1980); 3) *Ivesdale: A Photographic Essay*

602

by Raymond Bial (1982); 4) *Upon a Quiet Landscape: The Photographs of Frank Sadorus*, edited by Raymond Bial and Frederick A. Schlipf (1983); 5) *The History of Champaign County* by J.O. Cunningham, 1905 edition (1984); 6) *Combined 1893, 1913, and 1929 Atlases of Champaign County* edited by Frederick A. Schlipf (1984); 7) *Index to the Combined 1893, 1913, and 1929 Atlases of Champaign County* (1984); 8) hand-colored, limited, numbered edition of *The 1863 Alexander Bowman Map of Champaign County*; 9) *From Salt Fork to Chickamauga: Champaign County Soldiers in the Civil War* by Robert H. Behrens (1988). Other Library publications include *The Urbana Municipal Documents Center Manual* by Jean E. Koch, Howard C. Grueneberg, Jr., and Frederick A. Schlipf (1987). The Documents Center is a Library department which organizes, converts to microfiche, and indexes Urbana city documents.'' avg. press run 500-1.5M. 10 titles listed in the *Small Press Record of Books in Print* (20th Edition, 1991-92). avg. price, cloth: $12-$38; other: $6-$100 maps. Discounts: retail and wholesale schedules are available on request. Items 3, 7, 8, and 9 are short-discounted. Item 10 is available at retail only. Pages vary; size varies; of. Payment: usually 15% of net.

URBANUS/RAIZIRR, Cameron Drizhal, Peter Drizhal, PO Box 192561, San Francisco, CA 94119-2561. 1988. Poetry, fiction, art, interviews, reviews. *"Urbanus* seeks *quality* contemporary and progressive poetry. Does not want to see anything 'self-indulgent, cliched, rhymed.' Have recently published: Antler, Robert Peters, Martha Vertreace, Arthur Knight.'' circ. 300. 2/yr. Pub'd 1 issue 1990; expects 2 issues 1991, 2 issues 1992. sub. price: $10; per copy: $5; sample: $5 (postpaid). 48pp; 5½x8½; of. Reporting time: 4-8 weeks. Payment: 1 copy. Copyrighted, rights revert, but reserve the right to use material in a future "best of" anthology. Ads: $20/$10/quarter-page $5 (query about exchange ads).

Sherry Urie, Sherry Urie, RFD #3, Box 63, Barton, VT 05822, 802-525-4482. 1978. Poetry, fiction. "Manuscripts welcome. Vermont and other New England material given priority. Non-fiction preferred.'' avg. press run 2M. Expects 2 titles 1991, 2 titles 1992. 3 titles listed in the *Small Press Record of Books in Print* (20th Edition, 1991-92). avg. price, paper: $5.95. Discounts: 1-4 copies, 20%; 5-24 copies, 40%; 25-99 copies, 42%; 100 up, 50%. 200pp; 5½x8½; of. Reporting time: 4-6 weeks. Payment: arranged on an individual basis. Copyrights for author.

Urion Press, Alan Rosenus, PO Box 10085, San Jose, CA 95157, 408-867-7695. 1972. Fiction. "Reprints, fiction, history. Please send letter of inquiry first.'' avg. press run 2.5M. Expects 1 title 1991. 4 titles listed in the *Small Press Record of Books in Print* (20th Edition, 1991-92). avg. price, cloth: $14.95; paper: $7.95. Discounts: bookstores 40% on orders over 3, jobbers 50% on orders over 10. 250pp; of. Reporting time: 1 month. Copyrights for author.

US1 Poets' Cooperative (see also US1 WORKSHEETS), Rotating board, 21 Lake Drive, Roosevelt, NJ 08555, 609-448-5096. 1973. Poetry, fiction. avg. press run 750. Pub'd 1 title 1990; expects 1 title 1991, 1 title 1992. 2 titles listed in the *Small Press Record of Books in Print* (20th Edition, 1991-92). Discounts: inquire. 20pp; 11½x17; of. Reporting time: 2-3 months, query first. Copyrights for author. CLMP.

US1 WORKSHEETS, US1 Poets' Cooperative, Rotating panel, 21 Lake Drive, Roosevelt, NJ 08555-0057, 609-448-5096. 1973. Poetry, fiction, satire, parts-of-novels, long-poems. "Fiction should not be over 15 double-spaced pages. Poetry must be shorter than book length. A wide range of tastes represented in the rotating panel of editors. No restriction on subject or point of view. We read unsolicited mss., but accept very few.'' circ. 500. 1/yr. Pub'd 1 issue 1990; expects 1 issue 1991, 1 issue 1992. sub. price: $8 (2 double issues); per copy: $5 (double issue); sample: $4. Back issues: inquire. No. 1 and No. 2 have become quite rare. Discounts: inquire. 20-25pp; 11½x17; of. Reporting time: best to query first if we are reading at that time. Payment: copies. Copyrighted, reverts to author. No ads. CLMP.

Utah Geographic Series, R. Reese, L. Oswald, Box 8325, Salt Lake City, UT 84108. 1985. Non-fiction. "Full color books about Utah. 50% text (about 30,000-70,000 words each volume) and 50% color photos, maps, charts.'' avg. press run 10M. Pub'd 2 titles 1990; expects 2 titles 1991, 2 titles 1992. 5 titles listed in the *Small Press Record of Books in Print* (20th Edition, 1991-92). avg. price, cloth: $28.95; paper: $17.95. Discounts: 40% to retailers. 120pp; 11½x8¾. Payment: negotiated. Does not copyright for author. COSMEP, Utah Assn. of Publishers.

THE UTNE READER, Eric Utne, Publisher & Editor; Helen Cordes, Associate Editor; Jay Walljasper, Executive Editor; Lynette Lamb, Managing Editor, The Fawkes Building, 1624 Harmon Place, Minneapolis, MN 55403, 612-338-5040. 1984. Articles, art, photos, cartoons, interviews, satire, criticism, reviews, letters, news items, non-fiction. "The *Utne Reader* is an 'alternative *Reader's Digest'*. Each 144-page issue presents dozens of reprints, excerpts and reviews of articles selected from more than 1,000 independent magazines and newsletters. We don't accept unsolicited reviews, but we do accept unsolicited cartoons.'' circ. 225M. 6/yr. Pub'd 6 issues 1990; expects 6 issues 1991, 6 issues 1992. sub. price: $18; per copy: $4; sample: $4. Back issues: $4 most recent issues—up to $25 for older issues. Discounts: inquire. 144pp; 7⅜x10; web of. Reporting time: 2 months. Payment: $50 minimum honorarium to copyright holder of excerpted piece. Copyrighted, reverts to author. Pub's reviews: 60-100 in 1990. §All small circulation, independently-published periodicals

V

Vagabond Press, John Bennett, 605 East 5th Avenue, Ellensburg, WA 98926-3201, 509-962-8471. 1966. Poetry, fiction, articles, art, photos, interviews, reviews, letters, parts-of-novels, plays. "Query before submitting" avg. press run 1M. Pub'd 1 title 1990; expects 1 title 1991, 1 title 1992. 16 titles listed in the *Small Press Record of Books in Print* (20th Edition, 1991-92). avg. price, cloth: $10; paper: $5.95. Discounts: 20% trade; orders over $30, 40%; 20% book jobbers. 200pp; 6×9; of. Reporting time: 3-4 weeks. Payment: by agreement. Copyrights for author.

Vagrom Chap Books, Sparrow Press imprint (see also Sparrow Press), Felix Stefanile, Selma Stefanile, 103 Waldron Street, West Lafayette, IN 47906. 1954. Poetry. "By invitation only." avg. press run 500. Pub'd 1 title 1990; expects 1 title 1991, 1 title 1992. avg. price, paper: $6. Discounts: 20% 1, 40% +2. 48pp; 5½×8½; of, lp, also fine print items. Payment: $30, + 20% after cost. Copyrights for author. CCLM.

VAJRA BODHI SEA, Buddhist Text Translation Society, Bhikshuni Heng Liang, Coordinating Editor; Bhikshuni Heng Ching, Editor; Upasaka Chou Li-ren, Chinese Editor, 800 Sacramento Street, Gold Mountain Monastery, San Francisco, CA 94108, 415-421-6117. 1970. Poetry, articles, art, photos, interviews, reviews, letters, non-fiction. *"Vajra Bodhi Sea* is the monthly journal of the Dharma Realm Buddhist Association, printing translations of Buddhist texts, biographies of Buddhist Masters, feature articles, World Buddhist News, poetry, language lessons, and a calendar of Buddhist Holidays and events. For publishing operations: City of 10M Buddhas, PO Box 217, Talmage, CA 95481-0217. Beginning with the September 1978 issue, *Vajra Bodhi Sea* has been published bilingually (Chinese-English)." circ. 4M. 12/yr. Pub'd 12 issues 1990; expects 12 issues 1991, 12 issues 1992. sub. price: $40, $100 for 3 years; per copy: $5; sample: $5, free copies to universities and public libraries (sample copy one time only). Back issues: prices vary from $100 to $5 dependent on rarity of issues. Discounts: bulk, non-profit organization (the publication is a second class periodical). 48pp; 11×8½; of. Payment: none. Copyrighted, reverts to author. §Buddhism. No ads.

Vajra of Yoga Anand Ashram (see also MOKSHA JOURNAL), Yogi Ananda Viraj, Yogi Ananda Satyam, Steve Crimi, Rocco LoBosco, 49 Forrest Place, Amityville, NY 11701, 516-691-8475. 1989. Non-fiction. "Primarily interested in books pertaining to Samkhya and Yoga, although we will consider other manuscripts relating to liberation schools such as various forms of Buddhism, Sufism, Mystical Christianity, etc. We are not interested in 'self help' books of any kind. Our 'slant' is philosophical and the writing that interests us pertains to the concept of Moksha defined by Monier-Williams as 'liberation, release' (A Sanskrit-English Dictionary, 1899). Query before sending manuscript." avg. press run 500-1M. Expects 2 titles 1991, 2 titles 1992. 1 title listed in the *Small Press Record of Books in Print* (20th Edition, 1991-92). avg. price, paper: $10. 200pp; 5½×8½; †of. Reporting time: 5-10 weeks. Payment: after costs are met, profits split 50/50. Does not copyright for author.

Valentine Publishing & Drama Co., James L. Rodgers, Executive Director, PO Box 1378, Ashland, OR 97520-0046, 503-773-7035. 1981. "We are only interested in mss. on Shakespearean and pre-Twentieth Century world drama for now; full length mss.; monographs acceptable." avg. press run 3M-5M. Pub'd 1 title 1990; expects 3 titles 1991, 5 titles 1992. 2 titles listed in the *Small Press Record of Books in Print* (20th Edition, 1991-92). avg. price, cloth: $21.95; paper: $11.95. Universal discount schedule. 425pp; 5½×8½; of. Reporting time: 30 days. Payment: Author's Guild Contract. Copyrights for author if desired. Scholarly Publishers' Assn., PMA, Northwest Publishers Assoc.

Valkyrie Publishing House, Marjorie Schuck, Publisher & Editor, 8245 26th Avenue N, St. Petersburg, FL 33710, 813-345-8864. 1972. Poetry, fiction, non-fiction. "We are book publishers. In our nineteen years of active publishing, our complete list totals over 287 books, both cloth and paper, on such subjects as art, biography, juvenile, classical studies, fiction, folklore, health, history, how-to, humor, occult, philosophy, photography, poetry, religion, self-awareness, spiritual, and translations. We have enjoyed a cooperative publishing arrangement with the Lorber Verlag (publishers) of Bietigheim, Germany. Our major royalty book *Angel City*, by Patrick D. Smith, author of *Forever Island* and other novels, was produced by CBS-TV in 1980, in a two-hour feature movie and has been shown on television and Cable TV intermittently ever since. It has been translated into several foreign languages. Several other of our books have received major and notable reviews. Book orders accepted. No unsolicited manuscripts." avg. press run 1M-3M. Expects 2 titles 1991, 2 titles 1992. 24 titles listed in the *Small Press Record of Books in Print* (20th Edition, 1991-92). avg. price, cloth: $12.95; paper: $6.95. Discounts: 40% and up. 128-348pp; 5½×8½; of. Reporting time: 2-6

Payment: *by agreement and contract.* Copyrights for author. CLMP, COSMEP.

Valley House Gallery Press, Donald S. Vogel, 6616 Spring Valley Road, Dallas, TX 75240, 214-239-2441. 1989. "All books are related to the arts." avg. press run 5M. Expects 3 titles 1991. 4 titles listed in the *Small Press Record of Books in Print* (20th Edition, 1991-92). avg. price, cloth: $35; paper: $12. Discounts: 50%. 100pp; 6×8, 9×10; of. Reporting time: 6 months. Payment: 10%. Copyrights for author. Book Publishers of Texas.

Valley Lights Publications, John Ernst, Valley Light Center, 356 Little Mountain Rd, Trout Lake, WA 98650, 509-395-2092. 1981. Poetry, fiction, articles, art, photos, non-fiction. "This is strictly a metaphysical new age publishing house." avg. press run 2.5M-5M. Pub'd 1 title 1990; expects 1 title 1991, 1 title 1992. 1 title listed in the *Small Press Record of Books in Print* (20th Edition, 1991-92). avg. price, paper: $9.95. Discounts: 40% to retails stores. 300pp; 7×9; lp. Does not copyright for author.

VALLEY WOMEN'S VOICE, 321 Student Union, UMASS, Amherst, MA 01003, 413-545-2436. 1979. Poetry, fiction, articles, art, photos, cartoons, interviews, satire, criticism, reviews, letters, news items, non-fiction. "Please include a SASE if you want to see your less than 10-page, double-spaced, typed manuscript again. Our copy ranges from the personal to the theoretical; titles and short bios are always helpful. Recent contributors: Sarah Sloane, Marci Goodman, Mary Lewis. Writing about/by women only. Photos should be 5 X 7 or 8 X 10 b/w, more women in photo than men. No photos of men only" circ. 6M-8M. 11/yr. Pub'd 7 issues 1990; expects 12 issues 1991, 12 issues 1992. sub. price: $12; per copy: $1; sample: $1. Back issues: $1. Negotiable discount schedules; please inquire. 12-16pp; 12×17; of. Reporting time: as soon as possible or within 8 weeks. Payment: free copy of issue in which author is published. Not copyrighted. Pub's reviews: 6 in 1990. §Feminism, women's issues, lesbianism, racism. Ads: $490/$265/25¢.

THE VAMPIRE JOURNAL, Baker Street Publications, Sharida Rizzuto, Sidney J. Dragon, Thomas Schellenberger, PO Box 994, Metairie, LA 70004, 504-734-8414. 1983. Poetry, fiction, articles, art, photos, cartoons, interviews, satire, criticism, reviews, letters, long-poems, collages, plays, news items, non-fiction. circ. under 10M but growing. 2-4/yr. Pub'd 2-4 issues 1990; expects 2-4 issues 1991, 2-4 issues 1992. sub. price: $28 for 4 issues; per copy: $7.90; sample: $7.90. Back issues: $7.90. Discounts: trade with other like publications. 80-100pp, double issue 120-160pp; digest size; of, excellent quality photo copy, offset covers. Reporting time: 2-6 weeks. Payment: free copies, fees paid for articles, reviews artwork negotiable. Copyrighted, reverts to author. Pub's reviews: 16 in 1990. §Fiction, vampirism in film & literature, poetry. Ads: free. NWC, SPWAO, HWA, Literary Markets, Mystery Writers of America (MWA), Western Writers of America (WWA), Arizona Authors Associaiton (AAA).

Van Patten Publishing, George F. Van Patten, 4204 SE Ogden Street, Portland, OR 97206-8452, 503-775-3815. 1990. Photos, non-fiction. "Van Patten Publishing is interested in organic gardening" avg. press run 10M. Pub'd 1 title 1990; expects 2 titles 1991, 2 titles 1992. 3 titles listed in the *Small Press Record of Books in Print* (20th Edition, 1991-92). avg. price, cloth: $24.95; paper: $11.95. Discounts: 40% to bookstores and up to 60% to wholesalers. 200pp; 8½×11; of. Reporting time: 30 days. Payment: royalty rate set per title, paid twice a year. Does not copyright for author. PMA, Northwest Association of Book Publishers.

VANDELOECHT'S FICTION MAGAZINE, Mike Vandeloecht, Tracy Vandeloecht, Associate Editor, PO Box 515, Montross, VA 22520. 1991. Poetry, fiction. "Recent work by Logan McNeil, Hampton Creed, and Tazewell Roberts" circ. varies. 4/yr. Expects 4 issues 1991, 4 issues 1992. sub. price: $8; per copy: $2; sample: $2. 26pp; 8½×11. Reporting time: less than 10 days. Payment: 1 contributor's copy. Copyrighted, reverts to author. §Humor, fantasy, science fiction, horror, mystery, men's, women's, westerns. SPWAO.

Vanessapress, Liz Biesiot, Mary Beth Harder, Wanda Zimmerman, Sally Yarie, PO Box 81335, Fairbanks, AK 99708, 907-479-0172. 1984. Poetry, fiction, art, long-poems, non-fiction. "Publishes only manuscripts by women. We request samplers in any genre listed above; we request a $5 xeroxing fee and an SASE. Manuscripts must be neatly typed and be written from a feminist viewpoint. Our first book is *On Why the Quiltmaker Became a Dragon* by Sheila Nickerson. Our second book is *Tides of Morning,* an introductory anthology of four Alaskan women writers. The third book is *Bits of Ourselves,* women's experiences with cancer" avg. press run 1.25M. Expects 3 titles 1991. 3 titles listed in the *Small Press Record of Books in Print* (20th Edition, 1991-92). avg. price, paper: $7.95. Discounts: 40% to bookstores, ORDER THROUGH VANESSAPRESS, 55% through Inland Book Company & Bookpeople. 125pp; 6×9; of. Reporting time: 3 months. Payment: varies. Copyrights for author. AASP (Alaska Association of Small Presses).

Vanitas Press, March Laumer, Publisher, Platslagarevagen 4E1, 22230 Lund, Sweden. 1978. Poetry, fiction, art. "From 1965 to 1969 books were published under the name of *Opium Books.* Most recent releases pertain to "Oziana" themes. To contact the publisher directly, send to March Laumer, Plaatslagarevagen 4 E 1, 22230 Lund, Sweden." avg. press run 500. Pub'd 1 title 1990; expects 3 titles 1991, 3 titles 1992. 14 titles listed in the

Small Press Record of Books in Print (20th Edition, 1991-92). avg. price, cloth: $20 US; paper: $12 US. Discounts: all publications sold at production cost; no discounts. 200pp; 6×8; mi, of. Reporting time: 3-5 weeks. Payment: each case treated individually. Copyrights for author.

Vanity Press/Strolling Dog Press, Tuli Kupferberg, 160 6th Avenue, New York, NY 10013, 212-925-3823. 1980. Cartoons, satire, music. "Will accept little (if any) unsolicited work. Interested in aphoristic forms, cartoons, 'funny' advertisements, documents, ephemera (found materials)." avg. press run 5M. Pub'd 3 titles 1990; expects 2 titles 1991, 2 titles 1992. 7 titles listed in the *Small Press Record of Books in Print* (20th Edition, 1991-92). avg. price, paper: $1. Discounts: 40%. 32pp; 4¼×5½, 8½×11½; of. Reporting time: short. Does not copyright for author.

VANTAGE POINT, American Council for the Arts/ACA Books, Lisa Parr, 1285 Avenue of the Americas, 3rd Floor, Area M, New York, NY 10019, (212) 245-4510. 1984. Articles, art, photos, interviews, news items, non-fiction. circ. 2.5M. 5/yr. Pub'd 5 issues 1990; expects 5 issues 1991, 5 issues 1992. sub. price: available with ACA membership only and through special request. 16pp; 8½×10½. Reporting time: 3 weeks. Payment: varies. Copyrighted. No ads.

VDT NEWS, Louis Slesin, PO Box 1799, Grand Central Station, New York, NY 10163, 212-517-2802. 1984. Articles, news items. "We are a newsletter on the health effects of working with VDTs (video display terminals—or computers). We cover legislation, litigation, new research, labor agreements, etc...concerning possible radiation risks, repetition strain injuries and vision problems." circ. under 1M. 6/yr. Pub'd 6 issues 1990; expects 6 issues 1991, 6 issues 1992. sub. price: $87; per copy: $15; sample: $5. Back issues: $45 for a calendar year, $225 for a bound volume of 1984-1988. Discounts: $43.50/year for students. 8½×11; lp. Payment: none. Copyrighted, does not revert to author. Pub's reviews: 20 in 1990. §Computers, worker health and safety, epidemiology, non-ionizing radiation. Ads: $1,200/$750/$450 1/4 page/$275 1/8 page/$150 1/16 page.

VEGETARIAN JOURNAL, The Vegetarian Resource Group, Debra Wasserman, Charles Stahler, PO Box 1463, Baltimore, MD 21203, 301-366-VEGE (8343). 1982. Poetry, articles, art, cartoons, interviews, reviews, letters, news items, non-fiction. circ. 12M. 6/yr. Pub'd 6 issues 1990; expects 6 issues 1991, 6 issues 1992. sub. price: $20; per copy: $3; sample: $3. Back issues: inquire. Discounts: inquire. 36pp; 8½×11; of. Reporting time: 1 month. Payment: inquire. Copyrighted, we retain reprint rights. Pub's reviews: 8 in 1990. §Vegetarianism, animal rights, scientific nutrition, recipes. No ads.

The Vegetarian Resource Group (see also VEGETARIAN JOURNAL), Debra Wasserman, Charles Stahler, PO Box 1463, Baltimore, MD 21203, 301-752-VEGV. 1982. avg. press run 5M. Pub'd 1 title 1990; expects 2 titles 1991, 2 titles 1992. 5 titles listed in the *Small Press Record of Books in Print* (20th Edition, 1991-92). avg. price, paper: $8. Discounts: 40% bookstores. 80pp; 5×8½; of.

VEGETARIAN TIMES, Paul Obis, Sally Cullen, PO Box 570, Oak Park, IL 60303, 312-848-8100. 1974. Articles, cartoons, interviews. "Magazine covers all aspects of vegetarianism." circ. 165M. 12/yr. Pub'd 12 issues 1990; expects 12 issues 1991, 12 issues 1992. sub. price: $24.95; per copy: $3; sample: same. Discounts: contact us. 96pp; 8¼×10⅞; of. Reporting time: 2 months. Payment: on acceptance. Copyrighted. Pub's reviews: 50 in 1990. Ads: $3200/$2000/$2.40.

Vehicule Press, Simon Dardick, General Editor; Michael Harris, Poetry Editor; Linda Leith, Fiction Editor, PO Box 125, Place du Parc Station, Montreal, Quebec H2W 2M9, Canada, 514-844-6073. 1973. Poetry, fiction, non-fiction. "Publishers of Canadian literary works with occasional titles in the area of urban studies, politics, memoirs and feminism. Actively publish poetry in translation (French(Quebec)-English). Recent publications: *A Private Performance* by Kenneth Radu, *WSW (West South West)* by Erin Moure." avg. press run 1M-1.5M. Pub'd 12 titles 1990; expects 11 titles 1991, 10 titles 1992. 40 titles listed in the *Small Press Record of Books in Print* (20th Edition, 1991-92). avg. price, cloth: $25; paper: $12. Discounts: jobbers 20%; bookstores 40%; occasional short-discounted title 20%; please inquire. Poetry 76pp, other 300pp; 6×9; of. Reporting time: 2 months. Payment: generally 10-12%. Copyrights for author. Association of Canadian Publishers (ACP), 260 King St. E., 3rd Floor, Toronto, Canada M6K 1K3, Literary Press Group.

VELOCITIES, Andrew Joron, PO Box 9643, Berkeley, CA 94709. 1982. Poetry, art, photos, criticism, collages. ""A magazine of speculative poetry." Interested in poems traversing the space between surrealism and science fiction." circ. 500. 2/yr. Pub'd 1 issue 1990; expects 2 issues 1991, 2 issues 1992. sub. price: $6; per copy: $3.50; sample: $3.50. Back issues: none. Discounts: none. 44pp; 6×9; of. Reporting time: 1 month. Payment: contributors copies. Copyrighted, reverts to author. Ads: $300$15.

VELONEWS, John Wilcockson, Editor; Tim Johnson, Managing Editor, 1830 North 55th Street, Boulder, CO 80301. 1972. Articles, photos, cartoons, interviews, reviews, letters, news items, non-fiction. "We now do color editorial." circ. 35M. 18/yr. Pub'd 18 issues 1990; expects 18 issues 1991, 18 issues 1992. sub. price: $29.97; per copy: $2.50. Back issues: $4 each. Discounts: trade: 2 year sub for $52. 104pp; 14½×11; of. Reporting time:

several weeks. Payment: 10¢/word; $16.50-$100 for photos, $200 for color cover. Copyrighted, reverts to author. Pub's reviews: 18 in 1990. §Competitive cycling. Ads: $2340/$1495/$1 (4-color rates). ABC.

Ventana Press, Josef Woodman, Elizabeth Woodman, PO Box 2468, Chapel Hill, NC 27515, 919-942-0220. 1986. Non-fiction. "Street address: 110 E. Main Street, Carrboro, NC 27510. AutoCAD reference books, desktop publishing, various domestic travel, and regional cooking are of interest to Ventana Press." avg. press run 10M. Pub'd 12 titles 1990; expects 12 titles 1991, 15 titles 1992. 25 titles listed in the *Small Press Record of Books in Print* (20th Edition, 1991-92). avg. price, cloth: $19.95; paper: $22.95. Discounts: 1-4 20%, 5-14 40%, 15-24 42%, 25-49 43%, 50-99 44%, 100-499 45%. 270pp; 7⅜×9¼, 5½×8½; of, webb press. Reporting time: 1 month. Payment: negotiable. Copyrights for author. ABA, AAP, PMA, PAS.

Venture Perspectives Inc., Rick Charles, 4300 Stevens Creek Blvd., Suite 120, San Jose, CA 95129, 408-247-1325. 1983. Non-fiction. *"How to Start, Expand and Sell a Business* by James C. Coniskey. A complete guidebook for entrepreneurs" avg. press run 3M-5M. Pub'd 1 title 1990; expects 2 titles 1991, 4 titles 1992. 1 title listed in the *Small Press Record of Books in Print* (20th Edition, 1991-92). avg. price, paper: $17.95. Discounts: 40% 6 or more; 45% 25 or more; 50% 100 or more. 260pp; 8½×11. Reporting time: 30 days. Payment: negotiable. Copyrights for author.

Venture Press (see also LEAGUE SENTINAL), K.M. Thompson, Jerry Sibley, Editor, 54 Hindes Road, Harrow, Middlesex HA1 1SL, England, 06284-74994.

Venture Press, Thomas A. Williams, 104 South Respess Street, Washington, NC 27889. 1990. Non-fiction. "Venture Press publishes self-help and how-to titles in the fields of home business, legal do-it-yourself, writing and publishing." Expects 10 titles 1991, 10 titles 1992. 2 titles listed in the *Small Press Record of Books in Print* (20th Edition, 1991-92). avg. price, paper: $19.95; other: $24.95 ring binder. Discounts: trade 5+ 40%, wholesaler, standard terms. 96pp; 8½×11, 6×9; varies. Reporting time: 1 month. Payment: 10%-15% of net. Copyrights for author. PMA, PAS.

Venture Publishing, Inc., 1999 Cato Avenue, State College, PA 16801, 814-234-4561. 1979. avg. press run 2M-3M. Pub'd 6 titles 1990; expects 7 titles 1991, 8 titles 1992. 7 titles listed in the *Small Press Record of Books in Print* (20th Edition, 1991-92). avg. price, cloth: $25.95; paper: $16.95. Discounts: 20% jobber and educators. 300pp; 6×9; †of. Payment: varies. Copyrights for author.

VERBATIM, Verbatim Books, Laurence Urdang, 4 Laurel Heights, Old Lyme, CT 06371-1462, 203-767-8248. 1974. Articles, cartoons, interviews, reviews, letters, non-fiction. "All materials must deal with some aspect of language - any language, but preferably English. Writing in English only. Articles: 1500 words, max.; reviews: 1000 words, max." circ. 10M. 4/yr. Pub'd 4 issues 1990; expects 4 issues 1991, 4 issues 1992. sub. price: $16.50; per copy: $4.50; sample: free. Back issues: $16.50 for any four ppd; $4.50 for any one ppd. Discounts: Agents: 25%. 24pp; 8½×11; of. Reporting time: usually 2 weeks, sometimes 4-6 weeks. Copyrighted, does not revert to author. Pub's reviews: 16-20 in 1990. §Language. Ads: $400/$210/$125 per 1/4 page/$75 per 1/8 page.

Verbatim Books (see also VERBATIM), Laurence Urdang, 4 Laurel Heights, Old Lyme, CT 06371-1462, 203-434-2104. 1977. Non-fiction. "Reference, mainly." avg. press run 3M. Pub'd 1 title 1990; expects 1 title 1991. avg. price, cloth: $24.95. Discounts: 50% ppd for +4 copies; 55% ppd for +4 payment with order. 360pp; 6×9, 7×10, 8½×11, varies; of. Reporting time: 6 weeks. Payment: 10% of list price on trade sales; 5% on mail order; 50% of subsid. rts. sales. Copyrights for author.

Vergin Press (see also GYPSY), Belinda Subraman, S. Ramnath, c/o Belinda Subraman, 10708 Gay Brewer Drive, El Paso, TX 79935. 1984. Pub'd 2 titles 1990; expects 2 titles 1991, 2 titles 1992. 2 titles listed in the *Small Press Record of Books in Print* (20th Edition, 1991-92). avg. price, paper: $7. 8½×11. Reporting time: 6 weeks to 3 months. Copyrights for author.

VERSE, Henry Hart, Robert Crawford, David Kinloch, Henry Hart, English Dept., College of William & Mary, Williamsburg, VA 23185, 804-221-3922. 1984. Poetry, articles, interviews, criticism, reviews. "Articles on modern poets, about 20 pages long, most suitable. We publish a large number of translations of poetry, and poetry by British and American writers. Recent conributors: A.R. Ammons, James Dickey, Richard Eberhart, Donald Hall, Seamus Heaney, Galway Kinnell, William Heyen, John Hollander, James Merrill, Louis Simpson, Robert Pinsky, Charles Wright, Richard Kenney. Translations of Michel Deguy, Miroslav Holub, Philippe Jaccottet, Pier Pasolini, Tomas Transtromer." circ. 700. 3/yr. Pub'd 3 issues 1990; expects 3 issues 1991, 3 issues 1992. sub. price: $12; per copy: $4; sample: $4. Back issues: $4. 60pp; 6×8; of. Reporting time: 6 weeks. Payment: not yet, but we hope to pay when we get established. Not copyrighted. Pub's reviews: 6 in 1990. §Poetry, poetry criticism. Ads: $200/$100.

VERVE, Ron Reichick, PO Box 3205, Simi Valley, CA 93093. 1989. Poetry, fiction, photos, reviews, non-fiction. "Poetry max length 2 pages, fiction and non-fiction to 1000 words. Each issue has a theme, listed in guidelines." circ. 250. 4/yr. Pub'd 4 issues 1990; expects 4 issues 1991, 4 issues 1992. sub. price: $12; per copy: $3.50; sample: $3.50. Back issues: $4. Discounts: 40% 10 or more. 40pp; 5½×8½; of. Reporting time: 4-6 weeks after deadline. Payment: copy. Copyrighted, reverts to author. Pub's reviews: 1 in 1990. §Poetry. No ads.

Verve Press, Glyn Goldfisher, Assistant Editor, PO Box 1997, Huntington Beach, CA 92647. avg. press run 4M. 1 title listed in the *Small Press Record of Books in Print* (20th Edition, 1991-92). avg. price, paper: $8.95. Discounts: bookstores less than 5 20%, more 50%. 216pp; 5½×8½.

A VERY SMALL MAGAZINE, Beth Blevins, PO Box 221, Greenbelt, MD 20768. 1985. Poetry, fiction, articles, art, photos, cartoons, satire, letters, collages, non-fiction. "The keyword here is *short*. This is a *very* small magazine (4 X 5½) and a five-page article would nearly fill it up. Submissions should rarely be longer than 3 typed pages. Exceptions will be made if the material is extremely good & deserving of being the centerpiece of an issue. In the past, *AVSM* has devoted itself almost entirely to "themes"-women's diaries, anthologies of stupid poetry, myth. But because so much good material arrives (unsolicited) that doesn't fit any particular theme we've already defined, we are now determined to let every other issue be theme-less, a potpourri of interesting tidbits that creates its own framework. Finally, a word of warning to eager contributors: we rarely publish poetry-usually not more than one or two (very small) poems per issue. Also, a warning: our editor has been delinquent in both publishing the magazine & answering correspondence. Be patient. Because our publication should be more regular in the future, we are offering subscriptions of $5 for six issues—subscribers should get all six before the end of the decade!" circ. copied to order. Published sporadically. Pub'd 1 issue 1990; expects 4 issues 1991, 4 issues 1992. price per copy: $1; sample: $1. Discounts: $5/6 magazines. 20pp; 4×5½; xerox, of. Reporting time: 2 months (realistically, can average 6 months). Payment: in copies & fame. Copyrighted. §Books, movies, cultural heroes, implausible ideas.

Verygraphics (see also YELLOW SILK: Journal Of Erotic Arts), PO Box 6374, Albany, CA 94706, 415-841-6500.

Vesper Publishing, Frederick W. Gould, S.A., PO Box 150, Kenvil, NJ 07847, 201-927-9105; 1-800-732-0256. 1990. Non-fiction. "Primarily interested in how-to nonfiction. Booklets, manuals and books (20-400 pp.). In-house type setting and advertising departments. Also interested in distributing for other publishers." avg. press run 1M-5M. Pub'd 2 titles 1990; expects 2 titles 1991. 2 titles listed in the *Small Press Record of Books in Print* (20th Edition, 1991-92). Discounts: 3-199 40%, 200-499 50%, 500+ 40%+25%. 20-400pp; size varies; of. Reporting time: 4-8 weeks. Payment: royalty and payment. Copyrights for author. PMA.

Vesta Publications Limited (see also WRITER'S LIFELINE), Stephen Gill, Editor-in-Chief, PO Box 1641, Cornwall, Ont. K6H 5V6, Canada, 613-932-2135. 1974. Poetry, fiction, criticism, plays. avg. press run 1M. Pub'd 11 titles 1990; expects 10 titles 1991, 20 titles 1992. 102 titles listed in the *Small Press Record of Books in Print* (20th Edition, 1991-92). avg. price, cloth: $15; paper: $5; other: $3.50. Discounts: wholesalers 50%, libraries 10%, no shipping charges to American customers or other customers outside Canada. 120pp; 5×8; †of. Reporting time: 4-6 weeks. Payment: 10% paid annually. Copyrights for author. COSMEP, CPA.

Vestal Press Ltd, Grace Houghton, President, PO Box 97, 320 North Jensen Road, Vestal, NY 13851-0097, 607-797-4872. 1961. Non-fiction. "Vestal is recognized world-wide as the leading publisher of books on antique mechanical musical instruments. Also publish in theatres and early film history" avg. press run 2M. Pub'd 5 titles 1990; expects 8 titles 1991, 6 titles 1992. 44 titles listed in the *Small Press Record of Books in Print* (20th Edition, 1991-92). avg. price, cloth: $29.95; paper: $19.95. Discounts: Bookstores: 1-2 copies 33⅓%; 3-12 40%; 13-24 42½ %; 25-99 45%; 100+ 50%. 200pp; 8½×11, some smaller; of, lo. Reporting time: 2 months. Payment: special arrangements made with each, most often 10% of net on each title. Copyrights for author. COSMEP.

VIATOR: Medieval and Renaissance Studies, University of California Press, Mary Rouse, University of California Press, 2120 Berkeley Way, Berkeley, CA 94720, 415-642-4191. 1969. Non-fiction. "Editorial address: Center for Medieval & Renaissance Studies, Bunche Hall, University of CA, Los Angeles, CA 90024." circ. 400. 1/yr. Pub'd 1 issue 1990; expects 1 issue 1991, 1 issue 1992. sub. price: $45 (+ $5 foreign postage); per copy: $47. Back issues: $47. Discounts: foreign subs. agents 10%, one-time orders 10+ 30%, standing orders (bookstores): 1-99 40%, 100+ 50%. 220pp; 7×10; of. Payment: no. Copyrighted, does not revert to author. No ads accepted.

The Vic Press, Stan Oliner, 7684 E. Mercer Place, Denver, CO 80237-2123. 1957. avg. press run 500. Pub'd 2 titles 1990. avg. price, paper: $6.95. Discounts: 40%. 80pp; of. Does not copyright for author.

VICTIMOLOGY AN INTERNATIONAL JOURNAL, Emilio C. Viano, 2333 North Vernon Street, Arlington, VA 22207-4036, 703-528-3387. 1975. Articles, photos, interviews, reviews, letters, news items. circ. 2.5M. 4/yr. Pub'd 4 issues 1990; expects 4 issues 1991. 1 title listed in the *Small Press Record of Books in Print* (20th Edition, 1991-92). sub. price: $65 indiv., $105 instit.; per copy: $25; sample: $10. Back issues: $20. Discounts: 10% jobbers and subscription agencies; special 65% for complete set of back volumes. 200pp;

6½×10. Reporting time: 6-8 weeks. Payment: per story for nonacademics negotiable, query first. Copyrighted, magazine retains all rights. Pub's reviews: 57 in 1990. §Victimization in general, rape, spouse abuse, child abuse, consumerism, compensation to victims, genocide, etc. Environmental issues, prevention of victimization thru different measures. Ads: $175/$100/90¢ word $9 minimum. COSMEP, COSMEP-SOUTH, AAP.

Victory Press, 543 Lighthouse Avenue, Monterey, CA 93940-1422, 408-883-1725, 372-7046. 1988. avg. press run 300-5M. Pub'd 4 titles 1990; expects 1 title 1991, 2-4 titles 1992. 6 titles listed in the *Small Press Record of Books in Print* (20th Edition, 1991-92). avg. price, cloth: $8.95; paper: $8.95. Discounts: 40% for 5 or more, 55% 20 or more. COSMEP, PMA.

VIETNAM GENERATION: A Journal of Recent History and Contemporary Issues, Kali Tal, 2921 Terrace Drive, Chevy Chase, MD 20815, 301-608-0622; FAX 301-608-0761. 1988. Poetry, fiction, articles, art, photos, cartoons, interviews, criticism, reviews, letters, non-fiction. *"Vietnam Generation* provides a forum for interdisciplinary scholarship on all subjects of importance to the Vietnam Generation—those born between 1945 and 1960. Each issue is devoted to a single topic, contains no advertising or ephemera in the text, and can, therefore, be used as a teaching resource in college and university courses. Articles should run no more than 10,000 words, and can deal with any aspect of the Vietnam war, 1960s, counterculture, antiwar movement, veteran's issues, political trends, etc. We have a strong focus on gender, class, and race. We suggest that writers query us before submitting articles, since we select only those which fit into the special issues we are preparing. Contributors have included: Ruth Rosen, David Cortright, John A. Williams, Holly Near, Peter Davies, and many others." circ. 500. 4/yr. Pub'd 4 issues 1990; expects 4 issues 1991, 4 issues 1992. sub. price: $40 individual, $75 institutions; per copy: $12 for single issues; $16 for double issues; sample: $10. Back issues: 1989 issues $9 each, $30 for set. Discounts: $8 per issue for orders over 25, $14 for double issues. 160pp; 6×9; †desktop publishing. Reporting time: 1 month. Payment: copies of journal. Copyrighted, rights reverting can be arranged. Pub's reviews: 150 in 1990. §Vietnam war, 1960s, veteran's issues, feminist criticism, popular culture, CIA, military, Asian Americans, Indochina, Afro-Americans. Ads: $75/$40/$25 1/4 page.

VIETNAM WAR NEWSLETTER, Thomas W. Hebert, Box 469, Collinsville, CT 06022, 203-582-9784. 1979. Articles, interviews, reviews, letters, news items. "Not pro-war, not anti-war, pro Vietnam veteran!" circ. 2.5M. 12/yr. Pub'd 12 issues 1990; expects 12 issues 1991, 12 issues 1992. sub. price: $22.95; per copy: $1.75; sample: $1. Back issues: $1.50. Discounts: $39.95 for 2 year subscription; $54.95 for 3 years; $150 for life. 12pp; 8½×11; of. Payment: none. Copyrighted, reverts to author.

VIEWPOINT, Aaron Alpern, PO Box 1777, Tel Aviv 61016, Israel, 03/26645-7. 1986. Poetry, articles, art, photos, cartoons, interviews, criticism, reviews, letters, news items. "Published by Mapam (The United Worker's Party of Israel) and the Kibbutz Artzi Federation—Hashomer Hatzair. The paper reflects a socialist-zionist perspective on events in the Middle East and throught the Jewish world. Articles should be 400-750 words" circ. 10M. 10/yr. Pub'd 3 issues 1990; expects 10 issues 1991, 10 issues 1992. sub. price: $15; per copy: $2; sample: $1. 8-12pp; 11½×15¾; †newspaper-rotation. Reporting time: 1 month. Payment: limited, no set schedule as of yet. Not copyrighted. Pub's reviews. §Mideast, socialism, polisci, labor, women, peace. Ads: $1,000/$550/$300 1/4 page/$175 1/8.

VIEWS: The Journal of Photography in New England, Daniel Paul Younger, 602 Commonwealth Avenue, Boston, MA 02215. 1979. Articles, photos, interviews, reviews, news items. "Published by the Photographic Resource Center, same address, a not-for-profit art/educational organization." circ. 4M. 3/yr. Pub'd 3 issues 1990; expects 3 issues 1991, 3 issues 1992. sub. price: $30 includes membership, $15 subscription; per copy: $3; sample: free. Back issues: $3. 28-32pp; 38×27cm; of. Reporting time: 2 months. Payment: $30-$200. Copyrighted, reverts to author. Pub's reviews: 2-10 per issue in 1990. §Photography, artists' books, photographically illustrated books/mags. Ads: $450-$550/$260.

VIGIL, John Howard, 12 Priory Mead, Bruton, Somerset BA10 0DZ, United Kingdom, Bruton 813349. 1986. Poetry, fiction, articles, art, criticism. "As of May 1988 *Period Piece & Paberback* was absorbed by the title *Vigil*. Recent contributors include Roger Elkin, John Gonzalez, Peter Lambert, Mary Murray, Michael Newman, Colin Nixon, Max Moiprox, Ann Keith and Pamela Henderson." circ. 200. 3/yr. Pub'd 3 issues 1990; expects 3 issues 1991, 3 issues 1992. 1 title listed in the *Small Press Record of Books in Print* (20th Edition, 1991-92). sub. price: £3.50, $7.50; per copy: £1.50, $2.50. 40pp; size A5. Reporting time: 4 weeks USA. Payment: 2 copies. Copyrighted, reverts to author. Pub's reviews: 35 in 1990. §Poetry, fiction, writing. FAIM, ALP.

Villa Press, Betty Della Corte-Ryan, 4506 West Citros Way, Glendale, AZ 85301, 602-939-6801. 1985. Non-fiction. Expects 1 title 1991, 1 title 1992. avg. price, paper: $9.95. Discounts: 40%. 296pp; 8½×5½. Payment: all royalties going to the Faith House Shelter (victims of violence).

Village Books, Wendy Priesnitz, 195 Markville Road, Unionville, Ont. L3R4V8, Canada. 1976. Reviews, non-fiction. avg. press run 500-1M. Expects 2 titles 1991, 2 titles 1992. 1 title listed in the *Small Press Record of Books in Print* (20th Edition, 1991-92). avg. price, paper: $20. Discounts: retail: 40% - 10 copies minimum.

150pp; size varies; of. Reporting time: 2 months. Payment: varies. Copyrights for author.

THE VILLAGE IDIOT, Mother of Ashes Press, Joe M. Singer, Poet-in-Residence, PO Box 66, Harrison, ID 83833. 1970. Poetry, fiction, articles, art, photos, cartoons, interviews, satire, reviews, letters, collages, plays, news items, non-fiction. circ. less than 100. 3/yr. Pub'd 1 issue 1990; expects 3 issues 1991, 3 issues 1992. sub. price: $7.50; per copy: $3; sample: $3. Back issues: $15/5. 48pp; 5½×8¾; †of/mi. Reporting time: up to 3 months. Payment: at publication, contributor copy(ies). Copyrighted, reverts to author. Pub's reviews.

THE VINCENT BROTHERS REVIEW, Kimberly Willardson, Editor, Patrick Graf, Roger Willardson, Associate Editors, 1459 Sanzon Drive, Fairborn, OH 45324. 1988. Poetry, fiction, articles, art, photos, cartoons, interviews, satire, criticism, reviews, letters, parts-of-novels, collages, plays, non-fiction. "Because of our format, we prefer short pieces. We print black and white photos and art work only. Recent contributors include Herbert Woodward Martin, Carmine DiBiase, Laura E. Lehner, Gwen Strauss, Rafael Alvarez, Thomas Whissen, Kim Carey, Gregg Fry." circ. 250. 3/yr. Pub'd 3 issues 1990; expects 3 issues 1991, 3 issues 1992. sub. price: $12; per copy: $4.50; sample: $4.50. Back issues: $4.50. 60pp; 5½×8; of. Reporting time: 6-8 months. Payment: $10 on publication plus 1 copy. Copyrighted, reverts to author. Pub's reviews: 2 in 1990. §Lit mags; small press novels; poetry chapbooks; essay chapbooks. Ads: $75; 1/2 $45; Business card $25. Council of Literary Magazines and Presses (CLMP).

Vintage '45 Press, Susan L. Aglietti, Editor & Publisher, PO Box 266, Orinda, CA 94563-0266. 1983. "Submissions specifically relating to midlife women only please; and these must be by women writers. I publish anthologies only if these are books I originate. Query first." avg. press run 2M. Expects 1 title 1991. 1 title listed in the *Small Press Record of Books in Print* (20th Edition, 1991-92). avg. price, paper: $9.95. 150pp. Reporting time: 1 month. COSMEP.

VINTAGE NORTHWEST, Margie Brons, Editor; Enice Hunt, Assistant, PO Box 193, Bothell, WA 98041, 206-487-1201. 1980. Poetry, fiction, articles, art, satire, non-fiction. "We accept from authors over 50 years of age, and the physically handicapped." circ. 550. 2/yr. Pub'd 2 issues 1990; expects 2 issues 1991, 2 issues 1992. We are unable to take subscriptions as we are only volunteers. We do have a mailing list if people desire to be on it; price per copy: $2.50; sample: $2.50. Back issues: $2.50. 64pp; 7×8½; †typesetting. Reporting time: 3 months. Payment: copy. Not copyrighted. Ads: $75/$16 other.

VIOLENT VIRGINS, New Sins Press, Rane Arroyo, PO Box 7157, Pittsburgh, PA 15213. *"Violent Virgins* special one-poet issues; unsolicited submissions accepted with SASE. Recent contributors: Terri Jewell, B.Z. Niditch. See sample copy first! Checks/money orders must be made payable to Rane Arroyo" sample price: $1.

VIRGIN MEAT, Steve Blum, 2325 West Avenue, K-15, Lancaster, CA 93536, 805-722-1758. 1986. Poetry, fiction, art, cartoons, reviews. "Fiction: under 1,000 words only; non-violent, horror, vampires, ghosts, suspense and depression. Mildly erotic is fine. Poetry: free verse; short; dark and depressing. No references to modern objects." circ. 300. 4/yr. Pub'd 4 issues 1990; expects 3 issues 1991, 4 issues 1992. sub. price: $7 for 4 issues; per copy: $2; sample: $2. 24pp; 5½×8½; of. Reporting time: all replys go out in next day's mail. Payment: copy/copies. Not copyrighted. Pub's reviews: 100 in 1990. §Fiction, poetry, alternative, music—but will review anything as space allows. Ads: $7/$4/50¢ classifieds—40 words. Ad trades are available.

VIRGINIA LIBERTY, Marc Montoni, Christine Bregar, PO Box 28263, Richmond, VA 23228. Articles. "Typical submission length: 3/4 page (typed, double-spaced)." circ. 400. 6/yr. Pub'd 6 issues 1990; expects 6 issues 1991, 6 issues 1992. sub. price: $15; per copy: $1; sample: $1. Back issues: $1 each. Discounts: bulk $10/100 for classrooms or local affiliates for events. 4pp; web offset. Payment: none. Not copyrighted. Pub's reviews: 2 in 1990. §Libertarian. Ads: $75/$40/$25 1/4 page/$15 1/8 page/$10, classified ads free up to 60 words, individuals only.

THE VIRGINIA QUARTERLY REVIEW, Staige D. Blackford, Editor, One West Range, Charlottesville, VA 22903, 804-924-3124. 1925. Poetry, fiction, articles, satire, criticism, reviews. "Recent contributors: Harry Ashmore, George Garrett, Louis Simpson, William C. Havard, Nancy Hale, Edwin M. Yoder, Robert Coles, Mary Lee Settle." circ. 4.5M. 4/yr. Pub'd 4 issues 1990; expects 4 issues 1991, 4 issues 1992. sub. price: $15 individual, $22 institution; per copy: $5; sample: $5. Back issues: $5. Discounts: agent's commission: $3. 224pp; 5½×8; of. Reporting time: 6 weeks. Payment: essays & short stories, $10 per printed page; poetry $1 per line. Copyrighted, rights revert upon request. Pub's reviews: 23 essay, 374 brief in 1990. Ads: $150/$75.

Visa Books (Division of South Continent Corporation Pty Ltd), Louise N. Gold, PO Box 1024, Richmond North, Victoria 3121, Australia, 03-429-5599. 1975. Non-fiction. avg. press run 3M. Pub'd 5 titles 1990; expects 3 titles 1991, 5 titles 1992. avg. price, cloth: $30; paper: $20; other: $12. Discounts: trade 40%, jobber up to 55%. 240pp; 6×8½; of. Reporting time: 8 weeks. Copyrights for author. AIPA, RVHS.

VISIBILITIES, Susan T. Chasin, Publisher & Editor-in-Chief, PO Box 1169, Olney, MD 20830-1169. 1987. Poetry, fiction, articles, art, photos, cartoons, interviews, satire, criticism, reviews, news items, non-fiction. "Fiction: 1,200-2,400 words—must be life-affirming and contain lesbian themes and/or characters.

610

Contributors: Jenifer Levin, Lee Chiaramonte, Gloria Dickler. Interviews with: Marion Zimmer Bradley, Holly Near. Advertising rates subject to change—prefer having people contact us." circ. 7M. 6/yr. Pub'd 6 issues 1990; expects 6 issues 1991, 6 issues 1992. sub. price: $18/8 issues; per copy: $2.50; sample: $3.50. Back issues: $3.50. Discounts: to be determined. 32pp; 8×11; of. Reporting time: 3 months. Payment: 2 copies + $5. Copyrighted, reverts to author. Pub's reviews: 15 in 1990. §Anything with Lesbian themes.

Vision Quest Publishing, Linda Negleson, PO Box 2398, Aptos, CA 95001, 408-685-8728. 1986. Photos, cartoons, music, news items, non-fiction. avg. press run 2M. Pub'd 2 titles 1990; expects 3 titles 1991, 5 titles 1992. 1 title listed in the *Small Press Record of Books in Print* (20th Edition, 1991-92). avg. price, paper: $9.95. 128pp; 8½×5½; of. Payment: varies. Copyrights for author.

VISIONS, International, The World Journal of Illustrated Poetry, Black Buzzard Press, Bradley R. Strahan, Publisher, Poetry Editor; Shirley G. Sullivan, Associate Editor; Melissa Bell, Review Editor; Ursula Gill, Art Editor; Lane Jennings, Circulation, 1110 Seaton Lane, Falls Church, VA 22046. 1979. Poetry, art, photos, reviews. "We are looking for poetry that excites the imagination, that says things in fascinating new ways (even if they are the same old things), that hits people 'where they live.' We are open minded about poetry styles but send us only your best. You may include matching pen and ink illustrations. We don't care if you're a big name but we do expect poetry that is well worked (no poetasters please). We are always looking for good translations, particularly of work not previously rendered into English and from unusual languages such as Catalan, Basque, Telegu, Malayan, Breton, (please include original language version when submitting). Prefer poems under 60 lines (but will consider longer). Recent contributors: Ted Hughes, James Dickey, Marilyn Hacker, Marge Piercy, Kamal Boulata, Allen Ginsberg, Lee Upton, Medbh McGuckian, Knute Skinner, Andrei Codrescu, and Dennis Brutus. Please don't submit more than 8, or less than 3 poems at a time (not more than once a year unless requested). Strongly recommend getting a sample copy (cost $3.50) before submitting material. *Submissions without SASE will be trashed!* We are indexed in *The Index of American Periodical Verse*, the Roths periodical index *the American Humanities Index.* And Roths Index of poetry periodicals. We are also in *Ulrich's* periodicals listings." circ. 750. 3/yr. Pub'd 3 issues 1990; expects 3 issues 1991, 3 issues 1992. sub. price: $14/1 yr, $27/2 yrs., special rate for libraries only—3 yrs. $42; per copy: $4 add $2 per copy for Europe Airmail. $2.50 for airmail to Asia, Africa and the South Pacific or $1.50 for Airmail to Latin America and the Carribean; sample: $3.50 plus same postage as single copy. Back issues: quoted on request (a full backrun is still available). Discounts: bulk 30+ copies 30%. 54pp; 5½×8½; of. Reporting time: 3 days to 3 weeks, unless we are out of the country. Payment: 1 contributors copy, we hope to get money to pay contributors at least $5 per poem in '92. Copyrighted, reverts to author. Pub's reviews: 30 in 1990. §Poetry. Ads: individual & corporate benefactors get a mention on our inside back cover which may include Co. Logo. Inquire if interested. We are *nonprofit.* CLMP.

Vista Mark Publications, Gene Hines, 1401 Iroquois, PO Box 220, Chouteau, OK 74337, 918-476-6310. 1989. Articles, interviews. avg. press run 2.5M-5M. Pub'd 1 title 1990; expects 3 titles 1991, 5 titles 1992. 1 title listed in the *Small Press Record of Books in Print* (20th Edition, 1991-92). avg. price, paper: $4.95. Discounts: prepay 2-4 20%; 5-9 30%; 10-24 40%; 25-49 42%; 50-74 44%; 75-99 46%; 100-199 48%; 200+ 50%. 78pp; 5½×8½; of. Copyrights for author.

Vista Publishing Company, Alfred R. Ayme, 250 West 57th Street, #1527, New York, NY 10019, 212-942-3350. "Publishers & distributors of outdoors books mostly on camping, fishing, techniques, hiking & backpacking equipment and trail guides, bicycling tours in and around major cities. Adventurous trips to unusual places. Cooking and preparation of dehydrated foods (recipes)" avg. press run 3M-5M. Expects 2 titles 1991, 4 titles 1992. avg. price, paper: $7-$10. Discounts: 5+ copies 40%, 25+ 42%, 100+ 50%. 150-300pp; of. Reporting time: 4-8 weeks. Payment: paperback standard on net receipts. Copyrights for author.

Visual Studies Workshop (see also AFTERIMAGE), Joan Lyons, Cordinator, USW Press, Research Center, 31 Prince Street, Rochester, NY 14607, 716-442-8676. 1972. Art, photos, interviews, criticism, reviews, concrete art, news items. avg. press run 1M. Pub'd 12 titles 1990; expects 12 titles 1991, 12 titles 1992. 36 titles listed in the *Small Press Record of Books in Print* (20th Edition, 1991-92). avg. price, cloth: $18; paper: $10; other: $2 *Afterimage* (Tabloid). Discounts: 10% VSW members - Standard to bookstores. Pages vary; size varies; †of. Payment: varies. Copyrights for author.

THE VITAL FORCE, Liz Salada, Publisher; Lois Mahaney, Editor, 1477 155th Avenue, San Leandro, CA 94578, 415-278-3263. 1984. Poetry, articles, art, photos, cartoons, letters, news items. circ. 250+. 6/yr. Pub'd 6 issues 1990; expects 6 issues 1991, 6 issues 1992. sub. price: $20; per copy: $2.50; sample: free. Back issues: $2.50. 10pp; 8½×14; quick print. Payment: none. Copyrighted. No advertising. COSMEP, PMA, NAPRA.

Vitesse Press, Barbara George, Editorial Director, 28 Birge Street, Brattleboro, VT 05301, 802-254-2306. "We primarily publish how-to books on bicycle racing" avg. press run 3M. Pub'd 2 titles 1990; expects 4 titles 1991, 4 titles 1992. 14 titles listed in the *Small Press Record of Books in Print* (20th Edition, 1991-92). avg. price, cloth: $19.95; paper: $12.65. Discounts: 5-9 30% off retail, 10-24 40%, 25-49 41%, 50-99 43%, 100-249 45%,

611

250-499 50%, 500+ 55%. 197pp; 6×9; of. Reporting time: 2-4 weeks. Payment: 10% on net sales. Copyrights for author. Vermont Publishers Association.

Vitreous Group/Camp Colton, Kathleen Lundstrom, Camp Colton, Colton, OR 97017, 503-824-3150. 1983. Art, concrete art, non-fiction. "So far only in house, will consider outside material; glass art subjects." avg. press run 15M. Pub'd 1 title 1990; expects 1 title 1991. 3 titles listed in the *Small Press Record of Books in Print* (20th Edition, 1991-92). avg. price, paper: $30. Discounts: 35% booksellers, 50% distributors. 140pp; 8½×11; of. Reporting time: 1-2 months. Payment: negotiable. Copyrights for author. COSMEP.

VIV Publishing House, Vivian Wright, 600 East 137 Street, #13G, Bronx, NY 10454. 1 title listed in the *Small Press Record of Books in Print* (20th Edition, 1991-92).

Vivation Publishing Co., Phil Laut, Publisher, PO Box 8269, Cincinnati, OH 45208-0608, 513-321-4405. 4 titles listed in the *Small Press Record of Books in Print* (20th Edition, 1991-92).

Voice of Liberty Publications, David W. Lundberg, 3 Borger Place, Pearl River, NY 10965, (914) 735-8140. 1979. Plays, non-fiction. "The focus of V of L Publications is the individual. Books published by V of L will evaluate ideals, institutions, and processes in terms of their effects on the individual. A tenet held by the publisher is that individuals grow to their full stature when they have elbow room to control their own lives. The publisher believes that many current trends in government, economics, and society are destroying individual freedom. Alientation, violence, and self-destructive acts are the results of this loss. The objective of V of L Publications is to harness the power of the mind and the power of the printed word to increase individual liberty and thus increase the stature of the individual. No unsolicited ms considered." avg. press run 2M. Expects 1 title 1991. 1 title listed in the *Small Press Record of Books in Print* (20th Edition, 1991-92). avg. price, cloth: $10.95; paper: $7.95. Discounts: 2-5 copies, 20%; 6-11, 30%; 12-23, 40%. 224pp; 5½×8½; of.

A VOICE WITHOUT SIDES, dbqp, Ge(of Huth), po.ed.t, 317 Princetown Road, Schenectady, NY 12306-2022. 1987. Poetry, cartoons, collages, concrete art. "*A Voice Without Sides (VWOS)* is an irregular magazine publishing short avant-garde poetry and visual art in strange formats (in jars, on large self-stick labels, on erasers, etc. *VWOS* is a limited edition magazine, printing no more than 50 copies per issue" circ. 24-50. 2/yr. Pub'd 1 issue 1990; expects 2 issues 1991, 2 issues 1992. sub. price: can be any dollar amount—cost (which varies) will be subtracted when issue is mailed; per copy: $1-$4; sample: $1-$4. Discounts: none. 5pp; size varies; †rubberstamp, photocopying, handwriting, handtyping. Reporting time: 2 weeks. Payment: at least 2 copies; 1/4 of press run is divided among contributors. Copyrighted, reverts to author.

VOICES INTERNATIONAL, Clovita Rice, 1115 Gillette Drive, Little Rock, AR 72207, 501-225-0166. 1966. Poetry. "We look for poetry with haunting imagery and significant statement." circ. 350. 4/yr. Expects 4 issues 1991, 4 issues 1992. sub. price: $10 ($18 for 2 yrs); per copy: $2; sample: $2. Back issues: $2. 32pp; 6×9. Reporting time: 6 weeks. Payment: 1 free copy. Copyrighted, rights revert with request.

VOICES - ISRAEL, Mark Levinson, Editor-in-Chief; Gretti Izak, Associate Editor; Lila Julius, Associate Editor, c/o Mark Levinson, PO Box 5780, Herzliya 46101, Israel, 052-552411. 1972. Poetry. "*Voices Israel* is the only magazine in Israel devoted entirely to poetry in English. It calls for the submission of intelligible and feeling poetry concerned with the potentialities of the human spirit, and the dangers confronting it. It also seeks the peace of all mankind. Copyright to all poems is vested in the poets themselves; the only request of the Editorial Board is that if a poem is first printed in *Voices Israel*, that fact should be made known in any subsequent publications of it. No more than four poems to be submitted to each issue (one a year), size 11 X 8½ inch sheet (one) in seven copies, typewritten, to reach the Editor by the end of February each year." circ. 350. 1/yr. Pub'd 1 issue 1990; expects 1 issue 1991, 1 issue 1992. sub. price: $14 postpaid; per copy: $14 postpaid; sample: $10 postpaid. Back issues: $10 as available. Discounts: 33⅓% off to recognized booksellers only. No library discounts. 120pp; 8×6½, 20×16cm; †of. Reporting time: 6 months. Payment: none. Copyrighted, reverts to author. Ads: $30/$15. PEN.

VOICES OF YOUTH ON EDUCATION, SELF, CIVIC VALUES, Alvin J. Gordon, PO Box JJ, Sonoma, CA 95476, 707-938-8314. 1986. Poetry, articles, art, photos, cartoons, interviews, satire, letters, news items, non-fiction. "Published by the Meiklejohn Education Foundation. Produced by Educational Goals Study Group. We use material representing an intergenerational perspective on education, self development and citizenship. We emphasize material by young people. Articles are usually 600-800 words" circ. 2M. 2/yr. Expects 2 issues 1991, 2 issues 1992. sub. price: $9; per copy: $4.75. Back issues: orders of 10+ of current issue - $4 each, 10+ of back issues - $3.50 each. Discounts: 10% library. 64pp; 5½×8½; of. Copyrighted, does not revert to author. Pub's reviews: 2 in 1990. §education, citizenship, intergenerational issues. Ads: $100/$60/$40 quarter/back cover: $200 (2-color), $150 (b&w)/2nd & 3rd covers: $125 (b&w).

VOL. NO. MAGAZINE, Richard Weekley, Jerry Danielsen, Tina Landrum, Don McLeod, Los Angeles Poets' Press, 24721 Newhall Avenue, Newhall, CA 91321, 805-254-0851. 1983. Poetry, art, photos. "Limit of 4-6 submissions at a time. 80 lines or less preferably. Must relate to specified themes; 'Between a Poet and a Hard Spot' (Humor—August '91), 'Third World' (August '92), 'The Eros of Eros' (August '93). Solid, concise, adventuresome work wanted.'' circ. 300. 1/yr. Pub'd 2 issues 1990; expects 1 issue 1991, 1 issue 1992. 4 titles listed in the *Small Press Record of Books in Print* (20th Edition, 1991-92). sub. price: $5; per copy: $2.50; sample: $2.50. Back issues: $1.50. Discounts: 20%. 36pp; 7×8½; of. Reporting time: 1-5 months. Payment: 2 copies. Copyrighted, reverts to author. Ads: $30/$15.

Volcano Press, Inc, Ruth Gottstein, PO Box 270, Volcano, CA 95689, 209-296-3445; fax 209-296-4515. 1976. Articles, art, criticism, non-fiction. "All materials published in book form only.'' avg. press run 5M-10M. Pub'd 2 titles 1990; expects 2 titles 1991, 4 titles 1992. 11 titles listed in the *Small Press Record of Books in Print* (20th Edition, 1991-92). avg. price, paper: $14.95. Discounts: 1 copy 20% (prepaid 35%), 2-9 copies 35%, 10+ copies 40%. 200pp; 6×9 usually; of. Reporting time: 3 months. Payment: outright fee, or royalties. Copyrights for author. NCBPA, ABA.

THE VOLCANO REVIEW, Peninhand Press, Thomas Janisse, Editor & Publisher; Lee Warren, Fiction Editor; Cherryl Luallin, Associate Editor, 3665 SE Tolman, Portland, OR 97202. 1979. Fiction, art, interviews. "We publish fiction & art both national & international'' circ. 500. 1/yr. Expects 1 issue 1992. sub. price: $5; per copy: $6; sample: $3. Back issues: #1-#7 - $6. Discounts: 1-4 25%, 5 and over 40%. 104pp; 5½×8½; of. Reporting time: 2 weeks to 2 months; no unsolicited manuscripts at this time. Payment: copies. Copyrighted, reverts to author. CCLM.

VOLITION, Vortex Editions, Bonnie Lateiner, Editor, PO Box 314, Tenants Harbor, ME 04860. 1982. Poetry, fiction, parts-of-novels. "A magazine of prose and poetry edited by B. Lateiner. The dramatic presentation of each issue highlights the work of writers such as: Bobbie Louise-Hawkins, Stephen Emerson, Maureen Owen, Barrett Watten, Bill Berkson, Duncan McNaughton, Fielding Dawson, Lucia Berlin, and others. The covers of each issue are color-xeroxed to produce a vital textured magnetic appearance.'' circ. 400. 1/yr. Pub'd 2 issues 1990; expects 2 issues 1991, 2-3 issues 1992. sub. price: $12; per copy: $4; sample: $4. Discounts: trade available. 50pp; 7×8; mi, of, color xeroxed covers, offset text. Payment: 3 copies of issue. Copyrighted, reverts to author. CLMP.

THE VOLUNTARYIST, Carl Watner, Box 1275, Gramling, SC 29348, 803-472-2750. 1982. Articles, cartoons, interviews, criticism, letters. circ. 300. 6/yr. Pub'd 6 issues 1990; expects 6 issues 1991, 6 issues 1992. sub. price: $18, $20 overseas; per copy: $4; sample: $1. Back issues: 10 different issues $25. 8pp; 8½×11. Reporting time: 2 weeks. Payment: free subscription. Not copyrighted. Pub's reviews: 4 in 1990. Ads: $25 business card.

Volunteer Concepts, PO Box 27584, Austin, TX 78755, 512-472-2032. 1988. 1 title listed in the *Small Press Record of Books in Print* (20th Edition, 1991-92).

Volunteer Publications, M.E. Burton, Managing Editor, PO Box 240786, Memphis, TN 38124-0786, 901-682-4183. 1980. Poetry, fiction, criticism, long-poems, collages, non-fiction. avg. press run 500-1M. Expects 1 title 1991, 1+ titles 1992. 6 titles listed in the *Small Press Record of Books in Print* (20th Edition, 1991-92). avg. price, cloth: $12.95; paper: $6.95. Discounts: libraries and schools, less 25%; bookstores, 40%; wholesalers, distributors negotiable. 80pp; size varies; of, lp. Reporting time: 60 days. Payment: negotiable with author. Copyrights for author.

Vonpalisaden Publications Inc., 195 Spring Valley Road, Paramus, NJ 07652, 201-262-4919. 1986. Non-fiction. "Currently pet/hobby (dogs) animal book publisher (so far non-fiction only). *The Rottweiler: An International Study of the Breed,* by Dr. Dagmar Hodinar.'' avg. press run 5M. Pub'd 1 title 1990. 1 title listed in the *Small Press Record of Books in Print* (20th Edition, 1991-92). avg. price, paper: $25.95. Discounts: for resale: 1-9 copies 20%, 10-25 30%, 26-50 40%, 51-99 45%, 100+ 50% plus addit. 10% on net if displayed in catalogue. 350+pp; 6×9; lp.

THE VORTEX (A Historical and Wargamers Jornal), Axios Newletter, Inc., David Gorham, 806 South Euclid Street, Fullerton, CA 92632, 714-526-4952 & 714-526-1913. 1981. Fiction, articles, art, photos, cartoons, interviews, satire, criticism, reviews, letters, parts-of-novels, collages, concrete art, news items, non-fiction. "A historical + wargamers journal. Articles needed on politics and battles and wars, in the period between 1812 and 1930—especially Europe and America—Also articles on wargames, the people into wargames, and photos, art and cartoons on the same. Write for an intelligent lay reader rather than a professional historian, length 400-2.5M words. By-line given. Emphasis on articles that would interest wargamers!! Some poetry (on our subject matter).'' circ. 2.33M. 13/yr. Pub'd 13 issues 1990; expects 13 issues 1991, 13 issues 1992. sub. price: $15, $25/2 years; per copy: $2; sample: $2. Back issues: $2. Discounts: write for information (about 40% discount). 12pp; 8½×11; †of, li. Reporting time: 6-8 weeks. Payment: $20 to $100 depending on article. Copyrighted, reverts to author. Pub's reviews: 16 in 1990. §Wargames, military history. Ads: $160/$87.50/5¢. I.D.A., S.C.V., COSMEP.

Vortex Editions (see also VOLITION), Bonnie Lateiner, PO Box 314, Tenants Harbor, ME 04860. 1979. Parts-of-novels. "Vortex publishes post-modern progressive poetry and prose with emphasis on large range in styles. Contributing authors: Maureen Owen, Ed Friedman, Bill Berkson, Johanna Drucker, Michael Amnasan, Bobbie Louise Hawkins, Stephen Emerson, Alan Bernheimer, Barrett Watten, Carla Harryman, Simone O., Fielding Dawson, and Duncan McNaughton. NO unsolicited manuscripts." avg. press run 500-1M. Pub'd 2 titles 1990; expects 3 titles 1991, 3 titles 1992. 4 titles listed in the *Small Press Record of Books in Print* (20th Edition, 1991-92). avg. price, paper: $5. Discounts: trade available. 100pp; 6×9, 5×8, 7×8; of. Payment: arranged with respective authors according to demands of both author & publisher. Copyrights for author. CLMP.

VOYA (Voice of Youth Advocate), Scarecrow Press, Dorothy Brodrick, Editor, PO Box 4167, Metuchen, NJ 08840, 201-548-8600. 1978. circ. 4M. 6/yr. Pub'd 6 issues 1990; expects 6 issues 1991, 6 issues 1992. sub. price: $27; per copy: $4.50; sample: write for info. Back issues: $4.50. Discounts: write for info. 70pp; 8½×11. Copyrighted. Pub's reviews. §Young adult. Ads: write for info.

VOYAGES SF, StarLance Publications, James B. King, 50 Basin Drive, Mesa, WA 99343, 509-269-4497. 1987. Fiction, articles, art, parts-of-novels. "*Voyages SF Magazine* is primarily of interest to hobby enthusiasts of science-fiction adventure gaming, particularly role playing. Experience in role playing and a knowledge of particular games are necessary to write articles for submission to *Voyages SF*. We do, however, solicit short science-fiction from 2000 to 4000 words. We also solicit sf illustration, both black line and all mediums that reproduce well in b/w halftone. We review games and related products." circ. 1M. 4/yr. Pub'd 4 issues 1990; expects 4 issues 1991, 4 issues 1992. sub. price: $10; per copy: $2.75; sample: $3. Discounts: 50% to 62%, based on quantity. 36pp; 8½×11; of. Reporting time: 2-4 weeks. Copyrighted, reverts to author. Pub's reviews: 16 in 1990. §Game related only. Ads: $75; 1/2 $45. COSMEP.

W

W.D.C. PERIOD, Gordon Gordon, Chow Chow Productions, PO Box 50084, Washington, DC 20004-0084, 202-462-7229. 1984. Poetry, fiction, articles, art, photos, cartoons, interviews, criticism, reviews, music, letters. "Basically an 'anything goes' publication, although our most obvious focus is on alternative/punk music and culture as well as independent/underground cartoons and comic (books)" circ. 2M+. 4/yr. Pub'd 8 issues 1990; expects 4 issues 1991, 4 issues 1992. price per copy: $2 postpaid; sample: $2. Back issues: send SASE for info. 48+pp; 10×14; newsprint. Reporting time: varies. Payment: none. Copyrighted, reverts to author. Pub's reviews: lots in 1990. Ads: $100/$50/$25 1/4 page.

W.I.M. Publications, SDiane Bogus, Editor-in-Chief; T. Nelson Gilbert, Business Manager, 2215-R Market Street, Box 137, San Francisco, CA 94114, 408-253-3329. 1979. Poetry, long-poems. "We are now accepting four poetry or 'how-to' manuscripts during Spring, from April 1-June 30 (25-30 pages). Cover letter required. We are available for criticism of poetry and fiction. We make editorial suggestions. $5 per poem. $8 per page of fiction. We do reviews of small press poetry books upon approval. We offer our 3M name mailing list $30. We offer a poetry test for novice poets $10. We publish mail order lists/reports such as 'Women in Mail Order,' 'The Natural Headache Cure,' 'Where to Advertise in CA,' and a list of low budget advertising outlets in all 50 states. Write for catalog, enclose 5X7 SASE. We request $3 reading fee" avg. press run 1M. Pub'd 1 title 1990; expects 4 titles 1991, 4 titles 1992. 11 titles listed in the *Small Press Record of Books in Print* (20th Edition, 1991-92). avg. price, cloth: $10; paper: $9; other: $3 or less. Discounts: 40% with agency letterhead with order of 5 minimum (for individuals also). 48+pp; 5½×8½; of. Reporting time: acknowledgement upon receipt, report by personal letter at end of reading season (Aug 31). Payment: half or part of run to distribute and keep sales; 35% after first printing. Copyrights for author. COSMEP, IPW, FWG, SPWAO, IWWG, National Writers Union.

W.W. Publications (see also MINAS TIRITH EVENING-STAR), Philip W. Helms, PO Box 373, Highland, MI 48357-0373, 313-887-4703. 1967. Poetry, fiction, articles, art, photos, cartoons, interviews, satire, criticism, reviews, music, letters, long-poems, news items, non-fiction. "Send questions to: Paul S. Ritz, PO Box 901, Clearwater, FL 34617" avg. press run 200-500. Pub'd 2 titles 1990; expects 1 title 1991, 3 titles 1992. avg. price, paper: $3.50. 200pp; 8½×11; †of. Reporting time: 2 months. Payment: 5 free copies. Copyrights for author. ATS.

WALKING AND SINNING, J.D. Buhl, Accelerator Press, 1708 #4 Martin Luther King Jr. Way, Berkeley, CA 94709, 415-549-2815. 1989. Poetry, letters. circ. 100-500. 1/yr. Expects 1 issue 1991, 1 issue 1992. price per copy: $1; sample: free. Discounts: sold on a 60/40 basis in stores, same used for all other arrangements.

614

8-10pp; 4×5½; of. Reporting time: a long time. Payment: none. Copyrighted, reverts to author.

WALKING-STICK NOTES, Placebo Press, Cecil Curtis, 4051 East Olive Road #231, Pensacola, FL 32514, 904-477-3995. 1985. Articles, cartoons, reviews, news items, non-fiction. "Anything concerning walking-sticks (including canes, truncheons, sceptres, sticks, etc.) that may be of interest to makers, sellers, collectors, connoisuers, or others interested in any related fields, i.e. cane guns, sword sticks, music sticks, etc. Auction or sales notices & results. Museum collections. News items involving walking-sticks." 4/yr. Pub'd 4 issues 1990; expects 4 issues 1991, 4 issues 1992. sub. price: free for postage (sent 1st class mail); per copy: #10 SASE; sample: #10 SASE. Back issues: #10 SASE. 4pp; 8½×11; of. Reporting time: within 2 weeks. Payment: in copies. Not copyrighted. Pub's reviews: 6 in 1990. §Walking sticks and related items. No ads.

Walnut Publishing Co., Inc., Jeff Mackler, Alan Benjamin, Nat Weinstein, 3435 Army Street, Suite #308, San Francisco, CA 94110, 415-821-0511. 1987. Non-fiction. avg. press run 3M. Pub'd 2 titles 1990; expects 2 titles 1991. 4 titles listed in the *Small Press Record of Books in Print* (20th Edition, 1991-92). avg. price, paper: $8.95. Discounts: 40% for bookstores, distributors, schools, libraries, etc. 155pp; 6×9, varies; of, desktop layout. Reporting time: 1 month. Payment: varies. Copyrights for author.

Patrick Walsh Press, Barbara Nall, 2017 S. Ventura, Tempe, AZ 85282, 602-894-1230. 1980. Non-fiction. "Mostly non-fiction books under the broad umbrella of new age/transformational." avg. press run 5M. Pub'd 2 titles 1990; expects 3 titles 1991, 4 titles 1992. 1 title listed in the *Small Press Record of Books in Print* (20th Edition, 1991-92). avg. price, cloth: $14; paper: $8. 150pp. Reporting time: varies. Payment: varies. Copyrights for author. COSMEP, AAA (Arizona), ALA (Arizona).

Wampeter Press, George E. Murphy, Jr., Director, Box 2626, Key West, FL 33045-2626, 617-834-4137. 1977. "We are interested in books of poetry and fiction both by established writers and in "first" books by talented and actively-publishing lesser-known writers. Please do not send manuscripts; rather, send a sample of work from a ms and a list of publishing credits with a letter of inquiry. Recent books: *Matters of Life & Death: New American Stories*, Editor—Tobias Wolff. *New American Poets of the 80's* Edited by Myers & Weingarten, *The Esquire*, fiction reader by Rust Hills & Tom Jenks." avg. press run 2M. Pub'd 5 titles 1990; expects 7 titles 1991, 10 titles 1992. 9 titles listed in the *Small Press Record of Books in Print* (20th Edition, 1991-92). avg. price, cloth: $14.95; paper: $7.95. Discounts: 1-10, 30%; 11-25, 40%; 25+, 50%. 256pp; 6×9; of. Reporting time: 1 month. Payment: 10% of press run. Copyrights for author.

WANBLI HO, Gloria Dyc, PO Box 8, Sinte Gleska College, Mission, SD 57555, 605-856-2321. 1975. Poetry, fiction, articles, art, interviews, criticism, long-poems, non-fiction. "The purpose of *Wanbli Ho* is to encourage the development of Lakota writers and artists by providing an outlet for their work. The editors will also consider contributions from all Native American writers and from regional writers. The creative work should reflect the experiences of Native Americans and/or the land and people of the high plains region. Oral tradition texts are welcome. The first issue of *Wanbli Ho* (Eagle's Voice) edited by Roberta Hill Whiteman, was published in the mid-seventies. A Spring, 1986 issue, edited by visiting writer Simon Ortiz, featured work about the Black Hills. Recent contributors: Maurice Kenny, Joseph Bruchac, Barney Bush, Simon Ortiz, Diane Glancy, Laura Tohe. Submit unpublished work only." circ. 500. 1/yr. Pub'd 1 issue 1990; expects 1 issue 1991, 1 issue 1992. sub. price: $4.50; per copy: $4.50; sample: $4.50. Discounts: 40% off cover price for distributors. 75pp; 5×7; †of. Reporting time: please query for deadline, will report within 3 months of deadline. Payment: copies. Copyrighted, contributors may reprint with acknowledgement. Ads: $100/$50. CCLM.

The Wanderer's Ink, Jennifer S. Rothrock, 2 College Hill #1175, Westminster, MD 21157-4303. 1990. Fiction. "The Wanderer's Ink is concerned with developing a core of writers who are willing to tackle the many philosophical, and sociological problems of todays societies. Our motto is growth through fiction, and our goal is to educate and enlighten in a non-offensive way: good, clean, well written, and intriguing fiction." avg. press run 10M. Expects 2 titles 1991, 3 titles 1992. 1 title listed in the *Small Press Record of Books in Print* (20th Edition, 1991-92). avg. price, paper: $10.95. Discounts: 2-4 20%; 5-99 40%; 100+ 50%. 200pp; 6×9; lp. Reporting time: 2 months. Payment: 7-10%. Copyrights for author.

WANDERING WOLFS, Kinseeker Publications, Victoria Wilson, PO Box 184, Grawn, MI 49637, 616-276-6745. 1986. Articles, reviews, news items, non-fiction. circ. 50. 4/yr. Pub'd 4 issues 1990; expects 4 issues 1991, 4 issues 1992. sub. price: $10; per copy: $2.50; sample: $2.50. Back issues: $2.50. Discounts: none. 10pp; 8½×11; †xerox (photocopy). Reporting time: 2 weeks. Payment: varies. Not copyrighted. Pub's reviews: 3 in 1990. §Genealogy, particularly in Germany or areas Wolf(e) families settled.

Ward Hill Press, L. Dunlap, 514 Bay Street, Box 424, Staten Island, NY 10304, 718-816-9449. 1989. Poetry, art, non-fiction. "Only poetry suitable for children 10 and up, for inclusion in multicultural anthologies. Also nonfiction for children of the same age group, and with a multicultural, or progressive, approach. We are currently seeking biographies for a new series for middle readers and young adults. We also publish adult how-to in the automotive line." avg. press run 2M-5M. Pub'd 2 titles 1990; expects 4 titles 1991, 6 titles 1992. avg. price, paper: $12.95. Discounts: 1-4 copies 20%, 5-24 40%, 25-49 42%, 50-99 43%, 100+ 45%. 120pp;

6×9; of. Reporting time: 2-4 weeks. Payment: a small advance and a royalty based on net. Copyrights for author. PMA, COSMEP, MPE, ABA.

WARM FUZZY NEWSLETTER, Jalmar Press, Bradley L. Winch, President, 45 Hitching Post Dr. Bldg 2, Rolling Hills Estates, CA 90274, 213-547-1240. 1973. Non-fiction. "Educationally oriented books on self-concept/values; gifted + talented; parent involvement; parent/child relations; rigt-brain/whole-brain learning; conflict resolution; peace education" circ. 5M. 4/yr. Pub'd 2 issues 1990; expects 4 issues 1991, 6 issues 1992. sub. price: $5. 8½×11; of. Copyrighted, does not revert to author. PASCAL, COSMEP, ABA, NSSEA, CBA.

Warthog Press, Patricia Fillingham, 29 South Valley Road, West Orange, NJ 07052, 201-731-9269. 1979. Poetry, art, photos, music. "Warthog Press is interested in poetry that will bring poetry back to people, rather than using it as an academic exercise. We are interested in poetry that says something, and says it well." avg. press run 1M. Expects 4 titles 1991. 9 titles listed in the *Small Press Record of Books in Print* (20th Edition, 1991-92). avg. price, paper: $8. 64pp; 5½×8½; of. Reporting time: 1 month. Does not copyright for author.

WASCANA REVIEW, Joan Givner, Fiction Editor; Jeanne Shami, Poetry Editor; Kathleen Wall, Department of English, University of Regina, Regina, Sask S4S 0A2, Canada, 584-4316. 1966. circ. 300-500. 2/yr. sub. price: $8 ($7 Canadian); per copy: $4; sample: $4. Discounts: 20% for subscription agencies. 90pp. Reporting time: 2-3 months. Payment: poetry $10 per page; fiction, reviews, critical articles $3 per page. Copyrighted, reverts to author. Pub's reviews: 2 in 1990. Ads: Canadian books ones of local interest.

WASHINGTON INTERNATIONAL ARTS LETTER, James S. Duncan, PO Box 12010, Des Moines, IA 50312, 202-328-1900, 515-255-5577. 1962. "We publish financial information for the arts and artists. Federal actions and grants; private foundation and business corporation arts program information. And we have the following titles in books: *National Directory of Grants and Aid to Individuals*, 256pp, paper, 7th ed., $25.95; *National Directory of Arts Support by Private Foundations #5*, 1983, 336pp, paper, $79.95. *National Directory of Arts and Education Support By Business Corporations*, 160 pp, paper, $75, 3rd edition." circ. 15M. 10/yr. Pub'd 6 issues 1990; expects 10 issues 1991, 10 issues 1992. 3 titles listed in the *Small Press Record of Books in Print* (20th Edition, 1991-92). sub. price: individuals (personal address & check) $55, institutions $82; per copy: $10 (by mail only); sample: free. Back issues: $10. Discounts: departments & non-profits: 20% (off of $124 price). 6-8pp; 8½×11; of. Payment: none. Copyrighted. Pub's reviews: 350 in 1990. §All arts, and grants to them. Ads: classified word only - $5 per word, 5 line minimum, approx. 5 wds per line.

THE WASHINGTON MONTHLY, Charles Peters, 1611 Connecticut Avenue NW, Washington, DC 20009, 202-462-0128. 1969. Articles, art, photos, satire, reviews, letters, non-fiction. "Art & photos commissioned to accompany articles" circ. 30M. 10/yr. Pub'd 11 issues 1990; expects 11 issues 1991, 10 issues 1992. sub. price: $33; per copy: $3.50; sample: $4.50. Back issues: $4.50. 64pp; 7½×9¾; heatset, web offset. Reporting time: 2 months. Payment: 10¢/word. Copyrighted, does not revert to author. Pub's reviews: 60 in 1990. §Government, bureaucracy, politics, education, media, society. Ads: $2000/$1200/rates are lower for publishers.

THE WASHINGTON REPORT, Wm. A. Leavell, Editor, Editors Release Service, PO Box 10309, St. Petersburg, FL 33733, 813-866-1598. 1979. News items. "We are a political newsletter. We receive information from 'Sources' which we consider 'Confidential'. We do not pay for information and welcome all information regarding national politics." circ. 17M. 12/yr. Pub'd 12 issues 1990; expects 12 issues 1991, 12 issues 1992. sub. price: $25; per copy: $2.25; sample: free. Back issues: available upon request. Discounts: none. 4pp; 8½×11; of. Reporting time: timely. Payment: none. Not copyrighted. No ads.

WASHINGTON REVIEW, Clarissa Wittenberg, Editor; Mary Swift, Managing Editor; Pat Kolmer, Art Editor & Film Reviews; Beth Joselow, Literary Editor; Jeff Richards, Associate Literary Editor; Joe Ross, Associate Literary Editor; Ross Taylor, Associate Literary Editor; Anne Pierce, Dance Editor, PO Box 50132, Washington, DC 20091, 202-638-0515. 1975. Poetry, fiction, articles, art, photos, cartoons, interviews, satire, criticism, reviews, letters, parts-of-novels, plays, non-fiction. "Articles: 2,000 words at most. Review: 500-1,000 words. Interested in in-depth articles on all arts, with particular emphasis on DC. Recent contributors: E. Ethelbert Miller, Lee Fleming, Terence Winch, Carmen Delzell." circ. 10M. 6/yr. Pub'd 6 issues 1990; expects 6 issues 1991, 6 issues 1992. sub. price: $12/yr, $20/2 years; per copy: $2; sample: $2.50. Back issues: $3.50. Discounts: 15% bulk, 15% classroom, 10% agencies, 40% to bookstores for resale. 36pp; 11¼×16; of. Reporting time: 2 months. Payment: in issues. Copyrighted, reverts to author. Pub's reviews: 25 in 1990. §Arts, poetry, fiction, theater. Ads: $250/$175/$15 col. inch. COSMEP, CLMP.

THE WASHINGTON TROOPER, Grimm Press & Publishing Co., Inc., Bruce D. Grimm, Grimm Press & Publishing Co., Inc., PO Box 1523, Longview, WA 98632-0144, 206-577-8598. 1981. Articles, photos, cartoons, interviews, news items, non-fiction. "Additional address: 144 S.W. 153rd Street, Seattle, WA 98166. 500-2500 words, law enforcement related, highway and traffic safety issues" circ. 6.5M. 4/yr. Pub'd 4 issues 1990; expects 4 issues 1991, 4 issues 1992. sub. price: $9.97; per copy: $3.95; sample: $2.50. Discounts: 15% trade; 30% jobber. 64pp; 8½×11; of. Reporting time: 45 days. Payment: 3¢-6¢ per word. Copyrighted. §Law

616

enforcement, public safety. Ads: $925/$595/$99 1/12 page. COSMEP, CAOS.

Washington Writers' Publishing House, Jean Nordhaus, President; Sharon Negri, Treasurer, PO Box 15271, Washington, DC 20003, 202-543-1905. 1975. Poetry. "Open to poets in the Greater Washington Area only. A *cooperative* press." avg. press run 750. Pub'd 2 titles 1990; expects 2 titles 1991, 2 titles 1992. 28 titles listed in the *Small Press Record of Books in Print* (20th Edition, 1991-92). avg. price, paper: $8. Discounts: bulk orders-5 or more titles 40%; bookstores 20%. 64-72pp; 5½×8½; of. Reporting time: about 2 months, submissions are made only once a year, usually in the summers, with decisions made by the end of October. Payment: authors receive 50 copies. Does not copyright for author.

Water Mark Press, Coco Gordon, 138 Duane Street, New York, NY 10013, 212-285-1609. 1978. Poetry, art. "We are in process of changing format to artist books. 1983 publications: *Loose Pages,* Alison Knowles (pages of flax paper to sound & wear on the body,) deluxe limited edition of 10 hand copies, $3,600; *The Opaque Glass,* Barbara Roux (an artists bookwork both hand & machine made/xerox hand-colored, longpoem with visuals) edition 50 copies, $40. I focused in '83-'84 on new current literature (6 chapbooks) written in crossover genres. I produced three full-length traditional poetry books 1980-84 and feel that need has been filled by other presses. I use handmade papers designed specifically for parts, covers, or all of our publications, and sell to other presses-our papers from flax, linen and many plant fibers. No more unsolicited submissions please." avg. press run 50-600. Pub'd 2 titles 1990; expects 1 title 1991. 13 titles listed in the *Small Press Record of Books in Print* (20th Edition, 1991-92). avg. price, cloth: $29-$40; paper: $10; other: $100-$3,000 deluxe editions. Discounts: 1-2 copies 25%, 3+ 40%. size varies; of, lp. Payment: contributor's copies. Does not copyright for author. ALO, COSMEP.

Water Row Press (see also WATER ROW REVIEW), Cisco Harland, PO Box 438, Sudbury, MA 01776. 1985. Poetry, fiction, interviews, criticism, plays. "Our main focus are books and broadsides relative to the understanding and appreciation of the writings and times of 'Beat' writers. We are also seeking poetry and fiction from second generation 'Beats' and 'Outsiders'. Editions include signed limitations. Some recent contributors include Tom Clark, Arthur Knight, R. Crumb, Joy Walsh, William Burroughs. Any manuscripts which add to the understanding of Kerouac, Ginsberg, Bukowski are welcome. Tributes, poetry, dissertations, artwork. New poets' submissions always welcome." avg. press run 500-1M. Pub'd 5 titles 1990; expects 10 titles 1991, 10 titles 1992. 10 titles listed in the *Small Press Record of Books in Print* (20th Edition, 1991-92). avg. price, paper: $8. Discounts: 2-5 copies 20%, 6 or more 40%, distributors 50%. lp, of. Reporting time: 4-8 weeks. Payment: copies of work and additional payment on publication to be arranged. Copyrights for author. COSMEP.

WATER ROW REVIEW, Water Row Press, Cisco Harland, PO Box 438, Sudbury, MA 01776. 1986. Poetry, fiction, articles, interviews, criticism, reviews, parts-of-novels. "Recent contributors: William Burroughs, Charles Bukowski, Jeffrey Weinberg." circ. 2.5M. 4/yr. Pub'd 4 issues 1990; expects 4 issues 1991, 4 issues 1992. sub. price: $24; per copy: $6; sample: $6. Discounts: 2-10 20%, 11 or more 40%; of. Copyrighted. Pub's reviews: 12 in 1990. §Literature, fiction, poetry. COSMEP.

WATERBURY CHESS CLUB BULLETIN, Rob Roy, 54 Calumet Street, Waterbury, CT 06710-1201, 203-755-9749. 1976. Articles, photos, interviews, criticism, reviews, news items. "ISSN #0894-0606" circ. 600. 2/yr. Pub'd 2 issues 1990; expects 2 issues 1991, 2 issues 1992. sub. price: $2; per copy: $1; sample: same. Back issues: $1. 28pp; 5½×8; †Kodak copier. Reporting time: variable, see editor. Payment: none. Not copyrighted. Pub's reviews: 18 in 1990. §Chess and backgammon. Ads: inquire of editor.

Waterfront Books, Sherrill N. Musty, 98 Brookes Avenue, Burlington, VT 05401, 802-658-7477. 1983. Non-fiction. avg. press run 2.5M-5M. Pub'd 2 titles 1990; expects 2 titles 1992. 8 titles listed in the *Small Press Record of Books in Print* (20th Edition, 1991-92). avg. price, cloth: $15.95; paper: $12.95. Discounts: 50% to jobbers; 40% trade; 20% classroom and libraries. of. Reporting time: 2 months. Payment: standard 10%, 15% net, sometimes higher. Copyrights for author. Publisher's Marketing Association (PMA), American Booksellers Association (ABA), Association of Booksellers for Children.

Waterfront Center (see also WATERFRONT WORLD), Ann Breen, Co-Editor; Dick Rigby, Co-Editor, 1536 44th Street NW, Washington, DC 20007, 202-337-0356. 1981. Photos, letters, news items. "ISSN: 0733-0677" avg. press run 1.3M-1.5M. Pub'd 6 titles 1990; expects 6 titles 1991, 6 titles 1992. 10 titles listed in the *Small Press Record of Books in Print* (20th Edition, 1991-92). 40pp; 8½×11; of.

Waterfront Press, Kal Wagenheim, Co-Editor; Olga Jimenez Wagenheim, 52 Maple Avenue, Maplewood, NJ 07040, 201-762-1565. 1982. Poetry, fiction, plays, non-fiction. "Waterfront Press, specializes in fiction, poetry and non-fiction by Puerto Rican and other Hispanic writers, and includes translations from the Spanish. Its latest catalogue contains more than 20 in-print titles. Most are published by Waterfront, which also distributes selected titles from other publishers. Featured in the catalogue are an English translation of the classic 19th century Puerto Rican novel *La Charca*, by Manuel Zeno-Gandia and two works by Pedro Pietri: (Traffic Violations), poetry; and (The Masses are Asses), a play. Also featured is Harold Lidin's new 'History of the

Puerto Rican Independence Movement, Volume I(19th Century),' as well as nine research monographs published by the Hispanic Research Center of Fordham University, and fiction and non-fiction works from Editorial Cultural and Editorial Huracan, of Puerto Rico.'' avg. press run 1M-3M. Pub'd 3 titles 1990; expects 5 titles 1991, 5-6 titles 1992. 25 titles listed in the *Small Press Record of Books in Print* (20th Edition, 1991-92). avg. price, cloth: $18.95; paper: $12.95. Discounts: 20%; 40% on quantity orders. 200pp; 5½x8½; of. Reporting time: 60 days, send inquiry letter first. Payment: 10%-15%. Copyrights for author if requested.

WATERFRONT WORLD, Waterfront Center, Ann Breen, Co-Editor; Dick Rigby, Co-Editor, 1536 44th Street NW, Washington, DC 20007, 202-337-0356. 1981. Photos, news items. ''ISSN: 0733-0677'' circ. 1M-1.2M. 6/yr. Pub'd 6 issues 1990; expects 6 issues 1991, 6 issues 1992. sub. price: US: $35 individual, $55 organization; Canada: $45 individual, $65 organization; foreign: $55 individual, $75 organization; per copy: $6; sample: free. Back issues: $36/set. 40pp; 8½x11; of. Copyrighted. Pub's reviews: 20 in 1990. §urban design, architecture, city planning, economic development, real estate, boating. Ads: $250/year for professional card.

WaterMark, Incorporated, Leslie Cummins, Amy Gary, PO Box 1400, Columbiana, AL 35051, 205-879-7914. 1988. ''Additional address: 3250 Independence Drive, Birmingham, AL 35209.'' avg. press run 10M. Expects 6 titles 1991, 10 titles 1992. 6 titles listed in the *Small Press Record of Books in Print* (20th Edition, 1991-92). avg. price, cloth: $10.95; paper: $4.95. Discounts: see distributor, Publisher's Group West. 32pp; 8x9; of. Reporting time: 6 weeks. Payment: royalty percentage, illustrators-% and/or advance or flat fee. Copyrights for author. Publishers Association of the South.

Watermark Press, Harry S. Monesson, Alisa M. Hoffman, 315 Magnolia Rd., Pemberton, NJ 08068. 1988. Poetry, fiction, art, photos, long-poems, non-fiction. ''We are a service company helping self-publishers - editing = production. Books must be ordered from author since we don't do distribution.'' Pub'd 25 titles 1990; expects 30 titles 1991. 1 title listed in the *Small Press Record of Books in Print* (20th Edition, 1991-92). avg. price, cloth: $14.95; paper: $6.95; other: $4.95 saddle stitched. 160pp; 6x9; of. Reporting time: 4 weeks. Payment: none—they pay for publishing. We give ISBN #s, copyright application form—author files it himself.

Waterston Productions, Inc., Ellen Waterston, Carla Wigle, 115 N.W. Oregon Avenue #8, Bend, OR 97701, 503-385-7025; FAX 503-385-7663. 1989. Fiction. ''Children's fiction'' avg. press run 5M. Pub'd 1 title 1990; expects 4 titles 1991, 6 titles 1992. 6 titles listed in the *Small Press Record of Books in Print* (20th Edition, 1991-92). Discounts: wholesale 55%, 90 day net, 1 year return. 32pp; of. Reporting time: 6 weeks. Payment: negotiable. Copyrights for author. PMA, N.W. Pub. Association, N.W. Pub. Consortium, PNWBA.

WATERWAYS: Poetry in the Mainstream, Ten Penny Players, Inc., Bard Press, Barbara Fisher, Co-Editor; Richard Spiegel, Co-Editor, 393 St. Paul's Avenue, Staten Island, NY 10304-2127, 718-442-7429. 1978. Poetry. circ. 100-200. 11/yr. Pub'd 11 issues 1990; expects 11 issues 1991, 11 issues 1992. sub. price: $20; per copy: $2; sample: $2. Back issues: $2. 40pp; 7x4¼; †xerography. Reporting time: 1 month. Payment: copies. Copyrighted, reverts to author.

THE WAVE, Jason Mark Moskowitz, Publisher; Michael E. Napoliello, Editor-in-Chief, 300 1st Avenue, Spring Lake, NJ 07762-1903. 1982. Poetry, fiction, articles, art, photos, cartoons, interviews, satire, criticism, reviews, music, long-poems, concrete art, non-fiction. ''*The Wave* is a tabloid. We will print anything in the art, entertainment, intellectual categories. 99% of our material will only span 1 full page. We print art-repro's, drawings, all literary types. New Jersey writers, authors, and critics have an advantage.'' circ. 50M. 52/yr. Pub'd 26 issues 1990; expects 52 issues 1991, 52 issues 1992. sub. price: $25; per copy: $1; sample: $1 + 8 1/2 X 11 envelope with 3 22¢ stamps. Back issues: none, each issue is $1. 32-48pp; 9¾x16; †of. Reporting time: 3 weeks. Payment: $10-$200, but it is very dependent. Copyrighted. Pub's reviews: 12 in 1990. §Poetry, fiction, articles, art, photos, cartoons, interviews, satire, criticism, reviews, music, longpoems, concrete-art, non-fiction. Ads: $358/$200/$115 quarter page/$70 eighth page (inquire about discounts). CCE (Catalyst Communications Enterprises).

Wayfarer Publications (see also TAI CHI), Marvin Smalheiser, PO Box 26156, Los Angeles, CA 90026. 1981. Articles, interviews, reviews, letters, news items, non-fiction. avg. press run 5.2M. Pub'd 1 title 1990; expects 2 titles 1991, 3 titles 1992. 1 title listed in the *Small Press Record of Books in Print* (20th Edition, 1991-92). of. COSMEP.

Wayfinder Press, Jack W. Swanson, PO Box 217, Ridgway, CO 81432, 303-626-5452. 1980. Non-fiction. ''We specialize in history and guide books about the Southwest.'' avg. press run 3M. Pub'd 2 titles 1990; expects 2 titles 1991, 2 titles 1992. 8 titles listed in the *Small Press Record of Books in Print* (20th Edition, 1991-92). avg. price, paper: $11.50. Discounts: bookstores 40%, jobbers 50%. 272pp; 5½x8½; of. Reporting time: 10 days. Payment: quarterly. Copyrights for author. RMBPA (Rocky Mountain Book Publishers Association, 2928 Pearl Street, Boulder, CO 80301).

Wayland Press, Gary Schroeder, Joseph Hutchison, 675 South Sherman, Denver, CO 80209. 1985. Poetry, fiction. ''*Winegold*, short stories by Joe Nigg; *The Undersides Of Leaves*, poems by Joseph Hutchison;

618

Mistaken Lights, poems by Gary Schroeder; *Blessing*, poems by William Zaranka; *In A Wind We Cannot Hear*, poems by Michael Walton; *Redbud*, poems by Jilla Youngblood Smith; *The Year of Common Things*, poems by Kathleen Norris; *Handsigns for Rain*, poems by E.G. Burrows." avg. press run 500. Pub'd 1 title 1990; expects 2 titles 1991, 2 titles 1992. 10 titles listed in the *Small Press Record of Books in Print* (20th Edition, 1991-92). avg. price, cloth: $15; paper: $7. Discounts: 1-4 copies 15%; 5 or more 40%. 56pp; 5½×8½; of. Reporting time: 90 days. Payment: negotiable. Copyrights for author.

WCCF REPORTS, Robert A. Karch, PO Box 81101, Seattle, WA 98108-1462. 1986. Articles, photos, cartoons, interviews, satire, reviews, letters, news items, non-fiction. "Related to the art, skill and sport of correspondence chess; i.e., playing chess by mail" circ. 1.2M. 6/yr. Expects 4 issues 1991, 6 issues 1992. sub. price: $18; per copy: $3; sample: $2. Back issues: $2 each. 32pp; 8½×11; of. Reporting time: 4 weeks. Payment: yes, upon approval or if solicited, unsolicited at own risk. Copyrighted, reverts to author. Pub's reviews. Ads: $150/$80/$45 1/4 page/$24 1/8. WCCF.

WE ARE THE WEIRD, Mindy Irvin, Managing Editor; Mary Koon, Assistant Editor, PO Box 2002, Dallas, TX 75221, 214-692-8601. 1985. Poetry, fiction, art, photos, cartoons, satire, criticism, reviews, music, letters, news items, non-fiction. "Anything that makes us laugh will get our attention. We are most open to poems or short essays (500 words or less). They should be humorous or deal with popular culture, especially the fields of movies, music, and stand-up comedy." circ. 2.7M. 52/yr. Pub'd 22 issues 1990; expects 52 issues 1991, 52 issues 1992. sub. price: $35 or $19.95 for 24 weeks; per copy: $1.50; sample: 1 free. Back issues: $2. 8pp; 8½×11. Reporting time: 1 month. Payment: $25 maximum upon publication. Copyrighted, does not revert to author. Pub's reviews: 20 in 1990. §Popular culture—movies, music, stand-up comedy. Ads: $50 per inch (goes down with # of weeks).

WE MAGAZINE, We Press, Christopher Funkhouser, PO Box 1503, Santa Cruz, CA 95061, 408-427-9711. 1986. Poetry, fiction, art, photos, cartoons, criticism, music, letters. "We accept relevant contemporary writing and artwork. No long fiction. All art should be accompanied by a SASE. Recent contributors: Tuli Kupferberg, Allen Ginsberg, Eric Curkendall, Andy Clausen, Tory Miller, Dashka Slater, Ivan Arguelles, H.D. Moe, plus many others." circ. 500-1M. 4/yr. Pub'd 3 issues 1990; expects 3 issues 1991, 2 issues 1992. sub. price: $15; per copy: $5; sample: $5. Back issues: issues 1-9 $2. Discounts: will trade with other high quality publications. 28-50pp; 8½×11; †mi, of. Reporting time: 1-4 months. Payment: not as of yet, though cover artists have been paid. Copyrighted, reverts to author. No ads.

We Press (see also WE MAGAZINE), Christopher Funkhouser, Stephen Cope, PO Box 1503, Santa Cruz, CA 95061, 408-427-9711. 1986. Poetry, fiction, art, photos, cartoons, criticism, music, letters. "No long fiction (i.e. should be less than 5 pages); all material should be culturally/artistically relevant; all art should be accompanied with SASE (preferably with a cover note).Our most recent publication, *We Magazine Issue 14*, an audiomagazine, was released on compact disc April 1991." avg. press run 1M. Expects 4 titles 1991, 4 titles 1992. avg. price, paper: $5. 6-60pp; size varies; †mi, of. Reporting time: 1-4 months. Copyrights for author.

Weatherford Publications, Thomas Wilkinson, Editor and General Manager, 6447 Loma de Cristo Drive, El Paso, TX 79918-7314. 1988. 2 titles listed in the *Small Press Record of Books in Print* (20th Edition, 1991-92). avg. price, paper: $6.95.

WEBBER'S, Richard Cook, Peter Gebhardt, Peter Stewart, Ian Britain, 15 McKillop Street, Melbourne, Victoria 3000, Australia. 1989. Poetry, fiction, articles, criticism, reviews, non-fiction. circ. 1M. 2/yr. Pub'd 1 issue 1990; expects 2 issues 1991, 2 issues 1992. sub. price: $15; per copy: $7.50; sample: $7.50. Back issues: $8.50. Discounts: 40%. 100pp; 4×8. Reporting time: 1-2 months. Copyrighted, reverts to author. Pub's reviews: 5 in 1990. §history, biography, fiction. Ads: A$100/A$50. 407/12/15/73/46/700/814.

WEBSTER REVIEW, Nancy Schapiro, 470 East Lockwood, Webster University, Webster Groves, MO 63119, 314-432-2657. 1974. Poetry, fiction, articles, interviews, parts-of-novels, long-poems. "*Webster Review* publishes contemporary American and international literature. We are interested in fiction of any length, poetry, interviews, essays, and English translations of contemporary writing from all countries. Recent contributors have included: Gordon Lish, Carolyn Kizer, Yannis Ritsos, Charles Edward Eaton, Roald Hoffman." circ. 1.2M. 1/yr. Pub'd 2 issues 1990. sub. price: $5; per copy: $5; sample: free. Back issues: $2. Discounts: 25%. 128pp; 5½×8½; of. Reporting time: 1 month. Payment: 2 free copies. Copyrighted. CLMP.

Weems Concepts (see also THE BOTTOM LINE PUBLICATIONS; FELICITY; OMNIFIC; MY LEGACY), Kay Weems, Star Route, Box 21AA, Artemas, PA 17211, 814-458-3102. †Sharp copier.

Weidner & Sons, Publishing (see also LINGUISTIC REVIEW; JOURNAL OF AFRICAN LANGUAGES AND LINGUISTICS; JOURNAL OF ITALIAN LINGUISTICS; TROPICAL AND GEOTROPICAL MEDICINE), James H. Weidner, Box 2178, Riverton, NJ 08077, 609-486-1755. 1980. Poetry, fiction, parts-of-novels, non-fiction. "Weidner Associates and its publishing divisions (Foris Publications USA, Tycooly Publishing USA, and Weidner Publishing) is also the official distributor for publications of books in ornithology and conchology for the Delaware Museum of Natural History. Books published in the USA under the Bird-Sci Books imprint carry the ISBN 0-938198. Bird-Sci Books publishes in the arts and sciences; Foris in Europe publishes mostly books in linguistics. One of our best-selling authors is Noam Chomsky. Foris Publications USA and Tycooly Publishing USA a wholly owned subsidiary of Weidner Associates, Inc. (see *Literary Market Place*)." avg. press run 1M-5M. Pub'd 20 titles 1990; expects 30 titles 1991. 6 titles listed in the *Small Press Record of Books in Print* (20th Edition, 1991-92). avg. price, cloth: $40 U.S.; paper: $20 U.S. Discounts: 20%. Pages vary considerably; †of. Reporting time: 1-2 months. Payment: negotiable. Copyrights negotiable. COSMEP, AMWA, SSP.

WEIRDBOOK, W. Paul Ganley: Publisher, W. Paul Ganley, Box 149, Amherst Branch, Buffalo, NY 14226, 716-839-2415. 1968. Poetry, fiction, art. *"Weirdbook* is a modern "pulp magazine" similar to the old magazine *Weird Tales,* featuring fiction, art and verse" circ. 1,050. 1-2/yr. Expects 2 issues 1991, 2 issues 1992. sub. price: $25 for 7 issues; per copy: $6 + $1 postage; sample: $6. Back issues: send 25¢ stamp for catalog. Discounts: 40% or better depending on quantity. 64pp; 8½×11; of. Reporting time: up to 3 months. Payment: $10/page for art; fiction 1/2¢-1¢ per word; none for poetry. Copyrighted, reverts to author. No ads.

Samuel Weiser, Inc., B. Lunsted, PO Box 612, York Beach, ME 03910, 207-363-4393. 1955. Non-fiction. "Recent publications: *Inner Journeys* by Jay Earley; *Pranic Healing* by Choa Kok Sui; *Sefer Yetzirah* by Rabbi Aryeh Kaplan; *You Forever* by T. Lobsang Rampa; *Idiots in Paris* by Elizabeth Bennett; *Buddhist Reflections* by Lama Anagarika Govinda; *Astrology for Lovers* by Liz Greene; *What You Need is What You've Got* by Larry and Valere Althouse." avg. press run 4M. Pub'd 22 titles 1990; expects 19 titles 1991, 20 titles 1992. 102 titles listed in the *Small Press Record of Books in Print* (20th Edition, 1991-92). avg. price, cloth: $22.95; paper: $10.95. Normal trade discounts prevail. 240pp; 5⅜×8¼; of. Reporting time: 10-12 weeks. Payment: twice a year. Copyrights for author. B OF B/ABA.

Wellberry Press (see also REACHING OUT), Donald Caswell, 2022 E. Forest, Tallahassee, FL 32303, 904-386-5508. 1987. Poetry, non-fiction. "Queries only; unsolicited mss are unwelcome. Send outline. I am only interested in books on child welfare issues, health and diet, motivation, and literary reference. Author must know subject *and* market, have credentials, and be willing to rewrite if asked to. Poetry books published on author-subsidy basis only. Nonfiction books open to negotiation for advance, royalties, etc." avg. press run 500-1M. Pub'd 1 title 1990; expects 1 title 1991, 1 title 1992. avg. price, paper: $9.95. Discounts: 40% to bookstores, 20% to nonprofit groups. 100pp; 5×8; of. Reporting time: 1-3 months. Payment: by arrangement, none for poetry. Copyrights for author.

Wellcome Institute for the History of Medicine (see also MEDICAL HISTORY), 183 Euston Road, London NW1 2BN, England. 8 titles listed in the *Small Press Record of Books in Print* (20th Edition, 1991-92).

Wells & West, Publishers, R.E. Wells, Victor C. West, 1166 Winsor, North Bend, OR 97459, 503-756-6802. "Not accepting any at this time. For further information contact: Frank Walsh, Publishers Rep, 5770 Franson Court, Northbend, OR 97459. Ph. 503-756-5757" avg. press run 2M. Pub'd 1 title 1990. avg. price, paper: $5.95. Discounts: standard dealer's. 77pp; 5½×7½; of. Copyrights for author.

WELSH HISTORY REVIEW, University Of Wales Press, Kenneth O. Morgan, Ralph A. Griffiths, 6 Gwenuyth Street, Cathays, Cardiff CF2 4YD, Wales, Cardiff 231919. 1960. Articles. "Articles in English on various aspects of Welsh history." circ. 500. 2/yr. Pub'd 2 issues 1990; expects 2 issues 1991, 2 issues 1992. sub. price: £8; per copy: £4; sample: £4. Back issues: £4. Discounts: 10%. 120pp; size A5; of. Payment: none. Copyrighted, does not revert to author. Pub's reviews: 20 in 1990. §History, esp. Welsh history. Ads: £75/£37.50.

Wesley Press, Michael C. White, Editor; Alan Davis, Assistant Editor, English Department, Springfield College, Springfield, MA 01109. 1986. Fiction. "10,000 word short stories (no bias—serious fiction); previously unpublished only; send SASE for notification of acceptance/rejections; manuscripts *not* returned. Send manuscripts *only* after seeing our call for submissions (usually Sept.-Dec.) in *Poets & Writers* and AWP newsletters. American Fiction 87 had Ann Beattie as judge. AF 88 had Raymond Carver. Send $7.50 reading fee per story" avg. press run 2.5M. Pub'd 1 title 1990; expects 1 title 1991, 1 title 1992. 1 title listed in the *Small Press Record of Books in Print* (20th Edition, 1991-92). avg. price, cloth: $9.95; paper: $5.95. Discounts: 40% off for orders of 10 or more. 220pp; 5¾×8¼; lp. Reporting time: 2-3 months. Payment: $1,000, $500, $250, prizes, publication, and 2 free copies. Does not copyright for author.

Wesley Press (see also THE WESLEYAN ADVOCATE), Box 50434, Indianapolis, IN 46250-0434. 3 titles listed in the *Small Press Record of Books in Print* (20th Edition, 1991-92).

THE WESLEYAN ADVOCATE, Wesley Press, Wayne E. Caldwell, Box 50434, Indianapolis, IN 46250-0434, 317-576-1313. 1842. Articles, art, photos, cartoons, interviews, reviews, music, letters, news items, non-fiction. circ. 20M. 12/yr. Pub'd 18 issues 1990; expects 12 issues 1991, 12 issues 1992. sub. price: $12.50 US only; per copy: $2; sample: $2. Back issues: $2. Discounts: none. 36pp; 8½×11; †of. Reporting time:

1 week. Payment: general 2-3¢ per word, more for experienced writers. Copyrighted, reverts to author. Pub's reviews: 294 in 1990. §Christian experience, doctrine, Biblical. Ads: $500/$350/display col. inch $40. Evangelical Press Association.

West Anglia Publications, Helynn Hoffa, Editor; Wilama Lusk, Publisher, PO Box 2683, La Jolla, CA 92038, 619-457-1399. 1978. Poetry, fiction, art, photos, satire, long-poems, non-fiction. "We are a publishing company that assumes the cost of the book and pays the author in royalties or books. Baker and Taylor distributes our books. 'We look for excellence. We have recently printed poets John Theobald, Kathleen Iddings, and Gary Morgan. These are award winning poets whose books received excellent reviews.' Query with 5 poems, SASE. Cover letter should include previous publication credits and awards." avg. press run 500. Pub'd 2 titles 1990; expects 3 titles 1991, 3 titles 1992. 2 titles listed in the *Small Press Record of Books in Print* (20th Edition, 1991-92). avg. price, cloth: $18; paper: $9. Discounts: negotiable. 55-60pp; 5×8; †of. Reporting time: 1 month. Payment: negotiable. Copyrights for author.

WEST BRANCH, Karl Patten, Robert Taylor, Bucknell Hall, Bucknell University, Lewisburg, PA 17837, 717-524-1440 or 524-1554. 1977. Poetry, fiction, reviews. "*West Branch* continues to seek the best work being written today, both poetry and fiction. We believe that the most effective poems and stories make their way on terms established in the work itself; therefore we strive to read without prejudice all the prose and poetry sent to *West Branch*, trying to keep our own ideologies separate from our judgments of what constitutes 'the best work being written today.' Contributors to past issues include David Citino, Betsy Sholl, Harry Humes, Sally Jo Sorensen, Gary Fincke, Martha Collins, Victor Depta, Brigit Pegeen Kelly, Ken Poyner, Deborah Burnham, Julia Kasdorf, D. Nurkse, Anneliese Wagner, Barbara Crooker, Len Roberts, Layle Silbert, William F. Van Wert, Paul Shuttleworth, Molly Best Tinsley, Melissa Pritchard, Colette Inez, Timothy Russell, Earl Keener, William Kloefkorn, Emily Otis, David Ray, Doris Panoff, David Brooks, Jane Coleman, Steven Allaback, and others." circ. 500. 2/yr. Pub'd 2 issues 1990; expects 2 issues 1991, 2 issues 1992. sub. price: $7; per copy: $4; sample: $3. Discounts: 20-40% to bookstores. 96-118pp; 5½×8½; of. Reporting time: 4-6 weeks. Payment: 2 copies and a year's subscription. Copyrighted, reverts to author. Pub's reviews: 6 in 1990. §Small press fiction & poetry, primarily by writers who publish in West Branch. CLMP.

WEST COAST LINE: A Journal of Contemporary Writing and its Modernist Sources, Roy Miki, c/o English Department, Simon Fraser University, Burnaby, B.C. V5A 1S6, Canada. 1983. Articles, interviews, criticism, reviews. "Criticism, bibliography, reviews, and interviews concerned with contemporary Canadian and American writing; bpNichol on Gertrude Stein; Robin Blaser on Charles Olson; excerpts from Lewis Ellingham's in-progress biography of Jack Spicer; work by James Laughlin, Michael McClure, Robert Duncan, George Bowering, Robert Kroetsch, Steve McCaffery, Charles Bernstein, Lyn Hejinian, Bob Perelman." circ. 450. 3/yr. Pub'd 3 issues 1990; expects 3 issues 1991, 3 issues 1992. sub. price: $18 individuals, $24 institutions; per copy: $8; sample: $8. Back issues: $8. Discounts: $6 agents & jobbers. 130pp; 6×9; of. Reporting time: 2 months. Payment: 2 contributor's copies & modest royalty fee. Copyrighted, reverts to author. Pub's reviews: 3 in 1990. §Postmodern poetry, prose, criticism. Canadian Periodical Publisher's Association.

WEST END MAGAZINE, Gail Darrow Kaliss, PO Box 22433, Honolulu, HI 96822-0433. 1971. Poetry, fiction, photos, interviews. "We try to publish work of high literary quality which also serves to promote positive social and personal change" 1/yr. Expects 1 issue 1991, 1 issue 1992. sub. price: $10/4 issues; per copy: $3; sample: $2 (back issue). Back issues: $2 each issue in print, vol 3 no 1 thru vol 4 no 4. 48pp; 7×8½; of. Reporting time: 10 days to 6 months. Payment: in copies. Copyrighted, reverts to author.

West End Press, PO Box 27334, Albuquerque, NM 87125. 1976. Poetry, fiction, art, photos. "Politically progressive material favored." avg. press run 1.7M-3M. Pub'd 6 titles 1990; expects 6 titles 1991, 6 titles 1992. 29 titles listed in the *Small Press Record of Books in Print* (20th Edition, 1991-92). avg. price, paper: $8.95-$12.95. Discounts: 40% to stores; after 10 copies, 50%. 20% to faculty. 48-200pp; 5½×8½; of. Reporting time: up to 3 months. Payment: in copies, at least 10% of run. Copyrights for author.

WEST HILLS REVIEW: A WALT WHITMAN JOURNAL, William A. Fahey, Walt Whitman Birthplace Assn., 246 Old Walt Whitman Road, Huntington Station, NY 11746, (516) 427-5240. 1979. Poetry, articles, art, photos, criticism, collages, non-fiction. "No *West Hills Review* for 1990 (none printed in 1989). *West Hills Review: A Walt Whitman Journal* is conceived as a living memorial to America's great poet and devoted both to Whitman scholarship and to the contemporary poets whom he has inspired and touched. *The Review* emanates from his birthplace, West Hills Long Island, and publishes Whitman criticism, poems and prose pieces about Whitman, as well as what is best in contemporary American poetry. Some recent contributors: Gay Wilson Allen, Edwin H. Miller, Harold Blodgett, Roger Asselineau, William Stafford, David Ignatow, William Heyen, Robert Bly, Allen Ginsberg, Lawrence Ferlinghetti, Al Poulin Jr., Milton Kessler, John Logan, Richard Eberhart, Nobert Krapf, Raymond Roseliep, Norman Rosten." circ. 1M. 1/yr. Pub'd 1 issue 1990; expects 1 issue 1991, 1 issue 1992. sub. price: $6 + $1 handling; per copy: $6 + $1 handling; sample: $6 + $1 handling. Back issues: $2 + $1 handling. 128pp; 6×9; lp. Reporting time: 3 months. Payment: none. Copyrighted, reverts to author. §Whitman scholarship, contemporary poetry. No ads.

West of Boston, Norman Andrew Kirk, Editor, PO Box 2, Cochituate Station, Wayland, MA 01778. 1983. Poetry, art, photos, reviews, long-poems. "We believe in the power of poetry and in powerful poetry as well as literary works of international merit. 'Only the Best.'" avg. press run 1M. Pub'd 1 title 1990; expects 4 titles 1991, 4 titles 1992. 1 title listed in the *Small Press Record of Books in Print* (20th Edition, 1991-92). avg. price, cloth: varies. of. Reporting time: 1-2 months, SASE required. Payment: copies. Copyrights for author.

WESTART, Martha Garcia, PO Box 6868, Auburn, CA 95604, 916-885-0969. 1962. Articles, art, photos, interviews, criticism, reviews, letters. circ. 5M. 24/yr. Pub'd 24 issues 1990; expects 24 issues 1991. sub. price: $15; per copy: 75¢; sample: free. Back issues: available thru xerox University Microfilms. Discounts: on request. 16pp; 10×15; web, of. Reporting time: 2 weeks. Payment: 50¢ per column inch. Copyrighted, reverts to author. Pub's reviews: 10 in 1990. §Arts, art techniques, crafts, craft techniques. Ads: $420/$210/25¢ per word.

Westburg Associates, Publishers, John E. Westburg, General Editor; Mildred Westburg, General Editor; Martial R. Westburg, Art Consultant, 1735 Madison Street, Fennimore, WI 53809, 608-822-6237. 1964. Poetry, fiction, articles, art, criticism, reviews, collages, non-fiction. "Not open for discussion on use of any kind of material in liberal arts or humanities until 1992." avg. press run less than 1M. Pub'd 4 titles 1990; expects 2 titles 1991. 41 titles listed in the *Small Press Record of Books in Print* (20th Edition, 1991-92). avg. price, paper: $16.50. Discounts: special rates to jobbers, wholesalers, retailers. 180-240pp; 8½×11, 8½×5½, 9×6; of. Reporting time: not accepting new submissions until 1992. Payment: varies, but negotiable, generally no payment made except in copies. If author contributes 50% of printing and publishing costs, the author receives 200 copies of the published work for sale to his own list of readers and audiences (particularly in the case of poetry and drama). Copyrights for author.

Westchester House, Erin Wence, Editor, 218 South 95 Street, Omaha, NE 68114. 1986. Non-fiction. avg. press run 2M. Expects 2 titles 1991. 1 title listed in the *Small Press Record of Books in Print* (20th Edition, 1991-92). avg. price, cloth: $15. Discounts: 40% 5 or more. 320pp; 7×9½; of.

WESTERN AMERICAN LITERATURE, Thomas J. Lyon, English Dept., Utah State Univ., Logan, UT 84322-3200. 1966. Articles, interviews, criticism, reviews. "Send books for review to Dana Brunvand, Assistant Editor." circ. 900. 4/yr. Pub'd 4 issues 1990; expects 4 issues 1991, 4 issues 1992. sub. price: $15 individuals, $30 institutions, $23 for individuals who want to be members of the Western Literature Association; per copy: $5 individuals, $6 institutions; sample: $3. Back issues: $5. Discounts: 20% agency. 96pp; 6×9; of. Reporting time: 2 months. Payment: 1-3 copies, tear sheets (for articles); tear sheets only for reviewers. Copyrighted, does not revert to author. Pub's reviews: 100-120 in 1990. §Books by Western authors, about Western authors or Western literature. Ads: $75/$40. Western Literature Association.

WESTERN & EASTERN TREASURES, People's Publishing Co., Inc., Rosemary Anderson, 5440 Ericson Way, PO Box 1095, Arcata, CA 95521, 707-822-8442. 1965. Articles, photos. "How-to articles about metal detecting, gold prospecting, collecting coins, jewelry, artifacts, bottles. Usual length: 1,500 words." circ. 50M. 12/yr. Pub'd 12 issues 1990; expects 12 issues 1991, 12 issues 1992. sub. price: $16.95; per copy: $2.95; sample: $3. Back issues: 1-12 $3 ea., 13-23 $2.50, 24+ $2.25. Discounts: 25% agency. 80pp; 8×10; of. Reporting time: 2 months. Payment: 3¢/word + photos. Copyrighted, does not revert to author. Pub's reviews: 36 in 1990. §Treasure hunting, prospecting, ghost towns, travel. Ads: $750/$405.

WESTERN HUMANITIES REVIEW, Barry Weller, Editor; Larry Levis, Fiction Editor; Richard Howard, Poetry Editor; Pamela Houston, Managing Editor, University of Utah, Salt Lake City, UT 84112, 801-581-6070. 1947. Poetry, fiction, articles, art, interviews, satire, criticism, reviews, music, letters, parts-of-novels, long-poems, plays, concrete art, non-fiction. "We prefer 2-3M words; We print articles in the humanities, fiction, poetry, and film and book reviews. Recent contributors: Francine Prose, Charles Simic, Charles Wright, Carol Muske, David St. John, Thomas Lux, Joseph Brodsky, Sandra McPherson, John Hollander." circ. 1.5M. 4/yr. Pub'd 4 issues 1990; expects 4 issues 1991. sub. price: $24 (institutions) $18 (individuals); per copy: $5; sample: $5. Back issues: $5 for issues pub'd in 70s and 80s; $6 for earlier issues. Discounts: 25% to agents. 96pp; 6×9; photoset. Reporting time: 1-3 months. Payment: $150 for stories and articles; $50 for poems; $50 for reviews. Copyrighted, rights revert on request. Pub's reviews: 8 in 1990. §All but novels (we don't review them), poetry, scholarly works in any area of the humanities. We don't use ads.

WESTERN PUBLISHER, Paula von Loewenfeldt, Editor, PO Box 470361, San Francisco, CA 94123-1012. 1980. "Mini-reviews of forthcoming books, features and articles on publishing trades. Also covering magazines, newspapers, and trade journals" circ. 5M. 5-6/yr. Pub'd 4 issues 1990; expects 6 issues 1991, 10 issues 1992. sub. price: $20/yr, $35/2 years; per copy: $2; sample: same. Back issues: inquire. 16pp; 10×13¼; of. Reporting time: 1 month. Payment: negotiable. Copyrighted, does not revert to author. Pub's reviews: 120 in 1990. §All categories. Ads: $600/$300/$150 1/4 page/$1 word-10 word min.

Western Tanager Press, Hal Morris, Publisher, 1111 Pacific Avenue, Santa Cruz, CA 95060. 1979.

Non-fiction. "Western Tanager publishes hardcover and trade paperback originals and reprints. (Average about 4 titles a year; we receive 75 ms submissions annually.) We publish regional history (*California* and The West) and biographies. We also publish bicycling and hiking guides. 25% of books from first-time authors; 100% from unagented writers. *Query* the publisher before submitting manuscripts." avg. press run 5M. Pub'd 3 titles 1990; expects 3 titles 1991, 4 titles 1992. 25 titles listed in the *Small Press Record of Books in Print* (20th Edition, 1991-92). Discounts: 5 books 40%, 10-49 42%, 50-99 43%, 100 44%, 250 45%, 500 46%. Reporting time: 1-2 months; we publish on an average 6-8 months after acceptance. Payment: 10%. Copyrights for author. NCBA, PMA, California Hist. Society.

Westgate Press, Lorraine Chandler, Editor, 5219 Magazine Street, New Orleans, LA 70115-1858. 1979. Art, photos, collages, non-fiction. "Metaphysical material, occult science and philosophy, esoteric mss. in related areas. Presently we are publishing *The Book Of Azrael* by Leilah Wendell, 'an intimate and first person encounter with the True Personification of Death! This dark and melancholy Angel is revealed through the writings of His Earthbound 'Bride' as well as direct communications with the Angel of Death Himself! Never before and never again will a book of this nature be offered. *This is not fiction*. But rather an account of the journey of an ancient spirit from the beginning of time to the present and beyond!...A Divine Dance Macabre!' That should give you an idea of what we are interested in. We request that *only queries* be sent at this time with appropriate SASE." avg. press run 500-5M. Pub'd 3 titles 1990; expects 3 titles 1991, 4 titles 1992. 2 titles listed in the *Small Press Record of Books in Print* (20th Edition, 1991-92). avg. price, paper: $6.50 to $12.95; other: series folios @ $5 each. Discounts: 1-5 books 20%, 6-25 40%, 26-50 43%, 51-100 46%, 100+ 50%, discount applies to booksellers and others. 200+pp; 5×8; of. Reporting time: 1 month on ms., 2 weeks on query. Payment: negotiable on a project to project basis; no advance at present. Copyrights for author. AG/ALA, P&W Inc., NWC, PMA, NAPRA, ABE.

THE WESTMINSTER REVIEW, David Swerdlow, Managing Editor, Department of English, Westminster College, New Wilmington, PA 16172. 1983. Poetry, fiction, articles, art, photos, non-fiction. "*The Westminster Review* welcomes poetry and fiction. We are interested in all forms of work, but tend not to publish rhymed poetry. Manuscripts are read between September and May. SASE required." circ. 300. 2/yr. Pub'd 2 issues 1990; expects 2 issues 1991, 2 issues 1992. sub. price: $8; per copy: $5. Discounts: library & academic 20%, p/h added; retail 40%, p/h added; wholesale 1-5 copies 4%, 60% 50%, p/h added. 72pp; 9×6; of. Reporting time: 12 weeks. Payment: 2 copies. Copyrighted, reverts to author. Pub's reviews. §Poetry. Ads: $100/$60/not taken.

The Westphalia Press, Bill Nunn, 3749 Schott Road, Jefferson City, MO 65101-9028. 1984. Non-fiction. "Complete manuscript - 200-400 pages. We want to establish *The Westphalia Press* as the publisher of factually solid entertainingly written books of importance and value which otherwise might not be published. We want material which, while it may be 'provincial' in the sense that its locale is, say, Missouri, its appeal is universal. For those who might be familiar with it, we want to make *The Westphalia Press* a book-ish extension of *MISSOURI LIFE MAGAZINE* as it began when I founded it in 1973" avg. press run 2M-5M. Pub'd 2 titles 1990; expects 3 titles 1991, 4 titles 1992. 3 titles listed in the *Small Press Record of Books in Print* (20th Edition, 1991-92). avg. price, cloth: $20; paper: $9.95. Discounts: 40%. 128-192pp; 5½×7; of. Reporting time: 3 weeks. Payment: by arrangement. Copyrights for author. National Association of Independent Publishers.

Westport Publishers, Inc., Terry Faulkner, 4050 Pennsylvania, Suite 310, Kansas City, MO 64111, 816-756-1490. 1984. "Books published are trade paperbacks, with some hardcover books. Books have either a strong regional interest or are national in scope. Recent contributors include Dr. Edward Christophersen, J. Barrish, Dr. Harriet Barrish" avg. press run 3M. Pub'd 5 titles 1990; expects 12 titles 1991, 12 titles 1992. 11 titles listed in the *Small Press Record of Books in Print* (20th Edition, 1991-92). avg. price, cloth: $19.95; paper: $11.95. Discounts: 1 20%, 2-4 30%, 5-11 40%, 12-49 43%, 50-99 44%, 100+ 45%. 200pp; 6×9, 8½×11. Reporting time: 3-4 weeks. Payment: negotiable. Sometimes copyrights for author.

Westwind Press, A.S. Parrish, Director, Route 1, Box 208, Farmington, WV 26571. 1974. Fiction, art, non-fiction. "*An Edge of the Forest* (reissue), *The Bluegreen Tree* (first edition), (Speaking as a Writer (first edition). Very small staff, cannot consider unsolicited mss" Pub'd 1 title 1990; expects 1 title 1991. 3 titles listed in the *Small Press Record of Books in Print* (20th Edition, 1991-92). avg. price, cloth: $9; paper: $5. Discounts: libraries: 2-5, 10%; 6 and up, 25%; bookstores & jobbers: 1-4, 25%; 5 & up, 40%. 76-202pp; 6×9; of. Does not copyright for author. COSMEP.

WESTWORDS, David Woolley, 15 Trelawney Road, Peverell, Plymouth, Devonshire PL3 4JS, England, 262877. 1986. Poetry, fiction, art, photos, reviews, parts-of-novels. "Poems, pref. not more than 40 lines. Stories not more than 2,500 words. Photos pref. epec. b&w" circ. 400-500. 3/yr. Pub'd 3 issues 1990; expects 3 issues 1991, 3 issues 1992. sub. price: £6 (+ add'l p&p for USA); per copy: £1.75 (+ add'l p/h for US); sample: £1 (+ additional postage for USA, etc). Back issues: 1-8 for £8 + add'l p/h. 52pp; 6×8, A5; of, with colour cover. Reporting time: 2-3 months. Payment: free copy and extra copy or small fee. Copyrighted, reverts to author. Pub's reviews: 2-4 per issue in 1990. §Poetry, short stories, arts. Ads: £15/£8/£20 inside back cover/£25 back cover.

Wet Editions, Patti Chambers, Director, Box 2045, Times Square Station, New York, NY 10036. 1987. avg. press run 2M. Expects 1 title 1991, 2 titles 1992. 1 title listed in the *Small Press Record of Books in Print* (20th Edition, 1991-92). avg. price, paper: $6. 150pp; 7×8½; of. Payment: yes. Copyrights for author.

WEYFARERS, Guildford Poets Press, Jeffery Wheatley, Margaret Pain, Susan James, Martin Jones, 9 White Rose Lane, Woking, Surrey GU22 7JA, England. 1972. Poetry. "All kinds of poetry: free verse and rhymed/metred, serious and humorous; mostly 'mainstream modern.'" circ. 300. 3/yr. Pub'd 3 issues 1990; expects 3 issues 1991, 3 issues 1992. sub. price: £4, overseas £5 sterling or equivalent; per copy: £1.40 (overseas, £1.75 sterling or equivalent); sample: £1.40 (overseas, £1.75 sterling or equiv.). Back issues: £1 (overseas, £1.50 sterling or equiv.). 32pp; 8×6; of. Reporting time: 3-4 months maximum. Payment: free copy of issue sent. Copyrighted, reverts to author. Pub's reviews: approx. 53 brief reviews (inc mags) in 1990. §Poetry only. No ads.

Whalesback Books, W.D. Howells, Box 9546, Washington, DC 20016, 202-333-2182. 1988. Art, photos, non-fiction. "High quality photographic and graphic presentations of art, architecture and related subjects." avg. press run 2M-5M. Pub'd 1 title 1990; expects 1-2 titles 1991, 2 titles 1992. 1 title listed in the *Small Press Record of Books in Print* (20th Edition, 1991-92). avg. price, cloth: $45; paper: $28. Discounts: 1-3 20%, 4-10 40%, 11-50 50%, 50+ 60%, no shipping, no returns. 200pp; 9×12; of. Reporting time: acknowledgement immediate, decision 2-4 weeks. Payment: negotiable. Copyrights for author. SSP, PMA, Washington Book Publishers.

Wheat Forders, E.S. Lawrence, Denise de Faymonville, Renee K. Boyle, Box 6317, Washington, DC 20015-0317, 202-362-1588. 1974. Poetry, long-poems, non-fiction. "Interested in book-length analyses of the significance of discoveries in such sciences as quantum physics, evolutionary biology, analytical psychology, brain functions analysis as they relate to the modern metaphysical outlook, Metahistory and interpretations of modern times in light of one or other of its theories is also of interest as is the extension of A. Huxley's interpretations of the parallels in the Great Religions and the discovery of a common Mysticism below them all. Work must be interdisciplinary and show how all these sciences support a single world view. We print a series: Primers for the Age of Inner Space to which anyone having anything to contribute has equal access. We have been approached by the Accademy of Independent Scholars to print/publish certain books. We publish cooperatively with the author required to arrange for the sale of 150 books @ cover price. (for paperbacks this is in the range of $10-$20)." avg. press run 2M. Pub'd 2-4 titles 1990. 5 titles listed in the *Small Press Record of Books in Print* (20th Edition, 1991-92). avg. price, cloth: $15-$20; paper: $10-$15. Discounts: wholesalers 45%; libraries 25%; university classroom 45%; poor student, but interested, free on showing of need. 100-250pp; 5½×8½; of. Reporting time: 6-7 weeks. Payment: cooperative with author purchasing 100-150 copies via his connections. Copyrights for author. SP, AAP, AIS.

WHEAT LIFE, David A. Andersen, 109 East 1st Avenue, Ritzville, WA 99169, 509-659-0610. Articles, interviews, news items. circ. 14M. 11/yr. Pub'd 11 issues 1990; expects 11 issues 1991, 11 issues 1992. sub. price: $12. 22pp; 8⅜×10¾; web. Reporting time: 3 months. Copyrighted, reverts to author. Ads: $900/$540. AAEA, SMPG, WPA.

Wheel of Fire Press (see also CROOKED ROADS), Carl Bettis, Sharon Eiker, PO Box 32631, Kansas City, MO 64111. 1988. Poetry, fiction, articles, satire, long-poems, plays, non-fiction. "Prefer between 3,000 and 50,000 words. Since we don't do this for profit (fortunately), will only publish what really interests us. Politically and spiritually radical; William Blake a hero and guiding light. Recent works by Sharon Eiker, Carl Bettis, poets for Peace and Justice (among others)." avg. press run 500-1.2M. Pub'd 5 titles 1990; expects 7-8 titles 1991, 10-12 titles 1992. avg. price, paper: $5. Discounts: 20% for bulk orders. 70pp; 5½×8½; †laserprint and photocopy. Reporting time: 6-8 weeks. Payment: varies wildly, but we never try to do more for the press than recover costs. Copyrights for author.

Wherry Advertising Agency, PO Box 11081, Jacksonville, FL 32239, 904-398-7782. Non-fiction. avg. press run 5M. Pub'd 3 titles 1990. 1 title listed in the *Small Press Record of Books in Print* (20th Edition, 1991-92). avg. price, paper: $6. Discounts: 40%. 15pp; 8½×11; of.

WHETSTONE, Sandra Berris, Marsha Portnoy, Jean Tolle, Barrington Area Arts Council, PO Box 1266, Barrington, IL 60011, 708-382-5626. 1984. Poetry, fiction, art, photos, parts-of-novels, non-fiction. "Prefer to see 3-5 poems or up to 25 or 30 pages of fiction or non-fiction. Feature one guest artist; include SASE. Especially interested in showcasing Illinois writers but accept others. Recent contributors include: poetry—Martha Vertreace, Robert Klein Engler, Robin Behn, Paulette Roeske, Nance Van Winckel, Jeanne Murray Walker; fiction or non-fiction—Bill Brashler, John Jacob, Berniece Rabe, Bill Roorbach, Rebecca Rule, Barbara Scheiber; art—Gail Collier, Kent Belasco." circ. 500. 1/yr. Pub'd 1 issue 1990; expects 1 issue 1991, 1 issue 1992. sub. price: $5 + $1 p/h; per copy: $5 + $1 p/h; sample: $3 + $1 p/h. Back issues: $3 + $1 p/h. 96pp; 5⅞×9; of. Reporting time: 2-3 months. Payment: 2 copies plus eligible for annual *Whetstone* prize cash awards.

624

Not copyrighted. Coordinating Council of Literary Magazines (CCLM).

WHISKEY ISLAND MAGAZINE, Katherine Murphy, U.C. 7 Cleveland State University, Cleveland, OH 44115, 687-2056. 1978. Poetry, fiction, art, photos. "No simultaneous submissions please. We are most interested in Ohio and midwestern writers and artists for what we see as a regional magazine with a strong midwestern voice, but we are open to others" circ. 2M. 2/yr. Pub'd 2 issues 1990; expects 2 issues 1991, 2 issues 1992. sub. price: $5; per copy: $2.50; sample: $2.50. Back issues: $2. 84pp; 5½x8½; of. Reporting time: 3 months. Payment: 2 contributors copies. Copyrighted, reverts to author.

WHISPERING PALM, Doris Lamb, PO Box 6523, Lake Worth, FL 33466. 1991. Poetry, fiction, articles, art, cartoons, satire, reviews, letters, non-fiction. "Magazine *just* starting. Biases: liberal, optimistic, openminded, community spirited. Dislike very religious and very obscene poetry, etc. Prefer *short* or what lends itself to installments. Serves the South Florida area; takes submissions from everywhere." circ. 1M-2M. 12/yr. Expects 4 issues 1991, 12 issues 1992. sub. price: all issues, except those paid to contributors are given to those temporarily in need of income, to sell—homeless, layed off with family, etc. 30pp; 8½x5½. Reporting time: immediately to 4 months. Payment: copies, to best in issue—a *little* cash. Not copyrighted. Ads: $150 full page/$200 back page.

WHISPERING WIND MAGAZINE, Jack B. Heriard, 8009 Wales Street, New Orleans, LA 70126, 504-241-5866. 1967. Articles, art, photos, cartoons, interviews, reviews, letters, parts-of-novels, news items, non-fiction. "Magazine for those interested in the American Indian; his traditions and crafts, past and present." circ. 8M. 6/yr. Pub'd 6 issues 1990; expects 6 issues 1991, 6 issues 1992. sub. price: $15; per copy: $2.75; sample: $4. Back issues: included in each issue. Discounts: 5-9 $1.65, 10+ $1.37. 42pp; 8½x11; of. Reporting time: 4-8 weeks. Payment: copies. Copyrighted, reverts to author. Pub's reviews: 15 in 1990. §American Indian. Ads: $171/$88/45¢. AMA.

White Cliffs Media Company (see also WORLD MUSIC CONNECTIONS NEWSLETTER), Larry W. Smith, PO Box 561, Crown Point, IN 46307-0561, (219) 322-5537. 1985. Poetry, art, photos, music. "Current emphasis is on innovative publications in world and popular music. Cassettes often included. General trade titles also considered as is marketable poetry. Current title: *The New Folk Music* by Craig Harris." avg. press run varies. Pub'd 6 titles 1990; expects 3 titles 1991, 5 titles 1992. 5 titles listed in the *Small Press Record of Books in Print* (20th Edition, 1991-92). avg. price, cloth: $40; paper: $12.95; other: cassette $9.95. Discounts: follow industry standards. 180pp; 6x9; of. Reporting time: 1-3 months. Payment: varies. Copyrights for author. Mid-American Publisher's Association, Publisher's Marketing Association.

WHITE CLOUDS REVUE, Wind Vein Press, Scott Preston, Cameron Lindsley, PO Box 462, Ketchum, ID 83340, 726-3101. 1987. Poetry, art, music, news items. "It wasn't practical to produce our last publication, *Cloudline*, on even an every-other-year basis. *Cloudline* hasn't folded, but *White Clouds Revue* will be able to fill in the gaps between. We are a *regional* publication! We are not interested in a national 'readership', nor do we want to provide padding to the vitas of writers outside our area of enviropoetic interest. We are interested in work from divergent Western American traditions. Consider Ketchum as the epicenter of an earthquake, with concentric rings emanating from it. The farther away your rings, the less likely we are to publish you. We like *raw poems*" circ. 250. 2 or 3. Pub'd 3 issues 1990; expects 2 issues 1991, 2 issues 1992. sub. price: 4 issues for $12; per copy: $3.50; sample: $3.50. Discounts: write and ask. 32pp; 7x8. Reporting time: if we hate it, immediately; if we even halfway might consider it, at least 1 month. Payment: 2 copies. Copyrighted, reverts to author. Ads: $25/$15/we offer exchanges to selected small presses in our region.

The White Cross Press, Claude W. Horton, Sr., Route 1, Box 592, Granger, TX 76530, 512-859-2814. 1974. Fiction, non-fiction. "Manuscripts by invitation only." avg. press run 500. Expects 1 title 1991, 1-2 titles 1992. 3 titles listed in the *Small Press Record of Books in Print* (20th Edition, 1991-92). avg. price, cloth: $15.95; paper: $7.95. Discounts: bookstores (on consignment) 40%, 2 or more copies, returns permitted. 200pp; 6x9; lp. Payment: varies. Copyrights for author.

The White Ewe Press, Kevin Urick, P.O. Box 1614, Baltimore, MD 21203, 301-837-0794. 1976. Fiction. "I recently returned to school to earn another degree. Until I finish, 1987 or 1988, I will not be able to consider additional manuscripts" avg. press run 1M. Pub'd 3 titles 1990; expects 3 titles 1991. 14 titles listed in the *Small Press Record of Books in Print* (20th Edition, 1991-92). avg. price, cloth: $9.95; paper: $3.00. Trade policies upon request. 128pp; 5½x8½; of. Copyrights for author.

White Horse Press, W.L. Bushey, 306 South First Street, Cottage Grove, OR 97424, 503-942-0659. 1983. Poetry, fiction, art, interviews, letters, non-fiction. "Books are printed by hand, on hand-printing press, hand-set type. We take our time for fine editions, most things we wish to do, in limited edition, both cloth-paper editions are hand-printed. Emphasis on fine book printing-design-illustrations, binding. Plan reprint of rare works, classical literature" avg. press run 100-1M. Expects 2 titles 1991, 3-5 titles 1992. avg. price, cloth: varies; paper: varies. Discounts: 30-50% write for details. 24-150pp; size varies; †of, lp. Reporting time: 3 months. Payment: standard. Copyrights for author.

White Lilac Press, Susan K. Lundgren, PO Box 2556, Providence, RI 02906, 401-273-6678. 1988. "Plan to reprint books *about* music and musicians for both adults and children. (*Not* interested in publishing music.) Especially interested in Russian music and musicians." avg. press run 3M. Pub'd 1 title 1990; expects 3 titles 1991, 6 titles 1992. 3 titles listed in the *Small Press Record of Books in Print* (20th Edition, 1991-92). avg. price, paper: $9. Discounts: 20% to schools and libraries (2+ copies), 40% to dealers (5+ copies), 55% to jobbers. of. Copyrights for author.

White Mane Publishing Company, Inc., Martin K. Gordon, Executive Editor, 63 West Burd Street, PO Box 152, Shippensburg, PA 17257, 717-532-2237. 1987. Non-fiction. "White Mane specializes in military history (esp. the American Civil War period). Also, regional topics. Our authors are the top historians in their fields." avg. press run 3M-5M. Pub'd 10 titles 1990; expects 12 titles 1991, 15 titles 1992. avg. price, cloth: $24.95; paper: $9.95. Discounts: available on request. 200-300pp; 6×9. Reporting time: 60-90 days with guideline, proposal guidelines available on request. Payment: Twice yearly statements. Copyrights for author. ABA/BPA.

White Oak Press, Robert McGill, PO Box 188, Reeds Spring, MO 65737, 417-272-3507. 1986. "Recent contributors: Mary Hartmann, Jory Sherman, Leanne Potts." avg. press run 1.5M. Pub'd 2 titles 1990; expects 4 titles 1991. avg. price, paper: $8.95. 180pp; 5½×8½. Reporting time: 90 days. Payment: standard, although no advances. Copyrights for author. COSMEP, MAP.

White Pine Press, Dennis Maloney, Editor; David Lampe, Associate Editor; Elaine Maloney, Associate Editor, 76 Center Street, Fredonia, NY 14063, 716-672-5743. 1973. Poetry, fiction, long-poems, non-fiction. "White Pine Press continues to publish a variety of translations, poetry, fiction, and non-fiction. Do not send unsolicited ms without querying first. White Pine Press has published fine works of poetry, fiction, essays, non-fiction, and literature in translation from many languages." avg. press run 1M-2M. Pub'd 10 titles 1990; expects 10 titles 1991, 10 titles 1992. 79 titles listed in the *Small Press Record of Books in Print* (20th Edition, 1991-92). avg. price, cloth: $20; paper: $9-$10. Discounts: 2-4, 20%; 5 & over, 40%. 100-200pp; 5½×8½; of. Reporting time: 2 weeks to 1 month. Payment: copies, honorarium, royalties. Copyrights for author. PMA, CLMP, COSMEP, ILPA.

White Rose Press, John Patterson, 61 Cherokee Drive, Memphis, TN 38111, 525-1836. 1986. Non-fiction. avg. press run 1M. Expects 9 titles 1991, 9 titles 1992. avg. price, paper: $7.95. Discounts: 2-4 books 20%, 5-99 40%, 100+ 50%. 200pp; 6×9, 5×7; †of. Reporting time: 1 month. Payment: standard arrangements. Copyrights for author. PMA.

White Rose Publishing, 978 Amelia Avenue, San Dimas, CA 91773, 714-592-6303. 1990. Non-fiction. "The primary focuses of our books and other products are: 1. Marriage relationship/creative dating, 2. The care of infants and children, 3. The business of commercial radio." avg. press run 5M. Expects 1 title 1991, 5 titles 1992. avg. price, paper: $9.95. Discounts: 1-2 no discount; 3-199 40%; 200-499 50%; 500+ 40-25%. 200pp; 5½×8½; of. Reporting time: 1-2 months. Payment: 10%. Does not copyright for author.

White Urp Press (see also ABBEY), 5360 Fallriver Row Court, Columbia, MD 21044. 5 titles listed in the *Small Press Record of Books in Print* (20th Edition, 1991-92).

WHITE WALLS: A Journal of Language and Art, Susan Snodgrass, Managing Editor, PO Box 8204, Chicago, IL 60680. 1977. Art, photos, collages, concrete art. "We are interested in writings by visual artists, performance documentation and image/text work." circ. 1.4M. 3/yr. Pub'd 2 issues 1990; expects 3 issues 1991, 3 issues 1992. sub. price: $15, overseas $20; per copy: $6. Back issues: selected sets $20. Discounts: trade 40%, jobber 40%, classroom and bulk 20%. 80-88pp; 5½×8½; of. Reporting time: 1 month. Payment: $5/page, plus 5 contributors copies. Copyrighted, does not revert to author. §Writings by artists, concrete writing, essays, performance documentation. Ads: 1X: $180/$100; 3X 1-yr contract: $350/$250.

Whitehorse, Greg Davis, Knowledge Engineer, PO Box 6125, Boise, ID 83707. 1984. Non-fiction. Pub'd 1 title 1990; expects 3 titles 1991. 2 titles listed in the *Small Press Record of Books in Print* (20th Edition, 1991-92). avg. price, cloth: $39.95; paper: $24.95. Discounts: paper 2-4 10%, 5-9 15%, 10+ 20%; cloth 2-4 10%, 5-9 15%, 10+ 20%. 450-500pp; 8½×11; †of. Does not copyright for author.

Whitford Press, Ellen Taylor, Editor, 1469 Morstein Road, Westchester, PA 19380, 215-696-1001. 1972. Non-fiction. "Whitford Press now distributes for the Donning Company." avg. press run 5M. Pub'd 40 titles 1990; expects 40 titles 1991, 40 titles 1992. 4 titles listed in the *Small Press Record of Books in Print* (20th Edition, 1991-92). avg. price, paper: $15.95. Discounts: 1 10%, 2-4 20%, 5-24 40%, 25-49 42%, 50-99 43%, 100-249 44%, 250-499 45%, 500+ 46%. 200pp; 6½×9¼. Reporting time: 2 months or less (usually 1 month). Payment: royalties paid twice yearly. Copyrights for author. ABA, NEBA, COSMEP.

Albert Whitman & Company, Kathy Tucker, 6340 Oakton Street, Morton Grove, IL 60053-2723. 1919. Fiction, non-fiction. avg. press run 7.5M. Pub'd 25 titles 1990; expects 25 titles 1991, 25 titles 1992. avg. price, cloth: $10.75. Discounts: varies depending on type of customer, we should be contacted for specifics. 32pp; 8×9; of. Reporting time: 60 days. Payment: to be negotiated. Copyrights for author.

626

WALT WHITMAN QUARTERLY REVIEW, Ed Folsom, 308 EPB The University of Iowa, Iowa City, IA 52242, 319-335-0454; 335-0438. 1983. Articles, criticism, letters, non-fiction. "The *Walt Whitman Quarterly Review* is a literary quarterly begun in the summer of 1983. *WWQR* features previously unpublished letters and documents written by Whitman, critical essays dealing with Whitman's work and its place in American literature, thorough reviews of Whitman-related books, and an ongoing Whitman bibliography—one of the standard reference sources for Whitman studies. The journal is edited and published at The University of Iowa and the editorial board is made up of some of the most distinguished Whitman scholars including Gay Wilson Allen, Harold Aspiz, Arthur Golden, Jerome Loving, James E. Miller, Jr, Roger Asselineau. We offer an annual award—the Feinberg Award—to be given to the author of the best essay published in *WWQR* during the year. We also offer for sale selected back issues of the *Walt Whitman Review* (1955-1982). Please write for details." circ. 1M. 4/yr. Pub'd 4 issues 1990; expects 4 issues 1991, 4 issues 1992. sub. price: $12 individuals, $15 institutions ($3 postage charge on foreign subs); per copy: $3; sample: $3. Back issues: $3 each. Discounts: 10% to agencies for subscriptions, 40% to bookstores, 25% to classroom. 56pp; 6×9; of. Reporting time: 1-3 months. Payment: contributor copies. Copyrighted, reverts to author. Pub's reviews: 8 in 1990. §Whitman scholarship, 19th and 20th American and World literature that discusses Whitman, poetry collections that reveal Whitman influences. Ads: $100/$50.

Whitmore Publishing Company, Roy Sandstrom, Managing Editor, 35 Cricket Terrace, Ardmore, PA 19003, 215-896-6116. 1961. Non-fiction. "*Whitmore* focuses on books that will provide the reader insight and techniques to manage his or her life more effectively. *Whitmore* book subjects are as follows: community life, education, family planning, career planning, nutrition, philosophy, and self improvement" avg. press run 3M. Expects 3 titles 1991, 4 titles 1992. 8 titles listed in the *Small Press Record of Books in Print* (20th Edition, 1991-92). avg. price, cloth: $15.95; paper: $8.95. Discounts: 20% educational/library, 40% (5 or more copies), 30% (1-4) to bookstores. 128pp; 6×9; †of. Reporting time: 4 weeks. Payment: 10% of retail price. Copyrights for author.

The George Whittell Memorial Press, Jean Kelty, Editor; Kathleen Thomas, Managing Editor; Debra Brink, Production Editor, 3722 South Avenue, Youngstown, OH 44502, 216-783-0645. 1979. Poetry, fiction, art, reviews, non-fiction. "We publish primarily children's books though we are open to manuscripts aimed at a general audience. Manuscripts must be of a high literary quality; we will consider fiction, non-fiction and poetry. However, subject matter is limited to animals, nature study, ecology and the interrelationship and interdependence of all life. See *If You Have A Duck* as a sample of the attitudes which are necessary for publication. Length is open. Payment in copies. All manuscripts should be typed, double spaced, and must be accompanied by a SASE. Report in three months. Though we accept full manuscripts for consideration, queries are advisable." avg. press run 2M. Pub'd 1 title 1990; expects 1 title 1991, 2 titles 1992. avg. price, paper: $5.00-$10.00. Discounts: Straight 50% wholesalers, 40% retailers, 20% libraries and other organizations. 105pp; 8½×11, 6×9; †of/lo. Reporting time: 3 months. Payment: in copies. Copyrights for author. COSMEP.

WHOLE AGAIN RESOURCE GUIDE, SourceNet, Tim Ryan, Patricia J. Case, PO Box 6767, Santa Barbara, CA 93160, 805-494-7123. 1980. "An annotated, international directory of new age and alternative periodicals and resource materials in 38 chapters by specialists. Indexed by publisher, title, editor, subject, and place of publication. We do not accept unsolicited material or advertising. Annual update sheets available for SASE" Irregular. Pub'd 1 issue 1990. price per copy: $24.95 + $2 postage and handling. Back issues: $5. Discounts: 40% on 5 or more copies. 300pp; 8½×11; of.

THE WHOLE CHILE PEPPER, Out West Publishing, Dave DeWitt, PO Box 4278, Albuquerque, NM 87196, 505-889-3745. 1987. Articles, photos, cartoons, reviews, letters, news items. "Street address: 2425-C Monroe NE, Abq, NM 87110. All material must concern the preparation and eating of spicy foods" circ. 40M. 6/yr. Pub'd 4 issues 1990; expects 6 issues 1991, 6 issues 1992. 1 title listed in the *Small Press Record of Books in Print* (20th Edition, 1991-92). sub. price: $15.95; per copy: $2.95; sample: same. Back issues: set of six $15.95. Discounts: trade 40%, distributors 50%. 48pp; 8½×11; of, heat set web/coated stock. Reporting time: 2-4 weeks. Payment: negotiable. Copyrighted, does not revert to author. Pub's reviews: 16 in 1990. §Food and gardening. Ads: $1450/$875/+ $450 for color full page. COSMEP.

WHOLE EARTH REVIEW, Kelly Teevan, Director; Howard Bheingold, Editor, 27 Gate Five Road, Sausalito, CA 94965, 415-332-1716. 1974. Fiction, articles, cartoons, interviews, satire, reviews, letters, non-fiction. "Subscription address: Box 38, Sausalito, CA 94966. Credit card orders: 415-332-1716." circ. 50M. 4/yr. Pub'd 4 issues 1990; expects 4 issues 1991, 4 issues 1992. 2 titles listed in the *Small Press Record of Books in Print* (20th Edition, 1991-92). sub. price: $20; per copy: $6; sample: $7. Back issues: write for information. Discounts: distributors 1-49 copies 40%, 50+ 50%. 144pp; 7¾×10½; of. Reporting time: 3 months. Payment: ranges from $20 for suggestions and letters to $500 for a major article. Copyrighted, reverts to author. Pub's reviews: 300-400 in 1990. §Soft tech., craft, architecture, sports & travel, educational mat'ls, agriculture, small business, music, parenting, environment, politics, economics. Ads: 75¢/word-classified ads only (must be a subscriber). ABA, SMPG (Small Magazine Publishers Group).

WHOLE NOTES, Daedalus Press, Nancy Peters Hastings, PO Box 1374, Las Cruces, NM 88004, 505-382-7446. 1984. Poetry. *"Whole Notes* seeks original work from beginning and established writers. All forms are considered. Recent contributors include Ted Kooser, Carol Oles, Bill Kloefkorn, Roy Scheele, Keith Wilson, Don Welch." circ. 400. 2/yr. Pub'd 2 issues 1990; expects 2 issues 1991, 2 issues 1992. sub. price: $6; per copy: $3; sample: $3. Back issues: $3. Discounts: available upon request. 20-24pp; 5½×8½; of. Reporting time: immediately. Payment: 2 copies. Copyrighted, does not revert to author. Ads: $50/$25. CLMP.

Whole Person Associates Inc., Donald A. Tubesing, Nancy Loving Tubesing, 1702 East Jefferson Street, PO Box 3151, Duluth, MN 55803, 218-728-4077. 1977. avg. press run 5M-10M. 8 titles listed in the *Small Press Record of Books in Print* (20th Edition, 1991-92). avg. price, cloth: $16.95; paper: $12.95; other: $24.95. Discounts: normal trade for some books/professional discounts. Copyrights for author. PMA, Mid Ameno Publisher, ABA, Minn Insependent Publisher.

WICCAN/PAGAN PRESS ALLIANCE TRADE PAPER, Silver RavenWolf, Director; MindWalker, Publications, PO Box 1392, Mechanicsburg, PA 17055. 1989. *"The Trade* publishes articles on publishing, pagan publishing, pagan politics, and community news. No fiction. No poetry. However, the WPPA does offer a syndicated article service to over 122 various newsletters for fiction and poetry. Payment is between press and author, most often in contributing copies. Material must be *good* copy quality, double-spaced, no longer than 2 pages. Art work is also needed." circ. 350. 4/yr. Pub'd 4 issues 1990; expects 4 issues 1991, 4 issues 1992. sub. price: $15; per copy: $4; sample: $3. Back issues: do not carry. Discounts: 40% for bookstores and bulk mailings over 15. 30pp; 8½×11; †of. Reporting time: 1 month. Payment: 1 copy of the issue their work appears in. Copyrighted, reverts to author. Pub's reviews: approx. 30 in 1990. §Occult, new age, philosophy, Native American practices and religions. Ads: $30/$15/$10 1/4 page.

WICKED MYSTIC, Andre Scheluchin, PO Box 3087, Dept 222, Astoria, NY 11103, 718-545-6713. 1990. Poetry, fiction, articles, art, photos, cartoons, interviews, satire, criticism, reviews, music, letters, long-poems. circ. 500. 12/yr. Pub'd 12 issues 1990; expects 12 issues 1991, 12 issues 1992. sub. price: $39.95; per copy: $4; sample: $4. Back issues: $4. Discounts: trade. 60pp; 4¼×5½; †lp. Reporting time: 1-2 weeks. Payment: none. Copyrighted, reverts to author. Ads: $85/$50/$30 1/4 page/$20 business card.

WIDE OPEN MAGAZINE, Clif Simms, Editor; Lynn L. Simms, Co-Editor, Wide Open Press, 116 Lincoln Street, Santa Rosa, CA 95401, 707-545-3821. 1984. Poetry, fiction, articles, satire, letters, non-fiction. "We prefer short poems with punch, maximum 16 lines and we will consider all styles and forms. Previously published works are o.k. Maximum number per submission: five (5). Quarterly poetry contest—$150 in prizes. No entry fees. All poetry will be considered for prizes. Send for prose writer's guidelines" circ. 1M. 4/yr. Pub'd 4 issues 1990; expects 4 issues 1991, 4 issues 1992. sub. price: $24; per copy: $10; sample: $6. Discounts: 40%. 80pp; 8½×11; of, web press. Reporting time: 1-3 months poetry, 4 months prose. Payment: none for poetry, $5-$25 for prose. Copyrighted, reverts to author. Pub's reviews: 6 in 1990. §Self-help, solutions to current problems, about writing. Ads: $150/$85/50¢-min. 15 words.

Wide World Publishing/TETRA, Elvira Monroe, PO Box 476, San Carlos, CA 94070, 415-593-2839. 1976. Articles, photos, non-fiction. "Imprint—Math Products Plus." avg. press run varies. Pub'd 10 titles 1990; expects 8 titles 1991, 8 titles 1992. 28 titles listed in the *Small Press Record of Books in Print* (20th Edition, 1991-92). avg. price, paper: $5.95-$9.95. Discounts: 2-4 books 20%, 5-24 40%, 25-49 42%, 50-99 44%, 100+ 48%. 200pp; size varies; lp. Reporting time: 30 days. Payment: 10%. Copyrights for author. COSMEP, Publishers Marketing Association, American Booksellers Association, Museum Store Association.

THE WIDENER REVIEW, Michael Clark, Fiction Editor; Kenneth Pobo, Poetry Editor; Christopher Nielson, Essay & Reviews Editor, Humanities Division, Widener Univ., Chester, PA 19013, 215-499-4354. 1984. Poetry, fiction, interviews, reviews, parts-of-novels. circ. 250. 1/yr. Pub'd 1 issue 1990; expects 1 issue 1991, 1 issue 1992. sub. price: $4; per copy: $4; sample: $3. Discounts: 40% on 10 copies or more. 80pp; 5½×8½; of. Reporting time: 1-4 months. Payment: 2 copies of the magazine. Copyrighted, reverts to author. Pub's reviews: 1 in 1990. §Contemporary literature. Ads: $40/$25.

Wilchester Publishing Company, Michael J. Stich, 1407 W. Brooklake Court, #200, PO Box 820874, Houston, TX 77282-0874, 713-496-0788. 1988. Non-fiction. "Wilchester Publishing specializes in business subjects centering around real estate. The company is also interested in gardening manuscripts" avg. press run 1.5M. Expects 2 titles 1991, 3 titles 1992. 1 title listed in the *Small Press Record of Books in Print* (20th Edition, 1991-92). avg. price, paper: $19.95. 230pp; 6×9; lp. Reporting time: 120 days. Payment: negotiable. Copyrights for author.

Wild & Woolley, Pat Woolley, PO Box 41, Glebe NSW 2037, Australia, 02-692-0166. 1974. Fiction, cartoons, criticism. "Books by Australian authors only" avg. press run 5M. Pub'd 4 titles 1990; expects 5 titles 1991, 5 titles 1992. 26 titles listed in the *Small Press Record of Books in Print* (20th Edition, 1991-92). avg. price, cloth: $24.95; paper: $9.95. Discounts: 40% retail stores, through Australia In Print, Inc., 110 W. Ocean Blvd., Suite 901, Long Beach, CA 90802. 128pp; 5½×8½; of. Reporting time: 3 months. Payment: royalties. Copyrights for author. ABPA.

Wild East Publishing Co-operative Limited, Margaret McLeod, Shari Andrews, Joe Blades, Raymond Fraser, Jo-Anne Elder, PO Box 1135, Station A, Fredericton, NB E3B 5C2, Canada, 506-454-5127. 1987. Poetry, fiction, art, plays. "Publishes Atlantic Canadian writers and artists. Does not read unsolicited manuscripts (except for magazine)." avg. press run 500. Pub'd 4 titles 1990; expects 8 titles 1991, 8 titles 1992. 8 titles listed in the *Small Press Record of Books in Print* (20th Edition, 1991-92). avg. price, paper: $7. Discounts: Trade 40%; Libraries 20% on 4 or more. 52pp; 7×8½, 5½×8½, 8½×11; of. Reporting time: 2 months for magazine. Payment: 10% of press run.

THE WILD FOODS FORUM, Deborah A. Duchon, 4 Carlisle Way, NE, Atlanta, GA 30308, 404-876-1441. 1989. Articles, reviews, letters, news items, non-fiction. "Our bias is upbeat and outdoorsy, environmentally-friendly. *The Wild Foods Forum* is a newsletter for people who are interested in foraging, that is, eating dandelions and other wild things. Articles range in length from a few paragraphs to 1,000 words. Most contributors are avid foragers; Deborah Lee and Dr. Thomas Squier have been recent ones. I am especially interested in hearing from contributors who actually *teach* wild foods." circ. 500. 12/yr. Pub'd 12 issues 1990; expects 12 issues 1991, 12 issues 1992. sub. price: $15; per copy: $1.50; sample: $1.50. Back issues: $1.50. Discounts: negotiable. 8pp; 8½×11; †copier. Reporting time: 2 months. Payment: $10. Not copyrighted. Pub's reviews: 16 in 1990. §Foraging, wild foods, survival skills, medicinal plants, ethnobotany. Ads: $20/$10.

WILDFIRE: A NETWORKING MAGAZINE, Bear Tribe Publishing, Sun Bear, Matt Ryan, PO Box 9167, Spokane, WA 99209, 509-326-6561. 1985. Poetry, articles, art, photos, interviews, reviews. "Accurate but not scholastic short articles about native American spirituality, earth awareness, male and female energy, herbs. Some short poetry, some news" circ. 11M. 4/yr. Pub'd 3 issues 1990; expects 4 issues 1991, 4 issues 1992. sub. price: $15; per copy: $3.50-$3.75. Back issues: $4. Discounts: write to Bear Tribe. 70pp; 8½×11; of. Reporting time: 2-5 months ahead, Feb 15, May 15, Aug 15, Nov 15. Payment: copies only. Copyrighted. Pub's reviews: 6-8 in 1990. §American Indian religion, history, environment, new age, family and relationship, work and money, male and female energy, children, cultures. Ads: write for rates. COSMEP.

WILDFLOWER, Wildflower Press, Jeanne Shannon, PO Box 4757, Albuquerque, NM 87196-4757. 1981. Fiction. *"Wildflower* is in leaflet form. We are interested in short poems." circ. 75. 6-8/yr. Pub'd 6 issues 1990; expects 10 issues 1991, 10 issues 1992. sub. price: $5; per copy: $2; sample: $2. 8½×11; photocopied. Reporting time: 2-3 weeks. Payment: copies. Not copyrighted.

Wildflower Press (see also WILDFLOWER), Jeanne Shannon, PO Box 4757, Albuquerque, NM 87196-4757. 1981. Poetry. "Short poems on any subject, including haiku and imagistic poetry. Poems about the natural world, environmental concerns, etc., are always welcome." avg. press run 75. Pub'd 10 titles 1990; expects 10 titles 1991, 10 titles 1992. 1 title listed in the *Small Press Record of Books in Print* (20th Edition, 1991-92). avg. price, paper: $9.50. Discounts: 40% to bookstores. 8½×11; photocopied. Reporting time: 2-3 weeks. Payment: copies. Does not copyright for author.

Willamette River Press, Douglas Allen Conner, PO Box 605, Troutdale, OR 97060, 503-667-5548. 1991. Poetry. "Additional address: 731 S.E. 17th Street, Troutdale, OR 97060. Recent contributors: Martin Anderson, Alana Sherman. Biases: excellence is the *only* criteria. No unsolicited mss. at this time; query first, include bio and publishing credits and one poem. We expect this to be an enduring press and plan to publish work we think will endure in high quality editions. Annual competition in November; watch publ. like *Poets & Writers* for announcement of chapbook and collection competitions." avg. press run collections 500, chapbooks 250. Expects 6 titles 1991, 6 titles 1992. avg. price, paper: $10 collection; $6 chapbook. Discounts: 50%. 60-100pp collection, 38-50pp chapbook; 4½×6½; of. Reporting time: 3 months. Payment: payment arrangements made with author, honorarium and copies for winners of competitions. Copyrights for author.

WILLIAM AND MARY REVIEW, William Clark, Editor, Campus Center, College of William and Mary, Williamsburg, VA 23185, 804-253-4895. 1962. Poetry, fiction, art, photos, interviews, criticism, reviews, parts-of-novels, non-fiction. "The *Review* is a national literary magazine published without faculty supervision, but with college funding, by the students of William and Mary. In our most recent issues, we have published works by Cornelius Eady, Dana Gioia, David Ignatow, Phyllis Janowitz, Michael Mott, W.S. Penn, Valerie Smith, and Debbie Lee Wesselmann, among others" circ. 5M. 1/yr. Pub'd 1 issue 1990; expects 1 issue 1991, 1 issue 1992. sub. price: $4.50; per copy: $5; sample: $5. Back issues: $4.50 per issue. Discounts: 40% off list for trade. 115pp; 6×9; of. Reporting time: 2 months. Payment: 4 copies of issue. Copyrighted, reverts to author. §Current literature. Ads: $5000/$2500. CCLM.

Williamson Publishing Company, Inc., Susan Williamson, Box 185, Church Hill Road, Charlotte, VT 05445, 802-425-2102. 1983. Non-fiction. avg. press run 5M. Pub'd 8 titles 1990; expects 10 titles 1991, 10 titles 1992. 39 titles listed in the *Small Press Record of Books in Print* (20th Edition, 1991-92). avg. price, paper: $12.95. Discounts: 5 copies, 40%; 15, 42%; 25, 43%; 50, 44%; 100, 45%; 250, 46%; wholesalers-straight 50%; libraries 5+ 25%. 196-220pp; 6×9, 8¼×7¼, 8½×11; of. Payment: standard industry terms, 10% of net price, modest advances, pay twice a year. Copyrights for author. ABA, NEBA, VBPA (Vermont Book Publishers Association).

Williams-Wallace Publishers, Inc. (see also TIGER LILY MAGAZINE: The Magazine by Women of Colour), Gay Allison, PO Box 756, Stratford, Ontario N5A 3E8, Canada, 519-271-7045. 1979. Poetry, fiction, non-fiction. "Non-sexist: poetry 64 pages; fiction, maximum 164. Non-racist. Recent authors: Marjorie Agosin—non-fiction, Gay Allison—feminist poet, Dionne Brand-fiction, Theresa Lewis—non-fiction, Yeshim Ternar, Daniel David Moses" avg. press run 3M. Pub'd 7 titles 1990; expects 6 titles 1991, 7 titles 1992. avg. price, cloth: $12.95. Discounts: trade 40%, institution 20%. 164pp; 5½×8½. Reporting time: 3-5 months. Payment: 10%. Does not copyright for author. ACP.

Willow Bee Publishing House (see also WYOMING, THE HUB OF THE WHEEL...A Journey for Universal Spokesmen...), Dawn Senior, Managing & Art Editor; Lenore A. Senior, Associate Editor, PO Box 9, Saratoga, WY 82331, 307-326-5214. 1983. Poetry, non-fiction. "Query, with 5-10 sample pages. Do not send entire manuscript." avg. press run 500. Pub'd 2 titles 1990; expects 2 titles 1991, 2 titles 1992. 6 titles listed in the *Small Press Record of Books in Print* (20th Edition, 1991-92). avg. price, paper: $5.95. Discounts: 40% on 5 or more copies. 60pp; 7×8½; of. Reporting time: 3 months. Payment: varies. Copyrights for author. COSMEP, CLMP.

WILLOW SPRINGS, Nance Van Winckel, Editor, MS-1, Eastern Washington University, Cheney, WA 99004, 509-458-6429. 1977. Poetry, fiction, art, photos, interviews, criticism, reviews, parts-of-novels, long-poems, plays, non-fiction. "Michael Burkard, Russell Edson, Dara Wier, Thomas Lux, Alberto Rios, Carolyn Kizer, Madeline DeFrees, Peter Cooley, Yusef Komunyakaa, Donald Revell, William Stafford, Lee Upton, David Russell Young, William Van Wert. We encourage the submissions of translations from all languages and periods, as well as essays and essay-reviews." circ. 800. 2/yr. Pub'd 2 issues 1990; expects 2 issues 1991, 2 issues 1992. sub. price: $7; per copy: $4; sample: $4. Back issues: $4 each. Discounts: 40%. 96pp; 6×9; of. Reporting time: 1-3 months. Payment: 2 contributor copies, 1-yr subscription, small honorarium. Copyrighted, reverts to author. Pub's reviews: 3 in 1990. §Poetry, fiction, nonfiction. Ads: $100/$50. CLMP, COSMEP.

Willowood Press, Larry Greenwood, Judy Greenwood, PO Box 1846, Minot, ND 58702, 701-838-0579. 1980. Non-fiction. "Guides to library research for undergraduate and graduate university students specialized by subject and level of difficulty. University reference-bibliography; art." avg. press run 1M+. Expects 1 title 1991, 1 title 1992. 2 titles listed in the *Small Press Record of Books in Print* (20th Edition, 1991-92). avg. price, paper: $4.50-$30. Discounts: available on request. 180pp; 5½×8½, 8½×11; of. Reporting time: 1-2 months. Payment: yes. Copyrights for author. COSMEP.

Wilson & Crewe, Nancy Kenney, Publications Coordinator, 1548-D Adams Avenue, Costa Mesa, CA 92626. 1 title listed in the *Small Press Record of Books in Print* (20th Edition, 1991-92). avg. price, paper: $6.95.

WIN NEWS, Fran P. Hosken, Editor & Publisher, 187 Grant Street, Lexington, MA 02173, 617-862-9431. 1975. Interviews, news items. "*WIN News (Women's International Network)* has ongoing columns on women and health, women and development, women and media, environment, violence, united nations and more. International career opportunities are listed; an investigation on genital/sexual mutilations regularly reports; news from Africa, the Middle East, Asia & Pacific, Europe and the Americas are featured in every issue. You are invited to send news and participate! *WIN* is a non-profit organization. Contributions tax-deductible. We hope to hear from you soon. Deadline (next issue): April." circ. 1M-1.1M. 4/yr. Pub'd 4 issues 1990; expects 4 issues 1991, 4 issues 1992. 6 titles listed in the *Small Press Record of Books in Print* (20th Edition, 1991-92). sub. price: $40 (institution), $30 (individual), add $4 postage abroad, add $10 air abroad; per copy: $5; sample: $5. Back issues: $15/year. Discounts: available on request. 80pp; 7×11; of. Payment: none. Copyrighted. Pub's reviews: 18-20+ in 1990. §Women and international development, women's right world-wide. Ads: $200/$100/$50 1/4 page.

B. L. Winch & Associates, Bradley L. Winch, President, 45 Hitching Post Dr. Bldg 2, Rolling Hills Estate, CA 90274, 213-547-1240. 1971. Non-fiction. "Affiliated with Jalmar Press. Educationally oriented books on self-concept/values; self-esteem; parent involvement; parent-oriented self-help materials (infant to teen); affective curriculum guidebooks. Send all ms. to: Editor, 45 Hitching Post Drive, Building 2, Rolling Hills Estates, CA 90274." avg. press run 5M. Pub'd 4 titles 1990; expects 4 titles 1991, 4 titles 1992. 7 titles listed in the *Small Press Record of Books in Print* (20th Edition, 1991-92). avg. price, cloth: $16.95; paper: $9.95. Discounts: trade: 40%-45%; agent/jobber 40-50%. 150pp; 8½×11, 6×9; of. Reporting time: 12 weeks if interested, 3 weeks if no interest. Payment: royalty (5-12.5%) paid on semi-annual basis on net receipts, minimum advances as a general rule. Copyrights for author. PMA, NSSEA, EDSA, ABA, CBA.

WIND, Quentin R. Howard, RFD Rt. 1, Box 809K, Pikeville, KY 41501, 606-631-1129. 1971. Poetry, fiction, articles, reviews. "No set length on anything. No biases." circ. 425. 2/yr. Pub'd 2 issues 1990. sub. price: 3 issues $7 individual, $8 institutional, $12 foreign; per copy: $2.50; sample: $2.50. Back issues: $2.50.

Discounts: $1.50 per copy to contributors for extras. 80pp; 8½x5½; of. Reporting time: 2-4 weeks. Payment: copies only. Copyrighted, reverts to author. Pub's reviews: 25 in 1990. §Small presses only. CLMP, SSSL, AWP, Academy of American Poets.

Wind River Institute Press, Jim McDonald, 329 East 3rd Street, Loveland, CO 80537, 800-866-5000; 303-669-3442. 1985. Non-fiction. "Try to keep under 200pp. Non-fiction self-help, how-to. Bias: self-sufficiency in a complex, hurried world. See catalog/literature." avg. press run 5M. Pub'd 1 title 1990; expects 2 titles 1991, 3-4 titles 1992. 4 titles listed in the *Small Press Record of Books in Print* (20th Edition, 1991-92). avg. price, paper: $14.95. Discounts: 2 20%, 6 40%, 36 50%. 200pp; 5½x8½.

Wind Vein Press (see also CLOUDLINE; WHITE CLOUDS REVUE), Scott Preston, PO Box 462, Ketchum, ID 83340, 208-788-3704. 1981. "Wind Vein Press was formed to self-publish a chapbook in 1981. Now the time as appeared right to begin publishing works by others. I plan to publish thematic issues of the journal *Cloudline* on succeeding years. In this "off" year, I will be publishing *The Collected Early Books of Keith Wilson 1967-1972.* Several other projects have been, or are being, considered" 1 title listed in the *Small Press Record of Books in Print* (20th Edition, 1991-92).

WINDFALL, Windfall Prophets Press, Ron Ellis, c/o The Friends of Poetry, English Dept., UW-Whitewater, Whitewater, WI 53190, 414-472-1036. 1979. Poetry, art, photos. "We are interested in short, intense, highly crafted work in any form. Longer poems will also be considered. Copyrights revert to author." circ. 400. 1-2/yr. Pub'd 1 issue 1990; expects 1 issue 1991, 2 issues 1992. sub. price: $5; per copy: $3; sample: $3. Back issues: $2 each. Discounts: none. 50-60pp; 5½x8½; of. Reporting time: 2-4 weeks. Payment: 1 copy. Copyrighted, reverts to author. Pub's reviews: 1 in 1990. §All contemporary poetry collections. Ads: $100/$50/$20 quarter-page.

Windfall Prophets Press (see also WINDFALL), Ron Ellis, c/o The Friends of Poetry, English Dept., UW-Whitewater, Whitewater, WI 53190. 1979. Poetry, art, photos. "Windfall Prophets Press publishes chapbooks for which the poet must pay $300 toward production costs (subject to negotiation). Query with 2-3 samples. $10 reading fee for submission (if invited). Simultaneous submissions if crisp, clear copy or dot-matrix. Diskettes OK if ASCII text file on MS-Dos. Poet receives all copies except 20, is responsible for promotion and distribution of the chapbook under the Windfall Prophets logos. Some distribution help if resources permit. Definitely not a vanity operation." avg. press run 400. Pub'd 1 title 1990; expects 1 title 1991, 1 title 1992. 4 titles listed in the *Small Press Record of Books in Print* (20th Edition, 1991-92). avg. price, paper: $4. Discounts: Negotiated. 50-60pp; 5½x8½; of. Reporting time: 2-4 months. Payment: royalties go to author; author contributes to cost of publishing. Does not copyright for author.

Windflower Press, Ted Kooser, PO Box 82213, Lincoln, NE 68501. 1967. Poetry. "We are not currently accepting unsolicited manuscripts." 1 title listed in the *Small Press Record of Books in Print* (20th Edition, 1991-92). avg. price, cloth: $9.95; paper: $5.95. Discounts: 40% on orders over $20. 65pp; 5½x8½; of. Reporting time: 2 weeks. Payment: by contract. Copyrights for author.

THE WINDHAM PHOENIX, Michael J. Westerfield, Mark Svetz, PO Box 752, Willimantic, CT 06226. 1985. Poetry, fiction, articles, art, cartoons, interviews, satire, criticism, reviews, letters, parts-of-novels, plays, news items, non-fiction. "THE WINDHAM PHOENIX is a news/feature magazine serving northeastern Connecticut. Each month we publish several poems and at least one work of fiction as well as news stories, essays, opinion and reviews. Our bias is in favor of local writers, but we will publish high quality material regardless of the source. We also use a number of line drawings in each issue and are always on the lookout for suitable art" circ. 800. 10/yr. sub. price: $18; per copy: $2; sample: $2.50. Back issues: Vol. I, No. 1; $5. All others $2. Discounts: 20% discount to newsstands. 40pp; 6×9. Reporting time: 1-8 weeks. Payment: 5 contributor copies + one years subscription. Not copyrighted. Ads: $60/$30/quarter page: $15.

THE WINDHORSE REVIEW, John Castlebury, Samurai Press, Yarmouth, N.S., Canada. 1982. Poetry, fiction, art, photos, collages. "Poetry, calligraphy, photography, brush & ink, collage. Inscription reads, 'Has pluck, is on pitch, and does not mumble itself.' '*Windhorse* is an energy or force of upliftedness, arising from a connection with one's own genuine heart—beyond ego-mania,' (LLR). 'Being in the poetic world, we have something to wake up or excite in ourselves. There is a definite sense of gallantry, and a definite attitude of no longer fearing threats of any kind. By developing that attitude, we begin to help ourselves appreciate our world, which is already beautiful,' (CTR). Include bionote, SASE." circ. 500. 1/yr. Pub'd 1 issue 1990. sub. price: $5/1-yr, $9/2-yr; per copy: $5; sample: $5 check or stamps. Back issues: same. Discounts: 30% (5 copies or more). 28pp; 7×10½; of. Reporting time: 1-3 months. Payment: in copies. Copyrighted, reverts to author. Ads: $200/$125/$75 1/4 page/$40 1/8/$25 1/16.

THE WINDLESS ORCHARD, Robert Novak, c/o R. Novak, English Dept., Indiana University, Ft. Wayne, IN 46805, 219-481-6841. 1970. Poetry, art, photos, cartoons, criticism, reviews, letters. circ. 300. 2-4/yr. Pub'd 2 issues 1990; expects 2 issues 1991, 3 issues 1992. 2 titles listed in the *Small Press Record of Books in Print* (20th Edition, 1991-92). sub. price: $8 for 3 issues; per copy: $3; sample: $3. Back issues: $3. 56pp; 5½x8½;

of. Reporting time: 1 week to 4 months. Payment: 2 copies. Copyrighted. Pub's reviews: 0 in 1990. §Contempory poetry. CLMP.

Windmill Publishing Co., Ronald S. Barlow, 2147 Windmill View Road, El Cajon, CA 92020, 619-448-5390. 1979. Non-fiction. "We publish for collectors and advertise in 40 antiques & collectibles tabloids & magazines. Any submissions must have many photos & illustrations; all must be captioned and include current market value of the objects." avg. press run 20M. Pub'd 1 title 1990; expects 1 title 1991, 1 title 1992. 3 titles listed in the *Small Press Record of Books in Print* (20th Edition, 1991-92). avg. price, paper: $12.95. Discounts: 1-4 20%, 5-50 40%, 51-99 50%. 230pp; 9×12; of, perfect bound. Reporting time: 3 weeks. PMA.

Windom Books, PO Box 6444, Santa Fe, NM 87502, 505-983-3800. 1989. Poetry, fiction, art, photos, non-fiction. "Publishes books of high quality, fiction, non-fiction, and beautifully illustrated children's books. Query first. Enclose SASE." avg. press run 5M. Expects 5-7 titles 1992. 1 title listed in the *Small Press Record of Books in Print* (20th Edition, 1991-92). avg. price, cloth: $19.95; paper: $12.95. Discounts: 20-50%. Pages vary; size varies. Reporting time: 8 weeks. Payment: advance and royalties. Copyrights for author. COSMEP, PMA, Rocky Mountain Publishers.

Window Publications (see also THE AMARANTH REVIEW), Dana L. Yost, PO Box 56235, Phoenix, AZ 85079, 846-5567. 1988. Poetry, fiction, art, reviews, long-poems, non-fiction. avg. press run 1M. Pub'd 2 titles 1990; expects 2 titles 1991, 4 titles 1992. avg. price, paper: $7. Discounts: 40%. 150pp; 6×9; of. Reporting time: 8-12 weeks. Payment: 10% after all costs. Copyrights for author.

WindRiver Publishing Company, J. Brim Crow, PO Box 111003, Carrollton, TX 75011-1003, 214-869-7625. 1986. "Editorial and Corporate offices: Three Dallas Communications Complex, 6311 North O'Connor Road, Irving, TX 75039-3510. Recently published *Randolph Scott/The Gentleman From Virginia*, a hardcover filmography that was chosen by two book clubs. Will publish first work of fiction in August *Deadfall*. It is the first of a series about private investigator Ross McCarley and the first in our new series of "Illustrated Novels", a series of trade novels with 30-50 b/w photos illustrating the story. We welcome all queries" avg. press run 5M-10M. Expects 3 titles 1991, 5+ titles 1992. avg. price, cloth: $29.95 non-fiction film books, $20.95 illustrated novels. Discounts: 2-4 books 20%, 5+ 40%. 300pp; 8½×11, 6×9. Reporting time: 6 weeks. Payment: varies, usually standard. Copyrights for author. Texas Publishers Assoc., Publisher's Marketing Assoc., National Writer's Club, Southwestern Booksellers Association.

WINDSCRIPT, Saskatchewan Writers Guild, Cathy Wall, Managing Editor, 2049 Lorne Street, Regina, Saskatchewan S4P 2M4, Canada, 306-757-6310. 1983. Poetry, fiction, art. circ. 4M. 2/yr. Pub'd 2 issues 1990; expects 2 issues 1991, 2 issues 1992. sub. price: $6; per copy: $3; sample: $3. Discounts: 2 yr subscription $10; bulk subscriptions: 5 copies $2.50 ea., 10 $2 ea., 20+ $1.50 each. 52pp; 22×29.5cm; of. Reporting time: 3 months. Payment: contributor's copy. Copyrighted. Ads: $600/$325/$175 1/4 page/$100 1/8/$800 outside cover/$700 inside cover. Special rates for non-profit organizations.

Windsong Books International, Charles Shows, Box 867, Huntington Beach, CA 92648. Articles, cartoons. "Not seeking submissions at this time" avg. press run 5M. Expects 1 title 1991. 1 title listed in the *Small Press Record of Books in Print* (20th Edition, 1991-92). avg. price, cloth: $10.95; paper: $4.95. Discounts: standard. 224pp; 5½×8½; of.

Windsong Press, Sharon Haney, PO Box 644, Delta Jct., AK 99737, 907-895-4179. 1981. Poetry, fiction, articles, art, photos, letters, news items, non-fiction. "By personal solicitation only." avg. press run 1.5M. Expects 1 title 1991, 2 titles 1992. 2 titles listed in the *Small Press Record of Books in Print* (20th Edition, 1991-92). avg. price, paper: $7.95; other: 25¢/$1. Discounts: 40% bookstores, 30% authors. 100pp; 5½×8½; of. Reporting time: 1 month. Payment: individual contracts. Copyrights for author. AASP (Alaska Association of Small Presses), Alaska Press Women, Alaska Press Club.

Windsor Medallion Book Publishing Co., Judie Telfer, PO Box 223756, Carmel, CA 93922, 408-624-5655. 1987. Fiction. "We publish quality books for children, ages 6-15. Our projects are mostly fiction. Currently like to see samples of illustration/drawing any medium. Send photocopies-originals not necessary." avg. press run 5-15M. Pub'd 1 title 1990; expects 2 titles 1991, 2 titles 1992. avg. price, cloth: $12.95; paper: $3.95. 160pp. Reporting time: 2 months. PMA.

Windstar Books, Andrey P. Swystun, PO Box 1643, Virginia Beach, VA 23451, (804) 479-4502. 1986. Non-fiction. "Primary interest is in manuscripts that have a Christian basis, and are inspirational or prophecy related." avg. press run 10M+. Expects 2 titles 1991, 2+ titles 1992. 1 title listed in the *Small Press Record of Books in Print* (20th Edition, 1991-92). avg. price, paper: $7.95. Discounts: universal discount schedule by quantity. 50% off on 100+. 250pp; 5½×8½. Reporting time: 8 weeks. Payment: standard. Copyrights for author. COSMEP.

Wineberry Press, Elisavietta Ritchie, 3207 Macomb Street, NW, Washington, DC 20008, 202-363-8036: Editor's personal number. 1983. Poetry. "To order books: c/o The Writer's Center, 7815 Old Georgetown

632

Road, Bethesda, MD 20814. Press formed as collaborative to publish anthology *Finding The Name*, 1983. Published *20/20 Visionary Eclipse*, a chapbook of conceptual art by Judith McCombs in 1985; *No One Is Listening*, a pamphlet of poems by Elizabeth Follin-Jones in 1987; *Swimming Out of the Collective Unconscious*, a chapbook of poems by Maxine Combs in 1989; *Get With It, Lord: New & Selected Poems*, chapbook by Beatrice Murphy, 1990; *Horse and Cart: Stories from the Country* by Elisabeth Stevens, 1990. Can't handle unsolicited manuscripts—already have plenty I'd like to publish." avg. press run 500-2M. Pub'd 2 titles 1990; expects 1 title 1991. 4 titles listed in the *Small Press Record of Books in Print* (20th Edition, 1991-92). avg. price, paper: $3-$7.95 chapbooks. Discounts: 40% to booksellers. 32-200pp; 5½x8½. Reporting time: ASAP. Payment: copies (as many as they need). Does not copyright for author.

Wingbow Press, Randy Fingland, Stanton Nelson, 2929 Fifth Street, Berkeley, CA 94710, 415-549-3030. 1971. Poetry, fiction. avg. press run 5M. Pub'd 6 titles 1990; expects 3 titles 1991, 3 titles 1992. 27 titles listed in the *Small Press Record of Books in Print* (20th Edition, 1991-92). avg. price, cloth: $15; paper: $8; other: $10 per cassette. Discounts: 42% to bookstores, 10 or more assorted; 50% to wholesalers. 120-200pp; 5½x8½, 6x9, 8½x11; of. Reporting time: 2 months. Payment: royalty rate set per title, paid twice yearly. Copyrights for author. COSMEP.

Winn Books, Larry W. Winn, 5700 6th Avenue South, PO Box 80157, Seattle, WA 98108, 206-763-9544. 1984. Poetry, fiction, art. "Authors published: Jim Harrison, Thomas McGuane, Dan Gerber, Don Berry/Pegge Hopper, Russell Chatham" avg. press run 5M. Pub'd 3 titles 1990; expects 3 titles 1991, 3 titles 1992. avg. price, paper: $11.50; other: $685 ltd. ed. book & art/portfolio. Discounts: 40%. 85pp; 6x9; of, lp. Reporting time: 30 days. Payment: negotiated on a per case basis. Copyrights for author.

Winslow Publishing, Carolyn Winslow, Box 413, Station Z, Toronto, Ontario M5N 2Z5, Canada, 416-789-4733. 1981. Non-fiction. "After publishing for mail order only since 1981, we moved into book stores in 1986. Title range from *The Complete Guide To Companion Advertising* to *The No-Bull Guide To Getting Published And Making It As A Writer*. At present, most business is still in mail order, and we are always looking for new reps to drop ship for. Please send *Queries only* (no mss)—non-fiction only, which can be marketed through the mail. Books do *not* have to have Canadian content - we are well represented in the U.S., and will be expanding greatly in the next couple of years. (Someday we'll be a *Big* Press!) We are completely computerized, and would appreciate mss on disk." avg. press run 500-1M (mail order), (bookstore) 5M. Pub'd 4 titles 1990; expects 4 titles 1991, 4 titles 1992. 1 title listed in the *Small Press Record of Books in Print* (20th Edition, 1991-92). avg. price, paper: $9.95; other: cheaper mail-order paperback $5.95. Discounts: 40% on 5 or more copies of a title; also will drop-ship for mail order dealers for 50%. 160pp; 5½x8½; of, lp. Reporting time: 1-2 weeks. Payment: usual royalties, or purchase ms. outright. Copyrights for author. COSMEP, ABE (North American Bookdealers Exchange, Box 606, Cottage Grove, OR 97424).

Winston-Derek Publishers, Inc., J. Winston Peebles, General Editor; Marjorie E. Staton, Juvenile, Pennywell Drive, PO Box 90883, Nashville, TN 37209, 615-329-1319. 1976. Poetry, fiction, non-fiction. "We are looking for top-notch children's manuscripts. Good modern fiction with strong plots are always welcomed. Our non-fiction is slanted toward history and various types of Americana. Black history is highly needed." avg. press run 3M-5M. Pub'd 30 titles 1990; expects 35 titles 1991, 40 titles 1992. 47 titles listed in the *Small Press Record of Books in Print* (20th Edition, 1991-92). avg. price, cloth: $6.95; paper: $4.95; other: $10.95 special editions. Discounts: Bookstores 40% on 5 or more copies; Salesmen 5%-10%%. 150-350pp; 6½x9½; of, lp. Reporting time: 4-6 weeks. Payment: standard, some flexibility on certain manuscripts. Copyrights for author. SEBA, APA, CBA-ABA.

THE WIRE, Sharon Wysocki, 7320 Colonial, Dearborn Heights, MI 48127, 313-995-1171. 1981. Poetry, photos, collages. "Looking for language, experimental or short form erotic poetry only." circ. 100+. 2-3/yr. Pub'd 2-3 issues 1990; expects 2-3 issues 1991, 2-3 issues 1992. sub. price: $3.75; per copy: $1; sample: $1. Back issues: $1. 5-10pp; 8½x11; xerox. Reporting time: varies. Payment: copies. Not copyrighted.

WISCONSIN ACADEMY REVIEW, Faith B. Miracle, Editor, 1922 University Ave., Madison, WI 53705, 608-263-1692. 1954. Poetry, fiction, articles, art, photos, interviews, criticism, reviews. "We use poetry, short fiction, art and literary history, and book reviews that have Wisconsin connected author or subject, as well as scientific articles or political essays which have Wisconsin tie-in. Quarterly journal of the Wisconsin Academy of Sciences, Arts and Letters. If not Wisconsin return address, include Wisconsin connection with submission or query." circ. 1.5M. 4/yr. Expects 4 issues 1991. sub. price: $15; per copy: $4; sample: $2. Back issues: $3.50. Discounts: none. 48pp; 8½x11; of. Reporting time: 6-8 weeks. Payment: 5 copies. Copyrighted, rights revert only on request. Pub's reviews: 36 in 1990. §Wisconsin connected books by author or subject. No ads.

WISCONSIN RESTAURATEUR, Janice N. LaRue, 125 W. Doty, Madison, WI 53703. 1933. "8½ X 11" circ. 4.2M. 11/yr. Pub'd 11 issues 1990; expects 11 issues 1991, 11 issues 1992. sub. price: $17.50; per copy: $2; sample: same. Back issues: $2. 80pp; of, sheetfed. Reporting time: 4 weeks. Payment: $1.50-$30. Copyrighted, reverts to author. Pub's reviews: 6 in 1990. §Management trends, service, education (general), food service trends, *Foodseruice Liability and Law*. Ads: $574/$338/$229 1/4 page/$145 1/8/$20 classified/$50 boxed classified. ASAE, SRDS.

WISCONSIN REVIEW, Erin L. McGath, Editor, Box 158, Radford Hall, Univ. of Wisconsin-Oshkosh, Oshkosh, WI 54901, (414) 424-2267. 1966. Poetry, fiction, art, photos, cartoons, interviews, satire, reviews, collages, plays, non-fiction. "Poetry in all forms, fiction to 3,000 words, reviews, essays, interviews and artwork (black and white or color) suitable for offset printing. Artwork may be full-page (6 X 9"), half-page, or proportioned to run alongside poems. Photographs considered also. In poetry, we publish mostly free verse with strong images and fresh approaches. We want new turns of phrase. Poems should be single-spaced. In fiction, we look for strong characterization, fresh situations and clipped, hammering dialogue. Fiction should be typed and double-spaced. SASEs mandatory; we accept no responsibility for unsolicited manuscripts. Recent contributors include William Stafford, Antler, Kelly Cherry, Martin Rosenblum, Ronald Wallace, William Silver, G.E. Murray, Richard Kostelanetz" circ. 2M. 3/yr. Pub'd 3 issues 1990; expects 3 issues 1991, 3 issues 1992. 3 titles listed in the *Small Press Record of Books in Print* (20th Edition, 1991-92). sub. price: $6 (3 issues); per copy: $2; sample: $2. Back issues: varies. 64pp; 6×9; of. Reporting time: 3 months, never w/out SASE (mss held during summer months till fall); do not read mss during summer. Payment: 2 copies. Copyrighted, reverts to author. Pub's reviews: 0 in 1990. §Poetry, fiction, art. No ads.

WISCONSIN TRAILS, Wisconsin Trails, Howard Mead, Editor; Lucy Rhodes, Assistant Editor, PO Box 5650, Madison, WI 53705, 608-231-2444. 1960. Articles, photos. "Wisconsin Trails at present is interested in books about nature and the environment, heritage, and folklore, and guides to city and countryside as well as outdoor sports. Submissions should contain outline and sample chapters." circ. 55M. 6/yr. Pub'd 6 issues 1990; expects 6 +1 special issue issues 1991. sub. price: $19; per copy: $3.50, March/April Travel Planner Issue $3.95; sample: $3.50 plus $2 shipping/handling. Back issues: reg. issues $3.50/rare issues $4.50. Discounts: sub agency discount, all other universal disc. sched. 92+pp; 8½x11; of. Reporting time: 4 weeks. Payment: on publication. Copyrighted, reverts to author. Pub's reviews: 6 in 1990. §Outdoor sports, activities, anything dealing w/Wisconsin, photography. AAP, RPA, COSMEP.

Wisconsin Trails (see also WISCONSIN TRAILS), Howard Mead, Editor; Lucy Rhodes, Assistant Editor, P.O.Box 5650, Madison, WI 53705, 608-231-2444. 1975. Fiction, articles, art, photos, cartoons, interviews, non-fiction. "We conduct no major business by phone. Wisconsin Trails is interested in books about travel/environment/heritage/recreation: Wisconsin theme." avg. press run 7.5M. Expects 1-2 titles 1991. avg. price, cloth: $20; paper: $10. Universal Discount Schedule. 120-200pp; 8½x11; of. Reporting time: 2 months; queries, outline & sample chapters 1 month. Payment: varies. Copyrights for author. AAP, RPA, COSMEP.

Wise Owl Press, Mary J. Mooney-Getoff, Editor & Publisher, PO Box 377 (1475 Waterview Dr.), Southold, NY 11971, 516-765-3356. 1980. Non-fiction. "At present we are interested only in the following subjects: Laura Ingalls Wilder, Foods, Nutrition, Cooking, Travel, Long Island (New York), and it must fit into our standard length of about 40 pages, 5½ X 8½ inches. We also distribute books and booklets on the above subjects for other small presses. Our SAN is 217-5754." avg. press run 2.5M. Expects 2 titles 1991, 2 titles 1992. avg. price, paper: $5. Discounts: 40% over 10 copies; 10% to libraries and schools if prepaid. 40pp; 5½x8½; of. Reporting time: 2 months or shorter. Copyrights for author.

THE WISE WOMAN, Ann Forfreedom, 2441 Cordova Street, Oakland, CA 94602, 415-536-3174. 1980. Poetry, articles, art, photos, cartoons, interviews, reviews, music, news items, non-fiction. "Focus of *The Wise Woman*: feminist spirituality, feminist witchcraft, feminist issues. Includes articles, columns (such as *The War Against Women* and *The Rising of Women*). Annotated songs appropriate to subject, interviews (in *Inspirational Women of Our Time*), poems, art, wise sayings, cartoons by Bulbul. Send SASE with submissions if you want to get original material back." circ. small but influential. 4/yr. Pub'd 2 issues 1990; expects 2 issues 1991, 4 issues 1992. sub. price: $15/1 year, $27/2 years, $38/3 years (U.S. funds only); per copy: $4; sample: $4 (U.S. funds only). Back issues: $4 (U.S. funds only). 32pp; 8½x11; of. Reporting time: varies, try to reply promptly when SASE is included. Payment: copy of the issue. Copyrighted, rights revert, but TWW reserves the right to reprint. Pub's reviews: 5+ in 1990. §Feminist spirituality, psychic development, feminist issues, women's history. Ads: $40, no one classified word.

THE WISHING WELL, Laddie Hosler, Editor and Publisher, PO Box 713090, Santee, CA 92072-3090. 1974. Poetry, articles, art, photos, criticism, reviews, letters, news items, non-fiction. "*The Wishing Well* is the largest national/international magazine featuring hundreds of current self-descriptions, some with photos, (by code number) of loving women wishing to safely write/meet one another. Offers many original features not found elsewhere for women. Is a highly supportive, dignified, award winning publication serving women in 50 states and the world. We publish work by members, only. *Free info*." circ. 5M. 6/yr. Pub'd 6 issues 1990; expects 6 issues 1991, 6 issues 1992. 4-7 mo. membership: $55 + photo published $10 extra (optional); price per copy: $5; sample: $5. Back issues: from $1.50 to $5 depending on date of issue. Discounts: renewal $50 (membership) by next deadline date following current membership. 52pp; 7×8½; of. Payment: none. Copyrighted. Pub's reviews: 75 in 1990. §Women, book reviews (relating to readership), human rights, relating

634

to women, bi-sexual women, human relationships, growth, lesbian. Ads: query, $10 per inch one time (3¼" wide) $8 per inch 4 insertions or more. $1 word one time; 80¢ word 4 times in one year.

WITCHCRAFT DIGEST MAGAZINE (THE WICA NEWSLETTER), Leo Louis Martello, 153 West 80th Street, Suite 1B, New York, NY 10024. 1970. "Prospective contributors should familiarize themselves with our theology-philosophy as outlined in Dr. Martello's book *Witchcraft: The Old Religion;* or Patricia Crowther's *Witch Blood: Autobiography of a Witch High Priestess* or her *The Witches Speak.* We're Pre-Christian Pagans, naturalists, and the Old Religion has NOTHING to do with Christian-defined Satanism, devil-worship etc. Anyone sending in a self-addressed stamped envelope will receive our FREE lists of Old Religion books and publications" circ. 3.5M. 1/yr. sub. price: $1.50. Back issues: Witchcraft Digest $1.50 - WICA Newsletter 10 for $4.00. Discounts: 40%. 24pp; 8½×11; of. Reporting time: immediate. Payment: 1¢ per word. Pub's reviews. §Witchcraft, occult, psychology, religion. Ads: $100/$50/$.20.

WITHIN & BEYOND, Dan Latour, Co-Director; Missy Latour, Co-Director, PO Box 2683, Lafayette, LA 70502, 318-235-6535. 1984. Poetry, articles, art, interviews, reviews, letters, news items, non-fiction. circ. 870. 4/yr. Pub'd 5 issues 1990; expects 6 issues 1991, 6 issues 1992. sub. price: $10; per copy: $1.75; sample: $2. Back issues: not available. Discounts: free subscription to Cooperating, Spiritual Organizations (pref. non-profit). 14pp; 5½×8½; †mi, computer. Reporting time: within 3 weeks. Payment: none. Copyrighted, reverts to author. Pub's reviews: 14 in 1990. §Philosophy, psychology, new physics, sociology, metaphysical, health, nutrition. Ads: $45/$20/18¢.

WITHOUT HALOS, Frank L. Finale, Editor-in-Chief, PO Box 1342, Point Pleasant Beach, NJ 08742, 201-240-5355. 1983. Poetry. "Poetry not exceeding 2 pages. Prefer contemporary poetry. Featured essay and poetry by Stephen Dunn in Vol. VIII and Geraldine C. Little in Vol. VII. Last issue (Vol. VIII) had Thomas Reiter, Marvin Solomon, Gayle Elen Harvey, Harold Witt, Emilie Glen and Jean Hollander." circ. 1M. 1/yr. Pub'd 1 issue 1990; expects 1 issue 1991, 1 issue 1992. sub. price: $6.25; per copy: $5 + $1.25 p/h; sample: $5 + $1.25 p/h. Back issues: 1984-1987 $3, 1990 $4. 96pp; 5½×8½; of. Reporting time: within 3 months from deadline. Payment: 1 copy per poem. Copyrighted, reverts to author.

WITNESS, Peter Stine, 31000 Northwestern Hwy, Suite 200, Farmington Hills, MI 48018, 313-626-1110. 1987. Poetry, fiction, articles, art, photos, parts-of-novels, long-poems, non-fiction. "Highlights role of writer as witness, fiction, non-fiction essays, poetry. Special issues (sixties, holocaust, writings from prison, nature writings). Contributors: Joyce Carol Oates, Donald Hill, Madison Smartt Bell, Lynn Sharon Schwartz, Gordon Lish." circ. 2.8M. 3/yr. Pub'd 3 issues 1990; expects 3 issues 1991, 3 issues 1992. sub. price: $15; per copy: $6; sample: $5. Back issues: $5. Discounts: 40% to distributor/retailer. 160pp; 6×9; of. Reporting time: 2 months. Payment: $6/page for prose, $10/page for poetry. Copyrighted, reverts to author. Ads: $100/$50.

THE WITTENBERG REVIEW: An Undergraduate Journal of the Liberal Arts, Dr. Richard P. Veler, Wittenberg University, PO Box 720, Springfield, OH 45501, 513-327-7428. 1990. Poetry, fiction. "Chiefly research essays. Undergraduates from liberal arts colleges. Essays cover the range of academic disciplines" circ. 7M. 2/yr. Pub'd 2 issues 1990; expects 2 issues 1991, 2 issues 1992. sub. price: free. 150pp; 6×9. Reporting time: receipt 1 week; referees 4 weeks; Editorial Board twice annually. Payment: none. Copyrighted, does not revert to author.

Witwatersrand University Press (see also AFRICAN STUDIES; ENGLISH STUDIES IN AFRICA-A Journal of the Humanities), Professor W.D. Hammond-Tooke, African Studies; Professor G.I. Hughes, English Studies in Africa, WITS, 2050 Johannesburg, Republic of South Africa, 011-716-2029. 1923. Poetry, articles, criticism, reviews, non-fiction. avg. press run 1M. Pub'd 5 titles 1990; expects 4 titles 1991, 5 titles 1992. 42 titles listed in the *Small Press Record of Books in Print* (20th Edition, 1991-92). avg. price, paper: R30. Discounts: 25% to libraries, 30% to booksellers. 200pp; 15×21cm; of. Reporting time: up to 1 year. Payment: individual arrangement. Copyrights for author, press holds copyright.

Wizard Works, Jan O'Meara, PO Box 1125, Homer, AK 99603. 1988. Poetry, art, photos, cartoons, non-fiction. "Alaska subjects only. No unsolicited manuscripts without query first." avg. press run 1M. Pub'd 2 titles 1990; expects 1 title 1991, 2 titles 1992. 3 titles listed in the *Small Press Record of Books in Print* (20th Edition, 1991-92). avg. price, paper: $7.95. Discounts: library 20%, wholesale 1-5 20%, 6-199 40%, 200+ 50%. 100pp; 5½×8½; of. Payment: negotiable.

WLW JOURNAL: News/Views/Reviews for Women and Libraries, McFarland & Company, Inc., Publishers, Audrey Eaglen, Editor, Box 611, Jefferson, NC 28640, 919-246-4460. 1975. Articles, art, photos, cartoons, interviews, criticism, reviews, letters, news items. "*WLW Journal* contains news and information of interest to members of this feminist library workers organization and those interested in reviews of feminist materials. *WLW* is handled by major library periodical vendors including Ebsco, Faxon, Mc Gregor, etc" circ. 500. 4/yr. Pub'd 2 issues 1990; expects 4 issues 1991, 4 issues 1992. sub. price: $18 U.S., $22 foreign; per copy: $7. 32pp; 8¼×10¾; of. Reporting time: 2 months. Payment: $50 for 2-page article. Copyrighted, does not revert to author. Pub's reviews: 57 books/3 records in 1990. §Feminism, libraries & information services, worker's rights, sexism. Ads: $175/$100.

Wolcotts, Inc., Allen Hughes, 15126 Downey Avenue, Paramount, CA 90723, 213-630-0911, No. CA: 1-800-262-1538, Out of state: 1-800-421-2220. 1893. avg. press run 2M-5M. Expects 4 titles 1991, 5 titles 1992. 8 titles listed in the *Small Press Record of Books in Print* (20th Edition, 1991-92). avg. price, paper: $5.95-$24.95. Discounts: 40% to retailers, 55% distributors. 40-300pp; 8½×11; †lp. Reporting time: 30 days. Payment: yes. Copyrights for author.

Woldt Publishing, V.G McClintock, Chairman; P.J. Powers, Founder; Mary Savani, VP, 2516 Ridge Avenue, Sarasota, FL 34235, 813-388-2378. 1980. Poetry, fiction, art, photos, long-poems, collages, plays, non-fiction. "Imprints: Starbooks Press, Florida Literary Foundation Press, Woldt Books." avg. press run 1M. Pub'd 4 titles 1990; expects 6⅞ titles 1991. 8 titles listed in the *Small Press Record of Books in Print* (20th Edition, 1991-92). avg. price, paper: $9.95. Discounts: 55% Distributors; 40% Booksellers. 128-200pp; 5½×8½. Reporting time: 2-3 months. Payment: negotiable. Copyrights for author. ABA.

Wolfhound Press (see also PLANKTON), 68 Mountjoy Square, Dublin 1, Ireland, 740354. 1974. Fiction, art. avg. press run 3M. Pub'd 13 titles 1990. 142 titles listed in the *Small Press Record of Books in Print* (20th Edition, 1991-92). avg. price, cloth: £8.95 (IR); paper: £3.95 (IR). Pages vary; size varies; of. Reporting time: 12+ weeks. Payment: yes, vary with type of title. CLE - Irish Book Publishers Association.

Arnie Wolman Co. (see also CORVALLIS STREETS POETRY MAGAZINE), Arnold Wolman, President, Editor, Publisher, PO Box 2291, Corvallis, OR 97339, 758-8244. 1971. Poetry, fiction, articles, art, photos, reviews, parts-of-novels, long-poems, non-fiction. "In 1989 I published a book of poetry by Rochelle Holt of Cranford, NJ and some of my own works that were out of print, plus the 25th edition of Tickle, the Pickle, a children's book, and now I am working on a collection of poems that wil lbe called: Corvallis Street Poetry, a magazine. I am also beginning to get interested again in rebuilding my whole publishing house and publishing books again." avg. press run 100-10M. Pub'd 5 titles 1990; expects 10 titles 1991. 5 titles listed in the *Small Press Record of Books in Print* (20th Edition, 1991-92). avg. price, paper: $2.50 - $15; other: handmade books $100-$5,000. Discounts: 40-50%. 8-64pp; 5×8, 8×11; of/handmade. Reporting time: varies from 1 week to 3 months. Payment: 5-15% of retail price—To Distribution ONLY and other (special) arrangements. Does not copyright for author. COSMEP.

Wolsak & Wynn Publishers Ltd., Heather Cadsby, Maria Jacobs, Box 316, Don Mills Post Office, Don Mills, Ontario M3C 2S7, Canada, 416-222-4690. 1982. Poetry. avg. press run 500. Pub'd 5 titles 1990; expects 5 titles 1991, 5 titles 1992. 23 titles listed in the *Small Press Record of Books in Print* (20th Edition, 1991-92). avg. price, paper: $9 Can. Discounts: 40% trade. 80pp; 5½×8½; of. Reporting time: 4 months. Payment: as per contract. ACP, LPG.

THE WOLSKE'S BAY STAR, Francis Nied, RR 1 Box 186-A, Caledonia, MN 55921-9801. 1985. Poetry, fiction, articles, art, photos, cartoons, interviews, satire, criticism, reviews, music, letters, parts-of-novels, long-poems, collages, plays, concrete art, news items, non-fiction. circ. 1M+. Published when you least expect it. Pub'd 1 issue 1990. sub. price: $10; per copy: $2; sample: $2. Back issues: $2. 24pp; 8½×11; of. Payment: on occasion. Copyrighted, reverts to author. Pub's reviews: 1 in 1990. §Science, energy, health, agriculture, mysticism. Ads: $80/$45/available on request.

WOMAN OF POWER, Char McKee, Editor and Designer, PO Box 827, Cambridge, MA 02238-0827, 617-625-7885. 1984. Poetry, fiction, articles, art, photos, interviews, reviews. "A magazine of feminism, spirituality, and politics. Send for guidelines and upcoming themes." circ. 60M. 4/yr. Pub'd 4 issues 1990; expects 4 issues 1991, 4 issues 1992. sub. price: $26; per copy: $7; sample: $7 (includes postage). Back issues: $7. Discounts: 40% to bookstores. 88pp; 8⅜×11; of. Reporting time: 4 months. Payment: 2 copies and 1 year subscription. Copyrighted, reverts to author. Pub's reviews: 120 in 1990. §Occult, feminism, spirituality, politics, futurism, women, women of color, Third World women. Ads: $785/$525/45¢ per word.

WOMAN POET, Women-in-Literature, Inc., Elaine Dallman, Editor-in-Chief, PO Box 60550, Reno, NV 89506, 702-972-1671. 1978. Poetry, photos, interviews, criticism. "Unpublished fine poems of any length will be considered for our series of regional book/journals—*The West* (1980), *The East* (1982), *The Midwest* (1985), *The South* (1991). Interviews and critical reviews of featured poets. We have an international readership interested in fine women's poetry. Well-written articles will let readers have deeper insights into—How is good literature written? What kind of women write it? What is their education? What does it take to write and to write well? Other material of human interest about writers will be presented. Recent contributors: Josephine Miles, Ann Stanford, Madeline DeFrees, Marilyn Hacker, June Jordan, Marie Ponsot, Audre Lorde, Lisel Mueller, Judith Minty. We urge writers to inspect a copy before submitting. We are a non-profit corporation (literary-educational)—we welcome tax-deductible donations." circ. 4M. 1/yr. Expects 1 issue 1991, 1 issue 1992. sub. price: $12.95 plus $1.75 shipping and insurance per copy; per copy: $12.95 indiv. + $1.75 shipping and insurance; sample: $12.95 + $1.75 shipping and insurance. Discounts: 1, list; 2-4, 20%; 5-24, 40%; write for classroom rates; on approval copy on request to libraries, professors; prepaid only to individuals.

100-130pp; 8×9½; of. Reporting time: 3 weeks to 3 months. Payment: copies. Copyrighted, does not revert to author. Pub's reviews. §Of our studied poets. COSMEP.

WOMAN'S ART JOURNAL, Elsa Honig Fine, 1711 Harris Road, Philadelphia, PA 19118-1208, 615-584-7467. 1980. Articles, art, reviews. *"WAJ* is a semiannual publication devoted to women and issues related to women in all areas of the visual arts. It is concerned with recovering a lost heritage and with documenting the lives and work of contemporary women in the arts, many of whom have been neglected previously because of their sex. *WAJ* represents sound scholarship presented with clarity, and it is open to all ideas and encourages research from all people." circ. 2M. 2/yr. Pub'd 2 issues 1990; expects 2 issues 1991, 2 issues 1992. sub. price: $14 indiv., $18 instit.; per copy: $9; sample: $9. Back issues: $9. Discounts: Trade: $4.25 per issue plus mailing. 56pp; 8½×11; of. Reporting time: 6 months. Payment: none. Copyrighted. Pub's reviews: 16 in 1990. §Women in all areas of visual arts-Images of women. Ads: $475/$325/$625 full back color cover.

WOMEN AND ENVIRONMENTS, Weed Foundation Board Member—rotating editors, c/o Center for Urban and Community Studies, 736 Bathurst Street, Toronto, Ontario M5S 2R4, Canada, 416-516-2379. 1976. Articles, photos, interviews, reviews, letters, news items, non-fiction. "Women in Public Space. Single Parent Housing. Network Directory. Remote office work. Women's Roles in Distressing and Revitalizing Cities. Women as Urban Developers. Women, Nuclear Power and Energy. Women and the Environment." circ. 1M. 4/yr. Pub'd 1 issue 1990; expects 4 issues 1991, 4 issues 1992. sub. price: $20 individual, $30 institutional (plus $5 foreign overseas); per copy: $5; sample: $4. Back issues: $3-$4. Discounts: sub agents - 5% off price, bookstores - 20% of price. 32pp; 8½×11; of. Reporting time: 2-3 months. Payment: none. Copyrighted, reverts to author. Pub's reviews: 10 in 1990. §Women and housing, planning, work, natural environments. Ads: $225/$120/third page $95/quarter page $70/bus. card $45. CPPA.

WOMEN AND LANGUAGE, Anita Taylor, Executive Editor, Communication Dept, George Mason University, Fairfax, VA 22030. 1975. Articles, cartoons, interviews, criticism, reviews, news items, non-fiction. *"Women and Language* is an interdisciplinary research periodical. WL attends to communication, language, gender and women's issues. It reports books, journals, articles and research in progress; publishes short articles and speeches." circ. 500+. 2/yr. Pub'd 2 issues 1990; expects 2 issues 1991, 2 issues 1992. sub. price: $15 all US institutions, $10 US individuals; $13 Canada and $18 other foreign individuals (US funds only); $20 all international institutions; per copy: $8 special issues; $5 individual issues. Back issues: $75 for Vols 1-11. 60pp; 8½×11; of. Reporting time: 1 month. Payment: none. Copyrighted, reverts to author. Pub's reviews: 12 in 1990. §Women's studies, language, gender, linguistics, writing, communication, speech, public address. No ads.

WOMEN & THERAPY, Esther D. Rothblum, Ph.D., Ellen Cole, Ph.D., Dr. Esther Rothblum, Dept. of Psychology, University of Vermont, Burlington, VT 05405, (802) 656-2680. 1982. Articles, reviews, non-fiction. *"Women & Therapy* is the only professional journal that focuses entirely on the complex interrelationship between women and the therapeutic experience. The journal is devoted to descriptive, theoretical, clinical, and empirical perspectives on the topic of women and therapy. Women comprise the overwhelming majority of clients in therapy, yet there has been little emphasis on this area in the training of therapists or in the professional literature. *Women & Therapy* is designed to fill this void of information. The Journal will only consider articles not published elsewhere or submitted for publication consideration elsewhere. Your manuscript may be no longer than 10-20 pages double-spaced (including references and abstract). Lengthier manuscripts may be considered, but only at the discretion of the Editor." circ. 1M. 4/yr. Pub'd 4 issues 1990; expects 4 issues 1991, 4 issues 1992. sub. price: $32; sample: free. Back issues: ranges from $10 to $29. 120pp; 5½×8½. Payment: none. Copyrighted, does not revert to author. Pub's reviews: 6 in 1990. §Psychology of women, women's mental health.

WOMEN ARTISTS NEWS, Midmarch Arts Press, Cynthia Navaretta, Executive Editor; Rena Hausen, Editor, 300 Riverside Drive, New York City, NY 10025, 212-666-6990. 1975. Interviews, criticism, letters, collages, concrete art, news items. "300-500 word articles; emphasis on visual arts; coverage of dance, film, music, arts events, etc. Listing solo and group shows across the USA; opportunities for artists; artists' panels, symposia + conference reports; political news of interest to artists; interviews. 12 to 20 pages with b&w photos. Present ideas, philosophies and recent art phenomena. Frequently only publication of record reporting on N.Y. art-talk scene; many male subscribers." circ. 5M. 4/yr. Pub'd 5 issues 1990; expects 4 issues 1991. sub. price: $12 indiv, $16 inst.; per copy: $3 (including back issues), plus $0.70 postage; sample: $3, plus $0.70 postage. Back issues: on application. Discounts: jobber & agent 40%; bookstores, galleries 40%; classroom 40%. 40pp; 8½×11; of. Reporting time: 2-3 weeks. Payment: only in years when funded for payment to writers; pay regular regional contributors. Copyrighted, reverts to author. Pub's reviews: 35 in 1990. §Art, (visual arts, film, dance) women, arts legislation. Ads: $240/$125/$5/line, min. 5 lines. CCLM, COSMEP, Small Press.

WOMEN IN THE ARTS BULLETIN/NEWSLETTER, Women In The Arts Foundation, Inc., Jackie Skiles, c/o R. Crown, 1175 York Avenue #2G, New York, NY 10021, 212-691-0988. 1971. Articles, photos, interviews, letters, news items. "Length: 200 to 1,000 words—must be on women's art movement or topics relevant to women artists." circ. 1M. 4/yr. Pub'd 6 issues 1990; expects 4 issues 1991, 4 issues 1992. sub. price: $9 ($15 institution); per copy: $1; sample: free. Discounts: trade-free, subscription in exchange for free subscription. 8pp; 8½×11; of. Reporting time: 2-3 months. Payment: none. Copyrighted, reverts to author. Pub's reviews: 2 in 1990. §Women's visual art & writing. Ads: $110/$60.

Women In The Arts Foundation, Inc. (see also WOMEN IN THE ARTS BULLETIN/NEWSLETTER), Jackie Skiles, Editor, 325 Spring St, New York, NY 10013. 1971. 7 titles listed in the *Small Press Record of Books in Print* (20th Edition, 1991-92).

Women-in-Literature, Inc. (see also WOMAN POET), Elaine Dallman, Editor-in-Chief, PO Box 60550, Reno, NV 89506. 1978. Poetry, photos, interviews, criticism. "Unpublished fine poems of any length, by women, will be considered for our series of regional book/journals—the West (1980), the Midwest (1985), the East (1982), the South (1991). Interviews and critical reviews of featured poets. We have an international readership interested in fine women's poetry. Well-written articles will let readers have deeper insights into: How is good literature written? What kind of women write it? What is their education? What does it take to write and to write well? Other material of human interest about writers will be presented. Recent contributors: Madeline DeFrees, June Jordan, Judith Minty, Marilyn Hacker, Marie Ponsot, Andre Lorde, Lisel Mueller and Mona Van Duyn. We urge writers to inspect a copy before submitting. We are a non-profit corporation (literary-educational) and all donations to us are needed and are tax-deductible." avg. press run 4M. Expects 1 title 1991, 1 title 1992. 9 titles listed in the *Small Press Record of Books in Print* (20th Edition, 1991-92). avg. price, cloth: $19.95 + $1.75 shipping and insurance; paper: $12.95 + $1.75 shipping and insurance. Discounts: 1, list; 2-4, 20%; 5-24, 40%; write for classroom rates; on approval copy on request to libraries, professors; prepaid only to individuals. 100-130pp; 8×9½; of. Reporting time: 3 weeks to 3 months. Payment: copies. Does not copyright for author. COSMEP.

WOMEN'S PAGES, Charlotte White, PO Box 15828, Phoenix, AZ 85060-5828, 602-230-8668. 1975. Articles. "A directory of women's businesses, services and professions" circ. 10M. 2/yr. Pub'd 1 issue 1990; expects 1 issue 1991, 1 issue 1992. sub. price: $12; per copy: $4.95. 64pp; 8½×11; of. Copyrighted. Ads: $800/$450/quarter page $225/eighth page $150/list only $110.

Women's Press, Angela Robertson, Co-Managing Editor, 517 College Street, Ste. 233, Toronto, Ontario M6G 4A2, Canada. 1972. Fiction, art, non-fiction. avg. press run 3M. Expects 8-10 titles 1991. 41 titles listed in the *Small Press Record of Books in Print* (20th Edition, 1991-92). avg. price, paper: $11.00. Discounts: regular. 200pp. Reporting time: 3 months. Payment: varies. Copyrights for author. ACP, and Canadian Book Information Center (CBIC).

WOMEN'S RESEARCH NETWORK NEWS, National Council for Research on Women, Debra L. Schultz, Editor, Sara D. Roosevelt Memorial House, 47-49 East 65th Street, New York, NY 10021, 212-570-5001. "Includes News from the Council; News from Member Centers; News from International Centers; News from the Caucuses; Publications and Resources; Upcoming Events; Job Opportunities; Opportunities for Research, Study, and Affiliation as well as other news of interest to the women's research, action, policy, and funding communities." 4/yr. sub. price: $35 indiv., $100 organizations.

THE WOMEN'S REVIEW OF BOOKS, Linda Gardiner, Wellesley College, Center For Research On Women, Wellesley, MA 02181, 617-431-1453. 1983. Reviews. "Book reviews only; average length 2M words; only recent books by and about women. Some contributors: Jessie Bernard; Andrea Dworkin; Marge Piercy; Michele Wallace; Ann Snitow; Heidi Hartmann. Unsolicited material is not normally accepted" circ. 12M. 11/yr. Pub'd 11 issues 1990; expects 11 issues 1991, 11 issues 1992. sub. price: $16 individuals, $25 institutions; per copy: $2; sample: free. Back issues: $2. Discounts: 10 or more, 60% of cover price. 28pp; 10×15; of. Payment: varies; $50 minimum. Copyrighted, reverts to author. Pub's reviews: 170 in 1990. §Feminism, women's studies. Ads: $1210/$650/$25/65¢ per word. CCLM.

Women's Studies Librarian, University of Wisconsin System (see also FEMINIST COLLECTIONS: A QUARTERLY OF WOMEN'S STUDIES RESOURCES; FEMINIST PERIODICALS: A CURRENT LISTING OF CONTENTS; NEW BOOKS ON WOMEN & FEMINISM), Susan Searing, Linda Shult, Carolyn Wilson, 112A Memorial Library, 728 State Street, Madison, WI 53706, 608-263-5754. 1977. Articles, interviews, criticism, reviews, non-fiction. "In addition to the three periodicals listed above, we publish a series *Wisconsin Bibliographies in Women's Studies* and a directory, *Women's Studies in Wisconsin: Who's Who & Where* (5th edition, 1989)." avg. press run 1.1M. 8½×11; offset. Reporting time: 1-2 weeks. Payment: none. Does not copyright for author.

WOMEN'S STUDIES QUARTERLY, The Feminist Press at the City University of New York, Florence Howe, Publisher; Nancy Porter, Editor, The Feminist Press, 311 East 94 Street, New York, NY 10128, 212-360-5790. 1972. Poetry, articles, art, photos, cartoons, interviews, satire, criticism, reviews, letters, news items, non-fiction. "News, issues, events in women's studies; articles are from 1M to 3M words usually" circ.

638

1.5M. 2/yr. Pub'd 2 issues 1990; expects 2 issues 1991, 2 issues 1992. sub. price: $25 individuals, $35 institutions, foreign $30 individual, $40 institution; per copy: $13 (double issue); sample: $13 (double issue). Back issues: $3.50 per copy; 15 years for $150. 150pp; 5×8; of. Reporting time: 2-3 months. Payment: 2 copies of the issue. Copyrighted, does not revert to author. Pub's reviews: 3 in 1990. §Women's studies, nonsexist education at all levels and in all settings. Ads: $300/$150/$100 1/3 page.

Women's Times Publishing, Jane Lind, Box 215, Grand Marais, MN 55604, 707-829-0558. 1982. Poetry, non-fiction. "Editorial address: PO Box 2005, Sebastopol, CA 95473." avg. press run 3M. Pub'd 2 titles 1990; expects 1 title 1991, 2 titles 1992. 6 titles listed in the *Small Press Record of Books in Print* (20th Edition, 1991-92). avg. price, cloth: $14.95; paper: $7.95. Discounts: trade. 150pp; 5½×8½; of. Reporting time: 4 weeks. Payment: individual contracts. Copyrights for author. COSMEP (PO Box 703, San Francisco, CA 94101).

WOMENWISE, Editorial Committee, 38 South Main Street, Concord, NH 03301, 603-225-2739. 1977. Poetry, articles, art, photos, cartoons, interviews, reviews, letters, news items, non-fiction. "*WomenWise* is the quarterly of the NH Federation Feminist Health Centers. Its purpose is to share women's health resources and information. Articles should be 4-12 pages, double spaced, 1 inch margins. Recent contributors: Faith Hansen, Lois Shea, Elizabeth Conner." circ. 2.5M. 4/yr. Pub'd 4 issues 1990; expects 4 issues 1991, 4 issues 1992. sub. price: $10; per copy: $2.95; sample: $2.95. Back issues: $2.95. Discounts: bulk arrangements made. 12pp; 11×19; of. Reporting time: 1-3 months. Payment: 1 year subscription. Copyrighted, reverts to author. Pub's reviews: 4 in 1990. §Health, reproductive freedom and rights, lesbian liberation articles.

WONDER, Wonder Press, Walter Gammons, PO Box 58367, Louisville, KY 40268-0367. 1982. Fiction. "Only international science-fiction stories (2,000-6,000 words) are featured." circ. 2M. 4/yr. Expects 4 issues 1991, 4 issues 1992. sub. price: $26 US; per copy: $6.50 US; sample: $6.50 US. 80-100pp; 8½×11; †of. Reporting time: 3 months. Payment: contributors copies plus 1¢ per word. Copyrighted, reverts to author. Ads: inquire.

Wonder Comix (see also EMERALD CITY COMIX & STORIES), Nils Osmar, PO Box 95402, Seattle, WA 98145. 1985. "Shorter pieces have the best chance of being published. We accept about 5-10% of submissions, on the average. Looking for high quality writings and graphics" avg. press run 10M. Pub'd 1 title 1990; expects 1 title 1991, 1 title 1992. 8-12pp; 11×17; web press. Reporting time: 2-3 months.

Wonder Press (see also WONDER; SPECTRUM STORIES), Walter Gammons, PO Box 58367, Louisville, KY 40268-0367. 1982. Fiction, art, cartoons. "Anthologies of short stories 2M-7M words. Science fiction, fantasy, and horror." avg. press run 1M-2M. Pub'd 3 titles 1990; expects 6 titles 1991, 6 titles 1992. avg. price, paper: $6.50. Discounts: 50-55%. 80-100pp; 8½×11; †of. Reporting time: 2 months. Payment: varies, 1st NASR's get payment plus part of royalty. Copyrights for author.

WONDER TIME, Evelyn J. Beals, Editor; Robyn K. Ginter, Editorial Assistant, 6401 The Paseo, Kansas City, MO 64131, 816-333-7000. 1969. Poetry, fiction, photos. "Inspirational and character building for 6 and 7-year-old children." circ. 42M. 52/yr. Pub'd 52 issues 1990. sub. price: $6.75; sample: free with SASE. 4pp; 8¼×11. Reporting time: 8-12 weeks. Payment: $25 per story (400-550 words); poetry 25¢ per line, $3 minimum. Copyrighted, rights sometimes revert—we retain reprint rights.

Wonder View Press, Lani Nedbalek, Leon Nedbalek, 823 Olive Avenue, Wahiawa, HI 96786, 808-621-2288. 1984. Non-fiction. "We specialize in histories of Hawaii locales, peoples, and traditions. We are also doing packaging—editing, typesetting, printing and binding cookbooks and historical/local interest booklets for schools, nonprofit organizations, etc." avg. press run 1.5M. Pub'd 4 titles 1990; expects 5 titles 1991, 7 titles 1992. avg. price, paper: $6-$10. Discounts: libraries 20%, bookstores 40%. 100-200pp; 5½×8½, 8½×11; †of. Reporting time: 1 month. Payment: negotiable. Copyrights for author.

Wood River Publishing, Gary H. Schwartz, 680 Hawthorne Drive, Tiburon, CA 94920, 415-435-0677. 4 titles listed in the *Small Press Record of Books in Print* (20th Edition, 1991-92).

Wood Thrush Books, Walt McLaughlin, Publisher, Editor; Judy Ashley, Associate Editor, 25 Lafayette Place, #C, Burlington, VT 05401, 802-863-9767. 1985. Poetry, fiction, non-fiction. "Currently looking for non-fiction on outdoor/nature themes." avg. press run 100-500. Pub'd 1 title 1990; expects 1 title 1991, 1 title 1992. 7 titles listed in the *Small Press Record of Books in Print* (20th Edition, 1991-92). avg. price, paper: $5; other: $2.50 chapbooks. Discounts: 40%. 64-96pp; 8×5¼; of. Reporting time: 3 months. Payment: copies. Copyrights for author.

Woodbine House, Susan Stokes, Editor, 5615 Fishers Lane, Rockville, MD 20852, 301-468-8800. 1985. Non-fiction. "Full length mss - only non-fiction" avg. press run 5M-10M. Pub'd 5 titles 1990; expects 8 titles 1991, 8 titles 1992. 24 titles listed in the *Small Press Record of Books in Print* (20th Edition, 1991-92). avg. price, cloth: $16.95; paper: $14.95. Discounts: available on request. 300pp; 5½×8½, 8½×11, 6×9; of. Reporting time: 6 weeks. Payment: on an individual basis. Does not copyright for author. ABA.

Woodbridge Press, Howard Weeks, PO Box 6189, Santa Barbara, CA 93160, 805-965-7039. 1971. Non-fiction. avg. press run 7.5M. Pub'd 5 titles 1990; expects 4 titles 1991, 5 titles 1992. avg. price, cloth: $19.95; paper: $8.95. Discounts: 5-14 42%, 15-99 44%, 100-499 46%, 500 48%; wholesale 52%. 200pp; 6×9; of. Reporting time: 30 days. Payment: 10-12% net receipt. Copyrights for author. ABA.

Woodcock Press, Ruth M Morgan, PO Box 4744, Santa Rosa, CA 95402, 415-533-4399. 1981. Fiction, art. "24-48 pages. Quality illustrated books, artist's books; generally geared toward social and spiritual conciousness. Recent contribution: *'Ester: the Story of a Small Ghost'* by Ruth Lynn" avg. press run 1M. Pub'd 1 title 1990; expects 1 title 1991, 1 title 1992. 1 title listed in the *Small Press Record of Books in Print* (20th Edition, 1991-92). avg. price, cloth: $12.95. Discounts: bookstores & libraries: 40% off; distributors: 40-50% off. 24-48pp; 8½×11; of. Reporting time: 2 months. Payment: half upon agreement, half upon publication, royalties of 5% after first thousand printed. Copyrights for author. COSMEP.

Woods Hole Press, D. Shephard, PO Box 44, Woods Hole, MA 02543, 508-548-9600. 1973. Poetry, non-fiction. "Poetry of local interest only" avg. press run 500. Pub'd 1 title 1990; expects 2 titles 1991, 2 titles 1992. 6 titles listed in the *Small Press Record of Books in Print* (20th Edition, 1991-92). avg. price, paper: $5.50. Discounts: 1-5 copies 25%, 6+ 40%. 100pp; 5½×8½; †of. Payment: variable. Copyrights for author.

Woodsong Graphics Inc., Ellen P. Bordner, PO Box 304, Lahaska, PA 18931-0304, 215-794-8321. 1979. Fiction, non-fiction. "Full-length books only. We don't want heavily sexual material, and we cannot accept poetry at the present time. Otherwise, we're open to good writing of any kind. Novices with talent are always welcome, too." avg. press run 2.5M. Pub'd 6 titles 1990; expects 5 titles 1991. 11 titles listed in the *Small Press Record of Books in Print* (20th Edition, 1991-92). avg. price, cloth: $10/95; paper: $5.95. Discounts: 1-4 copies 35%; 5-24 40%; 25-49 45%; 50 or more 50%. 160pp; 5½×8½; of, usually paperback, perfect or comb binding, 4 color cover, laminated. Reporting time: 1 month on queries, several months on full ms. Payment: usually 10% to 15% on net. Copyrights for author.

Woodstead Press, Susan M. Donnell, President, 1755 Woodstead Court, The Woodlands, TX 77380, 713-292-5000. 1988. Non-fiction. avg. press run 5M. Pub'd 3 titles 1990; expects 4 titles 1991, 5 titles 1992. 3 titles listed in the *Small Press Record of Books in Print* (20th Edition, 1991-92). avg. price, cloth: $30; paper: $14.95. Discounts: bookstores 2-4 20%, 5+ 40%; education and library 5+ 20%; trade, distributors 1-4 20%, 5-24 40%, 25+ 50%. 300pp; †of. Reporting time: 3-4 weeks. Payment: 20% of net sale. Copyrights for author. COSMEP, Book Publishers of Texas.

THE WORCESTER REVIEW, Rodger C. Martin, 6 Chatham Street, Worcester, MA 01609, 603-924-7342. 1973. Poetry, fiction, art, photos, satire, criticism. "Submit up to five poems. Fiction to 4,000 words maximum. Literary articles and criticism should have a central New England connection. Photography: black and white glossy, minimum 5"x 7". Graphic art: black and white, minimum 5"x 7". Author's name should appear in upper left of each page." circ. 1M. 2/yr. Pub'd 1 issue 1990; expects 1 issue 1991, 1 issue 1992. sub. price: $10; per copy: $5; sample: $4. Back issues: Volume VII: $10, Volume V & VI: $25, earlier volumes: $100. Discounts: 20% on orders of 10 or more of current issues. 100pp; 6×9. Reporting time: 12-16 weeks. Payment: $10 per poem, $20 per fiction or article (dependent upon grants) + 2 contributor's copies. Copyrighted, reverts to author. Pub's reviews: 1 in 1990. §Central-New England writers. Ads: $100 benefactors/$50 patrons (Listings = 2 issues); Full page per issue $200/1/2 pg. $120.

Word Of Mouth Press, Allen Sacharov, c/o Sacharov, 528 Minnieford Avenue, Bronx, NY 10464-1232. 1982. Fiction, non-fiction. "A recent publication - *The Redhead Book* - was successfully promoted via The Today Show and Washington Post Syndication Service. In 1986 the company published *Offbeat-Careers: 50 Ways To Avoid Being A Lawyer* and a childrens book *Ozzie The Alligator*. We are always looking for an offbeat slant" avg. press run 3M. Pub'd 2 titles 1990; expects 3 titles 1991, 3 titles 1992. 2 titles listed in the *Small Press Record of Books in Print* (20th Edition, 1991-92). avg. price, paper: $7.95. Discounts: 60% to distributors. 160pp; 5½×8½; of. Reporting time: 1 month. Payment: 10% semi-annually. Copyrights for author. COSMEP, Network Of Independent Publishers/Greater New York.

The Word Works, Inc., Karren L. Alenier, President & Director of the Board; Barbara Goldberg, Editor-in-Chief & Director of the Board; Jim Beall, Grants Manager & Director of the Board; Robert Sargent, Treasurer & Director of the Board, PO Box 42164, Washington, DC 20015. 1974. Poetry. "We welcome inquiries including SASE" avg. press run 500. Pub'd 2 titles 1990; expects 2 titles 1991, 2 titles 1992. 21 titles listed in the *Small Press Record of Books in Print* (20th Edition, 1991-92). avg. price, paper: $8; other: $10 anthologies. Discounts: 40% for bookstores, 30% institutions (5+ copies). 54pp; 5½×8½; of. Reporting time: 3 months. Payment: 15% of run. Does not copyright for author.

Wordcraft, David Memmot, Editor & Publisher; Sue Memmot, Editor & Publisher, 953 N. Gale, Union, OR 97883, 503-562-5638. 1984. Poetry, fiction, art. "Wordcraft has, to date, published two chapbooks, *Prayers of Steel* by Misha and *The Magic Deer* by Conger Beasley, Jr. in the Wordcraft Speculative Writers Series. We are not reading unsolicited manuscripts. Manuscripts are read by invitation only." avg. press run 500. Pub'd 1 title

1990; expects 1 title 1991, 2 titles 1992. avg. price, paper: $5. Discounts: 40% to bookstores or anyone ordering 5 or more copies. 30-50pp; 7×8½; of. Payment: copies or percentage by arrangement. Copyrights for author.

Wordland, Steve Wergeland, Department ID-23, Box 26333, Santa Ana, CA 92799, 714-953-2900. 1981. Poetry, fiction, articles, cartoons, interviews, criticism, reviews, letters, plays, news items, non-fiction. "We'd like to become the best and most prolific producers of Biblical puzzles (all types). We need to see single-page and book-length manuscripts including - but not limited to - crosswords, word-searches, cryptograms, double-acrostics, etc. We will also create puzzles and poetry on assignment such as for company or personal birthdays, anniversaries, promotions, weddings, etc., and for publications with specialized audiences. We've also started a couple of huge puzzle projects for which we'll need assistance! A home computer would be a great help. Send SASE for details on books and other publications, especially our first two: *The World's Largest Biblical Crossword Puzzle!* and *Free! Thousands of Publications - 21 Ways"* avg. press run 1M. Expects 1 title 1992. 2 titles listed in the *Small Press Record of Books in Print* (20th Edition, 1991-92). avg. price, paper: $2 (3/$5). Discounts: trade-50%, the rest by arrangement. 4-120pp; 8½×11, 6×9; of. Reporting time: 4 weeks to 4 months. Payment: negotiable. Copyrights for author.

WORDS OF WISDOM, J.M. Freiermuth, Editor, c/o J.M. Freiermuth, 612 Front Street, Glendora, NJ 08029, 609-939-0454. 1981. Poetry, fiction, articles, photos, cartoons, interviews, satire, letters, non-fiction. "Fillers and anecdotes. *Words of Wisdom* is a monthly report of what's happening to the expat worker on the New Jersey littoral of the American coast. We report the facts, the fictions, the phantasies and the rumors—all the things you rarely see in the good news press. Contributors in the last three years include J.M. Freiermuth, Mikhammad Abdel-Ishara, Alan Davie, Darcy Cummings, Miriam M. Macko, Yvette Williams, Brian Walker, Sheila Seiler, Valerie Drach Weidman, Susan Doro, George E. White, Don Tetley, Henry J. Cummings, John Nestor, and Jeanne Carroll, but never Lyn Lifshin." circ. 75-125. 12/yr. Pub'd 12 issues 1990; expects 12 issues 1991, 12 issues 1992. sub. price: $8 individuals, $15 institutions; per copy: $1; sample: SASE. Back issues: $1 each, $8 per year, $79.95 for first 10 years. Discounts: 50% for creative writing classes and groups. 12-40pp; 5½×8½; †xerographic. Reporting time: usually in next mail to 1 month. Payment: copies, 1 year subscription. Not copyrighted. Pub's reviews: 1 in 1990. none.

The Wordtree, Dr. Henry G. Burger, Publisher, 10876 Bradshaw, Overland Park, KS 66210-1148, 913-469-1010. 1984. Non-fiction. "This word-pinpointing dictionary, called The Wordtree, analyzes each transitive verb. For example: To enlarge & develop = to grow, to grow & complete = to mature, etc. Since all parts are cross-referenced, you can look up any goal, and "ripple" your way to all its causes and effects." avg. press run 1M. Pub'd 1 title 1990. 1 title listed in the *Small Press Record of Books in Print* (20th Edition, 1991-92). avg. price, cloth: $149; paper: not available; other: $149. Discounts: sold directly 10% for 2-3 copies; also via any distributor 20%. 380pp; 8½×11; of, photo-offset. Reporting time: 1 month. Payment: not standardized. Copyrights for author. DSNA, EURALEX (European Assn. for Lexicography), Academie Europeene des sciences.

WordWorkers Press, Linda Bishop, PO Box 1363, Lancaster, PA 17603, 717-299-1380. 1989. Plays. "Devoted to publication of plays of high literary merit in progressive forms, both in anthologies and acting editions." avg. press run 2M. Pub'd 1 title 1990; expects 2 titles 1991, 3 titles 1992. 2 titles listed in the *Small Press Record of Books in Print* (20th Edition, 1991-92). avg. price, paper: $9.95. Discounts: text 35%, bookstores 40%, wholesalers 55%. 50-208pp; 6×9, 5½×8½; of. Reporting time: 4 months. Payment: negotiable. Copyrights for author. COSMEP.

Wordwrights Canada, Susan Ioannou, PO Box 456, Station O, Toronto, Ontario M4A 2P1, Canada. 1985. avg. press run 100-300. Pub'd 1 title 1990; expects 1 title 1992. 8 titles listed in the *Small Press Record of Books in Print* (20th Edition, 1991-92). avg. price, paper: $7. Discounts: only on orders of 10 or more—20%. 24-72pp; 5½×8½; of. Reporting time: 1 month. Payment: payment/honorarium on publication plus copies. Author owns copyright.

WORK-AT-HOME REPORT, Edwin Simpson, 12221 Beaver Pike, Jackson, OH 45640, 614-988-2331. 1983. Articles, interviews, reviews, news items, non-fiction. "8 X 11" circ. 10M. 6/yr. Pub'd 10 issues 1990; expects 6 issues 1991, 6 issues 1992. sub. price: $39; per copy: $3; sample: $3. Back issues: $3. Discounts: 40%. 16pp; 8½×11; of. Reporting time: 1-3 months. Payment: varies, $10-$50. Copyrighted, reverts to author. Pub's reviews: 25 in 1990. §Home based businesses, marketing, mail order. Ads: $300/$185/1 inch $16.

THE WORKBOOK, Southwest Research and Information Center, Kathy Newton, Editor, PO Box 4524, Albuquerque, NM 87106, 505-262-1862. 1974. Articles, reviews, news items. "Action oriented. Political position is progressive." circ. 3M. 4/yr. Pub'd 4 issues 1990; expects 4 issues 1991, 4 issues 1992. sub. price: $8.50/yr students and senior citizens, $12/yr individuals, $25/yr institutions; per copy: $3.50; sample: $2. Back issues: $2.50. Discounts: 40% to distributors. 48pp; 8½×11; of. Reporting time: 1 month. Payment: none. Copyrighted by Southwest Research & Information Center. Pub's reviews: 100 in 1990. §Environmental, consumer & social problems. Ads: $200/$125/$65 1/4 page/$35 1/8/no classified.

WORKERS' DEMOCRACY, Don Fitz, PO Box 24115, St. Louis, MO 63130, 314-727-8554 (nites). 1981. Poetry, fiction, articles, art, photos, cartoons, interviews, satire, criticism, reviews, letters, news items. "We welcome unsolicited articles, poetry, cartoons, satires, book reviews, letters-to-the editor, etc. which deal with worklife, workplace, struggles and actions of working people in their own behalf. Recent contributors include Paul Buhle, H.L. Mitchell, Stan Weir, Martin Glaberman, David Roediger, George Lipsitz, Peter Rachleff, Kim Scipes, Berry Craig, John Perotti, Bruce Allen and Tom Wetzel" circ. 500. 4/yr. Pub'd 4 issues 1990; expects 4 issues 1991, 4 issues 1992. sub. price: $6; per copy: $1.50; sample: free. Back issues: 50¢ #2-4, 75¢ #5-8, $1.25 #9-17, $1.50 #18-present. Discounts: 50% off 5 or more, 60% off 10 or more. 24pp; 8½×11; of. Reporting time: 1-2 months. Payment: self-actualization that comes from contributing to social knowledge. Copyrighted, rights revert if so requested. Pub's reviews: 6 in 1990. §Worklife, workplace struggles, self-organization of working people. Ads: exchange only.

WORKING AT HOME, Mrs. H.C. McGarity, PO Box 200504, Cartersville, GA 30120. 1987. Articles, news items. "This is a newsletter of how-to income suggestions for women who cannot get out to 'regular' jobs because of small children, tending elderly relatives, or other good reasons that curtail their activities. Began as adjunct to self-published book of home business income ideas for women who have limited incomes and are in real need of extra money." circ. 300. 4/yr. Pub'd 4 issues 1990; expects 3 issues 1991, 3-4 issues 1992. sub. price: $12/5 issues; per copy: $2.75; sample: $2.75. Discounts: available in bulk for seminars, groups, etc., upon inquiry 6 weeks ahead of event. 4-12pp; 8½×11; of. Reporting time: usually within 2 weeks. Payment: 4¢ per word upon acceptance; articles 250-500 words. Copyrighted, reverts to author. Pub's reviews: 15 in 1990. §Must be of interest to women seeking a home income venture, or starting one and in need of guidance in legal areas, or sources of information. Ads: $25/$15/$9 1/4 page/5¢ per word.

WORKING CLASSICS, Red Wheelbarrow Press, David Joseph, Editor; Carol Tarlen, Assistant Editor, 298 9th Avenue, San Francisco, CA 94118, 415-387-3412. 1981. Poetry, fiction, articles, art, photos, cartoons, interviews, satire, criticism, reviews, music, letters, parts-of-novels, long-poems, collages, plays, concrete art, news items, non-fiction. "In *WC* you'll find the authentic voices of working people with humor, insight, and life! We deal creatively with day-to-day concerns in the workplace and family. We look for a sense of history and of future, for visions with the ability to see the complications and contradictions in people's lives. We publish reviews of books and magazines, briefly. Recent contributors: Sesshu Foster, Julia Stein, Rane Arroyo, Myung-Hee Kim, Steve Rayshich, Mi Sidumo Hlatshwayo, Karen Brodine." circ. 2M. 2/yr. Expects 2 issues 1991, 2 issues 1992. sub. price: $10/4 issues; per copy: $2.50; sample: $3. Back issues: same. Discounts: free to workers on picket lines. 40% on consignment. 24pp; 8½×11; of. Reporting time: 1-3 months. Payment: copies. Copyrighted, reverts to author. Pub's reviews. §Art and literature of workers. Ads: $100/$60/$12.50 per column inch.

Working Press, Karen Eliot, 85 St. Agnes Place, Kennington, London SE11 4BB, England, 01 582 0023. 1987. Art, criticism, reviews, collages, concrete art. "Working Press is an umbrella under which books by and about working class artists can be published and promoted. Distribution worldwide by Counter Productions, PO Box 556, London SE5 0RL, United Kingdom. Write for full catalogue." avg. press run 1M. Pub'd 5 titles 1990; expects 5 titles 1991, 5 titles 1992. 12 titles listed in the *Small Press Record of Books in Print* (20th Edition, 1991-92). avg. price, paper: £6 + postage, $20 US institutions (air mail); other: £3 pamphlets, chapbooks, comix, etc. Discounts: 1/3 off to general trade shops ideally minimum of 5 books, 50% to major distributor in a country. 30-150pp; size A6, A3; of. Reporting time: 30 days. Payment: authors pay all production and printing cost; pay w.p. 10% cover price towards promotion etc. Copyrights for author. Small Presses Group (SPG), BM Bozo, London WC1N3XX U.K., Federation of Worker Writers and Community Publishers (FWWCP).

WORKSHOP, Small-Small Press, Tom Fallon, 226 Linden Street, Rumford, ME 04276, 364-7237. 1980. Articles, interviews, satire, criticism, reviews, letters, collages, concrete art, news items. "Experimental literature from Maine; one out-of-state writer per issue. Will consider regulation prose & poetry if accompanied by the same piece written as an experiment. Content, human experience preferred, but no biases. One page pieces, excerpts. One page articles relating actual experiment work, definitions, literary category, etc." circ. 300. 2/yr. Pub'd 1 issue 1990; expects 6 issues 1991, 6 issues 1992. sub. price: $3; per copy: $2; sample: $2. Back issues: $3. 48pp; 6×9; of, mi. Reporting time: 2 months. Payment: copies. Not copyrighted. Pub's reviews. §Experimental writing forms, articles, etc. MWPA (Maine Writers and Publishers Alliance).

WORLD HUMOR AND IRONY MEMBERSHIP SERIAL YEARBOOK (WHIMSY), Victor Raskin, English Department, Purdue University, West Lafayette, IN 47907, 317-494-3780. 1982. Poetry, articles, cartoons, satire. "The material must be read at the annual WHIM (World Humor and Irony Membership) conference. Papers will be extracted down to about three pages per author" circ. 1M. 1/yr. Pub'd 1 issue 1990; expects 1 issue 1991, 1 issue 1992. 1 title listed in the *Small Press Record of Books in Print* (20th Edition, 1991-92). sub. price: $10; per copy: $10; sample: $10. Back issues: $10. 350pp; 8½×11; †word star, daisy printwheel. Reporting time: immediate. Payment: none. Copyrighted, reverts to author. Ads: $100/$60/$35 1/4 page. Conference of Editors of Learned Journals (CELJ).

WORLD LETTER, Jon Cone, 2726 E. Court Street, Iowa City, IA 52245, 319-337-6022. 1991. Poetry, fiction, art, parts-of-novels, long-poems. "No unsolicited material is being accepted at this time. However, I am interested in hearing from translators. What sort of publication is *World Letter*? The best answer to this question would be supplied by purchasing a copy and enjoying it firsthand. In the absence of such extravagance I can only offer my unofficial motto: no axe to grind and no money with which to do it. I publish whatever I enjoy and pride myself on being open to a wide range of style and content. Past contributors: Chandler Brossard, Irving Stettner, Charles Bernstein, Morty Sklar, Vicki Ramirez, Mary Kessler, Thomas Wiloch, Jacob Rabinowitz, Chuck Miller, Cary Fagan, Jeffrey Zable, James Koehnline. Forthcoming contributors will include: Charles Bukowski, Clayton Eshleman, Lyn Lifshin, George Economou, Nina Barragan, James Laughlin, Irving Stettner, Carol Adderley, Kurt Nimmo." circ. 200. 1+. Expects 2 issues 1991, 2 issues 1992. sub. price: $8/2 issues indiv., $10/2 issues instit.; per copy: $5 indiv., $5 instit.; sample: $4 indiv., $5 instit. 48pp; 5½×8½ to 6½×10; of. Reporting time: 2-4 weeks or as soon as possible. Payment: none. Copyrighted, reverts to author.

WORLD MUSIC CONNECTIONS NEWSLETTER, White Cliffs Media Company, Larry W. Smith, PO Box 561, Crown Point, IN 46307-0561. 1987. "Art infor on world music/ethnomusicology." circ. 5M-10M. 4/yr. Pub'd 2 issues 1990; expects 4 issues 1991, 4 issues 1992. sub. price: currently free (promotional), subscription fee will eventually be charged. 2-8pp; 8½×11. Payment: currently none. Copyrighted, does not revert to author. Pub's reviews. §World music (ethnomusicology), folk music, pop music. Ads: under review. PMA, MAP.

World Music Press, Judith Cook Tucker, Editor & Publisher, PO Box 2565, Danbury, CT 06813, 203-748-1131; fax 203-743-0784. 1985. Photos, music, non-fiction. "We are looking for manuscripts of traditional music from non-Western cultures (particularly African, Native American, Latin American, Southeast Asian) with in-depth annotation, prepared with the participation and knowledge of the indigenous musicians from whose repertoires the material is drawn. Slant is definitely for use by educators, and should be accurate and authentic but not dry or scholarly in tone. Range: grades 3-12 in particular. Current authors include Ghanaian master musician Abraham Kobena Adzinyah, Dumisani Maraire (ethnomusicologist/musician from Zimbabwe). Book Series in this area is called *Songs from Singing Cultures*. *Vocal Traditions* choral series (choral pieces for school use inspired by or drawn from traditional music of many cultures, including Africa, Latin America, the rural south (US), Israel, Native America). Composers/arrangers include Lorre Wyatt, Pete Seeger, Dumisani Maraire." avg. press run 1.5M books, 1M-3M choral pieces. Pub'd 1,3 titles 1990; expects 3 books, 5 choral pcs. titles 1991, 3,5 titles 1992. 9 titles listed in the *Small Press Record of Books in Print* (20th Edition, 1991-92). avg. price, paper: $12.95; other: indiv. choral pcs. $.80-$1.20; cassette companion tapes $6-$10.95. Discounts: 20% on 2-5 books, 30% 6-10; 40% 11+ mixed titles ok; mixed books/tapes ok; S.T.O.P. orders ok. 150pp; 8½×11, 6×9; of. Reporting time: 1 month. Payment: 10% (nego.) royalty; small advance; every 6-months payments. Copyrights for author. PMA.

WORLD OF FANDOM MAGAZINE, Allen Shevy, Chris Mygrant, PO Box 9421, Tampa, FL 33604, 813-933-7424; 238-4643. 1987. Fiction, articles, art, photos, cartoons, interviews, reviews, music, non-fiction. "Physical address: 2525 W. Knollwood Street, Tampe, FL 33614-4334. We also publish a comic book called *RatFinkComics*. We will run most anything as long as it has to do with comic books, movies, music, or TV. Art is also acceptable." circ. 30M+. 4/yr. Pub'd 4 issues 1990; expects 4 issues 1991, 4 issues 1992. sub. price: $12, $20 foreign; per copy: $3, $5 foreign; sample: $3, $5 foreign (includes p/h). Back issues: upon request, based on copies in stock. Discounts: will trade with mags; wholesale 60 non-returnable, 55% returnable. 68pp; 8½×11; of. Payment: depends on content but usually complimentary copies. Copyrighted, reverts to author. Pub's reviews. §SciFi, horror, movie, music, TV, review comic books. Ads: $400/$225/$125 1/4 page/discounts for more than 1 issue.

World Peace University Publications, PO Box 10869, Eugene, OR 97440, 503-231-3771. 1986. avg. press run 3M. Pub'd 1 title 1990; expects 4 titles 1991, 4 titles 1992. 3 titles listed in the *Small Press Record of Books in Print* (20th Edition, 1991-92). avg. price, paper: $10.95. Discounts: 30% on 5 or more copies, 40% to wholesalers. 120pp; 5⅜×8½. Copyrights for author.

WORLD PERSPECTIVES, Esty Dinur, Box 3074, Madison, WI 53704, 608-241-4812. 1990. Articles, news items. "*World Perspectives* specializes in alternative news, views and analysis from shortwave radio sources from around the world. Topics covered include the arms race, disarmament, the Third World, covert operations, women's, environmental and labor issues, and other issues not covered by U.S. media." circ. 1M. 12/yr. Pub'd 12 issues 1990; expects 12 issues 1991, 12 issues 1992. sub. price: $19; per copy: $1.75; sample: $1.75 (subject to change soon). Back issues: $2. Discounts: classes may get a semester sub (5 issues) for $7.50. 32pp; 7×8½; of. Reporting time: generally not looking for submissions. Payment: none. Copyrighted, reverts to author. Ads: $62/$34/$20 1/4 page.

World Promotions, Lana Hinshaw Davis, Tom McKernan, 699 Sudden Valley, Bellingham, WA 98226. 1986. Fiction. avg. press run 5M. Expects 2 titles 1991, 3 titles 1992. 2 titles listed in the *Small Press Record of Books in Print* (20th Edition, 1991-92). avg. price, cloth: $17.95; paper: $9.95. Discounts: 2-4 10%, 5-24 20%, 25-49

30%, 50-99 40%, 100+ 50%. 350pp; 5½×8; of. Reporting time: 3-6 months. Does not copyright for author unless material needs copyrighting, or unless author requests.

WORLD RAINFOREST REPORT, Randy Hayes, Director; Joe Kane, Editor, Rainforest Action Network, 301 Broadway, Suite A, San Francisco, CA 94133, 415-398-4404. 1982. News items. "The *World Rainforest Report* is an international newsletter dealing with all aspects of tropical rainforest preservation. Recent contributors include Catherine Caufield, author of *In The Rainforest*, and Randy Hayes, the director of the Rainforest Action Network." circ. 18M. 4/yr. Pub'd 4 issues 1990; expects 4 issues 1991, 4 issues 1992. sub. price: $25; per copy: $1; sample: same. Back issues: $2. Discounts: bulk copies to environmental educators. 8-12pp. Reporting time: 10 days prior to publication. Payment: none. Not copyrighted. Pub's reviews: 12 in 1990. §Environmental, human rights, animal rights, tropical rainforest information. No ads.

World Transport Press (see also AIRLINERS; AIRLINERS MONTHLY NEWS), John Wegg, PO Box 52-1238, Miami, FL 33152, 305-477-7163. 1988. Articles, photos, interviews, satire, reviews. "Books on commercial aviation" avg. press run 8.5M. Pub'd 2 titles 1990; expects 1 title 1991, 1 title 1992. 2 titles listed in the *Small Press Record of Books in Print* (20th Edition, 1991-92). avg. price, cloth: $27.95. Discounts: contact publisher, 30-55%. 155pp; 8½×11; of. Reporting time: 3 months. Payment: contact publisher. Does not copyright for author. COSMEP.

World Wildlife Fund & The Conservation Foundation (see also RESOLVE NEWSLETTER; WORLD WILDLIFE FUND & THE CONSERVATION FOUNDATION LETTER; FOCUS), Allison Rogers, 1250 24th Street, NW, Washington, DC 20037, 202-293-4800. 1948. Photos, non-fiction. "World Wildlife Fund & The Conservation Foundation is a nonprofit environmental research organization based in Washington, D.C. It conducts interdisciplinary policy research on emerging issues in environmental and resource management, and publishes many of its findings in books or newsletters. Staff numbers approximately 200 and includes lawyers, scientists, economists, political scientists, engineers, and others. Staff writers only" avg. press run 2M. Pub'd 7 titles 1990; expects 6 titles 1991, 6 titles 1992. avg. price, cloth: $40; paper: $18. Discounts: bulk: 1-4 books, 0; 5-9, 20%; 10-99, 25%; 100+, 40%; booksellers: 1, 0; 2-4, 30%; 5-9,35%; 10-99, 40%; 100+, 50%. 150-200pp; 6×9; of. Copyrights for author.

WORLD WILDLIFE FUND & THE CONSERVATION FOUNDATION LETTER, World Wildlife Fund & The Conservation Foundation, Jonathan Adams, 1250 24th Street, NW, Washington, DC 20037, 202-293-4800. 1948. Articles, non-fiction. "*World Wildlife Fund & The Conservation Foundation Letter* covers a single environmental or resource topic, in-depth coverage that is thoughtful and well documented. Written for professionals and informed lay readers who need a clear perspective on a variety of environmental issues, domestic and world-wide, the *Letter* assumes no advocacy position but addresses controversy in a manner that is critical yet undogmatic. Also keeps readers apprised of World Wildlife Fund & The Conservation Foundation activities, new books, etc. Complimentary subscriptions available by writing the World Wildlife Fund & The Conservation Foundation" circ. 5M. 12/yr. Pub'd 6 issues 1990; expects 12 issues 1991, 12 issues 1992. sub. price: free; per copy: $1.50; sample: free. 8pp; 8½×11; of. Copyrighted.

World Wisdom Books, Inc., PO Box 2682, Bloomington, IN 47402, 812-332-1663. 1981. Non-fiction. avg. press run 3M. Pub'd 2 titles 1990; expects 2 titles 1991, 1 title 1992. 11 titles listed in the *Small Press Record of Books in Print* (20th Edition, 1991-92). avg. price, cloth: $37.50; paper: $10.95. Discounts: trade - 1-2 20%, 3-9 33%, 10-24 40%, 25+ 50%. 195pp; 8½×5½; photo offset. Reporting time: 3-6 months. Copyrights for author. COSMEP.

Worldwatch Institute (see also WORLDWATCH PAPERS), 1776 Massachusetts Ave NW, Washington, DC 20036, 202-452-1999. 1974. "Worldwatch Institute is a non-profit research organization attempting to identify emerging global trends and bring them to the public's attention through its Worldwatch Paper Series and work with the media. Current projects are annual "State of the World" reporting on progress toward a sustainable society. All research is done in-house. No submissions—all written in house." avg. press run 30M-33M. Pub'd 6 titles 1990; expects 7-8 titles 1991. 43 titles listed in the *Small Press Record of Books in Print* (20th Edition, 1991-92). avg. price, paper: $5. Discounts: $5 single copy; $4 for 2-5 copies; $3 for 6-20 copies; $2 for 21 or more. 70pp; 5⅜×8⅜. Copyrights for author.

WORLDWATCH PAPERS, Worldwatch Institute, 1776 Massachusetts Ave., N.W., Washington, DC 20036.

THE WORMWOOD REVIEW, The Wormwood Review Press, Marvin Malone, Editor; Ernest Stranger, Art Editor, PO Box 4698, Stockton, CA 95204-0698, 209-466-8231. 1959. Poetry, reviews, long-poems, collages, concrete art, news items. "Poetry and prose-poems to 300+ lines reflecting the temper and depth of present human scene. All types and schools from traditional-economic through concrete, dada and extreme avant-garde. Special fondness for prose poems/fables. Each issue has yellow-page section devoted to one poet or topic (e.g. Bukowski, Wantling, Jon Webb, Micheline, Crews, Locklin, Koertge, Dick Higgins, Ian Hamilton Finlay, Steve Richmond, John Currier, Wm. Burroughs, etc.)." circ. 700. 4/yr. Pub'd 4 issues 1990; expects 4 issues 1991, 4 issues 1992. sub. price: $8/yr, $10/yr institutions, $1.75 surcharge for all foreign; per copy: $4; sample: $4 postpaid, first class. Back issues: inquire. Discounts: $4 retail copy costs agent $2.40. 40-48pp; 5½×8½; of. Reporting time: 2-8 weeks. Payment: 3-5 copies or cash equivalent. Copyrighted, rights revert—author *must* request re-assignment; re-assignment without cost. Pub's reviews: 85 in 1990. §Poetry/experimental prose. No ads accepted.

The Wormwood Review Press (see also THE WORMWOOD REVIEW), Marvin Malone, Editor; Ernest Stranger, Art Editor, PO Box 4698, Stockton, CA 95204-0698, 209-466-8231. 1959. Poetry, reviews, long-poems, collages, concrete art. "Chapbook authors: Koertge, Locklin, David Barker, Phil Weidman, Crews, Wilma McDaniel, Steve Richmond, Charles Bukowski, Todd Moore, Dan Lenihan." avg. press run 700. Pub'd 1 title 1990; expects 1 title 1991, 1 title 1992. 11 titles listed in the *Small Press Record of Books in Print* (20th Edition, 1991-92). avg. price, paper: $4. Discounts: $4 retail copies cost agent $2.40. 40-48pp; 5½×8½; of. Reporting time: 2-8 weeks. Payment: 35 copies. Copyrights for author.

WREE-VIEW OF WOMEN, Jan Jamshidi, Editor, 198 Broadway, #606, New York, NY 10038. 1975. Poetry, articles, art, photos, cartoons, interviews, news items. circ. 5M. 4/yr. Pub'd 1 issue 1990; expects 3 issues 1991, 4 issues 1992. sub. price: $6; per copy: $2; sample: $2. Back issues: $2 if available. Discounts: 40% off bundles of 5 or more. 32pp. Reporting time: 1 month. Payment: none. Not copyrighted. Pub's reviews: 2-3 in 1990. §Books re: women, children, affirmative action, etc. Ads: $100 half-page or $10 per display column inch or 20¢ per word classified.

WRESTLING - THEN & NOW, Evan Ginzburg, PO Box 471, Oakland Gdns. Station, Flushing, NY 11364. 1990. Articles, interviews, satire, reviews, letters, news items, non-fiction. "Explores history of professional wrestling. Features warm reminisces, where are they now type features, interviews, etc." circ. 150+. 12/yr. Pub'd 11 issues 1990; expects 12 issues 1991, 12 issues 1992. sub. price: $12; per copy: $1.25; sample: free with SASE. Back issues: $1. 10pp; 8½×11; xerox. Reporting time: varies. Payment: none. Copyrighted, reverts to author. Pub's reviews: 6 in 1990. Ads: none.

Wright-Armstead Associates, Sara Ellen Messmer, Editor; Madrue Chavers-Wright, Publisher, 2410 Barker Avenue, Suite 14-G, Bronx, NY 10467, (212) 654-9445. 1985. Non-fiction. "Special interests: history, social science, ethnic studies. Interested in image-building among people of color. Recent title: *The Guarantee* is a biography of P.W. Chavers, Ohio journalist and industrialist, his move to Chicago torn with bank failures and race riots after WW1, his establishing a national bank, campaigning for economic freedom in the Black Belt midst power struggles. The impact on his health and well-being of his family, revealing the triumphs and tragedies of the 'Black Experience' in the urban midwest of the 'Roaring Twenties'. Considerable history of bank legislation to protect depositors accounts in national banks: P.W. Chavers' work with the *Federal Reserve Board*, his writing the earliest federal legislation to guarantee depositors' bank accounts in national banks, urban politics and economics, *The Crash; The Great Depression; The Bank Holiday*; the emergence of the *Federal Depositors Insurance Corporation*. Also *The Great Migration; Federal Douglass; Booker T. Washington; WEB DuBois; The Marcus Garvey & Jean Baptiste Point DeSaible Movements*; and ethnic diversity and multiculturalism in the early 20th century." 2 titles listed in the *Small Press Record of Books in Print* (20th Edition, 1991-92). Discounts: on multiple orders only: 20%, prepayment preferred. 450pp; 5½×8½; Braun-Brumfield.

WRIT, Roger Greenwald, Editor; Richard Lush, Associate Editor, Two Sussex Avenue, Toronto M5S 1J5, Canada, 416-978-4871. 1970. Poetry, fiction, parts-of-novels, long-poems. "We have an open policy: we're looking for good writing regardless of format or length; we'll print work that's intellectual and difficult if we think it's good and work that's 'experimental' or whatever if we think it's good. We've printed large amounts of fiction (numbers 4, 10, 13, & 15 were all-fiction issues). Interested in translations of modern and contemporary poetry and fiction not yet well known in English (enclose originals). Number 14 and 18 were all-translation issues, with much work from Scandinavia. Starting with Number 19, each issue features at least one translated poet: 19 has Pia Tafdrup (Denmark); 20 (Tribute to Joel Oppenheimer) has Gunnar Harding (Sweden). Ordinarily we print only work that has not yet appeared in print (new translations okay). You must send SASE with Canadian stamps or international coupons (not US stamps) and a phone number where you can be reached. If you have an account on USENET or bitnet, state site name and log-in name, but submit all work on paper, with clear, dark typing or printout (clear photocopies okay, but no simultaneous submissions)." circ. 700. 1/yr. Pub'd 1 issue 1990; expects 1 issue 1991, 1 issue 1992. sub. price: 2 issues—Canada $15 individuals, $18 institutions, same in U.S.; per copy: $7.50, U.S. $6 outside Canada (current issue); sample: $7.50. Back issues: $7.50, $10 #14, 18, 21 (outside Canada send same amount in U.S. funds); #6, 11, 12, 14, 16, 18, 19, 21 available only as part of complete run. Discounts: bookstores 40% of sale price, 25% on complete run, subscription agencies none, classroom & other bulk purchases-by arrangement. 96pp; 6×9; of. Reporting time: generally 8-12 weeks; we do not read May-August; allow 2-3 weeks each direction for Canada's infamous mail service, unless you use special delivery. Payment: copies only. Copyright by the authors. §Poetry, fiction, translations. Ads: $400/$250/or by exchange.

THE WRITE AGE (First Magazine of Writing Therapy), Bonnie Langenhahn, PO Box 722, Menomonee Falls, WI 53051, 414-255-7706. 1985. Poetry, fiction, interviews, non-fiction. "Prefer under 1,000 words. Because of the focus on writing as therapy (that includes pleasure!), a brief "Why I Write" statement must accompany each story/poem. What does it do for you *emotionally*? Bulk of magazine is by older people, but stories by physically/mentally disabled, people in transition of any age, are welcome. Also, articles by health care professionals and teachers using unique writing methods with groups. Query, do not send unsolicited manuscripts" circ. 400+. 2/yr. Pub'd 2 issues 1990; expects 2 issues 1991, 2 issues 1992. sub. price: $10.50; per copy: $4.95 + postage; sample: $4.50. Back issues: $4.50 includes mailing. Discounts: $50/6 subscriptions, $97.50/12 subscriptions *or* $50/12 magazines. 60pp; 7×8½; of. Reporting time: 2-6 weeks, usually less. Payment: 2 copies of magazine. Copyrighted, reverts to author. Pub's reviews: 2 in 1990. §Writing as therapy (journaling, letter-writing, memoirs). Ads: $125/$80/quarter page $45. COSMEP.

WRITE NOW!, Right Here Publications, Emily Jean Carroll, PO Box 1014, Huntington, IN 46750. 1990. Poetry, articles. "300 to 1200 words about writing, poetry, publishing, self-promotion. Recent guest columnists: Dennis Hensley, Liz Flaherty, Kenneth Hardin. Recent guest editor column: Denver Stull. Theme 'On Assignment' contests each issue." circ. 250+. 6/yr. Pub'd 6 issues 1990; expects 6 issues 1991, 6 issues 1992. sub. price: $12; per copy: $2; sample: $1.50. Discounts: inquire. 32pp; 5½×8½; of. Reporting time: 1-2 months. Copyrighted, reverts to author. Pub's reviews: 11 in 1990. §Writing, publishing, self-publishing. Ads: $30/$18/inserts-inquire.

The Write Press, Bob Hensler, 8518 12th Way North, St. Petersburg, FL 33702. 1988. Poetry, non-fiction. avg. press run 200-300. Pub'd 6 titles 1990; expects 6 titles 1991. avg. price, paper: $6. 28pp; 5½×8½; †mi, of. Payment: Author pays all costs. Copyrights for author.

Writers & Scholars International Ltd. (see also INDEX ON CENSORSHIP), Andrew Graham-Vooll, 39c Highbury Place, London N5 1QP, England, 071-359-0161. 34 titles listed in the *Small Press Record of Books in Print* (20th Edition, 1991-92).

THE WRITERS' BAR-B-Q, Tim Osburn, Becky Bradway, Gary Smith, Myra Epping, Marcia Womack, 924 Bryn Mawr Boulevard, Springfield, IL 62703, (217) 525-6987. 1986. Fiction, parts-of-novels, plays. "*The Writers' Bar-B-Q*, is looking for literate, unpretentious fiction. All subjects and genres are encouraged. Well-written and entertaining stories, long stories, plays and novel excerpts will be considered. Characterization and content is important. Be daring, be truthful, discover something—tell us a story. Contributors include Lowry Pei, Sharon Sloan Fiffer, Shannon Keith Kelley, Nolan Porterfield, Michael C. White, Martha M. Vertreace, Florri McMillan." circ. 1M. 1-2/yr. Pub'd 2 issues 1990; expects 2 issues 1991, 2 issues 1992. sub. price: $10, $14 3 issues, $18 4 issues; per copy: $5; sample: same. 110pp; 8½×11; of. Reporting time: 6 weeks-4 months. Payment: 3 copies. Copyrighted, reverts to author. Ads: $110/$65/$35. CCLM, Poets and Writers.

THE WRITERS' BLOC*, Deborah Holland, Box 212, Marysville, OH 43040, 513-642-8019. 1985. Poetry, fiction, articles, reviews. "Stories to 6,000 words, although the shorter the better to see print. Poetry to 30 lines. No shaped poetry at this time. Contributors: Russ Ramsey, Kenneth Geisert, Kenneth Schulze, Jill DiMaggio" circ. 300. 4/yr. Pub'd 4 issues 1990; expects 4 issues 1991, 4 issues 1992. sub. price: $10; per copy: $3; sample: $3. Back issues: $3. Discounts: we give a special price break to contributors who want to buy in quantity. 40pp; 6½×8½. Reporting time: varies, 6-12 weeks. Payment: contributor's copy. Copyrighted, reverts to author. Pub's reviews: 1 in 1990. §Short story or poetry anthologies, series novels, fiction. No non-fiction. Ads: inquire.

The Writer's Center (see also CAROUSEL; POET LORE), 7815 Old Georgetown Road, Bethesda, MD 20814, 301-654-8664. 1977.

WRITERS CONNECTION, Jan Stiles, 1601 Saratoga-Sunnyvale Road, Suite 180, Cupertino, CA 95014, 408-973-0227. 1983. Articles, criticism, letters, news items, non-fiction. "Publishes 1500-2000 word how-to articles on writing and publishing topics. Also includes columns, departments and features on such topics as markets, writing events, writers' exchange, and milestones." circ. 3M. 12/yr. Pub'd 12 issues 1990; expects 12 issues 1991, 12 issues 1992. sub. price: $12; per copy: $1.50 + 75¢ p/h each; sample: free. Back issues: $1.50 + 75¢ p/h each. Discounts: 50% to magazine dealers/distributors. 16pp; 8×10½; of. Reporting time: 2-6 weeks. Payment: in services only (memberships, subscriptions, seminars, ad listings). Copyrighted, reverts to author. Pub's reviews: approx. 7 in 1990. §Writing-related guides. Ads: call for details. COSMEP.

WRITERS' FORUM, Alex Blackburn, Editor-in-Chief; Lesley Craig, Fiction Editor; Bret Lott, Fiction Editor; Victoria McCabe, Poetry Editor, University of Colorado, Colorado Springs, CO 80933-7150, 719-593-3155; 599-4023. 1974. Poetry, fiction, parts-of-novels, long-poems. "We publish a book representing some of the best new American literature by authors, both established and unrecognized, especially but not necessarily resident in or associated with states west of the Mississippi. We will publish up to 5 poems, including long ones, by one author and fiction, including excerpts from novels, up to 15M words. Ranked third in nation for non-paying fiction market (Writer's Digest)." circ. 1M. 1/yr. Pub'd 1 issue 1990; expects 1 issue 1991, 1 issue 1992. sub.

price: $8.95; per copy: $8.95; sample: $5.95 for readers of *International Directory of Little Magazines & Small Presses, 24th Edition*. Back issues: Vols. 1-7 lowcost microfiche. Discounts: 20% libraries, 40% bookstores. 240pp; 5½x8½; of. Reporting time: 3-5 weeks. Payment: free copies only, thus far. Copyrighted, reverts to author. Ads: $175/$100. AWP, CLMP.

Writers Forum (see also AND; KROKLOK), Bob Cobbing, 89A Petherton Road, London N5 2QT, England, 071-226-2657. 1963. Poetry, fiction, art, photos, criticism, music, long-poems, concrete art. "Mainly members' work." avg. press run 200 but often reprinted. Pub'd 25 titles 1990; expects 20 titles 1991, 20 titles 1992. 87 titles listed in the *Small Press Record of Books in Print* (20th Edition, 1991-92). avg. price, paper: £1.50. Discounts: 1/3 off. 20pp; size varies; †photo-copy. Reporting time: 3 weeks. Payment: copies. Copyrights for author on request. ALP, COLP.

WRITERS GAZETTE NEWSLETTER, Trouvere Company, Brenda Williamson, Route 2, Box 290, Eclectic, AL 36024. 1980. Poetry, fiction, articles, art, photos, cartoons, interviews, satire, criticism, reviews, long-poems, news items, non-fiction. "Short story to 2,500 words, non-fiction to 1,500 words, poetry to 100 lines. Sometimes we go over these limits, but mostly we prefer under these limits. Except for poetry, fiction, satire, art and photos, material should be writer related" circ. 1.2M. 12/yr. Pub'd 12 issues 1990; expects 12 issues 1991, 12 issues 1992. sub. price: $9; per copy: $1; sample: $1. Discounts: 20% library, 10% all others. 36pp; 8½x11; of. Reporting time: 2-8 weeks. Payment: varies. Copyrighted, reverts to author. Pub's reviews: 12 in 1990. §Mostly writer related, except we do include novels, chapbooks, etc. especially from self-publishers. Reviews are staffwritten, send book. Ads: $30 1x/$17 1x/$10 1/4 page/$7 1/8/reading notices 10¢ per word. Discounts for multi. insertion on displays.

WRITER'S GUIDELINES MAGAZINE, Susan Salaki, Box 608, Pittsburg, MO 65724. 1988. Poetry, fiction, articles, art, cartoons, interviews, satire, criticism, reviews, letters, news items, non-fiction. circ. 1M. 6/yr. Pub'd 4 issues 1990; expects 6 issues 1991, 6 issues 1992. sub. price: $18; per copy: $4; sample: $4. Back issues: $4. 32pp; 8½x11; †mi. Reporting time: 2-4 weeks. Payment: from copies to 1¢ per word. Copyrighted, reverts to author. Pub's reviews: 30 in 1990. §Open to all areas. Ads: $45/$26/$89 back cover. CCC, SPWAO.

THE WRITER'S HAVEN, Marcella Owens, PO Box 413, Joaquin, TX 75954. 1990. Poetry, fiction, articles, criticism, reviews, letters, parts-of-novels, non-fiction. "Length of material: 8 pages, 12 pages sometimes. Contributors: Leona Griffin, Jean Werner, Gainelle Murray, C.E. Heffley, Wanda Windham, Sandra K. Wheeler, A.J. Speers." circ. 200. 6/yr. Expects 5 issues 1991, 6 issues 1992. sub. price: $12; per copy: $3; sample: $3. Back issues: $2. Discounts: $10 year. 8x11. Reporting time: 2-3 weeks. Payment: 2 free copies. Not copyrighted. Pub's reviews. §Writer-related gothics, mysteries, nonfiction (any subject). Ads: $4 for 2-inch line. ICS, NRI, BGTG.

Writer's Helper Publishing, PO Box 32006, Overland Park, KS 66212, 913-383-9894. 1990. 1 title listed in the *Small Press Record of Books in Print* (20th Edition, 1991-92).

Writers House Press (see also BEGINNING: THE MAGAZINE FOR THE WRITER IN THE COMMUNITY), Richard L. Collett, Jr., Editor, 1530 Bladensburg Road, Ottumwa, IA 52501-9066, 515-682-4305. 1982. Poetry, fiction, articles, art, photos, interviews, satire, criticism, reviews, music, letters, parts-of-novels, long-poems, plays, news items, non-fiction. "WE ARE NOT ACCEPTING MANUSCRIPTS AT THIS TIME. We publish high quality manuscripts on any topic. We currently have the following series: 1) Political & Social Affairs Series (books concerning politics & social problems); 2) Contemporary Studies in the Humanities (books concerning psychology, philosophy, history, new age subjects, holistic medicine, self-help books in personal development, etc. 3) Contemporary literature for children; 4) Contemporary Poets Series; 5) Poetry in Translation; 6) Fiction in Translation; and 7) Works in translation (other than poetry or fiction). Writers House Press is a Cooperative Press. We believe, as established authors published by major Houses have found, that when one has participated in the entire publishing process (writing, publishing, distributing) a greater sense of satisfaction is felt when seeing the final result on the bookstore shelves. In a Cooperative Royalty publishing venture the author shares in the investment and the profits. Traditional publishing houses keep the majority of the proceeds and leave the author with as little as 6% for paperbacks and 10% for hardbacks. As a participant in the publishing process, the author maintains more artistic control, assists in promotion and distribution plans, and shares equally in the financial success of the book. See specifics of financial arrangements under the Royalty and Payment Arrangement with Authors section below. Authors should first send a proposal with a sample chapter (or ten pages of poetry). The proposal should include information about the purpose of the book (if non-fiction), table of contents (if applicable), full text of any introduction or Foreword, story/plot outline, theme, potential audience, distribution ideas, copies of any reviews, personal background (including qualifications to write on a non-fiction subject), and any other information that may aid us in our decision. We are not a vanity press publishing any manuscript that comes with a check. All proposals must be submitted to a committee who will vote on whether to invite the submission of the entire manuscript. Expect one-two months for response to the proposal. Within three months of receiving the entire manuscript, we will notify the author if the work has been accepted for publication, at which time a

647

contract will be negotiated. All material and correspondence must include an SASE." avg. press run 500-1.5M. Pub'd 4 titles 1990; expects 4 titles 1991, 8 titles 1992. 8 titles listed in the *Small Press Record of Books in Print* (20th Edition, 1991-92). avg. price, cloth: $14.95-$24.95; paper: $5.95-$13.95; other: $3.95-$5.95. Discounts: Distributors: 1-5 copies 20%, 6-10 copies 25%, 11-25 copies 30%, 26-50 copies 35%, 51-100 copies 40%; Jobbers: 20%; Bookstores: 30%. Pages vary; 5½×8½, 6×9; of. Reporting time: 3 minutes to 3 months. As a cooperative venture the cost of publishing is shared as are the profits. We pay about 80% of the costs; the author pays about 20%. As a royalty house, the author receives a royalty of 14%-20%. In addition, the author may participate as his or her own distributor and receive up to 50% of the cover price in additional profits. Specific contract items may vary, depending on the needs of the particular book project. Copyrights for author.

WRITER'S INFO, Hutton Publications, Linda Hutton, PO Box 1870, Hayden, ID 83835, 208-772-6184. 1985. Poetry, articles, art, non-fiction. "Articles to 300 words & short poems all relating to writing." circ. 200. 12/yr. Pub'd 4 issues 1990; expects 12 issues 1991, 12 issues 1992. sub. price: $12; per copy: $1; sample: free for SAE plus 2 stamps. 6pp; 8½×14; of. Reporting time: 1 month. Payment: $1 and up for first rights. Copyrighted, reverts to author. No ads.

WRITERS INK, Writers Unlimited Agency, Inc, Writers Ink Press, David B. Axelrod, 186 North Coleman Road, Centereach, NY 11720, 516-736-6439. 1975. Articles, art, photos, cartoons, interviews, satire, criticism, reviews, collages. "Maximum article or story length 500 w. Though longer material might be serialized. Filler, humor for writers used. Limited to L.I. authors or items/ads of interest to L.I. literary scene. *No unsolicited manuscripts at present.*" circ. 2M. 0-4/yr. Pub'd 1 issue 1990; expects 1 issue 1991, 1 issue 1992. sub. price: $6; per copy: $1; No samples. Back issues: specific issues by request, free if available. Discounts: none-but free to worthy folks or groups—sold, $6.00 yearly rate direct by 1st class mail from WI. 4-12pp; 5×7; of. Reporting time: immediate (maximum 2 weeks) only if we are interested. No reply means no thanks. Payment: 50¢ col. inch or $2 per photo. Copyrighted, reverts to author. Pub's reviews: 1 in 1990. §All aids to writers, general interest and of course, L.I. works, mags., books. Ads: $15/$8/25¢. COSMEP, NESPA, LIPS, LA, EEAC, LIPS.

Writers Ink Press (see also WRITERS INK), 186 North Coleman Road, Centereach, NY 11720, 516-736-6439. 1982. Poetry. "No unsolicited mss. at this time." avg. press run 800. 6 titles listed in the *Small Press Record of Books in Print* (20th Edition, 1991-92). avg. price, cloth: $16; paper: $8; other: $6 chapbook. Discounts: 30% bookstores & distributors. 24-48pp; 5×7; of, desktop, IBM/pagemaker. Payment: 50% profit over cost, varies. Copyrights for author.

WRITERS' JOURNAL, Minnesota Ink, Inc., Valerie Hockert, Publisher & Managing Editor, 27 Empire Drive, Saint Paul, MN 55103-1861, 612-225-1306. 1980. "Articles on writing - inspirational and informative - 500-1.2M words. News, Book Reviews, Markets Report. *Writers' Journal* is a bi-monthly journal for writers and poets. Short story contest once a year...poetry contest twice a year. Cash prizes." circ. 35M. 6/yr. Pub'd 6 issues 1990; expects 6 issues 1991, 6 issues 1992. sub. price: $18; per copy: $3; sample: $4. Back issues: $2.50 each. Discounts: varies. 52pp; 8×10½; of. Reporting time: 3-4 weeks. Payment: to 3¢ per word. Copyrighted, reverts to author. Pub's reviews. §On writing, poetry, communications. Ads: $675/$355/80¢ classified word.

WRITER'S LIFELINE, Vesta Publications Limited, Stephen Gill, Editor, PO Box 1641, Cornwall, Ont. K6H 5V6, Canada. 1974. circ. 2M. 3/yr. Pub'd 3 issues 1990; expects 3 issues 1991, 3 issues 1992. sub. price: $18; per copy: $3; sample: $8 for 3 issues. Back issues: $1.50. Discounts: 30%. 36pp; 5¼×8¼; †of. Reporting time: 4-6 weeks. Payment: in copies at present. Copyrighted. Pub's reviews: 80 in 1990. §All, but particularly about writing and publishing. Ads: $150/$100/$15. COSMEP, CPPA.

WRITER'S N.W., Media Weavers, Blue Heron Publishing, Inc., Linny Stovall, Dennis Stovall, Route 3, Box 376, Hillsboro, OR 97124. 1987. Articles, interviews, reviews, news items, non-fiction. "Articles by assignment only." circ. 75M. 4/yr. Pub'd 1 issue 1990; expects 4 issues 1991, 4 issues 1992. sub. price: $10; per copy: $2; sample: $2. Back issues: $2. 12pp; 11×17; of. Payment: copies. Copyrighted, reverts to author. Pub's reviews: 25 in 1990. §Only books by writers from the Pacific Northwest or books published by NW presses. Ads: $1160, $660, $350 (1/4 page), $25 col., classified $7 1st, 2nd. Pac. NW Book Pub. Assoc. (PNBPA), NW Assoc. of Book Pub. (NABP), Pac. NW Booksellers (PNBA), Book Publicists NW (BPN).

THE WRITER'S NOOK NEWS, The Writers' Nook Press, Eugene Ortiz, 38114 3rd Street #181, Willoughby, OH 44094-6140, 216-975-8965. 1985. Articles, cartoons, news items. "The *Nook News* is a quarterly newsletter dedicated to giving freelance writers specific information for their immediate practical use in getting published and staying published. The *Nook News* is published for the enrichment of all writers, aspiring and established, and regardless of field or genre. It contains news; writing tips; books; reviews; legislative/tax updates; conference, contest, and market listings. I pay 6¢ per word for First North American Serial Rights to short, pithy articles (under 400 words). Articles must be specific, terse, and contain information my readers can put to immediate, practical use. Please, no poems, essays, or fiction." circ. 10M. 4/yr. Pub'd 4 issues 1990; expects 4 issues 1991, 4 issues 1992. sub. price: $18; per copy: $5; sample: $5. Discounts: anybody who wants to sell *TWNN* subscriptions gets 50% for initial sales. 12-16pp; 8½×11; †of. Reporting time: 2 weeks to 3 months. Payment: 6¢ per word. Not copyrighted. Pub's reviews: 6 in 1990. §Anything on the writing profession; send to Marcella Owens, PO Box 413, Joaquin, TX 75954. Ads: $506/$303.60/$177.10 1/4 page/unclassifieds 50¢/word. COSMEP.

The Writers' Nook Press (see also THE NOOK NEWS MARKET BULLETIN; THE WRITER'S NOOK NEWS; NOOK NEWS CONFERENCES AND KLATCHES BULLETIN; THE NOOK NEWS CONTESTS AND AWARDS BULLETIN; NOOK NEWS REVIEW OF WRITERS' PUBLICATIONS), Eugene Ortiz, Editor; Brian Sykes, Associate Editor, 38114 3rd Street #181, Willoughby, OH 44094, 216-975-8965. 1985. Articles, reviews, news items. Pub'd 4 titles 1990; expects 5 titles 1991, 5 titles 1992. avg. price, other: $4. Discounts: 50% to sales representatives. 12-16pp; 8½×11, 5½×8½. Payment: 1st North American Serial Rights. Does not copyright for author. COSMEP.

WRITERS' OWN MAGAZINE, Writers' Own Publications, Mrs. E.M. Pickering, 121 Highbury Grove, Clapham, Bedford, Beds MK41 6DU, England, (0234)365982. 1982. Poetry, fiction, articles, reviews, letters. circ. 150. 4/yr. sub. price: £5, overseas £7; per copy: £1.25, overseas £1.75; sample: £1.25 U.K. sterling, overseas £1.75. 49pp; 5¾×8½; †stencil duplicating. Reporting time: 2 weeks. Payment: copy work appears in. Copyrighted, reverts to author. Pub's reviews: about 50 in 1990. Ads: 15 pence per word.

Writers' Own Publications (see also WRITERS' OWN MAGAZINE), Mrs. E.M. Pickering, 121 Highbury Grove, Clapham, Bedford, Beds MK41 6DU, England. 1983. Poetry, non-fiction. "Poetry booklets 20-24 pages. Articles/humor/autobiography 40-95 pages." avg. press run 150. Pub'd 6 titles 1990; expects 6 titles 1991, 6 titles 1992. 11 titles listed in the *Small Press Record of Books in Print* (20th Edition, 1991-92). avg. price, paper: £1.50. Discounts: 33⅓% to booksellers or library. 5¾×8¼; †stencil duplicating. Reporting time: 2 weeks to 1 month, depending on length. Payment: profits or sales for sole author books. Copyrights for author.

Writers Publishing Service Co., William R. Griffin, Publisher, 1512 Western Avenue, Seattle, WA 98101, 206-284-9954. 1976. Poetry, articles, photos, cartoons, interviews, criticism, reviews, letters, news items, non-fiction. "Provides full spectrum of services from consultations, editing, printing, binding and marketing. Specialists in self-publishing and mail order marketing, we handle how to's, cookbooks, poetry, and family histories and other short run (under 2500 copies) editions. Also provide editorial and market analysis report on manuscript. We do all work in house including desk top publishing, printing, hard cover and perfect binding. For those not interested or appropriate for self-publishing, we assist in book proposal development and submission to trade publishers." avg. press run 250-1M. Pub'd 20 titles 1990; expects 28 titles 1991, 22 titles 1992. avg. price, cloth: $16; paper: $8.50; other: $12. Discounts: 20% on multiple copies. 200pp; 8×11, 8½×5½, 8½×7; †of. Reporting time: 6 weeks. Payment: varies, 6% to 15%. Copyrights for author. Northwest Publishers Association.

Writers Unlimited Agency, Inc (see also WRITERS INK), David B. Axelrod, 186 North Coleman Road, Centereach, NY 11720. 1975. avg. press run 800. Pub'd 3 titles 1990; expects 3 titles 1991. avg. price, cloth: $16; paper: $8; other: $6 chapbook. Discounts: 30% distributor/bookseller. 40pp; 5½×8½, 5×8; IBM/pagemaker to format. Reporting time: no unsolicited mss. Payment: varies. Copyrights for author. Affiliate of 3WS, World-Wide Writers Service.

WRITER'S VOICE, Poetry Magic Publications, Lisa Roose-Church, 1630 Lake Drive, Haslett, MI 48840, 517-339-8754. 1987. "We accept work from all areas. A subscription does not guarantee publication of your work. An SASE must accompany all work or work will be discarded. All work should be original, unpublished work of author submitting it. We will consider previously published work if date and name of publication is noted at the time of submission. We do not accept pornographic material but will consider sexual themes if done in taste. Again, we don't promise anything. We reserve the right to edit your short story/article for grammar, punctuation, etc. If work is not legible, it will be returned unread." 4/yr. Pub'd 4 issues 1990; expects 4 issues 1991, 4 issues 1992. sub. price: $13.50; per copy: $3.50; sample: $4.50 ppd. Discounts: work out at time of request. 6-8pp; 8½×11; photocopy. Reporting time: 2-4 months, sometimes less. Payment: 1 complimentary copy of issue work will appear in; up to $100. Copyrighted, reverts to author. Pub's reviews: 2 in 1990. §Subjects relating to poetry, writing; will consider just about anything with taste. Ads: $10¢-word 1 issue/15¢-word 2 issues/20¢-word 3 issues. United Amateur Press, National Writers Club, WICI.

Writers West Books, Douglas K. Emry, PO Box 16097, San Diego, CA 92116-0097. 4 titles listed in the *Small Press Record of Books in Print* (20th Edition, 1991-92).

WRITING, Jeff Derksen, Editor; Nancy Shaw, Assistant, PO Box 69609, Station K, Vancouver, B.C. V5K 4W7, Canada, 604-688-6001. 1980. Poetry, fiction, parts-of-novels, long-poems, plays. "Recent contributors: Charles Bernstein, Bruce Andrews, Norma Cole, Ron Silliman, Karen MacCormack, Steve McCaffery, Lyn Hejinian, Deanna Ferguson, Andrew Levy, Nancy Shaw, Julia Steele" circ. 800. 3/yr. Pub'd 4 issues 1990; expects 4 issues 1991, 4 issues 1992. sub. price: $15, $18 US; per copy: $6; sample: $6. Back issues: $5. Discounts: bookstores: 40%. 94pp; 6×9; of. Reporting time: 3 months. Payment: none. Copyrighted, reverts to author. Pub's reviews: new policy in 1990. §poetics. Canadian Magazine Publishers Association.

WTI Publishing Co., Richard White, Chief Editor, PO Box 41851, Los Angeles, CA 90041, 213-254-1326. 1976. Articles. "We are a branch of a Calif. *non-profit* corporation, incorporated since Jan. 1971. Our focus is educational — we research and educate in all aspects of survival: moral, physical (both wilderness and city related), economic, spiritual, psychological, etc. Our primary focus is to relay data to newspapers and magazines and direct to the public. We regularly send out columns & articles to various magazines and newspapers, so far only under our own staff authors' names or noms de plum. We also publish a line of greeting/holiday cards call Cogito Cards. We also print catalogs, flyers and newsletters for other people and organizations" avg. press run 100-5M. Pub'd 5 titles 1990; expects 14 titles 1991, 20 titles 1992. avg. price, paper: $8.50 books, $0.85-$3.95 tracts, pamphlets and booklets; $0.10-$1.70 catalogs, newsletters and sale flyers; other: $8.50-$85 poesic artworks. Discounts: 10%-20% libraries, retirees, fulltime students, and disabled (on SSI Disability); 40% to stores and dealers(minimum 10 copies); 50% to distributors (minimum 20 copies). 2-250pp; 5×7 to 8½×11; †mi, photocopy or computer printer. Reporting time: 4-6 weeks. Payment: we submit basic contract, negotiable with author. Copyrights for author.

WW Publishers (see also LIBERATION! Journal of Revolutionary Marxism), Vince Copeland, 46 West 21 Street, New York, NY 10010, 212-255-0352. 1960. Non-fiction. avg. press run 2M. Pub'd 6 titles 1990; expects 7 titles 1991, 8 titles 1992. 1 title listed in the *Small Press Record of Books in Print* (20th Edition, 1991-92). avg. price, paper: $1-$13. Discounts: 50% for orders of 10 or more. 20-400pp; 5×8. Copyrights for author.

WYOMING, THE HUB OF THE WHEEL...A Journey for Universal Spokesmen..., Willow Bee Publishing House, Lenore A. Senior, Managing Editor; Dawn Senior, Assistant & Art Editor, PO Box 9, Saratoga, WY 82331, 307-326-5214. 1985. Poetry, fiction, art, letters, parts-of-novels, non-fiction. "Themes: peace, the human race, positive relationships, and the human spirit. Send #10 SASE for information and guidelines." circ. 500. 1/yr. Pub'd 2 issues 1990; expects 2 issues 1991, 1 issue 1992. sub. price: $10; per copy: $6; sample: $4 #1-3, $5 #4-5. Discounts: 40% on 5 or more copies. 100pp; 6×9; of. Reporting time: 6-8 weeks. Payment: 1 copy. Copyrighted, reverts to author. COSMEP, CCLM.

X

X MAGAZINE, Jeff Hansen, Scott Berk, PO Box 1077, Royal Oak, MI 48068, 313-548-9929. 1989. Poetry, art, cartoons, interviews, satire, reviews, music, letters, non-fiction. "Music review 400 words. Humorous stories/articles 2,000 words, comics 2 pages. Biases: no fiction; well-researched humor; proudly Elvis-free. Contributors: M & Co., Bill Griffith, Matt Feazell, Matt Groening, Evan Dorkin" circ. 5M. 4/yr. Pub'd 6 issues 1990; expects 3 issues 1991, 4 issues 1992. sub. price: $11; per copy: $3; sample: $3. Back issues: #3-#6 $2 each. 24pp; 8½×11; of. Reporting time: 1 week, SASE required. Payment: artists $50 per page, writers depends on source material, no kill fees. Copyrighted, reverts to author. Pub's reviews. §Humor, music, satire. Ads: $200/$110/non-profit—free (w/space constraints).

XANADU: A LITERARY JOURNAL, Pleasure Dome Press (Long Island Poetry Collective Inc.), Pat Nesbitt, Editor; Mildred Jeffrey, Editor; Lois V. Walker, Business Manager; Barbara Lucas, Editor, Box 773, Huntington, NY 11743, 516-248-7716. 1975. Poetry, art, photos, long-poems. "Poetry, criticism, and essays on aesthetics. Poems to 60 lines are most welcome, though longer work will be considered. We like to see 3-5 poems by an individual at one time" circ. 300. 1/yr. Pub'd 1 issue 1990; expects 1 issue 1991, 1 issue 1992. sub. price: $5 (includes p/h); per copy: $5 (include p/h); sample: $5. Discounts: 10% on orders of $20 or more, in any combination of titles (Pleasure Dome Press also included.). 64pp; 5½×8½; of. Reporting time: 3-12 weeks. Payment: 1 copy per contributor. Copyrighted, reverts to author.

XAVIER REVIEW, Box 110C, Xavier University, New Orleans, LA 70125, 504-486-7411 X481. 1961. circ. 500. 2/yr. sub. price: $6; sample: $3. 60pp. Pub's reviews: 2 in 1990. §Southern ethnic, and Latin-American culture.

X-CALIBRE, Nemeton Publishing, Juli and Ken Taylor, PO Box 780, Bristol, BS99 5BB, United Kingdom, +44-272-715144. 1986. Poetry, art. "Only previously unpublished poetry and illustration. Entertains wide varieties of form, style and content, embraces the contemporary spirit without excluding the past. More than 50 contributors from around the world present a banquet of rich and rare delight. Printed spine. IRC for contributors' guidelines." circ. 500. 1/yr. Pub'd 1 issue 1990; expects 1 issue 1992. price per copy: £3.60 sterling + 20% overseas post and packing; sample: £3. Discounts: by negotiation. 112pp; 5¾×8¼; of. Reporting time: 1 month. Payment: £35% discount. Copyrighted, reverts to author.

XENOPHILIA, Omega Cat Press, Joy Oestreicher, 904 Old Town Ct., Cupertino, CA 95014, 408-257-0462.

1990. Poetry, art, long-poems. "To 20 pages, any style. Prefer surrealism; beat, punk, humor all okay. Poetry must have a geo-cultural emphasis (e.g., our society from alien viewpoints; celebrating other cultures, including past and future). Recent contributors: Andrew Gettler, David Chorlton, Denise Dumars, Lyn Lifshin, John Grey, David Kopaska-Merkel" circ. 100. Expects 1 issue 1991, 2 issues 1992. sub. price: $5; per copy: $3; sample: $3. 30pp; 5½×8½; of. Reporting time: 30 days. Payment: $5 per manuscript page/art: $35 for 5 b+w drawings. Copyrighted, reverts to author. SPWAO.

Xenos Books, Karl Kvitko, Box 52152, Riverside, CA 92517, 714-684-4107. 1986. Poetry, fiction, articles, art, interviews, satire, criticism, long-poems, collages, plays, non-fiction. avg. press run 300. Pub'd 2 titles 1990; expects 3 titles 1991, 4 titles 1992. 6 titles listed in the *Small Press Record of Books in Print* (20th Edition, 1991-92). avg. price, cloth: $19.95; paper: $9.95. 160-200pp; 5½×8¼, 8½×11; of. Reporting time: immediately. Payment: individual agreements. Copyrights for author if requested. R.R. Bowker.

XEROLAGE, Xexoxial Endarchy, Miekal And, Elizabeth Was, 1341 Williamson, Madison, WI 53703, 258-1305. 1985. Poetry, art, photos, collages, concrete art. "*Xerolage* is devoted to work of a single artist in each issue. 'Xerolage' is a word coined by Miekal And to suggest the new world of 8½ x 11 art propagated by xerox technology. 'The mimeo of the 80's.' The primary investigation of this magazine is how collage techniques of 20th century art, Visual and Concrete Poetry movements and the art of xerox have been combined. #1 DiMichele '(Above) At the Meeting of White Witches', #2 Michael Voo Doo, #3 Scott Helmes, #4 Joe Napora, #5 Antonio Nelos, #6 Serse Luigetti, 'Pataphysic Italy', #7 Vittore Baroni, 'Sangue Misto' (Mixed Blood), #8 Joe Schwind 'Heavy Equipment', #9 Elizabeth Was 'Ound', #10 Lloyd Dunn, #11 American Living, #12 Greg Evason, #13 Gaetano Colonna 'Capitani Pericolofi', #14 Malock" circ. 100+. 4/yr. Pub'd 4 issues 1990; expects 4 issues 1991, 4 issues 1992. sub. price: $10; per copy: $3; sample: $2.50 + $1 p/h. Back issues: $3. Discounts: 20% discount and free postage & shipping with multiple orders of 5 or more/per title. 24pp; 8½×11; †xerox. Reporting time: less than a month. Payment: 7 copies and discount to author/artist on subsequent copies. Not copyrighted.

Xexoxial Endarchy (see also A PERIODIC JOURNAL OF 'PATAPHYSICAL SUCCULENTOSOPHY; ANTI-ISOLATION/NEW ARTS IN WISCONSIN; THE ACTS THE SHELFLIFE; XEROLAGE), Miekal And, Elizabeth Was, 1341 Williamson, Madison, WI 53703. 1981. Poetry, fiction, articles, art, photos, interviews, criticism, reviews, music, letters, parts-of-novels, long-poems, collages, plays, concrete art, non-fiction. "Experimental or non-idiomatic, visual/verbal literature only" avg. press run 100-2M. Pub'd 10 titles 1990; expects 10 titles 1991, 10 titles 1992. avg. price, cloth: $10; paper: $5; other: $30 (color xerox deluxe). Discounts: 20% to booksellers with multiple order per title, no consignments. 50pp; †xerox. Reporting time: less than a month. Payment: copies & discount on additional copies. Does not copyright for author.

XTRAS, From Here Press, William J. Higginson, Penny Harter, Box 219, Fanwood, NJ 07023, (201) 889-7886. 1975. Poetry, fiction, criticism, parts-of-novels, long-poems, plays, non-fiction. "*Xtras*, a cooperative periodical/chapbook series, features writing in both verse and prose. Issues of *Xtras* are devoted to the work of one or a related group of writers who cooperate in publishing their own chapbooks, and receive a substantial number of copies in payment. Individual issues of *Xtras* feature poems by Penny Harter, W.J. Higginson, and Ruth Stone, haiku and sequences by Alan Pizzarelli, W.J. Higginson, Adele Kenny, and Elizabeth Searle Lamb, workshop writings by teens and elderly, haiku and short poems by Allen Ginsberg, diary in haiku-prose by Rod Tulloss, essays and long poems by WJH. Not reading unsolicited mss now" circ. 500-1M. 2-4/yr. Pub'd 3 issues 1990; expects 3 issues 1991, 3 issues 1992. sub. price: $12/4 issues, institutions $16/4 issues; per copy: $3-$4.95. Discounts: 40% to trade (5 mixed titles; titles can be mixed with From Here Press books). 28-72pp; 5½×8½; of. Reporting time: 1 month. Payment: a substantial number of copies. Copyrighted, reverts to author. No ads.

Xyzyx Information Corporation, Julia E. Fulton, 21116 Vanowen Street, Canoga Park, CA 91303, 818-883-8200. 1969. Non-fiction. "We publish How-to Books according to a very specialized format known as the Job Performance Aid (JPA)." avg. press run 10M. Expects 1 title 1991, 2 titles 1992. avg. price, paper: $25. Discounts: 2-9 10%; 10-49 20%; 50-99 30%; 100+ 40%. 800+pp; 9×7½; of. Reporting time: varies. Payment: varies.

Y

Y GWYDDONYDD, University Of Wales Press, Glyn O. Phillips, 6 Gwennyth St., Cathays, Cardiff CF2 4YD, Wales, Cardiff 231919. 1962. Articles. circ. 500. 3/yr. Pub'd 3 issues 1990; expects 3 issues 1991, 3 issues 1992. sub. price: £4/3 parts; per copy: £1.33; sample: £1.33. Back issues: £1. Discounts: booksellers

10%. 50pp; size A4; of. Payment: none. Copyrighted. Pub's reviews: 4 in 1990. §Science. Ads: £50/£25. UWP.

THE YALE REVIEW, Penelope Laurans, Editor; Wendy Wipprecht, Managing Editor, 1902A Yale Station, New Haven, CT 06520. 1911. Poetry, fiction, articles, criticism, reviews, non-fiction. "Advertising, subscription office: Yale University Press, 92A Yale Station, New Haven CT 06520." circ. 6M. 4/yr. Pub'd 4 issues 1990; expects 4 issues 1991. sub. price: $27 institutions, $18 individuals; per copy: $8 (includes postage and handling); sample: $8 (includes postage and handling). Back issues: on request. Discounts: distributor, 50%, agent 20% bookstores 10%. 160pp plus 16-24pp front matter; 6⅜×9⅛; of, lp. Reporting time: 1-3 months. Payment: on publication. Copyright Yale University, remaining so on publication by agreement with author or transfer of copyright to author. Pub's reviews: 6 in 1990. §Literature, history, fiction, poetry, economics, biography, arts & architecture, politics, foreign affairs. Ads: $250. CLMP.

Yankee Books, Linda Spencer, Senior Editor, PO Box 1248, 62 Bay View Street, Camden, ME 04843, 207-236-0933. 1989. Fiction, non-fiction. "Yankee Books is New England's leading regional publisher. We principally publish nonfiction books which we sell to bookstores and gift shops nationwide. Our principal subject matter is New England and its six New England States: Maine, New Hampshire, Vermont, Massachusetts, Rhode Island, and Connecticut—and with some books, the rest of the Northeast. We publish cookbooks, travel guides, humor, history, photography theme books, books on the environment and natural history, literary anthologies, and books about traditional New England crafts and skills. Our Yankee Classics series is a line of reprints gleaned from New England nonfiction and fiction." avg. press run 5M. Expects 30 titles 1991, 30 titles 1992. 37 titles listed in the *Small Press Record of Books in Print* (20th Edition, 1991-92). avg. price, cloth: $17.95; paper: $11.95; other: $29.95 theme photo books. Discounts: 20% library; 40-45% retail; 45-50% wholesale. 200pp; 6×9 usually; of. Reporting time: 6 weeks. Payment: negotiable. Copyrights for author. NEBA.

Yardbird Books, Richard Sassaman, PO Box 10214, State College, PA 16805, 814-237-7569. 11 titles listed in the *Small Press Record of Books in Print* (20th Edition, 1991-92).

YARROW, A JOURNAL OF POETRY, Harry Humes, Editor, English Dept., Lytle Hall, Kutztown State University, Kutztown, PA 19530, 683-4353. 1981. Poetry, interviews. "William Pitt Root, Fleda Jackson, Jared Carter, Gibbons Ruark, Jonathan Holden." circ. 350. 2/yr. Expects 2 issues 1991, 2 issues 1992. 2 titles listed in the *Small Press Record of Books in Print* (20th Edition, 1991-92). sub. price: $5/2yrs; per copy: $1.50; sample: $1. 40pp; 6×9; of. Reporting time: 1-2 months. Payment: 2 copies of mag. Not copyrighted.

Ye Galleon Press, Glen Adams, Box 287, Fairfield, WA 99012, 509-283-2422. 1937. avg. press run 500-1M. Pub'd 30 titles 1990; expects 35 titles 1991. avg. price, cloth: $10-$15; paper: $2.95-$9.95. Discounts: 10% to libraries; to the trade: single copies 25% or 2 or more of the same title 40%; 40% on 10 or more assorted singles. 5½×8½, 6×9, 7×10, 8½×11; †of. Reporting time: 30 days. Payment: few royalty deals. We can copyright for author. Pacific Northwest Book Publishers Association.

YE OLDE NEWES, Cy Stapleton, 3200 South John Redditt, Lufkin, TX 75901-0514, 409-637-7468. 1982. Articles. "Limited number of articles used on Renaissance period crafts, trades, etc. Slanted towards how-to" circ. 60M. 2/yr. Pub'd 2 issues 1990; expects 2 issues 1991, 2 issues 1992. sub. price: $5; per copy: $4; sample: $4. Back issues: not available. Discounts: $45 + shipping for ctn of 25. 88pp; 10×15; of. Reporting time: done in January and June each year. Payment: none. Copyrighted, reverts to author. Ads: $2,000/$1,200.

Years Press, F. Richard Thomas, Editor, Publisher; Leonora H. Smith, Associate Editor, Dept. of ATL, EBH, Michigan State Univ, E. Lansing, MI 48824-1033. 1973. Poetry. "Occasional publisher of chapbooks, usually solicited after hearing a reading. *Centering Magazine* has become a series of one-author chapbooks." avg. press run 300-400. Pub'd 1 title 1990; expects 2 titles 1991, 2 titles 1992. 8 titles listed in the *Small Press Record of Books in Print* (20th Edition, 1991-92). avg. price, paper: $5. 12-24pp; 7×8½; of. Reporting time: 1 month. Payment: 5 copies.

Yellow Moon Press, Robert B. Smyth, PO Box 1316, Cambridge, MA 02238-0001, 617-776-2230. 1978. Poetry, music, non-fiction. "Authors/Storytellers include: Coleman Barks, Robert Bly, Connie Marin, Elizabeth McKim, Lorraine Lee, Doug Lipman, Robert Smyth and Maggi Peirce. *Yellow Moon* is committed to publishing material related to oral traditions. It is our goal to make available material that both explores its history and breathes new life into the tradition." avg. press run varies with title. Pub'd 1 title 1990; expects 3 titles 1991, 3 titles 1992. 28 titles listed in the *Small Press Record of Books in Print* (20th Edition, 1991-92). avg. price, cloth: $12.95; paper: $3-$6; other: $9.95. Discounts: 2-4 copies 30%; 5+ 40%; 10+ 50%. 32-56pp; 6×9, 8½×11; of. Reporting time: 6-8 weeks. Payment: varies according to book. Copyrights for author. COSMEP.

THE YELLOW PAGES, Telstar Publishing, Kathleen Lee Mendel, 7810 Bertha Avenue, Parma, OH 44129-3110. 1990. Poetry, articles, reviews. "Reviews: 500 words or less; short poetry" circ. 125. 4/yr. Expects 3 issues 1991, 4 issues 1992. sub. price: $12; per copy: $4; sample: $4. Discounts: none. 20pp; 7×8½;

of. Reporting time: 1 month. Payment: none. Copyrighted, reverts to author. Pub's reviews: 12 in 1990. §Poetry. Ads: $50/$25/classified-4 lines $2.50 per issue.

The Yellow Press, Richard Friedman, Peter Kostakis, Art Lange, 5819 North Sacramento, Chicago, IL 60659. 1972. Poetry, fiction. "Titles list includes books by Ted Berrigan, Paul Carroll, Maxine Chernoff, Richard Friedman, Paul Hoover, Henry Kanabus, Alice Notley, Bob Rosenthal, and Barry Schechter. No unsolicited book mss. currently being accepted" avg. press run 1.5M. Pub'd 1 title 1990; expects 1 title 1991, 1 title 1992. 15 titles listed in the *Small Press Record of Books in Print* (20th Edition, 1991-92). avg. price, cloth: $7.95; paper: $5.95; other: signed: $10.00 (paper), $15.00 (cloth). Discounts: bulk only, available through: Small Press Distribution Inc., 1814 San Pablo Avenue, Berkeley, CA 94702. 80pp; 5½×8½; of. Payment: varies. Copyrights for author. SBD.

YELLOW SILK: Journal Of Erotic Arts, Verygraphics, Lily Pond, PO Box 6374, Albany, CA 94706, 415-644-4188. 1981. Poetry, fiction, art, photos, cartoons, satire, criticism, reviews, letters, parts-of-novels, long-poems, collages, non-fiction. "*Yellow Silk* is a journal of erotic literature & arts focusing on excellence of craft as well as erotic content. Not pornographic, *YS* has featured fiction, poetry, essays, reviews & fine arts by Gary Soto, Ntozake Shange, William Kotzwinkle, Mayumi Oda, Octavio Paz, Marge Piercy, Eric Gill, Bharati Mukherjee, photography by Jan Saudek and many more. Editorial policy 'All persuasions; no brutality'. Quality a more important consideration than length (but don't send novels for publication). Experimental and traditional forms combine in 'the erotic alternative'. No poetry submissions June 1 to August 31. SASE. Name, address, phone on each page." circ. 16M. 4/yr. Pub'd 3 issues 1990; expects 4 issues 1991, 4 issues 1992. sub. price: $28/$35 library (Faxon & EBSCO), out of U.S. add $6 surface, $20 air-mail (in U.S. money order or check written on U.S. bank); per copy: $7; sample: $7. Back issues: write for prices. 52pp; 8½×11; of. Reporting time: 3 months. Payment: copies and minimum $5-poem, $10-prose piece and subscription. Copyrighted, rights revert after 1 year except in case of anthology. Pub's reviews: 11 in 1990. §Eros as it appears in art, literature, design, architecture, etc. Ads: query. CLMP.

Yes International Publishers, Theresa King, PO Box 75032, St. Paul, MN 55175-0032, 612-293-8094. 1986. Non-fiction. "Books for self-transformation. Psychology, spirituality, health." avg. press run 3M. Expects 3 titles 1992. 7 titles listed in the *Small Press Record of Books in Print* (20th Edition, 1991-92). avg. price, paper: $13. Discounts: 40% wholesale, 50% distributors. 100-250pp; 6×9, 8½×11; of. Reporting time: 2 weeks to 1 month. Payment: 8% and up depending on saleability. Copyrights for author. PMA, COSMEP, MIPA, NAPRA, UMBA.

Yes Press, Glenn Gallaher, Editor, PO Box 91, Waynesboro, TN 38485. 1984. Poetry. avg. press run 1M. Pub'd 4 titles 1990; expects 8 titles 1991, 8 titles 1992. avg. price, paper: $12.95. Discounts: pre-print 10% off. 100pp; 8½×11; †of. Reporting time: 2 weeks. Payment: none. Copyrights for author.

Yes You Can Press, Mary Wilder, 1106 Second St. #331, Encinitas, CA 92024, 619-720-9151. 1989. Non-fiction. "We publish adult self-help books and specialize in belief systems. We are a highly specialized publishing company. We are not equipped to deal with unsolicited manuscripts." avg. press run 3M. Pub'd 2 titles 1990; expects 1 title 1991. 1 title listed in the *Small Press Record of Books in Print* (20th Edition, 1991-92). avg. price, paper: $7.50. Discounts: 50% Distributors; 40% trade; 25% on any order of 10 books. 100pp; 5½×8½; of. Payment: 7%. PMA, COSMEP.

YESTERDAY'S MAGAZETTE, Independent Publishing Co., Ned Burke, PO Box 15126, Sarasota, FL 34277, 813-922-7080. 1973. Poetry, fiction, articles, photos, interviews, letters, non-fiction. "Must be nostalgia-related—publish memories & believe that everyone has a yesterday. 1,000 word (max) usually. Departments include opinion, small talk, I Remember When..., comments from readers, quips & quotes, memories." circ. 6.5M. 6/yr. Pub'd 6 issues 1990; expects 6 issues 1991, 12 issues 1992. sub. price: 10; per copy: $2; sample: $1.50. Back issues: $2. Discounts: 50-100 $1/copy, 100-500 75¢/copy, 500+ 55¢/copy. 24pp; 8½×11; †of. Reporting time: 2-6 weeks. Payment: 1st choice story receives $10-$25, others contributors copies. Copyrighted, reverts to author. Pub's reviews: 2 in 1990. §nostalgia, biography, history, writing, writers humor. Ads: $400/$200/$1 per word.

Yoknapatawpha Press, Lawrence Wells, Co-Publisher; Dean Wells, Co-Publisher, Box 248, Oxford, MS 38655, 601-234-0909. 1975. "We specialize in books by Southern authors or about Southern-related subjects. Some of our publications have been limited editions. We are expanding in the trade book market. Returns by written permission, only invoices may be considered for return, not before 60 days from date of invoice and not after one year from invoice. We refund on pre-paid orders, only." avg. press run 5M. Pub'd 2 titles 1990; expects 2 titles 1991, 2 titles 1992. avg. price, cloth: $14.95; paper: $8.95; other: ltd editions $50.00. Discounts: STOP-35%, 1 book-20%, 5 books-40%, 25-41%, 50-42%, 250-43%, 100-44%, 250-45%- straight 20% on all limited editions. 200pp; 5½×8¼; of. Reporting time: 3-6 weeks. Payment: 10%, annually. Copyrights for author. Publisher's Association of the South.

The Yolla Bolly Press, Carolyn Robertson, James Robertson, PO Box 156, Covelo, CA 95428, 707-983-6130.

1974. Fiction, non-fiction. "This press functions in two ways. We are independent book producers, signing about eight to ten trade books which are edited and designed here, and published under the imprints of others (*Sierra Club Books, Little, Brown & Company, The Viking Press*, HBJ, etc. We also publish under the imprint *Carolyn and James Robertson, Publishers* a small number of limited editions each year, mostly dealing with West Coast literature and history." avg. press run 10M. Pub'd 10 titles 1990; expects 10 titles 1991, 10 titles 1992. avg. price, cloth: $40; paper: $20; other: limited editions: $300. For discounts on our trade books, it is necessary to consult publishers' schedules. Limited edition discounts:30% to selected booksellers, ˙non-returnable. Pages vary; size varies; †of, lp. Reporting time: we try to respond within 3 weeks. Payment: for trade editions, it varies, but generally we get (and pay) fairly high rates. For limited editions, we pay fees only, no royalties. Copyrights for author.

Youth Policy Institute, PO Box 40132, Washington, DC 20016, 202-298-6050. 1990. "We are not a self-publisher. We are a foundation-supported publisher of newsletters and quarterlies." 1 title listed in the *Small Press Record of Books in Print* (20th Edition, 1991-92). avg. price, paper: $19.95. Discounts: 40% bookstores, bulk; 60% wholesalers. 826pp; 6×9; of.

THE YOUTH REPORT, A NEWS MAGAZINE ON ADVOCACY FOR YOUTH, 2320 J Apalachee Parkway, Suite #494, Tallahassee, FL 32301-4939, 904-681-0019.

Z

Zagier & Urruty Publicaciones (see also ETICA & CIENCIA; FISICA; TIERRA DEL FUEGO MAGAZINE), Sergio Zagier, Dario Urruty, PO Box 94 Sucursal 19, Buenos Aires 1419, Argentina, 541-572-1050. 1985. Articles, photos, reviews, letters, news items, non-fiction. "We publish basically about travel and tourism (books, maps, guides, magazines) and about science. Manuscripts about traveling through South America and Antarctica are welcome. Spanish, English, German and French. We also are interested in photographies travel and adventour-oriented. Any length of manuscripts are considered." avg. press run 5M. Pub'd 6 titles 1990; expects 6 titles 1991, 12 titles 1992. 2 titles listed in the *Small Press Record of Books in Print* (20th Edition, 1991-92). avg. price, cloth: $20; paper: $15; other: $5 magazines. Discounts: 50% distributor, 30% bookstores, 20% travel companies. 128pp; 6×8; of. Reporting time: 6 weeks. Payment: On an individual basis depending on the kind of work. Copyrights for author.

Zahra Publications, M. Bilgrami, Hajj Ahmad Mikell, PO Box 730, Blanco, TX 78606, 512-833-5334. 1982. Articles, reviews, long-poems, non-fiction. avg. press run 3M. Pub'd 8 titles 1990; expects 12 titles 1991, 10 titles 1992. 20 titles listed in the *Small Press Record of Books in Print* (20th Edition, 1991-92). avg. price, cloth: $25; paper: $10. Discounts: per catalogue 40%. 250pp; 5½x8½; of. Payment: outright purchase of manuscripts.

Zed Books Ltd., 57 Caledonian Road, London N1 9BU, England, 071-837-4014. 1976. Non-fiction. avg. press run 2.5M. Pub'd 30 titles 1990; expects 40 titles 1991, 40 titles 1992. avg. price, cloth: $49.95; paper: $15.00. 256pp; of. Reporting time: 3 months. Payment: annually. Does not copyright for author. Publishers Association.

Zeitgeist Press, 4368 Piedmont Avenue, Oakland, CA 94611. 1988. Poetry. "We publish poetry from SF's Cafe Babar reading and do not read unsolicited manuscripts" avg. press run 500. Pub'd 8 titles 1990; expects 4 titles 1991, 4 titles 1992. avg. price, paper: $5. Discounts: 40%+ available for wholesale orders. 60pp; 5½x8½; of, photocopy. Payment: copies. Copyrights for author.

Paul Zelevansky, Lynn Zelevansky, Paul Zelevansky, 333 West End Avenue, New York, NY 10023, 724-5071. 1975. "Material used: work that mixes visual and verbal forms." avg. press run 500-1M. Pub'd 1 title 1990; expects 1 title 1991, 1 title 1992. 7 titles listed in the *Small Press Record of Books in Print* (20th Edition, 1991-92). avg. price, cloth: $20; paper: $9. Discounts: bookstores 40%. 80pp; 8½×11; of. Author has copyright of work; we have copyright of book.

ZENOS, Daniel Hope, Agis Melis, 59 B Ilkeston Road, Nottingham NG7 3GR, England. 1982. Poetry, fiction, art. "Primarily poetry and some short prose. Half the magazine is dedicated to translated poetry, taken from a particular area. Remainder is contemporary poetry. Have published, Greek, Yugoslavian, Turkish and Bulgerian poets. From the English speaking, Hooker, Scott, Seaton, Oxley, Stannerd, Skinner, Alen Bold, Magee, Porvin, Holloway, etc. Also B/W visuals suitable to A5 size production" circ. 1M. 3/yr. Pub'd 3 issues 1990; expects 3 issues 1991, 3 issues 1992. sub. price: £3; per copy: £1 + post/packing, usually £1.20; sample: £1 + post/packing, usually £1.20. Back issues: 50p-60p. Discounts: bookshops and very large orders at 80p. 48pp; 5¾x8; typeset and of. Reporting time: 1-3 months. Payment: free copy. Copyrighted, reverts to author. Pub's reviews: 70 in 1990. §Literature translation, poetry, art, events, competitions. Ads: £30/£15.

Zephyr Press, Ed Hogan, 13 Robinson Street, Somerville, MA 02145. 1980. Poetry, fiction, non-fiction. "We publish fiction of all lengths, from conventional to experimental in style; non-fiction trade titles with an interest in unusual travel subjects; and selected poetry collections. We no longer read unsolicited manuscripts except in the following circumstances: If we receive a query that interests us (it must include a brief summary of publications and professional credits, and a sample of the proposed work no longer than ten pages), we will request the full manuscript, accompanied by a $15 readers fee, and will provide a critique in return." avg. press run 1.5M. Pub'd 1 title 1990; expects 2 titles 1991, 4 titles 1992. 10 titles listed in the *Small Press Record of Books in Print* (20th Edition, 1991-92). avg. price, cloth: $18.95; paper: $10.95; other: $25, signed limited editions. Discounts: 40% to the trade (mixed orders over 4 copies); 20% classroom (orders of 10 or more copies of a title); 20% jobbers (2 or more books per order). 180pp; 5½×8½, 6×9; of. Reporting time: 2-12 weeks, sometimes longer if we are seriously considering publication. Payment: varies; usually 10% of publisher net on first printing. Copyrights for author. COSMEP.

ZERO HOUR, Jim Jones, PO Box 766, Seattle, WA 98111, 206-323-3648. 1988. Poetry, fiction, articles, art, photos, cartoons, interviews, satire, reviews, music, letters, news items, non-fiction. "*ZH* is a magazine devoted to popular culture: religion, literature, sex, music; in tabloid form. Contributions should be 1,500 words or less." circ. 3M. 3/yr. Expects 3 issues 1991, 3 issues 1992. price per copy: $4; sample: $4. Discounts: $1.50 per issue for distributors who take over 25 copies; $2 per copy for orders less than 25. 48pp; 10×16; web press. Payment: 5 copies of magazine or free 1/4 page ad. Copyrighted, reverts to author. Pub's reviews. §The occult, subculture, music, literature, sociology. Ads: $200/$120/$80 1/4 page/$40 1/8. Small Press Alliance.

ZERO ONE, Arthur Moyse, Jan Witte, 39 Minford Gardens, West Kensington, London W14 0AP, England. 1970. "An elitist magazine—anarchist orientated—ill-mannered and unapologetic. Will use any material without permission. Will willingly read and return material with a stamped returned envelope but all *Zero One* published material is either commissioned (unpaid) or simply stolen." circ. 350. 3/yr. Pub'd 3 issues 1990; expects 3 issues 1991, 3 issues 1992. sub. price: £3; per copy: £1. 300pp; 8×10; of. Payment: none. Not copyrighted. Pub's reviews: 6 in 1990. §Art, politics.

ZerOX Books (see also UNMUZZLED OX), Michael Andre, 105 Hudson Street, #311, New York, NY 10013. 1971. "ZerOx Books is an occasional imprint of Unmuzzled Ox Books." avg. press run 105. 6 titles listed in the *Small Press Record of Books in Print* (20th Edition, 1991-92). avg. price, other: $25. 8½×11; xerox.

ZINGSHEIM TIMES, Kinseeker Publications, Victoria Wilson, PO Box 184, Grawn, MI 49637, 616-276-6745. 1986. Articles, reviews, news items, non-fiction. circ. 20. 4/yr. Pub'd 4 issues 1990; expects 4 issues 1991, 4 issues 1992. sub. price: $3; per copy: 75¢; sample: same. Back issues: 75¢. Discounts: none. 4pp; 8½×11; †xerox (photocopy). Reporting time: 2 weeks. Payment: †varies. Not copyrighted. Pub's reviews: 3 in 1990. §Genealogy.

Zirlinson Publishing (see also THE GAME'S AFOOT), Shawn Tomlinson, 1036 Glacier Avenue, Pacifica, CA 94044. 1983. Poetry, fiction, articles, long-poems, non-fiction. "Zirlinson Publishing is part of Write Bastards Ink, a group of wide-ranging media including multimedia, audio, video and print. Most of our publications to date have been hard-edged poetry. Other volumes have included traditional and experimental fiction, opinion and non-fiction. We look for really hard-edged material you can't find anyplace else. Poetry contributors include: Shawn Tomlinson, O'BEE, J.D. Canell, Andy Gore and Mike Easterly. We look for the unusual in everything. We also publish several periodicals: *The Game's Afoot* (roleplaying games), *PIY* (self-publishing), *The Antediluvian Levee* (literary) and new one in late 1991: *The WOWZO Chronicles* (opinion)" avg. press run 50. Pub'd 6 titles 1990; expects 7 titles 1991, 9 titles 1992. avg. price, paper: $4.95. Discounts: up to 50%. 52pp; 5½×8½; †desktop publishing, laser printing. Reporting time: 1 month. Payment: after costs we split 50/50. Copyrights for author.

Zivah Publishers, Margaret Thompson, Nancy Dye, PO Box 13192, Albuquerque, AZ 87192-3192. 1988. "(All) material directed toward raising human consciousness, which is also acceptable to the Zivah partners. We work closely with our authors for top quality work." avg. press run 5M. Pub'd 3 titles 1990; expects 3-4 titles 1991, 3-4 titles 1992. avg. price, paper: $9. Discounts: 40% trade, 55% whslr./distr. 130pp; 5½×8½, 6×9; of. Payment: All individually structured. Copyrights for author. PMA, TBPA, NAPRA.

Zoland Books, Roland F. Pease, Jr., 384 Huron Avenue, Cambridge, MA 02138, 617-864-6252; FAX 617-661-4998. 1987. Poetry, fiction, photos, plays, non-fiction. avg. press run 1.5M. Pub'd 3 titles 1990; expects 4 titles 1991, 5 titles 1992. 9 titles listed in the *Small Press Record of Books in Print* (20th Edition, 1991-92). avg. price, cloth: $13.95; paper: $8.95. Discounts: trade 5/40%. 100pp; size varies; acid-free paper. Reporting time: 2 months. Payment: varies. Copyrights for author.

Zon International Publishing Co., William Manns, PO Box 47, Millwood, NY 10546. 1985. Art. avg. press run 15M. Pub'd 1 title 1990; expects 3 titles 1991, 6 titles 1992. 2 titles listed in the *Small Press Record of Books in Print* (20th Edition, 1991-92). avg. price, cloth: $40; paper: $15. Discounts: 1 copy 25%, 2-3 38%,

5-10 40%, 20-50 42%. 250pp; 9×12; of. Payment: flat fee. Does not copyright for author. ABA.

ZONE, Zone Books, Sanford Kwinter, Michel Feher, Hal Foster, Jonathan Crary, 611 Broadway, Suite 838, New York, NY 10012, 212-529-5674. 1985. Articles, art, photos, non-fiction. *"Zone* explores critical developments in modern culture. Each issue examines a single theme from a transdisciplinary perspective, with texts on art, literature, economics, history and philosophy, as well as photographic essays, historical and technical dossiers, artists projects and formal questionnaires. The theme of the first issue was the contemporary city. Future issues will explore the human body and technology, pragmatics, the global West, politics and time." circ. 7M. 1/yr. Expects 1 issue 1991. sub. price: varies; per copy: varies; sample: varies. Back issues: vary. Discounts: sold to trade through The MIT Press. 450pp; 7¼×9¼; of. Copyrighted, reverts to author. Ads: $900/$600 reg. rate, $600/$380 publisher or nonprofit.

Zone Books (see also ZONE), Jonathan Crary, Michel Feher, Sanford Kwinter, Hal Foster, 611 Broadway, Suite 838, New York, NY 10012, 212-529-5674. 1985. "No unsolicited mss" avg. press run 4M. Pub'd 2 titles 1990; expects 8 titles 1991, 8 titles 1992. 20 titles listed in the *Small Press Record of Books in Print* (20th Edition, 1991-92). avg. price, cloth: $45; paper: $25. Discounts: distributed by The MIT Press, contact MIT sales department. Pages vary; 6×9; of. Payment: negotiated.

ZONE 3, Malcolm Glass, David Till, PO Box 4565, Austin Peay State University, Clarksville, TN 37044, 648-7031/7891. 1986. Poetry. *"Zone 3* is primarily a poetry journal published in Tennessee but seeking submissions and readership nationwide and beyond. For title, see the planting zone map on back of seed package. Editors want poems that are deeply rooted in place, mind, heart, experience, rage, imagination, laughter, etc. First six issues include work by Joseph Bruchac, Dave Etter, Fincke, Frumkin, Locke, Marge Piercy, Aden Ross, Shuttleworth, Laurel Speer, Stafford, Upton, Wakoski, and translations from the Cree by Howard Norman. Published winter, spring, fall. Submissions deadlines: Sep. 1, Dec. 15, and Apr. 1" circ. 1M. 3/yr. Expects 2 issues 1991, 3 issues 1992. sub. price: $8/yr, $10 to libraries & institutions; per copy: $3; sample: $3. Back issues: $2. Discounts: 33%. 70pp; 6×9; of. Reporting time: 2-3 months. Payment: copies. Copyrighted, reverts to author. Pub's reviews. §poetry.

ZOOMAR, Barbara Jarvis, Publisher, PO Box 6920, Alexandria, VA 22306. 1991. Articles, art, cartoons, interviews, satire, criticism, reviews, collages, news items. "Currently there are no guidelines for contributors or concrete deadlines. *Zoomar* is a film magazine—psychotronic pop culture, blah, blah, with a mostly female staff and unlike many films mags isn't anti-gay, etc." Random cycle. Expects 3-6 issues 1991. sub. price: $10/6 issues; per copy: $2; sample: $2 US, $2.50 Canada & Mexico, $3 overseas. Back issues: same. Discounts: wholesale 10 copies of a single issue $13. 12-20pp; 8½×11; laser/photocopy. Reporting time: depends on author but I refuse late work. Payment: free issue. Copyrighted, rights reverting depends. Pub's reviews. §Psychotronic, pop culture stuff, s&m, b&d stuff, etc.

ZYX, Phrygian Press, Arnold Skemer, 58-09 205th Street, Bayside, NY 11364. 1990. Reviews. "We review fiction but are most interested in the innovative, i.e.: experimental-avant garde-oulipienne-surrealist-nouveau roman-nouveau nouveau roman-postmodern-postwakian-etc. etc. etc. (and critical works about them). We will review small press fiction not of this stripe provided that it does not reek of the Iowa MFA syndrome and has some redeeming features, such as an alluring Conradian locale, some provocative viewpoint, or perhaps powerful satire or nastiness, which will make us laugh. This is not intended to merely be a review but, if you will, a clearing house for authorial resources. We anticipate (perhaps too hopefully) that writers of experimental bent will be our major audience. Accordingly we will interest ourselves in publishing economics, changes in printing technology. Since, no doubt, many writers of the innovative stamp will be self publishing, this is as significant as literary values in the scheme of things. We contemplate that short essays might be included concerning works in progress, or contributor essays about certain tendencies and developments in innovative fiction. Possibly at some point, short excerpts from such works might be here published. Peripheral subjects such as semiotics (is it really peripheral?) would also be dealt with." circ. 333. 2/yr. Pub'd 1 issue 1990; expects 2-3 issues 1991, 2-3 issues 1992. price per copy: gratis; send 29¢ return postage; sample: gratis; send 29¢ return postage. 5pp; 8½×11; †Xerography. Not copyrighted. Pub's reviews: 40-50 projected in 1990.

ZYZZYVA, Howard Junker, Editor; Heather Hendrickson, Art, 41 Sutter Street, Suite 1400, San Francisco, CA 94104. 1985. "West Coast writers only. SASE. ISSN 8756-5633." circ. 3.5M. 4/yr. Pub'd 4 issues 1990; expects 4 issues 1991, 4 issues 1992. sub. price: $20; per copy: $7; sample: $8. 144pp; 6×9; of. Reporting time: prompt. Payment: $50-$250. Copyrighted, reverts to author. Ads: $450/$275/$150 1/4 page. CLMP.

ZZAJ-SYNCHRONOLOGY, Dick Metcalf, PO Box 2879, HQ, 19th SUPCOM, APO San Francisco, CA 96218, 82-53-628-5259. 1990. Poetry, articles, art, photos, cartoons, interviews, satire, reviews, music, letters, news items. "Primarily a networking vehicle for musicians and poets, emphasis is on promoting independent thought in an effort to decapitalize mass-producers." circ. 25. 4/yr. Pub'd 3 issues 1990; expects 4 issues 1991, 4 issues 1992. sub. price: $5; per copy: $2; sample: $1.50. Back issues: $2.50. 10pp; 8×11½; †xerox. Reporting time: 60-90 days. Payment: copies. Copyrighted, reverts to author. Pub's reviews. §Music, free thought, music reviews. Ads: $25/$15.

Regional Index

ALABAMA

WaterMark, Incorporated, PO Box 1400, Columbiana, AL 35051, 205-879-7914
Doctor Jazz Press, 617 Valley View Drive, Pelham, AL 35124-1525, 205-663-3403
ANGELSTONE, 316 Woodland Drive, Birmingham, AL 35209, 205-870-7281
Angelstone Press, 316 Woodland Drive, Birmingham, AL 35209, 205-870-7281
All American Press, PO Box 20773, Birmingham, AL 35216, (205) 822-8263
Druid Press, 2724 Shades Crest Road, Birmingham, AL 35216, 205-967-6580
Colonial Press, 3325 Burningtree Drive, Birmingham, AL 35226-2643
AURA Literary/Arts Review, Box 76, University Center, Birmingham, AL 35294, 205-934-3216
BIRMINGHAM POETRY REVIEW, English Department, University of Alabama-Birmingham, Birmingham, AL 35294, 205-934-8573
DREAMS AND NIGHTMARES, 4801 Cypress Creek, #1004, Tuscaloosa, AL 35405, 205-553-2284
Swallow's Tale Press, Route 2, Box 90D, Coatopa, AL 35470
ALABAMA REVIEW, PO Box 1209, University of Alabama, Tuscaloosa, AL 35486-1209
National Council of Teachers of English, Drawer AL, University of Alabama, University, AL 35486, 205-348-6488
THE BLACK WARRIOR REVIEW, P.O. Box 2936, University of Alabama, Tuscaloosa, AL 35487, 205-348-4518
COLLEGE ENGLISH, Drawer AL, University of Alabama, Tuscaloosa, AL 35487, 205-348-6488
OUTRE, 2251 Helton Drive #N7, Florence, AL 35630, (205) 767-3324
Thornwood Book Publishers, PO Box 1442, Florence, AL 35631, 205-766-6782
BRICK, PO Box 1153, Russellville, AL 35653
FPMI Communications, Inc., 3322 South Memorial Parkway, #40, Huntsville, AL 35801, 205-882-3042
Huntsville Literary Association, c/o English Department, University of Alabama, Huntsville, AL 35899
POEM, c/o English Department, University of Alabama, Huntsville, AL 35899
Trouvere Company, Route 2, Box 290, Eclectic, AL 36024
WRITERS GAZETTE NEWSLETTER, Route 2, Box 290, Eclectic, AL 36024
ALABAMA LITERARY REVIEW, Smith 253, Troy State University, Troy, AL 36082, 205-566-8112 Ext. 3307
DISCOMBOBULATION, PO Box 240474, Montgomery, AL 36124
NEGATIVE CAPABILITY, 62 Ridgelawn Drive East, Mobile, AL 36608, 205-460-6146
Negative Capability Press, 62 Ridgelawn Drive East, Mobile, AL 36608, 205-460-6146
CREATIVE KIDS, PO Box 6448, Mobile, AL 36660, 205-478-4700
GCT Inc., PO Box 6448, Mobile, AL 36660, 205-478-4700
THE GIFTED CHILD TODAY, PO Box 6448, Mobile, AL 36660, 205-478-4700
CAESURA, Caesura Press, English Dept. Auburn University, Auburn, AL 36849, 205-826-4620
SOUTHERN HUMANITIES REVIEW, 9088 Haley Center, Auburn Univ., Auburn, AL 36849, 205-844-9088
SCIENCE/HEALTH ABSTRACTS, PO Box 319, Ft. Mitchell, AL 36856, 404-288-5495

ALASKA

ALASKA QUARTERLY REVIEW, English Department, Univ. of Alaska, 3221 Providence, Anchorage, AK 99508, 907-786-1731
Intertext, 2633 East 17th Avenue, Anchorage, AK 99508
Rainforest Publishing, PO Box 101251, Anchorage, AK 99510, 907-373-7277
Sedna Press, 5522 Cope Street, Anchorage, AK 99518, 333-8324
Glacier House Publications, Box 201901, Anchorage, AK 99520, 907-272-3286
Circumpolar Press, Box 221955, Anchorage, AK 99522, 907-248-7323
ALASKA ASSOCIATION OF SMALL PRESSES, PO Box 821, Cordova, AK 99574
Fathom Publishing Co., Box 1690, Cordova, AK 99574, 907-424-3116
Wizard Works, PO Box 1125, Homer, AK 99603
ALASKA WOMEN, HCR 64 Box 453, Seward, AK 99664, 907-288-3168
Fireweed Press, PO Box 75418, Fairbanks, AK 99707-2136
THE...CHRONICLE, PO Box 80721, Fairbanks, AK 99708, 907-479-2966
Vanessapress, PO Box 81335, Fairbanks, AK 99708, 907-479-0172
EUTHANASIA ROSES, 759 Cranberry Ridge, Fairbanks, AK 99712, 907-457-8691
Windsong Press, PO Box 644, Delta Jct., AK 99737, 907-895-4179
Alaska Native Language Center, Box 900111, University of Alaska, Fairbanks, AK 99775-0120, 907-474-7874
THE NORTHERN ENGINEER, Institute of Northern Engineering, University of Alaska, Fairbanks, AK 99775, 907-474-6113
The Denali Press, 1704 Willow Drive, Juneau, AK 99801, 907-586-6014
EXPLORATIONS, English Dept., Alaska Univ. Southeast, 11120 Glacier Highway, Juneau, AK 99801
Old Harbor Press, PO Box 97, Sitka, AK 99835, 907-747-3584

ARIZONA

A as A Publishing, 212 1/2 E. Portland Street, Phoenix, AZ 85004-1837
Bomb Shelter Propaganda, PO Box 17686, Phoenix, AZ 85011, 602-279-3531
MALLIFE, PO Box 17686, Phoenix, AZ 85011, 602-279-3531
The Oryx Press, 4041 N. Central Avenue, Suite 700, Phoenix, AZ 85012-3330, 602-254-6156
Primer Publishers, 5738 North Central, Phoenix, AZ 85012, 602-234-1574
Golden West Publishers, 4113 North Longview, Phoenix, AZ 85014, 602-265-4392
HOWLING WIND, Strangelove Press, 6202 N. 16 Street #43, Phoenix, AZ 85016, 602-279-0462
UCS Press, 3531 W. Glendale Avenue, Suite 202, Phoenix, AZ 85051, 602-841-7176
WOMEN'S PAGES, PO Box 15828, Phoenix, AZ 85060-5828, 602-230-8668
Hunter Publishing, Co., P.O. Box 9533, Phoenix, AZ 85068, 602-944-1022
Barca De Vela Publishing, PO Box 37168, Phoenix, AZ 85069-7168, 602-864-9493

Fiesta Books Inc., PO Box 51234, Phoenix, AZ 85076-1234, 602-759-4555
THE AMARANTH REVIEW, PO Box 56235, Phoenix, AZ 85079, 846-5567
Window Publications, PO Box 56235, Phoenix, AZ 85079, 846-5567
THE PARADOXIST MOVEMENT, PO Box 42561, Phoenix, AZ 85080, 602-436-2126
SMARANDACHE FUNCTION JOURNAL, PO Box 42561, Phoenix, AZ 85080
Olde & Oppenheim Publishers, PO Box 61203, Phoenix, AZ 85082, 602-839-0560
NEW THOUGHT, International New Thought Alliance, 5003 East Broadway Road, Mesa, AZ 85206, 602-945-0744
Hallelujah Press Publishing Company, PO Box 496, Gilbert, AZ 85234-0496, 602-821-2287; 892-4309
Pussywillow Publishing House, Inc., PO Box 1806, Gilbert, AZ 85234
Ironwood Publishing Company, PO Box 8464, Scottsdale, AZ 85252, 602-443-1390
ARIZONA GREAT OUTDOORS, Box 6243, Scottsdale, AZ 85257, 602-945-6746
SINGLE SCENE, 7432 East Diamond, Scottsdale, AZ 85257, 602-945-6746
Power Publishing Group, 10943 E. Gary Road, Scottsdale, AZ 85259
Starfield Press, 10603 N. Hayden Road, Suite 114, Scottsdale, AZ 85260, 602-951-3115
Five Star Publications, PO Box 3142, Scottsdale, AZ 85271-3142, 602-941-0770
Blue Bird Publishing, 1713 East Broadway, #306, Tempe, AZ 85282, 602-968-4088
THE NORTHLAND QUARTERLY, 1522 E. Southern Avenue #2161, Tempe, AZ 85282-5678
Northland Quarterly Publications, Inc., 1522 E. Southern Avenue #2161, Tempe, AZ 85282-5678
Patrick Walsh Press, 2017 S. Ventura, Tempe, AZ 85282, 602-894-1230
Graham-Conley Press, 1936 E. Belmont Drive, Tempe, AZ 85284, 602-491-1177
D.I.N. Publications, PO Box 27568, Tempe, AZ 85285-1126
Bilingual Review/Press, Hispanic Research Center, Arizona State University, Tempe, AZ 85287-2702, 602-965-3867
BILINGUAL REVIEW/Revista Bilingue, Hispanic Research Center, Arizona State University, Tempe, AZ 85287-2702, 602-965-3867
HAYDEN'S FERRY REVIEW, Matthews Center, Arizona State University, Tempe, AZ 85287-1502, 602-965-1243
Villa Press, 4506 West Citros Way, Glendale, AZ 85301, 602-939-6801
ARIZONA COAST, Hale Communications, Inc., 912 Joshua Avenue, Parker, AZ 85344, 602-669-6464
ANIMAL TALES, PO Box 2220, Payson, AZ 85547-2220
Tortilla Press, 8 Mulberry Lane, Bisbee, AZ 85603, 602-432-7040
Synergetic Press Inc., PO Box 689, Oracle, AZ 85623, 602-622-0641
Personal Efficiency Programs, Inc., PO Box 249, Sierra Vista, AZ 85636-0249, 213-596-5242
Chax Press, 101 West 6th Street #4, Tucson, AZ 85701, 602-622-7109
Bean Avenue Publishing, PO Box 1055, Tucson, AZ 85702, 602-882-8323
TUCSON MOTOR NEWS, PO Box 1055, Tucson, AZ 85702
Treasure Chest Publications, Inc., PO Box 5250, Tucson, AZ 85703, 602-623-9558
EXPERIMENTAL BASEMENT, 3740 N. Romero Road #A-191, Tucson, AZ 85705, 602-293-3287
eXpEriMenTal presS, 3740 N. Romero Road #A-191, Tucson, AZ 85705, 602-292-3287
Harbinger House, 2802 N. Alvernon Way, Tucson, AZ 85712, 602-326-9595
Microdex Bookshelf, 1212 N. Sawtelle, Suite 120, Tucson, AZ 85716, 602-326-3502
Pepper Publishing, 433 North Tucson Boulevard, Tucson, AZ 85716, 602-881-0783
BOOKS OF THE SOUTHWEST, Box 40850, Tucson, AZ 85717, 602-326-3533
IRONWOOD, P.O. Box 40907, Tucson, AZ 85717
Ironwood Press, PO Box 40907, Tucson, AZ 85717
Peccary Press, Box 40850 Sun Station, Tucson, AZ 85717
ARIZONA QUARTERLY, Univ. Of Arizona, Tucson, AZ 85721, Main Library B541 602-621-6396
SONORA REVIEW, Dept. of English, University of Arizona, Tucson, AZ 85721, 602-621-8077; 621-1836
THE MATCH, PO Box 3488, Tucson, AZ 85722
Friends Of Tucson Pub Lib/The Maguey Press, c/o Tucson Public Library, PO Box 27470, Tucson, AZ 85726, 602-791-4391
NEWSLETTER INAGO, Inago Press, PO Box 26244, Tucson, AZ 85726-6244, 602-294-7031
NON COMPOS MENTIS, Scott K. Smith #74481, AZ State Prison, 10,000 S. Wilmot, Tucson, AZ 85777
Northland Publishing Company, PO Box N, Flagstaff, AZ 86002, 602-774-5251
GCBA Publishing, PO Box 292, Grand Canyon, AZ 86023, 602-638-2597
FOCUS: Library Service to Older Adults, People with Disabilities, 2255 Pine Drive, Prescott, AZ 86301, 602-778-3821
Hohm Press, PO Box 2501, Prescott, AZ 86302, 602-778-9189
Geoscience Press, Inc., 1040 Hyland Circle, Prescott, AZ 86303, 602-445-8058
THE LAS VEGAS INSIDER, Good 'n' Lucky, PO Box 1185, Chino Valley, AZ 86323-1185
SARU Press International, 559 Jordan Road, Sedona, AZ 86336
Little Buckaroo Press, PO Box 3016, West Sedona, AZ 86340, 602-282-6278
Zivah Publishers, PO Box 13192, Albuquerque, AZ 87192-3192

ARKANSAS

Lancer Militaria, Box 886, Mt. Ida, AR 71957, 501-867-2232
SLANT, A Journal of Poetry, UCA PO Box 5063, Conway, AR 72032, 501-450-3180
CRAZYHORSE, 2801 S. University, Dept. of English, Univ. of Arkansas-Little Rock, Little Rock, AR 72204, 501-569-3160
Silver Dollar Press, Plaza Towers, Suite 8B, 6115 W. Markham Street, Little Rock, AR 72205-3151, 501-753-4181
Rose Publishing Co., 2723 Foxcroft Road, #208, Little Rock, AR 72207-6513, 501-372-1666
VOICES INTERNATIONAL, 1115 Gillette Drive, Little Rock, AR 72207, 501-225-0166
CONTEXT SOUTH, Box 2244, State University, AR 72467, 501-972-6095
AQUATERRA, WATER CONCEPTS FOR THE ECOLOGICAL SOCIETY, Route 3, Box 720, Eureka Springs, AR 72632
Bear House Publishing, Route 2, Box 94, Eureka Springs, AR 72632-9505, 501-253-9351
LUCIDITY, Route 2, Box 94, Eureka Springs, AR 72632-9505, 501-253-9351
EPIPHANY: A JOURNAL OF LITERATURE, PO Box 2699, University of Arkansas, Fayetteville, AR 72701
NEBO, Department of English, Arkansas Tech University, Russellville, AR 72801, 501-968-0256

CALIFORNIA

The Bieler Press, USC-Research Annex 122, 3716 South Hope Street, Los Angeles, CA 90007-4377, 213-743-3939
THE DUCKBURG TIMES, 3010 Wilshire Blvd., #362, Los Angeles, CA 90010-1146, 213-388-2364
International Jewelry Publications, PO Box 13384, Los Angeles, CA 90013, 818-282-3781
Chicano Studies Research Center Publications, University of California-Los Angeles, 405 Hilgard Avenue, Los Angeles, CA 90024, 213-825-2642
Happy Rock Press, Phil Nurenberg, c/o: PO Box 24453, Los Angeles, CA 90024-0453
Institute of Archaeology Publications, University of California-Los Angeles, 405 Hilgard Avenue, Los Angeles, CA 90024-1510, 213-825-7411
JACARANDA REVIEW, English Department, Univ. of California-Los Angeles, Los Angeles, CA 90024, 213-825-4173
Jamenair Ltd., PO Box 241957, Los Angeles, CA 90024-9757, 213-470-6688
McKinzie Publishing Company, 11000 Wilshire Boulevard, PO Box 241777, Los Angeles, CA 90024, 213-934-7685
NEW GERMAN REVIEW: A Journal of Germanic Studies, Dept of Germanic Languages, University of CA, Los Angeles, CA 90024, (213) 825-3955
AZTLAN: A Journal of Chicano Studies, University of California-Los Angeles, 405 Hilgard Avenue, Los Angeles, CA 90025, 213-825-2642
Kalimat Press, 1600 Sawtelle Blvd., #34, Los Angeles, CA 90025-3114, 213-479-5668
Little Sam & Co. Press, 1415 Camden Avenue #403, Los Angeles, CA 90025, 213-473-3324
TAI CHI, PO Box 26156, Los Angeles, CA 90026, 213-665-7773
TUCUMCARI LITERARY REVIEW, 3108 W. Bellevue Avenue, Los Angeles, CA 90026
Wayfarer Publications, PO Box 26156, Los Angeles, CA 90026
A.R.A. JOURNAL, Dr. Miron Butariu, 4310 Finley Avenue, Los Angeles, CA 90027, 213-666-8379
Love Child Publishing, 6565 Sunset Blvd., Suite 318, Hollywood, CA 90028
HIDDEN SPRINGS REVIEW, PO Box 29613, Los Angeles, CA 90029, 213-664-0007
OVERSIGHT, PO Box 29292, Los Angeles, CA 90029-0292
QuikRef Publishing, 913 N. Sanborn Avenue, Los Angeles, CA 90029, 213-913-1430; fax 213-913-1066
Global Publishing Company, PO Box 35357, Los Angeles, CA 90035, 937-4356
GENII, PO Box 36068, Los Angeles, CA 90036
Moscow Publishing Enterprises, 326 South Highland Avenue, Los Angeles, CA 90036-3025, 213-934-2453/735-9969
Scojtia Publishing Company, 6457 Wilcox Station, PO Box 38002, Los Angeles, CA 90038, FAX 213-470-2667
BURWOOD JOURNAL, Box 41834, Los Angeles, CA 90041, 213-255-9502
Survival News Service, Box 41834, Los Angeles, CA 90041, 213-255-9502
WTI Publishing Co., PO Box 41851, Los Angeles, CA 90041, 213-254-1326
BRAIN/MIND BULLETIN, P O Box 42211, Los Angeles, CA 90042, 213-223-2500; 800-553-MIND
Clothespin Fever Press, 5529 N. Figueroa, Los Angeles, CA 90042, 213-254-1373
Interface Press, PO Box 42211, Los Angeles, CA 90042, 213-223-2500; 800-553-MIND
ANCIENT CONTROVERSY, PO Box 43822, Los Angeles, CA 90043
BLACK HERITAGE UNVEILED NEWSLETTER, PO Box 43822, Los Angeles, CA 90043
SPENCER'S BOOK WORLD, PO Box 43822, Los Angeles, CA 90043, 213-937-3099
Spencer's Int'l Enterprises Corp., PO Box 43822, Los Angeles, CA 90043, 213-937-3099
AMERICAN COLLEGIATE POETS, PO Box 44044-L, Los Angeles, CA 90044, (213) 755-1814
International Publications, PO Box 44044-L, Los Angeles, CA 90044, 213-755-1814
GOLD, SILVER AND URANIUM FROM SEAS AND OCEANS PROGRESS UPDATE, 7804 Vicksburg Avenue, Los Angeles, CA 90045, 213-645-7571
POETIC JUSTICE, 8220 Rayford Drive, Los Angeles, CA 90045
THIRD RAIL, PO Box 46127, Los Angeles, CA 90046, 213-850-7548
Third Rail Press, PO Box 46127, Los Angeles, CA 90046, 213-850-7548
Big Sky Press, 653 N. Laurel Avenue, Los Angeles, CA 90048, 213-653-0444
BLITZ, PO Box 48124, Los Angeles, CA 90048-0124, 818-360-3262
Bombshelter Press, 6421-1/2 Orange Street, Los Angeles, CA 90048, 213-651-5488
ONTHEBUS, Bombshelter Press, 6421 1/2 Orange Street, Los Angeles, CA 90048
Adams-Hall Publishing, PO Box 491002, Los Angeles, CA 90049, 213-399-7137; 800-888-4452
Interlink Press, Inc., 908 Kenfield Avenue, Los Angeles, CA 90049, (213) 472-2908
Spectrum Productions, 979 Casiano Rd., Los Angeles, CA 90049
INTERNATIONAL OLYMPIC LIFTER, PO Box 65855, Los Angeles, CA 90065, 213-257-8762
Red Eye Press, 4238 Glenwood Avenue, Los Angeles, CA 90065, 213-225-3805
FUGITIVE POPE, 3338 Sawtelle Drive, Apt. 20, Los Angeles, CA 90066, 213-398-3161
Mar Vista Publishing Company, 11917 Westminster Place, Los Angeles, CA 90066, 213-391-1721
Red Car Press, 12228 Venice Boulevard #458, Los Angeles, CA 90066
Bellwether Productions, Inc., 1888 Century Park, E, #1924, Los Angeles, CA 90067-1723, 213-392-1964
Illuminati, PO Box 67e07, Los Angeles, CA 90067
ORPHEUS, c/o Illuminati, PO Box 67e07, Los Angeles, CA 90067
AGAPE, 6940 Oporto Drive, Los Angeles, CA 90068, 213-876-6295
Author's Unlimited, 3324 Barham Boulevard, Los Angeles, CA 90068, 213-874-0902
Multiple Dimensions, 2305 Canyon Drive, Los Angeles, CA 90068-2411, 213-469-4454
Truth Center, 6940 Oporto Drive, Los Angeles, CA 90068, 213-876-6295
Hollywood Film Archive, 8344 Melrose Ave., Hollywood, CA 90069, 213-933-3345
POETRY/LA, PO Box 84271, Los Angeles, CA 90073, 213-472-6171
Lone Eagle Publishing Co., 2337 Roscomare Road #9, Los Angeles, CA 90077-1815, fax 213-471-4969; 800-FILMBKS
Acting World Books, PO Box 3044, Hollywood, CA 90078, 213-466-4297
THE AGENCIES-WHAT THE ACTOR NEEDS TO KNOW, PO Box 3044, Hollywood, CA 90078, 213-466-4297
THE HOLLYWOOD ACTING COACHES AND TEACHERS DIRECTORY, PO Box 3044, Hollywood, CA 90078, 213-466-4297
THE ADVOCATE, PO Box 4371, Los Angeles, CA 90078-4371, 213-871-1225
FILM THREAT VIDEO GUIDE, PO Box 3170, Los Angeles, CA 90078-3170, 818-848-8971; FAX 818-848-5956
Liberation Publications, Inc., PO Box 4371, Los Angeles, CA 90078-4371, 213-871-1225
CHIPS OFF THE WRITER'S BLOCK, PO Box 83371, Los Angeles, CA 90083

FICTION FORUM, PO Box 83371, Los Angeles, CA 90083
THE SOUTHERN CALIFORNIA ANTHOLOGY, Master of Professional Writing Program, WPH 404/Univ. of Southern Calif., Los Angeles, CA 90089-4034, 213-740-3252
Rossi, PO Box 2001, Beverly Hills, CA 90213, 213-556-0337
The Krsna Institute, PO Box 281, Culver City, CA 90232, 213-838-3535
DUMARS REVIEWS, PO Box 810, Hawthorne, CA 90251
Buddha Rose Publications, PO Box 902, Hermosa Beach, CA 90254, 213-543-3809
Human Futures, PO Box 893, Hermosa Beach, CA 90254
R & R Publishing, PO Box 308, Hermosa Beach, CA 90254, 213-374-5894
THE SCREAM OF THE BUDDHA, PO Box 902, Hermosa Beach, CA 90254, 213-318-6743
HIPPO, Chautauqua Press, 28834 Boniface Drive, Malibu, CA 90265-4206
CLIENT MAGAZINE, PO Box 3879, Manhattan Beach, CA 90266
JB & Me Publishing, PO Box 3879, Manhattan Beach, CA 90266
Blue Arrow Books, PO Box 1669, Pacific Palisades, CA 90272, 213-447-5951
POTPOURRI PARTY-LINE, 7336 Berry Hill, Palos Verdes, CA 90274-4404, 213-377-7040
B. L. Winch & Associates, 45 Hitching Post Dr. Bldg 2, Rolling Hills Estate, CA 90274, 213-547-1240
DIRECT RESPONSE, PO Box 2100, Rolling Hills Estates, CA 90274, 213-212-5727
Jalmar Press, 45 Hitching Post Drive, Building 2, Rolling Hills Estates, CA 90274, 213-547-1240
WARM FUZZY NEWSLETTER, 45 Hitching Post Dr. Bldg 2, Rolling Hills Estates, CA 90274, 213-547-1240
GALAXY CLASS, PO Box 7000-822, Redondo Beach, CA 90277, 213-529-8573
Los Arboles Publications, PO Box 7000-54, Rendondo Beach, CA 90277, 213-375-0759
Elysium Growth Press, 700 Robinson Road, Topanga, CA 90290, 213-455-1000
JOTS (Journal of the Senses), 814 Robinson Road, Topanga, CA 90290
Poet Papers, P.O. Box 528, Topanga, CA 90290
THE RECORD SUN, PO Box 528, Topanga, CA 90290
Beyond Baroque Foundation Publications, PO Box 2727, Venice, CA 90291, 213-822-3006
FOREHEAD: Writing & Art Journal, PO Box 2727, Venice, CA 90291, 213-822-3006
Acrobat Books, PO Box 870, Venice, CA 90294, 213-578-1055
THE REALIST (NEWSLETTER), Box 1230, Venice, CA 90294, 213-392-5848
TSUNAMI, PO Box 1442, Venice, CA 90294, 213-453-6303
The Spinning Star Press, 1065 E. Fairview Blvd., Inglewood, CA 90302, 213-962-3862
Ten Star Press, PO Box 2325, Inglewood, CA 90305-0325, 213-758-2123
Astro Artz, 1641 18th Street, Santa Monica, CA 90404-3807, 213-315-9383
Global Sports Productions, Ltd., 1223 Broadway Street #101, Santa Monica, CA 90404-2707
HIGH PERFORMANCE, 1641 18th Street, Santa Monica, CA 90404-3807, 213-315-9383
IBS Press, 744 Pier Avenue, #1, Santa Monica, CA 90405, (213) 450-6485
REASON MAGAZINE, 2716 Ocean Park Blvd., Suite 1062, Santa Monica, CA 90405, 213-392-0443
THE SANTA MONICA REVIEW, 1900 Pico Boulevard, Santa Monica, CA 90405
Corfa Books, PO Box 3658, Santa Monica, CA 90408-3658, 213-829-7039
Sharp & Dunnigan Publications, Incorporated, 2803 Gramercy Avenue, Torrance, CA 90501-5431, 916-891-6602
Lowen Publishing, PO Box 6870-19, Torrance, CA 90504-0870, 213-831-2770
Steel Balls Press, Box 807, Whittier, CA 90608, 213-693-0397
Morning Glory Press, 6595 San Haroldo Way, Buena Park, CA 90620
PAST TIMES: THE NOSTALGIA ENTERTAINMENT NEWSLETTER, 7308 Fillmore Drive, Buena Park, CA 90620
American Montessori Consulting, PO Box 5062, 11961 Wallingsford Road, Rossmoor, CA 90721, 213-598-2321
Wolcotts, Inc., 15126 Downey Avenue, Paramount, CA 90723, 213-630-0911, No. CA: 1-800-262-1538, Out of state: 1-800-421-2220
GREEN SYNTHESIS-A NEWSLETTER AND JOURNAL FOR SOCIAL ECOLOGY, DEEP ECOLOGY, BIOREGION-ALISM, ECOFEMINISM, AND THE GREEN MOVEMENT, Box 1858, San Pedro, CA 90733, 213-833-2633
R. & E. Miles, PO Box 1916, San Pedro, CA 90733, 213-833-8856
Singlejack Books, PO Box 1916, San Pedro, CA 90733, 213-548-5964
DEWITT DIGEST & REVIEW, Box 355, Seal Beach, CA 90740
Photography Research Institute Carson Endowment, 21237 S. Moneta Avenue, Carson, CA 90745
GUTS, PO Box 2730, Long Beach, CA 90801
CALIFORNIA STATE POETRY QUARTERLY (CQ), 1200 East Ocean Blvd #64, Long Beach, CA 90802, 213-495-0925
SAN MIGUEL REVIEW, 1200 E. Ocean Boulevard #64, Long Beach, CA 90802, 213-495-0925
PEARL, 3030 E. Second Street, Long Beach, CA 90803, 213-434-4523
Pearl Editions, 3030 E. Second Street, Long Beach, CA 90803, 213-434-4523
Applezaba Press, PO Box 4134, Long Beach, CA 90804, 213-591-0015
Twelvetrees Press/Twin Palms Publishers, 2400 North Lake Avenue, Altadena, CA 91001
Amen Publishing Co., Box 3612, Arcadia, CA 91006, 818-355-9336
Charlemagne Press, PO Box 771, Arcadia, CA 91006, 818-357-7236
Relocation Research/Emigrants, PO Box 1122, Sierra Madre, CA 91024, 818-568-8484
THE NOCTURNAL LYRIC, Box 2602, Pasadena, CA 91101
Trilogy Books, 155 S. El Molino Avenue, Suite 103, Pasadena, CA 91101, 818-440-0669
THE BULLISH CONSENSUS, 1111 S. Arroyo Parkway, Suite 410, PO Box 90490, Pasadena, CA 91109-0490, (818) 441-3457
NewSage Press, PO Box 41029, Pasadena, CA 91114, 213-641-8912
UMBRELLA, PO Box 40100, Pasadena, CA 91114, 818-797-0514
AMBASSADOR REPORT, PO Box 60068, Pasadena, CA 91116, 818-798-6112
Hope Publishing House, PO Box 60008, Pasadena, CA 91116, 818-792-6123; fax 818-792-2121
Golden West Books, PO Box 80250, San Marino, CA 91118-8250, 213-283-3446
Glendale House Publishing, 249 N. Brand Blvd., Suite 440, Glendale, CA 91203, 818-507-7475
SHIRIM, 2405 Hollister Terrace, Glendale, CA 91206
Triton Books + Gallery, 4409 Lowell Avenue, La Crescenta, CA 91214, 818-249-0793
THE AGE OF AQUARIUS, 7131 Owensmouth Avenue #066, Canoga Park, CA 91303-2008
Masefield Books, 7210 Jordan Avenue, Suite B54, Canoga Park, CA 91303
Xyzyx Information Corporation, 21116 Vanowen Street, Canoga Park, CA 91303, 818-883-8200

Festival Publications, 7944 Capistrano Avenue, West Hills, CA 91304
GOLDEN ISIS, 23233 Saticoy Street, Building 105, Box 137, West Hills, CA 91304
RED DANCEFLOOR, PO Box 3051, Canoga Park, CA 91306, 818-785-7650
Chatsworth Press, 9135 Alabama Avenue #B, Chatsworth, CA 91311-6913, 818-341-3156
MYRIAD, 11564 Poema Place #101, Chatsworth, CA 91311-1121
VOL. NO. MAGAZINE, Los Angeles Poets' Press, 24721 Newhall Avenue, Newhall, CA 91321, 805-254-0851
Brooke-Richards Press, 9420 Reseda Blvd., Suite 511, Northridge, CA 91324, 818-893-8126
Cerulean Press (Subsidiary of Kent Publications), 18301 Halsted St., Northridge, CA 91325
Kent Publications, Inc., 18301 Halsted Street, Northridge, CA 91325, 818-349-2080
SAN FERNANDO POETRY JOURNAL, 18301 Halstead Street, Northridge, CA 91325
Lord John Press, 19073 Los Alimos Street, Northridge, CA 91326, 818-363-6621
Santa Susana Press, University Libraries, CSUN, 18111 Nordhoff Street, Northridge, CA 91330, 818-885-2271
Brason-Sargar Publications, PO Box 872, Reseda, CA 91337, 818-701-0809
Excellence Enterprises, 15831 Olden Street #71, Sylmar, CA 91342, 818-367-8085
Double M Press, 16455 Tuba Street, Sepulveda, CA 91343, 818-360-3166
Baker Publishing, 16245 Armstead Street, Granada Hills, CA 91344
MEDITATION MAGAZINE, 17211 Orozco Street, Granada Hills, CA 91344, 818-366-5441
Stepping Stone Books, 17939 Chatsworth Street, Ste 102, Granada Hills, CA 91344, 818-368-4268
Aviation Book Company, 25133 Anza Drive, Suite E, Santa Clarita, CA 91355-2999
Panorama Publishing Company, 18607 Ventura Boulevard #310, Tarzana, CA 91356
PEDIATRIC MENTAL HEALTH, Pediatric Projects Inc., PO Box 571555, Tarzana, CA 91357, 818-705-3660
ATHENA, PO Box 5028, Thousand Oaks, CA 91360, 805-379-3185
CROSSCURRENTS, A QUARTERLY, 2200 Glastonbury Road, Westlake Village, CA 91361, 818-991-1694
Key Publications, PO Box 6375, Woodland Hills, CA 91365, 818-992-4657
Sun Eagle Publishing, PO Box 33545, Granada Hills, CA 91394, 818-360-2224
Perivale Press, 13830 Erwin Street, Van Nuys, CA 91401-2914, 818-785-4671
Caravan Press, 15445 Ventura Boulevard #10279, Sherman Oaks, CA 91403-3005
Life Energy Media, 14755 Ventura Blvd, Suite 1908, Sherman Oaks, CA 91403, 818-905-2747
Gain Publications, PO Box 2204, Van Nuys, CA 91404, 818-785-1895
Infinite Savant Publishing, PO Box 2321, Van Nuys, CA 91404, 213-293-7767
NATIONAL MASTERS NEWS, PO Box 2372, Van Nuys, CA 91404, 818-785-1895
SoftServe Press, 7000 Bianca Avenue, Van Nuys, CA 91406-3512, 818-996-7000; fax 818-996-0008
THE N.A. WAY, PO Box 9999, Van Nuys, CA 91409, 818-780-3951
New Saga Publishers, PO Box 56415, Sherman Oaks, CA 91413, 818-988-0940
Stone and Scott, Publishers, PO Box 56419, Sherman Oaks, CA 91413-1419, 818-904-9088
National Publishers, PO Box 16790, Encino, CA 91416
THE UNEXPLAINED, PO Box 16790, Encino, CA 91416
IDEAS IN INVESTING, 4525 Hazeltine Avenue #3, Van Nuys, CA 91423-2832
Independent Research Services of Irvine (IRIS/I), 4525 Hazeltine Avenue #3, Van Nuys, CA 91423-2832
DESIGNING NEW CIVILIZATIONS, 16255 Ventura Blvd., #605, Encino, CA 91436, 818-788-1136
Floricanto Press, 16161 Ventura Blvd, Ste 830, Encino, CA 91436, 818-990-1885
LECTOR, 16161 Ventura Blvd., #830, Encino, CA 91436, 818-990-1882
Recreation Sales Publishing, Inc., 150 E. Olive Avenue, Suite 110, Burbank, CA 91502, 818-843-3616
L.A. GANG BANG, 1212A N. San Fernando #244, Burbank, CA 91504
SOCIETE, 1317 N. San Fernando Blvd, Suite 310, Burbank, CA 91504
Technicians of the Sacred, 1317 N. San Fernando Blvd., Suite 310, Burbank, CA 91504
Ascension Publishing, Box 3001-323, Burbank, CA 91508, 818-848-8145
TEMBLOR: Contemporary Poets, 4624 Cahuenga Blvd. #307, North Hollywood, CA 91602, 818-761-6112
Dramaline Publications, SAN 285-239X, 10470 Riverside Drive, Suite #201, Toluca Lake, CA 91602, 818-985-9148
Hartford Press, 3960 Laurel Canyon Blvd, Suite 380, Studio City, CA 91604, 818-761-2952
Players Press, Inc., PO Box 1132, Studio City, CA 91604, 818-789-4980
Panjandrum Books, 5428 Hermitage Avenue, North Hollywood, CA 91607, 818-985-7259
PANJANDRUM POETRY JOURNAL, 5428 Hermitage Avenue, North Hollywood, CA 91607, 818-985-7259
Empire Publishing Service, PO Box 1344, Studio City, CA 91614-0344
THE ALTERED MIND, PO Box 1083, Claremont, CA 91711, 714-949-9531
Hunter House Inc., Publishers, PO Box 847, Claremont, CA 91711, 714-624-2277
THE PRAIRIE RAMBLER, PO Box 505, Claremont, CA 91711
LOUDER THAN BOMBS, 2313 Santa Anita Avenue, S. El Monte, CA 91733, 818-575-1887
Seminal Life Press, 2313 Santa Anita Avenue, S. El Monte, CA 91733, 818-575-1887
Royal Publishing, 18825 Hicrest Road, PO Box 1120, Glendora, CA 91740, 818-335-8069
SHARING IDEAS FOR PROFESSIONAL SPEAKERS, 18825 Hicrest Road, PO Box 1120, Glendora, CA 91740, 818-335-8069; fax 818-335-6127
Bookworm Publishing Company, PO Box 3037, Ontario, CA 91761
Auromere Books and Imports, 1291 Weber Street, Pomona, CA 91768, 714-629-8255
PURNA YOGA, 1291 Weber Street, Pomona, CA 91768, 714-629-8255
White Rose Publishing, 978 Amelia Avenue, San Dimas, CA 91773, 714-592-6303
Freelance Communications, P.O. Box 1895, Upland, CA 91785, 714-985-3465
Barr-Randol Publishing Co., 136A N. Grand Avenue, West Covina, CA 91791, 818-339-0270
PM (The Pedantic Monthly), Numedia, 912 North Bushnell Avenue, Alhambra, CA 91801-1206
CALYPSO: Journal of Narrative Poetry and Poetic Fiction, 1829 Arnold Way #503, Alpine, CA 91901-3708
!MEXICO WEST!, PO Box 1646, Bonita, CA 91908, 619-585-3033
Mexico West Travel Club, Inc., PO Box 1646, Bonita, CA 91908, 619-585-3033
Anaphase II, Box 6157, Chula Vista, CA 91909, 619-661-2528
NEW MOON RISING, 8818 Troy Street, Spring Valley, CA 91977, 619-466-8064
Sun Features Inc., PO Box 368-D, Cardiff, CA 92007, 619-753-3489
Gurze Books, Box 2238, Carlsbad, CA 92008, 619-434-7533
KENNETH COLEMAN'S FED TRACKER/REALITY THEORY NEWSLETTER, 4805 Courageous Lane, Carlsbad, CA 92008, 619-720-0107

661

Craftsman Book Company, 6058 Corte Del Cedro, Carlsbad, CA 92009, 619-438-7828
OneOff Publishing, 7578 Caloma Circle, Carlsbad, CA 92009-7714
UNARIUS LIGHT, 145 S. Magnolia Avenue, El Cajon, CA 92020, 619-447-4170
Windmill Publishing Co., 2147 Windmill View Road, El Cajon, CA 92020, 619-448-5390
SCRIPT IDEAS, 449 Santa Fe Drive #239, Encinitas, CA 92024, 619-944-5182
Yes You Can Press, 1106 Second St. #331, Encinitas, CA 92024, 619-720-9151
Rand Editions/Tofua Press, Po Box 2610, Leucadia, CA 92024, 619-753-2500
Belleridge Press, 28455 Meadow Mesa Lane, Escondido, CA 92026, 619-749-2122
Robert Erdmann Publishing, 28629 Meadow Glen Way West, Escondido, CA 92026-9503
Athelstan Publications, PO Box 8025, La Jolla, CA 92038-8025
La Jolla Poets Press, PO Box 8638, La Jolla, CA 92038, 619-457-1399
Laurence McGilvery, PO Box 852, La Jolla, CA 92038
Nuventures Publishing, PO Box 2489, La Jolla, CA 92038-2489, 800-338-9768
San Diego Poet's Press, c/o Kathleen Iddings, PO Box 8638, La Jolla, CA 92038, (619) 457-1399
West Anglia Publications, PO Box 2683, La Jolla, CA 92038, 619-457-1399
DREAM INTERNATIONAL QUARTERLY, 121 North Ramona Street #27, Ramona, CA 92065-6206, 619-789-3258
THE WISHING WELL, PO Box 713090, Santee, CA 92072-3090
Dominion Press, PO Box 37, San Marcos, CA 92079-0037, 619-746-9430
MASTER THOUGHTS, PO Box 37, San Marcos, CA 92079-0037, 619-746-9430
ORNAMENT, Ancient Contemporary Ethnic, PO Box 2349, San Marcos, CA 92079
THEOLOGIA 21, PO Box 37, San Marcos, CA 92079-0037, 619-746-9430
Arrow Publishing, 405 W. Washington St., Suite 26, San Diego, CA 92103, 619-296-3201
Mho & Mho Works, Box 33135, San Diego, CA 92103, 619-488-4991
Unified Publications, 1050 University Avenue, Suite 103-203, San Diego, CA 92103, 619-497-0573
LIVELY ARTS, PO Box 4906, San Diego, CA 92104
In One Ear Press, 3527 Voltaire Street, San Diego, CA 92106, 619-223-1871
Point Loma Publications, Inc., PO Box 6507, San Diego, CA 92106
Birth Day Publishing Company, PO Box 7722, San Diego, CA 92107, 619-296-3194
S. Deal & Assoc., 1629 Guizot Street, San Diego, CA 92107
THE FESSENDEN REVIEW, The Reginald A. Fessenden Educational Fund, Inc., Box 7272, San Diego, CA 92107, 619-488-4991
House of Fire Press, 1019 Agate Street, Suite D, San Diego, CA 92109, 619-488-1208
THE OCCASIONAL TUESDAY-ART NEWS, 3808 Rosecrans Street #134, San Diego, CA 92110
Recovery Publications, 1201 Knoxville Street, San Diego, CA 92110, 619-275-1350
Tuesday-Art Press, 3808 Rosecrans Street #134, San Diego, CA 92110
ACS Publications, PO Box 16430, San Diego, CA 92116, 619-297-9203
ASTROFLASH, PO Box 16430, San Diego, CA 92116
Marlborough Publications, PO Box 16406, San Diego, CA 92116, 619-280-8310
SENSOR, PO Box 16074, San Diego, CA 92116
Strawn Studios Inc., 4663 Utah Street, San Diego, CA 92116-3147, 515-224-4760
Writers West Books, PO Box 16097, San Diego, CA 92116-0097
ADOLESCENCE, 3089C Clairemont Dr., Suite 383, San Diego, CA 92117, 619-581-9449
FAMILY THERAPY, 3089C Clairemont Dr., Suite 383, San Diego, CA 92117, 619-581-9449
Libra Publishers, Inc., 3089C Clairemont Dr., Suite 383, San Diego, CA 92117, 619-581-9449
A.J. Books, 3415 Lebon Drive, #237, San Diego, CA 92122
LuraMedia, Inc., PO Box 261668, San Diego, CA 92126, 619-578-1948
The Rateavers, 9049 Covina Street, San Diego, CA 92126, 619-566-8994
AAS HISTORY SERIES, PO Box 28130, San Diego, CA 92128, 619-746-4005
ADVANCES IN THE ASTRONAUTICAL SCIENCES, PO Box 28130, San Diego, CA 92128, 619-746-4005
SCIENCE AND TECHNOLOGY, PO Box 28130, San Diego, CA 92128, 619-746-4005
Univelt, Inc., PO Box 28130, San Diego, CA 92128, 619-746-4005
Brenner Information Group, 9282 Samantha Court, San Diego, CA 92129, 619-538-0093
Cosmoenergetics Publications, PO Box 86353, San Diego, CA 92138, 619-295-1664
"STRICTLY NOTHING BUT" THE BLUES, PO Box 81383, San Diego, CA 92138, 619-222-0577
CRAZYQUILT LITERARY QUARTERLY, CrazyQuilt Press, PO Box 632729, San Diego, CA 92163-2729, 619-688-1023
Los Hombres Press, PO Box 632279, San Diego, CA 92163-2729, 619-234-6710
EMERGING, PO Box 7601, San Diego, CA 92167-0601, 619-225-0133
LP Publications (Teleos Institute), PO Box 7601, San Diego, CA 92167-0601, 619-225-0133
Blue Swan Communications, PO Box 9925, San Diego, CA 92169-0925, 619-272-5718
FICTION INTERNATIONAL, San Diego State University, San Diego, CA 92182, 619-594-5443, 594-6220
San Diego State University Press, San Diego State University, San Diego, CA 92182, 619-594-6220
Atticus Press, 720 Heber Avenue, Calexico, CA 92231-2408, 619-357-5512
ATTICUS REVIEW, 720 Heber Avenue, Calexico, CA 92231-2408, 619-357-5512
Insight Press, PO Box 25, Ocotillo, CA 92259
ETC Publications, 700 East Vereda Sur, Palm Springs, CA 92262-1608, 619-325-5352
MIND IN MOTION, A MAGAZINE OF POETRY AND SHORT PROSE, P.O. Box 1118, Apple Valley, CA 92307, 619-248-6512
FRIENDS OF PEACE PILGRIM, 43480 Cedar Avenue, Hemet, CA 92344, 714-927-7678
Tributary Press, PO Box 3246, Idyllwild, CA 92349, 714-659-3278
Let's Go Travel Publications, 135 W. Nuevo, Suite-B, Perris, CA 92370, 714-943-4459
The Borgo Press, Box 2845, San Bernardino, CA 92406, (714) 884-5813
THE PACIFIC REVIEW, Department of English, Calif State University, San Bernardino, CA 92407, 714-880-5824
The Aegis Group, 155 W. Hospitality Lane #230, San Bernardino, CA 92408, 714-381-4800
Drew Blood Press Ltd., 3410 First Street, Riverside, CA 92501, 714-788-4319
Dovehaven Press, Ltd., PO Box 4578, Riverside, CA 92514, 714-787-0971
LATIN AMERICAN PERSPECTIVES, PO Box 5703, Riverside, CA 92517-5703, 714-787-5508
Xenos Books, Box 52152, Riverside, CA 92517, 714-684-4107

662

FREE LUNCH, PO Box 7647, Laguna Niguel, CA 92607-7647
Career Publishing, Inc., PO Box 5486, Orange, CA 92613-5486, 714-771-5155; 800-854-4014
Sun, Man, Moon Inc., PO Box 5084, Huntington Beach, CA 92615, 213-598-5342
Brighton & Lloyd, PO Box 2903, Costa Mesa, CA 92626, 714-540-6466
Mazda Publishers, PO Box 2603, 2991 Grace Lane, Costa Mesa, CA 92626-2603, 714-751-5252
ORANGE COAST MAGAZINE, OCNL, Inc., 245-D Fischer Avenue, Suite 8, Costa Mesa, CA 92626, 714-545-1900
Wilson & Crewe, 1548-D Adams Avenue, Costa Mesa, CA 92626
Pandit Press, Inc., 24843 Del Prado, Suite 405, Dana Point, CA 92629, 714-240-7151
Frontline Publications, PO Box 1104, El Toro, CA 92630
GGL Educational Press, 1501 East Chapman, Suite 346, Fullerton, CA 92631, 714-860-1088
GORHAM, 800 South Euclid Street, Fullerton, CA 92632, 714-526-4952
THE VORTEX (A Historical and Wargamers Jornal), 806 South Euclid Street, Fullerton, CA 92632, 714-526-4952 &
    714-526-1913
Main Track Publications, 2119 Forestwood Court, Fullerton, CA 92633, 714-441-2041
AXIOS, 800 South Euclid Avenue, Fullerton, CA 92634, 714-526-4952; 526-1913
Axios Newletter, Inc., 800 South Euclid Avenue, Fullerton, CA 92634, 714-526-1913
SOUTH COAST POETRY JOURNAL, California State University, English Department, Fullerton, CA 92634
Verve Press, PO Box 1997, Huntington Beach, CA 92647
Aames-Allen Publishing Co., 1106 Main Street, Huntington Beach, CA 92648, 714-536-4926
Windsong Books International, Box 867, Huntington Beach, CA 92648
Iris Communication Group, 1278 Glenneyre, Suite 138, Laguna Beach, CA 92651, 714-497-2101
Nanny Goat Productions, Box 845, Laguna Beach, CA 92652, (714) 494-7930
Parkhurst Press, PO Box 143, Laguna Beach, CA 92652, 714-499-1032
Publitec Editions, 271-A Lower Cliff Drive, PO Box 4342, Laguna Beach, CA 92652, 714-497-6100; FAX 714-581-6465
Ability Workshop Press, 24861 Alicia Parkway #292, Laguna Hills, CA 92653, 714-661-5779
Newport House, 100-P Via Estrada, Laguna Hills, CA 92653, 714-770-8323
Info Net Publishing, PO Box 3789, San Clemente, CA 92674, 714-489-9267
RACE ACROSS AMERICA PROGRAM, PO Box 3789, San Clemente, CA 92674, 714-489-9267
Riegel Publishing, PO Box 3241, San Clemente, CA 92674, 714-498-5732
Kent P. Larsen, Inc., 30252 Pacific Island Drive #198, Laguna Niguel, CA 92677, 714-661-8865
Unique Adventures Press, PO Box 185, San Juan Capistrano, CA 92693, 714-661-3991
THE ELEPHANT-EAR, Irvine Valley Coll., School of Humanities, 5500 Irvine Center Drive, Irvine, CA 92720, (714)
    559-9300
Wordland, Department ID-23, Box 26333, Santa Ana, CA 92799, 714-953-2900
COMPUTER GAMING WORLD, PO Box 4566, Anaheim, CA 92803, (714) 535-4435
THE HAPPY THRASHER, PO Box 2246, Anaheim, CA 92814, 714-647-2307
ART/LIFE, PO Box 23020, Ventura, CA 93002, 805-648-4331
Art/Life Limited Editions, PO Box 23020, Ventura, CA 93002, 805-648-4331
Golden West Historical Publications, PO Box 1906, Ventura, CA 93002
Monroe Press, 362 Maryville Avenue, Ventura, CA 93003-1912
CONDITIONED RESPONSE, PO Box 3816, Ventura, CA 93006
Conditioned Response Press, PO Box 3816, Ventura, CA 93006
J & T Publishing, PO Box 6520, Ventura, CA 93006, 805-525-8533, FAX: 525-4033
JASON UNDERGROUND'S NOTES FROM THE TRASHCOMPACTOR, 2795 Via Vela, Camarillo, CA 93010,
    805-482-3220
SOUND CHOICE, PO Box 1251, Ojai, CA 93023, 805-646-6814
Times Change Press, PO Box 1380, Ojai, CA 93024-1380, 805-646-8595
Racz Publishing Co., PO Box 287, Oxnard, CA 93032, 805-642-1186
Gross Advertising Service, 3445 Leora Avenue, Simi Valley, CA 93063, 805-527-0525
BAKUNIN, 2025 Plato Court, Simi Valley, CA 93065, 805-526-8900
Silver Dawn Media, 1606 Arcane Street, Simi Valley, CA 93065
VERVE, PO Box 3205, Simi Valley, CA 93093
Bandanna Books, 319 Anacapa Street, Santa Barbara, CA 93101, 805-962-9915
Fithian Press, PO Box 1525, Santa Barbara, CA 93102, 805-962-1780
Able Publishing, 3463 State Street, Suite 219, Santa Barbara, CA 93105
El Montecito Oaks Press, Inc., 135 Santa Isabel Lane, Santa Barbara, CA 93108-2514, 805-969-5698
Santa Barbara Press, 223 Via Sevilla, Santa Barbara, CA 93109, 805-966-2060
El Camino Publishers, 340 Old Mill Road #225, Santa Barbara, CA 93110, 805-687-2959; 682-9340
McNally & Loftin, Publishers, 5390 Overpass Road, Santa Barbara, CA 93111, 805-964-5117
Quantal Publishing B, PO Box 1598, Goleta, CA 93116-1598, 805-964-7293
Capra Press, PO Box 2068, Santa Barbara, CA 93120, 805-966-4590; FAX 805-965-8020
FREEBIES MAGAZINE, PO Box 20283, Santa Barbara, CA 93120, 805-962-9135
John Daniel and Company, Publishers, PO Box 21922, Santa Barbara, CA 93121, (805) 962-1780
Red Hen Press, PO Box 3774, Santa Barbara, CA 93130, 805-682-1278
Para Publishing, PO Box 4232-Q, Santa Barbara, CA 93140-4232, 805-968-7277; fax 805-968-1379
PUBLISHING POYNTERS, PO Box 4232-Q, Santa Barbara, CA 93140-4232, 805-968-7277; fax 805-968-1379
SourceNet, PO Box 6767, Santa Barbara, CA 93160, 805-494-7123
Summer Stream Press, PO Box 6056, Santa Barbara, CA 93160-6056, 805-962-6540
WHOLE AGAIN RESOURCE GUIDE, PO Box 6767, Santa Barbara, CA 93160, 805-494-7123
Woodbridge Press, PO Box 6189, Santa Barbara, CA 93160, 805-965-7039
Joelle Publishing, Inc., PO Box 91229, Santa Barbara, CA 93190, 805-962-9887
The Rights' Press, PO Box 555, Coalinga, CA 93210, (209) 935-3772
DRY CRIK REVIEW, PO Box 51, Lemon Cove, CA 93244, 209-597-2512
Prima Facie, PO Box 3267, Visalia, CA 93278, 209-627-8757; FAX 209-733-2653
AMELIA, 329 'E' Street, Bakersfield, CA 93304, 805-323-4064
Amelia Press, 329 'E' Street, Bakersfield, CA 93304, 805-323-4064
CICADA, 329 'E' Street, Bakersfield, CA 93304, (805) 323-4064
SPSM&H, 329 'E' Street, Bakersfield, CA 93304, 805-323-4064

PF$ Publications, PO Box 9852, Bakersfield, CA 93309-9852, 805-834-3901
Blake Publishing, 2222 Beebee Street, San Luis Obispo, CA 93401, 805-543-6843
Sand River Press, 1319 14th Street, Los Osos, CA 93402, 805-543-3591
COFFEEHOUSE POETS' QUARTERLY, PO Box 15123, San Luis Obispo, CA 93406, 805-541-4553
Impact Publishers, Inc., PO Box 1094, San Luis Obispo, CA 93406, 805-543-5911
Santa Lucia Chapter - Sierra Club, PO Box 15755, San Luis Obispo, CA 93406, 805-473-1947
The Press of MacDonald & Reinecke, PO Box 840, Arroyo Grande, CA 93420-0840, 805-473-1947
Bear Flag Books, PO Box 840, Arroyo Grande, CA 93421-0840, 805-473-1947
KALDRON, An International Journal Of Visual Poetry and Language Art, PO Box 7164, Halcyon, CA 93421-7164, 805-489-2770
San Luis Quest Press, Box 666, Avila, CA 93424-5822, 805-543-8500
TIGER MOON, 1850 Chester Lane, Cambria, CA 93428, 815-927-3920
Tiger Moon, 1850 Chester Lane, Cambria, CA 93428, 815-927-3920
The Olive Press Publications, PO Box 99, Los Olivos, CA 93441
Maize Press, 961 Bakersfield, Pismo Beach, CA 93449, (805) 773-5977
THE ELECTRONIC PUBLISHING FORUM, PO Box 140, San Simeon, CA 93452
Serendipity Systems, PO Box 140, San Simeon, CA 93452
Puma Publishing Company, 1670 Coral Drive, Santa Maria, CA 93454, 805-925-3216
Alpenglow Press, PO Box 1841, Santa Maria, CA 93456, 805-928-4904
ASYLUM, PO Box 6203, Santa Maria, CA 93456
Asylum Arts, PO Box 6203, Santa Maria, CA 93456, 805-928-8774
Challenger Press, PO Box 919, Solvang, CA 93464, 805-688-4439
VIRGIN MEAT, 2325 West Avenue, K-15, Lancaster, CA 93536, 805-722-1758
SILVER WINGS, PO Box 1000, Pearblossom, CA 93553-1000, 805-264-3726
America West Publishers, PO Box 986, Tehachapi, CA 93581
THE JOURNAL OF PAN AFRICAN STUDIES, California Inst. of Pan African Studies, PO Box 13063, Fresno, CA 93794, 209-266-2550
Coastline Publishing Company, PO Box 223062, Carmel, CA 93922, 625-9388
Creative With Words Publications (CWW), PO Box 223226, Carmel, CA 93922-3226, 408-649-1682
Windsor Medallion Book Publishing Co., PO Box 223756, Carmel, CA 93922, 408-624-5655
Sea Challengers, 4 Somerset Rise, Monterey, CA 93940, 408-373-6306
Victory Press, 543 Lighthouse Avenue, Monterey, CA 93940-1422, 408-883-1725, 372-7046
The Boxwood Press, 183 Ocean View Blvd, Pacific Grove, CA 93950, 408-375-9110
Professional Publications, Inc., 1250 Fifth Avenue, Belmont, CA 94002
Chatham Publishing Company, PO Box 283, Burlingame, CA 94010, 415-348-0331
Down There Press, PO Box 2086, Burlingame, CA 94011-2086, 415-342-2536; 550-0912
Comforter Publishing, 515 Crocker Avenue, Daly City, CA 94014, 415-584-3329
The Archives Press, 334 State Street #536, Los Altos, CA 94022
Crisp Publications, Inc., 95 First Avenue, Los Altos, CA 94022, 415-949-4888
Ballena Press, 823 Valparaiso Avenue, Menlo Park, CA 94025, 415-323-9261
Markgraf Publications Group, PO Box 936, Menlo Park, CA 94025, 415-940-1299
Allergy Publications, PO Box 640, Menlo Park, CA 94026, 415-322-1663
C. Salway Press, PO Box 4115 A, Menlo Park, CA 94026, 415-368-7882; FAX 415-368-2287
Harvestman and Associates, PO Box 271, Menlo Park, CA 94026-0271, 415-326-6997 x1511
Korn Kompany, PO Box 7414, M, Menlo Park, CA 94026, 415-965-3524
Open Chain Publishing, PO Box 2634, Menlo Park, CA 94026, 415-323-2549
Perseverance Press, PO Box 384, Menlo Park, CA 94026, 415-323-5572
Tioga Publishing Co., 150 Coquito Way, Portola Valley, CA 94028, 415-854-2445
Poor Souls Press/Scaramouche Books, PO Box 236, Millbrae, CA 94030
GOOD CLEAN FUN, 1190 Maria Privada, Mountain View, CA 94040
Ocean View Books, Box 4148, Mountain View, CA 94040
Tilton House, 255 East Street #1, Mountain View, CA 94043-3752
BACKBOARD, 1131 Galvez Drive, Pacifica, CA 94044, 415-355-4640
backspace ink., 1131 Galvez Drive, Pacifica, CA 94044, 415-355-4640
Creatures At Large Press, PO Box 687, 1082 Grand Teton Drive, Pacifica, CA 94044, (415) 355-READ
THE GAME'S AFOOT, 1036 Glacier Avenue, Pacifica, CA 94044
Zirlinson Publishing, 1036 Glacier Avenue, Pacifica, CA 94044
DR. DOBB'S JOURNAL, 501 Galveston Drive, Redwood City, CA 94063-4728, 415-366-3600
M & T Publishing, 501 Galveston Drive, Redwood City, CA 94063-4728, 415-366-3600
Popular Medicine Press, PO Box 1212, San Carlos, CA 94070, 415-594-1855
Reference Service Press, 1100 Industrial Road, #9, San Carlos, CA 94070
Wide World Publishing/TETRA, PO Box 476, San Carlos, CA 94070, 415-593-2839
Technical Communications Associates, 1250 Oakmead Parkway, Suite 210, Sunnyvale, CA 94086
American Business Consultants, Inc., 1540 Nuthatch Lane, Sunnyvale, CA 94087-4999, 408-732-8931/738-3011
Soundboard Books, 1016 E. El Camino Real, Suite 124, Sunnyvale, CA 94087, 408-738-1705
Cin Publications, PO Box 11277, San Francisco, CA 94101
EFQ Publications, PO Box 4958, San Francisco, CA 94101
EROTIC FICTION QUARTERLY, PO Box 4958, San Francisco, CA 94101
ISSUES, PO Box 11250, San Francisco, CA 94101, 415-864-4800 X136
MAGICAL BLEND, PO Box 11303, San Francisco, CA 94101
Magical Blend, PO Box 11303, San Francisco, CA 94101
Night Horn Books, PO Box 11536, San Francisco, CA 94101-7536, 415-750-0660
See Sharp Press, PO Box 6118, San Francisco, CA 94101, 415-626-2160; FAX 626-2685
Chronicle Books, 275 Fifth Street, San Francisco, CA 94103, 415-777-7240
CRITICAL REVIEW: An Interdisciplinary Journal, 942 Howard Street, San Francisco, CA 94103, 415-465-4985
GLB Publishers, 935 Howard St., Suite B, San Francisco, CA 94103, 415-243-0229
Modular Information Systems, 2440 16th Street, Suite 221, San Francisco, CA 94103, 415-863-0493
Burning Books, 690 Market Street, Suite 1501, San Francisco, CA 94104, 415-788-7480

664

CREDIT REPORT, 44 Montgomery Street, 5th floor, San Francisco, CA 94104, 415-955-2650
CreditPower Publishing Co., 44 Montgomery Street, 5th Floor, San Francisco, CA 94104, 415-955-2650
PROCESSED WORLD, 41 Sutter Street, #1829, San Francisco, CA 94104, 415-626-2979
Sierra Club Books, 100 Bush Street, San Francisco, CA 94104, 415-291-1600
ZYZZYVA, 41 Sutter Street, Suite 1400, San Francisco, CA 94104
CALLBOARD, 657 Mission Street #402, San Francisco, CA 94105, 415-621-0427
JACOB'S LETTER, 121 Steuart Street, #402, San Francisco, CA 94105, (415) 387-1004
METAPHOR, 109 Minna St., Suite 153, San Francisco, CA 94105, 415-641-7231
POP VOID, 109 Minna Street, Suite 583, San Francisco, CA 94105, 415-362-1157
Pop Void Publications, 109 Minna Street, Suite 583, San Francisco, CA 94105, 415-362-1157
Rhapsody International, 109 Minna Street, Suite 153, San Francisco, CA 94105
Foghorn Press, PO Box 77845, San Francisco, CA 94107, 415-641-5777
Meridian Learning Systems, 665 Third Street, Ste. 340, San Francisco, CA 94107, 415-495-2300
PUCK!, 350 Townsend Street #409-A, San Francisco, CA 94107
Institute for Contemporary Studies/International Center for Economic Growth, 243 Kearny Street, San Francisco, CA 94108, 415-981-5353; 800-326-0236
Pacific Research Institute, 177 Post Street #500, San Francisco, CA 94108, 415-989-0833
VAJRA BODHI SEA, 800 Sacramento Street, Gold Mountain Monastery, San Francisco, CA 94108, 415-421-6117
THE EQUATOR, 509 Cultural Center, 509 Ellis Street, San Francisco, CA 94109, 415-561-0502
MIND MATTERS REVIEW, 1438 Pacific Avenue, San Francisco, CA 94109
Paris Press, 2040 Polk Street #291, San Francisco, CA 94109, 415-931-7603
SAN FRANCISCO REVIEW OF BOOKS, 1117 Geary, San Francisco, CA 94109, 415-771-1252
Sunlight Publishers, PO Box 640545, San Francisco, CA 94109, 415-776-0372
Taurean Horn Press, 1355 California #2, San Francisco, CA 94109
ACTS, 514 Guerrero, San Francisco, CA 94110-1017, 415-431-8297
BROOMSTICK: A PERIODICAL BY, FOR, AND ABOUT WOMEN OVER FORTY, 3543 18th Street, #3, San Francisco, CA 94110, 415-552-7460
Cottage Books, 731 Treat Avenue, San Francisco, CA 94110, 415-826-7113
CULTURE CONCRETE, 2141-C Mission Street #305, San Francisco, CA 94110-9839, 415-285-4286
THE ISLAND, 731 Treat Avenue, San Francisco, CA 94110, 415-826-7113
S.I.R.S. Caravan Publications, 65 Norwich Street, San Francisco, CA 94110, 415-285-0562
Walnut Publishing Co., Inc., 3435 Army Street, Suite #308, San Francisco, CA 94110, 415-821-0511
THE BOOKWATCH, 166 Miramar Avenue, San Francisco, CA 94112, 415-587-7009
Alamo Square Press, PO Box 14543, San Francisco, CA 94114, 415-252-0643
BAD NEWZ, PO Box 14318, San Francisco, CA 94114
Bakhtin's Wife Publications, 47 Noe #6, San Francisco, CA 94114, 415-978-9737
Design Enterprises of San Francisco, PO Box 14695, San Francisco, CA 94114
DIGIT, 47 Noe Street #6, San Francisco, CA 94114-1017, 415-978-9759
EPIPHANY JOURNAL, PO Box 14727, San Francisco, CA 94114, 415-431-4388
INDIGENOUS WORLD/EL MUNDO INDIGENA, 275 Grand View Avenue, No. 103, San Francisco, CA 94114, 415-647-1966
LESBIAN CONTRADICTION-A Journal of Irreverent Feminism, 584 Castro Street, Suite 263, San Francisco, CA 94114
Micro Pro Litera Press, PO Box 14045, San Francisco, CA 94114, (415) 863-3037
Not-For-Sale-Press or NFS Press, 243 Grand View Ave., San Francisco, CA 94114, 415-282-5372
THE OPERA COMPANION, #40 Museum Way, San Francisco, CA 94114, 415-626-2741
Permeable Press, 47 Noe Street, Suite 6, San Francisco, CA 94114-1017, 415-978-9759
Rock Steady Press, 2750 Market Street #102, San Francisco, CA 94114, 415-255-4518
W.I.M. Publications, 2215-R Market Street, Box 137, San Francisco, CA 94114, 408-253-3329
Five Fingers Press, PO Box 15426, San Francisco, CA 94115
FIVE FINGERS REVIEW, PO Box 15426, San Francisco, CA 94115-0426
KMT, A Modern Journal of Ancient Egypt, 1531 Golden Gate Avenue, San Francisco, CA 94115, 415-922-7263
KMT Communications, 1531 Golden Gate Avenue, San Francisco, CA 94115, 415-922-7263
e.g., 3232 Taraval St. #7, San Francisco, CA 94116, 415-661-0851
STIFLED YAWN: A Magazine Of Contemporary Writing, 3232 Taraval #7, San Francisco, CA 94116, 415-661-0851
Haight-Ashbury Publications, 409 Clayton Street, San Francisco, CA 94117, 415-565-1904
JOURNAL OF PSYCHOACTIVE DRUGS, 409 Clayton Street, San Francisco, CA 94117, 415-565-1904
THE SAN FRANCISCO ALMANAC, 1657 Waller Street, San Francisco, CA 94117, 800-352-5268
Scottwall Associates, Publishers, 95 Scott Street, San Francisco, CA 94117, 415-861-1956
Seismograph Publications, PO Box 170127, San Francisco, CA 94117
III Publishing, PO Box 170363, San Francisco, CA 94117-0363, 415-221-1441
COMPOST NEWSLETTER (CNL), 729 Fifth Avenue, San Francisco, CA 94118
REAL FICTION, 298-9th Avenue, San Francisco, CA 94118
Red Wheelbarrow Press, 298 9th Avenue, San Francisco, CA 94118, 415-387-3412
Reunion Research, 3145 Geary Boulevard #14, San Francisco, CA 94118, 209-336-2345
Synergistic Press, 3965 Sacramento St., San Francisco, CA 94118, 415-EV7-8180
WORKING CLASSICS, 298 9th Avenue, San Francisco, CA 94118, 415-387-3412
FINE PRINT: The Review for the Arts of the Book, PO Box 193394, San Francisco, CA 94119, 415-543-4455
URBANUS/RAIZIRR, PO Box 192561, San Francisco, CA 94119-2561
Ediciones El Gato Tuerto, PO Box 210277, San Francisco, CA 94121
EL GATO TUERTO, PO Box 210277, San Francisco, CA 94121, 504-866-8598
HARMONY: VOICES FOR A JUST FUTURE, PO Box 210056, San Francisco, CA 94121-0056, 415-221-8527
Sea Fog Press, Inc., 447 20th Avenue, San Francisco, CA 94121, 415-221-8527
The Communication Press, PO Box 22541, San Francisco, CA 94122, 415-386-0178
NEW METHODS JOURNAL (VETERINARY), PO Box 22605, San Francisco, CA 94122-0605, 415-664-3469
Rehab Publications, 1237 28th Avenue, PO Box 22606, San Francisco, CA 94122
Stratton Press, PO Box 22391, San Francisco, CA 94122, 415-759-5270
BALLOT ACCESS NEWS, 3201 Baker Street, San Francisco, CA 94123, 415-922-9779
National Poetry Association Publishers, Fort Mason Center, Building D, San Francisco, CA 94123, 415-776-6602

POETRY: USA QUARTERLY, Fort Mason Center, Building D, San Francisco, CA 94123, 415-776-6602
PUNCTURE, 1592 Union Street, #431, San Francisco, CA 94123, 415-771-5127
Schneider Educational Products, 2880 Green St., San Francisco, CA 94123, 415-567-4455
WESTERN PUBLISHER, PO Box 470361, San Francisco, CA 94123-1012
Alan Wofsy Fine Arts, PO Box 2210, San Francisco, CA 94126, 415-986-3030
INVISIBLE CITY, PO Box 2853, San Francisco, CA 94126
Red Hill Press, San Francisco + Los Angeles, PO Box 2853, San Francisco, CA 94126
Sierra Trading Post, PO Box 2497, San Francisco, CA 94126, 415-456-9378
HAIGHT ASHBURY LITERARY JOURNAL, 558 Joost Avenue, San Francisco, CA 94127
Pancake Press, 163 Galewood Circle, San Francisco, CA 94131, 415-648-3573
Second Coming Press, PO Box 31249, San Francisco, CA 94131, 415-991-2302
ANDROGYNE, 930 Shields, San Francisco, CA 94132, 586-2697
Androgyne Books, 930 Shields, San Francisco, CA 94132, 586-2697
City Lights Books, Attn: Bob Sharrard, Editor, 261 Columbus Avenue, San Francisco, CA 94133, 415-362-8193
CITY LIGHTS JOURNAL, 261 Columbus Avenue, San Francisco, CA 94133, 415-362-8193
Mercury House, 201 Filbert Street, #400, San Francisco, CA 94133, 415-433-7042; 433-7080 (Editorial)
RE/SEARCH, 20 Romolo, Suite B, San Francisco, CA 94133, 415-362-1465
Re/Search Publications, 20 Romolo, Suite B, San Francisco, CA 94133, 415-362-1465
WORLD RAINFOREST REPORT, Rainforest Action Network, 301 Broadway, Suite A, San Francisco, CA 94133, 415-398-4404
Crime and Social Justice Associates, Inc., PO Box 40601, San Francisco, CA 94140, 415-550-1703
GAY SUNSHINE JOURNAL, PO Box 40397, San Francisco, CA 94140, 415-824-3184
Gay Sunshine Press, Inc., PO Box 40397, San Francisco, CA 94140, 415-824-3184
Leyland Publications, PO Box 40397, San Francisco, CA 94140, 415-824-3184
TRADESWOMEN MAGAZINE, Tradeswomen Inc., PO Box 40664, San Francisco, CA 94140, 415-821-7334
LA BELLA FIGURA, PO Box 411223, San Francisco, CA 94141-1223
Malafemmina Press, PO Box 411223, San Francisco, CA 94141-1223
manic d press, PO Box 410804, San Francisco, CA 94141
Spinster's Book Company, PO Box 410687, San Francisco, CA 94141, 415-558-9586
COSMEP NEWSLETTER, PO Box 420703, San Francisco, CA 94142-0703, 415-922-9490
Creighton-Morgan Publishing Group, Po Box 470862, San Francisco, CA 94147-0862
CANTU'S COMEDY NEWSLETTER, PO Box 590634, San Francisco, CA 94159-0634, 415-668-2402
Sink Press, PO Box 590095, San Francisco, CA 94159-0095
Norton Coker Press, PO Box 640543, San Francisco, CA 94164-0543, 415-922-0395
TOOK, PO Box 640543, San Francisco, CA 94164-0543, 415-922-0395
Dropzone Press, PO Box 882222, San Francisco, CA 94188, 415-776-7164; FAX 415-921-6776
THE FEMINIST BOOKSTORE NEWS, PO Box 882554, San Francisco, CA 94188, 415-626-1556
Genny Smith Books, 1304 Pitman Avenue, Palo Alto, CA 94301, 415-321-7247
Accent on Music, PO Box 417, Palo Alto, CA 94302, 415-856-0987
Bull Publishing Co., P O Box 208, Palo Alto, CA 94302, 415-322-2855
Magical Music Express, PO Box 417, Palo Alto, CA 94302, 415-856-0987
RHODODENDRON, Guerilla Poetics, Inc., 879 Bell Street, East Palo Alto, CA 94303
Fresh Press, 3712 Ortega Court, Palo Alto, CA 94303, 415-493-3596
Lincoln Publishing Company, 3434 Janice Way, Palo Alto, CA 94303
T.H. Peek, Publisher, PO Box 50123, Palo Alto, CA 94303, 415-962-1010
Timeless Books, PO Box 50905, Palo Alto, CA 94303-0673, 604-227-9224
Hoover Institution Press, Stanford University, Stanford, CA 94305-6010, 415-723-3373
SEQUOIA, Storke Publications Bldg., Stanford, CA 94305
FOREFRONT—HEALTH INVESTIGATIONS, PO Box 60637, Palo Alto, CA 94306, 408-733-2010; 415-949-0919
Institute of Lesbian Studies, PO Box 60242, Palo Alto, CA 94306
Klutz Press, 2121 Staunton Court, Palo Alto, CA 94306, 415-857-0888
The Live Oak Press, PO Box 60036, Palo Alto, CA 94306, 415-853-0197
Trackless Sands Press, 3790 El Camino Real, Suite 104, Palo Alto, CA 94306, 415-855-8086
CEILIDH: AN INFORMAL GATHERING FOR STORY & SONG, PO Box 6367, San Mateo, CA 94403, 415-591-9902
Ceilidh, Inc., P.O. Box 6367, San Mateo, CA 94403, 415-591-9902
SORE DOVE, PO Box 6332, San Mateo, CA 94403
Sore Dove Publishers, PO Box 6332, San Mateo, CA 94403
Latham Foundation, Latham Plaza, 1826 Clement Avenue, Alameda, CA 94501-1397, 415-521-0920
THE LATHAM LETTER, Latham Foundation, Latham Plaza, 1826 Clement Avenue, Alameda, CA 94501-1397, 415-521-0920
SYBEX Computer Books, 2021 Challenger Drive, Alameda, CA 94501
Calgre Press, Division of Calgre Inc., PO Box 711, Antioch, CA 94509, 415-754-4916
Front Row Experience, 540 Discovery Bay Boulevard, Byron, CA 94514, 510-634-5710
Alta Napa Press, 1969 Mora Avenue, Calistoga, CA 94515, 707-942-4444
EGW Publishing Company, 1320 Galaxy Way, Concord, CA 94520
POPULAR WOODWORKING, 1320 Galaxy Way, Concord, CA 94520, 415-671-6852
CHILDREN'S ALBUM, PO Box 6086, Concord, CA 94524, 415-671-9852
NEEDLEPOINT PLUS, PO Box 5967, Concord, CA 94524, 415-671-9852
TOLE WORLD, PO Box 5986, Concord, CA 94524, 415-671-9852
TechWest Publications, 560 South Hartz #447, Danville, CA 94526, 415-838-2670
Philmar Press, PO Box 402, Diablo, CA 94528-0402, 415-837-3490
Downey Place Publishing House, Inc., PO Box 1352, El Cerrito, CA 94530, 415-529-1012
AFFAIRE DE COEUR, 5660 Roosevelt Place, Fremont, CA 94538, 415-357-5665
INFINITY LIMITED, A Journal for .e Somewhat Eccentric, PO Box 2713, Castro Valley, CA 94546, 415-581-8172
Royce Baker Publishing, Inc., 953 Mountain View Drive, Suite 511, Lafayette, CA 94549
Greenridge Press, 5869 Greenridge Road, Castro Valley, CA 94552, 415-881-4432
C & T Publishing, 5021 Blum Road #1, Martinez, CA 94553, 415-370-9600
The Public Safety Press, 1320 Trancas Street, Suite 211, Napa, CA 94558, 707-255-7597

Affinity Press, 73 Brookwood Road #18, Orinda, CA 94563-3310, 415-253-1889
THE MICHAEL CONNECTION, PO Box 1873, Orinda, CA 94563, 415-256-7639
ROMEO NEWSLETTER, 120 Village Square, Suite 148, Orinda, CA 94563, 415-254-7409
Vintage '45 Press, PO Box 266, Orinda, CA 94563-0266
Eagle Publishing Company, 7283 Kolb Place, Dublin, CA 94568, 415-828-1350
Brandywyne Books, 1555 Washington Avenue, San Leandro, CA 94577
THE VITAL FORCE, 1477 155th Avenue, San Leandro, CA 94578, 415-278-3263
SCHMAGA, 436 Indiana Street, Vallejo, CA 94590-4441
Devil Mountain Books, PO Box 4115, Walnut Creek, CA 94596, 415-939-3415
MIDNIGHT ZOO, 544 Ygnacio Valley Road #A273, PO Box 8040, Walnut Creek, CA 94596, 415-942-5116
Dirty Rotten Press, 4401 San Leandro Street #36, Oakland, CA 94601, 415-533-2051
THE WISE WOMAN, 2441 Cordova Street, Oakland, CA 94602, 415-536-3174
Cliffhanger Press, P.O. Box 29527, Oakland, CA 94604-9527, 415-763-3510
LEFT CURVE, PO Box 472, Oakland, CA 94604
RADIANCE, The Magazine For Large Women, PO Box 31703, Oakland, CA 94604, (415) 482-0680
Stone Circle Press, PO Box 44, Oakland, CA 94604, 415-658-1135; 893-2972
Star Rover House, 1914 Foothill Blvd., Oakland, CA 94606, 415-532-8408
THE BERKELEY MONTHLY, 1301 59th Street, Emeryville, CA 94608, 415-848-7900
Children's Book Press, 6400 Hollis Street #4, Emeryville, CA 94608-1028
Conari Press, 1339 61st Street, Emeryville, CA 94608, 415-596-4040
OWLFLIGHT MAGAZINE, c/o Unique Graphics, 1025 55th Street, Oakland, CA 94608
Unique Graphics, 1025 55th Street, Oakland, CA 94608, 415-655-3024
THE BLACK SCHOLAR: Journal of Black Studies and Research, PO Box 2869, Oakland, CA 94609, 415-547-6633
CONNEXIONS, 4228 Telegraph, Oakland, CA 94609, 415-654-6725
EyeDEA Books, 477 Rich Street, Oakland, CA 94609, 415-653-7190
INKBLOT, 439 49th Street #11, Oakland, CA 94609-2158
Inkblot Publications, 439 49th Street #11, Oakland, CA 94609-2158
New Harbinger Publications, Inc., 5674 Shattuck Avenue, Oakland, CA 94609, 415-652-0215
BLACKJACK FORUM, 414 Santa Clara Avenue, Oakland, CA 94610, 415-465-6452
R.G.E. Publishing, 414 Santa Clara, Oakland, CA 94610
S.E.T. FREE: The Newsletter Against Television, Box 10491, Oakland, CA 94610, 415-763-8712
Score, 491 Mandana Street #3, Oakland, CA 94610-2123, 415-268-9284
SCORE, 491 Mandana Street #3, Oakland, CA 94610-2123, 415-268-9284
Sea Urchin Press, PO Box 10503, Oakland, CA 94610-0503, 415-428-0178
SOCIAL JUSTICE: A JOURNAL OF CRIME, CONFLICT, & WORLD ORDER, PO Box 40601, San Francisco, CA 94610, 415-550-1703
Chance Additions, 3064 Richmond Boulevard, Oakland, CA 94611
Gravity Publishing, 6324 Heather Ridge, Oakland, CA 94611, 415-339-3774
JIMMY & LUCY'S HOUSE OF 'K', 3816 Piedmont #6, Oakland, CA 94611-5329, 415-848-8177
Zeitgeist Press, 4368 Piedmont Avenue, Oakland, CA 94611
Kirit N. Shah, 980 Moraga Avenue, Piedmont, CA 94611, 415-653-2076
THIRD WORLD RESOURCES, 464 19 Street, Oakland, CA 94612, 415-835-4692; 536-1876; fax 415-835-3017
Akiba Press, PO Box 13086, Oakland, CA 94661, 415-339-1283
LOCUS: The Newspaper of the Science Fiction Field, Box 13305, Oakland, CA 94661, 415-339-9196, 9198
Berkeley Poets Workshop and Press, PO Box 459, Berkeley, CA 94701, 415-843-8793
City Miner Books, P.O. Box 176, Berkeley, CA 94701, 415-841-1511
JUMP CUT, A Review of Contemporary Media, P.O. Box 865, Berkeley, CA 94701, 415-658-4482
MARION ZIMMER BRADLEY'S FANTASY MAGAZINE, PO Box 249, Berkeley, CA 94701, 415-601-9000
THE MOUNTAIN ASTROLOGER, PO Box 11292, Berkeley, CA 94701, 415-267-3274
NET, PO Box 795, Berkeley, CA 94701, 415-524-0345
The New Humanity Press, PO Box 215, Berkeley, CA 94701
Polymath Systems, PO Box 795, Berkeley, CA 94701, 415-524-0345
Rakhamim Publications, PO Box 7, Berkeley, CA 94701
Ronin Publishing, Inc., Box 1035, Berkeley, CA 94701, 415-540-6278
Synthetix, PO Box 1080, Berkeley, CA 94701, 415-428-9009
And/Or Press, Inc., PO Box 2246, Berkeley, CA 94702, 415-548-2124
Homeward Press, PO Box 2307, Berkeley, CA 94702, 412-526-3254
Key Curriculum Press, PO Box 2304, Berkeley, CA 94702, 415-548-2304
Rebis Press, P.O. Box 2233, Berkeley, CA 94702, 415-527-3845
AGADA, 2020 Essex Street, Berkeley, CA 94703, 415-848-0965
Ariel Vamp Press, PO Box 3496, Berkeley, CA 94703, 415-654-4849
Bay Area Poets Coalition, Inc., POETALK, 1527 Virginia Street, Berkeley, CA 94703, 415-845-8409
Embassy Hall Editions, 1630 University Avenue, Suite 42, Berkeley, CA 94703, 415-486-0187
THE GALLEY SAIL REVIEW, 1630 University Avenue, Suite 42, Berkeley, CA 94703, 415-486-0187
Open Books, 1631 Grant Street, Berkeley, CA 94703, 415-548-2208
POETALK, 1527 Virginia Street, Berkeley, CA 94703, 415-845-8409
I. Reed Books, PO Box 3288, Berkeley, CA 94703
Rolling House Publications, PO Box 3865, Berkeley, CA 94703-0865, 415-548-4228
SINISTER WISDOM, PO Box 3252, Berkeley, CA 94703
Tabor Sarah Books, 2419 Jefferson Avenue, Berkeley, CA 94703
This Press, c/o Small Press Distribution, Inc., 1731 Stuart Street, Berkeley, CA 94703-1624
TWISTED IMAGE NEWSLETTER, 1630 University Avenue #26, Berkeley, CA 94703, 415-644-8035
Dawn Sign Press, 2124 Kittredge Street #107, Berkeley, CA 94704-1436, 415-430-9419
Dharma Publishing, 2425 Hillside Avenue, Berkeley, CA 94704
GESAR-Buddhism in the West, 2425 Hillside Avenue, Berkeley, CA 94704, 415-548-5407
MEN'S REPORT, Center For Men's Studies, 2600 Dwight Way, Berkeley, CA 94704, (415) 549-0537
New Earth Publications, PO Box 4790, Berkeley, CA 94704
Personabooks, 2054 University Avenue, Suite 502, Berkeley, CA 94704

POETRY FLASH, PO Box 4172, Berkeley, CA 94704, 415-525-5476
Rodmell Press, 2550 Shattuck Avenue, #18, Berkeley, CA 94704, 415-841-3123
Ross Books, Box 4340, Berkeley, CA 94704, 415-841-2474
SCP NEWSLETTER, PO Box 4308, Berkeley, CA 94704
SHMATE, Box 4228, Berkeley, CA 94704
Shmate Press, Box 4228, Berkeley, CA 94704
STAR-WEB PAPER, Tom Fisher, P.O. Box 40029, Berkeley, CA 94704, 505-523-7923
Berkeley West Publishing, 2847 Shattuck Avenue, Berkeley, CA 94705
Judah Magnes Museum Publications, 2911 Russell Street, Berkeley, CA 94705
Oyez, PO Box 5134, Berkeley, CA 94705
Peaceable Kingdom Press, 2980 College Avenue #2, Berkeley, CA 94705, (415) 654-9989
POETICS JOURNAL, 2639 Russell Street, Berkeley, CA 94705, 415-548-1817
Poltroon Press, PO Box 5476, Berkeley, CA 94705, 415-654-4745
Regent Press, 2747 Regent Street, Berkeley, CA 94705, 415-548-8459
Carousel Press, PO Box 6061, Albany, CA 94706, 415-527-5849
THE LETTER EXCHANGE, The Readers' League, PO Box 6218, Albany, CA 94706, 415-526-7412
Silver Skates Publishing, 1020 Santa Fe Avenue, Albany, CA 94706, 415-528-1302
Verygraphics, PO Box 6374, Albany, CA 94706, 415-841-6500
YELLOW SILK: Journal Of Erotic Arts, PO Box 6374, Albany, CA 94706, 415-644-4188
Oceanides Press, 1320 Albina, Berkeley, CA 94706
AMERICAS REVIEW, Box 7681, Berkeley, CA 94707, 415-845-2089
Banyan Tree Books, 1963 El Dorado Avenue, Berkeley, CA 94707, 415-524-2690
BURNT SIENNA, PO Box 7495, Berkeley, CA 94707
Goldstein & Blair, PO Box 7635, Berkeley, CA 94707, (415) 524-4000
LANDSCAPE, PO Box 7107, Berkeley, CA 94707, 415-549-3233
MYSTERY READERS JOURNAL, PO Box 8116, Berkeley, CA 94707-8116, 415-339-2800
Parallax Press, PO Box 7355, Berkeley, CA 94707, (415) 525-0101
Stone Bridge Press, PO Box 8208, Berkeley, CA 94707
Ten Speed Press, PO Box 7123, Berkeley, CA 94707, 415-845-8414
BLUE UNICORN, 22 Avon Road, Kensington, CA 94707, 415-526-8439
Cayuse Press, 1523 Valley Road, Kensington, CA 94707, 415-525-8515
DESIGN BOOK REVIEW, 1418 Spring Way, Berkeley, CA 94708, 415-486-1956; fax 415-540-1057
Peachpit Press, Inc., 1085 Keith Avenue, Berkeley, CA 94708, 415-527-8555
ARTICHOKE HEART, 1419 Bonita Avenue, Berkeley, CA 94709, 415-526-4765
Community Resource Institute Press, 1442-A Walnut #51, Berkeley, CA 94709, 415-526-7190
Fallen Leaf Press, PO Box 10034, Berkeley, CA 94709, 415-848-7805
Heyday Books, Box 9145, Berkeley, CA 94709, 415-549-3564
Kelsey St. Press, PO Box 9235, Berkeley, CA 94709, 415-845-2260
New Seed Press, PO Box 9488, Berkeley, CA 94709
NEWS FROM NATIVE CALIFORNIA, PO Box 9145, Berkeley, CA 94709, (415) 549-3564
THE THREEPENNY REVIEW, PO Box 9131, Berkeley, CA 94709, 415-849-4545
TQS NEWS, PO Box 9275, Berkeley, CA 94709, 415-655-8036
TQS Publications (Tonatiuh - Quinto Sol International Inc.), PO Box 9275, Berkeley, CA 94709, 415-655-8036; FAX 415-601-6938
VELOCITIES, PO Box 9643, Berkeley, CA 94709
WALKING AND SINNING, Accelerator Press, 1708 #4 Martin Luther King Jr. Way, Berkeley, CA 94709, 415-549-2815
KINGFISHER, PO Box 9783, North Berkeley, CA 94709
ACROSTICS NETWORK, 1030-A Delaware Street, Berkeley, CA 94710, 415-549-0659
THE BERKELEY REVIEW OF BOOKS, 1731 10th Street, Apt. A, Berkeley, CA 94710, 415-528-8713
Illuminations Press, 2110 9th Street, Apt B, Berkeley, CA 94710, 415-849-2102
Nolo Press, 950 Parker Street, Berkeley, CA 94710, 415-549-1976
Wingbow Press, 2929 Fifth Street, Berkeley, CA 94710, 415-549-3030
AGRICULTURAL HISTORY, University of California Press, 2120 Berkeley Way, Berkeley, CA 94720, 415-642-4191
ASIAN SURVEY, University of California Press, 2120 Berkeley Way, Berkeley, CA 94720, 415-642-4191
BERKELEY POETRY REVIEW, 700 Eshleman Hall, University of California, Berkeley, CA 94720
BERKELEY WOMEN'S LAW JOURNAL, 2 Boalt Hall, Univ. of Ca., School of Law, Berkeley, CA 94720, 415-642-6263
CALIFORNIA LAW REVIEW, University of California Press, 2120 Berkeley Way, Berkeley, CA 94720, 415-642-4191
Chicano Studies Library Publications Unit, 3404 Dwinelle Hall, University of California, Berkeley, CA 94720, 415-642-3859
CLASSICAL ANTIQUITY, Univ of California Press, 2120 Berkeley Way, Berkeley, CA 94720, 415-642-4191
COMPUTING SYSTEMS, University of California Press, 2120 Berkeley Way, Berkeley, CA 94720, 415-642-4191
EASTERN EUROPEAN POLITICS & SOCIETIES, University of California Press, 2120 Berkeley Way, Berkeley, CA 94720, 415-642-4191
ECOLOGY LAW QUARTERLY, University of California Press, 2120 Berkeley Way, Berkeley, CA 94720, 415-642-4191
FILM QUARTERLY, University of California Press, 2120 Berkeley Way, Berkeley, CA 94720, 415-642-4191
HIGH TECHNOLOGY LAW JOURNAL, University of California Press, 2120 Berkeley Way, Berkeley, CA 94720, 415-642-4191
HISTORICAL STUDIES IN THE PHYSICAL & BIOLOGICAL SCIENCES, University of California Press, 2120 Berkeley Way, Berkeley, CA 94720, 415-642-4191
INDEX TO FOREIGN LEGAL PERIODICALS, University of California Press, 2120 Berkeley Way, Berkeley, CA 94720, 415-642-4191
INDUSTRIAL RELATIONS LAW JOURNAL, University of California Press, 2120 Berkeley Way, Berkeley, CA 94720, 415-642-4191
INTERNATIONAL TAX AND BUSINESS LAWYER, University of California Press, 2120 Berkeley Way, Berkeley, CA 94720, 415-642-4191
JOURNAL OF MUSICOLOGY, University of California Press, 2120 Berkeley Way, Berkeley, CA 94720, 415-642-4191
LA RAZA LAW JOURNAL, University of California Press, 2120 Berkeley Way, Berkeley, CA 94720
MEXICAN STUDIES/ESTUDIOS MEXICANOS, University of California Press, 2120 Berkeley Way, Berkeley, CA

94720, 415-642-4191
MOUNTAIN RESEARCH & DEVELOPMENT, University of California Press, 2120 Berkeley Way, Berkeley, CA 94720
MUSIC PERCEPTION, Univ of CA Press, 2120 Berkeley Way, Berkeley, CA 94720, 415-642-4191
NINETEENTH-CENTURY LITERATURE, University of California Press, 2120 Berkeley Way, Berkeley, CA 94720, 415-642-4191
19TH-CENTURY MUSIC, University of California Press, 2120 Berkeley Way, Berkeley, CA 94720, 415-642-4191
PACIFIC HISTORICAL REVIEW, Univ of California Press, 2120 Berkeley Way, Berkeley, CA 94720, 415-642-4191
THE PUBLIC HISTORIAN, University of California Press, 2120 Berkeley Way, Berkeley, CA 94720, 415-642-4191
REPRESENTATIONS, University of California Press, 2120 Berkeley Way, Berkeley, CA 94720, 415-642-4191
RHETORICA: A Journal of the History of Rhetoric, Univ of California Press, 2120 Berkeley Way, Berkeley, CA 94720, 415-642-4191
ROMANCE PHILOLOGY, University of California Press, 2120 Berkeley Way, Berkeley, CA 94720, 415-642-4191
SOCIAL PROBLEMS, University of California Press, 2120 Berkeley Way, Berkeley, CA 94720, 415-642-4191
University of California Press, 2120 Berkeley Way, Berkeley, CA 94720, 415-642-4191
VIATOR: Medieval and Renaissance Studies, University of California Press, 2120 Berkeley Way, Berkeley, CA 94720, 415-642-4191
Cosmic Circus Productions, 414 So 41st Street, Richmond, CA 94804, 415-451-5818
SPIRIT MAGAZINE, 414 S. 41st Street, Richmond, CA 94804, 415-451-5818
Gateway Books, 13 Bedford Cove, San Rafael, CA 94901-4472, 415-454-5215
Libertarian Publishers, PO Box 6022, San Rafael, CA 94903, 415-472-3294
New World Library, 58 Paul Drive, San Rafael, CA 94903
ProActive Press, 64 Via La Cumbre, Greenbrae, CA 94904, 415-461-7854
THE CONSTRUCTION CLAIMS CITATOR, PO Box 9838, San Rafael, CA 94912, 415-927-2155
CONTRACTOR PROFIT NEWS (CPN), PO Box 9838, San Rafael, CA 94912, 415-927-2155
Axiom Press, Publishers, PO Box L, San Rafael, CA 94913, 415-956-4859
Cassandra Press, PO Box 868, San Rafael, CA 94915, 415-382-8507
Cadmus Editions, PO Box 687, Tiburon, CA 94920
HJ Kramer, Inc, PO Box 1082, Tiburon, CA 94920
Wood River Publishing, 680 Hawthorne Drive, Tiburon, CA 94920, 415-435-0677
American Samizdat Editions, PO Box 886, Bolinas, CA 94924, 415-868-9224
Tombouctou Books, Box 265, Bolinas, CA 94924, 415-868-1082
JOURNAL OF SOCIAL BEHAVIOR AND PERSONALITY, PO Box 37, Corte Madera, CA 94925, 415-924-1612
Select Press, PO Box 37, Corte Madera, CA 94925, 415-924-1612
Context Publications, PO Box 2909, Rohnert Park, CA 94927, 707-576-0100
CIP Communications, 6585 Commerce Blvd, Suite E-292, Rohnert Park, CA 94928, 707-792-2223
CONSTRUCTION COMPUTER APPLICATIONS NEWSLETTER (CCAN), 6585 Commerce Blvd., Suite E-292, Rohnert Park, CA 94928, 707-792-2223
Construction Industry Press, 6585 Commerce Blvd #E-292, Rohnert Park, CA 94928, 415-927-2155
HELTER SKELTER, 979 Golf Course Drive, Suite 223, Rohnert Park, CA 94928, 408-624-7066
SONOMA MANDALA, Department of English, Sonoma State University, Rohnert Park, CA 94928, 707-664-2140
Inner Wealth Press, PO Box 487, Forest Knolls, CA 94933, 415-488-0771
Lexikos, PO Box 296, Lagunitas, CA 94938, 415-488-0401
K0SMOS, 20 Millard Road, Larkspur, CA 94939
Tamal Vista Publications, 222 Madrone Ave, Larkspur, CA 94939, 924-7289
AMC Publishing, 10 Milland Drive #B-4, Mill Valley, CA 94941-2546
Bicycle Books (Publishing) Inc., PO Box 2038, Mill Valley, CA 94941, 415-381-2515
POETS ON:, 29 Loring Avenue, Mill Valley, CA 94941
Symbiosis Books, 8 Midhill Drive, Mill Valley, CA 94941, 415-383-7722
GRDA Publications, PO Box 1407, Mill Valley, CA 94942
PROPHETIC VOICES, 94 Santa Maria Drive, Novato, CA 94947
Chandler & Sharp Publishers, Inc., 11A Commercial Blvd., Novato, CA 94949, 415-883-2353
AVEC, PO Box 1059, Penngrove, CA 94951, 707-762-2370
Old Adobe Press, PO Box 969, Penngrove, CA 94951
Small Helm Press, 622 Baker Street, Petaluma, CA 94952, (707) 763-5757
Ten Mile River Press, 3809 Spring Hill Road, Petaluma, CA 94952-9637, 707-964-5579
FLOATING ISLAND, PO Box 516, Point Reyes Station, CA 94956
Floating Island Publications, PO Box 516, Pt Reyes Sta, CA 94956
Redwood Press, PO Box 817, Pt. Reyes, CA 94956, 415-663-8733
Fels and Firn Press, 33 Scenic Ave., San Anselmo, CA 94960, 415-457-4361
SPECIALTY TRAVEL INDEX, 305 San Anselmo Avenue #313, San Anselmo, CA 94960-2660, 415-459-4900
Pergot Press, 1001 Bridgeway, Suite 227, Sausalito, CA 94965, 415-332-0279
The Post-Apollo Press, 35 Marie Street, Sausalito, CA 94965, 415-332-1458
WHOLE EARTH REVIEW, 27 Gate Five Road, Sausalito, CA 94965, 415-332-1716
In Between Books, PO Box 790, Sausalito, CA 94966, 383-8447
COYDOG REVIEW, PO Box 2608, Aptos, CA 95001, 408-761-1824
Vision Quest Publishing, PO Box 2398, Aptos, CA 95001, 408-685-8728
GALLERY WORKS, 218 Appleton Drive, Aptos, CA 95003
Aslan Publishing, PO Box 887, Boulder Creek, CA 95006-0887, 408-338-7504
BOTTOMFISH MAGAZINE, 21250 Stevens Creek Blvd., Cupertino, CA 95014, 408-996-4538, 996-4547
Omega Cat Press, 904 Old Town Ct., Cupertino, CA 95014, 408-257-0462
WRITERS CONNECTION, 1601 Saratoga-Sunnyvale Road, Suite 180, Cupertino, CA 95014, 408-973-0227
XENOPHILIA, 904 Old Town Ct., Cupertino, CA 95014, 408-257-0462
Pacific Information Inc., 979 Eaton Drive, Felton, CA 95018, 405-335-5599; fax 408-335-3327
The Crossing Press, PO Box 1048, Freedom, CA 95019-1048, 408-722-0711
The Atlantean Press, 354 Tramway Drive, Milpitas, CA 95035, 408-262-8478
ALCATRAZ, 133 Towne Terrace, Santa Cruz, CA 95060
Alcatraz Editions, 133 Towne Terrace, Santa Cruz, CA 95060
Greenhouse Review Press, 3965 Bonny Doon Road, Santa Cruz, CA 95060, 408-426-4355

THE LEFT INDEX, 511 Lincoln Street, Santa Cruz, CA 95060, 408-426-4479
Moving Parts Press, 220 Baldwin Street, Santa Cruz, CA 95060, 408-427-2271
Paperweight Press, 761 Chestnut Street, Santa Cruz, CA 95060, 408-427-1177
THE STONE, c/o Greenpeace, 1112-B Ocean, Santa Cruz, CA 95060, 408-429-9988
Western Tanager Press, 1111 Pacific Avenue, Santa Cruz, CA 95060
FAMILY LIFE EDUCATOR, PO Box 1830, Santa Cruz, CA 95061, 408-438-4060
HerBooks, PO Box 7467, Santa Cruz, CA 95061
Little People's Press, PO Box 7280, Santa Cruz, CA 95061, 408-429-9506
Network Publications, a division of ETR Associates, PO Box 1830, Santa Cruz, CA 95061, 408-438-4060
WE MAGAZINE, PO Box 1503, Santa Cruz, CA 95061, 408-427-9711
We Press, PO Box 1503, Santa Cruz, CA 95061, 408-427-9711
Embers Press, 2150 Portola Drive, Santa Cruz, CA 95062, 408-476-6164
C. Olson & Company, PO Box 5100, Santa Cruz, CA 95063-5100, 408-458-3365
Red Alder Books, Box 2992, Santa Cruz, CA 95063, 408-426-7082
STONE SOUP, The Magazine By Children, Box 83, Santa Cruz, CA 95063, 408-426-5557
QUARRY WEST, c/o Porter College, University of Calif, Santa Cruz, CA 95064, 408-429-2155
Spirit Press, 1951 Branciforte Drive, Santa Cruz, CA 95065
Mark Publishing, 5400 Scotts Valley Drive, Scotts Valley, CA 95066-3439, 408-438-7668
R & E Publishers, PO Box 2008, Saratoga, CA 95070, 415-494-1112/408-866-6303
Papier-Mache Press, 795 Via Manzana, Watsonville, CA 95076
T-J TODAY, 732 Cynthia Court, Watsonville, CA 95076, 408-728-3948
CCR Publications, 2745 Monterey Road #76, San Jose, CA 95111
MODERN LITURGY, 160 East Virginia Street, #290, San Jose, CA 95112, 408-286-8505
Resource Publications, Inc., 160 East Virginia Street #290, San Jose, CA 95112, 408-286-8505
Australian American Publishing, 228 Fragrant Harbor Court, San Jose, CA 95123, 408-226-4056
Occasional Productions, 5653 Orchard Park Drive, San Jose, CA 95123
Parrot Press, 767 Schiele Avenue, Unit A, San Jose, CA 95126
Venture Perspectives Inc., 4300 Stevens Creek Blvd., Suite 120, San Jose, CA 95129, 408-247-1325
Alchemist/Light Publishing, PO Box 5183, San Jose, CA 95150-5183, 408-723-6108
American Handwriting Analysis Foundation, PO Box 6201, San Jose, CA 95150
INDIA CURRENTS, Box 21285, San Jose, CA 95151, 408-274-6966
R.J. Bender Publishing, PO Box 23456, San Jose, CA 95153, 408-225-5777
THE MILITARY ADVISOR, PO Box 23456, San Jose, CA 95153, 408-225-5777
Urion Press, PO Box 10085, San Jose, CA 95157, 408-867-7695
Northern Star Press, PO Box 28814, San Jose, CA 95159
History West Publishing Company, PO Box 612066, San Jose, CA 95161, 408-259-8060
SAN JOSE STUDIES, c/o English, San Jose State University, San Jose, CA 95192, 408-924-4476
International Consulting Associates, Inc., 1020 N. Commerce, Stockton, CA 95202, 209-466-7678
Heritage West Books, 306 Regent Court, Stockton, CA 95204-4435, 209-464-8818
THE WORMWOOD REVIEW, PO Box 4698, Stockton, CA 95204-0698, 209-466-8231
The Wormwood Review Press, PO Box 4698, Stockton, CA 95204-0698, 209-466-8231
THE AUTOGRAPH COLLECTOR'S MAGAZINE, PO Box 55328, Stockton, CA 95205, (209) 473-0570
Pine Cone Press, 11362 Yankee Hill Road, PO Box 1494, Columbia, CA 95310, 209-532-2699
Lawco Ltd./Moneytree Publications, PO Box 2009, Manteca, CA 95336, 209-239-6006
GlenHill Productions, PO Box 62, Soulsbyville, CA 95372, 209-532-7045
Black Sparrow Press, 24 Tenth Street, Santa Rosa, CA 95401
WIDE OPEN MAGAZINE, Wide Open Press, 116 Lincoln Street, Santa Rosa, CA 95401, 707-545-3821
MALEDICTA: The International Journal of Verbal Aggression, PO Box 14123, Santa Rosa, CA 95402-6123
Maledicta Press, PO Box 14123, Santa Rosa, CA 95402-6123
Woodcock Press, PO Box 4744, Santa Rosa, CA 95402, 415-533-4399
Social Order Series, 7899 St. Helena Road, Santa Rosa, CA 95404, 707-539-0569
Clamshell Press, 160 California Avenue, Santa Rosa, CA 95405
Hoffman Press, PO Box 2996, Santa Rosa, CA 95405-0996, 707-538-5527
Pygmy Forest Press, PO Box 591, Albion, CA 95410-1036
Manroot Books, Box 762, Boyes Hot Springs, CA 95416
The Dawn Horse Press, PO Box 3680, Clearlake, CA 95422
THE LAUGHING MAN: The Alternative to Scientific Materialism and Religious Provincialism, PO Box 3680, Clearlake, CA 95422
The Yolla Bolly Press, PO Box 156, Covelo, CA 95428, 707-983-6130
Ocean Star Publications, 30200 North Highway 1, Fort Bragg, CA 95437, 707-964-7302
Q.E.D. Press, 155 Cypress Street, Fort Bragg, CA 95437, 707-964-9520
SPEX (Small Press Exchange), 155 Cypress Street, Fort Braggs, CA 95437, 707-964-9520
Borderland Sciences Research Foundation, P.O. Box 429, Gaberville, CA 95440, 724-2043
JOURNAL OF BORDERLAND RESEARCH, P.O. Box 429, Gaberville, CA 95440, 724-2043
AHA Books, PO Box 767, Gualala, CA 95445, 707-882-2226
MIRRORS - IN THE SPIRIT OF HAIKU, PO Box 1250, Gualala, CA 95445, 707-882-2226
The Quilt Digest Press, PO Box 1331, Gualala, CA 95445-1331, 704-884-4100
Bell Springs Publishing, Box 640 Bell Springs Road, Laytonville, CA 95454, 707-984-6746
Blue Lights Publications, c/o Vicki Werkley, 16563 Ellen Springs Drive, Lower Lake, CA 95457
Integral Publishing, PO Box 1030, Lower Lake, CA 95457, 707-928-5751
SPECTRUM REVIEW, PO Box 1030, Lower Lake, CA 95457, 707-928-5751
Mendocino Book Partnership, PO Box 1414, Mendocino, CA 95460-1414
RIDGE REVIEW, Box 90, Mendocino, CA 95460, 707-964-8465
Ridge Times Press, Box 90, Mendocino, CA 95460, 707-964-8465
Nolo Press - Occidental, PO Box 722, Occidental, CA 95465, 707-874-3105
Dawn Rose Press, 12470 Fiori Lane, Sebastopol, CA 95472, 707-874-2001
Misty Hill Press, 5024 Turner Road, Sebastopol, CA 95472, 707-823-7437
Alta Research, PO Box 1001-D, Sebastopol, CA 95473, 707-829-1001

CRCS Publications, PO Box 1460, Sebastopol, CA 95473-1460
Mina Press, PO Box 854, Sebastopol, CA 95473, 707-829-0854
Exile Press, 241 South Temelec Circle, Sonoma, CA 95476, 707-996-8684
Kay Productions, PO Box 1728, Sonoma, CA 95476, 707-935-1666
VOICES OF YOUTH ON EDUCATION, SELF, CIVIC VALUES, PO Box JJ, Sonoma, CA 95476, 707-938-8314
Buddhist Text Translation Society, City of 10,000 Buddhas, Talmage, CA 95481-0217, 707-462-0939
PROPER DHARMA SEAL, City of 10,000 Buddhas, Talmage, CA 95481-0217, 707-462-0939
SOURCE OF WISDOM, City of 10,000 Buddhas, Talmage, CA 95481-0217, 707-462-0939
GREEN EGG, PO Box 1542, Ukiah, CA 95482, 707-485-7787
Holmgangers Press, 95 Carson Court Shelter Cove, Whitethorn, CA 95489, 707-986-7700
Combs Vanity Press, 925 Lakeville Street, Suite 295, Petaluma, CA 95492, 707-795-4797
NORTHCOAST VIEW MONTHLY MAGAZINE, Blarney Publishing, PO Box 1374, Eureka, CA 95502, (707) 443-4887
ENVIRONMENTAL OPPORTUNITIES, PO Box 4957, Arcata, CA 95521, 707-839-4640
People's Publishing Co., Inc., 5440 Ericson Way, PO Box 1095, Arcata, CA 95521, 707-822-8442
WESTERN & EASTERN TREASURES, 5440 Ericson Way, PO Box 1095, Arcata, CA 95521, 707-822-8442
Seed Center, PO Box 1700, Redway, CA 95560-1700, 707-923-2524
STAR ROUTE JOURNAL, PO Box 1451, Redway, CA 95560, 707-923-3351
Tough Dove Books, PO Box 1999, Redway, CA 95560
Quintessence Publications & Printing Museum, 356 Bunker Hill Mine Road, Amador City, CA 95601, 209-267-5470
Gazelle Publications, 5580 Stanley Drive, Auburn, CA 95603, 916-878-1223
RIP OFF COMIX, PO Box 4686, Auburn, CA 95604, 916-885-8183
WESTART, PO Box 6868, Auburn, CA 95604, 916-885-0969
TOWARDS, 3442 Grant Park Drive, Carmichael, CA 95608, 916-485-9274
Helios House, 4905 Foster Way, PO Box 864, Carmichael, CA 95609-0864, 916-485-9588
LOS ANGELES REVIEW (OF LITERATURE & CURRENT AFFAIRS), 7536 Circuit Drive, Citrus Heights, CA 95610
NYCTICORAX, 8420 Olivine Avenue, Citrus Heights, CA 95610-2721
THE CALIFORNIA QUARTERLY, 100 Sproul Hall, Univ of Calif, Davis, CA 95616
J P Publications, 2952 Grinnel, Davis, CA 95616, 916-758-9727
PAINTED HILLS REVIEW, PO Box 494, Davis, CA 95617-0494, 916-756-5987
Panorama West Publishing, PO Box 2088, Davis, CA 95617-4638, 916-756-7177; FAX 916-756-7188
Earth-Song Press, 6553 Shadow Hawk Drive, Citrus Heights, CA 95621, 916-721-8719
Dragon's Teeth Press, 7700 Wentworth Springs Road, El Dorado Nat. Forest, Georgetown, CA 95634
Clay Press, Inc., PO Box 100, Herald, CA 95638, 916-448-1668
LLAMAS MAGAZINE, PO Box 100, Herald, CA 95638, 916-448-1668
MT. AUKUM REVIEW, PO Box 483, Mt. Aukum, CA 95656, 209-245-4016
Sierra Oaks Publishing Company, 1370 Sierra Oaks Lane, Newcastle, CA 95658-9791
Success Publishing Company, 9250 Greenback Lane, Suite 128, Orangevale, CA 95662
Bluestocking Press, PO Box 1014, Dept. LF, Placerville, CA 95667-1014, 916-621-1123
Prima Publishing, PO Box 1260, Rocklin, CA 95677, 916-624-5718
Volcano Press, Inc, PO Box 270, Volcano, CA 95689, 209-296-3445; fax 209-296-4515
Konocti Books, 23311 County Road 88, Winters, CA 95694
SIPAPU, 23311 County Road 88, Winters, CA 95694, 916-662-3364; 916-752-1032
Caddo Gap Press, 915 L Street, Suite C-414, Sacramento, CA 95814
EDUCATIONAL FOUNDATIONS, 915 L Street, Suite C-414, Sacramento, CA 95814
MOM...GUESS WHAT! NEWSPAPER & TYPESETTING, 1725 L Street, Sacramento, CA 95814-4023, 916-441-6397
POET NEWS, 1727 I Street, Sacramento, CA 95814, 916-448-6679
RADIUS/Resources for Local Arts, c/o CCA, 1212 P Street, Sacramento, CA 95814, 916-447-7811
Rural Arts Services, 1212 P Street, Sacramento, CA 95814-5808
TEACHER EDUCATION QUARTERLY, 915 L Street, Suite C-414, Sacramento, CA 95814
Samuel Powell Publishing Company, 2201 I Street, Sacramento, CA 95816, 916-443-1161
Travel Keys, PO Box 160691, Sacramento, CA 95816, 916-452-5200
BLUE LIGHTS, 4945 U Street, c/o Lil Sibley, Sacramento, CA 95817, 916-452-2024
TEC Publications, PO Box 189601, Sacramento, CA 95818, 916-457-4937
STUDIA MYSTICA, Calif. State Univ., 6000 J Street, Sacramento, CA 95819
Cougar Books, PO Box 22879, Sacramento, CA 95822, 916-442-1434
Hibiscus Press, P.O. Box 22248, Sacramento, CA 95822
MinRef Press, 8379 Langtree Way, Sacramento, CA 95823, 916-424-8465
Aspiring Millionaire, PO Box 661540, Sacramento, CA 95825, 916-973-8181
Flume Press, 4 Casita, Chico, CA 95926-2412, 916-342-1583
Heidelberg Graphics, 1116D Wendy Way, Chico, CA 95926, 916-342-6582
Moon Publications, Inc., 722 Wall Street, Chico, CA 95928, 916-345-5473; FAX 916-345-6751
Equality Press, 420-CSUC, Chico, CA 95929, 916-895-5605
Comstock Bonanza Press, 18919 William Quirk Memorial Drive, Grass Valley, CA 95945, 916-273-6220
OUT WEST, 10522 Brunswick Road, Grass Valley, CA 95945, 916-477-9378
Blue Dolphin Press, Inc., PO Box 1908, Nevada City, CA 95959, 916-265-6923
Gateways Books And Tapes, Box 370, Nevada City, CA 95959, 916-477-1116
Greensleeves Publishing, PO Box 339, Nevada City, CA 95959, 916-273-4646
INNER JOURNEYS, PO Box 370, Nevada City, CA 95959
MACROBIOTICS TODAY, 1511 Robinson Street, Oroville, CA 95965, 916-533-7702
George Ohsawa Macrobiotic Foundation Press, 1511 Robinson Street, Oroville, CA 95965-4841, 916-533-7702
Dustbooks, PO Box 100, Paradise, CA 95967, 916-877-6110; 800-477-6110; fax 916-877-0222
THE SMALL PRESS REVIEW, PO Box 100, Paradise, CA 95967-9999, 916-877-6110
United Lumbee Nation, P.O. Box 512, Fall River Mills, CA 96028, 916-336-6701
UNITED LUMBEE NATION TIMES, P.O. Box 512, Fall River Mills, CA 96028, 916-336-6701
Naturegraph Publishers, Inc., PO Box 1075, Happy Camp, CA 96039, 916-493-5353
HOME POWER MAGAZINE, PO Box 130, Hornbrook, CA 96044, 916-475-3179
THE JOURNAL OF THE ORDER OF BUDDHIST CONTEMPLATIVES, PO Box 199, Mt. Shasta, CA 96067,
916-926-4208

THE HORROR SHOW, Phantasm Press, 14848 Misty Springs Lane, Oak Run, CA 96069, 916-472-3540
Eagle Publishing, PO Box 403, Red Bluff, CA 96080, 916-520-1126
POCKET INSPIRATIONS, PO Box 796, Weaverville, CA 96093
The Blue Oak Press, PO Box 27, Sattley, CA 96124, 916-994-3397
Lahontan Images, PO Box 1093, Susanville, CA 96130, 916-257-6747
ZZAJ-SYNCHRONOLOGY, PO Box 2879, HQ, 19th SUPCOM, APO San Francisco, CA 96218, 82-53-628-5259

COLORADO

New Idea Press, Inc., 532 West Lois Way, Louisville, CO 80027-9543
Finesse Publishing Company, PO Box 657, Broomfield, CO 80038, 303-466-4734
GLASS ART, PO Box 1507, Broomfield, CO 80038-1507, 303-465-4965
Shiro Publishers, 8680 West Rice Place, Littleton, CO 80123
Arden Press, Inc., PO Box 418, Denver, CO 80201, 303-239-6155
Information Requirements Clearinghouse, 3801 E. Florida Avenue, Suite 400, Denver, CO 80201, 303-691-3600
PENCOM Press, 511 16th Street, Suite 630, Denver, CO 80202, 303-595-3991
ONE SHOT, Contract Station 6, Box 145, 1525 Sherman Street, Denver, CO 80203
Reading Matters, PO Box 300309, Denver, CO 80203, 303-757-3506
THE BLOOMSBURY REVIEW, 1028 Bannock Street, Denver, CO 80204, 303-892-0620
METROSPHERE, Campus Box 32, Metropolitan State College, Denver, CO 80204, 303-556-2495
The Global Press, 1510 York Street #204, Denver, CO 80206, 303-899-4918
HIGH PLAINS LITERARY REVIEW, 180 Adams Street, Suite 250, Denver, CO 80206, (303) 320-6828
AFRICA TODAY, c/o G.S.I.S, Univ of Denver, Denver, CO 80208
DENVER QUARTERLY, University of Denver, Denver, CO 80208, 303-871-2892
Now It's Up To You Publications, 157 S Logan, Denver, CO 80209, 303-777-8951
Wayland Press, 675 South Sherman, Denver, CO 80209
Arrowstar Publishing, 10134 University Park Station, Denver, CO 80210-0134, 303-692-6579
State of the Art Ltd., 1625 South Broadway, Denver, CO 80210, 303-722-7177
TAPLIGHT NEWSLETTER, 1827 E. Mississippi Avenue, Denver, CO 80210, 303-744-2677
PLEIADES MAGAZINE, Box 357, 6677 W. Colfax Avenue, Suite D, Lakewood, CO 80214, 303-237-3398
Old West Publishing Co., 1228 E. Colfax Avenue, Denver, CO 80218
SOUTH AMERICAN EXPLORER, PO Box 18327, Denver, CO 80218-1425, 303-320-0388
Saxifrage Books, 387 South Bryant Street, Denver, CO 80219-3020, 756-3548
Quiet Tymes, Inc., 2121 S. Oneida Street, Ste. 521, Denver, CO 80224, 303-757-5545
Tippy Reed Publishing, PO Box 260301, Lakewood, CO 80226, 303-797-6393
American Source Books, PO Box 280353, Lakewood, CO 80228, 303-980-0580
Cosmic Footnotes Publications, 2575 S. Syracuse Way, #J-203, Denver, CO 80231
LAUGHING BEAR NEWSLETTER, PO Box 36159, Bear Valley Station, Denver, CO 80236, 303-989-5614
Laughing Bear Press, PO Box 36159, Bear Valley Station, Denver, CO 80236, 303-989-5614
The Vic Press, 7684 E. Mercer Place, Denver, CO 80237-2123
Johnson Books, 1880 South 57th Court, Boulder, CO 80301, 303-443-1576
M.H. Macy & Company, PO Box 11036, Boulder, CO 80301, 303-666-8130
Pruett Publishing Company, 2928 Pearl, Boulder, CO 80301, 303-449-4919
RED DIRT, 1630 30th Street, Suite A-307, Boulder, CO 80301
VELONEWS, 1830 North 55th Street, Boulder, CO 80301
MUSCADINE, 909 Arapahoe, Boulder, CO 80302-4459, 303-443-9748
Rocky Mountain Writers Guild, Inc., 837 15th Street, Boulder, CO 80302-7623
THE UNDERGROUND FOREST - LA SELVA SUBTERRANEA, 1701 Bluebell Avenue, Boulder, CO 80302
HOME RESOURCE MAGAZINE, PO Box 12061, Boulder, CO 80303, 303-449-6126
Blue Poppy Press, 1775 Linden Avenue, Boulder, CO 80304, 303-442-0796
Last Generation/Underground Editions, 2965 13th Street, Boulder, CO 80304, 303-938-9346
MurPubCo, 3820 Lakebriar Drive, Boulder, CO 80304
NOTES FROM THE UNDERGROUND, 2965 13th Street, Boulder, CO 80304, 303-938-9346
Artemis Press, Inc., PO Box 4295, Boulder, CO 80306, 303-443-9289
Cottonwood Press, PO Box 1947, Boulder, CO 80306, (303) 433-4166
Grace and Goddess Unlimited, PO Box 4367, Boulder, CO 80306
Paladin Enterprises, Inc., PO Box 1307, Boulder, CO 80306, 303-443-7250
LivingQuest, PO Box 3306, Boulder, CO 80307, 303-444-1319
THE AMERICAN BOOK REVIEW, Publications Center Box 494, English Dept., Colorado University, Boulder, CO 80309, 303-492-8947
BLACK ICE, English Department Publications Center, Box 494, University of Colorado, Boulder, CO 80309-0001, 617-484-2048
EAST EUROPEAN QUARTERLY, Box 29 Regent Hall, University of Colorado, Boulder, CO 80309, 303-492-6157
Fiction Collective Two, Inc., Publications Center, Campus Box 494, Colorado Univ., Boulder, CO 80309-0494, 303-492-8947
Fulcrum, Inc., 350 Indiana Street, Suite 350, Golden, CO 80401, 303-277-1623
DAYSPRING, 18600 West 58 Avenue, Golden, CO 80403-1070, 303-279-2462
The Dayspring Press, Inc., 18600 West 58 Avenue, Golden, CO 80403-1070, 303-279-2462
FICTION FORUM, 18600 West 58 Avenue, Golden, CO 80403-1070, 303-279-2462
NEW ANGLICAN REVIEW, 18600 West 58 Avenue, Golden, CO 80403-1070, 303-279-2462
NEW CATHOLIC REVIEW, 18600 West 58 Avenue, Golden, CO 80403-1070, 303-279-2462
POET'S FORUM, 18600 West 58 Avenue, Golden, CO 80403-1070, 303-279-2462
Dormant Brain Research and Development Laboratory, PO Box 10, Black Hawk, CO 80422
Bibliographies Unlimited, PO Box 873, Conifer, CO 80433, 303-838-6964
Chockstone Press, PO Box 3505, Evergreen, CO 80439, 303-377-1970
Silver Forest Publishing, PO Box 3520, Evergreen, CO 80439, 303-674-5755
New World Marketing, 12963 West Chenango Drive, Morrison, CO 80465, 303-979-3506
Metagnosis Publications, PO Box 2777, Estes Park, CO 80517, 303-586-5940
COTTONWOOD MONTHLY, 305 West Magnolia, #398, Fort Collins, CO 80521, 303-493-1286

Cottonwood Press, Inc., 305 West Magnolia, Suite 398, Fort Collins, CO 80521, 303-493-1286
SALON: A Journal of Aesthetics, 305 W. Magnolia, Suite 386, Ft. Collins, CO 80521, 303-224-3116
The Old Army Press, PO Box 2243, Fort Collins, CO 80522, 303-484-5535
COLORADO REVIEW: A Journal of Contemporary Literature, 322 Eddy, English Department, Colorado State University, Fort Collins, CO 80523, 303-491-6428
Robinson Press, Inc., 1137 Riverside Drive, Ft. Collins, CO 80524, 303-482-5393
PHASE AND CYCLE, 3537 East Prospect, Fort Collins, CO 80525, 303-482-7573
Phase and Cycle Press, 3537 East Prospect, Fort Collins, CO 80525
Renaissance House Publishers (a division of Jende-Hagan, Inc.), PO Box 177, 541 Oak Street, Frederick, CO 80530, 303-833-2030
Alpine Publications, 214 19th Street, SE, Loveland, CO 80537, 303-667-2017
Wind River Institute Press, 329 East 3rd Street, Loveland, CO 80537, 800-866-5000; 303-669-3442
Iron Gate Publishing, PO Box 999, Niwot, CO 80544, 303-530-2551
Roberts Rinehart, Inc. Publishers, PO Box 666, Niwot, CO 80544-0666
HANDICAP NEWS, 3060 East Bridge Street, #342, Brighton, CO 80601-2724, 303-659-4463
COLORADO NORTH REVIEW, University Center, University of Northern Colorado, Greeley, CO 80639, 303-351-1333
Student Media Corporation, University Center, University of Northern Colorado, Greeley, CO 80639
Mountain Automation Corporation, PO Box 6020, Woodland Park, CO 80866, 719-687-6647
CULTWATCH RESPONSE, PO Box 1842, Colorado Springs, CO 80901
THE ELEVENTH MUSE, PO Box 2413, Colorado Springs, CO 80901
INFINITE ONION, PO Box 263, Colorado Springs, CO 80901, 719-473-2647
MedLife Communications, Inc., 3107 W. Colorado Ave. Ste. 266, Colorado Springs, CO 80904, 719-473-9205
Arjuna Library Press, 1025 Garner Street, D, Space 18, Colorado Springs, CO 80905-1774
JOURNAL OF REGIONAL CRITICISM, 1025 Garner Street, Box 18, Colorado Springs, CO 80905-1774
Seventh-Wing Publications, 515 East Washington Street, Colorado Springs, CO 80907, 719-471-2932
Nightingale Music, 11190 Black Forest Road, Colorado Springs, CO 80908, 719-495-3815
Piccolo Press, 6844 Raven Crest, Colorado Springs, CO 80919, 719-598-4587
HANG GLIDING, U.S. Hang Gliding Assoc., Inc., PO Box 8300, Colorado Springs, CO 80933, (805) 944-5333
WRITERS' FORUM, University of Colorado, Colorado Springs, CO 80933-7150, 719-593-3155; 599-4023
CURRENTS, National Organization for River Sports, Box 6847, Colorado Springs, CO 80934, 719-473-2466
Piccadilly Books, PO Box 25203, Colorado Springs, CO 80936, 719-548-1844
Pueblo Poetry Project, 1501 E. 7th Street, Pueblo, CO 81001
BLUE LIGHT REVIEW, PO Box 1621, Pueblo, CO 81002
Quick Books, PO Box 222, Pueblo, CO 81002
THE CLIMBING ART, PO Box 816, Alamosa, CO 81101, 719-589-5579
The FreeSolo Press, PO Box 816, Alamosa, CO 81101, 719-589-5579
Communication Creativity, 425 Cedar, PO Box 909, Buena Vista, CO 81211, 719-395-8659
Financial Awareness Corporation, PO Box 430, Buena Vista, CO 81211, 519-749-2164
Salt-Works Press, 18903 Spring Canyon Road, Montrose, CO 81401-7906
Earth Star Publications, PO Box 117, Paonia, CO 81428, 303-527-3257
HIGH COUNTRY NEWS, PO Box 1090, Paonia, CO 81428, 303-527-4898
THE STAR BEACON, PO Box 117, Paonia, CO 81428, 303-527-3257
Wayfinder Press, PO Box 217, Ridgway, CO 81432, 303-626-5452

CONNECTICUT

BROKEN STREETS, 57 Morningside Drive East, Bristol, CT 06010
Singular Speech Press, Ten Hilltop Drive, Canton, CT 06019, 203-693-6059
VIETNAM WAR NEWSLETTER, Box 469, Collinsville, CT 06022, 203-582-9784
Knowledge, Ideas & Trends, Inc. (KIT), 1131-0 Tolland Turnpike, Ste. 175, Manchester, CT 06040, 203-646-1621
Literary Publications Company, PO Box 652, Manchester, CT 06040, 203-688-5496
Newmark Publishing Company, PO Box 603, South Windsor, CT 06074, 203-282-7265
ABACUS, 181 Edgemont Avenue, Elmwood, CT 06110
Potes & Poets Press Inc, 181 Edgemont Avenue, Elmwood, CT 06110, 203-233-2023
Kumarian Press, Inc., 630 Oakwood Avenue, Suite 119, West Hartford, CT 06110-1529, 203-953-0214
Curbstone Press, 321 Jackson Street, Willimantic, CT 06226, 423-9190
THE WINDHAM PHOENIX, PO Box 752, Willimantic, CT 06226
SPRING: A Journal of Archetype and Culture, English Department, Box U-25, University of Connecticut, Storrs, CT 06268
ANGRY, 325 Captain's Walk, Room 301, New London, CT 06320, 442-1835
Tyger Press, 325 Captain's Walk, Room 301, New London, CT 06320, 442-1835
Protea Publishing Company, 604 South Canterbury Road, Canterbury, CT 06331, 203-546-9380
BOOK FORUM, Crescent Publishing Co., Inc., PO Box 585, Niantic, CT 06357
VERBATIM, 4 Laurel Heights, Old Lyme, CT 06371-1462, 203-767-8248
Verbatim Books, 4 Laurel Heights, Old Lyme, CT 06371-1462, 203-434-2104
Leete's Island Books, Box 3131, Branford, CT 06405-1731, 203-481-2536
The Globe Pequot Press, 138 W. Main Street, Box Q, Chester, CT 06412, 203-526-9571
THE CATALOG CONNECTION, PO Box 1427, Guilford, CT 06437
EMBERS, Box 404, Guilford, CT 06437, 453-2328
Telephone Books, 109 Dunk Rock Rd., Guilford, CT 06437, 203-453-1921
THE LATEST NEWS, 501 Durham Road, Madison, CT 06443
Sound View Press, 170 Boston Post Road, Madison, CT 06443, 203-245-2246
Alchemy Books, PO Box 479, Marlborough, CT 06447
Michael Shore Associates, 26 Golden Hill Street, Milford, CT 06460, 203-324-0799
THE ANIMALS' AGENDA, 456 Monroe Turnpike, Monroe, CT 06468, 203-452-0446
SAMISDAT, 456 Monroe Turnpike, Monroe, CT 06468, 203-452-0446
Samisdat, 456 Monroe Turnpike, Monroe, CT 06468
FROGPOND: Quarterly Haiku Journal, 87 Bayard Avenue, North Haven, CT 06473, 203-281-9653
THE SMALL PRESS BOOK REVIEW, PO Box 176, Southport, CT 06490, 203-268-4878
Cider Mill Press, P O Box 211, Stratford, CT 06497

THE SMALL POND MAGAZINE OF LITERATURE aka SMALL POND, PO Box 664, Stratford, CT 06497, 203-378-4066
THEATER, 222 York Street, New Haven, CT 06520, 203-436-1417
THE YALE REVIEW, 1902A Yale Station, New Haven, CT 06520
THE CONNECTICUT POETRY REVIEW, PO Box 3783, Amity Station, New Haven, CT 06525
Audacious Press, PO Box 1001, Bridgeport, CT 06601, 203-579-4322
THE QUAYLE QUARTERLY, PO Box 8593, Brewster Station, Bridgeport, CT 06605, 203-333-9399
Sanguinaria Publishing, 85 Ferris Street, Bridgeport, CT 06605, 203-576-9168
CONNECTICUT RIVER REVIEW: A National Poetry Journal, Robert Isaacs, Editor, PO Box 2171, Bridgeport, CT 06608
Life-Link Books, 360 Center Road, Easton, CT 06612-1606
WATERBURY CHESS CLUB BULLETIN, 54 Calumet Street, Waterbury, CT 06710-1201, 203-755-9749
Chicory Blue Press, 795 East Street North, Goshen, CT 06756, 203-491-2271
THE EAGLE, PO Box 579MO, Naugatuck, CT 06770, 203-274-7853
Maradia Press, 228 Evening Star Drive, Naugatuck, CT 06770, 203-723-0758
HOBO JUNGLE, Rucum Road, Roxbury, CT 06783, 203-354-4359
World Music Press, PO Box 2565, Danbury, CT 06813, 203-748-1131; fax 203-743-0784
Devin-Adair, Publishers, Inc., 6 North Water Street, Greenwich, CT 06830
Sea Sports Publications, PO Box 647, 10 Buckingham Place, Norwalk, CT 06852-0647, 203-866-5376
Black Swan Books Ltd., PO Box 327, Redding Ridge, CT 06876, 203-938-9548
Belhue Press, Box 1081, Ridgefield, CT 06877, 203-438-2528
The Bold Strummer Ltd., PO Box 2037, Westport, CT 06880-0037, 203-226-8230
Meckler Corporation, 11 Ferry Lane West, Westport, CT 06880, 203-226-6967; FAX 203-454-5840
SMALL PRESS: The Magazine & Book Review of Independent Publishing, 11 Ferry Lane West, Westport, CT 06880, 203-226-6967; FAX 203-454-5840
Magic Circle Press, 10 Hyde Ridge Rd, Weston, CT 06883
BP REPORT, PO Box 7430, Wilton, CT 06897
Knights Press, PO Box 6737, Stamford, CT 06901, 203-969-1699
9N-2N-8N NEWSLETTER, 154 Blackwood Lane, Stamford, CT 06903, 203-322-7283

DELAWARE

BLADES, Poporo Press, 182 Orchard Road, Newark, DE 19711-5208
THE D.H. LAWRENCE REVIEW, Department of English, University of Delaware, Newark, DE 19716, 302-454-1480/302-451-2361
En Passant Poetry Press, 4612 Sylvanus Drive, Wilmington, DE 19803
EN PASSANT/POETRY, 4612 Sylvanus Drive, Wilmington, DE 19803
Idea House Publishing Company, 2019 Delaware Avenue, Wilmington, DE 19806, 302-571-9570
The Middle Atlantic Press, PO Box 945, Wilmington, DE 19899, 302-654-9922

DISTRICT OF COLUMBIA

ASC NEWSLETTER, 730 11th Street NW, 2nd Floor, Washington, DC 20001, 202-347-2850
Selous Foundation Press, 325 Pennsylvania Avenue, SE, Washington, DC 20001
Gallaudet University Press, 800 Florida Avenue NE, Washington, DC 20002, 202-651-5488
Washington Writers' Publishing House, PO Box 15271, Washington, DC 20003, 202-543-1905
W.D.C. PERIOD, Chow Chow Productions, PO Box 50084, Washington, DC 20004-0084, 202-462-7229
MIDDLE EAST REPORT, 1500 Massachusetts Ave., NW, #119, Washington, DC 20005, 202-223-3677
THE POST, Publishers Syndication Int'l, 1377 K Street NW, Suite 856, Washington, DC 20005
Publishers Syndication Int'l (PSI), 1377 K Street NW, Suite 856, Washington, DC 20005
SCIENCE BOOKS & FILMS, 1333 H Street, Northwest, Washington, DC 20005, 202-326-6463
Three Continents Press, Inc., 1901 Pennsylvania Ave, NW, #407, Washington, DC 20006, 202-223-2554, 223-2604
AERIAL, P.O. Box 25642, Washington, DC 20007, (202) 333-1544
AMERICAN HIKER, 1015 31st Street NW, Washington, DC 20007, 703-385-3252
The American Hiking Society, 1015 31st Street, N.W., Washington, DC 20007, 703-385-3252
Institute for Palestine Studies, PO Box 25697 Georgetown Station, Washington, DC 20007, 202-342-3990; 800-874-3614; FAX 202-342-3927
JOURNAL OF PALESTINE STUDIES, PO Box 25697 Georgetown Station, Washington, DC 20007
Mage Publishers, Inc., 1032 29th Street, NW, Washington, DC 20007, 202-342-1642
The Media Institute, 3017 M Street NW, Washington, DC 20007, 202-298-7512
THE PLUM REVIEW, PO Box 3557, Washington, DC 20007
Stone Wall Press, Inc, 1241 30th Street NW, Washington, DC 20007, 202-333-1860
Waterfront Center, 1536 44th Street NW, Washington, DC 20007, 202-337-0356
WATERFRONT WORLD, 1536 44th Street NW, Washington, DC 20007, 202-337-0356
Wineberry Press, 3207 Macomb Street, NW, Washington, DC 20008, 202-363-8036: Editor's personal number
THE AMERICAN SCHOLAR, 1811 Q Street NW, Washington, DC 20009, 202-265-3808
BIG CIGARS, The P.O.N. Press, 1625 Hobart Street NW, Washington, DC 20009
The William Byrd Press, 1811 Q Street NW, Washington, DC 20009, 202-265-3808
Cheshire Books, 1855 Mintwood Place NW #2, Washington, DC 20009-1941
Island Press, 1718 Connecticut Avenue NW #300, Washington, DC 20009, 202-232-7933
LAMBDA BOOK REPORT, 1625 Connecticut Avenue NW, Washington, DC 20009, 202-462-7924
NUTRITION ACTION HEALTHLETTER, 1875 Connecticut Avenue NW #300, Washington, DC 20009, 202-332-9110
OFF OUR BACKS, 2423 18th Street, NW, 2nd Floor, Washington, DC 20009-2003, 202-234-8072
THE WASHINGTON MONTHLY, 1611 Connecticut Avenue NW, Washington, DC 20009, 202-462-0128
CHALLENGE: A Journal of Faith and Action in Central America, 1470 Irving Street NW, Washington, DC 20010, 202-332-0292
Epica, 1470 Irving Street NW, Washington, DC 20010, 202-332-0292
AMERICAN FORESTS, PO Box 2000, Washington, DC 20013, (202) 667-3300
DECENTRALIZE!, PO Box 1608, Washington, DC 20013-1608
Maisonneuve Press, PO Drawer 2980, Washington, DC 20013-2980, 301-277-4579
Starfish Press, 6525-32nd Street NW, PO Box 42467, Washington, DC 20015, 202-244-2178

Wheat Forders, Box 6317, Washington, DC 20015-0317, 202-362-1588
The Word Works, Inc., PO Box 42164, Washington, DC 20015
The Compass Press, Box 9546, Washington, DC 20016, 202-333-2182
FOLIO: A LITERARY JOURNAL, Dept. of Literature, American University, Washington, DC 20016, 202-885-2971
Whalesback Books, Box 9546, Washington, DC 20016, 202-333-2182
Youth Policy Institute, PO Box 40132, Washington, DC 20016, 202-298-6050
E Publications, PO Box 19033, Washington, DC 20036, 202-223-4060
Farragut Publishing Co., 2033 M Street N.W., Washington, DC 20036, 202-872-4009; fax 202-872-4703
Heavy Bro Publishing Company, 2021 L Street NW, Suite 250, Washington, DC 20036, 202-966-4276
MUSEUM & ARTS WASHINGTON, 1707 L Street NW #222, Washington, DC 20036-4201
The Preservation Press, 1785 Massachusetts Avenue, NW, Washington, DC 20036, 202-673-4057
Worldwatch Institute, 1776 Massachusetts Ave NW, Washington, DC 20036, 202-452-1999
WORLDWATCH PAPERS, 1776 Massachusetts Ave., N.W., Washington, DC 20036
Aangstrom Publishing Company, 600 New Hampshire Avenue NW, Ste. 450, Washington, DC 20037, 202-298-8929
The Devon Publishing Co., Inc., 2700 Vol Avenue NW, Washington, DC 20037
FOCUS, World Wildlife Fund, 1250 24th street, NW, Washington, DC 20037, 202-293-4800
RESOLVE NEWSLETTER, 1250 24th Street, NW, Washington, DC 20037, 202-293-4800
World Wildlife Fund & The Conservation Foundation, 1250 24th Street, NW, Washington, DC 20037, 202-293-4800
WORLD WILDLIFE FUND & THE CONSERVATION FOUNDATION LETTER, 1250 24th Street, NW, Washington, DC 20037, 202-293-4800
TURN-OF-THE-CENTURY WOMEN, c/o Department of English, Georgetown University, Washington, DC 20057
WASHINGTON REVIEW, PO Box 50132, Washington, DC 20091, 202-638-0515

FLORIDA

CIN-DAV, Inc., Route 1, Box 778, Starke, FL 32091, 904-964-5370; 904-392-1631
Luthers, 1009 North Dixie Freeway, New Smyrna Beach, FL 32168-6221, 904-423-1600; 423-9450
KALLIOPE, A Journal of Women's Art, 3939 Roosevelt Blvd, Florida Community College at Jacksonville, Jacksonville, FL 32205, 904-387-8211
GO MAGAZINE, 1139 N. Laura Street, Jacksonville, FL 32206, 904-354-4382
POETRY TODAY, 4950 Richard Street, Suite 60, Jacksonville, FL 32207
Wherry Advertising Agency, PO Box 11081, Jacksonville, FL 32239, 904-398-7782
HARP-STRINGS, 310 S. Adams Street, Beverly Hills, FL 32265
FLORIDA VOCATIONAL JOURNAL, 2003 Apalachee Parkway, Tallahassee, FL 32301, 904-487-2054
Loiry/Bonner Press, 2320 J Apalachee Parkway, Suite #494, Tallahassee, FL 32301-4939, 904-681-0019
THE YOUTH REPORT, A NEWS MAGAZINE ON ADVOCACY FOR YOUTH, 2320 J Apalachee Parkway, Suite #494, Tallahassee, FL 32301-4939, 904-681-0019
Anhinga Press, PO Box 10595, Tallahassee, FL 32302-5144, 904-575-5592
The Naiad Press, Inc., PO Box 10543, Tallahassee, FL 32302, 904-539-9322
REACHING OUT, 2022 East Forest Drive, Tallahassee, FL 32303, 904-386-5508
Wellberry Press, 2022 E. Forest, Tallahassee, FL 32303, 904-386-5508
RACONTEUR: A Journal of World History, 2020 W. Pensacola St., Unit 46, Suite 515, Tallahassee, FL 32304, 904-222-5029
RACONTEUR Publications, 2020 W. Pensacola St., Unit 46, Suite 515, Tallahassee, FL 32304, 904-222-5029
SNUG, 1327 High Road #Y-6, Tallahassee, FL 32304, 904-224-9196
SUN DOG: The Southeast Review, 406 Williams Bldg., English Dept., F.S.U., Tallahassee, FL 32306-1036, 904-644-4230
Children Of Mary, Fidelis Et Verus, RR 10, Box 13517, Tallahassee, FL 32310-9803, 904-576-0817; 800-749-1925
Apalachee Press, PO Box 20106, Tallahassee, FL 32316
APALACHEE QUARTERLY, PO Box 20106, Tallahassee, FL 32316
FIDELIS ET VERUS, PO Box 2421, Tallahassee, FL 32316
De-Feet Press, Inc., 2401 W. 15th Street, Panama City, FL 32401
THEMATIC POETRY QUARTERLY, Audio-Visual Poetry Foundation, 400 Fish Hatchery Road, Marianna, FL 32446, 904-482-3890
Red Key Press, PO Box 551, Port St Joe, FL 32456, 904-227-1305
HALF TONES TO JUBILEE, English Dept., 1000 College Blvd., Pensacola Jr. College, Pensacola, FL 32504, 904-484-1000 ext. 1400
THE PANHANDLER, The Panhandler Press, English Dept., Univ. Of West Florida, Pensacola, FL 32514, 904-474-2923
Placebo Press, 4051 East Olive Road, #231, Pensacola, FL 32514-6444, 904-477-3995
WALKING-STICK NOTES, 4051 East Olive Road #231, Pensacola, FL 32514, 904-477-3995
Triad Publishing Co. Inc., 1110 NW 8th Avenue Suite C, Gainesville, FL 32601, 904-373-5800
POETRY OF THE PEOPLE, PO Box 13077, Gainesville, FL 32604, 904-375-3324
JABBERWOCKY, Chimera Connections, Inc., 502 NW 75th Street #197, Gainesville, FL 32607-1608, 904-332-6586
Maupin House, PO Box 90148, Gainesville, FL 32607
Security Seminars Press, 5724 S.E. 4th Street, PO Box 70162, Ocala, FL 32670-0162, 904-694-6185
Editor's Desk, 709 Southeast 52nd Avenue, Ocala, FL 32671, 904-694-2303; 694-2289
EDITOR'S DESK, 709 Southeast 52nd Avenue, Ocala, FL 32671, 904-694-2303; 694-2289
JUNIOR EDITOR, 709 S.E. 52nd Avenue, Ocala, FL 32671, 904-694-2303; 694-2289
THE ORLANDO SPECTATOR, 2390 S. Orange Blossom Trail, Apopka, FL 32703-1870, 407-293-2722
BELLYWASH, PO Box 151481, Altamonte Springs, FL 32715, 407-339-6965
MIDDLE EASTERN DANCER, PO Box 181572, Casselberry, FL 32718-1572, 407-831-3402
SKYDIVING, PO Box 1520, DeLand, FL 32721, 904-736-9779; fax 904-736-9786
RECOVERY TODAY, PO Box 754, Goldenrod, FL 32733, 407-679-5622
DIAMOND HITCHHIKER COBWEBS, 118 E. Goodheart Avenue, Lake Mary, FL 32746
Nuclear Trenchcoated Subway Prophets Publications, 118 E. Goodheart Avenue, Lake Mary, FL 32746
JKM Publishing Company, 1418 Meadowlark Street, PO Box 521547, Longwood, FL 32752-1547, 407-767-5633
Prudhomme Press, PO Box 11, Tavares, FL 32778, 904-589-0100
Edge Publishing, PO Box 3621, Longwood, FL 32779, 407-788-6357
CRYSTAL RAINBOW, The Mirrored Image, 340 Granada Drive, Winter Park, FL 32789
Tax Property Investor, Inc., PO Box 4602, Winter Park, FL 32793, 407-671-0004

Sentinel Books, Sentinel Communications Co., 633 North Orange Avenue, Orlando, FL 32801, 407-420-5588
Moonlight Press, 3407 Crystal Lake Drive, Orlando, FL 32806
THE FLORIDA REVIEW, PO Box 25000, Eng. Dept., Central Florida Univ., Orlando, FL 32816, 305-823-2038
Bio-Probe, Inc., PO Box 580160, Orlando, FL 32858-0160, 407-299-4149
Arbiter Press, PO Box 592540, Orlando, FL 32859, 407-380-8617; 345-3803
American Malacologists, Inc., PO Box 2255, Melbourne, FL 32902-2255, 407-725-2260
LIVING OFF THE LAND, Subtropic Newsletter, PO Box 2131, Melbourne, FL 32902-2131, 305-723-5554
Pine & Palm Press, PO Box 2131, Melbourne, FL 32902-2131, 305-723-5554
" "...A DEAD BEAT POET PRODUCTION, 500 North River Oaks, Indialantic, FL 32903, 407-952-0563
The Speech Bin, Inc., 1766 20th Avenue, Vero Beach, FL 32960, 407-770-0007, FAX 407-770-0006
Good Life Products, Inc., 7709 NW 178th Street, Hialeah, FL 33015, 305-362-6998
COOKBOOK SERIES, 2131 Hollywood Boulevard, Hollywood, FL 33020, 305-925-5242
DIET & HEALTH SERIES, 2131 Hollywood Boulevard, Hollywood, FL 33020, 305-925-5242
Fell Publishers, Inc., 2131 Hollywood Boulevard, Hollywood, FL 33020, 305-925-5242
FELL'S HEALTH SERIES, 2131 Hollywood Boulevard, Hollywood, FL 33020, 305-925-5242
FINANCIAL PLANNING SERIES, 2131 Hollywood Boulevard, Hollywood, FL 33020, 305-925-5242
GOOD COOKING SERIES, 2131 Hollywood Boulevard, Hollywood, FL 33020, 305-925-5242
Hermetician Press, PO Box 1961, Hollywood, FL 33022-1381, 305-922-6726
Siftsoft, 12950 SW 4th Street, #H-306, Pembroke Pine, FL 33027
KEY WEST REVIEW, 9 Avenue G, Key West, FL 33042, 305-296-1365
RGM Publications, PO Box 2432, Key West, FL 33045-2432, 305-294-5710; 296-0809
Wampeter Press, Box 2626, Key West, FL 33045-2626, 617-834-4137
Paragraph Publications, PO Box 2954, Pompano Beach, FL 33062, 305-946-5230
ACTION DIGEST, PO Box 163001, Miami, FL 33116, 305-559-4652
J. Flores Publications, PO Box 163001, Miami, FL 33116, 305-559-4652
ATHA NEWSLETTER, 1676 SW 11th Street, Miami, FL 33135, (305) 541-0218
THE PERSONAL MAGNETISM HOME STUDY COURSE ON ALL HUMAN POWERS, 2870 Pine Tree Drive, Suite F2, Miami Beach, FL 33140, 305-538-8427
CRS Consultants Press, PO Box 490175, Key Biscayne, FL 33149
Grapetree Productions, Inc., Box 10CN, 600 Grapetree Drive, Key Biscayne, FL 33149, 361-2060
AIRLINERS, PO Box 52-1238, Miami, FL 33152, 305-477-7163
AIRLINERS MONTHLY NEWS, PO Box 52-1238, Miami, FL 33152, 305-477-7163
COMMON SENSE, PO Box 520191, Miami, FL 33152-0191, 305-221-0154
World Transport Press, PO Box 52-1238, Miami, FL 33152, 305-477-7163
The International Society of Dramatists, Box 1310, Miami, FL 33153, 305-531-1530
CARIBBEAN REVIEW, 9700 SW 67th Avenue, Miami, FL 33156, 305-284-8466
Moonsquilt Press, 16401 NE 4th Avenue, North Miami Beach, FL 33162, 305-947-9534
EARTHWISE LITERARY CALENDAR, PO Box 680-536, Miami, FL 33168
Earthwise Publications, PO Box 680-536, Miami, FL 33168, 305-940-7157 (S. Newhouse/Asst. Editor); FAX 305-687-8387
EARTHWISE REVIEW, PO Box 680-536, Miami, FL 33168, 305-688-8558
THOUGHTS FOR ALL SEASONS: The Magazine of Epigrams, 11530 S.W. 99th Street, Miami, FL 33176, 305-598-8599
THE CATHARTIC, PO Box 1391, Ft Lauderdale, FL 33302, 305-474-7120
Cassell Communications Inc., PO Box 9844, Ft. Lauderdale, FL 33310, 305-485-0795; 800-351-9278
FREELANCE WRITER'S REPORT, PO Box 9844, Ft. Lauderdale, FL 33310, 305-485-0795; 800-351-9278
THE SOUTH FLORIDA POETRY REVIEW, 7190 N.W. 21 Street, Room 103, Ft. Lauderdale, FL 33313, 305-742-5624
Distinctive Publishing Corp., PO Box 17868, Plantation, FL 33318-7868, 305-975-2413
Ashley Books, Inc., 4600 West Commercial Boulevard, Fort Lauderdale, FL 33319, 305-739-2221
Atlantic Publishing Company, 7458 N.W. 33rd Street, Lauderhill, FL 33319, 1-800-541-1336
FATHOMS BELOW, 1320 N.W. 76th Avenue, Plantation, FL 33322-4740
Success Publishing, 2812 Bayonne Drive, Palm Beach Gard., FL 33410-1432
Creative Concern Publications, 12066 Suellen Circle, West Palm Beach, FL 33414, 305-793-5854
PEDESTRIAN RESEARCH, Century Village, Dorchester Bldg A, Apt. 12A, West Palm Beach, FL 33417
Liberty Publishing Company, Inc., 440 S. Federal Highway #202, Deerfield Beach, FL 33441, 305-360-9000
PRISONER'S LEGAL NEWS, PO Box 1684, Lake Worth, FL 33460, 407-582-2701
WHISPERING PALM, PO Box 6523, Lake Worth, FL 33466
THE FINAL PAGE, 1806 South Kings Avenue, Brandon, FL 33511
PSYCH IT, 6507 Bimini Court, Apollo Beach, FL 33572
RESONANCE, PO Box 69, Sumterville, FL 33585, (904) 793-8748
WORLD OF FANDOM MAGAZINE, PO Box 9421, Tampa, FL 33604, 813-933-7424; 238-4643
TAMPA REVIEW, Box 19F, Tampa University, Tampa, FL 33606-1490, 813-253-3333 X621; 813-343-3633; FAX 813-251-0016 (use name, Richard Mathews)
ORGANICA, 4419 N. Manhattan Avenue, Tampa, FL 33614, 813-876-4879
HYPATIA: A Journal of Feminist Philosophy, University of South Florida, SOC 107, Tampa, FL 33620-8100, 904-974-5531
BLACK MULLET REVIEW, PO Box 22814, Tampa, FL 33622
Harrison Brown, Publishers, Inc., PO Box 151574, Tampa, FL 33684, 813-963-2959
Axelrod Publishing of Tampa Bay, 1304 De Soto Avenue, PO Box 14248, Tampa, FL 33690, 813-251-5269
The Write Press, 8518 12th Way North, St. Petersburg, FL 33702
THE RATIONAL FEMINIST, Box 28253, Kenneth City Station, St. Petersburg, FL 33709
Valkyrie Publishing House, 8245 26th Avenue N, St. Petersburg, FL 33710, 813-345-8864
Little Bayou Press, 1735 First Avenue North, St. Petersburg, FL 33713-8903, 813-822-3278
THE WASHINGTON REPORT, Editors Release Service, PO Box 10309, St. Petersburg, FL 33733, 813-866-1598
CORVETTE FEVER MAGAZINE, Dobbs Publishing Group, PO Box 6320, Lakeland, FL 33807, 813-646-5743
SPECTRUM, A Guide to the Independent Press and Informative Organizations, 762 Avenue 'N', S.E., Winter Haven, FL 33880, (813) 294-5555
Spectrum Publications, 762 Avenue 'N', S.E., Winter Haven, FL 33880, 813-294-5555
Sutherland Publishing, 16956-6 McGregor Boulevard, Fort Myers, FL 33908, 813-466-1626

NAUTICAL BRASS, PO Box 3966, Fort Myers, FL 33918-3966
Nautical Brass, PO Box 3966, N. Fort Myers, FL 33918-3966
The Runaway Spoon Press, Box 3621, Port Charlotte, FL 33949-3621, 813-629-8045
Marilee Publications, PO Box 2351, Bonita Springs, FL 33959, 813-992-1800
ALBATROSS, 125 Horton Avenue, Englewood, FL 33981
Anabiosis Press, 125 Horton Avenue, Englewood, FL 33981
CALLI'S TALES, The Quarterly for Animal Lovers of All Ages, Box 1224, Palmetto, FL 34220, 813-722-2202
United Press Inc., PO Box 4064, Sarasota, FL 34230
New Collage Press, 5700 North Trail, Sarasota, FL 34234, 813-359-4360
Woldt Publishing, 2516 Ridge Avenue, Sarasota, FL 34235, 813-388-2378
Pineapple Press, Inc., PO Drawer 16008, Southside Station, Sarasota, FL 34239, 813-952-1085
NEW COLLAGE MAGAZINE, 5700 N. Tamiami Trail, Sarasota, FL 34243-2197, 813-359-4360
Independent Publishing Co., PO Box 15126, Sarasota, FL 34277, 922-7080
NEW WRITER'S MAGAZINE, PO Box 5976, Sarasota, FL 34277
Professional Resource Exchange, Inc., Box 15560, Sarasota, FL 34277-1560, 813-366-7913
YESTERDAY'S MAGAZETTE, PO Box 15126, Sarasota, FL 34277, 813-922-7080
Biblia Candida, 4466 Winterville Road, Spring Hill, FL 34606, 904-686-3527
Selective Books, Inc., Box 1140, Clearwater, FL 34617
Sphinx Publishing, PO Box 2005, Clearwater, FL 34617, 813-446-6840
Owen Laughlin Publishers, PO Box 6313, Clearwater, FL 34618-6313, 813-797-0404
Lindsay Press Inc. of Florida, PO Box 6316, Clearwater, FL 34618-6316, 813-797-2512
Bolton Press, 3606 El Camino Court, Largo, FL 34641, 813-535-4668
Green Key Press, Box 3801, Seminole, FL 34642, 813-596-0215
Top Of The Mountain Publishing, 11701 Belcher Road South, Ste. 123, Largo, FL 34643-5117, 813-530-0110
DRAMATIKA, 429 Hope Street, Tarpon Springs, FL 34689, 813-937-0109
Dramatika Press, 429 Hope Street, Tarpon Springs, FL 34689, 813-937-0109
TeakWood Press, 160 Fiesta Drive, Kissimmee, FL 34743
Montebello Press, 3041 SW Montebello Place, Palm City, FL 34990

GEORGIA

IllumiNet Press, PO Box 746, Avondale Estates, GA 30002, 404-377-2590
Gallopade Publishing Group, 235 E. Ponce de Leon Avenue, Ste. 100, Decatur, GA 30030
BABY SUE, PO Box 1111, Decatur, GA 30031, 404-875-8951
PARNASSUS LITERARY JOURNAL, Kudzu Press, PO Box 1384, Forest Park, GA 30051
Cherokee Publishing Company, PO Box 1730, Marietta, GA 30061, 404-424-6210
THE DILETTANTE FORUM, 142 Woodlawn Drive, Marietta, GA 30067-4016
Harris Stonehouse Press, 142 Woodlawn Drive, Marietta, GA 30067-4016
Pando Publications, 540 Longleaf Drive, Roswell, GA 30075, 404-587-3363
Linwood Publishers, 481 Hambrick Road, Suite 16, Stone Mountain, GA 30083, 404-296-3950
WORKING AT HOME, PO Box 200504, Cartersville, GA 30120
THE OLD RED KIMONO, Humanities, Floyd College, Box 1864, Rome, GA 30163, 404-295-6312
THE OVERLOOK CONNECTION, PO Box 526, Woodstock, GA 30188, 404-926-1762
Oddo Publishing, Inc., PO Box 68, Fayetteville, GA 30214
PIGEON CREEK CLARION, Box 1014, Greenville, GA 30222
Ander Publications, View Pointe Lane, Suite 202, LaGrange, GA 30240
CATALYST, A Magazine of Heart and Mind, 34 Peachtree Street, Ste. 2330, Atlanta, GA 30303, 404-730-5785
Clarity Press, 3277 Roswell Road NE, Suite 469, Atlanta, GA 30305
Hilton Thomas Publishers, Inc., 2035 Northside Drive, Atlanta, GA 30305-3927, 404-390-9546
ATALANTA, PO Box 5502, Atlanta, GA 30307
THE WILD FOODS FORUM, 4 Carlisle Way, NE, Atlanta, GA 30308, 404-876-1441
THUNDER & HONEY, PO Box 11386, Atlanta, GA 30310
SAGE: A SCHOLARLY JOURNAL ON BLACK WOMEN, PO Box 42741, Atlanta, GA 30311-0741, 404-681-3643 ext.
  360
CREATIVE LOAFING, 750 Willoughby Street, Atlanta, GA 30312-1124, 404-873-5623
Dead Angel Press, 1206 Lyndale Drive SE, Atlanta, GA 30316, 404-624-1524
Milner Press, 715 Miami Circle, Suite 220, Atlanta, GA 30324, 404-231-9107
Peachtree Publishers, Ltd., 494 Armour Circle NE, Atlanta, GA 30324, 404-876-8761
MANGAJIN, 2531 Briarcliff Road #121, Atlanta, GA 30329, 404-634-3874
THE CHATTAHOOCHEE REVIEW, DeKalb College, 2101 Womack Road, Dunwoody, GA 30338-4497, 404-551-3019
JAMES DICKEY NEWSLETTER, 2101 Womack Road, Dunwoody, GA 30338, 404-551-3162
The Chicot Press, Box 53198, Atlanta, GA 30355, 404-640-9918
ART PAPERS, PO Box 77348, Atlanta, GA 30357, 404-588-1837
Independence Publishers Inc., PO Box 29905, Atlanta, GA 30359, 404-636-7092
FOXFIRE, Box B, Rabun Gap, GA 30568, 404-746-5828
Foxfire Press, Box B, Rabun Gap, GA 30568, 404-746-5828
The Power Within Institute, Inc., 130 West Tugalo Street, Toccoa, GA 30577-2360, 404-886-1220; 1-800-533-POWER
THE CLASSICAL OUTLOOK, Department of Classics, The University of Georgia, Athens, GA 30602, 404-542-9257
THE GEORGIA REVIEW, Univ. of Georgia, Athens, GA 30602, 404-542-3481
STATE AND LOCAL GOVERNMENT REVIEW, Carl Vinson Institute of Government, University of Georgia, Terrell
  Hall, Athens, GA 30602, 404-542-2736
BLUE HORSE, P.O. Box 6061, Augusta, GA 30906, 404-798-5628
Blue Horse Publications, PO Box 6061, Augusta, GA 30906, 404-798-5628
Plantagenet House, Inc., PO Box 271, Blackshear, GA 31516, 912-449-6601
SNAKE NATION REVIEW, 2920 North Oak, Vaidosta, GA 31602, 912-242-1503
MAXINE'S PAGES, Box 866, Manchester, GA 31816

HAWAII

Petroglyph Press, Ltd., 201 Kinoole Street, Hilo, HI 96720, 808-935-6006

Press Pacifica, Ltd., PO Box 47, Kailua, HI 96734, 808-261-6594
NEW AGE DIGEST, New Age Press, PO Box 1373, Keala Kekua, HI 96750, 808-328-8013
New Age Press, PO Box 2089, Keala Kekua, HI 96750, 808-328-8031
KIDS LIB NEWS, PO Box 1064, Kurtistown, HI 96760
Oness Press, PO Box 1064, Kurtistown, HI 96760
AIGA Publications, PO Box 148, Laie, HI 96762, 808-293-5277
Wonder View Press, 823 Olive Avenue, Wahiawa, HI 96786, 808-621-2288
Aka Press, PO Box 1372, Wailuku, HI 96793, 808-242-4173
Buddhist Study Center Press, 876 Curtis Street #3905, Honolulu, HI 96813, 808-536-7633
CHAMINADE LITERARY REVIEW, 3140 Waialae Avenue, Honoluu, HI 96816-1578, 808-735-4723
COMPUTER BOOK REVIEW, 735 Ekekela Place, Honolulu, HI 96817, 808-595-7089
Maeventec, 735 Ekekela Place, Honolulu, HI 96817, 808-595-7089
Petronium Press, 1255 Nuuanu Avenue, #1813, Honolulu, HI 96817
Mutual Publishing of Honolulu, 2055 N. King, Honolulu, HI 96819
HAWAI'I REVIEW, c/o Dept. of English, 1733 Donaghho Road, Honolulu, HI 96822, 808-956-8548
MANOA: A Pacific Journal of International Writing, English Department, University of Hawaii, Honolulu, HI 96822, 956-0370
WEST END MAGAZINE, PO Box 22433, Honolulu, HI 96822-0433
The Bess Press, PO Box 22388, Honolulu, HI 96823, 808-734-7159
COSMOPOLITAN CONTACT, PO Box 89300, Honolulu, HI 96830-9300
Cable Publishing, PO Box 75575, Honolulu, HI 96836, 808-536-6697
BAMBOO RIDGE, THE HAWAII WRITERS' QUARTERLY, PO Box 61781, Honolulu, HI 96839-1781
Bamboo Ridge Press, PO Box 61781, Honolulu, HI 96839-1781

IDAHO

Little Red Hen, Inc., PO Box 4260, Pocatello, ID 83205, 208-233-3755
THE REDNECK REVIEW OF LITERATURE, PO Box 730, Twin Falls, ID 83301, 208-734-6653
CLOUDLINE, PO Box 462, Ketchum, ID 83340, 208-788-3704
WHITE CLOUDS REVUE, PO Box 462, Ketchum, ID 83340, 726-3101
Wind Vein Press, PO Box 462, Ketchum, ID 83340, 208-788-3704
Honeybrook Press, PO Box 883, Rexburg, ID 83440, 208-356-5133
Confluence Press, Inc., Lewis-Clark State College, 8th Avenue & 6th Street, Lewiston, ID 83501-2698, 208-799-2336
Red Ink/Black Hole Productions, PO Box 104, Grangeville, ID 83530-0104
TAPJOE: The Anaprocrustean Poetry Journal of Enumclaw, PO Box 104, Grangeville, ID 83530
THE SIGNAL - Network International, PO Box 67, Emmett, ID 83617, 208-365-5812
Fry's Incredible Inquirys, HC76, Box 2207, Garden Valley, ID 83622
INCREDIBLE INQUIRY REPORTS, HC76, Box 2207, Garden Valley, ID 83622
Stonehouse Publications, Timber Butte Road, Box 390, Sweet, ID 83670, 208-584-3344
Straight Arrow Publishing, PO Box 1092, Boise, ID 83701-1092
EOTU, Magazine of Experimental Fiction, 1810 W. State, #115, Boise, ID 83702, FAX 208-342-4996
THE LIMBERLOST REVIEW, HC 33, Box 1113, Boise, ID 83706-9702
LISTEN, PO Box 7000, Boise, ID 83707, 208-465-2500
Whitehorse, PO Box 6125, Boise, ID 83707
Ahsahta, Boise State University, Department of English, Boise, ID 83725, 208-385-1246 or 1999
Boise State University Western Writers Series, Department of English, Boise State University, Boise, ID 83725, 208-385-1246
COLD-DRILL, 1910 University Drive, Boise, ID 83725, 208-385-1999
Cold-Drill Books, Dept. of English, Boise State University, Boise, ID 83725
DELIRIUM, Route one, Box 7x, Harrison, ID 83833, 714-689-3726
Mother of Ashes Press, PO Box 66, Harrison, ID 83833-0066
THE PRINTER'S DEVIL, PO Box 66, Harrison, ID 83833
THE VILLAGE IDIOT, PO Box 66, Harrison, ID 83833
Hutton Publications, PO Box 1870, Hayden, ID 83835, 208-772-6184
MYSTERY TIME ANTHOLOGY, PO Box 1870, Hayden, ID 83835, 208-772-6184
RHYME TIME POETRY NEWSLETTER, PO Box 1870, Hayden, ID 83835, 208-772-6184
WRITER'S INFO, PO Box 1870, Hayden, ID 83835, 208-772-6184
Ramalo Publications, 2107 N. Spokane Street, Post Falls, ID 83854
THE EMSHOCK LETTER, Randall Flat Road, PO Box 411, Troy, ID 83871, 208-835-4902

ILLINOIS

TWISTED, 22071 Pineview Drive, Antioch, IL 60002
WHETSTONE, Barrington Area Arts Council, PO Box 1266, Barrington, IL 60011, 708-382-5626
PC PUBLISHING, 950 Lee Street, Des Plaines, IL 60016, 708-296-0770
THE MIND'S EYE, Box 656, Glenview, IL 60025
SMS Publishing Corp., PO Box 2276, Glenview, IL 60025
DeerTrail Books, 637 Williams Court, PO Box 171, Gurnee, IL 60031, 312-367-0014
DECEMBER MAGAZINE, Box 302, Highland Park, IL 60035
OTHER VOICES, 820 Ridge Road, Highland Park, IL 60035, 708-831-4684
Black & White & Read All Over Publishing Co., PO Box 452, Lake Bluff, IL 60044, 312-295-1077
PF Publications, PO Box 6202, Lindenhurst, IL 60046, 708-356-0625
FULL DISCLOSURE, Box 903, Libertyville, IL 60048, 708-395-6200
Albert Whitman & Company, 6340 Oakton Street, Morton Grove, IL 60053-2723
Calibre Press, Inc., 666 Dundee Road, Suite 1607, Northbrook, IL 60062-2727, 312-498-5680
STORYQUARTERLY, PO Box 1416, Northbrook, IL 60065
MOONSTONE BLUE, PO Box 393, Prospect Heights, IL 60070, 708-392-2435
NIGHT ROSES, PO Box 393, Prospect Heights, IL 60070, 708-392-2435
P.O. Publishing Company, Box 3333, Skokie, IL 60076
Bolchazy-Carducci Publishers, Inc., 1000 Brown Street, Wauconda, IL 60084, 708-526-4344

BRILLIANT STAR, Baha'i National Center, Wilmette, IL 60091
Thorntree Press, 547 Hawthorn Lane, Winnetka, IL 60093, 708-446-3099
Crossroads Communications, PO Box 7, Carpentersville, IL 60110
HUBRIS, 1122-1/2 North 13th, Dekalb, IL 60115
Branyan Press, PO Box 764, Elburn, IL 60119, 312-442-7907
INTERLIT, 850 North Grove, Elgin, IL 60120, 708-741-2400
The Devonshire Publishing Co., PO Box 85, Elgin, IL 60121-0085, 708-242-3846; fax 708-879-0308
The Flying Pencil Press, PO Box 7667, Elgin, IL 60121
NOMOS: Studies in Spontaneous Order, 257 Chesterfield, Glen Ellyn, IL 60137, 708-858-7184
Amnos Publications, 2501 South Wolf Road, Westchester, IL 60154, 312-562-2744
Crossway Books, 9825 W. Roosevelt Road, Westchester, IL 60154, 312-345-7474
THE FICTION REVIEW, PO Box 72939, Roselle, IL 60172
FOX VALLEY LIVING, 707 Kautz Road, St. Charles, IL 60174, 708-377-7570
Theosophical Publishing House, 306 West Geneva Road, Wheaton, IL 60187, 312-665-0130
PERSONAL PUBLISHING, 21W550 Geneva, Wheaton, IL 60188-2279, (312) 250-8900
THE QUEST, PO Box 270, Wheaton, IL 60189, 312-668-1571
FORMATIONS, 625 Colfax Street, Evanston, IL 60201
HAMMERS, 1718 Sherman #205, Evanston, IL 60201
ILLINOIS LIBERTARIAN, 1111 Church Street, #405, Evanston, IL 60201, 708-475-0391
The Press of Ward Schori, 2716 Noyes Street, Evanston, IL 60201, 312-475-3241
Thunder & Ink, PO Box 7014, Evanston, IL 60201, 708-492-1823
THE SHAKESPEARE NEWSLETTER, 1217 Ashland Ave., Chicago, Evanston, IL 60202, 312-475-7550
Carlton Books, PO Box 333, Evanston, IL 60204, (312) 328-0400
Center for the Art of Living, Box 788, Evanston, IL 60204, 312-864-8664
Healthmere Press, Inc., PO Box 986, Evanston, IL 60204, 312-251-5950
SPORTS-NUTRITION NEWS, PO Box 986, Evanston, IL 60204, 312-251-5950
TRIQUARTERLY, Northwestern University, 2020 Ridge, Evanston, IL 60208, 708-491-7614
The Erie Street Press, 221 S. Clinton Avenue, Oak Park, IL 60302-3113, 708-848-5716
Alpine Guild, PO Box 183, Oak Park, IL 60303
The P. Gaines Co., Publishers, PO Box 2253, Oak Park, IL 60303, 312-524-1073
VEGETARIAN TIMES, PO Box 570, Oak Park, IL 60303, 312-848-8100
Cat's Pajamas Press, 527 Lyman, Oak Park, IL 60304
The Hosanna Press, 215 Gale, River Forest, IL 60305, 708-771-8259
Planning/Communications, 7215 Oak Avenue, River Forest, IL 60305-1935
Outrider Press, 1004 East Steger Road, Suite C-3, Crete, IL 60417-1362, 312-672-6630
IMAGINATION MAGAZINE, PO Box 781, Dolton, IL 60419
Meyerbooks, Publisher, P.O. Box 427, Glenwood, IL 60425, 708-757-4950
Contemporary Curriculums, PO Box 152, Lockport, IL 60441
Combat Ready Publishing, 6049 West 95th Street, Oak Lawn, IL 60453
The Counter-Propaganda Press, Box 365, Park Forest, IL 60466, 312-534-8679
Transport History Press, PO Box 201, Park Forest, IL 60466, 708-748-7855
THE CREATIVE WOMAN, Governors State University, University Park, IL 60466, 312-534-5000, Ext. 2524
Goodheart-Willcox Company, 123 W. Taft Drive, South Holland, IL 60473, (312) 333-7200
THE MCCALLUM OBSERVER, PO Box 165, Downers Grove, IL 60515-0165, 708-852-6518
Dalkey Archive Press, 5700 College Road, Lisle, IL 60532
THE REVIEW OF CONTEMPORARY FICTION, 5700 College Road, Lisle, IL 60532
FOLK ERA TODAY, 6 South 230 Cohasset Road, Naperville, IL 60540, 708-961-3559
POPULAR FOLK MUSIC TODAY, 6 South 230 Cohasset Rd., Naperville, IL 60540-3535, 608-961-3559
INQ Publishing Co., PO Box 10, N. Aurora, IL 60542, 708-801-0607
Celestial Otter Press, PO Box 658, Warrenville, IL 60555, 708-416-3111
MAGIC CHANGES, PO Box 658, Warrenville, IL 60555, 708-416-3111
NATIONAL HOME BUSINESS REPORT, PO Box 2137, Naperville, IL 60567
The Philip Lesly Company, 155 Harbor Drive, Suite 2201, Chicago, IL 60601
Morningstar, Inc., 53 West Jackson Blvd., Chicago, IL 60604, 312-427-1985
MUTUAL FUND SOURCEBOOK, 53 West Jackson Blvd., Chicago, IL 60604, 312-427-1985
MUTUAL FUND VALUES, 53 West Jackson Blvd., Chicago, IL 60604, 312-427-1985
Path Press, Inc., 53 West Jackson Blvd Suite 724, Chicago, IL 60604-3701, 312-663-0167
Lyceum Books, Inc., 59 E. Van Buren, Suite 703, Chicago, IL 60605, 312-922-1880
NEW ART EXAMINER, 1255 South Wabash Avenue #4, Chicago, IL 60605-2427, 312-836-0330
OYEZ REVIEW, Roosevelt University, 430 S. Michigan Avenue, Chicago, IL 60605, 312-341-2017
Triumph Books, 644 S. Clark Street, Chicago, IL 60605, 939-3330
Community Workshop on Economic Development, 100 South Morgan, Chicago, IL 60607
Academy Chicago Publishers, 213 West Institute Place, Chicago, IL 60610, 312-751-7302
The Consumer's Press, Inc., 1050 N. State Street #200, Chicago, IL 60610, 312-943-0770
Harper Square Press, 29 East Division Street, Chicago, IL 60610-2316, 312-337-1482
The Noble Press, Inc., 213 West Institute Place #508, Chicago, IL 60610, 312-642-1168
POETRY, 60 West Walton Street, Chicago, IL 60610, 312-280-4870
The Press of the Third Mind, 65 East Scott Street, Loft 6P, Chicago, IL 60610, 312-337-3122
Another Chicago Press, PO Box 11223, Chicago, IL 60611, 312-848-6333
Bonus Books, Inc., 160 East Illinois Street, Chicago, IL 60611, 312-467-0580
The Center For Study of Multiple Birth, 333 East Superior Street, #464, Chicago, IL 60611, 312-266-9093
STUDENT LAWYER, American Bar Association Press, 750 N. Lake Shore Drive, Chicago, IL 60611
ACM (ANOTHER CHICAGO MAGAZINE), 3709 N. Kenmore, Chicago, IL 60613, 312-248-7665
Left Field Press, 3709 North Kenmore, Chicago, IL 60613, 312-248-7665
INSECTS ARE PEOPLE TOO, PO Box 146486, Chicago, IL 60614, 312-772-8686
LIBIDO: The Journal of Sex and Sensibility, PO Box 146721, Chicago, IL 60614, 312-281-0805; 312-728-5979
MIND YOUR OWN BUSINESS AT HOME, Box 14850, Chicago, IL 60614, 312-472-8116
POETRY EAST, Dept. of English, DePaul Univ., 802 West Belden Avenue, Chicago, IL 60614, 312-341-5114

PRIMAVERA, 1448 E. 52nd St., Box 274, Chicago, IL 60615, 312-324-5920
CASE ANALYSIS, 401 E 32nd, #1002, Chicago, IL 60616, 312-225-9181
Progresiv Publishr, 401 E. 32nd #1002, Chicago, IL 60616, 312-225-9181
African American Images, 9204 Commercial, Suite 308, Chicago, IL 60617
AIM MAGAZINE, PO Box 20554, Chicago, IL 60620
P-FORM, 756 N. Milwaukee Avenue, Chicago, IL 60622, 312-666-7737
MATI, 5548 N. Sawyer, Chicago, IL 60625
Ommation Press, 5548 North Sawyer, Chicago, IL 60625
SALOME: A JOURNAL FOR THE PERFORMING ARTS, 5548 N. Sawyer, Chicago, IL 60625, 312-539-5745
THE PAPER BAG, PO Box 268805, Chicago, IL 60626-8805, 312-285-7972
The Paper Bag Press, PO Box 268805, Chicago, IL 60626-8805, 312-285-7972
RAMBUNCTIOUS REVIEW, Rambunctious Press, Inc., 1221 West Pratt Blvd., Chicago, IL 60626
CHICAGO REVIEW, 5801 South Kenwood, Chicago, IL 60637, 312-702-0887
DOCTOR-PATIENT STUDIES, 5627 S. Drexel, Chicago, IL 60637, 312-752-3562
GREY CITY JOURNAL, 5627 S. Drexel, Chicago, IL 60637, 312-752-3562
BOOK RIGHTS REPORT, 1947 W. Leland #2, Chicago, IL 60640, 312-769-3769
CORNERSTONE, 939 W. Wilson, Chicago, IL 60640, 312-989-2080
Empty Closet Enterprises, 5210 N. Wayne, Chicago, IL 60640, 312-769-9009
HOT WIRE: Journal of Women's Music & Culture, 5210 North Wayne, Chicago, IL 60640, 312-769-9009
DAUGHTER OF SARAH, 3801 North Keeler, Chicago, IL 60641, 312-736-3399
ANNA'S HOUSE: THE JOURNAL OF EVERYDAY LIFE, PO Box 438070, Chicago, IL 60643-8070, 312-881-4907
NEW AMERICAN WRITING, 2920 West Pratt, Chicago, IL 60645
Chicago Democratic Socialists Of America, 1608 N. Milwaukee #403, Chicago, IL 60647
THE DIGGER, Chicago DSA, 1608 N. Milwaukee #403, Chicago, IL 60647
ECOSOCIALIST REVIEW, Chicago DSA, 1608 N. Milwaukee, 4th Floor, Chicago, IL 60647, 312-752-3562
SOCIALISM AND SEXUALITY, Chicago DSA, 1608 N. Milwaukee #403, Chicago, IL 60647
RHINO, c/o Kay Meier, 8403 West Normal Avenue, Niles, IL 60648
Great Lakes Poetry Press, Box 56703, Harwood Heights, IL 60656, 312-631-3697
B-CITY, B-City Press, 619 West Surf Street, Chicago, IL 60657, 312-871-6175
GAY CHICAGO MAGAZINE, 3121 North Broadway, Chicago, IL 60657, 312-327-7271
Lake View Press, PO Box 578279, Chicago, IL 60657, 312-935-2694
The Teitan Press, Inc., 339 West Barry Avenue, Suite 16B, Chicago, IL 60657, 312-929-7892
The Yellow Press, 5819 North Sacramento, Chicago, IL 60659
Black Light Fellowship, PO Box 5369, Chicago, IL 60680, 312-722-1441
WHITE WALLS: A Journal of Language and Art, PO Box 8204, Chicago, IL 60680
Abrazo Press, c/o Movimiento Artistico Chicano, Inc., PO Box 2890, Chicago, IL 60690-2890, 312-935-6188
ECOS: A Journal of Latino People's Culture, PO Box 2890, Chicago, IL 60690-2890, 312-935-6188
THE ORIGINAL ART REPORT (TOAR), P.O. Box 1641, Chicago, IL 60690
Mortal Press, 2315 North Alpine Road, Rockford, IL 61107-1422, 815-399-8432
KUMQUAT MERINGUE, PO Box 5144, Rockford, IL 61125, 815-968-0713
2AM MAGAZINE, PO Box 6754, Rockford, IL 61125-1754, 815-397-5901
2AM Publications, PO Box 6754, Rockford, IL 61125-1754, 815-397-5901
MIDWEST POETRY REVIEW, PO Box 4776, Rock Island, IL 61201
OUROBOROS, 3912 24th Street, Rock Island, IL 61201
The Hegeler Institute, Box 600, La Salle, IL 61301, 815-223-1231
THE MONIST: An International Quarterly Journal of General Philosophical Inquiry., Box 600, La Salle, IL 61301, 815-223-2520
CRICKET, THE MAGAZINE FOR CHILDREN, PO Box 300, Peru, IL 61354, 815-224-6643
Sherwood Sugden & Company, Publishers, 315 Fifth Street, Peru, IL 61354, 815-223-1231; 815-223-2520
THE PRAIRIE GOLD RUSH, Route 1, Box 76, Walnut, IL 61376, 815-379-2061
FARMER'S MARKET, PO Box 1272, Galesburg, IL 61402
PLOTS, PO Box 371, Kewanee, IL 61443, 309-852-0332
Glenbridge Publishing Ltd., 4 Woodland Lane, Macomb, IL 61455, 309-833-5104
Illinois Heritage Press, PO Box 25, Macomb, IL 61455, 309-836-8916
MISSISSIPPI VALLEY REVIEW, Dept. of English, Western Illinois University, Macomb, IL 61455, 309-298-1514
Computer Musician Coalition, 1024 West Willcox Avenue, Peoria, IL 61604, 309-685-4843
The Ellis Press, PO Box 1443, Peoria, IL 61655, 507-537-6463
CLOCKWATCH REVIEW, James Plath, English Department, Illinois Wesleyan University, Bloomington, IL 61702, 309-556-3352
Clockwatch Review Press, Department of English, Illinois Wesleyan University, Bloomington, IL 61702, 309-556-3352
THE PIKESTAFF FORUM, PO Box 127, Normal, IL 61761, 309-452-4831
The Pikestaff Press, PO Box 127, Normal, IL 61761, 309-452-4831
THE CHAOS NETWORK, PO Box 4100, Urbana, IL 61801, 217-328-0032
MATRIX, c/o Channing-Murray Foundation, 1209 W Oregon, Urbana, IL 61801, 217-344-1176
Red Herring Press, c/o Channing-Murray Foundation, 1209 W. Oregon, Urbana, IL 61801, 217-344-1176
Stormline Press, Inc., PO Box 593, Urbana, IL 61801, 217-328-2665
The Urbana Free Library, 201 South Race Street, Urbana, IL 61801, 217-367-4057
Human Kinetics Pub. Inc., Box 5076, Champaign, IL 61820, 217-351-5076
Illinois Writers, Inc., PO Box 1087, Champaign, IL 61820, (217) 429-0117
ILLINOIS WRITERS NEWSLETTER, PO Box 1087, Champaign, IL 61820, 217-429-0117
ILLINOIS WRITERS REVIEW, PO Box 1087, Champaign, IL 61820, 217-429-0117
Leisure Press, PO Box 5076, Champaign, IL 61820
Life Enhancement, Box 5076, Champaign, IL 61820
THE SPORT PSYCHOLOGIST, Box 5076, Champaign, IL 61820, 217-351-5076
ADAPTED PHYSICAL ACTIVITY QUARTERLY (APAQ), Box 5076, Champaign, IL 61825-5076, 217-351-5076
COACHING VOLLEYBALL, Box 5076, Champaign, IL 61825-5076, 217-351-5076
COACHING WOMEN'S BASKETBALL, Box 5076, Champaign, IL 61825-5076, 217-351-5076
INTERNATIONAL JOURNAL OF SPORT BIOMECHANICS, Box 5076, Champaign, IL 61825-5076, 217-351-5076

JOURNAL OF SPORT AND EXERCISE PSYCHOLOGY, Box 5076, Champaign, IL 61825-5076, 217-351-5076
JOURNAL OF SPORT MANAGEMENT, Box 5076, Champaign, IL 61825-5076, 217-351-5076
JOURNAL OF TEACHING IN PHYSICAL EDUCATION, Box 5076, Champaign, IL 61825-5076, 217-351-5076
JOURNAL OF THE PHILOSOPHY OF SPORT, Box 5076, Champaign, IL 61825-5076, 217-351-5076
PLAY & CULTURE, Box 5076, Champaign, IL 61825-5076, 217-351-5076
QUEST, Box 5076, Champaign, IL 61825-5076, 217-351-5076
SOCIOLOGY OF SPORT JOURNAL, Box 5076, Champaign, IL 61825-5076, 217-351-5076
Mayhaven Publishing, 803 Buckthorn Circle, Mahomet, IL 61853, 217-586-4493
KARAMU, Department of English, Eastern Illinois Univ., Charleston, IL 61920, 217-581-6291
MODERN IMAGES, 1217 Champaign Avenue, Mattoon, IL 61938-3167
SOU'WESTER, English Dept., Southern Illinois University, Edwardsville, IL 62026-1438
GOOD READING MAGAZINE, PO Box 40, Litchfield, IL 62056, 217-324-3425
ILLINOIS MAGAZINE, PO Box 40, Litchfield, IL 62056
SUNSHINE MAGAZINE, PO Box 40, Litchfield, IL 62056, 217-324-3425
Sunshine Press, PO Box 40, Litchfield, IL 62056, 217-324-3425
OBLATES, 15 South 59th Street, 9978, Belleville, IL 62223-4694, 618-233-2238
INTUITIVE EXPLORATIONS, PO Box 561, Quincy, IL 62306-0561, 217-222-9082
SOMNIAL TIMES, Box 561, Quincy, IL 62306-0561, 217-222-4141
SHINING STAR, Shining Star Publications, PO Box 299, Carthage, IL 62321
NATURE SOCIETY NEWS, Purple Martin Junction, Griggsville, IL 62340, (217) 833-2323
Pollard Press, RR 01, Box 201, Niota, IL 62358-9782
High/Coo Press, 4634 Hale Dr, Decatur, IL 62526-1117, 317-567-2596
MAYFLY, 4634 Hale Drive, Decatur, IL 62526-1117
THE WRITERS' BAR-B-Q, 924 Bryn Mawr Boulevard, Springfield, IL 62703, (217) 525-6987
QSKY Publishing/Independent Publishing, P.O. Box 3042, Springfield, IL 62708, 217-528-0886

INDIANA

Polexii Press, PO Box 14, Goldsmith, IN 46045-0014
Crossroads Publications, Inc., PO Box 842, Greenwood, IN 46142, 317-639-5474
Persistence Press, 4734 Wentworth Blvd., Indianapolis, IN 46201, 317-357-9071
Knowledge Systems, Inc., 7777 West Morris Street, Indianapolis, IN 46231, 317-241-0749; 317-248-1503 (FAX)
Wesley Press, Box 50434, Indianapolis, IN 46250-0434
THE WESLEYAN ADVOCATE, Box 50434, Indianapolis, IN 46250-0434, 317-576-1313
Fir Publishing Company, PO Box 78436, Indianapolis, IN 46278, 317-872-4059
Perspectives Press, PO Box 90318, Indianapolis, IN 46290-0318, 317-872-3055
White Cliffs Media Company, PO Box 561, Crown Point, IN 46307-0561, (219) 322-5537
WORLD MUSIC CONNECTIONS NEWSLETTER, PO Box 561, Crown Point, IN 46307-0561
SKYLARK, 2233 171st Street, Purdue University Calumet, Hammond, IN 46323, 219-844-0520
CHESS IN INDIANA, 214 S. 4th Street, Elkhart, IN 46516, 219-293-2241
Cottage Publications, Inc., 24396 Pleasant View Drive, Elkhart, IN 46517, 219-875-8618
SPL Publishing Group, 11777 Park Lane North, Granger, IN 46530-8649, 219-272-0389
The Poet, 2314 West Sixth Street, Mishawaka, IN 46544-1594, 219-255-8606
GROUND WATER REVIEW, 730 East Smith Street, Warsaw, IN 46580, 219-269-7680
Talking Leaves Press, 730 East Smith Street, Warsaw, IN 46580, 219-269-7680
and books, 702 South Michigan, Suite 836, South Bend, IN 46601
Shield Publishing, Inc., 2940 Rue Renoir #111, South Bend, IN 46615
Greenlawn Press, 107 S. Greenlawn Avenue, South Bend, IN 46614, 219-234-5088
NEW HEAVEN/NEW EARTH, 107 S. Greenlawn Avenue, South Bend, IN 46617, 219-234-5088
Right Here Publications, PO Box 1014, Huntington, IN 46750, 219-356-4223
WRITE NOW!, PO Box 1014, Huntington, IN 46750
THE WINDLESS ORCHARD, c/o R. Novak, English Dept., Indiana University, Ft. Wayne, IN 46805, 219-481-6841
Riverside Productions, PO Box 26, Delphi, IN 46923, 317-564-6180
CountrySide Business Publications, PO Box 115, Galveston, IN 46932, 219-626-2131
Cottontail Publications, R 1, Box 198, Bennington, IN 47011, 812-427-3914
THE PRESIDENTS' JOURNAL, R 1, Box 198, Bennington, IN 47011, (812) 427-3914
Fire Buff House, PO Drawer 709, New Albany, IN 47150, 812-945-2617
THE MYSTERY FANCIER, 2024 Clifty Drive, Madison, IN 47250-1632, 812-273-6908
Indiana Publications, Inc., PO Box 1213, Seymour, IN 47274, 812-523-8889
BARNWOOD, 600 E. Washington Street, Muncie, IN 47305
The Barnwood Press, 600 E. Washington Street, Muncie, IN 47305
Friends United Press, 101 Quaker Hill Drive, Richmond, IN 47374, 317-962-7573
Frozen Waffles Press/Shattered Sidewalks Press; 25th Century Chapbooks, The Writer's Group, 329 West 1st Street #5, Bloomington, IN 47401, 812-333-6304 c/o Rocky
CANVAS CHAUTAUQUA MAGAZINE, PO Box 361, Bloomington, IN 47402, 812-333-4542
World Wisdom Books, Inc., PO Box 2682, Bloomington, IN 47402, 812-332-1663
Royal Purcell, Publisher, 806 West Second Street, Bloomington, IN 47403, 812-336-4195
Birdalone Books, 508 N. College Avenue, Suite #333, Bloomington, IN 47404-3831, 812-333-0167
Gaslight Publications, 626 N. College Avenue, Bloomington, IN 47404, 812-332-5169
INDIANA REVIEW, 316 North Jordan Avenue, Indiana University, Bloomington, IN 47405, 812-855-3439
Grayson Bernard Publishers, Inc., 223 S. Pete Ellis Drive, Suite 12, Bloomington, IN 47408, 812-331-8182
OPOSSUM HOLLER TAROT, RR 3 Box 109, Orleans, IN 47452-9649, 812-755-4788
Ramp Creek Publishing Inc, PO Box 3, Smithville, IN 47458, 812-334-1852
Storytime Ink International, PO Box 813, Newburgh, IN 47629, 812-853-6797
THE FORMALIST, 525 S. Rotherwood, Evansville, IN 47714
LIBRARY TIMES INTERNATIONAL, Future World Publishing Company, 8128 Briarwood Drive, Evansville, IN 47715-8302, 812-473-2420
MIRKWOOD, PO Box 4083, Terre Haute, IN 47804, 812-234-3133
Tunnel Publishing, PO Box 4083, Terre Haute, IN 47804, 812-234-3133

POETS' ROUNDTABLE, 826 South Center Street, Terre Haute, IN 47807, 812-234-0819
BLACK AMERICAN LITERATURE FORUM, Indiana State University, Dept. of English, Terre Haute, IN 47809, 812-237-2968
The Fair Press, PO Box 9, Bowling Green, IN 47833, 812-331-8529; 237-3213
SNOWY EGRET, PO Box 9, Bowling Green, IN 47833, 812-331-8529
STONE TALK, Box 44, Universal, IN 47884, 317-832-8918
TOAD HIWAY, Box 44, Universal, IN 47884, 317-832-8918
Toad Hiway Press, Box 44, Universal, IN 47884, 317-832-8918
Manrovian Press, Fandom House, 30 N. 19th Street, Lafayette, IN 47904
PABLO LENNIS, Fandom House, 30 N. 19th Street, Lafayette, IN 47904
SPARROW POVERTY PAMPHLETS, Sparrow Press imprint, 103 Waldron Street, West Lafayette, IN 47906
Sparrow Press, 103 Waldron Street, West Lafayette, IN 47906
Vagrom Chap Books, Sparrow Press imprint, 103 Waldron Street, West Lafayette, IN 47906
SYCAMORE REVIEW, Department of English, Purdue University, West Lafayette, IN 47907, 317-494-3783
WORLD HUMOR AND IRONY MEMBERSHIP SERIAL YEARBOOK (WHIMSY), English Department, Purdue University, West Lafayette, IN 47907, 317-494-3780

IOWA

Iowa State University Press, English Department, ISU, 203 Ross Hall, Ames, IA 50011
POET & CRITIC, 203 Ross Hall, Iowa State University, Ames, IA 50011
CSS Publications, PO Box 23, Iowa Falls, IA 50126, 515-282-4379; 648-2716
Chris Drumm Books, PO Box 445, Polk City, IA 50226, 515-984-6749
BLUE BUILDINGS, Department of English, Drake University, Des Moines, IA 50311-3005, 515-274-9103
The Electric Bank, Inc., 4225 University, Des Moines, IA 50311, 515-255-3552
WASHINGTON INTERNATIONAL ARTS LETTER, PO Box 12010, Des Moines, IA 50312, 202-328-1900, 515-255-5577
THE APPLE BLOSSOM CONNECTION, PO Box 325, Stacyville, IA 50476, 515-737-2269
Peak Output Unlimited, PO Box 325, Stacyville, IA 50476, 515-737-2269
THE NATIONAL FARM DIRECTORY, PO Box 1574, Fort Dodge, IA 50501, 515-955-2488
THE NORTH AMERICAN REVIEW, Univ. Of Northern Iowa, Cedar Falls, IA 50614, 319-273-6455
MASSEY COLLECTORS NEWS—WILD HARVEST, Box 529, Denver, IA 50622, 319-984-5292
IATROFON, 10 East Charles, Oelwein, IA 50662, 319-283-3491
JAG, 10 East Charles, Oelwein, IA 50662, 319-283-3491
MIDWEST CHAPARRAL, 1309 2nd Avenue SW, Waverly, IA 50677, 319-352-1716
The Pterodactyl Press, PO Box 205, Cumberland, IA 50843, 712-774-2244
RED POWER, Box 277, Battle Creek, IA 51006, 712-365-4873
The Middleburg Press, Box 166, Orange City, IA 51041, 712-737-4198
CRAMPED AND WET, 1012 29th, Sioux City, IA 51104
Ansuda Publications, Box 158, Harris, IA 51345
HOR-TASY, PO Box 158, Harris, IA 51345
THE PUB, Box 158, Harris, IA 51345
TRADITION, PO Box 438, Walnut, IA 51577, 712-784-3001
SEED SAVERS EXCHANGE, RR 3, Box 239, Decorah, IA 52101, 319-382-5990
THE ANNALS OF IOWA, 402 Iowa Avenue, Iowa City, IA 52240, 319-335-3916
CAMPUS REVIEW, 336 S. Clinton #16, Iowa City, IA 52240, 319-338-1532
PALIMPSEST, State Historical Society of Iowa, 402 Iowa Avenue, Iowa City, IA 52240, 319-335-3916
DADA/SURREALISM, 425 EPB, University of Iowa, Iowa City, IA 52242
THE IOWA REVIEW, 308 EPB, Univ. Of Iowa, Iowa City, IA 52242, 319-335-0462
WALT WHITMAN QUARTERLY REVIEW, 308 EPB The University of Iowa, Iowa City, IA 52242, 319-335-0454; 335-0438
COMMON LIVES / LESBIAN LIVES, PO Box 1553, Iowa City, IA 52244
IOWA WOMAN, PO Box 680, Iowa City, IA 52244, 319-987-2879
Middle Coast Publishing, PO Box 2522, Iowa City, IA 52244, 319-335-4078; 354-8944
Penfield Press, 215 Brown Street, Iowa City, IA 52245-1358
WORLD LETTER, 2726 E. Court Street, Iowa City, IA 52245, 319-337-6022
Dog Hair Press, PO Box 372, West Branch, IA 52358, 319-643-7324
LUNA TACK, PO Box 372, West Branch, IA 52358-0144, 319-643-7324
BEGINNING: THE MAGAZINE FOR THE WRITER IN THE COMMUNITY, 1530 Bladensburg Road, Ottumwa, IA 52501-9066, 515-682-4305
Writers House Press, 1530 Bladensburg Road, Ottumwa, IA 52501-9066, 515-682-4305
Ad-Lib Publications, 51 North Fifth Street, Fairfield, IA 52556, 515-472-6617
BOOK MARKETING UPDATE, PO Box 1102, Fairfield, IA 52556, 515-472-6130
Fairfield Press, PO Box 773, Fairfield, IA 52556, 515-472-7231
Open Horizons Publishing Company, PO Box 1102, Fairfield, IA 52556, 515-472-6130
21st Century Publications, 401 N. 4th Street, PO Box 702, Fairfield, IA 52556, 515-472-5105
CLASSIC IMAGES, PO Box 809, Muscatine, IA 52761
Limerick Publications, PO Box 1072, Muscatine, IA 52761

KANSAS

COTTONWOOD, Box J, Kansas Union, Univ. of Kansas, Lawrence, KS 66045, 913-864-3777
Editorial Research Service, P.O.Box 2047, Olathe, KS 66061, 913-829-0609
PEOPLE'S CULTURE, Box 5224, Kansas City, KS 66119
The Wordtree, 10876 Bradshaw, Overland Park, KS 66210-1148, 913-469-1010
Writer's Helper Publishing, PO Box 32006, Overland Park, KS 66212, 913-383-9894
JOURNAL OF THE WEST, 1531 Yuma (PO Box 1009), Manhattan, KS 66502, 913-539-1888
Sunflower University Press, 1531 Yuma, (Box 1009), Manhattan, KS 66502, 913-539-1888
KANSAS QUARTERLY, English Department, Kansas State University, Manhattan, KS 66506, 913-532-6716
LITERARY MAGAZINE REVIEW, English Department, Kansas State University, Manhattan, KS 66506, 913-532-6716

SCAVENGER'S NEWSLETTER, 519 Ellinwood, Osage City, KS 66523, 913-528-3538
LEFTHANDER MAGAZINE, Lefthanders International, PO Box 8249, Topeka, KS 66608, (913) 234-2177
Christmans, PO Box 510, Pittsburg, KS 66762, 417-842-3322
THE MIDWEST QUARTERLY, Pittsburg State University, Pittsburg, KS 66762, 316-231-7000-4369
E.T.M. Publishing, 305-B East 7th Street, Winfield, KS 67156, 316-221-4743
PAGES, 3610 Country Club, Wichita, KS 67208, 316-684-9487
MW PENPAL WORLD MAGAZINE, PO Box 3121, Hutchinson, KS 67501
Chiron Press, 1514 Stone, Great Bend, KS 67530-4027, 316-792-5025
CHIRON REVIEW, 1514 Stone, Great Bend, KS 67530-4027, 316-792-5025

KENTUCKY

THE AMERICAN VOICE, 332 West Broadway, #1215, Louisville, KY 40202, 502-562-0045
The Sulgrave Press, 2005 Longest Avenue], Louisville, KY 40204, 502-459-9713
KENTUCKY POETRY REVIEW, Bellarmine College, Louisville, KY 40205
Marathon International Book Company, Deptartment SPR, PO Box 33008, Louisville, KY 40232-3008, 502-935-3147
Devyn Press, 3600 Chamberlain Lane #230, Louisville, KY 40241, 502-895-1354
SPECTRUM STORIES, Box 58367, Louisville, KY 40268-0367
WONDER, PO Box 58367, Louisville, KY 40268-0367
Wonder Press, PO Box 58367, Louisville, KY 40268-0367
THE LOUISVILLE REVIEW, Univ. of Louisville, English Dept., 315 Bingham Humanities, Louisville, KY 40292, 502-588-6801
HORTIDEAS, Route 1, Box 302, Gravel Switch, KY 40328, 606-332-7606
APPALACHIAN HERITAGE, Hutchins Library, Berea College, Berea, KY 40404, 606-986-9341 ext. 5260
ANQ: A Quarterly Journal of Short Articles, Notes, and Reviews, University of Kentucky, English Department, Office Tower 1321, Lexington, KY 40506, 606-257-6975
LIMESTONE: A LITERARY JOURNAL, c/o Univ. of Kentucky, English Dept., 1215 Patterson Office Tower, Lexington, KY 40506
PSYCHOLOGY OF WOMEN QUARTERLY, Dept. of Educ. & Counseling Psychology, 237 Dickey Hall, Univ. of Kentucky, Lexington, KY 40506-0017
PIKEVILLE REVIEW, Humanities Department, Pikeville College, Pikeville, KY 41501, 606-437-4046
WIND, RFD Rt. 1, Box 809K, Pikeville, KY 41501, 606-631-1129
PLAINSONG, Box 8245, Western Kentucky University, Bowling Green, KY 42101, 502-745-5708

LOUISANA

BAKER STREET GAZETTE, PO Box 994, Metailie, LA 70004, 504-734-8414
HORIZONS WEST, PO Box 994, Metailie, LA 70004, 504-734-8414
Baker Street Publications, PO Box 994, Metairie, LA 70004, 504-734-8414
THE HAUNTED JOURNAL, PO Box 994, Metairie, LA 70004, 504-734-8414
HORIZONS BEYOND, PO Box 994, Metairie, LA 70004, 504-734-8414
NOCTURNAL NEWS, PO Box 994, Metairie, LA 70004, 504-734-8414
POISON PEN WRITERS NEWS, PO Box 994, Metairie, LA 70004, 504-734-8414
SLEUTH JOURNAL, PO Box 994, Metairie, LA 70004, 504-734-8414
THE VAMPIRE JOURNAL, PO Box 994, Metairie, LA 70004, 504-734-8414
Pendaya Publications, Inc., 510 Woodvine Avenue, Metairie, LA 70005, 504-834-8151
THEMA, THEMA Literary Society, Box 74109, Metairie, LA 70033-4109
BAHLASTI PAPER, PO Box 15038, New Orleans, LA 70115, 504-899-7439
Westgate Press, 5219 Magazine Street, New Orleans, LA 70115-1858
THE NEW LAUREL REVIEW, 828 Lesseps Street, New Orleans, LA 70117, 504-947-6001
RED BASS, 2425 Burgundy Street, New Orleans, LA 70117, 504-949-5256
CELFAN Editions Monographs, Dept. of French & Italian, Tulane University, New Orleans, LA 70118
LOWLANDS REVIEW, 6109 Magazine, New Orleans, LA 70118
NEW ORLEANS REVIEW, Loyola University, Box 195, New Orleans, LA 70118, 504-865-2294
REVUE CELFAN REVIEW, Department of French and Italian, Tulane University, New Orleans, LA 70118
Acre Press, 1521 N. Lopez Street, New Orleans, LA 70119
FELL SWOOP, 1521 N. Lopez Street, New Orleans, LA 70119
XAVIER REVIEW, Box 110C, Xavier University, New Orleans, LA 70125, 504-486-7411 X481
WHISPERING WIND MAGAZINE, 8009 Wales Street, New Orleans, LA 70126, 504-241-5866
The Gallery Press International, Inc., PO Box 56175, New Orleans, LA 70156, 504-246-7379
ON THE SPOT, PO Box 70614, New Orleans, LA 70172, 504-947-5165
Research & Discovery Publications, PO Box 761, Patterson, LA 70392
TREASURE HUNTING RESEARCH BULLETIN, PO Box 761, Patterson, LA 70392
21st Century Books, PO Box 5225, Lafayette, LA 70502, 318-233-6388
WITHIN & BEYOND, PO Box 2683, Lafayette, LA 70502, 318-235-6535
Kore, 420 Orangewood Drive, Lafayette, LA 70503-5228
Cajun Publishing, Route 4, Box 88, New Iberia, LA 70560, 318-365-6653; 364-2752
RIVERSIDE QUARTERLY, 807 Walters St #107, Lake Charles, LA 70605-4665, 318-477-7943
EXQUISITE CORPSE: A Monthly of Books and Ideas, English Department, Louisiana State University, Baton Rouge, LA 70803-5001, 504-388-2982; -2823
NEW DELTA REVIEW, c/o Dept. of English, Louisiana State University, Baton Rouge, LA 70803-5001, 504-388-4079
THE SOUTHERN REVIEW, 43 Allen Hall, Louisiana State University, Baton Rouge, LA 70803, 504-388-5108
The Everett Companies, Publishing Division, PO Box 5376, 813 Whittington Street, Bossier City, LA 71171, 318-742-6240; 800-423-7033
Readers International, Inc., PO Box 959, (US Book Service Department), Columbia, LA 71418

MAINE

Nicolas-Hays, Inc., Box 612, York Beach, ME 03910, 207-363-4393
Samuel Weiser, Inc., PO Box 612, York Beach, ME 03910, 207-363-4393
Tide Book Publishing Company, Box 101, York Harbor, ME 03911-0101, 207-363-4534

Pittore Euforico, PO Box 182, Bowdoinham, ME 04008, 207-666-8453
MAINE IN PRINT, 19 Mason Street, Brunswick, ME 04011, 207-729-6333
TBW Books, Inc., c/o Lois Burns, Gurnet Road, Brunswick, ME 04011
Mercer House Press, P.O. Box 681, Kennebunkport, ME 04046, 207-282-7116
Intercultural Press, Inc., PO Box 700, Yarmouth, ME 04096, 207-846-5168
THE CAFE REVIEW, c/o Yes Books, 20 Danforth Street, Portland, ME 04101
GREATER PORTLAND, PO Box 15490, Portland, ME 04101-7490, 207-772-2811
Astarte Shell Press, PO Box 10453, Portland, ME 04104, 207-871-1817
CRAWLSPACE, Box 10911, Portland, ME 04104
Green Timber Publications, PO Box 3884, Portland, ME 04104, 207-797-4180
OTTERWISE, PO Box 1374, Portland, ME 04104, 207-883-4426
The Kennebec River Press, Inc., 36 Old Mill Road, Falmouth, ME 04105-1637, 207-781-3002
Maelstrom Press, 8 Farm Hill Road, Cape Elizabeth, ME 04107
MAELSTROM REVIEW, 8 Farm Hill Road, Cape Elizabeth, ME 04107
Dirigo Books, Inc., PO Box 343, Bryant Pond, ME 04219, 207-665-2133
Soleil Press, RFD #1, Box 452, Lisbon Falls, ME 04252, 207-353-5454
Small-Small Press, 226 Linden Street, Rumford, ME 04276, 364-7237
WORKSHOP, 226 Linden Street, Rumford, ME 04276, 364-7237
KENNEBEC: A Portfolio of Maine Writing, University of Maine at Augusta, Augusta, ME 04330, (207) 622-7131
Tilbury House, Publishers, 132 Water Street, Gardiner, ME 04345, 207-582-1899
Health Educator Publications, Inc., 1580 Kirkland Road, Old Town, ME 04468, 207-827-3633
RAFALE, 126 College Avenue, Orono, ME 04469, (207) 581-3764
Puckerbrush Press, PO Box 39, Orono, ME 04473-0039, 207-866-4868
THE PUCKERBRUSH REVIEW, 76 Main St., Orono, ME 04473
UNBRIDLED LUST!, 8 Elm Street #2, Orono, ME 04473, 207-866-3535
Unbridled Lust! Publishing, 8 Elm Street #2, Orono, ME 04473, 207-866-3535
Blackberry, Chimney Farm, R.R. 1, Box 228, Nobleboro, ME 04555, 207-729-5083
BELOIT POETRY JOURNAL, Box 154, RFD 2, Ellsworth, ME 04605, 207-667-5598
The Latona Press, RFD 2, Box 154, Ellsworth, ME 04605
Acadia Publishing Company, PO Box 170, Bar Harbor, ME 04609, 207-288-9025
Organization for Equal Education of the Sexes, Inc. (OEES), PO Box 438, Blue Hill, ME 04614, 207-374-5110
HarCroft Publishing Company, Star Route Box 179, Hancock, ME 04640, 207-422-3383
SLOW DANCER, Alan Brooks, Box 3010, RFD 1, Lubec, ME 04652
Stone Man Press, Box 3010, RFD 1, Lubec, ME 04652, 207-733-2194
Brook Farm Books, PO Box 246, Bridgewater, ME 04735
THE BLACK FLY REVIEW, University of Maine at Fort Kent, Fort Kent, ME 04743, 207-834-3162
NORTHERN LIGHTS STUDIES IN CREATIVITY, University of Maine at Presque Isle, Presque Isle, ME 04769, 207-764-0311
Dunstan Press, 30 Linden Street, Rockland, ME 04841, 207-596-0064
International Marine Publishing Co., Box 220, Camden, ME 04843, 207-236-4837
Yankee Books, PO Box 1248, 62 Bay View Street, Camden, ME 04843, 207-236-0933
Conservatory of American Letters, PO Box 123, So. Thomaston, ME 04858, 207-354-6550
CAL NEWSLETTER, PO Box 123, South Thomaston, ME 04858
VOLITION, PO Box 314, Tenants Harbor, ME 04860
Vortex Editions, PO Box 314, Tenants Harbor, ME 04860
Dan River Press, PO Box 88, Thomaston, ME 04861
Northwoods Press, PO Box 88, Thomaston, ME 04861, 207-354-6550
Bern Porter Books, 22 Salmond Road, Belfast, ME 04915, 207-338-3763
BERN PORTER INTERNATIONAL, 22 Salmond Road, Belfast, ME 04915
SMALL PRESS NEWS, Weeks Mills, New Sharon, ME 04955
Stony Hills Productions, Weeks Mills, New Sharon, ME 04955
TRANET, Box 567, Rangeley, ME 04970, 207-864-2252
Nightshade Press, PO Box 76, Ward Hill, Troy, ME 04987, 207-948-3427
POTATO EYES, PO Box 76, Troy, ME 04987, 207-948-3427
NAKED MAN, c/o Mike Smetzer, R. 1, Box 2315, Unity, ME 04988
Naked Man Press, c/o Mike Smetzer, R. 1, Box 2315, Unity, ME 04988
North Country Press, PO Box 641, Unity, ME 04988, 207-948-2208

MARYLAND

THE IMMIGRANT, 4601 Barbara Drive, Beltsville, MD 20705
Maryland Historical Press, 9205 Tuckerman St, Lanham, MD 20706, 301-577-2436 and 557-5308
Rainfeather Press, 3201 Taylor Street, Mt. Rainier, MD 20712
Gryphon House, Inc., PO Box 275, 3706 Otis Street, Mt. Ranier, MD 20712, 301-779-6200
Heritage Books, Inc., 1540-E Pointer Ridge Place, Bowie, MD 20716, 301-390-7708
FEMINIST STUDIES, c/o Women's Studies Program, University of Maryland, College Park, MD 20742, 301-405-7413
LITERARY RESEARCH: A Journal of Scholarly Method & Technique, Department of English and World Literature, University of Maryland, College Park, MD 20742, 301-454-6953
A VERY SMALL MAGAZINE, PO Box 221, Greenbelt, MD 20768
Say When Press, PO Box 942, Greenbelt, MD 20770, 301-474-0352
Claycomb Press, Inc., PO Box 70822, Chevy Chase, MD 20813-0822, 301-656-1057
Park & Park Publishers, Inc., PO Box 71201, Chevy Chase, MD 20813, 301-656-6511
CAROUSEL, 7815 Old Georgetown Road, Bethesda, MD 20814-2415, 301-654-8664
THE FUTURIST, World Future Society, 4916 St. Elmo Avenue, Bethesda, MD 20814, 301-656-8274
Iranbooks, Inc., 8014 Old Georgetown Road, Bethesda, MD 20814, 301-986-0079
Paycock Press, PO Box 30906, Bethesda, MD 20814, 301-656-5146
POET LORE, The Writer's Center, 7815 Old Georgetown Road, Bethesda, MD 20814-2415, 301-654-8664
The Writer's Center, 7815 Old Georgetown Road, Bethesda, MD 20814, 301-654-8664
COMMON BOUNDARY, 7005 Florida Street, Chevy Chase, MD 20815, 301-652-9495

VIETNAM GENERATION: A Journal of Recent History and Contemporary Issues, 2921 Terrace Drive, Chevy Chase, MD 20815, 301-608-0622; FAX 301-608-0761
ARMED FORCES & SOCIETY, PO Box 27, Cabin John, MD 20818, (301) 320-2130
Gut Punch Press, PO Box 105, Cabin John, MD 20818
Seven Locks Press, P.O. Box 27, Cabin John, MD 20818, (301) 320-2130
VISIBILITIES, PO Box 1169, Olney, MD 20830-1169
PC Press, 6 Nelson Street, Rockville, MD 20850-3130, 301-294-7450
Kar-Ben Copies, Inc., 6800 Tildenwood Lane, Rockville, MD 20852, 301-984-8733; 800-4KARBEN (in USA)
Woodbine House, 5615 Fishers Lane, Rockville, MD 20852, 301-468-8800
Ariadne Press, 4817 Tallahassee Avenue, Rockville, MD 20853, 301-949-2514
Script Humanistica, 1383 Kersey Lane, Potomac, MD 20854, 301-294-7949; 614-340-1095
TRENDS & PREDICTIONS ANALYST, 12628 Black Saddle Lane, Germantown, MD 20874, 301-972-1980
Shann Press, PO Box 45, Germantown, MD 20875-0045, 301-972-3012
American Cooking Guild, 6-F East Cedar Avenue, Gaithersburg, MD 20877, 301-949-6787
QUANTUM: Science Fiction & Fantasy Review, 8217 Langport Terrace, Gaithersburg, MD 20877, 301-948-2514
Packet Press, 14704 Seneca Castle Court, Gaithersburg, MD 20878, 301-762-7145
BELLES LETTRES, 11151 Captain's Walk Ct., North Potomac, MD 20878, 301-294-0278
Garrett Park Press, PO Box 190, Garrett Park, MD 20896, 301-946-2553
CorkScrew Press, 2915 Fenimore Road, Silver Spring, MD 20902, 301-949-6787
MEDIA REPORT TO WOMEN, Communication Research Associates, Inc., 10606 Mantz Road, Silver Spring, MD 20903, 301-445-3230
THE NAUTILUS, PO Box 7279, Silver Spring, MD 20907-7279
NEGATIVE, 4508 Stone Crest Drive, Ellicott, MD 21043
ABBEY, 5360 Fallriver Row Court, Columbia, MD 21044
White Urp Press, 5360 Fallriver Row Court, Columbia, MD 21044
New Fantasy Publications, PO Box 2655, Columbia, MD 21045-1655
Swand Publications, 120 N. Longcross Road, Linthicum Heights, MD 21090, 301-859-3725
FIGHTING WOMAN NEWS, 11438 Z Cronridge Drive, Owings Mills, MD 21117, 301-363-4919
Stemmer House Publishers, Inc., 2627 Caves Road, Owings Mills, MD 21117
Aeolus Press, Inc., PO Box 466, Randallstown, MD 21133-0466, 301-922-1212; fax 301-922-4262
KITE LINES, PO Box 466, Randallstown, MD 21133-0466, 301-922-1212; fax 301-922-4262
Christian Classics, Inc., 77 W. Main, Box 30, Westminster, MD 21157, 301-848-3065
The Wanderer's Ink, 2 College Hill #1175, Westminster, MD 21157-4303
The Nautical & Aviation Publishing Co. of American, Inc., 101 W. Read St., Suite 314, Baltimore, MD 21201, 301-659-0220
Genealogical Publishing Co., Inc., 1001 North Calvert Street, Baltimore, MD 21202, 301-837-8271; 301-752-8492 fax
PASSAGER: A Journal of Remembrance and Discovery, 1420 N. Charles Street, Baltimore, MD 21202-5779, 301-625-3041
Dolphin-Moon Press, PO Box 22262, Baltimore, MD 21203
JEWISH VEGETARIANS OF NORTH AMERICA, Jewish Vegetarians, PO Box 1463, Baltimore, MD 21203, 301-366-VEGE
STREET VOICE, PO Box 22962, Baltimore, MD 21203, 301-332-1207
VEGETARIAN JOURNAL, PO Box 1463, Baltimore, MD 21203, 301-366-VEGE (8343)
The Vegetarian Resource Group, PO Box 1463, Baltimore, MD 21203, 301-752-VEGV
The White Ewe Press, P.O. Box 1614, Baltimore, MD 21203, 301-837-0794
Icarus Books, 1015 Kenilworth Drive, Baltimore, MD 21204, 301-821-7807
The New Poets Series, Inc., 541 Piccadilly Rd., Baltimore, MD 21204, 301-321-2863
The Galileo Press Ltd., 7215 York Road, Suite 210, Baltimore, MD 21212
CELEBRATION, 2707 Lawina Road, Baltimore, MD 21216, 301-542-8785
Bacchus Press Ltd., 1421 Jordan Street, Baltimore, MD 21217, 301-576-0762
ALTERNATIVE PRESS INDEX, Alternative Press Center, Inc., PO Box 33109, Baltimore, MD 21218, 301-243-2471
Columbia Publishing Company, Inc., 234 East 25th Street, Baltimore, MD 21218, 301-366-7070
Prospect Hill Press, 216 Wendover Road, Baltimore, MD 21218, 301-889-0320
SHATTERED WIG REVIEW, 523 East 38th Street, Baltimore, MD 21218, 301-243-6888
SOCIAL ANARCHISM: A Journal of Practice And Theory, 2743 Maryland Avenue, Baltimore, MD 21218, 301-243-6987
TRIBE: An American Gay Journal, 234 East 25th Street, Baltimore, MD 21218, 301-366-7070
DIRTY LINEN, PO Box 66600, Baltimore, MD 21239-6600, 301-583-7973; fax 301-665-5144
ZORA NEALE HURSTON FORUM, PO Box 550, Morgan State University, Baltimore, MD 21239
The Zora Neale Hurston Society, PO Box 550, Morgan State University, Baltimore, MD 21239
Barefoot Press, 1856 Cherry Road, Annapolis, MD 21401
CHESAPEAKE BAY MAGAZINE, 1819 Bay Ridge Avenue, Annapolis, MD 21403, 301-263-2662
Nightsun Books, 520 Greene Street, Cumberland, MD 21502, 301-722-2127
Acheron Press, Bear Creek at the Kettle, Friendsville, MD 21531, 301-746-5885
NIGHTSUN, School of Arts-Humanities, Frostburg S. University, Frostburg, MD 21532
Cornell Maritime Press, Inc., PO Box 456, Centreville, MD 21617, 301-758-1075
Celestial Gifts Publishing, PO Box 414, RD 1, Box 80F, Chester, MD 21619, 301-643-4466
THE MONOCACY VALLEY REVIEW, Mount St. Mary's College, Emmitsburg, MD 21727, 301-447-6122 X4832
Antietam Press, 51 East Antietam Street, Hagerstown, MD 21740, 301-797-5155
ANTIETAM REVIEW, 82 W. Washington Street, 3rd Floor, Hagerstown, MD 21740, 301-791-3132
INFORMATION RETRIEVAL AND LIBRARY AUTOMATION, PO Box 88, Mt. Airy, MD 21771, 301-829-1496
Lomond Publications Inc., PO Box 88, Mt. Airy, MD 21771, 301-829-1496

MASSACHUSETTS

Bergin & Garvey Publishers, 1420 South East Street, Amherst, MA 01002, 413-253-9980
Forty-Seven Books, c/o MFA Creative Writing Program, 452 Bartlett Hall, MA University, Amherst, MA 01002
Parable Press, 136 Gray Street, Amherst, MA 01002, 413-253-5634
Spring Street Press, 104 Spring Street, Amherst, MA 01002, 413-253-7748
Swamp Press, 323 Pelham Road, Amherst, MA 01002

TIGHTROPE, 323 Pelham Road, Amherst, MA 01002
LEGACY: A JOURNAL OF AMERICAN WOMEN WRITERS, Univ. of Massachusetts, Dept. of English, Bartlett Hall, Amherst, MA 01003, 413-545-4270
THE MASSACHUSETTS REVIEW, Memorial Hall, Univ. of Mass, Amherst, MA 01003, 413-545-2689
(ROWBOAT), c/o MFA Creative Writing Program, 452 Bartlett Hall, MA University, Amherst, MA 01003
VALLEY WOMEN'S VOICE, 321 Student Union, UMASS, Amherst, MA 01003, 413-545-2436
Amherst Writers & Artists Press, Inc., PO Box 1076, Amherst, MA 01004, 413-253-3307
Food For Thought Publications, PO Box 331, Amherst, MA 01004, 413-549-1114
Lynx House Press, PO Box 640, Amherst, MA 01004, 316-342-0755
PEREGRINE, PO Box 1076, Amherst, MA 01004
TRANSITIONS ABROAD: The Guide to Living, Learning, and Working Overseas, 18 Hulst Road, PO Box 334, Amherst, MA 01004, 413-256-0373
University of Massachusetts Press, Box 429, Amherst, MA 01004, 413-545-2217
Adastra Press, 101 Strong Street, Easthampton, MA 01027, 413-527-3324
Abundance Press, 70 Granby Heights, Granby, MA 01033, 413-467-2231
PARAGRAPH, Oat City Press, 1423 Northampton Street, Holyoke, MA 01040-1915, 413-533-8767
TRIVIA, A JOURNAL OF IDEAS, Box 606, North Amherst, MA 01059, 413-367-2254
Carnival Press, 351 Pleasant Street, Suite 277, Northampton, MA 01060
Benjamin Press, PO Box 112, Northampton, MA 01061
NEW ENGLAND ANTIQUES JOURNAL, Turley Publications, 4 Church Street, Ware, MA 01082, 413-967-3505
Little River Press, 10 Lowell Avenue, Westfield, MA 01085, 413-568-5598
POULTRY - A MAGAZINE OF VOICE, Box 4413, Springfield, MA 01101, 413-20435
Poultry, Inc., Box 4413, Springfield, MA 01101, 413-20435
DEAD OF NIGHT MAGAZINE, 916 Shaker Road #143, Longmeadow, MA 01106-2416
Mouvement Publications, 109 Forest Glen Road, Longmeadow, MA 01106, 607-272-2157
Wesley Press, English Department, Springfield College, Springfield, MA 01109
The Figures, 5 Castle Hill Avenue, Great Barrington, MA 01230-1552, 413-528-2552
Lindisfarne Press, PO Box 778, 195 Main Street, Great Barrington, MA 01230, 413-232-4377
Mad River Press, State Road, Richmond, MA 01254, 413-698-3184
Cottage Press, PO Box 1207, Stockbridge, MA 01262
OTISIAN DIRECTORY, PO Box 235, Williamstown, MA 01267-0235
THE PARTY'S OVER, PO Box 366, Williamstown, MA 01267
COMMUNITY ECONOMICS, 151 Montague City Road, Greenfield, MA 01301, 413-774-7956
Institute For Community Economics, 151 Montague City Road, Greenfield, MA 01301, 413-774-7956
JOURNAL OF COMPUTING IN HIGHER EDUCATION, PO Box 343, Ashfield, MA 01330, 413-628-3838
Paideia Publishers, PO Box 343, Ashfield, MA 01330
Millers River Publishing Co., Box 159, Athol, MA 01331, 617-249-7612
OSIRIS, Box 297, Deerfield, MA 01342
St. Bede's Publications, PO Box 545, Petersham, MA 01366, 508-724-3407
CASSIE'S EXPRESS, 112 Conway Street, So. Deerfield, MA 01373
Bookcraft, PO Box 605, Fiskdale, MA 01518-0605, 413-245-7459
THE BLOATED TICK, 24 Main Street, S. Grafton, MA 01560, 508-839-3221
Edgeworth & North Books, PO Box 812 West Side Station, Worcester, MA 01602-0812
Metacom Press, 1 Tahanto Road, Worcester, MA 01602-2523, 617-757-1683
ELDRITCH SCIENCE, 87-6 Park, Worcester, MA 01605
THE WORCESTER REVIEW, 6 Chatham Street, Worcester, MA 01609, 603-924-7342
Brick House Publishing Co., Inc., PO Box 2134, Acton, MA 01720, 508-635-9800
Artifact Press, Ltd., 900 Tanglewood Drive, Concord, MA 01742, 508-369-8933
CLIPS FROM BEAR'S HOME MOVIES, c/o Dancing Bear Productions, PO Box 733, Concord, MA 01742, 617-369-5592
Dancing Bear Productions, PO Box 733, Concord, MA 01742, 617-369-5592
Bliss Publishing Company, Inc., PO Box 920, Marlboro, MA 01752, 508-779-2827
Water Row Press, PO Box 438, Sudbury, MA 01776
WATER ROW REVIEW, PO Box 438, Sudbury, MA 01776
West of Boston, PO Box 2, Cochituate Station, Wayland, MA 01778
AIRPORT POCKET GUIDE UNITED STATES EDITION, 67 S. Bedford Street, Ste 400W, Burlington, MA 01803-5166
THE LONG STORY, 11 Kingston Street, North Andover, MA 01845, 508-686-7638
Discovery Enterprises, Ltd., 134 Middle Street, Suite 210, Lowell, MA 01852, 508-459-1720; fax 508-937-5779
Ithaca Press, PO Box 853, Lowell, MA 01853
Loom Press, Box 1394, Lowell, MA 01853
THE RUGGING ROOM BULLETIN, 10 Sawmill Drive, PO Box 824, Westford, MA 01886
Lighthouse Press, 50 Evans Road, Marblehead, MA 01945, 617-631-6416
Micah Publications, 255 Humphrey St, Marblehead, MA 01945, 617-631-7601
SOUNDINGS EAST, English Dept., Salem State College, Salem, MA 01970, 508-741-6000
Manifest Press, PO Box 2103, S. Hamilton, MA 01982, 508-468-3815
APPALACHIA, 5 Joy Street, Boston, MA 02108, 617-523-0636
Appalachian Mountain Club Books, 5 Joy Street, Boston, MA 02108, 617-523-0636
Beacon Press, 25 Beacon Street, Boston, MA 02108, 617-742-2110
Walter H. Baker Company (Baker's Plays), 100 Chauncy St., Boston, MA 02111, 617-482-1280
BOSTON REVIEW, 33 Harrison Avenue, Boston, MA 02111-2008, 617-350-5353
THE DROOD REVIEW OF MYSTERY, Box 8872, Boston, MA 02114, 617-232-0411
THE EUGENE O'NEILL REVIEW, Department of English, Suffolk University, Boston, MA 02114, 617-573-8272
NORTHEASTARTS MAGAZINE, J.F.K. Station, PO Box 6061, Boston, MA 02114
Sigo Press, PO Box 8748, Boston, MA 02114-0037, 617-523-2321
THE NEW ENGLAND QUARTERLY, 243 Meserve Hall, Northeastern University, Boston, MA 02115, 617-437-2734
The New England Quarterly, Inc., 243 Meserve Hall, Northeastern University, Boston, MA 02115, 617-437-2734
South End Press, 116 St. Botolph Street, Boston, MA 02115, 617-266-0629
D.B.A. Books, 323 Beacon Street, Boston, MA 02116, 617-262-0411
PLOUGHSHARES, Emerson College, 100 Beacon Street, Boston, MA 02116, 617-578-8753

Alyson Publications, Inc., 40 Plympton Street, Boston, MA 02118, 617-542-5679
BAY WINDOWS, 1523 Washington Street, Boston, MA 02118, 617-266-6670, X211
Harvard Common Press, 535 Albany Street, Boston, MA 02118, 617-423-5803
Good Gay Poets Press, Box 277, Astor Station, Boston, MA 02123
QUIMBY, PO Box 281, Astor Station, Boston, MA 02123, 617-723-5360
Quimby Archives, PO Box 281, Astor Station, Boston, MA 02123, 617-723-5360
Innerer Klang, 7 Sherman Street, Charlestown, MA 02129
SISYPHUS, 8 Asticou Road, Boston, MA 02130, 617-983-5291
SOJOURNER, THE WOMEN'S FORUM, 42 Seaverns Avenue, Jamaica Plain, MA 02130-1109, 617-524-0415
AMERICAN LIVING, PO Box 901, Allston, MA 02134, 617-522-7782
KOOKS MAGAZINE, PO Box 953, Allston, MA 02134
Out-Of-Kontrol Data Institute, PO Box 953, Allston, MA 02134
Primal Publishing, 107 Brighton Avenue, Allston, MA 02134, 617-787-0203
SINGLES ALMANAC, 138 Brighton Avenue #209, Boston, MA 02134, 617-254-8810
Eidos, PO Box 96, Boston, MA 02137, 617-262-0096
EIDOS: Erotic Entertainment for Women, Men, & Couples, PO Box 96, Boston, MA 02137, 617-262-0096
Basement Graphics, 37 Wendell Street, Cambridge, MA 02138, 617-868-0685
Cultural Survival, Inc., 53-A Church Street, Cambridge, MA 02138, 617-495-2562
CULTURAL SURVIVAL QUARTERLY, 53-A Church Street, Cambridge, MA 02138, 617-495-2562
DAEDALUS, Journal of the American Academy of Arts and Sciences, American Academy of Arts and Sciences, 136
   Irving Street, Cambridge, MA 02138, 617-491-2600
GET STUPID, 25 Grant Street, Cambridge, MA 02138, 617-661-1738
THE HARVARD ADVOCATE, 21 South St., Cambridge, MA 02138, 617-495-0737
HARVARD WOMEN'S LAW JOURNAL, Publications Center, Harvard Law School, Cambridge, MA 02138, (617)
   495-3726
JLA Publications, A Division Of Jeffrey Lant Associates, Inc., 50 Follen Street #507, Suite 507, Cambridge, MA 02138,
   617-547-6372
Zoland Books, 384 Huron Avenue, Cambridge, MA 02138, 617-864-6252; FAX 617-661-4998
THE ARK, 35 Highland Avenue, Cambridge, MA 02139-1015, 617-547-0852
The Ark, 35 Highland Avenue, Cambridge, MA 02139, 617-547-0852
Political Research Associates, 678 Massachusetts Avenue, Suite 205, Cambridge, MA 02139, 671-661-9313
Alice James Books, 33 Richdale Avenue, Cambridge, MA 02140, 617-354-1408
GROWING WITHOUT SCHOOLING, 2269 Massachusetts Avenue, Cambridge, MA 02140, 617-864-3100
Holt Associates, Inc., 2269 Massachusetts Avenue, Cambridge, MA 02140, 617-864-3100
PEACEWORK, 2161 Massachusetts Avenue, Cambridge, MA 02140, 617-661-6130
THE DRAMA REVIEW, MIT Press Journals, 55 Hayward, Cambridge, MA 02142, 617-253-2889
HOBO STEW REVIEW, 2 Eliot Street #1, Somerville, MA 02143
RADICAL AMERICA, 1 Summer Street, Somerville, MA 02143, 617-628-6585
BOSTON LITERARY REVIEW, PO Box 357, West Somerville, MA 02144
Zephyr Press, 13 Robinson Street, Somerville, MA 02145
Hermes House Press, Inc., 52 Lanark Rd, Brookline, MA 02146-1844, 617-566-9766
Branden Publishing Company, 17 Station Street, Box 843, Brookline Village, MA 02147, 617-734-2045; FAX
   617-734-2046
PENGUIN DIP, 94 Eastern Avenue #1, Malden, MA 02148
KELTICA: THE INTER-CELTIC JOURNAL, 96 Marguerite Avenue, Waltham, MA 02154, 617-899-2204
Story County Books, 155 Winthrop Street #2, Medford, MA 02155
LEGAL INFORMATION MANAGEMENT INDEX, Legal Information Services, P.O. Box 67, Newton Highlands, MA
   02161-0067, 508-443-4798
Arts End Books, Box 162, Newton, MA 02168
NOSTOC, Box 162, Newton, MA 02168
WIN NEWS, 187 Grant Street, Lexington, MA 02173, 617-862-9431
THE CIVIL WAR NEWS, PO Box C, Arlington, MA 02174-0001, 617-646-2010
THE NEW RENAISSANCE, An International Magazine of Ideas & Opinions, Emphasizing Literature & The Arts, 9 Heath
   Road, Arlington, MA 02174
STORIES, PO Box 1467, Arlington, MA 02174-0022
AAUG Press, 556 Trapelo Road, Belmont, MA 02178, (617) 484-5483
ARAB STUDIES QUARTERLY, 556 Trapelo Road, Belmont, MA 02178, (617) 484-5483
MIDEAST MONITOR, 556 Trapelo Road, Belmont, MA 02178, (617) 484-5483
THE WOMEN'S REVIEW OF BOOKS, Wellesley College, Center For Research On Women, Wellesley, MA 02181,
   617-431-1453
American Family Foundation, PO Box 336, Weston, MA 02193, 617-893-0930
CULT OBSERVER, PO Box 336, Weston, MA 02193, 617-893-0930
CULTIC STUDIES JOURNAL, PO Box 336, Weston, MA 02193, 617-893-0930
Mockingbird Press, PO Box 776, Needham Heights, MA 02194, 617-455-8940
American Poets In Profile Series, PO Box 2764, Boston, MA 02208
Ford-Brown & Co., Publishers, PO Box 2764, Boston, MA 02208-2764
Thunder City Press, PO Box 2764, Boston, MA 02208
Union Park Press, PO Box 2737, Boston, MA 02208
AGNI, Boston Univ-Creative Writing Program, 236 Bay State Road, Boston, MA 02215, 617-353-5389
FAG RAG, Box 15331, Kenmore Station, Boston, MA 02215, 617-426-4469
NUCLEAR TIMES, 401 Commonwealth Avenue, Boston, MA 02215, 617-266-1193
PARTISAN REVIEW, 236 Bay State Road, Boston, MA 02215, 617-353-4260
VIEWS: The Journal of Photography in New England, 602 Commonwealth Avenue, Boston, MA 02215
Blue Crane Books, PO Box 291, Cambridge, MA 02238, 617-926-8585
Broken Mirrors Press, Box 473, Cambridge, MA 02238
Health Alert Press, PO Box 2060, Cambridge, MA 02238, 617-497-4190
UNDERGROUND SURREALIST MAGAZINE, Underground Surrealist Studio, PO Box 2565, Cambridge, MA 02238,
   617-891-9569

WOMAN OF POWER, PO Box 827, Cambridge, MA 02238-0827, 617-625-7885
Yellow Moon Press, PO Box 1316, Cambridge, MA 02238-0001, 617-776-2230
FORCED EXPOSURE, PO Box 1611, Waltham, MA 02254, 617-924-3923
IMMANENT FACE, PO Box 492 New Town Branch, Boston, MA 02258
AMERICAN POP, 154 Woodland Drive, Hanover, MA 02339, 617-982-9567
Jones River Press, 20 Middle Street, Plymouth, MA 02360, 508-747-3899
MARTHA'S VINEYARD MAGAZINE, PO Box 66, Edgartown, MA 02539, 508-627-4311
Woods Hole Press, PO Box 44, Woods Hole, MA 02543, 508-548-9600
Great Point Press, Commercial Wharf, Nantucket Island, MA 02554, (617) 228-6566
SANDSCRIPT, c/o Lunn, 25 Harvard Street, Hyannis, MA 02601, 617-362-6078
Cape Cod Writers Inc, Box 333, Cummaquid, MA 02637
PROVINCETOWN ARTS, 650 Commercial Street, Provincetown, MA 02657, 508-487-3167

MICHIGAN

LIGHTWORKS MAGAZINE, PO Box 1202, Birmingham, MI 48012-1202, 313-626-8026
MIRAGE, Box 75, Clawson, MI 48017, 313-585-0006
WITNESS, 31000 Northwestern Hwy, Suite 200, Farmington Hills, MI 48018, 313-626-1110
TANDAVA, PO Box 689, East Detroit, MI 48021
Spelman Publishing, Inc., 26941 Pebblestone Road, Southfield, MI 48034-3333, FAX 313-355-3686
FROG GONE REVIEW, PO Box 46308, Mt. Clemens, MI 48046, 313-263-3399
JOURNAL OF SOUTH ASIAN LITERATURE, Center for International Programs, Oakland University, Rochester, MI 48063, 313-370-2154
Ridgeway Press, PO Box 120, Roseville, MI 48066
X MAGAZINE, PO Box 1077, Royal Oak, MI 48068, 313-548-9929
Poetic Page, PO Box 71192, Madison Heights, MI 48071-0192, 313-548-0865
POETIC PAGE, PO Box 71192, Madison Heights, MI 48071-0192, 313-548-0865
EAP DIGEST, Performance Resource Press, Inc., 1863 Technology Drive, Suite 200, Troy, MI 48083-4244, 313-588-7733; fax 313-588-6633
Anderson Press, 706 West Davis, Ann Arbor, MI 48103, 313-995-0125; 994-6182
NOTUS NEW WRITING, OtherWind Press, Inc., 2420 Walter Drive, Ann Arbor, MI 48103, 313-665-0703
Otherwind, 2420 Walter Drive, Ann Arbor, MI 48103, 313-665-0703
RIPPLES, 1426 Las Vegas, Ann Arbor, MI 48103
Shining Waters Press, 1426 Las Vegas, Ann Arbor, MI 48103
Falling Water Press, 213 South Main, Ann Arbor, MI 48104, 313-747-9810
Pebble Press, 1313 N. Main Street, Ann Arbor, MI 48104-1044, 313-665-7119
Pedagogic Press, 317 S. Division, Suite 92, Ann Arbor, MI 48104, 313-668-4948
CUTTING EDGE QUARTERLY, PO Box 3430, Ann Arbor, MI 48106, 313-995-8637
Pierian Press, PO Box 1808, Ann Arbor, MI 48106
REFERENCE SERVICES REVIEW, PO Box 1808, Ann Arbor, MI 48106, 313-434-5530
SERIALS REVIEW, PO Box 1808, Ann Arbor, MI 48106, 313-434-5530
SINCERE SINGLES, PO Box 1719, Ann Arbor, MI 48106, 313-476-6110
UMI Research Press, 300 North Zeeb Road, Ann Arbor, MI 48106, 313-973-9821
Aatec Publications, PO Box 7119, Ann Arbor, MI 48107, 313-995-1470
Axiom Information Resources, PO Box 8015, Ann Arbor, MI 48107, 313-761-4842
DuReve Publications, PO Box 7772, Ann Arbor, MI 48107, 313-662-3801
EDUCATION DIGEST, PO Box 8623, Ann Arbor, MI 48107, 313-769-1211
ENTRY, PO Box 7648, Ann Arbor, MI 48107, 313-663-4686
LEADERSHIP DIRECTIONS, Box 7715, Ann Arbor, MI 48107, 313-663-0889
MOTORBOOTY MAGAZINE, PO Box 7944, Ann Arbor, MI 48107
The Neither/Nor Press, Box 7774, Ann Arbor, MI 48107
North American Students of Cooperation, Box 7715, Ann Arbor, MI 48107, 313-663-0889
The Olivia and Hill Press, Inc., PO Box 7396, Ann Arbor, MI 48107, 313-663-0235; FAX 313-663-0235
Prakken Publications, PO Box 8623, Ann Arbor, MI 48107, 313-769-1211
PREVIEW: Professional and Reference Literature Review, Mountainside Publishing, Inc., PO Box 8330, Ann Arbor, MI 48107, 313-662-3925, FAX 313-662-4450
SCHOOL SHOP, PO Box 8623, Ann Arbor, MI 48107, 313-769-1211
IM-Press, 3030 Chelsea Circle, Ann Arbor, MI 48108, (313) 973-7338
MICHIGAN FEMINIST STUDIES, 234 W. Engineering, Women's Studies, University of Michigan, Ann Arbor, MI 48109
MICHIGAN QUARTERLY REVIEW, 3032 Rackham Bldg., University of Michigan, Ann Arbor, MI 48109, 313-764-9265
Michigan Romance Studies, Department of Romance Language, MLB, University of MI, Ann Arbor, MI 48109, 313-764-5373
RACKHAM JOURNAL OF THE ARTS AND HUMANITIES (RaJAH), 411 Mason Hall, University of Michigan, Ann Arbor, MI 48109, 313-763-2351
L.G.L.C. NEWSLETTER, PO Box 447, Chelsea, MI 48118, 313-475-9792
Libertarians for Gay and Lesbian Concerns (LGLC), PO Box 447, Chelsea, MI 48118-0953, 313-475-9792
Jayell Enterprises Inc., PO Box 2616, Fort Dearborn Station, Dearborn, MI 48123, 313-565-9687
AMATEUR COMPUTERIST, PO Box 4344, Dearborn, MI 48126, 313-278-0246
THE WIRE, 7320 Colonial, Dearborn Heights, MI 48127, 313-995-1171
Endeavor Publishing, 30064 Annapolis Circle, Inkster, MI 48141, 313-729-7836
THE MAC GUFFIN, Schoolcraft College, 18600 Haggerty Road, Livonia, MI 48152, 313-462-4400, ext. 5292
JOURNAL OF NARRATIVE TECHNIQUE, Eastern Michigan University, Ypsilanti, MI 48197, 313-487-0151
SULFUR, 210 Washtenaw, Ypsilanti, MI 48197-2526, 313-483-9787
FIFTH ESTATE, 4632 Second Avenue, Detroit, MI 48201, 313-831-6800
POETRY RESOURCE CENTER OF MICHIGAN (PRC) NEWSLETTER & CALENDAR, 111 East Kirby, Detroit, MI 48202, 313-399-6163
Harlo Press, 50 Victor, Detroit, MI 48203
THE SOUNDS OF POETRY, 8761 Avis, Detroit, MI 48209, 843-8478

STRUGGLE: A Magazine of Proletarian Revolutionary Literature, PO Box 13261, Harper Station, Detroit, MI 48213-0261
PANDORA, 2844 Grayson, Ferndale, MI 48220
Lotus Press, Inc., PO Box 21607, Detroit, MI 48221, 313-861-1280
MOVING OUT: A Feminist Literary & Arts Journal, PO Box 21249, Detroit, MI 48221
Asian Studies Center, Michigan State University, Michigan State University, Oakland University, East Lansing, MI 48224
ALL OF THE ABOVE, PO Box 36023, Grosse Pointe, MI 48236-0023
Moonbeam Publications, Inc., 18530 Mack Avenue, Grosse Pointe, MI 48236, 313-884-5255
The Lunchroom Press, PO Box 36027, Grosse Pointe Farms, MI 48236
MENU, PO Box 36027, Grosse Pointe Farms, MI 48236
Stabur Press, Inc., 23301 Meadow Park, Redford, MI 48239, 313-535-0572
Katydid Books, c/o English Dept, Oakland University, Rochester, MI 48309-4401
HOWLING DOG, Parkville Publishing, 8419 Rhode Drive, Utica, MI 48317
SAUL BELLOW JOURNAL, 6533 Post Oak Drive, West Bloomfield, MI 48322
MINAS TIRITH EVENING-STAR, PO Box 373, Highland, MI 48357-0373, 313-887-4703
W.W. Publications, PO Box 373, Highland, MI 48357-0373, 313-887-4703
NEW PAGES: Access to Alternatives in Print, PO Box 438, Grand Blanc, MI 48439, 313-743-8055; 313-742-9583
New Pages Press, PO Box 438, Grand Blanc, MI 48439
Bamberger Books, PO Box 1126, Flint, MI 48501-1126, 313-232-5396
OLD TYME BASEBALL NEWS, 2447 Judd Road, Burton, MI 48529, 313-744-2102; 616-348-2967
Mayapple Press, PO Box 5473, Saginaw, MI 48603-0473
Inquiry Press, 1880 North Eastman, Midland, MI 48640-8838, 517-631-3350
GHOST DANCE: The International Quarterly of Experimental Poetry, 526 Forest, E. Lansing, MI 48823
Ghost Dance Press, 526 Forest, E. Lansing, MI 48823
THE CENTENNIAL REVIEW, 312 Linton Hall, Mich. State Univ., E. Lansing, MI 48824-1044, 517-355-1905
Red Cedar Press, 325 Morrill Hall, Michigan State University, E. Lansing, MI 48824
RED CEDAR REVIEW, 325 Morrill Hall, Dept. of English, Mich. State Univ., E. Lansing, MI 48824, 517-355-9656
Years Press, Dept. of ATL, EBH, Michigan State Univ, E. Lansing, MI 48824-1033
Bennett & Kitchel, PO Box 4422, East Lansing, MI 48826
Grand River Press, PO Box 1342, East Lansing, MI 48826, (517) 332-8181
Poetry Magic Publications, 1630 Lake Drive, Haslett, MI 48840, 517-339-8754
WRITER'S VOICE, 1630 Lake Drive, Haslett, MI 48840, 517-339-8754
Gweetna Press, PO Box 106, Mt. Pleasant, MI 48858, 517-772-0139
HOOFSTRIKES NEWSLETTER, PO Box 106, Mt. Pleasant, MI 48858
Pennsylvania State University Press, Department of English, Central Michigan University, Mt. Pleasant, MI 48858, 517-774-3171
LANGUAGE ARTS JOURNAL OF MICHIGAN, Department of English, Central Michigan University, Mt. Pleasant, MI 48859
SHAW. THE ANNUAL OF BERNARD SHAW STUDIES, Department of English, Central Michigan University, Mt. Pleasant, MI 48859, 517-774-3171
MARKETS ABROAD, Strawberry Media, Inc., 2460 Lexington Drive, Owosso, MI 48867, 517-725-9027
Flower Press, 10332 Shaver Road, Kalamazoo, MI 49002, 616-327-0108
PASSAGES NORTH, Kalamazoo College, 1200 Academy Street, Kalamazoo, MI 49007, 616-383-5700; 616-383-8473
Rarach Press, 1005 Oakland Drive, Kalamazoo, MI 49008, 616-388-5631
RIVERRUN, Glen Oaks Community College, 62249 Shimmel Road, Centreville, MI 49032-9719, 616-467-9945 ext. 277
THE LETTER PARADE, PO Box 52, Comstock, MI 49041, 349-8817
Blue Mouse Studio, 26829 37th Street, Gobles, MI 49055, 616-628-5160
CLUBHOUSE, Your Story Hour, PO Box 15, Berrien Springs, MI 49103, (616) 471-9009
LEGACIES IN TIME, PO Box 1074, Jackson, MI 49204, 517-782-1075
Proving Grounds International, Inc., PO Box 1074, Jackson, MI 49204, 517-783-4243
OFF MAIN STREET, Ferris State College, Languages & Literature Dept., Big Rapids, MI 49307, (616) 796-8762
Betty Boyink Publishing, 818 Sheldon Road, Grand Haven, MI 49417, 616-842-3304
BIG SCREAM, 2782 Dixie S.W., Grandville, MI 49418, 616-531-1442
Nada Press, 2782 Dixie S.W., Grandville, MI 49418, 616-531-1442
Traveler's Health Publications, Inc., PO Box 2737, Grand Rapids, MI 49501, 800-735-8941; 616-942-1271
Wm.B. Eerdmans Publishing Co., 255 Jefferson Avenue, S.E., Grand Rapids, MI 49503, 616-459-4591
AVALOKA: A Journal of Traditional Religion and Culture, 249 Maynard NW, Grand Rapids, MI 49504
Gearhead Press, 565 Lincoln, Northwest, Grand Rapids, MI 49504, 459-7861 or 459-4577
THE ESCHEW OBFUSCATION REVIEW, 3922 Monte Carlo, Kentwood, MI 49512, 616-942-0056
Pen-Dec Press, 3922 Monte Carlo, Kentwood, MI 49512, 616-942-0056
Phanes Press, PO Box 6114, Grand Rapids, MI 49516, 616-281-1224
THE BANNER, 2850 Kalamazoo SE, Grand Rapids, MI 49560, (616) 241-1691
CRC Publications, 2850 Kalamazoo SE, Grand Rapids, MI 49560
THE DICK E. BIRD NEWS, PO Box 377, Acme, MI 49610, 800-255-5128
ARNOLD ANCESTRY, PO Box 184, Grawn, MI 49637, 616-276-6745
CARROLL CABLES, PO Box 184, Grawn, MI 49637, 616-276-6745
EWING EXCHANGE, PO Box 184, Grawn, MI 49637
FERGUSON FILES, PO Box 184, Grawn, MI 49637, 616-276-6745
GATHERING GIBSONS, PO Box 184, Grawn, MI 49637, 616-276-6745
Kinseeker Publications, PO Box 184, Grawn, MI 49637, 616-276-6745
NORTON NOTES, PO Box 184, Grawn, MI 49637, 616-276-6745
WANDERING WOLFS, PO Box 184, Grawn, MI 49637, 616-276-6745
ZINGSHEIM TIMES, PO Box 184, Grawn, MI 49637, 616-276-6745
Smiling Dog Press, 9875 Fritz, Maple City, MI 49664, 616-334-3695
Sylvan Books, PO Box 101, Maple City, MI 49664-0101, 616-228-6239
Avery Color Studios, Star Route, Box 275, AuTrain, MI 49806, 906-892-8251

MINNESOTA

Black Hat Press, Box 12, Goodhue, MN 55027, 612-923-4590

RAG MAG, Box 12, Goodhue, MN 55027, 612-923-4590
ST. CROIX REVIEW, Box 244, Stillwater, MN 55082, 612-439-7190
Majority, Inc., PO Box 2037, Saint Paul, MN 55102-0037, 612-224-3879
River Basin Publishing Co., 403 Laurel Avenue, St Paul, MN 55102, 612-291-0980
Minnesota Ink, Inc., 27 Empire Drive, Saint Paul, MN 55103-1861, 612-225-1306
WRITERS' JOURNAL, 27 Empire Drive, Saint Paul, MN 55103-1861, 612-225-1306
Michael E. Coughlin, Publisher, 1985 Selby Avenue, St Paul, MN 55104, 612-646-8917
THE DANDELION, 1985 Selby Ave, St Paul, MN 55104, 612-646-8917
Men & Women of Letters, 1672 Wellesley Avenue, St. Paul, MN 55105-2006, 612-699-1594
Ally Press, 524 Orleans St., St. Paul, MN 55107, 612-227-1567
KIDSCIENCE, 2215 Doswell Avenue, St. Paul, MN 55108
Artek Press, Inc., 3474 Ebba Street, White Bear Lake, MN 55110, 612-777-4829
ARTPAPER, 2402 University Avenue W., Ste. 206, Saint Paul, MN 55114-1701
Dos Tejedoras Fiber Arts Publications, PO Box 14238, St. Paul, MN 55114-0238, 612-646-7445
The Graywolf Press, 2402 University Avenue #203, St. Paul, MN 55114, 612-641-0077
Blue Sky Marketing, Inc., PO Box 21583, Saint Paul, MN 55121-0583, 612-456-5602
Marquette Books, 1037 Arbogast Street, Shoreview, MN 55126-8103
MINNESOTA LITERATURE, 1 Nord Circle, St. Paul, MN 55127, 612-483-3904
Pogo Press, Incorporated, 4 Cardinal Lane, St. Paul, MN 55127, 612-483-4692
THE LLEWELLYN NEW TIMES, PO Box 64383, St. Paul, MN 55164, 612-291-1970
Llewellyn Publications, PO Box 64383, St. Paul, MN 55164, 612-291-1970
Yes International Publishers, PO Box 75032, St. Paul, MN 55175-0032, 612-293-8094
Applied Publishing, PO Box 672, Chanhassen, MN 55317, 612-470-1837
Sang Froid Press, PO Box 272, Excelsior, MN 55331, 612-470-9986
HENNEPIN COUNTY LIBRARY CATALOGING BULLETIN, 12601 Ridgedale Drive, Secretary, Technical Services
   Division, Hennepin County Library, Minnetonka, MN 55343-5648, 612-541-8562
Non-Stop Books, PO Box 1354, Minnetonka, MN 55345-0354
Tessera Publishing, Inc., 9561 Woodridge Circle, Eden Prairie, MN 55347, 612-941-5053
Paul Maravelas, 15155 Co. Rd. 32, Mayer, MN 55360, 612-657-2237
The Book Peddlers, 18326 Minnetonka Boulevard, Deephaven, MN 55391, 612-475-3527
Point Publications, 3701 Shoreline Drive, Wayzata, MN 55391
Coffee House Press, 27 N. 4th Street, #400, Minneapolis, MN 55401, 612-338-0125
FREE SPIRIT: NEWS AND VIEWS ON GROWING UP, 400 First Avenue North, Suite 616, Minneapolis, MN 55401,
   612-338-2068
Free Spirit Publishing Inc., 400 First Avenue North, Suite 616, Minneapolis, MN 55401, 612-338-2068
NEW NORTH ARTSCAPE, 420 North 5th Street #990, Minneapolis, MN 55401-1378, 338-4974
New Rivers Press, Inc., 420 North 5th Street #910, Minneapolis, MN 55401, 612-339-7114
Pentagram Press, 212 North Second Street, Minneapolis, MN 55401, 612-340-9821
Redpath Press, 420 North 5th Street, Ste. 710, Minneapolis, MN 55401, (612) 332-1278
JAMES WHITE REVIEW; A Gay Men's Literary Quarterly, PO Box 3356, Traffic Station, Minneapolis, MN 55403,
   612-291-2913
Milkweed Editions, Box 3226, Minneapolis, MN 55403, 612-332-3192
THE UTNE READER, The Fawkes Building, 1624 Harmon Place, Minneapolis, MN 55403, 612-338-5040
Midwest Villages & Voices, 3220 Tenth Avenue South, Minneapolis, MN 55407, (612) 224-7687
MSRRT NEWSLETTER, 4645 Columbus Avenue South, Minneapolis, MN 55407, 612-541-8572; 823-1214
SteelDragon Press, Box 7253, Minneapolis, MN 55407, 612-721-6076
Thompson and Co. Inc., 4600 Longfellow Avenue South, Minneapolis, MN 55407-3638, 612-331-3963
THE EVERGREEN CHRONICLES, PO Box 8939, Minneapolis, MN 55408-8939
NEW UNIONIST, 621 West Lake Street, Rm 210, Minneapolis, MN 55408, 612-823-2593
PROFANE EXISTENCE, PO Box 8722, Minneapolis, MN 55408, 612-377-5269
SEZ: A Multi-Racial Journal of Poetry & People's Culture, PO Box 8803, Minneapolis, MN 55408, 612-822-3488
Shadow Press, U.S.A., PO Box 8803, Minneapolis, MN 55408, 612-822-3488
Culpepper Press, 2901 Fourth Street SE, Minneapolis, MN 55414, 617-378-2116
THE HEADWATERS REVIEW, PO Box 13682, Dinkytown Station, Minneapolis, MN 55414
MINNE HA! HA!, PO Box 14009, Minneapolis, MN 55414, 612-729-7687
Minne Ha! Ha!, PO Box 14009, Minneapolis, MN 55414
North Stone Press, PO Box 14098, Minneapolis, MN 55414
THE NORTH STONE REVIEW, PO Box 14098, Minneapolis, MN 55414
SING HEAVENLY MUSE! WOMEN'S POETRY AND PROSE, PO Box 13320, Minneapolis, MN 55414
STREAM LINES, MN JOURNAL OF CREATIVE WRITING, 207 Lind Hall, 207 Church Street, SE, Minneapolis, MN
   55414, 612-625-6872
Pathway Books, 700 Parkview Terrace, Golden Valley, MN 55416, 612-377-1521
Glenhurst Publications, Inc., Central Community Center, 6300 Walker Street, St. Louis Park, MN 55416, 612-925-3632
ARTPOLICE, 5228 43rd Avenue S, Minneapolis, MN 55417-2210, 612-331-1721
International Childbirth Education Association, Inc., PO Box 20048, Minneapolis, MN 55420-0048
The Place In The Woods, 3900 Glenwood Avenue, Golden Valley, MN 55422, 612-374-2120
READ, AMERICA!, 3900 Glenwood Avenue, Golden Valley, MN 55422, 612-374-2120
Inkling Publications, Inc., 824 Winnetka Avenue South, Minneapolis, MN 55426
1 BIT SHOE, 2760 Louisiana Court #9, St. Louis Park, MN 55426
MIP Company, PO Box 27484, Minneapolis, MN 55427
Studia Hispanica Editors, Attn: Luis Ramos-Garcia, 5626 W. Bavarian Pass, Fridley, MN 55432, 612-574-9460
St. John's Publishing, Inc., 6824 Oaklawn Avenue, Edina, MN 55435, (612) 920-9044
Johnson Institute, 7151 Metro Boulevard #250, Minneapolis, MN 55435, 612-944-0511
Balmy Press, Box 972, Minneapolis, MN 55440, 612-874-8108
CompCare Publishers, 2415 Annapolis Lane, Minneapolis, MN 55441, 612-559-4800; 800-328-3330
LIFTOUTS, 1503 Washington Avenue South, Minneapolis, MN 55454, 612-333-0031
Preludium Publishers, 1503 Washington Avenue South, Minneapolis, MN 55454, 612-333-0031
HURRICANE ALICE, 207 Church St. S.E., Minneapolis, MN 55455

THE FOOTLOOSE LIBRARIAN, Box 972, Minneapolis, MN 55458, 612-874-8108
Women's Times Publishing, Box 215, Grand Marais, MN 55604, 707-829-0558
Latin American Press, 103 Sixth Avenue North, Virginia, MN 55792
Holy Cow! Press, PO Box 3170, Mount Royal Station, Duluth, MN 55803
Whole Person Associates Inc., 1702 East Jefferson Street, PO Box 3151, Duluth, MN 55803, 218-728-4077
Pfeifer-Hamilton, 1702 E. Jefferson Street, Duluth, MN 55812, (218) 728-6807
POETRY MOTEL, 1619 Jefferson, Duluth, MN 55812
Suburban Wilderness Press, 1619 Jefferson, Duluth, MN 55812
LAKE SUPERIOR MAGAZINE, Lake Superior Port Cities, Inc., PO Box 16417, Duluth, MN 55816-0417, 218-722-5002
THE WOLSKE'S BAY STAR, RR 1 Box 186-A, Caledonia, MN 55921-9801
GREAT RIVER REVIEW, 211 W 7th, Winona, MN 55987
MANKATO POETRY REVIEW, Box 53, Mankato State University, Mankato, MN 56001, 507-389-5511
ARABIAN HORSE TIMES, Route 3, End of Eighth Street N.E., Waseca, MN 56093, (507) 835-3204
Knollwood Publishing Company, 505 Monongalia Avenue SW, Willmar, MN 56201, 612-382-6276
SUNDOG, Route 1, Box 57, Chokio, MN 56221, 612-324-7456
Spoon River Poetry Press, PO Box 6, Granite Falls, MN 56241
SPOON RIVER QUARTERLY, PO Box 6, Granite Falls, MN 56241
Plains Press, Southwest State University, Marshall, MN 56258, 507-537-6463
North Star Press of St. Cloud, Inc., PO Box 451, St. Cloud, MN 56302, 612-253-1636
STUDIO ONE, College of St. Benedict, St. Joseph, MN 56374
Ox Head Press, Rt. 3, Box 136, Browerville, MN 56438, 612-594-2454
LITTLE FREE PRESS, Route 1, Box 102, Cushing, MN 56443
LOONFEATHER: A magazine of poetry, short prose, and graphics, Bemidji Community Arts Center, 426 Bemidji Avenue, Bemidji, MN 56601, 218-751-4869; 243-2402
Loonfeather Press, 426 Bemidji Avenue, Bemidji, MN 56601, 218-751-4869; 243-2402
Truly Fine Press, PO Box 891, Bemidji, MN 56601
Monographics Press, Route 1, Box 81, Puposky, MN 56667, 218-243-2402

MISSISSIPPI

The Guild Bindery Press, Inc., PO Box 1827, Oxford, MS 38655, 601-234-2596
SOUTHERN READER, PO Box 1827, Oxford, MS 38655, 601-234-2596
Yoknapatawpha Press, Box 248, Oxford, MS 38655, 601-234-0909
MISSISSIPPI REVIEW, Box 5144, Southern Station, Hattiesburg, MS 39406-5144, 601-266-4321
SOUTHERN QUARTERLY: A Journal of the Arts in the South, Box 5078, Southern Station, USM, Hattiesburg, MS 39406-5078, 601-266-4370
NEW DAY PUBLICATIONS, Route 4, Box 10, Eupora, MS 39744, 258-2935

MISSOURI

Cornerstone Press, PO Box 388, Arnold, MO 63010-0388
IMAGE MAGAZINE, PO Box 388, Arnold, MO 63010-0388
Singing Bone Press, 2318 Albion Place, Saint Louis, MO 63104, 314-865-2789
The Patrice Press, 1701 South 8th Street, St. Louis, MO 63104-0519, 314-436-3242
RIVER STYX, #14 South Euclid, St. Louis, MO 63108, 314-361-0043
TAPAS, 4017A Shenandoah, St. Louis, MO 63110, 314-772-8237
WEBSTER REVIEW, 470 East Lockwood, Webster University, Webster Groves, MO 63119, 314-432-2657
Cave Books, 756 Harvard Avenue, Saint Louis, MO 63130, 314-862-7646
WORKERS' DEMOCRACY, PO Box 24115, St. Louis, MO 63130, 314-727-8554 (nites)
ST. LOUIS JOURNALISM REVIEW, 8380 Olive Boulevard, St. Louis, MO 63132, 314-991-1699
SECRETARIAL/OFFICE SERVICES QUARTERLY, 1421 Willow Brook Cove #4, St. Louis, MO 63146, 314-567-3636
CHARITON REVIEW, Northeast Missouri State University, Kirksville, MO 63501, 816-785-4499
Chariton Review Press, Northeast Missouri State University, Kirksville, MO 63501, 816-785-4499
Hickman Systems - New Age Books, 4 Woodland Lane, Kirksville, MO 63501, 816-665-1836
Ishtar Press, Inc., Lang. & Lit. Division, Northeast Missouri State Univ., Kirksville, MO 63501, 816-785-4185
PAINTBRUSH: A Journal of Poetry, Translations & Letters, Language & Literature Divison, Northeast Missouri State Univ., Kirksville, MO 63501, 816-785-4185/4481
Rabeth Publishing Company, Box 171, Kirksville, MO 63501, 816-665-8209
ALURA, PO Box 44, Novinger, MO 63559, 816-488-5216
COMMUNITIES, Route 1, Box 155, Rutledge, MO 63563, 816-883-5543
THE CAPE ROCK, English Dept, Southeast Missouri State University, Cape Girardeau, MO 63701, 314-651-2500
OVERLAND JOURNAL, Oregon-California Trails Association, PO Box 1019, Independence, MO 64051-0519, 816-252-2276
THE INTERNATIONAL UNIVERSITY POETRY QUARTERLY, 1301 S. Noland Road, Independence, MO 64055, 816-461-3633
The International University Press, 1301 S. Noland Rd., Independence, MO 64055, 816-461-3633
American Press, PO Box 127, Odessa, MO 64076
ODESSA POETRY REVIEW, RR 1 Box 39, Odessa, MO 64076
Odessa Press, R.R. 1, Box 39, Odessa, MO 64076
BkMk Press, University of Missouri-Kansas City, 109 Scofield Hall, Kansas City, MO 64110, 276-2558
NEW LETTERS, University of Missouri, Kansas City, MO 64110, 816-235-1168
ASHES, PO Box 5987, Westport Station, Kansas City, MO 64111
THE BEAST, PO Box 5987, Westport Station, Kansas City, MO 64111
CROOKED ROADS, PO Box 32631, Kansas City, MO 64111
Howling Dog Press, PO Box 5987, Westport Station, Kansas City, MO 64111
STILETTO, PO Box 5987, Westport Station, Kansas City, MO 64111
Westport Publishers, Inc., 4050 Pennsylvania, Suite 310, Kansas City, MO 64111, 816-756-1490
Wheel of Fire Press, PO Box 32631, Kansas City, MO 64111
Helicon Nine Editions, Box 22412, Kansas City, MO 64113, 913-722-2999
Star Publications, PO Box 22534, Kansas City, MO 64113, 816-523-8228

IRISH FAMILY JOURNAL, Box 7575, Kansas City, MO 64116, 816-454-2410
O'Laughlin Press (Irish Genealogical Foundation), Box 7575, Kansas City, MO 64116, 816-454-2410
WONDER TIME, 6401 The Paseo, Kansas City, MO 64131, 816-333-7000
Sheed & Ward, PO Box 419492, Kansas City, MO 64141-6492, 800-444-8910
THE LAUREL REVIEW, Department of English, Northwest Missouri State University, Maryville, MO 64468, 816-562-1265
GreenTree Press, 3715 Beck Road, Bldg. C, St. Joseph, MO 64506, 816-233-4765; FAX 816-279-8787
Rama Publishing Co., PO Box 793, Carthage, MO 64836-0793, 417-358-1093
The Westphalia Press, 3749 Schott Road, Jefferson City, MO 65101-9028
REVIEW LA BOOCHE, 110 South Ninth, Columbia, MO 65201, 874-9519
Cityhill Publishing, 4600 Christian Fellowship Road, Columbia, MO 65203, (314) 445-8567
American Audio Prose Library (non-print), PO Box 842, Columbia, MO 65205, 314-443-0361/447-2275
ANARCHY: A JOURNAL OF DESIRE ARMED, PO Box 1446, Columbia, MO 65205-1446, 314-442-4352
DISC GOLF WORLD NEWS, Disc Golf World, PO Box 30011, Columbia, MO 65205, (314) 874-2981
AFRO-HISPANIC REVIEW, Romance Languages, Univ. of Missouri, 143 Arts & Science Building, Columbia, MO 65211, 314-882-2030
THE MISSOURI REVIEW, 1507 Hillcrest Hall, University of Missouri-Columbia, Columbia, MO 65211, 314-882-4474
Timberline Press, Rt. 1, Box 1434, Fulton, MO 65251, 314-642-5035
LOST GENERATION JOURNAL, Route 5 Box 134, Salem, MO 65560, 314-364-5900; 729-5669
DIE FAT PIGGY DIE, PO Box 134, Waynesville, MO 65583, 319-774-2822
WRITER'S GUIDELINES MAGAZINE, Box 608, Pittsburg, MO 65724
White Oak Press, PO Box 188, Reeds Spring, MO 65737, 417-272-3507
SOM Publishing, division of School of Metaphysics, HCR 1, Box 15, Windyville, MO 65783, 417-345-8411
THRESHOLDS JOURNAL, HCR 1, Box 15, Windyville, MO 65783, 417-345-8411
Nucleus Publications, Route 2, Box 49, Willow Springs, MO 65793
Jack October, 1313 South Jefferson Ave., Springfield, MO 65807

MONTANA

THE AZOREAN EXPRESS, PO Box 249, Big Timber, MT 59011
THE BADGER STONE CHRONICLES, PO Box 249, Big Timber, MT 59011
BLACK JACK & VALLEY GRAPEVINE, Box 249, Big Timber, MT 59011
THE BREAD AND BUTTER CHRONICLES, PO Box 249, Big Timber, MT 59011
HILL AND HOLLER, Box 249, Big Timber, MT 59011
Seven Buffaloes Press, Box 249, Big Timber, MT 59011
Council For Indian Education, 517 Rimrock Road, Billings, MT 59102, 406-252-7451
AERO SUN-TIMES, 44 N. Last Chance Gulch #9, Helena, MT 59601, 406-443-7272
American & World Geographic Publishing, PO Box 5630, Helena, MT 59601, 406-443-2842
Great Blue Graphics, 312 Clarke, Helena, MT 59601
Falcon Press Publishing Company, PO Box 1718, Helena, MT 59624, 406-942-6597; 800-582-2665
Editorial Review, 1009 Placer Street, Butte, MT 59701, 406-782-2546
CORONA, Dept. of Hist. & Phil., Montana State University, Bozeman, MT 59717, 406-994-5200
Outlaw Books, PO Box 4466, Bozeman, MT 59772, 406-586-7248
PERCEPTIONS, 1317 South Johnson Street, Missoula, MT 59801-4805, 406-543-5875
Mountain Press Publishing Co., P.O. Box 2399, Missoula, MT 59806, 406-728-1900
BIKEREPORT, PO Box 8308, Missoula, MT 59807, (406) 721-1776
CUTBANK, English Dept., University of Montana, Missoula, MT 59812
FIJACTIVIST, PO Box 59, Helmville, MT 59843, 406-793-5550
GHOST TOWN QUARTERLY, PO Box 714, Philipsburg, MT 59858, 406-859-3365
New Worlds Press, Box 1458, Kalispell, MT 59903, 406-756-7067

NEBRASKA

TRANS-MISSOURI ART VIEW, 1506 Harney Street, Omaha, NE 68102
PalmTree Publishers, PO Box 3787, Omaha, NE 68105, 402-345-1617
The Penumbra Press, 920 S. 38th Street, Omaha, NE 68105, 402-346-7344
The Nemo Press, 5119 Leavenworth Street, Omaha, NE 68106, 402-342-1545
Westchester House, 218 South 95 Street, Omaha, NE 68114
AMERICAN DANE, Danish Brotherhood in America, 3717 Harney Street, Omaha, NE 68131-3844, 402-341-5049
Abattoir Editions, Library Room 100, University of Nebraska, Omaha, NE 68182, 402-554-2787
THE NEBRASKA REVIEW, ASH 215, University of Nebraska-Omaha, Omaha, NE 68182-0324
Astonisher Press, PO Box 80635, Lincoln, NE 68501, 402-477-2800
Windflower Press, PO Box 82213, Lincoln, NE 68501
Black Oak Press, PO Box 4663, University Place Station, Lincoln, NE 68504
JOURNAL OF VISION REHABILITATION, 2440 'O' Street, Suite 202, Lincoln, NE 68510, 402-474-2676
Media Periodicals, 2440 'O' Street #202, Lincoln, NE 68510
Media Publishing, 2440 'O' Street, Suite 202, Lincoln, NE 68510
TECHNICALITIES, 2440 'O' Street, Suite 202, Lincoln, NE 68510-1125, 402-474-2676
Foundation Books, PO Box 29229, Lincoln, NE 68529, 402-466-4988
PEBBLE, Department of English, University of Nebraska-Lincoln, Lincoln, NE 68588, 402-826-4038
PRAIRIE SCHOONER, 201 Andrews Hall, Univ. of Nebraska, Lincoln, NE 68588-0334
THE NIHILISTIC REVIEW, PO Box 1074, S. Sioux City, NE 68776, 402-494-3110
Pessimism Press, Inc., PO Box 1074, S. Sioux City, NE 68776, 402-494-3110
Sandhills Press, 219 S 19th Street, Ord, NE 68862
Omega Cottonwood Press, PO Box 524, Alma, NE 68920-0524

NEVADA

PEGASUS, Pegasus Publishing, 525 Avenue B, Boulder City, NV 89005
Bristlecone Publications, 2405 Whirlaway, Las Vegas, NV 89108, 702-648-4710
Tambra Publishing, PO Box 14161, Las Vegas, NV 89114-4161, 702-876-4232; FAX 702-876-5252

Crystal Publishers, Inc., 4947 Orinda Court, Las Vegas, NV 89120, 702-434-3037
A Thousand Autumns Press, 760 Hermosa Palms, Las Vegas, NV 89123, 702-361-0676
The Family of God, PO Box 19571, Las Vegas, NV 89132, 702-795-8511
INTERIM, Department of English, University of Nevada, Las Vegas, Las Vegas, NV 89154, 702-739-3172
Crystal Press, Ltd., PO Box 215, Crystal Bay, NV 89402, 702-831-3846
Duck Down Press, PO Box 1047, Fallon, NV 89406
SCREE, PO Box 1047, Fallon, NV 89406, 702-423-6643
DHARMA COMBAT, PO Box 20593, Sun Valley, NV 89433
WOMAN POET, PO Box 60550, Reno, NV 89506, 702-972-1671
Women-in-Literature, Inc., PO Box 60550, Reno, NV 89506
Delta Publishing Company, 316 California Avenue #134, Reno, NV 89509, 702-329-9995
Nevada Publications, 4135 Badger Circle, Reno, NV 89509, 702-747-0800
The Builders Publishing Company, PO Box 2122, Oasis, NV 89835
THE BUILDERS QUARTERLY, PO Box 2122, Oasis, NV 89835

NEW HAMPSHIRE

EUROPA 1992, Wolfe Publishing, PO Box 7599, S. Station, Nashua, NH 03060, 603-888-0338
RISING STAR, Star/Sword Publications, 47 Byledge Road, Manchester, NH 03104, 603-623-9796
Igneus Press, 310 N. Amherst Road, Bedford, NH 03110, 603-472-3466
SPECTRUM—The Wholistic News Magazine, 61 Dutile Rd., Laconia, NH 03246, 603-528-4710
O.ARS, 21 Rockland Road, Weare, NH 03281, 603-529-1060
O.ARS, Inc., 21 Rockland Road, Weare, NH 03281, 603-529-1060
COLOR WHEEL, 4 Washington Court, Concord, NH 03301
700 Elves Press, 4 Washington Court, Concord, NH 03301
WOMENWISE, 38 South Main Street, Concord, NH 03301, 603-225-2739
BONE & FLESH, c/o Lester Hirsh, PO Box 349, Concord, NH 03302-0349
MONADNOCK GAY MEN, PO Box 1124, Keene, NH 03431, 603-357-5544
William L. Bauhan, Publisher, PO Box 443, Dublin, NH 03444-0443, 603-563-8020
Torngat Books, PO Box 384, Dublin, NH 03444, 603-563-8338
CALLIOPE: World History for Young People, 30 Grove Street, Peterborough, NH 03458, 603-924-7209
COBBLESTONE: The History Magazine for Young People, 30 Grove Street, Peterborough, NH 03458, 603-924-7209
Cobblestone Publishing, Inc., 30 Grove Street, Peterborough, NH 03458, 603-924-7209
FACES: The Magazine About People, 30 Grove Street, Peterborough, NH 03458
NORTHERN NEW ENGLAND REVIEW, PO Box 825, Franklin Pierce College, Rindge, NH 03461, 603-899-5111
Portmanteau Editions, PO Box 159, Littleton, NH 03561
Stillpoint Publishing, Box 640, Walpole, NH 03608, 603-756-9281
TIMBERLINE/VISION ONE, Box 640, Walpole, NH 03608, 603-756-9281
Upstart Publishing Company, Inc., 12 Portland Street, Dover, NH 03820, 607-749-5071
TRAY FULL OF LAB MICE PUBLICATIONS, PO Box 303, Durham, NH 03824
THE SINGLE HOUND, Box 598, Newmarket, NH 03857, 603-659-2685

NEW JERSEY

CHRISTIAN*NEW AGE QUARTERLY, PO Box 276, Clifton, NJ 07011
Humana Press, PO Box 2148, Clifton, NJ 07015, 201-773-4389
The Kingston Press, Inc., P.O. Box 2759, Clifton, NJ 07015, 609-921-0609
Merging Media, 516 Gallows Hill Road, Cranford, NJ 07016, 276-9479
EXIT 13 MAGAZINE, 22 Oakwood Court, Fanwood, NJ 07023
From Here Press, Box 219, Fanwood, NJ 07023
XTRAS, Box 219, Fanwood, NJ 07023, (201) 889-7886
Tory Corner Editions, PO Box 8100, Glen Ridge, NJ 07028, 201-669-8367
Big River Publishing, 1321 Washington Street, Hoboken, NJ 07030, 201-798-7800
CHALK CIRCLE, PO Box 5038, Hoboken, NJ 07030, 201-420-9235
LONG SHOT, PO Box 6231, Hoboken, NJ 07030
TALISMAN: A Journal of Contemporary Poetry and Poetics, Box 1117, Hoboken, NJ 07030, 201-798-9093
Waterfront Press, 52 Maple Avenue, Maplewood, NJ 07040, 201-762-1565
LIPS, PO Box 1345, Montclair, NJ 07042
Caliban Press, 114 Westview Road, Montclair, NJ 07043, 201-744-4453
Saturday Press, Inc., PO Box 884, Upper Montclair, NJ 07043, 201-256-5053
SHERLOCKIAN TIDBITS, 12 Glenwood Rd., Upper Montclair, NJ 07043
Ultimate Secrets, Box 43033, Upper Montclair, NJ 07043, 201-857-6283
Consumer Education Research Center, PO Box 336, 350 Scotland Road, Orange, NJ 07050
Warthog Press, 29 South Valley Road, West Orange, NJ 07052, 201-731-9269
ASH, 121 Gregory Avenue, #B-7, Passaic, NJ 07055, 201-471-8378
PASSAIC REVIEW, Forstmann Library, 195 Gregory Avenue, Passaic, NJ 07055, 201-438-7118
OVERVIEW LTD., Box 211, Wood-Ridge, NJ 07075, 201-438-9069
THE RAT RACE RECORD, PO Box 1611, Union, NJ 07083
Smyrna Press, Box 1151, Union City, NJ 07087
NOOSPAPERS, Open Dialogues, Inc., 215 N. Avenue West, Suite 21, Westfield, NJ 07090, 201-249-0280
Open Dialogues, 215 North Avenue West, Suite 21, Westfield, NJ 07090, 201-249-0280
OPEN MAGAZINE, Open Dialogues, Inc., 215 North Avenue West, Suite 21, Westfield, NJ 07090, 201-249-0280
Tradition Books, 614 Lenox Avenue, Westfield, NJ 07090, 201-232-8587
LYRA, Lyra Society for the Arts, Inc., PO Box 3188, Guttenberg, NJ 07093, 201-861-1941
R. Karman, 6600 Boulevard East, West New York, NJ 07093
SENSATIONS, c/o 2 Radio Avenue, #A5, Secaucus, NJ 07094
Dragon Disks, PO Box 30, Newark, NJ 07101-1545
MENTERTAINMENT, PO Box 9445, Elizabeth, NJ 07202, 908-558-9000
ST. JOSEPH MESSENGER, PO Box 288, Jersey City, NJ 07303, 201-798-4141
New Atlantis Press, 473 Pavonia Avenue, Jersey City, NJ 07306, 201-653-8221

Alleluia Press, Box 103, 672 Franklin Turnpike, Allendale, NJ 07401, 201-327-3513
ANT SPOIM/SMASH APATHY, PO Box 1216, Fairlawn, NJ 07410
Lincoln Springs Press, PO Box 269, Franklin Lakes, NJ 07417
Haypenny Press, 211 New Street, West Paterson, NJ 07424
Chantry Press, PO Box 144, Midland Park, NJ 07432
HUG THE EARTH, A Journal of Land and Life, 42 Greenwood Avenue, Pequannock, NJ 07440
Hug The Earth Publications, 42 Greenwood Ave., Pequannock, NJ 07440
NATURALLY, PO Box 203, Pequannock, NJ 07440
ACCCA Press, 19 Foothills Drive, Pompton Plains, NJ 07444, 201-835-2661
FOOTWORK: THE PATERSON LITERARY REVIEW, Passaic County Community College, College Boulevard, Paterson, NJ 07509, 201-684-6555
HORIZONTES, P.C.C.C.-Cultural Affairs Dept., 1 College Boulevard, Paterson, NJ 07509, 201-684-6555
TATTOO ADVOCATE JOURNAL, PO Box 8390, Haledon, NJ 07538-0390, 201-790-0429
Sandhill Publications, 441 Woodland Place, Leonia, NJ 07605
NEW DIRECTIONS FOR WOMEN, 108 West Palisade Avenue, Englewood, NJ 07631, 201-568-0226
Feris-Lee, Press, PO Box 560, Lodi, NJ 07644, 201-778-4163
Vonpalisaden Publications Inc., 195 Spring Valley Road, Paramus, NJ 07652, 201-262-4919
ARARAT, Armenian General Benevolent Union, 585 Saddle River Road, Saddle Brook, NJ 07662
Ararat Press, Armenian General Benevolent Union, 585 Saddle River Road, Saddle Brook, NJ 07662
BRAVO, THE POET'S MAGAZINE, 1081 Trafalgar Street, Teaneck, NJ 07666
John Edwin Cowen, Ltd., 1081 Trafalgar Street, Teaneck, NJ 07666
FIRSTHAND, PO Box 1314, Teaneck, NJ 07666, 201-836-9177
Hermitage (Ermitazh), PO Box 410, Tenafly, NJ 07670-0410, 201-894-8247
Green Tiger Press, Inc., 200 Old Tappan Road #BLDG, Old Tappan, NJ 07675-7005
Magnificat Press, PO Box 365, Avon-By-The-Sea, NJ 07717, 908-988-8915
PORTENTS, 12 Fir Place, Hazlet, NJ 07730, (201) 888-0535
THE WAVE, 300 1st Avenue, Spring Lake, NJ 07762-1903
OIKOS: A JOURNAL OF ECOLOGY AND COMMUNITY, 55 Magnolia Avenue, Denville, NJ 07834
THE PEGASUS REVIEW, PO Box 134, Flanders, NJ 07836, 201-927-0749
Vesper Publishing, PO Box 150, Kenvil, NJ 07847, 201-927-9105; 1-800-732-0256
COKEFISH, PO Box 683, Long Valley, NJ 07853, 908-876-3824
JOURNAL OF NEW JERSEY POETS, County College of Morris, Randolph, NJ 07869, 201-328-5460
Polygonal Publishing House, PO Box 357, Washington, NJ 07882, 908-689-3894
Afta Press, 47 Crater Avenue, Wharton, NJ 07885, 201-828-5467
CROW—The Alternative Magazine, Afta Press, Inc., 47 Crater Avenue, Wharton, NJ 07885-2023, 201-828-5467
CROW MAGAZINE, 47 Crater Avenue, Wharton, NJ 07885, 201-828-5467
The Russian Writers' Club Publishing House, PO Box 579, East Hanover, NJ 07936
THE LITERARY REVIEW, Fairleigh Dickinson University, 285 Madison Avenue, Madison, NJ 07940, 201-593-8564
The Unicorn Publishing House, 120 American Road, Morris Plains, NJ 07950
PTOLEMY/BROWNS MILLS REVIEW, Box 908, Browns Mills, NJ 08015, 609-893-0896
B-SIDE MAGAZINE, PO Box 1860, Burlington, NJ 08016-7460
LININGTON LINEUP, 1223 Glen Terrace, Glassboro, NJ 08028-1315, 609-589-1571
WORDS OF WISDOM, c/o J.M. Freiermuth, 612 Front Street, Glendora, NJ 08029, 609-939-0454
Silver Apples Press, PO Box 292, Hainesport, NJ 08036
RED HOT WORK-AT-HOME REPORT, 15 Brunswick Lane, Willingboro, NJ 08046, 609-835-2347
Beyond Athletics, 414 Aspen Court, Medford, NJ 08055, (609) 654-4050
BIOLOGY DIGEST, 143 Old Marlton Pike, Medford, NJ 08055, 609-654-6500
Plexus Publishing, Inc., 143 Old Marlton Pike, Medford, NJ 08055, 609-654-6500
Watermark Press, 315 Magnolia Rd., Pemberton, NJ 08068
JOURNAL OF AFRICAN LANGUAGES AND LINGUISTICS, Box 2178, Cinnaminson, NJ 08077, 609-486-1755
JOURNAL OF ITALIAN LINGUISTICS, Box 2178, Cinnaminson, NJ 08077, 609-486-1755
LINGUISTIC REVIEW, Box 2178, Cinnaminson, NJ 08077, 609-486-1755
TROPICAL AND GEOTROPICAL MEDICINE, Box 2178, Cinnaminson, NJ 08077, 609-486-1755
Weidner & Sons, Publishing, Box 2178, Riverton, NJ 08077, 609-486-1755
Phillips Publications, Inc., PO Box 168, Williamstown, NJ 08094, 609-567-0695
THE MICKLE STREET REVIEW, PO Box 1493, Camden, NJ 08101, 609-541-8280
BLIND ALLEYS, Rutgers Univ, Box 29, Camden, NJ 08102, 609-757-6117
Seventh Son Press, Rutgers Univ, Box 29, Camden, NJ 08102, 609-757-6117
Still Waters Press, 112 W. Duerer Street, Galloway, NJ 08201, 609-652-1790
A COMPANION IN ZEOR, Route 5, Box 82, Ashland Avenue, Pleasantville, NJ 08232, 609-645-6938
UNIROD MAGAZINE, 4214 B. Filbert Avenue, Atlantic City, NJ 08401
Modern Learning Press/Programs for Education, PO Box 167, Rosemont, NJ 08530
Princeton Book Company, Publishers, PO Box 57, Pennington, NJ 08534, 609-737-8177
Center Book Publishers, Inc., 301 N. Harrison Street, Suite 298, Princeton, NJ 08540, 609-924-6328
QRL POETRY SERIES, Princeton University, 26 Haslet Avenue, Princeton, NJ 08540, 921-6976
Quarterly Review of Literature Press, Princeton University, 26 Haslet Avenue, Princeton, NJ 08540
US1 Poets' Cooperative, 21 Lake Drive, Roosevelt, NJ 08555, 609-448-5096
US1 WORKSHEETS, 21 Lake Drive, Roosevelt, NJ 08555-0057, 609-448-5096
Africa World Press, Inc., PO Box 1892, Trenton, NJ 08607, 609-771-1666, FAX 609-771-1616
Broken Rifle Press, PO Box 749, Trenton, NJ 08607, 201-846-3750
HARDWARE, The Magazine of SF Technophilia, 710 Adeline Street, Trenton, NJ 08611
THE KELSEY REVIEW, Humanities Division, Mercer County Community College, Trenton, NJ 08690, 609-586-4800 ext. 326
WITHOUT HALOS, PO Box 1342, Point Pleasant Beach, NJ 08742, 201-240-5355
Bell Publishing, 15 Surrey Lane, East Brunswick, NJ 08816, 201-257-7793
Devida Publication, 6 Darby Road, East Brunswick, NJ 08816-3407, 201-257-7257
New Voyage Books, 415 Route 18, Suite 234, East Brunswick, NJ 08816, 800-345-0096 (orders only)
Algamut Press, PO Box 2293, Edison, NJ 08818, 201-549-1543

694

AVSTAR Publishing Corp., PO Box 537, Lebanon, NJ 08833, 201-236-6210
Scarecrow Press, PO Box 4167, Metuchen, NJ 08840, 201-548-8600
VOYA (Voice of Youth Advocate), PO Box 4167, Metuchen, NJ 08840, 201-548-8600
BIG HAMMER, PO Box 1698, New Brunswick, NJ 08901, 908-249-2645
RARITAN: A Quarterly Review, 31 Mine Street, New Brunswick, NJ 08903, 201-932-7852
SOCIETY, Transaction, Rutgers University, New Brunswick, NJ 08903, 201-932-2280
As Is/So & So Press, 123 North 8th Avenue, Highland Park, NJ 08904, (201) 985-5565
Catbird Press, 44 North Sixth Avenue, Highland Park, NJ 08904, 908-572-0816
Dragon Cloud Books, 232 Volkert Street, Highland Park, NJ 08904-3119, (201) 985-5565
THE LOST PERUKE, PO Box 1525, Highland Park, NJ 08904
SO & SO, 232 Volkert Street, Highland Park, NJ 08904-3119, (201) 985-5565

NEW MEXICO

Duende Press, Box 571, Placitas, NM 87043, 505-867-5877
SOUTHWESTERN DISCOVERIES, 15 Calle Bienvenida, Tijeras, NM 87059, 505-247-8736
Intermountain Publishing, 1713 Harzman Road SW, Albuquerque, NM 87105, 505-242-3333
Southwest Research and Information Center, PO Box 4524, Albuquerque, NM 87106, 505-262-1862
THE WORKBOOK, PO Box 4524, Albuquerque, NM 87106, 505-262-1862
BOOK TALK, 8632 Horacio Pl NE, Albuquerque, NM 87111, 505-299-8940
EXUM Publishing, 5705 Cochiti Drive NW, Albuquerque, NM 87120, 505-881-4413
West End Press, PO Box 27334, Albuquerque, NM 87125
FRONTIERS: A Journal of Women Studies, Mesa Vista Hall 2142, University of New Mexico, Albuquerque, NM 87131-1586, 505-277-1198
Esoterica Press, PO Box 15607, Albuquerque, NM 87174-0607
NOTEBOOK/CUADERNO: A LITERARY JOURNAL, PO Box 15607, Albuquerque, NM 87174-0607
Amador Publishers, PO Box 12335, Albuquerque, NM 87195, 505-877-4395
Out West Publishing, PO Box 4278, Albuquerque, NM 87196, 505-266-8322
THE WHOLE CHILE PEPPER, PO Box 4278, Albuquerque, NM 87196, 505-889-3745
WILDFLOWER, PO Box 4757, Albuquerque, NM 87196-4757
Wildflower Press, PO Box 4757, Albuquerque, NM 87196-4757
DUSTY DOG, PO Box 1103, Zuni, NM 87327, 505-782-4958
Dusty Dog Press, PO Box 1103, Zuni, NM 87327, 505-782-4958
DUSTY DOG REVIEWS, PO Box 1103, Zuni, NM 87327, 505-782-4958
CENTER, 307 Johnson Street, Santa Fe, NM 87501
Center Press, 307 Johnson Street, Santa Fe, NM 87501
FISH DRUM MAGAZINE, 626 Kathryn Avenue, Santa Fe, NM 87501
William Gannon, Publisher, 2887 Cooks Road, Santa Fe, NM 87501, 505-438-3430
Red Crane Books, 826 Camino de Monte Rey, Santa Fe, NM 87501, 505-988-7070
American-Canadian Publishers, Inc., PO Box 4595, Santa Fe, NM 87502-4595, 505-983-8484
Ancient City Press, PO Box 5401, Santa Fe, NM 87502, 505-982-8195
PUBLIC LANDS ACTION NETWORK, PO Box 5631, Santa Fe, NM 87502
Teal Press, PO Box 4098, Santa Fe, NM 87502-4098
Windom Books, PO Box 6444, Santa Fe, NM 87502, 505-983-3800
Museum of New Mexico Press, PO Box 2087, Santa Fe, NM 87503, 505-827-6454
Aurora Press, PO Box 573, Santa Fe, NM 87504, 505-989-9804
Bear & Company, Inc., Box 2860, Santa Fe, NM 87504, 505-983-5968
Bennett Books, PO Box 1553, Santa Fe, NM 87504, 505-986-1428
COALITION FOR PRISONERS' RIGHTS NEWSLETTER, PO Box 1911, Santa Fe, NM 87504, 505-982-9520
Health Press, Box 1388, Santa Fe, NM 87504, 505-982-9373
John Muir Publications, Inc., PO Box 613, Santa Fe, NM 87504, 505-982-4078
Mystic Crystal Publications, PO Box 8029, Santa Fe, NM 87504, 505-984-1048
Ocean Tree Books, PO Box 1295, Santa Fe, NM 87504, 505-983-1412
EL PALACIO, PO Box 2087, Santa Fe, NM 87504-2087, 505-827-6451
The Rydal Press, PO Box 2247, Santa Fe, NM 87504-2247, 505-983-1680
Sunstone Press, PO Box 2321, Santa Fe, NM 87504-2321, 505-988-4418; fax 505-988-1025
Muso Press, 33 Fonda Road, Santa Fe, NM 87505-0232
Two Rivers Press, Route 9, Box 56, Santa Fe, NM 87505
ANT FARM, PO Box 15513, Santa Fe, NM 87506, 505-473-0290
BREAKFAST WITHOUT MEAT, PO Box 15927, Santa Fe, NM 87506
ORPHIC LUTE, 526 Paul Place, Los Alamos, NM 87544
Gallery West Associates, PO Box 1238, Ranchos de Taos, NM 87557, 505-751-0073
Minor Heron Press, 117 East Plaza, Taos, NM 87571, 505-758-0081
MUSIC OF THE SPHERES, PO Box 1751, Taos, NM 87571, (505) 758-0405
Taos Bluewater Press, PO Box 529, Taos, NM 87571, 505-758-5617
PENNYWHISTLE PEOPLE PAPER, Box 734, Tesuque, NM 87574, 505-982-2622
Pennywhistle Press, Box 734, Tesuque, NM 87574, 505-982-2622
Barn Owl Books, P.O. Box 226, Vallecitos, NM 87581, 505-582-4226
NEW MEXICO HUMANITIES REVIEW, New Mexico Tech, Humanities Department, Socorro, NM 87801, 505-835-5445
ENERGY UNLIMITED, PO Box 493, Magdalena, NM 87825-0493
PUERTO DEL SOL, Box 3E, New Mexico State University, Las Cruces, NM 88003, 505-646-2345
Bilingue Publications, PO Drawer H, Las Cruces, NM 88004, 505-526-1557
Daedalus Press, PO Box 1374, Las Cruces, NM 88004, 505-382-7446
WHOLE NOTES, PO Box 1374, Las Cruces, NM 88004, 505-382-7446
SURVIVE & WIN, 2011 Crescent, PO Drawer 537, Alamogordo, NM 88310, 505-434-0234

NEW YORK

Jubilee Press, Box 34, Det 10/ 7WS, APO New York, NY 09182-5000
Biblio Press, 1140 Broadway, R. 1507, New York, NY 10001, 212-684-1257

Carroll & Graf Publishers, Inc., 260 Fifth Avenue, New York, NY 10001, (212) 889-8772
Do-It-Yourself Legal Publishers, 298 Fifth Avenue #403, New York, NY 10001
Drama Book Publishers, 260 Fifth Avenue, New York, NY 10001, 212-725-5377; fax 212-725-8506
Routledge, 29 West 35th Street, New York, NY 10001
Theatre Arts, 29 West 35th Street, New York, NY 10001, 212-244-3336
Asian CineVision, Inc., 32 East Broadway, New York, NY 10002
The Groundwater Press, 151 Ridge Street, 1B, New York, NY 10002, 212-228-5750
Publications of Arts (Art Resources for Teachers & Students), 32 Market Street, New York, NY 10002, 212-962-8231
ADRIFT, 239 East 5th Street #4D, New York, NY 10003
Boz Publishing, 163 Third Ave., Suite 127, New York, NY 10003, 212-795-1800
CINEASTE MAGAZINE, 200 Park Avenue South, New York, NY 10003, 212-982-1241
Dembner Books, 61 4th Avenue, 3rd Floor, New York, NY 10003-5202
DoubLeo Publications, 227 East 11th St, New York, NY 10003, 212-473-2739
The Foundation Center, 79 Fifth Avenue, New York, NY 10003, 212-620-4230
JEWISH CURRENTS, 22 E 17th Street, Suite 601, New York, NY 10003, 212-924-5740
New York Zoetrope Inc., 838 Broadway, New York, NY 10003, 420-0590
ON GOGOL BOULEVARD: Networking Bulletin for Dissidents from East and West, 151 1st Avenue #62, New York, NY 10003, 718-499-7720; 212-206-8463
Pagan Press, 26 St. Mark's Place, New York, NY 10003, 212-674-3321
PARNASSUS: POETRY IN REVIEW, 41 Union Square West, Room 804, New York, NY 10003, 212-463-0889
Princeton Architectural Press, 37 East 7th Street, New York, NY 10003, 212-995-9620
THE PRINCETON JOURNAL: THEMATIC STUDIES IN ARCHITECTURE, 37 East 7th Street, New York, NY 10003, 212-995-9620
STROKER, 129 2nd Ave. No. 3, New York, NY 10003
Teachers & Writers Collaborative, 5 Union Square West, New York, NY 10003, 212-691-6590
TEACHERS & WRITERS MAGAZINE, 5 Union Square West, New York, NY 10003, 212-691-6590
Union Square Press, 5 East 16th Street, New York, NY 10003, 212-924-2800
CONTACT/11: A Poetry Review, PO Box 451, Bowling Green Station, New York, NY 10004
Contact II: Publications, PO Box 451, Bowling Green Station, New York, NY 10004
BOOKS AND RELIGION: A Quarterly Review, Trinity Church, 74 Trinity Place, New York, NY 10006
HEALTH/PAC BULLETIN, 17 Murray Street, New York, NY 10007, 212-767-8890
BETWEEN C & D, 255 East 7th Street, New York, NY 10009
GANDHABBA, Nalanda University Press, c/o Savage, 622 East 11th Street, New York, NY 10009
Hard Press, 632 East 14th Street, #10, New York, NY 10009
HOME PLANET NEWS, P.O. Box 415 Stuyvesant Station, New York, NY 10009, 718-769-2854
Home Planet Publications, PO Box 415 Stuyvesant Station, New York, NY 10009, 718-769-2854
IKON, PO Box 1355, Stuyvesant Station, New York, NY 10009
IKON, Inc., PO Box 1355, Stuyvesant Station, New York, NY 10009
ME MAGAZINE, PO Box 1132, Peter Stuyvesant Station, New York, NY 10009, 212-673-2705
SECONDS MAGAZINE, PO Box 2553, Stuyvesant Station, New York, NY 10009, 212-260-0481
The Segue Foundation, 303 East 8th Street, New York, NY 10009
SUBWAY, PO Box 2001, New York, NY 10009
TELOS, 431 East 12th Street, New York, NY 10009, 212-228-6479
Telos Press, 431 East 12th Street, New York, NY 10009, 212-228-6479
United Artists, Box 2616, Peter Stuyvesant Station, New York, NY 10009
AMERICAN DANCE GUILD NEWSLETTER, 33 West 21st Street, New York, NY 10010, 212-627-3790
LIBERATION! Journal of Revolutionary Marxism, 46 West 21 Street, New York, NY 10010, 212-255-0352
N. Y. HABITAT, 928 Broadway, New York, NY 10010, 212-505-2030
Pequod Press, 344 Third Ave, Apt 3A, New York, NY 10010, 212-686-4789
TURNSTILE, 175 5th Avenue, Suite 2348, New York, NY 10010
WW Publishers, 46 West 21 Street, New York, NY 10010, 212-255-0352
AEGEAN REVIEW, Wire Press, 220 West 19th Street, Suite 2A, New York, NY 10011
Amethyst Press, 70A Greenwich Avenue, New York, NY 10011-8307, 212-629-8140
THE AMICUS JOURNAL, 40 West 20th Street, New York, NY 10011, 212-727-2700
ANTAEUS, 26 West 17th Street, New York, NY 10011, 212-645-2214
BOX 749 MAGAZINE, 411 West 22nd Street, New York, NY 10011, 212-98-0519
CONJUNCTIONS, 33 W. 9th Street, New York, NY 10011
Excalibur Publishing, 434 Avenue of Americas, #790, New York, NY 10011, 212-777-1790
GUARDIAN, 33 W 17th St, New York, NY 10011, 212-691-0404
ISRAEL HORIZONS, 27 West 20th Street, Suite 902, New York, NY 10011, 212-255-8760, FAX 212-627-1287
THE KIBBUTZ JOURNAL, 27 West 20th Street, New York, NY 10011, 212-255-1338
Lumen Books, Inc., 446 West 20 Street, New York, NY 10011, 212-989-7944
MEDIA HISTORY DIGEST, 11 West 19th Street, New York, NY 10011, 212-675-4380
Oxbridge Communications, Inc., 150 Fifth Avenue, Suite 636, New York, NY 10011, 212-741-0231; 800-955-0231
Paragon House Publishers, 90 5th Avenue, New York, NY 10011, 212-620-2820
PORTABLE LOWER EAST SIDE, PO Box 30323, New York, NY 10011-0103
The Printable Arts Society, Inc., 411 West 22nd Street, New York, NY 10011, (212) 989-0519
PUBLISHING TRENDS & TRENDSETTERS, 150 Fifth Avenue, New York, NY 10011, 800-955-0231
RE:PRINT (AN OCCASIONAL MAGAZINE), c/o BOX 749 Magazine, 411 West 22nd Street, New York, NY 10011
RESPONSE: A Contemporary Jewish Review, 27 West 20th Street, 9th Floor, New York, NY 10011
SITES, 446 West 20 Street, New York, NY 10011
THEATRE DESIGN AND TECHNOLOGY, 10 West 19th Street #5A, New York, NY 10011-4206, 212-924-9088
U.S. Institute for Theatre Technology, Inc., 10 West 19th Street #5A, New York, NY 10011-4206, 212-924-9088
The Ecco Press, 26 West 17th Street, New York City, NY 10011, 212-645-2214
ART INFORMATION REPORT, 496 La Guardia Place, New York, NY 10012, 212-505-2004
BOMB MAGAZINE, 594 Broadway, Suite 1002A, New York, NY 10012, 212-431-3943
DIAL-A-POEM POETS LP'S, 222 Bowery, New York, NY 10012, 212-925-6372; fax 212-966-7574
Fotofolio, Inc., 536 Broadway, 2nd Floor, New York, NY 10012, 212-226-0923

LOVE AND RAGE, A Revolutionary Anarchist Newsmonthly, Box 3 Prince Street Station, New York, NY 10012
THE NONVIOLENT ACTIVIST, War Resisters League, 339 Lafayette Street, New York, NY 10012, 212-228-0450
P E N American Center, 568 Broadway, New York, NY 10012
Parabola Books, 656 Broadway, New York, NY 10012, 212-505-6200
PARABOLA MAGAZINE, 656 Broadway, New York, NY 10012-2317, 212-505-6200
Poets & Writers, Inc., 72 Spring Street, New York, NY 10012, 212-226-3586
POETS & WRITERS MAGAZINE, 72 Spring Street, New York, NY 10012, 212-226-3586
ZONE, 611 Broadway, Suite 838, New York, NY 10012, 212-529-5674
Zone Books, 611 Broadway, Suite 838, New York, NY 10012, 212-529-5674
Giorno Poetry Systems Records, 222 Bowery, New York City, NY 10012
THE AMERICAN JOURNAL OF PSYCHOANALYSIS, 233 Spring Street, New York, NY 10013, (212) 741-3087
Box Turtle Press, 184 Franklin Street, New York, NY 10013
CHILDREN'S LITERATURE IN EDUCATION, 233 Spring Street, New York, NY 10013, (212) 741-3087
Corporeal Studio Ltd., One Hudson Street, New York, NY 10013
ENSEMBLE, THE NEW VARIETY ARTS REVIEW, One Hudson Street, New York, NY 10013
The Future Press, PO Box 73, Canal Street, New York, NY 10013
Harbor Publishing Company, 80 N. Moore Street, Suite 4J, New York, NY 10013, 212-349-1818
HERESIES: A FEMINIST PUBLICATION ON ART AND POLITICS, Box 1306, Canal St. Station, New York, NY 10013, 212-227-2108
JOURNAL OF THEORETICAL PSYCHOLOGY, 80 N. Moore Street, Suite 4J, New York, NY 10013, 212-349-1818
M/E/A/N/I/N/G, 60 Lispenard Street, New York, NY 10013
MUDFISH, 184 Franklin Street, New York, NY 10013, 212-219-9278
Plenum Publishing Corporation, 233 Spring Street, New York, NY 10013
POLITICAL BEHAVIOR, 233 Spring Street, New York, NY 10013, (212) 741-3087
PRECISELY, PO Box 73, Canal Street, New York, NY 10013
RESEARCH IN HIGHER EDUCATION, 233 Spring Street, New York, NY 10013, (212) 741-3087
Thunder's Mouth Press, 54 Greene Street, Suite 4S, New York, NY 10013
UNMUZZLED OX, 105 Hudson Street #311, New York, NY 10013, 212-226-7170
THE URBAN REVIEW, 233 Spring Street, New York, NY 10013, (212) 741-3087
Vanity Press/Strolling Dog Press, 160 6th Avenue, New York, NY 10013, 212-925-3823
Water Mark Press, 138 Duane Street, New York, NY 10013, 212-285-1609
Women In The Arts Foundation, Inc., 325 Spring St, New York, NY 10013
ZerOX Books, 105 Hudson Street, #311, New York, NY 10013
EAR MAGAZINE, 131 Varick Street #905, New York City, NY 10013-1323, 212-807-7944
Bank Street Press, 24 Bank Street, New York, NY 10014, 212-255-0692
BLUE LIGHT RED LIGHT, 496A Hudson Street, Suite F42, New York, NY 10014, 201-432-3245
Cane Hill Press, 225 Varick Street, New York, NY 10014
Four Walls Eight Windows, PO Box 548, Village Station, New York, NY 10014, 212-226-4998
GAYELLOW PAGES, Box 292 Village Station, New York, NY 10014, 212-674-0120
The Institute of Mind and Behavior Press, PO Box 522, Village Station, New York, NY 10014, 212-595-4853
JH Press, PO Box 294, Village Station, New York, NY 10014, 255-4713
THE JOURNAL OF MIND AND BEHAVIOR, PO Box 522, Village Station, New York, NY 10014, 212-595-4853
THE MILITANT, 410 West Street, New York, NY 10014, 212-243-6392
ST. MAWR, 496a Hudson Street, Suite K118, New York, NY 10014, 212-787-7155
The Twickenham Press, 31 Jane Street, New York, NY 10014, 212-741-2417
COLLECTORS CLUB PHILATELIST, 22 East 35th Street, New York, NY 10016, 212-683-0559
Dawnwood Press, 387 Park Avenue South, 5th Floor, New York, NY 10016-8810, 212-532-7160; fax 212-213-2495; 800-367-9692
Limelight Editions, 118 East 30th Street, New York, NY 10016, 212-532-5525
NBM Publishing Company, 185 Madison Avenue #1502, New York, NY 10016, 212-545-1223; fax 212-545-1227
Philomel Books, 200 Madison, New York, NY 10016
AMERICAN THEATRE MAGAZINE, 355 Lexington Avenue, New York, NY 10017, 212-697-5230
AUM U.S.A. Co. Ltd., 8 East 48th Street #2E, New York, NY 10017-1005, 212-226-5030
Theatre Communications Group, 355 Lexington Avenue, New York, NY 10017, 212-697-5230
THE TRIBUNE, 777 United Nations Plaza, 3rd floor, New York, NY 10017, 212-687-8633
THE CHARIOTEER, 337 West 36 Street, New York, NY 10018, 212-279-9586
JOURNAL OF THE HELLENIC DIASPORA, 337 West 36th Street, New York, NY 10018, 212-279-9586
NAMBLA BULLETIN, Box 174, Midtown Station, New York, NY 10018, 212-807-8578
Pella Publishing Co, 337 West 36th Street, New York, NY 10018, 212-279-9586
AMERICA, 106 West 56th Street, New York, NY 10019, 212-581-4640
American Council for the Arts/ACA Books, 1285 Avenue of the Americas, Third Floor, New York, NY 10019, 212-245-4510
THE ARMCHAIR DETECTIVE, 129 West 56th Street, New York, NY 10019, 212-765-0902
The Armchair Detective Library, 129 West 56th Street, New York, NY 10019, 212-765-0923
Folder Editions, 260 West 52 Street #5L, New York, NY 10019, 212-459-9086
FYI, 1285 Avenue of the Americas, 3rd Floor, New York, NY 10019, 212-977-2544
THE NEW CRITERION, 850 Seventh Avenue, New York, NY 10019
UPDATE, 1285 Avenue of the Americas, 3rd Floor, Area M, New York, NY 10019, (212) 245-4510
VANTAGE POINT, 1285 Avenue of the Americas, 3rd Floor, Area M, New York, NY 10019, (212) 245-4510
Vista Publishing Company, 250 West 57th Street, #1527, New York, NY 10019, 212-942-3350
Americas Society, 680 Park Avenue, New York, NY 10021
DIAMOND INSIGHT, 790 Madison Avenue, Suite 602, New York, NY 10021, 212-570-4180; FAX 212-772-1286
Gai Saber Monographs, c/o GAU, Box 480, Lenox Hill Station, New York, NY 10021-0033, 212-864-0361
THE HUDSON REVIEW, 684 Park Avenue, New York, NY 10021, 212-650-0020
KAIROS, A Journal of Contemporary Thought and Criticism, c/o Mandell, 450 E. 63rd Street, Apt. 4C, New York, NY 10021, 212-758-3257
National Council for Research on Women, Sara D. Roosevelt Memorial House, 47-49 East 65th Street, New York, NY 10021, 212-570-5001

Odin Press, PO Box 536, New York, NY 10021, 212-744-2538
The Poetry Connection, 301 East 64 Street #6K, New York, NY 10021, 212-249-5494
THE POETRY CONNECTION, 301 East 64 Street #6K, New York, NY 10021, 212-249-5494
PSYCHOANALYTIC BOOKS, 211 East 70th Street, New York, NY 10021, 212-628-8792
REVIEW. LATIN AMERICAN LITERATURE & ARTS, Americas Society, 680 Park Avenue, New York, NY 10021, 212-249-8950
SCANDINAVIAN REVIEW, 725 Park Avenue, New York, NY 10021, 212-879-9779
te Neues Publishing Company, 15 East 76th Street, New York, NY 10021, 212-288-0265
WOMEN IN THE ARTS BULLETIN/NEWSLETTER, c/o R. Crown, 1175 York Avenue #2G, New York, NY 10021, 212-691-0988
WOMEN'S RESEARCH NETWORK NEWS, Sara D. Roosevelt Memorial House, 47-49 East 65th Street, New York, NY 10021, 212-570-5001
Carnival Enterprises, c/o H. Jaffee, 15th Floor, 350 Park Avenue, New York, NY 10022
CHAKRA, PO Box 8551, Dept. 106, FDR Station, New York, NY 10022
Fromm International Publishing Corporation, 560 Lexington Avenue, 21st Floor, New York, NY 10022, 212-308-4010
REAL PEOPLE, 950 Third Avenue, New York, NY 10022, 212-371-4932
Rivercross Publishing, Inc., 127 East 59th Street, New York, NY 10022, 421-1950
Alternative Press Syndicate, PO Box 1347, Ansonia Station, New York, NY 10023
AUFBAU, 2121 Broadway, New York, NY 10023, 212-873-7400
CENTRAL PARK, P.O. Box 1446, New York, NY 10023
Council on Interracial Books For Children, 1841 Broadway, New York, NY 10023, 212-757-5339
Gumbs & Thomas Publishers, Inc., 142 West 72nd Street, Suite #9, New York, NY 10023, 212-769-8022
INTERRACIAL BOOKS FOR CHILDREN BULLETIN, 1841 Broadway, New York, NY 10023, 212-757-5339
The Petrarch Press, 133 West 72nd Street #703, New York, NY 10023, 212-362-7668
The Photographic Arts Center, Ltd., 163 Amsterdam Avenue, New York, NY 10023, 212-838-8640
SPACE AND TIME, 138 West 70th Street 4-B, New York, NY 10023-4432
Space and Time Press, 138 West 70th Street 4-B, New York, NY 10023-4432
Upper West Side Publishing, PO Box 1512, New York, NY 10023, 212-289-7942
Paul Zelevansky, 333 West End Avenue, New York, NY 10023, 724-5071
Helikon Press, 120 West 71st Street, New York City, NY 10023
Classic Theatre For Children, Publishers, 225 West 83rd Street #11A, New York, NY 10024-4903
Creative Roots, Inc., PO Box 401, Planetarium Station, New York, NY 10024, 212-799-2294
GRAND STREET, Grand Street Publications, Inc., 50 Riverside Drive, New York, NY 10024, 212-496-6088
Guarionex Press Ltd., 201 West 77th Street, New York, NY 10024, 212-724-5259
LEFT BUSINESS OBSERVER, 250 West 85 Street, New York, NY 10024
THE NEW DANCE REVIEW, 32 W. 82nd Street #2F, New York, NY 10024, 212-799-9057
Psyche Press, PO Box 780, New York, NY 10024, 212-721-4466
WITCHCRAFT DIGEST MAGAZINE (THE WICA NEWSLETTER), 153 West 80th Street, Suite 1B, New York, NY 10024
Psychohistory Press, 2315 Broadway, New York City, NY 10024, 212-873-5900
THE JOURNAL OF PSYCHOHISTORY, 2315 Broadway, NY, NY 10024, 212-873-5900
CARIBBEAN NEWSLETTER, Box 20392, Park West Station, New York, NY 10025
KIOSK, Attn: Charles Ward, 317 West 106th Street #2-C, New York, NY 10025-3648
PEACE & DEMOCRACY NEWS, PO Box 1640, Cathedral Station, New York, NY 10025, 212-666-5924
PHOTOGRAPHY IN NEW YORK, PO Box 20351, Park West Station, New York, NY 10025, 212-787-0401
THE SPACE PRESS, Vernuccio Publications, 645 West End Avenue, New York, NY 10025, 212-724-5919
Synerjy, PO Box 1854/Cathedral Station, Cathedral Station, New York, NY 10025, 212-865-9595
SYNERJY: A Directory of Renewable Energy, Box 1854/Cathedral Station, New York, NY 10025, 212-865-9595
SZ/Press, PO Box 20075, Cathedral Finance Station, New York, NY 10025, 212-749-5906
Midmarch Arts Press, 300 Riverside Drive, New York City, NY 10025, 212-666-6990
WOMEN ARTISTS NEWS, 300 Riverside Drive, New York City, NY 10025, 212-666-6990
Langston Press, PO Box 1615, Morningside Station, New York, NY 10026, 212-932-1607
THE MANHATTAN REVIEW, c/o Philip Fried, 440 Riverside Drive, #45, New York, NY 10027
JEAN RHYS REVIEW, Box 568 Havemeyer Hall, Columbia University, New York, NY 10027, 212-854-2929
Semiotext Foreign Agents Books Series, 522 Philosophy Hall, Columbia University, New York, NY 10027, 212-280-3956
SEMIOTEXT(E), 522 Philosophy Hall, Columbia University, New York, NY 10027, 212-280-3956
TRANSLATION, Translation Ctr./412 Dodge, Columbia University, New York, NY 10027, 212-854-2305
Translation Center, 412 Dodge, Columbia University, New York, NY 10027, 212-854-2305
Again + Again Press, PO Box 20041, Cherokee Station, New York, NY 10028
Michael Kesend, Publishing, Ltd., 1025 Fifth Avenue, New York, NY 10028-0134, 212-249-5150
NETWORK, Box 810, Gracie Station, New York, NY 10028, 212-737-7536
Red Dust, PO Box 630, Gracie Station, New York, NY 10028, 212-348-4388
REMARK, PO Box 20041, Cherokee Station, New York, NY 10028
Scarf Press, 58 E 83rd Street, New York, NY 10028, 212-744-3901
FICTION, c/o Dept. of English, City College, 138th Street & Convent Ave., New York, NY 10031, 212-690-8170
AMERICAN BUDDHIST, 301 West Forty-Fifth Street, New York, NY 10036, 212-489-1075
DRAMATISTS GUILD NEWSLETTER, 234 West 44th Street, New York, NY 10036
Peter Lang Publishing, Inc., 62 West 45 Street, New York, NY 10036, 212-302-6740
POETRY NEW YORK, Ph.D. Program in English, CUNY, 33 West 42 Street, New York, NY 10036, (212) 642-2206
SOCIAL POLICY, 25 West 43rd Street, Room 620, New York, NY 10036, 212-642-2929
SOCIALISM AND DEMOCRACY, 33 West 42nd Street, New York, NY 10036, 212-790-4300
Wet Editions, Box 2045, Times Square Station, New York, NY 10036
ACTIVIST, DSA Youth Section, 15 Dutch Street, Suite 500, New York, NY 10038-3708
ART HAZARDS NEWS, 5 Beekman Street, New York, NY 10038, 212-227-6220
DEMOCRATIC LEFT, 15 Dutch Street, Suite 500, New York, NY 10038, 212-962-0390
WREE-VIEW OF WOMEN, 198 Broadway, #606, New York, NY 10038
Italica Press, Inc., 595 Main Street, #605, New York, NY 10044, 212-935-4230
ARISTOS, PO Box 1105, Radio City Station, New York, NY 10101, 212-678-8550

698

Forbes/Wittenburg & Brown, 250 West 57th Street, Suite 1527, New York, NY 10107, 212-969-0969
LILITH, 250 West 57th, #2432, New York, NY 10107, 212-757-0818
AMANECER IN ENGLISH, PO Box 37, Times Square Station, New York, NY 10108, 212-928-7600; FAX 212-927-2757
GRUE MAGAZINE, Hell's Kitchen Productions, PO Box 370, Times Square Station, New York, NY 10108
LUCHA/STRUGGLE, PO Box 37, Times Square Station, New York, NY 10108, 212-928-7600; FAX 212-928-2757
New York CIRCUS, Inc., PO Box 37, Times Square Station, New York, NY 10108, 212-928-7600
The Pilgrim Press/United Church Press, 475 Riverside Drive, 10th floor, New York, NY 10115, 212-870-2200
Gringo Guides, Inc., PO Box 7050, Grand Central Station, NY 10116
International Publishers Co. Inc., PO Box 3042, New York, NY 10116, 212-366-9816; fax 212-366-9820
TEMPORARY CULTURE, PO Box 8180, New York, NY 10116-4650
THE U*N*A*B*A*S*H*E*D LIBRARIAN, THE "HOW I RUN MY LIBRARY GOOD" LETTER, G.P.O. Box 2631, New York, NY 10116
Agathon Press, 225 West 34th Street, New York, NY 10122-0072
The Feminist Press at the City University of New York, 311 East 94 Street, New York, NY 10128, 212-360-5790
SOURCE: NOTES IN THE HISTORY OF ART, 1 East 87th Street, Suite 8A, New York, NY 10128, 212-369-1881
WOMEN'S STUDIES QUARTERLY, The Feminist Press, 311 East 94 Street, New York, NY 10128, 212-360-5790
Banner Press International, Inc., PO Box 21195, Midtown Station, New York, NY 10129, 212-459-4525
MANHATTAN POETRY REVIEW, F.D.R. PO Box 8207, New York, NY 10150, 212-355-6634
Mystery Notebook Editions, PO Box 1341, FDR Station, New York, NY 10150
New Liberty Press, Box 6598, New York, NY 10150, 212-750-8410
SCAREAPHANALIA, PO Box 489, Murray Hill Station, New York, NY 10156-0489
Ashod Press, PO Box 1147, Madison Square Station, New York, NY 10159, 212-475-0711
Globe Press Books, PO Box 2045, Madison Square Station, New York, NY 10159-2045, 914-962-4614
JOURNAL OF POLYMORPHOUS PERVERSITY, PO Box 1454, Madison Square Station, New York, NY 10159, 212-689-5473
CHELSEA, Box 5880, Grand Central Station, New York, NY 10163
MICROWAVE NEWS, PO Box 1799, Grand Central Station, New York, NY 10163, 212-517-2802
VDT NEWS, PO Box 1799, Grand Central Station, New York, NY 10163, 212-517-2802
LA NUEZ, PO Box 1655, New York, NY 10276, 212-260-3130
Slate Press, Box 1421, Cooper Station, New York, NY 10276
Image Industry Publications, 10 Bay Street Landing, #7F, Staten Island, NY 10301-2511, 718-273-3229
OUTERBRIDGE, English A324, College of Staten Island, 715 Ocean Terrace, Staten Island, NY 10301, 212-390-7654, 7779
Bard Press, 393 St. Paul's Avenue, Staten Island, NY 10304-2127, 718-442-7429
Ten Penny Players, Inc., 393 St. Paul's Avenue, Staten Island, NY 10304-2127, 718-442-7429
Ward Hill Press, 514 Bay Street, Box 424, Staten Island, NY 10304, 718-816-9449
WATERWAYS: Poetry in the Mainstream, 393 St. Paul's Avenue, Staten Island, NY 10304-2127, 718-442-7429
EMPIRE! The NYS Inmate Literary Arts Magazine, Arthur Kill Correctional Facility, 2911 Arthur Kill Road, Staten Island, NY 10309, 718-356-7333 ext 406
VIV Publishing House, 600 East 137 Street, #13G, Bronx, NY 10454
THOUGHT, A REVIEW OF CULTURE & IDEA, University Box L, Bronx, NY 10458, 212-579-2322
Bronx Books, PO Box 100, Bronx, NY 10463, (212) 548-4050
Word Of Mouth Press, c/o Sacharov, 528 Minnieford Avenue, Bronx, NY 10464-1232
Blind Beggar Press, Box 437 Williamsbridge Station, Bronx, NY 10467, 914-683-6792
Wright-Armstead Associates, 2410 Barker Avenue, Suite 14-G, Bronx, NY 10467, (212) 654-9445
PHILOSOPHY AND THE ARTS, PO Box 431, Jerome Avenue Station, Bronx, NY 10468
Philosophy and the Arts Press, PO Box 431, Jerome Avenue Station, Bronx, NY 10468
JOURNAL OF MENTAL IMAGERY, PO Box 240, Bronx, NY 10471
The Sheep Meadow Press, PO Box 1345, Riverdale-on-Hudson, NY 10471, 212-549-3321
DorPete Press, PO Box 238, Briarcliff Manor, NY 10510, 914-941-7029
NightinGale Resources, PO Box 322, Cold Spring, NY 10516, 212-753-5383
CROTON REVIEW, P.O. Box 277, Croton on Hudson, NY 10520
Giro Press, PO Box 203, Croton-on-Hudson, NY 10520, 914-271-8924
Earl M Coleman Enterprises, Inc, PO Box T, Crugers, NY 10521, 914-271-5124
The Purchase Press, PO Box 5, Harrison, NY 10528, 212-645-4442
Communication Trends Inc., 2 East Avenue, Larchmont, NY 10538
THE HUMAN ECOLOGY AND ENERGY BALANCING SCIENTIST, PO Box 737, Mahopac, NY 10541, 516-751-3105
Human Ecology Balancing Sciences, Inc., PO Box 737, Mahopac, NY 10541
Orbis Books, ATTN: Renee Turcott, Walsh Building, Maryknoll, NY 10545, 914-941-7590
Zon International Publishing Co., PO Box 47, Millwood, NY 10546
AMERICAN BOOK COLLECTOR, PO Box 1080, Ossining, NY 10562, 914-941-0409
The Moretus Press, Inc., PO Box 1080, Ossining, NY 10562, 914-941-0409
THE ROTKIN REVIEW, RR 4, Peekskill, NY 10566-9804
New Chapter Press, Old Pound Road, Pound Ridge, NY 10576, 914-764-4011
Northeast Sportsman's Press, PO Box 188, Tarrytown, NY 10591
Sleepy Hollow Press, 150 White Plains Road, Tarrytown, NY 10591, 914-631-8200
Peter Pauper Press, Inc., 202 Mamaroneck Avenue, White Plains, NY 10601, 914-681-0144
Pro/Am Music Resources, Inc., 63 Prospect Street, White Plains, NY 10606, 914-948-7436
ROOM, 29 Lynton Place, White Plains, NY 10606-2818
Papyrus Publishers, PO Box 466, Yonkers, NY 10704, 914-664-0840
Ultramarine Publishing Co., Inc., PO Box 303, Hastings-on-Hudson, NY 10706, 914-478-2522
Beaconlamp Books, PO Box 182, Bronxville, NY 10708, 914-699-7155
Stop Light Press, PO Box 970, Bronxville, NY 10708
Roblin Press, PO Box 152, Yonkers, NY 10710, 914-337-4576
Don Bosco Multimedia, 475 North Avenue, Box T, New Rochelle, NY 10802, 914-576-0122
CROSS CURRENTS: Religion & Intellectual Life, College of New Rochelle, New Rochelle, NY 10805, 914-654-5425
LACTUCA, PO Box 621, Suffern, NY 10901
HEAVEN BONE, PO Box 486, Chester, NY 10918, (914) 469-9018

Esquire Books, Inc., 50 Sand Street, Garnerville, NY 10923-1430
Popular Reality Press, PO Box 571, Greenwood Lake, NY 10925-0571
Library Research Associates, Inc., RD #5, Box 41, Dunderberg Road, Monroe, NY 10950, 914-783-1144
ON COURSE, 459 Carol Drive, Monroe, NY 10950
THE GOOFUS OFFICE GAZETTE, The Goofus Office, PO Box 259, Pearl River, NY 10965, 914-620-1416
Voice of Liberty Publications, 3 Borger Place, Pearl River, NY 10965, (914) 735-8140
Alms House Press, PO Box 668, Stony Point, NY 10980
SCIENCE AND NATURE, The Annual of Marxist Philosophy for Natural Scientists, Dialectics Workshop, 53 Hickory Hill, Tappan, NY 10983, 914-359-2283
HUMERUS, PO Box 222, Piermont, NY 10986, 914-358-2371
The First East Coast Theatre and Publishing Company, Inc., PO Box 32, Westtown, NY 10992, 914-726-4289
DIRECTORY MARKETPLACE, PO Box 301, West Nyack, NY 10994, 914-358-6213
Todd Publications, PO Box 301, West Nyack, NY 10994, 914-358-6213
Avery Publishing Group, Inc., 120 Old Broadway, Garden City Park, NY 11040, 516-741-2155
Obsessive Compulsive Anonymous, PO Box 215, New Hyde Park, NY 11040, 516-741-4901; FAX 212-768-4679
Bain-Dror International Travel, Inc. (BDIT), PO Box 1405, Port Washington, NY 11050, 513-944-5508; fax 516-944-7540
California Bound Books, PO Box 613, Port Washington, NY 11050, 1-800-475-7046
Odysseus Enterprises Ltd., PO Box 1548, Port Washington, NY 11050-0306, 516-944-5330; fax 516-944-7540
WICKED MYSTIC, PO Box 3087, Dept 222, Astoria, NY 11103, 718-545-6713
Low-Tech Press, 30-73 47th Street, Long Island City, NY 11103, 718-721-0946
Starlight Press, Box 3102, Long Island City, NY 11103
The Smith (The Generalist Assn., Inc.), 69 Joralemon Street, Brooklyn, NY 11201
Algol Press, PO Box 2730, Brooklyn, NY 11202-0056, 718-643-9011
ASSEMBLING, PO Box 1967, Brooklyn, NY 11202
Assembling Press, PO Box 1967, Brooklyn, NY 11202
LATEST JOKES NEWSLETTER, PO Box 023304, Brooklyn, NY 11202-0066, 718-855-5057
SCIENCE FICTION CHRONICLE, PO Box 2730, Brooklyn, NY 11202-0056, 718-643-9011 (phone & fax)
NETWORK AFRICA FOR TODAY'S WORLD CITIZEN, Pratt Station, PO Box 81, Brooklyn, NY 11205
FREE FOCUS, Wagner Press, 224 82nd Street, #1, Brooklyn, NY 11209, (718) 680-3899
OSTENTATIOUS MIND, Thursday Press, 224 82nd Street, #1, Brooklyn, NY 11209, 718-680-3899
THE POISONED PEN, 8801 Shore Road, 6A East, Brooklyn, NY 11209-5409, 718-833-8248
POSKISNOLT PRESS, 224-82nd Street, Apt. #2, Brooklyn, NY 11209
ALA Social Responsibilities Round Table, c/o Eubanks, Brooklyn College Library, Brooklyn, NY 11210
ALA/SRRT NEWSLETTER, c/o Eubanks, Brooklyn College Library, Brooklyn, NY 11210
THE LION AND THE UNICORN: A Critical Journal of Children's Literature, Dept of English, Brooklyn College, Brooklyn, NY 11210, 780-5195
Autonomedia, Inc., PO Box 568, Brooklyn, NY 11211, 718-387-6471
A DIFFERENT DRUMMER, 84 Bay 28th Street, Brooklyn, NY 11214, 718-372-4806
AGOG, 340 22nd Street, Brooklyn, NY 11215, 718-965-3871
THE BAD HENRY REVIEW, Box 150045, Van Brunt Station, Brooklyn, NY 11215-0001
44 Press, Inc., Box 150045, Van Brant Station, Brooklyn, NY 11215-0001
GIANTS PLAY WELL IN THE DRIZZLE, 326-A 4th Street, Brooklyn, NY 11215, 718-788-7927
Interlink Publishing Group, Inc., 99 Seventh Avenue, Brooklyn, NY 11215, 718-797-4292
OLD-HOUSE JOURNAL, 435 9th Street, Brooklyn, NY 11215, 718-636-4514
THE PROSPECT REVIEW, 557 10th Street, Brooklyn, NY 11215
SPIT, 529 2nd Street, Brooklyn, NY 11215, 718-499-7343
City Spirit Publications, 590 Pacific Street, Brooklyn, NY 11217, 718-857-1545
CONNECTICUT NATURALLY, 590 Pacific Street, Brooklyn, NY 11217, 718-857-1545
HANGING LOOSE, 231 Wyckoff Street, Brooklyn, NY 11217
Hanging Loose Press, 231 Wyckoff Street, Brooklyn, NY 11217
NEW JERSEY NATURALLY, 590 Pacific Street, Brooklyn, NY 11217, 718-857-1545
NEW YORK NATURALLY, 590 Pacific Street, Brooklyn, NY 11217, 718-857-1545
MILIM, 324 Avenue F, Brooklyn, NY 11218
POSTCARD ART/POSTCARD FICTION, 143 McGuinness Blvd., Brooklyn, NY 11222
Martha Rosler, 143 McGuinness Blvd., Brooklyn, NY 11222
Gryphon Publications, PO Box 209, Brooklyn, NY 11228
HARDBOILED DETECTIVE, PO Box 209, Brooklyn, NY 11228
PAPERBACK PARADE, PO Box 209, Brooklyn, NY 11228
LIBRARY OUTREACH REPORTER, 1671 East 16th Street, Suite 226, Brooklyn, NY 11229, 718-645-2396
Library Outreach Reporter Publications, 1671 East 16th Street, Suite 226, Brooklyn, NY 11229, 718-645-2396
THE LIT PAGE: The Magazine for Library Literacy, 1671 East 16th Street, Suite 226, Brooklyn, NY 11229, 718-645-2396
ON THE ROAD: Mobile Ideas for Libraries, 1671 East 16th Street, Suite 226, Brooklyn, NY 11229, 718-645-2396
Pinched Nerves Press, 1610 Avenue P, Apt. 6-B, Brooklyn, NY 11229
RELIX, PO Box 94, Brooklyn, NY 11229, 718-258-0009
Alchemy Press, 1789 Macdonald Avenue, Brooklyn, NY 11230, 212-303-8301; 718-339-4168
FRAGMENTS, 1789 Macdonald Avenue, Brooklyn, NY 11230, 718-339-0184
SUB ROSA, 454 37th Street (Basement), Brooklyn, NY 11232
STICKY CARPET DIGEST, 38-27 147th Street, Apt. #3, Flushing, NY 11354, 718-463-7756
THE PIPE SMOKER'S EPHEMERIS, 20-37 120th Street, College Point, NY 11356
CNL/WORLD REPORT, PO Box 81, Whitestone, NY 11357
Griffon House Publications/Bagehot Council, PO Box 81, Whitestone, NY 11357
PARIS REVIEW, 45-39 171 Place, Flushing, NY 11358, 539-7085
Barclay House, 35-19 215th Place, Bayside, NY 11361, 718-225-5178
L D A Publishers, 42-36 209 Street, Bayside, NY 11361, 212-224-9484
Phrygian Press, 58-09 205th Street, Bayside, NY 11364
ZYX, 58-09 205th Street, Bayside, NY 11364
WRESTLING - THEN & NOW, PO Box 471, Oakland Gdns. Station, Flushing, NY 11364
JEWISH LINGUISTIC STUDIES, 67-07 215 Street, Oakland Gardens, NY 11364-2523

700

THE SPIRIT THAT MOVES US, PO Box 820, Jackson Heights, NY 11372, 718-426-8788
The Spirit That Moves Us Press, Inc., PO Box 820, Jackson Heights, NY 11372, 718-426-8788
Celtic Heritage Press, Inc., PO Box 637, Woodside, NY 11377, 718-478-8162
THE LEDGE POETRY AND PROSE MAGAZINE, 64-65 Cooper Avenue, Glendale, NY 11385, 718-366-5169
THE NEW PRESS, 87-40 Francis Lewis Blvd #A-44, Queens Village, NY 11427, 718-217-1464
House of Hits, Inc., North American Airlines Bldg 75, Suite 250, JFK International Airport, Jamaica, NY 11430, 718-656-2650
ARBA SICULA, c/o Modern Foreign Languages, St. John's University, Jamaica, NY 11439-0002
Arba Sicula, Inc., c/o Modern Foreign Languages, St. John's University, Jamaica, NY 11439
SICILIA PARRA, c/o Modern Foreign Languages, St. John's University, Jamaica, NY 11439-0002, 718-331-0613
CONFRONTATION, English Department, C.W. Post of Long Island Univ., Greenvale, NY 11548, 516-299-2391
Programmed Press, 599 Arnold Road, West Hempstead, NY 11552-3918, 516-599-6527
Cross-Cultural Communications, 239 Wynsum Avenue, Merrick, NY 11566
MOKSHA JOURNAL, 49 Forrest Place, Amityville, NY 11701, 516-691-8475
Vajra of Yoga Anand Ashram, 49 Forrest Place, Amityville, NY 11701, 516-691-8475
QUEEN OF ALL HEARTS, 26 South Saxon Avenue, Bay Shore, NY 11706, 516-665-0726
WRITERS INK, 186 North Coleman Road, Centereach, NY 11720, 516-736-6439
Writers Ink Press, 186 North Coleman Road, Centereach, NY 11720, 516-736-6439
Writers Unlimited Agency, Inc, 186 North Coleman Road, Centereach, NY 11720
Parent Tapes, Inc., PO Box 1025, Commack, NY 11725, 516-543-7082
KEYSTROKES, PO Box 2014, Setauket, NY 11733, 516-751-7080
THE CULTURAL FORUM, PO Box 709, Holbrook, NY 11741, 516-472-2191
COLLECTRIX, 389 New York Avenue, Huntington, NY 11743, 516-424-6479
Maple Hill Press, Ltd., 174 Maple Hill Road, Huntington, NY 11743, 516-549-3748; fax 516-421-2550
NEWSLETTER, PO Box 773, Huntington, NY 11743
Pleasure Dome Press (Long Island Poetry Collective Inc.), Box 773, Huntington, NY 11743
XANADU: A LITERARY JOURNAL, Box 773, Huntington, NY 11743, 516-248-7716
General Hall, Inc., 5 Talon Way, Dix Hills, NY 11746-6238, (516) 243-0155
WEST HILLS REVIEW: A WALT WHITMAN JOURNAL, Walt Whitman Birthplace Assn., 246 Old Walt Whitman Road, Huntington Station, NY 11746, (516) 427-5240
Cube Publications Inc, 1 Buena Vista Road, Port Jefferson, NY 11777, 516-331-4990
Brook House Press, Inc., Mills Pond House, PO Box 52, St. James, NY 11780, 516-584-6948
IRISH LITERARY SUPPLEMENT, 114 Paula Boulevard, Selden, NY 11784, 516-698-8243
Irish Studies, 114 Paula Boulevard, Selden, NY 11784, 516-698-8243
Street Press, Box 772, Sound Beach, NY 11789
Panther Press Ltd., PO Box A-44, Wantagh, NY 11793, 516-783-5673
THE MINNESOTA REVIEW, Dept. of English, SUNY-Stony Brook, Stony Brook, NY 11794
TAPROOT, a journal of elder writers, Fine Arts Center 4290, University at Stony Brook, Stony Brook, NY 11794-0001, 516-632-6635
Carriage House Press, 1 Carriage Lane, East Hampton, NY 11937, 516-267-8773
Sagapress, Inc., Box 21, Sagaponack Road, Sagaponack, NY 11962, 516-537-3717
The Permanent Press/The Second Chance Press, RD 2, Noyac Road, Sag Harbor, NY 11963, 516-725-1101
Savant Garde Workshop, PO Box 1650, Sag Harbor, NY 11963-0060, 516-725-1414
Broadway Press, 12 W. Thomas Street, Shelter Island, NY 11964-1037, 516-749-3266
Wise Owl Press, PO Box 377 (1475 Waterview Dr.), Southold, NY 11971, 516-765-3356
Pushcart Press, PO Box 380, Wainscott, NY 11975, 516-324-9300
Starchand Press, Box 468, Wainscott, NY 11975
CWM, 112 South Market Street, Johnstown, NY 12095, 518-374-7143
Kitchen Table: Women of Color Press, PO Box 908, Latham, NY 12110-0908, 518-434-2057
Omega Press (formerly Sufi Order Publications), RD #1, Box 1030 D, New Lebanon, NY 12125
Sachem Press, PO Box 9, Old Chatham, NY 12136, 518-794-8327
FACTSHEET FIVE, 6 Arizona Avenue, Rensselaer, NY 12144-4502, 518-479-3707
INNOVATING, The Rensselaerville Institute, Rensselaerville, NY 12147, 518-797-3783
The Rensselaerville Systems Training Center, PO Box 157, Rensselaerville, NY 12147-0157, 518-797-3954
Rocky Top Publications, Div. of Rocky Top Supply, PO Box 33, Stamford, NY 12167
Trestletree Publications, PO Box 295, Albany, NY 12201, 518-452-2000
Harrow and Heston, Publishers, Stuyvesant Plaza, P.O. Box 3934, Albany, NY 12203
THE ALBANY REVIEW, Albany Review Associates, Inc., 80 Willett Street #1, Albany, NY 12210-1010
GROUNDSWELL, PO Box 12093, Albany, NY 12212-2093, 518-449-8069
TIN WREATH, PO Box 13401, Albany, NY 12212-3401
THE LITTLE MAGAZINE, English Department, State Univ. of New York at Albany, Albany, NY 12222
13th MOON, 1400 Washington Avenue, SUNY, English Department, Albany, NY 12222-0001, 212-678-1074
FOR POETS ONLY, PO Box 4855, Schenectady, NY 12304
ALABAMA DOGSHOE MOUSTACHE, 317 Princetown Road, Schenectady, NY 12306-2022
dbqp, 317 Princetown Road, Schenectady, NY 12306-2022
SOCKS, DREGS AND ROCKING CHAIRS, 317 Princetown Road, Schenectady, NY 12306-2022
THE SUBTLE JOURNAL OF RAW COINAGE, 317 Princetown Road, Schenectady, NY 12306-2022
A VOICE WITHOUT SIDES, 317 Princetown Road, Schenectady, NY 12306-2022
MILDRED, Mildred Publishing Company, Inc., 961 Birchwood Lane, Niskayuna, NY 12309, (518) 374-5410
McPherson & Company Publishers, PO Box 1126, Kingston, NY 12401, 914-331-5807
OXALIS, PO Box 3993, Kingston, NY 12401, 914-687-7942
Selah Publishing Co., PO Box 103, Accord, NY 12404, 201-249-9849
ART TIMES, PO Box 730, Mount Marion, NY 12456-0730, 914-246-6944
Spear Shaker Press, PO Box 308, Napanoch, NY 12458, 914-647-3608
SPEAR SHAKER REVIEW, PO Box 308, Napanoch, NY 12458, 914-647-3608
Raymond Saroff, Publisher, Box 269, Acorn Hill Road, Olive Bridge, NY 12461
Gull Books, Box 273 A, Prattsville, NY 12468, 518-299-3171
Step-Over Toe-Hold Press, PO Box 40, Rosendale, NY 12472, 914-658-8780

701

FOOTSTEPS, Box 75, Round Top, NY 12473
Footsteps Press, Box 75, Round Top, NY 12473
BITTERROOT, PO Box 489, Spring Glen, NY 12483
APKL Publications, PO Box 371, Woodstock, NY 12498
Ash Tree Publishing, PO Box 64, Woodstock, NY 12498, 914-246-8081
Beekman Publishers, Inc., Po Box 888, Woodstock, NY 12498, 914-679-2300
Ceres Press, PO Box 87, Woodstock, NY 12498
Journey Publications, PO Box 423, Woodstock, NY 12498, 914-657-8434
LIGHTNING SWORD, PO Box 371, Woodstock, NY 12498
The Overlook Press, Road 1, PO Box 496, Woodstock, NY 12498, 914-679-8571
TRUE FOOD, PO Box 87, Woodstock, NY 12498
Open Book Publications, A Division of Station Hill Press, Station Hill Road, Barrytown, NY 12507
Station Hill Press, Station Hill Road, Barrytown, NY 12507, 914-758-5840
RESONANCE, PO Box 215, Beacon, NY 12508, 914-838-1217
CHESS LIFE, United States Chess Federation, 186 Route 9W, New Windsor, NY 12553, (914) 562-8350
SCHOOL MATES, 186 Route 9W, New Windsor, NY 12553, 914-562-8350
U.S. Chess Federation, 186 Route 9W, New Windsor, NY 12553, 914-562-8350
THE PUBLIC RELATIONS QUARTERLY, PO Box 311, Rhinebeck, NY 12572, 914-876-2081
SATORI, Hands Off The Press, Inc., PO Box 318, Tivoli, NY 12583, 914-757-4443
Front Street Publishers, 22A Sheldon Drive, Poughkeepsie, NY 12603
INVESTMENT COLUMN QUARTERLY (newsletter), PO Box 233, Barryville, NY 12719, 914-557-8713
NAR Publications, PO Box 233, Barryville, NY 12719, 914-557-8713
THE SNAIL'S PACE REVIEW, RR#2, Box 363 Brownell Road, Cambridge, NY 12816, 518-692-9953
The Greenfield Review Press/Ithaca House, PO Box 308, Greenfield Center, NY 12833-0308, 518-584-1728
ADIRONDAC, Rd. #3, Box 3055, Lake George, NY 12845-9523, 518-668-4447
Adirondack Mountain Club, Inc., RR 3, Box 3055, Lake George, NY 12845, 518-668-4447
THE DUPLEX PLANET, PO Box 1230, Saratoga Springs, NY 12866, 518-587-5356
SALMAGUNDI, Skidmore College, Saratoga Springs, NY 12866, 518-584-5000
Passport Press, PO Box 1346, Champlain, NY 12919-1346, 514-937-3868
Aa To Zz Publishing Co., 506 Valley Drive East, Chittenango, NY 13037, 315-687-9631
Ed-U Press, Inc., 7174 Mott Road, Fayetteville, NY 13066
LAKE EFFECT, Lake County Writers Group, PO Box 59, Oswego, NY 13126, 315-342-3579
SOVIET SPACEFLIGHT REPORT, PO Box 25, Pulaski, NY 13142
Starwise Publications, PO Box 25, Pulaski, NY 13142
THE POETRY PEDDLER, PO Box 250, W. Monroe, NY 13167, 315-676-2050
Snowbound Press, PO Box 250, W. Monroe, NY 13167, 315-676-2050
CONSTRUCTIVE ACTION NEWSLETTER, Act/Action, B 1104 Ross Towers 710 Lodi St., Syracuse, NY 13203, 315-471-4644
THE PEACE NEWSLETTER, 924 Burnet Avenue, Syracuse, NY 13203, 315-472-5478
Syracuse Peace Council, 924 Burnet Avenue, Syracuse, NY 13203, 315-472-5478
Syracuse Cultural Workers, PO Box 6367, Syracuse, NY 13217, 315-474-1132
POETPOURRI, Comstock Writers' Group, Inc., Box 3737 Taft Road, Syracuse, NY 13220
Acorn Publishing, Box 7067-D, Syracuse, NY 13261, 315-689-7072
Sunstone Publications, RD 4, Box 700A, Cooperstown, NY 13326, 607-547-8207
GRAHAM HOUSE REVIEW, Box 5000, Colgate University, Hamilton, NY 13346
THE MAGE, Student Association, Colgate University, Hamilton, NY 13346, 315-824-1000 (ask for Student Publications)
North Country Books, Inc., 18 Irving Place, Utica, NY 13501, 315-735-4877
Ash Lad Press, 14 West Main Street, Canton, NY 13617, 315-386-8820
AKWEKON LITERARY JOURNAL, PO Box 223, Hagansburg, NY 13655, 518-358-9531
AKWEKON: A National Native American Literary & Arts Journal, PO Box 223, Hogansburg, NY 13655, 518-358-9531/9535
BLUELINE, State University College, English Dept., Potsdam, NY 13676, 315-267-2006
CADENCE: THE REVIEW OF JAZZ & BLUES: CREATIVE IMPROVISED MUSIC, Cadence Building, Redwood, NY 13679, 315-287-2852 (FAX 315-287-2860)
Akwesasne Notes, PO Box 196, Rooseveltown, NY 13683, 518-358-9531
THE WALLACE STEVENS JOURNAL, Clarkson University, Potsdam, NY 13699-5750, 315-268-3987
Birch Brook Press, RD 1 Box 620, Delhi, NY 13753, 212-353-3326
Occam Publishers, Albor Road, RR1 Box 187A, Marathon, NY 13803-9755, 607-849-3186
Serpent & Eagle Press, 273 Main Street, Oneonta, NY 13820, 607-432-5604
M.A.F. Press, Box 392, Portlandville, NY 13834
THIRTEEN, Box 392, Portlandville, NY 13834-0392, 607-286-7500
Almar Press, 4105 Marietta Drive, Vestal, NY 13850, 607-722-0265 (6251)
Vestal Press Ltd, PO Box 97, 320 North Jensen Road, Vestal, NY 13851-0097, 607-797-4872
MODERN INTERNATIONAL DRAMA, c/o Theatre Dept., S.U.N.Y., Binghamton, NY 13901, 607-777-2704
MSS/NEW MYTHS, SUNY, Binghamton, NY 13901
Bellevue Press, 60 Schubert Street, Binghamton, NY 13905
MOODY STREET IRREGULARS: A Jack Kerouac Magazine, PO Box 157, Clarence Center, NY 14032, 716-741-3393
Moody Street Irregulars, Inc., PO Box 157, Clarence Center, NY 14032, 716-741-3393
Textile Bridge Press, PO Box 157, Clarence Center, NY 14032
FOR PARENTS, Interpersonal Communication Services, Inc., 7052 West Lane, Suite #090163, Eden, NY 14057, 716-992-3316
White Pine Press, 76 Center Street, Fredonia, NY 14063, 716-672-5743
BOOMBAH HERALD, 15 Park Boulevard, Lancaster, NY 14086
The Edwin Mellen Press, PO Box 450, Lewiston, NY 14092, 716-754-2266
ELF: ECLECTIC LITERARY FORUM (ELF MAGAZINE), PO Box 392, Tonawanda, NY 14150, 716-695-7669
ORO MADRE, 44 North Pearl Street #44, Buffalo, NY 14202
Ruddy Duck Press, 44 North Pearl Street #44, Buffalo, NY 14202-1422
Potentials Development, Inc., 775 Main Street, Suite 604, Buffalo, NY 14203, 716-842-2658

702

EARTH'S DAUGHTERS: Feminist Arts Periodical, Box 622, Station C, Buffalo, NY 14209, 716-837-7778
PAUNCH, 123 Woodward Avenue, Buffalo, NY 14214, 716-836-7332
FREE INQUIRY, Council For Democratic & Secular Humanism, PO Box 5, Buffalo, NY 14215, 716-834-2921
The Clyde Press, 373 Lincoln Parkway, Buffalo, NY 14216, 716-875-4713/834-1254
Labor Arts Books, 1064 Amherst St., Buffalo, NY 14216, 716-873-4131
LIVING FREE, Box 29, Hiler Branch, Buffalo, NY 14223
Amherst Media, 418 Homecrest Drive, Amherst, NY 14226, 716-874-4450
THE HUMANIST, 7 Harwood Drive, PO Box 146, Amherst, NY 14226-0146, 716-839-5080
AMANITA BRANDY, PO Box 149, Amherst Branch, Buffalo, NY 14226-0149, 716-839-2415
CREATION/EVOLUTION JOURNAL, PO Box 146, 7 Harwood Drive, Buffalo, NY 14226, 716-839-5080
W. Paul Ganley: Publisher, P.O. Box 149, Amherst Branch, Buffalo, NY 14226, 716-839-2415
WEIRDBOOK, Box 149, Amherst Branch, Buffalo, NY 14226, 716-839-2415
THE $ENSIBLE SOUND, 403 Darwin Drive, Snyder, NY 14226, 716-681-3513
SLIPSTREAM, Slipstream Productions, Box 2071, New Market Station, Niagara Falls, NY 14301, 716-282-2616 (after 5 p.m., E.S.T.)
BOA Editions, Ltd., 92 Park Avenue, Brockport, NY 14420, 716-637-3844
State Street Press, PO Box 278, Brockport, NY 14420, 716-637-0023
SENECA REVIEW, Hobart & William Smith Colleges, Geneva, NY 14456, 315-781-3349
Citeaux Commentarii Cistercienses, c/o Br. Anthony Weber, Abbey of the Genesee, Piffard, NY 14533
CITEAUX: COMMENTARII CISTERCIENSES, c/o Br. Anthony Weber, Abbey of the Genesee, Piffard, NY 14533
Syzygy, Box 428, Rush, NY 14543, 716-226-2127
Stereopticon Press, 534 Wahlmont Drive, Webster, NY 14580, 716-671-2342
Bet Alpha Editions, PO Box 20042, Rochester, NY 14602, 716-442-0570
Adaptive Living, PO Box 60857, Rochester, NY 14606
AFTERIMAGE, 31 Prince Street, Rochester, NY 14607, 716-442-8676
Visual Studies Workshop, Research Center, 31 Prince Street, Rochester, NY 14607, 716-442-8676
StarMist Books, Box 12640, Rochester, NY 14612
THE ROUND TABLE: A Journal of Poetry and Fiction, PO Box 18673, Rochester, NY 14618
Center Press, 232 Post Avenue, Rochester, NY 14619-1313
EXIT, 232 Post Avenue, Rochester, NY 14619-1313, FAX 716-328-7016
BLAKE: AN ILLUSTRATED QUARTERLY, Dept. of English, Univ. of Rochester, Rochester, NY 14627, 716-275-3820
CAMERA OBSCURA: A Journal of Feminism and Film Theory, University of Rochester, R Rhees Library, Rochester, NY 14627
MIORITA...A Journal of Romanian Studies, Dept of F.L.L.L., Univ of Rochester, Dewey Hall 482, Rochester, NY 14627, 716-275-4258, 275-4251
Lion Press, PO Box 92541, Rochester, NY 14692, 716-381-6410
HEATHENZINE, 511 West Sullivan Street, Olean, NY 14760
Split Personality Press, 511 West Sullivan, Olean, NY 14760
TEMM POETRY MAGAZINE, 511 West Sullivan Street, Olean, NY 14760
Heart of the Lakes Publishing, PO Box 299, Interlaken, NY 14847-0299, 607-532-4997
Firebrand Books, 141 The Commons, Ithaca, NY 14850, 607-272-0000
McBooks Press, 908 Steam Mill Road, Ithaca, NY 14850, 607-272-2114
ILR Press, Cornell University, School of Indust. & Labor Relations, Ithaca, NY 14851-0952, 607-255-3061
RUBBERSTAMPMADNESS, PO Box 6585, Ithaca, NY 14851-6585
Snow Lion Publications, Inc., PO Box 6483, Ithaca, NY 14851, 607-273-8506; 607-273-8519; fax 607-273-8508
CAMELLIA, PO Box 4092, Ithaca, NY 14852
EPOCH, 251 Goldwin Smith Hall, Cornell Univ., Ithaca, NY 14853, 607-255-3385
Great Elm Press, 1205 County Route 60, Rexville, NY 14877
THE CIVIL ABOLITIONIST, Box 26, Swain, NY 14884, 607-545-6213
Oak Tree, Box 26, Swain, NY 14884, 607-545-6213

NORTH CAROLINA

The Jackpine Press, 1007 Paschal Drive, Winston-Salem, NC 27106, 919-759-0783
Greencrest Press Inc., Box 7745, Winston-Salem, NC 27109, 919-722-6463
THE CRESCENT REVIEW, PO Box 15065, Winston-Salem, NC 27113, 919-924-1851
Jamison Station Press, 802 West Street, Winston-Salem, NC 27127-5116
INTERNATIONAL POETRY REVIEW, PO Box 2047, Greensboro, NC 27402, 919-273-1711
Unicorn Press, PO Box 3307, Greensboro, NC 27402
March Street Press, 3006 Stonecutter Terrace, Greensboro, NC 27405
PARTING GIFTS, 3006 Stonecutter Terrace, Greensboro, NC 27405
Tudor Publishers, Inc., 3007 Taliaferro Road, Greensboro, NC 27408-2628, 919-282-5907
ELT Press, Department of English, University of North Carolina, Greensboro, NC 27412-5001, 919-334-5446
ENGLISH LITERATURE IN TRANSITION, 1880-1920, Department of English, University of North Carolina, Greensboro, NC 27412-5001, 919-334-5446
THE GREENSBORO REVIEW, Dept. of English, Univ. of North Carolina-Greensboro, Greensboro, NC 27412, 919-334-5459
The Carolina Wren Press, PO Box 277, Carrboro, NC 27510, 919-560-2738
Lollipop Power Books, PO Box 277, Carrboro, NC 27510, 919-560-2738
Signal Books, PO Box 940, Carrboro, NC 27510, 919-929-5985
CHANGE: The Journal of the Synergetic Society, 1825 North Lake Shore Dr, Chapel Hill, NC 27514, 919-942-2994
FORBIDDEN LINES, PO Box 23, Chapel Hill, NC 27514, 942-5386
INCITE INFORMATION, 1507 E. Franklin Street #530, Chapel Hill, NC 27514
Synergetics Press, 1825 North Lake Shore Drive, Chapel Hill, NC 27514, 919-942-2994
THE NEW RAIN MAGAZINE, PO Box 2087, Chapel Hill, NC 27515
New View Publications, PO Box 3021, Chapel Hill, NC 27515-3021
Ventana Press, PO Box 2468, Chapel Hill, NC 27515, 919-942-0220
THE SUN, A MAGAZINE OF IDEAS, 107 North Roberson Street, Chapel Hill, NC 27516, 919-942-5282
Meridional Publications, 7101 Winding Way, Wake Forest, NC 27587, 919-556-2940

NORTH CAROLINA LIBRARIES, 7101 Winding Way, Wake Forest, NC 27587, 919-556-2940
CAROLINA QUARTERLY, CB# 3520 Greenlaw Hall, Univ of N. Carolina, Chapel Hill, NC 27599-3520, 919-962-0244
The New South Company, 236 East Davie Street, Raleigh, NC 27601-1808
FARCE, Raleigh's Review of Alternative Arts, PO Box 543, Raleigh, NC 27602, 919-834-9203
The Paper Plant, PO Box 543, Raleigh, NC 27602, 919-834-9203
Alternating Crimes Publishing, PO Box 10363, Raleigh, NC 27605, 919-834-7542
SCREAM MAGAZINE, PO Box 10363, Raleigh, NC 27605, 919-834-7542
Acid Rain Foundation, Inc., 1410 Varsity Drive, Raleigh, NC 27606, 919-828-9443
Rockwell Publishing, 7905 Breda Court, Raleigh, NC 27606
The North Carolina Haiku Society Press, PO Box 14247, Raleigh, NC 27620, 919-231-4531
OBSIDIAN II: BLACK LITERATURE IN REVIEW, Dept. of English, Box 8105, NC State University, Raleigh, NC 27695-8105, 919-737-3870
POSTMODERN CULTURE, Box 8105, Raleigh, NC 27695, 919-737-2687
AFRICA NEWS, P.O. Box 3851, Durham, NC 27702, 919-286-0747
Crones' Own Press, PO Box 488, Durham, NC 27702, 919-688-3521
Institute for Southern Studies, PO Box 531, Durham, NC 27702
SOUTHERN EXPOSURE, PO Box 531, Durham, NC 27702, 919-688-8167
Jacar Press, 612 Bon Air Avenue, Durham, NC 27704-3302, 919-365-4188
AMERICAN LITERATURE, 304 E. Allen Building, Duke University, Durham, NC 27706, 919-684-3948
SIGNS: JOURNAL OF WOMEN IN CULTURE AND SOCIETY, Duke University, 207 East Duke Building, Durham, NC 27708, 919-684-2783
LADYSLIPPER CATALOG + RESOURCE GUIDE OF RECORDS, TAPES & VIDEOS BY WOMEN, PO Box 3124, Durham, NC 27715, 919-683-1570
Ladyslipper, Inc., PO Box 3124, Durham, NC 27715, 919-683-1570
TAR RIVER POETRY, Department of English, East Carolina University, Greenville, NC 27834, 919-752-6041
NORTH CAROLINA LITERARY REVIEW, English Department, East Carolina University, Greenville, NC 27858, 919-757-6041/6684
Pamlico Press, 1611 Oaklawn Avenue, Greenville, NC 27858, (919) 756-5964
Venture Press, 104 South Respess Street, Washington, NC 27889
CRUCIBLE, English Department, Barton College, Wilson, NC 27893, 237-3161 X217
LOBLOLLY: A LITERARY BIANNUAL OF THE VORTEX, 1310 Raleigh Road, Wilson, NC 27893, 919-237-2642
Star Books, Inc., 408 Pearson Street, Wilson, NC 27893, 919-237-1591
STARLIGHT, 408 Pearson Street, Wilson, NC 27893, 919-237-1591
SOUTHERN POETRY REVIEW, Department of English, UNC Charlotte, Charlotte, NC 28223, 704-547-4309; 704-547-2633
Guilt & Gardenias Press, PO Box 318, Fayetteville, NC 28302, 919-323-1776
Scots Plaid Press (Persephone Press), 22-B Pine Lake Drive, Whispering Pines, NC 28327-9388
Saint Andrews Press, c/o Saint Andrews College, Laurinburg, NC 28352-5598, 919-276-3652
PEMBROKE MAGAZINE, PO Box 60, PSU, Pembroke, NC 28372, 919-521-4214 ext 433
SANDHILLS/ST. ANDREWS REVIEW, 2200 Airport Road, Pinehurst, NC 28374, 919-692-6185
A CAROLINA LITERARY COMPANION, Community Council for the Arts, PO Box 3554, Kinston, NC 28501, (919) 527-2517
Sheer Joy! Press, PO Box 608, Pink Hill, NC 28572, 919-568-6101
SYNAESTHESIA, Route 3, Box 283, Hickory, NC 28602, (704) 327-9124
American Impressions, PO Box 3706, Hickory, NC 28603, 704-324-1416
HEMLOCKS AND BALSAMS, Box 128, Lees-McRae College, Banner Elk, NC 28604, 704-898-4284
Appalachian Consortium Press, University Hall, Appalachian State University, Boone, NC 28608, 704-262-2064, 704-262-2076
Third Lung Press, PO Box 361, Conover, NC 28613, 704-465-1254
THIRD LUNG REVIEW, PO Box 361, Conover, NC 28613, 704-465-1254
McFarland & Company, Inc., Publishers, Box 611, Jefferson, NC 28640, 919-246-4460
WLW JOURNAL: News/Views/Reviews for Women and Libraries, Box 611, Jefferson, NC 28640, 919-246-4460
BLACK MOUNTAIN REVIEW, PO Box 1112, Black Mountain, NC 28711-1112
Lorien House, PO Box 1112, Black Mountain, NC 28711, 704-669-6211
Celo Valley Books, 346 Seven Mile Ridge Road, Burnsville, NC 28714, 704-675-5918
Brain Books, 2075 Buffalo Creek Road, Lake Lure, NC 28746, 704-625-9153
INTERNATIONAL BRAIN DOMINANCE REVIEW, 2075 Buffalo Creek Road, Lake Lure, NC 28746, 704-625-9153
FIBERARTS, 50 College Street, Asheville, NC 28801, 704-253-0468
Altamont Press, Inc., 50 College Street, Asheville, NC 28801, 704-253-0468
French Broad Press, The Asheville School, Asheville, NC 28806, 704-255-7909

NORTH DAKOTA

NORTH DAKOTA QUARTERLY, University of North Dakota, PO Box 8237, Grand Forks, ND 58202, 701-777-3321
North Dakota Quarterly Press, University of North Dakota, PO Box 8237, Grand Forks, ND 58202, 701-777-3321
PLAINSWOMAN, PO Box 8027, Grand Forks, ND 58202, 701-777-8043
BLOODROOT, PO Box 891, Grand Forks, ND 58206-0891, 701-775-6079
Bloodroot, Inc., PO Box 891, Grand Forks, ND 58206-0891, 701-746-5858
PLAINS POETRY JOURNAL (PPJ), PO Box 2337, Bismarck, ND 58502
OBESITY & HEALTH: CURRENT RESEARCH AND RELATED ISSUES, Healthy Living Institute, RR 2, Box 905, Hettinger, ND 58639, 701-567-2845
Quill Books, PO Box 728-DB, Minot, ND 58702
Willowood Press, PO Box 1846, Minot, ND 58702, 701-838-0579

OHIO

Cumberland, 7652 Sawmill Road, Suite 194, Dublin, OH 43017
CUMBERLAND, 7652 Sawmill Road, Suite 194, Dublin, OH 43017
THE KENYON REVIEW, Kenyon College, Gambier, OH 43022, 614-427-3339
Ohio Chess Association, 224 East Broadway, Apt. B, Granville, OH 43023

704

Pudding House Publications, 60 North Main Street, Johnstown, OH 43031
PUDDING MAGAZINE: THE INTERNATIONAL JOURNAL OF APPLIED POETRY, 60 North Main Street, Johnstown, OH 43031
THE WRITERS' BLOC*, Box 212, Marysville, OH 43040, 513-642-8019
The Broken Stone, PO Box 246, Reynoldsburg, OH 43068
The Forces of Magic, PO Box 246, Reynoldsburg, OH 43068
Pebbles, PO Box 246, Reynoldsburg, OH 43068
THE BOOK REPORT: Journal for Junior & Senior High School Librarians, 5701 N. High Street, Suite One, Worthington, OH 43085, 614-436-7107; FAX 614-436-9490
LIBRARY TALK: The Magazine for Elementary School Librarians, 5701 N. High Street, Suite 1, Worthington, OH 43085, 614-436-7107; fax 614-436-9490
Linworth Publishing, Inc., 5701 N. High Street, Suite 1, Worthington, OH 43085, 614-436-7107; FAX 614-436-9490
COLUMBUS FREE PRESS, 1066 North High Street, Columbus, OH 43201-2440, 614-228-5796
NANCY'S MAGAZINE, N's M Publications, PO Box 02108, Columbus, OH 43202, 614-294-7935
The Biting Idge/Miracle Press (Chrysalis Publications), 581 South 6th Street, German Village, Columbus, OH 43206-1274
Amen-Ra Publishing Company, Box 3481, Columbus, OH 43210, 614-444-4460
THE JOURNAL: The Literary Magazine of the Ohio State University, OSU Dept. of English, 164 W. 17th Avenue, Columbus, OH 43210, 614-292-4076
THE MODERN LANGUAGE JOURNAL, Department of German, Ohio State University, Columbus, OH 43210-1229, 614-292-3748
Carpenter Press, PO Box 14387, Columbus, OH 43214
LOST AND FOUND TIMES, 137 Leland Ave, Columbus, OH 43214
Luna Bisonte Prods, 137 Leland Ave, Columbus, OH 43214, 614-846-4126
National Stereoscopic Association, Box 14801, Columbus, OH 43214, 614-263-4296
STEREO WORLD, Box 14801, Columbus, OH 43214, 614-263-4296
FREE PRESS NETWORK, PO Box 15548, Columbus, OH 43215, 614-236-1908
OHIOANA QUARTERLY, 1105 Ohio Dept Bldg., 65 S. Front St, Columbus, OH 43215, 614-466-3831
The Organization, Box 170, 400 N. High Street, Columbus, OH 43215, 614-447-8178
POLITICALLY INCORRECT, Box 170, 400 N. High Street, Columbus, OH 43215, 614-447-8178
THE SLEEPWALKER'S JOURNAL, 820 North Park Street, Columbus, OH 43215, 614-294-2922
Avalanche Press, PO Box 30815, Gahanna, OH 43230
COLUMBUS SINGLE SCENE, Box 30856, Gahanna, OH 43230, 614-476-8802
CORNFIELD REVIEW, English Dept, Ohio State Univ., 1465 Mount Vernon Avenue, Marion, OH 43302-5695, 614-389-6786
MID-AMERICAN REVIEW, Dept of English, Bowling Green State University, Bowling Green, OH 43403, 419-372-2725
THE DRAGONFANG, 9047 South River Rd., Waterville, OH 43566, 419-878-7246
11 X 13 - BROADSIDE, 32 Scott House, University of Toledo, Toledo, OH 43606
GLASS WILL, Department of English, University of Toledo, Toledo, OH 43606
MARK, Rm. 2514, Student Union, University of Toledo, Toledo, OH 43606, 419-537-2373
Toledo Poets Center Press, Department of English, University of Toledo, Toledo, OH 43606
TOWPATHS, 2121 Brookdale Road, Toledo, OH 43606, 419-531-9575
TOPICAL TIME, 1633 Park Ridge Lane, Toledo, OH 43614, 419-382-2719
Raven Rocks Press, 54118 Crum Road, Beallsville, OH 43716, 614-926-1705
REFLECTIONS, PO Box 368, Duncan Falls, OH 43734, 614-674-5209; 796-2595
Senay Publishing Inc., PO Box 397, Chesterland, OH 44026, 216-256-8519
BLACK RIVER REVIEW, 855 Mildred, Lorain, OH 44052, 216-244-9654
GENERATOR, 8139 Midland Road, Mentor, OH 44060, 216-951-3209
Generator Press, 8139 Midland Road, Mentor, OH 44060, 216-951-3209
FIELD, Rice Hall, Oberlin College, Oberlin, OH 44074
Mermaid Press, Box 183, Vermilion, OH 44089
NOOK NEWS CONFERENCES AND KLATCHES BULLETIN, 38114 Third Street, Suite 181, Willoughby, OH 44094, 216-975-8965
THE NOOK NEWS CONTESTS AND AWARDS BULLETIN, 38114 Third Street, Suite 181, Willoughby, OH 44094, 216-975-8965
THE NOOK NEWS MARKET BULLETIN, 38114 3rd Street #181, Willoughby, OH 44094, 216-975-8965
NOOK NEWS REVIEW OF WRITERS' PUBLICATIONS, 38114 Third Street, Suite 181, Willoughby, OH 44094, 216-975-8965
OHIO WRITER, PO Box 528, Willoughby, OH 44094-0528
THE WRITER'S NOOK NEWS, 38114 3rd Street #181, Willoughby, OH 44094-6140, 216-975-8965
The Writers' Nook Press, 38114 3rd Street #181, Willoughby, OH 44094, 216-975-8965
Cleveland State Univ. Poetry Center, Dept English, Cleveland State Univ., Cleveland, OH 44115, 216-687-3986
The Cobham and Hatherton Press, 1770 The Huntington Building, Cleveland, OH 44115, 216-589-4960
THE GAMUT, Cleveland State University, 1983 E. 24th Street, #FT1218, Cleveland, OH 44115-2440, 216-687-4679
WHISKEY ISLAND MAGAZINE, U.C. 7 Cleveland State University, Cleveland, OH 44115, 687-2056
Targeted Communications, PO Box 18002, Cleveland Heights, OH 44118-0002, 216-397-0268
Octavia Press, 3546 Edison Road, Cleveland, OH 44121, (216) 381-2853
THE ROCK HALL REPORTER, Big 'O' Publications, PO Box 24124, Cleveland, OH 44124
ADDICTION & RECOVERY, 4959 Commerce Parkway, Cleveland, OH 44128, 216-464-1210
Kenyette Productions, 16402 Cloverside Avenue, Cleveland, OH 44128-2120, 216-921-5029
RYAN'S REVIEW, 7810 Bertha Avenue, Parma, OH 44129-3110
Telstar Publishing, 7810 Bertha Avenue, Parma, OH 44129-3110
THE YELLOW PAGES, 7810 Bertha Avenue, Parma, OH 44129-3110
Step Ahead Press, A Heartlite Inc. Company, 6509 Brecksville Road, PO Box 31360, Cleveland, OH 44131, 216-526-6727
THE GATE, PO Box 43518, Richmond Heights, OH 44143
Oakhill Press, 7449 Oakhill Road, Cleveland, OH 44146-5901, 216-646-9999
IMPETUS, 4975 Comanche Trail, Stow, OH 44224, 216-688-5210
Implosion Press, 4975 Comanche Trail, Stow, OH 44224, 216-688-5210
Envirographics, Box 334, Hiram, OH 44234, (216) 527-5207

HIRAM POETRY REVIEW, Box 162, Hiram, OH 44234, 216-569-5331
Redeemer Resources, 4146 State Road, Medina, OH 44256-8408
KALEIDOSCOPE: INTERNATIONAL MAGAZINE OF LITERATURE, FINE ARTS, AND DISABILITY, UCPSH, 326
    Locust Street, Akron, OH 44302, 216-762-9755; 216-379-3349 (TDD)
THE MODEL & TOY COLLECTOR, 330 Merriman Road, Akron, OH 44303, 216-769-2523
Dumpster Press, PO Box 80044, Akron, OH 44308, 216-762-1279
DUMPSTER TIMES, PO Box 80044, Akron, OH 44308, 216-762-1279
Hampshire Books, 1660 Akron Peninsula Road #103, Akron, OH 44313-5156, 216-867-6868
THE THOMAS WOLFE REVIEW, Department of English, University of Akron, Akron, OH 44325, 216-972-7470
Alegra House Publishers, PO Box 1443-D, Warren, OH 44482, 216-372-2951
PIG IRON, P.O. Box 237, Youngstown, OH 44501, 216-783-1269
Pig Iron Press, P.O. Box 237, Youngstown, OH 44501
The George Whittell Memorial Press, 3722 South Avenue, Youngstown, OH 44502, 216-783-0645
OHIO CHESS BULLETIN, 128 Ertle Street Northeast, Massillon, OH 44646-3230, 216-832-8907
SOLO FLYER, 2115 Clearview NW, Massillon, OH 44646
Spare Change Poetry Press, 2115 Clearvi NE, Massillon, OH 44646
ARTFUL DODGE, Department of English, College of Wooster, Wooster, OH 44691
The Ashland Poetry Press, Ashland University, Ashland, OH 44805, 419-289-5110
Brennen Publishing Company, Ashland University, Clayton Hall, Ashland, OH 44805
AMERICAN SQUAREDANCE, Burdick Enterprises, PO Box 488, Huron, OH 44839, 419-433-2188
Bottom Dog Press, c/o Firelands College of BGSU, Huron, OH 44839, 419-433-5560
Cambric Press, 901 Rye Beach Road, Huron, OH 44839, 419-433-5660; 419-929-8767
Interalia/Design Books, PO Box 404, Oxford, OH 45056-0404, 513-523-6880
OXFORD MAGAZINE, 356 Bachelor Hall, Miami University, Oxford, OH 45056, 513-529-5221
STARWIND, PO Box 98, Ripley, OH 45167, 513-392-4549
Starwind Press, PO Box 98, Ripley, OH 45167, 513-392-4549
ST Publications/Book Division, 407 Gilbert Avenue, Cincinnati, OH 45202, 513-421-2050; fax 513-421-5144
STORY, 1507 Dana Avenue, Cincinnati, OH 45207, 513-531-2222
Vivation Publishing Co., PO Box 8269, Cincinnati, OH 45208-0608, 513-321-4405
Mosaic Press, 358 Oliver Road, Dept. 45, Cincinnati, OH 45215, 513-761-5977
THE LOOGIE, 435 Probasco #3, Cincinnati, OH 45220, 513-281-1353
CINCINNATI POETRY REVIEW, Dept of English (069), University of Cincinnati, Cincinnati, OH 45221, 513-556-3922
SPITBALL: The Literary Baseball Magazine, 6224 Collegevue, Cincinnati, OH 45224, 513-541-4296
AMBERGRIS, PO Box 29919, Cincinnati, OH 45229
THE VINCENT BROTHERS REVIEW, 1459 Sanzon Drive, Fairborn, OH 45324
THE ANTIOCH REVIEW, PO Box 148, Yellow Springs, OH 45387, 513-767-6389
Community Service, Inc., Box 243, Yellow Springs, OH 45387, 513-797-2161, 767-1461
COMMUNITY SERVICE NEWSLETTER, Box 243, Yellow Springs, OH 45387, 513-767-2161
MAIL ORDER SUCCESS NEWSLETTER, PO Box 14689, Dayton, OH 45413
Tomart Publications, PO Box 292102, Dayton, OH 45429, 513-294-2250
MAD RIVER: A Journal of Essays, Department of Philosophy, Wright State University, Dayton, OH 45435, 513-873-2173
Arlotta Press, 6340 Millbank Dr., Dayton, OH 45459
Kettering Foundation, 200 Commons Road, Dayton, OH 45459-2799, 513-434-7300
KETTERING REVIEW, 200 Commons Road, Dayton, OH 45459-2799, 513-434-7300
THE WITTENBERG REVIEW: An Undergraduate Journal of the Liberal Arts, Wittenberg University, PO Box 720,
    Springfield, OH 45501, 513-327-7428
OHIO RENAISSANCE REVIEW, PO Box 804, Infinity Press and Publications, Ironton, OH 45638, 614-532-0846
WORK-AT-HOME REPORT, 12221 Beaver Pike, Jackson, OH 45640, 614-988-2331
Bloody Twin Press, 4525 Blue Creek Road, Stout, OH 45684, 513-549-4162
OLD ABE'S NEWS, Route 2, Box 242, Vinton, OH 45686, 614-388-8895
Croissant & Company, P.O. Box 282, Athens, OH 45701-0282
THE OHIO REVIEW, Ellis Hall, Ohio University, Athens, OH 45701, 614-593-1900
BIRD WATCHER'S DIGEST, PO Box 110, Marietta, OH 45750, 614-373-5285
RIVERWIND, General Studies, Hocking Technical College, Nelsonville, OH 45764, 614-753-3591
COACHING SLO'PITCH SOFTBALL, PO Box 304, Lima, OH 45802
GDE Publications, PO Box 304, Lima, OH 45802
SLOWPITCH TIPS, PO Box 304, Lima, OH 45802
SOFTBALL ILLUSTRATED, PO Box 304, Lima, OH 45802
THE PRINTER, 337 Wilson Street, Findlay, OH 45840, 419-423-9184

OKLAHOMA

BYLINE, PO Box 130596, Edmond, OK 73013, 405-348-5591
Levite of Apache, 1005 N. Flood, #105, Norman, OK 73069, 405-366-6442
Poetry Around, 436 Elm, Norman, OK 73069, 405-329-9143
Point Riders Press, PO Box 2731, Norman, OK 73070
RENEGADE, Point Riders Press, PO Box 2731, Norman, OK 73070, 405-524-5733
CALLIGRAPHY REVIEW, 1624 24th Avenue SW, Norman, OK 73072, 405-364-8794
Pueblo Publishing Press, PO Box 850508, Yukon, OK 73085-0508, 405-354-7825
Cooper House Publishing Inc., PO Box 54947, Oklahoma City, OK 73154, 405-949-2020
POET MAGAZINE, PO Box 54947, Oklahoma City, OK 73154, 405-949-2020
Cedar Ridge Publications, 73 Cedar Ridge Road, Broken Arrow, OK 74011
Seabird Publishing, PO Box 624, Broken Arrow, OK 74013, 918-258-6209
Evans Publications Inc., 133 S. Main, PO Box 665, Perkins, OK 74059, 405-547-2144
CIMARRON REVIEW, 205 Morrill Hall, Oklahoma State University, Stillwater, OK 74078-0135, 405-744-9476
MIDLAND REVIEW, c/o English Department, Oklahoma State University, Stillwater, OK 74078
JAMES JOYCE QUARTERLY, University of Tulsa, 600 S. College, Tulsa, OK 74104
TULSA STUDIES IN WOMEN'S LITERATURE, 600 S. College, Tulsa, OK 74104, 918-631-2503
University of Tulsa, 600 South College, Tulsa, OK 74104

Garret Press, 4991 South Union Avenue, Tulsa, OK 74107-7839, 918-592-0729, 800-726-6265
Cardinal Press, Inc., 76 N Yorktown, Tulsa, OK 74110, 918-583-3651
NIMROD, Arts and Humanities Council of Tulsa, 2210 So. Main, Tulsa, OK 74114
Council Oak Books, 1428 S. St. Louis, Tulsa, OK 74120, 918-587-6454
Jigsaw Publishing House, 6830 S. Delaware Avenue, Tulsa, OK 74136-4501, 918-492-5112
New Levee Press, 3915 South 100 East Avenue, Tulsa, OK 74146-2434
Partners In Publishing, Box 50347, Tulsa, OK 74150, 918-584-5906
PIP COLLEGE 'HELPS' NEWSLETTER, Box 50347, Tulsa, OK 74150, 918-584-5906
HOBBY BOOKWATCH (MILITARY, GUN & HOBBY BOOK REVIEW), PO Box 52033, Tulsa, OK 74152,
    918-743-7048
Harrison House Publishers, PO Box 35035, Tulsa, OK 74153, 918-582-2126
MCN Press, PO Box 702073, Tulsa, OK 74170
Old World Travel Books, Inc., 2608 E. 74th, PO Box 700863, Tulsa, OK 74170, 918-493-2642
Vista Mark Publications, 1401 Iroquois, PO Box 220, Chouteau, OK 74337, 918-476-6310
Sparrow Hawk Press, PO Box 1274, Tahlequah, OK 74465, 918-456-3421

OREGON

Mocha Publishing Company, 8475 SW Morgan Drive, Beaverton, OR 97005, 503-643-7591
Hot Off the Press, 7212 S Seven Oaks, Canby, OR 97013
Vitreous Group/Camp Colton, Camp Colton, Colton, OR 97017, 503-824-3150
Centerplace Publishing Co., PO Box 901, Lake Oswego, OR 97034, 800-96-CHILD
Circa Press, PO Box 482, Lake Oswego, OR 97034, 503-636-7241
Culinary Arts Ltd., PO Box 2157, Lake Oswego, OR 97035, 503-639-4549
Jorvik Press, PO Box 18, Marylhurst, OR 97036-0018, 503-636-9244
Peel Productions, PO Box 185, Molalla, OR 97038-0185, 503-829-6849
DOG RIVER REVIEW, 5976 Billings Road, Parkdale, OR 97041, 503-352-6494
Trout Creek Press, 5976 Billings Road, Parkdale, OR 97041, 503-352-6494
Bicentennial Era Enterprises, PO Box 1148, Scappoose, OR 97056, 503-684-3937
Willamette River Press, PO Box 605, Troutdale, OR 97060, 503-667-5548
HearSay Press TM, Box 555, West Linn, OR 97068-2706, 503-655-5010
Beautiful America Publishing Company, 9725 South West Commerce Circle, PO Box 646, Wilsonville, OR 97070,
    503-682-0173
Doral Publishing, PO Box 596, Wilsonville, OR 97070, 503-694-5707
Alioth Press, PO Box 1554, Beaverton, OR 97075, 503-644-0983
Princess Publishing, PO Box 386, Beaverton, OR 97075, 503-646-1234
Sauvie Island Press, PO Box 751, Beaverton, OR 97075-0751, 503-626-4237
GAFF PRESS, PO Box 1024, 114 SW Willow Lane, Astoria, OR 97103, 503-325-8288
Beyond Words Publishing, Inc., 13950 NW Pumpkin Ridge Road, Hillsboro, OR 97123, 503-647-5109; 647-5114 FAX
Mountain Publishing, PO Box 1747, Hillsboro, OR 97123, 503-628-3995
Blue Heron Publishing, Inc., Media Weavers, Route 3, Box 376, Hillsboro, OR 97124, 503-621-3911
Media Weavers, Route 3, Box 376, Hillsboro, OR 97124, 503-621-3911
WRITER'S N.W., Route 3, Box 376, Hillsboro, OR 97124
Peavine Publications, Box 1264, McMinnville, OR 97128, 503-472-1933
Health Plus Publishers, PO Box 1027, Sherwood, OR 97140, 503-625-0589
The Florian Group, 5620 SW Riverside Lane #8, Portland, OR 97201
NORTHWEST MAGAZINE, THE OREGONIAN'S SUNDAY MAGAZINE, 1320 SW Broadway, Portland, OR 97201
Oriel Press, 2020 SW Kanan, Portland, OR 97201, 503-245-6696
ENFANTAISIE: La Revue des Jeunes, 2603 S.E. 32nd Avenue, Portland, OR 97202, (503) 235-5304
HUBBUB, 5344 S.E. 38th Avenue, Portland, OR 97202, 503-775-0370
MISSISSIPPI MUD, 1336 SE Marion Street, Portland, OR 97202, 503-236-9962
Mud Press, 1336 S.E. Marion Street, Portland, OR 97202
Peninhand Press, 3665 Southeast Tolman, Portland, OR 97202
Strawberry Hill Press, 3848 SE Division St, Portland, OR 97202-1641, 415-664-8112
THE VOLCANO REVIEW, 3665 SE Tolman, Portland, OR 97202
INFOCUS, 519 SW 3rd Avenue, #712, Portland, OR 97204-2519, 503-227-3393
Portland Entertainment Publishing, 114 Southwest Second, Portland, OR 97204, 503-299-6155
OREGON HISTORICAL QUARTERLY, 1230 S.W. Park Ave., Portland, OR 97205, 503-222-1741
Oregon Historical Society Press, 1230 S.W. Park Avenue, Portland, OR 97205, 503-222-1741
NRG, 6735 S E 78th, Portland, OR 97206
Van Patten Publishing, 4204 SE Ogden Street, Portland, OR 97206-8452, 503-775-3815
Continuing Education Press, Portland State University, PO Box 1491, 1633 SW Park, Portland, OR 97207
Continuing Education Publications, PO Box 1491, Portland State University, Portland, OR 97207
PORTLAND REVIEW, PO Box 751, Portland, OR 97207, 503-725-4533
STYLUS, PO Box 1716, Portland, OR 97207
CLINTON ST., Box 3588, Portland, OR 97208, 503-222-6039
Metamorphous Press, PO Box 10616, Portland, OR 97210, 503-228-4972
MR. COGITO, 2518 N.W. Savier Street, Portland, OR 97210, 503-233-8131, 226-4135
Mr. Cogito Press, 2518 N.W. Savier, Portland, OR 97210, 503-233-8131, 226-4135
Pallas Communications, 4226 NE 23rd Avenue, Portland, OR 97211, 503-284-2848
Coast to Coast Books Inc., 2934 NE 16th Avenue, Portland, OR 97212-3345, 503-232-9772
SIGN OF THE TIMES-A CHRONICLE OF DECADENCE IN THE ATOMIC AGE, 3819 NE 15th, Portland, OR 97212,
    206-323-6764
Studio 403, 3819 NE 15th, Portland, OR 97212, 206-323-6764
Ki**2 Books, PO Box 13322, Portland, OR 97213, (503) 256-3485
Beynch Press Publishing Company, 1928 S.E. Ladd Avenue, Portland, OR 97214, 503-232-0433
Leaping Mountain Press, PO Box 14663, Portland, OR 97214
Reliant Marketing & Publishing, PO Box 17456, Portland, OR 97217, 257-0211
Flying Pencil Publications, PO Box 19062, Portland, OR 97219, 503-245-2314

Paradise Publications, 8110 SW Wareham, Portland, OR 97223, 503-246-1555
Blue Water Publishing, Inc., PO Box 230893, Tigard, OR 97224, 503-684-9749
Timber Press, 9999 S.W. Wilshire, Portland, OR 97225, 503-292-0745
Communicom Publishing Company, 19300 NW Sauvie Island Road, Portland, OR 97231, 503-621-3049
Prescott Street Press, PO Box 40312, Portland, OR 97240-0312
Sa-De Publications Inc., PO Box 42607, Portland, OR 97242, 503-235-2759
AMERICAN INDIAN BASKETRY, PO Box 66124, Portland, OR 97266, 503-233-8131
HAPPINESS HOLDING TANK, 9727 SE Reedway Street, Portland, OR 97266-3738, 503-771-6779
Institute for the Study of Traditional American Indian Arts Press, PO Box 66124, Portland, OR 97266, 503-233-8131
Stone Press, 9727 SE Reedway Street, Portland, OR 97266-3738
Breitenbush Books, Inc., P.O. Box 82157, Portland, OR 97282
Heart Publishing & Production, PO Box 82037, Portland, OR 97282, 503-221-3989; 800-777-5458; FAX 503-774-4457
PENINHAND, PO Box 82699, Portland, OR 97282
Dimi Press, 3820 Oak Hollow Lane, SE, Salem, OR 97302, 503-364-7698; fax 503-364-9727
Grosvenor USA, PO Box 7084, Salem, OR 97303-0084, 503-393-2962
DARK TOME, PO Box 705, Salem, OR 97308, 503-371-8647
Doggerel Press, PO Box 985, Salem, OR 97308, 503-588-2926
Energeia Publishing, Inc., PO Box 985, Salem, OR 97308, 503-588-2926
Scareware, PO Box 705, Salem, OR 97308, 503-371-8647
Calapooia Publications, PO Box 160, Brownsville, OR 97327, 503-369-2439
THE REAPER, c/o Story Line Press, Three Oaks Farm, Brownsville, OR 97327-9718, 503-466-5352
Story Line Press, Three Oaks Farm, Brownsville, OR 97327-9718, 503-466-5352
Drift Creek Press, 1020 NW 34th, Corvallis, OR 97330, 503-754-6303
Oregon State University Press, 101 Waldo Hall, Corvallis, OR 97331, 503-737-3166
APAEROS, 960 SW Jefferson Avenue, Corvallis, OR 97333
Arrowood Books, PO Box 2100, Corvallis, OR 97339, 503-753-9539
CALYX: A Journal of Art and Literature by Women, PO Box B, Corvallis, OR 97339, 503-753-9384
Calyx Books, PO Box B, Corvallis, OR 97339
CORVALLIS STREETS POETRY MAGAZINE, PO Box 2291, Corvallis, OR 97339, 758-8244
Grapevine Publications, Inc., PO Box 2449, Corvallis, OR 97339-2449, 503-754-0583; fax 503-754-6508
THE GROWING EDGE MAGAZINE, PO Box 1027, Corvallis, OR 97339, 503-757-0027; FAX 503-757-0028
SINSEMILLA TIPS (Domestic Marijuana Journal), PO Box 1027, Corvallis, OR 97339-1027, 503-757-0027; 757-8477;
   fax 503-757-0028
Arnie Wolman Co., PO Box 2291, Corvallis, OR 97339, 758-8244
CALAPOOYA COLLAGE, PO Box 309, Monmouth, OR 97361, 503-838-6292
Gahmken Press, PO Box 1467, Newport, OR 97365
MESSAGE POST, Light Living Library, Po Box 190—DB, Philomath, OR 97370
L.A.N.D., 4466 Ike Mooney Road, Silverton, OR 97381, 503-873-8829
LIVING AMONG NATURE DARINGLY!, 4466 Ike Mooney Road, Silverton, OR 97381, 503-873-8829
MIDWIFERY TODAY, Box 2672, Eugene, OR 97402, 503-344-7438
BookNotes :(TM) Resources for Small & Self-Publishers, PO Box 3877, Eugene, OR 97403-0877
Castle Peak Editions, 1670 E. 27th Avenue, Eugene, OR 97403, 503-342-2975
Communitas Press, PO Box 3784, Eugene, OR 97403, 503-485-0776
NORTHWEST REVIEW, 369 P.L.C., University of Oregon, Eugene, OR 97403, 503-686-3957
Rainy Day Press, 1147 East 26th, Eugene, OR 97403, 503-484-4626
SILVERFISH REVIEW, PO Box 3541, Eugene, OR 97403, 503-344-5060
THE LAVENDER NETWORK, PO Box 5421, Eugene, OR 97405, 503-485-7285
Sandpiper Press, PO Box 286, Brookings, OR 97415, 503-469-5588
HEALING PATH, PO Box 599-DB, Coos Bay, OR 97420, 0114
BOOK DEALERS WORLD, PO Box 606, Cottage Grove, OR 97424-0026
HEARTSONG REVIEW, PO Box 1084, Cottage Grove, OR 97424
North American Bookdealers Exchange, PO Box 606, Cottage Grove, OR 97424-0026
White Horse Press, 306 South First Street, Cottage Grove, OR 97424, 503-942-0659
Conscious Living, PO Box 9, Drain, OR 97435
STRESS MASTER, PO Box 9, Drain, OR 97435
Castalia Publishing Company, PO Box 1587, Eugene, OR 97440, 503-343-4433
HEMLOCK QUARTERLY, PO Box 11830, Eugene, OR 97440
Hemlock Society, PO Box 11830, Eugene, OR 97440
POETIC SPACE: Poetry & Fiction, PO Box 11157, Eugene, OR 97440
PULPHOUSE: THE HARDBACK MAGAZINE, PO Box 1227, Eugene, OR 97440, 503-344-6742
Pulphouse Publishing, PO Box 1227, Eugene, OR 97440, 503-344-6742
World Peace University Publications, PO Box 10869, Eugene, OR 97440, 503-231-3771
Wells & West, Publishers, 1166 Winsor, North Bend, OR 97459, 503-756-6802
Cross Cultural Press, 1166 South 42nd St., Springfield, OR 97478, 503-746-7401
Keyboard Workshop, PO Box 700, Medford, OR 97501, 664-2317
Cove View Press, 375 Tudor Street, Ashland, OR 97520
Home Power, Inc., PO Box 275, Ashland, OR 97520, 916-475-3179
THE PATRIOT, PO Box 1172, Ashland, OR 97520, 503-482-2578
Quicksilver Productions, P.O.Box 340, Ashland, OR 97520, 503-482-5343
Runaway Publications, PO Box 1172, Ashland, OR 97520, 503-482-2578
SPROUTLETTER, Box 62, Ashland, OR 97520, 503-488-2326 (9-5 M-F Pac. Time)
Valentine Publishing & Drama Co., PO Box 1378, Ashland, OR 97520-0046, 503-773-7035
PSI Research/The Oasis Press, 300 North Valley Drive, Grants Pass, OR 97526, 800-221-4089 (CA); 800-228-2275
Angst World Library, PO Box 593, Selma, OR 97538-0593
Lions Head Press, PO Box 5202, Klamath Falls, OR 97601, 503-883-2101
THIS IS IMPORTANT, PO Box 323, Beatty, OR 97621, 503-533-2375
Waterston Productions, Inc., 115 N.W. Oregon Avenue #8, Bend, OR 97701, 503-385-7025; FAX 503-385-7663
Gilgal Publications, PO Box 3386, Sunriver, OR 97707, 503-593-8639

Synesis Press, PO Box 1843-N, Bend, OR 97709, 503-382-6517, fax 503-382-0750
SHOTS, Box 109, Joseph, OR 97846
HFH Publications, PO Box 81, LaGrande, OR 97850, 503-963-6410
The Bear Wallow Publishing Company, PO Box 370, Union, OR 97883, 503-562-5687
Wordcraft, 953 N. Gale, Union, OR 97883, 503-562-5638

PENNSYLVANIA

TAPROOT LITERARY REVIEW, 302 Park Road, Ambridge, PA 15003, 412-266-8476
PIG IN A PAMPHLET, 331 Ridge Point Circle #14, Bridgeville, PA 15017-1530
Pig In A Poke Press, 331 Ridge Point Circle #14, Bridgeville, PA 15017, 412-521-1237
THE ADROIT EXPRESSION, PO Box 73, Courtney, PA 15029
Chess Enterprises, Inc., 107 Crosstree Road, Coraopolis, PA 15108
D-Amp Publications, PO Box 1243, Coraopolis, PA 15108, 412-262-4531
EN PASSANT, 107 Crosstree Road, Coraopolis, PA 15108
Sports Support Syndicate, 1739 East Carson Street, Pittsburgh, PA 15203, 412-481-2497
STROKES, 1739 East Carson Street, Pittsburgh, PA 15203, 412-481-2497
SHOOTING STAR REVIEW, 7123 Race Street, Pittsburgh, PA 15208, 412-731-7039
THE PITTSBURGH QUARTERLY, 36 Haberman Avenue, Pittsburgh, PA 15211-2144, 412-431-8885
NEW SINS, PO Box 7157, Pittsburgh, PA 15213, 412-621-5611
New Sins Press, PO Box 7157, Pittsburgh, PA 15213
STAGE WHISPER, PO Box 7157, Pittsburgh, PA 15213
VIOLENT VIRGINS, PO Box 7157, Pittsburgh, PA 15213
5 AM, 1109 Milton Avenue, Pittsburgh, PA 15218
LATIN AMERICAN LITERARY REVIEW, 2300 Palmer Street, Pittsburgh, PA 15218, 412-351-1477
Latin American Literary Review Press, 2300 Palmer Street, Pittsburgh, PA 15218, 412-351-1477
ATROCITY, 2419 Greensburg Pike, Pittsburgh, PA 15221
Cleis Press, PO Box 8933, Pittsburgh, PA 15221
G'RAPH, 2419 Greensburg Pike, Pittsburgh, PA 15221
Motheroot Publications, PO Box 8306, Pittsburgh, PA 15221-0306
PROCEEDINGS OF THE SPANISH INQUISITION, 2419 Greensburg Pike, Pittsburgh, PA 15221
LILLIPUT REVIEW, 207 S. Millvale Ave. #3, Pittsburgh, PA 15224
Guyasuta Publishers, 1687 Washington Road, Pittsburgh, PA 15228
Mogul Book and FilmWorks, PO Box 2773, Pittsburgh, PA 15230, 412-461-0705
QP Publishing, Box 18281, Pittsburgh, PA 15236-0281, 412-885-1982
THE CONSTANTIAN, The Constantian Society, 123 Orr Road, Pittsburgh, PA 15241, 412-831-8750
THE PENNSYLVANIA REVIEW, English Department, 526 C. L., University of Pittsburgh, Pittsburgh, PA 15260
The Post-Industrial Press, PO Box 265, Greensboro, PA 15338
FLIPSIDE, Dixon Hall, California University of PA, California, PA 15419, 412-938-5946
THE PLOUGH, Hutterian Brethren, Spring Valley, Route 381, N. Farmington, PA 15437-9506, 412-329-1100; fax 412-329-0942
Backwoods Books, McClellan Lane, PO Box 9, Gibbon Glade, PA 15440, 412-329-4581
NATURALLY YOURS, McClellan Lane, PO Box 9, Gibbon Glade, PA 15440, 412-329-4581
THE RAYSTOWN REVIEW, RD1, Box 205, Schellsburg, PA 15559
The Fairfield Street Press, 308 North Fairfield Street, Ligonier, PA 15658, 412-238-0109
Herald Press, 616 Walnut Avenue, Scottdale, PA 15683, 412-887-8500
ON THE LINE, 616 Walnut Avenue, Scottdale, PA 15683
Jessee Poet Publications, RD #1, Portersville, PA 16051
POETS AT WORK, R.D. #1, Portersville, PA 16051
THEY WON'T STAY DEAD!, 11 Werner Road, Greenville, PA 16125, 412-588-3471
THE WESTMINSTER REVIEW, Department of English, Westminster College, New Wilmington, PA 16172
COLLAGES & BRICOLAGES, 212 Founders Hall, Clarion University of PA, Clarion, PA 16214, 814-226-2340
ALLEGHENY REVIEW, Box 32, Allegheny College, Meadville, PA 16335, 814-332-6553
Allegheny Press, Box 220, Elgin, PA 16413, 814-664-8504
THE HYPERBOREAN, 2024 North Manor Drive, Erie, PA 16505, 814-456-6819
Hyperborean Micropublications, 2024 North Manor Drive, Erie, PA 16505, 814-456-6819
Tower Press, RR 2 Box 411, Duncansville, PA 16635-9512
PIVOT, 221 South Barnard Street, State College, PA 16801, 212-222-1408
Venture Publishing, Inc., 1999 Cato Avenue, State College, PA 16801, 814-234-4561
The Carnation Press, PO Box 101, State College, PA 16804, 814-238-3577
Yardbird Books, PO Box 10214, State College, PA 16805, 814-237-7569
Libertarian Press, Inc./American Book Distributors, PO Box 137, Spring Mills, PA 16875, 814-422-8001
GREEN ZERO, PO Box 3104, Shiremanstown, PA 17011, 717-732-7191
Ultralight Publications, Inc., 1 Oakglade Circle, Hummelstown, PA 17036-9525, 717-566-0468
WICCAN/PAGAN PRESS ALLIANCE TRADE PAPER, PO Box 1392, Mechanicsburg, PA 17055
Shy City Press, 208 Reno St., #1, New Cumberland, PA 17070, 717-774-7627
TABULA RASA, 208 Reno St., #1, New Cumberland, PA 17070, 717-774-7627
PENNSYLVANIA PORTFOLIO, Dauphin County Library System, 101 Walnut Street, Harrisburg, PA 17101, 717-234-4961
THE BLUE GUITAR, 3022 North 5th Street, Harrisburg, PA 17110
FAT TUESDAY, 8125 Jonestown Road, Harrisburg, PA 17112, 717-469-7159
NEWS FROM THE WHITE HOUSE, PO Box 6088, Harrisburg, PA 17112, 215-987-3014
ANIMA: The Journal of Human Experience, 1053 Wilson Avenue, Chambersburg, PA 17201, 717-267-0087
Anima Publications, c/o Concocheague Associates, Inc., 1053 Wilson Avenue, Chambersburg, PA 17201, 717-267-0087
THE BOTTOM LINE PUBLICATIONS, Star Route, Box 21AA, Artemas, PA 17211, 814-458-3102
FELICITY, Star Route, Box 21AA, Artemas, PA 17211, 814-458-3102
MY LEGACY, Star Route, Box 21AA, Artemas, PA 17211, 814-458-3102
OMNIFIC, Star Route, Box 21AA, Artemas, PA 17211, 814-458-3102
Weems Concepts, Star Route, Box 21AA, Artemas, PA 17211, 814-458-3102

AMERICAN AMATEUR JOURNALIST, HC 80, Box 160, Big Cove Tannery, PA 17212, 717-573-4526
Camel Press, HC 80, Box 160, Big Cove Tannery, PA 17212, 717-573-4526
DUST (From the Ego Trip), HC 80, Box 160, Big Cove Tannery, PA 17212, 717-573-4526
White Mane Publishing Company, Inc., 63 West Burd Street, PO Box 152, Shippensburg, PA 17257, 717-532-2237
THE GETTYSBURG REVIEW, Gettysburg College, Gettysburg, PA 17325, 717-337-6770
Logbridge - Rhodes, Inc., PO Box 4511, Gettysburg, PA 17325-4511
MICROCOSM, PO Box 847, Hanover, PA 17331-0847
Quixsilver Press, PO Box 847, Hanover, PA 17331-0847
Americana & Collectibles Press, PO Box 1444, York, PA 17405, 717-848-1333
FESTIVAL QUARTERLY, PO Box 419, Intercourse, PA 17534, 717-768-7171
HOB-NOB, 994 Nissley Road, Lancaster, PA 17601
Underwood-Miller, Inc. & Brandywyne Books, 708 Westover Drive, Lancaster, PA 17601-1231, 717-285-2255
LANCASTER INDEPENDENT PRESS, PO Box 275, Lancaster, PA 17603, 717-394-8019
WordWorkers Press, PO Box 1363, Lancaster, PA 17603, 717-299-1380
Charter Oak Press, PO Box 7783, Lancaster, PA 17604, 717-898-7711
BUCKNELL REVIEW, Bucknell Hall, Bucknell University, Lewisburg, PA 17837, 717-524-1184
The Press of Appletree Alley, Box 608 138 South Third Street, Lewisburg, PA 17837
WEST BRANCH, Bucknell Hall, Bucknell University, Lewisburg, PA 17837, 717-524-1440 or 524-1554
FEELINGS, PO Box 2625, Lehigh Valley, PA 18001, 215-264-7594
SING OUT! The Folk Song Magazine, PO Box 5253, Bethlehem, PA 18015-5253, 215-865-5366
CREEPING BENT, 1023 Main Street, Apt. 5, Bethlehem, PA 18018, 215-866-5613
Log Cabin Publishers, PO Box 1536, Allentown, PA 18105, 215-434-2448
Pioneer Books, PO Box 704, Conyngham, PA 18219, 717-455-0757
DIARIST'S JOURNAL, 102 West Water Street, Lansford, PA 18232, 717-645-4692
Quotidian Publishers, Box D, Delaware Water Gap, PA 18327, (717) 424-5505
MILITARY IMAGES MAGAZINE, RR 1, Box 99A, Henryville, PA 18332-9801
Himalayan Publishers, RD 1, Box 400, Honesdale, PA 18431, 717-253-5551
KELTIC FRINGE, Box 251, RD #1, Uniondale, PA 18470, 717-679-2745
Kittatinny Press, Box 251, RD #1, Uniondale, PA 18470, 717-679-2745
Padakami Press, 23 Dana Street, Forty Fort, PA 18704, 717-287-3668; 800-338-5531
Ridge Row Press, 10 South Main Street, Montrose, PA 18801, 717-278-1141
Raw Dog Press, 128 Harvey Avenue, Doylestown, PA 18901, 215-345-6838
THE PRAGMATIST, Box 392, Forest Grove, PA 18922
Woodsong Graphics Inc., PO Box 304, Lahaska, PA 18931-0304, 215-794-8321
THE FREEDONIA GAZETTE, Darien B-28, New Hope, PA 18938, 215-862-9734
INDIVIDUAL LIBERTY, PO Box 338, Warminster, PA 18974, 215-675-6830
Society for Individual Liberty, PO Box 338, Warminster, PA 18974, 215-675-6830
Surrey Press, 224 Surrey Road, Warminster, PA 18974, 215-675-4569
Whitmore Publishing Company, 35 Cricket Terrace, Ardmore, PA 19003, 215-896-6116
Kurios Press, Box 946, Bryn Mawr, PA 19010, 215-527-4635
THE WIDENER REVIEW, Humanities Division, Widener Univ., Chester, PA 19013, 215-499-4354
Diane Publishing Company, 600 Upland Avenue, Upland, PA 19015, 215-499-7415
Black Bear Publications, 1916 Lincoln Street, Croydon, PA 19021-8026, 215-788-3543
BLACK BEAR REVIEW, Black Bear Publications, 1916 Lincoln Street, Croydon, PA 19021, 215-788-3543
Hellas, 304 South Tyson Avenue, Glenside, PA 19038
HELLAS: A Journal of Poetry & the Humanities, 304 South Tyson Avenue, Glenside, PA 19038, 215-884-1086
COME-ALL-YE, P.O. Box 494, Hatboro, PA 19040, 215-675-6762
Legacy Books (formerly Folklore Associates), PO Box 494, Hatboro, PA 19040, 215-675-6762
GAUNTLET: Exploring the Limits of Free Expression, 309 Powell Road, Springfield, PA 19064, 215-328-5476
MARQUEE, 624 Wynne Road, Springfield, PA 19064, 215-543-8378
International Information Associates, PO Box 773, Morrisville, PA 19067, 215-493-9214
Deltiologists of America, PO Box 8, Norwood, PA 19074, 215-485-8572
POSTCARD CLASSICS, PO Box 8, Norwood, PA 19074, 215-485-8572
Our Child Press, 800 Maple Glen Lane, Wayne, PA 19087, 215-964-0606
RECONSTRUCTIONIST, Federation of Reconstructionist Congregations and Havurot, Church Road & Greenwood Avenue, Wyncote, PA 19095, 215-887-1988
Reconstructionist Press, Church Road & Greenwood Avenue, Wyncote, PA 19095, 215-887-1988
AMRA, Box 8243, Philadelphia, PA 19101
Owlswick Press, Box 8243, Philadelphia, PA 19101, 215-EV2-5415
AMERICAN POETRY REVIEW, 1721 Walnut St., Philadelphia, PA 19103, 215-496-0439
BOULEVARD, Opojaz, Inc., 2400 Chestnut Street, #2208, Philadelphia, PA 19103, 215-561-1723
Morgan-Rand Publications, Inc., 2200 Sansom Street, Philadelphia, PA 19103-4350, 215-557-8200, 800-354-8673
Running Press, 125 South Twenty-Second Street, Philadelphia, PA 19103, 215-567-5080
ISI Press, 3501 Market Street, Philadelphia, PA 19104, 215-386-0100
Nordic Books, PO Box 1941, Philadelphia, PA 19105, 609-795-1887
Delancey Press, Inc., PO Box 40285, Philadelphia, PA 19106
NEW FRONTIER, 101 Cuthbert Street, Philadelphia, PA 19106, 215-627-5683
New Frontier Education Society, 46 North Front Street Side, Philadelphia, PA 19106, 215-627-5683
PAINTED BRIDE QUARTERLY, 230 Vine Street, Philadelphia, PA 19106, 215-925-9914
Singing Horse Press, PO Box 40034, Philadelphia, PA 19106
PENNSYLVANIA'S LITERARY NETWORK NEWSLETTER, 1204 Walnut Street, Philadelphia, PA 19107
WOMAN'S ART JOURNAL, 1711 Harris Road, Philadelphia, PA 19118-1208, 615-584-7467
Branch Redd Books, 4805 B Street, Philadelphia, PA 19120
BRANCH REDD REVIEW, 4805 "B" Street, Philadelphia, PA 19120
DESDE ESTE LADO/FROM THIS SIDE, PO Box 18458, Philadelphia, PA 19120
JOURNAL OF MODERN LITERATURE, Temple Univ., Philadelphia, PA 19122, 215-787-8505
AMERICAN WRITING: A MAGAZINE, 4343 Manayunk Avenue, Philadelphia, PA 19128, 215-483-7051
Nierika Editions, 4343 Manayunk Avenue, Philadelphia, PA 19128, 215-483-7051

NiceTown, 5201 Media Street, Philadelphia, PA 19131, 215-473-7575
RECON, P.O. Box 14602, Philadelphia, PA 19134
Recon Publications, PO Box 14602, Philadelphia, PA 19134
ASPECTS, 5507 Regent Street, Philadelphia, PA 19143, 215-726-9746
New Society Publishers, 4527 Springfield Avenue, Philadelphia, PA 19143, 215-382-6543
THE OTHER SIDE, 300 West Apsley Street, Philadelphia, PA 19144, 215-849-2178
THE COOL TRAVELER, PO Box 11975, Philadelphia, PA 19145, 215-440-0592
International Printing, G & S Enterprises, 1127 Watkins Street #303, Philadelphia, PA 19148, 215-463-0463
Concourse Press, PO Box 28600, Overbrook Station, Philadelphia, PA 19151, 215-649-2207
AXEFACTORY, 2653 Sperry Street, Philadelphia, PA 19152
Axefactory Press (A.K.A. The Axefactory), 2653 Sperry Street, Philadelphia, PA 19152
FANS OF HORROR, 2802 Shelley Road, Philadelphia, PA 19152, 215-677-8146
Whitford Press, 1469 Morstein Road, Westchester, PA 19380, 215-696-1001
Dufour Editions Inc., PO Box 449, Chester Springs, PA 19425-0049, 215-458-5005
YARROW, A JOURNAL OF POETRY, English Dept., Lytle Hall, Kutztown State University, Kutztown, PA 19530, 683-4353

RHODE ISLAND

Ampersand Press, Creative Writing Program, Roger Williams College, Bristol, RI 02809, 401-253-1040, ext. 2217
CALLIOPE, Creative Writing Program, Roger Williams College, Bristol, RI 02809, 401-253-1040, ext. 2217
Seacoast Information Services, 4446 South County Trail, Charlestown, RI 02813, 401-364-6419
MERLYN'S PEN: The National Magazine of Student Writing, Merlyn's Pen, Inc., PO Box 1058, East Greenwich, RI 02818, (401) 885-5175
DEVIANCE, PO Box 1706, Pawtucket, RI 02862
The Saunderstown Press, PO Box 307, Saunderstown, RI 02874, 401-295-8810
SAT SANDESH: THE MESSAGE OF THE MASTERS, 680 Curtis Corner Road, Wakefield, RI 02879, (401) 783-0662
CURLEY, PO Box 23521, Providence, RI 02903
Lost Roads Publishers, PO Box 5848, Weybosset Hill Station, Providence, RI 02903, 401-245-8069
Burning Deck Press, 71 Elmgrove Avenue, Providence, RI 02906
HAUNTS, Nightshade Publications, PO Box 3342, Providence, RI 02906, 401-781-9438
A NEW WORLD RISING, Box 33, 77 Ives Street, Providence, RI 02906
NORTHEAST JOURNAL, PO Box 2321, Providence, RI 02906
Tom Ockerse Editions, 37 Woodbury Street, Providence, RI 02906, 401-331-0783
Paradigm Press, 11 Slater Avenue, Providence, RI 02906
White Lilac Press, PO Box 2556, Providence, RI 02906, 401-273-6678
PRIVACY JOURNAL, PO Box 28577, Providence, RI 02908
Copper Beech Press, Box 1852 Brown Univ., English Department, Providence, RI 02912, 401-863-2393
GAVEA-BROWN, Center For Portuguese and Brazilian Studies, Brown University, Providence, RI 02912, 401-863-3042
Gavea-Brown Publications, Center For Portuguese and Brazilian Studies, Box 0, Brown University, Providence, RI 02912, 401-863-3042
THE LANGSTON HUGHES REVIEW, Box 1904, Brown University, Providence, RI 02912, 401-863-3137

SOUTH CAROLINA

R & M Publishing Company, PO Box 1276, Holly Hill, SC 29059, 804-732-4094, 804-520-5211
NOSTALGIA, A Sentimental State of Mind, PO Box 2224, Orangeburg, SC 29116
The Bench Press, 1355 Raintree Drive, Columbia, SC 29210, 803-781-7232
THE VOLUNTARYIST, Box 1275, Gramling, SC 29348, 803-472-2750
SOUTHERN LIBERTARIAN MESSENGER, Rt. 10 Box 52 A, Florence, SC 29501
SOUTH CAROLINA REVIEW, English Dept, Clemson Univ, Clemson, SC 29634-1503, 803-656-3229
SOULLESS STRUCTURES, 550 Pinewood Drive, Pendleton, SC 29670, 803-646-9048
THE DEVIL'S MILLHOPPER, 171 University Parkway, College of Humanities/USC at Aiken, Aiken, SC 29801-6399, 803-648-6851
The Devil's Millhopper Press, 171 University Parkway, College of Humanities/USC at Aiken, Aiken, SC 29801-6399, 803-648-6851

SOUTH DAKOTA

SOUTH DAKOTA REVIEW, Box 111, University Exchange, Vermillion, SD 57069, 605-677-5229/5966
Astro Black Books, P O Box 46, Sioux Falls, SD 57101, 605-338-0277
Ex Machina Publishing Company, Box 448, Sioux Falls, SD 57103
Tesseract Publications, 3001 West 57th Street, Sioux Falls, SD 57106-2652
PRAIRIE WINDS, Dakota Wesleyan University, Box 159, Mitchell, SD 57301
East Eagle Press, PO Box 812, Huron, SD 57350, 605-352-5875
WANBLI HO, PO Box 8, Sinte Gleska College, Mission, SD 57555, 605-856-2321

TENNESSEE

ZONE 3, PO Box 4565, Austin Peay State University, Clarksville, TN 37044, 648-7031/7891
AC Projects, Inc., Old Harding Road, Box 5106, Franklin, TN 37064, 615-646-3757
The Rheumatoid Disease Foundation, 5706 Old Harding Road, Franklin, TN 37064, 615-646-1030
Richard W. Smith Military Books, PO Box 2118, Hendersonville, TN 37077
RFD, PO Box 68, Liberty, TN 37095, 615-536-5176
AASLH Press, 172 Second Avenue N., Suite 202, Nashville, TN 37201, 615-255-2971
HISTORY NEWS, 172 Second Avenue N., Suite 102, Nashville, TN 37201, (615) 255-2971
The F. Marion Crawford Memorial Society, Saracinesca House, 3610 Meadowbrook Avenue, Nashville, TN 37205
THE ROMANTIST, Saracinesca House, 3610 Meadowbrook Avenue, Nashville, TN 37205
Depot Press, PO Box 60072, Nashville, TN 37206, 226-1890
Southern Resources Unlimited, 5632 Meadowcrest Lane, Nashville, TN 37209-4631, 615-356-3211
Winston-Derek Publishers, Inc., Pennywell Drive, PO Box 90883, Nashville, TN 37209, 615-329-1319
CUMBERLAND POETRY REVIEW, Poetics, Inc., PO Box 120128 Acklen Station, Nashville, TN 37212, 615-373-8948

POCKETS (Devotional Magazine for Children), 1908 Grand, PO Box 189, Nashville, TN 37212, 615-340-7333
Progressive Education, PO Box 120574, Nashville, TN 37212
PROGRESSIVE PERIODICALS DIRECTORY/UPDATE, PO Box 120574, Nashville, TN 37212
Pine Hall Press, PO Box 150657, Nashville, TN 37215
SOUNDMAKERS, PO Box 17999, Nashville, TN 37217, 615-834-0027
The Battery Press, Inc., PO Box 3107, Uptown Station, Nashville, TN 37219, 615-298-1401
Lionhouse Publishing Company, 804 25th Street, Suite 155, Cleveland, TN 37311, 615-339-5779
Southeastern FRONT, 565 17th Street, NW, Cleveland, TN 37311
SEWANEE REVIEW, Univ. of the South, Sewanee, TN 37375, 615-598-1246
Snowbird Publishing Company, PO Box 729, Tellico Plains, TN 37385, 615-546-7001; fax 615-524-8612
THE POETRY MISCELLANY, English Dept. Univ of Tennessee, Chattanooga, TN 37403, 615-755-4213; 624-7279
Timely Books, 4040 Mountain Creek Road, Suite 1304, Chattanooga, TN 37415, 615-875-9447
NOW AND THEN, P.O. Box 19, 180A, East Tennessee State Univ., Johnson City, TN 37614-0002, 615-929-5348
THE SOW'S EAR POETRY JOURNAL, 245 McDowell Street, Bristol, TN 37620, 615-764-1625
COMICS REVUE, PO Box 336 -Manuscript Press, Mountain Home, TN 37684-0336, 615-926-7495
Manuscript Press, PO Box 336, Mountain Home, TN 37684-0336, 615-926-7495
SWAMP ROOT, Box 1098, Route 2, Jacksboro, TN 37757, 615-562-7082
Fine Arts Press, PO Box 3491, Knoxville, TN 37927, 615-637-9243
Elm Publications, PO Box 23192, Knoxville, TN 37933, 615-966-5703
RIGHTING WORDS—THE JOURNAL OF LANGUAGE AND EDITING, Freedonna Communications, Drawer 9808, Knoxville, TN 37940
THE LAME MONKEY MANIFESTO, Box 8763, Knoxville, TN 37996-4800, 615-525-8243
KREATURE COMFORTS, 1916 Madison Avenue, Memphis, TN 38104, 901-274-1916
Ion Books, PO Box 111327, Memphis, TN 38111-1327, 901-323-8858
RACCOON, PO Box 111327, Memphis, TN 38111-1327, 901-323-8858
Redbird Press, Inc., PO Box 11441, Memphis, TN 38111, 901-323-2233
White Rose Press, 61 Cherokee Drive, Memphis, TN 38111, 525-1836
SINGLE TODAY, 2500 Mt. Moriah #185, Memphis, TN 38115, 901-365-3988
Volunteer Publications, PO Box 240786, Memphis, TN 38124-0786, 901-682-4183
Red Oak Press, 2447 Redbud Trail Drive, Germantown, TN 38138
RIVER CITY, Department of English, Memphis State University, Memphis, TN 38152, 901-454-4438
Mustang Publishing Co., PO Box 3004, Memphis, TN 38173, 901-521-1406
THE RED PAGODA, A JOURNAL OF HAIKU, 125 Taylor Street, Jackson, TN 38301, 901-427-7714 (after 6 p.m.)
Leadership Education and Development, Inc., 1116 West 7th Street, Suite 175, Columbia, TN 38401, 901-794-2985; 615-388-6135
Yes Press, PO Box 91, Waynesboro, TN 38485

TEXAS

Colormore, Inc., PO Box 111249, Carrollton, TX 75011-1249, 316-636-9326
Promontory Publishing, Inc., PO Box 117213, Carrollton, TX 75011-7213, 214-394-6020
Shadetree Publishing Inc., PO Box 110577, Carrollton, TX 75011, 214-341-3256
WindRiver Publishing Company, PO Box 111003, Carrollton, TX 75011-1003, 214-869-7625
Ide House, Inc., PO Box 160361, Las Colinas, TX 75016, 214-686-5332
NEW PATHWAYS, PO Box 475174, Garland, TX 75047-5174
INVERTED-A HORN, 401 Forrest Hill, Grand Prairie, TX 75051, 214-264-0066
Inverted-A, Inc., 401 Forrest HIll, Grand Prairie, TX 75051, 214-264-0066
J. Barnaby Distributors, 1709 Hawthorne Lane, Plano, TX 75074, (214) 422-2770
Mundus Artium Press, University of Texas at Dallas, Box 688, Richardson, TX 75083-0688
TRANSLATION REVIEW, Univ. of Texas-Dallas, Box 830688, Richardson, TX 75083-0688, 214-690-2093
Littlebooks, PO Box 863065, Plano, TX 75086, 214-727-6297
Oak Plantation Press, PO Box 640, Rockwall, TX 75087-0640, 214-722-BOOK
Newton-Cline Press, 421 Sam Rayburn Fwy, Sherman, TX 75090, 214-893-1818
Somesuch Press, 4800 Tower II, First Rep Bank Center, Dallas, TX 75201, 214-922-0022
Amrita Foundation, Inc., PO Box 8080, Dallas, TX 75205, 214-522-5224 (TX); 415-527-6813, 1-800-526-7746 (CA)
E-Heart Press, Inc., 3700 Mockingbird Lane, Dallas, TX 75205, 214-741-6915
HOT FLASHES, 5926 Marquita Avenue, Dallas, TX 75206-6116, 821-1308
SALAD, Box 64980-306, Dallas, TX 75206
C.C. Publishing Co., 5410 Davis, Dallas, TX 75211, 214-330-4845
THE STARK FIST OF REMOVAL, Church of the SubGenius, PO Box 140306, Dallas, TX 75214
MAAT, 1223 South Selva, Dallas, TX 75218, 214-324-3093
Steve Davis Publishing, PO Box 190831, Dallas, TX 75219, 214-558-4702
Still Point Press, 4222 Willow Grove Road, Dallas, TX 75220, 214-352-8282
Good Hope Enterprises, Inc., PO Box 2394, Dallas, TX 75221, 214-823-7666; fax 214-823-7373
WE ARE THE WEIRD, PO Box 2002, Dallas, TX 75221, 214-692-8601
Spring Publications Inc, PO Box 222069, Dallas, TX 75222, 214-943-4093, 4094
Adventure Printing Inc., 3441 Halifax Street, PO Box 29543, Dallas, TX 75229
Valley House Gallery Press, 6616 Spring Valley Road, Dallas, TX 75240, 214-239-2441
SOUTHWEST REVIEW, Southern Methodist University, 6410 Airline Road, Dallas, TX 75275, 214-373-7440
Billy Jack Ludwig Holding Co., Box 670954, Dallas, TX 75367, 214-980-7141; 980-8274; 502-7136 (mobile); 800-274-3011; fax 214-980-8517
Penumbra Publishing Co., PO Box 781681, Dallas, TX 75378-1681, 214-351-1726
LITERARY SKETCHES, PO Box 810571, Dallas, TX 75381-0571, 214-243-8776
BOTH SIDES NOW, Rt 6, Box 28, Tyler, TX 75704, 903-592-4263
Free People Press, Route 6, Box 28, Tyler, TX 75704
Scroll Publishing Co., Rt 19, Box 890, Tyler, TX 75706, 214-597-8023
YE OLDE NEWES, 3200 South John Redditt, Lufkin, TX 75901-0514, 409-637-7468
THE WRITER'S HAVEN, PO Box 413, Joaquin, TX 75954
THE IDEOLOGY OF MADNESS, PO Box 1742, Arlington, TX 76012

Bold Productions, PO Box 152281, Arlington, TX 76015, 817-468-9924
Tangram Press, PO Box 2249, 2063 Ravenswood, Granbury, TX 76048, 817-579-1777
Coker Publishing House, 625 N. Riverside Drive, Grapevine, TX 76051, 817-488-6764
THE DREAMWEAVER, PO Box 150692, Fort Worth, TX 76108, 817-332-1412
DESCANT, English Department, TCU, Box 32872, Fort Worth, TX 76129
EXPERIMENT IN WORDS, PO Box 470186, Fort Worth, TX 76147, 817-763-0158
BOOK NEWS & BOOK BUSINESS MART, PO Box 330309, Fort Worth, TX 76163, 817-293-7030
Premier Publishers, Inc., PO Box 330309, Fort Worth, TX 76163, 817-293-7030
AMERICAN LITERARY REVIEW: A National Journal of Poems and Stories, University of N. Texas Press, PO Box 13615, Denton, TX 76203, 817-565-2124
GRASSLANDS REVIEW, PO Box 13706, Denton, TX 76203, 817-565-2025/2127
Stone Drum Press, PO Box 233, Valley View, TX 76240
CROSS TIMBERS REVIEW, Cisco Junior College, Cisco, TX 76437, 817-442-2567
The White Cross Press, Route 1, Box 592, Granger, TX 76530, 512-859-2814
CONCHO RIVER REVIEW, Fort Concho Museum Press, English Dept., Angelo State Univ., San Angelo, TX 76909, 915-942-2253
Scribblers Publishing, Ltd., PO Box 90075-139, Houston, TX 77069, 713-440-5698
Gemini Publishing Company, 11543 Gullwood Drive, Houston, TX 77089, 713-484-2424
Lowy Publishing, 5047 Wigton, Houston, TX 77096, 713-723-3209
Quixote Press, 1810 Marshall, Houston, TX 77098
QUIXOTE, QUIXOTL, 1810 Marshall, Houston, TX 77098
THE AMERICA'S REVIEW, University of Houston, Houston, TX 77204-2090, 713-749-4768
Arte Publico Press, University of Houston, Houston, TX 77204-2090, 713-749-4768
Awareness Publications, PO Box 300792, Houston, TX 77230, 713-434-2845
Triad Press, PO Box 42006, Houston, TX 77242, 713-789-0424
Black Tie Press, PO Box 440004, Houston, TX 77244-0004, 713-789-5119
Gulf Publishing Company, PO Box 2608, Houston, TX 77252-2608, 713-529-4301
Affinity Publishers Services, PO Box 570213, Houston, TX 77257
Center For Self-Sufficiency, c/o Prosperity and Profits Unlimited, Box 570213, Houston, TX 77257
International Partners In Prayer, Publishing Division, Box 570122, Houston, TX 77257
Nunciata, Publishing Division, Box 570122, Houston, TX 77257
Scentouri, Publishing Division, c/o Prosperity + Profits Unlimited, Distribution Services, Box 570213, Houston, TX 77257
THE GOPHERWOOD REVIEW, Box 58784, Houston, TX 77258, 713-532-1622
Tafford Publishing, Inc., PO Box 271804, Houston, TX 77277, 713-529-3276
Wilchester Publishing Company, 1407 W. Brooklake Court, #200, PO Box 820874, Houston, TX 77282-0874, 713-496-0788
Space City Publications, PO Box 890263, Houston, TX 77289, 713-480-9102
THE TEXAS REVIEW, English Department, Sam Houston State University, Huntsville, TX 77341
Texas Review Press, English Department, Sam Houston State University, Huntsville, TX 77341
Woodstead Press, 1755 Woodstead Court, The Woodlands, TX 77380, 713-292-5000
TOUCHSTONE LITERARY JOURNAL, PO Box 8308, Spring, TX 77387-8308
Candle Publishing Company, PO Box 5009-136, Sugar Land, TX 77478, 713-242-6162
Julian Associates, 6831 Spencer Hwy, #203, Pasadena, TX 77505, 713-930-8551
NIGHT OWL'S NEWSLETTER, 6831 Spencer Hwy, #203, Pasadena, TX 77505, 713-930-8551
OUR WRITE MIND, 6831 Spencer Hwy, #203, Pasadena, TX 77505
Swan Publishing Company, 126 Live Oak, Alvin, TX 77511, 713-388-2547
Ledero Press, U. T. Box 99, Galveston, TX 77550-2783, 409-761-2091
Relampago Books Press, PO Box 307, Geronimo, TX 78115, 512-379-0797
CARTA ABIERTA, Center for Mexican American Studies, Texas Lutheran College, Seguin, TX 78155, 512-379-4161 X331
Tejas Art Press, 207 Terrell Road, San Antonio, TX 78209, 512-826-7803
Corona Publishing Co., 1037 S. Alamo, San Antonio, TX 78210
Myriad Moods, 202 Thoraine Boulevard, San Antonio, TX 78212-5243, 512-824-1185
THE BABY CONNECTION NEWS JOURNAL, Drawer 13320, San Antonio, TX 78213, 512-493-6278
Parent Education for Infant Development, Drawer 13320, San Antonio, TX 78213, 512-493-6278
THE GELOSOPHIST, Humor News & Views From Around The World, PO Box 29000, Suite 103, San Antonio, TX 78229
LONE STAR COMEDY MONTHLY, PO Box 29000, Suite 103, San Antonio, TX 78229
LONE STAR HUMOR, PO Box 29000 Suite #103, San Antonio, TX 78229
Lone Star Publications of Humor, PO Box 29000, Suite #103, San Antonio, TX 78229
Pedicard Press, 14305 Indian Woods, San Antonio, TX 78249-2047, 512-492-2045; FAX 800-443-9636
Helix Press, 4410 Hickey, Corpus Christi, TX 78413, 512-852-8834
Success Publications, PO Box 4608, McAllen, TX 78502-4608, 512-687-8747
Zahra Publications, PO Box 730, Blanco, TX 78606, 512-833-5334
Exanimo Press, PO Box 967, Cedar Park, TX 78613
Prickly Pear Press, 1402 Mimosa Pass, Cedar Park, TX 78613, 512-331-8825
JOURNAL FOR ANTHROPOSOPHY, HC01, Box 24, Dripping Springs, TX 78620, 413-256-0655
Shearer Publishing, 406 Post Oak Road, Fredericksburg, TX 78624, 512-997-6529
Dr. Homer W. Parker, P.E., 1601 Woodrock Drive, Round Rock, TX 78681, 512-255-0702
OFFICE NUMBER ONE, 1709 San Antonio Street, Austin, TX 78701, 512-320-8243
Thorp Springs Press, 1002 Lorrain Street, Austin, TX 78703-4829
AMERICAN ATHEIST, PO Box 140195, Austin, TX 78714-0195, 512-458-1244
American Atheist Press, PO Box 140195, Austin, TX 78714-0195, 512-458-1244
Keel Publications, PO Box 160155, Austin, TX 78716-0155
Nancy Renfro Studios, Inc., PO Box 164226, Austin, TX 78716, 1-800-933-5512; 572-327-9588
Roscher House, PO Box 201390, Austin, TX 78720, (512) 258-2288
LUCKY HEART BOOKS, 1909 Sunny Brook Drive, Austin, TX 78723-3449
SALT LICK, 1909 Sunny Brook Drive, Austin, TX 78723-3449
Salt Lick Press, 1909 Sunny Brook Drive, Austin, TX 78723-3449

AUSTIN SENIOR CITIZEN, Senior Service Press, 5600 Cedro Trail, Austin, TX 78731, 512-338-1712
Rental Business Press, 5600 Cedro Trail, Austin, TX 78731, 512-338-1712
TEXAS WINEMARKET NEWS, Cellar Press, 5600 Cedro Trail, Austin, TX 78731
MICROSOLUTIONS, 5211 Meadow Creek Drive, Austin, TX 78745-3015, 512-416-1644; FAX 512-416-1677
STONE DRUM: An International Magazine of the Arts, 3003 Riercrest Drive, Austin, TX 78746
Teri Gordon, Publisher, 10901 Rustic Manor Lane, Austin, TX 78750-1133, 512-258-8309
Hyde Park Publishing House, Inc., 3908 Avenue G, Austin, TX 78751, 512-467-9893
Erespin Press, 1705 Raven Drive, Austin, TX 78752
DIMENSION, Box 26673, Austin, TX 78755, 512-345-0622
RENT-TO-OWN ADVERTISING & PROMOTIONS PLANNER, PO Box 26505, Austin, TX 78755-0505, 512-338-1712
RENT-TO-OWN COLLECTIONS MANAGER, PO Box 26505, Austin, TX 78755-0505, 512-338-1712
RENT-TO-OWN LEGAL & FINANCIAL BULLETIN, PO Box 26505, Austin, TX 78755-0505, 512-338-1712
Volunteer Concepts, PO Box 27584, Austin, TX 78755, 512-472-2032
INTERVENTION IN SCHOOL AND CLINIC, 8700 Shoal Creek, Austin, TX 78758-6897, 512-451-3246
Multi Media Arts, PO Box 14486, Austin, TX 78761, 512-837-5503
ALL AVAILABLE LIGHT, PO Box 50174, Austin, TX 78763
CITY RANT, PO Box 50174, Austin, TX 78763, 512-477-2269
THE ICARUS REVIEW, PO Box 50174, Austin, TX 78763, 512-477-2269
McOne Press, PO Box 50174, Austin, TX 78763, 512-477-2269
S & S Press, PO Box 5931, Austin, TX 78763-5931
Plain View Press, Inc., PO Box 33311, Austin, TX 78764, (512) 441-2452
PRIVATE INVESTIGATOR'S CONNECTION: A Newsletter for Investigators, PO Box 33244, Austin, TX 78764, 512-832-0355
Thomas Publications, PO Box 33244, Austin, TX 78764, 512-832-0355
Argo Press, PO Box 4201, Austin, TX 78765-4201
ARGONAUT, PO Box 4201, Austin, TX 78765-4201
FIBERWORKS QUARTERLY, PO Box 49770, Austin, TX 78765, 512-343-6112
LIBRARY CURRENTS, Practical Perspectives, Inc., PO Box 4518, Austin, TX 78765-1349, 512-346-1426
AILERON, A LITERARY JOURNAL, PO Box 891, Austin, TX 78767-0891
NONVIOLENT ANARCHIST NEWSLETTER, Box 1385, Austin, TX 78767
Slough Press, Box 1385, Austin, TX 78767
Texas Monthly Press, PO Box 1569, Austin, TX 78767, 512-476-7085
THE ADVOCATE, HCR 2, Box 25, Panhandle, TX 79068, 806-335-1715
BUT A TWIST OF THE LIP, 1003 Avenue X, Apt. A, Lubbock, TX 79401, 806-744-7412
LIME GREEN BULLDOZERS (AND OTHER RELATED SPECIES), 1003 Avenue X, Apt. A, Lubbock, TX 79401, 806-744-7412
I. S. C. Press, 4450 Ridgemont Drive #1311, Abilene, TX 79606-2745
Selene Books, PO Box 220-253, El Paso, TX 79913
Skidmore-Roth Publishing, 1001 Wall Street, El Paso, TX 79915-1012
Weatherford Publications, 6447 Loma de Cristo Drive, El Paso, TX 79918-7314
Cinco Puntos Press, 2709 Louisville, EL Paso, TX 79930, 915-566-9072
GYPSY, c/o Belinda Subraman, 10708 Gay Brewer Drive, El Paso, TX 79935
Vergin Press, c/o Belinda Subraman, 10708 Gay Brewer Drive, El Paso, TX 79935
EDITOR'S DIGEST, PO Box 371371, El Paso, TX 79937, 915-595-2625
Rio Grande Press, PO Box 371371, El Paso, TX 79937, 915-595-2625
SE LA VIE WRITER'S JOURNAL, PO Box 371371, El Paso, TX 79937, 915-595-2625

UTAH

Gibbs Smith, Publisher, 1877 East Gentile Street, PO Box 667, Layton, UT 84041, 801-544-9800
MAGIC REALISM, PO Box 620, Orem, UT 84059-0620
Pyx Press, Box 620, Orem, UT 84059-0620
A THEATER OF BLOOD, PO Box 620, Orem, UT 84059-0620
Mountainwest Publishers, 5295 S. 300 W., Suite 475, Murray, UT 84107, 801-268-3232
Utah Geographic Series, Box 8325, Salt Lake City, UT 84108
ANCESTRY NEWSLETTER, PO Box 476, Salt Lake City, UT 84110, 801-531-1790
Ancestry Publishing, PO Box 476, Salt Lake City, UT 84110, 801-531-1790
THE BLACKLIST, PO Box 1417, Salt Lake City, UT 84110, 972-6739
GENEALOGICAL COMPUTING, PO Box 476, Salt Lake City, UT 84110, 801-531-1790
Signature Books, 350 South 400 East, #G4, Salt Lake City, UT 84111, 801-531-1483
QUARTERLY WEST, 317 Olpin Union, U. of Utah, Salt Lake City, UT 84112, 801-581-3938
WESTERN HUMANITIES REVIEW, University of Utah, Salt Lake City, UT 84112, 801-581-6070
Liberty Bell Press & Publishing Co., 4700 South 900 East, Suite 3-183, Salt Lake City, UT 84117, 801-943-8573
MANNA, 2966 West Westcove Drive, West Valley City, UT 84119
PAPER TOADSTOOL, 4946 West Point Way, West Valley, UT 84120, 801-972-8236
THE ABER BULLETIN, 1216 Lillie Circle, Salt Lake City, UT 84121, (801) 262-4586
DRAGONFLY: East/West Haiku Quarterly, PO Box 11236, Salt Lake City, UT 84147
Middlewood Press, PO Box 11236, Salt Lake City, UT 84147, 801-966-8034
Eagle's View Publishing, 6756 North Fork Road, Liberty, UT 84310, 801-393-4555 (orders); business phone 801-745-0903
WESTERN AMERICAN LITERATURE, English Dept., Utah State Univ., Logan, UT 84322-3200
Real People Press, Box F, Moab, UT 84532, 801-259-7578
CHASQUI, Dept of Spanish, Brigham Young University, Provo, UT 84602
ABBEY NEWSLETTER: Bookbinding & Conservation, 320 E. Center Street, Provo, UT 84606, 801-373-1598
Abbey Publications, 320 East Center, Provo, UT 84606, 801-373-1598
ALKALINE PAPER ADVOCATE, Abbey Publications, 320 East Center, Provo, UT 84606, 801-373-1598
GENERATIONS SANPETE: INDEX OF ORAL HISTORIES OF RURAL UTAH, PO Box 555, Fayette, UT 84630

VERMONT

New Victoria Publishers, PO Box 27, Norwich, VT 05055, 802-649-5297

714

EARTHTREKS DIGEST, Route 100, HCR 70, Box 7A, Plymouth, VT 05056, 802-672-3868
Five Corners Publications, Ltd., Route 100, HCR 70, Box 7A, Plymouth, VT 05056, 802-672-3868
Chelsea Green Publishing Company, PO Box 130, Post Mills, VT 05058, 802-333-9073
Countryman Press, PO Box 175, Woodstock, VT 05091, 802-457-1049
GemStone Press, LongHill Partners, Inc., PO Box 237, Woodstock, VT 05091, 802-457-4000
ANEMONE, PO Box 369, Chester, VT 05143
COLLABORATION, Sri Aurobindo Assn., PO Box 297, Saxtons River, VT 05154, 802-869-2789
Storey/Garden Way Publishing, Schoolhouse Road, Pownal, VT 05261, 802-823-5811
Amana Books, 58 Elliot Street, Brattleboro, VT 05301, 802-257-0872
LONGHOUSE, Green River R.F.D., Brattleboro, VT 05301
Longhouse, Green River R.F.D., Brattleboro, VT 05301
ProLingua Associates, 15 Elm Street, Brattleboro, VT 05301, 802-257-7779
THE SEARCH - JOURNAL FOR ARAB AND ISLAMIC STUDIES, PO Box 543, Brattleboro, VT 05301, 802-257-0872
Vitesse Press, 28 Birge Street, Brattleboro, VT 05301, 802-254-2306
Center for Arab and Islamic Studies, Box 543, Bratttleboro, VT 05301, 802-257-0872
The Green Street Press, PO Box 8119, Brattleboro, VT 05304-8119, 617-374-9923
MIRACLES MAGAZINE, PO Box 8118, Brattleboro, VT 05304
Tree Shrew Press, PO Box 8036, North Brattleboro, VT 05304
The Marlboro Press, Box 157, Marlboro, VT 05344, 802-257-0781
Threshold Books, RR4 Box 600, Putney, VT 05346, 802-387-4586 or 245-8300
TOWARD FREEDOM, 209 College Street, #202A, Burlington, VT 05401, 802-658-2523
Waterfront Books, 98 Brookes Avenue, Burlington, VT 05401, 802-658-7477
Wood Thrush Press, 25 Lafayette Place, #C, Burlington, VT 05401, 802-863-9767
WOMEN & THERAPY, Dr. Esther Rothblum, Dept. of Psychology, University of Vermont, Burlington, VT 05405, (802) 656-2680
CREATING EXCELLENCE, New World Publishing, Inc., PO Box 2048, South Burlington, VT 05407
Williamson Publishing Company, Inc., Box 185, Church Hill Road, Charlotte, VT 05445, 802-425-2102
Upper Access Inc., PO Box 457, 1 Upper Access Road, Hinesburg, VT 05461, 800-356-9315; 802-482-2988; fax 802-482-3125
GREEN MOUNTAINS REVIEW, Johnson State College, Box A-58, Johnson, VT 05656, 802-635-2356
STRAIGHTEDGE, 16 Chaplin Avenue, Rutland, VT 05701
Holistic Education Press, 39 Pearl Street, Brandon, VT 05733-1007, 802-247-8312
HOLISTIC EDUCATION REVIEW, 39 Pearl Street, Brandon, VT 05733-1007, 802-247-8312
Atrium Society Publications, PO Box 816, Middlebury, VT 05753, 802-388-0922
Paul S. Eriksson, Publisher, 208 Battell Building, Middlebury, VT 05753, 802-388-7303
Middlebury College Publications, Middlebury College, Middlebury, VT 05753, 802-388-3711 ext. 5075
NEW ENGLAND REVIEW, Middlebury College, Middlebury, VT 05753, 802-388-3711 ext. 5075
Inner Traditions International, One Park Street, Rochester, VT 05767, 802-767-3174
Sherry Urie, RFD #3, Box 63, Barton, VT 05822, 802-525-4482
Pigwidgeon Press, PO Box 706, Derby Line, VT 05830, 819-876-2538

VIRGIN ISLANDS

Mountaintop Books, PO Box 24031, Gallows Bay Station, Christiansted, VI 00824-0031, 809-773-3412
Eastern Caribbean Institute, PO Box 1338, Frederiksted, VI 00841, 809-772-1011
THE CARIBBEAN WRITER, Caribbean Research Institute, RR 2, Box 10,000, Univ of Virgin Islands, Kingshill, St. Croix, VI 00851, 809-778-0246 X20

VIRGINIA

CRYPTOSYSTEMS JOURNAL, 9755 Oatley Lane, Burke, VA 22015, 703-451-6664
PHOEBE, THE GEORGE MASON REVIEW, G.M.U. 4400 University Dr., Fairfax, VA 22030, 703-323-3730
WOMEN AND LANGUAGE, Communication Dept, George Mason University, Fairfax, VA 22030
THE (LIBERTARIAN) CONNECTION, Box 3343, Fairfax, VA 22038, 703-273-3297
THE SCIENCE FICTION CONVENTION REGISTER, Box 3343, Fairfax, VA 22038, 703-273-3297
Stripes Publishers, USA, PO Box 2109, Falls Church, VA 22042, 703-271-9155
Black Buzzard Press, 1110 Seaton Lane, Falls Church, VA 22046
BLACK BUZZARD REVIEW, 1110 Seaton Lane, Falls Church, VA 22046
VISIONS, International, The World Journal of Illustrated Poetry, 1110 Seaton Lane, Falls Church, VA 22046
ART CALENDAR, PO Box 1040, Great Falls, VA 22066, 703-430-6610
Strawberry Patchworks, 11597 Southington Lane, Herndon, VA 22070-2417, 703-709-0751
UP AGAINST THE WALL, MOTHER..., 4114 Wood Spice Lane, Lorton, VA 22079
RedBrick Press, PO Box 2184, Reston, VA 22090, 703-476-6420
DEANOTATIONS, 11919 Moss Point Lane, Reston, VA 22094
Dynamic Information Publishing, PO Box 1172, McLean, VA 22101-1172
EPM Publications, Inc., 1003 Turkey Run Road, McLean, VA 22101, 703-442-7810
Gifted Education Press/The Reading Tutorium, PO Box 1586, 10201 Yuma Court, Manassas, VA 22110-1586, 703-369-5017
Impact Publications, 10655 Big Oak Circle, Manassas, VA 22111, 703-361-7300
Imaginative Solutions, Box 3553, Merrifield, VA 22116-3553, 703-560-1013
THE INSIDER GUNNEWS, PO Box 2441, Merrifield, VA 22116, 202-832-0838
CROP DUST, Route 5, Box 75, Warrenton, VA 22186-8614, 703-642-6055
Crop Dust Press, Route 5, Box 75, Warrenton, VA 22186-8614, 703-642-6055
The Heather Foundation, Box 4, Waterford, VA 22190, 301-695-5276
BOGG, 422 N Cleveland Street, Arlington, VA 22201
Bogg Publications, 422 North Cleveland Street, Arlington, VA 22201
MINERVA: Quarterly Report on Women and the Military, 1101 S. Arlington Ridge Rd. #210, Arlington, VA 22202, 703-892-4388
Profile Press, 3004 S. Grant Street, Arlington, VA 22202, 703-684-6208
THE AHFAD JOURNAL: Women And Change, The Ahfad University for Women, 4141 N. Henderson Rd., Suite 1216,

Arlington, VA 22203, (703) 525-9045
GOING GAGA, 2630 Robert Walker Place, Arlington, VA 22207, 703-527-6032
VICTIMOLOGY AN INTERNATIONAL JOURNAL, 2333 North Vernon Street, Arlington, VA 22207-4036, 703-528-3387
The Gutenberg Press, c/o Fred Foldvary, 101 Mt. Vernon, Alexandria, VA 22301, 703-683-7769
COFFEE & DONUTS, PO Box 6920, Alexandria, VA 22306
THE FRONT STRIKER BULLETIN, The Retskin Report, 3417 Clayborne Avenue, Alexandria, VA 22306-1410, 703-768-3932; FAX 703-768-4719
ZOOMAR, PO Box 6920, Alexandria, VA 22306
Books for All Times, Inc., PO Box 2, Alexandria, VA 22313, 703-548-0457
EDUCATION IN FOCUS, PO Box 2, Alexandria, VA 22313, 703-548-0457
Editorial Experts, Inc., 66 Canal Center Plaza #200, Alexandria, VA 22314, 703-683-0683
THE EDITORIAL EYE, 66 Canal Center Plaza, Suite 200, Alexandria, VA 22314, 703-683-0683
Miles River Press, 1009 Duke Street, Alexandria, VA 22314, 703-683-1500
PARACHUTIST, 1440 Duke Street, Alexandria, VA 22314, 703-836-3495
Orchises Press, PO Box 20602, Alexandria, VA 22320-1602, 703-683-1243
UNION STREET REVIEW, PO Box 19078, Alexandria, VA 22320, 703-836-4549
VANDELOECHT'S FICTION MAGAZINE, PO Box 515, Montross, VA 22520
Pen & Ink Press, PO Box 235, Wicomico Church, VA 22579
Landon Publications, 1061-C South High Street, Harrisonburg, VA 22801
RE Publications, 246 Campbell Street, Harrisonburg, VA 22801, 703-433-0382
Cheops Books, 977 Seminole Trail, Suite 179, Charlottesville, VA 22901, 804-973-7670
CALLALOO, English Dept, Wilson Hall, University of Virginia, Charlottesville, VA 22903, (804) 924-6637; 924-6616
Callaloo Poetry Series, Department of English, University of Virginia, Charlottesville, VA 22903
dbS Productions, PO Box 1894, University Station, Charlottesville, VA 22903, 804-977-1581
THE VIRGINIA QUARTERLY REVIEW, One West Range, Charlottesville, VA 22903, 804-924-3124
Community Collaborators, PO Box 5429, Charlottesville, VA 22905, 804-977-1126
IRIS: A Journal About Women, Box 323, HSC, University of Virginia, Charlottesville, VA 22908, 804-924-4500
Shoe Tree Press, PO Box 219, Crozet, VA 22932-0219
Shepherd Publishers, 118 Pinepoint Road, Williamsburg, VA 23185-4436, 804-229-0661
Thirteen Colonies Press, 710 South Henry Street, Williamsburg, VA 23185, 804-229-1775
VERSE, Henry Hart, English Dept., College of William & Mary, Williamsburg, VA 23185, 804-221-3922
WILLIAM AND MARY REVIEW, Campus Center, College of William and Mary, Williamsburg, VA 23185, 804-253-4895
BOLD PRINT, 2211 Stuart Avenue, 1st Floor, Richmond, VA 23220
BOYS & GIRLS GROW UP, 904 Forestview Drive, Richmond, VA 23225
FOLK ART MESSENGER, PO Box 17041, Richmond, VA 23226, 804-355-6709
VIRGINIA LIBERTY, PO Box 28263, Richmond, VA 23228
ECA Associates, PO Box 15004, Great Bridge Station, Chesapeake, VA 23320, 804-547-5542
Inner Vision Publishing Company, PO Box 1117, Virginia Beach, VA 23451-0117
Windstar Books, PO Box 1643, Virginia Beach, VA 23451, (804) 479-4502
Hilltop Press, PO Box 4091, Virginia Beach, VA 23454
W.S. Dawson Co., PO Box 62823, Virginia Beach, VA 23462, 804-499-6271
The Donning Company / Publishers, 184 Business Park Drive #106, Virginia Beach, VA 23462-6533
The Hague Press, PO Box 385, Norfolk, VA 23501, 804-640-1694
THE HAGUE REVIEW, PO Box 385, Norfolk, VA 23501, 804-640-1694
INLET, Virginia Wesleyan College, Norfolk, VA 23502
REFLECT, 3306 Argonne Avenue, Norfolk, VA 23509, 804-857-1097
Associated Writing Programs, AWP c/o Old Dominion University, Norfolk, VA 23529-0079
AWP CHRONICLE, c/o Old Dominion University, Norfolk, VA 23529-0079
Heresy Press, 713 Paul Street, Newport News, VA 23605, 804-380-6595
IT GOES ON THE SHELF, 713 Paul Street, Newport News, VA 23605
Purple Mouth Press, 713 Paul Street, Newport News, VA 23605
Ask Publishing, PO Box 502, Newport News, VA 23607
Seascape Enterprises, PO Box 176, Colonial Heights, VA 23834, 804-526-7119
Brunswick Publishing Corporation, Rt. 1, Box 1A1, Lawrenceville, VA 23868, 804-848-3865
INTEGRAL YOGA MAGAZINE, Route 1, Box 172, Buckingham, VA 23921, 804-969-4801
ARTEMIS, PO Box 8147, Roanoke, VA 24014, 703-774-8440 or 977-3155
Crystal Spring Publishing, PO Box 8814, Roanoke, VA 24014, 703-982-2029
Lintel, Box 8609, Roanoke, VA 24014, 703-982-2265
THE HOLLINS CRITIC, P.O. Box 9538, Hollins College, VA 24020
THE LYRIC, 307 Dunton Drive, Southwest, Blacksburg, VA 24060, 703-552-3475
Pocahontas Press, Inc., 2805 Wellesley Court, Blacksburg, VA 24060-4126, 703-951-0467
McDonald & Woodward Publishing Company, PO Box 10308, Blacksburg, VA 24062, 703-951-9465
Rowan Mountain Press, PO Box 10111, Blacksburg, VA 24062-0111, 703-961-3315
SISTERS IN CRIME BOOKS IN PRINT, PO Box 10111, Blacksburg, VA 24062-0111, 703-961-3315
Commonwealth Press Virginia, 415 First Street, Box 3547, Radford, VA 24141
THE ROANOKE REVIEW, English Department, Roanoke College, Salem, VA 24153, 703-375-2367
Gong Enterprises, Inc., PO Box 1753, Bristol, VA 24203, 703-466-4672
CJE NEWSLETTER (Newsletter of the Coalition for Jobs & the Environment), 114 Court Street, PO Box 645, Abingdon, VA 24210-0645, 703-628-8996
Sterling-Miller, PO Box 2413, Staunton, VA 24401
SHENANDOAH, PO Box 722, Lexington, VA 24450, 703-463-8765
St. Andrew Press, PO Box 329, Big Island, VA 24526, 804-299-5956
PIEDMONT LITERARY REVIEW, RD 1, Box 512, Forest, VA 24551
PROOF ROCK, Proof Rock Press, PO Box 607, Halifax, VA 24558

716

WASHINGTON

Inspirational Publisher, 2500 So. 370th St., Suite 134, Federal Way, WA 98003, 206-874-2310
Resolution Business Press, 11101 N.E. Eighth Street, #208, Bellevue, WA 98004, 206-455-4611
Pickle Point Publishing, PO Box 4107, Bellevue, WA 98009, 206-462-6105
The Chas. Franklin Press, 7821 175th Street SW, Edmonds, WA 98020-1835, 206-774-6979
Hundman Publishing, 5115 Montecello Drive, Edmonds, WA 98020, 206-743-2607
MAINLINE MODELER, 5115 Montecello Drive, Edmonds, WA 98020, 206-743-2607
VINTAGE NORTHWEST, PO Box 193, Bothell, WA 98041, 206-487-1201
Sea Otter Press, PO Box 4484, Rolling Bay, WA 98061, 206-842-8148
Laughing Dog Press, 12509 SW Cove Road, Vashon, WA 98070, (206) 463-3153
LIGHTHOUSE, Lighthouse Publications, PO Box 1377, Auburn, WA 98071-1377
Blue Raven Publishing, PO Box 973, Woodinville, WA 98072, 206-485-0000
MEDIA SPOTLIGHT, Po Box 290, Redmond, WA 98073
Professional Counselor Books, PO Box 2079, Redmond, WA 98073, 206-867-5024; 800-622-7762
Shepherd Books, Box 2290, Redmond, WA 98073, 206-882-4500
Rainier Books, PO Box 2713, Kirkland, WA 98083-2713, 206-821-5676
ARTSFOCUS PERFORMING ARTS MAGAZINE, 1514 Western, Seattle, WA 98101, 206-624-6113
Left Bank Books, Box B, 92 Pike Street, Seattle, WA 98101, 206-522-8864
Sasquatch Books, 1931 2nd Avenue, Seattle, WA 98101, 206-623-3700
SIGNPOST, 1305 Fourth Avenue #512, Seattle, WA 98101, 206-625-1367
Writers Publishing Service Co., 1512 Western Avenue, Seattle, WA 98101, 206-284-9954
Bear Creek Publications, 2507 Minor Avenue East, Seattle, WA 98102, 206-322-7604
CATALYST, PO Box 20518, Seattle, WA 98102, 206-323-7268
Laocoon Books, PO Box 20518, Seattle, WA 98102, 206-323-7268
New Horizons Publishers, 737 Tenth Avenue East, Seattle, WA 98102, 206-323-1102
CRAB CREEK REVIEW, 4462 Whitman Avenue North, Seattle, WA 98103, 206-633-1090
Educare Press, PO Box 31511, Seattle, WA 98103, 206-781-2665
Entrepreneurial Workshops Publications, 4000 Aurora Building, Seattle, WA 98103, 206-633-5350
L'Epervier Press, 5419 Kensington Place North, Seattle, WA 98103, 206-547-8306
FINE MADNESS, PO Box 31138, Seattle, WA 98103-1138
GLOBE LITERARY, 3625 Greenwood North, Seattle, WA 98103
THE MONTANA REVIEW, 1620 N. 45th St., Seattle, WA 98103, 206-633-5929
Owl Creek Press, 1620 N. 45th St., Seattle, WA 98103, 206-633-5929
SEATTLE STAR, Starhead Comix, PO Box 30044, Seattle, WA 98103
The Square-Rigger Press, 1201 North 46th Street, Seattle, WA 98103-6610, 206-548-9385
ALWAYS JUKIN', 221 Yesler Way, Seattle, WA 98104
Always Jukin', 221 Yesler Way, Seattle, WA 98104
CHRYSANTHEMUM, 416-1/2 7th Avenue South, Seattle, WA 98104
Goldfish Press, 416-1/2 7th Avenue South, Seattle, WA 98104
Red Letter Press, 409 Maynard Avenue South #201, Seattle, WA 98104, 206-682-0990
MODERN LANGUAGE QUARTERLY, 4045 Brooklyn Ave. N.E., Seattle, WA 98105, 206-543-2992
HAIKU ZASSHI ZO, PO Box 17056, Seattle, WA 98107-0756
SEA KAYAKER, 6329 Seaview Avenue NW, Seattle, WA 98107, 206-789-1326
Silverleaf Press, Inc., PO Box 70189, Seattle, WA 98107
WCCF REPORTS, PO Box 81101, Seattle, WA 98108-1462
Winn Books, 5700 6th Avenue South, PO Box 80157, Seattle, WA 98108, 206-763-9544
ERGO! THE BUMBERSHOOT LITERARY MAGAZINE, One Reel/Bumbershoot, PO Box 9750, Seattle, WA 98109-0750, 206-622-5123
Frontier Publishing, 322 Queen Anne Avenue North, Seattle, WA 98109
Glen Abbey Books, Inc., PO Box 31329, Seattle, WA 98109, 206-548-9360; 800-782-2239
CLEANING BUSINESS MAGAZINE, PO Box 1273, Seattle, WA 98111-1273, (206) 622-4241
Cleaning Consultants Serv's, Inc., PO Box 1273, Seattle, WA 98111-1273
COSMIC KALUDO, PO Box 581, Seattle, WA 98111
Bruce Gould Publications, PO Box 16, Seattle, WA 98111
Rikki Leeson, PO Box 581, Seattle, WA 98111
REVIEWS UNLIMITED, PO Box 581, Seattle, WA 98111
TALES OF THE DESIGNERREAL UNIVERSE, PO Box 581, Seattle, WA 98111
ZERO HOUR, PO Box 766, Seattle, WA 98111, 206-323-3648
Pennypress, Inc., 1100 23rd Avenue East, Seattle, WA 98112, 206-325-1419
AMAZING HEROES, 7563 Lake City Way, Seattle, WA 98115
AMERICAN POETRY ANTHOLOGY, PO Box 51007, Seattle, WA 98115-1007
American Poetry Association, PO Box 51007, Seattle, WA 98115-1007, 408-429-1122
THE COMICS JOURNAL, 7563 Lake City Way, Seattle, WA 98115
Fantagraphics Books, 7563 Lake City Way, Seattle, WA 98115
Green Stone Publications, PO Box 15623, Seattle, WA 98115-0623, 206-524-4744
LOVE & ROCKETS, 7563 Lake City Way, Seattle, WA 98115
Fjord Press, PO Box 16501, Seattle, WA 98116, 206-625-9363
Argonauts/Misty Isles Press, 1616 NW 67th Street, Seattle, WA 98117, 206-783-5447
Bay Press, 115 West Denny Way, Seattle, WA 98119, 206-284-5913
Law Forum Press, 2318 Second Avenue, Seattle, WA 98121, 206-622-8240
The Real Comet Press, 3131 Western Avenue #410, Seattle, WA 98121-1028, 206-283-7827
The Seal Press, 3131 Western Avenue, Suite 410, Seattle, WA 98121-1028, 206-283-7844
Open Hand Publishing Inc., PO Box 22048, Seattle, WA 98122, 206-323-3868
Broken Moon Press, PO Box 24585, Seattle, WA 98124-0585, 206-548-1340
Dyad Services, Dept. 284, Box C34069, Seattle, WA 98124-1069, 604-734-0255
EMERGENCY LIBRARIAN, Dept. 284, PO Box C34069, Seattle, WA 98124-1069, 604-734-0255
Parenting Press, Inc., 11065 5th Avenue, NE, #F, Seattle, WA 98125, 206-364-2900

717

BAD HAIRCUT, 3115 SW Roxbury, Seattle, WA 98126
SUBTEXT, 1815 North 137th, Seattle, WA 98133, 206-782-4378
The Mountaineers Books, 1101 SW Klickitat Way, Suite 107, Seattle, WA 98134, 206-285-2665
BELLOWING ARK, PO Box 45637, Seattle, WA 98145, 206-545-8302
Bellowing Ark Press, PO Box 45637, Seattle, WA 98145, 206-545-8302
Black Heron Press, PO Box 95676, Seattle, WA 98145
EMERALD CITY COMIX & STORIES, PO Box 95402, Seattle, WA 98145, 206-527-2598
Fast Forward Publishing, PO Box 45153, Seattle, WA 98145-0153, 206-527-3112; fax 206-523-4829
LITERARY CENTER QUARTERLY, Box 85116, Seattle, WA 98145, 206-547-2503
Merrill Court Press, PO Box 85785, Seattle, WA 98145-1785
PAPER RADIO, PO Box 85302, Seattle, WA 98145-1302
Wonder Comix, PO Box 95402, Seattle, WA 98145
POETS. PAINTERS. COMPOSERS., 10254 35th Avenue SW, Seattle, WA 98146, 206-937-8155
Epicenter Press Inc., 18821 64th Ave NE, Seattle, WA 98155, 206-485-6822
Comprehensive Health Education Foundation (CHEF), 22323 Pacific Highway South, Seattle, WA 98198, 206-824-2907
Island Publishers, Box 201, Anacortes, WA 98221-0201, 206-293-3285/293-5398
National Lilac Publishing Co., 295 Sharpe Road, Anacortes, WA 98221-9729
JEOPARDY, Western Washington University, College Hall 132, Bellingham, WA 98225, 206-676-3118
Topping International Institute, 2622 Birchwood Ave, #7, Bellingham, WA 98225, 206-647-2703
THE BELLINGHAM REVIEW, 1007 Queen Street, Bellingham, WA 98226, 206-734-9781
Signpost Press Inc., 1007 Queen Street, Bellingham, WA 98226, 206-734-9781
World Promotions, 699 Sudden Valley, Bellingham, WA 98226
Blue Heron Press, PO Box 5182, Bellingham, WA 98227, 206-671-1155; 206-676-3954
Bright Ring Publishing, PO Box 5768-SP, Bellingham, WA 98227, 206-734-1601
COMPUTER EDUCATION NEWS, PO Box 5182, Bellingham, WA 98227, 206-676-3954
Post Point Press, PO Box 4393, Bellingham, WA 98227
THE UNINTELLIGENCER, PO Box 3194, Bellingham, WA 98227
Good Times Publishing Co., PO Box 8071-107, Blaine, WA 98230, 604-736-1045
Phoenix Publishing Inc., PO Box 10, Custer, WA 98240, 206-467-8219
Sweet Forever Publishing, PO Box 1000, Eastsound, WA 98245, (206) 376-2809
BLUEFISH, 4621 Westcott Drive, Friday Harbor, WA 98250-9733
Copyright Information Services, PO Box 1460-A, Friday Harbor, WA 98250, 217-356-7590
Umbrella Books, Po Box 1460-A, Friday Harbor, WA 98250-1460
Lone Star Press, PO Box 165, Laconner, WA 98257, 206-466-3377
Phoenix Publishing, 12811 52nd Place West, Mukilteo, WA 98275-3053
GREAT EXPEDITIONS MAGAZINE, Box 8000-411, Sumas, WA 98295, 604-852-6170
Brooding Heron Press, Bookmonger Road, Waldron Island, WA 98297
CACANADADADA REVIEW, PO Box 1283, Port Angeles, WA 98362, 206-325-5541
Olympic Publishing, Inc., 7450 Oak Bay Road, Port Ludlow, WA 98365, 206-437-2277
OLYMPIC TRAVEL GUIDE: YOUR GUIDE TO WASHINGTON'S OLYMPIC PENINSULA, PO Box 353, Port Ludlow, WA 98365, 206-437-2277
Copper Canyon Press, P.O. Box 271, Port Townsend, WA 98368
Esoterica, The Craft Press, 4545 San Juan Avenue, Port Townsend, WA 98368, 206-385-2318
LIBERTY, PO Box 1167, Port Townsend, WA 98368, 206-385-5097
The Lockhart Press, Box 1207, Port Townsend, WA 98368, 206-385-6412
Loompanics Unlimited, PO Box 1197, Port Townsend, WA 98368
Dragon Gate, Inc., 508 Lincoln Street, Townsend, WA 98368
Hound Dog Press, 10705 Woodland Avenue, Puyallup, WA 98373, (206) 845-8039
PORTRAITS POETRY MAGAZINE, 8312 123rd Street East, Puyallup, WA 98373, 206-848-5827
THE DESIGNMENT REVIEW, 4928 109th Street SW, Tacoma, WA 98499, 206-584-6309
Sovereign Press, 326 Harris Rd, Rochester, WA 98579
Upword Press, PO Box 1106, Yelm, WA 98597, 206-458-3619
Grimm Press & Publishing Co., Inc., PO Box 1523, Longview, WA 98632, (206) 577-8598
MASTERSTREAM, PO Box 1523, Longview, WA 98632, (206) 577-8598
THE WASHINGTON TROOPER, Grimm Press & Publishing Co., Inc., PO Box 1523, Longview, WA 98632-0144, 206-577-8598
THUNDERMUG REPORT, 110 Wildwood Drive, PO Box 206-876, Naselle, WA 98638, 206-484-7722
Tiptoe Literary Service, 110 Wildwood Drive, PO Box 206, Naselle, WA 98638, 206-484-7722
LYNX, PO Box 169, Toutle, WA 98649, 206-274-6661
Valley Lights Publications, Valley Light Center, 356 Little Mountain Rd, Trout Lake, WA 98650, 509-395-2092
Pandemic International Publishers Inc., POB 61849, Vancouver, WA 98666, 503-786-2949
Twin Peaks Press, PO Box 129, Vancouver, WA 98666, 206-694-2462 FAX 206-696-3210
DRUG INTERACTIONS AND UPDATES, PO Box 5077, Vancouver, WA 98668, 206-253-7123; FAX 206-253-8475
Directed Media, Inc., 246 N. Wenatchee Avenue, Box 3005, Wenatchee, WA 98801, 509-662-7693
ACTINIDIA ENTHUSIASTS NEWSLETTER, Friends of the Trees Society, PO Box 1064, Tonasket, WA 98855
HOME EDUCATION MAGAZINE, PO Box 1083, Tonasket, WA 98855, 509-486-1351
BRONG'S BUSINESS SUCCESS NEWS, PO Box 9, Ellensburg, WA 98926-0009, 509-962-8238
The Evergreen Press, PO Box 83, 1900 Brooklane Village #C-12, Ellensburg, WA 98926-0083, 509-962-3078
Vagabond Press, 605 East 5th Avenue, Ellensburg, WA 98926-3201, 509-962-8471
WILLOW SPRINGS, MS-1, Eastern Washington University, Cheney, WA 99004, 509-458-6429
Ye Galleon Press, Box 287, Fairfield, WA 99012, 509-283-2422
Ritz Publishing, 202 West 5th Avenue, Ritzville, WA 99169-1722, 509-659-4336
WHEAT LIFE, 109 East 1st Avenue, Ritzville, WA 99169, 509-659-0610
The Oxalis Group, PO Box 8051, Spokane, WA 99203, (509) 838-3295
Bear Tribe Publishing, PO Box 9167, Spokane, WA 99209, 509-326-6561
WILDFIRE: A NETWORKING MAGAZINE, PO Box 9167, Spokane, WA 99209, 509-326-6561
Arthur H. Clark Co., PO Box 14707, Spokane, WA 99214, 509-928-9540
StarLance Publications, 50 Basin Drive, Mesa, WA 99343, 509-269-4497

718

VOYAGES SF, 50 Basin Drive, Mesa, WA 99343, 509-269-4497
Earth-Love Publishing House, 302 Torbett, Suite 100, Richland, WA 99352, 509-943-9567

WEST VIRGINIA

Mountain State Press, c/o University of Charleston, 2300 MacCorkle, Charleston, WV 25304, 304-9471 ext 210
Carol Bryan Imagines, 1000 Byus Drive, Charleston, WV 25311
THE LIBRARY IMAGINATION PAPER!, 1000 Byus Drive, Charleston, WV 25311, 304-345-2378
The Bunny & The Crocodile Press, PO Box 416, Hedgesville, WV 25427-0416, 304-754-8847
Emily Press, 4639B Route 10, Barboursville, WV 25504-9650
Aegina Press, Inc., 59 Oak Lane, Spring Valley, Huntington, WV 25704, 304-429-7204
University Editions, Inc., 59 Oak Lane, Spring Valley, Huntington, WV 25704, 304-429-7204
Flax Press, Inc., PO Box 2395, Huntington, WV 25724, 304-525-1109
Power Publishing, PO Box 1805, Elkins, WV 26241, 304-636-8488
Westwind Press, Route 1, Box 208, Farmington, WV 26571

WISCONSIN

Affordable Adventures, Inc., PO Box 129, Brookfield, WI 53008-0129
FARMER'S DIGEST, PO Box 624, Brookfield, WI 53008-0624, 414-782-4480
Farmer's Digest Publishing Co., PO Box 624, Brookfield, WI 53008-0624, 414-782-4480
Name That Team!, PO Box 624, Brookfield, WI 53008-0624
Sun Designs, PO Box 206, Delafield, WI 53018, 414-567-4255
THE WRITE AGE (First Magazine of Writing Therapy), PO Box 722, Menomonee Falls, WI 53051, 414-255-7706
The Second Hand, PO Box 204, Plymouth, WI 53073, 414-893-5226
SEEMS, c/o Lakeland College, Box 359, Sheboygan, WI 53082-0359
Aroc Publishing, PO Box 550, Elm Grove, WI 53122-0550, 414-541-3407
Southport Press, Dept. of English, Carthage College, Kenosha, WI 53141, 414-551-8500 (252)
Tiare Publications, PO Box 493, Lake Geneva, WI 53147, 414-248-4845
WINDFALL, c/o The Friends of Poetry, English Dept., UW-Whitewater, Whitewater, WI 53190, 414-472-1036
Windfall Prophets Press, c/o The Friends of Poetry, English Dept., UW-Whitewater, Whitewater, WI 53190
THE CREAM CITY REVIEW, PO Box 413, English Dept, Curtin Hall, Univ. of Wisconsin, Milwaukee, WI 53201
"R"-Kids Publishing Co., PO Box 05796, Milwaukee, WI 53205, 414-453-4852
THE MID COASTER, 2750 North 45th Street, Milwaukee, WI 53210-2429
Cordelia Press, PO Box 11066, Milwaukee, WI 53211, 414-264-4018
THE MILWAUKEE UNDERGRADUATE REVIEW, PO Box 71079, Milwaukee, WI 53211
Ranger International Productions, Lion Publishing/Roar Recording, PO Box 71231, Milwaukee, WI 53211-7331, 414-332-7474
Sackbut Press, 2513 E Webster Place, Milwaukee, WI 53211
SQUARE ONE - A Magazine of Fiction, PO Box 11921, Milwaukee, WI 53211-0921
Hal Leonard Books, PO Box 13819, 8112 W. Bluemound Road, Milwaukee, WI 53213, 414-774-3630
BLANK GUN SILENCER, 1240 William Street, Racine, WI 53402, 414-639-2406
Gilgamesh Press Ltd., 205 6th Street, Racine, WI 53403-1255
Mother Courage Press, 1533 Illinois Street, Racine, WI 53405-3115, 414-634-1047
BELOIT FICTION JOURNAL, Box 11, Beloit College, Beloit, WI 53511, 608-363-2308
THE MAGAZINE OF SPECULATIVE POETRY, PO Box 564, Beloit, WI 53512
W.D. Hoard & Sons Company, 28 Milwaukee Avenue West, Fort Atkinson, WI 53538, 414-563-5551
HOARD'S DAIRYMAN, 28 Milwaukee Avenue West, Fort Atkinson, WI 53538, 414-563-5551
Dog-Eared Publications, PO Box 863, Middleton, WI 53562, 608-831-1410
CONVERGING PATHS, PO Box 63, Mt. Horeb, WI 53572
AURORA, PO Box 1624, Madison, WI 53701-1624, 233-0326
THE MADISON INSURGENT, PO Box 704, Madison, WI 53701-0704, 608-251-3967
MODERN HAIKU, PO Box 1752, Madison, WI 53701
NEW MOON, PO Box 2056, Madison, WI 53701-2056, 608-251-3854
SF**3, PO Box 1624, Madison, WI 53701-1624, 267-7483 (days); 255-9905 (evenings)
THE ACTS THE SHELFLIFE, 1341 Williamson, Madison, WI 53703, 608-258-1305
ANTI-ISOLATION/NEW ARTS IN WISCONSIN, 1341 Williamson, Madison, WI 53703
CANVAS, 6189 Helen C. White Hall, Madison, WI 53703
Center for Public Representation, 121 S. Pinckney Street, Madison, WI 53703-1999, 608-251-4008
CREATIVITY CONNECTION, Room 224 Lowell Hall, Wisconsin Univ., 610 Langdon Street, Madison, WI 53703, 608-262-4911
A PERIODIC JOURNAL OF 'PATAPHYSICAL SUCCULENTOSOPHY, 1341 Williamson, Madison, WI 53703, 608-258-1305
WISCONSIN RESTAURATEUR, 125 W. Doty, Madison, WI 53703
XEROLAGE, 1341 Williamson, Madison, WI 53703, 258-1305
Xexoxial Endarchy, 1341 Williamson, Madison, WI 53703
ART'S GARBAGE GAZZETTE, 214 Dunning, Madison, WI 53704, 608-249-0715
Art Paul Schlosser Books, Tapes, & Garbage Gazzette, 214 Dunning, Madison, WI 53704, 608-249-0715
WORLD PERSPECTIVES, Box 3074, Madison, WI 53704, 608-241-4812
Cooperative Children's Book Center, PO Box 5288, Madison, WI 53705, 608-262-3930
WISCONSIN ACADEMY REVIEW, 1922 University Ave., Madison, WI 53705, 608-263-1692
WISCONSIN TRAILS, PO Box 5650, Madison, WI 53705, 608-231-2444
Wisconsin Trails, P.O.Box 5650, Madison, WI 53705, 608-231-2444
CONTEMPORARY LITERATURE, 7141 Helen C. White Hall, University of Wisconsin, Madison, WI 53706
FEMINIST COLLECTIONS: A QUARTERLY OF WOMEN'S STUDIES RESOURCES, 112A Memorial Library, 728 State Street, Madison, WI 53706, 608-263-5754
FEMINIST PERIODICALS: A CURRENT LISTING OF CONTENTS, 112A Memorial Library, 728 State Street, Madison, WI 53706, 608-263-5754
THE MADISON REVIEW, Dept of English, H.C. White Hall, 600 N. Park Street, Madison, WI 53706, 263-3303
Medical Physics Publishing Corp., 1300 University Avenue, Suite 27B, Madison, WI 53706, 608-256-3300

NEW BOOKS ON WOMEN & FEMINISM, 112A Memorial Library, 728 State Street, Madison, WI 53706, 608-263-5754
Women's Studies Librarian, University of Wisconsin System, 112A Memorial Library, 728 State Street, Madison, WI 53706, 608-263-5754
STUDENT LEADERSHIP JOURNAL, PO Box 7895, Madison, WI 53707-7895, 608-274-4823 X425, 413
ABRAXAS, 2518 Gregory Street, Madison, WI 53711, 608-238-0175
Abraxas Press, Inc., 2518 Gregory Street, Madison, WI 53711, 608-238-0175
Ghost Pony Press, 2518 Gregory Street, Madison, WI 53711, 608-238-0175
CHANGING MEN, 306 N. Brooks #305, Madison, WI 53715, 608-256-2565
Feminist Mens' Publications, 306 N. Brooks #305, Madison, WI 53715, 608-256-2565
JOURNAL OF AESTHETICS AND ART CRITICISM, University of Wisconsin Press, 114 North Murray Street, Madison, WI 53715, 608-262-5839
MINORITY PUBLISHERS EXCHANGE, PO Box 9869, Madison, WI 53715, 608-244-5633
BASEBALL: OUR WAY, 5014 Starker Avenue, Madison, WI 53716, 608-241-0549
FOOTBALL: OUR WAY, 5014 Starker Avenue, Madison, WI 53716, 608-241-0549
Our Way Publications, 5014 Starker Avenue, Madison, WI 53716
BRILLIANT IDEAS FOR PUBLISHERS, PO Box 44237, Madison, WI 53744, 608-233-2669
RURAL NETWORK ADVOCATE, 6236 Borden Road, Boscobel, WI 53805
Westburg Associates, Publishers, 1735 Madison Street, Fennimore, WI 53809, 608-822-6237
PHOTOBULLETIN, PhotoSource International, Pine Lake Farm, Osceola, WI 54020, (715) 248-3800, Our Fax# 715-248-7394
THE PHOTOLETTER, PhotoSource International, Pine Lake Farm, Osceola, WI 54020, (715) 248-3800, Our Fax # 715-248-7394
PHOTOMARKET, PhotoSource International, Pine Lake Farm, Osceola, WI 54020, (715) 248-3800, Our Fax # 715-248-7394
PhotoSource International, Pine Lake Farm, Osceola, WI 54020, 715-248-3800, Fax 715-248-7394
SPWAO SHOWCASE, 309 North Humphrey Circle, Shawano, WI 54166
Druid Books, PO Box 231, Ephraim, WI 54211
Wm Caxton Ltd, Box 709, Sister Bay, WI 54234, 414-854-2955
DOOR COUNTY ALMANAK, 10905 Bay Shore Drive, Sister Bay, WI 54234, 414-854-2742
The Dragonsbreath Press, 10905 Bay Shore Drive, Sister Bay, WI 54234, 414-854-2742
George Sroda, Publisher, Amherst Jct., WI 54407, 715-824-3868
Evon Publishing, RT #1, Box 658, Elcho, WI 54428, 275-3887
Index House, PO Box 716, Stevens Point, WI 54481-6892, 715-341-2604
THE NORTHERN REVIEW, Academic Achievement Center, 2100 Main Street, Stevens Point, WI 54481, 715-346-3568
Pinery Press, P.O. Box 672, Stevens Point, WI 54481
Explorer's Guide Publishing, 4843 Apperson Drive, Rhinelander, WI 54501, 715-362-6029
Northword Press, Inc., PO Box 1360, Minocqua, WI 54548, 715-356-9800
Juniper Press, 1310 Shorewood Dr, La Crosse, WI 54601
NORTHEAST, 1310 Shorewood Dr., LaCrosse, WI 54601, 608-788-0096
THE HOWLING MANTRA, PO Box 1821, LaCrosse, WI 54602, 608-785-0810
Motorsport International Publishing Co. (MIPCO), R3 Box 6181, Sparta, WI 54656, 608-269-5591
Heritage Press WI, Rt 1, 89 SPR, Stoddard, WI 54658, 608-457-2734
Rhiannon Press, 1105 Bradley Avenue, Eau Claire, WI 54701, 715-835-0598
WISCONSIN REVIEW, Box 158, Radford Hall, Univ. of Wisconsin-Oshkosh, Oshkosh, WI 54901, (414) 424-2267
The Green Hut Press, 1015 Jardin Street East, Appleton, WI 54911, 414-734-9728
THE NEW AMERICAN, PO Box 8040, Appleton, WI 54913, 414-749-3784
SHENANDOAH NEWSLETTER, 736 West Oklahoma Street, Appleton, WI 54914
Pearl-Win Publishing Co., PO Box 300, Hancock, WI 54943, 715-249-5407
Aircraft Owner Organization, PO Box 337, Iola, WI 54945, 800-331-0038
Kitchen Sink Press, No. 2 Swamp Road, Princeton, WI 54968, 414-295-6922
THE SPIRIT, No. 2 Swamp Road, Princeton, WI 54968
STEVE CANYON MAGAZINE, No. 2 Swamp Road, Princeton, WI 54968, 414-295-6922

WYOMING

OWEN WISTER REVIEW, PO Box 4238, University Station, Laramie, WY 82071, 766-6190
Skyline West Press, PO Box 4281, University Station, Laramie, WY 82071, 307-742-4840
High Plains Press, Box 123, Glendo, WY 82213, 307-735-4370
Affiliated Writers of America, Inc., PO Box 343, Encampment, WY 82325, 307-327-5328
Willow Bee Publishing House, PO Box 9, Saratoga, WY 82331, 307-326-5214
WYOMING, THE HUB OF THE WHEEL...A Journey for Universal Spokesmen..., PO Box 9, Saratoga, WY 82331, 307-326-5214
Great Western Publishing Company, 1601 11th Street, Cody, WY 82414, 307-527-7480
Dooryard Press, 3645 Navarre Road, Casper, WY 82604, 307-235-9021
Alpine Press, PO Box 1930, Mills, WY 82644, 602-986-9457
Heirloom Publications, 4340 Hideaway Lane, PO Box 183, Mills, WY 82644, 307-235-3561
Achievement Press, Box 608, Sheridan, WY 82801, 307-672-8475
HOUSEWIFE-WRITER'S FORUM, PO Box 780, Lyman, WY 82937, 307-786-4513
Homestead Publishing, Box 193, Moose, WY 83012

ARGENTINA

ETICA & CIENCIA, PO Box 94 Suc. 19, Buenos Aires 1419, Argentina, 541-572-1050
FISICA, PO Box 94 Sucursal 19, Buenos Aires 1419, Argentina, 541-572-1050
TIERRA DEL FUEGO MAGAZINE, PO Box 94 Sucursal 19, Buenos Aires 1419, Argentina, 541-572-1050
Zagier & Urruty Publicaciones, PO Box 94 Sucursal 19, Buenos Aires 1419, Argentina, 541-572-1050

AUSTRALIA

ATINDEX, G.P.O. Box 2222T, Melbourne, Vic. 3001, Australia
CRAFTS NSW, 88 George Street, Sydney, N.S.W. 2000, Australia, 612-247-9126

720

THE CRITICAL REVIEW, Philosophy Dept, Research School of Social Science, Australian Nat'l Univ., GPO Box 4, Canberra, A.C.T. 2601, Australia
Elephas Books, 361 Orrong Road, Kewdalee WA 6105, Australia, 09 470 1080
English Language Literature Association, English Department, James Cook Univ-North Quensland, Townsville 4811, Australia
THE FAMOUS REPORTER, PO Box 319, Kingston, Tasmania 7051, Australia
Five Islands Press Cooperative Ltd., PO Box 1946, Wollongong, NSW 2500, Australia, 042-272875
GRASS ROOTS, PO Box 242, Euroa, Victoria 3666, Australia
HECATE, P.O. Box 99, St. Lucia, Queensland 4067, Australia
Hecate Press, PO Box 99, St. Lucia, QLD 4067, Australia
IDIOM 23, University College of Central Queensland, Rockhampton, Queensland, 4702, Australia, 0011-079-360655
IMAGO, Queensland Univ Technology, School of Communication, PO Box 2434, Brisbane Q1D 4001, Australia, (07)223 2111, FAX (07)229 1510
KYOCERA USER, G.P.O. Box 2222T, Melbourne, Vic. 3001, Australia
LINQ, English Dept., James Cook Univ.-North Queensland, Townsville 4811, Australia
Matilda Publications, 7 Mountfield Street, Brunswick, Melbourne, Victoria, Australia, 03-386-5604
Night Owl Publishers, PO Box 242, Euroa, Victoria 3666, Australia
John Noyce, Publisher, G.P.O. Box 2222T, Melbourne, Vic. 3001, Australia
OVERLAND, PO Box 14146, Melbourne 3000, Australia
P.I.E. (Poetry Imagery and Expression), PO Box 739, Parramatta, NSW 2124, Australia, 02 683-2971
Pinchgut Press, 6 Oaks Avenue, Cremorne, Sydney, N.S.W. 2090, Australia, 02-908-2402
POETRY AUSTRALIA, Market Place, Berrima, N.S.W. 2577, Australia
SCARP, PO Box 1144, Wollongong, NSW 2500, Australia, (042) 270985
SCRIPSI, Ormond College, University of Melbourne, Parkville, Victoria 3052, Australia, (03) 3476360; 3474784
SOCIAL CHANGE & INFORMATION SYSTEMS, G.P.O. Box 2222T, Melbourne, Vic. 3001, Australia
South Head Press, Market Place, Berrima, N.S.W. 2577, Australia
Graham Stone, GPO Box 4440, Sydney 2001, Australia, 02-3009879
STUDIO - A Journal of Christians Writing, 727 Peel Street, Albury, N.S.W. 2640, Australia
SUB STANDARD, PO Box 245, Willoughby, N.S.W. 2068, Australia, 6987071
Visa Books (Division of South Continent Corporation Pty Ltd), PO Box 1024, Richmond North, Victoria 3121, Australia, 03-429-5599
WEBBER'S, 15 McKillop Street, Melbourne, Victoria 3000, Australia
Wild & Woolley, PO Box 41, Glebe NSW 2037, Australia, 02-692-0166

BELGIUM

Atelier De L'Agneau, 39 Rue Louis Demeuse, 4400 Herstal, Belgium, (41) 363722
DE NAR, PO Box 104, 1210 Brussels 21, Belgium
MENSUEL 25, 39 Rue Louis Demeuse, 4400 Herstal, Belgium, (41) 363722
Nioba, Uitgevers, Maarschalk Gerardstraat 6, 2000 Antwerpen, Belgium, 03/232.38.62

BRITISH VIRGIN ISLANDS

MYCOPHILATELY, PO Box 704, Road Town-Tortola, British Virgin Islands
Vernon W. Pickering-Laurel Publications International, PO Box 704, Road Town-Tortola, British Virgin Islands

CANADA

Aardvark Enterprises, 204 Millbank Drive S.W., Calgary, Alta T2Y 2H9, Canada, 403-256-4639
ACTA VICTORIANA, 150 Charles Street West, Toronto, Ontario M5S 1K9, Canada, 416-585-4973
ALBERTA HISTORY, 95 Holmwood Ave NW, Calgary Alberta T2K 2G7, Canada, 403-289-8149
THE ALCHEMIST, PO Box 123, LaSalle, Quebec H8R 3T7, Canada
Alpha Beat Press, 68 Winter, Scarborough, Ont. M1K 4M3, Canada
ALPHA BEAT SOUP, Alpha Beat Press, 68 Winter, Scarborough, Ont. M1K 4M3, Canada, 416-261-7390
ANERCA/COMPOST, 3989 Arbutus Street, Vancouver, B.C. V6J 4T2, Canada, (604) 732-1648
ANIME SHOWER SPECIAL, 33, Prince Street #243, Montreal, Quebec H3C 2M7, Canada, 514-397-0342
Anjou, Two Sussex Avenue, Toronto M5S 1J5, Canada, 416-537-1569
Annick Press Ltd., 15 Patricia Avenue, Willowdale, Ontario M2M 1H9, Canada, 416-221-4802
THE ANTIGONISH REVIEW, St Francis Xavier University, Antigonish, Nova Scotia B2G1CO, Canada
Anvil Press, PO Box 1575, Station A, Vancouver, B.C. V6C 2P7, Canada
ARCTIC—Journal of the Arctic Institute of America, The Arctic Institute of N. America, University of Calgary, Calgary, Alberta T2N 1N4, Canada, 403-220-4050
ARIEL—A Review of International English Literature, The University of Calgary Press, Calgary, Alberta T2N 1N4, Canada, 403-220-4657
Arsenal Pulp Press, Ltd., #100-1062 Homer St., Vancouver, B.C. V6B 2W9, Canada, 604-687-4233
Art Metropole, 217 Richmond Street West, Toronto, Ontario M5V 1W2, Canada, (416) 362-l685
ARTISTAMP NEWS, PO Box 3655, Vancouver, B.C. V6B 3Y8, Canada, 604-876-6764
ATLANTIS: A Women's Studies Journal/Journal d'etudes sur la femme, Mount Saint Vincent University, Halifax, Nova Scotia, B3M 2J6, Canada
Banana Productions, PO Box 3655, Vancouver, BC V6B 3Y8, Canada, 604-876-6764
The Barbizon Foundation, Barbizon House, Rural Route One, Lumby, B.C. V0E 2G0, Canada, (604) 547-6621
BARBIZON MAGAZINE, Barbizon House, Rural Route One, Lumby, B.C. V0E 2G0, Canada, (604) 547-6621
BARDIC RUNES, 424 Cambridge Street South, Ottawa, Ontario K1S 4H5, Canada, 613-231-4311
BEAN ZINE, 1359 Oxford Avenue, Kingsville, Ontario N9Y 2S8, Canada, 519-733-4875
Betelgeuse Books, 193-55 McCaul Street, Toronto Ont. M5T 2W7, Canada
Between The Lines, 394 Euclid Avenue, Toronto, Ontario M6G 2S9, Canada, 416-925-8260
BikePress U.S.A./BikePress Canada, 492 Covey Hill Road, Franklin Centre, P.Q. J0S 1E0, Canada, 412-625-1180
Black Rose Books Ltd., 3981 St. Laurent Blvd., #444, Montreal, Que H2W 1Y2, Canada, 514-844-4076
BORDER/LINES, 183 Bathurst Street, #301, Toronto, Ontario M5T 2R7, Canada, 416-360-5249
Borealis Press Limited, 9 Ashburn Drive, Nepean Ontario, Canada, 613-224-6837
The Boston Mills Press, 132 Main Street, Erin, Ontario N0B 1T0, Canada, 519-833-2407

BOWBENDER, 65 McDonald Close, PO Box 912, Carstairs, Alberta T0M 0N0, Canada, 403-337-3023
BREAKTHROUGH!, 204 Millbank Drive S.W., Calgary, Alberta T2Y 2H9, Canada, 403-256-4639
BRICK: A Journal Of Reviews, Box 537, Station Q, Toronto, Ontario M4T 2M5, Canada, 519-666-0283
Brick Books, Box 38, Station B, London, Ontario N6K 4V3, Canada
Broken Jaw Press, M.A.P. Productions, 467 Waterloo Row, Suite 201, Fredericton, N.B. E3B 1Z6, Canada, 506-454-5127
BUDDHISM AT THE CROSSROADS, 86 Vaughan Road, Toronto, Ont. M6C 2M1, Canada, 416-658-0137
C.J.L. Press, Box 22006, 45 Overlea, Thorncliff Post Office, Toronto, Ont. M4H 1N9, Canada
C.S.P. WORLD NEWS, c/o Guy F. Claude Hamel, 1307 Bethamy Lane, Gloucester, Ont. K1J 8P3, Canada, 613-741-8675
Cacanadadada Press Ltd., 3350 West 21st Avenue, Vancouver, B.C. V6S 1G7, Canada, 604-738-1195
CANADIAN AUTHOR & BOOKMAN, 121 Avenue Road, Suite 104, Toronto, Ontario M5R 2G3, Canada, 416-926-8084
CANADIAN CHILDREN'S LITERATURE, Department of English, University of Guelph, Guelph, Ontario N1G 2W1, Canada
CANADIAN DIMENSION, 707-228 Notre dame Avenue, Winnipeg, Manitoba R3B IN7, Canada, 957-1519
CANADIAN FICTION MAGAZINE, PO Box 946, Station F, Toronto, Ontario M4Y 2N9, Canada
CANADIAN JOURNAL OF DRAMA AND THEATRE, Department of Drama, The University of Calgary, Calgary, Alberta T2N 1N4, Canada, 403-220-3849
CANADIAN JOURNAL OF LAW AND SOCIETY/Revue canadienne de droit et societe, Department des sciences juridiques, c.p. 8888, succ. A., Quebec Univ., Montreal, P.Q. H3C 3PA, Canada, 514-987-8397
CANADIAN JOURNAL OF PHILOSOPHY, Department of Philosophy, University of Alberta, Edmonton, Alberta T6G 2E5, Canada, 403-492-3307
CANADIAN JOURNAL OF PROGRAM EVALUATION/Le Revue canadienne d'evaluation de programme, Faculty of Social Welfare, The University of Calgary, Calgary, Alberta T2N 1N4, Canada, 403-220-6154
CANADIAN LITERATURE, University of British Columbia, 2029 West Mall, Vancouver, B.C. V6T 1Z2, Canada, 604-822-2780
CANADIAN MONEYSAVER, Box 370, Bath, Ontario K0H 1G0, Canada
CANADIAN PUBLIC POLICY- Analyse de Politiques, Room 039, MacKinnon Bldg., University of Guelph, Guelph, Ontario N1G 2W1, Canada, 519-824-4120 ext. 3330
CANADIAN SLAVONIC PAPERS, Centre for Russian and East European Studies, University of Toronto, Toronto, Ontario M5S 1A1, Canada
CANADIAN WOMAN STUDIES/les cahiers de la femme, 212 Founders College, York Univ., 400 Keele Street, Downsview, Ontario M3J 1P3, Canada, (416) 736-5356
THE CAPILANO REVIEW, 2055 Purcell Way, North Vancouver, B.C. V7J3H5, Canada, 604-986-1911; FAX 604-984-4985
Charnel House, c/o Crad Kilodney, PO Box 281, Station S, Toronto, Ontario M5M 4L7, Canada, 416-924-5670
CHASTITY AND HOLINESS, Box 22006, 45 Overlea, Thorncliff Post Office, Toronto, Ont. M4H 1N9, Canada, 423-6781
THE CHRISTIAN LIBRARIAN, Assoc. of Christian Librarians, Three Hills, Alberta T0M 2A0, Canada
THE CHURCH, FARM AND TOWN, Box 368, RR 4, Amherst, NS B4H 3Y2, Canada, 902-667-4006
Clover Press, Box 3236, Regina, Saskatchewan S4P 3H1, Canada
Coach House Press, 401 Huron Street (rear), Toronto, Ontario M5S 2G5, Canada, 416-979-7374
CODA: The Jazz Magazine, Box 87 Stn. J., Toronto, Ont. M4J4X8, Canada, 416-593-7230
CONNEXIONS DIGEST, 427 Bloor Street West, Toronto, Ontario M5S 1X7, Canada, 960-3903
Connexions Information Services, Inc., 427 Bloor Street West, Toronto, Ontario M5S 1X7, Canada, 416-960-3903
Coteau Books, 401-2206 Dewdney Avenue, Regina, Sask. S4R 1H3, Canada, 306-777-0170
CROSS-CANADA WRITERS' MAGAZINE, Cross-Canada Writers, Inc., Box 277, Station F, Toronto, Ontario M4Y 2L7, Canada
CROSSCURRENTS, 516 Ave K South, Saskatoon, Saskatchewan, Canada
THE DALHOUSIE REVIEW, Alan Andrews, Editor, Sir James Dunn Bldg. Suite 314, Halifax, Nova Scotia B3H 3J5, Canada
DESCANT, PO Box 314, Station P, Toronto, Ontario M5S 2S8, Canada
Dollarpoems, Box 5, Brandon University, Brandon, Manitoba R7A 6A9, Canada
DREAMS & VISIONS, Skysong Press, RR #1, Washago, Ontario L0K 2B0, Canada
Dundurn Press Ltd, 2181 Queen Street East #301, Toronto, Ontario M4E 1E5, Canada, 416-698-0454; FAX 416-698-1102
The E.G. Van Press, Inc., PO Box 6053, London ON N5V 2Y3, Canada, 519-453-4529
ECHOS DU MONDE CLASSIQUE/CLASSICAL VIEWS, Department of Classics, University of Calgary, Calgary, Alberta T2N 1N4, Canada, 403-220-5537
THE ECLECTIC MUSE, 340 West 3rd Street #107, North Vancouver, B.C. V7M 1G4, Canada, 604-984-7834
ECW Press, 307 Coxwell Avenue, Toronto, Ontario M4L 3B5, Canada, 416-694-3348
Edition Stencil, c/o Guy F. Claude Hamel, 1307 Bethamy Lane, Gloucester, Ont. K1J 8P3, Canada, 741-8675
Editions Ex Libris, C.P. 294, Sherbrooke, Quebec J1H 5J1, Canada, 819-565-7093
ELLIPSE, Univ. de Sherbrooke, Box 10, Faculte des Lettres et Sciences Humaines, Sherbrooke, Quebec J1K 2R1, Canada, 819-821-7277
ENCYCLOPEDIA BANANICA, PO Box 3655, Vancouver, B.C., V6B 3Y8, Canada, 604-876-6764
ENTROPY NEGATIVE, Box 65583, Vancouver 12, B.C. V5N 5K5, Canada
Escart Press, Environmental Studies, University of Waterloo, Waterloo, Ontario N2L 3G1, Canada, 519-885-1211 X3110
ESSAYS ON CANADIAN WRITING, 307 Coxwell Avenue, Toronto, Ontario M4L 3B5, Canada, 416-694-3348
EVENT, Douglas College, PO Box 2503, New Westminster, B.C. V3L 5B2, Canada, 604-527-5293
THE FIDDLEHEAD, Campus House, PO Box 4400, University of New Brunswick, Fredericton, NB E3B 5A3, Canada, 506-453-3501
FOCUS, 100 Richmond St., E, Suite 300, Toronto, Ontario M5C 2P9, Canada, 416-363-3388
The Folks Upstairs Press, 827A Bloor Street West, Toronto, Ontario M6G 1M1, Canada
FRASER FORUM, 626 Bute Street, 2nd Floor, Vancouver, BC V6E 3M1, Canada, 604-688-0221, FAX 604-688-8539
The Fraser Institute, 626 Bute Street, 2nd Floor, Vancouver, BC V6E 3M1, Canada, 604-688-0221, FAX 604-688-8539
FREELANCE, Box 3986, Regina, Saskatchewan S4P 3R9, Canada, 306-757-6310
FUSE MAGAZINE, 183 Bathurst Street, Main Floor, Toronto, Ont. M5T 2R7, Canada, 416-367-0159
GATES OF PANDRAGON, 33, Prince Street #243, Montreal, Quebec H3C 2M7, Canada, 514-397-0342
Gesture Press, 68 Tyrrel Avenue, Toronto M6G 2G4, Canada
THE GLOBAL FORUM MAGAZINE, International Relief Agency, Inc., 178 Jarvis Street, Suite 804, Toronto, Ontario M5B 2K7, Canada, 416-364-0124

722

Golden Sceptre, 45911 Silver Avenue, Sardis, British Columbia V2R 1V8, Canada, 604-858-6934; fax 604-858-0870
Grade School Press, 3266 Yonge Street #1829, Toronto, Ontario M4N 3P6, Canada, 416-487-2883
GRAIN, Box 1154, Regina, Sask. S4P 3B4, Canada, 306-757-6310
GREEN MULTILOGUE, 390 Jones Avenue, Toronto, Ont. M4J 3G3, Canada, 416-461-8467
GREEN'S MAGAZINE, Box 3236, Regina, Saskatchewan S4P 3H1, Canada
Growing Room Collective, Box 46160, Station G, Vancouver BC V6R 4G5, Canada, 604-321-1423
GUARD THE NORTH, Box 65583, Vancouver 12, B. C. V5N 5K5, Canada
Guernica Editions, Inc., PO Box 633, Station N.D.G., Montreal, Quebec H4A 3R1, Canada, 514-987-7411; FAX 514-982-9793
HEALTHSHARING: A Canadian Women's Health Quarterly, 14 Skey Lane, Toronto, Ontario M6J 3S4, Canada, 416-532-0812
Historical Society of Alberta, 95 Holmwood Ave. NW, Calgary, Alberta T2K 2G7, Canada
HMS Press, Box 340, Station B, London, Ont. N6A 4W1, Canada, 519-434-4740
HORIZONS INTERCULTURELS, Intercultural Institute of Montreal, 4917 St. Urbain, Montreal, Quebec H2T 2W1, Canada, 514-288-7229
HUNGRY ZIPPER, PO Box 3576, Cambridge, Ont. N3H 5C6, Canada
Ianus Publications, Inc., 33, Prince Street #243, Montreal, Quebec H3C 2M7, Canada, 514-397-0342
IMPULSE, 16 Skey Lane, Toronto, Ontario M6J 3S4, Canada, 1-416-537-9551
Infolib Resources, 469 Spadina Road, Suite 15, Toronto, Ontario M5P 2W6, Canada
INKSTONE, PO Box 67, Station H, Toronto, Ontario M4C 5H7, Canada, 962-6051
Inkstone Press, PO Box 67, Station H, Toronto, Ontario M4C 5H7, Canada
INNER SEARCH, PO Box 3577, Station C, Ottawa, Ontario K1Y 4J7, Canada
INTERCULTURE, Intercultural Institute of Montreal, 4917 St-Urbain, Montreal, Quebec H2T 2W1, Canada, 514-288-7229
INTERNATIONAL ART POST, PO Box 3655, Vancouver, B.C. V6B 3Y8, Canada
THE INTERNATIONAL FICTION REVIEW, Dept. of German & Russian, UNB, Fredericton, N.B. E3B 5A3, Canada, 506-453-4636
JOURNAL OF CANADIAN POETRY, 9 Ashburn Drive, Nepean Ontario K2E 6N4, Canada, (613) 224-6837
JOURNAL OF CANADIAN STUDIES/Revue d'etudes canadiennes, Trent University, Peterborough, Ont. K9J 7B8, Canada
JOURNAL OF CHILD AND YOUTH CARE, 117 Woodpark Boulevard, S.W. Calgary, Alberta T2W 2Z8, Canada, 403-281-2266 X436
K, 351 Dalhousie Street, Brantford, Ontario N3S 3V9, Canada, (416) 529-3125
KICK IT OVER, Kick It Over Collective, PO Box 5811, Station A, Toronto, Ontario M5W 1P2, Canada
LITERARY MARKETS, 4340 Coldfall Road, Richmond, B.C. V7C 1P8, Canada, 604-277-4829
THE MALAHAT REVIEW, PO Box 3045, Victoria, British Columbia V8W 3P4, Canada
MEDICAL REFORM, PO Box 366, Station J, Toronto, Ontario M4J 4Y8, Canada, 416-588-9167
Medical Reform Group, PO Box 366, Station J, Toronto, Ontario M4J 4Y8, Canada, 416-588-9167
Mr. Information, P.O. Box 955, Ganges, B.C. V1S 1E0, Canada, 604-653-9260
MONDO HUNKAMOOGA, PO Box 789, Station F, Toronto, Ontario M4Y 2N7, Canada
MUSICWORKS: THE CANADIAN AUDIO-VISUAL JOURNAL OF SOUND EXPLORATIONS, 1087 Queen Street West, Toronto, Ontario, Canada, 416-533-0192
New Star Books Ltd., 2504 York Avenue, Vancouver, B.C. V6K 1E3, Canada, 604-738-9429
NEWSLETTER (LEAGUE OF CANADIAN POETS), 24 Ryerson Avenue, Toronto, Ontario M5T 2P3, Canada, 416-363-5047
NEXT EXIT, 92 Helen Street, Kingston, Ontario K7L 4P3, Canada, 613-549-6790
ON BALANCE: MEDIA TREATMENT OF PUBLIC POLICY ISSUES, 626 Bute Street, 2nd Floor, Vancouver, BC V6E 3M1, Canada, 604-688-0221
Ontario Library Association, 100 Richmond St., E., Suite 300, Toronto, Ontario M5C 2P9, Canada, 416-363-3388
Oolichan Books, P.O. Box 10, Lantzville, B.C., V0R 2H0, Canada, 604-390-4839
OPEN ROAD, Box 6135, Station G, Vancouver, B.C. V6R 4G5, Canada
OUR GENERATION, 3981 St. Laurent Blvd., #444, Montreal, Quebec H2W 1Y5, Canada, 514-844-4076
PECKERWOOD, 1503-1465 Lawrence Avenue West, Toronto, Ont. M6L 1B2, Canada, 416-248-2675
Persona Publications, #1-3661 West 4th Avenue, Vancouver B.C., V6R 1P2, Canada, 604-731-9168
THE PIG PAPER, Pig Productions, 70 Cotton Drive, Mississauga, Ontario L5G 1Z9, Canada, (416) 278-6594
Plas Y Bryn Press, Box 97, West Hill, Ontario M1E 4R4, Canada, 416-282-1974
THE PLOWMAN, Box 414, Whitby, Ontario L1N 5S4, Canada, 416-668-7803
POETRY CANADA, PO Box 1061, Kingston, Ontario K7L 4Y5, Canada
The Poetry Group, Box 7074 North, Halifax, Nova Scotia B3K 4J5, Canada
POETRY HALIFAX DARTMOUTH, PO Box 7074 North, Halifax, Nova Scotia B3K 5J4, Canada
Porcepic Books, 4252 Commerce Circle, Victoria, B.C. V8Z 4M2, Canada, 604-727-6522
The Porcupine's Quill, Inc., 68 Main Street, Erin, Ontario N0B 1T0, Canada, 519-833-9158
POSTER-ZINE, 33, Prince Street #243, Montreal, Quebec H3C 2M7, Canada, 514-397-0342
THE POTTERSFIELD PORTFOLIO, PO Box 1135, Station A, Fredericton, New Brunswick E3B 5C2, Canada, 506-454-5127
Pottersfield Press, RR 2, Porters Lake, N.S. B0J 2S0, Canada
PRAIRIE FIRE, 423-100 Arthur Street, Winnipeg MB R3B 1H3, Canada, 204-943-9066
THE PRAIRIE JOURNAL OF CANADIAN LITERATURE, PO Box 997, Station G, Calgary, Alberta T3A 3G2, Canada
Prairie Journal Press, PO Box G 997, Station G, Calgary, Alberta T3A 3G2, Canada
Prairie Publishing Company, PO Box 2997, Winnipeg, MB R3C 4B5, Canada, 204-885-6496
Press Gang Publishers, 603 Powell Street, Vancouver, B.C. V6A 1H2, Canada, 604-253-2537
PRISM international, E455-1866 Main Mall, University of British Columbia, Vancouver BC V6T 1Z1, Canada, 604-822-2514
PROEM CANADA, 47 Gower Street, St. John, Afld., Canada, 705-749-5686
Proper Tales Press, PO Box 789, Station F, Toronto, Ontario M4Y 2N7, Canada
PROTOCULTURE ADDICTS, 33 Prince Street #243, Montreal, Quebec H3C 2M7, Canada, 514-397-0342
QUARRY MAGAZINE, Box 1061, Kingston, Ontario K7L 4Y5, Canada, 613-548-8429
Quarry Press, Box 1061, Kingston, Ontario K7L 4Y5, Canada

723

Quarterly Committee of Queen's University, Queen's University, Kingston, Ontario K7L 3N6, Canada
QUEEN'S QUARTERLY: A Canadian Review, Queen's University, Kingston, Ontario K7L 3N6, Canada, 613-545-2667
Ragweed Press, Inc., Box 2023, Charlottetown, Prince Edward Island C1A 7N7, Canada, 902-566-5750
RAMPIKE, 95 Rivercrest Road, Toronto, Ontario M6S 4H7, Canada, 416-767-6713
Les Recherches Daniel Say Cie., Box 65583, Vancouver 12, B.C. V5N 5K5, Canada
RESOURCE-MAG, FOR PUBLISHING PROFESSIONALS, 20 Tettenhall Road, Etobicoke, Ontario M9A 2C3, Canada, 416-231-7796
RESOURCES FOR FEMINIST RESEARCH/DOCUMENTATION SUR LA RECHERCHE FEMINISTE, 252 Bloor Street W., Toronto, Ontario M5S 1V6, Canada, 416-923-6641, ext. 2278
ROOM OF ONE'S OWN, PO Box 46160, Station G, Vancouver, British Columbia V6R 4G5, Canada, 604-327-1423
SACRED FIRE, PO Box 91980, West Vancouver, B.C. V7V 4S4, Canada, 604-922-8745
Salvo Books, Suite 465, 7305 Woodbine Avenue, Markham, Toronto, Ontario L3R 3V7, Canada, 416-493-9627
SAMIZDAT, 33, Prince Street #243, Montreal, Quebec H3C 2M7, Canada, 514-397-0342
Saskatchewan Writers Guild, Box 3986, Regina, Saskatchewan S4P 3R9, Canada, 306-757-6310
SCRIVENER, McGill University, 853 Sherbrooke Street W., Montreal, P.Q. H3A 2T6, Canada, 514-398-6588
Simon & Pierre Publishing Co. Ltd., Box 280, Adelaide St. P.O., Toronto, Ontario M5C2J4, Canada, 416-363-6767
Small Press International, PO Box 61, Lumby, B.C. V0E 2G0, Canada, (604) 547-6621
Sober Minute Press, PO Box 3576, Cambridge, Ont. N3H 5C6, Canada, 519-740-8166
Sororal Publishing, Box 2041, Winnipeg, MB, R3C 3R3, Canada, 204-774-9966
STUDIO NORTH, 78 Fox Run, Barrie, Ontario L4N 5A8, Canada, 705-734-0682
SUB-TERRAIN, PO Box 1575, Station A, Vancouver, B.C. V6C 2P7, Canada, 604-876-8710
Summerthought Ltd., PO Box 1420, Banff, Alberta T0L0C0, Canada, 762-3919; fax 403-762-4126
Sun Books, Box 28, Lennoxville, Quebec J1M 1Z3, Canada
Talon Books Ltd, 201/1019 East Cordova Street, Vancouver, BC, Canada, 604-253-5261
THE TEACHING LIBRARIAN, 100 Richmond Street, E, Suite 300, Toronto, Ontario M5C 2P9, Canada, 416-363-3388
THALIA: Studies in Literary Humor, Dept of English, Univ of Ottawa, Ottawa K1N 6N5, Canada, 613-230-9505
Theytus Books Ltd., PO Box 218, Penticton, B.C. V2A 6K3, Canada, 604-493-7181
THIS MAGAZINE, 16 Skey Lane, Toronto, Ontario M6J 3S4, Canada, 416-588-6580
Thistledown Press Ltd., 668 East Place, Saskatoon, Saskatchewan S7J 2Z5, Canada, 306-244-1722
Thunder Creek Publishing Co-operative, 401-2206 Dewdney Avenue, Regina, Sask. S4R 1H3, Canada, 306-777-0170
TIDEPOOL, 4 East 23rd Street, Hamilton, Ontario L8V 2W6, Canada, 416-383-2857
TIGER LILY MAGAZINE: The Magazine by Women of Colour, PO Box 756, Stratford, Ontario, Canada, 519-271-7045
TOWER, Dundas Public Library, 18 Ogilvie Street, Dundas, Ontario, L9H 2S2, Canada
Tower Press, Dundas Public Library, 18 Ogilvie Street, Dundas, Ontario, L9H 2S2, Canada
THE TOWNSHIPS SUN, Box 28, Lennoxville, Quebec J1M 1Z3, Canada
Trabarni Productions, 1531-550 Cottonwood Avenue, Coquitlam, BC V3J 2S1, Canada, 604-939-7910
Turnstone Press, 607-100 Arthur Street, Winnipeg R3B 1H3, Canada, 204-947-1555
TYRO MAGAZINE, 194 Carlbert Street, Sault St. Marie, Ontario P6A 5E1, Canada, 705-253-6402
Tyro Publishing, 194 Carlbert Street, Sault St. Marie, Ontario P6A 5E1, Canada, 707-253-6402
UNDERPASS, #574-21, 10405 Jasper Avenue, Edmonton, Alberta T5J 3S2, Canada
Underwhich Editions, PO Box 262, Adelaide Street Station, Toronto, Ontario M5C 2J4, Canada, 536-9316
UNION SHOP BLUFF, 205A Liverpool Street, Guelph, Ontario N1H 2L6, Canada, 519-767-1998
University of Calgary Press, 2500 University Drive NW, Calgary, Alberta T2N 1N4, Canada, 403-220-7578
UNIVERSITY OF WINDSOR REVIEW, c/o University of Windsor, Windsor, Ontario N9B3P4, Canada
Vehicule Press, PO Box 125, Place du Parc Station, Montreal, Quebec H2W 2M9, Canada, 514-844-6073
Vesta Publications Limited, PO Box 1641, Cornwall, Ont. K6H 5V6, Canada, 613-932-2135
Village Books, 195 Markville Road, Unionville, Ont. L3R4V8, Canada
WASCANA REVIEW, Department of English, University of Regina, Regina, Sask S4S 0A2, Canada, 584-4316
WEST COAST LINE: A Journal of Contemporary Writing and its Modernist Sources, c/o English Department, Simon Fraser University, Burnaby, B.C. V5A 1S6, Canada
Wild East Publishing Co-operative Limited, PO Box 1135, Station A, Fredericton, NB E3B 5C2, Canada, 506-454-5127
Williams-Wallace Publishers, Inc., PO Box 756, Stratford, Ontario N5A 3E8, Canada, 519-271-7045
THE WINDHORSE REVIEW, Samurai Press, Yarmouth, N.S., Canada
WINDSCRIPT, 2049 Lorne Street, Regina, Saskatchewan S4P 2M4, Canada, 306-757-6310
Winslow Publishing, Box 413, Station Z, Toronto, Ontario M5N 2Z5, Canada, 416-789-4733
Wolsak & Wynn Publishers Ltd., Box 316, Don Mills Post Office, Don Mills, Ontario M3C 2S7, Canada, 416-222-4690
WOMEN AND ENVIRONMENTS, c/o Center for Urban and Community Studies, 736 Bathurst Street, Toronto, Ontario M5S 2R4, Canada, 416-516-2379
Women's Press, 517 College Street, Ste. 233, Toronto, Ontario M6G 4A2, Canada
Wordwrights Canada, PO Box 456, Station O, Toronto, Ontario M4A 2P1, Canada
WRIT, Two Sussex Avenue, Toronto M5S 1J5, Canada, 416-978-4871
WRITER'S LIFELINE, PO Box 1641, Cornwall, Ont. K6H 5V6, Canada
WRITING, PO Box 69609, Station K, Vancouver, B.C. V5K 4W7, Canada, 604-688-6001

COLOMBIA

HORTICULTURA MODERNA, Apartado 20236, Cali, Valle, Colombia, 93-396206

ENGLAND

A, Flat 1, 41 Mapesbury Road, London NW2 4HJ, England
THE AFRICAN BOOK PUBLISHING RECORD, PO Box 56, Oxford 0X13EL, England, 0865-511428
AGENDA, 5 Cranbourne Court, Albert Bridge Road, London, England SW11 4PE, England, 071-228-0700
Agenda Editions, 5 Cranbourne Court, Albert Bridge Rd, London, England SW114PE, England, 01-228-0700
Allardyce, Barnett (Agneau 2), 14 Mount Street, Lewes, East Sussex, BN7 1HL, England, 0273 479393
Alphabox Press, Flat 1, 41 Mapesbury Road, London NW2 4HJ, England
AMBIT, 17 Priory Gardens, London, N6 5QY, England, 01-340-3566
AND, 89A Petherton Road, London N5 2QT, England, 01-226-2657
ANIMAL LIFE, RSPCA, Causeway, Horsham, West Sussex RH12 1HG, England, 0403-64181
ANIMAL WORLD, RSPCA, Causeway, Horsham, West Sussex RH12 1HG, England, 0403-64181

724

ANTI-APARTHEID NEWS, 13 Mandela Street, London NW1 0DW, England, 071 387 7966
Anvil Press Poetry, 69 King George St., London SE10 8PX, England, 01-858-2946
Applied Probability Trust, Department of Probability and Statistics, The University, Sheffield S3 7RH, England, England
AQUARIUS, Flat 10, Room A, 116 Sutherland Avenue, London W9, England
THE AUTHOR, 84 Drayton Gardens, London, England SW10 9SB, England
BALDER, c/o 60 Elmhurst Road, Reading, Berkshire RG1 5HY, England, 0734-323105 incl. Fax/answerphone
BB Books, 1 Spring Bank, Longsight Road, Copster Green, Blackburn, Lancs BB1 9EU, England, 0254 249128
BEAT SCENE, 27 Court Leet, Binley Woods, Coventry, Warwickshire CV3 2JO, England, 0203-543604
Beat Scene Press, 27 Court Leet, Binley Woods, Coventry, Warwickshire CV3 2JO, England, 0203-543604
THE BOUND SPIRAL, 72 First Avenue, Bush Hill Park, Enfield, Middlesex, EN1 1BW, England
BOUNDARY, 23 Kingsley Road, Runcorn, Cheshire, WA7 5PL, England, Runcorn 63624
THE BRADFORD POETRY QUARTERLY, 9, Woodvale Way, Bradford, West Yorkshire BD7 2SJ, England
BRITISH BOOK NEWS, 65 Davies Street, London W1Y 2AA, England, 01-930-8466
BULLETIN OF ANARCHIST RESEARCH, PO Box 556, London SE5 0RL, England
BULLETIN OF HISPANIC STUDIES, Dept. Of Hispanic Studies, The University, PO Box 147, Liverpool L69 3BX, England, 051 794 2774/5
Campaign For Press & Broadcasting Freedom, 9 Poland Street, London W1V 3DG, England, 01 437 0189; 01 437 2795
CANDELABRUM POETRY MAGAZINE, 9 Milner Road, Wisbech PE13 2LR, England, tel: 0945 581067
CERTAIN GESTURES, 55 Perowne Street, Aldershot, Hants. GU11 3JR, England, 316170
CHRISTIAN FAMILY, 37 Elm Road, New Malden, Surrey KT3 3HB, England, 01-942-9761
CLARITY, 26 Valleyside, Hemel Hempstead, Herts. HP1 2LN, England
COMMUNITY DEVELOPMENT JOURNAL, Foldyard House, Pinkhill House, Southfield Road, Naburn, York YO1 4RU, England, 0632-367142
THE COUNTRYMAN, Sheep Street, Burford, Oxford OX8 4LH, England, Burford 2258
Coxland Press, 60 Elmhurst Road, Reading, Berkshire RG1 5HY, England
The Curlew Press, Hare Cottage, Kettlesing, Harrogate, Yorkshire, England, Tel: Harrogate 770686
CURTAINS, 4 Bower Street, Maidstone, Kent ME16 8SD, England, 0622-63681
DESIGN AND TECHNOLOGY TEACHING, Unit 13/14, Trent Trading Pack, Botteslow St., Hanley, Stoke-on-Trent, Staffordshire ST1 3LY, England, 0203-523848
DOUBLE HARNESS, 74 Huntington Road, York, Y03 7RN, England
THE DURHAM UNIVERSITY JOURNAL, School of English/University of Durham, Elvet Riverside, New Elvet, Durham, DH1 3JT, England, 091-374 2000 Ext. 2744
Eight Miles High Home Entertainment, 44 Spa Croft Road, Teall Street, Ossett, W. Yorks WF5 0HE, England
Elm House Christian Communications Ltd, 37 Elm Road, New Malden, Surrey KT3 3HB, England, 01-942-9761
The Elvendon Press, 33 Elvendon Road, Goring-on-Thames, Reading, Berkshire RG8 0DP, England, (0491) 873227
Enitharmon Press, 22 Huntingdon Rd, East Finchley, London N2 9DU, England, 01 883 8764
Eon Publications, 2 Tewkesbury Drive, Grimsby, South Humberside DN34 4TL, England
EQUOFINALITY, 147 Selly Oak Road, Birmingham B30 1HN, England
ESCAPE, Escape Publishing, 156 Munster Road, London SW6 5RA, England, 01-731 1372
EUROPEAN JUDAISM, Kent House,, Rutland Gardens,, London SW7 1BX, England, 071-584-2754
EXETER STUDIES IN AMERICAN & COMMONWEALTH ARTS, Queens Bldg., Univ. of Exeter, Exeter EX4 4QH, England
FILM, 21 Stephen Street, London W1P 1PL, England, 01-255 1444
FIVE LEAVES LEFT, 12 Colne Road, Cowling, Keighley, West Yorkshire, BD22 0BZ, England
FOOLSCAP, 78 Friars Road, East Ham, London E6 1LL, England
FORESIGHT MAGAZINE, 44 Brockhurst Road, Hodge Hill, Birmingham B36 8JB, England, 021-783-0587
FOURTH WORLD REVIEW, 24 Abercorn Place, London, N.W.8, England
FREE LIFE, 1 Russell Chambers, The Piazza, Covent Garden, London WC2E 8AA, England, 01-836-6913
FREE PRESS, 9 Poland Street, London W1V 3DG, England, 01-437-2795; 01-437-0189
FREEDOM FORTNIGHTLY, In Angel Alley, 84B Whitechapel High St, London E1 7QX, England, 071 247 9249
Freedom Press, In Angel Alley, 84B Whitechapel High Street, London E1 7QX, England, 01-247-9249
FREELANCE MARKET NEWS, Cumberland House, Lissadell Street, Salford, Manchester M6 6GG, England
Freelance Press Services, Cumberland House, Lissadell Street, Salford, Manchester M6 6GG, England, 061 832-5079
Galloping Dog Press, 45 Salisbury Gardens, Newcastle upon Tyne, London, NE2 1HP, England
Gild of Saint George, Rose Cottage, 17 Hadassah Grove, Lark Lane, Liverpool L17 8XH, England, 051-728-9176
GLOBAL TAPESTRY JOURNAL, 1 Spring Bank, Salesbury, Blackburn, Lancs BB1 9EU, England, 0254 249128
GRANTA, 2-3 Hanover Yard, Noel Rd, London N1 88E, England, 071 704 9776, FAX: 071 704 0474
Granta Publications Ltd, 2-3 Hanover Yard, Noel Rd, London N1 8BE, England, (071) 704 9776
THE GROVE, Naturist Headquarters, Sheepcote, Orpington, BR5 4ET, England, 0689-871200
Guildford Poets Press, 9 White Rose Lane, Woking, Surrey, GU22 7JA, England
Hans Zell Publishers, PO Box 56, Oxford OX1 3EL, England, 0865-511428
HEART BREAK HOTELVIS, c/o 16 Powis Road, Brighton, Sussex BN7 3HJ, England
Hippopotamus Press, S22, Whitewell Road, Frome, Somerset BA11 4EL, England, 0373-66653
I WANT TO EAT YOUR STOMACH, 81 Castlerigg Drive, Burnley, Lancashire BB12 8AT, England, U.K. 0282 74321
ILLUMINATIONS, Ryde School, Queens Road, Ryde, Isle of Wight, PO33 3BE, England
Indelible Inc., BCM 1698, London WC1N 3XX, England, 0924-892-661
INDEX ON CENSORSHIP, 39c Highbury Place, London N5 1QP, England, 071-359-0161
THE INQUIRER, 1-6 Essex Street, London WC2R 3HY, England
Interim Press, 3 Thornton Close, Budleigh Salterton, Devon EX9 6PJ, England, 5231
IRON, 5 Marden Terrace, Cullercoats, North Shields, Tyne & Wear NE30 4PD, England, 091-2531901
Iron Press, 5 Marden Terrace, Cullercoats, North Shields, Tyne & Near NE30 4PD, England
ISSUE ONE, 2 Tewkesbury Drive, Grimsby, South Humberside DN34 4TL, England
Jackson's Arm, c/o Sunk Island Publishing, PO Box 74, Lincoln LN1 1QG, England
JAMES JOYCE BROADSHEET, School of English, University of Leeds, West Yorkshire LS2 9JT, England, 0532-459898
joe soap's canoe, 30 Quilter Road, Felixstowe, Suffolk IP11 7JJ, England, 0394 275569
JOE SOAP'S CANOE, 30 Quilter Road, Felixstowe, Suffolk IP11 7JJ, England, 0394 275569
THE JOURNAL OF COMMONWEALTH LITERATURE, PO Box 56, Oxford OX1 3EL, England, 0865-511428
Kawabata Press, Knill Cross House, Higher Anderton Road, Millbrook, Nr Torpoint, Cornwall, England

THE KEROUAC CONNECTION, 19 Worthing Road, Patchway, Bristol BS12 5HY, England
KRAX, 63 Dixon Lane, Leeds, Yorkshire LS12 4RR, England
KROKLOK, 89A Petherton Road, London N5 2QT, England, 01-226-2657
LABEL, 57 Effingham Road, Lee Green, London SE128NT, England, 01-690-9368
LANGUAGE INTERNATIONAL: THE MAGAZINE FOR THE LANGUAGE PROFESSIONS, Praetorius Limited, 5 East Circus Street, Nottingham NG1 5AH, England, 0602-411087
LEAGUE SENTINAL, 54 Hindes Road, Harrow, Middlesex HA1 1SL, England
LIBERAL DEMOCRAT NEWS, 4 Cowley Street, London SW1P3NB, England, 071222 7999; fax 071222 7904
Libertarian Books and the Libertarian Alliance, 1 Russell Chambers, The Piazza, Covent Garden, London WC2E 8AA, England, 01-836-6913
LINKS, 232 Cowley Road, Oxford OX4 1UH, England
LIVERPOOL NEWSLETTER, Rose Cottage, 17 Hadassah Grove, Lark Lane, Liverpool L17 8XH, England, 051-728-9176
Liverpool University Press, Dept. of Hispanic Studies, The University, PO Box 147, Liverpool L69 3BX, England, 051 794 . 2774/5
A LOAD OF BULL, Box 277, 52 Call Lane, Leeds, W. Yorkshire LS1 6DT, England
LONDON REVIEW OF BOOKS, Tavistock House South, Tavistock Square, London WC1H 9JZ, England, 01-388-6751
LORE AND LANGUAGE, The Centre for English Cultural Tradition and Language, The University, Sheffield S10 2TN, England, Sheffield 768555 ext 6296
The Mandeville Press, 2 Taylor's Hill, Hitchin, Hertfordshire SG4 9AD, England
Peter Marcan Publications, 31 Rowliff Road, High Wycombe, Bucks, HP12 3LD, England
MASSACRE, BCM 1698, London WC1N 3XX, England, 0924-892-661
MATHEMATICAL SPECTRUM, Dept of Probability and Statistics, The University, Sheffield S3 7RH, England
MEDICAL HISTORY, 183 Euston Road, London NW1 2BN, England
Melrose, 14 Clinton Rise, Beer, E. Devon EX12 3DZ, England, 0297-20619
The Menard Press, 8 The Oaks, Woodside Avenue, London N12 8AR, England
MINORITY RIGHTS GROUP REPORTS, 379 Brixton Road, London SW9 7DE, England, 071-9789498
MULTICULTURAL TEACHING FOR PRACTITIONERS IN SCHOOLS AND COMMUNITY, Unit 13/14, Trent Trading Pack, Botteslow St., Hanley, Stoke-on-Trent, Staffordshire ST1 3LY, England, 0782-274227
MUSIC AND LETTERS, Journals Subscription Department, Pinkhill House, Southfield Road, Eynsham, Oxford OX8 1JJ, England
MUSICAL OPINION, 2 Princes Road, St. Leonards-on-Sea, East Sussex TN37 6EL, England, 0424-715167; fax 0424-730052
National Poetry Foundation, 27 Mill Road, Fareham, Hampshire PO 16 OTH, England, 0329-822218
Naturist Foundation, Naturist Headquarters, Sheepcote, Orpington, BR5 4ET, England
N-B-T-V, Narrow Bandwidth Television Association, 1 Burnwood Dr., Wollaton, Nottingham, Notts NG8 2DJ, England, 0602-282896
New Broom Private Press, 78 Cambridge Street, Leicester, England
NEW DEPARTURES, Piedmont, Bisley, Stroud, Glos., England
NEW SPOKES, The Orchard House, 45 Clophill Road, Upper Gravenhurst, Bedfordshire MK45 4JH, England, 0462-711195
Northern House, 19 Haldane Terrace, Newcastle upon Tyne NE2 3AN, England, (0)91)2812614
NOTES & QUERIES, Journals Subscription Department, Pinkhill House, Southfield Road, Eynsham, Oxford OX8 1JJ, England
NOTTINGHAM MEDIEVAL STUDIES, Dept. of History, The University, Nottingham NG7 2RD, England
Oneworld Publications Ltd., 1C, Standbrook House, Old Bond Street, London, W1X 3TD, England, (0747) 51339
ORBIS, 199 The Long Shoot, Nuneaton, Warwickshire CV11 6JQ, England, 0203-327440
Panopticum Press London, 44, Howard Road, Upminster, England, (04022) 22100
PANURGE, PO Box 1QR, Newcastle-Upon-Tyne NE99 1QR, England, 091-232-7669
PAUSE, 27 Mill Road, Fareham, Hampshire PO 16 OTH, England, 0329-822218
PEACE NEWS "For Nonviolent Revolution", 55 Dawes Street, London SE17 1EL, England, 071-703 7189
Peace News Ltd, 55 Dawes Street, London SE17 1EL, England, 071-703 7189
PENNINE PLATFORM, Ingmanthorpe Hall Farm Cottage, Wetherby, West Yorks LS22 5EQ, England, 0937-584674
PEN:UMBRA, 1 Beeches Close, Saffron Walden Essex CB11 4BU, England
PHOENIX BROADSHEETS, 78 Cambridge Street, Leicester LE3 0JP, England, 547419
Plantagenet Productions, Westridge (Open Centre), Highclere, Nr. Newbury, Berkshire RG159PJ, England
PLANTAGENET PRODUCTIONS, Libraries of Spoken Word Recordings and of Stagescripts, Westridge (Open Centre), Highclere, Nr. Newbury, Royal Berkshire RG15 9PJ, England
POETIC LICENCE, 18 Stokesley Cres., Billingham, Cleveland, England
POETRY AND AUDIENCE, School of English, Cavendish Road, University of Leeds, Leeds Yorkshire, LS2 9JT, England
POETRY DURHAM, Dept. of English, Univ. of Durham, Elvet Riverside, New Elvet, Durham DH1 3JT, England, (091) 374-2730
POETRY NOTTINGHAM: The International Magazine of Today's Poetry, Summer Cottage, West Street, Shelford, Notts, NG12 1EJ, England, 0602 334540
Poetry Nottingham Society Publications, Summer Cottage, West Street, Shelford, Notts. NG12 1EJ, England
POETRY QUARTERLY, Hare Cottage, Kettlesing, Harrogate, Yorkshire, England, Tel: Harrogate 770686
POETRY REVIEW, 21 Earls Court Square, London SW5 9DE, England, 071-373-7861; fax 071-244-7388
Pressed Curtains, 4 Bower Street, Maidstone, Kent ME16 8SD, England, 0622-63681
PROMOTION, 8 Beaconview House, Charlemont Farm, W. Bromwich, West Midlands, B71 3PL, England
Protean Publications, 34 Summerfield Crescent, Flat 4, Edgbaston, Birmingham B16 OER, England
Purple Heather Publications, 12 Granby Terrace, Headingley, Leeds, West Yorkshire, LS6 3BB, England
PURPLE PATCH, 8 Beaconview House, Charlemont Farm, West Bromwich, West Midlands, England
QED, 1 Straylands Grove, York Y03 0EB, England, 904-424-381
RAVEN ANARCHIST QUARTERLY, In Angel Alley, 84B Whitechapel High Street, London E1 7QX, England
Red Candle Press, 9 Milner Road, Wisbech, PE13 2LR, England, tel: 0945 581067
THE RIALTO, 32 Grosvenor Road, Norwich, Norfolk, NR2 2PZ, England
Rivelin Grapheme Press, The Annex Kennet House, 19 High Street, Hungerford, Berkshire RG17 0NL, England, 0488-83480
Saqi Books Publisher, 26 Westbourne Grove, London W2 5RH, England, 071-221-9347; FAX 071-229-7692

726

SCILLONIAN MAGAZINE, c/o T. Mumford, St. Mary's, Isles of Scilly, Cornwall, England
SELF AND SOCIETY, 62 Southward Bridge Road, London, England
SEPIA, Knill Cross House, Higher Anderton Road, Millbrook, Nr Torpoint, Cornwall, England
SERIE D'ECRITURE, 83(b) London Road, Peterborough, Cambs. PE2 9BS, England
SMALL PRESS MONTHLY, Small Press Group of Britain, BM Bozo, London WC1N 3XX, England, 0234-211606
SMOKE, 40 Canning Street, Liverpool L8 7NP, England
SPARE RIB, 27 Clerkenwell Close, London EC1 0AT, England
Spectacular Diseases, 83(b) London Road, Peterborough, Cambs, England
SPECTACULAR DISEASES, 83(b) London Road, Peterborough, Cambs, England
Spredden Press, 55 Noel Road, London, England N1 8HE, England, 071-226-9098
SPUR, 25, Beehive Place, Brixton, London SW9 7QR, England
STAND MAGAZINE, 179 Wingrove Road, Newcastle-on-Tyne NE49DA, England, 091-273-3280
Stride Publications, 37 Portland Street, Newtown, Exeter, Devon EX1 2EG, England
Tharpa Publications Limited, 15 Bendemeer Road, London SWI5 1JX, England, 081-788-7792
THEATRE NOTEBOOK, Shakespeare Institute, University of Birmingham, Birmingham, London B15 2RX, England
THE THIRD HALF, "Amikeco", 16, Fane Close, Stamford, Lincs., PE9 1HG, England
THIRD WAY, 2 Chester House, Pages Lane, Muswell Hill, London NIO 1PR, England, 081-883-0372
Third Way Ltd., 2 Chester House, Pages Lane, Muswell Hill, London NIO 1PR, England, 081-883-0372
Third World First, 232 Cowley Road, Oxford OX4 1UH, England
TODAY, 37 Elm Road, New Malden, Surrey KT3 3HB, England, 01-942-9761
THE TOLL GATE JOURNAL, 12 Colne Road, Cowling, Keighley, West Yorkshire, BD22 OBZ, England
Trentham Books, Unit 13/14, Trent Trading Pack, Botteslow St., Hanley, Stoke-on-Trent, Staffordshire ST1 3LY, England, 0782 274227; fax 0782 281755
Trigon Press, 117 Kent House Road, Beckenham, Kent BR3 1JJ, England, 01-778-0534
TROUBLE & STRIFE, c/o Norwich Womens Centre, PO Box 8, Diss. Norfolk 1P22 3XG, England
21ST CENTURY CHRISTIAN MAGAZINE, 37 Elm Road, New Malden, Surrey KT3 3HB, England, 01-942-9761
'2D' (DRAMA AND DANCE), Knighton Fields Drama Centre, Herrick Road, Leicester LE2 6DJ, England, 0533-700850-701525
2D Publications, Knighton Fields Drama Centre, Herrick Road, Leicester LE2 6DJ, England, 0533-700850-701525
Venture Press, 54 Hindes Road, Harrow, Middlesex HA1 1SL, England, 06284-74994
Wellcome Institute for the History of Medicine, 183 Euston Road, London NW1 2BN, England
WESTWORDS, 15 Trelawney Road, Peverell, Plymouth, Devonshire PL3 4JS, England, 262877
WEYFARERS, 9 White Rose Lane, Woking, Surrey GU22 7JA, England
Working Press, 85 St. Agnes Place, Kennington, London SE11 4BB, England, 01 582 0023
Writers & Scholars International Ltd., 39c Highbury Place, London N5 1QP, England, 071-359-0161
Writers Forum, 89A Petherton Road, London N5 2QT, England, 071-226-2657
WRITERS' OWN MAGAZINE, 121 Highbury Grove, Clapham, Bedford, Beds MK41 6DU, England, (0234)365982
Writers' Own Publications, 121 Highbury Grove, Clapham, Bedford, Beds MK41 6DU, England
Zed Books Ltd., 57 Caledonian Road, London N1 9BU, England, 071-837-4014
ZENOS, 59 B Ilkeston Road, Nottingham NG7 3GR, England
ZERO ONE, 39 Minford Gardens, West Kensington, London W14 0AP, England

FINLAND

GOKOOMA, PO Box 63, 83501 Outokumpu, Finland
MY LIFE DEPENDS ON YOU, Kiilinpellont. 2, Rusko 21290, Finland
My Mother's House - Aitini Talo, Villa Remedia, Uusikyla, SF-16100, Finland, 358-18-631 136

FRANCE

'THE CASSETTE GAZETTE', An Audio Magazine, Atelier A2, 83 rue de la Tombe-Issoire, Paris 75014, France, 4327-1767
ELAN POETIQUE LITTERAIRE ET PACIFISTE, 31 Rue Foch, Linselles 59126, France, 20.03.48.59
FRANK: AN INTERNATIONAL JOURNAL OF CONTEMPORARY WRITING AND ART, BP 29, 94301 Vincennes Cedex, France, (1) 43-65-64-05
Handshake Editions, Atelier A2, 83 rue de la Tombe-Issoire, Paris 75014, France, 4327-1767
J'ECRIS, 85, rue des Tennerolles, Saint-Cloud 92210, France, (1) 47-71-79-63
LOLA-FISH, 36, Residence Jean Mace, 28300 Mainvilliers, France
Model-Peltex Association, 3 Rue Des Couples, 67000 Strasbourg, France
PELTEX, 3 Rue Des Couples, 67000 Strasbourg, France
SPHINX—WOMEN'S INTERNATIONAL LITERARY/ART REVIEW (IN ENGLISH), 175 Avenue Ledru-Rollin, Paris 75011, France, 43.67.31.92

GERMANY

Edition Gemini, Juelichstrasse 7, Huerth-Efferen D-5030, Germany, 02233/63550
Expanded Media Editions, PO Box 190136, Prinz Albert Str. 65, 5300 Bonn 1, Germany, 0228/22 95 83
Holger Harfst, Publisher, Postfach 5741, D8700 Wurzburg, Germany, 01149 931 411575
Maro Verlag, Riedingerstr. 24/6f, Augsburg, Germany, 0821-41 60 33

GREAT BRITAIN

IOTA, 67 Hady Crescent, Chesterfield, Derbyshire S41 0EB, Great Britain, 0246-276532
NUTSHELL, 8 George Marston Road, Ernsford Grange, Coventry CV3 2HH, Great Britain
Oriel, The Friary, Cardiff, Wales CF1 4AA, Great Britain, 0222-395548
Second Aeon Publications, 19 Southminster Road, Roath, Cardiff, Wales CF2 5AT, Great Britain, 0222-493093
TRIVIUM, Dept. Of History, St. David's University College, Lampeter, Dyfed SA48 7ED, Great Britain, 0570-422351 ext 244

GUATEMALA

CENTRAL AMERICA REPORT, Inforpress Centroamericana, 9a. Calle "A" 3-56, Zona 1, Ciudad de Guatemala, Guatemala, 29432,81997

HOLLAND

AT-SOURCE-TA, PO Box 41, 6700 AA Wageningen, Holland, 08370-12217/25033
PHILATELIC LITERATURE NEWS INTERNATIONAL, Brandespad 14, NL-3067 EB Rotterdam, Holland

HONG KONG

AREOPAGUS, Tao Fong Shan Road, PO Box 33, Shatin, New Territories, Hong Kong, 06- 10 54
ENERGY ASIA, 146 Prince Edward Road, West, 6th Floor, Kowloon, Hong Kong, 3-805294, 3-803029, 3-805794
Hong Kong Publishing Co., Ltd., 1801 World Trade Centre, Causeway Bay, Hong Kong, 5-8903067
PETROLEUM NEWS: Asia's Energy Journal, 146 Prince Edward Road, West, 6th Floor, Kowloon, Hong Kong, 3-805294, 3-803029, 3-805794
Petroleum News Southeast Asia Ltd., 146 Prince Edward Road, West, 6th Floor, Kowloon, Hong Kong, 3-805294, 3-803029, 3-805794
RENDITIONS, Chinese University of Hong Kong, Shatin, NT, Hong Kong
Renditions Paperbacks, Research Centre for Translation, Chinese University of Hong Kong, Shatin, NT, Hong Kong, 852-6952297/2399

INDIA

ASIAN LITERARY MARKET REVIEW, Kunnuparambil Buildings, Kurichy, Kottayam 686549, India, 91-4826-470
THE INDIAN WRITER, C-23, Anna Nagar East, Madras-600 102, Tamil Nadu, India, 615370
Jaffe Publishing Management Service, Kunnuparambil Buildings, Kurichy, Kottayam 686549, India, 91-4826-470
MANUSHI - a journal about women & society, C-202 Lajpat Nagar - I, New Delhi, New Delhi 110024, India, 6833022 or 6839158
Peacock Books, College Square, Cuttack , Orissa 753003, India, 0671-22733
Prakalpana Literature, P-40 Nandana Park, Calcutta-700034, West Bengal, India, 9137-77-7327
PRAKALPANA SAHITYA/PRAKALPANA LITERATURE, P-40 Nandana Park, Calcutta-700034, West Bengal, India, 9137-77-7327

IRELAND

AN SEANRUD, c/o Sunburst Press, 25 Newtown Avenue, Blackrock, Co. Dublin 882575, Ireland
Attic Press, 44 East Essex Street, Dublin 2, Ireland
The Dedalus Press, 24 The Heath, Cypress Downs, Dublin 6, Ireland
PLANKTON, 68 Moungjoy Square, Dublin 1, Ireland, 740354
Poetry Ireland Press, 44 Upper Mount, St. Dublin 2, Ireland
POETRY IRELAND REVIEW, 44 Upper Mount Street, Dublin 2, Ireland
THE SALMON, Bridge Mills, Galway, Ireland, tel: 62587
Salmon Publishing, Auburn, Upper Fairhill, Galway, Ireland, 62587
Sparkling Diamond Paperbacks, 66 St. Joseph's Place, Off Blessington Street, Dublin 7, Ireland
Sunburst Press, 25 Newtown Avenue, Blackrock, Co. Dublin 882575, Ireland
TRACKS, 24 The Heath, Cypress Downs, Dublin 6, Ireland
Wolfhound Press, 68 Mountjoy Square, Dublin 1, Ireland, 740354

ISLE OF MANN

CARN (a link between the Celtic nations), J.B. Moffatt-General Secretary, Celtic League-24, St. Germain's Place, Peel, Isle of Mann, 0306 2484 3135
Celtic League, J.B. Moffatt-General Secretary, Celtic League-24, St. Germain's Place, Peel, Isle of Mann, Dublin 373957

ISRAEL

THE OTHER ISRAEL, PO Box 956, Tel Aviv 61008, Israel, 972-3-5565804 (also fax)
VIEWPOINT, PO Box 1777, Tel Aviv 61016, Israel, 03/26645-7
VOICES - ISRAEL, c/o Mark Levinson, PO Box 5780, Herzliya 46101, Israel, 052-552411

ITALY

COOP. ANTIGRUPPO SICILIANO, Villa Schammachanat, Via Argentaria Km 4, Trapani, Sicily, Italy, 0923-38681
Sicilian Antigruppo/Cross-Cultural Communications, Villa Schammachanat, via Argenteria Km 4, Trapani, Sicily, Italy, 0923-38681
TRAPANI NUOVA, TERZA PAGINA, Villa Schammachanat, Via Argentaria Km 4, Trapani, Sicily, Italy

JAPAN

THE ABIKO QUARTERLY RAG, 8-1-8 Namiki, Abiko-shi, Chiba-ken 270-11, Japan, 0471-84-7904
AIKI NEWS, Lions Mansion #204, Tamagawa Gakuen 5-11-25, Machida-shi, Tokyo-to 194, Japan, 81(427)24-9119
Aiki News, Lions Mansion #204, Tamagawa Gakuen 5-11-25, Machida-shi, Tokyo-to 194, Japan, 81(427)9119
LIZZENGREASY, Dai Ni Kuroda Kopo #203, Funabashi 5-30-6, Setagaya-ku, Tokyo-to 156, Japan
New Cicada, 40-11 KUBO, Hobara, Fukushima 960-06, Japan
NEW CICADA, 40-11 KUBO, Hobara, Fukushima 960-06, Japan, 0245-75-4226
THE PLOVER (Chidori), PO Box 122, Ginowan City, Okinawa 901-22, Japan, 1-011-81-098-897-5042
POETRY KANTO, Kanto Gakuin University, Kamariya, Kanazawa-Ku, Yokohama 236, Japan
POETRY NIPPON, 11-2, 5-chome, Nagaike-cho, Showa-ku, Nagoya 466, Japan
The Poetry Nippon Press, 11-2, 5-Chome, Nagaike-cho, Showa-ku, Nagoya 466, Japan, 052-833-5724
PRINTED MATTER (Japan), 3-31-14-207 Ikebukuro Honcho, Toshima-ku, Tokyo 170, Japan
TELS PRESS, c/o The Second Story, Nakijima Bldg, 2nd Floor, 1-26-7 Umegaoka, Setagaya-ku, Tokyo 154, Japan, 03-706-5055
TSUBUSHI, 3-4-3-204 Togoshi, Shinagawa-ku, Tokyo 142, Japan, 03-3786-9782

KENYA

East African Publishing House, PO Box 30571, Nairobi, Kenya, 557417, 557788

LUXEMBOURG

Euroeditor, PO Box 212, Luxemburg, Luxembourg
NEW EUROPE, PO Box 212, Luxemburg, Luxembourg

MALAYSIA

ASIA-PACIFIC ENVIRONMENT NEWSLETTER, 43 Salween Road, 10050 Penang, Malaysia, (04) 375705, 376930
ENVIRONMENTAL NEWS DIGEST, 43 Salween Road, 10050 Penang, Malaysia
Sahabat Alam Malaysia (Friends of the Earth Malayasia), 43 Salween Road, 10050 Penang, Malaysia
SUARA SAM, 43 Salween Road, 10050 Penang, Malaysia, 04-376930, 375705

NEW ZEALAND

Brick Row Publishing Co. Ltd., PO Box 100-057, Auckland 10, New Zealand, 410-6993
BROADSHEET, P.O. Box 56-147, Dominion Rd., Auckland, New Zealand, 09-608-535
Islands, 4 Sealy Road, Torbay, Auckland 10, New Zealand, 4039007
ISLANDS, A New Zealand Quarterly of Arts & Letters, 4 Sealy Road, Torbay, Auckland 10, New Zealand, 4039007
TAKAHE, PO Box 13-335, Christchurch 1, New Zealand, 03-517973

NORWAY

Futurum Forlag, Hjelmsgt. 3, 0355 Oslo 3, Norway, +47 2 69 12 84
GATEAVISA, Hjelmsgt 3, 0355 Oslo 3, Norway, +47 2 69 12 84
IASP NEWSLETTER, International Association of Scholarly Publishers, PO Box 2959 Toyen, Universitets forlaget, 0608 Oslo 6, Norway

PEOPLE'S REPUBLIC OF CHINA

CHINESE LITERATURE, 24 Baiwanzhuang Road, Beijing 100037, People's Republic of China, 892554
Chinese Literature Press, 24 Baiwanzhuang Road, Beijing 100037, People's Republic of China

REPUBLIC OF SOUTH AFRICA

AFRICAN STUDIES, WITS, 2050 Johannesburg, Republic of South Africa
The Carrefour Press, PO Box 2629, Cape Town, 8000, Republic of South Africa
ENGLISH STUDIES IN AFRICA-A Journal of the Humanities, Witwatersrand University Press, WITS, 2050 Johannesburg, Republic of South Africa, 011-716-2029
NEW CONTRAST, S.A. Literary Journal Ltd, PO Box 3841, Cape Town, 8000, Republic of South Africa, 021-477468
Witwatersrand University Press, WITS, 2050 Johannesburg, Republic of South Africa, 011-716-2029

ROMANIA

ROMANIAN REVIEW, Piata Presei Libere 1, Bucharest, Romania, 173836

SCOTLAND

THE BIBLIOTHECK, c/o L.H. Davies, Glasgow Univ. Library, Hillhead Street, Glasgow G12 8QE, Scotland, 041-667-1011 X6732
CHAPMAN, 4 Broughton Place, Edinburgh EH1 3RX, Scotland, 031-557-2207
EDINBURGH REVIEW, 22 George Square, Edinburgh EH8 9LF, Scotland, 0315581117/8
The Findhorn Press, The Park, Findhorn, Forres, Morayshire IV360TZ, Scotland, 0309-30582
The Gleniffer Press, 11 Low Road, Castlehead, Paisley PA2 6AQ, Scotland, 041-889-9579
JUDY, D.C. Thomson & Company Limited, Albert Square, Dundee, Tayside DD1 9QJ, Scotland, 0382 23131
MIDNIGHT IN HELL (The Weirdest Tales of Fandom), The Cottage, Smithy Brae, Kilmacolm, Renfrewshire PA134EN, Scotland
ONE EARTH, Findhorn Foundation, The Park, Forres, Morayshire 1V36 0TZ, Scotland, 0309-30010
THE ORCADIAN, The Orcadian Limited, PO Box 18, Kirkwall, Orkney, Scotland

SRI LANKA

Karunaratne & Sons Ltd., 647, Kularatne Mawatha, Colombo 10, Sri Lanka, 941-692295
Path Press, Wye Estate, Ambegoda, Bandarawela, Sri Lanka, 057-2480

SWEDEN

INITIATIV, Tumstocksvagen 19, Taby S-18304, Sweden, 08-7567445
THE LUNDIAN, PO Box 722, 220 07 Lund, Sweden, fax: 046-138221
Modern Media, PO Box 722, 220 07 Lund, Sweden, fax: 046-138221
Tryckeriforlaget, Tumstocksvagen 19, Taby S-18304, Sweden, 08-7567445
Vanitas Press, Platslagarevagen 4E1, 22230 Lund, Sweden

SWITZERLAND

BIBLIOTHEQUE D'HUMANISME ET RENAISSANCE, Librairie Droz S.A., 11r.Massot, 1211 Geneve 12, Switzerland
Librairie Droz S.A., 11r.Massot, 1211 Geneve 12, Switzerland
TRANSNATIONAL PERSPECTIVES, CP 161, CH-1211 Geneva 16, Switzerland

THE NETHERLANDS

Cypres Publishing House, Heemraadschapslaan 33, Amstelveen, Holland 1181 T2, The Netherlands, 31-20-6410388
Kontexts Publications, Overtoom 444, 1054 JW Amsterdam, The Netherlands, 020-836665

UNITED KINGDOM

BRITISH JOURNAL OF AESTHETICS, Journal Subscription Department, Pinkhill House, Southfield Road, Eynsham, Oxford, OX8 1JJ, United Kingdom
British Society For Social Responsibility In Science, 25 Horsell Road, London N5 1XL, United Kingdom, 01-607-9615
CAMBRENSIS: THE SHORT STORY QUARTERLY MAGAZINE OF WALES, 41 Heol Fach, Cornelly, Bridgend, Mid-Glamorgan, CF334LN South Wales, United Kingdom, 0656-741-994

Deborah Charles Publications, 173 Mather Avenue, Liverpool L18 6JZ, United Kingdom, 051-724 2500
City Publications Ltd., 15 Mantilla Road, London SW17 8DY, United Kingdom, 01-767-1005
Claridge Press, 6 Linden Gardens, London W2 4ES, United Kingdom
ECONOMIC AFFAIRS, 2 Lord North Street, London SW1P 3LB, United Kingdom
FEMINIST REVIEW, 11 Carleton Gardens, Brecknock Road, London N19 5AQ, United Kingdom
Free Association Books (FAB), 26 Freegrove Road, London N7 9RQ, United Kingdom, 01-609-5646-0507
FREE ASSOCIATIONS: PSYCHOANALYSIS, GROUPS, POLITICS, CULTURE, 26 Freegrove Road, London N7 9RQ, United Kingdom, 01-609-5646
GREEN ANARCHIST, Box H, 34 Cowley Road, Oxford, Oxfordshire, United Kingdom, 0895-249406
Gwasg Gwalia, 14a Stryd Y Porth Mawr, Caernarfon, Gwynedd, Wales, United Kingdom, 0970 86 304
J.P.R. Instone Publications, 7 Winkley Street, London E2 6P4, United Kingdom
INTERNATIONAL JOURNAL FOR THE SEMIOTICS OF LAW, 173 Mather Avenue, Liverpool L18 6JZ, United Kingdom
JENNINGS MAGAZINE, 336 Westbourne Park Road, London W.11 1EQ, United Kingdom, 01-521-4349; 727-7810
Kozmik Press, 134 Elsenham Street, London SW18 5NP, United Kingdom, 874-8218
LAW AND CRITIQUE, 173 Mather Avenue, Liverpool L18 6JZ, United Kingdom
LIVERPOOL LAW REVIEW, 173 Mather Avenue, Liverpool L18 6JZ, United Kingdom
LOL, 14a Stryd Y Porth Mawr, Caernarfon, Gwynedd, Wales, United Kingdom, 0970 86 304
Lovely Publications, 81 Castlerigg Drive, Burnley, Lancashire BB12 8AT, United Kingdom
MEMES, c/o 38 Molesworth Road, Plympton Plymouth, Devonshire PL7 4NT, United Kingdom
Merlin Books Ltd., 40, East Street, Braunton, Devon EX33 2EA, United Kingdom
Mosquito Press, 27 A, Old Gloucester Street, London WC1N 3XX, United Kingdom
Nemeton Publishing, PO Box 780, Bristol, BS99 5BB, United Kingdom, +44-272-715144
New Hope International, 20 Werneth Avenue, Gee Cross, Hyde SK14 5NL, United Kingdom, 061-351 1878
NEW HOPE INTERNATIONAL REVIEW, 20 Werneth Avenue, Gee Cross, Hyde, Cheshire SK14 5NL, United Kingdom, 061-351 1878
NEW HOPE INTERNATIONAL ZINE, 20 Werneth Avenue, Gee Cross, Hyde, Cheshire SK14 5NL, United Kingdom, 061-351 1878
NNIDNID: SURREALITY, 3 Vale View, Ponsanooth, Truro, Cornwall, United Kingdom
NUMBERS, 6 Kingston Street, Cambridge, Cambs. CB1 2NU, United Kingdom, 0223 353425
Oasis Books, 12 Stevenage Road, London, SW6 6ES, United Kingdom
OTTER, Parford Cottage, Chagford, Newton Abbot TL13 8JR, United Kingdom
OUTPOSTS POETRY QUARTERLY, 22, Whitewell Road, Frome, Somerset BA11 4EL, United Kingdom
Oxford University Press, Journal Subscriptions Department, Pinkhill House, Southfield Road, Eynsham, Oxford OX8 1JJ, United Kingdom
The Phlebas Press, 2 The Stables, High Park, Oxenholme, Kendal, Cumbria LA9 7RE, United Kingdom
Pig Press, 7 Cross View Terrace, Durham DH1 4JY, United Kingdom, D. 3846914
Poetical Histories, 27 Sturton Street, Cambridge CB1 2QG, United Kingdom, 0223-327455
PSYCHOPOETICA, Department of Psychology, University of Hull, Hull HU6 7RX, United Kingdom
QUARTOS MAGAZINE, BCM Writer, 27 Old Gloucester Street, London WC1N 3XX, United Kingdom, 0559-371108
RADICAL SCIENCE SERIES, 26 Freegrove Road, London N7 9RQ, United Kingdom, 01-609-5646
Reality Studios, 4 Howard Court, Peckham Rye, London SE15 3PH, United Kingdom, 071-639-7297
SALISBURY REVIEW, 33 Canonbury Park South, London N1 2JW, United Kingdom
SCIENCE FOR PEOPLE, 25 Horsell Road, London N5 1XL, United Kingdom, 01-607-9615
Shearsman Books, c/o IPD (Independent Press Distribution), 12 Stevenage Road, London SW6 6ES, United Kingdom, 0752-779682
Slow Dancer, 58 Rutland Road, W. Bridgford, Nottingham NG2 5DG, United Kingdom, 0602-821518
Society Of Authors, 84, Drayton Gardens, London, England SW10 9SB, United Kingdom, 01-373-6642
STAPLE, Derbyshire College of HE, Mickleover, Derby, Derbyshire DE3 5GX, United Kingdom
THE T.E. LAWRENCE SOCIETY NEWSLETTER, 'Ambleside', 101 Hempstead Road, Kings Langley, Hertfordshire WD4 8BS, United Kingdom, 0923-263501
VIGIL, 12 Priory Mead, Bruton, Somerset BA10 0DZ, United Kingdom, Bruton 813349
X-CALIBRE, PO Box 780, Bristol, BS99 5BB, United Kingdom, +44-272-715144

WALES

BULLETIN OF THE BOARD OF CELTIC STUDIES, Univ. of Wales Press, 6 Gwennyth Street, Cathays, Cardiff CF2 4YD, Wales, 231919
CONTEMPORARY WALES, 6 Gwennyth Street, Cathays, Cardiff CF2 4YD, Wales, 231919
EFRYDIAU ATHRONYDDOL, 6 Gwennyth St., Cathays, Cardiff CF2 4YD, Wales, Cardiff 231919
IDO-VIVO, International Language (IDO) Society of GB, 10 Heol Salop, Penarth, De Morgannwg CF6 1HG, Wales, 0222-483545
International Language (IDO) Society of Great Britain, 10 Heol Salop, Penarth, De Morgonnwg CF6 1HG, Wales, 0222-497414
JOURNAL OF CELTIC LINGUISTICS, 6 Gwennyth Street, Cathays, Cardiff CF2 4YD, Wales, 231919
JOURNAL OF WELSH EDUCATION, 6 Gwennyth Street, Cathays, Cardiff CF2 4YD, Wales, 231919
LLEN CYMRU, 6 Gwennyth St., Cathays, Cardiff CF2 4YD, Wales, 0222-231919
MOMENTUM, Glan Llyn, Glyn Ceiriog, Liangollen, 31 Alexandra Road, Clwyd LL20 7AB, Wales, 069-172-320
POETRY WALES, Andmar House, Tondu Road, Bridgend, Mid Glamorgan CF31 4LJ, Wales
Poetry Wales Press, Ltd., Andmar House, Tondu Road, Bridgend, Mid Glamorgan CF31 4LJ, Wales
STUDIA CELTICA, University of Wales Press, 6 Gwennyth St., Cathays, Cardiff CF2 4YD, Wales, Cardiff 231919
University Of Wales Press, 6 Gwennyth St., Cathays, Cardiff CF2 4YD, Wales, 231919
WELSH HISTORY REVIEW, 6 Gwenuyth Street, Cathays, Cardiff CF2 4YD, Wales, Cardiff 231919
Y GWYDDONYDD, 6 Gwennyth St., Cathays, Cardiff CF2 4YD, Wales, Cardiff 231919

WEST INDIES

Sandberry Press, PO Box 507, Kingston 10, Jamaica, West Indies, 809-92-76423

Subject Index

Tombouctou Books
TOWARD FREEDOM
Unbridled Lust! Publishing
Unicorn Press
University of Calgary Press
VALLEY WOMEN'S VOICE
White Cliffs Media Company
Witwatersrand University Press
World Music Press
WORLD PERSPECTIVES
WORLD RAINFOREST REPORT
WRITER'S LIFELINE
Zed Books Ltd.

AGING

Barclay House
BELLES LETTRES
Bergin & Garvey Publishers
Blue Dolphin Press, Inc.
Borderland Sciences Research Foundation
COMPOST NEWSLETTER (CNL)
Crones' Own Press
Distinctive Publishing Corp.
FOREFRONT—HEALTH INVESTIGATIONS
Gateway Books
Harbinger House
Human Kinetics Pub. Inc.
Kitchen Table: Women of Color Press
Knowledge, Ideas & Trends, Inc. (KIT)
LuraMedia, Inc.
NiceTown
Papier-Mache Press
Parabola Books
PASSAGER: A Journal of Remembrance and Discovery
Potentials Development, Inc.
TAPROOT, a journal of elder writers
Tide Book Publishing Company
Unbridled Lust! Publishing
Williamson Publishing Company, Inc.
THE WRITE AGE (First Magazine of Writing Therapy)

AGRICULTURE

ACTINIDIA ENTHUSIASTS NEWSLETTER
AERO SUN-TIMES
AGRICULTURAL HISTORY
Alpine Press
ASSEMBLING
Assembling Press
AT-SOURCE-TA
THE AZOREAN EXPRESS
BLACK JACK & VALLEY GRAPEVINE
Cadmus Editions
Cheshire Books
The Chicot Press
CJE NEWSLETTER (Newsletter of the Coalition for Jobs
   & the Environment)
COMMUNITY DEVELOPMENT JOURNAL
Countryman Press
ENCYCLOPEDIA BANANICA
FARMER'S DIGEST
Farmer's Digest Publishing Co.
Fulcrum, Inc.
GRASS ROOTS
THE GROWING EDGE MAGAZINE
W.D. Hoard & Sons Company
HOARD'S DAIRYMAN
HORTICULTURA MODERNA
HORTIDEAS
JOURNAL FOR ANTHROPOSOPHY
Kumarian Press, Inc.
L.A.N.D.
Lahontan Images
LINKS
LIVING AMONG NATURE DARINGLY!
LOST GENERATION JOURNAL
MASSEY COLLECTORS NEWS—WILD HARVEST
Maupin House
Misty Hill Press

Name That Team!
THE NATIONAL FARM DIRECTORY
THE NEW RENAISSANCE, An International Magazine
   of Ideas & Opinions, Emphasizing Literature & The
   Arts
Night Owl Publishers
THE NORTHERN REVIEW
Oasis Books
OLD ABE'S NEWS
C. Olson & Company
Oregon Historical Society Press
Panorama West Publishing
PLAINSWOMAN
THE PRAIRIE GOLD RUSH
The Rateavers
RED POWER
THE REDNECK REVIEW OF LITERATURE
RFD
SINSEMILLA TIPS (Domestic Marijuana Journal)
TEXAS WINEMARKET NEWS
Third World First
Timber Press
THE TOWNSHIPS SUN
TRENDS & PREDICTIONS ANALYST
University of Calgary Press
Valkyrie Publishing House
Van Patten Publishing
WHEAT LIFE
Woodbridge Press
WORLD RAINFOREST REPORT
World Wildlife Fund & The Conservation Foundation
WORLD WILDLIFE FUND & THE CONSERVATION
   FOUNDATION LETTER
Worldwatch Institute
WTI Publishing Co.

AIDS

Barclay House
Bay Press
Star Books, Inc.

AIRPLANES

Aviation Book Company
R.J. Bender Publishing
Foundation Books
THE MILITARY ADVISOR

ALASKA

Alaska Native Language Center
ALASKA WOMEN
AMERICAN WRITING: A MAGAZINE
Ashley Books, Inc.
THE...CHRONICLE
Circumpolar Press
THE CLIMBING ART
" "...A DEAD BEAT POET PRODUCTION
The Denali Press
Epicenter Press Inc.
Fathom Publishing Co.
Fireweed Press
The FreeSolo Press
Glacier House Publications
Heyday Books
L.A.N.D.
Lone Star Press
MESSAGE POST
The Mountaineers Books
Naturegraph Publishers, Inc.
THE NORTHERN ENGINEER
Old Harbor Press
Pruett Publishing Company
Rainforest Publishing
Rocky Top Publications
Star Rover House
TechWest Publications
Windsong Press
Wizard Works

732

ALCOHOL, ALCOHOLISM

ADDICTION & RECOVERY
Bakhtin's Wife Publications
Challenger Press
CLUBHOUSE
Comprehensive Health Education Foundation (CHEF)
EAP DIGEST
Fell Publishers, Inc.
FELL SWOOP
Glen Abbey Books, Inc.
Gravity Publishing
Gurze Books
Haight-Ashbury Publications
THE HAPPY THRASHER
HEALING PATH
THE HUMAN ECOLOGY AND ENERGY BALANCING SCIENTIST
Human Ecology Balancing Sciences, Inc.
Johnson Institute
JOURNAL OF PSYCHOACTIVE DRUGS
Kent P. Larsen, Inc.
THE LETTER PARADE
THE N.A. WAY
New Idea Press, Inc.
NEWS FROM THE WHITE HOUSE
Omega Cottonwood Press
PARTING GIFTS
PEDESTRIAN RESEARCH
Professional Counselor Books
Publitec Editions
PUCK!
Quotidian Publishers
RedBrick Press
Rocky Top Publications
See Sharp Press
Seventh-Wing Publications
Skidmore-Roth Publishing
Star Books, Inc.
STREET VOICE
TEXAS WINEMARKET NEWS
Tyro Publishing

AMERICANA

ALWAYS JUKIN'
Always Jukin'
Americana & Collectibles Press
THE AUTOGRAPH COLLECTOR'S MAGAZINE
Avery Color Studios
Axelrod Publishing of Tampa Bay
Baker Street Publications
Beacon Press
BEAT SCENE
Blue Mouse Studio
The Borgo Press
Branden Publishing Company
BREAKTHROUGH!
CACANADADADA REVIEW
CAL NEWSLETTER
Cherokee Publishing Company
The Clyde Press
COMMON SENSE
Commonwealth Press Virginia
COMPOST NEWSLETTER (CNL)
Cottontail Publications
Cottonwood Press
Countryman Press
Crossroads Communications
Crossroads Publications, Inc.
DAYSPRING
Devil Mountain Books
Devin-Adair, Publishers, Inc.
Downey Place Publishing House, Inc.
Eagle's View Publishing
Escart Press
EUTHANASIA ROSES
Foundation Books
Fulcrum, Inc.

Gallery West Associates
Gallopade Publishing Group
Gaslight Publications
GAVEA-BROWN
GENERATIONS SANPETE: INDEX OF ORAL HISTORIES OF RURAL UTAH
GHOST TOWN QUARTERLY
Glenbridge Publishing Ltd.
The Globe Pequot Press
Heart of the Lakes Publishing
Heritage Books, Inc.
HORIZONS WEST
IMAGINATION MAGAZINE
THE IMMIGRANT
Independence Publishers Inc.
Indiana Publications, Inc.
International Publishers Co. Inc.
L.A.N.D.
THE LATEST NEWS
The Philip Lesly Company
THE LETTER PARADE
Lexikos
Little Bayou Press
Mayhaven Publishing
Media Publishing
Men & Women of Letters
Mendocino Book Partnership
Meyerbooks, Publisher
Middle Coast Publishing
Millers River Publishing Co.
Milner Press
Misty Hill Press
Mountain Press Publishing Co.
Museum of New Mexico Press
Mustang Publishing Co.
National Stereoscopic Association
The Neither/Nor Press
THE NEW AMERICAN
NOOSPAPERS
Nuventures Publishing
The Old Army Press
Omega Cottonwood Press
Oregon State University Press
EL PALACIO
THE PATRIOT
Peachtree Publishers, Ltd.
The Petrarch Press
Pioneer Books
The Place In The Woods
Pocahontas Press, Inc.
Pop Void Publications
The Preservation Press
THE PRESIDENTS' JOURNAL
The Quilt Digest Press
REAL PEOPLE
Redwood Press
Renaissance House Publishers (a division of Jende-Hagan, Inc.)
Runaway Publications
S & S Press
SCHMAGA
Seven Locks Press
Signal Books
Signature Books
Genny Smith Books
Southern Resources Unlimited
Star Rover House
Straight Arrow Publishing
Strawberry Hill Press
TATTOO ADVOCATE JOURNAL
Texas Monthly Press
Thirteen Colonies Press
Tioga Publishing Co.
TOWPATHS
TQS Publications (Tonatiuh - Quinto Sol International Inc.)
TRADITION
TUCUMCARI LITERARY REVIEW

THE UNDERGROUND FOREST - LA SELVA SUB-
TERRANEA
Vestal Press Ltd
WE MAGAZINE
We Press
Westburg Associates, Publishers
THE WESTMINSTER REVIEW
The Westphalia Press
White Mane Publishing Company, Inc.
Windmill Publishing Co.
Windsong Press
Woodbine House
Woodsong Graphics Inc.
Wright-Armstead Associates
Ye Galleon Press
ZOOMAR

THE AMERICAS

AKWEKON: A National Native American Literary &
Arts Journal
BELLES LETTRES
Between The Lines
In One Ear Press
Museum of New Mexico Press
The New Humanity Press
Signal Books
THIRD WORLD RESOURCES
Thirteen Colonies Press
TIERRA DEL FUEGO MAGAZINE
Tiptoe Literary Service
WORLD PERSPECTIVES
Zagier & Urruty Publicaciones

AMISH CULTURE

Author's Unlimited
" "...A DEAD BEAT POET PRODUCTION

ANARCHIST

ACTIVIST
Alchemy Books
ANARCHY: A JOURNAL OF DESIRE ARMED
ARTPAPER
ASSEMBLING
Assembling Press
THE AUTHOR
Autonomedia, Inc.
BAD NEWZ
Bakhtin's Wife Publications
BAKUNIN
BB Books
Black Rose Books Ltd.
Bomb Shelter Propaganda
BOTH SIDES NOW
BRICK
BULLETIN OF ANARCHIST RESEARCH
CHAKRA
Cheshire Books
City Lights Books
CLIPS FROM BEAR'S HOME MOVIES
COKEFISH
COMMON SENSE
Communitas Press
Cosmic Circus Productions
Michael E. Coughlin, Publisher
COYDOG REVIEW
CROOKED ROADS
Dancing Bear Productions
THE DANDELION
DE NAR
" "...A DEAD BEAT POET PRODUCTION
DHARMA COMBAT
DIAMOND HITCHHIKER COBWEBS
DIE FAT PIGGY DIE
Dumpster Press
DUMPSTER TIMES
EAR MAGAZINE
ECOSOCIALIST REVIEW
EXQUISITE CORPSE: A Monthly of Books and Ideas

FARCE, Raleigh's Review of Alternative Arts
FATHOMS BELOW
THE FICTION REVIEW
J. Flores Publications
FREEDOM FORTNIGHTLY
Freedom Press
FUSE MAGAZINE
The Future Press
Futurum Forlag
GATEAVISA
GET STUPID
GOING GAGA
GOKOOMA
GREEN ANARCHIST
GREEN MULTILOGUE
GREEN SYNTHESIS-A NEWSLETTER AND JOUR-
NAL FOR SOCIAL ECOLOGY, DEEP ECOLOGY,
BIOREGIONALISM, ECOFEMINISM, AND THE
GREEN MOVEMENT
GREY CITY JOURNAL
Gryphon Publications
THE HAPPY THRASHER
The Heather Foundation
Homeward Press
THE HYPERBOREAN
Hyperborean Micropublications
IllumiNet Press
INCITE INFORMATION
INFINITE ONION
JASON UNDERGROUND'S NOTES FROM THE
TRASHCOMPACTOR
KICK IT OVER
Last Generation/Underground Editions
Left Bank Books
LESBIAN CONTRADICTION-A Journal of Irreverent
Feminism
THE (LIBERTARIAN) CONNECTION
LIBERTY
LITTLE FREE PRESS
THE LOOGIE
Loompanics Unlimited
LOVE AND RAGE, A Revolutionary Anarchist News-
monthly
manic d press
Maryland Historical Press
THE MATCH
MEMES
Mermaid Press
NEGATIVE
The Neither/Nor Press
The New Humanity Press
THE NEW RENAISSANCE, An International Magazine
of Ideas & Opinions, Emphasizing Literature & The
Arts
New Society Publishers
THE NIHILISTIC REVIEW
NOMOS: Studies in Spontaneous Order
NONVIOLENT ANARCHIST NEWSLETTER
NOOSPAPERS
NOTES FROM THE UNDERGROUND
NRG
Nuclear Trenchcoated Subway Prophets Publications
OPEN ROAD
OPOSSUM HOLLER TAROT
THE OTHER ISRAEL
OTISIAN DIRECTORY
OUR GENERATION
Paladin Enterprises, Inc.
PARTING GIFTS
THE PARTY'S OVER
PAUNCH
Pessimism Press, Inc.
Pig Iron Press
POLITICALLY INCORRECT
Primal Publishing
PROCESSED WORLD
PROFANE EXISTENCE
Pygmy Forest Press

RAVEN ANARCHIST QUARTERLY
SAMISDAT
SCHMAGA
See Sharp Press
Semiotext Foreign Agents Books Series
SEMIOTEXT(E)
Smyrna Press
SOCIAL ANARCHISM: A Journal of Practice And
 Theory
Society Of Authors
SOULLESS STRUCTURES
SUB STANDARD
SUB-TERRAIN
SURVIVE & WIN
TEMPORARY CULTURE
III Publishing
Times Change Press
Unbridled Lust! Publishing
Vanity Press/Strolling Dog Press
THE VOLUNTARYIST
Wheel of Fire Press
WHITE CLOUDS REVUE
Working Press
WREE-VIEW OF WOMEN
ZERO ONE
Zirlinson Publishing

ANIMALS

Alpine Publications
Anaphase II
ANIMAL LIFE
ANIMAL TALES
ANIMAL WORLD
THE ANIMALS' AGENDA
ARABIAN HORSE TIMES
ASC NEWSLETTER
Ashley Books, Inc.
Avery Color Studios
Axelrod Publishing of Tampa Bay
BIRD WATCHER'S DIGEST
Blake Publishing
Blue Heron Press
BOWBENDER
CALLI'S TALES, The Quarterly for Animal Lovers of
 All Ages
Capra Press
Chelsea Green Publishing Company
THE CIVIL ABOLITIONIST
CJE NEWSLETTER (Newsletter of the Coalition for Jobs
 & the Environment)
DE NAR
Dog-Eared Publications
Doral Publishing
THE DREAMWEAVER
ECOSOCIALIST REVIEW
Falcon Press Publishing Company
FINE MADNESS
FISH DRUM MAGAZINE
FOCUS
Foundation Books
Gahmken Press
GCBA Publishing
THE HAPPY THRASHER
HFH Publications
Island Publishers
JEWISH VEGETARIANS OF NORTH AMERICA
JUDY
Michael Kesend, Publishing, Ltd.
L.A.N.D.
LAKE SUPERIOR MAGAZINE
THE LATHAM LETTER
LIVING AMONG NATURE DARINGLY!
LLAMAS MAGAZINE
Mayhaven Publishing
Micah Publications
Misty Hill Press
Mountain Press Publishing Co.
NATURE SOCIETY NEWS

Naturegraph Publishers, Inc.
The New Humanity Press
NEW METHODS JOURNAL (VETERINARY)
Oak Tree
Old Harbor Press
The Olive Press Publications
OTTERWISE
Parrot Press
Peel Productions
QuikRef Publishing
RESONANCE
Right Here Publications
Sierra Club Books
Gibbs Smith, Publisher
SNOWY EGRET
George Sroda, Publisher
Star Books, Inc.
Stillpoint Publishing
Stone Wall Press, Inc
STUDIO NORTH
TATTOO ADVOCATE JOURNAL
Texas Monthly Press
THEMATIC POETRY QUARTERLY
Trouvere Company
Univelt, Inc.
VEGETARIAN JOURNAL
VEGETARIAN TIMES
Vonpalisaden Publications Inc.
The George Whittell Memorial Press
Williamson Publishing Company, Inc.
Woodsong Graphics Inc.
WORLD RAINFOREST REPORT
WTI Publishing Co.
Zagier & Urruty Publicaciones

ANTHROPOLOGY, ARCHAELOGY

AFRICA TODAY
AFRICAN STUDIES
THE AHFAD JOURNAL: Women And Change
AMERICAN INDIAN BASKETRY
AMERICAN WRITING: A MAGAZINE
Ancient City Press
The Archives Press
Argonauts/Misty Isles Press
Arjuna Library Press
ARTPOLICE
Aspiring Millionaire
Bakhtin's Wife Publications
Ballena Press
Bergin & Garvey Publishers
Blue Dolphin Press, Inc.
Buddha Rose Publications
BULLETIN OF THE BOARD OF CELTIC STUDIES
CASE ANALYSIS
Cat's Pajamas Press
Cave Books
Celtic Heritage Press, Inc.
Chandler & Sharp Publishers, Inc.
Circumpolar Press
Citeaux Commentarii Cistercienses
CITEAUX: COMMENTARII CISTERCIENSES
THE CLASSICAL OUTLOOK
The Clyde Press
The Compass Press
COMPOST NEWSLETTER (CNL)
Cottonwood Press
Coxland Press
CREATION/EVOLUTION JOURNAL
Cultural Survival, Inc.
CULTURAL SURVIVAL QUARTERLY
DAEDALUS, Journal of the American Academy of Arts
 and Sciences
THE DALHOUSIE REVIEW
The Denali Press
DIE FAT PIGGY DIE
EAR MAGAZINE
ECHOS DU MONDE CLASSIQUE/CLASSICAL
 VIEWS

ENCYCLOPEDIA BANANICA
FACES: The Magazine About People
FESTIVAL QUARTERLY
Gavea-Brown Publications
GCBA Publishing
Glenbridge Publishing Ltd.
Harbor Publishing Company
The Heather Foundation
Hoffman Press
Hope Publishing House
HORIZONS WEST
Institute for the Study of Traditional American Indian Arts
  Press
Institute of Archaeology Publications
INTERCULTURE
International Information Associates
Johnson Books
JOURNAL OF THEORETICAL PSYCHOLOGY
KMT, A Modern Journal of Ancient Egypt
KMT Communications
LAKE SUPERIOR MAGAZINE
McPherson & Company Publishers
Metamorphous Press
Mockingbird Press
Moon Publications, Inc.
Museum of New Mexico Press
Nemeton Publishing
The New Humanity Press
NEWS FROM THE WHITE HOUSE
NightinGale Resources
THE NORTHERN REVIEW
Northland Publishing Company
Oneworld Publications Ltd.
Oregon Historical Society Press
OVERLAND JOURNAL
Paideia Publishers
EL PALACIO
Paragon House Publishers
Dr. Homer W. Parker, P.E.
T.H. Peek, Publisher
P-FORM
PLAY & CULTURE
Pop Void Publications
Pruett Publishing Company
Psyche Press
Psychohistory Press
PUCK!
Royal Purcell, Publisher
Rainier Books
Rand Editions/Tofua Press
THE REDNECK REVIEW OF LITERATURE
REPRESENTATIONS
Research & Discovery Publications
ROMANIAN REVIEW
Sang Froid Press
Santa Barbara Press
Sauvie Island Press
Scots Plaid Press (Persephone Press)
Talon Books Ltd
TATTOO ADVOCATE JOURNAL
Theytus Books Ltd.
TREASURE HUNTING RESEARCH BULLETIN
Unbridled Lust! Publishing
THE UNDERGROUND FOREST - LA SELVA SUB-
  TERRANEA
University of Calgary Press
Westburg Associates, Publishers
Whalesback Books
White Cliffs Media Company
THE WILD FOODS FORUM
Witwatersrand University Press
WORLD RAINFOREST REPORT
WTI Publishing Co.
Zagier & Urruty Publicaciones
ZONE
Zone Books

ANTIQUES

Almar Press
ALWAYS JUKIN'
Always Jukin'
Americana & Collectibles Press
Applied Publishing
ART INFORMATION REPORT
Aspiring Millionaire
COLLECTRIX
Countryman Press
CROP DUST
Fire Buff House
FOX VALLEY LIVING
GemStone Press
GREATER PORTLAND
HOBBY BOOKWATCH (MILITARY, GUN & HOBBY
  BOOK REVIEW)
Ironwood Publishing Company
LAKE SUPERIOR MAGAZINE
Levite of Apache
MASSEY COLLECTORS NEWS—WILD HARVEST
Mosaic Press
Myriad Moods
NAUTICAL BRASS
NEW ENGLAND ANTIQUES JOURNAL
Paperweight Press
THE PRINTER
The Quilt Digest Press
RED POWER
REFLECT
ROMANIAN REVIEW
Sleepy Hollow Press
SOUTHERN QUARTERLY: A Journal of the Arts in the
  South
13th MOON
Tomart Publications
Vestal Press Ltd
WALKING-STICK NOTES
Whalesback Books
Windmill Publishing Co.

APPALACHIA

Appalachian Consortium Press
APPALACHIAN HERITAGE
THE AZOREAN EXPRESS
BLACK JACK & VALLEY GRAPEVINE
CAL NEWSLETTER
CJE NEWSLETTER (Newsletter of the Coalition for Jobs
  & the Environment)
THE CLIMBING ART
Commonwealth Press Virginia
Emily Press
FOXFIRE
Foxfire Press
The FreeSolo Press
Great Elm Press
Institute for Southern Studies
Nightshade Press
NORTH CAROLINA LITERARY REVIEW
NOW AND THEN
PIKEVILLE REVIEW
Pocahontas Press, Inc.
POTATO EYES
Rowan Mountain Press
Signal Books
TRADITION
Vista Publishing Company

ARCHITECTURE

American Source Books
Applied Publishing
ARISTOS
ART INFORMATION REPORT
ART PAPERS
ASSEMBLING
Assembling Press
Bay Press

Beautiful America Publishing Company
Capra Press
Cheshire Books
Chronicle Books
Citeaux Commentarii Cistercienses
CITEAUX: COMMENTARII CISTERCIENSES
CJE NEWSLETTER (Newsletter of the Coalition for Jobs
   & the Environment)
Cottage Press
Craftsman Book Company
DESIGN BOOK REVIEW
THE DESIGNMENT REVIEW
The E.G. Van Press, Inc.
FOX VALLEY LIVING
FUSE MAGAZINE
Futurum Forlag
GATEAVISA
GRDA Publications
HOME RESOURCE MAGAZINE
Interalia/Design Books
Italica Press, Inc.
JOURNAL FOR ANTHROPOSOPHY
LAKE SUPERIOR MAGAZINE
Lumen Books, Inc.
MARQUEE
Maupin House
Midmarch Arts Press
MODERN LITURGY
Mosaic Press
Muso Press
Myriad Moods
THE NEW CRITERION
The New Humanity Press
New Levee Press
NewSage Press
THE NORTHERN ENGINEER
THE NORTHERN REVIEW
OLD-HOUSE JOURNAL
Ontario Library Association
Oregon Historical Society Press
The Oxalis Group
Pendaya Publications, Inc.
Pepper Publishing
The Preservation Press
Princeton Architectural Press
THE PRINCETON JOURNAL: THEMATIC STUDIES
   IN ARCHITECTURE
Professional Publications, Inc.
Rand Editions/Tofua Press
Sang Froid Press
SCHMAGA
Sentinel Books
SITES
Gibbs Smith, Publisher
SOUTHERN QUARTERLY: A Journal of the Arts in the
   South
STREAM LINES, MN JOURNAL OF CREATIVE
   WRITING
Synergistic Press
THEATRE DESIGN AND TECHNOLOGY
Thirteen Colonies Press
Three Continents Press, Inc.
Timber Press
THE UNDERGROUND FOREST - LA SELVA SUB-
   TERRANEA
Vestal Press Ltd
Waterfront Center
WATERFRONT WORLD
Whalesback Books
WOMEN AND ENVIRONMENTS
World Wildlife Fund & The Conservation Foundation
WTI Publishing Co.
ZONE
Zone Books

ARIZONA

Affiliated Writers of America, Inc.
ARIZONA GREAT OUTDOORS

Falcon Press Publishing Company
Fiesta Books Inc.
Harbinger House
Northland Publishing Company
The Patrice Press
Recreation Sales Publishing, Inc.
Tortilla Press
Treasure Chest Publications, Inc.

ARMENIAN

ARARAT
Blue Crane Books
Gilgamesh Press Ltd.
Panorama West Publishing
Saqi Books Publisher
Three Continents Press, Inc.
Zon International Publishing Co.

ARTHURIAN

Coxland Press
Nemeton Publishing
X-CALIBRE

ARTIFICIAL INTELLIGENCE

THE CHAOS NETWORK
DR. DOBB'S JOURNAL
DOCTOR-PATIENT STUDIES
Harbor Publishing Company
Infinite Savant Publishing
JOURNAL OF THEORETICAL PSYCHOLOGY
THE LETTER PARADE
M & T Publishing
Mockingbird Press
POLITICALLY INCORRECT
Unbridled Lust! Publishing

ARTS

Acrobat Books
ACTA VICTORIANA
ACTIVIST
THE ADVOCATE
AERIAL
Afta Press
Again + Again Press
AILERON, A LITERARY JOURNAL
AKWEKON: A National Native American Literary &
   Arts Journal
AKWEKON LITERARY JOURNAL
Alan Wofsy Fine Arts
ALASKA WOMEN
THE ALBANY REVIEW
Allardyce, Barnett (Agneau 2)
Altamont Press, Inc.
American Council for the Arts/ACA Books
AMERICAN LIVING
American-Canadian Publishers, Inc.
Americas Society
Anaphase II
Arden Press, Inc.
Argonauts/Misty Isles Press
ARISTOS
ART CALENDAR
ART HAZARDS NEWS
ART INFORMATION REPORT
Art Metropole
ART PAPERS
ART TIMES
ARTEMIS
ARTICHOKE HEART
ART/LIFE
Art/Life Limited Editions
ARTPAPER
ARTPOLICE
ASSEMBLING
Assembling Press
Asylum Arts
ATHA NEWSLETTER
Australian American Publishing

WE MAGAZINE
We Press
WESTART
Westburg Associates, Publishers
Westgate Press
THE WESTMINSTER REVIEW
WESTWORDS
Whalesback Books
White Cliffs Media Company
White Horse Press
WHITE WALLS: A Journal of Language and Art
Windmill Publishing Co.
Windom Books
Winn Books
WISCONSIN REVIEW
WITNESS
Wolfhound Press
WOMAN'S ART JOURNAL
WOMEN ARTISTS NEWS
WOMEN IN THE ARTS BULLETIN/NEWSLETTER
Woodcock Press
WREE-VIEW OF WOMEN
Writers House Press
WRITER'S LIFELINE
WTI Publishing Co.
Xenos Books
Xexoxial Endarchy
YELLOW SILK: Journal Of Erotic Arts
Yoknapatawpha Press
ZENOS
Zon International Publishing Co.

ASIA, INDOCHINA

ACTIVIST
AMC Publishing
ANIMA: The Journal of Human Experience
Anima Publications
AREOPAGUS
Argonauts/Misty Isles Press
ASIAN SURVEY
Autonomedia, Inc.
AXEFACTORY
Barclay House
BELLES LETTRES
Between The Lines
Buddha Rose Publications
The Carolina Wren Press
Chinese Literature Press
CICADA
Cross Cultural Press
Cultural Survival, Inc.
CULTURAL SURVIVAL QUARTERLY
Diane Publishing Company
ENERGY ASIA
FUSE MAGAZINE
The Global Press
GREY CITY JOURNAL
Hong Kong Publishing Co., Ltd.
Hoover Institution Press
INDIA CURRENTS
J P Publications
JOURNAL OF SOUTH ASIAN LITERATURE
Kitchen Table: Women of Color Press
LIBERATION! Journal of Revolutionary Marxism
LIZZENGREASY
MANOA: A Pacific Journal of International Writing
Moon Publications, Inc.
Moonsquilt Press
NET
The New Humanity Press
The Olive Press Publications
OPOSSUM HOLLER TAROT
Orbis Books
THE OTHER ISRAEL
PACIFIC HISTORICAL REVIEW
PETROLEUM NEWS: Asia's Energy Journal
Petroleum News Southeast Asia Ltd.
Polymath Systems

Publications of Arts (Art Resources for Teachers & Students)
RACONTEUR Publications
Readers International, Inc.
Redbird Press, Inc.
Salt Lick Press
SCHMAGA
Sharp & Dunnigan Publications, Incorporated
Snow Lion Publications, Inc.
SPECTRUM REVIEW
SUBTEXT
TANDAVA
TATTOO ADVOCATE JOURNAL
THIRD WORLD RESOURCES
TOWARD FREEDOM
TRANSITIONS ABROAD: The Guide to Living, Learning, and Working Overseas
Unbridled Lust! Publishing
Unicorn Press
Vesta Publications Limited
VIETNAM GENERATION: A Journal of Recent History and Contemporary Issues
Woodsong Graphics Inc.
WORDS OF WISDOM
WORLD PERSPECTIVES
WORLD RAINFOREST REPORT
Zed Books Ltd.

ASIAN-AMERICAN

Argonauts/Misty Isles Press
As Is/So & So Press
Avery Publishing Group, Inc.
BAMBOO RIDGE, THE HAWAII WRITERS' QUARTERLY
Bamboo Ridge Press
BELLES LETTRES
The Bess Press
Buddha Rose Publications
Buddhist Study Center Press
CHRYSANTHEMUM
Cottonwood Press
Council on Interracial Books For Children
Cross Cultural Press
Dragon Cloud Books
Esoterica Press
Frozen Waffles Press/Shattered Sidewalks Press; 25th Century Chapbooks
FUSE MAGAZINE
Goldfish Press
Heritage West Books
INDIA CURRENTS
International Information Associates
INTERRACIAL BOOKS FOR CHILDREN BULLETIN
Kelsey St. Press
Kitchen Table: Women of Color Press
LIZZENGREASY
MANOA: A Pacific Journal of International Writing
Mina Press
The New Humanity Press
THE NEW RENAISSANCE, An International Magazine of Ideas & Opinions, Emphasizing Literature & The Arts
New Star Books Ltd.
Northland Publishing Company
PACIFIC HISTORICAL REVIEW
The Place In The Woods
Reference Service Press
SEZ: A Multi-Racial Journal of Poetry & People's Culture
Shadow Press, U.S.A.
SO & SO
Stone Bridge Press
Strawberry Hill Press
Talon Books Ltd
Unbridled Lust! Publishing
VALLEY WOMEN'S VOICE
Vesta Publications Limited
VIETNAM GENERATION: A Journal of Recent History and Contemporary Issues

Ward Hill Press

ASTROLOGY

ACS Publications
THE AGE OF AQUARIUS
Alta Napa Press
Ashley Books, Inc.
ASPECTS
ASTROFLASH
Aurora Press
BALDER
Blue Dolphin Press, Inc.
BOTH SIDES NOW
Cassandra Press
COMPOST NEWSLETTER (CNL)
Cosmic Footnotes Publications
Cosmoenergetics Publications
Coxland Press
CRCS Publications
The Devonshire Publishing Co.
DoubLeo Publications
THE DREAMWEAVER
Esoterica, The Craft Press
EXUM Publishing
Hermetician Press
INNER SEARCH
JOURNAL FOR ANTHROPOSOPHY
Llewellyn Publications
Manifest Press
MOONSTONE BLUE
THE MOUNTAIN ASTROLOGER
The New Humanity Press
NIGHT ROSES
Ox Head Press
Pallas Communications
Quicksilver Productions
RADIANCE, The Magazine For Large Women
Ramp Creek Publishing Inc
Rio Grande Press
Sauvie Island Press
Kirit N. Shah
Sunstone Publications
TATTOO ADVOCATE JOURNAL
TEC Publications
TRENDS & PREDICTIONS ANALYST
Unbridled Lust! Publishing
Valley Lights Publications
Samuel Weiser, Inc.
Whitford Press
WITHIN & BEYOND
WTI Publishing Co.

ASTRONOMY

ASPECTS
BLUE LIGHTS
Blue Lights Publications
Infolib Resources
JOURNAL FOR ANTHROPOSOPHY
Mockingbird Press
The New Humanity Press
POLITICALLY INCORRECT
SOVIET SPACEFLIGHT REPORT
Starwise Publications
STRUGGLE: A Magazine of Proletarian Revolutionary
  Literature
Sunstone Publications
Univelt, Inc.

ATHEISM

American Atheist Press
DHARMA COMBAT
FREE INQUIRY
Hyperborean Micropublications
See Sharp Press

AUSTRALIA

Australian American Publishing
BELLES LETTRES

CRAFTS NSW
DAEDALUS, Journal of the American Academy of Arts
  and Sciences
THE FAMOUS REPORTER
Foxfire Press
J P Publications
OVERLAND
SCRIPSI
SPECTRUM, A Guide to the Independent Press and
  Informative Organizations
Spectrum Publications
Star Books, Inc.
STUDIO - A Journal of Christians Writing
TATTOO ADVOCATE JOURNAL
TechWest Publications
Three Continents Press, Inc.
Visa Books (Division of South Continent Corporation Pty
  Ltd)
Wide World Publishing/TETRA
Wild & Woolley
WORLD RAINFOREST REPORT

AUTOBIOGRAPHY

Academy Chicago Publishers
Adaptive Living
ALASKA WOMEN
ANNA'S HOUSE: THE JOURNAL OF EVERYDAY
  LIFE
BELLES LETTRES
Bonus Books, Inc.
BREAKTHROUGH!
Brunswick Publishing Corporation
Carroll & Graf Publishers, Inc.
Cave Books
Celo Valley Books
CRAWLSPACE
W.S. Dawson Co.
EPIPHANY: A JOURNAL OF LITERATURE
The Feminist Press at the City University of New York
Fromm International Publishing Corporation
Happy Rock Press
Hilltop Press
HORIZONS WEST
IMAGINATION MAGAZINE
Independence Publishers Inc.
Inspirational Publisher
JOURNAL FOR ANTHROPOSOPHY
L.A. GANG BANG
Limelight Editions
Lionhouse Publishing Company
LITTLE FREE PRESS
LuraMedia, Inc.
MANOA: A Pacific Journal of International Writing
NEW HOPE INTERNATIONAL REVIEW
The New Humanity Press
Omega Cottonwood Press
Oregon Historical Society Press
Parabola Books
P-FORM
POISON PEN WRITERS NEWS
Popular Reality Press
THE PRINTER
Prudhomme Press
Rebis Press
ROMANIAN REVIEW
SACRED FIRE
St. Bede's Publications
Signal Books
SLEUTH JOURNAL
Genny Smith Books
Spelman Publishing, Inc.
Star Books, Inc.
Three Continents Press, Inc.
Times Change Press
Tyro Publishing
Valley House Gallery Press
A VERY SMALL MAGAZINE
Wood Thrush Books

Xenos Books

AUTOS

Bonus Books, Inc.
CORVETTE FEVER MAGAZINE
EXUM Publishing
Motorsport International Publishing Co. (MIPCO)
Stone Press
TUCSON MOTOR NEWS
Ward Hill Press
Whitehorse

AVANT-GARDE, EXPERIMENTAL ART

ACTA VICTORIANA
ACTIVIST
THE ACTS THE SHELFLIFE
AILERON, A LITERARY JOURNAL
AMERICAN LIVING
American Poets In Profile Series
AMERICAN WRITING: A MAGAZINE
ANTI-ISOLATION/NEW ARTS IN WISCONSIN
Arden Press, Inc.
Arjuna Library Press
ART CALENDAR
ART INFORMATION REPORT
ART PAPERS
ART/LIFE
Art/Life Limited Editions
ARTPAPER
ART'S GARBAGE GAZZETTE
As Is/So & So Press
Astro Artz
Asylum Arts
Atelier De L'Agneau
Autonomedia, Inc.
Avalanche Press
B-CITY
BELLYWASH
BLACK BEAR REVIEW
Black Sparrow Press
Black Tie Press
BLANK GUN SILENCER
BORDER/LINES
Boz Publishing
Brook House Press, Inc.
Buddha Rose Publications
Burning Books
Castle Peak Editions
Center Press
CERTAIN GESTURES
CHAKRA
Chax Press
CITY RANT
COKEFISH
COLLAGES & BRICOLAGES
CRAFTS NSW
CURTAINS
DE NAR
" "...A DEAD BEAT POET PRODUCTION
DELIRIUM
DHARMA COMBAT
DIAMOND HITCHHIKER COBWEBS
DIE FAT PIGGY DIE
Dragon Cloud Books
Duende Press
DUMPSTER TIMES
EAR MAGAZINE
e.g.
The Electric Bank, Inc.
11 X 13 - BROADSIDE
EQUOFINALITY
EUTHANASIA ROSES
EXIT
EyeDEA Books
FARCE, Raleigh's Review of Alternative Arts
THE FICTION REVIEW
THE FINAL PAGE
FINE MADNESS

FORBIDDEN LINES
FORCED EXPOSURE
Ford-Brown & Co., Publishers
FRANK: AN INTERNATIONAL JOURNAL OF CON-
TEMPORARY WRITING AND ART
French Broad Press
Frozen Waffles Press/Shattered Sidewalks Press; 25th
Century Chapbooks
GET STUPID
GOING GAGA
GREEN ZERO
GREY CITY JOURNAL
Guilt & Gardenias Press
GYPSY
Helicon Nine Editions
HIGH PERFORMANCE
HOT FLASHES
HOWLING DOG
Howling Dog Press
HUBRIS
HUNGRY ZIPPER
ILLUMINATIONS
IMAGINATION MAGAZINE
IMPETUS
Implosion Press
Indelible Inc.
INKBLOT
Inkblot Publications
JIMMY & LUCY'S HOUSE OF 'K'
JOURNAL FOR ANTHROPOSOPHY
K
KALDRON, An International Journal Of Visual Poetry
and Language Art
Kelsey St. Press
KROKLOK
Last Generation/Underground Editions
LEFT CURVE
LIGHTWORKS MAGAZINE
LOBLOLLY: A LITERARY BIANNUAL OF THE
VORTEX
THE LOOGIE
LOST AND FOUND TIMES
LOST GENERATION JOURNAL
LOUDER THAN BOMBS
Luna Bisonte Prods
The Lunchroom Press
LYNX
manic d press
MASSACRE
MEMES
MENSUEL 25
MIDLAND REVIEW
Mortal Press
MUSICWORKS: THE CANADIAN AUDIO-VISUAL
JOURNAL OF SOUND EXPLORATIONS
NATURALLY
The Neither/Nor Press
NEW HOPE INTERNATIONAL REVIEW
NEW NORTH ARTSCAPE
NEW SINS
New Sins Press
NIGHT ROSES
THE NIHILISTIC REVIEW
NOOSPAPERS
NOTES FROM THE UNDERGROUND
NRG
Nuclear Trenchcoated Subway Prophets Publications
THE OCCASIONAL TUESDAY-ART NEWS
Tom Ockerse Editions
OHIO RENAISSANCE REVIEW
1 BIT SHOE
Open Book Publications, A Division of Station Hill Press
OUTRE
THE PAPER BAG
The Paper Bag Press
PAPER RADIO
THE PARADOXIST MOVEMENT
PARTING GIFTS

743

PEN:UMBRA
Pessimism Press, Inc.
P-FORM
Phrygian Press
Players Press, Inc.
POETS. PAINTERS. COMPOSERS.
Point Riders Press
The Press of the Third Mind
Pressed Curtains
THE PROSPECT REVIEW
PUCK!
RACKHAM JOURNAL OF THE ARTS AND HUMANI-
    TIES (RaJAH)
The Real Comet Press
RED BASS
RENEGADE
Re/Search Publications
ROMANIAN REVIEW
(ROWBOAT)
The Runaway Spoon Press
SALON: A Journal of Aesthetics
Savant Garde Workshop
Saxifrage Books
Art Paul Schlosser Books, Tapes, & Garbage Gazzette
SCHMAGA
Score
SCORE
SCREAM MAGAZINE
THE SCREAM OF THE BUDDHA
Scribblers Publishing, Ltd.
Seminal Life Press
Semiotext Foreign Agents Books Series
SEMIOTEXT(E)
Sink Press
SKYLARK
Slate Press
Small-Small Press
SO & SO
Sober Minute Press
SOUND CHOICE
Southeastern FRONT
THE SOUTHERN CALIFORNIA ANTHOLOGY
SPHINX—WOMEN'S INTERNATIONAL LITERARY/
    ART REVIEW (IN ENGLISH)
SPIT
THE STARK FIST OF REMOVAL
Station Hill Press
STIFLED YAWN: A Magazine Of Contemporary Writing
STILETTO
SUB ROSA
Synergetic Press Inc.
SZ/Press
TAPAS
TATTOO ADVOCATE JOURNAL
THIRD RAIL
Third Rail Press
TOAD HIWAY
TOOK
Tuesday-Art Press
Unbridled Lust! Publishing
UNDERPASS
UNION SHOP BLUFF
UNIROD MAGAZINE
UPDATE
VANTAGE POINT
VOLITION
Water Mark Press
THE WAVE
WE MAGAZINE
We Press
WHITE WALLS: A Journal of Language and Art
THE WIRE
Writers Forum
X MAGAZINE
XENOPHILIA
Xenos Books
XEROLAGE
Xexoxial Endarchy

YELLOW SILK: Journal Of Erotic Arts
ZERO HOUR
Zirlinson Publishing
ZONE
Zone Books
ZYX
ZZAJ-SYNCHRONOLOGY

AVIATION

Acorn Publishing
Aeolus Press, Inc.
AIRLINERS
AIRLINERS MONTHLY NEWS
Alta Research
Associated Writing Programs
THE AUTHOR
Avalanche Press
Aviation Book Company
AWP CHRONICLE
The Boston Mills Press
Eagle Publishing Company
Foundation Books
GATEAVISA
GCBA Publishing
HANG GLIDING
HOBBY BOOKWATCH (MILITARY, GUN & HOBBY
    BOOK REVIEW)
House of Hits, Inc.
KITE LINES
Paul Maravelas
Mountain Press Publishing Co.
Myriad Moods
The Nautical & Aviation Publishing Co. of American, Inc.
OVERLAND JOURNAL
Para Publishing
PARACHUTIST
The Patrice Press
Publitec Editions
R & R Publishing
Sharp & Dunnigan Publications, Incorporated
SKYDIVING
Society Of Authors
Sunflower University Press
TATTOO ADVOCATE JOURNAL
Texas Monthly Press
13th MOON
Ultralight Publications, Inc.
World Transport Press

AWARDS, FOUNDATIONS, GRANTS

American Impressions
ART CALENDAR
ARTPAPER
Caravan Press
DIAMOND HITCHHIKER COBWEBS
ENTRY
Festival Publications
FOLIO: A LITERARY JOURNAL
The Foundation Center
Nuclear Trenchcoated Subway Prophets Publications
P-FORM
POETIC SPACE: Poetry & Fiction
RADIUS/Resources for Local Arts
Reference Service Press
THE ROCK HALL REPORTER
Seven Locks Press
TATTOO ADVOCATE JOURNAL
VANTAGE POINT
WRITER'S LIFELINE

BEAT

Alpha Beat Press
ALPHA BEAT SOUP
BLANK GUN SILENCER
Chiron Press
CHIRON REVIEW
CITY RANT
" "...A DEAD BEAT POET PRODUCTION

DHARMA COMBAT
DIAMOND HITCHHIKER COBWEBS
Forty-Seven Books
NEW HOPE INTERNATIONAL REVIEW
THE NIHILISTIC REVIEW
Nuclear Trenchcoated Subway Prophets Publications
Omega Cottonwood Press
Pessimism Press, Inc.
P-FORM
(ROWBOAT)
SPIT
TAPAS
Trabarni Productions
Unbridled Lust! Publishing
XENOPHILIA

SAUL BELLOW

SAUL BELLOW JOURNAL

JOHN BERRYMAN

FINE MADNESS
Ultralight Publications, Inc.

BIBLIOGRAPHY

THE ABER BULLETIN
THE AFRICAN BOOK PUBLISHING RECORD
AMERICAN BOOK COLLECTOR
American Handwriting Analysis Foundation
AMERICAN LITERATURE
ANQ: A Quarterly Journal of Short Articles, Notes, and
   Reviews
Appalachian Consortium Press
ASSEMBLING
Assembling Press
BEAT SCENE
Bibliographies Unlimited
THE BIBLIOTHECK
Black Sparrow Press
Bluestocking Press
BookNotes :(TM) Resources for Small & Self-Publishers
The Borgo Press
Brennen Publishing Company
BRITISH BOOK NEWS
THE CHRISTIAN LIBRARIAN
Cottonwood Press
The F. Marion Crawford Memorial Society
W.S. Dawson Co.
The Denali Press
DIE FAT PIGGY DIE
DOCTOR-PATIENT STUDIES
Chris Drumm Books
Dundurn Press Ltd
EAR MAGAZINE
ECOSOCIALIST REVIEW
ECW Press
Edition Gemini
ELAN POETIQUE LITTERAIRE ET PACIFISTE
ELT Press
English Language Literature Association
ENGLISH LITERATURE IN TRANSITION, 1880-1920
ESSAYS ON CANADIAN WRITING
Ex Machina Publishing Company
Fallen Leaf Press
FEMINIST COLLECTIONS: A QUARTERLY OF WO-
   MEN'S STUDIES RESOURCES
FEMINIST PERIODICALS: A CURRENT LISTING OF
   CONTENTS
The Feminist Press at the City University of New York
FINE PRINT: The Review for the Arts of the Book
The Gleniffer Press
Gryphon Publications
Hans Zell Publishers
Heresy Press
Hoover Institution Press
THE HYPERBOREAN
ILLINOIS WRITERS REVIEW
Infolib Resources
International Information Associates

Ithaca Press
THE JOURNAL OF COMMONWEALTH LITERA-
   TURE
JOURNAL OF MODERN LITERATURE
Knowledge, Ideas & Trends, Inc. (KIT)
Latin American Press
THE LEFT INDEX
Library Research Associates, Inc.
LITERARY RESEARCH: A Journal of Scholarly Method
   & Technique
LOST GENERATION JOURNAL
Peter Marcan Publications
Mayhaven Publishing
Laurence McGilvery
Meyerbooks, Publisher
The Moretus Press, Inc.
MUSICWORKS: THE CANADIAN AUDIO-VISUAL
   JOURNAL OF SOUND EXPLORATIONS
THE MYSTERY FANCIER
Nevada Publications
NEW BOOKS ON WOMEN & FEMINISM
NEW HOPE INTERNATIONAL REVIEW
North Star Press of St. Cloud, Inc.
Norton Coker Press
NOTEBOOK/CUADERNO: A LITERARY JOURNAL
Ontario Library Association
Open Horizons Publishing Company
ORO MADRE
Panorama West Publishing
PAPERBACK PARADE
Placebo Press
Poltroon Press
Bern Porter Books
R & E Publishers
JEAN RHYS REVIEW
ROMANIAN REVIEW
THE ROMANTIST
Ruddy Duck Press
The Rydal Press
Saqi Books Publisher
SERIALS REVIEW
Signature Books
Smyrna Press
SOCIALISM AND DEMOCRACY
SPECTRUM, A Guide to the Independent Press and
   Informative Organizations
Spectrum Publications
Sunburst Press
Synerjy
SYNERJY: A Directory of Renewable Energy
TATTOO ADVOCATE JOURNAL
THE TEACHING LIBRARIAN
THIRD WORLD RESOURCES
Three Continents Press, Inc.
TOOK
THE UNDERGROUND FOREST - LA SELVA SUB-
   TERRANEA
Underwood-Miller, Inc. & Brandywyne Books
University of Calgary Press
Wise Owl Press
Witwatersrand University Press
Women's Studies Librarian, University of Wisconsin
   System
Woodbine House
Writers Publishing Service Co.

BICYCLING

Acorn Publishing
BEAN ZINE
The Bess Press
Bicycle Books (Publishing) Inc.
BikePress U.S.A./BikePress Canada
BIKEREPORT
Buddha Rose Publications
BURWOOD JOURNAL
Countryman Press
FOX VALLEY LIVING
The Globe Pequot Press

745

GREEN MULTILOGUE
Human Kinetics Pub. Inc.
Info Net Publishing
Leisure Press
THE LETTER PARADE
MESSAGE POST
Milner Press
The Mountaineers Books
Northland Publishing Company
Pruett Publishing Company
RACE ACROSS AMERICA PROGRAM
VELONEWS
Vista Publishing Company
Vitesse Press
Williamson Publishing Company, Inc.
WTI Publishing Co.

BILINGUAL

A.R.A. JOURNAL
THE ABER BULLETIN
Axelrod Publishing of Tampa Bay
Bandanna Books
Bilingual Review/Press
BILINGUAL REVIEW/Revista Bilingue
Black & White & Read All Over Publishing Co.
Branden Publishing Company
Broken Moon Press
Chandler & Sharp Publishers, Inc.
The Chicot Press
Coach House Press
Esoterica Press
Floricanto Press
GAVEA-BROWN
Gavea-Brown Publications
Helicon Nine Editions
Hoffman Press
Hope Publishing House
HORIZONS INTERCULTURELS
In One Ear Press
Interlink Publishing Group, Inc.
INTERNATIONAL POETRY REVIEW
Italica Press, Inc.
Kitchen Table: Women of Color Press
Langston Press
Latin American Literary Review Press
Latin American Press
LIZZENGREASY
LOLA-FISH
LOVE AND RAGE, A Revolutionary Anarchist News-
    monthly
Maize Press
Miles River Press
Minor Heron Press
New Idea Press, Inc.
NOTEBOOK/CUADERNO: A LITERARY JOURNAL
Nuventures Publishing
Ocean Tree Books
The Olivia and Hill Press, Inc.
THE PLOVER (Chidori)
Pocahontas Press, Inc.
POETRY NEW YORK
Rakhamim Publications
READ, AMERICA!
Salt Lick Press
Saqi Books Publisher
Scots Plaid Press (Persephone Press)
Serpent & Eagle Press
Smyrna Press
The Speech Bin, Inc.
Station Hill Press
Studia Hispanica Editors
Synergistic Press
THE UNDERGROUND FOREST - LA SELVA SUB-
    TERRANEA
Waterfront Press
Writers Forum
Xenos Books

BIOGRAPHY

THE ABER BULLETIN
Academy Chicago Publishers
Amen Publishing Co.
Anderson Press
THE ANNALS OF IOWA
ANQ: A Quarterly Journal of Short Articles, Notes, and
    Reviews
Appalachian Consortium Press
Arden Press, Inc.
ASSEMBLING
Assembling Press
THE AUTHOR
Author's Unlimited
AVSTAR Publishing Corp.
Barclay House
Beacon Press
BEAT SCENE
BELLES LETTRES
BELLOWING ARK
Black Sparrow Press
Bonus Books, Inc.
Don Bosco Multimedia
The Boxwood Press
Branden Publishing Company
Brennen Publishing Company
Brooke-Richards Press
Brunswick Publishing Corporation
Buddha Rose Publications
C.C. Publishing Co.
Calapooia Publications
Cambric Press
Camel Press
Capra Press
Carroll & Graf Publishers, Inc.
Celo Valley Books
THE CENTENNIAL REVIEW
Chandler & Sharp Publishers, Inc.
Chelsea Green Publishing Company
Cherokee Publishing Company
CIN-DAV, Inc.
Earl M Coleman Enterprises, Inc
Community Service, Inc.
COMMUNITY SERVICE NEWSLETTER
Cosmic Footnotes Publications
COTTONWOOD
Cottonwood Press
Countryman Press
COYDOG REVIEW
The F. Marion Crawford Memorial Society
CROSS TIMBERS REVIEW
Crossroads Communications
Crystal Press, Ltd.
CULTURE CONCRETE
W.S. Dawson Co.
DAYSPRING
De-Feet Press, Inc.
Discovery Enterprises, Ltd.
DOOR COUNTY ALMANAK
Double M Press
Dundurn Press Ltd
DUST (From the Ego Trip)
Earth Star Publications
Eastern Caribbean Institute
Edition Stencil
ELT Press
ENGLISH LITERATURE IN TRANSITION, 1880-1920
Epicenter Press Inc.
EPIPHANY: A JOURNAL OF LITERATURE
EPM Publications, Inc.
Robert Erdmann Publishing
ETC Publications
Evans Publications Inc.
The Everett Companies, Publishing Division
Ex Machina Publishing Company
Excellence Enterprises
Fell Publishers, Inc.

Fels and Firn Press
The Feminist Press at the City University of New York
Finesse Publishing Company
FISICA
Foundation Books
FOX VALLEY LIVING
THE FREEDONIA GAZETTE
Friends United Press
Fromm International Publishing Corporation
The Future Press
Gaslight Publications
Gavea-Brown Publications
Glacier House Publications
Glenbridge Publishing Ltd.
The Gleniffer Press
GOOD READING MAGAZINE
Great Blue Graphics
Grosvenor USA
Happy Rock Press
Harbinger House
Harrison House Publishers
HAWAI'I REVIEW
Heirloom Publications
Heresy Press
Heritage West Books
Hilltop Press
HMS Press
HORIZONS WEST
Icarus Books
ILLINOIS MAGAZINE
Institute for Southern Studies
International Publishers Co. Inc.
ISRAEL HORIZONS
Italica Press, Inc.
Ithaca Press
Jones River Press
JOURNAL FOR ANTHROPOSOPHY
JOURNAL OF MODERN LITERATURE
The Kennebec River Press, Inc.
The Kingston Press, Inc.
Kozmik Press
L.A.N.D.
LAKE SUPERIOR MAGAZINE
Latin American Press
The Latona Press
LEFTHANDER MAGAZINE
LEGACY: A JOURNAL OF AMERICAN WOMEN
    WRITERS
Levite of Apache
Libertarian Press, Inc./American Book Distributors
Library Research Associates, Inc.
Limelight Editions
LININGTON LINEUP
LOST GENERATION JOURNAL
Lowy Publishing
Maryland Historical Press
Mayhaven Publishing
Merlin Books Ltd.
Milner Press
Multiple Dimensions
Myriad Moods
NEW HOPE INTERNATIONAL REVIEW
The New Humanity Press
THE NEW PRESS
New Saga Publishers
NEW WRITER'S MAGAZINE
NORTH CAROLINA LITERARY REVIEW
North Country Books, Inc.
THE NORTHERN REVIEW
NOTEBOOK/CUADERNO: A LITERARY JOURNAL
Ocean Tree Books
The Olive Press Publications
Orbis Books
OREGON HISTORICAL QUARTERLY
Oregon Historical Society Press
Oregon State University Press
Organization for Equal Education of the Sexes, Inc.
    (OEES)

Pamlico Press
Panorama Publishing Company
Panorama West Publishing
Papyrus Publishers
Parable Press
Paragon House Publishers
Paragraph Publications
Path Press, Inc.
The Patrice Press
Peachtree Publishers, Ltd.
Pepper Publishing
Pinery Press
The Place In The Woods
THE PLOUGH
Pocahontas Press, Inc.
Poetry Wales Press, Ltd.
POISON PEN WRITERS NEWS
PORTLAND REVIEW
Prima Facie
PROMOTION
Protea Publishing Company
Pruett Publishing Company
Pussywillow Publishing House, Inc.
Quarterly Committee of Queen's University
QUEEN'S QUARTERLY: A Canadian Review
RADICAL AMERICA
REAL PEOPLE
Red Alder Books
RGM Publications
THE ROCK HALL REPORTER
Rockwell Publishing
ROMANIAN REVIEW
THE ROMANTIST
St. Bede's Publications
SALMAGUNDI
Saqi Books Publisher
Scentouri, Publishing Division
SCHMAGA
Scottwall Associates, Publishers
Sea Urchin Press
Shepherd Books
Sherwood Sugden & Company, Publishers
Signature Books
Simon & Pierre Publishing Co. Ltd.
SLEUTH JOURNAL
Gibbs Smith, Publisher
Society Of Authors
Soundboard Books
SOUTH DAKOTA REVIEW
Spredden Press
Star Books, Inc.
Star Rover House
Still Point Press
Straight Arrow Publishing
Strawberry Hill Press
STREAM LINES, MN JOURNAL OF CREATIVE
    WRITING
The Sulgrave Press
Sunburst Press
Surrey Press
Swand Publications
Synergistic Press
Talon Books Ltd
TATTOO ADVOCATE JOURNAL
TBW Books, Inc.
Tessera Publishing, Inc.
Texas Monthly Press
Thirteen Colonies Press
Three Continents Press, Inc.
Thunder's Mouth Press
Times Change Press
Tomart Publications
Tudor Publishers, Inc.
University of Massachusetts Press
Upword Press
THE VAMPIRE JOURNAL
Vestal Press Ltd
Villa Press

Ward Hill Press
Westburg Associates, Publishers
White Mane Publishing Company, Inc.
White Rose Press
Wolfhound Press
Woodbine House
Woodsong Graphics Inc.
World Promotions
THE WRITE AGE (First Magazine of Writing Therapy)
Xenos Books

BIOLOGY

American Malacologists, Inc.
Anaphase II
ASC NEWSLETTER
ASPECTS
Avery Publishing Group, Inc.
Blue Heron Press
BOWBENDER
Cave Books
Circa Press
THE CIVIL ABOLITIONIST
dbS Productions
The Denali Press
Dog-Eared Publications
FOCUS
FOREFRONT—HEALTH INVESTIGATIONS
Gahmken Press
Happy Rock Press
Homestead Publishing
Human Kinetics Pub. Inc.
Humana Press
International Information Associates
INTERNATIONAL JOURNAL OF SPORT BIOME-
  CHANICS
Island Press
KIDSCIENCE
THE LATHAM LETTER
The Latona Press
MIND MATTERS REVIEW
THE NAUTILUS
NEWS FROM THE WHITE HOUSE
THE NORTHERN REVIEW
Oregon State University Press
Dr. Homer W. Parker, P.E.
T.H. Peek, Publisher
RESONANCE
Rocky Top Publications
SCIENCE AND NATURE, The Annual of Marxist
  Philosophy for Natural Scientists
SNOWY EGRET
SURVIVE & WIN
TATTOO ADVOCATE JOURNAL
Tiger Moon
Tortilla Press
VDT NEWS
Weidner & Sons, Publishing
WHOLE EARTH REVIEW
Witwatersrand University Press
WORLD RAINFOREST REPORT

BIOTECHNOLOGY

THE CIVIL ABOLITIONIST
CJE NEWSLETTER (Newsletter of the Coalition for Jobs
  & the Environment)
ECOSOCIALIST REVIEW
FOREFRONT—HEALTH INVESTIGATIONS
GATEAVISA
THE HUMANIST
JOURNAL FOR ANTHROPOSOPHY
Mockingbird Press
New Idea Press, Inc.
THE NORTHERN REVIEW
Oak Tree
POLITICALLY INCORRECT
Stillpoint Publishing
TRENDS & PREDICTIONS ANALYST
Unbridled Lust! Publishing

Zed Books Ltd.

BIRDS

ANIMAL TALES
Capra Press
Chelsea Green Publishing Company
CJE NEWSLETTER (Newsletter of the Coalition for Jobs
  & the Environment)
THE DICK E. BIRD NEWS
Gahmken Press
Johnson Books
Milner Press
Naturegraph Publishers, Inc.
Northland Publishing Company
Parrot Press
SNOWY EGRET
STUDIO NORTH
Zagier & Urruty Publicaciones

BIRTH, BIRTH CONTROL, POPULATION

THE ABER BULLETIN
Alleluia Press
Aslan Publishing
Avery Publishing Group, Inc.
THE BABY CONNECTION NEWS JOURNAL
Bergin & Garvey Publishers
Cassandra Press
Children Of Mary
CJE NEWSLETTER (Newsletter of the Coalition for Jobs
  & the Environment)
Comforter Publishing
D.I.N. Publications
DOCTOR-PATIENT STUDIES
FIDELIS ET VERUS
The Chas. Franklin Press
Free Association Books (FAB)
FREE INQUIRY
HAWAI'I REVIEW
Humana Press
THE HUMANIST
Interlink Publishing Group, Inc.
International Childbirth Education Association, Inc.
Merlin Books Ltd.
NEW ANGLICAN REVIEW
NEW CATHOLIC REVIEW
NEWS FROM THE WHITE HOUSE
OFF OUR BACKS
Pandit Press, Inc.
Parent Education for Infant Development
Pennypress, Inc.
Rocky Top Publications
SACRED FIRE
SCIENCE/HEALTH ABSTRACTS
Skidmore-Roth Publishing
SPECTRUM, A Guide to the Independent Press and
  Informative Organizations
Spectrum Publications
Spirit Press
SURVIVE & WIN
Unbridled Lust! Publishing
WORLD RAINFOREST REPORT
WORLD WILDLIFE FUND & THE CONSERVATION
  FOUNDATION LETTER
Worldwatch Institute

BLACK

AFRICA NEWS
Africa World Press, Inc.
African American Images
AFRICAN STUDIES
AFRO-HISPANIC REVIEW
AIM MAGAZINE
Amen-Ra Publishing Company
Ashley Books, Inc.
ASSEMBLING
Assembling Press
Author's Unlimited
Banner Press International, Inc.

BLACK AMERICAN LITERATURE FORUM
Black Light Fellowship
THE BLACK SCHOLAR: Journal of Black Studies and
  Research
BORDER/LINES
The Borgo Press
CALLALOO
The Carolina Wren Press
CHRYSANTHEMUM
Clarity Press
CODA: The Jazz Magazine
Colonial Press
COTTONWOOD
Council on Interracial Books For Children
THE CRESCENT REVIEW
Cultural Survival, Inc.
CULTURAL SURVIVAL QUARTERLY
E Publications
Eastern Caribbean Institute
The Edwin Mellen Press
Esoterica Press
The Everett Companies, Publishing Division
The Feminist Press at the City University of New York
Five Fingers Press
FIVE FINGERS REVIEW
FREE PRESS
Garrett Park Press
Gay Sunshine Press, Inc.
General Hall, Inc.
Goldfish Press
Gumbs & Thomas Publishers, Inc.
Hilltop Press
Hope Publishing House
Independence Publishers Inc.
Institute for Southern Studies
International Publishers Co. Inc.
INTERRACIAL BOOKS FOR CHILDREN BULLETIN
THE JOURNAL OF PAN AFRICAN STUDIES
Kitchen Table: Women of Color Press
LANCASTER INDEPENDENT PRESS
Langston Press
LIBERATION! Journal of Revolutionary Marxism
LINKS
Lotus Press, Inc.
Love Child Publishing
LuraMedia, Inc.
Maryland Historical Press
McKinzie Publishing Company
Mercer House Press
THE MILITANT
Mina Press
MINORITY PUBLISHERS EXCHANGE
NETWORK AFRICA FOR TODAY'S WORLD CITI-
  ZEN
OBSIDIAN II: BLACK LITERATURE IN REVIEW
Open Hand Publishing Inc.
Orbis Books
Organization for Equal Education of the Sexes, Inc.
  (OEES)
PASSAGER: A Journal of Remembrance and Discovery
Path Press, Inc.
PENNYWHISTLE PEOPLE PAPER
Pennywhistle Press
The Place In The Woods
R & E Publishers
RADICAL AMERICA
Readers International, Inc.
Reference Service Press
SAGE: A SCHOLARLY JOURNAL ON BLACK
  WOMEN
SCHMAGA
Sea Urchin Press
SEZ: A Multi-Racial Journal of Poetry & People's Culture
Shadow Press, U.S.A.
SHOOTING STAR REVIEW
SPARE RIB
SPENCER'S BOOK WORLD
Spencer's Int'l Enterprises Corp.

SPIT
Star Books, Inc.
Strawberry Hill Press
STREET VOICE
STRUGGLE: A Magazine of Proletarian Revolutionary
  Literature
Syracuse Cultural Workers
TATTOO ADVOCATE JOURNAL
Texas Monthly Press
Textile Bridge Press
Third World First
Three Continents Press, Inc.
Times Change Press
Tippy Reed Publishing
Unbridled Lust! Publishing
Unicorn Press
University of Massachusetts Press
VALLEY WOMEN'S VOICE
VIETNAM GENERATION: A Journal of Recent History
  and Contemporary Issues
W.I.M. Publications
Ward Hill Press
White Cliffs Media Company
Winston-Derek Publishers, Inc.
Witwatersrand University Press
WOMEN ARTISTS NEWS
World Promotions
Wright-Armstead Associates
Youth Policy Institute

WILLIAM BLAKE

Bandanna Books
BLAKE: AN ILLUSTRATED QUARTERLY
CROOKED ROADS
FARCE, Raleigh's Review of Alternative Arts
JOURNAL FOR ANTHROPOSOPHY
KELTIC FRINGE
Nemeton Publishing
NEW DEPARTURES
NEW HOPE INTERNATIONAL REVIEW
Station Hill Press
TATTOO ADVOCATE JOURNAL
Unbridled Lust! Publishing
THE WAVE
Wheel of Fire Press
Arnie Wolman Co.

BOOK ARTS, CALLIGRAPHY

Abattoir Editions
THE ALBANY REVIEW
AMERICAN BOOK COLLECTOR
ART CALENDAR
ART PAPERS
As Is/So & So Press
Beacon Press
Bet Alpha Editions
BOOK MARKETING UPDATE
Branden Publishing Company
Broken Jaw Press
Caliban Press
CALLIGRAPHY REVIEW
CAROUSEL
Chiron Press
CHIRON REVIEW
Cold-Drill Books
CRAFTS NSW
The F. Marion Crawford Memorial Society
DIAMOND HITCHHIKER COBWEBS
Dragon Cloud Books
11 X 13 - BROADSIDE
FARCE, Raleigh's Review of Alternative Arts
FINE PRINT: The Review for the Arts of the Book
FUSE MAGAZINE
G'RAPH
Guilt & Gardenias Press
The Hosanna Press
IMAGINATION MAGAZINE
Interalia/Design Books

Iron Gate Publishing
IT GOES ON THE SHELF
KALDRON, An International Journal Of Visual Poetry
and Language Art
Laughing Dog Press
LIGHTWORKS MAGAZINE
LOLA-FISH
MAINE IN PRINT
The Moretus Press, Inc.
Mortal Press
Mother of Ashes Press
MUSEUM & ARTS WASHINGTON
NEW HOPE INTERNATIONAL REVIEW
The New Humanity Press
New Levee Press
NiceTown
Now It's Up To You Publications
Nuclear Trenchcoated Subway Prophets Publications
Tom Ockerse Editions
Open Horizons Publishing Company
PAPERBACK PARADE
POETS. PAINTERS. COMPOSERS.
THE PRINTER
THE PRINTER'S DEVIL
Rarach Press
RIGHTING WORDS—THE JOURNAL OF LAN-
GUAGE AND EDITING
ROMANIAN REVIEW
THE ROMANTIST
SALON: A Journal of Aesthetics
Sang Froid Press
Saqi Books Publisher
Saxifrage Books
SCHMAGA
SO & SO
SPIT
Still Point Press
Strawberry Hill Press
Stride Publications
TATTOO ADVOCATE JOURNAL
Tuesday-Art Press
UMBRELLA
Unbridled Lust! Publishing
Visual Studies Workshop
Water Mark Press

BOOK COLLECTING, BOOKSELLING

ALA/SRRT NEWSLETTER
Algol Press
AMERICAN BOOK COLLECTOR
Applied Publishing
ASIAN LITERARY MARKET REVIEW
Avalanche Press
BAKER STREET GAZETTE
Baker Street Publications
Bluestocking Press
BOOK DEALERS WORLD
BOOK MARKETING UPDATE
BOOK NEWS & BOOK BUSINESS MART
BOOK TALK
BookNotes :(TM) Resources for Small & Self-Publishers
BP REPORT
Children Of Mary
THE CIVIL WAR NEWS
The F. Marion Crawford Memorial Society
FIDELIS ET VERUS
FINE PRINT: The Review for the Arts of the Book
Food For Thought Publications
Gallopade Publishing Group
The Gleniffer Press
Gryphon Publications
THE HAUNTED JOURNAL
HORIZONS BEYOND
HORIZONS WEST
Inkling Publications, Inc.
Jaffe Publishing Management Service
LITERARY RESEARCH: A Journal of Scholarly Method
& Technique

Peter Marcan Publications
Mosaic Press
Myriad Moods
THE MYSTERY FANCIER
MYSTERY READERS JOURNAL
The New Humanity Press
NEW WRITER'S MAGAZINE
NORTH CAROLINA LITERARY REVIEW
Open Horizons Publishing Company
PAPERBACK PARADE
Para Publishing
THE PIPE SMOKER'S EPHEMERIS
POISON PEN WRITERS NEWS
Premier Publishers, Inc.
THE PRINTER
READ, AMERICA!
Roberts Rinehart, Inc. Publishers
THE ROMANTIST
SCHMAGA
SCIENCE FICTION CHRONICLE
Selective Books, Inc.
Signature Books
SLEUTH JOURNAL
Space City Publications
SPENCER'S BOOK WORLD
Spencer's Int'l Enterprises Corp.
SPEX (Small Press Exchange)
Stonehouse Publications
TATTOO ADVOCATE JOURNAL
TOOK
Trigon Press
UMBRELLA
THE VAMPIRE JOURNAL
Village Books
WESTERN PUBLISHER
Women's Studies Librarian, University of Wisconsin
System
Wright-Armstead Associates
WRITER'S N.W.

MINIATURE BOOKS

Bandanna Books
The Gleniffer Press
THE HOWLING MANTRA
MESSAGE POST
Ocean Tree Books
Ox Head Press
THE PRINTER
Quotidian Publishers
ROMANIAN REVIEW
Running Press
SALT LICK
Santa Susana Press
Serpent & Eagle Press
TATTOO ADVOCATE JOURNAL
Theosophical Publishing House
Tuesday-Art Press
White Horse Press
Arnie Wolman Co.

BOOK REVIEWING

ABRAXAS
Ad-Lib Publications
AFFAIRE DE COEUR
AFRICA TODAY
AFRICAN STUDIES
Afta Press
AIM MAGAZINE
AKWEKON: A National Native American Literary &
Arts Journal
AKWEKON LITERARY JOURNAL
ALA/SRRT NEWSLETTER
ALABAMA LITERARY REVIEW
THE ALBANY REVIEW
Algol Press
THE AMARANTH REVIEW
Anderson Press
ANERCA/COMPOST

THE ANNALS OF IOWA
ANQ: A Quarterly Journal of Short Articles, Notes, and Reviews
THE ANTIGONISH REVIEW
APPALACHIAN HERITAGE
Applied Publishing
ARISTOS
ARTPAPER
Arts End Books
ASPECTS
ASYLUM
ATALANTA
AT-SOURCE-TA
THE AUTOGRAPH COLLECTOR'S MAGAZINE
BACKBOARD
BAD NEWZ
BAKER STREET GAZETTE
Baker Street Publications
BEAT SCENE
BELLES LETTRES
BIBLIOTHEQUE D'HUMANISME ET RENAISSANCE
BLACK RIVER REVIEW
Black Rose Books Ltd.
THE BLOOMSBURY REVIEW
Bluestocking Press
BOOK MARKETING UPDATE
THE BOOK REPORT: Journal for Junior & Senior High School Librarians
BOOK TALK
BookNotes :(TM) Resources for Small & Self-Publishers
THE BOOKWATCH
BREAKTHROUGH!
BRICK: A Journal Of Reviews
C.S.P. WORLD NEWS
CACANADADADA REVIEW
CAL NEWSLETTER
CANADIAN AUTHOR & BOOKMAN
THE CATALOG CONNECTION
CATALYST, A Magazine of Heart and Mind
Chatham Publishing Company
Children Of Mary
CHILDREN'S ALBUM
THE CHRISTIAN LIBRARIAN
THE...CHRONICLE
Citeaux Commentarii Cistercienses
CITEAUX: COMMENTARII CISTERCIENSES
THE CIVIL ABOLITIONIST
THE CIVIL WAR NEWS
CJE NEWSLETTER (Newsletter of the Coalition for Jobs & the Environment)
THE CLASSICAL OUTLOOK
THE CLIMBING ART
COLLAGES & BRICOLAGES
COME-ALL-YE
COMPUTER BOOK REVIEW
CONTEXT SOUTH
COTTONWOOD
Council on Interracial Books For Children
Crime and Social Justice Associates, Inc.
CROW MAGAZINE
THE CULTURAL FORUM
CULTURE CONCRETE
The Curlew Press
CURLEY
CUTBANK
THE DALHOUSIE REVIEW
DAUGHTER OF SARAH
DECEMBER MAGAZINE
The Denali Press
DESIGN BOOK REVIEW
DEWITT DIGEST & REVIEW
DIAMOND HITCHHIKER COBWEBS
DIRECTORY MARKETPLACE
DR. DOBB'S JOURNAL
THE DROOD REVIEW OF MYSTERY
Earthwise Publications
EDITOR'S DIGEST
En Passant Poetry Press

EN PASSANT/POETRY
English Language Literature Association
ENGLISH LITERATURE IN TRANSITION, 1880-1920
EUTHANASIA ROSES
EXQUISITE CORPSE: A Monthly of Books and Ideas
THE FEMINIST BOOKSTORE NEWS
FEMINIST COLLECTIONS: A QUARTERLY OF WOMEN'S STUDIES RESOURCES
FESTIVAL QUARTERLY
FIBERWORKS QUARTERLY
FIDELIS ET VERUS
FINE MADNESS
FINE PRINT: The Review for the Arts of the Book
FOCUS
FORESIGHT MAGAZINE
FREE PRESS
The FreeSolo Press
Frozen Waffles Press/Shattered Sidewalks Press; 25th Century Chapbooks
FUSE MAGAZINE
The Future Press
THE GALLEY SAIL REVIEW
GATEAVISA
GAVEA-BROWN
GO MAGAZINE
G'RAPH
GRASS ROOTS
GREEN MOUNTAINS REVIEW
The Guild Bindery Press, Inc.
THE HAUNTED JOURNAL
HOBBY BOOKWATCH (MILITARY, GUN & HOBBY BOOK REVIEW)
HORIZONS BEYOND
HORIZONS INTERCULTURELS
HORIZONS WEST
HORTICULTURA MODERNA
THE ICARUS REVIEW
ILLINOIS WRITERS REVIEW
IMAGINATION MAGAZINE
IMPETUS
INNER SEARCH
INVERTED-A HORN
THE IOWA REVIEW
IRISH FAMILY JOURNAL
IRISH LITERARY SUPPLEMENT
ISSUES
JACARANDA REVIEW
JAMES JOYCE BROADSHEET
JASON UNDERGROUND'S NOTES FROM THE TRASHCOMPACTOR
JENNINGS MAGAZINE
JEWISH LINGUISTIC STUDIES
JOURNAL FOR ANTHROPOSOPHY
KALDRON, An International Journal Of Visual Poetry and Language Art
KALEIDOSCOPE: INTERNATIONAL MAGAZINE OF LITERATURE, FINE ARTS, AND DISABILITY
LAKE EFFECT
LAKE SUPERIOR MAGAZINE
LAMBDA BOOK REPORT
LANCASTER INDEPENDENT PRESS
LECTOR
LEFT BUSINESS OBSERVER
LEFTHANDER MAGAZINE
LIBERATION! Journal of Revolutionary Marxism
LIFTOUTS
LIGHTWORKS MAGAZINE
LITERARY CENTER QUARTERLY
LITERARY SKETCHES
LIVING AMONG NATURE DARINGLY!
LIZZENGREASY
LLAMAS MAGAZINE
LOLA-FISH
The Lunchroom Press
M & T Publishing
MARK
THE MATCH
Meckler Corporation

MENU
MID-AMERICAN REVIEW
MIDLAND REVIEW
Midmarch Arts Press
MIDNIGHT ZOO
Misty Hill Press
THE MODEL & TOY COLLECTOR
MODERN HAIKU
MONDO HUNKAMOOGA
THE MONOCACY VALLEY REVIEW
MUSEUM & ARTS WASHINGTON
THE MYSTERY FANCIER
MYSTERY READERS JOURNAL
NAKED MAN
THE NEBRASKA REVIEW
NEEDLEPOINT PLUS
The Neither/Nor Press
NEW ART EXAMINER
NEW CONTRAST
THE NEW DANCE REVIEW
NEW DAY PUBLICATIONS
NEW DEPARTURES
NEW HOPE INTERNATIONAL REVIEW
The New Humanity Press
NEW PAGES: Access to Alternatives in Print
NEW WRITER'S MAGAZINE
NEWS FROM THE WHITE HOUSE
NOCTURNAL NEWS
NORTH CAROLINA LITERARY REVIEW
NORTH DAKOTA QUARTERLY
North Stone Press
NORTHCOAST VIEW MONTHLY MAGAZINE
THE NORTHERN REVIEW
NORTHWEST REVIEW
NOSTOC
Nuclear Trenchcoated Subway Prophets Publications
OBSIDIAN II: BLACK LITERATURE IN REVIEW
OHIO RENAISSANCE REVIEW
OHIO WRITER
OHIOANA QUARTERLY
Omega Cottonwood Press
Ontario Library Association
ORGANICA
OTISIAN DIRECTORY
OUR GENERATION
PAINTED BRIDE QUARTERLY
PANDORA
Para Publishing
PENNYWHISTLE PEOPLE PAPER
Pennywhistle Press
THE PLOUGH
POETIC SPACE: Poetry & Fiction
POETRY CANADA
POETRY FLASH
POETRY QUARTERLY
POETS. PAINTERS. COMPOSERS.
POISON PEN WRITERS NEWS
POTATO EYES
PRECISELY
PREVIEW: Professional and Reference Literature Review
PSYCHOANALYTIC BOOKS
THE PUCKERBRUSH REVIEW
PUNCTURE
QUARRY WEST
Quarterly Committee of Queen's University
QUEEN'S QUARTERLY: A Canadian Review
Quixote Press
RADIANCE, The Magazine For Large Women
RAG MAG
RARITAN: A Quarterly Review
RED CEDAR REVIEW
THE REDNECK REVIEW OF LITERATURE
REMARK
RESOURCES FOR FEMINIST RESEARCH/DOCU-
MENTATION SUR LA RECHERCHE FEMINISTE
RHODODENDRON
RIGHTING WORDS—THE JOURNAL OF LAN-
GUAGE AND EDITING

Rio Grande Press
ROMANIAN REVIEW
THE ROMANTIST
(ROWBOAT)
SACRED FIRE
ST. CROIX REVIEW
ST. LOUIS JOURNALISM REVIEW
SALMAGUNDI
SALOME: A JOURNAL FOR THE PERFORMING
ARTS
SAN FRANCISCO REVIEW OF BOOKS
SANDSCRIPT
SCARP
SCHMAGA
SCIENCE FICTION CHRONICLE
SCREAM MAGAZINE
SCRIPSI
SCRIVENER
SE LA VIE WRITER'S JOURNAL
SEA KAYAKER
THE SIGNAL - Network International
SLEUTH JOURNAL
THE SMALL POND MAGAZINE OF LITERATURE
aka SMALL POND
SMALL PRESS: The Magazine & Book Review of
Independent Publishing
THE SMALL PRESS BOOK REVIEW
SMALL PRESS NEWS
THE SMALL PRESS REVIEW
SOCIAL JUSTICE: A JOURNAL OF CRIME, CON-
FLICT, & WORLD ORDER
SOUTHERN HUMANITIES REVIEW
SOUTHERN QUARTERLY: A Journal of the Arts in the
South
SOUTHERN READER
Southwest Research and Information Center
SOUTHWESTERN DISCOVERIES
SPENCER'S BOOK WORLD
Spencer's Int'l Enterprises Corp.
SPEX (Small Press Exchange)
SPHINX—WOMEN'S INTERNATIONAL LITERARY/
ART REVIEW (IN ENGLISH)
STONE DRUM: An International Magazine of the Arts
STUDIO - A Journal of Christians Writing
STYLUS
SURVIVE & WIN
Swamp Press
TALISMAN: A Journal of Contemporary Poetry and
Poetics
TATTOO ADVOCATE JOURNAL
THE TEACHING LIBRARIAN
THEATRE DESIGN AND TECHNOLOGY
THEY WON'T STAY DEAD!
THIRD WORLD RESOURCES
TIGHTROPE
TOAD HIWAY
TOLE WORLD
TOOK
TRADITION
TRIVIUM
UMBRELLA
THE UNDERGROUND FOREST - LA SELVA SUB-
TERRANEA
UNION STREET REVIEW
UNIROD MAGAZINE
UNITED LUMBEE NATION TIMES
THE VAMPIRE JOURNAL
VIETNAM GENERATION: A Journal of Recent History
and Contemporary Issues
VIEWPOINT
THE VIRGINIA QUARTERLY REVIEW
W.I.M. Publications
THE WASHINGTON MONTHLY
WATERBURY CHESS CLUB BULLETIN
THE WAVE
WESTWORDS
THE WHOLE CHILE PEPPER
WITHIN & BEYOND

Witwatersrand University Press
Women's Studies Librarian, University of Wisconsin System
THE WORKBOOK
WORLD OF FANDOM MAGAZINE
THE WRITERS' BLOC*
WRITERS GAZETTE NEWSLETTER
WRITER'S GUIDELINES MAGAZINE
THE WRITER'S HAVEN
WRITERS INK
WRITER'S LIFELINE
THE YELLOW PAGES
Zagier & Urruty Publicaciones
ZYX

BRITISH COLUMBIA

The Barbizon Foundation
BARBIZON MAGAZINE
Epicenter Press Inc.
Resolution Business Press
Small Press International

BRONTES

COLLAGES & BRICOLAGES
NEW HOPE INTERNATIONAL REVIEW
Unbridled Lust! Publishing

BUDDHISM

ACTIVIST
The Archives Press
AREOPAGUS
ASPECTS
Beacon Press
BUDDHISM AT THE CROSSROADS
Buddhist Study Center Press
Buddhist Text Translation Society
Communitas Press
DHARMA COMBAT
Dharma Publishing
DIAMOND HITCHHIKER COBWEBS
DIE FAT PIGGY DIE
Frozen Waffles Press/Shattered Sidewalks Press; 25th Century Chapbooks
GESAR-Buddhism in the West
GREY CITY JOURNAL
INDIA CURRENTS
INNER SEARCH
THE JOURNAL OF THE ORDER OF BUDDHIST CONTEMPLATIVES
Karunaratne & Sons Ltd.
The New Humanity Press
Nuclear Trenchcoated Subway Prophets Publications
Omega Cottonwood Press
Orbis Books
Path Press
PROPER DHARMA SEAL
Rodmell Press
Stone Bridge Press
Tharpa Publications Limited
Theosophical Publishing House
Tiger Moon
Unbridled Lust! Publishing
Valley Lights Publications

BUSINESS & ECONOMICS

Aames-Allen Publishing Co.
Adams-Hall Publishing
Ad-Lib Publications
The Aegis Group
AFRICA NEWS
Alchemy Books
Almar Press
Alpine Guild
Amana Books
Amen Publishing Co.
American Business Consultants, Inc.
Applied Publishing
Atlantic Publishing Company

Author's Unlimited
Awareness Publications
Axiom Press, Publishers
Barr-Randol Publishing Co.
Beekman Publishers, Inc.
Bell Publishing
Bell Springs Publishing
Between The Lines
Bicentennial Era Enterprises
Black Rose Books Ltd.
Bluestocking Press
BOOK MARKETING UPDATE
BOOK NEWS & BOOK BUSINESS MART
BookNotes :(TM) Resources for Small & Self-Publishers
The Boxwood Press
BREAKTHROUGH!
Brennen Publishing Company
Brenner Information Group
Brick House Publishing Co., Inc.
BRONG'S BUSINESS SUCCESS NEWS
THE BULLISH CONSENSUS
C.C. Publishing Co.
CANADIAN MONEYSAVER
CANADIAN PUBLIC POLICY- Analyse de Politiques
Center For Self-Sufficiency
CENTRAL AMERICA REPORT
THE CHAOS NETWORK
Charter Oak Press
The Chicot Press
CJE NEWSLETTER (Newsletter of the Coalition for Jobs & the Environment)
Claycomb Press, Inc.
CLEANING BUSINESS MAGAZINE
Cleaning Consultants Serv's, Inc.
Coast to Coast Books Inc.
Coastline Publishing Company
Communication Creativity
Communication Trends Inc.
COMMUNITY DEVELOPMENT JOURNAL
COMMUNITY ECONOMICS
Community Service, Inc.
COMMUNITY SERVICE NEWSLETTER
Community Workshop on Economic Development
Consumer Education Research Center
The Consumer's Press, Inc.
Council on Interracial Books For Children
Craftsman Book Company
CreditPower Publishing Co.
Creighton-Morgan Publishing Group
D.B.A. Books
DAEDALUS, Journal of the American Academy of Arts and Sciences
D-Amp Publications
Diane Publishing Company
DIRECT RESPONSE
DIRECTORY MARKETPLACE
Dynamic Information Publishing
Eastern Caribbean Institute
ECONOMIC AFFAIRS
Energeia Publishing, Inc.
Robert Erdmann Publishing
ETC Publications
EUROPA 1992
The Evergreen Press
Fell Publishers, Inc.
Feris-Lee, Press
Festival Publications
FRASER FORUM
The Fraser Institute
FREE LIFE
Freelance Communications
Gain Publications
The P. Gaines Co., Publishers
Gallopade Publishing Group
Glenbridge Publishing Ltd.
The Global Press
Global Publishing Company
Good Hope Enterprises, Inc.

Bruce Gould Publications
Grapevine Publications, Inc.
Gravity Publishing
Great Western Publishing Company
Gringo Guides, Inc.
Grosvenor USA
Gulf Publishing Company
Hartford Press
Harvard Common Press
The Heather Foundation
Hickman Systems - New Age Books
Hoover Institution Press
Human Kinetics Pub. Inc.
IDEAS IN INVESTING
ILR Press
Image Industry Publications
Impact Publications
Independent Research Services of Irvine (IRIS/I)
INFOCUS
Infolib Resources
Information Requirements Clearinghouse
INITIATIV
Institute For Community Economics
Institute for Contemporary Studies/International Center
    for Economic Growth
Interlink Press, Inc.
International Consulting Associates, Inc.
International Information Associates
International Publishers Co. Inc.
INTERNATIONAL TAX AND BUSINESS LAWYER
The International University Press
INVESTMENT COLUMN QUARTERLY (newsletter)
Iris Communication Group
Jamenair Ltd.
JLA Publications, A Division Of Jeffrey Lant Associates,
    Inc.
JOURNAL OF SPORT MANAGEMENT
Karunaratne & Sons Ltd.
Knowledge, Ideas & Trends, Inc. (KIT)
Knowledge Systems, Inc.
LAKE SUPERIOR MAGAZINE
LANCASTER INDEPENDENT PRESS
Kent P. Larsen, Inc.
LATIN AMERICAN PERSPECTIVES
Law Forum Press
Lawco Ltd./Moneytree Publications
Leadership Education and Development, Inc.
LEFT BUSINESS OBSERVER
LIBERTY
Liberty Publishing Company, Inc.
Life Energy Media
Lincoln Publishing Company
LITTLE FREE PRESS
LLAMAS MAGAZINE
Lomond Publications Inc.
Lone Eagle Publishing Co.
Billy Jack Ludwig Holding Co.
M.H. Macy & Company
MAIL ORDER SUCCESS NEWSLETTER
Mark Publishing
Markgraf Publications Group
Mayhaven Publishing
Meridian Learning Systems
Metamorphous Press
Miles River Press
MIND YOUR OWN BUSINESS AT HOME
Morgan-Rand Publications, Inc.
Morningstar, Inc.
Mountain Publishing
MUTUAL FUND SOURCEBOOK
MUTUAL FUND VALUES
Myriad Moods
THE NEW AMERICAN
The New Humanity Press
New View Publications
New World Library
New Worlds Press
North American Students of Cooperation

THE NORTHERN REVIEW
Nuventures Publishing
Oakhill Press
Olde & Oppenheim Publishers
ONE EARTH
Open Horizons Publishing Company
OUR GENERATION
The Oxalis Group
Panther Press Ltd.
Park & Park Publishers, Inc.
PC Press
Phoenix Publishing
Photography Research Institute Carson Endowment
Piccadilly Books
The Place In The Woods
Planning/Communications
Point Publications
Pop Void Publications
POPULAR WOODWORKING
THE PRAGMATIST
THE PRAIRIE GOLD RUSH
Prima Publishing
Princess Publishing
PROCESSED WORLD
Programmed Press
Promontory Publishing, Inc.
Prudhomme Press
PSI Research/The Oasis Press
Publitec Editions
Puma Publishing Company
QP Publishing
Quarterly Committee of Queen's University
QUEEN'S QUARTERLY: A Canadian Review
QuikRef Publishing
Rand Editions/Tofua Press
The Rensselaerville Systems Training Center
RENT-TO-OWN ADVERTISING & PROMOTIONS
    PLANNER
RENT-TO-OWN COLLECTIONS MANAGER
RENT-TO-OWN LEGAL & FINANCIAL BULLETIN
Resolution Business Press
Ronin Publishing, Inc.
ST. CROIX REVIEW
Salvo Books
Sang Froid Press
Sauvie Island Press
Scribblers Publishing, Ltd.
THE SEARCH - JOURNAL FOR ARAB AND ISLAMIC
    STUDIES
Shadetree Publishing Inc.
Shiro Publishers
Simon & Pierre Publishing Co. Ltd.
THE SMALL POND MAGAZINE OF LITERATURE
    aka SMALL POND
Social Order Series
SOCIETY
Society for Individual Liberty
SoftServe Press
SPECTRUM, A Guide to the Independent Press and
    Informative Organizations
Spectrum Publications
SPENCER'S BOOK WORLD
Spencer's Int'l Enterprises Corp.
SPL Publishing Group
State of the Art Ltd.
Stonehouse Publications
Success Publications
SYBEX Computer Books
Sylvan Books
Targeted Communications
TechWest Publications
Ten Speed Press
Three Continents Press, Inc.
THRESHOLDS JOURNAL
THUNDERMUG REPORT
Todd Publications
Trestletree Publications
Triumph Books

Tryckeriforlaget
Union Square Press
University of Calgary Press
UPDATE
Upstart Publishing Company, Inc.
VANTAGE POINT
VDT NEWS
Venture Perspectives Inc.
Venture Press
Vestal Press Ltd
Village Books
Waterfront Center
WATERFRONT WORLD
Wilchester Publishing Company
Williamson Publishing Company, Inc.
Wind River Institute Press
Winslow Publishing
Witwatersrand University Press
Woodstead Press
WORK-AT-HOME REPORT
Writers Publishing Service Co.

CALIFORNIA

ACTIVIST
Androgyne Books
Ariel Vamp Press
As Is/So & So Press
THE AZOREAN EXPRESS
Ballena Press
Buddha Rose Publications
Carousel Press
Castle Peak Editions
Chatham Publishing Company
Chronicle Books
THE CLIMBING ART
COYDOG REVIEW
Devil Mountain Books
DOCTOR-PATIENT STUDIES
Downey Place Publishing House, Inc.
Dragon Cloud Books
El Montecito Oaks Press, Inc.
THE ELEPHANT-EAR
Excellence Enterprises
Falcon Press Publishing Company
Foghorn Press
The FreeSolo Press
Gravity Publishing
GREY CITY JOURNAL
Gringo Guides, Inc.
Gulf Publishing Company
Heritage West Books
Heyday Books
L.A. GANG BANG
Lahontan Images
Lexikos
The Live Oak Press
McNally & Loftin, Publishers
Men & Women of Letters
Micro Pro Litera Press
Midmarch Arts Press
R. & E. Miles
National Stereoscopic Association
Naturegraph Publishers, Inc.
NORTHCOAST VIEW MONTHLY MAGAZINE
Old West Publishing Co.
ORANGE COAST MAGAZINE
Panorama West Publishing
PENNYWHISTLE PEOPLE PAPER
Pennywhistle Press
Pine Cone Press
PROCESSED WORLD
PROPHETIC VOICES
Pruett Publishing Company
The Pterodactyl Press
RADIUS/Resources for Local Arts
Rand Editions/Tofua Press
Recreation Sales Publishing, Inc.
Redwood Press

RELIX
Riegel Publishing
Sand River Press
SCHMAGA
Scottwall Associates, Publishers
Sierra Oaks Publishing Company
Silver Skates Publishing
Genny Smith Books
Gibbs Smith, Publisher
SO & SO
Spirit Press
Star Rover House
Sunburst Press
TATTOO ADVOCATE JOURNAL
Ten Speed Press
Volcano Press, Inc
Western Tanager Press
Wide World Publishing/TETRA
Arnie Wolman Co.

CALLIGRAPHY

Bet Alpha Editions
CRAFTS NSW
FINE PRINT: The Review for the Arts of the Book
G'RAPH
KELTIC FRINGE
NEW HOPE INTERNATIONAL REVIEW
The Square-Rigger Press

CANADA

Aardvark Enterprises
AKWEKON: A National Native American Literary &
    Arts Journal
AKWEKON LITERARY JOURNAL
The Barbizon Foundation
BARBIZON MAGAZINE
BELLES LETTRES
Betelgeuse Books
Between The Lines
Black Rose Books Ltd.
BORDER/LINES
Borealis Press Limited
The Boston Mills Press
BOWBENDER
BREAKTHROUGH!
CANADIAN CHILDREN'S LITERATURE
CANADIAN DIMENSION
CANADIAN LITERATURE
CANADIAN PUBLIC POLICY- Analyse de Politiques
Chatham Publishing Company
CONNEXIONS DIGEST
Coteau Books
DESCANT
Dundurn Press Ltd
EDITOR'S DIGEST
Epicenter Press Inc.
Escart Press
Falcon Press Publishing Company
FRASER FORUM
The Fraser Institute
FUSE MAGAZINE
GAVEA-BROWN
Gavea-Brown Publications
Grade School Press
HORIZONS INTERCULTURELS
Infolib Resources
JOURNAL OF CANADIAN STUDIES/Revue d'etudes
    canadiennes
L.A.N.D.
LAKE SUPERIOR MAGAZINE
LIZZENGREASY
New Star Books Ltd.
NEWSLETTER (LEAGUE OF CANADIAN POETS)
THE NORTHERN REVIEW
ON BALANCE: MEDIA TREATMENT OF PUBLIC
    POLICY ISSUES
OUR GENERATION
Pigwidgeon Press

Plas Y Bryn Press
Porcepic Books
POTATO EYES
Pottersfield Press
PRAIRIE FIRE
THE PRAIRIE JOURNAL OF CANADIAN LITERA-
TURE
Prairie Journal Press
Prairie Publishing Company
PROEM CANADA
Ragweed Press, Inc.
Resolution Business Press
Rio Grande Press
Rocky Top Publications
Salvo Books
SE LA VIE WRITER'S JOURNAL
Small Press International
Sororal Publishing
Talon Books Ltd
TANDAVA
TATTOO ADVOCATE JOURNAL
TechWest Publications
Thirteen Colonies Press
Thunder Creek Publishing Co-operative
TOOK
THE TOWNSHIPS SUN
Tyro Publishing
University of Calgary Press
WEST COAST LINE: A Journal of Contemporary
Writing and its Modernist Sources
Whole Person Associates Inc.

CAREERS

Able Publishing
Artek Press, Inc.
Aslan Publishing
Brick House Publishing Co., Inc.
C.C. Publishing Co.
Charter Oak Press
D-Amp Publications
Energeia Publishing, Inc.
Grace and Goddess Unlimited
Impact Publishers, Inc.
Iron Gate Publishing
Knowledge, Ideas & Trends, Inc. (KIT)
Lionhouse Publishing Company
Littlebooks
Love Child Publishing
Organization for Equal Education of the Sexes, Inc.
(OEES)
Planning/Communications
Professional Publications, Inc.
Prudhomme Press
The Saunderstown Press
Sun Features Inc.
Union Square Press
Vesper Publishing
Williamson Publishing Company, Inc.

CARIBBEAN

Affiliated Writers of America, Inc.
CARIBBEAN NEWSLETTER
THE CARIBBEAN WRITER
DESDE ESTE LADO/FROM THIS SIDE
Esoterica Press
Sandberry Press
SOCIETE
Three Continents Press, Inc.
Unbridled Lust! Publishing
University of Massachusetts Press
WORLD PERSPECTIVES

LEWIS CARROLL

THE...CHRONICLE
DAYSPRING
FINE MADNESS
Hope Publishing House
MOONSTONE BLUE

NEW HOPE INTERNATIONAL REVIEW
NIGHT ROSES
Tuesday-Art Press

CARTOONS

ACTIVIST
ALASKA WOMEN
ANIMAL TALES
ANIME SHOWER SPECIAL
ATROCITY
Bean Avenue Publishing
BEAN ZINE
BELLYWASH
THE CIVIL ABOLITIONIST
CRAWLSPACE
DIAMOND HITCHHIKER COBWEBS
DIE FAT PIGGY DIE
Doggerel Press
EDITOR'S DIGEST
EMERALD CITY COMIX & STORIES
ESCAPE
EUTHANASIA ROSES
THE FINAL PAGE
FORBIDDEN LINES
GOKOOMA
G'RAPH
GREY CITY JOURNAL
HEATHENZINE
Heavy Bro Publishing Company
Ianus Publications, Inc.
IMAGINATION MAGAZINE
LAKE SUPERIOR MAGAZINE
THE LOOGIE
Nuclear Trenchcoated Subway Prophets Publications
OFFICE NUMBER ONE
The Organization
OTISIAN DIRECTORY
PLOTS
PM (The Pedantic Monthly)
POLITICALLY INCORRECT
POSTER-ZINE
PROTOCULTURE ADDICTS
Rio Grande Press
SACRED FIRE
SALON: A Journal of Aesthetics
SCREAM MAGAZINE
SE LA VIE WRITER'S JOURNAL
SEA KAYAKER
Signature Books
Stabur Press, Inc.
Star Books, Inc.
SUB STANDARD
TAPAS
TWISTED IMAGE NEWSLETTER
Unbridled Lust! Publishing
UNDERGROUND SURREALIST MAGAZINE
A VERY SMALL MAGAZINE
WORLD OF FANDOM MAGAZINE
X MAGAZINE
Zirlinson Publishing

CATHOLIC

Magnificat Press

CAVES

Cave Books
McNally & Loftin, Publishers

CELTIC

THE ALTERED MIND
The Archives Press
BALDER
CARN (a link between the Celtic nations)
Celtic Heritage Press, Inc.
Celtic League
COMPOST NEWSLETTER (CNL)
Cottage Books
Coxland Press

The F. Marion Crawford Memorial Society
DAYSPRING
DeerTrail Books
DHARMA COMBAT
DIAMOND HITCHHIKER COBWEBS
Dufour Editions Inc.
EPIPHANY JOURNAL
Esoterica, The Craft Press
GREEN EGG
IRISH FAMILY JOURNAL
IRISH LITERARY SUPPLEMENT
THE ISLAND
KELTIC FRINGE
KELTICA: THE INTER-CELTIC JOURNAL
Lindisfarne Press
LLEN CYMRU
Nemeton Publishing
NEWS FROM THE WHITE HOUSE
Nuclear Trenchcoated Subway Prophets Publications
O'Laughlin Press (Irish Genealogical Foundation)
THE ROMANTIST
SCHMAGA
Stone Circle Press
STUDIA CELTICA
Sunburst Press
TATTOO ADVOCATE JOURNAL
Unbridled Lust! Publishing
University Of Wales Press
Wolfhound Press

GEOFFREY CHAUCER

The Cobham and Hatherton Press

CHICAGO

Academy Chicago Publishers
ACTIVIST
B-CITY
Crossroads Communications
ECOSOCIALIST REVIEW
GREY CITY JOURNAL
Path Press, Inc.
WHITE WALLS: A Journal of Language and Art

CHICANO/A

THE AMERICA'S REVIEW
Arte Publico Press
As Is/So & So Press
THE AUTHOR
AZTLAN: A Journal of Chicano Studies
BELLES LETTRES
Bilingual Review/Press
BILINGUAL REVIEW/Revista Bilingue
Bilingue Publications
BOOK TALK
THE BOTTOM LINE PUBLICATIONS
CARTA ABIERTA
Chicano Studies Library Publications Unit
Chicano Studies Research Center Publications
Cinco Puntos Press
Community Workshop on Economic Development
Council on Interracial Books For Children
The Denali Press
DESDE ESTE LADO/FROM THIS SIDE
Dragon Cloud Books
Esoterica Press
Friends Of Tucson Pub Lib/The Maguey Press
Hope Publishing House
INTERRACIAL BOOKS FOR CHILDREN BULLETIN
Kitchen Table: Women of Color Press
LECTOR
Maize Press
MEXICAN STUDIES/ESTUDIOS MEXICANOS
Mina Press
NOTEBOOK/CUADERNO: A LITERARY JOURNAL
Ocean Tree Books
PENNYWHISTLE PEOPLE PAPER
Pennywhistle Press
The Place In The Woods

Pocahontas Press, Inc.
R & E Publishers
READ, AMERICA!
Red Crane Books
RED DIRT
Reference Service Press
Relampago Books Press
SEZ: A Multi-Racial Journal of Poetry & People's Culture
Shadow Press, U.S.A.
SO & SO
Society Of Authors
STONE DRUM: An International Magazine of the Arts
Strawberry Hill Press
STRUGGLE: A Magazine of Proletarian Revolutionary
  Literature
TATTOO ADVOCATE JOURNAL
TQS NEWS
TQS Publications (Tonatiuh - Quinto Sol International
  Inc.)
VALLEY WOMEN'S VOICE
VIETNAM GENERATION: A Journal of Recent History
  and Contemporary Issues
Volcano Press, Inc
Ward Hill Press

CHILDREN, YOUTH

Acadia Publishing Company
Achievement Press
Ad-Lib Publications
Agathon Press
AKWEKON: A National Native American Literary &
  Arts Journal
AKWEKON LITERARY JOURNAL
Alchemy Books
Alegra House Publishers
Alyson Publications, Inc.
American Audio Prose Library (non-print)
American Montessori Consulting
Amherst Writers & Artists Press, Inc.
Ancient City Press
Annick Press Ltd.
THE APPLE BLOSSOM CONNECTION
Ashley Books, Inc.
Auromere Books and Imports
Axelrod Publishing of Tampa Bay
THE BABY CONNECTION NEWS JOURNAL
Barefoot Press
B-CITY
BEGINNING: THE MAGAZINE FOR THE WRITER IN
  THE COMMUNITY
Belleridge Press
The Bess Press
Black & White & Read All Over Publishing Co.
Black Oak Press
Blue Crane Books
Blue Heron Publishing, Inc.
Blue Mouse Studio
Blue Water Publishing, Inc.
Bluestocking Press
Bold Productions
The Book Peddlers
THE BOOKWATCH
BORDER/LINES
Don Bosco Multimedia
Bright Ring Publishing
Brighton & Lloyd
BRILLIANT STAR
Bristlecone Publications
Broken Moon Press
C. Salway Press
Cajun Publishing
CANADIAN CHILDREN'S LITERATURE
Carlton Books
Carnival Enterprises
The Carolina Wren Press
Carousel Press
CASSIE'S EXPRESS
Center for Public Representation

757

The Center For Study of Multiple Birth
Centerplace Publishing Co.
Chandler & Sharp Publishers, Inc.
CHILDREN'S ALBUM
CHILDREN'S LITERATURE IN EDUCATION
Christmas
Claycomb Press, Inc.
CLUBHOUSE
The Clyde Press
COBBLESTONE: The History Magazine for Young People
The Cobham and Hatherton Press
Colormore, Inc.
Commonwealth Press Virginia
Comprehensive Health Education Foundation (CHEF)
Conscious Living
Cooperative Children's Book Center
Coteau Books
Cougar Books
Council For Indian Education
Cove View Press
CREATIVE KIDS
Creative With Words Publications (CWW)
CRICKET, THE MAGAZINE FOR CHILDREN
The Crossing Press
Dawn Sign Press
" "...A DEAD BEAT POET PRODUCTION
Dharma Publishing
Discovery Enterprises, Ltd.
Double M Press
Dovehaven Press, Ltd.
Down There Press
Dufour Editions Inc.
Dundurn Press Ltd
Eagle's View Publishing
East Eagle Press
Ed-U Press, Inc.
ENFANTAISIE: La Revue des Jeunes
Epicenter Press Inc.
EUTHANASIA ROSES
Excalibur Publishing
Falcon Press Publishing Company
The Feminist Press at the City University of New York
Five Star Publications
The Flying Pencil Press
FOCUS
FOR PARENTS
Four Walls Eight Windows
FREE SPIRIT: NEWS AND VIEWS ON GROWING UP
Free Spirit Publishing Inc.
Front Row Experience
The Future Press
The Galileo Press Ltd.
Gallaudet University Press
Gallopade Publishing Group
Gazelle Publications
GCBA Publishing
THE GIFTED CHILD TODAY
Gifted Education Press/The Reading Tutorium
The Gleniffer Press
Goodheart-Willcox Company
Grade School Press
Grayson Bernard Publishers, Inc.
Green Tiger Press, Inc.
Green Timber Publications
Grosvenor USA
GROWING WITHOUT SCHOOLING
Gryphon House, Inc.
Guarionex Press Ltd.
Hallelujah Press Publishing Company
Harrison House Publishers
Haypenny Press
Herald Press
Hilton Thomas Publishers, Inc.
Holt Associates, Inc.
HOME EDUCATION MAGAZINE
Homestead Publishing
Hong Kong Publishing Co., Ltd.

HOUSEWIFE-WRITER'S FORUM
Human Kinetics Pub. Inc.
Impact Publishers, Inc.
In Between Books
Indelible Inc.
Independence Publishers Inc.
Infolib Resources
INQ Publishing Co.
Interlink Publishing Group, Inc.
INTERRACIAL BOOKS FOR CHILDREN BULLETIN
Ironwood Publishing Company
J. Barnaby Distributors
Jalmar Press
Jayell Enterprises Inc.
JOURNAL FOR ANTHROPOSOPHY
JOURNAL OF CHILD AND YOUTH CARE
Kar-Ben Copies, Inc.
Kay Productions
Kenyette Productions
KIDS LIB NEWS
KIDSCIENCE
Knollwood Publishing Company
Korn Kompany
HJ Kramer, Inc
LAKE EFFECT
LANCASTER INDEPENDENT PRESS
Langston Press
Levite of Apache
Libertarian Press, Inc./American Book Distributors
Liberty Publishing Company, Inc.
THE LION AND THE UNICORN: A Critical Journal of Children's Literature
Lions Head Press
Little Buckaroo Press
Little People's Press
The Live Oak Press
Lollipop Power Books
Los Arboles Publications
THE LUNDIAN
Mage Publishers, Inc.
Magic Circle Press
Magical Music Express
Mar Vista Publishing Company
Mayhaven Publishing
MedLife Communications, Inc.
MEN'S REPORT
Meridional Publications
MERLYN'S PEN: The National Magazine of Student Writing
Metamorphous Press
Miles River Press
Mina Press
Misty Hill Press
Modern Media
Monroe Press
Moonlight Press
Morning Glory Press
John Muir Publications, Inc.
National Lilac Publishing Co.
New Harbinger Publications, Inc.
New Idea Press, Inc.
New Seed Press
NightinGale Resources
The Noble Press, Inc.
Northland Publishing Company
Nuventures Publishing
Oddo Publishing, Inc.
Old Harbor Press
ON THE LINE
Oness Press
Oneworld Publications Ltd.
Ontario Library Association
Open Hand Publishing Inc.
Open Horizons Publishing Company
Oregon Historical Society Press
OTTERWISE
Our Child Press
Outlaw Books

Pando Publications
Parable Press
Parent Education for Infant Development
Parenting Press, Inc.
Partners In Publishing
Passport Press
Path Press, Inc.
Peaceable Kingdom Press
Peak Output Unlimited
PEDIATRIC MENTAL HEALTH
Peel Productions
Pennypress, Inc.
PEREGRINE
Persona Publications
Perspectives Press
Philmar Press
Philomel Books
Piccolo Press
Pinchgut Press
PIP COLLEGE 'HELPS' NEWSLETTER
The Place In The Woods
THE PLOUGH
Pocahontas Press, Inc.
POETS. PAINTERS. COMPOSERS.
The Preservation Press
Press Gang Publishers
PROEM CANADA
Professional Counselor Books
Prospect Hill Press
Quotidian Publishers
"R"-Kids Publishing Co.
RADIANCE, The Magazine For Large Women
Ragweed Press, Inc.
Rama Publishing Co.
THE RATIONAL FEMINIST
READ, AMERICA!
Red Crane Books
Red Hen Press
Redbird Press, Inc.
Redeemer Resources
Roberts Rinehart, Inc. Publishers
Riverside Productions
Running Press
RYAN'S REVIEW
Sandberry Press
The Saunderstown Press
Scarf Press
Schneider Educational Products
SCHOOL MATES
Sea Fog Press, Inc.
Seabird Publishing
Security Seminars Press
Seed Center
Sentinel Books
Seven Locks Press
Sheer Joy! Press
SHINING STAR
Shoe Tree Press
Sierra Oaks Publishing Company
Silver Forest Publishing
Simon & Pierre Publishing Co. Ltd.
Small-Small Press
Spirit Press
Sports Support Syndicate
Star Books, Inc.
Stillpoint Publishing
STONE SOUP, The Magazine By Children
Storytime Ink International
Stride Publications
Sunstone Publications
Surrey Press
Symbiosis Books
Tabor Sarah Books
TATTOO ADVOCATE JOURNAL
TechWest Publications
Theytus Books Ltd.
Thistledown Press Ltd.
Thunder & Ink

Thunder Creek Publishing Co-operative
Tilbury House, Publishers
Tilton House
Top Of The Mountain Publishing
Treasure Chest Publications, Inc.
Tributary Press
Unbridled Lust! Publishing
Valley Lights Publications
Vanitas Press
Village Books
Volcano Press, Inc
Volunteer Publications
Ward Hill Press
WARM FUZZY NEWSLETTER
Warthog Publishing
WaterMark, Incorporated
Waterston Productions, Inc.
Wellberry Press
THE WESLEYAN ADVOCATE
Westport Publishers, Inc.
White Rose Publishing
Albert Whitman & Company
The George Whittell Memorial Press
Williamson Publishing Company, Inc.
B. L. Winch & Associates
WINDSCRIPT
Windsor Medallion Book Publishing Co.
Witwatersrand University Press
Wolfhound Press
Arnie Wolman Co.
WONDER TIME
Woodbine House
Woodsong Graphics Inc.
Writers House Press
WTI Publishing Co.
Youth Policy Institute

CHINA

ACTIVIST
AREOPAGUS
AXEFACTORY
The Bess Press
GREY CITY JOURNAL
Harbinger House
Kitchen Table: Women of Color Press
Mockingbird Press
The New Humanity Press
The Olive Press Publications
Orbis Books
Signal Books
Small Helm Press
SUBTEXT
Synergetic Press Inc.
Unbridled Lust! Publishing

SRI CHINMOY

INDIA CURRENTS
TATTOO ADVOCATE JOURNAL

KATE CHOPIN

LEGACY: A JOURNAL OF AMERICAN WOMEN
   WRITERS

CHRISTIANITY

Alleluia Press
APKL Publications
AREOPAGUS
ART'S GARBAGE GAZZETTE
Beacon Press
Blue Dolphin Press, Inc.
Don Bosco Multimedia
C.J.L. Press
CHASTITY AND HOLINESS
Children Of Mary
CHRISTIAN*NEW AGE QUARTERLY
THE...CHRONICLE
Comforter Publishing
DAUGHTER OF SARAH

759

DHARMA COMBAT
E.T.M. Publishing
EPIPHANY JOURNAL
FIDELIS ET VERUS
Friends United Press
THE HUMANIST
ISSUES
Jack October
JASON UNDERGROUND'S NOTES FROM THE
  TRASHCOMPACTOR
KOOKS MAGAZINE
LIGHTNING SWORD
Lindisfarne Press
LuraMedia, Inc.
Magnificat Press
MEDIA SPOTLIGHT
New Hope International
NEW HOPE INTERNATIONAL REVIEW
The New Humanity Press
OFFICE NUMBER ONE
THE OTHER SIDE
OTISIAN DIRECTORY
Out-Of-Kontrol Data Institute
PANDORA
The Pilgrim Press/United Church Press
Ridgeway Press
St. Bede's Publications
The Saunderstown Press
Art Paul Schlosser Books, Tapes, & Garbage Gazzette
Sheer Joy! Press
Sherwood Sugden & Company, Publishers
SHINING STAR
Small Helm Press
Social Order Series
Sparrow Hawk Press
SPECTRUM, A Guide to the Independent Press and
  Informative Organizations
Spectrum Publications
Star Books, Inc.
Stride Publications
THIRD WAY
Thirteen Colonies Press
Tiger Moon
Unbridled Lust! Publishing
Wordland
WTI Publishing Co.

CHRISTMAS

Aslan Publishing
LuraMedia, Inc.
Out West Publishing
Star Books, Inc.
Waterston Productions, Inc.

CITIES

Big River Publishing
Black Rose Books Ltd.
BORDER/LINES
BURWOOD JOURNAL
Career Publishing, Inc.
Carousel Press
DAYSPRING
DESIGN BOOK REVIEW
Ex Machina Publishing Company
Gallopade Publishing Group
Italica Press, Inc.
K
LAKE SUPERIOR MAGAZINE
LANDSCAPE
Peter Marcan Publications
Mendocino Book Partnership
The New Humanity Press
THE NORTHERN REVIEW
Ocean Tree Books
OUR GENERATION
PEDESTRIAN RESEARCH
Perivale Press
Redbird Press, Inc.

Sandhill Publications
SCHMAGA
Sentinel Books
Survival News Service
TATTOO ADVOCATE JOURNAL
TEMPORARY CULTURE
Texas Monthly Press
Unbridled Lust! Publishing
THE UNDERGROUND FOREST - LA SELVA SUB-
  TERRANEA
THE URBAN REVIEW
Waterfront Center
WATERFRONT WORLD
WOMEN AND ENVIRONMENTS

CIVIL RIGHTS

ART'S GARBAGE GAZZETTE
BALLOT ACCESS NEWS
Beacon Press
THE...CHRONICLE
COMMON SENSE
Crime and Social Justice Associates, Inc.
Cultural Survival, Inc.
CULTURAL SURVIVAL QUARTERLY
Cypres Publishing House
DHARMA COMBAT
Floricanto Press
GAUNTLET: Exploring the Limits of Free Expression
GOKOOMA
THE HAPPY THRASHER
Independence Publishers Inc.
Kitchen Table: Women of Color Press
LANCASTER INDEPENDENT PRESS
LINKS
THE LOOGIE
NATURALLY
The New Humanity Press
New Worlds Press
Organization for Equal Education of the Sexes, Inc.
  (OEES)
THE OTHER ISRAEL
Path Press, Inc.
P-FORM
PRISONER'S LEGAL NEWS
ROMANIAN REVIEW
Art Paul Schlosser Books, Tapes, & Garbage Gazzette
SOCIAL JUSTICE: A JOURNAL OF CRIME, CON-
  FLICT, & WORLD ORDER
Third World First
Tiger Moon
Unbridled Lust! Publishing
Youth Policy Institute

CIVIL WAR

Cherokee Publishing Company
Crossroads Publications, Inc.
The Devonshire Publishing Co.
EPM Publications, Inc.
The Everett Companies, Publishing Division
The New Humanity Press
Woodbine House

CLASSICAL STUDIES

Anderson Press
BALDER
Bandanna Books
Bliss Publishing Company, Inc.
Branden Publishing Company
CLASSICAL ANTIQUITY
THE CLASSICAL OUTLOOK
Coxland Press
DAEDALUS, Journal of the American Academy of Arts
  and Sciences
THE DALHOUSIE REVIEW
The Devonshire Publishing Co.
DIE FAT PIGGY DIE
Dufour Editions Inc.
ECHOS DU MONDE CLASSIQUE/CLASSICAL

VIEWS
The Edwin Mellen Press
Erespin Press
Hellas
HELLAS: A Journal of Poetry & the Humanities
JOURNAL FOR ANTHROPOSOPHY
K0SMOS
Misty Hill Press
Moon Publications, Inc.
ROMANIAN REVIEW
Salt Lick Press
Station Hill Press
Sunburst Press
University of Calgary Press
Westburg Associates, Publishers
White Horse Press
Witwatersrand University Press
Xenos Books

PAUL CLAUDEL

COLLAGES & BRICOLAGES

CLOTHING

Eagle's View Publishing
Tuesday-Art Press

COLLECTIBLES

Americana & Collectibles Press
FOLK ART MESSENGER
FOX VALLEY LIVING
GemStone Press
Gryphon Publications
KREATURE COMFORTS
NiceTown
THE OVERLOOK CONNECTION
PAPERBACK PARADE
Placebo Press
Gibbs Smith, Publisher
THEY WON'T STAY DEAD!
Tomart Publications

COLOR

COLOR WHEEL
DIAMOND HITCHHIKER COBWEBS
DIGIT
Epicenter Press Inc.
JOURNAL FOR ANTHROPOSOPHY
JOURNAL OF BORDERLAND RESEARCH
LAKE SUPERIOR MAGAZINE
Nuclear Trenchcoated Subway Prophets Publications
WTI Publishing Co.

COLORADO

American Source Books
Crossroads Communications
Falcon Press Publishing Company
Greenridge Press
Homestead Publishing
Johnson Books
Mountain Automation Corporation
Old West Publishing Co.
PHASE AND CYCLE
Pruett Publishing Company
Recreation Sales Publishing, Inc.
Renaissance House Publishers (a division of Jende-Hagan, Inc.)
Rocky Mountain Writers Guild, Inc.
The Vic Press

COMICS

ACTIVIST
AGOG
AKWEKON: A National Native American Literary & Arts Journal
AKWEKON LITERARY JOURNAL
Alan Wofsy Fine Arts
Alternating Crimes Publishing
AMAZING HEROES

ANIME SHOWER SPECIAL
ASSEMBLING
Assembling Press
ATROCITY
BABY SUE
BAD NEWZ
BAKER STREET GAZETTE
Baker Street Publications
BEAN ZINE
BELLYWASH
BIG HAMMER
Bogg Publications
BOYS & GIRLS GROW UP
COLUMBUS FREE PRESS
THE COMICS JOURNAL
COMICS REVUE
Cosmic Circus Productions
DIAMOND HITCHHIKER COBWEBS
Dolphin-Moon Press
THE DUCKBURG TIMES
EMERALD CITY COMIX & STORIES
EUTHANASIA ROSES
Fantagraphics Books
FAT TUESDAY
FATHOMS BELOW
FISH DRUM MAGAZINE
FORBIDDEN LINES
The Future Press
Futurum Forlag
GATEAVISA
GATES OF PANDRAGON
GAUNTLET: Exploring the Limits of Free Expression
GET STUPID
GOOD CLEAN FUN
THE GOOFUS OFFICE GAZETTE
GREY CITY JOURNAL
THE HAUNTED JOURNAL
HEATHENZINE
HORIZONS BEYOND
Ianus Publications, Inc.
THE IDEOLOGY OF MADNESS
IMAGINATION MAGAZINE
IMPETUS
JUDY
Kitchen Sink Press
KREATURE COMFORTS
L.A. GANG BANG
LANCASTER INDEPENDENT PRESS
LESBIAN CONTRADICTION-A Journal of Irreverent Feminism
LIZZENGREASY
THE LOOGIE
LOVE & ROCKETS
MANGAJIN
Manuscript Press
MINNE HA! HA!
Mosaic Press
MOTORBOOTY MAGAZINE
NANCY'S MAGAZINE
NBM Publishing Company
The Neither/Nor Press
The New Humanity Press
Nuclear Trenchcoated Subway Prophets Publications
THE OVERLOOK CONNECTION
PIG IRON
Popular Reality Press
POSTER-ZINE
PROCESSED WORLD
PROTOCULTURE ADDICTS
QUIMBY
Quimby Archives
The Real Comet Press
RIP OFF COMIX
The Runaway Spoon Press
Scarf Press
SCHMAGA
THE SCIENCE FICTION CONVENTION REGISTER
SCREAM MAGAZINE

761

SLEUTH JOURNAL
SOUND CHOICE
THE SPIRIT
SPIRIT MAGAZINE
SPIT
Star Books, Inc.
StarLance Publications
SteelDragon Press
STEVE CANYON MAGAZINE
Synergetic Press Inc.
TATTOO ADVOCATE JOURNAL
THEY WON'T STAY DEAD!
Tiptoe Literary Service
Unbridled Lust! Publishing
UNDERGROUND SURREALIST MAGAZINE
THE UNINTELLIGENCER
UNIROD MAGAZINE
THE VAMPIRE JOURNAL
VIRGIN MEAT
Wild & Woolley
Woodbine House
WORLD OF FANDOM MAGAZINE
X MAGAZINE

COMMUNICATION, JOURNALISM

ACTIVIST
THE ALBANY REVIEW
Algol Press
AMATEUR COMPUTERIST
and books
ANTI-ISOLATION/NEW ARTS IN WISCONSIN
Arjuna Library Press
Astonisher Press
Autonomedia, Inc.
THE BABY CONNECTION NEWS JOURNAL
Bakhtin's Wife Publications
Banana Productions
Beacon Press
Beekman Publishers, Inc.
Between The Lines
Blue Heron Press
Blue Heron Publishing, Inc.
Bonus Books, Inc.
BORDER/LINES
Branden Publishing Company
BRILLIANT IDEAS FOR PUBLISHERS
BYLINE
Caddo Gap Press
Campaign For Press & Broadcasting Freedom
CANADIAN AUTHOR & BOOKMAN
Cassell Communications Inc.
THE CHRISTIAN LIBRARIAN
THE...CHRONICLE
Communication Creativity
Communication Trends Inc.
Communicom Publishing Company
Comprehensive Health Education Foundation (CHEF)
The Counter-Propaganda Press
CREATIVITY CONNECTION
CULTURE CONCRETE
DAEDALUS, Journal of the American Academy of Arts and Sciences
DAYSPRING
DE NAR
" "...A DEAD BEAT POET PRODUCTION
DIE FAT PIGGY DIE
Distinctive Publishing Corp.
DOUBLE HARNESS
EDITOR'S DIGEST
EXETER STUDIES IN AMERICAN & COMMONWEALTH ARTS
Free Association Books (FAB)
FREE INQUIRY
FREE PRESS
FREE PRESS NETWORK
Freelance Communications
FREELANCE WRITER'S REPORT
FUSE MAGAZINE

The Future Press
Futurum Forlag
Gallopade Publishing Group
GATEAVISA
General Hall, Inc.
G'RAPH
GREY CITY JOURNAL
Guarionex Press Ltd.
Hartford Press
INDEX ON CENSORSHIP
Intercultural Press, Inc.
INTERLIT
THE INTERNATIONAL UNIVERSITY POETRY QUARTERLY
Iris Communication Group
ISI Press
JLA Publications, A Division Of Jeffrey Lant Associates, Inc.
KALDRON, An International Journal Of Visual Poetry and Language Art
KETTERING REVIEW
Kumarian Press, Inc.
LANCASTER INDEPENDENT PRESS
LAUGHING BEAR NEWSLETTER
The Philip Lesly Company
LIGHTWORKS MAGAZINE
THE LOOGIE
LOST GENERATION JOURNAL
MARKETS ABROAD
Maupin House
MEDIA HISTORY DIGEST
MEDIA SPOTLIGHT
Mercer House Press
Metamorphous Press
The Middleburg Press
MIND MATTERS REVIEW
MINORITY RIGHTS GROUP REPORTS
MinRef Press
Multi Media Arts
MY LIFE DEPENDS ON YOU
NETWORK AFRICA FOR TODAY'S WORLD CITIZEN
New Harbinger Publications, Inc.
The New Humanity Press
New Levee Press
NEW PAGES: Access to Alternatives in Print
NEW WRITER'S MAGAZINE
New York Zoetrope Inc.
Newton-Cline Press
NOOK NEWS CONFERENCES AND KLATCHES BULLETIN
THE NOOK NEWS CONTESTS AND AWARDS BULLETIN
THE NOOK NEWS MARKET BULLETIN
NOOK NEWS REVIEW OF WRITERS' PUBLICATIONS
OHIO WRITER
ON BALANCE: MEDIA TREATMENT OF PUBLIC POLICY ISSUES
Open Horizons Publishing Company
Oxbridge Communications, Inc.
P.O. Publishing Company
Para Publishing
Parent Education for Infant Development
The Place In The Woods
Players Press, Inc.
Pocahontas Press, Inc.
Porcepic Books
PROCESSED WORLD
THE PUBLIC RELATIONS QUARTERLY
PUBLISHING TRENDS & TRENDSETTERS
PUNCTURE
QSKY Publishing/Independent Publishing
QUARTOS MAGAZINE
Quixote Press
RAMPIKE
RED BASS
RESOURCE-MAG, FOR PUBLISHING PROFESSION-

ALS
RIGHTING WORDS—THE JOURNAL OF LANGUAGE AND EDITING
Rio Grande Press
ROMANIAN REVIEW
THE ROTKIN REVIEW
S.E.T. FREE: The Newsletter Against Television
ST. LOUIS JOURNALISM REVIEW
San Luis Quest Press
Sang Froid Press
SE LA VIE WRITER'S JOURNAL
SINSEMILLA TIPS (Domestic Marijuana Journal)
SOCIALISM AND DEMOCRACY
SOUND CHOICE
SPECTRUM, A Guide to the Independent Press and Informative Organizations
Spectrum Publications
The Speech Bin, Inc.
SURVIVE & WIN
Targeted Communications
TATTOO ADVOCATE JOURNAL
Texas Monthly Press
Top Of The Mountain Publishing
TOWARD FREEDOM
THE TRIBUNE
Unbridled Lust! Publishing
Union Square Press
Univelt, Inc.
University of Calgary Press
VIETNAM GENERATION: A Journal of Recent History and Contemporary Issues
THE WASHINGTON MONTHLY
Winslow Publishing
WOMEN AND LANGUAGE
WRITERS CONNECTION
THE WRITER'S HAVEN
WRITERS' JOURNAL
WRITER'S LIFELINE
WRITER'S N.W.
THE WRITER'S NOOK NEWS
The Writers' Nook Press

COMMUNISM, MARXISM, LENINISM

Autonomedia, Inc.
Banner Press International, Inc.
Bergin & Garvey Publishers
CANADIAN SLAVONIC PAPERS
Children Of Mary
FIDELIS ET VERUS
Free Association Books (FAB)
FREE INQUIRY
FREE PRESS
GUARDIAN
Hoover Institution Press
International Publishers Co. Inc.
LEFT BUSINESS OBSERVER
LEFT CURVE
LIBERATION! Journal of Revolutionary Marxism
LOVE AND RAGE, A Revolutionary Anarchist Newsmonthly
THE MILITANT
MIND MATTERS REVIEW
Moscow Publishing Enterprises
THE NEW AMERICAN
The New Humanity Press
Orbis Books
PEOPLE'S CULTURE
POETRY OF THE PEOPLE
PRISONER'S LEGAL NEWS
PROCESSED WORLD
QUIXOTE, QUIXOTL
RADICAL AMERICA
ROMANIAN REVIEW
SALMAGUNDI
Semiotext Foreign Agents Books Series
SEMIOTEXT(E)
Small Helm Press
SOCIALISM AND DEMOCRACY

SPECTRUM, A Guide to the Independent Press and Informative Organizations
Spectrum Publications
STRUGGLE: A Magazine of Proletarian Revolutionary Literature
SURVIVE & WIN
Times Change Press
TOWARD FREEDOM
Unbridled Lust! Publishing
VIEWPOINT
Walnut Publishing Co., Inc.
WW Publishers
Xenos Books

COMMUNITY

THE ALBANY REVIEW
ARIZONA COAST
ASPECTS
AT-SOURCE-TA
Bear Tribe Publishing
Big River Publishing
Black Rose Books Ltd.
Bottom Dog Press
BREAKTHROUGH!
City Spirit Publications
CJE NEWSLETTER (Newsletter of the Coalition for Jobs & the Environment)
COMMUNITIES
Community Collaborators
COMMUNITY DEVELOPMENT JOURNAL
COMMUNITY ECONOMICS
Community Service, Inc.
COMMUNITY SERVICE NEWSLETTER
Community Workshop on Economic Development
COYDOG REVIEW
Crime and Social Justice Associates, Inc.
Devil Mountain Books
DOUBLE HARNESS
ECOSOCIALIST REVIEW
The Findhorn Press
Five Fingers Press
FIVE FINGERS REVIEW
FOX VALLEY LIVING
FOXFIRE
Foxfire Press
FRIENDS OF PEACE PILGRIM
Futurum Forlag
GATEAVISA
GRASS ROOTS
GREEN MULTILOGUE
Grosvenor USA
HANDICAP NEWS
The Heather Foundation
Herald Press
HORIZONS INTERCULTURELS
Impact Publishers, Inc.
Institute For Community Economics
Institute for Southern Studies
ISRAEL HORIZONS
JOURNAL FOR ANTHROPOSOPHY
THE JOURNAL OF PAN AFRICAN STUDIES
KETTERING REVIEW
THE KIBBUTZ JOURNAL
Knowledge Systems, Inc.
LAKE SUPERIOR MAGAZINE
LANCASTER INDEPENDENT PRESS
Langston Press
THE LUNDIAN
THE MADISON INSURGENT
Marlborough Publications
Mendocino Book Partnership
Modern Media
Naturist Foundation
New Age Press
Night Owl Publishers
North American Students of Cooperation
NORTHCOAST VIEW MONTHLY MAGAZINE
ONE EARTH

THE OTHER SIDE
OTTER
OUR GENERATION
Pigwidgeon Press
THE PLOUGH
ProActive Press
R & E Publishers
RADIUS/Resources for Local Arts
Rainfeather Press
Red Alder Books
RFD
RIDGE REVIEW
RURAL NETWORK ADVOCATE
SACRED FIRE
Seven Locks Press
SILVER WINGS
SOCIAL ANARCHISM: A Journal of Practice And
Theory
SOCIAL JUSTICE: A JOURNAL OF CRIME, CON-
FLICT, & WORLD ORDER
SOCIAL POLICY
Stillpoint Publishing
SURVIVE & WIN
Times Change Press
TRENDS & PREDICTIONS ANALYST
Trentham Books
Valley Lights Publications
Volcano Press, Inc
WHISPERING PALM
WILDFIRE: A NETWORKING MAGAZINE
THE WINDHAM PHOENIX
Witwatersrand University Press
Arnie Wolman Co.
WOMEN AND ENVIRONMENTS
Wright-Armstead Associates
Youth Policy Institute

COMPUTERS, CALCULATORS

Achievement Press
Adams-Hall Publishing
AIGA Publications
All American Press
AMATEUR COMPUTERIST
AMC Publishing
and books
Astonisher Press
Athelstan Publications
Autonomedia, Inc.
Avery Publishing Group, Inc.
Bell Publishing
Blue Heron Press
THE BOOKWATCH
Brenner Information Group
Calgre Press, Division of Calgre Inc.
CANADIAN AUTHOR & BOOKMAN
Career Publishing, Inc.
THE CHRISTIAN LIBRARIAN
CIP Communications
COMPUTER BOOK REVIEW
COMPUTER EDUCATION NEWS
COMPUTER GAMING WORLD
Computer Musician Coalition
COMPUTING SYSTEMS
CONSTRUCTION COMPUTER APPLICATIONS
NEWSLETTER (CCAN)
Construction Industry Press
CONTRACTOR PROFIT NEWS (CPN)
Copyright Information Services
Cove View Press
CRYPTOSYSTEMS JOURNAL
DAEDALUS, Journal of the American Academy of Arts
and Sciences
DR. DOBB'S JOURNAL
Dragon Disks
EXUM Publishing
Fast Forward Publishing
FISICA
Free Association Books (FAB)

Freelance Communications
Frontline Publications
Gallopade Publishing Group
GATEAVISA
GCBA Publishing
GENEALOGICAL COMPUTING
GGL Educational Press
Goldstein & Blair
Goodheart-Willcox Company
Grapevine Publications, Inc.
Harbor Publishing Company
Hartford Press
IM-Press
Infinite Savant Publishing
INFOCUS
INITIATIV
J.P.R. Instone Publications
Jamenair Ltd.
JOURNAL OF COMPUTING IN HIGHER EDUCATION
JOURNAL OF THEORETICAL PSYCHOLOGY
Kumarian Press, Inc.
Lion Press
M & T Publishing
Maple Hill Press, Ltd.
Mayhaven Publishing
Meckler Corporation
Microdex Bookshelf
MICROSOLUTIONS
Middle Coast Publishing
Modular Information Systems
MUSIC OF THE SPHERES
My Mother's House - Aitini Talo
NET
NEW HOPE INTERNATIONAL REVIEW
New Levee Press
NEW WRITER'S MAGAZINE
New York Zoetrope Inc.
OUR WRITE MIND
Pacific Information Inc.
Packet Press
Paladin Enterprises, Inc.
PalmTree Publishers
Dr. Homer W. Parker, P.E.
PC Press
PC PUBLISHING
Peachpit Press, Inc.
PERSONAL PUBLISHING
Polymath Systems
Porcepic Books
THE PRINTER'S DEVIL
PRIVACY JOURNAL
PROCESSED WORLD
Professional Resource Exchange, Inc.
Programmed Press
PUCK!
QSKY Publishing/Independent Publishing
The Rensselaerville Systems Training Center
Resolution Business Press
ST. MAWR
Scribblers Publishing, Ltd.
Seacoast Information Services
SMALL PRESS: The Magazine & Book Review of
Independent Publishing
STARWIND
Sun Features Inc.
Surrey Press
SURVIVE & WIN
SYBEX Computer Books
Synthetix
Targeted Communications
TATTOO ADVOCATE JOURNAL
Technical Communications Associates
TECHNICALITIES
TechWest Publications
Tiptoe Literary Service
Top Of The Mountain Publishing
Unbridled Lust! Publishing
VDT NEWS

Ventana Press
THE WAVE
White Cliffs Media Company
Whitehorse
WHOLE EARTH REVIEW
WORK-AT-HOME REPORT
Xyzyx Information Corporation
Zirlinson Publishing

JOSEPH CONRAD

ENGLISH LITERATURE IN TRANSITION, 1880-1920
NIGHT ROSES
Three Continents Press, Inc.
UMI Research Press

CONSERVATION

ABBEY NEWSLETTER: Bookbinding & Conservation
Abbey Publications
ADIRONDAC
Adirondack Mountain Club, Inc.
AMERICAN FORESTS
The American Hiking Society
THE AMICUS JOURNAL
THE ANIMALS' AGENDA
AQUATERRA, WATER CONCEPTS FOR THE ECO-
    LOGICAL SOCIETY
ARIZONA GREAT OUTDOORS
AT-SOURCE-TA
Beacon Press
BikePress U.S.A./BikePress Canada
BLACK MOUNTAIN REVIEW
Bliss Publishing Company, Inc.
BOWBENDER
The Boxwood Press
Brick House Publishing Co., Inc.
CAL NEWSLETTER
CALLI'S TALES, The Quarterly for Animal Lovers of
    All Ages
Cave Books
Chelsea Green Publishing Company
Cheshire Books
City Spirit Publications
CJE NEWSLETTER (Newsletter of the Coalition for Jobs
    & the Environment)
COMMUNITY ECONOMICS
CONNECTICUT NATURALLY
CURRENTS
Dog-Eared Publications
DOUBLE HARNESS
ECOSOCIALIST REVIEW
Envirographics
ENVIRONMENTAL OPPORTUNITIES
FOX VALLEY LIVING
Fulcrum, Inc.
Harbinger House
HIGH COUNTRY NEWS
HIPPO
HOME RESOURCE MAGAZINE
Homestead Publishing
IMMANENT FACE
Institute For Community Economics
Institute for Southern Studies
Island Press
Johnson Books
LANCASTER INDEPENDENT PRESS
THE LATHAM LETTER
The Latona Press
THE LETTER PARADE
Lexikos
MESSAGE POST
The Mountaineers Books
Naturist Foundation
NEW JERSEY NATURALLY
New Worlds Press
NEW YORK NATURALLY
THE NORTHERN ENGINEER
THE NORTHERN REVIEW
Oregon State University Press

PEDESTRIAN RESEARCH
Pineapple Press, Inc.
Pruett Publishing Company
Rainfeather Press
The Rateavers
Redwood Press
Roberts Rinehart, Inc. Publishers
Rocky Top Publications
ROMANIAN REVIEW
SAMISDAT
Sandhill Publications
Sang Froid Press
SCHMAGA
SEA KAYAKER
SEED SAVERS EXCHANGE
THE SMALL POND MAGAZINE OF LITERATURE
    aka SMALL POND
Genny Smith Books
SOULLESS STRUCTURES
Southern Resources Unlimited
SPECTRUM, A Guide to the Independent Press and
    Informative Organizations
Spectrum Publications
SPIT
Stone Wall Press, Inc
SURVIVE & WIN
Unbridled Lust! Publishing
The George Whittell Memorial Press
THE WILD FOODS FORUM
Wineberry Press
WISCONSIN RESTAURATEUR
Women's Times Publishing
WORLD RAINFOREST REPORT
Worldwatch Institute
Zagier & Urruty Publicaciones

CONSTUCTION

Brick House Publishing Co., Inc.
CIP Communications
CJE NEWSLETTER (Newsletter of the Coalition for Jobs
    & the Environment)
CONSTRUCTION   COMPUTER   APPLICATIONS
    NEWSLETTER (CCAN)
Construction Industry Press
CONTRACTOR PROFIT NEWS (CPN)
GRDA Publications
Name That Team!
The Olive Press Publications
ROMANIAN REVIEW

CONSUMER

Achievement Press
Almar Press
Alpenglow Press
and books
Barclay House
Blue Sky Marketing, Inc.
Bluestocking Press
Bomb Shelter Propaganda
Bonus Books, Inc.
THE BOOKWATCH
Branden Publishing Company
Brenner Information Group
THE BULLISH CONSENSUS
CANADIAN MONEYSAVER
THE CATALOG CONNECTION
Catbird Press
Center for Public Representation
Center For Self-Sufficiency
Ceres Press
COMMUNITY ECONOMICS
Consumer Education Research Center
The Consumer's Press, Inc.
The Counter-Propaganda Press
DRUG INTERACTIONS AND UPDATES
Fast Forward Publishing
FOX VALLEY LIVING
The Chas. Franklin Press

GCBA Publishing
GemStone Press
The Globe Pequot Press
Grapevine Publications, Inc.
Gravity Publishing
Guarionex Press Ltd.
Institute For Community Economics
Liberty Publishing Company, Inc.
Loiry/Bonner Press
MALLIFE
Maradia Press
MESSAGE POST
THE NATIONAL FARM DIRECTORY
The New Humanity Press
NUTRITION ACTION HEALTHLETTER
PEDESTRIAN RESEARCH
Prima Publishing
PRIVACY JOURNAL
RENT-TO-OWN COLLECTIONS MANAGER
Roblin Press
Shadetree Publishing Inc.
SINGLES ALMANAC
THE SMALL POND MAGAZINE OF LITERATURE
 aka SMALL POND
SPENCER'S BOOK WORLD
Spencer's Int'l Enterprises Corp.
Stratton Press
SURVIVE & WIN
Targeted Communications
TRUE FOOD
Upper Access Inc.
VEGETARIAN JOURNAL
Whitehorse
Winslow Publishing
Woodbine House

COOKING

Alchemy Books
American Cooking Guild
Anaphase II
Avery Color Studios
Axelrod Publishing of Tampa Bay
The Bess Press
Blue Crane Books
Blue Dolphin Press, Inc.
Blue Sky Marketing, Inc.
Ceres Press
Circumpolar Press
The Clyde Press
COMPOST NEWSLETTER (CNL)
COOKBOOK SERIES
Countryman Press
Culinary Arts Ltd.
S. Deal & Assoc.
Drift Creek Press
E-Heart Press, Inc.
EPM Publications, Inc.
Explorer's Guide Publishing
Farragut Publishing Co.
Fell Publishers, Inc.
Foghorn Press
Fresh Press
The Globe Pequot Press
GOOD COOKING SERIES
Teri Gordon, Publisher
Gravity Publishing
THE HAPPY THRASHER
HarCroft Publishing Company
Harvard Common Press
Hoffman Press
Infolib Resources
Island Publishers
JEWISH VEGETARIANS OF NORTH AMERICA
Kar-Ben Copies, Inc.
HJ Kramer, Inc
LAKE SUPERIOR MAGAZINE
Owen Laughlin Publishers
Liberty Publishing Company, Inc.

Lionhouse Publishing Company
LIZZENGREASY
New Chapter Press
NightinGale Resources
Northland Publishing Company
Oak Plantation Press
George Ohsawa Macrobiotic Foundation Press
Out West Publishing
Panorama Publishing Company
Pen & Ink Press
Penfield Press
Persona Publications
Pickle Point Publishing
Pigwidgeon Press
Quicksilver Productions
Red Crane Books
RedBrick Press
Running Press
Sasquatch Books
Sentinel Books
SPROUTLETTER
The Sulgrave Press
Talon Books Ltd
Tiptoe Literary Service
TRUE FOOD
Tudor Publishers, Inc.
Twin Peaks Press
Tyro Publishing
Upper Access Inc.
VEGETARIAN JOURNAL
The Vegetarian Resource Group
Ventana Press
Vista Publishing Company
Westport Publishers, Inc.
THE WILD FOODS FORUM
Williamson Publishing Company, Inc.
Windsong Press
Woodbridge Press
Yankee Books

CO-OPS

Carousel Press
CJE NEWSLETTER (Newsletter of the Coalition for Jobs
 & the Environment)
ECOSOCIALIST REVIEW
The New Humanity Press
New Society Publishers
North American Students of Cooperation
TRENDS & PREDICTIONS ANALYST
Unbridled Lust! Publishing
Arnie Wolman Co.

COUNTER-CULTURE, ALTERNATIVES, COM-MUNES

ACTIVIST
THE AGE OF AQUARIUS
THE ALTERED MIND
and books
AREOPAGUS
ARTISTAMP NEWS
ARTPAPER
Avalanche Press
BAD NEWZ
BAHLASTI PAPER
Bakhtin's Wife Publications
BARBIZON MAGAZINE
Bear Tribe Publishing
BEAT SCENE
BIG HAMMER
BORDER/LINES
BOTH SIDES NOW
CAMPUS REVIEW
CANVAS CHAUTAUQUA MAGAZINE
Cassandra Press
CHAKRA
Cheshire Books
City Spirit Publications
CJE NEWSLETTER (Newsletter of the Coalition for Jobs

& the Environment)
COMMUNITIES
COMMUNITY ECONOMICS
Community Workshop on Economic Development
COMPOST NEWSLETTER (CNL)
CONNECTICUT NATURALLY
CROOKED ROADS
The Denali Press
DHARMA COMBAT
DIAMOND HITCHHIKER COBWEBS
DIE FAT PIGGY DIE
ECOSOCIALIST REVIEW
The Edwin Mellen Press
EUTHANASIA ROSES
THE FICTION REVIEW
FIVE LEAVES LEFT
FUSE MAGAZINE
Futurum Forlag
GATEAVISA
Grace and Goddess Unlimited
GRASS ROOTS
GREEN MULTILOGUE
GREY CITY JOURNAL
THE GROWING EDGE MAGAZINE
GYPSY
HEATHENZINE
HIPPO
Homeward Press
HOWLING DOG
HUBRIS
IllumiNet Press
INFINITE ONION
INITIATIV
INKBLOT
Institute For Community Economics
INTERNATIONAL ART POST
JOURNAL FOR ANTHROPOSOPHY
JOURNAL OF BORDERLAND RESEARCH
THE KEROUAC CONNECTION
THE KIBBUTZ JOURNAL
KICK IT OVER
KIDS LIB NEWS
KREATURE COMFORTS
THE LAME MONKEY MANIFESTO
THE (LIBERTARIAN) CONNECTION
LIGHTWORKS MAGAZINE
LITTLE FREE PRESS
LIZZENGREASY
THE LOOGIE
Loompanics Unlimited
LOVE AND RAGE, A Revolutionary Anarchist News-
   monthly
MAXINE'S PAGES
MEMES
MESSAGE POST
Middle Coast Publishing
MINNE HA! HA!
Mr. Information
MSRRT NEWSLETTER
NATURALLY
NEW AGE DIGEST
NEW DEPARTURES
The New Humanity Press
NEW JERSEY NATURALLY
New Society Publishers
A NEW WORLD RISING
New Worlds Press
NEW YORK NATURALLY
NEWS FROM THE WHITE HOUSE
Nuclear Trenchcoated Subway Prophets Publications
Ocean Tree Books
Oness Press
OPEN ROAD
THE OTHER ISRAEL
THE OTHER SIDE
OTISIAN DIRECTORY
PEOPLE'S CULTURE
P-FORM

PIG IRON
THE PLOUGH
Pottersfield Press
PROCESSED WORLD
PROFANE EXISTENCE
Progressive Education
PROGRESSIVE PERIODICALS DIRECTORY/UPDATE
Purple Heather Publications
Quixote Press
RADICAL AMERICA
THE RAT RACE RECORD
RED DIRT
RESONANCE
RFD
RURAL NETWORK ADVOCATE
SACRED FIRE
Savant Garde Workshop
SCHMAGA
SCIENCE/HEALTH ABSTRACTS
Semiotext Foreign Agents Books Series
SEMIOTEXT(E)
SINSEMILLA TIPS (Domestic Marijuana Journal)
Small Press International
SMALL PRESS NEWS
SOUND CHOICE
SPECTRUM—The Wholistic News Magazine
SPECTRUM REVIEW
SPROUTLETTER
STAR ROUTE JOURNAL
THE STARK FIST OF REMOVAL
SURVIVE & WIN
Syracuse Cultural Workers
Targeted Communications
TATTOO ADVOCATE JOURNAL
Times Change Press
Unbridled Lust! Publishing
THE UNDERGROUND FOREST - LA SELVA SUB-
   TERRANEA
THE UNINTELLIGENCER
UNIROD MAGAZINE
Upper Access Inc.
Valley Lights Publications
VIETNAM GENERATION: A Journal of Recent History
   and Contemporary Issues
Ward Hill Press
Wheel of Fire Press
WHOLE EARTH REVIEW
WILDFIRE: A NETWORKING MAGAZINE
THE WRITERS' BAR-B-Q
Youth Policy Institute
ZERO HOUR
Zirlinson Publishing
ZZAJ-SYNCHRONOLOGY

CRAFTS, HOBBIES

ABBEY NEWSLETTER: Bookbinding & Conservation
Abbey Publications
Aeolus Press, Inc.
Alchemy Books
All American Press
Almar Press
Altamont Press, Inc.
AMERICAN AMATEUR JOURNALIST
American Council for the Arts/ACA Books
Americana & Collectibles Press
APPALACHIAN HERITAGE
ART CALENDAR
ART HAZARDS NEWS
ATHA NEWSLETTER
THE AUTOGRAPH COLLECTOR'S MAGAZINE
Baker Publishing
Bear Creek Publications
Bright Ring Publishing
Broadway Press
Capra Press
CHESS LIFE
Christmans
CLUBHOUSE

COLLECTRIX
COSMOPOLITAN CONTACT
Cottontail Publications
Council For Indian Education
CRAFTS NSW
Culinary Arts Ltd.
DESIGN AND TECHNOLOGY TEACHING
Design Enterprises of San Francisco
Dirigo Books, Inc.
Dos Tejedoras Fiber Arts Publications
Dundurn Press Ltd
DuReve Publications
Eagle's View Publishing
EPM Publications, Inc.
Robert Erdmann Publishing
ETC Publications
The Evergreen Press
FIBERARTS
FIBERWORKS QUARTERLY
THE FRONT STRIKER BULLETIN
GemStone Press
GENII
The Gleniffer Press
The Globe Pequot Press
GRASS ROOTS
Guarionex Press Ltd.
THE HAPPY THRASHER
HOBBY BOOKWATCH (MILITARY, GUN & HOBBY
   BOOK REVIEW)
HOB-NOB
Hunter Publishing, Co.
Index House
Interlink Publishing Group, Inc.
International Marine Publishing Co.
JUDY
KITE LINES
LAKE SUPERIOR MAGAZINE
Levite of Apache
Mark Publishing
Mayapple Press
Mayhaven Publishing
MCN Press
Mermaid Press
MESSAGE POST
Midmarch Arts Press
R. & E. Miles
THE MODEL & TOY COLLECTOR
Moon Publications, Inc.
Myriad Moods
Naturegraph Publishers, Inc.
NAUTICAL BRASS
N-B-T-V
NEEDLEPOINT PLUS
NEW HOPE INTERNATIONAL REVIEW
The New Humanity Press
Night Owl Publishers
NightinGale Resources
Northland Publishing Company
Open Chain Publishing
ORNAMENT, Ancient Contemporary Ethnic
Parabola Books
Pebble Press
Penfield Press
Petroglyph Press, Ltd.
Piccadilly Books
POPULAR WOODWORKING
Potentials Development, Inc.
POTPOURRI PARTY-LINE
THE PRAIRIE GOLD RUSH
THE PRESIDENTS' JOURNAL
THE PRINTER'S DEVIL
Profile Press
Prospect Hill Press
QSKY Publishing/Independent Publishing
The Quilt Digest Press
RE Publications
Robinson Press, Inc.
Rockwell Publishing

Rocky Top Publications
Ross Books
Scentouri, Publishing Division
Sierra Trading Post
ST Publications/Book Division
Storytime Ink International
Success Publishing
Sun Designs
Sunstone Press
Sunstone Publications
Sylvan Books
Tamal Vista Publications
Tambra Publishing
TATTOO ADVOCATE JOURNAL
Thirteen Colonies Press
Timber Press
TOLE WORLD
TRADITION
Twin Peaks Press
Ultimate Secrets
Ultralight Publications, Inc.
UNITED LUMBEE NATION TIMES
Vestal Press Ltd
Vitreous Group/Camp Colton
WALKING-STICK NOTES
WESTART
WHISPERING WIND MAGAZINE
Williamson Publishing Company, Inc.
WOMEN ARTISTS NEWS
Woodbine House
Woodsong Graphics Inc.
YE OLDE NEWES

CREATIVITY

THE EMSHOCK LETTER
IMAGINATION MAGAZINE
Savant Garde Workshop

CRIME

Academy Chicago Publishers
Carroll & Graf Publishers, Inc.
THE...CHRONICLE
COALITION FOR PRISONERS' RIGHTS NEWSLET-
   TER
Crime and Social Justice Associates, Inc.
CULTWATCH RESPONSE
Gryphon Publications
THE HAPPY THRASHER
HARDBOILED DETECTIVE
HEALING PATH
Lyceum Books, Inc.
MAXINE'S PAGES
THE MYSTERY FANCIER
Mystery Notebook Editions
The New Humanity Press
PAPERBACK PARADE
Pine Hall Press
SCREAM MAGAZINE
Security Seminars Press
SLEUTH JOURNAL
SOCIAL JUSTICE: A JOURNAL OF CRIME, CON-
   FLICT, & WORLD ORDER
THEY WON'T STAY DEAD!
Tudor Publishers, Inc.
Unbridled Lust! Publishing
Woldt Publishing

CRITICISM

ABRAXAS
ACTA VICTORIANA
AGADA
ALABAMA LITERARY REVIEW
ALASKA QUARTERLY REVIEW
THE ALBANY REVIEW
Algol Press
AMELIA
AMERICAN LITERATURE
American Poets In Profile Series

768

769

MODERN LANGUAGE QUARTERLY
THE MYSTERY FANCIER
The Neither/Nor Press
NEW ART EXAMINER
THE NEW DANCE REVIEW
NEW DEPARTURES
THE NEW ENGLAND QUARTERLY
The New England Quarterly, Inc.
NEW GERMAN REVIEW: A Journal of Germanic Studies
New Hope International
NEW HOPE INTERNATIONAL REVIEW
NEW HOPE INTERNATIONAL ZINE
The New Humanity Press
THE NEW PRESS
THE NIHILISTIC REVIEW
NORTH DAKOTA QUARTERLY
North Stone Press
NORTHEAST
NORTHERN LIGHTS STUDIES IN CREATIVITY
THE NORTHERN REVIEW
NOTEBOOK/CUADERNO: A LITERARY JOURNAL
NOTES FROM THE UNDERGROUND
Open Book Publications, A Division of Station Hill Press
ORO MADRE
OUTPOSTS POETRY QUARTERLY
Oyez
PARTISAN REVIEW
PAUNCH
THE PENNSYLVANIA REVIEW
PENNYWHISTLE PEOPLE PAPER
Pennywhistle Press
Pequod Press
Pessimism Press, Inc.
P-FORM
PHOEBE, THE GEORGE MASON REVIEW
PIG IRON
PLAINS POETRY JOURNAL (PPJ)
PLOUGHSHARES
POET & CRITIC
POETICS JOURNAL
POETRY FLASH
THE POETRY MISCELLANY
POETRY NOTTINGHAM: The International Magazine of Today's Poetry
POETRY WALES
POETS. PAINTERS. COMPOSERS.
THE POISONED PEN
PORTLAND REVIEW
POSTMODERN CULTURE
THE PRAIRIE JOURNAL OF CANADIAN LITERATURE
Prairie Journal Press
PRECISELY
Quarterly Committee of Queen's University
QUEEN'S QUARTERLY: A Canadian Review
Quixote Press
RACKHAM JOURNAL OF THE ARTS AND HUMANITIES (RaJAH)
RARITAN: A Quarterly Review
The Real Comet Press
Reality Studios
THE REDNECK REVIEW OF LITERATURE
REPRESENTATIONS
Re/Search Publications
REVUE CELFAN REVIEW
RIGHTING WORDS—THE JOURNAL OF LANGUAGE AND EDITING
THE ROCK HALL REPORTER
ROMANIAN REVIEW
THE ROMANTIST
(ROWBOAT)
Ruddy Duck Press
The Runaway Spoon Press
ST. CROIX REVIEW
ST. LOUIS JOURNALISM REVIEW
SALMAGUNDI
SALOME: A JOURNAL FOR THE PERFORMING ARTS
SALON: A Journal of Aesthetics
Samisdat
SCHMAGA
SCRIPSI
SCRIVENER
The Segue Foundation
Semiotext Foreign Agents Books Series
SEMIOTEXT(E)
SENECA REVIEW
SEWANEE REVIEW
THE SHAKESPEARE NEWSLETTER
Sherwood Sugden & Company, Publishers
THE SIGNAL - Network International
THE SINGLE HOUND
Slate Press
Sleepy Hollow Press
SOUTH DAKOTA REVIEW
SOUTHERN HUMANITIES REVIEW
SOUTHERN QUARTERLY: A Journal of the Arts in the South
SOUTHWESTERN DISCOVERIES
Station Hill Press
STEVE CANYON MAGAZINE
Still Point Press
Stride Publications
Studia Hispanica Editors
SURVIVE & WIN
TALISMAN: A Journal of Contemporary Poetry and Poetics
Talon Books Ltd
TATTOO ADVOCATE JOURNAL
TELOS
THALIA: Studies in Literary Humor
Theatre Communications Group
13th MOON
Three Continents Press, Inc.
THE THREEPENNY REVIEW
Thunder Creek Publishing Co-operative
TOOK
Tower Press
TSUNAMI
Turnstone Press
Unbridled Lust! Publishing
THE UNDERGROUND FOREST - LA SELVA SUBTERRANEA
Vesta Publications Limited
VIETNAM GENERATION: A Journal of Recent History and Contemporary Issues
VIEWPOINT
Volunteer Publications
W.D.C. PERIOD
WEST COAST LINE: A Journal of Contemporary Writing and its Modernist Sources
WEST HILLS REVIEW: A WALT WHITMAN JOURNAL
Westburg Associates, Publishers
WALT WHITMAN QUARTERLY REVIEW
WILLOW SPRINGS
Window Publications
THE WISHING WELL
Witwatersrand University Press
THE WORCESTER REVIEW
WORLD OF FANDOM MAGAZINE
Writers Forum
WRITERS GAZETTE NEWSLETTER
Xenos Books
THE YALE REVIEW
Yoknapatawpha Press
Zirlinson Publishing

CRYSTALS

Borderland Sciences Research Foundation
DHARMA COMBAT
THE DREAMWEAVER
Metagnosis Publications
Mystic Crystal Publications
Top Of The Mountain Publishing

TRENDS & PREDICTIONS ANALYST
Valley Lights Publications

CUBA

Affiliated Writers of America, Inc.
Ediciones El Gato Tuerto
EL GATO TUERTO
Esoterica Press
THE MILITANT
The Place In The Woods
Smyrna Press
SOCIETE
SUBTEXT
WORLD PERSPECTIVES

CULTS

The Archives Press
ASPECTS
Beacon Press
THE...CHRONICLE
COMPOST NEWSLETTER (CNL)
Coxland Press
CULT OBSERVER
CULTIC STUDIES JOURNAL
CULTWATCH RESPONSE
DHARMA COMBAT
DIAMOND HITCHHIKER COBWEBS
KOOKS MAGAZINE
THE LOOGIE
MAXINE'S PAGES
Nuclear Trenchcoated Subway Prophets Publications
OFFICE NUMBER ONE
OTISIAN DIRECTORY
Out-Of-Kontrol Data Institute
SOCIETE
Unbridled Lust! Publishing

CULTURE

ACTIVIST
AERIAL
ALASKA WOMEN
THE ALBANY REVIEW
AMERICAN POP
ARISTOS
ART CALENDAR
ARTPAPER
Autonomedia, Inc.
BALDER
Bay Press
Beacon Press
Bergin & Garvey Publishers
Between The Lines
Big River Publishing
Birch Brook Press
BORDER/LINES
Borealis Press Limited
BOSTON REVIEW
Brook House Press, Inc.
BUDDHISM AT THE CROSSROADS
CACANADADADA REVIEW
Chandler & Sharp Publishers, Inc.
THE CHAOS NETWORK
THE CHARIOTEER
CHILDREN'S ALBUM
CJE NEWSLETTER (Newsletter of the Coalition for Jobs
  & the Environment)
The Clyde Press
COLUMBUS FREE PRESS
THE COOL TRAVELER
CORONA
Coxland Press
COYDOG REVIEW
CRAWLSPACE
CULTURE CONCRETE
DAEDALUS, Journal of the American Academy of Arts
  and Sciences
DESCANT
DESDE ESTE LADO/FROM THIS SIDE

DHARMA COMBAT
DIAMOND HITCHHIKER COBWEBS
THE DRAMA REVIEW
Eastern Caribbean Institute
EUTHANASIA ROSES
Exile Press
FACES: The Magazine About People
Five Fingers Press
FIVE FINGERS REVIEW
Four Walls Eight Windows
FOX VALLEY LIVING
FUSE MAGAZINE
GATEAVISA
GREEN MOUNTAINS REVIEW
GREY CITY JOURNAL
Gumbs & Thomas Publishers, Inc.
HEALING PATH
Hope Publishing House
HORIZONS INTERCULTURELS
HORIZONTES
HURRICANE ALICE
IKON
IKON, Inc.
THE IMMIGRANT
IMPULSE
Integral Publishing
Intercultural Press, Inc.
INTERCULTURE
Interlink Publishing Group, Inc.
JOURNAL FOR ANTHROPOSOPHY
THE JOURNAL OF PAN AFRICAN STUDIES
K
KALDRON, An International Journal Of Visual Poetry
  and Language Art
THE KIBBUTZ JOURNAL
KMT, A Modern Journal of Ancient Egypt
KMT Communications
KREATURE COMFORTS
LAKE SUPERIOR MAGAZINE
LANCASTER INDEPENDENT PRESS
LEFT CURVE
LEGACIES IN TIME
THE LETTER PARADE
LINKS
LUNA TACK
Lyceum Books, Inc.
M.H. Macy & Company
THE MADISON INSURGENT
MAXINE'S PAGES
MEDIA SPOTLIGHT
METAPHOR
MIND MATTERS REVIEW
Naturegraph Publishers, Inc.
NETWORK AFRICA FOR TODAY'S WORLD CITI-
  ZEN
THE NEW DANCE REVIEW
NEW DEPARTURES
THE NEW ENGLAND QUARTERLY
The New England Quarterly, Inc.
NightinGale Resources
NORTH DAKOTA QUARTERLY
NORTHCOAST VIEW MONTHLY MAGAZINE
THE NORTHERN REVIEW
Northland Publishing Company
Nuclear Trenchcoated Subway Prophets Publications
OTISIAN DIRECTORY
Penfield Press
PEOPLE'S CULTURE
P-FORM
PIG IRON
Pittore Euforico
POETS. PAINTERS. COMPOSERS.
Pop Void Publications
POSTMODERN CULTURE
ProLingua Associates
Royal Purcell, Publisher
R & E Publishers
RACKHAM JOURNAL OF THE ARTS AND HUMANI-

771

TIES (RaJAH)
RADIANCE, The Magazine For Large Women
RADIUS/Resources for Local Arts
THE REDNECK REVIEW OF LITERATURE
REPRESENTATIONS
RE/SEARCH
Re/Search Publications
ROMANIAN REVIEW
ST. CROIX REVIEW
SALMAGUNDI
SCHMAGA
Semiotext Foreign Agents Books Series
SEMIOTEXT(E)
SHMATE
Shmate Press
THE SIGNAL - Network International
SINSEMILLA TIPS (Domestic Marijuana Journal)
Slate Press
Small Helm Press
Snowbird Publishing Company
TATTOO ADVOCATE JOURNAL
Texas Monthly Press
THIRD WAY
Third World First
Thunder Creek Publishing Co-operative
TOOK
TQS Publications (Tonatiuh - Quinto Sol International Inc.)
TRADITION
Unbridled Lust! Publishing
THE UNDERGROUND FOREST - LA SELVA SUB-TERRANEA
THE UTNE READER
VIETNAM GENERATION: A Journal of Recent History and Contemporary Issues
W.D.C. PERIOD
Ward Hill Press
Westburg Associates, Publishers
The Westphalia Press
Wheel of Fire Press
WHISPERING WIND MAGAZINE
WHITE WALLS: A Journal of Language and Art
WISCONSIN ACADEMY REVIEW
Working Press
XENOPHILIA
Xenos Books

DADA

A
ACTIVIST
AILERON, A LITERARY JOURNAL
AMERICAN LIVING
American-Canadian Publishers, Inc.
ANDROGYNE
ANERCA/COMPOST
Arjuna Library Press
ART INFORMATION REPORT
ART/LIFE
Art/Life Limited Editions
Asylum Arts
BAD NEWZ
Banana Productions
BELLYWASH
Black Tie Press
BLADES
BLANK GUN SILENCER
BLUE HORSE
Blue Horse Publications
Bomb Shelter Propaganda
CACANADADADA REVIEW
CHAKRA
COLLAGES & BRICOLAGES
DADA/SURREALISM
" "...A DEAD BEAT POET PRODUCTION
DHARMA COMBAT
DIAMOND HITCHHIKER COBWEBS
11 X 13 - BROADSIDE
THE EMSHOCK LETTER

FAT TUESDAY
THE FICTION REVIEW
FINE MADNESS
FORBIDDEN LINES
Forty-Seven Books
Frozen Waffles Press/Shattered Sidewalks Press; 25th Century Chapbooks
FUSE MAGAZINE
The Future Press
GET STUPID
GOING GAGA
THE GOPHERWOOD REVIEW
GREY CITY JOURNAL
GYPSY
Happy Rock Press
HIPPO
HUNGRY ZIPPER
IMPETUS
Indelible Inc.
INKBLOT
Inkblot Publications
JOURNAL OF REGIONAL CRITICISM
K
KALDRON, An International Journal Of Visual Poetry and Language Art
Kitchen Sink Press
Last Generation/Underground Editions
LIGHTWORKS MAGAZINE
THE LOOGIE
LOST AND FOUND TIMES
LOST GENERATION JOURNAL
Luna Bisonte Prods
MALLIFE
manic d press
MASSACRE
MEMES
My Mother's House - Aitini Talo
The Neither/Nor Press
NEW DEPARTURES
NNIDNID: SURREALITY
North Stone Press
NRG
Nuclear Trenchcoated Subway Prophets Publications
Ocean View Books
OTISIAN DIRECTORY
PANJANDRUM POETRY JOURNAL
PAPER RADIO
P-FORM
Phrygian Press
PIG IRON
Pig Iron Press
POETRY OF THE PEOPLE
POETS. PAINTERS. COMPOSERS.
The Press of the Third Mind
PROCESSED WORLD
Pygmy Forest Press
RAMPIKE
(ROWBOAT)
SALT LICK
Salt Lick Press
Savant Garde Workshop
SCHMAGA
SCREE
Sober Minute Press
Station Hill Press
Thunder City Press
TOAD HIWAY
UMI Research Press
Unbridled Lust! Publishing
Vortex Editions
WE MAGAZINE
We Press
Wheel of Fire Press
Wordcraft
X MAGAZINE
XENOPHILIA
Zirlinson Publishing
ZYX

773

NORTHERN LIGHTS STUDIES IN CREATIVITY
THE NORTHERN REVIEW
Nuclear Trenchcoated Subway Prophets Publications
OBSIDIAN II: BLACK LITERATURE IN REVIEW
THE PACIFIC REVIEW
Personabooks
PHOEBE, THE GEORGE MASON REVIEW
PIG IRON
The Pikestaff Press
Players Press, Inc.
Poetry Wales Press, Ltd.
Bern Porter Books
THE POTTERSFIELD PORTFOLIO
PRISM international
THE PROSPECT REVIEW
Quintessence Publications & Printing Museum
RACKHAM JOURNAL OF THE ARTS AND HUMANI-
TIES (RaJAH)
RAMBUNCTIOUS REVIEW
RAMPIKE
Resource Publications, Inc.
ROMANIAN REVIEW
The Runaway Spoon Press
SALOME: A JOURNAL FOR THE PERFORMING
ARTS
Sea Urchin Press
THE SHAKESPEARE NEWSLETTER
Simon & Pierre Publishing Co. Ltd.
SKYLARK
Slate Press
Smyrna Press
SOUTHERN QUARTERLY: A Journal of the Arts in the
South
Spectrum Productions
SPIT
STIFLED YAWN: A Magazine Of Contemporary Writing
STREAM LINES, MN JOURNAL OF CREATIVE
WRITING
STRUGGLE: A Magazine of Proletarian Revolutionary
Literature
Synergetic Press Inc.
Talon Books Ltd
Tejas Art Press
Ten Penny Players, Inc.
THEATER
Theatre Arts
Theatre Communications Group
THEATRE DESIGN AND TECHNOLOGY
Three Continents Press, Inc.
Thunder Creek Publishing Co-operative
TOOK
'2D' (DRAMA AND DANCE)
UMI Research Press
UPDATE
Valentine Publishing & Drama Co.
VANTAGE POINT
Vesta Publications Limited
Waterfront Press
Westburg Associates, Publishers
Wheel of Fire Press
Wild East Publishing Co-operative Limited
WordWorkers Press
Xenos Books

DREAMS

AMERICAN WRITING: A MAGAZINE
Asylum Arts
BEAN ZINE
Challenger Press
CITY RANT
COMPOST NEWSLETTER (CNL)
CRAWLSPACE
" "...A DEAD BEAT POET PRODUCTION
DHARMA COMBAT
DIAMOND HITCHHIKER COBWEBS
DREAM INTERNATIONAL QUARTERLY
THE DREAMWEAVER
THE EMSHOCK LETTER

Harbinger House
HEALING PATH
HJ Kramer, Inc
Last Generation/Underground Editions
Metagnosis Publications
NIGHT OWL'S NEWSLETTER
THE NOCTURNAL LYRIC
Nuclear Trenchcoated Subway Prophets Publications
Rebis Press
Scots Plaid Press (Persephone Press)
SOM Publishing, division of School of Metaphysics
SOMNIAL TIMES
THRESHOLDS JOURNAL
Thunder Creek Publishing Co-operative
Unbridled Lust! Publishing
WRITER'S GUIDELINES MAGAZINE

DRUGS

ACTIVIST
ADDICTION & RECOVERY
Afta Press
THE AGE OF AQUARIUS
AGOG
Alegra House Publishers
And/Or Press, Inc.
Ashley Books, Inc.
Author's Unlimited
Black Heron Press
CHAKRA
Challenger Press
Chandler & Sharp Publishers, Inc.
THE...CHRONICLE
THE CIVIL ABOLITIONIST
Comprehensive Health Education Foundation (CHEF)
Crime and Social Justice Associates, Inc.
CROW MAGAZINE
D.I.N. Publications
" "...A DEAD BEAT POET PRODUCTION
DHARMA COMBAT
DIAMOND HITCHHIKER COBWEBS
DRUG INTERACTIONS AND UPDATES
EAP DIGEST
ECOSOCIALIST REVIEW
FELL SWOOP
FOREFRONT—HEALTH INVESTIGATIONS
Futurum Forlag
GATEAVISA
GREY CITY JOURNAL
Haight-Ashbury Publications
Harbinger House
Holger Harfst, Publisher
HEALING PATH
Health Press
Human Kinetics Pub. Inc.
Johnson Institute
JOURNAL OF PSYCHOACTIVE DRUGS
THE LOOGIE
MAXINE'S PAGES
Mother of Ashes Press
THE N.A. WAY
NET
Nuclear Trenchcoated Subway Prophets Publications
Omega Cottonwood Press
OPOSSUM HOLLER TAROT
The Organization
OTISIAN DIRECTORY
Polymath Systems
Professional Counselor Books
Quotidian Publishers
R & E Publishers
Red Alder Books
Red Eye Press
The Rights' Press
Rocky Top Publications
SCHMAGA
SCIENCE/HEALTH ABSTRACTS
Scojtia Publishing Company
Scribblers Publishing, Ltd.

775

Seventh-Wing Publications
SINSEMILLA TIPS (Domestic Marijuana Journal)
Skidmore-Roth Publishing
SOCIAL JUSTICE: A JOURNAL OF CRIME, CON-
FLICT, & WORLD ORDER
Station Hill Press
Steel Balls Press
STREET VOICE
Tyro Publishing
Unbridled Lust! Publishing
Villa Press
Wild & Woolley
Arnie Wolman Co.
Woodsong Graphics Inc.

BOB DYLAN

and books
DHARMA COMBAT
JOURNAL FOR ANTHROPOSOPHY
Limelight Editions
OUROBOROS

EARTH, NATURAL HISTORY

ACTIVIST
ADIRONDAC
Adirondack Mountain Club, Inc.
Allegheny Press
Alpine Publications
The American Hiking Society
American Malacologists, Inc.
THE ANIMALS' AGENDA
APPALACHIA
Appalachian Mountain Club Books
AQUATERRA, WATER CONCEPTS FOR THE ECO-
LOGICAL SOCIETY
ASC NEWSLETTER
BARBIZON MAGAZINE
Barn Owl Books
Beacon Press
Bear Flag Books
Bear Tribe Publishing
BIRD WATCHER'S DIGEST
Blake Publishing
Bliss Publishing Company, Inc.
THE BOOKWATCH
Borderland Sciences Research Foundation
BOWBENDER
The Boxwood Press
Caliban Press
Capra Press
The Carnation Press
THE CHAOS NETWORK
Chelsea Green Publishing Company
Cheshire Books
CJE NEWSLETTER (Newsletter of the Coalition for Jobs
& the Environment)
Columbia Publishing Company, Inc.
Continuing Education Press, Portland State University
THE COUNTRYMAN
Countryman Press
CREEPING BENT
John Daniel and Company, Publishers
Dog-Eared Publications
DOUBLE HARNESS
DoubLeo Publications
Dustbooks
EARTHWISE LITERARY CALENDAR
ECOSOCIALIST REVIEW
ENCYCLOPEDIA BANANICA
ENVIRONMENTAL OPPORTUNITIES
EPIPHANY JOURNAL
ETC Publications
Exanimo Press
Falcon Press Publishing Company
FINE MADNESS
Fithian Press
Five Corners Publications, Ltd.
Flower Press

FOCUS
Fulcrum, Inc.
Gaslight Publications
Geoscience Press, Inc.
Glacier House Publications
The Globe Pequot Press
GRASS ROOTS
Great Elm Press
GREY CITY JOURNAL
THE HAPPY THRASHER
Harbinger House
Helix Press
Homestead Publishing
Island Press
JOURNAL FOR ANTHROPOSOPHY
JOURNAL OF BORDERLAND RESEARCH
Michael Kesend, Publishing, Ltd.
KIDSCIENCE
L.A.N.D.
LAKE SUPERIOR MAGAZINE
LANCASTER INDEPENDENT PRESS
The Latona Press
THE LLEWELLYN NEW TIMES
Llewellyn Publications
Lomond Publications Inc.
M.H. Macy & Company
McDonald & Woodward Publishing Company
!MEXICO WEST!
Mexico West Travel Club, Inc.
Misty Hill Press
Mountain Press Publishing Co.
The Mountaineers Books
Multi Media Arts
NATURALLY
NATURE SOCIETY NEWS
Naturegraph Publishers, Inc.
THE NAUTILUS
New Cicada
NEW CICADA
Night Owl Publishers
THE NORTHERN ENGINEER
THE NORTHERN REVIEW
Northland Publishing Company
Omega Cottonwood Press
Oregon State University Press
OTTERWISE
Papyrus Publishers
Dr. Homer W. Parker, P.E.
T.H. Peek, Publisher
Pineapple Press, Inc.
Pinery Press
POETRY OF THE PEOPLE
PUBLIC LANDS ACTION NETWORK
Pygmy Forest Press
Quarterly Committee of Queen's University
QUEEN'S QUARTERLY: A Canadian Review
Red Crane Books
Red Ink/Black Hole Productions
RedBrick Press
Ridge Times Press
Rocky Top Publications
SAMISDAT
Sand River Press
Sandhill Publications
Sang Froid Press
Sierra Club Books
Small Press International
Genny Smith Books
Gibbs Smith, Publisher
SNOWY EGRET
SOUTH AMERICAN EXPLORER
George Sroda, Publisher
Stemmer House Publishers, Inc.
Stillpoint Publishing
Stone Wall Press, Inc
STUDIO NORTH
Sunstone Publications
SURVIVE & WIN

Sutherland Publishing
Synergetic Press Inc.
TATTOO ADVOCATE JOURNAL
Tiger Moon
Timber Press
Timberline Press
Tortilla Press
Tough Dove Books
THE TOWNSHIPS SUN
University of Calgary Press
Weidner & Sons, Publishing
The Westphalia Press
White Rose Press
WHOLE EARTH REVIEW
THE WILD FOODS FORUM
WILDFIRE: A NETWORKING MAGAZINE
Williamson Publishing Company, Inc.
Wisconsin Trails
Witwatersrand University Press
Women's Times Publishing
Wood Thrush Books
Woodbine House
WORLD RAINFOREST REPORT
WORLD WILDLIFE FUND & THE CONSERVATION
    FOUNDATION LETTER
Zagier & Urruty Publicaciones

ECOLOGY, FOODS

Achievement Press
ACTIVIST
ADIRONDAC
Adirondack Mountain Club, Inc.
AERO SUN-TIMES
THE AGE OF AQUARIUS
All American Press
AMERICAN FORESTS
Anaphase II
Androgyne Books
THE ANIMALS' AGENDA
APPALACHIAN HERITAGE
AQUATERRA, WATER CONCEPTS FOR THE ECO-
    LOGICAL SOCIETY
Artemis Press, Inc.
Ash Tree Publishing
Aslan Publishing
AT-SOURCE-TA
BARBIZON MAGAZINE
Beacon Press
Black Rose Books Ltd.
Bliss Publishing Company, Inc.
Blue Dolphin Press, Inc.
THE BOOKWATCH
Bookworm Publishing Company
BORDER/LINES
The Boxwood Press
Bull Publishing Co.
BURWOOD JOURNAL
Caddo Gap Press
Capra Press
Cassandra Press
Ceres Press
Chelsea Green Publishing Company
Cheshire Books
Christmans
THE CHURCH, FARM AND TOWN
City Lights Books
City Spirit Publications
THE CIVIL ABOLITIONIST
CJE NEWSLETTER (Newsletter of the Coalition for Jobs
    & the Environment)
Communitas Press
COMMUNITY DEVELOPMENT JOURNAL
COMMUNITY ECONOMICS
COMPOST NEWSLETTER (CNL)
CONNECTICUT NATURALLY
Consumer Education Research Center
Continuing Education Press, Portland State University
THE COUNTRYMAN

CROOKED ROADS
The Crossing Press
Culinary Arts Ltd.
Cultural Survival, Inc.
CULTURAL SURVIVAL QUARTERLY
The Dawn Horse Press
DE NAR
Devin-Adair, Publishers, Inc.
DHARMA COMBAT
Dirigo Books, Inc.
Dog-Eared Publications
DOUBLE HARNESS
DuReve Publications
ECOLOGY LAW QUARTERLY
ECOSOCIALIST REVIEW
ELAN POETIQUE LITTERAIRE ET PACIFISTE
The Elvendon Press
ENCYCLOPEDIA BANANICA
ETC Publications
The Findhorn Press
Flower Press
Foghorn Press
FOREFRONT—HEALTH INVESTIGATIONS
FOX VALLEY LIVING
GRASS ROOTS
Gravity Publishing
Great Elm Press
GREEN SYNTHESIS-A NEWSLETTER AND JOUR-
    NAL FOR SOCIAL ECOLOGY, DEEP ECOLOGY,
    BIOREGIONALISM, ECOFEMINISM, AND THE
    GREEN MOVEMENT
GREY CITY JOURNAL
THE HAPPY THRASHER
Harbinger House
Healthmere Press, Inc.
Helix Press
Hoffman Press
Hope Publishing House
THE HUMAN ECOLOGY AND ENERGY BALANC-
    ING SCIENTIST
Human Ecology Balancing Sciences, Inc.
INFINITE ONION
Institute For Community Economics
Institute for Southern Studies
Island Press
JASON UNDERGROUND'S NOTES FROM THE
    TRASHCOMPACTOR
JEWISH VEGETARIANS OF NORTH AMERICA
JOURNAL FOR ANTHROPOSOPHY
JOURNAL OF BORDERLAND RESEARCH
JUDY
Knowledge Systems, Inc.
LANCASTER INDEPENDENT PRESS
Langston Press
THE LATHAM LETTER
The Latona Press
Lexikos
LINKS
LITTLE FREE PRESS
LIVING OFF THE LAND, Subtropic Newsletter
LOVE AND RAGE, A Revolutionary Anarchist News-
    monthly
MACROBIOTICS TODAY
M.H. Macy & Company
MESSAGE POST
THE MILITANT
Mina Press
MIND MATTERS REVIEW
Misty Hill Press
Moonsquilt Press
Mosaic Press
Naturegraph Publishers, Inc.
NEW FRONTIER
NEW JERSEY NATURALLY
New Society Publishers
A NEW WORLD RISING
NEW YORK NATURALLY
Newmark Publishing Company

Night Owl Publishers
NightinGale Resources
The Noble Press, Inc.
THE NORTH AMERICAN REVIEW
NUTRITION ACTION HEALTHLETTER
George Ohsawa Macrobiotic Foundation Press
OIKOS: A JOURNAL OF ECOLOGY AND COMMUN-
ITY
C. Olson & Company
ONE EARTH
Oregon State University Press
ORGANICA
OUR GENERATION
Pacific Research Institute
Panjandrum Books
PEACE NEWS "For Nonviolent Revolution"
Peavine Publications
PEDESTRIAN RESEARCH
PENNYWHISTLE PEOPLE PAPER
Pennywhistle Press
Persona Publications
Petroglyph Press, Ltd.
Pine & Palm Press
Pineapple Press, Inc.
POETRY OF THE PEOPLE
Royal Purcell, Publisher
R & M Publishing Company
RADICAL AMERICA
Rama Publishing Co.
Rand Editions/Tofua Press
THE RAT RACE RECORD
The Rateavers
Red Crane Books
RESOLVE NEWSLETTER
RESONANCE
ROMANIAN REVIEW
Martha Rosler
Ross Books
Rossi
Sandpiper Press
Sang Froid Press
Sanguinaria Publishing
Sasquatch Books
SCHMAGA
SCIENCE/HEALTH ABSTRACTS
Sierra Club Books
Singlejack Books
Small Press International
Social Order Series
Southwest Research and Information Center
SPECTRUM—The Wholistic News Magazine
SPROUTLETTER
Stillpoint Publishing
Stone Wall Press, Inc
Strawberry Patchworks
Sun Eagle Publishing
Sunstone Publications
Survival News Service
SURVIVE & WIN
Synesis Press
SZ/Press
Talon Books Ltd
TATTOO ADVOCATE JOURNAL
Ten Speed Press
Third World First
Times Change Press
THE TOWNSHIPS SUN
TRANSITIONS ABROAD: The Guide to Living,
Learning, and Working Overseas
TRENDS & PREDICTIONS ANALYST
TRUE FOOD
21st Century Publications
Twin Peaks Press
Unbridled Lust! Publishing
THE UNDERGROUND FOREST - LA SELVA SUB-
TERRANEA
THE UNEXPLAINED
United Lumbee Nation

UNITED LUMBEE NATION TIMES
University of Calgary Press
Upper Access Inc.
Van Patten Publishing
VEGETARIAN JOURNAL
The Vegetarian Resource Group
Village Books
Wheel of Fire Press
The George Whittell Memorial Press
WHOLE EARTH REVIEW
Wide World Publishing/TETRA
Wild & Woolley
THE WILD FOODS FORUM
Wise Owl Press
Woodbridge Press
Woodsong Graphics Inc.
THE WORKBOOK
WORLD PERSPECTIVES
WORLD RAINFOREST REPORT
World Wildlife Fund & The Conservation Foundation
WORLD WILDLIFE FUND & THE CONSERVATION
FOUNDATION LETTER
Worldwatch Institute
WTI Publishing Co.
Zed Books Ltd.

EDITING

THE EDITORIAL EYE
EPM Publications, Inc.
Oxbridge Communications, Inc.
PUBLISHING TRENDS & TRENDSETTERS

EDUCATION

A as A Publishing
AASLH Press
Abundance Press
Accent on Music
Achievement Press
African American Images
Agathon Press
Amana Books
AMATEUR COMPUTERIST
AMBASSADOR REPORT
American Audio Prose Library (non-print)
American Business Consultants, Inc.
American Montessori Consulting
APPALACHIAN HERITAGE
AQUATERRA, WATER CONCEPTS FOR THE ECO-
LOGICAL SOCIETY
Arrow Publishing
Artemis Press, Inc.
Ash Lad Press
Aslan Publishing
Associated Writing Programs
Athelstan Publications
AT-SOURCE-TA
AWP CHRONICLE
Barclay House
Bergin & Garvey Publishers
The Bess Press
Between The Lines
BILINGUAL REVIEW/Revista Bilingue
Blue Bird Publishing
Blue Dolphin Press, Inc.
Blue Heron Press
Bluestocking Press
THE BOOK REPORT: Journal for Junior & Senior High
School Librarians
Books for All Times, Inc.
Don Bosco Multimedia
The Boxwood Press
Brain Books
BRAIN/MIND BULLETIN
Branden Publishing Company
BREAKTHROUGH!
Brick Row Publishing Co. Ltd.
Bright Ring Publishing
BRONG'S BUSINESS SUCCESS NEWS

Brook Farm Books
Buddha Rose Publications
Caddo Gap Press
Calgre Press, Division of Calgre Inc.
Carnival Enterprises
Center for Public Representation
CHILDREN'S LITERATURE IN EDUCATION
Christmans
Circa Press
Circumpolar Press
Claridge Press
Classic Theatre For Children, Publishers
THE CLASSICAL OUTLOOK
Coast to Coast Books Inc.
COLUMBUS FREE PRESS
Community Collaborators
COMMUNITY DEVELOPMENT JOURNAL
Community Service, Inc.
COMMUNITY SERVICE NEWSLETTER
Computer Musician Coalition
Conscious Living
CONSTRUCTIVE ACTION NEWSLETTER
Consumer Education Research Center
Contemporary Curriculums
Continuing Education Press, Portland State University
Continuing Education Publications
Copyright Information Services
COTTONWOOD MONTHLY
Cottonwood Press, Inc.
Council For Indian Education
Council on Interracial Books For Children
CREATING EXCELLENCE
CREATION/EVOLUTION JOURNAL
Creative Concern Publications
D.B.A. Books
D.I.N. Publications
DAEDALUS, Journal of the American Academy of Arts
    and Sciences
Dawn Sign Press
DAYSPRING
DESIGN AND TECHNOLOGY TEACHING
Distinctive Publishing Corp.
Dormant Brain Research and Development Laboratory
Double M Press
Dovehaven Press, Ltd.
Dyad Services
Ed-U Press, Inc.
Educare Press
EDUCATION DIGEST
EDUCATION IN FOCUS
EDUCATIONAL FOUNDATIONS
El Camino Publishers
EMERGENCY LIBRARIAN
THE EMSHOCK LETTER
Energeia Publishing, Inc.
ETC Publications
FAMILY LIFE EDUCATOR
Fast Forward Publishing
The Feminist Press at the City University of New York
FLORIDA VOCATIONAL JOURNAL
FOCUS
FREE INQUIRY
FREE SPIRIT: NEWS AND VIEWS ON GROWING UP
Free Spirit Publishing Inc.
Front Row Experience
Gallaudet University Press
Gallopade Publishing Group
Gazelle Publications
GGL Educational Press
THE GIFTED CHILD TODAY
Gifted Education Press/The Reading Tutorium
Glenhurst Publications, Inc.
The Global Press
Grade School Press
Grapevine Publications, Inc.
Grayson Bernard Publishers, Inc.
Green Stone Publications
Greencrest Press Inc.

GROWING WITHOUT SCHOOLING
Gryphon House, Inc.
Guarionex Press Ltd.
THE HAPPY THRASHER
Health Alert Press
HFH Publications
Hilton Thomas Publishers, Inc.
HISTORY NEWS
Holistic Education Press
HOLISTIC EDUCATION REVIEW
Holt Associates, Inc.
HOME EDUCATION MAGAZINE
Hoover Institution Press
Hope Publishing House
House of Fire Press
Human Kinetics Pub. Inc.
THE HUMANIST
Image Industry Publications
Impact Publications
Impact Publishers, Inc.
IM-Press
In One Ear Press
Independence Publishers Inc.
INNOVATING
Institute for Southern Studies
Intercultural Press, Inc.
Interface Press
INTERNATIONAL BRAIN DOMINANCE REVIEW
International Consulting Associates, Inc.
The International University Press
INTERRACIAL BOOKS FOR CHILDREN BULLETIN
INTERVENTION IN SCHOOL AND CLINIC
Ironwood Publishing Company
J P Publications
Jalmar Press
Jamenair Ltd.
JOURNAL FOR ANTHROPOSOPHY
JOURNAL OF COMPUTING IN HIGHER EDUCATION
JOURNAL OF WELSH EDUCATION
Karunaratne & Sons Ltd.
Kettering Foundation
KETTERING REVIEW
Key Curriculum Press
KIDS LIB NEWS
KIDSCIENCE
LANGUAGE ARTS JOURNAL OF MICHIGAN
THE LATHAM LETTER
LIBRARY TALK: The Magazine for Elementary School
    Librarians
LINKS
Littlebooks
Log Cabin Publishers
THE LUNDIAN
Magical Music Express
Mar Vista Publishing Company
Maupin House
Mazda Publishers
Mercer House Press
Meridional Publications
Metamorphous Press
Miles River Press
MIND MATTERS REVIEW
MINORITY PUBLISHERS EXCHANGE
MODERN LITURGY
Modern Media
Monroe Press
Moonlight Press
Morning Glory Press
MT. AUKUM REVIEW
Multi Media Arts
MULTICULTURAL   TEACHING   FOR   PRACTI-
    TIONERS IN SCHOOLS AND COMMUNITY
Nancy Renfro Studios, Inc.
NAR Publications
Network Publications, a division of ETR Associates
THE NEW AMERICAN
New Society Publishers
THE NORTHERN REVIEW

Nucleus Publications
Nuventures Publishing
Oak Plantation Press
Occasional Productions
Odin Press
Oness Press
Oneworld Publications Ltd.
Organization for Equal Education of the Sexes, Inc.
  (OEES)
Pacific Information Inc.
Panorama Publishing Company
Parenting Press, Inc.
Dr. Homer W. Parker, P.E.
Partners In Publishing
PEACE NEWS "For Nonviolent Revolution"
Pedagogic Press
T.H. Peek, Publisher
Pepper Publishing
Pergot Press
Personal Efficiency Programs, Inc.
PIP COLLEGE 'HELPS' NEWSLETTER
The Place In The Woods
THE PLOUGH
Poetry Wales Press, Ltd.
Prakken Publications
ProLingua Associates
Proving Grounds International, Inc.
Pruett Publishing Company
Royal Purcell, Publisher
QED
Quarterly Committee of Queen's University
QUEEN'S QUARTERLY: A Canadian Review
QUEST
R & E Publishers
R & M Publishing Company
RADIANCE, The Magazine For Large Women
Rama Publishing Co.
Raven Rocks Press
Real People Press
Redbird Press, Inc.
Reference Service Press
RESEARCH IN HIGHER EDUCATION
Riverside Productions
ROMANIAN REVIEW
ST. CROIX REVIEW
Sang Froid Press
Scarecrow Press
SCHOOL SHOP
Sea Challengers
Sea Fog Press, Inc.
Security Seminars Press
Seven Locks Press
Sherwood Sugden & Company, Publishers
SHINING STAR
Michael Shore Associates
Simon & Pierre Publishing Co. Ltd.
SMS Publishing Corp.
SOCIAL POLICY
SOCIALISM AND DEMOCRACY
SPECTRUM, A Guide to the Independent Press and
  Informative Organizations
Spectrum Publications
The Speech Bin, Inc.
Sports Support Syndicate
STONE SOUP, The Magazine By Children
Storytime Ink International
Success Publishing
Sun Features Inc.
Sunstone Publications
Surrey Press
SURVIVE & WIN
Symbiosis Books
Targeted Communications
TEACHER EDUCATION QUARTERLY
Teachers & Writers Collaborative
TEACHERS & WRITERS MAGAZINE
TechWest Publications
Third World First

Top Of The Mountain Publishing
TQS NEWS
Trentham Books
'2D' (DRAMA AND DANCE)
Tyro Publishing
UNITED LUMBEE NATION TIMES
University of Calgary Press
UPDATE
THE URBAN REVIEW
VANTAGE POINT
Village Books
VOICES OF YOUTH ON EDUCATION, SELF, CIVIC
  VALUES
Patrick Walsh Press
WARM FUZZY NEWSLETTER
THE WASHINGTON MONTHLY
Waterfront Books
Wellberry Press
Westburg Associates, Publishers
Williamson Publishing Company, Inc.
B. L. Winch & Associates
WISCONSIN RESTAURATEUR
Witwatersrand University Press
WOMEN'S STUDIES QUARTERLY
Woodbine House
World Music Press
WRITER'S GUIDELINES MAGAZINE
Writers Publishing Service Co.
WTI Publishing Co.
Youth Policy Institute

EMPLOYMENT

Brick House Publishing Co., Inc.
C.C. Publishing Co.
CJE NEWSLETTER (Newsletter of the Coalition for Jobs
  & the Environment)
Edge Publishing
ENVIRONMENTAL OPPORTUNITIES
Harvard Common Press
Jamenair Ltd.
Mountainwest Publishers
Planning/Communications
Resolution Business Press
The Saunderstown Press
Michael Shore Associates
Sun Features Inc.
Union Square Press
Williamson Publishing Company, Inc.
Word Of Mouth Press

ENERGY

Aatec Publications
AERO SUN-TIMES
AFRICA NEWS
AQUATERRA, WATER CONCEPTS FOR THE ECO-
  LOGICAL SOCIETY
ASPECTS
AT-SOURCE-TA
THE BABY CONNECTION NEWS JOURNAL
Blue Dolphin Press, Inc.
Borderland Sciences Research Foundation
The Borgo Press
The Boxwood Press
Brick House Publishing Co., Inc.
BURWOOD JOURNAL
Capra Press
Cheshire Books
CJE NEWSLETTER (Newsletter of the Coalition for Jobs
  & the Environment)
Countryman Press
DESIGN BOOK REVIEW
DOUBLE HARNESS
ECOSOCIALIST REVIEW
ENERGY ASIA
ENERGY UNLIMITED
Free Association Books (FAB)
Grapevine Publications, Inc.
Gross Advertising Service

HIGH COUNTRY NEWS
Home Power, Inc.
HOME POWER MAGAZINE
HOME RESOURCE MAGAZINE
Hope Publishing House
Ide House, Inc.
Institute for Southern Studies
Island Press
JOURNAL OF BORDERLAND RESEARCH
LANCASTER INDEPENDENT PRESS
MESSAGE POST
Middle Coast Publishing
Misty Hill Press
THE NORTHERN ENGINEER
THE NORTHERN REVIEW
NRG
Odin Press
Oness Press
Parent Education for Infant Development
PEACE NEWS "For Nonviolent Revolution"
PEDESTRIAN RESEARCH
PETROLEUM NEWS: Asia's Energy Journal
Petroleum News Southeast Asia Ltd.
RESONANCE
Rocky Top Publications
THE SMALL POND MAGAZINE OF LITERATURE
aka SMALL POND
Southwest Research and Information Center
SPECTRUM, A Guide to the Independent Press and
Informative Organizations
Spectrum Publications
SURVIVE & WIN
Synerjy
SYNERJY: A Directory of Renewable Energy
TRENDS & PREDICTIONS ANALYST
UNBRIDLED LUST!
University of Calgary Press
Village Books
THE WASHINGTON MONTHLY
Whitehorse
THE WORKBOOK
Worldwatch Institute

ENGINEERING

ADVANCES IN THE ASTRONAUTICAL SCIENCES
AQUATERRA, WATER CONCEPTS FOR THE ECO-
LOGICAL SOCIETY
AT-SOURCE-TA
Borderland Sciences Research Foundation
Brenner Information Group
Center Book Publishers, Inc.
CRS Consultants Press
Grapevine Publications, Inc.
Gulf Publishing Company
International Information Associates
JOURNAL OF BORDERLAND RESEARCH
Karunaratne & Sons Ltd.
N-B-T-V
New Levee Press
THE NORTHERN ENGINEER
Nuventures Publishing
Dr. Homer W. Parker, P.E.
Pendaya Publications, Inc.
SCIENCE AND TECHNOLOGY
STARWIND
SURVIVE & WIN
Thompson and Co. Inc.
Univelt, Inc.
University of Calgary Press

ENGLAND

BALDER
Catbird Press
Coxland Press
DIAMOND HITCHHIKER COBWEBS
KELTIC FRINGE
NEW HOPE INTERNATIONAL REVIEW
NightinGale Resources

North Stone Press
Nuclear Trenchcoated Subway Prophets Publications
THE PRINTER
Spredden Press
Zephyr Press

ENGLISH

THE ABER BULLETIN
ACTA VICTORIANA
American Audio Prose Library (non-print)
ANQ: A Quarterly Journal of Short Articles, Notes, and
Reviews
Bliss Publishing Company, Inc.
Borealis Press Limited
CANADIAN AUTHOR & BOOKMAN
THE CENTENNIAL REVIEW
Chandler & Sharp Publishers, Inc.
CHILDREN'S ALBUM
COLLEGE ENGLISH
Combs Vanity Press
COTTONWOOD MONTHLY
Cottonwood Press, Inc.
COYDOG REVIEW
THE DALHOUSIE REVIEW
DAYSPRING
" "...A DEAD BEAT POET PRODUCTION
DEWITT DIGEST & REVIEW
Distinctive Publishing Corp.
Dragon Disks
THE EDITORIAL EYE
ENGLISH STUDIES IN AFRICA-A Journal of the
Humanities
FISH DRUM MAGAZINE
Front Row Experience
The Future Press
Gallaudet University Press
Gallopade Publishing Group
Teri Gordon, Publisher
GRANTA
Green Stone Publications
Holger Harfst, Publisher
IMAGINATION MAGAZINE
In One Ear Press
INTERRACIAL BOOKS FOR CHILDREN BULLETIN
THE IOWA REVIEW
JOURNAL OF NARRATIVE TECHNIQUE
LANGUAGE ARTS JOURNAL OF MICHIGAN
LEGACY: A JOURNAL OF AMERICAN WOMEN
WRITERS
LIZZENGREASY
Men & Women of Letters
MERLYN'S PEN: The National Magazine of Student
Writing
MIDLAND REVIEW
R. & E. Miles
Multi Media Arts
National Council of Teachers of English
THE NEBRASKA REVIEW
NEW CONTRAST
THE NEW CRITERION
THE NEW ENGLAND QUARTERLY
The New England Quarterly, Inc.
NEW HOPE INTERNATIONAL REVIEW
THE NORTHERN REVIEW
NOTES & QUERIES
PAUNCH
PEACE NEWS "For Nonviolent Revolution"
T.H. Peek, Publisher
Pennsylvania State University Press
Poet Papers
THE PRAIRIE JOURNAL OF CANADIAN LITERA-
TURE
Prairie Journal Press
THE PRINTER
ProLingua Associates
The Purchase Press
RAMPIKE
Readers International, Inc.

THE REDNECK REVIEW OF LITERATURE
REPRESENTATIONS
RIGHTING WORDS—THE JOURNAL OF LAN-
GUAGE AND EDITING
SALMAGUNDI
SALT LICK
SCRIVENER
THE SHAKESPEARE NEWSLETTER
SHAW, THE ANNUAL OF BERNARD SHAW STU-
DIES
Sherwood Sugden & Company, Publishers
Silver Dawn Media
Simon & Pierre Publishing Co. Ltd.
Sleepy Hollow Press
Spredden Press
Station Hill Press
Stone Circle Press
STREAM LINES, MN JOURNAL OF CREATIVE
WRITING
Studia Hispanica Editors
Sunburst Press
Talon Books Ltd
Thorp Springs Press
TOOK
University of Calgary Press
VIETNAM GENERATION: A Journal of Recent History
and Contemporary Issues
THE VIRGINIA QUARTERLY REVIEW
Waterfront Books
Weidner & Sons, Publishing
Westburg Associates, Publishers
Witwatersrand University Press
The Wordtree
WTI Publishing Co.
THE YALE REVIEW

ENTERTAINMENT

Acting World Books
THE AGENCIES-WHAT THE ACTOR NEEDS TO
KNOW
ARIZONA COAST
ATROCITY
THE AUTOGRAPH COLLECTOR'S MAGAZINE
Axiom Information Resources
BEAN ZINE
BREAKTHROUGH!
CADENCE: THE REVIEW OF JAZZ & BLUES:
CREATIVE IMPROVISED MUSIC
CIN-DAV, Inc.
COLUMBUS FREE PRESS
COMPUTER GAMING WORLD
" "...A DEAD BEAT POET PRODUCTION
DIAMOND HITCHHIKER COBWEBS
EDITOR'S DIGEST
Empty Closet Enterprises
THE EMSHOCK LETTER
ENSEMBLE, THE NEW VARIETY ARTS REVIEW
EUTHANASIA ROSES
Excalibur Publishing
Festival Publications
FILM THREAT VIDEO GUIDE
FOLK ERA TODAY
FOX VALLEY LIVING
FREE PRESS
THE GELOSOPHIST, Humor News & Views From
Around The World
GENII
Glendale House Publishing
GO MAGAZINE
GREATER PORTLAND
THE HAPPY THRASHER
THE HAUNTED JOURNAL
THE HOLLYWOOD ACTING COACHES AND
TEACHERS DIRECTORY
HOT WIRE: Journal of Women's Music & Culture
HOWLING WIND
Independence Publishers Inc.
JUDY

KREATURE COMFORTS
LIVELY ARTS
LONE STAR COMEDY MONTHLY
Love Child Publishing
Main Track Publications
THE MCCALLUM OBSERVER
MEDIA SPOTLIGHT
MENTERTAINMENT
Micro Pro Litera Press
MIDDLE EASTERN DANCER
Mustang Publishing Co.
The Neither/Nor Press
THE NEW DANCE REVIEW
NORTHCOAST VIEW MONTHLY MAGAZINE
Nuclear Trenchcoated Subway Prophets Publications
Nuventures Publishing
Oak Plantation Press
Open Horizons Publishing Company
PAST TIMES: THE NOSTALGIA ENTERTAINMENT
NEWSLETTER
Peachtree Publishers, Ltd.
P-FORM
THE PIG PAPER
Players Press, Inc.
Portland Entertainment Publishing
RE/SEARCH
Re/Search Publications
RGM Publications
Rio Grande Press
THE ROCK HALL REPORTER
SALOME: A JOURNAL FOR THE PERFORMING
ARTS
SCHMAGA
SE LA VIE WRITER'S JOURNAL
Sentinel Books
SINGLES ALMANAC
Sparkling Diamond Paperbacks
Strawberry Hill Press
Tambra Publishing
TATTOO ADVOCATE JOURNAL
Texas Monthly Press
T-J TODAY
TRADITION
THE VAMPIRE JOURNAL
Vestal Press Ltd
THE WAVE
Woldt Publishing
WORLD OF FANDOM MAGAZINE
WRESTLING - THEN & NOW
YE OLDE NEWES
ZOOMAR

ENVIRONMENT

The Book Peddlers
City Spirit Publications
DHARMA COMBAT
EARTHTREKS DIGEST
Envirographics
ENVIRONMENTAL OPPORTUNITIES
FOX VALLEY LIVING
GYPSY
HIGH COUNTRY NEWS
Island Press
LAKE SUPERIOR MAGAZINE
LITTLE FREE PRESS
THE LUNDIAN
Modern Media
John Muir Publications, Inc.
New Worlds Press
Gibbs Smith, Publisher
Theosophical Publishing House
Tilbury House, Publishers
TOWARD FREEDOM
TRANSITIONS ABROAD: The Guide to Living,
Learning, and Working Overseas
WHOLE EARTH REVIEW

EROTICA

ACTA VICTORIANA
AILERON, A LITERARY JOURNAL
ANIME SHOWER SPECIAL
APAEROS
ASH
Asylum Arts
ATROCITY
BORDER/LINES
CAL NEWSLETTER
Carroll & Graf Publishers, Inc.
CATALYST
CHAKRA
Chiron Press
CHIRON REVIEW
" "...A DEAD BEAT POET PRODUCTION
The Devonshire Publishing Co.
DIAMOND HITCHHIKER COBWEBS
DIE FAT PIGGY DIE
DoubLeo Publications
Down There Press
Eidos
EIDOS: Erotic Entertainment for Women, Men, &
  Couples
THE EMSHOCK LETTER
THE FINAL PAGE
GLB Publishers
THE HAPPY THRASHER
HEATHENZINE
HUBRIS
Laocoon Books
LIBIDO: The Journal of Sex and Sensibility
Lionhouse Publishing Company
THE LOOGIE
MEMES
MIP Company
Mogul Book and FilmWorks
Nemeton Publishing
NEW HOPE INTERNATIONAL REVIEW
THE NIHILISTIC REVIEW
NON COMPOS MENTIS
Omega Cottonwood Press
Parkhurst Press
Pessimism Press, Inc.
P-FORM
POETRY OF THE PEOPLE
The Press of the Third Mind
Quimby Archives
Red Alder Books
(ROWBOAT)
SCREAM MAGAZINE
Sheer Joy! Press
SPIT
SPSM&H
SQUARE ONE - A Magazine of Fiction
Thunder's Mouth Press
Trabarni Productions
TWISTED IMAGE NEWSLETTER
UNBRIDLED LUST!
UNION SHOP BLUFF
Woldt Publishing
X MAGAZINE
X-CALIBRE
YELLOW SILK: Journal Of Erotic Arts
Zirlinson Publishing

ESSAYS

Abattoir Editions
ACTA VICTORIANA
AERIAL
Amana Books
AMERICAN WRITING: A MAGAZINE
ANNA'S HOUSE: THE JOURNAL OF EVERYDAY
  LIFE
ARISTOS
ARTICHOKE HEART
Asylum Arts

Bandanna Books
Beacon Press
Blue Lights Publications
BOGG
Bomb Shelter Propaganda
Broken Moon Press
THE CAFE REVIEW
Chelsea Green Publishing Company
THE...CHRONICLE
CICADA
CIMARRON REVIEW
Cinco Puntos Press
Coffee House Press
COLLAGES & BRICOLAGES
Comforter Publishing
Confluence Press, Inc.
CONTEXT SOUTH
CRAWLSPACE
" "...A DEAD BEAT POET PRODUCTION
Devil Mountain Books
DHARMA COMBAT
DIE FAT PIGGY DIE
DUMPSTER TIMES
ELF: ECLECTIC LITERARY FORUM (ELF MAGA-
  ZINE)
EPIPHANY JOURNAL
Ex Machina Publishing Company
Exile Press
Folder Editions
FOLIO: A LITERARY JOURNAL
Fromm International Publishing Corporation
Futurum Forlag
GAFF PRESS
GAUNTLET: Exploring the Limits of Free Expression
THE GEORGIA REVIEW
THE GETTYSBURG REVIEW
GRASSLANDS REVIEW
Harbinger House
HAWAI'I REVIEW
Helicon Nine Editions
HIPPO
HOBO JUNGLE
HOBO STEW REVIEW
Illuminations Press
INNOVATING
INVERTED-A HORN
JOURNAL FOR ANTHROPOSOPHY
KALEIDOSCOPE: INTERNATIONAL MAGAZINE OF
  LITERATURE, FINE ARTS, AND DISABILITY
Kitchen Table: Women of Color Press
K0SMOS
LESBIAN CONTRADICTION-A Journal of Irreverent
  Feminism
Loonfeather Press
THE LUNDIAN
LuraMedia, Inc.
MEMES
MID-AMERICAN REVIEW
THE MILWAUKEE UNDERGRADUATE REVIEW
Modern Media
THE NEW DANCE REVIEW
NEW HOPE INTERNATIONAL REVIEW
NIGHT OWL'S NEWSLETTER
NON COMPOS MENTIS
NORTHEAST
THE NORTHERN REVIEW
NOTES FROM THE UNDERGROUND
OFFICE NUMBER ONE
Omega Cottonwood Press
1 BIT SHOE
OTISIAN DIRECTORY
Ox Head Press
OXALIS
Parabola Books
Pentagram Press
Permeable Press
P-FORM
Placebo Press

PORTLAND REVIEW
PRAIRIE SCHOONER
THE PROSPECT REVIEW
THE RATIONAL FEMINIST
RED DANCEFLOOR
REMARK
ROMANIAN REVIEW
(ROWBOAT)
St. Bede's Publications
SHENANDOAH
Signature Books
SKYLARK
Slough Press
SPIT
SPSM&H
Star Books, Inc.
Still Waters Press
STUDIO ONE
TAPAS
TURNSTILE
THE VINCENT BROTHERS REVIEW
Volunteer Publications
White Pine Press
WTI Publishing Co.
Xenos Books
Zirlinson Publishing

ETHICS

Aardvark Enterprises
ASPECTS
Bandanna Books
Beacon Press
Comforter Publishing
COMPOST NEWSLETTER (CNL)
DIE FAT PIGGY DIE
DOCTOR-PATIENT STUDIES
Wm.B. Eerdmans Publishing Co.
THE EMSHOCK LETTER
ETICA & CIENCIA
Humana Press
JEWISH VEGETARIANS OF NORTH AMERICA
Knowledge Systems, Inc.
THE LETTER PARADE
LIBERTY
Lindisfarne Press
Orbis Books
The Saunderstown Press
Snowbird Publishing Company
Zagier & Urruty Publicaciones

EUROPE

THE ABER BULLETIN
Alpenglow Press
Amana Books
BALDER
Catbird Press
CIMARRON REVIEW
Citeaux Commentarii Cistercienses
CITEAUX: COMMENTARII CISTERCIENSES
Coxland Press
EASTERN EUROPEAN POLITICS & SOCIETIES
ECOSOCIALIST REVIEW
Esoterica Press
EUROPA 1992
EXUM Publishing
Glenhurst Publications, Inc.
Heyday Books
Jorvik Press
Langston Press
Mercury House
Michigan Romance Studies
Midmarch Arts Press
Mustang Publishing Co.
NightinGale Resources
NOTEBOOK/CUADERNO: A LITERARY JOURNAL
Dr. Homer W. Parker, P.E.
Pergot Press
Rainier Books

(ROWBOAT)
SCHMAGA
Sharp & Dunnigan Publications, Incorporated
Gibbs Smith, Publisher
TATTOO ADVOCATE JOURNAL
TechWest Publications
Thirteen Colonies Press
TOWARD FREEDOM
Travel Keys
WORLD PERSPECTIVES
Zephyr Press

EUTHANASIA, DEATH

ASPECTS
Barclay House
Drew Blood Press Ltd.
THE...CHRONICLE
DOCTOR-PATIENT STUDIES
EUTHANASIA ROSES
GOKOOMA
THE HAPPY THRASHER
HEMLOCK QUARTERLY
Hemlock Society
THE HUMANIST
JOURNAL FOR ANTHROPOSOPHY
THE LOOGIE
THE NOCTURNAL LYRIC
Path Press
UNBRIDLED LUST!
Valley Lights Publications
Westgate Press
WICKED MYSTIC

FAMILY

Aardvark Enterprises
Abundance Press
African American Images
Alegra House Publishers
Alpenglow Press
Avery Publishing Group, Inc.
Axelrod Publishing of Tampa Bay
THE BABY CONNECTION NEWS JOURNAL
Belleridge Press
Bergin & Garvey Publishers
The Bess Press
Blue Sky Marketing, Inc.
Bolton Press
BREAKTHROUGH!
Bright Ring Publishing
C.C. Publishing Co.
CAL NEWSLETTER
Calgre Press, Division of Calgre Inc.
Carousel Press
Castalia Publishing Company
Center for Public Representation
Centerplace Publishing Co.
Challenger Press
Chandler & Sharp Publishers, Inc.
Christmans
Cold-Drill Books
Community Service, Inc.
COMMUNITY SERVICE NEWSLETTER
The Consumer's Press, Inc.
Cottage Books
COYDOG REVIEW
CREATING EXCELLENCE
Elm Publications
Equality Press
Robert Erdmann Publishing
Excalibur Publishing
FOR PARENTS
FREE   ASSOCIATIONS: PSYCHOANALYSIS,
    GROUPS, POLITICS, CULTURE
Front Row Experience
Gallopade Publishing Group
Grade School Press
Grosvenor USA
Guarionex Press Ltd.

Gumbs & Thomas Publishers, Inc.
Harrison House Publishers
Harvard Common Press
HARVARD WOMEN'S LAW JOURNAL
HEALING PATH
Heirloom Publications
Herald Press
Hilton Thomas Publishers, Inc.
HOME EDUCATION MAGAZINE
Hope Publishing House
Human Kinetics Pub. Inc.
Impact Publishers, Inc.
Jalmar Press
THE KIBBUTZ JOURNAL
KIDS LIB NEWS
Liberty Bell Press & Publishing Co.
Lighthouse Press
Lindsay Press Inc. of Florida
Mayhaven Publishing
McKinzie Publishing Company
MedLife Communications, Inc.
Monroe Press
Naturist Foundation
THE NEW AMERICAN
New Harbinger Publications, Inc.
NightinGale Resources
NOSTALGIA, A Sentimental State of Mind
Nucleus Publications
The Olive Press Publications
Oness Press
Oneworld Publications Ltd.
Our Child Press
Parent Education for Infant Development
Parent Tapes, Inc.
Parenting Press, Inc.
Perspectives Press
The Pilgrim Press/United Church Press
THE PLOUGH
Political Research Associates
Professional Counselor Books
Quiet Tymes, Inc.
Quotidian Publishers
RADIANCE, The Magazine For Large Women
Ramalo Publications
Rio Grande Press
ROMANIAN REVIEW
St. Bede's Publications
SCIENCE/HEALTH ABSTRACTS
Shadetree Publishing Inc.
SILVER WINGS
Skidmore-Roth Publishing
SPECTRUM, A Guide to the Independent Press and
    Informative Organizations
Spectrum Publications
Spirit Press
Star Books, Inc.
STARLIGHT
Stillpoint Publishing
Strawberry Hill Press
Success Publishing
Sunstone Publications
Tessera Publishing, Inc.
Texas Monthly Press
Tide Book Publishing Company
Villa Press
Village Books
Volcano Press, Inc
WARM FUZZY NEWSLETTER
THE WESLEYAN ADVOCATE
The Westphalia Press
White Rose Publishing
Williamson Publishing Company, Inc.
B. L. Winch & Associates
Woodbine House
Wright-Armstead Associates

FANTASY, HORROR

Academy Chicago Publishers

Afta Press
Alchemy Books
Algol Press
ALL OF THE ABOVE
Amador Publishers
AMRA
Ansuda Publications
Argo Press
ARGONAUT
Astonisher Press
Baker Street Publications
BARDIC RUNES
The Biting Idge/Miracle Press (Chrysalis Publications)
Black Tie Press
THE BOOKWATCH
The Borgo Press
Broken Mirrors Press
Harrison Brown, Publishers, Inc.
CAL NEWSLETTER
The Carolina Wren Press
Carroll & Graf Publishers, Inc.
COMPOST NEWSLETTER (CNL)
The F. Marion Crawford Memorial Society
Creatures At Large Press
CROW MAGAZINE
DARK TOME
DAYSPRING
DEAD OF NIGHT MAGAZINE
DELIRIUM
The Devonshire Publishing Co.
DIAMOND HITCHHIKER COBWEBS
DIE FAT PIGGY DIE
Distinctive Publishing Corp.
THE DRAGONFANG
DREAM INTERNATIONAL QUARTERLY
DREAMS AND NIGHTMARES
DREAMS & VISIONS
Chris Drumm Books
DuReve Publications
ELDRITCH SCIENCE
Embassy Hall Editions
EMERALD CITY COMIX & STORIES
THE EMSHOCK LETTER
EOTU, Magazine of Experimental Fiction
FANS OF HORROR
FELICITY
FOOTSTEPS
Footsteps Press
FORBIDDEN LINES
THE GAME'S AFOOT
W. Paul Ganley: Publisher
Garret Press
THE GATE
GATEAVISA
GAUNTLET: Exploring the Limits of Free Expression
GOLDEN ISIS
GRUE MAGAZINE
Gryphon Publications
THE HAUNTED JOURNAL
HAUNTS
THE HORROR SHOW
HOR-TASY
THE IDEOLOGY OF MADNESS
IMAGINATION MAGAZINE
Infinite Savant Publishing
INFINITY LIMITED, A Journal for the Somewhat
    Eccentric
INNER SEARCH
IT GOES ON THE SHELF
JABBERWOCKY
LEFT CURVE
THE LOOGIE
THE MAGAZINE OF SPECULATIVE POETRY
THE MAGE
MARION ZIMMER BRADLEY'S FANTASY MAGA-
ZINE
Micro Pro Litera Press
MICROCOSM

MIDNIGHT IN HELL (The Weirdest Tales of Fandom)
MIDNIGHT ZOO
MINAS TIRITH EVENING-STAR
THE MODEL & TOY COLLECTOR
MOONSTONE BLUE
Nemeton Publishing
The Nemo Press
New Fantasy Publications
NEW PATHWAYS
NIGHT ROSES
THE NOCTURNAL LYRIC
NOCTURNAL NEWS
NON COMPOS MENTIS
OHIO RENAISSANCE REVIEW
OTISIAN DIRECTORY
OUROBOROS
THE OVERLOOK CONNECTION
OWLFLIGHT MAGAZINE
Owlswick Press
PABLO LENNIS
PANDORA
PAPERBACK PARADE
PENGUIN DIP
PIG IRON
PLOTS
POISON PEN WRITERS NEWS
PORTENTS
PSYCHOPOETICA
PULPHOUSE: THE HARDBACK MAGAZINE
Pulphouse Publishing
Purple Mouth Press
QUANTUM: Science Fiction & Fantasy Review
Quixsilver Press
RGM Publications
RISING STAR
RIVERSIDE QUARTERLY
THE ROMANTIST
Sandpiper Press
Saxifrage Books
SCAREAPHANALIA
Scareware
SCAVENGER'S NEWSLETTER
SCHMAGA
SCIENCE FICTION CHRONICLE
SCREAM MAGAZINE
Scribblers Publishing, Ltd.
SPACE AND TIME
Space and Time Press
SPECTRUM STORIES
SPWAO SHOWCASE
SQUARE ONE - A Magazine of Fiction
StarLance Publications
STARWIND
SteelDragon Press
Tafford Publishing, Inc.
TAPAS
TATTOO ADVOCATE JOURNAL
THEY WON'T STAY DEAD!
Three Continents Press, Inc.
III Publishing
Tiptoe Literary Service
TWISTED
2AM MAGAZINE
2AM Publications
Tyro Publishing
Ultramarine Publishing Co., Inc.
UNBRIDLED LUST!
Unique Graphics
THE VAMPIRE JOURNAL
VANDELOECHT'S FICTION MAGAZINE
VIRGIN MEAT
W.W. Publications
WEIRDBOOK
Westgate Press
WICKED MYSTIC
Wonder Press
Wordcraft
WORLD OF FANDOM MAGAZINE

THE WRITERS' BAR-B-Q
X-CALIBRE
XENOPHILIA
YE OLDE NEWES
Zirlinson Publishing
ZOOMAR

FASHION

ALASKA WOMEN
Altamont Press, Inc.
Blue Swan Communications
COMPOST NEWSLETTER (CNL)
DIAMOND HITCHHIKER COBWEBS
FIBERARTS
FOX VALLEY LIVING
GemStone Press
NEEDLEPOINT PLUS
NIGHT ROSES
RADIANCE, The Magazine For Large Women
RAMPIKE
SCHMAGA
Shiro Publishers
Spirit Press
ST Publications/Book Division
Step Ahead Press, A Heartlite Inc. Company
TOLE WORLD
Twelvetrees Press/Twin Palms Publishers
UNBRIDLED LUST!

FEMINISM

Academy Chicago Publishers
ACTA VICTORIANA
AILERON, A LITERARY JOURNAL
AMERICAN WRITING: A MAGAZINE
Artemis Press, Inc.
ARTPAPER
As Is/So & So Press
Ashley Books, Inc.
Astarte Shell Press
ATALANTA
ATHENA
ATLANTIS: A Women's Studies Journal/Journal d'etudes
  sur la femme
Attic Press
Aunt Lute Books
Autonomedia, Inc.
Banner Press International, Inc.
Barclay House
Beacon Press
BELLES LETTRES
BERKELEY WOMEN'S LAW JOURNAL
Black Rose Books Ltd.
Blue Dolphin Press, Inc.
BORDER/LINES
CAMERA OBSCURA: A Journal of Feminism and Film
  Theory
CANADIAN WOMAN STUDIES/les cahiers de la femme
Cardinal Press, Inc.
The Carolina Wren Press
Center for Public Representation
Chicory Blue Press
Chiron Press
CHIRON REVIEW
Cleis Press
Clothespin Fever Press
COLLAGES & BRICOLAGES
COLUMBUS FREE PRESS
COMPOST NEWSLETTER (CNL)
Council on Interracial Books For Children
COYDOG REVIEW
THE CREATIVE WOMAN
Crones' Own Press
CULTURE CONCRETE
DAUGHTER OF SARAH
DE NAR
DESDE ESTE LADO/FROM THIS SIDE
DEVIANCE
DHARMA COMBAT

WOMEN ARTISTS NEWS
THE WOMEN'S REVIEW OF BOOKS
Women's Studies Librarian, University of Wisconsin System
WOMENWISE
WORLD PERSPECTIVES
THE WRITERS' BAR-B-Q
Zed Books Ltd.

FESTIVALS

Coxland Press
Festival Publications
FOX VALLEY LIVING

FICTION

A as A Publishing
Abattoir Editions
ABBEY
Academy Chicago Publishers
ACM (ANOTHER CHICAGO MAGAZINE)
Acrobat Books
ACTA VICTORIANA
THE ADROIT EXPRESSION
AEGEAN REVIEW
Aegina Press, Inc.
AFFAIRE DE COEUR
Affiliated Writers of America, Inc.
AGADA
Again + Again Press
AGNI
AILERON, A LITERARY JOURNAL
AIM MAGAZINE
AKWEKON: A National Native American Literary & Arts Journal
AKWEKON LITERARY JOURNAL
ALABAMA LITERARY REVIEW
THE ALBANY REVIEW
THE ALCHEMIST
Alchemy Books
ALL AVAILABLE LIGHT
ALLEGHENY REVIEW
Alta Napa Press
Alternating Crimes Publishing
Amador Publishers
Amana Books
THE AMARANTH REVIEW
AMBIT
AMELIA
Amelia Press
American Audio Prose Library (non-print)
AMERICAS REVIEW
Ampersand Press
AND
Androgyne Books
ANEMONE
Angst World Library
ANIMAL TALES
ANQ: A Quarterly Journal of Short Articles, Notes, and Reviews
ANTAEUS
ANTIETAM REVIEW
THE ANTIGONISH REVIEW
THE ANTIOCH REVIEW
APALACHEE QUARTERLY
THE APPLE BLOSSOM CONNECTION
Applezaba Press
Arbiter Press
Ariadne Press
ARISTOS
Arjuna Library Press
The Armchair Detective Library
Arrowood Books
Arsenal Pulp Press, Ltd.
Arte Publico Press
ARTEMIS
ARTFUL DODGE
ARTICHOKE HEART
Artifact Press, Ltd.

As Is/So & So Press
ASH
Ashley Books, Inc.
Ashod Press
Associated Writing Programs
ASYLUM
Asylum Arts
The Atlantean Press
ATROCITY
Attic Press
Atticus Press
ATTICUS REVIEW
Author's Unlimited
Avalanche Press
AVEC
Avery Color Studios
AWP CHRONICLE
THE AZOREAN EXPRESS
BAKER STREET GAZETTE
Baker Street Publications
Bakhtin's Wife Publications
BAKUNIN
Bamberger Books
Banana Productions
Bank Street Press
Barn Owl Books
Beacon Press
BEAT SCENE
Beekman Publishers, Inc.
BEGINNING: THE MAGAZINE FOR THE WRITER IN THE COMMUNITY
THE BELLINGHAM REVIEW
BELLOWING ARK
Bellowing Ark Press
BELOIT FICTION JOURNAL
The Bench Press
THE BERKELEY MONTHLY
Berkeley Poets Workshop and Press
BETWEEN C & D
Beyond Baroque Foundation Publications
Biblia Candida
BIG CIGARS
BIG HAMMER
BIG SCREAM
Bilingual Review/Press
Birdalone Books
The Biting Idge/Miracle Press (Chrysalis Publications)
BkMk Press
Black & White & Read All Over Publishing Co.
THE BLACK FLY REVIEW
Black Heron Press
BLACK ICE
BLACK JACK & VALLEY GRAPEVINE
BLACK MULLET REVIEW
Black Sparrow Press
THE BLACK WARRIOR REVIEW
Blue Bird Publishing
Blue Heron Publishing, Inc.
BLUE HORSE
Blue Horse Publications
BLUE LIGHT REVIEW
BLUELINE
BOLD PRINT
BOMB MAGAZINE
Bomb Shelter Propaganda
BONE & FLESH
Books for All Times, Inc.
BOSTON LITERARY REVIEW
Bottom Dog Press
BOULEVARD
BOX 749 MAGAZINE
Boz Publishing
Branden Publishing Company
Brandywyne Books
Breitenbush Books, Inc.
Broken Moon Press
Brook House Press, Inc.
Harrison Brown, Publishers, Inc.

Brunswick Publishing Corporation
Burning Deck Press
BYLINE
C.C. Publishing Co.
Cacanadadada Press Ltd.
CACANADADADA REVIEW
Cadmus Editions
Caliban Press
THE CALIFORNIA QUARTERLY
CALLIOPE
CALYPSO: Journal of Narrative Poetry and Poetic Fiction
Cambric Press
CANADIAN AUTHOR & BOOKMAN
CANADIAN FICTION MAGAZINE
Cane Hill Press
CANVAS
THE CAPILANO REVIEW
Capra Press
Caravan Press
CAROLINA QUARTERLY
The Carolina Wren Press
Carpenter Press
Carroll & Graf Publishers, Inc.
Castle Peak Editions
Catbird Press
Cave Books
Cayuse Press
CENTER
Center Press
Center Press
CHALK CIRCLE
CHAMINADE LITERARY REVIEW
Chance Additions
Chandler & Sharp Publishers, Inc.
CHARITON REVIEW
Charnel House
Chax Press
CHELSEA
Chelsea Green Publishing Company
Cheops Books
Chicory Blue Press
CHIPS OFF THE WRITER'S BLOCK
Chiron Press
CHIRON REVIEW
CICADA
CIMARRON REVIEW
Cinco Puntos Press
City Lights Books
CITY RANT
Claycomb Press, Inc.
Cleis Press
CLINTON ST.
CLOCKWATCH REVIEW
Clockwatch Review Press
Clothespin Fever Press
The Clyde Press
Coach House Press
Coffee House Press
Coker Publishing House
COLD-DRILL
COLLAGES & BRICOLAGES
Colonial Press
COLOR WHEEL
COLORADO REVIEW: A Journal of Contemporary
 Literature
Columbia Publishing Company, Inc.
Commonwealth Press Virginia
Communication Creativity
COMPOST NEWSLETTER (CNL)
Concourse Press
Confluence Press, Inc.
CONJUNCTIONS
Context Publications
Copper Beech Press
Corfa Books
Cornerstone Press
CORNFIELD REVIEW
Cosmic Footnotes Publications

Coteau Books
COTTONWOOD
Council Oak Books
Countryman Press
COYDOG REVIEW
CRAB CREEK REVIEW
CRAMPED AND WET
CRAWLSPACE
CRAZYHORSE
CRAZYQUILT LITERARY QUARTERLY
Creative Concern Publications
Croissant & Company
Crones' Own Press
CROOKED ROADS
CROP DUST
CROSS TIMBERS REVIEW
CROSSCURRENTS, A QUARTERLY
Crossroads Publications, Inc.
Crossway Books
CRUCIBLE
CULTURE CONCRETE
Curbstone Press
CURLEY
CURTAINS
CUTBANK
CUTTING EDGE QUARTERLY
CWM
Dalkey Archive Press
Dawnwood Press
DAYSPRING
Dead Angel Press
DEAD OF NIGHT MAGAZINE
DECEMBER MAGAZINE
DELIRIUM
Delta Publishing Company
Dembner Books
DESCANT
DESCANT
DESDE ESTE LADO/FROM THIS SIDE
The Devonshire Publishing Co.
DHARMA COMBAT
DIAMOND HITCHHIKER COBWEBS
THE DILETTANTE FORUM
DIMENSION
Distinctive Publishing Corp.
Dolphin-Moon Press
The Donning Company / Publishers
Dragon Cloud Books
Dragon Gate, Inc.
The Dragonsbreath Press
DREAM INTERNATIONAL QUARTERLY
DREAMS & VISIONS
Chris Drumm Books
Duck Down Press
Dufour Editions Inc.
DuReve Publications
Dustbooks
E.T.M. Publishing
Eagle's View Publishing
Earth Star Publications
EARTH'S DAUGHTERS: Feminist Arts Periodical
East Eagle Press
Eastern Caribbean Institute
The Ecco Press
Ediciones El Gato Tuerto
ELDRITCH SCIENCE
THE ELEPHANT-EAR
ELF: ECLECTIC LITERARY FORUM (ELF MAGA-
 ZINE)
ELT Press
EMERALD CITY COMIX & STORIES
THE EMSHOCK LETTER
English Language Literature Association
EOTU, Magazine of Experimental Fiction
EPOCH
Paul S. Eriksson, Publisher
EVENT
Excalibur Publishing

Tilbury House, Publishers
Timely Books
Tippy Reed Publishing
Tiptoe Literary Service
TOAD HIWAY
Toad Hiway Press
Tombouctou Books
TOOK
TOUCHSTONE LITERARY JOURNAL
TRAY FULL OF LAB MICE PUBLICATIONS
TRIQUARTERLY
Truly Fine Press
Tryckeriforlaget
TUCUMCARI LITERARY REVIEW
Tudor Publishers, Inc.
TURNSTILE
Turnstone Press
The Twickenham Press
Tyger Press
Tyro Publishing
Ultramarine Publishing Co., Inc.
UNBRIDLED LUST!
Unicorn Press
UNION STREET REVIEW
UNIROD MAGAZINE
United Artists
University Editions, Inc.
Urion Press
US1 WORKSHEETS
Valkyrie Publishing House
Valley House Gallery Press
THE VAMPIRE JOURNAL
Vanitas Press
Vehicule Press
VERVE
A VERY SMALL MAGAZINE
Vesta Publications Limited
THE VINCENT BROTHERS REVIEW
VIRGIN MEAT
THE VOLCANO REVIEW
VOLITION
Volunteer Publications
Vortex Editions
WASHINGTON REVIEW
Water Row Press
Waterfront Press
Wayland Press
WEIRDBOOK
Wesley Press
West Anglia Publications
WEST BRANCH
Westburg Associates, Publishers
THE WESTMINSTER REVIEW
Westwind Press
Wet Editions
Wheel of Fire Press
WHETSTONE
WHISKEY ISLAND MAGAZINE
The White Cross Press
The White Ewe Press
White Pine Press
The George Whittell Memorial Press
THE WIDENER REVIEW
Wild & Woolley
WILLOW SPRINGS
Window Publications
WindRiver Publishing Company
Windsong Press
Wineberry Press
WISCONSIN REVIEW
WITNESS
Woldt Publishing
Wolfhound Press
Woodcock Press
Woodsong Graphics Inc.
THE WORCESTER REVIEW
WORDS OF WISDOM
WRIT

THE WRITERS' BAR-B-Q
THE WRITERS' BLOC*
WRITERS CONNECTION
WRITERS' FORUM
WRITERS GAZETTE NEWSLETTER
WRITER'S GUIDELINES MAGAZINE
THE WRITER'S HAVEN
Writers House Press
WRITER'S INFO
WRITER'S LIFELINE
THE WRITER'S NOOK NEWS
WRITER'S VOICE
WRITING
Xenos Books
XTRAS
The Yellow Press
YELLOW SILK: Journal Of Erotic Arts
The Yolla Bolly Press
ZENOS
Zephyr Press
Zirlinson Publishing

FILM, VIDEO

Acting World Books
Afta Press
AFTERIMAGE
THE AGENCIES-WHAT THE ACTOR NEEDS TO
    KNOW
AKWEKON: A National Native American Literary &
    Arts Journal
AKWEKON LITERARY JOURNAL
Amherst Media
ANQ: A Quarterly Journal of Short Articles, Notes, and
    Reviews
Arden Press, Inc.
ART CALENDAR
ART PAPERS
ARTPAPER
THE AUTOGRAPH COLLECTOR'S MAGAZINE
Autonomedia, Inc.
Axiom Information Resources
BAKER STREET GAZETTE
Baker Street Publications
BEAT SCENE
Between The Lines
Blue Heron Press
BLUE LIGHTS
Blue Lights Publications
BOMB MAGAZINE
CAMERA OBSCURA: A Journal of Feminism and Film
    Theory
CANADIAN AUTHOR & BOOKMAN
CATALYST, A Magazine of Heart and Mind
Children Of Mary
THE...CHRONICLE
CINEASTE MAGAZINE
CLASSIC IMAGES
COLUMBUS FREE PRESS
Communicom Publishing Company
Copyright Information Services
COYDOG REVIEW
Creatures At Large Press
CROW—The Alternative Magazine
CROW MAGAZINE
CULTURE CONCRETE
dbS Productions
DEAD OF NIGHT MAGAZINE
DECEMBER MAGAZINE
Dembner Books
DESDE ESTE LADO/FROM THIS SIDE
DIAMOND HITCHHIKER COBWEBS
Empty Closet Enterprises
ENTRY
Excalibur Publishing
EXETER STUDIES IN AMERICAN & COMMON-
    WEALTH ARTS
Festival Publications
FIDELIS ET VERUS

FILM
FILM QUARTERLY
FILM THREAT VIDEO GUIDE
FREE PRESS
THE FREEDONIA GAZETTE
The Future Press
Gaslight Publications
GAUNTLET: Exploring the Limits of Free Expression
Glenhurst Publications, Inc.
GO MAGAZINE
Grosvenor USA
THE HAUNTED JOURNAL
THE HOLLYWOOD ACTING COACHES AND
   TEACHERS DIRECTORY
Hollywood Film Archive
HORIZONS BEYOND
HORIZONS WEST
HOT WIRE: Journal of Women's Music & Culture
IMAGINATION MAGAZINE
JOE SOAP'S CANOE
JOURNAL OF BORDERLAND RESEARCH
JUMP CUT, A Review of Contemporary Media
Kontexts Publications
KREATURE COMFORTS
Lake View Press
LANCASTER INDEPENDENT PRESS
Langston Press
THE LAS VEGAS INSIDER
LEFT CURVE
LIGHTWORKS MAGAZINE
Limelight Editions
Lone Eagle Publishing Co.
MANOA: A Pacific Journal of International Writing
McFarland & Company, Inc., Publishers
McPherson & Company Publishers
MEDIA SPOTLIGHT
MedLife Communications, Inc.
Midmarch Arts Press
MUSIC OF THE SPHERES
THE MYSTERY FANCIER
N-B-T-V
The Neither/Nor Press
THE NEW DANCE REVIEW
New Levee Press
NEW ORLEANS REVIEW
New York Zoetrope Inc.
NOCTURNAL NEWS
NORTHERN LIGHTS STUDIES IN CREATIVITY
Norton Coker Press
Nuclear Trenchcoated Subway Prophets Publications
OHIO RENAISSANCE REVIEW
ORGANICA
THE OVERLOOK CONNECTION
PAUNCH
P-FORM
Pittore Euforico
The Post-Industrial Press
POSTMODERN CULTURE
Prudhomme Press
QUANTUM: Science Fiction & Fantasy Review
RAMPIKE
RE/SEARCH
Re/Search Publications
RGM Publications
ST. LOUIS JOURNALISM REVIEW
SALMAGUNDI
SALON: A Journal of Aesthetics
SCAREAPHANALIA
SCHMAGA
SCRIPT IDEAS
The Segue Foundation
Slate Press
SLEUTH JOURNAL
THE SMALL PRESS BOOK REVIEW
SOUTHERN QUARTERLY: A Journal of the Arts in the
   South
STICKY CARPET DIGEST
Strawberry Hill Press

Sun Eagle Publishing
Tambra Publishing
TechWest Publications
THEATRE DESIGN AND TECHNOLOGY
THEY WON'T STAY DEAD!
Theytus Books Ltd.
THIRD RAIL
Third Rail Press
THIRD WAY
THE THREEPENNY REVIEW
TOOK
TQS Publications (Tonatiuh - Quinto Sol International
   Inc.)
TRIVIUM
UNBRIDLED LUST!
Union Square Press
THE VAMPIRE JOURNAL
Vestal Press Ltd
VIETNAM GENERATION: A Journal of Recent History
   and Contemporary Issues
Visa Books (Division of South Continent Corporation Pty
   Ltd)
WE ARE THE WEIRD
WindRiver Publishing Company
Windsong Books International
Woldt Publishing
WOMEN ARTISTS NEWS
WORLD OF FANDOM MAGAZINE
Zirlinson Publishing
ZOOMAR

F. SCOTT FITZGERALD

LOST GENERATION JOURNAL

FLORIDA

Pineapple Press, Inc.
Woldt Publishing

FOLKLORE

AFRICAN STUDIES
Akwesasne Notes
Alaska Native Language Center
AMERICAN SQUAREDANCE
AMERICAN WRITING: A MAGAZINE
Ancient City Press
Avery Color Studios
Axelrod Publishing of Tampa Bay
THE AZOREAN EXPRESS
BALDER
Ballena Press
Beacon Press
Bergin & Garvey Publishers
Birdalone Books
Blue Crane Books
Borealis Press Limited
CAL NEWSLETTER
CEILIDH: AN INFORMAL GATHERING FOR STORY
   & SONG
Celtic Heritage Press, Inc.
Children's Book Press
The Clyde Press
COME-ALL-YE
Commonwealth Press Virginia
COMPOST NEWSLETTER (CNL)
Coteau Books
Cottage Books
Council For Indian Education
Coxland Press
COYDOG REVIEW
Creative With Words Publications (CWW)
Crossroads Publications, Inc.
CULTWATCH RESPONSE
Depot Press
DIAMOND HITCHHIKER COBWEBS
E-Heart Press, Inc.
FOLK ERA TODAY
Foundation Books
FOX VALLEY LIVING

Gavea-Brown Publications
GENERATIONS SANPETE: INDEX OF ORAL HISTORIES OF RURAL UTAH
GRASS ROOTS
GREEN EGG
THE HAUNTED JOURNAL
Hoffman Press
HORIZONS WEST
THE IMMIGRANT
INFINITY LIMITED, A Journal for the Somewhat Eccentric
Institute for Southern Studies
IRISH LITERARY SUPPLEMENT
THE ISLAND
JEWISH LINGUISTIC STUDIES
Kar-Ben Copies, Inc.
KELTIC FRINGE
L.A.N.D.
LAKE SUPERIOR MAGAZINE
Legacy Books (formerly Folklore Associates)
Lexikos
The Lockhart Press
LORE AND LANGUAGE
Luna Bisonte Prods
MAGIC REALISM
Majority, Inc.
MALEDICTA: The International Journal of Verbal Aggression
Maledicta Press
Meyerbooks, Publisher
The Middle Atlantic Press
Misty Hill Press
Moonsquilt Press
Mosaic Press
Museum of New Mexico Press
Nemeton Publishing
NEW MOON RISING
Night Owl Publishers
NightinGale Resources
Northland Publishing Company
NOTEBOOK/CUADERNO: A LITERARY JOURNAL
The Olive Press Publications
Outlaw Books
Parabola Books
PARABOLA MAGAZINE
Perivale Press
Petroglyph Press, Ltd.
Pioneer Books
Placebo Press
Pocahontas Press, Inc.
Poetry Wales Press, Ltd.
Point Riders Press
Publications of Arts (Art Resources for Teachers & Students)
Rainy Day Press
Rand Editions/Tofua Press
Rarach Press
THE REDNECK REVIEW OF LITERATURE
RENEGADE
Research & Discovery Publications
REVIEW LA BOOCHE
ROMANIAN REVIEW
SCHMAGA
SEMIOTEXT(E)
Serpent & Eagle Press
SEZ: A Multi-Racial Journal of Poetry & People's Culture
Shadow Press, U.S.A.
Signal Books
SING OUT! The Folk Song Magazine
SKYLARK
Sleepy Hollow Press
SOCIETE
Stone Circle Press
Strawberry Hill Press
A THEATER OF BLOOD
Thornwood Book Publishers
Three Continents Press, Inc.
Thunder Creek Publishing Co-operative

Top Of The Mountain Publishing
TRADITION
TREASURE HUNTING RESEARCH BULLETIN
UMI Research Press
UNBRIDLED LUST!
THE UNDERGROUND FOREST - LA SELVA SUBTERRANEA
United Lumbee Nation
UNITED LUMBEE NATION TIMES
THE VAMPIRE JOURNAL
WALKING-STICK NOTES
Ward Hill Press
Westgate Press
Wheel of Fire Press
White Cliffs Media Company
WISCONSIN TRAILS
Witwatersrand University Press
Woodsong Graphics Inc.
THE WRITERS' BAR-B-Q
WTI Publishing Co.
Yellow Moon Press

FRANCE, FRENCH

THE ABER BULLETIN
AVEC
Catbird Press
The Chicot Press
Citeaux Commentarii Cistercienses
CITEAUX: COMMENTARII CISTERCIENSES
COLLAGES & BRICOLAGES
CURTAINS
ENFANTAISIE: La Revue des Jeunes
FRANK: AN INTERNATIONAL JOURNAL OF CONTEMPORARY WRITING AND ART
INTERNATIONAL POETRY REVIEW
LOST GENERATION JOURNAL
Michigan Romance Studies
OSIRIS
RAMPIKE
REVUE CELFAN REVIEW
Rio Grande Press
Scots Plaid Press (Persephone Press)
SE LA VIE WRITER'S JOURNAL
SERIE D'ECRITURE
Soleil Press
Station Hill Press
Synergistic Press
TRANSITIONS ABROAD: The Guide to Living, Learning, and Working Overseas
Unicorn Press

FUTURISM

ACTIVIST
THE ACTS THE SHELFLIFE
America West Publishers
And/Or Press, Inc.
Angst World Library
ART INFORMATION REPORT
BALDER
Banana Productions
THE CHAOS NETWORK
Cheshire Books
COLUMBUS FREE PRESS
COMPOST NEWSLETTER (CNL)
Coxland Press
DELIRIUM
Devin-Adair, Publishers, Inc.
DHARMA COMBAT
DIAMOND HITCHHIKER COBWEBS
DIE FAT PIGGY DIE
ECOSOCIALIST REVIEW
EUTHANASIA ROSES
Fast Forward Publishing
FELL SWOOP
Free Association Books (FAB)
THE FUTURIST
Futurum Forlag
Gallopade Publishing Group

796

THE GAME'S AFOOT
GATEAVISA
GREEN MULTILOGUE
GREEN SYNTHESIS-A NEWSLETTER AND JOUR-
    NAL FOR SOCIAL ECOLOGY, DEEP ECOLOGY,
    BIOREGIONALISM, ECOFEMINISM, AND THE
    GREEN MOVEMENT
GREY CITY JOURNAL
THE HUMAN ECOLOGY AND ENERGY BALANC-
    ING SCIENTIST
Human Ecology Balancing Sciences, Inc.
THE HUMANIST
JABBERWOCKY
KALDRON, An International Journal Of Visual Poetry
    and Language Art
Knowledge Systems, Inc.
Kumarian Press, Inc.
LITTLE FREE PRESS
THE LOOGIE
MESSAGE POST
Misty Hill Press
NET
Nuclear Trenchcoated Subway Prophets Publications
Nuventures Publishing
Ocean Tree Books
ON COURSE
OTISIAN DIRECTORY
PIG IRON
Polymath Systems
QUANTUM: Science Fiction & Fantasy Review
RAMPIKE
Rocky Top Publications
(ROWBOAT)
Savant Garde Workshop
SCHMAGA
Scribblers Publishing, Ltd.
Seventh-Wing Publications
SPECTRUM STORIES
SQUARE ONE - A Magazine of Fiction
Stillpoint Publishing
SURVIVE & WIN
UNARIUS LIGHT
UNBRIDLED LUST!
Vortex Editions
THE WAVE
WE MAGAZINE
We Press
WITHIN & BEYOND
WOMAN OF POWER
Worldwatch Institute
XENOPHILIA
XEROLAGE
Zirlinson Publishing

GAELIC

THE ALTERED MIND
Celtic Heritage Press, Inc.
Cottage Books
Coxland Press
The F. Marion Crawford Memorial Society
Esoterica, The Craft Press
THE ISLAND
KELTIC FRINGE
KELTICA: THE INTER-CELTIC JOURNAL
Nuventures Publishing
OTISIAN DIRECTORY
Poetry Ireland Press
POETRY IRELAND REVIEW
THE ROMANTIST
Stone Circle Press
Sunburst Press
Top Of The Mountain Publishing
Wolfhound Press

GAMES

ALL OF THE ABOVE
Author's Unlimited
Benjamin Press

BLACKJACK FORUM
Bronx Books
Capra Press
Carousel Press
Chess Enterprises, Inc.
CHESS IN INDIANA
CHESS LIFE
The Clyde Press
Commonwealth Press Virginia
COMPUTER GAMING WORLD
Devyn Press
Dirigo Books, Inc.
DISC GOLF WORLD NEWS
EN PASSANT
The Evergreen Press
Evon Publishing
Explorer's Guide Publishing
Foxfire Press
Front Row Experience
Gallopade Publishing Group
Guarionex Press Ltd.
Human Kinetics Pub. Inc.
Impact Publishers, Inc.
JUDY
KIDS LIB NEWS
Klutz Press
Liberty Publishing Company, Inc.
MEDIA SPOTLIGHT
Micro Pro Litera Press
MOMENTUM
Mustang Publishing Co.
Naturist Foundation
NET
OHIO CHESS BULLETIN
Oness Press
Pando Publications
PENGUIN DIP
Polymath Systems
The Preservation Press
R.G.E. Publishing
Salt Lick Press
SCHOOL MATES
THE SCIENCE FICTION CONVENTION REGISTER
The Second Hand
SHINING STAR
SLEUTH JOURNAL
UNBRIDLED LUST!
Village Books
THE VORTEX (A Historical and Wargamers Jornal)
VOYAGES SF
WATERBURY CHESS CLUB BULLETIN
WCCF REPORTS
Wordland
Zirlinson Publishing

GARDENING

ACTINIDIA ENTHUSIASTS NEWSLETTER
Blue Dolphin Press, Inc.
Blue Sky Marketing, Inc.
Bookworm Publishing Company
BURWOOD JOURNAL
Center For Self-Sufficiency
Chelsea Green Publishing Company
Cheshire Books
The Chicot Press
Christmans
CJE NEWSLETTER (Newsletter of the Coalition for Jobs
    & the Environment)
Countryman Press
DESIGN BOOK REVIEW
Devin-Adair, Publishers, Inc.
Dirigo Books, Inc.
Foxfire Press
Fulcrum, Inc.
Gallopade Publishing Group
The Globe Pequot Press
GRASS ROOTS
THE GROWING EDGE MAGAZINE

HOME RESOURCE MAGAZINE
HORTIDEAS
Interlink Publishing Group, Inc.
JOURNAL FOR ANTHROPOSOPHY
KIDSCIENCE
LAKE SUPERIOR MAGAZINE
Littlebooks
LIVING OFF THE LAND, Subtropic Newsletter
THE LLEWELLYN NEW TIMES
Llewellyn Publications
Mayhaven Publishing
Mermaid Press
THE NATIONAL FARM DIRECTORY
Naturegraph Publishers, Inc.
Newton-Cline Press
Night Owl Publishers
ON COURSE
Out West Publishing
Petroglyph Press, Ltd.
Pine & Palm Press
Pineapple Press, Inc.
POTPOURRI PARTY-LINE
Prospect Hill Press
Pruett Publishing Company
The Rateavers
Red Eye Press
RFD
Ross Books
Running Press
Sagapress, Inc.
Sandhill Publications
Sasquatch Books
SCHMAGA
SCIENCE/HEALTH ABSTRACTS
SEED SAVERS EXCHANGE
Sentinel Books
Shearer Publishing
Sierra Club Books
SINSEMILLA TIPS (Domestic Marijuana Journal)
SMS Publishing Corp.
SPECTRUM—The Wholistic News Magazine
SPROUTLETTER
Stone Bridge Press
Strawberry Hill Press
Ten Speed Press
Timber Press
Tortilla Press
Van Patten Publishing
Village Books
Whitehorse
THE WHOLE CHILE PEPPER
Wilchester Publishing Company
Williamson Publishing Company, Inc.
Woodbridge Press
Woodsong Graphics Inc.
WTI Publishing Co.

GAY

ACTIVIST
THE ADVOCATE
Afta Press
Alamo Square Press
Alyson Publications, Inc.
Amethyst Press
APAEROS
ARTPAPER
Ashley Books, Inc.
ATALANTA
Bakhtin's Wife Publications
Bay Press
BAY WINDOWS
Beacon Press
Belhue Press
Drew Blood Press Ltd.
BORDER/LINES
CHAKRA
Chandler & Sharp Publishers, Inc.
Chiron Press

CHIRON REVIEW
COLLAGES & BRICOLAGES
Columbia Publishing Company, Inc.
COLUMBUS FREE PRESS
Communitas Press
CROW MAGAZINE
DEVIANCE
The Devon Publishing Co., Inc.
Dragon Disks
Esoterica Press
THE EVERGREEN CHRONICLES
FAG RAG
Feminist Mens' Publications
THE FINAL PAGE
FIRSTHAND
Five Fingers Press
FIVE FINGERS REVIEW
FREE PRESS
FUSE MAGAZINE
Gai Saber Monographs
GAY CHICAGO MAGAZINE
Gay Sunshine Press, Inc.
GAYELLOW PAGES
GLB Publishers
Good Gay Poets Press
GREY CITY JOURNAL
Harbinger House
HerBooks
IKON
IKON, Inc.
Illuminati
Infolib Resources
Institute for Southern Studies
JAMES WHITE REVIEW; A Gay Men's Literary Quarterly
JH Press
Kitchen Sink Press
Kitchen Table: Women of Color Press
Knights Press
L.G.L.C. NEWSLETTER
LAMBDA BOOK REPORT
Langston Press
THE LAVENDER NETWORK
LIBERATION! Journal of Revolutionary Marxism
Libertarians for Gay and Lesbian Concerns (LGLC)
THE LOOGIE
Los Hombres Press
LuraMedia, Inc.
Mho & Mho Works
Mogul Book and FilmWorks
MOM...GUESS WHAT! NEWSPAPER & TYPESET-TING
MONADNOCK GAY MEN
Motheroot Publications
Multiple Dimensions
NAMBLA BULLETIN
New Levee Press
NEW SINS
New Society Publishers
New Star Books Ltd.
Odysseus Enterprises Ltd.
OFF OUR BACKS
OTISIAN DIRECTORY
Pagan Press
P-FORM
The Place In The Woods
The Preservation Press
PROCESSED WORLD
RADICAL AMERICA
Red Letter Press
RFD
Seismograph Publications
SHMATE
Shmate Press
SOCIALISM AND SEXUALITY
SPIT
Strawberry Hill Press
Syracuse Cultural Workers

Timely Books
Times Change Press
TRIBE: An American Gay Journal
Twelvetrees Press/Twin Palms Publishers
UNBRIDLED LUST!
Unified Publications
Union Park Press
VIETNAM GENERATION: A Journal of Recent History
  and Contemporary Issues
Volcano Press, Inc
W.I.M. Publications
THE WISHING WELL
Woldt Publishing
WOMENWISE

GENEALOGY

THE ABER BULLETIN
American Impressions
ANCESTRY NEWSLETTER
Ancestry Publishing
ARNOLD ANCESTRY
CARROLL CABLES
The Clyde Press
The Curlew Press
W.S. Dawson Co.
DeerTrail Books
DorPete Press
The Everett Companies, Publishing Division
EWING EXCHANGE
FERGUSON FILES
GATHERING GIBSONS
GENEALOGICAL COMPUTING
Genealogical Publishing Co., Inc.
GENERATIONS SANPETE: INDEX OF ORAL HIS-
  TORIES OF RURAL UTAH
Guarionex Press Ltd.
Heart of the Lakes Publishing
Heirloom Publications
Heritage Books, Inc.
IRISH FAMILY JOURNAL
Iron Gate Publishing
JEWISH LINGUISTIC STUDIES
KELTIC FRINGE
Kinseeker Publications
NORTON NOTES
NOTEBOOK/CUADERNO: A LITERARY JOURNAL
O'Laughlin Press (Irish Genealogical Foundation)
Panorama West Publishing
Pioneer Books
Plas Y Bryn Press
POETRY QUARTERLY
R & M Publishing Company
Scots Plaid Press (Persephone Press)
Thornwood Book Publishers
Tyro Publishing
The Urbana Free Library
WANDERING WOLFS
Wright-Armstead Associates
Writers Publishing Service Co.
ZINGSHEIM TIMES

GEOGRAPHY

American & World Geographic Publishing
Bear Flag Books
Big River Publishing
The Denali Press
Educare Press
Escart Press
EXIT 13 MAGAZINE
Falcon Press Publishing Company
Gallopade Publishing Group
LAKE SUPERIOR MAGAZINE
LANDSCAPE
Lexikos
THE NORTHERN REVIEW
Pinery Press
Plas Y Bryn Press
Rocky Top Publications

Talon Books Ltd
TeakWood Press
TIERRA DEL FUEGO MAGAZINE
TOWPATHS
THE UNDERGROUND FOREST - LA SELVA SUB-
  TERRANEA
University of Calgary Press
The Urbana Free Library
Utah Geographic Series
WHOLE EARTH REVIEW
Witwatersrand University Press
WOMEN AND ENVIRONMENTS
XENOPHILIA
Zagier & Urruty Publicaciones

GEOLOGY

Cave Books
JOURNAL FOR ANTHROPOSOPHY
Mountain Press Publishing Co.
THE NORTHERN REVIEW
Genny Smith Books

GERMAN

AUFBAU
R.J. Bender Publishing
DIMENSION
Dufour Editions Inc.
The Edwin Mellen Press
Friends Of Tucson Pub Lib/The Maguey Press
Fromm International Publishing Corporation
Holger Harfst, Publisher
INDIA CURRENTS
INTERNATIONAL POETRY REVIEW
JOURNAL FOR ANTHROPOSOPHY
THE MILITARY ADVISOR
NEW GERMAN REVIEW: A Journal of Germanic
  Studies
SCHMAGA
Sharp & Dunnigan Publications, Incorporated
Three Continents Press, Inc.
Top Of The Mountain Publishing
TRANSITIONS ABROAD: The Guide to Living,
  Learning, and Working Overseas
Unicorn Press
White Horse Press

GOVERNMENT

Amana Books
Beacon Press
Brenner Information Group
Chandler & Sharp Publishers, Inc.
Children Of Mary
CJE NEWSLETTER (Newsletter of the Coalition for Jobs
  & the Environment)
COLUMBUS FREE PRESS
THE CONSTANTIAN
Corfa Books
" "...A DEAD BEAT POET PRODUCTION
The Devonshire Publishing Co.
ECOSOCIALIST REVIEW
EUTHANASIA ROSES
The Evergreen Press
FIDELIS ET VERUS
FPMI Communications, Inc.
Futurum Forlag
Greensleeves Publishing
INNOVATING
KETTERING REVIEW
LITTLE FREE PRESS
M.H. Macy & Company
New Levee Press
New View Publications
THE NORTHERN REVIEW
Pacific Research Institute
Planning/Communications
The Rensselaerville Systems Training Center
SOCIETY
SOULLESS STRUCTURES

Pruett Publishing Company
RENEGADE
Sandhills Press
Skyline West Press
Thunder Creek Publishing Co-operative
TRADITION
WANBLI HO
WESTERN AMERICAN LITERATURE

GREAT LAKES

COLLAGES & BRICOLAGES
LAKE SUPERIOR MAGAZINE
THE NORTHERN REVIEW
Pfeifer-Hamilton
SKYLARK

GREEK

AEGEAN REVIEW
Bandanna Books
Bolchazy-Carducci Publishers, Inc.
THE CHARIOTEER
Educare Press
GROUND WATER REVIEW
JOURNAL OF THE HELLENIC DIASPORA
Kelsey St. Press
MIDDLE EASTERN DANCER
Pella Publishing Co
Talking Leaves Press
University of Calgary Press
Wide World Publishing/TETRA

GRIEVING

Barclay House
Comforter Publishing
HEALING PATH
New Idea Press, Inc.
New Liberty Press

GUIDANCE

C.C. Publishing Co.
Comforter Publishing
Energeia Publishing, Inc.
The Findhorn Press
Impact Publishers, Inc.
Knowledge, Ideas & Trends, Inc. (KIT)
HJ Kramer, Inc
Organization for Equal Education of the Sexes, Inc. (OEES)
Paragraph Publications
ROMEO NEWSLETTER
The Saunderstown Press
Small Helm Press
Star Books, Inc.
Stillpoint Publishing
Thunder Creek Publishing Co-operative
Williamson Publishing Company, Inc.

HAIKU

ACTA VICTORIANA
AHA Books
THE AMARANTH REVIEW
AMELIA
Amelia Press
BACKBOARD
BLACK BEAR REVIEW
CANADIAN AUTHOR & BOOKMAN
Chiron Press
CHIRON REVIEW
CICADA
CRAWLSPACE
CRAZYQUILT LITERARY QUARTERLY
DAYSPRING
DRAGONFLY: East/West Haiku Quarterly
DREAM INTERNATIONAL QUARTERLY
ELF: ECLECTIC LITERARY FORUM (ELF MAGA-
ZINE)
FROGPOND: Quarterly Haiku Journal
From Here Press

Frozen Waffles Press/Shattered Sidewalks Press; 25th
Century Chapbooks
HAIKU ZASSHI ZO
High/Coo Press
HMS Press
THE HOWLING MANTRA
HUNGRY ZIPPER
IDIOM 23
IMAGINATION MAGAZINE
INKSTONE
Inkstone Press
Insight Press
ISSUE ONE
K
Kenyette Productions
LILLIPUT REVIEW
Literary Publications Company
Little River Press
LIZZENGREASY
THE LOOGIE
Los Hombres Press
MATI
MAYFLY
Middlewood Press
MIDWEST CHAPARRAL
MIRRORS - IN THE SPIRIT OF HAIKU
MODERN HAIKU
THE MONOCACY VALLEY REVIEW
Muso Press
My Mother's House - Aitini Talo
New Cicada
NEW CICADA
New Hope International
NEW HOPE INTERNATIONAL REVIEW
The North Carolina Haiku Society Press
NORTHEAST
Omega Cottonwood Press
PARNASSUS LITERARY JOURNAL
THE PLOVER (Chidori)
POETRY HALIFAX DARTMOUTH
POETS' ROUNDTABLE
PORTLAND REVIEW
THE RED PAGODA, A JOURNAL OF HAIKU
REFLECTIONS
Scots Plaid Press (Persephone Press)
SKYLARK
Swamp Press
TANDAVA
TIGHTROPE
UNBRIDLED LUST!
THE UNDERGROUND FOREST - LA SELVA SUB-
TERRANEA
THE WAVE
West Anglia Publications
WILDFLOWER
Wildflower Press
XTRAS
Youth Policy Institute

HAWAII

Aka Press
BAMBOO RIDGE, THE HAWAII WRITERS' QUAR-
TERLY
Bamboo Ridge Press
The Bess Press
Beyond Words Publishing, Inc.
CHAMINADE LITERARY REVIEW
Robert Erdmann Publishing
Falcon Press Publishing Company
HAWAI'I REVIEW
MANOA: A Pacific Journal of International Writing
Mutual Publishing of Honolulu
NEW AGE DIGEST
Paradise Publications
Petroglyph Press, Ltd.
Petronium Press
Riegel Publishing
Unique Adventures Press

Wide World Publishing/TETRA
Winn Books
Wonder View Press

HEALTH

ADAPTED PHYSICAL ACTIVITY QUARTERLY (APAQ)
AIGA Publications
All American Press
Allergy Publications
Alpine Guild
Alta Napa Press
Amador Publishers
America West Publishers
Anaphase II
And/Or Press, Inc.
THE ANIMALS' AGENDA
Artemis Press, Inc.
Ash Tree Publishing
Ashley Books, Inc.
Aslan Publishing
Aurora Press
Avery Publishing Group, Inc.
Axelrod Publishing of Tampa Bay
Backwoods Books
Bellwether Productions, Inc.
Beyond Words Publishing, Inc.
Bio-Probe, Inc.
Blue Poppy Press
Blue Water Publishing, Inc.
Bonus Books, Inc.
Borderland Sciences Research Foundation
Branden Publishing Company
Bronx Books
Bull Publishing Co.
Caravan Press
Cassandra Press
Center for Public Representation
Ceres Press
Cin Publications
City Spirit Publications
THE CIVIL ABOLITIONIST
CLUBHOUSE
COACHING VOLLEYBALL
COACHING WOMEN'S BASKETBALL
COMMUNITY DEVELOPMENT JOURNAL
COMPOST NEWSLETTER (CNL)
Comprehensive Health Education Foundation (CHEF)
CONNECTICUT NATURALLY
Conscious Living
CONSTRUCTIVE ACTION NEWSLETTER
The Consumer's Press, Inc.
Cosmoenergetics Publications
Cougar Books
CountrySide Business Publications
CRCS Publications
The Crossing Press
D.I.N. Publications
Devida Publication
Devin-Adair, Publishers, Inc.
DIET & HEALTH SERIES
Dimi Press
Dirigo Books, Inc.
DOCTOR-PATIENT STUDIES
Down There Press
DuReve Publications
EAP DIGEST
ECOSOCIALIST REVIEW
Envirographics
Robert Erdmann Publishing
Esquire Books, Inc.
FAMILY LIFE EDUCATOR
Fell Publishers, Inc.
FELL'S HEALTH SERIES
The Findhorn Press
FOREFRONT—HEALTH INVESTIGATIONS
FORESIGHT MAGAZINE
The Chas. Franklin Press

Free Association Books (FAB)
Free Spirit Publishing Inc.
Gallaudet University Press
Garret Press
Glen Abbey Books, Inc.
Glenbridge Publishing Ltd.
Golden West Books
Grace and Goddess Unlimited
GRASS ROOTS
GREEN MULTILOGUE
THE GROVE
Gurze Books
Haight-Ashbury Publications
Harrow and Heston, Publishers
HEALING PATH
Health Alert Press
Health Educator Publications, Inc.
Health Plus Publishers
Health Press
Healthmere Press, Inc.
HEALTH/PAC BULLETIN
HEALTHSHARING: A Canadian Women's Health Quarterly
Herald Press
Hickman Systems - New Age Books
Himalayan Publishers
Hoffman Press
Hohm Press
Hope Publishing House
THE HUMAN ECOLOGY AND ENERGY BALANCING SCIENTIST
Human Ecology Balancing Sciences, Inc.
Human Kinetics Pub. Inc.
Hunter House Inc., Publishers
IBS Press
Impact Publishers, Inc.
INNER SEARCH
Inner Traditions International
INTEGRAL YOGA MAGAZINE
International Childbirth Education Association, Inc.
JEWISH VEGETARIANS OF NORTH AMERICA
Jigsaw Publishing House
Joelle Publishing, Inc.
Johnson Institute
Jones River Press
JOURNAL FOR ANTHROPOSOPHY
JOURNAL OF BORDERLAND RESEARCH
JOURNAL OF PSYCHOACTIVE DRUGS
JOURNAL OF TEACHING IN PHYSICAL EDUCATION
JOURNAL OF VISION REHABILITATION
Michael Kesend, Publishing, Ltd.
KIDS LIB NEWS
KIDSCIENCE
HJ Kramer, Inc
LANCASTER INDEPENDENT PRESS
Langston Press
Kent P. Larsen, Inc.
Leisure Press
Life Energy Media
Life Enhancement
Lion Press
Little Sam & Co. Press
LivingQuest
THE LLEWELLYN NEW TIMES
Llewellyn Publications
Billy Jack Ludwig Holding Co.
LuraMedia, Inc.
MACROBIOTICS TODAY
MATRIX
MEDICAL HISTORY
MEDICAL REFORM
Medical Reform Group
MedLife Communications, Inc.
Metamorphous Press
Meyerbooks, Publisher
Morning Glory Press
Mouvement Publications

National Lilac Publishing Co.
NATURALLY YOURS
Naturegraph Publishers, Inc.
Naturist Foundation
Network Publications, a division of ETR Associates
New Harbinger Publications, Inc.
NEW JERSEY NATURALLY
New Sins Press
NEW YORK NATURALLY
Newmark Publishing Company
Nicolas-Hays, Inc.
NIGHT OWL'S NEWSLETTER
Nucleus Publications
NUTRITION ACTION HEALTHLETTER
Oak Tree
OBESITY & HEALTH: CURRENT RESEARCH AND
    RELATED ISSUES
OFF OUR BACKS
George Ohsawa Macrobiotic Foundation Press
Oness Press
The Organization
Out West Publishing
Pallas Communications
Dr. Homer W. Parker, P.E.
Pathway Books
PENNYWHISTLE PEOPLE PAPER
Pennywhistle Press
Pergot Press
Persona Publications
THE PERSONAL MAGNETISM HOME STUDY
    COURSE ON ALL HUMAN POWERS
Perspectives Press
Petroglyph Press, Ltd.
PLAY & CULTURE
POLITICALLY INCORRECT
Popular Medicine Press
Publitec Editions
RADIANCE, The Magazine For Large Women
Rama Publishing Co.
RFD
The Rheumatoid Disease Foundation
Robinson Press, Inc.
Rodmell Press
Ross Books
Rossi
SACRED FIRE
Sanguinaria Publishing
SCIENCE/HEALTH ABSTRACTS
Seacoast Information Services
Skidmore-Roth Publishing
SMS Publishing Corp.
Snow Lion Publications, Inc.
SOM Publishing, division of School of Metaphysics
Spelman Publishing, Inc.
SPIT
SPORTS-NUTRITION NEWS
SPROUTLETTER
Star Books, Inc.
Steel Balls Press
Step Ahead Press, A Heartlite Inc. Company
Stillpoint Publishing
Strawberry Hill Press
STREET VOICE
Sun Eagle Publishing
Synesis Press
TAI CHI
TEC Publications
Ten Speed Press
Ten Star Press
Theosophical Publishing House
Thompson and Co. Inc.
THRESHOLDS JOURNAL
Tide Book Publishing Company
Topping International Institute
Traveler's Health Publications, Inc.
Triad Publishing Co. Inc.
TRUE FOOD
21st Century Publications

Twin Peaks Press
THE UNEXPLAINED
United Press Inc.
University of Calgary Press
Upper Access Inc.
Valkyrie Publishing House
Valley Lights Publications
VDT NEWS
VEGETARIAN JOURNAL
VEGETARIAN TIMES
THE VITAL FORCE
Volcano Press, Inc
Waterfront Books
THE WAVE
Wayfarer Publications
Samuel Weiser, Inc.
Wellberry Press
Whitford Press
THE WHOLE CHILE PEPPER
Whole Person Associates Inc.
WIN NEWS
WindRiver Publishing Company
Wingbow Press
Winston-Derek Publishers, Inc.
WITHIN & BEYOND
Woodbine House
Woodbridge Press
Yes International Publishers

ERNEST HEMINGWAY

THE CENTENNIAL REVIEW
COLLAGES & BRICOLAGES
LOST GENERATION JOURNAL
(ROWBOAT)
SCREAM MAGAZINE

HISTORY

Aardvark Enterprises
AAS HISTORY SERIES
AASLH Press
Academy Chicago Publishers
Affiliated Writers of America, Inc.
AFRICAN STUDIES
Akiba Press
ALBERTA HISTORY
Amana Books
AMATEUR COMPUTERIST
Amen Publishing Co.
AMERICAN AMATEUR JOURNALIST
AMERICAN ATHEIST
American Atheist Press
ANCESTRY NEWSLETTER
Ancestry Publishing
Anderson Press
THE ANNALS OF IOWA
Appalachian Consortium Press
Arden Press, Inc.
Argonauts/Misty Isles Press
Ariel Vamp Press
ARTISTAMP NEWS
Ashley Books, Inc.
ATHA NEWSLETTER
THE AUTOGRAPH COLLECTOR'S MAGAZINE
Autonomedia, Inc.
Avery Color Studios
Axios Newletter, Inc.
Baker Street Publications
BALDER
Bandanna Books
The Battery Press, Inc.
William L. Bauhan, Publisher
Beacon Press
Bear Flag Books
The Bear Wallow Publishing Company
Beautiful America Publishing Company
R.J. Bender Publishing
Benjamin Press
The Bess Press

Betelgeuse Books
Between The Lines
BIBLIOTHEQUE D'HUMANISME ET RENAISSANCE
Bicentennial Era Enterprises
Black Sparrow Press
Blue Water Publishing, Inc.
Bolchazy-Carducci Publishers, Inc.
BOOMBAH HERALD
The Borgo Press
The Boston Mills Press
Branden Publishing Company
BREAKTHROUGH!
Brick Row Publishing Co. Ltd.
Broken Rifle Press
BULLETIN OF THE BOARD OF CELTIC STUDIES
CAL NEWSLETTER
Calapooia Publications
Camel Press
CANADIAN SLAVONIC PAPERS
Capra Press
The Carnation Press
Carroll & Graf Publishers, Inc.
Celtic Heritage Press, Inc.
Cerulean Press (Subsidiary of Kent Publications)
Chandler & Sharp Publishers, Inc.
Chatham Publishing Company
Chelsea Green Publishing Company
Cherokee Publishing Company
CHESAPEAKE BAY MAGAZINE
Cheshire Books
THE...CHRONICLE
CINEASTE MAGAZINE
Citeaux Commentarii Cistercienses
CITEAUX: COMMENTARII CISTERCIENSES
THE CIVIL WAR NEWS
Arthur H. Clark Co.
Coach House Press
COBBLESTONE: The History Magazine for Young
    People
Colonial Press
Commonwealth Press Virginia
Communication Creativity
Communitas Press
The Compass Press
THE CONSTANTIAN
Cottonwood Press
Countryman Press
Coxland Press
Creative Roots, Inc.
CROSS TIMBERS REVIEW
Crossroads Communications
Crossroads Publications, Inc.
CULTURE CONCRETE
Cypres Publishing House
THE DALHOUSIE REVIEW
DAUGHTER OF SARAH
Dawnwood Press
W.S. Dawson Co.
DeerTrail Books
The Denali Press
Depot Press
The Devonshire Publishing Co.
Dharma Publishing
DOOR COUNTY ALMANAK
DorPete Press
Dufour Editions Inc.
THE DURHAM UNIVERSITY JOURNAL
DUST (From the Ego Trip)
E.T.M. Publishing
THE EAGLE
Eagle's View Publishing
EAST EUROPEAN QUARTERLY
Eastern Caribbean Institute
Edition Gemini
Editorial Review
Educare Press
The Edwin Mellen Press
El Montecito Oaks Press, Inc.

ENCYCLOPEDIA BANANICA
Epicenter Press Inc.
EPM Publications, Inc.
Erespin Press
Escart Press
Esoterica Press
Evans Publications Inc.
Falcon Press Publishing Company
Farragut Publishing Co.
Fathom Publishing Co.
The Feminist Press at the City University of New York
Fire Buff House
FISICA
Foundation Books
FOX VALLEY LIVING
Friends United Press
Fromm International Publishing Corporation
Frontier Publishing
Fulcrum, Inc.
Gallaudet University Press
Gallopade Publishing Group
Gaslight Publications
Gavea-Brown Publications
GCBA Publishing
GENEALOGICAL COMPUTING
Genealogical Publishing Co., Inc.
GHOST TOWN QUARTERLY
Glenhurst Publications, Inc.
Golden West Books
Golden West Historical Publications
GORHAM
GREATER PORTLAND
The Guild Bindery Press, Inc.
Gumbs & Thomas Publishers, Inc.
The Gutenberg Press
Happy Rock Press
Heart of the Lakes Publishing
Heritage Books, Inc.
Heritage West Books
Hermitage (Ermitazh)
High Plains Press
Historical Society of Alberta
HISTORICAL STUDIES IN THE PHYSICAL & BIOLO-
    GICAL SCIENCES
HISTORY NEWS
History West Publishing Company
HOBBY BOOKWATCH (MILITARY, GUN & HOBBY
    BOOK REVIEW)
Homeward Press
Hoover Institution Press
Hope Publishing House
HORIZONS WEST
House of Fire Press
Hunter Publishing, Co.
Icarus Books
Ide House, Inc.
ILLINOIS MAGAZINE
IMAGINATION MAGAZINE
Independence Publishers Inc.
Institute for Palestine Studies
Institute for Southern Studies
Institute of Archaeology Publications
Interlink Publishing Group, Inc.
INTERRACIAL BOOKS FOR CHILDREN BULLETIN
Island Publishers
ISRAEL HORIZONS
Italica Press, Inc.
J & T Publishing
Jamison Station Press
Jones River Press
JOURNAL FOR ANTHROPOSOPHY
THE JOURNAL OF PSYCHOHISTORY
JOURNAL OF THE WEST
The Kennebec River Press, Inc.
Kent Publications, Inc.
Michael Kesend, Publishing, Ltd.
The Kingston Press, Inc.
KMT, A Modern Journal of Ancient Egypt

KMT Communications
Lahontan Images
LAKE EFFECT
LAKE SUPERIOR MAGAZINE
LANDSCAPE
Latin American Press
The Latona Press
Levite of Apache
Lexikos
Library Research Associates, Inc.
LINKS
Littlebooks
Lorien House
Lyceum Books, Inc.
Majority, Inc.
Paul Maravelas
Peter Marcan Publications
Markgraf Publications Group
The Marlboro Press
Maryland Historical Press
Masefield Books
Mayhaven Publishing
McFarland & Company, Inc., Publishers
McNally & Loftin, Publishers
MEDICAL HISTORY
Mexico West Travel Club, Inc.
Meyerbooks, Publisher
Micro Pro Litera Press
THE MIDWEST QUARTERLY
R. & E. Miles
THE MILITARY ADVISOR
MILITARY IMAGES MAGAZINE
Millers River Publishing Co.
Mr. Information
MODERN LANGUAGE QUARTERLY
Moon Publications, Inc.
Mosquito Press
Mountain Automation Corporation
Mountain State Press
Museum of New Mexico Press
Name That Team!
National Stereoscopic Association
Naturegraph Publishers, Inc.
Nevada Publications
THE NEW ENGLAND QUARTERLY
The New England Quarterly, Inc.
New Star Books Ltd.
NightinGale Resources
NORTH CAROLINA LITERARY REVIEW
North Country Books, Inc.
North Star Press of St. Cloud, Inc.
THE NORTHERN REVIEW
Northland Publishing Company
NOTEBOOK/CUADERNO: A LITERARY JOURNAL
Nuventures Publishing
OLD ABE'S NEWS
The Old Army Press
Old Harbor Press
Omega Cottonwood Press
Oolichan Books
Open Hand Publishing Inc.
OREGON HISTORICAL QUARTERLY
Oregon Historical Society Press
Oregon State University Press
Organization for Equal Education of the Sexes, Inc.
  (OEES)
THE OTHER ISRAEL
OVERLAND JOURNAL
EL PALACIO
Paladin Enterprises, Inc.
PALIMPSEST
Pamlico Press
Panorama West Publishing
Paragon House Publishers
Park & Park Publishers, Inc.
The Patrice Press
Penfield Press
People's Publishing Co., Inc.

Phillips Publications, Inc.
Vernon W. Pickering-Laurel Publications International
Pine Cone Press
Pine Hall Press
Pineapple Press, Inc.
Pinery Press
Pioneer Books
The Place In The Woods
THE PLOUGH
Pocahontas Press, Inc.
Poetry Wales Press, Ltd.
Political Research Associates
The Post-Apollo Press
THE PRAIRIE GOLD RUSH
Prairie Publishing Company
Princeton Architectural Press
THE PRINCETON JOURNAL: THEMATIC STUDIES
  IN ARCHITECTURE
PROCESSED WORLD
Pruett Publishing Company
Psychohistory Press
THE PUBLIC HISTORIAN
QED
Quarterly Committee of Queen's University
QUEEN'S QUARTERLY: A Canadian Review
The Quilt Digest Press
RACONTEUR: A Journal of World History
RACONTEUR Publications
RADIANCE, The Magazine For Large Women
RADICAL AMERICA
Rand Editions/Tofua Press
Red Crane Books
Redwood Press
REPRESENTATIONS
REVIEW LA BOOCHE
Riegel Publishing
Ritz Publishing
ROMANIAN REVIEW
Rose Publishing Co.
Salvo Books
Sand River Press
Saqi Books Publisher
Sasquatch Books
The Saunderstown Press
SCHMAGA
Scojtia Publishing Company
Scottwall Associates, Publishers
Scroll Publishing Co.
Sea Otter Press
Sea Sports Publications
Sentinel Books
Serpent & Eagle Press
SEZ: A Multi-Racial Journal of Poetry & People's Culture
Shadow Press, U.S.A.
Sharp & Dunnigan Publications, Incorporated
Sherwood Sugden & Company, Publishers
SHMATE
Shmate Press
Signature Books
Silver Dawn Media
Sleepy Hollow Press
THE SMALL POND MAGAZINE OF LITERATURE
  aka SMALL POND
Genny Smith Books
Snowbird Publishing Company
SOCIALISM AND DEMOCRACY
SOUTHERN READER
Southern Resources Unlimited
SPECTRUM, A Guide to the Independent Press and
  Informative Organizations
Spectrum Publications
THE SPIRIT
Starfish Press
STEREO WORLD
Sterling-Miller
STEVE CANYON MAGAZINE
Still Point Press
Strawberry Hill Press

Strawn Studios Inc.
Summerthought Ltd.
Sun Books
Sunflower University Press
Sunstone Press
TBW Books, Inc.
Theytus Books Ltd.
Third World First
Thirteen Colonies Press
A Thousand Autumns Press
Thunder Creek Publishing Co-operative
TIERRA DEL FUEGO MAGAZINE
Times Change Press
Tippy Reed Publishing
TOWARDS
TOWPATHS
Transport History Press
TRIVIUM
Umbrella Books
UNBRIDLED LUST!
University of Calgary Press
University of Massachusetts Press
The Urbana Free Library
Urion Press
Vestal Press Ltd
VIATOR: Medieval and Renaissance Studies
The Vic Press
VIETNAM GENERATION: A Journal of Recent History
    and Contemporary Issues
VIETNAM WAR NEWSLETTER
THE VIRGINIA QUARTERLY REVIEW
Volcano Press, Inc
THE VORTEX (A Historical and Wargamers Jornal)
WALKING-STICK NOTES
Waterfront Books
Waterfront Press
Wayfinder Press
Wells & West, Publishers
WELSH HISTORY REVIEW
Westburg Associates, Publishers
Western Tanager Press
The White Cross Press
White Mane Publishing Company, Inc.
White Rose Press
Witwatersrand University Press
Wolfhound Press
Wonder View Press
Woodbine House
World Promotions
Wright-Armstead Associates
WW Publishers
Yankee Books
Ye Galleon Press
Youth Policy Institute
Zagier & Urruty Publicaciones
ZONE
Zone Books

SHERLOCK HOLMES

BAKER STREET GAZETTE
Baker Street Publications
Carroll & Graf Publishers, Inc.
ENGLISH LITERATURE IN TRANSITION, 1880-1920
THE GAME'S AFOOT
W. Paul Ganley: Publisher
Gaslight Publications
Gryphon Publications
THE MYSTERY FANCIER
PAPERBACK PARADE
SLEUTH JOURNAL
Zirlinson Publishing

HOLOCAUST

University of Massachusetts Press

HOLOGRAPHY

Blue Heron Press
MUSIC OF THE SPHERES

Poet Papers
RAMPIKE
Ross Books
THEATRE DESIGN AND TECHNOLOGY
UNBRIDLED LUST!

HOMEMAKING

Blue Sky Marketing, Inc.
The Book Peddlers
Center For Self-Sufficiency
Nunciata
Oak Plantation Press
Star Books, Inc.
Twin Peaks Press
WTI Publishing Co.

HOW-TO

Aames-Allen Publishing Co.
Accent on Music
Achievement Press
Acting World Books
ACTION DIGEST
Adams-Hall Publishing
The Aegis Group
Aeolus Press, Inc.
THE AGENCIES-WHAT THE ACTOR NEEDS TO
    KNOW
All American Press
Almar Press
Alpenglow Press
Altamont Press, Inc.
AMATEUR COMPUTERIST
Amen Publishing Co.
American Business Consultants, Inc.
American Impressions
American Montessori Consulting
Amherst Media
Anaphase II
ANCESTRY NEWSLETTER
Ancestry Publishing
and books
Anderson Press
Applied Business
Arlotta Press
Arrow Publishing
Ashley Books, Inc.
ATHA NEWSLETTER
Author's Unlimited
Avery Publishing Group, Inc.
Awareness Publications
Axelrod Publishing of Tampa Bay
BACKBOARD
Baker Publishing
Barclay House
Barn Owl Books
BEAN ZINE
Bear Creek Publications
Bell Springs Publishing
Beynch Press Publishing Company
Bicycle Books (Publishing) Inc.
The Biting Idge/Miracle Press (Chrysalis Publications)
Blue Arrow Books
Blue Bird Publishing
Blue Dolphin Press, Inc.
Blue Sky Marketing, Inc.
Bluestocking Press
Bonus Books, Inc.
BOOK NEWS & BOOK BUSINESS MART
BookNotes :(TM) Resources for Small & Self-Publishers
Bookworm Publishing Company
Brennen Publishing Company
Brenner Information Group
Brick House Publishing Co., Inc.
Bright Ring Publishing
Bronx Books
BURWOOD JOURNAL
BYLINE
Capra Press

Carousel Press
Cassandra Press
Celestial Gifts Publishing
Center for Public Representation
The Center For Study of Multiple Birth
Charter Oak Press
Chelsea Green Publishing Company
Cheshire Books
The Chicot Press
Christmans
Cin Publications
CLEANING BUSINESS MAGAZINE
Cleaning Consultants Serv's, Inc.
CLUBHOUSE
Communication Creativity
The Communication Press
Communicom Publishing Company
The Consumer's Press, Inc.
Cooper House Publishing Inc.
Cottage Press
Cottonwood Press
Countryman Press
CountrySide Business Publications
Crisp Publications, Inc.
Culinary Arts Ltd.
D-Amp Publications
DEAD OF NIGHT MAGAZINE
Design Enterprises of San Francisco
THE DESIGNMENT REVIEW
Devin-Adair, Publishers, Inc.
The Devonshire Publishing Co.
Devyn Press
Dimi Press
Distinctive Publishing Corp.
Do-It-Yourself Legal Publishers
Dos Tejedoras Fiber Arts Publications
Dragon Disks
Dundurn Press Ltd
Dustbooks
Dynamic Information Publishing
Eagle's View Publishing
Edgeworth & North Books
EDITOR'S DIGEST
El Camino Publishers
Elephas Books
THE EMSHOCK LETTER
Energeia Publishing, Inc.
Envirographics
EPM Publications, Inc.
Robert Erdmann Publishing
ETC Publications
Evon Publishing
Exanimo Press
EXUM Publishing
Fell Publishers, Inc.
FIBERARTS
Financial Awareness Corporation
Five Star Publications
J. Flores Publications
Flower Press
Forbes/Wittenburg & Brown
The P. Gaines Co., Publishers
Gazelle Publications
GCBA Publishing
Gemini Publishing Company
GemStone Press
GENEALOGICAL COMPUTING
Gilgal Publications
Glenbridge Publishing Ltd.
The Globe Pequot Press
Good Life Products, Inc.
Good Times Publishing Co.
Goodheart-Willcox Company
Grade School Press
Grapevine Publications, Inc.
GRASS ROOTS
Gravity Publishing
Great Western Publishing Company

Grosvenor USA
Guarionex Press Ltd.
Gumbs & Thomas Publishers, Inc.
HAPPINESS HOLDING TANK
Harlo Press
Harvard Common Press
Haypenny Press
Heavy Bro Publishing Company
Hemlock Society
HMS Press
Hoffman Press
THE HOLLYWOOD ACTING COACHES AND
    TEACHERS DIRECTORY
Human Kinetics Pub. Inc.
Hundman Publishing
Hunter Publishing, Co.
IMAGINATION MAGAZINE
IM-Press
Info Net Publishing
INFOCUS
Information Requirements Clearinghouse
Inkling Publications, Inc.
INQ Publishing Co.
Interlink Press, Inc.
Interlink Publishing Group, Inc.
International Information Associates
International Marine Publishing Co.
Iron Gate Publishing
Jalmar Press
Jamenair Ltd.
JLA Publications, A Division Of Jeffrey Lant Associates,
    Inc.
JUDY
Michael Kesend, Publishing, Ltd.
KITE LINES
Klutz Press
HJ Kramer, Inc
Kumarian Press, Inc.
L.A.N.D.
Kent P. Larsen, Inc.
LAUGHING BEAR NEWSLETTER
Lawco Ltd./Moneytree Publications
LEFTHANDER MAGAZINE
Lexikos
Liberty Bell Press & Publishing Co.
Liberty Publishing Company, Inc.
Lighthouse Press
Lion Press
Literary Publications Company
LITTLE FREE PRESS
Little Sam & Co. Press
Littlebooks
LIVING AMONG NATURE DARINGLY!
THE LLEWELLYN NEW TIMES
Llewellyn Publications
Log Cabin Publishers
Loiry/Bonner Press
Loompanics Unlimited
Love Child Publishing
Billy Jack Ludwig Holding Co.
MAINLINE MODELER
Maradia Press
Maupin House
Mayhaven Publishing
Meckler Corporation
Meridian Learning Systems
Mermaid Press
MESSAGE POST
Metamorphous Press
Microdex Bookshelf
Middle Coast Publishing
MIND YOUR OWN BUSINESS AT HOME
Mr. Information
Moon Publications, Inc.
Mother of Ashes Press
Mountainwest Publishers
John Muir Publications, Inc.
Mustang Publishing Co.

807

Myriad Moods
Naturegraph Publishers, Inc.
N-B-T-V
New Chapter Press
New Cicada
NEW CICADA
New Harbinger Publications, Inc.
New View Publications
NEW WRITER'S MAGAZINE
Newton-Cline Press
NiceTown
Night Owl Publishers
The Noble Press, Inc.
Nolo Press - Occidental
North American Bookdealers Exchange
The North Carolina Haiku Society Press
Nucleus Publications
Nunciata
Oak Plantation Press
Occasional Productions
OLD-HOUSE JOURNAL
Open Horizons Publishing Company
Paladin Enterprises, Inc.
Panjandrum Books
Panorama Publishing Company
Panther Press Ltd.
Para Publishing
Pathway Books
Pergot Press
THE PERSONAL MAGNETISM HOME STUDY
 COURSE ON ALL HUMAN POWERS
Piccadilly Books
Plas Y Bryn Press
POETRY HALIFAX DARTMOUTH
Poetry Magic Publications
Poets & Writers, Inc.
Point Publications
Pollard Press
POTPOURRI PARTY-LINE
Premier Publishers, Inc.
The Preservation Press
Prima Publishing
THE PRINTER'S DEVIL
Progresiv Publishr
Promontory Publishing, Inc.
PSI Research/The Oasis Press
The Public Safety Press
Publitec Editions
Puma Publishing Company
Pushcart Press
Q.E.D. Press
Quotidian Publishers
R & E Publishers
R & M Publishing Company
R & R Publishing
RACE ACROSS AMERICA PROGRAM
Racz Publishing Co.
Rainy Day Press
RE Publications
REAL PEOPLE
Red Eye Press
RED HOT WORK-AT-HOME REPORT
Reliant Marketing & Publishing
The Rensselaerville Systems Training Center
Reunion Research
Right Here Publications
Rio Grande Press
Roblin Press
Rockwell Publishing
ROMEO NEWSLETTER
Ronin Publishing, Inc.
Roscher House
Ross Books
Rossi
THE RUGGING ROOM BULLETIN
Running Press
S & S Press
St. John's Publishing, Inc.

Santa Barbara Press
The Saunderstown Press
Sauvie Island Press
Scentouri, Publishing Division
SCHMAGA
SCIENCE/HEALTH ABSTRACTS
Scojtia Publishing Company
Scribblers Publishing, Ltd.
SE LA VIE WRITER'S JOURNAL
SEA KAYAKER
Senay Publishing Inc.
Sentinel Books
Seven Locks Press
Shadetree Publishing Inc.
Shepherd Publishers
Shoe Tree Press
Michael Shore Associates
Siftsoft
Silver Dollar Press
SINGLES ALMANAC
SINSEMILLA TIPS (Domestic Marijuana Journal)
SMALL PRESS: The Magazine & Book Review of
 Independent Publishing
SMALL PRESS MONTHLY
SOFTBALL ILLUSTRATED
SOM Publishing, division of School of Metaphysics
Sororal Publishing
Southwest Research and Information Center
Space City Publications
SPEX (Small Press Exchange)
Sphinx Publishing
Spirit Press
ST Publications/Book Division
STARWIND
State of the Art Ltd.
Steel Balls Press
Step Ahead Press, A Heartlite Inc. Company
Sterling-Miller
Stone Wall Press, Inc
Stonehouse Publications
Storey/Garden Way Publishing
Strawberry Hill Press
STUDIO NORTH
Success Publishing
Sun Features Inc.
Sunstone Publications
Surrey Press
SURVIVE & WIN
Swan Publishing Company
Tamal Vista Publications
Tambra Publishing
Taos Bluewater Press
Tax Property Investor, Inc.
TechWest Publications
Ten Speed Press
Tide Book Publishing Company
Tiptoe Literary Service
Top Of The Mountain Publishing
Travel Keys
Trestletree Publications
Triad Press
Tudor Publishers, Inc.
Twin Peaks Press
Tyro Publishing
UCS Press
Ultimate Secrets
THE UNDERGROUND FOREST - LA SELVA SUB-
 TERRANEA
United Press Inc.
Upper Access Inc.
Van Patten Publishing
Ventana Press
Venture Press
Vesper Publishing
Vestal Press Ltd
Vision Quest Publishing
Vista Mark Publications
Vista Publishing Company

Vitesse Press
Vitreous Group/Camp Colton
Volunteer Concepts
Ward Hill Press
Waterfront Books
Weatherford Publications
WESTERN & EASTERN TREASURES
Westport Publishers, Inc.
Wherry Advertising Agency
WHISPERING WIND MAGAZINE
White Rose Publishing
Whitmore Publishing Company
Wilchester Publishing Company
THE WILD FOODS FORUM
Williamson Publishing Company, Inc.
Wind River Institute Press
Window Publications
WindRiver Publishing Company
Windsong Books International
Winslow Publishing
Woodsong Graphics Inc.
Wordwrights Canada
THE WORKBOOK
WORKING AT HOME
WRITERS GAZETTE NEWSLETTER
WRITER'S GUIDELINES MAGAZINE
Writers Publishing Service Co.
WRITER'S VOICE
Xyzyx Information Corporation

HUMAN RIGHTS

ACTIVIST
Alchemy Books
ASPECTS
Beacon Press
BLACK MOUNTAIN REVIEW
THE...CHRONICLE
Clarity Press
Comforter Publishing
COMMON SENSE
Crime and Social Justice Associates, Inc.
DE NAR
GREY CITY JOURNAL
Harbinger House
HEALING PATH
THE HYPERBOREAN
Hyperborean Micropublications
Independence Publishers Inc.
KETTERING REVIEW
Kitchen Table: Women of Color Press
LANCASTER INDEPENDENT PRESS
LIBERTY
THE LOOGIE
MR. COGITO
Mr. Cogito Press
NATURALLY
NEGATIVE
New Worlds Press
The Noble Press, Inc.
Orbis Books
PEACE & DEMOCRACY NEWS
THE PEACE NEWSLETTER
P-FORM
PRISONER'S LEGAL NEWS
ROMANIAN REVIEW
Savant Garde Workshop
Snowbird Publishing Company
SOCIAL JUSTICE: A JOURNAL OF CRIME, CON-
FLICT, & WORLD ORDER
SPECTRUM, A Guide to the Independent Press and
Informative Organizations
Spectrum Publications
Syracuse Cultural Workers
Syracuse Peace Council
Talon Books Ltd
THIRD WORLD RESOURCES
Thunder Creek Publishing Co-operative
UNBRIDLED LUST!

WORLD PERSPECTIVES

HUMANISM

ANGRY
ANIMA: The Journal of Human Experience
Anima Publications
Bandanna Books
Black Rose Books Ltd.
Blue Lights Publications
Caliban Press
CHANGING MEN
THE...CHRONICLE
CIMARRON REVIEW
COLLAGES & BRICOLAGES
COYDOG REVIEW
CREATING EXCELLENCE
CREATION/EVOLUTION JOURNAL
Dharma Publishing
DIE FAT PIGGY DIE
Dufour Editions Inc.
Eagle Publishing
EMERGING
Erespin Press
Esoterica Press
FREE INQUIRY
The Gleniffer Press
The Green Hut Press
GYPSY
THE HUMANIST
THE HYPERBOREAN
Hyperborean Micropublications
IASP NEWSLETTER
IMMANENT FACE
INTERRACIAL BOOKS FOR CHILDREN BULLETIN
JABBERWOCKY
Jalmar Press
JOURNAL FOR ANTHROPOSOPHY
Kumarian Press, Inc.
THE LATHAM LETTER
The Philip Lesly Company
Let's Go Travel Publications
THE LOOGIE
LP Publications (Teleos Institute)
Metamorphous Press
Mountaintop Books
NATURALLY
A NEW WORLD RISING
THE NORTHERN REVIEW
The Olive Press Publications
OUR GENERATION
Pagan Press
PEDESTRIAN RESEARCH
PEOPLE'S CULTURE
Pergot Press
PIG IRON
POETS ON:
THE PRAGMATIST
Royal Purcell, Publisher
R & E Publishers
RADIANCE, The Magazine For Large Women
The Rights' Press
ROMANIAN REVIEW
Savant Garde Workshop
Michael Shore Associates
SKYLARK
THE SMALL POND MAGAZINE OF LITERATURE
aka SMALL POND
Strawberry Hill Press
Times Change Press
Top Of The Mountain Publishing
UNBRIDLED LUST!
Villa Press
WARM FUZZY NEWSLETTER
Waterfront Books
Willow Bee Publishing House
B. L. Winch & Associates
THE WISHING WELL
WITHIN & BEYOND

WITNESS
WYOMING, THE HUB OF THE WHEEL...A Journey for Universal Spokesmen...
XENOPHILIA
Yes You Can Press

HUMOR

Again + Again Press
AKWEKON: A National Native American Literary & Arts Journal
ALASKA WOMEN
Alchemy Books
Alpenglow Press
AMELIA
Anaphase II
and books
ANIMAL TALES
Ariadne Press
Arsenal Pulp Press, Ltd.
ART'S GARBAGE GAZZETTE
Astonisher Press
ATROCITY
Attic Press
Author's Unlimited
Axelrod Publishing of Tampa Bay
BABY SUE
Bean Avenue Publishing
BELLES LETTRES
BELLYWASH
The Bess Press
Big River Publishing
BLADES
Blue Crane Books
Blue Dolphin Press, Inc.
BLUE HORSE
Blue Horse Publications
Blue Mouse Studio
Bogg Publications
Bomb Shelter Propaganda
Bonus Books, Inc.
BORDER/LINES
BREAKFAST WITHOUT MEAT
BREAKTHROUGH!
Brook Farm Books
C.C. Publishing Co.
CACANADADADA REVIEW
CANTU'S COMEDY NEWSLETTER
Catbird Press
Chiron Press
CHIRON REVIEW
THE...CHRONICLE
CIMARRON REVIEW
CLINTON ST.
COLLAGES & BRICOLAGES
The Communication Press
COMPOST NEWSLETTER (CNL)
CorkScrew Press
Cottage Press
Cottonwood Press, Inc.
Countryman Press
COYDOG REVIEW
CRAWLSPACE
Cube Publications Inc
DELIRIUM
The Devonshire Publishing Co.
DIE FAT PIGGY DIE
Distinctive Publishing Corp.
Doggerel Press
Down There Press
THE DUPLEX PLANET
Eagle's View Publishing
EDITOR'S DIGEST
e.g.
THE EMSHOCK LETTER
ENCYCLOPEDIA BANANICA
EUTHANASIA ROSES
Ex Machina Publishing Company
Excalibur Publishing

FAT TUESDAY
FILM THREAT VIDEO GUIDE
FINE MADNESS
THE FREEDONIA GAZETTE
Frontier Publishing
FUGITIVE POPE
Futurum Forlag
GAFF PRESS
GATEAVISA
Gateways Books And Tapes
THE GELOSOPHIST, Humor News & Views From Around The World
GET STUPID
Goldstein & Blair
GOOD READING MAGAZINE
THE GOOFUS OFFICE GAZETTE
Grapetree Productions, Inc.
Gravity Publishing
Green Stone Publications
Heavy Bro Publishing Company
HOUSEWIFE-WRITER'S FORUM
HOWLING DOG
HUMERUS
THE IDEOLOGY OF MADNESS
IMAGINATION MAGAZINE
THE IMMIGRANT
Independence Publishers Inc.
Independent Research Services of Irvine (IRIS/I)
Insight Press
JABBERWOCKY
Jigsaw Publishing House
JOURNAL OF POLYMORPHOUS PERVERSITY
JUDY
KALEIDOSCOPE: INTERNATIONAL MAGAZINE OF LITERATURE, FINE ARTS, AND DISABILITY
Keel Publications
Kitchen Sink Press
KRAX
KUMQUAT MERINGUE
LAKE EFFECT
LAKE SUPERIOR MAGAZINE
Langston Press
LATEST JOKES NEWSLETTER
THE LATEST NEWS
Ledero Press
LESBIAN CONTRADICTION-A Journal of Irreverent Feminism
Levite of Apache
Little Sam & Co. Press
LONE STAR COMEDY MONTHLY
LONE STAR HUMOR
Lone Star Publications of Humor
THE LOOGIE
THE LOST PERUKE
Lowy Publishing
MALEDICTA: The International Journal of Verbal Aggression
MALLIFE
MANNA
MARK
MASSACRE
Mayhaven Publishing
Mermaid Press
Metamorphous Press
Micro Pro Litera Press
R. & E. Miles
MINNE HA! HA!
Minne Ha! Ha!
Mortal Press
Mosaic Press
MOTORBOOTY MAGAZINE
THE MOUNTAIN ASTROLOGER
MurPubCo
Mustang Publishing Co.
Myriad Moods
Naked Man Press
NANCY'S MAGAZINE
Nanny Goat Productions

New Chapter Press
NEW HOPE INTERNATIONAL REVIEW
NEW WRITER'S MAGAZINE
Newport House
THE NIHILISTIC REVIEW
NON COMPOS MENTIS
THE NORTHERN REVIEW
NOSTALGIA, A Sentimental State of Mind
OFFICE NUMBER ONE
The Olive Press Publications
Omega Cottonwood Press
ON COURSE
Paladin Enterprises, Inc.
PARNASSUS LITERARY JOURNAL
Peachtree Publishers, Ltd.
Perivale Press
Pessimism Press, Inc.
PHASE AND CYCLE
Piccadilly Books
THE PIG PAPER
Pittore Euforico
PM (The Pedantic Monthly)
POETRY HALIFAX DARTMOUTH
POETRY OF THE PEOPLE
Pollard Press
Portmanteau Editions
POTATO EYES
POULTRY - A MAGAZINE OF VOICE
Poultry, Inc.
THE PRAIRIE JOURNAL OF CANADIAN LITERA-
TURE
Prairie Journal Press
PROCESSED WORLD
Puma Publishing Company
THE QUAYLE QUARTERLY
Quimby Archives
Ramalo Publications
RAMPIKE
Raw Dog Press
The Real Comet Press
Resource Publications, Inc.
Right Here Publications
Rio Grande Press
ROMANIAN REVIEW
Ronin Publishing, Inc.
The Runaway Spoon Press
SALAD
SALON: A Journal of Aesthetics
The Saunderstown Press
Say When Press
Art Paul Schlosser Books, Tapes, & Garbage Gazzette
SCHMAGA
SE LA VIE WRITER'S JOURNAL
Signature Books
SKYLARK
THE SMALL POND MAGAZINE OF LITERATURE
aka SMALL POND
SOUTHERN LIBERTARIAN MESSENGER
SPIT
SQUARE ONE - A Magazine of Fiction
Stabur Press, Inc.
Starchand Press
STIFLED YAWN: A Magazine Of Contemporary Writing
STORIES
Straight Arrow Publishing
STRUGGLE: A Magazine of Proletarian Revolutionary
Literature
Synergistic Press
Ten Speed Press
Texas Monthly Press
THALIA: Studies in Literary Humor
THOUGHTS FOR ALL SEASONS: The Magazine of
Epigrams
THRESHOLDS JOURNAL
Thunder Creek Publishing Co-operative
Times Change Press
TOOK
Top Of The Mountain Publishing

TURNSTILE
TWISTED IMAGE NEWSLETTER
Tyro Publishing
UNBRIDLED LUST!
THE UNDERGROUND FOREST - LA SELVA SUB-
TERRANEA
Valkyrie Publishing House
VANDELOECHT'S FICTION MAGAZINE
Vanity Press/Strolling Dog Press
Vestal Press Ltd
VOICES - ISRAEL
W.D.C. PERIOD
Waterfront Books
THE WAVE
WE ARE THE WEIRD
Wet Editions
Woodbine House
WORLD HUMOR AND IRONY MEMBERSHIP SER-
IAL YEARBOOK (WHIMSY)
THE WRITE AGE (First Magazine of Writing Therapy)
THE WRITERS' BLOC*
WTI Publishing Co.
X MAGAZINE
Yankee Books
Zirlinson Publishing

HUNGER

Comforter Publishing

HYPNOSIS

ASPECTS
THE...CHRONICLE
Grace and Goddess Unlimited
Llewellyn Publications
LuraMedia, Inc.
Top Of The Mountain Publishing
UNBRIDLED LUST!

IDAHO

CLOUDLINE
COLD-DRILL
Cold-Drill Books
THE EMSHOCK LETTER
Falcon Press Publishing Company
THE REDNECK REVIEW OF LITERATURE
Resolution Business Press
WHEAT LIFE
WHITE CLOUDS REVUE

ILLINOIS

ACTIVIST
Affordable Adventures, Inc.
Blue Water Publishing, Inc.
The Carnation Press
Crossroads Communications
The Devonshire Publishing Co.
ECOSOCIALIST REVIEW
FARMER'S MARKET
FOX VALLEY LIVING
GREY CITY JOURNAL
Heritage Press WI
Illinois Heritage Press
ILLINOIS MAGAZINE
Mayhaven Publishing
NIGHT ROSES
Stormline Press, Inc.
The Urbana Free Library
WHETSTONE
THE WRITERS' BAR-B-Q

IMMIGRATION

International Consulting Associates, Inc.

INDEXES & ABSTRACTS

ALTERNATIVE PRESS INDEX
American Handwriting Analysis Foundation
Anderson Press
The Borgo Press

CACANADADADA REVIEW
THE CHRISTIAN LIBRARIAN
CONNEXIONS DIGEST
THE DALHOUSIE REVIEW
The Denali Press
Ex Machina Publishing Company
Fallen Leaf Press
FEMINIST PERIODICALS: A CURRENT LISTING OF CONTENTS
GENERATIONS SANPETE: INDEX OF ORAL HISTORIES OF RURAL UTAH
Glacier House Publications
Graham-Conley Press
HORTIDEAS
Index House
International Information Associates
THE LEFT INDEX
LEGAL INFORMATION MANAGEMENT INDEX
LITERARY RESEARCH: A Journal of Scholarly Method & Technique
Little Buckaroo Press
Laurence McGilvery
NEW BOOKS ON WOMEN & FEMINISM
The Oryx Press
RE Publications
Resolution Business Press
SERIALS REVIEW
Signature Books
SOUTHWESTERN DISCOVERIES
Sterling-Miller
Sunburst Press
Three Continents Press, Inc.
Univelt, Inc.
The Urbana Free Library
Volcano Press, Inc
Women's Studies Librarian, University of Wisconsin System
The Wordtree

INDIA

CANVAS CHAUTAUQUA MAGAZINE
Erespin Press
Happy Rock Press
Jack October
The Krsna Institute
Mockingbird Press
Three Continents Press, Inc.
Tiger Moon
UNBRIDLED LUST!
Valley Lights Publications

INDIANA

CHESS IN INDIANA
SKYLARK

INDIANS

Argonauts/Misty Isles Press
Baker Street Publications
Beacon Press
Dusty Dog Press
Eagle's View Publishing
Epicenter Press Inc.
GREEN MULTILOGUE
Harbinger House
Heyday Books
HORIZONS WEST
INDIA CURRENTS
Kitchen Table: Women of Color Press
LAKE SUPERIOR MAGAZINE
Levite of Apache
THE NORTHERN REVIEW
Northland Publishing Company
Oregon State University Press
SHENANDOAH NEWSLETTER
Sierra Oaks Publishing Company
Gibbs Smith, Publisher
Snowbird Publishing Company
Tiger Moon

Treasure Chest Publications, Inc.
TRENDS & PREDICTIONS ANALYST
WHISPERING WIND MAGAZINE

INSPIRATIONAL

ALL AVAILABLE LIGHT
American Impressions
AREOPAGUS
Ascension Publishing
Aslan Publishing
Comforter Publishing
Dharma Publishing
Drift Creek Press
E.T.M. Publishing
Earth-Love Publishing House
ELF: ECLECTIC LITERARY FORUM (ELF MAGAZINE)
Fell Publishers, Inc.
IBS Press
International Partners In Prayer
JOURNAL FOR ANTHROPOSOPHY
HJ Kramer, Inc
Leadership Education and Development, Inc.
Lionhouse Publishing Company
LITTLE FREE PRESS
LuraMedia, Inc.
MANNA
New World Library
The Pilgrim Press/United Church Press
St. Bede's Publications
The Saunderstown Press
Shiro Publishers
SKYLARK
Star Books, Inc.
Stillpoint Publishing
SUNSHINE MAGAZINE
Sunshine Press
Theosophical Publishing House
Tiger Moon
Top Of The Mountain Publishing
Tyro Publishing
Valley Lights Publications
Yes You Can Press

INSURANCE

DOCTOR-PATIENT STUDIES
Maryland Historical Press
Publitec Editions
Stratton Press
VDT NEWS

INTERVIEWS

AGOG
BLUE LIGHTS
Blue Lights Publications
C.C. Publishing Co.
CALYPSO: Journal of Narrative Poetry and Poetic Fiction
Esoterica Press
THE FICTION REVIEW
THE HAPPY THRASHER
THE IDEOLOGY OF MADNESS
IMAGINATION MAGAZINE
INFINITE ONION
INNOVATING
ISSUES
LESBIAN CONTRADICTION-A Journal of Irreverent Feminism
THE LOOGIE
MEMES
THE NEW DANCE REVIEW
NIGHT OWL'S NEWSLETTER
Oxbridge Communications, Inc.
PENINHAND
Peninhand Press
P-FORM
PUBLISHING TRENDS & TRENDSETTERS
SACRED FIRE
The Saunderstown Press

Score
SECONDS MAGAZINE
SENSOR
Signature Books
SPIT
STAPLE
Sun Features Inc.
Thunder Creek Publishing Co-operative
THE VOLCANO REVIEW
Woldt Publishing
WORLD OF FANDOM MAGAZINE
Zirlinson Publishing

IOWA

THE ANNALS OF IOWA
As Is/So & So Press
CAMPUS REVIEW
Coffee House Press
Crossroads Communications
Dragon Cloud Books
Foundation Books
Heritage Press WI
IOWA WOMAN
LUNA TACK
Middle Coast Publishing
PALIMPSEST
Penfield Press
SO & SO

IRELAND

ADRIFT
The Archives Press
Attic Press
Beacon Press
BELLES LETTRES
Celtic Heritage Press, Inc.
Cottage Books
The F. Marion Crawford Memorial Society
Devin-Adair, Publishers, Inc.
Dufour Editions Inc.
FREE PRESS
IRISH FAMILY JOURNAL
IRISH LITERARY SUPPLEMENT
THE ISLAND
JAMES JOYCE BROADSHEET
KELTIC FRINGE
KELTICA: THE INTER-CELTIC JOURNAL
LINKS
MAXINE'S PAGES
NORTH DAKOTA QUARTERLY
Nuventures Publishing
O'Laughlin Press (Irish Genealogical Foundation)
PLANKTON
Poetry Ireland Press
POETRY IRELAND REVIEW
THE ROMANTIST
Sparkling Diamond Paperbacks
Stone Circle Press
Sunburst Press
Third World First
Three Continents Press, Inc.
Top Of The Mountain Publishing
TRANSITIONS ABROAD: The Guide to Living,
   Learning, and Working Overseas
UNBRIDLED LUST!
Zephyr Press

ITALIAN-AMERICAN

Malafemmina Press

ITALY

BELLES LETTRES
Blue Dolphin Press, Inc.
Catbird Press
The Clyde Press
THE COOL TRAVELER
Italica Press, Inc.
LA BELLA FIGURA

TRANSITIONS ABROAD: The Guide to Living,
   Learning, and Working Overseas

JAPAN

ACTIVIST
AIKI NEWS
Aiki News
ANIME SHOWER SPECIAL
AREOPAGUS
The Bess Press
Cross Cultural Press
ECOSOCIALIST REVIEW
The Global Press
GREY CITY JOURNAL
Ianus Publications, Inc.
LIZZENGREASY
MANGAJIN
NEW HOPE INTERNATIONAL REVIEW
POSTER-ZINE
PROTOCULTURE ADDICTS
Signal Books
Stone Bridge Press
TRANSITIONS ABROAD: The Guide to Living,
   Learning, and Working Overseas
TSUBUSHI
UNBRIDLED LUST!

ROBINSON JEFFERS

Castle Peak Editions
WESTERN AMERICAN LITERATURE

JEWELRY, GEMS

CRAFTS NSW
DIAMOND INSIGHT
Eagle's View Publishing
GemStone Press
International Jewelry Publications
Naturegraph Publishers, Inc.
ORNAMENT, Ancient Contemporary Ethnic

JOURNALS

ALL AVAILABLE LIGHT
Blue Sky Marketing, Inc.
CITY RANT
DIARIST'S JOURNAL
Dirty Rotten Press
Fromm International Publishing Corporation
Happy Rock Press
HEALING PATH
LuraMedia, Inc.
THE PROSPECT REVIEW
Scots Plaid Press (Persephone Press)
Signature Books
Trabarni Productions
UNIROD MAGAZINE
WHITE WALLS: A Journal of Language and Art

JAMES JOYCE

Bakhtin's Wife Publications
JAMES JOYCE BROADSHEET
JAMES JOYCE QUARTERLY
KELTIC FRINGE
Station Hill Press
UMI Research Press
University of Tulsa
THE WAVE

JUDIASM

AGADA
Amen Publishing Co.
ASPECTS
AUFBAU
Beacon Press
Bet Alpha Editions
Biblio Press
Carroll & Graf Publishers, Inc.
COMMON BOUNDARY
The Edwin Mellen Press

Bilingual Review/Press
BILINGUAL REVIEW/Revista Bilingue
Bolchazy-Carducci Publishers, Inc.
THE BOUND SPIRAL
The Boxwood Press
BULLETIN OF HISPANIC STUDIES
BULLETIN OF THE BOARD OF CELTIC STUDIES
CANADIAN AUTHOR & BOOKMAN
Chandler & Sharp Publishers, Inc.
The Chicot Press
Circumpolar Press
CITY RANT
Clamshell Press
THE CLASSICAL OUTLOOK
COLLAGES & BRICOLAGES
Cosmoenergetics Publications
The Counter-Propaganda Press
COYDOG REVIEW
CURTAINS
dbqp
S. Deal & Assoc.
DEWITT DIGEST & REVIEW
Dragon Cloud Books
11 X 13 - BROADSIDE
Farragut Publishing Co.
Fell Publishers, Inc.
Five Fingers Press
FIVE FINGERS REVIEW
FUSE MAGAZINE
Gallopade Publishing Group
Gavea-Brown Publications
GET STUPID
Teri Gordon, Publisher
GRAIN
GREEN ZERO
Gringo Guides, Inc.
Holger Harfst, Publisher
IDO-VIVO
In One Ear Press
JEWISH LINGUISTIC STUDIES
JOURNAL FOR ANTHROPOSOPHY
JOURNAL OF CELTIC LINGUISTICS
KALDRON, An International Journal Of Visual Poetry
   and Language Art
Kontexts Publications
LA NUEZ
LANGUAGE INTERNATIONAL: THE MAGAZINE
   FOR THE LANGUAGE PROFESSIONS
LIGHTNING SWORD
LINGUISTIC REVIEW
Literary Publications Company
Liverpool University Press
LORE AND LANGUAGE
MALEDICTA: The International Journal of Verbal
   Aggression
Maledicta Press
MANGAJIN
manic d press
Metamorphous Press
Michigan Romance Studies
MIND MATTERS REVIEW
THE MODERN LANGUAGE JOURNAL
MOKSHA JOURNAL
Moon Publications, Inc.
Multi Media Arts
NANCY'S MAGAZINE
NEW HOPE INTERNATIONAL REVIEW
NOTES & QUERIES
NOTES FROM THE UNDERGROUND
NRG
Tom Ockerse Editions
OHIO RENAISSANCE REVIEW
The Olivia and Hill Press, Inc.
Open Horizons Publishing Company
OSIRIS
PEN:UMBRA
Petroglyph Press, Ltd.
Pressed Curtains

PROCESSED WORLD
Progresiv Publishr
ProLingua Associates
THE PROSPECT REVIEW
Pygmy Forest Press
THE REDNECK REVIEW OF LITERATURE
RHETORICA: A Journal of the History of Rhetoric
RIGHTING WORDS—THE JOURNAL OF LAN-
   GUAGE AND EDITING
ROMANCE PHILOLOGY
ROMANIAN REVIEW
(ROWBOAT)
Salt Lick Press
Saqi Books Publisher
SCHMAGA
Score
SCORE
Kirit N. Shah
Sink Press
Slate Press
Gibbs Smith, Publisher
Snow Lion Publications, Inc.
SOCKS, DREGS AND ROCKING CHAIRS
Station Hill Press
Stone Bridge Press
THE SUBTLE JOURNAL OF RAW COINAGE
Talon Books Ltd
Thorp Springs Press
THE UNDERGROUND FOREST - LA SELVA SUB-
   TERRANEA
Univelt, Inc.
Vajra of Yoga Anand Ashram
VERBATIM
Verbatim Books
A VOICE WITHOUT SIDES
WE MAGAZINE
We Press
Weidner & Sons, Publishing
Witwatersrand University Press
WOMEN AND LANGUAGE
The Wordtree
WTI Publishing Co.
XEROLAGE

LAPIDARY

GemStone Press

LATIN AMERICA

ACTIVIST
AFRO-HISPANIC REVIEW
ALCATRAZ
Americas Society
Autonomedia, Inc.
Beacon Press
Bergin & Garvey Publishers
Between The Lines
CARIBBEAN REVIEW
CENTRAL AMERICA REPORT
CHALLENGE: A Journal of Faith and Action in Central
   America
CHASQUI
Cleis Press
CLINTON ST.
COLLAGES & BRICOLAGES
Communitas Press
Cultural Survival, Inc.
CULTURAL SURVIVAL QUARTERLY
CULTURE CONCRETE
DESDE ESTE LADO/FROM THIS SIDE
Ediciones El Gato Tuerto
EL GATO TUERTO
Epica
Esoterica Press
Floricanto Press
Gateway Books
Gay Sunshine Press, Inc.
Glenhurst Publications, Inc.
Grapevine Publications, Inc.

GREY CITY JOURNAL
Gringo Guides, Inc.
Grosvenor USA
Hoover Institution Press
Hope Publishing House
IKON
IKON, Inc.
In One Ear Press
INDIGENOUS WORLD/EL MUNDO INDIGENA
Interlink Publishing Group, Inc.
Jorvik Press
Kitchen Table: Women of Color Press
L.A.N.D.
LANCASTER INDEPENDENT PRESS
LATIN AMERICAN LITERARY REVIEW
LATIN AMERICAN PERSPECTIVES
Latin American Press
LECTOR
LIBERATION! Journal of Revolutionary Marxism
LINKS
LUCHA/STRUGGLE
MAXINE'S PAGES
THE MILITANT
Museum of New Mexico Press
New Earth Publications
NEW ORLEANS REVIEW
New Star Books Ltd.
NewSage Press
NOTEBOOK/CUADERNO: A LITERARY JOURNAL
Orbis Books
Paragon House Publishers
Passport Press
Publications of Arts (Art Resources for Teachers &
    Students)
RACONTEUR Publications
Readers International, Inc.
RED BASS
REVIEW. LATIN AMERICAN LITERATURE & ARTS
SALMAGUNDI
Sea Otter Press
SEZ: A Multi-Racial Journal of Poetry & People's Culture
Signal Books
SOCIETE
SOUTH AMERICAN EXPLORER
SPECTRUM, A Guide to the Independent Press and
    Informative Organizations
Spectrum Publications
Studia Hispanica Editors
SUBTEXT
Syracuse Cultural Workers
Third Rail Press
Third World First
THIRD WORLD RESOURCES
Three Continents Press, Inc.
Times Change Press
TOWARD FREEDOM
THE UNDERGROUND FOREST - LA SELVA SUB-
    TERRANEA
Unicorn Press
Waterfront Press
White Pine Press
World Music Press
WORLD RAINFOREST REPORT
Zagier & Urruty Publicaciones

LATINO

BILINGUAL REVIEW/Revista Bilingue
DESDE ESTE LADO/FROM THIS SIDE
Esoterica Press
International Consulting Associates, Inc.
Kitchen Table: Women of Color Press
Museum of New Mexico Press
New Sins Press
PASSAGER: A Journal of Remembrance and Discovery
THE SOUNDS OF POETRY
VALLEY WOMEN'S VOICE
Ward Hill Press

LATVIA

OTISIAN DIRECTORY

LAW

Adams-Hall Publishing
Alchemy Books
Amana Books
AMBASSADOR REPORT
AMERICAN ATHEIST
American Atheist Press
ART CALENDAR
Barr-Randol Publishing Co.
BULLETIN OF THE BOARD OF CELTIC STUDIES
Calibre Press, Inc.
CALIFORNIA LAW REVIEW
CANADIAN JOURNAL OF LAW AND SOCIETY/
    Revue canadienne de droit et societe
Catbird Press
Center for Public Representation
Charter Oak Press
THE CONSTRUCTION CLAIMS CITATOR
Construction Industry Press
COYDOG REVIEW
Crime and Social Justice Associates, Inc.
Do-It-Yourself Legal Publishers
ECOLOGY LAW QUARTERLY
Edgeworth & North Books
FIJACTIVIST
The P. Gaines Co., Publishers
Grand River Press
Gringo Guides, Inc.
Harrow and Heston, Publishers
HARVARD WOMEN'S LAW JOURNAL
HIGH TECHNOLOGY LAW JOURNAL
INDEX TO FOREIGN LEGAL PERIODICALS
INDIGENOUS WORLD/EL MUNDO INDIGENA
INDUSTRIAL RELATIONS LAW JOURNAL
Information Requirements Clearinghouse
Institute for Southern Studies
Interlink Press, Inc.
INTERNATIONAL JOURNAL FOR THE SEMIOTICS
    OF LAW
INTERNATIONAL TAX AND BUSINESS LAWYER
LAW AND CRITIQUE
Law Forum Press
LEGAL INFORMATION MANAGEMENT INDEX
LIVERPOOL LAW REVIEW
Lyceum Books, Inc.
MASTERSTREAM
MAXINE'S PAGES
THE NEW AMERICAN
Nolo Press
Nolo Press - Occidental
Northland Publishing Company
Dr. Homer W. Parker, P.E.
Pine Hall Press
PRISONER'S LEGAL NEWS
PRIVACY JOURNAL
Professional Resource Exchange, Inc.
R & E Publishers
RENT-TO-OWN LEGAL & FINANCIAL BULLETIN
RESOLVE NEWSLETTER
Seven Locks Press
Snowbird Publishing Company
SOCIAL JUSTICE: A JOURNAL OF CRIME, CON-
    FLICT, & WORLD ORDER
Social Order Series
Sphinx Publishing
Stratton Press
STUDENT LAWYER
Thomas Publications
Top Of The Mountain Publishing
THE WASHINGTON TROOPER
Weidner & Sons, Publishing
Wind River Institute Press
Wolcotts, Inc.

D.H. LAWRENCE

Black Sparrow Press
Black Swan Books Ltd.
THE D.H. LAWRENCE REVIEW
The Press of Appletree Alley
STAPLE
UMI Research Press

LEADERSHIP

Knowledge Systems, Inc.
Leadership Education and Development, Inc.
STUDENT LEADERSHIP JOURNAL

LESBIANISM

ACTIVIST
THE ADVOCATE
Alamo Square Press
Alyson Publications, Inc.
Amethyst Press
APAEROS
ATALANTA
Aunt Lute Books
BAY WINDOWS
Beacon Press
BELLES LETTRES
BORDER/LINES
CHAKRA
Chiron Press
CHIRON REVIEW
Cleis Press
Clothespin Fever Press
COLLAGES & BRICOLAGES
COMMON LIVES / LESBIAN LIVES
Context Publications
D.I.N. Publications
DAUGHTER OF SARAH
Empty Closet Enterprises
Esoterica Press
THE EVERGREEN CHRONICLES
THE FEMINIST BOOKSTORE NEWS
FEMINIST COLLECTIONS: A QUARTERLY OF WO-
    MEN'S STUDIES RESOURCES
FEMINIST PERIODICALS: A CURRENT LISTING OF
    CONTENTS
Firebrand Books
Five Fingers Press
FIVE FINGERS REVIEW
FREE PRESS
FUSE MAGAZINE
GATEAVISA
GAY CHICAGO MAGAZINE
GAYELLOW PAGES
GLB Publishers
GREY CITY JOURNAL
HerBooks
HOT WIRE: Journal of Women's Music & Culture
IKON
IKON, Inc.
Illuminati
Institute for Southern Studies
Institute of Lesbian Studies
JH Press
KICK IT OVER
Kitchen Table: Women of Color Press
L.G.L.C. NEWSLETTER
LAMBDA BOOK REPORT
THE LAVENDER NETWORK
LESBIAN CONTRADICTION-A Journal of Irreverent
    Feminism
Libertarians for Gay and Lesbian Concerns (LGLC)
THE LOOGIE
LuraMedia, Inc.
Motheroot Publications
Multiple Dimensions
The Naiad Press, Inc.
NEW BOOKS ON WOMEN & FEMINISM
NEW SINS

New Society Publishers
New Victoria Publishers
OFF OUR BACKS
The Organization
P-FORM
The Place In The Woods
POLITICALLY INCORRECT
PROCESSED WORLD
RADICAL AMERICA
THE RATIONAL FEMINIST
Red Letter Press
Sanguinaria Publishing
SCHMAGA
The Seal Press
SHMATE
Shmate Press
Silverleaf Press, Inc.
SINISTER WISDOM
SOCIALISM AND SEXUALITY
SPARE RIB
Spinster's Book Company
Syracuse Cultural Workers
Talon Books Ltd
13th MOON
Timely Books
Times Change Press
Tough Dove Books
TROUBLE & STRIFE
UNBRIDLED LUST!
THE UNDERGROUND FOREST - LA SELVA SUB-
    TERRANEA
VALLEY WOMEN'S VOICE
VIETNAM GENERATION: A Journal of Recent History
    and Contemporary Issues
VISIBILITIES
Volcano Press, Inc
W.I.M. Publications
THE WISHING WELL
THE WOMEN'S REVIEW OF BOOKS
Women's Studies Librarian, University of Wisconsin
    System
WOMEN'S STUDIES QUARTERLY
WOMENWISE
Working Press

LIBERTARIAN

ACTIVIST
Alchemy Books
ANARCHY: A JOURNAL OF DESIRE ARMED
ASPECTS
Autonomedia, Inc.
Bluestocking Press
Books for All Times, Inc.
'THE CASSETTE GAZETTE', An Audio Magazine
Cheshire Books
City Lights Books
Comforter Publishing
COMMON SENSE
Michael E. Coughlin, Publisher
THE DANDELION
DE NAR
" "...A DEAD BEAT POET PRODUCTION
FOREFRONT—HEALTH INVESTIGATIONS
Free Association Books (FAB)
FREE INQUIRY
GREY CITY JOURNAL
Handshake Editions
The Heather Foundation
THE HYPERBOREAN
Hyperborean Micropublications
ILLINOIS LIBERTARIAN
INCITE INFORMATION
INDIVIDUAL LIBERTY
KICK IT OVER
L.G.L.C. NEWSLETTER
THE (LIBERTARIAN) CONNECTION
Libertarian Press, Inc./American Book Distributors
Libertarian Publishers

Libertarians for Gay and Lesbian Concerns (LGLC)
LIBERTY
LITTLE FREE PRESS
LIVING FREE
Mermaid Press
Mustang Publishing Co.
MY LIFE DEPENDS ON YOU
THE NEW AMERICAN
New Saga Publishers
NOMOS: Studies in Spontaneous Order
The Organization
OTISIAN DIRECTORY
Pacific Research Institute
POLITICALLY INCORRECT
PROCESSED WORLD
RAMPIKE
SALON: A Journal of Aesthetics
SAMISDAT
SOUTHERN LIBERTARIAN MESSENGER
SPECTRUM, A Guide to the Independent Press and
  Informative Organizations
Spectrum Publications
SURVIVE & WIN
UNBRIDLED LUST!
VIRGINIA LIBERTY
Voice of Liberty Publications
THE VOLUNTARYIST

LIBRARIES

ALA/SRRT NEWSLETTER
American Audio Prose Library (non-print)
THE BIBLIOTHECK
BkMk Press
Bluestocking Press
Bookcraft
THE BOOK REPORT: Journal for Junior & Senior High
  School Librarians
BOOK TALK
BookNotes :(TM) Resources for Small & Self-Publishers
Caliban Press
THE CHRISTIAN LIBRARIAN
Cooperative Children's Book Center
Copyright Information Services
The Denali Press
Dundurn Press Ltd
Dyad Services
EDITOR'S DIGEST
EMERGENCY LIBRARIAN
FEMINIST COLLECTIONS: A QUARTERLY OF WO-
  MEN'S STUDIES RESOURCES
FEMINIST PERIODICALS: A CURRENT LISTING OF
  CONTENTS
FOCUS
FOCUS: Library Service to Older Adults, People with
  Disabilities
FUGITIVE POPE
The Gleniffer Press
Graham-Conley Press
HENNEPIN COUNTY LIBRARY CATALOGING BUL-
  LETIN
HOBBY BOOKWATCH (MILITARY, GUN & HOBBY
  BOOK REVIEW)
L D A Publishers
LEGAL INFORMATION MANAGEMENT INDEX
LIBRARY CURRENTS
THE LIBRARY IMAGINATION PAPER!
LIBRARY OUTREACH REPORTER
Library Outreach Reporter Publications
LIBRARY TALK: The Magazine for Elementary School
  Librarians
LIBRARY TIMES INTERNATIONAL
THE LIT PAGE: The Magazine for Library Literacy
LITERARY RESEARCH: A Journal of Scholarly Method
  & Technique
Masefield Books
McFarland & Company, Inc., Publishers
MSRRT NEWSLETTER
Nancy Renfro Studios, Inc.

NEW BOOKS ON WOMEN & FEMINISM
NORTH CAROLINA LIBRARIES
ON THE ROAD: Mobile Ideas for Libraries
Ontario Library Association
ORO MADRE
The Oryx Press
OUR WRITE MIND
Pacific Information Inc.
Dr. Homer W. Parker, P.E.
THE PRAIRIE JOURNAL OF CANADIAN LITERA-
  TURE
PREVIEW: Professional and Reference Literature Review
R & E Publishers
Rio Grande Press
THE ROTKIN REVIEW
Ruddy Duck Press
Scarecrow Press
SE LA VIE WRITER'S JOURNAL
SERIALS REVIEW
SIPAPU
SOCIAL CHANGE & INFORMATION SYSTEMS
THE TEACHING LIBRARIAN
TECHNICALITIES
TOOK
THE   U*N*A*B*A*S*H*E*D   LIBRARIAN,   THE
  "HOW I RUN MY LIBRARY GOOD" LETTER
University of Calgary Press
The Urbana Free Library
Willowood Press
WLW JOURNAL: News/Views/Reviews for Women and
  Libraries
Women's Studies Librarian, University of Wisconsin
  System
WRITER'S LIFELINE

LITERARY REVIEW

ACTA VICTORIANA
ADRIFT
AGENDA
AKWEKON: A National Native American Literary &
  Arts Journal
AKWEKON LITERARY JOURNAL
ALASKA QUARTERLY REVIEW
ALLEGHENY REVIEW
THE AMERICAN BOOK REVIEW
AMERICAN WRITING: A MAGAZINE
THE AMERICA'S REVIEW
ANERCA/COMPOST
ANQ: A Quarterly Journal of Short Articles, Notes, and
  Reviews
ANTAEUS
THE ANTIGONISH REVIEW
ARIEL—A Review of International English Literature
ARISTOS
ARIZONA QUARTERLY
ASYLUM
AURA Literary/Arts Review
AXEFACTORY
BACKBOARD
BAKER STREET GAZETTE
BARNWOOD
BEAT SCENE
BELLES LETTRES
BLACK AMERICAN LITERATURE FORUM
BLACK MULLET REVIEW
BOOK TALK
BOSTON REVIEW
Brick Row Publishing Co. Ltd.
BRITISH JOURNAL OF AESTHETICS
Brooding Heron Press
CACANADADADA REVIEW
CALYX: A Journal of Art and Literature by Women
Cambric Press
CANADIAN AUTHOR & BOOKMAN
CANADIAN FICTION MAGAZINE
CANADIAN LITERATURE
CATALYST, A Magazine of Heart and Mind
CENTER

PIKEVILLE REVIEW
THE PITTSBURGH QUARTERLY
PLAINSONG
PLOUGHSHARES
POETICS JOURNAL
POETRY CANADA
POETRY EAST
POETRY MOTEL
POETRY QUARTERLY
POSTMODERN CULTURE
POTATO EYES
POULTRY - A MAGAZINE OF VOICE
Poultry, Inc.
THE PRAIRIE JOURNAL OF CANADIAN LITERA-
  TURE
PRAIRIE SCHOONER
PRAKALPANA SAHITYA/PRAKALPANA LITERA-
  TURE
THE PROSPECT REVIEW
THE PUCKERBRUSH REVIEW
PURPLE PATCH
QUANTUM: Science Fiction & Fantasy Review
QUARTOS MAGAZINE
RACCOON
RACKHAM JOURNAL OF THE ARTS AND HUMANI-
  TIES (RaJAH)
THE RAYSTOWN REVIEW
THE REDNECK REVIEW OF LITERATURE
REMARK
THE REVIEW OF CONTEMPORARY FICTION
RHODODENDRON
JEAN RHYS REVIEW
Rio Grande Press
RIVERWIND
THE ROMANTIST
ROOM OF ONE'S OWN
Ruddy Duck Press
ST. LOUIS JOURNALISM REVIEW
SAMISDAT
SAN FRANCISCO REVIEW OF BOOKS
SAN MIGUEL REVIEW
SANDHILLS/ST. ANDREWS REVIEW
THE SANTA MONICA REVIEW
SE LA VIE WRITER'S JOURNAL
SEQUOIA
SHAW. THE ANNUAL OF BERNARD SHAW STU-
  DIES
SHENANDOAH
SMALL PRESS NEWS
SONORA REVIEW
SOUTHERN HUMANITIES REVIEW
SOUTHERN READER
THE SOUTHERN REVIEW
SOUTHWEST REVIEW
SPHINX—WOMEN'S INTERNATIONAL LITERARY/
  ART REVIEW (IN ENGLISH)
STAND MAGAZINE
STAR-WEB PAPER
Student Media Corporation
STUDIO - A Journal of Christians Writing
SULFUR
SYCAMORE REVIEW
TAKAHE
TALISMAN: A Journal of Contemporary Poetry and
  Poetics
THE TEXAS REVIEW
THALIA: Studies in Literary Humor
THIRD RAIL
Third Rail Press
13th MOON
THE THREEPENNY REVIEW
Thunder's Mouth Press
TOOK
TOWARDS
TRANSLATION REVIEW
TULSA STUDIES IN WOMEN'S LITERATURE
TURNSTILE
Two Rivers Press

THE UNDERGROUND FOREST - LA SELVA SUB-
  TERRANEA
UNION STREET REVIEW
University of Tulsa
UNIVERSITY OF WINDSOR REVIEW
UNMUZZLED OX
URBANUS/RAIZIRR
VIGIL
THE VINCENT BROTHERS REVIEW
THE VIRGINIA QUARTERLY REVIEW
VISIONS, International, The World Journal of Illustrated
  Poetry
W.I.M. Publications
WATER ROW REVIEW
THE WAVE
WEBSTER REVIEW
Westburg Associates, Publishers
WESTERN AMERICAN LITERATURE
WESTERN HUMANITIES REVIEW
WILLIAM AND MARY REVIEW
Window Publications
WITHIN & BEYOND
Witwatersrand University Press
WOMENWISE
THE WORCESTER REVIEW
THE WORMWOOD REVIEW
The Wormwood Review Press
WRITER'S GUIDELINES MAGAZINE
THE WRITER'S HAVEN
THE YALE REVIEW
YELLOW SILK: Journal Of Erotic Arts

LITERATURE (GENERAL)

Abattoir Editions
Acadia Publishing Company
Acheron Press
ACTA VICTORIANA
AEGEAN REVIEW
AERIAL
AGADA
AGOG
AILERON, A LITERARY JOURNAL
AKWEKON: A National Native American Literary &
  Arts Journal
AKWEKON LITERARY JOURNAL
ALCATRAZ
Alchemy Press
Alioth Press
Allardyce, Barnett (Agneau 2)
THE AMARANTH REVIEW
AMBERGRIS
American Audio Prose Library (non-print)
American Poets In Profile Series
THE AMERICAN VOICE
Americas Society
ANERCA/COMPOST
Anhinga Press
ANQ: A Quarterly Journal of Short Articles, Notes, and
  Reviews
Appalachian Consortium Press
Arbiter Press
ARIEL—A Review of International English Literature
ARISTOS
ASYLUM
Asylum Arts
AURA Literary/Arts Review
BAMBOO RIDGE, THE HAWAII WRITERS' QUAR-
  TERLY
Bamboo Ridge Press
Beacon Press
BEAT SCENE
Beat Scene Press
BEGINNING: THE MAGAZINE FOR THE WRITER IN
  THE COMMUNITY
BELLES LETTRES
Beyond Baroque Foundation Publications
THE BIBLIOTHECK
Bilingue Publications

Birch Brook Press
BkMk Press
Black Hat Press
Black Heron Press
BLACK MULLET REVIEW
Black Sparrow Press
Black Swan Books Ltd.
BLIND ALLEYS
Blind Beggar Press
BLOODROOT
Bloodroot, Inc.
THE BLOOMSBURY REVIEW
BLUE LIGHT RED LIGHT
Bluestocking Press
Bolton Press
Borealis Press Limited
BOTTOMFISH MAGAZINE
BOULEVARD
The Boxwood Press
Branden Publishing Company
Breitenbush Books, Inc.
Brick Row Publishing Co. Ltd.
BRILLIANT STAR
Broken Moon Press
Brook House Press, Inc.
BUCKNELL REVIEW
Buddha Rose Publications
Burning Books
CAL NEWSLETTER
CALAPOOYA COLLAGE
Caliban Press
CALLALOO
CALYX: A Journal of Art and Literature by Women
CANADIAN AUTHOR & BOOKMAN
Capra Press
CAROLINA QUARTERLY
The Carolina Wren Press
Carroll & Graf Publishers, Inc.
CATALYST
Cayuse Press
CENTRAL PARK
Cerulean Press (Subsidiary of Kent Publications)
Chandler & Sharp Publishers, Inc.
Chantry Press
CHELSEA
CHILDREN'S ALBUM
Chinese Literature Press
Chiron Press
CHIRON REVIEW
CIMARRON REVIEW
City Lights Books
Clothespin Fever Press
CNL/WORLD REPORT
Coach House Press
The Cobham and Hatherton Press
Coffee House Press
COLD-DRILL
COLLAGES & BRICOLAGES
Comforter Publishing
Concourse Press
CONJUNCTIONS
CORNFIELD REVIEW
CRAB CREEK REVIEW
CRAMPED AND WET
The F. Marion Crawford Memorial Society
CRAWLSPACE
CRAZYQUILT LITERARY QUARTERLY
CRICKET, THE MAGAZINE FOR CHILDREN
CROOKED ROADS
CROSS-CANADA WRITERS' MAGAZINE
CROSSCURRENTS, A QUARTERLY
CROTON REVIEW
CRUCIBLE
Cube Publications Inc
THE CULTURAL FORUM
CULTURE CONCRETE
Cumberland
CUMBERLAND

The Curlew Press
Dalkey Archive Press
Dan River Press
John Daniel and Company, Publishers
DAYSPRING
" "...A DEAD BEAT POET PRODUCTION
DECEMBER MAGAZINE
DELIRIUM
DESCANT
The Devonshire Publishing Co.
A DIFFERENT DRUMMER
DIMENSION
Directed Media, Inc.
DOG RIVER REVIEW
Double M Press
DREAMS & VISIONS
Dufour Editions Inc.
Dunstan Press
THE DUPLEX PLANET
THE DURHAM UNIVERSITY JOURNAL
EARTH'S DAUGHTERS: Feminist Arts Periodical
Earthwise Publications
Ediciones El Gato Tuerto
Edition Gemini
EFQ Publications
e.g.
E-Heart Press, Inc.
ELT Press
Endeavor Publishing
ENGLISH LITERATURE IN TRANSITION, 1880-1920
ENGLISH STUDIES IN AFRICA-A Journal of the
   Humanities
EPIPHANY: A JOURNAL OF LITERATURE
EROTIC FICTION QUARTERLY
Esoterica Press
Euroeditor
Exile Press
The Family of God
THE FAMOUS REPORTER
The Feminist Press at the City University of New York
FICTION
FINE MADNESS
The First East Coast Theatre and Publishing Company,
   Inc.
FISH DRUM MAGAZINE
Fithian Press
Fjord Press
THE FLORIDA REVIEW
Ford-Brown & Co., Publishers
FOREHEAD: Writing & Art Journal
Four Walls Eight Windows
FRAGMENTS
French Broad Press
Fromm International Publishing Corporation
FUSE MAGAZINE
The Future Press
The Galileo Press Ltd.
Galloping Dog Press
GAVEA-BROWN
Gavea-Brown Publications
THE GETTYSBURG REVIEW
GIANTS PLAY WELL IN THE DRIZZLE
GlenHill Productions
The Gleniffer Press
Globe Press Books
GO MAGAZINE
GRAND STREET
GRANTA
The Graywolf Press
Great Elm Press
Green Key Press
The Green Street Press
Griffon House Publications/Bagehot Council
Gringo Guides, Inc.
Growing Room Collective
Guernica Editions, Inc.
HAIGHT ASHBURY LITERARY JOURNAL
THE HARVARD ADVOCATE

HearSay Press TM
HEMLOCKS AND BALSAMS
Hermitage (Ermitazh)
Heyday Books
HOB-NOB
HOBO JUNGLE
THE HOLLINS CRITIC
Holmgangers Press
Holy Cow! Press
HOWLING DOG
Howling Dog Press
Humana Press
HURRICANE ALICE
The Zora Neale Hurston Society
Ianus Publications, Inc.
IDIOM 23
ILLUMINATIONS
Illuminations Press
IMAGINATION MAGAZINE
IMAGO
Indelible Inc.
Independence Publishers Inc.
THE INDIAN WRITER
INKBLOT
Inkblot Publications
Inkling Publications, Inc.
The Institute of Mind and Behavior Press
INTERRACIAL BOOKS FOR CHILDREN BULLETIN
Ion Books
THE IOWA REVIEW
IOWA WOMAN
Italica Press, Inc.
JAMES JOYCE BROADSHEET
J'ECRIS
JENNINGS MAGAZINE
JOURNAL FOR ANTHROPOSOPHY
THE JOURNAL OF MIND AND BEHAVIOR
JOURNAL OF MODERN LITERATURE
Jubilee Press
KALDRON, An International Journal Of Visual Poetry
    and Language Art
Kelsey St. Press
Kenyette Productions
Michael Kesend, Publishing, Ltd.
KEY WEST REVIEW
KEYSTROKES
Knowledge, Ideas & Trends, Inc. (KIT)
LA NUEZ
LANCASTER INDEPENDENT PRESS
LANGUAGE ARTS JOURNAL OF MICHIGAN
Laocoon Books
Last Generation/Underground Editions
LATIN AMERICAN LITERARY REVIEW
Latin American Literary Review Press
Laughing Bear Press
Laughing Dog Press
Leete's Island Books
LEFT CURVE
LIGHTNING SWORD
LIMESTONE: A LITERARY JOURNAL
Lincoln Springs Press
THE LION AND THE UNICORN: A Critical Journal of
    Children's Literature
LITERARY RESEARCH: A Journal of Scholarly Method
    & Technique
LOBLOLLY: A LITERARY BIANNUAL OF THE
    VORTEX
LOST GENERATION JOURNAL
Lotus Press, Inc.
LUCKY HEART BOOKS
Lumen Books, Inc.
LYRA
MAINE IN PRINT
Maisonneuve Press
Maize Press
THE MANHATTAN REVIEW
manic d press
MANOA: A Pacific Journal of International Writing

Marilee Publications
MARK
The Marlboro Press
Matilda Publications
Mayapple Press
Laurence McGilvery
McPherson & Company Publishers
Meckler Corporation
MEDIA SPOTLIGHT
MEMES
Men & Women of Letters
The Menard Press
Mercury House
Merging Media
MERLYN'S PEN: The National Magazine of Student
    Writing
METAPHOR
MICHIGAN QUARTERLY REVIEW
Michigan Romance Studies
THE MID COASTER
The Middleburg Press
Middlebury College Publications
R. & E. Miles
Milkweed Editions
Mina Press
MIND IN MOTION, A MAGAZINE OF POETRY AND
    SHORT PROSE
MINNESOTA LITERATURE
THE MINNESOTA REVIEW
Mockingbird Press
MOMENTUM
MOODY STREET IRREGULARS: A Jack Kerouac
    Magazine
Moody Street Irregulars, Inc.
Mortal Press
Moscow Publishing Enterprises
Motheroot Publications
Multi Media Arts
MUSCADINE
Mustang Publishing Co.
Mutual Publishing of Honolulu
NEGATIVE CAPABILITY
Negative Capability Press
The Neither/Nor Press
NEW COLLAGE MAGAZINE
New Collage Press
NEW CONTRAST
NEW DEPARTURES
NEW ENGLAND REVIEW
NEW EUROPE
NEW GERMAN REVIEW: A Journal of Germanic
    Studies
NEW HOPE INTERNATIONAL REVIEW
THE NEW LAUREL REVIEW
NEW ORLEANS REVIEW
THE NEW RENAISSANCE, An International Magazine
    of Ideas & Opinions, Emphasizing Literature & The
    Arts
New Rivers Press, Inc.
The New South Company
New Victoria Publishers
NEW WRITER'S MAGAZINE
NEWSLETTER
NEXT EXIT
Night Horn Books
Nightshade Press
NIGHTSUN
NINETEENTH-CENTURY LITERATURE
Nioba, Uitgevers
THE NORTH AMERICAN REVIEW
NORTH DAKOTA QUARTERLY
NORTHCOAST VIEW MONTHLY MAGAZINE
THE NORTHERN REVIEW
THE NORTHLAND QUARTERLY
Northland Quarterly Publications, Inc.
Norton Coker Press
NOTES & QUERIES
NOTES FROM THE UNDERGROUND

NOTUS NEW WRITING
NUTSHELL
Nuventures Publishing
O.ARS
O.ARS, Inc.
Oasis Books
ORO MADRE
OTHER VOICES
Otherwind
OVERLAND
The Overlook Press
OWEN WISTER REVIEW
THE PACIFIC REVIEW
Panopticum Press London
PARIS REVIEW
PARNASSUS LITERARY JOURNAL
Path Press, Inc.
PENNSYLVANIA'S LITERARY NETWORK NEWS-
   LETTER
PENNYWHISTLE PEOPLE PAPER
Pennywhistle Press
The Petrarch Press
Petronium Press
PIG IRON
Pigwidgeon Press
The Pikestaff Press
Placebo Press
Plain View Press, Inc.
Plantagenet House, Inc.
Pocahontas Press, Inc.
POETRY EAST
POETRY MOTEL
POETRY QUARTERLY
Poetry Wales Press, Ltd.
Poets & Writers, Inc.
The Post-Apollo Press
The Post-Industrial Press
POSTMODERN CULTURE
THE POTTERSFIELD PORTFOLIO
Pottersfield Press
THE PRAIRIE JOURNAL OF CANADIAN LITERA-
   TURE
Prairie Journal Press
Prakalpana Literature
PRAKALPANA SAHITYA/PRAKALPANA LITERA-
   TURE
PRECISELY
Primal Publishing
PROOF ROCK
PROPHETIC VOICES
PROVINCETOWN ARTS
THE PUB
THE PUCKERBRUSH REVIEW
Pushcart Press
Q.E.D. Press
Quarterly Committee of Queen's University
QUEEN'S QUARTERLY: A Canadian Review
QUIXOTE, QUIXOTL
RACKHAM JOURNAL OF THE ARTS AND HUMANI-
   TIES (RaJAH)
RAMPIKE
RARITAN: A Quarterly Review
Readers International, Inc.
REAL FICTION
Rebis Press
RED BASS
Red Key Press
THE REDNECK REVIEW OF LITERATURE
I. Reed Books
Regent Press
RENDITIONS
Renditions Paperbacks
RENEGADE
REVIEW. LATIN AMERICAN LITERATURE & ARTS
RIVER STYX
ROMANIAN REVIEW
THE ROMANTIST
ROOM OF ONE'S OWN

Rossi
(ROWBOAT)
Ruddy Duck Press
Running Press
The Rydal Press
SAMIZDAT
Sand River Press
SANDHILLS/ST. ANDREWS REVIEW
Santa Susana Press
Saqi Books Publisher
Savant Garde Workshop
Say When Press
SCANDINAVIAN REVIEW
SCARP
SCHMAGA
Score
SCORE
Scribblers Publishing, Ltd.
SCRIPSI
SCRIVENER
Sea Urchin Press
Second Coming Press
Selene Books
Seventh Son Press
Seventh-Wing Publications
SEWANEE REVIEW
SEZ: A Multi-Racial Journal of Poetry & People's Culture
Shadow Press, U.S.A.
Sherwood Sugden & Company, Publishers
SHMATE
Shmate Press
Shy City Press
Silver Skates Publishing
SINISTER WISDOM
SISYPHUS
SITES
Slate Press
SLIPSTREAM
THE SMALL POND MAGAZINE OF LITERATURE
   aka SMALL POND
SMALL PRESS: The Magazine & Book Review of
   Independent Publishing
SMALL PRESS NEWS
Small-Small Press
SMS Publishing Corp.
SOUTH DAKOTA REVIEW
THE SOUTHERN REVIEW
Southport Press
SOUTHWEST REVIEW
SPIT
SPRING: A Journal of Archetype and Culture
The Square-Rigger Press
Station Hill Press
THE WALLACE STEVENS JOURNAL
STIFLED YAWN: A Magazine Of Contemporary Writing
STILETTO
Still Point Press
Stone Circle Press
STORIES
STORY
STREAM LINES, MN JOURNAL OF CREATIVE
   WRITING
Stride Publications
STUDIO - A Journal of Christians Writing
Sunburst Press
SYNAESTHESIA
Synergistic Press
TABULA RASA
TAKAHE
Talon Books Ltd
TAPROOT, a journal of elder writers
Teal Press
THALIA: Studies in Literary Humor
THEMA
THIRD RAIL
Third Rail Press
13th MOON
This Press

Thorp Springs Press
THOUGHT, A REVIEW OF CULTURE & IDEA
THE THREEPENNY REVIEW
Threshold Books
Thunder Creek Publishing Co-operative
Tippy Reed Publishing
TOOK
TQS Publications (Tonatiuh - Quinto Sol International Inc.)
TRANSLATION
Translation Center
TRAPANI NUOVA, TERZA PAGINA
TRIQUARTERLY
Triton Books + Gallery
TRIVIA, A JOURNAL OF IDEAS
TRIVIUM
Two Rivers Press
Tyger Press
Tyro Publishing
THE UNDERGROUND FOREST - LA SELVA SUB-TERRANEA
Underwhich Editions
UNION SHOP BLUFF
University of Calgary Press
University of Massachusetts Press
Sherry Urie
Urion Press
Vagabond Press
Valentine Publishing & Drama Co.
THE VINCENT BROTHERS REVIEW
THE VIRGINIA QUARTERLY REVIEW
W.D.C. PERIOD
WATER ROW REVIEW
THE WAVE
Wayland Press
WE MAGAZINE
We Press
Weidner & Sons, Publishing
West Anglia Publications
West End Press
West of Boston
Westburg Associates, Publishers
WESTERN AMERICAN LITERATURE
WESTERN HUMANITIES REVIEW
Westwind Press
Wheel of Fire Press
White Horse Press
Windom Books
Window Publications
WINDSCRIPT
Wise Owl Press
WITNESS
WORKSHOP
THE WRITERS' BAR-B-Q
THE WRITERS' BLOC*
WRITERS GAZETTE NEWSLETTER
WRITER'S GUIDELINES MAGAZINE
Writers House Press
WRITER'S LIFELINE
YELLOW SILK: Journal Of Erotic Arts
Yoknapatawpha Press
Zephyr Press
Zoland Books

LONDON

BAKER STREET GAZETTE
Gaslight Publications
KELTIC FRINGE
Peter Marcan Publications
Zephyr Press

JACK LONDON

CHESAPEAKE BAY MAGAZINE
The Live Oak Press
Mutual Publishing of Honolulu
Star Rover House
WESTERN AMERICAN LITERATURE

LOS ANGELES

B-CITY
Excellence Enterprises
Happy Rock Press
Recreation Sales Publishing, Inc.

LOUISIANA

Cajun Publishing
The Chicot Press
Ocean Tree Books

H.P. LOVECRAFT

Algol Press
Baker Street Publications
THE...CHRONICLE
The F. Marion Crawford Memorial Society
THE GAME'S AFOOT
W. Paul Ganley: Publisher
Gryphon Publications
THE HAUNTED JOURNAL
MOONSTONE BLUE
Nemeton Publishing
OTISIAN DIRECTORY
THE OVERLOOK CONNECTION
PAPERBACK PARADE
THE ROMANTIST
SCIENCE FICTION CHRONICLE
SOCIETE
TATTOO ADVOCATE JOURNAL
UNBRIDLED LUST!
Zirlinson Publishing

BULWER LYTTON

The F. Marion Crawford Memorial Society
FINE MADNESS
THE ROMANTIST

MAGAZINES

Afta Press
ANGRY
ARTPAPER
BABY SUE
BAKER STREET GAZETTE
Baker Street Publications
BEAN ZINE
BEAT SCENE
BELLYWASH
THE BERKELEY MONTHLY
BOOK MARKETING UPDATE
BRILLIANT IDEAS FOR PUBLISHERS
THE...CHRONICLE
CLIENT MAGAZINE
CONFRONTATION
CROP DUST
CROW MAGAZINE
CULTURE CONCRETE
DE NAR
" "...A DEAD BEAT POET PRODUCTION
THE DILETTANTE FORUM
EDITOR'S DIGEST
Elysium Growth Press
FACTSHEET FIVE
THE FAMOUS REPORTER
FATHOMS BELOW
FEMINIST PERIODICALS: A CURRENT LISTING OF CONTENTS
THE FESSENDEN REVIEW
FIDELIS ET VERUS
FRANK: AN INTERNATIONAL JOURNAL OF CONTEMPORARY WRITING AND ART
W. Paul Ganley: Publisher
GATEAVISA
Gryphon Publications
HAPPINESS HOLDING TANK
THE HAUNTED JOURNAL
HEATHENZINE
Heidelberg Graphics

QED
R.G.E. Publishing
SCIENCE AND NATURE, The Annual of Marxist Philosophy for Natural Scientists
SMARANDACHE FUNCTION JOURNAL
Snowbird Publishing Company

MEDIA

ACTIVIST
American Audio Prose Library (non-print)
Beacon Press
BLUE LIGHTS
Blue Lights Publications
BOOK MARKETING UPDATE
BORDER/LINES
D.B.A. Books
DE NAR
Festival Publications
THE FINAL PAGE
FUSE MAGAZINE
GREY CITY JOURNAL
KETTERING REVIEW
LEFT BUSINESS OBSERVER
LEFT CURVE
LINKS
Mho & Mho Works
New Levee Press
Open Horizons Publishing Company
P-FORM
Progressive Education
PROGRESSIVE PERIODICALS DIRECTORY/UPDATE
PUBLISHING TRENDS & TRENDSETTERS
S.E.T. FREE: The Newsletter Against Television
ST. LOUIS JOURNALISM REVIEW
SPECTRUM, A Guide to the Independent Press and Informative Organizations
Spectrum Publications
Talon Books Ltd
THIRD WAY
Third World First
THE WASHINGTON MONTHLY
WORLD OF FANDOM MAGAZINE

MEDIEVAL

THE ALTERED MIND
BALDER
Beacon Press
Bear & Company, Inc.
Bolchazy-Carducci Publishers, Inc.
The Carnation Press
The Cobham and Hatherton Press
Coxland Press
The F. Marion Crawford Memorial Society
DIE FAT PIGGY DIE
The E.G. Van Press, Inc.
Erespin Press
Esoterica Press
Forty-Seven Books
Glenhurst Publications, Inc.
Ide House, Inc.
Italica Press, Inc.
JOURNAL FOR ANTHROPOSOPHY
NEW HOPE INTERNATIONAL REVIEW
NOTES & QUERIES
NOTTINGHAM MEDIEVAL STUDIES
Resource Publications, Inc.
THE ROMANTIST
(ROWBOAT)
SCHMAGA
Scribblers Publishing, Ltd.
Silver Dawn Media
UNBRIDLED LUST!
YE OLDE NEWES

MEDICINE

ADAPTED PHYSICAL ACTIVITY QUARTERLY (APAQ)
ADDICTION & RECOVERY

Alpine Guild
THE ANIMALS' AGENDA
Borderland Sciences Research Foundation
THE CIVIL ABOLITIONIST
dbS Productions
Distinctive Publishing Corp.
DOCTOR-PATIENT STUDIES
DRUG INTERACTIONS AND UPDATES
The Everett Companies, Publishing Division
FOREFRONT—HEALTH INVESTIGATIONS
Grace and Goddess Unlimited
Health Educator Publications, Inc.
Health Press
Human Kinetics Pub. Inc.
Humana Press
IBS Press
Jones River Press
JOURNAL OF POLYMORPHOUS PERVERSITY
Ledero Press
Life Enhancement
LINKS
MAXINE'S PAGES
MedLife Communications, Inc.
MIDWIFERY TODAY
New Idea Press, Inc.
THE NORTHERN REVIEW
OBESITY & HEALTH: CURRENT RESEARCH AND RELATED ISSUES
Persona Publications
Popular Medicine Press
RESONANCE
The Saunderstown Press
SCIENCE/HEALTH ABSTRACTS
Sun Eagle Publishing
Third World First
Triad Publishing Co. Inc.
Arnie Wolman Co.
WOMENWISE
The Write Press
Xenos Books

MEN

THE ADVOCATE
APAEROS
Beacon Press
Blue Dolphin Press, Inc.
CHANGING MEN
CLINTON ST.
COYDOG REVIEW
Down There Press
FIRSTHAND
Gemini Publishing Company
GLB Publishers
HEALING PATH
THE ICARUS REVIEW
JAMES WHITE REVIEW; A Gay Men's Literary Quarterly
THE LATHAM LETTER
Liberty Bell Press & Publishing Co.
McOne Press
MEN'S REPORT
MENTERTAINMENT
New Atlantis Press
Omega Cottonwood Press
The Place In The Woods
THE RATIONAL FEMINIST
Red Alder Books
RFD
ROMEO NEWSLETTER
SINGLE SCENE
SPECTRUM, A Guide to the Independent Press and Informative Organizations
Spectrum Publications
Steel Balls Press
Straight Arrow Publishing
Sun Features Inc.
Thunder Creek Publishing Co-operative
Times Change Press

Triad Press
Twelvetrees Press/Twin Palms Publishers
VIETNAM WAR NEWSLETTER
White Rose Publishing
Whole Person Associates Inc.
THE WRITERS' BAR-B-Q
Yellow Moon Press

H.L. MENCKEN

AILERON, A LITERARY JOURNAL
The Organization
POLITICALLY INCORRECT
THE PRINTER
Three Continents Press, Inc.

METAPHYSICS

ACS Publications
Alchemy Books
AREOPAGUS
Arjuna Library Press
Ascension Publishing
ASPECTS
ASTROFLASH
The Biting Idge/Miracle Press (Chrysalis Publications)
Blue Dolphin Press, Inc.
Borderland Sciences Research Foundation
Comforter Publishing
COMPOST NEWSLETTER (CNL)
Cosmoenergetics Publications
The Devonshire Publishing Co.
Dharma Publishing
Distinctive Publishing Corp.
THE DREAMWEAVER
EMERGING
THE EMSHOCK LETTER
Excellence Enterprises
Futurum Forlag
Gateways Books And Tapes
Golden Sceptre
Great Western Publishing Company
HEAVEN BONE
I. S. C. Press
IBS Press
INNER JOURNEYS
INNER SEARCH
Inner Vision Publishing Company
INTUITIVE EXPLORATIONS
JOURNAL FOR ANTHROPOSOPHY
JOURNAL OF BORDERLAND RESEARCH
JOURNAL OF REGIONAL CRITICISM
KOOKS MAGAZINE
HJ Kramer, Inc
Lorien House
Los Arboles Publications
LP Publications (Teleos Institute)
Metagnosis Publications
Mockingbird Press
NEW MOON RISING
Non-Stop Books
OFFICE NUMBER ONE
Omega Press (formerly Sufi Order Publications)
OTISIAN DIRECTORY
Out-Of-Kontrol Data Institute
Parabola Books
PARABOLA MAGAZINE
THE PERSONAL MAGNETISM HOME STUDY
    COURSE ON ALL HUMAN POWERS
Phanes Press
Ramp Creek Publishing Inc
THE REDNECK REVIEW OF LITERATURE
Rio Grande Press
Rolling House Publications
SACRED FIRE
Savant Garde Workshop
SOM Publishing, division of School of Metaphysics
Sunstone Publications
Synergetic Press Inc.
Tambra Publishing

Theosophical Publishing House
THRESHOLDS JOURNAL
Top Of The Mountain Publishing
TRENDS & PREDICTIONS ANALYST
UNBRIDLED LUST!
Upword Press
Valley Lights Publications
Samuel Weiser, Inc.
Westgate Press
Whitehorse
WTI Publishing Co.
Yes You Can Press

MICHIGAN

Avery Color Studios
Wm.B. Eerdmans Publishing Co.
FROG GONE REVIEW
Grand River Press
HOWLING DOG
LAKE SUPERIOR MAGAZINE
THE NORTHERN REVIEW
Northword Press, Inc.
SINCERE SINGLES
THE SOUNDS OF POETRY
TANDAVA

MIDDLE EAST

AAUG Press
Africa World Press, Inc.
Amana Books
ARAB STUDIES QUARTERLY
Beacon Press
Between The Lines
The Borgo Press
Esoterica Press
Hoover Institution Press
House of Hits, Inc.
INCITE INFORMATION
Infolib Resources
Institute for Palestine Studies
Interlink Publishing Group, Inc.
Iranbooks, Inc.
ISRAEL HORIZONS
JEWISH CURRENTS
Judah Magnes Museum Publications
THE KIBBUTZ JOURNAL
The Kingston Press, Inc.
KMT, A Modern Journal of Ancient Egypt
KMT Communications
Lake View Press
LIBERATION! Journal of Revolutionary Marxism
LINKS
Lions Head Press
M.H. Macy & Company
Mage Publishers, Inc.
Mazda Publishers
MIDDLE EAST REPORT
MIDDLE EASTERN DANCER
MIDEAST MONITOR
Moonsquilt Press
NET
Orbis Books
Political Research Associates
Polymath Systems
The Post-Apollo Press
RACONTEUR Publications
Readers International, Inc.
RECONSTRUCTIONIST
Relampago Books Press
Saqi Books Publisher
THE SEARCH - JOURNAL FOR ARAB AND ISLAMIC
    STUDIES
Smyrna Press
SPECTRUM, A Guide to the Independent Press and
    Informative Organizations
Spectrum Publications
SUBTEXT
Third World First

THIRD WORLD RESOURCES
Three Continents Press, Inc.
Times Change Press
TOWARD FREEDOM
UNBRIDLED LUST!
VIEWPOINT
VOICES - ISRAEL
WORDS OF WISDOM
WORLD PERSPECTIVES

MIDWEST

THE ANNALS OF IOWA
Avery Color Studios
Blue Bird Publishing
Cardinal Press, Inc.
Wm Caxton Ltd
CORNFIELD REVIEW
ECOSOCIALIST REVIEW
Wm.B. Eerdmans Publishing Co.
THE EVERGREEN CHRONICLES
FARMER'S MARKET
Foundation Books
Heritage Press WI
Homestead Publishing
HORIZONS WEST
IOWA WOMAN
THE LETTER PARADE
MANKATO POETRY REVIEW
Mayhaven Publishing
MIDLAND REVIEW
Misty Hill Press
THE NORTHERN REVIEW
Omega Cottonwood Press
THE PRAIRIE JOURNAL OF CANADIAN LITERA-
    TURE
Pruett Publishing Company
REVIEW LA BOOCHE
Right Here Publications
RIVERWIND
STREAM LINES, MN JOURNAL OF CREATIVE
    WRITING
Thompson and Co. Inc.
TRADITION
The Urbana Free Library
WESTERN AMERICAN LITERATURE
Westport Publishers, Inc.
WHETSTONE
THE WRITERS' BAR-B-Q

MILITARY, VETERANS

ACTION DIGEST
AUSTIN SENIOR CITIZEN
THE AUTOGRAPH COLLECTOR'S MAGAZINE
Avery Publishing Group, Inc.
The Battery Press, Inc.
Beacon Press
R.J. Bender Publishing
The Borgo Press
Brennen Publishing Company
Broken Rifle Press
Cedar Ridge Publications
THE CIVIL WAR NEWS
Combat Ready Publishing
Consumer Education Research Center
J. Flores Publications
Hampshire Books
HOBBY BOOKWATCH (MILITARY, GUN & HOBBY
    BOOK REVIEW)
Hope Publishing House
J & T Publishing
Kitchen Sink Press
LANCASTER INDEPENDENT PRESS
Lancer Militaria
Markgraf Publications Group
McKinzie Publishing Company
MCN Press
THE MILITARY ADVISOR
MILITARY IMAGES MAGAZINE

MINERVA: Quarterly Report on Women and the Military
Muso Press
The Nautical & Aviation Publishing Co. of American, Inc.
THE NIHILISTIC REVIEW
The Old Army Press
Paladin Enterprises, Inc.
Pessimism Press, Inc.
Phillips Publications, Inc.
The Place In The Woods
QSKY Publishing/Independent Publishing
RECON
Reunion Research
Salvo Books
Sharp & Dunnigan Publications, Incorporated
STEVE CANYON MAGAZINE
Texas Monthly Press
A Thousand Autumns Press
Thunder Creek Publishing Co-operative
Tippy Reed Publishing
The Urbana Free Library
VIETNAM GENERATION: A Journal of Recent History
    and Contemporary Issues
VIETNAM WAR NEWSLETTER
THE VORTEX (A Historical and Wargamers Jornal)
Woodbine House

HENRY MILLER

COLLAGES & BRICOLAGES
Happy Rock Press
UNBRIDLED LUST!

MINNESOTA

Applied Publishing
ARTPAPER
Blue Sky Marketing, Inc.
Falcon Press Publishing Company
Heritage Press WI
LAKE SUPERIOR MAGAZINE
MANKATO POETRY REVIEW
NEW NORTH ARTSCAPE
THE NORTHLAND QUARTERLY
Northword Press, Inc.
Open Horizons Publishing Company
Ox Head Press
POETRY MOTEL
Pogo Press, Incorporated
STREAM LINES, MN JOURNAL OF CREATIVE
    WRITING
Suburban Wilderness Press
SUNDOG
Thompson and Co. Inc.
Whole Person Associates Inc.
Women's Times Publishing

MISSOURI

Crossroads Communications
Falcon Press Publishing Company
The Patrice Press
ST. LOUIS JOURNALISM REVIEW
The Westphalia Press
Westport Publishers, Inc.
White Oak Press
WRITER'S GUIDELINES MAGAZINE

MONTANA

CUTBANK
Editorial Review
Falcon Press Publishing Company
Mountain Press Publishing Co.
Old West Publishing Co.
Pruett Publishing Company

MORMON

Signature Books

MOTIVATION, SUCCESS

Able Publishing
American Impressions

Axelrod Publishing of Tampa Bay
C.C. Publishing Co.
Challenger Press
Comforter Publishing
Robert Erdmann Publishing
Fell Publishers, Inc.
Harbinger House
Lionhouse Publishing Company
LITTLE FREE PRESS
Open Horizons Publishing Company
OUR WRITE MIND
RED HOT WORK-AT-HOME REPORT
The Saunderstown Press
Top Of The Mountain Publishing
Vesper Publishing
Youth Policy Institute

MOVIES

ACTIVIST
ATROCITY
BAKER STREET GAZETTE
BLUE LIGHTS
Blue Lights Publications
THE...CHRONICLE
" "...A DEAD BEAT POET PRODUCTION
EUTHANASIA ROSES
Excalibur Publishing
Festival Publications
FILM THREAT VIDEO GUIDE
THE FINAL PAGE
FUSE MAGAZINE
GAUNTLET: Exploring the Limits of Free Expression
GREY CITY JOURNAL
THE HAUNTED JOURNAL
Hollywood Film Archive
HORIZONS BEYOND
IMAGINATION MAGAZINE
Open Horizons Publishing Company
PAST TIMES: THE NOSTALGIA ENTERTAINMENT
  NEWSLETTER
P-FORM
Prudhomme Press
ROMANIAN REVIEW
SCAREAPHANALIA
SLEUTH JOURNAL
Tambra Publishing
THEY WON'T STAY DEAD!
UNBRIDLED LUST!
THE VAMPIRE JOURNAL
Vestal Press Ltd
W.D.C. PERIOD
WE ARE THE WEIRD
Woldt Publishing
WORLD OF FANDOM MAGAZINE
ZOOMAR

MUSIC

Accent on Music
ACTIVIST
Afta Press
AKWEKON: A National Native American Literary &
  Arts Journal
AKWEKON LITERARY JOURNAL
Allardyce, Barnett (Agneau 2)
THE ALTERED MIND
ALWAYS JUKIN'
Always Jukin'
AMERICAN POP
AMERICAN WRITING: A MAGAZINE
AND
Anderson Press
ANTI-ISOLATION/NEW ARTS IN WISCONSIN
ARISTOS
ARTSFOCUS PERFORMING ARTS MAGAZINE
ASPECTS
Astro Artz
BABY SUE
backspace ink.

BAD NEWZ
Bell Springs Publishing
BELLYWASH
Birdalone Books
Bliss Publishing Company, Inc.
BLITZ
The Bold Strummer Ltd.
BOOMBAH HERALD
BORDER/LINES
BREAKFAST WITHOUT MEAT
B-SIDE MAGAZINE
Buddha Rose Publications
Burning Books
BUT A TWIST OF THE LIP
CADENCE: THE REVIEW OF JAZZ & BLUES:
  CREATIVE IMPROVISED MUSIC
CANADIAN JOURNAL OF DRAMA AND THEATRE
THE...CHRONICLE
CIN-DAV, Inc.
City Publications Ltd.
CLOCKWATCH REVIEW
CODA: The Jazz Magazine
Columbia Publishing Company, Inc.
Computer Musician Coalition
CROSSCURRENTS
CROW MAGAZINE
Crystal Publishers, Inc.
DE NAR
" "...A DEAD BEAT POET PRODUCTION
DIE FAT PIGGY DIE
THE DILETTANTE FORUM
DIRTY LINEN
Dirty Rotten Press
Distinctive Publishing Corp.
Dragon's Teeth Press
EAR MAGAZINE
The Edwin Mellen Press
E-Heart Press, Inc.
Empty Closet Enterprises
EUTHANASIA ROSES
Exile Press
Fallen Leaf Press
THE FINAL PAGE
FOLK ERA TODAY
FORCED EXPOSURE
Fromm International Publishing Corporation
FUSE MAGAZINE
GATEAVISA
GAUNTLET: Exploring the Limits of Free Expression
Glenbridge Publishing Ltd.
GO MAGAZINE
GOKOOMA
GOOD CLEAN FUN
THE GOOFUS OFFICE GAZETTE
GREY CITY JOURNAL
GYPSY
THE HAPPY THRASHER
Harris Stonehouse Press
HearSay Press TM
HEARTSONG REVIEW
HIGH PERFORMANCE
HOBO JUNGLE
HOT WIRE: Journal of Women's Music & Culture
HOWLING DOG
HOWLING WIND
IMAGINATION MAGAZINE
Index House
Intermountain Publishing
JOURNAL FOR ANTHROPOSOPHY
JOURNAL OF MUSICOLOGY
JUDY
Keyboard Workshop
KREATURE COMFORTS
L.G.L.C. NEWSLETTER
LANCASTER INDEPENDENT PRESS
Legacy Books (formerly Folklore Associates)
Hal Leonard Books
LIGHTWORKS MAGAZINE

Limelight Editions
LIVELY ARTS
LuraMedia, Inc.
Magical Music Express
Main Track Publications
Peter Marcan Publications
MARK
MEMES
Metamorphous Press
Micro Pro Litera Press
MODERN LITURGY
Moon Publications, Inc.
MOTORBOOTY MAGAZINE
Multi Media Arts
MUSEUM & ARTS WASHINGTON
MUSIC AND LETTERS
MUSIC OF THE SPHERES
MUSIC PERCEPTION
MUSICAL OPINION
MUSICWORKS: THE CANADIAN AUDIO-VISUAL
  JOURNAL OF SOUND EXPLORATIONS
The Neither/Nor Press
NET
THE NEW CRITERION
THE NEW DANCE REVIEW
NEW HOPE INTERNATIONAL REVIEW
Nicolas-Hays, Inc.
Nightingale Music
19TH-CENTURY MUSIC
NOOSPAPERS
NORTHERN LIGHTS STUDIES IN CREATIVITY
THE NORTHERN REVIEW
Norton Coker Press
Omega Press (formerly Sufi Order Publications)
ONE SHOT
Open Book Publications, A Division of Station Hill Press
THE OPERA COMPANION
ORGANICA
OTISIAN DIRECTORY
PAST TIMES: THE NOSTALGIA ENTERTAINMENT
  NEWSLETTER
Piccolo Press
THE PIG PAPER
Polymath Systems
POPULAR FOLK MUSIC TODAY
Popular Reality Press
Potentials Development, Inc.
Pro/Am Music Resources, Inc.
PROFANE EXISTENCE
PUNCTURE
Ranger International Productions
Real People Press
RELIX
RE/SEARCH
Re/Search Publications
Resource Publications, Inc.
Riverside Productions
THE ROCK HALL REPORTER
ROMANIAN REVIEW
St. Andrew Press
ST. MAWR
SALON: A Journal of Aesthetics
Scarecrow Press
SCHMAGA
Scots Plaid Press (Persephone Press)
THE SCREAM OF THE BUDDHA
SECONDS MAGAZINE
See Sharp Press
Selah Publishing Co.
THE $ENSIBLE SOUND
SING OUT! The Folk Song Magazine
SOULLESS STRUCTURES
SOUND CHOICE
SOUNDMAKERS
SOUTHERN QUARTERLY: A Journal of the Arts in the
  South
The Spinning Star Press
SPIT

Station Hill Press
STICKY CARPET DIGEST
"STRICTLY NOTHING BUT" THE BLUES
STYLUS
Swand Publications
Tambra Publishing
THIRD WAY
Thirteen Colonies Press
Three Continents Press, Inc.
Thunder Creek Publishing Co-operative
T-J TODAY
TOOK
TRADITION
UMI Research Press
UNBRIDLED LUST!
Vestal Press Ltd
Vision Quest Publishing
White Cliffs Media Company
White Lilac Press
Wild & Woolley
Witwatersrand University Press
World Music Press
WORLD OF FANDOM MAGAZINE
Writers Forum
X MAGAZINE
Yellow Moon Press
ZERO HOUR
Zirlinson Publishing
ZZAJ-SYNCHRONOLOGY

MYSTERY

Academy Chicago Publishers
Amethyst Press
THE APPLE BLOSSOM CONNECTION
THE ARMCHAIR DETECTIVE
The Armchair Detective Library
BAKER STREET GAZETTE
Baker Street Publications
BALDER
BELLES LETTRES
Borderland Sciences Research Foundation
Carlton Books
Carroll & Graf Publishers, Inc.
Cliffhanger Press
Countryman Press
Coxland Press
THE DROOD REVIEW OF MYSTERY
DuReve Publications
GAUNTLET: Exploring the Limits of Free Expression
Gryphon Publications
HARDBOILED DETECTIVE
Hutton Publications
Infinite Savant Publishing
LININGTON LINEUP
THE MYSTERY FANCIER
Mystery Notebook Editions
MYSTERY READERS JOURNAL
New Victoria Publishers
New View Publications
NiceTown
OHIO RENAISSANCE REVIEW
PAPERBACK PARADE
Peak Output Unlimited
Perseverance Press
PLOTS
POISON PEN WRITERS NEWS
THE POST
SCREAM MAGAZINE
The Seal Press
SHERLOCKIAN TIDBITS
SISTERS IN CRIME BOOKS IN PRINT
SQUARE ONE - A Magazine of Fiction
UNBRIDLED LUST!
Valley House Gallery Press
VANDELOECHT'S FICTION MAGAZINE

MYTH, MYTHOLOGY

AMERICAN WRITING: A MAGAZINE

The Archives Press
Argonauts/Misty Isles Press
Aslan Publishing
Baker Street Publications
BALDER
Beacon Press
BLUE LIGHT RED LIGHT
COLLAGES & BRICOLAGES
COLOR WHEEL
Coxland Press
ENCYCLOPEDIA BANANICA
EPIPHANY: A JOURNAL OF LITERATURE
Esoterica Press
GREEN EGG
THE HAUNTED JOURNAL
INNER SEARCH
JOURNAL FOR ANTHROPOSOPHY
KELTIC FRINGE
K0SMOS
MAGIC REALISM
Metagnosis Publications
Mockingbird Press
NEW MOON RISING
THE NOCTURNAL LYRIC
Oregon State University Press
Parabola Books
Placebo Press
PUCK!
ROMANIAN REVIEW
SOCIETE
Stone Circle Press
The Teitan Press, Inc.
A THEATER OF BLOOD
Theosophical Publishing House
Three Continents Press, Inc.
Top Of The Mountain Publishing
Trabarni Productions
UNBRIDLED LUST!
THE VAMPIRE JOURNAL
WALKING-STICK NOTES
Ward Hill Press
WTI Publishing Co.
XENOPHILIA

NATIVE AMERICAN

AKWEKON: A National Native American Literary & Arts Journal
AKWEKON LITERARY JOURNAL
Akwesasne Notes
Alaska Native Language Center
ALBERTA HISTORY
American Audio Prose Library (non-print)
AMERICAN INDIAN BASKETRY
Ancient City Press
Arbiter Press
Arrowstar Publishing
Avery Color Studios
Baker Street Publications
Ballena Press
Beacon Press
Bear Tribe Publishing
BELLES LETTRES
Between The Lines
Blue Bird Publishing
Blue Crane Books
Blue Heron Press
BOOK TALK
BURWOOD JOURNAL
CANVAS CHAUTAUQUA MAGAZINE
Capra Press
Cat's Pajamas Press
CHRYSANTHEMUM
Cinco Puntos Press
CJE NEWSLETTER (Newsletter of the Coalition for Jobs & the Environment)
COLLAGES & BRICOLAGES
COMPOST NEWSLETTER (CNL)

Council For Indian Education
Council on Interracial Books For Children
THE CRESCENT REVIEW
Cultural Survival, Inc.
CULTURAL SURVIVAL QUARTERLY
" "...A DEAD BEAT POET PRODUCTION
DELIRIUM
The Denali Press
THE DREAMWEAVER
Dusty Dog Press
THE EAGLE
Eagle's View Publishing
Earth-Love Publishing House
Epicenter Press Inc.
Esoterica Press
ETC Publications
Frontier Publishing
Frozen Waffles Press/Shattered Sidewalks Press; 25th Century Chapbooks
Fulcrum, Inc.
Goldfish Press
GREEN MULTILOGUE
Heidelberg Graphics
HIGH COUNTRY NEWS
Historical Society of Alberta
HORIZONS WEST
Illuminations Press
INDIGENOUS WORLD/EL MUNDO INDIGENA
Institute for Southern Studies
Institute for the Study of Traditional American Indian Arts Press
INTERRACIAL BOOKS FOR CHILDREN BULLETIN
KICK IT OVER
Kitchen Table: Women of Color Press
L.A.N.D.
LAKE SUPERIOR MAGAZINE
Levite of Apache
Maryland Historical Press
McDonald & Woodward Publishing Company
McNally & Loftin, Publishers
The Middle Atlantic Press
Miles River Press
Minor Heron Press
Museum of New Mexico Press
Naturegraph Publishers, Inc.
THE NEW ENGLAND QUARTERLY
NEWS FROM NATIVE CALIFORNIA
NORTH DAKOTA QUARTERLY
Northland Publishing Company
Ocean Tree Books
Omega Cottonwood Press
Oregon Historical Society Press
Oregon State University Press
Organization for Equal Education of the Sexes, Inc. (OEES)
Parabola Books
Dr. Homer W. Parker, P.E.
PASSAGER: A Journal of Remembrance and Discovery
T.H. Peek, Publisher
The Place In The Woods
Pocahontas Press, Inc.
Pogo Press, Incorporated
Point Riders Press
Red Crane Books
RED DIRT
THE REDNECK REVIEW OF LITERATURE
Reference Service Press
RENEGADE
Sand River Press
SCREE
SEZ: A Multi-Racial Journal of Poetry & People's Culture
Shadow Press, U.S.A.
SHENANDOAH NEWSLETTER
Sierra Oaks Publishing Company
Genny Smith Books
Snowbird Publishing Company
SOUTH DAKOTA REVIEW
STRUGGLE: A Magazine of Proletarian Revolutionary

Literature

Syracuse Cultural Workers
Talon Books Ltd
Ten Speed Press
Texas Monthly Press
Theosophical Publishing House
Theytus Books Ltd.
Tilbury House, Publishers
Todd Publications
Treasure Chest Publications, Inc.
TRENDS & PREDICTIONS ANALYST
UNBRIDLED LUST!
Unicorn Press
United Lumbee Nation
UNITED LUMBEE NATION TIMES
Valley Lights Publications
VALLEY WOMEN'S VOICE
VIETNAM GENERATION: A Journal of Recent History
and Contemporary Issues
WANBLI HO
Ward Hill Press
WHISPERING WIND MAGAZINE
White Cliffs Media Company
WHITE CLOUDS REVUE
Whitford Press
WILDFIRE: A NETWORKING MAGAZINE
World Music Press
WTI Publishing Co.
Zagier & Urruty Publicaciones

NATURE

Envirographics
Falcon Press Publishing Company
Naturegraph Publishers, Inc.
Omega Cottonwood Press
Red Ink/Black Hole Productions
SKYLARK
TAPJOE: The Anaprocrustean Poetry Journal of Enum-
claw   .
WILDFLOWER
Wildflower Press

NEBRASKA

Omega Cottonwood Press

NETWORKING

Applied Publishing
AQUATERRA, WATER CONCEPTS FOR THE ECO-
LOGICAL SOCIETY
AT-SOURCE-TA
BACKBOARD
Big River Publishing
BookNotes :(TM) Resources for Small & Self-Publishers
BUT A TWIST OF THE LIP
Center for Public Representation
THE CHRISTIAN LIBRARIAN
CJE NEWSLETTER (Newsletter of the Coalition for Jobs
& the Environment)
CLEANING BUSINESS MAGAZINE
CONNEXIONS DIGEST
CREATING EXCELLENCE
DECENTRALIZE!
EDITOR'S DIGEST
FACTSHEET FIVE
Futurum Forlag
GGL Educational Press
GREEN MULTILOGUE
Greensleeves Publishing
THE HAPPY THRASHER
LIGHTWORKS MAGAZINE
MSRRT NEWSLETTER
MUSIC OF THE SPHERES
NETWORK
NETWORK AFRICA FOR TODAY'S WORLD CITI-
ZEN
New Society Publishers
A NEW WORLD RISING
NIGHT OWL'S NEWSLETTER

NOOSPAPERS
OUR WRITE MIND
POISON PEN WRITERS NEWS
REAL PEOPLE
Rio Grande Press
RURAL NETWORK ADVOCATE
SE LA VIE WRITER'S JOURNAL
Michael Shore Associates
SOCIETE
SOUND CHOICE
SPROUTLETTER
Stillpoint Publishing
SUBWAY
TRADESWOMEN MAGAZINE
Village Books
W.D.C. PERIOD
WOMEN'S PAGES

NEW AGE

ACS Publications
THE AGE OF AQUARIUS
American Handwriting Analysis Foundation
AREOPAGUS
Ascension Publishing
ASTROFLASH
Beacon Press
Blue Dolphin Press, Inc.
Blue Water Publishing, Inc.
Brason-Sargar Publications
Chiron Press
CHIRON REVIEW
CHRISTIAN*NEW AGE QUARTERLY
City Spirit Publications
COMMUNITIES
COMPOST NEWSLETTER (CNL)
CONVERGING PATHS
Cosmoenergetics Publications
Cottontail Publications
D.B.A. Books
Dawn Rose Press
Distinctive Publishing Corp.
THE DREAMWEAVER
E.T.M. Publishing
Earth-Love Publishing House
Esoterica, The Craft Press
Excalibur Publishing
The Findhorn Press
Futurum Forlag
Globe Press Books
GOLDEN ISIS
Grace and Goddess Unlimited
Great Western Publishing Company
GREEN EGG
Guarionex Press Ltd.
THE HAUNTED JOURNAL
HEAVEN BONE
HOWLING DOG
IBS Press
Idea House Publishing Company
IllumiNet Press
INNER SEARCH
INTUITIVE EXPLORATIONS
Jalmar Press
JOURNAL OF BORDERLAND RESEARCH
KOOKS MAGAZINE
HJ Kramer, Inc
LivingQuest
THE LOOGIE
Los Arboles Publications
MAGICAL BLEND
MEDITATION MAGAZINE
Metagnosis Publications
Mho & Mho Works
THE MICHAEL CONNECTION
Mr. Information
THE MOUNTAIN ASTROLOGER
MUSIC OF THE SPHERES
Mystic Crystal Publications

NEW FRONTIER
NEW MOON RISING
New World Library
A NEW WORLD RISING
NOCTURNAL NEWS
Ocean Tree Books
OFFICE NUMBER ONE
Omega Press (formerly Sufi Order Publications)
ONE EARTH
Out-Of-Kontrol Data Institute
Pallas Communications
Paragon House Publishers
Persona Publications
THE PERSONAL MAGNETISM HOME STUDY COURSE ON ALL HUMAN POWERS
Princess Publishing
Rakhamim Publications
Ramp Creek Publishing Inc
RFD
Rio Grande Press
Rolling House Publications
SCIENCE/HEALTH ABSTRACTS
Silver Forest Publishing
SOM Publishing, division of School of Metaphysics
SourceNet
Sparrow Hawk Press
SPECTRUM—The Wholistic News Magazine
SPROUTLETTER
Station Hill Press
Sun Eagle Publishing
Sunstone Publications
TAI CHI
TEC Publications
Theosophical Publishing House
Top Of The Mountain Publishing
TRENDS & PREDICTIONS ANALYST
UNBRIDLED LUST!
Unified Publications
Upper Access Inc.
Upword Press
Valley Lights Publications
WARM FUZZY NEWSLETTER
Samuel Weiser, Inc.
Westgate Press
Whitehorse
Whitford Press
WHOLE AGAIN RESOURCE GUIDE
WIDE OPEN MAGAZINE
B. L. Winch & Associates
Wingbow Press
Arnie Wolman Co.
Yes International Publishers
Zivah Publishers

NEW ENGLAND

Acadia Publishing Company
Beacon Press
Bliss Publishing Company, Inc.
Bookcraft
CAL NEWSLETTER
Carnival Press
Chelsea Green Publishing Company
THE CLIMBING ART
Countryman Press
Devin-Adair, Publishers, Inc.
The FreeSolo Press
Gavea-Brown Publications
The Globe Pequot Press
Great Point Press
Jones River Press
THE LATEST NEWS
The Latona Press
Mendocino Book Partnership
Midmarch Arts Press
Millers River Publishing Co.
Mockingbird Press
MONADNOCK GAY MEN
THE NEW ENGLAND QUARTERLY

The New England Quarterly, Inc.
North Country Press
Pigwidgeon Press
Pocahontas Press, Inc.
Sandhill Publications
SINGLES ALMANAC
Soleil Press
TechWest Publications
Thirteen Colonies Press
Union Park Press
University of Massachusetts Press
Sherry Urie
THE WORCESTER REVIEW
Yankee Books
Zephyr Press

NEW MEXICO

Ancient City Press
Cave Books
Falcon Press Publishing Company
Harbinger House
Jack October
KUMQUAT MERINGUE
Ocean Tree Books
Old West Publishing Co.
Pruett Publishing Company
Red Crane Books
Tortilla Press
TRENDS & PREDICTIONS ANALYST
TUCUMCARI LITERARY REVIEW

NEW YORK

AGOG
B-CITY
Chelsea Green Publishing Company
City Spirit Publications
Happy Rock Press
McBooks Press
PHOTOGRAPHY IN NEW YORK
Gibbs Smith, Publisher

NEW ZEALAND

Brick Row Publishing Co. Ltd.
ISLANDS, A New Zealand Quarterly of Arts & Letters
Starchand Press

NEWSLETTER

Abbey Publications
ALA/SRRT NEWSLETTER
Algol Press
ALKALINE PAPER ADVOCATE
AMATEUR COMPUTERIST
Amen Publishing Co.
AMERICAN DANCE GUILD NEWSLETTER
American Impressions
AQUATERRA, WATER CONCEPTS FOR THE ECO-LOGICAL SOCIETY
ARTISTAMP NEWS
ASC NEWSLETTER
BACKBOARD
BAHLASTI PAPER
BAKER STREET GAZETTE
Baker Street Publications
BASEBALL: OUR WAY
BLUE LIGHTS
Blue Lights Publications
BookNotes :(TM) Resources for Small & Self-Publishers
THE BOOKWATCH
The Boxwood Press
BP REPORT
THE BREAD AND BUTTER CHRONICLES
BRILLIANT IDEAS FOR PUBLISHERS
CARIBBEAN NEWSLETTER
CAROUSEL
Ceres Press
THE...CHRONICLE
Coast to Coast Books Inc.
COLUMBUS SINGLE SCENE

Community Service, Inc.
COMMUNITY SERVICE NEWSLETTER
CONSTRUCTION COMPUTER APPLICATIONS NEWSLETTER (CCAN)
Construction Industry Press
CONTRACTOR PROFIT NEWS (CPN)
COSMEP NEWSLETTER
CRYSTAL RAINBOW
CURRENTS
DE NAR
DIRECTORY MARKETPLACE
DOCTOR-PATIENT STUDIES
DoubLeo Publications
EARTHWISE REVIEW
THE EDITORIAL EYE
EDITOR'S DESK
ENCYCLOPEDIA BANANICA
ENSEMBLE, THE NEW VARIETY ARTS REVIEW
ENTRY
THE EUGENE O'NEILL REVIEW
FELICITY
FIDELIS ET VERUS
FLORIDA VOCATIONAL JOURNAL
FOCUS
FOCUS: Library Service to Older Adults, People with Disabilities
FOOTBALL: OUR WAY
FOR PARENTS
FOREFRONT—HEALTH INVESTIGATIONS
FREE SPIRIT: NEWS AND VIEWS ON GROWING UP
The Gleniffer Press
THE GOOFUS OFFICE GAZETTE
G'RAPH
Great Western Publishing Company
THE HAUNTED JOURNAL
HORIZONS BEYOND
HORIZONS INTERCULTURELS
IDEAS IN INVESTING
INNER JOURNEYS
INNER SEARCH
KENNETH COLEMAN'S FED TRACKER/REALITY THEORY NEWSLETTER
KEYSTROKES
LAUGHING BEAR NEWSLETTER
Laughing Bear Press
LITERARY MARKETS
Literary Publications Company
LOCUS: The Newspaper of the Science Fiction Field
MAIL ORDER SUCCESS NEWSLETTER
Meckler Corporation
MINORITY PUBLISHERS EXCHANGE
Mr. Information
MOODY STREET IRREGULARS: A Jack Kerouac Magazine
Moody Street Irregulars, Inc.
MSRRT NEWSLETTER
MW PENPAL WORLD MAGAZINE
NETWORK
NEW DAY PUBLICATIONS
NEW WRITER'S MAGAZINE
NEWSLETTER
NIGHT OWL'S NEWSLETTER
NOCTURNAL NEWS
OHIO WRITER
OLD ABE'S NEWS
THE ORIGINAL ART REPORT (TOAR)
Outlaw Books
Partners In Publishing
PEACEWORK
PENNSYLVANIA'S LITERARY NETWORK NEWSLETTER
THE PIG PAPER
PIP COLLEGE 'HELPS' NEWSLETTER
POETIC SPACE: Poetry & Fiction
POETRY RESOURCE CENTER OF MICHIGAN (PRC) NEWSLETTER & CALENDAR
Poets & Writers, Inc.
POETS & WRITERS MAGAZINE

POISON PEN WRITERS NEWS
Prima Publishing
PRIVACY JOURNAL
Progressive Education
PROGRESSIVE PERIODICALS DIRECTORY/UPDATE
PUBLISHING TRENDS & TRENDSETTERS
RED HOT WORK-AT-HOME REPORT
Rio Grande Press
THE ROCK HALL REPORTER
RURAL NETWORK ADVOCATE
SCIENCE FICTION CHRONICLE
SCRIPT IDEAS
SE LA VIE WRITER'S JOURNAL
SIPAPU
SMALL PRESS: The Magazine & Book Review of Independent Publishing
SMALL PRESS MONTHLY
Social Order Series
SOUTHERN LIBERTARIAN MESSENGER
SOUTHWESTERN DISCOVERIES
SPECTRUM, A Guide to the Independent Press and Informative Organizations
Spectrum Publications
THE STAR BEACON
THUNDERMUG REPORT
TQS NEWS
TRUE FOOD
VDT NEWS
Village Books
WASHINGTON INTERNATIONAL ARTS LETTER
WE ARE THE WEIRD
THE WILD FOODS FORUM
Window Publications
THE WISHING WELL
WORKSHOP
WRESTLING - THEN & NOW
WRITERS CONNECTION
THE WRITER'S NOOK NEWS
Writers Publishing Service Co.
WTI Publishing Co.
Zirlinson Publishing

NEWSPAPERS

ACTIVIST
BOOK MARKETING UPDATE
Children Of Mary
THE...CHRONICLE
CREATIVE LOAFING
DE NAR
FIDELIS ET VERUS
GREY CITY JOURNAL
KETTERING REVIEW
MIRKWOOD
The Neither/Nor Press
THE ORLANDO SPECTATOR
Oxbridge Communications, Inc.
P.O. Publishing Company
Progressive Education
PROGRESSIVE PERIODICALS DIRECTORY/UPDATE
PUBLISHING TRENDS & TRENDSETTERS
SPECTRUM, A Guide to the Independent Press and Informative Organizations
Spectrum Publications
SUBTEXT
Tunnel Publishing
THE WINDHAM PHOENIX

NICARAGUA

Esoterica Press
Laughing Dog Press
MAXINE'S PAGES
Orbis Books
Signal Books
UNBRIDLED LUST!
WORLD PERSPECTIVES

ANAIS NIN

COLLAGES & BRICOLAGES

DIARIST'S JOURNAL
Happy Rock Press
LOST GENERATION JOURNAL
UNBRIDLED LUST!

NON-FICTION

Aa To Zz Publishing Co.
Academy Chicago Publishers
Aegina Press, Inc.
Amana Books
Amen-Ra Publishing Company
American Handwriting Analysis Foundation
Anderson Press
Arden Press, Inc.
Argonauts/Misty Isles Press
Arjuna Library Press
Ask Publishing
Attic Press
Avery Color Studios
Axelrod Publishing of Tampa Bay
BAKER STREET GAZETTE
Baker Street Publications
Barca De Vela Publishing
Barr-Randol Publishing Co.
Beacon Press
R.J. Bender Publishing
Blue Crane Books
Bluestocking Press
Bolchazy-Carducci Publishers, Inc.
Bonus Books, Inc.
Books for All Times, Inc.
Brenner Information Group
Broken Rifle Press
Brunswick Publishing Corporation
BYLINE
C.C. Publishing Co.
Cacanadadada Press Ltd.
The Carolina Wren Press
Carousel Press
Carroll & Graf Publishers, Inc.
Catbird Press
Cave Books
Wm Caxton Ltd
THE CENTENNIAL REVIEW
Chandler & Sharp Publishers, Inc.
Chelsea Green Publishing Company
Children Of Mary
Chiron Press
CHIRON REVIEW
THE...CHRONICLE
CIMARRON REVIEW
CITY RANT
COLLAGES & BRICOLAGES
Columbia Publishing Company, Inc.
Combat Ready Publishing
Confluence Press, Inc.
Continuing Education Press, Portland State University
Continuing Education Publications
Cosmoenergetics Publications
Countryman Press
Steve Davis Publishing
W.S. Dawson Co.
Delta Publishing Company
Dembner Books
Double M Press
Dufour Editions Inc.
DuReve Publications
EAP DIGEST
East Eagle Press
Editions Ex Libris
EDITOR'S DIGEST
THE ELEPHANT-EAR
Elephas Books
ELF: ECLECTIC LITERARY FORUM (ELF MAGA-
ZINE)
Robert Erdmann Publishing
Paul S. Eriksson, Publisher
Excalibur Publishing

EXUM Publishing
The Fairfield Street Press
FARMER'S MARKET
FATHOMS BELOW
FIDELIS ET VERUS
Fir Publishing Company
FOLIO: A LITERARY JOURNAL
Fromm International Publishing Corporation
Front Row Experience
Futurum Forlag
GAFF PRESS
The Galileo Press Ltd.
Gateways Books And Tapes
GAUNTLET: Exploring the Limits of Free Expression
Glen Abbey Books, Inc.
The Globe Pequot Press
THE GOPHERWOOD REVIEW
Gravity Publishing
The Graywolf Press
Happy Rock Press
Harbinger House
THE HAUNTED JOURNAL
HEATHENZINE
HOB-NOB
Hoover Institution Press
HORIZONS BEYOND
Humana Press
Idea House Publishing Company
Illuminations Press
IllumiNet Press
IMAGINATION MAGAZINE
In One Ear Press
Independence Publishers Inc.
INNOVATING
Iron Gate Publishing
Italica Press, Inc.
Jalmar Press
Johnson Books
KALEIDOSCOPE: INTERNATIONAL MAGAZINE OF
    LITERATURE, FINE ARTS, AND DISABILITY
Kitchen Table: Women of Color Press
Knowledge, Ideas & Trends, Inc. (KIT)
Knowledge Systems, Inc.
K0SMOS
HJ Kramer, Inc
THE LAUREL REVIEW
Levite of Apache
Limelight Editions
Lionhouse Publishing Company
THE LOOGIE
LOONFEATHER: A magazine of poetry, short prose, and
    graphics
Los Arboles Publications
LuraMedia, Inc.
MANOA: A Pacific Journal of International Writing
Marquette Books
Mercury House
Metagnosis Publications
Metamorphous Press
Microdex Bookshelf
THE MILITARY ADVISOR
Milkweed Editions
Milner Press
THE MILWAUKEE UNDERGRADUATE REVIEW
Mr. Information
Monographics Press
Monroe Press
John Muir Publications, Inc.
Multi Media Arts
MW PENPAL WORLD MAGAZINE
NAR Publications
Naturegraph Publishers, Inc.
NAUTICAL BRASS
The Neither/Nor Press
New Worlds Press
Newmark Publishing Company
NIGHT OWL'S NEWSLETTER
NOCTURNAL NEWS

Nolo Press - Occidental
NON COMPOS MENTIS
The North Carolina Haiku Society Press
Northland Publishing Company
OHIO RENAISSANCE REVIEW
Omega Cottonwood Press
Orbis Books
Oregon Historical Society Press
Oregon State University Press
The Organization
OXALIS
P.O. Publishing Company
Paladin Enterprises, Inc.
PANDORA
Path Press, Inc.
Pathway Books
Penumbra Publishing Co.
Perspectives Press
PF Publications
Phanes Press
Piccadilly Books
POISON PEN WRITERS NEWS
POLITICALLY INCORRECT
Popular Medicine Press
PRISM international
PRIVATE INVESTIGATOR'S CONNECTION: A News-
    letter for Investigators
Prudhomme Press
Publitec Editions
Rabeth Publishing Company
The Real Comet Press
THE REDNECK REVIEW OF LITERATURE
Rio Grande Press
Rodmell Press
ROMANIAN REVIEW
St. Bede's Publications
Saqi Books Publisher
Raymond Saroff, Publisher
SCREAM MAGAZINE
SE LA VIE WRITER'S JOURNAL
Shield Publishing, Inc.
Shiro Publishers
Shoe Tree Press
Signal Books
Signature Books
SKYLARK
SLEUTH JOURNAL
Small Helm Press
Genny Smith Books
Snowbird Publishing Company
Social Order Series
SPECTRUM, A Guide to the Independent Press and
    Informative Organizations
Spectrum Publications
Spirit Press
SPIT
Spredden Press
Star Books, Inc.
State of the Art Ltd.
Summer Stream Press
Tambra Publishing
Ten Star Press
Theosophical Publishing House
Thunder Creek Publishing Co-operative
Thunder's Mouth Press
Times Change Press
Tippy Reed Publishing
Torngat Books
Trabarni Productions
TUCUMCARI LITERARY REVIEW
Tyger Press
Tyro Publishing
UNBRIDLED LUST!
THE UNDERGROUND FOREST - LA SELVA SUB-
    TERRANEA
UNION SHOP BLUFF
UNIROD MAGAZINE
University Editions, Inc.

Upper Access Inc.
THE VAMPIRE JOURNAL
Vestal Press Ltd
THE VINCENT BROTHERS REVIEW
Volunteer Publications
Ward Hill Press
THE WASHINGTON MONTHLY
Westgate Press
Westport Publishers, Inc.
White Mane Publishing Company, Inc.
White Rose Publishing
Whitehorse
Whitford Press
Williamson Publishing Company, Inc.
Willow Bee Publishing House
Window Publications
Woldt Publishing
Wood Thrush Books
Woodbine House
WRITERS GAZETTE NEWSLETTER
THE WRITER'S NOOK NEWS
WTI Publishing Co.
Xenos Books
Yes You Can Press
Zirlinson Publishing

NON-VIOLENCE

THE ANIMALS' AGENDA
ASPECTS
Bandanna Books
Broken Rifle Press
THE...CHRONICLE
CJE NEWSLETTER (Newsletter of the Coalition for Jobs
    & the Environment)
Communitas Press
DAUGHTER OF SARAH
DE NAR
DECENTRALIZE!
EUTHANASIA ROSES
Ex Machina Publishing Company
FRIENDS OF PEACE PILGRIM
GREEN MULTILOGUE
HARMONY: VOICES FOR A JUST FUTURE
HEALING PATH
JASON UNDERGROUND'S NOTES FROM THE
    TRASHCOMPACTOR
Kitchen Table: Women of Color Press
LANCASTER INDEPENDENT PRESS
MOKSHA JOURNAL
Path Press, Inc.
SOCIAL ANARCHISM: A Journal of Practice And
    Theory
UNBRIDLED LUST!
Vajra of Yoga Anand Ashram
Valley Lights Publications
THE VOLUNTARYIST
Ward Hill Press
Yes You Can Press

THE NORTH

ARCTIC—Journal of the Arctic Institute of America
Betelgeuse Books
THE NORTHERN REVIEW

NORTH AMERICA

University of Calgary Press

NORTH CAROLINA

CJE NEWSLETTER (Newsletter of the Coalition for Jobs
    & the Environment)
THE CRESCENT REVIEW
Ocean Tree Books
Pamlico Press
SCREAM MAGAZINE
Signal Books
Ventana Press

NOVELS

Aangstrom Publishing Company
Acadia Publishing Company
Amelia Press
American Audio Prose Library (non-print)
Asylum Arts
Baker Street Publications
Beacon Press
Belhue Press
BELLES LETTRES
Black Sparrow Press
Brunswick Publishing Corporation
C.C. Publishing Co.
Carroll & Graf Publishers, Inc.
Catbird Press
Cave Books
Celo Valley Books
Clarity Press
Claycomb Press, Inc.
Cleis Press
Coffee House Press
Confluence Press, Inc.
Crossroads Publications, Inc.
The Devonshire Publishing Co.
DIAMOND HITCHHIKER COBWEBS
Earth-Love Publishing House
Educare Press
Excalibur Publishing
Fir Publishing Company
Fromm International Publishing Corporation
Futurum Forlag
The Galileo Press Ltd.
THE HAUNTED JOURNAL
HORIZONS BEYOND
Idea House Publishing Company
ILLUMINATIONS
Independence Publishers Inc.
Italica Press, Inc.
J & T Publishing
MANOA: A Pacific Journal of International Writing
Mockingbird Press
Mogul Book and FilmWorks
New Victoria Publishers
Nuclear Trenchcoated Subway Prophets Publications
OUR WRITE MIND
Permeable Press
POISON PEN WRITERS NEWS
Saqi Books Publisher
Signal Books
SLEUTH JOURNAL
Slough Press
Gibbs Smith, Publisher
Stride Publications
Talon Books Ltd
Ten Star Press
Thunder Creek Publishing Co-operative
Turnstone Press
Tyro Publishing
THE VAMPIRE JOURNAL
The Wanderer's Ink
The White Cross Press
White Pine Press
Window Publications
World Promotions
Xenos Books

NUCLEAR ENERGY

CJE NEWSLETTER (Newsletter of the Coalition for Jobs
  & the Environment)
ECOSOCIALIST REVIEW
THE EQUATOR
LANCASTER INDEPENDENT PRESS
UNBRIDLED LUST!
WORLD PERSPECTIVES

OCCULT

Ability Workshop Press

THE AGE OF AQUARIUS

Alamo Square Press
America West Publishers
Artemis Press, Inc.
Ashley Books, Inc.
ASPECTS
Auromere Books and Imports
BAHLASTI PAPER
Baker Street Publications
BALDER
Beacon Press
Bennett Books
Borderland Sciences Research Foundation
BOTH SIDES NOW
Buddha Rose Publications
CAL NEWSLETTER
CANVAS CHAUTAUQUA MAGAZINE
Cassandra Press
Celestial Gifts Publishing
CHAKRA
THE...CHRONICLE
COMPOST NEWSLETTER (CNL)
Cosmoenergetics Publications
Coxland Press
The F. Marion Crawford Memorial Society
CRCS Publications
CULTWATCH RESPONSE
The Devonshire Publishing Co.
DIAMOND HITCHHIKER COBWEBS
DIE FAT PIGGY DIE
The Donning Company / Publishers
E.T.M. Publishing
Earth-Song Press
El Montecito Oaks Press, Inc.
EMERGING
THE EMSHOCK LETTER
Esoterica, The Craft Press
Free People Press
Fry's Incredible Inquirys
THE GATE
GATEAVISA
GOLDEN ISIS
Golden Sceptre
GREEN EGG
THE HAUNTED JOURNAL
HEAVEN BONE
Hermetician Press
Hickman Systems - New Age Books
Hong Kong Publishing Co., Ltd.
HORIZONS BEYOND
INCREDIBLE INQUIRY REPORTS
INKBLOT
INNER SEARCH
Inner Traditions International
JOURNAL FOR ANTHROPOSOPHY
KOOKS MAGAZINE
THE LLEWELLYN NEW TIMES
Llewellyn Publications
THE LOOGIE
LP Publications (Teleos Institute)
MAGICAL BLEND
Magical Blend
MAXINE'S PAGES
Melrose
MEMES
Metagnosis Publications
THE MICHAEL CONNECTION
Mr. Information
National Publishers
NEW MOON RISING
THE NOCTURNAL LYRIC
NOCTURNAL NEWS
Ocean Tree Books
OPOSSUM HOLLER TAROT
OTISIAN DIRECTORY
Out-Of-Kontrol Data Institute
Pallas Communications
THE PERSONAL MAGNETISM HOME STUDY

COURSE ON ALL HUMAN POWERS
Phoenix Publishing Inc.
POISON PEN WRITERS NEWS
Quantal Publishing B
THE QUEST
Quicksilver Productions
Quimby Archives
Ramp Creek Publishing Inc
REFLECT
Rio Grande Press
THE ROMANTIST
Sauvie Island Press
SCHMAGA
Scots Plaid Press (Persephone Press)
Seventh-Wing Publications
SOCIETE
SPIRIT MAGAZINE
THE STARK FIST OF REMOVAL
Station Hill Press
Strawberry Hill Press
Sun, Man, Moon Inc.
Tambra Publishing
TEC Publications
Technicians of the Sacred
The Teitan Press, Inc.
Top Of The Mountain Publishing
2AM MAGAZINE
2AM Publications
Tyro Publishing
UNBRIDLED LUST!
THE UNEXPLAINED
Valkyrie Publishing House
Valley Lights Publications
THE VAMPIRE JOURNAL
THE WAVE
Samuel Weiser, Inc.
Westgate Press
Whitford Press
WICCAN/PAGAN PRESS ALLIANCE TRADE PAPER
WICKED MYSTIC
THE WISE WOMAN
WITCHCRAFT DIGEST MAGAZINE (THE WICA NEWSLETTER)
WITHIN & BEYOND
WTI Publishing Co.
Zirlinson Publishing

OCEANOGRAPHY

American Malacologists, Inc.
Commonwealth Press Virginia
LAKE SUPERIOR MAGAZINE
POETRY OF THE PEOPLE
Rand Editions/Tofua Press

OHIO

AMBERGRIS
The Cobham and Hatherton Press
COLUMBUS SINGLE SCENE
GLASS WILL
Kenyette Productions
MAD RIVER: A Journal of Essays
Mermaid Press
Octavia Press
OHIO CHESS BULLETIN
OHIO WRITER
RIVERWIND
SCHMAGA
Toledo Poets Center Press
TOWPATHS
THE WRITER'S NOOK NEWS

OREGON

Calapooia Publications
Castle Peak Editions
Drift Creek Press
Epicenter Press Inc.
Flying Pencil Publications
Gahmken Press

The Mountaineers Books
Resolution Business Press
Riegel Publishing
WHEAT LIFE

OUTDOORS, SPORTS, BOATING

Acorn Publishing
ACTION DIGEST
ADAPTED PHYSICAL ACTIVITY QUARTERLY (APAQ)
Aeolus Press, Inc.
Affordable Adventures, Inc.
AIKI NEWS
Aiki News
Alchemist/Light Publishing
All American Press
Allegheny Press
AMERICAN HIKER
The American Hiking Society
APPALACHIA
Appalachian Mountain Club Books
ARIZONA GREAT OUTDOORS
Avery Color Studios
BASEBALL: OUR WAY
Bear Flag Books
Beyond Athletics
Bicycle Books (Publishing) Inc.
Bliss Publishing Company, Inc.
Blue Heron Press
Bonus Books, Inc.
BOWBENDER
Brooke-Richards Press
Brunswick Publishing Corporation
CANVAS CHAUTAUQUA MAGAZINE
Capra Press
Charter Oak Press
CHESAPEAKE BAY MAGAZINE
Chockstone Press
Chronicle Books
City Spirit Publications
THE CLIMBING ART
COACHING VOLLEYBALL
COACHING WOMEN'S BASKETBALL
CONNECTICUT NATURALLY
Countryman Press
Culpepper Press
CURRENTS
dbS Productions
S. Deal & Assoc.
Dirigo Books, Inc.
DISC GOLF WORLD NEWS
Edgeworth & North Books
Elysium Growth Press
ETC Publications
Explorer's Guide Publishing
Falcon Press Publishing Company
FIGHTING WOMAN NEWS
J. Flores Publications
Flying Pencil Publications
Foghorn Press
FOOTBALL: OUR WAY
The FreeSolo Press
Fulcrum, Inc.
GHOST TOWN QUARTERLY
Glacier House Publications
Glenhurst Publications, Inc.
Global Sports Productions, Ltd.
The Globe Pequot Press
GOOD READING MAGAZINE
GREATER PORTLAND
THE GROVE
HANG GLIDING
Harbinger House
Harvestman and Associates
Heyday Books
Hope Publishing House
Human Kinetics Pub. Inc.
ILLINOIS MAGAZINE

Info Net Publishing
INTERNATIONAL JOURNAL OF SPORT BIOME-
CHANICS
International Marine Publishing Co.
Johnson Books
Jones River Press
JOTS (Journal of the Senses)
JOURNAL OF SPORT AND EXERCISE PSYCHO-
LOGY
JOURNAL OF SPORT MANAGEMENT
JOURNAL OF TEACHING IN PHYSICAL EDUCA-
TION
JOURNAL OF THE PHILOSOPHY OF SPORT
JUDY
Keel Publications
Michael Kesend, Publishing, Ltd.
KITE LINES
Korn Kompany
LAKE SUPERIOR MAGAZINE
Ledero Press
Leisure Press
Liberty Publishing Company, Inc.
LLAMAS MAGAZINE
A LOAD OF BULL
Lone Star Press
Lyceum Books, Inc.
McNally & Loftin, Publishers
MESSAGE POST
!MEXICO WEST!
Mexico West Travel Club, Inc.
Millers River Publishing Co.
Mountain Press Publishing Co.
The Mountaineers Books
Mouvement Publications
Name That Team!
National Lilac Publishing Co.
NATIONAL MASTERS NEWS
Naturegraph Publishers, Inc.
Naturist Foundation
NEW JERSEY NATURALLY
NEW YORK NATURALLY
North Country Press
Northeast Sportsman's Press
OLD TYME BASEBALL NEWS
OLYMPIC TRAVEL GUIDE: YOUR GUIDE TO
WASHINGTON'S OLYMPIC PENINSULA
OUT WEST
Paladin Enterprises, Inc.
Papier-Mache Press
Para Publishing
PARACHUTIST
People's Publishing Co., Inc.
Plas Y Bryn Press
PLAY & CULTURE
Pruett Publishing Company
Publitec Editions
QUEST
RACE ACROSS AMERICA PROGRAM
Ramalo Publications
Recreation Sales Publishing, Inc.
Riegel Publishing
(ROWBOAT)
Running Press
Sandhill Publications
Santa Lucia Chapter - Sierra Club
Sauvie Island Press
Sea Sports Publications
Seascape Enterprises
Sentinel Books
Sierra Trading Post
SIGNPOST
SKYDIVING
Genny Smith Books
SOCIOLOGY OF SPORT JOURNAL
SOFTBALL ILLUSTRATED
SPECIALTY TRAVEL INDEX
SPITBALL: The Literary Baseball Magazine
THE SPORT PSYCHOLOGIST

Sports Support Syndicate
State of the Art Ltd.
Stone Wall Press, Inc
Stripes Publishers, USA
STROKES
STUDIO NORTH
Synergistic Press
Tamal Vista Publications
Ten Speed Press
Texas Monthly Press
Third Lung Press
Tilbury House, Publishers
Torngat Books
Unique Adventures Press
University of Calgary Press
Utah Geographic Series
Vista Publishing Company
THE VITAL FORCE
Vitesse Press
Waterfront Center
WESTERN & EASTERN TREASURES
Western Tanager Press
Whitford Press
Whole Person Associates Inc.
THE WILD FOODS FORUM
WISCONSIN TRAILS
Women's Times Publishing
Wood River Publishing
Wood Thrush Books
Woodsong Graphics Inc.
WORLD RAINFOREST REPORT
Zagier & Urruty Publicaciones

PACIFIC NORTHWEST

Arrowood Books
Ballena Press
Beautiful America Publishing Company
Blue Heron Press
BRONG'S BUSINESS SUCCESS NEWS
Calapooia Publications
Castle Peak Editions
Catbird Press
Chatham Publishing Company
Chronicle Books
THE CLIMBING ART
CLINTON ST.
Confluence Press, Inc.
Continuing Education Press, Portland State University
The Denali Press
Dog-Eared Publications
Editorial Review
Epicenter Press Inc.
Falcon Press Publishing Company
FINE MADNESS
Fjord Press
Flying Pencil Publications
The FreeSolo Press
Frontier Publishing
GAFF PRESS
Gahmken Press
Homestead Publishing
Island Publishers
Ki**2 Books
L.A.N.D.
Laughing Dog Press
Lions Head Press
LITERARY CENTER QUARTERLY
Lone Star Press
MASTERSTREAM
Mendocino Book Partnership
MESSAGE POST
The Mountaineers Books
New Horizons Publishers
THE NORTHERN REVIEW
OLYMPIC TRAVEL GUIDE: YOUR GUIDE TO
WASHINGTON'S OLYMPIC PENINSULA
OREGON HISTORICAL QUARTERLY
Oregon Historical Society Press

Oregon State University Press
POETIC SPACE: Poetry & Fiction
PORTRAITS POETRY MAGAZINE
Pygmy Forest Press
Q.E.D. Press
Rainforest Publishing
THE REDNECK REVIEW OF LITERATURE
Resolution Business Press
Riegel Publishing
Sasquatch Books
Sauvie Island Press
Sierra Oaks Publishing Company
SIGNPOST
SINSEMILLA TIPS (Domestic Marijuana Journal)
TAPJOE: The Anaprocrustean Poetry Journal of Enum-
claw
Tiptoe Literary Service
Umbrella Books
Wells & West, Publishers
WHEAT LIFE
WOMEN ARTISTS NEWS

PARENTING

Ascension Publishing
Aslan Publishing
THE BABY CONNECTION NEWS JOURNAL
Beacon Press
Bear Creek Publications
Belleridge Press
Bluestocking Press
The Book Peddlers
Bright Ring Publishing
Castalia Publishing Company
Centerplace Publishing Co.
Circumpolar Press
DAUGHTER OF SARAH
Distinctive Publishing Corp.
Double M Press
Down There Press
Robert Erdmann Publishing
Excalibur Publishing
Fast Forward Publishing
Free Spirit Publishing Inc.
Grayson Bernard Publishers, Inc.
Harbinger House
HEALING PATH
Human Kinetics Pub. Inc.
Impact Publishers, Inc.
INQ Publishing Co.
McBooks Press
MedLife Communications, Inc.
Monroe Press
John Muir Publications, Inc.
Oak Plantation Press
Orbis Books
Parent Education for Infant Development
Pedagogic Press
Perspectives Press
Professional Counselor Books
Quiet Tymes, Inc.
SACRED FIRE
SCIENCE/HEALTH ABSTRACTS
Star Books, Inc.
Thunder Creek Publishing Co-operative
Valley Lights Publications
Westport Publishers, Inc.
White Rose Publishing
Williamson Publishing Company, Inc.
Woodbine House
Youth Policy Institute

PEACE

THE ADVOCATE
THE AGE OF AQUARIUS
Amana Books
ASPECTS
Astarte Shell Press
Atrium Society Publications

Avery Publishing Group, Inc.
BAD HAIRCUT
Barclay House
Branden Publishing Company
Broken Rifle Press
CJE NEWSLETTER (Newsletter of the Coalition for Jobs
& the Environment)
COKEFISH
COLLAGES & BRICOLAGES
COLOR WHEEL
COMMUNITY ECONOMICS
CROOKED ROADS
CULTURE CONCRETE
DAUGHTER OF SARAH
" "...A DEAD BEAT POET PRODUCTION
The Denali Press
Epica
Free Spirit Publishing Inc.
FRIENDS OF PEACE PILGRIM
GREEN MULTILOGUE
GYPSY
THE HAPPY THRASHER
HARMONY: VOICES FOR A JUST FUTURE
The Heather Foundation
Herald Press
THE IMMIGRANT
Impact Publishers, Inc.
Institute For Community Economics
Institute for Palestine Studies
International Publishers Co. Inc.
ISRAEL HORIZONS
Jalmar Press
JASON UNDERGROUND'S NOTES FROM THE
TRASHCOMPACTOR
KICK IT OVER
Kitchen Table: Women of Color Press
HJ Kramer, Inc
L.A.N.D.
LANCASTER INDEPENDENT PRESS
LINKS
Lions Head Press
LITTLE FREE PRESS
M.H. Macy & Company
manic d press
THE MILITANT
Mockingbird Press
MUSIC OF THE SPHERES
NEGATIVE
New Age Press
NEW HOPE INTERNATIONAL REVIEW
New Society Publishers
Nolo Press - Occidental
THE NONVIOLENT ACTIVIST
Northland Quarterly Publications, Inc.
NUCLEAR TIMES
Ocean Tree Books
ONE EARTH
OPOSSUM HOLLER TAROT
Orbis Books
OTISIAN DIRECTORY
PEACE NEWS "For Nonviolent Revolution"
THE PEACE NEWSLETTER
PEACEWORK
THE PLOUGH
Proving Grounds International, Inc.
RADICAL AMERICA
RECON
RED DIRT
RFD
ROMANIAN REVIEW
Sandpiper Press
SCHMAGA
Sea Otter Press
Seven Locks Press
Social Order Series
SOUND CHOICE
Stillpoint Publishing
Sunstone Publications

Syracuse Cultural Workers
Syracuse Peace Council
Third World First
TOWARD FREEDOM
TRANSNATIONAL PERSPECTIVES
TRENDS & PREDICTIONS ANALYST
UNBRIDLED LUST!
THE UNDERGROUND FOREST - LA SELVA SUB-
TERRANEA
Valley Lights Publications
VIETNAM GENERATION: A Journal of Recent History
and Contemporary Issues
VOICES - ISRAEL
Ward Hill Press
WARM FUZZY NEWSLETTER
Wheel of Fire Press
Willow Bee Publishing House
B. L. Winch & Associates
WITHIN & BEYOND
WORLD PERSPECTIVES
WYOMING, THE HUB OF THE WHEEL...A Journey for
Universal Spokesmen...

PHILATELY, NUMISMATICS

ARTISTAMP NEWS
COLLECTORS CLUB PHILATELIST
INTERNATIONAL ART POST
Latin American Press
MYCOPHILATELY
PHILATELIC LITERATURE NEWS INTERNATIONAL
Vernon W. Pickering-Laurel Publications International
TOPICAL TIME
Vestal Press Ltd

PHILOSOPHY

A as A Publishing
Acheron Press
Affinity Press
Akwesasne Notes
Alleluia Press
Alta Napa Press
America West Publishers
AMERICAN ATHEIST
American Atheist Press
Anima Publications
Auromere Books and Imports
Autonomedia, Inc.
AVALOKA: A Journal of Traditional Religion and
Culture
Bennett Books
Berkeley West Publishing
Birdalone Books
Black Rose Books Ltd.
Blue Water Publishing, Inc.
BOOKS AND RELIGION: A Quarterly Review
BOTH SIDES NOW
The Boxwood Press
Brason-Sargar Publications
Brennen Publishing Company
BRITISH JOURNAL OF AESTHETICS
Buddha Rose Publications
Burning Books
C.C. Publishing Co.
C.S.P. WORLD NEWS
CANADIAN JOURNAL OF PHILOSOPHY
CANVAS CHAUTAUQUA MAGAZINE
'THE CASSETTE GAZETTE', An Audio Magazine
Celestial Gifts Publishing
Center for the Art of Living
Chandler & Sharp Publishers, Inc.
Children Of Mary
Circa Press
Claridge Press
COLLABORATION
COLLAGES & BRICOLAGES
Columbia Publishing Company, Inc.
Comforter Publishing
Community Service, Inc.

COMMUNITY SERVICE NEWSLETTER
COMPOST NEWSLETTER (CNL)
Concourse Press
Cosmoenergetics Publications
COSMOPOLITAN CONTACT
CREATION/EVOLUTION JOURNAL
CRITICAL REVIEW: An Interdisciplinary Journal
The Dawn Horse Press
Dawn Rose Press
" "...A DEAD BEAT POET PRODUCTION
DEWITT DIGEST & REVIEW
Dharma Publishing
DIE FAT PIGGY DIE
Dominion Press
Dragon's Teeth Press
Dufour Editions Inc.
THE DURHAM UNIVERSITY JOURNAL
Earth-Song Press
Edition Gemini
Editions Ex Libris
Educare Press
The Edwin Mellen Press
EFRYDIAU ATHRONYDDOL
THE EMSHOCK LETTER
THE EQUATOR
ETICA & CIENCIA
EUROPEAN JUDAISM
Exile Press
FAT TUESDAY
FIDELIS ET VERUS
The Findhorn Press
FISICA
Flax Press, Inc.
FREE INQUIRY
Free People Press
Futurum Forlag
Gearhead Press
GESAR-Buddhism in the West
GET STUPID
Gifted Education Press/The Reading Tutorium
Glenbridge Publishing Ltd.
GlenHill Productions
Goldfish Press
Gong Enterprises, Inc.
GREEN MULTILOGUE
Gringo Guides, Inc.
The Gutenberg Press
Handshake Editions
HarCroft Publishing Company
The Heather Foundation
The Hegeler Institute
Hermetician Press
Hickman Systems - New Age Books
Himalayan Publishers
THE HUMANIST
HYPATIA: A Journal of Feminist Philosophy
Idea House Publishing Company
IKON
IKON, Inc.
IllumiNet Press
INDIVIDUAL LIBERTY
INFINITY LIMITED, A Journal for the Somewhat
Eccentric
INNER SEARCH
Inquiry Press
Institute of Lesbian Studies
The Institute of Mind and Behavior Press
Integral Publishing
INTERCULTURE
International Information Associates
JOURNAL FOR ANTHROPOSOPHY
THE JOURNAL OF MIND AND BEHAVIOR
THE JOURNAL OF PAN AFRICAN STUDIES
JOURNAL OF REGIONAL CRITICISM
JOURNAL OF THE PHILOSOPHY OF SPORT
Journey Publications
K
KAIROS, A Journal of Contemporary Thought and

Criticism
Karunaratne & Sons Ltd.
K0SMOS
HJ Kramer, Inc
L.G.L.C. NEWSLETTER
The Philip Lesly Company
THE LETTER PARADE
THE (LIBERTARIAN) CONNECTION
Libertarian Press, Inc./American Book Distributors
LIBERTY
Lindisfarne Press
THE LLEWELLYN NEW TIMES
Llewellyn Publications
Los Arboles Publications
MACROBIOTICS TODAY
Maisonneuve Press
Metagnosis Publications
Mockingbird Press
MOKSHA JOURNAL
THE MONIST: An International Quarterly Journal of
    General Philosophical Inquiry.
Moonsquilt Press
Mortal Press
NET
NEW CONTRAST
THE NEW RAIN MAGAZINE
NEW THOUGHT
New Worlds Press
Nicolas-Hays, Inc.
NIGHTSUN
NORTHERN LIGHTS STUDIES IN CREATIVITY
Nucleus Publications
Occam Publishers
Ocean Star Publications
OFFICE NUMBER ONE
George Ohsawa Macrobiotic Foundation Press
The Olive Press Publications
Omega Press (formerly Sufi Order Publications)
ON COURSE
ONE EARTH
Oneworld Publications Ltd.
OUR GENERATION
Paideia Publishers
PalmTree Publishers
Parabola Books
PARABOLA MAGAZINE
Paragon House Publishers
Path Press
PAUNCH
PENNYWHISTLE PEOPLE PAPER
Pennywhistle Press
THE PERSONAL MAGNETISM HOME STUDY
    COURSE ON ALL HUMAN POWERS
Phanes Press
PHILOSOPHY AND THE ARTS
POETS. PAINTERS. COMPOSERS.
Polymath Systems
PROPHETIC VOICES
Quarterly Committee of Queen's University
QUEEN'S QUARTERLY: A Canadian Review
THE QUEST
RADIANCE, The Magazine For Large Women
Renaissance House Publishers (a division of Jende-Hagan,
    Inc.)
Rocky Top Publications
Rodmell Press
Rolling House Publications
ROMANIAN REVIEW
Runaway Publications
St. Bede's Publications
SALMAGUNDI
SAT SANDESH: THE MESSAGE OF THE MASTERS
Savant Garde Workshop
Say When Press
SCHMAGA
SCIENCE AND NATURE, The Annual of Marxist
    Philosophy for Natural Scientists
Scojtia Publishing Company

THE SCREAM OF THE BUDDHA
Seed Center
Selene Books
Semiotext Foreign Agents Books Series
SEMIOTEXT(E)
Seventh-Wing Publications
Sherwood Sugden & Company, Publishers
Signal Books
Slate Press
Snow Lion Publications, Inc.
Social Order Series
Society for Individual Liberty
Sovereign Press
SPECTRUM REVIEW
Station Hill Press
Stillpoint Publishing
Sunburst Press
SURVIVE & WIN
Syzygy
TAI CHI
TAPAS
TELOS
Telos Press
Theosophical Publishing House
THIRD WAY
THOUGHT, A REVIEW OF CULTURE & IDEA
Times Change Press
TOOK
Top Of The Mountain Publishing
TOWARDS
UNBRIDLED LUST!
University of Calgary Press
University of Massachusetts Press
Upword Press
Vajra of Yoga Anand Ashram
Valley Lights Publications
Vision Quest Publishing
The Wanderer's Ink
THE WAVE
Samuel Weiser, Inc.
Westgate Press
Wheel of Fire Press
Whitford Press
Whitmore Publishing Company
WITHIN & BEYOND
Witwatersrand University Press
Wood Thrush Books
World Wisdom Books, Inc.
WTI Publishing Co.
Xenos Books
Yes International Publishers
ZONE
Zone Books

PHOTOGRAPHY

THE ABER BULLETIN
ABRAXAS
ACM (ANOTHER CHICAGO MAGAZINE)
ACTA VICTORIANA
AFTERIMAGE
ALABAMA LITERARY REVIEW
THE ALBANY REVIEW
Alchemist/Light Publishing
All American Press
ALLEGHENY REVIEW
American & World Geographic Publishing
THE AMERICAN VOICE
Amherst Media
AND
ANTIETAM REVIEW
Appalachian Consortium Press
Arjuna Library Press
ART CALENDAR
ART INFORMATION REPORT
ART/LIFE
Art/Life Limited Editions
ARTPAPER
Australian American Publishing

Avery Color Studios
Axelrod Publishing of Tampa Bay
Banana Productions
Barefoot Press
Bay Press
The Bear Wallow Publishing Company
BEGINNING: THE MAGAZINE FOR THE WRITER IN THE COMMUNITY
Beyond Words Publishing, Inc.
BLACK MULLET REVIEW
THE BLACK WARRIOR REVIEW
BORDER/LINES
THE BREAD AND BUTTER CHRONICLES
Broken Jaw Press
Cacanadadada Press Ltd.
CACANADADADA REVIEW
Cambric Press
CANVAS
THE CAPE ROCK
Capra Press
Caravan Press
The Carnation Press
Chronicle Books
Clothespin Fever Press
Coach House Press
Coast to Coast Books Inc.
COTTONWOOD
CULTURE CONCRETE
" "...A DEAD BEAT POET PRODUCTION
DESCANT
DESDE ESTE LADO/FROM THIS SIDE
Devin-Adair, Publishers, Inc.
DOUBLE HARNESS
Double M Press
Druid Books
Duck Down Press
EARTHTREKS DIGEST
EARTHWISE LITERARY CALENDAR
Elysium Growth Press
THE EMSHOCK LETTER
ENTRY
Epicenter Press Inc.
The Erie Street Press
EVENT
EXETER STUDIES IN AMERICAN & COMMON- WEALTH ARTS
EyeDEA Books
Falcon Press Publishing Company
Farmer's Digest Publishing Co.
Festival Publications
Five Corners Publications, Ltd.
FLOATING ISLAND
FOLIO: A LITERARY JOURNAL
Fotofolio, Inc.
GALLERY WORKS
Ghost Pony Press
Gross Advertising Service
Guilt & Gardenias Press
Happy Rock Press
HORIZONTES
Hundman Publishing
IKON
IKON, Inc.
ILLINOIS MAGAZINE
INTERNATIONAL ART POST
J P Publications
JOTS (Journal of the Senses)
JOURNAL OF REGIONAL CRITICISM
Jubilee Press
Kenyette Productions
LAKE EFFECT
LEFT CURVE
LIBIDO: The Journal of Sex and Sensibility
LIGHTWORKS MAGAZINE
Lincoln Springs Press
LINKS
Lionhouse Publishing Company
LOST GENERATION JOURNAL

LUNA TACK
MAINLINE MODELER
MARK
Mark Publishing
Metamorphous Press
Midmarch Arts Press
MILDRED
MILITARY IMAGES MAGAZINE
Milkweed Editions
MR. COGITO
Mr. Cogito Press
MUSIC OF THE SPHERES
Muso Press
Mutual Publishing of Honolulu
National Stereoscopic Association
NEEDLEPOINT PLUS
NEW ORLEANS REVIEW
NewSage Press
NORTH CAROLINA LITERARY REVIEW
Northland Publishing Company
Not-For-Sale-Press or NFS Press
Omega Cottonwood Press
Open Book Publications, A Division of Station Hill Press
OVERSIGHT
Papier-Mache Press
Dr. Homer W. Parker, P.E.
PASSAGES NORTH
PAUNCH
P-FORM
PHOEBE, THE GEORGE MASON REVIEW
PHOTOBULLETIN
The Photographic Arts Center, Ltd.
PHOTOGRAPHY IN NEW YORK
Photography Research Institute Carson Endowment
THE PHOTOLETTER
PHOTOMARKET
PIG IRON
Plas Y Bryn Press
PORTABLE LOWER EAST SIDE
PRAIRIE WINDS
The Preservation Press
Pueblo Publishing Press
PUNCTURE
QUARRY WEST
Quimby Archives
R & R Publishing
Rainier Books
RAMPIKE
The Real Comet Press
Red Alder Books
Red Crane Books
RE/SEARCH
Re/Search Publications
RIVER STYX
Rock Steady Press
Ross Books
THE ROTKIN REVIEW
THE SALMON
Salt Lick Press
Salt-Works Press
Saxifrage Books
SCHMAGA
SCREE
SHOOTING STAR REVIEW
SHOTS
Sierra Club Books
Signal Books
SLIPSTREAM
Station Hill Press
STEREO WORLD
THE STONE
Stormline Press, Inc.
STREAM LINES, MN JOURNAL OF CREATIVE WRITING
Studia Hispanica Editors
STUDIO ONE
Talon Books Ltd
te Neues Publishing Company

843

Texas Monthly Press
Third World First
Thunder's Mouth Press
Tioga Publishing Co.
TOLE WORLD
TURNSTILE
Twelvetrees Press/Twin Palms Publishers
Two Rivers Press
UMBRELLA
UNION SHOP BLUFF
The Urbana Free Library
Valkyrie Publishing House
VIEWS: The Journal of Photography in New England
THE VINCENT BROTHERS REVIEW
Visual Studies Workshop
Warthog Press
WEST BRANCH
Whalesback Books
THE WINDLESS ORCHARD
THE WORCESTER REVIEW
Writers Forum
Writers House Press
Yankee Books
YELLOW SILK: Journal Of Erotic Arts
Zoland Books
Zon International Publishing Co.

PHYSICS

Borderland Sciences Research Foundation
THE CHAOS NETWORK
THE EMSHOCK LETTER
FISICA
Grapevine Publications, Inc.
JOURNAL OF BORDERLAND RESEARCH
JOURNAL OF REGIONAL CRITICISM
RESONANCE
SCIENCE AND NATURE, The Annual of Marxist
   Philosophy for Natural Scientists
Shadetree Publishing Inc.
UNBRIDLED LUST!
Zagier & Urruty Publicaciones

POETRY

A
Abattoir Editions
ABBEY
ABRAXAS
ACM (ANOTHER CHICAGO MAGAZINE)
Acre Press
ACTA VICTORIANA
ACTS
Adastra Press
THE ADROIT EXPRESSION
AEGEAN REVIEW
Aegina Press, Inc.
AERIAL
AGADA
Again + Again Press
THE AGE OF AQUARIUS
AGENDA
AGNI
AGOG
Ahsahta
AILERON, A LITERARY JOURNAL
AKWEKON: A National Native American Literary &
   Arts Journal
AKWEKON LITERARY JOURNAL
ALABAMA DOGSHOE MOUSTACHE
ALABAMA LITERARY REVIEW
THE ALBANY REVIEW
ALBATROSS
THE ALCHEMIST
Alchemy Press
Alice James Books
ALL AVAILABLE LIGHT
ALLEGHENY REVIEW
Alleluia Press
Ally Press

Alms House Press
Alpha Beat Press
ALPHA BEAT SOUP
Alphabox Press
Alta Napa Press
Alternating Crimes Publishing
ALURA
Amana Books
AMANITA BRANDY
THE AMARANTH REVIEW
AMBIT
AMELIA
Amelia Press
AMERICAN COLLEGIATE POETS
AMERICAN LITERARY REVIEW: A National Journal
   of Poems and Stories
AMERICAN POETRY ANTHOLOGY
AMERICAN POETRY REVIEW
American Poets In Profile Series
American Press
American Samizdat Editions
THE AMERICAN SCHOLAR
AMERICAN WRITING: A MAGAZINE
AMERICAS REVIEW
Amethyst Press
THE AMICUS JOURNAL
Ampersand Press
AND
ANDROGYNE
ANEMONE
ANERCA/COMPOST
ANGELSTONE
Angelstone Press
Anhinga Press
ANIMAL TALES
Anjou
Ansuda Publications
ANT FARM
ANTAEUS
Antietam Press
ANTIETAM REVIEW
ANTI-ISOLATION/NEW ARTS IN WISCONSIN
THE ANTIOCH REVIEW
Anvil Press Poetry
APALACHEE QUARTERLY
THE APPLE BLOSSOM CONNECTION
Applezaba Press
AQUARIUS
ARIEL—A Review of International English Literature
ARISTOS
THE ARK
The Ark
Arrowood Books
Arsenal Pulp Press, Ltd.
Arte Publico Press
ARTEMIS
ARTFUL DODGE
ARTICHOKE HEART
Artifact Press, Ltd.
ART/LIFE
Art/Life Limited Editions
Arts End Books
ART'S GARBAGE GAZZETTE
As Is/So & So Press
ASH
The Ashland Poetry Press
Ashley Books, Inc.
Ashod Press
Ask Publishing
Associated Writing Programs
Astro Black Books
ASYLUM
Atelier De L'Agneau
The Atlantean Press
Atticus Press
ATTICUS REVIEW
Audacious Press
AURA Literary/Arts Review

844

Author's Unlimited
AVEC
AWP CHRONICLE
AXEFACTORY
Axefactory Press (A.K.A. The Axefactory)
THE AZOREAN EXPRESS
BABY SUE
BACKBOARD
backspace ink.
BAD HAIRCUT
THE BAD HENRY REVIEW
THE BADGER STONE CHRONICLES
BAKER STREET GAZETTE
Baker Street Publications
Bakhtin's Wife Publications
BAKUNIN
Bank Street Press
Barclay House
Bard Press
BARNWOOD
The Barnwood Press
BB Books
B-CITY
Bear House Publishing
BEAT SCENE
BEGINNING: THE MAGAZINE FOR THE WRITER IN
  THE COMMUNITY
Belhue Press
Bellevue Press
THE BELLINGHAM REVIEW
BELLOWING ARK
Bellowing Ark Press
BELOIT POETRY JOURNAL
The Bench Press
Bennett & Kitchel
BERKELEY POETRY REVIEW
Berkeley Poets Workshop and Press
Beyond Baroque Foundation Publications
BIG CIGARS
BIG HAMMER
BIG SCREAM
Bilingual Review/Press
BIRD WATCHER'S DIGEST
BIRMINGHAM POETRY REVIEW
BITTERROOT
BkMk Press
Black Bear Publications
BLACK BEAR REVIEW
Black Buzzard Press
BLACK BUZZARD REVIEW
THE BLACK FLY REVIEW
BLACK JACK & VALLEY GRAPEVINE
BLACK MULLET REVIEW
Black Oak Press
BLACK RIVER REVIEW
Black Sparrow Press
Black Swan Books Ltd.
Black Tie Press
THE BLACK WARRIOR REVIEW
Blackberry
BLADES
BLANK GUN SILENCER
BLIND ALLEYS
Blind Beggar Press
Bloody Twin Press
BLUE BUILDINGS
Blue Crane Books
THE BLUE GUITAR
BLUE HORSE
Blue Horse Publications
BLUE LIGHT REVIEW
The Blue Oak Press
BLUE UNICORN
BLUELINE
BOA Editions, Ltd.
BOGG
Bogg Publications
BOLD PRINT

Bomb Shelter Propaganda
Bombshelter Press
BONE & FLESH
BOSTON LITERARY REVIEW
Bottom Dog Press
BOTTOMFISH MAGAZINE
BOULEVARD
THE BOUND SPIRAL
BOX 749 MAGAZINE
Boz Publishing
THE BRADFORD POETRY QUARTERLY
Branch Redd Books
BRANCH REDD REVIEW
BRAVO, THE POET'S MAGAZINE
BREAKTHROUGH!
Breitenbush Books, Inc.
Brick Books
Broken Jaw Press
Broken Moon Press
The Broken Stone
BROKEN STREETS
Brooding Heron Press
Brook House Press, Inc.
Brunswick Publishing Corporation
Buddha Rose Publications
The Bunny & The Crocodile Press
Burning Deck Press
BURNT SIENNA
BYLINE
Cacanadadada Press Ltd.
CACANADADADA REVIEW
Cadmus Editions
CAESURA
THE CAFE REVIEW
Cajun Publishing
CAL NEWSLETTER
CALAPOOYA COLLAGE
THE CALIFORNIA QUARTERLY
CALIFORNIA STATE POETRY QUARTERLY (CQ)
CALLIOPE
CALYPSO: Journal of Narrative Poetry and Poetic Fiction
CALYX: A Journal of Art and Literature by Women
Cambric Press
CANADIAN AUTHOR & BOOKMAN
CANADIAN LITERATURE
CANDELABRUM POETRY MAGAZINE
CANVAS
CANVAS CHAUTAUQUA MAGAZINE
THE CAPE ROCK
THE CAPILANO REVIEW
Caravan Press
Cardinal Press, Inc.
A CAROLINA LITERARY COMPANION
CAROLINA QUARTERLY
The Carolina Wren Press
Carpenter Press
THE CATHARTIC
Cat's Pajamas Press
CCR Publications
CEILIDH: AN INFORMAL GATHERING FOR STORY
  & SONG
CELEBRATION
Celestial Otter Press
Celo Valley Books
THE CENTENNIAL REVIEW
Center Press
CHALK CIRCLE
CHAMINADE LITERARY REVIEW
Chance Additions
Chantry Press
CHARITON REVIEW
Chariton Review Press
Chax Press
CHELSEA
Chicory Blue Press
Chiron Press
CHIRON REVIEW
CHRYSANTHEMUM

CICADA
CIMARRON REVIEW
CINCINNATI POETRY REVIEW
Cinco Puntos Press
City Lights Books
CITY RANT
Clamshell Press
Cleveland State Univ. Poetry Center
CLIPS FROM BEAR'S HOME MOVIES
CLOCKWATCH REVIEW
Clockwatch Review Press
Clothespin Fever Press
CLOUDLINE
Clover Press
Coach House Press
The Cobham and Hatherton Press
Coffee House Press
COFFEEHOUSE POETS' QUARTERLY
COKEFISH
COLD-DRILL
COLLABORATION
COLLAGES & BRICOLAGES
COLOR WHEEL
COLORADO REVIEW: A Journal of Contemporary
   Literature
Commonwealth Press Virginia
Concourse Press
CONDITIONED RESPONSE
Conditioned Response Press
Confluence Press, Inc.
CONJUNCTIONS
THE CONNECTICUT POETRY REVIEW
CONNECTICUT RIVER REVIEW: A National Poetry
   Journal
CONTACT/11: A Poetry Review
Contact II: Publications
CONTEXT SOUTH
COOP. ANTIGRUPPO SICILIANO
Cooper House Publishing Inc.
Copper Beech Press
Copper Canyon Press
Cordelia Press
Cornerstone Press
CORNFIELD REVIEW
Coteau Books
COTTONWOOD
Cottonwood Press, Inc.
John Edwin Cowen, Ltd.
COYDOG REVIEW
CRAB CREEK REVIEW
CRAMPED AND WET
The F. Marion Crawford Memorial Society
CRAWLSPACE
CRAZYHORSE
CRAZYQUILT LITERARY QUARTERLY
Creative With Words Publications (CWW)
CREEPING BENT
Croissant & Company
Crones' Own Press
CROP DUST
CROSS TIMBERS REVIEW
CROSSCURRENTS, A QUARTERLY
The Crossing Press
CROTON REVIEW
CRUCIBLE
CSS Publications
CULTURE CONCRETE
CUMBERLAND POETRY REVIEW
Curbstone Press
The Curlew Press
CURLEY
CURTAINS
CUTBANK
CUTTING EDGE QUARTERLY
CWM
Daedalus Press
THE DALHOUSIE REVIEW
Dancing Bear Productions

dbqp
DE NAR
Dead Angel Press
" "...A DEAD BEAT POET PRODUCTION
DEANOTATIONS
The Dedalus Press
DELIRIUM
DENVER QUARTERLY
DESCANT
DESCANT
DESDE ESTE LADO/FROM THIS SIDE
Devil Mountain Books
THE DEVIL'S MILLHOPPER
The Devil's Millhopper Press
DIAL-A-POEM POETS LP'S
THE DILETTANTE FORUM
DIMENSION
Dirty Rotten Press
Doctor Jazz Press
DOG RIVER REVIEW
Dollarpoems
Dolphin-Moon Press
Dooryard Press
DOUBLE HARNESS
Dragon Cloud Books
Dragon Gate, Inc.
DRAGONFLY: East/West Haiku Quarterly
Dragon's Teeth Press
DREAM INTERNATIONAL QUARTERLY
DREAMS AND NIGHTMARES
Druid Books
DRY CRIK REVIEW
Duck Down Press
Dufour Editions Inc.
DUMARS REVIEWS
DUSTY DOG
Dusty Dog Press
E Publications
EARTH'S DAUGHTERS: Feminist Arts Periodical
EARTHWISE LITERARY CALENDAR
Earthwise Publications
EARTHWISE REVIEW
The Ecco Press
THE ECLECTIC MUSE
Ediciones El Gato Tuerto
Editorial Review
Editor's Desk
EDITOR'S DESK
EDITOR'S DIGEST
The Edwin Mellen Press
e.g.
EL GATO TUERTO
ELAN POETIQUE LITTERAIRE ET PACIFISTE
ELDRITCH SCIENCE
The Electric Bank, Inc.
THE ELEPHANT-EAR
11 X 13 - BROADSIDE
THE ELEVENTH MUSE
ELF: ECLECTIC LITERARY FORUM (ELF MAGA-
   ZINE)
ELLIPSE
ELT Press
Embassy Hall Editions
Embers Press
EMERALD CITY COMIX & STORIES
Emily Press
THE EMSHOCK LETTER
En Passant Poetry Press
EN PASSANT/POETRY
Endeavor Publishing
English Language Literature Association
Enitharmon Press
L'Epervier Press
EPIPHANY: A JOURNAL OF LITERATURE
EPOCH
THE EQUATOR
EQUOFINALITY
Erespin Press

ERGO! THE BUMBERSHOOT LITERARY MAGA-
ZINE
The Erie Street Press
EUTHANASIA ROSES
EVENT
EXETER STUDIES IN AMERICAN & COMMON-
WEALTH ARTS
EXIT
EXIT 13 MAGAZINE
Expanded Media Editions
EXPERIMENT IN WORDS
EXPERIMENTAL BASEMENT
eXpEriMenTal presS
The Family of God
FARCE, Raleigh's Review of Alternative Arts
FARMER'S MARKET
FAT TUESDAY
FEELINGS
FELICITY
FELL SWOOP
THE FESSENDEN REVIEW
THE FIDDLEHEAD
FIELD
The Figures
Fine Arts Press
FINE MADNESS
The First East Coast Theatre and Publishing Company,
Inc.
FISH DRUM MAGAZINE
Fithian Press
5 AM
FIVE FINGERS REVIEW
Five Islands Press Cooperative Ltd.
FLOATING ISLAND
Floating Island Publications
THE FLORIDA REVIEW
Flume Press
Folder Editions
FOLIO: A LITERARY JOURNAL
The Folks Upstairs Press
FOOTWORK: THE PATERSON LITERARY REVIEW
FOR POETS ONLY
The Forces of Magic
Ford-Brown & Co., Publishers
FOREHEAD: Writing & Art Journal
THE FORMALIST
44 Press, Inc.
FRAGMENTS
FRANK: AN INTERNATIONAL JOURNAL OF CON-
TEMPORARY WRITING AND ART
FREE FOCUS
FREE LUNCH
French Broad Press
Friends Of Tucson Pub Lib/The Maguey Press
FROG GONE REVIEW
From Here Press
Front Street Publishers
Frozen Waffles Press/Shattered Sidewalks Press; 25th
Century Chapbooks
The Future Press
Gain Publications
The Galileo Press Ltd.
GALLERY WORKS
THE GALLEY SAIL REVIEW
Gallopade Publishing Group
Galloping Dog Press
THE GAMUT
GANDHABBA
W. Paul Ganley: Publisher
GAVEA-BROWN
Gavea-Brown Publications
Gay Sunshine Press, Inc.
Gearhead Press
GENERATOR
Generator Press
THE GEORGIA REVIEW
Gesture Press
THE GETTYSBURG REVIEW

GHOST DANCE: The International Quarterly of Experi-
mental Poetry
Ghost Dance Press
Ghost Pony Press
GIANTS PLAY WELL IN THE DRIZZLE
Gild of Saint George
GLASS WILL
GLB Publishers
GlenHill Productions
The Gleniffer Press
GO MAGAZINE
GOLDEN ISIS
Goldfish Press
GOOD CLEAN FUN
Good Gay Poets Press
THE GOPHERWOOD REVIEW
GRAHAM HOUSE REVIEW
GRAIN
GRASSLANDS REVIEW
The Graywolf Press
Great Elm Press
Great Lakes Poetry Press
GREAT RIVER REVIEW
The Green Hut Press
GREEN MOUNTAINS REVIEW
GREEN ZERO
The Greenfield Review Press/Ithaca House
Greenhouse Review Press
GREEN'S MAGAZINE
THE GREENSBORO REVIEW
GROUNDSWELL
The Groundwater Press
Guildford Poets Press
Gull Books
GUTS
GYPSY
The Hague Press
HAIGHT ASHBURY LITERARY JOURNAL
HAMMERS
HANGING LOOSE
Hanging Loose Press
HAPPINESS HOLDING TANK
HarCroft Publishing Company
Hard Press
Harper Square Press
HARP-STRINGS
Harris Stonehouse Press
THE HAUNTED JOURNAL
HAWAI'I REVIEW
HAYDEN'S FERRY REVIEW
HEATHENZINE
Helicon Nine Editions
Helikon Press
Hellas
HELLAS: A Journal of Poetry & the Humanities
HELTER SKELTER
HEMLOCKS AND BALSAMS
HERESIES: A FEMINIST PUBLICATION ON ART
AND POLITICS
Hermes House Press, Inc.
Hibiscus Press
HIDDEN SPRINGS REVIEW
High/Coo Press
Hippopotamus Press
HIRAM POETRY REVIEW
HMS Press
HOB-NOB
HOBO JUNGLE
HOBO STEW REVIEW
Hohm Press
Holy Cow! Press
HOME PLANET NEWS
Home Planet Publications
Homeward Press
Honeybrook Press
Hong Kong Publishing Co., Ltd.
HOOFSTRIKES NEWSLETTER
HORIZONTES

LUNA TACK
The Lunchroom Press
Lynx House Press
THE LYRIC
M.A.F. Press
MAAT
THE MAC GUFFIN
Mad River Press
THE MADISON REVIEW
Maelstrom Press
MAELSTROM REVIEW
THE MAGAZINE OF SPECULATIVE POETRY
THE MAGE
MAGIC CHANGES
MAGIC REALISM
Maize Press
MALLIFE
The Mandeville Press
MANHATTAN POETRY REVIEW
THE MANHATTAN REVIEW
manic d press
MANKATO POETRY REVIEW
MANNA
MANOA: A Pacific Journal of International Writing
Manroot Books
Marathon International Book Company
March Street Press
Marilee Publications
MARK
Markgraf Publications Group
Maro Verlag
MATI
MATRIX
Mayapple Press
MAYFLY
McOne Press
ME MAGAZINE
Melrose
MEMES
The Menard Press
MENSUEL 25
MERLYN'S PEN: The National Magazine of Student
   Writing
Metacom Press
METROSPHERE
THE MICKLE STREET REVIEW
MICROCOSM
MID-AMERICAN REVIEW
MIDLAND REVIEW
Midmarch Arts Press
MIDWEST CHAPARRAL
MIDWEST POETRY REVIEW
THE MIDWEST QUARTERLY
Midwest Villages & Voices
MILDRED
Milkweed Editions
THE MILWAUKEE UNDERGRADUATE REVIEW
MIND IN MOTION, A MAGAZINE OF POETRY AND
   SHORT PROSE
THE MIND'S EYE
Minor Heron Press
MIP Company
MISSISSIPPI REVIEW
MISSISSIPPI VALLEY REVIEW
MR. COGITO
Mr. Cogito Press
MODERN IMAGES
MOKSHA JOURNAL
MOMENTUM
THE MONOCACY VALLEY REVIEW
Monographics Press
THE MONTANA REVIEW
MOODY STREET IRREGULARS: A Jack Kerouac
   Magazine
Moody Street Irregulars, Inc.
Moonsquilt Press
MOONSTONE BLUE
Mortal Press

Mosaic Press
Mother of Ashes Press
Motheroot Publications
MT. AUKUM REVIEW
Moving Parts Press
MSS/NEW MYTHS
MUDFISH
Multi Media Arts
Mundus Artium Press
MUSIC OF THE SPHERES
MUSICWORKS: THE CANADIAN AUDIO-VISUAL
   JOURNAL OF SOUND EXPLORATIONS
Muso Press
MY LEGACY
My Mother's House - Aitini Talo
Myriad Moods
Nada Press
NAKED MAN
Naked Man Press
National Poetry Association Publishers
National Poetry Foundation
NEBO
THE NEBRASKA REVIEW
NEGATIVE CAPABILITY
Negative Capability Press
Nemeton Publishing
NEW AGE DIGEST
NEW AMERICAN WRITING
New Cicada
NEW CICADA
NEW COLLAGE MAGAZINE
New Collage Press
NEW CONTRAST
THE NEW CRITERION
NEW DAY PUBLICATIONS
NEW DELTA REVIEW
NEW DEPARTURES
New Earth Publications
NEW ENGLAND REVIEW
New Hope International
NEW HOPE INTERNATIONAL REVIEW
NEW HOPE INTERNATIONAL ZINE
THE NEW LAUREL REVIEW
NEW LETTERS
NEW MEXICO HUMANITIES REVIEW
NEW ORLEANS REVIEW
The New Poets Series, Inc.
THE NEW PRESS
THE NEW RAIN MAGAZINE
New Rivers Press, Inc.
NEW SINS
NEW SPOKES
NEW WRITER'S MAGAZINE
New York CIRCUS, Inc.
NEWSLETTER (LEAGUE OF CANADIAN POETS)
NEWSLETTER INAGO
NEXT EXIT
NIGHT OWL'S NEWSLETTER
NIGHT ROSES
Nightshade Press
Nightsun Books
THE NIHILISTIC REVIEW
NIMROD
Nioba, Uitgevers
NON COMPOS MENTIS
NOOSPAPERS
THE NORTH AMERICAN REVIEW
North Star Press of St. Cloud, Inc.
North Stone Press
NORTHCOAST VIEW MONTHLY MAGAZINE
NORTHEAST
NORTHEAST JOURNAL
NORTHEASTARTS MAGAZINE
Northern House
NORTHERN LIGHTS STUDIES IN CREATIVITY
NORTHERN NEW ENGLAND REVIEW
Northland Quarterly Publications, Inc.
NORTHWEST REVIEW

849

Northwoods Press
NOSTALGIA, A Sentimental State of Mind
NOSTOC
NOTEBOOK/CUADERNO: A LITERARY JOURNAL
NOTES FROM THE UNDERGROUND
NOTUS NEW WRITING
NOW AND THEN
Now It's Up To You Publications
NRG
NUMBERS
NUTSHELL
NYCTICORAX
O.ARS
O.ARS, Inc.
Oasis Books
OBSIDIAN II: BLACK LITERATURE IN REVIEW
Ocean Star Publications
Oceanides Press
Tom Ockerse Editions
ODESSA POETRY REVIEW
OFF MAIN STREET
OHIO RENAISSANCE REVIEW
THE OHIO REVIEW
Old Harbor Press
THE OLD RED KIMONO
The Olive Press Publications
Omega Cat Press
Omega Cottonwood Press
Ommation Press
ON COURSE
Oolichan Books
Open Book Publications, A Division of Station Hill Press
OPOSSUM HOLLER TAROT
ORBIS
Orchises Press
ORGANICA
The Organization
ORO MADRE
ORPHEUS
ORPHIC LUTE
OSIRIS
OSTENTATIOUS MIND
Otherwind
OTTER
OUR WRITE MIND
OUROBOROS
OUTERBRIDGE
Outlaw Books
OUTPOSTS POETRY QUARTERLY
OUTRE
Outrider Press
OVERVIEW LTD.
Owl Creek Press
Ox Head Press
OXALIS
The Oxalis Group
Oyez
OYEZ REVIEW
P.I.E. (Poetry Imagery and Expression)
THE PACIFIC REVIEW
PAGES
PAINTBRUSH: A Journal of Poetry, Translations & Letters
PAINTED BRIDE QUARTERLY
PAINTED HILLS REVIEW
PalmTree Publishers
Pancake Press
PANDORA
THE PANHANDLER
Panjandrum Books
PANJANDRUM POETRY JOURNAL
Panopticum Press London
THE PAPER BAG
The Paper Bag Press
The Paper Plant
PAPER RADIO
PAPER TOADSTOOL
Papier-Mache Press

Paradigm Press
PARIS REVIEW
PARNASSUS: POETRY IN REVIEW
PARNASSUS LITERARY JOURNAL
PARTING GIFTS
PASSAGER: A Journal of Remembrance and Discovery
PASSAGES NORTH
PASSAIC REVIEW
THE PATRIOT
PAUNCH
PAUSE
Paycock Press
Peacock Books
Peak Output Unlimited
PEARL
Pearl Editions
Pearl-Win Publishing Co.
Pebbles
PECKERWOOD
PEGASUS
THE PEGASUS REVIEW
PEMBROKE MAGAZINE
PENINHAND
Peninhand Press
PENNINE PLATFORM
THE PENNSYLVANIA REVIEW
PENNYWHISTLE PEOPLE PAPER
Pennywhistle Press
Pentagram Press
PEN:UMBRA
The Penumbra Press
Pequod Press
Perivale Press
Permeable Press
Pessimism Press, Inc.
The Petrarch Press
Petroglyph Press, Ltd.
Petronium Press
PHASE AND CYCLE
Phase and Cycle Press
The Phlebas Press
PHOEBE, THE GEORGE MASON REVIEW
PHOENIX BROADSHEETS
Piccolo Press
PIEDMONT LITERARY REVIEW
PIG IN A PAMPHLET
PIG IRON
Pig Iron Press
Pig Press
The Pikestaff Press
Pinched Nerves Press
Pinchgut Press
Pittore Euforico
THE PITTSBURGH QUARTERLY
PIVOT
Placebo Press
PLAINS POETRY JOURNAL (PPJ)
PLAINSONG
Pleasure Dome Press (Long Island Poetry Collective Inc.)
PLOUGHSHARES
THE PLOWMAN
THE PLUM REVIEW
POEM
The Poet
POET & CRITIC
POET LORE
POET MAGAZINE
POET NEWS
Poet Papers
POETIC JUSTICE
POETIC LICENCE
Poetic Page
POETIC PAGE
POETIC SPACE: Poetry & Fiction
Poetical Histories
POETPOURRI
POETRY
POETRY AND AUDIENCE

Poetry Around
POETRY AUSTRALIA
POETRY CANADA
The Poetry Connection
THE POETRY CONNECTION
POETRY DURHAM
POETRY EAST
POETRY FLASH
The Poetry Group
POETRY HALIFAX DARTMOUTH
Poetry Ireland Press
POETRY IRELAND REVIEW
POETRY KANTO
Poetry Magic Publications
THE POETRY MISCELLANY
POETRY MOTEL
POETRY NEW YORK
POETRY NIPPON
The Poetry Nippon Press
POETRY NOTTINGHAM: The International Magazine of
    Today's Poetry
Poetry Nottingham Society Publications
THE POETRY PEDDLER
POETRY QUARTERLY
POETRY REVIEW
POETRY: USA QUARTERLY
POETRY TODAY
POETRY WALES
Poetry Wales Press, Ltd.
POETRY/LA
POETS & WRITERS MAGAZINE
POETS AT WORK
POET'S FORUM
POETS ON:
POETS. PAINTERS. COMPOSERS.
POETS' ROUNDTABLE
Point Riders Press
POISON PEN WRITERS NEWS
Polexii Press
POLITICALLY INCORRECT
Poltroon Press
Porcepic Books
The Porcupine's Quill, Inc.
PORTABLE LOWER EAST SIDE
Bern Porter Books
Portmanteau Editions
PORTRAITS POETRY MAGAZINE
POSKISNOLT PRESS
The Post-Apollo Press
The Post-Industrial Press
POTATO EYES
Potes & Poets Press Inc
THE POTTERSFIELD PORTFOLIO
Power Publishing
PRAIRIE FIRE
THE PRAIRIE JOURNAL OF CANADIAN LITERA-
    TURE
Prairie Journal Press
PRAIRIE SCHOONER
PRAIRIE WINDS
Prakalpana Literature
PRAKALPANA SAHITYA/PRAKALPANA LITERA-
    TURE
Preludium Publishers
Prescott Street Press
The Press of Appletree Alley
Pressed Curtains
Prickly Pear Press
Primal Publishing
PRIMAVERA
Princess Publishing
PRINTED MATTER (Japan)
PRISM international
PROEM CANADA
PROMOTION
PROOF ROCK
Proper Tales Press
PROPHETIC VOICES

THE PROSPECT REVIEW
Protean Publications
PSYCHOPOETICA
The Pterodactyl Press
PTOLEMY/BROWNS MILLS REVIEW
THE PUB
Puckerbrush Press
THE PUCKERBRUSH REVIEW
Pudding House Publications
PUDDING MAGAZINE: THE INTERNATIONAL
    JOURNAL OF APPLIED POETRY
Pueblo Poetry Project
PUERTO DEL SOL
The Purchase Press
PURPLE PATCH
Pygmy Forest Press
QRL POETRY SERIES
QUARRY MAGAZINE
Quarry Press
QUARRY WEST
Quarterly Review of Literature Press
QUARTERLY WEST
QUARTOS MAGAZINE
Quick Books
Quill Books
Quintessence Publications & Printing Museum
QUIXOTE, QUIXOTL
Quixsilver Press
RACCOON
RACKHAM JOURNAL OF THE ARTS AND HUMANI-
    TIES (RaJAH)
RAG MAG
Ragweed Press, Inc.
Ramalo Publications
RAMBUNCTIOUS REVIEW
RAMPIKE
Ranger International Productions
Rarach Press
Raw Dog Press
Reality Studios
THE REAPER
Rebis Press
Red Alder Books
Red Candle Press
RED CEDAR REVIEW
RED DANCEFLOOR
RED DIRT
Red Dust
Red Herring Press
Red Hill Press, San Francisco + Los Angeles
Red Ink/Black Hole Productions
Red Key Press
THE REDNECK REVIEW OF LITERATURE
I. Reed Books
REFLECT
REFLECTIONS
RENEGADE
RE:PRINT (AN OCCASIONAL MAGAZINE)
RESONANCE
REVIEW LA BOOCHE
RFD
Rhiannon Press
RHINO
RHODODENDRON
RHYME TIME POETRY NEWSLETTER
THE RIALTO
Ridgeway Press
Right Here Publications
Rio Grande Press
RIPPLES
Rivelin Grapheme Press
RIVER CITY
RIVER STYX
RIVERRUN
Rock Steady Press
Rolling House Publications
THE ROMANTIST
ROOM

THE ROUND TABLE: A Journal of Poetry and Fiction
Rowan Mountain Press
(ROWBOAT)
Ruddy Duck Press
Runaway Publications
The Russian Writers' Club Publishing House
RYAN'S REVIEW
Sachem Press
SACRED FIRE
Sa-De Publications Inc.
Saint Andrews Press
ST. MAWR
SALAD
SALMAGUNDI
THE SALMON
Salmon Publishing
SALOME: A JOURNAL FOR THE PERFORMING
   ARTS
SALT LICK
Salt Lick Press
Salt-Works Press
SAMISDAT
Samisdat
San Diego Poet's Press
SAN FERNANDO POETRY JOURNAL
SAN MIGUEL REVIEW
Sandberry Press
Sandhills Press
SANDHILLS/ST. ANDREWS REVIEW
Sandpiper Press
SANDSCRIPT
Santa Susana Press
Saqi Books Publisher
SARU Press International
SATORI
Saturday Press, Inc.
The Saunderstown Press
Sauvie Island Press
Savant Garde Workshop
Saxifrage Books
Say When Press
SCARP
Art Paul Schlosser Books, Tapes, & Garbage Gazzette
SCHMAGA
Score
SCORE
Scots Plaid Press (Persephone Press)
SCREAM MAGAZINE
THE SCREAM OF THE BUDDHA
SCREE
Script Humanistica
SCRIVENER
SE LA VIE WRITER'S JOURNAL
Second Aeon Publications
Second Coming Press
SEEMS
The Segue Foundation
Seismograph Publications
Selene Books
Seminal Life Press
SENECA REVIEW
SENSATIONS
SENSOR
SEPIA
SEQUOIA
SERIE D'ECRITURE
Serpent & Eagle Press
Seven Buffaloes Press
700 Elves Press
SEZ: A Multi-Racial Journal of Poetry & People's Culture
Shadow Press, U.S.A.
SHATTERED WIG REVIEW
Shearsman Books
The Sheep Meadow Press
SHENANDOAH
Shining Waters Press
SHIRIM
Shy City Press

Sicilian Antigruppo/Cross-Cultural Communications
THE SIGNAL - Network International
Signature Books
Signpost Press Inc.
Silver Apples Press
SILVERFISH REVIEW
SING HEAVENLY MUSE! WOMEN'S POETRY AND
   PROSE
Singing Bone Press
Singular Speech Press
Sink Press
SISYPHUS
SKYLARK
SLANT, A Journal of Poetry
Slate Press
THE SLEEPWALKER'S JOURNAL
SLEUTH JOURNAL
SLIPSTREAM
SLOW DANCER
Slow Dancer
THE SMALL POND MAGAZINE OF LITERATURE
   aka SMALL POND
SMALL PRESS NEWS
Small-Small Press
Smiling Dog Press
SMOKE
Smyrna Press
THE SNAIL'S PACE REVIEW
Snowbird Publishing Company
Snowbound Press
SNOWY EGRET
SNUG
SO & SO
Sober Minute Press
SOCKS, DREGS AND ROCKING CHAIRS
Soleil Press
SOLO FLYER
SORE DOVE
Sore Dove Publishers
SOUNDINGS EAST
SOUNDMAKERS
THE SOUNDS OF POETRY
SOUTH CAROLINA REVIEW
SOUTH COAST POETRY JOURNAL
SOUTH DAKOTA REVIEW
THE SOUTH FLORIDA POETRY REVIEW
South Head Press
Southeastern FRONT
THE SOUTHERN CALIFORNIA ANTHOLOGY
SOUTHERN POETRY REVIEW
THE SOUTHERN REVIEW
SOUTHWEST REVIEW
SOUTHWESTERN DISCOVERIES
SOU'WESTER
THE SOW'S EAR POETRY JOURNAL
Spare Change Poetry Press
SPARROW POVERTY PAMPHLETS, Sparrow Press
   imprint
Sparrow Press
Spectacular Diseases
SPECTACULAR DISEASES
SPHINX—WOMEN'S INTERNATIONAL LITERARY/
   ART REVIEW (IN ENGLISH)
THE SPIRIT THAT MOVES US
The Spirit That Moves Us Press, Inc.
SPIT
SPITBALL: The Literary Baseball Magazine
Split Personality Press
SPSM&H
STAPLE
Star Books, Inc.
STARLIGHT
Starlight Press
StarMist Books
State of the Art Ltd.
State Street Press
Station Hill Press
Step-Over Toe-Hold Press

852

Warthog Press
WASHINGTON REVIEW
Washington Writers' Publishing House
Water Mark Press
Water Row Press
WATER ROW REVIEW
Waterfront Press
WATERWAYS: Poetry in the Mainstream
THE WAVE
Wayland Press
WE MAGAZINE
We Press
West Anglia Publications
WEST BRANCH
WEST COAST LINE: A Journal of Contemporary Writing and its Modernist Sources
WEST END MAGAZINE
WEST HILLS REVIEW: A WALT WHITMAN JOURNAL
West of Boston
Westburg Associates, Publishers
THE WESTMINSTER REVIEW
WESTWORDS
Wet Editions
WEYFARERS
Wheel of Fire Press
WHETSTONE
WHISKEY ISLAND MAGAZINE
WHISPERING PALM
White Cliffs Media Company
WHITE CLOUDS REVUE
White Horse Press
White Pine Press
The George Whittell Memorial Press
WHOLE NOTES
WICKED MYSTIC
WIDE OPEN MAGAZINE
THE WIDENER REVIEW
Wild East Publishing Co-operative Limited
WILDFLOWER
Wildflower Press
Willamette River Press
Willow Bee Publishing House
WILLOW SPRINGS
WIND
Wind Vein Press
WINDFALL
Windfall Prophets Press
Windflower Press
THE WINDLESS ORCHARD
Window Publications
Windsong Press
Wineberry Press
Winn Books
WISCONSIN REVIEW
THE WISHING WELL
WITHOUT HALOS
WITNESS
Woldt Publishing
Arnie Wolman Co.
Wolsak & Wynn Publishers Ltd.
WOMAN POET
Women-in-Literature, Inc.
Woods Hole Press
THE WORCESTER REVIEW
The Word Works, Inc.
Wordwrights Canada
WORLD LETTER
THE WORMWOOD REVIEW
The Wormwood Review Press
WRIT
THE WRITE AGE (First Magazine of Writing Therapy)
WRITE NOW!
The Write Press
THE WRITERS' BLOC*
WRITERS' FORUM
Writers Forum
WRITERS GAZETTE NEWSLETTER

THE WRITER'S HAVEN
Writers House Press
WRITER'S INFO
Writers Ink Press
WRITER'S LIFELINE
THE WRITER'S NOOK NEWS
Writers Publishing Service Co.
Writers Unlimited Agency, Inc
WRITER'S VOICE
WRITING
WTI Publishing Co.
WYOMING, THE HUB OF THE WHEEL...A Journey for Universal Spokesmen...
XANADU: A LITERARY JOURNAL
X-CALIBRE
XENOPHILIA
Xenos Books
XEROLAGE
XTRAS
YARROW, A JOURNAL OF POETRY
Years Press
Yellow Moon Press
THE YELLOW PAGES
The Yellow Press
YELLOW SILK: Journal Of Erotic Arts
Yoknapatawpha Press
Zeitgeist Press
ZENOS
Zirlinson Publishing
Zoland Books
ZONE 3
ZZAJ-SYNCHRONOLOGY

POLAND

MR. COGITO
Mr. Cogito Press
TAPJOE: The Anaprocrustean Poetry Journal of Enumclaw

POLITICAL SCIENCE

ACTIVIST
AFRICA TODAY
Agathon Press
Amana Books
THE ANIMALS' AGENDA
ARMED FORCES & SOCIETY
BALLOT ACCESS NEWS
Beacon Press
Bergin & Garvey Publishers
Between The Lines
The Borgo Press
BOSTON REVIEW
Branden Publishing Company
Brunswick Publishing Corporation
Buddha Rose Publications
CANADIAN DIMENSION
CANADIAN JOURNAL OF LAW AND SOCIETY/ Revue canadienne de droit et societe
CANADIAN PUBLIC POLICY- Analyse de Politiques
CANADIAN SLAVONIC PAPERS
CASE ANALYSIS
Chandler & Sharp Publishers, Inc.
Circa Press
Claridge Press
Clarity Press
CNL/WORLD REPORT
Earl M Coleman Enterprises, Inc
COMMUNITY DEVELOPMENT JOURNAL
The Compass Press
Corfa Books
The Counter-Propaganda Press
CRITICAL REVIEW: An Interdisciplinary Journal
CULTURE CONCRETE
" "...A DEAD BEAT POET PRODUCTION
The Denali Press
EAST EUROPEAN QUARTERLY
Eastern Caribbean Institute
EASTERN EUROPEAN POLITICS & SOCIETIES

ECOSOCIALIST REVIEW
FREE LIFE
FUSE MAGAZINE
Gild of Saint George
Glenbridge Publishing Ltd.
Golden West Historical Publications
GREEN MULTILOGUE
GREY CITY JOURNAL
Griffon House Publications/Bagehot Council
GYPSY
Harbinger House
The Heather Foundation
Hickman Systems - New Age Books
HOBBY BOOKWATCH (MILITARY, GUN & HOBBY
 BOOK REVIEW)
Hoover Institution Press
INVERTED-A HORN
Inverted-A, Inc.
KETTERING REVIEW
Kumarian Press, Inc.
L.G.L.C. NEWSLETTER
LIBERATION! Journal of Revolutionary Marxism
Libertarian Press, Inc./American Book Distributors
LITTLE FREE PRESS
LIVERPOOL NEWSLETTER
LUCHA/STRUGGLE
Lyceum Books, Inc.
M.H. Macy & Company
Maisonneuve Press
MEXICAN STUDIES/ESTUDIOS MEXICANOS
MIDDLE EAST REPORT
MIDEAST MONITOR
THE MILITANT
MINORITY RIGHTS GROUP REPORTS
New Star Books Ltd.
New Worlds Press
THE NIHILISTIC REVIEW
Pandit Press, Inc.
Paragon House Publishers
PEACEWORK
T.H. Peek, Publisher
Pessimism Press, Inc.
Poetry Wales Press, Ltd.
POLITICAL BEHAVIOR
Political Research Associates
PROCESSED WORLD
Q.E.D. Press
RADICAL AMERICA
RECON
ROMANIAN REVIEW
ST. CROIX REVIEW
Saqi Books Publisher
SCHMAGA
SCIENCE AND TECHNOLOGY
Selous Foundation Press
Seven Locks Press
SOCIAL POLICY
SOCIETY
SOUTHERN LIBERTARIAN MESSENGER
SPECTRUM, A Guide to the Independent Press and
 Informative Organizations
Spectrum Publications
STATE AND LOCAL GOVERNMENT REVIEW
Texas Monthly Press
TOWARD FREEDOM
TRANSNATIONAL PERSPECTIVES
UNBRIDLED LUST!
THE UNDERGROUND FOREST - LA SELVA SUB-
 TERRANEA
Univelt, Inc.
University of Calgary Press
University of Massachusetts Press
VIETNAM GENERATION: A Journal of Recent History
 and Contemporary Issues
THE VIRGINIA QUARTERLY REVIEW
Voice of Liberty Publications
THE WASHINGTON MONTHLY
Westburg Associates, Publishers

Witwatersrand University Press
Wright-Armstead Associates
WTI Publishing Co.
WW Publishers

POLITICS

A as A Publishing
Aardvark Enterprises
ACM (ANOTHER CHICAGO MAGAZINE)
ACTIVIST
Akwesasne Notes
ALCATRAZ
Amana Books
ANTI-APARTHEID NEWS
Arden Press, Inc.
ARTPAPER
ART'S GARBAGE GAZZETTE
Astarte Shell Press
Autonomedia, Inc.
BAD HAIRCUT
BALLOT ACCESS NEWS
Beacon Press
Beekman Publishers, Inc.
Between The Lines
BLACK MOUNTAIN REVIEW
Blue Crane Books
BOTH SIDES NOW
BREAKTHROUGH!
Brick Row Publishing Co. Ltd.
CANADIAN PUBLIC POLICY- Analyse de Politiques
CARIBBEAN NEWSLETTER
Center for Public Representation
CENTRAL AMERICA REPORT
CENTRAL PARK
CHALLENGE: A Journal of Faith and Action in Central
 America
Chandler & Sharp Publishers, Inc.
Chelsea Green Publishing Company
Cheshire Books
Children Of Mary
THE...CHRONICLE
CINEASTE MAGAZINE
City Lights Books
CLINTON ST.
COLUMBUS FREE PRESS
COMMON SENSE
Communitas Press
COMMUNITY DEVELOPMENT JOURNAL
The Compass Press
COMPOST NEWSLETTER (CNL)
THE CONSTANTIAN
CRITICAL REVIEW: An Interdisciplinary Journal
CROSSCURRENTS
Cultural Survival, Inc.
CULTURAL SURVIVAL QUARTERLY
CULTURE CONCRETE
DE NAR
" "...A DEAD BEAT POET PRODUCTION
DECEMBER MAGAZINE
DECENTRALIZE!
The Denali Press
DEVIANCE
Devin-Adair, Publishers, Inc.
DEWITT DIGEST & REVIEW
THE DIGGER
DIGIT
Dufour Editions Inc.
THE DURHAM UNIVERSITY JOURNAL
ECOSOCIALIST REVIEW
Editorial Research Service
Epica
EUTHANASIA ROSES
FAG RAG
FEMINIST REVIEW
FICTION INTERNATIONAL
FIDELIS ET VERUS
FIFTH ESTATE
Fir Publishing Company

Five Fingers Press
FIVE FINGERS REVIEW
FOREFRONT—HEALTH INVESTIGATIONS
Four Walls Eight Windows
Free Association Books (FAB)
FREE   ASSOCIATIONS: PSYCHOANALYSIS,
   GROUPS, POLITICS, CULTURE
Free People Press
FREE PRESS NETWORK
FULL DISCLOSURE
Gain Publications
GATEAVISA
Glenbridge Publishing Ltd.
Goldstein & Blair
GOOD CLEAN FUN
Good Hope Enterprises, Inc.
GRANTA
Greenlawn Press
GREY CITY JOURNAL
GUARDIAN
Guernica Editions, Inc.
HARMONY: VOICES FOR A JUST FUTURE
HERESIES: A FEMINIST PUBLICATION ON ART
   AND POLITICS
Heyday Books
Hoover Institution Press
IKON
IKON, Inc.
INCITE INFORMATION
INDIVIDUAL LIBERTY
Institute for Southern Studies
International Publishers Co. Inc.
The International University Press
INVERTED-A HORN
Inverted-A, Inc.
ISRAEL HORIZONS
J & T Publishing
JAG
Kettering Foundation
KETTERING REVIEW
THE KIBBUTZ JOURNAL
KICK IT OVER
Kitchen Table: Women of Color Press
L.A.N.D.
L.G.L.C. NEWSLETTER
LANCASTER INDEPENDENT PRESS
LATIN AMERICAN PERSPECTIVES
Left Bank Books
LEFT BUSINESS OBSERVER
LEFT CURVE
LIBERAL DEMOCRAT NEWS
LIBERATION! Journal of Revolutionary Marxism
THE (LIBERTARIAN) CONNECTION
Library Research Associates, Inc.
LINKS
LITTLE FREE PRESS
Lomond Publications Inc.
LOVE AND RAGE, A Revolutionary Anarchist News-
   monthly
LUCHA/STRUGGLE
Lyceum Books, Inc.
THE MADISON INSURGENT
MAXINE'S PAGES
The Menard Press
THE MILITANT
MIND MATTERS REVIEW
MINNE HA! HA!
Minne Ha! Ha!
MINORITY RIGHTS GROUP REPORTS
MR. COGITO
Mr. Cogito Press
Moon Publications, Inc.
Mosquito Press
Moving Parts Press
NAMBLA BULLETIN
NEW AGE DIGEST
THE NEW AMERICAN
THE NEW ENGLAND QUARTERLY

NEW HEAVEN/NEW EARTH
THE NEW PRESS
New Society Publishers
New Worlds Press
THE NONVIOLENT ACTIVIST
NOOSPAPERS
Northland Quarterly Publications, Inc.
NUCLEAR TIMES
OFF OUR BACKS
ON GOGOL BOULEVARD: Networking Bulletin for
   Dissidents from East and West
Oneworld Publications Ltd.
Oolichan Books
Open Hand Publishing Inc.
OPEN ROAD
ORGANICA
The Organization
P.O. Publishing Company
Pandit Press, Inc.
Panopticum Press London
Park & Park Publishers, Inc.
Path Press, Inc.
PEACE & DEMOCRACY NEWS
PEACEWORK
Pig Iron Press
Pine Hall Press
Pinery Press
Poetry Wales Press, Ltd.
POLITICALLY INCORRECT
POSTCARD ART/POSTCARD FICTION
POSTMODERN CULTURE
THE PRAGMATIST
PRISONER'S LEGAL NEWS
ProActive Press
PROCESSED WORLD
PROFANE EXISTENCE
PUNCTURE
Pygmy Forest Press
Quarterly Committee of Queen's University
THE QUAYLE QUARTERLY
QUEEN'S QUARTERLY: A Canadian Review
REASON MAGAZINE
RED BASS
Red Letter Press
RENT-TO-OWN LEGAL & FINANCIAL BULLETIN
RFD
The Rights' Press
River Basin Publishing Co.
Martha Rosler
THE ROTKIN REVIEW
ST. CROIX REVIEW
Saqi Books Publisher
SCANDINAVIAN REVIEW
Art Paul Schlosser Books, Tapes, & Garbage Gazzette
SCHMAGA
Sea Otter Press
Semiotext Foreign Agents Books Series
SEMIOTEXT(E)
SEZ: A Multi-Racial Journal of Poetry & People's Culture
SHMATE
Shmate Press
THE SMALL POND MAGAZINE OF LITERATURE
   aka SMALL POND
SOCIALISM AND SEXUALITY
Society for Individual Liberty
South End Press
SOUTHERN EXPOSURE
Sovereign Press
SPECTRUM, A Guide to the Independent Press and
   Informative Organizations
SPECTRUM—The Wholistic News Magazine
Spectrum Publications
SUB STANDARD
Syracuse Cultural Workers
Texas Monthly Press
THIRD WAY
Third World First
THIS MAGAZINE

THUNDERMUG REPORT
Thunder's Mouth Press
Tilbury House, Publishers
Times Change Press
Tippy Reed Publishing
Tiptoe Literary Service
TOWARD FREEDOM
University of Massachusetts Press
THE UTNE READER
VIETNAM GENERATION: A Journal of Recent History
    and Contemporary Issues
THE VIRGINIA QUARTERLY REVIEW
Voice of Liberty Publications
Walnut Publishing Co., Inc.
THE WASHINGTON MONTHLY
THE WASHINGTON REPORT
Waterfront Press
WEST END MAGAZINE
West End Press
Wheel of Fire Press
Witwatersrand University Press
WREE-VIEW OF WOMEN
WTI Publishing Co.
Youth Policy Institute
Zed Books Ltd.
ZERO HOUR

PORTUGAL

TRANSITIONS ABROAD: The Guide to Living,
    Learning, and Working Overseas

POST MODERN

ACTIVIST
THE ALTERED MIND
AMERICAN WRITING: A MAGAZINE
Asylum Arts
BLANK GUN SILENCER
COLLAGES & BRICOLAGES
THE COOL TRAVELER
" "...A DEAD BEAT POET PRODUCTION
FATHOMS BELOW
GREEN ZERO
GREY CITY JOURNAL
Last Generation/Underground Editions
LEFT CURVE
Mockingbird Press
NOTES FROM THE UNDERGROUND
P-FORM
POSTMODERN CULTURE
The Press of the Third Mind
Savant Garde Workshop
SENSOR
SPIT
UNBRIDLED LUST!
WHITE WALLS: A Journal of Language and Art
XENOPHILIA
ZYX

POSTCARDS

Barefoot Press
" "...A DEAD BEAT POET PRODUCTION
Deltiologists of America
Gesture Press
Now It's Up To You Publications
Omega Cottonwood Press
POSTCARD CLASSICS
Red Crane Books
Running Press
Trabarni Productions
Tuesday-Art Press
UNBRIDLED LUST!
Westgate Press

ELVIS PRESLEY

THE...CHRONICLE
COMPOST NEWSLETTER (CNL)
FUSE MAGAZINE
Glendale House Publishing

HEART BREAK HOTELVIS
KREATURE COMFORTS
Ocean Tree Books
Quimby Archives
(ROWBOAT)
UNBRIDLED LUST!

PRINTING

Abattoir Editions
Abbey Publications
Achievement Press
Ad-Lib Publications
ALASKA ASSOCIATION OF SMALL PRESSES
Algol Press
ALKALINE PAPER ADVOCATE
All American Press
Alpine Guild
AMERICAN AMATEUR JOURNALIST
AMERICAN BOOK COLLECTOR
Astonisher Press
BACKBOARD
Baker Street Publications
BOOK DEALERS WORLD
BOOK MARKETING UPDATE
BOOK NEWS & BOOK BUSINESS MART
BOOK TALK
BP REPORT
BRILLIANT IDEAS FOR PUBLISHERS
Caliban Press
CANADIAN AUTHOR & BOOKMAN
Cheshire Books
Circa Press
CLIENT MAGAZINE
Coast to Coast Books Inc.
The Cobham and Hatherton Press
Commonwealth Press Virginia
Communication Creativity
Cooperative Children's Book Center
COSMEP NEWSLETTER
The Denali Press
EDITOR'S DIGEST
FEMINIST COLLECTIONS: A QUARTERLY OF WO-
    MEN'S STUDIES RESOURCES
FINE PRINT: The Review for the Arts of the Book
GGL Educational Press
The Gleniffer Press
G'RAPH
Gringo Guides, Inc.
GYPSY
HAPPINESS HOLDING TANK
HORIZONS BEYOND
INFOCUS
Inkling Publications, Inc.
INTERLIT
Iris Communication Group
Iron Gate Publishing
ISI Press
JB & Me Publishing
J'ECRIS
Jessee Poet Publications
JLA Publications, A Division Of Jeffrey Lant Associates,
    Inc.
Laughing Dog Press
LOST GENERATION JOURNAL
Meckler Corporation
Middle Coast Publishing
MONDO HUNKAMOOGA
Mother of Ashes Press
Myriad Moods
NEW PAGES: Access to Alternatives in Print
Nordic Books
OHIO WRITER
The Oryx Press
OSTENTATIOUS MIND
Oxbridge Communications, Inc.
Para Publishing
PC PUBLISHING
Peachpit Press, Inc.

PELTEX
Plas Y Bryn Press
POETS. PAINTERS. COMPOSERS.
POISON PEN WRITERS NEWS
Poltroon Press
Premier Publishers, Inc.
THE PRINTER
THE PRINTER'S DEVIL
PUBLISHING POYNTERS
PUBLISHING TRENDS & TRENDSETTERS
PUCK!
Q.E.D. Press
QUARTOS MAGAZINE
RIGHTING WORDS—THE JOURNAL OF LANGUAGE AND EDITING
Rio Grande Press
THE ROMANTIST
ST. LOUIS JOURNALISM REVIEW
Sang Froid Press
Sauvie Island Press
SCHMAGA
Scojtia Publishing Company
Selective Books, Inc.
SEZ: A Multi-Racial Journal of Poetry & People's Culture
Shadow Press, U.S.A.
SMALL PRESS: The Magazine & Book Review of Independent Publishing
SMALL PRESS NEWS
Southeastern FRONT
Southport Press
SOUTHWESTERN DISCOVERIES
SPENCER'S BOOK WORLD
Spencer's Int'l Enterprises Corp.
SPEX (Small Press Exchange)
ST Publications/Book Division
Still Point Press
Stonehouse Publications
Success Publishing
Sunburst Press
TOOK
Trigon Press
Tuesday-Art Press
Twin Peaks Press
UMBRELLA
THE UNDERGROUND FOREST - LA SELVA SUBTERRANEA
Univelt, Inc.
W.I.M. Publications
WESTERN PUBLISHER
Winslow Publishing
Women's Studies Librarian, University of Wisconsin System
WRITERS CONNECTION
WRITER'S N.W.

PRISON

Ariel Vamp Press
The Carolina Wren Press
Center for Public Representation
COALITION FOR PRISONERS' RIGHTS NEWSLETTER
Coker Publishing House
COLLAGES & BRICOLAGES
Crime and Social Justice Associates, Inc.
The Devonshire Publishing Co.
EMPIRE! The NYS Inmate Literary Arts Magazine
Futurum Forlag
GATEAVISA
Herald Press
Institute for Southern Studies
Kitchen Table: Women of Color Press
LOVE AND RAGE, A Revolutionary Anarchist Newsmonthly
MAXINE'S PAGES
NON COMPOS MENTIS
OFF OUR BACKS
OUROBOROS
Pine Hall Press

The Place In The Woods
PRISONER'S LEGAL NEWS
Pygmy Forest Press
R & E Publishers
RFD
The Rights' Press
Signal Books
SOCIAL JUSTICE: A JOURNAL OF CRIME, CONFLICT, & WORLD ORDER
STROKER
Tower Press
UNBRIDLED LUST!
Volcano Press, Inc
Woldt Publishing

PROSE

Abattoir Editions
ACTA VICTORIANA
AGADA
AGOG
American Audio Prose Library (non-print)
ART/LIFE
Art/Life Limited Editions
ASH
Asylum Arts
Beacon Press
Bear House Publishing
Bomb Shelter Propaganda
Broken Moon Press
The Carolina Wren Press
CHAKRA
CIMARRON REVIEW
" "...A DEAD BEAT POET PRODUCTION
DREAM INTERNATIONAL QUARTERLY
ELF: ECLECTIC LITERARY FORUM (ELF MAGAZINE)
EUTHANASIA ROSES
THE FICTION REVIEW
FINE MADNESS
FOLIO: A LITERARY JOURNAL
The Graywolf Press
HAWAI'I REVIEW
HERESIES: A FEMINIST PUBLICATION ON ART AND POLITICS
IDIOM 23
IMAGINATION MAGAZINE
Independence Publishers Inc.
KALEIDOSCOPE: INTERNATIONAL MAGAZINE OF LITERATURE, FINE ARTS, AND DISABILITY
Kitchen Table: Women of Color Press
KUMQUAT MERINGUE
THE LEDGE POETRY AND PROSE MAGAZINE
Lincoln Springs Press
THE LOOGIE
MASSACRE
MEMES
Milkweed Editions
Monographics Press
New Hope International
NEW HOPE INTERNATIONAL REVIEW
New Rivers Press, Inc.
THE NIHILISTIC REVIEW
NON COMPOS MENTIS
NORTHEAST
THE NORTHERN REVIEW
NOTES FROM THE UNDERGROUND
OUR WRITE MIND
The Penumbra Press
Pessimism Press, Inc.
THE PITTSBURGH QUARTERLY
THE POTTERSFIELD PORTFOLIO
Power Publishing
PRAIRIE FIRE
The Press of Appletree Alley
THE PROSPECT REVIEW
Ramalo Publications
Rebis Press
ROMANIAN REVIEW

(ROWBOAT)
SHENANDOAH
SKYLARK
Small-Small Press
SPIT
Star Books, Inc.
TAPAS
Thunder Creek Publishing Co-operative
Tyro Publishing
UNBRIDLED LUST!
A VERY SMALL MAGAZINE
THE VINCENT BROTHERS REVIEW
Westgate Press
White Horse Press
WIDE OPEN MAGAZINE
Windsong Press
Writers Forum
WRITERS GAZETTE NEWSLETTER
THE WRITER'S HAVEN
THE WRITER'S NOOK NEWS
WYOMING, THE HUB OF THE WHEEL...A Journey for
  Universal Spokesmen...
Xenos Books
YELLOW SILK: Journal Of Erotic Arts
Zirlinson Publishing

PSYCHOLOGY

Ability Workshop Press
ADDICTION & RECOVERY
ADOLESCENCE
Affinity Press
AILERON, A LITERARY JOURNAL
Alamo Square Press
Alegra House Publishers
Alpenglow Press
Alpine Guild
AMBASSADOR REPORT
American Handwriting Analysis Foundation
THE AMERICAN JOURNAL OF PSYCHOANALYSIS
Anderson Press
ANIMA: The Journal of Human Experience
AREOPAGUS
Arrow Publishing
ART CALENDAR
Ash Lad Press
Atrium Society Publications
Beacon Press
Bergin & Garvey Publishers
Beynch Press Publishing Company
Birth Day Publishing Company
Blue Dolphin Press, Inc.
The Boxwood Press
Brain Books
BRAIN/MIND BULLETIN
Brason-Sargar Publications
Bronx Books
Brunswick Publishing Corporation
Buddha Rose Publications
CASE ANALYSIS
Castalia Publishing Company
Celestial Gifts Publishing
Celo Valley Books
Center for the Art of Living
Challenger Press
Chandler & Sharp Publishers, Inc.
CHANGE: The Journal of the Synergetic Society
THE CHAOS NETWORK
Chatsworth Press
Circa Press
Comforter Publishing
COMMON BOUNDARY
Conari Press
Concourse Press
Conscious Living
CONSTRUCTIVE ACTION NEWSLETTER
Cosmoenergetics Publications
Cottage Books
CRCS Publications

CREATING EXCELLENCE
Creative Roots, Inc.
Culpepper Press
The Devonshire Publishing Co.
DIE FAT PIGGY DIE
Dimi Press
Directed Media, Inc.
Distinctive Publishing Corp.
Dormant Brain Research and Development Laboratory
Down There Press
DREAM INTERNATIONAL QUARTERLY
Elm Publications
Elysium Growth Press
EMERGING
THE EMSHOCK LETTER
Robert Erdmann Publishing
ETC Publications
FAMILY THERAPY
Fell Publishers, Inc.
Feris-Lee, Press
Food For Thought Publications
FOREFRONT—HEALTH INVESTIGATIONS
Free Association Books (FAB)
FREE   ASSOCIATIONS: PSYCHOANALYSIS,
  GROUPS, POLITICS, CULTURE
FREE LIFE
Free Spirit Publishing Inc.
Fromm International Publishing Corporation
Garret Press
Gateways Books And Tapes
Gay Sunshine Press, Inc.
THE GIFTED CHILD TODAY
Gifted Education Press/The Reading Tutorium
Gilgal Publications
GLB Publishers
Glenbridge Publishing Ltd.
Globe Press Books
Grace and Goddess Unlimited
Gurze Books
Harbor Publishing Company
Holger Harfst, Publisher
HEALING PATH
Health Press
Hickman Systems - New Age Books
Himalayan Publishers
Human Kinetics Pub. Inc.
Humana Press
Hunter House Inc., Publishers
IBS Press
Impact Publishers, Inc.
INFINITY LIMITED, A Journal for the Somewhat
  Eccentric
Inner Vision Publishing Company
The Institute of Mind and Behavior Press
Interface Press
The International University Press
INTERVENTION IN SCHOOL AND CLINIC
Jalmar Press
Joelle Publishing, Inc.
JOTS (Journal of the Senses)
JOURNAL FOR ANTHROPOSOPHY
JOURNAL OF MENTAL IMAGERY
THE JOURNAL OF MIND AND BEHAVIOR
JOURNAL OF POLYMORPHOUS PERVERSITY
JOURNAL OF PSYCHOACTIVE DRUGS
THE JOURNAL OF PSYCHOHISTORY
JOURNAL OF SPORT AND EXERCISE PSYCHO-
  LOGY
JOURNAL OF THEORETICAL PSYCHOLOGY
Keel Publications
Knowledge Systems, Inc.
HJ Kramer, Inc
Libra Publishers, Inc.
Life Energy Media
Lindisfarne Press
Lindsay Press Inc. of Florida
LivingQuest
The Lockhart Press

LP Publications (Teleos Institute)
LuraMedia, Inc.
Metamorphous Press
Mr. Information
Monroe Press
Mother Courage Press
Mouvement Publications
MUSIC PERCEPTION
NET
New Atlantis Press
New Chapter Press
New Harbinger Publications, Inc.
New Idea Press, Inc.
New Liberty Press
New Saga Publishers
New View Publications
New Voyage Books
New World Library
Nicolas-Hays, Inc.
Northern Star Press
Nucleus Publications
Obsessive Compulsive Anonymous
Occasional Productions
Ocean Star Publications
Oceanides Press
Omega Press (formerly Sufi Order Publications)
ON COURSE
Oness Press
Oneworld Publications Ltd.
OSTENTATIOUS MIND
Paideia Publishers
Pallas Communications
PalmTree Publishers
Panorama Publishing Company
Parabola Books
Pathway Books
PEDIATRIC MENTAL HEALTH
Pergot Press
Perspectives Press
Phoenix Publishing
Polymath Systems
Princess Publishing
Professional Counselor Books
Professional Resource Exchange, Inc.
Progresiv Publishr
Promontory Publishing, Inc.
PSYCH IT
Psyche Press
PSYCHOANALYTIC BOOKS
Psychohistory Press
PSYCHOLOGY OF WOMEN QUARTERLY
PSYCHOPOETICA
Pudding House Publications
PUDDING MAGAZINE: THE INTERNATIONAL
   JOURNAL OF APPLIED POETRY
Quarterly Committee of Queen's University
QUEEN'S QUARTERLY: A Canadian Review
THE QUEST
R & E Publishers
RADIANCE, The Magazine For Large Women
Raven Rocks Press
Real People Press
Red Alder Books
Rio Grande Press
ROMANIAN REVIEW
Ross Books
The Runaway Spoon Press
San Luis Quest Press
The Saunderstown Press
Scojtia Publishing Company
SELF AND SOCIETY
Seventh-Wing Publications
Shepherd Books
Michael Shore Associates
Sigo Press
Skidmore-Roth Publishing
SOCIETY
SPECTRUM—The Wholistic News Magazine

SPECTRUM REVIEW
THE SPORT PSYCHOLOGIST
SPRING: A Journal of Archetype and Culture
Spring Publications Inc
Station Hill Press
Stepping Stone Books
Stillpoint Publishing
Sun, Man, Moon Inc.
SURVIVE & WIN
Tambra Publishing
TAPLIGHT NEWSLETTER
Targeted Communications
Theosophical Publishing House
Top Of The Mountain Publishing
Topping International Institute
Tudor Publishers, Inc.
Ultimate Secrets
UNARIUS LIGHT
UNBRIDLED LUST!
University of Calgary Press
Vesper Publishing
Villa Press
Vision Quest Publishing
Vivation Publishing Co.
Volcano Press, Inc
WARM FUZZY NEWSLETTER
Waterfront Books
Samuel Weiser, Inc.
Wellberry Press
Westport Publishers, Inc.
White Rose Publishing
Whitford Press
Whole Person Associates Inc.
Williamson Publishing Company, Inc.
B. L. Winch & Associates
Wind River Institute Press
Window Publications
Wingbow Press
WITHIN & BEYOND
Witwatersrand University Press
Woldt Publishing
WOMEN & THERAPY
Woodbine House
Woodsong Graphics Inc.
Wright-Armstead Associates
WTI Publishing Co.
Yes International Publishers
Yes You Can Press
Youth Policy Institute

PUBLIC AFFAIRS

THE ADVOCATE
THE ANIMALS' AGENDA
THE ANTIOCH REVIEW
AXIOS
Beacon Press
Big River Publishing
Borealis Press Limited
The Borgo Press
Camel Press
CANADIAN DIMENSION
CANADIAN PUBLIC POLICY- Analyse de Politiques
Capra Press
Center for Public Representation
Chandler & Sharp Publishers, Inc.
CJE NEWSLETTER (Newsletter of the Coalition for Jobs
   & the Environment)
COMMON SENSE
The Compass Press
Continuing Education Press, Portland State University
Corfa Books
COSMOPOLITAN CONTACT
Crossway Books
DEMOCRATIC LEFT
The Denali Press
DEWITT DIGEST & REVIEW
DIE FAT PIGGY DIE
DUST (From the Ego Trip)

Editorial Research Service
Farragut Publishing Co.
FREE LIFE
FREE PRESS
FULL DISCLOSURE
FUSE MAGAZINE
Gain Publications
Grosvenor USA
Hickman Systems - New Age Books
Hoover Institution Press
Impact Publications
Independence Publishers Inc.
Institute for Contemporary Studies/International Center
for Economic Growth
Institute for Southern Studies
International Publishers Co. Inc.
KETTERING REVIEW
Knowledge Systems, Inc.
Kumarian Press, Inc.
LEAGUE SENTINAL
LEFT BUSINESS OBSERVER
The Philip Lesly Company
LITTLE FREE PRESS
THE NEW AMERICAN
The Noble Press, Inc.
North American Students of Cooperation
Occam Publishers
The Olive Press Publications
THE OTHER ISRAEL
Dr. Homer W. Parker, P.E.
PARTISAN REVIEW
PEACE NEWS "For Nonviolent Revolution"
PEDESTRIAN RESEARCH
Pine Hall Press
Planning/Communications
THE PRAGMATIST
Prima Facie
PROCESSED WORLD
Progressive Education
PROGRESSIVE PERIODICALS DIRECTORY/UPDATE
THE PUBLIC RELATIONS QUARTERLY
Quixote Press
REASON MAGAZINE
RECON
The Rensselaerville Systems Training Center
RESOLVE NEWSLETTER
Seven Locks Press
THE SMALL POND MAGAZINE OF LITERATURE
aka SMALL POND
Social Order Series
SOCIAL POLICY
SPECTRUM, A Guide to the Independent Press and
Informative Organizations
SPECTRUM—The Wholistic News Magazine
Spectrum Publications
SPUR
TAPROOT, a journal of elder writers
Texas Monthly Press
THIRD WAY
Thorp Springs Press
THUNDERMUG REPORT
Timely Books
Tower Press
VDT NEWS
Voice of Liberty Publications
Volcano Press, Inc
THE WASHINGTON MONTHLY
World Wildlife Fund & The Conservation Foundation
WORLD WILDLIFE FUND & THE CONSERVATION
FOUNDATION LETTER
Worldwatch Institute
The Write Press

PUBLISHING

Aa To Zz Publishing Co.
Ad-Lib Publications
THE AFRICAN BOOK PUBLISHING RECORD
ASIAN LITERARY MARKET REVIEW

Baker Street Publications
Blue Heron Publishing, Inc.
Bold Productions
BOOK MARKETING UPDATE
BP REPORT
BRITISH BOOK NEWS
Chiron Press
CHIRON REVIEW
Communication Trends Inc.
CREATIVITY CONNECTION
D.B.A. Books
The Devonshire Publishing Co.
Editions Ex Libris
Editorial Experts, Inc.
THE EDITORIAL EYE
EDITOR'S DIGEST
THE ELECTRONIC PUBLISHING FORUM
EXUM Publishing
FINE PRINT: The Review for the Arts of the Book
FUSE MAGAZINE
G'RAPH
Hans Zell Publishers
IASP NEWSLETTER
Iron Gate Publishing
Jaffe Publishing Management Service
Littlebooks
LOCUS: The Newspaper of the Science Fiction Field
MAINE IN PRINT
MIRKWOOD
Morgan-Rand Publications, Inc.
Multi Media Arts
North American Bookdealers Exchange
Open Horizons Publishing Company
OUR WRITE MIND
Dr. Homer W. Parker, P.E.
Peachpit Press, Inc.
POISON PEN WRITERS NEWS
THE PRINTER
THE PRINTER'S DEVIL
PUBLISHING TRENDS & TRENDSETTERS
READ, AMERICA!
RED HOT WORK-AT-HOME REPORT
RESOURCE-MAG, FOR PUBLISHING PROFESSION-
ALS
RIGHTING WORDS—THE JOURNAL OF LAN-
GUAGE AND EDITING
Rio Grande Press
SCIENCE FICTION CHRONICLE
SMALL PRESS MONTHLY
SPECTRUM, A Guide to the Independent Press and
Informative Organizations
Spectrum Publications
Tiptoe Literary Service
Tunnel Publishing
WICCAN/PAGAN PRESS ALLIANCE TRADE PAPER
WRITE NOW!
Zirlinson Publishing

PUERTO RICO

DESDE ESTE LADO/FROM THIS SIDE
Floricanto Press
Kitchen Table: Women of Color Press
Waterfront Press

QUILTING, SEWING

Altamont Press, Inc.
Betty Boyink Publishing
C & T Publishing
Christmans
CRAFTS NSW
Eagle's View Publishing
FIBERARTS
Levite of Apache
Mayhaven Publishing
R. & E. Miles
The Quilt Digest Press
Silver Dollar Press
Success Publishing

Twin Peaks Press

QUOTATIONS

Anderson Press
Brason-Sargar Publications
FOXFIRE
IMAGINATION MAGAZINE
R. & E. Miles
NEW WRITER'S MAGAZINE
Open Horizons Publishing Company
PEDESTRIAN RESEARCH
R & E Publishers
Saxifrage Books
Sunburst Press
TOOK
UNBRIDLED LUST!

RACE

Amen-Ra Publishing Company
Beacon Press
Floricanto Press
FUSE MAGAZINE
Grosvenor USA
Independence Publishers Inc.
INDIA CURRENTS
LESBIAN CONTRADICTION-A Journal of Irreverent Feminism
MAXINE'S PAGES
MULTICULTURAL TEACHING FOR PRACTITIONERS IN SCHOOLS AND COMMUNITY
P-FORM
SOCIAL JUSTICE: A JOURNAL OF CRIME, CONFLICT, & WORLD ORDER
UNBRIDLED LUST!
University of Massachusetts Press
VALLEY WOMEN'S VOICE
Ward Hill Press
Youth Policy Institute

RADIO

American Audio Prose Library (non-print)
BOOK MARKETING UPDATE
EUTHANASIA ROSES
MAXINE'S PAGES
PAST TIMES: THE NOSTALGIA ENTERTAINMENT NEWSLETTER
Thunder Creek Publishing Co-operative
Tiare Publications
Vestal Press Ltd
White Rose Publishing

READING

GOOD READING MAGAZINE
Grayson Bernard Publishers, Inc.
THE HAPPY THRASHER
Maupin House
Multi Media Arts
NEW HOPE INTERNATIONAL REVIEW
Oak Plantation Press
Ontario Library Association
POISON PEN WRITERS NEWS
READ, AMERICA!
Thunder Creek Publishing Co-operative

REAL ESTATE

Ancient City Press
Applied Publishing
Axiom Press, Publishers
Barr-Randol Publishing Co.
Big River Publishing
Brenner Information Group
C.C. Publishing Co.
CANADIAN MONEYSAVER
Charter Oak Press
Consumer Education Research Center
Distinctive Publishing Corp.
Dropzone Press
Robert Erdmann Publishing

Grapevine Publications, Inc.
The Heather Foundation
LAKE SUPERIOR MAGAZINE
Markgraf Publications Group
N. Y. HABITAT
PF$ Publications
Rand Editions/Tofua Press
Relocation Research/Emigrants
Roscher House
Sphinx Publishing
Tax Property Investor, Inc.
TEC Publications
Technical Communications Associates
Upper Access Inc.
Wilchester Publishing Company

REFERENCE

Adams-Hall Publishing
Alan Wofsy Fine Arts
American Handwriting Analysis Foundation
ANCESTRY NEWSLETTER
Ancestry Publishing
Anderson Press
Appalachian Consortium Press
Applied Publishing
Arden Press, Inc.
Axiom Information Resources
Bacchus Press Ltd.
Barr-Randol Publishing Co.
Beacon Press
Biblio Press
Bibliographies Unlimited
Blue Heron Publishing, Inc.
Bluestocking Press
BookNotes :(TM) Resources for Small & Self-Publishers
The Borgo Press
Brenner Information Group
Broadway Press
Brunswick Publishing Corporation
Calgre Press, Division of Calgre Inc.
Center For Self-Sufficiency
Chicano Studies Library Publications Unit
THE CHRISTIAN LIBRARIAN
CONNEXIONS DIGEST
Cooperative Children's Book Center
Crisp Publications, Inc.
Steve Davis Publishing
The Denali Press
The Devon Publishing Co., Inc.
DIRECTORY MARKETPLACE
E.T.M. Publishing
Edgeworth & North Books
EDUCATION DIGEST
Energeia Publishing, Inc.
The Evergreen Press
Fallen Leaf Press
Farragut Publishing Co.
Feris-Lee, Press
Festival Publications
Foghorn Press
The Foundation Center
Garrett Park Press
Gaslight Publications
GENEALOGICAL COMPUTING
GGL Educational Press
GOLD, SILVER AND URANIUM FROM SEAS AND OCEANS PROGRESS UPDATE
Graham-Conley Press
Grapevine Publications, Inc.
Gravity Publishing
HearSay Press TM
Hilltop Press
Hollywood Film Archive
Human Kinetics Pub. Inc.
Index House
Infolib Resources
International Consulting Associates, Inc.
J P Publications

Knowledge, Ideas & Trends, Inc. (KIT)
L D A Publishers
Langston Press
Lexikos
Literary Publications Company
LITERARY RESEARCH: A Journal of Scholarly Method
    & Technique
The Lunchroom Press
Maledicta Press
Peter Marcan Publications
McFarland & Company, Inc., Publishers
Microdex Bookshelf
MINORITY PUBLISHERS EXCHANGE
MinRef Press
Mockingbird Press
Moonbeam Publications, Inc.
New Chapter Press
NEW HOPE INTERNATIONAL REVIEW
New York Zoetrope Inc.
Nolo Press
Nolo Press - Occidental
Open Horizons Publishing Company
The Oryx Press
Oxbridge Communications, Inc.
P E N American Center
Packet Press
Paradise Publications
Paragon House Publishers
People's Publishing Co., Inc.
Perivale Press
Poetry Wales Press, Ltd.
Poets & Writers, Inc.
Popular Medicine Press
Prakken Publications
The Preservation Press
PREVIEW: Professional and Reference Literature Review
Professional Publications, Inc.
Progressive Education
PROGRESSIVE PERIODICALS DIRECTORY/UPDATE
QuikRef Publishing
R & E Publishers
Racz Publishing Co.
Reference Service Press
REFERENCE SERVICES REVIEW
The Rensselaerville Systems Training Center
Reunion Research
Running Press
Scarecrow Press
Scojtia Publishing Company
Selah Publishing Co.
Senay Publishing Inc.
SERIALS REVIEW
Shoe Tree Press
SILVER WINGS
Sound View Press
Southwest Research and Information Center
SPECTRUM, A Guide to the Independent Press and
    Informative Organizations
Spectrum Publications
Sterling-Miller
Sunburst Press
Surrey Press
THE TEACHING LIBRARIAN
Theatre Communications Group
Todd Publications
TOOK
Twin Peaks Press
Univelt, Inc.
Upper Access Inc.
Ventana Press
Vestal Press Ltd
Volcano Press, Inc
WASHINGTON INTERNATIONAL ARTS LETTER
Weidner & Sons, Publishing
Willowood Press
WOMEN'S PAGES
Woodbine House
The Wordtree

THE WORKBOOK
THE WRITER'S NOOK NEWS

RELIGION

Aardvark Enterprises
THE ABER BULLETIN
Affinity Press
AFRICAN STUDIES
AGADA
AGAPE
Alleluia Press
Amana Books
AMBASSADOR REPORT
AMERICAN ATHEIST
American Atheist Press
Amnos Publications
ANIMA: The Journal of Human Experience
Anima Publications
AREOPAGUS
Ask Publishing
Astarte Shell Press
Author's Unlimited
AVALOKA: A Journal of Traditional Religion and
    Culture
Axelrod Publishing of Tampa Bay
AXIOS
Axios Newletter, Inc.
BALDER
Ballena Press
THE BANNER
Barclay House
Beacon Press
Bear & Company, Inc.
Bennett Books
Berkeley West Publishing
Bet Alpha Editions
Between The Lines
Biblio Press
Birth Day Publishing Company
Black Light Fellowship
Blue Dolphin Press, Inc.
Blue Water Publishing, Inc.
BOOKS AND RELIGION: A Quarterly Review
BOTH SIDES NOW
Branden Publishing Company
BREAKTHROUGH!
BRILLIANT STAR
Brunswick Publishing Corporation
Buddha Rose Publications
BUDDHISM AT THE CROSSROADS
Buddhist Study Center Press
C.J.L.
CANVAS CHAUTAUQUA MAGAZINE
Celtic Heritage Press, Inc.
THE CENTENNIAL REVIEW
CHAKRA
CHALLENGE: A Journal of Faith and Action in Central
    America
Charlemagne Press
CHASTITY AND HOLINESS
Children Of Mary
Christian Classics, Inc.
THE CHRISTIAN LIBRARIAN
CHRISTIAN*NEW AGE QUARTERLY
THE...CHRONICLE
Citeaux Commentarii Cistercienses
CITEAUX: COMMENTARII CISTERCIENSES
Cityhill Publishing
CLARITY
Clothespin Fever Press
CLUBHOUSE
Comforter Publishing
COMMON BOUNDARY
Commonwealth Press Virginia
Communitas Press
COMPOST NEWSLETTER (CNL)
CONVERGING PATHS
CORNERSTONE

Cosmic Footnotes Publications
Coxland Press
CRC Publications
CREATION/EVOLUTION JOURNAL
CROOKED ROADS
CROSS CURRENTS: Religion & Intellectual Life
Crossway Books
CULTWATCH RESPONSE
DAUGHTER OF SARAH
The Dawn Horse Press
Dawn Rose Press
" "...A DEAD BEAT POET PRODUCTION
DEVIANCE
The Devonshire Publishing Co.
Dharma Publishing
Dominion Press
DREAMS & VISIONS
Dunstan Press
The E.G. Van Press, Inc.
E.T.M. Publishing
Editorial Review
The Edwin Mellen Press
Wm.B. Eerdmans Publishing Co.
THE EMSHOCK LETTER
Epica
EPIPHANY JOURNAL
THE EQUATOR
Esoterica Press
EUROPEAN JUDAISM
Esoterica, The Craft Press
FESTIVAL QUARTERLY
FIDELIS ET VERUS
FISH DRUM MAGAZINE
Foundation Books
Foxfire Press
FREE INQUIRY
Free People Press
Friends United Press
Gilgal Publications
Golden Sceptre
Gong Enterprises, Inc.
GREEN EGG
Greenlawn Press
GREY CITY JOURNAL
Grosvenor USA
Hampshire Books
Harrison House Publishers
The Hegeler Institute
Herald Press
Hilltop Press
Hohm Press
Hope Publishing House
THE HUMANIST
Hunter House Inc., Publishers
Idea House Publishing Company
INNER SEARCH
Inner Traditions International
THE INQUIRER
Integral Publishing
The International University Press
ISSUES
JEWISH LINGUISTIC STUDIES
JEWISH VEGETARIANS OF NORTH AMERICA
JOURNAL FOR ANTHROPOSOPHY
THE JOURNAL OF THE ORDER OF BUDDHIST
   CONTEMPLATIVES
Kalimat Press
Kar-Ben Copies, Inc.
Karunaratne & Sons Ltd.
The Kingston Press, Inc.
KOOKS MAGAZINE
THE LAUGHING MAN: The Alternative to Scientific
   Materialism and Religious Provincialism
Lindisfarne Press
Lions Head Press
Little Red Hen, Inc.
THE LLEWELLYN NEW TIMES
Llewellyn Publications

Los Arboles Publications
LUCHA/STRUGGLE
LuraMedia, Inc.
M.H. Macy & Company
Majority, Inc.
Peter Marcan Publications
MASTER THOUGHTS
MAXINE'S PAGES
McKinzie Publishing Company
MEDIA SPOTLIGHT
Melrose
Meyerbooks, Publisher
MIND MATTERS REVIEW
Mr. Information
MODERN LITURGY
MOKSHA JOURNAL
THE MONIST: An International Quarterly Journal of
   General Philosophical Inquiry.
Moon Publications, Inc.
Moonsquilt Press
Myriad Moods
Naturegraph Publishers, Inc.
NEEDLEPOINT PLUS
NET
Nevada Publications
NEW ANGLICAN REVIEW
NEW CATHOLIC REVIEW
NEW HEAVEN/NEW EARTH
New Saga Publishers
NEW THOUGHT
NiceTown
NightinGale Resources
OBLATES
Occam Publishers
Ocean Star Publications
Ocean Tree Books
OFFICE NUMBER ONE
The Olive Press Publications
Omega Press (formerly Sufi Order Publications)
ON COURSE
Oneworld Publications Ltd.
Orbis Books
The Organization
THE OTHER SIDE
OTISIAN DIRECTORY
Out-Of-Kontrol Data Institute
PalmTree Publishers
Pandit Press, Inc.
Parable Press
Parabola Books
PARABOLA MAGAZINE
Paragon House Publishers
Path Press
Penfield Press
Peter Pauper Press, Inc.
The Petrarch Press
Phanes Press
PHILOSOPHY AND THE ARTS
The Pilgrim Press/United Church Press
THE PLOUGH
POCKET INSPIRATIONS
Poet Papers
POETS. PAINTERS. COMPOSERS.
Political Research Associates
POLITICALLY INCORRECT
Polymath Systems
Progresiv Publishr
PROPER DHARMA SEAL
Quantal Publishing B
QUEEN OF ALL HEARTS
THE QUEST
Quimby Archives
R & E Publishers
Rakhamim Publications
RECONSTRUCTIONIST
Redeemer Resources
Resource Publications, Inc.
Ridge Row Press

Ross Books
Sackbut Press
St. Andrew Press
St. Bede's Publications
ST. CROIX REVIEW
Saqi Books Publisher
SAT SANDESH: THE MESSAGE OF THE MASTERS
The Saunderstown Press
Scarf Press
SCHMAGA
Scojtia Publishing Company
SCP NEWSLETTER
Scroll Publishing Co.
The Second Hand
Sheed & Ward
Sheer Joy! Press
Sherwood Sugden & Company, Publishers
SHINING STAR
SHMATE
Shmate Press
Signature Books
Snow Lion Publications, Inc.
Social Order Series
SOCIETE
Sovereign Press
SPECTRUM, A Guide to the Independent Press and
  Informative Organizations
SPECTRUM—The Wholistic News Magazine
Spectrum Publications
SPECTRUM REVIEW
SPENCER'S BOOK WORLD
Spencer's Int'l Enterprises Corp.
SPL Publishing Group
Star Books, Inc.
THE STARK FIST OF REMOVAL
Stillpoint Publishing
STUDENT LEADERSHIP JOURNAL
STUDIA MYSTICA
STUDIO - A Journal of Christians Writing
Technicians of the Sacred
Tharpa Publications Limited
THEOLOGIA 21
Theosophical Publishing House
Thirteen Colonies Press
THOUGHT, A REVIEW OF CULTURE & IDEA
TODAY
TOLE WORLD
Top Of The Mountain Publishing
Truth Center
UNBRIDLED LUST!
THE UNDERGROUND FOREST - LA SELVA SUB-
  TERRANEA
University of Calgary Press
VAJRA BODHI SEA
Vajra of Yoga Anand Ashram
Valley Lights Publications
Vesta Publications Limited
VOICES - ISRAEL
THE WESLEYAN ADVOCATE
West Anglia Publications
Wheat Forders
Wheel of Fire Press
Windstar Books
WITCHCRAFT DIGEST MAGAZINE (THE WICA
  NEWSLETTER)
Witwatersrand University Press
WONDER TIME
World Wisdom Books, Inc.
WTI Publishing Co.
Yes International Publishers
Zahra Publications
ZONE
Zone Books

RENAISSANCE

Italica Press, Inc.

REPRINTS

Academy Chicago Publishers
Alan Wofsy Fine Arts
Anderson Press
Avery Color Studios
Axelrod Publishing of Tampa Bay
BAKER STREET GAZETTE
Beacon Press
BELLES LETTRES
Black Sparrow Press
Bliss Publishing Company, Inc.
BOTH SIDES NOW
Brandywyne Books
Carousel Press
Cherokee Publishing Company
Earl M Coleman Enterprises, Inc
COMPOST NEWSLETTER (CNL)
The Crossing Press
Edition Stencil
Evans Publications Inc.
Exanimo Press
The Feminist Press at the City University of New York
Free People Press
Fromm International Publishing Corporation
Great Point Press
THE HAPPY THRASHER
THE HAUNTED JOURNAL
Heritage Books, Inc.
Hickman Systems - New Age Books
House of Fire Press
IMAGINATION MAGAZINE
Indelible Inc.
Kitchen Table: Women of Color Press
THE LAUGHING MAN: The Alternative to Scientific
  Materialism and Religious Provincialism
Libertarian Press, Inc./American Book Distributors
Laurence McGilvery
Mountain Press Publishing Co.
Mutual Publishing of Honolulu
NEW AGE DIGEST
NOCTURNAL NEWS
THE NORTHERN ENGINEER
O'Laughlin Press (Irish Genealogical Foundation)
Oregon State University Press
Paladin Enterprises, Inc.
THE PIG PAPER
Pigwidgeon Press
PLOTS
Poets & Writers, Inc.
POISON PEN WRITERS NEWS
Press Pacifica, Ltd.
THE RECORD SUN
Renaissance House Publishers (a division of Jende-Hagan,
  Inc.)
RE:PRINT (AN OCCASIONAL MAGAZINE)
Sackbut Press
SALOME: A JOURNAL FOR THE PERFORMING
  ARTS
Santa Barbara Press
Saqi Books Publisher
Scojtia Publishing Company
Sherwood Sugden & Company, Publishers
SLEUTH JOURNAL
Genny Smith Books
SOCIETE
Sterling-Miller
Still Point Press
Graham Stone
STORIES
Sunburst Press
Texas Monthly Press
Timely Books
THE UNDERGROUND FOREST - LA SELVA SUB-
  TERRANEA
UNION SHOP BLUFF
UNITED LUMBEE NATION TIMES
University of Calgary Press

Happy Rock Press
Lexikos
Micro Pro Litera Press
MIND MATTERS REVIEW
Muso Press
PENNYWHISTLE PEOPLE PAPER
Pennywhistle Press
Pine Cone Press
PROCESSED WORLD
REAL FICTION
RELIX
THE SAN FRANCISCO ALMANAC
SCHMAGA
Scottwall Associates, Publishers
Spirit Press
Star Rover House
Volcano Press, Inc

SATIRE

ACTA VICTORIANA
Afta Press
AILERON, A LITERARY JOURNAL
AMELIA
AMERICAN LIVING
Anaphase II
Ashod Press
Astonisher Press
ATROCITY
BABY SUE
Bean Avenue Publishing
BELLYWASH
The Biting Idge/Miracle Press (Chrysalis Publications)
BLUE HORSE
Blue Horse Publications
BOYS & GIRLS GROW UP
Branden Publishing Company
CACANADADADA REVIEW
Chiron Press
CHIRON REVIEW
THE...CHRONICLE
The Cobham and Hatherton Press
COKEFISH
COLLAGES & BRICOLAGES
COMPOST NEWSLETTER (CNL)
Concourse Press
COYDOG REVIEW
CRAWLSPACE
CROW MAGAZINE
DELIRIUM
Delta Publishing Company
DREAM INTERNATIONAL QUARTERLY
Dumpster Press
EDITOR'S DIGEST
Erespin Press
EUTHANASIA ROSES
Exile Press
FAT TUESDAY
FELL SWOOP
THE FICTION REVIEW
FILM THREAT VIDEO GUIDE
THE FINAL PAGE
FINE MADNESS
Futurum Forlag
GAUNTLET: Exploring the Limits of Free Expression
GYPSY
THE HAPPY THRASHER
Harbinger House
HOBO JUNGLE
HUBRIS
HUMERUS
HUNGRY ZIPPER
I WANT TO EAT YOUR STOMACH
IMAGINATION MAGAZINE
THE IMMIGRANT
Independence Publishers Inc.
ISSUE ONE
JABBERWOCKY
JOURNAL OF POLYMORPHOUS PERVERSITY

K
KIDS LIB NEWS
Kitchen Sink Press
KOOKS MAGAZINE
LAKE EFFECT
LATEST JOKES NEWSLETTER
LONE STAR HUMOR
Lone Star Publications of Humor
THE LOOGIE
THE LOST PERUKE
Lowy Publishing
MASSACRE
Laurence McGilvery
Mermaid Press
THE MILWAUKEE UNDERGRADUATE REVIEW
MOMENTUM
MOTORBOOTY MAGAZINE
Mustang Publishing Co.
NAKED MAN
Naked Man Press
The Neither/Nor Press
Nemeton Publishing
NEW HOPE INTERNATIONAL REVIEW
OFFICE NUMBER ONE
Omega Cottonwood Press
OUROBOROS
Out-Of-Kontrol Data Institute
Ox Head Press
PM (The Pedantic Monthly)
Poor Souls Press/Scaramouche Books
Popular Reality Press
Portmanteau Editions
POTATO EYES
POULTRY - A MAGAZINE OF VOICE
Poultry, Inc.
THE QUAYLE QUARTERLY
Quimby Archives
THE REALIST (NEWSLETTER)
Rio Grande Press
The Saunderstown Press
SCHMAGA
Scribblers Publishing, Ltd.
SKYLARK
SQUARE ONE - A Magazine of Fiction
Star Rover House
THE STARK FIST OF REMOVAL
Station Hill Press
STICKY CARPET DIGEST
Straight Arrow Publishing
STRUGGLE: A Magazine of Proletarian Revolutionary
    Literature
SUB STANDARD
SUB-TERRAIN
III Publishing
Times Change Press
TOOK
Tributary Press
TURNSTILE
Tyro Publishing
UNBRIDLED LUST!
THE UNINTELLIGENCER
Vanitas Press
A VERY SMALL MAGAZINE
THE WAVE
WE ARE THE WEIRD
WIDE OPEN MAGAZINE
WORDS OF WISDOM
WORLD HUMOR AND IRONY MEMBERSHIP SER-
    IAL YEARBOOK (WHIMSY)
X MAGAZINE
X-CALIBRE

SCANDINAVIA

Coxland Press
Culinary Arts Ltd.
Fjord Press
Friends United Press
INITIATIV

867

Jorvik Press
MEMES
Nordic Books
Penfield Press
SCANDINAVIAN REVIEW
TRANSITIONS ABROAD: The Guide to Living,
    Learning, and Working Overseas
White Pine Press
Woodsong Graphics Inc.
Years Press

SCIENCE

AAS HISTORY SERIES
ADVANCES IN THE ASTRONAUTICAL SCIENCES
America West Publishers
American Handwriting Analysis Foundation
Anaphase II
Ander Publications
THE ANIMALS' AGENDA
ASC NEWSLETTER
AVSTAR Publishing Corp.
Bear & Company, Inc.
BIOLOGY DIGEST
Blue Heron Press
THE BOOKWATCH
Borderland Sciences Research Foundation
The Boxwood Press
BRAIN/MIND BULLETIN
Brenner Information Group
British Society For Social Responsibility In Science
BUCKNELL REVIEW
Caravan Press
Carnival Press
THE CENTENNIAL REVIEW
THE CHAOS NETWORK
Cheshire Books
Continuing Education Press, Portland State University
CREATION/EVOLUTION JOURNAL
CRYPTOSYSTEMS JOURNAL
DAEDALUS, Journal of the American Academy of Arts
    and Sciences
The Denali Press
The Devonshire Publishing Co.
Dog-Eared Publications
Dominion Press
Dormant Brain Research and Development Laboratory
DoubLeo Publications
ENERGY UNLIMITED
THE EQUATOR
Esquire Books, Inc.
ETICA & CIENCIA
Fast Forward Publishing
Fir Publishing Company
FOREFRONT—HEALTH INVESTIGATIONS
Free Association Books (FAB)
Frontline Publications
Geoscience Press, Inc.
GET STUPID
GGL Educational Press
GOLD, SILVER AND URANIUM FROM SEAS AND
    OCEANS PROGRESS UPDATE
Gong Enterprises, Inc.
Grapevine Publications, Inc.
Gross Advertising Service
The Heather Foundation
Helix Press
THE HUMAN ECOLOGY AND ENERGY BALANC-
    ING SCIENTIST
Human Ecology Balancing Sciences, Inc.
Human Kinetics Pub. Inc.
Humana Press
Hunter House Inc., Publishers
IASP NEWSLETTER
Infolib Resources
Inquiry Press
Interface Press
International Information Associates
ISI Press

Island Press
Island Publishers
JOURNAL FOR ANTHROPOSOPHY
JOURNAL OF BORDERLAND RESEARCH
JOURNAL OF POLYMORPHOUS PERVERSITY
JOURNAL OF VISION REHABILITATION
Kay Productions
KETTERING REVIEW
KIDSCIENCE
Lighthouse Press
MAD RIVER: A Journal of Essays
MEDICAL HISTORY
Medical Physics Publishing Corp.
Meridional Publications
MIND MATTERS REVIEW
MOONSTONE BLUE
Multi Media Arts
MY LIFE DEPENDS ON YOU
N-B-T-V
The Neither/Nor Press
NET
THE NEW RAIN MAGAZINE
THE NORTHERN ENGINEER
THE NORTHERN REVIEW
Orchises Press
ORGANICA
The Organization
Organization for Equal Education of the Sexes, Inc.
    (OEES)
PABLO LENNIS
Paideia Publishers
Dr. Homer W. Parker, P.E.
Peavine Publications
T.H. Peek, Publisher
Plexus Publishing, Inc.
POLITICALLY INCORRECT
Polymath Systems
Popular Medicine Press
PROCESSED WORLD
Progresiv Publishr
PSYCHOANALYTIC BOOKS
QED
QUANTUM: Science Fiction & Fantasy Review
Quarterly Committee of Queen's University
QUEEN'S QUARTERLY: A Canadian Review
THE QUEST
RADICAL SCIENCE SERIES
Rand Editions/Tofua Press
RESONANCE
Rocky Top Publications
Ross Books
SCIENCE AND NATURE, The Annual of Marxist
    Philosophy for Natural Scientists
SCIENCE AND TECHNOLOGY
SCIENCE BOOKS & FILMS
SCIENCE FOR PEOPLE
SCIENCE/HEALTH ABSTRACTS
Scojtia Publishing Company
Sea Challengers
SOVIET SPACEFLIGHT REPORT
STARWIND
Starwise Publications
Sunstone Publications
SURVIVE & WIN
Syzygy
Texas Monthly Press
Third Lung Press
THRESHOLDS JOURNAL
Timber Press
TOWARDS
UNBRIDLED LUST!
Univelt, Inc.
University of Calgary Press
VDT NEWS
Weidner & Sons, Publishing
Wheat Forders
Woodbine House
Woods Hole Press

WTI Publishing Co.
Zagier & Urruty Publicaciones

SCIENCE FICTION

AAS HISTORY SERIES
ACTIVIST
Algol Press
ALL OF THE ABOVE
Angst World Library
Argo Press
ARGONAUT
Ashley Books, Inc.
Astonisher Press
AURORA
Author's Unlimited
Avalanche Press
Baker Street Publications
Beacon Press
Blue Heron Press
BLUE LIGHT RED LIGHT
BLUE LIGHTS
Blue Lights Publications
BOMB MAGAZINE
THE BOOKWATCH
The Borgo Press
Broken Mirrors Press
CANADIAN AUTHOR & BOOKMAN
The Carolina Wren Press
Carpenter Press
Carroll & Graf Publishers, Inc.
CENTER
Center Press
Coach House Press
COLLAGES & BRICOLAGES
A COMPANION IN ZEOR
COMPOST NEWSLETTER (CNL)
Cosmic Circus Productions
The F. Marion Crawford Memorial Society
CRAZYQUILT LITERARY QUARTERLY
CULTURE CONCRETE
The Devonshire Publishing Co.
The Donning Company / Publishers
DREAM INTERNATIONAL QUARTERLY
DREAMS AND NIGHTMARES
Chris Drumm Books
DuReve Publications
Earth Star Publications
ECOSOCIALIST REVIEW
ELDRITCH SCIENCE
EMERALD CITY COMIX & STORIES
ENTROPY NEGATIVE
EOTU, Magazine of Experimental Fiction
Excellence Enterprises
FINE MADNESS
Fir Publishing Company
FISH DRUM MAGAZINE
FORBIDDEN LINES
Free Association Books (FAB)
Frozen Waffles Press/Shattered Sidewalks Press; 25th
  Century Chapbooks
The Future Press
Futurum Forlag
GALAXY CLASS
Gallopade Publishing Group
THE GAME'S AFOOT
GATEAVISA
GATES OF PANDRAGON
GREY CITY JOURNAL
Gryphon Publications
GUARD THE NORTH
HARDWARE, The Magazine of SF Technophilia
HAUNTS
HAWAI'I REVIEW
Heresy Press
HORIZONS BEYOND
Ianus Publications, Inc.
THE IDEOLOGY OF MADNESS
THE IMMIGRANT

Infinite Savant Publishing
INFINITY LIMITED, A Journal for the Somewhat
  Eccentric
Infolib Resources
INNER SEARCH
Inverted-A, Inc.
IT GOES ON THE SHELF
JABBERWOCKY
Kent Publications, Inc.
L.A.N.D.
LAKE SUPERIOR MAGAZINE
LOCUS: The Newspaper of the Science Fiction Field
Lorien House
THE MAGAZINE OF SPECULATIVE POETRY
THE MAGE
Manuscript Press
MATI
Mayhaven Publishing
MEMES
MIDNIGHT ZOO
THE MODEL & TOY COLLECTOR
MOONSTONE BLUE
Nemeton Publishing
The Nemo Press
NET
New Fantasy Publications
NEW MOON
NEW PATHWAYS
THE NOCTURNAL LYRIC
NON COMPOS MENTIS
Ocean View Books
OHIO RENAISSANCE REVIEW
OPOSSUM HOLLER TAROT
OTISIAN DIRECTORY
THE OVERLOOK CONNECTION
OWLFLIGHT MAGAZINE
Owlswick Press
PABLO LENNIS
PANDORA
PAPERBACK PARADE
PENGUIN DIP
PHOEBE, THE GEORGE MASON REVIEW
PIG IRON
Pig Iron Press
POISON PEN WRITERS NEWS
POLITICALLY INCORRECT
Polymath Systems
Porcepic Books
Pottersfield Press
PROTOCULTURE ADDICTS
PULPHOUSE: THE HARDBACK MAGAZINE
Pulphouse Publishing
Purple Mouth Press
QUANTUM: Science Fiction & Fantasy Review
RGM Publications
Rio Grande Press
RISING STAR
RIVERSIDE QUARTERLY
ROMANIAN REVIEW
THE ROMANTIST
SAMIZDAT
Savant Garde Workshop
SCAVENGER'S NEWSLETTER
SCIENCE FICTION CHRONICLE
THE SCIENCE FICTION CONVENTION REGISTER
Scojtia Publishing Company
Scribblers Publishing, Ltd.
SF**3
Shepherd Books
SOM Publishing, division of School of Metaphysics
SPACE AND TIME
Space and Time Press
SPECTRUM STORIES
SPIRIT MAGAZINE
SPIT
SPWAO SHOWCASE
SQUARE ONE - A Magazine of Fiction
StarLance Publications

STARWIND
SteelDragon Press
Graham Stone
Sweet Forever Publishing
Tafford Publishing, Inc.
TAPAS
III Publishing
Triton Books + Gallery
2AM MAGAZINE
2AM Publications
Ultramarine Publishing Co., Inc.
UNBRIDLED LUST!
Underwood-Miller, Inc. & Brandywyne Books
Unique Graphics
UNIROD MAGAZINE
Univelt, Inc.
VANDELOECHT'S FICTION MAGAZINE
VELOCITIES
VOYAGES SF
WONDER
Wonder Press
Woodsong Graphics Inc.
Wordcraft
WORLD OF FANDOM MAGAZINE
THE WRITERS' BAR-B-Q
WTI Publishing Co.
XENOPHILIA
Xenos Books
Zirlinson Publishing

SCOTLAND

Celtic Heritage Press, Inc.
DeerTrail Books
Dufour Editions Inc.
KELTIC FRINGE
THE NEW DANCE REVIEW
NEW HOPE INTERNATIONAL REVIEW
Penfield Press
Rowan Mountain Press
Stone Circle Press
Zephyr Press

SCOUTING

dbS Productions
Ramalo Publications

SELF-HELP

Able Publishing
Adams-Hall Publishing
American Impressions
Aroc Publishing
Ascension Publishing
Ask Publishing
Aslan Publishing
ASPECTS
Attic Press
Barclay House
Blue Dolphin Press, Inc.
Brason-Sargar Publications
C.C. Publishing Co.
Cable Publishing
Challenger Press
CompCare Publishers
Conari Press
Cooper House Publishing Inc.
CREATIVITY CONNECTION
D.B.A. Books
DuReve Publications
Earth-Love Publishing House
Envirographics
Esoterica, The Craft Press
The Evergreen Press
FREE SPIRIT: NEWS AND VIEWS ON GROWING UP
Free Spirit Publishing Inc.
Fulcrum, Inc.
Gateway Books
Glen Abbey Books, Inc.
Grace and Goddess Unlimited

GREEN MULTILOGUE
THE HAPPY THRASHER
Haypenny Press
HEALING PATH
Health Press
Human Kinetics Pub. Inc.
Humana Press
IBS Press
IDEAS IN INVESTING
Impact Publishers, Inc.
Inner Vision Publishing Company
Inner Wealth Press
Intermountain Publishing
INTUITIVE EXPLORATIONS
Knowledge, Ideas & Trends, Inc. (KIT)
Littlebooks
Los Arboles Publications
Billy Jack Ludwig Holding Co.
LuraMedia, Inc.
Maupin House
MedLife Communications, Inc.
Meridian Learning Systems
Metagnosis Publications
Monroe Press
New Liberty Press
New Voyage Books
New World Library
Obsessive Compulsive Anonymous
Open Horizons Publishing Company
Paragraph Publications
Persona Publications
Personal Efficiency Programs, Inc.
THE PERSONAL MAGNETISM HOME STUDY
  COURSE ON ALL HUMAN POWERS
Perspectives Press
Princess Publishing
Professional Counselor Books
Prudhomme Press
Publitec Editions
Recovery Publications
RED HOT WORK-AT-HOME REPORT
RURAL NETWORK ADVOCATE
SCIENCE/HEALTH ABSTRACTS
The Seal Press
Shiro Publishers
Shoe Tree Press
Siftsoft
SMALL PRESS MONTHLY
SOMNIAL TIMES
Sororal Publishing
Steel Balls Press
Stepping Stone Books
Stillpoint Publishing
TEC Publications
Top Of The Mountain Publishing
Tudor Publishers, Inc.
Tyro Publishing
Upper Access Inc.
Vesper Publishing
White Rose Publishing
Williamson Publishing Company, Inc.
Wind River Institute Press
Window Publications
Yes International Publishers
Yes You Can Press

SENIOR CITIZENS

Alpenglow Press
American Source Books
AUSTIN SENIOR CITIZEN
Barclay House
Bellwether Productions, Inc.
Brenner Information Group
BROOMSTICK: A PERIODICAL BY, FOR, AND
  ABOUT WOMEN OVER FORTY
The Carolina Wren Press
Center for Public Representation
Christmans

Stone Circle Press
STORY
Stride Publications
STRUGGLE: A Magazine of Proletarian Revolutionary Literature
STUDIO ONE
Talon Books Ltd
TANDAVA
TAPAS
TAPROOT LITERARY REVIEW
The Teitan Press, Inc.
A THEATER OF BLOOD
Thunder Creek Publishing Co-operative
Tiptoe Literary Service
TURNSTILE
Turnstone Press
2AM MAGAZINE
2AM Publications
UNBRIDLED LUST!
UNIROD MAGAZINE
THE VAMPIRE JOURNAL
THE VINCENT BROTHERS REVIEW
Volunteer Publications
White Pine Press
WONDER
WORDS OF WISDOM
WORLD LETTER
YELLOW SILK: Journal Of Erotic Arts
Zirlinson Publishing

SINGLES

Gateway Books
GOKOOMA
MIRAGE
Nunciata
ROMEO NEWSLETTER
RURAL NETWORK ADVOCATE
SINCERE SINGLES
SINGLE SCENE
SINGLE TODAY
Star Books, Inc.
Arnie Wolman Co.

SOCIAL WORK

Lyceum Books, Inc.

SOCIALIST

ACTIVIST
AIM MAGAZINE
Autonomedia, Inc.
Bergin & Garvey Publishers
Between The Lines
BORDER/LINES
Cardinal Press, Inc.
Children Of Mary
COLLAGES & BRICOLAGES
Crime and Social Justice Associates, Inc.
CROSSCURRENTS
DE NAR
DIE FAT PIGGY DIE
THE DIGGER
Dufour Editions Inc.
ECOSOCIALIST REVIEW
FIDELIS ET VERUS
Five Fingers Press
FIVE FINGERS REVIEW
Free Association Books (FAB)
FREE PRESS
GREY CITY JOURNAL
GUARDIAN
Homeward Press
Institute for Southern Studies
International Publishers Co. Inc.
ISRAEL HORIZONS
JEWISH CURRENTS
THE KIBBUTZ JOURNAL
Kitchen Table: Women of Color Press
LEFT CURVE

LIBERATION! Journal of Revolutionary Marxism
LINKS
LITTLE FREE PRESS
LOVE AND RAGE, A Revolutionary Anarchist News-monthly
MEMES
MIDDLE EAST REPORT
THE MILITANT
NEW UNIONIST
OTISIAN DIRECTORY
PEOPLE'S CULTURE
POETRY OF THE PEOPLE
PROCESSED WORLD
RADICAL AMERICA
RADICAL SCIENCE SERIES
RED DIRT
Red Letter Press
See Sharp Press
Singlejack Books
SLEUTH JOURNAL
Smyrna Press
SOCIAL JUSTICE: A JOURNAL OF CRIME, CON-FLICT, & WORLD ORDER
SOCIALISM AND DEMOCRACY
SOCIALISM AND SEXUALITY
South End Press
SPECTRUM, A Guide to the Independent Press and Informative Organizations
Spectrum Publications
Star Rover House
STRUGGLE: A Magazine of Proletarian Revolutionary Literature
SUB-TERRAIN
Third World First
Times Change Press
UNBRIDLED LUST!
VIEWPOINT
Zed Books Ltd.

SOCIETY

ADOLESCENCE
ANTI-APARTHEID NEWS
ARTPAPER
AZTLAN: A Journal of Chicano Studies
Between The Lines
BLACK MOUNTAIN REVIEW
Blue Bird Publishing
Borealis Press Limited
C.C. Publishing Co.
Carnival Press
CASE ANALYSIS
Center for Public Representation
Chandler & Sharp Publishers, Inc.
CHANGE: The Journal of the Synergetic Society
Chelsea Green Publishing Company
Chicano Studies Research Center Publications
COMMON SENSE
COMMUNITY ECONOMICS
Community Service, Inc.
COMMUNITY SERVICE NEWSLETTER
COSMOPOLITAN CONTACT
Crime and Social Justice Associates, Inc.
CROOKED ROADS
CROSSCURRENTS
CULTURE CONCRETE
Cumberland
CUMBERLAND
The Denali Press
The Edwin Mellen Press
ETC Publications
FAMILY THERAPY
GATEAVISA
GREEN SYNTHESIS-A NEWSLETTER AND JOUR-NAL FOR SOCIAL ECOLOGY, DEEP ECOLOGY, BIOREGIONALISM, ECOFEMINISM, AND THE GREEN MOVEMENT
Grosvenor USA
THE HAPPY THRASHER

HEALING PATH
The Heather Foundation
THE HUMAN ECOLOGY AND ENERGY BALANC-
ING SCIENTIST
Human Ecology Balancing Sciences, Inc.
Institute For Community Economics
Institute for Southern Studies
The Institute of Mind and Behavior Press
INTERCULTURE
The International University Press
JOURNAL FOR ANTHROPOSOPHY
THE JOURNAL OF MIND AND BEHAVIOR
K
Kettering Foundation
KETTERING REVIEW
THE KIBBUTZ JOURNAL
Knowledge Systems, Inc.
KOOKS MAGAZINE
The Philip Lesly Company
Libra Publishers, Inc.
LIZZENGREASY
THE LOOGIE
THE LUNDIAN
M.H. Macy & Company
MEN'S REPORT
THE MIDWEST QUARTERLY
Modern Media
New Society Publishers
The New South Company
The Noble Press, Inc.
NOOSPAPERS
Nucleus Publications
Occam Publishers
Oneworld Publications Ltd.
OSTENTATIOUS MIND
THE OTHER SIDE
Out-Of-Kontrol Data Institute
PEACE NEWS "For Nonviolent Revolution"
PIGEON CREEK CLARION
PROCESSED WORLD
Psyche Press
Red Alder Books
River Basin Publishing Co.
ROMANIAN REVIEW
SCANDINAVIAN REVIEW
SELF AND SOCIETY
SMALL PRESS NEWS
SOCIAL JUSTICE: A JOURNAL OF CRIME, CON-
FLICT, & WORLD ORDER
Social Order Series
SOCIAL POLICY
SOCIAL PROBLEMS
SOCIETY
Southwest Research and Information Center
Sovereign Press
SPECTRUM REVIEW
THOUGHTS FOR ALL SEASONS: The Magazine of
Epigrams
Times Change Press
Tippy Reed Publishing
TOOK
Tower Press
UNBRIDLED LUST!
THE UTNE READER
VICTIMOLOGY AN INTERNATIONAL JOURNAL
VIEWPOINT
Volcano Press, Inc
THE WASHINGTON MONTHLY
Westburg Associates, Publishers
Wheel of Fire Press
THE WORKBOOK
Youth Policy Institute
Zed Books Ltd.

SOCIOLOGY

Adaptive Living
AFRICA TODAY
African American Images

Agathon Press
AIM MAGAZINE
Appalachian Consortium Press
The Archives Press
AREOPAGUS
ARMED FORCES & SOCIETY
Big River Publishing
Black Rose Books Ltd.
BORDER/LINES
The Borgo Press
Broken Rifle Press
Buddha Rose Publications
CASE ANALYSIS
Center for Public Representation
Chandler & Sharp Publishers, Inc.
Cheshire Books
THE CHURCH, FARM AND TOWN
CINEASTE MAGAZINE
Claridge Press
Coker Publishing House
COMMUNITY DEVELOPMENT JOURNAL
Community Service, Inc.
COMMUNITY SERVICE NEWSLETTER
The Compass Press
CONTEMPORARY WALES
Crime and Social Justice Associates, Inc.
CRITICAL REVIEW: An Interdisciplinary Journal
CULTURE CONCRETE
DeerTrail Books
Distinctive Publishing Corp.
DOCTOR-PATIENT STUDIES
DorPete Press
Elm Publications
Elysium Growth Press
Feminist Mens' Publications
FREE LIFE
Gain Publications
GAVEA-BROWN
Gavea-Brown Publications
General Hall, Inc.
GREY CITY JOURNAL
Gumbs & Thomas Publishers, Inc.
Haight-Ashbury Publications
Harbor Publishing Company
Holger Harfst, Publisher
Harrow and Heston, Publishers
HearSay Press TM
The Heather Foundation
Human Kinetics Pub. Inc.
ILR Press
INFINITY LIMITED, A Journal for the Somewhat
Eccentric
Insight Press
Institute for Southern Studies
The Institute of Mind and Behavior Press
Interlink Publishing Group, Inc.
Jalmar Press
JOTS (Journal of the Senses)
JOURNAL FOR ANTHROPOSOPHY
THE JOURNAL OF MIND AND BEHAVIOR
THE JOURNAL OF PAN AFRICAN STUDIES
JOURNAL OF PSYCHOACTIVE DRUGS
JOURNAL OF THEORETICAL PSYCHOLOGY
KAIROS, A Journal of Contemporary Thought and
Criticism
Karunaratne & Sons Ltd.
KETTERING REVIEW
Knowledge Systems, Inc.
Kumarian Press, Inc.
LIZZENGREASY
Lyceum Books, Inc.
M.H. Macy & Company
Maisonneuve Press
Metamorphous Press
Mountain State Press
Multi Media Arts
New Atlantis Press
THE NEW ENGLAND QUARTERLY

New Idea Press, Inc.
OIKOS: A JOURNAL OF ECOLOGY AND COMMUN-
ITY
OneOff Publishing
OSTENTATIOUS MIND
OUR GENERATION
T.H. Peek, Publisher
PLAY & CULTURE
POLITICAL BEHAVIOR
Pop Void Publications
PROCESSED WORLD
Progresiv Publishr
Psyche Press
Royal Purcell, Publisher
QSKY Publishing/Independent Publishing
R & E Publishers
R & M Publishing Company
Reunion Research
ROMANIAN REVIEW
Saqi Books Publisher
SCHMAGA
SCIENCE AND TECHNOLOGY
Signature Books
SINGLE SCENE
Singlejack Books
Slate Press
Small Helm Press
SOCIAL JUSTICE: A JOURNAL OF CRIME, CON-
FLICT, & WORLD ORDER
SOCIAL POLICY
SOCIAL PROBLEMS
SOCIALISM AND DEMOCRACY
SOCIETY
SOCIOLOGY OF SPORT JOURNAL
SPECTRUM, A Guide to the Independent Press and
Informative Organizations
Spectrum Publications
Still Point Press
Ten Speed Press
THIRD WAY
Tide Book Publishing Company
Tower Press
UNBRIDLED LUST!
Univelt, Inc.
University of Massachusetts Press
VIETNAM GENERATION: A Journal of Recent History
and Contemporary Issues
Voice of Liberty Publications
The Wanderer's Ink
WARM FUZZY NEWSLETTER
Waterfront Books
B. L. Winch & Associates
WITHIN & BEYOND
Witwatersrand University Press
Youth Policy Institute
ZONE
Zone Books

SOLAR

Brick House Publishing Co., Inc.
CJE NEWSLETTER (Newsletter of the Coalition for Jobs
& the Environment)
Grapevine Publications, Inc.
GREEN MULTILOGUE
POETRY OF THE PEOPLE
UNBRIDLED LUST!

SOUTH

Appalachian Consortium Press
Arbiter Press
CAESURA
CANVAS CHAUTAUQUA MAGAZINE
A CAROLINA LITERARY COMPANION
The Carolina Wren Press
Cherokee Publishing Company
Colonial Press
The F. Marion Crawford Memorial Society
THE CRESCENT REVIEW

FOXFIRE
Foxfire Press
The Guild Bindery Press, Inc.
Gut Punch Press
Institute for Southern Studies
MAXINE'S PAGES
Midmarch Arts Press
Misty Hill Press
Ocean Tree Books
Peachtree Publishers, Ltd.
PIKEVILLE REVIEW
Redbird Press, Inc.
THE ROMANTIST
Rose Publishing Co.
Sentinel Books
Sherwood Sugden & Company, Publishers
Signal Books
SOUTHERN EXPOSURE
SOUTHERN QUARTERLY: A Journal of the Arts in the
South
SOUTHERN READER
Southern Resources Unlimited
Starchand Press
Third Lung Press
TRADITION
THE VIRGINIA QUARTERLY REVIEW

SOUTHWEST

Affiliated Writers of America, Inc.
Amador Publishers
Ancient City Press
ARIZONA COAST
Baker Street Publications
Ballena Press
BOOK TALK
BOOKS OF THE SOUTHWEST
Cardinal Press, Inc.
Cinco Puntos Press
CONCHO RIVER REVIEW
CROSS TIMBERS REVIEW
Duende Press
Dusty Dog Press
EDITOR'S DIGEST
Evans Publications Inc.
Fiesta Books Inc.
FISH DRUM MAGAZINE
Fulcrum, Inc.
Gallery West Associates
GCBA Publishing
Harbinger House
HORIZONS WEST
Insight Press
Johnson Books
KUMQUAT MERINGUE
Levite of Apache
MALLIFE
Minor Heron Press
Museum of New Mexico Press
THE NEW DANCE REVIEW
Northland Publishing Company
Ocean Tree Books
Old West Publishing Co.
Out West Publishing
Outlaw Books
EL PALACIO
Peccary Press
Pepper Publishing
Point Riders Press
Primer Publishers
Pruett Publishing Company
Red Crane Books
RENEGADE
Research & Discovery Publications
Rio Grande Press
The Rydal Press
SE LA VIE WRITER'S JOURNAL
Sierra Oaks Publishing Company
Gibbs Smith, Publisher

875

SOUTHWEST REVIEW
Still Point Press
Studia Hispanica Editors
Sunstone Press
TEXAS WINEMARKET NEWS
Treasure Chest Publications, Inc.
TREASURE HUNTING RESEARCH BULLETIN
TUCUMCARI LITERARY REVIEW
WESTERN AMERICAN LITERATURE
THE WHOLE CHILE PEPPER

SPACE

AAS HISTORY SERIES
ACTIVIST
ADVANCES IN THE ASTRONAUTICAL SCIENCES
BLUE LIGHTS
Blue Lights Publications
Blue Water Publishing, Inc.
Borderland Sciences Research Foundation
Brenner Information Group
Caliban Press
The Carolina Wren Press
COMPOST NEWSLETTER (CNL)
THE EMSHOCK LETTER
Futurum Forlag
GATEAVISA
GREY CITY JOURNAL
THE IMMIGRANT
INFINITY LIMITED, A Journal for the Somewhat
  Eccentric
JABBERWOCKY
JOURNAL OF BORDERLAND RESEARCH
KIDSCIENCE
MOONSTONE BLUE
NET
NRG
Polymath Systems
SCIENCE AND TECHNOLOGY
SOVIET SPACEFLIGHT REPORT
THE SPACE PRESS
THE STAR BEACON
STARWIND
Starwise Publications
Sunstone Publications
Texas Monthly Press
UNBRIDLED LUST!
WITHIN & BEYOND
Woodbine House

SPAIN

Amana Books
Esoterica Press
Michigan Romance Studies
Pocahontas Press, Inc.
White Pine Press

SPEAKING

Bonus Books, Inc.
Foundation Books

SPIRITUAL

Ability Workshop Press
Affinity Press
AGADA
Alamo Square Press
ALL AVAILABLE LIGHT
Amana Books
America West Publishers
APPALACHIAN HERITAGE
The Archives Press
AREOPAGUS
Artemis Press, Inc.
Ascension Publishing
Ash Tree Publishing
Aslan Publishing
ASPECTS
Astarte Shell Press
AUM U.S.A. Co. Ltd.

Auromere Books and Imports
Avalanche Press
AVALOKA: A Journal of Traditional Religion and
  Culture
Avery Publishing Group, Inc.
BALDER
Barclay House
Barn Owl Books
Beacon Press
Bear & Company, Inc.
Bear Tribe Publishing
Bennett Books
Bergin & Garvey Publishers
Beyond Words Publishing, Inc.
Birth Day Publishing Company
Borderland Sciences Research Foundation
BOTH SIDES NOW
Brason-Sargar Publications
Brunswick Publishing Corporation
Buddha Rose Publications
Buddhist Study Center Press
The Builders Publishing Company
THE BUILDERS QUARTERLY
Burning Books
Caravan Press
Cassandra Press
Celestial Gifts Publishing
CHAKRA
Children Of Mary
CHRISTIAN*NEW AGE QUARTERLY
Christmas
City Spirit Publications
Coastline Publishing Company
COLLABORATION
COLOR WHEEL
Comforter Publishing
COMMON BOUNDARY
CONNECTICUT NATURALLY
Cosmoenergetics Publications
Coxland Press
CRCS Publications
CRYSTAL RAINBOW
DAUGHTER OF SARAH
The Dawn Horse Press
Dawn Rose Press
The Devonshire Publishing Co.
Dharma Publishing
Double M Press
DREAM INTERNATIONAL QUARTERLY
DuReve Publications
E.T.M. Publishing
Earth Star Publications
Earth-Love Publishing House
Earth-Song Press
EMERGING
THE EMSHOCK LETTER
Esoterica, The Craft Press
Fell Publishers, Inc.
FIDELIS ET VERUS
The Findhorn Press
Flax Press, Inc.
FORESIGHT MAGAZINE
Friends United Press
Gateways Books And Tapes
Globe Press Books
Golden Sceptre
Great Western Publishing Company
GREEN MULTILOGUE
Greenlawn Press
Guarionex Press Ltd.
Happy Rock Press
HEALING PATH
HEARTSONG REVIEW
HEAVEN BONE
Helios House
Herald Press
Hickman Systems - New Age Books
Himalayan Publishers

Hohm Press
Hope Publishing House
IBS Press
INNER JOURNEYS
INNER SEARCH
Inner Vision Publishing Company
Inner Wealth Press
Integral Publishing
INTEGRAL YOGA MAGAZINE
JOURNAL FOR ANTHROPOSOPHY
JOURNAL OF BORDERLAND RESEARCH
THE JOURNAL OF THE ORDER OF BUDDHIST
   CONTEMPLATIVES
Journey Publications
Knowledge Systems, Inc.
HJ Kramer, Inc
Life Energy Media
Lindisfarne Press
LivingQuest
THE LLEWELLYN NEW TIMES
Llewellyn Publications
LP Publications (Teleos Institute)
LuraMedia, Inc.
M.H. Macy & Company
MAGICAL BLEND
Magical Blend
McOne Press
MEDIA SPOTLIGHT
Melrose
Metagnosis Publications
MIND MATTERS REVIEW
Mr. Information
MODERN LITURGY
Moon Publications, Inc.
Mortal Press
MUSIC OF THE SPHERES
MUSICWORKS: THE CANADIAN AUDIO-VISUAL
   JOURNAL OF SOUND EXPLORATIONS
Naturegraph Publishers, Inc.
NET
NEW ANGLICAN REVIEW
NEW CATHOLIC REVIEW
NEW FRONTIER
NEW HEAVEN/NEW EARTH
NEW JERSEY NATURALLY
NEW THOUGHT
New World Library
NEW YORK NATURALLY
Nicolas-Hays, Inc.
Non-Stop Books
NOSTALGIA, A Sentimental State of Mind
Nucleus Publications
OBLATES
Ocean Star Publications
Omega Cottonwood Press
Omega Press (formerly Sufi Order Publications)
ON COURSE
ONE EARTH
Oness Press
Oneworld Publications Ltd.
OTISIAN DIRECTORY
PalmTree Publishers
Parabola Books
PARABOLA MAGAZINE
Paragon House Publishers
Path Press
The Pilgrim Press/United Church Press
THE PLOUGH
POETS. PAINTERS. COMPOSERS.
Polymath Systems
RADIANCE, The Magazine For Large Women
Rakhamim Publications
Resource Publications, Inc.
RFD
Rio Grande Press
Rodmell Press
Rolling House Publications
S.I.R.S. Caravan Publications

SACRED FIRE
St. Andrew Press
St. Bede's Publications
Sandpiper Press
SAT SANDESH: THE MESSAGE OF THE MASTERS
SCP NEWSLETTER
THE SCREAM OF THE BUDDHA
Seed Center
Seventh-Wing Publications
Silver Forest Publishing
SOCIETE
SOM Publishing, division of School of Metaphysics
Sparrow Hawk Press
SPECTRUM—The Wholistic News Magazine
SPECTRUM REVIEW
THE STAR BEACON
Star Books, Inc.
STARLIGHT
Station Hill Press
Stillpoint Publishing
Stone Circle Press
Sunstone Publications
Sweet Forever Publishing
TAI CHI
TAPLIGHT NEWSLETTER
Theosophical Publishing House
Threshold Books
Tiger Moon
Timeless Books
Times Change Press
Top Of The Mountain Publishing
Tough Dove Books
Trabarni Productions
TRENDS & PREDICTIONS ANALYST
UNARIUS LIGHT
UNBRIDLED LUST!
Upper Access Inc.
Upword Press
Valkyrie Publishing House
Valley Lights Publications
Vision Quest Publishing
THE VITAL FORCE
Patrick Walsh Press
Wayfarer Publications
Samuel Weiser, Inc.
Wheat Forders
Whitford Press
WILDFIRE: A NETWORKING MAGAZINE
Windstar Books
THE WISE WOMAN
WITHIN & BEYOND
Arnie Wolman Co.
WOMAN OF POWER
WTI Publishing Co.
Yes International Publishers

STOICISM

Bandanna Books

STORYTELLING

Aardvark Enterprises
BREAKTHROUGH!
Circumpolar Press
Foundation Books
HOBO STEW REVIEW
KELTIC FRINGE
THE LUNDIAN
LuraMedia, Inc.
Modern Media
Moonlight Press
Open Horizons Publishing Company
Storytime Ink International
Stride Publications
Ward Hill Press
THE WOLSKE'S BAY STAR
WRITER'S GUIDELINES MAGAZINE
Yellow Moon Press

PLANTAGENET PRODUCTIONS, Libraries of Spoken
  Word Recordings and of Stagescripts
POETS. PAINTERS. COMPOSERS.
Prima Publishing
PUNCTURE
Quiet Tymes, Inc.
Ranger International Productions
RELIX
Resource Publications, Inc.
THE ROCK HALL REPORTER
St. Andrew Press
St. Bede's Publications
SCHMAGA
THE SMALL PRESS BOOK REVIEW
SOULLESS STRUCTURES
SOUND CHOICE
Station Hill Press
STONE TALK
Stride Publications
SUBTEXT
THEY WON'T STAY DEAD!
Timeless Books
TOAD HIWAY
Toad Hiway Press
TOOK
Top Of The Mountain Publishing
UMBRELLA
Underwhich Editions
UNIROD MAGAZINE
Vestal Press Ltd
VIRGIN MEAT
Vision Quest Publishing
W.D.C. PERIOD
White Rose Publishing
Wind River Institute Press
World Music Press
WORLD OF FANDOM MAGAZINE
Writers Forum
X MAGAZINE
Yellow Moon Press

TAROT

BALDER
Coxland Press
OTISIAN DIRECTORY
Ramp Creek Publishing Inc
UNBRIDLED LUST!
Samuel Weiser, Inc.

TAXES

Applied Publishing
Avery Publishing Group, Inc.
CANADIAN MONEYSAVER
CJE NEWSLETTER (Newsletter of the Coalition for Jobs
  & the Environment)
COMMON SENSE
Eastern Caribbean Institute
Robert Erdmann Publishing
Fir Publishing Company
GCBA Publishing
Gringo Guides, Inc.
Independent Research Services of Irvine (IRIS/I)
INTERNATIONAL TAX AND BUSINESS LAWYER
The Organization
POLITICALLY INCORRECT
THE PRAGMATIST
PSI Research/The Oasis Press
RENT-TO-OWN LEGAL & FINANCIAL BULLETIN
SPECTRUM, A Guide to the Independent Press and
  Informative Organizations
Spectrum Publications
Tax Property Investor, Inc.
Upper Access Inc.
Wolcotts, Inc.

TELEVISION

BAKER STREET GAZETTE
Between The Lines

BLUE LIGHTS
Blue Lights Publications
BOOK MARKETING UPDATE
COFFEE & DONUTS
Festival Publications
FUSE MAGAZINE
KOOKS MAGAZINE
OTISIAN DIRECTORY
Out-Of-Kontrol Data Institute
P-FORM
Prudhomme Press
S.E.T. FREE: The Newsletter Against Television
SCRIPT IDEAS
SLEUTH JOURNAL
Zirlinson Publishing

TENNESSEE

CJE NEWSLETTER (Newsletter of the Coalition for Jobs
  & the Environment)
Ocean Tree Books

TENNYSON, ALFRED LORD

COLLAGES & BRICOLAGES
Myriad Moods

TEXAS

AUSTIN SENIOR CITIZEN
Author's Unlimited
C.C. Publishing Co.
Clothespin Fever Press
CONCHO RIVER REVIEW
Corona Publishing Co.
EDITOR'S DIGEST
E-Heart Press, Inc.
Falcon Press Publishing Company
Gulf Publishing Company
Ledero Press
Midmark Arts Press
Milner Press
Myriad Moods
Quixote Press
Rio Grande Press
SALAD
SALT LICK
SE LA VIE WRITER'S JOURNAL
Shearer Publishing
Still Point Press
Studia Hispanica Editors
TEXAS WINEMARKET NEWS
WESTERN AMERICAN LITERATURE

TEXTBOOKS

Accent on Music
Applied Publishing
Arden Press, Inc.
Avery Publishing Group, Inc.
Barr-Randol Publishing Co.
Beacon Press
Bergin & Garvey Publishers
Beyond Athletics
Buddha Rose Publications
Calibre Press, Inc.
Chandler & Sharp Publishers, Inc.
Children Of Mary
Circumpolar Press
Classic Theatre For Children, Publishers
The Clyde Press
Communicom Publishing Company
Cosmic Footnotes Publications
The Counter-Propaganda Press
Crystal Publishers, Inc.
Directed Media, Inc.
Distinctive Publishing Corp.
Elysium Growth Press
FIDELIS ET VERUS
Finesse Publishing Company
Free Spirit Publishing Inc.
Front Row Experience

Gallaudet University Press
GGL Educational Press
Glenbridge Publishing Ltd.
Goodheart-Willcox Company
Grapevine Publications, Inc.
GRDA Publications
Human Kinetics Pub. Inc.
International Information Associates
ISI Press
Jamenair Ltd.
JOTS (Journal of the Senses)
L.A.N.D.
Literary Publications Company
MAXINE'S PAGES
Microdex Bookshelf
Mountain State Press
Multi Media Arts
New Harbinger Publications, Inc.
New View Publications
Oneworld Publications Ltd.
Organization for Equal Education of the Sexes, Inc. (OEES)
Panorama Publishing Company
Paragon House Publishers
Dr. Homer W. Parker, P.E.
T.H. Peek, Publisher
Pepper Publishing
Personal Efficiency Programs, Inc.
Prakken Publications
Princeton Book Company, Publishers
Professional Resource Exchange, Inc.
ProLingua Associates
The Rensselaerville Systems Training Center
Sandberry Press
Sauvie Island Press
Sherwood Sugden & Company, Publishers
Signal Books
Gibbs Smith, Publisher
ST Publications/Book Division
Tower Press
University of Calgary Press
Whitehorse
Witwatersrand University Press
Wordwrights Canada
Writers Publishing Service Co.

TEXTILES

CRAFTS NSW
NEW HOPE INTERNATIONAL REVIEW

THEATRE

Acting World Books
ACTIVIST
THE AGENCIES-WHAT THE ACTOR NEEDS TO KNOW
AMERICAN THEATRE MAGAZINE
Anderson Press
ANQ: A Quarterly Journal of Short Articles, Notes, and Reviews
ARISTOS
ARTSFOCUS PERFORMING ARTS MAGAZINE
As Is/So & So Press
Aspiring Millionaire
Astro Artz
Walter H. Baker Company (Baker's Plays)
BLIND ALLEYS
BOMB MAGAZINE
BORDER/LINES
Branden Publishing Company
Broadway Press
CALLBOARD
CANADIAN AUTHOR & BOOKMAN
CANADIAN JOURNAL OF DRAMA AND THEATRE
The Carolina Wren Press
Classic Theatre For Children, Publishers
CRAZYQUILT LITERARY QUARTERLY
" "...A DEAD BEAT POET PRODUCTION
Devil Mountain Books

THE DILETTANTE FORUM
Drama Book Publishers
THE DRAMA REVIEW
DRAMATIKA
Dramatika Press
DRAMATISTS GUILD NEWSLETTER
Dumpster Press
DUMPSTER TIMES
ENSEMBLE, THE NEW VARIETY ARTS REVIEW
THE EUGENE O'NEILL REVIEW
Excalibur Publishing
Gavea-Brown Publications
GO MAGAZINE
GREATER PORTLAND
GREY CITY JOURNAL
Grosvenor USA
Gumbs & Thomas Publishers, Inc.
Harris Stonehouse Press
HAWAI'I REVIEW
HIGH PERFORMANCE
THE HOLLYWOOD ACTING COACHES AND TEACHERS DIRECTORY
IDIOM 23
Indelible Inc.
Institute for Southern Studies
IRISH LITERARY SUPPLEMENT
ISSUE ONE
JH Press
JOURNAL FOR ANTHROPOSOPHY
Labor Arts Books
Limelight Editions
MARQUEE
MEDIA SPOTLIGHT
Micro Pro Litera Press
MODERN INTERNATIONAL DRAMA
THE MONOCACY VALLEY REVIEW
Moon Publications, Inc.
MUSIC OF THE SPHERES
THE NEW DANCE REVIEW
THE NORTHERN REVIEW
ORGANICA
PAST TIMES: THE NOSTALGIA ENTERTAINMENT NEWSLETTER
Personabooks
P-FORM
Players Press, Inc.
Pogo Press, Incorporated
THE PRAIRIE JOURNAL OF CANADIAN LITERATURE
Preludium Publishers
Prudhomme Press
Quintessence Publications & Printing Museum
RACKHAM JOURNAL OF THE ARTS AND HUMANITIES (RaJAH)
Resource Publications, Inc.
ROMANIAN REVIEW
SALOME: A JOURNAL FOR THE PERFORMING ARTS
Sea Urchin Press
Seventh Son Press
THE SHAKESPEARE NEWSLETTER
Simon & Pierre Publishing Co. Ltd.
Slate Press
SOUTHERN QUARTERLY: A Journal of the Arts in the South
Station Hill Press
SUB-TERRAIN
Talon Books Ltd
THEATER
Theatre Arts
Theatre Communications Group
THEATRE DESIGN AND TECHNOLOGY
THEATRE NOTEBOOK
THIRD RAIL
Third Rail Press
Three Continents Press, Inc.
THE THREEPENNY REVIEW
Tomart Publications

TOOK
TSUBUSHI
Waterfront Books
THE WAVE
Wet Editions
Wild East Publishing Co-operative Limited
WordWorkers Press

THEOSOPHICAL

El Montecito Oaks Press, Inc.
Metagnosis Publications
THE QUEST
Theosophical Publishing House

THIRD WORLD, MINORITIES

AAUG Press
ACTIVIST
AFRICA NEWS
AGADA
AKWEKON: A National Native American Literary &
Arts Journal
AKWEKON LITERARY JOURNAL
Akwesasne Notes
Amana Books
ARAB STUDIES QUARTERLY
ARTPAPER
ATHENA
Aunt Lute Books
Banner Press International, Inc.
Beacon Press
Between The Lines
Blind Beggar Press
BORDER/LINES
Broken Rifle Press
CARIBBEAN REVIEW
The Carolina Wren Press
CARTA ABIERTA
CHALLENGE: A Journal of Faith and Action in Central
America
Chandler & Sharp Publishers, Inc.
Children's Book Press
CHRYSANTHEMUM
CJE NEWSLETTER (Newsletter of the Coalition for Jobs
& the Environment)
Clarity Press
Communitas Press
COMMUNITY DEVELOPMENT JOURNAL
Council on Interracial Books For Children
Crime and Social Justice Associates, Inc.
CURLEY
DAUGHTER OF SARAH
DE NAR
The Denali Press
DESDE ESTE LADO/FROM THIS SIDE
Eastern Caribbean Institute
EMPIRE! The NYS Inmate Literary Arts Magazine
Epica
Esoterica Press
THE FEMINIST BOOKSTORE NEWS
The Feminist Press at the City University of New York
FREE PRESS
Frozen Waffles Press/Shattered Sidewalks Press; 25th
Century Chapbooks
Gay Sunshine Press, Inc.
Goldfish Press
GREY CITY JOURNAL
GUARDIAN
Hope Publishing House
HORIZONS INTERCULTURELS
IASP NEWSLETTER
IKON
IKON, Inc.
INDIA CURRENTS
Institute for Southern Studies
INTERCULTURE
INTERLIT
INTERRACIAL BOOKS FOR CHILDREN BULLETIN
Kitchen Table: Women of Color Press

Kumarian Press, Inc.
L.A.N.D.
Lake View Press
Langston Press
LECTOR
LEFT CURVE
LIBERATION! Journal of Revolutionary Marxism
LINKS
Lotus Press, Inc.
Maize Press
THE MILITANT
MINORITY PUBLISHERS EXCHANGE
MINORITY RIGHTS GROUP REPORTS
MR. COGITO
Mr. Cogito Press
NETWORK AFRICA FOR TODAY'S WORLD CITI-
ZEN
New Worlds Press
OBSIDIAN II: BLACK LITERATURE IN REVIEW
OFF OUR BACKS
Oneworld Publications Ltd.
Orbis Books
THE OTHER ISRAEL
Paragon House Publishers
Path Press
Path Press, Inc.
The Pilgrim Press/United Church Press
The Place In The Woods
Pocahontas Press, Inc.
POETS. PAINTERS. COMPOSERS.
PUCK!
RACONTEUR: A Journal of World History
RACONTEUR Publications
RADICAL AMERICA
Readers International, Inc.
RED DIRT
Red Letter Press
I. Reed Books
RENEGADE
REVUE CELFAN REVIEW
Ridge Times Press
ROMANIAN REVIEW
Saqi Books Publisher
SCHMAGA
Sea Urchin Press
SEZ: A Multi-Racial Journal of Poetry & People's Culture
Shadow Press, U.S.A.
Smyrna Press
SOCIAL JUSTICE: A JOURNAL OF CRIME, CON-
FLICT, & WORLD ORDER
THE SOUTHERN CALIFORNIA ANTHOLOGY
SPARE RIB
SPENCER'S BOOK WORLD
Spencer's Int'l Enterprises Corp.
Spinster's Book Company
SPIT
SPUR
STONE DRUM: An International Magazine of the Arts
STRUGGLE: A Magazine of Proletarian Revolutionary
Literature
SUBTEXT
Syracuse Cultural Workers
Talon Books Ltd
THIRD WAY
Third World First
THIRD WORLD RESOURCES
Three Continents Press, Inc.
Times Change Press
TOWARD FREEDOM
TRANSITIONS ABROAD: The Guide to Living,
Learning, and Working Overseas
TRANSNATIONAL PERSPECTIVES
UNBRIDLED LUST!
Unicorn Press
VALLEY WOMEN'S VOICE
VIEWPOINT
Volcano Press, Inc
W.I.M. Publications

Prescott Street Press
Pressed Curtains
PRISM international
Pygmy Forest Press
QRL POETRY SERIES
QUARRY WEST
RACKHAM JOURNAL OF THE ARTS AND HUMANI-
TIES (RaJAH)
Readers International, Inc.
RED DIRT
Red Hill Press, San Francisco + Los Angeles
RENDITIONS
Renditions Paperbacks
ROMANIAN REVIEW
SALMAGUNDI
THE SALMON
SALOME: A JOURNAL FOR THE PERFORMING
ARTS
SCANDINAVIAN REVIEW
The Seal Press
SEQUOIA
SEZ: A Multi-Racial Journal of Poetry & People's Culture
Singular Speech Press
SKYLARK
Spectacular Diseases
SPECTACULAR DISEASES
THE SPIRIT THAT MOVES US
SPIT
Station Hill Press
STONE TALK
STORIES
Studia Hispanica Editors
Sunburst Press
Swand Publications
Three Continents Press, Inc.
Threshold Books
TOAD HIWAY
Toad Hiway Press
TOOK
Top Of The Mountain Publishing
TOUCHSTONE LITERARY JOURNAL
Tradition Books
TRANSLATION
Translation Center
TRANSLATION REVIEW
Unicorn Press
Valkyrie Publishing House
Vehicule Press
VISIONS, International, The World Journal of Illustrated
Poetry
Waterfront Press
WEBSTER REVIEW
Westburg Associates, Publishers
White Pine Press
WILLOW SPRINGS
The Wordtree
WORLD LETTER
WRIT
WRITER'S GUIDELINES MAGAZINE
Writers House Press
Xenos Books
Yellow Moon Press
ZENOS
Zephyr Press
ZONE
Zone Books
ZONE 3

TRANSPORTATION, TRAVEL

ADIRONDAC
Adirondack Mountain Club, Inc.
Affordable Adventures, Inc.
AIRPORT POCKET GUIDE UNITED STATES EDI-
TION
Alchemist/Light Publishing
Alpenglow Press
Amana Books
American & World Geographic Publishing

American Source Books
ANNA'S HOUSE: THE JOURNAL OF EVERYDAY
LIFE
ARIZONA COAST
Author's Unlimited
Bain-Dror International Travel, Inc. (BDIT)
Basement Graphics
Bear Creek Publications
Bear Flag Books
The Bess Press
BikePress U.S.A./BikePress Canada
BLADES
Blake Publishing
The Boston Mills Press
BREAKTHROUGH!
Carousel Press
Catbird Press
Chandler & Sharp Publishers, Inc.
Charter Oak Press
Chatham Publishing Company
Chronicle Books
CJE NEWSLETTER (Newsletter of the Coalition for Jobs
& the Environment)
Colormore, Inc.
THE COOL TRAVELER
Cottage Publications, Inc.
Cottontail Publications
Countryman Press
Crossroads Communications
Crystal Spring Publishing
S. Deal & Assoc.
De-Feet Press, Inc.
Distinctive Publishing Corp.
EARTHTREKS DIGEST
ECOSOCIALIST REVIEW
EPM Publications, Inc.
Robert Erdmann Publishing
Esoterica Press
EXIT 13 MAGAZINE
Fiesta Books Inc.
Five Corners Publications, Ltd.
The Florian Group
Foghorn Press
THE FOOTLOOSE LIBRARIAN
GATEAVISA
Glacier House Publications
The Global Press
The Globe Pequot Press
Golden West Books
GOOD READING MAGAZINE
Great Blue Graphics
GREAT EXPEDITIONS MAGAZINE
Gringo Guides, Inc.
Gumbs & Thomas Publishers, Inc.
Harbinger House
Harvard Common Press
Harvestman and Associates
Heritage Press WI
ILLINOIS MAGAZINE
Interlink Publishing Group, Inc.
Italica Press, Inc.
J P Publications
Jamison Station Press
Ki**2 Books
Kozmik Press
Kurios Press
LAKE SUPERIOR MAGAZINE
THE LAS VEGAS INSIDER
Let's Go Travel Publications
Lexikos
Lion Press
LivingQuest
Markgraf Publications Group
The Marlboro Press
Maupin House
McDonald & Woodward Publishing Company
Mendocino Book Partnership
MESSAGE POST

!MEXICO WEST!
Mexico West Travel Club, Inc.
Millers River Publishing Co.
Mockingbird Press
Moon Publications, Inc.
Mountain Automation Corporation
Mountain Press Publishing Co.
The Mountaineers Books
John Muir Publications, Inc.
Mustang Publishing Co.
Nevada Publications
NEW HOPE INTERNATIONAL REVIEW
THE NORTHERN ENGINEER
Old World Travel Books, Inc.
The Olivia and Hill Press, Inc.
OLYMPIC TRAVEL GUIDE: YOUR GUIDE TO
    WASHINGTON'S OLYMPIC PENINSULA
OUT WEST
Pamlico Press
Paradise Publications
Dr. Homer W. Parker, P.E.
Passport Press
PEDESTRIAN RESEARCH
Pergot Press
Pine Cone Press
Plas Y Bryn Press
THE PRESIDENTS' JOURNAL
Prima Publishing
Rand Editions/Tofua Press
Recreation Sales Publishing, Inc.
Red Car Press
Redbird Press, Inc.
Riegel Publishing
Robinson Press, Inc.
Sasquatch Books
Scots Plaid Press (Persephone Press)
SEA KAYAKER
Sentinel Books
Shiro Publishers
Sierra Club Books
Signature Books
Small Helm Press
Genny Smith Books
Southern Resources Unlimited
SPECIALTY TRAVEL INDEX
Summerthought Ltd.
Synergistic Press
TeakWood Press
TechWest Publications
Tioga Publishing Co.
Torngat Books
TOWPATHS
Trackless Sands Press
TRANSITIONS ABROAD: The Guide to Living,
    Learning, and Working Overseas
Transport History Press
Travel Keys
Traveler's Health Publications, Inc.
Twin Peaks Press
Umbrella Books
Unique Adventures Press
University of Massachusetts Press
The Urbana Free Library
Ventana Press
THE WASHINGTON TROOPER
Wayfinder Press
Wide World Publishing/TETRA
Williamson Publishing Company, Inc.
Windsong Press
WOMEN AND ENVIRONMENTS
Woodbine House
Woodsong Graphics Inc.
WORDS OF WISDOM
Yankee Books
Zephyr Press

TREASURE

The Devon Publishing Co., Inc.

Foundation Books
Research & Discovery Publications
TREASURE HUNTING RESEARCH BULLETIN
Westport Publishers, Inc.

MARK TWAIN

COLLAGES & BRICOLAGES
THE PRINTER
Genny Smith Books
Star Rover House
X MAGAZINE

U.S. HISPANIC

BILINGUAL REVIEW/Revista Bilingue
COLLAGES & BRICOLAGES
Esoterica Press
International Consulting Associates, Inc.
Kitchen Table: Women of Color Press
Organization for Equal Education of the Sexes, Inc.
    (OEES)
Publications of Arts (Art Resources for Teachers &
    Students)
UNBRIDLED LUST!
Ward Hill Press

U.S.S.R.

Autonomedia, Inc.
Blue Crane Books
CANADIAN SLAVONIC PAPERS
Capra Press
Hoover Institution Press
International Publishers Co. Inc.
JOURNAL FOR ANTHROPOSOPHY
Kozmik Press
LIBERATION! Journal of Revolutionary Marxism
M.H. Macy & Company
MIP Company
Moscow Publishing Enterprises
Paragon House Publishers
PORTABLE LOWER EAST SIDE
Quixote Press
(ROWBOAT)
Semiotext Foreign Agents Books Series
SOCIALISM AND DEMOCRACY
SOVIET SPACEFLIGHT REPORT
SPECTRUM, A Guide to the Independent Press and
    Informative Organizations
Spectrum Publications
Starwise Publications
TRANSNATIONAL PERSPECTIVES
VIEWPOINT
Xenos Books
Zephyr Press

UTAH

Falcon Press Publishing Company
Signature Books
Gibbs Smith, Publisher

VEGETARIANISM

THE ALTERED MIND
Blue Dolphin Press, Inc.
CJE NEWSLETTER (Newsletter of the Coalition for Jobs
    & the Environment)
DE NAR
THE DREAMWEAVER
THE HAPPY THRASHER
INFINITE ONION
JASON UNDERGROUND'S NOTES FROM THE
    TRASHCOMPACTOR
JEWISH VEGETARIANS OF NORTH AMERICA
HJ Kramer, Inc
McBooks Press
Micah Publications
NEW FRONTIER
OTTERWISE
PROPER DHARMA SEAL
SCIENCE/HEALTH ABSTRACTS

Outlaw Books
PACIFIC HISTORICAL REVIEW
Point Riders Press
The Real Comet Press
THE REDNECK REVIEW OF LITERATURE
Redwood Press
Renaissance House Publishers (a division of Jende-Hagan, Inc.)
RENEGADE
Research & Discovery Publications
Robinson Press, Inc.
Sagapress, Inc.
Sand River Press
Santa Barbara Press
Seabird Publishing
Signature Books
Skyline West Press
Genny Smith Books
SOUTH DAKOTA REVIEW
Thunder Creek Publishing Co-operative
Tortilla Press
TREASURE HUNTING RESEARCH BULLETIN
TUCUMCARI LITERARY REVIEW
Utah Geographic Series
WANBLI HO
WESTERN AMERICAN LITERATURE
Wind Vein Press
World Promotions
WRITERS' FORUM
Zon International Publishing Co.

WHALING

THE ANIMALS' AGENDA
Blake Publishing
ECOSOCIALIST REVIEW
NAUTICAL BRASS

WALT WHITMAN

Barclay House
COLLAGES & BRICOLAGES
THE MICKLE STREET REVIEW
The Petrarch Press
WEST HILLS REVIEW: A WALT WHITMAN JOURNAL
WALT WHITMAN QUARTERLY REVIEW
WRITER'S GUIDELINES MAGAZINE

WICCA

Wild East Publishing Co-operative Limited

WINE, WINERIES

North Country Books, Inc.
The Organization
POLITICALLY INCORRECT
Sentinel Books

WISCONSIN

Affordable Adventures, Inc.
Baker Street Publications
Center for Public Representation
Crossroads Communications
DOOR COUNTY ALMANAK
Explorer's Guide Publishing
FEMINIST COLLECTIONS: A QUARTERLY OF WOMEN'S STUDIES RESOURCES
Heritage Press WI
LAKE SUPERIOR MAGAZINE
THE MILWAUKEE UNDERGRADUATE REVIEW
THE NORTHERN REVIEW
Northword Press, Inc.
Open Horizons Publishing Company
Pinery Press
Whole Person Associates Inc.
WISCONSIN ACADEMY REVIEW
Women's Studies Librarian, University of Wisconsin System

THOMAS WOLFE

BEAT SCENE
COLLAGES & BRICOLAGES
Croissant & Company
THE THOMAS WOLFE REVIEW

WOMEN

Academy Chicago Publishers
AGOG
THE AHFAD JOURNAL: Women And Change
ALASKA WOMEN
Alice James Books
American Audio Prose Library (non-print)
Ancient City Press
ANIMA: The Journal of Human Experience
APAEROS
Arden Press, Inc.
Ariadne Press
Ash Tree Publishing
Astarte Shell Press
ATALANTA
ATHENA
ATLANTIS: A Women's Studies Journal/Journal d'etudes sur la femme
Attic Press
Aunt Lute Books
AURORA
Autonomedia, Inc.
Bakhtin's Wife Publications
Barclay House
Beacon Press
BELLES LETTRES
Between The Lines
Biblio Press
BLOODROOT
Bloodroot, Inc.
Blue Dolphin Press, Inc.
Blue Poppy Press
BORDER/LINES
BROADSHEET
BROOMSTICK: A PERIODICAL BY, FOR, AND ABOUT WOMEN OVER FORTY
Calapooia Publications
CALYX: A Journal of Art and Literature by Women
CAMERA OBSCURA: A Journal of Feminism and Film Theory
CANADIAN WOMAN STUDIES/les cahiers de la femme
Cardinal Press, Inc.
The Carolina Wren Press
THE CENTENNIAL REVIEW
Center for Public Representation
The Center For Study of Multiple Birth
Chandler & Sharp Publishers, Inc.
Chicory Blue Press
Cleis Press
CLINTON ST.
Clothespin Fever Press
Cold-Drill Books
COLLAGES & BRICOLAGES
COMMON LIVES / LESBIAN LIVES
Communication Creativity
COMMUNITY DEVELOPMENT JOURNAL
COMPOST NEWSLETTER (CNL)
Conari Press
CONNEXIONS
Cottonwood Press
Council on Interracial Books For Children
CountrySide Business Publications
THE CREATIVE WOMAN
Crones' Own Press
DAUGHTER OF SARAH
DE NAR
Distinctive Publishing Corp.
Down There Press
Dundurn Press Ltd
DuReve Publications
EARTH'S DAUGHTERS: Feminist Arts Periodical

The Edwin Mellen Press
E-Heart Press, Inc.
Eidos
EIDOS: Erotic Entertainment for Women, Men, & Couples
Embers Press
Emily Press
English Language Literature Association
Esoterica Press
THE FEMINIST BOOKSTORE NEWS
FEMINIST COLLECTIONS: A QUARTERLY OF WOMEN'S STUDIES RESOURCES
FEMINIST PERIODICALS: A CURRENT LISTING OF CONTENTS
The Feminist Press at the City University of New York
FEMINIST REVIEW
FEMINIST STUDIES
FIGHTING WOMAN NEWS
Five Fingers Press
FIVE FINGERS REVIEW
Flower Press
FREE FOCUS
Friends United Press
Fromm International Publishing Corporation
FRONTIERS: A Journal of Women Studies
FUSE MAGAZINE
GAYELLOW PAGES
Gemini Publishing Company
GLB Publishers
Gross Advertising Service
Grosvenor USA
Growing Room Collective
GUARDIAN
Gurze Books
Harvard Common Press
HEALING PATH
HEALTHSHARING: A Canadian Women's Health Quarterly
HECATE
Hecate Press
Helicon Nine Editions
HerBooks
HERESIES: A FEMINIST PUBLICATION ON ART AND POLITICS
Hope Publishing House
HOUSEWIFE-WRITER'S FORUM
Human Kinetics Pub. Inc.
Hunter House Inc., Publishers
HURRICANE ALICE
HYPATIA: A Journal of Feminist Philosophy
IBS Press
Ide House, Inc.
IKON
IKON, Inc.
ILR Press
Impact Publishers, Inc.
Independent Research Services of Irvine (IRIS/I)
INDIGENOUS WORLD/EL MUNDO INDIGENA
Institute for Southern Studies
Institute of Lesbian Studies
International Childbirth Education Association, Inc.
International Publishers Co. Inc.
INTERRACIAL BOOKS FOR CHILDREN BULLETIN
IOWA WOMAN
IRIS: A Journal About Women
KALLIOPE, A Journal of Women's Art
Kelsey St. Press
Kenyette Productions
Kitchen Table: Women of Color Press
Knowledge, Ideas & Trends, Inc. (KIT)
Kumarian Press, Inc.
LADYSLIPPER CATALOG + RESOURCE GUIDE OF RECORDS, TAPES & VIDEOS BY WOMEN
LEGACY: A JOURNAL OF AMERICAN WOMEN WRITERS
LESBIAN CONTRADICTION-A Journal of Irreverent Feminism
LIBERATION! Journal of Revolutionary Marxism

LILITH
Lindsay Press Inc. of Florida
LINKS
Lion Press
LivingQuest
THE LLEWELLYN NEW TIMES
Llewellyn Publications
Lollipop Power Books
Lotus Press, Inc.
LUNA TACK
LuraMedia, Inc.
Magic Circle Press
Malafemmina Press
MANUSHI - a journal about women & society
MATI
Mayapple Press
McFarland & Company, Inc., Publishers
McKinzie Publishing Company
Merging Media
Midmarch Arts Press
MILDRED
MIND MATTERS REVIEW
MINERVA: Quarterly Report on Women and the Military
MINORITY RIGHTS GROUP REPORTS
Morning Glory Press
Motheroot Publications
MOVING OUT: A Feminist Literary & Arts Journal
The Naiad Press, Inc.
Nanny Goat Productions
NATURALLY
NEEDLEPOINT PLUS
NEW BOOKS ON WOMEN & FEMINISM
THE NEW DANCE REVIEW
NEW DIRECTIONS FOR WOMEN
New Victoria Publishers
NewSage Press
Northland Quarterly Publications, Inc.
Nucleus Publications
OFF OUR BACKS
The Olive Press Publications
Omega Cottonwood Press
Ommation Press
Oneworld Publications Ltd.
Organization for Equal Education of the Sexes, Inc. (OEES)
Pandit Press, Inc.
Papier-Mache Press
Paragraph Publications
PARTING GIFTS
PASSAGER: A Journal of Remembrance and Discovery
PF Publications
The Pilgrim Press/United Church Press
The Place In The Woods
Plain View Press, Inc.
PLAINSWOMAN
Political Research Associates
Portland Entertainment Publishing
POSTCARD ART/POSTCARD FICTION
THE PRAIRIE JOURNAL OF CANADIAN LITERATURE
Prairie Journal Press
Press Gang Publishers
Press Pacifica, Ltd.
PRIMAVERA
PROCESSED WORLD
PSYCHOLOGY OF WOMEN QUARTERLY
PUCK!
RACONTEUR Publications
RADICAL AMERICA
Rainier Books
Rama Publishing Co.
THE RATIONAL FEMINIST
REAL FICTION
Red Alder Books
Reference Service Press
RESOURCES FOR FEMINIST RESEARCH/DOCUMENTATION SUR LA RECHERCHE FEMINISTE
Rhiannon Press

888

Branden Publishing Company
Brunswick Publishing Corporation
Distinctive Publishing Corp.
GCBA Publishing
THE MILITARY ADVISOR
Muso Press
Dr. Homer W. Parker, P.E.
Path Press, Inc.
Renaissance House Publishers (a division of Jende-Hagan, Inc.)
Still Point Press
Thunder Creek Publishing Co-operative
White Mane Publishing Company, Inc.

WRITERS/WRITING

Ad-Lib Publications
American Audio Prose Library (non-print)
THE APPLE BLOSSOM CONNECTION
BAKER STREET GAZETTE
Baker Street Publications
Beacon Press
Bold Productions
BOOK MARKETING UPDATE
BORDER/LINES
THE BOUND SPIRAL
BYLINE
Capra Press
Chiron Press
CHIRON REVIEW
CIMARRON REVIEW
COLLAGES & BRICOLAGES
CREATIVITY CONNECTION
DESDE ESTE LADO/FROM THIS SIDE
EDITOR'S DIGEST
THE ELECTRONIC PUBLISHING FORUM
Elephas Books
11 X 13 - BROADSIDE
Esoterica Press
THE FINAL PAGE
Foundation Books
FUSE MAGAZINE
GLASS WILL
G'RAPH
Harbinger House
THE HAUNTED JOURNAL
HORIZONS WEST
HOUSEWIFE-WRITER'S FORUM
IMAGINATION MAGAZINE
Independence Publishers Inc.
Iron Gate Publishing
Last Generation/Underground Editions
Lindisfarne Press
MAINE IN PRINT
MEMES
Mockingbird Press
MUSEUM & ARTS WASHINGTON
New Hope International
NEW HOPE INTERNATIONAL REVIEW
NOOK NEWS CONFERENCES AND KLATCHES BULLETIN
THE NOOK NEWS CONTESTS AND AWARDS BULLETIN
NOOK NEWS REVIEW OF WRITERS' PUBLICATIONS
North Stone Press
THE NORTHERN REVIEW
Open Horizons Publishing Company
OUR WRITE MIND
PAPERBACK PARADE
Peak Output Unlimited
POET MAGAZINE
POET NEWS
POETIC PAGE
POISON PEN WRITERS NEWS
Rio Grande Press
SE LA VIE WRITER'S JOURNAL
SISTERS IN CRIME BOOKS IN PRINT
SLEUTH JOURNAL

Space City Publications
Toledo Poets Center Press
Tudor Publishers, Inc.
UNBRIDLED LUST!
THE VAMPIRE JOURNAL
WIDE OPEN MAGAZINE
Window Publications
Woldt Publishing
WRITE NOW!
WRITERS GAZETTE NEWSLETTER
WRITER'S GUIDELINES MAGAZINE
THE WRITER'S HAVEN
THE WRITER'S NOOK NEWS
The Writers' Nook Press
Zirlinson Publishing
ZYX

WYOMING

Affiliated Writers of America, Inc.
The Bear Wallow Publishing Company
Heirloom Publications
High Plains Press
Old West Publishing Co.
Pruett Publishing Company
Skyline West Press
The Vic Press

YOGA

AREOPAGUS
Borderland Sciences Research Foundation
CANVAS CHAUTAUQUA MAGAZINE
CRCS Publications
THE EMSHOCK LETTER
Himalayan Publishers
INDIA CURRENTS
INTEGRAL YOGA MAGAZINE
Metagnosis Publications
MOKSHA JOURNAL
NEW FRONTIER
Rodmell Press
SAT SANDESH: THE MESSAGE OF THE MASTERS
Ten Star Press
Theosophical Publishing House
Timeless Books
UNBRIDLED LUST!
Vajra of Yoga Anand Ashram
Valley Lights Publications
Samuel Weiser, Inc.
WTI Publishing Co.
Yes International Publishers

ZEN

ACTIVIST
AILERON, A LITERARY JOURNAL
Alamo Square Press
AMERICAN BUDDHIST
The Archives Press
AREOPAGUS
As Is/So & So Press
ASPECTS
AVALOKA: A Journal of Traditional Religion and Culture
Beacon Press
BEAT SCENE
Blue Dolphin Press, Inc.
Bottom Dog Press
Brennen Publishing Company
Buddha Rose Publications
BUDDHISM AT THE CROSSROADS
COMMON BOUNDARY
DIE FAT PIGGY DIE
Dragon Cloud Books
THE EMSHOCK LETTER
FAT TUESDAY
FISH DRUM MAGAZINE
Flax Press, Inc.
Frozen Waffles Press/Shattered Sidewalks Press; 25th Century Chapbooks

GET STUPID
GREY CITY JOURNAL
High/Coo Press
IllumiNet Press
INKBLOT
Mockingbird Press
MOKSHA JOURNAL
Muso Press
Nemeton Publishing
NEW FRONTIER
Omega Cottonwood Press
1 BIT SHOE
OPOSSUM HOLLER TAROT
PalmTree Publishers
Parallax Press
PARTING GIFTS
POETS. PAINTERS. COMPOSERS.
THE SCREAM OF THE BUDDHA
Scribblers Publishing, Ltd.
SO & SO
Theosophical Publishing House
UNBRIDLED LUST!
Vajra of Yoga Anand Ashram
Valley Lights Publications
THE WAVE
Samuel Weiser, Inc.
West Anglia Publications
White Pine Press